RHS
PLANT FINDER
2000-2001

DEVISED BY CHRIS PHILIP

PRINCIPAL EDITOR
TONY LORD

RHS EDITORS
JANET CUBEY
MIKE GRANT
ADRIAN WHITELEY

A Dorling Kindersley Book

Dorling  Kindersley

LONDON, NEW YORK, SYDNEY, DELHI, PARIS, MUNICH and JOHANNESBURG

Published by
Dorling Kindersley Limited
9 Henrietta Street
Covent Garden, London WC2E 8PS

British Library Cataloguing Publication Data.
A Catalogue record for this book is available from the British Library.

ISBN 0 7513 0811 0
ISSN 0961-2599

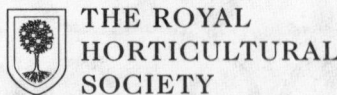

THE ROYAL HORTICULTURAL SOCIETY

Compiled by
The Royal Horticultural Society
80 Vincent Square
London SW1P 2PE
Registered charity no: 222879

www.rhs.org.uk

Illustrations by Murdo Culver
Maps by Alan Cooper

Printed and bound in Italy by Legoprint

**The Compiler and the Editors of the *RHS Plant Finder* have taken every care, in the time available,
to check all the information supplied to them by the nurseries concerned. Nevertheless, in a work of this
kind, containing as it does hundreds of thousands of separate computer encodings, errors and omissions
will, inevitably, occur. Neither the RHS, the Publisher nor the Editors can accept responsibility for
any consequences that may arise from such errors.**

If you find mistakes we hope that you will let us know so that the matter can be corrected in the next edition.

Front cover photographs clockwise from top left: *Nymphaea* 'Escarboucle', *Phlox paniculata* 'Eventide',
Gazania 'Cookei', *Cotoneaster lacteus*, *Osteospermum* 'Whirlygig', *Aeonium haworthii*,
Back cover photographs clockwise from top left: *Felicia amelloides* 'Santa Anita', *Rosa* 'Geranium',
Delphinium 'Sungleam', *Prunus* 'Shirofugen', *Buddleja globosa*, *Clematis* 'Vyvyan Pennell',
Ilex aquifolium 'Golden Milkboy', *Phormium* 'Sundowner', *Allium caeruleum*, *Narcissus* 'February Gold'

The publisher would like to thank the Harry Smith Collection for their kind permission
to reproduce their photograph of *Delphinium* 'Sungleam'.

See our complete catalogue at
www.dk.com

CONTENTS

SYMBOLS AND ABBREVIATIONS

SYMBOLS APPEARING TO THE LEFT OF THE NAME

*   Name not validated. Not listed in the appropriate International Registration Authority checklist nor in works cited in the Bibliography. For fuller discussion see The Naming of Plants on p.772

I   Invalid name. See *International Code of Botanical Nomenclature 1994* and *International Code of Nomenclature for Cultivated Plants 1995*. For fuller discussion see The Naming of Plants on p.772

N   Refer to Nomenclature Notes on p.754

¶   New plant entry in this edition

§   Plant listed elsewhere in the Plant Directory under a synonym

x   Hybrid genus

+   Graft hybrid genus

SYMBOLS APPEARING TO THE RIGHT OF THE NAME

✿   National Council for the Conservation of Plants and Gardens (NCCPG) Plant Collection exists for all or part of this genus. Full details of the NCCPG Plant Collections are contained in the *National Plant Collections™ Directory 2000* available from: NCCPG, The Stable Courtyard, RHS Garden Wisley, Woking, Surrey GU23 6QP

♀   The Royal Horticultural Society's Award of Garden Merit, see p.15.

®   Registered Trade Mark ⎫ Based on information

™   Trade Mark ⎬ supplied by nurseries

(d)   double-flowered

(F)   Fruit

(f)   female

(m)   male

(v)   variegated plant, see p.15

PBR   Plant Breeders Rights see p.14

For abbreviations relating to individual genera see **Classification of Genera** p.763
For **Collectors' References** see p.760
For symbols used in the **Nurseries** section see the reverse of the card insert

SYMBOLS AND ABBREVIATIONS USED AS PART OF THE NAME

x   hybrid species

aff.   affinis (allied to)

cl.   clone

cv(s)   cultivar(s)

f.   forma (botanical form)

g.   grex

sp.   species

subsp.   subspecies

subvar.   subvarietas (botanical subvariety)

var.   varietas (botanical variety)

GEOGRAPHICAL KEY TO CODES

The first letter of each nursery code represents the area of the country in which the nursery is situated.

C   **South West**
Bath & NE Somerset, Bournemouth, Channel Islands, City of Bristol, City of Plymouth, Cornwall, Devon, Dorset, Isles of Scilly, Poole, North Somerset, Somerset, South Gloucestershire, Swindon, Torbay, Wiltshire.

E   **Eastern**
Cambridgeshire, City of Peterborough, Essex, Lincolnshire, Norfolk, North Lincolnshire, NE Lincolnshire, Southend-on-Sea, Suffolk, Thurrock.

G   **Scotland**
All Scottish counties plus Orkney, Shetland.

I   **Northern Ireland & Republic of Ireland**

L   **London Area**
Bedfordshire, Bracknell Forest, Buckinghamshire, Hertfordshire, London, Luton, Middlesex, Milton Keynes, Reading, Slough, Surrey, West Berkshire, Windsor & Maidenhead, Wokingham.

M   **Midlands**
Birmingham, Cheshire, City of Derby, City of Leicester, City of Nottingham, City of Stoke-on-Trent, Coventry, Derbyshire, Dudley, Isle of Man, Leicestershire, Northamptonshire, Nottinghamshire, Oxfordshire, Rutland, Sandwell, Solihull, Staffordshire, Walsall, Warwickshire, Wirral, Wolverhampton.

N   **Northern**
Barnsley, Blackburn with Darwen, Bolton, Bradford, Bury, Calderdale, City of Kingston-upon-Hull, Cumbria, Darlington, Doncaster, Durham, East Riding of Yorkshire, Gateshead, Halton, Hartlepool, Kirklees, Knowlsley, Lancashire, Leeds, Liverpool, Manchester, Middlesborough, Newcastle-upon-Tyne, North Tyneside, North Yorkshire, Northumberland, Oldham, Redcar & Cleveland, Rochdale, Rotherham, St Helens, Salford, Sheffield, South Tyneside, Stockport, Stockton-on-Tees, Sunderland, Tameside, Trafford, Wakefield, Warrington, Wigan, York.

S   **Southern**
Brighton & Hove, City of Portsmouth, City of Southampton, East Sussex, Hampshire, Isle of Wight, Kent, Medway, West Sussex.

W   **Wales & the West**
All Welsh counties plus Gloucestershire (but not South Gloucestershire), Herefordshire, Shropshire, Telford & Wrekin, Worcestershire.

X   **Abroad**

USING THE PLANT DIRECTORY

The main purpose of the Plant Directory is to help the reader identify correctly the plant they seek and find its stockist. Each nursery has a unique identification code which appears to the right of the plant name. Turn to Nursery Details by Code (p.796) for the address, opening times and other details of the nursery. The first letter of each nursery code denotes its geographical region.

See p.6 or turn to the card insert towards the rear of the book to find your region code and then identify the nurseries in your area.

Another purpose of the Directory is to provide more information about the plant through the symbols and other information. For example, if it has an alternative names, is new to this edition or has received the RHS Award of Garden Merit.

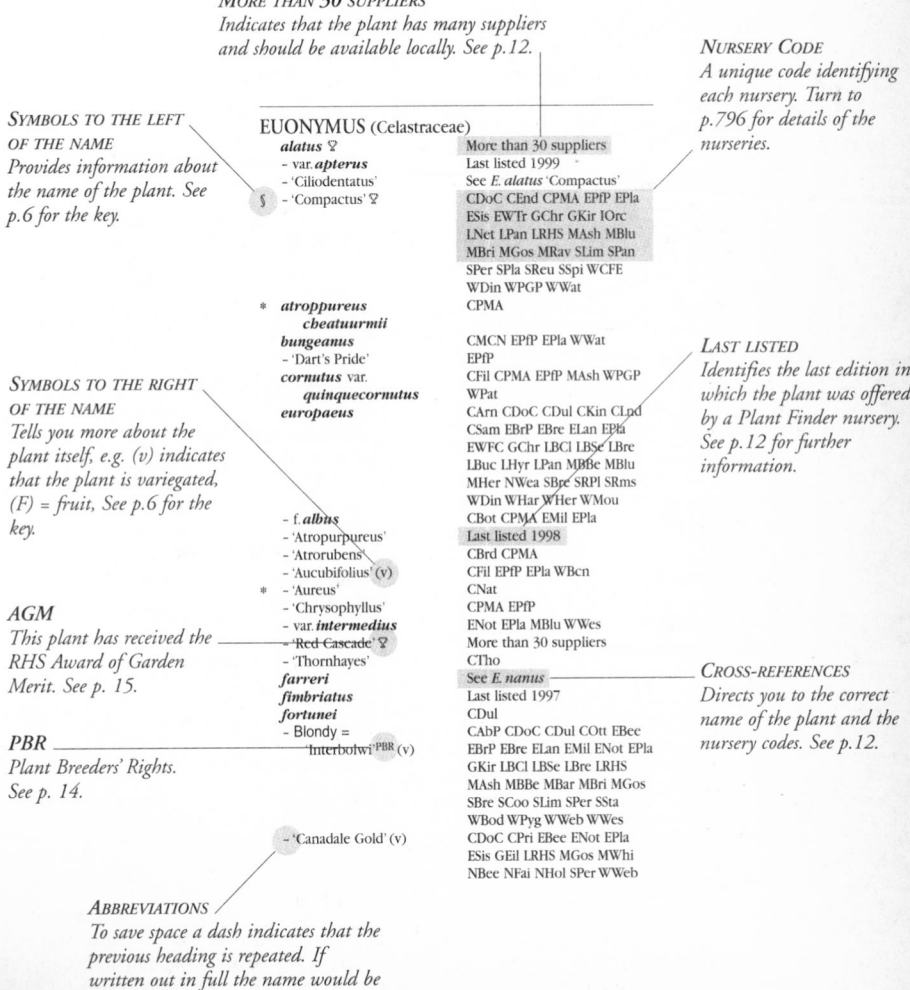

MORE THAN 30 SUPPLIERS
Indicates that the plant has many suppliers and should be available locally. See p.12.

NURSERY CODE
A unique code identifying each nursery. Turn to p.796 for details of the nurseries.

SYMBOLS TO THE LEFT OF THE NAME
Provides information about the name of the plant. See p.6 for the key.

SYMBOLS TO THE RIGHT OF THE NAME
Tells you more about the plant itself, e.g. (v) indicates that the plant is variegated, (F) = fruit, See p.6 for the key.

AGM
This plant has received the RHS Award of Garden Merit. See p. 15.

PBR
Plant Breeders' Rights. See p. 14.

LAST LISTED
Identifies the last edition in which the plant was offered by a Plant Finder nursery. See p.12 for further information.

CROSS-REFERENCES
Directs you to the correct name of the plant and the nursery codes. See p.12.

ABBREVIATIONS
To save space a dash indicates that the previous heading is repeated. If written out in full the name would be Euonymus fortunei 'Canadale Gold'.

EUONYMUS (Celastraceae)

alatus ♀	More than 30 suppliers
- var. apterus	Last listed 1999
- 'Ciliodentatus'	See E. alatus 'Compactus'
§ - 'Compactus' ♀	CDoC CEnd CPMA EPfP EPla
	ESis EWTr GChr GKir IOrc
	LNet LPan LRHS MAsh MBlu
	MBri MGos MRav SLim SPan
	SPer SPla SReu SSpi WCFE
	WDin WPGP WWat
* atroppureus	CPMA
cheatuurmii	
bungeanus	CMCN EPfP EPla WWat
- 'Dart's Pride'	EPfP
cornutus var.	CFil CPMA EPfP MAsh WPGP
quinquecornutus	WPat
europaeus	CArn CDoC CDul CKin CLnd
	CSam EBrP EBre ELan EPla
	EWFC GChr LBCI LBSe LBre
	LBuc LHyr LPan MBBe MBlu
	MHer NWea SBre SRPl SRms
	WDin WHar WHer WMou
- f. albus	CBot CPMA EMil EPla
- 'Atropurpureus'	Last listed 1998
- 'Atrorubens'	CBrd CPMA
- 'Aucubifolius' (v)	CFil EPfP EPla WBcn
* - 'Aureus'	CNat
- 'Chrysophyllus'	CPMA EPfP
- var. intermedius	ENot EPla MBlu WWes
- 'Red Cascade' ♀	More than 30 suppliers
- 'Thornhayes'	CTho
farreri	See E. nanus
fimbriatus	Last listed 1997
fortunei	CDul
- Blondy =	CAbP CDoC CDul COtt EBee
Interbolwi PBR (v)	EBrP EBre ELan EMil ENot EPla
	GKir LBCI LBSe LBre LRHS
	MAsh MBBe MBar MBri MGos
	SBre SCoo SLim SPer SSta
	WBod WPyg WWeb WWes
- 'Canadale Gold' (v)	CDoC CPri EBee ENot EPla
	ESis GEil LRHS MGos MWhi
	NBee NFai NHol SPer WWeb

INTRODUCTION

The *RHS Plant Finder* exists to put enthusiastic gardeners in touch with suppliers of plants, many of them unusual. The book is divided into two related sections – PLANTS and NURSERIES. PLANTS includes an A–Z Plant Directory of some 70,000 plant names, against which are listed a series of nursery codes. These codes point the reader to the full nursery details contained in the NURSERIES section towards the back of the book.

The *RHS Plant Finder* is comprehensively updated every year and provides the plant lover with the richest source of suppliers known to us, whether you are looking for plants locally, shopping from your armchair or touring the country in search of the rare and unusual.

> Simply because a nursery is listed against a given plant, it does not necessarily follow that the plant will be in stock throughout the year.
>
> TO AVOID DISAPPOINTMENT, WE SUGGEST THAT YOU ALWAYS:
>
> **Check with the nursery before visiting or ordering and always use the current edition of the book.**

AVAILABLE FROM THE COMPILER

APPLICATION FOR ENTRY

Nurseries appearing in the *RHS Plant Finder* for the first time this year are printed in bold type in the Nursery Index by Name starting on p.xxx.

If any other nursery wishes to be considered for inclusion in the next edition of the *RHS Plant Finder* (2001-02), please write for details to the Compiler at the address below. The closing date for new entries will be 31 January 2001.

PLANTS LAST LISTED IN EARLIER EDITIONS

Previously known as Plant Deletions
Plants cease to be listed for a variety of reasons but those listed in one or other of the last three editions are named in the Plant Directory, together with the date they were last listed. For more information turn to 'How to Use the Plant Directory' on p.12.

A booklet of the 19,000 or so plants last listed in earlier editions, and for which we currently have no known supplier, is available from the Compiler. Please send three £1 stamps.

BACK COPIES

For those who wish to find previously listed plants, back editions of the *RHS Plant Finder* are still available at £6.00 (incl. p&p) from the Compiler.

LISTS OF NURSERIES FOR PLANTS WITH MORE THAN 30 SUPPLIERS

To prevent the *RHS Plant Finder* from becoming still larger, if more than 30 nurseries offer the same plant we cease to print the nursery codes and instead list the plant as having 'more than 30 suppliers'. This is detailed more fully in 'How to Use the Plant Directory' on p.12.

If any readers have difficulty in finding such a plant, we will be pleased to send a full list of all the nurseries that we have on file as stockists. All such enquiries must include the full name of the plant being sought, as shown in the *RHS Plant Finder*, together with an A5 size SAE.

The above may all be obtained from:
The Compiler,
RHS Plant Finder,
RHS Garden Wisley,
Woking,
Surrey
GU23 6QB

NEW IN THIS EDITION

For the first time, plants covered by an active Plant Breeders' Rights grant are indicated in the *RHS Plant Finder*. Look for the intials PBR after the name. For further information see p.14.

THE RHS PLANT FINDER ON CD-ROM

The *RHS Plant Finder* is available in an electronic format as part of the *RHS Plant Finder CD-ROM*. It is available from **RHS Enterprises Ltd, RHS Garden Wisley, Woking, Surrey, GU23 6QB.**

THE RHS PLANT FINDER ONLINE

The *RHS Plant Finder* is now available on the Internet. Visit the Royal Horticultural Society's website, **www.rhs.org.uk**, and search the *RHS Plant Finder* database online.

ACKNOWLEDGMENTS

Generating the *RHS Plant Finder* from *BG-BASE*™ has involved an almost entirely new team this year, all of whom have risen to the challenge magnificently. In Plant Finder Compiler Clare Burgh's absence on maternity leave, Judith Merrick has co-ordinated the complex job of compiling nursery information and plant lists admirably, assisted by June Skinner. More nurseries have this year taken advantage of providing their information electronically, simplifying considerably the job of updating their listings. Our team has again been helped enormously by the efforts of Dr Kerry Walter of *BG-BASE* Inc. Senior Database Administrator Dr Andrew Sier and Horticultural Database Administrator Niki Simpson have left the RHS during the last year, though we still reap the benefits of their excellent and accurate work in the past. Christine Ellis has taken over from Niki and has been responsible for much of the name editing in this edition, assisted by Data Inputter Richard Sanford. The tight time schedule for production of the *RHS Plant Finder* has made it a particular blessing to have had the help of Wisley's botanists Janet Cubey, Mike Grant and Adrian Whiteley, who have made the first check on all new names this year. This has allowed me to concentrate on new names they could not find or verify and on entries from our last edition, while trying to ensure a consistent nomenclatural approach throughout. All our efforts are supervised by RHS Head of Botany, Dr Simon Thornton-Wood. I could not wish for more efficient and helpful colleagues. All who use The RHS Plant Finder owe them thanks and I am particularly grateful to them all for making the job of editing so much easier.

For the compilation of this edition, I am once more indebted to my colleagues on the RHS Advisory Panel on Nomenclature and Taxonomy: Chris Brickell, Susyn Andrews, James Compton, Stephen Jury, Sabina Knees, Alan Leslie, Simon Thornton-Wood, Piers Trehane and Adrian Whiteley, along with Mike Grant, Diana Miller and Janet Cubey, all of whom have provided much valuable guidance throughout the past year. Scores of nurseries have sent helpful information about asterisked plants which has proved immensely useful in verifying some of the most obscure names, as well as suggested corrections to existing entries. Some of these suggested corrections remain to be checked and entered in our next edition, though I have had to reject those that contravene the Codes of Nomenclature for reasons covered in The Naming of Plants (p.xxx). I am grateful, too, to our regular correspondents and to the RHS International Registrars, including Vicki Mathews who has checked new *Clematis* entries for this edition.

Artemisia	Dr J.D. Twibell ('94)
Bamboos	D. McClintock ('90-'94)
Bougainvillea	S. Read ('94)
Camellia	T.J. Savige, International Registrar, NSW, Australia ('96)
Cimicifuga	J. Compton ('94)
Cistus	R. Page ('97 & '99)
Conifers	P. Trehane, International Registrar, RHS Wisley ('94 & '99)
Cotoneaster	Jeanette Fryer, NCCPG Collection Holder ('99)
Cyclamen	Dr C. Grey-Wilson ('94)
Dahlia	R. Hedge, RHS Wisley ('96-'00)
Delphinium	Dr A.C. Leslie, International Registrar, RHS Wisley ('97-'00)
Dianthus	Dr A.C. Leslie, International Registrar, RHS Wisley ('91-'00)
Gesneriaceae	J.D. Dates, International Registrar ('94)
Hebe	Mrs J. Hewitt ('94-'99)
Hedera	P.Q. Rose & Mrs H. Key ('93) Alison Rutherford ('92-'94)
Hypericum	Dr N.K.B. Robson ('94-'97)
Ilex	Ms S. Andrews ('92-'98)
Iris	Mrs J. Hewitt ('95-'99)
Jovibarba & *Sempervivum*	P.J. Mitchell, International Registrar, Sempervivum Society ('98)

Lavandula	Ms S. Andrews ('92-'99)
Lilium	Dr A.C. Leslie, International Registrar, RHS Wisley ('91-'00)
Liriope	Dr P.R. Fantz ('99)
Narcissus	Mrs S. Kington, International Registrar, RHS ('91-'00)
Ophiopogon	Dr P.R. Fantz ('99)
Pelargonium	Mrs H. Key ('91-'95)
Pelargonium spp.	Mrs D. Miller ('93)
Polemonium	Mrs D. Nichol-Brown ('94)
Rhododendron	Dr A.C. Leslie, International Registrar, RHS Wisley ('91-'00)
Salvia	J. Compton ('94)
Zauschneria	P. Trehane ('94)

To all these, as well as the many readers and nurseries who have also made comments and suggestions, we are, once again, sincerely grateful.

Tony Lord
March 2000

PLANTS

WHATEVER PLANT YOU ARE LOOKING FOR,
MAYBE AN OLD FAVOURITE OR A MORE UNUSUAL
CULTIVAR, SEARCH HERE FOR A LIST OF THE
SUPPLIERS THAT ARE CLOSEST TO YOU.

HOW TO USE THE PLANT DIRECTORY

NURSERY CODES

Look up the plant you require in the alphabetical Plant Directory. Against each plant you will find one or more four-letter codes, for example SLan, each code representing one nursery offering that plant. The first letter of each code indicates the main area of the country in which the nursery is situated, based on their county. For this geographical key, refer to Symbols and Abbreviations p.6 and the card insert at the beginning of the NURSERIES section p.793.

Turn to the **Nursery Details by Code** starting on p.796 where, in alphabetical order of codes, you will find details of each nursery which offers the plant in question. If you wish to visit any of these nurseries you can find its location on one of the maps (following p.921). Mail order only nurseries are generally not indicated on the maps. For a fuller explanation of how to use the nursery listings please turn to p.793. Always check that the nursery you select has the plant in stock before you set out.

PLANTS WITH MORE THAN 30 SUPPLIERS

In some cases, against the plant name you will see the term 'more than 30 suppliers' instead of a nursery code. Clearly, if we were to include every plant listed by all nurseries, the *RHS Plant Finder* would become unmanageably bulky. We therefore ask nurseries to restrict their entries to only those plants that are not already well represented. As a result, if more than 30 nurseries offer any plant the Directory gives no nursery codes and the plant is listed instead as having 'more than 30 suppliers'. You should have little difficulty in locating these in local nurseries or garden centres. However, if you are unable to find such plants, we will be pleased to send a full list of all the nurseries that we have on file as stockists. Please see the Introduction on p.8 for details of how to obtain the lists.

> *Please, never use an old edition*

IF YOU HAVE DIFFICULTY FINDING YOUR PLANT

If you cannot immediately find the plant you seek, look through the various species of the genus. You may be using an incomplete name. The problem is most likely to arise in very large genera such as *Phlox* where there are a number of possible species, each with a large number of cultivars. A search through the whole genus may well bring success.

CROSS-REFERENCES

It may be that the plant name you seek is a synonym. Our intention is to list nursery codes only against the correct botanical name, where you find a synonym you will be cross-referred to the correct name. Sometimes you may find that the correct botanical name to which you have been referred is not listed. This is because it was last listed more than three years ago as explained below.

PLANTS LAST LISTED IN EARLIER EDITIONS

Previously known as Plant Deletions
It may also be that the plant you are seeking has no known suppliers and is thus not listed. In this edition, plants that were last listed in one or other of the three previous editions of the *RHS Plant Finder*, in a separate index called Plant Deletions, are here integrated into the Plant Directory. Against the plant name, instead of nursery codes, you will see the phrase 'last listed' together with a year e.g. '1997'. This indicates that the plant was last listed in the 1997-98 edition of the book. Plants which have received the AGM but which are not offered by any of the nurseries in the book, are also included in this way irrespective of when they were last listed.

The loss of a plant name from the Directory may arise for a number of reasons – the supplier may have gone out of business, or may not have responded to our latest questionnaire and has therefore been removed from the book. Such plants may well be still available but we have no current knowledge of their whereabouts. Alternatively, some plants may have been misnamed by nurseries in previous editions, but are now appearing under their correct name.

To obtain a booklet of plants last listed in earlier editions please see the Introduction on p.8.

Finding Fruit and Vegetables

If the plant name you are seeking is a fruit or vegetable, you will need to look it up by its botanical name, for which you may find the following list useful.

Almond	See *Prunus dulcis*
Añu	See *Tropaeolum tuberosum*
Apple	See *Malus domestica*
Apple, Crab	See *Malus*
Apricot	See *Prunus armeniaca*
Artichoke, Globe	See *Cynara cardunculus* Scolymus Group
Artichoke, Jerusalem	See *Helianthus tuberosus*
Avocado	See *Persea*
Banana	See *Musa*
Blackberry	See *Rubus fruticosus*
Blackcurrant	See *Ribes nigrum*
Blueberry	See *Vaccinium corymbosum*
Boysenberry	See *Rubus* Boysenberry
Bullace	See *Prunus insititia*
Butternut	See *Juglans cinerea*
Calamondin	See × *Citrofortunella*
Cape Gooseberry	See *Physalis*
Carambola	See *Averrhoa carambola*
Cardoon	See *Cynara cardunculus*
Cashew-nut	See *Anacardium occidentale*
Cherimoya	See *Annona cherimola*
Cherry, Duke	See *Prunus* × *gondouinii*
Cherry, Sour or Morello	See *Prunus cerasus*
Cherry, Sweet	See *Prunus avium*
Chestnut, Sweet	See *Castanea*
Citron	See *Citrus medica*
Cobnut	See *Corylus avellana*
Coconut	See *Cocos nucifera*
Coffee	See *Coffea*
Cranberry	See *Vaccinium macrocarpon*, *V. oxycoccos*
Custard Apple	See *Annona cherimola*, *A. reticulata*
Damson	See *Prunus insititia*
Date	See *Phoenix dactylifera*
Elderberry	See *Sambucus*
Fig	See *Ficus carica*
Filbert	See *Corylus maxima*
Gooseberry	See *Ribes uva-crispa* var. *reclinatum*
Granadilla	See *Passiflora quadrangularis*
Granadilla, Purple	See *Passiflora edulis*
Granadilla, Sweet	See *Passiflora ligularis*
Granadilla, Yellow	See *Passiflora laurifolia*
Grape	See *Vitis*
Grapefruit	See *Citrus* × *paradisi*
Guava, Common	See *Psidium guajava*
Guava, Purple or Strawberry	See *Psidium littorale*
Hazelnut	See *Corylus*
Hickory, Shagbark	See *Carya ovata*
Hildaberry	See *Rubus* 'Hildaberry'
Horned Melon	See *Cucumis metulifer*
Jostaberry	See *Ribes* × *culverwellii* Jostaberry
Jujube	See *Ziziphus jujuba*
Kaffir Plum	See *Harpephyllum caffrum*
Kiwano	See *Cucumis metulifer*
Kiwi Fruit	See *Actinidia deliciosa*
Kumquat	See *Fortunella*
Lemon	See *Citrus limon*
Lime	See *Citrus aurantiifolia*
Loganberry	See *Rubus* Loganberry Group
Loquat	See *Eriobotrya japonica*
Mandarin	See *Citrus reticulata*
Mango	See *Mangifera indica*
Medlar	See *Mespilus germanica*
Mulberry	See *Morus*
Natal Plum	See *Carissa macrocarpa*
Nectarine	See *Prunus persica* var. *nectarina*
Nut, Cob	See *Corylus avellana*
Nut, Filbert	See *Corylus maxima*
Olive	See *Olea europaea*
Orange, Sour or Seville	See *Citrus aurantium*
Orange, Sweet	See *Citrus sinensis*
Papaya (Paw Paw)	See *Carica papaya*
Passion Fruit	See *Passiflora*
Passion Fruit, Banana	See *Passiflora mollissima*
Paw Paw (False Banana)	See *Asimina triloba*
Peach	See *Prunus persica*
Pear	See *Pyrus communis*
Pear, Asian	See *Pyrus pyrifolia*
Pecan	See *Carya illinoinensis*
Pepino	See *Solanum muricatum*
Persimmon	See *Diospyros virginiana*
Persimmon, Japanese	See *Diospyros kaki*
Pineapple Guava	See *Acca sellowiana*
Pinkcurrant	See *Ribes rubrum* (P)
Plum	See *Prunus domestica*
Pomegranate	See *Punica granatum*
Pummelo	See *Citrus maxima*
Rhubarb	See *Rheum* × *hybridum*
Quince	See *Cydonia*
Raspberry	See *Rubus idaeus*
Redcurrant	See *Ribes rubrum* (R)
Satsuma	See *Citrus unshiu*
Seakale	See *Crambe maritima*
Shaddock	See *Citrus maxima*
Soursop	See *Annona muricata*

Strawberry	See *Fragaria*	Tummelberry	See *Rubus* 'Tummelberry'
Sunberry	See *Rubus* 'Sunberry'	Ugli	See *Citrus* x *tangelo* 'Ugli'
Tamarillo	See *Cyphomandra betacea*	Veitchberry	See *Rubus* 'Veitchberry'
Tamarind	See *Tamarindus indica*	Walnut	See *Juglans*
Tangelo	See *Citrus* x *tangelo*	Whitecurrant	See *Ribes rubrum* (W)
Tangerine	See *Citrus reticulata*	Wineberry	See *Rubus phoenicolasius*
Tangor	See *Citrus* x *nobilis* Tangor Group	Worcesterberry	See *Ribes divaricatum*
Tayberry	See *Rubus* Tayberry Group	Youngberry	See *Rubus* 'Youngberry'

ADDITIONAL PLANT NAME INFORMATION IN THE DIRECTORY

DESCRIPTIVE TERMS

Terms which appear after the main part of the name are shown in a smaller font to distinguish name parts that are cultivar authors, common names, collectors' codes and other descriptive terms. For example, *Penstemon* 'Sour Grapes' M. Fish, *Lobelia tupa* dark orange.

PLANT BREEDERS' RIGHTS AND TRADE DESIGNATIONS (SELLING NAMES)

For the first time, plants covered by an active Plant Breeders' Rights grant are indicated in the *RHS Plant Finder*. Grants are awarded by both UK and EU Plant Variety Rights offices. Because grants can come into force and lapse at any time, this book can only represent the situation at one point in time, but it is hoped that the information presented will act as a useful guide to growers and gardeners. UK grants represent the position as of the end of February 2000 and EU grants as of the end of December 1999.

Plants granted protection under Plant Breeders' Rights (PBR) legislation, and those with high-volume international sales, are often given a code or nonsense name for registration purposes. Under the rules of the International Code of Nomenclature for Cultivated Plants 1995 (ICNCP), such a name, established by a legal process, has to be regarded as the correct cultivar name for the plant.

Unfortunately, the names are often unpronounceable and usually meaningless, so the plants are given other names designed to attract sales when they are released. These are often referred to as selling names but are officially termed trade designations. Also, when a cultivar name is translated into a language other than that in which it was published, the translation is regarded as a trade designation in the same way as a PBR selling name. The name in its original language is the correct cultivar name.

While PBRs remain active it is a legal requirement for both names to appear on a label at point-of-sale. The reason for this may not appear obvious until it is realised that there is potentially no limit to the number of trade designations for any one plant. In reality, most plants are sold under only one trade designation, but some, especially roses, are sold under a number of names, particularly when cultivars are introduced to other countries. Usually, the registered or original cultivar name is the only way to ensure that the same plant is not bought unwittingly under two or more different trade designations. Although the use of trade designations goes against the principle that a cultivar should have only one correct name, the ICNCP has had to accommodate them and the *RHS Plant Finder* follows its recommendations. These are always to quote the cultivar name and trade designation together and to style the trade designation in a different typeface, without single quotation marks.

In the Plant Directory trade designations are listed in alphabetical order of the trade designation.

Further information on all matters concerning PBR in the UK can be obtained from:
Mr R Greenaway
Plant Variety Rights Office, White House Lane, Huntingdon Road, Cambridge CB3 0LF
Tel: (01223) 342350
Fax: (01223) 342386.

For details of plants covered by Community Rights contact the Community Plant Variety Office (CPVO):
Office Communautaire des Variétés Végétales, B.P. 2141, F-49021 Angers Cedex 02, France.
Tel: 00 33 (0)241 36 84 50
Fax: 00 33 (0)241 36 84 60
Internet: www.cpvo.fr

VARIEGATED PLANTS

Following a suggestion from the Variegated Plant Group of the Hardy Plant Society, we have added a (v) to those plants which are 'variegated' although this may not be apparent from their name. The dividing line between variegation and less distinct colour marking is necessarily arbitrary and plants with light veins, pale, silver or dark zones or leaves flushed in paler colours are not shown as being variegated unless there is an absolutely sharp distinction between paler and darker zones. For further details of the Variegated Plant Group, please write to
**Stephen Taffler,
18 Hayes End Manor,
South Pemberton,
Somerset TA13 5BE.**

♀ THE AWARD OF GARDEN MERIT

The Award of Garden Merit (AGM) is one of the highest accolades the Royal Horticultural Society can give to a garden plant and is of practical value for the ordinary gardener. Every AGM plant should have the following qualities:

* outstanding excellence for garden decoration or use
* available in the trade
* of good constitution
* requiring neither highly specialist growing conditions nor care.

A complete and categorised listing of over 6,000 AGM plants is available as *AGM Plants 2000* from **RHS Enterprises Ltd, RHS Garden Wisley, Woking, Surrey, GU23 6QB. Tel:(01483) 211320**

SUPPLEMENTARY KEYS TO THE PLANT DIRECTORY

NOMENCLATURE NOTES

These refer to plants in the Directory that are marked with a 'N' to the left of the name. The notes add further information to names which are complex or may be confusing. They start on p.754.

COLLECTORS' REFERENCES

Abbreviations (usually with numbers) following a plant name, refer to the collector(s) of the plant. These abbreviations are expanded, with a collector's name or expedition title, in the section Collectors' References starting on p.760.

A collector's reference may indicate a new, as yet unnamed range of variation within a species; their inclusion in the *RHS Plant Finder* supports the book's role in sourcing unusual plants.

Since the adoption of the *Convention on Biological Diversity* in 1993, collectors are normally required to have prior consent for the acquisition and commercialisation of collected material.

CLASSIFICATION OF GENERA

Genera including a large number of species or with many cultivars are often subdivided into groups, each based on a particular characteristic or combination of characteristics. Colour of flower or fruit and shape of flower are common examples, and, with fruit, whether a cultivar is grown for

culinary or dessert purposes. How such groups are named differs from genus to genus.

To help users of the *RHS Plant Finder* find exactly the plants they want, the majority of classifications used within cultivated genera are listed with codes and each species or cultivar is marked with the appropriate code in brackets after its name in the Plant Directory. The codes relating to edible fruits are listed with the more specialised classifications. These apply across several genera. To find the explanation of each code, simply look it up under the genus concerned in the Classification of Genera on p.763.

REVERSE SYNONYMS

It is likely that users of this book will come across names in certain genera which they did not expect to find. This may be because species have been transferred from another genus (or genera). In the list of Reverse Synonyms on p.767, the name on the left hand side is that of an accepted genus to which species have been transferred from the genus on the right. Sometimes all species will have been transferred, but in many cases only a few will be affected. Consulting Reverse Synonyms enables users to find the genera from which species have been transferred. If the right-hand genus is then found in the Plant Directory, the movements of species becomes clear through the cross-references in the nursery-code column.

THE PLANT DIRECTORY

A

ABELIA ✿ (Caprifoliaceae)

'Abghop'	See *A.* x *grandiflora* Hopleys = 'Abghop'
chinensis hort.	See *A.* x *grandiflora*
- R.Br.	CB&S CNic CPle EBee EPfP MAsh SMer SPer SSta WAbe WFar WHCG WPat WSHC WWat
§ Confetti = 'Conti'PBR (v)	CAbP CB&S CBlo CChe CDoC COtt CRos CWSG EBee ELan EPfP LAst LPan LRHS MAsh MCCP MGos NPro SBod SLim SMur SPer SPla SSta WRHF WWeb
'Conti'PBR	See *A.* Confetti = 'Conti'
'Edward Goucher' ♀	CB&S CDoC CPle CWit EBee ELan ENot LPan LRHS MGos NFla SEND SPer SPlb WBod WFar WPat WPyg WSHC WWal WWat WWeb
engleriana	CAbP CPle CSam EPla LRHS SEas SPan SPer WWat
floribunda ♀	CB&S CFil CLan CPle CSam CTrw EBee ELan EPfP IDee LRHS MRav SEas SMur SPer WAbe WBod WWat
graebneriana	Last listed 1997
§ x *grandiflora* ♀	More than 30 suppliers
- 'Aurea'	See *A.* x *grandiflora* 'Gold Spot'
- 'Compacta'	LRHS MAsh WWat
- dwarf form	CDoC
§ - 'Francis Mason' (v) ♀	More than 30 suppliers
§ - 'Gold Spot'	CB&S CBlo CDoC CKen CWSG EBee EPfP IOrc LHop MTis MWat SBod SEas SOWG WLRN WPat WPyg WWeb
- 'Gold Strike'	See *A.* x *grandiflora* 'Gold Spot'
- 'Goldsport'	See *A.* x *grandiflora* 'Gold Spot'
§ - Hopleys = 'Abghop'	LHop
- 'Panache' (v)	CLyn CPle
- 'Prostrata'	WWeb
- 'Sunrise' (v)	CAbP ELan LRHS MAsh NPro SMur SPer SPla SSta
- 'Variegata'	See *A.* x *grandiflora* 'Francis Mason'
rupestris Lindley	See *A. chinensis*
- hort.	See *A.* x *grandiflora*
schumannii	CAbP CB&S CBot CFil CHar CMCN CMHG CPle CSam EBee ELan ENot GKir LHop LRHS MAsh MBri SDry SEas SLim SLon SPer WBod WCFE WCot WHCG WPat WPyg WSHC WWat
- 'Bumblebees'	WGer
spathulata	LRHS WWat
triflora	CAbP CBot CFil CPle EPfP LFis LRHS SPla SSta WHCG WPat WSHC WWat
zanderi (Gräbn.) Rehd.	CTrw GQui

ABELIOPHYLLUM (Oleaceae)

distichum	More than 30 suppliers
- Roseum Group	CB&S CFil CPMA EBee EBrP EBre ELan GBuc GKir GOrc LBCl LBSe LBre LHop LRHS MAsh MBBe MRav SBre SEND SLon SSpi WPGP

ABELMOSCHUS (Malvaceae)

§ *manihot*	Last listed 1998

ABIES ✿ (Pinaceae)

alba	CDul EBee LCon MBar NWea
- 'Compacta'	CKen
- 'King's Dwarf'	CKen
- 'Microphylla'	CKen
¶ - 'Munsterland'	CKen
- 'Schwarzwald'	CKen
- 'Tortuosa'	CKen
amabilis	CAgr LCon WFro
- 'Spreading Star'	GKir LCon MAsh
x *arnoldiana*	MBar
balsamea	CAgr LCon NWea
- var. *balsamea*	WFro
- Hudsonia Group ♀	CDoC CFee CKen CMac EHul EPla GChr GKir IMGH IOrc LCon LLin LRHS MAsh MBar MBri MGos MOne NDlv NMen SLim SLon SSmi WDin
- 'Nana'	CKen EBrP EBre EHul EOrn LBCl LBSe LBee LBre LCon LRHS MAsh MBBe MBri SBre SRms WDin WStI
- 'Piccolo'	CKen GKir IMGH WGor
- 'Prostrata'	CBlo ECho LLin LRHS
¶ - 'Verkade's Prostrate'	CKen
borisii-regis	Last listed 1997
* - 'Pendula'	CKen
brachyphylla dwarf	See *A. homolepis* 'Prostrata'
bracteata	Last listed 1999
cephalonica	LCon NWea
§ - 'Meyer's Dwarf'	IMGH LCon LLin MAsh MBar SLim
- 'Nana'	See *A. cephalonica* 'Meyer's Dwarf'
cilicica	NWea
concolor ♀	CB&S CBlo CDoC CDul CTho ECGN GChr GKir IOrc LCon LPan LRHS MBar NWea WFro
- 'Archer's Dwarf'	CKen MGos
- 'Blue Spreader'	CKen MGos
§ - 'Compacta' ♀	CDoC CKen EOrn IMGH LCon LLin LNet LRHS MAsh MBar MGos SLim
- 'Fagerhult'	CKen
- 'Gable's Weeping'	CKen
- 'Glauca'	See *A. concolor* Violacea Group
- 'Glauca Compacta'	See *A. concolor* 'Compacta'
- 'Hillier Broom'	See *A. concolor* 'Hillier's Dwarf'
§ - 'Hillier's Dwarf'	CKen
- 'Husky Pup'	CKen
- (Lowiana Group) 'Creamy'	CKen

	- 'Masonic Broom'	CKen
	- 'Piggelmee'	CKen
*	- 'Swift's Silver'	LRHS WBcn WFro
§	- Violacea Group	CDoC CKen LCon MAsh MBar
	- 'Violacea Prostrata'	Last listed 1998
	- 'Wattezii'	CKen LLin
	- 'Wintergold'	CKen LCon
	delavayi var. *delavayi*	Last listed 1997
	- - Fabri Group	See *A. fabri*
	- 'Major Neishe'	CKen
	- 'Nana Headfort'	See *A. fargesii* 'Headfort'
	- S&F 360	ISea
	- S&F 656	ISea
§	*fabri*	LCon
§	*fargesii* 'Headfort'	CBlo LCon MBar
	firma	COIW NWea
	forrestii var.	Last listed 1999
	georgei S&F 519	
	fraseri	CDoC EWTr LCon NWea WFro WMou
	- 'Kline's Nest'	CKen
¶	- 'Raul's Dwarf'	CKen
	grandis ♀	CB&S CDul ENot GAri GChr Ilve IOrc LCon MBar NWea WDin WMou
	- 'Compacta'	CKen
	bolophylla	LCon
	bomolepis	CDoC CDul LCon NWea
§	- 'Prostrata'	CKen
	kawakamii	Last listed 1997
	koreana	More than 30 suppliers
	- 'Aurea'	See *A. koreana* 'Flava'
	- 'Blaue Zwo'	CKen MAsh
	- 'Blauer Pfiff'	MGos SLim
	- 'Cis'	CKen
	- 'Compact Dwarf'	LCon LLin MBar MGos WAbe
§	- 'Flava'	CDoC CKen ECho GAri IMGH LCon LLin MAsh MBar MBri NHol SLim
	- 'Gait'	CKen
	- 'Golden Dream'	CKen
	- 'Golden Wonder'	COtt
¶	- 'Green Carpet'	CKen
	- 'Inverleith'	CKen
	- 'Kohout'	CKen
¶	- 'Lippetal'	CKen
	- 'Luminetta'	CKen
	- 'Nisbet'	ECho IMGH LRHS
¶	- 'Oberon'	CKen
	- 'Piccolo'	CKen MAsh
	- 'Pinocchio'	CKen
	- 'Prostrata'	See *A. koreana* 'Prostrate Beauty'
§	- 'Prostrate Beauty'	ECho EOrn IMGH
	- 'Silberkugel'	CKen
	- 'Silberlocke' ♀	CBlo CDoC CKen EBrP EBre GAri GKir IOrc LBCl LBSe LBee LBre LCon LLin LPan LRHS MAsh MBBe MBar MBlu MBri MGos NHol SBre SLim SPer SSta
	- 'Silberperl'	CKen
	- 'Silberschmeltzer'	CDoC
	- 'Silver Show'	CKen
	- 'Starker's Dwarf'	CKen
*	- 'Threave'	CKen
	- 'Tundra'	CKen
*	- 'Wittboldt'	CKen
	lasiocarpa	NWea
	- var. *arizonica*	CLnd LCon LPan MBri SSta
	- - 'Argentea'	NWea
	- 'Arizonica Compacta'	CBlo CDoC CKen CMac EBrP EBre EHul IOrc LBCl LBSe LBee LBre LCon LLin LRHS MAsh MBBe MBar MBri MGos NHol SBre SLim SMad
	- 'Compacta' ♀	ECho GKir IMGH WGor
	- 'Day Creek'	CKen
	- 'Duflon'	CKen
	- 'Glauca'	See *A. concolor* Violacea Group
	- 'Green Globe'	CKen MBar NHol
*	- 'Kenwith Blue'	CKen
	- 'King's Blue'	CKen
	- 'Mulligan's Dwarf'	CKen
I	- 'Witch's Broom'	Last listed 1998
	magnifica	LCon LPan WFro
I	- 'Nana'	CKen
	marocana	See *A. pinsapo* var. *marocana*
	nobilis	See *A. procera*
	nordmanniana ♀	CDoC CDul EHul GChr LBuc LCon LPan LRHS MBar MGos NWea SLim WDin WFro WGer WTro WWal
	- 'Barabits' Compact'	MBar
	- 'Barabits' Spreader'	CKen
	- subsp. *equi-trojani* 'Archer'	CKen
	- 'Golden Spreader' ♀	CBlo CDoC CKen EBrP EBre EOrn IMGH LBCl LBSe LBee LCon LLin LRHS MAsh MBBe MBar MBri MGos SBre SLim SPer SSta
	- 'Jakobsen'	CKen
	- 'Pendula'	LPan MBri
	numidica	LPan
	- 'Glauca'	CKen
I	- 'Pendula'	LCon
I	- 'Prostrata'	LPan
	pindrow	CLnd
	pinsapo	GChr LCon LPan LRHS MBar NWea SEND
	- 'Aurea'	CKen
I	- 'Aurea Nana'	CKen
	- 'Glauca' ♀	CDoC CKen CTho GKir IOrc LCon LPan MBar NHol WDin
	- 'Hamondii'	CKen
I	- 'Horstmann'	CKen LLin NHol
	- 'Kelleriis'	LCon
§	- var. *marocana*	Last listed 1997
§	*procera* ♀	CDoC CDul EHul GAri GChr GIBF LCon LRHS MBar NWea WDin WGwG WMou
	- 'Blaue Hexe'	CKen SLim
	- Glauca Group	CDoC CMac EBrP EBre GKir IOrc LBCl LBSe LBre LCon LLin LPan LRHS MAsh MBBe MBar MBri MGos SBre SLim WGer
	- 'Glauca Prostrata'	GAri IOrc LBee LPan LRHS MBar MGos
	- 'Mount Hood'	Last listed 1998
	- 'Sherwoodii'	CKen
	religiosa	Last listed 1997
	Rosemoor form	CKen
	sachalinensis	NWea
	sibirica	LCon NWea
	squamata	Last listed 1998
	veitchii ♀	CB&S CDul LCon MBar NWea
	- 'Hedergott'	CKen
	- 'Heine'	CKen
I	- 'Pendula'	CKen

ABROMEITIELLA (Bromeliaceae)

brevifolia ♀	CFil

ABROTANELLA (Asteraceae)

sp.	ECho

ABRUS (Papilionaceae)
cantoniensis   Last listed 1997
precatorius   Last listed 1997

ABUTILON ✿ (Malvaceae)
'Alpha Glory'   Last listed 1997
'Amiti'   Last listed 1999
'Amsterdam'   ERea
'Ashford Red' ♀   IOrc LRHS SOWG SRms SYvo
                   WWeb
* 'Benary's Giant'   SYvo
'Bloomsbury Can-can' Last listed 1999
'Bloomsbury Rose' Last listed 1999
'Boule de Neige'   CBot EDAr ERea LCns LRHS
                   SOWG SYvo
'Canary Bird' ♀   CB&S CBot CGre CHal CPle EDAr
                   ELan ERea LRHS MLan SYvo WKif
'Cannington Carol' (v) ♀   ERea WSan WWol
'Cannington Peter' (v) ♀   CHal WWol
'Cannington Sally' (v)   SSte
'Cannington Sonia' (v)   ERea
'Cerise Queen'   Last listed 1999
'Cloth of Gold'   LRHS SOWG
'Cynthia Pike' (v) LRHS
§ 'Feuerglocke'   CSev LHop
Firebell   See A. 'Feuerglocke'
'Frances Elizabeth' LRHS SOWG
'Glenroy Snowdrift' Last listed 1999
globosum   See A. x *hybridum*
'Golden Fleece'   ERea IBlr
'Heather Bennington' LRHS SOWG
'Henry Makepeace' LRHS
'Hinton Seedling' CFil
§ x *hybridum*   CHEx
- 'Savitzii'   See A. 'Savitzii'
'J. Morris'   LRHS SMrm
'Kentish Belle' ♀ CAbb CB&S CFil CMHG CMac
                   CPle CSev CWit EBee ECot ECtt
                   EDAr ENot EPVP EPfP IOrc LRHS
                   NTow SBra SEas SLim SPer WWeb
                   CHal
'Lemon Queen'   Last listed 1999
'Louis Marignac'   LRHS SOWG
'Marion' ♀   CMac ERea
'Master Michael'   CB&S CBot CMHG CPle CRHN
megapotamicum ♀ EBee ECtt EDAr ELan ENot EPla
                   ERea GQui LRHS MGos MHer
                   MRav SMad SOWG SPer SRms
                   SSht SUsu WBod WCru WFar
                   WHar WSHC WWat
- 'Variegatum'   CAbb CB&S CBrm CFil CWit ECtt
                   ELan GQui IBlr IOrc LRHS MAsh
                   SAga SBod SEas SLim SOWG SPer
                   SPlb WCru WFar WHar
- 'Wisley Red'   Last listed 1997
x *milleri* ♀   CMac CPLG CRHN ELan ERea
                   IOrc SMrm SVen WSHC
- 'Variegatum'   CB&S CMHG CMac LRHS SEND
                   WWol
'Nabob' ♀   CFil CGre CHal CWit ERea LCns
                   LRHS MBri MTis SLdr SOWG SYvo
'Orange Glow' (v) ♀ Last listed 1995
'Orange King'   Last listed 1999
'Orange Vein'   CHal WWol
otocarpum   Last listed 1998
'Patrick Synge'   CFil CMHG CPle CWit ERea GOrc
                   LCns LRHS SLim SOWG SVen
'Peaches and Cream' LRHS
§ *pictum*   EHol ERea SYvo
- 'Thompsonii' (v) CHal ERea LCns LRHS MLLN SGar
                   SVen WDyG

'Pink Lady'   CB&S EDAr ERea GQui
'Red Bells'   EDAr GQui SVen
'Red Goblin'   Last listed 1998
'Rotterdam'   LCns
§ 'Savitzii' (v) ♀   CB&S CHal EDAr EPfP SOWG
                   SRms SVen
sellowianum   ERea
var. *marmoratum*
'Silver Belle'   Last listed 1999
'Simcox White'   WSPU
'Souvenir de Bonn' (v) ♀ EDAr EHol ERea LCns LRHS
                   MGrG MTis SMrm WWol
striatum hort.   See A. *pictum*
x *suntense*   CB&S CHEx CMHG CMac CPle
                   ELan ERea LHop LHyd NPer
                   SOWG SPer SSta WBod
- 'Jermyns' ♀   CEnd ECtt EPfP LRHS NEgg SSta
                   WEas WFar WPyg
- 'Ralph Gould'   ECGP SMrm
- 'Violetta'   CEnd MAvo SSta
theophrasti   MSal
vitifolium   CB&S CBot CBrm CFil ECot EPfP
                   ERea IOrc ISea MGos MHer NChi
                   NEgg SChu SHFr SYvo WKif
                   WWin WWye
- var. *album*   CAbb CB&S CMHG ELan EPfP
                   ISea LHop LHyd MAvo MHer
                   MLan SChu SEND SSpi SSta WBod
                   WWye
- 'Ice Blue'   CBot
- 'Simcox White'   WEas
- 'Tennant's White' ♀ CAbP CBot CEnd EPfP ERea LRHS
                   SOWG WCot WCru
- 'Veronica Tennant' ♀ CEnd ERea GOrc MSte SLon
                   WPyg

ACACIA ✿ (Mimosaceae)
acinacea   SPlb
adunca   SPlb
alpina   WCel
armata   See A. *paradoxa*
baileyana ♀   CB&S CTrG ECon ECot ELan EMil
                   ERea GQui IDee ISea LCns LRHS
                   SPar SPlb
- 'Purpurea' ♀   CAbb CB&S CBos CDoC CEnd
                   CGdn CGre CTbh CWSG CWit
                   EBee EMil EPfP ERea GQui LHop
                   LRHS MBlu MLan MTis SPer SPlb
                   WCot WMul
§ *binervia*   Last listed 1999
boormanii   ISea WCel
caffra   Last listed 1999
cardiophylla   Last listed 1999
catechu   ERea
cultriformis   Last listed 1999
cyanophylla   See A. *saligna*
dawsonii   Last listed 1999
dealbata ♀   CAbb CB&S CDoC CGre CHEx
                   CPle CTbh CWSG EBee ELan
                   ERea IOrc ISea LCns LPan LRHS
                   MGos MLan MWat SAPC SArc
                   SPer SPlb SRms WBod WNor
                   WPGP WPyg WStI
- 'Gaulois Astier' LRHS
- 'Mirandole'   Last listed 1997
- *prostrata*   Last listed 1998
- 'Rêve d'Or'   Last listed 1997
- *subalpina*   LPan LRHS NHol WCel WMul
                   WPGP
decora   Last listed 1999
decurrens   Last listed 1999
dunnii   Last listed 1998

erioloba		Last listed 1997
Exeter hybrid		CGre
farnesiana		Last listed 1998
filicifolia		LPan WCel
flexifolia		WCel
floribunda		Last listed 1998
- 'Lisette'		ELan EPfP LCns LRHS
frigescens		WCel
galpinii		WMul
gerrardii		Last listed 1999
glaucescens		See *A. binervia*
glaucoptera		Last listed 1998
bowittii		See *A. verniciflua*
julibrissin		See *Albizia julibrissin*
juniperina		See *A. ulicifolia*
karroo		CArn EPVP WMul
kybeanensis		WCel
longifolia		CB&S CHEx EOas IDee LRHS
		NPSI SRms SYvo WCFE
macradenia		SPlb
maidenii		Last listed 1998
mearnsii		CTrC WCel WMul
melanoxylon		ISea LHil LRHS WCel WHer
motteana		ECot ERea
mucronata		CB&S
obliquinervia		WCel
obtusifolia		Last listed 1998
§ **paradoxa**		EHol LCns LRHS
- var. **angustifolia**		Last listed 1999
¶ **pataczekii**		EPfP ERea SSpi
pendula		Last listed 1998
podalyriifolia		CFil WPGP
pravissima		CAbb CB&S CDoC CFil CGre
		CHEx CMFo CMHG CPle CTbh
		CTrC CWit EBee ERea GQui IDee
		LCns LHop LPan LRHS SAPC SArc
		SMur WCel WMul WNor WPGP
pycnantha		Last listed 1999
rebmanniana		Last listed 1998
retinodes ♀		CAbb CB&S CGre CPLG CPle
		ELan EPfP ERea GQui LRHS SEND
		WMul
riceana		CB&S CTrG GQui
rivalis		ERea
rotundifolia		Last listed 1999
rubida		LPan WCel WMul
salicina		Last listed 1999
§ **saligna**		LRHS WCot
senegal		ELau
sentis		See *A. victoriae*
sophorae		Last listed 1999
¶ **spectabilis**		SPlb
stricta		Last listed 1999
¶ **suaveolens**		SPlb
terminalis		Last listed 1998
tortilis		Last listed 1997
trinervis		Last listed 1999
§ **ulicifolia**		CPle CTrG CWit
§ **verniciflua**		Last listed 1999
verticillata		CTrG
¶ - riverine form		CGre
vestita		WCel
§ **victoriae**		ERea
xantbopbloea		WMul

ACAENA (Rosaceae)

adscendens Vahl	See *A. magellanica* subsp.
	laevigata
- Margery Fish	See *A. affinis*
- hort.	See *A. magellanica* subsp.
	magellanica, A. saccaticupula
	'Blue Haze'

- 'Glauca'		CMdw EMan LHop MBel NBir
		NFor
§ **affinis**		COIW ECha SDix
§ **anserinifolia** Druce		EBee ECha MRav NHol WPer
		WWin
§ - hort.		See *A. novae-zelandiae*
buchananii		CTri EBee EDAr EGoo ENot EPot
		GGar GTou LRHS MBar MBri
		MLLN NBro NFor NMGW SRms
		SSmi WHoo WLin WPer WPyg
caerulea		See *A. caesiiglauca*
§ **caesiiglauca**		CNic CRow CTri EBee GAbr
		GGar GTou MWat NBid NFor SBla
		SVal WEas WPer
- CC 451		Last listed 1999
fissistipula		EHoe GAri GGar WHer
glabra		Last listed 1997
glaucophylla		See *A. magellanica* subsp.
		magellanica
'Greencourt Hybrid'		CLyd
inermis		CLyd EBee EPot GMaP GTou
		MLLN SPlb SSmi WPer
§ **magellanica**		EHoe GAri GGar GTou WWin
subsp. **laevigata**		
§ - subsp. **magellanica**		GTou
microphylla ♀		EBee EBrP EBre ECha ESis LBCl
		LBSe LBee LBre LRHS MBBe MBar
		MBri MWat NMen SBre SHFr SIng
		SPlb SRms SSmi SVal WCcr WEas
		WMoo WPer
- Copper Carpet		See *A. microphylla*
		'Kupferteppich'
- 'Glauca'		See *A. caesiiglauca*
§ - 'Kupferteppich'		CLTr EBee EDAr EHoe GAbr GAri
		GGar GKir LRHS MBri MBro
		MCLN MRav MWgw NCat NVic
		SIng WPat WPer WPyg
- var. **pallideolivacea**		CRow
- 'Pewter Carpet'		EGoo SIng
- 'Pulchella'		EBee EBrP EBre EMan LBCl LBSe
		LBre LRHS MBBe SBre
minor		GGar
myriophylla		CInt EBee ECho EDAr EGoo
		EMFP MHar WPer
§ **novae-zelandiae**		CRow CTri EBee GAri GTou SDix
		SIng WPer
ovalifolia		CNic CRow EBee EDAr GTou
		SLod
pallida		Last listed 1998
'Pewter'		See *A. saccaticupula* 'Blue Haze'
pinnatifida		GTou NBro WPer
profundeincisa		See *A. anserinifolia* Druce
'Purple Carpet'		See *A. microphylla*
		'Kupferteppich'
saccaticupula		Last listed 1998
§ - 'Blue Haze'		CGle CLTr CLyd COIW EBee ECha
		EDAr EGoo EPot GGar GKir GTou
		LRHS MBar MBro MLLN MWhi
		NPer NVic SIng SPer SPlb SRms
		WFar WHoo WPer
sanguisorbae		See *A. anserinifolia* Druce
sericea		EBee NMen
viridior		See *A. anserinifolia* Druce

ACALYPHA (Euphorbiaceae)

bispaniolae	ERea
hispida ♀	LRHS MBri
pendula	See *A. reptans*
§ **reptans**	CHal LPVe

ACANTHOCALYX See MORINA

ACANTHOLIMON (Plumbaginaceae)
acerosum var. **acerosum** NWCA
- var. **brachystachyum**   Last listed 1999
androsaceum   See A. ulicinum
armenum   Last listed 1999
confertiflorum   Last listed 1999
glumaceum   MDHE MWat NMen WPat
hilariae   Last listed 1998
hohenackeri   Last listed 1999
trojanum   Last listed 1999
§ **ulicinum**   EPot NWCA
¶ **venustum** var. **venustum** SOkd

ACANTHOPANAX See ELEUTHEROCOCCUS

ACANTHUS ✿ (Acanthaceae)
balcanicus   See A. hungaricus
caroli-alexandri   EBlw LRHS
dioscoridis   LGre
- var. **perringii**   CGle CRDP EBee SBla SSte WCot
    WFar WPGP WPen WSel WViv
- smooth-leaved   Last listed 1999
hirsutus   EBee EMar EMon LGre MMil SCro
    SVal WCot
- JCA 109.700   SBla
- f. **roseus**   WFar
- subsp. **syriacus**   CGle CLon LGre
    JCA 106.500
§ **hungaricus**   More than 30 suppliers
- AL&JS 90097YU   Last listed 1998
longifolius   See A. hungaricus
mollis   More than 30 suppliers
- 'Fielding Gold'   CFir GCal NPro SDix
- free-flowering form   GCal
- 'Hollard's Gold'   CHad CRDP CWes GBin LPio
    MLLN MTed NDov SCob SWat
    WCot WFar
- Latifolius Group   CMGP EBee EFou EGar EMan EPla
    LRHS MRav MSte NHol SChu SPer
    SRms WWal
¶ - var. **niger**   EBrP EBre LBCl LBSe LBre MBBe
    SBre
¶ 'Rue Ledan'   LGre
spinosus ♀   More than 30 suppliers
- 'Lady Moore'   EBee EMon IBlr IHdy WCot WSPU
¶ - 'Royal Haughty'   EFou
- Spinosissimus Group   CGle CMHG CSpe ECha ELan
    EMan GCal LGre LPio MMil MRav
    SAga SBla SWat WCot WCru WFar
syriacus   EBee EMan GCal NLar NPro SAga
    SVal WViv

ACCA (Myrtaceae)
sellowiana (F)   CArn CB&S CDoC CGre CHEx
    CMHG CPle CSam CTrG EBee
    ELan EPla ERea GQui LCns LHil
    LPan LRHS LSpr MCCP MWat
    SLim SOWG WBod WPat WSHC
- 'Apollo' (F)   ERea
- 'Coolidge' (F)   ERea
- 'Mammoth' (F)   CB&S ERea
- 'Triumph' (F)   CB&S ERea
- 'Variegata' (F)   CGre

ACER ✿ (Aceraceae)
acuminatum   CMCN WNor
albopurpurascens   Last listed 1999
argutum   CMCN SFur WCwm WNor
barbinerve   CPMA EPfP SFur WNor

buergerianum   CB&S CBlo CDul CGre CLnd
    CMCN CPMA ECrN GAri GKir
    LRHS MBri STre WCwm WNor
    WWat
- 'Goshiki-kaede' (v)   CPMA LNet
- 'Integrifolium'   See A. buergerianum
    'Subintegrum'
- 'Naruto'   CMCN
§ - 'Subintegrum'   CMCN
- 'Tanchô'   LNet
* - 'Variegatum'   CMCN
caesium   Last listed 1999
calcaratum   CMCN
campbellii   CMCN LNet SFur
- subsp. **flabellatum**   CGre CMCN
- - var. **yunnanense**   CFil CMCN
- - - S&F 533   Last listed 1999
- subsp. **sinense**   See A. sinense
- subsp. **wilsonii**   See A. wilsonii
campestre ♀   More than 30 suppliers
- 'Carnival' (v)   CB&S CBlo CDul CEnd CMCN
    CPMA ELan EPfP GKir LNet LPan
    LRHS MAsh MBlu MBri MGos
    NHol SMad SPer WPGP WWeb
¶ - 'Commodore'   LPan
- 'Elsrijk'   CLnd
- 'Pendulum'   CBlo CEnd CTho
- 'Postelense'   CEnd CMCN CPMA GKir LNet
    MBlu NBea SLim SSpi
- 'Pulverulentum' (v)   CBlo CDoC CEnd CMCN CPMA
    GKir LNet SLim SMad SPer SSta
- 'Queen Elizabeth'   CDul
- 'Red Shine'   MGos
- 'Royal Ruby'   CB&S CMCN CPMA CTho LNet
    NBea SLim SSta
* - 'Ruby Glow'   CBlo CDoC CEnd GChr LRHS
    SPer
- 'Schwerinii'   CMCN
¶ - 'Silver Dawn' (v)   CPMA
- 'William Caldwell'   CEnd CTho LRHS
capillipes ♀   More than 30 suppliers
¶ - B&SWJ 4504   WHCr
- 'Candy Stripe'   GKir SSpi SSta
- var. **morifolium**   See A. morifolium
* - 'Variegatum'   CEnd
cappadocicum   CBlo CMCN CSam GChr LRHS
    MLan NWea WDin WNor WWes
- 'Aureum' ♀   More than 30 suppliers
- var. **mono**   See A. mono
- 'Rubrum' ♀   CBlo CDoC CDul CLnd CMCN
    EBee ECrN ENot EPfP GChr GKir
    IDee IOrc LNet LPan LRHS MBlu
    MGos MRav NBea SMHT SPer
    WDin
- subsp. **sinicum**   CFil CMCN EPfP WWes
carnea 'Variegatum'   Last listed 1997
carpinifolium   CLnd CMCN LNet SFur SSpi WGer
    WNor WPGP WWes
§ - B&SWJ 5086   WHCr
catalpifolium   See A. longipes subsp.
    catalpifolium
§ **caudatifolium**   CMCN WPGP
- B&SWJ 3531   WCru
§ aff. **caudatifolium**   WHCr
    CC 1744
§ - CC 1927   Last listed 1998
§ **caudatum**   SSpi
- subsp. **ukurunduense**   CMCN CPMA SFur WNor
cinerascens   CMCN
cinnamomifolium   See A. coriaceifolium
circinatum ♀   CB&S CDul CMCN CPMA CSam
    CTho ECtt EPfP GChr LNet NBea

	NFor NHol SSpi SSta WDin WFro WNor WWat
- 'Little Gem'	CMCN CPMA LNet
- 'Monroe'	CMCN LNet
- NJM 94038	Last listed 1998
cissifolium	CB&S CDoC CFil CMCN EPfP WNor
x *conspicuum*	CPMA EPfP
'Elephant's Ear'	
- 'Phoenix'	CPMA CTho EPfP GKir LNet LRHS MBlu MBri SSpi
- 'Silver Cardinal'	See *A.* 'Silver Cardinal'
§ - 'Silver Vein'	CMCN CPMA EBee EBrP EBre GKir LBCl LBSe LBre LNet LRHS MBBe MBlu SBre SSpi SSta WGer
§ *cordatum*	CMCN
§ *coriaceifolium*	CMCN WNor
crataegifolium	CMCN WNor
- 'Veitchii' (v)	CDoC CMCN CPMA EPfP GKir LNet SBrw SSpi SSta WBcn WPGP
creticum	See *A. sempervirens*
dasycarpum	See *A. saccharinum*
davidii	CAbP CB&S CBlo CDoC CDul CMCN CMHG CTrg EBee ECrN ENot EWTr GKir IOrc LPan LRHS MAsh MBar MGos MRav MWat NBea SLim SPer WDin WFro WOrn
- 'Ernest Wilson'	CB&S CBlo CMCN GKir LRHS
- 'George Forrest' ♀	CB&S CBlo CDul CMCN CTho EBee EBrP EBre ELan EPfP GChr GKir LBCl LBSe LBre LPan LRHS MAsh MBBe MBri MGos NBea NWea SBod SBre SBrw SEND WDin WOrn
- 'Karmen'	GKir LRHS MBri
- 'Rosalie'	CLyn EPfP GKir LRHS MBlu MBri WWes
- 'Serpentine' ♀	CB&S CDoC CMCN CPMA CTho EPfP GKir IHar LRHS MAsh MBlu MBri SSpi
- 'Silver Vein'	See *A.* x *conspicuum* 'Silver Vein'
diabolicum	CMCN
divergens	CMCN
elegantulum	CGre CMCN WFro WNor
erianthum	CDul CLnd SSpi SSta WNor
fabri	CMCN WNor
flabellatum	See *A. campbellii* subsp. *flabellatum*
§ *forrestii*	CDoC CDul CMCN EPfP NBea WNor
- 'Alice'	CB&S CLyn CMCN CPMA LNet MGos SMad SSpi SSta WBcn WPGP
- PB 57173	
franchetii	CMCN
§ x *freemanii* Autumn Blaze® = 'Jeffersred'	CDoC CPMA EPfP GChr IOrc
- 'Autumn Fantasy'	LNet MBlu
- 'Jeffersred'	See *A.* x *freemanii* Autumn Blaze = 'Jeffersred'
fulvescens	See *A. longipes*
ginnala	See *A. tataricum* subsp. *ginnala*
giraldii	Last listed 1999
glabrum	CLnd CMCN WNor
- subsp. *douglasii*	CLyn CMCN
globosum	See *A. platanoides* 'Globosum'
grandidentatum	See *A. saccharum* subsp. *grandidentatum*
griseum ♀	More than 30 suppliers
grosseri	CB&S CDul CMCN CTri GKir NEgg WFro WLRN
- var. *bersii* ♀	CBlo CDoC CDul CLnd CTho

	EBee ENot GGar GKir LRHS MAsh MBri MRav NBea NWea SLim SPer SRPl WCwm WDin WGer WNor WOrn WPyg WWat
¶ - 'Leiden'	CLnd
beldreichii	CLnd CMCN EPfP WShe
benryi	CB&S CGre CLnd CMCN ENot EPfP GKir LNet MAsh SFur WCwm WNor WWes
x *billieri*	CMCN
bookeri	CMCN
byrcanum	CMCN
japonicum	CDul CMCN GChr LNet LRHS MBar SSta WNor
§ - 'Aconitifolium' ♀	More than 30 suppliers
- 'Attaryi'	CMCN
- 'Aureum'	See *A. shirasawanum* 'Aureum'
- 'Ezo-no-momiji'	See *A. shirasawanum* 'Ezo-no-momiji'
- 'Filicifolium'	See *A. japonicum* 'Aconitifolium'
- 'Green Cascade'	CEnd CMCN CPMA ECho WPat
* - 'King Copse'	Last listed 1999
- 'Laciniatum'	See *A. japonicum* 'Aconitifolium'
- f. *microphyllum*	See *A. shirasawanum* 'Microphyllum'
- 'Ogurayama'	See *A. shirasawanum* 'Ogurayama'
- 'Ô-isami'	CMCN LNet
- 'Ô-taki'	ECho
- 'Vitifolium' ♀	CBlo CDoC CEnd CMCN CPMA ELan EMac EPfP GKir IOrc LNet LPan LRHS MAsh MBlu MBri MLan NPSI SPer SReu SSpi SSta WWeb
kawakamii	See *A. caudatifolium*
laevigatum	CMCN
lanceolatum	CMCN
laxiflorum	CLnd CMCN SFur SSta
lobelii Tenore	CLnd
- Bunge	See *A. turkestanicum*
§ *longipes*	CMCN
¶ - subsp. *amplum*	CMCN WCwm WShe
§ - subsp. *catalpifolium*	CMCN
macrophyllum	CFil CMCN EPfP GKir IDee ISea LHyd SMad
- 'Kimballiae'	CMCN
- NJM 94040	Last listed 1998
- 'Seattle Sentinel'	CMCN
* - 'Variegatum'	CMCN
mandschuricum	CMCN CPMA EPfP LNet MBlu SFur WNor WWoo
§ *maximowiczianum*	CB&S CLnd CMCN CSam CTho ELan GChr IOrc LNet LPan SSpi SSta WNor WWat WWes
maximowiczii	CMCN LRHS MBlu NWea WNor WNor
§ *metcalfii*	CFil CMCN EPfP ESis SSpi WGer WNor WPGP WWes
micranthum ♀	SFur WBod
miyabei	CMCN EPfP MAsh
§ *mono*	CMCN
- 'Hoshiyadori' (v)	WCwm WNor
- subsp. *mono*	CMCN
- 'Shufu-nishiki'	CB&S CFil CMCN GKir
monspessulanum	CMCN
§ *morifolium*	See *A. caudatifolium*
morrisonense	CBlo CCHP CDul CLnd CMCN ECrN ENot EWTr NWea SCrf WNor WTro
negundo	See *A. negundo* 'Variegatum'
- 'Argenteovariegatum'	CBlo CMCN MBar WPat
- 'Auratum'	CB&S MBar
- 'Aureovariegatum'	

- subsp. *californicum*	SFur WNor	
§ - 'Elegans' (v)	CBlo CDul CLnd CMCN COtt	
	EBee EBrP EBre ENot LBCl LBSe	
	LBre LPan LRHS MBBe SBre SPer	
- 'Elegantissimum'	See *A. negundo* 'Elegans'	
- 'Flamingo' (v) ♀	More than 30 suppliers	
- 'Kelly's Gold'	CB&S CBlo CTho EBee EMac	
	LRHS MAsh MGos SLim	
§ - 'Variegatum'	CB&S CBlo CLnd EBee ENot LPan	
	LRHS NBea NBee NWea SPer	
	WDin	
- var. *violaceum* ♀	CB&S CMCN WBcn	
nikoense	See *A. maximowiczianum*	
oblongum	CDoC CMCN	
§ *obtusifolium*	CCHP CMCN	
okomotoanum	CMCN	
oliverianum	CLyn CMCN EPfP SFur WNor	
opalus	CDul CMCN WCwm	
- subsp. *obtusatum*	Last listed 1999	
orientale	See *A. sempervirens*	
Pacific Sunset™	GKir LRHS MBri	
palmatum	CDul CLan CMCN CMHG EBee	
	ENot ESis GChr LHyr LNet LRHS	
	MBar MBlu MBro MLan NBee	
	NWea SBrw SPar SPer SSpi SSta	
	STre WFar WFro WHar WOrn	
	WPat WWat	
§ - 'Aka Shigitatsusawa'	CMCN CMac CPMA GKir LNet	
	LRHS MGos SSpi	
§ - 'Akaji-nishiki'	GKir LRHS MAsh MBri SPla	
- 'Akane'	LNet	
- 'Akegarasu'	CMCN LNet MBri	
- 'Aoba-jo'	CPMA WWes	
- 'Aoshime-no-uchi'	See *A. palmatum* 'Shinobugaoka'	
- 'Aoyagi'	CEnd CMCN CPMA LNet LRHS	
	MAsh WPat WWes	
§ - 'Arakawa'	CMCN LNet	
- 'Aratama'	CMCN CPMA WPat	
- 'Ariadne' (v)	CPMA	
- 'Asahi-zuru' (v)	CBlo CMCN CPMA EBee ECho	
	GKir LNet LPan LRHS MBri MGos	
	NHol NPSI SSta WWes	
- 'Atrolineare'	LNet	
- f. *atropurpureum*	More than 30 suppliers	
- 'Atropurpureum	CBlo CMCN CMac MBri	
Superbum'		
- 'Aureum'	CBlo CMCN CPMA ELan EPfP	
	LNet SBod SSpi	
- Autumn Glory Group	CPMA SSpi WWes	
* - 'Autumn Red'	LPan LRHS	
* - 'Autumn Showers'	CEnd	
- 'Azuma-murasaki'	CMCN CPMA	
- B&SWJ 4474	WCru	
* - 'Beni K Sport'	CPMA	
¶ - 'Beni-chidori'	CPMA	
¶ - 'Beni-hime'	CPMA	
- 'Beni-kagami'	CDul CEnd CMCN CPMA LNet	
	MGos WWes	
- 'Beni-kawa'	LNet	
- 'Beni-komachi'	CB&S CMCN CPMA ECho EMac	
	LNet LRHS MAsh WPat	
- 'Beni-maiko'	CBlo CEnd CMCN CPMA GKir	
	LNet LRHS MBri WPat WWes	
- 'Beni-otake'	CB&S CMCN CPMA ECho EMac	
	LNet LRHS MGos NPSI	
- 'Beni-schichihenge' (v)	CB&S CBlo CCHP CEnd CMCN	
	CPMA ELan EMac EPfP GKir LNet	
	LRHS MAsh NHol SMur SSta WPat	
- 'Beni-shidare Variegated'	CMCN CPMA LNet	
- 'Beni-shigitatsu-sawa'	See *A. palmatum* 'Aka	
	Shigitatsusawa'	
- 'Beni-tsukasa' (v)	CEnd CPMA GKir LNet LPan	

	LRHS MAsh SSpi WPGP WPat	
	WWes	
- 'Berry Dwarf'	WPat	
- 'Bloodgood' ♀	More than 30 suppliers	
- 'Bonfire'	See *A. palmatum* 'Akaji-nishiki'	
- 'Brocade'	CMCN WPat	
- 'Burgundy Lace' ♀	CB&S CBlo CDoC CEnd CMCN	
	CPMA EMil GKir IOrc LNet LRHS	
	MBlu MBri MGos NHol NPSI SPer	
	WPat WPyg	
- 'Butterfly' (v) ♀	More than 30 suppliers	
- 'Carminium'	See *A. palmatum* 'Corallinum'	
- 'Chirimen-nishiki' (v)	CMCN LNet	
- 'Chishio'	See *A. palmatum* 'Shishio'	
- 'Chishio Improved'	See *A. palmatum* 'Shishio	
	Improved'	
- 'Chitoseyama' ♀	CBlo CDul CEnd CMCN COtt	
	CPMA ELan EPfP LNet LRHS	
	MAsh MBar MBri MGos SMur SSpi	
	SSta WPat WWeb	
- 'Coonara Pygmy'	CMCN CPMA ECho EMac LNet	
	LRHS WPat WWes	
- 'Coral Pink'	CPMA	
§ - 'Corallinum'	CBlo CEnd CMCN CPMA GOrc	
	LNet LRHS MGos SSpi WPat	
N - var. *coreanum*	CMCN CSam WNor	
- 'Crippsii'	EMac EMil LRHS WWes	
- 'Deshôjô'	CB&S CBlo CMCN GKir LNet	
	LPan MBlu MGos NHol	
- var. *dissectum* ♀	CDoC CEnd EBee ENot EWTr	
	GKir IOrc LHyd LRHS MBar MBri	
	MGos NBee NHol NWea SBod	
	SBrw SReu SSoC WCFE WDin	
	WFar WNor WPat WPyg WStI	
	WWat	
- - 'Baldsmith'	CPMA	
- - 'Crimson Queen' ♀	CB&S CDoC CDul CEnd CMCN	
	CPMA GKir IOrc LNet LPan LRHS	
	MAsh MBar MBri MBro MGos	
	SPer SSta WFar WGer WNor WPat	
	WPyg WStI	
- - Dissectum	CB&S CPMA EBrP EBre ELan EPfP	
Atropurpureum Group	GKir LBCl LBSe LBre LHyd LNet	
	LPan LRHS MBBe MGos NBea	
	NWea SBre SBrw SLim SPer SReu	
	SSpi SSta WBod WDin WFar WPat	
	WWeb	
¶ - - - 'Pink Filigree'	LPan	
- - 'Dissectum Flavescens'	CEnd CMCN CMac CPMA ISea	
§ - - 'Dissectum Nigrum'	CBlo CPMA CTri GChr LNet LPan	
	LRHS MAsh MGos NBea NHol	
	WLRN WPat	
- - 'Dissectum	LNet LRHS NPSI	
Palmatifidum'		
- - 'Dissectum Rubrifolium'	CMCN	
§ - - 'Dissectum Variegatum'	COtt CPMA EPfP LNet LRHS	
	MAsh SSta	
- - Dissectum Viride Group	CB&S CDul CMCN CPMA ELan	
	EPfP ISea LNet LPan LRHS MAsh	
	MBro MDun NBea NBee NPSI	
	NPri SBrw SLim SPer SPla SSta	
	WBod WWeb	
- - 'Green Globe'	LPan LRHS	
¶ - - 'Green Lace'	LPan	
- - 'Green Mist'	CPMA	
- - 'Inaba-shidare' ♀	CB&S CDoC CEnd CMCN COtt	
	CPMA EMil EPfP GKir IMGH LNet	
	LPan LRHS MAsh MBar MBri	
	MGos NHol SBod SPer SRPI SReu	
	SSta WGer WPat WPyg WWeb	
* - - 'Lionheart'	CPMA ECho EMac EMil LNet	
	LRHS MDun MGos NPSI SPer	

¶ - - 'Nomura-nishiki' (v)	CPMA
¶ - - 'Octopus'	CPMA
- - 'Orangeola'	CPMA LNet WPat
- - 'Ornatum'	CDoC CMCN COtt CTri ECho EWTr IMGH LNet LPan LRHS MBar MGos NBea SBrw SPer SSoC WFar WGer WHar
- - 'Sunset'	CMCN CPMA WPat
¶ - - 'Zaaling'	CPMA ECho
- 'Eddisbury'	CPMA MGos SSta WBod WPat
- 'Effegi'	See *A. palmatum* 'Fireglow'
- 'Elegans'	EPfP MAsh
- 'Ever Red'	See *A. palmatum* var. *dissectum* 'Dissectum Nigrum'
- 'Filigree' (v)	CBlo CDoC CMCN CPMA EPfP GKir LNet LRHS MAsh MGos SSpi WPat
- 'Fior d'Arancio'	CEnd COtt CPMA WWes
§ - 'Fireglow'	CBlo CDoC CEnd CMCN CPMA EMil LPan LRHS MGos WPat WWes
- 'Fjellheim'	WPat
- 'Frederici Guglielmi'	See *A. palmatum* var. *dissectum* 'Dissectum Variegatum'
- 'Garnet' ♀	More than 30 suppliers
- 'Goshiki-kotohime' (v)	CMCN CPMA WPat
- 'Goshiki-shidare' (v)	CEnd CMCN CPMA ISea LNet
- 'Green Trompenburg'	CMCN CPMA LNet
§ - 'Hagoromo'	CDoC CMCN ECho LNet NPSI SPer
- 'Hanami-nishiki'	CMCN CPMA
- 'Harusame' (v)	CMCN LNet
- 'Hazeroino' (v)	CMCN
- var. *heptalobum*	CMCN
§ - 'Heptalobum Elegans'	CBlo CMCN LRHS SSpi
- 'Heptalobum Elegans Purpureum'	See *A. palmatum* 'Hessei'
§ - 'Hessei'	CEnd CMCN GKir LNet LRHS MAsh
- 'Higasayama' (v)	CB&S CDoC CEnd CMCN COtt CPMA LNet LRHS MGos NHol WPGP WPat WWes
- 'Hôgyoku'	CMCN CPMA
- 'Ichigyôji'	CDul CEnd CMCN CPMA LRHS WWeb
- 'Improved Shishio'	See *A. palmatum* 'Shishio Improved'
- 'Inazuma'	CB&S CDoC CMCN ECho LRHS MBri MGos SBod
- 'Jirô-shidare'	LNet LRHS WWeb
- 'Junihitoe'	See *A. shirasawanum* 'Junihitoe'
- 'Kagero' (v)	Last listed 1999
§ - 'Kagiri-nishiki' (v)	CDul CMCN CPMA LNet LRHS MGos NHol SPer WNor
- 'Kamagata'	CDoC CEnd CMCN CPMA EPfP LRHS MGos NPSI SSta WPat WWeb
- 'Karaori-nishiki' (v)	CMCN LNet
- 'Karasugawa' (v)	CMCN CPMA LNet
- 'Kasagiyama'	CEnd CMCN COtt CPMA LRHS ECho
- 'Kasen-nishiki'	ECho
- 'Kashima'	CMCN CPMA ECho LRHS WWes
- 'Katsura'	CB&S CDoC CEnd CMCN COtt CPMA ELan EPfP GKir LPan LRHS MAsh MBlu MBri MGos NHol SPer SRPl SSpi SSta WNor WWeb
- 'Ki-hachijô'	CMCN CPMA
- 'Kinran'	CMCN GKir LNet LRHS MAsh WPat WWeb
- 'Kinshi'	CEnd CMCN CPMA GKir LNet LRHS SSta WWeb WWes
- 'Kiri-nishiki'	CMCN CPMA ECho
- 'Kiyohime'	CDoC CMCN WPat
- 'Komache-hime'	CPMA
- 'Komon-nishiki' (v)	CPMA
- 'Koshibori-nishiki'	CPMA
§ - 'Koshimino'	CPMA LPan
- 'Kotohime'	CMCN CPMA
- 'Koto-ito-komachi'	CPMA ECho WPat
- 'Koto-no-ito'	CMCN LNet
¶ - 'Kurabu-yama'	CMCN
- 'Kurui-jishi'	LNet WPat
- 'Linearilobum' ♀	CMCN EPfP LHyd LNet LRHS MBlu NBea NHol WNor WPat
- 'Linearilobum Atropurpureum'	LRHS WNor
- 'Little Princess'	See *A. palmatum* 'Mapi-no-machihime'
- 'Lutescens'	CMCN CPMA ECho
- 'Maiko'	CMCN ECho
- 'Mama'	CMCN
§ - 'Mapi-no-machihime'	CDoC CEnd CMCN CPMA ELan GKir LNet LRHS MAsh NHol SMur WPat WWat WWeb WWes
- 'Masamurasaki'	WPat
- 'Masukagami' (v)	CEnd CPMA
- 'Matsukaze'	CMCN COtt CPMA WWes
* - 'Mikasayama'	WWeb
- 'Mikawa-yatsubusa'	CMCN CPMA EMac LRHS WPat WWes
- 'Mirte'	LNet
- 'Mizuho-beni'	CPMA
- 'Mizu-kuguri'	CMCN
- 'Momenshide'	WPat
¶ - 'Mon Papa'	CPMA
- 'Monzukushi'	CMCN
- 'Moonfire'	CMCN CPMA ELan EPfP GKir LNet LRHS MAsh SSpi WWeb
¶ - 'Murasaki-kiyohime'	CMCN CPMA ECho WPat
- 'Mure-hibari'	CMCN CPMA
- 'Murogawa'	CMCN CPMA
- 'Nicholsonii'	CMCN LPan LRHS WPat
- 'Nigrum'	CMCN LNet WPat
§ - 'Nishiki-gawa'	CMCN CPMA LNet
- 'Nishiki-momiji'	Last listed 1998
- 'Nomurishidare'	See *A. palmatum* 'Shôjô-shidare' misapplied
- 'Nomurishidare' Wada	SSpi
- 'Nuresagi'	CMCN CPMA LNet
- 'Ogon-sarasa'	CPMA
- 'Ô-kagami'	CDoC CEnd CMCN CPMA ECho EMac LNet LRHS MBlu MBri MGos SBod SSta
- 'Okukuji-nishiki'	CBlo CPMA LNet
- 'Okushimo'	CDoC CEnd CMCN CPMA LNet LRHS WPat
- 'Omato'	LNet
- 'Omurayama'	CDoC CEnd CMCN CPMA EPfP LNet LRHS MGos SSta WPat WWeb WWes
§ - 'Ô-nishiki'	CMCN LNet
- 'Orange Dream'	CMCN CPMA LNet LPan LRHS MBri WWes
- 'Oregon Sunset'	CMCN
- 'Orido-nishiki' (v)	CEnd CMCN COtt CPMA ELan EPfP LNet LRHS MAsh MGos NBea NBee SCoo SRPl SSta
- 'Ôsakazuki' ♀	More than 30 suppliers
- 'Ôshio-beni'	CPMA ECho
- 'Ôshû-beni'	CMCN
- 'Ôshû-shidare'	CMCN CPMA MBri WPat
- 'Otome-zakura'	CMCN
- 'Peaches and Cream' (v)	CPMA
- 'Pendulum Julian'	CMCN

	CMCN COtt EBee EBrP EBre ENot GKir IArd LBCl LBSe LBre LBuc LNet LRHS MAsh MBBe MBri MGos MLan SBre SLim WHar WLRN WOrn WWeb
- 'Cucullatum'	CMCN CTho
- 'Deborah'	CDul CLnd CTho EWTr LPan
- 'Dissectum'	CTho GKir
- 'Drummondii' (v) ♀	More than 30 suppliers
- 'Emerald Queen'	CDoC CLnd CMCN ENot EWTr WOrn
- 'Faassen's Black'	LPan
§ - 'Globosum'	CLnd CMCN EBee ENot LPan MGos
- 'Goldsworth Purple'	CLnd CMCN
- 'Laciniatum'	CEnd CMCN ENot GKir SPer
- 'Lorbergii'	See *A. platanoides* 'Palmatifidum'
- 'Olmsted'	ENot LNet
§ - 'Palmatifidum'	CSam
§ - 'Prigo'^PBR	See *A. platanoides* Princeton Gold = 'Prigo'
- Princeton Gold = 'Prigo'^PBR	CDoC EBee GKir LPan LRHS MBri
- 'Pyramidale Nanum'	Last listed 1999
- 'Royal Red'	CBlo CDul CMCN EBee ENot EWTr LPan MGos
- 'Schwedleri' ♀	CBlo CDul CLnd CMCN MGos NBee NWea SPer
- 'Summershade'	Last listed 1999
- 'Tharandt'	CMCN
¶ - 'Walderseei'	CLnd
pseudoplatanus	CB&S CBlo CDul CKin CLnd CMCN CTri ENot GChr GKir LBuc LHyr LPan MBar MGos NWea SPer WDin WHar WMou
§ - 'Atropurpureum' ♀	CBlo CDoC CDul CLnd CTho ENot IOrc NBee NWea SMHT WOrn
- 'Brilliantissimum' ♀	More than 30 suppliers
- 'Constant P.'	ENot
- 'Corstorphinense'	CMCN
- 'Erectum'	EBee ENot WOrn
- 'Erythrocarpum'	CMCN
N - 'Leopoldii' (v) ♀	CB&S CBlo CDoC CDul CLnd CMCN COtt CTho ECrN ELan ENot EPfP EWTr IOrc LPan MAsh NBea NBee SLim SPer WOrn
- 'Negenia'	Last listed 1998
- 'Nizetii' (v)	CMCN LRHS MBri
- 'Prinz Handjéry'	CB&S CBlo CDoC CDul CEnd CMCN CTri EWTr LNet LPan LRHS MAsh MBar MGos NWea SLim SPer WFoF WHar
- 'Simon-Louis Frères' (v)	CBlo CDul CEnd CLnd CMCN EBee EMui GChr LNet LPan LRHS MAsh MBri MDun MGos MWat NBea SLim SPer WFoF WHar
N - 'Spaethii' hort.	See *A. pseudoplatanus* 'Atropurpureum'
- 'Spring Gold'	MGos
- f. *variegatum*	Last listed 1999
- 'Worley' ♀	CB&S CBlo CDoC CDul CLnd CMCN COtt EBee ECrN ENot EPfP GChr IOrc LPan LRHS NBea NBee NWea SLim SPer WDin WHar WOrn
pseudosieboldianum	CFil CMCN GKir SSpi WNor WPGP
- MSF 861	Last listed 1998
pubipalmatum	WNor
pycnanthum	CMCN
robustum	CMCN WNor

rubescens	CLnd SFur
rubrum	CB&S CBlo CDoC CDul CGre CLnd CMCN CTri EBee ECrN GCHN GKir LHyr LRHS MGos MLan MWat NBea NBee NWea SLim SPer WDin WNor WWat
- 'Armstrong'	Last listed 1997
- 'Bowhall'	CMCN
- 'Columnare'	CMCN
- 'Elstead'	LNet
- 'Morgan'	CEnd
- October Glory® ♀	CBlo CDoC CDul CEnd CMCN CMHG CPMA CTho GChr GKir IOrc LPan LRHS MAsh MBlu MBri NWea SPer SSpi SSta WCwm WPat WWeb
- Red Sunset	CDoC CEnd CMCN CPMA CTho LPan LRHS MBlu MBri MSad SSpi SSta WCwm
- 'Schlesingeri'	CEnd CMCN CPMA EBee MBlu SSta
- 'Tilford'	SSta
§ **rufinerve** ♀	CB&S CBlo CDoC CDul CLnd CMCN CMHG CSam CTho CTri ENot EPfP ESis EWTr GChr IOrc LPan LRHS MBri NBea NBee NWea SPer SSpi WDin WGer WNor WOrn WPyg WStI
- 'Albolimbatum'	See *A. rufinerve* 'Hatsuyuki'
- 'Albomarginatum'	See *A. rufinerve* 'Hatsuyuki'
¶ - B&SWJ 5108	WHCr
- 'Erythrocladum'	CPMA LNet
§ - 'Hatsuyuki' (v)	CBlo CDoC CEnd CMCN CPMA ELan GKir LRHS SSpi WPGP
§ **saccharinum** ♀	CB&S CBlo CDul CLnd CMCN EBee ELan ENot EPfP EWTr GChr LHyr MGos MLan MWat NBee NWea SPer SRPl SSpi WDin WFar WNor
- 'Born's Gracious'	GChr IOrc
- 'Fastigiatum'	See *A. saccharinum* f. *pyramidale*
- f. *laciniatum*	CMCN EBee ENot LRHS MBlu MGos WDin
- 'Laciniatum Wieri'	CLnd CMCN CTho LPan MGos NBee
- f. *lutescens*	CDul CMCN CTho ENot MBlu NWea
§ - f. *pyramidale*	CBlo CDoC CLnd CMCN ENot EPfP IOrc LPan
saccharum	CAgr CDoC CDul CLnd CMCN EPfP LPan MLan NWea SPer WCwm WNor
- subsp. *barbatum*	See *A. saccharum* subsp. *floridanum*
§ - subsp. *floridanum*	CMCN
§ - subsp. *grandidentatum*	CMCN
§ - subsp. *leucoderme*	CMCN
§ - subsp. *nigrum*	CMCN
- - 'Temple's Upright'	CMCN LNet
- subsp. *skutchii*	CMCN
'Scanlon' ♀	CB&S CDul CEnd CLnd CMCN CTho LRHS WOrn
§ **sempervirens**	CFil CMCN
serrulatum	CMCN
- CC 1891	Last listed 1997
§ **shirasawanum**	CDul CMCN WNor
§ - 'Aureum' ♀	More than 30 suppliers
§ - 'Ezo-no-momiji'	CDul CMCN CPMA
§ - 'Junihitoe'	WNor
§ - 'Microphyllum'	CMCN LNet WNor
§ - 'Ogurayama'	CPMA LNet
- 'Palmatifolium'	CBlo CMCN CPMA MGos WStI

- var. **tenuifolium**	CLyn WNor
sieboldianum	CLnd CMCN CTri ECho EPfP ESis GAri SSpi WNor
- 'Sode-no-uchi'	CMCN
sikkimense	See *A. metcalfii*
subsp. **metcalfii**	
§ 'Silver Cardinal' (v)	CB&S CEnd CPMA LNet MGos SMad SSpi WWes
'Silver Vein'	See *A.* x *conspicuum* 'Silver Vein'
§ **sinense**	CMCN GIBF SFur WNor
- var. **pubinerve**	Last listed 1998
¶ sp. B&SWJ 6245	WHCr
¶ sp. B&SWJ 6341	WHCr
sp. CC 1648	Last listed 1997
spicatum	CMCN WNor
§ **stachyophyllum**	GQui
§ **sterculiaceum**	CMCN WPGP WWes
syriacum	See *A. obtusifolium*
taronense	CMCN
tataricum	CMCN
§ - subsp. **ginnala** ♀	CB&S CBlo CDul CLnd CMCN CTho EBee ECrN ELan ENot EPfP EPla GChr GKir IOrc LRHS MGos NBea NWea SLim SPer WDin WNor WWat
- - 'Durand Dwarf'	CMCN
- - 'Fire'	LNet
- - 'Flame'	CBlo CLnd CPMA EBee EPfP GKir LRHS MGos WWoo
- subsp. **semenowii**	CMCN
tegmentosum	CMCN CPMA SFur WNor WWoo
- subsp. **glaucorufinerve**	See *A. rufinerve*
tenellum	Last listed 1997
tenuifolium	CMCN
tetramerum	See *A. stachyophyllum*
thomsonii	Last listed 1998
trautvetteri	CMCN WNor WTro
triflorum	CLnd CMCN CTho EPfP GChr IArd IMGH LRHS NWea SFur SSpi WWat WWes
truncatum	CMCN GKir WCwm WNor WOTO
- 'Akaji-nishiki'	See *A. palmatum* 'Akaji-nishiki'
- 'Akikaze-nishiki' (v)	CPMA LNet SFur
tschonoskii	CDoC CMCN GQui WWes
- subsp. **koreanum**	CDoC CPMA SFur WNor
§ **turkestanicum**	CMCN
velutinum	CMCN
¶ - var. **vanvolxemii**	WPGP
villosum	See *A. sterculiaceum*
¶ 'White Tigress'	GKir
§ **wilsonii**	CMCN CSam SFur WNor WShe
x **zoeschense**	CMCN
- 'Annae'	CPMA IOrc

ACERAS (Orchidaceae)

anthropophorum	EFEx

ACERIPHYLLUM See MUKDENIA

x ACHICODONIA (Gesneriaceae)

§ 'Cornell Gem'	NMos
¶ 'Dark Velvet'	WDib

ACHILLEA ✿ (Asteraceae)

abrotanoides	Last listed 1999
ageratifolia ♀	ECha ECtt LBee LRHS MBro MTho NMen SRms SSca SSmi WByw WFar
- subsp. **ageratifolia**	Last listed 1998
§ - subsp. **aizoon**	WPer
- subsp. **serbica**	NBro
§ **ageratum**	CArn CSev ELau GBar GPoy IIve

	MChe MHer MSal SIde WGwG WHer WJek WOak WPer WWye
- 'W.B. Childs'	CGle CPlt CSpe EBee ECha EGle ELan GBuc LGre MArl MAvo MNrw MSte SUsu WCot WEas
'Alabaster'	CLon CRDP CSli EFou EMon EPPr GBuc LGre LRHS MBel NCiC
'Anblo'^PBR	See *A.* Anthea = 'Anblo'
§ Anthea = 'Anblo'^PBR	CHad CMGP CSpe CWit EBee EBrP EBre EGle EMan GKir GSki LBCl LBSe LBre LFis LGre LRHS MBBe MBro MCLN MLLN SBre SMad SWat WFar WWat
§ 'Apfelblüte'	More than 30 suppliers
Appleblossom	See *A.* 'Apfelblüte'
argentea hort.	See *A. clavennae*, *A. umbellata*
- Lamarck	See *Tanacetum argenteum*
aurea	See *A. chrysocoma*
'Bahama'	EBee EPPr GBuc NBro NFai
¶ 'Belle Epoque'	LGre
'Bloodstone'	CSli EGar EMan EPPr GMac WBea WWhi
brachyphylla	EPot
cartilaginea	EFou EGar MTed WCot WFar WMoo
- 'Silver Spray'	EBee SRCN WWpP
chamaemelifolia	WHil
§ **chrysocoma**	MWat NMen NTow SSmi
- 'Grandiflora'	CHad CHar MGrG NGdn
§ **clavennae**	CGle EPot GCHN LBee LPio LRHS MWat NMen NTow SBla SIng SMer SMrm SRms WAbe WCot WFar WKif
clypeolata Sibth. & Sm.	GOrP LPio NFla SPlb SRms
coarctata	NBir WElm WPer
'Coronation Gold' ♀	CBlo CDoC CWit EBee EFou ELan EMan ENot EPfP GKir GMac LAst LFis LGre LRHS MBri MCAu MCLN MChl MMil MWat MWgw SPer WEas
'Credo'	More than 30 suppliers
* 'Crimson King'	Last listed 1997
'Croftway'	SCro
decolorans	See *A. ageratum*
erba-rotta	EWTr NBro
subsp. **moschata**	
- subsp. **rupestris**	CMea MDHE SMer WPer
§ 'Fanal'	More than 30 suppliers
'Faust'	EFou
'Feuerland'	More than 30 suppliers
filipendulina	NSti SWat
- 'Cloth of Gold'	More than 30 suppliers
- 'Gold Plate' ♀	CDoC CHad EBee EBrP EBre ECha ECtt EFou ELan GKir LBCl LBSe LBre MBBe MCLN MLan MMil MWgw NOrc NTow SBre SCro SHel SPer SRms WCot WEas
- 'Parker's Variety'	COIW EGar EMil EMon GBuc LRHS MBri MLan NOak SRCN WFar WPnP
Flowers of Sulphur	See *A.* 'Schwefelblüte'
'Forncett Beauty'	CSli EFou NBrk SChu WWhi
'Forncett Bride'	CSli EFou
'Forncett Candy'	CSli EFou
I 'Forncett Citrus'	EFou
'Forncett Fletton'	CSli EBee EFou EGle EMar EPPr GBri LFis MBel MCAu NBrk NDov SAga SCro SHel SUsu WCot WViv
'Forncett Ivory'	CSli EFou
fraasii	WPer
glaberrima	NDov
¶ - hybrid	WCot

grandifolia — CBos CBre CPou CSam EBee EGle EMan EMar EMon GCal IHdy LEdu LGre LRHS MSte NBro NPSI NSti SMad SSvw WBea WFar WHal WHer WWye

'Great Expectations' — See *A.* 'Hoffnung'

'Hartington White' — EMon GBuc MWgw

'Hella Glashoff' — CSli EMon LGre NBrk SAga WCot

§ 'Hoffnung' — CBlo CMGP CSli EBee EBrP EBre ECtt EGle EMan GSki LBCl LBSe LBre LHop MBBe NBrk SBre SCro SPer SSpe WLRN WPer WWin

boloseriecea NS 747 — Last listed 1998

'Huteri' — CInt CLyd CPea ECtt EDAr EGoo EMNN EPot ESis GMaP LBee LRHS MBro MHer MRav NCat NFor NMen NNrd NRya SBla SChu SSmi WAbe WEas WFar WPer WWin

'Inca Gold' — CSli EBee ECha EGle EMan EPPr GBri MCLN SChu SUsu SWat

x *jaborneggii* — Last listed 1999

'Jambo' — Last listed 1998

'James Chapman' — Last listed 1997

x *kellereri* — MBro MDHE SAsh SSmi

'Kempsey Buttermilk' — Last listed 1999

x *kolbiana* — EMan MWat NHol NMen SDys SRms SSmi WHoo WLin WPat WWin

§ - 'Weston' — NTow

§ 'Lachsschönheit' — More than 30 suppliers

x *lewisii* — NMen

- 'King Edward' ♀ — CMHG CSam EBrP EBre ECha EDAr ESis LBCl LBSe LBee LBre LRHS MBBe MTho NBir NMGW NTow SBla SBre SChu SIng SSmi WFar

'Libella' — GBuc

'Lucky Break' — SDix

'Lusaka' — Last listed 1998

macrophylla — EBee EMar

'Marmalade' — CSli EFou EMon SMrm SUsu SWat

'Martina' — CDoC CM&M CSli EBee ECha EFou EGoo EMan EMar EMon EPPr GBuc GMac LAst LRHS MLLN NCat NOrc NTow SVil WPGP

'McVities' — CSli EFou EGle EPPr GBin LFis MLLN MSph SWat WCot WHal WRus WTin

millefolium — CArn CGle COld EEls ELau EWFC GBar GPoy MHew NHex NLan NMir SIde WHbs WHer WOak WSel WWye

- 'Burgundy' — Last listed 1998

- 'Carla Hussey' — MTed WFar

- 'Cerise Queen' — More than 30 suppliers

- 'Colorado' — CFri CM&M COlW CPou EWTr SRCN STes WBea

- dark red — CSli LRHS

- 'Fire King' — CHal

- 'Lansdorferglut' — LRHS MBri MRav MTed

- 'Lavender Beauty' — See *A. millefolium* 'Lilac Beauty'

§ - 'Lilac Beauty' — CBlo CGle CSli CSpe EBee ECha EMan EWTr LRHS MBel MRav SAga SUsu WElm WFar WHal WHoo WMaN WPer WWhi

* - 'Lilac Queen' — CMGP CSli MArl SWat

- 'Malmesbury' (v) — CNat

- 'Melanie' — Last listed 1999

- 'Paprika' — CBlo CElw CPar CRDP CSli EBee EGle GBuc GKir LRHS MAvo

---

MBNS MBel MBri MCLN MCli MLLN NFai SBod SMad SPla SRCN SWat WBro WByw WElm WMaN WPer WRus WWhi

* - 'Pastel Shades' — MNaF

¶ - 'Pink Trophy' — LBmB

- 'Red Beauty' — CSli EWTr LRHS MTis SAga SRms SWat WOve

- f. *rosea* — Last listed 1999

- 'Sammetriese' — CSli EFou EGle ELan EMon EPPr GBuc LRHS MAvo MSte SMad WElm WHoo WPnP WPyg WRHF WWhi

¶ - 'Summertime' — SBod

- 'Sweet Harmony' — Last listed 1997

- 'Tickled Pink' — WPer

- 'White Queen' — EWTr WPer

'Mondpagode' — CSli EGle EPPr LGre SAga

* 'Moonbeam' — GKir

'Moonlight' — MBro

'Moonshine' ♀ — More than 30 suppliers

'Moonwalker' — CBlo CSli EBee EWTr LRHS MLLN SIde WFar WPer WRHF

'Nakuru' — NCat

nobilis subsp. *neilreichii* — CElw CRDP CSli CSpe EGoo EMar EMon EPPr LFis MLLN SAga WCot WHal WOve

'Peter Davis' — See *Hippolytia herderi*

pindicola — EWes
  subsp. *integrifolia*

¶ 'Prospero' — LFis MBro MSte NDov WBea

ptarmica — CArn CKin ELau EWFC EWTr GBar IIve MChe MHer MHew MSal NEgg NMir SIde SPer WGwy WWye

* - 'Ballerina' — NCat NDov NLar

- 'Boughton Beauty' — NLar

- Innocence — See *A. ptarmica* 'Unschuld'

- 'Major' — Last listed 1998

- 'Nana Compacta' — ECha EFou EGle EPPr LRHS MBri MCAu NFor SMrm SPlb SUsu WCFE WCot WMaN

- 'Perry's White' — CBre EBee ECha EMon GCal NCat WByw WCot

- 'Stephanie Cohen' — CStr EBee GOrP MAvo MLLN MSph NDov WCot WMaN

N - (The Pearl Group) 'Boule de Neige' (clonal) (d) — CBlo CHal LRHS MBri NPer NSti SPer SPla WFar WGwG WLRN WWal

N - - seed-raised (d) — More than 30 suppliers

N - - 'The Pearl' (clonal) (d) — EWTr NBid SRms WEas WFar WHer WPnP WWat

§ - 'Unschuld' — NBir

I 'Rose Madder' — WCot

'Sandstone' — See *A.* 'Wesersandstein'

§ 'Schwefelblüte' — LFis NBir

'Schwellenburg' — EBee EGle EPPr

sibirica — LPio WElm

- AGS 1241 — Last listed 1999

¶ - var. *camschatica* — CBrm EPPr NChi SSvw WBea WHil

- 'Love Parade' — WHil

- 'Kiku-san' — Last listed 1998

'Smiling Queen' — Last listed 1998

'Summer Glory' — SCro

Summer Pastels Group — CM&M COlW EMan EMil GCHN GKir LRHS MFir NArg NBus NMir NOak NOrc SEas SRCN SRms SWat WLRN WPer WRha

'Summerwine' — CFri CPlt CSli EBee ECha EFou EGle EMar EPPr GBri LGre MNrw MRav NDov SAga SChu SCro

		SMad STes SUsu SWat WHil WMaN WRus
I	'Taygetea'	CBot CFri CGle CSam CSli ECha EFou ELan EMan EWTr GMaP MCAu MWat NSti SChu SDix SPer SUsu SWat WByw WCot WFar WKif WOve WPer WRus WSHC
	'Terracotta'	More than 30 suppliers
	'The Beacon'	See A. 'Fanal'
	tomentosa ♀	CTri ECha ECtt EPfP NEgg NNrd SWat
§	- 'Aurea'	CHal EBot ECtt ELau LPVe MOne MSCN NBro SIde SRCN SRms WPer WRos
	- 'Maynard's Gold'	See A. *tomentosa* 'Aurea'
§	*umbellata*	CLyd NTow
	- NS 390	Last listed 1997
	- 'Weston'	See A. x *kolbiana* 'Weston'
	'Walther Funcke'	CElw CHad CHea CLon CMdw CRDP CSli CSpe EBee EFou EGle EMan EMil EMon EPPr LFis LGre LRHS MBri MWat NDov NPro SAga SMrm SUsu WCot WHil WRus
§	'Wesersandstein'	CSli EBee EFou EMan EMon EPPr GMac LFis LRHS MAvo MBri SBod WCot WElm WMaN WPer WWhi
	'Wilczekii'	NChi SRms

x ACHIMENANTHA (Gesneriaceae)

	'Cerulean Mink'	See x *Smithicodonia* 'Cerulean Mink'
	'Dutch Treat'	NMos
	'Ginger Peachy'	NMos
	'Inferno'	NMos WDib
*	'Rose Bouquet'	NMos
	'Royal'	NMos

ACHIMENES (Gesneriaceae)

	'Adelaide'	Last listed 1998
	'Adèle Delahaute'	Last listed 1998
	'Adonis Blue'	Last listed 1998
	'Almandine'	NMos
	'Ambleside'	Last listed 1998
	'Ambroise Verschaffelt'	LAma NMos WDib
	'Ami Van Houtte'	NMos
	'Ann Marie'	NMos
	'Apricot Glow'	NMos
	'Aquamarine'	NMos
*	'Aries'	Last listed 1997
	'Bassenthwaite'	NMos
	'Bea'	Last listed 1998
	'Bernice'	NMos
	'Blauer Planet'	NMos
	'Bloodstone'	NMos
	'Blue Gown'	NMos
	'Brilliant'	NMos
	'Butterfield Bronze'	NMos
	'Buttermere'	NMos
	'Camberwell Beauty'	NMos
	'Cameo Rose'	NMos
	'Cameo Triumph'	NMos
	'Camille Brozzoni'	NMos
	candida	NMos
	'Carmine Queen'	NMos
	'Cascade Cockade'	NMos
	'Cascade Evening Glow'	NMos
	'Cascade Fairy Pink'	Last listed 1998
	'Cascade Fashionable Pink'	NMos
	'Cascade Rosy Red'	NMos
	'Cascade Violet Night'	NMos
	'Cattleya'	LAma

	'Chalkhill Blue'	Last listed 1998
	'Charm'	NMos
	'Clouded Yellow'	NMos
	'Compact Great Rosy Red'	NMos
	'Coniston Water'	NMos
	'Copeland Boy'	NMos
	'Copeland Girl'	NMos
	'Coral Sunset'	NMos
	'Cornell Favourite 'A''	NMos
	'Cornell Favourite 'B''	NMos
	'Crimson Beauty'	NMos
	'Crimson Glory'	NMos
	'Crimson Tiger'	Last listed 1998
	'Crummock Water'	NMos
	'Cupido'	NMos
	'Dentoniana'	Last listed 1998
	'Derwentwater'	NMos
	'Dorothy'	NMos
	'Dot'	NMos
	dulcis	NMos
	'Early Arnold'	NMos
	'Elke Michelssen'	NMos
	'English Waltz'	NMos
	erecta	WDib
	'Escheriana'	NMos
	'Flamenco'	NMos
	'Flamingo'	SDeJ
	flava	NMos
	'Fritz Michelssen'	NMos
	'Gary John'	NMos
	'Gary/Jennifer'	NMos
	'Grape Wine'	NMos
	'Grasmere'	NMos
	'Harry Williams'	LAma
§	'Harveyi'	NMos
	'Haweswater'	NMos
	'Hilda Michelssen'	NMos WDib
	'Honey Gold'	NMos
	'Ida Michelssen'	NMos
	'India'	NMos
§	'Jaureguia Maxima'	NMos
	'Jennifer Goode'	NMos
	'Jewell Blue'	NMos
	'Johanna Michelssen'	NMos
	'Jubilee Gem'	NMos
	'Lakeland Lady'	NMos
	'Lavender Fancy'	Last listed 1998
	'Little Beauty'	NMos
	'Little Red Tiger'	NMos
	longiflora	
	- 'Alba'	See A. 'Jaureguia Maxima'
	- 'Major'	NMos
	'Magnificent'	NMos
	'Marie'	NMos
	'Masterpiece'	NMos
	'Maxima'	LAma
	'Menuett '80'	NMos
	'Milton'	NMos
	misera	NMos
	'Moonstone'	NMos
	'Old Rose Pink'	LAma NMos
¶	'Orange Delight'	WDib
	'Orange Queen'	NMos
	'Pally'	NMos
	'Panic Pink'	NMos
	'Patens Major'	NMos
	'Patricia'	Last listed 1998
	'Paul Arnold'	NMos
	'Peach Blossom'	LAma NMos
	'Peach Glow'	NMos
	'Peacock'	Last listed 1998
	'Pearly Queen'	NMos

'Pendant Blue' NMos
'Pendant Purple' NMos
'Petticoat Pink' NMos
'Pink Beauty' NMos
'Pinocchio' NMos
'Prima Donna' NMos
'Pulcherrima' Last listed 1999
'Purple King' NMos
'Queen of Sheba' Last listed 1998
'Quickstep' NMos
'Rachael' NMos
'Red Admiral' NMos
'Red Giant' NMos
'Red Imp' Last listed 1998
'Red Top Hybrid' NMos
'Robin' NMos
'Rosenelfe' NMos
'Rosy Doll' NMos
'Rosy Frost' NMos
'Rydal Water' NMos
'Scafell' NMos
* *selloana* Last listed 1997
'Shirley Dwarf White' NMos
'Shirley Fireglow' See *A.* 'Harveyi'
'Show-off' NMos
'Silver Wedding' NMos
'Snow Princess' SDeJ
Snow White See *A.* 'Schneewittchen'
'Sparkle' NMos
'Stan's Delight' NMos WDib
'Sue' NMos
'Tango' NMos
'Tantivvy' Last listed 1998
'Tarantella' NMos
'Teresa' NMos
'Tiny Blue' NMos
'Topsy' NMos
'Troutbeck' NMos
'Ullswater' NMos
'Vanessa' NMos
'Viola Michelssen' NMos
'Violacea Semiplena' NMos
'Vivid' LAma NMos
'Warren' NMos
'Wastwater' NMos
'Wetterflow's Triumph' NMos
'White Admiral' NMos
'White Rajah' NMos
'Wilma' NMos
'Windermere' NMos

ACHLYS (Berberidaceae)
japonica WCru
triphylla EMar GBuc WCru

ACHNATHERUM See STIPA

ACHYRANTHES (Amaranthaceae)
bidentata CArn ELau IIve

ACIDANTHERA See GLADIOLUS

ACINOS (Lamiaceae)
§ *alpinus* CArn EBee SBla
- subsp. *meridionalis* EGle NTow
§ *arvensis* MBri MHer MSal
§ *corsicus* ESis LFis MBro NWCA SIde SRCN
WHoo WPat WWin

ACIPHYLLA (Apiaceae)
aurea GCal ITim NHar
- CC 464 Last listed 1997

colensoi Last listed 1998
* - *major* Last listed 1997
crenulata Last listed 1999
crosby-smithii Last listed 1997
dobsonii Last listed 1999
glaucescens NHar
hectoris Last listed 1999
horrida WCot
kirkii Last listed 1998
'Lomond' Last listed 1999
lyallii Last listed 1998
maxima Last listed 1999
monroi Last listed 1997
montana Last listed 1999
pinnatifida GCal GCrs NHar NMen
scott-thomsonii Last listed 1999
simplex EPot
squarrosa ECou GCal
subflabellata ECou GAbr GCal NHar SIng

ACNISTUS (Solanaceae)
australis See *Iochroma australe*

ACOELORRHAPHE (Arecaceae)
wrightii CBrP EOas LPal

ACONITUM ✿ (Ranunculaceae)
alboviolaceum GCal
anglicum See *A. napellus* subsp. *napellus*
Anglicum Group
anthora IHdy LPio MTis NLar
arcuatum B&SWJ 864 WCot WCru
N *autumnale* NBir
bartlettii B&SWJ 337 CFri EBee EMan WCru
'Blue Sceptre' EBrP EBre LBCl LBSe LBre MBBe
SBre SRms
'Bressingham Spire' ♀ More than 30 suppliers
x *cammarum* 'Bicolor' ♀ More than 30 suppliers
- 'Grandiflorum Album' LGre SAga
§ *carmichaelii* CArn CBot CGle CLon EBee EFou
EMan GAbr GKir GMac IBlr IHdy
LRHS MBro MRav NChi NFla
NFor NGdn NOrc SCro SRms
WBod WHoo WPnP
- 'Arendsii' More than 30 suppliers
- Wilsonii Group CHad CHar EBee GGar LGre
LRHS MBri MRav MSte MWat
NChi SAga SChu SSoC WFar
WOve WPer WWin WWye
§ - - 'Barker's Variety' CPou CRow EGle EMan GBuc
LGre MFir NHol NSti WCot
- - 'Kelmscott' ♀ EBee ECGN EGle EMon MSte
MWgw SAga SDix WByw WFar
WRHF
- - 'Spätlese' GCal WCot
- - 'The Grim Reaper' EMon
cilicicum See *Eranthis hyemalis* Cilicica
Group
compactum See *A. napellus* subsp. *vulgare*
deflexum Last listed 1998
'Eleonara' CFir EPfP GBuc GKir LRHS MCli
MRav WFar WHil
elliotii GBin
elwesii EBee GGar
episcopale CPIN GCrs NDov WCru WFar
aff. *episcopale* CLD 1426 GBuc LPio WCot WFar
ferox EBee
fischeri hort. See *A. carmichaelii*
fukutomei var. WCru
formosanum
B&SWJ 3057
gymnandrum Last listed 1997

§ *hemsleyanum* — CBot CGle CPlN CRow EBee GAbr IBlr LGre MFir MSCN NBid NSti SAga SMad WBor WBrE WCot WCru WEas WHoo WWhi
- dark blue — CMea
- *latisectum* — IBlr
heterophyllum — Last listed 1998
hyemale — See *Eranthis hyemalis*
'Ivorine' — More than 30 suppliers
japonicum — EBee
lamarckii — See *A. lycoctonum* subsp. *neapolitanum*
lycoctonum — EWll GCrs MCAu SRms SSoC
- 'Dark Eyes' — EBee ECGN NBrk WCot
§ - subsp. *lycoctonum* — CBlo GKir MSal SRms
- subsp. *moldavicum* — EBee
§ - subsp. *neapolitanum* — CBlo CLon EBee ELan EMFP EMan EMar EPfP GCal LAst LRHS MLLN NHol NLar NSti SWat WHil
§ - subsp. *vulparia* — CArn EBee ECGN ECha ECtt EFou EGar GCal GPoy IHdy LRHS MAvo MRav MSal WByw WEas WSan WWye
napellus — More than 30 suppliers
- 'Albiflorus' — See *A. napellus* subsp. *vulgare* 'Albidum'
- 'Bergfürst' — EBee LGre LPio MTed
- 'Blue Valley' — EBee EMan EPfP NPSI WHil
- 'Carneum' — See *A. napellus* subsp. *vulgare* 'Carneum'
§ - subsp. *napellus* Anglicum Group — CRow CSev EBee GBuc GSki IBlr MMal MSal MSte NSti WCot WPen
- 'Rubellum' — EBrP EBre EMar LBCl LBSe LBre MBBe MCli NBro NPri SBre WHil WPnP WSpi
- 'Sphere's Variety' — NOrc WPyg
- subsp. *tauricum* — Last listed 1998
§ - subsp. *vulgare* 'Albidum' — More than 30 suppliers
§ - - 'Carneum' — EBee ELan EMan EMon GKir GMac MLLN MRav WByw WCot WEas WElm WHer WHoo WKif WLin WWin WWye
¶ *napiforme* B&SWJ 943 — WCru
neapolitanum — See *A. lycoctonum* subsp. *neapolitanum*
'Newry Blue' — CHad EBee ELan GBuc GKir GSki IHdy LRHS MBri MRav MWll NHol SRms WFar WPer WRHF
orientale hort. — See *A. lycoctonum* subsp. *vulparia*
paniculatum — EBee MBri
- 'Roseum' — LRHS MBNS SPer SSvw
aff. *pendulum* KGB 762 — Last listed 1999
¶ 'Pink Sensation' — LGre
pyrenaicum — See *A. lycoctonum* subsp. *neapolitanum*
ranunculifolius — See *A. lycoctonum* subsp. *neapolitanum*
sczukinii — EMon WCru
seoulense B&SWJ 1005 — Last listed 1999
septentrionale — See *A. lycoctonum* subsp. *lycoctonum*
sp. ACE 1449 — GBuc
sp. B&SWJ 2652 from Sikkim, climbing — Last listed 1999
sp. B&SWJ 2954 from Nepal — WCru
'Spark's Variety' ♀ — More than 30 suppliers
spicatum — EBee
'Stainless Steel' — CBlo CHea CSpe GBri GKir GMaP LGre LRHS MBri MChl SCro WCot WHil

---

stapfianum B&L 12038 — Last listed 1997
¶ 'Tissington Pearl' — MTis
x *tubergenii* — See *Eranthis hyemalis* Tubergenii Group
variegatum — EBee
¶ *vilmorinianum* — MFir
volubile hort. — See *A. hemsleyanum*
vulparia — See *A. lycoctonum* subsp. *vulparia*

ACONOGONON See PERSICARIA

ACORUS ✿ (Araceae)
calamus — CAgr CArn CRow CWat EHon ELau EWFC GPoy LPBA MCCP MHew MSal MSta NDea SWat SWyc WHer WMAq WWeb
- 'Argenteostriatus' (v) — CB&S CBen CRow CWat EHon ECtt EHon EMFW EPfP GCal LHil LNor LPBA MSta NDea NOrc SLon SPer SWat SWyc WMAq
- 'Purpureus' — Last listed 1998
gramineus — CRow EMFW LPBA LRot MLan SWat WHer
- 'Hakuro-nishiki' (v) — CBod CChe CInt COtt CRow EBee EOrn GDea LRHS MCCP MMoz NBea NOGN SCob SLim SMad SPla SSoC SVil WMoo WRHF WRus
I - 'Licorice' — LRHS WBea WCHb WCot WWpP
- 'Masamune' (v) — EBee EPla GBri GCal LFis MSCN NPro WCFE WCot WLeb WSPU
N - 'Oborozuki' (v) — CRow EBee EGle EPla NPro
N - 'Ogon' (v) — More than 30 suppliers
- 'Pusillus' — CRow EBee EPPr EPla LHil NBro
- 'Variegatus' — More than 30 suppliers
- 'Yodo-no-yuki' (v) — CRow EBee EPla

ACRADENIA (Rutaceae)
frankliniae — CB&S CFil CMHG CPLG CPle CTrG GEil GGar IBlr LRHS SSpi WBod WPGP WSHC

ACRIDOCARPUS (Malpighiaceae)
natalitius — CPlN

ACROCLADIUM See CALLIERGON

ACTAEA (Ranunculaceae)
alba — See *A. pachypoda*, *A. rubra* f. *neglecta*
asiatica — EBee GBin
- B&SWJ 616 — WCru
erythrocarpa — See *A. rubra*
§ *pachypoda* ♀ — CBrd CLyd CPou CRow ECGN ECha EGle EPar EPla GPoy GTou IBlr LRHS MFir MSal NLar WCru WWat WWye
- f. *rubrocarpa* — EBee
§ *rubra* ♀ — More than 30 suppliers
- *alba* — See *A. pachypoda*, *A. rubra* f. *neglecta*
§ - f. *neglecta* — EBee GBuc GKir IHdy SMad SSpi WCru WWat
§ *spicata* — CRDP EBee GBuc GLil GPoy LRHS MSal MSte NLar NSti NWoo WCot WCru
- var. *rubra* — See *A. rubra*

ACTINELLA (Asteraceae)
scaposa — See *Tetraneuris scaposa*

ACTINIDIA ✿ (Actinidiaceae)

arguta	CAgr CFil CPlN WPGP
- B&SWJ 569	WCru
- 'Issai' (s-p/F)	CB&S EBee ERea LBuc MGos
- (m)	Last listed 1999
- 'Weiki'	MGos
callosa	CPlN
- var. *ephippioidea* B&SWJ 1790	WCru
- var. *formosana* B&SWJ 3806	WCru
chinensis hort.	See *A. deliciosa*
¶ *coriacea*	CPlN
§ *deliciosa*	CGre CMac CWit ELan EMil ERom MGos WCru WSHC WStI
- (f/F)	NBea WDin
- (m/F)	NBea WDin
- 'Atlas'	MBri SLim
- 'Blake' (s-p/F)	Last listed 1998
* - 'Boskoop'	Last listed 1999
- 'Bruno' (f/F)	SLim
- 'Hayward' (f/F)	CB&S CDoC CHEx CHad COtt CPlN EBee EBrP EBre ELan EMil EMui ERea IOrc LBCl LBSe LBre LRHS MAsh MBBe MBri MGos MWat SBre SDea SPer SSta WCru WStI
- 'Jenny' (s-p/F)	CMac LBuc LRHS MGos SDea
- 'Solo'	CDoC
- 'Tomuri' (m)	CB&S CDoC CHEx CHad COtt CPlN EBee EBrP EBre ELan EMil EMui ERea IOrc LBCl LBSe LBre LRHS MAsh MBBe MGos MWat SBre SPer SSht SSta WCru WStI
giraldii	CMac
kolomikta ♀	More than 30 suppliers
¶ - B&SWJ 4243	WCru
latifolia B&SWJ 3563	WCru
melanandra	CPlN
pilosula	CFil CPlN EMil GCal GOrc SBrw SLon WCru WPGP WSHC
polygama (F)	CPlN GKir
purpurea	CPlN
rubricaulis B&SWJ 3111	WCru
rufa B&SWJ 3525	WCru
sp. from China	Last listed 1999
tetramera B&SWJ 3664	Last listed 1999

ADELOCARYUM See LINDELOFIA

ADENOCARPUS (Papilionaceae)
decorticans	CTrC

ADENOPHORA ✿ (Campanulaceae)

'Afterglow'	See *Campanula rapunculoides* 'Afterglow'
* *asiatica*	WFar
aurita	CB&S CFir CMea CRDP EBee EMan EWll GGar MHar MLLN NCiC NSti NWoo SWat WCot
axilliflora	Last listed 1997
bulleyana	CBrd COIW EBee EBrP EBre ECGN EGle ELan EMan EOld EWTr GBuc GMac IBlr IHdy LBCl LBSe LBre LRHS MBBe MSCN NBid NPri SBre SRot WFar WHoo WLin WMoo WPer
* *campanulata*	WPer
coelestis	EBee EMan GCal SRot
- ACE 2455	EPot GBuc WCot
confusa	EBee EGar EMan GAbr LHop

	MAnH WFar WHer
coronopifolia	Last listed 1997
cymerae	EBee
divaricata	EMan WFoF
forrestii	WFar
- var. *bandeliana* KGB 86	Last listed 1998
himalayana	EGle GBri MNrw WCot WPer
khasiana	CBlo CFir CPea EBee EGle GAbr MNrw NFai NSti SCob WCot WPrP WWin
koreana	EBee
latifolia Fischer	EBee GBri NBir WElm
- hort.	See *A. pereskiifolia*
liliifolia	CHea EBee ECtt EEls ELan EMan GAbr GCal LRHS NBro NCat NPer NSti SCro SMrm SRot SWat WCot WFar WMaN WPer WPrP WPyg
§ *nikoensis*	EBee MNrw NBid NWCA
* - *alba*	Last listed 1999
§ - var. *stenophylla*	Last listed 1999
nipponica	See *A. nikoensis* var. *stenophylla*
§ *pereskiifolia*	CMGP EBee EGar NBus WCot WElm WPer
- 'Alba'	Last listed 1997
- var. *heterotricha*	Last listed 1997
- *uryuensis*	Last listed 1997
polyantha	CPea EBee EMan GAbr GBuc GMac LRHS MNrw SRms WPic WPrP
polymorpha	See *A. nikoensis*
potaninii	CFir CHea EBee EGle EGra EMan GBuc GMac IHdy MGrG MNrw NSti WFar WHal WMoo WWhi
- 'Alba'	Last listed 1997
- lilac	Last listed 1997
- white	WHal
remotiflora	Last listed 1998
sp. from Yunnan	Last listed 1997
stricta	LRHS MLan WWeb
- subsp. *sessilifolia*	EBee GMac
sublata	EBee EGar WFar
takedae	Last listed 1997
- var. *howozana*	EBee NSti
tashiroi	CLyd CNic EBee GAbr GBri GBuc MBro MNrw NBro SCob SCro SHel WHoo
triphylla	EMan GAbr GCal WFar
- var. *hakusanensis*	Last listed 1999
- var. *japonica*	EBee
- var. *puellaris*	Last listed 1997
uehatae	Last listed 1997
- B&SWJ 126	WCru

ADENOSTYLES (Asteraceae)
alpina	See *Cacalia glabra*

ADIANTUM ✿ (Adiantaceae)

aethiopicum	Last listed 1999
§ *aleuticum* ♀	CCuc CFil CLAP CRDP EFer ELan EMon IOrc NBro NBus NHol NMar SBla SCob WHal WPGP WRic WWat
- 'Laciniatum'	CFil SRms WRic
* - f. *minimum*	SCob SLon SRms
¶ - 'Miss Sharples'	CLAP LRHS NMar SPla SRms WRic
capillus-veneris	CHEx MWat
- 'Banksianum'	Last listed 1999
- 'Cornubiense'	Last listed 1999
- 'Mairisii'	See *A.* x *mairisii*
- 'Pointonii'	NMar
concinnum	Last listed 1998

cuneatum	See *A. raddianum*
diaphanum	NMar
edgeworthii	Last listed 1999
formosum	Last listed 1999
henslowianum	Last listed 1999
hispidulum	LRHS NMar SRms
jordanii	CFil
§ x *mairisii* ♀	NMar
* *monocolor*	MBri
pedatum ♀	CBos CCuc CFil CGle CHEx CLAP CRDP EBee EBrP EBre ECha EFer ELan EPVP LBCl LBSe LBre LRHS MBBe MBri NBus NHol SApp SBre SChu SPer SSpi SWat WPGP WWat
- var. *aleuticum*	See *A. aleuticum*
- Asiatic form	See *A. pedatum* 'Japonicum'
- 'Imbricatum'	CCuc ECha LRHS NHar NHol NMar SBla SRms
§ - 'Japonicum'	CBos CFil CLAP CMil CRDP EBee ELan LRHS MBri NBir SEas SRms SSpi WCru WHal WPGP WRic
- 'Roseum'	See *A. pedatum* 'Japonicum'
- var. *subpumilum*	See *A. aleuticum* 'Subpumilum'
peruvianum	MBri
pubescens	MBri NMar
§ *raddianum* ♀	CFil CHal NMar
- 'Brilliantelse' ♀	NMar
- 'Crested Majus'	NMar
- 'Crested Micropinnulum'	NMar
- 'Deflexum'	NMar
- 'Double Leaflet'	NMar
- 'Elegans'	NMar
- 'Feltham Beauty'	NMar
- 'Fragrans'	See *A. raddianum* 'Fragrantissimum'
- 'Fragrantissimum'	MBri NMar
- 'Fritz Luthi' ♀	CHal LRHS MBri NMar
- 'Gracilis'	See *A. raddianum* 'Gracillimum'
§ - 'Gracillimum'	NMar
- 'Grandiceps'	NMar
- 'Gympie Gold'	NMar
- 'Kensington Gem' ♀	NMar
- 'Legrand Morgan'	NMar
- 'Legrandii'	NMar
- 'Micropinnulum'	NMar
- 'Pacific Maid'	NMar
- 'Pacottii'	NMar
- 'Triumph'	NMar
- 'Tuffy Tips'	NMar
- 'Variegated Pacottii'	NMar
- 'Variegated Tessellate'	NMar
- 'Victoria's Elegans'	NMar
- 'Weigandii'	NMar
tenerum 'Green Glory'	NMar
venustum ♀	CCuc CFil CGle CLAP CRDP EFer EGle ELan EMon GCal NBus NMar SBla SDix SRms SSpi SWat WCot WEas WFib WPGP WRic
whitei	NMar

ADLUMIA (Papaveraceae)

fungosa	CGle CPlN CSpe EBrP EBre GAri IHdy LBCl LBSe LBre LRHS MBBe MCCP MLLN NSti SBre WCru WPnP

ADONIS (Ranunculaceae)

aestivalis	Last listed 1997
amurensis	EPar EPot LAma LRHS
- 'Flore Pleno' (d)	EBrP EBre EPar GKir LBCl LBSe LBre LRHS MBBe MBri MTed SBod SBre SPer WCot WFar

- 'Fukujukai'	ECha WFar
annua	EWFC MHew
brevistyla	EPot GCrs NSla NTow WAbe
dahurica	Last listed 1999
multiflora	WCru
pyrenaica	Last listed 1998
sutchuenensis	Last listed 1999
vernalis	EPar GPoy MMHG NCut NEgg WCot

ADOXA (Adoxaceae)

moschatellina	CKin EWFC WGwy WHer WShi WWye

ADROMISCHUS (Crassulaceae)

¶ *cooperi*	WEas

AECHMEA (Bromeliaceae)

chantinii ♀	Last listed 1996
fasciata ♀	LRHS MBri SSte
Foster's Favorite Group ♀	Last listed 1997
* *fulgens* var. *discolor* ♀	Last listed 1990
gamosepala	Last listed 1997
nudicaulis ♀	Last listed 1995
orlandiana ♀	Last listed 1995

AEGLE (Rutaceae)

sepiaria	See *Poncirus trifoliata*

AEGOPODIUM (Apiaceae)

podagraria 'Bengt'	EMon
- 'Dangerous' (v)	CHid CNat WCHb
- 'Hullavington' (v)	Last listed 1997
- 'Variegatum'	More than 30 suppliers

AEONIUM (Crassulaceae)

arboreum ♀	CAbb CHEx WHal WIvy WRos
* - 'Arnold Schwarzkopff'	CAbb CPLG CSpe ERea SAPC SArc SPet WIvy
- 'Atropurpureum' ♀	CHEx CWit ERav ERea IBlr LHil MBri MLan NPer SEND WEas
* - 'Magnificum'	SAPC SArc
- 'Variegatum'	LHil NPer
balsamiferum	CHEx CTbh LHil SArc SChr WHal
canariense	CAbb CHEx EBee LHil WHal
§ - var. *subplanum*	Last listed 1999
cuneatum	CTbh SAPC SPet SVen
* *decorum* 'Variegatum' (v)	Last listed 1998
'Dinner Plate'	CHEx
x *domesticum*	See *Aichryson* x *domesticum*
glandulosum	Last listed 1999
haworthii ♀	CHEx CHal CTbh CTrC LHil SSte
- 'Variegatum'	SChr
holochrysum	IBlr
§ x *hybridum*	Last listed 1999
laxum	Last listed 1999
lindleyi	SChr
manriqueorum	Last listed 1999
nobile	CAbb
percarneum	Last listed 1998
simsii	CHEx CHal CTbh SChr
spathulatum	Last listed 1999
subplanum	See *A. canariense* var. *subplanum*
tabuliforme ♀	Last listed 1998
undulatum ♀	CHEx
urbicum	CHEx
'Zwartkop' ♀	CHEx CTbh EOas NPer WCot WEas WHal WRos

AESCHYNANTHUS (Gesneriaceae)

'Big Apple'	WDib
Black Pagoda Group	WDib

'Fire Wheel'	WDib
hildebrandii	WDib
'Hot Flash'	WDib
lobbianus	See *A. radicans*
longicalyx	WDib
§ *longicaulis* ♀	LRHS WDib
marmoratus	See *A. longicaulis*
'Mira'	MBri
'Mona'	MBri
parvifolius	See *A. radicans*
I 'Pulobbia'	Last listed 1999
'Purple Star'	Last listed 1999
§ *radicans*	EBak MBri
- lobbianus	See *A. radicans*
'Rigel'	Last listed 1999
* *rigidus*	Last listed 1997
speciosus ♀	CHal WDib
* *- rubens*	Last listed 1999
'Topaz'	Last listed 1999

AESCULUS ✿ (Hippocastanaceae)

arguta	See *A. glabra* var. *arguta*
x *arnoldiana*	CDul CFil CMCN MBlu
- 'Autumn Splendor'	CLyn
assamica	WPGP
§ x *bushii*	CDul CFil CMCN CSam CTho
californica	CB&S CFil CMCN CSam CTho
	CTrw EPfP ERod IDee LFis SMad
	SSpi WPGP WWat
x *carnea*	CDul ELan MBar
- 'Aureomarginata'	ERod SMad WPat
- 'Briotii' ♀	More than 30 suppliers
- 'Marginata' (v)	CLyn
- 'Plantierensis'	CDul CTho ENot MBlu SMHT
	WPGP
* - 'Variegata' (v)	CDul CMCN LRHS MBlu
chinensis	CMCN MBlu
'Dallimorei'	EBee SMad WPGP
(graft-chimaera)	
§ *flava* ♀	CFil CMCN CTho EBee ENot
	GChr MMea SPer SSpi WCwm
	WPGP
- x *pavia*	See *A. x hybrida*
- f. *vestita*	CDul MBlu
georgiana	See *A. sylvatica*
glabra	CDul CFil CLnd CMCN CTho
	LRHS WPGP
§ - var. *arguta*	CFil CMCN GKir WPGP
- 'October Red'	CFil MBlu WPGP
glaucescens	See *A. x neglecta*
hippocastanum ♀	More than 30 suppliers
- 'Aureomarginata' (v)	GKir
§ - 'Baumannii' (d) ♀	CBlo CDoC CDul CLnd COtt EBee
	ECrN ENot EPfP ERod EWTr
	GChr GKir LPan LRHS MAsh
	MBlu MBri MGos NBee NWea
	SPer WDin WStI
- 'Digitata'	CDul CMCN GKir LRHS
- 'Flore Pleno'	See *A. hippocastanum*
	'Baumannii'
- 'Globosa'	See *A. hippocastanum*
	'Umbraculifera'
- 'Hampton Court Gold'	CB&S CDul CEnd CMCN GKir
	LPan
- 'Honiton Gold'	CTho
- 'Laciniata'	CDul CMCN ERod GKir IDee
	LRHS MBlu SMad
- 'Pyramidalis'	CLnd LPan
§ - 'Umbraculifera'	SMad
- 'Wisselink'	CMCN MBlu SMad
§ x *hybrida*	CFil SSpi WCwm WPGP
indica ♀	CDul CHEx CLnd CMCN CSam

	CTho CTrw EBee ELan ENot EC
	IOrc LRHS MBlu MBri NWea SLdr
	SPer SRPl SSpi WCwm WDin
	WPGP
- 'Sydney Pearce'	CDoC CEnd CFil CMCN ERod
	GKir IOrc MBlu MGos MMea
	SMad SPer SSpi WPGP
x *marylandica*	CDul
x *mississippiensis*	See *A. x bushii*
x *mutabilis* 'Harbisonii'	Last listed 1998
- 'Induta'	CFil CLnd LRHS MBlu MBri SSpi
	WPGP WWes
§ - 'Penduliflora'	CB&S CDul CEnd CFil CTho EPfP
	LRHS MBlu SMad
§ x *neglecta*	CB&S CDul CLnd CMCN
* - 'Autumn Fire'	CLyn SMad WPGP
- 'Erythroblastos' ♀	CB&S CDoC CEnd CFil CLnd
	CMCN CTho EBee EPfP ERod
	GKir LNet LRHS MBlu SMad SSpi
	WPGP WPat
parviflora ♀	CB&S CBlo CDul CFil CGre CLnd
	CMCN CTho EBee ELan ENot
	GChr IDee LNet LPan MBlu MGos
	NFla SMad SPer SSpi WDin WPGP
	WWat
§ *pavia* ♀	CB&S CDul CFil CLnd CMCN
	CTho EPfP GKir ISea LRHS SSpi
	WWoo
- 'Atrosanguinea'	CBlo CDul CEnd CFil CMCN
	ERod LRHS SMad SSpi WPGP
¶ - var. *discolor*	CFil WPGP
- - 'Koehnei'	CDoC LRHS MBri
- 'Penduliflora'	See *A. x mutabilis* 'Penduliflora'
- 'Rosea Nana'	CMCN MBlu
splendens	See *A. pavia*
§ *sylvatica*	CFil CLnd CTho WPGP
turbinata	CB&S CLnd CMCN IDee MBlu
	WCwm
¶ - var. *pubescens*	WPGP
wilsonii	CB&S
x *woerlitzensis*	WCwm

AETHIONEMA (Brassicaceae)

armenum	MLan WLin
coridifolium	NBus WPer
§ *euonomioides*	NTow
§ *grandiflorum* ♀	NBro NTow SBla SRms WPer
- Pulchellum Group ♀	CLyd EPot GKir MBro NMen
	WWin
iberideum	MOne MWat SRms
oppositifolium	CLyd GTou MBro MWat NMen
	WHoo WPyg
pulchellum	See *A. grandiflorum*
rotundifolium	SIng
schistosum	Last listed 1999
'Warley Rose' ♀	CLyd EDAr ELan EPot GKir LHop
	MBro MWat NFor NHol NMen
	NRya NWCA SIng SRms WHil
	WHoo WPat WPyg WWin
'Warley Ruber'	CLyd CNic EDAr NBir NHol SIng
	WAbe

AEXTOXICON (Aextoxicaceae)

punctatum	CGre

AFROCARPUS (Podocarpaceae)

falcatus	CGre ECou GCal

AGAPANTHUS ✿ (Alliaceae)

I 'Accebt'	Last listed 1997
¶ 'Accent'	WFar
§ *africanus* ♀	CElw CFri CStr EBee EPfP GSki

		IBlr LRHS MBNS NRog SAPC SArc SPar SWat WPer
*	- 'Albus' ♀	CB&S CDoC CHEx CHad EBee EMan EPfP EWTr GSki IBlr LFis LRHS MBNS NBlu SEND SPla SYvo WHil WPer
*	- 'Big Blue'	CDoC
	'Albatross'	ECha
I	*alboroseus*	Last listed 1997
*	'Albus'	CM&M MHer
I	'Albus Nanus'	Last listed 1999
I	'Albus Roseus'	Last listed 1999
	'Arctic Star'	ERav
	Ardernei hybrid	CBot CFil EBee ECha EWes GCal IBlr LGre MTed NCat SSpi WCot WPGP
	'Baby Blue'	CLyd IBlr LRHS SApp
	'Ballyrogan'	IBlr
¶	'Beeches Dwarf'	EBee
	'Ben Hope'	GBuc
	'Bethlehem Star'	ERav
¶	'Bicton Bluebell'	IBlr
	'Bleuet'	Last listed 1997
	'Blue Baby'	CB&S LRHS WFar
	'Blue Bird'	EBee
¶	'Blue Cascade'	IBlr
	'Blue Companion'	IBlr
¶	'Blue Fortune'	WGer
	'Blue Giant'	CBro EBee EWTr IBlr LRHS MTed NCut NHaw SPla SRPl SWat WFar WPyg
	'Blue Globe'	EBee EMan GMaP GMac LAst MCAu SCro
	'Blue Gown'	CPne
	'Blue Imp'	ECtt GBuc GSki IBlr MMHG NHol
	'Blue Mercury'	IBlr
	'Blue Moon'	CAvo CBro CHad ECha EGle IBlr LRHS MTed SEND SLod WCot
	'Blue Nile'	Last listed 1998
	'Blue Skies'	CB&S EBee
	'Blue Triumphator'	CBlo EBee EPfP EWll IBlr LBow LFis LRHS MTed WCot
	'Blue Velvet'	CPne
	'Bressingham Blue'	CBlo CBro CTri EBee EBrP EBre GCal IBlr LBCl LBSe LBre LRHS MBBe MRav MSte NVic SBre SSpe SWat
	'Bressingham Bounty'	EBrP EBre LBCl LBSe LBre MBBe SBre
	'Bressingham White'	CGle EBee EBrP EBre ECtt EFou GCHN GMac LBCl LBSe LBre LRHS MBBe MBri MCLN MRav MTed SBre SSpe SWat WRus WWat
	'Buckingham Palace'	CBro CFil EBee IBlr
	Cambourne hybrids	MBri
§	*campanulatus*	CGle CMGP CRDP EBee ELan ERav GDra GGar GSki ISea LRHS NChi SCro SLon SWat WCot WLRN
	- var. *albidus*	CHad CRDP EBee EBrP EBre ECha ELan EMan ENot IBlr LBCl LBSe LBre LHop LRHS MBBe MSte NFla NGdn NHol NSti NVic SBre SChu SPer SRPl SSpi WCot WFar
	- 'Albus Nanus'	See A. 'Albus Nanus'
	- bright blue	GCal
	- 'Buckland'	IBlr
¶	- subsp. *campanulatus* 'Albovittatus' (v)	CLAP CSam ECho LGre
	- 'Cobalt Blue'	ECha WCot
¶	- dwarf blue	WLin
	- 'Isis'	CBro CFir CTri EBee EBrP EBre ECha GBuc GCHN IBlr IHdy LBCl LBSe LBre LRHS MBBe SBre
	- 'Meibont' (v)	WCot
	- 'Oxbridge'	See A. 'Oxbridge'
	- 'Oxford Blue'	GBri IBlr
	- subsp. *patens* ♀	CPne EBee EMan GBri GBuc MTed SSpi SWat WHil
	- - - deep blue form	CFir IBlr
	- 'Premier'	IBlr
	- 'Profusion'	CBro EBrP EBre ECha IBlr LBCl LBSe LBre LRHS MBBe SBre SSpi WFar
§	- 'Rosewarne'	CB&S GQui IBlr
	- 'Slieve Donard Variety'	IBlr
	- 'Spokes'	IBlr
	- variegated	ECha NPer
	- 'Wedgwood Blue'	IBlr
	- 'Wendy'	IBlr
	- 'White Hope'	IBlr
	- 'White Triumphator'	WCot
	'Castle of Mey'	CFil CPlt EGle IBlr LGre LHyd MTho
	caulescens ♀	IBlr WCot
	- subsp. *angustifolius*	IBlr WCot WHil
	- subsp. *caulescens*	SWat
	'Cedric Morris'	ERav IBlr
	'Chandra'	IBlr
	'Charlie Morrell'	LHil
	'Cherry Holley'	Last listed 1999
¶	'Clarence House'	CBro
	coddii	EBee EMan IBlr LPio LRHS SVen
	comptonii	CAvo CFir CPou IBlr SYvo
	- subsp. *comptonii*	SWat
	- subsp. *longitubus*	SWat
	Danube	See A. 'Donau'
¶	'Dayspring'	CRow
	'Delft'	IBlr
	'Density'	IBlr
§	'Donau'	EBee MTed NCut WFar
	dyeri	IBlr
	'Eve'	EBee
	'Evening Star'	EBee ERav LRHS
	'Far Horizon'	Last listed 1999
	'Findlay's Blue'	EBee WCot
*	'Gayle's Lilac'	WCDu WCot
	giant hybrids	Last listed 1999
¶	'Glacier Stream'	WSpi WViv
	'Golden Rule' (v)	CFir CRow EBee IBlr LHil SSpi WPGP
	'Goliath'	ERav
§	Headbourne hybrids	More than 30 suppliers
	'Holbrook'	CSam
	'Hydon Mist'	LHyd
	'Ice Blue Star'	ERav
¶	'Ice Lolly'	WViv
	inapertus	CFil CRDP SBla SWat WCot
¶	- 'Graskop'	SWat
	- subsp. *bollandii*	CAvo GCal IBlr MSte SWat WCot WHil
	- subsp. *inapertus*	SWat WCot
	- subsp. *intermedius*	EBee GCal IBlr SWat
	- subsp. *pendulus*	IBlr
	Johannesberg hybrids	ECha
	'Kalmthout Blue'	EBee WWat
	'Kalmthout White'	MLan
	'Kew White'	SDix
	'Kingston Blue'	EBee ECha IBlr WFar
	'Kobold'	EBee SBod WFar
¶	'Lady Edith'	IBlr
	'Lady Moore'	EBee EGle IBlr
	'Lady Wimborne'	CPne

	'Leighton Blue'	MBri
	'Lilac Bells'	CPne
	'Lilac Time'	CPne
	'Lilliput'	More than 30 suppliers
	'Loch Hope' ♀	CFil CPne EBee WCot
	'Mabel Grey'	CPne
	'Magnifico'	IBlr
¶	'Malvern'	WWeb
*	'Marjorie'	CLCN
	'Midnight'	CHad LRHS
	'Midnight Blue'	CBos CGle EBee ECha ELan EPfP GCal IBlr LHil LPio LRHS SApp WFar WWeb
	'Midnight Star'	COtt ERav LRHS MSte WFar
	mixed giant hybrids	ERav
	mixed whites	ERav WCFE
	'Molly Howick'	Last listed 1998
	'Moonstar'	Last listed 1999
I	'Mooreanus' misapplied	GCal IBlr
	'Morning Star'	ERav
I	'Nix'	IBlr
	'Norman Hadden'	IBlr
	nutans	EBee IBlr LRHS WCot WHil
	- 'Albus'	GCal
§	'Oxbridge'	IBlr
	pale form	SRms
	Palmer's hybrids	See A. Headbourne hybrids
	'Penelope Palmer'	IBlr
	'Penny Slade'	Last listed 1998
	'Peter Pan'	CB&S CElw CMil CRow CSWP CTrC EBee EFou EOrc GBuc LRHS MRav SPla WFar WPyg WWat WWeb WWoo
	'Phantom'	CPne IBlr
	'Pinocchio'	LRHS NHol WWoo
	'Plas Merdyn Blue'	IBlr
	'Plas Merdyn White'	CFir IBlr
	'Podge Mill'	CLCN EGle
	'Polar Ice'	CFir EBee EFou GAri IBlr MCCP NHol WPyg
	praecox	CFil CLAP EBee IBlr SVen
	- 'Bangor Blue'	IBlr
	- 'Blue Formality'	IBlr
	- 'Dwarf White'	See A. white dwarf hybrids
	- 'Flore Pleno' (d)	EBee ECha IBlr LGre WCot WFar
	- subsp. *floribundus*	SWat WHil
	- - 'Saint Ivel'	Last listed 1998
	- subsp. *maximus* 'Albus'	CPou EWTr IBlr SSpi
	- 'Miniature Blue'	SWat
	- subsp. *minimus*	GSki IBlr SWat
	- - 'Adelaide'	SWat
	- - blue	SWat
I	- - 'Supreme'	IBlr
	- - white	SWat
	- 'Mount Stewart'	IBlr
§	- subsp. *orientalis*	CBlo CHEx CSut EBee ERea EWTr GSki IBlr SMad SWat WHil WPic
	- - var. *albiflorus*	CBro CPou CTrC ETub GSki LBow WHil
	- subsp. *praecox*	IBlr
	- - azure	SWat
¶	- - 'Variegatus' (v) ♀	SYvo WSPU
	- Slieve Donard form	IBlr
	- 'Storms River'	SWat WHil
	- 'Vittatus' (v)	WCot WFar
	'Pride of Bicton'	CPne
	'Purple Cloud'	CAbb CB&S CDoC CLAP CRos CTrC EBee ERea GSki IBlr LRHS SApp SMad SPla
¶	'Purple Star'	SVil
¶	'Queen Anne'	EBee
	'Queen Elizabeth The Queen Mother'	EBee
	'Rhône'	EFou IBlr WSpi
	'Rosemary'	EBee
	'Rosewarne'	See A. campanulatus 'Rosewarne'
	'Royal Blue'	CBro EBee ECtt GBuc LPio MTed NHol SVil
	'San Gabriel' (v)	EMon WCot
	'Sandringham'	CFil EBee IBlr WPGP
	'Sapphire'	IBlr
¶	'Sea Mist'	CB&S
	'Silver Mist'	CPne
¶	'Silver Sceptre'	IBlr
	'Sky Rocket'	EBee
	'Sky Star'	Last listed 1999
	'Snowball'	CB&S CLAP CPne SVen
*	'Snowdrop'	WCot
	'Snowy Baby'	CRos
	'Snowy Owl'	CLAP
¶	sp. from Johannesburg	ECha
	'Storm Cloud' (d)	Last listed 1997
	'Streamline'	CDoC CElw CFai CFri CLAP EBee EGle EMan EMil IBro LAst MMil MSte SDys SPla WCot WFar WRus
	'Sunfield'	LRHS WWeb
	'Tinkerbell' (v)	CAbb CB&S CBro CElw CMil CRos CSWP CStu EBee EMan EMil EPfP IOrc LRHS MRav MSph MTho NPer SCob SPla SUsu WAbe WFar WPGP
	'Torbay'	CElw IBlr SBla
¶	'Twilight'	IBlr
	umbellatus L'Hérit.	See A. africanus
	- Redouté	See A. praecox subsp. orientalis
	'Underway'	GCal IBlr
¶	white	GGar
	'White Christmas'	ERea
	'White Dwarf'	See A. white dwarf hybrids
§	white dwarf hybrids	CBlo CBro EBee ECha EFou EMan LPio LRHS WFar WHil WTre
	'White Ice'	CAbb CB&S EBee GQui SCro
	'White Superior'	CSpe EBee EMan MCAu SCro WWat
	'White Umbrella'	Last listed 1998
	'Windlebrooke'	EBee ECha WCDu
	'Windsor Castle'	IBlr
	'Windsor Grey'	EBee IBlr WPGP
	'Wolga'	EBee EFou
	'Woodcote Paleface'	LHil
	'Yves Klein'	IBlr
	'Zella Thomas'	LHyd

AGAPETES (Ericaceae)

	buxifolia	Last listed 1998
	'Ludgvan Cross'	CGre
	serpens ♀	CGre CPlN SLon
	- 'Nepal Cream'	CGre
	- 'Scarlet Elf'	CGre

AGARISTA (Ericaceae)

§	*populifolia*	WWat

AGASTACHE (Lamiaceae)

	anethiodora	See A. foeniculum
	anisata	See A. foeniculum
	barberi	Last listed 1999
	'Blue Fortune'	EBee EMon GBri LRHS NBro SOkh WFar WWeb
	breviflora	EBee
	camphor hyssop	EOHP
§	*cana*	CGle CM&M EBee EOHP LGre SAga SRCN WCot WElm WFar WRos WSan

– 'Cinnabar Rose'	WFar
– 'Heather Queen'	EOHP
cusickii	EBee
'Firebird'	More than 30 suppliers
§ *foeniculum*	CAgr CArn CGle CSev EBee ECha EFou ELan ELau EOHP EOld ERav GCHN GPoy LRHS MCAu MChe MHer MRav MTis NFai NFor SIde SPer SRms WFar WGwG WPer WWye
– 'Alabaster'	CB&S CGle EGoo ELau EMon SAga WCHb WWye
– 'Alba'	CBlo EFou EWTr MLLN SHDw SIde WFar
– 'Fragrant Delight'	WElm
'Globetrotter'	Last listed 1999
¶ 'Honey Bee Blue'	EWll
§ *mexicana*	CGle CSev EBee LHop MChe MHar WGwG WSan
– 'Carille Carmine'	CLTr EMan EMar MLLN
– 'Champagne'	CGle GBri LIck WCHb WPer WRus
– 'Mauve Beauty'	NNor SMrm WPer
aff. *mexicana* PC&H 153	Last listed 1998
– pink	MBri
– 'Rose Beauty'	SMrm
– 'Rosea'	See *A. cana*
nepetoides	CArn EBee MLan MSal
occidentalis	Last listed 1999
orange	Last listed 1999
pallidiflora	EBee SGar
var. *pallidiflora*	
palmeri	EBee
pringlei	EBee EMar SWat WOut
rugosa	CAgr CArn CFir CFri CSev EBee ELau EMan EOHP GBar GPoy LGre MLLN MSal SAga SWat WBea WCot WGwG WJek WPer WSel WWye
– 'Alba'	WBea
– 'Korean Zest' B&SWJ 735	EGoo EMan SUsu WCru
rupestris	LGre NTow WCot WKif
– JCA 1.025.050	Last listed 1998
scrophulariifolia	EBee
¶ 'Serpentine'	EMon
'Tangerine Dreams'	WCot
¶ 'Tutti-frutti'	EBrP EBre EHrv EMan LBCl LBSe LBre MBBe SBre
urticifolia	CArn EBee EPfP LRHS MSal WOut
– 'Alba'	EBee WPer
I – 'Liquorice'	CSam
– 'Liquorice Blue'	COlW ECtt EMan EMar GSki LRHS MLan MWgw NBid NGdn NLar SPer SWat WPer
– 'Liquorice White'	CM&M COlW CRDP CSam ECtt EMan GSki LRHS MWgw NLar NPSI SCro SPer SWat WOve
wrightii	Last listed 1998

AGATHAEA See FELICIA

AGATHIS (Araucariaceae)
australis	CFil CPLG

AGATHOSMA (Rutaceae)
crenulata	ELau
ovata	SVen
– 'Kleitijies Kraal'	Last listed 1997

AGAVE ✿ (Agavaceae)
americana ♀	CAbb CB&S CCtw CDoC CHEx CTrC CWSG EBee ECha ELau

	EOas GQui IBlr LCns LHil LPal LPan LRHS SAPC SArc SChr SMad WMul
– 'Marginata'	CBrP CFri CHal CInt EOas IBlr LHop MWst
– 'Mediopicta' ♀	CTbh MWst SAPC SArc WEas
– 'Mediopicta Alba' ♀	CBrP SChr
– 'Striata' (v)	Last listed 1998
– 'Variegata' ♀	CAbb CB&S CDoC CHEx CMdw CTbh CTrC CWSG ECha ELau EWes GQui LCns LEdu LRHS MLLN NMoo NPer SAPC SArc SChr SMad SPer SSoC WCot WEas WMul
angustifolia	Last listed 1998
arizonica	SChr
attenuata	SAPC SArc
§ *celsii*	CHEx CTbh SAPC SArc
– var. *albicans*	CCpl EOas
cerulata subsp. *nelsonii*	CTbh
chrysantha	CTrC
colorata	Last listed 1998
deserti	CCpl
¶ *elongata*	WCot
ferdinandi-regis	SChr
ferox	CTbh CTrC EPVP MWst
filifera ♀	CHEx CTrC EOas MWst SChr
franzosinii	CCtw CTrF
gigantea	See *Furcraea foetida*
goldmaniana	CCpl
guadalajarana 'Jalisco'	CCpl
havardiana	Last listed 1999
¶ *horrida*	SChr
lechuguilla	SChr
lophantha	CCpl
§ – var. *univittata*	EOas
mitis	See *A. celsii*
* *montana*	CFir
neomexicana	Last listed 1999
nizandensis	CCpl
palmeri	CTrC EOas
parryi	CDoC EOas EPVP SChr
– var. *couesii*	See *A. parryi* var. *parryi*
– var. *huachucensis*	CBrP CCpl
§ – var. *parryi*	CBrP CFir CTbh
– var. *truncata*	CCpl
parviflora ♀	Last listed 1989
potatorum ♀	SChr
– var. *verschaffeltii*	CTbh
salmiana var. *ferox*	SAPC SArc
¶ *scabra*	CTrC
schidigera	CBrP CFir GCal
schottii	CTbh
shawii	EOas
sisalana	CTrF MWst
striata	CCpl
stricta ♀	CCpl
toumeyana	CCpl SChr
univittata	See *A. lophantha* var. *univittata*
utahensis	EOas EPVP
– var. *discreta*	SChr
victoriae-reginae ♀	CBrP CTbh CTrC
xylonacantha	CHEx EOas

AGERATINA See EUPATORIUM

AGERATUM (Asteraceae)
¶ *corymbosum*	CSpe

AGLAONEMA (Araceae)
§ *crispum*	LRHS MBri
* – 'Marie'	MBri

'Malay Beauty'	MBri
roebelinii	See *A. crispum*
'Silver Queen' ♀	LRHS MBri

AGONIS (Myrtaceae)
| *flexuosa* | CPLG CTrC |
| *marginata* | Last listed 1998 |

AGRIMONIA (Rosaceae)
eupatoria	CArn CKin COld EBee ELau
	EWFC GPoy IIve MChe MGas
	MHer MHew NMir SIde SWat
	WCHb WGwy WHbs WHer WOak
	WWye
- 'Topas'	ELau
grandiflora	EBee
gryposepala	EBee
odorata (L.) Mill.	See *A. repens*
- hort.	See *A. procera*
pilosa	CArn EBee ELau IIve
§ *procera*	EWFC
§ *repens*	GBar MSal WCHb

AGROPYRON (Poaceae)
¶ *cristatum*	CBrm
glaucum	See *Elymus hispidus*
magellanicum	See *Elymus magellanicus*
pubiflorum	See *Elymus magellanicus*
scabrum	See *Elymus scabrus*

AGROSTEMMA (Caryophyllaceae)
coronaria	See *Lychnis coronaria*
githago	EWFC MHew MMal MSal WHer
	WJek WOak
- 'Purple Queen'	Last listed 1998

AGROSTIS (Poaceae)
calamagrostis	See *Stipa calamagrostis*
canina 'Silver Needles' (v)	CBre CBrm CCuc CHor CInt CPea
	EBee EGle EGra EHoe EMan
	EMon EPPr EWes GCal GKir LRHS
	MMoz MWhi WElm
karsensis	See *A. stolonifera*
nebulosa	CInt LIck SWal
§ *stolonifera*	Last listed 1997

AGROSTOCRINUM (Phormiaceae)
| *scabrum* | Last listed 1998 |

AICHRYSON (Crassulaceae)
| § x *domesticum* | CHEx CHal CTrC |
| - 'Variegatum' ♀ | CHal EBak LHil |

AILANTHUS (Simaroubaceae)
§ *altissima* ♀	CB&S CDul CHEx CLnd EBee
	EBrP EBre ECrN EMil ENot GKir
	IOrc LBCl LBSe LBre LPan MBBe
	MBlu MGos MPEx NBee SAPC
	SArc SBre SMad SPer SRPl WDin
	WNor WStI
- var. *sutchuenensis*	CFil
glandulosa	See *A. altissima*

AINSLIAEA (Asteraceae)
| *acerifolia* B&SWJ 4795 | WCru |

AIPHANES (Arecaceae)
| ¶ *aculeata* | LPal |

AJANIA (Asteraceae)
| § *pacifica* | CHal EBee ECtt ELan EMan EMar |
| | LRHS MRav NFai SPla WWal |

| *tibetica* JJH 9308103 | NWCA |
| * *xylorhiza* JJH 95095 | Last listed 1999 |

AJUGA (Lamiaceae)
bombycina	Last listed 1999
'Brockbankii'	Last listed 1998
chamaepitys	Last listed 1998
genevensis 'Alba'	Last listed 1998
- 'Tottenham'	MCli
metallica hort.	See *A. pyramidalis*
'Monmotaro San'	EGar
orientalis	Last listed 1999
§ *pyramidalis*	CFee CLyd ECha EGar EWTr LNor
	NBrk SCro WGwy WHer
- 'Metallica Crispa'	CRDP EBee EWTr EWes MBro
	NHar NRya WHil WOut WPnP
reptans	CKin ECtt ELau EWFC GPoy LGro
	LPBA LRHS MChe MHer MHew
	MMal MSal NBrk NMir SGar
	WRHF
- 'Alba'	CArn CNic CRow CTri EBee
	EWTr GCal MNrw NBro NCiC
	NFla NPro NSti SRms WAlt WByw
	WCHb WFar WHil WPer WWeb
	WWye
- 'Arctic Fox' (v)	CElw CLAP CMil CRDP CSpe
	GOrP MHar MLLN NDov NPSl
	NPro WCot WFar WSpi
- 'Argentea'	See *A. reptans* 'Variegata'
§ - 'Atropurpurea' ♀	More than 30 suppliers
- 'Braunherz' ♀	More than 30 suppliers
- 'Burgundy Glow' (v) ♀	More than 30 suppliers
* - 'Burgundy Red'	Last listed 1998
- 'Carol'	Last listed 1997
§ - 'Catlin's Giant' ♀	More than 30 suppliers
- 'Delight' (v)	ECot NNrd SBod WCer WEas
¶ - 'Ermine'	WCot
- 'Grey Lady'	WCot
- 'Harlequin' (v)	Last listed 1997
¶ - 'John Pierpoint'	WCot
- 'Julia'	EMon LNor
- 'Jumbo'	See *A. reptans* 'Jungle Beauty'
§ - 'Jungle Beauty'	CHid CRDP CRow CSev EBee
	ECtt EMan EOrc EPar EPfP GCal
	WCer WHen
- 'Macrophylla'	See *A. reptans* 'Catlin's Giant'
§ - 'Multicolor' (v)	More than 30 suppliers
- 'Palisander'	EBee GSki LRHS NSti
I - 'Pat's Selection' (v)	NDov
- 'Pink Elf'	CB&S CBre CLyd CMCo CMHG
	CNic CRow CTri EBee EMan
	EOrc LHop LRHS MRav NBro
	NOak SHel SIng SUsu SWat WBea
	WCer WFar WHoo WMoo WPer
	WPyg
- 'Pink Splendour'	CBre CMea CTri EBee MGed
	NChi WCer
- 'Pink Surprise'	CHid CNic CRow CSpe EBee
	EBrP EBre ECha EHoe EMar EMon
	EPla EPri GBar LBCl LBSe LBre
	LRHS MBBe MHer NRya SBre
	SCro SRPl SSvw WCHb WEas
	WFar WMoo
- 'Pink Towers'	LRHS
- 'Purple Brocade'	CStr WBro WByw
- 'Purple Torch'	EBee ECha MCli SLod WCer WEas
	WLin WOut
- 'Purpurea'	See *A. reptans* 'Atropurpurea'
- 'Rainbow'	See *A. reptans* 'Multicolor'
- 'Rosea'	CHal EBee NPro WHil
¶ - 'Rowden Royal Purple'	CRow
- 'Schneekerze'	MCli

- 'Silver Shadow'	MSCN NPro
- 'Tricolor'	See *A. reptans* 'Multicolor'
§ - 'Variegata'	More than 30 suppliers
'Variegated Glacier' (v)	ELau

AKEBIA (Lardizabalaceae)

longeracemosa B&SWJ 3606	
	WCru
x *pentaphylla*	CPIN EMil EPfP ERea GQui LRHS
	MAsh SBra SPer
quinata	More than 30 suppliers
- B&SWJ 4425	WCru
- cream form	EPfP LRHS MAsh SBra SPer WCru
¶ - variegated	WCru
trifoliata	CBlo CGdn CHEx CPIN EBee EPfP
	LRHS MAsh MDun WSHC
- B&SWJ 2829	WCru
- B&SWJ 5063	WCru

ALANGIUM (Alangiaceae)

chinense	CFil CMCN IDee SLon WBcn
	WPGP
platanifolium	CBot CFil CMCN EPla MBlu
	WPGP

ALBIZIA (Mimosaceae)

adianthifolia	Last listed 1998
distachya	See *Paraserianthes lophantha*
guachapele	Last listed 1998
§ *julibrissin*	CArn CFil CTrC ISea LRHS MLan
	MWat SPlb WMul
- f. *rosea* ♀	CB&S CGre CHEx CLnd CMCN
	CPle CTho CTrC EBee ELan GQui
	LPan LRHS MBri MCCP MTis
	SAPC SArc SDry SOWG SPer
	WNor WOTO WPGP WSHC
lophantha	See *Paraserianthes lophantha*

ALBUCA (Hyacinthaceae)

altissima	EBee
aurea	EBee
canadensis	EBee
caudata	Last listed 1998
cooperi	EBee
humilis	CStu EBee EPot ESis NMen NTow
	WAbe
juncifolia	EBee
nelsonii	CAvo
shawii	CStu EBee NSla SBla SOkd WAbe
spiralis	EBee
tortuosa S&SH 53	Last listed 1999
wakefieldii	Last listed 1998

ALCEA (Malvaceae)

'Arabian Nights'	SRCN WHer
'Blackcurrant Whirl'	WHer
'Double Moonlight'	SRCN WRHF
ficifolia	CGle EBee NBus NFai SSvw WHil
- 'Golden Eye'	Last listed 1998
pallida	EBee EMan
- HH&K 284	Last listed 1998
§ *rosea*	CGle MRav MWgw WFar WHil
- 'Black Beauty'	Last listed 1999
- Chater's Double Group (d)	CHad EBrP EBre ECtt EMan EPfP
	LBCl LBSe LBre LCot MBBe MBri
	NFor NNor SBre SCoo SPer SRob
	WHil WLRN WOve WRHF
¶ - - chamois (d)	WViv
¶ - - chestnut brown (d)	WViv
¶ - - pink (d)	WViv
¶ - - red (d)	WViv
¶ - - salmon pink (d)	WViv

¶ - - white (d)	WViv
¶ - - yellow (d)	WViv
- double apricot (d)	Last listed 1999
¶ - double pink (d)	MHer
¶ - double red (d)	MHer
¶ - double rose	NCut
¶ - double scarlet	NCut
- double white (d)	EBee LRHS MHer NCut
- double yellow (d)	EBee LRHS MHer NCut
- 'Lemon Light'	EBee
- Majorette Group	ECtt
* - 'Negrite'	Last listed 1998
- 'Nigra'	CArn CFri CGle CHad COIW EBee
	EGoo EMan EOld EOrc LRHS
	MBNS MCAu MHer MNrw MSte
	MTis MWgw MWll NFor NGdn
	NPri SPer SRCN SRob SSoC SSvw
	WOak
- single	COIW
- single pink	EBee LCot LRHS
- Summer Carnival Group	EMan WGor
- yellow	Last listed 1998
§ *rugosa*	CGle CHad CSam ECha ELan
	EMan EOrc MNrw MSte SDix
	WKif WPGP WRus
- *alba*	Last listed 1999

ALCHEMILLA ✿ (Rosaceae)

§ *abyssinica*	CGle CHid EMar GAbr GBuc MBel
	NDov WBro WHen
N *alpina* L.	More than 30 suppliers
- misapplied	See *A. conjuncta, A. plicatula*
aroanica	EBee
arvensis	See *Aphanes arvensis*
§ *conjuncta*	More than 30 suppliers
elisabethae	ECGP EMon MGrG NBrk WCHb
ellenbeckii	CFee EBee EBrP EBre EMon GBar
	GCHN GKir LBCl LBSe LBre
	MBBe MBar MHar MHer MLLN
	NChi NNrd NSti NWCA SBre SSca
	SWat WCHb WEas WFar WHen
	WPGP WPer WWat
epipsila	MSte NLar WPer
erythropoda ♀	More than 30 suppliers
faeroensis	EGle LBee NChi NFor WPer
- var. *pumila*	CLyd EBee LRHS
filicaulis 'Minima'	CNat
§ *fulgens*	CArn CBlo CBod EPPr EWTr GAri
	LFis WHen
glaucescens	CNat
hoppeana hort.	See *A. plicatula*
iniquiformis	EBee
lapeyrousei	EMon EPPr NChi SIng WPer
mollis ♀	More than 30 suppliers
I - 'Auslese'	EBee LRHS WHil
* - 'Robusta'	EBee ECha EMan EPla LRHS
	MTho NBrk SEND SMad SPlb SRPl
	SWat WFar WMoo WPnP
* - 'Senior'	GCal
¶ - 'Thriller'	EWTr NArg WSpi
- 'Variegata'	IBlr
monticola	WPer
'Mr Poland's Variety'	See *A. venosa*
pedata	See *A. abyssinica*
pentaphylla	EBee
§ *plicatula*	WPer
potentilloides	Last listed 1999
psilomischa	EBee EMon LRHS WCDu
pumila	EFou LRHS MGrG
robusta	Last listed 1997
saxatilis	WPer
speciosa	EBee SHel

N *splendens* See *A. fulgens*
¶ *straminea* EFou ERav
§ *venosa* EBee SCro SLod SPer WWat
aff. *venosa* EPla
vetteri EBee
vulgaris hort. See *A. xanthochlora*
§ *xanthochlora* CAgr EBee GBar GGar GPoy
MHew MSal NLar WHer WPer

ALECTRYON (Sapindaceae)
excelsus CHEx

ALISMA (Alismataceae)
lanceolatum Last listed 1998
plantago-aquatica CBen CKin CRow EHon EMFW
GBar LGuA LPBA MHew MSta
NDea SWat WMAq WWeb
- var. *parviflorum* CBen EMFW LPBA MSta SPlb
SWat WWeb

ALKANNA (Boraginaceae)
aucheriana Last listed 1997
orientalis Last listed 1998
tinctoria MSal
- HH&K 345 Last listed 1999

ALLAGOPTERA (Arecaceae)
arenaria Last listed 1999

ALLAMANDA (Apocynaceae)
§ *blanchetii* SOWG
cathartica CPIN ECon EPfP ERea LChe LRHS
MBri
- 'Birthe' MBri
* - 'Chocolate Swirl' Last listed 1998
- 'Grandiflora' CPIN
* - 'Hendersonii' ♀ LRHS SOWG
- 'Williamsii' Last listed 1998
'Halley's Comet' LChe
'Jamaican Sunset' LChe
neriifolia See *A. schottii*
§ *schottii* ♀ CPIN ECon LRHS SOWG
violacea See *A. blanchetii*

ALLIARIA (Brassicaceae)
petiolata CArn CKin CSev EWFC GPoy IIve
NLan WHbs WHer

ALLIUM ✿ (Alliaceae)
§ *acuminatum* GCHN NBir WCot
aflatunense hort. See *A. hollandicum*, *A. stipitatum*
- Fedtschenko EMon
akaka GCrs LBow
albidum See *A. denudatum*
albopilosum See *A. cristophii*
¶ *altaicum* GIBF
altissimum LBow NRog
- 'Goliath' EBee
amabile See *A. mairei* var. *amabile*
ambiguum See *A. roseum* var. *carneum*
amethystinum EBee
ampeloprasum CFil ECha WHer WPGP WShi
- var. *babingtonii* CNat GPoy IIve ILis MLLN WHer
WShi
amphibolum EBee
amplectens EBee GDra LRHS NRog
anceps Last listed 1998
§ *angulosum* EBee LEdu LLWP MMil WCot
angustitepalum See *A. rosenbachianum*
anisopodium EBee
atropurpureum EBee ECha ELan EMan EMon EPar
LBow LEdu LRHS MLLN NRog

SUsu WCot WRos
aucheri CLAP
azureum See *A. caeruleum*
¶ *balansae* SOkd
'Beau Regard' ♀ EBee LAma LBow MTed NRog
beesianum W.W. Smith ♀ CGle CLAP CLyd EBee EBur ESis
EWes MBro NBir NRya WCot
- hort. See *A. cyaneum*
brevicaule LRHS
bulgaricum See *Nectaroscordum siculum*
subsp. *bulgaricum*
§ *caeruleum* ♀ More than 30 suppliers
- *azureum* See *A. caeruleum*
caesium Last listed 1999
¶ - 'Tashkent' WCDu
callimischon CAvo CBro CStu NRog NRya
- subsp. *callimischon* Last listed 1998
- subsp. *haemostictum* CStu EPot LBow NRog SBla SIng
campanulatum Last listed 1998
canadense CArn EBee
cardiostemon MBel
§ *carinatum* EBee GCHN
§ - subsp. *pulchellum* ♀ More than 30 suppliers
- - f. *album* CAvo CBos CBro CSWP CStr EBee
ECha EGle EMon EPar EPot ETub
LBow LFis LLWP LRHS MMal
MNrw NRog NSti SUsu SYvo
WBea WCot WWin
- - 'Tubergen' EBee ETub
§ *carolinianum* GCrs GIBF
- CC 1935 Last listed 1999
cepa Last listed 1999
- Aggregatum Group ELau GPoy ILis
- 'Perutile' CArn GBar GPoy ILis MCoo MHer
SIde
- Proliferum Group CArn CSev ELau GBar GPoy ILis
LEdu MChe MHer NWoo SIde
WCHb WCer WHer WJek WOak
WSel
* - 'White Flower' WCot
cernuum More than 30 suppliers
- *album* Last listed 1997
- 'Hidcote' ♀ CLAP EMon MCLN WCot
- *roseum* CLyd
chamaemoly Last listed 1998
littorale AB&S 4387
cirrhosum See *A. carinatum* subsp.
pulchellum
¶ *commutatum* LEdu
cowanii See *A. neapolitanum* Cowanii
Group
crenulatum Last listed 1998
§ *cristophii* ♀ More than 30 suppliers
cupanii EBee
- subsp. *hirtovaginatum* Last listed 1997
cupuliferum Last listed 1998
§ *cyaneum* ♀ CArn CAvo CGle CGra CHea CInt
CLyd ERos GCrs GKir LBee LBow
LRHS NMen NNrd NRya NTow
SBla SRot SSca WBea WCDu
cyathophorum CPea GCrs NRog
§ - var. *farreri* CArn CAvo CBre CBro CHea CLyd
CNic EBee EPot ERos ESis GCHN
GCrs GGar GKir GSki LBow
LLWP MBro MRav NChi NFor
NMen NNrd NRya SIng WCot
§ *denudatum* EBee LBow
dichlamydeum CBro ERos LBow NRog
- JCA 11765 Last listed 1998
§ *drummondii* EBrP EBre ECha LBCl LBSe LBre
MBBe SBre
elatum See *A. macleanii*

ericetorum	EBee ERos
falcifolium	EBee NTow WCot
– JCA 11625	CLAP
farreri	See *A. cyathophorum* var. *farreri*
fetisowii	EBee
fimbriatum	EBee
– var. *abramsii*	Last listed 1997
'Firmament'	CAvo CMil EBee EMon LBow
	LRHS SPer WCot WPnP
fistulosum	CAgr CArn EBee EDAr ELau EPla
	GBar GPoy ILis LEdu MChe MHer
	NFor SIde WCHb WCer WCot
	WOak WPer WSel WWye
– 'Red Welsh'	IIve ILis
– 'Streaker' (v)	Last listed 1997
flavum ♀	CArn CAvo CBro CGle CHad
	CHea ECha EGle ELau EPar ETub
	GKir LAma LBow LHop MCLN
	NRog NSti SIng SPer SRob SYvo
	WBea WGor WPGP WPer
§ – 'Blue Leaf'	EBee EPot ERos GKir LEdu NBir
– subsp. *flavum*	EBee ELau LEdu
– – var. *minus* HH&K 273	Last listed 1999
– 'Glaucum'	See *A. flavum* 'Blue Leaf'
– 'Golden Showers'	MBNS
– var. *minus*	CNic EBee MTho NWCA SSca
– var. *nanum*	GKir NTow
– subsp. *tauricum*	EBee
forrestii	CLyd EBee GCrs
galanthum	EBee
geyeri	EBee WCot WLin
giganteum ♀	More than 30 suppliers
'Gladiator' ♀	CAvo CBro CFwr CHar EBee
	EMan EMon LAma LBow LRHS
	MLLN MSph NRog SPer WPnP
	WSel
glaucum	See *A. senescens* subsp.
	montanum var. *glaucum*
'Globemaster' ♀	CAvo CBro CHar CMea CRDP
	EBee ELan EMan ETub LAma
	LBow LRHS MMHG SMrm SPer
	WBry WPnP
'Globus'	EBee EPot LRHS
goodingii	CNic EBee
¶ *gultschense*	GIBF
guttatum	EBee
subsp. *sardoum*	
haematochiton	WCot
heldreichii	EBee
hierochuntinum S&L 79	Last listed 1998
'His Excellency'	CBlo EBee ECho LBow LRHS
§ *hollandicum* ♀	CAvo CBro CFri CGle CHar EBee
	ECha EMan EPar EPfP LAma LBow
	LRHS MDun MLLN MMal MNrw
	MWat NFai NOrc NRog NSti SChu
	SPer STes SUsu WHil WPer WSel
– 'Purple Sensation' ♀	More than 30 suppliers
– 'Purple Surprise'	EBee LRHS
hookeri ACE 2430	EPot WCot
humile	CLyd
hyalinum	EBee NRog
– pink	WCot
§ *insubricum* ♀	EBee ERos GCrs MS&S NBir
'Ivory Queen'	EBee
jajlae	See *A. rotundum* subsp. *jajlae*
jepsonii	Last listed 1997
jesdianum	CBro LBow MLLN
* – *album*	EBee
– 'Michael Hoog'	See *A. rosenbachianum* 'Michael
	Hoog'
– 'Purple King'	CMil LBow
kansuense	See *A. sikkimense*

karataviense ♀	More than 30 suppliers
kharputense	Last listed 1999
ledebourianum	EBee
libani	EBee WPer
¶ *longicuspis*	GIBF
loratum	EPar
'Lucy Ball'	CAvo EBee EMon ETub LAma
	LBow LRHS MLLN NRog
§ *macleanii*	CArn EBee ELau EMan EMon EPar
	LAma LBow LRHS NRog
macranthum	CLyd EBee EBrP EBre GCHN LBCl
	LBSe LBre MBBe MSte SBre WLin
macrochaetum	LAma
mairei	CElw CInt CLyd EBee ERos EWes
	GCHN LLWP LRHS MBar MDHE
	NBus NMen NRya SOkh WCDu
§ – var. *amabile*	CLyd EBee ERos NRya NTow
– – pink	NBir
'Mars'	CMea EBee LBow LRHS MLLN
maximowiczii	EBee ECho EWes
moly ♀	CArn CBro CGle EBee ELau EPar
	ETub GBuc IMGH LAma LBow
	LRHS MBri MMal MRav NRog
	NRya NSti SRms WBea WCHb
	WCot WPer WWin
– 'Jeannine' ♀	CBro EBee EPot LBow MLLN
	WBea WPGP
'Mont Blanc'	EBee ELan LBow
montanum	See *A. senescens* subsp.
	montanum
'Mount Everest'	CAvo CBro CMea CMil EBee EMar
	ETub LBow LRHS SPer WCot
multibulbosum	See *A. nigrum*
murrayanum Reg.	See *A. acuminatum*
– misapplied	See *A. unifolium*
§ *narcissiflorum* Villars	CLyd GCrs NMGW NMen NSla
	NSti NWCA
§ – hort.	See *A. insubricum*
neapolitanum	CAgr CArn CGle CLTr CM&M
	EBee EGar EPar LAma LBow LRHS
	MBri NRog NSti SRms WPer
§ – Cowanii Group	CBro CHar EBee IMGH LRHS
	MNrw WBea WCot WLin WRHF
	WRos
– 'Grandiflorum'	EBee EPla LRHS MLLN MNrw
	NRog WBea
nevii	Last listed 1999
§ *nigrum*	CAvo CBos CBro EBee EMan EMar
	EMon EPar LAma LBow LRHS
	MLLN MNrw MRav NBir NRog
	SPer SRob WCot
nutans	CBod EBee IIve LBow LEdu MBct
	NGHP SHDw WHal WJek
nuttallii	See *A. drummondii*
§ *obliquum*	EBee ECha EGle GSki LRHS SBea
	SUsu WCot WTin
odorum L.	See *A. ramosum* L.
oleraceum	WHer
olympicum	MBro
– ES 13	Last listed 1999
§ *oreophilum* ♀	CArn CAvo CBro CMdw EBee
	ECha ECtt ELau EPar GSki IMGH
	LAma LBow LRHS MLLN MMal
	NMGW NRog NRya SRms WBea
	WCot WPer
– 'Agalik'	LRHS
– 'Zwanenburg' ♀	CBro CMea EPot LBow NMen
	NRog WBea
¶ *oreoprasum*	GIBF
orientale	EPot
ostrowskianum	See *A. oreophilum*
pallens	CBre EBee ERav LBow MTho NBir

§ *paniculatum* — CAvo EBee ECha EPot LEdu MMil NRog
- subsp. *fuscum* — Last listed 1998
paradoxum — LRHS NBir NRog
- var. *normale* — CBro CRDP EBee EMon LBow NMen WCot
- PF 5085 — Last listed 1998
pedemontanum — See *A. narcissiflorum* Villars
peninsulare — Last listed 1997
perdulce — Last listed 1998
polyastrum — GCHN
polyphyllum — See *A. carolinianum*
porrum 'Saint Victor' — Last listed 1999
pskemense — GIBF
pulchellum — See *A. carinatum* subsp. *pulchellum*
pyrenaicum hort. — See *A. angulosum*
- Costa & Veyrada — EBee ELan EMan
§ *ramosum* L. — ELau ETub LAma NGHP WJek WPer
§ - Jacquin — See *A. obliquum*
'Rien Poortvliet' — CArn EBee LAma LBow LRHS NRog
* *romarovianum* — EBee
§ *rosenbachianum* — CArn CBro CHar EBee EMan EPar EPot LAma MLLN NCat NRog SUsu
- 'Akbulak' — LRHS
- 'Album' — ECha ECho EPar EPot LAma MLLN NRog WCot
§ - 'Michael Hoog' — EBee LBow LRHS
- 'Purple King' — EBee LRHS
- 'Shing' — EBee LRHS WIvy
roseum — CArn CLTr CMea EBee ECtt ELau EMon ERos LAma LBow LRHS NRog WBea WPer
- *album* — Last listed 1997
- B&S 396 — Last listed 1998
§ - var. *bulbiferum* — WCot
§ - var. *carneum* — EBee
- 'Grandiflorum' — See *A. roseum* var. *bulbiferum*
§ *rotundum* subsp. *jajlae* — EBee LLWP WPer
- subsp. *rotundum* — Last listed 1998
rubens — GCHN WPer
sanbornii var. *sanbornii* — Last listed 1998
sarawschanicum — Last listed 1997
sativum — CArn EEls ELau MHer SIde WJek WOak WSel WWye
* - *aureum* — GPoy
¶ - golden — IIve
¶ - Mexican — IIve
- var. *ophioscorodon* — GPoy IIve ILis
- 'Printanor' — CBod
- 'Thermidrome' — CBod
saxatile — EBee
scabriscapum — Last listed 1998
schmitzii — EMon
schoenoprasum — More than 30 suppliers
- 'Black Isle Blush' ♀ — GPoy
- 'Corsican White' — EMon SUsu
- fine-leaved — ELau IIve WRha
- 'Forescate' — CBod CM&M EBee ECha EFou ELau EWes GBar GCHN GCal LNor LRHS MLLN NHol SSpe SSvw WBea WCHb WCot
¶ - 'Forncett Purple' — EFou
- 'Grolau' — Last listed 1999
- medium leaved — ELau
- 'Pink Perfection' ♀ — GPoy
- 'Polyphant' — EBee WCHb WRha
- *roseum* — Last listed 1999
- var. *sibiricum* — GBar GPoy MBri SDix WSel WShi

- 'Silver Chimes' — CMil ELau SHDw
- 'Wallington White' — GBar MBro
- white — CArn CMea CSWP ECha ELau LEdu LGre MBro MHer MSte NBir SIde SSvw WBea WCHb WCot WEas WHer WRha WWye
schubertii — CArn CAvo CBro CMil EBee ELan ELau EMar EMon EOrc EPar EPot ETub LAma LBow LRHS MBNS MBri MLLN MNrw NChi NRog SMrm SUsu WCot WHil
scorodoprasum — WCHb
- subsp. *jajlae* — See *A. rotundum* subsp. *jajlae*
scorzonerifolium var. *xericiense* — WCot
senescens — CArn CBro CTri EBee ECGP ELau EPar ERos ESis GCHN LBow MRav NChi SRms SSca SSpe SSvw WBea
- var. *calcareum* — CPLG EBee
§ - subsp. *montanum* — EGar EGoo EPot ERav LEdu MBro NMen SDix SIng WAbe
§ - - var. *glaucum* — CLyd CMea CPBP CStr EBee EBrP EBre ECha EMan EPar EPla ESis GCHN LBCl LBSe LBow LBre LEdu LRHS MBBe MBel NTow SBre SIng WCot WHer WPer WWye
- subsp. *senescens* — EMon MLLN SUsu
sessiliflorum — GCrs
sibthorpianum — See *A. paniculatum*
siculum — See *Nectaroscordum siculum*
¶ *siebeanum* — EBee
§ *sikkimense* — CHea EBee ERos GDra GIBF GKir MBro NMen NNrd NSla NWCA SBea SBla WBea WLRN WPer
- ACE 1363 — Last listed 1997
siskiyouense — Last listed 1998
sphaerocephalon — More than 30 suppliers
splendens — EBee
stellatum — EBee EBrP EBre LBCl LBSe LBre LRHS MBBe SBre
stellerianum — GCHN WPer
- var. *kurilense* — CLyd
§ *stipitatum* — EBee EMon LAma LBow LRHS MBro MLLN NRog WCot WHoo
- 'Album' — CBro EBee EMon LAma LBow LRHS NRog
- 'Glory of Pamir' — EBee LRHS
stracheyi — WCot
strictum — EBee IIve
subhirsutum — CLyd EBee
subvillosum — EBee WCot
szovitsii — Last listed 1998
tanguticum — EBee EBrP EBre GCHN GKir LBCl LBSe LBre MBBe SBre
textile — Last listed 1998
thunbergii — CAvo CLTr CMea CStu EBee GCrs NBir
- 'Nanum' — EPot
- 'Ozawa' — EFou NMen SBla
tibeticum — See *A. sikkimense*
togashii — EBee
* *tournefortii* — EBee
tricoccum — Last listed 1998
triquetrum — CAvo CGle CLTr EBee ELan ELau EMan ERav GGar IBlr ILis LAma LBow MMal NBir NRog NSti SIng SLod SYvo WBea WBor WCHb WCot WCru WHer WPer WPnP WShi WWin
tuberosum — More than 30 suppliers

- purple/mauve	ELau
- variegated (v)	ELau
turkestanicum	Last listed 1999
§ *unifolium*	CAvo CBro CGle EBee EMan ETub
	LAma LBow LLWP LRHS MBri
	MLLN MNrw MRav NBir NCat
	NRog NRya NSti SPer STes WBea
	WCot WFar WPer
ursinum	CArn CAvo CKen CKin EBrP EBre
	ELau EWFC GPoy LAma LBCl
	LBSe LBre MBBe MHew NGHP
	NMir NRog SBre WCDu WCHb
	WGwy WHen WShi WWye
validum	Last listed 1998
victorialis	Last listed 1998
vineale	CArn EBee ELau MHew WHer
	WPer
violaceum	See *A. carinatum*
virgunculae	LBow SBla
wallichii	CLyd CPea CPou EMon GBuc
	LAma NBir WTin
- B 445	WLin
zaprjagaevii	EBee LEdu
zebdanense	CStu EBee ERos LAma LBow
	LRHS MNrw

lanata	CMCN
maritima	Last listed 1998
maximowiczii	CMCN
- AGSJ 334	Last listed 1999
nepalensis	WCwm WFro
nitida	CFil CGre CMCN IDee
oregana	See *A. rubra*
¶ *orientalis*	GIBF
rhombifolia	Last listed 1998
§ *rubra*	CBlo CDoC CDul CKin CLnd
	CMCN CTho ELan ENot GAri
	GChr IOrc LBuc NWea WDin
	WMou
- 'Pinnatifida'	See *A. rubra* f. *pinnatisecta*
§ - f. *pinnatisecta*	CTho MBlu
§ *rugosa*	CMCN
serrulata	See *A. rugosa*
§ *sieboldiana*	CGre
sinuata	See *A. viridis* subsp. *sinuata*
x *spaethii* ♀	CDoC CDul CTho IOrc SRPl
subcordata	CLnd
tenuifolia	See *A. incana* subsp. *incana*
viridis	CMCN GAri NWea
- subsp. *crispa* var. *mollis*	CMCN
§ - subsp. *sinuata*	CAgr CMCN NWea WPic

ALLOCASUARINA (Casuarinaceae)

crassa	Last listed 1999
§ *littoralis*	CGre
monilifera	ECou
nana	CTrC
§ *verticillata*	CTrC

ALNUS ✿ (Betulaceae)

cordata ♀	More than 30 suppliers
- wild origin	Last listed 1998
crispa	See *A. viridis* subsp. *crispa*
firma	CMCN
- var. *sieboldiana*	See *A. sieboldiana*
fruticosa	See *A. viridis* subsp. *fruticosa*
glutinosa	CB&S CBlo CDoC CDul CKin
	CLnd CSam EBee ECrN ENot
	GChr GKir IOrc LBuc LHyr LPan
	MGos MPEx NBee NRog NWea
	SHFr SPer WDin WMou WOrn
	WStI
- 'Aurea'	CDul CEnd CTho LRHS MBlu SSpi
	WWat
- 'Imperialis' ♀	CDoC CDul CEnd CLnd CPMA
	CTho EBee ELan ENot EPfP GChr
	GKir LPan LRHS MAsh MBri
	MGos NBee NPSI SMHT SPer SSpi
	WDin WWat
- f. *incisa*	ELan
- 'Laciniata'	CDoC CDul CLnd CTho GChr
	IDee IOrc MBlu
- 'Pyramidalis'	CTho
- 'Razzmatazz' (v)	CPMA
hirsuta	CMCN CTho GKir
incana	CBlo CDoC CKin CLnd CMCN
	EBee ECrN EMac ENot GKir IOrc
	LBuc MBar MGos NRog NWea
	SPer WDin WMou WOrn
- 'Aurea'	CB&S CDul CLnd COtt CTho
	EBee ECrN ELan ENot EPfP EPla
	GKir IOrc LPan LRHS MBar MBlu
	MBri MGos SPer SSpi WDin WOrn
§ - subsp. *incana*	Last listed 1999
- 'Laciniata'	CDul CTho ENot WDin
- 'Pendula'	Last listed 1998
- subsp. *tenuifolia*	See *A. incana* subsp. *incana*
japonica	SMac

ALOCASIA ✿ (Araceae)

x *amazonica* ♀	ERea MBri MNew
- 'Polly'	MNew
'Aquino'	MNew
x *argyraea*	MNew
'Black Velvet'	MNew
'Black Widow'	MNew
'Crinkles'	MNew
cucullata	MNew WMul
culionensis	MNew
cuprea	MNew
- 'Blackie'	Last listed 1998
- 'Greenback'	Last listed 1998
'Elaine'	MNew
gageana	MNew WMul
'Green Shield'	MNew
'Green Velvet'	MNew
guttata var. *imperialis*	MNew
'Hilo Beauty'	MNew
lancifolia	MNew
longiloba	MNew
lowii var. *veitchii*	See *A. veitchii*
macrorrhiza	EOas MNew WMul
- 'Jungle Gold'	Last listed 1999
- 'Lutea'	MNew WMul
- 'Variegata'	MNew
maximiliana	MNew
michotitziana	MNew
'Mindanao'	MNew
nigra	See *A. plumbea* 'Nigra'
odora	MNew WMul
plumbea	MNew
§ - 'Nigra'	MNew WMul
- white	MNew
porphyroneura	MNew
portei	MNew
'Portora'	MNew WMul
'Quilted Dreams'	MNew
sanderiana 'Nobilis'	MNew
x *sedenii*	MNew
'Tigrina Superba'	MNew
'Uhinkii'	WMul
§ *veitchii*	Last listed 1998
¶ *villeneuvei*	WMul
watsoniana	MNew
wentii	MNew

¶ *wenzelii*   WMul
I *whinkii*   See *A.* 'Uhinkii'
  'White Knight'   MNew
  zebrina   MNew
  - 'Reticulata'   MNew

ALOE (Aloaceae)

  arborescens   CAbb CHEx CTrC CTrF EOas
                            MBro WCot
* - var. *ferox*   CTrF
  aristata ♀   CHEx CHal EOas MBri MBro
                            SAPC SArc WHer
  bakeri ♀   Last listed 1995
  barbadensis   See *A. vera*
  boylei   CCpl CFir
  brevifolia   CRoM CTbh EOas SArc
  broomii   EOas
¶ *camperi*   CTrF
  - 'Maculata'   CTrC CTrF MBri
¶ *castanea*   CTrC
  ciliaris   CHEx ERea
¶ - var. *tidmarshii*   CTrF
¶ *comosa*   CTrF
  cooperi   CAbb
¶ *dawei*   CTrF
  dichotoma   CAbb GBin
  ecklonis   CCpl CTrC
  erinacea   Last listed 1997
  ferox   CCtw CTrC EOas SChr
¶ *globuligemma*   CTrF
  gracilis   CCpl
  grandidentata   CCpl CTrF
  greatheadii var. *davyana* CCpl CCtw
¶ *grisea*   CTrF
  humilis   IBlr
  jacksonii   CCpl
¶ *juvenna*   CTrF
  karasbergensis   Last listed 1998
¶ *lineata* var. *muirii*   CTrF
¶ *marlothii*   CTrF
  melanacantha ♀   Last listed 1995
  mitriformis   CCpl CTrF SChr SEND
  pachygaster   CCpl
  parvibracteata   CTrF
  plicatilis   CTrC EOas
  pluridens   CTrF
  polyphylla   Last listed 1999
  pratensis   CFir CTrC
  raubii ♀   Last listed 1995
  reitzii   CCpl CTrC
¶ *rupestris*   CTrF
  saponaria   CHEx CRoM
  somaliensis ♀   Last listed 1995
  striata   CTrF
  striatula   CFil CHEx CTrC CTrF EOas IBlr
                            SAPC SArc SChr
  - var. *caesia*   IBlr
  succotrina   CTrF
  variegata ♀   CTrF SSte
  veitchii   CTrC
§ *vera* ♀   CArn COld ECon ELau EOHP
                            EOas ERea GPoy ILis LChe LPJP
                            MSal NMoo NPer SIde SRCN
                            WHer WOak
  - grey form   CTrF
  'Walmsley's Blue'   MBri

ALOINOPSIS (Aizoaceae)

¶ *bilmari* 'Laingsburg'   CTrC
  lueckhoffii   Last listed 1997

ALONSOA (Scrophulariaceae)

  acutifolia   Last listed 1997
  - *candida*   Last listed 1998
  - coral   GPin
  linearis   LCot
  meridionalis   EWTr NCut WBea
* - 'Salmon Beauty'   NCut
  'Pink Beauty'   Last listed 1999
  unilabiata   CSpe
  warscewiczii ♀   EBee ECtt ELan ERea LRHS WWin
  - pale form   See *A. warscewiczii* 'Peachy-keen'
§ - 'Peachy-keen'   CSpe ECtt EMan LRHS SAga

ALOPECURUS (Poaceae)

  alpinus   CCuc CInt EHoe EMon LRHS
  - subsp. *glaucus*   CBrm EHoe MWhi
  lanatus   CInt NBea NRya
  pratensis   CKin NOrc
  - 'Aureovariegatus'   More than 30 suppliers
N - 'Aureus'   CMGP ECha EGle EGra GBin
                            LRHS MRav MWhi NArg NBro
                            NSti SCob WByw WPer WRHF
                            WWin
  - 'No Overtaking' (v)   EMon EPPr LRHS

ALOPHIA (Iridaceae)

  drummondii   ERos
  lahue   See *Herbertia lahue*

ALOYSIA (Verbenaceae)

  chamaedrifolia   CPle
  citriodora   See *A. triphylla*
§ *triphylla* ♀   More than 30 suppliers

ALPINIA (Zingiberaceae)

  formosana   EOas WMul
  galanga   Last listed 1999
§ *hainanensis*   LEur
  japonica   EOas MSal
  katsumadai   See *A. hainanensis*
  luteocarpa   Last listed 1998
¶ *officinarum*   CArn
  speciosa   See *A. zerumbet*
§ *zerumbet*   Last listed 1999
  - 'Variegata' (v)   EOas WMul

ALSOBIA See EPISCIA

ALSTROEMERIA ✿ (Alstroemeriaceae)

  'Aimi'   COtt EBee LRHS MBri SBai WViv
  angustifolia P&W 6574 Last listed 1998
  'Apollo' ♀   COtt GKir LRHS MGrG SBai SPer
                            WLRN WViv
  aurantiaca   See *A. aurea*
§ *aurea*   CGle CGre EBee ELan EMar EPfP
                            EWoo LAst MRav NCat NFla NLar
                            NMGW NSti SDys SRms WCot
  - 'Cally Fire'   GCal WCot
  - 'Dover Orange'   CB&S CDoC CGle CTri EBee
                            EMan EPfP LRHS SMrm SPer SRPl
  - 'Golden Bob'   ELan
  - 'Lutea'   EWTr LRHS SPer SPlb
  - 'Orange King'   CBlo ENot EPfP EWll LRHS MTed
                            NLar SDeJ
  brasiliensis   CGle CLAP CMil GCal LPio WCot
  'Bridesmaid'   Last listed 1999
  'Charm'   LRHS
  'Coronet' ♀   COtt EBee LRHS SBai SPer SPla
                            WViv
  'Dayspring Delight' (v) CLAP WTin
§ Diana, Princess of   SSmt

Wales = 'Stablaco'PBR
diluta subsp. *diluta* — Last listed 1998
Doctor Salter's hybrids — ECGP EFou MNrw SRms
'Evening Song' — LRHS MBri SBai WViv
exserens — SBla
- F&W 7207 — WCot
- JCA 14415 — Last listed 1998
'Firefly' — LRHS MBri SBai WViv
'Fortune' — LRHS
¶ 'Friendship' ♀ — WViv
garaventae — Last listed 1998
§ H.R.H. Princess Alexandra = 'Zelblanca' ♀ — SSmt
§ H.R.H. Princess Alice = 'Staverpi'PBR ♀ — SSmt
haemantha — CLAP
- 'Rosea' — EBee WCot
I 'Hatch Hybrid' — Last listed 1997
'Hawera' — Last listed 1999
Hawera Seedlings — GCal
hookeri — ECho MTho
'Inca Charm' — WWeb
¶ 'Inca Delight' — WWeb
¶ 'Inca Dream' — WWeb
'Inca Gold' — WWeb
Inca hybrids — CB&S
¶ 'Inca Ice' — WWeb
¶ 'Inca Moonlight' — WWeb
'Inca Salsa' — WWeb
'Inca Spice' — WWeb
'Inca Sunset' — WWeb
¶ 'Inca Surprise' — WWeb
¶ 'Inca Tropic' — WWeb
ligtu hybrids ♀ — More than 30 suppliers
- variegated hybrid — CRDP
- var. *ligtu* — EBee LGre WFar
'Little Eleanor'PBR — COtt GKir LRHS SBai SPla WViv
'Little Miss Charlotte' — CB&S COtt LRHS MBri SBai WViv
¶ Little Miss Isabel — WViv
'Little Miss Lucy' — CB&S COtt LRHS SBai
'Little Miss Matilda' — CB&S COtt LRHS MBri SBai WViv
'Little Miss Rosanna' — COtt LRHS SBai WViv
'Little Miss Teresa' — MBri
magnifica — Last listed 1999
  subsp. *maxima*
- RB 94012 — Last listed 1998
Manon — See A. Princess Marie-Louise = 'Zelanon'
Margaret = 'Stacova' — Last listed 1997
Marie-Louise — See A. Princess Marie-Louise = 'Zelanon'
'Marina' — LRHS SBai SPer SPla WViv
'Marissa' — EBee LIck LRHS MBri SBai SVil WViv
'Mars' — LRHS
Meyer hybrids — MLLN MTho
'Orange Gem' ♀ — COtt LRHS NCat SBai WViv
'Orange Glory' ♀ — COtt EBee IArd LRHS SBai SPla WViv
pallida — CBro
- F&W 7241 — Last listed 1997
- JCA 12407 — Last listed 1998
- JCA 14335 — Last listed 1998
patagonica P&W 6226 — NTow
§ *paupercula* — CSev
pelegrina — MTho WCot WPnP
- 'Alba' — ELan MRav
- var. *humilis* — WCot
- 'Rosea' — ELan
'Pink Perfection' — LRHS MGrG
presliana — CPou

  subsp. *australis*
- - JCA 12590 — SSpi
- subsp. *presliana* — SBla
- RB 94103 — WCot
Princess® Alice PBR — See A. H.R.H. Princess Alice = 'Staverpi'
Princess® Angela = 'Staprilan'PBR — COtt SSmt
¶ Princess® Astrid = 'Stabopink'PBR — SSmt
§ Princess® Beatrix = 'Stadoran' — SSmt
§ Princess® Carmina = 'Stasilva' ♀ — SSmt
§ Princess® Caroline = 'Stakaros' — SSmt
§ Princess® Charlotte = 'Staprizsa'PBR — SSmt
¶ Princess® Daniela — MMil SSmt
Princess® Elizabeth PBR — See A. Queen Elizabeth The Queen Mother = 'Stamoli'
Princess® Emily = 'Staprimil'PBR — SSmt
§ Princess® Frederika = 'Stabronza' — SSmt
§ Princess® Grace = 'Starodo'PBR ♀ — SSmt
§ Princess® Ileana = 'Stalvir'PBR — SSmt
§ Princess® Juliana = 'Staterpa' ♀ — SSmt
¶ Princess® Leyla — MMil
¶ Princess® Margaret — MMil
Princess® Margarita — Last listed 1999
§ Princess® Marie-Louise = 'Zelanon' — SSmt
* Princess® Marilene — COtt SSmt
§ Princess® Mira = 'Stapripur'PBR ♀ — SSmt
§ Princess® Monica = 'Staprimon'PBR — COtt SSmt
* Princess® Morana — COtt SSmt
¶ Princess® Oxana — LIck
¶ Princess® Pamela — SPla SSmt
Princess® Paola — COtt SSmt
Princess® Ragna — See A. Princess Stephanie = 'Stapirag'
§ Princess® Sarah = 'Stalicamp' — SSmt
§ Princess® Sissi = 'Staprisis'PBR — COtt SSmt
§ Princess® Sophia = 'Stajello'PBR — SSmt
§ Princess® Stephanie = 'Stapirag' — COtt SSmt
¶ Princess® Suzanna — MMil SSmt
Princess® VictoriaPBR — See A. 'Victoria'
¶ Princess® Violet — SSmt
Princess® Zsa ZsaPBR — See A. Princess Charlotte = 'Staprizsa'
pseudospathulata — EBee
- RB 94010 — WCot
§ *psittacina* — CBro CGle CHad CRDP EBee EHrv ELan EPar ERav ERos EWoo GCal MHer MSte NChi SSoC SSpi WCot WFar WPGP WPnP WSHC WSan
¶ - dark flowered — LHop
- variegated — CLAP CMil CRDP EBee EGar ELan EMar EMon EPPr LPio LRHS MGrG MRav WCot WFar WHil WRus

pulchella Sims | See *A. psittacina*
pulchra | LPio SBla
- BC&W 4751 | Last listed 1998
- BC&W 4762 | Last listed 1998
pygmaea | MTho
§ Queen Elizabeth The | LIck MWst SPla SSmt
Queen Mother = |
'Stamoli'PBR |
'Red Beauty' | EBee GKir LRHS MBri MGrG NBir
| NCat SBai SPer SPla WViv
'Red Elf' | GKir LRHS MBri SBai WViv
'Regina'PBR | See *A.* 'Victoria'
revoluta JCA 14378 | Last listed 1998
'Selina' | EBee LRHS MTed SBai SPer SPla
| WViv
short purple | WCot
simsii | Last listed 1998
'Solent Arrow' | Last listed 1997
'Solent Candy' | GKir WFar
'Solent Crest' ♀ | LRHS WFar
'Solent Dawn' | LRHS WFar
'Solent Glow' | Last listed 1997
'Solent Haze' | Last listed 1998
'Solent Mist' | Last listed 1997
'Solent Pride' | WFar
'Solent Rose' ♀ | Last listed 1998
'Solent Wings' | Last listed 1997
sp. F&W 7975 | Last listed 1998
spathulata RB 94015 | WCot
'Spring Delight' (v) | WCot
'Stablaco'PBR | See *A.* Diana, Princess of Wales
| = 'Stablaco'
'Stabronza' | See *A.* Princess Frederika =
| 'Stabronza'
'Stadoran' | See *A.* Princess Beatrix =
| 'Stadoran'
'Stajello'PBR | See *A.* Princess Sophia =
| 'Stajello'
'Stalicamp' | See *A.* Princess Sarah =
| 'Stalicamp'
'Stalvir'PBR | See *A.* Princess Ileana = 'Stalvir'
'Stamoli'PBR | See *A.* Queen Elizabeth The
| Queen Mother = 'Stamoli'
'Stapirag' | See *A.* Princess Stephanie =
| 'Stapirag'
'Staprimon'PBR | See *A.* Princess Monica =
| 'Staprimon'
'Stapripur'PBR | See *A.* Princess Mira = 'Stapripur'
'Staprisis'PBR | See *A.* Princess Sissi = 'Staprisis'
'Staprizsa'PBR | See *A.* Princess Charlotte =
| 'Staprizsa'
'Starodo'PBR | See *A.* Princess Grace = 'Starodo'
I 'Staroko' | See *A.* Princess Caroline =
| 'Starakos'
'Stasilva' | See *A.* Princess Carmina =
| 'Stasilva'
'Staterpa' | See *A.* Princess Juliana =
| 'Staterpa'
'Staverpi'PBR | See *A.* H.R.H. Princess Alice =
| 'Staverpi'
'Sunstar' | LRHS
'Tessa' | LRHS MBri SBai WViv
umbellata F&W 8497 | Last listed 1998
- JCA 14348 | Last listed 1998
'Verona' | LRHS
versicolor F&W 8721 | WHil
§ 'Victoria'PBR | SSmt
violacea | See *A. paupercula*
'White Apollo' | EBee MBri SPla
'Yagana' | GOrP
'Yellow Friendship' ♀ | COtt EBee GKir LRHS MBri SBai
| SPer SPla WLRN WViv

Yellow KingPBR | See *A.* Princess Sophia =
| 'Stajello'
'Yellow Queen' | WFar
'Zelanon' | See *A.* Princess Marie-Louise =
| 'Zelanon'
'Zelblanca' | See *A.* H.R.H. Princess
| Alexandra = 'Zelblanca'

ALTERNANTHERA (Amaranthaceae)
lehmannii | Last listed 1998

ALTHAEA (Malvaceae)
armeniaca | EBee GBuc NCat WCot
cannabina | CRDP EBee GBri GCal MAvo
| MBro MFir NFor SMad SOkh
| WEas WHal WHoo WPGP WWat
| WWhi
officinalis | CAgr CArn CKin CSev ECoo ELan
| ELau EWFC EWTr GBar GMac
| GPoy ILis LHop MChe MHer
| MHew MMil MPEx MSal NDea
| NFai SIde SMer WGwy WOak
| WPer WWye
- *alba* | EBee EGar NLar WHer WHil
§ - 'Romney Marsh' | CStr EWll GCal MRav SMad WCot
| WSHC
rosea | See *Alcea rosea*
rugosostellulata | See *Alcea rugosa*

ALTINGIA (Hamamelidaceae)
chinensis | CMCN

ALYOGYNE (Malvaceae)
hakeifolia | CSpe ECou ERea
§ ***huegelii*** | EDAr EMan LCns LHil LRHS SYvo
- 'Santa Cruz' | CSpe EOrc ERea LHop SBrw
| SOWG

ALYSSOIDES (Brassicaceae)
utriculata | GDea MBNS WCot WPer WWin
- var. ***graeca*** | Last listed 1998

ALYSSUM (Brassicaceae)
argenteum hort. | See *A. murale*
caespitosum | NWCA
corningii | Last listed 1999
corymbosum | See *Aurinia corymbosa*
cuneifolium | Last listed 1998
- var. ***pirinicum*** | Last listed 1998
idaeum | LBee LRHS
markgrafii | CLyd
montanum | CArn ECha GAbr MWat SPlb
| SRms
§ - 'Berggold' | CB&S CTri EMan EPfP GChr
| GMaP LPVe LRHS NPri WLRN
- Mountain Gold | See *A. montanum* 'Berggold'
§ ***murale*** | Last listed 1998
oxycarpum | NMen SBla
propinquum | Last listed 1997
pulvinare | CInt
purpureum | Last listed 1998
pyrenaicum | NWCA
repens | Last listed 1997
saxatile | See *Aurinia saxatilis*
serpyllifolium | CLyd ESis MOne NWCA
spinosum | CMea MBro WAbe WFar
§ - 'Roseum' ♀ | ECha EDAr ELan EPot ESis LBee
| LRHS LSpr MWat NHol NMen
| NWCA SBla WAbe WCot WPat
| WPer WWin
- 'Strawberries and Cream' | WAbe
stribrnyi | Last listed 1998

tortuosum   Last listed 1999
wulfenianum   NMen NRya NTow

AMANA See TULIPA

x AMARCRINUM (Amaryllidaceae)
memoria-corsii   Last listed 1998
- 'Howardii'   EBee LPio LRHS WCot

x AMARINE (Amaryllidaceae)
'Fletcheri'   Last listed 1998
tubergenii   LPio
- 'Zwanenburg'   CAvo

x AMARYGIA (Amaryllidaceae)
parkeri   Last listed 1998
§ - 'Alba'   CAvo

AMARYLLIS (Amaryllidaceae)
§ *belladonna*   CB&S CBro CFil CHEx CStu EPar
                     ERav ETub GVer LAma LBow
                     LRHS MBri NRog SDeJ SPer SSpi
                     WCot WGer WWat
- 'Bloemfontein'   CAvo
- 'Johannesburg'   CAvo EMon LRHS WCot
- 'Kimberley'   EMon
- 'Major'   CAvo
- 'Parkeri Alba'   See x *Amarygia parkeri* 'Alba'
- 'Purpurea'   EBee ETub WCot

AMBROSIA (Asteraceae)
mexicana   Last listed 1997

AMBROSINA (Araceae)
bassii S&L 315   Last listed 1998

AMELANCHIER ✿ (Rosaceae)
alnifolia   CAgr CDul CPle CTho EBee EPla
¶ - 'Northline' (F) ESim
¶ - 'Obelisk'   WWeb
§ - var. *pumila*   CPle CTho EPla GBin GSki LHop
                     MSte NHol SMad SSta WAbe WDin
                     WNor
- 'Smokey'   CBlo ESim
* *alpina*   Last listed 1999
arborea   WNor
bartramiana   CTho SSta
canadensis   More than 30 suppliers
- 'Micropetala'   Last listed 1999
x *grandiflora*   CDoC CEnd LRHS
  'Autumn Brilliance'
- 'Ballerina' ♀   More than 30 suppliers
- 'Robin Hill'   LBuc LPan LRHS MAsh MGos
                     SLim SMad
- 'Rubescens'   CEnd CPMA LPan LRHS MRav
laevis   CB&S CDul SPer
¶ - 'Snow Cloud'   MBri
lamarckii ♀   More than 30 suppliers
lucida   SSta
I *ovalis* 'Edelweiss' CBlo CEnd COtt CPMA GKir
                     LRHS MBri MGos SMur
pumila   See A. *alnifolia* var. *pumila*
rotundifolia 'Helvetia' CDoC CEnd GKir LRHS MBri
                     WEas
'Snowflake'   CBlo CEnd CPMA GKir LRHS
                     MAsh MBri NPro SLim SSta
spicata   Last listed 1998

AMIANTHUM (Melianthaceae)
muscitoxicum   Last listed 1998

AMICIA (Papilionaceae)
zygomeris   CAbb CBot CHEx CMdw CPle
                     CSpe EBee EMan GBuc GCal LHil
                     SMrm SSoC WEas WSHC WWye

AMMI (Apiaceae)
majus   MSal
visnaga   CSpe ELau GPoy IIve MSal

AMMOBIUM (Asteraceae)
alatum   Last listed 1999

AMMOCHARIS (Amaryllidaceae)
coranica   WCot

AMMOPHILA (Poaceae)
arenaria   GQui

AMOMYRTUS (Myrtaceae)
§ *luma*   CDoC CGre CLan CPle CTbh
                     CTrG CTrw EPfP IDee ISea SArc
                     WBod WPic WWat

AMORPHA (Papilionaceae)
canescens   CB&S CBlo CPle EBrP EBre EMan
                     EPfP GKir LBCl LBSe LBre LRHS
                     MBBe MWhi NSti SBre SEND
fruticosa   CAgr CB&S CFil CPle IOrc LEdu
                     MNrw SHFr SLon SPlb

AMORPHOPHALLUS (Araceae)
bulbifer   LAma LRHS WCru WMul
corrugatus B&SWJ 5244 WCru
kiusianus   Last listed 1999
¶ *konjac*   LEur
rivierei   GCal LBlo WMul
¶ *stipitatus*   LEur

AMPELOCALAMUS (Poaceae - Bambusoideae)
scandens   CFil EPla ISta

AMPELODESMOS (Poaceae)
mauritanicus   CBrm COlW EBee EHoe EMan
                     GBin GOrP LEdu LRHS MCCP
                     NOGN WLRN

AMPELOPSIS (Vitaceae)
aconitifolia   CPIN SBra
arborea   CPIN
bodinieri   CPIN
brevipedunculata   See A. *glandulosa* var.
                     brevipedunculata
chaffanjonii   CPIN SMur
§ *glandulosa* var. CB&S GAri MGrG SLim SPer
  brevipedunculata WDin WWat
- - B&SWJ 1094   Last listed 1999
- - f. *citrulloides* WCru
  B&SWJ 1173
§ - - 'Elegans' (v) More than 30 suppliers
- - 'Tricolor'   See A. *glandulosa* var.
                     brevipedunculata 'Elegans'
- var. *hancei* B&SWJ 1793 Last listed 1999
- - B&SWJ 3855   WCru
- var. *heterophylla* Last listed 1999
  B&SWJ 667
* - var. *maximowiczii* CPIN
henryana   See *Parthenocissus henryana*
megalophylla   CB&S CBot CFil CGre CHEx CPIN
                     EBee ELan EPfP LRHS SPer WBcn
                     WCru WNor WOVN WPGP WWat
orientalis   CPIN

sempervirens hort.   See *Cissus striata*
sinica   WCru
sp. from Taiwan   Last listed 1997
   B&SWJ 1173
thunbergii   CPlN
- B&SWJ 1863   Last listed 1999
tricuspidata 'Veitchii'   See *Parthenocissus tricuspidata*
   'Veitchii'

AMPHICOME See INCARVILLEA

AMSONIA (Apocynaceae)
ciliata   CFir EBee ECGN LFis LGre LRHS
   NCat SMrm WFar WPer
eastwoodiana   EBee
hubrichtii   EBee EMan
illustris   EBee LRHS MSte SMac WTin
jonesii   EBee WFar
§ *orientalis* ♀   CFri CHad CHea CMil EBee ECha
   EFou EGle EMan EPar ERea LGre
   LHop LRHS LSpr MBri MCAu
   MHar MRav SCro SMrm SUsu
   WFar WHil WPGP WPnP WWin
tabernaemontana   CFir CHad CLyd EBee ECGN ECha
   ELan EMan EMil EWTr GBuc LGre
   LRHS MMil MNrw NDov SAga
   SOkh SRms SSca WCot WFar WHil
   WPer
* - *galacticifolia*   EBee
- var. *salicifolia*   EBee EGle EOrc GKir GSki LRHS
   MSte
tomentosa   EBee

AMYGDALUS See PRUNUS

ANACAMPTIS (Orchidaceae)
pyramidalis   EFEx WHer

ANACARDIUM (Anacardiaceae)
occidentale (F)   Last listed 1999

ANACYCLUS (Asteraceae)
pyrethrum   GPoy
- var. *depressus*   CGle EBrP EBre ELan EMNN EMar
   ESis GKir GMaP GTou LBCl LBSe
   LBre LRHS MBBe NFor NHol
   NLAp NVic NWCA SBla SBre SIng
   SRms WFar WHoo WLin WPer
   WWin
- - 'Golden Gnome'   MSCN SGar
- - 'Silberkissen'   Last listed 1997

ANAGALLIS (Primulaceae)
alternifolia var. *repens*   Last listed 1999
arvensis   EWFC MHer MSal WEas WHbs
¶ - subsp. *arvensis*   EWFC
   f. *azurea*
- var. *caerulea*   Last listed 1999
foemina   MSal
linifolia   See *A. monellii* subsp. *linifolia*
§ *monellii* ♀   CNic ECtt EPot LRHS SBla SUsu
   WWin
§ - subsp. *linifolia*   Last listed 1999
- 'Sunrise'   CPBP LRHS SBla SUsu
'Skylover'   EMan
tenella   EWFC
- 'Studland' ♀   EDAr EPot LRHS NMen NWCA
   SBla SIng WAbe

ANANAS (Bromeliaceae)
comosus   LRHS
- var. *variegatus*   MBri

ANAPHALIS (Asteraceae)
alpicola   EPot MTed NMen
margaritacea   COIW ECtt EMon EOld EWTr
   GBin GGar GMaP MBri MLLN
   NBid NBro NOak SMer SPar SRms
   SSpe WByw WFar
§ - var. *cinnamomea*   CGle ELan EMon WEas
§ - 'Neuschnee'   CTri GKir LFis MGed MWgw
   NArg NHol NMir NPri SPla WBea
   WPer
- New Snow   See *A. margaritacea* 'Neuschnee'
§ - var. *yedoensis* ♀   CBre CTri EBee ECha ECot EFou
   EGle EPar MWat SDix SPer WBrE
   WLRN
nepalensis B&SWJ 1634   Last listed 1998
- var. *monocephala*   CGle EBee ELan EMon MCAu
   MWat NSti SRms
- - CC&McK 550   Last listed 1997
nubigena   See *A. nepalensis* var.
   monocephala
sinica subsp. *morii*   Last listed 1998
sp. ACE 1503   WCot
sp. ACE 1832   WCot
¶ *subumbellata*   EBrP EBre LBCl LBSe LBre MBBe
   SBre
triplinervis ♀   CGle EBee EFou ELan ENot GGar
   GKir GMaP LHrt MBrN MHer
   MLLN MRav MWgw NBro NFla
   NFor NSti NVic SPer SRms SSpe
   SWat WByw WCot WEas WFar
   WHoo WRus WWin
- CC 1620   GGar WCot
¶ - dwarf   GMac
§ - 'Sommerschnee' ♀   EBee EBrP EBre ECha ECot ECtt
   EFou EGle LBCl LBSe LBre LRHS
   MBBe MBri MCLN MTis MWgw
   NFor SAga SBre SChu SLon SPer
   WBea WElm WPer WWal
- Summer Snow   See *A. triplinervis*
   'Sommerschnee'
yedoensis   See *A. margaritacea* var.
   yedoensis

ANARRHINUM (Scrophulariaceae)
bellidifolium   EBee NPri
¶ *orientale*   WLin

ANCHUSA (Boraginaceae)
angustissima   See *A. leptophylla* subsp. *incana*
arvensis   MHew
§ *azurea*   GKir NCut NOrc WPer
- 'Blue Angel'   CBlo EMan EWll GKir LRHS
- 'Dropmore'   CBlo COIW CTri EBee EPfP EWTr
   LRHS MWgw NBus NOrc NPer
   SIde SRms WOve WPer
- ES 33   Last listed 1999
- 'Feltham Pride'   ECtt GKir GMaP NCut NPer
   WElm WFar WHoo WOve WPGP
   WPer WPyg
- 'Kingfisher Blue'   Last listed 1998
- 'Little John'   COtt ECot LRHS MChl SAga SRms
- 'Loddon Royalist' ♀   More than 30 suppliers
- 'Morning Glory'   Last listed 1998
- 'Opal'   CGle EBee ECot EMan EPfP LHop
   LRHS MWat SMrm SPla WElm
   WLRN
- 'Royal Blue'   LRHS
barrelieri   MLLN
caespitosa hort.   See *A. leptophylla* subsp. *incana*
capensis   EBee
cespitosa Lamarck ♀   ELan EPot EWes SBla SIng

italica	See *A. azurea*
laxiflora	See *Borago pygmaea*
§ *leptophylla*	CRDP EBee EMFP EMan EMar
subsp. *incana*	GBri LRHS WCot
myosotidiflora	See *Brunnera macrophylla*
officinalis	CArn MHew MSal SIde
sempervirens	See *Pentaglottis sempervirens*
undulata	EBee

ANDRACHNE (Euphorbiaceae)
¶ *colchica*	WCot

ANDROCYMBIUM (Colchicaceae)
europaeum MS 510	Last listed 1998
gramineum SB&L 26	Last listed 1998
punicum S&L 325	Last listed 1998
rechingeri	Last listed 1998

ANDROMEDA (Ericaceae)
glaucophylla	IOrc MBar SBrw
polifolia	CMHG CSam EMil GCrs GKir
	IOrc SBrw WBod WDin WFar
- 'Alba'	ELan GChr LRHS MAsh MBar
	MBro MDun MGos MRav NHar
	NHol SBod SBrw SPer SPlb WAbe
	WLin WPat WPyg WWin
- 'Blue Ice'	EPfP GKir LRHS MAsh SPer SSpi
	SSta
- 'Compacta' ♀	CHor EMil EPot EWTr GCHN
	GCrs GGar GKir IMGH LRHS
	MAsh MBar MBri MGos NHar
	NHol NMen SPer SReu SRms WPat
	WPyg WSHC WWin
* - 'Compacta Alba' ♀	Last listed 1992
- 'Grandiflora'	ITim LRHS MAsh MBri MDun
	MGos SBod SPer
- 'Hayachine'	EPot
- 'Kirigamine'	LRHS MAsh MBri MGos NHol
	WPat WPyg
- 'Macrophylla' ♀	EPot GCrs GDra ITim MBro NDlv
	NHar NHol SSta WAbe WPat WPyg
- 'Major'	Last listed 1999
- 'Minima'	Last listed 1999
- 'Nana'	ELan EPfP EPot GKir LNet LRHS
	MAsh MGos NMen SPer STre
	WAbe WLRN WStI WWat WWeb
- 'Nikko'	CBlo GBuc MAsh MGos NHol
	WPat WPyg
- 'Red Winter'	CBlo CRos LRHS
- 'Shibutsu'	GAri MGos SSta

ANDROPOGON (Poaceae)
gerardii	CBrm COIW EBrP EBre ECGN
	EHoe EMan EMon EPPr GBin LBCl
	LBSe LBre LGre LRHS MAnH
	MBBe SBre WHal WPer
ischaemum	See *Bothriochloa ischaemum*
saccharoides	Last listed 1997
scoparius	See *Schizachyrium scoparium*
¶ *virginicus*	CBrm LGre

ANDROSACE (Primulaceae)
albana	EWes NWCA
armeniaca	Last listed 1999
var. *macrantha*	
axillaris ACE 1060	WAbe
barbulata	CMea GCHN
bulleyana	Last listed 1999
- ACE 2198	EPot
cantabrica	Last listed 1999
carnea	CPBP GCHN LRHS MNrw NHar
	NMen SIng WWin

- *alba*	LBee LRHS MBro NHar NWCA
	WLin
- subsp. *brigantiaca*	GTou MBro NHar NMen NSla SIng
	WAbe WHoo
- var. *halleri*	See *A. carnea* subsp. *rosea*
- subsp. *laggeri* ♀	ECho EPot GCrs GTou NHar NSla
	WPat
- - 'Andorra'	WAbe
- x *pyrenaica*	CGra EPot GCHN NHar NMen
	SOkd
§ - subsp. *rosea* ♀	CPBP GDra NTow
- - x *carnea*	NHol
subsp. *laggeri*	
chamaejasme	CGra
ciliata	GTou NMen WAbe
cylindrica	CGra CPBP EPot GCHN GCrs
	GTou LRHS NHar NMen SBla SIng
	WFar
- x *hirtella*	GTou LRHS NHar NMen SIng
	WAbe
¶ - 'Val d'Ossue'	EPot
delavayi	Last listed 1999
foliosa	Last listed 1997
geraniifolia	CPLG EBee ECha GCHN IHdy
	WAbe WCru
- ex CC&McK 109	Last listed 1999
globifera	NHar NMen WAbe
hausmannii	GCHN GTou
hedraeantha	CLyd EPot MWat NMen NWCA
	WAbe WLin
x *heeri*	Last listed 1997
¶ - white	GCHN SBla
himalaica	Last listed 1999
hirtella	EPot GCHN GTou NHar NTow
¶ *hookeriana* CC 2813	MDCh
jacquemontii	See *A. villosa* var. *jacquemontii*
lactea	GCHN GTou MHar WAbe
§ *lactiflora*	CNic
§ *laevigata*	CGra WAbe
- var. *ciliolata*	GTou
- - NNS 94-38	Last listed 1999
- 'Gothenburg' AM	WPat
§ - var. *laevigata*	Last listed 1999
'Packwood'	
lanuginosa ♀	CLyd CMea CPBP EPot GCrs LRHS
	MBro MWat NMen NWCA SBla
	SDys SIng WAbe WWin
- CC 1271	NTow
- compact form	EPot
- 'Leichtlinii'	Last listed 1998
- 'Wisley Variety'	Last listed 1999
limprichtii	See *A. sarmentosa* var. *watkinsii*
x *marpensis*	EPot
mathildae	GTou NMen NWCA WHoo
- x *carnea*	NMen
microphylla	See *A. mucronifolia* Watt
§ *mollis*	CPBP EPot SIng
§ *montana*	CGra NWCA WLin
§ *mucronifolia* hort.	See *A. sempervivoides*
§ *mucronifolia* Watt	EPot GTou
- CHP&W 296	NWCA
- Schacht's form	Last listed 1999
- x *sempervivoides*	EPot
- SEP 284	Last listed 1999
muscoidea	EPot NWCA WAbe
- C&R 188	GTou
- f. *longiscapa*	GCrs NWCA
- f. *muscoidea*	Last listed 1997
- Schacht's form	CPBP SBla
- SEP 132	Last listed 1998
§ *nivalis*	NTow
primuloides	See *A. studiosorum*

* – white	Last listed 1998
pubescens	EPot GCHN LRHS SBla SIng
pyrenaica	CGra GCHN GTou ITim LRHS
	NHar NMen NTow SBla SIng
	WAbe
rigida ACE 2336	EPot
– KGB 168	EPot
robusta	Last listed 1998
* – subsp. *purpurea*	WAbe
rotundifolia	GCHN GTou LRHS WCru
sarmentosa Wall.	EDAr ELan GTou ITim LBee MBro
	MWat NMen NNrd SRms SSmi
	WAbe WHoo WPyg
– 'Brilliant'	Last listed 1997
¶ – CC 2727	MDCh
– CC 407	LRHS
– 'Chumbyi'	See *A. studiosorum* 'Chumbyi'
¶ – from Namche, Nepal	WAbe
I – Galmont's form	See *A. studiosorum* 'Salmon's Variety'
– misapplied	See *A. studiosorum*
– 'Salmon's Variety'	See *A. studiosorum* 'Salmon's Variety'
¶ – 'Sherriffii'	EPot GCHN GCrs MBro NHar SBla SRms WLin WWin
§ – var. *watkinsii*	EPot MBro MTed NHar NMen WLin
– var. *yunnanensis*	See *A. mollis*
– – misapplied	See *A. studiosorum*
§ *sempervivoides* ♀	CLyd ECha EDAr ELan GCHN GCrs GDra LBee LRHS MBro NDlv NHar NHol NMen NWCA SBla SIng SRms WHoo WLin WPat WPyg WWin
– scented	MBro
– 'Susan Joan' (v)	WAbe
sericea	Last listed 1999
sp. CD&R 2477	WCru
spinulifera	Last listed 1997
§ *studiosorum* ♀	GCHN NCat
* – alba	Last listed 1998
¶ – 'Chumbyi'	EHol MBro MOne NHol NTow NWCA SBla SRms WPat
– 'Doksa'	EPot GCrs NMen SOkd WAbe
§ – 'Salmon's Variety'	CMea CTri
tapete	Last listed 1999
– ACE 1725	EPot
vandellii	CGra EPot GCHN GTou
villosa	Last listed 1998
– var. *arachnoidea*	Last listed 1998
– – 'Superba'	NMen
– var. *congesta*	CGra
§ – var. *jacquemontii*	LRHS NHar NMen NTow NWCA SBla
– – lilac	EPot
– – pink	EPot MTed
– subsp. *taurica*	CLyd EPot
– – 'Palandoken'	Last listed 1999
vitaliana	See *Vitaliana primuliflora*
watkinsii	See *A. sarmentosa* var. *watkinsii*
yargongensis ACE 1722	EPot

ANDRYALA (Asteraceae)
agardhii	NNrd NTow NWCA WPat
lanata	See *Hieracium lanatum*

ANEMARRHENA (Asphodelaceae)
asphodeloides	EBee MSal WCot

ANEMIA (Schizaeaceae)
phyllitidis	Last listed 1999

ANEMONE ✿ (Ranunculaceae)
altaica	GAbr SRms WCot
apennina ♀	CAvo CLAP EPar SCro SRms WTin
– var. *albiflora*	CLAP CRDP EBee EPot ERos LRHS
– double	Last listed 1999
– 'Petrovac' CE&H 538	EBee EPot LRHS WCot
baicalensis	NSti
baldensis	CGle EBee ECho GAbr LBee LHop LRHS NBur NMen NOak SRms
barbulata	Last listed 1999
blanda ♀	EBrP EBre EOrc GKir LAma LBCl LBSe LBre MBBe MBri MBro NChi NFla NRog SBre SChu WBea WBro WCot WFar WPer WShi
– blue	CAvo CBro CMea CTri ELan EPar EPot ETub GAbr GKir LAma LRHS MBri MBro SRms WFar
– 'Blue Shades'	LRHS WHil WPGP
– 'Charmer'	EPar EPot LRHS MBNS MNrw NMen
– 'Ingramii' CE&H 626 ♀	EMan EPar GBri LAma NRog SGar SRms WCot
– 'Pink Star'	CBro EPot EWTr LAma LRHS MBNS NBir NRog SRms
– 'Radar' ♀	CAvo CBro CLAP CMea EPar EPot LAma MNrw NBir NMen NRog SRms SVal
– var. *rosea* ♀	CAvo CFwr ELan LAma MLLN WFar WPer
– 'Violet Star'	EPot LRHS
– 'White Splendour' ♀	CAvo CBro CElw CGle CMea ECha ELan EOrc EPar EPot ETub EWTr GAbr GKir LAma LFis LRHS MBro MNrw NChi NMen NRog SChu SRms WCot WFar WHil WPGP WPer WRus
¶ 'Bressingham Beauty'	EWTr
canadensis	CBos CElw CHar CSpe EBee EBrP EBre ECGP GAbr LBCl LBSe LBre MBBe MBrN MNrw MTis NBur NSti NWoo SBre WCot WElm WRos WSan
caroliniana	CGle CLyd EBee EBrP EBre EPla EPot ESis GAbr GBuc GCrs LBCl LBSe LBre LRHS MBBe NOak SBre WCru
caucasica	EPot SBla
coronaria	GVer
– De Caen Group	LAma LRHS NRog WFar
§ – – 'Die Braut'	CGle MNrw NRog
– – 'His Excellency'	See *A. coronaria* (De Caen Group) 'Hollandia'
§ – – 'Hollandia'	MNrw
– – 'Mister Fokker'	ETub LAma MNrw NRog
– – The Bride	See *A. coronaria* (De Caen Group) 'Die Braut'
– – 'The Governor'	GSki MDun MNrw NRog
– 'Jerusalem'	WFar
– (Mona Lisa Group) 'Sylphide'	MNrw NRog
– MS 783	Last listed 1998
– MS&CL 613	Last listed 1998
– Saint Bridgid Group (d)	LAma MBri NRog SDeJ WFar
– – 'Creagh Castle'	Last listed 1997
– – 'Lord Lieutenant' (d)	MDun MNrw NBir NBur NRog
– – 'Mount Everest' (d)	MNrw NBir
– – 'The Admiral' (d)	ETub MNrw NBir NRog
– Saint Piran Group	SDeJ
crinita	EBee

cylindrica   CFir CGle CSWP EBee EBlw GAbr MNrw

decapetala   GCal

demissa   GAbr NRya

drummondii   CHar CLyd EBee EBrP EBre GAbr LBCl LBSe LBre LRHS MBBe MBrN NBur NPri SBre

elongata B&SWJ 2975   WCru

eranthoides   WCot

fasciculata   See *A. narcissiflora*

flaccida   CBro CRDP EBee EPot GMac LGre LRHS SIng WCot WCru WFar

x *fulgens*   ECha NWCA SVal

- 'Annulata Grandiflora'   Last listed 1998

- 'Multipetala'   ETub NRog

- Saint Bavo Group   CBro

globosa   See *A. multifida*

'Guernica'   ECho GBuc SRot

hepatica   See *Hepatica nobilis*

§ *hortensis*   CMil SBla WCot WWat

- *alba*   Last listed 1998

- subsp. *heldreichii*   EBee

- JCA 161.003   Last listed 1999

- MS 958   Last listed 1998

§ *hupehensis*   CBlo CBot EBee EWll GKir LFis LRHS NOrc SVal WCot WFar

¶ - f. *alba*   CMil WPGP

§ - 'Bowles' Pink' ♀   CBlo CMil CRDP EBee EGle EPPr LRHS MAnH MBro MWat WCot WCru WHoo WMaN WPGP

- 'Crispa'   See *A.* x *hybrida* 'Lady Gilmour'

- 'Eugenie'   CGle CMil CStr EBee EMan LRHS SSca

- 'Hadspen Abundance' ♀   More than 30 suppliers

§ - var. *japonica*   CGle CPou GCal NCiC NFor WCru WEas

- - 'Bodnant Burgundy'   LRHS

§ - - 'Bressingham Glow'   More than 30 suppliers

§ - - 'Pamina' ♀   More than 30 suppliers

- - Prince Henry   See *A. hupehensis* var. *japonica* 'Prinz Heinrich'

§ - - 'Prinz Heinrich' ♀   More than 30 suppliers

§ - - 'Rotkäppchen'   CBos CLon EMan EWTr GCal LBuc MRav NBrk NSti

- 'Praecox'   CBel EBee EWTr GBri LRHS MBNS MBri MCLN NGdn NHol NSti SCro SLod WAbb WCru WHal WWal WWin

- 'September Charm'   See *A.* x *hybrida* 'September Charm'

- 'Splendens'   CBlo CMHG COIW CPLG EBee EMan LAst LRHS LSyl MBri NCiC NCut NHol SPer SSca SWal WAbb WBro WFar WHal WPyg WRHF

- 'Superba'   GKir WKif

§ x *hybrida*   CAvo CGle EBee EPar MBro NCih NOak SChu SGar SPla SRms WAbe WBod WCru WFar WHil WHoo WRHF

- 'Alba' hort. (UK)   See *A.* x *hybrida* 'Honorine Jobert'

- 'Andrea Atkinson'   CMGP EBee EGar EMan EPfP GMac LAst LRHS MBri MBro NCut NHol NPSI NPri NSti SChu SMrm WFar WHil WHoo WLRN

- 'Bowles' Pink'   See *A. hupehensis* 'Bowles' Pink'

- 'Bressingham Glow'   See *A. hupehensis* var. *japonica* 'Bressingham Glow'

- 'Coupe d'Argent'   EGar

- 'Elegans' ♀   EFou EGar MRav SWat WCru

§ - 'Géante des Blanches' ♀   CBlo CBos CLon CMil EBee ECtt EGar GKir GMac LRHS MAnH MBro MSph WFar WHoo

§ - 'Honorine Jobert' ♀   More than 30 suppliers

§ - 'Königin Charlotte' ♀   More than 30 suppliers

- 'Kriemhilde'   EBee GCal GMac

§ - 'Lady Gilmour'   CAvo CBel CBos CElw CFai CFri CRDP CSpe EBee EGle EHol EMan GCal GKir GMaP GMac LRHS MAnH MCCP MTis NChi NEgg NHol NSti SAga WCot WCra WCru WOve

- 'Lady Gilmour' misapplied   See *A.* x *hybrida* 'Margarete'

- 'Loreley'   CBlo CBos CHad EBee EGle EMan LAst LRHS MBNS MCLN MWat NCut NPSI SMrm SPer WHil

- 'Luise Uhink'   CBlo CGle CHor CPou NBir SSpi WCot WEas

§ - 'Margarete'   More than 30 suppliers

- 'Max Vogel'   LGre MTed WBcn WHil

- 'Monterosa'   See *A.* x *hybrida* 'Margarete'

- 'Pamina'   See *A. hupehensis* var. *japonica* 'Pamina'

- Prince Henry   See *A. hupehensis* var. *japonica* 'Prinz Heinrich'

- 'Prinz Heinrich'   See *A. hupehensis* var. *japonica* 'Prinz Heinrich'

- 'Profusion'   LRHS MTis NCut NHaw WCot WPyg WRus

- Queen Charlotte   See *A.* x *hybrida* 'Königin Charlotte'

- 'Richard Ahrens'   CDoC EBee EGle EMan GBuc GKir GMaP GMac LGre LHop LRHS MBel MBri NHol NOrc SCro SMrm SWat WCot WCru WFar WHil WPnP WWal

- 'Rosenschale'   CBos EGle GCal MBri WCru WFar

- 'Rotkäppchen'   See *A. hupehensis* var. *japonica* 'Rotkäppchen'

§ - 'September Charm' ♀   More than 30 suppliers

- 'Serenade'   CFri EBee EFou EGle EMan EPfP LRHS MBri MTed NBir NCut NHol NPSI SSvw SVil WFar WHil WWat

* - 'Thomas Ahrens'   Last listed 1997

- Tourbillon   See *A.* x *hybrida* 'Whirlwind'

§ - 'Whirlwind'   More than 30 suppliers

- 'White Queen'   See *A.* x *hybrida* 'Géante des Blanches'

- Wirbelwind   See *A.* x *hybrida* 'Whirlwind'

japonica   See *A.* x *hybrida*, *A. hupehensis*

x *lesseri*   CBrm CFri CGle CLyd ECha ELan EPri ESis GCrs GMac MBri MBro NMen NSti NWoo SBla SMad SPer SRms WBea WCru WFar WHoo WPat WWin

§ - red   CFir CSpe EBee GAbr MBNS MRav NBur NFor NSla SGar WHil

leveillei   CHar CMil CRDP EBee ELan GAbr GMac LGre LRHS MFir MHar MLLN MTis WAbe WCot WCru WSan WSpi

§ x *lipsiensis*   CAvo CBro CLon CRDP CStu EBee ECha EGle EPar EPot ERos GCHN LGre MRav MTho NFla NTow NWCA SUsu WAbe WCru WFar WHal WLin WPGP

- 'Pallida' ♀   CBos CHad CPlt CRDP ERos GCrs NPar NRar WAbe WCot WRus

N *magellanica* hort.   See *A. multifida*

§ *multifida*   More than 30 suppliers

- var. *globosa*   WWhi

- 'Major'   CFir CLyd CRDP EBee LAst MBro MMal NHol NWCA SAga SBla SMad WCFE WCot WHil WMoo

- pink	WSan
- f. *polysepala*	GAbr
- misapplied red	See *A.* x *lesseri* red
* - 'Rubra'	LAst NDlv NSti
¶ - white	EBrP EBre LBCl LBSe LBre MBBe SBre
§ *narcissiflora*	ECGP GGar GSki LSyl NHar SVal
- *citrina*	EBrP EBre LBCl LBSe LBre MBBe SBre
nemorosa ♀	CAvo CBro CCuc CElw CGle CKin EBee ELau EOld EPar EPot ETub EWFC IMGH LAma LBow LSyl MMal MNaF MSal NHar NHol SCob SIng SRms SSpi WCot WFar WShi
N - 'Alba Plena' (d)	CBro CCuc CHea CSWP EBee ECha EPot ERos GBuc GGar GMac IMGH LRHS MTho NMGW NMen NTow SIng SUsu WAbb WCot WCru WEas WFar WHil WRus
- 'Allenii' ♀	CBro CHea CLAP CSpe EBee ECha EPar EPot ERos GMac LGre LSyl MRav NHar NMen NPar NRya NTow SIng SSpi WAbe WCot WCru WPGP
- 'Amy Doncaster'	SCro
- 'Atrocaerulea'	EPar EPot GBuc IBlr NHol WCru
- 'Blue Beauty'	CLAP EPot ERos GBuc IBlr NMen WAbe WCru
- 'Blue Bonnet'	CElw GBuc WCot
- 'Blue Eyes' (d)	CBos CLAP CRDP EGle IBlr NPar SUsu WCot WCru
- 'Blue Queen'	EPot
- 'Bowles' Purple'	EBee EPar EPot GMac IBlr NHar NPar NRar NRya NTow SIng WAbe WCot WCru WFar WIvy WPGP
- 'Bracteata'	NDov
- 'Bracteata Peniflora' (d)	EBee ECha EGle EPot GBuc IBlr LHop MBro NWoo WAbe WCot WCru WFar
- 'Buckland'	IBlr
- 'Caerulea'	EPot
- 'Cedric's Pink'	EGle IBlr WCot WCru
- 'Danica'	Last listed 1999
- 'Dee Day'	CLAP EPPr GBuc NPar WAbe
- 'Flore Pleno' (d)	EBee EBrP EBre EOrc EPar GKir GMaP LBCl LBSe LBre MBBe MBro NBir NRar SBre WMaN WPGP
- 'Green Fingers'	ECho EPot GBuc LGre WAbe WCru WIvy
- 'Hannah Gubbay'	CLAP CRDP EBee EGle EPar IBlr WAbe
- 'Hilda'	CLAP EGle EPar EPot GBuc NDlv NMen NRya NTow WAbe
- 'Knightshayes Vestal' (d)	MRav WCot WIvy
- 'Lady Doneraile'	CLAP EBee ECha NTow WCru WFar
- 'Leeds' Variety' ♀	CRDP EGle EPot LGre MTho NHar NHol WCot
- 'Lychette'	CAvo EBee EGle EPar EPot GBuc IBlr LGre WAbe WCru
- 'Monstrosa'	EBee EPar EPot
- 'Parlez Vous'	CMil EBee EGle WCru
- 'Pentre Pink'	CBos EGle IBlr MTho WAbe WCru WIvy
- 'Picos Pink'	Last listed 1999
- pink	CPlt EPot LGre WCru
- x *ranunculoides*	See *A.* x *lipsiensis*
- 'Robinsoniana' ♀	More than 30 suppliers
- 'Rosea'	CGle EPot GMac NRar WCru
- 'Royal Blue'	CBos CLAP CMea CMil CNic CRDP EBee ECha EPar EPot GBuc GMac LAma NHol NMen SLod SUsu WAbe WCru WFar WTin
¶ - 'Tomas'	GMac
- 'Vestal' ♀	More than 30 suppliers
- 'Virescens' ♀	CAvo CMea MTed NPar NRar SIng WAbe WIvy WLin
- 'Viridiflora'	CFri CMil CRDP EBee GKir GMac LGre MCCP MRav MTho NSti SSpi SUsu WCot WCru WFar
- 'Westwell Pink'	WCot
- 'Wilks' Giant'	EBee WCot WCru
- 'Wilks' White'	CLAP EGle EPar EPot
- 'Wyatt's Pink'	CAvo CLAP LGre WAbe WCru
obtusiloba	CRDP GBuc GCrs GDra GTou IMGH MTho NHar SBla SRms
- *alba*	CRDP GDra LSyl NHar NHol NMen SBla WAbe
¶ - yellow	SBla
¶ 'Orange King'	MNaF
palmata	CPou GAbr WCru
- 'Alba'	Last listed 1998
- MS 413	Last listed 1998
parviflora	CHea
patens	See *Pulsatilla patens*
pavonina	ECha ERos MTho SBla SSca SVal
polyanthes	EBrP EBre GTou LBCl LBSe LRHS MBBe SBre
pseudoaltaica	WCru
- L 2084 blue	SBla
- L 2085 white	SBla
- purple	Last listed 1999
- white	Last listed 1999
pulsatilla	See *Pulsatilla vulgaris*
ranunculoides ♀	More than 30 suppliers
* - *laciniata*	GBuc
- 'Pleniflora' (d)	CHea CLAP CRDP EBee ECha EPar EPot MRav WCot WFar WIvy
richardsonii	CPla
riparia	See *A. virginiana* var. *alba*
rivularis	More than 30 suppliers
- CLD 573	WLin
rupicola	NBir SRot
x *seemannii*	See *A.* x *lipsiensis*
* *sherriffii*	Last listed 1997
sp. B&SWJ 1452	WCru
sp. from China PLW12/93	WCot
stellata	See *A. hortensis*
sulphurea	See *Pulsatilla alpina* subsp. *apiifolia*
sylvestris	More than 30 suppliers
§ - 'Elise Fellmann' (d)	CLAP CRDP LGre WCot
- 'Flore Pleno'	See *A. sylvestris* 'Elise Fellmann'
- 'Macrantha'	CLAP CRDP EBee GCHN LAst LRHS NCut NPSI SAga SMrm SSpi WCot WPGP
tetrasepala	Last listed 1998
§ *tomentosa*	CBel CGle CMGP EBee ECha EMan EOld GGar LRHS SCro SMrm SRms SWat WGwG WRha WWal WWhi
- 'Robustissima'	CGle EBee EFou EGra ENot EPfP LRHS MBri MChl MWgw NCut NHol NPri NSti SPer SPla WAbb WFar
trifolia	CRDP EBee ECha EPPr EPot ERos GAbr GMac NMen SUsu WCot
- 'Semiplena' (d)	WCot
trullifolia	CPlt CRDP GCrs NHar SBla
- *alba*	GGar GTou

- blue form	GTou
- SBEC 797	Last listed 1999
vernalis	See *Pulsatilla vernalis*
virginiana	CFir EBee GBin MSte MTed NBur NChi WFar WHil
§ - var. *alba*	Last listed 1999
§ *vitifolia* hort.	See *A. tomentosa*
§ *vitifolia* DC.	Last listed 1999
- B&SWJ 1452	Last listed 1999
- B&SWJ 2320	WCru
- CC&McK 43	CGle

ANEMONELLA (Ranunculaceae)

thalictroides	CElw CFir CGra CLAP CRDP CStu EFEx EPar GGar IMGH LAma NHar NMen NTow SBla SMrm WAbe WCot WCru WFar WLin WWat
- 'Alba Plena' (d)	NHar
- 'Amelia'	GCrs NPar SOkd
- 'Betty Blake'	GCrs NHar
- 'Cameo'	CLAP EFEx MS&S
- 'Double Green'	EFEx
- double pink (d)	NHar SAga SBla
- 'Full Double White'	EFEx SAga
- 'Green Hurricane'	EFEx
- 'Oscar Schoaf' (d)	MS&S NHar WAbe
- pink	CElw CLAP CRDP EPar GBuc LPio
¶ - f. *rosea*	LEur
- semi-double white (d)	CLAP CRDP EPar SBla WCot

ANEMONOPSIS (Ranunculaceae)

macrophylla	CBro CRDP EBee ECha EMan GCal IHdy LGre LRHS MNrw MTho NLar NTow SBla SSpi WCot WCru

ANEMOPAEGMA (Bignoniaceae)

chamberlaynii	CPIN

ANEMOPSIS (Saururaceae)

californica	CRDP EOHP

ANETHUM (Apiaceae)

graveolens	CArn EOHP GPoy LRHS MChe MHer MMal SIde WCer WPer WSel WWye
- 'Dukat'	CSev ELau GPoy MChe WGwG
- 'Fern Leaved'	CBod WGwG WJek
- 'Sowa'	EOHP

ANGELICA (Apiaceae)

acutiloba	EBee NChi SBla
- JCA via P.Kelaidis	Last listed 1999
archangelica	CArn CFri CGle CSev ECha EEls ELan ELau GAbr GBar GPoy LHrt MBri MCLN MChe MHer MHew MTis NBid NBro NFai SChu SIde SWat WHbs WOak WOve WPer WSel WWye
- 'Corinne Tremaine' (v)	MAvo NDov NEgg NSti SPer WCHb WCot
arguta	EBee
atropurpurea	CHad CSpe EBee ECGN ECoo EGar EWll GBar LGre MFir MHer MLLN MNrw MSal MSte NBur NGHP NLar SWat WCHb WHil
¶ *daburica*	CArn IIve
gigas	More than 30 suppliers
- B&SWJ 4170	WCru
grayi	EBee
* *hispanica*	CSpe EBee EWll MCCP MLLN

	NSti SSca STes WCHb WCru WElm
montana	See *A. sylvestris*
pachycarpa	CRDP EBee EFou EMan EOHP LPio NChi SDix SWat WHil
polymorpha sinensis	EOHP GPoy MSal
razulii	EBee
saxatilis	EBee IIve
§ sp. PC&H 129	WBry
§ *sylvestris*	CAgr CArn CKin EWFC GBar MSal WCHb WGwy WHer
* - 'Purpurea'	CMea CSpe EWes GKir MSph WCot
taiwaniana	EBee EBrP EBre LBCl LBSe LBre MBBe SBre SWat
'Vicar's Mead'	IBlr LGre

ANGELONIA (Scrophulariaceae)

gardneri	EMan LHil
¶ Imperial Star = 'Mandiana'[PBR]	EDAr
sp.	EDAr
'Stella Gem'	EDAr LFis LRHS

ANIGOZANTHOS (Haemodoraceae)

'Bush Ranger'	Last listed 1998
flavidus	CB&S EOHP MBri SOWG WCot
- red	SSoC
- yellow	LHil WBrE
humilis ♀	Last listed 1998
manglesii ♀	CTrC WBrE WPer
- 'Bush Dawn'	Last listed 1998

ANISACANTHUS (Acanthaceae)

wrightii	Last listed 1998

ANISODONTEA (Malvaceae)

§ *capensis*	CB&S CChe EBee ELan ERea GKir IBlr LRHS MAsh MBNS NBir NBrk SBod SChu SMrm SOWG SRms SVen WBod WEas
- 'Tara's Pink'	LGre LHop MAsh SAga SMrm
elegans	CSpe
huegelii	See *Alyogyne huegelii*
§ x *hypomadara* (Sprague) Bates	CMHG CSev ECtt NPer SEas SRms WPer
§ - hort.	See *A. capensis*
julii	WSan
malvastroides	CSev LHil
scabrosa	CAbb CChe EMil SAga

ANISOTOME (Apiaceae)

cauticola	Last listed 1999
flexuosa	NHar
haastii	Last listed 1999
imbricata	GDra
latifolia	Last listed 1997
pilifera	Last listed 1998

ANNONA (Annonaceae)

cherimola (F)	CTrG LBlo
muricata (F)	LBlo
reticulata (F)	WMul
squamosa (F)	LBlo

ANODA (Malvaceae)

cristata 'Opal Cup'	EMon

ANOIGANTHUS (Amaryllidaceae)

luteus	See *Cyrtanthus luteus*

ANOIGANTHUS See CYRTANTHUS

ANOMALESIA See GLADIOLUS

ANOMATHECA (Iridaceae)

cruenta	See *A. laxa*
¶ *grandiflora*	WHil
§ *laxa*	CInt CMHG CStu ECha ELan EMan EPot ERos IMGH LGre MNrw MTho NMen NPer SDix SIng SMac SRms SSpi STes WAbe WCru WFar WPat WPer WWin
- var. *alba*	ELan EPot ERos LGre MHar MTho NMen NPer SSpi WAbe WWeb
- *alba-maculata*	CPea LRHS
- blue	ERos
- 'Joan Evans'	CCuc CElw CNic CStu ELan EPot ERos NMen SRms WAbe
- red spot	Last listed 1998
viridis	CPou ERos LBow MNrw NMGW

ANOPTERUS (Escalloniaceae)

glandulosus	IBlr WCru

ANREDERA (Basellaceae)

§ *cordifolia*	CPlN CRHN IIve LRHS WCot WPer

ANTENNARIA (Asteraceae)

aprica	See *A. parvifolia*
dioica	CTri CGHN GPoy LRHS MBro MHer NBus SRms WFar WLow WPyg WWye
- 'Alba'	EHoe GAbr NFla WFar
- 'Alex Duguid'	CNic CPlt GCrs LBee LRHS SAga SBla SIng WAbe
- 'Aprica'	See *A. parvifolia*
§ - var. *hyperborea*	LGro SSmi
- 'Minima'	EPot GCrs MBro MWat NBro NHar NMen NNrd SIng WAbe
- 'Nyewoods Variety'	EPot GDra NTow
- red	SIng
- var. *rosea*	See *A. rosea*
* - 'Rubra'	CTri ECha EDAr GAri MBro MHer NMen NNrd SBla SHel SSmi WHen
- *tomentosa*	See *A. dioica* var. *hyperborea*
¶ 'Joy'	SBla
macrophylla hort.	See *A. microphylla*
§ *microphylla*	EDAr EHoe EMNN ESis LGro MBar NFla NHar NHol NMen SRms SSmi WBea WEas WPat WPer
- 'Plena' (d)	SRms
neglecta var. *gaspensis*	SIng
§ *parvifolia*	CLyd CNic CTri ESis GCHN GDra MBar NEgg NHar WMoo WPer
- var. *rosea*	See *A. microphylla*
plantaginifolia	EBee
¶ 'Red Wonder'	WWeb
§ *rosea* ♀	GKir MHer NLAp NVic SAga SPlb

ANTHEMIS ✿ (Asteraceae)

aizoon	See *Achillea ageratifolia* subsp. *aizoon*
arvensis	EWFC
N 'Beauty of Grallagh'	CBre CMea GCal GMac LFis MAvo NCat NGdn SDix SHel SOkh WCot
biebersteinii	See *A. marschalliana* subsp. *biebersteiniana*
'Blomit'	See *A.* Susanna Mitchell = 'Blomit'
carpatica	CGle GCHN MCCP NBro
- 'Karpatenschnee'	GKir GMaP

cretica	Last listed 1998
§ - subsp. *cretica*	CLyd EBee
- - NS 754	NWCA
frutescens	See *Argyranthemum frutescens*
N 'Grallagh Gold'	CGle CLon CMil EBee ECha EGar EMon EOrc EWes GKir LHop LRHS MBri MSCN MWat NCat NFla NPer SAga SMrm SRPl WBea WEas WFar
§ *marschalliana*	EBee ECha EDAr EPot ESis LBee LRHS MSte NOak NTow SIng SSmi WPer
§ - subsp. *biebersteiniana*	CHea
montana	See *A. cretica* subsp. *cretica*
nobilis	See *Chamaemelum nobile*
punctata subsp. *cupaniana* ♀	More than 30 suppliers
- - 'Nana'	EMon GKir NPer
rudolphiana	See *A. marschalliana*
sachokiana	Last listed 1999
sancti-johannis	CGle EBee ECoo EGar EGle EGoo EMar MBri MGed MHer NArg NOak NPer SPer SRms SSvw WBea WElm WPer WWpP
§ Susanna Mitchell = 'Blomit'	EBee EBrP EBre EPfP GKir LBCl LBSe LBre LFis LRHS MArl MBBe MGrG MSph NCat NFla NHaw SBre WEas
'Tetworth'	CStr EBee ECha ELan EMon EPPr GBuc GMac LRHS MMil MSte NGdn SChu SMad WCot WFar WPer
tinctoria	CArn CGle EBee ELan ELau EMon EWFC GKir GMac GPoy LRHS MChe MHer MHew MMal NEgg NFor NPer SIde WAbe WBea WByw WJek WOak WWye
- 'Alba'	CGle EBee ECha EMar GCal GKir LGre LRHS MHer MWgw SChu SHar WHen WLRN WPer
* - 'Compacta'	EFou EWes SAsh SMrm
- dwarf form	EBee GMac LRHS SOkh SUsu WCot WWpP
- 'E.C. Buxton'	More than 30 suppliers
- 'Eva'	EMon LRHS NCat NDov WEas
- 'Gold Mound'	Last listed 1997
- 'Grallagh Gold'	See *A.* 'Grallagh Gold'
- 'Kelwayi'	CGle CHor EBee ECtt EMar EWTr GCHN GKir LAst LRHS MBNS NBid NBro NFai NPer SAga SLon SMer SPer SPla SRms WBea WFar WHen WOve WPer
- 'Lemon Maid'	EPPr SChu SUsu
- 'Pride of Grallagh'	See *A.* 'Beauty of Grallagh'
- 'Sauce Béarnaise'	EMon WCra
- 'Sauce Hollandaise'	More than 30 suppliers
- subsp. *tinctoria*	NCat
- 'Wargrave Variety'	More than 30 suppliers
triumfettii	NPer
tuberculata	LRHS NChi SBla SIng

ANTHERICUM (Anthericaceae)

algeriense	See *A. liliago* var. *major*
baeticum	EBee
* *bovei*	Last listed 1998
* *fistulosum*	EBee
liliago	More than 30 suppliers
§ - var. *major* ♀	CAvo CFri EBee ECha EPla GDra IBlr LGre SSpi WCot
ramosum	CAvo EBee ECGN ECha ELan EMan EPot ERos EWes GBin GDra LGre LRHS MBrN MBro MLLN

	NBid NBir NWCA SHel SIng
	SMrm WPer
- JCA 166.300	WLin
- *plumosum*	See *Trichopetalum plumosum*
saundersiae	WCot

ANTHOCERCIS (Solanaceae)
| *littorea* | Last listed 1998 |

ANTHOLYZA (Iridaceae)
coccinea	See *Crocosmia paniculata*
crocosmioides	See *Crocosmia latifolia*
paniculata	See *Crocosmia paniculata*
ringens	Last listed 1999

ANTHOXANTHUM (Poaceae)
| *odoratum* | CArn CKin ELau GBar GIBF GPoy |
| | NNor WWye |

ANTHRISCUS (Apiaceae)
cerefolium	CArn CSev EOHP GPoy ILis LRHS
	MChe MHer MMal SIde SLod
	WGwG WHbs WJek WOak WPer
	WSel WWye
- 'D'Hiver de Bruxelles'	Last listed 1998
sylvestris	WShi
- 'Broadleas Blush'	CNat
- 'Hullavington' (v)	CNat
- 'Moonlit Night'	EHoe
- 'Ravenswing'	More than 30 suppliers

ANTHURIUM (Araceae)
amazonicum	MBri
andraeanum	MBri
- 'Acropolis'	MBri
'Flamingo'	MBri
scherzerianum	MBri
- 'Rosemarie'	MBri

ANTHYLLIS (Papilionaceae)
cytisoides	Last listed 1998
hermanniae	Last listed 1999
- 'Compacta'	See *A. hermanniae* 'Minor'
§ - 'Minor'	EPot NSla SBla WLin
montana	Last listed 1999
- subsp. *atropurpurea*	LRHS
- 'Rubra' ♀	CInt ECho EDAr EGle EPot MHer
	NFor NMen WWin
vulneraria	CFee CKin CMil EWFC GTou
	MChe MWat NMir NPri SSpi
	WHer WPer
- var. *coccinea*	CGdn CMil CNic CSpe EBee EGar
	EMar GGar MBro MCCP MNrw
	MSCN MSte MTho NMen NSla
	NWCA SUsu WElm WPGP
- var. *iberica*	Last listed 1999
* - 'Peach'	Last listed 1999

ANTIGONON (Polygonaceae)
| *leptopus* | CPIN LChe SOWG |
| - 'Album' | CPIN |

ANTIRRHINUM (Scrophulariaceae)
asarina	See *Asarina procumbens*
barrellieri	EBee
braun-blanquetii	CNic CPea EBee EMan MCAu
	MLLN MOne SAga WCot
'Bridesmaid'	Last listed 1999
¶ Chandelier Primrose Vein	LFis
¶ 'Dark Star'	CSpe
'Deep Pink'	Last listed 1999
glutinosum	See *A. hispanicum* subsp.

	hispanicum
§ *hispanicum*	CGle EBee NBir SBla
- 'Avalanche'	CHal ECtt EMan MLan SCoo
§ - subsp. *hispanicum*	CMea CSam CSpe EDAr EMan
roseum	WKif
majus 'Black Prince'	CHad SAga
- subsp. *linkianum*	Last listed 1999
- subsp. *majus*	EWll
- 'Taff's White' (v)	CSpe LRHS
molle	CSpe EBee ECtt EOrc MSte MTho
	NBir NPer NWCA SAga SRCN
	SUsu WPyg
- pink	CSWP EOrc MSte MTho
'Pink Candelabra'	LFis
'Powys Pride' (v)	EWll MCCP WHer WSan
pulverulentum	CSam ESis LGre LHop MArl WKif
sempervirens	ESis SBla WAbe WPat
siculum	EBee
'Starlight'	Last listed 1999
'Sugar Buttons'	Last listed 1999
'Summer Eyes'	Last listed 1999
'Torbay Rock'	EWll
'White Monarch'	Last listed 1997

APHANES (Rosaceae)
| § *arvensis* | MSal WWye |

APHELANDRA (Acanthaceae)
alexandri	Last listed 1997
squarrosa	CHal LRHS MBri
- 'Dania' (v)	MBri

APHYLLANTHES (Aphyllanthaceae)
| *monspeliensis* | CFee ECho SBla |

APIOS (Papilionaceae)
§ *americana*	CPIN EMon LEdu WCot WCru
	WSHC
tuberosa	See *A. americana*

APIUM (Apiaceae)
graveolens	CArn CBod ELau EOHP EWFC
	GPoy IIve MHer MSal SIde WJek
¶ - (Secalinum Group)	EOHP
'Par-cel'	
- - 'Zwolsche Krul'	MMal
nodiflorum	Last listed 1997
prostratum	Last listed 1997

APIUM x PETROSELINUM (Apiaceae) See APIUM
graveolens Secalinum Group

APOCYNUM (Apocynaceae)
| *androsaemifolium* | Last listed 1998 |
| *cannabinum* | CArn GPoy MSal WWye |

APONOGETON (Aponogetonaceae)
distachyos	CBen CRow CWat EHon ELan
	EMFW LPBA MSta NDea SLon
	SWat SWyc WMAq WWeb

APTENIA (Aizoaceae)
cordifolia	CHEx CSev EOas NPer SChr
	SEND SSte SVen WRos
- 'Variegata'	LHil MRav SHFr

AQUILEGIA ✿ (Ranunculaceae)
akitensis hort.	See *A. flabellata* , *A. flabellata*
	var. *pumila*
'Alaska'	LCTD LEur
* *alba variegata*	WEas
alpina	CBot CMea EBee ECtt EDAr ELau

	GAbr GCHN GKir GTou LRHS
	LSyl MHer MLan MWll NFor SPer
	SRPl SRms WFar WHen WOve
	WPer WRHF WStl WWin
- 'Alba'	CBlo LEur MLLN MWll NOak
- 'Carl Ziepke'	LEur
- 'Hensol Harebell'	See A. 'Hensol Harebell'
'Alpine Blue'	Last listed 1998
amaliae	See A. *ottonis* subsp. *amaliae*
* *anemoniflora*	NCut NEgg
aragonensis	See A. *pyrenaica*
§ *atrata*	CGle CPou EBee ECGN EGar
	EMan GCHN GSki LEur NOak
	SHel WPer WRos
atrovinosa	Last listed 1999
aurea Janka	CLTr EBee LEur
- misapplied	See A. *vulgaris* golden-leaved
baicalensis	See A. *vulgaris* Baicalensis Group
'Ballerina'	CMil EBee GMac LRHS MLLN
	NFai WCot WHer
barnebyi	CMea CMil CPou GBin LRHS
	MLLN NSti
bernardii	NOak
bertolonii ♀	CFee CGle CPlt EMNN GCrs
	GTou LEur LHop LRHS MBro
	NHar NMen NOak SBla SRms
	WHoo WPat WPyg
- *alba*	NWCA
Biedermeier Group	CM&M EBee EMil GAbr GKir
	LPVe LRHS MBNS NNor NOrc
	SRob WPer
'Blue Berry'	CMHG EBee MBro NHar WLin
	WPat
'Blue Bonnet'	CMGP EBee EGar EMan NPSI
	WElm
'Blue Jay' (Songbird Series)	CFai EMar LEur NPri SPer
'Blue Jewel'	Last listed 1998
§ 'Blue Star' (Star Series)	EBee ECtt GCHN LRHS NPSI
	WElm WPer
¶ 'Bluebird' (Songbird Series)	LCTD LEur
'Branching Red'	LEur
brevicalcarata	CHar CMil GBin
buergeriana	CLTr CPou EBee GAbr GBin LEur
	MCCP WPer
- f. *flavescens*	Last listed 1999
- var. *oxysepala*	See A. *oxysepala*
'Bunting' (Songbird Series)	EMar EWll LEur
canadensis ♀	CGle CMHG EBee EDAr ELan
	GSki LEur LRHS MHer MLLN NBid
	NBir NBro NOak NSti NWCA
	SRms WCru WOve WPer
- 'Corbett'	GBuc LCTD WHil
- 'Nana'	CInt GAri LCTD MSte
'Cardinal' (Songbird Series)	CFai EMar LEur SPer
cazorlensis	See A. *pyrenaica* subsp.
	cazorlensis
'Celestial Blue'	EBee ELan
§ *chaplinei*	CBot EBee GAbr LEur NBir WEas
chrysantha	CFri CHea EBee EBrP EBre ECGN
	GAbr GBin GCHN LBCl LBSe LBre
	LEur MBBe MGrG MLLN NBus
	NHar NOak SBre SPla SRms WBrE
	WCot WCru WEas WOve WPer
- var. *chaplinei*	See A. *chaplinei*
- 'Flore Pleno' (d)	EBee
- 'Yellow Queen'	CSpe EBee LEur LRHS NSti SSvw
	WHil
clematiflora	See A. *vulgaris* var. *stellata*
coerulea ♀	CGle EMan GAbr GCHN NCat
	SRms
- ex RMRP 940134	LEur
- 'Mrs Nicholls'	EPar MBri

- var. *ochroleuca*	EBee GCHN
- var. *pinetorum*	Last listed 1997
'Colorado' (Swan Series)	EMar LEur
'Cream Edge'	Last listed 1998
¶ 'Crimson Shower'	MNaF
'Crimson Star'	CBlo CHea EBrP EBre EOld EPfP
	GKir LBCl LBSe LBre LEur MBBe
	MLLN NBus NHaw SBre SPer
desertorum	LEur NTow SMac
discolor	CCuc GSki GTou LHop LRHS
	MBro NMen NWCA WPat
'Dorothy'	LCTD LHop LRHS
¶ 'Dorothy in White'	LCTD
'Double Chocolate'	LRHS
'Double Quilled Purple'	Last listed 1999
Double Rubies (d)	EMan SCro WElm
§ 'Dove' (Songbird Series)	CFai EWll LCTD LEur MHer SPer
	SWat
I 'Dragonfly'	CB&S EPfP GAbr GAri GMaP
	LNor MBri NMir NOak WFar
	WPer
'Dwarf Fairyland'	Last listed 1999
'Eastgrove'	WEas
ecalcarata	See *Semiaquilegia ecalcarata*
'Edelweiss'	SBla
einseleana	GSki WHer
elegantula	GAbr LEur
- JJA 11390	Last listed 1998
eximia	LCTD SBla
'Firecracker'	LEur
'Firewheel'	See A. *vulgaris* var. *stellata*
	'Firewheel'
§ *flabellata* ♀	CGle CMil CTri GAri GCHN LEur
	MBro WPat WPer
§ - f. *alba*	CTri ELan GCHN LEur NWCA
	SRms WEas
- 'Blue Angel'	CB&S EDAr LEur WPer
- Cameo Series	EDAr SMrm WHil WRos
- 'Cameo Blue and White'	EDAr NCut
- 'Cameo Blue'	EDAr LEur
(Cameo Series)	
- 'Cameo Blush'	EDAr NCut
(Cameo Series)	
- 'Cameo Pink and White'	EDAr MHer NCut
(Cameo Series)	
- 'Cameo Pink'	EDAr LEur
(Cameo Series)	
¶ - 'Cameo Rose and White'	ESis NCut
(Cameo Series)	
- 'Cameo White'	EDAr LEur NCut
(Cameo Series)	
- Cameo Series mixed	EDAr EWll WGor
- 'Jewel'	ECho WHil
- 'Ministar'	CFri CHor CM&M EDAr ESis GKir
	GSki LEur LRHS MBNS MBro
	MHer MRav NOak NVic SRms
	SRot SSpe WFar WHil WHoo WPer
	WPyg WWin
- 'Nana Alba'	See A. *flabellata* var. *pumila* f.
	alba
§ - var. *pumila* ♀	CCuc ECha GAbr GDra GTou
	LHop LRHS NNrd NOak SBla SIng
	SRms WAbe WCru WFar WHil
	WPer
§ - - f. *alba* ♀	CBot CGle ECha ESis GDra LEur
	LHop LRHS MBNS MHer MSte
	NBus SRCN SRms WWin
- - 'Flora Pleno'	WLin
- - f. *kurilensis*	CGle GCal GDra MSte
- - 'Silver Edge'	CMil CPla MNrw NFai NLar WCot
* - - 'Snowflakes'	WRha

- soft pink — Last listed 1999
* - 'White Angel' — MLan NPro WPer
flavescens — WPer
- var. *miniana* — Last listed 1999
§ - var. *rubicunda* — Last listed 1999
formosa — CBot CLon EBee GCHN LCTD NChi NPri NSti NWCA SBla SUsu WCru WPer
- ex NNS 9343 — Last listed 1999
- var. *formosa* — LEur
- var. *pauciflora* — Last listed 1999
- var. *truncata* — CGle CRDP EBee GBuc LEur MLLN WCru
- var. *wawawensis* RMRP 950136 — LEur
§ *fragrans* — CGle CHar CPou ECGN GAbr GBin GCHN GCrs LEur LSyl MBro MCLN MTho NOak STes WCra WHoo WMaN WOve WPGP WPic WRha
* - 'Alba' — Last listed 1999
- ex CC&MR 96 — Last listed 1997
- ex KBE 48 — Last listed 1997
- white — LEur
glandulosa — CMHG EBee LEur SSte WEas
glauca — See *A. fragrans*
§ 'Goldfinch' — CBot EMar EWll LEur
(Songbird Series)
'Graeme's Green' — NFai
grata — GCHN LEur LGre WCot
§ 'Hensol Harebell' ♀ — CGle CPou CSWP EBee MBro MFir NBus SRms WHoo WPyg
hirsutissima — See *A. viscosa* subsp. *hirsutissima*
'Ice Blue' — Last listed 1999
'Irish Elegance' — EGoo WRha
japonica — See *A. flabellata* var. *pumila*
Jewel hybrids — CSpe EMNN WPer
jonesii — Last listed 1999
- x *saximontana* — Last listed 1998
¶ 'Kansas' — LEur
karelinii — LEur MAvo SRob
kitaibelii — Last listed 1999
'Koralle' — CLTr GBin LEur
'Kristall' — EPri MWll NOak STes WHil
kubistanica — EBee
laramiensis — CGra CPBP LEur NWCA WAbe
* 'Lavender and White' — CFai
(Songbird Series)
longissima — CGle CHar CMea CSam GAbr GBri GBuc LCTD LEur LSyl MBro MHer MLLN SBla STes WEas WHil WHoo WLin
long-spurred hybrid, white — Last listed 1999
'Lovebird' — LEur
'Magpie' — See *A. vulgaris* 'William Guiness'
¶ 'Maxi' — WHil
McKana Group — EBrP EBre ELan ENot GAbr GCHN GMaP LAst LBCl LBSe LBre LHop LRHS MAvo MBBe NFor NGdn NOak NVic SBre SPer SPlb SRms WPer
'Mellow Yellow' — CPla ECGP ECoo GBuc LEur MBNS MLLN MSCN MWll NCut STes WBea WPer WPnP WViv
micrantha — GCHN
aff. *micrantha* JCA 1.061.350 — Last listed 1998
¶ 'Milk and Honey' — CBre CFwr SSte
¶ 'Mobius' — LEur
moorcroftiana — CPou
- CC 1371 — CPLG
- CC 1414 — Last listed 1997

Mrs Scott-Elliot hybrids — CBlo COIW EBee EHol EMan GAbr LEur LIck LNor MBri MLan SLon SPer WFar
Music Series ♀ — CHor NOak SMrm SRms WByw
'Music Pink and White' (Music Series) — Last listed 1999
'Music Red and White' (Music Series) — LEur
'Music White' (Music Series) — Last listed 1999
¶ 'Nevada' — LCTD
nigricans — See *A. atrata*
nivalis — SBla
'Nuthatch' (Songbird Series) — EMar
'Olympia' red and gold — LEur
§ *olympica* — EMan EWes LGre MLLN WPer
'Orange Flaming Red' — LHop
ottonis — LEur LHop
§ - subsp. *amaliae* — SSca WLin
§ *oxysepala* — CGle EBee LEur NBus
'Petticoats' — Last listed 1999
'Phyll's Bonnet' — GCal
'Pink Bonnet' — GCal
'Pink Jewel' — CMHG
pubescens — EBee LEur WLin
pubiflora — GCHN
- CC&MR 96 — WLin
'Purple Emperor' — LRHS
§ *pyrenaica* — CLTr CTri NHar
§ - subsp. *cazorlensis* — GCHN
'Quilled Violets' — CMil
'Red Hobbit' — CSpe LEur LRHS NOrc
§ 'Red Star' (Star Series) — EBee ECtt GCHN LEur NBus NOak NPSI SPer WHil WPer WRus
¶ 'Redwing' (Songbird Series) — LEur
§ 'Robin' (Songbird Series) — CBot CFai EMar LCTD LEur NPri SWat
rockii — GAbr SIng
- CLD 0437 — Last listed 1997
- KGB 176 — Last listed 1997
'Roman Bronze' — CPla EBee EBrP EBre EGoo EMan GBin LAst LBCl LBSe LBre LEur LRHS MAnH MBBe MCCP MCLN MLLN MWrn NOak NPSI NPro SBre SPla SSte STes WCot WUnu WViv WWhi
* 'Rose Red' — Last listed 1997
rubicunda — See *A. flavescens* var. *rubicunda*
saximontana — GCHN GNor GTou LRHS NWCA
§ 'Schneekönigin' — GCHN NOak WHen WPer WViv
scopulorum — CGra LCTD NWCA
- subsp. *perplexans* — Last listed 1998
* *secundiflora* — Last listed 1998
shockleyi — CPou GBuc MLan NTow NWCA
sibirica — LEur WPer
'Silver Queen' — EBee LRHS WRus
'Simone's White' — EBee LEur
skinneri — CBel CMil ECtt GAbr GBin GSki IHdy LCTD LGre MCLN MHer NBus NRya SCro STes WCot WCru WHil WRha
Snow Queen — See *A.* 'Schneekönigin'
Songbird Series — CSpe MLLN NPri SWat WLRN
sp. CDC&C 253 from Korea — Last listed 1999
stellata — See *A. vulgaris* var. *stellata*
'Stoulton Blue' — EBee WSPU
'Sunburst Ruby' — CHar CMil CPla LEur MCCP MWrn NOak NPro WPrP
'Sweet Lemon Drops' — CPla

'Sweet Surprise'	NCut
thalictrifolia	CLTr EBee
- JCA 174.400	Last listed 1999
transsilvanica	Last listed 1998
triternata	CMil EBee NNor NWCA
turczaninovii	Last listed 1999
¶ *vicaria*	LCTD
viridiflora	CBot CFri CGle CHar CMea CRDP
	CStr CTri EBee GBuc GCHN LEur
	MTho MTis NHar NHol SAga SBea
	SBla WCot WCru WEas WFar WHil
	WPat WPer WPnP
§ *viscosa* subsp.	EBee
hirsutissima	
vulgaris	CArn CMHG EBee GAbr GPoy
	LEur LHrt LLWP MCAu MChe
	MHew NBro SPlb WGwG WOak
	WPer WShi WWye
- 'Adelaide Addison'	CGle CPlt ECha ELan GBri GBuc
	GMac LRHS NFai WEas WFar
	WRha WViv
- var. *alba*	CArn CLTr CMea EMan LLWP
	MCAu SEND SGar WByw
- 'Aureovariegata'	See *A. vulgaris* Vervaeneana
	Group
§ - Baicalensis Group	GCHN
- 'Blue Star'	See *A.* 'Blue Star' (Star Series)
* - 'Cap de Rossiter'	CRow
- 'Christa Barlow'	CB&S LRHS
- *clematiflora*	See *A. vulgaris* var. *stellata*
- 'Crystal Star'	LRHS
- 'Dorothy Rose'	EBee LEur SAga
- 'Double Pleat' (d)	WHer
- 'Double Pleat'	EBee WHil WPer
blue/white	
- 'Double Pleat'	EBee WHil WPer
pink/white	
- 'Dove'	See *A.* 'Dove' (Songbird Series)
- var. *flore-pleno* (d)	CLTr LLWP WByw WHen WPer
- - black (d)	WCot
- - blue	WCot
- - 'Burgundy' (d)	CMil
- - pale blue	LLWP
- - pink	GGar
- - 'Powder Blue'	Last listed 1998
- - purple (d)	LLWP
- - red (d)	GGar
¶ - - 'Tower Light Blue'	WMoo
(Tower Series)	
- - white (d)	GAbr LGre LLWP NOak
- 'Gold Finch'	See *A.* 'Goldfinch' (Songbird
	Series)
§ - golden-leaved	CMea ECho
- 'Grandmother's Garden'	EWll LRHS
- 'Granny's Gold'	CMHG LRHS MBri
- 'Heidi'	CBot EBee EWll NCut WPer
- f. *inversa*	Last listed 1999
- 'Jane Hollow'	CMil CPou CRow EBee MLLN
	NCut
- 'Magda'	WRha
- 'Magpie'	See *A. vulgaris* 'William Guiness'
- 'Michael Stromminger'	LEur MNrw WPer
- 'Miss Coventry'	Last listed 1997
- 'Mrs Fincham'	Last listed 1999
- Munstead White	See *A. vulgaris* 'Nivea'
§ - 'Nivea' ♀	CBel CBot CGle CHad CPou
	CSam EBee ECha ELan GAbr LAst
	MBro MCLN NChi NFai SBla
	WHoo
- Olympica Group	See *A. olympica*
- 'Patricia Zavros'	Last listed 1998
- 'Pink Spurless'	See *A. vulgaris* var. *stellata* pink

- 'Pink Storm'	MNrw
- Pom Pom Series	CMil MCCP
- 'Pom Pom Crimson'	NBro NBur WCot
(Pom Pom Series)	
- 'Pom Pom Rose'	Last listed 1998
(Pom Pom Series)	
- 'Pom Pom Violet'	Last listed 1999
(Pom Pom Series)	
- 'Pom Pom White'	CLTr
(Pom Pom Series)	
- 'Primivera'	CFri
- 'Purple Emperor'	MBri
- 'Red Star'	See *A.* 'Red Star' (Star Series)
- 'Robin'	See *A.* 'Robin' (Songbird Series)
- 'Rose Barlow'	GCal WHen WViv
- 'Silver Edge'	GBri
- 'Slaty Grey'	Last listed 1999
- 'Snowdust'	EHoe
§ - var. *stellata*	CGle CHid EBee ECGN ECtt ELan
	EMan GCHN LEur MBNS MHer
	MTis NBro NFai WPer WPic WWin
- - 'Belhaven Blue'	EGoo
- - 'Bicolor Barlow' (d)	GCal WViv
- - 'Black Barlow' (d)	CB&S CFri CHad EBee ECGP
	EGoo EPar EWll GCal GMaP NCut
	NOrc SCro SSoC SSte WViv
- - 'Blue Barlow' (d)	EWll GCal GMaP NCut SPla SUsu
	WPer WViv
- - double	Last listed 1998
- - double blue	Last listed 1999
§ - - 'Firewheel'	CMil EBee EBrP EBre LBCl LBSe
	LBre LRot MBBe NEgg NFai SBre
	WUnu
- - 'Green Barlow'	WViv
- - 'Greenapples'	CFri CLTr CMil EBee LEur LHop
	MAnH MAvo MCCP MLLN NPro
	SIng WBar WCot WHer
- - 'Iceberg'	CMil MAnH NPro WSpi
- - 'Melton Rapids'	WBea
- - 'Nora Barlow' (d) ♀	More than 30 suppliers
§ - - pink	EBrP EBre GBin LBCl LBSe LBre
	LEur MBBe SBre
- - purple	LEur LLWP
- - red	LLWP
- - 'Royal Purple'	MWll MWrn NBro STes
- - 'Ruby Port'	CM&M EBee EMan GCal GKir
	LEur LGre MBri MCAu MNrw
	MTis NBus NChi SLod SRCN
	SSvw STes WHen WRus WWhi
¶ - - 'Ruby Port' crimped	NDov
- - 'Sunlight White'	LEur SWat WMaN WPer
§ - - white	CGle CLTr GCHN LEur LHop
	NBro WFar WHal
* - - 'Woodside Blue'	EBlw
* - - 'Woodside Pink'	EBlw
- 'Strawberry Ice Cream'	EBee GBri NBro WElm
- 'The Bride'	CBlo EBee MBro
- variegated foliage	See *A. vulgaris* Vervaeneana
	Group
§ - Vervaeneana Group (v)	More than 30 suppliers
- - double white (d/v)	CHad
- - 'Graeme Iddon' (v)	EBee GBuc MBri MLLN NBrk NFai
	NMGW
- - 'Woodside'	See *A. vulgaris* Vervaeneana
	Group
- - 'Woodside Blue' (v)	EGoo MWll NCut SRob
¶ - - 'Woodside Red' (v)	MWll WCra
- - 'Woodside White' (v)	MWll NBir NCut
- 'Westfaeld'	MNrw MTed NDov NOak
- 'White Barlow'	GCal SCro WViv
* - 'White Bonnets'	EBee EBrP EBre LBCl LBSe LBre
	MBBe NPSI SBre SRos

- 'White Spurless'   See *A. vulgaris* var. *stellata* white
- 'White Star'   See A. 'White Star' (Star Series)
§ - 'William Guiness'   More than 30 suppliers
- 'William Guiness Doubles' MCCP
- 'Wishy Washy'   Last listed 1998
white   Last listed 1998
§ 'White Star' (Star Series)   EBee ECtt GCHN MTis NBus NPSI
  SPer WHil WPer
'White Swan'   CMil LEur
yabeana   CHid GBin
'Yellow Star' (Star Series)   LEur

ARABIS (Brassicaceae)

albida   See *A. alpina* subsp. *caucasica*
alpina   CB&S SPlb
§ - subsp. *caucasica*   GDea WFar
- - 'Corfe Castle'   Last listed 1997
§ - - 'Flore Pleno' (d) ♀   CHad CTri ECha ECtt ELan EOrc
  GAbr LGro MFir MHer MTho
  NChi NFla SBod SRms WByw
  WEas WFar WWin
- - 'Gillian Sharman' (v)   NCat
- - 'Goldsplash' (v)   Last listed 1998
- - 'Pink Pearl'   LRHS MHer NPri WFar
- - 'Pinkie'   EMNN
¶ - - 'Rosea'   MRav NBir SRms WFar WMoo
§ - - 'Schneehaube' ♀   ECtt EMNN GKir LRHS MBNS
  MBar MHer NMir NOrc SGar
  SRms WLRN WPer
- - Snowcap   See *A. alpina* subsp. *caucasica*
  'Schneehaube'
- - 'Snowdrop'   MRav NPri SMer WFar
- - 'Variegata'   ECha EHoe ELan EPot LBee LHop
  MBri MHer MTho NFor SRms
  WByw WEas WFar WPat WWin
androsacea   EPot GTou WLRN
x *arendsii* 'Compinkie'   ECtt SPlb SRms WLRN
- 'La Fraicheur'   Last listed 1997
- 'Rosabella' (v)   ECha GKir LRHS MBNS
- 'Rose Frost'   Last listed 1997
aubrietoides   Last listed 1999
blepharophylla   GAbr MWat NTow
§ - 'Frühlingszauber' ♀   CB&S CPea CTri GDra GKir LPVe
  MOne MWat NNrd NPri SGar
  SRms WFar WGor WGwG
- Spring Charm   See *A. blepharophylla*
  'Frühlingszauber'
bryoides   EPot GTou LBee LRHS MDHE
  NMen NTow
- *olympica*   Last listed 1997
¶ *carduchorum*   NMen
caucasica   See *A. alpina* subsp. *caucasica*
* 'Cloth of Gold'   Last listed 1997
§ *collina* subsp. *rosea*   WUnu
cypria   Last listed 1998
ferdinandi-coburgi   EGar EPot GKir MGed MRav NBro
  NBus WEas
- 'Aureovariegata'   CTri EDAr EHoe GKir LGro LRHS
  SPet
- 'Old Gold'   EDAr EPot ESis GKir LBee LHop
  LRHS MBar MHer MRav NEgg
  NHar NNrd NVic SBla SHel SRms
  SSmi WFar WHoo WMoo WPat
  WRHF WWin
- 'Variegata'   See *A. procurrens* 'Variegata'
glabra   WPer
¶ *kawasakiana*   WUnu
x *kellereri*   NMen NTow
'Pink Snow'   GKir
§ *procurrens* 'Variegata' ♀   ECha ELan ESis EWes GKir GTou
  LBee LHop LRHS MBar MHer
  MTho MWat NFor NHar NWCA

  SBla SHFr SHel SPlb SRms SSmi
  WFar
rosea   See *A. collina* subsp. *rosea*
rubella   See *Minuartia rubella*
§ *scabra*   CNat
Snow Cap   See *A. alpina* subsp. *caucasica*
  'Schneehaube'
sp. double white   CFee
stricta   See *A. scabra*
x *sturii*   NTow
x *suendermannii*   Last listed 1998

ARACHNIODES (Dryopteridaceae)

aristata   WRic
simplicior   NMar WCot WRic
standishii   LEur WRic

ARAIOSTEGIA (Davalliaceae)

pseudocystopteris   SSpi

ARALIA ✿ (Araliaceae)

armata B&SWJ 3137   WCru
bipinnata   CFil
cachemirica   CHad EBee EWes GCal MBro
  NBid NLar SDix WHoo WTin
californica   EBee GCal GPoy LGre MSal NLar
  WCru
chinensis hort.   See *A. elata*
- L.   CSam MBNS MSal SPer SRCN
continentalis   GCal
- CC 1035   Last listed 1997
cordata   EBee EWes GAbr GCal NLar
¶ - B&SWJ 5511   WCru
decaisneana   WCru
  B&SWJ 3588
- CC 1925   CPLG
§ *elata* ♀   CBrm CDoC CDul CHEx CLnd
  EBee ELan ENot EWTr GChr IOrc
  LEdu LNet LPan MBlu MGos NBea
  NBee NFla NFor SArc SPer SSpi
  WDin WNor WPic
- 'Albomarginata'   See *A. elata* 'Variegata'
- 'Aureovariegata'   CB&S CDoC ELan ENot IOrc LNet
  LRHS MBri NMoo WDin WPat
  WPyg
- 'Silver Umbrella'   EPfP MGos
§ - 'Variegata' ♀   CB&S CBot CDoC EMil ENot EPfP
  IOrc LNet LRHS MBlu MBri NBea
  NMoo WDin WPat WPyg
nudicaulis   EBee
racemosa   EBee ELau GCal GPoy LEdu MLLN
  MNrw MSal MSte NLar SRms
  WHal WWye
sieboldii de Vriese   See *Fatsia japonica*
spinosa   WHer

ARAUCARIA (Araucariaceae)

angustifolia   Last listed 1998
§ *araucana*   More than 30 suppliers
¶ *cunninghamii*   CGre
excelsa hort.   See *A. heterophylla*
§ *heterophylla* ♀   LRHS MBri WNor
imbricata   See *A. araucana*

ARAUJIA (Asclepiadaceae)

¶ *angustifolia*   CPIN
grandiflora   Last listed 1998
graveolens   CPIN
sericifera   CFri CHEx CMHG CMac CPIN
  CRHN EMil ERea GQui SGar SLon
  SSpi WBor WSHC

ARBUTUS ✿ (Ericaceae)

andrachne	CDul CFil ISea LRHS
x *andrachnoides* ♀	CAbP CB&S CFil CMHG CPMA
	ELan GKir IOrc LHop LNet LPan
	SAPC SArc SBrw SPer SReu SSpi
	SSta WBod WHCG WPGP WWat
canariensis	CHEx
glandulosa	See *Arctostaphylos glandulosa*
'Marina'	CAbP CFil CPMA CRos ELan EPfP
	GKir LRHS MAsh SMad SPer SReu
	SSpi SSta WPGP WPat WWat
menziesii ♀	CFil CMCN CPMA EPfP EWes
	GChr LNet SLon SMad SSpi WPGP
	WWat
– NJM 94046	Last listed 1998
unedo ♀	More than 30 suppliers
¶ – 'Atlantic'	MBri WGer
– 'Compacta'	CB&S CBlo CDoC EBrP EBre
	GChr GKir LBCl LBSe LBre LPan
	LRHS MAsh MBBe MGos SBre
– 'Elfin King'	LRHS SSpi SSta
– 'Quercifolia'	SReu SSta WPat WPyg
– f. *rubra* ♀	More than 30 suppliers
xalapensis	Last listed 1997

ARCHONTOPHOENIX (Arecaceae)

alexandrae	CRoM LPal
cunninghamiana ♀	CBrP CRoM LPal

ARCTANTHEMUM (Asteraceae)

§ *arcticum*	EBee EFou MSte NBrk
– 'Roseum'	EFou
– 'Schwefelglanz'	EFou WCot

ARCTERICA See PIERIS

ARCTIUM (Asteraceae)

lappa	CAgr CArn CKin GBar GPoy Ilve
	MChe MHer MSal NHex SIde
	WHer
minus	CKin EWFC MSal
¶ – 'Plus'	WAlt
pubens	CKin
tomentosum	Ilve

ARCTOSTAPHYLOS (Ericaceae)

* *californica*	Last listed 1999
crustacea var. *rosei*	See *A. tomentosa* subsp. *rosei*
§ *glandulosa*	SArc
manzanita	SMad
x *media* 'Snow Camp'	Last listed 1999
– 'Wood's Red'	GEil GKir MBar MGos SBrw WFar
myrtifolia	GAri MBar
nevadensis	MBar NRya SReu SSta
* – var. *coloradensis*	GKir
nummularia	Last listed 1999
patula	SMad
stanfordiana C&H 105	GGGa
§ *tomentosa* subsp. *rosei*	SMad
uva-ursi	CArn EBee ENot GPoy IOrc MBar
	MGos NFor SBod SBrw SEas SLon
	SPer SSta WBod WDin
– 'Massachusetts'	ELan EWTr GKir GQui LRHS
	MAsh SMur SReu SSta
– 'Point Reyes'	SBrw
– 'Snowcap'	MAsh
– 'Vancouver Jade'	CDoC CEnd EPfP GChr GKir
	LRHS MAsh MBar MGos NHol
	SBrw SReu SSta
* – 'Variegata'	Last listed 1998

ARCTOTIS (Asteraceae)

grandiflora	EWTr
x *hybrida* 'African Sunrise'	LRHS
– 'Apricot'	CHEx LRHS MSte SAga SMrm
– 'Bacchus'	SMrm
– 'China Rose'	SAga SMrm SUsu
– 'Flame' ♀	CHad CPlt CSpe LRHS MLan MSte
	NCiC SAga SChu SMrm SUsu
	WEas
– 'Harlequin'	CBrm
* – 'Mahogany' ♀	MSte SAga SUsu
– 'Midday Sun'	LRHS
– 'Pink'	SChu
* – 'Raspberry'	Last listed 1998
– 'Red Devil'	CHEx LRHS SMrm WLRN
– 'Red Magic' ♀	Last listed 1999
– 'Rosita'	Last listed 1999
– 'Tangerine'	Last listed 1997
– 'Terracotta'	MSte
– 'Torch'	Last listed 1999
– white	CHEx LRHS
– 'Wine'	LRHS MSte WEas WLRN
– 'Yellow'	Last listed 1999
'Prostrate Raspberry'	CSpe

ARDISIA (Myrsinaceae)

crenata	LRHS MBri
maclurei B&SWJ 3772	LRHS WCru

ARECA (Arecaceae)

catechu	MBri
concinna	LPal
¶ *vestiaria*	LPal

ARECASTRUM See SYAGRUS

ARENARIA (Caryophyllaceae)

aggregata	SIng SPlb
subsp. *erinacea*	
alfacarensis	See *A. lithops*
balearica	CInt EPar GCHN LBee LRHS
	MCCP SIng SRms
bertolonii	LRHS
¶ *congesta* var. *crassula*	CGra
festucoides	GCrs GTou WLRN
grandiflora	Last listed 1999
hookeri	Last listed 1999
– subsp. *desertorum*	Last listed 1999
– – NNS 93-53	Last listed 1997
kingii	Last listed 1997
ledebouriana	MWat NTow
§ *lithops*	CLyd
magellanica	See *Colobanthus quitensis*
montana ♀	More than 30 suppliers
nevadensis	Last listed 1998
norvegica	GKir
– subsp. *anglica*	Last listed 1998
obtusiloba	See *Minuartia obtusiloba*
pinifolia	See *Minuartia circassica*
procera subsp. *glabra*	NMen
pseudacantholimon	Last listed 1998
pulvinata	See *A. lithops*
pungens	Last listed 1998
purpurascens	EDAr EMNN ESis NMen NSla
	NWCA SRms WHoo
– 'Elliott's Variety'	NHol WPat
recurva	See *Minuartia recurva*
roseiflora ACE 1526	Last listed 1999
rubella	See *Minuartia rubella*
¶ – 'Popcorn' (d)	CGra
sp. ex CC 1363	Last listed 1999

tetraquetra — EGle GCrs IMGH NMen NWCA
§ - subsp. *amabilis* — EPot LRHS NHar NMen NNrd NSla NTow SIng WLin
- var. *granatensis* — See *A. tetraquetra* subsp. *amabilis*
tmolea — NMen
verna — See *Minuartia verna*

ARENGA (Arecaceae)
engleri — CBrP EOas EPVP LPal

ARGEMONE (Papaveraceae)
grandiflora — ELan
mexicana — ELan WHer WWin
ochroleuca — Last listed 1998

ARGYLIA (Bignoniaceae)
adscendens — Last listed 1997

ARGYRANTHEMUM ✿ (Asteraceae)
'Anastasia' — LIck WPnn
'Apricot Surprise' — See *A.* 'Peach Cheeks'
'Beauty of Nice' — WEas
§ 'Blizzard' (d) — EPri LIck LLWP LRHS SMer
'Bofinger' — LIck
Boston Yellow daisy — See *A. callichrysum*
'Bridesmaid' — Last listed 1999
broussonetii — LIck
'Butterfly' — LIck LRHS MBNS SVil WWol
§ *callichrysum* — LIck
§ - 'Etoile d'Or' — LIck
- 'Penny' — LIck
- 'Prado' — LIck
- Yellow Star — See *A. callichrysum* 'Etoile d'Or'
'Camilla Ponticella' — LIck
canariense hort. — See *A. frutescens* subsp. *canariae*
- 'Saimi' — CPne
'Champagne' — LIck
'Cheek's Peach' — See *A.* 'Peach Cheeks'
'Chelsea Princess' — Last listed 1997
* *compactum* — LIck
'Comtesse de Chambord' — LIck
'Cornish Gold' ♀ — LIck LRHS MBNS MMil
coronopifolium — LIck
'Donington Hero' ♀ — LIck
double cream (d) — LHil LIck
double white (d) — LIck SCro
'Edelweiss' (d) — ECtt LHil LIck LRHS WEas WHen
'Flamingo' — See *Rhodanthemum gayanum*
§ *foeniculaceum* hort. — CTri EHol ELan LRHS WEas WHen WKif
- pink — See *A.* 'Petite Pink'
§ *foeniculaceum* (Willd.) Webb & Sch.Bip. — CHal GMac
§ - 'Royal Haze' ♀ — CLTr GMac LIck LRHS NPer SLon SMer SUsu
'Frosty' — LIck WWol
§ *frutescens* — CHEx ECtt EMan LHil LIck LRHS NFai SGar WEas
* - 'Album Plenum' (d) — SEND
§ - subsp. *canariae* ♀ — CHal LIck
§ - subsp. *frutescens* — Last listed 1997
- x *maderense* — LHil
- subsp. *succulentum* — LIck
  'Margaret Lynch'
- 'Sugar and Ice'^PBR — LIck
¶ - 'Sugar Button'^PBR (d) — LIck
- 'Summer Pink'^PBR — CHal LIck WLRN
'Fuji Sundance' — LIck SSte
'George' — LHil LIck
'Gill's Pink' — CElw ECtt GMac LHil LIck LLWP MFir SAga WCot WPnn

'Golden Treasure' — LIck
§ *gracile* — LHil WEas
- 'Chelsea Girl' ♀ — CInt CLTr ECtt EHol LIck LRHS MSte SYvo
'Harvest Snow' — LIck MBNS
'Hopleys Double Cream' (d) — LIck
'Hopleys Double Yellow' (d) — Last listed 1999
§ 'Jamaica Primrose' ♀ — CB&S CBot CHEx ELan EWTr GMac LIck LRHS MHar SAga SCro SHFr SRms WBod WEas WHen WPnn
'Jamaica Snowstorm' — See *A.* 'Snow Storm'
'Lemon Chiffon' — LIck
'Lemon Delight' — LIck
'Lemon Meringue' (d) — ECtt LIck
'Lemon Soufflé' — LIck
'Levada Cream' ♀ — LIck
'Leyton Treasure' — Last listed 1999
'Lilliput' — LIck
§ *maderense* ♀ — CHal CLTr CSam IBlr LHil LIck LRHS MSte SCro SUsu WEas
- pale — LIck
'Mary Cheek' (d) ♀ — LHil LIck LRHS WPnn
'Mary Wootton' (d) — ECtt LIck SSte
mawii — See *Rhodanthemum gayanum*
'Mike's Pink' — LIck
'Mini-snowflake' — See *A.* 'Blizzard'
'Mini-star Yellow' — Last listed 1997
§ 'Mrs F. Sander' (d) — ECtt LIck
'Nevada Cream' — See *A.* 'Qinta White'
ochroleucum — See *A. maderense*
¶ 'Patches Pink' — LIck
§ 'Peach Cheeks' (d) — CHal LIck LRHS MSte NFai SAga SRms WWol
§ 'Petite Pink' ♀ — ECtt EMan EPri GMac LAst LIck MSte SMer SRms WEas WHen
'Pink Australian' (d) — CLTr LHil LIck LRHS
'Pink Break' — CHal LIck
I 'Pink Dahlia' — LIck
'Pink Delight' — See *A.* 'Petite Pink'
'Pink Pixie' — LIck
'Powder Puff' (d) — CLTr ECtt LIck LRHS MRav NFai SCro WPnn
prostrate double pink — LIck
§ 'Qinta White' (d) ♀ — ECtt LHil LIck WEas
'Rising Sun' — LIck
'Rollason's Red' — Last listed 1999
'Rosa Dwarf' — LIck
'Royal Haze' — See *A. foeniculaceum* Webb 'Royal Haze'
'Royal Yellow' — LIck SAga
'Saute' — LIck
'Silver Leaf' — LIck WLRN
'Silver Queen' — See *A. foeniculaceum* hort.
single pink — CLTr LIck
§ 'Snow Storm' ♀ — CB&S GMac LAst LIck NFai WHer WPnn
'Snowflake' (d) — CHEx ECtt LHil LRHS MSte WHen
'Snowflake' misapplied — See *A.* 'Mrs F. Sander'
'Starlight' — LIck
'Sugar Baby'^PBR — GMac LIck LRHS WLRN
§ 'Sugar Lace' — LIck
¶ 'Summer Angel'^PBR — CHal LIck
¶ 'Summer Eyes' — LIck
'Summer Melody'^PBR — CElw CSpe LIck MMil
¶ 'Summer Stars Pink' (d) — LIck
¶ 'Sweety' — LIck
'Tenerife' — LIck MSte
'Tony Holmes' — LIck
'Vancouver' (d) ♀ — CB&S CBot CElw LHil LIck LRHS MBNS NGdn SChu SRms WEas WHen WPnn WWol

* 'Vera'	LIck
'Wellwood Park'	ECtt LIck
'Weymouth Pink'	LIck
'Weymouth Surprise'	LIck
'White Spider'	LIck SSte
'Whiteknights' ♀	LIck
'Yellow Australian' (d)	LIck LRHS

ARGYREIA (Convolvulaceae)
nervosa	CPlN

ARGYROCYTISUS See CYTISUS

ARISAEMA (Araceae)
amurense	CCuc CFil CFir CLAP EBee EBot EPot GCal GDra NHar SSpi WFar WPGP
- B&SWJ 762	Last listed 1999
- B&SWJ 947	WCru
- subsp. robustum	WCru
B&SWJ 1186	
- subsp. serratum	WCru
B&SWJ 711	
angustatum	LAma
var. amurense	
- var. peninsulae	LAma WCru
B&SWJ 841	
- - f. variegatum	WCru
B&SWJ 4321	
- var. serratum	LAma
auriculatum	LAma WCru
bathycoleum	LAma WCru
brevipes	LAma WCru
candidissimum ♀	CAvo CBro CElw CFil CFir CLAP CRDP CStu EBee EMan EPar EPot ETub GBuc GCal GCrs LAma LAst LHil LRHS NHar SBla SSpi WCot WCru WHal WIvy WPGP
- green	LAma
- white	LAma
ciliatum	CRDP CStu EBee LAma NHar NLar SBla SSpi WCot
- CT 369	CFil WCru WPGP
concinnum	EBee EPot GNor LAma WCru WViv
consanguineum	CBro CFil CGle CMea EPot ETub LAma NWoo SSpi WCru WPGP
- B&SWJ 071	WCru
* - bicolour	LEur
- CLD 1519	GKir NHar
costatum	CFil CHEx EPot GBuc LAma WCru WPGP
dilatatum	LAma WCru
dracontium	CArn CLAP EBee EBot EPot LAma WCru
du-bois-reymondiae	LAma WCru
echinatum	EPot
elephas	EPot LAma WCru
erubescens	EPot LAma
exappendiculatum	CFil EPar EPot WCru WPGP
fargesii	CLAP EPot LAma WCru
flavum	CBro CCuc CFil CHEx CLAP CMea EBee EPot GCal GCrs LAma LRHS NMen SIng SSpi WCot WCru WPGP
- CC 1782	WCot
- subsp. intermedium	Last listed 1997
- tall	CLAP
¶ - subsp. tibeticum	LEur
formosanum	LAma
- B&SWJ 280	WCru
- B&SWJ 390	CPou WCot

- var. bicolorifolium	WCru
B&SWJ 3528	
- f. stenophyllum	WCru
B&SWJ 1477	
franchetianum	EPot WCru
fraternum	WCot
galeatum	EBee EPot LAma WCru WViv
§ griffithii	EBee EPar EPot GGar LAma SSpi WCru WViv
helleborifolium	See A. tortuosum
heterophyllum	WCru
B&SWJ 2028	
inkiangense	LAma WCru
intermedium	EPot LAma
- var. biflagellatum	Last listed 1998
- - HWJCM 161	WCru
iyoanum	Last listed 1999
jacquemontii	CBro CFil CLAP EPot GBuc GCrs GKir LAma WCot WCru
- B&SWJ 2719	WCru
japonicum	See A. serratum
¶ kelung-insularis	WCru
B&SWJ 256	
kiushianum	CFil EFEx SOkd WCru
* laxiflorum	SSpi
lingyunense	EPot LAma WCru
lobatum	LAma WCru
maximowiczii	Last listed 1999
§ nepenthoides	CBro EBee EPar EPot LAma WViv
- B&SWJ 2614b	WCru
ochraceum	See A. nepenthoides
* ochresia	EPot
ostiolatum	EPot
ovale	CLAP
polyphyllum	WCru
B&SWJ 3904	
propinquum	EPot LAma WCru
purpureogaleatum	LAma
quinatum	Last listed 1997
- f. pusillum	Last listed 1997
- f. zebrinum	Last listed 1997
rhizomatum	LAma WCru
rhombiforme	LAma WCru
ringens hort.	See A. robustum
ringens (Thunberg) Schott	CCuc EFEx LAma WCot WPGP
- f. glaucescens	Last listed 1999
- f. praecox B&SWJ 1515	WCru
- f. sieboldii B&SWJ 551	WCru
§ robustum	CFil SSpi WPGP
- B&SWJ 711	WCru
saxatile	LAma WCru
sazensoo	WCru
§ serratum	CFil LAma SSpi WCru
- GG 89394	Last listed 1999
- GG 89399	Last listed 1999
- GG 89404	Last listed 1999
§ sikokianum	CBro CFil EFEx EPot ETub GCrs LAma SSpi WCru WPGP
- var. serratum	Last listed 1999
- variegated	WCot WCru
sp. CLD 12482*	Last listed 1998
speciosum	EBee EPar EPot LAma SSpi WCru WViv
- B&SWJ 2403	WCru
- var. mirabile	WCru
B&SWJ 2712	
* - var. sikkimense	LAma
taiwanense	CFil WCot
- B&SWJ 269	WCru
- B&SWJ 356	CPou
- var. brevipedunculatum	WCru
B&SWJ 1859	

- f. *cinereum* B&SWJ 1912   WCru
¶ - silver leaf   WCot
tashiroi   Last listed 1999
ternatipartitum   WCru
thunbergii   EFEx
- subsp. *autumnale*   WCru
   B&SWJ 1425
- subsp. *thunbergii*   WCru
- subsp. *urashima*   CLAP EFEx LAma SSpi WCru
§ *tortuosum*   CBro CFil CLAP EBee EPar EPot
   GKir LAma SBla WCru
- CC 1452   CPou
- (high alt.form)   WCru
   B&SWJ 2386
- (low alt. form)   WCru
   B&SWJ 2298
tosaense   Last listed 1999
- GG 91224   WCru
triphyllum   CFil CHEx CLAP EBee EBot EPPr
   EPar EPot GGar LAma LRHS MSal
   NMen SLod SSpi WCru WPGP
- var. *atrorubens*   WPGP
§ *utile*   EPot LAma WViv
¶ - HWJCM 161   WCru
verrucosum   See *A. griffithii*
- var. *utile*   See *A. utile*
* *vulgare* var. *typicum*   Last listed 1999
yamatense   Last listed 1999
- subsp. *sugimotoi*   WCru
yunnanense   LAma
zanlanscianense   Last listed 1998

ARISARUM ✿ (Araceae)
proboscideum   More than 30 suppliers
- MS 958   EMar
vulgare   CRDP
- subsp. *simorrhinum*   Last listed 1998
   S&F 396/347
- subsp. *vulgare* JRM 1396   Last listed 1998

ARISTEA (Iridaceae)
africana   SWat
confusa   SWat
ecklonii   CAvo CFil CPLG CPou GSki LFis
   SLod SWat WCot WWin
ensifolia   EMon SWat WCDu
- S&SH 88   Last listed 1999
grandis   WCot
lugens   Last listed 1999
macrocarpa   EBee
§ *major*   CAbb CFir EMan GSki SWat
- pink   CGre
sp. JCA 15812   SSpi
spiralis   SWat
thyrsiflora   See *A. major*
woodii   Last listed 1999

ARISTIDA (Poaceae)
purpurea   Last listed 1997

ARISTOLOCHIA ✿ (Aristolochiaceae)
baetica   CPIN WCru
californica   CPIN
chrysops   CPIN
clematitis   CArn GPoy MHew MSal NHex
   WCot WCru WWye
contorta   SMad
debilis   CPIN
durior   See *A. macrophylla*
elegans   See *A. littoralis*
fimbriata   CPIN
gigantea   CPIN LChe

grandiflora   CPIN
griffithii B&SWJ 2118   WCru
heterophylla B&SWJ 3109 WCru
kaempferi   CPIN
- B&SWJ 293   WCru
§ *labiata*   CPIN
§ *littoralis* ♀   CPIN SOWG
longa subsp. *paucinervis* WCru
§ *macrophylla*   CBot CHEx CPIN EBee EPla EWTr
   IDee SLim SPer WCru
manshuriensis   CPIN
- B&SWJ 962   WCru
paucinervis S&F 235   Last listed 1998
peruviana   CPIN
pistolochia   Last listed 1999
ringens Vahl.   CPIN
- Link & Otto   See *A. labiata*
rotunda   CPIN
sempervirens   CPIN
sipho   See *A. macrophylla*
tagala   CPIN WMul
tomentosa   CFil CPIN SSta WCru
trilobata   CPIN
watsonii   CPIN

ARISTOTELIA (Elaeocarpaceae)
§ *chilensis*   IDee WPic
- 'Variegata'   CB&S CCHP CFee CPLG CPle
   EPla MMil SLim WEas WLRN
   WPyg
fruticosa   Last listed 1998
- (f)   ECou
- (m)   ECou
macqui   See *A. chilensis*
peduncularis   Last listed 1997
serrata   ECou

ARMERIA (Plumbaginaceae)
§ *alliacea*   ECha WPer
- f. *leucantha*   NBro SRms WMoo
§ *alpina*   MWat
Bee's hybrids   WMoo
'Bee's Ruby' ♀   EWTr MBri WPer
caespitosa   See *A. juniperifolia*
¶ *euscadiensis*   ESis
formosa hybrids   CMCo CTri ELan EMan IBlr LFis
   MNrw NMir WRha
§ *girardii*   NNrd
¶ 'Joystick Lilac Shades'   CFri
   (Joystick Series)
¶ Joystick Series   NArg
§ *juniperifolia* ♀   CLyd EBrP EBre ECtt EDAr ELan
   EMNN ESis LBCl LBSe LBee LBre
   LRHS MBBe MHer MTho NFla
   NMen NNrd NVic NWCA SBla
   SBre SIng SRms WWin
- 'Alba'   CMea EDAr ELan LRHS MHer
   NHar NMen NPri SRms WAbe
   WWin
- 'Beechwood'   LBee LRHS SBla SSmi
- 'Bevan's Variety' ♀   CPla EBrP EBre ECha ELan GCrs
   GKir LBCl LBSe LBre LRHS MBBe
   MBro MNrw MWat NHar NHol
   NMen NNrd NRya SBre SRms
   SRot SSmi WAbe WPyg
- dark   EWes GDra SBla WAbe
¶ - x *maritima*   SIng
- rose   EPot
- spiny dwarf   EDAr EPot
§ *maritima*   CArn CKin EBrP EBre EWTr GKir
   LBCl LBSe LBee LBre LRHS MBBe
   MBar MRav NArg NCat NFor SBre

- 'Alba' — SIde WBea WCFE WOak CArn CB&S CBrm CLTr ECha EDAr ELan EPot ESis EWTr LBee LPVe LRHS MBar MBri NArg NChi NFor NMir NRya NVic SHel SRms WBea WHen WLin WMoo WPer WWin WWye
- subsp. *alpina* — See *A. alpina*
- 'Bloodstone' — CB&S CTri ECot ELan LBee LRHS MWat
- 'Corsica' — CMea CTri ECha EPot IMGH MHar MHer MOne NBir NRya SMer WFar
- Düsseldorf Pride — See *A. maritima* 'Düsseldorfer Stolz'
§ - 'Düsseldorfer Stolz' — CPBP EBrP EBre ECha EDAr ELan GKir LBCl LBSe LBre LNor LRHS MBBe MBri MBro NHar NMen NNrd NPro SBre SIng WBea WHen WPat WWye
- 'Glory of Holland' — EPot
- 'Laucheana' — CBod NOak WHoo WMoo WPyg
* - 'Pink Lusitanica' — EMar WPer
- 'Ruby Glow' — CTri GAri
- 'Snowball' — NOak
- 'Splendens' — EMNN EMil EPfP ESis GCHN LFis LRHS MHer MLan MMal MOne MWgw NHar NMir NRya NVic SWal WFar WPer WWin
- 'Vindictive' ♀ — CB&S CMea CTri EDAr EPfP GKir LGro
'Nifty Thrifty' (v) — CBod CLyd CMea ECGP EDAr EWes GKir LAco LRHS NMen NPSI SCoo SRot WHen WMoo WPat WWeb
'Ornament' — ECtt LFis WFar WHen
plantaginea — See *A. alliacea*
pseudarmeria — ELan MLan MNrw WEas
rumelica — Last listed 1999
setacea — See *A. girardii*
sp. from Patagonia — MDCh
tweedyi — CLyd GTou
* *variegata* 'Stephen Taffler' LFis
vulgaris — See *A. maritima*
welwitschii — SRms

ARMORACIA (Brassicaceae)

§ *rusticana* — CArn COld CSev ELau GPoy ILis MBri MHer MSal NGCt NGHP NPri SIde WCer WGwR WHer WJek WOak WSel WWye
- 'Horwood' — Last listed 1999
- 'Variegata' — EBee ELau EMar EMon GBar GCal GOrP LFis LHop LRHS NGHP NSti SCob SMad SPla WBar WCHb WCot WHal WLRN WSel

ARNEBIA (Boraginaceae)

densiflora — Last listed 1997
echioides — See *A. pulchra*
longiflora — See *A. pulchra*
§ *pulchra* — Last listed 1998

ARNICA (Asteraceae)

angustifolia — EBee SRms
  subsp. *alpina*
- subsp. *iljinii* — EBee NBir
chamissonis — EBee ELau GBar MNrw MSal SIde WJek WPer WRha WWye
¶ *chionopappa* — EBee
cordifolia — Last listed 1997
frigida — EBee

---

lessingii — EBee MDCh
longifolia — EBee
montana — CArn EBee EOHP GBar GPoy GTou MChe MHer NSti SRms SWat WJek WPer WWye
- yellow — MLan
nevadensis — EBee
sachalinensis — EBee

ARONIA (Rosaceae)

arbutifolia — CB&S CGre CPle CTri EPfP EPla GBin IOrc MBlu MWhi SLdr SLon WDin WWat
- 'Erecta' — CDul EBee EBrP EBre ELan EPfP GChr LBCl LBSe LBre LHop LRHS MBBe MBNS MBlu SBre SLPl SMac SRms SSpi WWat
melanocarpa — CB&S CMCN CMHG CSam EBrP EBre ELan EPla EWTr GKir LBCl LBSe LBre LPan LRHS MAsh MBBe MBar MBlu MRav SBre SSpi WCwm WDin WFro WHCG WWat
- 'Autumn Magic' — CAbP CBlo CFai CPMA CSam EPfP LRHS MAsh MBlu NFla NLar NPSI SPer WBod WRHF WWat
¶ - var. *elata* — EPla
¶ - 'Nero' (F) — CAgr
- 'Red Viking' — NPSI
- 'Viking' — CAgr EBee EPfP LBuc MAsh WLRN WShe WWes
x *prunifolia* — CAgr CB&S CDoC CMHG GKir SPer WHCG WWat
- 'Brilliant' — COtt EBee MAsh MCoo SPer SRPl WBcn WWat

ARRHENATHERUM (Poaceae)

elatius subsp. *bulbosum* SPer
- - 'Variegatum' — More than 30 suppliers

ARTEMISIA ✿ (Asteraceae)

§ *abrotanum* ♀ — More than 30 suppliers
* - 'Variegata' — EWll WShe
absinthium — CArn CSev EEls ELau EWFC EWTr GPoy LRHS MBar MChe MHer MLLN MWgw NFor NGCt NSti SIde SPer SWat WCer WHbs WOak WPer WWye
- 'Corinne Tremaine' (v) — WHer
¶ - 'Creeping Silver' — IIve
- 'Huntingdon' — CHad EEls
- 'Lambrook Giant' — EEls
- 'Lambrook Mist' ♀ — COtt CSev EBee ECha EEls ELan ELau EPPr EPfP GBri LRHS MAvo MBel MCAu MRav NCiC NSti NWoo SCob SWat WJek WLRN WRus WWat
- 'Lambrook Silver' ♀ — More than 30 suppliers
- 'Silver Ghost' — EEls
* - 'Variegata' — Last listed 1999
afra — EEls GBar
§ *alba* — CSWP CSev EEls EMan EMon GBar GPoy ILis MHer NBur NGCt NSti SIde SMad WCer WPer WRha
§ - 'Canescens' ♀ — More than 30 suppliers
annua — CArn EEls MSal SIde WJek WWye
¶ *anomala* — EEls
arborescens — CArn CDul CGle CMHG CTri ECha EEls ENot NFai NSti SDry SPer WDin WHer WMoo
- 'Brass Band' — See *A.* 'Powis Castle'
- 'Faith Raven' — CArn EEls GBuc NFai SRPl WHer WRus

- 'Porquerolles'	EEls
arctica	EBee EEls
argyi	EEls
§ *armeniaca*	EEls WWin
assoana	See *A. caucasica*
atrata	EEls
¶ *barrelieri*	EEls
brachyloba	MLLN WCHb
brachyphylla	ELau
caerulescens	See *Seriphidium caerulescens*
californica	EEls
campestris	EBlw EEls MChe MHer WCer
subsp. *borealis*	WRha WSel
- subsp. *campestris*	EEls
- subsp. *maritima*	EEls
- - Welsh form	EEls
camphorata	See *A. alba*
cana	See *Seriphidium canum*
canariensis	See *A. thuscula*
canescens hort.	See *A. alba* 'Canescens'
- Willd.	See *A. armeniaca*
capillaris	EBee EEls SMrm
§ *caucasica* ♀	CGlc CPBP EBee EBrP EBre EDAr
	EEls ELau EWes GCHN GKir LBCl
	LBSe LBre LGro MBBe MBrN
	MRav NDov SBla SBre SIng SRms
	SRot WCHb WEas WPer WWat
- *caucasica*	EEls ESis WFar
chamaemelifolia	CArn EEls EGar MHer NTow SIde
	WPer WWye
cretacea	See *Seriphidium nutans*
discolor Dougl. ex Besser	See *A. michauxiana*
douglasiana	EEls
- 'Valerie Finnis'	See *A. ludoviciana* 'Valerie Finnis'
dracunculus	CArn CGle CHad CSev ECha EDAr
	EEls ELan ELau GAbr GBar GPoy
	MBar MChe MHer MMal MRav
	NFor SCob SIde WCer WEas WFar
	WOak WPer WSel WWye
- *dracunculoides*	CArn EEls GBar NPri WGwG
eriantha	Last listed 1999
ferganensis	See *Seriphidium ferganense*
filifolia	EEls
fragrans Willd.	See *Seriphidium fragrans*
frigida ♀	EEls GBar ILis WHCG
genipi	EEls
glacialis	ECha EEls EGar NBur
gmelinii	EBee EEls GBar IIve
gnaphalodes	See *A. ludoviciana*
gorgonum	EEls
gracilis	See *A. scoparia*
N *granatensis* hort.	MSte
herba-alba	EEls
kawakamii B&SWJ 088	CFee EEls WCru
kitadakensis	EEls
- 'Guizhou'	See *A. lactiflora* Guizhou Group
laciniata	EEls
lactiflora ♀	CGle ECha ECtt EEls EFou ELan
	ELau EMon EPar EWTr MLLN
	MRav NFor NGdn NOrc NSti SDix
	SPer SRms WFar WWye
- dark form	See *A. lactiflora* Guizhou Group
§ - Guizhou Group	More than 30 suppliers
¶ - 'Jim Russell'	CElw EWes LGre NDov
- *purpurea*	See *A. lactiflora* Guizhou Group
- 'Variegata'	See *A. vulgaris* 'Variegata'
lagocephala	EEls SMrm WCot
lanata Willd. non Lam.	See *A. caucasica*
laxa	See *A. umbelliformis*
§ *ludoviciana*	CGle EBee EEls ELan ELau EOld
	GBar GCHN GMac GOrc MBrN
	MWat NBid NFor NOak NOrc

	SEas SIde SRCN SRms WCFE
	WOve WWin WWye
N - var. *latifolia*	See *A. ludoviciana* subsp.
	ludoviciana var. *latifolia*
- var. *latiloba* NNS 96-20	Last listed 1999
- subsp. *ludoviciana*	EBee ECha EEls EGle NFai WCot
var. *incompta*	WHer
§ - - var. *latiloba*	CHor EBee EEls EHoe GBuc LHop
	LRHS MBro MRav NBro NOak
	NSti SAga WByw WCot WHoo
	WPer
- subsp. *mexicana* var. *albula*	
	EBee EEls WFar
- 'Silver Queen' ♀	More than 30 suppliers
N - 'Valerie Finnis' ♀	More than 30 suppliers
mansburica	WCot
maritima	See *Seriphidium maritimum*
§ *michauxiana*	EBee EEls
molinieri	CSev EEls
mutellina	See *A. umbelliformis*
niitakayamensis	EEls GBar WWat
nitida	EEls
¶ *norvegica*	EEls
nova	See *Seriphidium novum*
nutans	See *Seriphidium nutans*
palmeri A. Gray	See *Seriphidium palmeri*
- hort.	See *A. ludoviciana*
pamirica	EEls
aff. *parviflora* CLD 1531	EEls EMon
pedemontana	See *A. caucasica*
pontica ♀	More than 30 suppliers
N 'Powis Castle' ♀	More than 30 suppliers
princeps	EEls
procera Willd.	See *A. abrotanum*
pursbiana	See *A. ludoviciana*
pycnocephala	EEls SMad
'David's Choice'	
ramosa	EEls
'Rosenschleier'	EBee EFou EMon LGre SRCN
rutifolia	EEls
schmidtiana ♀	ECha ECot EEls EFou EGar EMan
	EPot GKir LHop MNrw MWat
	NOrc SOkh SRms WOve
- 'Nana' ♀	More than 30 suppliers
§ *scoparia*	EEls
selengensis	EEls
sieberi	EEls
sp. Guiz 137	See *A. lactiflora* Guizhou Group
splendens Willd.	EBrP EBre ELan LBCl LBSe LBre
	LGre MBBe NSti SBre WEas
- hort.	See *A. alba* 'Canescens'
stelleriana	CGle ECha EEls GMaP LFis MBel
	MCAu MHer MTho NBro NFla
	NFor NSti SHel SPer SRms SSvw
	WEas WPer
N - 'Boughton Silver'	CArn CHad EBee EEls EFou EGle
	EGoo EHoe ELan GAbr GBri GKir
	LGre LRHS MAsh MRav MSCN
	NSti NTow WFar WPer WWat
	WWye
N - 'Mori'	See *A. stelleriana* 'Boughton
	Silver'
¶ - 'Mori's Form'	GMac
- 'Nana'	ECha EEls EMan
- 'Prostata'	See *A. stelleriana* 'Boughton
	Silver'
- 'Silver Brocade'	See *A. stelleriana* 'Boughton
	Silver'
taurica	EEls
§ *thuscula*	EEls
¶ *tilesii*	IIve
tridentata	See *Seriphidium tridentatum*

§	*umbelliformis*	EEls
	vallesiaca	See *Seriphidium vallesiacum*
	verlotiorum	EEls GBar
*	*versicolor*	Last listed 1999
	vulgaris	CArn EEls ELau EWFC GBar GPoy MChe MHer SIde WHbs WHer WJek WOak WWye
	- 'Byrne's Variegated'	EGle EMan EMon
	- 'Cragg-Barber Eye' (v)	EBee EEls EGar MGrG NPro WAlt WBar WCHb WCot WHer WRha
	- 'Crispa'	ELau EMon
	- 'Obelisk'	EEls EFou
	- 'Oriental Limelight' (v)	CSpe CWes EBee ECtt EDAr EEls EFou LHop LRHS MBri MMil NPri WFar WHer WJek WSpi WWoo
	- 'Peddar's Gold' (v)	EPPr EWes
§	- 'Variegata'	CBre CWit EBee EEls ERav GBar GLil LFis NBir NSti SLod SMad WAlt WBea WCHb WCot WFar WHer WHil WJek WPer WRha
	- 'Woolaston' (v)	WAlt
	x *wurzellii*	EEls

ARTHROPODIUM (Anthericaceae)

	candidum	CBot CPea CRow ECha ECou EPPr EPla EPot GBin IMGH MBrN MSCN NCat NWCA SBea SIng SRot WEas WHal WPer WRos
	- *maculatum*	CInt SPlb WElm
	- *purpureum*	CB&S EBee EMan EPPr GBri GCal GGar LHil LRHS LRot MMoz NEgg SCob SSoC STes WCot WFar WPrP
*	*carlesii*	CRHN
	cirratum	CAbb ECou EPPr ERea GBri LHil MLan SVen WHal WHil WMul WSHC
	- 'Matapouri Bay'	CB&S CDoC EMan
	milleflorum	ECou NWoo

ARUM ✿ (Araceae)

¶	*alpinum*	CFil WPGP
§	*besserianum*	Last listed 1998
§	*concinnatum*	CFil CLAP EBee EMon EPot EWes LAma SChr SSpi WPGP
	- subsp. *albispathum*	WCot
¶	- purple	LEur
	cornutum	See *Sauromatum venosum*
	creticum	CBot CBro CFir ECha EPar IBlr MMil MRav MTho NLar NTow SSpi WPGP
	- FCC form	CLAP SBla WCot
	- yellow	NBir NPar WFar WIvy
	cyrenaicum	CStu
§	*dioscoridis*	CStu EBee EPot MTho NRog WCot WPGP
§	- var. *dioscoridis*	Last listed 1997
¶	- - JCA 195.200	EMon
	- JCA 195.157	WCot
	- var. *liepoldtii*	See *A. dioscoridis* var. *dioscoridis*
	- var. *smithii*	See *A. dioscoridis* var. *dioscoridis*
	dracunculus	See *Dracunculus vulgaris*
	elongatum	Last listed 1998
	hygrophilum	EMon
	idaeum	CLAP SSpi
	italicum	CGdn CGle CTri EBee EWTr LAma LRHS MBri MTho NLar NRog SEND SWat WAbe WByw WCot WFar WPnP WShi
	- subsp. *albispathum*	CFil CStu EBee EMon EPot LAma NRog WCot WPGP
	- black spotted	WFar
	- 'Cyclops' EAF 7701	CHid CLAP EBee MNrw NMen

		WCot
	- 'Green Marble'	SBla WFar
	- subsp. *italicum*	EPla
	- - 'Bill Baker'	EMon
§	- - 'Marmoratum' ♀	More than 30 suppliers
¶	- - 'Sparkler'	WCot
	- - 'Tiny'	GCal
§	- - 'White Winter'	CAvo CRDP EMon GBuc WCot WRus WSPU
	- 'Nancy Lindsay'	EMon WPrP
	- subsp. *neglectum*	CAvo CBos CHad CLAP CRDP EBee Emon MAvo NCat SMad WCot WFar WHal WWeb
	'Chameleon'	
¶	- - 'Miss Janay Hall' (v)	WCot
	- NL 1234	CLAP WTin
	- 'Pictum'	See *A. italicum* subsp. *italicum* 'Marmoratum'
	- 'Spotted Jack'	MNrw WCot
	korolkowii	NRog
	maculatum	CArn CKin EOld EPar EPot EWFC GPoy LAma LSyl MMal MRav MSal NHex WHer WShi WWye
	- 'Painted Lady' (v)	WCot
	- 'Pleddel'	MRav WCot
*	- 'Variegatum'	GPoy
	nickelii	See *A. concinnatum*
§	*nigrum*	WCot
	orientale	EPot NTow
	- subsp. *besserianum*	See *A. besserianum*
	- subsp. *sintenisii*	LEur
	palaestinum	WCot
	petteri hort.	See *A. nigrum*
	pictum	CAvo CLAP CRDP EWTr LAma LRHS NRog WCot WIvy
	- ACL 321/78	EMon
	- CL 28	Last listed 1998
	- 'Taff's Form'	See *A. italicum* subsp. *italicum* 'White Winter'
	purpureospathum	SBla
	rupicola var. *virescens*	WCot
*	*sintenisii*	WCot
¶	'Streaked Spectre'	EMon

ARUNCUS ✿ (Rosaceae)

	aethusifolius	More than 30 suppliers
	asiaticus	EBee
	dioicus	CWes ECGP EGle EMil EPfP EWTr GGar GKir LRHS MBel MCAu MNaF NCut NGdn SPlb SRPl WByw WCot
§	- (m) ♀	More than 30 suppliers
	- Child of Two Worlds	See *A. dioicus* 'Zweiweltenkind'
	- 'Glasnevin'	CRow CSev ECha ECtt EGol EMan LFis LRHS MBri MRav NDov NHol
	- var. *kamtschaticus*	EWes NHol
	- - AGSJ 238	NHol
	- 'Kneiffii'	More than 30 suppliers
§	- 'Zweiweltenkind'	CBrm ECGN GSki LFis MBro MCli WPer
	plumosus	See *A. dioicus*
*	*sinensis*	EWll
	sp. AGSJ 214	NHol
	sylvestris	See *A. dioicus*

ARUNDINARIA ✿ (Poaceae - Bambusoideae)

	amabilis	See *Pseudosasa amabilis*
	anceps	See *Yushania anceps*
	angustifolia	See *Pleioblastus chino* f. *angustifolius*
	auricoma	See *Pleioblastus auricomus*
	chino	See *Pleioblastus chino*
	disticha	See *Pleioblastus pygmaeus* var. *distichus*

falconeri	See *Himalayacalamus falconeri*
fangiana	EPla
fargesii	See *Bashania fargesii*
fastuosa	See *Semiarundinaria fastuosa*
fortunei	See *Pleioblastus variegatus*
fungbomii	See *Schizostachyum fungbomii*
gigantea	EPla SDry WJun
hindsii	See *Pleioblastus hindsii* hort.
hookeriana hort.	See *Himalayacalamus falconeri* 'Damarapa'
– Munro	See *Himalayacalamus hookerianus*
humilis	See *Pleioblastus humilis*
japonica	See *Pseudosasa japonica*
jaunsarensis	See *Yushania anceps*
maling	See *Yushania maling*
marmorea	See *Chimonobambusa marmorea*
murieliae	See *Fargesia murieliae*
nitida	See *Fargesia nitida*
oedogonata	See *Clavinodum oedogonatum*
palmata	See *Sasa palmata*
pumila	See *Pleioblastus humilis* var. *pumilus*
pygmaea	See *Pleioblastus pygmaeus*
quadrangularis	See *Chimonobambusa quadrangularis*
simonii	See *Pleioblastus simonii*
spathiflora	See *Thamnocalamus spathiflorus*
§ *tecta*	EPla SDry
tessellata	See *Thamnocalamus tessellatus*
vagans	See *Sasaella ramosa*
variegata	See *Pleioblastus variegatus*
veitchii	See *Sasa veitchii*
viridistriata	See *Pleioblastus auricomus*
'Wang Tsai'	See *Bambusa multiplex* 'Fernleaf'

ARUNDO (Poaceae)

donax	CAbb CFil CHEx CInt CPla CRow ECha EFul EPla EWes GKir LPBA LPan MBlu SAPC SApp SArc SDix SMad SSoC WGer WHal WHil WMul
¶ – 'Golden Chain'	EMan
– 'Macrophylla'	CRow EPla LEdu LPJP
– 'Variegata'	See *A. donax* var. *versicolor*
§ – var. *versicolor* (v)	More than 30 suppliers
¶ – yellow variegated	EOas
pliniana	CRow EMon LEdu

ASARINA (Scrophulariaceae)

antirrhiniflora	See *Maurandella antirrhiniflora*
barclayana	See *Maurandya barclayana*
erubescens	See *Lophospermum erubescens*
hispanica	See *Antirrhinum hispanicum*
lophantha	See *Lophospermum erubescens*
lophospermum	See *Lophospermum erubescens*
§ *procumbens*	CGle EBee EMan EWTr GDra GKir GTou IMGH MPEx MSCN MTho NFor NHex NWCA SBea SHFr SHel SIng SLod SRCN SRms SSpi WCot WCru WFar WGwG WHer WPer WWin
– 'Alba'	SRms
– dwarf	WCot
purpusii	See *Maurandya purpusii*
scandens	See *Lophospermum scandens*
'Victoria Falls'	See *Maurandya* 'Victoria Falls'

ASARUM ✿ (Aristolochiaceae)

albomaculatum B&SWJ 1726	WCru
arifolium	CHid CLAP EPar
asaroides	Last listed 1999
asperum	Last listed 1999
* *campaniforme*	LAma WCru
canadense	CArn EBee EPot GPoy LRHS MSal WCru
caudatum	CHid CLAP CRow EBee EGar EMan EPla NBro NLar NSti NWCA SRms WCot WCru WFar WPGP
caudigerum	LAma
– B&SWJ 1517	WCru
caulescens	CLAP LAma WCru
chinense	WCru
costatum	Last listed 1999
debile	LAma WCru
delavayi	LAma WCru
epigynum B&SWJ 3443	WCru
– 'Silver Web' B&SWJ 3442	WCru
europaeum	CLAP CNat CTri EBee ECha EFou EMar EPar EPla ERos GGar GPoy LSpr MGrG MSal MWgw NBro NHex NSti SMac SMad WCot WCru WEas WFar WHer WWat WWye
forbesii	WCru
hartwegii	CLAP EMan EPar EPot ERos GBuc MTed WCru
heterophyllum	Last listed 1999
hexalobum	Last listed 1999
hirsutisepalum	Last listed 1999
infrapurpureum B&SWJ 1994	WCru
kiusianum	Last listed 1999
kumageanum	Last listed 1999
lemmonii	EGar WCru
leptophyllum B&SWJ 1983	WCru
macranthum	Last listed 1999
– B&SWJ 1691	WCru
maculatum B&SWJ 1114	WCru
magnificum	LAma WCru
maximum	LAma MTed WCot WCru
megacalyx	Last listed 1999
minamitanianum	Last listed 1999
nipponicum	Last listed 1999
¶ *pulchellum*	EPar LEur
rigescens	Last listed 1999
sakawanum	Last listed 1999
shuttleworthii	CLAP WCru
– 'Callaway'	Last listed 1999
sieboldii	WCru
splendens	EBee EMan EPPr LAma MCCP SBla WCot WCru WHer
stellatum	Last listed 1999
subglobosum	Last listed 1999
taipingshanianum B&SWJ 1688	WCot WCru
takaoi	Last listed 1999

ASCLEPIAS (Asclepiadaceae)

'Cinderella'	CSev EBee LBuc NCut SGar WOve WWin
curassavica	CHal CSev LRHS SHFr SSte SUsu WMul
§ *fascicularis*	Last listed 1999
fasciculata	See *A. fascicularis*
fruticosa	See *Gomphocarpus fruticosus*
incarnata	CAgr CInt CMea CSev EBee ELan

	EWll GKir MRav MSal MTis SPer
	WPer
- 'Alba'	EMon
- 'Ice Ballet'	CSev EBee EMan EMar EWll LRHS
	MMil NChi SWat WLin WWin
- 'Soulmate'	EPfP EWll
- 'White Superior'	Last listed 1997
physocarpa	See *Gomphocarpus physocarpus*
purpurascens	CArn EBee SRCN SSte
rotundifolia	EBee
speciosa	CAgr EBee
syriaca	CAgr CArn EBee LRHS MLLN
	MSte SHFr WPer
tuberosa	CAgr CArn CB&S COIW EBee
	ELau EMan GKir GPoy LRHS
	MHer MMHG MNrw MRav MSal
	NCut SAga SCob SLod WPer
	WWin
- Gay Butterflies Group	CInt MLan SMrm
- 'Hello Yellow'	Last listed 1999
verticillata	Last listed 1999

ASIMINA (Annonaceae)
triloba	CAgr IDee LEdu SMad WNor
¶ - 'Davis' (F)	CAgr
¶ - 'Overleese' (F)	CAgr

ASKIDIOSPERMA (Restionaceae)
chartaceum	CCpl GOrP
esterbuyseniae	CTrC WNor
paniculatum	LHil

ASPARAGUS (Asparagaceae)
asparagoides ♀	CPlN ERea
§ - 'Myrtifolius'	CHal SYvo
cochinchinensis	EBee ELau WCru
B&SWJ 3425	
densiflorus 'Myersii' ♀	CHal ERea LHil LRHS MBri SRms
- Sprengeri Group ♀	CHal LRHS MBri SRms
falcatus	LRHS MBri SEND
officinalis	CHEx ERea SEND
- 'Backlim'	EMui
- 'Butler'	SDea
- 'Cito' (m)	SDea
- 'Dariano'	SDea
- 'Franklim'	EMui MRav
plumosus	See *A. setaceus*
pseudoscaber	EBee WCot
'Spitzenschleier'	
¶ 'Purple Jumbo'	LEdu
¶ *retrofractus*	WPGP
scandens	CPlN
schoberioides	GCal
§ *setaceus* ♀	CHal LRHS MBri
- 'Nanus'	LPVe
- 'Pyramidalis'	MBri SRms
sp. B&SWJ 871	WCru
verticillatus	Last listed 1999

ASPERULA (Rubiaceae)
§ *arcadiensis* ♀	CLyd EPot NWCA SBla SIng
- JCA 210.100	NTow
aristata subsp. *scabra*	EBee ECha ELan EMar EMon
- subsp. *thessala*	See *A. sintenisii*
cyanchica	MHew
daphneola	CPBP ECho SBla SIng
gussonei	CLyd CMea EDAr EMNN EPot ESis
	LBee LRHS MBro MWat NDlv
	NMen NWCA SBla SIng SSmi
	WAbe WPat
hexaphylla	Last listed 1998
hirta	Last listed 1999

§ *lilaciflora*	IMGH SSmi
- var. *caespitosa*	See *A. lilaciflora* subsp. *lilacifl.*
§ - subsp. *lilaciflora*	CLyd CPBP EDAr EPot ESis LRHS
	NMen NWCA WWin
nitida	ECho NNrd
- subsp. *puberula*	See *A. sintenisii*
odorata	See *Galium odoratum*
¶ *orientalis*	WPGP
§ *sintenisii* ♀	CLyd CPBP EPot LBee LRHS MBro
	NMen NTow NWCA SBla SIng
	SSmi WAbe WHoo
suavis	Last listed 1999
suberosa Sibth. & Sm.	CPBP ECho
- hort.	See *A. arcadiensis*
taurina subsp. *caucasica*	CPLG EMon EOrc MBro NSti
	WCHb WCot
taygetea NS 723	NWCA
tinctoria	CArn EOHP GBar GPoy MChe
	MHer MHew MSal SIde SRms
	WCHb WSel

ASPHODELINE (Asphodelaceae)
§ *brevicaulis*	Last listed 1997
liburnica	CBro ECGN ECGP ECha ELan
	EMan EMar ERos MBel MBro
	MRav MWat SAga SEND SSpi
	WCot WFar WGwG WPer
§ *lutea*	More than 30 suppliers
§ - 'Gelbkerze'	LRHS MNrw SMrm
- Yellow Candle	See *A. lutea* 'Gelbkerze'
rigidifolia	EBee
taurica	EMan SMrm SVal WPer

ASPHODELUS (Asphodelaceae)
acaulis	EWoo WAbe
- S&F 37	Last listed 1998
§ *aestivus*	EBee SWat WPer
albus	CArn CBlo CBot EBee ECGN
	ECha EWTr LGre MWll NBid NPri
	SOkh SPlb SRms WCot WPer
- subsp. *albus*	Last listed 1997
brevicaulis	See *Asphodeline brevicaulis*
cerasiferus	See *A. ramosus*
fistulosus	EMar EPPr MDCh NBir SAga
	WCDu WCot WPer WWin
lusitanicus	See *A. ramosus*
luteus	See *Asphodeline lutea*
microcarpus	See *A. aestivus*
§ *ramosus*	EBee ECGN ECGP EGoo EMan
	MNrw MTho WCot WPer

ASPIDISTRA (Convallariaceae)
¶ *attenuata* B&SWJ 377	WCru
¶ *caespitosa* 'Jade Ribbons'	WCot
elatior ♀	CHEx CHal EBak ERav IBlr LHil
	LRHS MBri NRog SAPC SArc SCob
	SMad SRms WCot
- 'Milky Way' (v)	WCot WViv
- 'Variegata' ♀	CHal EMon IBlr MTho NBir WCot
lurida	IBlr
- 'Irish Mist' (v)	IBlr

ASPLENIUM ✿ (Aspleniaceae)
adiantum-nigrum	CCuc EMon LRHS NHar SPer
	SRms
§ *aethiopicum*	EBee
§ *australasicum*	WRic
f. *robinsonii*	
bulbiferum ♀	ECon LCns NMar
canariense	NMar
§ *ceterach*	SRms WHer
dareoides	GDra IMGH SOkd

flabellifolium	WRic
fontanum	NHar
forisiense	Last listed 1998
furcatum Thunb.	See *A. aethiopicum*
monanthes	WRic
nidus ♀	LRHS MBri
oblongifolium	Last listed 1998
platyneuron	CFil
robinsonii	See *A. australasicum* f. *robinsonii*
ruta-muraria	SRms
§ *scolopendrium* ♀	More than 30 suppliers
- var. *americanum*	Last listed 1999
- 'Angustatum'	CBlo CLAP CMil EBee LRHS MBri NHar NHol SSoC WCru
- 'Capitatum'	SRms
* - 'Circinatum'	CCuc CRow WPGP
- 'Conglomeratum'	SRms
¶ - 'Cornutoabruptum'	NMar
- Crispum Group	CCuc CFil CLAP CRDP CRow EBrP EBre ECha EFer ELan EMon LBCl LBSe LBre MBBe MBri NBus NHar NHol SBre SRms WFib WPGP
- 'Crispum Bolton's Nobile' ♀	NBro NMar WFib WPGP WRic
- Crispum Cristatum Group	CLAP
- Crispum Fimbriatum Group	GQui
- - 'Drummondiae'	Last listed 1999
- (Crispum Group) 'Golden Queen'	CRow
- Cristatum Group	CFil CHEx CLAP CRDP CRow EBee ELan EMar EMon GCHN IOrc LRHS MBri MRav NBus NDlv NHar NHol NMar SNut SPer SPla SRms SSoC SWat WCot WFib WGor WRic
- Fimbriatum Group	CLAP WRic
- 'Furcatum'	CLAP EBee EFer EMar
- 'Kaye's Lacerated' ♀	CLAP CRow EFer EGol ELan EMon NHar NHol NMar SChu WFib WRic
- Laceratum Group	SRms
- Marginatum Group	EMon NMar SWat WPGP
- - 'Irregulare'	CRDP NHar NHol SChu SRms WFib
- 'Muricatum'	CLAP CRDP NMar SChu WFib WRic
- 'Ramocristatum'	CRow NMar
- Ramomarginatum Group	CLAP EFer ELan EMon SRms WRic
- 'Sagittatocristatum'	EFer WPGP
- 'Spirale'	Last listed 1997
- Undulatum Group	CLAP EFou EGol NBir NBus NHar NMar NPar SRms SSpi SWat WPnP WRic
- Undulatum Cristatum Group	MBri NDlv WRic
septentrionale	SRms
terrestre	SRms
trichomanes ♀	CCuc CFil CHea CLAP EBee EBrP EBre EFer ELan EMon GGar LBCl LBSe LBre LRHS MBBe MBri MLan NDlv NHar NHol NMar SBre SLon SNut SRms WFib WPGP WRic
¶ - 'Bipinnatum'	WRic
- Cristatum Group	SRms
- Grandiceps Group	EFer
- Incisum Group	CLAP EBee EFer EMon IOrc NHar NHol NMar NOrc SMad WFib
- 'Incisum Moule'	WRic
- subsp. *pachyrachis*	NMar

- 'Ramocristatum'	Last listed 1999
- 'Stuart Williams'	WRic
viride	SRms

ASTARTEA (Myrtaceae)

fascicularis	CPLG LRHS SOWG

ASTELIA (Asteliaceae)

banksii	CB&S CBos CSpe LEdu WAbe WDyG
§ *chathamica* ♀	More than 30 suppliers
- 'Silver Spear'	See *A. chathamica*
cunninghamii	See *A. solandri*
fragrans	CFil ECou IBlr LEdu WCot WDyG
graminea	IBlr
graminifolia	See *Collospermum microspermum*
grandis	CHEx IBlr LEdu
nervosa	CAbb CFil IBlr LEdu SAPC SArc SVen WCot WPGP
nivicola	IBlr
- 'Red Gem'	IBlr LEdu
§ *solandri*	CFil CHEx IBlr LEdu LHil

ASTER ✿ (Asteraceae)

acris	See *A. sedifolius*
§ *albescens*	CGre CPle CPne GOrc ISea WSHC
- AIC337	WCot
alpigenus	Last listed 1998
alpinus ♀	EBrP EBre EMNN GCHN GKir LBCl LBSe LBre LRHS MBBe MNrw NMen SBre SRms WFar WPer WStl WWin
- var. *albus*	EPfP EWTr GCHN MWll NPri WPer WPnP
- Dark Beauty	See *A. alpinus* 'Dunkle Schöne'
- var. *dolomiticus*	NSla
§ - 'Dunkle Schöne'	EBee GKir NFai NOak SRms WPer
- 'Goliath'	MAvo
- 'Happy End'	CM&M EMil MAvo NFai NOak NPri SRms WCot WPnP
- 'Märchenland'	MAvo
- 'Trimix'	ESis GKir LFis NArg NBir NVic SRms WFar
- violet	WPer
- 'White Beauty'	NFai SRms SSca
* - 'Wolfii'	SRms
amelloides	See *Felicia amelloides*
amellus	EBot MBct MHer NFor
- 'Blue King'	LFis LRHS MBri MCAu MLLN NFai WCot
- 'Breslau'	MTed
- 'Brilliant'	EBee ECtt EFou EGle EMan LFis LRHS MBri MLLN MRav MWat SMer SMrm SPer WOld WWin
- 'Butzemann'	EBee
- 'Doktor Otto Petschek'	WFar WViv
- Empress	See *A. amellus* 'Glücksfund'
- 'Forncett Flourish'	EFou GMac
- 'Framfieldii' ♀	WFar WOld
§ - 'Glücksfund'	Last listed 1998
- 'Grunder'	WOld
- 'Jacqueline Genebrier' ♀	CHar CMil EGle EPPr SChu SMrm SUsu WIvy WOld
- 'Joseph Lakin'	Last listed 1999
- 'King George' ♀	More than 30 suppliers
- 'Kobold'	LRHS WFar WOld
- 'Lac de Genève'	LFis LRHS WCot WFar WOld
- 'Lady Hindlip'	MTed WEas
* - 'Mary Ann Neil'	LFis
¶ - 'Mira'	WByw
- 'Moerheim Gem'	EFou WEas WOld

- 'Mrs Ralph Woods' WOld
- 'Nocturne' EGle EPPr ERou LFis NBrk SMrm
  WCot WOld
- 'Peach Blossom' WCot
- 'Pink Pearl' WFar
- Pink Zenith See *A. amellus* 'Rosa Erfüllung'
§ - 'Rosa Erfüllung' More than 30 suppliers
- 'Rotfeuer' EFou
- 'Rudolph Goethe' EGle EGra EMil EPri LRHS MLLN
  MRav MWhi NFla NVic STes WCot
  WEas WFar WMoo WOld WWye
- 'Schöne von Ronsdorf' LBuc
- September Glow' EBee EFou EGle
- 'Sonia' ECha EFou EGle LFis MBri MCAu
  NFla WFar WOld
- 'Sonora' EBee EGle LGre NHol SAga WOld
- 'Sternkugel' NBrk WOld
- 'Ultramarine' WFar
- 'Vanity' GBuc WOld
§ - 'Veilchenkönigin' ♀ More than 30 suppliers
N - Violet Queen See *A. amellus* 'Veilchenkönigin'
- 'Weltfriede' WOld
'Anja's Choice' EMon LGre WOld WPrP
asper See *A. bakerianus*
asperulus LGre SUsu
§ *bakerianus* CMGP EBee NOak WFar WPer
'Barbara Worl' Last listed 1999
capensis 'Variegatus' See *Felicia amelloides* variegated
§ *carolinianus* WOld
'Cha-Cha' Last listed 1998
¶ *ciliolatus* EBrP EBre LBCl LBSe LBre MBBe
  SBre
'Climax' EBee ECha GBuc GCal MRav NSti
  WCot WOld
coelestis See *Felicia amelloides*
coloradoensis NSla
* 'Connecticut Snow Fleure' CSam
'Coombe Fishacre' ♀ CGle COIW EMan ERou GCal LFis
  LGre LRHS MBel MBri MBro MMil
  MRav NFai SAga SHel SPla SSvw
  WByw WCot WEas WFar WOld
  WOve WWye
cordifolius WFar
- 'Aldebaran' LGre NBrk
- 'Chieftain' ♀ LGre MTed SAga WCot WIvy
  WOld
- 'Elegans' EBee EFou EGar MBri NSti WCot
  WIvy WMoo WOld
- 'Ideal' EFou WOld WPer
- 'Little Carlow' See *A*. 'Little Carlow' (*cordifolius*
  hybrid)
- 'Little Dorrit' See *A*. 'Little Dorrit' (*cordifolius*
  hybrid)
- 'Photograph' See *A*. 'Photograph'
- 'Silver Queen' WHil WOld
- 'Silver Spray' CElw EFou EMan ERou GMaP
  GMac LGre MBro MLLN MWat
  NBro WEas WHoo WOld WPer
  WPyg
- 'Sweet Lavender' ♀ ERou LFis NBrk WOld
corymbosus See *A. divaricatus*
§ 'Dark Pink Star' WOld
'Deep Pink Star' See *A*. 'Dark Pink Star'
delavayi EBee EGle SUsu WCot
- CLD 0494 Last listed 1997
diffusus See *A. lateriflorus*
diplostephioides EBee SSpi
§ *divaricatus* More than 30 suppliers
N *dumosus* SHel WPer
¶ 'Dwarf Blue' EWTr
eatonii EBee
'Edo-murasaki' WCot

ericoides CBrm CGle CSam ERav NWCA
  WWin
- 'Blue Star' ♀ CM&M EFou EGar EWTr GBuc
  LRHS MBel MLLN NBrk NFai NSti
  SChu SHel SPer WCot WOld
- 'Blue Wonder' CGle EOrc NBrk
- 'Brimstone' ♀ EBee EPPr MRav WOld
- 'Cinderella' CHor COIW EGar EPPr GBuc
  GMac NFla NSti WCot WOld
- 'Cirylle' EFou
- 'Constance' NBrk WOld
* - 'Dainty' Last listed 1997
- 'Enchantress' ERou
- 'Erlkönig' EBee EFou EMan EPPr GAbr
  GMac LAst LRHS MMil MSte
  MWgw SChu SPla SSpe SWat
  WOld WPer WWin
- 'Esther' CGle CHea ECha EFou EGle ELan
  EMan EMou EOrc EPri ERou LFis
  MSte NBrk SDix WOld
- 'Golden Spray' ♀ EBee EFou EWTr NFai NSti SHel
  WFar WLRN WOld
- 'Herbstmyrte' EWTr GBuc MLLN
- 'Hon. Edith Gibbs' Last listed 1999
- 'Hon. Vicary Gibbs' See *A*. 'Hon. Vicary Gibbs'
  (*ericoides* hybrid)
- 'Kaytie Fisher' LFis
- 'Maidenhood' WOld
- 'Monte Cassino' See *A. pringlei* 'Monte Cassino'
- 'Pink Cloud' ♀ More than 30 suppliers
- f. *prostratus* EMon EOrc EPot ERav LRHS SCro
  WFar
§ - - 'Snow Flurry' CBre EBee ECha EFou EGle EMan
  EPPr MLLN MNrw NBrk SCob
  SUsu WBor WCot WEas WOld
  WRus
- 'Rosy Veil' GMac NBrk NGdn WByw WCot
  WIvy WOld WPrP
- 'Ruth McConnell' NSti
- 'Schneegitter' MLLN MSte
- 'Schneetanne' EWTr
- 'Sulphurea' MWat
- 'White Heather' EGar EMou GMac MBro NFai
  WByw WCot WIvy WOld WPyg
  WRHF
- 'Yvette Richardson' MSte WOld
'Fanny's Fall' EBee EMan LRHS NDov
farreri EBee GCHN NBro NLar SSpi
- 'Blue Moon' Last listed 1999
§ *flaccidus* EBee GKir LRHS WCot
foliaceus EBee
- var. *cusickii* Last listed 1997
x *frikartii* EBee EBrP EBre EFou EGle ELan
  EPar ERou GCHN LAst LBCl LBSe
  LBre MBBe MBro MRav NFla SBre
  SChu SRms SSoC WByw WEas
  WOld WPer WWin
- 'Eiger' NBrk WOld
- 'Flora's Delight' EBrP EBre EFou EMan ERou GKir
  LBCl LBSe LBre MBBe MRav SBre
  SPer WOld
- 'Jungfrau' GMaP LRHS MMil MTed NCut
  SCob WOld
N - 'Mönch' ♀ More than 30 suppliers
- Wonder of Stafa See *A*. x *frikartii* 'Wunder von
  Stäfa'
§ - 'Wunder von Stäfa' ♀ CEnd CMGP EBee EGle EMan
  GBuc GKir GMaP GMac LFis
  LHop LRHS MBNS MBri SChu
  SCob WLRN WOld WPnP
glebnii Last listed 1999
'Hama-otome' Last listed 1999

'Herfstweelde'	CMil EBee EFou EGar EMon GBuc LGre LRHS MBri MBro MSte SLod SUsu WFar WOld
x *herveyi*	CElw EBee EMan EMon EPPr LGre LRHS SAga WOld
himalaicus	EBee GCHN GTou SRms
– CC&McK 145	GCHN NWCA
'Hittlemaar'	EBee EPPr WCot
§ 'Hon. Vicary Gibbs'	CBre CHea EBee GMac LFis MSte
(*ericoides* hybrid)	NBrk WCot WOld
hybridus luteus	See x *Solidaster luteus*
ibericus	EBee
§ 'Kylie' ♀	CBre CMGP EBee EMon GBuc LFis LRHS MAvo MBro MSte NBrk SCro WCot WFar WHoo WOld WPrP WTin
laevis	EBee EMon GKir MSte SMad
– 'Arcturus'	CFir CLTr EBee EGar LRHS MBri MLLN MMil NSti SSvw WCot WFar
– 'Blauhügel'	GCal
– 'Calliope'	CHad CSam EBee ECha EMan GCal GMac IHdy LGre LPio MBNS MBri MBro MMil MSte NOak SAga SMrm SUsu WCot WEas WFar WIvy WKif WLin WOld
– var. *geyeri*	MNrw
lanceolatus Willd.	WCot
– Kuntze	See *Pyrrocoma lanceolata*
– 'Edwin Beckett'	CBre EMan GMac LFis NBrk WOld
§ *lateriflorus*	CGle EBee ERav ESis MNes MRav MWat WMaN WOld WPer
– 'Bleke Bet'	WCot WOld
– 'Buck's Fizz'	EFou ELan NLar SPla WOld
¶ – 'Chaevis Callsope'	EWTr
– 'Daisy Bush'	Last listed 1997
– 'Datschii'	WFar
– 'Delight'	MLLN WCot
– 'Horizontalis' ♀	More than 30 suppliers
– 'Jan'	WCot WOld
– 'Lady in Black'	CBos CBot CElw CHid CLTr CSpe EBee EFou EGle EMan LGre LRHS MGrG MSte NSti SAga SMrm SSvw WCot WHil WOld
– 'Lovely'	EBee EFou EMan LFis LRHS MBro MLLN NOak WOld
– 'Prince'	More than 30 suppliers
– 'Rubrifolius'	MBel
linariifolius	EBee
§ *linosyris*	LFis MSte NLar NSti SPer WCot WHer WOld
– 'Goldilocks'	See *A. linosyris*
§ 'Little Carlow'	More than 30 suppliers
(*cordifolius* hybrid) ♀	
§ 'Little Dorrit'	CBre GMac MBro MLLN NBro NOak WLRN WOld
(*cordifolius* hybrid)	
maackii	EBee
macrophyllus	CFee CPou EBee ELan EMon LRHS MBel NSti SPer WOld
– 'Albus'	EMon EPPr WFar WIvy WOld
– 'Twilight'	CGle CMea EBee EFou EGle EMan EOrc EPPr EPla GCal GMac LLWP MBro MLLN MSte SUsu WCot WFar WIvy WOld WRHF
¶ 'Midget'	NNor
¶ *miyagii*	SIng
mongolicus	See *Kalimeris mongolica*
natalensis	See *Felicia rosulata*
novae-angliae	ELau WOld
– 'Andenken an Alma Pötschke' ♀	More than 30 suppliers
– 'Andenken an Paul Gerbe'	Last listed 1999
¶ – 'Annabelle de Chazal'	WOld
– Autumn Snow	See *A. novae-angliae* 'Herbstschnee'
– 'Barr's Blue'	EFou LRHS MBNS MCAu MSte MTed MWat NFla NSti WFar WOld
– 'Barr's Pink'	CBre EFou LFis LRHS MCAu MRav MWat NFla SHel WEas WFar WOld WPer WPyg
– 'Barr's Violet'	EGle NFor SRms WCot WHoo WOld WPer WTin
– 'Bishop Colenso'	EFou
– 'Christopher Harbutt'	EGle ERou WOld
– 'Crimson Beauty'	EGar EMon EPPr GMac LRHS MWat WOld
– 'Festival'	Last listed 1998
– 'Forncett Jewel'	Last listed 1997
– 'Harrington's Pink' ♀	More than 30 suppliers
§ – 'Herbstschnee'	More than 30 suppliers
¶ – 'John Davies'	WOld
– 'Lachsglut'	LRHS
– 'Lou Williams'	WOld
– 'Lye End Beauty'	CPou EBee EGle EMon EOrc LRHS MAvo MFir MRav MSte MWat NFor SChu WCot WOld
¶ – 'Millenium Star'	WOld
– 'Mrs S.T. Wright'	EFou EGar EGle EMon ERou GMac LFis MBrN WFar WFoF WOld
* – 'Mrs S.W. Stern'	WOld
– 'Pink Parfait'	EFou WCot WOld
– 'Pink Victor'	CTri EPPr LRHS NFai NLar SEND
– 'Primrose Upward'	WCot
– 'Purple Cloud'	EMon EPPr ERou GMac LHop LRHS MHer MWat MWgw WFoF WPrP
– 'Purple Dome'	EBee EBrP EBre EFou EGle ELan EMon LBCl LBSe LBre LRHS MBBe MBri MBro MCAu MNrw NBlu SAga SBre SEND SSpe SSvw SUsu WCot WFar WMoo WOld WPnP WPrP
– 'Quinton Menzies'	WOld
– 'Red Cloud'	EFou NFai WOld
– 'Rosa Sieger'	CBre CPlt EBrP EBre EFou EGle EMon LBCl LBSe LBre MBBe MGrG SBre SChu SUsu WByw WOld WViv
– 'Rose Williams'	WOld
– 'Roter Stern'	Last listed 1998
– 'Rubinschatz'	WOld
– 'Rudelsburg'	LBuc
– 'Sayer's Croft'	EBee EFou EGle EMon LRHS MBri MWat WCot WHoo WOld
– September Ruby	See *A. novae-angliae* 'Septemberrubin'
§ – 'Septemberrubin'	CBlo CMea ECtt EGle EMon ERou LHop LRHS MRav MSte NFai SChu SMer SUsu WCot WEas WFar WHoo WOld WPnP WPyg WWin
– 'Treasure'	CBre CLTr EBee EFou WFar WOld
– 'Violetta'	CAbx CBre EFou EGle EMon LGre LRHS MAvo MSte MTed NFai WOld WPrP WWye
– 'W. Bowman'	Last listed 1998
N *novi-belgii*	SEas WHer
– 'Ada Ballard'	CBlo EBee EMan ENot ERou GCHN LRHS MBel SPer WLRN WOld WWye
– 'Albanian'	CElw WOld
– 'Alderman Vokes'	ERou WOld
– 'Alex Norman'	ERou LRHS WOld
– 'Algar's Pride'	ERou LGre NBro WOld
– 'Alice Haslam'	CBlo CM&M CMGP EBee ECtt

EFou EOld GBri GKir LRHS MBri
MFir MWgw NOrc NPri SSpe STes
WByw WLRN WOld WOve WPer
WRHF

- 'Alpenglow' — WOld
- 'Anita Ballard' — WOld
- 'Anita Webb' — ERou GBri NBir NOak WOld
- 'Anneke' — EPfP SHel
- Antwerp Pearl — See A. *novi-belgii* 'Antwerpse Parel'
- 'Apollo' — CB&S LCaP LRHS NBus NPri
- 'Apple Blossom' — SHel WOld
- 'Arctic' — ERou WOld
- 'Audrey' — CMGP EBee ECtt EFou ERou GCHN GKir GMaP LRHS MBNS MBri MLLN MWgw NBro NOrc SChu SEas SMer STes SUsu WBar WByw WCot WOld
- 'Autumn Beauty' — WOld
- 'Autumn Days' — WOld
- 'Autumn Glory' — CSam ERou WOld
- 'Autumn Rose' — CHea WOld
- 'Baby Climax' — WOld
- 'Beauty of Colwall' — WOld
- 'Beechwood Challenger' — ERou MOne WOld
- 'Beechwood Charm' — WOld
- 'Beechwood Rival' — Last listed 1999
- 'Beechwood Supreme' — ERou WOld
- 'Bewunderung' — NBro WOld
- 'Blandie' — CBlo CHea CTri EBee EFou ERou MSte MWat NBro SHel WLRN WOld
- 'Blauglut' — EFou NBro WOld
- 'Blue Baby' — WPer WWye
- 'Blue Bouquet' — ERou SRms WByw WOld
- 'Blue Boy' — CHea WOld
- 'Blue Danube' — WOld
- 'Blue Eyes' — CElw ERou EWTr LGre NOak SAga WOld WWye
- 'Blue Gown' — EGar ERou GCal WOld
¶ - 'Blue Lagoon' — CAbx CBlo CWes LRHS MBri WOld
- 'Blue Patrol' — ERou NOak WOld
- 'Blue Radiance' — WOld
- 'Blue Whirl' — ERou NBro WOld
- 'Bonanza' — WOld
- 'Boningale Blue' — MTed WOld
- 'Boningale White' — ERou MAvo WOld
- 'Bridesmaid' — SHel WOld
- 'Brightest and Best' — NBrk WOld
- 'Caborn Pink' — LLWP
- 'Cameo' — WOld
- 'Cantab' — WOld
- 'Cantonese Queen' (v) — EMon
- 'Carlingcott' — ERou MOne NOak WOld
- 'Carnival' — CBlo CM&M EBee EFou ERou MBri NHaw NOrc SHel SPer SSpe WOld
- 'Cecily' — NBro WLin WOld
- 'Charles Wilson' — WOld
- 'Chatterbox' — CFwr ECtt LRHS MBri MRav MWat SChu SRms WOld
- 'Chelwood' — WOld
- 'Chequers' — CBlo CBrm CM&M EBee ECot EMan ERou WLRN WOld
- 'Christina' — See A. *novi-belgii* 'Kristina'
- 'Christine Soanes' — EFou WOld
- 'Cliff Lewis' — ERou NBro WOld
- 'Climax Albus' — See A. 'White Climax'
- 'Cloudy Blue' — CElw WOld
- 'Colonel F.R. Durham' — ERou MBro
- 'Coombe Delight' — ERou

- 'Coombe Gladys' — ERou MBri WOld
- 'Coombe Joy' — ERou NOak WLRN WOld
- 'Coombe Margaret' — MLLN WOld
- 'Coombe Pink' — ERou
- 'Coombe Queen' — WOld
- 'Coombe Radiance' — ERou WOld
- 'Coombe Ronald' — ERou MWat WOld
- 'Coombe Rosemary' — ECtt ERou LRHS MBri NLar NOak WOld WRHF
- 'Coombe Violet' — LGre MWat WOld
- 'Countess of Dudley' — WOld WPer
- 'Court Herald' — EFou WOld
- 'Crimson Brocade' — CTri ELan ENot EPfP ERou LRHS MBri MRav MWat SHel SPer WOld
- 'Dandy' — CBlo EBee ECot ELan EMar LRHS MBro NGdn SChu SEas WByw WOld
- 'Daniela' — CHea WOld
- 'Daphne Anne' — WOld
- 'Dauerblau' — WOld
- 'Davey's True Blue' — CTri EBee EFou EMan ERou MBri WLRN WOld
- 'David Murray' — WOld
- 'Dazzler' — WOld
- 'Destiny' — WOld
- 'Diana' — CNic EMan ERou NBro WOld WViv
- 'Diana Watts' — ERou WOld
- 'Dietgard' — WOld
- 'Dolly' — NBir WOld
- 'Dusky Maid' — MBri SHel WOld
- 'Elizabeth' — CElw WOld
- 'Elizabeth Bright' — WOld
- 'Elizabeth Hutton' — WOld
- 'Elsie Dale' — WOld
- 'Elta' — WOld
- 'Erica' — CElw MWat WOld
- 'Ernest Ballard' — ERou WOld
- 'Eva' — WOld
- 'Eventide' — CB&S CElw CTri ENot ERou MBro NOak SPer WLRN WMoo WOld WRHF
- 'F.M. Simpson' — ERou WElm
- 'Fair Lady' — ERou MWat WOld
- 'Faith' — WOld
- 'Farrington' — WOld
- 'Fellowship' — CB&S CElw CFir CMGP CPar EBee EFou ENot ERou GCHN LRHS MWat SAga SEas SMer SPer SRms WByw WCot WEas WHil WOld
- 'Fontaine' — WOld
- 'Freda Ballard' — EBee EPPr ERou GCHN LRHS MWat WLRN WOld
- 'Freya' — WOld
- 'Fuldatal' — EFou SHel WOld
- 'Gayborder Blue' — WOld
- 'Gayborder Royal' — CFir ERou MOne SHel WOld
- 'Gayborder Splendour' — Last listed 1998
- 'Glory of Colwall' — WOld
- 'Goliath' — WOld
- 'Grey Lady' — WOld
- 'Guardsman' — ERou GKir LRHS MBri WOld
- 'Gulliver' — WOld
- 'Gurney Slade' — ERou GKir LRHS MBri WOld
- 'Guy Ballard' — ERou
- 'Harrison's Blue' — ERou LGre SAga WOld WPer
- 'Heinz Richard' — CBlo CM&M COIW EBee ECha EFou LRHS MBri NBir NGdn SChu WLRN WOld
- 'Helen' — WOld
- 'Helen Ballard' — CHea CPlt CStr ERou NBrk WOld

- 'Herbstgruss vom Bresserhof' — EWTr LRHS MBro
- 'Herbstpurzel' — Last listed 1999
- 'Hilda Ballard' — ERou WOld
- 'Ilse Brensell' — WOld
- 'Irene' — WOld
- 'Isabel Allen' — WOld
- 'Janet McMullen' — Last listed 1998
- 'Janet Watts' — ERou NBro WOld
- 'Jean' — MWat SHel WOld
- 'Jean Gyte' — WOld
- 'Jenny' — More than 30 suppliers
- 'Jollity' — WOld
- 'Judith' — Last listed 1999
- 'Julia' — WOld
- 'Karminkuppel' — WOld
- 'Kassel' — MBro
- 'King of the Belgians' — WOld
- 'King's College' — CElw GKir LRHS MBri WOld
§ - 'Kristina' — CFri COlW EBrP EBre ECha ECtt EFou ERou GKir LBCl LBSe LBre LLWP LRHS MBBe MBro MCLN MOne NBrk SBre SSpe WCot WLin WOld WRHF
- 'Lady Evelyn Drummond' — WOld
- 'Lady Frances' — WOld
- 'Lady in Blue' — COlW EBee ECtt ELan ENot EOld EPla GCHN GKir LRHS MBNS MWat NMir NVic SEas SPer SRms SSpe STes SUsu SWat WByw WFar WHil WMoo WOld WPer WWin
- 'Lady Paget' — WOld
- 'Lassie' — CHea ERou LFis MLLN MWat WOld
- 'Lavanda' — WLRN
- 'Lavender Dream' — WOld
- 'Lawrence Chiswell' — LGre SHel WOld
- 'Lilac Time' — WByw WLin WOld
- 'Lisa Dawn' — WOld
- 'Little Boy Blue' — CB&S ERou NBus WOld
- 'Little Man in Blue' — WOld
- 'Little Pink Beauty' — COlW EBee ECtt EFou ELan ERou GCHN GChr GKir LRHS MBNS MBri MRav NFai NMir NVic SEas SHel SPer SRPl SSpe STes SUsu SWat WMoo WOld WWin
- 'Little Pink Lady' — ERou SAga WLin WOld
- 'Little Pink Pyramid' — LLWP SRms
- 'Little Red Boy' — CB&S CBlo ERou MBel WOld
- 'Little Treasure' — WOld
- 'Lucy' — WOld
- 'Mabel Reeves' — Last listed 1997
- 'Madge Cato' — NOak WOld
- 'Malvern Castle' — ERou
- 'Mammoth' — WOld
- 'Margaret Rose' — NCiC NOrc WLRN WOld
- 'Margery Bennett' — ERou GBri NOak WOld
- 'Marie Ann Neil' — Last listed 1997
- 'Marie Ballard' — CB&S CElw CHea CSam CTri ENot ERou GKir GMaP MAvo MBri MFir MWat NBro NOrc SEas SHel SMer SPer SRms STes SWat WEas WOld WPer
- 'Marie's Pretty Please' — WOld
- 'Marjorie' — SEas WOld
- 'Marjory Ballard' — WOld
- 'Martonie' — WOld WPer
- 'Mary Ann Neil' — WOld
- 'Mary Deane' — CHea WOld WPer
- 'Mauve Magic' — MBri
- 'Melbourne Belle' — NOak WOld
- 'Melbourne Magnet' — CHea ERou WOld

- 'Michael Watts' — ERou WOld
- 'Mistress Quickly' — CAbx CPou CTri ERou MBel MBri NOak SHel WOld
- 'Mittelmeer' — EFou
- 'Mount Everest' — ERou WOld WPer
- 'Mrs Leo Hunter' — NOak WOld
- 'Newton's Pink' — Last listed 1999
- 'Niobe' — ELan
- 'Nobilis' — WOld
- 'Norman's Jubilee' — ERou MTed NBir WOld
- 'Norton Fayre' — Last listed 1997
- 'Nursteed Charm' — WOld
- 'Oktoberschneekuppel' — EMan ERou LRHS MBri NBro
- 'Orlando' — ERou WCot WOld
- 'Pacific Amarant' — SRos
- 'Pamela' — ERou WOld
- 'Patricia Ballard' — CBlo CElw CTri ERou GKir LFis MWat NBro SMer SPer SSpe WByw WLRN WLin WOld WPer
- 'Peace' — WOld
- 'Percy Thrower' — CMGP ERou WByw WLRN WOld
- 'Peter Chiswell' — MBri WOld
- 'Peter Harrison' — CFwr GMaP GMac NBir NBrk NBro WOld WPer
- 'Peter Pan' — EBee LCaP NBus WOld
- 'Picture' — WOld
- 'Pink Gown' — WOld
- 'Pink Lace' — ERou MBNS MBro MLLN WByw WOld WPer
- 'Pink Pyramid' — WOld
- 'Plenty' — ERou LRHS MBri WOld
- 'Porzellan' — CBre CElw CM&M CMGP EMan EMar
- 'Pride of Colwall' — ERou MWat
- 'Priory Blush' — CHea ERou NBrk NOak WLRN WOld
- 'Professor Anton Kippenberg' — CBlo EBee EFou EMan EPPr ERou GCHN GKir GMaP GMac LRHS MBri MHer NBro NFai NPri SHel SPer WOld
- 'Prosperity' — ERou GKir NOak WOld
* - 'Prunella' — ERou WOld
- 'Purple Dome' — ECha LFis WHoo WOld
- 'Queen Mary' — ERou WOld
- 'Queen of Colwall' — WOld
- 'Ralph Picton' — WOld
- 'Raspberry Ripple' — CBlo CPar EBee ECot EMan EMar ERou EWes NCiC SEas WLRN WOld WRha
I - 'Rector' — See A. novi-belgii 'The Rector'
- 'Red Robin' — MWat
- 'Red Sunset' — CB&S ERou MBro SRms WOld
* - 'Reitlinstal' — Last listed 1997
- 'Rembrandt' — GKir
- 'Remembrance' — GKir LRHS MBri WOld
- 'Reverend Vincent Dale' — WOld
- 'Richness' — ERou LGre NOak SAga SHel WOld
- 'Robin Adair' — WOld
- 'Roland Smith' — WOld
- 'Rose Bonnet' — CMGP EFou EMan ENot LRHS MWat SPlb WLRN
- 'Rose Bouquet' — WOld
- 'Rosebud' — CBlo SEas WEas WOld
- 'Rosemarie Sallmann' — Last listed 1998
- 'Rosenwichtel' — EBee EFou EMar GAri MCLN NLar SAga WLRN WOld
- 'Royal Blue' — Last listed 1999
- 'Royal Ruby' — ECtt WOld
- 'Royal Velvet' — ENot ERou WOld
- 'Rozika' — EFou WOld
- 'Rufus' — ERou NOak WOld
- 'Sailor Boy' — EFou ERou LFis WLRN WOld

– 'Saint Egwyn'	WOld	
– 'Sam Banham'	ERou NBro	
– 'Sandford White Swan'	ERou GKir LLWP LRHS MBel MBri WPer	
– 'Sandford's Purple'	Last listed 1997	
– 'Sarah Ballard'	ERou MWat WOld	
§ – 'Schneekissen'	EBee ECtt EGoo EMan EMar EPla GMaP MHer NPri NTow SAga SEND SMer SPer STes WLRN WMoo WOld	
– 'Schöne von Dietlikon'	CWes EFou NOak WLRN WOld	
– 'Schoolgirl'	ERou GKir LRHS MBri WOld	
– 'Sheena'	ERou LRHS MBri WOld	
§ – 'Silberteppich'	GMac	
– Silver Carpet	See A. novi-belgii 'Silberteppich'	
– Snow Cushion	See A. novi-belgii 'Schneekissen'	
– 'Snowdrift'	EBee WOld	
– 'Snowsprite'	CB&S EBee EMan EPfP MWat NBro NOrc SWat WOld	
– 'Sonata'	EBee ERou GMaP NOak SPer WOld	
– 'Sophia'	ERou NOak WOld	
– 'Starlight'	ENot ERou LRHS MBNS WOld WRHF	
– 'Steinebrück'	WOld	
– 'Sterling Silver'	CElw ERou NOak WByw WOld	
– 'Storm Clouds'	EFou LFis	
¶ – 'Strahlenmeer'	EFou	
– 'Sunset'	CAbx WOld	
¶ – 'Susan'	WOld	
– 'Sweet Briar'	CElw WOld	
– 'Tapestry'	WOld	
– 'Terry's Pride'	WOld	
– 'The Archbishop'	WOld	
– 'The Bishop'	ERou WOld	
– 'The Cardinal'	ERou WOld	
– 'The Choristers'	WOld	
– 'The Dean'	ERou NHaw WOld	
§ – 'The Rector'	WOld	
– 'The Sexton'	ERou WOld	
– 'Thundercloud'	LGre WOld	
– 'Timsbury'	WOld	
– 'Tony'	WOld	
– 'Tosca'	LFis	
– 'Tovarich'	GMac NBrk WOld	
– 'Triumph'	Last listed 1997	
– 'Trudi Ann'	NBir WOld	
– 'Twinkle'	NBro WOld	
– 'Victor'	EMan WOld	
¶ – 'Vignem'	NSti	
– 'Violet Lady'	ERou MBro WOld	
– 'Violetta'	Last listed 1999	
– 'Waterperry'	MWat	
– 'Weisse Wunder'	EFou WOld	
– 'White Ladies'	CBlo EBee ECtt EFou ERou GAri GMaP LLWP LRHS MWat NOrc SHel SMer SPer WLRN	
– 'White Swan'	CPou EMon EPPr LGre NOak WEas WOld WPrP	
– 'White Wings'	WOld	
– 'Winston S. Churchill'	COlW CTri EBee ELan ENot ERou GMaP LRHS MWat NOrc NSti SEas SHel SPer SPlb SSpe WMoo WOld WPnP	
oblongifolius	WOld	
– 'Fanny's Aster'	WOld	
'Ochtendgloren' (pringlei hybrid) ♀	EBee EBrP EBre EFou EGle EMon EPPr GBuc GKir LBCl LBSe LBre LGre LRHS MBBe MBri MSte NSti SAga SBre WCot WFar WHil WMaN WOld WWye	
Octoberlight	See A. 'Oktoberlicht'	

§ 'Oktoberlicht'	EBee EMon WOld	
pappei	See Felicia amoena	
'Pearl Star'	GMac WOld	
petiolatus	See Felicia petiolata	
§ 'Photograph' ♀	MBri MWat NBrk WFar WOld	
§ pilosus var. demotus ♀	EBee ECha EGar EMon EPPr EWes GGar MLLN MRav MSte SCro SDys SHel SMad SMrm SPla WFar WRus	
'Pink Cassino'		
'Pink Star'	EFou EMan GKir GMac LGre LRHS MBri MRav MWgw NPri NSti NWoo SDys WCot WFar WOld	
'Plowden's Pink'	WOld	
'Poollicht'	EFou	
§ pringlei 'Monte Cassino' ♀	More than 30 suppliers	
I – 'Phoebe'	WCot	
– 'Pink Cushion'	Last listed 1998	
§ ptarmicoides	CBlo CFee CM&M EBee EFou EMon MBrN MLLN WCot WOld WPer	
purdomii	See A. flaccidus	
pyrenaeus 'Lutetia'	CHea EBee ECha EFou EGar EMan EOrc EPPr GCal GMac LRHS MBri MMil MSte NLar SHel WCot WFar WOld WOve	
radula	EBee EGar EMan EMon EPPr GCal LRHS NBrk NSti WCot WOld	
'Ringdove' (ericoides hybrid) ♀	CBlo CBre EBee EFou ERou GMac LRHS MMil MNrw MTis MWat MWgw NSti NVic WCot WEas WLRN WOld	
'Rosa Star'	SHel WOld	
rotundifolius 'Variegatus'	See Felicia amelloides variegated	
¶ × salignus	WOld	
* sativus atrocaeruleus	Last listed 1998	
scaber	EBee WPGP	
scandens	See A. carolinianus	
schreberi	CHea WCot	
§ sedifolius	CHea EBee ELan EMan EPPr LFis MSte MWat NBid SDix WEas WFar WOld WPer	
– 'Nanus'	ECha EFou EOrc ERou LFis LRHS MBri MBro MLLN NBir NFai NLar NSti SMrm SPer WByw WCot WFar WOld	
– 'Snow Flurries'	See A. ericoides f. prostratus 'Snow Flurry'	
§ sibiricus	WOld	
'Snow Star'	SHel WOld	
¶ souliei	EBee	
sp. CC&McK 145	Last listed 1997	
spathulifolius	Last listed 1997	
spectabilis	WOld	
stracheyi	EBee NTow	
subspicatus	WPer	
¶ 'Sunhelene'	WViv	
¶ 'Sunplum'	WViv	
¶ 'Sunqueen'	WViv	
¶ 'Sunsky'	WViv	
tataricus	WOld	
– 'Jindai'	WCot	
thomsonii 'Nanus'	CGle CSam EBee EBrP EBre EFou EGle GCHN LBCl LBSe LBre LFis LGre MBBe MBro NNrd SAga SBre SPer SUsu WCot WEas WFar WHil WHoo WOld WSHC	
tibeticus	See A. flaccidus	
§ tongolensis	EBee EPfP GKir MLLN SAga SEas SRms WCot WFar WWin	
– 'Berggarten'	CHar EBrP EBre GKir GMac LBCl LBSe LBre LFis LRHS MBBe MBri	

	MMil NHaw SBre SCro SUsu WAbe WFar
- 'Dunkleviolette'	GBuc NBro SRms
- 'Lavender Star'	CBlo EFou GBuc SRms
- 'Leuchtenburg'	ERou
- 'Napsbury'	CBlo ERou GKir LRHS MCli
- 'Sternschnuppe'	Last listed 1998
- Summer Greeting	See *A. tongolensis* 'Sommergrüss'
- 'Wartburgstern'	CMdw CMil EBee EGar EMan EPfP GKir LFis LRHS MBri MCli NPri SPla WFar WGwG WLRN WPer
tradescantii L.	CGle CLTr EBee EFou ELan EMan MBNS MFir MWgw NOak NSti SCou SHel SMad WEas WOld
- hort.	See *A. pilosus* var. *demotus*
trinervius subsp.	SSvw
ageratoides 'Asran'	
tripolium	WHer
turbinellus hort. ♀	CAbx CPlt EBee ECGN EFou EMan EMon GBuc GMac LGre LRHS MBNS MBro NBrk NTow SChu SDix SMrm WCot WFar WHer WHoo WOld
umbellatus	CBre CLTr EMon EPPr NSti SRms WCot WOld WPrP
vahlii	GAbr
vimineus Lamarck	See *A. lateriflorus*
- 'Ptarmicoides'	See *A. ptarmicoides*
§ 'White Climax'	EFou MTed WCot WOld
'Yvonne'	CBre EBee

ASTERANTHERA (Gesneriaceae)
| *ovata* | CDoC CFil CGre CPIN GGGa GGar GOrc WAbe WBod WCru WGwG WSHC WWal WWat |

ASTERISCUS (Asteraceae)
'Gold Coin'	See *A. maritimus*
* 'Golden Dollar'	LRHS NPri
§ *maritimus*	LIck WCot

ASTEROMOEA (Asteraceae)
| *mongolica* | See *Kalimeris mongolica* |
| *pinnatifida* | See *Kalimeris pinnatifida* |

ASTEROPYRUM (Ranunculaceae)
| *cavaleriei* | WCru |

ASTILBE ✿ (Saxifragaceae)
'America'	MDun
'Aphrodite'	CCuc CMCo CPlt ENot LAst LFis
(*simplicifolia* hybrid)	MBri NFla NHol NMir NPro SChu SPla SSpi WGor
x *arendsii*	CPea MBro MHer NFor WPer
- 'Amethyst'	CBlo CCuc CHor CMGP CMHG CTri EBee LRHS MCli NFai NPSI SEas SMer SPer WFar WMoo
- 'Anita Pfeifer'	CMHG GKir LRHS MBri WFar WPnP
- 'Bergkristall'	CMHG EMil
§ - 'Brautschleier' ♀	CMHG CTri ECtt EFou ENot EPfP GCHN LRHS MWat NFai NPSI SMer WPnP
- 'Bressingham Beauty'	CDoC CMHG EBee EBrP EBre ECtt EHon ELan EMan ENot EPar EWTr GCHN GKir GMaP LBCl LBSe LBre LSyl MBBe MBri MCLN MRav NFla NHol NSti SBre SEas SPer SSpe
- Bridal Veil	See *A.* x *arendsii* 'Brautschleier'
- 'Bumalda'	CFir CMCo COtt GCHN LRHS

	MBri NDlv SSpi WFar WWat
- 'Cattleya'	CCuc CMHG EBee EFou LCaP WFar
* - 'Cattleya Dunkel'	CMHG
- 'Ceres'	CCuc CMHG MWat NHol
§ - 'Diamant'	CHor CMHG EBee LAst LFis LRHS MBri NGdn SEas WFar
- Diamond	See *A.* x *arendsii* 'Diamant'
- 'Drayton Glory'	See *A. rosea* 'Peach Blossom'
- 'Eliblo' PBR	See *A.* x *arendsii* Elizabeth Bloom = 'Eliblo'
§ - Elizabeth Bloom = 'Eliblo' PBR	EMan EPGN GCHN GSki LRHS MCLN SVil WFar WHil
- 'Ellie'	See *A.* x *arendsii* 'Ellie van Veen'
§ - 'Ellie van Veen'	CCuc EMan EPGN LRHS MBri MCLN NPSI NPro SVil
- 'Erica'	CBlo CHor CMHG CTri EWll GKir LRHS MBri MDun MRav
- 'Fanal' ♀	More than 30 suppliers
§ - 'Federsee'	CB&S CMGP CMHG ECha ELan ENot LRHS SPer WFar WLRN
§ - 'Feuer'	CCuc CMGP CMHG CSam EBee ECha ELan EPfP GCHN NHol NVic SPer
- Fire	See *A.* x *arendsii* 'Feuer'
- 'Gertrud Brix'	CB&S CCuc EPar NGdn WRus
- 'Gladstone'	See *A.* 'W.E. Gladstone' (japonica hybrid)
- 'Gloria'	CMHG CTri LPBA LRHS MBri WFar
§ - 'Gloria Purpurea'	CBlo CCuc CHor CMHG GKir LRHS MBri MDun MTed NHol WRHF
- Glow	See *A.* x *arendsii* 'Glut'
§ - 'Glut'	CMHG GKir LRHS MBri NHol SRms WFar
- 'Granat'	CCuc CDoC CHor CMHG EBee MCli WLRN WWin
- 'Grete Püngel'	GKir LRHS MBri MLLN
- 'Harmony'	CMHG
- Hyacinth	See *A.* x *arendsii* 'Hyazinth'
§ - 'Hyazinth'	CDoC CFai CMHG EBee ELan GAbr LRHS MCli NFai NHol WWal
- 'Irrlicht'	CB&S CGle CMHG EHon ELan EPfP EPla EWTr GGar GKir LHop LPBA LRHS MBri NDea SEas SPer SWat WWpP
- 'Kvele'	CMHG MBri WFar WViv
§ - 'Lachskönigin'	CMHG MWat
¶ - 'Moerheim's Glory'	MChl
- 'Mont Blanc'	Last listed 1998
- 'Obergärtner Jürgens'	EBee EMan EPGN NCut SAga
- 'Paul Gaärder'	CMHG
- 'Pink Curtsy'	Last listed 1998
- Pink Pearl	See *A.* x *arendsii* 'Rosa Perle'
- 'Queen of Holland'	See *A.* 'Queen of Holland' (japonica hybrid)
- Red Light	See *A.* x *arendsii* 'Rotlicht'
§ - 'Rosa Perle'	CMHG ECha NHol
§ - 'Rotlicht'	CCuc CMHG CPlt ECot LRHS MBNS MBri NPro NSti WFar WGor
- Salmon Queen	See *A.* x *arendsii* 'Lachskönigin'
- 'Sarma'	MBri
- 'Snowdrift'	CCuc CMHG EBee EBrP EBre ECha EFou EPGN EPla EWTr GAri GCHN GKir LBCl LBSe LBre LRHS LRot MBBe MBNS MCli NFor NOak NOrc NPro SBre SMer SWat WHil
- 'Solferino'	CMHG
- 'Spartan'	See *A.* x *arendsii* 'Rotlicht'
- 'Spinell'	CBlo MWat WPnP

- 'Venus'	CCuc CSam EBee ECha ECtt EFou EGra GKir MCLN NHaw NHol NOrc NVic SPer SSpe SWat WFar WMoo WViv
- 'Walküre'	CMHG
- 'Washington'	See *A.* 'Washington' (*japonica* hybrid)
§ - 'Weisse Gloria'	CCuc CMHG EBee ECha EPar EWTr LPBA NMGW NSti SLod SPla
- 'Weisse Perle'	Last listed 1998
- White Gloria	See *A.* x *arendsii* 'Weisse Gloria'
- 'White Queen'	GChr NHol NWoo
- 'William Reeves'	CMHG MFir NHol
- 'Zuster Theresa'	LRHS MBri
astilboides	NHol WCot
'Atrorosea'	MBri SRms
(*simplicifolia* hybrid)	
'Avalanche'	EPGN
'Betsy Cuperus'	CMHG MCli NCut
(*thunbergii* hybrid)	
'Bonn' (*japonica* hybrid)	CB&S EPar LPBA SCoo SRms WRus
'Bremen' (*japonica* hybrid)	CMHG LPBA
§ 'Bronce Elegans'	CB&S CMGP COtt ECha EFou
(*simplicifolia* hybrid) ♀	EPar GKir GSki LAst LRHS MBNS MGrG MMal NFla NHar NHol NOrc SChu SPer WBea WFar WHoo WWat
* *bumalda* 'Bronze Pygmy'	EMan
* 'Carmine King'	Last listed 1997
'Carnea'	Last listed 1997
(*simplicifolia* hybrid)	
'Catherine Deneuve'	See *A.* x *arendsii* 'Federsee'
'Cherry Ripe'	See *A.* x *arendsii* 'Feuer'
chinensis	CMHG GKir IBlr LRHS MHer MMal MPEx
- var. *davidii*	CMHG
- 'Finale'	NHol SPer SRms WEas WFar WWat
- 'Frankentroll'	CMHG
- 'Intermezzo'	EBee GMaP
§ - var. *pumila* ♀	More than 30 suppliers
- - 'Serenade'	CCuc LBuc LRHS MBri WFar
- 'Purperkerze'	EBee MBri
- 'Purple Glory'	CMHG
- 'Spätsommer'	CMHG
- var. *taquetii*	NSti
- - Purple Lance	See *A. chinensis* var. *taquetii* 'Purpurlanze'
§ - - 'Purpurlanze'	CMCo CMHG ECha EFou EGra EMan LPBA GKir LRHS MBri MCAu MRav NBir NCat NCiC NPro WFar WWin
§ - - 'Superba' ♀	CCuc CGle CMHG CRow ECha ENot GCHN MLLN MNrw MSte NDea NFai NFor NHol SDix SPer SRms WEas
- 'Veronica Klose'	GKir LRHS MBri NLar NPro
- 'Visions'	CCuc EBee EMan LRHS MBri NPSl NPro WFar
Cologne	See *A.* 'Köln' (japonica hybrid)
'Crimson Feather'	See *A.* x *arendsii* 'Gloria Purpurea'
x *crispa*	IBlr
- 'Gnom'	CMCo NHar
- 'Lilliput'	CMGP EBee GKir LRHS NHar NLar NPro SRPl
§ - 'Perkeo' ♀	More than 30 suppliers
- 'Peter Pan'	See *A.* x *crispa* 'Perkeo'
- 'Snow Queen'	LRHS NHar NMen NPro WFar
'Darwin's Dream'	LRHS MBri
'Darwin's Surprise'	Last listed 1997

'Deutschland'	CB&S CMHG EBee EMan EPGN
(*japonica* hybrid)	GCHN GKir LSyl MBNS MBri MCLN MGrG MRav NBir NFor NHol NVic SEas SPer SPla SRms SSpi STes SWat WEas WHoo WMoo WWal WWin
'Dunkellachs'	CBlo CCuc CM&M EBee GCHN
(*simplicifolia* hybrid)	MBel MBri MDun SPla WViv
'Düsseldorf'	CCuc CMGP CMHG EPar GGar
(*japonica* hybrid)	LRHS MBri SPer SSea WRus
'Dutch Treat'	CMea
(*japonica* hybrid) (v)	
'Emden' (*japonica* hybrid)	Last listed 1999
'Etna' (*japonica* hybrid)	CB&S CMHG EBee EGle EGra GBri SRms WPnP WRus
'Europa' (*japonica* hybrid)	CBlo EBee EMil EPGN GGar LPBA NFai NOak SPla SSpe WHil
§ *glaberrima*	EPar GCal NMen
- var. *saxatilis* ♀	CLyd CRow ELan GAri GCHN GDea IMGH MBro NOak NSla NWoo SAga SSmi WAbe WHal WOve WPrP
- *saxosa*	See *A.* 'Saxosa'
* - - *minor*	Last listed 1998
'Glenroy Elf'	Last listed 1999
grandis	CMHG SSca
'Hennie Graafland'	CB&S CMCo COtt EFou GKir
(*simplicifolia* hybrid)	MBNS
'Inshriach Pink'	CMHG EBee EFou EHoe ELan
(*simplicifolia* hybrid)	GCHN GChr GCrs GDra GKir LRHS MBri NBir NCiC NHar NHol NMen NNrd NOak SMad WCot WFar WHal
* *japonica* 'Pumila'	NHol
- var. *terrestris*	See *A. glaberrima*
'Jo Ophorst'	CCuc CMHG ECha EMan GCHN
(*davidii* hybrid)	LPBA MRav NGdn SPer WLRN WWal
'Koblenz' (*japonica* hybrid)	CCuc MBri
§ 'Köln' (*japonica* hybrid)	EMil LPBA NFai WFar
koreana	WCot
'Koster'	LPBA
'Kriemhilde'	Last listed 1998
'Lady Digby'	LPBA
* *lilacina*	MBro
'Maggie Daley'	COtt EBee EPGN
'Mainz' (*japonica* hybrid)	EMil GCHN
microphylla	CMHG NHol
- pink	CMHG NHol
'Moerheimii'	CMHG
(*thunbergii* hybrid)	
'Montgomery'	CCuc CHor ECha LRHS MBri NFai
(*pitardii* x *japonica*)	NGdn NHol
Ostrich Plume	See *A.* 'Straussenfeder' (*thunbergii* hybrid)
'Peaches and Cream'	LRHS MBri MRav
'Peter Barrow'	SIng SRms
(*glaberrima* hybrid)	
'Professor van der Wielen' (*thunbergii* hybrid)	CCuc CGle CMHG EFou EGle EMan GCHN GCal GGar LAst MCAu MCli MSte SDix SMer SPer SRms SSpi WWat
pumila	See *A. chinensis* var. *pumila*
* 'Queen'	LPBA
§ 'Queen of Holland'	MCli
(*japonica* hybrid)	
* 'Red Admiral'	NFor
'Red Sentinel'	CB&S CCuc EPGN EPar GCHN
(*japonica* hybrid)	MCli NHar NHol NOrc SPla SVil
'Rheinland'	CCuc CMHG EPGN EPfP GCHN
(*japonica* hybrid) ♀	LPBA MBro NArg NPri SMad SSea STes WEas WFar WHoo WRus

rivularis	CFil CMHG WCot
§ x *rosea* 'Peach Blossom'	CB&S CM&M EMan EPGN EPar EWTr GCHN MBel MBro MGrG NArg NBir NFai NHol NSti SEas SHel SRPl WFar
- 'Queen Alexandra'	SPla WFar
'Rosea'	NHol WFar
(*simplicifolia* hybrid)	
Rosemary Bloom = 'Rosblo'	EBee
§ 'Saxosa'	EPot ESis GAri GGar NMGW SPla
* - x *glaberrima*	Last listed 1997
* 'Showstar'	LRHS NCut
simplicifolia ♀	CGle CRow GKir NHar NMen WFar
- 'Alba'	GGar NHol
- Bronze Elegance	See *A.* 'Bronce Elegans' (*simplicifolia* hybrid)
- 'Darwin's Snow Sprite'	EBee ECho GKir LRHS MBri NHol NPri WFar
- x *glaberrima*	GDra NHar
- 'Jacqueline'	EBee LBuc NCut NLar
* - 'Nana Alba'	NPro
- 'Praecox Alba'	CBlo MCli NFla NHol WLin
sp. CLD 1559	Last listed 1997
'Sprite' (*simplicifolia* hybrid) ♀	More than 30 suppliers
§ 'Straussenfeder' (*thunbergii* hybrid) ♀	CCuc CM&M CMGP CMHG CTri EBee EFou EMan EPfP EPla GCHN GCal GMaP LAst LRHS MCli NHol SSpi WLRN WPnP WViv
'Superba'	See *A. chinensis* var. *taquetii* 'Superba'
thunbergii	Last listed 1998
'Vesuvius' (*japonica* hybrid)	CB&S CBlo CCuc CHor GKir LSyl MBel MDun MGrG NFai NSti WLin
§ 'W.E. Gladstone' (*japonica* hybrid)	CBlo CMea GCHN MSte NBlu NCiC NHol WGor WWeb
§ 'Washington' (*japonica* hybrid)	EPGN MCli WHil
'Willie Buchanan' (*simplicifolia* hybrid)	More than 30 suppliers
Wisley form	CPla
'Yakushima'	GCHN
* *yakusimanum* pink	Last listed 1998

ASTILBOIDES (Saxifragaceae)

§ *tabularis*	More than 30 suppliers

ASTRAGALUS (Papilionaceae)

alopecuroides	Last listed 1999
alpinus	Last listed 1998
arnotianus	Last listed 1997
arnottii JCA 14169	Last listed 1999
¶ *canadensis*	GKir
centralpinus	Last listed 1998
cicer	Last listed 1999
danicus	Last listed 1998
detritalis	Last listed 1998
falcatus	Last listed 1999
glycyphyllos	CAgr CArn CNat EBee IIve MSal WWye
§ *massiliensis*	NTow
membranaceus	CArn ELau EOHP IIve MSal
¶ *norvegicus*	MAvo
odoratus	Last listed 1997
purshii	Last listed 1998
tragacantha hort.	See *A. massiliensis*
utahensis	Last listed 1999
§ *whitneyi* var. *confusus*	Last listed 1998
* - var. *lenophyllus* NNS 93-98	Last listed 1997

- var. *sonneanus*	See *A. whitneyi* var. *confusus*

ASTRANTHIUM (Asteraceae)

beamanii	Last listed 1997

ASTRANTIA ✿ (Apiaceae)

bavarica	CElw EBee EBlw EMan EMar GCal WCot
§ 'Buckland'	CElw CPlt EBee ECha EMon GBuc GCal LGre MTed MTho NDov NPro SSpe SSpi WCru WFar WHal WLin WMoo WPnP
carniolica	EMon EOld
- *major*	See *A. major*
- var. *rubra*	See *A. major rubra*
- 'Variegata'	See *A. major* 'Sunningdale Variegated'
helleborifolia hort.	See *A. maxima*
§ *major*	More than 30 suppliers
- *alba*	CMHG CRow EBee ECGN ECha EFou EGle LLWP MRav NBir NCat NGdn NPer WPnP
- subsp. *biebersteinii*	EBee EMon NBir
- 'Buckland'	See *A.* 'Buckland'
- 'Canneman'	CLon EBee EMon EWes MBct NSti WCot
- 'Claret'	CBos CLAP CRDP EBee EBrP EBre ECha EMon EOld EPPr GBuc GKir LBCl LBSe LBre LGre LRHS MBBe MBro SAga SBre WCot WFar WPnP WRus
- 'Elmblut'	EBlw EMon
- 'Hadspen Blood'	More than 30 suppliers
- 'Hillview Red'	CElw SHel
- subsp. *involucrata*	CLon EBee GCHN LRHS MBro NHol SCro SWat WFar
- - 'Barrister'	CFil CSam EBee GBuc SSpi WFar WPGP
- - 'Margery Fish'	See *A. major* subsp. *involucrata* 'Shaggy'
- - 'Moira Reid'	EBee GBri WRus
¶ - - 'Orlando'	EBlw
§ - - 'Shaggy' ♀	More than 30 suppliers
- 'Lars'	More than 30 suppliers
- 'Lars' seedlings	GCal MBel
- 'Maureen'	NOak
- 'Primadonna'	CFri CSam EBee EGle EHrv EMan MBNS MSte MTis NArg NCut NLar SCro SPlb WFar WHil WMoo WPer WWat
- 'Roma'[PBR]	EFou EMon LGre MBri SAga
- *rosea*	More than 30 suppliers
- 'Rosensinfonie'	EOld GLil GMaP MCli MWrn NCut WFar WMoo WPyg WViv
§ - *rubra*	More than 30 suppliers
- 'Ruby Cloud'	ECGN EHrv MBro WFoF
- 'Ruby Wedding'	CBlo CBos CGle CLon EBee EBrP EBre EHrv EMon EOld GBuc LBCl LBSe LBre LGre MBBe MRav MTho MWrn NFor SBla SBre SUsu SVil WCot WFar WPGP WPnP
¶ - 'Snowstar'	SVil
- 'Starburst'	EBee NCot
§ - 'Sunningdale Variegated' ♀	More than 30 suppliers
- 'Titoki Point'	EBlw WCot
- 'Variegata'	See *A. major* 'Sunningdale Variegated'
§ *maxima* ♀	More than 30 suppliers
- 'Mark Fenwick'	NBir
* - *rosea*	LBmB

minor	EPla WCru
'Rainbow'	NLar
rubra	See *A. major rubra*

ASYNEUMA (Campanulaceae)

canescens	EBee EBrP EBre EMan LBCl LBSe LBre LFis MBBe MLLN NCut NFai SBre WWin
limonifolium	SOkd
- subsp. *pestalozzae*	Last listed 1999
lobelioides	Last listed 1999
pulvinatum	CPBP LRHS SIng WAbe
- Mac&W 5880	EPot
trichostegium	EPot

ASYSTASIA (Acanthaceae)

bella	See *Mackaya bella*
§ *gangetica*	CSev LHil SYvo
violacea	See *A. gangetica*

ATHAMANTA (Apiaceae)

macedonica	EBee NChi
subsp. *arachnoidea*	
- - JCA 224105	Last listed 1999
turbith	Last listed 1999
- subsp. *haynaldii*	NTow SOkh
¶ *vestina*	LGre
- JCA 224300	SSpi

ATHANASIA (Asteraceae)

parviflora	CPLG

ATHEROSPERMA (Monimiaceae)

moschatum	CB&S CGre CPLG WSHC WWat

ATHROTAXIS (Taxodiaceae)

cupressoides	CKen MBar WCwm
laxifolia	CDoC CKen MBar WCwm
selaginoides	CDoC CTrG EPot WCwm

ATHYRIUM ✿ (Woodsiaceae)

filix-femina ♀	More than 30 suppliers
* - *congestum cristatum*	WFib
- 'Corymbiferum'	GQui LSyl NHar NMar SRms
- 'Crispum Grandiceps Kaye'	SRms
- Cristatum Group	CLAP EBlw EFer ELan EMon LRHS NHol SCob SWat WFib WRic
§ - Cruciatum Group	CBos CLAP CRDP CRow EBee EGol ELan EMar EMon EPfP GAri GGar MWgw NHar NHol NOGN SLon SRms WFib WRic
- 'Fieldii'	CCuc CLAP CRow EFer NHar NHol SChu SRms WFib
- 'Frizelliae' ♀	More than 30 suppliers
- 'Frizelliae Capitatum'	CCuc CLAP CRow NMar WFib WPGP
- 'Frizelliae Cristatum'	SRms
- 'Grandiceps'	NHar NMar SRms
- 'Minutissimum'	CBos CCuc CFil CLTr CPlt CRDP ECha EFou EGol EHon ELan EMon GCHN LPBA NMar SCob WFib WPGP
- 'Percristatum'	EMon
- Plumosum Group	CFil CLAP GQui NMar WFib
- 'Plumosum Axminster'	CFil CRDP
- 'Plumosum Cristatum'	NMar
- 'Plumosum Percristatum'	GQui NMar
- Ramocristatum Group	NMar
- 'Rotstiel'	CLAP MBri MSCN
- 'Setigerum Cristatum'	NMar WRic
* - *superbum* 'Druery'	WFib

- 'Vernoniae' ♀	CCuc CLAP EBee EFer ELan EMon LHil LRHS MBri WRic
- 'Vernoniae Cristatum'	CLAP GBin NHol NMar SPer WFib
- Victoriae Group & cl.	See *A. filix-femina* Cruciatum Group
flexile	Last listed 1999
goeringianum 'Pictum'	See *A. niponicum* var. *pictum*
niponicum	CCuc SLdr
¶ - 'Genuflect' (v)	EMon
- f. *metallicum*	See *A. niponicum* var. *pictum*
§ - var. *pictum* ♀	More than 30 suppliers
- - crested	Last listed 1998
* - - 'Cristatoflabellatum'	CLAP ELan EMon
otophorum ♀	CRDP EMon NHol NMar SChu SRms WPGP WRic
- var. *okanum*	CFil CLAP EBee EFer ELan EMar LHil LRHS MBri NBus NHar NHol SNut WAbe WCot WCru
proliferum	See *Diplazium proliferum*
vidalii	CFil CLAP MBri WRic

ATRACTYLODES (Asteraceae)

japonica	EFEx
macrocephala	EFEx

ATRAGENE See CLEMATIS

ATRIPLEX (Chenopodiaceae)

canescens	CAgr WDin
halimus	CAgr CB&S CBot CGle ECha EHoe ENot LRHS MRav NBir NBrk NLar SLon SPer SWat WCot WDin WHCG WHer WPGP
hortensis	MChe
- gold-leaved	EOHP MLan WCot WJek
- var. *rubra*	CArn CGle CHad CRDP CSpe EGra ELan EOHP MChe MGed MHer NChi SIde WCHb WCot WEas WGwG WHer WJek WKif WOak WWye
portulacoides	See *Halimione portulacoides*

ATROPA (Solanaceae)

bella-donna	CArn GBar GPoy Ilve MSal WWye
- var. *lutea*	MSal
mandragora	See *Mandragora officinarum*

ATROPANTHE (Solanaceae)

§ *sinensis*	MSal

AUBRIETA ✿ (Brassicaceae)

¶ 'Alba'	EDAr
albomarginata	See *A.* 'Argenteovariegata'
'Alix Brett'	CMea CPBP EBrP EBre EDAr ELan LBCl LBSe LBre LRHS MBBe NPer SAga SBre
¶ *anamasica*	SBla
'April Joy'	ECot EDAr ELan LRHS SRms
§ 'Argenteovariegata'	CSpe EDAr ELan LRHS MHer SAga SBla SRms WAbe WPyg WWeb
'Astolat' (v)	GCHN LRHS MOne NSla SAga SBla SRms WPat
§ 'Aureovariegata'	CMea EBrP EBre EDAr EGle ELan LBCl LBSe LBre LRHS MBBe MHer NFla NPer SAga SBla SBre SIng WAbe WFar
'Barker's Double' (d)	LRHS
'Belisha Beacon'	ECtt EMNN LRHS MBri
Bengal hybrids	GAbr WGor
Blaue Schönheit	See *A.* 'Blue Beauty'
¶ 'Bläumeise'	CWes
'Blue Cascade'	ECho ECtt EPfP GKir LPVe SPlb WGor

'Blue Emperor' — CWes
'Blue Gown' — EDAr
'Blue King' — Last listed 1999
¶ 'Blue Midnight' — EDAr
* 'Blue Mist' — ECho EDAr
¶ 'Blue Sky' — EDAr
§ 'Bob Saunders' (d) — CMea CTri EBrP EBre ECtt LBCl
LBSe LBre LRHS MBBe SBre
'Bonfire' — ECho
* 'Bonsul' — Last listed 1997
'Bordeaux' — Last listed 1999
'Bressingham Pink' (d) — CMea CTri EBrP EBre ECtt ELan
LBCl LBSe LBre LRHS MBBe SBre
'Bressingham Red' — EBrP EBre LBCl LBSe LBre LRHS
MBBe SBre
canescens — EPot NTow
- subsp. *macrostyla* — Last listed 1999
Cascade Series mixed — WFar
columnae macrostyla — Last listed 1998
* *deltoidea* 'Gloria' — WPat
- 'Nana Variegata' — CLyd CPBP EPot MTho WGor
- *rosea* — Last listed 1998
- 'Tauricola' — WPyg
- 'Tauricola Variegata' — Last listed 1997
- Variegata Group — ECtt EPot ESis GKir LHop
LRHS MTho NMen NSla SIng
WFar WPat
'Doctor Mules' ♀ — CTri EBrP EBre EDAr GKir LBCl
LBSe LBre LRHS MBBe SBre SIng
SRms WPat
'Doctor Mules Variegata' — CWes EDAr LGro LRHS MHer
NEgg
Double Stock-flowered — MTed
  Group pink
'Dream' — ECtt SIng
'Elsa Lancaster' — EMNN EPot GCrs NMen NSla
'Fire King' — Last listed 1999
§ 'Frühlingszauber' — SRms WGor
'Gloriosa' — EDAr NEgg SIng
'Godstone' — Last listed 1999
'Golden Carpet' — SIng
'Golden King' — See *A*. 'Aureovariegata'
gracilis — Last listed 1998
§ - subsp. *scardica* — NTow SSca
* 'Graeca' — NPri
'Graeca Superba' — Last listed 1998
'Greencourt Purple' — EDAr ELan EMNN GAbr LRHS
MOne MWat SIng WWin
'Gurgedyke' — ECho ELan SIng SRms
¶ 'Hamburger Stadtpark' — ECho EDAr
¶ 'Harknoll Red' — EPot
'Hartswood' — SIng
'Hartswood Purple' — Last listed 1997
¶ Hemswell Purity = — ECho
  'Snow Maiden'PBR
'Hendersonii' — SRms
'Ina den Ouden' — Last listed 1999
'J.S. Baker' — SRms
'Joan Allen' — EDAr LRHS
'Joy' (d) — EMNN SIng
'Lavender Gem' — Last listed 1998
'Leichtlinii' — ECho WPyg
'Lemon and Lime' — LRHS
'Lilac Cascade' — Last listed 1997
'Little Gem' — ECho
'Lodge Crave' — SIng
macedonica — EPot
'Magician' — ECtt
'Mars' — SRms
'Mary Poppins' — Last listed 1998
'Maurice Prichard' — EMNN LRHS
'Mrs Lloyd Edwards' — Last listed 1999

'Mrs Rodewald' — CMea EDAr EMNN LAco NEgg
SRms
'Novalis Blue' ♀ — SRms WLRN
'Oakington Lavender' — ECho EDAr ELan LRHS
parviflora — Last listed 1998
'Pennine Glory' — Last listed 1997
'Pennine Heather' — Last listed 1997
'Pike's Variegated' — ECho SRms
pinardii — Last listed 1999
'Prichard's A1' — WPyg
'Purity' — LRHS
'Purple Cascade' — ECtt EMNN EPfP GCHN LRHS
SCoo SPlb SRms WFar WGor
'Purple Charm' — SRms
'Purple Emperor' — SIng
'Red Carpet' — EBrP EBre EDAr ELan EMNN EPot
LBCl LBSe LBre LGro LRHS MBBe
SBre SIng SRms WWin
'Red Carpet Variegated' — CMea LRHS
'Red Cascade' — ECtt EMNN GCHN GKir SCoo
SPlb
'Red Dyke' — SIng
* 'Red King' — Last listed 1998
'Riverslea' — SIng
'Rosanna Miles' — SIng
'Rose Queen' — CMea LBee LRHS SMrm
'Rosea Splendens' — Last listed 1999
'Royal Blue' (Royal Series) — LRHS MHer NNrd
'Royal Red' (Royal Series) — ESis LRHS MHer SRms WFar WGor
'Royal Violet' (Royal Series) — ECho LRHS MHer WPer
'Sauerland' — MTed
scardica subsp. *scardica* — See *A*. *gracilis* subsp. *scardica*
'Schloss Eckberg' — Last listed 1999
'Schofield's Double' — See *A*. 'Bob Saunders'
'Silberrand' — ECha ECtt EDAr NSla
¶ 'Somerford Lime' — WWeb
Spring Charm = — See *A*. 'Frühlingszauber'
  'Frühlingszauber'
¶ 'Swan Red' (v) — EPot
thessala — Last listed 1998
'Toby Saunders' — ECho
'Triumphante' — CTri LRHS
'Wanda' — ECho ELan SIng
'Whitewell Gem' — NNrd SRms

AUCUBA ✿ (Aucubaceae)

japonica (m) — CB&S CBlo CDoC CHEx ELan
SReu
- (f) — CDul EMac GKir SMer
- 'Angelon' — Last listed 1999
- 'Crassifolia' (m) — CHig SAPC SArc
- 'Crotonifolia' (f/v) ♀ — More than 30 suppliers
- 'Dentata' — WCru
- 'Fructu-albo' (f/v) — SPer
- 'Gold Dust' (f/v) — CLan LRHS MAsh WWeb
- 'Gold Splash' (v) — CBlo
- 'Golden King' (m/v) — CB&S CBlo CCHP CDoC CTrw
EBee ENot EPfP GKir LNet LRHS
MAsh MGos MWat SLim SPla
- 'Golden Spangles' (v) — CB&S CBlo CDoC EBee ECot SSht
- 'Goldstrike' (v) — CBlo CDoC EBee EHoe LNet
LRHS
- 'Hillieri' (f) — CLan
- 'Lance Leaf' (m) — SLon WCru
- 'Latiomaculata' (v) — Last listed 1998
- f. *longifolia* ♀ — CHig CMac LRHS MAsh SAPC
SArc SDix WCru
- - 'Salicifolia' (f) — ENot EPla LRHS MBri SLon SMad
SPer WBcn WCru WDin WPGP
- 'Maculata' hort. — See *A. japonica* 'Variegata'
- 'Marmorata' — LRHS
- 'Nana Rotundifolia' (f) — EPla LRHS

- 'Picturata' (m/v)	CB&S CBlo CMac CPne EBee ENot EPfP EPla LRHS SAga SPer WCFE WFar
- 'Rozannie' (f/m)	CB&S CBlo CDoC ELan ENot EPla GKir LRHS MAsh MBlu MBri MGos MLan MRav MWat NBee NFla SLim SMac SMad SPer SPla SReu WDin WStI
- 'Speckles'	GSki
- 'Sulphurea Marginata' (f/v)	CB&S CDoC CHEx CMac EPla LRHS MBri SPer WBcn WBod WGwG
§ - 'Variegata' (f/v)	More than 30 suppliers
- Windsor form	EPla LRHS MAsh MBri
- 'Wykehurst' (v)	LRHS

AULAX (Proteaceae)
cancellata	Last listed 1999

AURINIA (Brassicaceae)
§ *corymbosa*	Last listed 1998
§ *saxatilis* ♀	EBrP EBre EWTr GKir LBCl LBSe LBre MBBe MBar MWat SBre SIng SPlb WFar
- 'Citrina' ♀	CHal ECha ECtt EGar GMaP IMGH MWat SRms WPyg
- 'Compacta'	CTri EBrP EBre ECtt ENot LBCl LBSe LBre MBBe MBro NFor SBre WHoo
- 'Dudley Nevill'	EMan LRHS MSCN MWat SBla WFar
- 'Dudley Nevill Variegated'	EBrP EBre ECha EGar EWes LBCl LBSe LBee LBre MBBe MHer NBir SBla SBre WFar
- 'Flore Pleno' (d)	WCot WEas
- Gold Ball	See *A. saxatilis* 'Goldkugel'
- 'Gold Dust'	ECtt LGro MOne MWat SRms
- 'Golden Queen'	ECtt MHer
§ - 'Goldkugel'	EMNN GKir LRHS NVic SRms WLRN
- 'Silver Queen'	WEas
- 'Variegata'	Last listed 1999

AUSTROCEDRUS (Cupressaceae)
§ *chilensis*	CGre CKen CMCN CPne

AVENA (Poaceae)
candida	See *Helictotrichon sempervirens*
sterilis	Last listed 1998

AVENULA See HELICTOTRICHON

AVERRHOA (Oxalidaceae)
carambola (F)	LBlo

AYAPANA See EUPATORIUM

AZALEA See RHODODENDRON

AZARA ✿ (Flacourtiaceae)
alpina	CFil
- G&P 5015	WPGP
- S&F 4583	Last listed 1997
dentata	CB&S CFil CGre CMac CPle ERea GKir SMac WPGP WSHC
- 'Variegata'	CCHP ERea LRHS
* *integerrima*	GQui
integrifolia	CFil SLon SPan WPGP
- 'Variegata'	CFil SBrw
lanceolata	CB&S CFil CMCN CPle CTri EPfP EPla GKir IOrc ISea SPan SPer WGer WPGP WPic WTro WWat

- G 3502	WPGP
microphylla ♀	CB&S CBrm CChe CDul CFil CGre CMCN CMHG CPle EBee EPla IOrc ISea LRHS NSti SArc SBra SBrw SDry SSpi WBod WFar WPGP WSHC WWat
- 'Variegata'	CAbb CB&S CDoC CFil CGre CMac CPle EBee EHoe EPfP EPla GQui IOrc ISea LHop MLan SBrw SPan SSpi STre WCru WFar WGer WPGP WSHC WWat
N *paraguayensis*	CPle CPne GAri GKir IDee ISea
* *patagonica*	Last listed 1997
petiolaris	CFil CPle EPfP NFla SPan WGer WPic
- G&P 5026	WPGP
serrata	More than 30 suppliers
- 'Patagonica'	ISea
sp. from Chile	CGre
uruguayensis	CFil CGre GKir

AZOLLA (Azollaceae)
caroliniana Willd.	See *A. filiculoides*
- auct. non Willdenow	See *A. mexicana*
§ *filiculoides*	CBen CRow ECoo EHon EMFW LGuA LPBA MSta NArg SCoo SWat SWyc WRic WStI
§ *mexicana*	WWeb

AZORELLA (Apiaceae)
compacta	Last listed 1999
filamentosa	ECou
glebaria hort.	See *A. trifurcata*
- A.Gray	See *Bolax gummifera*
gummifera	See *Bolax gummifera*
lycopodioides	GCHN
§ *trifurcata*	CPar CTri EPfP EPot GAbr GKir GTou MNaF SDys SIng SSmi WAbe WByw WPer
- 'Nana'	CNic GGar MBro MTho MWat NHol NMen NNrd SDys SSmi WPat

AZORINA (Campanulaceae)
§ *vidalii*	CBot CSpe ERea SAPC SAga SArc SVen WPer
- 'Rosea'	Last listed 1999

B

BABIANA (Iridaceae)
ambigua	Last listed 1998
angustifolia	CGrW
'Blue Gem'	CGrW LBow
cedarbergensis	Last listed 1998
disticha	See *B. plicata*
dregei	CGrW
ecklonii	Last listed 1998
hybrids	CGrW LBow
'Laura'	Last listed 1998
nana	CGrW
odorata	CGrW
patula	LBow
§ *plicata*	CGrW SYvo
pulchra	LBow
pygmaea	Last listed 1998
rubrocyanea	CGrW
scabrifolia	Last listed 1998
secunda	Last listed 1998

¶ *sinuata*	CGrW
striata	Last listed 1998
stricta	CGrW WCot WHil
- 'Purple Star'	CGrW CPLG
- 'Tubergen's Blue'	CGrW
¶ *truncata*	CGrW
tubulosa	CGrW
villosa	CGrW
villosula	Last listed 1998
'White King'	Last listed 1998
'Zwanenburg's Glory'	CGrW

BACCHARIS (Asteraceae)
genistelloides	SMad WCot
glomeruliflora	Last listed 1999
halimifolia	CB&S CPle GQui
- 'Twin Peaks'	SDry
magellanica	ECou
patagonica	CBlo GEil LGre LSpr SAPC SAga SArc WBod WKif WPen
'Sea Foam' ex RB 94142	NFla SMad

BACOPA (Scrophulariaceae)
caroliniana	EOHP
'Snowflake'	See *Sutera cordata* 'Snowflake'

BAECKEA (Myrtaceae)
camphorosmae	Last listed 1998
gunniana	CPLG
virgata	CPLG CTrC SPan

BAHIA (Asteraceae)
ambrosioides	SVen

BAILLONIA (Verbenaceae)
juncea	CPle WSHC

BALBISIA (Geraniaceae)
peduncularis	WFoF

BALDELLIA (Alismataceae)
ranunculoides	CRow EMFW EMan
- f. *repens*	CRDP EMan

BALLOTA (Lamiaceae)
acetabulosa	ECGP ECha EFou EGoo EMan LRHS MBel NTow SDix SPar WCot WWat WWeb
'All Hallows Green'	CFee CGle EBee ECtt EFou EGoo GBuc GKir LAst LHop LRHS MBri NGdn NSti SBla SChu SRPl WHen WWat
hirsuta	CGle
nigra	CArn EBee MChe MHer MHew MSal SIde WHer WWye
§ - 'Archer's Variegated' (v)	CFri CHar EBee ECoo EGar EGle EMan EMar EWes GBri MGrG MLLN MSCN SAga WCot WRus WSan
- 'Intakes White'	MInt
- 'Variegata'	See *B. nigra* 'Archer's Variegated'
- 'Zanzibar' (v)	EMon
pseudodictamnus ♀	More than 30 suppliers
¶ - 'Candia'	SBla

BALSAMITA See TANACETUM

BALSAMORHIZA (Asteraceae)
sagittata	Last listed 1999

BAMBUSA ✿ (Poaceae - Bambusoideae)
eutuldoides	CB&S

glaucescens	See *B. multiplex*
gracilis	See *Drepanostachyum falcatum*
gracillima	CB&S COtt EPla
§ *multiplex*	EFul GKir LJus
- 'Alphonse Karr'	CB&S COtt EBee EPla GKir ISta LJus NMoo SCob SDry WGer
* - 'Elegans'	NMoo
§ - 'Fernleaf'	CAbb CB&S CHEx COtt EFul EPla ISta LJus SCob SDry
¶ - 'Golden Goddess'	NMoo
- 'Wang Tsai'	See *B. multiplex* 'Fernleaf'
oldhamii	Last listed 1997
pubescens	See *Dendrocalamus strictus*
textilis	WJun
tuldoides	Last listed 1998
ventricosa	CAbb ISta LJus SDry
vulgaris	Last listed 1997
- 'Vittata'	Last listed 1997
- 'Wamin'	Last listed 1997

BANISTERIOPSIS (Malpighiaceae)
caapi	Last listed 1998

BANKSIA (Proteaceae)
aspleniifolia	Last listed 1999
baxteri	CCpl
burdettii	Last listed 1997
caleyi	CCpl
canei	CCpl
coccinea	CGre CTrC
conferta	CTrC
ericifolia	CGre CTrC SOWG
- var. *macrantha*	Last listed 1999
grandis	CTrC SOWG
hookeriana	Last listed 1998
integrifolia	CB&S CPLG CTrC GQui
marginata	CTrC ECou SPlb
media	CCpl CTrC
¶ *menziesii*	CTrC
ornata	Last listed 1998
¶ *paludosa*	SPlb
praemorsa red	CCpl
quercifolia	CGre
robur	Last listed 1998
saxicola	Last listed 1999
serrata	SOWG
serratifolia	CPla
speciosa	CTrC
spinulosa	CTrC
- var. *collina*	CCpl CTrC
- var. *cunninghamii*	CCpl
- var. *spinulosa*	Last listed 1998

BAPTISIA (Papilionaceae)
arachnifera	Last listed 1997
australis ♀	More than 30 suppliers
- dark blue form	Last listed 1997
- 'Exaltata'	ELan GBuc LHop LRHS
¶ - var. *minor*	LGre
¶ - 'Navy Blue'	EFou
§ *bracteata*	EBee EBrP EBre LBCl LBSe LBre MBBe SBre
§ *lactea*	CMdw CPle EBee EBrP EBre LBCl LBSe LBre MBBe NBir SBre WCot
leucantha	See *B. lactea*
leucophaea	See *B. bracteata*
megacarpa	Last listed 1997
pendula	EBee EMan
tinctoria	CArn CPle MSal WPyg

BARBAREA (Brassicaceae)
praecox	See *B. verna*

rupicola	WPer
§ *verna*	CArn GPoy MHer SIde WHer
	WWye
vulgaris 'Variegata'	CArn CBrm CElw CGle CHal EBee
	EHoe ELan EMan EMon GAbr
	MFir MSCN NBid NBro NHex
	NOak NSti SDys SIng WBea WByw
	WCHb WCot WMoo WOve WPnP
	WSan

BARLERIA (Acanthaceae)

cristata	Last listed 1997
* - *rosea*	Last listed 1997
greenii	Last listed 1997
obtusa	Last listed 1998
- pink	Last listed 1997
repens	Last listed 1998
- 'Blue Prince'	Last listed 1997
- 'Rosea'	Last listed 1997
suberecta	See *Dicliptera suberecta*

BARLETTINA See EUPATORIUM

BASHANIA (Poaceae - Bambusoideae)

§ *fargesii*	EPla GKir ISta LJus SEND WJun
I *qingchengshanensis*	CFil EPla

BASSIA (Chenopodiaceae)

scoparia	MSal
- f. *trichophylla* ♀	LPVe

BASUTICA (Thymelaeaceae)

aff. *aberrans* JJ&JH 940178NWCA

BAUERA (Cunoniaceae)

¶ *rubioides* pink	ECou

BAUHINIA (Papilionaceae)

alba	See *B. variegata*
corymbosa	CPlN LRHS SOWG
galpinii	CPlN SOWG
glabra	CPlN
monandra	SOWG WMul
natalensis	CSpe
vahlii	CPlN
§ *variegata*	MPEx WMul
¶ *yunnanensis*	SOWG

BEAUFORTIA (Myrtaceae)

micrantha	SOWG
orbifolia	SOWG
sparsa	CTrC SOWG

BEAUMONTIA (Apocynaceae)

grandiflora	CPlN LChe LRHS SOWG

BEAUVERDIA See LEUCOCORYNE

BECCARIOPHOENIX (Arecaceae)

madagascariensis	LPal

BECKMANNIA (Poaceae)

eruciformis	Last listed 1997

BEDFORDIA (Asteraceae)

¶ *linearis*	CCpl
salicina	ECou

BEGONIA ✿ (Begoniaceae)

'Abel Carrière'	CHal ER&R
acerifolia	See *B. vitifolia*
¶ *acetosa*	ER&R
acida	ER&R

aconitifolia	ER&R
acutifolia	ER&R
'Aladdin'	ER&R
albopicta (C)	CHal EBak ER&R LRHS
- 'Rosea'	CHal WDib
¶ *alice-clarkiae*	ER&R
'Allan Langdon' (T)	CBla
'Alleryi' (C)	ER&R
alnifolia	ER&R
'Alto Scharff' ♀	ER&R
'Alzasco' (C)	ER&R
ampla	ER&R
'Amy' (T)	CBla
angularis	See *B. stipulacea*
'Anita Roseanna' (C)	ER&R
'Anna Christine' (C)	ER&R
'Anniversary' (T)	CBla
§ *annulata*	ER&R
'Apollo' (T)	CBla
'Apricot Delight' (T)	CBla
'Aquarius'	ER&R
'Argentea' (R)	EBak MBri
x *argenteoguttata* (C)	CHal ER&R
'Aries'	ER&R
'Arthur Mallet'	ER&R
'Aruba'	ER&R
'Autumn Glow' (T)	ER&R
'Aya' (C)	WDib
'Baby Perfection'	WDib
'Bahamas'	ER&R
¶ 'Bantam Delight'	ER&R
'Barbara Ann' (C)	ER&R
¶ 'Barbara Parker'	ER&R
'Barclay Griffiths'	ER&R
'Beatrice Haddrell'	CHal ER&R WDib
* *benichoma*	WDib
'Benitochiba' (R)	ER&R
'Bernat Klein' (T)	CBla
'Bess'	ER&R
'Bessie Buxton'	ER&R
'Bethlehem Star'	ER&R WDib
§ 'Bettina Rothschild' (R)	CHal ER&R WDib
'Beverly Jean'	ER&R
'Billie Langdon' (T)	CBla
'Black Knight'	CHal
¶ 'Black Raspberry' (R)	ER&R
'Blanc de Neige'	ER&R
'Bokit'	ER&R WDib
'Bonaire'	CHal
'Boomer' (C)	ER&R
'Bouton de Rose' (T)	NRog SDeJ
bowerae	CHal ER&R LRHS
§ - var. *nigramarga*	ER&R
'Boy Friend'	ER&R
bracteosa	ER&R
brevirimosa	ER&R
'Brown Twist'	WDib
'Bunchii'	ER&R
'Burgundy Velvet'	ER&R WDib
'Burle Marx' ♀	CHal ER&R LChe WDib
'Bush Baby'	CHal
'Buttermilk' (T)	CBla
'Calico Kew'	ER&R
'Calla Queen' (S)	ER&R
'Camelliiflora' (T)	NRog
'Can-can' (R)	See *B.* 'Herzog von Sagan'
'Can-can' (T)	CBla
'Carol Mac'	ER&R
'Carol Wilkins of Ballarat' (T)	CBla
'Carolina Moon' (R)	ER&R
carolineifolia	LHil WDib

carrieae	ER&R
x *carrierei*	See *B.* Semperflorens Cultorum Group
'Cathedral'	ER&R WDib
¶ 'Cat's Paw'	SYvo
'Chantilly Lace'	CHal ER&R
'Charles Chevalier'	ER&R
'Charles Jaros'	ER&R
'Charm' (S)	CHal ER&R WDib
'Cherry Feast'	Last listed 1999
'Chocolate Box'	ER&R
'Chocolate Chip'	ER&R
'Christmas Candy'	ER&R WDib
'Chumash'	ER&R
'Clara' (R)	MBri
'Cleopatra' ♀	CHal ER&R MRav WDib
'Clifton'	ER&R
coccifera	Last listed 1997
coccinea (C)	ER&R WDib
compta	See *B. stipulacea*
'Comte de Lesseps' (C)	WDib
conchifolia	ER&R
var. *rubrimacula*	
'Concord'	ER&R
'Connee Boswell'	ER&R WDib
convolvulacea	ER&R
cooperi	ER&R
* 'Coppelia'	CBla
x *corallina*	EBak
§ - 'Lucerna' (C)	CHal EBak ER&R
- 'Lucerna Amazon' (C)	CHal IBlr
'Corbeille de Feu'	CHal ER&R
'Cowardly Lion' (R)	ER&R
¶ *crassicaulis*	ER&R
'Crestabruchii'	ER&R
'Crimson Cascade'	CBla
* 'Crystal Cascade'	CBla
cubensis	ER&R
cucullata	CHal ER&R
'Curly Locks' (S)	CHal
'Dancin' Fred'	ER&R
'Dancing Girl'	ER&R
'Dannebo'	MBri
'D'Artagnan'	ER&R
'Dawnal Meyer' (C)	ER&R WDib
'De Elegans'	ER&R
'Decker's Select'	ER&R
decora	ER&R
deliciosa	ER&R
'Dewdrop' (R)	ER&R WDib
diadema	ER&R
'Di-anna' (C)	ER&R
dichotoma	ER&R
dichroa (C)	ER&R
'Di-erna'	ER&R
dietrichiana Irmsch.	ER&R
'Digswelliana'	ER&R
¶ *dipetala*	ER&R
discolor	See *B. grandis* subsp. *evansiana*
¶ *domingensis*	ER&R
'Don Miller'	ER&R
'Doublet Pink'	ER&R
'Doublet Red'	ER&R
'Doublet White'	ER&R
dregei (T)	ER&R
'Druryi'	ER&R
'Dwarf Houghtonii'	ER&R
* 'Ebony' (C)	CHal ER&R
echinosepala	ER&R
'Edinburgh Brevirimosa'	ER&R
¶ *edmundoi*	ER&R
egregia	ER&R

'Elaine'	ER&R
§ 'Elaine Wilkerson'	ER&R
'Elaine's Baby'	See *B.* 'Elaine Wilkerson'
'Elda'	ER&R
'Elda Haring' (R)	ER&R
'Elizabeth Hayden'	ER&R
'Elsie M. Frey'	ER&R
'Emerald Giant' (R)	ER&R WDib
'Emma Watson'	CHal ER&R
'Enchantment'	ER&R
'Enech'	ER&R
'English Knight'	ER&R
'English Lace'	ER&R
epipsila	ER&R
x *erythrophylla* 'Bunchii'	ER&R
§ - 'Helix'	CHal ER&R
'Essie Hunt'	ER&R
'Esther Albertine' (C) ♀	CHal ER&R
¶ 'Eureka' (T)	CBla
'Evening Star'	ER&R
'Exotica'	ER&R
'Fairy'	ER&R
'Fairylight' (T)	CBla
feastii 'Helix'	See *B.* x *erythrophylla* 'Helix'
fernando-costae	ER&R
'Festiva' (T)	CBla
§ 'Feuerkönigin' (S)	ER&R
'Filigree'	ER&R
'Fire Flush'	See *B.* 'Bettina Rothschild'
'Firedance' (T)	CBla
'Fireworks' (R)	ER&R WDib
'Five and Dime'	ER&R
¶ 'Flamboyant' (T)	ER&R
Flaming Queen	See *B.* 'Feuerkönigin'
'Flamingo'	ER&R
'Flamingo Queen'	ER&R
'Flo'Belle Moseley' (C)	ER&R WDib
'Florence Carrell'	ER&R
'Florence Rita' (C)	ER&R
foliosa	CHal ER&R WDib
- var. *amplifolia*	CHal ER&R
§ - var. *miniata* 'Rosea'	CDoC CHal LRHS
'Fred Bedson'	ER&R
friburgensis	WDib
'Frosty' (T)	ER&R
'Frosty Fairyland'	ER&R
'Fuchsifoliosa'	ER&R
fuchsioides ♀	CDoC EBak ER&R GPin LIck LRHS MArl NPri SDix SYvo WDib WEas
- 'Rosea'	See *B. foliosa* var. *miniata* 'Rosea'
'Full Moon' (T)	CBla
'Fuscomaculata'	ER&R
gehrtii	ER&R
¶ *geranioides*	ER&R
glabra	ER&R
glaucophylla	See *B. radicans*
'Gloire de Sceaux'	ER&R
goegoensis	ER&R
'Gold Cascade'	CBla
'Gold Doubloon' (T)	CBla
'Goldilocks' (T)	CBla
'Good 'n' Plenty'	ER&R
'Granada'	ER&R
§ *grandis* subsp. *evansiana*	CDoC CGle CHEx CHal EBee ELan EMan EOas ER&R GCal LEdu LHil MLLN MSte MTho NCiC SDix SIng SMad SSpi WCot WCru WFar WHen
- - var. *alba* hort.	CDoC CHal EBee EMon ER&R GCal LHil MSte MTho SMad SSpi WCot WPGP

	– – 'Claret Jug'	WPGP
	– 'Maria'	EBee
	– 'Simsii'	WFar
*	'Great Beverly'	ER&R
	'Grey Feather'	ER&R
	griffithii	See *B. annulata*
	'Gustav Lind' (S)	CHal ER&R SSad
	'Guy Savard' (C)	WDib
	'Gypsy Maiden' (T)	CBla
	haageana	See *B. scharffii*
¶	*handelii*	ER&R
*	'Happy Heart'	ER&R
*	'Harry's Beard'	ER&R
	hatacoa	ER&R
	– silver	ER&R
	– spotted	ER&R
¶	'Hazel's Front Porch' (C)	ER&R
	'Helen Teupel' (R)	ER&R WDib
	'Her Majesty' (R)	ER&R
§	'Herzog von Sagan' (T)	ER&R
	x *hiemalis* 'Elatior'	LRHS
	hispida var. *cucullifera*	ER&R
	'Holmes Chapel'	ER&R
	homonyma (T)	ER&R
	'Honeysuckle' (C)	ER&R
	hydrocotylifolia	ER&R
	hypolipara	ER&R
	imperialis	ER&R
	incarnata (C)	ER&R
	– 'Metallica'	See *B. metallica*
	'Ingramii'	ER&R
	integerrima	CEqu
	'Interlaken' (C)	ER&R
	'Irene Nuss' (C) ♀	ER&R
¶	'Ivanhoe' (T)	CBla
	'Ivy Ever'	ER&R
	'Jean Blair' (T)	CBla
	'Jelly Roll Morton'	ER&R
	'Joe Hayden'	ER&R
	'John Tonkin' (C)	ER&R
¶	*johnstonii*	ER&R
	'Jumbo Jeans'	ER&R
	'Jumbo Jet' (C)	ER&R
	'Kagaribi' (C)	ER&R
	kellermanii (C)	ER&R
	'Kentwood' (C)	ER&R
	kenworthyae	ER&R
	kingiana	WDib
¶	'Kookaburra' (T)	CBla
*	'Krakatoa'	CBla
	'La Paloma' (C)	WDib
	'Lady Carol'	CHal
	'Lady Clare'	ER&R
*	'Lady France'	ER&R MBri
¶	'Lady Rowena' (T)	CBla
	'Lady Snow'	CHal
	'Lana' (C)	ER&R
*	'Lancelot'	CBla
	'Lawrence H. Fewkes'	ER&R
	leathermaniae (C)	ER&R
¶	'Legia'	ER&R
	'Lenore Olivier' (C)	ER&R
	'Leopard'	ER&R MBri
	'Lexington'	ER&R
	'Libor' (C)	ER&R
	'Lime Swirl'	ER&R
	limmingheana	See *B. radicans*
	'Linda Harley'	ER&R
	'Linda Myatt'	ER&R
	lindeniana	ER&R
	listada ♀	CHal ER&R MBri WDib
	'Lithuania'	ER&R

	'Little Brother Montgomery'	CHal ER&R WDib
	'Little Darling'	ER&R
	'Lois Burks' (C)	CHal ER&R WDib
	'Loma Alta'	ER&R
	'Looking Glass' (C)	ER&R WDib
	'Lospe-tu'	ER&R
	'Lou Anne'	CBla
	'Lubbergei' (C)	ER&R
	'Lucerna'	See *B.* x *corallina* 'Lucerna'
	'Lulu Bower' (C)	ER&R
	luxurians	ER&R SYvo
	– 'Ziesenhenne'	ER&R
¶	*lyman-smithii*	ER&R
	'Mabel Corwin'	ER&R
	macdougallii	CHal WDib
	var. *purpurea*	
	macrocarpa	ER&R
	'Mac's Gold'	ER&R
	maculata ♀	ER&R
	– 'Wightii' (C)	CHal CSpe ER&R WDib
	'Mad Hatter'	ER&R
	'Madame Butterfly' (C)	ER&R
	'Magic Carpet'	ER&R
	'Magic Lace'	ER&R
	'Majesty' (T)	CBla
	manicata	ER&R WDib
	'Maphil'	MBri
*	'Mardi Gras'	CBla
	'Margaritae'	ER&R
	'Marmaduke'	CHal WDib
	'Marmorata' (T)	LRHS NRog
	'Martha Floro' (C)	ER&R
	'Martin Johnson' (R)	WDib
	'Martin's Mystery'	ER&R
	masoniana ♀	CHal ER&R ERea LRHS WDib
I	'Matador' (T)	CBla
*	'Maurice Amey'	ER&R
	mazae	ER&R
	'Medora' (C)	ER&R
*	'Melissa' (T)	CBla
	'Merry Christmas' (R) ♀	ER&R
	metachroa	ER&R
§	*metallica* ♀	CHal ER&R
¶	*meyeri-johannis*	GCal
	'Midnight Sun'	ER&R
	'Midnight Twister'	ER&R
	'Mikado' (R)	ER&R
¶	*minor*	ER&R
	'Mirage' ♀	ER&R
	mollicaulis	ER&R
	'Moon Maid'	ER&R
*	'Moulin Rouge'	CBla
	'Mr Steve' (T)	CBla
	'Mrs Hashimoto' (C)	ER&R
	multinervia	ER&R
	'Munchkin' ♀	ER&R WDib
*	'Mystic'	ER&R
	'Mystique'	ER&R
	natalensis (T)	ER&R
	'Nell Gwynne' (T)	CBla
	'Nelly Bly'	ER&R
	nelumbifolia	ER&R
	nigramarga	See *B. bowerae* var. *nigramarga*
	'Nokomis' (C)	ER&R
	'Norah Bedson'	ER&R
	'Northern Lights' (S)	ER&R
	obscura	ER&R
	'Obsession'	ER&R
¶	*odorata*	ER&R
	'Odorata Alba'	ER&R
	olbia	ER&R
	'Old Gold' (T)	ER&R

'Oliver Twist'	ER&R
'Ophelia' (T)	CBla
'Orange Cascade' (T)	CBla
'Orange Dainty'	ER&R
'Orange Rubra' (C) ♀	CHal ER&R
'Orpha C. Fox' (C)	ER&R
'Orrell' (C)	ER&R
'Othello'	ER&R
¶ 'Otto Forster'	ER&R
¶ *oxyphylla*	ER&R
'Panasoffkee'	ER&R
'Panther'	ER&R
'Papillon' (T)	ER&R
* 'Parilis'	ER&R
partita	ER&R
'Passing Storm'	ER&R
'Patricia Ogdon'	ER&R
'Paul Harley'	ER&R
'Paul-bee'	ER&R
paulensis	ER&R
pearcei	ER&R
'Peggy Stevens' (C)	ER&R
* 'Penelope Jane'	ER&R
'Persephone' (T)	CBla
¶ 'Persian Brocade'	ER&R
'Piccolo'	ER&R
'Pickobeth' (C)	ER&R
'Picotee' (T)	CSut NRog
¶ 'Picotee Pink'	ETub
'Pinafore' (C) ♀	ER&R
'Pink Champagne' (R)	CBla WDib
'Pink Nacre'	CHal ER&R
'Pink Parade' (C)	ER&R
'Pink Spot Lucerne' (C)	ER&R SYvo
plagioneura	ER&R
polyantha	ER&R
¶ *polygonoides*	ER&R
popenoei	ER&R
'Potpourri'	ER&R
'Président Carnot' (C)	ER&R SYvo
'Preussen'	ER&R
'Primrose' (T)	CBla
'Princess of Hanover' (R)	ER&R
¶ *prismatocarpa*	ER&R
procumbens	See *B. radicans*
pustulata 'Argentea'	ER&R
¶ 'Queen Mother' (R)	ER&R
'Queen Olympus'	ER&R WDib
'Quinebaug'	ER&R
§ *radicans* ♀	CHal ER&R LRHS MBri
'Raquel Wood'	ER&R
'Raspberry Swirl' (R) ♀	CHal ER&R WDib
ravenii B&SWJ 1954	WCru
'Raymond George Nelson' ♀	ER&R
* 'Razzmatazz'	WDib
'Red Berry' (R)	ER&R
'Red Planet'	ER&R WDib
'Red Reign'	ER&R
'Red Robin'	WDib
'Red Spider'	ER&R
'Regal Minuet' (R)	WDib
'Regalia'	ER&R
rex	LRHS MBri
'Richard Robinson'	ER&R
'Richmondensis'	ER&R LHil
'Ricinifolia'	ER&R
'Ricky Minter' ♀	ER&R
¶ 'Rip van Winkle'	ER&R
¶ 'Robin' (R)	ER&R
¶ 'Roi de Roses' (R)	ER&R
roxburghii	ER&R

'Roy Hartley' (T)	CBla
'Royal Lustre'	ER&R
'Royalty' (T)	CBla
'Saber Dance' (R)	ER&R
'Sachsen'	ER&R
salicifolia (C)	ER&R
sanguinea	ER&R
'Scarlet Pimpernel' (T)	CBla
'Scarlett O'Hara' (T)	CBla ER&R
'Sceptre' (T)	CBla
scharffiana	ER&R
§ *scharffii*	CHal EBak ER&R LChe
'Scherzo'	CHal ER&R
'Sea Coral' (T)	CBla
semperflorens hort.	See *B.* Semperflorens Cultorum Group
§ Semperflorens Cultorum Group	MBri
– double (d)	CHal
'Serlis'	ER&R
serratipetala	CHal EBak ER&R MBri WDib
* *sheperdii*	CHal WDib
'Silver Cloud'	ER&R WDib
* 'Silver Dawn'	ER&R
'Silver Jewell'	WDib
'Silver Mist' (C)	ER&R
'Silver Points'	ER&R
'Silver Sweet' (R)	ER&R
'Silver Wings'	ER&R
sinensis	WCot
* 'Sir Charles'	ER&R
'Sir John Falstaff'	ER&R
Skeezar Group	ER&R
– 'Brown Lake'	ER&R
– 'Snowcap' (S)	ER&R WDib
solananthera ♀	CHal ER&R LCns WDib
sonderiana	ERea
'Sophie Cecile' (C) ♀	CHal ER&R
'Speculata' (R)	ER&R
'Spellbound'	ER&R WDib
'Spindrift'	ER&R
'Spotches'	ER&R
¶ 'Stained Glass' (R)	WDib
§ *stipulacea*	CHal ER&R
§ – 'Bat Wings'	Last listed 1998
subvillosa (S)	ER&R
'Sugar Candy' (T)	CBla
sutherlandii ♀	CAvo CHEx CHal EBak ER&R ERea ERos LHil LRHS NBir NChi NPer SDix SYvo WCot WCru WDib WEas WHer
– 'Papaya'	CSpe
'Swan Song'	ER&R
'Sweet Dreams' (T)	CBla
'Sweet Magic'	CHal ER&R
'Swirly Top' (C)	ER&R
'Switzerland' (T)	Last listed 1998
'Sylvan Triumph' (C)	ER&R
'Tahiti' (T)	CBla
'Tapestry' (R)	ER&R
* *taya*	WDib
'Tea Rose'	ER&R
teuscheri (C)	ER&R
'Texastar'	ER&R WDib
'The Wiz'	ER&R
thelmae	ER&R
'Thrush' (R)	Last listed 1998
'Thunderclap'	CHal ER&R
thurstonii ♀	CHal ER&R
'Tiger Paws' ♀	CHal ER&R MBri
'Tingley Mallet' (C)	ER&R
'Tiny Bright' (R)	ER&R

'Tiny Gem' ER&R
'Tom Ment' (C) ER&R
'Tom Ment II' (C) ER&R
'Tondelayo' (R) ER&R
* 'Tribute' ER&R
tripartita (T) ER&R
'Trout' (C) Last listed 1997
'Two Face' ER&R WDib
ulmifolia ER&R
undulata (C) CHal ER&R
'Universe' ER&R
venosa CHal ER&R
'Venus' CHal ER&R
x *verschaffeltii* ER&R
'Vesuvius' WDib
'Viaudii' ER&R
'Viau-Scharff' ER&R
§ *vitifolia* ER&R
'Weltoniensis' ER&R
'Weltoniensis Alba' (T) ER&R
* 'White Cascade' ER&R
'Witch Craft' (R) ER&R
'Withlacoochee' ER&R WDib
wollnyi ER&R
'Wood Nymph' (R) ER&R
'Yellow Sweety' (T) CBla
'Zuensis' ER&R
'Zulu' (T) CBla

BELAMCANDA (Iridaceae)
chinensis CAbb CArn CBro EBee EGoo
EMan GPoy LHop LRHS MAnH
MAvo MChl MLLN MSal NTow
SYvo WBea WCru WPer WWye
- 'Dwarf Orange' Last listed 1999
- 'Hello Yellow' MSte
* - 'Pumila Campbellii' Last listed 1998
* - 'Yellow Bird' Last listed 1999

BELLEVALIA (Hyacinthaceae)
brevipedicellata MS 746 Last listed 1998
dubia WCot
forniculata GTou
gracilis WCot
hackelii MS 439 Last listed 1998
kurdistanica Last listed 1999
longistyla Last listed 1998
maura S&F 387 Last listed 1998
nivalis CL 101 Last listed 1998
§ *paradoxa* EPar ERos NRog WCot
pycnantha hort. See *B. paradoxa*
romana MTho NRog WHil
- JCA 523 Last listed 1998
sessiliflora Last listed 1998
sp. PD 20493 Last listed 1998

BELLIS (Asteraceae)
perennis CKin EWFC MHew
- 'Alba Plena' (d) ECho ELan
- 'Alice' CGle CLTr WSan
- 'Annie' CGle
- 'Aucubifolia' (v) Last listed 1998
- 'Capel Ulo' Last listed 1999
- 'Dawn Raider' Last listed 1997
- 'Dresden China' ♀ CElw CLTr ELan GAbr MTho SIng
WAlt WOut WRus
§ - 'Habanera White With NBrk
Red Tips'
(Habanera Series)
- Hen and Chicken See *B. perennis* 'Prolifera'
- 'Jocelyn Castle' (d) WAlt
- 'Lipstick' See *B. perennis* 'Habanera White

(Habanera Series) With Red Tips' (Habanera Series)
- 'Miniskirt' WAlt
- 'Miss Mason' CGle GAbr NPro SIng WRus
- 'Monstrosa' Last listed 1999
- 'Odd Bod' CBos CNat WAlt
- 'Parkinson's Great White' CLTr GAbr
- 'Pomponette' ♀ Last listed 1999
§ - 'Prolifera' CBos WAlt
- 'Rob Roy' ♀ CBos CGle
- 'Robert' CLTr GAbr
- 'Rusher Rose' EPfP
- 'Single Blue' See *B. rotundifolia* 'Caerulescens'
- 'Stafford Pink' Last listed 1999
- 'Super Enorma' Last listed 1997
rotundifolia CInt
§ - 'Caerulescens' CNic CSev ELan GAbr NBir NBro
NMGW WOut WPat

BELLIUM (Asteraceae)
bellidioides NHol
crassifolium canescens CInt CRDP WPer
minutum CNic ESis MTho NPro

BELOPERONE See JUSTICIA

BENSONIELLA (Saxifragaceae)
oregona EBee EMon LRHS NCat WCru

BERBERIDOPSIS (Flacourtiaceae)
beckleri CFil ISea
corallina More than 30 suppliers

BERBERIS ✿ (Berberidaceae)
aggregata CAgr EPla GKir MNrw NBir SEas
SPer SRms
amurensis 'Flamboyant' WBcn
- var. *latifolia* WCru
B&SWJ 4353
x *antoniana* LRHS MBri
aquifolium See *Mahonia aquifolium*
- 'Fascicularis' See *Mahonia* x *wagneri*
'Pinnacle'
N *aristata* CAgr CArn CMCN SMrm
atrocarpa CPle
bealei See *Mahonia japonica* Bealei
Group
bergmanniae SLPl
brevipedunculata Bean See *B. prattii*
x *bristolensis* EPla LRHS MBri SLon SPla SRms
buchananii WCwm
var. *tawangensis*
buxifolia CBlo CPle GGar SCob WCFE
- 'Nana' hort. See *B. buxifolia* 'Pygmaea'
N - 'Pygmaea' CAbP CDoC CTri EBee EMil ENot
GKir LRHS MBNS MBar MBri
MRav NHol SLim SMer SPer STre
WDin WFar WPyg WStl
calliantha ♀ CBlo CChe CPle WWat
candidula EBee EBrP EBre ENot GKir IOrc
LBCl LBSe LBre MBBe MBar MGos
NFla NFor NHol SBre SLon SPer
WDin WGwG WStl WWat
- 'Jytte' See *B.* 'Jytte'
x *carminea* 'Barbarossa' SPer
- 'Buccaneer' ENot EPfP GKir WWes
- 'Pirate King' CBlo ENot LRHS MBri MRav SEas
SPer
chilensis WPic
chitria Last listed 1998
chrysosphaera WWat
§ *concinna* IMGH
congestiflora Last listed 1999

coxii	GBin GGar GKir WCwm
darwinii ♀	More than 30 suppliers
dictyophylla ♀	CFil CPMA CPle EPfP EPla GKir
	LRHS MBri MGos SLon SPer SPla
	SSpi WCwm WGer WPGP WPat
	WSHC
dulcis 'Nana'	See *B. buxifolia* 'Pygmaea'
empetrifolia	CPle NFor SIng
- JCA 14165	Last listed 1999
erythroclada	See *B. concinna*
¶ 'Fireball'	CMac
x *frikartii* 'Amstelveen' ♀	CBlo CDoC CMac CSam EBee
	EBrP EBre ELan ENot EPfP GChr
	GKir LBCl LBSe LBre MBBe MBNS
	SBre SCob WFar
- 'Telstar' ♀	CDoC ENot GChr LBuc LRHS
	MBri MRav NPro SCob WStI
gagnepainii	CCHP GChr GKir SLPl WGwG
- hort.	See *B. gagnepainii* var. *lanceifolia*
- 'Fernspray'	EPfP EPla GKir LRHS MBri MRav
	SBod SRms WBod
§ - var. *lanceifolia*	CB&S CTri EBee ENot EPla GGar
	IOrc MBar MGos MWhi NFor
	NHol NWea WFar WHCG WLRN
	WWal
- 'Purpurea'	See *B.* x *interposita* 'Wallich's
	Purple'
'Georgei'	CCHP CMHG GKir LRHS MAsh
	WBcn
glaucocarpa	ELan EPfP EPla LRHS WPat
'Goldilocks' ♀	CAbP CFil CMHG CPMA EPfP
	LRHS MBlu MBri WBcn WGer
	WPGP
¶ *gyalaica*	GIBF
hookeri	CB&S GKir
- var. *latifolia*	See *B. manipurana*
- var. *viridis*	GKir
x *hybridogagnepainii*	CBlo ELan SPer
'Chenaultii'	
hypokerina	CMac
insignis	WWat
- subsp. *insignis* var. *insignis* B&SWJ 2432	
	WCru
integerrima	Last listed 1998
§ x *interposita*	CBlo CDoC EBee ENot GGar
'Wallich's Purple'	MBar WCFE WLRN WStI
jamesiana	CMac GAbr SLon
julianae	CB&S CDoC CSam EBee ELan
	ENot EPla EWTr GChr GKir IOrc
	MBar MBri MGos MRav NBee
	NFla NFor NWea SHFr SLPl SPer
	WDin WFar WHCG WHar WSHC
- 'Mary Poppins'	LRHS MBri
§ 'Jytte'	MWhi
kawakamii	SLPl
knightii	See *B. manipurana*
koreana	CFil CMCN CSam ECtt EPfP EPla
	GBin WPGP
- 'Red Tears'	LRHS
lempergiana	CMCN CPle
¶ *lepidifolia*	GBin
linearifolia	WPat
- 'Jewel'	GKir
- 'Orange King'	CB&S CDoC CMac EBee ELan
	ENot EPfP GChr GKir LRHS MAsh
	MGos NBee NHol SPer SSta WDin
	WHar WPat WPyg WStI
'Little Favourite'	See *B. thunbergii* 'Atropurpurea
	Nana'
x *lologensis*	IMGH IOrc MGos WDin
- 'Apricot Queen' ♀	CB&S GKir LRHS MAsh MBri
	MGos NBee NEgg SPer SSta WDin

	WPyg WStI WWeb
- 'Mystery Fire'	CAbP CBlo CDoC COtt ECtt GKir
	IOrc LRHS MAsh MBar MBlu MBri
	MGos NBee NEgg SCoo SPla
	WHar
- 'Stapehill'	CSam ELan ENot EPfP GKir LRHS
	MAsh MBri SSpi WBcn
lycium	CAgr CPle WHCr
- CC 1729	CPLG GGar
macrosepala var.	WCru
macrosepala	
B&SWJ 2124	
§ *manipurana*	CGre EBee ENot
x *media* Park Jewel	See *B.* x *media* 'Parkjuweel'
§ - 'Parkjuweel' ♀	CB&S CBlo EBee ENot EPfP GKir
	IArd MRav SRms WLRN
- 'Red Jewel' ♀	CBlo CChe CDoC CMac EBrP
	EBre EPfP EPla LBCl LBSe LBre
	LRHS MBBe MBri MGos MWat
	SBre SEas SPer WBod WFar WWal
morrisonensis	CFil CPle WPGP
x *ottawensis*	MWhi WStI
- 'Auricoma'	LRHS MAsh MBri MGos
- 'Decora'	Last listed 1998
- f. *purpurea*	EBee GKir LRHS MBri MGos NFla
	SBod WDin WHar
§ - 'Silver Miles' (v)	EHoe EPfP LNet LRHS MBel MBri
	MCCP MRav SLon WFar WPat
§ - 'Superba' ♀	CB&S CBlo CChe CDoC CSam
	CTri EBee ELan ENot EWTr GChr
	GGar GOrc LHop LRHS MBar
	MGos NBee NFor NHol SLim SPer
	SPla SRms WBod WDin WFar
	WGwG WHar
§ *panlanensis*	EBee ENot MBar WWes
patagonica	Last listed 1999
poiretii	CPle
polyantha hort.	See *B. prattii*
- Hemsley	Last listed 1998
§ *prattii*	CMHG MBri MWat
¶ - var. *laxipendula*	SMad
pruinosa	CFil CPle
'Red Tears'	CBlo CPMA CSam MBlu MBri
	MGos MLan SPer WGwG WHCG
replicata	Last listed 1998
'Rubrostilla' ♀	EBee EPla GKir
x *rubrostilla* 'Cherry Ripe'	CMac
- 'Wisley'	LRHS
sanguinea hort.	See *B. panlanensis*
sargentiana	CPle ENot NFor SLPl SLon WTro
sherriffii	WCwm
sieboldii	LRHS WPat WPyg WWat
sp. ACE 2237	EPot
sp. B&L 12060	Last listed 1999
sp. C&S 1571	Last listed 1998
sp. C&S 1651	Last listed 1998
x *stenophylla* ♀	CB&S CChe CDoC EBee ELan
	ENot GChr GGar GKir ISea LBuc
	LRHS MBar MBri MGos MLan
	MWat NDlv NHol NWea SMer
	SPer SRPl WBod WCFE WDin
	WFar WHar WWin
- 'Autumnalis'	CBlo SCob
- 'Claret Cascade'	CBlo EBee EPfP EWTr GKir LRHS
	MAsh MBri MGos SEas SPer WBod
	WFar WGwG
- 'Coccinea'	MGos
- 'Corallina'	WBcn
- 'Corallina Compacta' ♀	CFee CLyd ELan EPfP EPot ESis
	GKir LHop LRHS MAsh MBlu
	MBro NHol NRya SChu SIng SPer
	SRms WPat WPyg

- 'Cornish Cream' — See *B.* x *stenophylla* 'Lemon Queen'
- 'Crawley Gem' — CBlo CMHG ESis LNet LRHS MBar MBri MGos WFar WLRN WStI
- Cream Showers™ — See *B.* x *stenophylla* 'Lemon Queen'
- 'Etna' — ELan LRHS MAsh
- 'Irwinii' — CBlo CMHG CMac CTri ENot GKir IOrc MBar MBri MGos NHol SCob SLon SPer WDin WFar
N - 'Lemon Queen' — LRHS SEas SMer SPer
- 'Nana' — SRms
- 'Pink Pearl' — CMHG LBuc LRHS MBri MGos
taliensis — Last listed 1999
temolaica — CFil CPMA EPfP GKir LRHS MBlu MBri NEgg SPer SPla SSpi SSta WAbe WDin WPat WWat
- S&F 95186 — ISea
thunbergii ♀ — CBlo CDoC CTri ENot GChr GKir LBuc NWea SMer SPer SPlb WBod WDin WFar WStI
- f. *atropurpurea* — CB&S CPle EBrP EBre ENot EWTr GKir LAst LBCl LBSe LBre LBuc MBBe MBar MBri MGos MWat NFor NWea SBre SGar SPer SRCN WBod WDin WFar WWin
§ - 'Atropurpurea Nana' ♀ — More than 30 suppliers
- 'Atropurpurea Superba' — See *B.* x *ottawensis* 'Superba'
- 'Aurea' — More than 30 suppliers
- 'Bagatelle' ♀ — More than 30 suppliers
- Bonanza Gold = 'Bogozam'^PBR — CAbP CB&S CBlo CDoC COtt EBee ELan EPfP LRHS MAsh MBri SMur WSpi
- 'Carmen' — LRHS MGos
- 'Carpetbagger' — IOrc WHar
- 'Crimson Pygmy' — See *B. thunbergii* 'Atropurpurea Nana'
- 'Dart's Purple' — LRHS MAsh MBri WFar
- 'Dart's Red Lady' — CBlo CPMA EBee EBrP EBre ECtt ELan ENot ESis GKir IOrc LBCl LBSe LBre LRHS MAsh MBBe MBri MRav SBre SLim SPer SPla WDin WFar WPat
- 'Erecta' — CMac ENot LRHS MBar MGos MRav SCob SPer WBod WCFE WDin
- 'Golden Ring' — CChe CDoC EBee ECtt EHoe EMil GOrc LRHS MBNS MBar MBri MGos MTis NHol SChu SEND SLim SPer SPla WDin WHCG WHar WPat WPyg WSHC
- 'Green Carpet' — CBlo EBrP EBre ENot GKir IOrc LBCl LBSe LBre LRHS MBBe MBar MBlu SBre SLon
- 'Green Mantle' — See *B. thunbergii* 'Kelleriis'
- 'Green Marble' — See *B. thunbergii* 'Kelleriis'
- 'Green Ornament' — Last listed 1999
- 'Green Ring' — EWTr
- 'Harlequin' (v) — More than 30 suppliers
- 'Helmond Pillar' — More than 30 suppliers
§ - 'Kelleriis' — CBlo CDoC EPfP EPla GKir GOrc MBar MBel MGos SRms WFar WStI
- 'Kobold' — CBlo ENot ESis GKir LRHS MAsh MBar MBri MGos NHol SEas SPer SPla WFar WLRN WPat WPyg
- 'Pink Attraction' — CBlo
- 'Pink Queen' (v) — CBlo EBee ENot EPfP LRHS MAsh MGos WHar WPat
- 'Pow-wow' — MGos MMil MTis WBcn
- 'Red Chief' ♀ — More than 30 suppliers
- 'Red King' — EHol MRav WDin
- 'Red Pillar' — More than 30 suppliers

- 'Red Rocket' — EMil MGos
- 'Rose Glow' (v) ♀ — CB&S CDoC CMHG EBee ELan ENot EWTr GChr GKir LAst LHop LRHS MBar MBri MGos MTis MWat NFor NHol SLim SMad SPer SReu SSpi WBod WDin WFar WGwG WHCG WPat
- 'Silver Beauty' (v) — CB&S CBlo CMHG CSam EBee ELan LRHS MBri MGos SBod WHCG
- 'Silver Mile' — See *B.* x *ottawensis* 'Silver Miles'
* - 'Silver Queen' — CBlo CHor
- 'Somerset' — WWat
* - 'Tricolor' (v) — CMac EHoe WFar WPat WPyg WSHC
tsangpoensis — SLPl
valdiviana — CFil EPfP EPla WPGP
veitchii — SLPl
verruculosa ♀ — CB&S CLan EBee ENot GChr GGar GKir LAst LHop MBar MGos NFor NHol NWea SPer SPla SRms WBod WCFE WDin WFar WGwG WWal WWat
vulgaris — CArn GPoy MSal
- 'Atropurpurea' — Last listed 1999
wallichiana B&SWJ 2432 — Last listed 1997
wardii — CB&S
wilsoniae ♀ — CB&S CBlo CFil CLan CPle EBee EBrP EBre ENot EPla GChr IOrc LBCl LBSe LBre MBBe MBar MWat MWhi NWea SBre SPer WDin WFar
- ACE 2462 — Last listed 1999
- blue — GKir LRHS MBri NPro WFar WGer
- 'Graciella' — EPla LRHS MBri NPro
- var. *guhtzunica* — EPla EWes
- L 650 — WPGP
- var. *parvifolia* — CPle

BERCHEMIA (Rhamnaceae)
racemosa — CPlN WSHC
scandens — CPlN

BERGENIA ✿ (Saxifragaceae)
'Abendglocken' — CMil ECGP ECha EPfP LFis LGro LRHS MBri MTis MWat NHol NSti SChu SWat WFar WWoo
§ 'Abendglut' — CB&S CGle CMHG EBee ECha ECtt ELan EWTr GKir LRHS MBNS MBri MRav NDea NFla NHol NOrc SCob SPer SPla SRms SSpi SWat WByw WCot WFar WHoo
'Admiral' — ECha EGle EPla SCob
afghanica — IHdy
'Apple Court White' — Last listed 1998
'Baby Doll' — COtt EBee EBrP EBre ECha EFou EGle EPla GKir GSki LBCl LBSe LBre LHop LRHS MAvo MBBe MCAu NBir NHol NOrc NPer NPro NSti SBre SCob SPla WCot WRus WWeb
§ 'Ballawley' ♀ — ECha IBlr IHdy MCAu NDea NVic SSpi SWat
¶ 'Ballawley Guardsman' — MTed
N Ballawley hybrids — CMGP EBee EPar GKir LGro NSti SDix SPer SWat WCot WWoo
'Bartók' — MTed SSpi
beesiana — See *B. purpurascens*
'Beethoven' — CLAP CPlt EBee ECha EGle EPPr EPla IHdy NBir NPar SSpi SWat WCot WPGP
Bell Tower — See *B.* 'Glockenturm'

'Bizet' — MTed SSpi
'Borodin' — SCob
'Brahms' — SCob
'Bressingham Bountiful' — GKir SCob SPer WCot
'Bressingham Ruby'PBR — CTri EBee EBrP EBre ECGP ECha EGar EPla GAri GKir LBCl LBSe LBre LRHS MBBe MCAu MRav MTed NBid NBir SBre SPer SWat WCot WPGP
'Bressingham Salmon' — CHar EBee EGle ELan EPfP EWTr GMaP LRHS MBri MRav NHol SCob SPer WCot
'Bressingham White' ♀ — More than 30 suppliers
'Britten' — LPio SBla
ciliata — CBos CFee CHEx CLAP CMil EBee ECha GCal IHdy LEdu MRav NBir NLar SDix SLon SPer SSpi SUsu WCot WEas WPGP WPer
- × crassifolia — See B. × schmidtii
- ficifolia — Last listed 1998
- f. ligulata — CCuc CHEx CLAP ECha EPla GGar LEdu MWgw NBid NBir NSti SCob SSpi WCot WPer
- - - B&SWJ 2693 — WCru
¶ - - CC 1793 — GGar
¶ - - ex CC 2049 — MDCh
- 'Wilton' — WCot
'Claire Maxine' — GCal
cordifolia — More than 30 suppliers
- 'Purpurea' ♀ — CB&S CDoC EBee ECha ELan ENot EPla EWTr GKir LBuc LGro LRHS MBNS MBri MCLN MRav NBir SDix SPer SPla SRms SWat WPnP
- 'Redstart' — CBlo NOak
- 'Tubby Andrews' (v) — CRDP GBri MBel MLLN NEgg NPro WCot
- 'Winterglut' — GMaP
crassifolia — CB&S CGle EMan EPla SRms SSca WByw
- 'Autumn Red' — ECha EPla
- DF 90028 — EMon
- 'Orbicularis' — See B. × schmidtii
- var. pacifica — CFil EBee WWoo
'Croesus' — IHdy
* cyanea — WCot
'David' — EMon
delavayi — See B. purpurascens var. delavayi
'Delbees' — See B. 'Ballawley'
emeiensis — Last listed 1999
'Eric Smith' — CLAP ECha EPar EPla GCal IHdy WCot
'Eric's Best' — Last listed 1998
'Eroica' — CSpe EBee ECha EMan EMon EPla GBin NCut
'Evening Glow' — See B. 'Abendglut'
'Frau Holle' — EFou
§ 'Glockenturm' — GCal
JCA mixed red clones — CNic
'Jo Watanabe' — ECha EPla
'Lambrook' — See B. 'Margery Fish'
§ 'Margery Fish' — ECha EPla SPer SPla
milesii — See B. stracheyi
§ 'Morgenröte' ♀ — CB&S CMGP EBee ECha EMan EMil EPfP GKir LRHS MBri MCLN NDea NHol NSti SPer SRms SWat WCFE
Morning Red — See B. 'Morgenröte'
¶ 'Mozart' — CLAP
'Mrs Crawford' — ECha SCob
'Oeschberg' — Last listed 1998
'Opal' — ECha EPla

'Perfect' — Last listed 1999
'Profusion' — IHdy SPer
'Pugsley's Pink' — CBlo CMil ECha LPio WLRN
'Pugsley's Purple' — Last listed 1997
§ purpurascens ♀ — ECha EPla ERav GDra GKir GSki MBro MHer NHol SDix SPer WByw WCot WPyg WWin
- 'Ballawley' — See B. 'Ballawley'
§ - var. delavayi — MBri SRms WPnP
- - CLD 1366 — WPer
- hybrid — Last listed 1997
aff. purpurascens — WCot
  ACE 2175
'Purpurglocken' — GCal
'Red Beauty' — CBlo LRHS
'Rosette' — LPio NFai
'Rosi Klose' — CGle ECha EMon EPPr EPla EWes GCal MBel MBri MRav
'Rotblum' — EBee ECtt EPla GBin GMaP LAst LFis LNor NCut NGdn NOrc NPri NVic WFar WPer WRHF
§ × schmidtii ♀ — EBee EWll NBir NFla SDix WCot
'Schneekissen' — EGle LAst MCAu MRav SLon SWat WElm WLRN
§ 'Schneekönigin' — CGle ECha EPla LPio MRav WGer
§ 'Silberlicht' ♀ — More than 30 suppliers
Silberlight — See B. 'Silberlicht'
Snow Queen — See B. 'Schneekönigin'
'Snowblush' — SSpi
§ stracheyi — CFee ECha EGle EGoo SApp SCob SDix WEas WPyg
- Alba Group — CGle CRDP ECha EMan EPfP GCal MBel NDea NWoo SCob WLRN WSHC
- KBE 151 — NHol
- KBE 209 — NHol
'Sunningdale' — CB&S CDoC CMGP EBee ECha ELan EMan EPPr EPar EPla EWTr GMaP LRHS MCAu MLLN MRav NBir NFla SChu SCob SPer SRPl SSpi SWat
'Winter Fairy' — Last listed 1998
'Wintermärchen' — CM&M CMGP CMHG EBee ECha ECtt EGle ELan EMan EPPr EPfP EPla ERav LRHS MBri MCli MSte NHol NSti SSea SWat WRus WWeb
'Winterzauber' — MTed

BERGERANTHUS (Aizoaceae)
¶ glenensis — EDAr
scapiger — SChr SDys

BERKHEYA (Asteraceae)
cuneata — Last listed 1998
macrocephala — WCot
maritima — Last listed 1998
multijuga — Last listed 1999
¶ purpurea — WCot

BERLANDIERA (Asteraceae)
lyrata — EMan EMon GCal

BERNEUXIA (Diapensiaceae)
thibetica — IBlr

BERULA (Apiaceae)
erecta — EHon WWpP

BERZELIA (Bruniaceae)
lanuginosa — CTrC

BESCHORNERIA (Agavaceae)
septentrionalis	WCot
tubiflora	CFil CHEx EOas LEdu WPGP
yuccoides ♀	CB&S CFil CHEx CTrC IBlr LHil
	MSte SAPC SArc SChr WMul

BESSERA (Alliaceae)
elegans	ETub LRHS WCot

BETA (Chenopodiaceae)
trigyna	EMon
vulgaris	WHer
- 'Bull's Blood'	CSpe EMan

BETONICA See STACHYS

BETULA ✿ (Betulaceae)
alba L.	See *B. pendula*, *B. pubescens*
albosinensis ♀	CB&S CBlo CDul CGre CMCN
	CSam EBee ELan EPfP GAri GChr
	GIBF GKir NWea WCwm WDin
	WFro WNor WOrn WWoo
- 'Bowling Green'	CTho
- 'China Ruby'	GKir LRHS MAsh MBri
- 'Chinese Garden'	CTho
- clone F	CTho
- 'Kenneth Ashburner'	CTho
- misapplied F 19505	See *B. utilis* F 19505
- var. **septentrionalis** ♀	CDoC CEnd CLnd CTho EBee
	ENot EPfP ELan ENet LRHS MAsh
	MBlu MBri MRav SPer SSpi SSta
	WWat
- W 4106	Last listed 1998
§ **allegbaniensis**	CDul CGre CLnd CMCN CSam
	IOrc
alnoides	WNor
apoiensis	CGre SSta
austrosinensis	WNor
borealis	See *B. pumila*
§ x **caerulea**	CLnd CTho WWat
caerulea-grandis	See *B.* x *caerulea*
chichibuensis	EPla SBir WHer
chinensis	CMCN WNor
- S016	WHCr
¶ 'Conyngham'	CTho MBlu
cordifolia	See *B. papyrifera* var. *cordifolia*
costata Trautvetter	CDoC CLnd CTho ELan ENot
	EPfP WDin WFro WOrn
- 'Fincham Cream'	EPfP GKir
¶ **daburica**	CBlo CMCN LRHS WNor WWoo
¶ - B&SWJ 4247	WHCr
- 'Maurice Foster'	CTho
- 'Stone Farm'	CTho
delavayi B&L 12260	Last listed 1997
ermanii	More than 30 suppliers
- 'Blush'	See *B. ermanii* 'Grayswood Hill'
- from Hokkaido, Japan	CSam
§ - 'Grayswood Hill' ♀	CEnd CTho GKir LPan LRHS MBri
	MGos SMad SPer SSta STre
	WWat
- 'Hakkoda Orange'	CTho
- var. **saitoana**	Last listed 1999
subvar. **genuina**	
- var. **subcordata**	CSam
'Fetisowii'	CDul CLnd CTho GKir IMGH
	LPan LRHS MAsh MBlu SSta
fontinalis	See *B. occidentalis*
forrestii Yu 10561	Last listed 1997
fruticosa	See *B. bumilis*
glandulifera	See *B. pumila*
glandulosa	Last listed 1999

globispica	Last listed 1997
grossa	CDul CLnd CMCN GAri GIBF
'Hergest'	CBlo COtt EPfP GKir LRHS MAsh
	MBri MGos WHCr
§ **bumilis**	CLnd CMCN GQui SBir
'Inverleith'	See *B. utilis* var. *jacquemontii*
	'Inverleith'
jacquemontii	See *B. utilis* var. *jacquemontii*
kamtschatica	See *B. bumilis*
§ **kenaica**	CTho
lenta	CFil CLnd CMCN EPfP SBir
§ - subsp. **uber**	CMCN
litvinovii	Last listed 1997
luminifera	CPMA
lutea	See *B. allegbaniensis*
§ **mandsburica**	CLnd EBee EWes GChr GKir
var. *japonica*	WFro WShe WWoo
- — 'Whitespire Senior'	CDoC CDul ELan LRHS MBlu
maximowicziana	CLnd CMCN CTho GAri NWea
	SSta WFro WNor
§ **medwedewii** ♀	CDul CFil CLnd CMCN CTho
	EBee EPfP EPla GAri GIBF NWea
	SBir SSta WPGP WWat
- from Winkworth	CTho
- 'Gold Bark'	MBlu
megrelica	See *B. medwedewii*
§ **michauxii**	MBro NHol WPyg
x **minor**	Last listed 1998
nana	CBlo ELan ESis IOrc MBar MWhi
	NSla SIng SMac SRms SSta STre
	WPer
- 'Glengarry'	EPot GAri GBin
- var. **michauxii**	See *B. michauxii*
§ **neoalaskana**	WNor
nigra ♀	CB&S CBlo CDoC CDul CGre
	CLnd CMCN CTho EBee ENot
	GChr GKir IOrc LHyr LPan LRHS
	MAsh NWea SMad SPer SSta WDin
	WFro WGer WNor WOrn
- 'Heritage'	CDoC CDul CEnd CLnd EBee
	ENot GChr GKir LPan LRHS MBlu
	MBri SSpi SSta WDin WWat
- Wakehurst form	EPfP GKir LRHS MBri
§ **occidentalis**	MAsh
papyrifera	More than 30 suppliers
- var. **commutata**	Last listed 1997
- subsp. **bumilis**	See *B. neoalaskana*
- var. **kenaica**	See *B. kenaica*
- 'Occidentalis'	See *B. occidentalis*
- 'Saint George'	CTho WWat
- 'Vancouver'	CTho
§ **pendula** ♀	More than 30 suppliers
¶ - 'Bangor'	GKir MBri
- f. **crispa**	See *B. pendula* 'Laciniata'
- 'Dalecarlica'	SMHT
N - 'Dalecarlica' hort.	See *B. pendula* 'Laciniata'
- 'Fastigiata'	CBlo CDoC CDul CEnd CLnd
	CTho EBee ELan ENot GChr LPan
	MGos SPer WOrn
* - 'Golden Beauty'	CDoC CDul CEnd LRHS MBlu
- 'Golden Cloud'	CLnd IOrc
- 'Gracilis'	CTho EMil
§ - 'Laciniata' ♀	CB&S CBlo CDoC CDul CEnd
	CLnd CMCN CTho EBee ENot
	EWTr GChr GKir IOrc LPan LRHS
	MAsh MBri MGos MRav NBea
	NBee NWea SPer SSpi SSta WDin
	WMou WPyg WWes
- 'Purpurea'	CBlo CLnd CTho EBee EBrP EBre
	ECrN ELan ENot EWTr GKir IOrc
	LBCI LBSe LBre LPan LRHS MBBe
	MBar MBlu MGos NBea SBre SPer

- 'Tristis' ♀	SSpi WDin WOrn
	CB&S CBlo CDoC CDul CEnd
	CLnd CTho CTri EBee ECrN EMil
	ENot GChr GKir IMGH IOrc LPan
	LRHS MGos NBea NWea SLim
	SPer SSpi SSta WDin WFar WMou
	WOrn WPyg
- 'Youngii' ♀	More than 30 suppliers
platyphylla	CMCN GAri NWea WFro
- var. *japonica*	See *B. mandshurica* var. *japonica*
- var. *kamtschatica*	See *B. mandshurica* var. *japonica*
populifolia	CFil CMCN GAri
potaninii	Last listed 1998
§ *pubescens*	CDul CKin CLnd GChr GKir GTre
	IOrc LNet LPan NBee NWea SLPl
	WDin WFar WMou
- 'Arnold Brembo'	CTho
§ *pumila*	Last listed 1998
raddeana	CFil SBir WNor WPGP
- 'Hugh McAllister'	CTho
resinifera Britton	See *B. neoalaskana*
saposhnikovii	Last listed 1997
schmidtii	CMCN
'Snow Queen'	CBlo CDul CEnd COtt EMui EPfP
	GKir IMGH LBuc LRHS MAsh
	MBri MDun MGos MLan SCoo
	SLim
szechuanica	Last listed 1998
- 'Liuba White'	CTho
tianschanica	WNor WShe
'Trost's Dwarf'	CBlo GChr GQui IOrc MGos SPer
	WPyg
uber	See *B. lenta* subsp. *uber*
x *utahensis*	Last listed 1998
utilis	CBlo CLnd CMCN CMHG CTho
	EBee EMil ENot LNet LRHS MAsh
	MBar MRav NBee NWea SPer SSta
	WDin WFro WNor WOrn
- BL&M 100	CTho
- CC 1409	Last listed 1997
- DB 319	Last listed 1998
§ - F 19505	CTho
- 'Fascination'	GKir LNet LRHS SPer SRPl SSpi
- 'Forrest's Blush'	GKir LRHS MAsh MBri
- 'Gregory Birch'	Last listed 1997
N - var. *jacquemontii*	More than 30 suppliers
- - 'Doorenbos' ♀	CDoC CLnd LPan MBlu MGos
	NEgg SSta
- - 'Grayswood Ghost'	CBlo CEnd CLnd CTho EBee EPfP
	GKir LPan LRHS SMad SPer SRPl
	SSpi SSta WWat
§ - - 'Inverleith'	CEnd EBee GKir LRHS MBri SSpi
	WWat
- - 'Jermyns' ♀	CDul CLnd CTho ECot EPfP GKir
	LNet LRHS MBlu SPer SRPl SSpi
	SSta WWat
- - 'Silver Shadow' ♀	CLnd CTho EPfP GKir LNet LRHS
	MBlu MBri SPer SSpi SSta WWat
- - wild origin	Last listed 1998
- 'Knightshayes'	CTho
- McB 1257	CTho
- 'Moonbeam'	GKir SSpi
- var. *occidentalis*	CTho
'Kyelang'	
- var. *prattii*	CEnd CGre CTho GKir
- 'Ramdang River'	CTho MBlu
- S&F 48	ISea
- S&L 5380	Last listed 1997
¶ - Sch 2168	MBri
- 'Schilling'	LRHS
- 'Silver Queen'	SSpi
¶ - 'Thyangboche Monastery'	MDun

- 'Trinity College'	GKir SRPl SSpi
verrucosa	See *B. pendula*

BEYERIA (Euphorbiaceae)
¶ *viscosa*	CCpl

BIARUM ✿ (Araceae)
arundanum	Last listed 1998
bovei S&L 132	Last listed 1998
carduchorum	GCrs
carratracense S&F 233	Last listed 1998
davisii	CLAP GCrs LAma LRHS
- subsp. *davisii*	Last listed 1998
MS 785/735	
- subsp. *marmarisense*	Last listed 1998
dispar	WCot
- AB&S 4455	Last listed 1998
- S&L 295	Last listed 1998
ditschianum	Last listed 1999
eximium FF 1024	Last listed 1998
- PD 26644	Last listed 1998
ochridense	WCot
- M&T 4629	Last listed 1998
pyrami PB	Last listed 1998
- S&L 584	Last listed 1998
spruneri S&L 229	SSpi
tenuifolium	CLAP CStu EPot SSpi
- AB&S 4356	GCrs
- subsp. *idomenaeum*	Last listed 1998
MS 758	

BIDENS (Asteraceae)
atrosanguinea	See *Cosmos atrosanguineus*
aurea	CGle ECtt EMan LIck LRHS NFai
	SCoo
cernua	MSal
ferulifolia ♀	CLTr CSev ECtt LHil LRHS MFir
	NPer SChu SMer SMrm WWol
¶ - 'Goldie'	NPri
heterophylla	CMil CStr EBee EMan EMon EPPr
	EWes GCal LHil MAnH MGrG
	MNrw SAga SBla SChu SGar SLod
	SMrm STes SUsu WBor WFar
	WWye
- CD&R 1230	Last listed 1999
- cream	MSte
- 'Hannay's Lemon Drop'	CMea CStr GBri MAvo MNrw
	MSte STes
humilis	See *B. triplinervia* var.
	macrantha
integrifolia	SMad
ostruthioides	Last listed 1999
pilosa	EBee
polylepis	Last listed 1998
sp. CD&R 1515	CGle CLAP
tripartita	EWFC MSal
§ *triplinervia*	LHop
var. *macrantha*	

BIGNONIA (Bignoniaceae)
capreolata	CPIN GOrc SBra SPer SSta WCru
	WSHC
lindleyana	See *Clytostoma callistegioides*
unguis-cati	See *Macfadyena unguis-cati*

BILDERDYKIA See FALLOPIA

BILLARDIERA (Pittosporaceae)
bicolor	CPIN
* *cordata*	Last listed 1997
cymosa	SOWG
erubescens	Last listed 1997

longiflora ♀ — More than 30 suppliers
- 'Cherry Berry' — CGre CPlN EBee ECou ELan LPio LRHS MAsh SBra SLim SMur SPan
- *fructu-albo* — CGre CPlN EBee ELan EWes GOrc LPio LRHS MAsh SBra SLim SPan SPer
- red berried — CPle CSam
scandens — ECou

BILLBERGIA (Bromeliaceae)
decora — GBin
nutans — CHEx CHal CMdw EBak ECon EGra EOas EPVP GBin IBlr LCns LRHS MBri SAPC SArc SRms SSte SVen WGwG
* - 'Variegata' — LHil WCot
pyramidalis var. *striata* (v) — Last listed 1998
x *windii* ♀ — CHEx CHal EBak ECon LCns LRHS SRms

BISCUTELLA (Brassicaceae)
frutescens — WWin

BISMARCKIA (Arecaceae)
nobilis — LPal

BISTORTA See PERSICARIA

BIXA (Bixaceae)
orellana — ELau MSal

BLANDFORDIA (Blandfordiaceae)
grandiflora — Last listed 1998
punicea — Last listed 1999

BLECHNUM (Blechnaceae)
alpinum — See *B. penna-marina* subsp. *alpinum*
¶ *australe* — WRic
brasiliense — WRic
cartilagineum — CFil CRDP WRic
N *chilense* ♀ — CCuc CFil CHEx CRow IBlr LSyl NVic SAPC SArc SChu SDix SLod SSpi WAbe WPGP WRic
colensoi — Last listed 1999
discolor — LPal NMar
fluviatile — Last listed 1999
gibbum — LRHS MBri WRic
§ *glandulosum* — NMar
indicum — Last listed 1999
magellanicum misapplied — See *B. chilense*
minus — NMar WRic
¶ - 'Cristatum' — WRic
- x *wattsii* — Last listed 1999
moorei — NMar
nudum — CFil CRDP CTrC MCCP NMoo WRic
occidentale — Last listed 1999
- *nanum* — See *B. glandulosum*
patersonii — Last listed 1999
penna-marina ♀ — CBro CCuc CFil EFer EMon EPVP EPar GCHN GGar LEdu MBri NHar NMar NRya NVic NWCA SChu SDix SIng SSpi WAbe WEas WPGP WRic
§ - subsp. *alpinum* — CFil NMar WPGP
- 'Cristatum' — CCuc CFil EFer GDra GGar NHar WAbe WPGP WRic
spicant ♀ — More than 30 suppliers
- 'Cristatum' — WRic
- 'Heterophyllum' — Last listed 1998

- *incisum* — See *B. spicant* 'Rickard's Serrate'
§ - 'Rickard's Serrate' — Last listed 1999
- Serratum Group — CFil
N *tabulare* (Thunb.) Kuhn ♀ — Last listed 1999
- misapplied — See *B. chilense*
vulcanicum — Last listed 1998
¶ *wattsii* — WRic

BLEPHILIA (Lamiaceae)
¶ *ciliata* — Ilve

BLETILLA ✿ (Orchidaceae)
Brigantes g. — EPot
* Brigantes g. 'Moonlight' — Last listed 1999
Coritani g. — EPot LAma WCot
formosana — EPot LAma
* - *alba* — EPot
hyacinthina — See *B. striata*
ochracea — EPot LAma WCot
Penway Dragon g. — EPot
* Penway Imperial g. — EPot
Penway Paris g. — EPot
Penway Princess g. — EPot
Penway Rainbow g. — EPot
* Penway Rose g. — EPot
Penway Starshine g. — EPot
Penway Sunset g. — EPot WCot
§ *striata* — EBee EBrP EBre ERea ERos GKir IBlr LAma LBCl LBSe LBre LEdu LHop LRHS MBBe MBri MSal NHol NRog SBre SCob SIng SLon SStn WCot WFar
- *alba* — See *B. striata* var. *japonica* f. *gebina*
- 'Albostriata' — EBee ELan IBlr LAma NHol NRog WCot
- var. *japonica* — EPot
§ - - f. *gebina* — IBlr LAma LRHS NHol NRog SSpi WCot WFar
- - - variegated — EPot
szetschuanica — EPot LAma
'Yokohama' — EPot LAma

BLOOMERIA (Alliaceae)
crocea — Last listed 1999

BOCCONIA (Papaveraceae)
cordata — See *Macleaya cordata*
microcarpa — See *Macleaya microcarpa*

BOEHMERIA (Urticaceae)
biloba — Last listed 1999
nivea — MSal

BOENNINGHAUSENIA (Rutaceae)
albiflora — IHdy WCot
- B&SWJ 1479 — WCru WTin
- S&SH 108 — Last listed 1999
japonica B&SWJ 4876 — WCru

BOLAX (Apiaceae)
glebaria — See *Azorella trifurcata*
§ *gummifera* — EPot ITim NWCA WAbe

BOLBOSCHOENUS (Cyperaceae)
§ *maritimus* — LPBA

BOLTONIA (Asteraceae)
asteroides — CBlo CFee CGle CSam EBee ECoo EMon GMac LRHS MCAu NBrk NBro NGdn NSti SLon SWat WDyG WLRN WPrP WRHF

- var. *latisquama*	CGle CHea GMaP LRHS MBel MBrN MRav MSte MWat SMad SPer SSvw WCot WFar WHal
- - 'Nana'	CBre EBee EMan EPPr GOrP LRHS MBro MLLN MRav MWgw NBid NBrk NBro NFai NPri WMoo WPer WPrP
- 'Pink Beauty'	EMon
- var. *recognita*	EMon LRHS
- 'Snowbank'	ELan EMan MBel MCli
¶ *decurrens*	EBee
incisa	See *Kalimeris incisa*

BOLUSANTHUS (Papilionaceae)
speciosus	Last listed 1997

BOMAREA (Alstroemeriaceae)
caldasii ♀	CFil CHEx CPlN CRHN ERea SOWG SSpi WBor WPGP WSHC WTre
edulis	ERea
hirtella	CHEx CPlN CRHN SSpi WCot WHil WIvy WSPU
- JCA 13676	WCot
multiflora	CPlN
ovata	ERea
patacocensis	Last listed 1998
sp. RCB/Eq A-5	WCot
sp. RCB/Eq C-1	WCot
sp. RCB/Eq X-2	WCot

BONGARDIA (Berberidaceae)
chrysogonum	CAvo LRHS NRog WCot

BOOPHANE (Amaryllidaceae)
disticha	Last listed 1997
guttata	Last listed 1997

BORAGO ✿ (Boraginaceae)
alba	EOHP MChe WBry WCHb WGwG
laxiflora	See *B. pygmaea*
officinalis	CArn CSev EDAr ELau GKir GPoy LRHS MBri MChe MHer MHew MMal NFai SIde WGwG WHer WOak WPer WSel WWye
- 'Alba'	CBre CGle CSev ELau EMon ILis MHer MMal NBid NChi WCHb WHer WJek WPer WRha WSel
* - 'Bill Archer' (v)	CNat GOrP
- 'Variegata' (v)	EMon
§ *pygmaea*	CArn CFri CHid CSev CSpe ELan EMan EMon ERav GBar LHop MFir MHar MHer MHew MTho NChi NLar NSti SChu STes SWat WCHb WOak WPrP WWin WWye

BORINDA (Poaceae)
albocerea	CFil EPla

BORNMUELLERA (Brassicaceae)
tymphaea	Last listed 1998

BORONIA (Rutaceae)
'Heaven Scent'	CB&S
heterophylla	CB&S CMHG CSWP ECou ERea SAga
megastigma	CB&S
- brown	Last listed 1998
- 'Brown Meg'	CB&S
¶ *serrulata*	ECou
'Southern Star'	Last listed 1998

BOTHRIOCHLOA (Poaceae)
§ *bladhii*	EPPr
caucasica	See *B. bladhii*
§ *ischaemum*	CCuc EHoe EPPr EWes LEdu MCCP WDyG WHal WPrP

BOTRYOSTEGE See ELLIOTTIA

BOUGAINVILLEA (Nyctaginaceae)
'Ailsa Lambe'	See *B.* (Spectoperuviana Group) 'Mary Palmer'
* 'Alabama Sunset'	CWDa
'Alexandra'	LChe MBri
'Alison Davey'	LRHS
'Amethyst'	ERea MBri
'Apple Blossom'	See *B.* 'Elizabeth Doxey'
'Asia'	ERea
'Audrey Grey'	See *B.* 'Elizabeth Doxey'
'Aurantiaca'	See *B.* 'Lindleyana'
'Aussie Gold'	See *B.* 'Carson's Gold'
'Barbara Karst'	CWDa ERea LRHS SGrm
'Begum Sikander'	CWDa
'Betty Lavers'	ERea
§ 'Blondie'	CWDa
'Bridal Bouquet'	See *B.* x *buttiana* 'Cherry Blossom'
'Brilliance'	CWDa ERea LRHS
'Brilliant' misapplied	See *B.* x *buttiana* 'Raspberry Ice'
x *buttiana* 'Afterglow'	CWDa SGrm
- 'Audrey Grey'	See *B.* 'Elizabeth Doxey'
§ - 'Cherry Blossom' (d)	CWDa ERea LCns
§ - 'Daphne Mason'	ERea
§ - 'Enid Lancaster'	ECon ERea LRHS
- 'Golden Glow'	See *B.* x *buttiana* 'Enid Lancaster'
§ - 'Golden McLean'	CWDa
§ - 'Jamaica Red'	ERea
- 'Killie Campbell' ♀	ERea LChe MBri
- 'Lady Mary Baring'	See *B.* 'Lady Mary Baring'
§ - 'Louise Wathen'	CWDa ECon LCns LRHS
§ - 'Mahara' (d)	CWDa ERea SOWG
- 'Mahara Double Red'	See *B.* x *buttiana* 'Mahara'
- 'Mahara Off-white'	See *B.* x *buttiana* 'Cherry Blossom'
- 'Mahara Pink'	See *B.* 'Los Banos Beauty'
§ - 'Mardi Gras' (v)	CWDa ERea
§ - 'Mrs Butt' ♀	CWDa ERea
§ - 'Mrs McLean'	ERea
¶ - 'Orange Ice' (v)	SGrm
§ - 'Poultonii'	ERea
- 'Poultonii Variegata'	Last listed 1998
§ - 'Poulton's Special' ♀	ERea LChe
§ - 'Rainbow Gold'	ERea
§ - 'Raspberry Ice' (v)	ERea LCns LRHS SGrm SOWG
§ - 'Rosenka'	CWDa ERea SGrm
§ - 'Roseville's Delight' (d)	ERea LCns LRHS SOWG
§ - 'Scarlet Glory'	ERea
§ - Texas Dawn	ERea
'California Gold'	See *B.* x *buttiana* 'Enid Lancaster'
§ Camarillo Fiesta™ (*spectabilis* hybrid)	CWDa ERea SOWG
'Captain Caisy'	CWDa ERea
§ 'Carson's Gold' (d)	CWDa
'Cherry Blossom'	See *B.* x *buttiana* 'Cherry Blossom'
§ 'Chiang Mai Beauty'	ERea
'Coconut Ice' (v)	CWDa LCns SOWG
'Crimson Lake' misapplied	See *B.* x *buttiana* 'Mrs Butt'
'Dania'	LRHS MBri
'Danica Rouge'	Last listed 1998
'Dauphine'	See *B.* 'Los Banos Beauty'
'David Lemmer'	CWDa ERea

'Delicate' See B. 'Blondie'
'Dixie' ERea
'Donyo' CWDa ERea LCns
'Double Yellow' See B. 'Carson's Gold'
'Durban' See B. glabra 'Jane Snook'
§ 'Elizabeth Angus' CWDa ERea LRHS SGrm
§ 'Elizabeth Doxey' ERea
'Elizabeth' ERea
   (spectabilis hybrid)
* 'Elsbet' CWDa
'Enchantment' See B. (Spectoperuviana Group)
   'Mary Palmer's Enchantment'
'Fair Lady' See B. 'Blondie'
'Flamingo Pink' See B. 'Chiang Mai Beauty'
'Floribunda' CWDa
'Gillian Greensmith' ERea
glabra ♀ CPlN ERea LCns LRHS MBri SPlb
   WMul
- A ERea
§ - 'Doctor David Barry' CWDa ERea
- 'Elizabeth Angus' See B. 'Elizabeth Angus'
§ - 'Harrissii' (v) CWDa ERea LRHS MBri SVen
§ - 'Jane Snook' CWDa ERea
- 'Jennifer Fernie' See B. 'Jennifer Fernie'
§ - 'Magnifica' ERea
§ - 'Pride of Singapore' ERea
§ - 'Sanderiana' ERea LPan
¶ - small-leaved SGrm
'Gladys Hepburn' ERea
'Gloucester Royal' CWDa
* 'Glowing Flame' (v) CWDa
¶ gold SGrm
'Golden Doubloon' See B. x buttiana 'Roseville's
   Delight'
'Golden Glow' See B. x buttiana 'Enid Lancaster'
'Golden MacLean' See B. x buttiana 'Golden
   McLean'
* 'Golden Tango' CWDa
* 'Granada' LChe
'Harrissii' See B. glabra 'Harrissii'
'Hawaiian Scarlet' See B. 'San Diego Red'
'Hugh Evans' See B. 'Blondie'
'Indian Flame' See B. 'Partha'
'Isabel Greensmith' CWDa ERea LCns
* 'Jamaica Gold' LChe LRHS
'Jamaica Orange' CWDa ERea LRHS
'Jamaica Red' See B. x buttiana 'Jamaica Red'
'James Walker' ERea SGrm
'Jane Snook' See B. glabra 'Jane Snook'
§ 'Jennifer Fernie' ERea LRHS
'Juanita Hatten' CWDa ERea SGrm
'Kauai Royal' See B. 'Elizabeth Angus'
'Klong Fire' See B. x buttiana 'Mahara'
'La Jolla' ERea
§ 'Lady Mary Baring' ERea LCns LRHS SOWG
'Lavender Girl' CWDa ERea
'Lemmer's Special' See B. 'Partha'
'Limberlost Beauty' See B. x buttiana 'Cherry
   Blossom'
§ 'Lindleyana' Last listed 1999
'Little Caroline' CWDa SOWG
'Lord Willingdon' See B. 'Pixie'
   misapplied
§ 'Los Banos Beauty' (d) CWDa ERea
I 'Louis Wathen' See B. x buttiana 'Louise Wathen'
'Magnifica' See B. glabra 'Magnifica'
'Mahara Double Red' See B. x buttiana 'Mahara'
   (x buttiana)
'Mahara Off-white' See B. x buttiana 'Cherry
   (x buttiana) Blossom'
'Mahara Orange' See B. x buttiana 'Roseville's
   (x buttiana) Delight'

'Mahara Pink' See B. 'Los Banos Beauty'
'Mahara White' See B. x buttiana 'Cherry
   Blossom'
'Manila Magic Red' See B. x buttiana 'Mahara'
'Mardi Gras' (x buttiana) See B. x buttiana 'Mardi Gras'
¶ 'Margaret Schuetz' SGrm
'Mary Palmer's See B. (Spectoperuviana Group)
   Enchantment' 'Mary Palmer's Enchantment'
'Meriol Fitzpatrick' ERea
¶ 'Miami Pink' SGrm
* 'Michael Lemmer' CWDa
'Mini-Thai' See B. 'Pixie'
* 'Mischief' CWDa
§ 'Miss Manila' CWDa ERea
'Mrs Butt' See B. x buttiana 'Mrs Butt'
'Mrs Helen McLean' See B. x buttiana 'Mrs McLean'
'Mrs McLean' See B. x buttiana 'Mrs McLean'
¶ Ms Alice™ SGrm
Natalii Group CWDa ERea
'Nina Mitton' CWDa ERea
'Ninja Turtle' (v) Last listed 1997
* 'Orange Cotton' LCns
'Orange Glow' See B. Camarillo Fiesta
   (spectabilis hybrid)
'Orange King' See B. x buttiana 'Louise Wathen'
'Orange Stripe' (v) ERea
'Pagoda Pink' See B. 'Los Banos Beauty'
§ 'Partha' CWDa
'Pearl' Last listed 1997
'Penelope' See B. (Spectoperuviana Group)
   'Mary Palmer's Enchantment'
pink ECon
'Pink Champagne' See B. 'Los Banos Beauty'
'Pink Clusters' CWDa ERea
¶ pink single SGrm
§ 'Pixie' ERea SGrm
'Poultonii' See B. x buttiana 'Poultonii'
'Poultonii Special' See B. x buttiana 'Poulton's
   Special'
'Pride of Singapore' See B. glabra 'Pride of Singapore'
'Princess Mahara' See B. x buttiana 'Mahara'
'Purple Robe' CWDa ERea
'Rainbow Gold' See B. x buttiana 'Rainbow Gold'
'Ralph Sander' LCns
'Raspberry Ice' (v) See B. x buttiana 'Raspberry Ice'
'Ratana Orange' Last listed 1997
'Ratana Red' Last listed 1997
'Red Diamond' ERea
'Red Fantasy' (v) Last listed 1997
'Red Glory' CWDa ERea
* 'Reggae Gold' (v) CWDa
'Robyn's Glory' See B. x buttiana Texas Dawn
'Rose Parme' ERea
'Rosenka' See B. x buttiana 'Rosenka'
'Royal Purple' CWDa ERea SGrm
'Rubyana' CWDa ERea LChe LCns LRHS
   SOWG
§ 'San Diego Red' ECon ERea GQui LCns LRHS
   SGrm SOWG
'Sanderiana' See B. glabra 'Sanderiana'
'Scarlet Glory' See B. x buttiana 'Scarlet Glory'
Scarlett O'Hara See B. 'San Diego Red'
'Sea Foam' SGrm
¶ Silhouette™ SGrm
'Singapore Pink' See B. glabra 'Doctor David
   Barry'
'Singapore White' CWDa ERea
'Smartipants' See B. 'Pixie'
'Snow Cap' See B. (Spectoperuviana Group)
   'Mary Palmer'
§ spectabilis variegated Last listed 1998
- 'Wallflower' CWDa

§ Spectoperuviana Group (v) ERea
- 'Makris'   Last listed 1997
§ - 'Mary Palmer'   CWDa LRHS
¶ - 'Mary Palmer   SGrm
    Variegated' (v)
§ - 'Mary Palmer's   CWDa ERea
    Enchantment'
§ - 'Mrs H.C. Buck'   CWDa ERea LCns
  'Summer Snow'   CWDa
¶ 'Sundown Orange'   SGrm
  Surprise   See *B.* (Spectoperuviana Group)
                             'Mary Palmer'
§ 'Suwannee' (v)   SGrm
  'Tango'   See *B.* 'Miss Manila'
* 'Tango Supreme'   CWDa
§ 'Temple Fire'   ERea LRHS SGrm SOWG
  'Thai Gold'   See *B.* x *buttiana* 'Roseville's
                             Delight'
* 'Tom Thumb'   CWDa
* 'Tropical Bouquet'   CWDa
  'Tropical Rainbow'   See *B.* x *buttiana* 'Raspberry Ice'
* 'Turkish Delight'   CWDa ECon EPfP LChe LCns
  'Variegata' (*glabra*)   See *B. glabra* 'Harrissii' , *B. glabra*
                             'Sanderiana Variegata'
  'Vera Blakeman'   CWDa ECon ERea LCns LRHS
  'Wac Campbell' (d)   CWDa SOWG
  'Weeping Beauty'   ERea
* 'White Cascade'   CWDa
  White Stripe   See *B.* 'Suwannee'

BOUSSINGAULTIA (Basellaceae)
baselloides Hook.   See *Anredera cordifolia*

BOUTELOUA (Poaceae)
curtipendula   CBrm CCuc EMon
§ *gracilis*   CBrm CCuc CInt EBee EBrP EBre
                          EMan EMon LBCl LBSe LBre
                          MBBe MCCP MLLN MMal MMoz
                          NBea NSti SBre SLod SPla SSvw
                          SUsu WLRN WPGP WPer

BOUVARDIA (Rubiaceae)
longiflora   ERea LChe LR
                          HS SOWG

BOWENIA (Boweniaceae)
serrulata   CBrP
spectabilis   CBrP CRoM

BOWIEA (Hyacinthaceae)
volubilis   CHal CPlN

BOWKERIA (Scrophulariaceae)
citrina   CGre CPle
gerrardiana   CGre

BOYKINIA (Saxifragaceae)
aconitifolia   EBee EBrP EBre GTou LBCl LBSe
                          LBre LFis MBBe MGrG MLLN
                          MRav NBur NLar NRya SBre SSpi
                          STes WCru WMoo WPrP
elata   See *B. occidentalis*
heucheriformis   See *B. jamesii*
§ *jamesii*   CGra GCrs MBro NNrd NWCA
                          WAbe
major   WCru
§ *occidentalis*   GGar NLar WCru
rotundifolia   EBee GBin GBuc GCHN GDea
                          SLon WCru
- JLS 86269LACA   EMon EPPr
tellimoides   See *Peltoboykinia tellimoides*

BRACHYCHILUM See HEDYCHIUM

BRACHYCHITON (Sterculiaceae)
acerifolius   Last listed 1998
bidwillii   Last listed 1999
populneus   Last listed 1997

BRACHYGLOTTIS ✿ (Asteraceae)
§ *bidwillii*   CB&S CDoC SDry WAbe WCru
§ *buchananii*   GEil SDry WSHC
- 'Silver Shadow'   GChr GKir
§ *compacta*   EBee ECha ECou EPfP GKir LRHS
                          MAsh MWgw SDry SPer WEas
- x *monroi*   ECou LRHS
  'Drysdale'   EPfP GGar GKir LRHS MAsh MBri
                          MRav MTed SDry SLon SPan SPla
                          WWat
§ (Dunedin Group)   CPle EGoo EPla SDry WEas WSHC
  'Moira Reid' (v)
§ - 'Sunshine' ♀   CChe CDoC CDul EBee EGoo
                          ELan ENot EWTr GChr GKir IBlr
                          LAst LGro LHop LRHS MAsh
                          MGos NBee NPer SLim SPer SPla
                          SPlb SRms SSht WCFE WDin WFar
                          WHen WTro
§ *elaeagnifolia*   ISea
  'Frosty'   ECou
N *greyi*   CTrG EBee EHol ISea MBar MWhi
                          WEas
§ *huntii*   CPle SPer
§ *kirkii*   Last listed 1998
N *laxifolia*   Last listed 1999
¶ 'Leith's Gold'   CTrC
§ 'Leonard Cockayne'   SLim SPer
§ *monroi* ♀   CCHP CChe CSam EBee ECou
                          EGoo EHoe EHol ELan GGar GKir
                          IBlr IOrc LAst LHop MBar MLLN
                          MRav SBrw SCoo SMer SPan SPar
                          SPer WEas WTro WWat
- 'Clarence'   ECou
  repanda   CHEx CPle CTrG SBrw
- x *greyi*   CDoC CPle LHil SAPC SArc
- 'Purpurea'   CTrC
§ *rotundifolia*   CDoC CPle EPfP IBlr SBrw WCru
                          WEas
  'Silver Waves'   ECou
§ *spedenii*   CFee GCrs GGar GTou
I 'Sunshine Improved'   WSPU
  'Sunshine Variegated'   See *B.* (Dunedin Group) 'Moira
                          Reid'

BRACHYLAENA (Asteraceae)
discolor   Last listed 1997

BRACHYPODIUM (Poaceae)
phoenicoides   Last listed 1997
pinnatum   EHoe EPPr
sylvaticum   CBod CKin EHul WPer

N BRACHYSCOME (Asteraceae)
  'Blue Mist'   GPin LRHS
  'Harmony'   LHil
  iberidifolia   Last listed 1999
  'Lemon Drops'   LRHS
  'Lemon Mist'   GPin LRHS
  melanocarpa   Last listed 1999
  multifida   EMan MBri WWol
  nivalis var. *alpina* See *B. tadgellii*
  'Pink Mist'   GPin LHil LRHS
  rigidula   ECou MDHE
  'Strawberry Mousse'   LHil LRHS NPri

§ *tadgellii*　　　　IMGH MTPN
'Tinkerbell'　　　　LRHS
¶ 'Violet Splendor'　　CGdn

BRACHYSTACHYUM (Poaceae - Bambusoideae)
densiflorum　　　EPla SDry

BRACTEANTHA (Asteraceae)
bracteata 'Dargan　　CMHG CSev SRms WEas
Hill Monarch'
¶ - 'Eastgrove Sherbert'　WEas
- 'Skynet'　　　　Last listed 1999
§ 'Coco'　　　　CMHG EBee GMac WCot WEas

BRAHEA (Arecaceae)
aculeata　　　CBrP LPal
armata　　　CBrP CRoM CTrC EOas EPVP LPal
　　　　　LPan MWst SAPC SArc
brandegeei　　LPal
edulis　　　CRoM CTrC EPVP LPal MWst

BRASSAIA See SCHEFFLERA

BRASSICA (Brassicaceae)
japonica　　　See *B. juncea* var. *crispifolia*
§ *juncea* var. *crispifolia*　CArn WJek
oleracea　　　WHer
* - *botrytis aparagoides*　CAgr
* *rapa* var. *japonica*　WJek
* - var. *purpurea*　WJek

BRASSIOPHOENIX (Arecaceae)
schumannii　　Last listed 1999

BRAVOA (Agavaceae)
geminiflora　　See *Polianthes geminiflora*

BREYNIA (Euphorbiaceae)
nivosa (v)　　Last listed 1999
- 'Rosea Picta' (v)　ECon

BRICKELLIA (Asteraceae)
¶ *eupatorioides*　IIve

x BRIGANDRA (Gesneriaceae)
calliantha　　NTow
- 'Tinneys Rose'　GCrs

BRIGGSIA (Gesneriaceae)
aurantiaca　　GCrs
muscicola　　NWCA

BRIMEURA (Hyacinthaceae)
§ *amethystina*　CAvo EBot ERos LRHS WCot
- 'Alba'　　　CAvo EBot ERos LRHS NMen
　　　　　NRog
§ *fastigiata*　　ERos

BRIZA (Poaceae)
maxima　　　COIW CRDP EGoo EPla LIck NSti
　　　　　WByw WHal WHer WRos WWye
- from Rhodes　Last listed 1999
media　　　More than 30 suppliers
- Elatior Group　Last listed 1997
- 'Limouzi'　　CElw EBee EMan EMon EPPr
　　　　　GCal LGre LRHS MSph SApp SDys
　　　　　SOkh WPGP
* - 'Luz'　　　NCat
minor　　　SWal
subaristata　　WHal
triloba　　　CInt EMan EPPr EWes GBin
　　　　　NOGN WHal

BRODIAEA (Alliaceae)
§ *californica*　　CNic ERos NMen
- var. *leptandra*　WCot
capitata　　　See *Dichelostemma capitatum*
coronaria subsp. *rosea*　Last listed 1998
'Corrina'　　　See *Triteleia* 'Corrina'
* *crocea* var. *aurea*　Last listed 1999
elegans　　　WCot
ida-maia　　　See *Dichelostemma ida-maia*
jolonensis　　Last listed 1997
laxa　　　See *Triteleia laxa*
leptandra　　Last listed 1997
§ *minor*　　　WCot
peduncularis　See *Triteleia peduncularis*
purdyi　　　See *B. minor*
stellaris　　Last listed 1999
terrestris　　Last listed 1997
volubilis　　Last listed 1997

BROMUS (Poaceae)
catharticus　　See *B. unioloides*
inermis 'Skinner's Gold' (v)　CBrm EBee EGar EHoe EMan
　　　　　EMon EPPr EPla EWes EWsh
　　　　　MAvo MGed MMoz
morrisonensis　Last listed 1998
　B&SWJ 294
ramosus　　　CKin EHoe EPPr
§ *unioloides*　　Last listed 1997

BROUSSONETIA (Moraceae)
papyrifera　　CB&S CFil CMCN ELan IDee LEdu
　　　　　LPan MLan MPEx SLon SPer
　　　　　WPGP WSPU
- 'Laciniata'　　Last listed 1999

BROWALLIA (Solanaceae)
speciosa 'Major'　MBri
- 'Silver Bells'　MBri

BRUGMANSIA (Solanaceae)
§ *arborea*　　　CArn CHEx SRms
aurea　　　CHEx LRHS
- 'Golden Queen'　ERea
x *candida*　　EBak ERea SSte
- x *aurea*　　Last listed 1999
- 'Blush'　　　ERea
- 'Ecuador Pink'　EPfP ERea
§ - 'Grand Marnier' ♀　CBot CHEx CMdw ECon ECot
　　　　　ELan EPfP ERea LRHS SOWG
　　　　　SSoC SVen WCot WEas
§ - 'Knightii' (d) ♀　CHEx CHal CSev EBak ECon ELan
　　　　　EPfP ERea LRHS SOWG WCot
- pink　　　Last listed 1997
- 'Plena'　　　See *B.* x *candida* 'Knightii'
- 'Primrose'　ERea
§ - 'Variegata'　ERea
§ *chlorantha*　　Last listed 1997
hybrids　　　Last listed 1997
§ x *insignis*　　LRHS
* - 'Orange'　　Last listed 1998
§ - pink　　　CHEx EPfP
'La Fleur Lilas'　See *Datura metel* 'La Fleur Lilas'
'Margaret Lewington'　Last listed 1999
meteloides　　See *Datura inoxia*
'Panache'　　　Last listed 1999
* pink　　　LIck WWol
rosei　　　See *B. sanguinea* subsp.
　　　　　sanguinea 'Flava'
§ *sanguinea* ♀　CHEx EBak ERea SOWG SVen
　　　　　WCot WHer
- 'Golden Queen'　Last listed 1997

- 'Rosea'　　　　　　　See *B.* x *insignis* pink
§ - subsp. *sanguinea* 'Flava' CHEx
§ *suaveolens* ♀　　　　CHEx ELan ERea IDee LRHS
* - hybrid pink　　　　　Last listed 1999
* - hybrid white　　　　　Last listed 1998
- 'Myles Challis'　　　　Last listed 1999
- *rosea*　　　　　　　See *B.* x *insignis* pink
- 'Variegata'　　　　　ERea
- x *versicolor*　　　　See *B.* x *insignis*
'Variegata Sunset'　　See *B.* x *candida* 'Variegata'
versicolor hort.　　　See *B. arborea*
- Lagerh.　　　　　　ERea LPan SOWG
yellow　　　　　　　LIck WWol
* 'Yellow Trumpet'　　　EPfP LRHS

BRUNFELSIA (Solanaceae)

americana　　　　　LChe SYvo
calycina　　　　　　See *B. pauciflora*
eximia　　　　　　　See *B. pauciflora*
jamaicensis　　　　CSpe
latifolia　　　　　　ECon
§ *pauciflora* ♀　　　　ELan LRHS MBri SYvo
- 'Floribunda'　　　　LChe LCns LRHS SOWG
- 'Macrantha'　　　　LCns SOWG
undulata　　　　　LChe

BRUNIA (Bruniaceae)

albiflora　　　　　　Last listed 1999

BRUNNERA (Boraginaceae)

§ *macrophylla* ♀　　　More than 30 suppliers
- 'Alba'　　　　　　　See *B. macrophylla* 'Betty
　　　　　　　　　　　　Bowring'
§ - Aluminium Spot =　　More than 30 suppliers
　'Langtrees'
§ - 'Betty Bowring'　　　CBos CElw CHad CLAP CPlt
　　　　　　　　　　　　CRDP CRow ECha EGle EMon
　　　　　　　　　　　　GBuc MHar MTed WCru WFar
　　　　　　　　　　　　WHal WPGP
§ - 'Dawson's White' (v)　More than 30 suppliers
- 'Gordano Gold' (v)　　EHoe
- 'Hadspen Cream' (v) ♀ More than 30 suppliers
- 'Langford Hewitt' (v)　CLAP
- 'Langtrees'　　　　See *B. macrophylla* Aluminium
　　　　　　　　　　　　Spot = 'Langtrees'
- 'Variegata'　　　　See *B. macrophylla* 'Dawson's
　　　　　　　　　　　　White'

x BRUNSCRINUM (Amaryllidaceae)

'Dorothy Hannibel'　　Last listed 1998

BRUNSVIGIA (Amaryllidaceae)

grandiflora　　　　Last listed 1997
gregaria　　　　　Last listed 1997
multiflora　　　　　See *B. orientalis*
§ *orientalis*　　　　　Last listed 1998
radulosa　　　　　Last listed 1998
rosea 'Minor'　　　See *Amaryllis belladonna*

BRYONIA (Cucurbitaceae)

dioica　　　　　　EWFC GPoy MHew MSal

BRYOPHYLLUM See KALANCHOE

BUCHLOE (Poaceae)

dactyloides　　　　Last listed 1997

BUDDLEJA ✿ (Buddlejaceae)

agathosma　　　　CBot CFil CPle WEas WHar WPGP
　　　　　　　　　　　　WSHC
albiflora　　　　　CPle SLon
alternifolia ♀　　　More than 30 suppliers

- 'Argentea'　　　　CBot CDoC CPle ELan ERav ERea
　　　　　　　　　　　　LRHS MBNS MBro MHar MRav
　　　　　　　　　　　　NFla NSti SPer SPla SSpi WHCG
　　　　　　　　　　　　WPat WSHC WWat
asiatica ♀　　　　CBot CBrm CPIN CPle ECon ERea
　　　　　　　　　　　　LCns LRHS SLon
- B&SWJ 2679　　　Last listed 1999
auriculata　　　　CAbb CB&S CBlo CBot CCHP
　　　　　　　　　　　　CDoC CGre CLTr CMCN CPle
　　　　　　　　　　　　CRHN CWit ERea GQui NSti SDix
　　　　　　　　　　　　SOWG SPer WCru WHCG WPGP
australis　　　　　CPle
* 'Butterfly Ball'　　　SLon WBcn WPer
caryopteridifolia　　EHol SLon
colvilei　　　　　CAbb CB&S CDoC CFil CPle
　　　　　　　　　　　　CTrw CWit EPfP SBrw SPlb WAbe
　　　　　　　　　　　　WCot WEas WSpi
- B&SWJ 2121　　　WCru
- C&S 1577　　　　Last listed 1998
- 'Kewensis'　　　　CBot CGre CRHN IBlr SLon SMad
　　　　　　　　　　　　WBod WCru WPGP WSHC
cordata　　　　　Last listed 1999
coriacea　　　　　CPle SLon
§ *crispa*　　　　　CB&S CBot CDoC CPle ECha
　　　　　　　　　　　　ELan ERav IMGH LRHS SBra SBrw
　　　　　　　　　　　　SDry SOWG SPer SSpi SSta WAbe
　　　　　　　　　　　　WCot WFar WHCG WKif WPGP
　　　　　　　　　　　　WSHC WSpi WWat
- L 1544　　　　　CFil WPGP
crotonoides　　　SLon
　amplexicaulis
curviflora　　　　Last listed 1999
davidii　　　　　CArn CKin MBro NWea SGar
　　　　　　　　　　　　SHFr STre WDin
- 'African Queen'　　SPer SRPl
- var. *alba*　　　　NSti
- 'Black Knight' ♀　　More than 30 suppliers
- 'Blue Horizon'　　GCHN MHar SEND SLon WCot
　　　　　　　　　　　　WMoo WRHF
- 'Border Beauty'　　GKir SEas
§ - 'Charming'　　　MBri WMoo WSHC
- 'Dartmoor' ♀　　　More than 30 suppliers
- 'Dart's Blue Butterfly'　MBri SRPl
- 'Dart's Ornamental White' CBlo EBee MBri
- 'Dart's Papillon Blue'　SLPl
- 'Dart's Purple Rain'　CBlo MBri
- 'Dubonnet'　　　SLon
- 'Empire Blue' ♀　　CB&S CDoC EBee ECtt ELan ENot
　　　　　　　　　　　　EWTr GChr GKir GOrc LRHS
　　　　　　　　　　　　MAsh MRav MWat NBee NPer
　　　　　　　　　　　　NWea SPer SPlb WBod WDin
　　　　　　　　　　　　WGwG WPyg WStI WWeb
- 'Fascinating'　　　CBlo CTri MAsh SBod
- 'Flaming Violet'　　SLon
- 'Fortune'　　　　Last listed 1998
- 'Glasnevin Blue'　　CTri NSti SDix SMrm SPer
- 'Golden Sunset'　　Last listed 1997
- 'Gonglepod'　　　SLon
- 'Harlequin' (v)　　More than 30 suppliers
- 'Ile de France'　　CB&S CBlo GKir MGos MWat
　　　　　　　　　　　　NWea SRms
- 'Les Kneale'　　　Last listed 1999
§ - 'Masquerade =　　CBlo ENot EPfP MGos MGrG
　'Notbud'[PBR] (v)　　SLon WGor WLRN WStI WWes
§ - 'Nanho Blue'　　　More than 30 suppliers
- 'Nanho Petite Indigo'　See *B. davidii* 'Nanho Blue'
- 'Nanho Petite Purple'　See *B. davidii* 'Nanho Purple'
§ - 'Nanho Purple'　　CDoC CHar CMHG EBee EGoo
　　　　　　　　　　　　ELan ENot EPfP GChr GKir LRHS
　　　　　　　　　　　　MAsh MBar MBel MBri SLim SLon
　　　　　　　　　　　　SPer SPlb WHar WSHC
- var. *nanhoensis*　　CBlo CPle GCHN MWhi SEND

- - *alba*	SIde SPer WHCG CBlo CChe ELan EPfP GKir LFis MBar SPer SRPl SRms WWat
- - blue	GKir LHil MBri SLon SPer SRPl WWat
- - purple	CPLG GKir
- 'Notbud'PBR	See *B. davidii* Masquerade = 'Notbud'
- 'Orchid Beauty'	CBlo MBNS NCut NPro
- 'Peace'	CChe CDoC EBee ENot EPfP NPer SPer
- Petite Indigo™	See *B. davidii* 'Nanho Blue'
- Petite Plum™	See *B. davidii* 'Nanho Purple'
- 'Pink Beauty'	CLTr GKir WHCG WWat
- 'Pink Charming'	See *B. davidii* 'Charming'
- 'Pink Pearl'	SLon
* - 'Pixie Blue'	MAsh NCut WWeb
- 'Pixie Red'	CLyn EBee MAsh NCut NPri SLon WShe WWeb
* - 'Pixie White'	CLyn MAsh MBNS NCut WShe WWeb
- 'Purple Prince'	NCut
- 'Purple Rain'	Last listed 1998
- 'Royal Purple'	GKir SLim
- 'Royal Red' ♀	More than 30 suppliers
- 'Salicifolia'	GEil
- Santana = 'Thia' (v)	COtt LRHS MAsh
- 'Silver Butterfly'	Last listed 1999
- 'Summer Beauty'	CBlo CCHP GKir LRHS MBri MGos NPro WBcn
- 'Variegata'	LRHS SMrm
- 'White Ball'	LRHS MBNS SLon
- 'White Bouquet'	CBlo EWTr GKir GOrc LAst LRHS MBel MHer MWat NWea SBod SEND SEas SLim SMer SPer SReu WLRN WWeb
- 'White Butterfly'	LRHS SLon
- 'White Cloud'	EPar GQui IOrc SRms WGwG
- 'White Harlequin' (v)	CLTr CRow SLon WCFE WCot WEas WWat
- 'White Perfection'	Last listed 1997
- 'White Profusion' ♀	CB&S CSam EBee ECtt ELan EWTr GCHN GChr LFis LRHS MBar MGos NBee NBrk NFla NFor NWea WBod WCFE WDin WEas WFar WHCG WHar WPnP WPyg WStl WWin
- 'White Wings'	SLon
§ *delavayi*	CMil CPle ERea SPan WCru
fallowiana Balf. f.	CB&S CPle LRHS NFor SPla SReu
- ACE 2481	LRHS WAbe
- var. *alba* ♀	CBlo CBot CDoC CMHG CPle ELan ENot ERav LRHS MBel MRav NSti SLon SRPl SSta WAbe WCru WEas WPGP WSHC WWat
- CLD 1109	CFil WPGP
- misapplied	See *B.* 'West Hill'
farreri	CBot CPle MSte SOWG WBod
forrestii	CBot CHEx CPle SVen WCru
- KR 2737	WCru
globosa ♀	More than 30 suppliers
- 'Cannington Gold'	CBlo
- 'Lemon Ball'	WBcn
heliophila	See *B. delavayi*
indica	CPle SLon
japonica	CPle
* 'Lady Curzon'	WRHF
x *lewisiana*	Last listed 1999
- 'Margaret Pike'	CBot SOWG
limitanea	SLon
lindleyana	CB&S CBot CFil CGre CMCN CPle

'Lochinch' ♀	CRHN EBee ELan EPla ERea MRav MTis SChu SMac SOWG SPan SPer SPla SSpi WCFE WCot WCru WFar WHCG WPGP WSHC WWeb
longifolia	More than 30 suppliers
loricata	CChe CAbb CBot CGre CPle CStr ERea GQui SOWG SPan SVen WCFE WPGP
- CD&R 190	Last listed 1999
macrostachya	CFil CPle
- SBEC 360	NHex WPGP
§ *madagascariensis*	CPle CRHN SOWG SVen WCot WWat
myriantha	GQui SPan
nappii	SLon
nepalensis	CPLG
nicodemia	See *B. madagascariensis*
nivea	CBot CMCN CPle MHar SOWG SPan
- pink	SLon
- var. *yunnanensis*	CPle MSte WCFE
aff. *nivea* L. 860	WPGP
officinalis	CBot CDoC CPle CRHN EHol ERea LFis SVen
paniculata	SLon
parvifolia MPF 148	WPGP
pichinchensis	CFil
x *pikei*	SDys
§ - 'Hever'	CHal CPle GQui SPer
'Pink Delight' ♀	More than 30 suppliers
pterocaulis	CGre
saligna	CGre CPle CTrC SLon
salviifolia	CAbb CBot CFil CGre CPle CRHN CSWP CSam CTbh CTrG EBee EGar ELan GQui SBrw SDry SPan SPer SSoC WCot WHer WLRN
- Burtt 6139	WPGP
- white	CDoC CRHN
sp. ACE 2522	Last listed 1999
sp. TS&BC 94062	Last listed 1997
sp. TS&BC 94287	Last listed 1997
sp. TS&BC 94408	Last listed 1999
stenostachya	Last listed 1999
sterniana	See *B. crispa*
tibetica	See *B. crispa*
tubiflora	CBot ERea SLon SOWG
¶ *venenifera* B&SWJ 6036	WCru
- B&SWJ 895	WCru
§ 'West Hill'	SLon
x *weyeriana*	CBlo CLTr CRHN CSam EBee ECtt EOrc EPar GOrc MAsh MNrw MTis MWat NBir NSti SEas SPlb SSte WEas WFar WHCG WPyg WSHC
* - 'Flight's Fancy'	EPla EWes
- 'Golden Glow' (v)	CBlo CChe CDoC CMil CTri EPfP GCHN GOrc LAst MBri NFor SHel SLon SPla WPyg WTro WWeb WWin
- 'Lady de Ramsey'	SEND WPer
- 'Moonlight'	CPle CRow LAst SCob
- 'Sungold' ♀	CBrm CDoC CPle EBee ELan EPfP EWTr GKir IOrc LHrt MBel MBlu MCCP MGos MLLN NFla SLon SPer SSht WBod WCot WHar
- 'Trewithen'	Last listed 1999
* - 'Variegata'	CPMA

BUGLOSSOIDES (Boraginaceae)

§ *purpurocaerulea*	CKin CMHG EBee ECha EEls ELan EMar EMon EWTr GOrP LFis

LRHS MAvo MBro MHew MSal
MSte NChi SAga WFar WRHF
WWin WWye

BULBINE (Asphodelaceae)
bulbosa   Last listed 1999
caulescens   See *B. frutescens*
§ *frutescens*   CPea CSev EMan EWll LHil MWhi
                   WCot WHal WWin
- yellow   LHil WCot
semibarbata   EBee NBro WPer

BULBINELLA (Asphodelaceae)
angustifolia   WCot
cauda-felis   Last listed 1999
eburnifolia   Last listed 1999
floribunda   Last listed 1998
hookeri   CRDP EBee EBrP EBre ECou EPPr
                   GAbr GCrs GDra GGar ITim LBCl
                   LBSe LBee LBre MBBe MFir NDlv
                   NHar SBre SRms SYvo WCot WPer
nutans var. *nutans* EEls
rossii   WLin

BULBINOPSIS See BULBINE

BULBOCODIUM (Colchicaceae)
vernum   EPot ERos ETub GCrs LAma LRHS
                   MBri MNrw NRog

BUNIUM (Apiaceae)
bulbocastanum   LEdu

BUPHTHALMUM (Asteraceae)
§ *salicifolium*   CSam CSev EBee ELan EPfP EWTr
                   GKir GMaP LRHS MBri NBid NBro
                   NFla NGdn NNor NOrc NTow
                   SPer SRms SWat WCot WFar WPer
- 'Alpengold'   EBee ECha GKir
- 'Dora'   EBee EMan SUsu WCot WWal
- 'Sunwheel'   EFou EWll LRHS NPri
speciosum   See *Telekia speciosa*

BUPLEURUM (Apiaceae)
angulosum   CBos CFil CLon CLyd CMil CNic
                   CRDP SMrm WCot WCru WFar
                   WPGP
- copper   See *B. longifolium*
barceloi   Last listed 1999
falcatum   CGle CLTr CLyd ECGP ECha ELau
                   EPPr MBro MLLN MWgw NFla
                   NSti SChu SMrm WFar WWat
fruticosum   CB&S CBot CFil CPle LRHS MHar
                   SBla SChu SCob SDix SPer SRPl
                   SSpi WCot WCru WEas WFoF
                   WKif WPGP WPat WSHC WSpi
                   WStI WWat
* *griffithii*   MSal
komarovianum   SMrm
§ *longifolium*   CElw CRDP EBee GBin GGar
                   NChi NSti WCot WWhi
longiradiatum   WCru
  B&SWJ 729
multinerve   Last listed 1998
ranunculoides   CFri CLyd EBee SMrm
rotundifolium   EWFC MSal SMrm WPGP
salicifolium   CFil CPle
spinosum   WCru
stellatum   GGar LRHS
tenue B&SWJ 2973 WCru

BURCHARDIA (Colchicaceae)
umbellata   Last listed 1998

BURSARIA (Pittosporaceae)
spinosa   CPLG CPle ECou GQui SLon SPlb

BUTIA (Arecaceae)
capitata   CBrP CHEx CRoM CTbh CTrC
                   EGln EOas EPVP LPJP LPal LPan
                   SAPC SArc SEND WMul
yatay   CRoM LPal

BUTOMUS (Butomaceae)
umbellatus ♀   CBen CRow CWat ECha ECoo
                   ECtt EHon EMFW LPBA MSta
                   NDea SLon SWat SWyc WFar
                   WMAq WShi
- 'Rosenrot'   CRow SWyc
- 'Schneeweisschen' CRow LLWG SWyc

BUXUS ✿ (Buxaceae)
aurea 'Marginata' See *B. sempervirens* 'Marginata'
balearica   CFil CGre EPla SDry SLan WPGP
                   WSHC WWat
bodinieri   EPla SLan WWat
- 'David's Gold'   WEas WSHC
glomerata   SLan
'Green Gem'   EPla LEar NHol SLan
'Green Mountain'   SLan
'Green Velvet'   LPan NHol SLan WWeb
harlandii hort. EPla GAri LEar SIng SLan SRiv
- 'Richard'   SLan STre
henryi   SLan
japonica 'Nana' See *B. microphylla*
jaucoensis   Last listed 1999
leonii   SLan
macowanii   SLan
macrophylla   See *B. sinica* var. *insularis* 'Winter
  'Asiatic Winter' Gem'
§ *microphylla*   CBlo CSWP GDra LPan MHer
                   NHol NWea SIde SIng SLan STre
§ - 'Compacta'   CFil SLan SRiv
- 'Curly Locks'   EPla GAri MHer NHol SLan
- 'Faulkner'   CChe EBee EMil ENot EPfP EPla
                   ERea LEar LHop LPan LRHS MBlu
                   MBri NFla NHol SLan SRiv WBcn
                   WLRN WWeb
- 'Grace Hendrick Phillips' SLan
¶ - 'Green Jade'   SLan
- 'Green Pillow'   CLTr NHol SLan SRiv
- 'Helen Whiting' SLan
- var. *insularis* See *B. sinica* var. *insularis*
- var. *japonica* SLan
- - 'Aurea'   Last listed 1997
- - 'Gold Dust'   SLan
- - 'Morris Dwarf' SLan
- - 'Morris Midget' IArd NHol SLan
- - 'National'   SLan WPGP
- - 'Variegata'   Last listed 1998
- - f. *yakushima* SLan
- 'John Baldwin'   SLan SRiv WBcn
- var. *koreana*   See *B. sinica* var. *insularis*
- var. *riparia*   See *B. riparia*
- var. *sinica*   See *B. sinica*
- 'Winter Gem'   See *B. sinica* var. *insularis* 'Winter
                   Gem'
'Newport Blue'   See *B. sempervirens* 'Newport
                   Blue'
§ *riparia*   EPla SLan
* *rugulosa* var. *intermedia* SLan
sempervirens ♀   More than 30 suppliers

§ - 'Angustifolia' EPla MHer NHol SLan SMad
¶ - 'Arborescens' LPan
- 'Argentea' See *B. sempervirens*
'Argenteovariegata'
§ - 'Argenteovariegata' CBlo EPfP GKir MRav SLan WBcn
WFar WSHC
- 'Aurea' See *B. sempervirens*
'Aureovariegata'
- 'Aurea Maculata' See *B. sempervirens*
'Aureovariegata'
- 'Aurea Marginata' See *B. sempervirens* 'Marginata'
- 'Aurea Pendula' (v) EPla SLan SLon WWye
§ - 'Aureovariegata' More than 30 suppliers
¶ - 'Bentley Blue' NHol
- 'Blauer Heinz' CSev EMil LEar LRHS MAsh MBri
MHer MTed SLan SRiv
§ - 'Blue Cone' GBin LEar NHol
- 'Blue Spire' See *B. sempervirens* 'Blue Cone'
- clipped ball LPan
- clipped pyramid LPan
§ - 'Elegantissima' (v) ♀ More than 30 suppliers
- 'Gold Tip' See *B. sempervirens* 'Notata'
¶ - 'Golden Frimley' (v) LHop
§ - 'Graham Blandy' LEar LPan NHol SLan SRiv WBcn
- 'Greenpeace' See *B. sempervirens* 'Graham
Blandy'
- 'Handsworthiensis' EBee EMil LEar SEND SLan SPer
- 'Handsworthii' CBlo CTri ERea NWea SRms
- subsp. *byrcana* SLan
- 'Ickworth Giant' SLan
- 'Inverewe' SLan
- 'Japonica Aurea' See *B. sempervirens* 'Latifolia
Maculata'
- 'Kensington Gardens' SLan
- 'Kingsville' See *B. microphylla* 'Compacta'
- 'Kingsville Dwarf' See *B. microphylla* 'Compacta'
- 'Lace' NHol NSti SLan
§ - 'Langley Beauty' SLan WBcn
- 'Langley Pendula' See *B. sempervirens* 'Langley
Beauty'
- 'Latifolia Macrophylla' GAbr SEas SLan SLon
§ - 'Latifolia Maculata' ♀ CAbP CChe EBee EPfP EPla GDra
LEar LRHS NHol NPer SEas SLan
SRiv STre
* - 'Latifolia Pendula' SLan
- 'Longifolia' See *B. sempervirens* 'Angustifolia'
§ - 'Marginata' ECtt EPla GBar GCHN GKir LHop
MRav NHol NSti SHFr SLan SLon
SRPl WHar WOak WStl
- 'Memorial' GAbr MHer NHol SLan
- 'Myosotidifolia' CFil CMHG EPla NPro SLan SRiv
WPGP WWat
- 'Myrtifolia' CBot EPla MHer NHol SLan
§ - 'Newport Blue' MTed
§ - 'Notata' (v) CSWP ERea GKir MAsh SBrw
SHel SPlb WGor WWal
- 'Parasol' MHer SLan
- 'Pendula' CGre CMHG EPla GKir SLan SLon
SMad WWat
I - 'Pendula Esveld' Last listed 1998
- 'Prostrata' NHol NWea SLan
- 'Pyramidalis' GAbr NBee SLan SMad SRPl
- 'Rosmarinifolia' MRav SLan
- 'Rotundifolia' CLnd EBee LPan MHer NFla SIde
SLan WDin WLRN
- 'Salicifolia Elata' SLan
- 'Silver Beauty' (v) CB&S EMil MGos
- 'Silver Variegated' See *B. sempervirens*
'Elegantissima'
- 'Suffruticosa' ♀ More than 30 suppliers
I - 'Suffruticosa Blue' NHol SVil
- 'Suffruticosa Variegata' CB&S EOHP ERea SRms

- 'Vardar Valley' NPro SLan SRiv
* - 'Variegata' EPfP LRHS SLon
- 'Waterfall' SLan
§ *sinica* SLan WWat
§ - var. *insularis* EPla
- - 'Filigree' EPla NHol SLan WWat
- - 'Justin Brouwers' CSev MHer SLan SRiv
- - 'Pincushion' SLan
- - 'Tide Hill' SLan WBcn
- - 'Winter Beauty' Last listed 1997
§ - - 'Winter Gem' ENot MHer MRav NHol SLPl SLan
wallicbiana CFil EPla SLan WPGP WWat

C

CACALIA (Asteraceae)
atriplicifolia EBee GOrP
firma B&SWJ 4650 WCru
§ *glabra* Last listed 1999
¶ *kiusiana* B&SWJ 5911 WCru

CACCINIA (Boraginaceae)
macrantha IHdy
macranthera var. Last listed 1999
crassifolia

CAESALPINIA (Caesalpiniaceae)
decapetala S&SH 380 Last listed 1999
gilliesii CBot EBee LRHS SOWG
pulcherrima LChe SPlb
- f. *flava* LChe

CAIOPHORA (Loasaceae)
acuminata Last listed 1998
coronata Last listed 1998
§ *lateritia* Last listed 1999
prietea Last listed 1998

CALADENIA (Orchidaceae)
Fairy Floss g. Last listed 1999
latifolia Last listed 1999
menziesii Last listed 1999

CALADIUM (Araceae)
§ *bicolor* (v) MBri
x *hortulanum* See *C. bicolor*
§ *lindenii* (v) MBri

CALAMAGROSTIS (Poaceae)
N x *acutiflora* 'Karl Foerster' CCuc CElw CFri CLon CMea EBee
ECGN ECha EGle EHoe EPPr EPla
GCal GGar GKir GOrn LGre LPan
LRHS MMoz NBea NSti SApp
SCob SDix SMer SPer WWat
WWye
- 'Overdam' (v) More than 30 suppliers
- 'Stricta' EPPr EWsh GKir LGre
argentea See *Stipa calamagrostis*
§ *arundinacea* More than 30 suppliers
§ *brachytricha* CBrm CCuc CElw CHar CKno
EBee ECGN ECha EGle EPGN
EPPr EPla EWes EWsh GBin GOrn
LEdu LGre LHrt LRHS MMoz
NOGN SAga SAsh SMad SMrm
SUsu WHal WPGP
emodensis LPan SApp
§ *epigejos* CInt CNat EMan EPPr GBin LGre
NHol NOGN SWal
- CLD 1325 EPla

varia   EHoe

CALAMINTHA ✿ (Lamiaceae)

alpina   See *Acinos alpinus*
clinopodium   See *Clinopodium vulgare*
cretica   CLyd EMon GBar LHop MGrG
    WPer WWye
- *variegata*   WEas
* 'Fritz Kuhn'   EMan
§ *grandiflora*   More than 30 suppliers
- 'Variegata'   CGle CRow EBee ELan EMan
    EMon EWTr LFis LHop MBro
    MGrG SCob SCro SHDw STes
    WBea WByw WCHb WFar WHer
    WHoo WMaN WRus
megalantha   EMon
§ *nepeta*   CAgr CArn CFri CLon EBee ECha
    ECoo EWFC LAst LGre LRHS
    MCAu MFir MGrG MHer MPEx
    MRav MSte MWgw NBir NBro
    SBla SWat WFar WHal WPer WWin
    WWye
- subsp. *glandulosa*   LRHS WHoo
    ACL 1050/90
- - 'White Cloud'   CGle CHea CSpe EBrP EBre
    ECGN EFou GBar GBuc LBCl LBSe
    LBre LGre LLWP MBBe MBro
    MCAu MSte NTow SBre SLod
    WHoo WMaN WRus WWye
- 'Gottfried Kuehn'   MRav
§ - subsp. *nepeta*   CGle CSev EBee EFou ELan EMon
    EWTr GBar GMac LHop MBri
    MHer MTho NFla NOak NSti SHel
    SPer SRPl SUsu WCHb WHoo
    WRus WSHC WWat WWhi
- - 'Blue Cloud'   CGle CHea CHor EBee ECGN
    ECha EFou LGre MCAu NTow
    SAga SHel SLod SWat WCot
    WMaN WRus WWye
nepetoides   See *C. nepeta* subsp. *nepeta*
officinalis   SRCN
§ *sylvatica*   CAgr NLar
- subsp. *ascendens*   MLLN NCat
- HH&K 163   CElw GBri
I - 'Menthe'   SSvw
vulgaris   See *Clinopodium vulgare*

CALAMOVILFA (Poaceae)

longifolia   Last listed 1997

CALAMUS (Arecaceae)

¶ *acanthospathus*   LPal

CALANDRINIA (Portulacaceae)

caespitosa   Last listed 1998
discolor   LRHS
grandiflora   MLLN WWin
sericea   Last listed 1998
- *alba*   Last listed 1998
sibirica   See *Claytonia sibirica*
umbellata   NPri NWCA SBla WPer WWin
* - *amarantha*   EDAr
¶ - 'Ruby Tuesday'   NPri

CALANTHE (Orchidaceae)

amamiana   EFEx
arisanenesis   EFEx
aristulifera   EFEx LAma
bicolor   See *C. discolor* var. *flava*
biloba   LAma
brevicornu   LAma
caudatilabella   EFEx

chloroleuca   LAma
discolor   EFEx LAma WCot
§ - var. *flava*   CLAP LAma
Grouville g.   SStn
bamata   EFEx
berbacea   LAma
Hizen g.   Last listed 1997
Ishi-zuchi g.   Last listed 1997
japonica   EFEx
Kozu g.   WCot
Kozu hybrids   Last listed 1999
mannii   EFEx LAma
masuca   LAma
nipponica   EFEx LAma
puberula   LAma
reflexa   EFEx LAma WCot
Saint Aubin g.   SStn
Satsuma g.   Last listed 1997
§ *sieboldii*   EFEx LAma LRHS WCot
- Takane hybrids   Last listed 1999
striata   See *C. sieboldii*
tokunoshimensis   EFEx
tricarinata   EFEx LAma WCot
vestita   SStn

CALATHEA (Marantaceae)

albertii   MBri
§ *crocata*   LRHS MBri
'Exotica'   MBri
¶ 'Gemengd'   CHal
'Greystar'   MBri
§ *lancifolia* ♀   Last listed 1990
lietzei   MBri
- 'Greenstar'   MBri
§ *majestica*   LRHS MBri
makoyana ♀   LRHS MBri
* 'Mavi Queen'   MBri
metallica   MBri
* 'Misto'   MBri
oppenheimiana   See *Ctenanthe oppenheimiana*
orbiculata   See *C. truncata*
ornata   See *C. majestica*
picturata 'Argentea'   MBri
- 'Vandenheckei'   MBri
roseopicta   LRHS MBri
§ *truncata*   MBri
veitchiana   LRHS MBri
warscewiczii   MBri
'Wavestar'   LRHS MBri
zebrina ♀   MBri

CALCEOLARIA (Scrophulariaceae)

acutifolia   See *C. polyrhiza*
alba   CPla WCot WElm WLin
arachnoidea   NWCA NWoo
x *banksii*   EBee GQui MFir WCot
bicolor   WCot WWat
§ *biflora*   CLyd EDAr GDra GTou MHer
    WPat
- 'Goldcrest Amber'   WPer
'Camden Hero'   WWat
chelidonioides   MTho
x *clibranii*   Last listed 1999
crenatiflora   NWoo
cymbiflora   Last listed 1998
ericoides   EBee
- JCA 13818   Last listed 1998
falklandica   CGra NLAp NWCA SRms WPer
    WWin
fiebrigiana   Last listed 1998
filicaulis   Last listed 1998
fothergillii   NArg

'Goldcrest' | ECtt EPfP LRHS SRms
'Hall's Spotted' | Last listed 1999
beliantbemoides | Last listed 1998
JCA 13911
birsuta | Last listed 1998
'Hort's Variety' | Last listed 1998
byssopifolia JCA 13648 | Last listed 1998
§ **integrifolia** ♀ | CB&S EBee ELan EMar EMon
| ERav MFir NRog SAga SChu SIng
| SLon SPer SRms WAbe WWat
- var. **angustifolia** ♀ | SDry
- bronze | SPer WAbe
- 'Sunshine' ♀ | CChe
'John Innes' | EBur ECho ESis WCot
'Kentish Hero' | CB&S CElw CHal EBee ELan EOrc
| LHil NPer SChu WCot
lagunae-blancae | Last listed 1998
lanigera | Last listed 1998
mendocina | Last listed 1998
mexicana | SHFr
nivalis JCA 13888 | Last listed 1998
aff. **pavonii** | LHil
perfoliata JCA 13736 | Last listed 1998
pinifolia | Last listed 1999
- JCA 14450 | Last listed 1999
pinnata | Last listed 1998
plantaginea | See C. biflora
§ **polyrbiza** | ECho NNrd NRya NWCA
purpurea | Last listed 1998
rugosa | See C. integrifolia
scabiosifolia | See C. tripartita
¶ 'Snowballs' | NArg
sp. ex P&W 6276 | Last listed 1998
sp. JCA 14128 | Last listed 1998
sp. JCA 14172 | Last listed 1998
'Stamford Park' | Last listed 1999
tenella | ECtt EDAr ELan EPot NMen
| NWCA WAbe
§ **tripartita** | Last listed 1998
uniflora var. **darwinii** | ECho GTou NMen SIng
volckmannii | Last listed 1998
'Walter Shrimpton' | EDAr EPot EWes NWCA

CALDCLUVIA (Cunoniaceae)
paniculata | Last listed 1998

CALEA (Asteraceae)
zacatecbicbi | Last listed 1998

CALENDULA (Asteraceae)
officinalis | CArn ELau EWTr GPoy MChe
| MHer MHew MSal SIde WHbs
| WHer WJek WOak WSel WWye
- 'Fiesta Gitana' ♀ | WJek
- 'Prolifera' | WHer
- 'Variegata' (v) | MSal

CALLA ✿ (Araceae)
aethiopica | See Zantedeschia aethiopica
palustris | CBen CRow CWat ECoo EHon
| EPfP LGuA LPBA MCCP MSta
| NDea SWat SWyc WMAq WWeb

CALLIANDRA (Mimosaceae)
brevipes | See C. selloi
* **emarginata minima** | LRHS SOWG
§ **selloi** | Last listed 1999

CALLIANTHEMUM (Ranunculaceae)
anemonoides | GCrs NHar
coriandrifolium | SBla
kernerianum | GCrs

CALLICARPA (Verbenaceae)
americana var. **lactea** | Last listed 1997
bodinieri | EWTr NBir
- var. **giraldii** | GBin MRav NFla SSta WBod WDin
| WWeb
- - 'Profusion' ♀ | More than 30 suppliers
cathayana | Last listed 1997
dichotoma | CBlo CPle CTrG LRHS MNes
| WBod WCru WOTO WSHC WWat
| WWin
¶ - f. **albifructa** | GIBF
japonica | Last listed 1999
- 'Leucocarpa' | CB&S CBlo CPle EPfP LRHS MRav
| SPan SPer WBcn WWat
kwangtungensis | CMCN
* **trichotoma** | GEil

CALLICOMA (Cunoniaceae)
serratifolia | Last listed 1999

CALLIRHOE (Malvaceae)
digitata | EBee
involucrata | EBee EMan SMad
triangulata | EBee EMan MAvo

CALLISIA (Commelinaceae)
elegans ♀ | CHal
§ **navicularis** | CHal CInt
repens | CHal LRHS MBri

CALLISTEMON ✿ (Myrtaceae)
brachyandrus | Last listed 1998
'Burning Bush' | CB&S SOWG
chisholmii | SOWG
citrinus | CPle EBee ECot ECou EPVP ERav
| ERom GGar GOrc GSki LRHS
| NPer SOWG SPlb SSte SUsu
| WDCP WGwG WHar WWal WWin
- 'Albus' | See C. 'White Anzac'
- 'Canberra' | SOWG
- 'Firebrand' | LRHS SMur
- 'Horse Paddock' | SOWG
- 'Mauve Mist' | CB&S LRHS MAsh SOWG SSta
- 'Reeve's Pink' | SOWG
- 'Splendens' ♀ | More than 30 suppliers
- 'Yellow Queen' | Last listed 1999
coccineus | CGre MSCN
comboynensis | SOWG
'Dawson River Weeper' | SOWG
flavescens | SOWG
flavovirens | SOWG
glaucus | See C. speciosus
¶ 'Injune' | SOWG
'Kings Park Special' | EHol LRHS SOWG
laevis hort. | See C. rugulosus
lanceolatus | CGre
linearifolius | Last listed 1998
linearis ♀ | CBlo CMac CTrC CTri ECou ELan
| EPVP EPfP EPla IOrc LHil LRHS
| MHer SBrw SEas SLim SLon
| SOWG SPlb SRCN SRms SSpi
| WNor
macropunctatus | CGre SOWG SPlb
pachyphyllus | CGre SOWG
- var. **viridis** | Last listed 1998
pallidus | CGre CHEx CMHG CMac CPle
| CWit ELan EPfP IDee LRHS SMur
| SOWG SPan SPer SPlb SSta SSte
- lilac | Last listed 1998
paludosus | See C. sieberi
- pink form | Last listed 1998

pearsonii	SOWG
'Perth Pink'	GSki SOWG SSte
phoeniceus	SOWG
pinifolius	CGre SOWG
– green form	Last listed 1999
– red	Last listed 1999
¶ – 'Sockeye'	SOWG
– yellow	Last listed 1999
pityoides	CGre ECou SOWG WAbe
– alpine form	Last listed 1998
– from Brown's	ECou
Swamp, Australia	
polandii	SOWG
recurvus	Last listed 1998
'Red Clusters'	CB&S ELan ERea GGar GSki LRHS
	SMur SOWG
rigidus	More than 30 suppliers
'Royal Sceptre'	Last listed 1998
§ *rugulosus*	LRHS SOWG
salignus ♀	CDoC CHEx CTrC CTri EPfP GSki
	IOrc ISea LEur MCCP MHer SHFr
	SLim SLod SOWG SPer WDCP
	WGwG WSHC
– 'Ruber'	Last listed 1999
§ *sieberi* ♀	CGre CMHG CTrC ECou EPfP
	GSki LEur NBir SOWG SPan SPlb
	SSpi
§ *speciosus*	CTrC SMur SOWG SPan WLRN
subulatus	CDoC ECou MCCP NLar SAPC
	SArc SOWG SPan SPlb WDCP
teretifolius	SOWG
viminalis	SOWG SPlb
– 'Captain Cook' ♀	ECou ERea LCns LRHS SBrw
	SOWG
– 'Hannah Ray'	NPer SOWG
– 'Harkness'	SOWG
– 'Little John'	CB&S CWSG LRHS SBrw SOWG
– 'Malawi Giant'	SOWG
'Violaceus'	WDCP
viridiflorus	CGre CPle ECou GGar GQui IBlr
	LEur MCCP NCut SBrw SOWG
	SRCN WCru WDCP WWat
§ 'White Anzac'	LRHS SOWG SSte

CALLITRICHE (Callitrichaceae)

autumnalis	See *C. hermaphroditica*
§ *hermaphroditica*	EMFW WMAq
§ *palustris*	CBen ECoo EHon SWyc
verna	See *C. palustris*

CALLITRIS (Cupressaceae)

monticola	Last listed 1998
oblonga	CGre
rhomboidea	CGre

CALLUNA ✿ (Ericaceae)

vulgaris	CKin LRHS MGos MMal
– 'Adrie'	Last listed 1998
– 'Alba Argentea'	Last listed 1998
– 'Alba Aurea'	ECho MBar
– 'Alba Carlton'	Last listed 1998
– 'Alba Dumosa'	Last listed 1998
– 'Alba Elata'	ECho MBar
– 'Alba Elegans'	Last listed 1998
– 'Alba Elongata'	See *C. vulgaris* 'Mair's Variety'
– 'Alba Erecta'	Last listed 1998
– 'Alba Jae'	MBar
– 'Alba Minor'	Last listed 1998
– 'Alba Multiflora'	Last listed 1998
– 'Alba Pilosa'	Last listed 1998
§ – 'Alba Plena' (d)	CMac ECho LRHS MBar WStI
– 'Alba Praecox'	Last listed 1998
– 'Alba Pumila'	MBar
§ – 'Alba Rigida'	LRHS MBar
– 'Alec Martin' (d)	Last listed 1998
– 'Alex Warwick'	Last listed 1998
– 'Alexandra'^PBR	LRHS NHol SCoo
– 'Alicia'^PBR	ECho LRHS
– 'Alieke'	Last listed 1998
– 'Alison Yates'	MBar
– 'Allegretto'	Last listed 1998
– 'Allegro' ♀	LRHS MBar MOke NHol SBod
	WStI
– 'Alportii'	CMac GDra MBar MOke WStI
– 'Alportii Praecox'	ECho LRHS MBar
– 'Alys Sutcliffe'	Last listed 1998
– 'Amanda Wain'	ECho
– 'Amethyst'^PBR	ECho NHol
– 'Amilto'	ECho NHol
– 'Amy'	Last listed 1998
– 'Andrew Proudley'	MBar
– 'Anette'^PBR	ECho LRHS NHol SCoo
– 'Angela Wain'	ECho
– 'Anna'	Last listed 1998
– 'Annabel' (d)	Last listed 1998
– 'Anne Dobbin'	Last listed 1998
– 'Anneke'	Last listed 1998
– 'Annemarie' (d) ♀	CMac EBrP EBre ENot GChr LBCl
	LBSe LBre LRHS MBBe MGos
	NHol SBre SCoo
– 'Anthony Davis' ♀	MBar MOke NHol SBod
– 'Anthony Wain'	Last listed 1998
– 'Anton'	Last listed 1998
– 'Apollo'	Last listed 1998
– 'Applecross' (d)	Last listed 1999
– 'Arabella'^PBR	LRHS NHol
– 'Argentea'	MBar
– 'Ariadne'	Last listed 1998
– 'Arina'	ECho LRHS MBri MOke
– 'Arran Gold'	MBar
– 'Ashgarth Amber'	Last listed 1998
– 'Ashgarth Amethyst'	Last listed 1998
– 'Ashgarth Shell Pink'	Last listed 1998
– 'Asterix'	Last listed 1998
– 'Atalanta'	Last listed 1998
– 'Atholl Gold'	CMac
– 'August Beauty'	ECho MOke
– 'Aurea'	ECho LRHS
– 'Autumn Glow'	ECho
– 'Baby Ben'	Last listed 1998
– 'Barbara Fleur'	Last listed 1998
– 'Barja'	Last listed 1998
– 'Barnett Anley'	ECho
– 'Battle of Arnhem' ♀	MBar
– 'Beechwood Crimson'	Last listed 1999
– 'Ben Nevis'	Last listed 1998
– 'Beoley Crimson'	GDra LRHS MBar MGos
– 'Beoley Gold' ♀	CB&S CTri EBrP EBre EPfP GChr
	GKir LBCl LBSe LBre LRHS MBBe
	MBar MBri MGos MOke NHol
	SBod SBre WStI
– 'Beoley Silver'	Last listed 1999
– 'Bernadette'	Last listed 1998
– 'Betty Baum'	Last listed 1998
– 'Blazeaway'	CMac CTri GDra GKir LRHS MBar
	MBri NHar NHol SBod WStI
– 'Blueness'	Last listed 1998
– 'Bognie'	Last listed 1999
– 'Bonfire Brilliance'	MBar NHar SBod
– 'Boreray'	Last listed 1999
– 'Boskoop'	CMac EBrP EBre LBCl LBSe LBre
	LRHS MBBe MBar MBri NHol
	SBod SBre
– 'Bradford'	Last listed 1998

- 'Braemar'	Last listed 1999
- 'Braeriach'	Last listed 1998
- 'Branchy Anne'	Last listed 1998
- 'Bray Head'	MBar
- 'Brightness'	Last listed 1998
- 'Brita Elisabeth' (d)	Last listed 1998
- 'Bud Lyle'	Last listed 1998
- 'Bunsall'	CMac
- 'Buxton Snowdrift'	Last listed 1998
- 'C.W. Nix'	ECho MBar
- 'Caerketton White'	ECho GChr
- 'Caleb Threlkeld'	ECho NHol
- 'Calf of Man'	Last listed 1998
- 'Californian Midge'	LRHS MBar MGos NHol
- 'Carl Röders' (d)	Last listed 1998
- 'Carmen'	ECho
- 'Carngold'	Last listed 1998
- 'Carole Chapman'	MBar
- 'Carolyn'	Last listed 1998
- 'Catherine Anne'	LRHS
- 'Celtic Gold'	Last listed 1998
- 'Chindit'	Last listed 1998
- 'Christina'	Last listed 1998
- 'Cilcennin Common'	Last listed 1998
- 'Citronella'	Last listed 1998
- 'Clare Carpet'	Last listed 1998
- 'Coby'	Last listed 1998
- 'Coccinea'	CMac ECho MBar
- 'Colette'	Last listed 1998
- 'Con Brio'	LRHS
- 'Copper Glow'	Last listed 1998
- 'Coral Island'	MBar MGos
- 'Corrie's White'	Last listed 1998
- 'Cottswood Gold'	Last listed 1998
- 'County Wicklow' (d) ♀	CTri EBrP EBre EPfP GChr GKir
	LBCl LBSe LBre LRHS MBBe MBar
	MBri MGos MOke NHar NHol
	SBod SBre
- 'Craig Rossie'	Last listed 1998
- 'Crail Orange'	Last listed 1998
- 'Cramond' (d)	ECho GDra LRHS MBar
- 'Cream Steving'	ECho
- 'Crimson Glory'	LRHS MBar NDlv WStI
- 'Crimson Sunset'	WStI
- 'Crowborough Beacon'	Last listed 1998
- 'Cuprea'	EOrn EPfP GDra LRHS MBar MBri
	MOke NHol SBod WStI
- 'Cuprea Select'	Last listed 1998
- 'Dainty Bess'	LRHS MBar NHol SBod WStI
- 'Dark Beauty'PBR (d)	EBrP EBre EOrn LBCl LBSe LBre
	LRHS MBBe MBar MGos NDlv
	NHol SBre WStI
- 'Dark Star' (d) ♀	CMac EBrP EBre EPfP LBCl LBSe
	LBre LRHS MBBe MBar MGos
	MOke NHar NHol SBre SCoo
- 'Darkness' ♀	CB&S CTri EOrn LRHS MBar MBri
	MGos MOke NHar NHol SBod
	SCoo WStI
- 'Darleyensis'	Last listed 1998
- 'Dart's Amethyst'	Last listed 1998
- 'Dart's Beauty'	Last listed 1998
- 'Dart's Brilliant'	Last listed 1998
- 'Dart's Flamboyant'	Last listed 1999
- 'Dart's Gold'	ECho MBar NHar
- 'Dart's Hedgehog'	ECho
- 'Dart's Parakeet'	Last listed 1999
- 'Dart's Parrot'	ECho NHar
- 'Dart's Silver Rocket'	Last listed 1998
- 'Dart's Squirrel'	Last listed 1998
- 'David Eason'	ECho
- 'David Hagenaars'	Last listed 1998
- 'David Hutton'	MBar

- 'David Platt' (d)	Last listed 1998
- 'Denny Pratt'	Last listed 1998
- 'Desiree'	Last listed 1998
- 'Devon' (d)	Last listed 1998
- 'Diana'	Last listed 1998
- 'Dickson's Blazes'	Last listed 1998
- 'Dirry'	Last listed 1999
- 'Doctor Murray's White'	See C. vulgaris 'Mullardoch'
- 'Doris Rushworth'	Last listed 1998
- 'Drum-ra'	GDra MBar SRms
- 'Dunkeld White'	Last listed 1998
- 'Dunnet Lime'	SPlb
- 'Dunnydeer'	Last listed 1998
- 'Dunwood'	MBar
§ - 'Durfordii'	ECho
- 'E.F. Brown'	Last listed 1999
- 'E. Hoare'	MBar
- 'Easter-bonfire'	NHol
- 'Eckart Miessner'	Last listed 1998
- 'Edith Godbolt'	Last listed 1999
- 'Elaine'	ECho
- 'Elegant Pearl'	MBar SBod
- 'Elegantissima'	MOke
- 'Elegantissima Lilac'	Last listed 1998
- 'Elegantissima Walter Ingwersen'	See C. vulgaris 'Walter Ingwersen'
- 'Elkstone'	MBar
- 'Ellen'	Last listed 1998
- 'Else Frye' (d)	Last listed 1998
- 'Elsie Purnell' (d) ♀	EHol LRHS MBar MGos MOke
	NHol SBod SPlb WStI
- 'Emerald Jock'	Last listed 1999
- 'Emma Louise Tuke'	ECho
- 'Eric Easton'	Last listed 1998
- 'Eskdale Gold'	Last listed 1998
- 'Fairy'	CMac MOke
- 'Falling Star'	Last listed 1998
- 'Feuerwerk'	Last listed 1998
§ - 'Finale' ♀	MBar
- 'Findling'	Last listed 1998
- 'Fire King'	MBar
- 'Firebreak'	ECho MBar
- 'Firefly' ♀	CBrm CMac EBrP EBre EOrn EPfP
	GKir LBCl LBSe LBre LRHS MBBe
	MBar MBri MOke NHar SBod SBre
	WStI
- 'Firestar'	Last listed 1998
- 'Flamingo'	EBrP EBre LBCl LBSe LBre LRHS
	MBBe MBar MBri MOke NHar
	NHol SBre
- 'Flatling'	NHol
- 'Flore Pleno' (d)	MBar
- 'Floriferous'	Last listed 1998
- 'Florrie Spicer'	Last listed 1998
- 'Fokko' (d)	Last listed 1998
- 'Fortyniner Gold'	Last listed 1998
- 'Foxhollow Wanderer'	MBar MOke
- 'Foxii'	ECho LRHS MBar
- 'Foxii Floribunda'	ECho LRHS MBar
- 'Foxii Lett's Form'	See C. vulgaris 'Velvet Dome', 'Mousehole'
- 'Foxii Nana'	LRHS MBar NDlv NHar NHol SBod
- 'Foya'	Last listed 1998
- 'Fred J. Chapple'	GKir LRHS MBar MBri MOke SBod WStI
- 'Fréjus'	Last listed 1998
- 'French Grey'	Last listed 1999
- 'Fritz Kircher'PBR	NHol
- 'Gerda'	LRHS
- 'Ginkels Glorie'	Last listed 1998
- 'Glasa'	Last listed 1998

- 'Glen Mashie'   Last listed 1998
- 'Glencoe' (d)   LRHS MBar MBri MOke NHar
- 'Glendoick Silver'   Last listed 1998
- 'Glenfiddich'   MBar
- 'Glenlivet'   MBar
- 'Glenmorangie'   MBar
- 'Gnome Pink'   Last listed 1998
- 'Gold Charm'   Last listed 1998
- 'Gold Finch'   Last listed 1998
- 'Gold Flame'   LRHS MBar SBod
- 'Gold Hamilton' (d)   ECho
- 'Gold Haze' ♀   CB&S CMac EBrP EBre EPfP LBCl
         LBSe LBre LRHS MBBe MBar MBri
         MOke NHol SBod SBre SCoo WStI
- 'Gold Knight'   ECho EOrn LRHS MBar SBod
- 'Gold Kup'   MBar
- 'Gold Mist'   ECho LRHS NDlv
- 'Gold Spronk'   Last listed 1998
- 'Goldcarmen'   ECho
- 'Golden Blazeaway'   ECho
- 'Golden Carpet'   CB&S EOrn LRHS MBar MBri
         MGos MOke NDlv NHar NHol
         SRms WStI
- 'Golden Dew'   Last listed 1998
- 'Golden Dream' (d)   Last listed 1998
- 'Golden Feather'   LRHS MBar MGos SBod
- 'Golden Fleece'   Last listed 1999
- 'Golden Max'   NHar
- 'Golden Rivulet'   LRHS MBar
- 'Golden Turret'   ECho LRHS
- 'Golden Wonder' (d)   ECho
- 'Goldsworth Crimson'   ECho
- 'Goldsworth Crimson   MBar
    Variegated'
- 'Grasmeriensis'   MBar
- 'Great Comp'   MBar
- 'Grey Carpet'   LRHS MBar SBod
- 'Grijsje'   Last listed 1998
- 'Grizzly'   Last listed 1998
- 'Grönsinka'   Last listed 1998
- 'Guinea Gold'   ECho LRHS MBar MBri
§ - 'H.E. Beale' (d)   CB&S CTri EBrP EBre GDra LBCl
         LBSe LBre LRHS MBBe MBar MBri
         MGos MOke NDlv NHar NHol
         SBod SBre
- 'Hamlet Green'   MBar
- 'Hammondii'   SBod WStI
- 'Hammondii Aureifolia'   LRHS MBar MBri MOke
- 'Hammondii Rubrifolia'   LRHS MBar MBri MOke NHar
- 'Harlekin'   Last listed 1998
- 'Harry Gibbon' (d)   Last listed 1998
- 'Harten's Findling'   Last listed 1998
- 'Hatjes Herbstfeuer' (d)   Last listed 1998
- 'Hayesensis'   Last listed 1998
- 'Heidberg'   Last listed 1998
- 'Heidepracht'   Last listed 1998
- 'Heidesinfonie'   Last listed 1998
- 'Heideteppich'   Last listed 1998
- 'Heidezwerg'   Last listed 1998
- 'Helen Gill'   Last listed 1998
- 'Herbert Mitchell'   Last listed 1998
- 'Hester'   Last listed 1998
- 'Hetty'   Last listed 1998
- 'Hibernica'   MBar
- 'Hiemalis'   MBar
- 'Hiemalis Southcote'   See C. vulgaris 'Durfordii'
- 'Highland Cream'   SDys
- 'Highland Rose'   ECho LRHS SPlb
- 'Highland Spring'   SDys
- 'Hilda Turberfield'   Last listed 1998
- 'Hillbrook Orange'   MBar
- 'Hillbrook Sparkler'   Last listed 1998

- 'Hinton White'   Last listed 1998
- f. hirsuta   GKir
- 'Hirsuta Albiflora'   Last listed 1998
- 'Hirsuta Typica'   ECho
- 'Hirta'   MBar SBod
- 'Hollandia'   Last listed 1998
- 'Holstein'   Last listed 1998
- 'Hookstone'   MBar
- 'Hoyerhagen'   Last listed 1998
§ - 'Hugh Nicholson'   NHar
- 'Humpty Dumpty'   ECho NHol
- 'Hypnoides'   Last listed 1998
- 'Ide's Double' (d)   SBod
- 'Inchcolm'   Last listed 1998
- 'Ineke'   MBar
- 'Ingrid Bouter' (d)   Last listed 1998
- 'Inshriach Bronze'   MBar
- 'Iris van Leyen'   ECho LRHS
- 'Islay Mist'   Last listed 1998
- 'Isobel Frye'   MBar
- 'Isobel Hughes' (d)   MBar
- 'J.H. Hamilton' (d) ♀   CB&S CTri GDra LRHS MBar MBri
         MGos NHol SBod SRms WStI
- 'Jan'   Last listed 1998
- 'Jan Dekker'   LRHS MGos NHol SBod
- 'Janice Chapman'   ECho MBar
- 'Japanese White'   Last listed 1998
- 'Jenny'   Last listed 1998
- 'Jill'   Last listed 1998
- 'Jimmy Dyce' (d) ♀   SBod
- 'Joan Sparkes' (d)   LRHS MBar WStI
- 'Jochen'   Last listed 1998
- 'John F. Letts'   LRHS MBar MGos SBod SRms
         WStI
- 'Johnson's Variety'   ECho MBar
- 'Josefine'   Last listed 1998
- 'Joseph's Coat'   Last listed 1998
- 'Joy Vanstone' ♀   CMac LRHS MBar MBri MGos
         MOke NHol
- 'Julia'   Last listed 1999
- 'Julie Ann Platt'   Last listed 1998
- 'Julie Gill'   Last listed 1997
- 'Karin Blum'   Last listed 1998
- 'Kermit'   Last listed 1998
- 'Kerstin'   ECho LRHS NHol SPlb
- 'Kinlochruel' (d) ♀   CMac EPfP GChr GDra LRHS
         MBar MBri MGos MOke NHar
         NHol SBod SRms
- 'Kirby White'   LRHS MBar MBri NDlv NHol
- 'Kirsty Anderson'   LRHS MOke
- 'Kit Hill'   MBar
- 'Kuphaldtii'   MBar
- 'Kuppendorf'   Last listed 1998
- 'Kynance'   MBar
- 'Lady Maithe'   Last listed 1998
- 'Lambstails'   MBar
- 'L'Ancresse'   Last listed 1998
- 'Late Crimson Gold'   Last listed 1998
- 'Lemon Gem'   Last listed 1998
- 'Lemon Queen'   Last listed 1998
- 'Leprechaun'   ECho
- 'Leslie Slinger'   LRHS MBar
- 'Lewis Lilac'   Last listed 1998
- 'Liebestraum'   Last listed 1998
- 'Lime Glade'   ECho
- 'Limelight'   Last listed 1998
- 'Llanbedrog Pride' (d)   MBar
- 'Loch Turret'   EOrn MBar MBri MOke
- 'Loch-na-Seil'   MBar
- 'London Pride'   Last listed 1998
- 'Long White'   ECho MBar
- 'Lüneberg Heath'   Last listed 1998

- 'Lyle's Late White' Last listed 1999
- 'Lyle's Surprise' MBar
- 'Lyndon Proudley' Last listed 1998
§ - 'Mair's Variety' ♀ GDra LRHS MBar
- 'Mallard' Last listed 1998
- 'Manitoba' Last listed 1998
- 'Marie' Last listed 1998
- 'Marion Blum' MBar
- 'Marleen' MBar NHol SBod
- 'Marlies' NHol
- 'Martha Hermann' Last listed 1998
- 'Masquerade' MBar
- 'Matita' Last listed 1998
- 'Mauvelyn' Last listed 1998
- 'Mazurka' Last listed 1998
- 'Melanie' ECho LRHS NHol
- 'Mick Jamieson' (d) Last listed 1998
- 'Mies' Last listed 1998
- 'Minima' MBar
- 'Minima Smith's Variety' MBar
- 'Mini-öxabäck' Last listed 1998
- 'Minty' Last listed 1998
- 'Mirelle' Last listed 1999
- 'Miss Muffet' NHol
- 'Molecule' MBar
- 'Monika' (d) Last listed 1998
- 'Moon Glow' Last listed 1998
§ - 'Mousehole' LRHS MBar MOke NHol
- 'Mousehole Compact' See C. vulgaris 'Mousehole'
- 'Mrs Alf' Last listed 1998
- 'Mrs E.Wilson' (d) Last listed 1998
- 'Mrs Neil Collins' Last listed 1998
- 'Mrs Pat' LRHS MBar MOke NHol
- 'Mrs Ronald Gray' MBar
- 'Mullach Mor' Last listed 1998
§ - 'Mullardoch' MBar
- 'Mullion' ♀ MBar MOke
- 'Multicolor' CB&S EOrn LRHS MBar MOke
   NDlv NHol SBod SRms
§ - 'My Dream' (d) EPfP LRHS MBar NHol SCoo
- 'Nana' Last listed 1997
- 'Nana Compacta' ESis LRHS MBar MOke SRms
- 'Natasja' Last listed 1998
- 'Naturpark' MBar
- 'Nico' Last listed 1998
- 'Nordlicht' Last listed 1998
- 'October White' Last listed 1999
- 'Oiseval' Last listed 1998
- 'Old Rose' Last listed 1998
- 'Olive Turner' ECho
- 'Olympic Gold' Last listed 1998
- 'Orange and Gold' ECho LRHS
- 'Orange Carpet' Last listed 1998
- 'Orange Max' Last listed 1998
- 'Orange Queen' ♀ LRHS MBar SBod
- 'Öxabäck' MBar
- 'Oxshott Common' GQui MBar
- 'Pallida' ECho
- 'Parsons' Gold' Last listed 1998
- 'Parsons' Grey Selected' Last listed 1998
- 'Pat's Gold' Last listed 1998
- 'Peace' Last listed 1998
- 'Pearl Drop' MBar
- 'Penhale' Last listed 1998
- 'Penny Bun' Last listed 1998
- 'Pepper and Salt' See C. vulgaris 'Hugh Nicholson'
- 'Perestrojka' ECho NHol
- 'Peter Sparkes' (d) CMac EOrn GDra LRHS MBar
   MBri MGos MOke NHar NHol
   SBod SRms
- 'Petra' Last listed 1998

- 'Pewter Plate' MBar
- 'Pink Beale' See C. vulgaris 'H.E. Beale'
- 'Pink Dream' (d) Last listed 1998
- 'Pink Gown' Last listed 1999
- 'Plantarium' Last listed 1998
- 'Platt's Surprise' (d) Last listed 1998
- 'Prizewinner' Last listed 1999
- 'Prostrata Flagelliformis' Last listed 1998
- 'Prostrate Orange' MBar
- 'Punch's Dessert' Last listed 1998
- 'Pygmaea' MBar
- 'Pyramidalis' ECho LRHS
- 'Pyrenaica' MBar
- 'R.A. McEwan' Last listed 1998
- 'Radnor' (d) ♀ LRHS MBar MGos MOke NHar
   SBod
- 'Radnor Gold' (d) MBar
- 'Ralph Purnell' MBar NHar SBod
- 'Ralph Purnell Select' Last listed 1998
- 'Ralph's Pearl' Last listed 1998
- 'Ralph's Red' Last listed 1998
- 'Randall's Crimson' Last listed 1998
- 'Rannoch' Last listed 1998
- 'Red Carpet' LRHS MBar MOke
- 'Red Favorit' (d) LRHS SBod
- 'Red Fred' MGos NHol SCoo
- 'Red Haze' CBrm CMac EPfP LRHS MBar
   MOke NHol SBod WStI
- 'Red Max' Last listed 1998
- 'Red Pimpernel' Last listed 1999
- 'Red Rug' Last listed 1998
- 'Red Star' (d) ♀ LRHS MBar MOke NHol
- 'Red Wings' Last listed 1998
- 'Redbud' ECho
- 'Reini' ECho NHol
- 'Rica' Last listed 1998
- 'Richard Cooper' MBar
- 'Rieanne' Last listed 1998
- 'Rigida Prostrata' See C. vulgaris 'Alba Rigida'
- 'Rivington' Last listed 1998
- 'Robber Knight' ECho
- 'Robert Chapman' ♀ CBrm CMac EBrP EBre EOrn
   GChr LBCl LBSe LBre LRHS MBBe
   MBar MBri MGos MOke NHar
   NHol SBod SBre
- 'Rock Spray' Last listed 1998
- 'Roland Haagen' ♀ MBar MOke NHar
- 'Roma' ECho LRHS MBar
- 'Romina' ECho NHol
- 'Ronas Hill' GDra
- 'Roodkapje' Last listed 1998
- 'Rosalind' LRHS MBar MOke NHol
- 'Rosalind, Crastock Heath'
   Last listed 1998
- 'Rosalind, Underwood's' ECho LRHS
- 'Rosea' Last listed 1998
- 'Ross Hutton' Last listed 1998
- 'Roswitha' ECho
- 'Rotfuchs' Last listed 1998
- 'Ruby Slinger' LRHS MBar SBod
- 'Rusty Triumph' SBod
- 'Ruth Sparkes' (d) CMac LRHS MBar MOke NHol
   SBod
- Saint Kilda Group Last listed 1997
- 'Saint Nick' MBar
- 'Salland' Last listed 1998
- 'Sally Anne Proudley' MBar
- 'Salmon Leap' MBar NHol
- 'Sam Hewitt' Last listed 1998
- 'Sampford Sunset' CSam
- 'Sandhammaren' Last listed 1998
- 'Sandwood Bay' Last listed 1998

- 'Sarah Platt' (d) — ECho
- 'Scaynes Hill' — Last listed 1998
- 'Schurig's Sensation' (d) — LRHS MBar MBri MOke NHar
- 'Scotch Mist' — Last listed 1998
- 'Sedloňov' — Last listed 1998
- 'September Pink' — Last listed 1998
- 'Serlei' — LRHS MBar MOke
- 'Serlei Aurea' ♀ — LRHS MBar SBod
- 'Serlei Grandiflora' — MBar
I - 'Serlei Lavender' — ECho
- 'Serlei Purpurea' — Last listed 1998
- 'Serlei Rubra' — Last listed 1998
- 'Sesam' — Last listed 1998
- 'Shirley' — CMac MBar
- 'Silver Cloud' — CMac MBar
- 'Silver Fox' — ECho
- 'Silver King' — LRHS MBar
- 'Silver Knight' — EBrP EBre EOrn LBCl LBSe LBre LRHS MBBe MBar MBri MGos MOke NHar NHol SBod SBre SPlb WStI
- 'Silver Queen' ♀ — EBrP EBre GChr LBCl LBSe LBre LRHS MBBe MBar MBri MOke NHar NHol SBod SBre SRms
- 'Silver Rose' ♀ — LRHS MBar
- 'Silver Sandra' — Last listed 1998
- 'Silver Spire' — MBar
- 'Silver Stream' — LRHS MBar SBod
- 'Sir Anthony Hopkins' — ECho
- 'Sir John Charrington' ♀ — CB&S CMac EBrP EBre EOrn GDra GKir LBCl LBSe LBre LRHS MBBe MBar MBri MGos MOke NHol SBod SBre WStI
- 'Sirsson' — MBar MBri
- 'Sister Anne' ♀ — EBrP EBre LBCl LBSe LBre LRHS MBBe MBri MGos MOke NDlv NHol SBod SBre SRms
- 'Skipper' — ECho MBar
- 'Snowball' — See C. vulgaris 'My Dream'
- 'Snowflake' — Last listed 1998
- 'Soay' — MBar SBod
- 'Sonja' (d) — Last listed 1999
- 'Sonning' (d) — Last listed 1998
- 'Sonny Boy' — Last listed 1998
- 'Spicata' — Last listed 1998
- 'Spicata Aurea' — MBar
- 'Spider' — ECho
- 'Spitfire' — LRHS MBar NHol WStI
- 'Spook' — Last listed 1998
- 'Spring Cream' ♀ — EBrP EBre LBCl LBSe LBre LRHS MBBe MBar MBri MGos MOke NHar NHol SBod SBre WStI
- 'Spring Glow' — CMac LRHS MBar MBri MOke NHar SBod
- 'Spring Torch' — CB&S EBrP EBre EOrn GDra LBCl LBSe LBre LRHS MBBe MBar MBri MGos MOke NHar NHol SBod SBre SCoo WStI
- 'Springbank' — MBar
- 'Stag's Horn' — Last listed 1998
- 'Stefanie' — Last listed 1998
- 'Stranger' — Last listed 1998
- 'Strawberry Delight' (d) — CB&S NHol
- 'Summer Elegance' — Last listed 1998
- 'Summer Orange' — LRHS MBar NHol
- 'Sunningdale' — See C. vulgaris 'Finale'
- 'Sunrise' — LRHS MBar MGos MOke NHol SBod WStI
- 'Sunset' ♀ — CBrm EBrP EBre GDra LBCl LBSe LBre LRHS MBBe MBar NHol SBod SBre SRms WStI
- 'Sunset Glow' — Last listed 1998

- 'Talisker' — ECho
- 'Tenella' — Last listed 1998
- 'Tenuis' — ECho MBar
- 'Terrick's Orange' — Last listed 1998
- 'The Pygmy' — Last listed 1998
- 'Tib' (d) ♀ — CB&S CMac LRHS MBar MBri MGos MOke NDlv SBod SRms WStI
- 'Tino' — Last listed 1998
- 'Tom Thumb' — MBar
- 'Tomentosa Alba' — Last listed 1998
- 'Tom's Fancy' — Last listed 1998
- 'Torogay' — Last listed 1998
- 'Torulosa' — Last listed 1998
- 'Tremans' — Last listed 1998
- 'Tricolorifolia' — LRHS NHol SBod
- 'Underwoodii' ♀ — ECho LRHS MBar
§ - 'Velvet Dome' — LRHS MBar MGos SBod
- 'Velvet Fascination' — ECho EPfP LRHS MBar MGos NHol
- 'Violet Bamford' — Last listed 1998
- 'Visser's Fancy' — Last listed 1998
§ - 'Walter Ingwersen' — Last listed 1998
- 'Westerlee Gold' — Last listed 1998
- 'Westerlee Green' — Last listed 1998
- 'Westphalia' — Last listed 1998
- 'White Bouquet' — See C. vulgaris 'Alba Plena'
- 'White Carpet' — MBar
- 'White Coral' (d) — ECho MGos SDys
- 'White Gold' — Last listed 1998
- 'White Gown' — GDra
- 'White Lawn' ♀ — EOrn LRHS MBar MGos NDlv NHol SRms
- 'White Mite' — ECho LRHS MBar
- 'White Princess' — See C. vulgaris 'White Queen'
§ - 'White Queen' — MBar
- 'White Star' (d) — LRHS
- 'Whiteness' — SDys
- 'Wickwar Flame' ♀ — CB&S CBrm CMac EBrP EBre EOrn EPfP GDra LBCl LBSe LBre LRHS MBBe MBar MBri MGos MOke NHar NHol SBod SBre WGwG WStI
- 'Wingates Gem' — Last listed 1998
- 'Wingates Gold' — Last listed 1998
- 'Winter Chocolate' — LRHS MBar MBri MGos MOke NDlv NHol SBod WStI
- 'Winter Fire' — Last listed 1998
- 'Winter Red' — Last listed 1998
- 'Wollmers Weisse' (d) — Last listed 1998
- 'Wood Close' — Last listed 1998
- 'Yellow Basket' — Last listed 1998
- 'Yellow Dome' — Last listed 1999
- 'Yellow One' — Last listed 1998
- 'Yvette's Gold' — Last listed 1998
- 'Yvette's Silver' — Last listed 1998
- 'Yvonne Clare' — Last listed 1998

CALOCEDRUS (Cupressaceae)
§ **decurrens** ♀ — CB&S CDoC CDul CMac CTho CTri EBrP EBre EHul ENot EOrn EPfP GKir IOrc LBCl LBSe LBre LCon LPan MBBe MBar MBlu MBri MGos NWea SBre SLim SPer WFro
- 'Aureovariegata' (v) — CBlo CDoC CKen IOrc LCon LLin LNet LPan LRHS MAsh MBar MBlu MBri NHol NLar SLim
- 'Berrima Gold' — CKen EPfP LRHS
§ - 'Depressa' — CKen
- 'Intricata' — CKen
- 'Nana' — See C. decurrens 'Depressa'
- 'Pillar' — CKen LRHS MBri

CALOCEPHALUS (Asteraceae)
brownii	See *Leucophyta brownii*

CALOCHORTUS (Liliaceae)
albus	EPot LRHS
- var. *rubellus*	ECho EPot GCrs LAma
amabilis	Last listed 1999
amoenus	Last listed 1999
apiculatus	Last listed 1999
argillosus	EPot
barbatus	EPot NWCA
- var. *chihuahuaensis*	Last listed 1997
bruneaunis	Last listed 1998
caeruleus	Last listed 1999
catalinae	EPot
clavatus	EPot
- var. *avius*	EPot
concolor	Last listed 1999
eurycarpus	See *C. nitidus*
excavatus	Last listed 1999
greenei	Last listed 1999
gunnisonii	Last listed 1999
howellii	Last listed 1998
¶ *invenustus*	EPot
kennedyi	Last listed 1997
- JA 9312	Last listed 1999
leichtlinii	Last listed 1999
luteus	EPot LAma WLin
- 'Golden Orb'PBR	CBro ETub GCrs LRHS WCot WPnP
macrocarpus	Last listed 1998
monophyllus	EPot
§ *nitidus*	Last listed 1999
obispoensis	EPot
palmeri	EPot
plummerae JA 94-104	Last listed 1999
pulchellus	Last listed 1998
splendens	LAma
striatus	Last listed 1999
- JA 93-21	Last listed 1999
superbus	CBro EPot GCrs LRHS WPnP
tolmiei	Last listed 1998
umbellatus	Last listed 1997
umpquaensis	GCrs
uniflorus	EPot GCrs LRHS WCot
venustus	CBro EPot GCrs LAma LRHS WLin WPnP
vestae	WCot WLin
¶ 'Violet Queen'	CBro

CALOMERIA (Asteraceae)
§ *amaranthoides*	WJek

CALONYCTION See IPOMOEA

CALOPHACA (Papilionaceae)
grandiflora	Last listed 1998

CALOPOGON (Orchidaceae)
tuberosus	SSpi

CALOPSIS (Restionaceae)
¶ *paniculata*	CTrC

CALOSCORDUM (Alliaceae)
§ *neriniflorum*	EBee EBur

CALOTHAMNUS (Myrtaceae)
blepharospermus	SOWG
gilesii	SOWG
homolophyllus	SOWG
pinifolius	CCpl
quadrifidus	SOWG
rupestris	SOWG
sanguineus	SOWG
validus	SOWG SPlb

CALOTROPIS (Asclepiadaceae)
gigantea	CInt

CALPURNIA (Papilionaceae)
aurea	Last listed 1997

CALTHA ✿ (Ranunculaceae)
'Auenwald'	CLAP CRDP CRow
'Honeydew'	CLAP CRDP CRow EBee GBuc NCat
howellii	WLin
introloba	SWat
laeta	See *C. palustris* var. *palustris*
leptosepala	CLAP CRow
- NNS 9420	EPot
natans	CRow
palustris ♀	More than 30 suppliers
- var. *alba*	More than 30 suppliers
- 'Flore Pleno' (d) ♀	More than 30 suppliers
- var. *himalensis*	GCrs NTow WCot
- 'Marilyn'	CLAP CRDP NCat
- 'Multiplex' (d)	COtt WLin WViv
§ - var. *palustris*	CBen CBre CRDP CRow ECha EHon ELan EMFW EMon EPar GAri GGar LPBA MSta NDea SLon SSpi SWat WFar WMAq
- - 'Plena' (d)	COIW CRow CSam CWat ENot EPfP GDea LRHS WElm WFar WMAq WWat
- var. *radicans*	CRow EMFW GCrs SSpi
- 'Semiplena' (d)	EMon
- 'Stagnalis'	CRow SWyc
- 'Tyermannii'	CRow
- 'Wheatfen'	Last listed 1997
N *polypetala* Hochst.	CLAP EBee EMFW
N - hort.	See *C. palustris* var. *palustris*
sagittata	CRow
- JCA 2.198.200	SSpi
scaposa ACE 2139	EPot
'Susan'	CRow

CALYCANTHUS (Calycanthaceae)
chinensis	CPle SRPl
fertilis	See *C. floridus* var. *glaucus*
- 'Purpureus'	See *C. floridus* var. *glaucus* 'Purpureus'
floridus	CArn CB&S CBlo CFil CMCN CPMA CPle EBee ELan EPfP GVer IOrc LRHS MBNS MBlu MDun MWhi SPan SPer WBod WDin WLRN WWat WWin
§ - var. *glaucus*	CFil EBee EPfP LBuc MBel MBlu SPer WSHC
§ - - 'Purpureus'	CPMA MBlu NEgg
- var. *laevigatus*	See *C. floridus* var. *glaucus*
occidentalis	CArn CB&S CCHP CFil CGre CMCN CPle EMil LRHS MBlu SSpi

CALYDOREA (Iridaceae)
speciosa	See *C. xiphioides*
§ *xiphioides*	EWes

CALYPSO (Orchidaceae)
bulbosa	Last listed 1997

CALYPTRIDIUM (Portulacaceae)
umbellatum   See *Spraguea umbellata*

CALYSTEGIA (Convolvulaceae)
¶ **affinis**   CPlN
collina subsp. **venusta**   WCot
hederacea   WFar
§ - 'Flore Pleno' (d)   CPlN CSpe EBee ECha ELan EMon
        EOrc EPar GMac LHop MTho
        SMad WCot WFar WHer WWin
japonica 'Flore Pleno'   See *C. hederacea* 'Flore Pleno'
macrostegia subsp.   WCot
    cyclostegia
pulchra   WCru
silvatica 'Incarnata'   EBee EMon EOrc EWes
tuguriorum   Last listed 1997

CAMASSIA ✿ (Hyacinthaceae)
cusickii   More than 30 suppliers
- 'Zwanenburg'   EBee LRHS WCDu
esculenta   See *C. quamash*
fraseri   See *C. scilloides*
leichtlinii hort.   See *C. leichtlinii* subsp. *suksdorfii*
N - 'Alba' hort.   See *C. leichtlinii* subsp. *leichtlinii*
* - 'Alba Plena'   Last listed 1998
- 'Blauwe Donau'   See *C. leichtlinii* subsp. *suksdorfii*
        'Blauwe Donau'
- Blue Danube   See *C. leichtlinii* subsp. *suksdorfii*
        'Blauwe Donau'
- 'Electra'   ECha LPio MRav
§ - subsp. **leichtlinii** ♀   More than 30 suppliers
N - 'Plena' (d)   ECha
- 'Semiplena' (d)   CAvo CBro CFai CLAP CMea CMil
        CRDP EBee EMon EPar LPio LRHS
        MBNS SAga WCot WIvy WPnP
§ - subsp. **suksdorfii**   CAvo CBro EPPr EPar GBuc LBow
        LRHS MLan SAga SPer
§ - - 'Blauwe Donau'   EMon LAma LBow LRHS MGed
- - Caerulea Group   CBro CHad CHar CMdw CMea
        CMil CRDP EBee ECha ELan EMan
        EMon EOld EPar EPfP EWTr ISea
        LAma LRHS MMal MNrw NRog
        SAga SGar SUsu WAbb WCot WHil
        WHoo WPGP
§ **quamash**   CAvo CBro CHar CLAP EBee ECha
        EMon EPar ETub EWTr GSki LAma
        LBow LEdu LRHS MBri MTho
        NBir NRog SPar SRms WBea
        WByw WFar WLin WShi
- 'Blue Melody' (v)   CBro CMea CMil EBee GBuc
        LRHS WCot WHil WPnP
- subsp. **linearis**   NHol
- 'Orion'   CBro CLAP CMea CSWP EMon
        GBuc LRHS MAvo WCot
§ **scilloides**   MBri

CAMELLIA ✿ (Theaceae)
'Auburn White'   See *C. japonica* 'Mrs Bertha A.
        Harms'
'Barbara Clark'   CTrG LRHS MGos SCog
    (*saluenensis* x
    reticulata)
¶ 'Barbara Hillier' x *C.*   CDoC
    japonica 'Juno'
'Barbara Hillier'
    (*reticulata* x *japonica*)   CTre SStn
'Bertha Harms Blush'   See *C. japonica* 'Mrs Bertha A.
        Harms'
'Betty Ridley' (hybrid)   SStn
'Black Lace' (*reticulata* x   CDoC CTrh MBri SCam SCog SLdr
    williamsii)   SStn WGwG WLRN

'Bonnie Marie' (hybrid)   CCHP CTre SCog SStn
'Charles Cobb'   See *C. japonica* 'Mrs Charles
        Cobb'
'China Lady' (*reticulata* x   Last listed 1997
    granthamiana)
'Christmas Daffodil'   Last listed 1999
    (*japonica* hybrid)
chrysantha   See *C. nitidissima* var.
        nitidissima
'Cinnamon Cindy' (hybrid)   CDoC
'Contessa Lavinia Maggi'   See *C. japonica* 'Lavinia Maggi'
'Cornish Clay'   ISea
'Cornish Snow' (*japonica*   CB&S CCHP CDoC CGre COtt
    x *cuspidata*) ♀   CSam CTre CTrh EPfP GGGa IOrc
        ISea LNet LRHS SBrw SReu SSpi
        SSta SStn WCwm WWat
'Cornish Spring' (*japonica*   CB&S CDoC COtt CPne CTre
    x *cuspidata*) ♀   CTrh EPfP LRHS WBcn WLRN
        WWat
'Corsica'   Last listed 1998
crapnelliana   CGre
cuspidata   CGre CTre LRHS
'Czar'   See *C. japonica* 'The Czar'
¶ 'Dainty Dale' (hybrid)   NBlu
'Delia Williams'   See *C.* x *williamsii* 'Citation'
'Diamond Head' (*japonica*   LRHS MAsh
    x *reticulata*)
'Doctor Clifford Parks'   CDoC CTre SCog
    (*reticulata* x
    japonica) ♀
'Donckelaeri'   See *C. japonica* 'Masayoshi'
'Dorothy James' (hybrid)   SStn
'El Dorado' (*pitardii* x   CTrG CTrh ECle LRHS
    japonica)
'Extravaganza' (*japonica*   CB&S CTrh IArd SBod SCog SStn
    hybrid)   WBcn
'Fairy Wand' (hybrid)   CDoC
'Faustina Lechi'   See *C. japonica* 'Faustina'
'Felice Harris' (*sasanqua*   SCog
    x *reticulata*)
'First Flush' (*cuspidata* x   Last listed 1997
    saluenensis)
* 'Fishtail White'   Last listed 1997
'Forty-niner' (*reticulata* x   CB&S CDoC SCog
    japonica) ♀
'Fragrant Pink' (*rusticana*   CTrh
    x *lutchuensis*)
'Francie L' (*saluenensis* x   CDoC CGre CTre CTrh SSta
    reticulata)
'Frau Minna Seidel'   See *C. japonica* 'Otome'
'Freedom Bell' (hybrid) ♀   CDoC CTrG CTre CTrh GGGa
        ISea MAsh MBri SBrw SCog SStn
'Gay Baby' (hybrid)   MGos
granthamiana   Last listed 1997
grijsii   CTrh
hiemalis 'Chansonette'   SCog SLdr
§ - 'Dazzler'   CCHP CDoC CTre CTrh SCog
        SStn
- 'Kanjirô'   CTrh
- 'Shôwa-no-sakae'   SCog
- 'Sparkling Burgundy'   CB&S CTre LHyd SCog SStn
'Hooker' (hybrid)   CDoC
'Howard Asper'   Last listed 1997
    (*reticulata* x *japonica*)
'Imbricata Rubra'   See *C. japonica* 'Imbricata'
'Innovation' (x *williamsii*   CB&S CDoC CTre LRHS MGos
    x *reticulata*)   SStn
'Inspiration' (*reticulata*   CB&S CDoC CGre CMHG CMac
    x *saluenensis*) ♀   CTrG CTre CTrh EPfP GGGa GKir
        ISea LHyd LRHS MBri MGos SBod
        SBrw SCam SCog SLdr SSpi SStn
        WBod

japonica 'Aaron's Ruby' CB&S CDoC COtt CTre SStn
- 'Ada Pieper' CTrh
- 'Adelina Patti' CB&S CDoC CTre CTrh SCog SStn WCwm
¶ - 'Adelina Patti' carmine sport SStn
- 'Adolphe Audusson' ♀ More than 30 suppliers
- 'Adolphe Audusson Special' CB&S
§ - 'Akashigata' ♀ CDoC CTrG CTre CTrw ENot EPfP LRHS MAsh MWat SReu SSta SStn
§ - 'Akebono' CTrw
- 'Alba Plena' CDoC CGre CMac CTre CTrh ENot IOrc LHyd LNet LRHS SBod SCog SPer SStn
- 'Alba Simplex' CB&S CGre CMac CTre CTrh ELan EPfP IOrc LHyd LNet LRHS SBod SCog SPer SSta SStn WLRN WStI
§ - 'Albertii' WBod
- 'Alexander Hunter' ♀ CTre LHyd MAsh SBod SStn
- 'Alice Wood' Last listed 1998
§ - 'Althaeiflora' CB&S CDoC CGre CTre SStn WBod
- 'Ama-no-gawa' Last listed 1997
- 'Anemoniflora' CB&S CDoC CTrG CTre EBee ELan LRHS SBod SLdr SPer WBod
- 'Angel' CB&S CDoC CTre SCog SStn
- 'Angela Cocchi' Last listed 1998
- 'Ann Sothern' CTrh
- 'Annie Wylam' CTrh SCog
§ - 'Apollo' CB&S CDoC CSam CTrG CTrh EPfP LRHS MAsh MGos SBrw SPer SStn WBcn WBod
§ - 'Apple Blossom' ♀ CGre CMac ELan LRHS SStn
- 'Arabella' Last listed 1997
- 'Arajishii' See C. rusticana 'Arajishii'
* - 'Augustine Supreme' CMac
- 'Augusto Leal de Gouveia Pinto' CTre SStn
- 'Australis' CTrh WBod
- 'Ave Maria' CTrh
- 'Azurea' CGre
- 'Baby Sis' Last listed 1999
- 'Ballet Dancer' ♀ CDoC LRHS MGos SLdr SStn WBcn WGwG
- 'Barbara Woodroof' Last listed 1997
- 'Baron Gomer' See C. japonica 'Comte de Gomer'
- 'Baronne Leguay' LRHS SStn
- 'Beau Harp' SStn WBod
- 'Bella Romana' SStn WBod
- 'Benidaikagura' SStn
- 'Benihassaku' SStn
- 'Benten' (v) CTrG CTrw
- 'Berenice Boddy' ♀ CB&S CTrh SStn
- 'Berenice Perfection' LRHS SStn
- 'Bertha Raressi' WBod
- 'Betty Foy Sanders' CTrh
- 'Betty Sheffield' CCHP CDoC CGre COtt CTrG CTre MGos SBod SCog
- 'Betty Sheffield Blush' Last listed 1998
- 'Betty Sheffield Coral' Last listed 1997
- 'Betty Sheffield Pink' CTrG SStn
- 'Betty Sheffield Supreme' CB&S CDoC CGre LRHS SCog
- 'Betty Sheffield White' Last listed 1997
- 'Bienville' Last listed 1997
- 'Billie McCaskill' SStn
¶ - 'Black Tie' CBrm MAsh
- 'Blackburnia' See C. japonica 'Althaeiflora'
- 'Blaze of Glory' CDoC CGre CTrh WBcn

§ - 'Blood of China' CB&S CDoC COtt EBee LRHS MAsh SBod SPer SStn WBod WCwm
- 'Bob Hope' ♀ CB&S CDoC CGre CTre CTrh ECle LRHS MAsh MGos SCog SStn
- 'Bob's Tinsie' ♀ CB&S CDoC CGre CTre CTrw ECle EPfP LRHS
§ - 'Bokuhan' CCtw CGre CTre SStn
- 'Bonomiana' Last listed 1998
- 'Brushfield's Yellow' CB&S CDoC CGre CMHG COtt ECle GKir IArd IMGH MGos SPer SSta SStn
- 'Bush Hill Beauty' See C. japonica 'Lady de Saumarez'
§ - 'C.M. Hovey' ♀ CMHG CMac CTrh EPfP MAsh MNes SStn WBcn WBod WGwG
- 'C.M.Wilson' ♀ CMac CTre SStn
N - 'Campbellii' WBod
- 'Campsii Alba' LRHS WStI
- 'Can Can' CB&S CDoC CTrG SCam SCog SSht
- 'Canon Boscawen' CTrG
- 'Cara Mia' CB&S CTre SStn WBod
- 'Cardinal Variegated' SStn
- 'Cardinal's Cap' CGre
- 'Carolyn Tuttle' CDoC
- 'Carter's Sunburst' ♀ CB&S CDoC CTrh EPfP SStn
- 'Cécile Brunazzi' SCog
- 'Chandleri' SStn
- 'Chandleri Elegans' See C. japonica 'Elegans'
- 'Charlie Bettes' SStn
- 'Charlotte de Rothschild' CTrh CTri MBri
- 'Cheerio' Last listed 1997
- 'Cheryll Lynn' CTrh MAsh SStn WBod
- 'Christmas Beauty' WBod
- 'Cinderella' CDoC CTre SCog SStn
- 'Clarise Carleton' CTre CTrh
- 'Clarissa' SStn
§ - 'Coccinea' LRHS
- 'Colonel Firey' See C. japonica 'C.M. Hovey'
- 'Colonial Dame' Last listed 1997
- 'Commander Mulroy' CTrh SStn WBcn
- 'Compton's Brow' See C. japonica 'Gauntlettii'
§ - 'Comte de Gomer' CGre ELan EPfP LRHS SLdr SSta WBcn
- 'Conrad Hilton' Last listed 1997
- 'Conspicua' CB&S
§ - 'Coquettii' ♀ CB&S CCHP CDoC CTre WBod
- 'Coral Pink Lotus' SStn
- 'Coral Queen' SStn
- 'Countess of Orkney' CTre WBcn
- 'Daikagura' CDoC
- 'Dainty' CB&S WBcn
- 'Daitairin' See C. japonica 'Dewatairin'
- 'Dear Jenny' CB&S CTrG CTre SCog
- 'Debbie' CDoC WGwG
- 'Debutante' CB&S CGre CMac CTre CTrh LHyd LRHS MAsh MBri SStn WBcn WBod
- 'Deep Secret' CDoC
- 'Desire' CB&S CDoC CMHG CTrh ECle LRHS SCog
- 'Devonia' CB&S EPfP LHyd LRHS WBod
§ - 'Dewatairin' CMac SStn WBod
- 'Dixie Knight' CDoC LRHS SCam SLdr SSta
- 'Dobreei' CMac WBod WGer WWal
- 'Doctor Burnside' CB&S CMHG CTrh SCog SStn
- 'Doctor Tinsley' ♀ CDoC CGre CTrh LRHS SStn WBcn
- 'Dona Herzilia de Freitas Magalhaes' CTre SStn WBcn
- 'Dona Jane Andresson' SStn

- 'Donckelarii'   See *C. japonica* 'Masayoshi'
- 'Donnan's Dream'   CTrh
- 'Double Rose' (d)   Last listed 1998
- 'Doutor Balthazar   Last listed 1997
  de Mello'
- 'Drama Girl' ♀   CB&S CDoC CGre CTre CTrw
  IOrc LRHS SBod SStn WBod
- 'Duc de Bretagne'   ISea
- 'Duchesse Decazes'   CB&S COtt CTre SStn
- 'Duchesse Decazes Pink'   SStn
¶ - 'Duckyls Belle'   SStn
- 'Effendee'   See *C. sasanqua* 'Rosea Plena'
- 'Eleanor Grant'   SStn
- 'Eleanor Hagood'   CB&S CGre WBcn
§ - 'Elegans' ♀   CB&S CDoC CGre CHig CMac
  CTrG CTre ENot EPfP IOrc LHyd
  LRHS MAsh MWat SBod SBrw
  SCog SLdr SPer SReu SSta SStn
  WBcn
- 'Elegans Champagne'   CTrh LRHS SCog WBcn
- 'Elegans Splendor'   CTre SStn WBcn
- 'Elegans Supreme'   CGre CTre
- 'Elegant Beauty'   See *C. x williamsii* 'Elegant
  Beauty'
- 'Elisabeth'   WBod
- 'Elizabeth Arden'   CTre WBod
- 'Elizabeth Dowd'   CB&S SCog
- 'Elizabeth Hawkins'   CTre CTrh EBee WLRN
- 'Ella Drayton'   SCog
- 'Ellen Sampson'   Last listed 1998
- 'Emmett Barnes'   SStn
- Emmett Pfingstl™ (v)   SStn WBcn
- 'Emperor of Russia'   CB&S CDoC ELan LRHS SStn
  WBod
- 'Erin Farmer'   CB&S SCog
- 'Eugene Bolen'   SStn
- 'Eugène Lizé'   SStn
- 'Evelyn'   SStn
- 'Eximia'   WBod
- 'Extravaganza Pink'   SStn
- 'Faith'   MAsh SStn
- 'Fashionata'   SCam SStn
- 'Fatima'   CTre
§ - 'Faustina'   Last listed 1997
- 'Feast Perfection'   CDoC
§ - 'Fimbriata'   SStn
- 'Fimbriata Alba'   See *C. japonica* 'Fimbriata'
- 'Finlandia Variegated'   Last listed 1998
- 'Fire Dance'   CTrh
- 'Fire Falls'   LRHS
- 'Flame'   CB&S CDoC WBod
¶ - 'Flashlight'   MAsh
§ - 'Fleur Dipater'   SStn
- 'Flowerwood'   SStn
- 'Forest Green'   ELan LRHS MAsh SBrw SCog
- 'Frans van Damme'   SStn
- 'Fred Sander'   EBee SStn
¶ - 'Frizzle White'   WBod
- 'Frosty Morn'   CB&S
- 'Furo-an'   MAsh SStn
§ - 'Gauntlettii'   SStn WBod
- 'Gay Chieftain'   WBod
- 'Geisha Girl'   CDoC SStn
- 'Général Lamoricière'   CDoC
- 'Giardino Franchetti'   CGre CMHG
§ - 'Gigantea'   SStn WBod
§ - 'Gigantea Red'   IOrc
- 'Giuditta Rosani'   CDoC
- 'Gladys Wannamaker'   Last listed 1998
- 'Glen 40'   See *C. japonica* 'Coquettii'
- 'Gloire de Nantes' ♀   CB&S CGre MNes SStn WBcn
* - 'Golden Wedding'   LRHS MAsh

- 'Goshoguruma'   WBod
- 'Grace Bunton'   CB&S CDoC SCam
- 'Granada'   SCog
- 'Grand Prix' ♀   CDoC CTrh CTrw LRHS SLdr SSta
  SStn WBod
- 'Grand Slam' ♀   CB&S CDoC CMac CTre CTrh
  LRHS MAsh SStn WBcn
- 'Grand Sultan'   SStn
- 'Great Eastern'   CDoC WBod
- 'Guest of Honor'   CB&S COtt LRHS
- 'Guilio Nuccio' ♀   CB&S CDoC CTrG CTre EBee
  IArd LRHS MGos SCog SPer SStn
  WBod
- 'Gus Menard'   SStn
- 'Gwenneth Morey'   CB&S CTre EPfP SStn
- 'H.A. Downing'   SStn
§ - 'Hagoromo' ♀   CDoC CGre ELan ENot EPfP LRHS
  MAsh SPer SStn WBcn WBod
  WWat
- 'Hakurakuten' ♀   CCHP CDoC CTre CTrh EHol ISea
  SBod SCog SStn WBod
- 'Hanafûki'   CDoC CTre LRHS SStn WBod
- 'Hanatachibana'   SStn WBcn
- 'Hatsuzakura'   See *C. japonica* 'Dewatairin'
- 'Hawaii'   CB&S CMac CTre CTrh LRHS
  SCog SStn
- 'Henry Turnbull'   SStn
- Herme   See *C. japonica* 'Hikarugenji'
- 'High Hat'   CB&S LHyd SLdr SStn WBod
§ - 'Hikarugenji'   CDoC SCam
- 'Hime-otome'   SStn
- 'Hinomaru'   CMac LRHS
- 'Holly Bright'   CTrh
§ - 'Imbricata'   CCHP CTre ENot MAsh MGos
  SCog
- 'Imbricata Alba'   SBrw SCog SSta SStn
- 'In the Pink'   Last listed 1998
- 'Italiana Vera'   Last listed 1998
- 'J.J. Whitfield'   CMac SStn
- 'Jack Jones Scented'   CMHG
- 'Janet Waterhouse'   CB&S SCog SStn WWat
§ - 'Japonica Variegata'   CGre CMHG WBcn
- 'Jean Clere'   CTrG MGos SStn WBcn
- 'Jean Lyne'   Last listed 1997
- 'Jingle Bells'   Last listed 1998
- 'Joseph Pfingstl'   CDoC CGre CTre LRHS SLdr SStn
  WBod
- 'Joshua E.Youtz'   LHyd LRHS
- 'Jovey Carlyon' (hybrid)   CDoC
- 'Joy Sander'   See *C. japonica* 'Apple Blossom'
§ - 'Julia Drayton'   LRHS MAsh SStn
- 'Julia France'   CB&S
- 'Juno'   CB&S
- 'Jupiter' ♀   CB&S CDoC CMac CTre CTrh
  CTri CTrw EBee EPfP ISea LHyd
  LNet LRHS MAsh MGos SCog SStn
  WBod
- 'Just Sue'   CDoC
- 'Justine Heurtin'   SStn
- 'K. Sawada'   Last listed 1997
- 'Katherine Nuccio'   SStn
- 'Katie'   Last listed 1998
- 'Kay Truesdale'   SStn
- 'Kellingtoniana'   See *C. japonica* 'Gigantea'
- 'Kenny'   CB&S WBod
- 'Kewpie Doll'   CDoC CTrh SCog
- 'Kick-off'   CB&S CTrh SStn
- 'Kimberley'   CB&S EPfP SCog WBcn WBod
  WLRN
- 'King's Ransom'   CDoC CMac LHyd WBod
§ - 'Kingyo-tsubaki'   CGre SSta
- 'Kinsekai'   See *C. rusticana* 'Kinsekai'

- 'Kitty' SCog
- 'Kitty Berry' CTrh SStn
- 'Kokinran' SStn
§ - 'Konronkoku' ♀ CDoC SCog SStn WBcn
- 'Kouron-jura' See *C. japonica* 'Konronkoku'
- 'Kramer's Beauty' LRHS SCog
- 'Kramer's Supreme' CBrm CCHP CDoC CGre CTrG
LNet MGos SBod SBrw SCog SStn
WCot WLRN
§ - 'Kumasaka' WBod
- 'La Graciola' See *C. japonica* 'Odoratissima'
- 'La Pace' SStn
- 'La Pace Rubra' SStn
- 'Lady Campbell' SStn
- 'Lady Clare' See *C. japonica* 'Akashigata'
§ - 'Lady de Saumarez' ♀ CDoC LNet SBod SStn
- 'Lady de Saumarez' white CGre
- 'Lady Erma' CB&S
- 'Lady Loch' CCHP CTre CTrh MGos SCog SStn
- 'Lady Mackinnon' MAsh
- 'Lady Marion' See *C. japonica* 'Kumasaka'
- 'Lady McCulloch' Last listed 1997
- 'Lady Vansittart' CB&S CBrm CDoC CSam CTrG
CTre EBee ELan ENot EPfP ISea
LHyd LNet LRHS SBod SBrw SCog
SPer SStn WBcn WBod
§ - 'Lady Vansittart Pink' MGos SBod SCam SLdr
- 'Lady Vansittart Red' See *C. japonica* 'Lady Vansittart
Pink'
- 'Lady Vansittart Shell' See *C. japonica* 'Yours Truly'
- 'Lanarth' CTre
- 'Latifolia' CTre
- 'Laurie Bray' CGre
§ - 'Lavinia Maggi' ♀ CDoC CGre CTrG CTre CTrh
ELan EPfP IOrc LHyd LPan LRHS
MBri MGos SBod SBrw SCog SPer
SReu SRms SSta SStn
- 'Lavinia Maggi Rosea' SCog SStn
- 'L'Avvenire' Last listed 1997
§ - 'Le Lys' SStn
- 'Lemon Drop' CTrh
- 'Lily Pons' CTrh
- 'Lipstick' CTrh
- 'Little Bit' CB&S CDoC CTrh SSta
- 'Little Bo Peep' CTrh
- 'Little Red Riding Hood' Last listed 1999
- 'Little Slam' Last listed 1999
- 'Look-away' Last listed 1997
- 'Lotus' See *C. japonica* 'Gauntlettii'
- 'Lovelight' CTrh ISea SCog WCot
- 'Lucy Hester' CTre
- 'Lulu Belle' Last listed 1999
- 'Ma Belle' CMHG SCog
- 'Mabel Blackwell' SStn
- 'Madame Charles Blard' Last listed 1998
- 'Madame de Cannart SStn
d'Hamale'
- 'Madame de Strekaloff' CMac SStn
- 'Madame Lebois' CB&S SStn
- 'Madame Lourmand' Last listed 1998
- 'Madame Martin Cachet' CMHG
- 'Madge Miller' CTre ELan LRHS
- 'Magic City' Last listed 1997
- 'Magnoliiflora' See *C. japonica* 'Hagoromo'
- 'Magnoliiflora Alba' See *C. japonica* 'Miyakodori'
- 'Maiden's Blush' CMac SCog WLRN
- 'Man Size' CDoC ECle
- 'Margaret Davis' CDoC CTrG ECle IMGH MGos
SStn
- 'Margaret Davis Picotee' CB&S CGre CMHG CTrh CTrw
MGos SCog SPer SSta WBcn
- 'Margaret Rose' SStn

- 'Margaret Short' MAsh
- 'Margarete Hertrich' Last listed 1997
- 'Margherita Coleoni' CB&S SBod SBrw SStn WBcn
WBod
- 'Marguérite Gouillon' ISea SStn
- 'Marian Mitchell' SStn
- 'Mariana' Last listed 1999
¶ - 'Mariann' CTrh
- 'Marie Bracey' CB&S SStn
- 'Marinka' CB&S
- 'Mariottii Rubra' Last listed 1997
- 'Marjorie Magnificent' CDoC LRHS MAsh
- 'Mark Alan' CTrh
- 'Maroon and Gold' CDoC WBcn
- 'Mars' ♀ CB&S CDoC CTre LRHS MWat
SBrw SCam SLdr SStn
- 'Mary Costa' CB&S CGre CTrh
- 'Mary J.Wheeler' CTrw
§ - 'Masayoshi' ♀ CDoC CMac CTrG IOrc LHyd
LNet SStn
- 'Masquerade' SStn
- 'Masterpiece' SStn
§ - 'Mathotiana' CTrw LRHS
- 'Mathotiana Alba' ♀ CB&S CDoC CMac LRHS SPer
SReu SSta SStn
- 'Mathotiana Purple King' See *C. japonica* 'Julia Drayton'
§ - 'Mathotiana Rosea' CB&S CMac CTre LNet LRHS
SBod SBrw SStn WBod
- 'Mathotiana Supreme' CDoC LRHS SStn
- 'Matterhorn' CTrh LRHS MAsh WBcn
- 'Mattie Cole' CDoC CGre CTre SStn
- 'Mattie O'Reilly' CTre
- 'Melody Lane' Last listed 1997
- 'Mercury' ♀ CB&S CDoC CMac COtt CTrG
GGGa LRHS MWat SPer WBod
- 'Mercury Variegated' CMHG
- 'Midnight' CB&S CDoC CGre CMHG SCog
SStn
- 'Midnight Magic' Last listed 1998
- 'Midnight Serenade' CDoC CTrh MAsh SStn
- 'Midsummer's Day' CB&S
- 'Mikado' CDoC
§ - 'Mikenjaku' CTrG ENot LNet LRHS MAsh
SBrw SCam SStn WBod
- 'Minnie Maddern Fiske' SStn
- 'Miss Charleston' ♀ CB&S SStn
- 'Miss Lyla' SStn
- 'Miss Universe' CGre CTrh
- 'Mississippi Beauty' CTrh
§ - 'Miyakodori' EPfP LRHS
- 'Momiji-gari' Last listed 1997
- 'Mona Lisa' SStn
- 'Monsieur Faucillon' CB&S
- 'Monstruosa Rubra' See *C. japonica* 'Gigantea Red'
- 'Monte Carlo' CDoC
- 'Moonlight Bay' Last listed 1997
- 'Morning Glow' WBod
- 'Moshe Dayan' EBee
§ - 'Mrs Bertha A. Harms' CGre
§ - 'Mrs Charles Cobb' LPan
- 'Mrs D.W. Davis' ♀ CB&S CGre CTrw LRHS SStn
- 'Mrs Sander' See *C. japonica* 'Gauntlettii'
- 'Mrs Tingley' SStn
- 'Mrs William Thompson' NBlu WBod
I - 'Mutabilis' WBcn
- 'Nagasaki' See *C. japonica* 'Mikenjaku'
- 'Nigra' See *C. japonica* 'Konronkoku'
- 'Nobilissima' CB&S CDoC CMac CTrG CTre
CTrh CTri ECle ENot ISea LRHS
MAsh MWat SBod SBrw SCog
SPer SSta SStn WBcn WBod WWeb
- 'Nuccio's Cameo' CDoC CTrh MAsh

- 'Nuccio's Gem' ♀	CDoC ELan LHyd LRHS SCog SSta SStn
- 'Nuccio's Jewel' ♀	CDoC COtt CTre CTrh IMGH LRHS MGos SCog SPer WBcn
- 'Nuccio's Pearl'	CB&S LRHS SCog WBcn
§ - 'Odoratissima'	CTrG WBod
- 'Onetia Holland'	CB&S CDoC CTre CTrw SLdr
§ - 'O-niji'	Last listed 1999
- 'Onore Del Monte'	WBod
- 'Optima Rosea'	CB&S CTrG EBee ENot
§ - 'Otome'	SBrw WBod
- 'Painted Lady'	Last listed 1997
- 'Paolina'	Last listed 1997
- 'Paolina Maggi'	CDoC ECle SCog SStn
- 'Patricia Ann'	CTrh
- 'Paulette Goddard'	SStn
- 'Pauline Winchester'	Last listed 1997
- 'Paul's Apollo'	See C. japonica 'Apollo'
- 'Peachblossom'	See C. japonica 'Fleur Dipater'
- 'Pearl Harbor'	SStn
- 'Pensacola Red'	Last listed 1998
- 'Pink Champagne'	CTre LRHS SBod WBod
- 'Pink Clouds'	CB&S
- 'Pink Pagoda'	SStn
- 'Pink Perfection'	See C. japonica 'Otome'
- 'Pink Star'	WBod
- 'Pirate's Gold' (v)	Last listed 1997
- 'Pompone'	Last listed 1997
- 'Pope Pius IX'	See C. japonica 'Prince Eugène Napoléon'
- 'Powder Puff'	CTre
- 'Preston Rose'	CB&S CDoC CTre LRHS SStn WBcn
- 'Pride of Descanso'	See C. japonica 'Yukibotan'
- 'Primavera'	CTrh SStn
- 'Prince Albert'	See C. japonica 'Albertii'
§ - 'Prince Eugène Napoléon'	SStn
- 'Prince of Orange'	SStn
- 'Princess Baciocchi'	CB&S
- 'Princess du Mahe'	CMac
- 'Professor Sargent'	Last listed 1997
- 'Purple Emperor'	See C. japonica 'Julia Drayton'
- 'R.L. Wheeler' ♀	CB&S CDoC CGre CTre CTrw MAsh SCog SStn WBod
- 'Rafia'	CDoC SLdr
- 'Rainbow'	See C. japonica 'O-niji'
- 'Red Cardinal'	SStn
- 'Red Dandy'	CDoC SCam SStn
- 'Red Ensign'	Last listed 1997
- 'Reg Ragland'	CDoC SStn
- 'Reigyoku'	See C. rusticana 'Reigyoku'
- 'Robert Strauss'	SStn
- 'Roger Hall'	LRHS SCog WOTO
- 'Rôgetsu'	CB&S CGre SStn WBod
- 'Roman Soldier'	CB&S
- 'Rose Dawn'	WBod
- 'Roza Harrison'	LHyd
- 'Rubescens Major' ♀	CB&S CGre ISea LHyd SStn WBod
- 'Ruddigore'	CTrh LRHS
- 'Sabrina'	Last listed 1997
- 'Saint André'	CMac
- 'Sally Harrell'	SStn
- 'San Dimas'	CDoC CTrh SLdr SSta WBcn
- 'Saturnia'	CDoC COtt EBee
- 'Sawada's Dream'	ISea SStn
- 'Scented Red'	CDoC
- 'Scentsation' ♀	CMHG COtt CTre SCog
- 'Sea Gull'	CTrh SStn
- 'Seiji'	CMac
- 'Serenade'	CMHG
- 'Shin-akebono'	See C. japonica 'Akebono'
- 'Shiro Chan'	SStn WBcn

- 'Shirobotan'	CTrG EPfP GQui SCam SCog WBod
- 'Shiro-daikagura'	See C. rusticana 'Shiro-daikagura'
- 'Sierra Spring'	Last listed 1997
- 'Silver Anniversary'	CB&S CMHG CTrG CTrh ELan GQui LRHS MAsh MGos SBod SCog SLdr SReu SSta SStn
- 'Silver Ruffles'	SStn
- 'Silver Triumph'	SStn
- 'Silver Waves'	Last listed 1997
- 'Simeon'	CDoC
¶ - 'Smiling Beauty'	WBod
- 'Snow Goose'	Last listed 1997
- 'Snowflake'	WBod
- 'Snowman'	SStn
¶ - 'Southern Charm'	MAsh
- 'Souvenir de Bahuaud-Litou' ♀	CB&S CGre CTre SCog SStn WBod WWat
- 'Spencer's Pink'	CB&S CTre CTrw LRHS SStn
¶ - 'Splendens Carlyon'	MAsh
- 'Spring Fever'	SStn
- 'Spring Formal'	Last listed 1998
- 'Spring Sonnet'	Last listed 1997
- 'Strawberry Blonde'	CDoC
- 'Strawberry Swirl'	Last listed 1997
- 'Sweetheart'	CDoC
- 'Sylva'	CPne SStn
- 'Sylvia'	CMac LRHS WBod
- 'Takayama'	SStn
- 'Tammia'	COtt
- 'Tarô'an'	CDoC
- 'Temple Incense'	Last listed 1999
- 'Teresa Ragland'	SStn
- 'Teringa'	CCtw CDoC CTre
§ - 'The Czar'	CB&S CTre CTrw ISea
- 'The Mikado'	CDoC CGre CTre SCog
- 'The Pilgrim'	Last listed 1997
¶ - 'Theo's Mini'	SStn
- 'Thomas Cornelius Cole'	CTre
- 'Tick Tock Blush'	CDoC SCam
- 'Tickled Pink'	CDoC
- 'Tiffany'	CB&S CDoC CTre LHyd LNet LRHS SStn
- 'Tinker Bell'	CGre
- 'Tinker Toy'	CTrh
- 'Tom Thumb'	CMHG CTrh SRms SStn
- 'Tomorrow'	CB&S CDoC CTre CTrw EBee LRHS MAsh WBod
- 'Tomorrow Park Hill'	SStn
§ - 'Tomorrow Variegated'	CDoC
- 'Tomorrow's Dawn'	CB&S SStn
- 'Touchdown'	SStn
- 'Tregye'	CB&S
- 'Trewithen White'	CSam
§ - 'Tricolor' ♀	CB&S CDoC CGre CMHG CMac CTrh ENot IOrc LRHS MAsh SBrw SCam SCog SPer SStn WGwG WPnP
- 'Tricolor Red'	See C. japonica 'Lady de Saumarez'
- 'Tricolor Superba'	Last listed 1997
- 'Twilight'	LRHS SStn
- 'Valtevareda'	CGre WBod
- 'Victor de Bisschop'	See C. japonica 'Le Lys'
- 'Victor Emmanuel'	See C. japonica 'Blood of China'
- 'Ville de Nantes'	CB&S CDoC SSta WBcn
- 'Ville de Nantes Red'	SStn
- 'Virginia Carlyon'	CB&S CCHP CCtw CDoC CTre
- 'Virginia Robinson'	SStn
- 'Virgin's Blush'	SStn
¶ - 'Visconti Nova'	MAsh

- 'Vittorio Emanuele II'   CTrh
- 'Warrior'   CCHP CDoC COtt CTre SStn
¶ - 'White Empress'   WBod
- 'White Giant'   CDoC
- 'White Nun'   SCog SStn
- 'White Swan'   CB&S CMac COtt CTre MAsh SStn
- 'White Tulip'   CGre
- 'Wilamina'   CTrh LRHS
- 'Wildfire'   SStn
- 'William Bartlett'   CTrh
- 'William Honey'   CTrh
* - 'Wisley White'   IArd
- 'Woodville Red'   Last listed 1997
§ - 'Yours Truly'   CB&S CMac CTre CTrh LHyd
   LRHS SBod SCog WBcn
§ - 'Yukibotan'   Last listed 1997
- 'Yukimi-guruma'   WBod
§ - 'Yukishiro'   CTrw
- 'Zoraide Vanzi'   WBod
'Jury's Yellow'   See C. x williamsii 'Jury's Yellow'
kissi   CGre CTrh
'Kôgyoku'   See C. sasanqua 'Kôgyoku'
'Lasca Beauty' (reticulata   Last listed 1997
   x japonica) ♀
'Lavender Queen'   See C. sasanqua 'Lavender
   Queen'
'Leonard Messel'   CB&S CDoC CGre CMHG CTrG
   (reticulata x   CTre CTrh ECle ENot GGGa LHyd
   williamsii) ♀   LRHS MGos SBod SBrw SCog SPer
   SReu SStn WBod WCwm WStI
'Lila Naff'   CTre
   (reticulata hybrid)
lutchuensis   CTrh
'Madame Victor   See C. japonica 'Le Lys'
   de Bisschop'
§ maliflora (d)   CB&S
'Mandalay Queen'   Last listed 1994
   (reticulata hybrid) ♀
'Night Rider' (hybrid)   CDoC
'Nijinski' (reticulata hybrid)   CDoC ISea
§ nitidissima   Last listed 1997
   var. nitidissima
oleifera   CCHP CSam CTre CTrh LRHS
   SCog SStn WWat
'Pink Spangles'   See C. japonica 'Mathotiana
   Rosea'
'Polar Ice' (oleifera hybrid)   CDoC SCog
'Portuense'   See C. japonica 'Japonica
   Variegata'
'Quintessence' (japonica   SCog
   x lutchuensis)
reticulata   CGre CTre
- 'Arch of Triumph' ♀   CTrG
- 'Captain Rawes' ♀   CTre
- 'Mary Williams'   CB&S
- 'Ming Temple'   CTre
- 'Nuccio's Ruby'   Last listed 1997
- 'William Hertrich'   CB&S CGre CTre
rosiflora   CTre
'Royalty'   CB&S CTrG CTre
   (japonica x reticulata)
§ rusticana 'Arajishi'   CB&S CDoC CMac COtt CTre
   SCam SCoo SStn WBod WLRN
   WWal
§ - 'Kinsekai' (v)   SStn
§ - 'Reigyoku' (v)   SStn
§ - 'Shiro-daikagura'   WBod
saluenensis   CGre CTre CTrh
- 'Baronesa de Soutelinho'   Last listed 1997
- 'Exbury Trumpet'   CTre
- x japonica   See C. x williamsii
- 'Trewithen Red'   CTrw WBod

- 'William's Lavender'   WBod
'Salutation' (saluenensis   CB&S CDoC CGre CTre ISea SStn
   x reticulata)
sasanqua   CSam ISea LPan LRHS
I - 'Alba'   SCog
I - 'Apple Blossom'   MAsh
¶ - 'Baronesa de Soutelinho'   SCam
- 'Ben'   Last listed 1998
- 'Bert Jones'   LRHS
- 'Bettie Patricia'   SCog
¶ - 'Cleopatra'   LPan
- 'Cotton Candy'   CDoC
- 'Crimson King' ♀   CGre GQui LRHS SBod SCog
- 'Dazzler'   See C. hiemalis 'Dazzler'
- 'Flamingo'   See C. sasanqua 'Fukuzutsumi'
- 'Flore Pleno'   See C. maliflora
- 'Fuji-no-mine'   CTrh
§ - 'Fukuzutsumi'   CBrm CDoC COtt CTrG LHyd
   SBod SBrw SCog SStn WCwm
- 'Gay Sue'   CTrh
- 'Hugh Evans'   CB&S CDoC COtt CTre CTrh
   LHyd SBrw SCog SSta SStn
- 'Jean May'   CB&S CDoC COtt CTre SBod
   SCog SPer SSta SStn
- 'Kenkyô'   SCog SSta SStn
§ - 'Kôgyoku'   Last listed 1999
§ - 'Lavender Queen'   SStn
- 'Little Liane'   SCog
- 'Little Pearl'   Last listed 1999
- 'Lucinda'   SCog
- 'Mignonne'   CTrh
- 'Mine-no-yuki'   SCog
- 'Narumigata' ♀   CB&S CDoC CMac COtt CTrw
   EBee LHyd MAsh SBod SCam
   SCog SLdr SSta SStn WBod
   WCwm WPnP WSHC
- 'Navajo'   CTrh
- 'Nodami-ushiro'   Last listed 1999
- 'Nyewoods'   CMac
- 'Papaver'   SStn
- 'Paradise Blush'   SCog
- 'Paradise Glow'   SCog
- 'Paradise Hilda'   SCog
- 'Paradise Pearl'   SCog
- 'Paradise Petite'   SCog
- 'Paradise Venessa'   SCog
- 'Peach Blossom'   CB&S
- 'Plantation Pink'   ECle LRHS SBrw SCog
- 'Rainbow'   CBrm CTrG CTrh ISea SCog SSta
   SStn
- 'Rosea'   SSta SStn
§ - 'Rosea Plena'   CB&S CMac CTre CTrw
- 'Sasanqua Rubra'   CMac
- 'Sasanqua Variegata'   SSta SStn WWat
- 'Setsugekka'   SStn
- 'Shishigashira'   CTrh
- 'Snowflake'   SSta SStn
- 'Tanya'   CTrh
¶ - 'Winter's Snowman'   SStn
'Satan's Robe' (reticulata   CDoC CTre
   hybrid) ♀
¶ 'Scented Sun'   CTrh
'Scentuous' (japonica   SCog WBcn
   x lutchuensis)
'Show Girl' (sasanqua   CDoC CTre CTrh SBod SCog
   x reticulata)   WBod
§ sinensis   CGre CTre LRHS
'Snow Flurry'   DoC SCog SStn
   (oleifera hybrid)   C
'Splendens'   See C. japonica 'Coccinea'
'Spring Festival'   CDoC CHig CMHG MGos
   (cuspidata hybrid) ♀

'Spring Mist' (*japonica*   CMHG CTrh
   x *lutchuensis*)
'Strawberry Parfait'   ECle
'Swan Lake' (hybrid)   CTrG LRHS SCog
taliensis   CB&S CGre CTre
'Tarôkaja' (Wabisuke)   SStn
tbea   See *C. sinensis*
'Tinsie'   See *C. japonica* 'Bokuhan'
'Tiny Princess' (*japonica*   CB&S
   x *fraterna*)
'Tom Knudsen'   CTre CTrh EPfP SBrw
   (*reticulata* x *japonica*)
'Tomorrow Supreme'   See *C. japonica* 'Tomorrow
   Variegated'
transnokoensis   CTre CTrh
'Tricolor Sieboldii'   See *C. japonica* 'Tricolor'
'Tristrem Carlyon'   CB&S CDoC CTrG CTre LRHS
   (*reticulata* hybrid) ♀   WBod
tsaii ♀   CGre
'Usu-ôtome'   See *C. japonica* 'Otome'
'Valley Knudsen'   Last listed 1997
   (*saluenensis* x
   reticulata)
vernalis 'Hiryû'   SCog SStn
- 'Kyô-nishiki'   SCog
- 'Yuletide'   Last listed 1999
§ x *williamsii*   CGre
- 'Anemone Frill'   Last listed 1998
- 'Anticipation' ♀   More than 30 suppliers
- 'Anticipation Variegated'   SCog
- 'Ballet Queen'   CB&S CDoC LRHS MGos WBod
- 'Ballet Queen Variegated'   CDoC SCog SSta
- 'Bartley Number Five'   CMac
- 'Beatrice Michael'   CB&S CMac CTre SStn
- 'Bow Bells'   CDoC CGre CMac CTre CTrh
   GKir LHyd LRHS SCog WWat
- 'Bowen Bryant' ♀   CGre CTre CTrh CTrw GGGa
   SCog
- 'Bridal Gown'   Last listed 1997
- 'Brigadoon' ♀   CDoC CMHG CTrG CTre CTrh
   CTri CTrw EPfP GGGa GKir IOrc
   LHyd LRHS MBri MGos SCog
   WBod WWal
- 'Burncoose'   CB&S
- 'Burncoose Apple   CB&S
   Blossom'
- 'C.F. Coates'   CTre MNes SSta
- 'Caerhays'   CB&S CTre
- 'Carnation'   MAsh
- 'Carolyn Williams'   CB&S
- 'Celebration'   CB&S
§ - 'Charity'   Last listed 1998
- 'Charlean'   SCam SStn
- 'Charles Colbert'   CTrh
- 'Charles Michael'   CB&S CGre SStn
- 'Charles Puddle'   WBod
- 'China Clay' ♀   CB&S CDoC CTrG CTre LHyd
   LRHS SBod SCog WBcn WWal
§ - 'Citation'   CB&S CGre CMac CTrw WBod
- 'Clarrie Fawcett' ♀   CDoC CTre
- 'Contribution'   CTrh
- 'Crinkles'   CGre
- 'Daintiness' ♀   CDoC CTre LRHS SStn
- 'Dark Nite'   CMHG CPne
- 'Debbie' ♀   More than 30 suppliers
- 'Debbie's Carnation'   CMHG
- 'Donation' ♀   More than 30 suppliers
- 'Dream Boat'   CB&S LRHS
- 'Dresden China'   CDoC
- 'E.G. Waterhouse'   CB&S CDoC CGre CMHG CTrG
   CTrh CTri CTrw EPfP GKir LHyd
   LRHS MAsh SBod SCam SCog SSta

   SStn WBcn WBod WCwm WWeb
- 'E.T.R. Carlyon' ♀   CB&S CDoC CTre EPfP LRHS
   MAsh
§ - 'Elegant Beauty'   CB&S CGre CTrG CTre CTrh
   CTrw LRHS SBod SBrw SCog
   WCwm
- 'Elizabeth Anderson'   CTrh
- 'Elizabeth de Rothschild'   SStn
- 'Ellamine'   CB&S
- 'Elsie Jury' ♀   CB&S CDoC CGre CMac CTrG
   CTrw GQui IOrc LHyd LRHS
   MGos SBod SCog SPer SStn WBcn
   WBod WGwG WWal
- 'Empire Rose'   Last listed 1997
- 'Exaltation'   LRHS
- 'Francis Hanger'   CB&S CDoC CTre CTrh CTrw
   IOrc LHyd LRHS SBod SCog SSpi
   SStn WGwG WWal
- 'Free Style'   SStn
- 'Galaxie' ♀   CB&S CTrh EPfP ISea
- 'Garden Glory'   CTre CTrh
- 'Gay Time'   CTre
- 'George Blandford' ♀   CB&S CMHG CMac CTre
- 'Glenn's Orbit' ♀   CB&S CDoC CGre CTre CTrw
   WBcn
- 'Golden Spangles' (v)   CB&S CDoC CGre CMac CTrG
   CTre CTrh ELan EPfP GKir GOrc
   IOrc LHyd LRHS MAsh MBri
   MGos MNes SPer SReu SSta SStn
   WBcn
- 'Grand Jury'   CB&S CTre MGos SStn
- 'Gwavas'   CB&S CCHP CDoC CTre
- 'Hilo'   CTrw
- 'Hiraethlyn' ♀   CB&S CTre LHyd SStn WBod
- 'Hope'   Last listed 1999
- 'J.C. Williams' ♀   CB&S CGre CMac CSam CTre
   CTrw EBee ENot EPfP IOrc ISea
   LHyd LRHS SBod SCog SPer SSpi
   SStn WBod
- 'Jean Claris'   CDoC
- 'Jenefer Carlyon' ♀   CTre LRHS
- 'Jill Totty'   CTrh
- 'Joan Trehane' ♀   CTrw
- 'Joyful Bells'   Last listed 1997
- 'Jubilation'   Last listed 1998
- 'Julia Hamiter' ♀   CB&S CGre CTrw SStn
§ - 'Jury's Yellow'   CB&S CDoC CTrG CTrh CTrw
   ECle ELan EPfP GOrc GQui IOrc
   LHyd LRHS MAsh MBri MGos
   SBod SCog SPer SSta SStn WBcn
   WWat
- 'Laura Boscawen'   CTrG CTrh
- 'Les Jury'   SCog SPer
- 'Margaret Waterhouse'   COtt CTre
- 'Mary Christian' ♀   CB&S COtt CTre EPfP LHyd LRHS
   SStn WBod
- 'Mary Jobson'   CB&S CDoC CTre SStn WWat
- 'Mary Larcom'   CPne CTre
- 'Mary Phoebe Taylor'   CB&S CDoC CTrG CTre CTrh
   CTrw SBod SCog WBod
- 'Mildred Veitch'   CGre CTre
- 'Mirage'   CTrh SStn
- 'Mona Jury'   Last listed 1998
- 'Monica Dance'   CB&S
- 'Muskoka' ♀   CB&S CTrh ISea SStn WCwm
- 'New Venture'   CB&S
- 'November Pink'   CB&S CTre EHol GKir
- 'Opal Princess'   Last listed 1999
- 'Parkside'   CTre
* - 'Phillippa'   SStn
- 'Phillippa Forward'   CMac
- 'Red Dahlia'   SStn

- 'Rendezvous'	CDoC LRHS SCam SLdr
- 'Rose Court'	WBod
- 'Rose Parade' ♀	LRHS
- 'Rose Quartz'	LRHS
- 'Rosemary Williams'	CB&S CTre CTrw
- 'Rosie Anderson'	LRHS MAsh
- 'Ruby Bells'	CMHG
- 'Ruby Wedding'	CTrh ECle GQui LRHS SPer
- 'Saint Ewe' ♀	CB&S CDoC CGre CTrG CTre
	CTrh CTri CTrw EPfP GChr LHyd
	LRHS MBri MGos SBod SBrw
	SCog SPer SStn WBod
- 'Saint Michael' ♀	CB&S
- 'Sayonara'	CTre SCog
- 'Senorita'	CTrh LHyd
- 'Taylor's Perfection'	CTrw
- 'The Duchess of Cornwall'	CDoC CTre
- 'Tiptoe' ♀	CTrh LRHS SStn
- 'Tregrehan'	COtt
- 'Twinkle Star'	Last listed 1999
- 'Water Lily' ♀	CB&S CDoC CTre CTrh CTrw
	EPfP LRHS MGos SStn WBcn
	WBod
- 'Wilber Foss'	CB&S CDoC CGre CTre CTrh
	CTrw SCam SStn
- 'William Carlyon'	CTre
- 'Wood Nymph'	CTre
- 'Yesterday'	CTre SMur
'Winter's Fire' (hybrid)	CDoC
'Winter's Interlude'	SCog
(oleifera x sinensis)	
'Winter's Toughie'	CDoC SCog SStn
(C. ?oleifera	
x sasanqua)	
'Winton' (cuspidata	CB&S CDoC SStn WWat
x saluenensis)	
'Yukihaki'	See C. japonica 'Yukishiro'

CAMISSONIA See OENOTHERA

CAMPANULA ✿ (Campanulaceae)

adsurgens	Last listed 1997
aizoides	Last listed 1997
alaskana	See C. rotundifolia var. alaskana
§ alliariifolia	More than 30 suppliers
- 'Ivory Bells'	See C. alliariifolia
allionii	See C. alpestris
§ alpestris	GTou NMen
- 'Grandiflora'	Last listed 1998
- JCA 250500	SBla
- 'Rosea'	MTPN
alpina	Last listed 1999
- subsp. orbelica	See C. orbelica
americana	Last listed 1997
ancbusiflora	NWCA
andrewsii	Last listed 1997
- subsp. andrewsii	Last listed 1997
argaea	Last listed 1999
argyrotricha	Last listed 1998
- CC&McK 477	Last listed 1999
arvatica ♀	CLyd EPot GCHN LBee LRHS
	NHar NNrd NTow WPat
- 'Alba'	CGra CLyd EPot LBee LRHS NMen
	WAbe WLin WPat
- x cochleariifolia	WBea
atlantis	LRHS
aucheri	EBur NSla SSca
autraniana	Last listed 1997
'Avalon'	SAsh
§ 'Balchiniana' (v)	WEas
barbata	CSam EBee ELan GCHN GDra
	GTou MSte NWCA WMoo WPer

- var. alba	EBee NBur
baumgartenii	EBee
bellidifolia	NBir SSte
bertolae	Last listed 1997
§ betulifolia ♀	CGra CSam EMon GCHN GDra
	MBro NHar NHol NMGW NNrd
	SIng WHoo WPat
- JCA 252.005	SBla
- x troegerae	Last listed 1997
biebersteiniana	Last listed 1997
'Birch Hybrid' ♀	CMHG EDAr ELan EMNN ESis
	GCHN GDra GKir LBee LRHS
	MBro NHar SCro SIng WCra WFar
	WPyg
§ bluemelii	Last listed 1998
bononiensis	EBee EMon NBrk SRms WUnu
bornmuelleri	Last listed 1999
'Bumblebee'	CGra
'Burghaltii' ♀	More than 30 suppliers
§ buseri	Last listed 1997
calaminthifolia	CGra EBur
§ carnica	EBee ECho MSte
carpatha	SBla
carpatica ♀	CGle EBee EWTr GAri GDra MBar
	MBri NBro SPlb SRms SWat
	WMoo WWin
- f. alba	CGle EWTr LPVe MBro NFor SPlb
	SWat
- - 'Bressingham White'	CBlo EBrP EBre GCHN GDra GKir
	LBCl LBSe LBre MBBe SBla SBre
	WHoo
- - 'Snowdrift'	Last listed 1998
§ - - 'Weisse Clips'	CPri EBee ECtt EDAr ELan EMNN
	EPar ERav ESis GKir GTou LRHS
	NBur NFla NMen SPer SPla SRPl
	SRms STes WFar WOve WPer
§ - 'Blaue Clips'	EBee ECtt EDAr ELan EMNN EPar
	EPfP ESis GKir GTou LRHS MBNS
	NFla NMen SPer SPla SRms STes
	WFar WGwG WOve WPer WRHF
- blue	Last listed 1999
- 'Blue and White Uniform'	Last listed 1999
- Blue Clips	See C. carpatica 'Blaue Clips'
- 'Blue Moonlight'	EBee EBrP EBre EBur GKir LBCl
	LBSe LBre LRHS MBBe SBre SMer
- 'Caerulea'	CB&S
- 'Chewton Joy'	CLyd EBrP EBre GCHN GKir LBCl
	LBSe LBre LRHS MBBe MBro SBre
	WLin
- 'Ditton Blue'	GDra GMaP
- dwarf	EPot
- 'Harvest Moon'	Last listed 1997
- 'Karpatenkrone'	EBee
- 'Kathy'	GBuc LRHS SAsh
- 'Lavender'	Last listed 1997
- 'Mattocks' Double' (d)	WCot
- 'Maureen Haddon'	EBrP EBre GCHN GKir LBCl LBSe
	LBre LRHS MBBe NWCA SBre
- 'Mrs V. Frère'	Last listed 1997
- 'Queen of Sheba'	Last listed 1999
- 'Queen of Somerville'	NNrd NWoo
- 'Riverslea'	Last listed 1997
- 'Suzie'	EWes SBla
- var. turbinata	EBee GDra LRHS MTho NSla
	SRms WPer
- - f. alba	Last listed 1998
- - - 'Hannah'	EBrP EBre GCHN GDra LBCl LBSe
	LBre LRHS MBBe SBre
- - - 'Snowsprite'	Last listed 1997
§ - - 'Craven Bells'	Last listed 1997
- - 'Georg Arends'	CLyd SAsh
- - 'Isabel'	GCHN LRHS

- - 'Jewel'   LBee LRHS
- - 'Karl Foerster'   CMil CTri EBrP EBre GBuc GCHN GKir LBCl LBSe LBre LRHS MBBe MTho NNrd SBre SMer WFar WHoo
- - 'Pallida'   GDra
- - 'Wheatley Violet'   GCHN LBee LRHS SBla
- White Clips   See *C. carpatica* f. *alba* 'Weisse Clips'
§ **cashmeriana**   EBur GCHN NTow NWCA
celsii   Last listed 1999
cenisia   Last listed 1999
cephallenica   See *C. garganica* subsp. *cephallenica*
cervicaria   EBee
§ **cespitosa**   Last listed 1999
§ **chamissonis**   GBuc NNrd NSla SBla WPat
§ - 'Major'   CPBP EDAr EMNN EPot EWes LBee MBro NMGW SIng
- 'Oyobeni'   NHar SUsu WLin
§ - 'Superba' ♀   EBur EGle ELan GDra IMGH MTho NMen NRya NSla SSmi
chorubensis   CGra
§ **cochleariifolia** ♀   CSpe EDAr ELan EMNN ESis EWTr GCHN GKir GTou MBro MFir MTho MWat NHar SIng SSvw WFar WHoo WPer WWhi WWin
- var. *alba*   CSpe EDAr EMNN EPot GCHN LRHS MBro MWat NChi NHar NMen NNrd NRya SBla SRms WAbe WHoo WPer
- - 'Bavaria White'   NHar
¶ - - double white (d)   CRDP
- - 'White Baby' (Baby Series)   EPfP LRHS NPri SCob
- 'Bavaria Blue'   NHar
- 'Blue Baby' (Baby Series)   LRHS SCob
- 'Blue Tit'   EPot GBuc
- 'Cambridge Blue'   EBrP EBre GCHN LBCl LBSe LBee LBre LRHS MBBe SBre SSmi WAbe
- 'Elizabeth Oliver' (d)   More than 30 suppliers
- 'Flore Pleno' (d)   ECtt NMen NNrd WRHF
- 'Miss Willmott'   CBrd CLyd EBur MTho NBir NTow
- 'Oakington Blue'   CTri LRHS MBro
- var. *pallida*   SRms
- - 'Miranda'   LRHS WCot WIvy
- - 'Silver Chimes'   MBro
- 'R.B. Loder' (d)   Last listed 1999
- 'Temple Bells'   MBro
- 'Tubby'   CLyd CMea CPlt CRDP ECho GCHN LRHS MHer MTho SAga SRms
- 'Warleyensis'   See *C. x haylodgensis* 'Warley White'
collina   CTri GBri MBro NHar NPri WHoo WPer WPyg
'Constellation'   Last listed 1999
coriacea JCA 253.800   Last listed 1997
'Covadonga'   CMea CPBP LRHS MBro
'Craven Bells'   See *C. carpatica* var. *turbinata* 'Craven Bells'
crispa JCA 253.901   Last listed 1997
dasyantha   See *C. chamissonis*
divaricata   Last listed 1997
'E.K. Toogood'   CBre CElw CPBP EBee ECtt EMNN MDHE MWat NBro NFai NHar NHol NNrd SBla SCro SMac SMrm SRms WRHF WWpD
elatines   EBee EBrP EBre LBCl LBSe LBre MBBe NNrd NOak SBre

- var. *elatinoides*   WMoo
- - JCA 254.300   Last listed 1998
'Elizabeth'   See *C. takesimana* 'Elizabeth'
ephesia   Last listed 1997
erinus   Last listed 1997
eriocarpa   See *C. latifolia* 'Eriocarpa'
excisa   LBee
§ 'Faichem Lilac'   MWll NChi NLar NPro WBar WCot WPer WSan
fenestrellata   MTho NBro SRms SSmi WAbe
- subsp. *fenestrellata*   Last listed 1997
§ - subsp. *istriaca*   Last listed 1997
'Fergusonii'   CMil
finitima   See *C. betulifolia*
foliosa   WPer
formanekiana ♀   CHar CSam EBur ECoo EDAr EMan MLLN NWCA WSan
fragilis   EBur SOkd WPer
- subsp. *cavolinii*   Last listed 1999
- 'Hirsuta'   Last listed 1997
'G.F. Wilson' ♀   EBee EBur EGle
garganica ♀   EPfP ESis GAbr MBro MRav NFla NFor NHar SIng WFar WMaN WMoo WPer
- 'Aurea'   See *C. garganica* 'Dickson's Gold'
- 'Blue Diamond'   EDAr ELan EMNN ESis LHop SCro WAbe WLRN
§ - subsp. *cephallenica*   NBro NNrd
§ - 'Dickson's Gold'   More than 30 suppliers
- 'Hirsuta'   SRms
- subsp. *istriaca*   See *C. fenestrellata* subsp. *istriaca*
- 'Major'   SRms
- 'W.H. Paine' ♀   CLyd EBrP EBre ECho EDAr LBCl LBSe LBre LRHS MBBe NMen NSla SAga SBre WHoo
gieseckiana   Last listed 1997
§ 'Glandore'   NCat NMen
glomerata   CBot CKin EBee EDAr EWFC GKir GTou LRHS MBNS MBrN MFir MMal NBid NBro NFai NLan NMir NRya SOkh STes WBea WByw WFar WGwG WMoo WOve WWin WWye
- var. *acaulis*   EBee EMNN EMan EOld GCHN GKir LRHS MBNS MBro MHer NArg NOak NTow SEas SPla SSca WFar WHil WMoo WPer WPyg WWin
- var. *alba*   More than 30 suppliers
§ - - 'Alba Nana'   Last listed 1999
§ - - 'Schneekrone'   EBee EBrP EBre ECha EFou EWTr LBCl LBSe LBre LRHS MBBe MCli MGrG NBrk NFor NOak SBre WBea WFar
- 'Caroline'   EBrP EBre EMil EMon LBCl LBSe LBre LRHS MBBe MRav SBre SCro SOkh SPer SSvw WCot WHal WHil
- Crown of Snow   See *C. glomerata* var. *alba* 'Schneekrone'
- var. *daburica*   CTri EBee EWTr MHer MOne NLar NOak WBea WMoo WPer
- 'Joan Elliott'   CMGP EBee ECha GBuc LRHS MRav MWat NBrk
- 'Nana Alba'   See *C. glomerata* var. *alba* 'Alba Nana'
- 'Purple Pixie'   Last listed 1998
- 'Superba' ♀   More than 30 suppliers
¶ - 'White Barn'   EBee ECha NBrk NOak
grossekii   EBee EBrP EBre EPPr GBuc LBCl LBSe LBre MBBe MNrw SBre
hagielia   Last listed 1997

'Hallii' — ESis LRHS MBro NWCA WPat
hawkinsiana — Last listed 1999
- JCA 256002 — Last listed 1998
x **haylodgensis** sensu stricto hort. — See *C.* x *haylodgensis* 'Plena'
§ - 'Marion Fisher' (d) — MBro SUsu WAbe WHoo
§ - 'Plena' (d) — CElw ELan EPot LBee LHop LRHS MBro NBro NHar SBla SIng SRms SSmi WAbe WCot WEas WHoo WKif WPyg
§ - 'Warley White' (d) — CSpe EBur ELan EPot NNrd SIng
- 'Yvonne' — EDAr LRHS NNrd WFar WPer
hemschinica — Last listed 1997
'Hemswell Starlight' — CLyd EDAr NPro
hercegovina — NTow SIng
- 'Nana' — CPBP NNrd SBla WAbe
herminii — Last listed 1999
heterophylla — Last listed 1997
hierosolymitana — Last listed 1997
'Hilltop Snow' — CGra
iconia — Last listed 1997
§ **incurva** — CFri CGle CPou EBee EBur ELan EMan GAbr GBin GBuc MAvo MMil MNrw MTho NBrk NBro NFla NOak SMrm WBea WByw WElm WPer WUnu
- **alba** — WPer
- 'Blue Ice' — WWin
- JCA 256.800 — Last listed 1998
x **innesii** — See *C.* 'John Innes'
isophylla ♀ — MBri SIng SYvo WEas
- 'Alba' ♀ — SIng SYvo WEas
- 'Flore Pleno' (d) — EBur
- 'Mayi' ♀ — CSpe LHil
- 'Mayi' misapplied — See *C.* 'Balchiniana'
- 'Variegata' — See *C.* 'Balchiniana'
jaubertiana — CGra
'Joe Elliott' ♀ — EWes LRHS SBla
§ 'John Innes' — CLyd MGed
justiniana — Last listed 1997
kemulariae — ESis GCHN WPer
- **alba** — MAvo
'Kent Belle' — More than 30 suppliers
kladniana — Last listed 1997
kolenatiana — GCHN
laciniata — Last listed 1998
lactiflora — More than 30 suppliers
- **alba** — See *C. lactiflora* white
N - 'Alba' ♀ — EMil GKir GMac MAvo STes
- 'Blue Avalanche' — CBos SMrm
- 'Blue Cross' — COtt EBee EFou GKir GMac LRHS NLar WCot
- 'Loddon Anna' ♀ — More than 30 suppliers
- 'Pouffe' — CDoC EBee ECha EGle ELan GKir GMac LRHS MBro MGrG MRav NBro NFla NGdn SCro SPer SPla SWat WHoo WPyg WRus WWin
- 'Prichard's Variety' ♀ — More than 30 suppliers
- 'Senior' — EFou
- 'Splash' — MGrG
- 'Superba' ♀ — GKir MCLN WCot
- 'Violet' — EBee SWat WPer
§ - white — CBot EBee ECha EFou EGle MBro NBir NBrk SPer SPla WHoo WOut WPer
- 'White Pouffe' — More than 30 suppliers
lanata — EBee GAbr WBea WUnu
lasiocarpa — CPBP EBur LRHS WFar
- 'Talkeetna' — Last listed 1998
§ **latifolia** — CAgr CArn CKin CSev EBee ECha EWTr GAbr GGar LEdu LRHS MCLN MWgw NBid NChi NFla NFor NMir NOrc NTow NVic SAga SMer SPer WCer WEas WFar WLin WMoo WWat
* - 'Amethyst' — CFri EWTr
- 'Brantwood' — CGle CMil EBee EBrP EBre ECoo EGle EMan EMar LBCl LBSe LBre MBBe MBel MFir MSte MWat NBrk NChi NOak NPro SBre SCro SMer SPer SSpe WCot WWin
§ - 'Eriocarpa' — MWrn
- 'Gloaming' — GKir LRHS MBri WCot
- 'Lavender' — Last listed 1999
- var. **macrantha** — More than 30 suppliers
- - **alba** — CBos CM&M CMil EBee ECha ECtt EMan EPri LGre LHop LRHS MRav SPla STes WCot WMoo WPer WPyg WWat
- 'Roger Wood' — MWgw WCot
- white — CGle EBrP EBre LBCl LBSe LBre LRHS MBBe MBro MCLN MRav MSte NTow SBre SPer SSpi WEas WHoo WRus
- 'White Ladies' — Last listed 1999
§ **latiloba** — CBre CElw CGle CMHG GKir LGro MBro MFir NChi NWoo WByw WCot WEas WHoo WWin
- 'Alba' ♀ — CBre CElw CGle CHar CPlt EFou EGle ELan GAbr GCal GMac NChi SHel WEas WLin WMaN
- 'Hidcote Amethyst' ♀ — CElw CHad COlW CSpe EBee EFou ELan GAbr GCal GMac LGre LRHS MBel MBri MBro MCAu MGrG NBir NSti SPer WCot WEas WFar WHil WHoo WKif WLin WMaN
- 'Highcliffe Variety' ♀ — CMGP EBee ECha EFou EGle EMan EPfP MBel MBri MRav NSti SPer SPla SSpe SSpi WCot WEas WKif WLRN
* - 'Highdown' — MLLN WFar
- 'Percy Piper' ♀ — CSam EBee ELan GBri GKir GMac LRHS MBri MCAu MNrw MRav MSCN NBrk NBro NFor WByw WFar WHil WLin
- 'Splash' — MAvo MTed WCot
¶ **ledebouriana** — EHyt
lingulata — EBee
linifolia — See *C. carnica*
longestyla — Last listed 1997
'Lynchmere' — EWes MBro NTow
lyrata — Last listed 1997
makaschvilii — EBee NBur
marchesettii — EBee
'Marion Fisher' — See *C.* x *haylodgensis* 'Marion Fisher'
§ **medium** 'Calycanthema' ♀ — Last listed 1997
- 'Cup and Saucer' — See *C. medium* 'Calycanthema'
¶ - white — SMrm
mirabilis — Last listed 1997
'Mist Maiden' — CFee CLyd CMHG GAri LRHS NNrd NTow WFar
moesiaca — EWTr NBur
mollis — Last listed 1997
- var. **gibraltarica** — NTow
morettiana — Last listed 1999
muralis — See *C. portenschlagiana*
myrtifolia — Last listed 1999
'Mystery'[PBR] — CFri CFwr CSpe EBee EMan MBNS NCut SRCN WHil
nitida — See *C. persicifolia* var. *planiflora*
- var. **planiflora** — See *C. persicifolia* var. *planiflora*
'Norman Grove' — CLyd EGle EPot LBee LRHS MNaF

oblongifolioides	Last listed 1997
ochroleuca	CBel CMea CRDP EBee EFou EGar GCal LAst LRHS NSti SCro SWat WCFE WCot WHal WUnu
olympica Boissier	Last listed 1998
– hort.	See *C. rotundifolia* 'Olympica'
§ *orbelica*	Last listed 1997
oreadum	Last listed 1997
orphanidea	Last listed 1997
ossetica	See *Symphyandra ossetica*
pallida	Last listed 1997
– subsp. *tibetica*	See *C. casbmeriana*
parryi	Last listed 1999
parviflora Lam.	See *C. sibirica*
patula	CBrm GBin LSyl MHew NLar
– subsp. *abietina*	EBee MDCh
'Paul Furse'	LRHS NSti WLin WWin
pelviformis	MNrw
peregrina	EBee
persicifolia	More than 30 suppliers
– *alba*	More than 30 suppliers
§ – 'Alba Coronata' (d)	CFir CMil CStr EBrP EBre EMon GBri LBCl LBSe LBre LRHS MBBe MBro MCAu MTis NBir NBrk SBre SPer WEas WFar
– 'Alba Plena'	See *C. persicifolia* 'Alba Coronata'
– 'Bennett's Blue' (d)	EOrc LFis WCDu
– 'Best China'	MAvo
– blue	EMan EOrc MMal MRav NCut SPlb WEas WFar
– 'Blue Bell'	CBlo
– 'Blue Bloomers' (d)	CMil EBee EBrP EBre EMon EWes GBri LBCl LBSe LBre MAvo MBBe MSph SBre SUsu WCot WPnP WRHF
– blue cup-in-cup (d)	WLin WRus WWin
– 'Boule de Neige' (d)	CHea CLon CM&M EBee EGle LFis NBrk NMGW NOak NRya WCot WEas WPGP WPnP
– 'Caerulea Coronata'	See *C. persicifolia* 'Coronata'
* – 'Caerulea Plena' (d)	ELan MBNS WEas
– 'Capel Ulo' (v)	WHer
– 'Carillon'	GBri NBrk
§ – 'Chettle Charm' PBR	More than 30 suppliers
§ – 'Coronata' (d)	CHea EBrP EBre GMac LBCl LBSe LBre MBBe MDun MRav SBre SGar WShe
N – cup and saucer white (d)	CBlo CElw CLyd ELan NBrk WByw WHil WPer
– double blue (d)	CLon CSWP EOrc NBro NFai WByw WCot WEas WRHF
– double powder blue (d)	Last listed 1998
– double white (d)	EBee ELan NChi WMoo
– 'Eastgrove Blue'	Last listed 1999
– 'Fleur de Neige' (d) ♀	CGle CMea CSam EBee LRHS MBro MLLN MSph NOak WHoo WLin WPyg
– 'Flore Pleno' (d)	NBir
– 'Frances' (d)	CHar CLAP EBee EMon GBri MAvo MRav WLin WMaN WPnP
– 'Frank Lawley' (d)	EBee EBrP EBre EFou LBCl LBSe LBre LRHS MBBe SBre
– 'Gawen'	See *C. persicifolia* 'Hampstead White'
– 'George Chiswell' PBR	See *C. persicifolia* 'Chettle Charm'
– 'Grandiflora Alba'	GBuc SMrm SSca
– 'Grandiflora Caerulea'	NLar
§ – 'Hampstead White' (d)	More than 30 suppliers
– 'Hetty'	See *C. persicifolia* 'Hampstead White'
– Irish double white (d)	EMon SAga
– 'Moerheimii' (d)	EOrc EPar MBel NBir NDov WHal

	WHil WIvy WWin
– var. *nitida*	See *C. persicifolia* var. *planiflora*
– 'Peach Bells'	MBNS NOak
– 'Perry's Boy Blue'	NPer
– 'Pike's Supremo'	See *C.* 'Pike's Supremo'
§ – var. *planiflora*	CPBP CSpe EBee GTou NHar NTow WAbe
§ – – f. *alba*	WAbe WSan WWin
– 'Pride of Exmouth' (d)	CGle CHar CHea CPou CSam EBee ELan EMon GOrP LHop LLWP LRHS MArl MBro MRav NFor NOak NVic WCot WFar WHil WHoo WLin WPnP WRHF
– subsp. *sessiliflora*	See *C. latiloba*
– 'Snowdrift'	SRms
– 'Telham Beauty' misapplied	CDoC CHea COtt EBee EFou ELan EPri EWTr GKir LHop LRHS LRot MFir MRav SAga SMer SMrm SPer SRCN SRms WBea WCot WCra WMoo WPer WRus
¶ – 'Tinpenny Blue'	WTin
– 'Wedgwood'	Last listed 1999
N – 'White Cup and Saucer' (d)	NBrk WFar WWhi WWye
– 'White Queen' (d)	CMGP NBur NFai WEas
– 'Wortham Belle' (d)	CGle CSev EBee EGle EMan EPri GBri GCal LFis LHop LRHS MAvo MBel MCAu MCLN MMil MTis NCat NSti SChu SPer SPla SWat WHil WLRN WMoo WRus
petraea	Last listed 1997
petrophila	CLyd
§ 'Pike's Supremo' (d)	NBir
pilosa	See *C. chamissonis*
piperi	CGra NWCA SBla
– 'Marmot Pass'	Last listed 1998
– 'Townsend Ridge'	Last listed 1999
– 'Townsend Violet'	Last listed 1999
planiflora	See *C. persicifolia* var. *planiflora*
§ *portenschlagiana* ♀	CAgr CElw ELan ENot EPar GAbr LGro LRHS MHar MHer MMal MWat NBro NDlv NRya NVic SBla SDix SIng SPer SRms SSmi WAbe WCru WEas WFar WMoo WPyg WWin
– 'Lieselotte'	GBuc MDHE
– 'Major'	CMCo GMaP SRms WFar
– 'Resholdt's Variety'	CMea CSam EBrP EBre EDAr EFou GCHN LBCl LBSe LBre LHop LRHS MBBe MChl NCat SBre WLRN WPer
poscharskyana	More than 30 suppliers
– 'Blauranke'	EWes GAri GCHN MDHE
– 'Blue Gown'	EGle GMaP GMac
– 'E.H. Frost'	CBre ECtt EDAr EGle EMNN EMou ESis EWTr GMac LHop LNor LRHS MBro MWat NBro NCat NHol NNrd NRya SAga SCro SIng SRms SSmi WBea WFar WPer
– 'Glandore'	See *C.* 'Glandore'
¶ – 'Lilacina'	EPPr NDov SCro SHel SIng
¶ – 'Lisduggan Variety'	More than 30 suppliers
– 'Stella' ♀	EBrP EBre ECha EGle EMNN ENot EPPr ESis GCHN GChr LBCl LBSe LBre LRHS MAvo MBBe MRav NBro NCat SBre SChu SDix SIng WFar WPyg
– variegated	EHoe IBlr
– white	WFar
primulifolia	CFri EBee EBlw ECoo ELan EMan GBuc LFis LRHS MBro MMal MMil MNrw MTis MWrn NFai NFla NSti SMac SPer SSca STes WPer WPyg

	WSan WWin
- 'Blue Spires'	GKir LRHS MBri NPro
'Priory'	Last listed 1999
x *pseudoraineri*	EBee EBur EDAr EWes NMen
	NNrd SSmi
pulla	CLyd CPlt CRDP EBur EDAr ELan
	EMNN EPot ESis MBro MTho NFla
	NHar NMGW SSmi WCot WCru
	WFar WPat WPer
- *alba*	CPBP CRDP EBee EBur EDAr
	EMNN EPot LBee LRHS MBro
	NHar NMGW NNrd WCru WPat
x *pulloides*	CLyd EBrP EBre EDAr LBCl LBSe
	LBee LBre MBBe SBre
punctata	More than 30 suppliers
- f. *albiflora*	GKir LHop LRHS MBri MBro
	MLLN MOne NChi SCro WBro
	WFar WHil WWin
- - 'Nana Alba'	CMil EBee GBin GCal GMac LRHS
	NBur NCut NFla WCot WMoo
I - 'Beetroot'	EBee EMon WPGP
- var. *bondoensis*	CHar CPea EBee EPPr MBel MBrN
	MNrw NLar NSti SAga WBea
	WCot WHil WLin WMoo WUnu
¶ - - 'Bossy Boots'	EFou
- - white	WUnu
- f. *impunctata*	Last listed 1997
¶ - var. *microdonta*	EBrP EBre LBCl LBSe LBre MBBe
	SBre
¶ - 'Millennium'	WFar
- 'Milly'	EMon
* - 'Nana'	Last listed 1997
- 'Pallida'	Last listed 1997
¶ - 'Pink Eclipse'	MAvo WFar
¶ - 'Reifrock'	EFou
- 'Rosea'	CGle LPio MBri SRms WHil WSan
- f. *rubriflora*	More than 30 suppliers
¶ - - 'Wine 'n' Rubies'	CElw CStr EMan MAvo
- var. *takesimana*	See *C. takesimana*
- 'White Hose-in-hose'	MAvo WFar
* 'Purple Dwarf'	Last listed 1998
pusilla	See *C. cochleariifolia*
pyramidalis	CBot CMGP CSpe EBee EPfP
	EWTr LIck MBNS MHer NOrc
	SRob WPer
- *alba*	CM&M CMGP CSpe EBee EWTr
	LPio MCAu NCut SIde WPer
	WRHF
¶ - lavender blue	NCut
x *pyraversi*	Last listed 1997
raddeana	CElw CLyd CMdw CRDP GCHN
	MBro NBus NLar SCro SSmi WFar
raineri ♀	CFee CPBP EPot LRHS MBro
	NMen NOak NWCA SBla WPyg
* - *alba*	Last listed 1997
- 'Nettleton Gold'	EPot
ramosissima	Last listed 1997
§ *rapunculoides*	CArn CBrm EBee EGoo GAbr
	LRot MCli MLLN SWat WBea
	WHer WPer
§ - 'Afterglow'	CStr MAvo WCot
- 'Alba'	CStr EMon LRHS MAvo WBar
	WPnP
rapunculus	ILis MGed
'Rearsby Belle'	Last listed 1998
recurva	See *C. incurva*
reiseri	EBee
retrorsa	Last listed 1997
rhomboidalis Gorter	See *C. rapunculoides*
rigidipila	Last listed 1997
¶ 'Rosanna's Rainbow' (v)	WBar
rotundifolia	CArn CKin EWTr MBro MHer

	MHew NBid NChi NLan NMir
	NNrd NSti SIde SPlb SRms SSvw
	WBea WElm WGwy WJek WOve
	WPer
§ - var. *alaskana*	NWCA
- var. *alba*	EBee MBro NChi WHoo WPyg
- 'Jotunheimen'	CGra
§ - 'Olympica'	CInt EBee EBur EMan EPfP GAbr
	GCHN LFis MBNS MHar NPri SEas
	WFar
- 'Superba'	SCro
rupestris	CPBP EBee EBur SSca
– NS 401	NWCA
rupicola	Last listed 1997
– JCA 262.400	SBla
samarkandensis	Last listed 1997
'Sarastro'	CElw CLAP CMil EBee EFou EGle
	EMon EPPr GBuc LGre MAvo
	SAga SUsu WCot WPnP
sarmatica	CGle CHea EBee ECoo EMan
	GAbr GBuc LCot MBct MBrN
	NOak SMrm SRCN SRms WMaN
	WPer WPic
sartorii	CPBP EBur WWin
saxatilis ♀	Last listed 1997
- subsp. *saxatilis*	Last listed 1999
saxifraga	EBur EPot GCHN LRHS
scabrella	CGra NWCA
* *scardica*	Last listed 1997
scheuchzeri	NNrd
sclerotricha	Last listed 1997
scouleri	NWCA
serrata	Last listed 1997
shetleri	CGra
§ *sibirica*	LFis WPer
- subsp. *taurica*	Last listed 1997
- white	NLar
siegizmundii	GMac
'Southern Seedling'	Last listed 1997
sp. from Iran	CElw EMon
sp. from Morocco	Last listed 1999
sp. JCA 6872	Last listed 1997
sp. JCA 8363	Last listed 1997
sp. JJH 918638	Last listed 1997
sparsa	Last listed 1997
spathulata	Last listed 1997
- subsp. *spathulata*	NNrd
- subsp. *spruneriana*	Last listed 1997
speciosa	EBee STes
spicata	MNrw
sporadum	Last listed 1998
'Stansfieldii'	CPBP EBur EPot NMen NNrd
	WPat
stevenii	CGra
- subsp. *beauverdiana*	Last listed 1997
sulphurea	Last listed 1997
'Swannbles'	See *C. punctata* x *Symphyandra*
	ossetica, 'Swannbles'
§ *takesimana*	More than 30 suppliers
* - *alba*	EBee GKir LPio MAvo NCut NFla
	NPSI WCot WIvy WOut WRus
	WUnu
- dark form	GKir LFis
§ - 'Elizabeth'	More than 30 suppliers
teucrioides	Last listed 1999
thessala	Last listed 1999
thyrsoides	EBee GDra GTou ITim MNrw
	MTis NBur NWCA WHal WPer
- subsp. *carniolica*	SGar
tommasiniana ♀	LBee LRHS SAsh WLin
topaliana	Last listed 1998
- subsp. *cordifolia*	Last listed 1997

trachelium	CGle CKin EBee ECoo EOrc EWFC GAbr MBNS MHew MNrw MRav NLan SCou SIde SSca WByw WCot WFar WHer WPer
- var. *alba*	CGle CPea EBee LFis LSyl MFir MNrw MWll NPar SCou SHel SSca STes WCot WFar WMaN WMoo WPer WWhi
- 'Alba Flore Pleno' (d)	CFir CGle CHar CHea CLon CPou EBee EFou EMan LGre LPio SMac WBro WByw WCot WFar WHil WHoo WMaN WRus WSan
- 'Bernice' (d)	More than 30 suppliers
- 'Faichem Lilac'	See *C.* 'Faichem Lilac'
- lilac-blue	CBlo NCut NOrc
transsilvanica	Last listed 1997
trautvetteri	Last listed 1997
trichocalycina	Last listed 1997
tridentata	NTow WPer
troegerae	LBee LRHS SBla
tubulosa	See *C. buseri*
'Tymonsii'	CPBP EBur ECho ESis LBee LRHS NBir NNrd
uniflora	Last listed 1997
'Van-Houttei'	CBos CElw CHar CMil CPlt CStr EBee EMan EMon GCal LGre MBro MSte NBrk SAga SUsu WCot WFar WPGP WPer
versicolor	EBee GAbr LFis
- G&K 3347	EMon
- NS 745	NWCA
'Victor Cohen'	Last listed 1999
vidalii	See *Azorina vidalii*
waldsteiniana	CPBP EPot LBee LRHS NTow SSmi WFar
- JCA 266.000	MBro
'Warley White'	See *C.* x *haylodgensis* 'Warley White'
'Warleyensis'	See *C.* x *haylodgensis* 'Warley White'
x *wockei* 'Puck'	EBee EBur EPot LBee LRHS MBro MNaF NHar NMen NSla NWCA SSmi WAbe WPat
xylocarpa	Last listed 1997
zoysii	CGra LRHS

CAMPANULA x SYMPHYANDRA
(Campanulaceae)
§ *C. punctata* x *S. ossetica*, 'Swannbles'
CPou EGle EMan GMac NCat WCot

CAMPANUMOEA See CODONOPSIS

CAMPSIS (Bignoniaceae)
* *atrosanguinea*	LRHS
grandiflora	CB&S CHEx CPIN EBee EBrP EBre ELan ENot EPfP GSki IMGH LBCl LBSe LBre LRHS MAsh MBBe MGos SBre SPer WCFE
radicans	CArn CB&S CBot CHEx CMac CPIN CRHN EBee ELan EOld EWTr GQui LPan LRHS MGrG MHer MWat NBea NFla SLon SPer SPlb SYvo WDin
¶ - 'Atrosanguinea'	CPIN
- 'Flamenco'	CB&S CBlo CDoC CPIN EBee ELan EQui GSki IOrc LRHS MAsh NBea SBra SLim WBro WCru
§ - f. *flava* ♀	CDoC CHEx CPIN EBee ELan IMGH IOrc LHop LRHS MAsh MBri MCCP MGos MWat NBea

	NSti SBra SLim SPer SSoC SSta WSHC
¶ - 'Indian Summer'	MGos WWeb
- 'Yellow Trumpet'	See *C. radicans* f. *flava*
¶ x *tagliabuana*	EWTr
- 'Madame Galen' ♀	More than 30 suppliers

CAMPTOSORUS See ASPLENIUM

CAMPTOTHECA (Cornaceae)
acuminata	ISea

CAMPYLANDRA See TUPISTRA

CANANGA (Annonaceae)
odorata	ERea

CANARINA (Campanulaceae)
canariensis ♀	CPlN CPle

CANDOLLEA See HIBBERTIA

CANNA ✿ (Cannaceae)
'Adams Orange'	CHEx
'Aida'	Last listed 1999
altensteinii	LBlo
'Angele Martin'	Last listed 1999
'Argentina'	Last listed 1998
'Assaut'	CHEx EBot LPio SVen
'Australia'	Last listed 1999
'Black Knight'	EBee GBuc LAma LLWG LPio NMoo WCot
brasiliensis	WCot
- 'Rosea'	WMul
'Brillant'	CHEx NCut
'Cerise Davenport'	CFir
'Champion'	CHEx
'Cherry Red'	Last listed 1999
'Chinese Coral'	CHEx LHil
'City of Portland'	EPVP NCut
'Cleopatra'	Last listed 1999
coccinea	LBlo
'Côte d'Or'	Last listed 1999
cream speckled	Last listed 1999
'Creamy White'	CHEx
Crozy hybrids	Last listed 1998
'Délibáb'	Last listed 1997
'Di Bartolo'	LPio
'Durban' (v)	CFil CSpe LBlo LHil LPJP WCot WHal WMul
edulis	LBlo
¶ - 'Newlyn Green'	CHEx
x *ehemanii*	CGre CHEx SVen
x *ehemanii* x *iridiflora*	LHil WMul
'En Avant'	EBot
'Endeavour'	CFil LPJP MSta WMAq WMul WPGP
'Erebus'	MSta WMAq
'Étoile du Feu'	Last listed 1999
'Extase'	Last listed 1999
Firebird	See *C.* 'Oiseau de Feu'
flaccida	LBlo
'Florence Vaughan'	Last listed 1999
'General Eisenhower'	Last listed 1999
x *generalis*	CB&S CHEx
glauca	SDix
'Gnom'	Last listed 1999
'Golden Lucifer'	CSpe LAma MBri MRav
'Heinrich Seidel'	CHEx
'Hercule'	Last listed 1999
hybrids	LBow
§ *indica*	CB&S CGdn CHEx CSev EBot

	EFul ERav LHil LPio SAPC SArc SYvo
- 'Purpurea'	CBos CFil EBot ECha EOrc EPVP ERav LEdu LHil SArc SDix SLon WCot WDyG WMul WPGP WPic
'Ingeborg'	NCut
'Intrigue'	Last listed 1999
iridiflora	CSev CWit EBot EOas SAPC SArc SDix
'Jivago'	Last listed 1999
¶ 'Kansas City' (v)	WCot
'King Hakon'	Last listed 1999
I 'King Humbert' (blood-red)	SYvo WCot
King Humbert (orange-red)	See *C.* 'Roi Humbert'
'King Midas'	CHEx LBlo SVen WCot
'Königin Charlotte'	Last listed 1999
'La Bohème'	NCut
'La Gloire'	Last listed 1999
'Lafayette'	Last listed 1999
'Lesotho Lill'	CHad LHil
'Libération'	Last listed 1999
'Louis Cayeux'	EBot
'Louise Cottin'	ETub LPio
'Lucifer'	EBee LRHS NCut NPer SYvo
lutea	Last listed 1999
¶ 'Madeira'	LHil
'Malawiensis Variegata'	See *C.* 'Striata'
'Melanie'	CHEx
'Meyerbeer'	Last listed 1999
'Mrs Oklahoma'	Last listed 1999
'Mrs Tim Taylor'	Last listed 1999
musifolia	CHEx EBot EPVP LBlo LHil LPJP SDix WMul
'Mystique'	Last listed 1999
'Nectarine'	Last listed 1999
§ 'Oiseau de Feu'	MBri SVen
'Oiseau d'Or'	LHil
'Orange Beauty'	SVen
'Orange Perfection'	CFir CHEx
'Orchid'	EBee LAma MBri
'Panache'	CFil
'Perkeo'	CHEx LHil
'Picadore'	Last listed 1999
'Picasso'	EBee LAma SVen SYvo
'Pink Paradise'	LHil
'Pink Sunburst' (v)	LLWG WCot
'President'	CHEx EBee EBot LAma LHil LPio MBri NCut
'Pretoria'	See *C.* 'Striata'
'Primrose Yellow'	Last listed 1997
'Pringle Bay' (v)	Last listed 1999
'Professor Lorentz'	CFil LBlo WPGP
'Ra'	MSta WMAq
'Richard Wallace'	CHEx EBee EBot LPio NCut
§ 'Roi Humbert'	LHil NCut NMoo SVen
'Roi Soleil'	CFil CHEx WPGP
'Roitelet'	CHEx
'Rosemond Coles'	CHEx SYvo
'Saladin'	LHil
'Salmon'	Last listed 1997
'Sémaphore'	Last listed 1999
'Shenandoah'	Last listed 1999
'Singapore Girl'	SVen
speciosa	LBlo
'Strasbourg'	CHEx NPer WPGP
§ 'Striata' (v)	CFil CSev CSpe EBee EBot EOrc LBlo LHil LPJP LPio MSta NPSI SVen SYvo WCot WHal WMul WSPU
'Striped Beauty' (v)	LHil
'Stuttgart' (v)	WCot
'Talisman'	SVen

'Taney'	MSta WMAq
'Tango'	CHEx
'Taroudant'	Last listed 1999
'Tashkent Red'	CHad LHil
'Tirol'	LHil SVen
'Tropical Rose'	LRHS WMul
'Tropical Rose' red	Last listed 1999
Tropicanna = 'Phasion'PBR (v)	COtt LPio LRHS NPer WCot
* 'Variegata' (v)	LAma LRHS NCut WCot
'Verdi'	LHil LLWG
warscewiczii	LBlo SYvo WMul
'Wyoming'	CHad EBee EBot EOas LAma LBlo LHil LPio NCut SLod SYvo WCot WMul
'Yellow Humbert'	CSev LAma LHil

CANTUA (Polemoniaceae)

buxifolia	CB&S CFee CFil CPle ERea GQui LHil LRHS SOWG
¶ - 'Alba'	WPGP

CAPSICUM (Solanaceae)

annuum	MBri
* - 'Janne'	MBri

CARAGANA (Papilionaceae)

arborescens	CBlo CDul ENot EPfP GChr GKir IOrc MBar MWhi NFla NWea SRCN WDin WStI
- 'Lorbergii' ♀	CDoC CEnd CLnd EPfP EWTr GChr GKir IOrc MBlu SEas SLim WFoF
- 'Pendula'	CBlo CLnd EBee ELan ENot EPfP GKir LRHS MAsh MBar MBlu NBee NEgg NPri SLim SPer WDin WStI
- 'Walker'	CB&S CBlo CDoC CDul COtt EBee EBrP EBre ELan EMil EPfP GKir IOrc LBCl LBSe LBre LPan LRHS MAsh MBBe MBar MBlu MBri MGos SBre SLim SMad SPer WOrn WStI
aurantiaca	MBar
brevispina	Last listed 1999
franchetiana	Last listed 1998
frutex 'Globosa'	SPer
jubata	SMad
microphylla	WNor

CARDAMINE ✿ (Brassicaceae)

alba	WEas
asarifolia L.	Last listed 1999
- hort.	See *Pachyphragma macrophyllum*
bulbifera	CLAP CRDP IBlr NDov NRya NWoo SIng WCot WCru
diphylla	CLAP WCot WFar
enneaphylla	IBlr SSpi SVal WCru
glanduligera	CElw EGle EPPr WCru
§ *heptaphylla*	CLAP ELan EPar GBri IBlr MBri MRav SSpi SWat WCru WHoo
- Guincho form	CFir IBlr
- white	CPlt WCot
§ *kitaibelii*	CLAP EPar GAbr IBlr NHol SSpi WCru
laciniata	SVal SWat WCot WCru
latifolia Vahl	See *C. raphanifolia*
macrophylla	CLAP COtt SDys SSpi SWat WCot WCru WFar WIvy
§ *microphylla*	CLAP GCrs IMGH WCot
x *paxiana*	Last listed 1997

pentaphylla	CGle EBee EBrP EBre ECha EGle
	ELan EMar EPar EPla ERos GAbr
	GCrs GGar GMaP LBCl LBSe LBre
	MBBe MBri MRav MS&S SBre SSpi
	SVal WCot WCru
* – 'Alba'	ECha
– bright pink	CLAP
pratensis	CArn CKin CRow EBrP EBre
	EMan EWFC EWTr LBCl LBSe
	LBre MBBe MGas MHer MHew
	MMal NDea NMir NOrc SBre SIde
	SWat WFar WGwy WHbs WHer
	WShi WWye
– 'Edith' (d)	CGle CLAP CMil CRow EPPr GAri
	GBuc MNrw NChi WPrP
– 'Flore Pleno' (d) ♀	CBre CFee CGle CNat CRow
	CSpe EBee ECha EWTr GAbr GKir
	LRHS MCLN MHer MNrw MRav
	MTho NBid NBro NLar NSti SUsu
	SWat WAlt WEas WFar WHoo
	WRus
– 'William' (d)	CGle CMea EPPr GBuc MNrw
	WFar WPrP
quinquefolia	CElw CGle CLAP CMea EBee EGle
	EMar EPPr EPar NCat SCro SDys
	SUsu WCot WCru WFar WPGP
	WRha WWye
§ *raphanifolia*	CBre CGle CRow EBee ECha
	EMan EOrc GAbr GBuc GCal
	GGar IBlr MFir MRav NBro NCat
	NVic SSpi SWat WBor WCru
trifolia	CGle CRDP EBee ECha EGle
	EMan EPar ERos GAbr GCal GMaP
	LBee LRHS MBar MSCN NBro
	NChi NFor NRya NVic SWat WCot
	WCru WFar WHer WWye
* – *digitata*	MTho
waldsteinii	CElw CLon CPlt CStu EGle EPPr
	SSpi WCru WHoo WTin

CARDIANDRA (Hydrangeaceae)

formosana B&SWJ 2005	WCru

CARDIOCRINUM (Liliaceae)

cordatum	Last listed 1998
– var. *glehnii*	Last listed 1999
giganteum ♀	More than 30 suppliers
¶ – B&SWJ 2419	WCru
– var. *yunnanense*	CFil EPfP GGGa IBlr SSpi WAbe
	WCru WPGP

CARDIOSPERMUM (Sapindaceae)

grandiflorum	CPlN

CARDUNCELLUS (Asteraceae)

mitissimus	SIng

CARDUUS (Asteraceae)

benedictus	See *Cnicus benedictus*
nutans	GKir

CAREX (Cyperaceae)

acutiformis	GKir
albida	CBrm CCuc CInt CPea EBee EHoe
	EMan EPPr EPla GKir GOrn LHrt
	LRHS SCob WCDu
appressa	SApp
arenaria	NNor
atrata	CBrm CCuc CHar EBrP EBre
	EHoe EMar EMon EPPr EPla ESis
	LBCl LBSe LBre LHrt LRHS MBBe
	SBre

aurea	GDea GKir
baccans	EPla GCal
berggrenii	More than 30 suppliers
binervis	Last listed 1998
boottiana	EPPr EWes GGar
brunnea	EHoe EPPr EWes WDyG
– 'Variegata'	CCuc EBee EHoe GGar SAga
	SCob WCot WLeb WRus
buchananii	More than 30 suppliers
– 'Viridis'	EBee EHoe ELan EMan EPPr EPla
	LRHS WHer WWoo
caryophyllea 'The Beatles'	CBrm CCuc CElw CMea EBee
	EGoo EHoe EPPr EPla ESis LPan
	LRHS MCCP MMoz NBro NHol
¶ *chathamica*	EMan NSti SMac
¶ 'China Blue'	SApp
comans	More than 30 suppliers
– bronze	More than 30 suppliers
– 'Frosted Curls'	More than 30 suppliers
¶ – 'Kupferflamme'	EFou
– 'Small Red'	EBrP EBre GKir LBCl LBSe LBre
	LRHS MAsh MBBe MMoz SBre
	SWal WLeb
§ *conica*	GKir LHil MBri SPer
– 'Hime-kan-suge'	See *C. conica* 'Snowline'
§ – 'Snowline' (v)	More than 30 suppliers
crinata	MNrw
crus-corvi	EBee EPPr
dallii	CInt EBee ECou EPPr EWes
demissa	CCuc CInt EBee EHoe EPPr GBin
	WWye
depauperata	CCuc EHoe EMon EPla WWye
digitata	WWye
dipsacea	CBrm CElw CRow EBee ECou
	EHoe EMan EMon EPGN EWsh
	GBri GCal GOrn LHrt MAvo MBel
	MBrN MCLN MLLN MMoz MNrw
	MWhi NChi NWCA SAga WHal
	WPer WWye
dissita	CCuc CInt
¶ *disticha*	GDea
divulsa	GBin GDea
– subsp. *leersii*	Last listed 1997
dolichostachya	CBod EBee EMon EPPr EPla GBin
'Kaga-nishiki' (v)	LRHS MAvo MMoz WCot WLeb
§ *elata* 'Aurea' (v) ♀	More than 30 suppliers
– 'Bowles' Golden'	See *C. elata* 'Aurea'
– 'Knightshayes'	MMoz WCot
'Evergold'	See *C. oshimensis* 'Evergold'
ferruginea	GBin
firma	NNrd
– 'Variegata'	EPar EPot MAsh MDHE MTho
	MWat NHar NMen NTow NWCA
	SChu SIng SRot WAbe
§ *flacca*	CBrm CFri CInt EBee EHoe EMan
	EPPr GBin GDea GKir MSCN
– 'Bias' (v)	CKin CNat EBee EMan EMon
	EPPr EPla GKir LRHS MMoz WCot
§ – subsp. *flacca*	EHul EWes MMoz MTed SHel
	WWye
flaccosperma	SApp
flagellifera	More than 30 suppliers
– 'Rapunzel'	EBee WPGP
flava	EHoe GDea
forsteri	See *C. pseudocyperus*
fortunei 'Variegata'	See *C. morrowii* 'Variegata'
fraseri	EHoe GBin
fuscula	Last listed 1997
glauca Bosc. ex Boott	EPla
– Scopoli	See *C. flacca* subsp. *flacca*
grayi	CBrm CCuc CElw CInt CRDP
	EGar EHoe EMar EMon EPPr EPla

GCal LEdu LRHS MCCP MTho
WCot WPer WRus WWye

§ **bachijoensis** — EMon EPPr EPla LRHS WFar
  'Happy Wanderer' — SLPl
hirta — CKin EPPr
hispida — EPPr GOrP LHrt
hordeistichos — EBee EPPr
humilis 'Hexe' — Last listed 1997
§ 'Ice Dance' (v) — EFou SApp WCot
intumescens — EBee
kaloides — CCuc EBee EHoe EMar EMon
  LRHS

'Kan-suge' — See C. morrowii
'Little Red' — EPla GKir WMoo
¶ **lupulina** — CBrm
lurida — CBod CBrm EPGN GBin MCCP
macloviana — CInt EBee EPPr
* **marylandica** — EBrP EBre LBCl LBSe LBre MBBe
  SBre

montana — EPPr
§ **morrowii** Boott — GCHN IBlr MWhi WPyg
§ - hort. — See C. oshimensis, C. bachijoensis
- 'Evergold' — See C. oshimensis 'Evergold'
- 'Fisher's Form' (v) — More than 30 suppliers
- 'Gilt' — EMon EPPr LRHS MAvo
- 'Ice Dance' — See C. 'Ice Dance'
- 'Nana Variegata' — NBir NWoo WPGP
N - 'Variegata' — More than 30 suppliers
muricata — CBrm CKin GDea
muskingumensis — More than 30 suppliers
¶ - 'Little Midge' — EFou EPPr GKir
- 'Oehme' (v) — CBel CHar EBrP EBre EMan EMon
  EPPr EPla GBin LBCl LBSe LBre
  MBBe MTed SBre SUsu WCot
  WDyG WLeb

- 'Silberstreif' (v) — EMon EPPr
- 'Small Red' — Last listed 1998
- 'Wachtposten' — GCal MFir
nigra — CBrm CKin EHon EPPr EWFC
  GAbr GSki
- 'On-line' (v) — EMon EPPr EPla GBin LRHS MAvo
  MMoz WCot WPrP
- subsp. **tornata** — Last listed 1998
obnupta — CBrm EBee
ornithopoda — EPot
- 'Aurea' — See C. ornithopoda 'Variegata'
§ - 'Variegata' — More than 30 suppliers
§ **oshimensis** — IBlr
§ - 'Evergold' (v) ♀ — More than 30 suppliers
- 'Variegata' — NBir SCob
otrubae — CKin
ovalis — CCuc CInt CKin
pallescens — GBin WWye
- 'Wood's Edge' (v) — CNat
panicea — EHoe EMar EPPr EPla MMoz SApp
paniculata — CBrm CInt EBee
pauciflora — EPPr
pendula — More than 30 suppliers
- 'Moonraker' (v) — CBot CFil CHar EBee EPla LEdu
  MAnH SApp WLeb
petriei — CCuc CWSG EBee ECha ECoo
  EHoe ELan EPPr EPot EWsh GAbr
  GAri GOrn LAst LLWP MBNS
  MCLN MMoz MSCN NVic SPla
  SSoC WCot WFar WPer

- dwarf — EWes
phyllocephala — EHoe WCot
- 'Sparkler' (v) — More than 30 suppliers
pilulifera 'Tinney's
  Princess' (v) — EBee EHoe EPot IBlr LRHS MCCP
  NHol WCot
plantaginea — CCuc CFil CHEx EGar EHoe EMar
  EMon EPPr EPla GBin LRHS NBea

SCob WCot WDyG WFar WHil
WPGP
¶ **platyphylla** — WWye
§ **pseudocyperus** — CBrm CCuc CInt CKin ECGN
  EGar EHoe EHon EPPr EPla EWFC
  GBin GCHN GDea MLLN MNrw
  MSCN MSta SBea SRms SUsu SWal
  SWyc WLeb WPer WWye
pulicaris — CKin
reinii — EBee
remota — CKin EPPr GBin WWye
riparia — EMFW EPPr LPBA MMal MWhi
  WFar WShi WWeb
- 'Bowles' Golden' — See C. elata 'Aurea'
- 'Variegata' — More than 30 suppliers
* **saxatilis** 'Variegata' — CInt EMon
secta — ECou EHoe EPPr GOrn MNrw
  WDyG WLRN WMoo
- var. **tenuiculmis** — CBod CBrm CCuc EHoe EMon
  EOld EPPr EWsh GBin GGar
  LRHS MAvo MWhi NHol
siderosticha — CFil EPla EPot GAri MTed WPGP
  WPer
- 'Kisokaido' (v) — EMon EPPr
- 'Shima-nishiki' (v) — EBee EMan EMon WCot
- 'Variegata' — More than 30 suppliers
'Silver Sceptre' (v) — More than 30 suppliers
solandri — EBee EPPr SHel WDyG
sp. from Uganda — GCal LEdu
sp. from Wellington, — EWes
  New Zealand
spissa — MNrw
stenocarpa — EBee
stricta Lamarck — EPPr EPla
- Goodenough — See C. elata
- 'Bowles' Golden' — See C. elata 'Aurea'
sylvatica — CKin ECGN MBrN WWye
testacea — More than 30 suppliers
- 'Old Gold' — LRot SMer SPlb WFar
texensis — EPPr MMoz
trifida — CCuc CInt EBee EHoe EPla EWTr
  EWsh GAbr GCHN GCal GGar
  LHrt LRHS MAnH MBel MMoz
  MNrw MWhi SCob SPla WCot
  WHal WLeb WWye
¶ **umbrosa** subsp. — EMon
  sabynensis 'Thinny
  Thin' (v)
uncifolia — ECou
vulpina — CKin EPPr SBea

CARICA (Caricaceae)
papaya (F) — Last listed 1998

CARISSA (Apocynaceae)
bispinosa — Last listed 1998
grandiflora — See C. macrocarpa
§ **macrocarpa** (F) — CSpe ECon ERea LCns

CARLINA (Asteraceae)
acanthifolia — MAvo NSla
- subsp. **cyanara** — NWCA
  JJA 274.101
acaulis — CM&M EBee ELan GKir MBel NSti
  NWCA SPlb WElm WFar WJek
  WPer WPyg
- bronze — EMan GCal NChi
- var. **caulescens** — See C. acaulis subsp. simplex
§ - subsp. **simplex** — EBee ECGP ECha EMan EMar
  GBuc GMaP LRHS MBri NPSI NPri
  SMad SPer WFar WJek WPer
- - bronze — MAvo NSla

corymbosa	Last listed 1997
vulgaris	CArn CKin EWFC WPer
- 'Silver Star'	Last listed 1998

CARMICHAELIA (Papilionaceae)
'Abundance'	ECou
'Angie'	ECou
angustata 'Buller'	ECou
appressa	ECou
- 'Ellesmere'	ECou
§ *arborea*	ECou
- 'Grand'	ECou
arenaria	Last listed 1998
astonii	ECou
- 'Ben More'	ECou
- 'Chalk Ridge'	ECou
australis	ECou
- Aligera Group	SVen
- 'Bright Eyes'	ECou
- 'Cunningham'	ECou
- Flagelliformis Group	ECou SVen
- 'Mahurangi'	ECou
- Ovata Group	ECou
- 'Solander'	ECou
'Charm'	ECou
'Clifford Bay'	ECou
corrugata	ECou
'Culverden'	ECou
curta	ECou
enysii	CTri ITim MBro
- AGS 27	Last listed 1998
- 'Pringle'	Last listed 1998
exsul	ECou
fieldii 'Westhaven'	ECou
flagelliformis 'Roro'	ECou
glabrata	CPLG CPle
grandiflora	Last listed 1999
'Hay and Honey'	ECou
juncea Nigrans Group	ECou
kirkii	ECou
- x *astonii*	Last listed 1998
- hybrid	Last listed 1998
'Lilac Haze'	ECou
monroi	ECou
- 'Rangitata'	ECou
- 'Tekapo'	ECou
nana	ECou
- 'Desert Road'	ECou
- 'Pringle'	ECou
- 'Waitaki'	ECou
nigrans 'Wanaka'	ECou
odorata	ECou SVen
- Angustata Group	ECou
- 'Green Dwarf'	ECou
- 'Lakeside'	ECou
- 'Riverside'	ECou
ovata 'Calf Creek'	ECou
'Parson's Tiny'	ECou
petriei	ECou SMad
- 'Aviemore'	ECou
- 'Lindis'	ECou
- 'Pukaki'	ECou
- Virgata Group	ECou
'Porter's Pass'	ECou
robusta	Last listed 1998
'Spangle'	ECou
suteri	Last listed 1997
'Tangle'	ECou
uniflora	ECou
- 'Bealey'	ECou
violacea	Last listed 1997
'Weka'	ECou

williamsii	ECou
'Yellow Eyes'	ECou

x CARMISPARTIUM (Papilionaceae)
astens	See x *C. hutchinsii*
§ *hutchinsii*	ECou
¶ - 'Butterfly'	ECou
- 'County Park'	ECou
¶ - 'Delight'	ECou
- 'Pink Beauty'	ECou
¶ - 'Wingletye'	ECou

CARPENTERIA (Hydrangeaceae)
californica ♀	CBot CPMA CSam ELan ENot
	EPfP EWTr GKir GQui IOrc LHop
	LNet LRHS MAsh MBri MGos
	MRav MWhi SBrw SMur SPer
	SReu SSpi SSta WHCG WHar WPat
	WSHC WWat
- 'Bodnant'	LRHS
- 'Elizabeth'	CPMA GKir LRHS MAsh MBri
	SMur SPla SSpi SSta
¶ - 'Eskimo'	SSpi
- 'Ladhams' Variety'	CB&S CPMA EPfP WSPU

CARPINUS ✿ (Corylaceae)
betulus ♀	More than 30 suppliers
- 'Columnaris'	CLnd CTho LRHS MBri
* - 'Columnaris Nana'	CMCN
§ - 'Fastigiata' ♀	More than 30 suppliers
- 'Frans Fontaine'	CDul CMCN CTho EBee GKir
	IOrc MBlu SSta
- 'Horizontalis'	CMCN
- 'Incisa'	GAri
- 'Pendula'	CDul CEnd CTho EBee GAri
- 'Purpurea'	CDul ENot
- 'Pyramidalis'	See *C. betulus* 'Fastigiata'
caroliniana	CLnd CMCN SMad WNor
caucasica	Last listed 1997
* *comptoniifolia*	Last listed 1998
cordata	CMCN WCwm WDin
coreana	CDul CMCN CTho SFur WNor
fargesii	See *C. viminea*
henryana	WDin
japonica	CDul CEnd CMCN EPfP GKir
	LBuc MBlu SFur SMad WDin
laxiflora	GAri SMad WNor
- var. *macrostachya*	See *C. viminea*
mollicoma	Last listed 1999
omeiensis	Last listed 1999
orientalis	CMCN WNor
polyneura	CMCN WNor
* *schisiensis*	WCwm
x *schuschaensis*	Last listed 1997
tschonoskii	CMCN
turczaninowii	CDul CMCN WDin WNor WOTO
	WShe
§ *viminea*	CBlo CDoC CEnd CMCN EPfP
	WNor

CARPOBROTUS (Aizoaceae)
§ *edulis*	CAgr CHEx CTrC EOas IBlr SAPC
	SArc SChr SEND WHer
muirii	CTrC EOas
quadrifidus	EOas
sauerae	CTrC EOas

CARPODETUS (Escalloniaceae)
serratus	Last listed 1997

CARTHAMUS (Asteraceae)
tinctorius	EOHP MChe MSal

CARUM (Apiaceae)

carvi	CArn ELau GPoy IIve MChe MHer SIde WGwG WHer WJek WOak WPer WSel WWye
copticum	MSal
petroselinum	See *Petroselinum crispum*

CARYA ✿ (Juglandaceae)

cordiformis ♀	CMCN EPfP
¶ *floridana*	CMCN
glabra	CMCN
N *illinoinensis* (F)	CMCN
laciniosa 'Henry' (F)	Last listed 1999
- 'Stephens' (F)	Last listed 1999
myristiciformis	CMCN
ovata (F) ♀	CAgr CLnd CMCN CTho MBlu SSpi
pallida	CMCN
tomentosa	Last listed 1997

CARYOPTERIS ✿ (Verbenaceae)

* x *bungei*	Last listed 1999
x *clandonensis*	CB&S CSam CTrw EBee ELan ENot MWat NBir SHel WBod WCFE WDin WFar WHCG WHar WSHC WStl WWat WWin WWye
- 'Arthur Simmonds'	CBlo EBee ECha EPfP GKir LFis LHop LRHS SPer WGor WRHF
- 'Dark Night'	LRHS MBri WBcn
- 'Ferndown'	CChe CDoC EBee EBrP EBre ELan EWTr GKir GOrc LBCl LBSe LBre LFis LHop LRHS MAsh MBBe MGos SBre SLim SPer SPla SReu SRms SSpi WFar WWeb
- 'First Choice'	CAbP CRos ELan EPfP GKir LRHS MAsh MWat SChu SMad SMrm SMur SPer SUsu WBcn WRus
- 'Heavenly Blue' ♀	More than 30 suppliers
- 'Kew Blue'	More than 30 suppliers
- 'Longwood Blue'	EPfP GCal LRHS MAsh WBcn
- 'Newleaze'	LHop
* - 'Pershore'	LRHS MBri MTis WCFE WCot WSPU
- 'Worcester Gold'	More than 30 suppliers
* 'Dark Prince'	Last listed 1998
divaricata	CFil CPle EBee EMon
- 'Electrum'	EMon
- 'Jade Shades'	EMon
- variegated (v)	Last listed 1998
§ *incana*	CPle EBee EBrP EBre ELan EPfP ERav LBCl LBSe LBre LFis MBBe MSte MWhi SBre SPer WCot WOTO WSHC
- pink form	LRHS
- weeping form	ELan GBuc GCal LFis SMrm SPan SRms WLeb WPat
mastacanthus	See *C. incana*

CARYOTA (Arecaceae)

'Hymalaya'	LPal
mitis	LPal
obtusa	LPal
ochlandra	LPal
ophiopellis	Last listed 1999
urens	LPal

CASSANDRA See CHAMAEDAPHNE

CASSIA (Caesalpiniaceae)

corymbosa Lam.	See *Senna corymbosa*
§ *javanica*	Last listed 1999
marilandica	See *Senna marilandica*
nodosa	See *C. javanica*
obtusifolia	See *Senna obtusifolia*
siamea	See *Senna siamea*

CASSINIA (Asteraceae)

aculeata	Last listed 1998
aureonitens	Last listed 1998
leptophylla	CDoC CPLG SPer
- subsp. *fulvida*	CB&S ECou EHoe EMil GKir GOrc GTou IOrc MBar MBlu NFor SPer STre WBcn WBod WTro
- subsp. *vauvilliersii*	CDoC GEil NFor SPer
- - var. *albida*	CB&S EGoo EPfP LRHS SPer WBod WGer
- - CC 570	NWCA
- - 'Silberschmelze'	SOWG
N *retorta*	CDoC ECou
- yellow	Last listed 1998
'Ward Silver'	CBot ECou EMan EWes GSki MBel NFor SPan

CASSINIA x HELICHRYSUM (Asteraceae)

* *C.* sp. x *H.* sp.	WKif WSHC

CASSIOPE ✿ (Ericaceae)

* 'Askival'	ITim
'Askival Arctic Fox'	GCrs
'Askival Freebird'	See *C.* Freebird Group
'Askival Snowbird'	GCrs
'Askival Snow-wreath'	See *C.* Snow-wreath Group
'Askival Stormbird'	GCrs
'Badenoch'	ECho EPot GAri GDra GKir LRHS MDun NDlv NHar WAbe
'Bearsden'	CMHG GAri GDra MBar NDlv NHar WPat WPyg
'Edinburgh' ♀	CMHG EPfP GAbr GChr GCrs GDra GKir MBar MBro NDlv NHar NHol NMen WAbe WPat WPyg
§ Freebird Group	GCrs
'George Taylor'	Last listed 1999
* *inermis*	NMen
'Kathleen Dryden'	GDra
lycopodioides ♀	EPot GCrs GDra GTou IMGH MBar MGos NHar NHol
- 'Beatrice Lilley'	EPot GAri GChr GKir GTou LRHS MBar MDun NDlv NHar NHol WAbe WPat WPyg
- 'Jim Lever'	WAbe
- 'Rokujô'	GCrs NHol
'Medusa'	GDra GTou LRHS NHar NHol WPat WPyg
mertensiana	ECho GTou MBar NDlv NMen SRPl SRms
- 'California Pink'	Last listed 1998
- var. *californica*	GKir WAbe
- dwarf	Last listed 1999
- var. *gracilis*	CMHG GKir LRHS MGos NHar NHol
- - dwarf	EPot
'Muirhead' ♀	CMHG EPot GDra GKir GTou IMGH MBar MDun NDlv NHar NHol NMen SRms WAbe WPat WPyg
'Randle Cooke' ♀	CMHG EPot EWes GChr GCrs GDra GKir GTou MBar MBro MDun NDlv NHar NHol SRms WAbe WPat WPyg
selaginoides LS&E 13284	GAri GNor WAbe
§ Snow-wreath Group	GCrs
§ *stelleriana*	Last listed 1998

tetragona	GKir GTou LRHS MBar SRms
- var. *saximontana*	NHol
wardii	GKir
- x *fastigiata* Askival strain	GCrs

CASTANEA ✿ (Fagaceae)

'Layeroka' (F)	CAgr LEdu
* 'Marigoule'	Last listed 1997
mollissima	CMCN GAri
x *neglecta*	CTho ESim
sativa ♀	CB&S CDoC CHEx CKin CLnd EBee ECrN ENot EWTr GChr GKir IOrc LBuc LHyr LPan LRHS MBar MBri MGos MWat NRog NWea SPer WDin WFar WHar WMou WOrn WStl WWes
§ - 'Albomarginata'	CBlo CDoC CDul CTho EBee EBrP EBre EPfP IMGH LBCl LBSe LBre LRHS MBBe MBlu MBri MGos NBea NBee SBre SLim SMad SPer WWes
- 'Anny's Red'	MBlu
- 'Anny's Summer Red'	CDul
- 'Argenteovariegata'	See *C. sativa* 'Albomarginata'
- 'Aspleniifolia'	CB&S CDoC CDul MBlu WPGP
- 'Aureomarginata'	See *C. sativa* 'Variegata'
- 'Bournette' (F)	Last listed 1998
* - 'Corkscrew'	LPan
* - 'Doré de Lyon'	Last listed 1997
- 'Glabra'	Last listed 1999
- 'Marron de Lyon' (F)	CEnd CTho EMui EPfP LRHS MBlu MCoo SLim
¶ - 'Thompson' (F)	ESim
§ - 'Variegata'	CAbP CB&S CFil CMCN COtt ELan EMil EPfP LPan LRHS MAsh WPGP
- 'Vincent van Gogh'	SMad
seguinii	LEdu LRHS
'Simpson'	CAgr LEdu

CASTANOPSIS (Fagaceae)

cuspidata	CMCN

CASUARINA (Casuarinaceae)

cunninghamiana	IDee
equisetifolia	CGre
glauca	Last listed 1999
littoralis	See *Allocasuarina littoralis*
stricta	See *Allocasuarina verticillata*

CATALPA ✿ (Bignoniaceae)

bignonioides ♀	More than 30 suppliers
- 'Aurea' ♀	More than 30 suppliers
- 'Nana'	Last listed 1997
- 'Purpurea'	See *C. x erubescens* 'Purpurea'
- 'Variegata'	CLnd EBee EPfP LNet LRHS MBro NHol SLim SPer WPat WPyg
bungei	CTho LPan WNor
- 'Purpurea'	ELan
x *erubescens*	Last listed 1999
§ - 'Purpurea' ♀	More than 30 suppliers
fargesii	CFil CLnd
- f. *duclouxii*	CFil CTho
ovata	CBlo CGre CHEx CMCN CTho SFur WPGP
speciosa	CB&S CHEx CLnd CMCN CTho EWTr LRHS SPer
- 'Pulverulenta' (v)	CB&S CDoC CEnd CMCN LRHS SPer WStl

CATANANCHE (Asteraceae)

caerulea	More than 30 suppliers
- 'Alba'	CGle CPou EBee ECha EPar EPfP GKir LIck LRHS NBid NBir NPri SPer SUsu WPer WWhi
- 'Bicolor'	CM&M CSev EMan EMon EWTr LRHS MHer MNrw NFai SLon STes WElm WHer WHoo WPnP WWal
- 'Major' ♀	ENot EWTr LRHS MWat SRms WEas
* - 'Stargazer'	NArg
caespitosa	SBla

CATAPODIUM (Poaceae)

§ *rigidum*	Last listed 1997

CATHA (Celastraceae)

edulis	Last listed 1998

CATHARANTHUS (Apocynaceae)

roseus ♀	EOHP GPoy MBri
- Ocellatus Group	MBri

CATOPSIS (Bromeliaceae)

berteroana	WMEx

CAULOPHYLLUM (Berberidaceae)

thalictroides	CArn CRDP EBee LRHS WCot WCru
- subsp. *robustum*	WCru

CAUTLEYA (Zingiberaceae)

§ *gracilis*	WCot WMul
lutea	See *C. gracilis*
spicata	CHEx IBlr MTed
¶ - CCW106	EMan GCal
- 'Robusta'	CHEx CRDP EMan GCal SMad SSoC WCru

CAYRATIA (Vitaceae)

japonica	Last listed 1999
- B&SWJ 570	Last listed 1999

CEANOTHUS ✿ (Rhamnaceae)

'A.T. Johnson'	CBlo EBee ENot EOld LCaP MAsh NFai SLim SPer SRPl SRms SSoC WGwG
americanus	CArn CPle MSal
- 'Fincham'	CKno
arboreus	SAPC SArc
- 'Owlswood Blue'	LRHS
- 'Trewithen Blue' ♀	More than 30 suppliers
'Autumnal Blue' ♀	More than 30 suppliers
'Basil Fox'	LRHS WBcn
'Blue Boy'	Last listed 1997
'Blue Buttons'	LRHS
* 'Blue Carpet'	Last listed 1998
'Blue Cushion'	CB&S CBlo CDoC EBee ECtt LHop LRHS MBel MGos SEas WWat
'Blue Jeans'	CAbP CBlo EBee LRHS MAsh SPan WAbe
'Blue Mist'	Last listed 1997
* 'Blue Moon'	LRHS
'Blue Mound' ♀	CDoC CLan CTrw EBee EBrP EBre EMil ENot EWTr GChr GKir LBCl LBSe LBre LRHS MBBe MGos MRav NFor NHol SBre SLim SPer SPla SReu SSpi WBod WSHC WWat WWeb

* 'Blue Star'	Last listed 1999
'Burkwoodii' ♀	CB&S CMac CTri EBrP EBre EWTr
	GKir IOrc LBCl LBSe LBre LRHS
	MAsh MBBe MBri MGos SBre SPer
	SRPl SReu WFar
'Burtonensis'	Last listed 1997
'Cascade' ♀	CB&S EBee ENot GGar GKir IOrc
	LAst LRHS MAsh MBri MGos
	MWat NFor SLon SPer SRPl WAbe
	WBod WHCG WSHC WStl
'Comtesse de Paris'	See C. x delileanus 'Comtesse de
	Paris'
'Concha'	More than 30 suppliers
crassifolius var. planus	Last listed 1998
* - 'Plenus'	Last listed 1999
§ cuneatus var. rigidus	CPle EBee LRHS SDry SRms
- - 'Snowball'	EBee ELan EPfP GSki LRHS MAsh
	MGos SPan WBcn
cyaneus	CGre CPle
'Cynthia Postan'	CAbP CMHG CPle CWSG EBee
	EBrP EBre EPfP GOrc IArd ISea
	LBCl LBSe LBre LRHS MAsh MBBe
	MBlu MBri MWat NPri SBre WAbe
	WPat
'Dark Star'	CB&S CBlo CChe CDoC CMHG
	CTbh CWSG EPfP EWll GOrc
	LRHS MAsh NPro SOWG SPla
	SReu SSta WPat
'Delight' ♀	CBlo EBee ELan EPla EWTr IOrc
	LRHS MGos NFla SPer WAbe
	WBod WFar WWat
x delileanus	CKno
§ - 'Comtesse de Paris'	CKno MRav WBcn
- 'Gloire de Versailles' ♀	More than 30 suppliers
- 'Henri Desfossé'	CBlo CKno CPle ELan LRHS MRav
	SOWG SPer WDin WKif
- 'Indigo'	CKno NFla
- 'Topaze' ♀	CB&S CBlo CKno CPle ELan EMil
	EPfP ISea LRHS MRav SLon SOWG
	WHar WKif WWeb
dentatus hort.	See C. x lobbianus
- Torrey & A.Gray	ENot IOrc MAsh MGos SPer WPyg
- var. floribundus	ELan LRHS SDix
- 'Prostratus'	Last listed 1999
* - 'Superbus'	EBee
'Diamond Heights'	See C. griseus var. horizontalis
	'Diamond Heights'
'Dignity'	Last listed 1999
divergens	CPle
'Edinburgh' ♀	CBlo CMHG EPfP LRHS MAsh
	MGos NCut WBod WWeb
'Edward Stevens'	Last listed 1997
¶ 'El Dorado' (v)	WWeb
* 'Elan'	Last listed 1997
'Eleanor Taylor'	LRHS
'Fallen Skies'	CAbP LRHS MAsh
foliosus	CPle
- var. austromontanus	CTrw SPan
'Frosty Blue'	COtt LRHS
'Gentian Plume'	LRHS SMad
* 'Gloire Porrectus'	Last listed 1997
gloriosus	CFai CPle EWes IOrc LRHS SAga
	SDry WWat
- 'Anchor Bay'	COtt ELan EPfP LRHS MAsh SCob
	SLon SOWG SPan
- 'Emily Brown'	EBee
§ griseus var. horizontalis	LRHS MAsh SPer WWeb
'Diamond Heights' (v)	
- - 'Hurricane Point'	WFar
¶ - - 'Silver Surprise' (v)	WWeb
- - 'Yankee Point'	CB&S CBlo CChe CDoC CMHG

	CMac EBee EMil GKir LHop LRHS
	MAsh MBel MBri MGos MRav
	NFai SEas SLim SPer WAbe WBod
	WDin
- 'Santa Ana'	Last listed 1997
bearstiorum	CPle LRHS
impressus	CB&S CBlo CLan CMHG CPle
	EBee ENot GOrc LRHS MAsh
	MRav SPer SPla WAbe WCFE WEas
	WFar WPyg WWeb
integerrimus var.	Last listed 1998
macrothyrsus	
N 'Italian Skies' ♀	CB&S CBlo CChe CDoC CLan
	CMHG CMac CSam EBee EMil
	LHop LRHS MAsh MBri MGos
	MRav SEas SLim SLon SPer SPlb
	SRPl SWal WBod WGwG WWeb
'Joyce Coulter'	CB&S EBee ISea
'Julia Phelps'	CMHG EBee WEas WLRN WSPU
'Ken Taylor'	CRos LRHS MAsh
§ x lobbianus	CB&S CBrm CTri EBee EWTr
	LRHS MRav NHol NSti SPlb WBod
- 'Russellianus'	CAbP LCaP MGos WSPU
maritimus 'Point Sierra'	Last listed 1997
'Mary Lake'	Last listed 1997
x mendocinensis	Last listed 1998
oliganthus	Last listed 1998
§ - var. sorediatus	Last listed 1998
x pallidus	CFai WBcn
- 'Golden Elan'	CKno SBrw WBcn
- 'Marie Simon'	CB&S CBlo CBot CChe CKno
	CPle EBee ELan EMil EPfP GEil
	LHop LRHS MBel MBri MRav NFla
	NFor SEas SMer SPer SRms WBod
	WCFE WFar WKif WPyg WSHC
	WWeb
- 'Marie Simon	CPMA
Variegated' (v)	
- 'Perle Rose'	CB&S CBlo CMac CPle
	EPfP IOrc LRHS MAsh MTis
	SOWG SPer SPla WKif WSHC
papillosus	WBod
- var. roweanus	CPle GAri WEas WWat
'Percy Picton'	LRHS
'Picnic Day'	Last listed 1997
'Pin Cushion'	CWSG EBee EPfP LRHS SPla WPat
	WRHF WSPU WWat
'Point Millerton'	See C. thyrsiflorus 'Millerton
	Point'
prostratus	GSki LBuc MAsh SDry SMad
	WAbe WEas WWin
'Puget Blue' ♀	More than 30 suppliers
purpureus	CPle LBuc LCaP WWeb
ramulosus	LRHS
'Ray Hartman'	SMad SSoC WBcn
repens	See C. thyrsiflorus var. repens
rigidus	See C. cuneatus var. rigidus
'Sierra Blue'	EBee
'Snow Flurries'	CB&S CBlo EMil EPfP EWTr LAst
	MBel MGos SPan SRPl WAbe WFar
	WGwG WRHF WSPU WWat
	WWeb
sorediatus	See C. oliganthus var. sorediatus
'Southmead' ♀	CBlo CDoC CTri EBee ECtt EMil
	EPfP EWTr GBuc IOrc ISea LRHS
	MAsh MBel MBri MGos NCut
	NFla WBod WDin WHCG WPat
	WWat
spinosus	SVen
'Thundercloud'	Last listed 1997
thyrsiflorus	CB&S CBlo CMac CTri EPfP LRHS
	MAsh MBri NFai NHol SPer SRms

	WDin WFar WHar
- 'Borne Again' (v)	WBcn
§ - 'Millerton Point'	CBlo CChe CPMA CPle CWSG
	EBee EMil LRHS MAsh MBlu MBro
	SLim SPla WWeb
§ - var. *repens* ♀	More than 30 suppliers
- 'Skylark'	CBlo CDoC CMHG CPle CRos
	CTbh EBee ELan GKir LHop LNet
	LRHS MAsh MBri NPro SDix SLim
	SLon SReu SSta WFar WWat
	WWeb
'Tilden Park'	LRHS
* 'Underway'	Last listed 1999
x *veitchianus*	CBlo CMac EBee ENot GChr
	LRHS MAsh MBar NHol SPer SSta
	WWeb
verrucosus	Last listed 1998
'White Cascade'	LRHS SPan
§ Zanzibar = 'Pershore	CWSG EBee EPla LRHS MGos
Zanzibar' PBR (v)	MTis MWat NEgg SCoo WOVN
	WSPU

CEDRELA (Meliaceae)

sinensis	See *Toona sinensis*

CEDRONELLA (Lamiaceae)

§ *canariensis*	CArn CGle CInt CSev GBar GPoy
	IBlr IIve ILis MChe MHer MMal
	MSal NHex SIde SOWG SWat
	WCer WHer WOak WPer WSel
	WWye
mexicana	See *Agastache mexicana*
triphylla	See *C. canariensis*

CEDRUS (Pinaceae)

atlantica	CDul CGre CTho EHul GKir LCon
	MBar NWea SLim SPar WMou
	WPGP
- 'Aurea'	CDoC CMac LCon LLin LPan
	LRHS MAsh MBar MGos SSta
	WDin WHar
- 'Fastigiata'	CDoC CMac EHul LCon MBar
	MBri MGos SLim
- Glauca Group ♀	More than 30 suppliers
- - 'Saphir Nymphe'	CKen
- - 'Silberspitz'	CKen
- 'Glauca Fastigiata'	CKen LPan
- 'Glauca Pendula'	CDoC CKen EHul EOrn EPfP
	GChr GKir IMGH IOrc LCon LNet
	LPan LRHS MBar MBri MGos
	NBee NBlu SLim SMad SSta WGer
	WOrn WWes
- 'Pendula'	CDul CMac ECho GAri
brevifolia ♀	CDoC ECho LCon LPan MBar
	MBri MGos
- 'Epstein'	LCon MBar
- 'Hillier Compact'	CKen
- 'Kenwith'	CKen
deodara ♀	CDoC CDul CMac CSam CTho
	EHul ENot GKir IOrc LBee LCon
	LHyr LPan LRHS MAsh MBar MBri
	MGos NBee NWea SLim SPer STre
	WDin WFar WMou WPGP WPyg
	WWat WWeb
- 'Albospica' (v)	LCon
- 'Argentea'	MBar MGos
- 'Aurea' ♀	CDoC CDul CTho EHul EOrn
	GKir IMGH ISea LBee LCon LLin
	LPan LRHS MAsh MBar MBri
	MGos SLim WDin WFro WOrn
I - 'Aurea Pendula'	Last listed 1997
- 'Blue Dwarf'	CKen LCon LLin MAsh

* - 'Blue Mountain Broom'	CKen
- 'Blue Triumph'	LPan
- 'Cream Puff'	CSli ECho LCon LLin MAsh MBar
	MGos
- 'Feelin' Blue'	CDoC CKen COtt CSli EBrP EBre
	EPla GKir IMGH LBCl LBSe LBee
	LBre LCon LLin LPan LRHS MAsh
	MBBe MBar MBri MGos NHol
	SBre SCoo SLim WStI WWeb
- 'Gold Cone'	MGos
- 'Gold Mound'	CKen GAri LCon
- 'Golden Horizon'	CDoC CKen EBrP EBre EHul EOrn
	GKir IMGH IOrc LBCl LBSe LBee
	LBre LCon LLin LPan LRHS MAsh
	MBBe MBar MBri MGos SBre SLim
	SPer WDin WPyg WWeb
- 'Karl Fuchs'	CDoC EBrP EBre GKir LBCl LBSe
	LBre LPan LRHS MBBe MBri SBre
	WGor
- 'Kashmir'	CSli
- 'Kelly Gold'	CDoC GKir LPan MBri
- 'Klondyke'	LCon SBir
- 'Lime Glow'	Last listed 1999
- 'MacPenny's Seedling'	Last listed 1997
- 'Mountain Beauty'	CKen
- 'Nana'	CKen
- 'Nivea'	CKen
- 'Pendula'	CDoC EHul LCon LPan MBar
	MGos MWat WGor WStI
- 'Pygmy'	CKen
¶ - 'Raywood's Prostrate'	CKen
- 'Roman Candle'	CSli ECho EOrn
- 'Scott'	CKen
- 'Silver Mist'	CKen
- 'Verticillata Glauca'	Last listed 1997
* 'Home Park'	CKen
libani ♀	More than 30 suppliers
- 'Comte de Dijon'	EHul LCon LLin SLim
- Nana Group	CKen ECho LCon
- 'Sargentii'	CDoC CKen EHul EOrn IMGH
	LCon LLin LRHS MAsh MBar MBri
	MGos SLim SSta
- 'Taurus'	MBar

CELASTRUS (Celastraceae)

angulatus	CPIN
orbiculatus	CB&S CDoC CMac CPIN EBee
	EMil GBin GEil LRHS MRav NSti
	SLon SRPl SReu SSta WBod WFar
	WGwG WSHC
- 'Diana' (f)	NBea SSta
- 'Hercules' (m)	NBea
- Hermaphrodite Group ♀	CBrm CSam EPla GOrc GSki
	MCCP MGrG SBra SDix SPan SPer
	SSpi WTro WWat
- JLS 88018WI	Last listed 1997
- var. *papillosus*	WCru
B&SWJ 591	
- var. *punctatus*	WCru
B&SWJ 1931	
scandens	CMac CPIN ELan IMGH MSal
	SMur

CELMISIA ✿ (Asteraceae)

adamsii	IBlr
allanii	GCrs IBlr
alpina	GAbr IBlr
- large-leaved	IBlr
angustifolia	GCrs GNor IBlr
- silver-leaved	IBlr
argentea	EPot GCrs GNor GTou IBlr NDlv
	NHar WAbe

asteliifolia	IBlr
Ballyrogan hybrids	IBlr
bellidioides	EPot EWes GCrs GGar IBlr NEgg
	NHar NHol NMen WAbe
bonplandii	GNor IBlr
brevifolia	GNor IBlr
coriacea	GCal IBlr MDun NFor NHar WEas
- 'Harry Bryce'	IBlr
¶ *costiniana*	IBlr
dallii	GNor IBlr
densiflora	GCrs IBlr NLAp
- silver-leaved	IBlr
discolor	IBlr
durietzii	IBlr
'Edrom'	Last listed 1998
glandulosa	IBlr
gracilenta	GCrs IBlr NSla SOkd
- CC 563	NWCA
graminifolia	IBlr
haastii	IBlr
hectorii	GGar GNor IBlr ITim
holosericea	IBlr
hookeri	GCal IBlr
¶ *inaccessa*	IBlr
incana	GCrs IBlr
Inshriach hybrids	IBlr
insignis	IBlr
Jury hybrids	IBlr
¶ *latifolia*	IBlr
¶ - large-leaved	IBlr
lindsayi	Last listed 1997
longifolia	GCrs GNor SSpi
- large-leaved	Last listed 1999
- small-leaved	IBlr
mackaui	IBlr
monroi	IBlr
morganii	IBlr
prorepens	IBlr
¶ *pugioniformis*	IBlr
ramulosa	GNor SIng
§ - var. *tuberculata*	GCrs GTou IBlr ITim WAbe
saxifraga	IBlr
semicordata	EPot NHar NSla
- subsp. *aurigans*	EPot
- 'David Shackleton'	IBlr
- subsp. *stricta*	GCrs IBlr
* *sericifolia*	Last listed 1999
sericophylla	IBlr
- large-leaved	IBlr
sessiliflora	EPot GTou IBlr ITim
- 'Mount Potts'	IBlr
spectabilis	IBlr MDun NEgg NHar WCot WHil
- var. *angustifolia*	IBlr
- subsp. *magnifica*	IBlr
¶ *tomentella*	IBlr
traversii	GNor IBlr NHar
verbascifolia	IBlr
viscosa	IBlr
§ *walkeri*	GCrs GTou IBlr
webbiana	See *C. walkeri*

CELOSIA (Amaranthaceae)

argentea var. *cristata*	MBri
- var. *cristata* Plumosa	MBri
Group	

CELSIA See VERBASCUM

x CELSIOVERBASCUM See VERBASCUM

CELTIS (Ulmaceae)

africana	CGre

aurantiaca	Last listed 1998
australis	CB&S CDul GKir LPan LRHS
	MWat SSta
bungeana	IDee
caucasica	Last listed 1997
jessoensis	CMCN
julianae	WCwm WNor
laevigata	CMCN
occidentalis	ELan EPfP EWTr LRHS SSta
- var. *pumila*	WNor
sinensis	CMCN CPle WNor
tournefortii	CMCN

CENOLOPHIUM (Apiaceae)

denudatum	SDix

CENTAUREA (Asteraceae)

¶ *achtarovii*	SOkd
alba	EBee
- HH&K 228A	Last listed 1999
argentea	CBot
atropurpurea	EMon NLar SGar
bella	CBot CGle CHad CSam CSev
	EBee EMar EOld EOrc GCal GKir
	LAst LFis LGre LHop LRHS MBri
	MGrG MRav NBro NFor NGdn
	NNrd NSti SHel SMrm SWat WAbe
	WFar
benoistii	CHad ECGN EMan EMar
'Blue Dreams'	CSpe EMon LRHS MGrG MLLN
	SUsu
cana	See *C. triumfettii* subsp. *cana*
candidissima hort.	See *C. cineraria*
- Lamarck	See *C. rutifolia*
cheiranthifolia	EBee ECha EMon GCal MBct
	WFar
§ - var. *purpurascens*	EMon LRHS MAvo
§ *cineraria*	SRms WCot WEas
- subsp. *cineraria* ♀	EBee
cyanus	EWFC MHer MHew MMal NArg
	SYvo WFar WJek
cynaroides	See *Leuzea centauroides*
dealbata	CBot COIW ECtt EOld EWTr
	GAbr LRHS MBro MFir MHer
	MMal NArg NBro NFai NMir
	NOak NOrc SCro WByw WFar
	WOve WPer WWin
- 'Steenbergii'	More than 30 suppliers
debeauxii subsp.	Last listed 1998
nemoralis	
declinata	Last listed 1999
drabifolia	Last listed 1997
- subsp.	Last listed 1999
austro-occidentalis	
¶ *fischeri* Willd.	EMon
glastifolia	EBee EMon GCal LRHS MLLN
	WCot WPGP
gymnocarpa	See *C. cineraria*
¶ 'Hoar Frost'	EMon
hypoleuca 'John Coutts'	More than 30 suppliers
jacea	NBid WCot
kerneriana subsp.	Last listed 1999
kerneriana HH&K 297	
kotschyana	EBee
¶ *lactifolia*	EBee
macrocephala	More than 30 suppliers
marschalliana HH&K 271	Last listed 1999
- HH&K 276	Last listed 1998
montana	More than 30 suppliers
- *alba*	More than 30 suppliers
§ - *carnea*	CElw CMea EBee ECha EMon
	MAvo NChi NFla SAga SCro STes

- 'Gold Bullion' — SUsu WHal WRus WWin
EBee EGar EMon EPPr MAvo NBir
WBcn
- 'Grandiflora' — GGar LRHS MBri
¶ - 'Joyce' — EMon
- 'Lady Flora Hastings' — CBot CElw CSam EBee GMac
MAvo MTed SCro
- 'Ochroleuca' — CElw EBee EGle EGoo EMon
MLLN
- 'Parham' — CElw CMGP CPou CSev EBee
EMan GCal LFis LLWP LRHS MBel
MBro MCLN MSCN NCiC NSti
SChu SHel SMrm SPer SPla SPlb
SSvw SWat WLRN
- 'Purple Prose' — EMon
- *purpurea* — MRav
- *rosea* — See *C. montana carnea*
* - *violacea* — IBlr
- 'Violetta' — CPou NBir
nervosa — See *C. uniflora* subsp. *nervosa*
nigra — CArn CKin COld EBee EMan
EWFC EWTr MHew MNaF MOne
NLan NMir NNor SBea SRob WJek
WMoo
- var. *alba* — CArn CBre
- subsp. *rivularis* — ECha
orientalis — ECha LGre NBro NLar WPer
ornata — Last listed 1998
pannonica subsp. — Last listed 1999
    pannonica HH&K 259
parilica NS 699 — NWCA
phrygia — EBee GBuc MGed MHar MNrw
SSvw WFar WPer WRos
pulcherrima — EBee ECha EGle EMon MLLN
NOak WByw WPer
'Pulchra Major' — See *Leuzea centauroides*
rhapontica — See *Leuzea rhapontica*
rigidifolia — SMer
rothrockii — EWTr WSan
rupestris — LGre SBla WBar WWin
ruthenica — WCot
§ *rutifolia* — EBee
salonitana — EMon WCot
scabiosa — CArn CKin CPea ECoo EWFC
EWTr MChe MHer MMal MNrw
MWhi NBid NLan SIde SMrm
WJek WPer
- f. *albiflora* — CNat EBee EBlw EMan EMon LAst
LRHS NPSI WCot
- 'Nell Hill' — CNat
seridis subsp. *maritima* — Last listed 1997
simplicicaulis — CElw CInt CMea CNic CPlt CRDP
EBee EGle GAbr GBri MBel MBro
MFir MTho NChi NMen SBla
SRms SRot WCot WEas WHoo
WPGP WPer
solstitialis subsp. — Last listed 1998
    solstitialis HH&K 179
¶ *stenolepis* subsp. — CMil
    razgradensis
    HH&K 297
thracica — EBee SAga WCot
§ *triumfettii* subsp. *cana* — CNic CPea CRDP NNrd SBla
'Rosea' — WWin
- subsp. *stricta* — EBee EMon EPPr GBuc MSte
NMGW SCro WFar WPGP
- - from Macedonia — LFis
§ *uniflora* subsp. *nervosa* — CSam EBee EMan GGar MGas
MHar NBid NBro WBea WPer
- - JCA 287.000 — EMan

CENTAURIUM (Gentianaceae)
chloodes — See *C. confertum*
§ *confertum* — MNrw
erythraea — CArn EWFC GPoy MChe MHer
MHew MSal SIde WWye
scilloides — CInt LRHS MBro MTho NFor
NHol NMen NWCA WWin

CENTELLA (Apiaceae)
§ *asiatica* — CArn EOHP ILis MSal

CENTRADENIA (Melastomataceae)
¶ *floribunda* — SYvo
inaequilateralis 'Cascade' — CHal CInt CLTr ECtt EMan GPin
LHil LPVe MBri NFai SHFr WCot
WLRN

CENTRANTHUS (Valerianaceae)
¶ *macrosiphon* — EBee
§ *ruber* — More than 30 suppliers
§ - 'Albus' — More than 30 suppliers
- *atrococcineus* — ECha EMan SPer WPer
- var. *coccineus* — CB&S CLTr EBee EGoo ELan ENot
EPfP GAbr GKir LGre LIck LRHS
MCAu MRav MWat NFai SEND
SMrm SRPl WCot
- mauve — LGre
- 'Pretty Betsy' — NPri
* - 'Roseus' — NCut
'White Cloud' — MTis

CEPHALANTHERA (Orchidaceae)
falcata — EFEx
longibracteata — EFEx

CEPHALANTHUS (Rubiaceae)
occidentalis — CB&S CBlo CPle EMil LFis MBNS
MBlu MBro SPer SSta WPat

CEPHALARIA (Dipsacaceae)
§ *alpina* — CElw CGle ECha EDAr EMan
EMar GCHN GKir LAst LRHS
MBel MHer MNrw NFla NGdn
NLar NNrd SMer SOkh SRms
SWat WCot WFar WLin WPer
- 'Nana' — CMil NMen NWCA WPyg
ambrosioides — MLLN
dipsacoides — CNat EBee ECha EMon LGre
flava — EBee EBrP EBre GKir LBCl LBSe
LBre LFis MBBe SBre
galpiniana subsp. — EBee
    simplicior
§ *gigantea* — More than 30 suppliers
* *graeca* — EBee
leucantha — CHea COIW EBee EBot EGar
EWTr GBuc MLLN NLar SHel STes
WElm WWhi
litvinovii — EMon
natalensis — EBee
radiata — EBee EMou
sp. from Nepal 2800m — CSam
tatarica — See *C. gigantea*
tchihatchewii — IHdy
uralensis — Last listed 1999

CEPHALIPTERUM (Asteraceae)
drummondii — Last listed 1998

CEPHALOPHYLLUM (Aizoaceae)
alstonii — Last listed 1999

CEPHALOTAXUS (Cephalotaxaceae)
fortunei — CAgr CGre SLon
barringtonii — ECho LEdu LLin MRav SMur
- var. *drupacea* — Last listed 1999
- 'Fastigiata' — CDoC CKen EHul EOrn EPla GKir
LCon LPan LRHS MAsh MBar MBri
SLim SSmi WGer
- 'Gimborn's Pillow' — MBar
- 'Korean Gold' — CKen
- 'Prostrata' — MBar

CEPHALOTUS (Cephalotaceae)
follicularis — CSWC EAnd EEls GTro WMEx

CERASTIUM (Caryophyllaceae)
alpinum — CMea SRms
- var. *lanatum* — EGoo EWes NTow NWCA WPer
candidissimum — EWes
theophrasti — Last listed 1998
tomentosum — CHal CTri EFer EPfP EWTr GKir
IMGH LGro MHer NFor NPri SIng
SPer SPlb WCar WFar WLRN WPer
- var. *columnae* — CBlo EBrP EBre ECha ECho EHoe
EPfP EWes LBCl LBSe LBre MBBe
SBre SRms WCot
- 'Silberteppich' — EGoo LFis

CERATOCAPNOS (Papaveraceae)
¶ *heterocarpa* — CSpe

CERATONIA (Caesalpiniaceae)
siliqua — CFil MSal

CERATOPHYLLUM (Ceratophyllaceae)
demersum — CBen CRow EHon EMFW LGuA
NDea SWat SWyc WMAq

CERATOSTIGMA ✿ (Plumbaginaceae)
abyssinicum — EBee ELan ERav
griffithii — CB&S CBot CChe CDoC CPle
EBee EBrP EBre ECtt ELan GOrc
IOrc LBCl LBSe LBre LRHS MBBe
MCCP MRav MWat SBre SEas SPer
SSta WAbe WBod WDin WSHC
WWat WWeb
- 'Album' — Last listed 1999
- S&F 149/150 — ISea
minus — CPLG WCot
§ *plumbaginoides* ♀ — More than 30 suppliers
ulicinum — Last listed 1998
willmottianum ♀ — More than 30 suppliers
- Forest Blue = 'Lice'[PBR] — CAbP EBee ELan ENot EPfP GChr
GKir LHop LRHS MAsh NPro
SCoo SPer SPla SReu WPat WWeb

CERATOTHECA (Pedaliaceae)
triloba — SUsu SWat

CERCIDIPHYLLUM ✿ (Cercidiphyllaceae)
japonicum ♀ — More than 30 suppliers
- 'Boyd's Dwarf' — SSta
- 'Heronswood Globe' — CPMA
- f. *pendulum* — CBlo CDul CEnd CFil CMCN EBee
EPfP GKir LBuc LPan LRHS MAsh
MBlu MBri NBea SPer SRPl SSpi
WDin WPGP WWes
- Red Fox — See *C. japonicum* 'Rotfuchs'
§ - 'Rotfuchs' — CB&S CEnd CMCN CPMA CTho
EPfP GKir LRHS MAsh MBlu SMad
SSpi WGer WPGP
- 'Ruby' — CPMA

magnificum ♀ — CEnd CFil CMCN EPfP MBlu SSpi
WWat
- Og 95.111 — CDoC
- Og 95.144 — CFil EPla WPGP
¶ - f. *pendulum* — CPMA

CERCIS (Caesalpiniaceae)
canadensis — CAgr CB&S CBrm CLnd CMCN
EMil EPfP GIBF LRHS MCCP
MGos SPer WHCG WNor WPat
- 'Forest Pansy' ♀ — More than 30 suppliers
* - 'Gigantea' — MBlu
§ - var. *occidentalis* — CAgr SOWG
- 'Royal White' — EPfP MBlu
- 'Rubye Atkinson' — MBlu
chinensis — LRHS MCCP NPSI WOTO
- f. *alba* — Last listed 1997
- 'Avondale' — CEnd CPMA EBee EMil EWes
LNet MBlu MGos
griffithii — WPGP
occidentalis — See *C. canadensis* var.
occidentalis
¶ *reniformis* 'Oklahoma' — CPMA
- 'Texas White' — CPMA
siliquastrum ♀ — More than 30 suppliers
- f. *albida* — CB&S CBlo CBot CLnd CTho EPfP
LPan LRHS SMHT SPer
- 'Rubra' — LRHS

CERCOCARPUS (Rosaceae)
ledifolius — CPLG

CERINTHE (Boraginaceae)
glabra — CPea EMan EWll SRms WWye
¶ 'Golden Bouquet' — NPSI SPer
'Kiwi Blue' — CHar SPer
major — EWll SRCN WEas WSan
- 'Purpurascens' — More than 30 suppliers

CEROPEGIA (Asclepiadaceae)
africana — Last listed 1999
ampliata — Last listed 1999
barklyi — CHal
lanceolata — See *C. longifolia*
linearis subsp. *woodii* ♀ — CHal IBlr MBri SRms
§ - - 'Lady Heart' (v) — CInt
- - 'Variegata' — See *C. linearis* subsp. *woodii*
'Lady Heart'
§ *longifolia* — Last listed 1998
pubescens B&SWJ 2531 — WCru
radicans — Last listed 1999
stapeliiformis ♀ — Last listed 1998

CEROXYLON (Arecaceae)
alpinum — LPJP LPal
¶ *ceriferum* — LPal
quindiuense — Last listed 1997
utile — Last listed 1997
ventricosum — LPal

CESTRUM (Solanaceae)
aurantiacum — CB&S CPle ERea LHil
auriculatum — SOWG
x *cultum* — CPle
§ *elegans* ♀ — CDoC CHal ECon LCns LHil LRHS
SOWG WBod WMul
fasciculatum — CB&S CPle GQui LHil SMad
SOWG
¶ - 'Penlee' — LHil
'Newellii' ♀ — CAbb CB&S CDoC CHEx CMHG
CSev CTbh EBak ECon ELan ERea
ERom GQui LCns LRHS NPSI

nocturnum	SOWG SYvo WBor WSHC CB&S CPle EBak ECon ELan EOHP ERea LHil LRHS MSal
parqui ♀	SOWG SYvo WMul CAbb CGre CMHG CPle ECha ECon ELan EPfP ERea LHil MBel SBrw SDix SLon SMrm SOWG SSte SUsu SYvo WCot WKif WPen WSHC
- 'Cretan Purple'	Last listed 1997
- hybrid	LHil
psittacinum	CGre CPle
purpureum	See *C. elegans*
roseum	ECon
- 'Ilnacullin'	CGre EHol ERea
* *splendens*	SOWG
violaceum misapplied	See *Iochroma cyaneum* 'Trebah'
- 'Woodcote White' misapplied	See *Iochroma cyaneum* 'Woodcote White'

CETERACH (Aspleniaceae)

officinarum	See *Asplenium ceterach*

CHAENACTIS (Asteraceae)

ramosa	Last listed 1999

CHAENOMELES (Rosaceae)

x *californica*	CAgr
- 'Enchantress'	Last listed 1997
cathayensis	CTho EMon EPla SPan WBcn WHer
'James Pilger'	GAbr
§ *japonica*	ENot GOrc MBar NEgg NFor SEND WDin WOTO
- f. *alba*	Last listed 1997
- var. *alpina*	Last listed 1999
- 'Orange Beauty'	Last listed 1997
- 'Sargentii'	CB&S CBlo CFai CMac COtt NEgg NPro SPan
'John Pilger'	NPro SPan
lagenaria	See *C. speciosa*
maulei	See *C. japonica*
sinensis	See *Pseudocydonia sinensis*
§ *speciosa*	CSam MBar NFor NWea WNor
- 'Apple Blossom'	See *C. speciosa* 'Moerloosei'
- 'Aurora'	LRHS MBri
- 'Cardinalis'	CGre
- 'Contorta'	WCot
- 'Falconnet Charlet' (d)	MRav WLRN
- 'Geisha Girl'	More than 30 suppliers
- 'Grayshott Salmon'	CLyn MCCP NCiC NHol NPro SLim SMac SPan WLeb WWat
- 'Knap Hill Radiance'	CBlo
§ - 'Moerloosei' ♀	CDoC CSam EBee ELan ENot GGar GKir GOrc IMGH LAst LRHS MAsh MBri MRav NPSI NSti SIng SLim SPer SPla SSta WDin WGwG WMoo WWat WWeb
- 'Nivalis'	More than 30 suppliers
- 'Port Eliot'	WBcn WWeb
- 'Rosea Plena' (d)	WBcn
- 'Rosemoor Seedling'	GAri
- 'Rubra Grandiflora'	CBlo MGos
- 'Simonii' (d)	CB&S CBlo EBee EHol ENot LRHS MBri MGos MRav NFla NWea SPer WWat
- 'Snow'	CChe CSam ISea MRav MWat SEas SPla SRms WLRN WRHF WStI
- 'Umbilicata'	ENot MRav SPer SRms WWes
- 'Yukigoten'	LRHS SLim WBcn
x *superba*	NFor
- 'Boule de Feu'	CCHP CTri ECtt
- 'Cameo' (d)	CBot CChe EPfP LAst LRHS MBri

	NPri SEas SLPl WLRN WWat
- 'Clementine'	CBlo
- 'Coral Sea'	NFor
- 'Crimson and Gold' ♀	More than 30 suppliers
- 'Elly Mossel'	CB&S CBlo CMac GKir SMer WLRN
- 'Ernst Finken'	WSPU
- 'Etna'	CBlo NCut
¶ - 'Fascination'	EMac
- 'Fire Dance'	CBlo CMac EBee ECtt EGra ENot EOld LRHS MAsh NBee NHol SPer WLRN
- 'Hever Castle'	Last listed 1999
- 'Hollandia'	CBlo MGos SRms
- 'Issai White'	LRHS MBri
- 'Jet Trail'	CB&S CBlo EBee ELan ENot LAst LRHS MBri MCCP MGos MRav NPro
- 'Knap Hill Scarlet' ♀	CBlo CDoC EBee EBrP EBre ECot ENot EPfP GKir IOrc LBCI LBSe LBre LHop LRHS MBBe SBre SEND SLim SPer SRms STre WBod WDin WStI WTro WWat
- 'Lemon and Lime'	CLyn EBee ELan ENot MGos MRav NSti SPan SPer WBcn
- 'Nicoline' ♀	CB&S CBlo EBee ENot EPfP LRHS MBri MWat NEgg NPri SBra WDin WStI
- 'Ohio Red'	WBod WTro
¶ - 'Orange Trail'	MBri
- 'Pink Lady' ♀	More than 30 suppliers
¶ - 'Pink Trail'	MBri
- 'Red Trail'	EBee ENot MRav
- 'Rowallane' ♀	CBlo EBee ELan ENot EPfP GAri MRav SEas SPer WLRN
¶ - 'Salmon Horizon'	EWTr WBcn
- 'Texas Scarlet'	GKir MBri
- 'Tortuosa'	CBlo GOrc SPan WWat
- 'Vermilion'	MBNS
§ - 'Yaegaki' (d)	Last listed 1997

CHAENORHINUM (Scrophulariaceae)

glareosum	Last listed 1999
§ *origanifolium*	EBee ESis GDea Llck LRHS NWCA SPlb WWin
- 'Blue Dream'	CSpe EMan GBri LRHS MDHE MNrw NPri SCob WElm WFar WPer WWal
¶ - subsp. *cadevallii*	EBee

CHAEROPHYLLUM (Apiaceae)

hirsutum	CRow ELan NBrk
- 'Roseum'	More than 30 suppliers

CHAMAECRISTA (Caesalpiniaceae)

¶ *fasciculata*	EBee

CHAMAECYPARIS ✿ (Cupressaceae)

formosensis	CKen LRHS
funebris	See *Cupressus funebris*
lawsoniana	CDul EHul GAri GChr MBar NWea WDin WMou
- 'Albospica' (v)	EHul GKir MBar MWat SBod WFar
- 'Albospica Nana'	See *C. lawsoniana* 'Nana Albospica'
- 'Albovariegata' (v)	ECho EHul EOrn LBee LRHS MBar SRms
- 'Albrechii'	ENot
- 'Allumii Aurea'	See *C. lawsoniana* 'Alumigold'
- 'Allumii Magnificent'	CB&S MAsh WWeb
§ - 'Alumigold'	CB&S CDoC CSli GKir GPin LCon MAsh MBar MGos SBod SLim

- 'Alumii' — SMer SPer WGwG WStI WWeb CMac CTri EHul ENot GChr GKir MAsh MBar MGos NWea SLim SMer SPer WStI
- 'Argentea' — See *C. lawsoniana* 'Argenteovariegata'
§ - 'Argenteovariegata' (v) — CMac GKir LCon SLim
- 'Aurea' — CDul
I - 'Aurea Compacta' — ECho
- 'Aurea Densa' ♀ — CBlo CKen CMac CNic CSli CTri EHul EOrn GAri GKir LCon MAsh MBar MGos SBod SSmi STre WGor
- 'Aureovariegata' — MBar WBcn
§ - 'Barabits' Globe' — MBar
- 'Barry's Gold' — EOrn
§ - 'Bleu Nantais' — CBrm CKen CMac CTri EHul EOrn GChr GKir LBee LCon LLin LNet LRHS MAsh MBar MGos MWat SBod SLim SSmi WCFE
- 'Blom' — CKen EHul LRHS MBri
- 'Blue Gem' — LBee NHol
§ - 'Blue Gown' — CBlo CTri EHul LBee MBar MGos SRms
§ - 'Blue Jacket' — MBar
- 'Blue Nantais' — See *C. lawsoniana* 'Bleu Nantais'
- 'Blue Surprise' — CKen EHoe EHul EOrn LCon LLin LRHS MAsh MBar NPro WFar
- 'Bowleri' — Last listed 1997
- 'Brégéon' — CKen
- 'Broomhill Gold' — CBrm CDoC CMac CSli EBrP EBre EHul ENot GKir LBCl LBSe LBre LCon LLin LNet LRHS MAsh MBBe MBar MBri MGos MWat NHol SBod SBre SLim SPer WCFE WDin WWeb
- 'Buckland Gem' — Last listed 1999
* - 'Burkwood's Blue' — MBar
- 'Caudata' — CKen MBar WBcn
- 'Chantry Gold' — CBlo CKen EHul SLim
§ - 'Chilworth Silver' ♀ — EBrP EBre EHul EOrn EPot GKir LBCl LBSe LBee LBre LRHS MAsh MBBe MBar MBri MGos SBod SBre SLim SPer SRms WDin WFar WGwG WStI
- 'Chingii' — EHul
- 'Columnaris' — CB&S CDoC CMac EBrP EBre ENot EPfP GKir IOrc LBCl LBSe LBee LBre LRHS MBBe MBar MBri MGos MOke NBee NBlu NWea SBre SLim WCFE WFar
- 'Columnaris Aurea' — See *C. lawsoniana* 'Golden Spire'
N - 'Columnaris Glauca' — EBrP EBre EHul EOrn GChr GKir LBCl LBSe LBre LCon LPan MAsh MBBe MGos MWat SBod SBre SPer WDin WFar WStI
- 'Crawford's Compact' — CMac
- 'Cream Crackers' — EHul
¶ - 'Cream Glow' — CKen
- 'Croftway' — EHul
- 'Delorme' — Last listed 1998
- 'Dik's Weeping' — GKir SMad
- 'Dorset Gold' — CMac
- 'Dow's Gem' — LCon
- 'Drummondii' — Last listed 1998
- 'Duncanii' — EHul
- 'Dutch Gold' — EHul GKir MAsh
- 'Dwarf Blue' — See *C. lawsoniana* 'Pick's Dwarf Blue'
- 'Eclipse' — CKen
N - 'Elegantissima' — CKen CMac
- 'Ellwoodii' ♀ — More than 30 suppliers
- 'Ellwood's Empire' — EHul LRHS MBri

- 'Ellwood's Gold' ♀ — More than 30 suppliers
- 'Ellwood's Gold Pillar' — CDoC EHul EOrn LBee LLin MAsh MBri MGos NHol SLim SSmi WGwG WLRN WPat
§ - 'Ellwood's Nymph' — CBlo CKen CSli EOrn MBar SLim WGor WWeb
§ - Ellwood's Pillar = 'Flolar' More than 30 suppliers
- 'Ellwood's Pygmy' — CMac ECho MBar NHol
- 'Ellwood's Silver' — MAsh WFar WGor
- 'Ellwood's Silver Threads' CMac GKir
* - 'Ellwood's Treasure' — WCFE
- 'Ellwood's Variegata' — See *C. lawsoniana* 'Ellwood's White'
§ - 'Ellwood's White' (v) — CBlo CBrm CKen CMac CSli EHul EOrn GPin LRHS MAsh MBar MBri WFar
I - 'Emerald' — CKen MBar MBri NHol
- 'Emerald Spire' — CBlo CDoC CMac CTri MAsh NHol
- 'Empire' — CBlo
- 'Erecta Aurea' — CSli ECho EHul LBee LRHS MAsh MBar
- 'Erecta Filiformis' — MBar
§ - 'Erecta Viridis' — CB&S CMac CTrG CTri GKir LCon MBar MWat NEgg NWea SBod WCFE WDin WFar WStI
- 'Ericoides' — EHul
- 'Erika' — MBar
- 'Fantail' — Last listed 1998
- 'Filiformis Compacta' — EHul
- 'Fleckellwood' — CSli EHul GPin LLin MAsh MBar MGos SAga SBod SLim SMer WLRN WStI
- 'Fletcheri' ♀ — CB&S CMac EHul ENot GKir LBee LCon LRHS MAsh MBar MGos NBee NWea SBod SLim SMer SPer WDin WFar WStI
- 'Fletcheri Aurea' — See *C. lawsoniana* 'Yellow Transparent'
- 'Fletcheri Nana' — CBlo
- 'Fletcher's White' — ECho EHul LRHS MBar MBri WBcn
- 'Flolar' — See *C. lawsoniana* Ellwood's Pillar = 'Flolar'
- 'Forsteckensis' — CKen CSli EHul EOrn GKir LLin MBar MGos MOne NWea SLim SMer SRms SSmi WFar WGwG
I - 'Forsteckensis Aurea' — CBlo
- 'Fraseri' — CMac LCon MBar NWea WDin
- 'Gail's Gold' — CKen
- 'Gilt Edge' — CKen
- 'Gimbornii' ♀ — CDoC CMac EBrP EBre EHul EOrn GChr GKir LBCl LBSe LBee LBre LCon LLin LRHS MAsh MBBe MBar MBri SBod SBre SLim SRms WCFE
- 'Glauca' — CDul
- 'Glauca Spek' — See *C. lawsoniana* 'Spek'
- 'Globosa' — MGos
- 'Globus' — See *C. lawsoniana* 'Barabits' Globe'
- 'Gnome' — CDoC CMac CNic EHul EOrn EPot ESis GAri MBar MGos NHol SBod SLim WAbe
- 'Gold Flake' — CBlo MBar MBri MGos
- 'Gold Splash' — CBlo CKen GPin MBar
- 'Golden Guinea' — Last listed 1998
- 'Golden King' — MAsh MBar
§ - 'Golden Pot' — CBrm CDoC CKen CMac CSli EHul EOrn GKir LBee LCon LRHS MBar MGos MOke MWat SBod SMer WGwG WWeb
§ - 'Golden Queen' — CMHG EHul

– 'Golden Showers'	CKen EHul
§ – 'Golden Spire'	LRHS MAsh MBar MBri MGos
– 'Golden Triumph'	CBlo EHul
– 'Golden Wonder'	CDoC CMac CSli EHul IOrc LBee
	LBuc LCon LNet LRHS MAsh
	MBar MGos NWea SRms WFar
	WStI
– 'Goldfinger'	CKen
– 'Grant's Gold'	EHul
– 'Grayswood Feather'	CDoC CKen CTri EHul GKir LBee
	LCon LRHS MAsh MBar MBri
	MGos SLim SMer WWeb
– 'Grayswood Gold'	CBlo CKen EHul EOrn LBee LLin
	LRHS MAsh MBar MGos
– 'Grayswood Pillar' ♀	CBlo CMac EHul EOrn GKir LBee
	LCon LRHS MBar MGos
* – 'Grayswood Spire'	CMac
– 'Green Globe'	CBlo CDoC CKen CNic CSli EBrP
	EBre EHul EOrn EPot LBCl LBSe
	LBee LBre LCon LLin LRHS MAsh
	MBBe MBar MBri SAga SBod SBre
	WDin
§ – 'Green Hedger' ♀	CMac EHul ENot GKir LBuc MAsh
	MBar SBod SRms WFar
§ – 'Green Pillar'	CBrm CCHP CKen CTri GAri
	GChr IOrc LBee LRHS MBar
	MGos MWat
– 'Green Spire'	See *C. lawsoniana* 'Green Pillar'
– 'Green Wall'	Last listed 1998
– 'Greycone'	CKen LBee LRHS
– 'Hillieri'	MBar
– 'Hogger's Blue Gown'	See *C. lawsoniana* 'Blue Gown'
* – 'Hogger's Gold'	CBlo
– 'Howarth's Gold'	GAri GKir LRHS MBri
* – 'Imbricata'	MBlu
– 'Imbricata Pendula'	CKen LCon SMad
– 'Intertexta' ♀	CMHG EHul LCon WBcn WCwm
– 'Ivonne'	EHul MGos NBlu
– 'Jackman's Green Hedger'	See *C. lawsoniana* 'Green Hedger'
– 'Jackman's Variety'	See *C. lawsoniana* 'Green Pillar'
– 'Kelleriis Gold'	EHul LPan MBar
– 'Killiney Gold'	Last listed 1998
– 'Kilmacurragh' ♀	CMac ENot GKir LCon LLin MAsh
	MBar MGos NWea WCwm
– 'Kilworth Column'	CBlo LLin MGos
– 'Kingswood'	LRHS MBri
– 'Knowefieldensis'	CMac EHul LLin WBcn
– 'Lane' hort.	See *C. lawsoniana* 'Lanei Aurea'
§ – 'Lanei Aurea' ♀	CDoC CMac CSli EHul ENot EPfP
	GKir LCon MAsh MBar MGos
	NWea WFar
– 'Lemon Flame'	Last listed 1999
– 'Lemon Pillar'	CBlo
– 'Lemon Queen'	CBlo EHul LBee LCon LRHS
– 'Limelight'	CKen EHul EPot MGos
– 'Little Spire'	CDoC CMHG EBrP EBre EOrn
	EPla GKir LBCl LBSe LBee LBre
	LCon LLin LRHS MAsh MBBe
	MBar MBri MGos SBre SLim WGor
– 'Lombartsii'	EHul WFar
– 'Lutea' ♀	CMac EHul LCon MGos SBod
§ – 'Lutea Nana' ♀	CBlo CKen CMac EHul MAsh
	MBar MGos MOne WGwG WLRN
§ – 'Lutea Smithii'	EHul MBar
– 'Luteocompacta'	CKen LBee LRHS MGos
– 'Lycopodioides'	EHul MBar SSmi
* – 'MacPenny's Gold'	CMac
– 'Magnifica Aurea'	Last listed 1997
– 'Milford Blue Jacket'	See *C. lawsoniana* 'Blue Jacket'
§ – 'Minima'	MBar SRms WCFE
– 'Minima Argentea'	See *C. lawsoniana* 'Nana

	Argentea'
– 'Minima Aurea' ♀	More than 30 suppliers
– 'Minima Densa'	See *C. lawsoniana* 'Minima'
– 'Minima Glauca' ♀	More than 30 suppliers
– 'Moonlight'	CBlo MBar MGos
– 'Nana'	MBar
§ – 'Nana Albospica' (v)	CKen EHul EOrn GKir LBee LCon
	LLin LRHS MAsh MBar MGos
	NPro SLim SPla WFar WGwG WStI
§ – 'Nana Argentea'	CKen CMac CSli ECho EHul EOrn
	EPfP GPin WGor
– 'Nana Lutea'	See *C. lawsoniana* 'Lutea Nana'
– 'New Silver'	CBlo
– 'Nidiformis'	CBlo EHul LBee LRHS MBar NWea
	SRms
– 'Nyewoods'	See *C. lawsoniana* 'Chilworth
	Silver'
– 'Nymph'	See *C. lawsoniana* 'Ellwood's
	Nymph'
– 'Pearl Nova'	CBlo
§ – 'Pelt's Blue' ♀	CBlo CDoC CKen CSli EHul LBee
	LCon LRHS MAsh MBar MBri
	MGos NBee SCoo SLim WLRN
– 'Pembury Blue' ♀	More than 30 suppliers
– 'Pendula'	LCon LLin MBar
§ – 'Pick's Dwarf Blue'	CBlo EHul MBar MBri NHol WGor
– Pot of Gold™	See *C. lawsoniana* 'Golden Pot'
– 'Pottenii'	CDoC CMac CSli EHul IOrc LBee
	LCon LRHS MAsh MBar MGos
	NBee NWea SBod SMer SPer
	WDin WFar WStI
– 'Pygmaea Argentea' (v) ♀	CDoC CKen CMac EBrP EBre
	EHul EOrn EPfP EPla GChr GKir
	LBCl LBSe LBee LBre LCon LLin
	LRHS MAsh MBBe MBar MBri
	SBod SBre SLim SPla SSmi WCFE
	WDin
– 'Pygmy'	CBlo CNic CSli EHul GAri MBar
	SLim WLRN
– 'Pyramidalis Lutea'	CKen
I – 'Reid's Own Number One'	Last listed 1997
– 'Rijnhof'	EHul GAri LBee LLin WBcn
– 'Rogersii'	EOrn MBar SRms WFar
– 'Romana'	ENot MAsh MBri
– 'Royal Gold'	CSli ECho EHul EOrn
– 'Silver Queen' (v)	CKen MBar NWea WBcn
– 'Silver Threads' (v)	CMac CSli EBrP EBre EHul ENot
	EOrn EPla GKir LBCl LBSe LBee
	LBre LLin LRHS MAsh MBBe MBar
	MBri MGos MWat SBod SBre SLim
	WStI WWeb
– 'Silver Tip' (v)	EHul GPin SLim
– 'Smithii' Dallimore	See *C. lawsoniana* 'Lutea Smithii'
& Jackson	
– 'Snow Flurry' (v)	EHul
– 'Snow White' PBR (v)	CDoC EBrP EBre EHul EPla GKir
	LBCl LBSe LBee LBre LCon LLin
	LRHS MAsh MBBe MBar MBri
	MGos SBre SLim SPla WGor
	WWeb
– 'Somerset'	CBlo CMac MBar
§ – 'Spek'	CB&S MBar
– 'Springtime'PBR	CDoC EHul EOrn LCon LRHS
	MAsh MGos SLim WGor WWeb
– 'Stardust' ♀	CChe CDoC CMac CSli EHul ENot
	GKir IOrc LCon LPan LRHS MAsh
	MBar MBri MGos MWat SBod
	SLim SMer SPer WDin
– 'Stewartii'	CMac CTri ENot GChr MBar
	MGos NWea SBod SMer SPer WStI
– 'Stilton Cheese'	MBar
* – 'Summer Cream'	EHul

- 'Summer Snow' (v) — CB&S CDoC EHoe EHul ENot GKir IOrc LBee LLin LRHS MAsh MBar MBri MGos SBod SLim SPla SRms WCFE WFar WGwG WStI WWeb
- 'Sunkist' — CKen MAsh WFar
- 'Sylvia's Gold' — EOrn
- 'Tamariscifolia' ♀ — CDoC EHul LCon MBar SBod WCFE WDin WFar WGwG WLRN WStI
- 'Temple's White' — CKen
- 'Tharandtensis Caesia' — EOrn MBar WFar
- 'Tilford' — EHul
- 'Treasure' (v) — CKen CSli EBrP EBre EHoe EHul EOrn EPfP EPla LBCl LBSe LBee LBre LCon LLin LRHS MBBe MBar MBri MGos NHol SBre SLim WGor
- 'Triomf van Boskoop' — MBar
- 'Van Pelt's Blue' — See C. lawsoniana 'Pelt's Blue'
- 'Versicolor' (v) — MBar
- 'Westermannii' (v) — CMac EHul LCon SBod SLim
- 'White Spot' (v) — CDoC CKen CSli EBrP EBre EHul LBCl LBSe LBee LBre LCon LRHS MBBe MBar MBri MGos SBre SLim WStI
- 'Winston Churchill' — CBlo LCon MAsh MBar MGos NWea SBod
- 'Wisselii' ♀ — CDoC CKen CMac CTrG EHul ENot GChr GKir LBee LCon LLin LRHS MAsh MBar NBlu NWea SBod SRms WCFE WDin
- 'Wisselii Nana' — CKen EHul
- 'Wissel's Saguaro' — CKen LRHS MAsh
- 'Witzeliana' — CBlo ECho EOrn GPin LRHS MAsh MBar MBri MGos WGer WGor
- 'Wyevale Silver' — MBar
- 'Yellow Cascade' — ECho GPin
- 'Yellow Queen' — See C. lawsoniana 'Golden Queen'
- 'Yellow Success' — See C. lawsoniana 'Golden Queen'
§ - 'Yellow Transparent' — CDoC CMac CSli CTri LCon MBar MGos SBod SLim SPer WGor
- 'Yvonne' — CBlo LCon LLin LRHS MAsh MBar MBri SLim SPla WWeb

leylandii — See x Cupressocyparis leylandii
nootkatensis — MBar SMer
- 'Aurea' — GKir MAsh
- 'Aureovariegata' (v) — EHul SLim WBcn
- 'Compacta' — CBlo CTri MBar
- 'Glauca' — CTho LCon MBar
- 'Gracilis' — EHul
- 'Jubilee' — SLim SMad
- 'Lutea' — CMHG CMac CTri LCon MBar NWea SLim
- 'Nidifera' — MBar WCwm
- 'Pendula' ♀ — More than 30 suppliers
I - 'Pendula Speech House' — Last listed 1999
- 'Variegata' (v) — MBar SLim WBcn

obtusa 'Albospica' (v) — ECho EHul
- 'Albovariegata' (v) — CKen
- 'Aurea' — CDoC
- 'Aureovariegata' — See C. obtusa 'Opaal'
- 'Aurora' — CKen EOrn LCon
* - 'Autumn Gold' — MBar
- 'Bambi' — CKen EOrn MGos
- 'Barkenny' — CKen
- 'Bartley' — CKen EPot
- 'Bassett' — CKen
- 'Bess' — CKen

- 'Caespitosa' — CKen EPot
- 'Chabo-yadori' — CBlo CDoC EHul EOrn LCon LLin MAsh MBar MGos NHol SBod SLim WStI
- 'Chilworth' — CKen LCon MAsh MBar MGos
- 'Chima-anihiba' — CKen
- 'Chirimen' — CKen
- 'Clarke's Seedling' — MGos
- 'Confucius' — CBlo EHul NHol
- 'Contorta' — EOrn EPot LCon MBar
¶ - 'Cooper's Gem' — EPot
§ - 'Coralliformis' — CMac ECho EOrn LCon LLin MBar NHol SMur WGwG
§ - 'Crippsii' ♀ — CB&S CDoC CKen CMHG CMac EHul EOrn LCon MAsh MBar MGos NHol SBod SLim SPla
- 'Crippsii Aurea' — See C. obtusa 'Crippsii'
- 'Dainty Doll' — CKen EOrn
- 'Densa' — See C. obtusa 'Nana Densa'
- 'Drath' — CBlo CDoC MBar WBcn
- 'Elf' — CKen
- 'Ellie B' — CKen EOrn
- 'Ericoides' — CKen ECho EOrn GPin
- 'Erika' — ECho EOrn GChr GPin WBcn
- 'Fernspray Gold' — CBlo CDoC CKen CMac CSli CTri EHul ENot EOrn LCon LLin MAsh MBar NHol SBod SLim SPer WWeb
- 'Flabelliformis' — CKen
- 'Gimborn Beauty' — MGos
- 'Golden Fairy' — CKen EOrn
- 'Golden Filament' (v) — CKen
- 'Golden Nymph' — CKen CSli EOrn MGos
- 'Golden Sprite' — CKen EBrP EBre EPot LBCl LBSe LBre MBBe MGos SBre
- 'Goldilocks' — ECho EHul
- 'Gracilis Aurea' — CKen
- 'Graciosa' — See C. obtusa 'Loenik'
¶ - 'Green Diamond' — CKen
- 'Hage' — CKen EOrn EPot LCon MGos
- 'Hypnoides Nana' — CKen EOrn
- 'Intermedia' — CKen EOrn EPot MGos
- 'Ivan's Column' — CKen
- 'Juniperoides' — CKen EOrn
- 'Juniperoides Compacta' — CKen EPot
- 'Kamarachiba' — CKen SLim WBcn
- 'Kanaamihiba' — MBar
- 'Konijn' — EHul EOrn WLRN
- 'Kosteri' — CDoC CKen CMac EBrP EBre EHul EOrn EPot LBCl LBSe LBee LBre LCon LLin MAsh MBBe MBar MGos NDlv SBre SIng SLim WStI
- 'Laxa' — Last listed 1999
- 'Leprechaun' — Last listed 1999
- 'Little Markey' — CKen EOrn
§ - 'Loenik' — EOrn MBar NHol
- 'Lycopodioides' — EOrn EPot
- 'Lycopodioides Aurea' — SLim
- 'Marian' — CKen
§ - 'Mariesii' (v) — CKen CSli EOrn LCon
- 'Minima' — CKen MGos SMer
- 'Nana' ♀ — CBlo CKen CMac EPot GAri GChr LBee LCon LRHS MBar MGos NHol SIng
- 'Nana Albospica' — ECho
- 'Nana Aurea' ♀ — CDoC CMac CNic CSli EBrP EBre EHul EOrn EPot GKir GPin LBCl LBSe LBre LLin MAsh MBBe MBar MGos MWat NHol NPro NWea SBre SIng SMer WBod WStI WWeb
- 'Nana Compacta' — EOrn LCon NHol
§ - 'Nana Densa' — CKen CMac

	- 'Nana Gracilis' ♀	More than 30 suppliers
I	- 'Nana Gracilis Aurea'	EHul SMur
I	- 'Nana Lutea'	CBlo CDoC CKen EBrP EBre EHul EOrn EPfP EPla LBCl LBSe LBee LBre LCon LLin LRHS MAsh MBBe MBar MBri MGos NDlv NHol SBod SBre SLim SMer SPla SSmi WGer
	- 'Nana Pyramidalis'	CBlo
	- 'Nana Rigida'	See C. obtusa 'Rigid Dwarf'
	- 'Nana Variegata'	See C. obtusa 'Mariesii'
§	- 'Opaal' (v)	MBar WBcn
	- 'Pygmaea'	EBrP EBre EHul ENot EOrn LBCl LBSe LBre LCon LLin MAsh MBBe MBar MGos SBod SBre SLim SPla
	- 'Pygmaea Aurescens'	MBar SIng
	- 'Reis Dwarf'	Last listed 1997
	- 'Repens'	EOrn WBcn
§	- 'Rigid Dwarf'	CKen EHul EOrn EPot IMGH LBee LCon LRHS MBar WLRN
*	- 'Saint Andrew'	CKen
	- 'Snowflake' (v)	CKen EOrn MGos WBcn WGor
	- 'Snowkist' (v)	CKen
	- 'Spiralis'	CKen MBar
	- 'Stoneham'	CKen EPot LCon MBar
	- 'Tempelhof'	CKen EHul EOrn GKir LCon LLin LRHS MAsh MBar MGos NDlv SBod SLim SMer SPla WStl WWeb
	- 'Tetragona Aurea' ♀	CMac EGra EHul EOrn EPot GPin IMGH MBar MGos SBod SLim WGer
	- 'Tonia' (v)	CBlo CDoC CKen CWSG EHul EOrn MAsh MBri NHol SLim WLRN
	- 'Torulosa'	See C. obtusa 'Coralliformis'
	- 'Tsatsumi Gold'	CKen
	- 'Verdon'	CKen
	- 'Watchi'	Last listed 1997
	- 'Wissel'	CKen EOrn
¶	- 'Wyckoff'	CKen
	- 'Yellowtip' (v)	CKen EHul LCon MBar MGos

pisifera — Last listed 1999

	- 'Aurea Nana' misapplied	See C. pisifera 'Strathmore'
	- 'Avenue'	CBlo EHul LCon LLin
	- 'Baby Blue'	SLim
	- 'Blue Globe'	CKen EOrn
	- 'Blue Tower'	CBlo
	- 'Boulevard' ♀	More than 30 suppliers
	- 'Compacta'	ECho EOrn MLan NDlv
	- 'Compacta Variegata'	ECho EHul EOrn MBar NDlv
	- 'Curly Tops'	CDoC CKen GKir LCon MGos SLim WBcn
	- 'Devon Cream'	LBee LLin LRHS MAsh MBar NHol SBod
	- 'Filifera'	CBlo CMac EBrP EBre GKir LBCl LBSe LBre MBBe MBar SBod SBre SLim SLon WFar
	- 'Filifera Aurea' ♀	CGdn CGre CKen CMac EBrP EBre EHul EOrn GKir LBCl LBSe LBee LBre LCon LLin LNet LRHS MAsh MBBe MBar MBri NBee NWea SBod SBre SRms WCFE WDin WFar
	- 'Filifera Aureovariegata' (v)	CMac CSli EBrP EBre EHul GAri LBCl LBSe LBre LLin MBBe MBar SBre SLim
	- 'Filifera Nana'	CDoC EBrP EBre EHul EOrn GKir LBCl LBSe LBre MBBe MBar MBri MOne NDlv SBre SPer STre WDin WFar
	- 'Filifera Sungold'	See C. pisifera 'Sungold'
	- 'Fuiri-tsukomo'	CKen

*	- 'Gold Cascade'	MGos
	- 'Gold Cushion'	CKen
	- 'Gold Dust'	See C. pisifera 'Plumosa Aurea'
	- 'Gold Spangle'	EHul EOrn MAsh MBar MGos SBod WFar
	- 'Golden Mop' ♀	CKen EHul LCon MAsh WAbe
	- 'Hime-himuro'	CKen
	- 'Hime-sawara'	CKen EOrn
	- 'Nana'	CKen CNic EBrP EBre EHul EPfP GAri GPin IOrc LBCl LBSe LBre LLin MAsh MBBe MBar MWat NDlv NHol SBod SBre SMer WFar
I	- 'Nana Albovariegata'	CBlo CDoC EOrn LRHS MBar MBri NPro SBod
§	- 'Nana Aureovariegata'	CDoC CMac CSli EHul IMGH IOrc LBee LCon LRHS MAsh MBar MBri NDlv NHol SBod SLim SSmi WFar
I	- 'Nana Compacta'	CMac SRms
	- 'Nana Variegata'	CNic CSli ECho LBee LRHS MAsh MBar SLim SPer
I	- 'Parslorii'	CKen
	- 'Pici'	CKen
	- 'Plumosa'	SRms
	- 'Plumosa Albopicta' (v)	MBar SBod
§	- 'Plumosa Aurea'	CKen EHul GKir MAsh MBar NWea WDin WFar
	- 'Plumosa Aurea Compacta'	CBlo CKen CMac GAri NDlv
I	- 'Plumosa Aurea Compacta Variegata'	CMac
	- 'Plumosa Aurea Nana'	CBlo CDoC ENot MAsh MBar MGos NBee NDlv SMer WGwG
I	- 'Plumosa Aurea Nana Compacta'	CMac SBod
	- 'Plumosa Aurescens'	CMac
§	- 'Plumosa Compressa'	CDoC CKen CNic EHul EOrn ESis LBee LCon MBar MGos NDlv SLim WGor WGwG
	- 'Plumosa Densa'	See C. pisifera 'Plumosa Compressa'
	- 'Plumosa Flavescens'	EHul GPin LRHS MBar NDlv
I	- 'Plumosa Juniperoides'	CKen EHul EOrn MBar NDlv SLim
	- 'Plumosa Purple Dome'	See C. pisifera 'Purple Dome'
I	- 'Plumosa Pygmaea'	ECho MGos MLan NDlv WGor
§	- 'Plumosa Rogersii'	CDoC EHul EOrn LRHS MBar MGos SBod WGor
§	- 'Purple Dome'	CSli EHul EOrn MBar MGos WLRN
	- 'Rogersii'	See C. pisifera 'Plumosa Rogersii'
	- 'Silver and Gold' (v)	CBlo CSli EHul MBar
	- 'Silver Lode' (v)	CKen EOrn
	- 'Snow' (v)	CKen CMac EOrn GAri MBar SBod SIng SMer
	- 'Snowflake'	CKen EHul
	- 'Spaan's Cannon Ball'	CKen
	- 'Spindrift'	Last listed 1998
§	- 'Squarrosa'	GAri MBar NWea WDin WFar WGor
N	- 'Squarrosa Argentea'	Last listed 1999
	- 'Squarrosa Dumosa'	CKen CSli EHul MBar
	- 'Squarrosa Intermedia'	EHul LLin MBar MGos
I	- 'Squarrosa Lombarts'	CMac CSli EBrP EBre EHul EOrn LBCl LBSe LBee LBre LCon LLin MBBe MBar NPro SBod SBre SSmi WGwG
	- 'Squarrosa Lutea'	CKen MAsh MBar NPro
	- 'Squarrosa Sulphurea'	CDoC CSli EBrP EBre EGra EHul EOrn EPfP LBCl LBSe LBee LBre LCon LLin LRHS MAsh MBBe MBar NBee SBod SBre SLim SPer WDin WFar

- 'Squarrosa Veitchii'   See *C. pisifera* 'Squarrosa'
§ - 'Strathmore'   CKen EHul LLin MAsh MBar NHol
§ - 'Sungold'   CDoC CKen CSli CTri EGra EHul
   ENot LCon LLin LRHS MAsh MBar
   MBri NDlv NWea SBod SLim
- 'Tama-himuro'   CKen LLin MGos SLim
- 'White Beauty' (v)   CKen
* - 'White Brocade'   CMac
- 'White Pygmy'   EOrn EPot MAsh SAga
thyoides 'Andelyensis' ♀   CBlo CDoC CMac EHul EOrn
   GAri LLin MBar
- 'Andelyensis Nana' ♀   CKen WPyg
- 'Aurea'   EHul MBar WBcn
- 'Conica'   CKen CSli MAsh
- 'Ericoides' ♀   CBlo CDoC CKen CMac CSam
   CSli CTri EHul EOrn LBee LLin
   MAsh MBar MWat NDlv SBod
   SPer WDin WFar WGwG WPyg
§ - 'Glauca'   EOrn
- 'Kewensis'   See *C. thyoides* 'Glauca'
¶ - 'Little Jamie'   CKen
- 'Purple Heather'   LRHS SMur
- 'Red Star'   See *C. thyoides* 'Rubicon'
§ - 'Rubicon'   CBlo CKen CMac CSli EBrP EBre
   EHul EOrn EPla ESis LBCl LBSe
   LBee LBre LCon LLin LRHS MAsh
   MBBe MBar MGos NDlv SBod
   SBre SLim SPla WFar WGer
- 'Schumaker's Blue Dwarf'   EPla WBcn
- 'Top Point'   CKen EOrn LCon MBri SLim
- 'Variegata' (v)   CDoC ECho EHul MBar

CHAMAECYTISUS (Papilionaceae)
§ *albus*   ENot GKir GQui WDin WStI
¶ *austriacus*   GEil
danubialis HH&K 327   Last listed 1999
glaber   Last listed 1997
§ *hirsutus*   CFil WLin WPGP
- var. *demissus*   See *C. polytrichus*
- subsp. *hirsutissimus*   WLin
§ *polytrichus* ♀   EPot MHar
proliferus   Last listed 1998
§ *purpureus*   CAbP EBee EBrP EBre ELan EWTr
   GKir IOrc LBCl LBSe LBre LHop
   MBBe MBar MBri MGos MRav
   NWea SBre SPer SRPl WBod WDin
   WFar WPat
- f. *albus*   EPfP EWTr MBar SPer WBcn
§ - 'Atropurpureus' ♀   ENot WLin NHol SPer
- 'Incarnatus'   See *C. purpureus* 'Atropurpureus'
pygmaeus C&W 3818   Last listed 1998
§ *supinus*   MNrw SHFr SPan SRms

CHAMAEDAPHNE (Ericaceae)
§ *calyculata*   CB&S EBee GEil LRHS SPer WSHC
- 'Nana'   CMHG MBar MGos SRPl

CHAMAEDOREA (Arecaceae)
cataractarum   CBrP
costaricana   Last listed 1997
elegans ♀   LPal MBri
erumpens   See *C. seifrizii*
linearis   LPal
metallica Cook ♀   LPal
- hort.   See *C. microspadix*
§ *microspadix*   CRoM LPJP LPal
radicalis   CBrP EPVP LPJP LPal
§ *seifrizii* ♀   LPal

CHAMAELIRIUM (Melanthiaceae)
luteum   Last listed 1999

CHAMAEMELUM (Asteraceae)
§ *nobile*   CArn CBrm CSev EDAr ELau GBar
   GDea GKir GMac GPoy MBar
   MBri MHer MMal NNrd SGar SIde
   SPlb SRms WJek WOak WPer WSel
   WWye
¶ - dwarf   GBar
   double-flowered (d)
¶ - dwarf   GBar
- 'Flore Pleno' (d)   More than 30 suppliers
- 'Treneague'   More than 30 suppliers

CHAMAENERION See EPILOBIUM

CHAMAEPERICLYMENUM See CORNUS

CHAMAEROPS (Arecaceae)
excelsa Thunb.   See *Rhapis excelsa*
- hort.   See *Trachycarpus fortunei*
humilis ♀   More than 30 suppliers
§ - var. *argentea*   CBrP LPal WMul
- var. *cerifera*   See *C. humilis* var. *argentea*
- silver back   Last listed 1999

CHAMAESCILLA (Anthericaceae)
corymbosa   Last listed 1998

CHAMAESPARTIUM See GENISTA

CHAMBEYRONIA (Arecaceae)
macrocarpa   CBrP LPal

CHAMELAUCIUM (Myrtaceae)
uncinatum   ECon LRHS

CHARA (Charophyceae)
vulgaris   Last listed 1999

CHASMANTHE (Iridaceae)
aethiopica   CPou MBel SYvo
bicolor   CPou
floribunda   CTrF LBow
- var. *duckittii*   Last listed 1998

CHASMANTHIUM (Poaceae)
§ *latifolium*   More than 30 suppliers

CHEILANTHES (Adiantaceae)
distans   WRic
eatonii   Last listed 1997
feei   Last listed 1998
lanosa   Last listed 1999
§ *nivea*   Last listed 1998
tomentosa   LHil WRic

CHEIRANTHUS See ERYSIMUM

CHELIDONIUM (Papaveraceae)
japonicum   See *Hylomecon japonica*
majus   CArn CFri CKin CRow ELau
   EWFC GPoy MChe MGas MHer
   MHew MSal NHex SIde WCHb
   WHer WShi WWye
- 'Bowles' Variety'   EBee
- 'Flore Pleno' (d)   CBre CGle CRow ECoo ELan
   GCHN GGar NBrk NBro NFla NSti
   WCHb WCot WHer WOve
- var. *laciniatum*   CInt EMon GBar GGar NBid NSti
   WCHb
- 'Laciniatum Flore   CRow EBee EMar IBlr WCot
   Pleno' (d)

CHELONE (Scrophulariaceae)

barbata	See *Penstemon barbatus*
§ *glabra*	CArn CHea EBee ECha EFou ELan ELau EWTr GCal GGar GPoy LRHS MBNS MBel MHew MSal NBro NHol SChu SCro SPer SPlb SRms WFar WPer WPnP WWat WWye
lyonii	NCut NLar SHFr WShi
obliqua	More than 30 suppliers
- var. *alba*	See *C. glabra*
- *rosea*	LRHS

CHELONOPSIS (Lamiaceae)

moschata	EBee ECha EMan WPGP

CHENOPODIUM (Chenopodiaceae)

ambrosioides	WJek
bonus-henricus	CArn ELau GAbr GBar GPoy ILis LRHS MChe MHer SIde WCHb WHer WOak WPer WSel WWye
botrys	MSal

CHIASTOPHYLLUM (Crassulaceae)

§ *oppositifolium* ♀	More than 30 suppliers
- 'Frosted Jade'	See *C. oppositifolium* 'Jim's Pride'
- 'Jim's Pride' (v)	More than 30 suppliers
simplicifolium	See *C. oppositifolium*

CHILIOTRICHUM (Asteraceae)

diffusum	CPle ECou GDra GEil GKir GSki IMGH ISea SMad SPer
- 'Siska'	CB&S EBee IMGH LRHS SPan WWes

CHILOPSIS (Bignoniaceae)

linearis	Last listed 1998

CHIMAPHILA (Pyrolaceae)

maculata	Last listed 1997
umbellata	Last listed 1997

CHIMONANTHUS (Calycanthaceae)

fragrans	See *C. praecox*
nitens	CMCN
§ *praecox*	More than 30 suppliers
¶ - 'Fragrance'	ERea
- 'Grandiflorus' ♀	CEnd ENot
- var. *luteus* ♀	CBlo CEnd CPMA ENot EPfP LRHS SPer WWat
- 'Mangetsu'	SSta
- 'Trenython'	CEnd CPMA SSta
yunnanensis	CGre EPfP
zhejiangensis	EPfP

CHIMONOBAMBUSA (Poaceae)

falcata	See *Drepanostachyum falcatum*
hookeriana hort.	See *Himalayacalamus falconeri* 'Damarapa'
macrophylla f. *intermedia*	EPla SDry
§ *marmorea*	CFil EOas EPla ISta LJus MMoz SDry WJun WPGP
- 'Variegata'	CFil EFul EPla ISta LJus MTed SDry WJun WPGP
§ *quadrangularis*	CFil EFul EPfP EPla ERod GAri ISta LJus NMoo SDry WJun WPGP
- f. *nagaminea* (v)	EPla
- 'Svow' (v)	EPla ISta SDry
§ *tumidissinoda*	EPla ERod ISta NDov SDry WJun WPGP

CHIOGENES See GAULTHERIA

CHIONANTHUS (Oleaceae)

retusus	CMCN EPfP IDee WWat
virginicus	CB&S CBlo CEnd CFil CMCN CPMA ELan EPfP GKir IMGH IOrc LRHS MBel MBlu MBri SBrw SMad SPer SSpi SSta WDin WHCG WPGP WWat

CHIONOCHLOA (Poaceae)

conspicua	CElw CFil ELan EMan EWes GAbr GAri LEdu MFir MNrw NBir NOGN SApp SMad WHer WLRN WPGP WRHF WWye
- 'Rubra'	See *C. rubra*
flavescens	GBin GSki
flavicans	CInt EBee EMan EWsh GAbr MBel SMad WPrP
§ *rubra*	CCuc CElw CFil CPLG EBee EHoe EMon EPPr EPla EWes GOrP LEdu MMoz SApp SCob SUsu WCot WPGP

CHIONODOXA ✿ (Hyacinthaceae)

cretica	See *C. nana*
§ *forbesii*	CBro CNic EPar EPot ETub LRHS SRms WPer WShi
- 'Alba'	EPar LAma NRog
- 'Blue Giant'	EPot LRHS
- 'Pink Giant'	CAvo CBro ELan EPar EPfP EPot ETub LAma LRHS NEgg WCot
- 'Rosea'	EPar LAma NRog
§ - Siehei Group ♀	CBro
gigantea	See *C. luciliae* Gigantea Group
luciliae hort.	See *C. forbesii*
- Boissier ♀	CAvo CBro EPar EPot LAma MBri NRog
- 'Alba'	CBro ECho LRHS
§ - Gigantea Group	ELan EPar EPot LAma LRHS NEgg NRog SRms
- - 'Alba'	EPar EPot GCrs LRHS
* *mariesii*	Last listed 1999
§ *nana*	CAvo
sardensis ♀	CBro EPar EPot LAma LRHS MBNS NEgg NRog WPer
siehei	See *C. forbesii* Siehei Group

CHIONOGRAPHIS (Liliaceae)

japonica	EFEx

CHIONOHEBE (Scrophulariaceae)

armstrongii	EPot ITim
§ *densifolia*	EPot GCrs MNaF NSla WPat
pulvinaris	GCrs ITim NHar NSla WAbe

x CHIONOSCILLA (Hyacinthaceae)

§ *allenii*	Last listed 1999

CHIRITA (Gesneriaceae)

¶ 'Aiko'	WDib
¶ 'Diane Marie'	WDib
linearifolia	WDib
sinensis ♀	CHal WDib
¶ - 'Hisako'	WDib

CHIRONIA (Gentianaceae)

baccifera	Last listed 1997

x CHITALPA (Bignoniaceae)

¶ *tashkentensis*	CEnd MBlu

CHLIDANTHUS (Amaryllidaceae)
fragrans   CFwr CStu ECho NRog WCot

CHLORANTHUS (Chloranthaceae)
fortunei   SBla WCru
japonicus   WCru
oldbamii B&SWJ 2019   EBee WCru
serratus   EBee WCru

CHLORIS (Poaceae)
¶ *virgata*   EBee EPPr

CHLOROPHYTUM (Anthericaceae)
comosum 'Mandanum' (v) CHal
- 'Variegatum' ♀   CHal LChe LRHS MBri SRms
- 'Vittatum' (v) ♀   SRms
¶ *krookianum*   WHil
§ *laxum* 'Bichetii' (v)   WCot
- 'Variegatum'   See *C. laxum* 'Bichetii'
§ *majus*   WCot
nepalense B&SWJ 2393   WCru

CHOISYA (Rutaceae)
'Aztec Pearl' ♀   More than 30 suppliers
dumosa var. *arizonica*   SDry
- var. *mollis*   SLon
¶ 'Goldfingers'   MBri WWeb
ternata ♀   More than 30 suppliers
- 'Brica'PBR   See *C. ternata* Sundance = 'Lich'
§ - Moonshine = 'Walcho'PBR LRHS MAsh
- MoonsleeperPBR   See *C. ternata* Sundance = 'Lich'
§ - Sundance = 'Lich'PBR ♀ More than 30 suppliers
- 'Walchoi'PBR   See *C. ternata* Moonshine = 'Walcho'

CHONDROPETALUM (Restionaceae)
mucronatum   CCpl CTrC
tectorum   CAbb CTrC WMul WNor

CHONDROSUM (Poaceae)
gracile   See *Bouteloua gracilis*

CHONEMORPHA (Apocynaceae)
¶ *fragrans*   CPlN

CHORDOSPARTIUM (Papilionaceae)
muritai   ECou
- 'Huia Gilpen'   ECou
- 'Ron Feron'   ECou
- 'Wayne Nichols'   ECou
stevensonii   CPle ECou EPfP SMad
- 'Duncan'   ECou
- 'Kiwi'   ECou
- 'Miller'   ECou

CHORIZEMA (Papilionaceae)
cordatum ♀   CPlN
dicksonii   Last listed 1998
diversifolium   CPlN ERea
ilicifolium   CAbb CB&S CPlN CSPN CWSG ERea GQui SBra

CHRYSALIDOCARPUS (Arecaceae)
lutescens   See *Dypsis lutescens*

CHRYSANTHEMOPSIS See RHODANTHEMUM

CHRYSANTHEMUM ✿ (Asteraceae)
Adorn = 'Yoado' (22d)   MCol
'Agnes Ann' (29K)   MCol
'Aimee Jane' (24b)   MCol

'Alan Rowe' (5a)   Last listed 1997
'Albert Broadhurst' (24b)   NHal
'Albert's Yellow' (29Rub)   MCol MMil
'Alexis' (5a)   Last listed 1997
'Aline' (29K)   Last listed 1997
'Alison' (29c)   LRHS
'Alison Kirk' (23b)   MCol NHal
'Allouise' (25b) ♀   MCol NHal
Allure = 'Yoall' (22d)   Last listed 1997
alpinum   See *Leucanthemopsis alpina*
'Amber Chessington' (25a) NHal
'Amber Enbee Wedding' (29d) ♀   Last listed 1997
¶ 'Amber Gigantic' (1)   WIvo
¶ 'Amber Matlock' (24b)   NHal
'Amber Yvonne Arnaud' (24b) ♀   Last listed 1995
'American Beauty' (5b)   Last listed 1998
'Amy Shoesmith' (15a)   MCol
'Anastasia' (28)   CElw CHid CLTr ECtt EMan EPPr GMac LHop MCol MMil MRav NBrk NFai NSti SEas SRms WCot WEas WFar WPer WRHF WWin
N 'Anastasia Variegated' (28/v) CSam MBel WCot WHer
'Anastasia White' (28)   WCot WIvy
'Angelic' (28)   MCol
'Angora' (25b) ♀   MCol
'Anja's Bouquet'   Last listed 1998
'Ann Brook' (23b)   Last listed 1997
'Anna Marie' (18c) ♀   MCol
'Annapurna' (3b)   Last listed 1997
'Anne' (29K)   Last listed 1997
'Anne, Lady Brocket'   CLTr EMon GBuc MBel MNrw NBrk WCot WMaN
'Apollo' (29K)   EFou EMon EWll LRHS SMer
'Apricot' (29Rub)   EBrP EBre ECtt EFou EPPr GKir LBCl LBSe LBre MBBe MFir MRav NFla SBre SSoC
'Apricot Alexis' (5a)   Last listed 1997
'Apricot Chessington' (25a) NHal
'Apricot Chivenor' (9c)   Last listed 1999
'Apricot Courtier' (24a)   NHal
'Apricot Enbee Wedding' (29d)   See *C.* 'Bronze Enbee Wedding'
'Apricot Harry Gee' (1)   WIvo
'Apricot Margaret' (29c) ♀ MCol
'Archie Benson' (3b)   NHal
'Arctic' (9c)   MCol
arcticum L.   See *Arctanthemum arcticum*
argenteum   See *Tanacetum argenteum*
'Audrey Shoesmith' (3a)   Last listed 1997
'Aunt Millicent' (29K)   MCol
'Autumn Days' (25b)   MCol NHal
'Autumn Sonata'   Last listed 1997
'Babs' (28)   MMil
'Baden Locke' (24b)   Last listed 1997
'Bagley Cream' (3b)   MCol
'Bagley Glow' (4b)   MCol
'Bagley Pink' (14b)   MCol
'Balcombe Perfection' (5a) MCol NHal WWol
balsamita   See *Tanacetum balsamita*
'Barbara Ward' (7b)   MCol
Barbara = 'Yobarbara' PBR (22)   EPfP MCol NHal WLRN WWol
'Beacon' (5a) ♀   MCol NHal
'Belair' (9c)   MCol
¶ 'Bella Pink' (29)   WWol
¶ 'Bella Rosella' (29)   WWol
¶ 'Bella Yellow' (29)   WWol
'Belle' (29K)   LRHS
¶ 'Benjamin Joseph' (24b)   WWol
'Beppie' (29e)   MCol

¶ 'Beppie Bronze' (29)   WWol
¶ 'Beppie Purple' (29)   WWol
'Bernadette Wade' (23a)   NHal
'Bertos'   Last listed 1997
'Bessie Rowe' (25a)   MCol
'Betty' (29K)   MCol
'Betty Wiggins' (25b)   MCol
'Bill Bye' (1)   Last listed 1999
'Bill Wade' (25a)   MCol NHal
* 'Billy Bell' (25a)   WWol
'Black Magic' (24b)   MCol
'Bob Dear' (25a)   MCol
'Bonnie Jean' (9d)   Last listed 1997
'Bo-peep' (28)   MCol
Bravo = 'Yobra' PBR (22c)   ♀ EPfP MCol NHal
* 'Breitner's Supreme'   MCAu MNrw
'Brenda Rowe' (5a)   MCol
'Brietner' (24b)   MCol
'Bright Eye' (28)   MCol WPer
'Bright Golden   Last listed 1997
   Princess Anne' (4b)
'Brightness' (29K)   NFai SChu SUsu
'Broadacre' (7a)   MCol
'Broadway Mandy' (29c)   Last listed 1999
'Bronze Beauty' (25b)   WFar
'Bronze Belair' (9c)   MCol
'Bronze Bornholm' (14b)   MCol
¶ 'Bronze Carlene   WWol
   Welby' (15b)
'Bronze Cassandra' (5b) ♀ NHal
'Bronze Dee Gem' (29c)   NHal
§ 'Bronze Elegance' (28b)   CLTr CM&M CSam EBee EFou
   ELan EMan EMon LRHS MLLN
   NGdn NSti SPer SPla SRms WEas
   WIvy WMaN WWat
'Bronze Elite' (29d)   Last listed 1997
§ 'Bronze Enbee   MCol NHal WWol
   Wedding' (29d) ♀
'Bronze Fairy' (28a)   MCol
'Bronze John   NHal
   Wingfield' (14b)
'Bronze John   Last listed 1997
   Wingfield' (24b)
'Bronze Margaret' (29c) ♀ MCol NHal
'Bronze Maria' (18a)   MCol
'Bronze Matlock' (24b)   NHal
'Bronze Max Riley' (23b)   NHal
'Bronze Mayford   MCol NHal WWol
Perfection' (5a) ♀
'Bronze Mei-kyo'   See C. 'Bronze Elegance'
'Bronze Pamela'   See C. 'Pamela'
'Bronze Pennine Goal' (29c) Last listed 1998
'Bronze Yvonne   MCol
Arnaud' (24b)
'Bronzetti'   Last listed 1997
'Brown Eyes' (29K)   Last listed 1999
'Bruera' (24b)   NHal
'Bryan Kirk' (4b)   NHal WWol
§ 'Buff Margaret' (29c)   Last listed 1997
'Buff Peter Rowe' (23b)   NHal
'Bullfinch' (12a)   Last listed 1998
'Bunty' (28)   LRHS
'Butter Milk' (25c)   MCol
'Cameo' (28a) ♀   MCol
'Candid' (15b)   MCol
'Candlewick   MCol
Limelight' (29d) ♀
'Candylite' (14b)   MCol
'Carlene Welby' (25b)   NHal
'Carmine Blush'   EFou WCot
'Caroline Barclay' (14a)   WWol
I 'Cassandra' (5b)   NHal

'Challenger' (25b)   MCol
'Charles Tandy' (5a)   Last listed 1997
'Charles Wood' (15a)   Last listed 1997
'Cheddar' (13a)   MCol
'Cherry Chessington' (25a) NHal
'Cherry Enbee   Last listed 1999
Wedding' (29d)
'Cherry Margaret' (29c)   NHal
¶ Cheryl = 'Yocheryl' (22)   WWol
'Chessington' (25a)   MCol NHal
'Chester Globe' (23b)   NHal
'Chesterfield' (15b)   WWol
'Chestnut Talbot   NHal
Parade' (29c) ♀
'Chivenor' (9c)   MCol
'Christine Hall' (25a)   MCol
'Christopher Lawson' (24b) NHal
cinerariifolium   See *Tanacetum cinerariifolium*
'Citrus' (29K)   EFou
'Clara Curtis' (29Rub)   More than 30 suppliers
'Clare Dobson' (25b)   MCol
'Clare Louise' (24b)   Last listed 1997
'Clarette'   SLon
'Claudia' (24c)   MCol
clusii   See *Tanacetum corymbosum*
   subsp. *clusii*
coccineum   See *Tanacetum coccineum*
¶ 'Coconut Ice'   EWTr
'Colossus' (24a)   MCol NHal
'Columbine' (29d/K)   Last listed 1997
* 'Consort' (25b)   WWol
'Copper Margaret' (29c)   Last listed 1998
'Copper Nob' (29K)   Last listed 1998
'Cornetto' (25b)   MCol NHal
'Corngold' (5b)   NHal
corymbosum   See *Tanacetum corymbosum*
'Cossack' (2)   WWol
'Cottage Apricot'   CHea EMan EWoo GMac LHop
   MBNS MNrw SMrm SUsu WCot
   WEas WRHF
'Cottage Pink'   See C. 'Emperor of China'
'Cottingham' (25a)   MCol
'Courtier' (24a)   NHal
¶ 'Cream Duke of Kent' (1)   WIvo
'Cream Elegance' (9c)   Last listed 1999
¶ 'Cream Enbee   WWol
Wedding' (29d)
'Cream John Hughes' (3b)   Last listed 1999
'Cream Margaret' (29c) ♀ NHal
¶ 'Cream Patricia Millar' (14b)NHal
'Cream Pauline White' (15a)Last listed 1997
'Cream West   Last listed 1997
Bromwich' (14a)
'Creamist' (25b) ♀   MCol
'Cricket' (25b)   MCol
'Crimson Yvonne   MCol
Arnaud' (24b) ♀
Dana =   NHal
'Yodana' PBR (25b) ♀
'Daniel Cooper' (29Rub)   MCol
'Danielle' (29d)   MCol
* 'Daphne'   Last listed 1997
¶ 'Dark Red Mayford   WWol
Perfection' (4b) ♀
¶ 'Dark Tripoli'   WWol
Dark Triumph =   Last listed 1999
'Dark Yotri' PBR (22)
¶ 'David McNamara' (3b)   WWol
'David Shoesmith' (25a)   MCol
'Dawn Jackson' (29d)   MCol
'Deane Dainty' (9f) ♀   MCol
'Debbie' (29c/K)   Last listed 1997

Debonair = 'Yodebo' [PBR] (22c)¿ — EPfP MCol NHal WLRN

'Dee Candy' (29c) — Last listed 1999

'Dee Crimson' (29c) — Last listed 1999

'Dee Gem' (29c) ♀ — NHal

'Dee Pink' (29c) — Last listed 1997

¶ 'Delta Orange' (29) — WWol

* 'Delta Pink' (29) — WWol

* 'Delta White' (29) — WWol

¶ 'Delta Yellow' (29) — WWol

'Denise' (28b) ♀ — MCol WLRN

'Dennis Fletcher' (25a) — Last listed 1998

'Derek Bircumshaw' (28a) — MCol

'Deva Glow' (25a) — MCol

§ 'Doctor Tom Parr' (28) — CGle EFou ELan EMon MBel MFir NBrk SUsu

'Domingo' (4b) — Last listed 1999

Donna = 'Yodon' [PBR] (22f) — MCol

'Doreen Burton' (25b) — MCol

'Doreen Hall' (15a) — MCol

'Doreen Statham' (4b) — NHal WWol

'Doris' (29K) — Last listed 1997

'Dorothy Stone' (25b) — NHal

'Dorridge Beauty' (24a) — NHal WWol

'Dorridge Bolero' (24a) — Last listed 1998

'Dorridge Celebration' (3b) — Last listed 1999

'Dorridge Crystal' (24a) — NHal WWol

'Dorridge Dawn' (4b) — Last listed 1998

'Dorridge Flair' (3b) — Last listed 1999

'Dorridge King' (4b) — Last listed 1998

'Dorridge Velvet' (4b) — NHal

'Dorridge Vulcan' (23b) — WWol

'Dragon' (9c) — Last listed 1999

'Duchess of Edinburgh' (30Rub) — CGle CPlt CSam EBrP EBre ECtt ELan EMan EMon GKir GMac LBCl LBSe LBre LRHS MBBe MBNS MBri MCol MFir MTis SBre SEas SSpe SSvw SUsu WEas WMaN WPyg WRHF

'Duke of Kent' (1) — NHal WIvo

'Dulverton' (24c) — Last listed 1997

'Early Bird' (24b) ♀ — MCol

'Eastleigh' (24b) ♀ — Last listed 1995

'Ed Hodgson' (25a) — MCol NHal

'Edelgard' — WMaN

'Edelweiss' (29K) — EFou GMac

'Egret' (23b) — Last listed 1998

¶ 'Elaine Johnson' (3b) — NHal

'Elegance' (9c) — MCol WWol

¶ 'Elegance Yellow' (9e) — WWol

'Elizabeth Burton' (5a) — WWol

'Elizabeth Lawson' (5b) — NHal

'Elizabeth Shoesmith' (1) — NHal

'Ellen' (29c) — NHal WWol

'Emily Peace' (25a) — Last listed 1997

Emily = 'Yoemily' (22) ♀ — MCol

* 'Emma Jane' (25a) — WWol

'Emma Lou' (23a) — MCol NHal

§ 'Emperor of China' (29Rub) — CElw CGle CSam EBee ECha EFou EMan GCal LGre LRHS MBel MCol MNrw MRav MSte NBrk NFai NFla NFor SAga SChu SSvw WEas WFar WHoo WMaN WRus

'Enbee Dell' (29d) — MCol

'Enbee Frill' (29d) — MCol

'Enbee Sunray' (29d) — EFou

'Enbee Wedding' (29d) ♀ — MCol NHal WWol

Encore = 'Yoenco' (22) — Last listed 1998

¶ Erica = 'Yoerica' (22) — WWol

'Ermine' (23a) — MCol NHal

¶ 'Erntekranz' — EFou

'Eston Fancy' (5a) — NHal

'Evelyn Bush' (25b) — MCol

* 'Evesham Vale' (24b) — WWol

'Eye Level' (5a) — NHal

'Fairway' (15a) — Last listed 1999

'Fairweather' (3b) — MCol

'Fairy' (28) — MCol

* 'Fairy Rose' (29K) — MCol

'Fairy Rose' (4b) — LRHS

'Felicity' (15b) — Last listed 1998

'Fellbacher Wein' (29K) — EFou

'Feu de l'Automne' — EFou

¶ 'Fiamma' — WWol

'Fieldfare' (22) — NHal

Fiery Barbara = 'Fiery Yobarbara' [PBR] (22c) — WLRN

¶ 'Fitton's Reward' (1) — WIvo

¶ 'Flame Enbee Wedding' (29d) — MCol

'Flamingo' (9f) — Last listed 1998

§ 'Fleet Margaret' (29c) ♀ — Last listed 1998

'Flo Cooper' (25a) ♀ — Last listed 1989

'Flying Saucer' (6a) — MCol

foeniculaceum hort. — See *Argyranthemum foeniculaceum* hort.

foeniculaceum (Willd.) Desf. — See *Argyranthemum foeniculaceum* (Willd.) Webb & Sch.Bip.

'Formcast' (24a) — NHal

'Foxdown' (25b) — MCol

'Foxy Valerie' [PBR] (22c) — Last listed 1998

'Frances Jeavons' — EBee

'Fred Brocklehurst' (25a) — MCol

'Fred Shoesmith' (5a) — MCol WWol

¶ 'Fred Taylor' (3) — WIvo

'Fresha' (25a) — Last listed 1998

Frolic = 'Yofro' [PBR] (22c) — MCol

frutescens — See *Argyranthemum frutescens*

'Fulfen' (24b) — NHal

'Gala Princess' (24b) — Last listed 1997

'Galaxy' (9d) ♀ — MCol

'Gambit' (24a) — MCol NHal

'Gary Scothern' (25b) — Last listed 1997

'Gay Anne' (4b) — Last listed 1997

'Gazelle' (23a) — MCol

* 'Geischa Fontaine' (29f) — WWol

'Geordie' (25b) — MCol

'George Griffiths' (24b) ♀ — NHal

'Gerry Tull' (29d) — NHal

'Gertrude' (19c) — MCol

'Gigantic' (1) — NHal WIvo

Ginger = 'Yogin' (22c) — WLRN

'Gingernut' (5b) — MCol NHal

'Gladys' (4b) — EBee ELan EWoo

'Gloria' (29K) — MCol

'Gloria' (25a) — Last listed 1997

'Glowing Lynn' [PBR] (22c) — WLRN

'Gold Chessington' (25a) — Last listed 1998

'Gold Enbee Frill' (29d) — Last listed 1997

'Gold Enbee Wedding' (29d) ♀ — MCol NHal

'Gold Foil' (5a) — Last listed 1999

¶ 'Gold John Wingfield' (14b) — NHal

'Gold Margaret' — See *C.* 'Golden Margaret'

'Golden Anemone' (29K) — Last listed 1997

'Golden Angora' (25b) — MCol

'Golden Cassandra' (5b) ♀ — NHal

'Golden Courtier' (24a) — NHal

'Golden Creamist' (25b) ♀ — MCol

'Golden Elegance' (5a) — Last listed 1999

'Golden Gigantic' (1) — WIvo

'Golden Honeyball' (15b) — MCol

'Golden Ivy Garland' (5b) — MCol

	'Golden Lady' (3b)	WWol
§	'Golden Margaret' (29c) ♀	MCol NHal
	'Golden Mayford Perfection' (5a) ♀	MCol NHal WWol
	'Golden Pamela' (29c)	NHal
	'Golden Pixton' (25b)	MCol
	'Golden Plover' (22)	NHal
	'Golden Saskia' (7b)	MCol
	'Golden Seal' (7b)	EMon GBuc MCol NBrk
	'Golden Shoesmith Salmon' (4a) ♀	Last listed 1987
	'Golden Taffeta' (9c)	Last listed 1997
	'Golden Treasure' (28a)	MCol
	'Golden Wedding' (29K)	MCol
	'Goldengreenheart'	EFou WCot
	Goldmine = 'Yogol' (22c) ♀	Last listed 1995
	'Goodlife Sombrero' (29a)	♀NHal
	'Grace Fraser' (15b)	WWol
	'Grace Riley' (24a)	MCol
	'Grandchild' (29c)	LRHS MCol
§	*grandiflorum*	MNrw SRms
¶	'Green Boy' (10b)	WWol
*	'Green Envy' (10b)	WWol
	'Green Nightingale' (10)	WWol
	'Green Satin' (5b)	WWol
	'Grenadier' (24b)	MCol
	Grenadine = 'Yogrena' (22c) ♀	NHal
	'Halloween' (4b)	Last listed 1997
	'Handford Pink' (29K)	Last listed 1997
¶	'Hanenburg'	WWol
*	'Happy Days' (15b)	WWol
	'Happy Geel'	Last listed 1997
	haradjanii	See *Tanacetum haradjanii*
¶	'Harmony'	WWol
	'Harold Lawson' (5a)	NHal
	'Harry Gee' (1)	WIvo WWol
	'Harry Wilson' (3b)	NHal
	'Harry Woolman' (3b)	NHal
	Harvest Emily = 'Harvest Yoemily' PBR (22c)	MCol NBlu
	'Harvey' (29K)	MCol
	'Hayley Griffin' (25a)	Last listed 1999
*	'Hazel' (29K)	LRHS
	'Hazel Macintosh' (5a)	NHal
	'Hazy Days' (25b)	NHal
	'Heather James' (3b)	MCol NHal
	Heather = 'Yoheather' PBR (22)	WLRN
	'Hedgerow' (7b)	MCol
	'Heide' (29c) ♀	MCol NHal
	Hekla = 'Yohek' (30)	MCol
	'Helen' PBR (29K)	Last listed 1997
	'Hesketh Knight' (5b)	NHal
	Holly = 'Yoholly' (22b) ♀	MCol NHal WLRN
	'Honey' (25b)	EMan LRHS SMer
	'Honey Enbee Wedding' (29d)	NHal
	'Honeyball' (25b)	MCol
	'Horace Martin'	LRHS
	'Horningsea Pink' (19d)	EPPr
	hosmariense	See *Rhodanthemum hosmariense*
	'Ian' (29K)	Last listed 1997
	'Imp' (28)	MCol
	'Innocence' (29Rub)	CElw CGle CSam EBee EFou ELan EMon GMac LGre MBel MNrw MRav NFai NGdn NSti SAga SEas SPla
	'Irene' (29K)	CElw
*	'Iris Morris' (4b)	WWol
¶	'Ivor Mace' (1)	NHal WIvo

	'Ivy Garland' (5b)	MCol
¶	'Ja Dank'	WWol
¶	'Jan Horton' (3b)	WWol
	'Janice' PBR (7a)	Last listed 1997
	'Janice Shreeve' (24a)	Last listed 1999
	'Jante Wells' (28)	EMon MBel MCol MFir WEas
	Jennifer = 'Yojennifer' PBR (22c)	Last listed 1999
	'Jessica' (29c)	Last listed 1997
	'Jessie Cooper'	See *C.* 'Mrs Jessie Cooper'
	'Jessie Habgood' (1)	WIvo
	'Jimmy Motram' (1)	Last listed 1999
	'Joan' (25b)	LRHS
	'John Cory' (3b)	NHal
	'John Harrison' (25b)	NHal
	'John Hughes' (3b)	MCol NHal
	'John Lewis' (24b)	Last listed 1997
	'John Riley' (14a)	Last listed 1997
	'John Wingfield' (14b)	MCol NHal
	'Julia' (28)	CLTr EFou GMac
	'Julie Lagravère' (28)	EFou EMon GBuc MBel
	'June Buglass' (3b)	Last listed 1998
	'June Rose' (24b)	Last listed 1999
	'June Wakley' (25b)	MCol
	'Karen Riley' (25a)	Last listed 1997
	'Kay Woolman' (13b)	NHal WWol
	'Ken Lyons' (7b)	MCol
	'Keystone' (25b)	MCol
	'Kimberley Marie' (15b)	NHal
	x *koreanum*	See *C. grandiflorum*
¶	'Kota Kinabalu' (1)	WIvo
	'Lady in Pink' (29Rub)	GBuc
	'Lakelanders' (3b)	NHal WWol
¶	'Lameet' (29)	WWol
¶	'Lancashire Fold' (1)	WIvo
¶	'Lancashire Lad' (1)	WIvo
	'Lantern' (15b)	Last listed 1998
	'Laser' (24b)	WWol
	Laurie = 'Yolaurie' (22c)	Last listed 1999
	Legend = 'Yoleg' (22)	NHal
	'Leading Lady' (25b)	WWol
	'Lemon Heide' (29c)	MCol
	'Lemon Margaret' (29c) ♀	NHal
	leucanthemum	See *Leucanthemum vulgare*
¶	'Leviathan' (1)	WIvo
¶	'Lilac Chessington' (25a)	NHal
	'Lilian Hoek' (29c)	MCol
	'Lilian Jackson' (7b)	Last listed 1999
	'Lilian Shoesmith' (5b)	Last listed 1997
	Linda = 'Lindayo' PBR (22c)	MCol WLRN
	'Lindie' (28)	EFou
	'L'Innocence' (29K)	WMaN
	Lisa = 'Yolisa' PBR (22c)	MCol
	'Little Dorrit' (29K)	LRHS MBNS MCol
	'Liverpool Festival' (23b)	MCol
	'Long Island Beauty' (6b)	♀MCol
	'Long Life' (25b)	MCol
	'Lorna Wood' (13b)	NHal
¶	'Louisa Pockett' (1)	WIvo
	'Louise' (25b)	LRHS
	'Louise Park' (24a)	NHal
	'Lucy Simpson' (29K)	MCol MMil WMaN
	'Lundy' (2)	NHal
¶	'Luv Purple'	WWol
	'Lyndale' (25b)	MCol
	'Lynmal's Choice' (13b)	MCol
	Lynn = 'Yolynn' PBR (22c)	♀ NHal WLRN
	macrophyllum	See *Tanacetum macrophyllum*
	'Mac's Delight' (25b)	MCol
	'Madeleine' (29c) ♀	Last listed 1998
	'Malcolm Perkins' (25a)	NHal
	'Mancetta Bride' (29a) ♀	Last listed 1995

'Mancetta Comet' (29a)	NHal	
¶ 'Mancetta Symbol' (5b)	NHal	
'Mandarin' (5b)	CGle EFou	
maresii	See *Rhodanthemum bosmariense*	
'Margaret' (29c) ♀	MCol NHal	
'Maria' (28a)	MCol	
'Mariann' (12a)	Last listed 1998	
'Marie Brunton' (15a)	Last listed 1997	
'Marion' (25a)	Last listed 1998	
¶ 'Mark Woolman' (1)	NHal WIvo	
'Martha'	LRHS MBNS	
'Martin Riley' (23b)	MCol	
'Mary' (29K)	MCol WMaN	
'Mary Stevenson' (25b)	MCol	
'Mary Stoker' (29Rub)	More than 30 suppliers	
'Mason's Bronze' (7b)	MCol	
¶ 'Matador' (14a)	WWol	
'Matlock' (24b)	MCol NHal	
'Matthew Woolman' (4a)	Last listed 1997	
'Maureen' (29K)	Last listed 1997	
'Mauve Gem' (29K)	Last listed 1997	
'Mavis' (28a) ♀	MCol	
mawii	See *Rhodanthemum gayanum*	
'Max Riley' (23b) ♀	NHal	
maximowiczii	EMon	
maximum Ramond	See *Leucanthemum maximum* (Ramond) DC	
- hort.	See *Leucanthemum* x *superbum*	
'May Shoesmith' (5a) ♀	NHal	
'Mayford Perfection' (5a) ♀	MCol NHal WWol	
'Medallion' (9c)	MCol	
'Megan Woolman' (3b)	WWol	
Megan = 'Yomegan' (22d)	WLRN	
'Mei-kyo' (28b)	CGle CHar CM&M CMea EBee ECtt EFou ELan EMan EMon MBel MLLN MRav NFai SPer SPla SRms WBor WEas WFar WWat	
'Membury' (24b) ♀	MCol NHal	
¶ 'Michelle Preston' (13b)	NHal	
¶ 'Migoli'	WWol	
'Minaret' (3b)	Last listed 1999	
¶ 'Minstreel Bronze' (9)	WWol	
¶ 'Minstreel Dark' (9)	WWol	
'Minstrel Boy' (3b)	MCol	
Mirage = 'Yomira' (22b) ♀	Last listed 1997	
'Miss Prim' (24b)	MCol	
'Moira' (29K)	LRHS	
'Molly Lambert' (5a)	Last listed 1999	
¶ 'Monica Bennett' (1)	WIvo	
'Moonlight' (29d/K)	LRHS	
'Morning Star' (12a)	Last listed 1998	
'Mottram Barleycorn' (29d)	Last listed 1997	
'Mottram Minstrel' (29d)	MCol	
'Mottram Sentinel' (29d)	MCol	
'Mottram Twotone' (29d)	MCol	
§ 'Mrs Jessie Cooper' (29Rub)	EFou ELan EMon GMac MNrw MSte NBir NBrk SChu SEas WCot WHoo WLRN	
'Music' (23b)	MCol NHal	
'My Love' (7a)	MCol	
'Myss Madi' (29c) ♀	Last listed 1999	
'Myss Rosie' (29c)	Last listed 1997	
naktongense	See *C. zawadskii* var. *latilobum*	
'Nancy Perry' (19Rub)	CElw CSam ELan EMan EMon MCol MRav SChu SEas	
§ *nankingense*	EMon WFar	
'Nantyderry Sunshine' (28b) ♀	CElw CMea CSpe EFou LRHS MAvo MNrw MWgw SMrm SPla WCot WEas WMaN WPer WPrP WRha WWat	
Naomi =	Last listed 1997	
'Yonaomi' PBR (22f)		
'Naru' (9c)	Last listed 1999	
'Nathalie' (19c) ♀	Last listed 1995	
'National Celebration' (25b)	Last listed 1999	
'Nell Gwyn' (29Rub)	MCol	
Nicole =	MCol NHal WLRN WWol	
'Yonicole' PBR (22c) ♀		
nipponicum	See *Nipponanthemum nipponicum*	
'Nora Brook' (25b) ♀	Last listed 1987	
'Nudazzler' (9d)	MCol	
'Nurobin' (9d)	MCol	
'Nurosemary' (9d) ♀	MCol	
'Old Cottage Yellow'	Last listed 1998	
'Orange Allouise' (25b)	MCol NHal	
'Orange Corfu' (9a)	Last listed 1998	
'Orange Enbee Wedding' (29d)	NHal	
'Orange Fairway' (15b)	Last listed 1999	
'Orangeade' (24b)	MCol	
'Orno' (29b) ♀	Last listed 1996	
pacificum	See *Ajania pacifica*	
'Packwell' (24b)	Last listed 1997	
§ 'Pamela' (29c)	NHal	
'Panache' (5a)	MCol	
¶ 'Pandion'	WWol	
'Parkfield Tigger' (29c)	NHal	
parthenium	See *Tanacetum parthenium*	
¶ 'Pascal Dark' (29)	WWol	
'Pat Davison' (25b)	NHal	
'Patricia' (29c)	WWol	
'Patricia Millar' (14b)	NHal	
'Paul Boissier' (30Rub)	CElw CGle EFou ELan EMan EMon LGre MBel MBro NSti WCot WEas WHoo	
'Pauline White' (15a)	NHal	
'Payton Blaze' (29c)	MCol	
'Payton Dale' (29c) ♀	MCol NHal	
'Payton Lady' (29c)	MCol	
'Payton Pixie' (29c)	Last listed 1997	
'Payton Prince' (29c) ♀	Last listed 1995	
'Payton Snow' (29c)	MCol	
'Peach Allouise' (25b) ♀	NHal	
'Peach Cassandra' (5b)	MCol	
'Peach Courtier' (24a)	NHal	
'Peach Enbee Wedding' (29d) ♀	MCol	
'Peach Margaret'	See *C.* 'Salmon Margaret'	
Peachy Lynn =	WLRN	
'Peachy Yolynn' PBR (22c)		
'Pearl Celebration' (24a)	NHal	
'Peggy' (28a)	Last listed 1997	
¶ 'Peggy Anne' (1)	WIvo	
'Pelsall Imperial' (3a)	Last listed 1998	
'Pennine Alfie' (29f) ♀	Last listed 1989	
'Pennine Autumn' (29c)	MCol	
'Pennine Bouquet' (29e)	Last listed 1999	
'Pennine Calypso' (29b) ♀	Last listed 1993	
'Pennine Canary' (29c) ♀	Last listed 1998	
'Pennine Charm' (29b)	Last listed 1998	
'Pennine Cheer' (29c)	Last listed 1998	
'Pennine Claret' (29c)	Last listed 1998	
'Pennine Click' (29c)	Last listed 1998	
'Pennine Club' (29d) ♀	Last listed 1999	
I 'Pennine Coconut' (29)	WWol	
'Pennine Coffee' (29c)	Last listed 1999	
'Pennine Colt' (29d)	Last listed 1999	
'Pennine Crystal' (29c)	MCol WWol	
'Pennine Dancer' (29d)	Last listed 1998	
'Pennine Dart' (29d)	NHal	
'Pennine Dell' (29d)	Last listed 1999	

'Pennine Digger' (29c)	Last listed 1998	
'Pennine Eagle' (29c)	Last listed 1999	
'Pennine Fizz' (29d)	Last listed 1997	
'Pennine Flute' (29f) ♀	Last listed 1992	
'Pennine Gambol' (29a) ♀	Last listed 1993	
'Pennine Gift' (29c)	MCol NHal	
'Pennine Ginger' (29c) ♀	NHal	
'Pennine Gipsy' (29c)	Last listed 1998	
'Pennine Glory' (29c) ♀	MCol	
'Pennine Goal' (29c) ♀	WWol	
¶ 'Pennine Grant'	WWol	
'Pennine Hannah' (29d)	Last listed 1997	
'Pennine Hayley' (29d)	Last listed 1998	
'Pennine Jade' (29d) ♀	Last listed 1998	
¶ 'Pennine Jane'	WWol	
'Pennine Jessie' (29d)	Last listed 1999	
'Pennine Jude' (29a) ♀	Last listed 1993	
'Pennine Lace' (29f) ♀	Last listed 1995	
'Pennine Lotus' (29c) ♀	Last listed 1992	
'Pennine Magic' (29c) ♀	Last listed 1993	
'Pennine Magnet' (29a) ♀	Last listed 1999	
'Pennine Marie' (29a) ♀	MCol NHal	
'Pennine Oriel' (29a) ♀	MCol NHal	
'Pennine Pageant' (29d)	NHal	
'Pennine Panda' (29d)	Last listed 1999	
¶ 'Pennine Passion' (29c)	WWol	
'Pennine Phyllis' (29b) ♀	Last listed 1992	
¶ 'Pennine Pilot'	WWol	
¶ 'Pennine Point'	WWol	
'Pennine Polo' (29d) ♀	MCol NHal WWol	
'Pennine Posy' (29f)	Last listed 1999	
'Pennine Pride' (29d)	Last listed 1997	
'Pennine Punch' (29a)	Last listed 1997	
'Pennine Purple' (29c)	MCol	
'Pennine Ranger' (29d)	NHal	
'Pennine Ray' (29d)	Last listed 1997	
'Pennine Ritz' (29d)	Last listed 1997	
'Pennine Romeo' (19c)	NHal	
'Pennine Saffron' (29c)	Last listed 1999	
'Pennine Sally' (29c)	Last listed 1998	
'Pennine Signal' (29d) ♀	Last listed 1993	
'Pennine Silver' (29c) ♀	Last listed 1992	
'Pennine Ski' (29c)	MCol	
'Pennine Slumber' (29c)	Last listed 1998	
'Pennine Soldier' (29d) ♀	Last listed 1999	
'Pennine Sparkle' (29f)	Last listed 1997	
'Pennine Splash' (29d)	NHal	
'Pennine Sprite' (29d)	Last listed 1997	
'Pennine Sun' (29d) ♀	Last listed 1996	
¶ 'Pennine Sunlight' (19d)	WWol	
'Pennine Swan' (29c)	MCol NHal	
'Pennine Sweetheart' (29c) ♀		
	Last listed 1990	
'Pennine Swing' (29d)	NHal	
'Pennine Tango' (29d) ♀	Last listed 1996	
¶ 'Pennine Toy'	WWol	
'Pennine Twinkle' (29a) ♀	Last listed 1994	
'Pennine Whistle' (29f) ♀	Last listed 1994	
'Pennine Wine' (29c)	Last listed 1998	
'Percy Salter' (24b)	MCol	
'Perry's Peach'	MNrw NPer SUsu	
'Peter Fraser' (14b)	Last listed 1998	
'Peter Pan' (24b)	Last listed 1998	
'Peter Rowe' (23b)	MCol NHal	
'Peter Sare' (29d)	EBrP EBre GMac LBCl LBSe LBre	
	LRHS MBBe SBre	
'Peter White' (23a)	MCol	
'Peterkin'	CHea EBrP EBre ECtt EMon GMac	
	LBCl LBSe LBre LRHS MBBe	
	MNrw SBre	
'Phil Houghton' (1)	WIvo WWol	
'Phillip McNamara' (3b)	Last listed 1999	

'Piecas'	Last listed 1997	
'Pink Champagne' (4b)	Last listed 1997	
'Pink Duke' (1)	NHal	
¶ 'Pink Duke of Kent' (1)	WIvo	
'Pink Favorite' (5b)	MCol	
'Pink Gin' PBR (9c) ♀	Last listed 1996	
'Pink Honeysuckle	Last listed 1998	
Time' (5b)		
'Pink Ice' (5b)	MCol WRha	
'Pink John Wingfield' (24b)	MCol NHal	
'Pink Margaret' (29c) ♀	Last listed 1999	
¶ 'Pink Marvellous' (29f)	WWol	
¶ 'Pink Nurosemary' (9d) ♀	MCol	
'Pink Overture' (15b)	MCol	
'Pink Pennine Cheer' (29c)	Last listed 1998	
'Pink Progression'	GMac MWgw NBir NBrk	
¶ 'Pink Tripoli'	WWol	
'Pink World of Sport' (25a)	Last listed 1997	
'Pixton' (25b)	MCol	
'Playmate' (29K)	MCol	
'Polar Gem' (3a)	MCol NHal	
'Polaris' (9c)	Last listed 1997	
* 'Pompon Bronze' (28)	WWol	
* 'Pompon Pink' (28)	WWol	
* 'Pompon Purple' (28)	WWol	
* 'Pompon Yellow' (28)	WWol	
'Poppet' (28a) ♀	Last listed 1987	
'Pot Black' (14b)	Last listed 1998	
praeteritum	See *Tanacetum praeteritum*	
'Primrose Alison Kirk' (23b)	MCol NHal	
'Primrose Allouise' (24b) ♀	NHal	
'Primrose Anemone' (29K)	Last listed 1997	
'Primrose Angora' (25b)	MCol	
'Primrose Bill Wade' (25a)	Last listed 1999	
'Primrose	NHal	
Chessington' (25a)		
'Primrose Courtier'	See *C.* 'Yellow Courtier'	
'Primrose Cricket' (25b)	MCol	
'Primrose Dorothy	NHal	
Stone' (25b)		
'Primrose Dorridge	NHal	
Crystal' (24a)		
'Primrose Enbee	NHal	
Wedding' (29d)		
'Primrose Ermine' (23a)	NHal	
¶ 'Primrose Jessie	WIvo	
Habgood' (1)		
'Primrose John	NHal	
Hughes' (3b)		
'Primrose Margaret'	See *C.* 'Buff Margaret'	
'Primrose Mayford	MCol NHal	
Perfection' (5a) ♀		
'Primrose Pennine	Last listed 1997	
Oriel' (29a)		
'Primrose West	NHal	
Bromwich' (14a)		
'Prince Bishop' (25a)	NHal	
'Princess' (29K)	LRHS	
'Princess Anne' (4b)	MCol	
'Promise' (25a)	MCol NHal	
¶ 'Pryce Thompson' (25b)	NHal	
ptarmiciflorum	See *Tanacetum ptarmiciflorum*	
'Purleigh White' (28b)	EFou GMac LRHS MAvo NSti SPla	
	WCot WMaN WRha	
'Purple Fairie' (28b)	MCol	
'Purple Glow' (5a)	NHal	
'Purple Margaret' (29c)	NHal	
'Purple Pennine	Last listed 1992	
Wine' (29c) ♀		
'Purple Wessex	Last listed 1997	
Charm' (29d)		
'Queenswood' (5b)	MCol	

'Quill Elegance' (9f)   MCol
¶ 'Rachel'   WWol
'Rachel Fairweather' (3a)   NHal
'Rachel Knowles' (25a)   MCol
Radiant Lynn = 'Radiant   MCol NHal WLRN
   Yolynn' PBR (22c)
'Ralph Lambert' (1)   WIvo
'Raquel' (29K)   MCol
Raquel =   WWol
   'Yoraquel' PBR (22c)
'Rayonnante' (11)   MCol
¶ 'Rebecca' (14b)   WWol
'Red Balcombe   NHal WWol
   Perfection' (5a)
¶ 'Red Bella' (29c)   MCol
'Red Carlene Welby' (25b)   Last listed 1998
'Red Chempak Rose' (14b)   Last listed 1997
'Red Claudia' (29c)   Last listed 1997
'Red Early Bird' (24b)   MCol
'Red Eye Level' (5a)   Last listed 1997
'Red Formcast' (24a)   NHal
'Red Galaxy' (9d)   Last listed 1999
'Red Gambit' (24a)   NHal
'Red Mayford   MCol
   Perfection' (5a)
'Red Pamela' (29c)   NHal
'Red Payton Dale' (29c)   MCol
'Red Pennine Gift' (29c)   NHal
'Red Pennine Jade' (29d) ♀ Last listed 1992
'Red Pheasant'   Last listed 1997
'Red Resilient' (4b) ♀   Last listed 1991
'Red Rosita' (29c)   MCol
'Red Shirley Model' (3a)   NHal
'Red Shoesmith Salmon' (4a) Last listed 1997
¶ 'Red Tripoli'   WWol
'Red Wendy' (29c) ♀   MCol WWol
'Redall' (4c)   MCol
'Regal Mist' (25b)   MCol
'Regalia' (24b) ♀   MCol
Remarkable = 'Yorema' (30) MCol
'Resilient' (4b) ♀   Last listed 1991
¶ 'Revert'PBR   WWol
'Riley's Dynasty' (14a)   NHal
'Robeam' (9c) ♀   Last listed 1998
Robin = 'Yorobi' (22c)   MCol NHal
'Roblaze' (9c)   Last listed 1999
'Roger Kirby' (15a)   NHal
'Rolass' (9c)   Last listed 1999
'Romano Mauve'   Last listed 1997
'Romantika'   EFou GMac
'Romany' (2)   CElw WEas
'Romark' (9c)   MCol
'Rose Broadway   MCol
   Mandy' (29c)
'Rose Enbee Wedding' (29d) MCol NHal WWol
'Rose Mayford   MCol NHal WWol
   Perfection' (5a) ♀
'Rose Patricia Millar' (14b) NHal
'Rosedew' (25a) ♀   Last listed 1987
roseum   See Tanacetum coccineum
'Rosita' (28b)   MCol
'Roswan' (9c)   Last listed 1999
¶ Roxanne =   WWol
   'Yoroxanne' (22)
'Roy Coopland' (5b) ♀   Last listed 1997
'Royal Cardinal' (9c)   MCol
'Royal Command' (29Rub) EBee EMon MNrw NBro
Royal Lynn =   MCol WLRN
   'Royal Yolynn' PBR (22c)
I 'Rozette'   Last listed 1997
¶ 'Rubaiyat'   WWol
rubellum   See C. zawadskii

'Ruby Enbee   MCol NHal WWol
   Wedding' (29d) ♀
'Ruby Mound' (29c/K)   CElw CMdw EFou LGre LRHS
   MCol MTis WEas
'Ruby Raynor' (29Rub)   MCol
'Rumpelstilzchen'   CElw CMea EBee EMan EMar
   EPPr MNrw SAga WPer
'Russet Gown'   EBee
'Rybronze' (9d)   Last listed 1999
'Ryfinch' (9d)   MCol
'Ryflare' (9c)   Last listed 1997
'Ryflash' (9d)   MCol
'Rylands Gem' (24b) ♀   MCol
'Rylands Victor' (23c)   MCol
'Rynoon' (9d) ♀ ·   MCol
'Ryred'   MCol
'Rystar' (9d) ♀   Last listed 1991
'Rytorch' (9d)   MCol
'Salmon Cassandra' (5b) ♀ Last listed 1997
'Salmon Chessington' (25a) NHal
'Salmon Enbee   NHal
   Wedding' (29d) ♀
'Salmon Fairie' (28a) ♀   MCol
¶ 'Salmon Lilac Prince' (1)   WIvo
§ 'Salmon Margaret' (29c) ♀ MCol
'Salmon Pauline White' (15a) Last listed 1997
'Salmon Pennine   Last listed 1992
   Gambol' (29a) ♀
'Salmon Pennine   Last listed 1992
   Wine' (29c) ♀
'Salmon Rylands Gem' (24b) MCol
'Salmon Susan Rowe' (24b) MCol
'Salmon Talbot   Last listed 1995
   Parade' (29c) ♀
'Salmon Venice' (24b)   Last listed 1997
'Salurose'   Last listed 1997
'Sam Vinter' (5a)   MCol NHal
Sandy = 'Yosandy' (30)   MCol
Sarah = 'Yosar' PBR (22f)   WLRN
'Sarah's Yellow'   CSam
'Saskia' PBR (7b)   MCol
'Satin Pink Gin' PBR (9c) ♀ Last listed 1996
'Scarlet Medallion' (9c)   MCol
'Scottie' (24b)   Last listed 1999
'Sea Urchin' (29c)   MCol
'Seashell' (28b)   MCol
'Seatons Flirt' (3b)   Last listed 1998
'Setron'   Last listed 1998
¶ 'Shamrock' (10b)   WWol
'Sheila' (29K)   Last listed 1997
Shelley = 'Yoshelley' (22b) WWol
'Shining Light' (29f/K)   MCol
'Shirley' (25b)   Last listed 1997
'Shirley Primrose' (1)   WIvo
'Shoesmith's   Last listed 1995
   Salmon' (4a) ♀
'Silver Gigantic' (1)   NHal WIvo
'Simon Mills' (2)   Last listed 1999
¶ 'Smokey' (29)   WWol
'Snowbound' (29K)   Last listed 1997
'Snowdon' (5b/9c) ♀   Last listed 1987
Soft Lynn = 'Soft   NHal WLRN
   Yolynn' PBR (22c)
'Solarama' (9e)   Last listed 1999
'Sonnenschein'   LHop WHen
'Sonya' (29K)   Last listed 1997
Sophia =   WLRN
   'Yosophia' PBR (22c)
'Southway Sanguine' (29d) NHal
¶ 'Southway Snoopy' (29d)   NHal
'Southway Sonar' (29d)   NHal
'Southway Stomp' (29d)   NHal

¶ 'Southway Strontium' (29d) NHal
'Southway Sure' (29d) ♀   Last listed 1999
'Sparta' (9c)   Last listed 1999
'Spartan Fire'   WWol
'Spartan Glory' (25b)   WWol
'Spartan Leo' (29c)   WWol
¶ 'Spartan Linnet'   WWol
'Spartan Magic' (29d)   Last listed 1998
'Spartan Moon' (25b)   WWol
'Spartan Rose' (29c)   Last listed 1998
¶ 'Spartan Seagull'   WWol
'Spartan Sunrise' (29c)   WWol
'Spartan Torch'   WWol
'Spartan White' (29c)   Last listed 1998
'Spencer's Cottage' (13b)   MCol
* 'Spoons'   SCro
'Stan's Choice' (29K)   MCol
'Stardust' (24b)   MCol
'Starlet' (29f/K)   LRHS MCol
'Stella' (29c)   EFou GMac
'Stockton' (3b)   NHal
'Stoke Festival' (25b)   MCol
'Stuart Jackson' (25a)   Last listed 1998
'Stunning Lynn' PBR (22c)   WLRN
'Sun Spider' (30)   Last listed 1997
'Sun Valley' (5a)   MCol
'Sunbeam' (28)   EBrP EBre EFou LBCl LBSe LBre LRHS MBBe SBre
'Suncharm Bronze' (22a)   Last listed 1997
'Suncharm Pink' (22a)   Last listed 1997
'Suncharm Red' (22a)   Last listed 1997
'Suncharm Yellow' (22a)   Last listed 1997
Sundoro = 'Yosun' PBR (22d) NHal
'Sunflight' (25b)   MCol
Sunny Denise = 'Sunny Yodenise' (22)   Last listed 1999
Sunny Linda = 'Sunny Lindayo' (22c)   WLRN WWol
¶ 'Sunny Tripoli' PBR   WWol
'Susan Rowe' (24b)   MCol
'Sutton White' (25a)   WWol
'Suzanne Marie' (24a)   MCol
'Swalwell' (25b) ♀   Last listed 1995
'Taffeta' (9c)   MCol
'Talbot Bolero' (29c)   MCol NHal
'Talbot Bouquet' (29a) ♀   Last listed 1995
'Talbot Parade' (29c) ♀   MCol NHal
'Tang' (12a)   Last listed 1998
'Tapestry Rose' (29K)   CGle CMea EMon MMil MNrw NBrk
'Tapis Blanc'   Last listed 1997
Target = 'Yotarget' PBR (22) MCol NHal WLRN
'The Favourite' (5b)   MCol
'Thoroughbred' (24a)   NHal WWol
'Tickle Pink' (29f/K)   Last listed 1997
'Toledo' (25a)   MCol WWol
'Tom Blackshaw' (25b)   MCol NHal
'Tom Parr'   See C. 'Doctor Tom Parr'
'Tom Snowball' (3b)   NHal
'Tommy Trout' (28)   MCol
'Tone Gambol' (29a)   MCol
'Tone Sail' (29a)   MCol
'Topsy' (29c/K)   Last listed 1997
'Tracy Waller' (24b)   NHal
Triumph = 'Yotri' (22)   NHal
'Tundra' (4a)   Last listed 1999
uliginosum   See *Leucanthemella serotina*
'Universiade' (25a)   NHal
'Vagabond Prince'   CSam MBro WHoo
'Valerie' (9f/10)   Last listed 1998
'Vanity Pink' (7b)   MCol
'Vanity Primrose' (7b)   MCol

'Venice' (24b)   NHal
'Venus' (29K)   CBlo LRHS MBro
'Vera Smith' (3b)   MCol
* 'Veria'   Last listed 1997
'Victor Rowe' (5b) ♀   MCol
'Virginia' (29K)   WWol
'Vrenelli'   EFou
'Wedding Day' (29K)   CElw CStr EMan EMon GBuc MBro MFir MMil MNrw NFla NFor SRms SUsu WCot WHoo WMaN WOve WRus
'Wedding Sunshine' (29K) LRHS MMil
welwitschii   See *Xanthophthalmum segetum*
'Wembley' (24b)   Last listed 1998
'Wendy' (29c) ♀   MCol
¶ 'Wendy Bronze'   WWol
'Wendy Tench' (29d)   Last listed 1997
'Wessex Dawn' (29d)   MCol
'Wessex Eclipse' (29c)   MCol
'Wessex Ivory' (29d)   MCol
'Wessex Shell' (29d) ♀   Last listed 1990
'Wessex Sunshine' (29d)   MCol
'Wessex Tang' (29d) ♀   Last listed 1995
'West Bromwich' (14a)   NHal
§ *weyrichii*   EBrP EBre LBCl LBSe LBre LFis LRHS MBBe MHer MTho NMen NNrd NWCA SBla SBre SRms SSmi WCot
'White Allouise' (25b) ♀   NHal
'White Beppie' (29e)   MCol
'White Bouquet' (28)   MCol WWol
'White Cassandra' (5b)   NHal
'White Enbee Wedding' (29d)   Last listed 1997
'White Fairweather' (3b)   Last listed 1998
'White Gem' (25b)   Last listed 1997
'White Gloss' (29K)   LRHS SMer
¶ 'White Lancashire Fold' (1) WIvo
'White Lilac Prince' (1)   WIvo
'White Margaret' (29c) ♀   MCol NHal
¶ 'White Marvellous' (29f)   WWol
'White Nurosemary' (9d)   Last listed 1999
¶ 'White Papino'   WWol
'White Rachel Knowles' (25a)   Last listed 1999
'White Rayonnante' (11)   MCol
'White Sands' (9a) ♀   MCol
'White Skylark' (22)   NHal
'White Sonja' (29c)   MCol
'White Spider' (10a)   MCol
'White Taffeta' (9c)   MCol
'White Tower'   MNrw
'William Florentine' (15a)   NHal
'Win' (9c)   Last listed 1999
'Windermere' (24a)   NHal
'Wine Carlene Welby' (25b)NHal
'Winnie Bramley' (23a)   WWol
'Winning's Red' (29Rub)   EMon NBro SMad WWin
'Winter Queen' (5b)   NHal
'Woolley Globe' (25b)   MCol
'Woolman's Century' (1)   WWol
'Woolman's Perfecta' (3a)   Last listed 1997
'Woolman's Prince' (3a)   WWol
'Woolman's Star' (3a)   WWol
'Woolman's Venture' (4b)   NHal
'World of Sport' (25a)   Last listed 1997
'Yellow Alfreton Cream' (5b)   Last listed 1997
'Yellow Allison Kirk' (23b) Last listed 1999
'Yellow Allouise' (25b)   NHal
'Yellow Beppie' (29e)   MCol
§ 'Yellow Courtier' (24a)   NHal

'Yellow Danielle' (29d)   MCol
¶ 'Yellow Dorothy   NHal
    Stone' (25b)
¶ 'Yellow Duke of Kent' (1)   WIvo
    'Yellow Ellen' (29c)   NHal WWol
    'Yellow Flying Saucer' (6a) MCol
    'Yellow Fred Shoesmith' (5a) WWol
    'Yellow Galaxy' (9d) ♀   MCol
    'Yellow Gingernut' (25b)   MCol NHal
    'Yellow Hammer' (12a)   Last listed 1997
    'Yellow Hazy Days' (25b)   NHal
    'Yellow Heather James' (3b) MCol
    'Yellow Heide' (29c) ♀   MCol NHal
    'Yellow John Hughes' (3b) ♀
        MCol NHal
    'Yellow John   MCol NHal
        Wingfield' (14b)
    'Yellow Lilian Hock' (29c)   MCol
    'Yellow Margaret' (29c) ♀   MCol NHal
    'Yellow May Shoesmith' (5a) NHal
    'Yellow Mayford   MCol NHal
        Perfection' (5a) ♀
    'Yellow Megan   WWol
        Woolman' (3b)
    'Yellow Pennine   MCol NHal
        Oriel' (29a) ♀
    'Yellow Percy Salter' (24b) MCol
    'Yellow Phil Houghton' (1) WIvo WWol
    'Yellow Plover' (22)   NHal
* 'Yellow Pom' (28)   LRHS
    'Yellow Resilient' (5b) ♀   Last listed 1991
    'Yellow Roswan' (9c)   Last listed 1999
    'Yellow Sands' (9d)   MCol
    'Yellow Spider' (10a)   MCol
* 'Yellow Stardust' (24b)   MCol
    'Yellow Starlet' (29f/K)   MCol
    'Yellow Taffeta' (9c)   MCol
    'Yellow Talbot Parade' (29c) NHal
    Yellow Triumph = 'Yellow   WLRN
        Yotri' [PBR] (22)
    'Yellow Whitby' (5b)   MCol
§ *yezoense* ♀   EBee ELan EMan EMon MBel SPla
        WEas
    - 'Roseum'   EBee MBel MNrw NSti WPGP
    'Yvonne Arnaud' (24b) ♀   MCol
§ *zawadskii*   WFar WHer WPyg
§ - var. *latilobum*   EBee
    Zesty Barbara = 'Zesty   Last listed 1999
        Yobarbara' [PBR] (22c)

CHRYSOCOMA (Asteraceae)
ciliata JJH 9401633   NWCA
coma-aurea   Last listed 1998

CHRYSOGONUM (Asteraceae)
australe   EBee
virginianum   CHal CMea CRDP EBee ECha
    EMan EMar LRHS MRav SCob SPer
    WFar WHal

CHRYSOPOGON (Poaceae)
gryllus   EBee EMon LRHS WPGP

CHRYSOPSIS (Asteraceae)
villosa   See *Heterotheca villosa*

CHRYSOSPLENIUM (Saxifragaceae)
alternifolium   Last listed 1999
davidianum   CBre CGle EBee ECha EGle EMan
    EPar EPot LSpr NBir NSla SMac
    WCru WGer WHil WWat
    - SBEC 231   NHol NWoo

oppositifolium   EBee EMNN GAri GDra GGar
    WHer WShi

CHRYSOTHEMIS (Gesneriaceae)
pulchella ♀   CHal

CHUSQUEA ♣ (Poaceae - Bambusoideae)
argentina   ISta
¶ *coronalis*   WJun
culeou ♀   CDoC CEnd CFil CGre CHEx EFul
    EOas EPfP EPla IOrc ISta LJus
    LRHS MMoz MNes MWht SArc
    SDix SDry SSta WJun WNor WPGP
    - 'Breviglumis'   See *C. culeou* 'Tenuis'
§ - 'Tenuis'   EPla ERod ISta LJus SDry WJun
        WNor
¶ *cumingii*   WJun
liebmannii   Last listed 1998
montana   CFil EPla ISta WPGP
nigricans   ISta
¶ *pittieri*   WJun
quila   CFil ISta SDry WPGP
ramosissima   CFil SDry
¶ *sulcata*   WJun
¶ *uliginosa*   WJun
valdiviensis   ISta WJun

CICERBITA (Asteraceae)
§ *alpina*   GOrP NBid NHex NLar SPlb
macrorhiza B&SWJ 2970   WCot WCru
plumieri   MAvo WCot
- 'Blott' (v)   LSpr WCot
sp. B&SWJ 5162   EBee WCru

CICHORIUM (Asteraceae)
intybus   More than 30 suppliers
- f. *album*   CGle CPou CRDP EBee ECha
    ECoo EGle EMan EMon EPfP LAst
    LHop LRHS MCAu MRav MSte
    NSti SRPl SWat WCHb
- 'Roseum'   CBos CGle CHad CRDP CSpe
    EBee ECGP ECha ECoo ECot EGle
    ELan EMan EMon GBri LAst LHop
    LRHS MCAu MRav SPer SWat
    WCHb WWal WWin
spinosum   SOkd

CIMICIFUGA ♣ (Ranunculaceae)
acerina   See *C. japonica*
§ *americana*   MSal SRms
arizonica   SAga SBla
cordifolia Pursh   See *C. americana*
—(DC.)Torrey & A.Gray   See *C. rubifolia*
dahurica   EBee GAbr GCal LRHS MCli MSal
    SWat WCru
elata   EBee WCru
foetida   GBin GPoy
- B&SWJ 2966   WCru
frigida B&SWJ 2657   WCru
§ *japonica*   CLAP CRow EBrP EBre GAbr
    GCal LBCl LBSe LBre LFis LGre
    LRHS MBBe NDov SBre WCot
    WRus
racemosa ♀   More than 30 suppliers
- var. *cordifolia*   See *C. rubifolia*
* - 'Purple Torch'   Last listed 1999
- 'Purpurea'   See *C. simplex* var. *simplex*
    Atropurpurea Group
ramosa   See *C. simplex* var. *simplex*
    'Prichard's Giant'
§ *rubifolia*   EBee EMan GMaP LGre MBel
    MSal NCut WCru WWat

simplex	CBot CFil CMea EWTr GKir IHdy LRHS MBri SPer SWat WCot WCru WWat
¶ - from Hokkaido, Japan	GCal
¶ - 'James Compton'	CLAP CMil EBrP EBre LBCl LBSe LBre MBBe SBre
- var. *matsumurae* 'Elstead' ♀	CBos CFil CRow ECha EPar GCal LGre MRav SSpi WPGP
- - 'Frau Herms'	EBee ECha GKir LGre MRav
- - 'White Pearl'	More than 30 suppliers
- 'Silver Axe'	GCal
§ - var. *simplex* Atropurpurea Group	More than 30 suppliers
¶ - - 'Bernard Mitchell'	MTed
- - 'Brunette'	More than 30 suppliers
- - 'Prichard's Giant'	CPlt EBee GAri GBuc GCal LGre LRHS MBri MRav WFar
- - 'Scimitar'	LGre
sp. B&SWJ 343	Last listed 1998
* *taiwanensis* B&SWJ 3413	EBee WCru
¶ *yesoensis*	LGre
yunnanensis ACE 1880	GBuc WCot

CINERARIA (Asteraceae)

maritima	See *Senecio cineraria*

CINNAMOMUM (Lauraceae)

campbora	CB&S CFil CHEx CTrG ERea GQui LPan
¶ *japonicum*	CFil WPGP

CIONURA (Asclepiadaceae)

§ *erecta*	CPIN
oreopbila	CPIN GCal

CIRCAEA (Onagraceae)

lutetiana	CKin EWFC MHew MSal WHer WShi
- 'Caveat Emptor' (v)	CHid EMon WCot WHer

CIRSIUM (Asteraceae)

acaule	CKin
* *atro roseum*	SWat
diacantha	See *Ptilostemon diacantha*
dissectum	Last listed 1998
eriophorum	Last listed 1998
erisitbales	Last listed 1999
belenioides	See *C. heterophyllum*
§ *heterophyllum*	EMon
japonicum 'Early Rose Beauty'	MTis
* - 'Pink Beauty'	CSpe EWTr GKir WElm WFar WWpP
- 'Rose Beauty'	ELan EWTr LRHS MBri WElm WFar
oleraceum	NLar
palustre	Last listed 1998
¶ *purpuratum*	WCot WPGP
rivulare 'Atropurpureum'	CElw CFri CGle CHid CPlt EBee EGle ELan EMan EMon EPPr LGre MCLN MGrG MTed MTis NBid NBir NSti NTow SSpi WBar WByw WCHb WCot WEas WPGP
spinosissimum	EBee
ugoense	EBee
vulgare	CKin
- variegated	WAlt
- white	WAlt

CISSUS (Vitaceae)

adenopoda	CPIN
antarctica ♀	LRHS MBri

discolor	CHal
hypoglauca	Last listed 1998
pedata B&SWJ 2371	WCru
rhombifolia ♀	MBri
- 'Ellen Danica' ♀	CHal LRHS MBri
§ *striata*	CB&S CDoC CHEx CPIN CSPN CTrC EBee EMan EMil EPla IMGH LRHS SBra SLim SLon WCot WCru WSHC WWat

CISTUS ✿ (Cistaceae)

x *aguilarii*	CChe CSam CTri EBee EWTr SPan WGer WOve WSHC
- 'Maculatus' ♀	More than 30 suppliers
albanicus	See *C. sintenisii*
albidus	CArn CFil EGoo MLLN SDry SMrm SPan SSpi WHer
algarvensis	See *Halimium ocymoides*
'Ann Baker'	LGre MBri SLPl SPan
'Anne Palmer'	CHor EPfP NBrk WAbe
¶ x *argenteus* 'Blushing Peggy Sammons'	WSPU
- 'Peggy Sammons' ♀	More than 30 suppliers
atriplicifolius	See *Halimium atriplicifolium*
'Barnsley Pink'	See *C.* 'Grayswood Pink'
'Blanche'	See *C. ladanifer* 'Blanche'
¶ x *bornetianus* 'Jester'	SPan
'Candy Stripe' (v)	GBri MCCP NPro SPer
x *canescens*	Last listed 1999
- f. *albus*	CCHP LGre LRHS MBri NSti SPan WGer WHCG
'Chelsea Bonnet'	CFai EBee GMaP MSte SLim SPan SPla SRPl SUsu SVen WBod WPen
'Chelsea Pink'	See *C.* 'Grayswood Pink'
§ *clusii*	CHar MAsh
coeris	See *C.* x *hybridus*
x *corbariensis*	See *C.* x *hybridus*
creticus	CDoC GMaP MBel SPan
- subsp. *creticus*	CMHG EBee EGoo ELan EPfP GEil LRHS MBNS MBel MSte SPer WAbe WGer WWin
- - f. *albus*	MBel
- - - 'Tania Compton'	LGre SPan
* - - *lasithii*	WAbe
§ - subsp. *incanus*	LGre MNrw WHCG
§ x *crispatus* 'Warley Rose'	CLon GMaP LRHS MBri NSti SPan WAbe
§ *crispus* L.	GOrc LGre NFor SPan WAbe WEas WGer
- hort.	See *C.* x *pulverulentus*
- 'Prostratus'	See *C. crispus* L.
- 'Sunset'	See *C.* x *pulverulentus* 'Sunset'
§ x *cyprius* ♀	CArn CSpe EBee ECtt ELan ENot EWTr LAst LHop LRHS MBel MGos MRav MWat MWhi NBrk NSti SDix SEND SLPl SRms WBod WDin WFar WGer WPnn WWeb
- 'Albiflorus'	WBcn
- 'Tania Compton'	See *C. creticus* subsp. *creticus* f. *albus* 'Tania Compton'
§ x *dansereaui*	CHar CMHG CSam EBee ENot IOrc LGre LRHS MRav MSte NSti SPer WPat WPyg WWat
- 'Albiflorus'	See *C.* x *dansereaui* 'Portmeirion'
- 'Decumbens' ♀	More than 30 suppliers
- 'Jenkyn Place'	MBri SLPl SPan SUsu
§ - 'Portmeirion'	MBri
'Elma' ♀	CMHG ELan EPfP LGre LRHS MAsh MWgw SDry SPan SPer SPla WAbe WGer WHCG
§ x *florentinus* Lamarck	CLTr EBee IOrc LRHS NFor SChu WSHC

§ - hort.	See x *Halimiocistus* 'Ingwersenii'
- 'Fontfroide'	SPan
formosus	See *Halimium lasianthum*
Golden Treasure =	EBee EPfP LRHS MCCP MGos
'Nepond' PBR (v)	MWat NPro SLim SMur SPer SPla
§ 'Grayswood Pink'	CDoC CMHG EBee ELan EPla
	GCal GKir GMaP GOrc LRHS
	MAsh MBri MGos MHer MLLN
	MSte NSti SCoo SEND SLim SMrm
	SOkh SPlb SRms WAbe WGer
	WHCG
halimifolius	See *Halimium halimifolium*
hirsutus Lam. 1786	See *C. inflatus*
- var. *psilosepalus*	See *C. inflatus*
§ x *hybridus* ♀	More than 30 suppliers
incanus	See *C. creticus* subsp. *incanus*
- subsp. *creticus*	See *C. creticus* subsp. *creticus*
- subsp. *incanus*	See *C. creticus* subsp. *incanus*
§ *inflatus*	CPle NWoo SDry SEND WAbe
	WBod WHar WHer
ingwerseniana	See x *Halimiocistus* 'Ingwersenii'
'Jessamy Beauty'	SLPl SPan
'Jessamy Bride'	SLPl
'John Hardy'	SPan
ladanifer L. ♀	CB&S CFil CTri ECha ELan IMGH
	IOrc LRHS MBel MRav NFor NSti
	SChu SPer SPla WBod WEas WFar
	WHar WSHC WWye
- hort.	See *C.* x *cyprius*
- var. *albiflorus*	CB&S SPan SSpi
§ - 'Blanche'	LGre LRHS WKif
§ - 'Paladin'	LGre WAbe
- Palhinhae Group	See *C. ladanifer* var. *sulcatus*
- 'Pat'	CGre ELan EPfP LRHS
§ - var. *sulcatus* ♀	CFai CLTr LGre LRHS MSte SDry
	WAbe WCot
lasianthus	See *Halimium lasianthum*
laurifolius ♀	CFil EBee ENot EPfP ESis LPio
	MGos MNrw NBir NSti SLPl SLon
	SPan SPer WEas WHar WWal
x *laxus* 'Snow Queen'	See *C.* x *laxus* 'Snow White'
§ - 'Snow White'	CAbP CDoC EBee ELan LAst LGre
	LHop LRHS MAsh MBel MBri
	MSte NPer NPro NSti SAga SChu
	SLPl SLim SLon SPan SPer SSht
	SSpi WKif WWeb
x *ledon*	SLPl SUsu
libanotis	CSam MAsh NFor
'Little Gem'	LRHS MAsh MBri SPan
x *longifolius*	See *C.* x *nigricans*
x *loretii* Rouy & Fouc.	See *C.* x *stenophyllus*
- hort.	See *C.* x *dansereaui*
x *lusitanicus* Maund.	See *C.* x *dansereaui*
'Merrist Wood Cream'	See x *Halimiocistus wintonensis*
	'Merrist Wood Cream'
monspeliensis	CPle EPfP EWTr GOrc LPio LRHS
	MAsh SPan SPer SSpi
- CMBS 62	WPGP
§ x *nigricans*	EBee EHol SPan SRPl
x *oblongifolius*	LRHS
'Barr Common'	
x *obtusifolius* Sweet	CInt EPfP EWes MAsh MBel SMer
- hort.	See *C.* x *nigricans*
ochreatus	See *C. symphytifolius* subsp. *leucophyllus*
ocymoides	See *Halimium ocymoides*
osbeckiifolius	Last listed 1999
'Paladin'	See *C. ladanifer* 'Paladin'
palhinhae	See *C. ladanifer* var. *sulcatus*
parviflorus hort.	See *C.* 'Grayswood Pink'
- Lamarck	CBot ECha LGre LHop NSti SChu SPer WSHC

'Peggy Sammons'	See *C.* x *argenteus* 'Peggy Sammons'
x *platysepalus*	LGre SUsu
populifolius	CCHP CMHG ECha SPer SSta WAbe
- var. *lasiocalyx*	See *C. populifolius* subsp. *major*
§ - subsp. *major* ♀	CPle EPfP IOrc LGre SMrm SPan
psilosepalus	See *C. inflatus*
§ x *pulverulentus* ♀	CTri EBee EPfP MBel MMHG
	SChu SCro SWal WDin WLRN
	WSHC
§ - 'Sunset'	More than 30 suppliers
- 'Warley Rose'	See *C.* x *crispatus* 'Warley Rose'
§ x *purpureus* ♀	More than 30 suppliers
- 'Alan Fradd'	CBlo EBee ENot LRHS MAsh MBri
	MGos MGrG MTis MWgw NBrk
	SAga SCoo SCro SEND SLim SLod
	SMrm SPan SPla WGer WGwG
	WWal
- 'Betty Taudevin'	See *C.* x *purpureus*
* - f. *stictus*	WSPU
¶ x *rallettii*	SPan
¶ x *rodiaei* 'Jessica'	WSPU
rosmarinifolius	See *C. clusii*
sabucii	See x *Halimiocistus sabucii*
salviifolius	CArn CB&S CPle EMil ISea LRHS
	NSla SPan SRCN SSpi WHCG
	WLRN WWeb
- 'Avalanche'	GMaP LHop LRHS MRav WAbe
- x *monspeliensis*	See *C.* x *florentinus*
- 'Prostratus'	ELan LGre LHop LRHS NPro SRPl
	WHCG WWat
¶ 'Silver Ghost'	SCoo SPan
N 'Silver Pink'	More than 30 suppliers
'Silver Pink' misapplied	See *C.* 'Grayswood Pink'
§ *sintenisii*	GCHN
x *skanbergii* ♀	CB&S CHar CLTr CSpe EBee ELan
	ENot IMGH LFis LHop LRHS
	MAsh MGos MWat MWgw NBir
	NBrk NFai NSti SDix SDys SEas
	SPer WCFE WEas WFar WGwG
	WWal WWat WWin
§ 'Snow Fire'	ELan LGre LRHS MAsh MBri SLPl
	SPan SSpi SUsu WGer WSPU
'Snowflake'	See *C.* 'Snow Fire'
§ x *stenophyllus*	LGre NSti SPan SPer SUsu WKif
'Stripey'	Last listed 1999
symphytifolius	WPGP
§ - subsp. *leucophyllus*	CFil
- - MSF 98.019	WPGP
'Tania Compton'	See *C. creticus* subsp. *creticus* f. *albus* 'Tania Compton'
'Thornfield White'	Last listed 1998
¶ 'Thrive'	WWeb
tomentosus	See *Helianthemum nummularium* subsp. *tomentosum*
x *verguinii*	LGre LHop LRHS SPan WAbe
¶ - 'Albiflorus'	See *C.* x *dansereaui* 'Portmeirion'
- var. *albiflorus* misapplied	
villosus	See *C. creticus* subsp. *creticus*
wintonensis	See x *Halimiocistus wintonensis*

CITHAREXYLUM (Verbenaceae)
quadrangulare Jacquin	See *C. spinosum*
¶ *spicatum*	CPle
§ *spinosum*	CPLG

x CITROFORTUNELLA (Rutaceae)
§ *floridana*	CGOG
- 'Eustis' (F)	ECon ERea SCit

- 'Lakeland' (F)	ERea
Lemonquat (F)	SCit
Limequat	See x *C. floridana*
§ *microcarpa* (F) ♀	CAgr CGOG EPfP ERea ETub LCns MBri SCit WOTO
§ - 'Tiger' (v/F)	CB&S ECon EPfP ERea LCns SCit
- 'Variegata'	See x *C. microcarpa* 'Tiger'
mitis	See x *C. microcarpa*
Procimequat (F)	SCit
reticulata (F)	SCit
swinglei 'Tavares' (F)	ERea

X CITRONCIRUS (Rutaceae)

Citremon	CAgr LEdu
'Swingle' (F)	SCit
webberi 'Benton'	SCit
- 'C-32'	LEdu
- 'C-35'	Last listed 1999
- 'Carrizo'	CAgr SCit
- 'Rusk'	LEdu SCit
- 'Troyer'	LEdu

CITRONELLA (Icacinaceae)

§ *gongonha*	Last listed 1997
mucronata	See *C. gongonha*

CITRUS ✿ (Rutaceae)

amblycarpa Djeruk lime (F)	ERea
aurantiifolia (F)	SCit
- 'Indian Lime' x *limon* (F)	ERea
- 'La Valette' x *limon* (F)	ECon EPfP ERea
aurantium (F)	SCit
- 'Aber's Narrowleaf' (F)	SCit
- 'Bigaradier Apepu' (F)	SCit
- 'Bittersweet' (F)	SCit
- 'Bouquet de Fleurs'	CGOG ERea SCit
- 'Bouquetier de Nice'	Last listed 1999
- 'Bouquetier de Nice à Fleurs Doubles' (d)	SCit
- 'Gou-tou Cheng' (F)	SCit
- var. *myrtifolia* 'Chinotto' (F)	CGOG ERea SCit
- 'Sauvage' (F)	SCit
- 'Seville' (F)	CGOG ERea
- 'Smooth Flat Seville' (F)	SCit
- 'Willowleaf' (F)	SCit SPer
bergamia Bergamot	CGOG ERea
- 'Fantastico'	SCit
Calamondin	See x *Citrofortunella microcarpa*
deliciosa	See *C.* x *nobilis*
Ichang Lemon (F)	LEdu
ichangensis (F)	SCit
jambhiri 'Milam'	SCit
- Red Rough Lemon (F)	SCit
- Rough Lemon (F)	SCit
- Schaub Rough Lemon (F)	SCit
japonica	See *Fortunella japonica*
junos	LEdu
kinokuni	SCit
Kumquat	See *Fortunella margarita*
latifolia 'Bearss' (F)	CGOG ERea
- 'Tahiti' (F)	ECon ERea LChe LCns SPer
* x *latipes*	Last listed 1997
limettoides (F)	SCit
limon (F)	CGOG LPan
- 'Eureka Variegated' (F)	SCit
- 'Fino' (F)	CGOG SCit
§ - 'Garey's Eureka' (F)	EPfP ERea LCns
- 'Imperial' (F)	ERea
- 'Lemonade' (F)	ERea SCit
- 'Lisbon' (F)	ERea

- 'Quatre Saisons'	See *C. limon* 'Garey's Eureka'
- 'Toscana'	EPfP
- 'Variegata' (F)	ERea
- 'Verna' (F)	CGOG SCit
- 'Villa Franca' (F)	ERea
- 'Yen Ben' (F)	SCit
x *limonia* 'Rangpur' (F)	ERea
macrophylla	SCit
madurensis	See *Fortunella japonica*
maxima (F)	ERea SCit
medica (F)	SCit
- 'Cidro Digitado'	See *C. medica* var. *digitata*
§ - var. *digitata* (F)	CGOG ERea SCit
- 'Ethrog' (F)	ECon ERea SCit
- var. *sarcodactylis*	See *C. medica* var. *digitata*
x *meyeri* 'Meyer' (F)	CB&S CGOG ECon EPfP ERea GTwe LCns LHop LRHS SCit SPer
microcarpa Philippine Lime	See x *Citrofortunella microcarpa*
mitis	See x *Citrofortunella microcarpa*
natsudaidai	SCit
§ x *nobilis* (F)	LPan
- 'Blida' (F)	ERea SCit
- 'Ellendale' (F)	SCit
- 'Murcott' (F)	ERea SCit SPer
- Ortanique Group (F)	CGOG ECon EPfP SCit
- 'Silver Hill Owari' (F)	ERea
- Tangor Group (F)	ERea
x *paradisi* (F)	LPan
- 'Foster' (F)	ERea
- 'Golden Special' (F)	ERea
- 'Marsh' (F)	CGOG
- 'Navel' (F)	EPfP SCit
- 'Red Blush' (F)	CGOG
- 'Star Ruby' (F)	CGOG ECon ERea LCns SCit
- 'Wheeny' (F)	SCit
pennivesiculata (F)	SCit
'Ponderosa' (F)	CGOG ERea LChe SCit
reshni Cleopatra Mandarin (F)	SCit
reticulata (F)	LBlo
- 'Arrufatina' (F)	CGOG
- 'Dancy' (F)	SCit
- 'Fina' (F)	SCit
- 'Hernandina' (F)	CGOG SCit
- (Mandarin Group) 'Clementine' (F)	ERea LCns
- - 'Comun' (F)	Last listed 1999
- - 'De Nules' (F)	CGOG ECon SCit
- - 'Encore' (F)	ERea
- - 'Fortune' (F)	CGOG ECon SCit
- - 'Tomatera' (F)	CGOG
- 'Marisol' (F)	CGOG SCit
- 'Nour' (F)	CGOG SCit
- 'Nova'	See *C.* x *tangelo* 'Nova'
- 'Orogrande'	CGOG
- Satsuma Group	See *C. unshiu*
- 'Suntina'	See *C.* x *tangelo* 'Nova'
sinensis (F)	ERea LBlo LPan SAPC SArc
- 'Egg' (F)	ERea
- 'Embiguo' (F)	ERea
- 'Harwood Late' (F)	ERea
- 'Jaffa'	See *C. sinensis* 'Shamouti'
- 'Lane Late' (F)	CGOG SCit
- 'Malta Blood' (F)	ECon ERea
- 'Midknight' (F)	ERea
- 'Moro Blood' (F)	ERea SCit
- 'Navelate' (F)	CGOG SCit
- 'Navelina' (F)	CGOG ECon ERea SCit
- 'Newhall' (F)	CGOG SCit
- 'Parson Brown' (F)	ERea
- 'Prata' (F)	ERea

- 'Ruby' (F)	ERea
- 'Saint Michael' (F)	ERea
- 'Salustiana' (F)	CGOG SCit
- 'Sanguinelli' (F)	CGOG ERea SCit
§ - 'Shamouti' (F)	ERea
- 'Succari' (F)	SCit
- 'Tarocco' (F)	SCit
- 'Thomson' (F)	ERea
- 'Valencia' (F)	ECot ERea
- 'Valencia Late' (F)	CGOG ECon ERea LChe SCit
- 'Washington' (F)	CGOG ERea GTwe LCns SCit
tachibana	SCit
* x *tangelo* 'Minneoki' (F)	LBlo
- 'Minneola' (F)	CGOG SCit
- 'Nocatee' (F)	SCit
§ - 'Nova' (F)	CGOG SCit
- 'Orlando' (F)	SCit
- 'Samson' (F)	SCit
- 'Seminole' (F)	ERea
- 'Ugli' (F)	LBlo SCit
§ *unshiu* (F)	ERea SPer
- 'Clausellina' (F)	CGOG ECon ERea
- 'Hashimoto' (F)	CGOG SCit
- 'Okitsu' (F)	CGOG SCit
- 'Owari' (F)	CGOG SCit
volkameriana	ERea SCit

CLADIUM (Cyperaceae)

mariscus	EWFC

CLADOTHAMNUS See ELLIOTTIA

CLADRASTIS (Papilionaceae)

kentukea ♀	CArn CB&S CLnd CMCN CPle CTho ELan EPfP MBlu NBea SMac SPer SSpi WBod WDin WNor WWat
sinensis	WWat

CLARKIA (Onagraceae)

concinna	Last listed 1998
* *repens*	CSpe

CLAVINODUM (Poaceae - Bambusoideae)

§ *oedogonatum*	EPla SDry WJun

CLAYTONIA (Portulacaceae)

alsinoides	See *C. sibirica*
australasica	See *Neopaxia australasica*
caespitosa	Last listed 1997
caroliniana	LAma NRog
§ *megarhiza* var. *nivalis*	GDra MAsh NWCA
§ *nevadensis*	EMar
parvifolia	See *Naiocrene parvifolia*
§ *perfoliata*	CArn EWFC GPoy ILis WCHb WHer
§ *sibirica*	CAgr CArn CElw CNic CRow CSpe ECoo EEls EMan NBid NBus WHen WRHF WWye
- 'Alba'	NBid WCot
virginica	EPot LAma MBro NRog WMoo

CLEMATIS ❀ (Ranunculaceae)

'Abundance' (Vt)	CDoC CElw CPev CRHN CSPN CSam EBee EOrc ERob ESCh ETho GMac IOrc LPri LRHS MBri MCad NBea NHol NTay SBra SDix SPer WSHC WTre WWeb
'Ada Sari' (L)	Last listed 1998
addisonii	EBee ERob ESCh ETho NHaw WTre
aethusifolia	CPlN CSPN LPri MBri NTay SBra
afoliata	WTre CB&S CPev ECou ERob ESCh ETho WTre
'Aino' (Vt)	ERob
'Akaishi'	ERob ESCh MCad NBrk NTay WTre
akebioides	CPlN EBee LRHS MCad NBrk SBra SLim SPer WCru WFar
'Akemi' (L)	ERob ESCh MCad NTay WTre
'Akeshina'	MCad
§ Alabast™ = 'Poulala' PBR (Fl)	CBlo EBee EMil ERob ESCh ETho LPri MCad NTay WTre
'Alba Luxurians' (Vt) ♀	More than 30 suppliers
albicoma	Last listed 1999
'Albiflora'	CSPN ECtt ETho GMac MCad
I 'Albina Plena' (A/d)	ESCh ETho NBrk SPla
'Alice Fisk' (P)	EBee ESCh LPri MCad NBea NBrk NHaw NTay SBra WGor
'Aljonushka'	More than 30 suppliers
'Allanah' (J)	CRHN EBee EPfP ERob ESCh ETho GKir LPri MCad MGos NBea NTay SBra SEas SLim SPla WBod WStI WTre
§ *alpina* (A) ♀	CMac CPev ECtt GDra GKir GSki IOrc MBar MCad MWhi NEgg NPer NSti SLim SPlb WFar
- 'Albiflora'	See *C. alpina* subsp. *sibirica*
¶ - 'Aquarius'	LPri
- 'Burford White' (A)	EBee ESCh LPri MCad NBrk
- 'Columbine' (A)	CPev EBee ENot EOrc ETho LBuc LPri MBar MCad NBea NTay SDix SLim WTre WWeb
- 'Columbine White'	See *C. alpina* 'White Columbine'
- 'Constance' (A)	CBlo CSPN EBee EPfP ESCh ETho LPri LRHS MBri NSti NTay SBra SPer SRms WPGP WTre WWeb
- 'Foxy' (A)	EBee EPfP ERob ESCh ETho GMac LPri MBri NBrk NTay WTre
- 'Frances Rivis' (A) ♀	More than 30 suppliers
- 'Frankie' (A)	CDoC CSPN EBee EBrP EBre ELan ERob ESCh ETho LBCl LBSe LBre LPri LRHS MBBe MBri NTay SBra SBre SLim WGor WTre WWeb
- 'Jacqueline du Pré' (A)	CHad CPev CSPN EBee EOrc ERob ESCh ETho GMac IHar LPri MBri MCad MGos NBea NTay SBra WTre WWeb
- 'Jan Lindmark'	See *C. macropetala* 'Jan Lindmark'
- 'Odorata' (A)	ERob ESCh MGos NBea
§ - 'Pamela Jackman' (A)	CDoC CSPN EBee ELan ESCh GChr GKir IHar IOrc LAst LFis LPri LRHS MBri MCad MGos NBea NHol NSti NTay SBra SDix SHFr SLim SPer WTre WWeb
- 'Pink Flamingo' (A)	CBlo CElw CMHG CSPN EBee EBrP EBre ECtt ELan ENot ERob ESCh ETho GMac LBCl LBSe LBre LPri LRHS MBBe MBri NEgg NPri NSti NTay SBre SMur WTre WWeb
- 'Rosy Pagoda' (A)	ELan EOrc EPfP ERob ESCh ETho LPri LRHS MCad NBea NBir NHaw WTre
- 'Ruby' (A)	CMHG CPev EBee ELan ESCh ETho GChr LPri LRHS MBri MCad MGos NBea NEgg NHol NSti SBra SChu SDix SLim SPer SReu WTre WWeb
§ - subsp. *sibirica* (A)	CPev ERob MCad NTay
- - 'Riga' (A)	ERob ETho WTre
§ - - 'White Moth' (A)	CBlo CElw CSPN ELan ESCh ETho IHar LPri LRHS MBri MCad

- 'Tage Lundell' — MGos NBrk NHol NTay SBra SLim SPer SRms WTre
- 'Tage Lundell' — See *C.* 'Tage Lundell'
- 'Violet Purple' (A) — ERob
§ - 'White Columbine' (A) ♀ — CRHN EPfP ERob ESCh ETho MBri MCad MGos NBea WTre
- 'Willy' (A) — More than 30 suppliers
'Alpinist' (L) — ERob
'Ametistina' (A) — ERob
'André Devillers' — See *C.* 'Directeur André Devillers'
I 'Andromeda' (Fl) — ERob ESCh ETho LPri NTay WTre
'Anita' (Ta) — EBee EMil ERob ESCh ETho MCad NTay SBra SLim WTre
'Anna' (P) — ERob ESCh MCad NTay
'Anna German' — ERob
§ Anna Louise™ = 'Evithree' PBR (P) — CSPN EBee ERob ESCh ETho LPri LRHS MBri MCad NTay SLim WTre
'Annabel' (P) — ERob LPri MCad WTre
'Annamieke' (Ta) — ERob ESCh MGos NTay SBra WTre
* 'Anniversary' — ESCh
'Anouchka' (L) — EBrP EBre LBCl LBSe LBre MBBe SBre
'Aotearoa' — ERob
apiifolia — CPev ERob ESCh NTay WTre
- B&SWJ 4838 — WCru
'Arabella' (D) — CElw CHad CPev CPou CSPN EBee ERob ESCh ETho LRHS MBri MCAu MCad MGrG NBea NBrk NHaw NTay SBra SMur SPer SPla WCru WSHC WTre WWat WWeb
§ Arctic Queen™ = 'Evitwo' PBR (Fl) — CSPN EBee EBrP EBre ESCh ETho LBCl LBSe LBre LPri LRHS MBBe MBri MCad NBea NTay SBre SLim SPer WLRN WTre WWeb WWes
aristata — CPiN MCad
armandii — More than 30 suppliers
- 'Apple Blossom' — CB&S CPev CPou CSPN EBee ERob ESCh ETho EWTr GQui IHar IOrc LBuc LPri LRHS MCad MGos NBea NHol NTay SBra SLim SPer SReu SSoC SSta WStI WTre
- var. *biondiana* — ERob MNes SBla WTre
- 'Bowl of Beauty' — ERob ESCh MCad MGos SPer
- 'Jeffries' — LRHS
- 'Meyeniana' — ERob ESCh MCad SPer WTre
- 'Snowdrift' — CB&S CPev CSam ELan EPfP ERob ESCh EWTr LPri LRHS MCad MGos NTay SBra SEas SLim SPer SReu SRms WTre
- Treasure's form — WTre
x *aromatica* — ERob ESCh ETho GMac LFis LPri LRHS MCad NBea NTay SBra WTre
'Asagasumi' (L) — ERob MCad
'Asao' (P) — CElw CRHN EBee EBrP EBre ELan ERob ESCh ETho LAst LBCl LBSe LBre LPri LRHS MBBe MCad NBea NTay SBre SLim SPer SSoC WTre WWeb
'Ascotiensis' (J) ♀ — CPev CSPN EBee EBrP EBre ESCh ETho LBCl LBSe LBre LPri LRHS MBBe MCad NBea NTay SBra SBre SDix SLim SPer WStI WTre
'Ashitaka' — MCad
§ 'Aureolin' (Ta) ♀ — EBee EBrP EBre EPfP ERob ETho LBCl LBSe LBre LRHS MBBe MBar MCad MGos NBrk NHol SBra SBre SLim WPGP WTre
'Aurora Borealis' — MCad
australis — Last listed 1998
'Bagatelle' (P) — ESCh MCad
¶ 'Baltyk' (P) — ERob ESCh
'Barbara Dibley' (P) — CPev CTri EBee ERob ESCh LPri LRHS MCad NBea NTay SBod SBra SDix SLim WBar WBod WTre
'Barbara Jackman' (P) — CPev CRHN CSam EBee ECtt ENot ERob ETho EWTr GKir LPri LRHS MBar MBri MCad NBea NTay SBra SLim SPer WFar WFoF WStI WTre
barbellata (A) — ERob MCad
- 'Pruinina' — See *C.* 'Pruinina'
¶ 'Basil Bartlett' — ECou
'Beata' (L) — MCad
'Beauty of Richmond' (L) — ESCh MCad NBea SDix SPer WTre
'Beauty of Worcester' (Fl/L) — CPev CSPN EBee EBrP EBre ELan ESCh ETho GKir LAst LBCl LBSe LBre LPri LRHS MAsh MBBe MBar MCad NBea NEgg NHaw NTay SBra SBre SDix SLim SPer WTre
'Bees' Jubilee' (P) ♀ — More than 30 suppliers
'Bella' (J) — ERob MCad NTay
'Belle Nantaise' (L) — CPev EBee EBrP EBre EPfP ERob ESCh ETho LBCl LBSe LBre LPri LRHS MBBe MCad NBea NTay SBre WTre
'Belle of Woking' (Fl/P) — More than 30 suppliers
'Benedictus' (P) — Last listed 1997
'Bessie Watkinson' — WTre
'Betina' (A) — ERob ESCh ETho IHar LPri MCad WTre
'Betty Corning' (VtxT) — CHad CSPN EBee EBrP EBre EMil EOrc EPfP ERob ESCh ETho LBCl LBSe LBre LFis LPri LRHS MBBe MCad NBea NBrk NTay SBra SBre SLon WSHC WTre
'Betty Risdon' — ERob ETho NBea
¶ 'Big Bird' (A/d) — ERob
'Big Horns' — Last listed 1998
§ 'Bill MacKenzie' (Ta) ♀ — More than 30 suppliers
'Black Madonna' (P) — Last listed 1999
'Black Prince' (Vt) — ELan EPfP ERob ESCh LPri NBrk NTay WTre
§ 'Blekitny Aniol' (J/Vt) — CRHN ERob ESCh ETho IHar LPri MCad MGrG NBrk NTay SBra SLim SPer WTre
Blue Angel — See *C.* 'Blekitny Aniol'
'Blue Belle' (Vt) — CElw CPou CRHN EBee ELan ESCh LPri LRHS MBri MCad NBea NBrk NSti NTay SBra SLim WTre WWat WWeb
'Blue Bird' (A/d) — CPiN CRHN ECtt GChr IOrc LPri MCad NBea NHol SBra SPer SPla SRms WTre
'Blue Boy' (D) — See *C.* x *eriostemon* 'Blue Boy'
'Blue Boy' (L/P) — See *C.* 'Elsa Späth'
'Blue Dancer' (A) — CAbP CBlo ESCh ETho GKir LPri MWat NBrk NTay WTre WWeb WWes
¶ 'Blue Eclipse' — WTre
¶ 'Blue Eyes' — ERob ESCh
'Blue Gem' (L) — ERob ESCh MCad NTay SBra SLim WTre
¶ Blue Light™ (L/d) — ENot MCad
§ Blue Moon™ = 'Evirin'PBR — EBee EBrP EBre ESCh ETho LBCl LBSe LBre LRHS MBBe NBea NPri NTay SBre
Blue Rain = 'Sinij Dozhdj' (D) — ERob ESCh MBri WTre
'Blue Ravine' (P) — EPfP ERob ESCh ETho MCad NTay WTre
x *bonstedtii* (H) — ESCh
- 'Côte d'Azur' (H) — WTre
- 'Crépuscule' (H) — ERob ESCh NTay SRms WCot WTre

'Boskoop Beauty' (PxL) ERob MCad NBrk
'Boulevard' Last listed 1999
'Bracebridge Star' (L/P) ECtt ERob ESch SBra
brachiata SBra SDix
brachyura ERob
'Bravo' (Ta) ERob NTay WTre
¶ 'Broughton Bride' ERob
§ 'Brunette' (A) ERob ESCh ETho IHar LPri MBri
MCad MGos NBrk NTay SBra
WTre
buchananiana Finet & See *C. rehderiana*
Gagnepain
buchananiana DC. WTre
- S&SH 373 Last listed 1999
¶ 'Budapest' (I) ESCh SBra
'Burford Bell' ERob WTre
* 'Burford Princess' ERob
'Burford Variety' (Ta) ERob ESCh LPri MCad NBea NTay
WTre
'Burma Star' (P) CElw CPev ERob ESCh ETho
MCad NBrk
'C.W. Dowman' (P) ERob
'Caddick's Cascade' MCad
'Caerulea Luxurians' ERob ESCh WTre
* *calanthe* Last listed 1997
calycina See *C. cirrhosa*
campaniflora CBot CElw CPev CSPN CStu EBee
EOrc EPla ERob ESCh ETho MCad
MWhi NBea NBrk NSti NWCA
SBra SDix SIng SLim SPer WPGP
WTre
- 'Lisboa' ERob ESCh ETho NBrk SBra
WSHC WTre
'Campanulina Plena' (A) ERob
'Candy Stripe' ERob ESCh GKir
'Capitaine Thuilleaux' See *C.* 'Souvenir du Capitaine
Thuilleaux'
'Cardinal Wyszynski' See *C.* 'Kardynał Wyszynski'
'Carmen Rose' (A) ERob
'Carmencita' (Vt) ERob ETho NBrk NTay WTre
'Carnaby' (L) More than 30 suppliers
'Carnival Queen' ERob NTay WTre
'Caroline' (J) CPev ESCh ETho IHar MCad NBrk
NTay SBra WTre
¶ 'Caroline Lloyd' (Vt) ERob
* x *cartmanii* hort. (Fo) Last listed 1998
§ - 'Avalanche' PBR (Fo) ERob LRHS NPri SBla SPer
- 'Blaaval'PBR See *C.* x *cartmanii* 'Avalanche'
- 'Joe' (Fo) CB&S EOrc ESCh ETho EWes
GCrs ITim LBee LPri LRHS MAsh
MBri MCad MGos MLan NBrk
NHar NMen SAga SBra SIng SMad
SMrm SPer WAbe WHil WTre
'Cassiopeia' (PxL) Last listed 1997
¶ 'Celebration' MCad
'Centre Attraction' ESCh MCad
'Chalcedony' (FlxL) CPev ERob ESCh ETho LPri MCad
MGos NBrk NTay SBra WTre
'Charissima' (P) CPev ERob ESCh ETho IHar LPri
MBri MCad NTay SPet WTre
chiisanensis CB&S ERob ESCh MCad SBra
WCwm WHil WTre
- 'Lemon Bells' LRHS
- 'Love Child' ERob ESCh ETho NTay WTre
chinensis hort. See *C. terniflora*
- Retz ERob MCad WTre
'Christian Steven' (J) ERob ESCh MCad
chrysantha Last listed 1997
- var. *paucidentata* See *C. hilariae*
N *chrysocoma* Franchet CPev ELan ERob ETho LPri MBNS
MBar MCad NHol SBra SDix WCru
WTre

- ACE 1093 CPou
- B&L 12237 NBea WTre
- hybrid ERob NTay
- hort. See *C. montana* var. *sericea*
'Cicciolina' (Vt) ERob
§ *cirrhosa* CBot CPev ELan ESCh GSki LPri
LRHS MCad MGos NTay SArc
WTre
- var. *balearica* ♀ More than 30 suppliers
- 'Freckles' ♀ More than 30 suppliers
- 'Jingle Bells' EPfP ERob ESCh ETho LFis LPri
LRHS NBea NTay WTre
- subsp. *semitriloba* ERob
- 'Wisley Cream' More than 30 suppliers
§ 'Citra' (A) ERob ESCh ETho NTay WSHC
coactilis ERob
'Colette Deville' (J) EPfP ERob ESCh MCad NBea
NTay
columbiana LFis
- var. *columbiana* Last listed 1998
§ - var. *tenuiloba* ESCh SOkd
'Columella' (A) ERob
'Comtesse de Bouchaud' (J) ♀
More than 30 suppliers
connata CPlN ERob ESCh NBrk SBra WTre
¶ - CC&Mc 37 NWCA
- HWJCM 132 WCru
'Corona' (PxL) CBlo CPev CSPN EBee ELan ERob
LAst LPri LRHS MBar MCad NBea
NHaw NTay SBra SLim WTre
'Corry' (Ta) ERob ESCh MCad NBrk WTre
¶ 'Cotton Candy' ERob
'Countess of Lovelace' (P) CSPN EBee EBrP EBre ERob ESCh
ETho LBCl LBSe LBre LPri LRHS
MBBe MBar MCad MGos MSte
NBea NTay SBra SBre SDix SPer
WTre
County Park Group (Fo) ECou
¶ - 'Fairy' (Fo/f) ECou
§ - 'Pixie' (Fo/m) ECou ECre ESCh IHar LRHS MGos
WTre
'Crimson King' (L) CTri ESCh MAsh MCad NTay
SBod SBra WGor WTre
§ *crispa* CPou ERob ETho MCad NBea
NTay SBra WSHC WTre
§ - 'Cylindrica' CBlo MCad NBrk
- hybrid ERob
- 'Rosea' See *C. crispa* 'Cylindrica'
cunninghamii See *C. parviflora*
'Cyanea' EBee ERob ESCh GMac LPri MBri
NTay WTre
x *cylindrica* CSPN ESCh MCad NBrk NTay
WTre
'Daniel Deronda' (P) ♀ More than 30 suppliers
'Dawn' (L/P) CPev CSPN EBee ERob ESCh
ETho LPri LRHS MCad NBea NTay
SBra SLim SPer SPla WGwG WTre
'Debutante' ETho
'Denny's Double' (d) ERob ESCh MCad NBrk NTay
WTre
denticulata WTre
¶ 'Diana' ERob
dioscoreifolia See *C. terniflora*
§ 'Directeur André ERob MCad
Devillers' (P)
'Doctor Ruppel' (P) ♀ More than 30 suppliers
'Doggy' (Vt) ERob
'Dominika' (J) ERob ESCh NTay
'Dorath' ESCh WTre
'Dorota' ERob
'Dorothy Tolver' ERob ESCh ETho
'Dorothy Walton' (J) CBlo CRHN CSPN EBee ERob

	ESCh ETho IHar LPri MCad NBrk NHaw NTay SBra SLim WTre
douglasii	See *C. hirsutissima*
'Dr Lebel'	ERob NTay
'Duchess of Albany' (T) ♀	More than 30 suppliers
'Duchess of Edinburgh' (Fl)	More than 30 suppliers
'Duchess of Sutherland' (Vt/d)	CPev CRHN CSPN ESCh LPri LRHS MAsh MCad NBea NTay SBra WTre
x *durandii* (D) ♀	More than 30 suppliers
'Early Sensation' (Fo)	COtt ECtt ELan EPfP ESCh ETho IHar LRHS MBlu MCad MGos NBea NPro NTay SBra SCoo WFoF WTre
'Ebba'	MCad
'Edith' (L) ♀	CSPN EBee EBrP EBre ECtt ERob ESCh ETho LBCl LBSe LBre LPri LRHS MAsh MBBe MCad NBea NBrk NTay SBra SBre SLim WGor WGwG WTre
'Edomurasaki' (L)	EBee ERob ESCh LPri MBri NTay WTre
'Edouard Desfossé' (P)	ESCh ETho NTay WTre
'Edward Prichard'	ERob ESCh NBea NBrk NHaw WTre
'Eetika' (Vt)	ERob
'Ekstra' (J)	ERob ESCh
¶ 'Eleanor'	ECou
¶ 'Elf'	CPev
'Ellenbank White'	Last listed 1997
§ 'Elsa Späth' (L/P) ♀	More than 30 suppliers
'Elvan' (Vt)	CPev CRHN ERob ESCh MCad NBea NBrk NTay WTre
'Emajõgi' (L)	Last listed 1997
'Emilia Plater' (Vt)	CRHN ERob ESCh ETho LPri MBri MCad NBea NBrk SBra WBcn WTre
'Empress of India' (P)	EBrP EBre ERob ESCh LBCl LBSe LBre LPri MBBe MCad NTay SBre WTre
'Entel' (J)	ERob WTre
§ x *eriostemon* (D)	CSPN EBee EOrc EPfP ESCh GKir LFis LRHS MBNS MCad MSte NBrk NHaw NHol SBra SDix SGar SPer SPla WCot WTre
§ - 'Blue Boy' (D)	EPfP ERob ESCh ETho LFis MBri MCad MGos NBrk NHaw NTay SBra WTre
§ - 'Hendersonii' (D)	More than 30 suppliers
'Ernest Markham' (J/V) ♀	More than 30 suppliers
'Esperanto' (J)	MCad
'Etoile de Malicorne' (P)	EBee ERob ESCh ETho LRHS MCad NBea WGor WTre
'Etoile de Paris' (P)	CBlo ERob ESCh ETho NTay SBra WTre
'Etoile Nacrée'	ESCh
'Etoile Rose' (T)	More than 30 suppliers
'Etoile Violette' (Vt) ♀	More than 30 suppliers
'Europa'	ERob
Evening Star™ = 'Evista'	ETho NTay
'Eximia' (A)	ERob
'Fair Rosamond' (L/P)	CPev EBee EPfP ERob ESCh ETho LPri LRHS MBri MCad NHaw NTay SBod SBra SDix SLim SPla WTre
'Fairy Queen' (L)	ERob ESCh LPri MCad NTay SBra
fargesii	See *C. potaninii*
x *fargesioides*	See *C.* 'Paul Farges'
fasciculiflora	CBot CGre CMHG CPIN CRHN LRHS MCad SLon SSpi WTre WWat
- L 657	CFil SAga WCru WPGP

fauriei (A)	ERob
finetiana hort.	See *C. indivisa*
- L.	Last listed 1998
'Firefly'	ERob ESCh NTay
'Fireworks' (P) ♀	COtt CSPN EBee EBrP EBre ECtt ENot ESCh ETho LAst LBCl LBSe LBre LRHS MBBe MBri MCad MGos NBea NPri NTay SBra SBre SLim WFoF WGor WStI WTre WWeb
'Flamingo' (L)	ERob MCad
flammula	More than 30 suppliers
* - *rotundiflora*	Last listed 1999
- 'Rubra Marginata'	See *C.* x *triternata* 'Rubromarginata'
§ 'Floralia' (A/d)	CSPN EBee ELan EOrc ESCh LPri LRHS MBri MCad NBea NTay SLim WTre
florida	ERob ESCh ETho
- 'Bicolor'	See *C. florida* 'Sieboldii'
- 'Flore Pleno' (d)	CPev CSPN EBrP EBre ELan EOrc ESCh ETho GMac LBCl LBSe LBre LRHS MBBe MCad NBea NHol NTay SBod SBra SBre SPer SPla SSoC WTre
¶ - 'Plena'	CPIN
§ - 'Sieboldii'	More than 30 suppliers
foetida	ESCh WTre
forrestii	See *C. napaulensis*
§ *forsteri*	CB&S CSPN CSam EOrc ERob ESCh ETho GSki IDee LPri MCad NBrk NTay SBra WCru WPGP WSHC WTre
- x *indivisa*	WCru
'Four Star' (L)	LPri MCad
'Frau Mikiko' (P)	ERob
'Fryderyk Chopin'	ERob ESCh WTre
'Fuji-musume' (L)	ERob ESCh ETho LPri MCad NBrk SBra WTre
'Fujinami' (L)	ERob
fusca hort.	See *C. japonica*
fusca Turczaninow	ERob MCad WTre
¶ - B&SWJ 4229	WCru
- var. *coreana* f. *umbrosa* B&SWJ 700	WTre
- dwarf	Last listed 1998
§ - subsp. *fusca*	ESCh
- var. *kamtschatica*	See *C. fusca* subsp. *fusca*
- *koreana*	See *C. koreana*
- var. *mandshurica*	Last listed 1999
§ - var. *violacea*	EPfP ERob ESCh ETho MCad NBea SBra WSHC WTre
'G. Steffner' (A)	NBrk
'Gabrielle' (P)	ERob ESCh MCad WTre
¶ 'Gemini'	ESCh
'Général Sikorski' (L) ♀	More than 30 suppliers
gentianoides	ERob MCad WAbe
'Georg' (A/d)	ERob NTay
'Georg Ots' (J)	ERob
'Gillian Blades' (P) ♀	CRHN CSPN EBee EBrP EBre ELan EPfP ERob ESCh ETho LAst LBCl LBSe LBre LRHS MBBe MBri MCad NBea NBrk NHaw NPri NTay SBra SBre SLim SPer SSoC WTre
'Gipsy Queen' (J) ♀	More than 30 suppliers
'Gladys Picard' (P)	ERob ESCh MCad SLim WTre
glauca hort.	See *C. intricata*
glaucophylla	Last listed 1999
glycinoides	GSki
'Glynderek' (L)	ERob ESCh MCad NTay SBra WTre
'Golden Harvest' (Ta)	ERob ESCh MBri WPnP WTre
§ Golden Tiara® =	EBee ERob ESCh ETho LPri LRHS

'Kugotia' PBR (Ta)	MAsh MCad MGos NBea NTay SPer WTre WWeb
'Gornoe Ozero'	ERob ESCh
gouriana	ERob ESCh NTay WTre
- subsp. *lishanensis* B&SWJ 292	WCru
'Grace' (Ta)	ERob ETho WTre
gracilifolia	ERob ESCh WTre
'Grandiflora Sanguinea' (Vt)	ERob SLim
'Grandiflora Sanguinea' Johnson	ee C. 'Södertälje' S
grata hort.	See C. x *jouiniana*
- Wallich	CPev ERob MCad NBrk WTre
- CC 1895	Last listed 1999
'Gravetye Beauty' (T)	CElw CPev CPlN CSPN EBee ELan EOrc ERob ESCh ETho GKir LAst LFis LPri LRHS MBri MCad NBea SBra SDix SLim SMad SPer SReu SRms SSta WSHC WTre
'Gravetye Seedling' (T)	Last listed 1997
'Green Velvet' (Fo)	CPlN ECou
grewiflora B&SWJ 2956	WCru
'Guernsey'	Last listed 1997
'Guernsey Cream' (P)	CBlo CSPN CSam EBee EBrP EBre EMil ESCh ETho LBCl LBSe LBre LPri LRHS MBBe MBri MCad NBea NTay SBra SBre SLim WLRN WTre WWeb WWes
'Guiding Star'	ERob MCad NTay SBra
'H.F.Young' (L/P) ♀	More than 30 suppliers
¶ 'Hagelby White' (Vt)	ESCh
'Hagley Hybrid' (J)	More than 30 suppliers
'Hainton Ruby' (P)	ERob
'Haku-ôkan' (L)	CPev CSPN EBee EBrP EBre ERob ESCh ETho EWTr LBCl LBSe LBre LPri LRHS MAsh MBBe MCad NBea NTay SBod SBra SBre SLim WTre WWeb
'Hanaguruma' (P)	ESCh ETho MCad NHaw NTay WTre
'Hanna' (Vt)	ERob ETho
'Harmony'	ERob
'Haru-no-hoshi'	Last listed 1997
'Haruyama'	ESCh MCad
Havering hybrids (Fo)	ECou
'Heather Herschell'	CElw CPev ERob
'Helen Cropper' (P)	ERob ESCh ETho MCad NBrk
'Helios' (Ta)	EBee ENot EPfP ERob ESCh ETho IHar LPri LRHS MBri MCad MGos NBea NBrk NTay SBra WTre
'Helsingborg' (A) ♀	CB&S CSPN EBee ECtt ELan ENot ERob ESCh ETho LPri LRHS MBri MCad NBea NHol NSti NTay SBra SPla WTre WWes
hendersonii Standley	See C. x *eriostemon*
- Koch	See C. x *eriostemon* 'Hendersonii'
'Henryi' ♀	More than 30 suppliers
henryi var. *morii* B&SWJ 1668	WCru WTre
heracleifolia (H)	CB&S CBot CPou ECtt ESCh GKir GSki MCad NLar WHil WTre
- 'Alan Bloom' (H)	LRHS
I - 'Alba' (H)	ESCh
- B&SWJ 4560 (H)	WCru
- B&SWJ 5073 (H)	WCru
N - 'Campanile' (H)	CPev ERob ESCh LPri MCad NBea NBir NTay SDix
I - 'Cassandra' (H)	EFou
¶ - 'China Purple' (H)	MBri WHil
N - 'Côte d'Azur' (H)	ESCh MCAu MCad MTed NCiC WPnP
- var. *davidiana* (H)	CPev CPle ETho NBea NHol SPla SRms WTre
- - 'Wyevale' (H) ♀	More than 30 suppliers
- 'Jaggards' (H)	Last listed 1997
- 'New Love' (H)	ESCh ETho MGos
- 'Purple Spider' (H)	GKir
- 'Roundway Blue Bird' (H)	CBot
'Herbert Johnson' (P)	CPev ESCh ETho MCad NBea NBrk SBra
hexapetala hort.	See C. *recta* subsp. *recta* var. *lasiosepala*
- DC.	See C. *forsteri*
'Hidcote Purple' (L)	MCad NTay
'Hikarugenji'	ERob ESCh MCad NTay
§ *hilariae*	ERob ESCh NTay
§ *hirsutissima*	WCru
- var. *scottii*	ERob
'Honora' (P)	ESCh MCad WTre
hookeriana	WTre
'Horn of Plenty' (L/P) ♀	CSPN EBee ERob ESCh ETho LRHS MCad NBea NPri NTay SBra SLim WTre
'Huldine' (Vt)	More than 30 suppliers
'Huvi'	ERob
§ 'Hybrida Sieboldii' (L)	CRHN EBee ERob ESCh ETho LPri MCad NBea NBrk NTay SBra SLim WTre WWat
'Hythe Egret'	Last listed 1999
ianthina	See C. *fusca* var. *violacea*
* - var. *kuripoensis*	ERob
¶ 'Ice Maiden'	ESCh
'Ideal' (L)	ERob
'Ilka' (P)	ERob
'Imperial' (P/d)	ERob ESCh ETho WTre
§ *indivisa*	CPev LPri LRHS MCad SBra WTre
- (f)	MCad
- (m)	MCad
§ - var. *lobata*	MGrG WTre
¶ 'Inglewood' (P)	ERob
integrifolia	More than 30 suppliers
- 'Alba'	CBot ECtt LRHS NHaw NTay SLim SPer WSHC
§ - var. *albiflora*	CHad EBee ESCh ETho GBuc LPri MBel MBri MCad NBea NBir NBrk SBra WCru WTre
- 'Amy'	ERob ESCh
* - 'Cascade'	Last listed 1999
* - 'Finnis Form'	SChu
- 'Floris V'	ERob
I - 'Hendersonii' hort.	CHar ERob ETho LRHS WTre
- 'Hendersonii' Koch	See C. x *eriostemon* 'Hendersonii'
- subsp. *integrifolia* var. *latifolia*	ERob
- 'Lauren'	ERob
- 'Olgae'	CHad CPev CSPN EBee ESCh ETho LPri MCad NBea NBrk NTay SBra SLim WTre
- 'Pangbourne Pink'	CHad EBee EOrc ESCh ETho GBuc LRHS MCad NBea NBrk NHaw NTay SBra WCru WTre
- 'Pastel Blue'	CPev ERob ESCh ETho MCad NBea
- 'Pastel Pink'	CPev ERob ESCh ETho MCad
- 'Rosea' ♀	CBot CHar CLon CM&M CPev CSPN EBee ERob ESCh ETho LPri LRHS MBri MCad MTho NBea NBrk NTay SLim SSoC WSHC WTre
- 'Tapestry'	CPev ERob MCad NTay SBra WTre
- white	See C. *integrifolia* var. *albiflora*
§ *intricata*	CSPN EPfP MCad NSti WTre
- 'Harry Smith'	ERob
'Iola Fair' (P)	ESCh ETho

'Ishobel' (P)   ERob ESCh LPri MCad NBrk

ispahanica   See *C. orientalis* L.

'Ivan Olsson' (PxL)   ERob ESCh ETho LPri

'Jackmanii' ♀   More than 30 suppliers

'Jackmanii Alba' (J)   CPev EBee EBrP EBre ELan ERob ESCh ETho EWTr LAst LBCl LBSe LBre LPri LRHS MBBe MBar MCad NBea NBrk NTay SBre SDix SLim SPer WTre

'Jackmanii Rubra' (J)   CPev ERob LPri MAsh MCad NBea SLim WLRN WTre

N 'Jackmanii Superba' (J)   More than 30 suppliers

'Jacqueline'   LRHS

'James Mason'   CMHG CPev ESCh ETho MCad NBea NTay WTre

§ 'Jan Pawel II' (J)   CBlo CMHG CMac EBee EBrP EBre ECtt ELan ESCh ETho GKir GMac IHar LBCl LBSe LBre LPri LRHS MBBe MCad NBea NTay SBra SBre SLim SPer WTre

Jánis Ruplēns No. 1   ERob

§ *japonica*   CPev ERob ESCh MCad NBea NBrk NHaw NTay SBra WTre

- var. *obvallata*   See *C. obvallata*

'Jashio'   MCad

'Jasper'   ERob WTre

'Jennifer Valentine'   MCad

'Jenny Caddick' (Vt)   ERob ESCh ETho MCad NHaw WTre

'Jim Hollis' (Fl)   ERob ESCh MCad NTay WTre

'Joan Gray'   ERob

'Joan Picton' (P)   ESCh ETho LPri MAsh MCad NBea NTay SBra WTre

'Joanna' (Fo)   Last listed 1997

'John Gould Veitch' (Fl)   ERob ESCh MCad

* 'John Gudmunsson'   ERob ESCh

'John Huxtable' (J)   CDoC CPev CRHN EPfP ERob ESCh ETho EWTr LPri LRHS MBri MCad NBea NBrk NHaw NTay SBra SDix SLim WGor WTre

John Paul II   See *C.* 'Jan Pawel II'

¶ 'John Treasure'   WTre

'John Warren' (L)   ERob ESCh ETho EWTr LPri LRHS MCad NBea NTay SBod SBra SLim SPer WTre WWeb

'Jorma' (J)   ERob MCad

§ Josephine™ =   COtt ESCh ETho LPri LRHS MBNS
'Evijohill'^PBR   NPri NTay SPer WWeb

§ x *jouiniana*   EBee EBrP ESCh GBuc GOrc MBlu MCad NHol SEas SPer WGwG WSHC WTre

§ - 'Mrs Robert Brydon'   EBee EPfP ERob ETho MCad NBrk NFla NTay SBra SHel WHil WTre

- 'Praecox' ♀   More than 30 suppliers

'Jubileinyi 70'   ERob ESCh

¶ 'Juuli' (I)   ERob

'Kaaru' (Vt)   ERob WTre

'Kacper' (L)   ESCh ETho LPri MCad NTay WTre

'Kaiu'   ERob ESCh WTre

§ 'Kakio' (P)   CDoC EBee ENot ERob ESCh ETho GKir LAst LPri LRHS MBri MCad NBea NTay SBra SLim SPer WLRN WTre

'Kaleidoscope'   MCad

'Kalina' (P)   ERob ESCh

'Kamilla'   ERob ESCh

§ 'Kardynal Wyszynski' (J)   CBlo CRHN ESCh LPri MCad MGos NBea NTay SBra WTre

'Kasmu'   ERob WTre

'Kasugayama' (L)   ERob MCad WTre

'Katherine'   MCad

'Kathleen Dunford' (Fl)   ERob ESCh LPri LRHS MAsh

   MCad NBea NHaw NTay SBra SLim WTre

'Kathleen Wheeler' (P)   CMac CPev ERob ESCh ETho LPri LRHS MCad NBea NTay SBra SDix SLim WTre

'Keith Richardson' (P)   CPev ESCh LPri MCad NBea NBrk NTay SBra WTre

'Ken Donson' (L) ♀   CBlo CElw EBee EPfP ERob ESCh ETho MBri MCad NBrk NTay SBod SBra

'Kermesina' (Vt)   More than 30 suppliers

¶ 'Ketu'   ERob

'Kiev' (Vt)   ERob

'King Edward VII' (L)   EBee EPfP ERob ESCh ETho LPri LRHS NBea NBrk NTay SBra WGor WStl WTre

'King George V' (L)   ERob ESCh NBrk SBra

¶ 'Kinokawa' (P)   ERob

'Kiri Te Kanawa'   CPev EPfP ERob ESCh ETho MCad NBea NBrk NTay SBra WTre

kirilovii   ERob GSki

'Kirimäe' (P)   ERob

'Kjell'   ERob

'Klaara' (P)   ERob

'Kommerei' (Vt)   ERob WTre

'Königskind' (P)   ERob ESCh MCad NTay WTre

'Königskind Rosa' (P)   ERob

§ *koreana*   ERob ETho MCad NBea NHol WHer WTre

- 'Brunette'   See *C.* 'Brunette'

- *citra*   See *C.* 'Citra'

- var. *fragrans*   Last listed 1999

- f. *lutea*   MCad NBrk

- 'Shiva'   ERob

'Kosmiczeskaja Melodija' (J)   ERob ESCh MCad NTay

¶ 'Kotkas' (J/L)   ERob

'Kuba' (P)   ERob

'Kyllus' (L)   ERob NTay

ladakhiana   CPev EBee EPfP ESCh ETho GQui MCad NBea NBir NTay SBra WCru WTre

'Lady Betty Balfour' (J/Vt)   CPev CSPN EBee EBrP EBre ERob ESCh ETho EWTr GKir LBCl LBSe LBre LPri LRHS MBBe MBNS MBri MCad NBea NHaw NTay SBra SBre SDix SLim WFar WTre WWal

'Lady Caroline Nevill' (L)   CPev CRHN EBee ERob ESCh ETho LPri MCad NBea NTay SBra WTre

'Lady in Red'   LPri

¶ 'Lady Katherine' (d)   ESCh

'Lady Londesborough' (P)   CPev CSPN ELan ESCh ETho LPri LRHS MCad NBea NBrk NHaw NTay SBra SDix SLim WLRN WTre

'Lady Northcliffe' (L)   CPev CTri EPfP ERob ESCh ETho ISea LPri LRHS MAsh MCad NBea NTay SBra SDix SLim WTre

'Ladybird Johnson' (T)   CPev ERob ESCh ETho MCad NBrk NTay SBra WTre

'Lanuginosa Candida'   MCad

lasiandra   ERob WTre

¶ - white   ERob

lasiantha   ESCh

'Lasurstern' (P) ♀   More than 30 suppliers

'Laura' (L)   ERob ESCh MCad WTre

'Laura Denny' (P)   MCad NBrk

'Lavender Lace'   ERob MCad WTre

'Lawsoniana' (L)   CElw ESCh ETho LAst LPri MAsh MBar MCad NBea NBrk NTay SBra SLim WTre

'Lemon Chiffon' (P)   EBee ERob ETho MCad NBea NBrk NTay SBra SLim

§ Liberation™ = 'Evifive'PBR EBee ERob ESCh ETho LPri LRHS
                           MBri NTay SBra WTre
§ *ligusticifolia*   ERob GSki NHaw WHil
   'Lilacina Floribunda' (L) EBee ESCh LPri LRHS MBNS MBar
                           MCad NBea NBrk NHaw NTay
                           SBra SLim WTre
   'Lilactime'   CBlo ERob ESCh LPri NBea
   'Lincoln Star' (P)   CMac CPev CRHN EBee EBrP
                           EBre ERob ESCh GKir LAst LBCl
                           LBSe LBre LPri LRHS MBBe MBar
                           MCad NBea NBrk NTay SBra SBre
                           SDix SLim SPer WTre
   'Lincolnshire Lady' (A) NTay WPen
   'Little Joe'   Last listed 1998
   'Little Nell' (Vt)   More than 30 suppliers
   'Lord Herschell'   CPev
   'Lord Nevill' (P) ♀   CMHG CPev CRHN EBrP EBre
                           ESCh IHar LBCl LBSe LBre LPri
                           LRHS MBBe MBri MCad NBea
                           NTay SBod SBra SBre WTre
   'Louise Rowe' (Fl)   EBee EBrP EBre ELan ERob ESCh
                           ETho IHar LBCl LBSe LBre LPri
                           LRHS MBBe MCad MGos NBea
                           NTay SBra SBre SLim SPla WTre
   'Lucey' (J)   NTay
   'Lucie' (P)   ESCh MCad NBea WTre
   'Lunar Lass' (Fo)   ECho ESCh ETho LBee LRHS
                           MCad NHar SIng WAbe WTre
   'Lunar Lass' x *foetida* EBee ECou EPot
I 'Lunar Lass Variegata' (Fo) ECho
   'Luther Burbank' (J)   ERob ESCh MCad NBea NTay
                           WTre
   macropetala (A/d)   CB&S CElw CPev EBee ELan ENot
                           ERob ESCh GDra GKir LAst LPri
                           LRHS MBar MCad MGos MWat
                           NBea NEgg SBod SDix SLim
                           WBod WTre WWat WWin
   - 'Alborosea' (A/d)   ERob ESCh NTay
   - 'Anders' (A/d)   Last listed 1997
   - 'Ballerina' (A/d)   MCad
   - 'Ballet Skirt' (A/d)   ERob ESCh ETho LRHS MCad
                           MGos WTre
   - 'Blue Lagoon'   See *C. macropetala* 'Lagoon'
§ - 'Chili' (A)   ERob NBrk NTay
   - 'Floralia'   See *C.* 'Floralia'
   - 'Harry Smith'   See *C. macropetala* 'Chili'
§ - 'Jan Lindmark' (A/d)   CSPN EBee EOrc ERob ESCh
                           ETho GMac LRHS MBri MCad
                           MGos NBea NBir NTay SBra SLim
                           WCru WGor WTre
§ - 'Lagoon' (A/d)   ECle ERob LRHS MBri NBea NBrk
                           NSti SBra SLim SMur WCru WTre
* - 'Lord Neville'   Last listed 1999
   - 'Maidwell Hall'   CDoC CMac EBee EBrP EBre
     hort. (A/d) ♀   ERob ESCh ETho LBCl LBSe LBre
                           LFis LPri LRHS MBBe MCad MGos
                           NBea NBrk NHol SBra SBre SPer
                           SPla WPGP WSHC WTre
   - 'Markham's Pink' (A/d) ♀ More than 30 suppliers
   - 'Pauline' (A/d)   ERob ETho NBea NBrk NTay SBra
   - 'Pearl Rose' (A/d)   ERob
   - 'Purple Spider' (A/d) CElw ERob ESCh ETho GKir
                           LRHS MBri NBea SBra SPer WTre
                           WWeb
   - 'Rosea' (A/d)   Last listed 1997
   - 'Salmonea' (A/d)   Last listed 1997
   - 'Snowbird' (A/d)   CPev ERob ESCh ETho NBea
                           NHol SBra WTre
   - 'Vicky' (A/d)   Last listed 1999
   - 'Wesselton' (A/d)   ERob ESCh ETho MCad NHol
                           WTre
   - 'White Lady' (A/d)   ERob ESCh GKir SBra SDix WTre

   - 'White Moth'   See *C. alpina* subsp. *sibirica*
                           'White Moth'
   - 'White Swan'   See *C.* 'White Swan'
   - 'White Wings' (A/d)   ESCh
   'Madame Baron Veillard' (J) CMHG CPev CSPN EBee EBrP
                           EBre ECtt ESCh ETho IHar LAst
                           LBCl LBSe LBre LPri LRHS MBBe
                           MBar MCad NBea NBrk NTay SBra
                           SBre SDix SLim SRPl WTre
   'Madame Edouard   CDoC CPev CRHN CTri EPfP
     André' (J) ♀   ERob ESCh ETho LPri LRHS MCad
                           NBea NTay SBra SDix SLim SPla
                           WTre
   'Madame Grangé' (J) ♀   CPev CRHN CSPN EBee EPfP
                           ESCh ETho LPri LRHS MCad NBea
                           NBrk NHaw NTay SBod SBra SDix
                           SLim WTre
   'Madame Julia   More than 30 suppliers
     Correvon' (Vt) ♀
   'Madame le Coultre'   See *C.* 'Marie Boisselot'
   'Madame van Houtte' (L) ERob ESCh MCad
   'Magnus Johnson' (A)   ERob
   'Majojo' (Fo)   ESCh WTre
   'Mammut' (P)   ERob ESCh WTre
§ *mandschurica*   ERob ETho GCal GSki LEur MCad
                           NTay SBra WTre
   - B&SWJ 1060   WCru
   marata   GCrs WTre
   - 'Temple Prince' (m)   Last listed 1997
   - 'Temple Queen' (f)   Last listed 1997
   'Marcel Moser' (P)   CPev ESCh MCad NBrk NTay SBra
                           WTre
   'Margaret Hunt' (J)   CBlo CMHG CSPN ELan ERob
                           ESCh ETho LPri LRHS MCad NBea
                           NBrk NHaw NTay SBra SPla WTre
   'Margaret Wood' (P)   ERob ESCh MCad NTay
   'Margot Koster' (Vt)   CDoC CRHN EBee EBrP EBre
                           EPfP ESCh ETho LBCl LBSe LBre
                           LPri LRHS MBBe MBri MCad
                           NBea NHaw NTay SBra SBre SLim
                           WSHC WTre
§ 'Marie Boisselot' (L) ♀   More than 30 suppliers
   'Marie Louise Jensen' (J) ESCh MCad NTay WTre
   marmoraria ♀   CPBP EPot GCrs GNor LRHS
                           MCad NHar NSla SBla WAbe WFar
                           MGos NHar
   - x *cartmanii* hort.   MGos NHar
     'Joe' (Fo)
   - hybrid   LBee LRHS NHar
   - x *petriei* (f)   GCrs
   'Marmori'   ERob ESCh
   'Mary Claire'   ERob
§ 'Maskarad' (Vt)   CBlo CSPN EBee EBrP EBre ERob
                           ESCh ETho LBCl LBSe LBre MBBe
                           NBrk SBra SBre WLRN WTre
                           WWeb
   Masquerade (Vt)   See *C.* 'Maskarad' (Vt)
   'Masquerade' (P)   LRHS MBri NTay SMur
   'Matka Siedliska' (Fl)   ERob ESCh WTre
§ 'Matka Teresa'   ERob ESCh MCad WTre
¶ 'Matka Urszula   ERob
     Ledóchowska'
   'Matthais' (PxL)   Last listed 1997
   'Maureen' (L)   CPev CSPN ESCh ETho LPri MCad
                           NBea SBra WTre
   mauritiana   ERob
   maximowicziana   See *C. terniflora*
   'Meeli' (J)   MCad
¶ 'Memm' (A/d)   ERob
§ 'Mevrouv Oud' (P)   ESCh
   'Mia' (P)   ERob
   microphylla   ECou MCad
   'Miikla' (J)   ERob ESCh WTre

'Mikelite' (P) — ERob

'Miniseelik' (J) — ERob

'Minister' (P) — ESCh MCad

'Minuet' (Vt) ♀ — CElw CHad CRHN CSPN EBee EBrP EBre ERob ESCh ETho IOrc LBCl LBSe LBre LPri LRHS MBBe MBri MCad NBea NHol NTay SBra SBre SLim SPer WSHC WTre WWeb

'Miriam Markham' (J) — CPev ERob ESCh MCad NBea NHaw WTre

'Miss Bateman' (P) ♀ — More than 30 suppliers

'Miss Crawshay' (P) — CPev EBee ERob ESCh MCad NBea NHaw NTay SBra SLim WTre

N *montana* — CB&S CPev EBee ECtt ENot ESCh EWTr GChr GKir LPri MBar MCad MGos MWat NBea NEgg NHol SBod SBra SDix SLim SSta WAbe WFar WTre WWeb

- *alba* — See *C. montana*

- 'Alexander' — CBlo CDoC CPou ERob ESCh LPri LRHS MCad MGos NTay SBra SRPl WCru WTre

¶ - 'East Malling' — ESCh

¶ - 'Elten' — ESCh

- 'Fragrant Spring' — EBee ERob ESCh ETho MCad MGos NTay SBra WBcn WTre

- 'Gothenburg' — EBee EPfP ERob ESCh ETho NBea NTay SBra WTre WWes

- f. *grandiflora* ♀ — More than 30 suppliers

§ - 'Hidcote' — ERob ESCh SBra WTre

- 'Jacqui' (d) — ERob ESCh ETho LPri LRHS SBra WWeb

¶ - 'Jenny Keay' (d) — ERob ESCh SBra

- 'Lilacina' — ESCh IHar WTre

- 'Mrs Margaret Jones' (d) — EHol ERob ESCh NBrk NTay SBra SPla WTre

- 'New Dawn' — ERob ESCh IHar MCad NTay SBra WTre

- 'Odorata' — CDoC EBee EPfP ERob ETho GSki MCad MGos NTay SBra SLim WGor

* - 'Olga' — ESCh IHar

- 'Peveril' — CPev ERob ESCh ETho IHar MCad NBea NBrk SBra

- 'Pleniflora' (d) — ESCh ETho MCad MGos SBra WTre

- var. *rubens* ♀ — More than 30 suppliers

- - 'Broughton Star' (d) — CBlo CElw CGre CHad CPou CRHN CSPN EBee ELan ERob ESCh ETho EWTr GMac ISea LFis LPri MBlu MBri MCad MGos NBea NHaw SBra SLim SMad WCot WTre WWeb

- - 'Continuity' — ETho MCad NTay SBra SDix SLim WSHC WTre

- - 'Elizabeth' ♀ — More than 30 suppliers

- - 'Freda' ♀ — More than 30 suppliers

- - 'Marjorie' (d) — More than 30 suppliers

- - 'Mayleen' — CBlo CElw CHad CPou EBee EBrP EBre ESCh ETho LBCl LBSe LBre LPri LRHS MBBe MBri MCad MGos NBea NTay SBra SBre SLim SPer WPen WTre WWat WWeb

- - 'Odorata' — ESCh SLim WTre

- - 'Picton's Variety' — CDoC CPev ETho LPri MCad NBea NHol NTay SBra SPer SPla SRms WTre

- - 'Pink Perfection' — CDoC EBee EBrP EBre ECtt ELan ERob ESCh ETho GOrc LAst LBCl LBSe LBre LPri LRHS MBBe MCad NBea NBrk NHaw NHol NTay SBra SBre SLim SPer WStl WTre WWeb

§ - - 'Superba' — CBlo CMHG EBee ECtt GKir SLim

- - 'Tetrarose' ♀ — More than 30 suppliers

- - 'Vera' — CSPN EBee ERob ESCh ETho GMac LRHS MCad NBea NBir NBrk NTay SBra SEas SLim SPla WCru WTre

- - 'Warwickshire Rose' — CElw EBee ESCh ETho GKir MCad NBea NBrk NHaw NHol NPro NTay SBra WCot WPGP WPen WSHC WTre WWeb

- 'Rubens Superba' — See *C. montana* var. *rubens* 'Superba'

§ - var. *sericea* ♀ — CBot CElw CPev CSam CTri ECtt ERob ESCh GKir LPri LRHS MCad NBea NBrk NPro NTay SBra SLim SLon SRms WCru WFoF WHil WTre WWeb

- 'Snow' — Last listed 1997

- 'Spooneri' — See *C. montana* var. *sericea*

- 'Veitch's Form' — CBot

- var. *wilsonii* — More than 30 suppliers

¶ - - 'Hergist' — ESCh

'Monte Cassino' (J) — ERob ESCh IHar MCad WTre

¶ 'Moonbeam' (Fo) — EBrP EBre ECou EOrc ESCh GKir LBCl LBSe LBre MBBe MGos NBrk NTay SBra SBre SIng SMrm SPer WHil

§ 'Moonlight' (P) — CPev EBee ERob ESCh LPri MCad NBea NBrk SBra SPer WTre

'Moonman' (Fo) — WTre

* 'Morning Cloud' — MCad

Mother Theresa — See *C.* 'Matka Teresa'

'Mrs Bush' (L) — ERob ESCh LRHS MCad NBea WTre WWes

'Mrs Cholmondeley' (L) ♀ — More than 30 suppliers

'Mrs George Jackman' (P) ♀ — CPev EBee ERob ESCh ETho LPri MBri MCad NBea NBrk NTay SBra SLim WStl WTre

'Mrs Hope' (L) — CPev ERob ESCh MAsh MCad NBea NBrk NTay SBra WTre

'Mrs James Mason' — CPev ESCh ETho MCad NBea NHaw NTay SBra WBcn WTre

'Mrs N. Thompson' (P) — More than 30 suppliers

'Mrs Oud' — See *C.* 'Mevrouv Oud'

'Mrs P.B. Truax' (P) — CMHG EBee ERob ESCh ETho LPri LRHS MCad NBea NTay SBra SDix SLim WLRN WTre

'Mrs Robert Brydon' — See *C.* x *jouiniana* 'Mrs Robert Brydon'

'Mrs Spencer Castle' (Vt) — CPev ERob ESCh LPri MAsh MCad NBea NTay SBra WTre

'Mrs T. Lundell' (Vt) — ERob ESCh ETho MCad NBea NBrk NTay WTre

'Mukle' — MCad

'Multi Blue' — More than 30 suppliers

'Muly' — MCad

'Musa China' (L) — MCad

¶ 'My Angel' (Ta) — ELan ENot ESCh ETho IHar MBri MCad MGos SBra SPer WTre

'Myôjô' (P) — CSPN ERob ESCh ETho LPri LRHS MCad NTay WTre

'Myôkô' (L) — CBlo MCad

'Nadezhda' (P) — ERob NTay

§ *napaulensis* — CB&S CPev CPIN EBee ERob ESCh IBlr LPri LRHS MCad NBea NTay SBra SHFr SLim WCru WLRN WSHC WTre

'Natacha' (P) — ERob ESCh MCad WTre

'Negristka' — LPri

'Negritjanka' (J) — ERob ESCh MBri NHaw WTre

'Negus' (J)	ERob ESCh
'Nelly Moser' (L/P) ♀	More than 30 suppliers
'New Love'	MGos
New Zealand hybrids	ECou
'Nikolai Rubtsov'	ERob ESCh LPri MCad NTay WTre
'Niobe' (J) ♀	More than 30 suppliers
¶ 'Norfolk Queen'	ESCh
'North Star'	See *C.* 'Pôhjanael'
'Nuit de Chine'	ERob ESCh MCad
obscura	Last listed 1999
§ *obvallata*	Last listed 1999
§ *occidentalis*	Last listed 1999
- var. *dissecta*	Last listed 1999
- var. *occidentalis*	Last listed 1999
ochotensis	ERob ESCh MCad SDys
ochroleuca	Last listed 1999
¶ 'Ola Howells' (A/d)	ERob
'Olimpiada-80' (L)	ESCh NTay SPla
* 'Opaline'	MCad
§ *orientalis* hort.	See *C. tibetana* subsp. *vernayi*
- 'Sherriffii'	See *C. tibetana* subsp. *vernayi* LS&E 13342
- 'Orange Peel'	See *C. tibetana* subsp. *vernayi* 'Orange Peel'
§ *orientalis* L.	EPfP ESCh GSki IMGH LRHS MCad NHol SBod SBra SReu WTre
- 'Bill MacKenzie'	See *C.* 'Bill MacKenzie'
- var. *daurica*	Last listed 1999
- var. *orientalis*	CStr ERob ETho WTre
* - 'Rubromarginata'	CPev
- var. *tenuifolia*	ERob ESCh
- var. *tenuiloba*	See *C. columbiana* var. *tenuiloba*
'Otto Froebel' (L)	ESCh ETho MCad NTay
'Paala'	ERob
'Paddington'	ERob ETho
'Pagoda' (PxVt)	CDoC CPev CRHN CSPN EBee EOrc EPfP ESCh ETho LFis LRHS MBri MCad NBea NHol NTay SBra SLim SPla SRms WSHC WTre WWat
¶ 'Päkapikk' (Vt)	ERob
'Pamela'	ERob ESCh WTre
'Pamela Jackman'	See *C. alpina* 'Pamela Jackman'
¶ 'Pamiat Serdtsa' (I)	ERob ESCh ETho WTre
paniculata Gmelin	See *C. indivisa*
- Thunb.	See *C. terniflora*
- 'Lobata'	See *C. indivisa* var. *lobata*
* 'Paola'	MCad NTay
'Parasol'	ERob ESCh NTay WTre
§ *parviflora*	ERob
- x *forsteri*	ESCh WTre
* 'Pastel Princess'	ERob MCad NTay
¶ 'Pat Coleman'	ETho
patens	NBea WTre
- Chinese form	ERob ESCh
- Japanese form	ERob ESCh
§ Patricia Ann Fretwell = 'Parfar'	CPev ERob LPri LRHS MCad NBea WWeb
§ 'Paul Farges'	CB&S CSPN EOrc ERob ETho LFis LRHS MBri MCad NBrk NHol NTay SBra SLim WTre
'Pendragon'	ERob
'Pennell's Purity' (L)	ERob MCad
'Percy Picton' (P)	MAsh WTre
'Perle d'Azur' (J) ♀	More than 30 suppliers
'Perrin's Pride' (Vt)	EBee ERob ESCh ETho LRHS MCad NBrk NTay WTre
'Peter Pan' (P)	ERob
peterae	ERob
- var. *trichocarpa*	ERob EWTr
§ Petit Faucon™ = 'Evisix'PBR	CBlo EBee EBrP EBre ECtt ERob ETho LBCl LBSe LBre LPri LRHS

	MBBe MBri NBea NTay SBra SBre SPer WPGP WTre
petriei	ECou ESCh NHar WTre
- x *foetida*	ECou
- x *forsteri*	Last listed 1998
- 'Limelight' (m)	Last listed 1999
- x *marmoraria*	Last listed 1999
- x *parviflora*	Last listed 1997
- 'Princess' (f)	ECou
'Peveril Peach'	CPev
'Peveril Pearl' (P)	CPev ERob ESCh ETho LPri LRHS MCad NTay WWeb
'Peveril Pendant'	CPev
'Phil Mason'	Last listed 1999
phlebantha	Last listed 1999
I 'Phoenix' (P)	ESCh
pierotii	ERob WTre
'Piilu' (P)	CB&S ELan ERob ESCh ETho IHar MCad SBra WTre
'Pink Champagne'	See *C.* 'Kakio'
'Pink Fantasy' (J)	CPev CSPN CTri EBee EBrP EBre ERob ESCh ETho EWTr IHar LBCl LBSe LBre LPri LRHS MAsh MBBe MBar MCad NBea NBrk NTay SBra SBre SLim WTre WWeb
'Pink Pearl'	MCad NBrk
¶ 'Pirko' (Vt)	ERob
¶ Pistachio™ = 'Evirida' PBR (Fl)	ESCh ETho NPri
§ *pitcheri*	CPev CPlN ERob ESCh MCad NBrk NSti NTay WSHC WTre
'Pixie'	See *C.* (County Park Group) 'Pixie'
§ 'Pôhjanael' (J)	ERob ESCh MCad SLim WTre
'Polish Spirit' (Vt) ♀	More than 30 suppliers
§ *potaninii*	ELan MCad MWll NSti WSHC
§ - var. *potaninii*	CGle CPev EPfP ERob MCad MGed NBea NTay SDix SLon WHil
- var. *souliei*	See *C. potaninii* var. *potaninii*
'Prairie River' (A)	ERob ETho WTre
'Pribaltika' (J)	ERob
'Prince Charles' (J)	CElw CHad CPou EBee EBrP EBre ELan ESCh ETho LBCl LBSe LBre LPri LRHS MBBe MCad NBea NBir NHaw NTay SBra SBre SDix SLim SPer SPla WSHC WTre WWat
'Prince Philip' (P)	ERob ESCh SBra WTre
§ 'Princess Diana' (T)	CBlo CElw CHad CPev CRHN ERob ESCh ETho LRHS MCad MGos MWat NBrk NHaw NTay SBra SLim WTre WWat
§ 'Princess of Wales' (L)	ERob EWTr LPri LRHS MBri MCad MGrG NBea SBra WSHC WTre
'Prins Hendrik' (L/P)	ERob ESCh MCad WGor WTre
'Propertius' (A)	ERob
'Proteus' (Fl)	CPev CSPN EBee EBrP EBre ELan ESCh ETho IHar LAst LBCl LBSe LBre LPri LRHS MBBe MBNS MCad NBea NTay SBra SBre SDix SLim SPer SPla WSHC WTre WWeb
§ 'Pruinina' (A)	ERob NTay WTre
psilandra B&SWJ 3650	WCru
¶ 'Pulmapäev' (L)	ERob
'Purple Haze'	CRHN
quadribracteolata	ECou
'Queen Alexandra' (P)	ERob ESCh MCad
'Radostj' (J)	ESCh
¶ 'Ragamuffin'	ERob
'Rahvarinne'	See *C.* 'Hybrida Sieboldii'
'Ramona'	WCru
ranunculoides	
CD&R 2345	

- KGB 111	Last listed 1998
recta	CFee CHad CPev CSPN ECtt ERob ETho GKir LPri LRHS MBel MBro MCad MLLN MNrw NBea NLar NWCA SPer WByw WHil WPer WPyg WTre WWye
- 'Grandiflora'	Last listed 1999
- 'Peveril'	CPev ERob ESCh NBrk
- 'Purpurea'	More than 30 suppliers
§ - subsp. *recta* var. *lasiosepala*	ERob
* - 'Velvet Night'	CBos CElw CSpe EBee EMan ERob GBin LAst LFis MBri MLLN MMil MTis NChi NDov SMrm WCot WTre
'Red Ballon' (Ta)	ERob
'Red Cooler'	ERob ESCh MCad WTre
'Red Pearl' (P)	ERob
§ *rehderiana* ♀	More than 30 suppliers
¶ 'Reiman' (L/J)	ERob
reticulata	ERob
'Rhapsody'	CPev EBee EPfP ERob ETho IHar LRHS MBri MCad NBrk NHaw NTay SBra WBar WSHC WTre
'Richard Pennell' (P) ♀	CMac CPev EBee ERob ESCh ETho LPri LRHS MBri MCad NBea NBrk NTay SBra SDix SLim WTre
¶ 'Ristimagi'	ERob
'Rodomax' (A)	ESCh
'Roguchi'	LPri
¶ 'Roko' (J)	ERob
'Roko-Kolla' (J)	ERob ESCh ETho NBrk WWes
'Romantika' (J)	EBee ELan ERob ESCh ETho LPri NTay SBra SPer WTre
'Roogoja' (L)	ERob
'Rose Supreme'	MCad
'Rosie O'Grady' (A)	EBee ELan EOrc ESCh ETho IHar LPri MBar MCad MGos NBea NHol NSti SBra SPer WTre
* 'Rosugyana'	MCad
'Rouge Cardinal' (J)	More than 30 suppliers
'Royal Velours' (Vt) ♀	More than 30 suppliers
§ Royal Velvet™ = 'Evifour'PBR	CSPN EBee ESCh ETho LRHS MBri MCad NTay SLim WTre WWeb
'Royalty' (LxP) ♀	CGdn CSPN EBee EBrP EBre ELan ERob ESCh ETho LBCl LBSe LBre LPri LRHS MBBe MCad NBea NBir NTay SBra SBre SDix SLim SPer WBod WTre
'Ruby Anniversary'	MCad
'Ruby Glow' (L)	EPfP ERob ESCh MCad NTay SBra WLRN WStI WTre WWeb
'Ruby Lady'	LPri
'Rüütel' (J)	ERob ESCh ETho MCad NTay
'Saalomon' (J)	ERob
¶ 'Sakala'	ERob
'Sally Cadge' (P)	ERob MCad
'Samantha Denny'	ERob NBea NBrk NRib NTay WTre
'Sander' (H)	ERob ESCh WTre
'Saruga'	MCad
'Satsukibare'	ERob ESCh MCad WTre
'Saturn' (Vt)	ECle ERob ESCh MCad NBea SBra SPla WTre
'Scartho Gem' (P)	CPev EBee EPfP ERob ESCh LRHS MCad NBea NTay SBra WTre
'Schneeglanz' (P)	MCad
'Sealand Gem' (L)	CPev EBee ESCh ETho LAst MCad NBea NHaw NTay SBra SLim WTre
¶ 'Semu' (J)	ERob ESCh
'Serebrjannyj Ruczejok'	MCad

'Serenata' (J)	ERob LPri MCad NBea NTay
serratifolia	CLon CPev ELan ESCh ETho LPri MCad NSti NTay SDix WTre
'Sheila Thacker'	ETho
'Sherriffii' (Ta)	ERob ESCh
¶ 'Shirakihane'	NBrk
¶ 'Shirayukihime' (L)	ESCh
'Shogun'	MCad
¶ 'Shorty' (Ta)	ESCh
'Sho-un' (L)	EBee ERob ESCh ETho NTay
'Sialia' (A/d)	ESCh NTay
sibirica	See *C. alpina* subsp. *sibirica*
'Signe' (Vt)	ERob ESCh ETho MCad WTre
¶ 'Siirus' (L)	ERob
¶ 'Silmakivi' (L/J)	ERob
'Silver Lining'	MCad
'Silver Moon' (L) ♀	CSPN ERob ESCh ETho LPri LRHS MAsh MCad NBea NPri NTay SBra WTre WWeb
'Simi'	MCad
simsii Britt. & A.Br.	See *C. pitcheri*
- Sweet	See *C. crispa*
¶ 'Sinee Plamia' (J)	ERob
'Sir Garnet Wolseley' (P)	ERob ESCh NBea NBrk NTay SBod SBra WTre
'Sir Trevor Lawrence' (T)	CPev CSPN EBee EBrP EBre ERob ESCh ETho LBCl LBSe LBre LFis LPri LRHS MBBe MCad NBea NHaw NHol NTay SBod SBra SBre SDix SLim SPer WPGP WTre
'Sizaja Ptitsa' (I)	Last listed 1997
smilacifolia subsp. *andersonii*	Last listed 1998
'Snow Queen'	CBlo CSPN EBee EBrP EBre EPfP ESCh ETho LBCl LBSe LBre LPri LRHS MBBe MBri MCad NBea NTay SBra SBre WTre WWeb
'Snowdrift'	See *C.* 'Paul Farges'
§ 'Södertälje' (Vt)	CRHN CSPN EBrP EBre ERob ESCh ETho LBCl LBSe LBre LPri MBBe MCad NBea NTay SBra SBre WLRN WSHC WTre
'Solveig' (P)	ERob
songarica	CBlo CSPN ESCh LFis LRHS MCad NBea NBrk NHol NTay SBra WSHC
- var. *songarica*	ERob WTre
- 'Sundance'	ERob WTre
'Souvenir de J.L. Delbard' (P)	ERob ESCh NBea NBrk NTay SBra
§ 'Souvenir du Capitaine Thuilleaux' (P)	CPev EBee ECtt ESCh ETho GKir LAst LPri MBri MCad NBea NTay SBra SLim SPer WTre
sp. ACE 16807*	Last listed 1999
sp. B&SWJ 1243	Last listed 1999
'Special Occasion'	ESCh ETho NBea NTay WWeb
spooneri	See *C. montana* var. *sericea*
- 'Rosea'	See *C.* x *vedrariensis* 'Rosea'
'Sputnik' (J)	EPfP ERob NTay WTre
stans	CHea CMdw CPou EOrc EPfP ERob ESCh ETho GSki LEur LRHS MCli NBea SIng SSca WHil WTre
- 'Rusalka'	ERob WTre
'Star Fish' (L)	ERob ESCh WTre
'Star of India' (P/J) ♀	CBlo CPev CRHN EBee EBrP EBre ERob ESCh ETho IHar LBCl LBSe LBre LPri LRHS MBBe MBri MCad NBea NTay SBra SBre SDix SLim SPer WTre
'Stasik' (J)	ERob
'Strawberry Roan' (P)	NTay
§ Sugar Candy™ = 'Evione' PBR (P)	CBlo EBee EBrP EBre EMil ERob ESCh ETho LBCl LBSe LBre LPri

Summer Snow — MAsh MBBe MBri NPri NTay SBra SBre SLim SRPl WTre WWeb WWes

See *C.* 'Paul Farges'

'Sunset' (J) — EBee ESCh ETho LRHS MAsh MBri MCad NBea NPri NTay SBra SMur WLRN

'Susan Allsop' (L) — CPev ERob ESCh MCad WTre

'Sylvia Denny' (Fl) — CSPN EBee EBrP EBre ELan ERob ESCh ETho EWTr IHar LAst LBCl LBSe LBre LPri LRHS MBBe MBar MBri MCad NBea NBrk NHaw NTay SBod SBra SBre SLim SPer WTre

'Sympathia' (L) — ERob ESCh IHar MCad SGar WTre

'Syrena' (J) — ESCh ETho

§ 'Tage Lundell' (A) — CSPN ECle ERob MCad NBea NBrk NTay WCru WTre

'Tango' (T) — EBee ERob ESCh ETho MBri MCad NBrk NTay SBra WCru WTre

tangutica — More than 30 suppliers

- 'Aureolin' — See *C.* 'Aureolin'
- 'Bill MacKenzie' — See *C.* 'Bill MacKenzie'
- dwarf — Last listed 1998
- 'Gravetye Variety' — CBlo ERob ESCh NHol WTre
- 'Lambton Park' — EPfP ERob ESCh ETho LPri LRHS MCad NBea NBrk NTay SBra SPla WTre
- var. *obtusiuscula* — Last listed 1998
- 'Radar Love' — MWhi
'Tartu' (L) — ERob
tasbiroi B&SWJ 1423 — WCru WTre
'Tateshina' (P) — MCad
'Teksa' (J) — ERob
'Tentel' (J) — ERob
tenuiloba — See *C. columbiana* var. *tenuiloba*
§ *terniflora* — CPev CPIN EBee EHol EPfP ESCh ETho LPri LRHS MCad NBea NBrk NHaw NSti NTay SBra SLim SPer WCru

- Caddick's form — Last listed 1999
- var. *mandshurica* — See *C. mandshurica*
- var. *robusta* — See *C. terniflora* var. *terniflora*
§ - var. *terniflora* — ERob ESCh WTre
'Teshio' (Fl) — ERob ESCh ETho LPri MCad SBra WTre

'Tevia' — MCad
texensis — MCad NBea
¶ - 'Red Five' — CPev
- 'The Princess of Wales' — See *C.* 'Princess Diana'
'The Bride' (J) — ERob ESCh MCad NBrk NHaw NTay SBra WTre

'The Comet' — ERob
* 'The First Lady' — ERob ESCh ETho MCad NTay WTre

'The President' (P) ♀ — More than 30 suppliers
'The Princess of Wales' (L) — See *C.* 'Princess of Wales' (L)
'The Princess of Wales' (T) — See *C.* 'Princess Diana' (T)
'The Vagabond' (P) — ELan ERob ETho LPri MCad NBea NBrk NHaw NTay SBra WLRN WTre

thunbergii hort. — See *C. terniflora*
'Thyrislund' — ESCh WTre
Tibetan mix — ERob ESCh
§ *tibetana* — CMac CPev ELan ETho MBar MCad MNrw NTay SLim SPer WSHC
§ - subsp. *vernayi* ♀ — CMHG CNic EBee EPfP ERob GKir MCad MSte NBea NSti SBra SPer WCru WWin

- - CC&McK 193 — NWCA

- - var. *laciniifolia* — ERob ESCh NHol WTre
§ - - LS&E 13342 — CPev EPfP ERob ESCh LRHS MCad NBea NBrk NHol NSti SBra SDix SLim SPer WTre
§ - - 'Orange Peel' — CB&S CDoC EBee ENot ERob ESCh ETho GKir IOrc LAst LBuc MCad SLim WTre

'Titania' (PxL) — EPfP ERob
tongluensis HWJCM 076 — WCru
'Treasure Trove' — ESCh MBri SPer WTre
'Trianon' (P) — ERob MCad NBrk
¶ 'Trine' (Vt) — ERob
§ x *triternata* — More than 30 suppliers
'Rubromarginata' ♀
* 'Tsuzuki' — ERob ESCh NBea NTay SPla
tubulosa 'Alba' — ERob
'Tuczka' (J) — ERob
'Twilight' (J) — CSPN EBee ECle ESCh ETho MAsh MCad NBea NTay SBra SLim WTre

'Ulrique' (P) — ERob NTay
uncinata — CPev SDix
- B&SWJ 1893 — WCru WTre
¶ - var. *ovatifolia* — ERob
'Valge Daam' (L) — ERob ESCh MCad
'Vanessa' (J) — ERob
'Vanilla Cream' — ECou
x *vedrariensis* — MCad NBrk
- 'Dovedale' — CPev
- 'Hidcote' — See *C. montana* 'Hidcote'
- 'Highdown' — ERob MCad NBrk NHol SBra WTre
§ - 'Rosea' — CTrw ERob ESCh MCad NBrk WSHC

veitchiana — ERob
'Velutinea Purpurea' (J) — ERob
'Venosa Violacea' (Vt) ♀ — CElw CRHN CSPN EBee ELan EOrc ERob ESCh ETho GMac LPri LRHS MCad NBea NHol NSti SBra SDix SPer WFar WSHC WTre WWeb

vernayi — See *C. tibetana* subsp. *vernayi*
'Veronica's Choice' (L) — CPev EBee ELan ERob ESCh ETho LRHS MBri MCad MGos NBea NHaw NTay SBra WTre

versicolor — ERob ESCh
verticillaris — See *C. occidentalis*
¶ 'Vetke' (J) — ERob
N 'Victoria' (J) — CPev EBrP EBre ERob ESCh ETho LAst LBCl LBSe LBre LPri LRHS MBBe MCad NBea NHaw NTay SBra SBre SDix SLim WTre

'Ville de Lyon' (Vt) — More than 30 suppliers
§ Vino™ = 'Poulvo' (J) — CBlo EBee ERob ESCh ETho IHar LRHS MBri MCad NBea NTay WTre

I 'Viola' (J) — ECle ERob ESCh ETho MCad NBea NBrk NTay SPla WBcn WTre
'Violet Charm' (L) — CBlo ERob ESCh ETho LPri NBrk NTay SBra WTre
'Violet Elizabeth' (P) — ESCh MCad NBrk NTay SBra WTre
'Violetta' (P) — ERob
viorna — CPIN ERob ESCh LPri MNrw NBea SPer WSHC WTre
virginiana Hooker — See *C. ligusticifolia*
- hort. — See *C. vitalba*
§ *vitalba* — CArn CPev ERob ESCh EWFC EWTr MBar MCad MHer NTay WGwy WHer WTre

viticella — CPev ERob ESCh ETho EWTr LPri MBNS MCad NBea NHaw SBra SDix WSHC WStI WTre

– 'Brocade'	CPev
I – 'Danae'	ERob WTre
* – 'Foxtrot'	ERob WTre
– 'Mary Rose' (d)	CPev ERob ESCh SBra WTre
– 'Purpurea Plena Elegans' (d) ♀	More than 30 suppliers
– 'Rosea' (Vt)	ERob
'Viticella Rubra' (Vt)	EWTr NBrk
'Vivienne'	ESCh ETho
'Vivienne Lawson'	ESCh NTay WTre
'Voluceau' (Vt)	CPou CRHN EBee ELan ERob ESCh LAst MCad NBea NTay SBra SLim SPer WStI WTre
'Vostok' (J)	ERob ESCh NTay WTre
'Vyvyan Pennell' (Fl/P) ♀	More than 30 suppliers
'W.E. Gladstone' (L)	CPev EBee ENot ERob ESCh ETho GKir LPri LRHS MCad NBea NTay SBra SDix SPer WTre
'W.S. Callick' (P)	ERob ESCh ETho MCad WTre
'Wada's Primrose' (P)	More than 30 suppliers
'Walenburg' (Vt)	ERob SBra
'Walter Pennell' (Fl/P)	CPev ESCh ETho LPri MCad NBea NTay SBra WGor WTre
'Warszawska Nike' (J)	CElw CRHN ELan EPfP ERob ESCh ETho EWTr IHar LPri MCad MGos MSte NBea NTay SBra SPer WStI WTre
'Western Virgin'	ERob ESCh NTay WTre
'Westerplatte' (P)	ERob ESCh NBea WTre
§ 'White Swan' (A)	CSPN EBee ERob ESCh ETho LPri LRHS MBri MCad MGos NBea NHol NSti SBra SLim SPer SSoC WFoF WPGP WPnP WTre
'White Tokyo' (A)	MGos
'Wilhelmina Tull' (L)	ERob ESCh MCad NBrk WTre
'Will Goodwin' (L) ♀	CB&S EBee EBrP EBre ELan EPfP ERob ESCh ETho LAst LBCl LBSe LBre LPri LRHS MBBe MBri MCad NBea NBrk SBra SBre SLim WStI WTre
'William Kennett' (L)	CMHG CPev CSPN EBee ELan ESCh ETho LAst LPri LRHS MBNS MBar MBri MCad MGos NBea NTay SBod SBra SDix SLim SPer WTre
'Wistaria Purple' (A)	Last listed 1999
'Wolga' (P)	MCad
'Xerxes'	See C. 'Elsa Späth'
'Yellow Queen'	See C. 'Moonlight'
'Yorkshire Pride'	ERob MCad
'Yukikomachi' (LxJ)	ERob ESCh MCad WTre
'Yukiokoshi' (Fl)	ERob
'Yvette Houry' (L)	ERob ESCh MCad NHaw NTay WTre
'Zingaro' (Vt)	ERob
'Zolotoi Jubilei' (J)	ERob ESCh

CLEMATOPSIS (Ranunculaceae)

scabiosifolia	Last listed 1999

CLEMENTSIA See RHODIOLA

CLEOME (Capparaceae)

arborea	Last listed 1997
§ bassleriana	CSpe MLan SMrm SWat WSan
sp.JCA 13931	Last listed 1998
spinosa hort.	See C. bassleriana

CLERODENDRUM (Verbenaceae)

bungei ♀	More than 30 suppliers
§ chinense 'Pleniflorum' (d) ERea LHil	
fragrans var. pleniflorum See C. chinense 'Pleniflorum'	

myricoides 'Ugandense'	CPIN CSpe ECon ELan EPfP ERea LChe LCns LRHS SOWG WMul
philippinum	See C. chinense 'Pleniflorum'
quadriloculare	LChe
sp. SF 96243	ISea
speciosissimum	LChe
x speciosum	CPIN LChe SOWG
splendens ♀	LCns SOWG
thomsoniae ♀	CPIN ELan LChe LCns LRHS MBri SOWG SYvo
– 'Variegatum'	ECon
trichotomum	More than 30 suppliers
– 'Carnival' (v)	CFil CPMA ELan EPfP EWes GKir LRHS MAsh MBri SBrw SLim SMad SMur SPer SSta WWeb WWes
– var. fargesii ♀	CAbb CB&S CBlo CBrm CHEx CPMA ELan GKir IOrc LHop MBNS MBlu MGos MRav NFla SMac SPer SRPl SSpi WBod WCot WEas WPat WPyg WWat

CLETHRA (Clethraceae)

acuminata	WWoo
alnifolia	CB&S CBlo CBrm CDul CGre CMHG CTrG GCHN GChr GKir IOrc MBar SBrw SMur SPer SRPl SRms SSpi WBod WDin WFar WWat WWin
– 'Alba'	Last listed 1998
– 'Fingle Dwarf'	SReu SSta
– 'Hummingbird'	EPfP GKir IMGH LRHS MAsh SBrw SSht SSpi
– 'Paniculata' ♀	CDoC WWat
– 'Pink Spire'	CB&S CGdn EBee ELan EPfP GOrc MRav NBee SBrw SCoo WFar WLRN WPyg WStI WWat
– 'Rosea'	CBot CTri GKir IMGH IOrc MBar MBlu MGos SPer WSHC WWat
* – 'Ruby Spice'	CDoC GKir LRHS MBri SBrw SMur SPer
arborea	CB&S CFil CHEx CMHG CPle CTre
barbinervis ♀	CB&S CFai CMCN EPfP IMGH MBel MBlu SBrw SPan SPer WBod WSHC WWat
delavayi ♀	CBrd GGGa GQui
– C&H 7067	GGGa
– CNW 815	ISea
fargesii	EPfP MGos
monostachya	GGGa

CLEYERA (Theaceae)

fortunei	See C. japonica 'Fortunei'
– 'Variegata'	See C. japonica 'Fortunei'
§ japonica 'Fortunei' (v)	CDoC CFil CGre CHal CMac WWat
– var. japonica	WPGP

CLIANTHUS (Papilionaceae)

formosus	Last listed 1998
§ puniceus ♀	CAbb CB&S CBrm CCHP CCtw CDoC CHEx CPIN CTrw EBee ECou EMil ERea GGar LCns LRHS SBrw SHFr SLon SOWG SPer SSoC WBrE WCru WSHC
§ – 'Albus' ♀	CBot CCHP CCtw CSpe CTrw EBee ELan EMil ERea IOrc LCns LRHS SBrw SDry SDys SOWG SPer SSoC
– 'Flamingo'	See C. puniceus 'Roseus'
¶ – 'Kaka King'	CB&S

- var. *maximus*	ECou
- 'Red Admiral'	See *C. puniceus*
- 'Red Cardinal'	See *C. puniceus*
§ - 'Roseus'	ELan EMil ERea LRHS SBrw SPer SVen
- 'White Heron'	See *C. puniceus* 'Albus'

CLINOPODIUM (Lamiaceae)

acinos	See *Acinos arvensis*
ascendens	See *Calamintha sylvatica*
calamintha	See *Calamintha nepeta*
grandiflorum	See *Calamintha grandiflora*
§ *vulgare*	CArn CKin ECoo EOHP EWFC GBar MGas MHer MHew NMir SIde WHer

CLINTONIA (Convallariaceae)

andrewsiana	CBro GDra GGGa SSpi WCot WCru
borealis	CBro WCru
udensis	Last listed 1999
umbellulata	CBos WCru
uniflora	CBro EBee

CLITORIA (Papilionaceae)

mariana	CPIN

CLIVIA ✿ (Amaryllidaceae)

¶ *caulescens*	ERea
¶ x *cyrtanthiflora*	ERea
gardenii	ERea
miniata ♀	CB&S CHal LRHS SRms SYvo WCot
- var. *citrina*	Last listed 1997
- - 'New Dawn'	ERea
- hybrids	ERea LAma LHil MBri SEND
- 'Striata'	ERea
nobilis	ERea IBlr

CLYTOSTOMA (Bignoniaceae)

§ *callistegioides*	CPIN ERea

CNEORUM (Cneoraceae)

tricoccon	CFil SRCN SSpi

CNICUS (Asteraceae)

§ *benedictus*	CArn GPoy MHer MSal SIde WHer WWye
diacantha	Last listed 1997

COBAEA (Cobaeaceae)

pringlei CD&R 1323	Last listed 1999
scandens ♀	CPIN NFai WPen
- f. *alba* ♀	CBos WPen
trianea	ERea

COCCINIA (Cucurbitaceae)

¶ *birtella*	SPlb
rebmannii	Last listed 1999

COCCOTHRINAX (Arecaceae)

crinita	LPal

COCCULUS (Menispermaceae)

carolinus	CPIN EPla
§ *orbiculatus*	Last listed 1999
trilobus	See *C. orbiculatus*

COCHLEARIA (Brassicaceae)

armoracia	See *Armoracia rusticana*
glastifolia	MSal NBur
officinalis	MHer MSal WHer WWye

COCOS (Arecaceae)

nucifera (F)	Last listed 1999
plumosa	See *Syagrus romanzoffiana*
weddelliana	See *Lytocaryum weddellianum*

CODIAEUM ✿ (Euphorbiaceae)

variegatum var. *pictum* 'Excellent' (v)	LRHS
- var. *pictum* 'Gold Moon' (v)	Last listed 1999
- - 'Gold Sun' (v)	Last listed 1999
- - 'Goldfinger' (v)	Last listed 1999
- - 'Juliette' (v)	Last listed 1999
- - 'Louise' (v)	Last listed 1999
- - 'Mrs Iceton' (v)	Last listed 1999
- - 'Petra' (v)	LRHS MBri
- - 'Sunny Star' (v)	Last listed 1999

CODONANTHE (Gesneriaceae)

gracilis	EBak WDib
'Paula'	WDib

x CODONATANTHUS (Gesneriaceae)

'Sunset'	WDib
'Tambourine'	WDib

CODONOPSIS ✿ (Campanulaceae)

affinis HWJCM 70	LEur WCru
bhutanica	EBee LEur
bulleyana	EBee MTPN NLar SMac WCot WSan
cardiophylla	EBee GDra LEur MNrw WLin
clematidea	More than 30 suppliers
convolvulacea ♀	CBlo CPIN EBee GBuc GNor MTho NHar NSla WCru WHoo WPGP
- 'Alba'	See *C. grey-wilsonii* 'Himal Snow'
- ex J&JA 4220705	LEur NWCA
- Forrest's form	See *C. forrestii* Diels
dicentrifolia	EBee
- HWJCM 267	WCru
§ *forrestii* Diels	CNic EBee NHar NTow WCru
§ - hort.	See *C. grey-wilsonii*
§ *grey-wilsonii*	CLAP EBee GCrs
§ - 'Himal Snow'	CLAP GCrs IMGH NHar SBla
bandeliana	See *C. tubulosa*
§ *javanica* B&SWJ 380	WCru
kawakamii	Last listed 1999
- B&SWJ 1592	WCru
§ *lanceolata*	CPIN CRDP EBee GAri LEur MCCP MGrG NChi NHar NLar
- B&SWJ 562	LEur WCot WCru
¶ - dark red	LEur
lancifolia B&SWJ 3835	LEur WCru
meleagris Diels	NHar WCru
§ - hybrid	EBee
- misapplied	See *C. meleagris* hybrid
mollis	CBlo EBee GSki LEur NLar WCru WFar
nepalensis Grey-Wilson	See *C. grey-wilsonii*
obtusa	EBee NChi
ovata	CBot CFir CGle CHid CLyd EBee EPri GBuc GDra MTho NBro NChi SBla SChr SRms SSca WCru WEas
pilosula	EBee GAri GPoy MLLN MNrw MSal MTho WCru
rotundifolia	CPIN EBee GBin LEur
§ - var. *angustifolia*	EBee LEur SSoC
- CC 2015	Last listed 1999
silvestris	EBee

sp. ACE 1687	Last listed 1997	
subsimplex	CLyd	
tangshen Oliver	CArn CGre CPIN GBuc GPoy MCCP MNrw MSal MTho NChi NSti SHFr WCru	
- misapplied	See *C. rotundifolia* var. *angustifolia*	
thalictrifolia MECC 93	WCru	
§ **tubulosa**	CPIN EBee EMan LEur NCut WCot WCru	
ussuriensis	See *C. lanceolata*	
vinciflora	CFir LEur SBla SSca WCot WCru	
viridiflora	CFri EBee LEur MHar WWhi	
viridis	Last listed 1999	
- S&L 4962	Last listed 1998	

COELOGLOSSUM (Orchidaceae)
viride — EFEx

COFFEA (Rubiaceae)
arabica — LCns LRHS

COIX (Poaceae)
lacryma-jobi — CBrm MSal

COLCHICUM ✿ (Colchicaceae)

agrippinum ♀	CAvo CBro CFee EPar EPot LAma MRav NBir NMGW NRog NRya WTin	
algeriense AB&S 4353	Last listed 1998	
'Antares'	LAma	
atropurpureum	CBro EBot EPot LAma	
¶ - Drake's form	SSpi	
'Attlee'	EPot LAma LRHS	
'Autumn Herald'	LAma LRHS	
N 'Autumn Queen' ♀	CBro EPot LAma LRHS	
§ **autumnale**	CArn CAvo CBro CFee EPot GPoy LAma LRHS NMGW NRya WShi	
* - 'Albopilosum'	NBir	
- 'Alboplenum'	CBro CSWP EPot ETub LAma NMGW	
- 'Album'	CAvo CBro CSWP EPar EPot ETub GAbr LAma LRHS NBir WPnP WShi	
- 'Atropurpureum'	WShi	
- var. **major**	See *C. byzantinum*	
- var. **minor**	See *C. autumnale*	
- 'Nancy Lindsay' ♀	CBro EPot NMGW	
§ - 'Pleniflorum' (d)	CBro EPar EPot LAma LRHS	
- 'Roseum Plenum'	See *C. autumnale* 'Pleniflorum'	
baytopiorum	EPot	
- PB 224	Last listed 1998	
'Beaconsfield'	Last listed 1997	
§ **bivonae**	CBro CLAP ECha LAma NMGW	
§ **boissieri**	EPot	
- S&L 468	Last listed 1998	
bornmuelleri Freyn	CAvo CBro EPar EPot LAma	
- hort.	See *C. speciosum* var. *bornmuelleri* hort.	
bowlesianum	See *C. bivonae*	
§ **byzantinum** ♀	CAvo CBro EBot EPar EPot LAma LRHS MBri NRog	
- **album**	CBro EBot EPot LRHS	
chalcedonicum	Last listed 1997	
cilicicum	CBro EPot ETub GAbr LAma LRHS	
- Bowles' form	Last listed 1997	
- 'Purpureum'	LAma	
'Conquest'	See *C.* 'Glory of Heemstede'	
corsicum	EPar LAma	
cupanii	Last listed 1999	
* - var. **cousturieri**	Last listed 1999	
- Glossophyllum Group	Last listed 1999	

- MS 977	Last listed 1998	
- var. **pulverulentum**	Last listed 1999	
'Daendels'	LAma LRHS	
deserti-syriaci SB&L 155	Last listed 1998	
'Dick Trotter'	GKir LAma LRHS	
'Disraeli'	CBro LRHS	
doerfleri	See *C. bungaricum*	
'E.A. Bowles'	LAma LRHS	
fasciculare	Last listed 1998	
§ **giganteum**	EPot LAma	
§ 'Glory of Heemstede'	ECha LAma	
hierosolymitanum	LAma	
§ **bungaricum**	CBro EPot LAma	
- f. **albiflorum**	Last listed 1999	
'Huxley'	EPot	
illyricum	See *C. giganteum*	
kesselringii	CLAP	
kotschyi	LAma	
laetum hort.	See *C. parnassicum*	
- Stev.	EHyt	
'Lilac Wonder'	CBro ECha EPot GAbr LAma LRHS MBri NMGW NRog WCot	
lingulatum	NRog WTin	
- S&L 217	Last listed 1998	
'Little Woods'	Last listed 1997	
§ **longiflorum**	LAma	
lusitanicum	LAma	
- HC 2273	Last listed 1998	
luteum	LAma NRog	
- CC 2020	Last listed 1999	
macedonicum	GCrs	
macrophyllum	LAma	
- S&L 578	Last listed 1998	
micranthum	LAma	
- AB&S 4522	Last listed 1997	
neapolitanum	See *C. longiflorum*	
* - **macranthum**	Last listed 1998	
¶ 'Octoberfest'	EPot	
parlatoris	Last listed 1998	
- Rix 2127	Last listed 1998	
§ **parnassicum**	CBro CLAP ECha EPot LRHS	
peloponnesiacum	Last listed 1998	
'Pink Goblet' ♀	CBro EPot LAma LRHS	
polyphyllum	LAma	
'Prinses Astrid'	LAma	
procurrens	See *C. boissieri*	
psaridis S&L 198	Last listed 1998	
pusillum	Last listed 1999	
- MS 803/833	Last listed 1998	
'Rosy Dawn' ♀	CBro ECha EPot LAma LRHS	
sfikasianum	Last listed 1999	
sibthorpii	See *C. bivonae*	
speciosum ♀	CAvo CBro EBrP EBre EPot LAma LBCl LBSe LBre LRHS MBBe NBir SBre SYvo WCot WShi	
- 'Album' ♀	CAvo CBro CFee ECha EPar LAma LRHS MBri NBir NMGW	
- 'Atrorubens'	ECha GDra LAma LRHS	
§ - var. **bornmuelleri**	LRHS	
- var. **illyricum**	See *C. giganteum*	
- 'Maximum'	LAma LRHS	
- 'Rubrum'	Last listed 1998	
stevenii	Last listed 1999	
- SB&L 120	Last listed 1998	
szovitsii	Last listed 1999	
tenorei ♀	LAma NBir WCot	
'The Giant'	CAvo CBro ECha EPot ETub LAma LRHS NMGW NRog	
troodii ♀	Last listed 1998	
turcicum	Last listed 1997	
umbrosum	Last listed 1998	
variegatum	CBro LAma	

- S&L 594	Last listed 1998
'Violet Queen'	CBro CFee EPot LAma LRHS
'Waterlily' (d) ♀	CAvo CBro CLyd EBrP EBre EPar
	EPot ETub LAma LBCl LBSe LBre
	LRHS MBBe MBri NBir NMGW
	NRog SBre WCot
'William Dykes'	EPot LAma LRHS
'Zephyr'	LAma LRHS

COLEONEMA (Rutaceae)
album	SAga SBrw WPat
pulchrum	CSpe CTrC ECre NSti
¶ 'Sunset Gold'	CSpe CTrC

COLEUS See PLECTRANTHUS, SOLENOSTEMON

COLLETIA (Rhamnaceae)
armata	See *C. hystrix*
cruciata	See *C. paradoxa*
ferox	Last listed 1998
§ *hystrix*	CB&S CPle GBin GGar SAPC SArc
	SLon SMad SOWG
- 'Rosea'	CAbb CGre CPle SAPC SPan
	WSHC
§ *paradoxa*	CB&S CCHP CGre CHEx CPle
	CTri EPla LPJP SAPC SArc SMad
	WWat
- x *spinosissima*	SMad

COLLINSIA (Scrophulariaceae)
bicolor Benth.	See *C. heterophylla*
§ *heterophylla*	Last listed 1997

COLLINSONIA (Lamiaceae)
canadensis	CArn EBee ELan ELau EMan MSal
	WWye

COLLOMIA (Polemoniaceae)
biflora	Last listed 1997
debilis	NWCA
- var. *larsenii*	See *C. larsenii*
grandiflora	LCot
§ *larsenii*	GTou

COLLOSPERMUM (Asteliaceae)
§ *microspermum*	IBlr

COLOBANTHUS (Caryophyllaceae)
acicularis	Last listed 1999
apetalus	Last listed 1998
- var. *alpinus*	Last listed 1997
buchananii	Last listed 1998
canaliculatus	CPBP NTow
muelleri	Last listed 1997
§ *quitensis*	NWCA
sp. CC 465	NWCA

COLOCASIA (Araceae)
¶ *affinis* var. *jeningsii*	WMul
antiquorum	See *C. esculenta*
§ *esculenta* ♀	CHEx EOas WMul
- 'Black Magic'	EOas WMul
- 'Fontanesii'	WMul
- 'Illustris'	WMul
- 'Nigrescens'	WMul

COLQUHOUNIA (Lamiaceae)
coccinea ♀	CArn CHEx CHal CWit EMil MRav
	WCru WHer WPGP WSHC
- var. *mollis*	See *C. coccinea* var. *vestita*
§ - var. *vestita*	CB&S CCHP CFai CFil CGre CPle
	CTrC EBee EPfP IMGH MSte SBra

SEND SLPl WPGP WPat

COLUMNEA (Gesneriaceae)
'Aladdin's Lamp'	CHal WDib
'Apollo'	LRHS WDib
x *banksii*	CHal WDib
'Bold Venture'	WDib
* 'Bonfire'	WDib
§ 'Broget Stavanger' (v)	WDib
'Chanticleer' ♀	CHal MBri WDib
I 'Firedragon'	WDib
'Gavin Brown'	WDib
gloriosa	EBak
'Heidi'	Last listed 1999
hirta ♀	MBri WDib
- 'Variegata'	See *C.* 'Light Prince'
'Inferno'	WDib
'Katsura'	MBri SOWG WDib
I 'Kewensis Variegata' ♀	MBri
§ 'Light Prince' (v)	WDib
'Merkur'	WDib
microphylla 'Variegata'	MBri
I 'Midnight Lantern'	WDib
'Rising Sun'	WDib
'Robin'	WDib
schiedeana	CHal MBri WDib
'Starburst'	Last listed 1998
'Stavanger' ♀	CHal EBak WDib
'Stavanger Variegated'	See *C.* 'Broget Stavanger'
'Winifred Brown'	WDib
Yellow Dragon Group	CHal

COLUTEA (Papilionaceae)
arborescens	More than 30 suppliers
§ *buhsei*	SLPl SOWG
x *media*	CHad EMil MBel MBlu MNrw
	SRCN
- 'Copper Beauty'	CB&S EPfP GEil MGos SPer WPat
orientalis	CPle EPfP
persica hort.	See *C. buhsei*

COMARUM See POTENTILLA

COMBRETUM (Combretaceae)
erythrophyllum	CGre
paniculatum	CPlN

COMMELINA (Commelinaceae)
coelestis	See *C. tuberosa* Coelestis Group
dianthifolia	CFee CInt CRDP EBee EMon
	GBuc GCal GCrs GKir MTho
	NMen NTow SSad SYvo WCDu
	WCot WPer
- 'Sapphirino'	EMon
tuberosa	CAvo ELan EPfP EWTr GBuc
	MLan NSti SLod
- 'Alba'	EBee ELan EMon MLLN MSte
	WHer WPer
- 'Axminster Lilac'	WPer
§ - Coelestis Group	CFri CInt EBee ECha EMan ETub
	MLLN NFai SAga SRms SYvo WFar
	WHer WPGP WPer WWin
¶ - - 'Hopleys Variegated' (v) LHop
- 'Snowmelt'	MGrG
virginica L.	IBlr
- hort.	See *C. erecta*

COMMIPHORA (Burseraceae)
opobalsamum	LEdu

COMPTONIA (Myricaceae)
peregrina	CMac WCru

CONANTHERA (Tecophilaeaceae)
campanulata Last listed 1998

CONICOSIA (Aizoaceae)
pugioniformis CTrF

CONIOGRAMME (Adiantaceae)
intermedia NMar
japonica Last listed 1999

CONIOSELINUM (Apiaceae)
morrisonense B&SWJ 173 WCru
schugnanicum EBee

CONIUM (Apiaceae)
maculatum 'Golden Nemesis' (v)
  Last listed 1999

CONOPODIUM (Apiaceae)
majus CKin WShi

CONRADINA (Lamiaceae)
verticillata CFee

CONSOLIDA (Ranunculaceae)
§ *ajacis* EWFC MSal
  ambigua See *C. ajacis*
  regalis ECoo

CONVALLARIA ✿ (Convallariaceae)
japonica See *Ophiopogon jaburan*
keiskei CLAP
majalis ♀ More than 30 suppliers
§ - 'Albostriata' (v) CFil CHEx CLAP CRDP CRow
  EBee ECha ELan EMon EPar MRav
  MTho NBir SIng SLod SSvw
  WCHb WCot WCru WEas WHer
  WPGP
- 'Berlin Giant' EBee WCot
- 'Dorien' EBee EFou
- 'Flore Pleno' (d) EPar WCot
- 'Fortin's Giant' CAvo CBro CLAP CMea CRDP
  CRow EGar EPar EPla ERav MRav
  WCot WPGP
- 'Gerard Debureaux' (v) See *C. majalis* 'Green Tapestry'
§ - 'Green Tapestry' (v) CRow
* - 'Haldon Grange' EMon WCot
- 'Hardwick Hall' (v) CAvo CLAP CRDP CRow ECha
  EHoe EPar EPla EPot MTed NPar
  NRar WCot
- 'Hofheim' (v) CRow
¶ - 'Plant Pips' NPSI
- 'Prolificans' CAvo CBro CLAP CRDP CRow
  EMon EPar EPot ERos MRav SIng
  SSvw
- var. *rosea* More than 30 suppliers
- 'Variegata' CBlo CBro EPar EPla ERav SMac
- 'Vic Pawlowski's Gold' (v) CRow SBla WCHb
montana LRHS
transcaucasica EBee WHer

CONVOLVULUS (Convolvulaceae)
althaeoides CBos CBot CFil CFri CHad CMil
  CPle ECGP LRHS MNes MNrw
  MTho SBla SChu SHFr SMad
  WAbb WCru WEas WHal WPGP
  WWin
§ - subsp. *tenuissimus* CGle CSWP CSpe EBee EMar EPPr
  EWes LHop MBri MHer MWat
  NTow SUsu WCFE WCot
arvensis Last listed 1997

§ *boissieri* CFir NWCA SBla SIng WAbe
cantabricus Last listed 1998
chilensis CPBP EMan
- RB 94080 Last listed 1998
cneorum ♀ More than 30 suppliers
elegantissimus See *C. althaeoides* subsp.
  tenuissimus
incanus WCru
lineatus EMan ESis LBee LRHS MBro MTho
  NMen NNrd NWCA SBla SMrm
  SRot
mauritanicus See *C. sabatius*
nitidus See *C. boissieri*
remotus Last listed 1998
§ *sabatius* ♀ CB&S CFri CGle CHEx CHad CHal
  CHar CSam ECha ECtt ELan EMan
  ERea GCHN LHop LRHS SAga
  SBla SDix SHFr SIng SRCN SYvo
  WCFE WEas WWin
- dark CMHG CSpe ELan EMan LFis LHil
  LHop LIck LLWP MSte SMrm
  SUsu

x COOPERANTHES See ZEPHYRANTHES

COOPERIA See ZEPHYRANTHES

COPERNICIA (Arecaceae)
alba LPal
prunifera Last listed 1999

COPROSMA ✿ (Rubiaceae)
acerosa 'Live Wire' (f) ECou
areolata ECou
atropurpurea (f) ECou
- (m) ECou
baueri See *C. repens*
'Beatson's Gold' (f/v) CB&S CBot CChe CGre CHal CLTr
  CMHG CTrG EBee EMil EPVP
  ERea GEil GOrc GQui IOrc MSCN
  NFai SBrw STre WHen WSHC
'Blue Pearls' (f) ECou
'Brunette' (f) ECou
§ *brunnea* ECou
- 'Blue Beauty' (f) ECou
- (m) x *kirkii* Last listed 1998
- 'Violet Fleck' (f) ECou
'Bruno' (m) ECou
cheesemanii (f) ECou
- (m) ECou
- 'Hanmer Red' (f) ECou
- 'Mack' (m) ECou
- 'Red Mack' (m) ECou
'Chocolate Soldier' (m) ECou
'Coppershine' CB&S ERea
crassifolia (m) x *repens* ECou
x *cunninghamii* (f) ECou
x *cunninghamii* ECou
  x *macrocarpa* (m)
depressa ECou
- 'Orange Spread' (f) ECou
'Evening Glow' LHop
foetidissima Forster Last listed 1997
'Green Girl' (f) ECou
'Hinerua' (f) ECou
'Indigo Lustre' (f) ECou
'Jewel' (f) ECou
¶ 'Kirke Blue' SSht
x *kirkii* 'Kirkii' (f) CInt ECou ERea STre
- 'Kirkii Variegata' (f) CB&S CBot CDoC CGre CTrC
  EBee ECou ERea GEil GQui LHop
  LRHS SEas SLon SOWG SPan STre

'Kiwi-gold' (v)	WBrE WSHC ECou ERea
'Lemon Drops' (f)	ECou
linariifolia	ECou
lucida (f)	ECou
- (m)	Last listed 1997
macrocarpa (f)	ECou
- (m)	ECou
¶ 'Middlemore'	CDoC
nitida (f)	ECou
- (m)	ECou
parviflora (m)	ECou
- purple fruit (f)	ECou
- red fruit (f)	ECou
- white fruit (f)	ECou
'Pearl Drops' (f)	ECou
'Pearl's Sister' (f)	ECou
'Pearly Queen' (f)	ECou
petriei	ECou
- AGS 50	Last listed 1998
- 'Don' (m)	ECou
- 'Lyn' (f)	ECou
'Pride'	CDoC CTrC
propinqua	EPla SDry WSHC
- (f)	ECou
- (m)	ECou
- var. *latiuscula* (f)	ECou
- - (m)	ECou
'Prostrata' (m)	ECou
pseudocuneata (m)	ECou
pumila	Last listed 1997
§ *repens*	CDoC
§ - (f)	CHEx ECou
- (m)	CB&S ECou SEND
- 'Apricot Flush' (f)	ECou
- 'Brownie' (f)	Last listed 1998
- CC 543	CPLG
- 'County Park Purple' (f)	ECou ERea
- 'Exotica' (f/v)	ECou
- 'Marble King' (m/v)	ECou
- 'Marble Queen' (m/v)	ECou LHil WCot WLRN
- 'Orangeade' (f)	ECou
- 'Painter's Palette'	CB&S ECou
- 'Picturata' (m/v)	ECou ERea
- 'Pink Splendour' (m/v)	CB&S CDoC ECou ERea LHop
- 'Rangatiri' (f)	ECou
- 'Silver Queen' (m/v)	ECou SVen
- 'Variegata' (m)	ECou LHil
rhamnoides	Last listed 1997
rigida	ECou
robusta	ECou SDry
- 'Cullen's Point' (f)	ECou
- 'Sally Blunt' (f)	ECou
- 'Steepdown' (f)	ECou
- 'Tim Blunt' (m)	ECou
* - 'Variegata' (m)	ECou
- 'William' (m)	ECou
- 'Williamsii Variegata' (f/m)	Last listed 1999
- 'Woodside' (f)	ECou
rotundifolia	ECou
'Roy's Red'	ECou
rugosa (f)	ECou
I 'Snowberry' (f)	ECou
tenuifolia (m)	ECou
'Tuffet' (f)	Last listed 1997
'Violet Drops' (f)	ECou
virescens	ECou
'Walter Brockie'	CGre CHal SVen
'White Lady' (f)	ECou
'Winter Bronze' (f)	ECou

COPTIS (Ranunculaceae)
japonica var. *dissecta*	Last listed 1999
quinquefolia	Last listed 1999
¶ - B&SWJ 1677	WCru

x CORALIA (Papilionaceae)
'County Park'	ECou
'Essex'	ECou
'Havering'	ECou

CORALLOSPARTIUM (Papilionaceae)
crassicaule	ECou

CORDYLINE (Agavaceae)
australis ♀	More than 30 suppliers
- 'Albertii' (v) ♀	CB&S CHEx ERea GQui LNet MBri MCCP NMoo SAPC SArc
* - 'Atropurpurea'	CB&S
* - 'Black Tower'	CB&S ELan LRHS MAsh MGos WGer
* - 'Coffee Cream'	CBrm CTor EBee EGln ELan EPVP GGar IOrc LEdu LRHS MAsh MBlu SPer WBod WGer
- 'Pink Stripe' (v)	CB&S CDoC COtt CTor ELan EPVP IOrc LRHS SPla WGer WPat
- 'Purple Tower'	CB&S CBlo CDoC COtt CTor CTrC EBee EMil EPfP EWTr IOrc LRHS MWst SLim SPla WLRN WPat WWeb
- Purpurea Group	CB&S CBot CChe CHEx CHar EBee EBrP EBre ENot EOld ERea GGar GOrc GQui IOrc ISea LAst LBCl LBSe LBre LRHS MBBe MGos NCut SBre SEND SPer WFar WGer WStI
- 'Red Star'	CAbb CB&S CBlo COtt CTor EBee EGln ENot EPfP LAst LHil LRHS MCCP MLan NHol NPer SPar WBod WCFE WCot WLRN WStI WWes
- 'Sundance'	CB&S CBlo CDoC CEnd CTor CWit EBee EGln EPVP EPfP IOrc LAst LEdu LRHS MAsh MBri MCCP NCut NPer SLim SMer SPla SRPl SWat WCot WFar WPyg WStI WWes
* - 'Torbay Coffee Cream'	Last listed 1999
- 'Torbay Dazzler' (v)	More than 30 suppliers
- 'Torbay Green'	CTor
* - 'Torbay Razzle Dazzle'	CTor
- 'Torbay Red'	CAbb CB&S CBrm CDoC CHEx COtt CSam CTor EBee ELan EPVP EPfP IOrc LPan LRHS MAsh MBlu MBri SEas SPla WPat WWeb
- 'Torbay Sunset'	COtt CTor ELan IOrc LRHS
- 'Torbay Surprise'	CTor
- 'Variegata'	CBot CHEx
* *autumn*	NCut
banksii	ECou IHdy WLRN
baueri	Last listed 1997
¶ 'Dark Star'	MCCP
'Dollar Princess'	EOld
fruticosa 'Atom'	MBri
- 'Baby Ti' (v)	MBri
- 'Calypso Queen'	MBri
- 'Kiwi'	MBri
- 'Orange Prince'	MBri
- 'Red Edge'	MBri
- 'Yellow King'	MBri
'Green Goddess'	CB&S EPVP MWst
§ *indivisa*	CBrP CHEx CTrC EBak IHdy LEdu

	LPan LRHS MBri SPlb WGer WMul WPGP
kaspar	CHEx LHil SAPC
parryi 'Purpurea'	Last listed 1999
¶ 'Red Fountain'	ENot
§ *stricta*	CHEx MBri

COREOPSIS ✿ (Asteraceae)

auriculata Cutting Gold	See *C. auriculata* 'Schnittgold'
§ - 'Schnittgold'	CBlo CFri CMea CWit EOld LFis NCut SHel WPer
- 'Superba'	Last listed 1998
'Baby Gold'	EPfP LRHS MBNS NNor
Baby Sun	See *C.* 'Sonnenkind'
'Goldfink'	EBrP EBre EMan GKir GSki LBCl LBSe LBre LRHS MBBe MBrN MNrw MRav SBre SIng SRms
grandiflora	EWTr SRPl SRob SWat
- 'Astolat'	CMGP CStr EMon MNrw
- 'Badengold'	CB&S EMil EWTr
I - 'Calypso' (v)	CWSG LRHS MAsh SCoo WWeb
- 'Domino'	EBee EMan LHop NCut NOak SMrm WShe
- 'Early Sunrise'	CBrm COlW CSam EBee ECtt EWTr GMaP LRHS MHer MMal MTis NFai NMir NPer SAga SGar SMer WHen WHoo WPer WPyg WRHF
- Flying Saucers = 'Walcoreop'	LRHS SCoo
- 'Kelvin Harbutt'	CStr EMan
- 'Mayfield Giant'	CBlo EBee EFou EMan EWTr EWll LRHS MGrG MNrw MWat NFla NPri SMer SRms SWat
§ - 'Rotkehlchen'	Last listed 1997
- Ruby Throat	See *C. grandiflora* 'Rotkehlchen'
- variegated	Last listed 1998
integrifolia	WCot
lanceolata	COlW EFou GDea
- 'Lichtstad'	Last listed 1997
- 'Sterntaler'	CFir EBee EFou EMil EPar GKir LRHS NCut NOrc SLod WPer
latifolia	EBee
¶ *maritima*	EBee
maximilianii	See *Helianthus maximiliani*
palmata	EBee EMon WCot
pubescens	EBee
rosea	EGar MBel NLar NPro SRPl WFar
- 'American Dream'	CB&S CBrm CHor CRDP EBee EGle ELan EMan EMil EWTr GGar GKir LHop LRHS MCCP MCLN MCli MMil NBro NFai SHel SMad SPer SPlb WAbe WFar WPyg
- f. *leucantha*	CStr
- 'Nana'	Last listed 1999
§ 'Sonnenkind'	ECtt EMil EPar GMaP LRHS MHer NBro WPer
Sun Child	See *C.* 'Sonnenkind'
'Sunburst'	CBlo COlW COtt EOHP LRHS NFai NOak SLod SRCN WOve WPer
'Sunray'	CB&S CDoC COlW EBee ECtt EOld EPar GKir LPVe LRHS MBri MFir MNrw NFai NGdn NOak NOrc SIde SPlb SRCN SRms WPer WWal WWeb WWye
¶ 'Tequila Sunrise' (v)	EFou WCot
tinctoria	MSal SIde WHer
- var. *atkinsoniana*	WPer
tripteris	CPou EBee EGar EMan EMon LGre SAga SMrm SSvw
verticillata	CMea CTri ECha ENot EOld LFis

	LRHS MBrN MBro MFir MHer MWat NFai NPer SDix SRPl SRms SSpe SWat WAbe WHal WPyg
- 'Alba'	Last listed 1998
- 'Golden Gain'	CMGP EBee EBrP EBre EFou EMan EPla GBri GKir GSki LBCl LBSe LBre LHop LRHS MArl MBBe MLLN MMil NGdn NHol SBre WWal
- 'Golden Shower'	See *C. verticillata* 'Grandiflora'
§ - 'Grandiflora' ♀	CB&S CHor CSev EBee EBrP EBre EFou ELan GMaP LBCl LBSe LBre MBBe MBri MCLN MRav NFor NGdn NHol NOak NVic SBre SChu SMad SPer SPla SSpe WWal WWin
- 'Moonbeam'	More than 30 suppliers
- 'Rosea'	CHar
- 'Zagreb'	More than 30 suppliers

CORIANDRUM (Apiaceae)

sativum	CArn EDAr EOHP GPoy ILis LRHS MChe SIde WOak WPer WWye
- 'Cilantro'	CSev GAbr MHer WHer
- 'Leisure'	CBod CSev MMal NPri WGwG
- 'Santo'	ELau WJek

CORIARIA ✿ (Coriariaceae)

intermedia B&SWJ 019	WCru
japonica	CPle WCru
- B&SWJ 2833	WCru
kingiana	ECou WCru
§ *microphylla*	WCru
myrtifolia	CFil CPle GCal GSki WCot WCru WWat
napalensis	GCal SLon WCru WWat
ruscifolia	WCru
- HCM 98178	WCru
sarmentosa	GCal WCru
* *terminalis fructu-rubro*	Last listed 1997
- var. *xanthocarpa*	CCHP CPle CTrG EBee EMan GBuc GCal IBlr NHol NPSI SSpi WCot WCru WGwG WWat
thymifolia	See *C. microphylla*

CORNUS ✿ (Cornaceae)

alba	CDoC CKin CLnd CTri ENot GChr GKir IOrc MBar NWea SRms WDin WMou WStI WWat
* - 'Albovariegata'	ENot
- 'Argenteovariegata'	See *C. alba* 'Variegata'
- 'Aurea' ♀	More than 30 suppliers
- 'Elegantissima' (v) ♀	More than 30 suppliers
- 'Gouchaultii' (v)	CB&S CBlo EBee GKir LCaP LPan MBar SPer SRms WDin
¶ - 'Hessei'	LRHS
- 'Hessei' misapplied	See *C. sanguinea* 'Compressa'
- 'Ivory Halo'	EBee EBrP EBre GKir LBCl LBSe LBre LRHS MBBe MGos NMoo SBre SPer WGer
- 'Kesselringii'	More than 30 suppliers
- 'Siberian Pearls'	CB&S COtt ELan MBlu MGos NEgg NMoo SSta
§ - 'Sibirica' ♀	More than 30 suppliers
- 'Sibirica Variegata'	CDoC CMac EBee EBrP EBre EPla GOrc IOrc LBCl LBSe LBre LPan LRHS MAsh MBBe MBlu MBri MGos NBee NEgg SBre SLim SPer SSpi SSta WFar WPyg WWeb
- 'Spaethii' (v) ♀	More than 30 suppliers
§ - 'Variegata'	CB&S CBlo MNaF SPer WWal WWin

- 'Westonbirt'	See *C. alba* 'Sibirica'
alternifolia	CBlo CMCN CMHG COtt CPMA
	ELan EWTr GKir IOrc LPan LRHS
	SBrw SPer SSpi WWat
§ - 'Argentea' (v) ♀	More than 30 suppliers
- 'Variegata'	See *C. alternifolia* 'Argentea'
amomum	CB&S EPla NHol WBcn WWat
angustata	SPer
§ 'Ascona'	CPMA CRos ELan EPfP LNet LRHS
	MBlu MBri SBrw SPer SSpi SSta
	WPat WWes
australis	EPla
baileyi	See *C. stolonifera* 'Baileyi'
§ *canadensis* ♀	More than 30 suppliers
candidissima	See *C. racemosa*
capitata	CB&S CDoC CGre CMac CPMA
	CTbh CTrG CTri IDee IHdy IOrc
	LRHS SEND SSpi WAbe WGer
	WPGP
- ACE	Last listed 1999
- 'Rag Doll' (v)	CPMA
chinensis	Last listed 1997
controversa	CB&S CBlo CDoC CDul CFee
	CMCN CPMA CTho EBee ELan
	EMil GChr IOrc LPan MBar MBlu
	NDlv NPSI NWea SBrw SLPl SPer
	SReu SSht SSpi SSta WDin WHar
	WPGP WWat
- 'Pagoda'	CBlo CEnd CPMA MBlu SMur SSpi
- 'Variegata' ♀	CDoC CDul CLnd CPMA CTho
	EBee ENot GKir IMGH ISea LRHS
	MAsh MBar MGos NBee NMoo
	NPSI NWea SBrw SLon SPla SRPl
	WPGP WStl
- 'Variegata' Frans type	CB&S CBot CEnd CPMA CRos
	EBre EBre ELan EMil ERom IOrc
	LBCl LBSe LBre LNet LPan MBBe
	MBlu MBri SBre SPer SReu SSta
	WDin WHCG WPat WSHC WWat
'Eddie's White Wonder' ♀	CB&S CDoC CEnd CFil CPMA
	CRos CTbh CTho ECho ELan
	GKir IMGH IOrc LNet LPan LRHS
	MBlu MBri MGos SBrw SLim SPer
	SRPl SReu SSpi SSta WDin WPat
	WPyg
florida	CBlo CMCN CTho ELan EPfP
	GOrc IOrc ISea LRHS MBar SBrw
	SPer SRPl SReu SSta WBod WLRN
	WNor WWat WWoo
- 'Alba Plena' (d)	CPMA LPri
- 'Apple Blossom'	CMac CPMA
- 'Cherokee Brave'	LRHS SSpi SSta
- 'Cherokee Chief' ♀	CAbP CB&S CCHP CEnd COtt
	CPMA EPfP IArd IMGH LPan
	LRHS MBel MGos SLim SPer WAbe
	WPat
- 'Cherokee Princess'	CPMA CRos ELan LPan LRHS
	MAsh MGos SMur SSta
- 'Clear Moon'	LPan
- 'Cloud Nine'	CB&S CDoC COtt CPMA EMil
	LPan LRHS MGos SLdr SLim SSpi
	WPat
* - 'Daniela'	Last listed 1998
- 'Daybreak' (v)	CEnd COtt CPMA LPan MGos
	WPat
- 'First Lady'	CB&S CPMA ECho LPan
- 'Fragrant Cloud'	Last listed 1998
- 'G.H. Ford' (v)	CPMA
- 'Golden Nugget'	CPMA
- 'Green Glow' (v)	CPMA
¶ - 'Junior Miss'	CPMA
- 'Junior Miss Variegated' (v)	CPMA

- 'Moonglow'	CPMA
- 'Pendula'	CPMA
- 'Pink Flame' (v)	CPMA
- 'Purple Glory'	CPMA
- 'Rainbow' (v)	CAbP CB&S COtt CPMA ELan
	EPfP LPan LRHS MAsh MBri MGos
	NBee NEgg NPSI SPer SSta WAbe
	WDin WPat
- 'Red Giant'	CAbP CPMA CRos ELan EPfP
	LRHS MAsh SMur SSpi SSta
- 'Royal Red'	CPMA
- f. *rubra*	CB&S CBlo CDoC EPfP LPan
	LRHS MGos NEgg SPer SSta WAbe
	WGer WNor WPyg WWoo
- 'Spring Song'	CMac CPMA ECho LRHS MBri
- 'Stoke's Pink'	CEnd COtt CPMA ECho LNet
- 'Sunset' (v)	CEnd COtt CPMA MGos SPer
	WPat
- 'Sweetwater'	CPMA
- 'Tricolor'	See *C. florida* 'Welchii'
§ - 'Welchii' (v)	CEnd CPMA
- 'White Cloud'	CPMA LRHS
foemina	See *C. stricta*
'Greenlight'	WWeb
hemsleyi	CNat EPla
bessei misapplied	See *C. sanguinea* 'Compressa'
'Kelsey's Dwarf'	See *C. stolonifera* 'Kelseyi'
kousa	CB&S CDoC CDul CMCN CTbh
	CTho ECrN ELan EMil ERom GKir
	ISea LNet LRHS MBar MWat NFor
	SBrw SPer WAbe WDin WHCG
	WHar WStl WWat
* - *angustifolia*	SPer
¶ - 'Autumn Rose'	EPfP
- 'Beni-fuji'	CPMA
- 'Boltinc'ks Beauty'	LRHS SSpi SSta
- 'Bonfire' (v)	CPMA
- var. *chinensis* ♀	More than 30 suppliers
- - 'Bodnant Form'	CEnd CPMA
- - 'China Girl'	CAbP CEnd COtt CPMA CRos
	ELan EPfP GKir LPan LRHS MAsh
	MBlu MBri MGos SLim SPer SSta
	WPGP WPyg
¶ - - 'Greta's Gold' (v)	CPMA
- - 'Milky Way'	CPMA
¶ - - 'Snowflake'	CPMA
¶ - - Spinners form	CPMA
¶ - - 'White Dusted'	EPfP
¶ - - 'White Fountain'	LPan
¶ - - 'Wieting's Select'	CPMA
¶ - 'Doubloon'	CPMA
- 'Elizabeth Lustgarten'	SSpi SSta
¶ - 'Gold Cup' (v)	CPMA
- 'Gold Star' (v)	CAbP CB&S CDoC CEnd CMac
	COtt CPMA CTho ELan EPfP IOrc
	LRHS MAsh MBri MGos SPer SPla
	SSpi SSta
¶ - 'John Slocock'	SSpi
- 'Lustgarten Weeping'	LRHS SSpi
- 'Madame Butterfly'	CEnd CPMA ELan LRHS MAsh
	SSpi
¶ - 'Moonbeam'	CPMA
- 'National'	CPMA MGos
* - 'Nicole'	CDoC LPan
- 'Radiant Rose'	CPMA
- 'Rosea'	CPMA CTho
- 'Satomi' ♀	CB&S CDoC CEnd CFil COtt
	CPMA ELan GKir LNet LPan LRHS
	MAsh MBri MGos SLdr SLim SPer
	SRPl SReu SSpi SSta WDin WPGP
	WPat
- 'Schmetterling'	CPMA

- 'Snowboy' (v) | CB&S CEnd COtt CPMA LRHS NBee NEgg
- 'Southern Cross' | CPMA
- 'Summer Majesty' | CPMA
- 'Sunsplash' (v) | CPMA
- 'Temple Jewel' (v) | CPMA LRHS
- 'Triple Crown' | CPMA
- 'Tsukubanomine' | CPMA
- 'Weaver's Weeping' | COtt CPMA
macrophylla | CMCN WCwm
mas ♀ | More than 30 suppliers
- 'Aurea' (v) | CAbP CPMA ELan EPfP GKir LPan MAsh MBri MCCP SLim SPan SPer SSpi SSta WAbe WDin WPat WWat
§ - 'Aureoelegantissima' (v) | CFil CPMA LNet LRHS MAsh MBri MBro NHol SPer WCot WPGP WPat WSHC
- 'Elegantissima' | See *C. mas* 'Aureoelegantissima'
- 'Golden Glory' | CB&S CPMA MBlu MBri
- 'Variegata' ♀ | CB&S CBot CDoC CMCN CPMA EBee EPfP GKir IOrc LNet LRHS MAsh MBlu MBri MGos NEgg SBrw SSpi WCot WDin WFar WPat WWat
N 'Norman Hadden' ♀ | CAbP CDoC CMac CPMA CRos CSam CTbh CTho EPfP GKir LRHS MAsh MBel SBrw SHFr SLim SSpi SSta WAbe WPat WWat
nuttallii | CB&S CCHP CDoC CTho ELan EPfP GOrc LPan LRHS MBro SBrw SSta WDin WNor WWat WWoo
- 'Ascona' | See *C.* 'Ascona'
- 'Colrigo Giant' | CPMA SSpi
- 'Gold Spot' (v) | CBlo CMac CPMA EPfP IOrc LPan LRHS MGos WWes
- 'Monarch' | CPMA LPan SPer WWes
- 'North Star' | CPMA CRos
- 'Portlemouth' | CEnd CPMA LRHS MAsh
obliqua | CFil WPGP
§ *occidentalis* | EPla
officinalis | CMCN EPfP LPan LRHS MBri WCwm WDin WWat
'Ormonde' | CPMA ECho LRHS SBrw SSpi WWes
'Pink Blush' | CPMA
'Porlock' ♀ | EPfP LRHS WDin
pubescens | See *C. occidentalis*
pumila | NHol WDin
§ *racemosa* | WWat
rugosa | WNor
I x *rutgersiensis* 'Aurora' | CPMA
§ - Celestial™ = 'Rutdan' | CPMA
- Constellation™ = 'Rutcan' | CPMA
- Galaxy™ | See *C.* x *rutgersiensis* Celestial = 'Rutdan'
- 'Ruth Ellen' | CPMA
- 'Stellar Pink' | CPMA
sanguinea | CB&S CBlo CDul CKin CLnd CSam CTri EBrP EBre ENot GChr LBCI LBSe LBre LBuc LHyr MAsh MBBe MDun MHer MPEx NFor NWea SBre SMer SPer WDin WGwG WHar WMou
§ - 'Compressa' | EPla MBro NHol WPat WPyg WShe
- 'Midwinter Fire' | More than 30 suppliers
§ - 'Winter Beauty' | CDoC CDul EMil EPfP GChr IOrc LHop LRHS MBro NHol SEas WPat WPyg WWat
- 'Winter Flame' | See *C. sanguinea* 'Winter Beauty'
- 'Winter Flame Anny' | MBlu
sp. CLD 613 | EPla

stolonifera | CArn EPla MGos SMer
§ - 'Baileyi' | Last listed 1999
- 'Flaviramea' ♀ | More than 30 suppliers
§ - 'Kelseyi' | CB&S CBlo CMac CWit EBee EPla ESis GKir IOrc MBNS MBar MRav NPro SBod SLPl SPer WLRN WWat
- Kelsey's Gold = 'Roseo' | Last listed 1997
- 'Sunshine' | CSpe
§ - 'White Gold' (v) | CAbP CBlo CDoC CPMA ENot EPla IOrc LNet LRHS MBri MGos NPro SPer WBcn WWeb
- 'White Spot' | See *C. stolonifera* 'White Gold'
§ *stricta* | Last listed 1998
x *unalaschkensis* | Last listed 1997
walteri | CMCN WCwm WWat

COROKIA (Escalloniaceae)

. *buddlejoides* | CAbb CDoC CMHG CPle ECou MGrG SBrw SOWG WBod WCru WTro
- var. *linearis* | Last listed 1998
'Coppershine' | CB&S CMHG
cotoneaster | CAbP CHor CMac CPle CTrw ECou ELan EMan ENot EPot MBlu MGos NHol SBrw SDry SLon SMur SPar SPer SSta WBod WBrE WCot WFar WOTO WPat WWat WWes
- 'Little Prince' | CB&S
- 'Ohau Scarlet' | ECou
- 'Ohau Yellow' | ECou
- 'Swale Stream' | ECou
- 'Wanaka' | ECou
macrocarpa | CDoC CPle ISea SDix SPer WSHC
- x *buddlejoides* | Last listed 1998
x *virgata* | CAbP CB&S CMHG CPle CSam CTrC EBee ECou ELan IOrc ISea LRHS MBlu MCCP MWhi SAPC SArc SBrw SPer WLeb WSHC WTro WWal
- 'Bronze King' | CDoC CMil CPle CWit SPer SVen
- 'Bronze Knight' | MHar
- 'Bronze Lady' | Last listed 1999
- 'Cheesemanii' | ECou
- 'County Park Lemon' | ECou SOWG
¶ - 'County Park Orange' | ECou
- 'County Park Purple' | ECou
¶ - 'County Park Red' | ECou
* - 'Dartonii' | MBlu
* - 'Frosted Chocolate' | CB&S SBrw
- 'Havering' | ECou
- 'Pink Delight' | CDoC EPfP
* - *purpurea* | Last listed 1998
- 'Red Wonder' | CBlo CMHG CTrC EBee ERea LRHS SAga SBrw SDry SEND SOWG WCot WDin WLeb
* - 'Sunsplash' | CB&S
- 'Virgata' | CChe ECou
- 'Yellow Wonder' | CB&S CMHG CTrC EBee ECot ECou EMan GEil GGar WDin

CORONILLA (Papilionaceae)

cappadocica | See *C. orientalis*
comosa | See *Hippocrepis comosa*
¶ *coronata* | EBrP EBre LBCI LBSe LBre MBBe SBre
emerus | See *Hippocrepis emerus*
glauca | See *C. valentina* subsp. *glauca*
globosa | SUsu
minima | NTow SBla
§ *orientalis* | NWCA WWin
- var. *orientalis* | Last listed 1998

valentina	CMac CRHN CSPN CSam EMil
	LHop SBra SDix SVen WSHC
§ - subsp. *glauca* ♀	CB&S CBot CFee CGle CMac CPle
	CSam CTri EBee ELan ENot ERea
	IOrc LRHS MWhi NTow SPer
	SRCN SRms WAbe WHCG WPic
- - 'Citrina' ♀	CB&S CBot CDoC CElw CSam
	ELan LGre LHop LRHS MCCP
	MLan NPer SBrw SChu SMur SPer
	SVil WAbe WCot WHCG WKif
	WPGP WRus WSHC WSpi
* - - 'Pygmaea'	WCot
- - 'Variegata'	More than 30 suppliers
§ *varia*	CAgr CStr NLar SRCN WViv
- HH&K 334	Last listed 1999

CORREA (Rutaceae)

alba	CDoC CSev ECou ERea SMur
- 'Pinkie'	ECou ERea LHop SOWG
backhouseana ♀	CAbb CDoC CPle CTrG CTri ECre
	ERea GCal GQui IDee IOrc LCns
	LHil LHop SAga SLon SOWG
	WAbe WBod WCot WSHC WSPU
baeuerlenii	CMHG SOWG
calycina	ERea
decumbens	CPle ECon ECou GSki LCns SMur
	SOWG WSHC
'Dusky Bells'	CDoC CPle CSWP CWSG ECou
	ERea LCns LHop SOWG WCFE
'Dusky Maid'	CAbb
'Harrisii'	See C. 'Mannii'
lawrenceana	CAbb CDoC CTrC CWSG GQui
	SEND WAbe WLRN
- *rosea*	Last listed 1998
§ 'Mannii' ♀	CLTr CSam CSev EBee ECou ERea
	EWTr IDee IOrc MNes SBrw
	SOWG SVen WAbe WSHC WWat
'Marian's Marvel'	CAbb CMHG CTrC ERea GQui
	LCns LHil LRHS SOWG SVen
	WAbe WLRN
'Peachy Cream'	CDoC
pulchella	CDoC CTri ERea GQui LRHS
	MNes SOWG WAbe
§ *reflexa*	CB&S CPle ECou SOWG WBor
- var. *reflexa*	Last listed 1998
- *virens*	WEas
- 'Yanakie'	CPle SOWG
speciosa	See C. *reflexa*
viridiflora	GQui

CORTADERIA (Poaceae)

argentea	See C. *selloana*
§ *fulvida*	EBrP EBre EGar EWes IBlr IHdy
	LBCl LBSe LBre LRHS MBBe
	MNrw SBre SMad
§ *richardii* hort.	See C. *fulvida*
§ *richardii* (Endlicher) Zotov	
	CCuc CHEx CPLG EBrP EBre
	EFou EHoe ELan EPla EWes GAbr
	GAri GGar IBlr LBCl LBSe LBre
	MBBe SAPC SArc SBre WBea
	WCot WPic
§ *selloana*	CB&S CHEx CTri ELan ENot EPfP
	GChr GKir LNet MBar MRav NArg
	NBee NBir NFor SAPC SArc SPlb
	WStI
§ - 'Albolineata' (v)	CBrm CMil EHoe EWes EWsh
	LRHS MWht SCob SEND SLim
	SMad SPla WLRN WLeb WMoo
	WPat
§ - 'Aureolineata' (v) ♀	CB&S CBrm CCuc CDoC CMac
	CMil EHoe ELan ENot EPfP LRHS

	MAsh MBri MGos MMoz MRav
	SCob SEas SLim SPer WFar WLeb
	WPGP WPat
- 'Gold Band'	See C. *selloana* 'Aureolineata'
- 'Monstrosa'	Last listed 1999
- 'Pink Feather'	CBlo GChr GKir MAsh MWat
	NEgg SRms SWal WFar WLow
	WPyg WStI
- 'Pumila' ♀	More than 30 suppliers
- 'Rendatleri'	CB&S CDoC EHoe ELan EPfP
	LRHS MAsh SCob SEND SEas
	SLim SMad SPer WLRN
- 'Roi des Roses'	CBlo
- 'Rosea'	CHEx GSki LRHS MBar MGos
	NArg
- 'Silver Comet'	EBrP EBre LBCl LBSe LBre MBBe
	SBre WWoo
- 'Silver Fountain'	ELan EPfP LRHS MAsh SPer
- 'Silver Stripe'	See C. *selloana* 'Albolineata'
- 'Sunningdale Silver' ♀	CB&S CBlo CDoC CMac EBrP
	EBre ECha ECtt EHoe ELan ENot
	GKir LBCl LBSe LBre LRHS MAsh
	MBBe MBri MGos MWat SBre
	SCob SEas SLim SMad SPer WPyg
- 'White Feather'	CBlo CHEx MAsh WFar WLow
Toe Toe	See C. *richardii* (Endlicher) Zotov

CORTUSA (Primulaceae)

altaica	GCal
brotheri	EBee NWCA
matthioli	CGle EBee EPfP GGar GTou LBee
	LRHS NMGW NMen NWCA SRms
	WAbe WFar WWhi
- 'Alba'	ECGN EPPr LRHS NHar NLar
	NWCA SRms WLin
- var. *congesta*	EBee
- subsp. *pekinensis*	CFir CLyd EBee GDra GSki IMGH
	LSyl NDov NHar NMen SRms
	WOve
- var. *yezoensis*	Last listed 1999
turkestanica	EBee WAbe

CORYBAS (Orchidaceae)

diemenicus	Last listed 1999
incurvus	Last listed 1999

CORYDALIS (Papaveraceae)

* *afghanica*	GKir
§ *aitchisonii* subsp. *aitchisonii*	
	Last listed 1997
alexeenkoana	CLAP EPot
- subsp. *vittae*	See C. *vittae*
* *alta*	CPla
ambigua hort.	See C. *fumariifolia*
- Cham. & Schldt.	ETub
angustifolia	EPot GCrs
¶ - 'Georgian White'	EHyt
¶ *blanda* subsp. *blanda*	GCrs
- subsp. *oxelmannii*	GCrs
- subsp. *parnassica*	EPot GCrs
'Blue Dragon'	LRHS MBNS
'Blue Panda'	See C. *flexuosa* 'Blue Panda'
bracteata	GCrs LRHS
- *alba*	Last listed 1997
- 'Marina'	Last listed 1998
¶ - white	WWst
bulbosa auct. non DC.	See C. *cava*
—(L.) DC.	See C. *solida*
buschii	CElw GCrs IMGH LRHS SBla WAbe
cashmeriana	EPot GCrs GTou IMGH NHar
	NHol NMen NNrd SBla WAbe
	WIvy

- 'Kailash'	GBuc
caucasica	EPot GCrs GDra LAma
- var. *alba* misapplied	See *C. malkensis*
§ *cava* ♀	CGle EBot EPar EPot EWTr GGar LAma WCot WShi
- *albiflora*	EPar EPot SBla
- subsp. *marschalliana*	NMen
¶ *chaerophylla*	IBlr
- B&SWJ 2951	WCru
cheilanthifolia	More than 30 suppliers
chionophila	Last listed 1998
conorhiza	EPot
darwasica	GCrs
decipiens	See *C. solida* subsp. *incisa*
elata	More than 30 suppliers
- 'Blue Summit'	EBrP EBre LBCl LBSe LBre MBBe SBla SBre
erdelii	GCrs
firouzii	EPot
flexuosa	CFee CMil CSpe EBee ECGN EDAr EGle ELan EMar EMou GMac MArl MBel MBro MGrG MNrw MTho NNrd SChu WAbe WCFE WHil WRus WSHC WWin
- 'Balang Mist'	CBos SBla SOkh SUsu
§ - 'Blue Panda'	CBos CElw EPfP EWes GCrs GMaP IBlr LPio LRHS SSpi WAbe WCot
- CD&R 528	CGle LGre MBro MRav NHar NRya SAga WCot WRHF
- 'China Blue' CD&R 528c	More than 30 suppliers
- 'Copperhead'	Last listed 1999
- 'Nightshade'	CElw GAri GBuc MAvo MCCP NCot NDov SWat WCot WCra WFar WIvy WRHF WSpi
I - 'Norman's Seedling'	EPPr WCot WPGP
- 'Père David' CD&R 528b	More than 30 suppliers
- 'Purple Leaf' CD&R 528a	More than 30 suppliers
§ *fumariifolia*	EPot LAma MTho NRog
glauca	See *C. sempervirens*
glaucescens	EPot GCrs LRHS
- 'Medeo'	GCrs
gracilis	Last listed 1999
haussknechtii	GCrs
henrikii	EPot GCrs
heterocarpa	Last listed 1999
integra	GCrs
intermedia	EPot
* *itacifolia*	Last listed 1999
kashgarica	EPot
kusnetzovii	GCrs
ledebouriana	WWst
linstowiana	CLon EDAr EMan EMar EMon EPPr IBlr LGre NWCA SAga
- CD&R 605	CLAP CMdw
ludlowii	Last listed 1997
§ *lutea*	CB&S EDAr ELan EMar EWTr GBuc IBlr IMGH LGro MMal NFai NPer NPri NVic SBea SEND SRms SYvo WBea WCot WCru WHen
macrocentra	WWst
¶ *magadanica*	EHyt
§ *malkensis* ♀	EPot GCrs NBir NHar NTow WCot
nariniana white	Last listed 1999
nevskii	See *C. aitchisonii* subsp. *aitchisonii*
nobilis	NEgg
nudicaulis	GCrs
ochotensis	EMar NLar WCot
- B&SWJ 3138	WCru
§ *ochroleuca*	CElw CRow EBee EMar EPot ESis

	MBro MCLN MTho NEgg WBro WCru WHal WMoo
ophiocarpa	CGle EBee EHoe ELan EMan EMar EWTr GAri GCal GGar IBlr LSyl NArg NFla SOkh WBea WCot WElm WFoF WOve WPrP
oppositifolia subsp. *oppositifolia*	GCrs
ornata	Last listed 1999
¶ - white	WWst
paczoskii	EPot GCrs LRHS WAbe
- RS 12180	WCot
pallida	NDov
- B&SWJ 395	WCru
parnassica	Last listed 1999
paschei	GCrs
popovii	GCrs
pseudofumaria alba	See *C. ochroleuca*
pumila	EPot GCrs LRHS NTow
- *alba*	EPot
rosea	IBlr
ruksansii	EPot GCrs
rupestris	Last listed 1997
§ *saxicola*	EPot
scandens	See *Dicentra scandens*
schanginii	EPot
- subsp. *ainii*	EPot GCrs
- subsp. *schanginii*	Last listed 1999
scouleri	NBir WCot
seisumsiana	GCrs
§ *sempervirens*	CInt EMar MLan NFai WBea WCot WCru WHer WPat WRos WSan WWin
- *alba*	ELan WFoF
- 'Rock Harlequin'	Last listed 1997
¶ *sewerzowii*	WWst
smithiana	CMdw EDAr WFar WTin WUnu
- ACE 154	CPBP EMar EPot GBuc NCot NMen WCot
aff. *smithiana* CLD 385	EDAr
§ *solida* ♀	CBro CElw CGle CMea CRDP EBee ELan EMan EPar EPot EWTr GCrs GGar IBlr LAma LRHS MMal MRav NFla NHar NMen NNrd NRog NRya WAbe WCot WFar WHil WPnP WShi
¶ - 'Blue Dream'	GCrs
- BM 8499	NHol
- from Penza	GCrs
- 'Harkov'	GCrs LRHS
- 'Ice Pink'	EPot
§ - subsp. *incisa*	CMea EPot LRHS MNrw MTho
¶ - 'Ivory'	EHyt
¶ - 'Lilac Time'	EHyt
¶ - 'Maxima'	GCrs
- MS 881	Last listed 1998
¶ - 'Munich Sunrise'	EHyt
¶ - 'Punk Lips'	EHyt
¶ - 'Rozula'	EHyt
* - 'Smokey Blue'	Last listed 1998
- 'Soft Pink'	EPot
- subsp. *solida* 'Beth Evans' ♀	CBro WCot
- - 'Blue Pearl'	GCrs
- - 'Blushing Girl'	GCrs
- - 'Evening Shade'	GCrs
- - 'Highland Mist'	GCrs NHar
¶ - - 'Munich Sunrise'	NRya
- - 'Prasil Sunset'	WCot
- - 'Snowstorm'	EHyt
- - 'White Knight'	GCrs
¶ - subsp. *subremota*	WWst

- f. *transsylvanica*   CLAP EPot GCrs LRHS NBir NHar
       NMen NPar NRya WAbe WCot
- - 'Dieter Schacht'   GCrs LAma
- - 'George Baker' ♀   CBro CMea CRDP EPar EPot GCrs
       LAma LRHS MTho NHar NMen
       WCot
- - 'Lahovice'   GCrs
- - 'Nettleton Pink'   EPot
- 'White King'   LRHS
sp. from Sichuan, China   NCot
speciosa   Last listed 1997
taliensis ACE 2443   EPot
tauricola   EPot
thalictrifolia Franchet   See *C. saxicola*
tomentella   CPBP EPot
¶ *triternata*   GCrs
¶ *turtschaninovii*   WWst
uniflora   GCrs
verticillaris   Last listed 1999
§ *vittae*   Last listed 1999
wendelboi   EPot GCrs
¶ - subsp. *congesta*   WWst
- - 'Abant Wine'   EPot
wilsonii   CBot EDAr GCHN GCal IBlr MTho
       NTow NWCA SBla WEas
zetterlundii   Last listed 1998

CORYLOPSIS ✿ (Hamamelidaceae)

§ *glabrescens*   CPMA LRHS SMur SPer WNor
       WWes
- var. *gotoana*   CPMA EPfP LRHS MAsh SMur
       SPer SSpi SSta WBod WWat
himalayana KR 990   Last listed 1998
pauciflora ♀   CB&S CDoC CEnd CPMA EBee
       EBrP EBre EMil ENot EWTr IOrc
       LBCl LBSe LBre LRHS MAsh MBBe
       MBel MBri MGos NBee SBre SBrw
       SLim SPer SReu SSpi SSta WBod
       WWat
platypetala   See *C. sinensis* var. *calvescens*
- var. *laevis*   See *C. sinensis* var. *calvescens*
sinensis   EMil SSta WShe
§ - var. *calvescens*   CB&S CPMA LRHS
§ - - f. *veitchiana* ♀   CBlo CPMA EPfP LRHS SMur
       WBod
- - - 'Purple Selection'   CPMA
§ - var. *sinensis* ♀   CDoC CPMA CWit EPfP LAst
       SMad SRPl SReu WAbe WBod
       WWat
- - 'Spring Purple'   CAbP CMac CPMA EPfP LHop
       LRHS MBri SBrw SPer SSpi SSta
       WDin WWat
sp. from Chollipo,   LRHS
   South Korea
spicata   CB&S CBlo CDoC CPMA IMGH
       LRHS MBlu MBri SCoo SLim SRPl
       WBod
veitchiana   See *C. sinensis* var. *calvescens* f.
       veitchiana
willmottiae   See *C. sinensis* var. *sinensis*

CORYLUS ✿ (Corylaceae)

avellana (F)   More than 30 suppliers
- 'Aurea'   CBlo CEnd COtt CTho ELan ENot
       EPfP GChr GKir LBuc LRHS MAsh
       MBlu MBri MGos NHol SLim SPer
       SPla SSta WDin WPyg
- 'Bollwylle'   See *C. maxima* 'Halle'sche
       Riesennuss'
- 'Contorta' ♀   More than 30 suppliers
· - 'Cosford Cob' (F)   CBlo CDoC CTho CTri ERea ESim
       GKir GTwe LBuc LRHS MBlu MBri

       MGos NRog SDea SKee SPer
¶ - 'Fortin' (F)   ESim
§ - 'Fuscorubra' (F)   CMac GKir IOrc MAsh MRav
§ - 'Heterophylla'   CEnd CTho GKir WMou WWes
- 'Laciniata'   See *C. avellana* 'Heterophylla'
- 'Merveille de Bollwyller'   See *C. maxima* 'Halle'sche
       Riesennuss'
- 'Nottingham Prolific'   See *C. avellana* 'Pearson's
       Prolific'
§ - 'Pearson's Prolific' (F)   EBee ERea ESim GTwe LBuc SDea
- 'Pendula'   MBlu WMou
- 'Purpurea'   See *C. avellana* 'Fuscorubra'
- 'Webb's Prize Cob' (F)   ERea GTwe IOrc NRog SDea
       WMou
colurna ♀   CAgr CBlo CDul CFil CLnd CMCN
       CTho EBee ECrN ENot EPfP GChr
       GKir IOrc LHyr LPan LRHS MGos
       NBee NWea SKee SLPl SPer WDin
       WMou WOrn
* - 'Te Terra Red'   CEnd CMCN MBlu SMad WMou
§ x *colurnoides*   Last listed 1998
¶ - 'Chinoka' (F)   ESim
¶ - 'Laroka' (F)   ESim
maxima (F)   CDul CLnd EMui GTwe NWea
       SDea WDin
* - 'Annise Summer Red'   Last listed 1997
- 'Butler' (F)   CBlo ERea GTwe LRHS MBri SKee
       WPyg
- 'Ennis' (F)   ERea GTwe LRHS SDea SKee
- 'Fertile de Coutard'   See *C. maxima* 'White Filbert'
- 'Frizzled Filbert' (F)   EMil ERea
- 'Frühe van Frauendorf'   See *C. maxima* 'Red Filbert'
- 'Grote Lambertsnoot'   See *C. maxima* 'Kentish Cob'
- 'Gunslebert' (F)   CBlo ERea GChr GKir GTwe
       LRHS MBri SDea SKee WPyg
- Halle Giant   See *C. maxima* 'Halle'sche
       Riesennuss'
§ - 'Halle'sche Riesennuss' (F)   ERea GTwe SKee
§ - 'Kentish Cob' (F)   CBlo CDoC CTho EBrP EBre ERea
       ESim GTwe IOrc LBCl LBSe LBre
       LBuc LRHS MBBe MBlu MGos
       NBee NRog SBre SDea SFam SKee
       SPer SRms WHar WPyg
- 'Lambert's Filbert'   See *C. maxima* 'Kentish Cob'
- 'Longue d'Espagne'   See *C. maxima* 'Kentish Cob'
- 'Monsieur de Bouweller'   See *C. maxima* 'Halle'sche
       Riesennuss'
- 'Purple Filbert'   See *C. maxima* 'Purpurea'
§ - 'Purpurea' (F) ♀   More than 30 suppliers
§ - 'Red Filbert' (F)   CBlo CEnd ERea GKir GTwe IOrc
       LRHS MBlu MBri NRog SKee SLim
- 'Red Zellernut'   See *C. maxima* 'Red Filbert'
- 'Spanish White'   See *C. maxima* 'White Filbert'
- 'Tonne de Giffon' (F)   Last listed 1997
§ - 'White Filbert' (F)   ERea GTwe NRog SKee WHar
- 'White Spanish Filbert'   See *C. maxima* 'White Filbert'
- 'Witpit Lambertsnoot'   See *C. maxima* 'White Filbert'
¶ *sieboldiana* var.   CMCN
   mandshurica
x *vilmorinii*   WMou

CORYNEPHORUS (Poaceae)

canescens   CBrm CCuc EBee EHoe EMan
       EPla GBin MCCP MLLN

CORYNOCARPUS (Corynocarpaceae)

laevigatus   CHEx ECou MBri
- 'Picturatus'   CHEx
- 'Variegatus'   CHEx

COSMOS (Asteraceae)

§ *atrosanguineus*   More than 30 suppliers

* **bipinnatus** 'Sonata' ♀   Last listed 1994

COSTUS (Zingiberaceae)
§ **cuspidatus**	LChe
igneus	See *C. cuspidatus*
malortieanus	LChe
¶ **pictus**	LEur WMul
speciosus	ELau GPoy LHil·NRog WMul
- tetraploid	Last listed 1997
¶ **spicatus**	LEur
spiralis	LChe

COTINUS (Anacardiaceae)
americanus	See *C. obovatus*
§ **coggygria** ♀	More than 30 suppliers
- 'Foliis Purpureis'	See *C. coggygria* Rubrifolius Group
¶ - Golden Spirit™ = 'Ancot'PBR	ELan ENot EPfP MGos SCoo SPer WWeb
- 'Notcutt's Variety'	CBlo CMac EBee EBrP EBre ELan ENot GKir LBCl LBSe LBre MAsh MBBe MRav NSti SBre WWes
- 'Pink Champagne'	CPMA
- Purpureus Group	ENot
- 'Red Beauty'	LRHS MBri
- 'Royal Purple' ♀	More than 30 suppliers
§ - Rubrifolius Group	CB&S EBee GKir LRHS NFor SChu SDix SPer SPla WHCG
¶ - 'Sheffield Park'	MAsh
- 'Velvet Cloak'	CBlo CPMA ELan EPfP GKir LRHS MAsh MGos MRav SLon SPer SPla SReu SSta WHCG WPat WPyg
'Flame' ♀	CBlo CPMA EBee ELan EPfP IOrc LRHS MAsh MGos SLim SPla WPat WWat WWeb
'Grace' ♀	More than 30 suppliers
§ **obovatus** ♀	CGre CMCN CMHG CPMA CPle ELan ENot EPfP MRav SPer SSpi SSta WWat WWes

COTONEASTER ✿ (Rosaceae)
acuminatus	SRms WPGP
acutifolius var. laetevirens	See *C. laetevirens*
adpressus ♀	CBlo EPfP EPla GDra GKir LRHS MGos NCut NFor NHar NWea
§ - 'Little Gem'	GAri LRHS MBri SRms
- var. **praecox**	See *C. nanshan*
- 'Tom Thumb'	See *C. adpressus* 'Little Gem'
affinis	SRms
afghanicus CC 738	WLRN
albokermesinus	SRms
altaicus	SRms
ambiguus	SRms
amoenus	SLPl SRms
- 'Fire Mountain'	LRHS NPro WFar
§ **apiculatus**	CSWP GKir LRHS MAsh MBar MBri SRms WRHF
armenus	SRms
§ **ascendens**	SRms
assadii	SRms
assamensis	SRms
§ **astrophoros**	MBlu SIng SRms WBod
atropurpureus	SRms
§ - 'Variegatus' ♀	CBot CDul EBee EHoe ELan ENot EPot GChr GKir IOrc LRHS MBNS MBar MBri MGos NBee NFla NHol SLim SPer SRms WDin WRHF WSHC WWal WWat WWin
bacillaris	SRms
boisianus	SRms
bradyi	SRms

§ **bullatus** ♀	CDul ENot GChr GlBF GKir MGos NFor SEND SLon SPer SRms WCwm WSHC WWat
N - 'Firebird'	CBlo LRHS SPer SRms
- f. **floribundus**	See *C. bullatus*
- var. **macrophyllus**	See *C. rebderi*
buxifolius Wallich ex Lindley	ESis SRms
- blue-leaved	See *C. lidjiangensis*
- 'Brno'	See *C. marginatus* 'Brno'
- f. **vellaeus**	See *C. astrophoros*
calocarpus	SRms
cambricus	CNat SRms
canescens	SRms
§ **cashmiriensis** ♀	SRms
cavei	SRms
chailaricus	SRms
chengkangensis	SRms
cinerascens	SRms
§ **cochleatus**	CChe EBee EPot ESis GAri GDra GKir MBar MGos NFla NMen SReu SRms WCot WEas WRHF WWat
§ **congestus**	CFee GKir IOrc LRHS MBar MBri MBro MGos MRav NFor SPer SPlb SRms WBod WHar WWat WWin
- 'Nanus'	CLyd CMHG CNic ELan EOrn ESis LRHS MAsh MBro MOne NFor NHol NNrd SPla SRms WPat WPyg WWat
conspicuus	CB&S CSam SRms
- 'Decorus' ♀	CDoC CMHG EBee EHol ENot EPfP GKir GOrc IOrc LRHS MBar MGos MRav NFor NHol NWea SLim SPer SPlb WDin WPyg WStI WWes
- 'Flameburst'	LRHS MBri
§ - KR 3407	CDoC
- 'Red Alert'	SRms
- 'Red Glory'	SRms
- 'Winter Jewel'	See *C. x suecicus* 'Winter Jewel'
cooperi	SRms
crispii	SRms
aff. **crispii**	SRms
cuspidatus	SRms
N **dammeri** ♀	CBlo CChe CDul CMHG EBee ELan ENot GChr GKir ISea LBuc LRHS MBar MGos NFor NWea SIng SMac SPer SRPl SRms WBod WDin WFar WHar WWat WWin
§ - 'Major'	CBlo NFla SPla WCFE
§ - 'Mooncreeper'	CChe CDoC LRHS
- 'Oakwood'	See *C. radicans* 'Eichholz'
- var. **radicans** hort.	See *C. dammeri* 'Major'
- var. **radicans** C.K.Schneid.	See *C. radicans*
- 'Streibs Findling'	See *C. procumbens*
dielsianus	NWea SPer SRms
- 'Rubens'	SRms
discolor	SRms
distichus	See *C. nitidus*
- var. **tongolensis**	See *C. splendens*
divaricatus	ENot EPla NWea SLon SRms WFar WWat
'Donald Lowndes'	See *C. integrifolius* 'Donald Lowndes'
duthieanus	SRms
- 'Boer'	See *C. apiculatus*
elegans	SRms
ellipticus	SRms
'Erlinda'	See *C. x suecicus* 'Erlinda'
¶ **falconeri**	SRms

fangianus	SRms
floccosus	CBlo GKir GOrc LRHS MBri
	NWea SPer SRms WLRN WWat
forrestii	SRms
franchetii	More than 30 suppliers
- S&F 96051	ISea
- var. *sternianus*	See *C. sternianus*
frigidus	CBlo GAri NWea SRms
N - 'Cornubia' ♀	More than 30 suppliers
- 'Fructu Luteo'	GKir IBlr LRHS MBri SRms WWes
- 'Notcutt's Variety'	ELan ENot WWes
§ - 'Pershore Coral'	GKir LRHS MBri
- 'Saint Monica'	MBlu
- 'Sherpa'	Last listed 1997
froebelii	SRms
gamblei	SRms
gangbobaensis	SRms
giraldii	SRms
glabratus	SLPl SRms
glacialis	SRms
glaucophyllus	SEND SMad SRms
- TW 332	Last listed 1997
§ *glomerulatus*	MBar SRms
goloskokovii	SRms
gracilis	SRms
griffithii	SRms
harrovianus	EPla SLPl SRms
barrysmithii	SRms
bebephyllus	SRms
benryanus	SRms
- 'Anne Cornwallis'	WBcn
'Herbstfeuer'	See *C. salicifolius* 'Herbstfeuer'
bessei	SRms
'Highlight' (aff. *sheriffii*)	See *C. pluriflorus*
bissaricus	SRms
§ *bjelmqvistii*	LBuc SRms WRHF
- 'Robustus'	See *C. hjelmqvistii*
- 'Rotundifolius'	See *C. hjelmqvistii*
borizontalis ♀	More than 30 suppliers
- 'Tangstedt'	ENot
- 'Variegatus'	See *C. atropurpureus* 'Variegatus'
- var. *wilsonii*	See *C. ascendens*
bsingsbangensis	SRms
bumifusus	See *C. dammeri*
bummelii	SRms
§ 'Hybridus Pendulus'	CBlo CDoC CSam EBee ELan
	GChr GKir IOrc LNet LPan LRHS
	MAsh MBar MBri MGos MRav
	MWat NWea SLim SPer SRPl SRms
	WBod WHCG WHar WJas WStI
§ *bylmoei*	SLPl SRms
ignavus	SLPl SRms
induratus	SLPl SRms
insculptus	SRms
insolitus	SRms
integerrimus	SRms
§ *integrifolius*	CMHG EPfP EPla ESis GKir LNet
	LRHS MAsh MBar MWhi NHol
	NMen SRms STre WMoo WWat
§ - 'Donald Lowndes'	SRPl
juranus	SRms
kitaibelii	SRms
kweitschoviensis	SRms
lacteus ♀	CBlo CTri EBee ELan ENot EPla
	GChr GKir IOrc LBuc LPan LRHS
	MGos MRav SEND SEas SLon SPer
	SPla SRPl SRms WCFE WDin WFar
	WWat
- 'Golden Gate'	Last listed 1997
- 'Variegatus'	CEnd
§ *laetevirens*	SRms
langei	SRms

laxiflorus	SRms
§ *lidjiangensis*	SRms WCot
§ *linearifolius*	CLyd EHol GKir LRHS SRms
lucidus	SRms
ludlowii	SRms
§ *mairei*	GChr SRms
- Yu 14144	Last listed 1999
marginatus	SRms
§ - 'Blazovice'	SRms
§ - 'Brno'	SRms
marquandii	EPla SRms
megalocarpus	SRms
§ *meiopbyllus* ♀	SRms
melanocarpus	SRms
microphyllus	CChe CLan ENot IOrc ISea MBar
Wallich ex Lindley ♀	MBri MGos NFor NWea SDix SPer
	SRms STre WBod WDin WWal
	WWat
- hort.	See *C. purpurascens*
- var. *cochleatus*	See *C. cochleatus*
- var. *cochleatus*	See *C. cashmiriensis*
misapplied	
- 'Donard Gem'	See *C. astrophoros*
- 'Inermis'	GKir
- KR 3407	See *C. conspicuus* KR 3407
- 'Teulon Porter'	See *C. astrophoros*
- var. *thymifolius*	See *C. linearifolius*
- -	See *C. integrifolius*
miniatus	SRms
mongolicus	SRms
monopyrenus	SRms
'Mooncreeper'	See *C. dammeri* 'Mooncreeper'
morrisonensis	SRms
moupinensis	EBee SRms
mucronatus	SRms
multiflorus Bunge	SRms
¶ 'My Pet'	NLAp
§ *nansban*	EBee NWea SRms WSPU
- 'Boer'	See *C. apiculatus*
nepalensis	SRms
newryensis	SRms
niger	SRms
nitens	SRms
nitidifolius	See *C. glomerulatus*
§ *nitidus*	SRms
nummularius	SRms
obscurus	SRms
oliganthus	SRms
otto-schwarzii S&F 636	ISea
ovatus	SRms
pannosus	SLPl SRms WWat
paradoxus	SRms
parkeri	SRms
peduncularis	SRms
pekinensis	SRms
permutatus	See *C. pluriflorus*
perpusillus	GAri MBri SRms WFar
'Pershore Coral'	See *C. frigidus* 'Pershore Coral'
§ *pluriflorus*	ECtt SRms
poluninii	SRms
polyanthemus	SRms
praecox 'Boer'	See *C. apiculatus*
§ *procumbens*	ESis LRHS MAsh SRms
- 'Queen of Carpets'	CBlo CDoC EBee EBrP EBre ECtt
	GKir LBCl LBSe LBre LRHS MBBe
	MBri MGos MRav SBre SEas SRms
- 'Seattle'	SRms
prostratus	SRms
- 'Arnold Forster'	SRms
przewalskii	SRms
pseudoambiguus	SRms
§ *purpurascens*	WOTO

pyrenaicus	See *C. congestus*
racemiflorus	SRms
§ *radicans*	LRHS SRms
§ - 'Eichholz'	EBee ECtt ENot EPfP GKir LRHS MGos WWeb
§ *rebderi*	SRms
¶ *rokujodaisanensis*	SRms
roseus	SRms
'Rothschildianus'	See *C. salicifolius* 'Rothschildianus'
rotundifolius	SLon SRms
'Royal Beauty'	See *C.* x *suecicus* 'Coral Beauty'
rugosus	SRms
'Saldam'	Last listed 1999
salicifolius	CBlo CLnd EMil GKir LRHS NFor SLim SMad SRms WDin WFar
- Autumn Fire	See *C. salicifolius* 'Herbstfeuer'
§ - 'Avonbank'	CBlo CEnd MAsh WLRN WSPU
- 'Elstead'	SPer
- 'Exburyensis'	CB&S CBlo CDoC CDul CSam CTrw EBee EBrP EBre GKir LRHS LBSe LBre LNet LRHS MAsh MBBe MBri MGos MWat SBre SPer SRms WDin WFar WHCG WWat WWeb WWin
- 'Gnom'	CBlo EPfP GOrc LNet LRHS MAsh MBar MBlu MBri MGos MRav NFor SRms WFar WWat
§ - 'Herbstfeuer'	CBlo EBee ECtt EHol GChr GKir MGos MWat NFor SPla SRms
- 'Merriott Weeper'	CDoC WWat
- Park Carpet	See *C. salicifolius* 'Parkteppich'
§ - 'Parkteppich'	CBlo GKir NWea SPer
- 'Pendulus'	See *C.* 'Hybridus Pendulus'
- 'Red Flare'	SPer SRPl
- 'Repens'	CBlo CCHP CChe EPfP NFor NWea SPer SRms WFar
§ - 'Rothschildianus' ♀	CBlo CTri EBee EBrP EBre ECtt ELan EMil ENot GChr GKir GOrc LBCl LBSe LBre LRHS MAsh MBBe MBar MRav SBre SEas SLim SPla WJas WMoo
- var. *rugosus* hort.	See *C. bylmoei*
- 'Scarlet Leader'	LRHS MBri
salwinensis	SLPl SRms
sandakpbuensis	SRms
saxatilis	SRms
scandinavicus	SRms
schantungensis	SRms
schlechtendalii 'Blazovice'	See *C. marginatus* 'Blazovice'
- 'Brno'	See *C. marginatus* 'Brno'
serotinus Hutchinson	CAbP EPla SLPl SRms
- misapplied	See *C. meiophyllus*
shansiensis	LRHS MBri SRms
sherriffii	SRms
sikangensis	GBin SLon SRms
simonsii ♀	CChe CDoC EBee EBrP EBre ELan GChr GKir IOrc LBCl LBSe LBre LBuc LRHS MBBe MBar MGos NBee NWea SBre SRms WDin WFar WHar
soczavianus	SRms
§ *splendens* ♀	LRHS SRms WWat
- 'Sabrina'	See *C. splendens*
staintonii	SRms
§ *sternianus* ♀	ENot EPfP GKir LRHS MBar MBri SLPl SRms WBod
- ACE 2200	EPot MNaF
suavis	SRms
subadpressus	SRms
§ x *suecicus* 'Coral Beauty'	More than 30 suppliers
§ - 'Erlinda' (v)	CEnd MBar SMad SRms

¶ - 'Ifor'	SLPl
¶ - 'Juliette'	NBlu
- 'Jürgl'	SRms
- 'Skogholm'	CTri GChr GKir LPan LRHS MBar MGos MWat NWea SIng SPer SRms WDin WHar WStI WWin
§ - 'Winter Jewel'	CBlo
talgaricus	SRms
tengyuebensis	SRms
tomentellus	SRms
tomentosus	SRms WWat
transens	SRms
tripyrenus	SRms
turbinatus	SRms
turcomanicus	SRms
veitchii	SRms
vernae	SRms
verruculosus	SRms
vestitus	SRms
villosulus	EHol SRms
vilmorinianus	SRms
wardii W. W. Smith	IOrc NBee
- hort.	See *C. mairei*
x *watereri*	CBlo CCHP CDul CLnd EBee GChr LHyr LNet LRHS MAsh MGos NWea SPla WCFE WDin WJas WWeb
- 'Avonbank'	See *C. salicifolius* 'Avonbank'
¶ - 'Coral Bunch'	MBri
- 'Cornubia'	See *C. frigidus* 'Cornubia'
- 'Goscote'	MGos
- 'John Waterer' ♀	EPfP LRHS MGos SRms WBod
- 'Pendulus'	See *C.* 'Hybridus Pendulus'
- 'Pink Champagne'	CAbP GKir LRHS MBri SPer
wilsonii	SRms
zabelii	SRms
- 'Magyar'	SRms

COTULA (Asteraceae)

atrata	See *Leptinella atrata*
- var. *dendyi*	See *Leptinella dendyi*
coronopifolia	CBen CSev CWat LPBA MSta NDea SWat SWyc WWpP
bispida	More than 30 suppliers
lineariloba	CHea CPBP ECha EWes LBee LHop LRHS
minor	See *Leptinella minor*
pectinata	See *Leptinella pectinata*
perpusilla	See *Leptinella pusilla*
'Platt's Black'	See *Leptinella squalida* 'Platt's Black'
potentilloides	See *Leptinella potentillina*
pyretbrifolia	See *Leptinella pyretbrifolia*
reptans	See *Leptinella scariosa*
rotundata	See *Leptinella rotundata*
scariosa	See *Leptinella scariosa*
sericea	See *Leptinella albida*
serrulata	See *Leptinella serrulata*
sp. C&H 452	NWCA
squalida	See *Leptinella squalida*

COTYLEDON (Crassulaceae)

chrysantha	See *Rosularia chrysantha*
gibbiflora var. *metallica*	See *Echeveria gibbiflora* var. *metallica*
oppositifolia	See *Chiastophyllum oppositifolium*
orbiculata	CStu LHil SDix
- var. *oblonga*	CTrC EBee SChr WCot
- S&SH 40	Last listed 1998
* *pomedosa*	MBri
* - 'Variegata'	MBri

simplicifolia	See *Chiastophyllum oppositifolium*
undulata	WEas

COWANIA (Rosaceae)
stanburyana	Last listed 1997

COXELLA (Apiaceae)
dieffenbachii	GCal

CRAIBIODENDRON (Ericaceae)
yunnanense	Last listed 1999

CRAMBE (Brassicaceae)
abyssinica	Last listed 1997
cordifolia ♀	More than 30 suppliers
filiformis	WCot
koktebelica	Last listed 1998
maritima	CGle CSev EBee ECGP ECha EMan EMar GKir GPoy MAvo MLLN MSal MWgw NFor NSti SPer SWat WCot WCru WHer WHoo WPer WWye
- 'Lilywhite'	CAgr ILis WCot WHer
orientalis	ECha WCot
tatarica	CAgr CArn EGar EMan NLar WPer
- HH&K 236	Last listed 1999

CRASPEDIA (Asteraceae)
globosa	Last listed 1998
lanata var. *elongata*	Last listed 1998
uniflora	Last listed 1998

CRASSULA (Crassulaceae)
anomala	SChr
arborescens	GAri SRms STre
argentea	See *C. ovata*
brachystachya	Last listed 1999
coccinea	CHEx CTrC EDAr
dejecta x *coccinea*	CHEx
falcata ♀	IBlr LHil MBri WCot
* *galanthea*	Last listed 1998
§ *helmsii*	EHon EMFW NDea WWeb
justi-corderoyi	CHal
lactea	CHal STre
lanceolata subsp. *lanceolata*	Last listed 1999
§ *milfordiae*	CTri GKir MBar MOne MWat NBir SSmi WPer
monstrosa	Last listed 1998
muscosa	STre
- 'Variegata'	Last listed 1997
natalensis	Last listed 1999
§ *ovata* ♀	CHEx CHal EBak GBin MBri NPer
- 'Basutoland'	Last listed 1999
- 'Blue Bird'	GBin LHil
* - 'Coral'	Last listed 1999
- 'Hummel's Sunset' (v) ♀	CHal
* - *nana*	STre
* - 'Riversii'	Last listed 1998
- 'Variegata'	CHal EBak
pellucida subsp. *marginalis*	CHal
* - subsp. *marginalis* 'Variegata'	CHal
peploides	Last listed 1998
perforata	CHal
- 'Variegata'	CHal
portulacea	See *C. ovata*
recurva	See *C. helmsii*
rupestris ♀	MBri
rupicola	GAri

§ *sarcocaulis*	CHEx CHal CTri ELan EOas EPot ESis GTou MHar MTho NMen NVic NWCA SIng SRms SRot SSmi STre WAbe WCot WEas WLow WPat WSHC WWin
- *alba*	CHal SHFr SIng STre WPer
- 'Ken Aslet'	SIng STre
schmidtii	CHal EDAr MBri
I - 'Desert Rose'	EDAr
¶ - 'Desert Ruby'	EDAr
sedifolia	See *C. milfordiae*
sediformis	See *C. milfordiae*
¶ *setulosa*	CTrC
socialis	CHal
tetragona	Last listed 1998
* *tomentosa* 'Variegata'	LHil
'Très Bon'	STre
vaginata	CTrF

CRATAEGUS ✿ (Rosaceae)
arnoldiana	CAgr CEnd CLnd CTho SEND SLPl
'Autumn Glory'	CBlo CEnd CLnd EBee EBrP EBre GKir LBCl LBSe LBre LRHS MBBe MGos SBre
azarolus	CAgr LEdu .
- 'White Italian' (F)	Last listed 1998
champlainensis	CTho
chungtienensis ACE 1624	SSpi
N *coccinea*	NWea
cordata	See *C. phaenopyrum*
crus-galli hort.	See *C. persimilis* 'Prunifolia'
crus-galli L.	CBlo CDoC CLnd CTho EBee GKir LBuc MAsh SPer WDin WJas WMou
- var. *pyracanthifolia*	CTho
x *durobrivensis*	CLnd CTho
ellwangeriana	Last listed 1998
eriocarpa	CLnd
flabellata	CEnd GKir SSpi
gemmosa	CEnd CTho GKir
x *grignonensis*	CB&S CDul CLnd EBee ENot GChr MAsh MCoo SPer WJas WPyg
jonesiae	EPfP
§ *laciniata*	CBlo CDul CEnd CLnd CMCN EBee EPfP GKir LRHS MAsh MBri MCoo NWea SLPl SLim SSpi WCFE WJas WMou
§ *laevigata*	WMou
- 'Coccinea Plena'	See *C. laevigata* 'Paul's Scarlet'
- 'Crimson Cloud'	CBlo CDoC CEnd CLnd EBee ELan EMui ENot EPfP GChr GKir LRHS MAsh MBri MGos MRav MWat NWea SCoo SLim SLon SPer WGor WJas WOrn WPyg
- 'Flore Pleno'	See *C. laevigata* 'Plena'
- 'Mutabilis'	CTho
§ - 'Paul's Scarlet' (d) ♀	More than 30 suppliers
- 'Pink Corkscrew'	CTho GAri MBlu
§ - 'Plena' (d)	CB&S CBlo CDoC CDul CTho EBee GChr LPan LRHS MAsh MBri MWat NWea SFam SLim SPer WDin WMou WOrn
- 'Punicea'	CBlo
- 'Rosea Flore Pleno' (d) ♀	CBlo CDoC CDul CLnd CTho EBee EBrP EBre ELan ENot EWTr GKir LBCl LBSe LBre LPan LRHS MAsh MBBe MBar MBri MGos MWat NWea SBre SPer WDin WJas WOrn WStI
x *lavalleei*	CBlo CLnd CTri EBee ENot EPfP

	GChr GKir MAsh SMHT SPer SRPl WDin WOrn
- 'Carrierei' ♀	CBlo CDoC CDul CSam CTho EPfP GKir IOrc LPan LRHS MBri NWea SRPl
x *media* 'Gireoudii' (v)	CCHH CEnd LNet MBlu MGos WMou WPat
mexicana	See *C. pubescens* f. *stipulacea*
mollis	EPfP
monogyna	CB&S CDoC CKin CLnd CSam EBrP EBre ELan ENot EPfP GChr GKir GTre LBCl LBSe LBre LBuc LHyr LRHS MBBe MBar MBri MGos NBee NWea SBre SPer SRPl WDin WMou
- 'Biflora'	CDul CEnd CTho EBee MAsh MGos NWea SLim WMou WPGP WSPU
- 'Compacta'	MBlu
- 'Ferox'	CTho
- 'Flexuosa'	LNet
- 'Pendula Rosea'	SMHT
- 'Stricta'	CDul CLnd CTho EBee ENot GKir WOrn WSpi
- 'Variegata'	CDul EBee LNet WBcn WSPU
x *mordenensis* 'Toba' (d)	CBlo CDoC CDul CLnd CTho LPan
opaca (F)	CAgr
orientalis	See *C. laciniata*
oxyacantha	See *C. laevigata*
pedicellata	CDul CLnd CTho EPfP
§ *persimilis* 'Prunifolia' ♀	More than 30 suppliers
* - 'Prunifolia Splendens'	LPan
§ *phaenopyrum*	CDul CLnd CMCN CTho EPfP SLPl SSpi WMou
pinnatifida	WWat
- var. *major*	CBlo CEnd GKir
- - 'Big Golden Star'	CTho ESim
* 'Praecox'	CBlo
prunifolia	See *C. persimilis* 'Prunifolia'
§ *pubescens* f. *stipulacea*	CMCN
punctata	SLPl
schraderiana	CLnd CTho
succulenta var. *macracantha*	Last listed 1997
tanacetifolia	CLnd CTho MBlu SSpi
wattiana	CLnd CTho

x CRATAEMESPILUS (Rosaceae)
grandiflora	CLnd CTho

CRAWFURDIA (Gentianaceae)
speciosa	Last listed 1997
- B&SWJ 2102	WCru
- HWJCM 135	WCru

CREMANTHODIUM (Asteraceae)
arnicoides	GCan

CRENULARIA See AETHIONEMA

CREPIS (Asteraceae)
aurea	EPar GAbr GGar IBlr
incana ♀	More than 30 suppliers
rubra	LRHS WCot
sibirica	Last listed 1999

CRINITARIA See ASTER

CRINODENDRON (Elaeocarpaceae)
§ *hookerianum* ♀	More than 30 suppliers
patagua	CB&S CEnd CGre CLTr CPle

	CSam EPfP GKir GQui IDee LRHS MBel MDun SLon SPer SRPl WAbe WBod WSHC

CRINUM (Amaryllidaceae)
amoenum	Last listed 1998
§ *bulbispermum*	CFil CFir ELan WCot
- 'Album'	EBee ECha EMan
capense	See *C. bulbispermum*
'Ellen Bosanquet'	CFir
moorei	CAvo CB&S CFir LBlo NRog SChr
- f. *album*	WMul
pedunculatum R.Br.	Last listed 1998
§ x *powellii* ♀	More than 30 suppliers
- 'Album' ♀	CAvo CHEx CPne ECha ELan EMan ERav ETub EWes LAma LBow LPio LRHS NPSI NRog SPar SSpi WCot WCru WPic
- 'Longifolium'	See *C. bulbispermum*
- 'Roseum'	See *C.* x *powellii*
yemense	Last listed 1998

CRIOGENES See CYPRIPEDIUM

CRITHMUM (Apiaceae)
maritimum	CArn EBee GPoy MGrG MSal NLar WWye

CROCOSMIA ✿ (Iridaceae)
'Amberglow'	CElw CGle CWes EWoo IBlr MBNS WFar WRus
aurea	CAvo CPou SIng SSpi
- hort.	See *C.* x *crocosmiiflora* 'George Davison' Davison
- var. *aurea*	GCal IBlr
- var. *maculata*	IBlr
- var. *pauciflora*	IBlr
bicolor	WHil
§ Bressingham Beacon = 'Blos'	CMHG EBee EBrP EBre IBlr LBCl LBSe LBre LRHS MBBe NHol SBre SLod SLon WBea WRHF
'Bressingham Blaze'	CMHG EBee EBrP EBre EGar GCal GKir IBlr IHdy LBCl LBSe LBre LRHS MBBe MBri NOak SBre WCot WWin
¶ 'Cadenza'	IBlr
'Carnival'	IBlr
¶ 'Chinatown'	IBlr
N 'Citronella' misapplied	See *C.* 'Honey Angels'
'Comet'	CAbx GBuc IBlr IBro MAvo WMaN WWhi
I 'Corona'	IBlr
x *crocosmiiflora*	CLTr COlW CTri EGra EPla IBlr MBel MCli NCut NOrc SPlb SWat WCHb WCot WFar WRHF WShi WWye
- 'A.J. Hogan'	IBlr
- 'Apricot Queen'	IBlr
- 'Baby Barnaby'	CAbx CBos IBlr
- 'Babylon'	CBre CBro CPou EBee IBlr LRHS MBri WFar WHil WPer WWhi
- 'Burford Bronze'	IBlr
- 'Canary Bird'	CBlo CBro CRow CSam EBee GAbr GCHN GCal GKir GMac IBlr LRHS WHil
- 'Carmin Brillant'	More than 30 suppliers
- 'Citronella' J.E. Fitt	CBro CSam EPfP GKir LRHS SCob WRha
¶ - 'Colwall'	CPou
- 'Constance'	CBre CBro CSam EBee IBlr LRHS MBri NFai WCHb WFar WWoo

- 'Corten'	IBlr
§ - 'Croesus'	CAvo EGra GBri IBlr IBro MAvo SCro WCot WHal WHil
- 'Custard Cream'	GKir IBlr IBro LRHS MBri WCot
- 'Debutante'	CMil IBlr MCLN WCot WMaN WRus WWhi
- 'Dusky Maiden'	CAvo CBos CElw CHad CHea CMHG CMil CSpe EBee ECGN GCHN IBlr LAst MCLN MMil MRav MTis NHol NPri NSti SApp SLod SPer SPla SWat WCDu WCot WMaN WRus WWoo
§ - 'E.A. Bowles'	CAbx CPou IBlr
- 'Eastern Promise'	CAbx CAvo CBre EBee GKir IBlr
- 'Elegans'	CElw IBlr
§ - 'Emily McKenzie'	More than 30 suppliers
- 'Firebrand'	IBlr MCLN WCot
- 'Flamethrower'	IBlr
§ - 'George Davison' Davison	CBre CGle CM&M CPou CRow EMan EWTr GCal IBlr LAst LEur LRHS MCCP NHol SCro WBro WCot WHil WHoo WLin WMoo
§ - 'Gerbe d'Or'	CBos CRow CSpe EBee ECGN ECGP GBri GCal GKir GMac IBlr IBro IHdy LRHS MAvo MBri NCut NHol SDys SLod SOkh SSpe SUsu WCot WFar WHil WLin WPGP WViv
- 'Gloria'	IBlr
§ - 'Golden Glory'	CSam EMar EPar IBlr LRHS STes WCot
- 'Golden Sheaf'	EGar GBri GMac IBlr SDys WBea
- 'Goldfinch'	IBlr IBro
- 'Hades'	IBlr
- 'Highlight'	IBlr
- 'His Majesty'	CBos CGle CLTr CMil CPou CRDP CRow CSam CSpe EBee EGar GKir IBlr IBro LRHS MBri NHol SAga SCro SDys WGer WMaN WPer WPrP WWhi
§ - 'Jackanapes'	More than 30 suppliers
- 'James Coey' J.E.Fitt	CFil CHad COIW CRow EBee ECha EMar GCal GMac IBlr LAma LAst LRHS MCLN NHol NOrc NRog NWCA SIng SLod SPer WFar WLin
* - 'Jesse van Dyke'	IBlr
§ - 'Jessie'	CBos CElw EBee GCal IBlr LRHS MBri WCot WHil WPer
- 'Kiatschou'	CFil EBee ECha EGar IBlr SDys SLod
- 'Lady Hamilton'	More than 30 suppliers
- 'Lady McKenzie'	See C. x crocosmiiflora 'Emily McKenzie'
- 'Lady Oxford'	CFil EBee EBrP EBre ECha EGar EMan GCal IBlr IBro LBCl LBSe LBre MBBe SBre WCot
- 'Lutea'	EBrP EBre EGar EGra IBlr LBCl LBSe LBre MBBe SBre
- 'Marjorie'	CAvo LAma WCot
- 'Mephistopheles'	IBlr
- 'Météore'	EBee GGar NCut NOrc
- 'Morning Light'	CBos IBlr
§ - 'Mrs Geoffrey Howard'	CBos CGle CPlt CSam EBee EGar GBri IBlr IBro IHdy MAvo SUsu WCot WCru WMaN WPGP WWhi
- 'Mrs Morrison'	See C. x crocosmiiflora 'Mrs Geoffrey Howard'
- 'Newry seedling'	See C. x crocosmiiflora 'Prometheus'
- 'Nimbus'	GBri IBlr WCot
§ - 'Norwich Canary'	More than 30 suppliers
- 'Polo'	EBee
- 'Princess'	See C. x crocosmiiflora 'Red Knight'
- 'Princess Alexandra'	IBlr WCHb WWoo
- 'Prolificans'	IBlr
§ - 'Prometheus'	IBlr
§ - 'Queen Alexandra' J.E. Fitt	CBos ECha EGar IBlr IBro LAma LHop SWat WHal WPer
- 'Queen Charlotte'	IBlr
- 'Queen Mary II'	EBee EMan IBlr WHil
- 'Queen of Spain'	CBos CRos EBee EBrP EBre GKir IBlr IBro LBCl LBSe LBre LRHS MBBe MLLN NCut SBre SCro SMad SUsu WCra WHil
- 'Red King'	EBee IBlr NCut
§ - 'Red Knight'	CAvo IBlr IBro WCot WHil
- 'Rheingold'	See C. x crocosmiiflora 'Golden Glory'
- 'Rose Queen'	IBlr
- 'Saracen'	EGar IBlr MAvo SSpi WCot WFar WPer
- 'Sir Matthew Wilson'	EBrP EBre EGar EGra GBri IBlr LBCl LBSe LBre MBBe SBre
- 'Solfatare' ♀	More than 30 suppliers
- 'Solfaterre Coleton Fishacre'	See C. x crocosmiiflora 'Gerbe d'Or'
- 'Star of the East'	More than 30 suppliers
§ - 'Sulphurea'	CBos CRos CRow CSam EBee EOrc GCal GGar GKir IBlr LAma LHop MBel MBri MCLN NHol SDix SIng SOkh SPer WAbe WCot WEas WHal WHil WPer WTin
- 'Sultan'	CBro CElw CGle EGar IBlr LPio WCot WFar WPGP
* - 'Tiger'	CElw IBlr
- 'Venus'	CBre CPou EBee EBrP EBre EGar EGra IBlr LBCl LBSe LBre MBBe SBre WLin
- 'Vesuvius' W. Pfitzer	CElw GCal IBlr LRHS MBri WFar
- 'Voyager'	IBlr
- 'Culzean Peach'	GCal WCot
¶ 'D.H. Houghton'	IBlr
'Darkleaf Apricot'	See C. x crocosmiiflora 'Gerbe d'Or'
¶ 'Eclatant'	IBlr
'Eldorado'	See C. x crocosmiiflora 'E.A. Bowles'
'Emberglow'	More than 30 suppliers
¶ 'Etoile de Feu'	IBlr
'Fandango'	IBlr
'Festival Orange'	NCat
* 'Feuerser'	NHol
'Fire King' misapplied	See C. x crocosmiiflora 'Jackanapes'
'Firebird'	CBlo EBrP EBre GBuc IBlr LBCl LBSe LBre LRHS MBBe MBri NHol SBre SMer WBea WCot
'Fireglow'	CCuc IBlr WPer
fucata	IBlr
- 'Jupiter'	See C. 'Jupiter'
- plicate leaf form	IBlr
* 'Fusilade'	IBlr
'George Davison' hort.	See C. x crocosmiiflora 'Golden Glory', 'Sulphurea'
Golden Fleece Lemoine	See C. x crocosmiiflora 'Gerbe d'Or'
'Golden Fleece' M. Wickenden	Last listed 1997
¶ 'Goldsprite'	IBlr
'Honey Angels'	EBee EBrP EBre EGar EMar GKir GMac LBCl LBSe LBre MAvo

		MBBe MBel MLan NChi NCut NSti NTow SBre SCro SPla SUsu WBod WBro WCot WPer
	'Jennine'	WHil
	'Jenny Bloom'	CAvo CFil EBee EBrP EBre EGar GBuc GCal GKir LBCl LBSe LBre LRHS MBBe NBir SBre WWoo
§	'Jupiter'	CAvo CBlo CBos CHar CM&M CPou EBee EFou EGar IBlr LRHS NHol WHal WLin
	'Kiaora'	IBlr
	'Lady Wilson' hort.	See C. x crocosmiiflora 'Norwich Canary'
	'Lana de Savary'	EGar IBlr WCot
	'Late Cornish'	See C. x crocosmiiflora 'Queen Alexandra' J.E. Fitt
	'Late Lucifer'	SDix
§	latifolia	IBlr
	- 'Castle Ward Late'	CBos CLAP CPou CRow EBee ECha EGar GCal IBlr MSte SDys SUsu
	- 'Vulcan' T.Smith	GKir IBlr
	'Lord Nelson'	Last listed 1997
	'Lucifer' ♀	More than 30 suppliers
¶	'Malahide Castle'	CBos
	'Mandarin'	IBlr
§	'Marcotijn'	EBee EBrP EBre EGar EMan EWoo GCal IBlr LBCl LBSe LBre MBBe MBel NCut SBre WGwG
	'Mars'	CMil EBee EGar GBuc GCal GGar IBlr IBro LRHS MBel NCut NFai NHol SPlb SUsu WCHb WCot WFar WGer WPGP WPer WWoo
§	masoniorum ♀	More than 30 suppliers
	- 'Auricorn'	IBlr
	- 'Dixter Flame'	IBlr SDix
	- 'Fern Hill'	IBlr
	- 'Flamenco'	CHad GKir IBlr IBro LRHS MBri MTed
	- 'Minotaur'	IBlr
	- red	IBlr
	- Rowallane orange	IBlr
	- 'Rowallane Yellow'	CAvo EBrP EBre GBri GCHN GKir IBlr LBCl LBSe LBre LRHS MBBe MBri NHol SBre WCot
	mathewsiana	IBlr
	aff. mathewsiana	IBlr
	'Merryman'	WRus
	'Mistral'	IBlr LRHS WCot
	'Mount Stewart'	See C. x crocosmiiflora 'Jessie'
	'Mount Usher'	CAvo EGar GCal IBlr LRHS WHil
	'Mr Bedford'	See C. x crocosmiiflora 'Croesus'
	Old Hat	See C. 'Walberton Red'
	'Orangeade'	EBee EBrP EBre GBri IBlr LBCl LBSe LBre MAvo MBBe SBre SUsu
*	'Orangerot'	NCut
§	paniculata	CAvo CB&S CElw CPou EBee EMar GAbr GGar IBlr LRHS NHol NOrc NTow SAPC SChu SIng WCot WPen WPyg WShi
	- brown/orange	IBlr
	- 'Major'	CTri
	- x masoniorum	IBlr
	'Shocking'	
¶	- x pottsii	WHil
	- red	EBrP EBre IBlr LBCl LBSe LBre MBBe SBre
*	- 'Ruby Velvet'	IBlr
	aff. paniculata	IBlr
	pearsei	IBlr
I	'Pepper'	IBlr
	'Plaisir'	IBlr MBri WFar

	pottsii	CAvo CFee CRow EGar GBin IBlr LEur SLod WFar WHil
	- CD&R 109	CBre CLAP CPou
	- 'Culzean Pink'	EBee EBrP EBre GBuc GKir IBlr LBCl LBSe LBre MBBe SBre WHil
	- deep pink	IBlr
	- 'Grandiflora'	IBlr
¶	'Rayon d'Or'	IBlr
	'Red Star'	NFai
	rosea	See Tritonia disticha subsp. rubrolucens
	'Rowden Bronze'	See C. x crocosmiiflora 'Gerbe d'Or'
	'Rowden Chrome'	See C. x crocosmiiflora 'George Davison' Davison
	'Saturn'	See C. 'Jupiter'
	'Severn Sunrise'	More than 30 suppliers
	'Short Red'	Last listed 1998
	'Sonate'	NCut NHol SPlb WPer
	'Spitfire'	More than 30 suppliers
	'Tangerine Queen'	CAbx EBrP EBre EGra IBlr LBCl LBSe LBre MBBe SBre
¶	'Vic's Yellow'	SGar SMrm SSpe
*	'Voyager'	WWoo
I	'Vulcan' A.Bloom	CMdw CMil EBrP EBre EWoo IBlr LBCl LBSe LBre LRHS MBBe SAga SBre WFar
§	'Walberton Red'	EBee IBlr SUsu
§	Walberton Yellow =	SSpi
	'Walcroy'PBR	
	'Zeal Giant'	IBlr
	'Zeal Tan'	CElw IBlr NCat WCot
	Zeal unnamed	IBlr

CROCUS ✿ (Iridaceae)

	abantensis	ERos LRHS
	adanensis	ERos
	'Advance'	CAvo CBro EPar EPot LAma NRog
§	aerius	LAma
	- 'Cambridge'	Last listed 1999
	alatavicus	EPot LRHS
	albiflorus	See C. vernus subsp. albiflorus
§	ancyrensis	CAvo CBro CMea EPar EPot ETub LAma NRog WShi
	- 'Golden Bunch'	LRHS
§	angustifolius ♀	CAvo CBro EBot EBrP EBre EPot ERos LAma LBCl LBSe LBre LRHS MBBe NRog SBre
	- 'Minor'	EPot LAma
	antalyensis	EPot
	asturicus	See C. serotinus subsp. salzmannii
	asumaniae	EPot ERos LRHS
	aureus	See C. flavus subsp. flavus
	banaticus ♀	CBro EPot ERos GCrs LAma NHol NMGW WCot
	- albus	EPot ERos
	baytopiorum	EPot ERos LRHS
	biflorus	LAma NRog
	- subsp. adamii	CLAP ERos LAma
	- subsp. alexandri	EPot ERos LAma LRHS NRog
§	- subsp. biflorus	ERos LAma
	- - MS 984/957	Last listed 1998
§	- - 'Parkinsonii'	ERos
	- subsp. crewei	ERos
	- subsp. isauricus	ERos LRHS
	- subsp. melantherus	ERos WWst
	- - S&L 226	Last listed 1998
	- 'Miss Vain'	CAvo LAma LRHS
	- var. parkinsonii	See C. biflorus subsp. biflorus 'Parkinsonii'
	- subsp. pulchricolor	LAma

- subsp. *tauri*	WWst
- subsp. *weldenii*	Last listed 1997
- - 'Albus'	ERos LAma LRHS
- - 'Fairy'	CAvo CBro EPot ERos LAma LRHS
¶ - WM 9908	MPhe
'Big Boy' (*speciosus* x *pulchellus*)	Last listed 1999
biliottii	See *C. aerius*
boryi ♀	CAvo EPot LRHS
- CE&H 582	Last listed 1998
- PJC 168	Last listed 1997
- VHH 1546	Last listed 1998
cambessedesii	CLAP ERos SBla
- PB 91	Last listed 1998
§ *cancellatus* subsp. *cancellatus*	EPot ERos LAma
- var. *cilicicus*	See *C. cancellatus* subsp. *cancellatus*
- subsp. *mazziaricus*	CNic ERos LRHS
- subsp. *pamphylicus*	ERos LRHS
candidus var. *subflavus*	See *C. olivieri* subsp. *olivieri*
§ *cartwrigbtianus* ♀	CAvo CBro LAma LRHS
N - 'Albus' ♀	CLAP EPot ERos
- CE&H 613	Last listed 1997
- S&L 484	Last listed 1998
caspius	Last listed 1998
chrysanthus ♀	Last listed 1994
- 'Ard Schenk'	LAma LRHS
- 'Aubade'	EPot
- 'Blue Bird'	CBro EPar EPot LAma LRHS
- 'Blue Giant'	Last listed 1999
- 'Blue Pearl' ♀	CAvo CBro CMea EPar EPot ETub LAma LRHS MBri NBir NRog WShi
- 'Blue Peter'	LAma
- 'Brass Band'	LAma LRHS
- 'Canary Bird'	NFor LAma LRHS
- 'Cream Beauty' ♀	CAvo CBro EBrP EBre EPar EPot ETub EWal LAma LBCl LBSe LBre LRHS MBBe MBri NBir NRog SBre
- 'Dorothy'	EPot LAma LRHS NRog
- 'E.A. Bowles' ♀	LAma
- 'E.P. Bowles'	CBro EPot LAma LRHS MBri NRog
- 'Elegance'	LAma LRHS
- 'Eye-catcher'	EPot LAma LRHS
- var. *fuscotinctus*	LAma MBri NRog WShi
- 'Gipsy Girl'	CBro EPot LAma LRHS MBri NRog
- 'Gladstone'	Last listed 1997
- 'Goldilocks'	EPot LAma LRHS
- 'Herald'	LAma LRHS
- 'Ladykiller' ♀	CBro EBrP EBre EPar EPot LAma LBCl LBSe LBre LRHS MBBe MBri NRog SBre
- 'Moonlight'	CAvo CBro ETub LAma LRHS NRog
- 'Prins Claus'	CAvo EPot LAma LRHS WShi
- 'Prinses Beatrix'	EPot LAma LRHS NRog
- 'Romance'	CAvo EPot LAma LRHS
- 'Saturnus'	EPot LAma LRHS NRog
- 'Sky Blue'	Last listed 1999
- 'Skyline'	CAvo CBro EPot GCrs LRHS
- 'Snow Bunting' ♀	CAvo CBro EPar EWal LAma LRHS NBir NRog
- 'Spring Pearl'	CBro LAma LRHS
- 'Sunkist'	Last listed 1997
- 'Uschak Orange'	Last listed 1997
- 'Warley'	CAvo NRog
- 'White Beauty'	LAma
- 'White Triumphator'	CBro EPot LAma NBir NRog
- 'Zenith'	LAma
- 'Zwanenburg Bronze' ♀	EBrP EBre EPar EPot EWal LAma LBCl LBSe LBre LRHS MBBe NRog SBre

'Cloth of Gold'	See *C. angustifolius*
clusii	See *C. serotinus* subsp. *clusii*
corsicus ♀	EPot ERos LAma
cvijicii	EPot
cyprius	Last listed 1997
dalmaticus	EPot LAma
danfordiae	ERos LRHS
'Dutch Yellow'	See *C.* x *luteus* 'Golden Yellow'
etruscus ♀	ERos
- B&S 334	Last listed 1998
* - 'Rosalind'	EPot
- 'Zwanenburg'	EPot LAma WCot
flavus	See *C. flavus* subsp. *flavus*
§ - subsp. *flavus* ♀	EPot LAma LRHS
- M&T 4578	Last listed 1998
fleischeri	EPot ERos LAma NMen
gargaricus	EPot ERos LRHS
- subsp. *herbertii*	Last listed 1997
'Golden Mammoth'	See *C.* x *luteus* 'Golden Yellow'
goulimyi ♀	CAvo CBro EPar EPot ERos LAma LRHS WCot
- 'Albus'	See *C. goulimyi* 'Mani White'
- deep colour	Last listed 1999
- var. *leucanthus*	Last listed 1999
§ - 'Mani White' ♀	CAvo
- S&L 197	Last listed 1998
'Haarlem Gem'	LAma WCot
§ *hadriaticus* ♀	CAvo CLAP EPot ERos LAma LRHS
- B&M 8039	Last listed 1997
- BM 8124	Last listed 1998
- var. *chrysobelonicus*	See *C. hadriaticus*
- f. *lilacinus*	EPot
hermoneus LB 1	Last listed 1998
hyemalis S&L 50	Last listed 1998
imperati ♀	CNic ERos
- subsp. *imperati*	Last listed 1999
- - 'De Jager'	CAvo EPot ETub LAma LRHS WCot
- - MS 965	Last listed 1998
- subsp. *suaveolens*	ERos LRHS
- - MS 962	Last listed 1998
x *jessoppiae*	ERos WWst
karducborum	CBro LAma NRog
korolkowii	EPar EPot ERos LAma LRHS
- 'Agalik'	Last listed 1997
- 'Dytiscus'	Last listed 1997
- 'Golden Nugget'	EPot
- 'Kiss of Spring'	EPot
- 'Mountain Glory'	Last listed 1997
- 'Unicoloratus'	WWst
- 'Varzob'	Last listed 1997
- 'Yellow Princess'	EPot
- 'Yellow Tiger'	Last listed 1997
kosaninii	ERos
kotschyanus ♀	EPar
- 'Albus'	LRHS SRms
- subsp. *cappadocicus* ♀	LRHS
- CM&W 2720	Last listed 1998
§ - subsp. *kotscbyanus*	CBro CLAP EPot LAma LRHS NRog WCot
- var. *leucopharynx*	ECha LRHS
laevigatus ♀	CLAP LRHS
- CE&H 612	Last listed 1998
- 'Fontenayi'	CAvo CBro EPot ETub LAma LEdu LRHS
- form	LAma
- from Crete	LRHS
'Large Yellow'	See *C.* x *luteus* 'Golden Yellow'
lazicus	See *C. scharojanii*
ligusticus	EPar
longiflorus ♀	CAvo CBro EPot ERos LRHS

– MS 968/974/967	Last listed 1999
§ x *luteus* 'Golden Yellow' ♀	EPot ETub LAma LRHS
§ – 'Stellaris'	EBot EPot ERos
malyi ♀	CAvo CLAP EPot GCrs LRHS
– CE&H 519	Last listed 1997
'Mammoth Yellow'	See *C.* x *luteus* 'Golden Yellow'
medius ♀	CBro ECha EPot ERos LAma LRHS
	NMGW NRog WCot
michelsonii	WWst
minimus	CBro CMea EPot ERos LAma
	LRHS
¶ *nevadensis*	WWst
niveus	CAvo CBro CLAP EPot ERos ETub
	LAma LRHS WCot
– blue	Last listed 1999
– PJC 164	Last listed 1997
– S&L 194	Last listed 1998
nudiflorus	CAvo CBro CLAP EPot ERos LAma
	LRHS NHol NMen
– MS 872	Last listed 1998
ochroleucus ♀	CBro EBot EBrP EBre EPot ERos
	LAma LBCl LBSe LBre LRHS MBBe
	NRog SBre
olivieri	ERos LAma
– subsp. *balansae*	Last listed 1997
– – 'Zwanenburg'	EPot
– subsp. *istanbulensis*	EPot
§ – subsp. *olivieri*	LAma LRHS
oreocreticus	Last listed 1999
– PB 137	Last listed 1998
pallasii	Last listed 1999
– subsp. *pallasii*	ERos
pelistericus	EPot
pestalozzae	EPot ERos
– var. *caeruleus*	EPot ERos
pulchellus ♀	EPot ERos GCrs LAma MMal
	WCot
– *albus*	Last listed 1999
– CE&H 558	Last listed 1997
– M&T 4584	Last listed 1998
'Purpureus'	See *C. vernus* 'Purpureus
	Grandiflorus'
reticulatus	CLAP
– subsp. *reticulatus*	EPot
robertianus ♀	LRHS
rujanensis	Last listed 1997
salzmannii	See *C. serotinus* subsp.
	salzmannii
sativus	CArn CAvo CBod CBro ELan
	EOHP EPar EPot ETub GPoy GVer
	LAma LRHS MBri MSal NBir NRog
– var. *cartwrightianus*	See *C. cartwrightianus*
– var. *cashmirianus*	Last listed 1999
scardicus	EPot
scepusiensis	See *C. vernus* subsp. *vernus* var.
	scepusiensis
§ *scharojanii*	EPot
– var. *flavus*	Last listed 1997
§ *serotinus* subsp. *clusii* ♀	CBro EPot LAma
§ – subsp. *salzmannii*	CBro EPar EPot ERos LAma LRHS
– – AB&S 4326	Last listed 1998
– – 'Albus'	Last listed 1997
– – MS 343	Last listed 1998
– – S&F 218	Last listed 1998
sibiricus	See *C. sieberi*
§ *sieberi* ♀	EPot ERos
§ – 'Albus' ♀	CAvo CBro EPot LAma LRHS WLin
– subsp. *atticus*	EPot LAma LRHS
– 'Bowles' White'	See *C. sieberi* 'Albus'
– 'Firefly'	CBro EPot LAma LRHS NRog
– 'Hubert Edelsten' ♀	EPot ERos LAma
– f. *pallidus*	Last listed 1998

– subsp. *sublimis*	CAvo CBro EPot ERos ETub GCrs
'Tricolor' ♀	LAma LRHS NMen WCot
– 'Violet Queen'	CBro LAma LRHS MBri NRog
¶ *siebeanus*	WWst
sp. WM 9803 from	Last listed 1999
Slovenia	
sp. WM 9809 from Bosnia	MPhe
speciosus ♀	CAvo CBro EBrP EBre EPar ETub
	GCHN LAma LBCl LBSe LBre
	LRHS MBBe NMGW NRog SBre
	WHoo WShi
– 'Aitchisonii'	CBro LAma LRHS
– 'Albus' ♀	CBro CMea ECha EPar EPot LRHS
– 'Artabir'	CBro EPot LRHS
– 'Cassiope'	EPot LAma LRHS
– 'Conqueror'	CBro ETub LAma LRHS
– subsp. *ilgazensis*	EPot
– 'Oxonian'	EMon EPar EPot LAma LRHS
x *stellaris*	See *C.* x *luteus* 'Stellaris'
susianus	See *C. angustifolius*
suterianus	See *C. olivieri* subsp. *olivieri*
thomasii B&S 364	Last listed 1998
– MS 978/982	Last listed 1998
tommasinianus ♀	CAvo CBro EPar EPot ETub LAma
	MBri MRav NMGW WShi
– f. *albus*	CBro EPot LAma LRHS
– 'Barr's Purple'	LAma LRHS
– 'Bobbo'	Last listed 1999
– 'Eric Smith'	CLAP
– 'Lilac Beauty'	EPot LAma
– PF 6584	Last listed 1998
– var. *pictus*	LAma LRHS
– purple tips	Last listed 1997
– var. *roseus*	CBro CLAP EPot LAma NMGW
– 'Ruby Giant'	CAvo CBro CNic EPar EPot ETub
	LAma LRHS NMGW NRog WShi
– 'Whitewell Purple'	CAvo CBro EPot LAma LRHS MBri
	NMGW NRog
tournefortii ♀	CAvo CBro CLAP EPot ERos LAma
	LRHS
vallicola	Last listed 1999
veluchensis	EPot
– JCA 354.002	CLAP
veneris PB 198	Last listed 1998
§ *vernus* subsp. *albiflorus*	EPot ERos LAma
– 'Enchantress'	EPot LAma
– 'Flower Record'	EPot NBir
– 'Graecus'	EPot ERos
– 'Grand Maître'	LAma NRog
– 'Jeanne d'Arc'	CBro EPot ETub LAma NBir NRog
– 'King of the Blues'	NRog
– 'Paulus Potter'	NRog
– 'Peter Pan'	NRog
– 'Pickwick'	EPot ETub LAma NBir NRog
§ – 'Purpureus Grandiflorus'	CBro EPot LAma NRog
– 'Queen of the Blues'	CBro EPot NRog
– 'Remembrance'	EPot ETub LAma NBir NRog
– 'Sky Blue'	NRog
– 'Snowstorm'	LAma
– 'Striped Beauty'	LAma NRog
– 'Vanguard'	CBro EPot ETub LAma NRog
– subsp. *vernus* 'Grandiflorus'	
	See *C. vernus* 'Purpureus
	Grandiflorus'
§ – – Heuffelianus Group	EPot WWst
* – – *napolitanus*	ERos
§ – – var. *scepusiensis*	EPot ERos
– – 'Victor Hugo'	NRog
– WM 9615 from	Last listed 1998
E Slovenia	
versicolor	Last listed 1999
– 'Picturatus'	CAvo EBrP EBre EPot ERos ETub

	LAma LBCl LBSe LBre LRHS MBBe SBre
'Yellow Mammoth'	See C. x luteus 'Golden Yellow'
'Zephyr' ♀	CBro EPot ERos ETub ITim LAma LRHS
zonatus	See C. kotschyanus subsp. kotschyanus

CROSSANDRA (Acanthaceae)
| infundibuliformis | MBri |

CROTALARIA (Papilionaceae)
| capensis | Last listed 1997 |
| cunninghamii | Last listed 1998 |

CROWEA (Rutaceae)
| exalata x saligna | CPLG |

CRUCIANELLA (Rubiaceae)
| stylosa | See Phuopsis stylosa |

CRUCIATA (Rubiaceae)
| § laevipes | CKin EWFC NMir WGwy |

CRYPTANTHUS (Bromeliaceae)
bivittatus ♀	CHal
- 'Pink Starlight' (v) ♀	MBri
- 'Roseus Pictus'	CHal
bromelioides	MBri
- var. tricolor (v) ♀	Last listed 1990
fosterianus ♀	Last listed 1992
'It' (v) ♀	Last listed 1992
* 'Red Starlight' (v)	MBri
x roseus 'Le Rey'	MBri
- 'Marian Oppenheimer'	MBri
zonatus ♀	Last listed 1992

CRYPTOCARYA (Lauraceae)
| alba | CGre |

CRYPTOGRAMMA (Adiantaceae)
| ¶ acrostichoides | EFer |
| crispa | CCuc SRms WHer |

CRYPTOMERIA (Taxodiaceae)
fortunei	See C. japonica var. sinensis
japonica ♀	CDul GAri IOrc ISea LCon STre WFro WNor WPGP
- Araucarioides Group	EHul
- 'Aritaki'	Last listed 1997
- 'Bandai-sugi' ♀	CBlo CDoC CKen CMac EHul EOrn ESis LCon LLin MBar MGos MOne NDlv SLim STre WStI
- 'Barabits Gold'	MGos
- 'Compressa'	CBlo CDoC CKen CNic CSli EHul EPfP ESis LBee LCon LLin LRHS MBar MBri MGos MOne SLim SPer SSmi WGwG WLRN
§ - 'Cristata'	CDoC CMac ELan EOrn LCon LLin MBar SLon WWeb
* - 'Cristata Compacta'	EOrn
- Elegans Group	CB&S CBrm CDoC CHig CMac CTri EHul ELan ENot EOrn GChr GKir IOrc LCon LLin LNet LPan MBar MGos MWat SBod SLim SPer WDin WFar WPyg WWin
- 'Elegans Aurea'	CB&S CBlo CDoC CSli CTri EHul LCon LLin MBar MBri SBod SRms STre WDin WPyg WTro
- 'Elegans Compacta' ♀	CBlo CCmP CDoC CSli EHul EOrn IMGH LBee LCon LRHS MBNS MBar MBri SLim WWeb

- 'Elegans Nana'	CBlo LBee LRHS NFla SLim SPer SRms
- 'Elegans Viridis'	CBlo SLim
- 'Globosa'	CDoC EOrn SRms
- 'Globosa Nana' ♀	EHul ERom LBee LCon LLin LPan LRHS MBar NDlv SLim WGor
- 'Golden Promise'	EOrn MAsh SLim WGor
- 'Jindai-sugi'	CMac MBar NDlv
- 'Kilmacurragh'	CKen EHul MBar NWea SLim
- 'Knaptonensis' (v)	LLin
- 'Kohui Yatsubusa'	CKen
* - 'Konijn Yatsubusa'	CKen
- 'Koshiji-yatsubusa'	EOrn LCon MBar MBri
- 'Koshyi'	CKen
- 'Little Diamond'	CKen
- 'Littleworth Dwarf'	See C. japonica 'Littleworth Gnom'
§ - 'Littleworth Gnom'	LCon
- 'Lobbii Nana' hort.	See C. japonica 'Nana'
§ - 'Mankichi-sugi'	CBlo
- 'Monstrosa'	MBar
- 'Monstrosa Nana'	See C. japonica 'Mankichi-sugi'
§ - 'Nana'	CDoC CMac CTri EBrP EBre EGra EHul EOrn EPfP LBCl LBSe LBre LLin LRHS MBBe SBod SBre WLRN
¶ - 'Pipo'	CKen
- 'Pygmaea'	CBlo LCon MBar MGos SRms
- 'Rasen-sugi'	COtt GAri LCon SLim SMad
- 'Sekkan-sugi'	CB&S CBlo CSli EBrP EBre EHul EOrn EPla GAri LBCl LBSe LBee LBre LCon LLin LRHS MAsh MBBe MBar MBri MGos SAga SBre SLim SMad WPyg
- 'Sekka-sugi'	See C. japonica 'Cristata'
§ - var. sinensis	CMCN NOGN
* - - 'Vilmoriniana Compacta'	EOrn
§ - 'Spiralis'	CDoC CGre CKen CMac EHul EOrn EPfP IOrc LBee LCon LLin LRHS MBar SLim SPer SSmi WFar WWeb
§ - 'Spiraliter Falcata'	CBlo CDoC MBar
§ - 'Tansu'	CBlo EHul EOrn LCon LLin MBar NHol SLim WFar
- 'Tenzan-sugi'	CKen SOkd
- 'Tilford Cream'	MAsh
- 'Tilford Gold'	EGra EHul EOrn GPin LLin MBar MGos NDlv NHol WBcn
- 'Vilmorin Gold'	CKen EOrn MBri
- 'Vilmorin Variegated'	Last listed 1997
- 'Vilmoriniana' ♀	More than 30 suppliers
- 'Viminalis'	NHol
- 'Winter Bronze'	CKen
- 'Yatsubusa'	See C. japonica 'Tansu'
- 'Yore-sugi'	See C. japonica 'Spiralis', 'Spiraliter Falcata'
- 'Yoshino'	CKen
sinensis	See C. japonica var. sinensis

CRYPTOTAENIA (Apiaceae)
canadensis	MRav
japonica	CPou LFis MHer WHer WJek
- f. atropurpurea	CGle CLTr CPla EBee ECha ECoo EHoe EMan EMar EMon GCal GGar LRHS LSpr MNrw SUsu WCHb WCot WCru WEas WFar

CTENANTHE (Marantaceae)
§ amabilis ♀	CHal MBri
* 'Greystar'	MBri
lubbersiana ♀	CHal LRHS MBri

§ *oppenheimiana* LRHS MBri
- 'Tricolor' ♀ Last listed 1990
setosa MBri
'Stripe Star' MBri

CTENIUM (Poaceae)
concinnum Last listed 1999

CUCUBALUS (Caryophyllaceae)
baccifer MNrw

CUCUMIS (Cucurbitaceae)
metulifer (F) Last listed 1998

CUCURBITA (Cucurbitaceae)
'Cerrano' Last listed 1998
ficifolia Last listed 1998

CUDRANIA (Moraceae)
tricuspidata LEdu

CUMINUM (Apiaceae)
cyminum CArn SIde WGwG

CUNILA (Lamiaceae)
origanoides EOHP

CUNNINGHAMIA (Taxodiaceae)
konishii Last listed 1999
§ *lanceolata* CB&S CDoC CGre CMCN LCon
LLin MDun SLim SMad SSta STre
WNor WPGP
§ - 'Bánó' SLim
- 'Compacta' See *C. lanceolata* 'Bánó'
* - 'Coolwijn's Compact' CKen
- 'Glauca' SLim
- 'Little Leo' CKen
- Og 91.1101 Last listed 1997
sinensis See *C. lanceolata*
unicaniculata See *C. lanceolata*

CUNONIA (Cunoniaceae)
capensis CTrC

CUPHEA (Lythraceae)
caeciliae CHal CLTr
cyanaea CMHG CSev LHil MLLN SAga
SDix SOWG SSte SVen
birtella CMHG EBee LHil LHop SDys
SOWG
byssopifolia ♀ CFee CHal CPle CTre GQui MBri
SAga SBrw SOWG SRms STre
- 'Alba' CLTr LIck MLan NPri SAga SOWG
STre
- 'Riverdene Gold' CHal CLTr EMan
- 'Rob's Mauve' Last listed 1999
- 'Rosea' LIck NPri
§ *ignea* ♀ CHal CLTr ELan MBri NPri SOWG
SRms
- 'Variegata' CHal EBee LHil SLod SOWG
lanceolata Last listed 1999
llavea See *C. x purpurea*
macrophylla Last listed 1999
¶ *melvilla* ERea
miniata hort. See *C. x purpurea*
platycentra See *C. ignea*
§ x *purpurea* WWol
violacea Last listed 1998

x CUPRESSOCYPARIS ✿ (Cupressaceae)
§ *leylandii* More than 30 suppliers
§ - 'Castlewellan' More than 30 suppliers

- 'Galway Gold' See x *C. leylandii* 'Castlewellan'
- 'Golconda'PBR Last listed 1997
- 'Gold Rider' ♀ CDoC EHul IOrc LBee LPan MAsh
MBar MBri MGos NMoo SLim
SPer WHar WLRN
- 'Haggerston Grey' ♀ Last listed 1992
§ - 'Harlequin' (v) CMHG LCon MBar SLim WHar
WWeb
- 'Herculea' CDoC LPan MGos WWeb
- 'Hyde Hall' CTri EOrn EPla ESis LBee SBod
WLRN
- 'Leighton Green' GChr
* - 'Medownia' Last listed 1998
- 'Michellii' Last listed 1997
- 'Naylor's Blue' CMac SEND
- 'New Ornament' Last listed 1997
- 'Olive's Green' CDoC COtt EHul IOrc LCon LPan
SCoo WHar
- 'Robinson's Gold' ♀ CDul CMac EHul GAri GQui LBee
LCon MBar NWea SBod SLim
WFar WHar WStI
- 'Silver Dust' (v) MBri NEgg SRms WFar
- 'Variegata' See x *C. leylandii* 'Harlequin'
¶ - 'Winter Sun' WCFE
notabilis ♀ WCwm
ovensii EHul WCwm

CUPRESSUS (Cupressaceae)
arizonica var. *arizonica* Last listed 1999
- - 'Arctic' CBlo LRHS MAsh MBri
- 'Conica Glauca' ENot LHyr MBar
- var. *glabra* 'Aurea' CBlo ECho EHul LCon LPan MAsh
MBar SLim SPer WGer
- - 'Blue Ice' CB&S CBlo CDoC CMHG EHul
EOrn LCon LLin LRHS MAsh MBar
MBri MGos SLim SPer WGer
WLRN
- - 'Compacta' CKen
- - 'Conica' CKen NBlu SBod WWat
I - - 'Fastigiata' CB&S EHul LCon LPan MBar
* - - 'Lutea' EOrn
- 'Pyramidalis' ♀ CBlo CMac EPfP LRHS MAsh
WCwm
I - 'Sulfurea' CKen
bakeri CMHG
cashmeriana ♀ CB&S CHEx ERea LCon LPan
SLim SPer WNor
chengiana Last listed 1997
duclouxiana CMHG
dupreziana WCwm
§ *funebris* CMCN
¶ *gigantea* KR 3353 CDoC
glabra 'Arctic' See *C. arizonica* var. *arizonica*
'Arctic'
goveniana GAri MBar
- var. *abramsiana* WCwm
guadalupensis CMHG
lusitanica WCwm
- var. *benthamii* WCwm
'Knightiana'
- 'Brice's Weeping' CKen
- 'Glauca Pendula' CBlo CKen EPfP LCon MAsh MBri
WCwm
- 'Pygmy' CKen
macrocarpa CDoC CHEx EHul GChr SEND
- 'Barnham Gold' SBod SRms
- 'Compacta' CKen
- 'Donard Gold' ♀ CMac EOrn MBar
- 'Gold Spread' ♀ CDoC ECho EHul EOrn LBee
LCon LLin LRHS SLim WBcn
WGer
- 'Goldcrest' ♀ CB&S CDoC CMac EHul ENot

	EOrn IOrc LBee LCon LLin LPan
	LRHS MBar MBri MGos SBod SLim
	SPer WAbe WCFE WDin WFar
	WPyg
- 'Golden Cone'	CKen CMac ECho LRHS
- 'Golden Pillar'	CBlo CDoC CMac EHul EOrn
	LBee LCon LLin LRHS MAsh MBar
	MBri MWat SLim SPer WDin WGer
	WLRN WPyg WWeb
- 'Greenstead Magnificent'	MAsh SLim
- 'Horizontalis Aurea'	CTri EHul MBar WBcn
- 'Lohbrunner'	CKen
- 'Lutea'	CB&S CDoC CMac ECho
- 'Pygmaea'	CKen
- 'Sulphur Cushion'	CKen
- 'Wilma'	EHul EOrn LBee LCon LRHS
	MGos SCoo WBcn WWeb
- 'Woking'	CKen
sempervirens	CB&S CMCN CTho EHul ERom
	GChr LEdu LHyr LLin
- 'Garda'	CDoC
- 'Green Pencil'	CKen EPfP LRHS WWat
- 'Pyramidalis'	See *C. sempervirens* Stricta Group
- var. *sempervirens*	See *C. sempervirens* Stricta Group
§ - Stricta Group ♀	CArn CMCN CSWP EHul EPfP
	GAri GVer LCon LLin LPan LRHS
	SAPC SArc WCFE
- 'Swane's Gold' ♀	CDoC CKen CMHG EHul EOrn
	EPfP LBee LCon LLin MAsh SLim
- 'Totem Pole'	CBlo CDoC CKen EHul EOrn EPfP
	LLin MAsh SEND SLim WBcn
	WGor

CURCUMA (Zingiberaceae)

amada	GPoy
aromatica	GPoy
¶ *australasica*	LEur
elata	EOas
longa	ELau GPoy
¶ 'Maroon Beauty'	LEur
petiolata	EOas WMul
¶ - variegated (v)	WMul
zedoaria	GPoy LAma LRHS WMul

CURTONUS See CROCOSMIA

CUSSONIA (Araliaceae)

paniculata	WMul
spicata	WMul

CYANANTHUS (Campanulaceae)

§ *chungdienensis*	Last listed 1998
delavayi	WCru
- ACE 2449	Last listed 1999
incanus	Last listed 1997
inflatus	Last listed 1998
integer hort.	See *C. microphyllus*
integer Wallich	Last listed 1997
- 'Sherriff's Variety'	GDra NHar WCot WLin
lobatus ♀	CPla GBuc IMGH SBla
- 'Albus'	EPot EWes SBla WAbe
- 'Dark Beauty'	WCot
- dark	EWes GDra WAbe
- giant	EPot GCrs GDra GTou MNaF SBla
	WAbe
- var. *insignis*	Last listed 1997
- x *microphyllus*	EPot NWCA WAbe
longiflorus ACE 1963	Last listed 1997
macrocalyx	WAbe
§ *microphyllus* ♀	CPla EPot GDra GMaP NSla SBla
	WAbe
sherriffii	WAbe

sp. ACE 1813	WCot
spathulifolius	Last listed 1997
- CLD 1492	Last listed 1997
I *zhongdienensis*	See *C. chungdienensis*

CYANELLA (Tecophilaeaceae)

orchidiformis	LBow

CYANOTIS (Commelinaceae)

somaliensis ♀	CHal

CYATHEA (Cyatheaceae)

albifrons	Last listed 1997
* *atrox*	WRic
australis	EOas GQui LPal WMul WRic
brownii	EOas WMul WRic
celebica	Last listed 1997
cooperi	CB&S EOas LJus WMul WRic
* - 'Brentwood'	Last listed 1999
¶ - 'Revolutum'	WRic
cunninghamii	WRic
dealbata	CAbb CB&S CBrP CTrC GQui
	LJus LPal WMul WRic
dregei	EOas EPVP WMul WRic
incisoserrata	WMul WRic
intermedia	Last listed 1997
lepifera	LPal
lunulata	WRic
* 'Marleyi'	WRic
medullaris	CAbb CB&S CTrC EOas LBlo LJus
	WMul WRic
¶ *milnei*	LPal WRic
rebeccae	Last listed 1997
robertsiana	Last listed 1997
smithii	CAbb CTrC LJus WMul WRic
¶ sp. from New Guinea	WRic
¶ *spinulosa*	WRic
tomentosissima	CBrP WMul WRic
woollsiana	Last listed 1997

CYATHODES (Epacridaceae)

§ *colensoi*	EPot MBar MBri MGos NHar NHol
	SBrw SLon SPer SSpi WAbe WBod
	WPat WWat
empetrifolia	EPot
fasciculata	See *Leucopogon fasciculatus*
fraseri	See *Leucopogon fraseri*
juniperina	ECou SReu
§ *parviflora*	ECou
parvifolia	ECou

CYBISTETES (Amaryllidaceae)

longifolia	Last listed 1998

CYCAS (Cycadaceae)

cairnsiana	Last listed 1997
circinalis	CRoM LPal
kennedyana	See *C. papuana*
media	CRoM LPal
panzihihuaensis	CRoM LPal
§ *papuana*	Last listed 1997
revoluta ♀	CAbb CB&S CBrP CHEx CRoM
	CTrC EPVP EPfP LCns LPal LPan
	LRHS MBri MWst NMoo SAPC
	SArc SEND SPar WMul WNor
- x *taitungensis*	CBrP
§ *rumphii*	CBrP LPal LRHS
siamensis	LPal
simplicipinna	LPal
taitungensis	CBrP LPal
thouarsii	See *C. rumphii*

CYCLAMEN ✿ (Primulaceae)

africanum	CBro CElm CLCN EBee EBrP EBre EJWh EPot ITim LAma LBCl LBSe LBre LRHS MAsh MBBe SBre STil WAbe WIvy
balearicum	CBro CElm CLCN EBrP EBre EJWh EPot LAma LBCl LBSe LBre LRHS MAsh MBBe SBre STil
cilicium ♀	More than 30 suppliers
- f. *album*	CAvo CBro CElm CLCN EBrP EBre EJWh GCrs LAma LBCl LBSe LBre LCTD LRHS MAsh MBBe SBre STil WCot
§ *coum* ♀	More than 30 suppliers
- var. *abchasicum*	See *C. coum* subsp. *caucasicum*
* - Blanchard's form pink-flowered	Last listed 1998
- 'Broadleigh Silver'	LCTD
- BS 8927	Last listed 1997
- BSBE	CPBP STil
§ - subsp. *caucasicum*	EPot ERos GCrs LAma SSpi STil
- subsp. *coum*	CBro
- - f. *albissimum*	LCTD
- - - 'Golan Heights'	STil
- - 'Atkinsii'	CBro MBro
- - f. *coum* 'Crimson King'	SDeJ
- - - 'Dusky Maid'	LCTD
- - - 'Linnett Jewel'	LCTD
- - - 'Linnett Rose'	LCTD
- - - Nymans Group	EPot LCTD MAsh SBla
- - - Pewter Group ♀	CMil CPBP ERos MAsh MTho NPar SSpi WIvy WPyg
- - - - bicoloured	EJWh
- - - - 'Blush'	STil
- - - - 'Maurice Dryden'	CAvo CBro CGle CPBP GBuc GCrs LAma LCTD LRHS MAsh SSpi STil WAbe WIvy
- - - - red	CLCN LAma LCTD WPat
- - - - 'Tilebarn Elizabeth'	MAsh STil
- - - - white	Last listed 1997
- - - plain-leaved red	STil
- - - 'Roseum'	CAvo CBel CElm GBuc LAma LBow SDeJ STil SUsu
- - - Silver Group	CBro LRHS NSla SSpi WAbe
- - - - bicolor	CElm LCTD
- - - - 'Heavy Metal'	LCTD
- - - - red	CAvo EBrP EBre EPot LBCl LBSe LBre MBBe MTho NHar SBre STil WHoo
- - - - 'Silver Star'	LCTD
- - - - 'Sterling Silver'	LCTD
- - - 'Turkish Princess'	Last listed 1998
- - - 'Urfa'	EPot
¶ - - f. *pallidum*	GCrs
- - - 'Album'	CAvo CBot CElm EPot ERos ITim LAma MAsh NHol SDeJ SIng STil WAbe WHoo WNor WPat
- - - 'Marbled Moon'	LCTD STil
- dark pink	CAvo EDAr
- subsp. *elegans*	STil
- forms	CLyd EDAr GKir LAma LCTD MBro MS&S WWat
- M&T 4051	Last listed 1998
- marbled leaf	EDAr WHoo
- 'Meaden's Crimson'	EPot LCTD
* - *merymana*	CElm
- plain-leaved	CElm EPot LCTD WAbe
- red	EDAr GKir
- scented	CElm
- TK form	ERos
creticum	CBro CLCN EJWh LAma MAsh STil

- x *repandum*	See *C.* x *meiklei*
cyprium	CAvo CBro CElm CLCN EBrP EBre EJWh EPot LAma LBCl LBSe LBre LRHS MAsh MBBe NSla SBla SBre STil WIvy
- 'E.S.'	CElm LCTD MAsh STil
europaeum	See *C. purpurascens*
fatrense	See *C. purpurascens* subsp. *purpurascens* from Fatra, Slovakia
graecum	CBro CElm CFil CLCN CStu EJWh EPot ESis LAma LRHS MAsh SSpi STil WIvy
- f. *album*	CAvo CBro CElm EJWh LAma LRHS MAsh STil
- subsp. *anatolicum*	STil
§ *hederifolium* ♀	More than 30 suppliers
- x *africanum*	Last listed 1999
- arrow-head form	Last listed 1997
- var. *confusum*	MAsh STil
- forms	CElm EDAr LAma LCTD MS&S
- var. *hederifolium*	More than 30 suppliers
f. *albiflorum*	
- - - Bowles' Apollo Group	CLCN CMil LCTD
§ - - - - 'Artemis'	STil
- - - - 'White Bowles' Apollo'	See *C. hederifolium* var. *hederifolium* f. *albiflorum* (Bowles' Apollo Group) 'Artemis'
- - - 'Coquette'	Last listed 1999
- - - 'Cotswold White'	Last listed 1999
- - - 'Nettleton Silver'	See *C. hederifolium* var. *hederifolium* f. *albiflorum* 'White Cloud'
- - - 'Perlenteppich'	EDAr GMaP LCTD
§ - - - - 'White Cloud'	CElm EPot MAsh STil WIvy
- - f. *hederifolium*	CElm CLAP ITim LCTD MAsh SBla
Bowles' Apollo Group	SSpi STil
- - - 'Fairy Rings'	LCTD MAsh
- - - 'Green Elf'	Last listed 1997
- - - red	WPyg
- - - 'Rosenteppich'	EDAr GBuc GMaP LCTD
- - - 'Ruby Glow'	LCTD MAsh WCot
- - - 'Silver Cloud'	CBel CBro CLAP CLCN LCTD MAsh SSpi STil WAbe WCot WIvy
- - - 'Silver Shield'	LCTD
- - - 'Stargazer'	Last listed 1999
- 'San Marino Silver'	LCTD
- scented	CLCN STil
- silver-leaved	CAvo CElm CMil EPot LCTD LRHS MAsh STil SUsu
x *hildebrandii*	WIvy
ibericum	See *C. coum* subsp. *caucasicum*
intaminatum	CAvo CBro CLCN CSWP EJWh EPot ERos LAma LRHS MAsh NMen NSla NTow SBla STil WAbe WIvy
- EKB 628a	EPot
- patterned-leaved	CElm EJWh LCTD STil
- pink	STil
- plain-leaved	CElm STil
latifolium	See *C. persicum*
libanoticum ♀	CAvo CBro CElm CLCN EBrP EBre EJWh EPot ERos LAma LBCl LBSe LBre LCTD LRHS MAsh MBBe NMen SBla SBre SIng STil WCot
§ x *meiklei*	CBro
mirabile ♀	CAvo CBro CLCN EBrP EBre EJWh EPot GCrs LAma LBCl LBSe LBre LRHS MAsh MBBe NMen SBla SBre SIng STil WAbe WIvy
- silver-leaved	CElm
- 'Tilebarn Anne'	STil

- 'Tilebarn Jan' — STil
- 'Tilebarn Nicholas' — MAsh STil
neapolitanum — See *C. hederifolium*
orbiculatum — See *C. coum*
parviflorum — EJWh EPot LAma MAsh NMen STil
peloponnesiacum — See *C. repandum* subsp. *peloponnesiacum*
§ **persicum** — CBro CElm CFil CLCN CPBP EJWh LAma LRHS MAsh NMen STil
- CSE 90560 — STil
¶ - var. **persicum** f. **puniceum** from Lebanon — STil
- - - 'Tilebarn Karpathos' — STil
- RRL N8/65 — Last listed 1998
- S&L 55 — Last listed 1998
pseudibericum ♀ — CAvo CBro CLCN EBrP EBre EJWh EPot LAma LBCl LBSe LBre LCTD LRHS MAsh MBBe SBla SBre SIng STil WIvy
- 'Roseum' — CLCN LCTD MAsh STil
- scented form — Last listed 1997
§ **purpurascens** ♀ — CBro CElm CFil CLCN CMea EBrP EBre EJWh LAma LBCl LBSe LBre LRHS MAsh MBBe MBro MS&S NMen SBla SBre SIng SSpi STil WHoo WIvy WPat
- f. **album** — SBla
- var. **fatrense** — See *C. purpurascens* subsp. *purpurascens* from Fatra, Slovakia
- form — Last listed 1997
- 'Lake Garda' — CFil MAsh SSpi WPGP
§ - subsp. **purpurascens** from Fatra, Slovakia — GCrs STil
- silver-leaved — LCTD
- silver-leaved from Limone, Italy — SBla SSpi
repandum — CAvo CBro CElm CFil CLCN EBrP EBre EJWh ERos LAma LBCl LBSe LBre LCTD LRHS MAsh MBBe SBla SBre SIng SSpi STil WHer
- JCA 5157 — SSpi
§ - subsp. **peloponnesiacum** ♀ — EJWh MAsh
I - - f. **albiflorum** — STil
§ - - var. **peloponnesiacum** — CBro CElm CLCN LCTD SSpi STil
- - var. **vividum** — STil
- 'Pelops' misapplied — See *C. repandum* subsp. *peloponnesiacum* var. *peloponnesiacum*
- subsp. **repandum** f. **album** — CLCN EJWh MAsh SBla STil
- subsp. **rhodense** — CLCN LAma LCTD MAsh SSpi STil
- WM 9709 — Last listed 1999
roblfsianum — CBro CElm CFil CLCN EJWh LRHS MAsh STil
x **saundersii** — CLCN EJWh STil
'Super Puppet' — Last listed 1997
trochopteranthum — CAvo CBro CElm CLCN EJWh EPot GKir LAma LRHS MAsh NRog SBla SIng STil WAbe WIvy
- 'Pink Swirl' — Last listed 1997
- 'Red Devil' — Last listed 1997
x **wellensiekii** — STil

CYCLANTHERA (Cucurbitaceae)
pedata — Last listed 1999

CYDISTA (Bignoniaceae)
aequinoctialis — CPlN

CYDONIA ✿ (Rosaceae)
japonica — See *Chaenomeles speciosa*
oblonga (F) — Last listed 1999
- 'Bereczcki' — See *C. oblonga* 'Vranja'
- 'Champion' (F) — SKee WJas
- 'Early Prolific' — Last listed 1997
- 'Isfahan' — SKee
- 'Le Bourgeaut' (F) — Last listed 1999
* - 'Lescovacz' — MGos WJas
- 'Ludovic' — WJas
- 'Lusitanica' — See *C. oblonga* Portugal = 'Lusitanica'
- 'Meech's Prolific' (F) — CSam CTho EMui ERea ESim GKir GTwe LRHS MBlu MWat SDea SFam SKee SPer
- pear-shaped — CBlo CTri NRog
§ - Portugal = 'Lusitanica' (F) — CBlo GTwe NRog SKee WJas
- 'Seibosa' (F) — SKee
- 'Shams' — SKee
§ - 'Vranja' (F) ♀ — CDoC CEnd CMac CTho EBee EBrP EBre EMui ERea EWTr GTwe LBCl LBSe LBre LBuc LEdu LRHS MBBe MBri MGos NRog SBre SDea SFam SKee SPer WDin WJas WMou

CYMBALARIA (Scrophulariaceae)
aequitriloba — Last listed 1997
- 'Alba' — GGar
§ **hepaticifolia** — EDAr LBee LRHS NNrd WCru WPer
- 'Alba' — CNic
§ **muralis** — CKin EWFC EWTr GAbr MBar MHer MWat NMir NPri WGor WHer
- 'Albiflora' — See *C. muralis* 'Pallidior'
§ - 'Globosa Alba' — CHal EDAr EPot MDHE
- 'Globosa Rosea' — Last listed 1999
¶ - 'Kenilworth White' — WGwG
¶ - 'Len's Favourite' — MGas
- 'Nana Alba' — GAbr MDHE MLan NNrd NPri NWCA WPer
§ - 'Pallidior' — CMea ESis MBar MHar NHar NVic WWin
- 'Rosea' — WFar
§ **pallida** — CMea LBee LRHS NHar NSla SBla SPlb WByw WCru WFar WPer
- 'Alba' — LBee
§ **pilosa** — ECtt EMNN GAbr NNrd NSti WLRN
- 'Alba' — Last listed 1998

CYMBIDIUM ✿ (Orchidaceae)
ensifolium 'Kwanyin Susin' — Last listed 1999
- var. **rubrigemmum** — Last listed 1999
- 'Tehku Susin' — Last listed 1999
goeringii — Last listed 1999
- 'Chun Chien' — Last listed 1999
* - var. **formosanum** — Last listed 1999
- 'Tow Tow Shang' — Last listed 1999
kanran — Last listed 1997
sinense — Last listed 1999
* - var. **album** — Last listed 1998

CYMBOPOGON (Poaceae)
citratus — CArn COld CSev ELau GPoy MCCP MChe MHer MSal NPri SHDw SIde SWal WCHb WGwG WHer WJek
martinii — GPoy MSal

nardus	CArn GPoy MSal

CYMOPHYLLUS (Cyperaceae)
fraseri	EPla

CYMOPTERUS (Apiaceae)
terebinthinus	Last listed 1999

CYNANCHUM (Asclepiadaceae)
* *acuminatifolium*	Last listed 1998
sp. B&SWJ 1924	WCru

CYNARA (Asteraceae)
§ *baetica* subsp.	ECha
maroccana	
§ *cardunculus* ♀	More than 30 suppliers
– ACL 380/78	EMon SWat
– 'Cardy'	CBot EGoo EMan MLLN MWat
	NChi SMrm SWat WWhi
– dwarf	SDix WCot
– 'Florist Cardy'	COIW NLar NPSI SRob WBry
– New House Farm strain	Last listed 1999
– Scolymus Group	CB&S CHEx CHad EPfP ERav
	EWes GCal GPoy ILis LRHS MBri
	SMrm SPer WByw WHer WOak
– – 'Brittany Belle'	Last listed 1999
– – 'Green Globe'	CBod CBot CSev EBee MWat NPSI
	NPer NVic WWpP
– – 'Gros Camus de	WBar WCot
Bretagne'	
– – 'Gros Vert de Lâon'	EBee WCot
– – 'Large Green'	NLar WCot
– – 'Purple Globe'	CArn NPSI
– – 'Violetto di Chioggia'	WHer
¶ – 'Vert de Vaux en Velin'	LPio
hystrix	See *C. baetica* subsp. *maroccana*

CYNODON (Poaceae)
aethiopicus	EBee EHoe LGre

CYNOGLOSSUM (Boraginaceae)
amabile ♀	ELan MGed SRms
– 'Firmament'	SRms
– f. *roseum*	Last listed 1998
dioscoridis	CBot CGle NLar WPer WWin
glochidiatum	Last listed 1998
grande	CFee EBee SCro
hungaricum	Last listed 1997
¶ 'Mystery Rose'	WPGP
nervosum	CArn CBot CGle EBee EBrP EBre
	ECtt EFou EMil EPar EWTr LBCl
	LBSe LBre LRHS MBBe MRav MTis
	MWgw NChi SBre SLon SPer
	SRms SWat WCHb WCot WWhi
	WWin
officinale	CArn EWFC MChe MHer MHew
	MSal NSti SIde WCHb WCer WHer
	WWye
wallichii	CFee EBee
zeylanicum	EBee

CYNOSURUS (Poaceae)
cristatus	CKin

CYPELLA (Iridaceae)
aquatilis	MSta
§ *coelestis*	WCot WPer
herbertii	CGle LAma
¶ *peruviana*	EMan
plumbea	See *C. coelestis*

CYPERUS (Cyperaceae)
§ *albostriatus*	CHal CInt MBri
– 'Nanus'	Last listed 1999
alternifolius hort.	See *C. involucratus*
– 'Compactus'	See *C. involucratus* 'Nanus'
§ *cyperoides*	MBri
diffusus hort.	See *C. albostriatus*
§ *eragrostis*	CBrm CCuc CElw CHad CHal
	CMil CRow EBee ECha EHoe EPPr
	EPla GKir MCCP MSCN NBid
	NCut NOGN NSti SDix SPlb SUsu
	SWat WAbb WMAq
esculentus	CInt IBlr
fuscus	CCuc CElw CInt EBee EPPr EPla
	NCut NSti WHal
§ *giganteus*	CInt LLWG
glaber	EMan NCut
haspan hort.	See *C. papyrus* 'Nanus'
§ *involucratus* ♀	CBen CHEx CHal CInt EBak EHon
	EMFW EOas ERea LCns LGuA
	MBri MSta NBea SArc SSte SUsu
	SWat SYvo WFar WMAq WMul
	WWeb WWye
– 'Gracilis'	EBak MBri
§ – 'Nanus'	EPla MSCN
longus	CBen CCuc CHad CRow CWat
	EBee EHoe EHon EMFW EMon
	EPPr LGuA LPBA MHew MSta
	NDea NSti SMad SSoC SWat SWyc
	WHal WMAq WWeb WWye
nanus	CHEx
obtusiflorus subsp.	Last listed 1998
sphaerocephalus	
papyrus	CHEx CHad CInt EOas ERea LCns
	LGuA LLWG LPan MBri MSta
	SAPC SArc SLdr WMul
– 'Mexico'	See *C. giganteus*
§ – 'Nanus'	CInt ERea LPal WMul
rotundus	CWes EPGN MCCP
sumula hort.	See *C. cyperoides*
ustulatus	Last listed 1997
vegetus	See *C. eragrostis*

CYPHOMANDRA (Solanaceae)
betacea (F)	GPoy LBlo WMul
– 'Goldmine' (F)	ERea
– 'Oratia Red' (F)	ERea

CYPRIPEDIUM (Orchidaceae)
acaule	Last listed 1999
– x *pubescens*	Last listed 1999
Aki g.	CHdy
¶ x *andrewsii*	CHdy
x *barbeyi*	Last listed 1998
calceolus	CHdy
candidum	Last listed 1999
– x *macranthos*	Last listed 1998
cordigerum x *reginae*	CHdy
debile	EFEx
Emil g.	CHdy XFro
flavum	CHdy
– red unspotted	EFEx
* – var. *speciosum*	Last listed 1997
– yellow spotted	EFEx
§ *formosanum*	EFEx LAma SSpi
– x *pubescens*	CHdy
franchetii	CHdy
Gisela g.	CHdy XFro
¶ *guttatum*	EFEx
– var. *yatabeanum*	See *C. yatabeanum*
Hank Small g.	Last listed 1997

henryi	CHdy EFEx
himalaicum	EFEx
§ *japonicum*	EFEx LAma
- var. *formosanum*	See *C. formosanum*
- var. *japonicum*	See *C. japonicum*
Karl Heinz g.	CHdy
kentuckiense	CHdy
- x *reginae*	CHdy
macranthos	CHdy EFEx
- dark pink form from Wou-long, China	Last listed 1998
- green-flowered	EFEx
- var. *hotei-atsumorianum*	
	EFEx
- light pink form from Man-chou, China	Last listed 1998
- var. *rebunense*	EFEx
- var. *speciosum*	EFEx
margaritaceum	EFEx
Maria g.	Last listed 1998
montanum	EFEx
parviflorum	CHdy GCrs
- var. *makasin*	GCrs
- var. *pubescens*	CHdy GCrs LAma
- - Aitkin form	GCrs
- - dwarf form	GCrs
passerinum	Last listed 1999
¶ **Philipp g.**	XFro
reginae	CHdy GCrs LAma
segawae	CHdy EFEx
tibeticum	CHdy EFEx
¶ x *ventricosum*	XFro
§ *yatabeanum*	EFEx

CYRILLA (Cyrillaceae)

racemiflora	CPle

CYRTANTHUS (Amaryllidaceae)

§ *brachyscyphus*	EBee MTis SHFr WHil WSPU
breviflorus	WHil
clavatus	Last listed 1997
§ *elatus* ♀	CBro CHal CSev CSpe CStu EBot ERea LAma LBow LRHS MBri MCCP NChi NRog SCou SLon SRms SYvo WCot WHer
- 'Delicatus'	LBow
* - 'Snow Queen'	WCot
epiphyticus	Last listed 1999
falcatus	MLan
§ *luteus*	WCDu
mackenii	CPne NRog
- var. *cooperi*	Last listed 1998
montanus	Last listed 1997
obliquus	Last listed 1997
obrienii	Last listed 1997
* *ochroleucus*	WCot
'Stutterheim Variety'	
parviflorus	See *C. brachyscyphus*
* 'Pink Diamond'	CBro LRHS
purpureus	See *C. elatus*
sanguineus	Last listed 1998
smithiae	Last listed 1997
'Snow White'	CBro
speciosus	See *C. elatus*
spiralis	Last listed 1997
staadensis	Last listed 1997

CYRTOMIUM (Dryopteridaceae)

§ *caryotideum*	GQui NMar
§ *falcatum* ♀	CHEx CHal CLAP CRDP EBee EFer ELan MBri NMar NOrc SDix SRms SVen WRic WWat

- 'Butterfieldii'	Last listed 1999
- 'Rochfordianum'	CRow WFib
§ *fortunei* ♀	CFil CHal CHid CLAP EBee EFer EPVP GBin IOrc NBus NDlv NHar NHol NMar SChu SRms WFib WRic
- var. *clivicola*	NBus NDlv NHar WHil WRic
lonchitoides	WRic
macrophyllum	CFil CLAP NMar WCru WRic

CYRTOSTYLIS (Orchidaceae)

reniformis	Last listed 1998
robusta	Last listed 1998

CYSTICAPNOS (Papaveraceae)

pruinosa	Last listed 1999

CYSTOPTERIS ✿ (Woodsiaceae)

alpina	Last listed 1997
bulbifera	CCuc CLAP EFer EPot GQui NMar WEas
diaphana	WRic
dickieana	CLAP EMon GAri LGuA MCLN NHar NMar NVic WFib
fragilis	CCuc CGdn ECha EFer EMon GQui NBro NMar SRms WRic
- 'Cristata'	CLAP
- var. *sempervirens*	WRic
tennesseensis	WRic

CYTISOPHYLLUM (Papilionaceae)

§ *sessilifolium*	Last listed 1998

CYTISUS (Papilionaceae)

albus hort.	See *C. multiflorus*
- Hacq.	See *Chamaecytisus albus*
'Andreanus'	See *C. scoparius* f. *andreanus*
¶ 'Apricot Gem'	NBlu
ardoinoi ♀	GDra MBro
battandieri ♀	More than 30 suppliers
- 'Yellow Tail' ♀	CEnd LRHS MBri MGos WPGP WSPU
x *beanii* ♀	ELan ENot ESis GKir LRHS MAsh MBar NFor SLon SPer SRms WDin
- 'Osiris'	EPfP
'Boskoop Glory'	CBlo SPer
'Boskoop Ruby' ♀	CBlo CDoC EBee EGra EOld EPfP GKir GSki LRHS NWoo WLRN
'Burkwoodii' ♀	CB&S CDoC EBee ENot GCHN GChr GKir LRHS MWhi NFla WFar WPyg WStl
'Butterfly'	CB&S
canariensis	See *Genista canariensis*
'Compact Crimson'	CDoC EBrP EBre ECle LBCl LBSe LBre MBBe SBre
'Cottage'	EPot GDra IMGH MBro NHol WAbe WBod
'Cottage Gold'	Last listed 1999
'Criterion'	Last listed 1999
'Dainty'	WGwG
'Dainty Maid'	CEnd
'Daisy Hill'	CBlo
§ *decumbens*	CBlo CLyd IOrc MAsh MBro NHar WLin WWin
demissus	See *Chamaecytisus polytrichus*
¶ 'Donard Gem'	CDoC WWeb
'Dorothy Walpole'	CBlo CMHG
'Dragonfly'	CBlo IOrc
'Dukaat'	EBee MAsh WBcn WLRN
'Eastern Queen'	Last listed 1997
'Firefly'	CBlo
'Fulgens'	CBlo EPfP MAsh MBar SPer WLRN

'Golden Cascade' — CB&S CBlo CDoC ELan LRHS WGwG WLRN
'Golden Showers' — Last listed 1999
'Golden Sunlight' — CBlo EBee ELan ENot EPfP WStI
'Goldfinch' — CB&S CBlo CDoC CHar EBee ENot GKir MBri MWat NPri SMer WAbe WWeb
hirsutus — See *Chamaecytisus hirsutus*
'Hollandia' ♀ — CB&S CDoC EBee EBrP EBre EWTr GCHN GChr GKir LBCl LBSe LBre LRHS MBBe MBar MGos NFla SBre SPer WDin WStI WWeb WWin
x *kewensis* ♀ — More than 30 suppliers
- 'Niki' — CAbP CBlo EPfP GKir LRHS MAsh MBri MGos SPan SPer WGer
'Killiney Red' — CBlo CChe ENot EWTr GKir IOrc MBri WRHF
'Killiney Salmon' — CBlo CChe EBee ENot MAsh
'La Coquette' — CBlo CDoC CMHG EBee EGra LRHS MBar MWat SPlb WLRN
'Lena' ♀ — CDoC EBee EBrP EBre EGra GAri GChr GKir GOrc LBCl LBSe LBre LRHS MAsh MBBe MBar MBri MGos MTis SBre WBod WFar WStI WWeb
leucanthus — See *Chamaecytisus albus*
'Lord Lambourne' — CBlo CChe
'Luna' ♀ — EBee LRHS
maderensis — See *Genista maderensis*
'Maria Burkwood' — CBlo EPfP
'Minstead' ♀ — CBlo EBee EBrP EBre ECle ELan EPfP LBCl LBSe LBre MBBe SBre SPer WAbe
monspessulanus — See *Genista monspessulana*
'Moonlight' — EWTr SPer WGwG
'Moyclare Pink' — CMHG
'Muldean' — WWeb
§ *multiflorus* ♀ — GKir SRms WBod
- 'White Bouquet' — MBri
'Newry Seedling' — LRHS
nigrescens — See *C. nigricans*
§ *nigricans* — CFil CPle ENot SPer WPGP
- 'Cyni' — ELan EPfP GEil IArd LRHS MAsh NFla SPer SSpi
'Palette' — LRHS MBar SPer
'Porlock' ♀ — CB&S CDoC CLan CSPN CTre CWSG CWit ELan SEND SMac SPla WBod WWeb
x *praecox* — See *C.* x *praecox* 'Warminster'
- 'Albus' — More than 30 suppliers
- 'Allgold' ♀ — CB&S CChe CDoC CMHG EBee EBrP EBre ENot GKir LBCl LBSe LBre LRHS MAsh MBBe MBar MBri MRav SBre SLon SPer SPla SReu SRms SSta WAbe WBod WDin WFar WGwG
- 'Canary Bird' — See *C.* x *praecox* 'Goldspeer'
- 'Frisia' — CB&S GAri MBar NFla WBod
§ - 'Goldspeer' — CBlo ENot SEND
§ - 'Warminster' ♀ — CChe CHar EBee ELan ENot EWTr GCHN GChr GDra GKir LAst LRHS MAsh MBar MBri MGos MRav MWat NFla NWea SPer SRms WAbe WWat WWin
'Princess' — LRHS MBri WBcn
procumbens — LHop NBid
purgans — CBlo CPle
purpureus — See *Chamaecytisus purpureus*
racemosus hort. — See *Genista* x *spachiana*
Red Favourite — See *C.* 'Roter Favorit'
'Red Wings' — CBlo GCHN GKir MGos SPer

WAbe WStI
§ 'Roter Favorit' — CBlo EWTr MBar WGor
scoparius — CAgr CArn CBlo CKin ENot EWFC GChr IIve LEdu MCoo NWea SRms WDin
§ - f. *andreanus* ♀ — CBlo CDoC EBee EGra ENot EPfP GChr GKir MGos NFor
- - 'Splendens' — CB&S CBlo SPer WStI
- 'Cornish Cream' ♀ — CBlo ECot EPfP GKir SPer
§ - subsp. *maritimus* — GSki MBri MMHG MRav SLPl WGer
- 'Pastel Delight' — Last listed 1998
- var. *prostratus* — See *C. scoparius* subsp. *maritimus*
sessilifolius — See *Cytisophyllum sessilifolium*
§ *striatus* — Last listed 1999
supinus — See *Chamaecytisus supinus*
'Windlesham Ruby' — CChe CDoC EBee ELan EPfP GKir LRHS MAsh MBar SMer SPer WDin WPyg WWeb
'Zeelandia' ♀ — CB&S CHar EBee ENot EPfP EWTr GChr GKir LRHS MBar MRav MWat SEND SMer SPer WAbe WRHF

D

DABOECIA ♣ (Ericaceae)
§ *cantabrica* — GAri
§ - f. *alba* — CB&S CMac MBar MBri MGos MOke NHol SBod WStI
- 'Alba Globosa' — EPfP MBar
* - 'Arielle' — Last listed 1999
- 'Atropurpurea' — MGos MOke NHol WBod WStI
- 'Barbara Phillips' — MBar
- 'Bicolor' ♀ — EPfP MGos MOke NHar
- 'Blueless' — EPfP
- f. *blumii* 'Pink Blum' — Last listed 1998
- - 'White Blum' — ECho
- 'Bubbles' — Last listed 1998
- 'Celtic Star' — Last listed 1998
- 'Charles Nelson' (d) — MBar MOke
- 'Cherub' — Last listed 1998
- 'Cinderella' — MBar
- 'Cleggan' — Last listed 1998
- 'Covadonga' — MBar
- 'Creeping White' — Last listed 1998
- 'Cupido' — MGos
- 'David Moss' ♀ — MBar SBod
- 'Donard Pink' — See *D. cantabrica* 'Pink'
- 'Early Bride' — Last listed 1999
- 'Eskdale Baron' — Last listed 1998
- 'Eskdale Blea' — Last listed 1998
- 'Eskdale Blonde' — Last listed 1998
- 'Glamour' — Last listed 1998
- 'Globosa Pink' — Last listed 1998
- 'Harlequin' — Last listed 1998
- 'Heather Yates' — MOke
- 'Hookstone Purple' — MBar MGos MOke NHol
- 'Lilacina' — MBar
§ - 'Pink' — MBar NMen SRms
- 'Pink Lady' — MBar
- 'Polifolia' — MOke SRms
- 'Porter's Variety' — ECho MBar MOke NHar
- 'Praegerae' — CMac GKir MBar MGos NHol
- 'Purpurea' — ECho MBar
- 'Rainbow' (v) — MBar
- 'Rodeo' — Last listed 1998
- 'Rosea' — MBar

- subsp. *scotica* 'Bearsden' MBar
- - 'Ben' — Last listed 1998
- - 'Cora' — MBar
- - 'Goscote' — MGos
- - 'Jack Drake' ♀ — GChr MBar MBri MOke
- - 'Red Imp' — Last listed 1998
- - 'Robin' — Last listed 1998
- - 'Silverwells' ♀ — GChr MBar MBri NHar
- - 'Tabramhill' — MBar
- - 'William Buchanan' ♀ — CMac EHol GChr GKir MBar MBri MGos MOke NHar NHol NMen SBod
- - 'William Buchanan Gold' — MBar MBri
- - 'Snowdrift' — MBar
- - 'Tinkerbell' — ECho GChr
- - 'Waley's Red' ♀ — GQui MBar SDys
- - 'White Carpet' — Last listed 1998
- - 'Wijnie' — Last listed 1998

DACRYCARPUS (Podocarpaceae)
§ *dacrydioides* — ECou
- - 'Dark Delight' — ECou

DACRYDIUM (Podocarpaceae)
bidwillii — See *Halocarpus bidwillii*
cupressinum — CDoC CPLG ECou SMad
franklinii — See *Lagarostrobos franklinii*
laxifolium — See *Lepidothamnus laxifolius*

DACTYLIS (Poaceae)
glomerata 'Variegata' — CBod CCuc EGle EMan EMon ENot EPPr EPla GCHN IBlr LPan MCCP MMoz NBid NBro NCat NSti WCot

DACTYLORHIZA (Orchidaceae)
aristata — EFEx
- x *fuchsii* — EFEx
* - *punctata* — EFEx
x *braunii* — ECha IBlr
cordigera — CHdy
§ *elata* ♀ — CEnd CHdy CLAP EPar GCrs IBlr LAma MDun SSpi
- 'Lydia' — CLAP GCrs
- (m) x *majalis* (f) — Last listed 1999
* - *variegata* — Last listed 1999
Eskimo Nell g. — CHdy
Estella g. (*elata* x *foliosa*) — EPot GCrs
Florina g. (*iberica* x *saccifera*) — Last listed 1997
§ *foliosa* ♀ — CBro CFir CHdy ERos GCrs GKir IBlr LRHS MBri MDun MNrw MTho NHar
- x *saccifera* — CHdy EPot
§ *fuchsii* — CHdy EPot ERos GBuc GCrs MNrw NHar NRya SSpi SUsu WHer WShi
* - *alba* — Last listed 1998
- 'Bressingham Bonus' — WTin
- 'Cruickshank' — NHar
Glendora g. (*elata* x *incarnata*) — CHdy
x *grandis* — CHdy
hybrids — Last listed 1999
incarnata — CFir EBee EPot GCrs LAma NCut SPer SSpi WWol
- subsp. *cruenta* — Last listed 1997
Larissa g. x *purpurella* — Last listed 1999
§ *maculata* — CHdy CHid EBee EPar EPot GCrs IBlr LAma NCut NRog SPer SWyc WHer WShi WWol

- subsp. *ericetorum* — Last listed 1997
¶ - 'Madam Butterfly' — CBro
- 'Strawberry Fields' — EPot
maderensis — See *D. foliosa*
Madonna g. (*majalis* x *sambucina*) — CHdy
§ *majalis* — CHdy EBee EPot LAma NCut SPer SSpi
- *alba* — Last listed 1999
- var. *bowmanii* — Last listed 1999
- subsp. *occidentalis* — Last listed 1999
- subsp. *praetermissa* — See *D. praetermissa*
mascula — See *Orchis mascula*
nieschalkiorum — Last listed 1999
§ *praetermissa* — CHdy EPot SSpi
purpurella — CHdy EBee NCut SPer SSpi WWol
saccifera — CHdy
sambucina — CHdy
'Tinney's Spotted' — NHar
traunsteineri — Last listed 1999

DAHLIA ✿ (Asteraceae)
'Abridge Natalie' (SWL) — Last listed 1997
'Akita' (Misc) — WAba
¶ 'Allan Sparkes' (SWL) ♀ — LAyl
'Alloway Cottage' (MD) — NHal
'Alltami Cherry' (SBa) — Last listed 1997
'Alltami Classic' (MD) — NHal
'Alltami Corsair' (MS-c) — LAyl
'Alltami Cosmic' (LD) — NHal
'Almand's Climax' (GD) ♀ — LBut WAba
'Alstergruss' (Col) — NRog
'Alva's Doris' (SS-c) ♀ — LAyl
'Alva's Supreme' (GD) ♀ — LBut NHal
'Amaran Candyfloss' (SD) — Last listed 1999
'Amaran Relish' (LD) — NHal
'Amaran Royale' (MinD) — Last listed 1997
¶ 'Amber Festival' (SD) — NHal
'Amberglow' (MinBa) — LAyl
'Amberley Jean' (SD) — Last listed 1999
'Amberley Victoria' (MD) — Last listed 1999
'American Copper' (GD) — Last listed 1999
'Amgard Delicate' (LD) — Last listed 1999
'Amira' (SBa) — NHal
'Amy Campbell' (MD) — NHal
* 'Anaïs' — Last listed 1999
* 'Anatol' (LD) — CSut
'Andrew Magson' (SS-c) ♀ — NHal
'Andrew Mitchell' (MS-c) — NHal
* 'Andries Amber' (MinS-c) — LBut
'Andries' Orange' (MinS-c) — LBut
'Anglian Water' (MinD) — NHal
'Anniversary Ball' (MinBa) — LAyl
'Apricot Beauty' (MS-c) — NHal
'Apricot Honeymoon Dress' (SD) — WAba
'Apricot Jewel' (SD) — LAyl
'Arabian Night' (SD) — CHad CLTr EBee EMan LAst LRHS MSte NDov NPSI NRog SDeJ WAba WCot WSpi
'Athalie' (SC) — Last listed 1999
¶ 'Audacity' (MD) — LAyl
'Aurwen's Violet' (Pom) — NHal
'Autumn Lustre' (SWL) ♀ — CBos LAyl
'Aylett's Dazzler' (MinD) ♀ — Last listed 1995
'B.J. Beauty' (MD) — LAyl NHal WAba
¶ 'Baby Royal' (SD) — CHad
'Bach' (MC) — LRHS
'Barat Joy' (MD) — Last listed 1999
'Barbarossa' (LD) — Last listed 1999
'Barbary Aegean' — Last listed 1999
'Barbary Ball' (SBa) — Last listed 1999

'Barbarry Banker' (MinD)　LAyl
¶ 'Barbarry Bluebird' (MinD)　NHal
¶ 'Barbarry Carousel' (SBa)　WAba
'Barbarry Choice' (SD)　WAba
'Barbarry Fern' (SD)　Last listed 1999
'Barbarry Flag' (MinD)　NHal
'Barbarry Gaiety' (MinD)　Last listed 1997
'Barbarry Gateway' (MinD)　Last listed 1997
'Barbarry Ideal' (MinD)　Last listed 1998
'Barbarry Majestic' (SBa)　Last listed 1999
'Barbarry Oracle' (SD)　WAba
'Barbarry Orange' (SD)　WAba
'Barbarry Pinky' (SD)　Last listed 1997
'Barbarry Snowball' (MinBa)　Last listed 1999
'Barbarry Suffusion' (MinBa)　NHal
'Barbarry Ticket' (SD)　WAba
'Barbarry Token' (SD)　Last listed 1999
'Baret Joy' (LS-c)　NHal WAba
'Bea' (SWL)　WAba
'Bednall Beauty'　CFri CGle CLTr CRDP CSpe EBee
　(Misc/DwB) ♀　EWes LAst LHil SAga SDys WCot
'Ben Huston' (GD)　WAba
'Berwick Wood' (MD)　NHal
'Biddenham Fire' (SD)　Last listed 1998
'Biddenham　Last listed 1999
　Strawberry' (SD)
'Biddenham Sunset' (MS-c)　Last listed 1999
'Bill Homberg' (GD)　Last listed 1997
'Bishop of Llandaff'　More than 30 suppliers
　(Misc) ♀
'Black Diamond' (Ba)　CHad
'Black Fire' (SD)　LAyl
'Black Monarch' (GD)　NHal
'Blewbury First' (MinD)　Last listed 1999
'Blithe Spirit' (LD)　CSut
'Bloom's Amy' (MinD)　NHal
I 'Blossom' (Pom)　CSut
'Blue Beard'　CSut
'Bonaventure' (GD)　NHal
'Bonne Esperance' (Sin/Lil)　LBut
'Border Princess' (SC/DwB)　SDeJ
'Bracken Ballerina' (SWL)　LAyl NHal WAba
'Brackenhill Flame' (SD)　NHal
'Brackenridge　WAba
　Ballerina' (SWL)
'Brandaris' (MS-c)　Last listed 1999
'Brandysnap' (SD) ♀　Last listed 1999
'Bridal Bouquet' (Col)　NHal
'Burnished Bronze'　Last listed 1997
　(Misc/DwB) ♀
'Butterball' (MinD/DwB) ♀　Last listed 1999
'Calgary' (SD)　Last listed 1997
'Cameo' (WL)　LBut
* 'Canary Fubuki' (MD)　CSut
'Candy Cane' (MinBa)　Last listed 1999
'Candy Cupid' (MinBa) ♀　LBut NHal WAba
'Candy Keene' (LS-c)　NHal
'Carolina Moon' (SD)　LAyl NHal
'Carstone Cobblers' (SBa)　NHal WAba
'Carstone Ruby' (SD)　NHal
¶ 'Carstone Suntan' (MinC)　NHal
'Charlie Two' (MD)　LAyl LBut NHal WAba
'Cherry Wine' (SD)　Last listed 1999
'Cherwell Goldcrest' (SS-c)　NHal
'Chessy' (Sin/Lil)　LBut LRHS
'Cheyenne' (SS-c)　Last listed 1999
'Chimborazo' (Col)　LAyl
'Christmas Carol' (Col)　NHal
'Christopher　Last listed 1999
　Nickerson' (MS-c) ♀
'Christopher Taylor' (SWL)　NHal WAba
'Clair de Lune' (Col) ♀　LBut NHal

'Clarion' (MS-c)　SDeJ
'Classic A.1' (MC)　LAyl
'Clint's Climax' (LD)　WAba
coccinea　CFil CGle CPou EBee EMan LAst
　　SMad WAba WCot
– hybrids　Last listed 1998
¶ – × merckii　EWes
'Color Spectacle' (LSD)　CSut
'Connie Bartlam' (MD)　NHal
'Conway' (SS-c) ♀　Last listed 1998
¶ 'Copper Queen' (MinD)　NHal
* 'Coral Puff'　LRHS
'Cornel' (SBa)　LBut NHal WAba
'Corona' (SS-c/DwB)　Last listed 1999
¶ 'Corrie Vigor' (SS-c)　NHal
'Corrine' (SWL)　WAba
'Corton Bess' (SD)　Last listed 1997
'Cream Alva's' (GD) ♀　Last listed 1993
'Cream Beauty' (SWL)　Last listed 1999
'Cream Delight' (SS-c)　Last listed 1997
'Cryfield Bryn' (SS-c)　NHal
'Cryfield Keene' (LS-c)　Last listed 1999
'Crystal Ann' (MS-c)　Last listed 1999
'Curiosity' (Col)　LAyl LBut NHal
'Czardas'　GCal
'Daddy's Choice' (SS-c)　Last listed 1999
'Dad's Delight' (MinD)　Last listed 1998
'Daleko Jupiter' (GS-c)　NHal WAba
'Dana Iris' (SS-c) ♀　Last listed 1998
'Dancing Queen' (S-c)　Last listed 1997
'Danjo Doc' (SD)　NHal
'Danum Meteor' (GS-c)　WAba
'Dark Splendour' (MC)　Last listed 1998
'Davar Donna' (MS-c) ♀　Last listed 1995
'Davenport Anita' (MinD)　Last listed 1998
'Davenport Honey' (MinD)　NHal
'Davenport Lesley' (MinD)　Last listed 1997
'Davenport Sunlight' (MS-c)　NHal
¶ 'Dave's Kiss' (MinBa)　NHal
'David Digweed' (SD)　NHal
'David Howard' (MinD) ♀　CB&S CGle CHad CMGP EBee
　　EBrP EBre ELan EMan EPfP LAst
　　LAyl LBCl LBSe LBre LHil LRHS
　　MBBe MMil NHal SAga SBre SPer
　　SPla WAba WCot WLRN WWol
'Dawn Sky' (SD)　LAyl
'Daytona' (SD)　CSut
'Dazzler' (MinD/DwB)　Last listed 1999
'Deborah's Kiwi' (SC)　NHal
'Debra Anne Craven' (GS-c)　NHal
'Denise Willow' (Pom)　WAba
'Doctor Caroline　Last listed 1993
　Rabbitt' (SD) ♀
'Doktor Hans Ricken' (SD)　CSut WAba
'Doris Day' (SC)　LBut NHal NRog WAba
'Doris Knight' (SC)　LBut
'Downham Royal' (MinBa)　Last listed 1999
'Duet' (MD)　LRHS NRog
'Dusky Harmony' (SWL)　LBut
'Dutch Baby' (Pom)　WAba
'Earl Marc' (SC)　LBut
'East Anglian' (SD)　Last listed 1999
'East Court' (Sin)　Last listed 1999
'Easter Sunday' (Col)　Last listed 1999
'Eastwood　NHal WAba
　Moonlight' (MS-c)
'Eastwood Star' (MS-c)　WAba
'Edge of Gold' (GD)　CSut
'Edinburgh' (SD)　NRog
'Elizabeth Hammett' (MinD)　WAba
'Ella Britton' (MinD)　EBee EMan LRHS NDov
'Ellen Huston' (Sin/DwB)　♀CHad EBee EMan LRHS MBri

	NHal SAga
'Elma E' (LD)	NHal WAba
'Elmbrook Chieftain' (GD)	Last listed 1998
'Emory Paul' (LD)	Last listed 1997
'Ernie Pitt' (SD)	Last listed 1998
'Esther'	MBri
'Eveline' (SD)	ETub LRHS SDeJ
'Evelyn Foster' (MD)	NHal
'Evening Mail' (GS-c) ♀	Last listed 1995
'Exotic Dwarf' (Sin/Lil)	NHal
'Explosion' (SS-c)	Last listed 1999
'Extase' (MD)	LRHS
'Ezau' (GD)	CSut
¶ 'Fairway Spur' (GD)	NHal
'Fascination' (SWL/DwB)	♀ CBos CHad LAyl MSCN NHal
	SChu WCot
'Fashion Monger' (Col)	NHal
'Fermain' (MinD)	NHal
* 'Fernhill Suprise' (SD)	LBut
'Fidalgo Magic' (MD)	WAba
'Fidalgo Supreme' (MD)	NHal
* 'Figaro White'	Last listed 1997
'Figurine' (SWL) ♀	LAyl NHal
'Finchcocks' (SWL) ♀	LAyl
'Fiona Stewart' (SBa)	Last listed 1999
* 'Fire Mountain'	NHal
(MinD/DwB)	
'Firebird' (Sin)	LRHS NRog WAba
'Flutterby' (SWL)	Last listed 1998
* 'Fluttering'	Last listed 1997
'Foreman's Jubilee' (GS-c)	Last listed 1999
'Formby Supreme' (MD)	Last listed 1998
'Forncett Furnace' (B)	GCal
'Frank Holmes' (Pom)	WAba
¶ 'Frank Lovell' (GS-c)	WAba
'Freya's Thalia' (Sin/Lil) ♀	LBut
'Frigoulet'	CSut
* 'Friquolet'	Last listed 1999
¶ 'Funny Face' (Misc)	WAba
'Fusion' (MD)	Last listed 1999
'Gaiety' (SD/DwB)	Last listed 1999
'Gala Parade' (SD)	NHal
¶ 'Gallery Degas' PBR (MinD)	WWol
¶ 'Gallery Singer' PBR (MinD)	WWol
'Garden Festival' (SWL)	LAyl NHal
'Garden Party'	LAyl
(MC/DwB) ♀	
Gateshead Festival =	NHal
'Peach Melba' (SD)	
'Gay Mini' (MinD)	LBut
'Gay Princess' (SWL)	LAyl
§ 'Geerling's Indian	NHal
Summer' (MS-c) ♀	
'Geerlings Queeny' (SC) ♀	Last listed 1995
'Gerrie Hoek' (SWL)	LBut LRHS NRog
'Gina Lombaert' (MS-c)	LRHS WAba
'Glenbank Twinkle' (MinC)	NHal
'Glorie van Heemstede'	LAyl LBut LRHS NHal NRog
(SWL) ♀	
'Go American' (GD)	NHal
'Gold Crown' (LS-c)	NRog
'Gold Diable' (SS-c) ♀	Last listed 1995
'Golden Emblem' (MD)	SDeJ
'Golden Impact' (MS-c)	NHal
'Golden Symbol' (MS-c)	WAba
'Good Earth' (MC)	Last listed 1999
'Good Hope' (MinD)	Last listed 1997
'Grand Prix' (GD)	CSut
'Grand Willo' (Pom)	WAba
'Grenadier' (SWL)	EBee WAba WCot
'Grenidor Pastelle' (MS-c)	LBut NHal WAba
¶ 'Gurtla Twilight' (Pom)	NHal

'Gypsy Boy' (LD)	Last listed 1999
'Halam Portia' (SWL)	WAba
'Hamari Accord' (LS-c) ♀	LAyl NHal WAba
'Hamari Bride' (MS-c) ♀	LAyl
'Hamari Girl' (GD)	NHal
'Hamari Gold' (GD) ♀	NHal
'Hamari Katrina' (LS-c)	LRHS WAba
'Hamari Rosé' (MinBa) ♀	LAyl NHal
'Hamari Sunshine' (LD) ♀	NHal
'Hamilton Lillian' (SD) ♀	WAba
'Hans Radi' (Misc)	WAba
'Hans Ricken' (SD)	Last listed 1997
* 'Haresbrook'	CMil EBee EMan WAba WCot
	WSpi
* 'Hartenaas' (Col/DwB)	NRog
'Harvest Amanda' (Sin/Lil) ♀	LBut
'Harvest Brownie' (Sin/Lil)	LBut
§ 'Harvest Dandy' (Sin/Lil)	Last listed 1999
§ 'Harvest Imp' (Sin/Lil)	LBut
§ 'Harvest Inflammation'	LBut
(Sin/Lil) ♀	
§ 'Harvest Red Dwarf'	LBut
(Sin/Lil) ♀	
§ 'Harvest Samantha'	LBut NHal
(Sin/Lil) ♀	
§ 'Harvest Tiny Tot' (Sin/Lil) ♀	LBut NHal
'Hayley Jayne' (SC)	CSut WAba
'Hazard' (MS-c)	NRog
I 'Hazel' (Sin/Lil)	Last listed 1997
'Henriette' (MC)	CSut
'Highgate Gold' (MS-c)	Last listed 1997
'Hilda Clare' (Col)	Last listed 1997
'Hillcrest Albino' (SS-c) ♀	Last listed 1998
'Hillcrest Blaze' (SS-c) ♀	Last listed 1995
¶ 'Hillcrest Delight' (MD)	NHal
'Hillcrest Desire' (SC) ♀	LAyl NHal WAba
'Hillcrest Divine' (MinD)	NHal
'Hillcrest Heights' (LS-c)	WAba
'Hillcrest Hillton' (LS-c)	NHal
'Hillcrest Royal' (MC) ♀	NHal
'Hillcrest Suffusion' (SD)	NHal
'Hillcrest Ultra' (SD)	Last listed 1999
'Hit Parade' (MS-c)	CSut NRog
'Honey' (Anem/DwB)	LRHS NRog
'Honeymoon Dress' (SD)	NHal
'House of Orange' (MD)	SDeJ
'Hugh Mather' (MWL)	Last listed 1999
'Ice Cream Beauty' (SWL) ♀	Last listed 1995
'Imp'	See D. 'Harvest Imp'
imperialis (B)	EMon EWes GCal WCot
- 'Alba' (B)	EMon
- pink double (B)	WCot
'Inca Dambuster' (GS-c)	LBut NHal
'Inca Matchless' (MD)	WAba
'Inca Metropolitan' (LD) ♀	Last listed 1987
'Inflammation'	See D. 'Harvest Inflammation'
'Inglebrook Jill' (Col)	LAyl NHal
'Iris' (Pom)	LBut WAba
'Jaldec Joker' (SC) ♀	Last listed 1995
'Jamie' (SS-c)	NHal
'Jane Horton' (Col)	LBut
'Jason' (SS-c)	WAba
'Jean Fairs' (MinWL)	LBut
'Jean McMillan' (SC)	NHal
'Jeanette Carter' (MinD) ♀	Last listed 1999
'Jeanne d'Arc'	Last listed 1999
'Jescot Jess' (MinD)	LBut
'Jescot Julie' (O)	LBut
'Jescot Lingold' (MinD)	CSut WAba
'Jescot Nubia' (SS-c)	CBos
'Jessica' (S-c)	CSut
'Jessica Crutchfield'(SWL) ♀	Last listed 1995

'Jessie G' (SBa) — LBut NHal
'Jessie Ross' (MinD/DwB) — Last listed 1998
'Jill Day' (SC) — LBut
* 'Jill's Blush' (MS-c) — Last listed 1997
'Jill's Delight' (MD) ♀ — Last listed 1999
'Jim Branigan' (LS-c) — NHal
'Joan Beecham' (SWL) — LAyl
'Jocondo' (GD) — NHal
'Johann' (Pom) — LBut NHal
'John Prior' (SD) — Last listed 1999
'John Street' (SWL) ♀ — LBut
'Jomanda' (MinBa) ♀ — LBut NHal
'Jorja' (MS-c) — NHal
'Jo's Choice' (MinD) — LBut
'Karenglen' (MinD) ♀ — LBut NHal
¶ 'Karras' (SS-c) — NHal
'Kathleen's Alliance' (SC) ♀ LAyl NHal
'Kathryn's Cupid' (MinBa) ♀ — NHal WAba
'Katie Dahl' (MinD) — NHal
'Keith's Choice' (MD) — NHal WAba
'Kelsea Carla' (SS-c) — NHal
'Keltie Peach' (MD) — NHal
'Kenn Emerland' (MS-c) — Last listed 1999
'Kenora Canada' (MS-c) — Last listed 1999
'Kenora Challenger' (LS-c) — NHal WAba
'Kenora Fireball' (MinBa) — NHal
'Kenora Moonbeam' (MD) — Last listed 1997
'Kenora Petite' (MinS-c) — WAba
'Kenora Sunset' (MS-c) — LAyl LBut NHal
'Kenora Superb' (LS-c) — NHal
'Kenora Valentine' (LD) ♀ — LAyl NHal WAba
'Kenora Wildfire' (LD) — WAba
'Ken's Coral' (SWL) — NHal
¶ 'Ken's Rarity' (SWL) — NHal
'Kidd's Climax' (GD) ♀ — LBut NHal WAba
'Kimi' (O) — Last listed 1998
'Kim's Marc' (SC) — LBut
'Kiwi Gloria' (SC) — NHal WAba
'Klankstad Kerkrade' (SC) — Last listed 1999
'Klondike' (MS-c) — CSut WAba
'Kochelsee' (MinD) — Last listed 1999
* 'Kogano Fubuki' (MD) — CSut
'Kotare Jackpot' (SS-c) — LAyl
'Kym Willo' (Pom) — LBut
I 'Kyoto' (SWL) — WAba
¶ 'L.A.T.E.' (MinBa) — NHal
'La Cierva' (Col) — LBut
'La Corbière' (MinBa) — Last listed 1997
'Lady Kerkrade' (SC) — Last listed 1997
'Lady Linda' (SD) — LBut NHal WAba
'Lady Sunshine' (SS-c) — Last listed 1998
'L'Ancresse' (MinBa) — LAyl NHal WAba
* 'Laura's Choice' (SD) — Last listed 1999
'Lauren's Moonlight' (MS-c) NHal
'Lavender Athalie' (SC) — Last listed 1999
¶ 'Lavender Line' (SC) — NHal
¶ 'Le Castel' (D) — WCot
'Lemon' (Anem) — WAba
'Lemon Cane' (Misc) — WAba
'Lemon Elegans' (SS-c) ♀ — LBut NHal WAba
'Lemon Zing' (MinBa) — NHal
* 'Life Force' — Last listed 1998
'Lilac Shadow' (S-c) — Last listed 1998
§ 'Lilac Taratahi' (SC) — NHal
'Lilac Time' (MD) — LRHS SDeJ
'Lilianne Ballego' (MinD) — NHal
'Linda's Chester' (SC) — LBut NHal
¶ 'Lismore Carol' (Pom) — NHal
¶ 'Lismore Chaffinch' (MinD) NHal
'Lismore Moonlight' (Pom) NHal
'Lismore Sunset' (Pom) — LAyl NHal WAba

'Lismore Willie' (SWL) ♀ — LAyl LBut NHal WAba
'Little Dorrit' (Sin/Lil) ♀ — LBut
'Little Dream' (S-c) — SDeJ
'Little Sally' (Pom) — Last listed 1999
'Little Tiger' — NRog
¶ 'Longwood Dainty' (DwB) NHal
'Love's Dream' (SWL) — Last listed 1999
'Lynda Windsor' (Sin) — CRDP
¶ 'Mabel Ann' (GD) — NHal
'Madame Simone Stappers' (WL) — EBee MSCN
'Madame Vera' (SD) — LBut
'Maelstrom' (SD) — Last listed 1999
¶ 'Magenta Magic' (Sin/DwB) NHal
'Majestic Kerkrade' (SC) — Last listed 1998
'Majuba' (MD) — NRog SDeJ
¶ 'Maltby Whisper' (SC) — NHal
'Margaret Ann' (MinD) — LAyl LBut
¶ 'Margie' (SD) — WAba
'Mariner's Light' (SS-c) ♀ — Last listed 1997
'Mariposa' (Col) — WAba
'Mark Damp' (LS-c) — Last listed 1999
'Mark Hardwick' (GD) — NHal
'Mark Lockwood' (Pom) — WAba
'Marlene Joy' (MS-c/Fim) — NHal WAba
¶ 'Martin's Red' (Pom) — NHal
'Martin's Yellow' (Pom) — NHal WAba
'Mary Eveline' (Col) — NHal
'Mary Hammett' (MinD) — WAba
'Mary Layton' (Col) — Last listed 1999
'Mary Pitt' (MinD) — NHal
'Matilda Huston' — NHal
'Maxine Bailey' (SD) — Last listed 1997
merckii — CGle CHad ERav EWes GCal GMac LHil LRHS MNrw NSti WPer WWin
- *alba* — CFil CHad EBee WPGP WPer
- compact — CBos CFil EMan WPGP
- 'Edith Eddleman' — CFil
'Meredith's Marion Smith' (SD) — Last listed 1999
'Mi Wong' (Pom) — NHal
¶ 'Midnight Sun' (MinD) — NHal
'Mikado' (MD) — Last listed 1999
'Mini' (Sin/Lil) — LBut
* 'Minley Carol' (Pom) — LAyl NHal WAba
'Minley Iris' (Pom) — LBut
'Minley Linda' (Pom) — LBut
'Mistill Contessa' (MinD) — NHal
'Monk Marc' (SC) — LBut
'Monkstown Diane' (SC) — Last listed 1999
'Moonfire' (Misc/DwB) — CFir EBee EBrP EBre ECle EMan LAyl LBCl LBSe LBre LRHS MBBe MMil MSte NCut NGdn NHal SBre SDys SPer SSea SUsu WAba WCot WHer WWol
'Moonlight' (SD) — MBri
'Moor Place' (Pom) — CBos NHal WAba WCot
'Morning Dew' (SC) — SDeJ
'Morning Kiss' (LSD) — SDeJ
'Mount Noddy' (Sin) — SAga
'Mrs McDonald Quill' (LD) NHal
'Murdoch' — CBos EBee LAst WAba WCot WSpi
'Murillo' — MBri NRog
'My Love' (SS-c) — LRHS NRog
* 'Myuma Fubuki' (MD) — CSut
'Nagano' (MD) — Last listed 1999
'Nargold' (MS-c/Fim) — LAyl
'Nationwide' (SD) ♀ — Last listed 1993
'Neal Gillson' (MD) — Last listed 1999
¶ 'Nenekazi' (MS-c/Fim) — NHal

'Nepos' (SWL) | LBut
'New Baby' (MinBa) | NRog
'Nicola Jane' (Pom) ♀ | NHal
I 'Night Queen' (Pom) | CSut
'Nina Chester' (SD) | WAba
¶ 'Nonette' (SWL) | WAba
'Noreen' (Pom) | NHal
'Oakwood Diamond' (SBa) | LBut
'Omo' (Sin/Lil) ♀ | LBut
'Orange Keith's | NHal
   Choice' (MD) |
'Orange Mullett' | Last listed 1999
   (MinD/DwB) ♀ |
'Orange Nugget' (MinBa) | LRHS
I 'Orange Queen' (MC) | CSut
'Oreti Duke' (Pom) | NHal
'Orfeo' (MC) | NRog
I 'Orion' (MD) | Last listed 1998
'Ornamental Rays' (SC) | LBut
'Pablo' | WWol
'Pacific Argyle' (SD) | NHal
'Pacific Revival' (Pom) | NHal
∗ 'Park Fever' | Last listed 1997
'Park Princess' (SC/DwB) | LRHS NHal SDeJ
'Paul Chester' (SC) | Last listed 1999
'Peace Pact' (SWL) | WAba
'Peach Cupid' (MinBa) ♀ | LBut NHal WAba
'Peachette' (Misc/Lil) ♀ | LBut
'Pearl of Heemstede' | LAyl NHal
   (SD) ♀ |
'Pearl Sharowean' (MS-c) | WAba
'Pensford Marion' (Pom) | WAba
'Periton' (MinBa) | Last listed 1999
I 'Peter' (LD) | LRHS
'Phill's Pink' (SD) ♀ | Last listed 1995
I 'Phoenix' (MD) | WAba
'Pinelands' | NHal
   Morgenster' (S-c) |
'Pink Jupiter' (GS-c) | NHal
'Pink Pastelle' (MS-c) ♀ | NHal
'Pink Paul Chester' (SC) ♀ | Last listed 1995
'Pink Sensation' (SC) | LBut
'Pink Shirley Alliance' (SC) | LAyl
∗ 'Pink Silvia' | Last listed 1997
'Pink Suffusion' (SD) | NHal
'Pink Surprise' (LS-c) | SDeJ
'Pink Symbol' (MS-c) | Last listed 1999
pinnata soft yellow | CGle
'Piper's Pink' (SS-c/DwB) ♀ | Last listed 1999
I 'Pippa' (MinWL) | LBut
'Plum Surprise' (Pom) | Last listed 1999
'Polventon' (SD) | Last listed 1997
'Polventon Supreme' (SBa) | Last listed 1998
'Pomponnette' (Anem) | Last listed 1999
'Pontiac' (SC) | LAyl
'Pop Willo' (Pom) | Last listed 1999
I 'Poppet' (Pom) | WAba
'Porcelain' (SWL) ♀ | LBut NHal
'Potgieter' (MinBa) | NRog
'Preference' (SS-c) | Last listed 1999
'Preston Park' (Sin/DwB) ♀ | LAyl NHal
'Pretty Little Princess' | Last listed 1995
   (SS-c) ♀ |
'Pride of Berlin' | See D. 'Stolze von Berlin'
'Primrose Diane' (SD) | NHal WAba
'Procyon' (SD) | LRHS
'Promotion' (MC) | SDeJ
'Purple Gem' | LRHS NRog
∗ 'Quantum Leap' | WCot
'Radfo' (SS-c) | NHal WAba
'Raffles' (SD) | LAyl
'Raiser's Pride' (MC) | NHal WAba

'Rebecca Lynn' (MinD) | Last listed 1999
'Red Balloon' (SBa) | NHal
'Red Diamond' (MD) | NHal
'Red Dwarf' | See D. 'Harvest Red Dwarf'
∗ 'Red Fubuki' (MD) | CSut
'Red Velvet' (SWL) | LAyl
I 'Reedley' (SWL) | LBut
'Regal Boy' (SBa) | WAba
'Reginald Keene' (LS-c) | NHal
'Requiem' (SD) | CSut WAba
'Rhonda' (Pom) | LBut NHal
'Rhonda Suzanne' (Pom) | LBut
'Richard Marc' (SC) | LBut
'Rip City' (MS-c) | CSut
'Risca Miner' (SBa) | WAba
I 'Roberta' (SD) | WAba
'Robin Hood' (SBa) | WAba
'Rockliffe' (MinD) | Last listed 1999
'Rokesly Mini' (MinC) ♀ | Last listed 1995
'Rose Jupiter' (GS-c) | LRHS NHal
'Rothesay Herald' (SD/DwB) | Last listed 1998
'Rothesay Reveller' (MD) | Last listed 1998
'Rothesay Robin' (SD) | WAba
'Rotterdam' (MS-c) | SDeJ
I 'Roxy' | CMil EBee ECle EMan LAst LRHS
 | NCut NGdn WAba WCot
'Royal Blush' (MinD) | Last listed 1997
'Ruby Wedding' (MinD) | Last listed 1999
'Ruskin Belle' (MS-c) | Last listed 1998
'Ruskin Diane' (SD) | LBut NHal WAba
'Ruskin Lilo' (SD) | WAba
∗ 'Ruskin Tangerine' (SBa) | Last listed 1999
'Rustig' (MD) | WAba
'Ryedale Rebecca' (GS-c) | Last listed 1997
'Safe Shot' (MD) | NRog
'Saint Moritz' (SS-c) | Last listed 1997
'Salmon Athalie' (SC) | Last listed 1997
'Salmon Beauty' (D) | SDeJ
'Salmon Keene' (LS-c) | NHal WAba
'Salmon Symbol' (MS-c) | WAba
'Salsa' (Pom) ♀ | Last listed 1999
'Sam Huston' (GD) | NHal WAba
'Samantha' | See D. 'Harvest Samantha'
'Satellite' (MS-c) | SDeJ
'Scarlet Kokarde' (MinD) | Last listed 1999
'Scarlet Rotterdam' (MS-c) | WAba
'Scaur Swinton' (MD) | LAyl NHal
'Scottish Relation' (SS-c) ♀ | Last listed 1996
'Scottish Rhapsody' (MS-c) | Last listed 1999
'Seattle' (SD) | Last listed 1999
'Seikeman's Feuerball' | WAba
   (MinD) |
'Senzoe Ursula' (SD) | Last listed 1999
'Shandy' (SS-c) | LAyl NHal
sherffii | CHad CHal EBee MCCP MNrw
- x *coccinea* | CHad
'Sherwood Standard' (MD) | NHal WAba
'Sherwood Titan' (GD) | Last listed 1999
'Shirley Alliance' (SC) | WAba
'Shooting Star' (LS-c) | Last listed 1997
∗ 'Show and Tell' | Last listed 1997
'Siemen Doorenbos' | NRog
   (Anem) |
'Silver City' (LD) | NHal
'Silver Years' | Last listed 1999
¶ 'Sir Alf Ramsey' (GD) | NHal
'Small World' (Pom) ♀ | LAyl LBut NHal WAba
¶ 'Smoots' (SC/Fim) | NHal
'Sneezy' (Sin) | LRHS
¶ 'Snip' (MinS-c) | WAba
'Snowstorm' (MD) | SDeJ
'So Dainty' (MinS-c) ♀ | LAyl WAba

'Sonia'   Last listed 1998
* 'Spacemaker'   SDeJ
¶ 'Spartacus' (LD)   WAba
§ 'Stolze von Berlin' (MinBa) NRog WAba
  'Stoneleigh Cherry' (Pom)   LAyl LBut
  'Suffolk Punch' (MD)   LAyl LBut
* 'Suitzus Julie' (DwB)   NHal
  'Summer Night' (MC)   CHad CPlt
  'Summer Night' (SC)   NHal
  'Sunray Glint' (MS-c)   WAba
  'Superfine' (SC)   WAba
  'Swanvale' (SD)   NHal
  'Sweet Sensation' (MS-c)   Last listed 1999
  'Sweetheart' (SD)   ETub LRHS
  'Sylvia's Desire' (SC)   NHal
  'Sympathy' (SWL)   NHal WAba
I 'Tally Ho' (Misc)   EBee EMan LRHS MBri NCut
                                          WCot
  'Taratahi Lilac'   See *D.* 'Lilac Taratahi'
¶ 'Taratahi Ruby' (SWL)   NHal
  'Tender Moon' (SD)   Last listed 1999
  'Thomas A. Edison' (MD)   CSut
  'Tiny Tot'   See *D.* 'Harvest Tiny Tot'
  'Tommy Doc' (SS-c)   NHal WAba
  'Tomo' (SD)   NHal
  'Top Choice' (GS-c)   SDeJ
* 'Topaz Puff'   LRHS
I 'Tranquility' (Col)   NHal
  'Trelawny' (GD)   WAba
  'Trendy' (SD)   SDeJ
  'Trengrove Jill' (MD)   LAyl
  'Trengrove Tauranga' (MD)   Last listed 1998
  'Trevelyn Kiwi' (S-c)   NHal
  'Tui Orange' (SS-c)   NHal WAba
  'Twiggy' (SWL)   LRHS
  'Twilight Time' (MD)   LRHS
  'Union Jack' (Sin)   WAba
  'Vaguely Noble' (SBa)   NHal
  'Vazon Bay' (MinBa)   CSut
  'Vera's Elma' (LD)   NHal
  'Veritable' (MS-c)   SDeJ
  'Vicky Crutchfield' (SWL)   LAyl LBut
  'Walter Hardisty' (GD) ♀   Last listed 1988
  'Walter James' (SD)   Last listed 1997
  'Wanda's Capella' (GD)   NHal WAba
  'Wandy' (Pom) ♀   WAba
  'Warkton Willo' (Pom)   Last listed 1997
  'Welcome Guest' (MS-c)   WAba
  'Wendy's Place' (Pom)   Last listed 1999
  'Weston Nugget' (MinC)   LBut WAba
  'Whale's Rhonda' (Pom)   WAba
  'White Alva's' (GD) ♀   NHal
  'White Ballet' (SD) ♀   LAyl LBut NHal
  'White Kerkrade' (SC)   Last listed 1997
  'White Klankstad' (SC)   Last listed 1999
¶ 'White Knight' (MinD)   NHal
  'White Linda' (SD)   NHal
  'White Moonlight' (MS-c)   LAyl LBut NHal WAba
  'White Perfection' (LD)   CSut SDeJ
  'White Polventon' (SBa)   NHal
  'White Swallow' (SS-c)   NHal
  'Willo's Flecks' (Pom)   WAba
  'Willo's Surprise' (Pom)   NHal
  'Willo's Violet' (Pom)   WAba
¶ 'Willowfield Mick' (LD)   NHal
  'Winkie Colonel' (GD)   NHal
  'Winston Churchill' (MinD)   LBut
  'Wittemans Superba'   LAyl NHal
    (SS-c) ♀
  'Wootton Cupid' (MinBa)   ♀LAyl LBut NHal WAba
  'Wootton Impact' (MS-c) ♀   LBut NHal
  'Worton Bluestreak' (SS-c)   LBut

  'Yellow Cheer' (SD/DwB)   SDeJ
  'Yellow Frank Hornsey'   WAba
    (SD)
  'Yellow Hammer'   LAyl NHal SChu
    (Sin/DwB) ♀
  'Yellow Impact' (MS-c)   Last listed 1999
  'Yellow Linda's Chester'   NHal
    (SC)
  'Yellow Spiky' (MS-c)   Last listed 1997
  'Yellow Star' (MS-c)   CSut
  'Yellow Symbol' (MS-c)   LBut
  'Yelno Enchantment' (SWL)LAyl
  'Yelno Harmony' (SD) ♀   LBut
  'Yelno Velvena' (SWL)   LAyl
  'York and Lancaster' (MD)   EMon
  'Yorkie' (MS-c)   WAba
I 'Yvonne' (MWL)   NHal WAba
* 'Zakuro Fubuki' (MD)   CSut
  'Zorro' (GD) ♀   LBut NHal WAba

DAIS (Thymelaeaceae)
  cotinifolia   CPle

DAISWA See PARIS

DALEA (Papilionaceae)
  fremontii   Last listed 1998
  purpurea   Last listed 1999

DALECHAMPIA (Euphorbiaceae)
  dioscoreifolia   CPIN

DAMPIERA (Goodeniaceae)
  diversifolia   CSpe

DANAE (Ruscaceae)
§ *racemosa* ♀   CB&S CDoC CFil EBee EMon
                                          ENot GCal LHop LRHS MRav
                                          MSte NFla SAPC SArc SDry SPer
                                          SPla SRms SSpi SSta WSpi WWeb

DAPHNE ✿ (Thymelaeaceae)
  acutiloba   CPMA ERea GBri LRHS SAga SBrw
                                          SSta WCru
  albowiana   CFil CPMA SSpi SSta WCru WPGP
                                          WPat WWes
¶ 'Alison Carver'   CPMA
  alpina   CPMA NNrd SBla WCru
  altaica   CPMA
  'Anton Fahndrich'   SBla
  arbuscula ♀   CPMA EPot SBla WPat
  - subsp. *arbuscula*   SBla
    f. *albiflora*
I 'Aureamarginata Alba'   CPMA
  'Beauworth'   CPMA GCrs SBla SSta
  bholua   CPMA ERea GGGa LHop LRHS
                                          MDun SBrw SReu SSta WCru
                                          WRus WSpi
I - 'Alba'   CB&S CFil CPMA LRHS SBla SSta
                                          WCru WPGP
¶ - 'Darjeeling'   CFil CPMA ELan EPfP LRHS MAsh
                                          SBla SBrw SMur SSpi SSta WCru
                                          WPGP WPat WWat
  - var. *glacialis*   WCru
  - - 'Gurkha' ♀   CPMA SSta
¶ - 'Glendoick'   EPfP MAsh
  - 'Jacqueline Postill' ♀   CEnd CPMA EPfP GKir LRHS
                                          MAsh MBlu MBri MDun MGos
                                          SBla SSpi SSta WAbe WCru WGer
                                          WPat WWat
  - 'Peter Smithers'   SBla SSta
¶ - Wakehurst form   CPMA

blagayana	CBlo CFil CPMA EPot SBla SRms WCru WPGP
* - ***nana***	ITim
'Bramdean'	SBla
x ***burkwoodii*** ♀	CB&S CBlo IOrc SLon WCFE WDin WGwG WRHF
- 'Albert Burkwood'	CB&S CPMA MDun NWea SBla
- 'Astrid' (v)	COtt CPMA ELan LHop LNet LRHS MBlu MGos SBrw SLim SMur SPer SSta WDin WPyg WStI WWeb WWes
¶ - 'Brigg's Moonlight' (v)	LRHS MAsh SPer
§ - 'Carol Mackie' (v)	CPMA GGGa LRHS MAsh MDun SBla SSta
- 'G.K. Argles' (v)	CBlo CFil CPMA EPfP LRHS MAsh MDun MGos MLan MWst SBla SSta WPGP WPat WWes
- 'Gold Strike' (v)	CPMA
- 'Lavenirei'	CPMA
- 'Somerset'	More than 30 suppliers
§ - 'Somerset Gold Edge' (v)	CPMA
§ - 'Somerset Variegated'	SBla
I - 'Variegata'	IMGH WBod WPat
- 'Variegata' broad cream edge	See *D.* x *burkwoodii* 'Somerset Variegated'
- 'Variegata' broad gold edge	See *D.* x *burkwoodii* 'Somerset Gold Edge'
- 'Variegata' narrow gold edge	See *D.* x *burkwoodii* 'Carol Mackie'
caucasica	CPMA SBla
¶ aff. ***caucasica***	SBla
'Cheriton'	CPMA GCrs SBla SSta WBcn
cneorum	CB&S CBlo CEnd CFil CPMA ELan ENot EPfP EWTr LRHS MDun MGos NBee NEgg SBod SMur SReu SSta WPat WSpi WStI WWeb WWin
- f. ***alba***	CPMA SBla
- var. ***arbuscula*** x ***verlotii***	CPMA
- 'Blackthorn Triumph'	SBla
- 'Eximia' ♀	CPMA EPot GCrs IOrc LNet MAsh MBel MDun MGos MWst SRms WAbe
- 'Grandiflora'	See *D.* x *napolitana* 'Maxima'
* - 'Poszta'	CPMA SAga SBla WCru
- var. ***pygmaea***	CPMA EPot SBla WPat
- - 'Alba'	CPMA SBla WPat
- 'Rose Glow'	CPMA
- 'Rubrum'	EPot
¶ - 'Stasek'	SBla
- 'Variegata'	CB&S CPMA EPot LHop MGos MMil NWCA SIng WAbe
- 'Velký Kosir'	CPMA SBla
collina	See *D. sericea* Collina Group
- x ***petraea***	SSta
'Fragrant Cloud' (aff. ***acutiloba***) CD&R 626	CPMA SBla
genkwa	CPMA LRHS SBla SBrw
giraldii	CPMA EPot GCrs MGrG SSpi WCru
x ***hendersonii***	CPMA
- 'Appleblossom'	CPMA SBla
- 'Blackthorn Rose'	SBla
- CDB 11660	Last listed 1999
- 'Ernst Hauser'	CPMA GCrs SBla
- 'Fritz Kummert'	CPMA SBla
- 'Rosebud'	SBla
x ***houtteana***	CBot CPMA LRHS NBir SSta WCru
x ***hybrida***	CPMA SBla
japonica 'Striata'	See *D. odora* 'Aureomarginata'
jasminea	CPMA ECho SBla SIng WPat
- AM form	Last listed 1998
jezoensis	CPMA SBla
juliae	CPMA SBla
'Kilmeston'	CPMA SBla
kosaninii	GKir
laureola	CPMA CSWP EPfP GCrs GPoy MBro MGos NPer NSti SSta WSpi WWat WWye
- var. ***cantabrica***	SChu
- 'Margaret Mathew'	EPot SBla
- subsp. ***philippi***	CBlo CPMA CWSG EPfP IMGH LHop LRHS MAsh SBrw SChu SPer SSpi SSta WCot WCru WPat WWat
'Leila Haines' x ***arbuscula***	CPMA SBla
longilobata	WCru WPat WWat
- 'Peter Moore'	CPMA
x ***manteniana***	SSpi
- 'Manten'	CPMA SLon
¶ x ***mauerbachii*** 'Perfume of Spring'	CPMA SBla
'Meon'	CPMA SBla
mezereum	More than 30 suppliers
- f. ***alba***	CFil CPMA GAbr GKir IOrc LHop LRHS MBar MGos NChi NNrd SBla SPer SRms SSta WAbe WCru WPGP WPat WPyg WTin WWat
- 'Bowles' Variety'	CBot CPMA EPot SPer
- 'Rosea'	SRms
- var. ***rubra***	CB&S CBlo CFil CPMA ELan EPfP GVer IOrc LNet MGos NBee NBlu SBod SPer SReu SSta WAbe WCru WDin
- 'Variegata'	LHop
x ***napolitana*** ♀	CPMA LNet LRHS MGos MWst SSta WWat
§ - 'Maxima'	MAsh MGos
odora	CBlo CPMA CPle ERea GOrc LRHS LSpr MAsh MGos SBrw SChu SSta WSel WStI
§ - f. ***alba***	CB&S CPMA ERea LRHS MGos SSta
§ - 'Aureomarginata'	More than 30 suppliers
- 'Banana Split'	Last listed 1998
- 'Clotted Cream'	CPMA
¶ - 'Geisha Girl' (v)	SPer
- var. ***leucantha***	See *D. odora* f. *alba*
- 'Marginata'	See *D. odora* 'Aureomarginata'
- var. ***rubra***	CPMA LRHS SBrw SSta
- 'Sakiwaka'	CPMA
- 'Walberton' (v)	LRHS
* - 'Zuiko-nishiki'	WCru
oleoides	CPMA GCrs IMGH LNet SBla
petraea	EPot SBla
- 'Alba'	See *D. petraea* 'Tremalzo'
- 'Grandiflora' ♀	EPot GCrs SBla WAbe WPat
§ - 'Tremalzo'	SBla
pontica ♀	CB&S CFil CPMA CPle EPfP LRHS SBrw SDix SSpi SUsu WCru WPGP WPat WWat
pseudomezereum	WCru
retusa	See *D. tangutica* Retusa Group
'Richard's Choice'	CPMA
rodriguezii	Last listed 1998
x ***rollsdorfii*** 'Arnold Cihlarz'	CPMA SBla
- 'Wilhelm Schacht'	CPMA SBla
'Rosy Wave'	SBla
§ ***sericea*** ♀	CPMA SBla SRms
§ - Collina Group	CPMA EPfP SRms SSpi SSta WWat
x ***suendermannii***	SBla
tangutica ♀	More than 30 suppliers
§ - Retusa Group ♀	CPMA EPot GAbr GChr GKir

	GMaP LHop MBri MGos NRya SAga SBla SReu SRms SSta SUsu WCru WPyg
x *thauma*	SBla
- 'Aymon Correvon'	CPMA SBla
'Tichborne'	CPMA SBla
¶ *velenovskyi*	SBla

DAPHNIPHYLLUM (Daphniphyllaceae)

glaucescens B&SWJ 4058	WCru
himalense var.	CB&S CDoC CFil CHEx CMCN
macropodum	CPle EOas EPfP EPla MBlu SAPC SArc SBrw SDix SLPl SMad SSpi SSta WPGP WShe
– – B&SWJ 581	WCru
humile B&SWJ 2898	WCru
teijsmannii B&SWJ 3805	WCru

DARLINGTONIA (Sarraceniaceae)

| *californica* ♀ | CFil CSWC EAnd EEls EFEx GTro WMEx |

DARMERA (Saxifragaceae)

| § *peltata* ♀ | More than 30 suppliers |
| - 'Nana' | ECha MFir MTed NHol NLar SWat WCot WFar |

DASYLIRION (Agavaceae)

§ *acrotrichum*	CHEx SAPC SArc
glaucophyllum	EPVP
gracile Planchon	See *D. acrotrichum*
longissimum	Last listed 1999
texanum	EOas
wheeleri	CAbb CRoM CTrC

DASYPHYLLUM (Asteraceae)

| *diacanthoides* | CGre |

DATISCA (Datiscaceae)

| *cannabina* | CArn GCal SMrm WCot WPic |

DATURA (Solanaceae)

arborea	See *Brugmansia arborea*
chlorantha	See *Brugmansia chlorantha*
cornigera	See *Brugmansia arborea*
§ *inoxia*	EBak ERea MSal SOWG SYvo
- 'Evening Fragrance'	SPar
- subsp. *inoxia*	Last listed 1998
metel	ERea
- black	Last listed 1997
* - 'Cherub'	GQui
§ - 'La Fleur Lilas'	Last listed 1997
meteloides	See *D. inoxia*
rosea	See *Brugmansia* x *insignis* pink
rosei	See *Brugmansia sanguinea*
sanguinea	See *Brugmansia sanguinea*
stramonium	CArn EWFC MHew MSal SSte SYvo WHer WWye
- var. *chalybaea*	MSal
suaveolens	See *Brugmansia suaveolens*
versicolor	See *Brugmansia versicolor* Lagerh.
- 'Grand Marnier'	See *Brugmansia* x *candida* 'Grand Marnier'

DAUCUS (Apiaceae)

| *carota* | CArn CKin EWFC IIve MHew WHer |

DAVALLIA ✿ (Davalliaceae)

| *canariensis* ♀ | CFil CGre |
| I *fejeensis* | See *D. solida* var. *fejeensis* |

§ *mariesii* ♀	CFil MBri WCot WRic
- var. *stenolepis*	NMar
pyxidata	See *D. solida* var. *pyxidata*
§ *solida* var. *fejeensis*	MBri
§ - var. *pyxidata*	NMar
tasmanii	CFil
trichomanoides	NMar WRic
¶ - f. *barbata*	NMar
- var. *lorrainei*	NMar

DAVIDIA (Davidiaceae)

| *involucrata* ♀ | More than 30 suppliers |
| - var. *vilmoriniana* ♀ | CB&S CGre ELan EPfP LNet LRHS MAsh MGos NBee SPer SRPl WBod WOrn |

DEBREGEASIA (Urticaceae)

| *longifolia* | Last listed 1999 |

DECAISNEA (Lardizabalaceae)

fargesii	CBrd CDoC CPle EBee ELan EPla EWTr IDee MBNS MBel MBlu MCCP MDun MWhi NArg NTow SBrw SMad SPar SPer WBod WBor WDin WGer WHer WWat
- 'Harlequin' (v)	Last listed 1997
insignis	WNor

DECODON (Lythraceae)

| *verticillatus* | EMon |

DECUMARIA (Saxifragaceae)

| *barbara* | CB&S CDoC CFil CGre CHEx CMac CPlN CTrC EBee EMil EPfP EPla GEil GOrc LRHS MBlu SBra SLim SLon SSta WCru WSHC WWat |
| *sinensis* | CHEx CPlN EPfP SBra SSpi WSHC |

DEGENIA (Brassicaceae)

| *velebitica* | NTow |

DEINANTHE (Hydrangeaceae)

bifida	WCru
- B&SWJ 5012	WCru
caerulea	EBee WCru WPGP

DELAIREA (Asteraceae)

| § *odorata* | CHEx |

DELONIX (Caesalpiniaceae)

| *regia* | LBlo SOWG |

DELOSPERMA (Aizoaceae)

§ *aberdeenense*	CHEx
* *album*	CHEx
ashtonii	EOas NTow SChr WPer
'Basutoland'	See *D. nubigenum*
congestum	Last listed 1999
cooperi	CFai EDAr EOas NHol NSla NTow SChr SIng SMad WPat WPer WPyg WWoo
* *deschampsii*	WWeb
floribundum	CTrC
lineare	NBir
lydenburgense	IBlr SChr
* *macei*	Last listed 1997
macellum	EOas
mariae	Last listed 1997
§ *nubigenum*	CHEx CHal CTrC EDAr ELan EOas EPot GGar LNor LRHS NHol NNrd SIng SSmi WHoo WPer WPyg

WWin
sutherlandii   EDAr EOas WPyg
uncinatum   EOas

DELPHINIUM ✿ (Ranunculaceae)

'Abendleuchten'   LGre
'Agnes Brookes'   ERou
alabamicum   Last listed 1998
'Alice Artindale'   CBos CHad CPlt EGle LGre MRav
                SAga SMrm WSan
'Alie Duyvensteyn'   EFou
ambiguum   See *Consolida ajacis*
andesicola   Last listed 1998
'Ann Kenrick'   MWoo
'Ann Woodfield'   MWoo
'Anne Page'   ERou
Astolat Group   More than 30 suppliers
'Augenweide'   EFou
Avon strain   MWoo
'Barbara Nason'   Last listed 1997
barbeyi   EBee
'Basil Clitheroe'   Last listed 1998
beesianum   Last listed 1998
 - ACE 1361   GBin
Belladonna Group   ELan SRPl WHil
 - 'Atlantis'   EBrP EBre ECha EFou LBCl LBSe
                LBre LGre LRHS MBBe MBri SAga
                SBre SMrm SWat WViv
 - 'Ballkleid'   EFou
 - 'Blue Shadow'   LRHS
 - 'Capri'   Last listed 1998
 - 'Casa Blanca'   CBlo CGle CPlt EBee EFou EWTr
                LRHS NArg SMrm SRPl SWat
                WLRN WPer
 - 'Cliveden Beauty'   CBlo CGle EBee EFou EWTr GBri
                LRHS SMrm SWat WLRN WPer
I - 'Freedom'   LRHS
 - 'Kleine Nachtmusik'   EFou
 - 'Moerheimii'   EFou MTis
 - 'Peace'   EBrP EBre LBCl LBSe LBre LRHS
                MBBe SBre
 - 'Piccolo'   EBee EBrP EBre EFou LBCl LBSe
                LBre LRHS MBBe MTis SBre SWat
                WViv
 - 'Pink Sensation'   See *D.* x *ruysii* 'Pink Sensation'
 - 'Völkerfrieden'   EBee EBrP EBre EFou LBCl LBSe
                LBre LRHS MBBe MBri MRav NPri
                NPro SBre WRus
x ***bellamosum***   CBlo CBot CMGP EBee EFou
                EWTr GBri LRHS SMrm SPla SWat
                WLRN WPer WViv
'Berghimmel'   Last listed 1998
'Beryl Burton'   ERou
'Betty Baseley'   ERou
bicolor   EBee
Black Knight Group   More than 30 suppliers
'Blauwal'   LGre SWat
Blue Bird Group   CB&S EBee ELan EPfP EWTr GAbr
                GKir LRHS MBri MBro MCAu
                MRav NFor NMir NPri NVic SMer
                SPer SPla WFar
'Blue Butterfly'   See *D. grandiflorum* 'Blue
                Butterfly'
'Blue Dawn' ♀   CBla ERou
Blue Fountains Group   EMan GKir LRHS MBri NBee
                NOak SPer SRms WStI
Blue Heaven Group   Last listed 1997
Blue Jade Group   CBla ERou
'Blue Jay'   CB&S CMGP EBee EBrP EBre
                ENot EOld EWTr LBCl LBSe LBre
                LRHS MBBe MCAu MMal NBir
                NPri SBre SPer WLRN

'Blue Lagoon'   CBla
'Blue Mirror'   WViv
'Blue Nile' ♀   CBla ERou MWoo
Blue Springs Group   NOrc WShe WViv
'Blue Tit'   CBla ERou MWat
'Blue Triumph'   WPyg
'Blue Triumphator'   LRHS
§ ***brachycentrum***   Last listed 1998
'Browne's Lavender'   Last listed 1997
'Bruce' ♀   EFou ERou MWoo WCFE
brunonianum   CLyd EBee NLAp
bulleyanum   EBee
'Butterball'   CBla
californicum   Last listed 1998
Cameliard Group   CB&S CMGP EBee EBrP EBre ECtt
                ELan EMan GAbr LBCl LBSe LBre
                LRHS MBBe NCut NPri SBre SPer
                SRPl WLRN
'Can-can' ♀   ERou
cardinale   EBee EWTr LEur
'Carl Topping'   ERou
carolinianum   Last listed 1998
 - subsp. *virescens*   See *D. virescens*
cashmerianum   EBee MTho NTow
 - 'Gladys Hull'   Last listed 1998
'Cassius' ♀   CBla ERou MWoo
caucasicum   See *D. speciosum*
'Celebration'   Last listed 1997
* 'Centurion Sky Blue'   Last listed 1999
ceratophorum   EBee
chamissonis   See *D. brachycentrum*
cheilanthum   Last listed 1999
'Chelsea Star'   CBla ERou WViv
'Cherry Blossom'   Last listed 1999
'Cherub'   CBla ERou MWoo
chinense   See *D. grandiflorum*
'Christel'   EFou
'Circe'   ERou
'Clack's Choice'   ERou WViv
'Claire' ♀   MWoo
¶ 'Clear Springs Blue'   WWeb
    (Clear Springs Series)
'Clear Springs Lavender'   Last listed 1998
    (Clear Springs Series)
'Clear Springs Mid Blue'   Last listed 1998
    (Clear Springs Series)
'Clear Springs Rose Pink'   Last listed 1998
    (Clear Springs Series)
'Clifford Lass'   MWoo
'Clifford Pink'   CBla MWoo
'Clifford Sky' ♀   MWoo
Connecticut Yankees Group CBlo CFri NOak
'Conspicuous' ♀   CBla ERou MWoo
'Constance Rivett' ♀   ERou
¶ 'Cottage Garden Blue   MDCh
    and White'
aff. ***crassifolium***   Last listed 1999
'Cressida'   ERou
'Cristella'   ERou
'Crown Jewel'   CBla EFou ERou WCFE
¶ x ***cultorum***   CFri
'Cupid'   CBla ERou
'Daily Express'   ERou
'Darling Sue'   Last listed 1997
'David's Magnificent'   WEas
decorum   Last listed 1998
delavayi   Last listed 1999
 - CLD 895   Last listed 1999
* 'Delfy Blue'   WViv
¶ 'Delfy Light Blue'   WViv
¶ 'Delfy White'   WViv
'Demavand'   ERou

'Dolly Bird'	CBla ERou
'Dora Larkan'	Last listed 1997
'Dreaming Spires'	SRms
'Duchess of Portland'	ERou
dwarf dark blue	LRHS
dwarf lavender	LRHS
dwarf pink	LRHS
dwarf sky blue	LRHS
'Eamonn Andrews'	ERou
elatum	EWTr GCal SRms
'Elmfreude'	Last listed 1998
'Emily Hawkins' ♀	ERou MWoo
'Eva Gower'	ERou
exaltatum	Last listed 1999
'F.W. Smith'	WPyg
'Fanfare' ♀	CBla ERou
'Father Thames'	ERou
'Faust' ♀	CBla ERou MWat MWoo
'Fenella' ♀	CBla MWoo WCFE
'Finsteraarhorn'	EFou
'Foxhill Nina'	Last listed 1997
'Fred Yule'	ERou
Galahad Group	More than 30 suppliers
'Garden Party'	CBla
'Gemma'	MWoo
geraniifolium	NTow
geyeri	EBee
'Gillian Dallas' ♀	CBla ERou MWoo
'Giotto' ♀	Last listed 1995
glareosum	Last listed 1999
glaucum	Last listed 1998
'Gletscherwasser'	LGre
'Gordon Forsyth'	CBla ERou MWoo
'Gossamer'	Last listed 1998
§ *grandiflorum*	EBee ESis EWTr SMrm
– ACE 1606	Last listed 1999
– 'Azure Fairy'	Last listed 1999
§ – 'Blauer Zwerg'	CGle EBee EPfP WRus
§ – 'Blue Butterfly'	CBot CSpe EBee EBrP EBre EBur
	EWTr LBCl LBSe LBre LRHS MBBe
	MWgw NOrc SBla SBre SCoo SPlb
	WPer WWin
– Blue Dwarf	See *D. grandiflorum* 'Blauer
	Zwerg'
* – 'Tom Pouce'	Last listed 1999
– 'White Butterfly'	EBee
Guinevere Group	CB&S EBee EBrP EBre ECtt EMan
	EOld EWTr GAbr LBCl LBSe LBre
	LPVe LRHS MBBe MBri MMal
	MRav MWat NBir NFor NPri SBre
	SPer SPla WFar WRHF WViv
'Guy Langdon'	ERou
'Harlekijn'	Last listed 1998
'Harmony'	ERou
himalayae	Last listed 1998
'Honey Bee'	Last listed 1997
hotulae	EBee
hybridum	Last listed 1998
'Icecap'	Last listed 1997
Ivory Towers Group	ECtt
'James Nuttall'	ECha
'Joyce Roffey'	ERou
'Judy Knight'	ERou MWat
'Kathleen Cooke' ♀	Last listed 1997
'Kestrel'	ERou
King Arthur Group	CB&S EBee ECtt EHol ELan ENot
	EPfP GAbr GKir MBri MCAu
	MOne MRav MWat NFla NPri
	SMer SPer WFar
'Lady Guinevere'	ERou WPyg
§ 'Langdon's Royal Flush' ♀	CBla MWoo
'Leonora'	ERou

likiangense	EBee
* 'Lilac Arrow'	Last listed 1998
'Lilian Bassett' ♀	ERou MWoo
'Loch Leven' ♀	CBla ERou MWoo
'Loch Nevis'	Last listed 1997
'Lord Butler' ♀	CBla
'Lorna'	ERou
§ *luteum*	CPBP EDAr SBla WIvy
Magic Fountains Series	EBee EBrP EBre EWTr GKir LBCl
	LBSe LBre MBBe MTis NCut NPri
	SBre SMrm SPlb STes WGor WRHF
'Magic Fountains Sky Blue'	LRHS
(Magic Fountains Series)	
'Margaret Farrand'	ERou
'Marie Broan'	ERou
'Max Euwe'	Last listed 1998
menziesii	EBee ERos NWCA
'Michael Ayres' ♀	CBla ERou MWoo
'Micky'	Last listed 1998
'Mighty Atom' ♀	CBla ERou MWoo
'Min' ♀	ERou MWoo
'Molly Buchanan'	CBla ERou
montanum	Last listed 1998
'Moonbeam'	CBla
'Morning Cloud'	ERou
'Mother Teresa'	ERou
'Mrs Newton Lees'	ERou LBuc WPyg
'Mrs T. Carlile'	ERou
multiplex	Last listed 1998
muscosum	Last listed 1998
* 'Mystique'	CBla ERou
'Nar'	Last listed 1998
nelsonii	Last listed 1998
New Century hybrids	CB&S EBrP EBre LBCl LBSe LBre
	LRHS MBBe SBre
'Nicholas Woodfield'	MWoo
'Nimrod'	CBla ERou
'Nobility'	CBla ERou
nudicaule	CBot CFwr EBee EDAr EPfP LRHS
	MBNS MHer SGar SRot
– var. *luteum*	See *D. luteum*
nuttallianum	Last listed 1998
occidentale	Last listed 1998
'Olive Poppleton'	CBla MWoo
'Oliver' ♀	ERou MWoo
* *orfordii*	EBee NWCA
'Our Deb' ♀	MWoo
oxysepalum	EBee
Pacific hybrids	ENot EWTr GKir LRHS NOak
	SRms
* 'Pandora'	CBla
* 'Parade'	EFou
parryi	Last listed 1998
'Patricia Johnson'	ERou
Percival Group	LRHS
'Pericles'	CBla
'Perlmutterbaum'	LGre
Pink Dream Group	Last listed 1997
'Pink Ruffles'	CBla ERou
pogonanthum	Last listed 1999
'Polar Sun'	ERou
'Princess Caroline'	CB&S
przewalskii	Last listed 1998
pseudograndiflorum	Last listed 1999
ACE 2243	
'Purity'	ERou
'Purple Ruffles'	ERou
'Purple Sky'	Last listed 1998
'Purple Triumph'	ERou
'Purple Velvet'	CBla
pylzowii	CLyd EBee MBro NNrd
pyramidatum	Last listed 1998

'Pyramus' ERou
'Rakker' Last listed 1999
'Red Rocket' CB&S
requienii CBot EBee ERav MTho NBir WCot
WEas WPen
- variegated Last listed 1997
'Rona' Last listed 1997
'Rosemary Brock' ♀ ERou MWoo
Round Table Mixture CSam
'Royal Copenhagen' Last listed 1998
'Royal Flush' See *D.* 'Langdon's Royal Flush'
'Royal Velvet' Last listed 1997
'Rubin' LGre
'Ruby' CBla
§ x **ruysii** 'Pink Sensation' CBot ERou EWTr GBri MTed
NBro NPri STes WHil WPGP WPyg
WRus
'Sabrina' CBla ERou
'Samantha' ERou
'Sandpiper' ♀ Last listed 1997
'Sarah Edwards' Last listed 1997
scaposum Last listed 1998
'Schildknappe' EFou LBuc LGre SMrm
'Schönbuch' Last listed 1999
scopulorum EBee
§ **semibarbatum** CBot NPri
'Sentinel' ERou
'Shimmer' CBla ERou
'Silver Jubilee' ERou
'Silver Moon' ERou
'Sky Beauty' Last listed 1997
* 'Sky Fantasie' Last listed 1998
'Skyline' CBla ERou
Snow White Group NOak
'Snowdon' Last listed 1998
'Solomon' ERou
¶ 'Sommerabend' LGre
Southern Aristocrats Group WPyg
Southern Consort Group CBlo WPyg
Southern Countess Last listed 1999
Group ♀
Southern Countrymen Last listed 1996
Group ♀
Southern Debutante Group CBlo WPyg
Southern Jesters Group CBlo WPyg
Southern Ladies Group WPyg
Southern Maidens Group ♀ Last listed 1999
Southern Minstrels Group Last listed 1999
Southern Royals Group CBlo WPyg
sp. ACW Last listed 1998
sp. CLD 349 Last listed 1998
sp. from Czech Republic CGra
* 'Space Fantasy' Last listed 1998
§ **speciosum** EBee
'Spindrift' ♀ EFou
stapeliosmum EBee WCru
B&SWJ 2954
staphisagria EBee ELau EOHP MHew MSal
* - 'Variegatum' Last listed 1998
'Strawberry Fair' CBla ERou MWat WViv
suave EBee
'Summer Haze' ERou
Summer Skies Group CB&S CMGP EBee ECtt EMan
EPfP EWTr LRHS MBri MCAu
MTis MWat MWgw NBir NFla
NPri SMer SPer SRPl WFar WHoo
'Summerfield Ariane' MWoo
'Summerfield Diana' MWoo
'Summerfield Miranda' ♀ MWoo
'Summerfield Oberon' MWoo WCot
'Summerfield Viking' MWoo
'Sungleam' ♀ CBla CFir ERou EWTr MWat WRus

'Sunkissed' MWoo
'Swan Lake' ERou
tatsienense EBee GDra MBro MTho NWCA
SRms STes WHoo WPyg
- 'Album' EWes
'Tessa' ERou
'Thamesmead' ♀ Last listed 1996
'Thelma Rowe' ♀ Last listed 1991
'Thundercloud' ERou
'Tiddles' ♀ CBla
'Titania' CBla
trichophorum Last listed 1998
tricorne ERos GCrs LRHS
'Turkish Delight' CBla ERou LRHS
uliginosum EBee
¶ **variegatum** J&JA 304500 SBla
'Vespers' CBla ERou
vestitum EBee GCan
§ **virescens** Last listed 1998
- subsp. **wootonii** See *D. wootonii*
'Walton Beauty' MWoo
'Walton Gemstone' ♀ CBla MWat MWoo
'Watkin Samuel' ERou
¶ 'West End' WWeb
¶ 'West End Blue' MBri
'White Ruffles' CBla
§ **wootonii** Last listed 1998
yunnanense Last listed 1998
'Yvonne' EFou
zalil See *D. semibarbatum*
Zeeland Series light Last listed 1996
blues ♀

DENDRANTHEMA ❀ (Asteraceae)
cultivars See *Chrysanthemum*
nankingense See *Chrysanthemum*
nankingense
pacificum See *Ajania pacifica*

DENDRIOPOTERIUM See SANGUISORBA

DENDROBENTHAMIA See CORNUS

DENDROBIUM ❀ (Orchidaceae)
moniliforme Last listed 1999

DENDROCALAMUS (Poaceae - Bambusoideae)
giganteus Last listed 1997
§ **strictus** Last listed 1997

DENDROMECON (Papaveraceae)
rigida CB&S CFil EPfP LRHS SBra SMad
SMrm SMur SSpi WPGP

DENDROSERIS (Asteraceae)
littoralis Last listed 1998

DENNSTAEDTIA (Dennstaedtiaceae)
davallioides WRic

DENTARIA (Brassicaceae)
californica EBee EPar WCru
diphylla EPar WCru
microphylla See *Cardamine microphylla*
pinnata See *Cardamine heptaphylla*
polyphylla See *Cardamine kitaibelii*

DERMATOBOTRYS (Scrophulariaceae)
saundersii LHil

DERRIS (Papilionaceae)
elliptica CPIN

DERWENTIA See PARAHEBE

DESCHAMPSIA (Poaceae)

cespitosa	CBrm CKin CNat COlW EPPr EWTr GDea GOrn LBuc LHrt MBar MBrN MHar MWhi NArg NHol NNor WCFE WGwG WPer WPnP
- subsp. *alpina*	EHoe EMon EPPr LRHS
- Bronze Veil	See *D. cespitosa* 'Bronzeschleier'
§ - 'Bronzeschleier'	More than 30 suppliers
- 'Fairy's Joke'	See *D. cespitosa* var. *vivipara*
- Gold Dust	See *D. cespitosa* 'Goldstaub'
- Golden Dew	See *D. cespitosa* 'Goldtau'
- Golden Pendant	See *D. cespitosa* 'Goldgehänge'
- Golden Shower	See *D. cespitosa* 'Goldgehänge'
- Golden Veil	See *D. cespitosa* 'Goldschleier'
§ - 'Goldgehänge'	CCuc ECtt EGar EHoe EMan EMon EPPr EPfP EPla GCal LRHS NBir NHol NPro NSti SLPl
§ - 'Goldschleier'	CBrm EBee EBrP EBre ECGP ECha EFou EHoe EMon EPPr EPla EWsh GAri GCHN GGar GKir GOrn LBCl LBSe LBre LGre LRHS MBBe MCLN NHar NOak SApp SBre SCob WPGP
§ - 'Goldstaub'	EFou WCot
§ - 'Goldtau'	More than 30 suppliers
- 'Morning Dew'	ECoo WFar
¶ - 'Northern Lights' (v)	EFou
- subsp. *paludosa*	EMon EPPr
- var. *parviflora*	Last listed 1997
- 'Tauträger'	Last listed 1999
§ - var. *vivipara*	CNat EBrP EBre ECtt EHoe EMon EPPr EPla LBCl LBSe LBre LHil LRHS MBBe MMHG NBid NBro NHol NOGN NSti SBre WPrP
flexuosa	CBrm CCuc CPea EHoe EMon EPPr EPla EWTr LHrt LRHS MBri SSca WPer
- 'Tatra Gold'	More than 30 suppliers
media	Last listed 1997
- bronze	Last listed 1997
setacea bronze	Last listed 1997

DESFONTAINIA (Loganiaceae)

§ *spinosa* ♀	More than 30 suppliers
- 'Harold Comber'	CMac MDun WBod WCru WDin WGer
- *hookeri*	See *D. spinosa*

DESMANTHUS (Mimosaceae)

illinoensis	Last listed 1998
leptolobus	Last listed 1998

DESMAZERIA (Poaceae)

rigida	See *Catapodium rigidum*

DESMODIUM (Papilionaceae)

callianthum	CMac CSam EPfP LRHS WLRN WSHC
canadense	EBee WHil
§ *elegans*	CB&S CFil CMCN CPle EPfP GOrc IDee SSpi WBod WSHC
¶ *glutinosum*	EBee
podocarpum B&SWJ 1269	WCru
praestans	See *D. yunnanense*
styracifolium	Last listed 1997
tiliifolium	See *D. elegans*
§ *yunnanense*	CHEx CPle EPfP LRHS WCru WSHC

DEUTZIA ♀ (Hydrangeaceae)

calycosa	CFil
- 'Dali' SBEC 417	SDys WPGP
chunii	See *D. ningpoensis*
compacta	CFil WBod WPGP WWat
- 'Lavender Time'	GSki NSti SEas SPan WCFE
corymbosa	CFil
crenata 'Flore Pleno'	See *D. scabra* 'Plena'
- var. *nakaiana*	SIng
- - 'Nikko'	CB&S EBee EBrP EBre EPla ESis EWTr EWes GKir GOrc LBCl LBSe LBre LRHS MAsh MBBe MBar MGos MHer SBre SMad SPlb WHCG WSHC WWeb WWin
§ - var. *pubescens*	CFil WPGP
x *elegantissima*	CBlo EBee ENot ISea MRav NFla SReu SRms
- 'Fasciculata'	EPfP SPer WWin
- 'Rosealind' ♀	More than 30 suppliers
glabrata	WPGP
- B&SWJ 617	WCru
glomeruliflora	CFil EPla WPGP
gracilis	CBlo CDoC CHar CTri EBee EPfP EWTr GQui MBar MBel MRav MWat NBee SEas SLod SPer WBod WDin WFar WGwG WStI WWal WWat
- 'Aurea'	LBuc
- 'Carminea'	See *D.* x *rosea* 'Carminea'
§ - 'Marmorata'	CBlo CPMA WHCG WWes
- 'Rosea'	See *D.* x *rosea*
- 'Variegata'	See *D. gracilis* 'Marmorata'
hookeriana	GGGa ISea WWat
x *hybrida* 'Contraste'	MBri SPer
- 'Joconde'	ECtt GSki LRHS MBri WFar WKif
- 'Magicien'	CBrm CCHP CDoC CHar CMHG CSam EBrP EBre ECtt ENot EPla LBCl LBSe LBre MBBe MBel NFla NHol SBre SEas SLon SPer SSta WFar WHCG WHar WPGP WPat
- 'Mont Rose' ♀	More than 30 suppliers
- 'Perle Rose'	WLRN
x *kalmiiflora*	CB&S CMil EPla GKir GQui LRHS MBar MBel MBri MGos MGrG MRav MWhi NFor SLPl SPer SRms WDin
x *lemoinei*	CBot
longifolia	CCHP CFil SAga WPGP
- 'Veitchii' ♀	CPle GQui MRav SMrm WCFE
§ - 'Vilmoriniae'	MRav
x *magnifica*	CB&S ELan EWTr GEil GQui IOrc LRHS NFla SPan SRms WHCG WHar WStI WWeb WWin
- 'Rubra'	See *D.* 'Strawberry Fields'
monbeigii	ENot GKir WWat
§ *ningpoensis*	CB&S CEnd CFil CWSG EBee NHol NSti SMac SPan SPer SSta WPGP WWat
'Pink Pompon'	See *D.* 'Rosea Plena'
pubescens	See *D. crenata* var. *pubescens*
pulchra	CFai CFil CHar CPle EPfP GKir GOrc NPro SLon SMac SMrm SPer SSpi WHCG WPGP WWat
- B&SWJ 3870	WCru
purpurascens	WPyg
§ x *rosea*	CTrw EBee ENot EWTr LRHS MBar MWat NFla SMer SRms SWal WFar WHCG WKif WStI WWin
- 'Campanulata'	EBee ENot GSki
§ - 'Carminea' ♀	CChe GChr MRav SDix SPer SRms SSta WDin WFar WPyg

- 'Floribunda' — Last listed 1997
§ 'Rosea Plena' (d) — CCHP CDoC CHar EPfP GKir GSki LRHS MAsh MGos MGrG SEas SLim SSta WBod WCFE
scabra — GKir NPro
§ - 'Candidissima' (d) — CBlo CMHG GQui MBri MRav SMer SPer WBod WCFE
- 'Codsall Pink' — CB&S EBee MRav
§ - 'Plena' (d) — CB&S CCHP CChe EBee ECtt ELan EPfP EWTr IMGH LRHS MRav NFla SPer WPyg WWal
- 'Pride of Rochester' (d) — EBee EBrP EBre EHol ENot GChr LBCl LBSe LBre MBBe MBar MRav SBre SLon SPla WDin WHar WLRN
- 'Punctata' (v) — CFai EHoe SRms WFar
- 'Variegata' — EPla NPro NSti SLim WPGP WSHC
schneideriana — LRHS
setchuenensis — EPfP GGGa GQui SSpi SSta WHCG WSHC
- var. corymbiflora ♀ — CB&S CBot CDoC CFil EPfP EPla WBcn WKif WPGP WWat
sp. CC 1231 — Last listed 1997
staminea — CFil WPGP
§ 'Strawberry Fields' ♀ — CEnd CFai CFil CHar EBee EPla GKir LAst LRHS MAsh MBlu MBri MRav MTis NPro SBod SLon SPan WBod WKif WLRN
taiwanensis — CFil WPGP
'Tourbillon Rouge' — SRPl
x wellsii — See D. scabra 'Candidissima'
x wilsonii — SRms

DIANELLA ✿ (Phormiaceae)

caerulea — EBee ECou EGar ELan GBuc
- var. petasmatodes — LHil
- 'Variegata' — See D. tasmanica 'Variegata'
ensifolia — CInt
intermedia — IBlr WWat
- 'Variegata' — Last listed 1999
nigra — CFil CPou ECou SVen WCot
revoluta — ECou GKir IBlr
tasmanica — CElw CFee CFil CFir CGle CHEx CNic CRow EBee ECou ECre GBuc GGar IBlr LEdu MHar SAga SApp SArc SLod SSpi WSHC WWat
§ - 'Variegata' — CB&S CCtw CFir CPou CRDP ECou EGra ELan EMan EPPr EWes GQui IBlr LEdu WCot WCru

DIANTHUS ✿ (Caryophyllaceae)

acicularis — Last listed 1999
'Ada Florence' — Last listed 1998
'Admiral Crompton' (pf) — NGil
'Admiral Lord Anson' (b) — WKin
'Admiration' (b) — SHay
'Afton Water' (b) — Last listed 1998
'Alan Hardy' (pf) — Last listed 1998
'Alan Titchmarsh' (p) — NGil SBai WSpi
'Albatross' (p) — SChu
'Albert Portman' (p) — Last listed 1999
'Albus' — SYvo
'Aldridge Yellow' (b) — SAll
'Alfriston' (p) ♀ — Last listed 1989
'Alice' (p) — EBee EMFP EPfP SAll SHay WKin
'Alice Forbes' (b) — SAll SHay
'Alice Lever' (p) — WAbe
'Allen's Ballerina' (p) — Last listed 1999
§ 'Allen's Huntsman' (p) — CBlo
§ 'Allen's Maria' (p) — CBlo EDAr NCiC
'Alloway Star' (p) — EMFP WKin
'Allspice' (p) — CLTr CLyd CThr EMFP MBro

MRav SChu SSvw WEas WHoo WKin WPyg WWhi WWye
'Allspice Sport' (p) — WKin
Allwoodii Alpinus Group (p) — CNic SRms
'Allwood's Crimson' (pf) — SHay
alpinus ♀ — CGle CGra CLyd GKir GTou LBee LRHS NMen NWCA SBla SRms WHen WPer
- 'Adonis' — Last listed 1998
- 'Albus' — CPBP LBee LRHS SBla WAbe WLin
§ - 'Joan's Blood' ♀ — CLyd CPBP EPot ESis LRHS MBro NHar NMen SAga SBla WAbe WHoo WLRN WPyg
- 'Millstream Salmon' — CLyd
- 'Rax Alpe' — Last listed 1999
'Alyson' (p) — SAll
* 'Amalfi' (pf) — SAll
'Amarinth' (p) — MNrw
'Ambervale' (pf) — NGil
amurensis — EBrP EBre EMon GCal LBCl LBSe LBre LRHS MBBe SBre WPer
- 'Siberian Blue' — SRCN
anatolicus — CLyd CTri EGle LBee LRHS MHer WAbe WPer
'Andrew' (p) — SHay
'Angelo' (b) — SAll
'Ann Franklin' (pf) ♀ — Last listed 1999
'Ann Unitt' (pf) ♀ — Last listed 1998
'Annabelle' (p) — CLyd EMFP EMil LRHS MMal SChu
'Annette' (pf) — EDAr LFis LRHS
'Annie Claybourne' (pf) — NGil
'Anniversay' (p) — NGil SBai
anomala — Last listed 1997
'Antique' — Last listed 1999
'Apricot Sue' (pf) — SHay
'Archfield' — Last listed 1997
'Arctic Star' (p) — CMea EBee EDAr LRHS MBNS NHol
arenarius — CMea CNic GCHN LPVe MHer SHel SPlb WPer WWin
'Argus' — CMil SChu WKin
Arizona (pf) — SAll
* 'Arlene' (b) — SAll
armeria ♀ — CKin EWFC NEgg SIng WHer WPer
'Arnhem Spirit' (pf) — Last listed 1998
arpadianus — MDHE NHol
¶ - var. pumilus — NWCA
'Arthur' (p) — EMFP WKin
'Arthur Leslie' (b) — SAll
§ x arvernensis (p) ♀ — CNic ECha EPot GAbr MBro SAga SIng
'Ashley' (p) — SAll
'Audrey Robinson' (pf) — NGil
'Audrey's Frilly' — SChu WKin
'Aurora' (b) — SHay
'Autumn Tints' (b) — SAll
'Auvergne' — See D. x arvernensis
'Avon Dasset' — EDAr
'Baby Treasure' (p) — CLyd ECho NHol
'Badenia' (p) — CLyd LBee LRHS SChu
'Bailey's Apricot' (pf) — Last listed 1997
'Bailey's Celebration' (p) — SBai
Bailey's Yellow Delight® (p) — Last listed 1998
'Ballerina' (p) — SHay
'Barbara Evelyn' (pf) — NGil
barbatus — Last listed 1997
- Nigrescens Group (p,a) ♀ — CBre CHad CSpe LFis NDov SUsu WCot

I - 'Sooty'   EBee SSca WHer WUnu
- 'Wee Willie'   Last listed 1997
'Barleyfield Rose' (p)   CLyd NHar
'Barlow' (pf)   Last listed 1999
basuticus   Last listed 1998
- subsp. *basuticus*   CSpe
- ECN 058   Last listed 1999
'Bath's Pink'   GKir GMac LRHS
§ 'Bat's Double Red' (p)   EMFP SChu SSvw WKin
'Beauty of Cambridge' (b)   SAll
'Beauty of Healey' (p)   CLTr EMFP WKin
'Becka Falls' (p)   SHay SRms
'Becky Robinson' (p) ♀   CThr EDAr LAco SAga SAll SHay
                                   WWhi
'Bella'   CPBP
'Belle of Bookham' (b)   SAll
'Berlin Snow'   CLyd EPot ESis ITim LBee NMen
'Bet Gilroy' (b)   SHay
'Betty Buckle' (p)   SChu
'Betty Day' (b)   Last listed 1999
'Betty Dee' (pf)   NGil
'Betty Morton' (p) ♀   CLyd CPri MBro NBus SBla SMrm
                                   SSvw WHoo WKif WKin WPyg
'Betty Tucker' (b)   SHay
'Betty's Choice' (pf)   NGil
'Betty's Delight' (pf)   NGil
'Bibby's Cerise' (pf)   Last listed 1997
'Bill Smith' (pf)   Last listed 1997
'Binsey Red' (p)   EMFP WKin
Black and White Minstrels   CLyd WKin
    Group
¶ Blakeney seedling (p)   WKin
* 'Blue Carpet'   WPer
'Blue Hedgehog'   Last listed 1997
'Blue Hills' (p)   CLyd ECho ELan LBee LRHS
                                   MWat SChu
'Blue Ice' (b)   SAll SHay
'Blush'   See *D.* 'Souvenir de la Malmaison'
'Bobby' (p)   SAll
'Bobby Ames' (b)   SHay
'Bob's Highlight' (pf)   NGil
'Bombardier' (p)   EBrP EBre LBCl LBSe LBre MBBe
                                   SBre
'Bookham Fancy' (b)   SAll SHay
'Bookham Grand' (b)   SHay
'Bookham Lad' (b)   SAll
'Bookham Lass' (b)   Last listed 1998
'Bookham Perfume' (b)   SBai SHay
'Bookham Sprite' (b)   SAll SHay
'Bourboule'   See *D.* 'La Bourboule'
'Bovey Belle' (p) ♀   CLTr CSam CThr EBrP EBre LBCl
                                   LBSe LBre LRHS MBBe NGil SBai
                                   SBre WSpi
'Boydii' (p)   CLyd
'Bransgore' (p)   CLyd MBro WPyg
'Brecas' (pf)   See *D.* Dona = 'Brecas'
'Bressingham Pink' (p)   ECtt
brevicaulis   NWCA
- *brevicaulis*   Last listed 1998
- Mac&W 5849   Last listed 1998
'Brian Tumbler' (b)   SAll
'Bridal Veil' (p)   CThr EMFP GAbr SChu SSvw
                                   WKin
'Brigadier' (p)   SRms WWin
'Brilliant'   See *D. deltoides* 'Brilliant'
§ Brilliant Gipsy® =   MWst SSmt
    'Stagispan'
'Brilliant Star' (p)   CPBP EDAr
'Brimstone' (b)   SHay
'Bruce Parker' (p)   Last listed 1998
'Brympton Red' (p)   CThr ECha EFou EMFP EOrc
                                   MRav SBla SChu SMrm WEas WKif

                                   WKin WWhi
'Bryony Lisa' (b) ♀   Last listed 1995
§ 'Caesar's Mantle' (p)   WKin
caesius   See *D. gratianopolitanus*
callizonus   CPBP ESis NWCA
'Calypso' (pf)   Last listed 1999
'Calypso Star' (p)   EBee EDAr MBNS
'Camelford' (p)   WKin
'Camilla' (b)   CLyd CThr EGoo EMFP WKin
'Can-can' (pf)   ECtt
'Candy' (p)   See *D.* 'Sway Candy'
'Candy Clove' (b)   SAll SHay
'Cannup's Pride' (pf)   Last listed 1997
capitatus subsp.   Last listed 1998
    andrzejowskianus
'Carinda' (p)   SHay
'Carlotta' (p)   SHay
'Carmen' (b)   SHay
'Carmine Joy'   EDAr
'Carmine Letitia   EDAr
    Wyatt' [PBR] (p)
'Caroline Bone' (b)   SHay
'Caroline Clove' (b)   SHay
'Carolyn Hardy' (pf)   Last listed 1997
carthusianorum   CHad CMdw EWTr GSki MNrw
                                   MSte SRCN SSvw WPer
- subsp. *vaginatus*   Last listed 1998
caryophyllus   CArn GBar IIve MPEx WOak
* 'Casper' (pf)   SAll SYvo
'Casser's Pink' (p)   GBuc
'Catherine Glover' (b)   SAll SHay
* 'Catherine Tucker'   WEas
'Catherine's Choice'   See *D.* 'Rhian's Choice'
caucaseus   Last listed 1999
'Cecil Wyatt' (p)   CThr EBee EDAr EMFP
§ 'Cedric's Oldest' (p)   SChu WKin
'Champagne' (pf)   Last listed 1999
'Charcoal'   WCot
'Charity' (p)   Last listed 1998
'Charles' (p)   SAll
'Charles Edward' (p)   SAll
'Charles Musgrave'   See *D.* 'Musgrave's Pink'
'Charlotte'   SAll SHay
'Charm' (b)   SHay
'Chastity' (p)   EMFP GAbr GCHN MBro SBla
                                   SChu WHoo WKin WPyg
Cheddar pink   See *D. gratianopolitanus*
'Cherry Clove' (b)   SAll
'Cherry Moon'   LRHS NPSI
'Cherryripe' (p)   SHay
'Cheryl'   See *D.* 'Houndspool Cheryl'
'Chetwyn Doris' (p) ♀   NGil SBai
chinensis (p,a)   MBri WHer
'Chris Crew' (b) ♀   SBai
'Christine Hough' (b)   SAll
'Christopher' (p)   CBlo EBrP EBre GCHN LBCl LBSe
                                   LBre LRHS MBBe SAll SBre SHay
'Christopher Tautz' (b) ♀   Last listed 1995
'Circular Saw' (p)   CInt SChu
'Clara' (pf)   NGil
'Clara's Flame' (p)   Last listed 1998
'Clara's Lass' (p)   NGil
'Clare' (p)   SAll SHay
'Claret Joy' (p) ♀   CThr EBrP EBre EDAr EMFP LBCl
                                   LBSe LBre MBBe NGil SBai SBre
                                   SRms WSpi
'Clarinda' (b)   SAll
'Clifford Pink'   WKin
'Clockface' (p)   Last listed 1999
'Clunie' (b)   SAll SHay
§ 'Cockenzie Pink' (p)   CLTr CThr EMFP GAbr SAll WEas
                                   WKin

'Cocomo Sim' (pf)	Last listed 1998	
'Colin's Shot Salmon' (pf)	NGil	
'Constance' (p)	CBlo SAll	
'Constance Finnis'	See *D.* 'Fair Folly'	
'Consul' (b)	SAll	
'Copperhead' (b)	SHay	
'Coronation Ruby' (p) ♀	NGil SBai	
'Coste Budde' (p)	CLyd WEas WKin	
'Cranborne Seedling' (p)	WKin	
'Cranmere Pool' (p) ♀	CMea CThr EBrP EBre EDAr ELan	
	LBCl LBSe LBre LRHS MBBe	
	MBNS MCAu MWat NGil SBai	
	SBre SHay SMrm WSpi WWol	
'Cream Lass' (pf)	NGil	
'Cream Sue' (pf)	SHay	
¶ *cretaceus*	NWCA	
'Crimson Ace' (p)	SHay	
'Crimson Chance'	Last listed 1997	
'Crimson Joy' (p)	EDAr	
'Crimson Tempo' PBR (pf)	SBai SHay	
'Crimson Velvet' (b)	SHay	
crinitus	SHFr SSca	
'Crompton Bride' (pf)	Last listed 1998	
'Crompton Classic' (pf)	NGil	
'Crompton Princess' (pf)	NGil	
'Crompton Wizard' (pf)	Last listed 1997	
'Crossways' (p)	NHar	
'Crowley's Pink Sim' (pf)	Last listed 1997	
cruentus	MAnH MSte	
'Dad's Choice' (p)	SBai WSpi	
'Dad's Favourite' (p)	CGle CThr EMFP EOrc SAll SChu	
	SHay SRms SSvw WEas WHoo	
	WKin WWhi	
'Daily Mail' (p)	NGil SBai SChu	
'Dainty Clove' (b)	Last listed 1997	
'Dainty Dame' (p)	CMea COlW CSpe CTri EDAr ESis	
	GMaP LRHS NBus NHol NMen	
	SAga SBla SChu SMrm WLRN	
	WWoo	
'Dainty Lady' (b)	SBai	
'Damask Superb' (p)	CLyd EMFP MBro WKin	
'Daphne' (p)	SAll	
'Dark Pierrot' (pf) ♀	Last listed 1995	
'Dark Tempo' PBR (pf)	SBai SHay	
'Darling' (b)	SAll	
'Dartington Double' (p)	NHol	
'Dartington Laced'	GAbr WKin	
'Dartmoor Forest' (p)	Last listed 1998	
'David' (p)	CPri EPfP SAll SHay	
'David Saunders' (b) ♀	SBai	
'Dawlish Charm' (p)	CThr SBai	
'Dawlish Joy' (p)	CThr EDAr	
'Dawn' (b)	SAll SHay	
* 'Dazzler'	Last listed 1999	
'Debi's Choice' (p)	Last listed 1997	
'Deep Purple' (pf)	Last listed 1997	
Delphi (pf)	SBai SHay	
deltoides ♀	CArn CSev ECha ELau EPfP EWFC	
	GBar SIng SPlb SRms WFar WJek	
	WOak WSel	
- 'Albus'	CNic ECha EPfP EWTr GBar GSki	
	MBar NBlu SRms SWat WPer	
	WRos WSel	
- 'Bright Eyes'	Last listed 1999	
§ - 'Brilliant'	CNic CSev GTou LPVe MNrw	
	NVic SRms SWat WGor WOve	
- 'Broughty Blaze'	Last listed 1998	
- 'Dark Eyes'	EWes	
- *degenii*	Last listed 1997	
- 'Erectus'	EPfP	
- Flashing Light	See *D. deltoides* 'Leuchtfunk'	
§ - 'Leuchtfunk'	CPri EBrP EBre ECtt EMNN GDra	

		GKir GTou LBCl LBSe LBre LGro
		LRHS MBBe MOne NHar NMir
		SBre SHel SRms WEas WFar WHen
		WPer WRos
- 'Microchip'		NHar SRms SSca WFar
- 'Nelli' (p)		Last listed 1999
* - 'Red Eye'		Last listed 1999
- *splendens*		EPfP
'Denis' (p)		ELan NCiC SAll SBai WSpi
'Desert Song' (b)		SAll
'Desmond'		WRus
'Devon Blossom' (p) ♀		Last listed 1995
'Devon Blush' (p)		EBrP EBre LBCl LBSe LBre LRHS
		MBBe SBre
'Devon Charm' (p)		LRHS
'Devon Cream' PBR (p)		CThr EBee EBrP EBre EMFP LBCl
		LBSe LBre LRHS MBBe SBre SRms
		WLRN
'Devon Dove' PBR (p) ♀		CLyd CMea CThr EBee EBrP EBre
		EGra EPfP LBCl LBSe LBre LFis
		MBBe SBre SRms
'Devon General' PBR (p) ♀		CThr CTri EBee EBrP EBre LBCl
		LBSe LBre LRHS MBBe SBre
'Devon Glow' PBR (p) ♀		CLTr CThr EBrP EBre EMFP EPfP
		LBCl LBSe LBre LRHS MBBe SBre
		SRms WLRN WWeb
'Devon Joy' (p)		CMea CThr LRHS SRms
'Devon Magic' PBR (p)		CBlo SRms
'Devon Maid' PBR (p) ♀		CThr EBee EPfP
'Devon Pearl' PBR (p)		CBlo CThr
'Devon Pride' (p) ♀		EBrP EBre LBCl LBSe LBre MBBe
		SBre
'Devon Violet'		Last listed 1999
'Devon Wizard' PBR (p) ♀		EBee EMFP LRHS SRms WLRN
		WWeb
'Dewdrop' (p)		CInt CMea CTri ECtt EDAr ESis
		GCHN LRHS MHer NBir NGdn
		NHar NMen SAll SChu SMrm
		WAbe WFar WKin WLRN WPer
'Diana'		See *D.* Dona = 'Brecas'
'Diane' (p) ♀		CThr EBrP EBre EDAr ELan EMFP
		LBCl LBSe LBre MBBe NGil SAga
		SAll SBai SBre SHay WEas WPer
		WSpi WWal
* 'Diane Cape'		SAll
'Dianne' (pf)		EDAr
'Dick Portman' (p)		Last listed 1998
'Diplomat' (b)		SAll
'Doctor Archie		SHay
Cameron' (b)		
'Doctor Ramsey'		Last listed 1999
§ Dona = 'Brecas' (pf)		LRHS SAll SBai
'Dora'		CLyd LRHS SChu
'Doris' (p) ♀		More than 30 suppliers
'Doris Allwood' (pf)		NGil SHay
'Doris Elite' (p)		SAll
'Doris Galbally' (b)		SBai
'Doris Majestic' (p)		SAll
'Doris Ruby'		See *D.* 'Houndspool Ruby'
'Doris Supreme' (p)		SAll
'Downs Cerise' (b)		SHay
drenovskianus		Last listed 1999
§ 'Dubarry' (p)		CTri ECtt EWes WGor WPer
'Duchess of Fife' (p)		Last listed 1999
'Duchess of		WMal
Westminster' (M)		
* 'Duet'		Last listed 1999
'Dunkirk' (b)		Last listed 1998
'Dunkirk Spirit' (pf) ♀		Last listed 1998
'Dusky' (p)		WKin
'Dwarf Vienna'		CPri
'E.J. Baldry' (b)		SHay

'Earl of Essex' (p) — CThr EHol EMFP SAll SHay WKin
'Ebor II' (b) — SAll
echiniformis — GKir
'Edenside Scarlet' (b) — SHay
'Edenside White' (b) — SAll
'Edna' (p) — SAll
* 'Eilat' (pf) — Last listed 1999
'Eileen' (p) — SAll
'Eileen Lever' (p) — MDHE SBla WAbe
'Eileen Neal' (b) ♀ — Last listed 1989
'Eileen O'Connor' (b) ♀ — SBai
'Elfin Star' (p) — EDAr
'Elizabeth' (p) — CFee CGle CThr LHop
'Elizabeth Jane' (p) — EMFP
'Elizabeth Pink' — SMrm
'Elizabethan' (p) — SBla WKin
* 'Elizabethan Pink' — CNic
'Emile Paré' (p) — SChu WKin
'Emperor' — See *D.* 'Bat's Double Red'
'Enid Anderson' (p) — SChu WKin
'Enid Burgoyne' — WKin
eretmopetalus — Last listed 1998
erinaceus — CMea EMNN EPot GCHN GCrs
  GTou ITim LRHS MBro MOne
  NHar NWCA WAbe WPer WWin
 - var. *alpinus* — CLyd EPot GKir NSla SIng
'Erycina' (b) — SAll
'Ethel Hurford' — WHoo WKin
'Eudoxia' (b) — SAll
'Eva Humphries' (b) — SAll SBai SHay
'Evening Star' (p) — CPBP EDAr WWol
'Excelsior' (p) — CBlo CThr NFor
'Exquisite' (b) — SAll
§ 'Fair Folly' (p) — CThr NBus SChu SSvw WEas
  WKin
'Fair Lady' (p) — Last listed 1998
'Falcon' (pf) — SBai
'Fanal' (p) — NBir WKin
* 'Fancy Magic' (pf) — CBlo SAll
'Farnham Rose' (p) — CLTr SChu
'Fenbow Nutmeg Clove' (b) — SChu WKin
'Fettes Mount' (p) — CLTr CLyd GAbr WCot WKin
'Fiery Cross' (b) — SAll SHay
'Fimbriatus' (p) — MBro WHoo WKin WPyg
'Fingo Clove' (b) — SAll
'Fiona' (p) — SAll
'Firecrest Rose' — Last listed 1998
'Firewitch' — LRHS
'First Lady' (b) — SAll
'Flame' (p) — SHay
'Flame Sim' (pf) — Last listed 1999
'Flanders' (b) ♀ — Last listed 1989
'Fleur' (p) — SAll
'Forest Edge' (b) — SBai
'Forest Glow' (b) — SAll
'Forest Sprite' (b) — SAll SBai
'Forest Treasure' (b) — SAll SBai
'Forest Violet' (b) — SAll
'Fortuna' (p) — SAll
'Fountain's Abbey' (p) — EMFP WIvy WKin
'Fragrant Ann' (pf) ♀ — NGil SHay
¶ 'Fragrant Frills' — WWeb
'Fragrant Phyllis' (pf) — NGil
'Fragrant Rose' (pf) — NGil
* *fragrantissimus* — LRHS
'Frances Isabel' (p) ♀ — SAll
'Frances King' (pf) — Last listed 1998
'Frances Sellars' (b) — SHay
'Frank's Frilly' (p) — CThr WKin
'Freckles' (p) — CThr SHay
'Freda' (p) — SAll
'Freeland Crimson — Last listed 1998
  Clove' (b)

'French' — Last listed 1997
freynii — CLyd EWes NDlv SAga SBla SSca
* 'Frilly' — Last listed 1997
N fringed pink — See *D. superbus*
furcatus — NWCA
'Fusilier' (p) — CMea EBrP EBre ECtt EDAr EMFP
  GCrs GKir LBCl LBSe LBre LRHS
  MBBe MBar MHer NWCA SAga
  SAll SBre SChu WAbe WFar WKin
  WPat WWol
'G.J. Sim' (pf) — Last listed 1998
'G.W. Hayward' (b) — Last listed 1997
¶ 'Gail Tilsley' (b) — SHay
'Galil' (p) — SAll
'Garland' (p) — CMea CTri LRHS WGor
'Garnet' (p) — CPri SChu
'Gatekeeper' (p) — GCHN
'Gaydena' (b) — SAll
'George Allwood' (pf) — NGil
§ 'Giant Gipsy® = 'Stagigi' — MWst SSmt
giganteus — IBlr MNrw WKin
'Gingham Gown' (p) — CLyd NBir NBrk SBla
'Gipsy Clove' (b) — SHay
Gipsy King — See *D.* Giant Gipsy = 'Stagigi'
Gipsy Maiden — See *D.* White Gipsy = 'Stagiwit'
Gipsy Monarch — See *D.* Brilliant Gipsy = 'Stagispan'
Gipsy Prince — See *D.* Violet Gipsy = 'Staviolet'
Gipsy Queen — See *D.* Salmon Gipsy = 'Stadarpi'
Gipsy Rascal — See *D.* Rondo = 'Stagirond'
Gipsy Rogue® — See *D.* Scarlet Gipsy = 'Stagilon'
glacialis — GMaP GTou NHar NHol
 - subsp. *gelidus* — CGra NMen
'Glebe Cottage White' — CGle
'Gloriosa' (p) — WKin
'Glorious' (p) — SHay
'Gold Fleck' — EDAr LBee LRHS
'Golden Cross' (b) ♀ — SBai
'Golden Rain' (pf) — Last listed 1999
'Golden Sceptre' (b) ♀ — SBai
'Grandma Calvert' (p) — SAll
graniticus — WPer
'Gran's Favourite' (p) ♀ — CLTr CMea EBee EBrP EBre
  ECtt EDAr EMFP EWTr LBCl
  LBSe LBre LFis LRHS MBBe
  MWat NGil SAga SBai SBla
  SBre SChu SHay SRms WEas
  WKin WWye
§ *gratianopolitanus* ♀ — CArn CTri ELau GCHN GTou
  LRHS MHer MMal MNrw MRav
  NBid NOak SIde SRms WKin
  WPer WWye
 - 'Albus' — CLyd
 - 'Corinne Tremaine' (p) — Last listed 1998
 - 'Emmen' (p) — Last listed 1998
 - 'Fellerhexe' (p) — WEas
 - 'Flore Pleno' (d) — EMFP MInt
¶ - from Cheddar — CLyd
* - 'Karlik' (p) — Last listed 1999
§ - 'Princess Charming' (p) — Last listed 1999
 - red (p) — GAbr
 - 'Rosenfeder' (p) — WPer
 - 'Splendens' (p) — WPer
§ - 'Tiny Rubies' (p) — ECho WAbe WFar WKin
'Gravetye Gem' (b) — SRms WPyg
'Gravetye Gem' (p) — WKin
¶ 'Greensides' (p) — CLyd
'Grenadier' (p) — ECho ELan
'Grey Dove' (b) ♀ — Last listed 1989
'Greytown' (b) — Last listed 1999
'Gwendolen Read' (p) — SHay
'Gypsy Star' (p) — EDAr MBNS
haematocalyx — NWCA WAbe WPer

- 'Alpinus'	See *D. haematocalyx* subsp. *pindicola*
§ - subsp. *pindicola*	CLyd CPBP EMFP NHol WPat
'Hannah Louise' (b) ♀	SBai
'Harlequin' (p)	ECtt EMFP WPer
'Harmony' (b)	SAll SHay
¶ 'Harry Oaks' (p)	WKin
'Harry Wilcock' (pf)	Last listed 1998
'Havana' PBR (pf)	SBai SHay
'Haytor'	See *D.* 'Haytor White'
'Haytor Rock' (p) ♀	CThr EBee EBrP EBre EMFP EPfP LBCl LBSe LBre MBBe SBre SHay
§ 'Haytor White' (p) ♀	CThr EBee EBrP EBre EDAr EMFP EPfP GCHN LBCl LBSe LBre LRHS MBBe NGil SBai SBre SChu SHay SRms WCot WEas WWhi
'Hazel Ruth' (b) ♀	SBai
I 'Heath' (b)	WKin
'Heidi' (p)	EPfP
'Helen' (p)	CThr SAll SHay
'Helena Hitchcock' (p)	CThr
'Herbert's Pink' (p)	WKin
'Hereford Butter'	Last listed 1999
¶ 'Hereford Butter Market'	SChu WKin
'Hidcote' (p)	CLyd CTri ELan EMFP LRHS MWat NBus NMen SBla SIng WKin WLRN WWin
'Hidcote Red'	ECho LBee LRHS
* Highgates hybrid	CLyd
'Highland Fraser' (p)	GAbr MBro SAll SChu SRms WEas WHoo WKif WWin
Highland hybrids	Last listed 1999
'Highland Queen' (p)	WKin
'Hilda Scholes' (p)	Last listed 1999
* 'Hi-lite' (pf)	SAll
¶ 'Hoffman's Red'	EFou
¶ 'Hoo House' (p)	WKin
'Hope' (p)	CLyd EMFP NCat SChu WKin
'Horsa' (b)	SHay
§ 'Houndspool Cheryl' (p) ♀	CPri EBee EMFP EPfP LRHS NGil SRms WWeb WWol
§ 'Houndspool Ruby' (p) ♀	COlW CThr EDAr EMFP EPfP MBNS MCAu MWat NOak SAga SBai WEas WSpi WWeb WWol
'Howard Hitchcock' (b) ♀	SBai
'Huntsman'	See *D.* 'Allen's Huntsman'
'Ian' (p)	CLTr CThr NGil SAll SBai SHay WSpi
'Ibis' (b)	SHay
'Icomb' (p)	CLyd CTri SRms WHoo WKin WPer WPyg
'Impulse' PBR (pf)	SBai
'Ina' (p)	SRms
Incas® (pf) ♀	SBai
'Inchmery' (p)	CLTr CLyd CMil EBrP EBre EMFP LBCl LBSe LBre MBBe NFor SAll SBre SChu SHay SSvw WEas WHoo WKin WWhi
'India Star' (p)	EDAr
Indios® (pf) ♀	SBai
¶ 'Ine' (p)	CPri
'Inga Bowen' (p)	Last listed 1997
'Inglestone' (p)	CTri NHar SBla WLin WPer
'Inshriach Dazzler' (p) ♀	CInt CLyd CMea CPBP EBrP EBre ECtt EDAr GAbr GCHN GCrs GDra GKir ITim LBCl LBSe LBee LBre MBBe NDlv NHar NHol NPri SBla SBre SIng SSvw WAbe WHal WKin
'Inshriach Startler' (p)	CFee CLyd CMea
'Ipswich Pink' (p)	LGro LRHS
'Irene Della-Torré' (b) ♀	SBai

'Ivonne Orange' (pf)	SBai SHay
'J.M. Bibby' (pf)	Last listed 1998
'Jacqueline Ann' (pf) ♀	Last listed 1999
'James Portman' (p)	SBai
'Jane Austen' (p)	NBrk SChu WKin WPer
'Jane Coffey' (b)	SHay
'Janelle Welch' (pf)	Last listed 1998
'Janet Walker' (p)	Last listed 1997
japonicus	LCot
* 'Jenny Spillers'	Last listed 1997
'Jenny Wyatt' (p)	SHay
'Jess Hewins' (pf)	NGil
'Jessica' (pf)	SAll
'Jo Emma' (pf)	NGil
'Joan Randal' (pf)	Last listed 1999
'Joan Schofield' (p)	CLyd NHol WWol
'Joan Siminson' (p)	WKin WWhi
'Joanne' (pf)	Last listed 1998
'Joanne's Highlight' (pf)	NGil
'Joan's Blood'	See *D. alpinus* 'Joan's Blood'
'Joe Vernon' (pf)	NGil
'John Ball' (p)	CLTr EMFP WKin
'John Faulkner' (pf) ♀	Last listed 1998
'John Gray' (p)	Last listed 1997
'John Grey' (p)	WKin
'John Partridge' (p)	SBai WSpi
'Joker' (pf)	Last listed 1997
'Joy' (p) ♀	CThr EBee EBrP EBre EDAr EMFP EPfP LBCl LBSe LBre LRHS MBBe NGil SBai SBre SHay SRms
'Judy' (p)	Last listed 1999
'Julian' (p)	SAll
¶ 'Katherine' (p)	WWeb
'Kathleen Hitchcock' (b) ♀	SBai
'Kesteven Chambery' (p)	CLyd WPer
'Kesteven Chamonix' (p)	CLyd WPer
'Kesteven Kirkstead' (p) ♀	CLyd CSWP
'Kestor' (p)	Last listed 1999
'King of the Blacks' (p,a)	CHad ELan MRav
kitaibelii	See *D. petraeus* subsp. *petraeus*
'Kiwi Pretty' (p)	CThr
knappii	CLyd CPou EGar ELan GCHN MLLN MNrw NOak SRot SSca WPer WWin WWye
- 'Yellow Harmony' (p,a)	LRHS NPri WHer
'Kosalamana'	See *D. Salamanca* = 'Kosalamana'
§ 'La Bourboule' (p) ♀	EDAr ELan EMNN EPot GAbr GKir LBee LRHS MBar MBro MWat NHol NMen NPri SBla SRms SSmi WFar WKin WPat WWin
'La Bourboule Albus' (p)	CTri EDAr EPot SBla WFar WWin SChu WKin
'Laced Hero' (p)	Last listed 1999
laced hybrids (p)	Last listed 1999
'Laced Joy' (p)	CThr EDAr EMFP SAll SChu SHay WKin
'Laced Monarch' (p)	COlW CThr EBee EBrP EBre EDAr EMFP GCHN LBCl LBSe LBre LRHS MBBe MBro NGil SAga SAll SBai SBre SChu SPlb SRms WKin WSpi
'Laced Mrs Sinkins' (p)	SBai WSpi
'Laced Prudence'	See *D.* 'Prudence'
'Laced Romeo' (p)	EMFP SAll SChu SHay WKin
'Laced Treasure' (p)	CLTr CThr SAll
'Lady Granville' (p)	SSvw WKin
'Lady Salisbury' (p)	EMFP SAsh WKin
§ 'Lady Wharncliffe' (p)	CLTr CMil EMFP WKin
'L'Amour' (b)	SAll
'Lancing'	Last listed 1999
'Lancing Lady' (b)	SAll
'Lancing Monarch' (b)	SAll SHay
langeanus	SIng

– NS 255	NWCA
'Laura' (p)	SAll SHay
'Lavender Clove' (b)	SAll SBai SHay
'Lavender Lady' (pf)	NGil
'Lawley's Red' (p)	WKin
'Leiden' (b)	SAll SBai
'Lemsii' (p) ♀	CLyd ECtt EMFP GCHN NMen NVic WPer WPyg WWye
'Lena Sim' (pf)	Last listed 1998
'Leslie Rennison' (b)	SAll SHay
'Letitia Wyatt' (p) ♀	CMea CThr EDAr LFis
'Leuchtkugel'	ECho
Liberty® (pf)	SBai SHay
'Lightning' (pf)	SAll
'Lilac Clove' (b)	Last listed 1998
¶ 'Linfield Annie's Fancy' (pf)	NGil
'Lior' (pf)	Last listed 1999
'Little Diane' (p)	Last listed 1997
'Little Gem' (pf)	WKin
'Little Jock' (p)	More than 30 suppliers
'Little Miss Muffet' (p)	Last listed 1998
'Liz Rigby' (b)	Last listed 1997
'London Brocade' (p)	NBrk EMFP
'London Delight' (p)	CThr EMFP SHay WKin
'London Glow' (p)	CThr SAll WKin
* 'London Joy'	Last listed 1997
'London Lovely' (p)	CLTr CThr SAll SSvw WKin
'London Poppet' (p)	CThr LAco SAll WHoo WKin
'Louise's Choice' (p) ♀	Last listed 1993
'Loveliness' (p)	CBre
lumnitzeri	EPot WPer
lusitanicus	Last listed 1997
'Lustre' (b)	SAll SHay
'Mab'	WKin
¶ 'Mabel Appleby'	SHel
'Madame Dubarry'	See *D.* 'Dubarry'
'Madonna' (p)	SBai SHay WKin
'Maisie Neal' (b) ♀	Last listed 1989
Malaga® (pf) ♀	NGil SAll SBai SHay
'Mambo' (pf)	SAll SBai SHay
'Mandy' (p)	SAll
'Manningtree Pink'	See *D.* 'Cedric's Oldest'
Manon® (pf)	Last listed 1997
'Marcato' PBR (pf)	SBai
'Marg's Choice' (p) ♀	Last listed 1999
'Maria'	See *D.* 'Allen's Maria'
'Marmion' (M)	WMal
'Mars' (p)	ECtt ELan GAbr NBus SAll SChu WAbe WFar WWye
'Marshwood Melody' (p)	CThr SBai WSpi
'Marshwood Mystery' (p)	CThr WKin
'Mary Jane Birrel' (pf)	Last listed 1997
¶ 'Mary Mottram'	CLyd
'Mary Simister' (b)	SAll
* 'Mary's Gilliflower'	EMFP WKin
'Master Stuart' (b)	SBai
'Matador' (b)	SHay
'Maudie Hinds' (b)	SBai
'Maureen Lambert' (pf) ♀	Last listed 1998
'Maybole' (b)	SAll SHay
'Maythorne' (p)	SRms
'Mendip Hills' (b)	SAll SHay
'Mendlesham Belle' (p)	EMFP
'Mendlesham Frilly' (p)	EMFP
'Mendlesham Glow' (p)	EMFP
'Mendlesham Maid' (p)	EMFP
¶ 'Mendlesham Minx' (p)	EMFP
'Mendlesham Moll' (p)	EMFP
¶ 'Mendlesham Saint Helen's' (p)	EMFP
'Mercury' (p)	SAll
'Merlin Clove' (b)	SBai SHay

'Messines Pink' (p)	SAll
'Michael Saunders' (b) ♀	SBai
'Michelangelo' (pf)	Last listed 1997
microlepis	ITim NMen NWCA WAbe
– f. *albus*	NSla WAbe
– ED 791562	Last listed 1998
– 'Leuchtkugel'	ECho ITim SBla WAbe
– var. *musalae*	CLyd CMea MDHE NHar WLin
'Miss Sinkins' (p)	EDAr GKir
* 'Misty Morn'	Last listed 1998
* 'Molly Blake'	Last listed 1998
* 'Momoko' (pf)	SAll
'Monarch' (pf)	Last listed 1997
'Mondriaan' (pf)	Last listed 1999
'Monica Wyatt' (p) ♀	CThr EBrP EBre EDAr GKir LBCl LBSe LBre LFis LRHS MBBe NGil SAga SBai SBre SChu SHay SRms
monspessulanus	NEgg NWCA WPer
'Montrose Pink'	See *D.* 'Cockenzie Pink'
'Moortown Plume'	WKin
'Moulin Rouge'	CMea SChu
'Mrs Clark'	See *D.* 'Nellie Clark'
'Mrs Elmhurst' (p)	Last listed 1999
¶ 'Mrs Gumbly' (p)	WKin
'Mrs Holt' (p)	EMFP
'Mrs Jackson' (p)	CLTr CLyd SAsh
'Mrs Macbride' (p)	NCat WKin
'Mrs N. Clark'	See *D.* 'Nellie Clark'
'Mrs Perkins' (b)	SAll
'Mrs Roxburgh'	WKin
'Mrs Shaw' (p)	Last listed 1999
'Mrs Sinkins' (p)	More than 30 suppliers
'Munot'	Last listed 1999
Murcia® (pf)	SBai
'Murray's Laced Pink' (p)	WKin WSPU
N 'Musgrave's Pink' (p)	CGle CLTr CSam CThr ECha EMFP SAll SBla SChu SSvw WEas WKin
'Musgrave's White'	See *D.* 'Musgrave's Pink'
myrtinervius	CLTr CLyd ITim NWCA WPer
'Mystery' (pf)	SAll
'N.M. Goodall' (p)	Last listed 1999
'Nan Bailey' (p)	SBai
* 'Napoleon'	SAll
'Napoleon III' (p)	WKif
nardiformis	WPer
'Natalie Saunders' (b) ♀	SBai
'Nautilus' (b)	SAll SHay
neglectus	See *D. pavonius*
§ 'Nellie Clark' (p)	CLyd MWat SChu
'New Tempo' (p)	SBai SHay
'Nichola Ann' (b) ♀	SAll
'Nicol' (pf)	Last listed 1998
'Night Star' (p)	CMea SChu WWol
nitidus	CLyd NBir WPer
nivalis	NMen
noeanus	See *D. petraeus* subsp. *noeanus*
'Nonsuch' (p)	EMFP NBrk WKin
'Northland' (pf)	NGil SHay
'Nyewoods Cream' (p)	CTri EBrP EBre EMFP ESis GKir LBCl LBSe LBee LBre LRHS MBBe MBar MBro MRav NHar NHol NMen SBre WPat WPer WRHF
§ 'Oakington' (p)	CTri EBrP EBre EMNN GCHN LBCl LBSe LBre LRHS MBBe MRav MWat SBre SChu WKin
'Oakington Rose'	See *D.* 'Oakington'
'Oakwood Dainty' (p)	CLyd
'Oakwood Erin Mitchell' (p)	Last listed 1999
'Oakwood Gillian Garforth' (p) ♀	NGil SBai

'Oakwood Romance' (p) ♥ NGil
'Oakwood Rose Parker' (p) Last listed 1999
'Oakwood Splendour' (p) ♥ EDAr NGil
* 'Odino'   SAll
'Old Blush'   See *D.* 'Souvenir de la Malmaison'
'Old Clove Red' (b)   LFis
'Old Crimson Clove' (b)   Last listed 1997
'Old Dutch Pink' (p)   CLTr CMil SChu WKin
'Old Fringed Pink' (p)   WKin
'Old Fringed White' (p)   CLTr EMFP
'Old Irish' (p)   WKin
'Old Mother Hubbard' (p) ♥ CFee
'Old Red Clove' (p)   MHar WCot
§ 'Old Square Eyes' (p)   CInt CLyd EOrc MNrw SAga SAll
    SBla WEas WKin
'Old Velvet' (p)   CLTr GCal SChu WKin
'Oliver' (p)   SAll
* 'Olivia' (pf)   SAll
'Omagio' (pf)   SAll
* 'Ondina' (pf)   SAll
* 'Opera'   SAll
* 'Orange Magic' (pf)   SAll
'Orange Maid' (b)   SAll
'Orchid Beauty' (pf)   Last listed 1997
'Oscar' (b)   SAll
'Osprey' (b)   SHay
'Paddington' (p)   CThr EMFP SChu WKin
'Painted Beauty' (p)   CLTr CSam CThr EMFP NBir
'Painted Lady' (p)   CLyd CThr NHol SAll SChu WKin
'Paisley Gem' (p)   CLTr CThr SChu WKif WKin
palinensis B&SWJ 3770   Last listed 1999
§ Pastel Gipsy® = 'Stagipast' SSmt
'Patchwork'   Last listed 1997
'Patricia' (b)   SHay
'Patricia Bell'   See *D. turkestanicus* 'Patricia Bell'
'Paul' (p)   EBrP EBre LBCl LBSe LBre MBBe
    SBai SBre WSpi
'Paul Hayward' (p)   SHay
§ *pavonius* ♥   CLyd EWes GTou NWCA SBla
    WPer
- *roysii*   See *D.* 'Roysii'
Pax® (pf)   SAll SBai SHay
'Peach' (p)   SHay
'Pearl'   SAll
'Perfect Clove' (b)   SHay
'Peter Wood' (b) ♥   Last listed 1989
§ *petraeus*   EWes NHol WPat
§ - subsp. *noeanus*   CGra CLyd CPBP ESis WAbe WPat
    WPer
- - *albus*   WLin
§ - subsp. *petraeus*   NOak WPer
'Petticoat Lace' (p)   EMFP SHay
'Phantom' (b)   SHay
'Pheasant's Eye' (p)   EMFP SSvw WKin
'Philip Archer' (b)   SHay
* 'Picton's Propeller' (p)   CMil GBuc
Pierrot® = 'Kobusa' (pf) ♥ SBai
'Pike's Pink' (p) ♥   CMea CPBP CSpe EBee EDAr
    ELan GCHN LBee LFis LHop LRHS
    MHer MRav MWat NEgg NHol
    NMen NNrd SAll SBla SChu SIng
    SRPl SRms SSmi SSvw WEas WKin
    WLin WLin
pindicola   See *D. haematocalyx* subsp.
    pindicola
pinifolius   Last listed 1998
'Pink Bizarre' (b)   SHay
'Pink Damask' (p)   GAbr
* 'Pink Dona' (pf)   SAll SBai SHay
'Pink Doris' (pf)   NGil
* 'Pink Fringe'   NSla
'Pink Jewel' (p)   CInt CLyd CMea CTri EDAr LBee

LRHS MHer NHol NMen SAll
    SChu SIng WEas
'Pink Mist Sim' (pf)   Last listed 1997
'Pink Monica Wyatt' (p)   CThr
'Pink Mrs Sinkins' (p)   CLTr ECha EMFP GAri SAll SBai
    SChu WHoo WKin
'Pink Pearl' (p)   CBlo CThr EDAr SAll WLRN
'Pink Sim' (pf)   SAll
'Pixie' (b)   EPot NHol
'Pixie Star' PBR (p)   EDAr
plumarius   NMir SRms SSvw WByw WGor
    WGwG WMoo WPer
- 'Albiflorus'   SRms WPer
pontederae   NDlv WPer
'Portsdown Fancy' (b)   SHay
'Portsdown Lass' (b)   Last listed 1998
'Portsdown Perfume' (b)   Last listed 1999
'Prado' PBR (pf)   SAll SBai SHay
preobrazhenskii   Last listed 1999
'Pretty'   LRHS
'Pretty Lady' (p)   Last listed 1999
'Prince Charming' (p)   CLyd ELan EMNN ITim NMen
    NPri SAga SRms WPer
'Princess Charming'   See *D. gratianopolitanus*
    'Princess Charming'
'Princess of Wales' (M)   WMal
'Priory Pink' (p)   SAll
§ 'Prudence' (p)   CThr LAco SAll WHoo WKin
'Pudsey Prize' (p)   Last listed 1999
'Pummelchen' (p)   ITim
'Purley King' (p)   CThr
'Purple Frosted' (pf)   Last listed 1997
'Purple Jenny' (p)   SAll
'Purple Pacal' (pf)   SBai SHay
'Purple Pierrot' (pf)   SBai
'Purple Rendez-vous' (pf)   SAll
pygmaeus   NBro WTin
- B&SWJ 1510   NCiC NHol
- B&SWJ 3533   Last listed 1999
'Queen of Hearts' (p)   CLyd EBrP EBre LBCl LBSe LBre
    LRHS MBBe NBus SBre SMrm
    WPer
§ 'Queen of Henri' (p)   ECtt EDAr GMaP LBee LRHS
    MHer NHol NNrd SBla SChu WFar
    WKin
'Queen of Sheba' (p)   CThr EMFP SChu SSvw WKin
'Rachel' (p)   Last listed 1999
'Raeden Pink' (p)   Last listed 1997
'Raggio di Sole' (pf)   SAll SBai
'Rainbow Loveliness' (p,a)   NBir SAll SSca WHil
'Ralph Gould' (p)   ECho
Ramona® (pf)   SBai
'Red and White' (p)   WKin
'Red Denim' (p)   Last listed 1999
'Red Emperor' (p)   Last listed 1997
'Red Penny' (p)   Last listed 1999
* 'Red Rimon' (pf)   SAll
'Red Velvet'   CLyd CSWP LRHS SAsh SMrm
'Red-edged Skyline' (pf)   Last listed 1998
'Reiko' (pf)   SAll
'Reine de Henri'   See *D.* 'Queen of Henri'
'Rembrandt' (p)   Last listed 1997
'Rendez-vous' PBR (pf)   SAll SBai
'Renoir' (b)   SAll SHay
'Revell's Lady Wharncliffe'   See *D.* 'Lady Wharncliffe'
§ 'Rhian's Choice' (p) ♥   Last listed 1996
'Riccardo' (b) ♥   SBai
'Richard Gibbs' (p)   WWin
'Rimon' (pf)   SAll
'Rivendell' (p)   NHar NSla WAbe
'Robert' (p)   SAll
'Robert Baden-Powell' (b)   SHay

'Roberta' (pf) — SAll
* 'Robin Ritchie' — WHoo WKin WWhi
'Robin Thain' (b) — SAll SBai SHay
'Rodrigo' (pf) — Last listed 1998
§ Rondo® = 'Stagirond' — SSmt
'Ron's Joanne' (pf) — Last listed 1999
'Roodkapje' (p) — WKin
'Rosalind Linda' (pf) — Last listed 1997
'Rose de Mai' (p) — CBre CLTr CLyd CMil CSam CSev EMFP LLWP SAll SChu SSvw WEas WHoo WHoo
'Rose Joy' (p) ♀ — CThr EBee EDAr EMFP EPfP NGil SBai SHay SRms
'Rose Monica Wyatt' PBR (p) ♀ — CThr
'Rose Perfection' (pf) — Last listed 1999
'Rosealie' (p) — SHay
'Royal Scot' (p) ♀ — Last listed 1998
'Royalty' (p) — SHay
§ 'Roysii' (p) — WPer
'Rubin' (pf) — WEas
'Ruby' — See D. 'Houndspool Ruby'
'Ruby Doris' — See D. 'Houndspool Ruby'
'Ruby Wedding' (p) — GCHN
rupicola — Last listed 1998
'Russling Robin' — See D. 'Fair Maid of Kent'
'Sahara' (pf) — SAll
'Saint Edith' (p) — WKin
'Saint Nicholas' (p) — EMFP SChu WKin
'Saint Winifred' — SChu WKin
§ Salamanca = 'Kosalamana' (pf) — SBai
'Sally Anne Hayward' (b) — SHay
'Salmon Clove' (b) — Last listed 1998
§ Salmon Gipsy® = 'Stadarpi' — SSmt
'Sam Barlow' (p) — CPri CThr EMFP SAll SChu SHay WKin WWye
Sammy — CLyd
'Samuel Doby' (p) — Last listed 1997
'Sandra Neal' (b) ♀ — SBai
'Santa Claus' (b) — SAll SHay
'Sappho' (b) — Last listed 1997
'Scania' (pf) — SHay
scardicus — Last listed 1999
'Scarlet Fragrance' (b) — SHay
§ Scarlet Gipsy® = 'Stagilon' — SSmt
'Scarlet Joanne' (pf) — Last listed 1999
scopulorum perplexans — NTow
seguieri — GSki MNrw WMoo WPer
serotinus — SIng
'Shaston' (b) — Last listed 1998
'Shaston Scarletta' (b) — SHay
'Shaston Superstar' (b) — Last listed 1997
'Sheila's Choice' (p) ♀ — Last listed 1993
¶ Shiplake seedling (p) — WKin
'Shot Silk' (p) — NGil
'Show Aristocrat' (p) — SAll
'Show Beauty' (p) — Last listed 1998
'Show Portrait' (p) — NFor
simulans — CLyd EWes
'Sir Arthur Sim' (pf) — Last listed 1998
'Sir Cedric Morris' — See D. 'Cedric's Oldest'
'Sir David Scott' (p) — WKin
* 'Six Hills' — CLyd WPat
Smiling Gipsy — See D. Violet Gipsy = 'Staviolet'
'Snow Clove' (b) — SHay
'Snowbird' (pf) — SAll
'Snowfire' — SChu
'Snowshill Manor' (p) — WPer
* 'Sofia' (pf) — SAll
'Solomon' (p) — CThr WKin

¶ 'Solomon's Hat' (p) — WKin
'Solway Hannah Scholes' (pf) — Last listed 1998
'Solway Splash' (pf) — Last listed 1997
'Solway Sunset' (pf) — Last listed 1998
'Solway Surprise' (pf) — NGil
'Solway Susan' (pf) — Last listed 1998
'Solway Sweetheart' (pf) — Last listed 1998
'Sops-in-wine' (p) — CLTr CSam CThr ECha EMFP GCal GMac LNor MNrw SAll SChu SHay WKin WWhi
'Southmead' (p) — ECho
§ 'Souvenir de la Malmaison' (M) — WMal
sp. ACW 2116 — CLyd LBee WPer
sp. B&SWJ 1414 — Last listed 1998
sp. J Watson — Last listed 1998
'Spangle' (b) — SAll
'Spangled Star' (p) — EDAr MBNS
'Spencer Bickham' (p) — EMFP EPot MNrw WKin
'Spetchley' — Last listed 1997
spiculifolius — CLyd
'Spinfield Happiness' (b) ♀ — Last listed 1995
'Spring Beauty' (p) — LPVe NBir NFla WHer
'Spring Star' (p) — ECtt NPri SAga
'Square Eyes' — See D. 'Old Square Eyes'
squarrosus — EPot GKir LBee NWCA
* – *alpinus* — ECho
– 'Nanus' — CNic ELan EWes LRHS
'Squeeks' (p) — SChu
'Staccato' (pf) — SBai
'Stadarpi' — See D. Salmon Gipsy = 'Stadarpi'
'Stagigi' — See D. Giant Gipsy = 'Stagigi'
'Stagilon' — See D. Scarlet Gipsy = 'Stagilon'
'Stagipast' — See D. Pastel Gipsy = 'Stagipast'
'Stagirond' — See D. Rondo = 'Stagirond'
'Stagispan' — See D. Brilliant Gipsy = 'Stagispan'
'Stagiwit' — See D. White Gipsy = 'Stagiwit'
'Stan Stroud' (b) — SHay
'Startler' (p) — Last listed 1997
'Staviolet' — See D. Violet Gipsy = 'Staviolet'
sternbergii — Last listed 1998
– JJH 931078 — NWCA
'Storm' (pf) — Last listed 1999
'Strathspey' (b) — SAll SHay
'Strawberries and Cream' (p) — CThr EBee EBrP EBre EDAr EMFP EWTr LBCl LBSe LBre LHop LRHS MBBe NGil NOrc SBai SBre SHay
* *strictus pulchellus* — Last listed 1999
§ *subacaulis* — GAbr NHar NWCA
'Sue Randall' (pf) — Last listed 1999
suendermannii — See D. *petraeus*
* 'Sullom Voe' — Last listed 1998
'Sunray' (p) — SAll SHay
'Sunstar' (b) — SAll SHay
§ *superbus* — MTho WKin WPer WWhi WWin WWye
– 'Crimsonia' — WPer
– var. *longicalycinus* — MNrw MSte
– – B&SWJ 3230 — Last listed 1998
I – 'Primadonna' — WPer
* – 'Rose' — WPer
– 'Snowdonia' — WPer
'Susan' (p) — EWTr SAll
'Susannah' (p) — SAll
* 'Susan's Seedling' (p) — SAll
'Swanlake' (p) — SHay
'Swansdown' (p) — NFor
'Sway Belle' (p) — CThr NCiC SBai WSpi
§ 'Sway Candy' (p) — Last listed 1999
'Sway Gem' (p) — SBai
'Sway Joy' (p) — SBai

'Sway Lass' (p) SBai
'Sway Melody' (p) SBai
'Sway Mist' (p) Last listed 1999
'Sway Pearl' (p) NGil SBai
'Sway Ripple' (p) SBai
'Sway Sunset' (p) SBai
'Sweet Sophie' (pf) NGil
'Sweet Sue' (b) SAll SHay
'Sweetheart Abbey' (p) CThr EMFP SChu SSvw WKin
sylvestris CLyd EPot
 - subsp. *tergestinus* SSvw
 - 'Uniflorus' Last listed 1998
'Syston Beauty' (p) WKin
'Tamsin' (p) ♀ SBla WKin
'Tamsin Fifield' (b) ♀ Last listed 1995
'Tangerine Sim' (pf) Last listed 1997
* 'Tasty' (pf) Last listed 1999
'Tatra Bull's-eye' (p) GCal
tatsiense Last listed 1999
'Tayside Red' (M) WMal
'Telstar' (pf) NPer
'Tempo' (pf) ♀ SBai SHay
* *tenerifa* MBri
'Terra' PBR (pf) SHay
'Terry Sutcliffe' (p) WKin
'Texas' (pf) SAll
the Bloodie pink See *D.* 'Caesar's Mantle'
'Theo' (pf) SAll
'Thomas' (p) EFou NBrk SAll SChu WEas
'Thomas Lee' (b) SAll
'Thora' (M) WMal
'Tinnington Secret Garden' Last listed 1998
'Tiny Rubies' See *D. gratianopolitanus* 'Tiny Rubies'
'Toledo' (p) EMFP WKin
'Tom Portman' (p) Last listed 1997
'Tony's Choice' (pf) NGil
'Torino' (pf) Last listed 1999
'Tracy Barlow' (b) SHay
'Tracy Jardine' (pf) Last listed 1998
'Treasure' (p) SHay
'Trevor' (p) SAll
'Trisha's Choice' (p) ♀ Last listed 1993
'Tundra' PBR (pf) SBai
turkestanicus CLyd NBir
§ - 'Patricia Bell' (p) CSam
'Tweedale Seedling' GBuc
Tyrolean trailing carnations SAll
'Uncle Teddy' (b) ♀ SBai
uniflorus Last listed 1998
'Unique' (p) EMFP MBro SChu SSvw WHoo WKin
'Ursula Le Grove' (p) CLTr CLyd EMFP SChu WHoo WIvy WKin
'V.E. Jubilation' (pf) ♀ Last listed 1998
'Valda Wyatt' (p) ♀ CThr EBee EDAr ELan EMFP EPfP GCHN GKir LHop LRHS NGil SAll SBai SChu SRms WSpi WWol
Valencia (pf) SBai
Van Gogh (pf) Last listed 1997
'Velvet and Lace' Last listed 1997
'Vera Woodfield' (pf) Last listed 1998
'Vermeer' Last listed 1998
'Violet Clove' (b) SHay
§ Violet Gipsy = 'Staviolet' MWst SSmt
'Visa' (pf) SAll
¶ *viscidus* MDCh
'W.A. Musgrave' See *D.* 'Musgrave's Pink'
'W.H. Brooks' (b) SAll
'Waithman Beauty' (p) CLyd CMil CTri ECha GAbr MBar MBro MHar SAll WEas WHoo

'Waithman's Jubilee' (p) WKin WPer WPyg WWye GCHN NBrk NCat SRms
'Warden Hybrid' (p) CMea CTri EBee ECtt EDAr EMNN EPfP ESis GAbr LRHS MOne NHol WAbe WLRN WWol
'Warrior' (b) CBlo
'Wedding Bells' (pf) NGil
'Weetwood Double' (p) WPer
'Welcome' (b) SHay
weyrichii CLyd ECho NMen SIng WPer
'Whatfield Anona' (p) CLyd EGle ELan SAll
'Whatfield Beauty' CLyd ECho ECtt EDAr ELan LRHS SAll
'Whatfield Brilliant' (p) CLyd
'Whatfield Can-can' CLyd CMea CPBP CPri EDAr EMFP ESis GKir LFis LRHS MOne NHol SAll WAbe WWol
¶ 'Whatfield Cerise' CLyd
'Whatfield Cyclops' CLyd CPBP EDAr LRHS MBro MOne SAll SChu WKin WLRN
'Whatfield Dawn' CLyd ECho ELan NNrd SAll
'Whatfield Dorothy Mann' (p) ECho ELan SAll
'Whatfield Fuchsia' (p) CLyd SAll
'Whatfield Gem' (p) CLyd EBrP EBre ELan EMFP ESis GCal LBCl LBSe LBre LRHS MBBe MBro MOne MWgw NHol NMen SAll SBre WFar WHoo WKin WPer
'Whatfield Joy' (p) CLyd EBee EDAr ELan EPot ESis LBee LRHS MHer MOne NHol NMen NPri SAll
'Whatfield Magenta' (p) CLyd CPBP EGle ELan EPot ESis LBee LRHS MOne NHol NNrd SAll SChu WAbe WEas WLin
'Whatfield Mini' (p) EDAr LAco SAll SRms WPer
'Whatfield Miss' (p) SAll
'Whatfield Misty Morn' (p) CLyd ECho ELan
'Whatfield Peach' (p) SAll
'Whatfield Pom Pom' (p) CLyd
'Whatfield Pretty Lady' (p) ECho ELan SAll
'Whatfield Rose' (p) ECho SAll
'Whatfield Ruby' (p) CLyd EGle ELan EMFP LRHS SAll WPer
¶ 'Whatfield Smokey Joe' CLyd
'Whatfield Supergem' CLyd ECho ELan EPot SAll
'Whatfield White' (p) CLyd ECho ELan LRHS SAll SRms WGwG
'Whatfield White Moon' (p) ECho
'Whatfield Wink' EGle
'Whatfield Wisp' (p) CM&M CPBP CTri EGle ELan NBir NMen WFar WLRN
'White Barn' (p) ECha
'White Joy' PBR (p) ♀ EDAr EMFP
'White Ladies' (p) CThr ELan EMFP ENot SAll WKin
'White Liberty' (pf) SBai SHay
'White Lightning' (pf) SAll
'White Sim' (pf) Last listed 1997
'Whitecliff' (b) SAll SHay
'Whitehill' (p) ♀ EPot MHer NHol NMen NWCA NWoo WPat WWin
'Whitesmith' (b) ♀ SAll
'Whitford Belle' (p) SBai
'Widecombe Fair' (p) ♀ CLTr CMea CSam CThr CTri EBrP EBre ECtt EDAr LBCl LBSe LBre LRHS MBBe SAll SBre SRms
* 'Wild Velvet' (p) WKin
'William Brownhill' (p) CMil EMFP SChu WKin
'William Sim' (pf) Last listed 1997
'Winsome' (p) SHay
'Woodfield's Jewel' (p) Last listed 1998
'Yellow Dusty Sim' (pf) Last listed 1997

'Yellow Rendez-vous' (pf)   SBai
'Yorkshireman' (b)   SAll SHay
'Zebra' (b)   SAll SBai SHay
zederbaueri   NWCA SBla SIng
'Zodiac' (pf)   Last listed 1997
'Zoe's Choice' (p) ♀   CPri

DIAPENSIA (Diapensiaceae)
lapponica var. *obovata*   WAbe

DIARRHENA (Poaceae)
japonica   Last listed 1997

DIASCIA ✿ (Scrophulariaceae)
'Alys'   Last listed 1999
anastrepta   EOrc MSCN WPer WWye
 - HWEL 0219   NWCA
'Andrew'   Last listed 1999
'Appleby Appleblossom'   EOrc EPot LLWP MLLN SChu SIng
    SSvw WRus
'Appleby Apricot'   EMar EWTr MSCN NDov NGdn
'Apricot' hort.   See *D. barberae* 'Hopleys Apricot'
'April Fool'   LLWP
* 'Aquarius'   SChu WPen
barberae   CInt EBrP EBre ELan GAri LBCl
    LBSe LBre MBBe SBre SEas WOve
 - 'Belmore Beauty' (v)   CElw EBrP EBre ECtt EMan EMar
    EWes LBCl LBSe LBre LLWP MAvo
    MBBe MHer SBre SGar WByw
 - 'Blackthorn Apricot' ♀   More than 30 suppliers
§ - 'Fisher's Flora' ♀   CGle EPot LFis NBro NHar NMen
    WFar WOve WWin WWye
¶ - 'Fisher's Flora' x 'Lilac   ECtt EDAr SCoo SHFr
    Belle'
§ - 'Hopleys Apricot'   CLTr EPfP LHop MLLN NBrk
 - HWEL 037   Last listed 1999
§ - 'Ruby Field' ♀   CB&S CGle EBee ECha ECtt EDAr
    ELan EMNN EMan GCHN GKir
    LAst LHop LRHS MBNS MBri
    MHer NEgg NLAp NSti SBla SPer
    SRms WCFE WFar WWol
'Bloomsbury Ice'   Last listed 1998
'Blue Bonnet'   ECtt EMan EPot GMac LHop SChu
    WFar
'Blush'   See *D. integerrima* 'Blush'
* 'Chalgrave Beauty'   EMan
¶ 'Coldham'   LHop SDys
§ Coral Belle = 'Hecbel'PBR   CElw CPBP CSpe EBee ECtt EMan
    EOrc EPot EWes GMac LAst LLWP
    LRHS MDHE MMil MTis NCiC
    NHar SChu SIng SMac SSoC SUsu
    WEas WFar WLRN WPer WWol
cordata hort.   See *D. barberae* 'Fisher's Flora'
cordifolia   See *D. barberae* 'Fisher's Flora'
'Cotswold Beauty'   LFis
'Crûg Variegated'   EPot MAvo MLLN WCot WCru
    WPat WPer
'Dainty Duet'   ECtt MGed SChu WPer
'Dark Eyes' ♀   SChu
¶ 'Eclat'   NBlu WFar
elegans   See *D. fetcaniensis*, *D. vigilis*
'Elizabeth' ♀   LFis NFai NHar WSPU
'Emma'   CMea LHop LLWP NHar SChu
    SIng SUsu
felthamii   See *D. fetcaniensis*
§ *fetcaniensis*   CFri CMHG CSpe EBee LHil LHop
    NDov NPer SChu SCro SPer WCru
    WHal WPer WWin
 - 'Pitlochrie Pink'   GDea
* 'Fiona'   Last listed 1997
flanaganii   See *D. stachyoides*, *D. vigilis*
'Frilly' ♀   ECtt NBrk SChu

'Garden News'   Last listed 1999
'Hecbel'PBR   See *D.* Coral Belle = 'Hecbel'
'Hecsyd'   See *D.* Sydney Olympics =
    'Hecsyd'
'Hector Harrison'   See *D.* 'Salmon Supreme'
'Hector's Hardy' ♀   EOrc GDea GMaP LLWP
'Ice Cracker'   CElw CLTr CMea CSpe CWes ECtt
    EMan EOrc EPot EWTr GMac LAst
    LHop LRHS MBNS SAsh SIng
    WHal WWol
'Iceberg'   Last listed 1999
§ *integerrima* ♀   CSam CSpe ECha ELan EMan
    EOrc LFis LGre LHil LLWP MBNS
    MBro MFir NSti SChu SHel SMrm
    SPla
 - 'Alba'   See *D. integerrima* 'Blush'
§ - 'Blush'   CElw CMil CSam CSpe EGoo
    EMan EMar GMac LHil NHar SGar
    SMrm
 - from Lesotho   Last listed 1999
 - 'Harry Hay'   CGle
 - 'Ivory Angel'   See *D. integerrima* 'Blush'
integrifolia   See *D. integerrima*
'Jack Elliott'   See *D. vigilis* 'Jack Elliott' ex JE
    8955
'Jackpot'   EPot MDHE
'Jacqueline's Joy'   CGle CMea EMan GMac NCiC
    NHar NNrd NPer SAga SChu
    SMrm WBar WFar
'Joyce's Choice' ♀   CFri CHar EOrc EPot EWes GCal
    LGre LLWP LRHS MBri MSCN
    NCiC SChu SUsu WByw WCot
    WLRN WWol
'Kate'   LHil LRHS SChu SIng SMrm
'Katherine Sharman' (v)   CElw EMan EMon EPPr LRHS
    MAvo SUsu WWeb
'Lady Valerie' ♀   CElw EWes GMac LHil LLWP MBri
    MGed MLLN NHar SLod WPer
    WWin
'Lavender Bell'   Last listed 1997
'Lilac Belle' ♀   CB&S CLTr CSam EBee ECtt ELan
    GMac LAst LHil LLWP LRHS MHer
    MMil NHar SEas SIng SLod SMrm
    SPlb WFar WPer WWin
'Lilac Dream'   WWin
'Lilac Lace' (v)   NHar
'Lilac Mist' ♀   CLTr LGre MLLN NBur NHar NPer
    NSti NWoo SChu SDix SLod SSoC
    SUsu WPen
'Lilac Queen'   WEas
lilacina   CLTr EMan GAri LRHS WPer
    WWye
'Little Charmer'   MBro WHoo
'Little Emma'   Last listed 1999
'Little Fiona'   Last listed 1999
'Louise'   CSpe EOrc EPot GBuc MRav NHar
    SMrm
'Lucy'   EPot GMac LLWP NHar
'Lucy' x *mollis*   SChu SDys SIng SUsu
megatbura   Last listed 1998
'Megavil'   EPot
mollis   Last listed 1999
'Orangeade'   LLWP
'Pale Face'   NHar
patens   CLyd
'Patio Wine'   Last listed 1998
'Paula'   Last listed 1999
'Penlyn'   Last listed 1999
personata   Last listed 1998
'Pink Queen'   ECtt LRHS
'Pink Spires'   Last listed 1997
'Pink Spot'   SIng

* 'Pisces'	SChu SIng
* 'Pitlochrie Pink'	Last listed 1997
purpurea	Last listed 1999
racemulosa	Last listed 1999
'Red Ace'	CElw CSpe EPot MDHE NPer
	SIng WWol
'Red Start'	ECtt EOrc GMac LAst LFis
	LHop LLWP MDHE NCiC
	NHar SChu SIng SUsu SVil
	WFar WLRN WWeb WWin
	WWoo
rigescens ♀	More than 30 suppliers
§ - 'Anne Rennie'	Last listed 1999
- x *integerrima*	WLRN
- x *lilacina*	CElw CFri MArl NCat SOkh
- pale form	See *D. rigescens* 'Anne Rennie'
'Ruby Field'	See *D. barberae* 'Ruby Field'
'Ruby's Pink'	EOrc
'Rupert Lambert' ♀	CElw CLTr GBuc GMac LHil LLWP
	LRHS MBro NBur NHar NSti SChu
	SLod WHoo WLin WPat WPer
	WPyg
§ 'Salmon Supreme'	CGle CLTr EBee ECtt ELan EWTr
	LFis LGre LHil LLWP LRHS MMil
	NHar NPer SChu SHel SMrm
	SRms WEas WFar WPer WRus
'Selina's Choice'	EPot GBuc SChu
§ *stachyoides*	ELan LHop MBNS NDov NPer
	WPer
'Stella'	Last listed 1999
'Strawberry Sundae'PBR	EWTr
'Super Salmon'	EPot
¶ 'Susan'	CSpe MBNS WFar
§ Sydney Olympics =	EPot LHil LLWP MLLN NHar
'Hecsyd'	WLRN WPer
tugelensis	CGle WFar
'Twinkle' ♀	CLyd CPBP CSpe EBee ECtt EDAr
	EMan EPot EWTr EWes GMac
	LAst LHil LLWP LRHS MLLN NBir
	NFai NHar NHol NNrd NPer SChu
	SIng WEas WFar WPer WWin
	WWol
* 'Twins Gully'	GCal
* *variegata*	Last listed 1999
§ *vigilis* ♀	More than 30 suppliers
§ - 'Jack Elliott' ex JE 8955	CB&S CFri CLTr CSev CSpe EBee
	EBrP EBre ITim LBCl LBSe LBre
	LHop MBBe SBre SHel WCFE
	WLRN WPer
'Wendy'	LHop
'White Cloud'	LLWP SChu WSPU
'Woodcote'	LHil

DIASCIA x LINARIA See NEMESIA CAERULEA

DICENTRA ✿ (Papaveraceae)

'Adrian Bloom'	EBee EBlw EBrP EBre EPla EWTr
	LBCl LBSe LBre LRHS LRot MBBe
	MBNS MCLN MCli NArg NCat
	NCut NOak NSti SBre SPer WFar
'Bacchanal'	More than 30 suppliers
'Boothman's Variety'	See *D.* 'Stuart Boothman'
'Boothman's White'	GKir WWeb
'Bountiful'	CGle CMHG CRow EBee EMan
	GKir GMaP LRHS MBro MChl
	MLLN MRav NArg NFor NSti SCoo
	SPer WMoo WRHF
'Brownie'	GBuc MCLN NCat NGdn NSti
canadensis	EPot GBuc MSal MTho NSti WCot
'Catforth Filigree'	NCat
chrysantha	Last listed 1999
'Coldham'	WCru WTin

cucullaria	CBos CElw CRDP CRow CSWP
	CStu EBee EPar EPot ERos GBuc
	GCrs IMGH LGre LRHS MRav
	MTho NHar NMen NSti NTow
	NWCA WAbe WCot WCru WLin
- 'Pittsburg'	CBos EBee WCot
* 'Dark Stuart Boothman'	ECGN EWTr NOak
eximia hort.	See *D. formosa*
—(Ker-Gawl.) Torrey	EBee MTho MWat SWat
- 'Alba'	See *D. eximia* 'Snowdrift'
§ - 'Snowdrift'	CLAP CLon CM&M CSpe CTri
	EBee ELan EPfP GKir LRHS MBro
	MTho NWoo SCob SDys SRms
	SSpi WBar WHoo WMoo WPnP
	WWat WWeb
§ *formosa*	More than 30 suppliers
§ - *alba*	CGle CHad CRow ECha ELan
	MCAu MCLN NBir NCot NFor
	NOak NSti NVic SChu SCob SPer
	SRPl SRms STes WByw WCru
	WFar WRus
* - 'Aurora'	CHid EBee EFou EMan EWTr
	GBin LRHS MCAu MCLN MRav
	NCut SCob
- dark	WMoo
- 'Furse's Form'	EBee NCat NOak WCot
- subsp. *oregana*	CLAP CRow EPPr EPar GCal NCat
	NChi NOak NSti WAbb WByw
	WCru WWin
- - 'Rosea'	MBel NPar
'Fusd'PBR	See *D.* Snowflakes = 'Fusd'
'Langtrees' ♀	More than 30 suppliers
'Luxuriant' ♀	More than 30 suppliers
macrantha	CAvo CFil CFri CGle CHad CRDP
	CRow EBee ECha EPfP LGre
	MRav MTho SAga SSpi WCru
	WPGP
macrocapnos	CB&S CFir CPIN CRow EBee
	EMan GBuc GQui IHdy LFis LRHS
	MTho SMrm WCru WLRN WTre
* *maculata*	LAma
'Pearl Drops'	More than 30 suppliers
peregrina	CMGP GCrs GTou
§ *scandens*	CFri CGle CHar CMil CPIN CRHN
	CRow CSpe EBee EPfP ERav GCal
	IHdy MCCP MSCN MTho NLar
	SSea SSpi WSHC WSPU WWhi
- B&SWJ 2427	WCru
¶ 'Silversmith'	CFil
§ Snowflakes = 'Fusd'PBR	EBrP EBre EWes GAbr GCHN
	GKir LBCl LBSe LBre LRHS MBBe
	MCCP MRav NHaw NMen SBre
	WCer
spectabilis ♀	More than 30 suppliers
- 'Alba' ♀	More than 30 suppliers
¶ - 'Gold Heart'PBR	CHad EMan EPfP GBri GKir
	MGrG SAga SPla WFar
'Spring Morning'	CElw CGle CMHG CMil CRow
	CSam EGle EMon EPPr IBlr NSti
	SChu SSpi WEas WRHF WRus
§ 'Stuart Boothman' ♀	More than 30 suppliers
thalictrifolia	See *D. scandens*
torulosa	NArg

DICHELOSTEMMA (Alliaceae)

§ *capitatum*	NTow
congestum	CAvo EBee ERos LRHS MNrw
	WCot
§ *ida-maia*	CAvo CFwr EBee EPot ETub LRHS
	SMrm
multiflorum	GBin
volubile	CPIN

DICHOPOGON (Anthericaceae)
strictus   EBee

DICHOTOMANTHES (Rosaceae)
tristaniicarpa   CFil

DICHROA (Hydrangeaceae)
febrifuga   CAbb CB&S CCHP CDoC CEnd
                              CFil CGre CMil EMan ERav EWes
                              GBri GQui LRHS SLon SOWG
                              WCru WOVN WPGP WWat
versicolor   Last listed 1999
¶ - B&SWJ 6565   WCru

DICHROMENA See RHYNCHOSPORA

DICKSONIA ✿ (Dicksoniaceae)
antarctica ♀   More than 30 suppliers
brackenridgei   Last listed 1997
* *conjugata*   Last listed 1997
fibrosa ♀   CAbb CB&S CBrP CHEx LJus
                              WMul WRic
* *juxtaposita*   Last listed 1997
* *neorosthornii*   Last listed 1997
sellowiana   LPal WMul WRic
squarrosa ♀   CAbb CB&S CBrP CTrC EOas
                              EPVP ERea LBlo LJus NMoo SAPC
                              WMul WRic
youngiae   WMul WRic

DICLIPTERA (Acanthaceae)
§ *suberecta*   CB&S CHal EHol ERea SMrm
                              SOWG SUsu

DICRANOSTIGMA (Papaveraceae)
lactucoides   EBee

DICTAMNUS (Rutaceae)
albus ♀   More than 30 suppliers
§ - var. *purpureus* ♀   More than 30 suppliers
fraxinella   See *D. albus* var. *purpureus*

DICTYOLIMON (Plumbaginaceae)
macrorrhabdos   Last listed 1998

DICTYOSPERMA (Arecaceae)
album   CRoM LPal MBri

DIDYMOCHLAENA (Dryopteridaceae)
lunulata   See *D. truncatula*
§ *truncatula*   CHal MBri

DIEFFENBACHIA (Araceae)
'Camille' (v)   LRHS
'Compacta' (v)   LRHS

DIERAMA ✿ (Iridaceae)
argyreum   CFil CPla EBee IBlr WSan
- JCA 3.140.400   Last listed 1999
'Ariel'   IBlr
'Black Knight'   IBlr
'Blush'   IBlr
'Candy Stripe'   CPla CRow GBri MCCP SMad
                              STes
cooperi   GBri IBlr
- white, S&SH 20   Last listed 1999
* 'Donard Legacy'   GBri IBlr
§ *dracomontanum*   CBro CElw CFil CGle CLon
                              CMHG CPou CRDP CRow EBee
                              ECGN ECtt GCal IBlr LGre MHar
                              NBir SAga SBla SWat WAbe WCDu

WCot WCru WHil WHoo WPGP
WRHF WUnu
- dwarf lilac   CM&M GCal
- dwarf pale pink   CM&M GCal
- dwarf pink   Last listed 1998
¶ *dubium*   IBlr WHil
- x *robustum*   EBee
ensifolium   See *D. pendulum*
erectum   EBee
floriferum   CBro IBlr
¶ *galpinii*   WHil
grandiflorum   IBlr
igneum   More than 30 suppliers
- CD&R 278   CPou CRDP
¶ *insigne*   WHil
jucundum   EBee GBri GBuc MLLN
latifolium   CPla EBee IBlr WSan
lepidum JCA 3.952.800   Last listed 1999
'Mandarin'   IBlr
medium   CFil CLon EBee GSki LPio NSti
                              SMrm SWat WAbe WCot WPGP
'Milkmaid'   IBlr
mossii   EBee
'Pamina'   IBlr
'Papagena'   IBlr
'Papageno'   IBlr
pauciflorum   CFil CFir CHid CLon CM&M CMil
                              CRDP CStu EBee ECGP LGre
                              WAbe WCot WHil
¶ - CD&R 197   CPBP
- JCA 3.143.500   SMad
§ *pendulum*   More than 30 suppliers
'Pretty Flamingo'   IBlr
'Puck'   ECha GCal IBlr LRHS MLLN MRav
pulcherrimum   More than 30 suppliers
- var. *album*   ECha GBuc LPio MNrw SMad
                              WPen
- 'Blackbird'   CM&M EBee EPfP EPla IBlr LPio
                              LRHS SUsu WPGP
- x *dracomontanum*   Last listed 1998
- dwarf forms   GCal GSki WWhi
- 'Pearly Queen'   CRow
- 'Peregrine'   WPGP
- pink   NCut
- Slieve Donard hybrids   CFri EBrP EBre GBri GCal GMac
                              LBCl LBSe LBre LHop MAnH
                              MBBe SBre STes WHil WRHF
                              WSan
pumilum hort.   See *D. dracomontanum*
'Queen of the Night'   IBlr
reynoldsii   EBee IBlr WCot WHil
robustum   CFil CPou GBri IBlr WAbe WCot
                              WHil
- S&SH 49   Last listed 1999
- S&SH 63   Last listed 1999
- white S&SH 18   Last listed 1999
¶ 'Sarastro'   IBlr
¶ 'September Charm'   IBlr
sertum   CBro
* 'Snowbells'   MAvo STes WWhi
sp. CD&R 192   CRow
sp. CD&R 96   Last listed 1999
sp. from Lesotho   GCal
sp. JCA 15555   Last listed 1999
sp. SH 85   Last listed 1999
'Tamino'   IBlr
'Titania'   IBlr
trichorhizum   GBri IBlr WCot WHil
'Tubular Bells'   IBlr
'Violet Ice'   IBlr
'Westminster Chimes'   IBlr

DIERVILLA ✿ (Caprifoliaceae)

lonicera	CGdn CPle SMac SPan WFar WWat
middendorffiana	See Weigela middendorffiana
rivularis	Last listed 1998
sessilifolia	CB&S CHar CPle CSpe EPar EPfP GOrc IMGH IOrc MBel SLon WBod WCFE WCot WHCG WRus WSHC WWin
- 'Butterfly'	GKir LRHS MBri
x splendens	CMHG CPle EBee EHoe ELan ENot EPla IOrc LHop LRHS MBNS MBar MRav MTis NArg NHol SEas SLPl SPer SSta WDin WTro

DIETES (Iridaceae)

bicolor	CAbb CHEx CPne EMan ERea
grandiflora	CArn CPne EMan ERea LEdu SVen
§ iridioides	CGle CNic CSWP EBee GBin LEdu LRHS MSte WPer

DIGITALIS ✿ (Scrophulariaceae)

ambigua	See D. grandiflora
apricot hybrids	See D. purpurea 'Sutton's Apricot'
'Butterfingers'	LEur WCot
'Butterfingers' x ferruginea	Last listed 1999
'Butterfingers' x laevigata subsp. laevigata	LEur
'Butterfingers' x obscura	LEur
campanulata alba	Last listed 1998
cariensis	WDCP
ciliata	CFir CFri EBee ELan MLLN NOak SBla SCou
cream hybrids	EFou
davisiana	CBel CBot CLon EBee EGle EWTr MWgw NOak SCou SSoC STes WDCP WHil WMoo WPer
dubia	CBot EBee NBir SRob WCHb WDCP WGor
'Electrum'	Last listed 1999
eriostachya	See D. lutea
ferruginea	More than 30 suppliers
- 'Gelber Herold'	CBel CBot CLon EBee EMan EPfP EWTr LGre LRHS MSte NLar SMrm WDCP WGor WHil
- 'Gigantea'	CBot CPou EBee ECGN GCal LRHS NNor NPri SMrm SSoC WBea
- x grandiflora	LEur
- var. schischkinii	EBee GCal NArg
'Flashing Spires'	See D. lutea 'Flashing Spires'
* floribunda	EBee
fontanesii	EBee GMac MBct WBro WViv
'Frosty'	Last listed 1997
x fulva	EBee MLLN NBir
'Glory of Roundway'	CBot CPlt EBee LEur MAnH MHer MRav SOkh SWat WCot WFar WPGP WSan WWeb
§ grandiflora ♀	More than 30 suppliers
- 'Carillon'	ECle EMar LEur MSte MTis NPri NPro SRob WBro WGor WPer
- 'Dropmore Yellow'	Last listed 1997
* - 'Dwarf Carillon'	Last listed 1999
- 'Temple Bells'	CBlo EMar LSyl SSoC SWat WPer
beywoodii	See D. purpurea subsp. beywoodii
'John Innes Tetra'	CFri CHad CLon CMil CSam ECoo LEur LRHS MBNS NArg STes WBry WGor WPGP WPer WRus WWhi WWin

kisbinskyi	See D. parviflora
laevigata	CBel CBot CHad CSam EBee ECGN EDAr GAbr GMac LGre LRHS MSte NBro NSti SSoC WCHb WHer WPer
- subsp. graeca	CMdw EBee LEur SSoC WGor
- subsp. laevigata	LEur
- - x obscura	LEur
lamarckii hort.	See D. lanata
- Ivanina	EBee WPer
§ lanata ♀	More than 30 suppliers
- HH&K 177	Last listed 1999
- HH&K 178	Last listed 1999
leucophaea	EGoo EMar
§ lutea	More than 30 suppliers
- subsp. australis	LEur SHFr WDCP
- Brickell's form	CBel EBee MSte
- ex NS 676	LEur
§ - 'Flashing Spires' (v)	CFri CPla EMan NPro WBar
* - floribunda	Last listed 1999
- subsp. lutea	Last listed 1999
- 'Yellow Medley'	LEur WCot
x macedonica from Macedonia	Last listed 1999
¶ x media	ECGN
x mertonensis ♀	More than 30 suppliers
¶ - 'Summer King'	WGor
micrantha	See D. lutea subsp. australis
'Molten Ore'	ESis
nervosa	WDCP
obscura	CBot CFir CGle CLon EBee ECtt LAst LEur LRHS NOak SBla SSoC SSpi WCHb WCot WDCP WElm WGor WHer WHil WPer
* - 'Dusky Maid'	NArg
- x Isoplexis canariensis	Last listed 1999
orientalis	See D. grandiflora
§ parviflora	More than 30 suppliers
x purpurascens 'Aurora'	Last listed 1999
purpurea	CArn CKin EBrP EBre EDAr EFou ENot EWFC GPoy LBCl LBSe LBre MBBe MHer MMal NArg NFor NLan NMir NPri SBre SCou SIde SPlb SRCN WGwG WOak WPer WWye
- f. albiflora	More than 30 suppliers
- - unspotted	EMar
- 'Campanulata'	SGar
* - 'Campanulata Alba'	MHer
- 'Chedglow' (v)	CNat WCHb
* - 'Danby Lodge'	Last listed 1997
* - dwarf red	WGor
- Excelsior Group	CB&S CBot CTri EBrP EBre EMan GMaP LBCl LBSe LBre MBBe MBri MWat NFai NFla NMir NVic SBre SMer SPer SRms WGor
- - primrose	LEur SPer
- - (Suttons; Unwins) ♀	CBrm MRav
- - white	Last listed 1999
- Foxy Group	CBlo CBot GKir MBNS MRav NFai SRms SRob WHen WPer
- Giant Spotted Group	COtt CSam GKir LRHS SCoo WHil WPer WRus
- - pink	Last listed 1999
- - purple	Last listed 1999
- - white	Last listed 1999
- Glittering Prizes Group	LRHS NCut SWat
- - maroon	Last listed 1999
- - white	Last listed 1999
- Gloxinioides Group	EBee ELan EPfP NRya SHFr WUnu
¶ - - 'Isabellina'	CBot WPer WViv
- - 'The Shirley' ♀	ECtt MWat WBry WGor

§ - subsp. *beywoodii*   CSam CSpe EBee EGoo ELan
                    EMar ESis GBuc SPer SRob WCHb
                    WCot WLRN WOut WPer WPnP
                    WWin
  - subsp. *mariana*   EBee
  - subsp. *nevadensis*   CBot
  - 'Pam's Choice'   CSpe EMar
  - peloric   WViv
  - 'Primrose Carousel'   EBee LEur STes WElm
§ - 'Sutton's Apricot' ♀   More than 30 suppliers
* - 'Sutton's Giant Primrose'   CBot EBee EMar NCut WBry
                    WDCP WWeb
  - white cen-type mutant   Last listed 1999
* 'Roundway Gold'   Last listed 1998
  sibirica   CFri EBee GBuc MLLN NBur SCou
                    WPer
* *stewartii*   EBee EMan
  'Strawberry Crush'   Last listed 1998
  thapsi   CBot EDAr EOld ESis MLLN SBla
                    SMrm WCHb WPer WSel
  - JCA 410.000   EBee
  trojana   EBee GBuc LEur LFis LRHS NPri
                    SCou SLod WHil WPer WWin
* *tuberosa*   Last listed 1999
  Vesuvius hybrids   Last listed 1999
  viridiflora   CFri EBee ECtt EDAr GAbr LEur
                    MBNS MHer MWhi NBro NPri
                    NSti WCHb WElm WHer WOut
                    WPer WWin
  - HH&K 308   Last listed 1999
¶ - 'Moss Green'   NArg

DIONAEA (Droseraceae)
  muscipula   CSWC EAnd LRHS WMEx
  - 'Royal Red'   CSWC
  - 'Spider'   Last listed 1999

DIONYSIA (Primulaceae)
  'Agnes'   Last listed 1998
  'Annielle'   Last listed 1999
  archibaldii   Last listed 1997
  aretioides ♀   EPot WAbe
  - 'Gravetye'   ECho
  - 'Paul Furse'   Last listed 1999
  - 'Phyllis Carter'   CPBP ECho EPot
  - 'Susan Hale'   Last listed 1999
  curviflora   EPot
  - x *tapetodes* MK 2   Last listed 1998
  denticulata   Last listed 1998
¶ 'Emmely'   EHyt
¶ 'Eric Watson'   EHyt
  'Ewesley Epsilon'   Last listed 1999
¶ 'Ewesley Theta'   EHyt
  'Francesca'   EHyt
  involucrata   CGra
¶ *lamingtonii*   EHyt
  'Markus'   CGra
  'Monika' MK 8809/1   CGra
  'Nan Watson'   Last listed 1999
¶ 'Schneeball'   EHyt
¶ 'Sonate'   EHyt
  tapetodes   Last listed 1998
¶ - 'Brimstone'   EHyt
* - CGW No. 1   Last listed 1998
  - ENF 5   Last listed 1999
  - farinose   ECho
  - 'Peter Edwards'   EPot
    (Hewer 1164)
  - 'Sulphur'   Last listed 1999

DIOON (Zamiaceae)
  edule   CBrP CRoM LPal

  - var. *angustifolium*   CBrP
  - var. *edule*   CTrC
  mejiae   LPal
  rzedowskii   CBrP LPal
  spinulosum   CBrP LPal

DIOSCOREA (Dioscoreaceae)
  batatas   CPlN IIve MSal WCru
  deltoidea   WCru
  dregeana   Last listed 1999
  elephantipes   Last listed 1999
  nipponica   EBee IIve
  quinqueloba   WCru
  villosa   MSal

DIOSMA (Rutaceae)
  ericoides   LBuc
  - 'Pink Fountain'   LRHS
  - 'Sunset Gold'   CCHP CInt LBuc LRHS SCoo

DIOSPHAERA (Campanulaceae)
  asperuloides   See *Trachelium asperuloides*

DIOSPYROS (Ebenaceae)
  austroafricana   Last listed 1998
  duclouxii   CFil SSpi
  kaki (F)   CAgr CGre CMCN LPan LRHS
                    SSpi WDin
  lotus   CAgr CB&S CFil CMCN CTho
                    LPan SMac SSpi WPGP
  rhombifolia   CFil
  virginiana (F)   CAgr CB&S CMCN EPfP SMac
                    SSpi

DIPCADI (Hyacinthaceae)
  lividum S&F 1   Last listed 1998
  serotinum   Last listed 1997

DIPELTA (Caprifoliaceae)
  floribunda   CBot CBrm CFil CPMA EPfP GKir
                    LRHS MAsh MBlu SSpi WBod
                    WPGP WWat
  ventricosa   CFil CPLG CPMA CPle EPfP LRHS
                    MBlu WPGP WWat
  yunnanensis   CFil EPfP LRHS SPla WPGP WWes

DIPHYLLEIA (Berberidaceae)
  cymosa   CRDP EBee ECha EMan EOld EPar
                    MSal WCru
  grayi   WCru
  sinensis   WCru

DIPIDAX See ONIXOTIS

DIPLACUS See MIMULUS

DIPLADENIA See MANDEVILLA

DIPLARCHE (Ericaceae)
  multiflora   GKir

DIPLARRHENA (Iridaceae)
  Helen Dillon's form   EMan
§ *latifolia*   CAvo CFil GGar LBee WAbe WCot
  moraea   CFil CHid CNic EBee EMan GCal
                    GGar IBlr ILis LFis LRHS SSpi
                    WAbe WCot WHal WPGP WWin
  - *minor*   Last listed 1999
  - 'Slieve Donard'   CLAP CRDP
  - West Coast form   See *D. latifolia*

DIPLAZIUM (Woodsiaceae)
§ *proliferum*   Last listed 1999

DIPLOTAXIS (Brassicaceae)
tenuifolia   Last listed 1997

DIPOGON (Papilionaceae)
§ *lignosus*   CPIN

DIPSACUS (Dipsacaceae)
§ *fullonum*   CArn CHal CKin CLTr EWFC
                  EWTr GBar MChe MHer MHew
                  NBid NBro NMir SIde WBea
                  WByw WCer WHer WOak WWye
- subsp. *fullonum*   WJek
inermis   EBee ECha EMon GBar GCan
              NBid NPSI WFar
- CC&McK 567   Last listed 1999
laciniatus   SRCN SRob WMoo
pilosus   CKin EBee EWFC
sativus   NHex
sylvestris   See *D. fullonum*

DIPTERACANTHUS See RUELLIA

DIPTERONIA (Aceraceae)
sinensis   CB&S CFil CMCN CSam GKir
              LRHS MAsh SSpi WNor WShe

DISA (Orchidaceae)
aurata   GCrs
Diores g.   GCrs
x *kewensis*   GCrs
'Kirstenbosch Pride'   GCrs
tripetaloides   GCrs
uniflora   GCrs

DISANTHUS (Hamamelidaceae)
cercidifolius ♀   CAbP CB&S CFil CPMA EPfP GCal
                      GKir IDee IMGH LRHS MAsh
                      MBel MBlu MBri MGos SPer SReu
                      SSpi SSta WBod WDin WPat WWat

DISCARIA (Rhamnaceae)
¶ *chacaye*   WPGP
toumatou   Last listed 1998

DISELMA (Cupressaceae)
archeri   CKen CNic MBar

DISPHYMA (Aizoaceae)
crassifolium   SChr

DISPOROPSIS (Convallariaceae)
arisanensis B&SWJ 1490   EBee WCru WFar
aspera   EBee WCru
longifolia B&SWJ 5284   WCru
§ *pernyi*   More than 30 suppliers
sp. from Philippines   EBee
  B&SWJ 3891

DISPORUM (Convallariaceae)
¶ *bodinieri*   LEur
cantoniense   WCot WCru
¶ - B&L 12512   SBla
- B&SWJ 1424   WCru
- var. *cantoniense* f.   EBee WCru
  brunneum B&SWJ 5290
- var. *kawakamii*   Last listed 1998
- - B&SWJ 350   WCru
flavens   CFil CRDP EBee EBrP EBre EPPr

                  EPar EPfP GKir LBCl LBSe LBre
                  LGre MBBe SBre SUsu WCot WFar
                  WPGP WSHC
- B&SWJ 872   WCru
* *flavum*   SOkd
hookeri   EPar GKir WCot WCru
- var. *oreganum*   CBro EBee GTou IBlr WCru
lanuginosum   CBro GCrs WCot WCru
lutescens   EBee WCru
maculatum   CLAP CRDP EPar LGre SMac
megalanthum   EPPr
  CD&R 2412b
nantauense B&SWJ 359   EBee WCot WCru
sessile   WCru
- 'Variegatum'   More than 30 suppliers
- var. *yakushimense*   WCru
shimadae B&SWJ 399   WCru
smilacinum   EBee EPar WCru
* - 'Aureovariegatum'   WCot WCru
- B&SWJ 713   WCru
smithii   CFil CRDP EBee EPPr EPar EPot
              ERos GCrs NBir NHar NMen
              WCot WCru WPGP WWat
sp. B&SWJ 872   Last listed 1999
taiwanense B&SWJ 1513   WCru
uniflorum   WCru
- B&SWJ 651   WCot WCru
viridescens   WCru

DISSOTIS (Melastomataceae)
canescens   Last listed 1997

DISTICTIS (Bignoniaceae)
buccinatoria   CPIN
'Mrs Rivers'   CPIN

DISTYLIUM (Hamamelidaceae)
myricoides   CFil CMCN EPfP WWat
racemosum   CB&S CFil CTre EPfP GSki LRHS
                SReu SSta WSHC WWat

DIURANTHERA See CHLOROPHYTUM

DIURIS (Orchidaceae)
corymbosa from   Last listed 1999
  S. Australia
- from W. Australia   Last listed 1999
- yellow   Last listed 1999
drummondii 'Buttery'   Last listed 1999
Earwig g.   Last listed 1999
lanceolata   Last listed 1999
'Pioneer Big Ears'   Last listed 1999
punctata 'Old Vic'   Last listed 1999
sulphurea 'Golden   Last listed 1999
  Dragon'

DIZYGOTHECA See SCHEFFLERA

DOBINEA (Podoaceae)
vulgaris B&SWJ 2532   WCru

DODECATHEON ✿ (Primulaceae)
alpinum   GCrs IMGH NHar NRya SRms
                WViv
- JCA 11744   SBla
amethystinum   See *D. pulchellum*
clevelandii   NTow
- subsp. *insulare*   CNic EBee LRHS NWCA
- subsp. *patulum*   LRHS
conjugens   EBee
- JCA 11133   Last listed 1999
cusickii   See *D. pulchellum* subsp. *cusickii*

dentatum ♀	CElw CNic CPBP EPar IMGH LRHS MBro MTho NMen NSla WAbe WFar
- subsp. *ellisiae*	GCrs
frigidum	WAbe
§ *hendersonii* ♀	CBro EBee EPar NPar SBla SRms
- 'Inverleith' ♀	Last listed 1995
- subsp. *parvifolium*	GNor
integrifolium	See *D. hendersonii*
§ *jeffreyi*	EBee EBlw LRHS MBro NHar NMen NWCA WAbe
- 'Rotlicht'	NHar SRms
* x *lemoinei*	EPot WAbe
§ *meadia* ♀	More than 30 suppliers
- f. *album* ♀	CB&S CBro CCuc CLon CSWP EBee ECha EFou EGle ELan EOrc EPar EWTr GDra LAma LHop LRHS MLLN MTho NHol NMen SIng SPer SRms WPnP
- from Cedar County	WAbe
* - 'Goliath'	Last listed 1997
- membranaceous	WAbe
- 'Millard's Clone'	EPar
- 'Queen Victoria'	WPnP
- red shades	Last listed 1997
- 'Splendidum' ♀	Last listed 1995
pauciflorum (Dur.) E. Greene	See *D. meadia*
- hort.	See *D. pulchellum*
poeticum	MBro NTow
§ *pulchellum* ♀	CBro EBee EPar EPot GDra LRHS MBro MNrw NHar NMen NRya NWCA SBla SIng WAbe
- *album*	Last listed 1997
§ - subsp. *cusickii*	CNic LRHS NWCA SRms
- subsp. *pulchellum* 'Red Wings'	CLon CMea EBrP EBre EPot EWTr GDra LBCl LBSe LBre MBBe MBro SBre WHoo WLin WPyg
- *radicatum*	See *D. pulchellum*
- 'Sooke's Variety'	WAbe
radicatum	See *D. pulchellum*
redolens	EBee WAbe
- NNS 95-224	Last listed 1999
tetrandrum	See *D. jeffreyi*

DODONAEA (Sapindaceae)

humilis (f)	Last listed 1997
- (m)	Last listed 1997
viscosa	CArn CMFo ECou IBlr LHil SPlb
- subsp. *angustifolia*	Last listed 1998
- subsp. *cuneata*	Last listed 1998
- subsp. *linearis*	Last listed 1998
- 'Purpurea'	CAbb CB&S CDoC CGre ECou ERea

DOLICHOS (Papilionaceae)

lignosus	See *Dipogon lignosus*

DOLICHOTHRIX (Asteraceae)

§ *ericoides*	WHer

DOMBEYA (Sterculiaceae)

burgessiae	LRHS SOWG

DONDIA See HACQUETIA

DOODIA (Blechnaceae)

aspera	GQui NMar
§ *caudata*	NMar
heterophylla	Last listed 1999
media	GQui NMar WRic
mollis	NMar

* *rubra*	Last listed 1999
squarrosa	See *D. caudata*

DORONICUM ✿ (Asteraceae)

austriacum	EBee EPri MSCN NCat SMac WCot
carpetanum	CSam
catatactarum	EBee GOrP
caucasicum	See *D. orientale*
clusii	Last listed 1999
§ *columnae*	EBee GDra
cordatum	See *D. columnae*
§ x *excelsum* 'Harpur Crewe'	CElw CGle LRHS MCAu MCLN MRav NPer NTow NVic WCot WEas
'Finesse'	CBlo EPfP LRHS NOak SRms WMoo
§ 'Frühlingspracht' (d)	CElw CRDP GDra LRHS MInt SPer SPla SRms WEas
grandiflorum	EBee
'Little Leo'	COIW LRHS MHer NEgg WHil WWeb
'Miss Mason' ♀	LRHS MBNS MBri SPer
§ *orientale*	CBlo EMar ENot EPfP LRHS MOne MSCN NBid NCiC SMac SWat WByw WOve
- 'Goldcut'	SPla WLRN
- 'Magnificum'	COIW CSam EBee EMan GChr GKir GMaP LAst LPVe LRHS MFir MHer MWat NArg NFai NFla NMir NOak SMer SPer SRms WBea WFar WPer WPnP WPyg WWal WWin
pardalianches	CMea ECha GGar MHew MLLN SDys WCot WRHF
- 'Goldstrauss'	EWTr
plantagineum 'Excelsum'	See *D.* x *excelsum* 'Harpur Crewe'
'Riedels Goldkranz'	LRHS MBct MBri MWhi WCot
Spring Beauty	See *D.* 'Frühlingspracht'

DORYANTHES (Agavaceae)

excelsa	CTrC
palmeri	CHEx

DORYCNIUM See LOTUS

DORYOPTERIS (Adiantaceae)

pedata	MBri

DOUGLASIA (Primulaceae)

laevigata	See *Androsace laevigata*
montana	See *Androsace montana*
nivalis	See *Androsace nivalis*
vitaliana	See *Vitaliana primuliflora*

DOVEA (Restionaceae)

macrocarpa	CCpl

DOVYALIS (Flacourtiaceae)

caffra (F)	LBlo

DOXANTHA See MACFADYENA

DRABA (Brassicaceae)

acaulis	Last listed 1999
aizoides	EBrP EBre ECha ELan GCHN GCrs GDra GKir LBCl LBSe LBre LRHS MBBe MHer MOne MWat NRya SBre SIng SRms WLow WWin
- 'Compacta'	Last listed 1997
aizoon	See *D. lasiocarpa*
alticola JJH 119.94	Last listed 1999
§ *aspera*	WAbe

bertolonii Nyman — See *D. aspera*
- Thell. — See *D. brachystemon*
- Boissier — See *D. loeseleurii*
bruniifolia — EBrP EBre EBur EGle EWes LBCl LBSe LBre LRHS MBBe MTho NWCA SBre SSmi
- subsp. *bruniifolia* — CGra
bryoides — See *D. rigida* var. *bryoides*
cappadocica — Last listed 1999
cinerea — Last listed 1998
compacta — See *D. lasiocarpa* Compacta Group
cretica — NMen
cusickii — CGra CPBP
cuspidata — Last listed 1999
dedeana — ECho EWes WAbe
- subsp. *mawii* — NTow
densifolia — Last listed 1999
- JJA 11826 — NWCA
dubia — Last listed 1998
glacialis var. *pectinata* — Last listed 1999
baynaldii — Last listed 1997
bispanica — NMen
- subsp. *lebrunii* — Last listed 1998
boppeana — Last listed 1999
imbricata — See *D. rigida* var. *imbricata*
§ *incana* — MOne WPyg
§ - Stylaris Group — Last listed 1998
kitadakensis — GCHN
§ *lasiocarpa* — NArg WAbe
§ - Compacta Group — ECho
§ *loeseleurii* — Last listed 1999
lonchocarpa — Last listed 1998
longisiliqua ♀ — ITim MDCh SBla SIng
- EMR 2551 — EPot
magellanica — Last listed 1998
mollissima — CGra EPot GTou NMen NWCA
oligosperma — CGra NWCA WLin
* - var. *bastere* — Last listed 1999
- NNS 94-40 — Last listed 1999
oreades CC&McK 804 — Last listed 1999
oreibata — Last listed 1999
ossetica var. *racemosa* — Last listed 1999
pamirica — ITim
parnassica — GCHN
paysonii — Last listed 1999
- var. *treleasei* — WAbe WLin
polytricha — GTou
repens — See *D. sibirica*
rigida — CMea MLan MOne MTho SSmi
§ - var. *bryoides* — 'CGra MBro NWCA SOkd
- - HZ 82-97 — Last listed 1999
- - JJH 960858 — Last listed 1998
§ - var. *imbricata* — MBro NHol NTow SSmi WLin
- - f. *compacta* — EPot
- var. *rigida* — CNic
rosularis — CGra EPot SIng WLin
sakuraii — EDAr
x *salomonii* — EPot
sauteri — GCHN
scardica — See *D. lasiocarpa*
§ *sibirica* — CNic
sp. CC 1911 — WCot
sp. F&W 8173 from Peru — Last listed 1997
sphaeroides — CGra
streptocarpa — Last listed 1998
stylaris — See *D. incana* Stylaris Group
talassica — Last listed 1997
* *thymbriphyrestus* — CPBP
ussuriensis — WPer
ventosa — CNic GTou NTow
yunnanensis — Last listed 1999

- ex JJH 90856 — Last listed 1997

DRACAENA ✿ (Agavaceae)
congesta — See *Cordyline stricta*
draco — ECre
fragrans — MBri
- (Compacta Group) 'Compacta Purpurea' — MBri
- - 'Compacta Variegata' — MBri
- (Deremensis Group) 'Lemon Lime' (v) — LRHS MBri
- - 'Warneckei' (v) ♀ — MBri
- - 'Yellow Stripe' (v) — MBri
* - *glauca* — MBri
- 'Janet Craig' — MBri
- 'Massangeana' (v) ♀ — MBri
indivisa — See *Cordyline indivisa*
marginata (v) ♀ — LRHS MBri
- 'Colorama' (v) — MBri
reflexa 'Variegata' ♀ — Last listed 1995
sanderiana (v) ♀ — LRHS MBri
* *schrijveriana* — MBri
steudneri — MBri
stricta — See *Cordyline stricta*

DRACOCEPHALUM (Lamiaceae)
altaiense — See *D. imberbe*
argunense — CPBP CPlt CRDP EBee GKir LBee LFis LGre LRHS SAga SBla SCro SHFr SOkh SRms SRot SSoC WCru WPat WPer WWin
* - 'Album' — EBee
¶ *austriacum* — WLin
botryoides — CPBP EBee NWCA
calophyllum ACE 1611 — Last listed 1997
- var. *smithianum* — Last listed 1998
forrestii — CLyd EPot ESis SBla
grandiflorum — CRDP EBee ESis NLar
bemsleyanum — EBee WPat
§ *imberbe* — EBee GKir
isabellae — EBee
mairei — See *D. renatii*
moldavica — MSal SIde
nutans — EBee ESis NLar
oblongifolium — Last listed 1998
palmatum — EBee Ilve
aff. *paulsenii* JJH 9209334 — Last listed 1997
peregrinum — EBee
prattii — See *Nepeta prattii*
§ *renatii* — EBee MSal
rupestre — EBee EPPr MBri
ruyschianum — EMan EMon MLLN NWCA
sibiricum — See *Nepeta sibirica*
tanguticum — NLar
virginicum — See *Physostegia virginiana*
wendelboi — CPea EBee GBri MLLN NBir NBus WPat WPer WWin

DRACUNCULUS ✿ (Araceae)
canariensis — CAvo
- MS 934 — Last listed 1998
¶ *muscivorus* — CFir
§ *vulgaris* — CGle CHid CLAP EBee EBot EMon EPar EPot LEdu LRHS MCCP MGrG MRav SDix SEND SMad SSoC WCot WCru WHal WPnP

DRAPETES (Thymelaeaceae)
dieffenbachii — Last listed 1998
lyallii — Last listed 1998

DREGEA (Asclepiadaceae)
§ **sinensis** CB&S CBot CBrd CGre CPln
CSam ELan EPfP ERav ERea EWes
GQui LRHS SBra SOWG WCot
WCru WSHC WWat WWeb

DREPANOSTACHYUM (Poaceae - Bambusoideae)
§ **falcatum** CTrC ISta LJus WJun
falconeri hort. See *Himalayacalamus falconeri*
bookerianum See *Himalayacalamus bookerianus*
§ **kbasianum** CFil ISta WPGP
§ **microphyllum** ISta SDry WJun

DRIMIOPSIS (Hyacinthaceae)
maculata Last listed 1998

DRIMYS (Winteraceae)
aromatica See *D. lanceolata*
colorata See *Pseudowintera colorata*
granatensis CFil
§ **lanceolata** More than 30 suppliers
- (f) ECou GEil GGar SPer
- (m) CDoC ECou GGar
- 'Mount Wellington' GCal
- 'Suzette' MBlu
§ sp. CPla
winteri CAbb CB&S CDoC CFil CHEx
CMac CPle CSam CTrG CTrw
EPfP IArd IOrc SArc SBrw SLim
SPer SRPl WBrE WCwm WDin
WGer WSHC WWat
- var. *andina* CFil CMHG EPfP GGGa SSpi
WPGP WWat
§ - var. *chilensis* CFil CGre CHEx CLan WBod
WCru WPGP
- 'Fastigiata' Last listed 1999
- Latifolia Group See *D. winteri* var. *chilensis*

DROSANTHEMUM (Aizoaceae)
bellum Last listed 1999
bicolor EOas
floribundum CHEx EOas
bispidum CHEx CHal EBrP EBre ECtt EDAr
ELan EOas EPot IMGH LBCl LBSe
LBre LRHS MBBe MBro MTho
NMen NNrd NTow NWCA SBre
SIng WPat WPyg
micans EOas
speciosum EOas
striatum Last listed 1999
* **sutherlandii** Last listed 1999

DROSERA (Droseraceae)
adelae EAnd WMEx
admirabilis Last listed 1999
aliciae EAnd WMEx
andersoniana EFEx
anglica CSWC WMEx
x **badgerupii** WMEx
'Lake Badgerup'
'Beermullah' WMEx
binata GTro WMEx
§ - subsp. *dichotoma* Last listed 1998
- 'Extrema' WMEx
- 'Multifida' GTro WMEx
- T form EAnd
browniana EFEx
bulbigena EFEx
bulbosa WMEx
- subsp. *bulbosa* EFEx

- subsp. *major* EFEx
x *californica* 'California WMEx
Sunset'
capensis EAnd GTro LRHS WMEx
¶ - 'Albino' EAnd GTro WMEx
- narrow-leaved WMEx
- red Last listed 1999
capillaris WMEx
cuneifolia WMEx
dichotoma See *D. binata* subsp. *dichotoma*
dielsiana WMEx
erythrorrhiza EFEx WMEx
- subsp. *collina* EFEx WMEx
- subsp. *erythrorrhiza* EFEx
- subsp. *magna* WMEx
- subsp. *squamosa* EFEx
filiformis var. *filiformis* EAnd WMEx
- var. *tracyi* Last listed 1997
gigantea EFEx WMEx
graniticola EFEx
bamiltonii WMEx
beterophylla EFEx WMEx
intermedia WMEx
loureirii EFEx
macrantha EFEx WMEx
- subsp. *macrantba* EFEx
¶ - subsp. *planchonii* NEgg
macrophylla subsp. EFEx
macrophylla
¶ **marcbantii** subsp. EFEx
prophylla
'Marston Dragon' CSWC WMEx
menziesii Last listed 1997
- subsp. *basifolia* EFEx
- subsp. *menziesii* EFEx
- subsp. *tbysanosepala* EFEx
modesta EFEx
orbiculata EFEx WMEx
peltata EFEx WMEx
- subsp. *auriculata* Last listed 1997
platypoda EFEx WMEx
pulcbella WMEx
- giant Last listed 1997
- x *nitidula* WMEx
ramellosa EFEx
rosulata EFEx WMEx
rotundifolia CSWC WMEx
salina EFEx
scorpioides CSWC
slackii CSWC WMEx
spatulata WMEx
- Kansai WMEx
- Kanto WMEx
stolonifera WMEx
- subsp. *compacta* EFEx
- subsp. *bumilis* EFEx
- subsp. *porrecta* EFEx
- subsp. *rupicola* EFEx
- subsp. *stolonifera* EFEx
stricticaulis WMEx
tubaestylus EFEx WMEx
villosa Last listed 1997
zonaria EFEx WMEx

DRYANDRA (Proteaceae)
armata Last listed 1998
* **aromatica** Last listed 1998
formosa CCpl
nivea Last listed 1997
nobilis Last listed 1997
praemorsa Last listed 1997
quercifolia Last listed 1999

DRYAS (Rosaceae)

drummondii	CGra EPot SBla WAbe
- 'Grandiflora'	Last listed 1998
* - 'Grandiflora'	NHar
E.B.Anderson'	
grandis	Last listed 1997
§ *integrifolia*	CMea EPot GDra IMGH NHar
	NMGW NMen WAbe
- 'Greenland Green'	WAbe
octopetala ♀	CAgr CGle CLyd CSam EDAr
	GCHN GDra GKir GTou IMGH
	LHop MBro MWat NChi NFla
	NFor NHar NVic SBla SIng SRms
	WAbe WCFE WCot WEas WWin
¶ - 'Harry Bush'	NHar
- 'Minor' ♀	CLyd EDAr LBee LRHS MBro
	NMen NWCA NWoo SRms WAbe
	WPyg
x *suendermannii* ♀	CMHG EBrP EBre ELan EPfP GTou
	LBCl LBSe LBre LRHS MBBe MBro
	MNaF NHol NMen NWCA SBre
	SMrm WAbe WPyg
tenella	See *D. integrifolia*

DRYOPTERIS ✿ (Dryopteridaceae)

aemula	EFer SRms
§ *affinis* ♀	CCuc CFil CLAP CRow EBee
	ECha EFou EPar EPfP GGar LHil
	LSyl NHol NMar SCob SRms WFib
	WRic
§ - subsp. *borreri*	EFer IOrc MBri NBus
- subsp. *cambrensis*	EFer
- 'Congesta'	CLAP EBee GKir SLon WFib WWat
- 'Congesta Cristata'	CLAP EBrP EBre LBCl LBSe LBre
	LRHS MBBe MBri NHar NHol SBre
- Crispa Group	CLAP GBin IOrc LAst LRHS SCob
	SMac SRPl
§ - 'Crispa Gracilis' ♀	CCuc CLAP CMil EFer ELan EMon
	LHil MBri NBir NBus SPer SPla
	SRms WRic
§ - 'Cristata' ♀	More than 30 suppliers
- 'Cristata Angustata' ♀	CLAP EFer ELan EMon GBin IOrc
	NDlv NHol NMar SCob SRms
	WFib WPGP WRic
- 'Cristata The King'	See *D. affinis* 'Cristata'
¶ - 'Grandiceps Askew'	CCuc NMar WFib
* - 'Insubrica'	EFer
- 'Linearis Cristata'	Last listed 1997
- 'Pinderi'	CLAP EFer EFou ELan MBri NOrc
	SCob WGor
- Polydactyla Group	GQui NMar
* - 'Polydactyla	CCuc CLAP CRDP CRow NHol
Mapplebeck' ♀	SRms
- 'Revolvens'	EFer SRms WRic
aitoniana	Last listed 1999
atrata hort.	See *D. cycadina*
austriaca hort.	See *D. dilatata*
blanfordii	CFil WPGP
borreri	See *D. affinis* subsp. *borreri*
buschiana	Last listed 1999
carthusiana	CBlo CFil CLAP EFer NBus NHar
	SRms WRic
- 'Cristata'	NVic
clintoniana	CFil NBus WPGP WRic
x *complexa* 'Stablerae'	CLAP EFer GQui NMar WFib
	WPGP WRic
conjugata	WRic
corleyi	WRic
crassirhizoma	Last listed 1998
crispifolia	EFer
cristata	EFer MLan WRic

§ *cycadina* ♀	CCuc CFil CLAP CRDP EBee EFer
	ELan EMar EMon EPfP GCal IOrc
	LRHS MCCP MDun NBir NBus
	NHol NMar SEas SMac SPla WCot
	WFib WGor WRic WWat
darjeelingensis	Last listed 1999
dickinsii	EMon WRic
§ *dilatata* ♀	CCuc CKin EBee ECha EFer ELan
	EMon GCHN MGas MWgw NBus
	NHol NMar SCob SRms WFib
	WRic WWat WWye
- 'Crispa Whiteside' ♀	CFil CLAP CMil EBee EFer ELan
	EMon MBri MDun NBus NCiC
	NHar NHol NLar SCob SPlb WFib
	WHil WPGP WRic WWoo
- 'Grandiceps'	CLAP CMHG CRDP CRow EFer
	EMon MBri NHar NHol NVic
	SChu WFib WRic
- 'Lepidota Crispa Cristata'	CLAP LRHS
- 'Lepidota Cristata' ♀	CCuc CLAP CMHG CRDP EFer
	ELan EMon IOrc NHar NHol
	NMar SCob SRms WFib WRic
- 'Lepidota Grandiceps'	CLAP NMar
* - 'Recurvata'	CLAP
¶ - 'Revolvens'	WRic
erythrosora ♀	More than 30 suppliers
* - 'Prolifera' ♀	CBos CLAP CRDP EBee EMon
	GCal GMaP LHil MSte NBir NCiC
	NDlv NHar NHol NRib WFib
	WRic
expansa	EMon
filix-mas ♀	EBee EFou EPfP GKir GMaP IIve
	LHil LPBA LRHS MCLN MDun
	NBus SMac SPer SRCN SRPl WShi
	WWat WWye
- 'Barnesii'	CBlo CCuc CLAP EBee EFer MSte
	NBus NDlv NHar NMar SCob
	WRic
- 'Bollandiae'	WRic
* - 'Corymbifera Crispa'	EFer
- 'Crispa'	EHon NHol SCob WFib
- 'Crispa Congesta'	See *D. affinis* 'Crispa Gracilis'
- 'Crispa Cristata'	More than 30 suppliers
- 'Crispatissima'	CCuc EFer MDun SRms
- 'Cristata' ♀	CCuc CFil CKin CRow EBrP EBre
	EFer EHon ELan EGir IOrc LBCl
	LBSe LBre MBBe NMar NOak
	NOrc SBre SCob SWat WFib WRic
	WWye
- Cristata Group	EFer NMar SCob SPer WFib WRic
- - 'Fred Jackson'	CCuc CLAP NHol WFib
* - 'Cristata Grandiceps'	EFer
- 'Cristata Jackson'	SPlb
- 'Cristata Martindale'	CLAP CRDP CRow EFer GQui
	NHol NMar SRms WFib
- 'Depauperata'	CCuc CFil CLAP CRDP SChu
	WFib WPGP
- 'Euxinensis'	CCuc CLAP
- 'Furcans'	CLAP
- 'Grandiceps Group	SCob
- 'Grandiceps Wills' ♀	CRow EMon NHol NMar SChu
	WFib WRic
- 'Linearis'	CMHG CRow EBee EFer EHon
	ELan EMar EMon IOrc MBri NBus
	SCob SRms
- 'Linearis Congesta'	CFil WPGP
- 'Linearis Cristata'	NMar WRic
- 'Linearis Polydactyla'	CLAP CMil EBee IMGH MDun
	NHar NMar SCob SLdr SMac
	SMad WHil
- 'Multicristata'	NMar
- Polydactyla Group	GAri NMar WFib

- 'Polydactyla Dadds'	IOrc MBri WFib
¶ *formosana*	EFer
fragrans	Last listed 1998
* *fructuosa*	Last listed 1997
goldieana	CLAP EBee GMaP NBir NBus NHar NMar SCob WGwG WRic
guanchica	CFil
hawaiiensis	Last listed 1998
hirtipes	See *D. cycadina*
hondoensis	CFil
lacera	NHar
lepidopoda	Last listed 1998
marginalis	CLAP NOGN WRic
§ *nigropaleacea*	Last listed 1998
odontoloma	See *D. nigropaleacea*
oreades	SRms
paleacea	CLAP
pallida	CFil
pseudomas	See *D. affinis*
x *remota*	SRms WRic
shiroumensis	Last listed 1997
sieboldii	CCuc CFil CLAP EBee ELan MDun NHar NHol NMar NOGN SChu SRms WFib WPGP WRic
sp. from Emei Shan, China	WPGP
stenolepis	WRic
stewartii	NHar
tokyoensis	CLAP NHar WFib WRic
x *uliginosa*	Last listed 1999
uniformis	CLAP
wallichiana ♀	More than 30 suppliers

DUCHESNEA (Rosaceae)

chrysantha	See *D. indica*
§ *indica*	CAgr CSWP EMan GAbr IBlr MRav NHol NPri NSti SRms SSca WBor WCer WOak
- CC 2007	Last listed 1999
- 'Dingle Variegated'	Last listed 1997
§ - 'Harlequin' (v)	EMan EMon GBar GBuc MCCP MNrw MTho NSti
- 'Snowflakes'	CRow EBee
- 'Taff's Silverline' (v)	Last listed 1998
- 'Variegata'	See *D. indica* 'Harlequin'

DUDLEYA (Crassulaceae)

cymosa	NTow
- JCA 11777	CNic
- subsp. *pumila*	NWCA WCot
farinosa	CHEx IBlr
- NNS 93-240	Last listed 1999
lanceolata NNS 95230	Last listed 1999
pulverulenta	Last listed 1997
¶ *saxosa* subsp. *collomiae*	EBee

DUMASIA (Papilionaceae)

truncata B&SWJ 4905	WCru

DUNALIA (Solanaceae)

australis	See *Iochroma australe*
- blue	See *Iochroma australe* 'Bill Evans'
- white	See *Iochroma australe* 'Andean Snow'

DURANTA (Verbenaceae)

§ *erecta*	LRHS
- 'Variegata'	Last listed 1998
plumieri	See *D. erecta*
repens	See *D. erecta*
* *stenostophylla*	CSpe

DYCKIA (Bromeliaceae)

remotiflora	SChr

DYMONDIA (Asteraceae)

margaretae	LRHS WAbe

DYPSIS (Arecaceae)

§ *decaryi*	CBrP LBlo LPal
decipiens	CBrP LPal
§ *leptocheilos*	Last listed 1999
§ *lutescens* ♀	CRoM EPVP LPal LRHS MBri
utilis	LPal

DYSOSMA See PODOPHYLLUM

E

EBENUS (Papilionaceae)

cretica	Last listed 1997

ECBALLIUM (Cucurbitaceae)

elaterium	MHew MSal WHer

ECCREMOCARPUS (Bignoniaceae)

ruber	See *E. scaber* f. *carmineus*
scaber ♀	CB&S CPlN CRHN CTrG EBee ELan EMil ENot EWTr GAbr GCHN GKir LIck LRHS MBri MNrw NChi NPer SLim SPer SRms SYvo WBrE WFar
¶ - apricot	EMar
- f. *aureus*	CMHG CNic EPfP MAsh NLar SDys SHFr
§ - f. *carmineus*	CMHG CNic EPfP GCHN GGar MAsh NLar SSoC SUsu WCot WElm WPyg
- f. *roseus*	CBot CGle EPfP MAsh

ECHEVERIA ✿ (Crassulaceae)

affinis	MBri
agavoides ♀	MRav WBrE
* - 'Metallica'	MBri
* 'Black Knight'	LHil WCot
* 'Black Prince'	CHEx NPer WCot
derenbergii ♀	CHEx
x *derosa*	LHil
* 'Duchess of Nuremberg'	Last listed 1998
elegans ♀	CHEx CHal EOas LHil MBri SAPC
* 'Frank Reinelt' ♀	LHil
§ *gibbiflora* var. *cristata*	LHil
§ - var. *metallica* ♀	WEas
glauca Bak.	See *E. secunda* var. *glauca*
- *cristata*	See *E. gibbiflora* var. *cristata*
harmsii ♀	CSWP LHil NTow
* 'Harry Butterfield'	Last listed 1998
'Imbricata'	CHEx
nodulosa	LHil
'Paul Bunyon'	CHal
peacockii	EPfP
¶ 'Perle d'Azur'	CTrC
'Perle von Nürnberg' ♀	Last listed 1999
prolifica	CCpl
pulvinata ♀	CHal
* - 'Frosty'	Last listed 1999
secunda	LHil
§ - var. *glauca*	IBlr NBir SArc
- - 'Gigantea'	NPer

setosa ♀	CHEx
'Warfield Wonder' ♀	WEas

ECHINACEA ✿ (Asteraceae)

angustifolia	CArn EBee EMan GPoy MHer
	MSal WCot WHer WOak WWye
- 'Mecklenburg Select'	EBee
¶ 'Greenheart'	LGre
pallida	CBot CMil EBee EGar ELan EMan
	EWTr GPoy LFis MAnH MSal
	NCut NPri NSti SMad SSoC SSvw
	WCot WMoo
paradoxa	CArn CPou EHrv EMan MAnH
	MSal NArg NChi SDys WBea WCot
	WHil
§ **purpurea**	More than 30 suppliers
- Bressingham hybrids	EBee EBrP EBre ELan LBCl LBSe
	LBre LRHS MBBe SBre SPer SPla
	WFar
- dark stemmed	SAga
- 'Green Edge'	Last listed 1998
¶ - 'Kim's Knee High'	CFai COtt EBee EBrP EBre EMan
	GBin LAst LBCl LBSe LBre MBBe
	MLLN NDov NPSI NSti SBre SDys
	SMad SUsu WCot WMaN WWhi
- 'Leuchtstern'	CHar CMdw ECGN EOld GSki
	LRHS MWll SMrm SWat WOve
	WPer
- 'Magnus'	More than 30 suppliers
¶ - 'Pink Flamingo'	EWTr
- 'Robert Bloom'	ECGN EHrv LGre LRHS MCLN
	NDov NPSI SVal WCot
- 'Rubinstern'	CFri COtt EBee EMan LGre NDov
	NPSI WMaN WRus WWhi
- 'The King'	Last listed 1997
- 'Verbesserter Leuchtstern'	NLar
- 'White Lustre'	EBrP EBre ECha LBCl LBSe LBre
	LCaP LRHS MBBe WMoo SBre
	SRCN WFar
- 'White Swan'	More than 30 suppliers
simulata	Last listed 1998
¶ **tennesseensis**	IIve

ECHINODORUS (Alismataceae)

§ **cordifolius**	LLWG
¶ - 'Marble Queen' (v)	LLWG
radicans	See E. cordifolius

ECHINOPS (Asteraceae)

albus	See E. 'Nivalis'
§ **bannaticus**	EBee ERav LLWP LRHS SMer
	WCot
* - 'Albus'	EPfP EWll LAst LRHS NSti SPer
§ - 'Blue Globe'	COIW EBee ECGN EMan EOld
	EPfP GCal LAst LFis LRHS MCli
	NChi SCoo SSca WHil WLRN
	WPer WWal
- 'Taplow Blue' ♀	More than 30 suppliers
commutatus	See E. exaltatus
§ **exaltatus**	EBee MWgw NBir
maracandicus	GCal WCot
microcephalus	EGar
- HH&K 285	Last listed 1999
§ 'Nivalis'	CBre EBee ECGP ECha ELan EPla
	GAbr GCal MWgw SEND
oxyodontus HH&K 145	Last listed 1999
- HH&K 153	Last listed 1998
- HH&K 235	Last listed 1998
* **perringii**	GCal
ritro hort.	See E. bannaticus
§ **ritro** L. ♀	CB&S ECha ECtt ELan ENot EWTr
	GCHN MArl MCAu NBro NCut

	NFai NFor NVic SEND SPer SPlb
	SRms SSvw WEas WFar WOve
	WPer WWin WWye
- 'Charlotte'	Last listed 1998
- 'Moonstone'	CRow
- subsp. **ruthenicus** ♀	ECGP ELan EWTr EWll GBuc
	LRHS MRav WBro WPGP
- 'Veitch's Blue'	CHad CM&M CPlt EBee ECha
	EFou EMan EMon GCal GKir GLil
	LRHS MBri MCAu MCLN MCli
	MMil MRav MWat NCat SAga SPer
	SRPl SSpe WCot WLRN WWeb
- 'Veitch's Blue' misapplied	See E. ritro L.
sphaerocephalus	ELan EMan EMon IBlr MSCN NBid
	SSca WBea WByw WLRN WPer
- 'Arctic Glow'	More than 30 suppliers
strigosus	EBee
tournefortii	EGar
tschimganicus	EBee

ECHINOSPARTUM See GENISTA

ECHIUM (Boraginaceae)

¶ **albicans**	EWll
boissieri	EGoo IHdy
§ **candicans**	CAbb CCtw CGdn CHEx CSpe
	CTbh CTrF ECre EWll LHil MNrw
	SAPC SArc SRob SVen WCHb
fastuosum	See E. candicans
italicum	NLar
¶ **lusitanicum**	EWll
* **nebrum**	GBri
nervosum	Last listed 1999
§ **pininana**	CAbb CCtw CHEx CTbh CTrC
	CTrF EBee ECre ELan EOas EWes
	IHdy NBur SAPC SArc SChr SGar
	SYvo WCHb WHer
- x **wildpretii**	EWll
pinnifolium	See E. pininana
russicum	CFir EBee ECGN EGoo LGre
	MAvo NLar WHil
x **scilloniense**	SYvo
simplex	Last listed 1997
sp. from Greece	WHer
* **virescens**	Last listed 1999
vulgare	CArn CKin ECGN EEls ELan
	EOHP EWFC MChe MHer MHew
	MMal MSal NLar NMir SIde WBrE
	WCHb WHer WJek WWye
- Drake's form	WElm
webbii	CGre
wildpretii	CAbb CHEx IHdy SAPC SVen
	WHer

ECLIPTA (Asteraceae)

alba	See E. prostrata
§ **prostrata**	MSal

EDGEWORTHIA (Thymelaeaceae)

§ **chrysantha**	CB&S CCHP CEnd CPMA EPfP
	LBuc LPan LRHS WSHC
- B&SWJ 1048	WCru
I - 'Grandiflora'	EPfP
- 'Rubra'	CPMA
papyrifera	See E. chrysantha

EDRAIANTHUS (Campanulaceae)

* **angustifolius**	MWll
croaticus	See E. graminifolius
dalmaticus	NTow SBla
dinaricus	Last listed 1998
§ **graminifolius** ♀	CHea ECtt EHyt MOne NHar

- albus	NHol NMen NWCA SRot WFar WPer WWin See *E. graminifolius* subsp. *niveus*
§ - subsp. *niveus*	WHil
parnassicus	NMen
§ *pumilio* ♀	CLyd EPot LRHS NHar NMen NTow SBla SIng
serbicus	Last listed 1998
§ *serpyllifolius*	Last listed 1998
§ - 'Major'	WAbe

EGERIA (Hydrocharitaceae)
§ *densa* — CBen SWyc

EHRETIA (Boraginaceae)
§ *acuminata* var. *obovata*	CGre
dicksonii	CFil CHEx WPGP
ovalifolia	See *E. acuminata* var. *obovata*
thyrsiflora	See *E. acuminata* var. *obovata*

EHRHARTA (Poaceae)
thunbergii — EBee

EICHHORNIA (Pontederiaceae)
'Azure'	Last listed 1998
crassipes	CBen CWat EMFW LPBA MSta NDea
- 'Major'	Last listed 1999

ELAEAGNUS ✿ (Elaeagnaceae)
angustifolia	CAgr CBlo CBot CSam EWTr LPan MBar MBlu MCoo MRav SPer SRPl SRms WDin WGer WWat
- Caspica Group	See *E.* 'Quicksilver'
argentea	See *E. commutata*
§ *commutata*	CAgr CBot CMCN CPle EHoe ENot EPar IMGH IOrc LHop MBlu MTis MWhi NFor SLPl SPer WRus WWat
x *ebbingei*	More than 30 suppliers
I - 'Aurea'	Last listed 1997
- 'Coastal Gold' (v)	CAbP CB&S CBlo CDoC COtt EBee EMil ENot LBuc LRHS MAsh MBri MGos SLim SReu SRms SSta WPat WStI WWes
- 'Gilt Edge' (v) ♀	More than 30 suppliers
- 'Gold Splash'	CDoC CWSG MBri
- 'Limelight' (v)	More than 30 suppliers
- 'Salcombe Seedling'	LRHS MBri
- 'Southern Seedling'	CHEx
¶ *glabra*	EPfP
- 'Reflexa'	See *E.* x *reflexa*
macrophylla	CLan CSam ENot NFor SDry WWat
multiflora	CDul IDee LEdu SPer WPGP
- 'Gigantea'	ELan
parvifolia ♀	EBee ENot EPfP
pungens	ERom EWTr NBir
- 'Argenteovariegata'	See *E. pungens* 'Variegata'
- 'Aureovariegata'	See *E. pungens* 'Maculata'
- 'Dicksonii' (v)	CBlo CCHP LNet LRHS SLon SPer SRms SSpi WBcn
- 'Forest Gold' (v)	CAbP ELan LRHS MAsh
- 'Frederici' (v)	CB&S CBlo CDoC CMHG CMac EHoe ELan EPla ERav MAsh MBri MRav NHol SCob SLim SPer SSpi WHCG WPat WWat
- 'Goldrim' (v)	CBlo COtt EPfP GOrc LRHS MAsh MBri MGos SCob SLim
§ - 'Maculata' (v) ♀	More than 30 suppliers
§ - 'Variegata'	CB&S CBlo CMac EBee IOrc LRHS

§ 'Quicksilver' ♀	MBri NBir SCob SPer SRPl WHCG WLRN More than 30 suppliers
§ x *reflexa*	CFil WHCG WWat
umbellata	CAgr CDul CPle IDee MBlu SPan SPer WHCG WWat
- *borealis*	Last listed 1999

ELATOSTEMA (Urticaceae)
repens var. *pulchrum* ♀	CHal MBri
- var. *repens*	CHal

ELEGIA (Restionaceae)
caespitosa	CTrC
capensis	CFee CFir CHEx CTrC WMul WNor
cuspidata	CTrC
equisetacea	CFee CTrC LHil WNor
fenestrata	Last listed 1998
grandis	LHil
grandispicata	LHil

ELEOCHARIS (Cyperaceae)
acicularis	ELan EMFW NDea SWyc
¶ *dulcis* variegated	CRow
palustris	EMFW MSta SWyc

ELEPHANTOPUS (Asteraceae)
tomentosus — Last listed 1997

ELETTARIA (Zingiberaceae)
cardamomum	CArn CHEx ELau EOas GPoy MBri MSal WCot WJek WMul

ELEUTHEROCOCCUS (Araliaceae)
¶ *nikaianus* B&SWJ 5027	WCru
pictus	See *Kalopanax septemlobus*
senticosus	GPoy
septemlobus	See *Kalopanax septemlobus*
§ *sieboldianus*	MRav
- 'Aureomarginatus'	Last listed 1998
§ - 'Variegatus'	CBot EBee ELan EPfP IHar IOrc MBlu MGos MRav WHer WSHC

ELINGAMITA (Myrsinaceae)
johnsonii — CHEx ECou

ELISENA (Amaryllidaceae)
longipetala — See *Hymenocallis longipetala*

ELLIOTTIA (Ericaceae)
bracteata	See *Tripetaleia bracteata*
pyroliflorus	SSta WAbe
racemosa	Last listed 1999

ELLISIOPHYLLUM (Scrophulariaceae)
pinnatum B&SWJ 197 — WCru

ELMERA (Saxifragaceae)
racemosa — Last listed 1998

ELODEA (Hydrocharitaceae)
canadensis	CBen EHon EMFW SWyc WMAq
crispa	See *Lagarosiphon major*
densa	See *Egeria densa*

ELSHOLTZIA (Lamiaceae)
ciliata	Last listed 1998
fruticosa	CArn WWye
stauntonii	CArn CB&S CBot CFee EBee ECha EMan EOHP EPri EWTr GPoy IMGH MTis SLPl SRCN WHil

- 'Alba'	WSHC WWye CBot NEgg WWye

ELYMUS (Poaceae)

arenarius	See *Leymus arenarius*
canadensis	CBrm CCuc CKno EHoe EWsh WMoo
- f. *glaucifolius*	GCal SLim
cinereus	EPPr
farctus	EPPr
giganteus	See *Leymus racemosus*
glaucus hort.	See *E. hispidus*
§ *hispidus*	CBrm CCuc CInt EBee EBlw ECoo EGle EGoo EHoe EMan EPPr EPla ESis EWTr LHop LHrt LRHS MBri MMoz NHol NPSI NSti SCob SOkh SPer SUsu WCFE WPrP WWye
N *magellanicus*	More than 30 suppliers
§ *scabrus*	SMrm
tenuis	CCuc SMad
villosus var. *arkansanus*	EPPr EPla NOGN

ELYTROPUS (Apocynaceae)

chilensis	GKir

EMBOTHRIUM ✿ (Proteaceae)

coccineum	CFil CHEx CTrG EPfP IOrc LRHS MAsh SDry SReu WBrE WNor WPGP WPat WPyg
- Lanceolatum Group	CDoC CEnd CGre ELan EPfP GGar GKir GOrc LRHS MDun SBrw SSpi SSta WPic WWat
- - 'Inca Flame'	CDoC CDul CEnd COtt CPMA LRHS MDun NDlv SBrw SMur SSta WPat WWat
* - - 'Inca King'	LRHS
- - 'Ñorquinco' ♀	CB&S GGar IOrc LRHS MBri MDun SSpi WBod WCru WPyg
- Longifolium Group	CB&S IBlr IOrc ISea MDun

EMINIUM (Araceae)

albertii	LAma

EMMENOPTERYS (Rubiaceae)

henryi	CFil CGre CLyn EPfP SMad WPGP

EMPETRUM (Empetraceae)

luteum	MBar
nigrum	GAri GPoy MBar
- 'Bernstein'	NHar NHol
* - 'Gold'	Last listed 1998
- var. *japonicum*	GTou
- 'Lucia'	MGos
¶ - 'Tore'	NHar
rubrum	WAbe
sp. from Falklands	WWat

ENCELIOPSIS (Asteraceae)

argophylla	EBee
covillei	EBee

ENCEPHALARTOS (Zamiaceae)

¶ *altensteinii*	CRoM
¶ *cycadifolius*	LPal
¶ *ghellinckii*	LPal
¶ *kisambo*	LPal
¶ *lehmannii*	LPal
natalensis	LPal
¶ *senticosus*	LPal
¶ *villosus*	LPal

ENCHYLAENA (Chenopodiaceae)

tomentosa	Last listed 1998

ENDYMION See HYACINTHOIDES

ENKIANTHUS ✿ (Ericaceae)

campanulatus ♀	More than 30 suppliers
- var. *campanulatus* f. *albiflorus*	CWSG LRHS SMur SPer SSpi
- var. *palibinii*	CGre GAri GChr GGGa GKir LRHS MAsh MGos NHol SBrw SSpi SSta WBrE WNor WPat WWat
- 'Red Bells'	CAbP CBlo CDoC COtt CWSG EBee EPfP GKir GOrc LRHS MBri MDun MGos NDlv SBrw SPer SSht SSpi SSta WAbe
- var. *sikokianus*	CFai CWSG GAri GGGa
* - 'Variegatus'	LRHS MAsh
cernuus	GKir
- var. *matsudae*	GAri
- f. *rubens* ♀	CB&S EPfP GAri GGGa LRHS MAsh SSpi SSta WDin WNor WPic
chinensis	CPLG EPfP GAri GGGa LRHS MAsh SSta WCwm WNor WWat
deflexus	CFil LRHS MAsh SSta WPGP
perulatus ♀	CBrm CFil EMil EPfP GAri GKir LRHS MBar SBrw SSpi SSta WWat WWes

ENSETE (Musaceae)

¶ *glaucum*	WMul
§ *ventricosum*	CAbb CBot CHEx CRoM EOas LBlo LCns LPal LPan SAPC SArc WKif WMul
- 'Atropurpureum'	CHEx
§ - 'Maurelii'	EOas EPVP LCns SArc WMul
- 'Rubrum'	See *E. ventricosum* 'Maurelii'

ENTELEA (Tiliaceae)

arborescens	CHEx CTrC ECou

ENTEROLOBIUM (Mimosaceae)

cyclocarpum	Last listed 1999

EOMECON (Papaveraceae)

chionantha	More than 30 suppliers

EPACRIS (Epacridaceae)

paludosa	GCrs GGGa IMGH SReu
petrophila	GCrs GGGa WPat
- Baw Baw form	Last listed 1997

EPHEDRA (Ephedraceae)

alte	WCot
americana var. *andina*	SArc
distachya	GPoy NFor WWye
equisetina	SMad
- JJH 920912	Last listed 1998
- JJH 9308135	NWCA
fedtschenkoi	Last listed 1999
fragilis	SDry
gerardiana	Last listed 1998
- KR 0853	EPla
- var. *sikkimensis*	CStu EPla SDry WPer
likiangensis	Last listed 1999
§ *major*	SDry WHer
minima	MTPN NWCA
monosperma	Last listed 1998
nebrodensis	See *E. major*
nevadensis	GBin GPoy MSal
przewalskii	Last listed 1998

sinica	MSal	
¶ sp.	SAPC	
viridis	CArn ELau GBin MSal	

EPIDENDRUM (Orchidaceae)
criniferum	Last listed 1997

EPIGAEA (Ericaceae)
asiatica	Last listed 1999
gaultherioides	GCrs GGGa
repens	IMGH

EPILOBIUM (Onagraceae)
§ *angustifolium*	CGle CKin GBar NNrd SWat WHer
§ - var. *album*	More than 30 suppliers
- 'Isobel'	CHea CSpe LFis MRav MTed NHex WAbb WCot
- f. *leucanthum*	See *E. angustifolium* var. *album*
- 'Stahl Rose'	CBot CHid CMea EBee EMar EMon EWes GCal LGre LPio NHex SUsu SWat WPGP WSHC
californicum hort.	See *Zauschneria californica*
- Haussknecht	See *Zauschneria californica* subsp. *angustifolia*
canum	See *Zauschneria californica* subsp. *cana*
§ *chlorifolium*	NChi SAga
- var. *kaikourense*	See *E. chlorifolium*
crassum	CPBP ESis GBuc MBNS NArg NWoo WMoo WWin
§ *dodonaei*	CGle EBee EMan LFis MLLN MTho WBea WCot WMoo WSHC WWin
fleischeri	CLyd CPou EDAr SAga WSHC
garrettii	See *Zauschneria californica* subsp. *garrettii*
N *glabellum*	CGle CHea CMea CSpe EMan ESis GKir GMac LGre LHop LRHS MWat NBir NMen SAga SUsu WAbe WCru WEas WFar WOve WSpi WWhi WWin
- 'Sulphureum'	EBee NChi
hirsutum	CKin SWat
- *album*	NSti WAlt
- 'Caerphilly Castle' (d)	WAlt
- 'Pistils at Dawn'	WAlt
- *roseum*	WRha
- 'Well Creek' (v)	CElw ECha EMan EMar GOrP LFis MCLN MLLN SWat WBar WCHb WCot WOve WPer
latifolium	Last listed 1998
luteum	Last listed 1999
microphyllum	See *Zauschneria californica* subsp. *cana*
montanum	Last listed 1998
- variegated	Last listed 1998
obcordatum	CLTr CLyd NMen NWCA SSca
¶ *obscurum*	IIve
¶ - variegated	WAlt
rosmarinifolium	See *E. dodonaei*
* *spathulifolium*	Last listed 1999
x *subhirsutum*	WAlt
tasmanicum	CLyd
tetragonum	Last listed 1997
villosum	See *Zauschneria californica* subsp. *mexicana*
wilsonii hort.	See *E. chlorifolium*

EPIMEDIUM ✿ (Berberidaceae)
acuminatum	CElw CFil CLAP EBee EFEx GLil LEur LGre SChu WAbe WPGP

- L 575	CBos CLon CRDP EHrv MSte SBla SSpi WAbe WPnP
'Akakage'	GLil
'Akebono'	GLil
alpinum	CMGP EMon EPar GBuc LEur NHol SMac SMer SPer WMoo
¶ 'Amanagawa'	SBla
Asiatic hybrids	SChu WPnP
'Beni-chidori'	GLil
'Beni-kujaku'	GBuc GLil
'Black Sea'	GLil
brevicornu Og 88.010	SBla
- f. *rotundatum* Og 82.010	SBla
x *cantabrigiense*	CBlo EBee ECtt EGle EMan EOrc EPla GCHN GKir GLil LEur LRHS MBri MBro MRav MWgw NHol SMac SPer WAbe WCru
¶ *chlorandrum*	LEur
¶ - Og 94.003	SBla
cremeum	See *E. grandiflorum* subsp. *koreanum*
davidii	CRDP EBee ECha GBri MBro MSte SSpi WAbe WFar WHal WPGP WPnP
- EMR 4125	CElw CLAP EHrv SAga SBla
diphyllum	CBos CLTr CRDP EHrv LGre NDov SAga WHal
- dwarf white	GLil
dolichostemon	CBos LEur SBla WAbe
- Og 81.010	SBla
ecalcaratum Og 93.082	SBla
elongatum	LEur
'Enchantress'	CBos EBee ECha EGle GBuc LEur SSpi WAbe WHal
fangii	SSpi
- Og 81.007	Last listed 1998
fargesii	SBla
¶ - 'Pink Constellation' Og 93.023	SBla
flavum Og 92.036	SBla
franchetii 'Brimstone Butterfly' Og 87.001	SBla WAbe
'Genpei'	GLil
§ *grandiflorum* ♀	More than 30 suppliers
- 'Album'	CLAP EPot IMGH
- var. *coelestre*	GLil
- 'Crimson Beauty'	CLAP CLTr EBee ECha EMan GBuc LEur LGre SAga SChu SUsu WCru WHal
¶ - 'Crimson Queen'	WPGP
- 'Elfenkönigin'	EBee LRHS WAbe
- 'Koji'	EGle
- subsp. *koreanum*	CFil CLAP CLon CPla CRDP ECha EFEx GLil LGre MBro NDov NHar SUsu WAbe WPGP
- 'La Rocaille'	SBla
- lilac	CHad CPlt CRDP LGre SAga WFar
- 'Lilacinum'	SBla
- 'Lilafee'	More than 30 suppliers
- 'Mount Kitadake'	EGle GLil SSpi WAbe
- 'Nanum' ♀	CBos CLyd CMil CRDP EBee EHrv EPot LGre NHar NMen NTow NWCA SAga SBla SChu WAbe WCru WPGP
- 'Nanum Freya'	Last listed 1999
- pink	EHrv
- 'Rose Queen' ♀	More than 30 suppliers
§ - 'Roseum'	CHid CLAP EBrP EBre GBri LBCl LBSe LBre MBBe NDov SBre
- 'Rubinkrone'	EBee EMar GBin GLil NHol WOVN

- 'Shikinomai'	LEur WAbe
¶ - 'Sirius'	SBla
- f. *violaceum*	CFir CLAP CLTr SBla SChu WAbe WPnP
- 'White Queen' ♀	CBos CFir CLon CPlt CRDP EHrv GLil LGre NOak SBla SSpi WAbe WRus
bigoense	EBee
'Kaguyahime'	SBla WAbe
latisepalum Og 91.002	SBla
leptorrhizum	CLAP EBee EGle EMon GLil LEur NBrk SWat WAbe WPGP
- Og Y 44	CRDP SAga SSpi
'Little Shrimp'	CLyd CTri EBee EGle LEur MBro WPat
macranthum	See *E. grandiflorum*
membranaceum	CBos WAbe
¶ - Og 93047	SBla
ogisui Og 91.001	SBla SSpi WAbe
x *omeiense*	WBcn
¶ - 'Emei Shan' Og 82001	SBla
- 'Stormcloud' Og 82.002	SBla
pauciflorum Og 92.123	SBla
x *perralchicum* ♀	CBro EBee EMan EMon EPot GBuc GKir GMaP MBel NFla SIng SLPl SSpi WPGP WPnP WRus WSHC
- 'Frohnleiten'	More than 30 suppliers
- 'Wisley'	CElw EHrv LEur MBro MTed NDov SBla SOkh
perralderianum	CFil CSam EBee EGle ELan EMan ENot EPar GKir LEur LGro MBro MFir NHar SBla SCro SRPl SRms SSpi WAbe WCru WHen WLin WPGP WPnP WWat WWin
- 'Weihenstephan'	Last listed 1997
pinnatum	CWes GLil GMaP WHal
§ - subsp. *colchicum* ♀	More than 30 suppliers
- - L 321	SBla
- *elegans*	See *E. pinnatum* subsp. *colchicum*
platypetalum Og 93.085	SBla
pubescens Og 91.003	SBla WAbe
pubigerum	CBlo CHid CLTr EBee ECha EGar EGle EMan GAbr GLil IMGH MWgw NHol NPri SCob WHil WLin
rhizomatosum Og 92.114	SBla
x *rubrum* ♀	More than 30 suppliers
sagittatum	EFEx GLil
'Sasaki'	GBuc GLil
sempervirens	SBla
setosum	CElw CFil EBee ECha EHrv LEur MSte SMac SSpi WAbe
'Shiho'	GLil
'Sohayaki'	EBee GLil
stellulatum 'Wudang Star' L 1193	EHrv EWes WAbe
'Sunset'	GLil
¶ 'Tama no Genpei'	LEur
'Tamabotan'	GBuc GLil WCot
x *versicolor*	CBlo LEur
- 'Cupreum'	SAga SSpi
- 'Neosulphureum'	CBro CFir CLAP EBee EMon SBla SSpi WHil WViv
- 'Sulphureum' ♀	More than 30 suppliers
- 'Versicolor'	ECha EHrv LGre NHar SAga SBla
x *warleyense*	CBos EBee ECha EFou ELan EMan EPot GCHN GKir GLil LFis LGre LRHS MBro NHar SAga SBla SIng SUsu WAbe WFar WHal WPGP WRus WWin
- 'Orangekönigin'	EBee EBrP EBre EGle EPar GBuc LBCl LBSe LBre LEur LPio LRHS MBBe MBel MCAu MMil NHol SAga SBre SLPl SPla WAbe WHil WPnP
wushanense 'Caramel' Og 92.009	SBla
¶ - Og 93.019	SBla
x *youngianum*	CB&S EGle EPot WCru
- 'Lilacinum'	See *E.* x *youngianum* 'Roseum'
- 'Merlin'	CBos CFir EBee ECha EHrv EMan EMar GLil SBla SChu WAbe
- 'Niveum' ♀	More than 30 suppliers
§ - 'Roseum'	More than 30 suppliers
- 'Typicum'	CLon EGle WAbe
- white	NMen

EPIPACTIS (Orchidaceae)

gigantea	CAvo CBro CFil CHdy CMea EBee EBrP EBre ECha ELan EMan EPar EPot ERos GCrs LBCl LBSe LBre MBBe MTho NHar NMen SBla SBre WAbe WCru WFar
- 'Enchantment'	Last listed 1997
- x *palustris*	Last listed 1997
* - 'Serpentine Night'	IBlr
- x *veratrifolia*	See *E.* Lowland Legacy g.
helleborine	Last listed 1999
§ Lowland Legacy g.	Last listed 1997
* Lowland Legacy g. 'Edelstein'	Last listed 1999
* - 'Frankfurt'	Last listed 1999
palustris	CHdy WHer WShi
'Renate'	Last listed 1999
* Sabine g. 'Frankfurt'	Last listed 1999
thunbergii	EFEx GCrs
* *veratrifolia* 'Jerusalem'	Last listed 1997

EPIPREMNUM (Araceae)

§ *aureum* ♀	CHal EBak LBlo MBri
- 'Marble Queen' (v)	CHal LRHS
§ *pinnatum*	LRHS MBri
* - 'Aztec' ♀	Last listed 1995

EPISCIA (Gesneriaceae)

'Country Kitten'	CHal
cupreata	CHal
§ *dianthiflora*	CHal MBri SRms WDib
* 'Iris August'	MBri
'Pink Panther'	CHal
* *primeria*	MBri
* 'San Miguel'	CHal MBri WDib

EQUISETUM ✿ (Equisetaceae)

arvense	MSal
'Bandit'	EMon
x *bowmanii*	CNat
* *camtschatcense*	CInt SMad WHil
¶ x *dycei*	CNat
giganteum	CNat
hyemale	CInt CNat EPla MCCP SPlb WHal WWye
§ - var. *affine*	CNat ELan EMon EPla MTed WMAq
- var. *robustum*	See *E. hyemale* var. *affine*
¶ - 'Yellow Streaks' (v)	CNat
ramosissimum var. *japonicum*	EMFW MCCP WWeb
scirpoides	CInt CNat EMFW EMon MCCP WHal WMAq WWeb
sylvaticum	CNat
telmateia	CNat

ERAGROSTIS (Poaceae)

abyssinica	See *E. tef*
¶ *airoides*	EMan WRos
capensis	EBee EPPr EWes
cbloromelas	CMHG LGre
curvula	CCuc CElw CFil CInt CKno CSpe
	EBee ECGN ECha ECoo EHoe
	EMan EMon EPPr GBin LGre
	LRHS MCCP NChi NOGN SUsu
	WCot WKif WPic WRos WWye
- S&SH 10	CCuc CRDP MSte WPGP
¶ - 'Totnes Burgundy'	WPGP
¶ 'Silver Needles'	EBrP EBre LBCl LBSe LBre MBBe
	SBre
¶ *spectabilis*	CBrm
§ *tef*	LIck SWal
tricbodes	GBin WPer

ERANTHEMUM (Acanthaceae)

pulcbellum	LHil

ERANTHIS (Ranunculaceae)

§ *byemalis* ♀	CBro CMea ELan EMon EPar EPot
	ETub EWFC LAma LRHS MBri
	MBro MHew NRog SRms SUsu
	WCot WMaN WPnP WShi
§ - Cilicica Group	CBro EMon EPar EPot ERav LAma
	LRHS NRog WCot WPGP
- 'Flore Pleno' (d)	EPot
§ - Tubergenii Group	EPot
- - 'Guinea Gold' ♀	GCrs LRHS
pinnatifida	EFEx GCrs
stellata	WCru

ERCILLA (Phytolaccaceae)

volubilis	CAbb CFee CGre CPLG CPIN
	CPle CSam GOrc SBrw SPer WCot
	WCru WPic WSHC

EREMAEA (Myrtaceae)

beaufortioides	SOWG
pauciflora	SOWG

EREMOPHILA (Myoporaceae)

maculata	CPLG

EREMURUS (Asphodelaceae)

§ *aitcbisonii*	EBee LAma LRHS NRog
- 'Albus'	WCot
'Brimstone Beauty'	NRog
* 'Brutus'	EBrP EBre LAma LBCl LBSe LBre
	MBBe MMHG NFor SBre
bungei	See *E. stenophyllus* subsp.
	stenophyllus
elwesii	See *E. aitcbisonii*
'Emmy Ro'	EBee LBow LRHS NRog
'Harmony'	LBow NRog WViv
bimalaicus	CBot CHar EBee ELan EMan EPar
	ETub EWTr LAma LBow LRHS
	MHer NEgg NLar NRog SMad SPer
	WCra WPyg
'Image'	LBow NRog WViv
x *isabellinus* 'Cleopatra'	CHar CMea CSWP CSpe EBee
	EMon GCHN LAma LBow LPio
	LRHS MBNS MCli MHer MLLN
	MMHG NPSI NRog SPer WCot
	WPGP
- 'Pinokkio'	EBee EMan ETub EWTr LAma
	MHer NRog WPGP WPyg
- Ruiter hybrids	CBlo CSWP EBee ECot ELan EMan
	EMon EPar LAma LAst LRHS

	MLLN NFla NRog SPer WCra WViv
- Shelford hybrids	CB&S CBlo CBro EBee ELan EMan
	EMon LAma LBow LRHS MLLN
	MMHG MNrw NOak SDeJ WPen
lactiflorus	Last listed 1999
'Moneymaker'	EBee EBrP EBre EWTr LAma LBCl
	LBSe LBre LRHS MBBe NRog SBre
'Oase'	CHar EBee EBrP EBre ELan EMan
	EWTr LBCl LBSe LBow LBre LRHS
	MBBe NRog SBre SPer
'Obelisk'	CMea EBee LBow LPio LRHS
	NRog SPer WViv
¶ 'Paradiso'	EBee
'Rexona'	NRog
robustus	More than 30 suppliers
- pink	NPSI SWat
'Roford'	NRog
'Romance'	EBee LBow LPio LRHS NRog
	WViv
stenopbyllus	CBro EBot EWTr LRHS MGrG
	NFai SMrm WPGP WWeb
- subsp. *aurantiacus*	LFis
§ - subsp. *stenopbyllus*	CMea EBee EBrP EBre ELan EMan
	EMon EOld EPar ETub EWTr
	LAma LBCl LBSe LBow LBre
	MBBe MHer MLLN MNrw NEgg
	NFla NFor NOak NRog SBre SPer
	WPyg
¶ *tianscbanicus*	SBla

ERIANTHUS See SACCHARUM

ERICA ✿ (Ericaceae)

arborea	CTrG SAPC SLon
§ - 'Albert's Gold' ♀	CB&S CMac EBrP EBre ELan EPfP
	GChr GKir IOrc LBCl LBSe LBre
	LRHS MAsh MBBe MBar MBri
	MOke NHol SBod SBre SBrw SPer
	SPla
- var. *alpina* ♀	CDoC CMac ENot EPfP GKir IOrc
	LRHS MBar NHar NHol SBod
	SBrw SDys SPar SPer SReu SSta
	WWat
- 'Arbora Gold'	See *E. arborea* 'Albert's Gold'
- 'Arnold's Gold'	See *E. arborea* 'Albert's Gold'
- 'Estrella Gold' ♀	CDoC CMac EBrP EBre ELan EPfP
	LBCl LBSe LBre LRHS MAsh MBBe
	MBar MGos NHar NHol SBod SBre
	SBrw SPer SPla SSta SVil WStI
- 'Picos Pygmy'	SDys
- 'Spring Smile'	Last listed 1998
australis ♀	CB&S ELan LRHS MBar
- 'Castellar Blush'	NHol SBrw
- 'Holehird'	Last listed 1998
- 'Mr Robert' ♀	EPfP LRHS MBar
- 'Riverslea' ♀	GAri IOrc LRHS MBar MOke NHol
	SBod SPer
bauera	Last listed 1998
canaliculata ♀	CB&S CGre SBod
carnea 'Accent'	Last listed 1998
- 'Adrienne Duncan' ♀	MBar MBri MGos MOke NDlv
	NHol SBod
- 'Alan Coates'	MBar
- 'Alba'	Last listed 1999
- 'Altadena'	MBar
- 'Amy Backhouse'	CMac
- 'Amy Doncaster'	See *E. carnea* 'Treasure Trove'
- 'Ann Sparkes' ♀	CMac EBrP EBre EOrn GChr LBCl
	LBSe LBre LGro MBBe MBar MBri
	MGos MOke MWat NHol SBod
	SBre SPla
- 'Atrorubra'	CMac MBar NHol

- 'Aurea'   CB&S CMac LGro MBar MBri
                         MOke NDlv NHol SBod
- 'Barry Sellers'   LRHS NHol
- 'Bell's Extra Special' ECho
- 'Beoley Pink'   Last listed 1999
- 'C.J. Backhouse'   Last listed 1999
- 'Carnea'   MBar MOke NHol
- 'Catherine'   Last listed 1998
- 'Cecilia M. Beale'   MBar NHol
- 'Challenger' ♀   EBrP EBre EPfP LBCl LBSe LBre
                         MBBe MBar MBri MGos NHol
                         SBre
- 'Christine Fletcher'   Last listed 1999
- 'Clare Wilkinson'   Last listed 1999
- 'David's Seedling'   Last listed 1999
- 'December Red'   CB&S CMac EBrP EBre EOrn EPfP
                         LBCl LBSe LBre MBBe MBar MBri
                         MOke MWat NHol SBod SBre SPla
- 'Dommesmoen'   Last listed 1998
- 'Early Red'   Last listed 1999
- 'Eileen Porter'   CMac MBar
- 'Foxhollow' ♀   CMac EBrP EBre GChr GDra GKir
                         IArd LBCl LBSe LBre LGro MBBe
                         MBar MBri MGos MOke MWat
                         NHar NHol SBod SBre
- 'Foxhollow Fairy'   CB&S CBrm MBar SRms
- 'Gelber Findling'   Last listed 1999
- 'Golden Starlet' ♀   CMac EOrn EPfP LGro MBar
                         MGos NHol
- 'Gracilis'   ECho MBar NDlv NHol
- 'Heathwood'   CB&S MBar NHol SRms
- 'Hilletje'   NHol
- 'Ice Princess'   EPfP NHol SPla
- 'Isabell'   LRHS SPla
- 'Jack Stitt'   MBar
- 'James Backhouse'   ECho NDlv NHol
- 'January Sun'   EOrn NHol
- 'Jason Attwater'   Last listed 1998
- 'Jean'   LRHS NHol
- 'Jennifer Anne'   MBar
- 'John Kampa'   EOrn MBar NHol
- 'John Pook'   Last listed 1998
- 'King George'   CMac CTri GChr MBar MGos
                         MWat NHar NHol SBod SPla
- 'Lake Garda'   NHol
- 'Late Pink'   Last listed 1999
- 'Lesley Sparkes'   MBar
- 'Little Peter'   Last listed 1999
- 'Lohse's Rubin'   ECho NDlv
- 'Loughrigg' ♀   CMac CTri EOrn GDra GKir MBar
                         MOke NHol SBod WStI
- 'March Seedling'   CB&S EBrP EBre GDra LBCl LBSe
                         LBre MBBe MBar MBri MGos
                         MOke NHol SBod SBre SPla WStI
- 'Margery Frearson'   Last listed 1998
- 'Martin'   Last listed 1999
- 'Moonlight'   Last listed 1998
- 'Mrs Sam Doncaster'   ECho MBar SBod
- 'Myretoun Ruby' ♀   CB&S CMac EBrP EBre GChr
                         GDra GKir LBCl LBSe LBre LGro
                         MBBe MBar MBri MGos MOke
                         NDlv NHar NHol SBod SBre SPla
- 'Nathalie'   ECho LRHS
- 'Orient'   Last listed 1999
- 'Pallida'   Last listed 1999
- 'Pink Beauty'   See E. carnea 'Pink Pearl'
- 'Pink Cloud'   Last listed 1999
- 'Pink Mist'   LRHS
§ - 'Pink Pearl'   MBar
- 'Pink Spangles' ♀   CB&S CMac EBrP EBre GChr
                         GDra LBCl LBSe LBre MBBe MBar
                         MBri MGos MOke NHol SBod

                         SBre
- 'Pirbright Rose'   ECho MGos SBod
- 'Polden Pride'   Last listed 1999
- 'Porter's Red'   ECho LRHS MBar
- 'Praecox Rubra' ♀   CB&S GChr GDra LGro MBar
                         MGos MOke NHol
- 'Prince of Wales'   ECho NHol
- 'Queen Mary'   ECho SBod
- 'Queen of Spain'   MBri MOke
- 'R.B. Cooke' ♀   CBrm EOrn EPfP MBar MBri SPla
- 'Red Rover'   Last listed 1999
- 'Robert Jan'   Last listed 1998
- 'Rosalie'   CB&S IArd LRHS NHol SPla
- 'Rosalinde Schorn'   NHol
- 'Rosantha'   NHol
- 'Rosea'   ECho
- 'Rosy Gem'   ECho MBar
- 'Rosy Morn'   Last listed 1999
- 'Rotes Juwel'   ECho LRHS
- 'Rubinteppich'   Last listed 1999
- 'Rubra'   Last listed 1998
- 'Ruby Glow'   CTri MBar MOke NDlv NHol
- 'Scatterley'   Last listed 1998
- 'Schatzalp'   Last listed 1998
- 'Schneekuppe'   NHol
- 'Schneesturm'   Last listed 1999
§ - 'Sherwood Creeping' MBar
- 'Sherwoodii'   See E. carnea 'Sherwood
                         Creeping'
- 'Smarts Heath'   ECho NHol
- 'Snow Queen'   CMac MBar SBod
- 'Spring Cottage Crimson' MBar
- 'Spring Day'   Last listed 1998
- 'Springwood Pink'   CBrm CMac CTri GDra LGro
                         MBar MBri MGos MOke MWat
                         NHol SBod
- 'Springwood White' ♀   CB&S CBrm CMac EBrP EBre
                         GChr GDra GKir LBCl LBSe LBre
                         LGro MBBe MBar MBri MGos
                         MOke MWat NHar NHol SBod
                         SBre
- 'Startler'   LRHS MBar NHol SBod
- 'Sunshine Rambler' ♀   MBar MGos NHol SPla
- 'Thomas Kingscote'   MBar
§ - 'Treasure Trove'   CMac NHol
- 'Tybesta Gold'   NHol
- 'Urville'   See E. carnea 'Vivellii'
- 'Viking'   NHol
§ - 'Vivellii' ♀   CMac CTri EBrP EBre GDra GKir
                         LBCl LBSe LBre MBBe MBri MBri
                         MOke MWat NDlv NHar NHol
                         SBod SBre
- 'Vivellii Aurea'   Last listed 1999
- 'Walter Reisert'   Last listed 1999
- 'Wanda'   MBar
- 'Wentwood Red'   Last listed 1999
- 'Westwood Yellow' ♀   CMac EBrP EBre LBCl LBSe LBre
                         LGro MBBe MBar MBri MGos
                         NHar NHol SBod SBre SPla
- 'White Glow'   CMac ECho EOrn
- 'White March Seedling' Last listed 1998
- 'Whitehall'   LRHS NHol
- 'Winter Beauty'   MGos MOke NDlv NHol
- 'Winter Gold'   Last listed 1999
- 'Winter Melody'   Last listed 1998
- 'Winter Rubin'   Last listed 1998
- 'Winter Snow'   ECho
- 'Winterfreude'   NHol
- 'Wintersonne'   ECho LGro NHol
ciliaris alba   Last listed 1998
- 'Aurea'   CMac MBar SRms
- 'Camla'   MBar

- 'Corfe Castle' ♀ — MBar
- 'David McClintock' ♀ — MBar
- 'Globosa' — ECho
- 'Maweana' — Last listed 1998
- 'Mrs C.H. Gill' ♀ — CMac GChr MGos
- 'Ram' — Last listed 1998
- 'Rotundiflora' — Last listed 1998
- 'Stapehill' — Last listed 1998
- 'Stoborough' ♀ — GChr MBar
- 'White Wings' — Last listed 1999
- 'Wych' — Last listed 1998
cinerea f. *alba* — CMac
- 'Alba Major' — ECho MBar
- 'Alba Minor' ♀ — EOrn GChr MBar MBri MOke NHar NHol
- 'Alette' — Last listed 1998
- 'Alfred Bowerman' — Last listed 1998
- 'Alice Anne Davies' — Last listed 1998
- 'Angarrack' — Last listed 1998
- 'Anja Blum' — Last listed 1998
- 'Ann Berry' — MBar SBod
- 'Apple Blossom' — Last listed 1998
- 'Apricot Charm' — MBar SBod
- 'Aquarel' — Last listed 1998
- 'Ashdown Forest' — Last listed 1998
- 'Ashgarth Garnet' — MBar
- 'Atrococcinea' — Last listed 1997
- 'Atropurpurea' — ECho MBar NDlv
- 'Atrorubens' — MBar NHar SRms
- 'Atrorubens, Daisy Hill' — Last listed 1998
- 'Atrosanguinea' — MBar SBod
- 'Atrosanguinea Reuthe's Variety' — ECho
- 'Atrosanguinea Smith's Variety' — ECho
- 'Baylay's Variety' — MBar
- 'Blossom Time' — MBar
- 'Brick' — Last listed 1998
- 'Bucklebury Red' — Last listed 1998
- 'C.D. Eason' ♀ — CB&S CMac EPfP GChr GDra GKir MBar MBri MGos MOke NHol SBod
§ - 'C.G. Best' ♀ — CMac MBar
- 'Cairn Valley' — Last listed 1998
- 'Caldy Island' — MBar
- 'Carnea' — Last listed 1998
- 'Carnea Underwood's Variety' — Last listed 1998
- 'Celebration' — ECho
- 'Cevennes' ♀ — CMac MBar MOke
- 'Champs Hill' — Last listed 1998
- 'Cindy' ♀ — MBar MOke NHol
- 'Coccinea' — ECho
- 'Colligan Bridge' — MBar
- 'Constance' — MBar
- 'Contrast' — LRHS MBar
- 'Daphne Maginess' — Last listed 1999
- 'Discovery' — Last listed 1998
- 'Doctor Small's Seedling' — Last listed 1998
- 'Domino' — MBar MGos MOke
- 'Duncan Fraser' — ECho MBar
- 'Eden Valley' ♀ — CMac GChr GKir MBar MGos NHol SRms
- 'England' — ECho
- 'Felthorpe' — Last listed 1998
- 'Fiddler's Gold' ♀ — MBar MBri MOke NDlv NHar NHol
- 'Flamingo' — Last listed 1998
- 'Foxhollow Mahogany' — MBar
- 'Frances' — Last listed 1998
- 'Fred Corston' — Last listed 1998
- 'G. Osmond' — MBar MOke

- 'Glasnevin Red' — MBar NHar
- 'Glencairn' — MBar NHol
- 'Godrevy' — Last listed 1998
- 'Golden Charm' — CMac ECho GChr NHol
- 'Golden Drop' — EOrn GChr MBar MBri MOke NHol SBod
- 'Golden Hue' ♀ — CB&S CMac MBar MOke NDlv NHol .
- 'Golden Sport' — ECho MGos NHar
- 'Golden Tee' — Last listed 1998
- 'Graham Thomas' — See *E. cinerea* 'C.G. Best'
- 'Grandiflora' — MBar
- 'Guernsey Lime' — MBar
- 'Guernsey Pink' — Last listed 1998
- 'Guernsey Plum' — Last listed 1998
- 'Guernsey Purple' — Last listed 1998
- 'Hardwick's Rose' — MBar
- 'Harry Fulcher' — MBri MGos MOke
- 'Heatherbank' — Last listed 1998
- 'Heathfield' — Last listed 1998
- 'Heidebrand' — MBar
- 'Hermann Dijkhuizen' — Last listed 1998
- 'Honeymoon' — MBar
- 'Hookstone Lavender' — Last listed 1998
- 'Hookstone White' ♀ — GDra MBar NDlv
- 'Hutton's Seedling' — Last listed 1998
- 'Iberian Beauty' — Last listed 1998
- 'Jack London' — Last listed 1999
- 'Janet' — ECho MBar
- 'Jersey Wonder' — Last listed 1998
- 'Jim Hardy' — Last listed 1998
- 'John Ardron' — Last listed 1998
- 'John Eason' — Last listed 1998
- 'Joseph Murphy' — MBar
- 'Joseph Rock' — Last listed 1998
- 'Josephine Ross' — MBar
- 'Joyce Burfitt' — Last listed 1999
- 'Jubilee' — ECho
- 'Katinka' — MBar NHol
- 'Kerry Cherry' — Last listed 1998
- 'Knap Hill Pink' ♀ — ECho MBar
- 'Lady Skelton' — MBar
- 'Lavender Lady' — Last listed 1998
- 'Lilac Time' — ECho MBar
- 'Lilacina' — ECho MBar MOke
- 'Lime Soda' — CMac MBri
- 'Lorna Anne Hutton' — Last listed 1998
- 'Maginess Pink' — Last listed 1999
- 'Marina' — Last listed 1998
- 'Michael Hugo' — Last listed 1999
- 'Miss Waters' — MBar
- 'Mrs Dill' — ECho MBar
- 'Mrs E.A. Mitchell' — LRHS MOke SPlb
- 'Mrs Ford' — MBar
- 'My Love' — MBar MBri MOke
- 'Nell' — MBar
- 'Nellie Dawson' — Last listed 1998
- 'Newick Lilac' — MBar MOke
- 'Next Best' — MBar
- 'Novar' — Last listed 1998
- 'Old Rose' — Last listed 1998
- 'P.S. Patrick' ♀ — MBar
- 'Pallas' — Last listed 1998
- 'Pallida' — Last listed 1998
- 'Patricia Maginess' — Last listed 1999
- 'Peñaz' — Last listed 1998
- 'Pentreath' ♀ — MBar MBri MOke
- 'Pink Foam' — MBar
- 'Pink Ice' ♀ — CB&S CMac EBrP EBre EPfP GDra LBCl LBSe LBre MBBe MBar MBri MGos MOke NDlv NHar NHol SBod SBre

- 'Plummer's Seedling'   MBar
- 'Prostrate Lavender'   Last listed 1998
- 'Providence'   LRHS
- 'Purple Beauty'   MBar MGos MOke
- 'Purple Robe'   ECho LRHS
- 'Purple Spreader'   Last listed 1998
- 'Purpurea'   Last listed 1998
- 'Pygmaea'   MBar
- 'Red Pentreath'   Last listed 1998
- 'Rijneveld'   Last listed 1998
- 'Robert Michael'   Last listed 1998
- 'Rock Pool'   MBar NHol
- 'Rock Ruth'   Last listed 1998
- 'Romiley'   EOrn MBar MBri MOke
- 'Rosabella'   MBar
- 'Rose Queen'   ECho
- 'Rosea'   Last listed 1998
* - 'Rosea Splendens'   Last listed 1998
- 'Rozanne Waterer'   Last listed 1998
- 'Ruby'   CMac MBar
- 'Sandpit Hill'   MBar
- 'Schizopetala'   MBar
- 'Sea Foam'   MBar
- 'Sherry'   MBar
- 'Smith's Lawn'   Last listed 1998
- 'Snow Cream'   MBar
- 'Son of Cevennes'   MGos
- 'Spicata'   Last listed 1998
- 'Splendens'   Last listed 1999
- 'Startler'   MBri MOke
- 'Stephen Davis' ♀   EBrP EBre LBCl LBSe LBre MBBe
                       MBar MBri MOke NHol SBod SBre
- 'Steven Leitch'   ECho
- 'Strawberry'   Last listed 1998
- 'Sue Lloyd'   Last listed 1998
- 'Summer Gold'   ECho LRHS NDlv
- 'Tilford'   Last listed 1998
- 'Tom Waterer'   MBar
- 'Uschie Ziehmann'   Last listed 1998
- 'Velvet Night' ♀   CMac GChr MBar MBri MOke
                       NHar NHol SRms
- 'Victoria'   MBar
- 'Violetta'   Last listed 1999
- 'Vivienne Patricia'   MBar
- 'W.G. Notley'   Last listed 1998
- 'West End'   Last listed 1998
- 'White Dale'   ECho MBar
- 'Windlebrooke' ♀   MBar MGos NHol
- 'Wine'   Last listed 1998
- 'Yvonne'   ECho
cruenta   Last listed 1998
curviflora   Last listed 1998
x *darleyensis* 'Ada S.   MBar SBod
  Collings'
- 'Alba'   See *E.* x *darleyensis*
             'Silberschmelze'
- 'Archie Graham'   Last listed 1998
§ - 'Arthur Johnson' ♀   CB&S CMac EBrP EBre LBCl LBSe
                         LBre MBBe MBar MBri MGos
                         MOke NHol SBod SBre SPla SRms
- 'Cherry Stevens'   See *E.* x *darleyensis* 'Furzey'
§ - 'Darley Dale'   CMac EBrP EBre EOrn EPfP LBCl
                    LBSe LBre MBBe MBar MBri
                    MOke NHol SBod SBre
- 'Dunreggan'   Last listed 1999
- 'Dunwood Splendour'   See *E.* x *darleyensis* 'Arthur
                         Johnson'
- 'Epe'   Last listed 1999
- 'Erecta'   Last listed 1999
§ - 'Furzey' ♀   CB&S CMac EOrn MBar MBri
                 MGos MOke NDlv NHar NHol
                 SBod SRms

- 'George Rendall'   CB&S CMac CTri NHol WGwG
- 'Ghost Hills' ♀   CBrm EBrP EBre GDra LBCl LBSe
                    LBre MBBe MBar MOke NHol
                    SBod SBre
- 'J.W. Porter' ♀   EOrn MBar MOke NDlv
§ - 'Jack H. Brummage'   CMac CTri EBrP EBre EOrn IArd
                         LBCl LBSe LBre MBBe MBar MBri
                         MGos MOke NHar NHol SBod
                         SBre SPla
- 'James Smith'   MBar
- 'Jenny Porter' ♀   CMac EOrn MBar MBri MOke
- 'Kramer's Rote' ♀   CBrm CMac CTri EBrP EBre EOrn
                       GChr LBCl LBSe LBre MBBe MBar
                       MBri MGos MOke NDlv NHol
                       SBre SPla
- 'Margaret Porter'   CB&S CMac GChr SBod
- 'Mary Helen'   CB&S CBrm EOrn LRHS MGos
                 NHol
- Molten Silver   See *E.* x *darleyensis*
                   'Silberschmelze'
- 'Mrs Parris' Red'   Last listed 1998
- 'Norman R. Webster'   Last listed 1999
- 'Pink Perfection'   See *E.* x *darleyensis* 'Darley Dale'
§ - 'Silberschmelze'   CB&S CTri EBrP EBre EOrn EPfP
                       GChr GDra GKir LBCl LBSe LBre
                       MBBe MBar MBri MGos MOke
                       NDlv NHol SBod SBre
* - 'Silver Bells'   CMac EOrn
- 'Spring Surprise'[PBR]   CB&S
- 'W.G. Pine'   Last listed 1999
- 'White Glow'   CTri EOrn NHol WGwG
- 'White Perfection' ♀   EBrP EBre EOrn IArd LBCl LBSe
                         LBre MBBe MBar MBri NHol SBre
                         SPla WGwG
discolor   Last listed 1999
doliiformis   Last listed 1998
§ *erigena*   Last listed 1998
- 'Alba'   CMac MBar
- 'Brian Proudley' ♀   MBar
- 'Brightness'   CB&S EPfP GChr MBar MBri
                 MOke NDlv NHar NHol SBod
- 'Coccinea'   Last listed 1999
- 'Ewan Jones'   IOrc MBar
- 'Glauca'   Last listed 1999
- 'Golden Lady' ♀   CMac EOrn MBar MBri MGos
                    MOke NHol SBod
- 'Hibernica'   GKir
- 'Hibernica Alba'   MBar
- 'Irish Dusk' ♀   EBrP EBre LBCl LBSe LBre MBBe
                   MBar MBri MGos MOke NHar
                   NHol SBod SBre SPla SRms
- 'Irish Salmon' ♀   CMac EOrn GChr MBar NDlv
- 'Irish Silver'   MBar MBri
- 'Ivory'   Last listed 1999
- 'Maxima'   Last listed 1998
- 'Mrs Parris' Lavender'   Last listed 1998
- 'Mrs Parris' White'   Last listed 1998
- 'Nana'   Last listed 1998
- 'Nana Alba'   MBar
- 'Nana Compacta'   Last listed 1998
- 'Rosea'   ECho MBar
- 'Rosslare'   Last listed 1998
- 'Rubra'   ECho NDlv
- 'Rubra Compacta'   Last listed 1997
- 'Superba'   CMac MBar MGos MOke SBod
- 'W.T. Rackliff' ♀   CB&S EBrP EBre EOrn EPfP GKir
                      LBCl LBSe LBre MBBe MBar MBri
                      MGos MOke NHol SBre SPla
                      SRms
- 'W.T. Rackliff Variegated'   Last listed 1998
fontana   Last listed 1998
formosa   CGre

glomiflora   Last listed 1999
gracilis   ECho
x *griffithsii*   NHol
- 'Ashlea Gold'   Last listed 1998
§ - 'Heaven Scent' ♀   LRHS
§ - 'Valerie Griffiths'   CBrm LRHS MBar NHol SBod
  'Heaven Scent'   See E. x *griffithsii* 'Heaven Scent'
bibernica   See E. *erigena*
x *biemalis*   Last listed 1998
x *krameri*   SDys
laeta   Last listed 1997
lusitanica ♀   CB&S CMac CTrG MAsh MBar
                                NHol SBod SBrw
- 'George Hunt'   ELan LRHS NHol SBod SPer
* - 'Sheffield Park'   ELan LRHS SPer
mackayana subsp.   Last listed 1998
    andevalensis
- 'Ann D. Frearson' (d)   Last listed 1999
- 'Doctor Ronald Gray'   MBar MBri MOke SBod
- 'Donegal'   Last listed 1998
- 'Errigal Dusk'   Last listed 1998
- 'Galicia'   Last listed 1999
- 'Lawsoniana'   Last listed 1998
- 'Maura' (d) ♀   Last listed 1998
- 'Plena' (d)   MBar MOke
- 'Shining Light' ♀   SDys
- 'William M'Calla'   Last listed 1998
mammosa   Last listed 1998
manipuliflora   MBar
- 'Aldeburgh'   Last listed 1999
§ - 'Cascade'   Last listed 1998
- 'Corfu'   Last listed 1999
- 'Don Richards'   Last listed 1999
- 'Elegant Spike'   Last listed 1998
- 'Ian Cooper'   Last listed 1999
- 'Korcula'   Last listed 1999
- x *vagans* 'Valerie   See E. x *griffithsii* 'Valerie
  Griffiths'   Griffiths'
- 'Waterfall'   See E. *manipuliflora* 'Cascade'
mediterranea   See E. *erigena*
multiflora 'Formentor'   Last listed 1998
x *oldenburgensis*   SDys
  'Ammerland'
- 'Oldenburg'   Last listed 1998
pageana   Last listed 1998
patersonia   Last listed 1997
plukenetii   CGre
x *praegeri*   See E. x *stuartii*
scoparia subsp. *azorica*   Last listed 1998
- subsp. *maderincola*   Last listed 1998
  'Madeira Gold'
§ - subsp. *scoparia* 'Minima' MBar
- - - 'Pumila'   See E. *scoparia* subsp. *scoparia*
                                'Minima'
sparsa   Last listed 1999
speciosa   SBod
sphaeroidea   CGre
spiculifolia   EPot GChr ITim MBar NDlv
- 'Balkan Rose'   GCrs NHol
§ x *stuartii*   MBar SBod
- 'Connemara'   Last listed 1998
- 'Irish Lemon' ♀   MBar NHar NHol SBod
- 'Irish Orange'   MBar NHol SBod
- 'Nacung'   Last listed 1998
- 'Pat Turpin'   Last listed 1998
§ - 'Stuartii'   Last listed 1999
terminalis ♀   CMac ENot IOrc MBar SBod SRms
                                WPic
- *stricta*   See E. *terminalis*
- 'Thelma Woolner'   MBar
tetralix   CKin SRms
- 'Afternoon'   Last listed 1998

- 'Alba'   Last listed 1998
- 'Alba Mollis' ♀   CMac EOrn GChr MBar MBri
                                MOke NHar NHol SBod
- 'Alba Praecox'   Last listed 1998
- 'Allendale Pink'   Last listed 1998
- 'Ardy'   Last listed 1998
- 'Bala'   Last listed 1999
- 'Bartinney'   MBar
- 'Con Underwood' ♀   CMac EBrP EBre EOrn GChr GKir
                                LBCl LBSe LBre MBBe MBar MBri
                                MOke NHol SBod SBre SRms
- 'Curled Roundstone'   Last listed 1998
- 'Dänemark'   Last listed 1998
- 'Daphne Underwood'   Last listed 1998
- 'Darleyensis'   Last listed 1998
- 'Dee'   Last listed 1998
- 'Delta'   MBar
- 'Foxhome'   MBar
- 'George Frazer'   Last listed 1998
- 'Hailstones'   MBar
- 'Helma'   Last listed 1998
- 'Hookstone Pink'   GKir MOke NHar
- 'Humoresque'   Last listed 1998
- 'Ken Underwood'   MBar
- 'L.E. Underwood'   MBar NHol
- 'Mary Grace'   Last listed 1998
- 'Melbury White'   MBar
- 'Morning Glow'   See E. x *watsonii* 'F. White'
- 'Pink Glow'   Last listed 1998
- 'Pink Pepper'   Last listed 1998
- 'Pink Star' ♀   CMac EBrP EBre GChr LBCl LBSe
                                LBre MBBe MBar NHol SBre
- 'Rosea'   Last listed 1998
- 'Rubra'   Last listed 1998
§ - 'Ruby's Variety'   MBar
- 'Ruby's Velvet'   See E. *tetralix* 'Ruby's Variety'
- 'Ruth's Gold'   CMac MBar NHol
- 'Salmon Seedling'   Last listed 1998
- 'Silver Bells'   MBar
- 'Stardome'   Last listed 1998
- 'Swedish Yellow'   Last listed 1998
- 'Terschelling'   Last listed 1998
- 'Tina'   Last listed 1999
- 'Trixie'   Last listed 1998
- 'White House'   Last listed 1998
umbellata   MBar
vagans 'Alba Nana'   See E. *vagans* 'Nana'
- 'Birch Glow' ♀   EPfP SBod
- 'Carnea'   Last listed 1998
- 'Charm'   Last listed 1998
- 'Chittendenii'   Last listed 1998
- 'Cornish Cream' ♀   EPfP MBar NHol
- 'Cream'   MOke NHar
- 'Diana Hornibrook'   MBar MOke NHar
- 'Diana's Gold'   Last listed 1998
- 'Fiddlestone' ♀   MBar
- 'French White'   MBar SBod
- 'George Underwood'   MBar
- 'Golden Triumph'   ECho MBar NHol
- 'Grandiflora'   MBNS MBar
- 'Holden Pink'   MOke NHar
- 'Hookstone Rosea'   MBar
- 'Ida M. Britten'   MBar
- 'J.C. Fletcher'   Last listed 1998
- 'Kevernensis Alba' ♀   MBar SBod SRms
- 'Leucantha'   Last listed 1998
- 'Lilacina'   CMac MBar
- 'Lyonesse' ♀   CB&S CMac EBrP EBre GChr LBCl
                                LBSe LBre MBBe MBar MBri MGos
                                MOke NHol SBod SBre SRms
- 'Miss Waterer'   MBar
- 'Mrs D.F. Maxwell' ♀   CB&S CMac EBrP EBre GChr GKir

LBCl LBSe LBre MBBe MBar MBri
MGos MOke NHar NHol SBod
SBre SRms
- 'Mrs Donaldson'   Last listed 1998
§ - 'Nana'   ECho MBar
- 'Pallida'   Last listed 1999
- 'Peach Blossom'   MBar
- 'Pyrenees Pink'   CMac MBar MOke NHar
- 'Rosea'   ECho
- 'Rubra'   ECho MBar
- 'Rubra Grandiflora'   Last listed 1997
- 'Saint Keverne'   CB&S CMac GKir IArd MBar
MGos MOke NHar NHol SBod
- 'Summertime'   MBar
- 'Valerie Proudley' ♀   CB&S CMac EBrP EBre EOrn
GChr GDra GKir LBCl LBSe LBre
MBBe MBar MBri MGos MOke
MWat NHar NHol SBod SBre
SRms
- 'Valerie Smith'   Last listed 1998
- 'Viridiflora'   MBar
- 'White Giant'   Last listed 1998
- 'White Lady'   ECho MBar
- 'White Rocket'   MBar
- 'White Spire'   Last listed 1998
- 'Yellow John'   ECho MBar
x **veitchii**   Last listed 1999
- 'Brockhill'   SDys
- 'Exeter' ♀   ELan EPfP GAri LRHS MAsh MBar
NHol
- 'Gold Tips' ♀   MAsh MBar MBri MGos MOke
NHar
- 'Pink Joy'   GAri MAsh MBri MOke NHar
NHol SBrw SVil
versicolor   CGre
verticillata   SBod
viridescens   CGre
x **watsonii** 'Cherry Turpin' Last listed 1998
- 'Ciliaris Hybrida'   Last listed 1998
- 'Dawn' ♀   MBar MBri NHar SBod
- 'Dorothy Metheny'   Last listed 1998
§ - 'F.White'   MBar
- 'Gwen'   MBar
- 'H. Maxwell'   Last listed 1999
- 'Mary'   Last listed 1998
- 'Pink Pacific'   Last listed 1998
- 'Rachel'   Last listed 1999
- 'Truro'   Last listed 1998
x **williamsii** 'Cow-y-Jack'   Last listed 1998
- 'David Coombe'   Last listed 1998
- 'Gold Button'   MBar
- 'Gwavas'   MBar SBod
- 'Ken Wilson'   SDys
- 'Lizard Downs'   Last listed 1998
- 'P.D. Williams' ♀   ECho MBar

ERIGERON ✿ (Asteraceae)
acer   CKin EWFC WHer
- var. **debilis**   Last listed 1998
- HH&K 269A   Last listed 1999
'Adria'   EBee EBrP EBre GBuc LBCl LBSe
LBre LRHS MBBe MMil SBre SPer
§ **alpinus**   EHol GCHN GKir GTou LBee
LRHS MOne
'Amity'   EBee EBrP EBre EFou GCHN
GMac LBCl LBSe LBre MBBe SBre
SMer
aphanactis NNS 93-249   Last listed 1997
argentatus   Last listed 1997
atticus   Last listed 1997
aurantiacus   EDAr EHol EPfP EWTr GMaP
LHop MBNS MCCP MHer NBro

NOak SSca
§ **aureus**   WAbe
§ - 'Canary Bird' ♀   CPBP EGle EPfP GCrs LRHS NBir
NHar NMen NPSI SBla SPer SRot
WAbe WLin
¶ - NNS 96-87   NWCA
* 'Azure Beauty'   CMGP EPfP LRHS NPro
Azure Fairy   See E. 'Azurfee'
§ 'Azurfee'   EBee ELan GAbr GKir GMaP
MBNS MCLN MHer MWhi NFai
NMir NOak SMer SPer SPla SSca
WHen WPer WWin
'Birch Hybrid'   Last listed 1999
Black Sea   See E. 'Schwarzes Meer'
bloomeri   Last listed 1998
- NNS 92-108   Last listed 1997
¶ blue   WBar
'Blue Beauty'   LRHS NCut SRms
borealis   GCHN
'Charity'   CGle EFou EGar LRHS SSpe
WLRN
chrysopsidis   EPfP LRHS NWCA SBla WAbe
'Grand Ridge' ♀
compactus var. **consimilis** Last listed 1998
- var. **consimilis**   Last listed 1998
NNS 93-252
compositus   CGra GAbr GCHN ITim NWCA
SRms WPer
§ - var. **discoideus**   EBur GKir NMen SPlb WPer
- var. **glabratus**   Last listed 1999
- 'Mount Adams Dwarf'   Last listed 1999
- 'Rocky'   Last listed 1999
* **daicus**   Last listed 1997
Darkest of All   See E. 'Dunkelste Aller'
'Dignity'   EBee EDAr EFou EGle ELan
GCHN LFis MWat SMer SPer SSpe
SUsu WCot WFar WPGP
'Dimity'   CGle ECha EPPr MBri SUsu WAbe
WFar WWin
§ 'Dunkelste Aller' ♀   More than 30 suppliers
elegantulus   NSla
* **epirocticus**   Last listed 1997
* - NS 462   NWCA
'Felicity'   CElw EFou MBel SRms
flettii   EBee GCHN WPer WWin
'Foersters Liebling' ♀   CMGP EBee EGle GKir LAst LRHS
MBri MNrw MWat NFla NGdn
SHel WByw WCot
formosissimus   EBee
'Four Winds'   EBrP EBre ECtt EDAr ELan EMan
ESis EWes LBCl LBSe LBre LHop
LRHS MBBe MRav NGdn NMen
SBre WPer
from Big Horns   CGra
'Gaiety'   EBee MCAu
¶ **glauca** 'Sea Breeze'   NBlu NPri
glaucus   COIW CSam EHol EWTr GMaP
NCat NVic SMrm WBea WCot
WFar WLRN
- 'Albus'   CSev LHop LRHS WPer
- 'Elstead Pink'   CSev CTri EBee EBrP EBre LBCl
LBSe LBre MBBe NFai SBre SPla
WEas WFar
- pink   NCat
* - 'Roger Raiche'   Last listed 1997
- 'Roseus'   CB&S CHal ECha
¶ 'Goat Rocks'   GCrs
howellii   EBee ECha
§ **karvinskianus** ♀   More than 30 suppliers
§ **kennedyi alpigenus**   Last listed 1998
NS 93-276
leiomerus   EFou EPot GCrs LBee NWCA

linearis	NMen NWCA WAbe WCot WPat
'Mrs F.H. Beale'	EFou SCro
mucronatus	See *E. karvinskianus*
multiradiatus	Last listed 1999
'Nachthimmel'	EBee
nanus	NWCA WPat WPer WPyg
oreganus	EBee EBrP EBre LBCl LBSe LBre
	MBBe SBre
§ *peregrinus*	NOak
§ - subsp. *calliantbemus*	Last listed 1997
pbiladelpbicus	CElw CGle NBir NBro SUsu
'Pink Beauty'	NCut
Pink Jewel	See *E.* 'Rosa Juwel'
Pink Triumph	See *E.* 'Rosa Triumph'
pinnatisectus	NWCA WPer
polymorpbus	Last listed 1998
'Profusion'	See *E. karvinskianus*
'Prosperity'	CGle EFou
pygmaeus	Last listed 1998
pyrenaicus hort.	See *E. alpinus*
- Rouy	See *Aster pyrenaeus*
'Quakeress'	CElw CGle CSam EBee EBrP EBre
	EFou EMan EMon GCHN GKir
	GMac LBCl LBSe LBre LRHS MBBe
	MBel MRav NBro SAga SBre SHel
	SMer SMrm SSpe WCot WFar
	WLin WRHF
§ 'Rosa Juwel'	CM&M EBee ENot GAbr GCHN
	GKir LPVe LRHS MBNS MHer
	NBir NMir NOak SEND SMer SPer
	SPla SRms WHen WPer
§ 'Rosa Triumph'	EFou MBel MCAu SPla
'Rosenballett'	EBrP EBre LBCl LBSe LBre MBBe
	NBrk SBre
roseus	Last listed 1997
'Rotes Meer'	EBee ELan LRHS MAvo MBri
	NTow
rotundifolius	See *Bellis rotundifolia*
'Caerulescens'	'Caerulescens'
salsuginosus	See *E. peregrinus*
(Richardson) A. Gray	
- misapplied	See *Aster sibiricus, E. peregrinus*
	subsp. *calliantbemus*
§ 'Schneewittchen'	CGle CMGP EBee EFou EGar ELan
	EMan GMac LAst LHop LRHS
	MBel MCAu MMil MRav MWat
	MWgw NSti NVic SCro SPla
	WLRN
'Schöne Blaue'	Last listed 1999
§ 'Schwarzes Meer'	EFou GKir LRHS NGdn SPer SPla
	SUsu WCot
scopulinus	LRHS
'Serenity'	Last listed 1997
simplex	LRHS MWat NMen NNrd
'Snow Queen'	WFar
Snow White	See *E.* 'Schneewittchen'
'Sommerabend'	Last listed 1999
'Sommerneuschnee'	ECha NPri SHel
sp. dwarf from Idaho, USA	Last listed 1998
sp. from Bald Mountains	NWCA
* 'Spanish Daisy'	GPin LAst
speciosus	EBee SMer SSvw
- var. *macrantbus*	Last listed 1999
'Strahlenmeer'	EBee ECGP LRHS WLRN
* *strictus* from Ireland	Last listed 1997
trifidus	See *E. compositus* var. *discoideus*
tweedyi	NBro
uncialis var. *conjugans*	CGra
uniflorus	NNrd
'Unity'	MWat
vagus	WWin
- JCA 8911	Last listed 1999

¶ 'Wayne Roderick'	SMac
'White Quakeress'	CBos CElw CMea EGle GBuc
	SLod WRHF
'Wuppertal'	CBlo EBee EGar EGle EMan LRHS
yukonensis	Last listed 1999

ERINACEA (Papilionaceae)

§ *antbyllis* ♀	SIng SOkd
pungens	See *E. antbyllis*

ERINUS (Scrophulariaceae)

alpinus ♀	CMHG CMea EBot ECtt ESis
	EWFC GKir GTou MBro MWat
	NBro NFor NHol SIng SRms WAbe
	WEas WFar WPer WPyg WWin
- var. *albus*	CBot GTou MBro NMen NWCA
	SRms WAbe WHoo WPer WPyg
- 'Dr Hähnle'	CNic EBrP EBre ECGP EDAr GKir
	LBCl LBSe LBre LRHS MBBe
	NMen SBre SGar SRms WHoo
	WPyg WRHF
- 'Mrs Charles Boyle' ♀	MBro WPyg
* *olivana*	EWes

ERIOBOTRYA (Rosaceae)

deflexa	CFil CHEx
japonica (F) ♀	CAbb CB&S CBot CFil CGre
	CHEx CMCN EPfP ERea ERom
	GQui IDee LBlo LPan LRHS MRav
	SArc SDry SLon SPer SSta WHer
	WMul WNor WPGP WSHC WWat
- 'Benlehr' (F)	Last listed 1998
- 'Mrs Cookson' (F)	Last listed 1998

ERIOCAPITELLA See ANEMONE

ERIOCEPHALUS (Asteraceae)

africanus	WJek

ERIOGONUM (Polygonaceae)

breedlovei var.	CGra
breedlovei	
brevicaule var. *nanum*	NWCA
cespitosum	CPBP NTow NWCA
- subsp. *douglasii*	See *E. douglasii*
- NNS 94-44	Last listed 1999
compositum	Last listed 1999
var. *leiantbum*	
croceum	Last listed 1997
§ *douglasii*	WLin
- NNS 95-238	Last listed 1999
flavum	CGra WPer
giganteum	Last listed 1998
beracleoides var. *minus*	See *E. umbellatum* var. *minus*
jamesii	WPat WPyg
kennedyi var. *alpigenum*	CGra
- var. *austromontanum*	NTow
libertini	Last listed 1999
lobbii var. *lobbii*	Last listed 1998
ochrocepbalum	Last listed 1998
ovalifolium	NTow
- var. *depressum*	NWCA
- - NNS 94-47	Last listed 1998
panguicense	Last listed 1998
var. *alpestre*	
pauciflorum	Last listed 1997
subsp. *nebraskense*	
rosense	Last listed 1999
saxatile	Last listed 1998
siskiyouense	Last listed 1997
subalpinum	EPot
thymoides	Last listed 1999

umbellatum	ECha EPot LRHS NLAp SIng
- var. **haussknechtii**	See *E. umbellatum* var.
	polyanthum
- var. **humistratum**	SBla
§ - var. **minus**	Last listed 1999
§ - var. **polyanthum**	Last listed 1999
- var. **porteri**	NWCA
- var. **subalpinum**	Last listed 1997
- var. **torreyanum**	CMea MBro NHol WLin WPat
- var. **umbellatum**	LBee
ursinum	Last listed 1998

ERIOPHORUM (Cyperaceae)

angustifolium	CBen CBrm COlW CWat EGle
	EHoe EHon EMFW EPPr EPla
	EWFC GCHN GOrn LPBA MCCP
	MMoz MSta NDea SWat WCot
	WHal WHer WMAq WPer WWeb
latifolium	LPBA
vaginatum	CRow EHoe SWyc

ERIOPHYLLUM (Asteraceae)

lanatum	CHal EBee ECGP ECha EPfP GAbr
	MBNS MWat NArg NBid SBla
	SMrm WEas WWin
- 'Bella'	NLar
* - 'Pointe'	EBee EWll GSki MCCP SSca

ERIOSTEMON (Rutaceae)

myoporoides	See *Philotheca myoporoides*

ERITRICHIUM (Boraginaceae)

§ **canum**	NTow
nanum	CGra
rupestre	See *E. canum*
- var. **pectinatum**	NEgg NWCA
* **sibiricum**	Last listed 1997
strictum	See *E. canum*

ERODIUM ✿ (Geraniaceae)

absinthoides	GCHN LRHS MDHE NChi
- var. **amanum**	See *E. amanum*
- blue	GCHN
§ **acaule**	GCHN NMGW NRog
alnifolium	GCHN
§ **amanum**	GCHN LRHS MBri
'Ardwick Redeye'	MDHE
balearicum	See *E.* x *variabile* 'Album'
battandierianum	GCHN
§ 'Bidderi'	MDHE NChi WAbe
boissieri	GCHN
botrys	Last listed 1998
brachycarpum	GCHN
'Caroline'	WHoo WTin
carvifolium	CElw EBee EPPr GCHN GKir
	LRHS MBri MDHE MHar NMGW
	NWCA WPnn
§ **castellanum**	CLyd EBee ESis GCHN GKir NBro
	NMen NRog NSti SBla SRms
celtibericum	MDHE
- 'Peñagolosa'	Last listed 1999
chamaedryoides	See *E. reichardii*
§ **cheilanthifolium**	GCHN GMaP MDHE WMaN
- 'Bidderi'	See *E.* 'Bidderi'
chrysanthum	More than 30 suppliers
- pink	CGle EPPr LGre SMrm SUsu
- sulphureum	WPnn WShe
ciconium	Last listed 1998
§ **cicutarium**	EWFC GCHN
§ - subsp. **cicutarium**	GCHN
corsicum	CGle EBur MDHE MTho NMen
	NRog WAbe

- 'Album'	GCHN MDHE
§ 'County Park'	CLyd CMea CPlt ECha ECou EDAr
	EWes GCHN GMaP MBri MDHE
	MMil MOne NChi NDlv NMen
	NRog NRya SAga SBla SChu SIng
	SMrm SRms WKif WPnn
crinitum	GCHN
danicum	Last listed 1998
daucoides hort.	See *E. castellanum*
- Boiss. ex I. Kreeger 4593	Last listed 1999
'Eileen Emmett'	GCHN MDHE
'Elizabeth'	GCHN WPnn
§ **foetidum**	EGle GCHN LFis MDHE MHer
	MWat NMen NRog NSla
- 'County Park'	See *E.* 'County Park'
- 'Pallidum'	See *E.* 'Pallidum'
- 'Roseum'	GCal MWat SBla
'Frans Choice'	See *E.* 'Fran's Delight'
§ 'Fran's Delight'	CMea MBro MDHE WHoo
'Géant de Saint Cyr'	CElw EMon WCot
N **glandulosum** ♀	CMea EDAr GCHN GCal LHop
	MBro MHer MTis NRog SAga SBla
	SRms WBea WEas WKif WPat
	WWhi
¶ - 'Emma'	MDHE
- 'Espiguette'	Last listed 1999
gruinum	EBee ECoo GCHN LFis SBla SRCN
	SSca WPat WPnn WSan
guicciardii	EDAr
N **guttatum**	CGle EMan EWTr LPio MWat
	NMen NTow SAga SRms WHal
	WPer WSHC
'Helen'	GCHN
I **hirtum** (Forssk.) Willd.	Last listed 1998
x **hybridum** hort.	See *E.* 'Sara Francesca'
- Sünderm.	EGle EWes WAbe WHal
hymenodes L'Hér.	See *E. trifolium*
jahandiezianum	GCHN
'Julie Ritchie'	MDHE WElm WHoo
'Katherine Joy'	EWes MDHE NChi NDlv NRog
	WAbe
x **kolbeanum** 'Nadia'	MBri
x **kolbianum**	MBro MDHE NChi SMrm WAbe
	WElm WHoo WPnn WPyg
- 'Natasha'	CMHG ECha EMan EPot EPri
	EWes GCHN GKir LBee LRHS
	MDHE MHer NChi NHol NMGW
	NMen NRog SChu SMrm SWat
	WAbe WFar WKif
'Las Meninas'	CPlt CRDP GCHN
x **lindavicum**	MDHE WPnn
- 'Charter House'	GCHN WPnn
- pink	WPnn
macradenum	See *E. glandulosum*
malacoides	GCHN
manescaui	More than 30 suppliers
- dwarf form	Last listed 1999
moschatum	Last listed 1998
- Guitt 88041904	GCHN
munbyanum	GCHN
neuradifolium	GCHN
Guitt 86040601	
'Nunwood Pink'	GCHN MDHE
§ 'Pallidum'	CHal CSam
pelargoniiflorum	CBot CGle CHar CRDP EBee
	EMou ESis EWes GCHN LFis
	MTho NBro NChi NLar SAga
	SRCN SRms STes SUsu WEas WFar
	WHil WKif WPGP WPer WPnP
	WPnn WPyg WRus WWin
petraeum (Gouan) Willd.	See *E. foetidum*
- subsp. **crispum**	See *E. cheilanthifolium*
misapplied	

- subsp. *glandulosum*	See *E. glandulosum*
'Pickering Pink'	GCHN MDHE NMen NRog SWat
pimpinellifolium	See *E. cicutarium*
'Princesse Marion'	GCHN
* 'Purple Haze'	CSpe
'Rachel'	See *E.* x *willkommianum* 'Rachel'
¶ *recoderi*	GCHN
I 'Red Eve'	Last listed 1998
§ *reichardii*	CElw ESis GMaP IMGH LBee
	LRHS MHer MTho NRog SAga
	SBla SRms SWat WPnn
¶ - 'Bianca'	SVil
- 'Derek'	ECho
- JR 961	GCHN
- JR 962	GCHN
- JR 963	GCHN
- JR 964	GCHN
* - 'Rubrum'	Last listed 1998
rodiei	GCHN
¶ - x *glandulosum*	MDHE
romanum	See *E. acaule*
§ *rupestre*	CBot CMea ECho ECtt GCHN
	MDHE NDlv WPnn
salzmannii	See *E. cicutarium* subsp.
	cicutarium
§ 'Sara Francesca'	MDHE NSla
§ *saxatile*	GCHN NNrd NRog
sebaceum 'Polly'	GCHN
'Spanish Eyes'	CWes MBri MDHE SAga SMrm
'Stephanie'	CElw CLyd EGle EWes GCHN
	LBee LRHS MDHE NBir NChi
	NHol SAsh
supracanum	See *E. rupestre*
tordylioides	GCHN
trichomanifolium L'Hér.	EWes LBee LRHS MHer WPnn
- hort.	See *E. cheilanthifolium*, *E.*
	saxatile
§ *trifolium*	CMCo ELan LFis MMil NChi
	NCiC NMGW NSti SIng SSpi
	WCru WHal WHoo
- Guitt 85051701	GCHN
- var. *montanum*	GCHN
valentinum	See *E. saxatile*
- 'Alicante'	Last listed 1997
§ x *variabile*	Last listed 1999
§ - 'Album'	CMHG EDAr EMNN EPot GBuc
	GMac LBee MBar MHer MTho
	NHar NHol NMen NVic NWCA
	SBla SHFr SRms SUsu WAbe
	WEas WPat WPer WPnn WWin
I - 'Bishop's Form'	CMHG ECtt EDAr EMNN EPot
	ESis GMac LPio LRHS MBar
	MBro MHer NBro NHar NHol
	NMen NNrd NRog NTow SBla
	SRms WHoo WPat
- 'Flore Pleno' (d)	ECtt EDAr ELan EOrc ESis
	EWes MHer NMen NRog
	SHFr SIng SRms WAbe
	WPer WPnn
- 'Roseum' ♀	CBot CNic ECho EDAr ELan
	EOrc LRHS MHer NRog
	NWCA SIng SRms WAbe
	WPer WWin
I 'Westacre Seedling'	EWes
'Whiteleaf'	CElw MDHE
x *wilkommianum*	NRog
§ x *willkommianum* 'Rachel'	GCHN MDHE

ERPETION See VIOLA

ERUCA (Brassicaceae)

vesicaria subsp. *sativa*	CArn CBod ELau GPoy MChe

	MHer SIde WHer WJek WOak
	WSel WWye

ERYNGIUM ✿ (Apiaceae)

§ *agavifolium*	More than 30 suppliers
- HCM 98048	Last listed 1999
alpinum ♀	CB&S CElw CGle EBee ECha EFou
	EGle ELan EMon EPar GKir LPio
	MBro MCLN MLLN MTho MTis
	NBir NChi NSti SPer SRms SWat
	WEas WHoo WOve WPGP
- 'Amethyst'	CRDP GBuc LRHS MBri MCli
	MTed NLar WCot
- 'Blue Star'	CB&S CBot CHar EBee ECGN
	EHrv EMar GCal GKir GMac GSki
	LGre MWll SPla SSpi WHoo WLin
	WPer
- 'Holden Blue'	CPlt
- 'Opal'	LRHS
- 'Slieve Donard'	IBlr LAst LFis LRHS SPer
- 'Superbum'	CBot CRDP CSam ECGN EHrv
	GSki MNrw SBla SMad SRms
	WCot
amethystinum	CBot EBee ECGN ECha EGle EHrv
	EMan EWes GSki LGre MNrw
	NSla SChu SMad SSca WLRN WPer
biebersteinianum Nevski	See *E. caucasicum*
* - from Kashmir	Last listed 1997
bourgatii	More than 30 suppliers
- Graham Stuart	CSpe EMar GBin MAvo MBel
Thomas's selection	NDov WCot
- 'Oxford Blue' ♀	CLon CMea CMil CRDP EBee
	EHrv EPar LGre LPio MMil NTow
	SSoC SSpi WCot WEas
¶ - 'Picos Blue'PBR	CGle EHrv LGre LPio WCot
bromeliifolium hort.	See *E. agavifolium*
caeruleum	EMon EWTr EWes LGre MNrw
	NChi NFai SIng
campestre	CBot MAvo NChi NLar SRCN
	WPer
§ *caucasicum*	EBee ECGN GBuc
creticum	CFri EBee EGar EMon EWes MAvo
	NBir NBro
decaisneanum	See *E. pandanifolium*
Delaroux	See *E. proteiflorum*
dichotomum	EMon EPPr LGre NChi
ebracteatum	CLon GCal LGre
- var. *poterioides*	LGre
§ *eburneum*	CBot CRoM EBee EBrP EBre ECha
	ECoo EMon EWes GBuc LBCl
	LBSe LBre LEdu LGre LRHS MBBe
	MGrG MSCN MWgw NBro NChi
	SBre WCot WFar WPic
foetidum	CArn EOHP GPoy
'Forncett Ultra'	EFou WPGP
§ *giganteum* ♀	More than 30 suppliers
- 'Silver Ghost' ♀	CMea EBee EGle EHrv EMon LGre
	MWll NLar SDix SMrm SUsu SWat
	WAbe WCot WHal
glaciale	CFil NSla
- JJA 461.000	Last listed 1999
horridum	EBrP EBre EWTr EWes LBCl LBSe
	LBre LEdu LGre LRHS MBBe MBro
	MFir MNrw NBro SArc SBre WHer
	WWhi WWin
humile	CPne
'Jos Eijking'PBR	EBee EMan GKir LRHS MCLN
	MRav SPer
leavenworthii	Last listed 1999
maritimum	CArn CBot CPou CSpe ECha
	GPoy LGre WAbe WSel
Miss Willmott's ghost	See *E. giganteum*

x *oliverianum* ♀ — CHad CMea CRDP CSam EBee EFou EHrv ELan EMan GAbr GBuc GMac IHdy LGre LRHS MAvo MBro MCAu MCli SDix SMad SPer WByw

§ *pandanifolium* — CLon CMHG CRoM EBee EWes GBin GCal IBlr MAnH MSCN NSti SAPC SArc SCob SMad SPer WBrE WCot WPGP

- purple — LGre SDix WPGP

planum — More than 30 suppliers

- 'Bethlehem' ♀ — CLon GCal LRHS WPyg WSpi

§ - 'Blauer Zwerg' — CLon EFou GLil LRHS MCAu SCoo SWat WPyg

- 'Blaukappe' — CBot CFir CHar ECGP GBri LGre LRHS MBro NCut NLar SMad SMrm SSca WElm WFar WHoo WOve WPGP WPyg WWhi

¶ - 'Blue Candle' — WSpi

- Blue Dwarf — See *E. planum* 'Blauer Zwerg'

- 'Blue Ribbon' — CHad CRDP EBee EMan LAst LCaP LRHS SWat

- 'Flüela' — CGle CLon CPar EBee EMan EWes GCal LPio LRHS MRav NGdn SPla SWat WWal

- 'Seven Seas' — CFir CMil EBee EBlw LHop LRHS MBel MRav SChu SPla SRPl SWat WCot WHil WLRN WPer

- 'Silverstone' — CFwr EBee GCal GSki LRHS NCiC NPri

- 'Tetra Petra' — EBee MCCP WPer

- violet blue — GCal

§ *proteiflorum* — CRDP GBin GCal LRHS SCob SWat

serra — CRoM EWes MAnH

sp. CD&R — EWes

sp. RB 94054 — NSti

spinalba — CBot GSki LPio WPer

tricuspidatum — CBlo EBrP EBre LBCl LBSe LBre LRHS MBBe SBre WPer

x *tripartitum* ♀ — More than 30 suppliers

- 'Variegatum' — WCot

* *umbelliferum* — Last listed 1997

* *umbellulatum* — EMon

variifolium — More than 30 suppliers

venustum — EBee LGre NChi

yuccifolium — CArn CB&S CHEx EBee EBot EBrP EBre ECoo EOld EWes GCal GKir LBCl LBSe LBre LHil LPio MBBe MSCN NChi SBre SCob SMad WCot WHer

x *zabelii* — CBos CRDP EBee ELan GCal GMac LGre MFir NBir NTow WEas WPGP

- 'Donard Variety' — CLon GCal GKir LRHS MAvo MBri SWat

- 'Jewel' — CLon MAvo SUsu SWat

¶ - 'Spring Hill Seedling' — MAvo

- 'Violetta' — CBos CGle CLon CPlt ELan GBuc MTed SWat WHoo

ERYSIMUM ✿ (Brassicaceae)

§ *alpestre* — Last listed 1999

- J. Jurasek 222/96 — Last listed 1998

alpinum hort. — See *E. hieraciifolium*

amoenum — Last listed 1997

'Anne Marie' — ELan MRav SOkh

¶ 'Apricot Twist' — CFai CSpe

arenicola var. *torulosum* See *E. torulosum*

arkansanum — See *E. helveticum*

§ *asperum* — Last listed 1999

'Aunt May' — SMrm

'Bowles' Mauve' ♀ — More than 30 suppliers

'Bowles' Purple' — ISea

'Bowles' Yellow' — GBuc NSti SMer

'Bredon' ♀ — EBee ECoo ELan EOld EPfP GAbr GKir LRHS MAsh MMil NPer SAga SCob SRPl SUsu WFar WKif WRus

'Butterscotch' — CFee CFri CGle CLTr CMil CSam NHaw WEas WMaN WWhi

capitatum — CLyd NMen

'Cheerfulness' — MBri

cheiri — EWFC IBlr MHer MMal WCot WHer

N - 'Baden-Powell' (d) — Last listed 1999

- 'Bloody Warrior' (d) — CBot CElw ECtt ELan GBuc NPer NSla WEas WMaN

- 'Deben' — CBot

- 'Harpur Crewe' (d) ♀ — CBot CFee CGle CSam ELan EPot GKir LRHS MBri MMil MTho NPer SAga SChu SRms WCot WEas WFar WHoo WPat WPyg WWin

- 'Helen Louise' — Last listed 1997

- 'Jane's Derision' — CNat

'Chelsea Jacket' ♀ — CLTr CM&M EBee ECGP GAbr GBri LRHS MMil MRav NSti SAga WEas WHil WMaN WOve

'Chequers' — WPer

* 'Clent Calcutt' — Last listed 1997

concinnum — See *E. suffrutescens*

'Constant Cheer' ♀ — CElw CPlt CSam CSpe EGoo GAbr GBuc GMac LRHS NFai NPer NSti SAga WEas WFar WHil WKif WPat WPer WRha WRus

cuspidatum — Last listed 1998

'Devon Cream' — SAga WWoo

'Devon Gold' — See *E.* 'Plant World Gold'

'Devon Sunset' — CGle CM&M CSam CSpe MSCN MSte NHaw SAga SChu SLod SUsu WMaN WRus WSan

'Dorothy Elmhirst' — See *E.* 'Mrs L.K. Elmhirst'

dwarf lemon — WHoo

'Ellen Willmott' — Last listed 1999

'Emm's Variety' — NCat

gelidum J. Jurasek 220/96 — Last listed 1999

* - var. *kotschyi* — NWCA

* 'Gingernut' — NPer

'Glowing Embers' — MAsh SOkh

'Gold Flame' — MWat

'Golden Gem' — WLRN WPer

'Golden Jubilee' — ECho NTow

§ *helveticum* — CNic ECoo GTou NPri SGar SRms

§ *hieraciifolium* — WLRN

humile — WCot

'Jacob's Jacket' — CGle CLTr CMil CPea LFis MBNS MHer MSCN NPer SAga SChu WEas WMaN WWin

'John Codrington' — CBel CGle CMHG CMil CPlt CSam GBuc LRHS MHer MRav NFai NFla NGdn NPer SAga SChu SUsu WHoo WKif WLin

'Joseph's Coat' — WViv

'Jubilee Gold' — EWll GCrs

'Julian Orchard' — CElw EBlw GMac NCiC SChu SUsu WHil WRus WWhi

kotschyanum — CGra CLyd LBee LRHS MDHE NMen NTow NWCA SRms WAbe WPat

* 'Lady Roborough' — GBuc

* 'Lewis Hart' — Last listed 1998

linifolium — CPea EBur ECoo SRms WGor

§ - 'Variegatum' — CArn CBrm CGle CSam EBee ELan EOrc EPot LAst LFis LHil LRHS MAsh MHer MSCN NPer

	SAga SCob SCro SPer SRot WAbe
	WCot WHoo WPGP
'Mayflower'	Last listed 1997
¶ *menziesii* subsp. *yadonii*	NWCA
'Mill Cottage Dawn'	CMil
'Mill Cottage Dusk'	CMil
'Miss Hopton'	NPer NTow WEas
'Moonlight'	CBrm CSam GBuc LBee LNor
	LRHS MHer MSCN MTho NBrk
	NFor SChu SRms WCot WEas
	WHil WMaN WPer
§ 'Mrs L.K. Elmhirst'	CElw LFis NPer SHel WCot WMaN
mutabile	CElw CHar CInt CLTr CMea CTri
	EGoo EOrc MFir MRav NBir
	WMaN
- 'Variegatum'	WEas WHoo
nivale	CElw
'Onslow Seedling'	Last listed 1999
'Orange Flame'	CMHG ECha ELan EPot LBee
	LHop MBar NPer SMrm WPer
	WRHF
perofskianum	SLon WEas
Perry's hybrid	NPer
'Perry's Peculiar'	NBur NPer
'Perry's Pumpkin'	NPer
§ 'Plant World Gold'	LRHS
'Plant World Lemon'	EPri LRHS
'Primrose'	WCot WPer
§ *pulchellum*	ESis MWat NHol WPat WPyg
- *aurantiacum*	Last listed 1997
- 'Variegatum'	EBee NFla WCot
aff. *pulchellum*	NWCA
JJH 9309143	
pumilum DC.	See *E. helveticum*
'Rosemoor'	MRav NCat
'Rufus'	CSam NHaw SAga
rupestre	See *E. pulchellum*
§ *scoparium*	EBee ECGP SChr
'Scorpio'	Last listed 1999
semperflorens	Last listed 1997
sintenisianum	See *E. alpestre*
'Sissinghurst Variegated'	See *E. linifolium* 'Variegatum'
sp. from Madeira	CPLG
'Sprite'	CLyd CMHG CMea CTri EDAr
	EPot NPer SMrm
'Stonyford Gem'	MSCN
§ *suffrutescens*	EBee ESis NPer SUsu
'Sunbright'	NCat
'Sunshine'	Last listed 1998
§ *torulosum*	Last listed 1999
* 'Tricolor'	WHil
'Turkish Bazaar'	Last listed 1999
'Valerie Finnis'	Last listed 1999
N 'Variegatum'	CB&S WWin
'Wembdon Bravery'	Last listed 1998
'Wenlock Beauty' ♀	CBel CSam MTho MTis NDov
	NFai NGdn SAga SChu SRms SUsu
	WByw WCot WMaN WPer WRus
	WWhi
'Wenlock Beauty Variegated'	CSam
wheeleri	EBee ECoo NPer
¶ 'White Dame'	CElw
witmannii	Last listed 1997
'Yellow Bird'	Last listed 1999

ERYTHRAEA See CENTAURIUM

ERYTHRINA (Papilionaceae)

caffra	Last listed 1998
corallodendron	SSoC
crista-galli ♀	CAbb CB&S CBot CGre CHEx
	EBee ELan EOas ERea GQui LRHS

	MLan SMur SOWG SPan SPlb
	SSoC
- 'Compacta'	SMad
fusca	Last listed 1998
§ *humeana*	Last listed 1999
indica	See *E. variegata*
latissima	Last listed 1998
lysistemon	SOWG
princeps	See *E. humeana*
§ *variegata*	Last listed 1997
vespertilio	SOWG

ERYTHRONIUM ✿ (Liliaceae)

albidum	CLAP CWoo EBee EPot GBuc
	LAma NRog
americanum	CArn CAvo CBro CLAP CRDP
	CWoo EBee ECha EPot GCrs
	LAma MLLN MS&S MSal NRog
	SSpi WCru
¶ 'Beechpark'	IBlr
'Blush'	IBlr
californicum ♀	CLAP CWoo GCrs MS&S NRog
	WAbe WCru WPnP
- J&JA 13216	CLAP
¶ - Plas Merdyn form	IBlr
§ - 'White Beauty' ♀	CAvo CBro CCuc CLAP EBee
	ECha EMon EPot ETub GBuc
	GCrs GGar LAma LBow LPio
	LRHS MCCP MDun MTho NHar
	NSti SIng SMac SSpi SUsu WAbe
	WCru WKif WPnP WShi
caucasicum	CLAP NRog
citrinum	CWoo MPhe WLin
- J&JA 13462	CLAP CWoo
'Citronella'	CBro CLAP EBee ERos GBuc
	LAma LBow LRHS MMHG MS&S
	NDlv NHar NRog WAbe WCru
cliftonii hort.	See *E. multiscapoideum* Cliftonii
	Group
dens-canis ♀	More than 30 suppliers
- 'Charmer'	EPot WWst
- 'Frans Hals'	CLAP EPar EPot ERos GBuc GCrs
	IMGH LAma LRHS MTho NMen
	NRog WCru
- from Serbia, white	MPhe
- from Slovenia	CLAP
- JCA 470.001	CLAP
- 'Lilac Wonder'	EPar EPot IMGH LAma LRHS
	MTho NRog WWst
- var. *niveum*	EPot ERos LAma
* - - 'Plenum'	WWst
- 'Old Aberdeen'	CLAP CRDP NPar
- 'Pink Perfection'	EPar EPot ERos GCrs LAma LRHS
	NHar NRog WCru WHil
- 'Purple King'	EPot ERos GCrs IMGH LAma
	NHar NRog WCru
- 'Rose Queen'	CAvo CBro EPar EPot ERos ETub
	GBuc GCrs IMGH LAma LRHS
	MAvo MLLN MTho NHar NHol
	NRog NSti WAbe
- 'Snowflake'	CAvo CLAP CMea CRDP ECha
	EPar EPot ERos IMGH LAma LRHS
	MLLN NBir NHar NRog SSpi
	WAbe WCru
- 'White Splendour'	CBro NEgg
- WM 9615 from	MPhe
E Slovenia	
elegans	WPGP
¶ 'Flash'	IBlr
§ *grandiflorum*	GCrs MS&S MWll NHar
- subsp. *chrysandrum*	See *E. grandiflorum*
- J&JA 11394	CLAP

- MP&S 007	CLAP SSpi
helenae	CLAP CWoo IBlr WPGP
hendersonii	CLAP CWoo LAma MPhe MS&S WLin
- J&JA 12945	CLAP CWoo SSpi
- JCA 11116	CLAP
howellii	CLAP GCrs MPhe WLin WPGP
- J&JA 13428	CWoo
- J&JA 13441	CLAP
japonicum	CBro EBee EFEx LAma LBow NMen NRog WCru
'Jeannine'	WCru
'Joanna'	CBro CLAP CRDP LAma
'Kondo'	CCuc EBee EPot ERos GBuc GMaP LAma LRHS MBro MS&S MTho NHar NRog SLod WAbe WCru WHil
mesochoreum	IBlr
'Minnehaha' ♀	Last listed 1997
moerheimii	Last listed 1997
* - 'Semiplena'	Last listed 1998
§ *multiscapoideum*	CLAP CWoo MPhe WLin
§ - Cliftonii Group	CLAP MPhe WLin
- - J&JA 13525	CLAP CWoo SSpi
- JCA 12700	SSpi
oregonum	CLAP CWoo MS&S WCru
- subsp. *leucandrum*	CLAP MPhe MS&S WLin
- - J&JA 13494	CWoo SSpi
'Pagoda' ♀	More than 30 suppliers
purdyi	See *E. multiscapoideum*
revolutum ♀	CBro CLAP CRDP CWoo EPot GGar IBlr LBow MS&S NWoo SBla SSpi WCru
- Johnsonii Group	CNic CWoo NHar SSpi WCot WCru
- 'Knightshayes Pink'	CLAP
- 'Pink Beauty'	WNor
¶ - Plas Merdyn form	IBlr
- 'White Beauty'	See *E. californicum* 'White Beauty'
sibiricum	GCrs
- 'Altai Snow'	Last listed 1999
- 'White Fang'	Last listed 1998
'Sundisc'	ECha EPot MS&S MTho NRog
tuolumnense ♀	CAvo CBro CLAP EBee EBrP EBre EMon EPar EPot ERos GCrs LAma LBCl LBSe LBow LBre LRHS MBBe MCCP MDun MS&S NHar NRog SBre WAbe

ESCALLONIA ✿ (Escalloniaceae)

'Alice'	CRsw SLPl SPer
§ *alpina*	CRsw
'Apple Blossom' ♀	More than 30 suppliers
'Bantry Bay'	CB&S
§ *bifida*	CDoC CGre CPle CRsw CWit LRHS SPan WSHC WWat
'C.F. Ball'	CTri EBee EHol ELan GCHN GChr GEil IOrc LBuc MGos NFla NWea SEND SLim SRms WAbe WBod WDin WFar WHer WMoo WPic WStI
'Cardinalis'	CRsw NCut
'Compacta Coccinea'	CRsw
'Dart's Rosy Red'	CBlo NHol SLPl
'Donard Beauty'	CBlo CChe CRsw CSam SRms
'Donard Brilliance'	CRsw MGos WPic
'Donard Gem'	CRsw
'Donard Radiance' ♀	CB&S CChe CDoC CRsw CSam EBee ENot EPfP GChr GKir ISea LRHS MGos MWat NHol SBod SLim SMer SPer SRPl SRms WBod

	WDin WFar WGer
'Donard Rose'	CRsw
'Donard Scarlet'	CRsw
'Donard Seedling'	More than 30 suppliers
'Donard Star'	CDoC CRsw EBee ENot EPfP IOrc MGos NWea SLPl WCFE WGwG WWeb
'Donard Surprise'	NFor
'Donard White'	CPri CRsw
'Edinensis' ♀	CMHG ECtt EMil ENot EPfP EWTr GChr MBar NFla SEND SLim SRms WDin WGer WMoo WWat
'Erecta'	CBlo EPfP
x *exoniensis*	SRms
fonkii	See *E. alpina*
'Glasnevin Hybrid'	CRsw
'Glory of Donard'	CRsw ENot
* *gracilis alba*	CRsw
'Gwendolyn Anley'	CLTr CMHG SBod SLPl SPer WPic WWat
'Hopleys Gold'[PBR]	See *E. laevis* 'Gold Brian'
illinita	CPle CRsw WPGP
'Iveyi' ♀	More than 30 suppliers
§ *laevis*	CRsw CTrw SDry SPan
§ - 'Gold Brian'[PBR]	CMHG CRsw CSam EBrP EBre EHoe ELan ENot EPla IOrc LBCl LBSe LBre LRHS MBBe MGos MWat SBre SPer WBod WHar WStI
- 'Gold Ellen' (v)	CBlo CChe CRsw CWSG EBee EBrP EBre EMil EPfP GOrc LBCl LBSe LBre LRHS MBBe MBri MCCP MGos MRav NHol SAga SBre SCoo SEND SLim SPer SPla
Lanarth no.1	CRsw
'Langleyensis' ♀	CCHP CTri GOrc MWat MWhi NFor NWea SBod WDin WFar WHar WPic WSHC
leucantha	CGre CRsw
littoralis	Last listed 1999
mexicana	CBot CFil WPGP WWat
x *mollis*	CPle CRsw SPer
montevidensis	See *E. bifida*
'Newry'	CRsw SPer
organensis	See *E. laevis*
'Peach Blossom' ♀	CChe CDoC CPle CRsw CSam EBee ELan EMil ENot EPfP EWTr GKir LRHS MBNS MBri MGos SLPl SLim SPer SRms WFar WGwG WWal WWeb
'Pink Elf'	CBlo ECtt IOrc LRHS MBri NCut WLRN
'Pink Pearl'	CRsw
'Pride of Donard' ♀	CB&S CBlo CDoC CRsw EBee EPfP IOrc LHop LRHS NPri SPla SRms WGwG WWeb
pulverulenta	CRsw WPic
punctata	See *E. rubra*
'Rebecca'	CRsw GOrc
'Red Dream'	CBlo CChe CFai EBee EBrP EBre IOrc LBCl LBSe LBre LRHS MAsh MBBe MBri MGos NFla NPro SBre SCoo SRms WFar WGer WLRN WStI
'Red Dwarf'	Last listed 1998
'Red Elf'	More than 30 suppliers
'Red Hedger'	CBlo CCHP CDoC CDul CTrG GGar LRHS MGos MTis SCoo WGwG
resinosa	CB&S CPle CRsw SAPC SArc
revoluta	CPle CRsw SDry
rosea	CRsw
§ *rubra*	CRsw GGar

- 'Crimson Spire' ♀	More than 30 suppliers
- 'Ingramii'	CCHP CChe CMHG CRsw NWea SBod
§ - var. *macrantha*	CB&S CChe CDoC CDul CHEx CSam EBee GChr GGar GKir IArd LRHS MBri MHer NWea SLim SPer SPla SRms WBod WDin WGer WGwG WPic WStl WWal
- 'Pygmaea'	See *E. rubra* 'Woodside'
- var. *uniflora*	SDry
§ - 'Woodside'	CPle EHol EPfP GChr NHol SIng SRPl SRms WHCG
'Saint Keverne'	CRsw
'Silver Anniversary'	CB&S CBlo CRsw EPfP MGos MRav WBcn WWeb
'Slieve Donard'	CBlo CRsw EBee ENot EPfP MGos MRav SLPl SRPl SRms WFar WWeb
x *stricta* 'Harold Comber'	CRsw
tucumanensis	CGre CPle CRsw
virgata	CPle CRsw
viscosa	CPle CRsw WCwm
'William Watson'	CRsw

ESCHSCHOLZIA (Papaveraceae)

californica ♀	EWTr
¶ - 'Jersey Cream'	CSpe
¶ - var. *maritima*	CGdn

ETLINGERA (Zingiberaceae)

¶ *elatior*	LBlo

EUCALYPTUS ✿ (Myrtaceae)

acaciiformis	CMFo WDCP
aggregata	CMFo SAPC SArc SPer WCel WDCP WMul WTro
albens	Last listed 1999
alpina	Last listed 1998
amygdalina	Last listed 1998
approximans	WCel
subsp. *approximans*	
archeri	CDoC CMFo EPfP GAri GKir GQui ISea LPan WBod WCel WOVN WPGP
botryoides	Last listed 1999
§ *bridgesiana*	CMFo ELau
brookeriana	Last listed 1998
caesia	WDCP
cameronii	Last listed 1998
camphora	CMFo WCel
cinerea	CMFo CTrC GQui IOrc SPlb WCel WDCP
citriodora	ELau EOHP GQui MHer WCel WGwG WHer WLRN WNor
coccifera ♀	CBrm CDoC CHEx CMFo CTho EBee ELan EPfP GAri GKir GOrc IOrc LPan LRHS MAsh MCCP NEgg SEND SPla SPlb SSpi WBod WCel WDCP WHer WNor
- silver-leaved	WCel
consideniana	NEgg
cordata	CGre CMFo CMHG NEgg WCel
crenulata	GQui LPan WCel
¶ *cypellocarpa*	SPlb
dalrympleana ♀	More than 30 suppliers
deanei	WCel
debeuzevillei	See *E. pauciflora* subsp. *debeuzevillei*
delegatensis	CMFo CMHG GAri IOrc WCel WTro
divaricata	See *E. gunnii divaricata*
dives	CMFo
¶ *erythrocorys*	WDCP

* *eximia nana*	EOHP NEgg SPlb WDCP WTro
ficifolia	CB&S CGre WDCP
fraxinoides	WCel WDCP
¶ *gamophylla*	SPlb
glaucescens	CDoC CGre CMFo CMHG CTho EPfP EWes GKir GQui LPan LRHS NEgg SAPC SArc SPer WCel WDCP WGer
globulus ♀	CHEx CMFo CTrC ELau GAri ISea MSal WCel
goniocalyx	WCel
§ *gregsoniana*	CDoC ISea NFor SPlb WCel
gunnii ♀	More than 30 suppliers
§ - *divaricata*	EPfP GQui LPan LRHS NHol WCel WGer
* - 'Silver Drop'	Last listed 1998
- white	CMFo
haemastoma	Last listed 1997
johnstonii	CMFo GAri SPer WDCP
kitsoniana	CBrm WCel
kruseana	Last listed 1997
kybeanensis	CMFo GQui WBod WCel
lehmannii	SOWG
leucoxylon	WCel
- subsp. *megalocarpa*	SPlb
§ - 'Rosea'	WDCP
macarthurii	WCel
macrandra	Last listed 1998
macrocarpa	SPlb
macroryncha	SPlb
mannifera subsp. *elliptica*	WCel
- subsp. *maculosa*	Last listed 1997
melliodora	ELau
mitchelliana	LRHS WCel
moorei	WSHC
* - *nana*	CBlo MWat WDCP WNor WShe
neglecta	WCel
nicholii	CB&S CBrm CMFo EPfP EWes GKir GQui LPan WBod WCel WDCP WGer WMul WOVN
niphophila	See *E. pauciflora* subsp. *niphophila*
nitens	CMFo CMHG GAri GKir LPan LRHS SAPC SArc SPlb WBod WCel WDCP
§ *nitida*	CGre CMFo CMHG EOHP WCel WDCP WNor
nova-anglica	CMFo CMHG GAri
obliqua	CMFo
olsenii	CMFo
ovata	Last listed 1998
parvifolia ♀	CB&S CDoC CDul CLnd CMFo CTrC EPfP GAri GKir ISea LPan LRHS MAsh SDry SEND WBod WCel WDCP
pauciflora	CBlo CDoC CMFo CTho CTri EBee EBrP EBre ELan EPfP GAri LBCl LBSe LBre LPan MBBe SBre SEND SPar SPer WBod WCel WDCP WNor
- subsp. *acerina*	WCel
§ - subsp. *debeuzevillei*	CBrm CDoC CMFo CTho EPVP EPfP EWes GGar GKir GQui LRHS MCCP SAPC SArc WCel WMul WPGP
- subsp. *bedraia*	WCel
- var. *nana*	See *E. gregsoniana*
§ - subsp. *niphophila* ♀	More than 30 suppliers
- - 'Pendula'	CMHG GAri LPan LRHS NHol WCel WPGP
perriniana	CB&S CHEx CMFo EBee ELan

	ENot EPfP GKir IBlr LPan LRHS
	SDry SPer SPla SPlb WBod WCel
	WMul WNor WPat
phoenicea	SOWG
polyanthemos	Last listed 1997
preissiana	Last listed 1998
pulchella	Last listed 1997
pulverulenta	CBlo CBrm CGre CMFo GAri
	LRHS WCel WDCP WGer
¶ - Baby Blue®	WCel
radiata	CMFo ELau WDCP
regnans	GAri ISea WDCP
remota	Last listed 1997
risdonii	GAri WNor WShe
roduayi	WDCP
rubida	CGre CMFo CMHG IOrc WCel
	WDCP
sideroxylon	SPlb
- 'Rosea'	SPlb
sieberi	Last listed 1997
simmondsii	See *E. nitida*
stellulata	CMFo GAri MCCP WCel WDCP
stricta	WDCP
stuartiana	See *E. bridgesiana*
sturgissiana	NEgg WDCP
subcrenulata	CMFo CMHG EPfP GAri GKir
	GQui ISea LPan WBod WCel
tenuiramis	CGre WDCP
urnigera	CGre CMFo GAri GChr GKir ISea
	LPan LRHS WCel WDCP
vernicosa	LPan WCel
- subsp. *johnstonii*	CMHG GAri WCel
viminalis	CArn CMFo GAri ISea WCel
	WDCP
youngiana	ISea

EUCHARIDIUM See CLARKIA

EUCHARIS (Amaryllidaceae)

§ *amazonica*	LAma LRHS NRog SDeJ
x *grandiflora*	LBow
Plan. & Lind.	
- hort.	See *E. amazonica*

EUCODONIA (Gesneriaceae)

'Adele'	NMos WDib
andrieuxii	NMos
- 'Naomi'	CHal NMos WDib
'Cornell Gem'	See x *Achicodonia* 'Cornell Gem'
'Tintacoma'	NMos
verticillata 'Frances'	NMos

EUCOMIS (Hyacinthaceae)

§ *autumnalis*	CAbb CAvo CBro CPou CRHN
	CSWP CTrC EBee GBin GSki
	LAma LPio MCCP WHil
- subsp. *amaryllidifolia*	Last listed 1999
- subsp. *clavata*	WHil
bicolor	More than 30 suppliers
- 'Alba'	CAvo GSki LPio
- hybrids	Last listed 1999
§ *comosa*	CAvo CB&S CBro CHEx CRHN
	EBee EBot EMan GSki LAma
	LBow LRHS NRog SYvo WCot
	WCru WEas WLRN
- purple-leaved	EBot
¶ - 'Sparkling Burgundy'	WCot
hybrid	Last listed 1999
montana	CCtw WHil
pallidiflora	CHEx EBee LEdu
pole-evansii	CFir CTrC EBee GBin GCal MMil
	NEgg NPSI WCot WCru WHil

	WLRN
punctata	See *E. comosa*
regia	EBee
* *reichenbachii*	MWll
undulata	See *E. autumnalis*
zambesiaca	GBin GCal LBow WHil
'Zeal Bronze'	CDoC CFil CMHG CRHN EPfP
	GCal LGre LPio MCCP NSti WCot
	WCru WPGP

EUCOMMIA (Eucommiaceae)

ulmoides	CFil CMCN CPle SMad

EUCRYPHIA ✿ (Eucryphiaceae)

'Castlewellan'	ISea
cordifolia	CB&S CCHP CFil CGre CTrw ISea
	WBod
- Crarae hardy form	GGGa
- x *lucida*	CB&S CBrm CFai CGre IOrc ISea
	SPer WAbe WDin
glutinosa ♀	CDul CGre EBee ELan EPfP GKir
	ISea LHyd LRHS MAsh MBri NBir
	SBrw SPer SSpi SSta WBod WDin
	WNor WPat
- Plena Group (d)	ISea
x *hillieri* 'Winton'	CGre CMHG ISea SSpi
x *intermedia*	CDul CGre CSam CTrC CTrG
	ELan GCHN GGGa GOrc NHol
	SBrw SPer SRms SSpi WDin WPat
	WWat
- 'Rostrevor' ♀	CB&S CLan CMHG CPMA ELan
	EPfP GChr GGar IArd ISea LRHS
	MAsh MBel NRib SBrw SLon SPer
	SReu SSta WCwm WPic WSHC
lucida	CFil CGre ELan EPfP GGGa GSki
	ISea SBrw WBod WNor WPGP
	WWat
- 'Ballerina'	CPMA ISea LRHS SReu
- 'Gilt Edge' (v)	CFil ISea WPGP
- 'Leatherwood Cream' (v)	ISea SBrw SSta
- 'Pink Cloud'	CAbP CDoC CFil CMHG CPMA
	ELan EPfP ISea LRHS SBrw SPer
	SSpi SSta WPGP WWat
- 'Spring Glow' (v)	ISea
milliganii	CAbP CDoC CFil CGre CMHG
	EBee GQui ISea LHop LRHS MBlu
	SBrw SPer SRms SSpi SSta WAbe
	WPGP WSHC WWat
moorei	CB&S CFil CGre ELan ISea SBrw
x *nymansensis*	CB&S CDul CFil CTrG EBrP EBre
	EMil EPfP LBCl LBSe LBre MAsh
	MBBe SAPC SArc SBre SReu SRms
	SSpi WBrE WHCG WStI
- 'George Graham'	GGGa ISea WBod
- 'Mount Usher'	IOrc ISea
- 'Nymansay' ♀	More than 30 suppliers
N 'Penwith'	CDoC CPMA IMGH ISea LPan
	SBrw SPer SSpi WGer WWat
wilkiei	ISea

EUGENIA (Myrtaceae)

australis	LHil
myrtifolia	CSev STre
- 'Variegata'	Last li\sted 1997

EUMORPHIA (Asteraceae)

* *canescens*	Last listed 1999
prostrata	Last listed 1999
sericea	NFor WSHC

EUNOMIA See AETHIONEMA

EUODIA (Rutaceae)
daniellii See *Tetradium daniellii*
hupehensis See *Tetradium daniellii*
  Hupehense Group

EUONYMUS (Celastraceae)
alatus ♀ More than 30 suppliers
- var. *apterus* Last listed 1999
- 'Ciliodentatus' See *E. alatus* 'Compactus'
§ - 'Compactus' ♀ CDoC CEnd CPMA EPfP EPla ESis
  EWTr GChr GKir IOrc LNet LPan
  LRHS MAsh MBlu MBri MGos
  MRav SLim SPan SPer SPla SReu
  SSpi WCFE WDin WPGP WWat
* *atroppureus* CPMA
  cheatuurmii
bungeanus CMCN EPfP EPla WWat
- 'Dart's Pride' EPfP
cornutus var. CFil CPMA EPfP MAsh WPGP
  quinquecornutus WPat
europaeus CArn CDoC CDul CKin CLnd
  CSam EBrP EBre ELan EPla EWFC
  GChr LBCl LBSe LBre LBuc LHyr
  LPan MBBe MBlu MHer NWea
  SBre SRPl SRms WDin WHar
  WHer WMou
- f. *albus* CBot CPMA EMil EPla
- 'Atropurpureus' Last listed 1998
- 'Atrorubens' CBrd CPMA
- 'Aucubifolius' (v) CFil EPfP EPla WBcn
* - 'Aureus' CNat
- 'Chrysophyllus' CPMA EPfP
- var. *intermedius* ENot EPla MBlu WWes
- 'Red Cascade' ♀ More than 30 suppliers
- 'Thornhayes' CTho
farreri See *E. nanus*
fimbriatus Last listed 1997
fortunei CDul
- Blondy = CAbP CDoC CDul COtt EBee
  'Interbolwi'[PBR] (v) EBrP EBre ELan EMil ENot EPla
  GKir LBCl LBSe LBre LRHS MAsh
  MBBe MBar MBri MGos SBre
  SCoo SLim SPer SSta WBod WPyg
  WWeb WWes
- 'Canadale Gold' (v) CDoC CPri EBee ENot EPla ESis
  GEil LRHS MGos MWhi NBee
  NFai NHol SPer WWeb
- 'Coloratus' CBlo CLan EBee EHol ENot MBar
  MBlu NCut SLon SPer WDin
  WGwG WTro WWal
- 'Country Gold' CBlo
- 'Croftway' SCro
- 'Dart's Blanket' CBlo EGoo ELan ENot EPla MRav
  MWhi SLPl SSta WDin
* - 'Emerald Carpet' Last listed 1997
- 'Emerald Cushion' ENot NCut SPer WShe
- 'Emerald Gaiety' (v) ♀ More than 30 suppliers
- 'Emerald 'n' Gold' (v) ♀ More than 30 suppliers
- 'Emerald Surprise' LRHS MBri NHol NPro
- 'Gold Spot' See *E. fortunei* 'Sunspot'
- 'Gold Tip' See *E. fortunei* Golden Prince
§ - 'Golden Pillar' (v) EBee EHoe EHol EPla ERav ESis
  MDHE WCot
§ - Golden Prince CWSG EBee ENot EPla IOrc LRHS
  MBar MRav NFai NHol SLim SPer
  WGor WGwG WStI
- 'Harlequin' (v) CB&S COtt CWSG EBee EHoe
  ELan GOrc LBuc LHop LRHS
  MAsh MBar MBlu MGos MRav

  NPro SAga SIng SLim SMad SPer
  SRPl SSta WCot WFar WWal
  WWeb
- 'Highdown' EMon WWat
- 'Hort's Blaze' Last listed 1997
- 'Kewensis' CMHG CNic CPle EBee ENot EPfP
  MBar MRav MWat SAPC SArc
  SBod WCot WCru WWat
- 'Minimus' CBlo CTri EPla ESis LRHS MGos
  NFai NHol NPro SMrm SPan SPla
  WFar WPer
* - 'Minimus Variegatus' ECho SPlb
§ - var. *radicans* CPlN
- 'Sheridan Gold' EBee ECtt EHoe EPla MRav NHol
  SEas
- 'Silver Gem' See *E. fortunei* 'Variegatus'
- 'Silver Pillar' (v) EHoe ENot ERav ESis LRHS WFar
- 'Silver Queen' (v) ♀ More than 30 suppliers
- 'Sunshine' (v) CAbP CBlo ELan EPla LRHS MAsh
  NCut NPro
§ - 'Sunspot' (v) More than 30 suppliers
- 'Tustin' EPla SLPl
§ - 'Variegatus' CMHG ENot MBar NFor SPer
  SRms STre WCot WDin WPat
  WPyg
- 'Variegatus' EM '85 NSti
- var. *vegetus* EPla SPer
grandiflorus CPMA EPfP WWat
hamiltonianus CMCN SSpi
- 'Fiesta' Last listed 1997
- subsp. *hians* See *E. hamiltonianus* subsp.
  sieboldianus
- 'Indian Summer' EBee EPfP MBlu
- 'Red Elf' CPMA
§ - subsp. *sieboldianus* CDul CMCN CPMA CTho EBee
  EPfP GKir MRav SLPl SMrm SPan
  SRms
- - 'Coral Charm' CPMA SMrm SMur
- 'Winter Glory' CBlo CPMA EPfP LRHS WWes
- var. *yedoensis* See *E. hamiltonianus* subsp.
  sieboldianus
hibarimisake See *E. japonicus* 'Hibarimisake'
japonicus EBee ENot EPfP LRHS SAPC SArc
  SPer WDin
- 'Albomarginatus' CB&S CBlo CTri MBar NBrk SEND
  SRms WSHC WWeb
* - 'Argenteus Compactus' LPan
- 'Aureopictus' See *E. japonicus* 'Aureus'
- 'Aureovariegatus' See *E. japonicus* 'Ovatus Aureus'
§ - 'Aureus' (v) CB&S CBrm CDoC CMHG EBee
  ENot EPla ERav GOrc LPan LRHS
  MBri SEas SHFr SLon SMac SPer
  WDin WHar WWeb
- 'Bravo' CDoC EBee EGra EHoe EMil LRHS
  MBri NHol SPer
- 'Chedju' (v) WBcn
- 'Chollipo' CBlo ELan EPla LRHS MAsh
* - 'Compactus' LPan
- Thunb. 'Duc d'Anjou' CB&S EBrP EBre EHoe ELan EPla
  Carrière (v) ESis EWes LBCl LBSe LBre LPan
  MAsh MBBe SBre SDry SMad
- 'Duc d'Anjou' hort. See *E. japonicus* 'Viridivariegatus'
- 'Golden Maiden' CBlo ELan EPfP LRHS MAsh
- 'Golden Pillar' See *E. fortunei* 'Golden Pillar'
- 'Harvest Moon' Last listed 1999
§ - 'Hibarimisake' EPla SBla
§ - 'Latifolius EBee EHoe EHol EPfP EPla LRHS
  Albomarginatus' ♀ MNrw MRav SPer
- 'Luna' See *E. japonicus* 'Aureus'
- 'Macrophyllus Albus' See *E. japonicus* 'Latifolius
  Albomarginatus'
- 'Maiden's Gold' COtt

- 'Marieke' — See *E. japonicus* 'Ovatus Aureus'
- 'Mediopictus' — MBri
- 'Microphyllus' — CDoC EMil LCaP STre WGwG WShe
§ - 'Microphyllus Albovariegatus' — CDoC CLTr CMHG EBee ELan EMil EPfP EPla EPot LRHS MBar MBrN MGos MRav NHol SAga SBla SLim SLon SPla SRms SSca WCot WHCG WPat WPyg WSHC WStI WWat
§ - 'Microphyllus Aureovariegatus' — CBlo CDoC EMil LPan MWhi NHol SEas WPat WPyg WWin
- 'Microphyllus Aureus' — See *E. japonicus* 'Microphyllus Pulchellus'
§ - 'Microphyllus Pulchellus' (v) — CB&S CDoC CMHG EBee ENot EPfP EPla EPot LHop LRHS MBar MNrw MRav NDlv NHol SAga SEas WBod WHCG WPyg WWeb
- 'Microphyllus Variegatus' — See *E. japonicus* 'Microphyllus Albovariegatus'
§ - 'Ovatus Albus' (v) — EBee
§ - 'Ovatus Aureus' (v) ♀ — CChe CDoC CMHG CTri EBee ENot EPfP ESis LPan LRHS MBar MGos SEas SLim SPer SPlb SRPl SRms SWal WDin WPat WStI
- 'Président Gauthier' (v) — CDoC EBee LPan LRHS MGos NCut SPer WGer
- 'Pulchellus Aureovariegatus' — See *E. japonicus* 'Microphyllus Aureovariegatus'
- 'Robustus' — EPla
- 'Silver King' — CBlo WRHF
* - 'Silver Princess' — Last listed 1998
- 'Susan' — EBee EGra EPla
§ - 'Viridivariegatus' — GEil LRHS
kiautschovicus — CBrd EPla
latifolius — CMCN EPMA EPfP
- x *hamiltonianus* — Last listed 1997
macropterus — EPla
myrianthus — CBrd EPfP MBlu WCot WWat
§ *nanus* — CCHP CNic CPMA CPle EHol EMon EPla ESis MBlu MBro NHol WPyg
- var. *turkestanicus* — EPla ESis SPan SRms WWat
obovatus — Last listed 1999
oresbius — CPMA WPGP
oxyphyllus — CBrd CMCN CPMA EPfP GKir SLon WDin WMou WWat
§ *pendulus* — CGre CHEx
phellomanus — CDul EBee EPfP GDra GKir LNet LRHS MAsh MBNS MBar MBlu MBri SPan WDin WWat
¶ - 'Silver Surprise' (v) — CPMA
§ *planipes* ♀ — CDul CMHG CPle CTho CWit EBee ELan ENot EPfP EPla GChr GKir IMGH MBNS MBel MBlu MBri NHol NWea SPan SPer SSpi WCFE WNor WPGP WWat
radicans — See *E. fortunei* var. *radicans*
'Rokojõ' — CLyd MBro NWCA WPat
rosmarinifolius — See *E. nanus*
sachalinensis hort. — See *E. planipes*
sanguineus — CPMA EPfP
sp. B&L 12543 — EPla ESis EWes
tingens — CFil SLon WAbe WWat
velutinus — Last listed 1997
verrucosus — CPMA EPfP EPla WWes
yedoensis — See *E. hamiltonianus* subsp. *sieboldianus*

EUPATORIUM (Asteraceae)

§ *album* — CHad NBid WPer
- 'Braunlaub' — EBee EMan EMar EMon GKir LPio

LRHS MCli NSti SSpi
altissimum — CBot CGle EPar MSal SRms
- JLS 88029 — Last listed 1998
aromaticum — CArn CSev EBee LFis MBel MLLN MRav MWgw NBro NSti SPer SWat WCHb WPer WWye
cannabinum — CArn CKin ECoo EHon ELan EMFW EMar EOld EWFC GBar GGar GPoy MBNS MHer MHew MMal MRav MSal MSta NBir NMir NSti SRob SWat SWyc WCer WGwG WOak WPer WWye
- 'Album' — EMon
- 'Flore Pleno' (d) — CSev EBee ECGP ECha EFou EGar EGle EMan EMar EMon GCal LFis LRHS MBel MFir MLLN MRav MSph MSte NBrk NDov NSti SLon SWat WAlt WCot WWat
- 'Not Quite White' — WAlt
- 'Spraypaint' — CNat
capillifolium — CWit MLLN SAPC SAga SArc SDix SMrm WCot
- 'Elegant Feather' — CElw CSpe EMan EMar EWes MSCN SMad SUsu WTin
chinense — Last listed 1997
coelestinum — EMan
* *cyclophyllum* — EBee EBrP EBre LBCl LBSe LBre MBBe SBre
fistulosum — Last listed 1997
* - 'Atropurpureum' — WHil WPer
fortunei — CArn CPLG EMon
* - 'Variegatum' — EMan WCot
hyssopifolium — EBee
* - 'Bubba' — Last listed 1997
§ *ligustrinum* ♀ — CB&S CDoC CElw CLan CPle CTbh CTri CWit EBee ECha ELan EMan EPla GEil IOrc LGre LRHS SAga SDix SLim SMrm SPer SUsu WCHb WFar WHil WRus WSHC
maculatum — See *E. purpureum* subsp. *maculatum*
madrense — CLTr
micranthum — See *E. ligustrinum*
occidentale — Last listed 1999
perfoliatum — CAgr CArn GPoy MNrw MSal NCut WPer WWye
purpureum — More than 30 suppliers
- 'Album' — GKir LGre
¶ - 'Bartered Bride' — GKir
§ - subsp. *maculatum* — CSam EBrP EBre EMon GCal LBCl LBSe LBre LFis MBBe NLar SBre SSpi STes WPer
- - 'Album' — EMon EWTr NSti SUsu
- - 'Atropurpureum' ♀ — More than 30 suppliers
- - 'Berggarten' — GCal
- - 'Gateway' — CRow GCal
- - 'Glutball' — CHid SMad
- - 'Riesinschirm' — LGre LRHS MTed SMad SWat WElm
- 'Purple Bush' — CHad ECha LGre NBrk SUsu
rotundifolium — Last listed 1997
rugosum — CGle CSam EBrP EBre ELan EMar EOrc EPfP GBar LBCl LBSe LBre LEdu LGre MBBe MFir NLar SAga SBre SDys SPer WCHb
- *album* — See *E. album*
- 'Brunette' — Last listed 1999
- 'Chocolate' — More than 30 suppliers
* 'Snowball' — SMrm
§ *sordidum* — EMan ERav ERea GCal LHil SYvo
triplinerve — EGar MSte
* *variabile* 'Variegatum' — CHid EMan EPPr NSti WCot

weinmannianum — See *E. ligustrinum*

EUPHORBIA ✿ (Euphorbiaceae)

acanthothamnos — LGre
altissima — MSte SPan
'Amber Glow' — Last listed 1999
amygdaloides — CKin CRow EWFC GKir NWit SSpi WCer WWye
- 'Brithembottom' — CSam
- 'Craigieburn' — EBee EGle EMan EWes GBri GCal NDov SUsu
§ - 'Purpurea' — More than 30 suppliers
§ - var. *robbiae* ♀ — More than 30 suppliers
- - x *characias* — WCot
- - 'Pom Pom' — WCot
¶ - - 'Redbud' — EPla
- 'Rubra' — See *E. amygdaloides* 'Purpurea'
- 'Variegata' — GBuc
balsamifera — Last listed 1998
¶ *barrelieri* — NWit
biglandulosa — See *E. rigida*
¶ *boissieri* — EMon
brittingeri — EGar NWit
¶ - Baker's form — EPPr
broteroi — SPan WCot
canariensis — Last listed 1999
capitata — CLyd WPat
capitulata — ELan EWes MBro MTho NMen NWit SMrm WWin
ceratocarpa — EGar EWes GBuc NWit SMad SPan WCHb WOve WSHC
characias — More than 30 suppliers
- 'Amber Eye' — IBlr
- Ballyrogan hybrids — IBlr
- 'Black Pearl' — CDoC CFir CMil EFou GKir IArd NHol SPan SSvw WOVN
- 'Blue Wonder' — CDoC EBee EFou GBin GMaP
- subsp. *characias* ♀ — GAbr WCru
- - 'Blue Hills' — CLon EFou EGar EGle GBuc GCal IBlr SMrm SPan WRus
- - 'Burrow Silver' PBR (v) — CBot CRDP MLLN SCob SPar SWat
- - 'Green Mantle' — IBlr NWit
- - 'H.E. Bates' — NBir
- - 'Humpty Dumpty' — CMdw COtt EBee EBrP EBre EFou GKir GMaP LBCl LBSe LBre LRHS MBBe NPer SBre SChu SMad SMrm SPan SPer SSvw WCot WGer WHil WOVN WWhi
- - 'Percy Picton' — SPan
- - 'Perry's Winter Blusher' — ECtt NPer NWit
- dwarf — SMrm
- 'Forescate' — CSWP EBee EMil LRHS MChl MRav NGdn NHol SCro SMrm SPer SRPl WFar WGer WRus WSpi
- 'Goldbrook' — CM&M CSev EBee EMan LFis LRHS NPSI SPla SRPl SWat
- 'Golden Wonder' — IBlr
- JCA 475.500 — Last listed 1998
- 'Jenetta' — Last listed 1999
- 'Portuguese Velvet' — More than 30 suppliers
- 'Sombre Melody' — IBlr
- 'Spring Splendour' — EBee EWes NLar SPan
- 'Starbright' — EFou
- 'Variegata' — CRow SMad
- 'Whistleberry Gold' — LRHS
- 'Whistleberry Jade' — LRHS
- subsp. *wulfenii* ♀ — More than 30 suppliers
- - 'Bosahan' (v) — CB&S EGar SPan
- - 'Emmer Green' (v) — ECha EWes GBri MGrG SBla SWat WCDu WCot WFoF WRus
- - JCA 475.603 — Last listed 1999

- - 'Jimmy Platt' — MWll SRms SRob
§ - - 'John Tomlinson' ♀ — CBlo CMil EBee ECha EPla EWes MBro MSte MWll SChu SUsu WCot WEas WOve
- - Kew form — See *E. characias* subsp. *wulfenii* 'John Tomlinson'
- - 'Lambrook Gold' ♀ — CMHG CRow CSam EBee ECtt EGar EGle EPar LRHS MBri MBro MRav MWat NPer SPan SVal WCot WGer WHoo WPyg WRus WWat
- - 'Lambrook Yellow' — EMon GBuc LPio SMur SVal WSPU
- - Margery Fish Group — CDoC EBee EFou EGle EMan EPla LRHS MCLN MFir MLLN NCat NPSI SMrm SPer SWat
- - 'Minuet' — Last listed 1997
- - 'Perry's Tangerine' — EWes NPer
§ - - 'Purple and Gold' — CMil CPou EWes MGrG NDov SBla SPan WCot WRus
- - 'Purpurea' — See *E. characias* subsp. *wulfenii* 'Purple and Gold'
- - var. *sibthorpii* — SPan WCot
'Charam' PBR — See *E.* Redwing = 'Charam'
clava — GBin
clavarioides var. *truncata* — EBee WCot
cognata — ECGN NWit
- CC&McK 607 — EWes GCHN
- CC&McK 724 — EBee GBin
confinalis — GBin
conifera — Last listed 1998
corallioides — EBee EBrP EBre ECha EGar ELan EMan EPPr IBlr LBCl LBSe LBre LRHS MBBe NFai NFla NPer NPri NSti SBre SHFr SPer SRCN SSca WBrE WHer WLin
§ *cornigera* — More than 30 suppliers
- CC 720 — CPou
corollata — Last listed 1998
cylindrica — Last listed 1998
cyparissias — More than 30 suppliers
- 'Baby' — WFar
- 'Betten' — See *E.* x *gayeri* 'Betten'
- 'Bushman Boy' — EGar GBri IBlr
- 'Clarice Howard' — See *E. cyparissias* 'Fens Ruby'
- clone 2 — Last listed 1999
§ - 'Fens Ruby' — More than 30 suppliers
- 'Orange Man' — EBee ECoo EFou EGar EMon EWes GBin GBri IBlr LRHS MBro MHer NBrk NHol NSti SPan SPla SWat WElm WGer
- 'Purpurea' — See *E. cyparissias* 'Fens Ruby'
- red — SPan
- 'Red Devil' — CBre IBlr NCat NWit SChu WOve
- 'Tall Boy' — EGar EMar EMon EWes GBri IBlr LRHS SPan
dendroides — GBin
§ *donii* — EGle ELan EWes IBlr NWit SDix SVal
dulcis — CElw CGle CRow ECha ECtt EFou ELan EPar NBrk NBro NHex NOak NSti SMac WByw WHen WWat
- 'Chameleon' — More than 30 suppliers
I - 'Nana' — CBlo EWll GBin NHol
epithymoides — See *E. polychroma*
§ *erubescens* — Last listed 1999
esula — CGle
¶ - Baker's form — NWit
§ Excalibur = 'Froeup' PBR — EBee ELan EMan GBin LHop LRHS LRot MBri MCCP MLan MTis NEgg NFor NSti SPan SPla SSpi SVil

fasciculata — Last listed 1998
fimbriata — Last listed 1998

'Froeup'^PBR See *E.* Excalibur = 'Froeup'
fulgens CHal
'Garblesham Enchanter' EPPr
§ x *gayeri* 'Betten' EMan GCal
'Giant Green Turtle' CMil
glauca CFee IBlr WCot
'Golden Foam' See *E. stricta*
griffithii CFri CRow GKir NBrk NBro NCat
  SSpi SWat WAbb WGer
- 'Dixter' ♀ More than 30 suppliers
¶ - 'Dixter Flame' NWit
- 'Fern Cottage' CElw CRDP EFou EWes GAbr
  SMrm SPan SUsu WHal
- 'Fireglow' More than 30 suppliers
- 'King's Caple' EGar NWit
- 'Robert Poland' CSWP
- 'Wickstead' EBee EGar LRHS SMrm WViv
* *hiemale* Last listed 1997
horrida Last listed 1998
hyberna EBee GBri IBlr MLLN NMen NWit
  SWat WLin
ingens GBin
jacquemontii EBee EMan LPio NWit WWat
x *keysii* MBri
lathyris CRow EBlw ELan EMar ERav
  EWFC MHer MHew NBid NCat
  NHex NPer SIde SMad SRms SSoC
  WEas WWye
leucocephala GBin
longifolia D. Don See *E. donii*
- Lamarck See *E. mellifera*
- hort. See *E. cornigera*
macrostegia See *E. erubescens*
mammillaris Last listed 1998
x *martinii* ♀ More than 30 suppliers
- 'Red Dwarf' CElw EOrc SPan
melanocarpa CEnd
§ *mellifera* More than 30 suppliers
meloformis Last listed 1998
milii ♀ CHal EBak SRms SVal
- 'Koenigers Aalbäumle' MBri
* 'Variegata' CHal
¶ - yellow CHal
monteiroi Last listed 1998
myrsinites ♀ More than 30 suppliers
nereidum EWes NWit
nicaeensis CFil EBee EMan EOrc GCal LGre
  LHop LRHS MLLN SCro SMrm
  SPer SSpi SUsu WCot WPGP WWat
¶ - subsp. *glareosa* NWit
oblongata CB&S CFil EBee EBrP EBre ELan
  EMan EMon EWes GBuc IBlr LBCl
  LBSe LBre LRHS MBBe SBre
  WCHb WWat
¶ - DJH 200.651 WPGP
obtusifolia Last listed 1998
palustris ♀ More than 30 suppliers
- 'Walenburg's Glorie' EBee EGar EWTr GBin LRHS MBri
  MRav NBrk SMad SPan SUsu SWat
  WCot
- 'Zauberflöte' SRms SRob
¶ x *paradoxa* NWit
¶ *paralias* NWit
pekinensis MSal NWit
pilosa Last listed 1999
- 'Major' See *E. polychroma* 'Major'
pithyusa CBot CGle EBee ECha EGar ELan
  EMan EMon LHop MArl MLLN
  MSCN NFla SBla SPan WCot
  WOve WRus WWat WWhi
§ *polychroma* ♀ More than 30 suppliers
- 'Candy' More than 30 suppliers

- 'Emerald Jade' EBee GBri IBlr
§ - 'Lacy' (v) CDoC CMil CSpe CStr EBee EGle
  ELan EMan ERav EWes LRHS
  MCCP MGrG MMil NBir SMad
  SPan SPla SUsu WCot WHer WHil
  WSan
§ - 'Major' ♀ CMHG EBrP EBre ECha ELan EPPr
  GCal LBCl LBSe LBre LGre LPio
  LRHS MBBe NCat SAga SBre SPan
  SPer WCot WEas
- 'Midas' CFee EGle NWit SMrm
- 'Orange Flush' NWit WHoo
- 'Purpurea' See *E. polychroma* 'Candy'
* - 'Senior' Last listed 1999
- 'Sonnengold' EGar EWes GCal LRHS MBro
  WHoo WPyg WSHC
- 'Variegata' See *E. polychroma* 'Lacy'
portlandica CNic EMar GBin MBri NWit WHer
§ x *pseudovirgata* EMan IBlr LHop NWit SPan
pugniformis MBri
pulcherrima LRHS MBri
'Purple Preference' EPPr
§ Redwing = 'Charam'^PBR EBee ELan EMan ENot LPan LRHS
  MRav NSti SCoo SPer WGer
reflexa See *E. seguieriana* subsp.
  niciciana
resinifera Last listed 1998
§ *rigida* CBot CBro CFil CMil EBee ECGN
  EGle EMan EPfP EWes GCal MLLN
  SBla SMrm WCot WPGP WSHC
¶ - 'Sardis' NWit
robbiae See *E. amygdaloides* var. *robbiae*
sarawschanica EBee LGre NWit SMrm WCot
schillingii ♀ More than 30 suppliers
schoenlandii Last listed 1998
seguieriana EBee ECha EMan ERav GBin NLar
  SUsu
§ - subsp. *niciciana* CBot CGle CMHG EBee ECha
  ELan EMon ERav IBlr MArl MBro
  MLLN NBir SBla SDix SMrm SUsu
  WCra WEas WHoo WPGP WRus
  WWat
serrulata See *E. stricta*
sikkimensis More than 30 suppliers
soongarica MSte NWit
spinosa SMad
§ *stricta* CRow EBee ECha ELan EMan
  GBri IBlr MCCP MCLN MFir NArg
  NBro NCat NSti WElm WWat
stygiana CFil CTrF NWit SAga
* *submammillaris* MBri
  'Variegata'
susannae Last listed 1998
terracina WCot
transvaalensis Last listed 1998
uralensis See *E. x pseudovirgata*
villosa GBin MBro NWit
§ *virgata* EMFP EWes NSti NWit SPan
  WCHb WCot
'Virgile' Last listed 1998
x *waldsteinii* See *E. virgata*
wallichii Kohli See *E. cornigera*
- Hook.f. CSam EBrP EBre EMan IBlr LBCl
  LBSe LBre LRHS MBBe MBri NFla
  NOrc SBre SMrm SSoC WAbb
  WHil WWat
- misapplied See *E. donii*
* 'Welsh Dragon' Last listed 1997
zoutpansbergensis Last listed 1998

EUPTELEA (Eupteleaceae)
franchetii See *E. pleiosperma*

§ *pleiosperma*   EPfP SSpi
  polyandra   CFil CGre WPGP

EURYA (Theaceae)
  japonica   CCHP CFil WPGP
  - 'Variegata' misapplied   See *Cleyera japonica* 'Fortunei'

EURYOPS (Asteraceae)
  abrotanifolius   EBee LHil SVen
§ *acraeus* ♀   CBot CHea CPle ELan EPot GCHN
                             GTou LBee LHop LRHS MBro
                             MWat NFor NMen NWCA SBla
                             SIng WAbe WWin
  candollei   CTrC WAbe WCot
§ *chrysanthemoides*   CB&S CMHG CPne CSam EBee
                             ERav ERea IBlr LHil MMil MSte
                             WPer
  decumbens   NMen NSla
  aff. *decumbens*   NWCA
    JJ&JH 9401309
  evansii   See *E. acraeus*
  grandiflorus   Last listed 1997
  pectinatus ♀   CB&S CDoC CHEx CInt CMHG
                             CSam CSev CTrG ERea GGar IBlr
                             LHil LRHS MBlu MFir MLLN
                             MNrw MRav SBrw SDry SMrm
                             SOWG SPar SYvo WCFE WEas
                             WHer WPer WWye
  'Sonnesheim'   CHal WWol
  speciosissimus   Last listed 1997
  tysonii   CPle EWes GGar WCot
  virgineus   CB&S CTrC EBee GGar IBlr SVen

EUSTEPHIA (Amaryllidaceae)
  jujuyensis   Last listed 1997

EUSTOMA (Gentianaceae)
§ *grandiflorum*   LRHS MBri
  russellianum   See *E. grandiflorum*

EUSTREPHUS (Philesiaceae)
  latifolius   CPIN ECou

EUTERPE (Arecaceae)
  edulis   LPal

EVOLVULUS (Convolvulaceae)
  convolvuloides   ERea
  glomeratus 'Blue Daze'   See *E. pilosus* 'Blue Daze'
§ *pilosus* 'Blue Daze'   ERea SSad

EWARTIA (Asteraceae)
  nubigena   Last listed 1999
  planchonii   NLAp SOkd WAbe

EXACUM (Gentianaceae)
  affine   LRHS MBri
  - 'Rococo'   MBri

EXOCHORDA (Rosaceae)
  alberti   See *E. korolkowii*
  giraldii   CBlo CBrm CPle
  - var. *wilsonii*   CBlo CSam EBee EBrP EBre EPfP
                             GEil GKir GOrc LBCl LBSe LBre
                             LHop LRHS MAsh MBBe MBNS
                             MBlu MBri SBre SEas SSpi SSta
§ *korolkowii*   CGre
  x *macrantha*   GOrc WAbe
  - 'The Bride' ♀   More than 30 suppliers
  racemosa   CGre EHol ISea LHop MGos
                             MWhi NLar SPer SRPl WHCG
¶ *serratifolia*   EPfP

- 'Snow White'   CPMA MBlu

F

FABIANA (Solanaceae)
  imbricata   CAbP CDoC CLan EBee EMil EPfP
                             GKir GQui LRHS MAsh MBar
                             MBel SAga SBra SBrw SLon SPan
                             SPer WAbe
  - 'Prostrata'   EBee EPVP EPfP GCal LRHS SBrw
                             SDry SPer SSpi WWat WWin
  - f. *violacea* ♀   CB&S CFee CGre CTri EBee EMil
                             EPfP EPla ESis GQui LRHS MBar
                             SAga SBrw SPan SPer WKif WSHC

FAGOPYRUM (Polygonaceae)
  cymosum   See *F. dibotrys*
§ *dibotrys*   EBee ELan LEdu NSti

FAGUS ✿ (Fagaceae)
§ *crenata*   CMCN WNor
  - 'Mount Fuji'   MBlu
  engleriana   CBlo CMCN
  grandifolia   CMCN LPan
  - var. *caroliniana*   CLyn
  japonica   CMCN LRHS
  lucida   CMCN
  orientalis   CMCN CTho LRHS
  sieboldii   See *F. crenata*
  sylvatica ♀   More than 30 suppliers
§ - 'Albomarginata'   CDul CMCN GKir IOrc MBlu
                             SMHT
  - 'Albovariegata'   See *F. sylvatica* 'Albomarginata'
  - 'Ansorgei'   CDul CEnd CLnd CMCN GKir
                             LRHS MBlu MBri
¶ - 'Argenteomarmorata'   CDul
N - Atropurpurea Group   More than 30 suppliers
  - - 'Swat Magret'   LPan SMad
  - 'Aurea Pendula'   CEnd CMCN MBlu SMad
  - 'Birr Zebra'   CEnd
  - 'Black Swan'   CBlo CDul CEnd CMCN GChr
                             LPan LRHS MBlu MBri SLim SMad
                             WGer WGor
  - 'Bornyensis'   CMCN
  - 'Cochleata'   CMCN LRHS
  - 'Cockleshell'   CDul CMCN CTho GKir LRHS
                             MBri
  - 'Comptoniifolia'   See *F. sylvatica* var. *heterophylla*
                             'Comptoniifolia'
  - 'Cristata'   CDul CMCN GAri MBlu
N - Cuprea Group   NWea
  - 'Dawyck' ♀   More than 30 suppliers
  - 'Dawyck Gold' ♀   CAbP CB&S CBlo CDoC CDul
                             CEnd CMCN COtt CTho EBee
                             GChr GKir IOrc LPan LRHS MAsh
                             MBar MBlu MBri NBea NWea
                             SLim SMad SPer SSpi WOrn
  - 'Dawyck Purple' ♀   CAbP CBlo CDoC CDul CEnd
                             CMCN COtt CTho GChr GKir
                             IOrc LPan LRHS MAsh MBar MBlu
                             MBri MGos NBea NWea SCrf SLim
                             SMad SPer SSpi WOrn
  - 'Fastigiata' misapplied See *F. sylvatica* 'Dawyck'
  - 'Felderbach'   CLyn LRHS MBlu
  - 'Franken' (v)   MBlu SMad
  - 'Frisio'   CEnd CMCN
  - 'Grandidentata'   CMCN LPan LRHS
  - 'Greenwood'   CDul LRHS MBlu
* - 'Haaren'   CMCN LRHS

* - 'Haven'	Last listed 1998
- var. *heterophylla*	CBlo CLnd CTho GAri ISea NWea WOrn
- - 'Aspleniifolia' ♀	CDoC CDul CEnd CMCN COtt EBee ELan EMil ENot EPfP EPla GKir IOrc LPan LRHS MAsh MBar MBri SLim SPer WDin WMou WNor
§ - - 'Comptoniifolia'	CMCN
- - f. *laciniata*	CMCN GKir LRHS MBlu
- 'Horizontalis'	CLyn CMCN
- 'Interrupta'	SMad
- 'Luteovariegata'	CEnd CMCN
- 'Mercedes'	CDul CLyn CMCN GKir LRHS MBlu MBri
- 'Miltonensis'	CDul CMCN LRHS
N - 'Pendula' ♀	CB&S CBlo CDoC CDul CEnd CLnd CMCN CTho ELan ENot EWTr GChr GKir IOrc LPan MBar NWea SMad SPer WDin WHar WMou WOrn WPyg WStl
- 'Prince George of Crete'	CDul CEnd CMCN CTho GKir LRHS
- 'Purple Fountain' ♀	CBlo CDoC CEnd CMCN COtt EBee ELan EMil IOrc LPan LRHS MAsh MBar MBlu MBri MGos MWhi NBee SLim SPer WPyg WWeb
- Purple-leaved Group	See *F. sylvatica* Atropurpurea Group
- 'Purpurea Nana'	CMCN LRHS
- 'Purpurea Pendula'	CDul CEnd CMCN CTho EBee ELan ENot GChr IOrc LPan LRHS MAsh MBar MBlu MGos MWat NWea SLim SPer WDin WHar WPyg WStl
§ - 'Purpurea Tricolor' (v)	CBlo CDoC CEnd CMCN EWTr GChr GKir IOrc LPan LRHS MBar MGos NBea NBee SLim SMer SPer WDin WPyg
- 'Quercifolia'	CDul CMCN GKir
I - 'Quercina'	CMCN LRHS
- 'Red Obelisk'	CDul CMCN LPan MBlu
- 'Remillyensis'	CMCN
- 'Riversii' ♀	CB&S CBlo CDoC CDul CEnd CLnd CMCN CTho EBee ELan EMil ENot IOrc LPan LRHS MAsh MBri MGos NWea SLim SMer SPer SSta WDin WHar WOrn WStl
- 'Rohan Gold'	CDul CEnd CMCN EBee GKir LPan LRHS MBlu MBri
- 'Rohan Obelisk'	CEnd EBee IArd LRHS MBlu
I - 'Rohan Pyramidalis'	CDul CEnd CMCN LRHS
- 'Rohan Trompenburg'	CMCN LRHS MBlu
- 'Rohanii'	CAbP CB&S CBlo CDoC CDul CEnd CLnd CMCN COtt CTho EBee ECrN ELan EMil EWTr IMGH IOrc LRHS MBlu NBee SLim SPer WDin WOrn
- 'Roseomarginata'	See *F. sylvatica* 'Purpurea Tricolor'
- 'Rotundifolia'	CDoC CTho NWea
- 'Silver Wood'	CMCN LRHS MBlu
- 'Spaethiana'	CMCN LRHS
- 'Striata'	CMCN
- 'Tortuosa Purpurea'	CMCN CTho MBlu
- 'Tricolor' (v)	CB&S CCHP CDul CLnd EBee ELan EWTr MAsh SLim WDin
- 'Tricolor' misapplied	See *F. sylvatica* 'Purpurea Tricolor'
- 'Viridivariegata'	CMCN
- 'Zlatia'	CB&S CBlo CDoC CDul CLnd CMCN COtt CTho EBee ELan

ENot GKir IOrc LPan LRHS MBar MBri MGos NBee SLim SPer WDin WOrn WStl

FALKIA (Convolvulaceae)

¶ *repens*	CFir

FALLOPIA (Polygonaceae)

aubertii	See *F. baldschuanica*
§ *baldschuanica* ♀	More than 30 suppliers
¶ - Summer Sunshine = 'Acofal'	NEgg
x *bohemica*	CHEx CRow WCot
'Spectabilis' (v)	
§ *japonica*	CRow
§ - var. *compacta*	CRow EBee EPfP NLar NPri SMrm WBea WFar WMoo WPnP
* - - 'Midas'	IBlr
¶ - - f. *rosea*	WWeb
I - - 'Variegata'	CRow EMan EWes IBlr SMad
- 'Crimson Beauty'	CRow
§ *multiflora*	CArn EOHP MSal
- var. *hypoleuca* B&SWJ 120	GOrP WCot WCru
sachalinensis	CHEx CRow EBee EWes

FARFUGIUM (Asteraceae)

§ *japonicum*	CHEx MTho
- 'Argenteum' (v)	CFir CHEx WCot WFar WHal WHil WSan
- 'Aureomaculatum' (v) ♀	CAbb CBos CFir CHEx EBrP EBre EGar EHoe LBCl LBSe LBre LHil MBBe MSCN MTho SBre SLod SMad SWat WCot WFar WHal WHer WHil WMul WSan
- 'Crispatum'	CAbb CBos CFir CHid EBee EMan GCal MTPN MTed NChi NCut SMad SWat WCDu WCot WFar WHil WPrP WSpi
- 'Kinkan' (v)	WCot
tussilagineum	See *F. japonicum*

FARGESIA (Poaceae - Bambusoideae)

¶ *contracta*	EPla
denudata	EPla
dracocephala	CCtw CDoC CFil EPfP EPla GCal ISta LJus MMoz MWht SDry WCru WJun WNor WPGP
¶ *frigida*	EPla
fungosa	CFil ISta WJun WPGP
§ *murieliae* ♀	More than 30 suppliers
* - *dana*	Last listed 1998
- 'Harewood'	GBin MCCP MMoz
- 'Jumbo'	EMil EPfP EPla GBin ISta LRHS MCCP MMoz MWht WJun
§ - 'Leda' (v)	SDry
- 'Simba'	More than 30 suppliers
§ *nitida* ♀	More than 30 suppliers
- 'Anceps'	EPla
- 'Eisenach'	CFil EPla ISta LRHS MMoz WCru
¶ - from Jiuzhaigou, China	EPla
- 'Nymphenburg'	CPMA EPla GKir GOrc ISta LPan LRHS MMoz MWhi NPri
¶ - 'Wakehurst'	EPla
robusta	EFul EPfP EPla ISta LJus MMoz MWht SDry SLPl WJun WNor
- 'Red Sheath'	EPla ERod MMoz WJun
rufa	EPla ISta WJun WNor
spathacea hort.	See *F. murieliae*
utilis	CAbb CDDB EPla ERod ISta LJus MMoz SDry WJun WNor
yulongshanensis	CFil EPla WPGP

FARSETIA (Commelinaceae)
clypeata — See *Fibigia clypeata*

FASCICULARIA (Bromeliaceae)
andina — See *F. bicolor*
§ *bicolor* — CFil CFir CGre CHEx EBak ECre EGra EWes GCal GGar IBlr LHil LHop MFir NPer SAPC SArc SChr SSpi SSta WAbe WBor WCot WEas WGer WPic
§ - subsp. *canaliculata* — CFil LEdu WPGP
kirchhoffiana — See *F. bicolor* subsp. *canaliculata*
pitcairniifolia hort. — See *F. bicolor*

x FATSHEDERA (Araliaceae)
lizei ♀ — CB&S CBot CDoC CHEx EBee EPVP EPla GKir GQui IBlr LRHS MBri MGrG MWat NRog SArc SBra SDix SDry SLon SMac SPer SPla SPlb SSoC WCFE WDin WWal WWat
§ - 'Annemieke' (v) ♀ — CBot CHEx CSWP EPfP EPla IBlr MBri SBra SMac SMad SPer
§ - 'Aurea' (v) — EPfP LRHS SBra SDry SEND
- 'Aureopicta' — See x *F. lizei* 'Aurea'
- 'Lemon and Lime' — See x *F. lizei* 'Annemieke'
- 'Maculata' — See x *F. lizei* 'Annemieke'
- 'Pia' — CSWP LRHS MBri
* - 'Silver Prusca' — EPla
- 'Variegata' ♀ — CB&S CMHG ELan EPfP IBlr LRHS MBri MGrG SBra SDry SEND SMer SPer SPla WFar WWat

FATSIA (Araliaceae)
§ *japonica* ♀ — More than 30 suppliers
- 'Variegata' ♀ — CB&S CBot EPVP EPla LRHS MBri MGos SArc SPer
papyrifera — See *Tetrapanax papyrifer*

FAUCARIA (Aizoaceae)
tigrina — MBri

FAURIA See NEPHROPHYLLIDIUM

FEIJOA See ACCA

FELICIA (Asteraceae)
§ *amelloides* — CHEx CHal CLTr ERea ESis LRHS SChu SRms
- 'Astrid Thomas' — CSam CSpe LHil
- 'Read's Blue' — CHad CSev CSpe LHil LIck
- 'Read's White' — ERea GMac LHil MSte WEas
§ - 'Santa Anita' ♀ — CHal CSev CTri ECtt EOrc ERea LHil LIck SCro WEas
- 'Santa Anita' large flowered — LHil
- 'Santa Anita Variegated' ♀ — Last listed 1996
§ - variegated — ECtt ERea IBlr LHil LIck MBNS MBri MSte NPer SHFr SPar SRms SUsu WEas
- variegated, white flower — LIck
amethystina — See *F.* 'Snowmass'
§ *amoena* — CCHP CHEx CHal CInt CTri LHil MHar NCiC SRms
- 'Variegata' — CTri EOrc NCiC SChu SIng
bergeriana — Last listed 1998
capensis — See *F. amelloides*
- 'Variegata' — See *F. amelloides* variegated
coelestis — See *F. amelloides*
drakensbergensis — NTow
¶ *erigeroides* — CHal

filifolia — CTrC SPan
natalensis — See *F. rosulata*
pappei — See *F. amoena*
§ *petiolata* — ECha EMan ERea IBlr LHil NSti SGar SSpi WCot WWin
§ *rosulata* — EBee EMan EMon ESis GKir MHer MTho NBro NMen NNrd SRms SSmi WWin
§ 'Snowmass' — Last listed 1997
uliginosa — CFee CMHG CMea EDAr EWes GCrs GGar GTou LRHS MDHE MTho

FERRARIA (Iridaceae)
§ *crispa* — LBow
uncinata — Last listed 1998
undulata — See *F. crispa*

FERREYRANTHUS (Asteraceae)
excelsus — Last listed 1998

FERULA (Apiaceae)
assa-foetida — CArn EBee MSal
chiliantha — See *F. communis* subsp. *glauca*
§ *communis* — CArn CHad CRDP CSpe EBee ECha GKir IHdy LEdu LGre NBid NChi NLar NSti SDix SMad SMrm WCot WHal
- 'Gigantea' — See *F. communis*
- subsp. *glauca* — CMil EBee SDix SRCN WCot WPGP WSHC
'Giant Bronze' — See *Foeniculum vulgare* 'Giant Bronze'
tingitana — Last listed 1999
* - 'Cedric Morris' — EBee ECha

FESTUCA (Poaceae)
alpina — Last listed 1997
amethystina — CBrm CCuc EBee EHoe EMon EPPr EPla EPot ESis EWsh GBin GBri LHrt LRHS MBri MBro MCLN MNrw MWhi NCiC NHol NOak NVic SBea SPer WPer
- 'Aprilgrün' — EHoe
- 'Bronzeglanz' — Last listed 1997
ampla — Last listed 1997
arundinacea — CKin EWTr
californica — Last listed 1997
¶ *cinerea* — CStr
curvula subsp. *crassifolia* — EPPr EPla NHol
dalmatica — Last listed 1997
dumetorum — Last listed 1997
elatior 'Demeter' — Last listed 1997
elegans — EPPr
erecta — EHoe EPPr EPla
eskia — CCuc EBee EHoe EPPr EPla ESis GAri GKir GOrn LRHS MWhi NCut NEgg NHol SPer SVil WCot WPer
extremiorientalis — Last listed 1997
filiformis — EHoe EMon EPPr LRHS
¶ 'Fromefield Blue' — EHul
§ *gautieri* — CCuc ELan EPPr EPfP GBin GIBF LHil MBar MBrN NOrc SCob SPer WFoF
- 'Pic Carlit' — EMon EPPr
gigantea — CKin GBin
glacialis — EHoe NHol
- 'Czakor' — Last listed 1997
glauca — More than 30 suppliers
I - 'Auslese' — EWTr NCut WBar

- 'Azurit'	EHoe EMon EPPr EPla EWes LRHS NHol SCob
§ - 'Blaufuchs' ♀	More than 30 suppliers
§ - 'Blauglut'	EBee EBrP EBre EGar EHoe EHul EOrc EPGN EPla GAri GKir LBCl LBSe LBre LRHS MBBe MWgw NFla NHar NHol SBre SCob SHel WGer WLRN
- Blue Fox	See F. glauca 'Blaufuchs'
- Blue Glow	See F. glauca 'Blauglut'
- 'Elijah Blue'	More than 30 suppliers
- 'Golden Toupee'	More than 30 suppliers
- 'Harz'	CBrm CCuc EBee EBrP EBre EGar EHoe EMil EMon EPla GKir IBlr LBCl LBSe LBre MAnH MBBe MBar NBea SBre SCob WPnP
§ - 'Meerblau'	CCuc
* *minima*	ESis WPGP
- 'Pallens'	See F. longifolia
- Sea Blue	See F. glauca 'Meerblau'
- Sea Urchin	See F. glauca 'Seeigel'
§ - 'Seeigel'	CBrm CCuc EBee EBrP EBre EGar EGle EHoe EPPr EPla GKir LBCl LBSe LBre LHil MAvo MBBe MBel MBri MMoz NPro SAga SBre SCob SHel
- Select	See F. glauca 'Auslese'
- 'Seven Seas'	See F. valesiaca 'Silbersee'
- 'Silberreiher'	EBee EPPr
heterophylla	Last listed 1997
* *hogar*	EHoe
idahoensis	EPPr
juncifolia	Last listed 1997
§ *longifolia*	CKin EPPr
mairei	CCuc CLTr EHoe EMon EPPr IBlr LRHS WDyG
novae-zelandiae	GBin NNor
ovina	CBrm EHoe NOrc SPla WPer
- subsp. *coxii*	EHoe
I - 'Kulturform'	EBee
- 'Söhrewald'	EPPr
* - 'Tetra Gold'	GKir SAga
paniculata	EGle EHoe EMon EPla GOrn LRHS
pulchella	EBee EPPr
punctoria	CBrm CCuc CMea EBee ECha EHoe EMon EPPr EWsh MRav NHar SDys SIng SSmi
rubra 'Jughandles'	Last listed 1998
- var. *nankotaizanensis* B&SWJ 3190	EBee WCru
- 'Variegata'	Last listed 1998
- var. *viridis*	NHol
sclerophylla	Last listed 1997
scoparia	See F. gautieri
sp. B&SWJ 1555	Last listed 1998
¶ *tatrae*	CBrm GBin
tenuifolia	CKin
valesiaca	GOrn WFar
- var. *glaucantha*	EGra EPPr LPan LRHS MBri
§ - 'Silbersee'	CCuc CInt CSam EBee ECha EFou EHoe EPPr EPla ESis EWsh IBlr LRHS MBar MBri MCLN MNrw MSte NBee NCat NHol NOak SCob SIng SRms WFar
- Silver Sea	See F. valesiaca 'Silbersee'
¶ *violacea*	WRos
vivipara	CCuc CInt EGoo EHoe EMon EPPr LEdu LRHS NBid NHol
* 'Willow Green'	CBlo CBod MSte SCob SPlb

FIBIGIA (Brassicaceae)

§ *clypeata*	Last listed 1999

¶ - 'Select'	NArg
¶ *triquetra*	EBee

FICUS ✿ (Moraceae)

¶ *afghanistanica*	ERea
australis hort.	See F. rubiginosa 'Australis'
benghalensis	MBri
benjamina ♀	CHal EBrP EBre LBCl LBSe LBre LRHS MBBe MBri SBre SRms
- 'Exotica'	LRHS MBri
- 'Golden King'	LRHS MBri
- var. *nuda*	Last listed 1999
- 'Starlight' (v)	LRHS MBri
I *binnendijkii* 'Alii'	CHal
¶ *capitola* 'Long'	ERea
carica (F)	CHEx GAri LHyr LPan MBri SArc
¶ - 'Abbey Slip' (F)	CHEx
- 'Adam' (F)	ERea
- 'Alma' (F)	ERea
- 'Angélique' (F)	ERea
- 'Beall' (F)	ERea
- 'Bellone' (F)	ERea
- 'Bifère' (F)	ERea
- 'Black Ischia' (F)	ERea
¶ - 'Black Jack' (F)	ESim
- 'Black Mission' (F)	ERea
- 'Boule d'Or' (F)	ERea
- 'Bourjassotte Grise' (F)	ERea SDea
- 'Breva' (F)	CGOG
- 'Brown Turkey' (F) ♀	More than 30 suppliers
- 'Brunswick' (F)	CGre EBee ERea GBon GTwe LRHS MCCP MCoo SLim WCot
- 'Castle Kennedy' (F)	ERea GTwe
- 'Col de Dame' (F)	ERea
- 'Conandria' (F)	ERea
§ - 'Desert King' (F)	ESim
- 'Figue d'Or' (F)	ERea
- 'Goutte d'Or' (F)	ERea
- 'Grise de Saint Jean' (F)	ERea
- 'Grise Ronde' (F)	ERea
- 'Grosse Grise' (F)	ERea
- 'Kaape Bruin' (F)	ERea
- 'Kadota' (F)	ERea
- 'King' (F)	See F. carica 'Desert King'
- 'Lisa' (F)	ERea
- 'Longue d'Août' (F)	ERea
- 'Malcolm's Giant' (F)	ERea
- 'Malta' (F)	ERea
- 'Marseillaise' (F)	ERea GTwe SDea
- 'Negro Largo' (F)	ERea
¶ - 'Newlyn Harbour' (F)	CHEx
- 'Noir de Provence'	See F. carica 'Reculver'
- 'Osborn's Prolific' (F)	ERea
- 'Palmata'	Last listed 1999
- 'Panachée' (F)	ERea
- 'Pastilière' (F)	ERea
¶ - 'Peter's Honey' (F)	ERea
- 'Petite Grise' (F)	ERea
- 'Pied de Boeuf' (F)	ERea
- 'Pittaluse' (F)	ERea
- 'Précoce Ronde de Bordeaux' (F)	ERea
§ - 'Reculver' (F)	ERea
- 'Rouge de Bordeaux' (F)	ERea SDea
- 'Saint Johns' (F)	ERea
- 'San Pedro Miro' (F)	ERea
¶ - 'Snowden' (F)	ERea
- 'Sollies Pont' (F)	ERea
- 'Sugar 12' (F)	ERea
- 'Sultane' (F)	ERea
- 'Tena' (F)	ERea
¶ - 'Troiano' (F)	ERea

¶ - 'Trojano' (F)   ERea
- 'Verte d'Argenteuil' (F)   ERea
- 'Violette Dauphine' (F)   ERea
- 'Violette de Sollies' (F)   ERea
- 'Violette Sepor' (F)   ERea
- 'White Genoa'   See *F. carica* 'White Marseilles'
- 'White Ischia' (F)   ERea
§ - 'White Marseilles' (F)   CCHP EPfP ERea LRHS MCoo
    SDea
    cyathistipula   MBri
    deltoidea   MBri
    var. *diversifolia*
    elastica   LRHS SEND
- 'Robusta'   MBri
- 'Schrijveriana' (v) ♀   Last listed 1991
    foveolata Wallich   See *F. sarmentosa*
    lyrata ♀   MBri
    microcarpa   STre
- 'Hawaii' (v)   CHal
    natalensis subsp.   Last listed 1999
      leprieurii 'Westland'
    pumila ♀   CB&S CHEx CHal EBak LRHS
    MBri SAPC SArc
- 'Minima'   CFee
- 'Sonny' (v)   CHal MBri
- 'Variegata'   CHEx CHal MBri WCot
    radicans 'Variegata'   See *F. sagittata* 'Variegata'
    rubiginosa ♀   Last listed 1994
§ - 'Australis'   MBri
- 'Variegata'   CHal
§ *sagittata* 'Variegata'   MBri
§ *sarmentosa*   MBri

FILIPENDULA ✿ (Rosaceae)
    alnifolia 'Variegata'   See *F. ulmaria* 'Variegata'
    camtschatica   CFir CMCo CRow EBee ECoo
    ELan MHar MTed NBid NDea
    NLar NMir NPSI SMac WCot WFar
    WWat
- *rosea*   IBlr LHop NBrk SMad
    digitata 'Nana'   See *F. multijuga*
    hexapetala   See *F. vulgaris*
- 'Flore Pleno'   See *F. vulgaris* 'Multiplex'
    'Kahome'   CMCo CRow EBee GBuc GCHN
    GKir GMaP LAst LPan LRHS MBro
    NHol NLar NMir NOrc NSti NTow
    SPer WCot WFar WHil WMoo
    kiraishiensis   EBee WCru
    B&SWJ 1571
§ *multijuga*   CRow GCal MBro MCli SAsh
    WElm WFar WHoo WPyg
    palmata   ECha EFou MCli WFar
- 'Alba'   GCal
- 'Digitata Nana'   See *F. multijuga*
- dwarf   CLAP
- 'Elegantissima'   See *F. purpurea* 'Elegans'
- 'Nana'   See *F. multijuga*
- *purpurea*   See *F. purpurea*
- 'Rosea'   CGle IBlr NBir WCHb
- 'Rubra'   CBlo MRav NGdn
- *rufinervis* B&SWJ 941   WCru
§ *purpurea* ♀   CMea CRow EBrP EBre ECha
    EFou EGar GGar LBCl LBSe LBre
    LRHS MBBe MBel MTis NFla SBre
    SSoC WCru WFar
- f. *albiflora*   CBre GAbr LGre NDov
§ - 'Elegans'   CHea CRow EBee ECha EMil GCal
    GGar LAst NArg NCat NFai NFla
    NPSI SAsh SCob SWat
- 'Plena'   EBee LCaP NLar
    'Queen of the Prairies'   See *F. rubra*
§ *rubra*   CBlo CRow LAst LSyl NWoo STes

    WFar WWat
§ - 'Venusta' ♀   More than 30 suppliers
- 'Venusta Magnifica'   See *F. rubra* 'Venusta'
§ *ulmaria*   CArn CKin EBee ECoo EHon ELau
    EWFC EWTr GBar GMaP GPoy
    LRHS MChe MHer MHew MMal
    MTho NHol NLan NMir SIde SWat
    WFar WGwG WOak WPer WShi
    WWye
- 'Aurea'   More than 30 suppliers
- 'Flore Pleno' (d)   CBre CMil CRDP CRow EHon
    GKir LAst LRHS MBel MCli NBid
    NFai NHol NSti SPer SWat WCot
    WLRN
- 'Rosea'   CRDP IBlr
§ - 'Variegata'   More than 30 suppliers
§ *vulgaris*   CArn CFee CKin EBee ECtt EWFC
    GBar LAst LPBA LRHS MChe
    MHew MSal MWgw NArg NBro
    NFai NMir NOrc SIde SWat WBea
    WByw WPer WWye
- 'Grandiflora'   EPPr LRHS MTed NCat WCot
§ - 'Multiplex' (d)   CGle CRow CSpe EBee ECha EGle
    ELan EOrc GAbr GKir LRHS
    MCLN MHer MRav MTho NBid
    NDea NFla NHol SEas SPer SRms
    WCot WEas WFar WLin WRus
    WWat WWye
- 'Plena'   See *F. vulgaris* 'Multiplex'

FINGERHUTHIA (Poaceae)
    sesleriiformis S&SH 1   CInt

FIRMIANA (Sterculiaceae)
    simplex   CHEx IDee LPan

FITTONIA (Acanthaceae)
    albivenis Argyroneura   CHal LRHS
      Group ♀
- Verschaffeltii Group ♀   CHal LRHS

FITZROYA (Cupressaceae)
    cupressoides   CDoC CMac GAri IOrc LCon
    MBar SLim SLon WCwm

FOENICULUM (Apiaceae)
    vulgare   CArn CHad EBot ECha EDAr EEls
    ELan ELau GBar GMaP GPoy
    LRHS MChe MHer MMal MSal
    NBid SIde SPer SPlb SRCN WByw
    WCer WOak WPer WSel WWye
- 'Bronze'   See *F. vulgare* 'Purpureum'
- var. *dulce*   CSev SIde WGwG
§ - 'Giant Bronze'   CGle ELan GKir WHen
§ - 'Purpureum'   More than 30 suppliers
- 'Smokey'   EFou IIve MRav WOve

FOKIENIA (Cupressaceae)
    hodginsii   Last listed 1997

FONTANESIA (Oleaceae)
    phillyreoides   Last listed 1998

FONTINALIS (Sphagnaceae)
    antipyretica   EMFW

FORESTIERA (Oleaceae)
    neomexicana   See *F. pubescens*
§ *pubescens*   CB&S CFil

FORSYTHIA (Oleaceae)
    'Arnold Dwarf'   CBlo GKir SRms

N 'Beatrix Farrand' CTri EBee ECtt GKir LRHS MGos
MWat NFor SEas SPer SRms
WLRN WMoo
§ Boucle d'Or® = COtt ENot
'Courtacour'PBR
'Courtadic' See *F.* Melissa = 'Courtadic'
'Courtaneur'PBR See *F.* Mêlée d'Or = 'Courtaneur'
'Courtasol'PBR See *F.* Marée d'Or = 'Courtasol'
'Fiesta' (v) CPle EBee EBrP EBre ENot GKir
IOrc LAst LBCl LBSe LBre LRHS
MAsh MBBe MBar MBel MBri
MGos MRav MTis NPro NWea
SBre SLim SLod SPer SSta WCot
WHer
giraldiana CPle SRms WBcn WBod
'Gold Cluster'PBR See *F.* Melée d'Or
Gold Curl®PBR See *F.* Boucle d'Or = 'Courtacour'
'Gold Splash' Last listed 1998
Gold Tide®PBR See *F.* Marée d'Or = 'Courtasol'
'Golden Bells' EMil LRHS MBri
'Golden Nugget' CBlo EBrP EBre EPfP ESis IOrc
LBCl LBSe LBre LRHS MAsh MBBe
SBre SLon SMer SPer WCFE WWeb
'Golden Times' (v) CBlo EHoe EPla EWes IOrc LRHS
MBri MGos NPro SCoo SEas SMad
SPla WBcn WBod WCot
¶ 'Golden Times Allgold' WBcn
x *intermedia* Last listed 1999
- 'Arnold Giant' CBlo MBlu SPan WBod
- 'Courtalyn'PBR See *F.* x *intermedia* Week-End =
'Courtalyn'
- 'Densiflora' NWea
- Goldzauber LRHS MBri
- 'Karl Sax' CChe GKir WLRN
* - 'Liliane' Last listed 1999
- 'Lynwood' ♀ CB&S CBlo CChe CDoC EBee
ELan ENot GChr GKir ISea LRHS
MBar MBri MGos NBee NFla NFor
NWea SLon SPer SRPl SReu SSta
WBod WDin WFar WWeb
- 'Lynwood' LA '79 MLan
- 'Minigold' ECtt EPfP GEil LRHS MAsh MGos
MWat SEas SRms WPyg WRHF
WStI WWeb
- 'Spectabilis' CBlo ELan EWTr GChr GKir IOrc
LBuc MBar NBee NFla NWea SPer
WDin WRHF WTro WWal
- 'Spectabilis Variegated' CPle LRHS MBNS NPro SPan SRPl
WCot WPyg
- 'Spring Glory' EBee CBlo ENot LPan LRHS MBri
- 'Variegata' CBlo NSti NWea SPer SSta
§ - Week-End® = CBlo ENot EPfP GAri LPan MBri
'Courtalyn'PBR ♀ MGos NWea SLim SPlb
§ Marée d'Or = COtt EBee ENot LRHS MBri MGos
'Courtasol'PBR MRav SPer WLRN
§ Mêlée d'Or® = EBee ENot LRHS SPer
'Courtaneur'PBR
§ Melissa = 'Courtadic' NWea
'Northern Gold' CB&S EPfP
ovata EMon EPla
- 'Tetragold' CB&S CBlo MBar NBee NFla
NWea
'Paulina' CBlo ESis GAri
* *pumila* EWes
* 'Spring Beauty' Last listed 1999
suspensa ♀ CB&S CTri ENot EPfP IIve IOrc
LRHS Frsca MSal MWat NWea
SEas SLon SPer WStI
- f. *atrocaulis* CPle GAri NWea
- 'Cynthia Barber' (v) Last listed 1997
- 'Decipiens' WBod
- var. *fortunei* WWal

- 'Hewitt's Gold' EMon
- 'Nymans' EPfP GKir MBri MRav NSti NWea
SLPl SMad
§ - 'Taff's Arnold' (v) CBlo CFwr CMil CPMA MBri
WBcn WSPU
- 'Variegata' See *F.* *suspensa* 'Taff's Arnold'
'Tremonia' EBee NFor
viridissima NFor NWea
- 'Bronxensis' EPar EPot ESis NBir NNrd NWea
SMad SRot WAbe WPyg
- var. *koreana* Last listed 1999
* - - 'Variegata' Last listed 1999
- 'Weber's Bronx' MBar NWea

FORTUNELLA (Rutaceae)

x *crassifolia* (F) SCit
- 'Meiwa' (F) ERea
'Fukushu' (F) ECon ERea SCit
hindsii (F) SCit
§ *japonica* (F) SArc SCit
§ *margarita* (F) CGOG LPan MBri SCit SPer
- 'Nagami' (F) ECon ERea

FOTHERGILLA (Hamamelidaceae)

gardenii CB&S CPMA EBrP EBre ELan EPfP
GKir IOrc LBCl LBSe LBre MAsh
MBBe MBlu MBri SBre SPer SSpi
SSta WDin WWat
- 'Blue Mist' CAbP CDoC CPMA CSam EBee
ELan EPfP GKir IOrc LRHS MAsh
MBel MBlu MBri MGos SBrw SPer
SPla SReu SSpi SSta WWat
'Huntsman' CAbP GKir LRHS MAsh SBrw SSta
major ♀ More than 30 suppliers
- Monticola Group CDoC CGdn CPMA ELan ENot
EPfP IMGH LRHS MBar MBri
NDlv SBrw SChu SPer SSpi SSta
WBod WBrE WHar WSHC
'Mount Airy' CDoC CPMA SBrw

FRAGARIA ✿ (Rosaceae)

alpina See *F.* *vesca* 'Semperflorens'
- 'Alba' See *F.* *vesca* 'Semperflorens Alba'
x *ananassa* (F) NRog
- 'Aromel' (F) ♀ CWSG GTwe LRHS MBri SDea
- 'Auchincruive Climax' (F) EMui
- 'Bogota' PBR (F) GTwe LRHS NBee
- 'Bolero'PBR (F) EMui GTwe
- 'Bounty' (F) Last listed 1997
- 'Calypso' (F) CSut EMui GTwe LRHS
- 'Cambridge CMac CWSG EMui GKir GTwe
Favourite' (F) ♀ LRHS MBri NRog SDea WWeb
- 'Cambridge Late Pine' (F) CWSG EMui GTwe LRHS
- 'Cambridge Rival' (F) LRHS
- 'Cambridge Sentry' (F) EMui
- 'Cambridge Vigour' (F) GKir GTwe LRHS NBee NRog
SDea
- 'Elsanta' PBR (F) CTri CWSG EMui GKir GTwe
IArd LRHS NRog SDea
- 'Elvira' PBR (F) EMui
* - 'Emily' (F) CSut EMui GTwe LRHS
- 'Eros' PBR (F) EMui GTwe NRog
- 'Evita' PBR (F) EMui
- 'Florence' (F) EMui GTwe LRHS
- 'Fraise des Bois' See *F.* *vesca*
* - 'Franny Karan' (F) WGor
* - 'Fresca' (F) WGor
- 'Gorella' (F) LRHS WWeb
- 'Hapil' PBR (F)¿ EMui GTwe LRHS NRog WLRN
- 'Honeoye' (F) ♀ EMui GTwe LRHS
- 'Korona' PBR (F) CSut
- 'Kouril' (F) LRHS

- 'Laura'[PBR] (F)	EMui GTwe LRHS
- 'Maraline' (F)	EMui
- Marastil (F)	EMui
- 'Maxim' (F)	EMui
- 'Melody' (F)	Last listed 1998
- 'Ostara' (F)	Last listed 1998
- 'Pandora' [PBR] (F)	Last listed 1999
- 'Pantagruella' (F)	LRHS
- 'Pegasus' [PBR] (F) ♀	EMui GTwe LRHS NRog
- pink-flowered	CFee
- 'Rapella' [PBR] (F)	Last listed 1999
- 'Redgauntlet' (F)	GTwe LRHS NRog
- 'Rhapsody' [PBR] (F) ♀	EMui GTwe LRHS
- 'Royal Sovereign' (F)	CMac EMui GTwe LRHS
- 'Serenata' (F)	NBur
- 'Sophie' (F)	CSut GTwe LRHS
- 'Symphony' [PBR] (F) ♀	EMui
- 'Talisman' (F)	LRHS
- 'Tamella' (F)	EMui GTwe LRHS NRog
- 'Tango' [PBR] (F)	EMui
- 'Totem' (F)	GTwe
§ - 'Variegata' (F)	CGle CLTr CMea CSev EBee EMon EPla GBar LRHS MCCP MCLN MHar MRav NEgg NHol NSti SCob SIng SPer WBea WOak WRha WRus
- 'Viva Rosa' (F)	EMui SSte
'Baron Solemacher' (F)	WHer
'Bowles' Double'	See *F. vesca* 'Multiplex'
chiloensis (F)	CAgr EMon LEdu NDov
- 'Chaval'	CHid ECGP ECha EGoo EMon EPPr MRav MWgw NWoo SIng GCal LBuc WByw WEas
N - 'Variegata'	
- x *virginiana*	CArn
daltoniana	NHol
- CC&McK 390	Last listed 1997
- CC&McK 559	GCHN
indica	See *Duchesnea indica*
'Lipstick'	EBee NDov
nubicola	GPoy
Pink Panda = 'Frel' [PBR] (F)	CM&M CTri EBee EBrP EBre ECtt EGra GKir LBCl LBSe LBre LEdu LRHS MAsh MBBe MBri MOne NHol NLar SBre SHFr SIng SPer WByw WEas WElm WFar WLRN WMaN
'Red Ruby'	CMGP EBee EBrP EBre ECGP EMar GAri GKir LBCl LBSe LBre LRHS MBBe MCAu MNrw NLar SBre SPer WMoo
* 'Ruby Surprise'	LRHS
sp. from Taiwan	WHer
'Variegata'	See *F.* x *ananassa* 'Variegata'
§ *vesca* (F)	CAgr CArn CKin ECoo EWFC GPoy LRHS LSyl MGas MHer MHew NMir SIde SPlb WGwG WJek WOak WPer WShi WWye
- 'Alexandra' (F)	CArn CBod ELau GAbr LRHS MCHe SIde WCHb WHer
- 'Flore Pleno'	See *F. vesca* 'Multiplex'
- 'Fructu Albo' (F)	CRow WAlt WPer
- 'Mara Des Bois' [PBR] (F)	EMui GTwe
- 'Monophylla' (F)	CRow EMon LRHS NHol SIde WHer
§ - 'Multiplex' (d)	CGle CRow CSev EMon EMou GAbr MInt MRav NHex NHol NSti SSvw WAlt WCHb WHer WOak WWye
§ - 'Muricata'	CFee CLTr CPou CRow GAbr LEdu NBrk WAlt WCer WHer WWye
* - 'Pineapple Crush'	WHer

- 'Plymouth Strawberry'	See *F. vesca* 'Muricata'
- 'Rügen' (F)	CHal WHoo WPyg
§ - 'Semperflorens' (F)	CLTr ILis MBNS NBrk WAlt WHer WOak
§ - 'Semperflorens Alba' (F)	WOak
N - 'Variegata'	EHoe ELau EPar LAst MSCN MWgw SMac WPer WSel
¶ *virginiana*	CAgr

FRANCOA (Saxifragaceae)

appendiculata	CGre EBee EMFP EMan EMar GMac GOrP LPio MGrG SGar SSca SYvo WHer WPic
Ballyrogan strain	IBlr
'Confetti'	CMCo EBee LFis MGrG MTed SOkh WCot WPGP
* dwarf purple	EBee
'Purple Spike'	See *F. sonchifolia* Rogerson's form
§ *ramosa*	CGle CMCo CSpe CTri EBee GAbr GBri GBuc IBlr LFis LRHS MAvo MBct MGed MNrw MWat NBro NRog SAga SDix STes WCru WFar
* - 'Alba'	See *F. ramosa*
§ *sonchifolia*	More than 30 suppliers
- 'Alba'	CPlt CRDP CSpe EBee LHop SUsu WCot
¶ - 'Dr Tom Smith'	
§ - Rogerson's form	CGle CNic CRDP CSpe EMar EPPr GBuc GGar IBlr LFis LPio MAvo MGrG MSCN NBur SDix SOkh SUsu WCot WSan

FRANKENIA (Frankeniaceae)

laevis	CHal CTri SRms
thymifolia	CHal CInt CMHG EPar EPot ESis GCHN LRHS MBar MHer MWat SAga SIng SPlb SSmi WFar WPer WPyg WWin

FRANKLINIA (Theaceae)

alatamaha	CB&S CTho EPfP LHyd SLPl SMac SSpi WNor

FRAXINUS ✿ (Oleaceae)

americana	CDul CMCN WLRN
- 'Autumn Purple'	CBlo CDul CEnd CTho EBee MAsh MBlu
- 'Rose Hill'	CTho
§ *angustifolia*	CLnd CMCN CTho
- 'Elegantissima'	CTho
- 'Flame'	See *F. angustifolia* Raywood = 'Flame'
- var. *lentiscifolia*	CTho
§ - 'Monophylla'	CLnd CTho
¶ - subsp. *oxycarpa*	GIBF
§ - Raywood = 'Flame' ♀	CB&S CBlo CDoC CDul CEnd CLnd CTho EBee ECrN ELan ENot EWTr GChr GKir IOrc LRHS MAsh MBlu MGos NBee NWea SMHT SMad SPer WDin WJas WOrn
* - 'Variegata'	CPMA MGos
bungeana	CMCN
chinensis	CDul CLnd CMCN CTho
- subsp. *rhynchophylla*	GKir
elonza	CTho
excelsior ♀	CB&S CBlo CDoC CDul CKin CLnd EBee ECrN EMac ENot EWTr GChr GKir GTre LBuc LHyr LPan MBar MGos NBee NWea SPer WDin WMou WOrn WStI
- 'Allgold'	CEnd SMad
- 'Aurea Pendula'	CEnd CMCN GKir LRHS

- 'Crispa' — Last listed 1999
- f. *diversifolia* — CDul CLnd CTho WMou
- 'Diversifolia Pendula' — See *F. excelsior* 'Heterophylla Pendula'
- 'Geessink' — ENot SLPl
§ - 'Heterophylla Pendula' — Last listed 1999
- 'Jaspidea' ♀ — More than 30 suppliers
- 'Nana' — EMon WPat
- 'Pendula' ♀ — CBlo CDoC CDul CEnd CLnd CTho EBee ELan ENot GChr GKir IMGH IOrc LPan LRHS MAsh MBlu MBri NBee NWea SLim SPer WDin WJas WMou WOrn WStI
- 'Pendula Wentworthii' — Last listed 1998
- R.E. Davey' — CDul CNat CTho
- 'Stanway Gold' — Last listed 1997
- 'Stripey' — Last listed 1997
¶ - variegated — CDul
- 'Westhof's Glorie' ♀ — CDoC CDul CLnd EBee ENot GKir WDin WJas WOrn
bolotricha — CTho
¶ *insularis* var. *benryana* — CFil WPGP
mariesii — See *F. sieboldiana*
nigra — CFil CMCN
- 'Fallgold' — CBlo CEnd
ornus ♀ — CBlo CDul CLnd CMCN CTri ECrN ELan ENot EPfP GChr GKir IOrc LPan LRHS MBri NBee NWea SPer SSta WDin WFar WTro WWat
- 'Arie Peters' — CDul WStI
- 'Obelisk' — MBri
- Sch 3177 — WHCr
oxycarpa — See *F. angustifolia* subsp. *oxycarpa*
pennsylvanica — CDul CLnd CMCN
- 'Aucubifolia' — CTho
- 'Patmore' — CBlo
- 'Summit' — CTho
- 'Variegata' — CBlo CLnd CTho EBee EPfP GKir LPan LRHS MAsh MBri SSta
quadrangulata — WDin WWoo
§ *sieboldiana* — CDoC CFil CLnd CPMA MBlu SSpi WPGP
spaethiana — Last listed 1998
'Veltheimii' — See *F. angustifolia* 'Monophylla'
velutina — CDul CLnd CMCN CTho SLPl

FREESIA (Iridaceae)
alba Foster — See *F. lactea*
- (G.L.Mey.) Gumbl. — WHil
- Watson — See *F. caryophyllacea*
§ *caryophyllacea* — WHil
'Diana' — Last listed 1999
double mixed (d) — ETub
elimensis — Last listed 1998
'Fantasy' (d) — Last listed 1999
hybrids — CSut NRog
§ *lactea* — Last listed 1999
'Romany' (d) — Last listed 1999
'White Swan' — Last listed 1999
xanthospila — LBow

FREMONTODENDRON (Sterculiaceae)
'California Glory' ♀ — More than 30 suppliers
californicum — CAbb CHEx EBee ELan EMil EWTr IOrc MBlu MBri MDun MWhi SLim SOWG SPlb SRPl WAbe WBod WCFE WDin WNor WStI WWin
§ - subsp. *decumbens* — Last listed 1999
'Ken Taylor' — LRHS
mexicanum — CGre

'Pacific Sunset' — CPMA EBee ENot EPfP LHop LRHS MBri SBra SBrw SMur SPer

FREYLINIA (Scrophulariaceae)
cestroides — See *F. lanceolata*
§ *lanceolata* — CPle CTre

FRITILLARIA ✿ (Liliaceae)
acmopetala ♀ — CAvo CBro EPar EPot ERos EWal GCrs ITim LAma LRHS MDun MNaF MS&S MTho NMen NRog NWCA WCot WLin
- subsp. *wendelboi* — LAma WCot
§ *affinis* — EWal GCrs LAma MS&S NHar WLin
§ - var. *gracilis* — LAma SPer WLin
- 'Limelight' — EBee EPot GCrs
- 'Sunray' — GCrs NHar
§ - var. *tristulis* — NMen
- 'Vancouver Island' — EBee EPot
- 'Wayne Roderick' — EPot GCrs
* *albidiflora* — LAma
alburyana — EPot GCrs
arabica — See *F. persica*
armena — EPot GCrs LAma
assyriaca — See *F. uva-vulpis*
atropurpurea — Last listed 1998
aurea — CLAP EPot GCrs MS&S NMen
- 'Golden Flag' — ETub WWst
biflora — CLAP
- 'Martha Roderick' — CAvo CBro CMea EBrP EBre EPot ETub EWal LAma LBCl LBSe LBre MBBe MCli MS&S NMen SBla SBre WWst
§ *bithynica* — CBro CLAP EPot GCrs LAma MS&S NMen
brandegeei — EWal LAma
bucharica — CAvo CLAP EPot
- 'Aman Kutan' — Last listed 1999
camschatcensis — CAvo CBro CRDP ECha EFEx EPar EPot ETub GCrs GKir GNor LAma MS&S MTho NDov NHar NMen NRog SSpi WAbe WCru WLin
* - *alpina aurea* — GCrs
- 'Aurea' — Last listed 1999
- black — GBuc GKir
- f. *flavescens* — EFEx LAma
- from Alaska — GCrs
- *multiflora* — Last listed 1999
¶ - yellow — WWst
carduchorum — See *F. minuta*
carica — CAvo EPot GCrs MS&S NMen
- subsp. *serpenticola* — EPot GCrs
caucasica — CLAP LAma
'Chatto' — Last listed 1998
cirrhosa — GKir WWst
¶ - brown — GKir
¶ - green — GKir
citrina — See *F. bithynica*
§ *collina* — WWst
conica — EPot GCrs NHar
crassifolia — EPot LAma MS&S
- subsp. *crassifolia* — CGra
§ - subsp. *kurdica* — EPot GCrs NMen SSpi
davisii — CMea EPot ETub LAma LRHS MNaF NHar NMen
delphinensis — See *F. tubiformis*
drenovskyi — CLAP EPot
eastwoodiae — EPot GCrs LAma WLin
ebrhartii — EPot GCrs SBla
elwesii — Last listed 1999
ferganensis — See *F. walujewii*

fleischeriana	GCrs WWst
forbesii	GCrs
gentneri	Last listed 1999
glauca	LAma MS&S NMen
* - 'Golden Flag'	NMen
- 'Goldilocks'PBR	CAvo CMea EPot ETub LRHS NMen WHil
graeca	CBro CHar EPot GCrs LRHS MTho NMen
- subsp. *graeca*	Last listed 1998
- subsp. *ionica*	See *F. graeca* subsp. *thessala*
§ - subsp. *thessala*	MS&S MTho WCot WLin
§ *grayana*	EPot MS&S NMen
- tall	CLAP
gussichiae	CLAP MS&S
* *halabulanica*	LAma
hermonis subsp. *amana*	CAvo EPot GCrs LAma LRHS NMen WLin
¶ - from Jebel esh Sharqui Mtns, Lebanon	WWst
hispanica	See *F. lusitanica*
hupehensis	EPot GCrs LAma
imperialis	CAvo CHEx EBot ECGP MBri NRog
- 'Aureomarginata' (v)	CMea EBee EPar LAma LBow LRHS MBri NRog
- 'Aurora'	CAvo CHar EBrP EBre EMon EPar ETub EWTr LAma LBCl LBSe LBow LBre LRHS MBBe MBNS MCli MWat NCut NRog SBre WPnP
- 'Crown upon Crown'	See *F. imperialis* 'Prolifera'
- 'Lutea'	CHar CMGP CMea EBot EMon EWTr LRHS NFor WPnP
- 'Lutea Maxima'	See *F. imperialis* 'Maxima Lutea'
- 'Maxima'	See *F. imperialis* 'Rubra Maxima'
§ - 'Maxima Lutea' ♀	CBro CHEx EBee EBrP EBre EPar EPfP ETub LAma LBCl LBSe LBow LBre LRHS MBBe MCli MLLN NRog SBre
§ - 'Prolifera'	EBot EPar LAma LBow LRHS MLLN
- 'Rubra'	CMGP EBee EMon EPar ETub LAma LBow MCli NBir NCut NRog
§ - 'Rubra Maxima'	CBro CHar EBot EMon EPfP EPot EWTr LAma LRHS MLLN
- 'Sulpherino'	EBee LRHS
- 'The Premier'	EMon EPar LAma LRHS
¶ - 'William Rex'	EPot
involucrata	CAvo GCrs LAma MS&S
ionica	See *F. graeca* subsp. *thessala*
japonica var. *koidzumiana*	EFEx
karadaghensis	See *F. crassifolia* subsp. *kurdica*
I *karelinii*	LAma WWst
¶ *kittaniae*	GCrs
kotschyana	NMen WWst
lanceolata	See *F. affinis* var. *tristulis*
latakiensis	Last listed 1997
§ *latifolia*	EPot GCrs LAma
- var. *nobilis*	See *F. latifolia*
liliacea	LAma
§ *lusitanica*	CLAP GCrs LAma MS&S SBla WLin
- MS 440	Last listed 1998
lutea Bieb.	See *F. collina*
macrocarpa SB&L 258	Last listed 1998
meleagris ♀	More than 30 suppliers
- 'Aphrodite'	CAvo EPot WCot
- 'Jupiter'	LRHS
- 'Mars'	LRHS

- var. *unicolor* subvar. *alba* ♀	CBro CHar EBee EPot ETub GBuc LAma LBow LRHS MBri MBro MS&S NHar NRya SUsu WCru WShi
§ *messanensis*	GCrs LAma MS&S SBla
- from Ólimbos, Greece	WLin
- subsp. *gracilis*	GCrs MS&S
- subsp. *messanensis*	CBro
michailovskyi ♀	CAvo CBro CHar EBee EPar EPot ETub EWal GBuc GCrs LAma LRHS MBri MDun MNrw MTho MTis NMen NRog SLod SYvo WAbe WHoo WPyg WSel
micrantha	LAma
minima	Last listed 1998
- JCA 500.100	Last listed 1998
§ *minuta*	EPot GCrs MS&S NMen
montana	GCrs LRHS MS&S NMen
nigra hort.	See *F. pyrenaica*
obliqua	EPot GCrs
olivieri	CLAP GCrs
§ *orientalis*	WWst
pallidiflora ♀	CAvo CBro CLAP EPar EPot ERos EWal LAma LRHS MDun MLLN MS&S MTho NHar NMen NSla SSpi SYvo WCru WLin
¶ - double (d)	LAma
§ *persica*	CHar EBee EBot EPar EPot LAma LRHS MBNS MBri MCli MNaF NMen WSel
- 'Adiyaman' ♀	CAvo CBro EBee EBrP EBre ELan EMon ETub LBCl LBSe LBow LBre LFis LRHS MBBe NRog SBre
- S&L 118	Last listed 1998
phaeanthera	See *F. affinis* var. *gracilis*
pinardii	EPot NMen
pluriflora	EPot
- JA 94109	Last listed 1999
pontica	CAvo CBro CLAP CMea EBee EPar EPot ERos EWal GKir ITim LAma LRHS MCli MDun MLLN MS&S MTho NMen NSla SBla SIng SSpi SUsu WCru WLin
pudica	CMea ETub GCrs LAma MMal MS&S MTho NHar NMen WLin
* - 'Fragrant'	EPot GCrs
- 'Richard Britten'	GCrs NMen
puqiensis	LAma
purdyi	CAvo CLAP EPot GCrs MS&S NMen
§ *pyrenaica* ♀	CBro CLAP GCrs LAma MS&S NHar NMen NSla SChu SSpi SUsu WCru
¶ - 'Lutea'	EHyt
raddeana	CLAP LAma MS&S
recurva	Last listed 1998
- 'Sensational'PBR	LAma
rhodocanakis	EPot GCrs
- subsp. *argolica*	WWst
- JCA 502.600	Last listed 1998
roderickii	See *F. grayana*
roylei	MS&S
rubra major	See *F. imperialis* 'Rubra Maxima'
ruthenica	ERos MS&S NMen SBla
sewerzowii	EPot LAma LRHS
sibthorpiana	CBro EPot GCrs
spetsiotica	GCrs
sphaciotica	See *F. messanensis*
stenanthera	EPot GCrs LAma
striata	Last listed 1998
stribrnyi	WWst
tachengensis	See *F. yuminensis*

tenella	See *F. orientalis*
thunbergii	EPar EPot LRHS NMen
¶ *tortifolia*	LAma
§ *tubiformis*	GCrs GKir WLin
tuntasia	GCrs
usuriensis	LAma
§ *uva-vulpis*	CAvo CBro CMea EBee EPar EPot
	ETub EWal ITim LAma LEdu LRHS
	MDun MNrw MTho NWCA SIng
	SSpi WCot WCru WHil WLin
verticillata	CAvo CBro EBot ECha EPar EPot
	GCrs LAma MS&S MTho NHar
§ *walujewii*	EPot LAma WWst
whittallii	EPot GCrs MS&S
§ *yuminensis*	LAma
zagrica	Last listed 1998

FUCHSIA ✿ (Onagraceae)

'A.M. Larwick'	CSil EBak EKMF
'A.W.Taylor'	EBak
'Aalt Groothuis'	EGou
'Abbé Farges'	CLoc CSil EBak ECtt EDAr EKMF
	EPts MWhe NArc SKen SLBF
'Abbey Hill'	MWar
'Abbigayle Reine'	NArc
'Abigail'	EGou EKMF
'Achievement' ♀	CLoc CSil LCla MJac NArc SKen
'Ada Perry'	ECtt NArc
'Adagio' (d)	CLoc
'Ada's Love'	EKMF
'Adinda'	EGou LCla
'Admiration'	CSil
'Adrian Young'	Last listed 1999
'Ailsa Garnett'	EBak
'Aintree'	NArc
'Airedale'	MJac NArc
'Ajax'	Last listed 1998
'Alabama Improved'	SKen
'Aladna'	Last listed 1998
'Aladna's Sanders'	NArc
'Alan Ayckbourn'	CSil NArc
'Alan Stilwell'	Last listed 1998
'Alan Titchmarsh'	EPts SLBF
'Alaska' (d)	CLoc EBak EKMF NArc WGwG
'Albertina'	LCla
'Albertus Schwab'	LCla
'Alde'	CSil EGou NArc
'Alf Thornley'	CSil LAco MWhe NArc
'Alfie'	CSil
'Alfred Rambaud'	CDoC CSil NArc
'Algerine'	SLBF
'Alice Ashton' (d)	EBak EKMF NArc
'Alice Doran'	CDoC LCla SLBF SWal
'Alice Hoffman'	CDoC CLoc CPri CSil EBak EBee
	EDAr EGou EKMF EPts LCla LRHS
	LVER MBar MBri MGos MJac
	MWat MWhe NArc SKen SPer
	SSea WGwG
'Alice Mary'	EBak EKMF EMan
'Alice Rowell'	EKMF
'Alice Stringer'	ECtt
'Alice Travis'	EBak
'Alipatti'	EKMF
'Alison Ewart'	CLoc EBak MJac MWhe NArc
'Alison June'	Last listed 1999
'Alison Patricia'	CSil EBak EKMF EMan LCla MAld
	MJac MWar MWhe SLBF
'Alison Reynolds'	LCla MWar NArc
¶ 'Alison Ruth Griffin'	EGou
'Alison Ryle'	CSil EBak
'Alison Sweetman'	CSil EKMF MJac MWhe SKen
'Allure'	EPts

'Alma Hulscher'	Last listed 1998
'Alma Muir'	Last listed 1997
§ *alpestris*	CDoC EBak EGou EKMF LCla
'Alton Water'	EGou
'Alwin'	CSil MWhe NArc
'Alyce Larson' (d)	EBak MJac NArc WGwG
'Amanda Bridgland'	EKMF
'Amanda Jones'	EKMF MWhe NArc
'Ambassador'	EBak SKen
'Amelie Aubin'	CLoc EBak EKMF NArc
'America'	EBak NArc
'American Dream'	NArc
'American Flaming Glory'	CSil NArc
'Amethyst Fire'	CSil
'Amigo'	EBak NArc
§ *ampliata*	EGou EKMF LCla
'Amy Lye'	CLoc CSil EBak EKMF NArc SKen
§ 'Andenken an Heinrich	CDoC CLoc EBak ECtt EKMF LCla
Henkel'	MWhe
'André Le Nostre' (d)	EBak NArc
andrei	EGou EKMF LCla
'Andrew'	EBak EKMF NArc
'Andrew Carnegie' (d)	CLoc
'Andrew George'	MJac
'Andrew Hadfield'	CSil EKMF MWar NArc SLBF
'Andrew Ryle'	NArc
N 'Andromeda'	CSil
'Angela Leslie' (d)	CLoc EBak EKMF NArc
'Angela Rippon'	MJac MWhe NArc
'Angelina'	Last listed 1999
'Angel's Dream'	CSil
'Angel's Flight' (d)	EBak
'Anita'	CSil EKMF EPts LCla MAld MWar
	MWhe NArc SLBF SYvo
'Anj'	Last listed 1997
'Anjo' (v)	EGou EKMF NArc SLBF SSea
'Ann Adams'	CSil MJac
'Ann Howard Tripp'	CLoc CSil MBri MJac MWhe NArc
'Ann Lee' (d)	EBak
'Ann Roots'	EGou
'Anna Douling'	Last listed 1997
'Anna of Longleat'	CLoc EBak EMan NArc SKen
'Annabel' (d) ♀	CDoC CGre CLoc CSil EBak
	EKMF EMan EPts LCla LRHS LVER
	MAld MBri MJac MWar MWhe
	NArc NFai SLBF SSea WGwG
'Annabelle Stubbs'	ECtt
'Anne Strudwick'	EGou
'Annie Earle'	EKMF
'Anthea Day' (d)	CLoc
'Anthonetta'	Last listed 1997
'Antigone'	SLBF
'Antonella Merrills'	EKMF
¶ *apetala*	EGou
'Aphrodite' (d)	CLoc EBak NArc
'Applause' (d)	CLoc CSil EBak ECtt EKMF EMan
	EPts LVER MAld MJac NArc
'Apple Blossom'	EKMF
aprica hort.	See *F.* x *bacillaris*
– Lundell	See *F. microphylla* subsp. *aprica*
'Aquarius'	MWhe
'Arabella'	CSil MWhe
'Arabella Improved'	EKMF
arborea	See *F. arborescens*
§ *arborescens*	CDoC CLoc CSil EBak ECre EGou
	EKMF ERea LCla LRHS NArc SLBF
	SMrm SYvo WCot WGwG
'Arcadia'	MWar
'Arcadia Aubergine'	NArc
'Arcadia Gold'	ECtt MWhe NArc WGwG
'Arcadia Lady'	MJac NArc
'Arcady'	CLoc

'Archie Owen'   Last listed 1998
'Arel's Avondzon'   NArc
'Ariel'   CSil NArc
'Army Nurse' ♀   CDoC CLoc CSil EKMF GCHN
                       LVER MWhe NArc SLBF SPet
'Art Deco'   NArc
¶ 'Ashley'   LCla
'Ashley Jane'   MAld
'Ashmore'   NArc
'Athela'   EBak
'Atlantic Crossing'   Last listed 1997
'Atlantic Star'   EKMF MJac NArc WGwG
'Atlantis'   MJac NArc
'Atomic Glow' (d)   EBak NArc
'Aubergine'   CLoc SLBF SSea
'Audray'   NArc
'Audrey Booth'   EGou
'Audrey Hepburn'   EKMF NArc
'Augustin Thierry'   MWhe
'Aunt Juliana' (d)   EBak
'Auntie Bertha'   EPts
'Auntie Jinks' (d)   CSil EBak ECtt EKMF LCla MJac
                       MWar MWhe NArc SLBF WGwG
* aureifolia   Last listed 1998
'Aurora Superba'   CLoc CSil EBak EKMF SLBF
'Australia Fair' (d)   CLoc CSil EBak NArc WGwG
§ austromontana   EBak
'Autumnale'   CDoC CLoc CSil EBak ECtt EKMF
                       EMan LCla LRHS LVER MWhe
                       NArc SKen SLBF SMrm SPet SSea
'Avalanche' (d)   CLoc CSil EBak EKMF NArc
'Avocet'   CLoc EBak NArc
'Avon Celebration'   CLoc
'Avon Gem'   CLoc CSil
'Avon Gold'   CLoc
'Axel of Denmark'   Last listed 1998
ayavacensis   EKMF LCla
'Azure Sky'   EKMF MJac
'Babette'   EKMF
'Babs'   Last listed 1999
'Baby Blue Eyes'   CDoC CSil SLBF
'Baby Bright'   CSil EPts LCla SLBF
'Baby Chang'   CSil EGou LCla MWhe
'Baby Face'   NArc
'Baby Girl'   EKMF
'Baby Pink'   CSil NArc
'Baby Thumb'   CSil
§ x bacillaris   CDoC CWit EBak EWes MBlu
                       SLBF SRms SSoC
§ – 'Cottinghamii'   CDoC CSil WPen WSHC
§ – 'Oosje'   See F. 'Oosje'
§ – 'Reflexa'   CTrC GQui SVen
'Bagworthy Water'   CLoc
'Baker's Tri'   EBak
'Balcony Queen'   Last listed 1999
'Balkonkönigin'   CLoc CSil EBak ECtt
'Ballet Girl' (d)   CLoc CSil EBak ECtt EKMF LCla
                       SLBF SPet
'Bambini'   CSil EPts WGwG
'Banks Peninsula'   GQui
'Banzai'   Last listed 1998
'Barbara'   CLoc CSil EBak EKMF MJac MWar
                       MWhe NArc SKen WCot WEas
¶ 'Barbara Evans'   MWar
'Barbara Pountain'   LVER
'Barbara Windsor'   EPts MAld MJac
'Baron de Ketteler'   CSil EKMF NArc
'Baroness van Dedem'   CSil
'Baroque Pearl'   EKMF NArc
'Barry M. Cox'   CSil EGou
'Barry's Queen'   CSil EBak EKMF SPet
'Bart Simpson'   Last listed 1998

'Bashful'   CSil EDAr EPts LCla LRHS NArc
'Basketfull'   CSil NArc
'Beacon'   CDoC CLoc CSil EBak EKMF
                       EMan LCla LRHS MBri MJac
                       MWhe NArc SRob SSea WStI
'Beacon Rosa'   CLoc CSil EGou EKMF EMan LCla
                       LRHS MAld MBri MJac MWar
                       MWhe NArc SKen SLBF
'Bealings' (d)   CLoc CSil ECtt EGou EMan MBri
                       MJac MWhe NArc
'Beatrice Burtoft'   EKMF
'Beau Nash'   CLoc
'Beautiful Bobbie'   SLBF
'Beauty of Bath' (d)   CLoc EBak NArc
'Beauty of Clyffe Hall' CSil EBak EKMF
'Beauty of Exeter'   COtt CSil EBak EKMF NArc
'Beauty of Prussia'   CDoC CLoc CSil ECtt
'Beauty of Swanley'   EBak
'Beauty of Trowbridge' CDoC LCla NArc
'Becky'   EGou
'Becky Jane'   CSil
'Bella Forbes' (d)   CLoc CSil EBak EKMF NArc
'Bella Rosella'   ECtt EPts MJac WWol
                       CSil EGou EKMF SCoo SLBF
'Belsay Beauty'   MJac NArc
'Belvoir Beauty'   CLoc MJac
'Belvoir Lakes'   ECtt
'Ben de Jong'   LCla MJac SLBF
'Ben Gunn'   Last listed 1999
'Ben Jammin'   CLoc EGou EPts LCla
¶ 'Ben Jiggins'   EGou
N 'Beranger' (d)   CSil EBak EKMF
'Berba's Coronation'   EKMF NArc
'Berba's Happiness'   CSil
'Berba's Inge Mariel' ECtt
'Berba's Ingrid'   MAld
'Bergnimf'   LCla NArc WGwG
'Berliner Kind' (d)   CSil EBak EKMF
'Bermuda'   CSil EKMF
'Bernadette'   Last listed 1999
¶ 'Bernie's Big-un' (d) MJac
'Bertha Gadsby'   EKMF
'Beryl Shaffery'   EGou
'Beryl's Choice'   Last listed 1998
'Beth Robley'   CSil
'Betsy Ross' (d)   EBak NArc
'Bette Sibley'   CSil
'Betty Jean'   EGou
'Beverley'   CSil EBak EKMF EPts
'Bewitched' (d)   EBak NArc
'Bianca'   SMur
'Bicentennial'   CLoc CSil EBak EGou EKMF EPts
                       LVER MJac MWar MWhe SKen
                       SSea
'Big Charles'   EGou
'Big Slim'   EGou
'Bill Gilbert'   Last listed 1999
'Bill Stevens'   EKMF
'Billy Green' ♀   CDoC CLTr CLoc CSil EBak ECtt
                       EKMF EPts LCla LRHS MAld MJac
                       MWar MWhe NArc SKen SLBF
                       WHen
'Bishop's Bells'   CSil MJac NArc
'Bits'   NArc
'Bittersweet'   CSil ECtt NArc
'Black Beauty'   CSil
'Black Prince'   CDoC CSil MWar NArc
I 'Blanche Regina'   MJac MWhe
'Bland's New Striped' EBak EKMF EPts NArc SLBF
'Blazeaway'   MBri MWar
'Blood Donor'   EKMF MJac
'Blowick'   EMan MBri MWhe NArc SWal

'Blue Beauty' (d) — CSil EBak EKMF NArc
'Blue Bush' — CSil EKMF MJac NArc
'Blue Butterfly' — EBak NArc
'Blue Eyes' — Last listed 1999
'Blue Gown' (d) — CDoC CLoc CSil EBak EKMF LCla LRHS LVER MWhe NArc SKen
'Blue Halo' — Last listed 1997
'Blue Ice' — CSil MWhe
'Blue Lace' — CSil
N 'Blue Lagoon' — Last listed 1999
'Blue Lake' — CSil ECtt LVER
'Blue Mink' — EBak
'Blue Mirage' — CSil LCla MWar WGwG
'Blue Mist' (d) — EBak
'Blue Pearl' (d) — EBak NArc
'Blue Petticoat' (d) — CLoc
'Blue Pinwheel' — CSil EBak
'Blue Sails' — NArc
'Blue Satin' — COtt LVER MAld MWhe NArc
'Blue Tit' — CSil
'Blue Veil' (d) — CLoc CSil EKMF LVER MJac MWar SKen SLBF
'Blue Waves' (d) — CLoc CSil EBak EGou EKMF EMan MJac MWar MWhe NArc SPet WGwG
'Blush of Dawn' — CLoc CSil EBak EGou EKMF EPts LVER MAld MWar NArc WGwG
'Blythe' — EPts SLBF
'Bob Pacey' — Last listed 1998
'Bob Paisley' — Last listed 1999
'Bobby Boy' (d) — EBak
'Bobby Dazzler' — CSil ECtt EKMF NArc
'Bobby Shaftoe' — EBak EKMF MWhe NArc
'Bobby Wingrove' — EBak NArc
'Bobby's Girl' — EPts
'Bobolink' (d) — EBak NArc
'Bob's Best' — CSil EPts LVER MJac
'Bob's Choice' — WLow
'Boerhaave' — EBak
§ *boliviana* Britton — See *F. sanctae-rosae*
§ *boliviana* Carrière — CAbb CDoC CLoc CSil EBak EKMF LCla LHil NArc SYvo
§ - var. *alba* ♀ — CDoC CLoc CPne CSil EBak EGou EKMF LCla LHil MWar MWhe NArc
- 'Alba' — See *F. boliviana* Carrière var. *alba*
- var. *boliviana* — EGou LRHS
- var. *luxurians* — See *F. boliviana* Carrière var. *alba*
- f. *puberulenta* — See *F. boliviana* Carrière
'Bon Accorde' — CLoc CSil EBak EKMF EPts LCla MJac SSea
'Bon Bon' (d) — CSil EBak NArc
'Bonita' — MJac NArc
'Bonnie Doan' — NArc
'Bonnie Lass' — CSil EBak NArc
'Bonny' (d) — CLoc
'Bookham Beauty' (d) — SLBF
'Bora Bora' (d) — CSil EBak EKMF
'Borde Hill' (d) — EPts SLBF
'Border Princess' — EBak LCla
'Border Queen' ♀ — CDoC CLoc CSil EBak EKMF EMan LCla MAld MJac MWar NArc WWol
'Border Reiver' — EBak NArc
'Börnemanns Beste' — CDoC CLoc CSil EBak EKMF LCla SKen
'Bouffant' — CLoc CSil MJac
'Bountiful' (d) — CGre CLoc CSil EKMF MWhe NArc SKen
'Bouquet' — CSil EKMF LCla
'Bouvigne' — NArc
'Bow Bells' — CLoc CSil MAld MJac MWhe NArc

'Boy Marc' — EGou LCla
'Brandt's Five Hundred Club' — CLoc EBak EKMF
'Breckland' — EBak MJac NArc
'Breeders' Delight' — MBri
'Breeder's Dream' (d) — EBak NArc
'Brenda' (d) — CLoc CSil EBak NArc
'Brenda Pritchard' — ECtt LVER
'Brenda White' — CLoc NArc
'Brentwood' — EBak
brevilobis — CSil EGou EKMF
'Brian A. McDonald' — EGou
'Brian Breary' — EGou LCla
'Brian C. Morrison' — EGou EKMF LCla
'Brian Ellis' — NArc
'Brian Kimberley' — EGou EKMF LCla
'Brian Soames' — EBak
'Brian Stannard' — EGou LCla
'Bridal Pink' — Last listed 1999
'Bridal Veil' (d) — EBak NArc
'Bridesmaid' (d) — CSil EBak NArc SPet
'Brigadoon' — CLoc EBak
'Brightling' — Last listed 1999
'Brighton Belle' — CDoC CSil EGou EWll LCla NArc WGwG
N 'Brilliant' — CDoC CLoc CSil EBak EKMF LCla LHil MGos MWhe
'Briony Caunt' — CSil EKMF
'British Jubilee' — CSil EKMF NArc
'British Sterling' — NArc
'Brodsworth' — CSil
'Bronze Banks Peninsula' — EKMF
'Brookwood Belle' ♀ — EPts LCla MAld MJac SLBF SYvo
'Brookwood Dale' — MWhe
'Brookwood Joy' — CSil EGou MJac NArc SLBF
'Brookwood Lady' — MWhe
'Brutus' ♀ — CDoC CLoc CSil EBak EKMF EMan EPts LCla LRHS MWat MWhe NArc SKen WGwG WStI
'Bryan Breary' — EKMF
'Bubble Hanger' — NArc
'Buddha' — EBak
'Bugle Boy' — EGou LCla
'Bunny' — CSil EBak NArc
'Burma Star' — Last listed 1999
'Burton Brew' — MJac
'Buttercup' — CLoc CSil EBak NArc
'Butterfly' — Last listed 1999
'Byron Rees' — EGou
'C.J. Howlett' — CSil EBak EKMF
'Caballero' (d) — EBak
'Cable Car' — Last listed 1997
'Caesar' (d) — EBak NArc
'Caledonia' — CSil EBak EKMF
'Calumet' — Last listed 1998
'Cambridge Louie' — CSil EBak LCla MAld MBri MWar MWhe NArc
'Camel Estuary' — NArc
'Camelot' — NArc
campii — EGou EKMF LCla
* - var. *rubra* — EGou
campos-portoi — CDoC CSil EGou EKMF LCla
'Cancun' — MJac
'Candlelight' (d) — CGre CLoc CSil EBak NArc SLBF
'Candy Kisses' — Last listed 1998
'Candy Stripe' — CLoc
canescens Bentham — Last listed 1998
- Munz — See *F. ampliata*
'Canny Bob' — MJac NArc
'Capri' (d) — CSil EBak NArc
'Captain Al Sutton' — EGou
'Cara Mia' — CLoc CSil

'Caradela' MAld MJac SLBF
'Cardinal' CLoc EKMF NArc
'Cardinal Farges' CLoc CSil EKMF NArc SKen SLBF SPet SSea
'Carillon van Amsterdam' MWhe
'Carioca' EBak
'Carisbrooke Castle' EKMF
'Carl Drude' Last listed 1999
'Carl Wallace' EKMF MJac
'Carla Johnston' CLTr CLoc EKMF EPts LCla LVER MAld MBri MJac MWar MWhe NArc SSea SYvo
'Carlisle Bells' NArc
'Carmel Blue' CDoC CLTr CLoc CSil EKMF LCla MWar MWhe NArc WGwG
'Carmen' CDoC CSil EKMF
'Carmen Maria' NArc
'Carmine Bell' CSil EKMF
'Carnea' CSil
'Carnival' (d) NArc
'Carnoustie' (d) EBak EGou NArc
'Carol Grace' (d) CLoc NArc
¶ 'Carol Lynn Whittemore' (d) SLBF
'Carol Nash' (d) CLoc
'Carol Roe' EKMF
'Caroline' CGre CLoc CSil EBak EPts MWhe NArc SLBF
'Cascade' CLoc CSil ECtt EKMF EMan LCla MBri MJac MWar MWhe NArc SPet SSea
'Casper Hauser' CSil EGou EKMF NArc
'Catherina' EKMF
'Catherine Bartlett' EKMF NArc
'Catherine Claire' Last listed 1998
'Cathie MacDougall' (d) EBak NArc
'Cecil Glass' EKMF
'Cecile' CSil ECtt EGou EKMF EPts LCla LVER MJac MWar MWhe NArc SLBF
'Celadore' (d) CSil LVER MJac NArc SKen
'Celebration' CLoc CSil EGou
'Celia Smedley' ♀ CGre CLoc CSil EBak EGou EKMF EPts LCla LVER MAld MBri MJac MWar MWhe NArc SKen SLBF
'Centerpiece' EBak
'Central Scotland' LCla
'Ceri' CLoc NArc
'Cerrig' NArc
'Chameleon' CSil NArc SPet WGwG
'Champagne Celebration' CLoc
'Chandleri' EKMF NArc SLBF
'Chang' CLoc CSil EBak EKMF LCla LRHS MWar MWhe NArc SLBF
'Chantry Park' EGou LCla
'Charisma' NArc
'Charles Edward' CSil EKMF
'Charlie Gardiner' EBak LAco MWhe NArc
'Charlie Girl' EBak
'Charlotte Clyne' MJac
'Charming' CDoC CLoc CSil EBak EKMF GCHN MJac MWar NArc
'Chase Delight' Last listed 1999
'Checkerboard' ♀ CLoc CSil EBak ECtt EGou EKMF LCla LVER MAld MJac MWar MWhe NArc SKen SLBF SSea SYvo WEas WGwG
'Cheeky Chantalle' SLBF
'Cheers' EKMF MWar MWhe
¶ 'Cherry' PBR WWol
'Cherry Pie' Last listed 1998
'Cheryl' MJac
'Chessboard' CLoc CSil

'Chillerton Beauty' ♀ CDoC CLTr CLoc CSil CTri ECtt EKMF LCla LRHS MJac MWhe NArc SLBF SPer WBod
'China Doll' (d) EBak MWhe NArc
'China Lantern' CLoc CSil EBak EKMF
'Chiquita Maria' NArc
'Chris' Last listed 1998
¶ 'Chris Nicholls' EKMF
'Christ Driessen' Last listed 1998
'Christina Becker' NArc
'Christine Bamford' EGou
'Christine Shaffery' EGou
'Christmas Ribbons' Last listed 1998
cinerea EKMF LCla
'Cinnabarrina' SLBF
¶ 'Cinpetio' LCla
'Circe' EBak EKMF NArc
'Circus' EBak
'Circus Spangles' COtt CSil ECtt EKMF MWar SCoo SMur SWal
'Citation' CLoc CSil EBak EKMF MJac SSea
'City of Adelaide' (d) CLoc CSil MWhe
'City of Leicester' CSil LCla SPet
'Claire Belle' Last listed 1999
'Claire de Lune' EBak NArc
'Claire Evans' (d) CLoc
'Claire Oram' CLoc SSea
¶ 'Claudia' (d) MWar
'Cliantha' MJac MWhe NArc
'Clifford Gadsby' (d) EBak NArc
'Cliff's Hardy' CSil EKMF LCla NArc
'Cliff's Own' CSil NArc
'Cliff's Unique' CSil EPts MWar
'Clifton Beauty' MJac
'Clifton Charm' CSil EPts MJac
'Clipper' CSil
'Cloth of Gold' CLoc EBak MJac MWhe SKen SSea
'Cloverdale Jewel' CSil EBak ECtt LCla MWhe NArc
'Cloverdale Joy' EBak
'Cloverdale Pearl' ♀ CSil EBak EKMF EMan ENot LCla MJac MWhe NArc WPyg
'Coachman' CLoc CSil EBak EKMF EMan EPts LCla MAld MWar MWhe NArc SLBF WGwG
coccinea CDoC CGre CSil EGou EKMF LCla NArc
'Coconut Ice' NArc
x colensoi CDoC ECou EKMF LCla SHFr
'Colin Chambers' EGou
'Collingwood' CLoc EBak NArc
'Colne Fantasy' EKMF EPts
'Colne Greybeard' CSil NArc
'Come Dancing' CSil ECtt LCla NArc SKen
N 'Comet' (d) CLoc CSil EBak NArc
'Conchilla' EBak
'Confection' NArc
'Congreve Road' Last listed 1999
'Connie' (d) CSil EBak EKMF
'Conspicua' CSil EBak EGou EKMF NArc SKen NArc
'Constable Country' NArc
'Constance' (d) CDoC CLoc CSil EGou EKMF LCla MJac MWar MWhe NArc SKen SLBF
'Constance Comer' MJac
N 'Constellation' (d) CLoc EBak MWhe NArc
'Continental' EGou NArc
'Coombe Park' MJac
'Copycat' CSil
'Coquet Bell' EBak NArc
'Coquet Dale' EBak EGou MJac MWhe NArc
'Coquet Gold' CSil ECtt NArc
'Coral Baby' Last listed 1999
'Coral Seas' EBak

§	'Coralle' ♀	CLoc EBak EGou EKMF EMan EPts LCla MJac MWar MWhe NArc SKen SLBF
	'Corallina' ♀	CDoC CLoc CSil EBak EHol EKMF LVER MWhe NArc SPet SSea WFar WLow WWat
I	'Corallina Variegata'	CSil
	cordifolia Bentham	CTre EBak EKMF
	– hort.	See *F. splendens*
	'Core'ngrato' (d)	CLoc EBak
	'Cornelia Smith'	EGou LCla
	'Cornwall Calls'	Last listed 1998
	'Corsage'	NArc
	'Corsair' (d)	CSil EBak EKMF NArc
§	*corymbiflora* Ruiz & Pav.	CDoC CLoc EBak EGou EKMF
	– *alba*	See *F. boliviana* Carrière var. *alba*
	– misapplied	See *F. boliviana*
	'Cosmopolitan' (d)	CSil EBak NArc
	'Costa Brava'	CLoc EBak NArc
¶	'Cotta 2000'	EKMF
	'Cotta Bella'	EKMF NArc
	'Cotta Bright Star'	EKMF LCla NArc
¶	'Cotta Carousel'	EKMF
¶	'Cotta Christmas Tree'	EKMF
	'Cotta Fairy'	EKMF
	'Cotta Princess'	EKMF
	'Cotta Vino'	EKMF NArc SLBF
	'Cottinghamii'	See *F. x bacillaris* 'Cottinghamii'
	'Cotton Candy' (d)	CLoc CSil ECtt EGou EPts LCla MWhe
	'Countdown Carol'	EPts
	'Countess of Aberdeen'	CLoc CSil EBak EGou EKMF NArc SLBF
	'Countess of Maritza' (d)	CLoc
	'County Park'	ECou EWes
	'Court Jester' (d)	CLoc EBak NArc
	'Cover Girl'	EBak MWhe NArc SPet
	'Coverdale Jewel'	Last listed 1997
	'Coxeen'	EBak
	'Crackerjack'	CLoc EBak
	crassistipula	EGou EKMF LCla
	'Creampuff'	NArc
	'Crescendo'	CLoc
	'Crinkley Bottom'	EKMF EPts LCla LVER MJac SLBF
	'Crinoline' (d)	EBak NArc
	'Crosby Serendipidy'	CLoc
	'Crosby Soroptimist'	CSil MWar MWhe
	'Cross Check'	EMan MBri MJac NArc
	'Crusader'	CSil
	'Crystal Blue'	EBak NArc
	'Crystal Stars'	NArc
	'Cupcake'	NArc
	'Cupid'	CSil EBak NArc
	'Curly Q'	CSil EBak NArc
	'Curtain Call' (d)	CLoc EBak NArc
	'Cutie Karen'	SLBF
¶	x *cuzco*	LCla
	cylindracea	CSil EKMF LCla
	– (f)	EGou
	– (m)	EGou
	'Cymon'	CSil MWhe
	'Cymru'	NArc
	'Cyril Holmes'	NArc
	cyrtandroides	EGou EKMF
	'Daffodil Dolly'	NArc
	'Dainty'	EBak
	'Dainty Lady'	EBak
	'Daisy Bell'	CLoc CSil EBak ECtt EKMF LCla MJac MWhe NArc SPet SSea WGwG
	'Dalton'	EBak NArc
	'Dancing Bloom'	EPts

	'Dancing Flame' (d)	CLoc CSil EKMF EMan EPts LCla LVER MAld MBri MJac MWar MWhe NArc SLBF SYvo WGwG
	'Daniel Austin'	MJac
¶	'Daniella'	SLBF
	'Danish Pastry'	NArc
	'Danny Boy' (d)	CLoc EBak EKMF EMan MWhe NArc
	'Daphne Arlene'	CSil
	'Dark Eyes' (d) ♀	CLoc CSil EBak EGou EKMF EMan LVER MAld MBri MJac MWar MWhe NArc NFai NHaw SLBF SSea WGwG WWol
	'Dark Lady'	MWhe
¶	'Dark Mystery'	SLBF
¶	'Dark Night' (d)	CSil
	'Dark Secret' (d)	EBak NArc
	'Dark Treasure'	CDoC CSil EKMF
	'Darreen Dawn'	Last listed 1997
	'David'	CSil EGou EKMF EOHP LCla MWhe SKen SLBF
	'David Alston' (d)	CLoc EBak
	'David Lockyer' (d)	CLoc
	'David Ward'	EKMF
	'Dawn'	EBak SKen
	'Dawn Carless'	EGou
¶	'Dawn Fantasia' (v)	EPts SLBF
	'Dawn Sky' (d)	EBak
	'Dawn Star' (d)	CSil LVER MJac MWhe NArc
	'Dawn Thunder'	NArc SMur
	'Dawning'	Last listed 1998
	'Day by Day'	Last listed 1999
	'Day Star'	EBak
	'Daytime Live'	EKMF
	'De Groot's Moonlight'	EGou SLBF
	'De Groot's Pipes'	Last listed 1998
	'Debby' (d)	EBak NArc
	'Deben'	EWll
	'Deben Petite'	CDoC CSil EWll LCla
	'Deben Rose'	NArc WGwG
	'Deborah Mitchell'	WGwG
	'Deborah Street'	CLoc
N	*decussata*	EBak EGou EKMF LCla
	'Dee Copley' (d)	EBak NArc
	'Dee Star'	NArc
	'Deep Purple'	CLoc CSil ECtt EKMF MJac SCoo SLBF
	'Delaval Lady'	CSil
	'Delicia'	Last listed 1999
	'Delilah'	EKMF MJac
	'Delta's Bride'	EGou SLBF
	'Delta's Delight'	Last listed 1998
	'Delta's Dream'	LCla NArc WGwG
	'Delta's Drop'	EGou
	'Delta's Groom'	EGou
	'Delta's K.O.'	LCla NArc
¶	'Delta's Matador'	SLBF
	'Delta's Night'	EGou
	'Delta's Paljas'	Last listed 1997
	'Delta's Parade'	LCla MWar NArc
	'Delta's Song'	NArc SLBF
	'Delta's Sprinkler'	NArc
	'Delta's Symphonie'	Last listed 1998
	'Delta's Trick'	Last listed 1998
	'Delta's Wonder'	CSil
§	*denticulata*	CDoC CLoc CSil EBak EGou EKMF ERea LCla NArc SAga SKen SLBF WGwG
	dependens	See *F. corymbiflora* Ruiz & Pav.
	'Derby Imp'	NArc
	'Derby Star'	CSil
	'Desperate Daniel'	EKMF EPts LCla

'Destiny'	Last listed 1997
'Deutsche Perle'	Last listed 1998
'Devonshire Dumpling' (d)	CGre CLTr CLoc CSil EBak ECtt
	EGou EKMF EMan EPts LCla LVER
	MAld MBri MJac MWar MWhe
	NArc NHaw SKen SLBF
'Diablo' (d)	CSil EBak
'Diamond Celebration'	EKMF MWar
'Diamond Wedding'	Last listed 1997
'Diana' (d)	EBak
'Diana Wills'	MWhe SKen
'Diana Wright'	CSil EKMF LHil WSPU
'Diane Brown'	EKMF MWhe SSea
'Dick Swinbank'	EKMF
'Die Fledermaus'	NArc
'Dilly-Dilly'	ECtt
'Dimples'	CSil MBri
'Diny Hetterscheid'	LCla
'Dipton Dainty'	CLoc CSil EBak LCla NArc
'Dirk van Delen'	MWhe
'Display' ♀	CDoC CLoc CSil EBak EBee ECtt
	EKMF EMan LCla LRHS LVER
	MBri MJac MWar MWhe NArc
	SLBF SSea WGwG WStI
'Doc'	CSil EDAr
'Docteur Topinard'	CLoc EBak EKMF
'Doctor'	See F. 'The Doctor'
'Doctor Brendan Freeman'	LAco NArc
'Doctor Foster'	CDoC CLoc CSil CTri EBak ENot
	NArc WEas
'Doctor Olson' (d)	CLoc EBak
'Doctor Robert'	EKMF EPts MBri MJac MWhe
	NArc
§ 'Dollar Princess' (d) ♀	CDoC CLoc CSil EBak EBee ECtt
	EGou EKMF EMan EPts LCla LRHS
	MAld MBri MJac MWar MWhe
	NArc NFai SChu SKen SLBF SPlb
	WFar WGwG WStI
'Dolly Daydream'	EKMF NArc
'Domacin'	Last listed 1998
'Dominique'	EKMF
'Dominyana'	EBak EKMF LCla
'Don Peralta'	EBak
'Dopey'	CSil EDAr
'Doreen Gladwyn'	Last listed 1999
'Doreen Redfern'	CLoc CSil EKMF MJac MWhe
	NArc
'Doris Coleman'	EMan
'Doris Hobbs'	EKMF
'Doris Joan'	CSil
'Dorking Delight'	LCla
'Dorothea Flower'	CLoc CSil EBak EKMF
'Dorothy'	CSil LCla SLBF
'Dorothy Day' (d)	CLoc
'Dorothy Hanley'	Last listed 1999
'Dorothy M. Goldsmith'	Last listed 1999
'Dorothy Shields'	LCla MAld MJac
'Dorrian Brogdale'	EGou LCla
'Dove House'	EKMF
¶ 'Dr Foster'	EKMF
'Drake 400' (d)	CLoc
'Drame'	CDoC CSil EBak EKMF LCla LHil
	NArc KSen SPet SSea WLow
'Drum Major'	EBak NArc
'Du Barry'	EBak NArc
'Duchess of Albany'	CLoc CSil EBak NArc
'Duchess of Cornwall'	CSil
'Duet'	CSil SMur
N 'Duke of Wellington' (d)	CLoc
'Dulcie Elizabeth' (d)	CSil EBak LCla MJac MWar NArc
'Dusky Beauty'	CSil MJac NArc
'Dusky Rose' (d)	CLoc CSil EBak MJac MWhe NArc

	WGwG
'Dutch King Size'	EGou
'Dutch Mill'	CLoc EBak
'Duyfken'	NArc
'Earre Barré'	EGou
'East Anglian'	CLoc EBak NArc
'Easter Bonnet' (d)	CLoc
'Easterling'	NArc
'Ebbtide' (d)	CLoc EBak NArc
'Echo'	CLoc LRHS
'Ed Largarde'	EBak EKMF
'Edale'	CSil
'Eden Beauty'	NArc
'Eden Lady'	CLoc NArc SPet
'Eden Princess'	MJac MWhe
'Edith'	CSil EKMF LCla SLBF
'Edith Emery'	Last listed 1999
'Edith Hall'	Last listed 1999
'Edith Jack'	Last listed 1999
'Edna W. Smith'	CSil ECtt
'Edwin J. Goulding'	EGou EKMF LCla
'Eileen Raffill'	EBak
'Eileen Saunders'	CSil EBak
'Eira Goulding'	EGou
'El Camino' (d)	CSil MWhe NArc NFai
'El Cid'	CLoc CSil EBak EKMF NArc
'Elaine Ann'	CInt EPts LHil MJac
'Eleanor Clark'	EKMF LCla NArc
'Eleanor Leytham'	EBak EKMF LCla NArc
'Eleanor Rawlins'	CSil EBak EKMF NArc SKen
'Elfin Glade'	CLoc CSil EBak EKMF
'Elfrida'	CSil EKMF
'Elfriede Ott'	CLoc EBak EKMF MWhe
'Elisabeth Honorine'	NArc
N 'Elizabeth'	EBak EKMF NArc
'Elizabeth Broughton'	EKMF
'Elizabeth Tompkins'	EKMF MJac
'Elizabeth Travis'	EBak
'Ellen Morgan'	EBak
'Elma'	LCla
'Elsa'	ECtt LRHS
'Elsie Downey'	NArc
'Elsie Mitchell'	CSil MWhe NArc
¶ 'Elsie Vert' (d)	SYvo
¶ 'Elysée'	EKMF
§ 'Emile de Wildeman'	EBak EKMF LVER MWar
'Emily Austen'	EKMF MJac NArc
'Emma Louise'	NArc
'Emma Massey'	Last listed 1997
'Emma Rowell'	EKMF
'Empress of Prussia' ♀	CDoC CLoc CSil EBak ECtt EKMF
	EMan LRHS NArc SLBF SSea
'Enchanted' (d)	EBak MWar
encliandra subsp.	EKMF LCla
encliandra	
* – var. *gris*	EGou
§ – subsp. *tetradactyla*	EKMF
'Enfant Prodigue'	CDoC CLoc CSil EKMF
'Englander'	Last listed 1998
'English Rose'	CSil
¶ 'Enid Joyce'	SLBF
'Enstone'	See F. magellanica var. molinae
	'Enstone'
'Eppsii'	CSil
'Erica Julie'	MWhe NArc
¶ 'Eric's Everest' (d)	EKMF
'Eric's Hardy'	CSil
'Eric's Majestic'	EKMF MJac
'Erika Frohmann'	Last listed 1999
'Erika Köth'	CSil LCla
'Ernest Rankin'	CSil EKMF NArc
'Ernestine'	MWhe

'Ernie Bromley' EGou NArc SLBF
'Eroica' NArc
'Errol' CLoc
'Estelle Marie' CLoc CSil EBak EGou EKMF MBri
MJac MWar MWhe SLBF SSea
'Esther Divine' CSil
'Eternal Flame' CSil EBak MBri MWhe NArc SKen
'Eureka Red' Last listed 1999
'Eurydice' (d) CLoc
'Eusebia' EKMF MJac NArc
'Eva Boerg' CLoc CSil EBak ECtt EKMF EMan
LCla MBri MWar MWhe NArc
NFai SKen SPet SWal WGwG WKif
'Eva Dayes' EKMF SLBF
'Eva Twaites' EGou LCla
'Evanson's Choice' Last listed 1999
'Eve Hollands' Last listed 1998
'Evelyn Stanley' Last listed 1998
'Evelyn Steele Little' EBak
'Evening Sky' (d) EBak NArc
'Evensong' CLoc CSil EBak MWhe NArc
'Excalibur' EGou NArc
excorticata CB&S CDoC CSil CTre CTrw
ECou EGou EKMF GOrP LCla
WPGP WSHC
'Exton Beauty' NArc
'Fabian Franck' LCla
'Fairy Floss' Last listed 1998
'Fairytales' NArc
'Falklands' CSil
'Falling Stars' CLoc CSil EBak ECtt MWhe
'Fan Dancer' (d) EBak
'Fancy Flute' CSil NArc
'Fancy Free' MBri WLRN
'Fancy Pants' CLoc EBak EGou
'Fanfare' CDoC EBak EKMF EWll LCla NArc
'Fascination' See *F.* 'Emile de Wildeman'
'Fashion' EBak
'Fasna 1100' NArc
'Favourite' EBak
'Fenman' EPts MJac NArc
'Fergie' LCla
'Festival' MWhe
'Festival Lights' Last listed 1998
'Festoon' EBak
'Fey' EKMF
¶ 'Ffion' EPts
'Fiery Spider' EBak NArc
'Figaro' Last listed 1998
§ 'Filigraan' NArc
Filigree See *F.* 'Filigraan'
'Fine Lady' Last listed 1998
'Finn' EGou EPts
'Fiona' CLoc CSil EBak EGou NArc
'Fiona Jane' EKMF
'Fiona Lynn' Last listed 1998
'Fiona Pitt' Last listed 1998
'Fire Mountain' (d) CLoc CSil ECtt MWhe NArc SKen
SSea
'Firecracker' MJac MWar WWeb
'Firefly' NArc
'Firefox' NArc
'Firelite' EBak NArc
'Firenza' MWar
'First Lady' NArc
'First Love' Last listed 1999
'First Success' EKMF LCla SLBF
'Flair' (d) CLoc
'Flame' EBak
'Flamenco Dancer' CLoc ECtt
'Flash' ♀ CDoC CLoc CSil CTri EBak EKMF
LCla MAld MJac MWhe NArc SLBF

WFar WStl
'Flashlight' EGou
¶ 'Flashlight Ameliore' CSil
'Flat Jack o' Lancashire' CSil ECtt EKMF
'Flavia' (d) EBak
'Flirtation Waltz' (d) CGre CLoc CSil EBak EKMF EMan
LVER MAld MJac MWhe NArc
SPet SSea
'Flocon de Neige' EBak EKMF NArc
'Floral City' (d) CLoc EBak NArc
'Florence Mary Abbott' EGou EMan
'Florence Turner' CSil EBak EKMF MWhe SKen
'Florentina' (d) CLoc CSil EBak EKMF NArc
'Floretta' Last listed 1998
'Fluffy Frills' CSil
'Flyaway' (d) EBak NArc
'Fly-by-night' NArc
'Flying Cloud' (d) ♀ CLoc CSil EBak EKMF MBri NArc
'Flying Scotsman' (d) CLoc CSil EBak EGou EKMF EPts
LVER MJac NArc SLBF
'Folies Bergères' EBak
'Foline' NArc
'Foolke' EBak EPts LHil
'Forest King' NArc
¶ 'Forfar's Pride' EGou
¶ 'Forget-me-not' CLoc CSil EBak EKMF NArc
'Formosissima' Last listed 1998
'Fort Bragg' (d) EBak NArc
'Forward Look' MWhe
'Fountains Abbey' EMan NArc
'Foxgrove Wood' CSil EBak EKMF EPts LCla MAld
SLBF
¶ 'Foxy Lady' EKMF
'Frances Haskins' MWhe
'Frank Sanford' NArc
'Frank Saunders' CSil LCla
'Frank Unsworth' ECtt EKMF MJac MWar NArc
'Frankie's Magnificent EPts
Seven'
'Frau Hilde Rademacher' (d) CDoC CSil EBak EKMF EMan
LVER NArc SLBF
'Frauke' NArc
'Fred Swales' CSil EKMF LCla
'Fred's First' CSil
'Freefall' EBak
'Freeland Ballerina' Last listed 1997
'Friendly Fire' (d) CLoc EKMF NArc
'Friendship' Last listed 1998
'Frosted Flame' CLoc CSil EKMF LCla MJac MWar
MWhe NArc SKen SSea
'Frühling' (d) CSil EBak
* *fuchsia* Last listed 1999
I 'Fuchsia Fan' Last listed 1998
'Fuchsiade '88' CLoc EBak EKMF LCla MWhe
'Fuchsiarama' EKMF
'Fuchsiarama '91' NArc
'Fuji San' CDoC EGou EPts LCla
'Fuksie Foetsie' CDoC CSil EGou EKMF LCla
WGwG
fulgens ♀ CDoC EKMF LCla LHil MWhe
NArc SYvo
- 'Gesneriana' See *F.* 'Gesneriana'
* - var. *machoacans* EKMF
I - var. *michocan* Last listed 1999
* - var. *minuata* EKMF
- 'Rubra Grandiflora' See *F.* 'Rubra Grandiflora'
* - 'Variegata' CLoc CSil EGou EKMF LCla
'Fulpila' EGou LCla
'Für Elise' (d) EBak
furfuracea EKMF
'Gala' (d) EBak NArc
'Galadriel' EGou

'Galahad'	NArc	
'Garden News' (d) ♀	CDoC CLoc CSil ECtt EGou EKMF EPts LCla LRHS LVER MAld MGos MJac MWar MWhe NArc SKen SLBF WFar WLow	
'Garden Week'	LVER MWhe	
'Gartenmeister Bonstedt' ♀	CDoC CLoc CSil EBak EKMF EPts LCla LRHS MLan NArc SKen SSea WEas WGwG	
'Gay Anne'	EKMF NArc	
'Gay Fandango' (d)	CLoc CSil EBak ECtt LCla NArc	
'Gay Future'	EKMF	
'Gay Parasol' (d)	CLoc EGou MJac	
'Gay Paree' (d)	EBak	
'Gay Senorita'	EBak	
'Gay Spinner'	CLoc	
gehrigeri	EBak EGou EKMF LCla	
'Geisha Girl'	CSil	
'Gelre'	Last listed 1997	
'Gemma Fisher'	EPts	
'Général Charles de Gaulle'	EGou LCla	
'Général Monk' (d)	CDoC CSil EBak ECtt EKMF EMan LVER MBri NArc WCot	
'Général Voyron'	CSil	
'General Wavell'	NArc WGwG	
'Genii' ♀	More than 30 suppliers	
'Geoffrey Smith'	CSil ECtt EKMF	
'Georg Börnemann'	NArc	
'Georgana' (d)	MWhe	
'George Barr'	CSil EKMF LRHS NArc	
'George Johnson'	CDoC NArc SPet WGwG	
'George Travis' (d)	EBak	
¶ 'Georgie Girl'	EGou	
'Gerald Drewitt'	CSil	
'Geraldine'	CSil	
'Gerda Manthey'	Last listed 1999	
'Gerharda's Aubergine'	EKMF	
'Gerharda's Kiekeboe'	Last listed 1999	
'Gerharda's Sophie'	Last listed 1997	
§ 'Gesneriana'	CLoc CSil EBak EGou	
'Ghislaine'	Last listed 1998	
'Giant Pink Enchanted' (d)	CLoc EBak NArc	
'Gilda'	CSil NArc	
'Gillian Althea'	NArc	
'Gilt Edge'	CLoc CSil	
'Gina's Gold'	Last listed 1999	
'Gingham Girl'	MJac	
'Giovanna and Wesley'	EGou	
'Gipping'	Last listed 1998	
¶ 'Gipsy Princess'	CLoc	
'Girls Brigade'	EKMF	
'Gladiator' (d)	CSil EBak EKMF LCla NArc	
'Gladys Haddaway'	LCla	
'Gladys Miller'	CLoc	
glaziouana	CDoC CSil EGou EKMF LCla SLBF SYvo	
'Glenby'	NArc	
'Gleneagles'	EGou	
'Glitters'	EBak EKMF NArc	
§ 'Globosa'	CAgr EBak EKMF	
'Gloria Johnson'	EKMF NArc	
'Glow'	CSil EBak EKMF	
'Glowing Embers'	EBak NArc	
Glowing Lilac	CSil ECtt EMan NArc	
'Glyn Jones'	EKMF	
'Goena-Goena'	CSil	
'Gold Brocade'	CSil NArc SPet	
'Gold Crest'	EBak	
'Gold Leaf'	Last listed 1997	
'Golden Anniversary' (d)	CLoc EBak EGou EKMF EMan LVER MAld MJac SSea	
'Golden Arrow'	EGou LCla LHil NArc	
'Golden Border Queen'	CLoc	
'Golden Dawn'	CLoc EBak ECtt NArc	
'Golden Drame'	Last listed 1997	
'Golden Eden Lady'	MWhe	
'Golden Herald'	SLBF SSea	
'Golden Jessimae'	NArc	
'Golden La Campanella'	CLoc ECtt MBri SSea	
'Golden Lena'	CSil EKMF EMan	
'Golden Marinka' ♀	CLoc CSil EBak ECtt EKMF LRHS MBri MWhe SPet	
'Golden Melody'	CSil	
'Golden Penny Askew'	Last listed 1999	
'Golden Runner'	Last listed 1999	
'Golden Swingtime'	CSil ECtt EGou LRHS MBri MJac MWhe NArc NHaw SSea WGwG WLow	
'Golden Tolling Bell'	Last listed 1997	
'Golden Treasure' (v)	CLoc CSil ECtt EKMF MBri MWar	
'Golden Vergeer'	EGou SLBF	
'Golden Wedding'	EKMF	
'Goldsworth Beauty'	CSil LCla	
'Golondrina'	CSil EBak MWhe	
'Goody Goody'	EBak	
'Gordon Thorley'	EKMF MWhe	
'Gordon's China Rose'	LCla	
'Gorgeous Gemma'	SLBF	
'Gottingen'	CSil EBak EKMF LCla	
'Göttinger Ruhm'	NArc	
'Governor 'Pat' Brown' (d)	EBak	
'Graaf Christian'	EGou	
'Grace Darling'	EBak MWhe	
'Grace Durham'	Last listed 1998	
gracilis	See *F. magellanica* var. *gracilis*	
'Graf Spee'	Last listed 1998	
'Graf Witte'	CDoC CLTr CSil NArc SKen WGwG	
'Grand Duchess'	EGou LCla	
'Grand Duke'	Last listed 1999	
'Grand Prix'	CSil NArc SKen	
'Grand Slam'	SKen	
'Grandad Fred' (d)	SLBF	
'Grandma Sinton'	CLoc CSil EMan LCla MBri MJac MWhe NArc SKen	
'Grandpa George'	CSil LCla	
'Grandpa Jack'	SLBF	
'Grasmere'	Last listed 1999	
'Grayrigg'	CSil EKMF EPPr	
'Great Ouse'	EPts	
'Great Scott' (d)	CLoc CSil SKen	
'Green 'n' Gold'	EBak	
'Greenpeace'	EKMF LCla	
'Greg Walker'	Last listed 1999	
'Greta'	CSil EGou	
'Gretna Chase'	MBri MWhe	
'Grey Lady'	CSil	
'Grietje'	EGou	
'Groene Kan's Glorie'	CGre EKMF NArc	
'Grumpy'	CSil EDAr EHol EPts LRHS MBri MWhe NArc	
'Gruss aus dem Bodethal'	CLoc EBak EGou EKMF EPts	
'Guinevere'	EBak	
'Gustave Doré' (d)	CSil EBak EKMF NArc	
'Guy Dauphine'	EBak	
¶ 'Gwen Burralls' (d)	EKMF	
'Gwen Dodge'	EGou LCla WGwG	
'Gwen Wakelin'	NArc	
'Gwen Wallis'	EGou	
'Gwendoline'	EGou	
'Gypsy Girl'	NArc	
'H.G. Brown'	CSil EBak EKMF MWhe	
'Halsall Beauty'	MBri	
'Halsall Belle'	MBri	

'Halsall Pride'	MBri
'Hampshire Beauty'	MJac
'Hampshire Blue'	CDoC CSil NArc SSea
'Hampshire Pride'	WGwG
'Hampshire Prince'	CSil LVER
'Hampshire Treasure'	CSil
'Hanna'	CSil
'Hannah Gwen'	EKMF
'Hannah Louise'	CInt EPts
'Hannah Williams'	CLTr
'Hans van Beek'	NArc
'Happiness'	CSil
'Happy'	CSil EDAr EPts LCla MWhe NArc
'Happy Anniversary'	CLoc EKMF NArc
'Happy Fellow'	CLoc CSil EBak EKMF
'Happy Wedding Day' (d)	CLoc CSil ECtt EKMF LCla LRHS
	MWar MWhe SSea WLow
'Hapsburgh'	EBak
'Harlow Car'	EKMF NArc WGwG
'Harlyn'	NArc
N 'Harmony'	EBak
'Harnser's Flight'	CSil EGou LCla
'Harriett'	Last listed 1999
'Harrow Pride'	CSil
'Harry Dunnett'	EBak
'Harry Gray' (d)	CLoc CSil EBak ECtt EMan EPts
	LCla MBri MJac MWar MWhe
	NArc SKen SLBF SSea WGwG
	WLow
hartwegii	CDoC CSil EGou EKMF LCla
'Hathersage'	EBak
'Hathor'	EGou
hatsbachii	CDoC CSil
hatschbachii	EGou EKMF LCla
'Haute Cuisine' (d)	CLoc CSil EGou EKMF EMan
	LVER MWhe NArc
'Hawaiian Night'	NArc
'Hawaiian Princess'	ECtt
'Hawaiian Sunset'	SLBF
'Hawkshead'	CDoC CGle CInt CLoc CSil ECha
	EGou EKMF ELan EPts GCal GOrc
	GQui LCla LHil LRHS MBri MGos
	MJac MWhe NArc SChu SLBF
	SMac SMrm WCot
'Hayley Marie'	SLBF
* 'Hazel'	EKMF MWhe SWal
'Heart Throb' (d)	EBak
'Heathfield'	CDoC
'Heavenly Hayley'	SLBF
'Hebe'	EBak MWhe
'Heidi Ann' (d) ♀	CDoC CLoc CSil EBak EKMF
	EMan EPts LCla LRHS MBri MJac
	MWar MWhe NArc SLBF SSea
	WGwG
'Heidi Weiss'	NArc
'Heinrich Henkel'	See *F.* 'Andenken an Heinrich
	Henkel'
'Heirloom'	ECtt EKMF
'Helen Clare' (d)	CLoc EBak NArc
'Helen Elizabeth'	Last listed 1999
'Helen Spence'	NArc
'Hellan Devine'	MJac
'Hello Dolly'	CLoc
'Hemsleyana'	See *F. microphylla* subsp.
	hemsleyana
'Henri Poincaré'	CDoC EBak EKMF
'Henriette Prins'	Last listed 1998
'Herald' ♀	CDoC CSil EBak EKMF MWhe
	NArc SLBF WGwG WLow
'Herbe de Jacques'	EKMF SKen
'Heritage'	CLoc CSil EBak EKMF NArc
'Herman de Graaff'	EGou

'Hermiena'	CLoc CSil EGou EKMF LCla MAld
	MWar MWhe NArc SLBF WGwG
'Heron'	CSil EBak EKMF SKen
'Hessett Festival' (d)	CSil EBak EGou MWhe NArc
'Heston Blue'	EKMF NArc
'Hi Jinks'	EBak
'Hiawatha'	NArc
hidalgensis	See *F. microphylla* subsp.
	hidalgensis
'Hidcote Beauty'	CDoC CLoc CSil EBak EKMF
	MWhe NArc SKen SLBF SSea
	SYvo WGwG
'Hidden Beauty'	NArc
'Hidden Treasure'	EGou
'Highland Pipes'	CSil EKMF LCla NArc
'Hilda May Salmon'	NArc
'Hindu Belle'	EBak
'Hinnerike'	CSil EKMF LCla NArc
'Hiroshige'	LCla
'His Excellency' (d)	CSil EBak
'Hobo'	EGou
'Hobson's Choice'	MWar SLBF
'Hokusai'	EKMF
'Holly's Beauty'	EKMF MWar SMur WGwG WWol
'Hollywood Park'	EBak
'Horatio'	CSil ECtt MJac
'Hot Coals'	CSil ECtt EGou EPts MWhe
'Howlett's Hardy'	CDoC CLoc CSil EBak ECtt EKMF
	GCHN LRHS MBri NArc
'Hula Girl' (d)	CSil EBak EKMF MJac MWar
	MWhe SLBF SPet
'Humboldt Holiday'	EKMF NArc
'Hummeltje'	Last listed 1999
'Huntsman'	CDoC ECtt EKMF MWhe WGwG
	WLRN
'Ian Brazewell' (d)	CLoc
'Ian Leedham'	EBak EKMF
'Ice Cream Soda'	EBak NArc
'Iceberg'	CSil EBak NArc
'Icecap'	CSil EKMF MBri NArc
'Iced Champagne'	CLoc EBak MJac NArc
'Ichiban' (d)	CLoc
'Ida' (d)	EBak
'Igloo Maid' (d)	CLoc CSil EBak EKMF MJac
	MWhe NArc SPet SSea
'Impala'	EGou
'Imperial Crown'	CSil
'Imperial Fantasy'	NArc
'Impudence'	CLoc CSil EBak SSea
'Impulse' (d)	CLoc EKMF NArc SKen SLBF
'Ina'	Last listed 1999
'Independence'	Last listed 1999
'Indian Maid' (d)	EBak EKMF LVER NArc SKen
	WGwG
'Inferno'	EKMF
¶ *inflata*	EGou
'Ingleore'	Last listed 1998
'Ingram Maid'	Last listed 1999
'Insa'	NArc
'Insulinde'	CDoC CSil EGou EKMF LCla
	MAld MWar NArc SLBF WWol
'Intercity'	NArc
'Interlude' (d)	EBak
'Iolanthe'	Last listed 1998
'Irene L. Peartree'	EGou LCla
'Irene van Zoeren'	MAld NArc
'Iris Amer' (d)	CLoc CSil EBak
'Irma'	Last listed 1998
'Isabel Ryan'	CSil
'Isis'	CSil
'Isle of Mull'	NArc
'Isle of Purbeck'	MJac

'Italiano'   MJac
'Ivy Grace'   CSil
'Ixion'   NArc
'Jaap Brummel'   Last listed 1998
'Jack Acland'   ECtt SKen
'Jack Rowlands'   EGou
'Jack Shahan' ♀   CDoC CLoc CSil EBak EKMF
                              EMan LCla MBri MJac MWar
                              MWhe NFai SLBF SSea WGwG
'Jack Stanway'   CSil EGou MWar WEas
¶ 'Jack Wilson'   CSil
'Jackie Bull'   EBak
'Jackpot' (d)   EBak
'Jackqueline'   CSil EKMF LCla NArc
'Jam Roll'   LVER
'Jamboree' (d)   EBak NArc
'James Lye' (d)   EBak EKMF SKen
'James Shurvell'   CSil
'James Travis' (d)   CDoC CSil EBak EKMF LCla
'Jan Bremer'   NArc
'Jan S. Kamphuis'   EGou
'Jane Humber'   EKMF LCla MJac NArc
'Jane Lye'   EBak
'Janet Goodwin'   NArc
'Janet Williams'   CSil
'Janice Ann'   EKMF LCla
¶ 'Janice Perry's Gold'   CLoc
'Janie'   CLyn
'Janneke   EGou SLBF
    Brinkman-Salentijn'
'Jap Van't Veer'   LCla SLBF
'Jasper's Likkepot'   NArc
'Jayess Wendy'   Last listed 1998
'Jayne Louise Mills'   NArc
'Jean Baker'   CSil
'Jean Campbell'   EBak
'Jean Clark'   Last listed 1999
'Jean Dawes'   Last listed 1998
'Jean Pidcock'   NArc
'Jeane'   EKMF
'Jennie Rachael'   NArc
'Jennifer Hampson'   CSil
'Jennifer Haslam'   LCla
'Jennifer Lister'   CSil EKMF
'Jenny May'   SLBF
'Jenny Sorensen'   CSil EKMF LCla MAld MJac MWar
                              NArc SLBF
'Jess'   LCla NArc SLBF
'Jessica's Dream' (d)   SLBF
'Jessimae'   NArc
N 'Jester'   CLoc CSil
'Jet Fire' (d)   CSil EBak NArc
'Jiddles'   SLBF
'Jill Storey'   EKMF
'Jill Whitworth'   CDoC
'Jim Coleman'   NArc
'Jim Dodge'   EPts LCla
'Jim Missin'   MAld
'Jim Muncaster'   EKMF NArc
jimenezii   EGou EKMF LCla
 – hybrid   EKMF
'Jimmy Carr'   EKMF
'Jimmy Cricket'   EKMF
¶ 'Jingle Bells'   MWhe
¶ 'Jinlye'   EKMF
'Joan Barnes'   CSil
'Joan Cooper'   CLoc CSil EBak EKMF
'Joan Gilbert'   CSil
'Joan Goy'   EKMF EPts MJac MWhe
'Joan Knight'   CLoc
'Joan Leach'   CSil
'Joan Margaret'   MJac

'Joan Morris'   SLBF
'Joan Pacey'   EBak EKMF NArc
'Joan Paxton'   LCla
'Joan Smith'   CSil EBak LCla SYvo
'Joan Young'   Last listed 1999
'Jo-Anne Fisher'   EPts
'Joe Kusber' (d)   CSil EBak MJac NArc SKen
'Joe Nicholls'   EKMF
'Joel'   SLBF
'John Boy'   EGou
'John E. Caunt'   CSil EKMF
'John Grooms'   CLoc EKMF LAco MJac MWar
'John Lockyer'   CLoc EBak NArc
'John Maynard Scales'   CDoC EGou LCla MJac MWhe
                              NArc
'John Oram'   Last listed 1998
'John Pitt'   Last listed 1998
'John Suckley'   EBak
'Johnny'   CLoc SSea
'Jomam'   CLoc MWar NArc SLBF
'Jon Oram'   CLoc
'Jose's Joan'   NArc
'Joy Bielby'   EKMF NArc
'Joy Patmore' ♀   CLoc CSil EBak EKMF EPts LCla
                              MBri MWar MWhe NArc SKen
                              SLBF
¶ 'Joyce Hill'   SLBF
'Joyce Maynard'   MJac
'Joyce Sinton'   EKMF EMan MBri MWar NArc
'Joyce Storey'   EKMF
'Joyce Wilson'   LCla
'Jubie-Lin'   Last listed 1998
'Jubilee Quest'   MWar SLBF
'Judith Alison Castle'   GCHN
'Julchen'   Last listed 1998
'Jules Daloges' (d)   EBak EKMF
'Julia'   CSil EKMF
'Julie'   Last listed 1999
'Julie Horton'   Last listed 1998
'Julie Marie'   CSil MJac NArc
'June Gardner'   EKMF
'June Spencer'   EGou
N 'Juno'   EBak
juntasensis   EGou EKMF
'Jupiter Seventy'   EBak
'Justin's Pride'   CSil EKMF
'Kaboutertje'   EKMF
'Kaleidoscope' (d)   CSil EBak NArc
'Karen Bielby'   EKMF
'Karen Bradley'   MJac NArc
'Karen Isles'   EKMF SLBF
'Karen Louise' (d)   CLoc
'Karin de Groot'   EKMF NArc
'Karin Siegers'   CSil
¶ 'Karin van der Sande'   EGou
'Kate Harriet' (d)   LCla WGwG
'Kath van Hanegem'   EGou
'Kathleen Muncaster'   EKMF
'Kathleen Smith'   ECtt EKMF NArc
'Kathryn Maidment'   EKMF NArc
'Kathy Louise'   EMan
'Kathy's Prince'   ECtt EKMF NArc
'Kathy's Sparkler'   CSil EGou EKMF
'Katie Elizabeth Ann'   MWar
'Katinka'   EGou EKMF LCla
¶ 'Katjan'   EKMF
'Katrina' (d)   CLoc EBak NArc
'Katrina Thompsen'   CLoc EKMF EPts LCla MAld MWar
                              SLBF SSea
'Katy James'   EKMF SLBF
'Kay Riley'   Last listed 1998
'Keele '92'   Last listed 1999

'Keepsake' (d) — CLoc CSil EBak
¶ 'Keesje' — SLBF
'Kegworth Beauty' — Last listed 1999
'Kegworth Carnival' — LCla NArc
'Kegworth Delight' — Last listed 1997
'Kegworth Supreme' — MJac
'Kelly Jo' — LCla
'Kelly Rushton' — Last listed 1997
¶ 'Kelly Stableford' — EGou
'Ken Goldsmith' — EPts LCla
'Ken Jennings' — MJac
'Ken Sharp' — NArc
'Kenny Dalglish' — CSil EKMF
'Kernan Robson' (d) — CLoc EBak NArc
'Kerry Anne' — EPts
'Kevin Stals' — LCla
'Keystone' — EBak
'Khada' — MWhe
'Kim Wright' — MWhe
'Kimberly' — EBak
'King George V' — MBlu
'King of Bath' — EBak
'King of Hearts' (d) — EBak
'King's Ransom' (d) — CLoc CSil EBak EKMF LRHS MWhe NArc SPet
'Kiss 'n' Tell' — MJac MWhe NArc
'Kit Oxtoby' — ECtt EGou EKMF EMan LCla LVER MJac NArc SKen SYvo
'Kiwi' (d) — EBak
'Klassic' — Last listed 1998
'Kleine Gärtnerin' — Last listed 1997
'Kleine Sandra' — EGou
'Knight Errant' — CSil SSea
'Knockout' — CSil EKMF
'Kolding Perle' — CSil EKMF
'Komeet' — Last listed 1999
'Königin der Frühe' — NArc
'Kon-Tiki' — CLoc CSil EKMF NArc
'Koralle' — See F. 'Coralle'
'Kwintet' — EBak LCla MJac SKen
'Kyoto' — EKMF
'La Apache' — Last listed 1998
'La Bianca' — EBak
'La Campanella' ♀ — CDoC CLoc CSil EBak ECtt EKMF EMan EPts LCla MAld MBri MJac MWar MWhe NArc NFai SLBF WGwG
'La Fiesta' (d) — EBak NArc
'La France' (d) — EBak EKMF
N 'La Neige' (d) — CSil EBak EKMF LCla
'La Porte' (d) — CLoc
'La Rosita' (d) — CSil EBak EGou SLBF
N 'La Traviata' (d) — EBak
'Lace Petticoats' (d) — EBak EKMF NArc
'Lady Beth' (d) — NArc
'Lady Boothby' — CHEx CSil EBak EKMF NArc SKen SLBF SMrm
'Lady Framlingham' — EPts
'Lady Heytesbury' — EKMF
'Lady in Grey' — EKMF
'Lady in Pink' — Last listed 1999
'Lady Isobel Barnett' — CLoc CSil EBak EKMF LCla MBri MJac MWar MWhe NArc
'Lady Kathleen Spence' — CSil EBak MWhe NArc SPet
'Lady Love' — Last listed 1999
'Lady Patricia Mountbatten' — CSil EKMF EMan MWhe NArc WGwG
'Lady Ramsey' — EBak MJac NArc
'Lady Rebecca' (d) — CLoc
'Lady Thumb' ♀ — More than 30 suppliers
'Lady's Smock' — EKMF
'Lakeland Princess' — EBak NArc

'Lakeside' — CLoc EBak
'Lambaba' — WWol
'Lambada' — EKMF MJac MWhe SLBF
'Lamme Goedzak' — Last listed 1997
'Lancashire Lad' — CDoC LCla MWar
'Lancashire Lass' — EMan MBri NArc WLRN
'Lancelot' — EBak
'Land van Beveren' — MWar NArc SLBF SYvo
'Lark' — EPts
'L'Arlésienne' — CLoc
'Lassie' (d) — CDoC CLoc EBak NArc
N 'Laura' — CLoc CSil EKMF EPts MWar MWhe SLBF
'Laura Amanda' — EPts
'Lavender Ann' — EGou
'Lavender Blue' — Last listed 1999
'Lavender Kate' (d) — CLoc EBak MJac
'Lavender Lace' — MWhe
'Lavender Lady' — CSil MAld
'Lazy Lady' — EBak
'Le Berger' — Last listed 1999
'Lechlade Apache' — EGou LCla
'Lechlade Chinaman' — CDoC CSil LCla
'Lechlade Debutante' — EGou EKMF LCla
'Lechlade Fire-eater' — LCla
¶ 'Lechlade Gordon' — WGwG
'Lechlade Gorgon' — CDoC CSil EKMF LCla NArc
'Lechlade Magician' — CDoC CSil EKMF LCla NArc
'Lechlade Maiden' — CSil LCla
'Lechlade Martianess' — EGou EKMF LCla
'Lechlade Potentate' — EGou LCla
'Lechlade Rocket' — EGou EKMF LCla
'Lechlade Tinkerbell' — LCla
'Lechlade Violet' — CDoC CSil EKMF
'Lee Anthony' — CSil
'Leica' — EKMF MJac
'Leicestershire Silver' — MJac NArc
'Len Bielby' — CDoC EKMF LCla
'Lena' ♀ — CDoC CLoc CSil EBak EKMF EPts LRHS LVER MBri MJac MWhe NArc NFai SKen SPer SSea WEas WGwG
'Lena Dalton' (d) — CLoc EBak EKMF MJac MWhe NArc
'Leonhart von Fuchs' — EGou LCla
'Leonora' ♀ — CLoc CSil EBak EKMF LCla MBri MWar MWhe NArc SLBF SWal WGwG
'Lesley' — LCla
¶ 'Lesson Nancy' — MWar
'Lett's Delight' — EGou EPts
'Letty Lye' — EBak
'Leverhulme' — See F. 'Leverkusen'
§ 'Leverkusen' — CDoC CLoc CSil EBak EGou LCla MJac MWhe WGwG
'Li Kai Lin' — CSil
N 'Liebesträume' (d) — EBak
'Liebriez' — CDoC CSil EBak EKMF EPts NArc SPet
* 'Lilac' — CSil EBak
'Lilac Dainty' — CSil
'Lilac Lady' — MJac
'Lilac Lustre' (d) — CGre CLoc CSil EBak EKMF NArc
'Lilac Princess' — MJac
'Lilac Queen' (d) — EBak
¶ 'Lilian' — EKMF
'Lillian Annetts' (d) — LCla SLBF
'Lillibet' (d) — CLoc CSil EBak NArc WGwG
'Lillydale' — CSil
'Lilo Vogt' — NArc WGwG
¶ 'Lime Lite' (d) — MJac
'Linda Goulding' — CSil EBak EGou MAld MWar

	MWhe NArc SSea
'Linda Grace'	EKMF MJac
'Lindisfarne'	CLoc EBak EKMF LCla MJac
	MWar NArc
'Linet'	Last listed 1997
'Lisa'	CDoC CSil EPts
'Lisa Ashton'	NArc
'Lisa Jane'	MWhe
'Lisa Rowe'	CSil
'Lisi'	NArc
'Little Beauty'	EKMF MWhe NArc
'Little Gene'	EBak
'Little Jewel'	MWar SKen
¶ 'Little Orphan Annie'	LCla
'Little Ouse'	EGou MWhe
'Little Ronnie'	MWhe
'Little Witch'	EGou EKMF LCla SLBF
'Lively Lady'	Last listed 1998
'Liver Bird'	NArc
'Liz' (d)	CSil EBak EKMF NArc
'Lochinver'	CSil SYvo
'Locky'	CLoc EBak SLBF SPet SSea
'Logan Garden'	See *F. magellanica* 'Logan Woods'
'Lolita' (d)	EBak
'Lonely Ballerina' (d)	CLoc
'Long Distance'	Last listed 1997
'Long Preston'	Last listed 1998
'Long Wings'	CSil EKMF LCla MAld NArc SYvo
'Look East'	EGou
'Lora Fairclough'	MJac NArc
'Lord Byron'	CLoc EBak EKMF NArc
'Lord Derby'	NArc
¶ 'Lord Jim'	EGou
'Lord Lonsdale'	CSil EBak EPts LCla MWhe NArc
'Lord Roberts'	CLoc CSil NArc SKen
'Lorelei'	EPts
'Lorna Swinbank'	CLoc NArc
'Lorraine's Delight'	Last listed 1998
'Lottie Hobby'	CDoC CInt CLoc CMGP CSil ECtt
	EKMF EPts GEil LCla LRHS MAld
	MHar MWhe NArc WBod WCot
	WFoF WPyg
'Lou Rinzema'	Last listed 1998
'Louise Emershaw' (d)	CSil EBak MJac
'Louise Foster'	MWar
'Louise Nicholls'	EKMF
'Lovable' (d)	EBak
'Love in Bloom'	EGou
'Loveliness'	CLoc CSil EBak EKMF MWhe
'Lovely Linda'	SLBF
'Love's Reward'	CLoc CSil EKMF EPts LCla MAld
	MJac MWar MWhe SLBF
I 'Loxensis' ♀	EBak EGou EKMF LCla
* *loxensis* var. *rubra*	EGou
'Loxhore Angelus'	CSil
'Loxhore Calypso'	EKMF
'Loxhore Cancan'	CSil
'Loxhore Cavalcade'	Last listed 1998
'Loxhore Chorale'	CSil
'Loxhore Clarion'	Last listed 1997
'Loxhore Cotillon'	CSil
¶ 'Loxhore Fairy Dancer'	CSil
'Loxhore Herald'	CSil
'Loxhore Lullaby'	CSil
'Loxhore Mazurka'	CSil
'Loxhore Minuet'	CSil
'Loxhore Operetta'	CSil
'Loxhore Posthorn'	CSil LCla
'Loxhore Tarantella'	CSil
'Lubbertje Hop'	Last listed 1998
'Lucille'	NArc
'Lucky Strike'	CLoc CSil EBak NArc

'Lucy Harris'	CSil
'Lucy Locket'	MJac
'Lula Bell'	Last listed 1999
'Lunter's Trots'	NArc
'Luscious'	Last listed 1999
'Lustre'	EBak NArc
lycioides hort.	See *F.* 'Lycioides'
– Andrews	CSil EBak EGou EKMF
§ 'Lycioides'	CSil LCla
'Lye's Elegance'	CSil
'Lye's Excelsior'	EBak LCla
'Lye's Own'	EBak SYvo
'Lye's Perfection'	EKMF
'Lye's Unique'	CDoC CLTr CLoc CSil EBak EDAr
	EGou EKMF EPts LCla MAld MJac
	MWar MWhe NArc SKen SLBF
	SYvo
· 'Lylac Sunsa'	EKMF
'Lynette' (d)	CLoc
'Lynn Ellen' (d)	EBak NArc
'Lynne Marshall'	CSil
'Mabel Greaves'	CSil
'Machu Picchu'	CLoc CSil EKMF EPts LCla MWar
	NArc
macrophylla	EKMF
macrostigma	Last listed 1999
'Madame Aubin'	EKMF
'Madame Butterfly' (d)	CLoc
'Madame Cornélissen' ♀	CDoC CLoc CSil EBak EBee EKMF
	ENot GChr LRHS LVER MBar MBri
	MGos MJac MWhe NArc SPer
	WFar WGwG
'Madame Eva Boye'	EBak EKMF
'Madelaine Sweeney'	MBri
'Maes-y-Groes'	EKMF
magdalenae	EKMF
magellanica	CCHP CDoC COld EKMF EMil
	GOrc LHil LRHS MWgw MWhi
	NFor NPer SPer WFar WOak
	WRha WWat
– 'Alba'	See *F. magellanica* var. *molinae*
I – 'Alba Aureovariegata'	CDoC EPfP LRHS MBri SPer SSea
– 'Alba Variegata'	CSil EKMF NHaw WEas
– 'Americana Elegans'	CSil
– 'Comber'	CSil
– var. *conica*	CDoC CSil EKMF
¶ – 'Exmoor Gold' (v)	CSil
– 'Fire Gold'	LRHS
– 'Globosa'	See *F.* 'Globosa'
§ – var. *gracilis* ♀	CDoC CHEx CLoc CSil EKMF
	EWTr LRHS MWhe NArc WBod
	WPic
– – 'Aurea'	CBot CDoC CMHG CSil CTre
	EBee EGou EHoe EKMF ELan
	ENot GCHN GQui LAst LCla LRHS
	MWat MWhe SDix SKen SLBF
	SPer SPla SSea WFar WGwG
	WHen WRus
§ – – 'Tricolor' (v)	CDoC CSil EGou EHol EKMF EPts
	EWes GChr GOrc LCla LRHS
	MAld SKen SLBF SRms SSea WCFE
– – 'Variegata' ♀	CGle CMHG CSil CTre EBak EBee
	EGou ENot LCla LHil LRHS MGos
	MRav NArc SChu SDix SIng SPer
	WEas
§ – 'Logan Woods'	CLTr CSil EKMF GCal SMrm
– 'Longipedunculata'	CDoC CSil EKMF
– var. *macrostema*	CSil EKMF
– – 'Variegata'	EGou
§ – var. *molinae*	CDoC CGle CHad CSil EBak EDAr
	EGou EKMF ELan EWTr GGar
	ISea LCla LVER MBlu MNrw

§ – – 'Enstone'	MWgw MWhe NChi NFai NFor NPer NSti SKen SMac SPer WBod WEas WOak WPGP EGou
– – 'Golden Sharpitor'	WCot
– – 'Mr Knight's Blush'	EOld
§ – – 'Sharpitor' (v)	CB&S CDoC CSil CTre EBak ECha EGou EKMF Elan GGar LRHS MBar MBri MRav MWat NPer SMrm SPer SSea WCFE WFar WKif WRus WSHC
– var. *myrtifolia*	CDoC CSil
– var. *prostrata*	CSil
– var. *pumila*	CDoC CSil EWes GCal SBla SIng SPer SRot
– 'Riccartonii'	See *F.* 'Riccartonii'
§ – 'Thompsonii' ♀	CDoC CSil ECGP EKMF GCal MBel SAga SKen
§ – 'Versicolor' (v) ♀	More than 30 suppliers
'Magic Flute'	CLoc CSil MJac
'Maharaja' (d)	EBak NArc
'Maike'	NArc
'Majebo'	NArc
'Major Heaphy'	EBak EKMF MWhe NArc
'Malibu Mist'	CSil EGou EKMF LCla LVER NArc
'Mama Bleuss' (d)	EBak NArc
'Mancunian'	CSil EGou LCla NArc
N 'Mandarin'	EBak NArc
'Mandi'	EGou EKMF EWll LCla SLBF
'Mandy'	Last listed 1998
'Mantilla'	CDoC CLoc CSil EBak EKMF LCla MJac MWhe NArc
'Maori Pipes'	CSil EGou
'Marbled Sky'	NArc
'Marco Jan'	Last listed 1998
'Marcus Graham' (d)	CLoc EGou EKMF LCla MWar MWhe NArc SLBF
'Marcus Hanton'	CSil LCla NArc
'Mardi Gras' (d)	EBak WGwG
'Margaret' (d) ♀	CDoC CLoc CSil CTri EBak EGou EKMF ENot GCHN LCla LVER MWar MWhe NArc SKen SLBF SSea WGwG WStI
'Margaret Brown' ♀	CDoC CLTr CLoc CSil CTri EBak EDAr EKMF LCla MWar MWhe NArc SLBF WLow WStI
'Margaret Davidson' (d)	CLoc
'Margaret Dawson'	Last listed 1999
'Margaret Hazelwood'	EKMF
'Margaret Kendrick'	Last listed 1999
'Margaret Pilkington'	CGre EKMF MJac MWar NArc SSea
'Margaret Roe'	CDoC CSil EBak EKMF MJac NArc
'Margaret Rose'	MJac
'Margaret Susan'	EBak
'Margarite Dawson'	CSil NArc
'Margery Blake'	CSil EBak EKMF
'Maria Landy'	EKMF EMan LCla MWar NArc WWol
'Maria Merrills'	EKMF EMan NArc
'Marietta'	Last listed 1998
'Marilyn Olsen'	CSil EPts LCla MAld MWar NArc
'Marin Belle'	EBak NArc
'Marin Glow' ♀	CLoc CSil EBak EKMF MWhe NArc SLBF SYvo
'Marinka' ♀	CLoc CSil EBak ECtt EKMF EMan LCla LVER MAld MBri MJac MWar MWhe NArc NFai SKen SLBF SSea SSte WGwG WWol
'Marjory Almond'	Last listed 1998
'Mark Kirby' (d)	EKMF
'Marlea's Vuurbol'	EGou

'Marlene Gilbee'	Last listed 1999
'Martha Franck'	Last listed 1998
'Martin Hayward'	SKen
'Martin's Catherina'	EGou
'Martin's Choice'	EGou
'Martin's Cinderella'	EGou
'Martin's Double Delicate'	EGou
'Martin's Midnight'	Last listed 1998
¶ 'Martin's Tiny'	EGou
'Martin's Yellow Suprise'	CLoc EGou EKMF LCla SLBF WGwG
'Marton Smith'	MWhe
'Marty' (d)	EBak
'Mary' ♀	CDoC CLoc CSil EGou EKMF EPts LCla LRHS MAld MLan MWar MWhe NArc SKen SLBF SSea WGwG
'Mary Caunt'	EKMF
'Mary Ellen Guffey'	SLBF
'Mary Fairclo'	EGou
'Mary Joan'	EKMF
¶ 'Mary Jones' (d)	EKMF
'Mary Lockyer' (d)	CLoc EBak NArc
'Mary Neujean'	Last listed 1999
'Mary Poppins'	LCla NArc
'Mary Reynolds'	Last listed 1998
'Mary Thorne'	CSil EBak EKMF
'Mary Wright'	MWhe
'Masquerade' (d)	EBak EKMF EMan MWhe NArc
'Matador'	CSil
mathewsii	EGou EKMF
'Matthew Morrison'	EGou
'Maureen'	NArc
'Maureen Ward'	EKMF
'Mauve Beauty'	CSil EGou EKMF
'Mauve Lace'	CSil
'Mauve Wisp'	NArc
'Max Jaffa'	CSil NArc
¶ 'May Gibson'	MWar
'May Rogers'	Last listed 1998
'Mayblossom' (d)	ECtt SPet
'Mayfayre' (d)	CLoc
'Mayfield'	MWhe NArc
'Maytime'	Last listed 1998
'Meadowlark'	EBak ECtt EKMF NArc
'Meditation'	CLoc CSil
'Meike Meursing'	LAco SPet
'Melanie'	CDoC MWar NArc SLBF
'Melody'	CSil EBak MWhe NArc
'Melody Ann' (d)	EBak
'Melting Moments'	EKMF NArc
'Memo'	Last listed 1998
'Mendocino Mini'	EKMF
'Menna'	NArc
'Mercurius'	CSil
'Merlin'	CSil LCla
'Merry England'	Last listed 1999
'Merry Mary' (d)	CSil EBak EKMF NArc
'Mexicali Rose'	CLoc
'Michael'	CSil EPts
'Michael Kurtz'	NArc
'Michele Wallace'	Last listed 1998
michoacanensis	Last listed 1998
'Micky Goult'	CLoc CSil EKMF EPts LCla MAld MJac MWhe NArc SSea
'Microchip'	SLBF
microphylla	CB&S CDoC CElw CGle CLoc CSam CSil CTre EBak EDAr ERav ERea MWhe SLon SSea STre WCru WEas
§ – subsp. *aprica*	EKMF LCla
§ – subsp. *hemsleyana*	CDoC CSil EGou EKMF LCla

	MWhe SKen
§ - subsp. *bidalgensis*	CSil CTbh EGou EKMF LCla SLBF
	SVen
- Kew form	CDoC
- subsp. *microphylla*	CSil EKMF WWat
- subsp. *quercetorum*	CDoC EKMF LCla
'Midas'	MBri NArc
'Midnight Sun' (d)	CSil EBak EPts NArc
'Midwinter'	NArc
'Mieke Alferink'	Last listed 1998
'Mieke Meursing'	CLoc CSil EBak ECtt EKMF MJac
	MWar MWhe NArc SLBF
'Miep Aalhuizen'	EGou EKMF LCla
N 'Mikado'	EGou
'Mike Oxtoby'	EKMF
'Millrace'	LCla
'Mimi Kubischta'	NArc
'Mina Knudde'	NArc
'Ming'	CLoc
'Miniature Jewels'	SLBF
N *minimiflora*	See *F. microphylla* subsp.
	bidalgensis
'Minirose'	CSil EKMF LRHS MWar MWhe
	SKen
'Minnesota'	EBak
'Minutifolia'	CLyn
'Mipam'	SLBF
'Mirjana'	NArc
'Mischief'	CSil NArc
'Miss Aubrey'	Last listed 1998
'Miss California'	CLoc EBak ECtt EKMF MBri
	MWhe NArc SKen
'Miss Debbie'	MJac
'Miss Great Britain'	CSil
¶ 'Miss Lye'	CSil
'Miss Marilyn'	Last listed 1998
'Miss Muffett'	Last listed 1998
'Miss Vallejo' (d)	EBak NArc
'Mission Bells'	CDoC CLoc CSil EBak EKMF LCla
	NArc SKen WGwG
'Mistoque'	CDoC CSil NArc
'Misty Blue'	CSil NArc
'Misty Haze'	CSil LVER MWar
'Misty Pink'	EKMF NArc
'Moira Ann'	ECtt
'Molesworth' (d)	CSil EBak EKMF MJac MWhe
	NArc SPet
'Mollie Beaulah'	CSil ECtt EKMF NArc
'Molly Chatfield'	NArc
'Money Spinner'	CLoc EBak
'Monica Dare'	EGou
'Monsieur Thibaut'	ENot LCla
'Monte Rosa'	CLoc
'Monterey'	MWhe
'Montevideo'	EGou
'Montrose Village'	CSil MWhe
'Monty Python'	Last listed 1998
'Monument'	CSil
'Mood Indigo'	CSil LVER MWar NArc SLBF
	WGwG
'Moonbeam' (d)	CLoc CSil MWhe
'Moonlight Sonata'	CLoc EBak MJac NArc
'Moonraker'	CSil NArc
'Moonshot'	SKen
'Morcott'	NArc
'More Applause' (d)	CLoc EKMF LVER MWhe NArc
'Morning Cloud'	NArc
'Morning Glow'	NArc
'Morning Light' (d)	CLoc CSil EBak NArc SPet
'Morning Mist'	EBak NArc
'Morning Star'	MBri
'Morrells' (d)	EBak

'Moth Blue' (d)	CSil EBak NArc SPet
'Mountain Mist'	EKMF MJac
'Moyra'	EKMF
'Mr A. Huggett'	CLoc CSil EKMF EPts LCla MWhe
	NArc SPet
'Mr P.D. Lee'	MWhe
'Mr W. Rundle'	EBak NArc
'Mrs Churchill'	CLoc
'Mrs Janice Morrison'	EGou
'Mrs John D. Fredericks'	CSil
'Mrs Lawrence Lyon'	EBak
'Mrs Lovell Swisher'	CDoC CSil EBak EKMF LCla MJac
	MWhe NArc
'Mrs Marshall'	CSil EBak NArc SLBF
'Mrs Popple' ♀	More than 30 suppliers
'Mrs Susan Brookfield'	NArc
'Mrs Victor Reiter'	CSil
'Mrs W. Castle'	CSil NArc WGwG
'Mrs W.P. Wood' ♀	CDoC CLoc EKMF NArc
'Mrs W. Rundle'	CLoc CSil EBak EKMF LRHS MAld
	MWhe NArc SLBF
'Multa'	LAco SWal SYvo
'Muriel'	CLoc EBak ECtt EKMF MWhe
	NArc
'Musi'	Last listed 1998
'My Dear'	Last listed 1998
'My Fair Lady' (d)	CLoc CSil EBak NArc
'My Honey'	CSil NArc
'Mystique'	Last listed 1999
'Nancy Darnley'	EKMF
'Nancy Lou' (d)	CDoC CGre CLoc EKMF EPts LCla
	LVER MAld MJac MWar MWhe
	NArc SLBF
'Nancy Scrivener'	NArc
'Nanny Ed'	MBri
'Natalie Jones'	Last listed 1998
'Natasha Sinton'	CLoc CSil ECtt EKMF EMan LCla
	LVER MAld MBri MJac MWar
	MWhe NArc SLBF WGwG WLRN
'Native Dancer' (d)	EBak
'Naughty Nicole'	SLBF
'Nautilus' (d)	EBak
'Navato'	Last listed 1999
'Navy Blue'	CSil NArc
'Neapolitan'	CDoC EPts MWhe SKen SLBF
'Neil Clyne'	MWhe
'Nell Gwyn'	CLoc CSil EBak NArc
'Nellie Nuttall' ♀	CLoc CSil EBak EKMF EPts LCla
	LRHS MAld MWar MWhe NArc
	SLBF SPet SSea
'Neopolitan'	CLoc CSil EGou LCla NArc
'Nettala'	EGou
'Neue Welt'	CSil EBak EKMF
'Neville Young'	Last listed 1999
'New Fascination' (d)	EBak NArc SKen
'Nice 'n' Easy'	LVER MBri MJac MWar MWhe
	NArc
'Nicholas Hughes'	NArc
'Nicis Findling'	CSil EKMF EPts LCla NArc
'Nicky Veerman'	Last listed 1998
'Nicola'	CLoc EBak
N 'Nicola Claire'	NArc SLBF
'Nicola Jane' (d)	CDoC CSil EBak EDAr EKMF EPts
	LCla LRHS MBri MJac MWhe
	NArc SLBF
'Nicolette'	MJac
'Night and Day'	Last listed 1997
'Nightingale' (d)	CLoc CSil EBak NArc
§ *nigricans*	EGou EKMF LCla
- × *gehrigeri*	EKMF
'Nimue'	EGou NArc
'Nina Wills'	EBak

'Niobe' (d)	EBak
'Niula'	EKMF LCla
'No Name' (d)	EBak
'Norah Henderson'	NArc
'Norfolk Belle'	Last listed 1998
'Norfolk Ivor'	EGou
'Norma Nield'	Last listed 1998
'Norman Greenhill'	Last listed 1997
'Norman Mitchinson'	Last listed 1999
'Normandy Bell'	CSil EBak SPet
'North Cascades'	Last listed 1999
¶ 'Northern Dancer' (d)	EKMF
'Northern Pride'	Last listed 1999
'Northilda'	NArc
'Northumbrian Belle'	EBak EDAr MJac NArc WGwG
'Northway'	CLoc LCla MJac MWhe NArc
'Norvell Gillespie' (d)	EBak
'Novato'	EBak NArc
'Novella' (d)	EBak NArc
'Noyo Star'	CSil
'Nunthorpe Gem'	CSil NArc
'Nuwenspete'	Last listed 1998
obconica	EGou EKMF LCla
'Obcylin'	EGou LCla
'Obergärtner Koch'	EKMF LCla NArc
'Ocean Beach'	EPts NArc
'Oddfellow'	CSil NArc
'Oetnang'	SCoo
'Old Somerset'	LCla
'Ole 7 Up'	MAld
'Olive Moon'	SLBF
'Olive Smith'	CSil EPts LCla MAld MJac MWhe NArc
'Olympia'	CSil EKMF MWhe
'Olympic Lass' (d)	EBak NArc
'Olympic Sunset'	Last listed 1997
¶ 'Onward'	EKMF
§ 'Oosje'	CSil LCla
'Opalescent' (d)	CLoc
'Orange Cocktail'	EKMF
'Orange Crush'	CLoc CSil EBak MWar MWhe NArc
'Orange Crystal'	CSil EBak EKMF MJac MWhe NArc NFai SKen
'Orange Drops'	CLoc CSil EBak EKMF EPts MWhe NArc SKen SYvo
¶ 'Orange Flair'	CLoc CSil EBak EKMF MJac MWhe NArc SLBF SSea
'Orange King' (d)	CLoc CSil EGou EMan SSea
'Orange Mirage'	CLoc CSil EBak LVER MAld MWhe NArc
'Orangeblossom'	CSil LCla NArc SLBF
'Oranje van Os'	MJac MWhe
'Orient Express'	CDoC CSil EGou LCla MWar MWhe NArc
Oriental Flame	EKMF NArc
'Oriental Sunrise'	MWhe
'Ornamental Pearl'	CLoc EBak NArc SLBF
'Ortenburger Festival'	NArc
'Orwell'	EGou
'Other Fellow'	CSil EBak EKMF EPts LCla MJac MWhe NArc SLBF SYvo
'Our Darling'	CSil MWhe NArc
¶ 'Our Nan' (d)	MJac
'Our Ted'	EGou
'Overbecks'	See *F. magellanica* var. *molinae* 'Sharpitor'
'Overbecks Ruby'	GBuc WCot
'P.J.B.'	LAco LCla NArc
'Pabbe's Teudebel'	Last listed 1998
'Pabbe's Tudebekje'	CSil
pachyrrhiza	EKMF

'Pacific Grove' (d)	EBak
'Pacific Queen' (d)	CLoc EBak NArc
'Pacquesa' (d) ♀	CDoC CSil EBak EKMF EPts MJac MWar MWhe NArc SPet
'Padre Pio'	MJac
'Pale Flame'	MWhe NArc
pallescens	EGou EKMF LCla
'Pam Plack'	LCla
'Pamela Hutchinson'	MAld NArc
'Pamela Knights'	EBak
'Pan'	EGou LCla NArc
'Pan America' (d)	EBak
¶ 'Panache'	LCla
'Pangea'	LCla
paniculata	CBot CDoC CEnd CLTr CSam CTbh EBak EGou EKMF LCla NArc SHFr SLBF SLod SMrm WCot WFoF
* - var. *mixensis*	Last listed 1997
'Pantaloons'	EBak NArc
'Panylla Prince'	CDoC EKMF EPts LCla SLBF
'Papa Bleuss' (d)	CLoc EBak
'Papoose'	CDoC CSil EBak EKMF LCla NArc
'Paramour'	NArc
¶ 'Partridge Lake'	MWar
'Party Frock'	CLoc CSil EBak LCla LVER NArc
parviflora hort.	See *F.* x *bacillaris*
- Lindley	EBak
'Pastel'	EBak
'Pat Crofts'	NArc
'Pat Meara'	CLoc EBak
'Pathetique' (d)	CLoc
'Patience' (d)	CSil EBak EGou MJac NArc
'Patio Party'	Last listed 1999
'Patio Princess'	CDoC CSil LCla MBri MJac MWhe NArc SSea
N 'Patricia'	CSil EBak
'Patricia Ann'	MWar
'Patricia Joan Yates'	EGou
'Patty Evans' (d)	EBak NArc
'Patty Sue'	MBri MWar WLRN
'Paul Berry'	CSil EKMF SLBF
'Paul Cambon' (d)	EBak EKMF NArc
'Paul Roe'	EKMF MJac
¶ 'Paul Storey'	EKMF
'Paula Jane' ♀	CLoc LCla MBri MJac MWar MWhe SLBF
'Paula Johnson'	Last listed 1997
'Pauline Rawlins' (d)	CLoc EBak
'Paulus'	SLBF
'Paxos Trail'	MAld
PC&H 247	CFee
'Peace' (d)	EBak
'Peaches 'n' Cream'	Last listed 1998
'Peachy'	EGou EKMF MJac WWol
'Peachy Keen' (d)	EBak
'Peacock' (d)	CLoc
'Pee Wee Rose'	CSil EBak EKMF NArc
¶ 'Peggy Cole'	EPts
'Peggy King'	CDoC CSil EBak EKMF LCla MWhe NArc
'Peloria' (d)	CLoc EBak NArc
'Pennine'	MBri MWar
'People's Princess'	MJac
'Peper Harow'	EBak
'Pepi' (d)	CLoc EBak SPet
'Peppermint Candy'	EKMF MJac SCoo WGwG
'Peppermint Stick' (d)	CDoC CLoc CSil EBak EKMF EMan LCla LRHS LVER MBri MJac MWhe NArc SKen SSea
'Perestroika'	Last listed 1998
'Perky Pink' (d)	EBak EPts LCla MWhe NArc SKen

'Perry Park' EBak LAco MBri MJac NArc
'Perry's Jumbo' NBir NPer
perscandens CSil EGou EKMF LCla SVen
'Personality' EBak NArc
'Peter Bielby' EGou EKMF LCla MWar SLBF
'Peter Crooks' CSil LCla NArc
'Peter James' CSil EKMF
'Peter Pan' CSil EHol SIng SPer
'Peter Sanderson' EKMF MJac NArc
petiolaris CDoC EGou EKMF LCla
'Petit Fleur' CSil
'Petit Four' CSil
'Petit Point' Last listed 1999
'Petite' (d) EBak NArc
'Petronella' Last listed 1999
'Pharaoh' CLoc
'Phénoménal' (d) CSil EBak EKMF EPts LRHS SKen
¶ 'Phillip Taylor' MJac
'Phyllis' ♀ CDoC CLoc CSil EBak EKMF EPts
 LCla LHil MJac MWhe NArc NFai
 SKen SLBF SPet WGwG
'Phyrne' (d) CSil EBak EKMF NArc
'Piet G.Vergeer' NArc
'Piet Heemserke' LCla
pilaloensis EKMF
¶ x ***pilcopata*** LCla
'Pinch Me' (d) CSil EBak EKMF LVER
'Pink Aurora' CLoc CSil
'Pink Ballet Girl' (d) CLoc EBak ECtt NArc
'Pink Bon Accorde' CLoc NArc
'Pink Bouquet' Last listed 1998
'Pink Chiffon' NArc
'Pink Cloud' CLoc EBak NArc
'Pink Cornet' LCla
'Pink Crystal' Last listed 1998
'Pink Darling' CLoc EBak MWhe
'Pink Dessert' EBak NArc
'Pink Domino' EKMF
'Pink Fairy' (d) CSil EBak NArc SPet
'Pink Fandango' CLoc
'Pink Fantasia' CLoc CSil EBak EGou EKMF EPts
 LCla LRHS MAld MJac MWar
 MWhe SSea WCot
'Pink Flamingo' CLoc EBak NArc
'Pink Galore' (d) CLoc CSil EBak EKMF EMan LCla
 LVER MAld MBri MJac MWhe
 NFai NHaw SKen SSea WGwG
'Pink Goon' CDoC CSil EKMF LCla LRHS SLBF
'Pink Jade' EBak EKMF
'Pink la Campanella' CSil EMan MAld MBri MWar
 MWhe NArc WGwG WLRN
'Pink Lace' CSil
N 'Pink Lady' MWhe
'Pink Marshmallow' (d) CLoc CSil EBak EKMF EMan LCla
 LVER MAld MJac MWar MWhe
 NHaw SLBF WGwG
'Pink Panther' EKMF MJac MWar
N 'Pink Pearl' CSil EBak EKMF LVER SWal SYvo
'Pink Picotee' LCla MJac
'Pink Pineapple' Last listed 1999
'Pink Profusion' EBak
'Pink Quartet' (d) CLoc CSil EBak NArc
'Pink Rain' CSil EKMF MJac NArc
'Pink Slipper' CLoc
'Pink Spangles' EMan MBri NHaw SSea WGwG
'Pink Surprise' MJac NArc
'Pink Temptation' CLoc EBak
'Pinkmost' ECtt EKMF
'Pinto' (d) CDoC NArc
'Pinto de Blue' EGou
'Pinwheel' (d) CLoc CSil EBak
'Piper' CDoC CSil MWar

'Piper's Vale' EGou LCla SLBF
¶ 'Pippa Rolt' EPts SLBF
'Pirbright' EKMF
'Pixie' CDoC CLoc CSil EBak EKMF MJac
 MWhe NArc SLBF
'Pixie Bells' CInt
* ***platyphylla*** Last listed 1999
'Playford' EBak NArc
'Plenty' CSil EBak
'Ploughman' Last listed 1998
'Plumb-bob' EGou EKMF
'Poacher' Last listed 1998
'Pop Whitlock' (v) EKMF NArc SSea
'Popely Pride' EGou
'Popsie Girl' EGou LCla SLBF
'Port Arthur' (d) EBak EKMF NArc
'Postiljon' CSil EBak EKMF NArc SPet
N 'Powder Puff' (d) CLoc CSil ECtt EKMF LRHS LVER
 MBri NArc
N 'Prelude' (d) CLoc CSil EBak NArc
'President' CDoC CSil EBak EKMF LCla SKen
'President B.W. Rawlins' EBak
§ 'President Elliot' CSil EKMF MWhe
'President George Bartlett' EKMF MJac SLBF
¶ 'President Joan Morris' (d) SLBF
'President Leo Boullemier' CSil EBak ECtt EKMF LCla MJac
 NArc WGwG
'President Margaret Slater' CDoC CLoc CSil EBak EMan MJac
 MWhe NArc SLBF
'President Moir' Last listed 1999
'President Norman Hobbs' EKMF MWar NArc
'President Roosevelt' CDoC ECtt
'President Stanley Wilson' EBak ECtt EPts
'President Wilf Sharp' NArc
'Preston Belle' Last listed 1998
'Preston Field' CSil SLBF SSea
'Preston Guild' CDoC CLoc CSil EBak EKMF
 LRHS MWar MWhe NArc NPer
 SLBF
'Pride of the West' CSil EBak EKMF
'Prince of Orange' CLoc CSil EBak EKMF NArc
'Prince of Peace' CSil
'Princess Dollar' See *F*. 'Dollar Princess'
'Princess of Bath' CLoc
'Princess Pamela' SLBF
'Princess Pat' EKMF
'Princessita' CSil EBak ECtt EKMF EMan MJac
 MWar MWhe NArc
pringsheimii EGou
'Priscilla Spek' Last listed 1998
procumbens CDoC CGre CLoc CNic CSil EBak
 ECou EGou EKMF ERea ESis
 GCHN GGar LCla MHar MWhe
 NArc NWCA SHFr SLBF SSea SSoC
 SYvo WBod WGwG
I - 'Argentea' CLoc CSil EKMF GCal GGar
 - 'Variegata' See *F. procumbens* 'Argentea'
'Prodigy' See *F*. 'Enfant Prodigue'
'Profusion' MWhe
'Prosperity' (d) ♀ CDoC CLoc CSil EBak EBee EGou
 EKMF ENot EPts LCla LRHS LVER
 MAld MJac MWar MWhe NArc
'Prove Thyself' EGou
N 'Pumila' CCHP CTri EKMF ELan NArc SVen
 SWal
'Purbeck Mist' EKMF
'Purperklokje' CLTr CSil EBak EGou EKMF LCla
 NArc
'Purple Emperor' CLoc
'Purple Graseing' Last listed 1999
'Purple Heart' (d) CLoc CSil EBak SKen
'Purple Patch' MBri MWar WLRN

'Purple Pride'	MBri	
'Purple Rain'	CLoc EKMF	
'Purple Showers'	CSil NArc	
'Purple Splendour'	CDoC CSil	
'Pussy Cat'	CLoc CSil EBak EKMF LCla	
'Putney Pride'	EPts	
'Put's Folly'	EBak MJac	
putumayensis	CSil EBak	
'Quasar' (d)	CDoC CLoc CSil EKMF EPts LRHS LVER MJac MWhe NHaw SLBF SPet WGwG	
'Queen Mabs'	EBak	
'Queen Mary'	CLoc CSil EBak EKMF	
'Queen of Bath'	EBak	
'Queen of Derby'	LCla MAld	
'Queen of Hearts'	CSil	
N 'Queen Victoria' (d)	EKMF	
'Queen's Park' (d)	EBak	
'Query'	CSil EBak EKMF NArc	
'Quintet'	Last listed 1999	
'R.A.F.' (d)	CLoc CSil EBak ECtt EKMF EPts LCla LVER MWar NArc SKen SLBF SSea	
'Rachel Craig'	MWar	
'Rachel Sinton'	EMan MBri WLRN	
'Radcliffe Beauty'	MWhe	
'Radcliffe Bedder'	CDoC CSil EKMF SKen	
'Radings Gerda'	EGou	
'Radings Inge'	EKMF	
'Rading's Juma'	Last listed 1998	
'Radings Karin'	CDoC	
'Radings Magma'	Last listed 1998	
'Radings Mapri'	EKMF	
'Rading's Marjorie'	Last listed 1998	
'Radings Mia'	Last listed 1998	
'Radings Michelle'	CSil	
'Raintree Legend'	NArc	
'Ralph Oliver'	EGou	
'Ralph's Delight'	EGou	
'Rambling Rose' (d)	CLoc CSil EBak ECtt MJac NArc	
'Rambo'	NArc	
'Rams Royal'	LCla LVER MJac NArc	
'Rascal'	MWar	
'Raspberry' (d)	CLoc CSil EBak LCla MWhe NArc	
'Ratatouille'	CSil EKMF NArc	
ravenii	EGou EKMF	
'Ravensbarrow'	NArc	
'Ravenslaw'	EKMF	
'Ray Redfern'	MJac	
'Raymond Scopes'	Last listed 1998	
'Razzle Dazzle' (d)	EBak	
'Reading Show'	CSil EPts LCla SLBF	
'Rebecca Williamson'	MJac MWhe NArc	
'Rebekah Sinton'	EBak MBri MWar	
'Red Ace'	CSil	
'Red Imp'	CDoC CSil	
'Red Jacket' (d)	EBak NArc	
'Red Rain'	EKMF	
'Red Ribbons' (d)	EBak	
'Red Rover'	EGou SLBF	
'Red Rum'	CSil SPet	
'Red Shadows' (d)	CLoc CSil EBak MJac MWhe NArc WGwG	
'Red Spider'	CLoc CSil EBak EKMF EMan MWar MWhe NArc NHaw SKen SSea WGwG	
'Red Sunlight'	Last listed 1999	
'Red Wing'	CLoc	
'Reflexa'	See *F.* x *bacillaris* 'Reflexa'	
'Reg Dickenson'	MJac	
'Reg Gubler'	SLBF	
'Regal'	CLoc	

'Regal Robe'	CSil	
regia	CSil	
- var. *alpestris*	See *F. alpestris*	
- subsp. *regia*	CDoC CSil EKMF LCla	
- subsp. *reitzii*	CDoC CSil EKMF LCla WGwG	
- subsp. *serrae*	CSil EKMF	
'Reinholt Leuthardt'	Last listed 1999	
'Remembrance'	CSil EKMF EPts LCla SSea	
'Remus'	CSil NArc	
'Requiem'	CLoc	
'Reverend Doctor Brown' (d)	EBak NArc	
'Reverend Elliott'	See *F.* 'President Elliot'	
¶ 'Rex Graham'	SYvo	
N 'Rhapsody' (d)	CLoc	
'Rhombifolia'	CSil	
¶ 'Rianna Foks'	EGou	
'Riant'	NArc	
§ 'Riccartonii' ♀	More than 30 suppliers	
'Riccartonii Variegated'	WEas	
'Richard John'	EGou NArc	
'Richard John Carrington'	CSil	
'Ridestar' (d)	CLoc CSil EBak EMan MJac MWhe	
'Rina Felix'	EGou	
'Ringwood Market'	ECtt EKMF EPts LCla MJac MWhe NArc	
'Robbie'	EGou EKMF NArc	
'Robert Lutters'	NArc	
'Robin'	Last listed 1997	
'Robin Hood'	CSil	
'Rocket Fire'	Last listed 1999	
'Rodeo'	EGou	
'Rolla' (d)	EBak EGou EKMF NArc	
¶ 'Rolt's Bride' (d)	EKMF	
'Rolt's Ruby'	EKMF EPts NArc	
'Roman City' (d)	CLoc	
'Romance'	Last listed 1999	
'Romany Rose'	CLoc	
'Ron Chambers Love'	EGou	
'Ron Ewart'	EKMF MWhe	
'Ron Venables'	Last listed 1997	
'Ronald L. Lockerbie' (d)	CLoc EKMF SMur	
'Ron's Ruby'	MWhe	
'Roos Breytenbach'	CDoC CSil EGou EKMF LCla	
'Rosamunda'	CLoc	
'Rose Aylett' (d)	EBak	
'Rose Bradwardine' (d)	EBak NArc	
'Rose Churchill'	LCla MBri MJac	
'Rose Fantasia'	CLoc CSil EGou EKMF EPts LCla LRHS MAld MJac MWar MWhe SLBF SSea	
'Rose Lace'	Last listed 1998	
'Rose Marie' (d)	CLoc NArc	
'Rose of Castile' ♀	CDoC CLoc CSil EBak EKMF LCla LRHS MJac MWhe NArc	
'Rose of Castile Improved'	CSil EBak EKMF LCla MJac MWar SPet	
'Rose of Denmark'	CLoc CSil EBak EGou EKMF MBri MJac MWar MWhe NHaw WGwG WLRN	
'Rose Reverie' (d)	EBak NArc	
'Rose Winston'	EKMF MWhe	
rosea Ruiz & Pav.	See *F. lycioides* Andrews	
- hort.	See *F.* 'Globosa'	
'Rosebud' (d)	EBak NArc	
'Rosecroft Beauty'	CSil EBak EKMF MWhe NArc SKen SSea	
'Rosemary Day'	CLoc	
'Roslyn Lowe'	CDoC CSil NArc	
'Ross Lea'	CSil	
'Rosy Frills'	CSil LCla MJac MWhe NArc	
'Rosy Morn' (d)	CLoc EBak	

Rosy Ruffles — EKMF
'Rough Silk' — CLoc CSil EBak
'Roy Walker' (d) — CLoc EKMF LVER MJac MWar NArc
'Royal and Ancient' — Last listed 1998
'Royal Mosaic' — Last listed 1999
'Royal Orchid' — EBak
'Royal Purple' — CSil EBak EKMF MBri NArc
'Royal Touch' (d) — EBak
'Royal Velvet' (d) ♀ — CLTr CLoc CSil EBak EKMF EMan EPts LCla LRHS LVER MAld MJac MWar MWhe NArc NHaw SKen SLBF SWal WGwG
'Royal Wedding' — CSil LCla NArc
'Rozientje' — NArc
'Rubicon' — NArc
§ 'Rubra Grandiflora' — EBak EKMF LCla MWar SLBF SMrm
'Ruby' — Last listed 1998
'Ruby Wedding' — CSil EGou EKMF LCla SLBF SSea
'Ruddigore' — NArc
'Ruffles' (d) — CSil EBak NArc
§ 'Rufus' — CDoC CLoc CSil CTri EBak EDAr EHol EKMF EPts LCla LRHS MJac MWar MWhe NArc SKen SLBF WGwG
'Rufus the Red' — See F. 'Rufus'
'Ruth' — CSil
'Ruth Brazewell' — CLoc
'Ruth King' (d) — EBak ECtt WGwG
'Rutland Water' — NArc
'Sailor' — MJac SLBF
'Sally Ann' — Last listed 1998
'Salmon Cascade' — CSil EBak ECtt EKMF EMan EPts LCla MJac MWar MWhe NArc SLBF SSea
'Salmon Glow' — MJac MWhe NArc
'Sampson's Delight' — Last listed 1999
'Sam's Song' — MJac
'Samson' (d) — EBak
'San Diego' — CSil NArc
'San Francisco' — EBak
'San Leandro' J. Rowell' — EBak NArc
'San Mateo' (d) — EBak
§ sanctae-rosae — EBak EGou EKMF LCla
'Sandboy' — CSil EBak
¶ 'Sanguinea' — EKMF
'Sanrina' — EKMF
'Santa Cruz' (d) — CSil EBak EGou EKMF LCla MWhe NArc SSea
'Santa Lucia' (d) — CLoc EBak NArc
'Santa Monica' (d) — EBak
'Sapphire' (d) — CSil EBak NArc
'Sara Helen' (d) — CLoc EBak
'Sarah Eliza' — MJac
'Sarah Greensmith' — EKMF NArc
'Sarah Jayne' — CSil EBak NArc
'Sarong' (d) — CSil EBak NArc
'Saskia' — EKMF NArc SLBF
'Satchmo' — Last listed 1999
'Satellite' — CLoc EBak EKMF NArc
'Saturnus' — CSil EBak SPet
scabriuscula — EGou EKMF LCla
scandens — See F. decussata
'Scarborough Rock' — NArc
'Scarborough Rosette' — EGou
'Scarcity' — CDoC CSil EBak MWhe NArc
'Scarlett O'Hara' — EGou
'Schiller' — EKMF
'Schneeball' — CSil EBak EKMF NArc
'Schneewittchen' Hoech — CSil EKMF
'Schneewittchen' Klein — CSil EBak EPts

'Schönbrunner Schuljubiläum' — EBak LCla
'Schöne Wilhelmine' — Last listed 1998
'Scotch Heather' — NArc
'Sea Shell' (d) — EBak NArc
'Seaforth' — EBak EKMF
'Sealand Prince' — CDoC CSil ECtt EKMF LCla NArc
'Sebastopol' (d) — CLoc EKMF
serratifolia Ruiz & Pavón — See F. denticulata
  - Hooker — See F. austromontana
sessilifolia — EGou EKMF LCla
'Seventh Heaven' (d) — CLoc EGou
'Severn Queen' — CSil
'Shady Lady' — NArc
'Shangri-La' (d) — EBak
'Shanley' — NArc
'Sharon Allsop' — CSil MWhe WGwG
'Sharon Caunt' — CSil EKMF
'Sharpitor' — See F. magellanica var. molinae 'Sharpitor'
'Shawn Rushton' — Last listed 1999
'Shawna Ree' — Last listed 1999
'Sheila Crooks' (d) — EBak EMan MAld MJac MWhe
'Sheila Kirby' — MJac
'Sheila Mary' — EKMF MJac
'Shell Pink' — CSil
'Shelley Lyn' — NArc SKen
'Shellford' ♀ — CLoc CSil EBak EKMF EMan EPts LCla MAld MJac MWar MWhe NArc SLBF SSea
'Shining Knight' — Last listed 1999
'Shirley Halladay' — EKMF
'Shooting Star' (d) — EBak
'Showtime' — CSil
'Shugborough' — EKMF MJac MWar MWhe
'Shy Lady' —
'Sierra Blue' (d) — CLoc EBak EKMF NArc
'Silver Anniversary' — EKMF NArc
'Silver Dawn' — CSil EKMF EPts MWhe SLBF
'Silver Dollar' — MWhe NArc SKen WGwG
'Silver Pink' — CSil
'Silverdale' — CDoC CSil EKMF MWhe
'Simon J. Rowell' — Last listed 1999
simplicicaulis — EBak EGou EKMF LCla
'Sincerity' (d) — CLoc CSil
'Sinton's Standard' — MBri MWar
'Sir Alfred Ramsey' — EBak MJac MWhe
'Sir Matt Busby' — EKMF MJac MWar
N 'Siren' (d) — EBak NArc
'Sister Ann Haley' — CSil EKMF EPts
'Sleepy' — CSil EDAr MBri NArc
'Sleigh Bells' — CLoc CSil EBak EKMF MWhe NArc
'Small Pipes' — EKMF LCla NArc
'Smokey Mountain' — EKMF MJac MWar NArc
'Smoky' — Last listed 1999
'Sneezy' — CSil EDAr EHol MWhe NArc
'Snow Burner' — MJac WWol
'Snow Country' — Last listed 1997
'Snow Goose' — EGou
'Snow White' — CSil NArc SMur WGwG
§ 'Snowcap' ♀ — CDoC CLoc CSil EBak EKMF EMan EPts GKir LCla LRHS LVER MAld MBNS MBri MGos MJac MWar MWhe NArc NFai NPer SKen SLBF SSea SYvo WGwG WStI
'Snowdon' — Last listed 1999
N 'Snowdrift' — CLoc EBak
'Snowfire' (d) — CLoc CSil ECtt EGou EKMF MAld MJac MWhe NArc WGwG
'Snowflake' — EKMF SLBF

'Snowstorm'　　　　　　CSil ECtt SPet
'Snowy Summit'　　　　　CSil SMur WGwG
'So Big'　　　　　　　　EKMF NArc
Software　　　　　　　　NArc
'Son of Thumb' ♀　　　　CChe CDoC CLoc CPri CSil EKMF
　　　　　　　　　　　　EMan EPts GCHN LAst LCla LRHS
　　　　　　　　　　　　MAld MBri MGos MJac MWhe
　　　　　　　　　　　　NArc SIng SLBF SSea
¶ 'Sonata'　　　　　　　　CLoc CSil EBak NArc
'Sonia Ann Bary'　　　　 Last listed 1998
'Sophie Claire'　　　　　 LCla
'Sophie Cochrane'　　　　NArc
'Sophie Louise'　　　　　EKMF MWar
¶ 'Sophie Wilson'　　　　 SLBF
'Sophie's Surprise'　　　　EGou EKMF
'Sophisticated Lady' (d)　 CLoc CSil EBak ECtt EKMF EPts
　　　　　　　　　　　　LVER MJac MWar NArc SPet
'Soroptimist International' MWar
'South Gate' (d)　　　　　CLoc CSil EBak EKMF EMan MBri
　　　　　　　　　　　　MJac MWar MWhe NArc NHaw
　　　　　　　　　　　　WGwG WWol
'South Lakeland'　　　　 Last listed 1998
'South Seas'　　　　　　 EBak NArc
'Southlanders'　　　　　 EBak
'Southwell Minster'　　　 EKMF NArc
'Space Shuttle'　　　　　 CLoc CSil EKMF LCla MWhe NArc
'Sparky'　　　　　　　　EPts LCla MWhe
'Speciosa'　　　　　　　EBak EKMF LCla MWhe
'Spellbinder'　　　　　　EGou
'Spion Kop' (d)　　　　　CSil EBak EKMF MJac MWar
　　　　　　　　　　　　MWhe NArc NFai

§ *splendens* ♀　　　　　 CDoC CFee CLoc CSil EBak EGou
　　　　　　　　　　　　EKMF LCla MWar NPer SMrm
 - 'Karl Hartweg'　　　　 CDoC
'Sporty'　　　　　　　　MJac
'Spring Bells'　　　　　　MWhe
'Squadron Leader' (d)　　 EBak EPts LVER
'Square Peg'　　　　　　NArc
'Stanley Cash' (d)　　　　CLoc CSil EKMF LVER MWar
　　　　　　　　　　　　MWhe NArc SCoo
'Stan's Choice'　　　　　CSil
'Star of Pink'　　　　　　MWhe
'Star Rose'　　　　　　　EKMF
'Stardust'　　　　　　　CSil EBak LCla MJac MWhe NArc
'Starlight'　　　　　　　Last listed 1998
'Steeley'　　　　　　　　MWhe
'Steirerblut'　　　　　　LCla
'Stella Ann'　　　　　　 CSil EBak EGou EPts LCla MAld
　　　　　　　　　　　　NArc
'Stella Marina' (d)　　　　CLoc EBak
'Sterretje'　　　　　　　Last listed 1999
¶ 'Stewart Taylor'　　　　 MJac
'Stoney Creek'　　　　　 Last listed 1999
'Stormy Sunset'　　　　　NArc
¶ 'Straat Magelhaen'　　　 LCla
'Straat Napier'　　　　　EGou SLBF
'Strawberry Delight' (d)　 CLoc CSil EBak ECtt EKMF LVER
　　　　　　　　　　　　MJac MWhe NArc
'Strawberry Mousse'　　　LVER
'Strawberry Sundae' (d)　 CLoc CSil EBak NArc
'Strawberry Supreme'　　 CSil EKMF
'String of Pearls'　　　　CLoc CSil EKMF LCla MJac NArc
　　　　　　　　　　　　SKen SLBF SSea
'Stuart Joe'　　　　　　 EKMF
'Sugar Almond'　　　　　MJac
'Sugar Blues'　　　　　　EBak NArc
Sugarbush　　　　　　　See F. 'Suikerbossie'
§ 'Suikerbossie'　　　　　MJac NArc
* 'Summer Daffodil'　　　 EGou
'Summerwood'　　　　　 Last listed 1998
'Sunkissed' (d)　　　　　COtt EBak
'Sunlight Path'　　　　　LCla

'Sunningdale'　　　　　　LCla
'Sunny'　　　　　　　　 COtt
'Sunny Smiles'　　　　　 CSil EKMF NArc
'Sunray' (v)　　　　　　 CLTr CLoc COlW EBak EGou
　　　　　　　　　　　　EKMF EPts LRHS MAld MAsh
　　　　　　　　　　　　MBel MWhe NArc NSti SKen SPla
　　　　　　　　　　　　WWeb
'Sunset'　　　　　　　　CLoc CSil EBak MWhe NArc SKen
　　　　　　　　　　　　SPer
'Supernova'　　　　　　 NArc
'Supersport'　　　　　　 EGou
'Superstar'　　　　　　　CSil EPts SSea
'Surrey Symphony'　　　　Last listed 1998
'Susan'　　　　　　　　 COtt LCla MWhe
'Susan Arnold'　　　　　 Last listed 1999
'Susan Diana'　　　　　　Last listed 1998
'Susan Ford'　　　　　　 CSil NArc SPet WGwG
'Susan Green'　　　　　　CSil EBak EKMF EMan LCla MAld
　　　　　　　　　　　　MJac MWar MWhe NArc WGwG
'Susan McMaster'　　　　 CLoc
'Susan Olcese'　　　　　 EBak NArc
'Susan Skeen'　　　　　　MJac
'Susan Travis'　　　　　　CLoc CSil EBak EKMF MWhe
　　　　　　　　　　　　NArc SKen SPet
'Susan Young'　　　　　　Last listed 1999
'Swanley Gem' ♀　　　　 CLoc EBak EKMF MWhe SLBF
　　　　　　　　　　　　SSea
'Swanley Pendula'　　　　CLoc
'Swanley Yellow'　　　　 EBak NArc
'Sweet Leilani' (d)　　　　CLoc CSil EBak NArc
'Sweet Sixteen' (d)　　　　CLoc
N 'Sweetheart'　　　　　　EBak NArc
'Swingtime' (d) ♀　　　　CGre CLoc CSil EBak EKMF EMan
　　　　　　　　　　　　EPts LCla LRHS LVER MAld MGos
　　　　　　　　　　　　MJac MWar MWhe NArc NFai
　　　　　　　　　　　　NHaw SKen SLBF SYvo WGwG
　　　　　　　　　　　　WWol
'S'Wonderful' (d)　　　　 CLoc EBak
sylvatica Benth.　　　　 EKMF LCla
 - Munz　　　　　　　　 See F. nigricans
'Sylvia Barker'　　　　　 EGou LCla MAld MJac MWar
'Sylvia Foster'　　　　　 NArc
'Sylvy'　　　　　　　　 CSil MWhe NArc
'Symphony'　　　　　　　CLoc EBak
'T' Vorske'　　　　　　　Last listed 1998
'Taco'　　　　　　　　　EGou EKMF LCla
'Taddle'　　　　　　　　EMan MJac NArc SLBF WGwG
'Taffeta Bow' (d)　　　　 CLoc CSil EKMF LVER
'Taffy'　　　　　　　　 EBak
'Tam O'Shanter'　　　　　Last listed 1999
'Tamino'　　　　　　　　Last listed 1998
'Tamworth'　　　　　　　CLoc EBak LCla MJac NArc SSea
'Tangerine'　　　　　　　CLoc CSil EBak MWar MWhe
　　　　　　　　　　　　NArc SSea
'Tania Leanne'　　　　　 NArc
'Tantalising Tracy'　　　　SLBF
'Tanya'　　　　　　　　 CLoc EKMF
'Tanya Bridger' (d)　　　 EBak NArc
'Tarra Valley'　　　　　　EGou LCla MWhe NArc
'Task Force'　　　　　　 CSil NArc
'Tausendschön' (d)　　　　CLoc ECtt EKMF NArc
'Tear Fund'　　　　　　　Last listed 1998
'Ted Heath'　　　　　　　NArc
'Ted Perry'　　　　　　　CSil
'Television'　　　　　　　NArc
'Tempo Doelo'　　　　　 Last listed 1998
N 'Temptation'　　　　　　CGre CLoc CSil EBak ECtt
'Tennessee Waltz' (d) ♀　 CGre CLoc CSil EBak EKMF EMan
　　　　　　　　　　　　EPts LCla LRHS LVER MAld MJac
　　　　　　　　　　　　MWar MWhe NArc SChu SKen
　　　　　　　　　　　　SLBF SPer SPla WEas WGwG
'Terrysue'　　　　　　　 EKMF

tetradactyla		See *F. encliandra* subsp. *tetradactyla*
	'Teupels Erfolg'	NArc
	'Texas Longhorn' (d)	CLoc CSil EBak EKMF NArc
	'Thalia' ♀	CDoC CGre CLoc CSam CSil EBak ECtt EGou EKMF EMan EPts ERea LCla LRHS LVER MAld MBri MJac MWar MWhe NArc SKen SLBF SPla SUsu WBod WEas WGwG
	'Thamar'	CLoc CSil EGou EKMF EPts MWar MWhe SWal SYvo
	'That's It' (d)	EBak NArc
	'The Aristocrat' (d)	CLoc EBak WGwG
§	'The Doctor'	CLoc CSil EBak EKMF MWhe NArc
	'The Jester' (d)	EBak
	'The Madame' (d)	EBak NArc
	'The Patriot'	EKMF NArc
	'The Rival'	EKMF
	'The Tarns'	CSil EBak EKMF NArc NCiC
	'Therese Dupois'	CSil
	'Théroigne de Méricourt'	EBak EKMF NArc
	'Thilco'	EKMF
	'Think Pink'	WGwG
	'This England'	CSil NArc
	'Thistle Hill'	EKMF
	'Thompsonii'	See *F. magellanica* 'Thompsonii'
	'Thornley's Hardy'	CSil EKMF EMan LCla NArc
	'Three Cheers'	CLoc EBak
	'Three Counties'	EBak
	'Thumbelina'	Last listed 1998
	'Thunderbird' (d)	CLoc EBak
	thymifolia	ESis GMac GQui LHop SHFr SIng SMrm WKif
	- subsp. *minimiflora*	EGou EKMF LCla
	- subsp. *thymifolia*	EGou EKMF LCla
	'Tiara'	EBak
N	'Tiffany' (d)	EBak
	tillettiana	EGou EKMF
	'Tillingbourne'	LCla
	'Tillmouth Lass'	EKMF
	'Timlin Brened'	CSil EBak LCla MWhe NArc
	'Timothy Titus'	EGou LCla SLBF
	'Tina's Teardrops'	SLBF
	'Ting-a-ling'	CLoc CSil EBak EKMF LVER MAld MWhe NArc SLBF SPet SSea
N	'Tinker Bell'	CSil EBak EDAr EKMF NArc WLRN
	'Tintern Abbey'	NArc
¶	'Tjingjara'	LCla
	'Toby Bridger' (d)	CLoc EBak NArc
	'Tolling Bell'	CSil EBak EKMF MJac MWhe NArc WGwG
	'Tom Coulson'	EGou
	'Tom H. Oliver' (d)	EBak
	'Tom Knights'	EBak EKMF MWhe NArc WGwG
	'Tom Redfern'	Last listed 1999
	'Tom Thorne'	EBak
	'Tom Thumb' ♀	More than 30 suppliers
	'Tom West' (v)	CBrm CDoC CGre CInt CLoc CMHG CSil EBak EGou EKMF LCla LHil LHop LRHS LVER MAld MJac MWar MWhe NArc SAga SKen SLBF SMrm SSea WCot WEas
	'Tom Woods'	LCla MWhe
	'Tony Galea'	LCla
	'Tony Porter'	MJac
	'Tony's Treat'	EPts
	'Toos'	Last listed 1998
	'Topaz' (d)	CLoc EBak NArc
	'Topper'	EMan NArc
	'Torch' (d)	CLoc CSil EBak MJac NArc

	'Torchlight'	CSil EPts LCla
	'Torvill and Dean' (d)	CDoC CLoc CSil EGou EKMF EPts LRHS LVER MJac MWar MWhe NArc SKen
	'Towi'	NArc
	'Tracid'	CLoc CSil
	'Tracie Ann'	EKMF
	'Trail Blazer'	CLoc CSil EBak MJac NArc
	'Trailing Queen'	CSil EBak EKMF MJac NArc
	'Trase' (d)	CCHP CDoC CSil EBak EKMF EPts LVER NArc
	'Traudchen Bonstedt'	CDoC CLoc CSil EBak EKMF EPts LCla MWhe NArc SLBF SPet
	'Traviata'	NArc
	'Treasure'	EBak
	'Trés Long'	EGou
	'Trewince Twilight'	NArc
	'Tricolor'	See *F. magellanica* var. *gracilis* 'Tricolor'
	'Tricolorii'	See *F. magellanica* var. *gracilis* 'Tricolor'
	'Trientje'	LCla
	'Trio'	CLoc SSea
	triphylla	EBak EGou EKMF LCla LRHS SVen
	'Tristesse' (d)	CLoc EBak MJac NArc
	'Troika' (d)	EBak EKMF
	'Troon'	NArc
	'Tropic Sunset'	CSil MBri MWhe NArc
	'Tropicana' (d)	CLoc EBak NArc
	'Troubadour'	CLoc
	'Trudy'	CSil EBak EKMF NArc SPet
	'Truly Treena'	SLBF
	'Trumpet Voluntary'	Last listed 1998
N	'Trumpeter'	CDoC CLoc CSil EBak EKMF EPts LCla MJac MWhe NArc
	'TSJ'	Last listed 1998
	'Tsjiep'	Last listed 1999
¶	'Tumbling Waters' (d)	LVER
	'Tuonela' (d)	CLoc CSil EBak EKMF MWhe NArc
	'Tutone'	MJac NArc
	'Tutti-frutti' (d)	CLoc MWhe
	'Tutu'	NArc
	'T'Vosk'	NArc
	'Twink'	EGou
	'Twinkling Stars'	CSil EKMF MJac NArc
	'Twinny'	EKMF SLBF
	'Twirling Square Dancer'	Last listed 1998
	'Twist of Fate'	EKMF
	'Two Tiers'	EKMF NArc WGwG
	'UFO'	CSil NArc
	'Uillean Pipes'	Last listed 1998
	'Ullswater' (d)	EBak LVER NArc
	'Ultramar' (d)	EBak NArc
¶	'Uncle Charlie'	CDoC CLoc EBak EKMF WEas
	'Uncle Jinks'	SPet
	'Uncle Steve'	EBak NArc
	'University of Liverpool'	MJac NArc
	'Upward Look'	EBak EKMF SSea
	'Vale of Belvoir'	Last listed 1998
	'Valentine'	EBak
	'Valerie Ann' (d)	EBak
	'Valiant'	EBak
	'Vanessa'	CLoc
	'Vanessa Jackson'	CLoc CSil MJac MWhe NArc WGwG
	'Vanity Fair' (d)	CLoc EBak NArc
	vargarsiana	CDoC EGou EKMF LCla
	'Variegated Brenda White'	EKMF MWar NArc
	'Variegated La Campanella'	MWhe
	'Variegated Lottie Hobby' (v)	CSil EKMF LCla MAld

'William Grant' — EGou
'William Jay' — Last listed 1998
'Wilson's Colours' — EPts
'Wilson's Joy' — Last listed 1999
'Wilson's Pearls' — CSil LAco NArc SLBF WGwG
'Wilson's Sugar Pink' — EPts LCla MJac
'Win Oxtoby' — EKMF NArc
'Wine and Roses' (d) — EBak NArc
'Wingrove's Mammoth' — CSil NArc
'Wings of Song' (d) — CSil EBak NArc
'Winifred' — NArc
'Winston Churchill' ♀ — CLoc CSil EBak EKMF EMan EPts LCla LRHS LVER MBri MJac MWar MWhe NArc NFai SPlb
¶ 'Winter's Touch' — EKMF
'Woodnook' — CSil
'Woodside' — CSil
* 'Woodside Gem' — NArc
  wurdackii — CSil EKMF ERea
* 'Xcuzco' — EKMF
'Xmas Tree' — Last listed 1999
'Y Me' — Last listed 1998
'Ymkje' — EKMF LCla SLBF
'Yolanda Franck' — CSil
'Yorkshire Rally' — Last listed 1998
'Yuletide' — CSil
'Zara' — CSil MWhe
'Zets Bravo' — WGwG
'Ziegfield Girl' (d) — EBak NArc
'Zulu King' — EGou NArc
'Zulu Queen' — EGou
'Zwarte Dit' — Last listed 1998
'Zwarte Snor' — NArc

FUMANA (Cistaceae)
procumbens — Last listed 1997
thymifolia — Last listed 1999

FUMARIA (Papaveraceae)
lutea — See *Corydalis lutea*
officinalis — MSal

FURCRAEA (Agavaceae)
bedinghausii — CFil CGre EOas WMul WPGP
§ *foetida* — Last listed 1999
§ - var. *mediopicta* — Last listed 1998
  - 'Variegata' — See *F. foetida* var. *mediopicta*
gigantea — See *F. foetida*
longaeva — CAbb CB&S CCtw CHEx CTor CTrC CTrF LHil SAPC SArc
selloa — LHil
  - var. *marginata* — CHEx LHil

G

GAGEA (Liliaceae)
fibrosa — Last listed 1997
lutea — EPot
pratensis — EPot

GAILLARDIA (Asteraceae)
aristata hort. — See *G.* x *grandiflora*
¶ - 'Maxima Aurea' — NCut
'Bremen' — EPfP LRHS NCut NNor NPri
'Burgunder' — More than 30 suppliers
'Dazzler' ♀ — CHar CTri EBee ECtt ELan EMan ENot EOld EPfP LRHS MBri MCAu NCut NFor NLar SPer SRCN WGor WPer WStI

§ 'Fackelschein' — CBrm NFai SRCN WBro WHer
Goblin — See *G.* 'Kobold'
§ 'Goldkobold' — ELan EPar MHer
§ x *grandiflora* — EMan NOak
  - 'Aurea' — LRHS WLRN
  - 'Aurea Plena' (d) — EBee MWhi
  - giant hybrids — WFar
§ 'Kobold' — CB&S COIW EBee EBrP EBre ECtt EMan GAbr GKir LBCl LBSe LBre LRHS MBBe MBri MHer MRav NBus SBre SCoo SOkh SPer SPla SPlb SRms STes WFar WWin
'Mandarin' — EBrP EBre LBCl LBSe LBre LRHS MBBe MRav SBre SRms
Monarch Group — NCut
'Nana Nieske' — NTow
* New Giant hybrids — Last listed 1998
  suavis — Last listed 1999
* 'Summer Fire' — Last listed 1999
'Tokajer' — EBee EPfP MCAu NCut NLar
Torchlight — See *G.* 'Fackelschein'
'Wirral Flame' — EPar
Yellow Goblin — See *G.* 'Goldkobold'

GALACTITES (Asteraceae)
tomentosa — CRDP ECha EHrv ELan EMan EMar LRHS MAvo SGar SUsu WBea WCot WEas WSan WWye

GALANTHUS ✿ (Amaryllidaceae)
x *allenii* — CAvo CBro EMor LRHS
alpinus — CLAP LAma
'Anglesey Abbey' — EMor
'Anne of Geierstein' — EMor
'Armine' — CAvo EMor LFox
¶ 'Athenae' — CBro
'Atkinsii' ♀ — CAvo CBro CLAP EMon EMor EOrc EPar EPot ERav LAma LFox MBri MRav NBir SChr SDix WPGP WRus WWat WWye
'Augustus' — CAvo CBel CFee EMor ERos LFox WIvy
'Barbara's Double' (d) — EMor
'Benhall Beauty' — CAvo EMor LFox
'Benton Magnet' — EMor
'Bertram Anderson' — EMor LFox
'Bitton' — CBro CLAP LFox WRus WTin
bortkewitschianus — CBro GCrs LFox
'Brenda Troyle' — CBel CBro CLAP EPar EPot LFox WIvy WRus
byzantinus — See *G. plicatus* subsp. *byzantinus*
cabardensis — See *G. transcaucasicus*
'Cassaba' — See *G. elwesii* 'Cassaba'
caucasicus ♀ — CAvo CBro ECha EMor EPot ERav LAma LFox MTho
  - hort. — See *G. elwesii* var. *monostictus*
  - 'Comet' — See *G. elwesii* 'Comet'
  - var. *hiemalis* — See *G. elwesii* var. *monostictus* 'Hiemalis'
  - 'John Tomlinson' — See *G. elwesii* 'John Tomlinson'
  - late-flowering — LRHS
  - 'Mrs McNamara' — See *G. elwesii* 'Mrs McNamara'
'Charmer Flore Pleno' (d) — EMor
'Clare Blakeway-Phillips' — EMor
'Colesbourne' — EMor
corcyrensis — See *G. reginae-olgae* subsp. *vernalis*
  spring-flowering — *vernalis*
  - winter-flowering — See *G. reginae-olgae* subsp. *reginae-olgae* Winter-flowering Group
'Cordelia' (d) — EMon EMor LFox
'Curly' — EMor

'David Shackleton'	EMor
'Desdemona'	CLAP EPot LFox WIvy
'Dionysus' (d)	CBro CLAP EMor EPot LFox LRHS MBri NBir WRus
'Double Scharlokii' (d)	Last listed 1998
'Edinburgh Ketton'	EMor
§ *elwesii* ♀	CAvo CBro EBee EMon EMor EOrc EPot ERav ERos LAma LFox LRHS MBri NBir NRog SRms WCot WIvy WShi
§ – 'Cassaba'	CAvo EPot
§ – 'Comet'	EMor
– 'Flore Pleno' (d)	LFox
– 'Grumpy'	Last listed 1998
§ – 'John Tomlinson'	EMor
* – 'Magnus'	CLAP
§ – var. *monostictus*	EMon
§ – – 'Hiemalis'	CBro ECha EMon EMor LAma WCot
§ – 'Mrs McNamara'	EMor
§ – 'Ransom's Dwarf'	EMor
§ – 'Washfield Colesbourne'	EMor
– var. *whitallii*	CLAP
– 'Zwanenburg'	EMon
'Falkland House'	EMor
'Fieldgate Superb'	EMor
* 'Finale'	ECha
fosteri	CAvo CBro LAma LRHS
– PD 256830	EMor
'Foxton'	EMor
'Galatea'	CLAP EMon EMor LFox LRHS WIvy
§ *gracilis*	CAvo CBro CLAP EMor EPar ERav LFox MTho WIvy
– 'Corkscrew'	EMor
graecus hort.	See *G. gracilis*
– Orph. ex Boiss.	See *G. elwesii*
'Grayling'	EMor
Greatorex double (d)	CLAP EMon SSvw
'Heffalump'	EMor
'Hill Poë' (d)	CAvo CBro EMor EPar LFox
'Hippolyta' (d)	CAvo CBro CElw CLAP ECha EMor EPar EPot LFox WIvy
'Icicle'	EMor
ikariae ♀	EOrc EPar EPot ERav LAma
– subsp. *ikariae* Butt's form	EMor
– Latifolius Group	See *G. platyphyllus*
– Woronowii Group	CAvo CLAP EMon GCrs LAma
¶ 'Imbolc'	EMor
'Jacquenetta' (d)	CBro CLAP EMor EPot WPGP
'John Gray'	CBel CBro EMon EMor LFox
'Ketton'	CAvo CBro CElw EMor ERav LFox LRHS WIvy
'Kingston Double' (d)	CLAP
'Kite'	CBro EMor
'Lady Beatrix Stanley' (d)	CAvo CBro CLAP ECha EMon EMor EPar EPot ERav LAma LRHS MTho NHar
latifolius	See *G. platyphyllus*
'Lavinia' (d)	CAvo CElw ERav WRus
'Lime Tree'	CBel CLAP EPot LFox
'Little Dorrit'	EMor
lutescens	See *G. nivalis* 'Sandersii'
'Magnet' ♀	CAvo CBel CBro CFee CLAP EMor EPot ERav LAma LFox NHar WPGP WRus
'Maidwell C'	EMor
'Maidwell L'	CAvo EMor LFox
'Melvillei'	NHar
'Merlin'	EMor EOrc LFox NHar WIvy WRus

'Mighty Atom'	CFee EMor ERav LFox
'Moccas'	Last listed 1999
'Modern Art'	EMor
'Mrs Thompson'	ECha EMor WIvy
'Mrs Wrightson's Double' (d)	EMor
'Neill Fraser'	LFox
'Nerissa' (d)	EPot
nivalis ♀	CBro CKin CNic ELan EMor EOld EPar EPot ERav ETub EWFC LAma LFox LRHS MBri MMal NRog SRms WCot WShi
– var. *angustifolius*	CBro EHyt
– 'Appleby'	Last listed 1999
– 'April Fool'	LFox
– 'Blewbury Tart' (d)	CAvo
– 'Blonde Inge'	EMor
– subsp. *cilicicus*	See *G. peshmenii*
– dwarf	LFox
– 'Flore Pleno' (d) ♀	CBro EBrP EBre EPar EPla EPot ERav ETub LAma LBCI LBSe LBre LFox LRHS MBBe NMGW NRog NRya SBre SRms WCot WHen WShi WWye
– 'Greenish'	EMor
¶ – 'Hambutt's Orchard'	EMor LFox
– subsp. *imperati* 'Ginns'	CLAP EMor LFox WRus
– JRM 3139	EMor
– 'Lady Elphinstone' (d)	CAvo CBro CRow EMor EPar EPot ERav GCrs LAma LFox MRav MTho NHar
– 'Lutescens'	See *G. nivalis* 'Sandersii'
– 'Pewsey Vale' (d)	EMor
¶ – Poculiformis Group	EMon
– – 'Sandhill Gate' (d)	EMor
– 'Pusey Green Tip' (d)	CAvo CBro CElw CLAP EMor EPar EPot ERav GCrs ITim LFox LRHS MRav WPGP
– 'Rushmere Green'	EMor
§ – 'Sandersii'	CBro CRDP EMor EPot GCrs SSpi
§ – 'Savill Gold'	EMor
§ – Scharlockii Group	CAvo CBel EMon EMor EOrc LAma LFox NHar
– 'Sibbertoft White'	EMor
– 'Tiny'	Last listed 1999
– 'Tiny Tim'	EPot NRya
§ – 'Virescens'	CLAP EMor
– 'Viridapicis'	CAvo CBro ECha EMor EPar EPot ERav LAma LFox LRHS WIvy WPGP WRus WShi
– 'Walrus' (d)	EMor
– 'Warei'	EMor LFox
– WM 9615 from E. Slovenia	Last listed 1998
– WM 9630 from C. Hungary	Last listed 1997
§ – 'Wonston Double'	EMor
'Ophelia' (d)	CAvo CBro EMor EOrc EPar EPot ERav LAma LFox WRus
* 'Paradise Double'	EPar
* 'Paradise Giant'	EPar
'Peg Sharples'	EMor ERav
§ *peshmenii*	Last listed 1998
§ *platyphyllus*	CAvo CBro EMor EOrc EPot LAma LFox LRHS
plicatus ♀	CAvo CFee EMon LFox LRHS
– 'Baxendale's Late'	EMor
§ – subsp. *byzantinus*	CAvo CBro EMor EOrc EPar LFox LRHS
– – early	WIvy
– – LP 17	EMor
– – 'Sophie North'	GCrs

- - 'Three Ships'	EMor
- - 'Trym'	EMor
- 'Finale'	Last listed 1999
- 'Gerard Parker'	EMor
- large	EOrc
- 'Ron Ginns'	LFox
- 'Warham'	CBro EMor EOrc EPot WPGP
- 'Wendy's Gold'	EMon EMor GCrs
'Primrose Warburg'	EMor
'Ransom's Dwarf'	See *G. elwesii* 'Ransom's Dwarf'
reginae-olgae	CAvo CBro EBee EMor EPot ERos
	ETub LAma SSpi
- from Sicily	ERav
¶ - subsp. *reginae-olgae*	ERav
- - 'Cambridge' ♀	EMor
§ - - Winter-flowering Group	CBro EMor ERav LAma LFox
§ - subsp. *vernalis*	EMon EMor EPot GCrs LRHS
- - AJM 75	EMor
- - CE&H 541	Last listed 1999
¶ - WM 9901	MPhe
¶ - WM 9908	MPhe
rizehensis	CBro WIvy
'Robin Hood'	EMor LFox LRHS
'S. Arnott' ♀	CAvo CBel CBro CElw CLAP ECha
	EMor EPar EPot ERav GVer LAma
	LFox NBir NHar WPGP
'Sally Ann'	LFox
'Scharlockii'	See *G. nivalis* Scharlockii Group
sp. WM 9803 from Slovenia	Last listed 1999
sp. WM 9808 from Hungary	MPhe
sp. WM 9809 from Croatia	MPhe
sp. WM 9817 from Bosnia	MPhe
¶ 'St Anne's'	WIvy
'Straffan'	CAvo CBel CBro EMor EOrc EPar
	EPot ERav LAma LFox LRHS NHar
	WRus
¶ 'Sybil Roberta'	NHar
¶ 'Sybil Roberts'	GCrs
¶ 'The Linns'	GCrs
'The Pearl'	EMor
'Three Leaves'	EMor
'Titania' (d)	CBro EMor
§ *transcaucasicus*	CBro EMon ERav LRHS
'Trotter's Merlin'	EMor
'Tubby Merlin'	EMor LFox
'Washfield Colesbourne'	See *G. elwesii* 'Washfield
	Colesbourne'
¶ 'Washfield Warham'	EMon LRHS
'William Thomson'	LFox
'Winifrede Mathias'	EMor LFox
'Wonston Double' (d)	See *G. nivalis* 'Wonston Double'

GALAX (Diapensiaceae)

aphylla	See *G. urceolata*
§ *urceolata*	CFil IBlr SSpi WCru

GALEGA (Papilionaceae)

bicolor	CMdw CWit EBee EGar EGle
	EMFP EWes IBlr MSte NBir NBrk
	NChi NLar SRms STes SWat WFar
'Duchess of Bedford'	CFir EBee MTis NCat
x *hartlandii*	IBlr MRav WHoo WWhi
- 'Alba' ♀	CPlt EBee EFou EGle EMar EMon
	EWes GBar GBri GCal IBlr LGre
	MArl MAvo MBel MRav MTis
	MWgw NBrk NBro SAga SOkh
	SWat WCot WMaN WPGP WPer
	WWhi
- 'Candida'	CGle CWit
- 'Lady Wilson'	CGle CPlt CWit EGle EMan EWes
	MArl MAvo MRav NBrk NDov
	NLar WCot WFoF WHoo WPen

	WRus
'Her Majesty'	See *G.* 'His Majesty'
§ 'His Majesty'	EBee EGle EMan LFis MArl MAvo
	MRav NBrk NLar SAga SWat WBea
	WBry WCot WMaN WPGP
officinalis	More than 30 suppliers
- 'Alba'	CBot CHad CMdw COlW CStr
	EGle ELan ELau EMan EMar IBlr
	LFis MBrN NChi NLar WBea
	WByw WCHb WEas WHer WOve
	WPyg WRus WWye
orientalis	CGle EBee ECGP ECha GCal LRHS
	MArl MBel MRav SWat WAbb
	WCot

GALEOBDOLON See LAMIUM

GALEOPSIS (Lamiaceae)

segetum	Last listed 1997
speciosa	Last listed 1997
tetrahit 'Contrast' (v)	WAlt
- 'Dirbach Variegated'	MInt

GALIUM (Rubiaceae)

aquaticum var. *crispum*	Last listed 1999
'Krause Münze'	
aristatum	MLLN WCot
cruciata	See *Cruciata laevipes*
mollugo	CArn CKin MSal WCHb
§ *odoratum*	More than 30 suppliers
palustre	CKin
saxatile	IIve
tinctorium	WOak
verum	CArn CKin EWFC IIve MChe
	MGas MHer MHew MMal MSal
	NLan NMir SIde WCHb WGwy
	WHbs WHer WOak

GALPINIA (Lythraceae)

transvaalica	Last listed 1998

GALTONIA (Hyacinthaceae)

§ *candicans*	More than 30 suppliers
princeps	CAvo CBro CHea EBee EBrP EBre
	ECha ERos GBuc LBCl LBSe LBre
	LPio LRHS MBBe SBre WBro WCot
regalis	EBee GCal MWll WCot WHil
viridiflora ♀	CAvo CB&S CBot CBrm CBro
	CEnd CHar CHea CSam EBee
	EBrP EBre ECha ELan GCHN GCal
	LAst LBCl LBSe LBre LRHS MBBe
	MTis NBid NChi NHol SAga SBre
	WCot WWat
- S&SH 3	Last listed 1999

GAMOLEPIS See STEIRODISCUS

GARDENIA (Rubiaceae)

§ *augusta*	EBak ELau EPfP LRHS MBri
- 'Veitchiana'	Last listed 1997
florida	See *G. augusta*
globosa	See *Rothmannia globosa*
grandiflora	See *G. augusta*
* 'Grandiflora Star'	LChe
jasminoides	See *G. augusta*
thunbergia	Last listed 1997

GARRYA ✿ (Garryaceae)

elliptica	More than 30 suppliers
- (m)	CDoC EHol NBlu SLim WBod
	WFar WGwG
- (f)	WPat

- 'James Roof' (m) ♀ More than 30 suppliers
fremontii ISea WLRN
x *issaquahensis* CAbP CCHP CDoC CEnd CFai
  'Glasnevin Wine' CPMA EBee ELan EPfP GKir GOrc
   IMGH IOrc LRHS MAsh MBlu
   MBri NHol SMur SPer SSht SSta
   WWat
- 'Pat Ballard' (m) CPMA ELan EPfP GKir LRHS
   MAsh NHol SLim SPer SReu SSta
x *thuretii* MGos WWat

GARULEUM (Asteraceae)
woodii JCA 324000 CPBP

GASTERIA ✿ (Liliaceae)
armstrongii CCpl
excelsa CCpl
verrucosa CCpl

x GAULNETTYA See GAULTHERIA

GAULTHERIA ✿ (Ericaceae)
adenothrix Last listed 1999
antipoda SSta
- x *macrostigma* Last listed 1998
crassa Last listed 1999
- x *depressa* Last listed 1999
cuneata ♀ EPot GCrs GDra LRHS MBar
   MGos NDlv SSta WAbe
- 'Pinkie' EPfP GKir LRHS MAsh
depressa Last listed 1999
§ *eriophylla* SReu
§ *fragrantissima* Last listed 1999
furiens See *G. insana*
  'Glenroy Maureen' MCCP
glomerata var. *petraea* SSta
griffithiana BM&W 69 Last listed 1999
hispidula MDun MGos
hookeri IBlr
- B 547 Last listed 1999
humifusa Last listed 1999
§ *insana* WPic
itoana MBar MGos WAbe
- B&SWJ 1576 WCru
littoralis Last listed 1999
macrostigma Last listed 1999
miqueliana MGos MMHG NHar WWat
mucronata CMHG ELan ENot EPfP MBar
   NWea
- (m) CDoC CTri ELan GGar GKir MAsh
   MBar MBri MGos MRav NHol SEas
   SPer SRms WPat
- 'Alba' (f) MAsh MBar MGos MRav
- 'Atrococcinea' (f) WPat WPyg
- 'Barry Lock' (f) WPat WPyg
- 'Bell's Seedling' (f) ♀ CChe CDoC CTri EPfP GGar GKir
   LRHS MAsh MGos SPer SReu SSta
   WPat WPyg
- C 9510 Last listed 1999
- 'Cherry Ripe' (f) GKir IOrc SEas
- 'Crimsonia' (f) ♀ CB&S CChe CTri ELan EPfP GKir
   LRHS MAsh MBar MGos SEas
   SLon SPer SReu SRms WPat WPyg
- 'Indian Lake' NHol SEas
- 'Lilacina' (f) CBlo MGos NCut WGwG
- 'Lilian' (f) CBlo CTri EBee ENot EPfP GKir
   GSki LRHS NHol SEas WLRN
- Mother of Pearl See *G. mucronata* 'Parelmoer'
- 'Mulberry Wine' (f) ♀ CBlo EPfP GKir IOrc LRHS NHol
   NHol SEas
- 'October Red' (f) NHol SEas
§ - 'Parelmoer' (f) CB&S CBlo CBrm ELan ENot EPfP
   GKir SEas SPer WPat WPyg

- 'Pink Pearl' (f) ♀ MAsh NHol SRms WLRN
- RB 94095 GTou
- 'Rosalind' (f) SEas WWeb
- 'Rosea' (f) MBar MGos
- 'Rosie' (f) SBod
- 'Sea Shell' (f) ♀ IOrc
§ - 'Signaal' (f) CBlo CBrm CDoC EBee ELan
   ENot EPfP GKir LRHS MGos SBrw
   SPer WLRN WPat
- Signal See *G. mucronata* 'Signaal'
§ - 'Sneeuwwitje' (f) CBlo CChe CDoC ENot EPfP GSki
   LRHS NHol SPer WPat
- Snow White See *G. mucronata* 'Sneeuwwitje'
- 'Stag River' (f) GDra MGos NCut
- 'Thymifolia' (m) CChe EPfP GAri SPla
- 'White Pearl' (f) GKir IOrc WLRN
- 'Wintertime' (f) ♀ CBrm ELan MGos SRms WWeb
§ *myrsinoides* SRms
nana Colenso See *G. parvula*
nummularioides GAri NMen SReu
- B 673 Last listed 1999
§ - var. *elliptica* SSta
- *minor* Last listed 1999
- 'Minuta' See *G. nummularioides* var.
   elliptica
ovalifolia See *G. fragrantissima*
I *paraguayensis* Last listed 1999
§ *parvula* Last listed 1998
  'Pearls' GCrs WAbe
phillyreifolia CMHG SSta WPic
  'Pink Champagne' SSta
poeppigii WPyg
* - *racemosa* SSta
procumbens ♀ More than 30 suppliers
prostrata See *G. myrsinoides*
- *purpurea* See *G. myrsinoides*
pumila GAri GCrs IMGH MBar MGos
   NHar NHol NMen
§ - C&W 5226 Last listed 1999
- 'E.K. Balls' EPot NHar
pyroloides GCrs
- BM&W 5 Last listed 1999
rupestris Last listed 1999
schultesii Last listed 1998
shallon CB&S CDoC EBee ENot EWTr
   GBar GChr GKir GOrc MBar
   MGos SPer SRms WDin WFar
   WFro WTro
- dwarf Last listed 1999
sinensis MDun
tasmanica ECou GCrs GDra IMGH MBar
- x *pumila* Last listed 1999
- white-berried Last listed 1998
- yellow-berried Last listed 1999
thymifolia SReu
trichophylla GCrs MDun NMen
willisiana See *G. eriophylla*
x *wisleyensis* LRHS MAsh SRms SSta WBod
   WPat WPyg
- 'Pink Pixie' CMHG EPfP GKir GOrc LRHS
   MAsh MBar MCCP MGos SBrw
   SIng SPer SSta
- 'Wisley Pearl' CB&S CDoC GDra GKir IBlr
   IMGH MBar MGos NHar SBrw
   SPer SReu WBod WPat
yunnanensis SReu

GAURA (Onagraceae)
lindheimeri ♀ More than 30 suppliers
- 'Corrie's Gold' (v) CHar CMea CSpe CWSG EBee
   ECha ECtt EHoe ELan EMan EMar
   EOrc EPfP EWTr LGre LHil LPio

	LRHS MHer MLLN MSCN SAga
	SPer SUsu WCDu WRus WWeb
- 'Jo Adela' (v)	CWes EGoo ELan EMan SUsu
	WWol
- 'Siskiyou Pink'	More than 30 suppliers
- 'The Bride'	CMGP COIW CTri EBee EFou
	EMar EWTr LRHS MArl MLan
	MNrw MWgw NFai NGdn SMrm
	STes WOve
- 'Whirling Butterflies'	CElw CHar CSam CSpe EBee
	EGoo EMan EMil EMon EPfP
	EWTr LFis LPio MChl MCli MLLN
	SAga SAsh SBod SEas SIng SLod
	SMad SMrm SWat WWoo
I 'Variegata'	Last listed 1999

GAUSSIA (Arecaceae)
maya	LPal

GAYLUSSACIA (Ericaceae)
brachycera	GGGa
ursinum	Last listed 1997

GAZANIA (Asteraceae)
'Aztec' ♀	CCHP CHal LHil LLWP LRHS
	NCiC NHaw SUsu
¶ 'Bicton Cream'	CHal
'Bicton Orange'	LRHS NPri
'Blackberry Ripple'	CGdn EBee LAst NCiC
'Blaze of Fire'	LRHS
'Brodick'	Last listed 1997
'Christopher'	CHal LHil MSte NCiC
'Circus'	LHil LRHS
'Cookei' ♀	CSpe GBin MSte WCot WEas
'Cornish Pixie'	CHal
cream	CHal NCiC
'Cream Beauty'	LRHS MSte SAga SUsu
'Cream Dream'	LAst
crimson and green	MSte
Daybreak Series	LPVe
'Daybreak Bronze'	LIck MLan
(Daybreak Series)	
'Daybreak Red Stripe'	LIck
(Daybreak Series)	
'Dorothy' ♀	LRHS
double yellow	See G. 'Yellow Buttons'
'Dwarf Orange'	LLWP
'Evening Sun'	LHil LRHS
'Flash'	WEas
'Freddie'	SMrm
'Garden Sun'	MLan
* *grayii*	CHal
* 'Hazel'	LRHS MSte
hybrids	Last listed 1999
krebsiana	Last listed 1997
'Lemon Beauty'	Last listed 1999
linearis RMRP 95-0283	NTow
'Magenta'	Last listed 1998
'Magic'	LRHS
'Michael' ♀	LRHS
Mini Star Series	CBrm
'Mini Star White'	SRms
'Mini Star Yellow'	Last listed 1998
'Northbourne' ♀	LHil
'Orange Beauty'	ELan LRHS
'Orange Magic'	WLRN
'Patricia Morrow'	Last listed 1997
'Red Velvet'	MSte
§ *rigens*	LRHS MBri
- var. *uniflora* ♀	MSte WEas
- - 'Variegata'	CBot
- 'Variegata' ♀	ELan LRHS WLRN

'Silver Beauty'	CBot LRHS
'Silverbrite'	CHal LLWP
splendens	See *G. rigens*
'Sundance'	Last listed 1997
'Talent' ♀	CHal COIW
§ 'The Serpent'	Last listed 1998
'Tiger'	GBin LRHS NCiC
§ 'Yellow Buttons' (d)	CHal LRHS WLRN

GEISSORHIZA (Iridaceae)
aspera	Last listed 1998
inflexa	Last listed 1998
monantha	Last listed 1998
radians	Last listed 1998
splendidissima	Last listed 1997
tulbaghensis	Last listed 1997

GELASINE (Iridaceae)
azurea	See *G. coerulea*
§ *coerulea*	WCot
uruguaiensis	Last listed 1998

GELIDOCALAMUS (Poaceae - Bambusoideae)
fangianus	See *Drepanostachyum*
	microphyllum

GELSEMIUM (Loganiaceae)
rankinii	CMCN CPIN CPle WCru
sempervirens ♀	CArn CLTr CMCN CPIN ERea
	IDee LCns SOWG
- 'Flore Pleno' (d)	CPIN ERea
- 'Pride of Augusta'	CMCN

GENISTA (Papilionaceae)
aetnensis ♀	CB&S CMCN CMHG CPle CSam
	EBee ELan ENot IOrc LRHS MBri
	MLan MNrw MWat SAPC SArc
	SDix SMad SPer SRCN SRms SSpi
	SSta WBod WDin WSHC WWat
anglica 'Cloth of Gold'	Last listed 1997
§ *canariensis*	CGre ERea LCns WAbe
cinerea	CBlo SPer WCFE
decumbens	See *Cytisus decumbens*
delphinensis	See *G. sagittalis* subsp.
	delphinensis
'Emerald Spreader'	See *G. pilosa* 'Yellow Spreader'
fragrans	See *G. canariensis*
hispanica	CB&S EBee EBrP EBre ELan ENot
	GChr GKir IOrc LBCl LBSe LBre
	LRHS MBBe MBar MGos MWat
	NFla SBre SLim SPer SRms WAbe
	WCFE WDin WGwG WHar WPyg
	WRHF WStI
- 'Compacta'	EHol EPla ESis
§ *horrida*	SIng
humifusa	See *G. pulchella*
lydia ♀	More than 30 suppliers
monosperma	See *Retama monosperma*
§ *monspessulana*	Last listed 1998
pilosa	CTri ENot EPot ISea LNet MBar
	MBro MGos MWhi NHar NMen
	SPer WWin
- 'Goldilocks'	CBlo ECtt MBar NHar SLon WBod
	WWeb
- 'Lemon Spreader'	See *G. pilosa* 'Yellow Spreader'
* - *major*	Last listed 1998
- var. *minor*	GKir GTou IMGH WAbe
- 'Procumbens'	CMea GDra NHol WPat WPyg
- 'Vancouver Gold'	CB&S EBee ELan ENot EPfP GChr
	GKir GOrc IOrc LAst LBuc LRHS
	MAsh MGos MNrw NHar NPro
	SRPl SRms WGor WHar WStI

		WWat WWeb
§	- 'Yellow Spreader'	CB&S CLTr CMHG ECtt GOrc
		WBod WRHF WWeb
	'Porlock'	Last listed 1997
§	*pulchella*	CTri MBro
	sagittalis	EPfP NFor NWoo SLon SPer SRCN
§	- subsp. *delphinensis* ♀	Last listed 1999
	- *minor*	See *G. sagittalis* subsp.
		delphinensis
§	x *spachiana* ♀	CTri GEil
	striata	See *Cytisus striatus*
	subcapitata	Last listed 1997
	- dwarf form	Last listed 1999
	tenera	Last listed 1999
	- 'Golden Shower' ♀	SLPl
	tinctoria	CArn CKin EWFC GBar GPoy ILis
		MBar MChe MHer MHew MSal
		NFor SIde WDin WHer WOak
		WWye
	- 'Flore Pleno' (d) ♀	CLyd CMHG GChr MGos NHar
		NMen NPro WHar WWeb
	- 'Humifusa'	EPot NHar NWCA
	- var. *humilior*	Last listed 1998
	- var. *prostrata*	WOak
	- 'Royal Gold' ♀	CCHP EBee ECtt ENot GChr
		MGos MRav SPan SPer SPlb SRms
		WBod WWeb
	tournefortii	Last listed 1999
	umbellata	Last listed 1998
	villarsii	See *G. pulchella*

GENTIANA ✿ (Gentianaceae)

§	*acaulis* ♀	More than 30 suppliers
	- f. *alba*	WLin
	- Andorra form	Last listed 1997
	- 'Belvedere'	WAbe
	- 'Coelestina'	GCrs
	- 'Dinarica'	See *G. dinarica*
	- Excisa Group	Last listed 1998
	- 'Holzmannii'	NNrd
	- 'Krumrey'	EPot
	- *occidentalis*	See *G. occidentalis*
	- 'Rannoch'	EPot MBro NMen NNrd
	- 'Undulatifolia'	NHar
	- 'Velkokvensis'	Last listed 1999
	algida	Last listed 1998
	- white	Last listed 1998
	'Alpha'	See *G.* x *hexafarreri* 'Alpha'
	'Amethyst'	GCrs NDlv NHar SBla WAbe
	andrewsii	Last listed 1998
	angustifolia	GCrs NTow
	- 'Montagne d'Aurouze'	Last listed 1999
	'Ann's Special'	GCrs GKir GMaP NHar NHol
	asclepiadea ♀	More than 30 suppliers
	- var. *alba*	CBot CFil CHea CLyd GBuc GGar
		GMac LRHS MBri MBro MTho
		SPer SRms WCot WCru WHoo
		WWat
	- 'Knightshayes'	MBro WHoo
	- 'Nymans'	Last listed 1999
	- pale blue	CFil WPGP
	- 'Phyllis'	CLyd GBuc MBro WHoo
	- 'Pink Cascade'	Last listed 1998
	- 'Rosea'	GBuc GKir MNrw WHoo
	'Barbara Lyle'	WAbe
	bavarica var. *subacaulis*	Last listed 1997
	bellidifolia	GTou
	x *bernardii*	See *G.* x *stevenagensis* 'Bernardii'
	bisetaea	SRms
	'Black Boy'	Last listed 1998
	'Blauer Diamant'	GCrs NHar
	'Blauer Zwerg'	NHar

	'Blue Flame'	GCrs GDra NHar WAbe
	'Blue Heaven'	GCHN GDra NHar WAbe
	'Blue Sea'	NHar
	'Blue Shell'	NHar
	'Blue Silk'	EWes GCrs NHar WAbe
	'Blue Spot'	Last listed 1999
	burseri	NChi
§	- var. *villarsii*	EBee NChi
N	*cachemirica*	CSam GTou LRHS
	'Cairngorm'	EWes GAbr GCrs GKir GMaP
		NDlv NHar SUsu
¶	*calycosa* NNS 96-109	NWCA
	Cambrian hybrids	Last listed 1998
	x *caroli*	LRHS NHar SBla WAbe
	'Christine Jean'	GTou NDlv NHar SIng
	clusii	EPot GCrs SBla WAbe
	- *alba*	GCrs
	- subsp. *clusii*	Last listed 1999
	- subsp. *costei*	WAbe
¶	- purple	CNic
	coelestis CLD 1087	EPot GCrs WAbe
	'Compact Gem'	EPot GCrs MNaF NHar WAbe
	corymbifera	GCrs
	crassicaulis	EBee
	- SBEL 220	Last listed 1999
§	*cruciata*	GTou MTho WLRN
§	*dahurica*	CPea GCal LRHS NCut NHar
	'Dark Hedgehog'	GCrs
	decumbens	CSam GCal WFar WLin
	depressa	MTho WAbe
	'Devonhall'	GCrs
§	*dinarica*	CLyd MTho WAbe
	Drake's strain	GDra GKir LRHS
	'Dumpy'	EPot GCrs NHar WAbe WPat
	'Dusk'	GDra NHar
	'Eleanor'	Last listed 1999
	'Elizabeth'	EWes GCrs MOne NDlv NHar
	x *farorna*	Last listed 1998
	farreri	EWes GKir WAbe
	- 'Duguid'	WAbe
	'Fasta Highlands'	NBir
	fetisowii	EBee
	freyniana	SOkd
	froelichii	Last listed 1999
	gelida	CSam GAbr MBro
	Glamis Strain	GCrs GMaP NDlv NHar
	'Glen Isla'	EWes MOne NHar
	'Glen Moy'	EWes GMaP MOne
	'Glendevon'	WAbe
§	*gracilipes*	ECho LRHS MSte MWat SPlb
		SRms
	- 'Yuatensis'	See *G. wutaiensis*
	grossheimii	WWin
	x *hascombensis*	See *G. septemfida* var.
		lagodechiana 'Hascombensis'
	'Henry'	WAbe
	x *hexafarreri*	EDAr GKir NHar
§	- 'Alpha'	GCHN IMGH NHar
	hexaphylla	NHar
	'Indigo'	Last listed 1998
	Inshriach hybrids	GDra GMaP MOne NHar NHol
	'Inverleith' ♀	EWes GKir IMGH MBri MBro
		MOne NHar NHol SPlb WGor
		WPat
	ishizuchii	EDAr
	japonica Maxim.	See *G. thunbergii*
	'John Aitken'	GCrs
	'Juwel'	NHar
	kauffmanniana	Last listed 1997
	kesselringii	See *G. walujewii*
	'Kirriemuir'	EWes GCrs NDlv
	'Kobold'	Last listed 1998

	WAbe WPat WPyg
- subsp. *angulosa*	See *G. verna* subsp. *balcanica*
§ - subsp. *balcanica* ♀	CLyd CPla EDAr ELan GAbr GCrs
	GTou MBro MTho NHar NHol
	SBla SRms WAbe WHoo WPat
	WPyg
¶ - var. *oschtenica*	WAbe
- x *pumila*	Last listed 1999
- slate blue	NHar NHol WPat
- subsp. *tergestina*	CPBP
'Violette'	GCrs
'Vip'	Last listed 1999
waltonii	ECho EWes
§ *walujewii*	Last listed 1999
wellsii	See *G.* x *macaulayi* 'Wells's
	Variety'
§ *wutaiensis*	CNic ECho GAbr SSca
yakushimensis	GCrs

GENTIANELLA (Gentianaceae)

cerastioides JCA 14003	Last listed 1999
hirculus JCA 13880/93	Last listed 1997
sp. K&LG 94/63	Last listed 1998

GENTIANOPSIS (Gentianaceae)

| sp. ACE 2331 | Last listed 1998 |

GERANIUM ✿ (Geraniaceae)

aconitifolium L'Héritier	See *G. rivulare*
albanum	CElw CFri CMCo CSev EBee EGra
	EMan EMar EMou EOrc EPPr
	GCHN GOrP MNrw NSti SCou
	SDix SRGP STes WBea WByw
	WCru WMoo WPnP
albiflorum	CMCo EBee EPPr GCHN IMGH
	LRHS MWhe NCat SCou SDys
	WMoo WPnP
anemonifolium	See *G. palmatum*
'Ann Folkard' ♀	More than 30 suppliers
'Anne Thomson'	More than 30 suppliers
antrorsum	EBee SDys
argenteum	CElw
'Aria'	Last listed 1999
aristatum	CBel CPou EBee EMan EMar EOrc
	EPPr EWes GCHN MNrw MSph
	NCot SCou SRGP STes WCra
	WCru WHil WMoo WPGP WPer
	WPnP
- NS 649	NWCA WHil
armenum	See *G. psilostemon*
asphodeloides	More than 30 suppliers
§ - subsp. *asphodeloides* white	
	CElw ECGP EMan EOrc EPPr
	SCou SRGP WFar WHen WMoo
	WPnP WRus WWpP
- 'Catforth Sam'	NCat
- subsp. *crenophilum*	CElw SCou
- 'Prince Regent'	CFri CHid EGle EPPr GCHN LPio
	NCat SCou WPnP
- subsp. *sintenisii*	Last listed 1997
- 'Starlight'	CElw GCHN MBro SCou SHel
	WCra WPnP
atlanticum Hook.f.	See *G. malviflorum*
'Baby Blue'	See *G. himalayense* 'Baby Blue'
'Bertie Crûg'	CHid CSpe EMan EPPr SIng SRms
	SRot SWat WCot WCru WHoo
	WWin
'Bethany'	Last listed 1998
biflorum	EBee
biuncinatum	EMar SCou WWin
'Black Ice'	GBuc GKir WCru WPnP
'Blue Cloud'	CElw CHil EBee EGle EPPr LGre

	NBrk SCou SHel SMrm SUsu
	WPnP WWpP
'Blue Pearl'	EPPr NHaw NSti SCou SRGP
	WPnP
§ 'Blue Sunrise'	EBee EBrP EBre GKir LBCl LBSe
	LBre LPio LRHS MBBe MCLN
	MWhe NHaw SAga SBre SCou
bohemicum	CFri EBee EMan GCHN NSti SCou
	SHel SRGP WBea WByw WCru
	WHen WHer WPnP
- DS&T 89077T	Last listed 1998
- 'Orchid Blue'	EMar LRHS
'Brookside'	More than 30 suppliers
brutium	GCHN WHen
brycei	EBee GOrP MNrw
'Buxton's Blue'	See *G. wallichianum* 'Buxton's
	Variety'
caeruleatum	EBee EPPr
caffrum	CMCo CPla EMan EPPr GBuc
	GCHN MNrw NBus NSti SCou
	SRGP STes WBea WCru WEas
	WPnP
californicum	GBuc NWCA WCru
canariense	CBod CGre CPla CSev CSpe CTbh
	EBee EMar EWes GKir LPio SCou
	SRGP WCru WElm WPnP
candicans hort.	See *G. lambertii*
§ x *cantabrigiense*	More than 30 suppliers
- 'Berggarten'	EBee EPPr
- 'Biokovo'	More than 30 suppliers
- 'Cambridge'	More than 30 suppliers
- 'Karmina'	CElw CHil CMCo EBee EGle EPPr
	EPla MBro MCli MNrw NBus
	SCou SHel WHoo WMoo WPnP
- 'Show Time'	CMCo SCro WHal WPnP
- 'St Ola'	More than 30 suppliers
¶ - 'Westray'	SCro
carolinianum	SCou
cataractarum	GCHN MNrw SCou WCru
- subsp. *pitardii*	SRGP
'Chantilly'	CElw CHar CMCo CMil CSam
	EBee EGra EMan EPPr GAbr
	GCHN GCal MBro MNrw NBir
	NBus NCat NFai NPro SCou SCro
	SUsu WBea WCra WCru WMoo
	WPnP WPrP
'Chocolate Candy'[PBR]	CWSG WWeb
* 'Chocolate Pot'	CHil NArg
cinereum	CGle CSev ENot GKir SIng
- 'Apple Blossom'	See *G.* x *lindavicum* 'Apple
	Blossom'
- 'Ballerina' ♀	More than 30 suppliers
¶ - 'Carol'[PBR]	EPPr MBri WWeb
- subsp. *cinereum*	GCHN SWat WCru
var. *cinereum*	
- - - 'Album'	GCHN WCru
- hybrids	MLLN WCru
- 'Janette'[PBR]	COtt EBrP EBre GKir LBCl LBSe
	LBre LRHS MAsh MBBe MBri
	NCat SBre SPer WCra WWeb
- 'Laurence Flatman'	More than 30 suppliers
- subsp. *nanum*	NCat
- var. *ponticum*	Last listed 1998
- 'Souvenir de René	LPio SUsu
Macé'[PBR]	
- subsp. *subcaulescens*	More than 30 suppliers
var. *subcaulescens* ♀	
- - - 'Giuseppii'	More than 30 suppliers
- - - 'Glühwein'	NPar
- - - 'Signal'	NPar

- - - 'Splendens' ♀ — CSpe EBee EBrP EBre EDAr EFou GCHN LBCl LBSe LBre LFis LRHS MBBe MBNS MTis MWhe NSla NSti SAga SBre SRGP SRms SWat WCru WFar WIvy WPnP WRus EPPr NPar
- - - 'Violaceum' — EPPr NPar
'Claridge Druce' — See *G.* x *oxonianum* 'Claridge Druce'
clarkei x *collinum* — EMan GOrP
- 'Kashmir Blue' — See *G.* 'Kashmir Blue'
- 'Kashmir Pink' — More than 30 suppliers
§ - 'Kashmir Purple' — More than 30 suppliers
§ - 'Kashmir White' ♀ — More than 30 suppliers
- Raina 82.83 — SCou
'Coffee Time' — SCro
collinum — CFri CHil CMCo GBuc GCHN LLWP MNrw NBus NCat NDov SCou SCro SRGP SUsu WCru WHen WIvy WPnP
columbinum — SCou
'Coombland White' — CElw CHil CMCo EBee EPPr LPio MAvo MNrw NPro NSti SCou SCro SDys SRGP WCru WHoo WMoo WPGP WPnP
'Crûg Pewter' — CSpe MBri NPSI
Crûg strain — CFri CHid CSev CSpe EMan GGar GKir LRHS MCCP MDun MHer MTis NPSI NSti SRPl STes SVil WCot WCru WPnP WWat
I 'Crûg's Darkest' — WCru
§ 'Cyril's Fancy' — EBee EPPr NCat SCro SUsu
dahuricum — WCru
dalmaticum ♀ — More than 30 suppliers
- 'Album' — CHil EDAr ELan EPot GKir LRHS MBro MHer MTho MWhe NHol SCou SIng SRGP SRms SRot WAbe WCra WCru WFar WHCG WPnP WWat WWin
- 'Bressingham Pink' — GKir
- x *macrorrhizum* — See *G.* x *cantabrigiense*
delavayi hort. — See *G. sinense*
- Franchet — CBot WCru
'Delight' — CHil
'Dilys' — CElw CMil CStr EBee EGra EPPr GCHN LLWP LPio MBro MCLN MNrw MWhe NBus NCat NGdn SCou SHel SRGP SUsu WBea WCru WFar WHal WHen WMoo WPnP WRus
dissectum — EWFC MSal SCou SIde
'Distant Hills' — CHil GBuc GCHN
'Diva' — CElw CMCo CMil EBee EGle EPPr GOrP NCat NSti SCou SCro SRGP SUsu WCot WCru WPnP
donianum CC 1074 — Last listed 1997
- HWJCM 311 — WCru
drakensbergense — CStr
'Dusky Crûg' — WCru
'Dusky Rose' — CFai EPfP GKir LRHS MBNS SAga SCou WPnP
'Elizabeth Ross' — CElw EPPr LRHS MAvo MNrw NBus WCru WMoo WWhi
'Elizabeth Wood' — EMan
endressii ♀ — CBre CElw CFri CSev EBee ECha EMou EOrc EWTr GCHN GDra LGro LRHS MBNS MMal MTho NBro NFai NFor NPer SCou SHel SPlb SRGP SRms WByw WEas WFar WGwG WHal
- 'Album' — See *G. endressii* 'Mary Mottram'
- 'Betty Catchpole' — EPPr NCat

- 'Castle Drogo' — CHil EPPr MChl NCat NFai SRGP WBea WPnP
- dark — NBus
§ - 'Mary Mottram' — CBos CElw CMCo EPPr GOrP MCLN MMil NBir NCat NSti SCro SHel WCot WEas WPnP WWpP
- 'Prestbury White' — See *G.* x *oxonianum* 'Prestbury Blush'
- 'Priestling's Red' — CElw CMCo EDAr EGra EMar SMrm
- 'Rose' — CHil SCob WPer WPnP WShe
erianthum — CFri EMan GBuc GCHN MCLN MSte MWhe NBus NCat NFai NLar SCou SIng SRGP STes WBea WCru WElm WPnP
- 'Calm Sea' — CElw EBee EPPr GBuc GCHN GOrP SHel SUsu WCru WMoo
- 'Neptune' — NCat SUsu WCra WCru
eriostemon Fischer — See *G. platyanthum*
§ *farreri* ♀ — CBot CFri CLyd EBee EGle GBri GBuc GCHN GCal LRHS MNrw NBir NWCA SBla SCou SWat WCru
¶ 'Flamingo' — MTPN
flanaganii — GCHN
fremontii — GBuc GCHN SCou
'Gillian Perrin' — Last listed 1999
goldmannii — SSpi
gracile — CElw CFri CHil EBee EMou EOrc EPla GBuc GCHN GMaP MBro MCLN MNrw NBir NChi SCou SCro SRGP WCra WCru WHal WMoo WPGP WPnP WPrP
- 'Blanche' — CElw EPPr SCou
- 'Blush' — CElw CHil CMCo EMan EPPr NCat SHel WBea
grandiflorum — See *G. himalayense*
- var. *alpinum* — See *G. himalayense* 'Gravetye'
gymnocaulon — CHil CMCo EBee EMan EMar EPPr GCHN LRHS NCat NSti SCou SLod STes WBea WCru WElm
'Harmony' — NCat
harveyi — CFri CHar CHil CMea CPBP CSpe EBee EMan EWes GBin LAco LGro LHop MBro MNrw WCra WCru WKif WPGP WPat WPnn
hayatanum — CAbP CHil
- B&SWJ 164 — CBod EBee EPPr GOrP NSti SCou WCru WMoo WWpP
§ *himalayense* — More than 30 suppliers
- *alpinum* — See *G. himalayense* 'Gravetye'
§ - 'Baby Blue' — CBel CBos CElw EBee EGle EPPr GBuc GCHN GCal MBri MBro MCLN MNrw NBrk NBus NCat NSti SCou SCro SHel SSoC WBea WBro WCru WHen WMoo WPnP
- 'Birch Double' — See *G. himalayense* 'Plenum'
¶ - 'Devil's Blue' — SCro
- 'Frances Perry' — SMur
§ - 'Gravetye' ♀ — More than 30 suppliers
- 'Irish Blue' — More than 30 suppliers
- *meeboldii* — See *G. himalayense*
- 'Pale Irish Blue' — GCal
§ - 'Plenum' (d) — More than 30 suppliers
hispidissimum — Last listed 1998
ibericum — CFri LRHS MCLN SRGP STes WFar
- subsp. *jubatum* — CElw CFri EBee EBrP EBre EGle EPPr GCHN GCal GKir LBCl LBSe LBre MBBe MMal MNrw NBus SBre SCou SRms WBea WCru WMoo WPnP
- - x *libani* — Last listed 1998

- - x *renardii*	GCal
- misapplied	See G. x *magnificum*
- var.*platypetalum* Boiss.	See G. *platypetalum* Fischer & Meyer
- - hort.	See G. x *magnificum*
incanum	CMHG CSev CSpe ECoo EWes GCHN MNrw NBir NTow SCou SMrm SRGP WCot WHal WHoo
- var.*incanum*	GCHN
- var.*multifidum*	EPPr GCHN LLWP SUsu SWat WCru WFar
- white form	SRGP
'Ivan'	CElw CHil CMCo CMil EBee EPPr GBuc LGre LRHS NBus NCat SAga SCou SCro WCot WPGP WPen WPnP WRus
'Johnson's Blue' ♀	More than 30 suppliers
'Joy'	CBos CElw CHad CHil CMCo CStr EBee ECGP EGle EPPr GCHN MAvo MCLN MChl MNrw MWrn NBir NChi NHaw NPro NSti SCou SCro SRGP SUsu SCra WCru WMoo WPGP WPnP
§ 'Kashmir Blue'	EBee EPPr GCHN NCat NMGW SCro WMoo WPnP
§ 'Kate'	CElw EGle GCHN GOrP NBus NChi WCru WPnn
'Kate Folkard'	See G. 'Kate'
§ 'Khan'	CBos CHil EPPr GCHN NBus NCat NDov SLod WCru WMoo
kishtvariense	CMCo EBee EBrP EBre ECoo EMan EOrc EPPr GCHN GCal LBCl LBSe LBre LPio LRHS MBBe MNrw MRav NDov NHol NSti SBre SCou SSpi WCru WMoo WOVN WPGP WPnP
- 'Blackthorn Garnet'	Last listed 1997
koraiense	CAbP CBod EMan
- B&SWJ	WMoo WWat
- B&SWJ 797	WCru
- B&SWJ 878	EBee SCou WCru
koreanum	CFil CMil CSpe EBee GCHN GKir GOrP LRHS NBus SPar SSpi STes SUsu WBea WCru WFar WMoo WPGP WPnP
- B&SWJ 602	SCou WCru
§ *kotschyi* var. *charlesii*	EBee SCou WCru WPnP
krameri	EMan GBin NSti
- B&SWJ 1142	EBee NCat WCru
§ *lambertii*	CFri EWes GBuc GCan GKir LPio MNrw NBir NChi WEas
- CC 1077	Last listed 1999
- hybrid	Last listed 1998
- 'Swansdown'	EMan GBuc GCHN GMac MNrw NBus WCru WPnP
lanuginosum	EMar SCou SRGP WUnu
libani	EBee EBrP EBre EMou GBuc GCHN GCal LBCl LBSe LBre LLWP MBBe MBel MTho MWhe NBus NSti SBre SCou SCro WByw WCot WCra WCru WEas WPGP WPnP
- x *peloponnesiacum*	CRDP
'Libretto'	EBee NCat WCru
x *lindavicum*	Last listed 1998
§ - 'Alanah'	Last listed 1998
§ - 'Apple Blossom'	CLyd CMea EDAr EPot GBuc GKir LPio MBel NBus NChi SAga SAsh SRGP SVil WAbe WCra WCru WHCG WWin
- 'Lissadell'	SBla

linearilobum subsp. *transversale*	EBee EPPr WCru
§ 'Little David'	EBee EPPr SUsu
'Little Devil'	See G. 'Little David'
'Little Gem'	CHil EBee EBrP EBre EFou GCHN GKir LBCl LBSe LBre LRHS MBBe MRav MWhe NBus NChi NDov NPro SBre SCou SCro SDys SHel SUsu WCru WFar WPnP
lucidum	EPPr EWFC GCHN MSal NCat NDov NSti SCou WElm
x *luganense*	SCou
'Lydia'	GOrP SRGP
§ *macrorrhizum*	More than 30 suppliers
- AL & JS 90179YU	CHid EPPr
- 'Album' ♀	More than 30 suppliers
- 'Bevan's Variety'	More than 30 suppliers
- 'Bulgaria'	EPPr NBus
- 'Czakor'	More than 30 suppliers
- 'Ingwersen's Variety' ♀	More than 30 suppliers
- 'Lohfelden'	CElw CHil EGle EPPr GCHN MBro SDys SHel SRGP SUsu WCra WCru WMoo WPnP WRHF
- 'Mount Olympus'	See G. macrorrhizum 'White-Ness'
- 'Mount Olympus White'	See G. macrorrhizum 'White-Ness'
- 'Pindus'	CElw CHil EBrP EBre EPPr GCHN LBCl LBSe LBre MBBe MBro NBus NCat NSti SBre SCou SDys SHel SRGP SUsu WCru WMoo WPnP
- 'Ridsko'	CElw CFee CHil CMCo EBee EGle EOrc EPPr GCHN GCal NBro NCat NDov SCou SCro SDys SHel SRGP WCru WHen WPnP
- *roseum*	See G. macrorrhizum
- 'Spessart'	CRos EBee EBrP EBre EPPr GKir LBCl LBSe LBre MBBe MBel MGed NBee NTow SBre SCob SCou SIng SRPl WCra WCru WFar WOVN WPnP WPyg WRHF
- 'Variegatum'	CElw CHil CRDP EBee ECha EFou ELan GCal GKir LRHS MBri MCLN MTho NBid NBir NFai SCob SIng WBea WCot WEas WFar WHCG WHen WHil WPnP WWin
- 'Velebit'	CBel CElw CFri CHil EPPr GCHN GOrP MSte NBus SRGP WCru WMoo WWgP
§ - 'White-Ness'	CBos CElw CFri CLAP CLTr EBee EMon EPPr GCHN NCat NPro SRGP WCot WCru WFar WHal WMoo WPGP WPnP
macrostylum	CElw CMil CPou EBee GCHN MBro SCou WCot WCru WPGP WPer
- 'Leonidas'	See G. tuberosum 'Leonidas'
¶ - 'Uln Oag Triag'	NCat
maculatum	More than 30 suppliers
- f.*albiflorum*	CElw CGle CHil CRDP EGle EMon EMou GCHN GCal MBel MBro MNrw NBid NSti SCou SHel SSpi SUsu WCra WCru WMaN WMoo WPnP WPrP
- 'Chatto'	CMCo CMil CSpe EBee EFou EMar EMil EPPr LRHS MBro MCli MNrw MRav MTis NHol SCob STes SWat WCra WFar WPnP WRus WWat
¶ - *purple*	EPPr
- 'Shameface'	EBee EPPr NBrk SHel WPnP
maderense ♀	More than 30 suppliers

§ x *magnificum* ♀ — More than 30 suppliers
- Clone C — CMHG NCat NSti
¶ - 'Rosemoor' — CFri
magniflorum — CHil GCHN NBid WBea WCru
§ *malviflorum* — More than 30 suppliers
- pink — CMil EBee SCro WCru WMoo
¶ - Spanish form — EPPr EWes
'Maxwelton' — CHil
microphyllum — See *G. potentilloides*
molle — EWFC MSal SCou
- *album* — Last listed 1997
§ x *monacense* — CElw CHil CMCo EBee EFou ELan
EMar EPla GGar GKir LRHS MBel
MWat MWhe NFai NSti SCou SCro
SSea SWat WBea WByw WCra
WCru WHer WPnP
- var. *anglicum* — CHil EBrP EBre ECtt EGle EOld
EOrc EPPr GAbr GCHN LBCl LBSe
LBre MBBe MBel MBro MWhe
NBus NSti SBre SCou SCro SHel
WMoo WPnP
- dark — WMoo
- var. *monacense* — CElw WFar WHen
§ - 'Muldoon' — More than 30 suppliers
§ - 'Variegatum' — More than 30 suppliers
'Money Peniche' — LPio
'Mourning Widow' — See *G. phaeum* var. *phaeum*
multisectum — WCru
nakaoanum HWJCM 504 — Last listed 1999
napuligerum hort. — See *G. farreri*
- Franchet — NSla
'Natalie' — NCat
nepalense — CMCo EMan NBus SCou SHel
SRGP SRms WHer WMoo WPnP
nervosum — CElw CHar CMCo CSev EBee
EMou MCCP NBus NLar NPro
NSti SCou STes WElm WPnP
WWhi
'Nicola' — CElw CHil EBee EGle EPPr NCat
SHel SLod SUsu
'Nimbus' — More than 30 suppliers
nodosum — More than 30 suppliers
- dark — See *G. nodosum* 'Swish Purple'
- 'Julie's Velvet' — WHoo
- pale — See *G. nodosum* 'Svelte Lilac'
¶ - pink — WPrP
§ - 'Svelte Lilac' — CElw CFri EBee ECGP EGle EMan
EMon EPPr GCal LRHS MBro
NBrk NCat NSti SCou SHel SMrm
SRGP SSea SWat WBea WCot
WCru WFar WMoo WPnP WPrP
§ - 'Swish Purple' — CBos CElw EBee EPPr MSte NCiC
SHel SIng SLod SRGP SWat WCot
WCru WFar WHen WMoo WPGP
- 'Whiteleaf' — CBos CElw CLTr EBee ECoo EGle
EPPr MBro NBrk NBur NBus NPro
SAga SWat WBea WCru WFar
WMoo WPnP
- 'Whiteleaf' seedling — EMar SHel
'Nora Bremner' — SUsu WPnP
ocellatum — CBre EBee NSti SCou
oreganum — CElw CMCo EMou EOrc GCHN
NBrk SCou SCro WCru
§ *orientalitibeticum* — More than 30 suppliers
'Orion' — Last listed 1999
'Orkney Pink' — More than 30 suppliers
ornithopodon — EBee
x *oxonianum* — EBrP EBre LBCl LBSe LBre MBBe
SAga SBre SCou SHel WCru
WMoo
- 'A.T. Johnson' ♀ — More than 30 suppliers
- 'Breckland Sunset' — CElw EBee EPPr SCou

- 'Bregover Pearl' — CBre CElw CHil CMCo EBee EPPr
MBro NCat SCou SHel SRGP
WMoo
- 'Bressingham Delight' — CElw CMCo EBee EBrP EBre
EWTr GKir LBCl LBSe LBre LRHS
MBBe MCLN MWhe NBus SBre
SCou SHel SRGP WPnP
- 'Buttercup' — CElw EMan EPPr
I - 'Cally Seedling' — EBee EGle EPPr EWes GCal WPnP
§ - 'Claridge Druce' — More than 30 suppliers
- 'Coronet' — EBee EGle EPPr NBrk SHel WBea
WMoo
- 'Crûg Star' — CElw CHil WPnP
- 'David McClintock' — CElw CHil EBee EMan EPPr MTed
NBus SCou WFar WMoo WWpP
- 'Dawn Time' — SCro
- 'Elworthy Misty' — CElw
- 'Frank Lawley' — CElw CHil CMCo EBee EPPr
GBuc GMac LLWP MBro NBus
NCat NChi NHex NSti SCou SCro
SHel SRGP WBea WMoo WPnP
- 'Fran's Star' — See *G. sanguineum* 'Fran's Star'
- 'Hexham Pink' — NCat
- 'Hollywood' — More than 30 suppliers
¶ - 'Jester' (v) — WCot
- 'Julie Brennan' — CElw EBee EPPr GCal NBus NCat
NGdn SRGP WBea WMoo WPnP
WWpP
- 'Kate Moss' — CHil EPPr GCHN GCal NBus NCat
NChi NDov NHex NSti WBar
WWpP
- 'Kingston' — See *G. versicolor* 'Kingston'
- 'Lace Time' — CBre CElw CHil CMCo CSev EBee
EPPr GMac LFis MBro MNrw
MWhe MWrn NBus NCot NOak
SCro SDys SHel SLod WBea WMoo
- 'Lady Moore' — CElw CHil CMCo EBee EMar EPPr
EPla GAbr GBuc GCHN MBro
MNrw MWhe NBro NBus NCot
SCou SCro SHel SRGP WBea WBor
WEll WHen WPnP
- 'Lambrook Gillian' — CElw CHil EBee EGle EPPr MBro
SCou SHel SRGP WBea WPnP
- 'Lasting Impression' — EPPr
- 'Miriam Rundle' — CElw CHil CMdw EBee EFou
EOrc EPPr MNrw NBus SCou
SDys SHel SRGP WBea WCru
WMoo WPnP
- 'Mrs Charles Perrin' — Last listed 1997
- 'Old Rose' — CElw CHil CMCo EBee EGle EPPr
GCHN GKir LRHS MBri NBus
NCat NCiC SCou SHel SLod SRGP
WBea WCru WMoo WPnP
- pale — Last listed 1998
- 'Pat Smallacombe' — CElw CHil EPPr LRot NBus NCat
NDov SHel SRGP WBea WCru
WMoo
- 'Phoebe Noble' — CBel CBre CElw CHil CMCo CMil
EBee EGle EMar EPPr LRHS MBri
MBro MNrw NBus NCat NSti
SAga SCou SCro SHel SRGP SSpe
SUsu WBea WCra WPnP
- 'Phoebe's Blush' — CElw EPPr GMac NCat NChi SHel
WBea
- 'Pink Lace' — Last listed 1998
§ - 'Prestbury Blush' — CBre CElw CMCo EBee EGle
EOrc EPPr GCHN NPar SCou SHel
WBea WCot WCru WMoo WWin
- 'Prestbury White' — See *G. x oxonianum* 'Prestbury
Blush'
- 'Rebecca Moss' — More than 30 suppliers
- 'Red Sputnik' — CElw EPPr GOrp

- 'Rohina Moss'   Last listed 1997
- 'Rose Clair'   CElw CFri CHid CHil CMCo CMil
                                EBee EGle EMou EOrc GCHN
                                GKir LRHS MCLN MWhe NFai
                                NSti SChu SCou SHel SRPl WBea
                                WCru WEas WElm WHen WMoo
                                WPer
I - 'Rosemary'   SCou WWpP
  - 'Rosemary Verey'   SHel
  - 'Rosenlicht'   CElw CHil CSev EBee EFou EMon
                                EMou EPPr LRHS MBro MCAu
                                MCLN MRav NBus NCat NEgg
                                NLar NTow SChu SCou SHel
                                SMrm SRGP SRPl SSpi WBea
                                WCru WMoo WPGP WPnP
  - x *sessiliflorum* subsp.   CHil SAga
    novae-zelandiae
    'Nigricans'
  - 'Sherwood'   More than 30 suppliers
  - 'Southcombe Double' (d)   CElw CHil CM&M CMCo CPla
                                CSev CStr EGle EMar EMou EPPr
                                GMac MCLN MFir NCat NFai
                                NGdn SRGP SUsu WBea WByw
                                WCru WHal WHen WMoo WWhi
                                WWin
§ - 'Southcombe Star'   CMCo EGar EOrc EPPr GAbr GCal
                                LAst MBel MBro MFir NBrk NBro
                                NBus NGdn NSti SHel SLod SRGP
                                WBea WCru WFar WHal WHen
                                WMoo WPer WPnP
  - 'Stillingfleet'   See *G.* x *oxonianum* 'Stillingfleet
                                Keira'
§ - 'Stillingfleet Keira'   GCHN NSti
  - 'Summer Surprise'   EBee EPPr NBus NCat SCro SRGP
                                SUsu
¶ - 'Susan'   EPPr EWes GOrP
  - 'Susie White'   CElw EPPr
§ - f. *thurstonianum*   More than 30 suppliers
¶ - - 'Armitageae'   CElw EPPr GOrP MBro NBus
                                NCat SHel SRGP
  - 'Thurstonianum   Last listed 1997
    Isherwood'
  - 'Trevor's White'   EBee EGle NCat
  - 'Wageningen'   CBre CElw CHil CMCo EBee EGar
                                EGle EMar GCal GMac LGre LRHS
                                MAvo MBri MMil NBus NCat
                                NGdn NPro SAga SCou SHel
                                SRGP WBea WCru WHal WHen
                                WHer WMoo
  - 'Walter's Gift'   More than 30 suppliers
  - 'Wargrave Pink' ♀   More than 30 suppliers
  - 'Waystrode'   CElw CMCo EBee EPPr SHel
¶ - white   SSea
  - 'Winscombe'   More than 30 suppliers
  'Pagoda'   EOrc MNrw SUsu
§ *palmatum* ♀   More than 30 suppliers
  palustre   CElw CHil EBee EMar EMou EOrc
                                EPPr GCHN LLWP MBel MNrw
                                NBro NBus NChi NHol NSti SCou
                                SRGP STes WCra WCru WHen
                                WMoo WPnP
  'Pamir'   CHil
  papuanum   GCHN WCru
  'Patricia'   More than 30 suppliers
  'Patricia Josephine'   MCAu
  peloponnesiacum   CStr EBee GGar WPGP
  - NS 660   CElw CPou
  'Persian Carpet'   NLar
  phaeum   More than 30 suppliers
  - 'Album'   More than 30 suppliers
¶ - 'Alec's Pink'   LLWP
  - 'All Saints'   CElw EMon WPrP

  - 'Aureum'   See *G. phaeum* 'Golden Spring'
  - black   See *G. phaeum* var. *phaeum*
  - 'Blue Shadow'   CElw EPPr
  - 'Calligrapher'   CElw EBee EGle EPPr NBrk SCou
                                SHel WBea WMoo WPnP
  - 'Charles Perrin'   CElw CHid
  - dark   CElw SCou WOut
¶ - 'David Bromley'   EMon
§ - 'Golden Spring'   NBus NCat NChi NPro
  - 'Hannah Perry'   CBel CElw CHil EBee EPPr LLWP
                                WBea WBro
  - var. *bungaricum*   CHil EGar EPPr MFir NBus NCat
                                SCou SHel WBea WCru WWpP
  - 'Langthorns Blue'   CElw CFri CHil CMCo CMea CSev
                                ELan EPPr MNrw NBus NCat
                                SCro WBar WBea WEll WHal
                                WHen WPnP WPrP
§ - 'Lily Lovell'   More than 30 suppliers
  - 'Little Boy'   CElw EMon NCat
  - var. *lividum*   More than 30 suppliers
  - - 'Joan Baker'   More than 30 suppliers
  - - 'Majus'   CElw CFri CHil EMon EPPr EPfP
                                GCal LGre LLWP NBus NSti SAga
                                SCou SCro SWat WBea WEll WFar
¶ - 'Margaret Wilson' (v)   EPPr SUsu
  - 'Mierhausen'   CCuc CElw CGle
  - 'Mourning Widow'   See *G. phaeum* var. *phaeum*
  - 'Night Time'   EPPr LLWP MBro SCro SHel WBea
§ - var. *phaeum*   CMil EPPr GBin GCal MWhe NCat
                                SCro SHel SRms WBea WCru
                                WHen WMoo WPGP
  - purple   EBee MDun
  - red   MRav MTed
  - 'Rose Air'   CFri EBee EPPr GOrP NBrk NBus
                                WMoo WPnP
  - 'Rose Madder'   CElw CFri CHad CHil CM&M
                                CMCo EBee EGle EPPr GBuc
                                GCal LGre LHop LLWP MBro
                                MCLN MNrw SCou SHel WBea
                                WMoo WPnP
  - 'Samobor'   More than 30 suppliers
  - 'Saturn'   Last listed 1998
  - 'Small Grey'   CHil
  - 'Stillingfleet Ghost'   EBee NBus NCat NChi NHex NSti
                                SCou
  - 'Taff's Jester' (v)   CElw CHad CMCo NBus NSti
                                SCro SHel WBea WCot WCru
                                WHer
  - 'Variegatum'   More than 30 suppliers
  'Phillippe Vapelle'   More than 30 suppliers
¶ 'Pink Delight'   CElw
  'Pink Spice'[PBR]   CHil MRav MWhe MWrn NHar
§ *platyanthum*   CGle CHil EMou EPPr GCHN
                                GCal GKir MNrw NChi NSti SCou
                                SRGP WCot WCru WHCG WHen
                                WMoo WPer
  - giant   SCou SGar
  - var. *reinii*   NCat
  - - f. *onoei*   WCru
§ *platypetalum* Fisch.   CElw EBrP EBre ELan EMou ENot
    & C.A. Mey.   EPPr GAri GCHN GKir LBCl LBSe
                                LBre MBBe MBri NBir NCat NFla
                                NSti SBre SCou SRms SWat WCru
                                WMoo
  - 'Georgia Blue'   CFil CLTr SSpi WCru WMoo
                                WPGP WPnP
  - Franchet   See *G. sinense*
  - misapplied   See *G.* x *magnificum*
§ *pogonanthum*   CElw EMan GBuc GCHN GCal
                                MNrw NBir SCou WCru WMoo
  polyanthes   CFri CMCo EBee EMan GAbr GAri

§ **potentilloides**

pratense
- 'Bittersweet'
- 'Blue Chip'
- 'Bodenfalle'
- 'Catforth Carnival'
- CC&McK 442
- 'Cluden Ruby'
- 'Cluden Sapphire'

- 'Flore Pleno'

- from Nepal
- 'Gay Hellyer'
* - 'Himalayanum'
- Midnight Reiter strain
¶ - 'Misty Morn' (d)
- 'Mrs Kendall Clark' ♀
- 'Nunwood Purple'
§ - 'Plenum Caeruleum' (d)
- 'Plenum Purpureum'

§ - 'Plenum Violaceum' (d) ♀
- subsp. **pratense**
  f. **albiflorum**
- - - 'Galactic'
- - - 'Plenum Album' (d)
- - - 'Silver Queen'

- - - 'Whimble White'
¶ - 'Purple-haze'
- 'Rectum Album'
- 'Rosalyn' (d)
§ - 'Rose Queen'

- 'Roseum'
- 'Spinners'
- 'Splish-splash'

- subsp. **stewartianum**
- - 'Elizabeth Yeo'

- - ex CC 31
- 'Striatum'
- 'Striatum' pale
- Summer Skies =
  'Gernic' PBR (d)

- Tibetan Border form
¶ - 'Victor Reiter Junior'
- 'Wisley Blue'

- 'Yorkshire Queen'

'Prelude'
'Priestley's Pink'
'Prima Donna'
procurrens

GBuc GDra GOrP GTou MSph
WCru WElm WPnP
CHil GCHN MNrw NBir NBus
NHex
More than 30 suppliers
CHil EBee EMon NBrk
SHel
Last listed 1998
Last listed 1998
CMCo GTou
GCHN
CAbP CBod CHil EBee EFou GAbr
GCHN GKir LRHS MBri MWhi
NCut NHol NPSI NPro NSti WCru
WFar
See *G. pratense* 'Plenum
Violaceum'
Last listed 1998
SCro
LGro WCru
CSpe WCot WHil
NCat
More than 30 suppliers
CHil
More than 30 suppliers
See *G. pratense* 'Plenum
Violaceum'
More than 30 suppliers
More than 30 suppliers
CHil CMCo EMar MBro MCli
MWll SRGP WCru WHen WMoo
CElw CStr WCot
CBre CFri CGle CHil EBee ELan
EMou EOrc EPPr EWTr GCHN
MBel MBro MCLN MMal MNrw
MWhe MWll NBrk SCou SOkh
SRGP STes WBea WFar WHen
WMoo WPnP WPyg WUnu
WWhi
CPla
See *G. clarkei* 'Kashmir White'
EWes
CBel CGle CHil CMea EBee ELan
EOrc GOrP MBro MNrw MRav
NBir NCat NHex NHol NLar NSti
SHel SSpi STes WBea WCru WHen
WHoo WPnP WUnu
See *G. pratense* 'Rose Queen'
See *G.* 'Spinners'
CBod CBrm CFri CSpe EBee EMan
GCal GKir LRHS MDun MLLN
MMal NSti SPer WHil WRHF
CElw CFri MRav WCru WPnP
EBee SAga SCou SCro SUsu
WWpP
Last listed 1997
More than 30 suppliers
CBre
CStr CTri EBee EBrP EBre GKir
LBCl LBSe LBre LRHS MBBe
MCLN MWhe NBus SBre SCou
SPer
EBee
NSti
CMCo EBee SCou SCro SHel
SRGP WHal WPnP
EBee EPPr NBus NCat NGdn
NHex NSti SHel
CElw NCat WBea
Last listed 1999
Last listed 1999
More than 30 suppliers

pseudosibiricum
§ **psilostemon** ♀
- 'Bressingham Flair'
- 'Gold Leaf'
- hybrid
pulchrum

punctatum hort.
- 'Variegatum'
purpureum
pusillum
pylzowianum

pyrenaicum

- f. **albiflorum**

- 'Bill Wallis'
- 'Isparta'
'Rambling Robin'

rectum

- 'Album'
'Red Admiral'
'Red Dwarf'
* 'Red Madder'
reflexum

- dark
regelii

- CC 806
renardii ♀
- blue
- 'Tcschelda'

§ - 'Whiteknights'

¶ - 'Zetterlund'
richardsonii

x **riversleaianum**
- 'Jean Armour'
- 'Mavis Simpson'
- 'Russell Prichard' ♀
§ **rivulare**

SCou
More than 30 suppliers
More than 30 suppliers
WCot
CElw WCru
CBel CElw CFri CMea CSev CSpe
EBee ECre EOrc EPPr GCHN LPio
MMal MNrw NLar NPro NSti
SCou SRGP STes SWat WCot
WCru WPer
See *G.* x *monacense* 'Muldoon'
See *G.* x *monacense* 'Variegatum'
SCou
CKin MSal SCou
GCHN MBro MMal NBid NNrd
NRya SDys SHFr SHel SRGP SSmi
WBea WByw WCru WFar WHal
WHen WMoo WPnP
CElw CHil CKin CM&M CRDP
CSev EBee EOrc EPPr EWFC
GAbr GCHN MHew NFla NSti
SCou WBea WHen WOut
CElw CFri EBee EMou EOrc ESis
GAbr GCHN LLWP MHer MNrw
MTho NBir NSti SCou SCro SHel
SUsu WBea WCra WHen WMoo
WPer WWin
More than 30 suppliers
CElw
CElw EBee EMan EMar EPPr
WCot WCru
CMCo EBee EPPr GOrP NBus
NCat SCou WCru WMoo
See *G. clarkei* 'Kashmir White'
NCat
CElw CHil GCHN WMoo
Last listed 1998
CFri CHid CHil CMCo CSev EMan
EPPr GCHN LFis MCLN NCat
NHol SCou SCro WCru WHCG
WHal WMoo WOve WPnP
Last listed 1998
CElw CMCo CSam EBee EMan
EMar EOrc EPPr GCHN GMac
MBel NSla SAga SHel WCra WCru
WMoo WPnP
CPou WCot
More than 30 suppliers
See *G. renardii* 'Whiteknights'
CElw CFai CHil CMCo EBee EFou
EMan EMil LBuc LPio MAvo MBri
NBus SBod SCob SPla SWat WRus
CElw CHil EGra EMou GCHN
LRHS MBro MRav NBir NBus
NPro SMac WBea WCru WEas
WIvy WMoo WPnP WWin
More than 30 suppliers
CElw CGra CHil CMCo EBee
EMan GCHN GCal MNrw NBir
NBus NCat NLar NSti SCou SCro
SRGP SRms WBea WCru WMoo
WPnP WPrP
SCou WCru WMoo
CHil EPPr GCHN WCru WMoo
More than 30 suppliers
More than 30 suppliers
CElw CFri CMCo EMan GCHN
GKir GOrP MBro NSti STes WBea
WHCG

- 'Album'   CHil MBro
robertianum   CKin EEls ELau EPPr EWFC MChe
                         MHer SCou SIde SRCN SRms
                         WHbs WHen WJek
§ - 'Album'   EPPr MHar MHer NSti SCou SIde
                         SRCN SRms WAlt
- f.*bernettii*   See *G. robertianum* 'Album'
- 'Celtic White'   CBre CHil ECoo EMon EPPr GCal
                         NBus NCat NDov NHex NSti
                         SRGP WAlt WElm WHen WPnP
¶ - subsp.*celticum*   WAlt
robustum   CElw CFri CGle EBee EMan EMar
                         EOrc EPPr EPri GCHN LRHS
                         MNrw MSph NBro NCat NChi
                         SCou SRGP STes WBea WByw
                         WCot WCra WCru WElm WFar
                         WHal WHer WPGP WWin
- Hannays' form   CElw CMea CSpe
- x *incanum*   CMea MAnH WCru
- 'Norman Warrington'   WHer
- S&SH 14   CElw CMea SUsu WBea WCru
'Rosanne'   MCLN NBus SCou
'Rosie Crûg'   CElw CFri CHid EBee EMan EMar
                         EPPr MDun SPla WCot WCru
                         WPnP WRus WWhi
rotundifolium   SCou
¶ 'Rozanne'   EBrP EBre GKir LBCl LBSe LBre
                         MBBe MWhe SBre
rubescens   CSpe EMar EMou EPPr GGar
                         MNrw NBir NBro NCat NSti SCou
                         SRGP SUsu WCra WCru WHal
                         WWye
rubifolium   CAbP CBod EBee EMan LRHS
                         MBri MCCP NBrk NBus NPri
                         SCou SSpi WCru WGwy WMoo
                         WOut
ruprechtii   CElw CHar CHil CMCo CRDP
                         EBee EBrP EBre ECoo EMan EMar
                         GCHN GMac LBCl LBSe LBre
                         MBBe MNrw NBus NCat SBre
                         SCou SRGP WBea WElm WPer
                         WPnP WUnu WWin
'Salome'   More than 30 suppliers
sanguineum   More than 30 suppliers
- 'Alan Bloom'   CMCo EBee EBrP EBre GKir LBCl
                         LBSe LBre LRHS MBBe MCLN
                         SBre SIng SMer
- 'Album' ♀   More than 30 suppliers
- 'Alpenglow'   CHil SRGP WCru
- 'Ankum's Pride'   CBlo CFri CGle CHil CMCo CRDP
                         EBee EDAr EGle EMon EPPr LRHS
                         MCLN WCot WCru WWat
- 'Aviemore'   NCat
- 'Barnsley'   CElw SCou SHel WWpP
- 'Belle of Herterton' CHil CMCo EPPr GCHN NChi
                         NPro SHel WCru
- 'Bloody Graham'   EGle MWhe NHaw SHel WMoo
- 'Catforth Carnival'   NCat
- 'Cedric Morris'   CElw CFil CHil ECha EFou EGle
                         EGra EPPr ERav LPio MRav MTho
                         SCou SCro SHel SRGP SUsu WCot
                         WCru WHen WPnP
- 'Elliott's Variety'   Last listed 1997
- 'Elsbeth'   CElw CHil CMCo CMil CRDP
                         EBee EPPr EWes GBuc GCHN
                         MCLN NBus NCat NHol SCob
                         SCou SHel SRGP WCru WFar
                         WHal WMoo WPnP WSan
§ - 'Fran's Star'   WCru
- 'Glenluce'   More than 30 suppliers
- 'Hampshire Purple'   See *G. sanguineum* 'New
                         Hampshire'

- 'Holden'   CElw CMea EPPr SCou SHel
                         WCru
¶ - 'Joanna'   SCou
- 'John Elsley'   More than 30 suppliers
- 'Jubilee Pink'   CHil EGar EPPr GCal NBus SBla
                         SCou SHel WCru
- var.*lancastrense*   See *G. sanguineum* var.*striatum*
- 'Leeds Variety'   See *G. sanguineum* 'Rod Leeds'
I - 'Lloyds Form'   SHel
- 'Max Frei'   More than 30 suppliers
- 'Minutum'   SCou WCru WPnP
- 'Nanum'   CMea EPar NHol NMen NNrd
                         WCru
§ - 'New Hampshire'   CHil WCru
- 'Nyewood'   CMCo ECGP EMon EPPr GCHN
                         IMGH MLLN SCou SEND SRGP
                         WCru
- 'Plenum'   EPPr WPnP
* - var.*prostratum* hort. EDAr
* - - (Cav.) Pers.   See *G. sanguineum* var.*striatum*
- 'Purple Flame'   WCru
§ - 'Rod Leeds'   LPio WHal
- 'Sara'   WHen WPnP
- 'Shepherd's Warning' ♀ More than 30 suppliers
¶ - 'Shepherd's Warning' GCal
       seedlings
§ - var.*striatum* ♀   More than 30 suppliers
- - deep pink   SCro
- - 'Farrer's Form'   EPPr GBuc WCru WMoo
- - 'Splendens'   CElw CSev ECha ELan ENot EPPr
                         LBee LHop MRav MWat NBid
                         NChi SAga SCou SSmi WCru WEas
                         WWhi
- x *swatense*   WMoo
- 'Vision'   WPnP
- 'Westacre Poppet'   EWes
¶ 'Sarah Louisa'   NPar
'Sea Fire'   CElw CMCo GCHN MNrw MTho
                         SCro SHel WMoo
'Sea Pink'   CElw GAbr GCHN MNrw MTho
                         NHar WHal WMoo WPnn
'Sea Spray'   CPlt EBee EMan EPPr EWes GBuc
                         GCHN MNrw MSte MTho MWrn
                         SWat WCra WCru WMoo WPnP
                         WPnn WPrP
seemannii   Last listed 1998
¶ 'Sellindge Blue'   CElw
sessiliflorum   CFri ECou EPar NHar SAga SCou
                         SIng
- 'Maria'   WByw
- subsp.*novae-zelandiae* GCHN SWat WCru
       green-leaved
- - 'Nigricans'   More than 30 suppliers
- - 'Nigricans' x *traversii* CBos CRDP EBee ESis GCHN
       var.*elegans*   NCat SWat WCru WFar
§ - - 'Porter's Pass'   CFri CHil CMea EHoe EWes GBri
                         GBuc GCHN MBro MHar MNrw
                         NBir NBus NChi NHex SCou SPlb
                         SWat WCru WFar WPGP WPnP
- - 'Porter's Pass' hybrid Last listed 1998
- - red-leaved   See *G. sessiliflorum* subsp. *novae-*
                         zelandiae 'Porter's Pass'
- - 'Rubrum'   SCou
¶ 'Sheilagh Hannay'   CStr
shikokianum   CHil EBee NChi SRGP STes WBea
                         WPnP
- var.*kaimontanum*   WCru
- var.*quelpaertense*   EBee
- - B&SWJ 1234   WCru
- var.*yoshiianum*   CElw GBuc GCHN NCat WCru
                         WMoo
sibiricum   GCHN SCou

'Silver Pink' LRHS
¶ 'Silver Shadow' SPer
§ *sinense* CBel CElw CFri CHil CLTr CPou
EBee EMou GCHN GCal LRHS
NChi NLar NSti NWCA SCou
SRGP SSoC STes WCru WHCG
WHal WHer WMaN WMoo WPGP
WPer WPnP WWhi
'Sirak' CBos CElw CFri CHil CLAP EBee
EGle EMan EPPr GCal GOrP
MAvo NCat SAga SCou SHel SUsu
WBea WPGP WPnP
soboliferum CAbP CBod CBos CHil EBee EBrP
EBre ELan EMan GCHN GCal
GMac LBCl LBSe LBre LRHS MBBe
NBir NCut NDlv NSti SBre SCou
SCro SPla WCru WGwy WWat
'Sonata' Last listed 1999
'Southcombe Star' See *G.* x *oxonianum* 'Southcombe
Star'
sp. from Pamirs, EBee EPPr WPnP
Tadzhikistan
¶ sp. from Sikkim NWCA
§ 'Spinners' More than 30 suppliers
'Stanhoe' CHil EMan EMar EPPr MAvo
MWgw SCou SCro WBea
stapfianum var. *roseum* See *G. orientalitibeticum*
'Stephanie' NCat
'Strawberry Frost' CElw CFri CMil EBee EMan EMar
EMil LFis MMil MTis NPSI WCot
'Sue Crûg' CBos CElw CHid CHil EBee EGle
EPPr GAbr GCHN MAvo MChl
MTis NBus NChi NCut NSti SCro
SDys SRGP SUsu WBea WByw
WCot WCru WMoo WPGP WPnP
WWin
'Summer Cloud' EPPr SRGP
suzukii B&SWJ 016 EBee EPPr WCru
swatense CBos CHil EMou SCou SWat
WCru
'Sydney Wharf' Last listed 1999
sylvaticum CM&M CSev EMou EWFC GKir
GMac MSCN MSal NBid NHex
SCou SRGP SSpi WCra WHal
WHen WMoo WPer WShi
- f. *albiflorum* CBel CBot CBre CElw CMil ELan
EMar EMou GCHN MBro MWhe
NSti SCou SSpi WCru WWin
- 'Album' ♀ More than 30 suppliers
- 'Amy Doncaster' More than 30 suppliers
- 'Angulatum' CElw CHil CPlt EBee EPPr LGre
SCou WMoo WPnP
- 'Baker's Pink' CElw CFri CHil CMCo CMea CMil
EBee EGle EMou GCHN MBro
MCLN MRav NCat NChi SCou
SHel SMrm SSpi WBea WCru WFar
WHCG WLin WMoo WPGP WPnP
WTin
- 'Birch Lilac' CElw CFri CHil CMCo EBee EGar
EMou EPPr EPfP GBuc GCal LRHS
NBus NCat NHol NSti SCou SHel
SMad SWal WBea WCra WFar
WMoo WPnP
¶ - 'Caerulatum' EMon
- 'Cyril's Fancy' See *G.* 'Cyril's Fancy'
¶ - deep pink EMou
- 'Mayflower' ♀ More than 30 suppliers
- 'Meran' EBrP EBre LBCl LBSe LBre LRHS
MBBe SBre
- 'Ray's Pink' CHil
- f. *roseum* CFri CHil CMCo EBee ECGP EGle
EMou GCHN GGar GKir NCat

SCro WPnP
- 'Silva' CElw CGle EBee EGle EMan
GCHN GOrP LRHS MChl MRav
NBrk NCut SCou SWat WCru
WPnP
- subsp. *sylvaticum* CGle CHil CMea EGle EPPr GCHN
var. *wanneri* MBro MRav NCat SCou SCro
WCru WWpP
¶ 'Terre Franche' CFri
§ *thunbergii* CFri CLTr CMCo CSam EBee EMar
EMou GCHN GGar LAst LGro
MMal MNrw MRav NBid NFai
NOak NSti SCou WCra WHen
WPer WPnP
- dark CSev EBee NCut
- pink EPPr SCou SRGP WCru
- purple Last listed 1999
- white EPPr NCot SRGP
thurstonianum See *G.* x *oxonianum* f.
thurstonianum
transbaicalicum CElw EBee EMan EPPr GCHN
LRHS MBri MMal MNrw SCro
SRGP WPGP WPnP
traversii CBot CLyd CPBP EBee EGle EWes
MMal NBus WRos WSan
- 'Big White' GCal WPnP
- var. *elegans* CFee CFri CSpe EBee GCHN LGre
LRHS MNrw NWCA SCou SRGP
WCra WCru WEas WHCG WKif
WPGP WPnP
- 'Sea Spray' EBee EBrP EBre LBCl LBSe LBre
MBBe NGdn SBre SCou
tripartitum Last listed 1998
tuberosum More than 30 suppliers
- var. *charlesii* See *G. kotschyi* var. *charlesii*
§ - 'Leonidas' CPou ETub LRHS
- subsp. *linearifolium* WCru
- M&T 4032 Last listed 1998
- pink WCru WPnP
- S&L 99 Last listed 1998
'Verguld Saffier' See *G.* 'Blue Sunrise'
versicolor More than 30 suppliers
- album CBel CElw CFri MGas MWhe
NBus WBea WHer WPnP
§ - 'Kingston' EBee EPPr GOrP
- 'Knighton' EBee
§ - 'Snow White' CHil EBee EOrc EPPr GMac
MNrw NBrk NMGW SCou SHel
WCru WMoo WPnP
- 'The Bride' EBee EGra EMan EMar EPPr
- 'White Lady' See *G. versicolor* 'Snow White'
¶ 'Victor Reiter' CBos CElw CHad CSpe SAga
SMrm WCot WCru
violareum See *Pelargonium* 'Splendide'
viscosissimum GCal LRHS MMal SCou SRGP STes
WOut WPnP
- rose pink NBir
wallichianum CBod CBos CLTr CMCo CPou
EBee ECGP EWTr LRHS NBir
NChi NSti SBla SUsu WAbe WBea
WCra WFar WHen WMoo WPyg
WWat
§ - 'Buxton's Variety' ♀ More than 30 suppliers
- 'Chadwell's Pink' EBee GOrP MAvo
- magenta GCHN
- pink CAbP CFri EMan GBuc WCru
WWat
- purple WCru
- 'Syabru' CElw CHar CMea EBee EMar EMil
GBuc LFis MNrw NLar NSti SAga
SCou SSpi WCot WCru WFar
WMoo WPnP WSpi

¶ 'Wednesday's Child'   WFar
  'Welsh Guiness'   NCat WCru
  wilfordii hort.   See *G. thunbergii*
  - Maximowicz   Last listed 1999
  'Wisley Hybrid'   See *G.* 'Khan'
  wlassovianum   More than 30 suppliers
¶ - 'Blue Star'   NPro
  yesoense   EBee EPPr GBin GCHN LFis NBir
                            NBus NChi NSti SCou SWat WCru
                            WFar WHal WOut WPnP WPrP
  - var. *nipponicum*   WCru
  - white   EBee NWCA
  yoshinoi   CFri CMCo EBee EMar EMou EPPr
                            EWes GAri GBuc GMac NBus
                            NPro SHel SRGP STes SUsu SWat
                            WMoo WPnP
  yunnanense Franchet   CElw GGar MNrw SCou
  - misapplied   See *G. pogonanthum*

GERANIUM hort. See PELARGONIUM

GERBERA (Asteraceae)
  jamesonii   Last listed 1998

GESNERIA (Gesneriaceae)
  cardinalis   See *Sinningia cardinalis*
  x *cardosa*   See *Sinningia* x *cardosa*

GEUM ✿ (Rosaceae)
  'Abendsonne'   CElw
  aleppicum   CFee EBee WMoo
  - CLD 610   Last listed 1997
  alpinum   See *G. montanum*
  andicola   EBee
¶ 'Apricot Beauty'   CFai
  'Beech House Apricot'   More than 30 suppliers
¶ - 'Blazing Sunset' (d)   NArg
N 'Borisii'   More than 30 suppliers
  'Borisii' x *montanum*   LHop
  bulgaricum   CMea GKir LRHS MNrw NBir
                            NPro NRya NTow WByw WPnP
                            WPrP
  calthifolium   CSam EBee EBrP EBre EPPr GKir
                            LBCl LBSe LBre MBBe MCCP
                            MOne NBro NCut SBea SBre
                            WElm
  canadense   Last listed 1998
  capense from Lesotho   CSpe
  - JJ&JH 9401271   EBee EWes
  - S&SH 33   WCot
  'Carlskaer'   CElw CLon EBee GCal MAvo
                            MNrw NTow SAga SDys SMrm
                            WPGP WPnP
§ *chiloense*   EBee
  - 'Farncombe'   Last listed 1999
  - P&W 6513   GBri MSte
  coccineum hort.   See *G. chiloense*
  coccineum Smith   CPlt WRha
  - NS 653   Last listed 1999
  'Coppertone'   CElw CGle CLon COlW CPla
                            EBee ECha ECtt ELan EMan GCal
                            GMac IBlr LFis MCLN MNrw
                            MRav NBir NBro NCat NRya SAga
                            SPer SUsu WHoo WMoo WPGP
                            WSan WWhi
  'Dingle Apricot'   MNrw MRav MTed NBir
  'Dolly North'   CHea EBee EGar EPPr GAbr GBri
                            GGar LAco LRHS MAvo MBNS
                            MBri MCAu MNrw MRav NBro
                            NCat NFai WHal
I 'Farmer John Cross'   CBre EBee MAvo MNrw MTPN
                            WHal

  'Feuermeer'   MSte NPro
  'Fire Opal' ♀   CPlt CSam MNrw NBir
  'Georgeham'   CPla
  'Georgenburg'   More than 30 suppliers
  'Glencoe'   Last listed 1999
* *hybridum luteum*   MBel NSti
  x *intermedium*   CBre CHor EBee EGle EMan
                            EMon EPPr LRHS MCLN MNrw
                            NLar SChu SCro WLRN WWin
  - 'Muriel' (v)   MInt
  'Karlskaer'   EGle LPio SUsu
  'Lady Stratheden' ♀   More than 30 suppliers
  'Lemon Drops'   CBre CElw CGle EBee ECha EGol
                            ELan EPPr GBri GMac MNrw
                            MRav MSte NCat NChi NCot
                            SChu SUsu WFar WMoo WPGP
                            WPrP
  'Lionel Cox'   More than 30 suppliers
  macrophyllum   EBee EMan GBar MNrw NBus
                            WMoo
  magellanicum   EBee
* 'Mandarin'   CFir GCal
  'Marika'   CBre CHid CRow EBee MAvo
                            MNrw NBrk SChu
  'Marmalade'   LGre MAvo MNrw
§ *montanum* ♀   CFri EBrP EBre GTou LBCl LBSe
                            LBre MBBe MBro NBid NBir NBro
                            NDlv NFla NRya SBea SBre SIng
                            SRms SSca WBea WMoo WPer
                            WWin
  - 'Maximum'   MNrw
  'Mrs J. Bradshaw' ♀   More than 30 suppliers
  'Mrs W. Moore'   GBri MLLN MNrw NCat NChi
                            NPro
  'Nordek'   GMac MBri MNrw
* 'Orangeman'   MNrw
  parviflorum   CPou EGar EOld MBro MLLN
                            MNrw MPro NBus NCut NLar
  pentapetalum   CGle MNrw WAbe
  - 'Flore Pleno'   WAbe
  'Present'   EBee
  'Prince of Orange'   CElw EGar GAbr MNrw WFar
                            WMoo
  'Prinses Juliana'   CBos CElw EBee EFou EGar EMan
                            EMar GCal GMac LRHS MBri
                            MCLN MRav NCat NCut NDov
                            WCot WFar WHal WPnP
  pseudococcineum   Last listed 1999
  pyrenaicum   MNrw NBus NWCA
  quellyon   See *G. chiloense*
  'Red Wings'   CM&M EFou EGar EMar GCal
                            MAvo WCra WRus
  reptans   See *Sieversia reptans*
  x *rhaeticum*   EBee MNrw NMen WPic
  rhodopeum   EBee MNrw
  'Rijnstroom'   LBuc MBel MTed NFai WCra
  rivale   More than 30 suppliers
  - 'Album'   More than 30 suppliers
  - apricot   LGro WPrP WWin
  - 'Cream Drop'   NWoo
  - cream, from Tien Shan, CFee
    China
  - lemon   CRDP EMan
* - 'Leonard's Double'   ECtt WElm
  - 'Leonard's Variety'   More than 30 suppliers
  - 'Marmalade'   NChi
  roylei   EBee
  'Rubin'   EBee EFou EGar EPPr LRHS MBNS
                            MBel MCAu MCLN MNrw NDov
                            NGdn SCro SLod SPla SSpe WCot
                            WElm
  'Sigiswang'   EFou GAbr MFir MNrw MSte

'Tangerine'   GAri GGar MNrw MRav
x *tirolense*   EBee
triflorum   CPBP EBee EBlw EMan EOld EPla
                                   GKir GTou LGre LPio LRHS MBri
                                   MNrw MRav MTis NLar SRot
                                   WFar WHil WLin WMoo WRus
- var. *campanulatum*   EDar NChi NPro NRya NTow
urbanum   CArn CKin ELau EWFC GBar
                                   GPoy MChe MGas MHew MNaF
                                   NLan NPri SIde SWat WHbs WHer
                                   WMoo WPic
- 'Checkmate' (v)   EMon
'Werner Arends'   EBee GCal LRHS MAvo MBri
                                   MRav WFar

GEVUINA (Proteaceae)
avellana   CB&S CGre CHEx CTrG CTrw
                                   GSki

GIBASIS (Commelinaceae)
¶ *pellucida*   ERea

GILIA (Polemoniaceae)
aggregata   See *Ipomopsis aggregata*
californica   See *Leptodactylon californicum*
¶ *capitata*   CGdn

GILLENIA (Rosaceae)
stipulata   CHea CPlt CRDP EMon GCal LGre
                                   MTPN SVal
trifoliata ♀   CArn CFil CRDP CSpe ECGN
                                   ECha EFou ELan EMon EPar GPoy
                                   LGre LRHS MCAu MSal MTis NSti
                                   SBod SChu SIng SPer SUsu WByw
                                   WCot WCru WEas WHoo WPnP
                                   WRus WWye

GINKGO ✿ (Ginkgoaceae)
biloba ♀   More than 30 suppliers
- 'Autumn Gold' (m)   CDoC CDul CEnd LNet LRHS
                                   MBlu MBri MGos SMad WPGP
¶ - 'Barabits Sztráda'   MBlu
- 'Fairmount' (m)   MBlu
- 'Fastigiata' (m)   CCHP CMCN MGos WMou
- 'Hekt Leiden'   CMCN
- 'Horizontalis'   CMCN MBlu
- 'Icho'   MBlu
- 'King of Dongting' (f)   GKir LRHS MBlu MBri WMou
- Pendula Group   CEnd CMCN EPfP LPan MBlu
                                   WMou
- 'Princeton Sentry' (m)   LRHS MBlu MBri SMad
I - 'Prostrata'   CPMA WWes
- 'Saratoga' (m)   CEnd CMCN CPMA LCon LNet
                                   LRHS MBlu MGos
- 'Tit'   CMCN EPfP LNet
- 'Tremonia'   CDoC LCon LNet LRHS MBlu
                                   MBri
- 'Tubifolia'   CMCN MBlu
- 'Umbrella'   CDul CMCN
- Variegata Group (v)   CMCN CPMA EPfP LNet MBlu

GLADIOLUS ✿ (Iridaceae)
'Acapulco' (L)   Last listed 1999
acuminatus   CGrW
'Advantage' PBR (L)   CGrW
alatus   CGrW
'Alba' (N)   CGrW
¶ 'Alexandra' (P)   CGrW
'Alice' (Min)   Last listed 1999
'Aloha' (L)   CSut
'Amanda Mahy' (N)   CBro CGrW NRog
'Ambiance' PBR (L)   CGrW

'Amsterdam' (G)   CGrW
'Anchorage' (L)   CGrW
'Andre Viette'   WCot
'Angel of Mine' (S)   CGrW
angustus   GCal
'Anitra' (P)   CGrW
'Anna Leorah' (L)   CGrW
antakiensis   CPou
'Antica' (L)   CGrW
'Applause' (L)   NRog
'Apricot Perfection' (P)   CGrW
* 'Arabian Night'   CAvo CSut
'Ashram' (M)   Last listed 1999
'Athelney Aztec' (P)   CGrW
'Athelney Sunburst' (L)   CGrW
'Atom' (S/P)   CBro EBee ETub
atroviolaceus   WPGP
'Aubrey Lane' (M)   CGrW
¶ 'August Days' (L)   CGrW
aurantiacus   GCal WCot
¶ *aureus*   CGrW
'Avalanche' (B)   Last listed 1999
'Baltica' (L)   Last listed 1999
'Barn Owl' (L)   CGrW
¶ Barnard hybrids   CGrW
'Beauty of Holland' PBR (L)   CGrW
'Belair' (S)   CGrW
'Bell Boy' (B)   Last listed 1999
'Beryl Jones' (L)   CGrW
'Bettine' (S)   CGrW
'Bewitched' (L)   CGrW
'Black Lash' (S)   CGrW
'Blackpool' (M)   NRog
blandus var. *carneus*   See *G. carneus*
'Blue Beauty' (L)   Last listed 1999
'Blue Dart' (M)   CGrW
'Blue Frost' (L)   CGrW
'Blue Tina' (Min)   CGrW
'Blue Tit' (P)   CGrW
¶ 'Blues' PBR   CGrW
'Bombay' (G)   CGrW
bonaespei   WCot
* 'Bread and Butter'   CSut
'Brenda Jo' (S)   Last listed 1999
'Bronzed Beauty' (S)   CGrW
'Burrowbridge Beauty' (P)   CGrW
byzantinus   See *G. communis* subsp.
                                   byzantinus
'Cairngorm' (P)   Last listed 1999
callianthus ♀   CSWP EWTr MSCN WCot WWhi
§ - 'Murieliae' ♀   CAvo CBro EBee ETub LAma
                                   LBow NRog SDeJ STes
'Cambourne' (Min)   NRog
¶ 'Candy Cane' (L)   CGrW
cardinalis   CAvo CFil CGrW CRDP EBee
                                   EMan EPla GCal IBlr SAga SSpi
                                   WCot WPGP
carinatus   CGrW NRog
'Carine' (N)   CGrW
'Carla Gabor' (L)   Last listed 1999
carmineus   CGrW LBow
§ *carneus*   CBro CGrW CPou EMan GCal
                                   LRHS NRog WCot WHal WHil
'Carquirenne' (G)   CGrW
'Cartago' (L)   CGrW
¶ 'Carved Ivory' (M)   CGrW
¶ *caryophyllaceus*   WHil
'Centrepiece' (M)   CGrW
'Cerise Spire' (M)   CGrW
'Charm' (N/Tub)   CAvo CBro CGrW
'Charmer' (L)   CGrW
'Charming Beauty' (Tub)   LRHS NRog

'Charming Lady' (Tub)	CGrW LRHS
'Chartres' (B)	Last listed 1999
'Chiltern Beauty' (L)	CGrW
'Chiquita' (M)	CSut
'Chloe' (M)	Last listed 1999
'Chloe's Dream' (S)	Last listed 1999
'Christabel' (L)	CGrW ERos
'Christofel' (N)	Last listed 1999
'Cimarosa' PBR (L)	CGrW
citrinus	See *G. tricbonemifolius*
'City Lights'	Last listed 1998
¶ 'Clarence's Choice' (L)	CGrW
'Columbine' (P)	CGrW LRHS NRog
x *colvillei*	ECha IBlr
'Comet' (N)	CGrW ETub NRog
communis	LAma
§ - subsp. *byzantinus* ♀	More than 30 suppliers
'Coral Dream' (L)	CGrW
'Cordoba' (L)	CGrW
'Corrinna' (P)	Last listed 1999
'Côte d'Azur' (G)	Last listed 1997
crassifolius	Last listed 1999
'Cream of the Crop' (M)	Last listed 1999
'Creme de Mint' (S)	CGrW
'Crimson Fire' (G)	Last listed 1999
cunonius	Last listed 1998
'Curload Champion' (P)	CGrW
§ *dalenii*	CGrW CPou ERos GCal IBlr SSpi WCot
* - 'Hookeri Rubra'	Last listed 1999
* - f. *rubra*	CGrW
'Dame Edna II' (L)	CGrW
'Dawn Jane' (S)	Last listed 1999
'Desirée' (B)	LRHS
'Devotion' (G)	CGrW
'Don Juan'	CGrW CSut
'Drama' (L)	CGrW
'Dyanito' (B/S)	Last listed 1999
'Eastbourne' (S/B)	Last listed 1999
ecklonii	Last listed 1997
'Edna' (S)	CGrW
¶ 'Elaine' (S)	CGrW
'Elin' (M)	CGrW
'Elvira' (N)	CGrW LAma NRog WPGP
'Emerald Spring' (S)	CGrW
equitans	CGrW
'Esperanto' (M)	Last listed 1999
'Essex' (P)	CGrW
'Esta Bonita' (G)	CGrW
'Estonia' PBR (G)	CGrW
'Eugenie' (M)	CGrW
'Eurovision' (L)	Last listed 1998
'Fair Lady' (Tub)	NRog
'Fidelio' (L)	LAma
'Final Touch' (G)	CGrW
'Finesse' (L)	CGrW
'Fingerprints' (L)	CGrW
¶ 'Flevo Cosmic' (Min)	CGrW
'Flevo Fire' PBR (M)	CGrW
'Flevo Maitre' (L)	CGrW
¶ 'Flevo Souvenir' PBR (L)	CGrW
'Florence C' (M)	CGrW
floribundus	CGrW LBow
'Flowersong' (L)	LAma
'Frank's Perfection' (P)	Last listed 1999
'Frosty Pink'	Last listed 1997
garnieri	CGrW SSpi
'Georgette' (B)	LAma
'Giallo Antico' (L)	Last listed 1998
'Gillian' (L)	LBow
'Golden Melody' (M)	CGrW
'Good Luck' (N)	CAvo CBro
gracilis	CGrW EBee
'Grand Finale' (L)	CGrW
'Grand Prix' PBR (L)	Last listed 1999
grandis	See *G. liliaceus*
'Granny White' (S/P)	Last listed 1999
¶ 'Green Star' (L)	CGrW
'Green Woodpecker' (M) ♀	CGrW LAma NRog
'Greyfriars' (P)	CGrW
'Guernsey Glory' (N)	CGrW NRog
'Halley'	CBro
'Hastings' (P)	Last listed 1999
'Heidi' (S)	CGrW
'Hi-era' (L)	Last listed 1999
'High Brow' (G)	CGrW
'High Style' (L)	CGrW
¶ 'Hi-Lite' (L)	CGrW
'Holland Pearl' (B)	CGrW LAma LRHS NRog
'Hradec Kralove' (L)	CGrW
'Hunting Song' (L)	LAma NRog
buttonii	CGrW
¶ *byalinus*	CGrW
'Ice Cap' (L)	CGrW
illyricus	CFil CGrW CSam EBee WPGP
- 'Mallorca'	CGrW
imbricatus	CGrW ERos GBuc GCrs
'Impressive' (N)	NRog
'Inca Queen' (L)	CGrW
§ *italicus*	CGrW WPGP
'Ivanhoe' (P)	Last listed 1999
'Ivory Beauty' (L)	Last listed 1999
'Ivory Tower' (G)	CGrW
'Jacksonville Gold' (L)	LAma
'Jeannie Rose' (S)	CGrW
'Jennifer Kay' (S)	Last listed 1999
¶ 'Jester' (L)	CSut
¶ 'Jo Ann' (L)	CGrW
'Joyce' (P)	CGrW
'Judy Jean' (S)	CGrW
'Jupiter' (B)	LRHS
§ *kotscbyanus*	GCrs
'Kristin' (L)	CGrW
'La Petite' (Min)	Last listed 1999
¶ 'Lada' (G)	CGrW
'Lady Eleanor' (P)	Last listed 1999
'Lady Godiva' (P/S)	LAma NRog
'Lady Lucille' (M)	CGrW
'Lavender Flare' (S)	CGrW
'Lavender Ruffles' (L)	Last listed 1999
'Leonore' (S)	LAma LRHS
§ *liliaceus*	CGrW LBow
¶ 'Lime Green' (P)	CGrW
¶ 'Little Jude' (P)	CGrW
'Little Wiggy' (P)	CGrW
'Lorena' (B)	Last listed 1999
'Lowland Queen' (L)	CGrW CSut
'Lowri' (M)	CGrW
'Madonna' (L)	CSut
'Magistral' PBR (L)	Last listed 1999
¶ 'Margaret' (P)	CGrW
'Margaret Lyall' (L)	CGrW
marlotbii	CGrW
'Mary Housley' (L)	LAma LRHS
'Meersen' (L)	CGrW
'Mileesh' (L)	CGrW
'Mirella' (N)	CGrW MRav NRog
'Miss America' (M)	Last listed 1999
'Mondiale' (G)	CGrW
'Moon Mirage' (G)	CGrW
'Moonshine' (G)	CGrW
'Mother's Day' (G)	Last listed 1999
¶ 'Mr Chris' (S)	CGrW
¶ 'Mrs Rowley' (P)	CGrW

'Murieliae'   See *G. callianthus* 'Murieliae'
'My Love' (L)   CSut LAma
natalensis   See *G. dalenii*
'Nathaly' (N)   CGrW
nerineoides   Last listed 1998
'Nicholas' (S)   CGrW
'Nova Lux' (L)   LAma LRHS NRog
'Nymph' (N)   CAvo CGrW ETub LAma NRog
'Obelisk' (P)   NRog
§ *oppositiflorus*   CPou WCot
   - subsp. *salmoneus*   See *G. oppositiflorus*
'Orange Rascal' (Min)   CGrW
orchidiflorus   CGrW CSWP LBow
'Oscar' (G)   LAma NRog
palustris   ERos
papilio   More than 30 suppliers
§ - Purpureoauratus Group   CBro CGle CSam EMan ERos GKir
                                IBlr MFir SRms
pappei   CGrW
'Parade' (G)   CGrW
'Pauline Johnson' (S)   CGrW
¶ 'Peace' (L)   CGrW
'Perky' (Min)   LAma
'Perseus' (P/Min)   LAma
'Peter Pears' (L)   LAma LRHS NRog
¶ 'Phyllis M' (L)   CGrW
'Picturesque' (P)   NRog
'Pink Elf' (S)   Last listed 1999
'Pink Ice' (L)   CGrW
'Pink Lady' (L)   CGrW
'Plum Splash' (S)   CGrW
'Plum Tart' (L)   LRHS
'Pole Position' (L)   CGrW
'Praha' (L)   LAma LRHS NRog
'Pretty Woman' (L)   CGrW
primulinus   See *G. dalenii*
Primulinus hybrids   SDeJ
'Princess Margaret Rose'   LAma
   (Min)
'Prins Claus' (N)   CBro CFwr CGrW EBee LAma
                                LRHS NRog
priorii   CGrW LBow
'Priscilla' (L)   LAma LRHS SLod
'Pulchritude' (M)   CGrW
punctulatus   LBow
   - var. *punctulatus*   ERos
¶ 'Purple Prince' (M)   CGrW
'Purple Princess' (M)   Last listed 1999
purpureoauratus   See *G. papilio* Purpureoauratus
                                Group
quadrangularis   Last listed 1998
'Queen's Blush' (L)   CGrW
'Queen's Lace' (M)   Last listed 1999
'Rachelle' (L)   CGrW
'Ramona'   Last listed 1997
'Red Jewel' (P/S)   CGrW
I 'Red Papilio'   CGrW
'Richards' Renown' (M)   CGrW
'Richmond' (B)   NRog
'Rob Roy' (P)   Last listed 1999
'Robinetta' (*recurvus*   CGrW LAma NRog
   hybrid) ♀
'Roncalli' (L)   CGrW
'Rooster' (P)   CGrW
'Rose Elf' (S)   CGrW
'Rougex'   Last listed 1998
¶ 'Roxborough' (P)   CGrW
'Sabrina' (M/N)   Last listed 1999
'Sabu'   LRHS
saccatus   CGrW
'Safari' (Min/B)   Last listed 1998
'Sailor's Delight' (L)   CGrW

'Sally's Orange' (P)   CGrW
'Samantha' (N)   CGrW
'San Remo' PBR (L)   CGrW
saundersii   CFil CGrW WPGP
'Scarlet Lady' (P)   CGrW
'Scarlet Opening' (L)   CGrW
'Scarlet Perfection' (P)   Last listed 1999
'Sceptre' (L)   CGrW
'Scrimshaw' (S)   CGrW
¶ 'Scrimshaw's Sister' (S)   CGrW
scullyi   CGrW LBow
segetum   See *G. italicus*
sericeovillosus   CGrW
'Sharkey' (G)   CGrW
'Shawna' (Min)   CGrW
'Silent Snow' (M)   CGrW
'Silver Jubilee' (G)   Last listed 1999
'Silver Shadow' PBR (S)   CGrW
'Sirael' (L)   Last listed 1999
'Snow Castle' (S)   Last listed 1999
'Song' (L)   CGrW
splendens   CGrW
'Stephanie' (L)   CGrW
'Stromboli' (L)   CGrW
¶ 'Sulphurous' (M)   CGrW
'Sweet Shadow'   Last listed 1999
'Tan Royale' (P)   CGrW
tenellus   CGrW
'Tesoro' (M)   CGrW
'The Bride' (x *colvillei*) ♀   CAvo CBos CBro CGle CGrW
                                CHad CMil EBee EBrP EBre GBri
                                LAma LBCl LBSe LBre MBBe NRog
                                SBre SLod SPlb
'Titania' (L)   Last listed 1999
'Tommy O' (S)   CGrW
'Topaz' (L)   CGrW
'Tout à Toi'   Last listed 1999
'Trader Horn' (G)   CGrW LAma LRHS NRog
§ *trichonemifolius*   CGrW LBow
tristis   CBro CFee CGrW CPou CRow
                                EBee ECha ELan EMan GMac
                                LBow NRog SAga SDix SSpi WAbe
                                WBor WCot WHal WPGP
   - var. *concolor*   CGrW ERos WCot WHer
'Uganda'   CSut
undulatus   CGrW CSWP ERos LBow
¶ 'Veerle'   CSut
'Velvet Eyes' (M)   CGrW
'Velvet Joy' (P)   LAma
'Vera Lynn'   SLod
'Verve' (L)   CGrW
'Vicki Cream' (L)   Last listed 1999
'Victor Borge' (L)   LRHS NRog
'Victoria' (M)   CGrW
¶ 'Video' (L)   CGrW
'Vienna' (L)   CGrW
violaceolineatus   Last listed 1998
'Violetta' (M)   CGrW CSut
virescens   LBow WCot
'Visionary' (L)   Last listed 1999
'Walter P' (G)   Last listed 1999
'Warmunda' (N)   Last listed 1999
watsonioides   CPou ERos
'Welcome' (L)   CGrW
¶ 'White Baby' (S)   CGrW
'White City' (P/S)   LAma LRHS
'White Friendship' (L)   LAma NRog
'White Knight' (L)   Last listed 1999
'White Prosperity' (L)   LRHS
'White Willie' (S)   CGrW
'Wind Song' (L)   LAma
'You'll Be Lucky' (L)   Last listed 1999

GLANDULARIA (Verbenaceae)
pulchella — See *Verbena tenera*

GLAUCIDIUM (Glaucidiaceae)
palmatum ♀ — CFir EFEx EMan GCrs GDra NHar NSla NWCA WAbe WCot WCru
- 'Album' — See *G. palmatum* var. *leucanthum*
§ - var. *leucanthum* — EFEx GCrs

GLAUCIUM (Papaveraceae)
* *caucasicum* — Last listed 1997
§ *corniculatum* — CBot CGle CHar EBee EBrP EBre LBCI LBSe LBre MBBe MWgw SBre SEND SSca SUsu WCot WEas WPGP WPyg
flavum — CArn CGle CSpe ECha EMFP EWFC GKir LRHS MHer SMrm SSca WHer WRos WWin
- *aurantiacum* — See *G. flavum* f. *fulvum*
§ - f. *fulvum* — EBee ECha EMFP EMan EPPr LPio MGed NFai SDix
- orange — See *G. flavum* f. *fulvum*
- red — See *G. corniculatum*
grandiflorum — EBee WRos WWin
phoenicium — See *G. corniculatum*

GLAUX (Primulaceae)
maritima — WPer
- dwarf form — NWCA

GLECHOMA (Lamiaceae)
hederacea — CArn CKin EWFC GBar GPoy IIve MHer MHew NBro NMir WCer WHbs WHer WWye
- 'Barry Yinger Variegated' (v) — CRow EBee
- 'Little Crown' (v) — WAlt
- 'Rosea' — GBar LRHS
- 'Spot Check' (v) — EPPr
§ - 'Variegata' — CHal CRow EPfP ILis LRHS MBri MRav
hirsuta AL&JS 90069YU — Last listed 1998

GLEDITSIA (Caesalpiniaceae)
caspica — CB&S
japonica — EPfP SMad
koraiensis — Last listed 1999
sinensis — SMad
triacanthos — CAgr CDul CPle ENot IOrc LEdu LPan MWhi SPlb WNor
- 'Elegantissima' (v) — SPer
- 'Emerald Cascade' — CBlo CEnd CLnd CPMA LRHS
- f. *inermis* — CAgr WNor
- 'Rubylace' — CB&S CBlo CDoC CDul CEnd CLnd CMCN COtt EBee ELan EPfP EWTr LBuc LPan LRHS MAsh MBar MBlu MBri MGos MRav SMad SMer SPer SSpi WDin WOrn
- 'Shademaster' — ENot
- 'Skyline' — LPan
- 'Sunburst' ♀ — More than 30 suppliers

GLIRICIDIA (Leguminosae)
sepium — Last listed 1999

GLOBBA (Zingiberaceae)
marantina — LChe LEur
winitii — LChe LRHS

GLOBULARIA (Globulariaceae)
bellidifolia — See *G. meridionalis*
bisnagarica — EBee WLin
- NS 695 — Last listed 1999
cordifolia ♀ — CTri EDAr IMGH LBee LRHS MBro MTho NHar NHol NMen NTow SBla SIng WHoo WMoo
- NS 696 — NWCA
- *purpurascens* — Last listed 1998
incanescens — EBee LBee LRHS WWin
§ *meridionalis* — CFee CLyd CPBP EWes ITim MBro MWat NHar NMen NWCA SBla SMrm
- 'Hort's Variety' — CTri NNrd NTow WAbe
nana — See *G. repens*
nudicaulis — EBot MBro NHar SBla
- 'Alba' — WIvy
§ *punctata* — LFis LRHS MBro NTow NWCA SRms WHil WHoo
pygmaea — See *G. meridionalis*
§ *repens* — CLyd CNic MBro MTho NMen
spinosa — Last listed 1998
stygia — NSla
trichosantha — CFee EDAr GAbr SMrm SRms WHil WPer
vulgaris — CInt

GLORIOSA (Colchicaceae)
lutea — See *G. superba* 'Lutea'
rothschildiana — See *G. superba* 'Rothschildiana'
§ *superba* ♀ — LAma MBri NRog SDeJ
§ - 'Lutea' — LAma LBow LRHS NRog
§ - 'Rothschildiana' — CB&S CHal CPIN CRHN CStu ETub LAma LBow LRHS SOWG SRms SYvo

GLOXINIA (Gesneriaceae)
'Chic' — NMos
* *latifolia* — Last listed 1999
'Medusa' — WDib
perennis — NMos
sylvatica — CHal WDib
- 'Bolivian Sunset' — WDib

GLUMICALYX (Scrophulariaceae)
flanaganii — EBee GCrs SIng
- HWEL 0325 — NWCA
goseloides — CFee SSpi WPat
lesuticus — EBee
montanus — EBee WCot
nutans — EBee SIng

GLYCERIA (Poaceae)
aquatica variegata — See *G. maxima* var. *variegata*
grandis — Last listed 1997
maxima — CBod
§ - var. *variegata* — More than 30 suppliers
spectabilis 'Variegata' — See *G. maxima* var. *variegata*

GLYCYRRHIZA (Papilionaceae)
acanthocarpa — Last listed 1999
echinata — CAgr CArn CPLG EWTr MSal
§ *glabra* — CAgr CArn ELau EOHP MHer MSal WHer WJek WWye
- 'Poznan' — GPoy
glandulifera — See *G. glabra*
lepidota — EBee
uralensis — CArn EBee ELau EOHP GPoy MHer MSal
yunnanensis — LGre

GLYPTOSTROBUS (Taxodiaceae)
§ *pensilis* Last listed 1999

GNAPHALIUM (Asteraceae)
'Fairy Gold' See *Helichrysum*
  thianschanicum 'Goldkind'
norvegicum Last listed 1997

GODETIA See **CLARKIA**

GOMPHOCARPUS (Asclepiadaceae)
§ *fruticosus* Last listed 1998
§ *physocarpus* CArn MSte

GOMPHOLOBIUM (Papilionaceae)
polymorphum Last listed 1998

GOMPHOSTIGMA (Buddlejaceae)
virgatum EBee EPPr LPio MSte NCut NPSI
  WCot WKif

GONIOLIMON (Plumbaginaceae)
¶ *incanum* EBee
§ – 'Blue Diamond' CM&M
§ *tataricum* EMan
§ – var. *angustifolium* EBee LFis SRms WByw WPer

GOODIA (Papilionaceae)
lotifolia Last listed 1999

GOODYERA (Orchidaceae)
biflora EFEx
bachijoensis var. *yakushimensis*
  EFEx
oblongifolia Last listed 1997
pubescens EFEx LRHS WCru
schlechtendaliana EFEx

GORDONIA (Theaceae)
axillaris CDoC

GOSSYPIUM (Malvaceae)
herbaceum MSal

GRAPTOPETALUM (Crassulaceae)
bellum MBri SChr
– 'Super Star' Last listed 1998
§ *paraguayense* CHal EOas

GRATIOLA (Scrophulariaceae)
officinalis CArn EHon EMan MHer MHew
  MSal NLar WHer WMoo WSel
  WWye

GREENOVIA (Crassulaceae)
aizoon NTow
§ *aurea* SIng

GREVILLEA ✿ (Proteaceae)
alpina CFee CPle EBee GQui SMur
  SOWG
– Olympic® Flame CB&S CCHP CDoC CPLG CTrw
  LHil SOWG
✳ 'Apricot Queen' Last listed 1999
aspleniifolia SOWG
  'Robyn Gordon'
australis var. *brevifolia* CPLG
banksii Last listed 1998
– 'Canberra Hybrid' See G. 'Canberra Gem'
– var. *forsteri* SOWG SPlb
'Bonnie Prince Charlie' CPLG SOWG

§ 'Canberra Gem' ♀ CDoC CGre CPLG CPle CTrG
  CWSG ECou LCns LHil LHop
  LRHS MBri MBro SAga SDry
  SMrm SOWG SSpi WAbe WCru
  WGer WPat
'Clearview David' LRHS SOWG
'Cranbrook Yellow' CDoC CPLG LHil
crithmifolia CPLG SOWG
curviloba CPLG
'Desert Flame' CPLG
'Honey Gem' SOWG
intricata SOWG
juniperina CTrC
– 'Aurea' Last listed 1998
– 'Molonglo' CPLG
– f. *sulphurea* ♀ CB&S CChe CDoC CFil CHEx
  COtt CPLG CTrG CTrw EPfP
  GQui SOWG WAbe WBod WPat
lanigera CPLG
¶ – 'Mount Tamboritha' CPLG
¶ – prostrate SOWG
'Mason's Hybrid' SOWG
monticola CPLG
'Moonlight' SOWG
'Orange Marmalade' SOWG
'Poorinda Peter' CPLG
prostrata 'Aurea' CPLG
robusta ♀ CHal CTrC MBri SOWG SPlb
rosmarinifolia ♀ CChe CDoC CFil CHEx COtt
  CTrG CTrw EBee EPfP GOrc
  GQui LAst MTis MWat SArc SLim
  SLon SOWG SPlb SSta WAbe
  WCru WPic WSHC
¶ – 'Desert Flame' CPLG
– 'Jenkinsii' CB&S CPLG
'Sandra Gordon' SOWG
§ x *semperflorens* CB&S CCHP CDoC CGre CPLG
  SOWG
'Sid Reynolds' CPLG
thelemanniana CPLG
thyrsoides CB&S SDry
tolminsis See G. x *semperflorens*
tridentifera CPLG
victoriae SSpi
– 'Mount Annan' Last listed 1999
williamsonii SOWG

GREWIA (Tiliaceae)
¶ *occidentalis* ECou

GREYIA (Greyiaceae)
radlkoferi Last listed 1998
sutherlandii CHEx CTrF

GRINDELIA (Asteraceae)
§ *camporum* EBee EMan GBar WCot WPer
  WWye
chiloensis CAbb EBee IBlr LLWP NDov SDix
  SDry SMad
robusta See G. *camporum*
sp. G&K 4423 Last listed 1997
squarrosa Last listed 1999
stricta CArn

GRISELINIA (Griseliniaceae)
✳ 'Crinkles' SDry
littoralis ♀ More than 30 suppliers
– 'Bantry Bay' (v) CAbP CDoC CHEx CLan CWSG
  EBee EHoe ELan IOrc ISea LRHS
  SAga SEND SLim SPer WCru WFar
– 'Dixon's Cream' (v) CB&S EPVP EPfP GQui MAsh
  SAga SDry SLon SMac WCru

- 'Green Jewel' (v)   CB&S CCHP CPMA SDry
SPla
- 'Luscombe's Gold'   CPne
- 'Variegata'   More than 30 suppliers
lucida   Last listed 1998
ruscifolia   Last listed 1999
scandens   CPle WSHC
* *serrata*   Last listed 1998

GUELDENSTAEDTIA (Papilionaceae)
himalaica B&SWJ 2631   WCru

GUICHENOTIA (Sterculiaceae)
ledifolia   Last listed 1998

GUIHAIA (Arecaceae)
¶ *argyrata*   EPVP

GUNDELIA (Asteraceae)
tournefortii   Last listed 1999

GUNNERA (Gunneraceae)
arenaria   IBlr
chilensis   See *G. tinctoria*
dentata   CFee CPla IBlr SCob
flavida   CFee CPla CRow EBee EPla GGar
IBlr SCob
fulvida   IBlr
hamiltonii   CCuc CHEx CPla CRow CStu
EBee ECha ECou EMan GGar IBlr
MDCh SCob
magellanica   More than 30 suppliers
¶ - 'Osorno'   SSpi
manicata ♀   More than 30 suppliers
monoica   CRow EBee GAbr GGar IBlr
prorepens   CFee CPla CTre EBee ECha
EMan EPla IBlr SCob SSpi
WWat WWye
scabra   See *G. tinctoria*
§ *tinctoria*   CBen CCuc CFil CHEx CRow
CTrG CWSG EBee ECha EHon
EPla GGar LRHS NOrc SDix SSpi
SWat WCru WLRN WPGP WPat
WWat WWeb
- 'Nana'   IBlr

GUTIERREZIA (Asteraceae)
spathulata F&W 8005   CPBP

GUZMANIA (Bromeliaceae)
'Amaranth'   MBri
'Cherry'   Last listed 1999
'Claret'   See *Neoregelia* Claret Group
dissitiflora   Last listed 1999
'Exodus'   MBri
Festival Group   Last listed 1999
'Gran Prix'   MBri
lindenii   Last listed 1999
lingulata ♀   Last listed 1999
- 'Empire'   MBri
- var. *minor* ♀   MBri
Marlebeca Group   MBri
monostachya ♀   MBri
musaica ♀   Last listed 1992
'Orangeade'   MBri
sanguinea ♀   MBri
* 'Surprise'   MBri
'Vulkan'   MBri
* 'Witten Lila'   Last listed 1999

GYMNADENIA (Orchidaceae)
conopsea   CHdy EFEx

GYMNOCARPIUM (Woodsiaceae)
dryopteris ♀   CCuc EFer EMar EMon EPar EPot
LSyl MBri MWgw NBus NMar
NWCA SDix SRms SSca WAbe
WFib WNor WRic WWat
- 'Plumosum' ♀   CBos CCuc CFil EBee EMon GQui
LHil NHar NHol NMar NVic SChu
SLod SLon WAbe WFib WHal
fedtschenkoanum   Last listed 1999
oyamense   NMar WRic
robertianum   EFer SRms WRic

GYMNOCLADUS (Caesalpiniaceae)
chinensis   WNor
dioica   CAgr CB&S CDul CFil CSam CTho
EBee ELan EPfP GBin MBlu MBri
SMad SPer SSpi WDin WGer
WNor WPGP

GYMNOGRAMMA See GYMNOPTERIS

GYMNOPTERIS (Adiantaceae)
vestita   EMon

GYMNOSPERMIUM (Berberidaceae)
§ *albertii*   GCrs WCot
altaicum   GCrs

GYNANDRIRIS (Iridaceae)
setifolia   Last listed 1998
sisyrinchium   EBee
- MS 416   Last listed 1998
* - *purpurea* AB&S 4447   Last listed 1998

GYNERIUM (Poaceae)
argenteum   See *Cortaderia selloana*

GYNURA (Asteraceae)
§ *aurantiaca* 'Purple Passion' ♀
MBri
sarmentosa hort.   See *G. aurantiaca* 'Purple
Passion'

GYPSOPHILA (Caryophyllaceae)
acutifolia   ELan LPio
altissima   CPou EBee MNrw
aretioides   LRHS NMen NNrd NWCA
§ - 'Caucasica'   CNic CPBP EBur EPot NDlv NHar
SIng WLin
- 'Compacta'   See *G. aretioides* 'Caucasica'
briquetiana   WPat
- Mac&W 5920   Last listed 1999
bungeana   Last listed 1998
cerastioides   CTri EMNN EMan EWTr GCHN
GTou LBee LHop LRHS MRav
NMen NWCA SPlb WAbe WElm
WMoo WPer WPnn WWin
* - *farreri*   Last listed 1999
dubia   See *G. repens* 'Dubia'
fastigiata   EBee EGar EMan WPer
'Festival' PBR (Festival   EBrP EBre LBCl LBSe LBre MBBe
Series)   SBre
'Festival Happy' (Festival   LRHS
Series)
'Festival Pink' (Festival   GMac LRHS WFar WHil
Series)
glomerata HH&K 221   Last listed 1998
- HH&K 275   Last listed 1999
gracilescens   See *G. tenuifolia*

muralis 'Garden Bride'   LIck
- 'Gypsy Pink' (d)   LIck
nana   SIng
- 'Compacta'   CLyd CPBP
oldhamiana   CBlo MLLN MTed
pacifica   EBee ECtt GBuc IIve MAnH MWll NBro NCut NEgg NOak WHer WPer

§ *paniculata*   CBlo CTri EBee EWTr GKir LRHS NFor NMir SRms SWat WBod
- 'Bristol Fairy' (d) ♀   CB&S CSam EBee EBrP EBre ECha EFou EGle ELan EMan ENot GKir LBCl LBSe LBre LRHS MBBe MBel MBri MCAu MTis NFai NFla NOrc SBre SMad SPer SRms WHoo
- 'Compacta Plena' (d)   EBee EFou EGle ELan EPfP GCal LHop MMil SMrm SPer SPla SRms SSpe WLRN WPer
- double pink (d)   GKir
- double white (d)   Last listed 1998
- 'Flamingo' (d)   CB&S EBee ECha ECot ECtt EFou EWTr LRHS MBri SPer
¶ - 'Magic Gilboa'[PBR]   COtt
- 'Magic Golan'[PBR]   COtt
- 'Perfekta'   EBee
§ - 'Schneeflocke' (d)   CBlo CMGP CTri EBee ECtt LFis LRHS MWat NPri NVic SEas SRms WPer WViv
- 'Snow White'   NOrc
- Snowflake   See *G. paniculata* 'Schneeflocke'
§ *petraea*   SIng
repens ♀   CSpe EMil GKir GTou LBee MHer MOne MWat SPlb WFar WPer
- 'Dorothy Teacher' ♀   CLyd CMea EMNN LHop LRHS SIng WEas WGor WPat WPyg
§ - 'Dubia'   CLyd ECha EDAr EHol ELan EMNN EPot ESis MHer SBod SRms WLin WPer WWin
- 'Fratensis'   ELan EMNN ESis ITim NMen WLin
- 'Letchworth Rose'   EWes
- Pink Beauty   See *G. repens* 'Rosa Schönheit'
§ - 'Rosa Schönheit'   EBee EBrP EBre ECha EGar EPot EWes LBCl LBSe LBre LRHS MBBe SBre SMrm SPer
- 'Rose Fountain'   NHol WPat WPyg
- 'Rosea'   CSpe EFou EMNN ESis GKir LBuc LFis LPVe LRHS MWat MWll NFor NMen NNrd NOak NWCA SBla SLon SRPl SRms SSvw WFar WHal WHoo
- white   CHor CM&M CTri EFou ELan ESis MWll NFor WPer
§ 'Rosenschleier' (d) ♀   EBee EBrP EBre ECha EFou EGoo ELan GKir LBCl LBSe LBre LFis MBBe MCAu MRav MTis NFla SBre SMer SMrm SOkh SRms SWat WEas WHoo WMaN
'Rosy Veil'   See *G.* 'Rosenschleier'
stevenii   EBee
§ *tenuifolia*   CLyd CPBP EPot ITim LBee LRHS MBro MWat NDlv NHol NMen SIng
transylvanica   See *G. petraea*
Veil of Roses   See *G.* 'Rosenschleier'
'White Festival'[PBR]   WFar

H

HAASTIA (Asteraceae)
pulvinaris   Last listed 1999

HABENARIA (Orchidaceae)
radiata   See *Pecteilis radiata*

HABERLEA (Gesneriaceae)
ferdinandi-coburgii   CGle CLAP GNor NWCA SIng WAbe
rhodopensis ♀   CElw CNic CStu EPar GCrs GNor IMGH MBro MSte MWat NHar NRya NWCA SBla SIng SRms WAbe
- 'Virginalis'   CElw CLAP GDra NHar NMen SBla SIng SOkd

HABLITZIA (Chenopodiaceae)
tamnoides   Last listed 1999

HABRANTHUS (Amaryllidaceae)
andersonii   See *H. tubispathus*
brachyandrus   CBro SRms
gracilifolius   CBro ERos SIng
howardii   Last listed 1997
martinezii   CBro
§ *robustus*   CBro EBee LAma LRHS MBri NRog NWCA
texanus   CBro ERos SIng
§ *tubispathus*   CBro CPea CStu ERos LBee LBow NWCA WCot WWin

HACQUETIA (Apiaceae)
§ *epipactis* ♀   CElw CRDP CSam EGle ELan EMan EMar EPot GGar GKir LHop LSpr MWgw NBro NMen NWCA SBla SIng SMac SOkh SSpi WAbe WCot WCru WFar WHil WRus WWat WWin
- 'Thor' (v)   EMon

HAEMANTHUS (Amaryllidaceae)
albiflos   CAvo CHEx CHal CStu LAma LHil SRms
coccineus   Last listed 1998
crispus   Last listed 1997
deformis   Last listed 1997
humilis subsp. *hirsutus*   Last listed 1999
   S&SH 72
kalbreyeri   See *Scadoxus multiflorus* subsp. *multiflorus*
katherinae   See *Scadoxus multiflorus* subsp. *katherinae*
natalensis   See *Scadoxus puniceus*
sanguineus   NRog

HAKEA (Proteaceae)
baxteri   CCpl
bucculenta   LRHS
clavata   CCpl
dactyloides   Last listed 1998
§ *drupacea*   CCpl CTrC
epiglottis   CTrC ECou
gibbosa   Last listed 1998
laurina   CTrC
lissocarpha   CCpl
§ *lissosperma*   CDoC CFil CPLG CTrC ECou LRHS WPGP
microcarpa   CPle
¶ *nodosa*   CCpl
§ *salicifolia*   CB&S LRHS SPlb
- 'Gold Medal'   CTrC
saligna   See *H. salicifolia*
sericea hort.   See *H. lissosperma*
- pink   CTrC

suaveolens | See *H. drupacea*
teretifolia | CTrC

HAKONECHLOA (Poaceae)
macra | CFil CPla EBrP EBre EHoe EMon EPar EPla LBCl LBSe LBre LGre LRHS MBBe MRav NFai NOGN SBre SCob WPGP
§ - 'Alboaurea' | More than 30 suppliers
* - 'Albolineata' | EMon LRHS
- 'Aureola' ♀ | More than 30 suppliers
* - 'Mediovariegata' | CCuc CFil EPPr EPla SCob SSpi WPGP
- 'Variegata' | See *H. macra* 'Alboaurea'

HALENIA (Gentianaceae)
elliptica | Last listed 1998

HALESIA ✿ (Styracaceae)
§ **carolina** | CAgr CBlo CBrm CDoC CDul CEnd CLnd CMCN CPMA CTho ELan EWTr GGGa GKir IMGH IOrc LPan LRHS MBel MBri MDun MGos SMer SSta WBod WDin WHar WWat
diptera | CMCN MBlu
monticola | CB&S CDul CMCN COtt EBrP EBre ELan EPfP GGGa LBCl LBSe LBre LRHS MAsh MBBe MBri NSti SBre SPer SReu SSpi WNor
- var. **vestita** ♀ | CAbP CDoC CPMA CSam CTho CWSG CWit EPfP GChr GKir IMGH IOrc LPan LRHS MBlu SBrw SPer SSht SSpi SSta WPat
- - f. **rosea** | CB&S EPfP SSta
tetraptera | See *H. carolina*

x HALIMIOCISTUS (Cistaceae)
algarvensis | See *Halimium ocymoides*
§ 'Ingwersenii' | CB&S CDoC CMHG EWes MWhi NHol SIng SPan SPer SRms WBod WPer
revolii hort. | See x *H. sahucii*
§ **sahucii** ♀ | CDoC EBee EBrP EBre ECha ELan GCHN LBCl LBSe LBre LFis LHop MAsh MBBe MBNS MGrG MRav MWat SBre SDys SEas SPan SPer WCFE WFar WHoo WKif WWin
- 'Ice Dancer' (v) | CDoC MAsh SPer
'Susan' | See *Halimium* 'Susan'
§ **wintonensis** ♀ | More than 30 suppliers
§ - 'Merrist Wood Cream' ♀ | More than 30 suppliers

HALIMIONE (Chenopodiaceae)
§ **portulacoides** | EEls

HALIMIUM ✿ (Cistaceae)
N **alyssoides** | CSam GCHN
§ **atriplicifolium** | Last listed 1998
§ **calycinum** | EBee ELan GCHN LRHS MAsh MBel SAga SCoo SLim SPan SSpi WAbe WCFE WPyg
commutatum | See *H. calycinum*
formosum | See *H. lasianthum*
N **halimifolium** | WSHC
§ **lasianthum** ♀ | CB&S CTri CWit EBee ELan EPfP GCHN LGre LRHS MAsh MBel MRav MTis SEas SLim SPer WBod WEas WPyg WWat WWin
- f. **concolor** | CCHP LHop SDry SPan WDin WWin
- subsp. **formosum** | CHar GEil MBri SDix WSHC

- 'Sandling' | EGoo ELan EPfP LRHS MAsh SPan
libanotis | See *H. calycinum*
§ **ocymoides** ♀ | CB&S CCHe CDoC EBee EGoo ELan EPfP LGre LRHS MAsh MBel MMHG MWat SLon SPan SPer WBod WHar WSHC
x **pauanum** | LGre LRHS MAsh
x **santae** | LGre
§ 'Susan' ♀ | CDoC EBee ELan LHop LRHS MAsh MBro NFai SPan SPer WAbe WPat WPyg WSHC
§ **umbellatum** | LGre LRHS MBri SAga SPer WKif WTro
wintonense | See x *Halimiocistus wintonensis*

HALIMODENDRON (Papilionaceae)
balodendron | CB&S EMil EPfP MBlu SPer SRPl

HALLERIA (Scrophulariaceae)
lucida | CGre CPLG

HALOCARPUS (Podocarpaceae)
§ **bidwillii** | CDoC ECou

HALORAGIS (Haloragaceae)
colensoi | ECou
erecta | CPle ECou SRCN SVen
- 'Rubra' | EBee WCot WPer
- 'Wellington Bronze' | CFri CPea ECoo EMan EMar GAri GSki LEdu MBNS MCCP MGed MWll NChi NCut NFor NSti SDys SMad SOkh SSca SWal WElm WHer WMoo WOut

HAMAMELIS ✿ (Hamamelidaceae)
§ 'Brevipetala' | CB&S GKir IOrc MAsh MBri NHol LRHS
x **intermedia** 'Allgold' | LRHS
- 'Angelly' | SSta
¶ - 'Aphrodite' | EPfP
- 'Arnold Promise' ♀ | CDoC CEnd CMac COtt EBee ELan GKir IOrc ISea LNet LPan LRHS MAsh MBri MGos MLan NBee NHol SBrw SLim SPer SPla SRPl SReu SSpi SSta WCFE WOrn
- 'Aurora' | Last listed 1998
- 'Barmstedt Gold' ♀ | EPfP GKir LRHS MAsh MBri MGos NHol SReu SSta
- 'Carmine Red' | MGos SMur SPer WNor
- 'Copper Beauty' | See *H. x intermedia* 'Jelena'
- 'Diane' ♀ | More than 30 suppliers
§ - 'Feuerzauber' | CMac GKir IOrc LBuc NFla SPer WOrn WPyg
* - 'Fire Cracker' | Last listed 1997
- 'Gimborn's Beauty' | Last listed 1998
- 'Hiltingbury' | LRHS SSpi
§ - 'Jelena' ♀ | CB&S CDoC CEnd CMac ELan ENot EWTr GKir GOrc IArd IMGH IOrc LNet LPan LRHS MAsh MBri MGos NHol SBrw SPer SReu SSoC SSpi SSta WCFE WDin WPGP WWat
- 'Luna' | SSta
- Magic Fire | See *H. x intermedia* 'Feuerzauber'
- 'Moonlight' | Last listed 1999
- 'Orange Beauty' | CB&S CBlo EPfP LRHS MGos
¶ - 'Orange Peel' | EPfP
- 'Pallida' ♀ | More than 30 suppliers
- 'Primavera' | CBlo EPfP IOrc MAsh NHol SSta
- 'Ruby Glow' | CB&S CBlo ECho LRHS MGos SPer SSta
- 'Strawberries and Cream' | EPfP
- 'Sunburst' | CBlo CDoC EPfP SSta

- 'Vesna'	CBlo EPfP LRHS MBlu SSta
§ - 'Westerstede'	CBlo COtt EBee IOrc LPan LRHS
	MAsh MGos NHol NWea SLim
	WDin WHar
japonica	GKir WWat
- 'Arborea'	WNor
- var. *flavopurpurascens*	Last listed 1999
- 'Sulphurea'	LRHS
- 'Zuccariniana'	CB&S CBlo
mollis ♀	CB&S CEnd ELan ENot EWTr
	GKir ISea LNet LRHS MAsh MBar
	MBri MGos NFla NHol NWea
	SBrw SLim SPer SRPl SReu SSpi
	SSta WDin WFar WPGP WPat
	WWat
- 'Boskoop'	SSta
- 'Brevipetala'	See *H.* 'Brevipetala'
- 'Coombe Wood'	Last listed 1997
- 'Goldcrest'	CAbP CBlo
- 'Nymans'	Last listed 1998
- 'Select'	See *H.* x *intermedia*
	'Westerstede'
- 'Superba'	Last listed 1998
- Wilson clone	Last listed 1998
vernalis	WDin
- 'Carnea'	Last listed 1998
- 'Christmas Cheer'	Last listed 1997
- Compact form	Last listed 1997
- 'Orange Glow'	Last listed 1998
- 'Pendula'	Last listed 1998
- 'Red Imp'	Last listed 1998
- 'Sandra' ♀	CB&S EPfP GKir LRHS MBri MGos
	SPer SReu SSpi SSta
- f. *tomentella*	Last listed 1998
virginiana	CB&S CBlo GPoy WDin WWat

HANABUSAYA (Campanulaceae)
asiatica	EBee

HANNONIA (Amaryllidaceae)
besperidum S&F 21	Last listed 1998

HAPLOCARPHA (Asteraceae)
rueppellii	MBro NBro SIng SRms SRot WHil
	WPer

HAPLOPAPPUS (Asteraceae)
acaulis	See *Stenotus acaulis*
brandegeei	See *Erigeron aureus*
coronopifolius	See *H. glutinosus*
§ *glutinosus*	CFwr CMHG CSev ECha ECtt
	LRHS MMil MNaF MTho NTow
	NWCA SAga SRms SSmi WAbe
lanceolatus	See *Pyrrocoma lanceolata*
lyallii	See *Tonestus lyallii*
microcepbalus	WPer
- AJW 93/559	Last listed 1997
prunelloides	LBee NNrd
rebderi	Last listed 1998

HARDENBERGIA (Papilionaceae)
comptoniana ♀	CPlN CSpe
* - *rosea*	ERea
violacea ♀	CAbb CPlN CSpe CTrC ECon
	ELan EMil ERea GKir GQui
	LChe LCns LRHS SEND SMur
	SPer
- 'Alba'	See *H. violacea* 'White Crystal'
- 'Happy Wanderer'	EBee EMil ERea LRHS SLon
	SOWG
- 'Rosea'	CB&S EBee
§ - 'White Crystal'	EBee ECon ERea SPer

HARPEPHYLLUM (Anacardiaceae)
caffrum (F)	LBlo

HARRIMANELLA See CASSIOPE

HASTINGSIA (Hyacinthaceae)
alba	EBee
¶ - NNS 98-310	WCot

HAWORTHIA ✿ (Aloaceae)
x *cuspidata*	Last listed 1998
reinwardtii	CHal

HEBE ✿ (Scrophulariaceae)
albicans ♀	CChe CLan CLyn EBee ECou ELan
	ENot ESis EWTr GKir LRHS MBar
	MBel MBri MGos NSti SMer SPer
	SSmi WBod WFar WHCG WWat
	WWin
- 'Cobb'	ECou
- 'Cranleigh Gem'	ECou NDlv NFai
- 'Pewter Dome'	See *H.* 'Pewter Dome'
* - 'Pink Elephant'	CAbP CDoC CLyn EPfP GKir LAst
	LRHS MAsh SPer WWeb
- prostrate	See *H. albicans* 'Snow Cover'
- 'Red Edge'	See *H.* 'Red Edge'
* - 'Snow Carpet'	CLyn
§ - 'Snow Cover'	ECou EWes NDlv SPar SWal
- 'Snow Drift'	See *H. albicans* 'Snow Cover'
- 'Snow Mound'	ECou
§ - 'Sussex Carpet'	ECou ESis
§ 'Alicia Amherst' ♀	CBlo CLyn EHol LRHS SPer SRms
	WLRN
allanii	See *H. amplexicaulis* var. *birta*
'Amanda Cook' (v)	EHoe ESis NPer SDry
amplexicaulis	CNic
- clone 4	STre
§ - var. *birta*	ESis GDra GEil MBro NDlv NHol
	NTow
§ 'Amy'	CLyn ESis IOrc MBel MHer NFai
	NPer NSti SPer WSHC
x *andersonii*	CLyn CPri
- 'Argenteovariegata'	See *H.* x *andersonii* 'Variegata'
§ - 'Aurea'	ECou SDry
- 'Aureovariegata'	See *H.* x *andersonii* 'Aurea'
* - 'Compacta'	Last listed 1998
¶ - 'Heida'	SWal
§ - 'Variegata'	CLyn ECou IOrc NSti NTow SDry
	SRCN SRms WCot WEas WLRN
'Andressa Paula'	CLyn
'Anne Pimm' (v)	WSHC
anomala hort.	See *H.* 'Imposter'
—(Armstr.) Cockayne	See *H. odora*
'Aoira'	See *H. recurva* 'Aoira'
§ *armstrongii*	CMHG ECou EHoe EOrn EPfP
	GKir MBar NDlv NFor SPan WDin
	WPer
- yellow	Last listed 1997
'Arthur'	ECou
astonii	Last listed 1998
'Autumn Beauty'	CPri
'Autumn Blush'	Last listed 1999
'Autumn Glory'	More than 30 suppliers
'Autumn Joy'	SPlb
'Autumn Queen'	Last listed 1998
'Azurea'	See *H. venustula*
'Azurens'	See *H.* 'Maori Gem'
'Baby Marie'	More than 30 suppliers
'Balfouriana'	WHCG
barkeri	ECou
'Barnettii'	Last listed 1999

'Beatrice'	ECou NDlv
¶ 'Bicolor Wand'	CLyn
§ x *bishopiana*	CFai ECou ESis LRHS MAsh
- 'Champagne'	See *H.* x *bishopiana*
'Blonde'	Last listed 1998
'Blue Clouds' ♀	ECou ESis LRHS MLan NDlv SPer
	SSmi WCFE WRus
'Blue Diamond'	Last listed 1998
I 'Blue Shamrock'	MBri
'Blue Wand'	Last listed 1999
'Bluebell'	Last listed 1998
'Blush Wand'	Last listed 1999
bollonsii	ECou MSte
'Boscawenii'	CTrG MGos
'Bowles' Variety'	See *H.* 'Bowles's Hybrid'
§ 'Bowles's Hybrid'	CLyn CPri EBee ECou LRHS MGos
	MRav NBee NFai NFor SRms
	WAbe WEas
brachysiphon	CLyn EBee ENot EPfP GOrc MGos
	MWhi SPer WDin WHCG
- 'White Gem'	See *H.* 'White Gem'
	(*brachysiphon* hybrid)
'Bracken Hills'	Last listed 1997
breviracemosa	ECou
* 'Brill Blue'	CLyd NMen WWin
'Brockiei'	Last listed 1998
buchananii	ECou ESis GDra GKir GTou MBar
	MDHE MGos MHer MTho NDlv
	NFai NFor NPer WPer
- 'Christchurch'	ECou
- 'Minima'	Last listed 1997
§ - 'Minor'	CLyd EPot ESis GCHN GCrs GNor
	LBee MBar NBir NDlv NHar
	NMen NNrd NWCA SIng
- 'Nana'	See *H. buchananii* 'Minor'
- 'Ohau'	ECou
- 'Otago'	ECou
§ - 'Sir George Fenwick'	LRHS MBro WHoo
- 'Wanaka'	ECou
buxifolia (Benth.)	EBrP EBre ENot GCHN GGar LBCl
Ckn. & Allan	LBSe LBre MBBe NFai NSti NWea
	SBre SPer WDin WStI
- hort.	See *H. odora*
- 'Champagne'	See *H.* x *bishopiana*
* - (Benth.) Ckn. & Allan	Last listed 1997
patens	
N 'C.P. Raffill'	ECou
§ 'Caledonia'	CLyn ECou ESis GAbr LRHS MAsh
	MBri MGos MSte NDlv NFai NHol
	NPer SPer SSmi WEas WFar WPat
	WPer WPyg
'Candy'	ECou
§ *canterburiensis*	ECou
N 'Carl Teschner'	See *H.* 'Youngii'
'Carnea'	Last listed 1997
'Carnea Variegata'	CLyn ECou ESis SBod SPer
carnosula	EBee ECou EHoe ESis GGar LRHS
	MBrN MGos NBir NFor SPer SSte
	WBod WPer
'Cassinioides'	Last listed 1999
catarractae	See *Parahebe catarractae*
I 'Chalk's Buchananii'	CNic SBla
* 'Charming White'	EBee LRHS MAsh
chathamica	CLyn CNic ECou ESis GGar MHer
	MMHG NMen SDry
cheesemanii	Last listed 1999
'Christabel'	CLyn ECou ESis
§ 'Christensenii'	ECou NDlv
ciliolata	Last listed 1998
coarctata	ECou
cockayneana	ECou
colensoi	ECou ESis

- 'Glauca'	See *H.* 'Leonard Cockayne'
'Colwall'	CBlo CLyd CSam ECho ESis WHen
* 'Colwall Blue'	Last listed 1997
* 'Coral Blue'	Last listed 1998
* 'Coral Pink'	WWeb
corriganii	ECou
corstorphinensis	Last listed 1997
'County Park'	CLyd ECou ECtt ESis EWes MGos
	MMil NDlv NHol NMen SWal
'Craig Park'	Last listed 1998
'Cranleighensis'	ECou MHer
'Crawii'	ECou
'Cressit'	Last listed 1997
'Cupins'	See *H. propinqua* 'Cupins'
cupressoides	CLyn CMHG ECou EPPr GKir
	MBar NBid NDlv NFor SEND
	WDin WGwG
- 'Boughton Dome' ♀	CSam ECha ECou EHoe EMNN
	ESis GCHN GTou LHil LRHS
	MAsh MBro MGos MHer MTho
	NCat NMen SAga SUsu WAbe
	WCFE WCot WEas WHoo WPer
	WSHC
- 'Golden Dome'	ESis
- 'Nana'	ECou
darwiniana	See *H. glaucophylla*
'David Hughes'	NFai
'Dazzler' PBR (v)	CAbP LRHS SPer WWeb
* 'Deans Fya'	ESis
'Debbie'	ECou
decumbens	CLyd CNic ECou ESis EWes GDra
	NHol
* 'Denise'	CLyn ENot WWeb
'Diamond'	CLyn
'Diana'	ECou
* 'Dianne'	CLyn
dieffenbachii	ECou SVen
diosmifolia	CAbP CBot CDoC CLan ECou ESis
	SMrm
- 'Marie'	ECou ESis
divaricata	ECou
- 'Marlborough'	ECou
- 'Nelson'	ECou
x *divergens*	CLan NDlv
'Dorothy Peach'	See *H.* 'Watson's Pink'
'Douglasii'	Last listed 1999
'E.A. Bowles'	CBlo ECou
'E.B. Anderson'	See *H.* 'Caledonia'
'Early Blue'	CSpe NBir
'Edinensis'	CNic CPri ECou GEil GKir NFor
	WPer WSHC WSPU
'Edington'	CHal CLyn ECou LRHS SCoo SPer
	WCFE
elliptica	ECou IBlr
- 'Anatoki'	CLTr ECou
- 'Bleaker'	ECou
- 'Charleston'	ECou
- 'Dwarf Blue'	Last listed 1997
- 'Kapiti'	ECou
- 'Variegata'	See *H.* x *franciscana* 'Variegata'
'Emerald Dome'	NMen WPer
'Emerald Gem'	See *H.* 'Emerald Green'
§ 'Emerald Green' ♀	CChe CLyn CSam EBee ERav ESis
	GKir LRHS MAsh MBar MBri
	MBro MGos MHer MTis MWat
	NDlv NHol NMen NWCA SEas
	SPlb WAbe WPat WPer WPyg
epacridea	ESis EWes GTou NDlv NHol
	NMen WAbe
'Eveline'	See *H.* 'Gauntlettii'
'Evelyn'	Last listed 1997
evenosa	ECou LRHS

'Eversley Seedling'   See *H.* 'Bowles's Hybrid'
'Fairfieldii'   EHol IBlr NMen WAbe
'Fairlane'   ECou
'Fragrant Jewel'   CLyn SEND SMrm
x *franciscana*   CHEx ECou LRHS
§ - 'Blue Gem' ♀   CLan CLyn CPri ENot ESis GGar
       LPVe LRHS MGos NBir NFai NPer
       NWea SPer SPlb SRms WBod
       WGer WHar
  - 'Jura'   Last listed 1998
  - 'Lavender Queen'   CLyn
  - 'Purple Tips' misapplied   See *H. speciosa* 'Variegata'
  - 'Red Gem'   Last listed 1997
  - 'Tresco Magenta'   ECou
§ - 'Variegata' ♀   CHEx CLyn EBee EBrP EBre ECou
       ELan ENot ESis LBCl LBSe LBre
       LRHS MBBe MBar MGos NFai
       NPer NSti SBre SPer WBod WHar
       WStI
  - 'White Gem'   SRms
'Franjo'   ECou SSmi
fruticeti   Last listed 1997
* 'Garths Glory'   Last listed 1999
§ 'Gauntlettii'   CChe CLyn CPri LRHS NBir SPer
       SVen
gibbsii   Last listed 1999
'Gibby'   ECou
N *glaucophylla*   ECou SBod
  - 'Clarence'   ECou NDlv
'Glaucophylla Variegata'   CChe CLyn CNic ECou ESis MBel
       MHer NDlv NFai NSti SPer WHer
       WKif WRus
'Glengarriff'   NHol
§ 'Gloriosa'   IOrc NCiC
'Gnome'   CBlo CLyn
'Godefroyana'   See *H. pinguifolia* 'Godefroyana'
gracillima   CBlo ECou SRPl
'Gran's Favourite'   CLyn ECou
'Great Orme' ♀   More than 30 suppliers
'Green Globe'   See *H.* 'Emerald Green'
'Greensleeves'   CBlo CLyn CSam ECou EPfP ESis
       LRHS MGos NDlv NFai
'Gruninard's Seedling'   Last listed 1999
haastii   CBlo ECou NFor
'Hadspen Pink'   CLyn
'Hagley Park'   CLyn EGoo EHol ESis LHil LRHS
       MAsh MMil SAga SMrm WCot
       WEas WHCG
§ 'Hartii'   MRav NFai SPer
'Havering Green'   ECou
'Headfortii'   CLyn
hectorii   CBlo ESis GTou NDlv NFla
  - var. *demissa*   NDlv
'Heidi'   ESis
'Hidcote'   Last listed 1998
'Hielan Lassie'   CLyn
'Highdownensis'   ECou
'Hinderwell'   NPer
'Hinerua'   ECou NNor
bookeriana   See *Parahebe bookeriana*
bulkeana ♀   CBot ELan LHil MBel NBir NFai
       SAga WAbe WEas WHCG WHoo
       WKif WPat
  - 'Averil'   Last listed 1998
  - 'Lilac Hint'   Last listed 1999
  - 'Sally Blunt'   Last listed 1998
§ 'Imposter'   CLyn ECou ESis NFai SRms
'Inspiration'   CDoC ECou LRHS
insularis   CBlo ECou
'Jack's Surprise'   ECou
'James Platt'   ECou ESis
'James Stirling'   See *H. ochracea* 'James Stirling'

'Jane Holden'   CLyn SBla WSHC
'Janet'   CPri SGar
¶ 'Jannas Blue'   CLyn ELan MAsh
'Jasper'   CNic ECou ESis
'Jewel'   Last listed 1999
'Joan Lewis'   ECou ESis
'Joanna'   ECou
§ 'Johny Day'   CLyn ECou
'Joyce Parker'   ECou NDlv
'Judy'   CLyn ECou
'June Small'   CNic
'Karo Golden Esk'   ECou
'Killiney Variety'   Last listed 1999
'Kirkii'   CBlo EBee EMil LNor LRHS MWhi
       NFai SPer
'Knightshayes'   See *H.* 'Caledonia'
'La Séduisante'   See *H. speciosa* 'La Seduisante'
'Lady Ardilaun'   See *H.* 'Amy'
laevis   See *H. venustula*
laingii   CNic ECou
latifolia   See *H.* x *franciscana* 'Blue Gem'
lavaudiana   ESis
* 'Lavender Lady'   Last listed 1997
'Lavender Queen'   Last listed 1997
'Lavender Spray'   See *H.* 'Hartii'
leiophylla   Last listed 1997
§ 'Leonard Cockayne'   CBlo MOne NFai WSHC
ligustrifolia   Last listed 1999
'Lilac Haze'   Last listed 1998
'Lindleyana'   Last listed 1999
'Lindsayi'   CLyd CLyn ECou NDlv
§ 'Loganioides'   CFai CTri ECou ESis GAbr MHer
       NFor SSmi WPer
'Longacre Variety'   ECou
'Lopen' (v)   CLyn ECou EWes
'Louise'   CPri
lyallii   See *Parahebe lyallii*
lycopodioides   ESis EWes
  - 'Aurea'   See *H. armstrongii*
  - var. *patula*   Last listed 1998
  - 'Peter Pan'   MBro SRms
'Lynash'   CLyn
§ 'Macewanii'   CMHG ECou ESis NDlv NFai
       WHCG
mackenii   See *H.* 'Emerald Green'
macrantha ♀   CLyn EPla ESis GAbr GCHN GCrs
       GGar ITim LGre LRHS MAsh MTis
       NFor NMen SIng SPer SRms WAbe
       WPat WSHC WWin
  - var. *brachyphylla*   Last listed 1999
macrocarpa   ECou
  - var. *brevifolia*   ECou EWes
  - var. *latisepala*   ECou
¶ - var. *macrocarpa*   CLyn
§ 'Maori Gem'   CHEx EWes NFai SCoo SMrm
       WBod WLRN
'Margery Fish'   See *H.* 'Primley Gem'
'Margret'[PBR]   COtt EBee EBrP EBre ECtt EMil
       LBCl LBSe LBre LRHS MAsh MBBe
       MBNS MBel MGos MHer NMen
       SBre SCoo SEas SMrm SPer SRPl
       WStI WWhi
'Marjery Joan'   LFis
'Marjorie'   CChe CLyn EBee ECou ECtt ENot
       GOrc LRHS MGos MRav NDlv
       NFai NFor NPer NWea SBod SPer
       SRPl WDin
matthewsii   ECou
'Mauve Queen'   CLyn EHol
'Mauvena'   SPer
'McEwanii'   See *H.* 'Macewanii'
'McKean'   ECou

'Megan'	ECou	
'Menzies Bay'	Last listed 1998	
'Mercury'	See *H. pimeleoides* 'Mercury'	
'Midsummer Beauty' ♀	More than 30 suppliers	
'Milmont Emerald'	See *H.* 'Emerald Green'	
'Mini'	Last listed 1998	
* *minima* 'Calvin'	Last listed 1998	
'Miss E. Fittall'	ECou	
'Mist Maiden'	ESis	
'Monica'	ECou GCHN NDlv NHol	
'Monticola'	Last listed 1997	
* 'Moppets Hardy'	SPer	
'Morning Clouds'	Last listed 1998	
§ 'Mrs Winder' ♀	More than 30 suppliers	
x *myrtifolia*	NFai	
'Mystery'	ECou	
'Nantyderry'	CHal MBel MSCN MWgw NMen WEas WLRN WWat	
§ 'Neil's Choice'	CLyn ECou EWes MBri MSte NFai	
'Netta Dick'	ECou	
'Nicola's Blush'	More than 30 suppliers	
'Northumbria Beauty'	Last listed 1999	
'Northumbria Gem'	NFor	
obtusata	ECou	
ochracea	ECou MGos MMal NFla SPer SWal WBod	
§ - 'James Stirling' ♀	More than 30 suppliers	
'Oddity'	ECou	
§ *odora*	CBlo CChe EBee ECou EPfP MWhi WIvy	
- 'New Zealand Gold'	CNic CSam ECou ESis GKir LRHS NDlv NFai SAga SLon SPan SPer WPyg WStI	
* - *patens*	MGos WHCG	
- prostrate	ECou	
- 'Stewart'	ECou	
- 'Wintergreen'	EBee	
'Oratio Beauty'	CLyn LRHS MAsh NFai WLRN	
'Orientale'	Last listed 1998	
'Otari Delight'	CMHG	
'Pageboy'	ECou NDlv	
parviflora hort.	See *H.* 'Bowles's Hybrid'	
§ - var. *angustifolia* ♀	ECou EPla EWes MTed SAPC SArc SDix SHFr	
- 'Holdsworth'	CLyn SDys	
- 'Palmerston'	ECou	
¶ 'Pascal'	ECou MBri	
'Patti Dossett'	See *H. speciosa* 'Patti Dossett'	
pauciflora hort.	See *H.* 'Christensenii'	
- Simpson & Thomson	Last listed 1998	
pauciramosa	ECou ESis NTow SRms	
'Paula'	ECtt	
'Penny Day'	Last listed 1998	
perfoliata	See *Parahebe perfoliata*	
'Perryhill Lilac'	SPer	
* 'Perry's Cerise'	NFai	
'Perry's Rubyleaf'	NPer	
* 'Peter Chapple'	EPot	
'Petra's Pink'	CLyn ECou EOrc ESis LRHS MAsh SWal	
petriei	Last listed 1999	
§ 'Pewter Dome' ♀	More than 30 suppliers	
'Pimeba'	NHol	
pimeleoides	ECou MWhi	
- 'Glauca'	MHer NPer	
- 'Glaucocaerulea'	ECou NDlv SPer WKif	
§ - 'Mercury'	ECou	
- var. *minor*	ECou WPat	
- - 'Elf'	ECou	
- - 'Imp'	ECou	
- 'Quicksilver' ♀	More than 30 suppliers	
- var. *rupestris*	ECou ESis	

pinguifolia	CLyn ECou NDlv SPlb WFar	
- 'Dobson'	CLyn	
- 'Forma'	Last listed 1998	
§ - 'Godefroyana'	SWal	
- 'Hutt'	ECou	
- 'Mount Dobson'	ECou NHol	
- 'Pagei' ♀	More than 30 suppliers	
- 'Sutherlandii'	CDoC CLyn CNic EBee ECou ESis GCHN GDra GGar LEdu LRHS MBar MWhi NBee NDlv NFai NSti	
§ - 'Wardiensis'	CMHG	
'Pink Elephant'	EBee ELan ESis GKir LAst LHop LRHS SCoo SEas SPer	
'Pink Fantasy'	LRHS MAsh WWeb	
'Pink Paradise'[PBR]	ELan EPfP LRHS MAsh	
'Pink Payne'	See *H.* 'Gauntlettii'	
'Pink Pearl'	See *H.* 'Gloriosa'	
'Pink Wand'	CLTr LHop WGer	
'Polly Moore'	Last listed 1999	
poppelwellii	ITim WAbe	
'Porlock Purple'	See *Parahebe catarractae* 'Delight'	
'Port e Vullen'	Last listed 1998	
§ 'Primley Gem'	CNic ESis LRHS	
'Princess'	Last listed 1998	
propinqua	ESis NMen	
§ - 'Aurea'	Last listed 1999	
§ - 'Cupins'	CLyd ESis SIng WBcn	
- 'Minor'	NDlv	
'Prostrata'	NDlv	
* 'Pulchella'	CSam	
* 'Purple Elf'	SPer	
'Purple Emperor'	See *H.* 'Neil's Choice'	
'Purple Picture'	ECou ECtt LRHS NFai SDry	
Purple Pixie = 'Mohawk'[PBR]	COtt LRHS MGos WLRN	
'Purple Princess'	CLyn	
§ 'Purple Queen'	EPfP LRHS MAsh SPla	
I 'Purple Shamrock' (v)	MAsh SPer	
'Purple Tips' misapplied	See *H. speciosa* 'Variegata'	
rakaiensis ♀	CChe CLyn ECou EHoe ELan ENot EWTr GAbr GKir ISea LHop LRHS MAsh MBar MBri MGos MWat NBir SPer SRPl STre WAbe WBod WCFE WDin WFar WHCG WPer WWin	
ramosissima	ESis GTou	
raoulii	GBri GKir WAbe WHoo WSHC	
- var. *maccaskillii*	ESis	
- 'Mount Hutt'	GTou	
- var. *pentasepala*	ESis	
§ *recurva*	CLyn CNic CSam EBee ECou ESis GGar GKir LRHS MBri NBee NFai NFor NHol SHFr SRms WBod WDin WPer WRus	
§ - 'Aoira'	CPri ECou NDlv	
- 'Boughton Silver' ♀	LRHS MBNS SDry	
- green-leaved	Last listed 1998	
- 'White Torrent'	ECou	
§ 'Red Edge' ♀	More than 30 suppliers	
'Red Ruth'	See *H.* 'Gauntlettii'	
rigidula	ECou ESis NMen	
'Ritt'	ESis	
'Ronda'	ECou	
'Rosie'[PBR]	LRHS MMHG NBee NFai SCoo SPer WEas WLRN	
* 'Royal Blue'	CLyn	
'Royal Purple'	See *H.* 'Alicia Amherst'	
salicifolia	CChe CLTr CLyn CNic CPri EBee ECou ELan ENot EPfP GCHN LGro NFai NFor SPer SPlb SRms WFar WHCG WTro	

- 'Snow Wreath'   See *H.* 'Snow Wreath'
salicornioides   ECou
- 'Aurea'   See *H. propinqua* 'Aurea'
'Sapphire'   CDoC CLyn CPri ECou ESis EWTr
                          GKir LRHS MAsh MBar MGos
                          NBlu NCiC SCoo SMrm WGer
'Sarana'   CLyn ECou
selaginoides hort.   See *H.* 'Loganioides'
'Silver Dollar' (v)   CAbP CFai CLyn CM&M ELan
                          EPfP GKir LPan LRHS MAsh NPri
                          SPer SPla WWeb
'Silver Gilt'   Last listed 1999
'Silver Wings' (v)   ECou NFai
'Simon Delaux' ♀   CLyn CSam ECou LRHS NCiC
                          SPer WEas
§ 'Snow Wreath' (v)   IBlr
speciosa   Last listed 1999
- 'Dial Rocks'   Last listed 1999
- 'Johny Day'   See *H.* 'Johny Day'
§ - 'La Seduisante' ♀   CLTr CLyn ECou ENot IOrc MGed
                          MLan MRav SEND WSHC
§ - 'Patti Dossett'   CLTr CLyn
§ - 'Purple Queen'   See *H.* 'Purple Queen'
- 'Rangatira'   ECou EWes
- 'Ruddigore'   See *H. speciosa* 'La Seduisante'
§ - 'Variegata' (v)   CHal CLyn IBlr NPer SDry SWal
                          WEas
'Spender's Seedling'   CLyn ECou EPfP GOrc LRHS
                          MWgw NBee SEND SPer SRms
                          STre
'Spender's Seedling' hort. See *H. parviflora* var. *angustifolia*
'Spring Glory'   EBrP EBre LBCl LBSe LBre LRHS
                          MBBe SBre
stricta   CLyn ECou
- var. *egmontiana*   CLyn ECou
- var. *macroura*   ECou EPla SDry
subalpina   CLan EBee EBrP EBre ECou ESis
                          LBCl LBSe LBre MBBe MOne MTis
                          NDlv SBre
subsimilis   SBla
- var. *astonii*   ESis
'Summer Blue'   CLyn
'Susan'   ECou
'Sussex Carpet'   See *H. albicans* 'Sussex Carpet'
tetrasticha   Last listed 1999
* - AGS 74   Last listed 1999
'Tiny Tot'   CLyd ESis MTho
'Tom Marshall'   See *H. canterburiensis*
topiaria   More than 30 suppliers
* - 'Doctor Favier'   CLyn
'Torlesse'   ECou
townsonii   CLyn ECou
traversii   CBlo ECou MSte SRms
- - 'Mason'   ECou
- - 'Woodside'   ECou
'Trenchant Rose'   CBlo
'Tricolor'   See *H. speciosa* 'Variegata'
'Trixie'   CLyn CNic ECou
tumida   SBla
'Underway'   Last listed 1998
urvilleana   ECou
'Veitchii'   See *H.* 'Alicia Amherst'
§ *venustula*   ECou ESis LRHS MBri NDlv SMrm
                          WPer
- 'Blue Skies'   ECou NFai
- 'Patricia Davies'   CLTr ECou NDlv
vernicosa   CLyn CNic EBee ECou ESis GDra
                          LRHS MBar MBri MGos MHer
                          NBee NDlv NFai NFor NHol NPer
                          NPro NTow SPer SPlb SSmi WAbe
                          WGwG WHCG
¶ 'Vogue'   MAsh

'Waikiki'   See *H.* 'Mrs Winder'
'Walter Buccleugh'   ECou
'Wardiensis'   See *H. pinguifolia* 'Wardiensis'
'Warley Pink'   CLyn
'Warleyensis'   See *H.* 'Mrs Winder'
§ 'Watson's Pink'   CLTr ECou GOrc SPer SUsu WKif
¶ 'Whistleberry Sapphire' SWal
'White Diamond'   SPer
§ 'White Gem'   ECou ECtt ESis EWTr MGos NBee
  (*brachysiphon* hybrid) NDlv NFor NPer WEas WStl
* 'White Grape'   CM&M
'White Heather'   LRHS MTPN
'White Summer'   Last listed 1997
'White Wand'   NFai
* 'White Wings'   Last listed 1998
'Willcoxii'   See *H. buchananii* 'Sir George
                          Fenwick'
'Wingletye'   CLyn CNic ECou EGoo ESis GGar
                          LRHS MBri MGos MWhi NDlv
                          NNor WAbe WGwG WPer WPyg
'Winter Glow'   CLyd COtt ECou GOrc NFai
'Wiri Blush'   CLyn
'Wiri Charm'   CAbP CDoC COtt EBee ECle EMil
                          ENot EPfP ESis IOrc LRHS MLan
                          MTis SVil WGer WWeb
'Wiri Cloud'   CAbP ELan EPfP ESis GGar IOrc
                          LRHS MAsh MGed MTis NBee
                          WWeb
'Wiri Dawn'   CAbP CB&S CLyn COtt ELan EPfP
                          ESis EWes IOrc LRHS MAsh
                          MWgw NFai SVil WLRN WWeb
'Wiri Gem'   CLyn EMil LRHS
'Wiri Icing Sugar'   CLyn
'Wiri Image'   CB&S CDoC CLyn COtt EBee EMil
                          IOrc LRHS
'Wiri Joy'   CLyn LRHS
'Wiri Mist'   CLyn COtt EBee EMil ESis IOrc
                          LRHS NFai WBod WLRN
'Wiri Splash'   CDoC COtt EMil LRHS MAsh
                          WWeb
'Wiri Vision'   COtt ESis LRHS
§ 'Youngii'   CLyn CPri EBee ECha ECou ECtt
                          ELan EMNN ENot ESis EWTr GGar
                          GKir LRHS MAsh MBar MGos
                          MHer NBee NMen NWCA SMer
                          SPer SPlb SRCN SRms SSmi WEas
                          WWin

HECHTIA (Bromeliaceae)
tillandsioides   LHil

HEDEOMA (Lamiaceae)
pulegioides   Last listed 1998

HEDERA ✿ (Araliaceae)
algeriensis   See *H. canariensis* hort.
¶ 'Anita'   CHal
§ *azorica*   CWhi WFib WWat
- 'Aurea'   Last listed 1998
- 'Pico'   CWhi WFib
- 'Variegata'   WCot
§ *canariensis* hort.   CDoC CHEx SAPC SArc WFib
§ - 'Willdenow'   Last listed 1997
- 'Algeriensis'   See *H. canariensis* hort.
- 'Argyle Street'   WFib
- var. *azorica*   See *H. azorica*
- 'Cantabrian'   See *H. maroccana* 'Spanish
                          Canary'
* - 'Casablanca'   CWhi
* - 'Etna'   CWhi
§ - hort. 'Gloire de Marengo' (v) ♀
                          More than 30 suppliers

¶ – hort. 'Gloire de Marengo' arborescent (v)
    SPer
 – 'Marginomaculata' ♀   CDoC EPfP LRHS NEgg WCot
    WFib WWeb
* – 'Mirandela'   CWhi
 – 'Montgomery'   EBee LRHS WFib
* – 'Nevada'   CWhi
 – 'Ravensholst' ♀   CMac NSti WFib WWat
 – 'Stauss'   WFib
 – hort. 'Variegata'   See *H. canariensis* hort. 'Gloire de
    Marengo'

chinensis   See *H. nepalensis* var. *sinensis*
 – *typica*   See *H. nepalensis* var. *sinensis*
§ ***colchica*** ♀   CBlo CHEx EBee ENot EPfP LRHS
    SPer WCFE WDin WFib
* – 'Arborescens Variegata'   Last listed 1999
 – 'Dentata' ♀   CBlo CHEx CWhi EPla LBuc LPri
    SEas WCru WFib
 – 'Dentata Aurea'   See *H. colchica* 'Dentata Variegata'
§ – 'Dentata Variegata' ♀   More than 30 suppliers
 – 'My Heart'   See *H. colchica*
 – 'Paddy's Pride'   See *H. colchica* 'Sulphur Heart'
§ – 'Sulphur Heart' (v) ♀   More than 30 suppliers
 – 'Variegata'   See *H. colchica* 'Dentata Variegata'
cristata   See *H. helix* 'Parsley Crested'
§ ***cypria***   EPla WCot WFib
§ ***helix***   CKin CTri CWhi EWFC GChr
    LRHS MBar MGos NWea WFib
    WHer
 – 'Abundance'   See *H. helix* 'California'
 – 'Adam' (v)   CBlo CCHP CPri CWhi LAst MAsh
    MBri MTho NCiC WByw WFib
    WLeb WWat WWeb
I – 'Ahorn'   CWhi WFib
 – 'Albany'   See *H. hibernica* 'Albany'
 – 'Alpha'   CWhi
 – 'Alte Brücke'   CWhi WFib
 – 'Alte Heidelberg'   CWhi WFib
 – 'Amberwaves'   WFib
I – 'Ambrosia' (v)   CWhi WFib
 – 'Anchor'   CWhi
§ – 'Angularis'   CWhi ECot
 – 'Angularis Aurea' ♀   CWhi EBee EHoe EPfP EPla NBir
    NCiC SLim WFib
 – 'Anne Borch'   See *H. hibernica* 'Anna Marie'
 – 'Anne Marie'   See *H. hibernica* 'Anna Marie'
 – 'Annette'   See *H. helix* 'California'
 – 'Appaloosa'   WCot WFib
 – 'Aran' misapplied   See *H. helix* 'Rutherford's Arran'
 – 'Arapahoe'   NGCt WFib
 – 'Arborescens'   CNat EPla
 – 'Ardingly' (v)   CWhi MWhi NBea WFib
 – 'Arran'   See *H. helix* 'Rutherford's Arran'
 – 'Asterisk'   CWhi EPla NBrk NCat WBro WFib
    WLeb
 – 'Astin'   CWhi WFib
 – 'Atropurpurea' ♀   CBlo CNat CWhi EPPr EPla MBar
    NCiC NHol WFib
 – 'Aurea Densa'   See *H. helix* 'Aureovariegata'
§ – 'Aureovariegata'   CMac CNic CWhi WFib
 – 'Avon' (v)   WFib
 – 'Baby Face'   CWhi
 – 'Baccifera'   CWhi WFib
 – 'Baden-Baden'   CWhi WFib
 – var. *baltica*   CWhi WFib
 – 'Barabits' Silver'   EPla
 – 'Big Deal'   CWhi
 – 'Bill Archer'   CWhi EPla WFib
 – 'Bird's Foot'   See *H. helix* 'Pedata'
 – 'Blodwen' (v)   WFib
 – 'Bodil' (v)   CWhi SHFr WFib
 – 'Boskoop'   CWhi WFib

 – 'Bowles Ox Heart'   WFib
 – 'Bredon'   WFib WSPU
 – 'Brigette'   See *H. helix* 'California'
 – 'Brightstone'   WFib
§ – 'Brokamp'   CWhi NFai SLPl WFib
 – 'Bruder Ingobert' (v)   CWhi NCat WFib
 – 'Buttercup' ♀   More than 30 suppliers
 – 'Butterflies'   WFib
§ – 'Caecilia' (v)   CB&S CBlo CMac ELan EPfP
    LHop LRHS MAsh NFai NPro NSti
    SPer WCDu WCot WCru WFib
    WLRN WLeb
N – 'Caenwoodiana'   See *H. helix* 'Pedata'
 – 'Caenwoodiana Aurea'   CWhi WFib
 – 'Calico'   See *H. helix* 'Schäfer Three'
§ – 'California'   CWhi MBri NSti WFib
 – 'California Fan'   CWhi
 – 'California Gold' (v)   CCuc CWhi NPro WFib
 – 'Caristian'   WFib
 – 'Carolina Crinkle'   CNat CWhi EPla MWhi NBrk
    WBro WFib
 – 'Cascade'   WFib
 – 'Cathedral Wall'   WFib
§ – 'Cavendishii' (v) ♀   CWhi NBrk SRms WCru WFib
    WLRN
§ – 'Ceridwen' (v)   CRHN CWhi MBri SPlb WFib
 – 'Chedglow' fasciated   CNat
 – 'Cheltenham Blizzard'   CNat
 – 'Chester' (v)   CWhi MAsh MBri WFib WWat
 – 'Chicago'   CBlo WFib
 – 'Chicago Variegated'   See *H. helix* 'Harald'
 – 'Christian'   See *H. helix* 'Direktor Badke'
 – 'Chrysanna'   WFib
 – 'Chrysophylla'   CWhi EPla
 – 'Cleeve'   WFib
 – 'Clotted Cream'   See *H. helix* 'Caecilia'
 – 'Cockle Shell'   CWhi WFib
 – 'Congesta' ♀   CWhi EPla EPot GDra MTho
    SRms SSmi STre WFib WLeb
 – 'Conglomerata'   CWhi ELan EPla MBar MBri MBro
    NBir NFor NRya SMad SPer SRms
    WAbe WFib WPyg
 – 'Conglomerata Erecta'   CSWP SLon SRms WCFE WFib
 – 'Corrugata'   WFib
 – 'Crenata'   CWhi WFib
 – 'Crispa'   MRav NFor
 – 'Cristata'   See *H. helix* 'Parsley Crested'
 – 'Cristata Melanie'   See *H. helix* 'Melanie'
 – 'Curleylocks'   See *H. helix* 'Manda's Crested'
 – 'Curley-Q'   See *H. helix* 'Dragon Claw'
 – 'Curvaceous' (v)   WCot WFib
 – 'Cuspidata Major'   See *H. hibernica* 'Cuspidata
    Major'
 – 'Cuspidata Minor'   See *H. hibernica* 'Cuspidata
    Minor'
 – 'Cyprus'   See *H. cypria*
* – 'Dead Again'   WCot
 – 'Dean' (v)   WFib
 – 'Deltoidea'   See *H. hibernica* 'Deltoidea'
 – 'Denmark' (v)   WFib
 – 'Denticulata'   CWhi WFib
 – 'Diana'   CWhi
 – 'Dicke von Stauss'   CWhi
§ – 'Direktor Badke'   CWhi WFib
 – 'Discolor'   See *H. helix* 'Minor Marmorata'
¶ – 'Dolly'   NGCt
 – 'Domino' (v)   CWhi EPla EWes WFib WLeb
§ – 'Donerailensis'   CWhi GAri NFai WFib WPer
¶ – 'Don's Papillion'   CNat
 – 'Dovers'   CCuc WFib
§ – 'Dragon Claw'   CWhi EPla NBrk NCiC WCot
    WCru WFib WLeb

- 'Duckfoot'	CCuc CDoC CHal CInt CLTr CSWP CWhi MTho MWhi NFai NSti WBro WFib WLeb WOut WWat	
- 'Dunloe Gap'	EPla	
- 'Edison'	CWhi	
- 'Elegance'	CWhi WFib	
- 'Elfenbein' (v)	CWhi WFib	
- 'Emerald Gem'	See *H. helix* 'Angularis'	
- 'Emerald Globe'	CWhi WFib	
- 'Emerald Jewel'	See *H. helix* 'Pittsburgh'	
- 'Erecta' ♀	CMac CNat CTri CWhi EMFP EPfP EPla GAri MBar MGos MTho MWhi NChi NRya SPer WCot WFar WFib WPat WWye	
- 'Erin'	See *H. helix* 'Pin Oak'	
- 'Ester'	See *H. helix* 'Harald'	
- 'Eugen Hahn' (v)	CWhi EPla WFib	
§ - 'Eva' (v) ♀	CMac CWhi MBri MGos NBir WFib	
- 'Evesham'	WFib	
- 'Fallen Angel'	CWhi WFib	
- 'Fan'	CWhi	
- 'Fantasia' (v)	CMac CWhi WFib	
- 'Faye' (v)	WCot	
- 'Ferney'	WFib	
- 'Filigran'	CWhi SMad WFib WHer WLeb	
- 'Flamenco'	CWhi WFib	
- 'Flava' (v)	CWhi	
- 'Fleur de Lis'	CNat CWhi WFib	
- 'Florida'	WFib	
- 'Fluffy Ruffles'	CWhi EPla WLeb	
* - 'Francis'	MBri	
- 'Fringette'	See *H. helix* 'Manda Fringette'	
- 'Frosty' (v)	Last listed 1997	
- 'Gavotte'	CWhi MTho NGCt WFib	
- 'Gertrud Stauss' (v)	CWhi MBri NCat WFib	
- 'Glache' (v)	SHFr WFib	
- 'Glacier' (v) ♀	More than 30 suppliers	
- 'Glacier Improved' (v)	NBea	
- 'Glymii'	CWhi EPla SLPl WFib	
- 'Gold Harald'	See *H. helix* 'Goldchild'	
- 'Gold Nugget'	CWhi	
§ - 'Goldchild' (v) ♀	More than 30 suppliers	
- 'Goldcraft' (v)	CWhi WFib	
- 'Golden Ann'	See *H. helix* 'Ceridwen'	
* - 'Golden Arrow'	LRHS MAsh	
- 'Golden Curl' (v)	Last listed 1999	
- 'Golden Ester'	See *H. helix* 'Ceridwen'	
- 'Golden Gate' (v)	MBri	
- 'Golden Gem'	NPro	
- 'Golden Ingot' (v)	CPri CWhi ELan EPla MAsh MBar MGos MWhi NFai NGCt WFib WLeb	
- 'Golden Kolibri'	See *H. helix* 'Midas Touch'	
- 'Golden Mathilde' (v)	CHal	
- 'Golden Medal'	WCot WFib	
- 'Golden Snow' (v)	MBri	
- 'Goldfinger'	See *H. helix* 'Goldstern'	
- 'Goldheart'	See *H. helix* 'Oro di Bogliasco'	
§ - 'Goldstern' (v)	CWhi MWhi WFib WLeb WWat	
- 'Goldwolke' (v)	SLPl	
- 'Gracilis'	See *H. hibernica* 'Gracilis'	
§ - 'Green Feather'	CWhi EGoo ESis WFib WOak	
§ - 'Green Finger'	See *H. helix* 'Très Coupé'	
§ - 'Green Ripple'	CB&S CChe CMac CTri CWhi EBee ENot GKir IOrc LRHS MAsh MBar MWht NBro NCat NCiC NPro SEND SEas SLim SPer SPlb WFib WHen WLeb	
- 'Green Spear'	See *H. helix* 'Spear Point'	
- 'Hahn's Green Ripple'	See *H. helix* 'Green Ripple'	

- 'Hamilton'	See *H. hibernica* 'Hamilton'	
§ - 'Harald' (v)	CBlo CDoC CWhi LAst MAsh MBNS MBri NGCt NSti WFib WLeb	
- 'Harlequin' (v)	CPri WFib	
- 'Harrison'	CWhi	
- 'Harry Wood'	See *H. helix* 'Modern Times'	
* - 'Hazel' (v)	WFib	
- 'Heise' (v)	CWhi WFib	
- 'Heise Denmark' (v)	WFib	
- 'Helvetica'	CWhi NGCt	
- 'Helvig'	See *H. helix* 'White Knight'	
¶ - 'Henrietta'	CStr	
- 'Heron'	Last listed 1998	
- subsp. ***hibernica***	See *H. hibernica*	
- 'Hispanica'	See *H. maderensis* subsp. *iberica*	
- 'Hite's Miniature'	See *H. helix* 'Merion Beauty'	
- 'Holly'	See *H. helix* 'Parsley Crested'	
- 'Hullavington'	CNat	
- 'Humpty Dumpty'	MBar	
- 'Ideal'	See *H. helix* 'California'	
- 'Imp'	See *H. helix* 'Brokamp'	
- 'Ingelise'	See *H. helix* 'Sagittifolia Variegata'	
- 'Ingrid'	See *H. helix* 'Harald'	
- 'Innuendo'	WFib	
- 'Itsy Bitsy'	See *H. helix* 'Pin Oak'	
- 'Ivalace' ♀	CB&S CNat CWhi EBee ECha EPla ESis GOrc MAsh MNrw MRav MWhi MWht NBid NChi NFai NSti NWoo SEas SRms WFib WLeb	
- 'Jack Frost' (v)	Last listed 1999	
- 'Jane's Findling' (v)	CNat	
- 'Jasper'	WFib	
- 'Jerusalem'	See *H. helix* 'Schäfer Three'	
- 'Jester's Gold'	EPfP EPla LRHS MBri MGos NEgg WWeb	
- 'Jubilee' (v)	CPri CWhi WCFE WFar WFib WLeb	
- 'Knülch'	EPla MWat WFib	
- 'Kolibri' (v) ♀	CBlo CChe CDoC CMac CPri CWhi EBee EBrP EBre EMil EPfP LAst LBCl LBSe LBre MAsh MBBe MBar MBri NCiC NPro SBre WFib WWeb	
- 'Königers Auslese'	CRHN CWhi EPla NBea SLPl WFib	
- 'Kurios'	CNat CWhi	
- 'La Plata'	CWhi	
§ - 'Lady Kay'	WFib	
- 'Lalla Rookh'	CWhi NBrk WFib WLeb	
- 'Lemon Swirl' (v)	CWhi WFib	
- 'Leo Swicegood'	CSWP CWhi EPla MWhi WFib	
- 'Light Fingers'	CCuc EPla MAsh WFib	
* - 'Lime Regis'	CWhi NGCt	
- 'Limey'	CWhi	
- 'Little Diamond' (v) ♀	CDoC CLTr CSam CTri CWhi EBee EHoe ELan EPla GChr GOrc LHop LRHS MAsh MBar MBri MGos MHar MWht NCiC SLon SRPl WAbe WFib WWat	
- 'Little Gem'	CWhi WFib	
- 'Little Luzii' (v)	WFib	
- 'Little Picture'	WFib	
- 'Little Witch'	EPla	
- 'Liz'	See *H. helix* 'Eva'	
- 'Liziz' (v)	WFib	
- 'Lopsided'	Last listed 1998	
- 'Lucy Kay'	See *H. helix* 'Lady Kay'	
§ - 'Luzii' (v)	CBlo EBee EHoe EPla MBar MGos NFai NSti SPer WByw WFib	
- 'Maculata'	See *H. helix* 'Minor Marmorata'	
- 'Malvern'	WFib	
§ - 'Manda Fringette'	CWhi MTho NFai WFib WLeb	

	WFib WLeb
§ - 'Tricolor' (v)	CB&S CBlo CMac CRHN CTri
	CWhi EPfP EPla LRHS MAsh
	MGos MWht SBra SLim SMer
	WCFE
- 'Trinity' (v)	WFib
- 'Tristram' (v)	CWhi WFib
- 'Triton'	CWhi MBar MTho WFib
- 'Troll'	CWhi WLeb
- 'Trustee'	CWhi
- 'Tussie Mussie' (v)	CWhi WFib
- 'Ursula' (v)	CSWP NChi WFib
- 'Ustler'	CWhi
* - 'Variegata'	Last listed 1998
* - 'Verity'	CWhi
¶ - 'Very Merry'	NGCt
I - 'Victoria'	MAsh WWeb
- 'Walthamensis'	CWhi WFib
- 'White Knight' (v)	CWhi MBri WFib
- 'White Kolibri'	MBri
- 'Whitehall'	WFib
- 'Wichtel'	CWhi
- 'William Kennedy' (v)	CWhi WFib WLeb
- 'Williamsiana' (v)	CWhi
- 'Woeneri'	CWhi SLPl WFib
- 'Woodsii'	See H. helix 'Modern Times'
- 'Yellow Ripple'	CPri EPla
- 'Zebra' (v)	CWhi NCat NGCt WFib
§ hibernica ♀	CB&S CBlo CNat CWhi EBee
	GCHN GChr GKir LBuc LRHS
	MBar MRav NBea NFor NWea
	SBra SPer SRms WDin WFib WLeb
	WStI WWat
§ - 'Albany'	WFib
§ - 'Anna Marie' (v)	CMac CPri CWhi GOrc LRHS
	MBri WFib WLeb
- 'Aracena'	EPla
§ - 'Cuspidata Major'	CWhi WFib
§ - 'Cuspidata Minor'	CWhi WFib
§ - 'Dealbata' (v)	CMac CWhi GOrc WFib
§ - 'Deltoidea'	CCuc CWhi EPla MBri MWht
	NGCt WCot WFib
- 'Digitata'	WFib
I - 'Digitata Crûg Gold'	WCru
§ - 'Gracilis'	CWhi WFib
§ - 'Hamilton'	WFib
- 'Helena' (v)	WFib
* - 'Lactimaculata'	CWhi
- 'Lobata Major'	SRms
- 'Maculata' (v)	EPla WSHC
- 'Palmata'	WFib
- 'Rona'	CWhi WFib
- 'Sulphurea' (v)	CWhi WFib
- 'Tess'	EPla WFib
- 'Variegata'	CPri CWhi MBar SLim WWat
¶ 'Jake'	CHal
maderensis	WFib
§ - subsp. iberica	WFib
maroccana 'Morocco'	WFib
- 'Spanish Canary'	WFib WSHC
nepalensis	WBcn WFib
- CC&MR 460	Last listed 1997
- var. nepalensis 'Suzanne'	MBar WFib
§ - var. sinensis	CWhi WFib
- - L 555	EPla
pastuchovii	CWhi WFib
- from Troödos, Cyprus	See H. cypria
* - 'Volga'	CWhi
§ rhombea ♀	CWhi WCot WFib
- var. formosana	WFib
- 'Japonica'	See H. rhombea
- var. rhombea 'Variegata'	NGCt WFib

HEDYCHIUM ✿ (Zingiberaceae)

aurantiacum	LHil WMul
¶ 'Carnival'	LEur
chrysoleucum	CGle LAma LBow LPio
coccineum ♀	CB&S CFil CHEx LAma LBow
	LChe LHil MNrw
- var. angustifolium	WMul
- var. aurantiacum	LAma LBow
- 'Tara' ♀	CDoC CFil CGle EBee EOas EPfP
	LEdu LPio MNrw MSte SAPC SArc
	WCru WMul WPGP
coronarium	CAvo CGle CHEx EBot LBow
	LChe LRHS MSte NFai SLon SYvo
	WMul
¶ - 'Andromeda'	LEur WMul
- var. flavescens	See H. flavescens
- var. maximum	CFir
densiflorum	CBrd CFil CHEx CTre EOas EPla
	LHil SDix SSpi WCru WMul WPGP
- 'Assam Orange'	CBrm CDoC CFil CGle CHEx CInt
	EBee EOas GCal LChe LEdu LPio
	MSte WCru WMul WPGP
- 'Stephen'	CBrd CFil MNrw
¶ 'Elizabeth'	WMul
ellipticum	LAma LBow WCru WMul
¶ 'Filagree'	CFir LEur
§ flavescens	CFil LAma LHil WCru WMul
	WPGP
forrestii	CFil CGle CHEx CTre EOas LPJP
	LPio MNrw MSte SAPC SArc
	WMul WPGP
- B&SWJ 2303	WCru WPGP
gardnerianum ♀	CCtw CFil CFir CGre CHEx CLTr
	EBee EBot EOas ERea LAma LBow
	LChe LEdu LPio LRHS MSte SAPC
	SArc SSoC SYvo WCru WMul
	WPGP
'Goldflame'	CFir
greenei	CDoC CFil CFir CGle CHEx EBee
	EBot EOas LBow LEdu LPio
	MNrw MSte SArc SDix SYvo
	WCot WCru WMul WPGP
¶ 'Kinkaku'	LEur
¶ 'Lemon Sherbert'	CFir
longicornutum	MSte
'Luna Moth'	CFil WMul
muluense	WMul
pradhanii	CFir WMul
x raffillii	MNrw WCot
* 'Shamshiri'	Last listed 1999
spicatum	CBrd CFil CFir CHEx CMdw EOas
	GPoy LHil MSte WCru WMul
thyrsiforme	CFil WMul
villosum	LAma WMul
¶ 'White Starburst'	LEur
yunnanense	CFil EOas WCot WCru WMul
	WPGP

HEDYSARUM (Papilionaceae)

coronarium	CArn CGle CPle CSev CSpe EBee
	EHrv ELan MBrN MSte MTis
	SRCN WCot WHal WOve
hedysaroides	EMan SPlb
multijugum	CB&S LBuc MBlu SPer WSHC
- var. apiculatum	ELan
occidentale	Last listed 1998

HEIMERLIODENDRON See PISONIA

HEIMIA (Lythraceae)

salicifolia	CArn CPle ELan GEil MBlu MSal
	MWhi SOWG SPan WWye

HELENIUM (Asteraceae)

autumnale	CBlo CMea CTri EWTr MBNS MBel MSal NBus NChi SEas SSvw WBea WLin WMoo
- 'All Gold'	WPer
- JLS 88007WI	EMon
- 'Praecox'	Last listed 1998
- 'Sunset Shades'	WElm
'Baudirektor Linne'	CWit EPPr GKir LRHS SCro
* 'Biedermeier'	CAbx CRDP EFou
bigelovii	WByw
'Blütentisch'	MBri SUsu SVil WWeb
'Bressingham Gold'	CElw
'Bruno'	CHar CRDP EBrP EBre EGle ELan GKir LBCl LBSe LBre LRHS MArl MBBe MChl MMil MRav NGdn SBre SMrm SOkh
'Butterpat'	EBee EFou EPPr GKir GMaP LRHS MBel MCLN MMil MRav NFai NFla NPri SChu
'Chipperfield Orange'	CBlo CElw CHad CPlt EFou EMan LRHS MArl MMil NGdn NVic SRPl SSvw WCot WLRN
'Coppelia'	CSam EBee EBrP EBre EMan GKir LBCl LBSe LBre MBBe MBro NFla NGdn SBre WHoo
Copper Spray	See H. 'Kupfersprudel'
'Crimson Beauty'	CMea EBrP EBre LBCl LBSe LBre LRHS MBBe MBel MBri MLLN MTis SBre
'Croftway Variety'	SCro
Dark Beauty	See H. 'Dunkelpracht'
'Die Blonde'	EGle LGre SAga
§ 'Dunkelpracht'	EPPr LGre SAga WCot
'Feuersiegel'	EGar LGre
'Flammendes Käthchen'	EBrP EBre LBCl LBSe LBre LGre LRHS MBBe SAga SBre
flexuosum	EBee
'Gold Fox'	CSam CWit
Golden Youth	See H. 'Goldene Jugend'
§ 'Goldene Jugend'	CElw EGar ELan LRHS MRav SSpe WCot WEas
* 'Goldlackzwerg'	EBee
'Goldrausch'	CAbx EFou SCro
boopesii	More than 30 suppliers
'Indianersommer'	MBel
'July Sun'	SSpe
'Kanaria'	CAbx CElw EFou EPPr NCat
'Karneol'	EFou LRHS SOkh
¶ 'Kleiner Fuchs'	SCro
'Königstiger'	EBrP EBre LBCl LBSe LBre MBBe SBre
§ 'Kupfersprudel'	EBrP EBre LBCl LBSe LBre LRHS MBBe MRav SBre
'Kupferzwerg'	CAbx LGre SOkh
'Mahogany'	See H. 'Goldlackzwerg'
'Margot'	EFou
'Moerheim Beauty'	More than 30 suppliers
Pipsqueak = 'Blopip'	EFou GKir LRHS MCLN
'Pumilum Magnificum'	CSam EFou EGle EPar EPfP LRHS MBri MWat SCro SPer SUsu WByw
Red and Gold	See H. 'Rotgold'
'Riverton Beauty'	Last listed 1999
'Riverton Gem'	ECtt
§ 'Rotgold'	CBlo CM&M EBrP EBre ECGN ECtt LBCl LBSe LBre LRHS MBBe MHer MSCN NArg NOak SBre SRms STes WHil WLRN WPer
'Rubinkuppel'	CAbx LGre SUsu
'Rubinzwerg'	LGre MBri SCro SOkh SUsu WWeb

'Sahin's Early Flowerer'	CElw EFou GBri MLLN NCut SOkh WCot
'Septemberfuchs'	EBee EFou EPPr SCro
'Sonnenwunder'	CWit EBee ECha EGar EGle
'Sunshine'	WSan
'The Bishop'	CBlo CSam EBee EFou EGar EMan EWTr LFis LRHS MBri MCLN MLLN MRav MTis NBro NCut NFai SChu WHil
¶ 'Tigerskonigin'	WWeb
'Waldtraut'	CBlo CM&M CMGP CSam EBee ECot EFou EGar EGle ELan GKir LEdu MRav NOak SAga SCro SMad SPer SSvw
¶ 'Wesergold'	EFou WLin
'Wonadonga'	EFou EGar
'Wyndley'	CB&S CBos CMGP CSam EBee EBrP EBre ECGN EFou EGar EGle LBCl LBSe LBre LRHS MBBe MBel MCAu MMil MRav SBre SChu SEas WCot WEas WFar
'Zimbelstern'	CElw CMil EBrP EBre EGar GKir LBCl LBSe LGre MBBe MRav SAga SBre SOkh WFar

HELIAMPHORA (Sarraceniaceae)

heterodoxa	WMEx
- x **ionasii**	WMEx
- x **minor**	WMEx
- x **nutans**	WMEx
minor	WMEx
nutans	WMEx
tatei	WMEx

HELIANTHELLA (Asteraceae)

§ **quinquenervis**	EBee EBrP EBre EMan GCal LBCl LBSe LBre MBBe MBel MSte NPer NTow SBre WFar

HELIANTHEMUM ✿ (Cistaceae)

'Alice Howarth'	CFul CWes EWes MBro MDHE SRms WHoo WPnn WPyg
alpestre serpyllifolium	See H. nummularium subsp. glabrum
'Amabile Plenum' (d)	CFul EPfP GAbr GCal GDra MBNS NCut
* 'Amber'	CFul GAbr
'Amy Baring' ♀	CFul EBrP EBre EGle GAbr GDra GKir LBCl LBSe LBre LHop LRHS MBBe NMen SBre WPer
'Annabel'	CFul CPri ECha EDAr EPfP GAbr GCHN NMGW SBla SChu SIde SMer WPer
apenninum	MDHE NTow WPer
- var. **roseum**	Last listed 1999
'Apricot'	SBla SBod
'Apricot Blush'	WAbe
'Baby Buttercup'	CFul CLyd CMea GAbr MBro NPro WPat
'Barbara'	Last listed 1998
'Beech Park Red'	CFul CLTr CMea ECtt ESis GAbr LBee LRHS MBro MDHE MMil MWat MWgw SChu WCer WHoo WKif WPyg
'Ben Afflick'	CFul CPri LBee LRHS MBNS MDHE MHer SAga SBod SRms WCer WPnn
'Ben Alder'	CFul CPri GAbr LFis MDHE MHer SSca
'Ben Dearg'	CFul CMea CPri ECtt EMNN GAbr MDHE SBod SRms
'Ben Fhada'	CB&S CFul CMea COlW CPBP

	CPri EDAr EMNN ESis EWTr GAbr GDra GKir LBee LRHS MHer SAga SBla SBod SRms WAbe WEas WPer WPnn WRHF WWin
'Ben Heckla'	CFul CPri CSam ECtt GAbr GCHN GKir LRHS MSte SBla WEas WPer
'Ben Hope'	CFul CPri EDAr EMNN EPfP GAbr GDra LRHS SAga SGar SRms WPer WWin
'Ben Lawers'	Last listed 1998
'Ben Ledi'	CB&S CFul CInt CMea CPri EDAr EMNN ESis GAbr GCHN GDra LHop LRHS MBar MHer NSla NVic SBod WAbe WCFE WCer WHoo WPer WPnn WWin
'Ben Lomond'	Last listed 1999
¶ 'Ben Macdhui'	CFul CPri GAbr
¶ 'Ben Mhor'	CFul
'Ben More'	CB&S CPri ECtt EDAr EMNN GAbr GDra GKir GTou LRHS MWat SBod SIng SSmi WPat WWin
'Ben Nevis'	CFul CPri CTri ECha EGoo GAbr GDra MDHE MHer SBla SRms WPyg WWin
'Ben Vane'	CFul COIW CPri GAbr LRHS MDHE
¶ 'Bentley'	CFul
'Birch White'	GAbr MDHE SIng
'Bishopsthorpe'	Last listed 1997
'Boughton Double Primrose' (d)	CFul CGle EDAr ELan EWes GAbr GCal GMac LHop LRHS SBla SChu SMer SUsu WEas WHoo WPen WSHC
'Broughty Beacon'	CFul CPri GAbr GDra MDHE WGor
'Broughty Sunset'	CFul CLTr CPri CSam GAbr MBro MDHE NBir WHoo WPyg
'Brown Gold' (d)	Last listed 1997
'Bunbury'	CFul CMea MBrN MDHE MWhi
* 'Butter and Eggs'	CInt SRms
'Butterball' (d)	MDHE
canum	SBla WPer
- subsp. *balcanicum*	NTow
'Captivation'	CFul CPri EGoo GAbr
'Cerise Queen' (d)	CFul EBrP EBre ECha EDAr GAbr GKir GMac LBCl LBSe LBre LRHS MBBe MBro NCut SBre SDix SRms WHoo WPer WPnn WPyg
chamaecistus	See *H. nummularium*
'Cheviot'	CFul CMea MBro MDHE WEas WHoo WPer WPyg WSHC WWat
¶ 'Chichester'	CFul
'Chocolate Blotch'	CFul CLTr COIW ECtt EDAr EOrc GAbr GKir LFis LRHS MHar MHer SChu SEND WPer
'Coppernob'	CFul
'Cornish Cream'	CFul CLTr EWes GAbr LBee LRHS
croceum	Last listed 1998
cupreum	CFul CInt EFou GAbr NHol
'David'	EGoo
'Doctor Phillips'	Last listed 1999
double apricot (d)	GAbr SAga
double cream (d)	ECha ECtt EGar MDHE WFar
double orange (d)	LHop MBNS NCut
double pale pink (d)	Last listed 1999
double pale yellow	NWoo
double pink (d)	CLTr GAbr MWat NWoo WFar
double primrose (d)	CLTr MDHE
double red (d)	ECha NChi
double yellow (d)	ECha
¶ 'Eden Vane'	NCat
'Elaine'	ELan
¶ 'Elfenbeinglanz'	EWTr
'Elisabeth'	EGoo
'Etna'	CFul
'Fairy'	EDAr EGle MDHE NPro
* 'Fire'	NCat
§ 'Fire Dragon' ♀	CFul CPea CPri CSam CTri EGle ELan GAbr GCHN GKir LRHS MWgw MWhi NWCA SBla SChu SRms WAbe WPyg
'Fireball'	See *H.* 'Mrs C.W. Earle'
'Firefly'	Last listed 1999
'Firegold'	WAbe
'Flame'	CPri
'Georgeham'	CFul CLTr CSam EDAr ELan GAbr LBee LHop LRHS MDHE SBla SMer SRms WEas WGor WHoo WPer
georgicum	Last listed 1999
'Gloiriette'	SIng
§ 'Golden Queen'	CFul CPri ECtt EDAr ENot EPfP EWTr GAbr LRHS MBNS MWhi SChu WPer WPyg
'Henfield Brilliant' ♀	More than 30 suppliers
'Hidcote Apricot'	CFul GAbr MDHE MMHG MTis
'Highdown'	CLTr GAbr SRms
'Highdown Apricot'	CFul MDHE NCat
¶ 'Highdown Peach'	CFul
'Honeymoon'	LRHS MDHE SAga SBla SIde WLRN
'John Lanyon'	LRHS MDHE
'Jubilee' (d) ♀	CFul CPri CSam ECtt EDAr ELan EMNN GAbr LFis LHop MMal NBid NChi NFor SBla SDix SRms WAbe WEas WHoo WWin
I 'Jubilee Variegatum'	CFul GAbr
'Karen's Silver'	WAbe
'Kathleen Druce' (d)	CFul CPri EWes GAbr MWat WHoo
¶ 'Lawrenson's Pink'	EWTr
ledifolium	WPer
I 'Linton Rose'	NBir
'Lucy Elizabeth'	CFul CPri GAbr
lunulatum	CInt CLyd ESis LBee LRHS MBro NHol NMen WAbe WPat WWin
'Magnificum'	EHol MDHE MWat
'Moonbeam'	Last listed 1999
§ 'Mrs C.W. Earle' (d) ♀	CFul CInt CLTr COIW CPri CSam CTri ECtt EDAr ELan ESis EWTr GAbr LAst LFis LHop LRHS MBrN SBla SDix SIng SRms WAbe WPer WWin
'Mrs C.W. Earle Variegated' (d)	Last listed 1999
'Mrs Clay'	See *H.* 'Fire Dragon'
'Mrs Croft'	SBla WPer
'Mrs Hays'	GMac
'Mrs Jenkinson'	Last listed 1998
'Mrs Lake'	Last listed 1998
'Mrs Moules'	SRms
'Mrs Mountstewart Jenkinson'	MBro
mutabile	MWhi SPlb WPer
§ *nummularium*	CKin EWFC GPoy IIve MDHE MHer MMal NMir NWCA SIde WPat WWye
§ - subsp. *glabrum*	CFul GAbr MBro NHol NMGW NMen WPat WPer WPyg
- subsp. *grandiflorum* 'Variegatum'	MWat
* - 'Lemon Queen'	NCat WBcn
§ - subsp. *tomentosum*	CFul GAbr MWat
oelandicum	NWCA

- subsp. *alpestre*   CLyd MBro NMen NNrd NTow
SRms SSmi WPer
- subsp. *piloselloides*   CLyd WWin
'Old Gold'   CFul CLTr EBrP EBre GAbr LBCl
LBSe LBre LRHS MBBe MHar SBre
SRms WAbe WPer WPnn
¶ 'Ovum Supreme'   CFul
pilosum   LRHS
'Pink Beauty'   WBcn
¶ 'Pink Double'   EWTr
'Pink Glow'   WPer
'Pink Perfection'   CSam
'Praecox'   CFul CMea CTri GAbr LBee LRHS
SMer SRms WHoo WPer WPyg
'Prima Donna'   CFul
'Prostrate Orange'   SRms
'Raspberry Ripple'   CFul EBrP EBre EDAr EGle ELan
ENot EWTr GAbr GCHN GKir
GMac LAst LBCl LBSe LBre LFis
LHop LRHS MBBe MTis NChi
NEgg SBre SRms WAbe WHoo
WPat WWin
'Red Dragon'   GKir WAbe
'Red Orient'   See *H.* 'Supreme'
'Regenbogen'   Last listed 1999
§ 'Rhodanthe Carneum' ♀   CMea CSam EDAr EFou ELan
ENot EWTr GAbr GCHN GKir
GTou LBee LGro LHop LRHS
MBrN MRav MTis MWat NHol
NMir SBla SSmi WAbe WEas WHoo
WLin WSHC WWin
§ 'Rosa Königin'   EMNN GAbr GKir LBee LRHS
MDHE MHer WAbe
'Rose of Leeswood' (d)   CFul CMea ELan GAbr GMac LBee
LRHS MBro MHar MHer NChi
NEgg SAga SMrm SRms WEas
WHoo WKif WPyg WSHC WWin
Rose Queen   See *H.* 'Rosa Königin'
¶ 'Rosenburg'   NCat
'Roxburgh Gold'   SRms
'Rushfield's White'   WRus WShe
¶ 'Ruth'   LBuc
'Saint John's College
Yellow'   CFul CLTr COIW CSam EDAr
GAbr LRHS MBNS SSmi WFar
WPer
'Salmon Bee'   Last listed 1997
'Salmon Queen'   CElw CFul CPri ECtt EMNN GAbr
GKir LBee LRHS MHar MSCN
NPri SAga SRms WPer WRHF
WWin
¶ 'Schnee' (d)   EGoo
serpyllifolium   See *H. nummularium* subsp.
glabrum
'Shot Silk'   CFul EWes MDHE
'Silvery Salmon' (v)   WAbe
'Snow Queen'   See *H.* 'The Bride'
'Snowball'   Last listed 1997
'Southmead'   CFul GAbr
'Sterntaler'   CFul GAbr GDra MDHE SIng
SRms WLin
'Sudbury Gem'   CFul COIW CPri CTri EBrP EBre
ECha GAbr GKir LBCl LBSe LBre
LHop LRHS MBBe NSla SBre SMer
WPer WPnn
x *sulphureum*   SDys
'Sulphureum Plenum' (d)   EPfP
'Sunbeam'   CSam EMNN GAbr MDHE SRms
'Sunburst'   CFul GAbr
§ 'Supreme'   CFul CLTr EDAr ELan EPfP EWes
GAbr LBee LHop LRHS MWat
SDix SRms WPer
'Tangerine'   CFul GAbr

§ 'The Bride' ♀   More than 30 suppliers
'Tigrinum Plenum' (d)   ESis EWes LBee LRHS MDHE
NPro WWin
'Tomato Red'   ECha NSla SMrm
tomentosum   See *H. nummularium*
umbellatum   See *Halimium umbellatum*
'Venustum Plenum' (d)   CInt MBro WEas
'Voltaire'   CFul EMNN GAbr MDHE MOne
NPri SWal WWin
'Watergate Rose'   MWat NBir NCat
'Welsh Flame'   WAbe
'White Queen'   Last listed 1997
'Windermere'   Last listed 1999
¶ 'Windmill Gold'   CPri
'Wisley Pink'   See *H.* 'Rhodanthe Carneum'
'Wisley Primrose' ♀   More than 30 suppliers
'Wisley White'   CFul CPri CSam CTri ECha EGoo
EWTr GAbr MBro WHoo WPyg
'Wisley Yellow'   EDAr GKir
'Yellow Queen'   See *H.* 'Golden Queen'

HELIANTHUS ✿ (Asteraceae)

angustifolius   Last listed 1998
atrorubens   LFis LRHS MBel MBri MRav WFar
'Capenoch Star' ♀   CElw CStr EBee EFou EMan GBuc
LFis LRHS MArl MBel MCAu MFir
MLLN MRav NDov SDix SMad
WByw WCot WFar WLRN
¶ 'Capenoch Supreme'   EBrP EBre LBCl LBSe LBre MBBe
SBre
cusickii   EBee
decapetalus   CStr LFis NFla WCot WWye
*   - 'Kastle Kobena'   Last listed 1997
- 'Maximus'   SRms
- 'Morning Sun'   CBlo CTri MLLN WCot
- 'Soleil d'Or'   CTri ECtt WCot
- 'Triomphe de Gand'   CBos CStr GBri LGre LRHS MRav
MTed MWat SAga SSvw WFar
divaricatus   EBee
x *doronicoides*   CFee SRms
'First Light'   Last listed 1997
giganteus 'Sheila's   CBre CElw CStr GBri WCot
Sunshine'
'Golden Pyramid'   Last listed 1997
grosseserratus   LGre
'Gullick's Variety'   CBre CStr EBee EFou EPfP IBlr
LFis LLWP NBro NPSI NSti STes
WCot
x *kellermanii*   CStr EMon LGre MTed SAga SMad
§ x *laetiflorus*   EBee ELan EMan EMon NChi
NOrc WCot
- var. *rigidus*   See *H. pauciflorus*
*   - 'Superbus'   IBlr NPSI
§ 'Lemon Queen'   More than 30 suppliers
'Limelight'   See *H.* 'Lemon Queen'
§ 'Loddon Gold' ♀   CBlo EBee EBrP EBre ECtt EFou
ELan EMan EPfP IBlr LBCl LBSe
LBre LFis LRHS MBBe MChl MRav
MTis NVic SAga SBre SLon WCot
WMoo WWye
§ *maximiliani*   EBee ECGN LRHS MAnH MSte
¶ *microcephalus*   NPSI
mollis   EBee WCot
'Monarch' ♀   CStr LFis MFir SDix SMad SVal
WCot WOve
nuttallii   EMon MTed WCot
occidentalis   EMon IBlr LRHS WPer
orgyalis   See *H. salicifolius*
§ *pauciflorus*   EMon
quinquenervis   See *Helianthella quinquenervis*
rigidus hort.   See *H.* x *laetiflorus*
-     See *H. pauciflorus*

§ **salicifolius** — CRDP CStr ECGN ECha EMan EMon LFis LGre LRHS MAnH MBri MLLN MSte MWat NSti SDix SMad SSpe WCot WHil WWye
scaberrimus — See *H.* x *laetiflorus*
- C&D 137 — WCot
strumosus — IIve WCot
'Summer Gold' — Last listed 1997
tuberosus — GPoy NRog
- 'Dwarf Sunray' — IIve
- 'Fuseau' — CAvo IIve LEdu

HELICHRYSUM ✿ (Asteraceae)

alveolatum — See *H. splendidum*
ambiguum — EFou MRav NOak
angustifolium — See *H. italicum*
- Cretan form — See *H. microphyllum* (Willd.) Cambess.
arenarium — MWll SSmi
§ **argyrophyllum** — Last listed 1997
§ **arwae** — EPot SBla WAbe
asperum — See *Ozothamnus purpurascens*
basalticum — CStu
bellidioides — ECha GGar IMGH LRHS NMen SMer WCru WPer
bellum — CStu NHol
chionophilum — NWCA
'Coco' — See *Bracteantha* 'Coco'
confertum — Last listed 1998
cooperi — Last listed 1999
coralloides — See *Ozothamnus coralloides*
'County Park Silver' — See *Ozothamnus* 'County Park Silver'
dasyanthum — Last listed 1999
doerfleri — NMen
'Elmstead' — See *H. stoechas* 'White Barn'
ericifolium — See *Ozothamnus purpurascens*
ericoides — See *Dolichothrix ericoides*
fontanesii — LHil SPer WHer
frigidum — CPBP EPot GNor LRHS NNrd NWCA SBla SMrm WAbe
gmelinii — Last listed 1999
heldreichii — CGra EPot NHol SMrm
- NS 127 — NWCA
hookeri — See *Ozothamnus hookeri*
hypoleucum — Last listed 1999
§ **italicum** ♀ — CArn ECha ELau GCHN GPoy LGro LRHS MBar MBri MHer MMal NBid NChi SMac SPar SPer SRCN SRms WCer WDin WEas WHCG WOak WOve WWat WWye
- 'Dartington' — CBod WJek WSel
- subsp. **microphyllum** — See *H. microphyllum* (Willd.) Cambess.
- 'Nanum' — See *H. microphyllum* (Willd.) Cambess.
§ - subsp. **serotinum** — CBrm CChe CTri EBee EGoo EPfP GPoy MAsh MRav NFla SLim SMer SPer SPla SRms STre WPer WSel WWeb
lanatum — See *H. thianschanicum*
ledifolium — See *Ozothamnus ledifolius*
lingulatum JJ&JH 9401733 — Last listed 1999
lobbii — Last listed 1998
marginatum hort. — See *H. milfordiae*
¶ - DC. JJ&JH 9401733 — NWCA
§ **microphyllum** (Willd.) Cambess. — CSam ELau GBar NPri NWoo SIde WSel WTro WWye
§ - hort. — See *Plecostachys serpyllifolia*
§ - Benth. & Hooker — See *Ozothamnus microphyllus*
§ **milfordiae** ♀ — EDAr EPot NHar NHol NMen

NNrd NSla NWCA SBla SIng SRms WAbe WPat
¶ **montanum** — NWCA
'Mo's Gold' — See *H. argyrophyllum*
orientale — EPot NHol SMer WAbe
pagophilum — CPBP GCrs ITim
- JJ&JH 9401304 — NWCA
- JJH from Lesotho — Last listed 1998
'Pale Skynet' — GCal
§ **petiolare** ♀ — EBak ECtt EWTr LPVe MRav
- 'Aureum' — See *H. petiolare* 'Limelight'
- 'Goring Silver' — CHal LHil NPri
§ - 'Limelight' ♀ — CHal ECtt MRav SLod
- 'Roundabout' (v) — GPin LHil NPri
- 'Variegatum' ♀ — CHal ECtt MRav
petiolatum — See *H. petiolare*
plicatum — MBNS MWhi NWCA
plumeum — ITim
populifolium — WHer
praecurrens — ITim NWCA
aff. **praecurrens** — Last listed 1997
purpurascens — See *Ozothamnus purpurascens*
rosmarinifolium — See *Ozothamnus rosmarinifolius*
§ 'Schwefellicht' — CSam EBee ECha EFou EGle LRHS MBri MCLN MRav MWgw NFla SChu SMer SPer SRPl SWat WEas WSHC WWal WWat
scorpioides — Last listed 1998
selago — See *Ozothamnus selago*
¶ - var. **tumidum** — NSla
serotinum — See *H. italicum* subsp. *serotinum*
serpyllifolium — See *Plecostachys serpyllifolia*
sessile — See *H. sessilioides*
§ **sessilioides** — EPot ITim NHar NNrd NSla NTow NWCA
§ **sibthorpii** — CSev LHil LRHS NMen NTow NWCA SSmi WAbe
'Silver Bush' — Last listed 1998
* 'Skynet' — GCal GMac
sp. from Drakensburg Mountains, South Africa — GAbr NHol NWCA
sp. H&W 336 — Last listed 1998
§ **splendidum** ♀ — CFee CSam ECha EHoe EPfP GAbr GCHN LHil NBro NFor SDix SLon SPer WBrE WDin WHer WPer WWat
stoechas — CArn
§ - 'White Barn' — ECha LPio WEas
Sulphur Light — See *H.* 'Schwefellicht'
'Sussex Silver' — NPro
§ **thianschanicum** — EMan ENot NWCA SRms
- Golden Baby — See *H. thianschanicum* 'Goldkind'
§ - 'Goldkind' — EPfP GKir LFis NBir NPri WMoo
thyrsoideum — See *Ozothamnus thyrsoideus*
trilineatum — See *H. splendidum*
aff. **trilineatum** JJ&JH 9401783 — NWCA
tumidum — See *Ozothamnus selago* var. *tumidus*
virgineum — See *H. sibthorpii*
woodii — See *H. arwae*

HELICHRYSUM x RAOULIA (Asteraceae)
H. sp. x *R.* 'Rivulet' — Last listed 1997
H. sp. x *R.* 'Silver Streams' — Last listed 1997

HELICODICEROS (Araceae)
muscivorus — WCot

HELICONIA (Heliconiaceae)

bibai	LChe WMul
¶ *bourgaeana*	LPal
§ 'Bucky'	WMul
¶ 'Golden Torch'	LChe
guyana	See *H.* 'Bucky'
'Guyana Red'	See *H.* 'Bucky'
¶ *lingulata* 'Fan'	LPal
¶ *orthotrica* 'She'	WMul
* - 'Total Eclipse'	WMul
psittacorum	LChe
rostrata	LBlo LChe LPal WMul
- dwarf	WMul
¶ *strica* 'Cooper's Sharonii'	WMul
stricta 'Dwarf Jamaican'	LChe WMul

HELICTOTRICHON (Poaceae)

filifolium	Last listed 1997
pratense	EHoe EMon EPPr LRHS
§ *sempervirens* ♀	More than 30 suppliers
- 'Berlin Oxblood'	Last listed 1998
- var. *pendulum*	EMon EPPr LRHS SPla
¶ - 'Saphirsprudel'	EMon EPPr
* *splendens*	SSoC

HELIOPHILA (Brassicaceae)

carnosa	Last listed 1998
longifolia	Last listed 1997

HELIOPSIS ✿ (Asteraceae)

Golden Plume	See *H. helianthoides* var. *scabra* 'Goldgefieder'
helianthoides	CStr EMon EWTr
- 'Benzinggold'	EFou MRav SMrm
- 'Hohlspiegel'	EBee EBrP EBre ECha EMan LBCl LBSe LBre MBBe MBri SBre WLRN
- 'Limelight'	See *Helianthus* 'Lemon Queen'
- var. *scabra*	CBlo EPfP EWTr
- - Ballerina	See *H. helianthoides* var. *scabra* 'Spitzentänzerin'
- - Golden Plume	See *H. helianthoides* var. *scabra* 'Goldgefieder'
§ - - 'Goldgefieder' ♀	EMan EPfP LRHS MBel WBea WRus
- - 'Goldgrünherz'	EBrP EBre LBCl LBSe LBre LRHS MBBe MBri SBre WCot
- - 'Goldspitze'	EBee
- - 'Incomparabilis'	MWgw
- - 'Light of Loddon'	MWat SVal
- - New hybrids	NLar SSvw
§ - - 'Sommersonne'	CHar CM&M EBee EBrP EBre ECGN ECtt EFou EMan GMaP LBCl LBSe LBre MBBe MRav NArg NFai NMir NPer SBre SPer SRCN SRms WFar WPer WWin
§ - - 'Spitzentänzerin'	LRHS MBri
- - Summer Sun	See *H. helianthoides* var. *scabra* 'Sommersonne'
- - 'Sunburst'	WPyg
- 'Sonnenglut'	LRHS MBri
¶ Loraine Sunshine = 'Helhan' (v)	EBrP EBre EFou LBCl LBSe LBre LRHS MBBe SBre WCot

HELIOTROPIUM ✿ (Boraginaceae)

§ *amplexicaule*	EBee SMrm SSad
anchusifolium	See *H. amplexicaule*
§ *arborescens*	CArn EPfP SYvo
* - 'Album'	LChe
¶ - 'The Queen'	ERea
'Chatsworth' ♀	CHad CPle CSev EHol EMan ERea LHil MSte SGar SIde SSad SUsu WEas WPen
'Dame Alice de Hales'	ERea
'Gatton Park'	ERea LHil LRHS MRav SMrm SSad
'Lord Roberts'	ERea SYvo
* 'Marine'	CGdn CSpe LIck SRCN
* 'Midnight'	Last listed 1997
'Mrs J.W. Lowther'	Last listed 1997
'Netherhall White'	ERea
'P.K. Lowther'	ERea WEas
peruvianum	See *H. arborescens*
'President Garfield'	LHil SMrm
'Princess Marina' ♀	CSev EMan ERea LHil LRHS MSte SSad WEas WWol
'The Speaker'	Last listed 1999
'W.H. Lowther'	LChe SYvo
'White Lady'	CHal CSev CSpe EHol ERea LHil SSad WSpi WWol
'White Queen'	LHil

HELIPTERUM (Asteraceae)

albicans	See *Leucochrysum albicans*
anthemoides	See *Rhodanthe anthemoides*

HELLEBORUS ✿ (Ranunculaceae)

§ *argutifolius* ♀	More than 30 suppliers
- from Italy	EHrv
- mottled-leaved	See *H. argutifolius* 'Pacific Frost'
§ - 'Pacific Frost' (v)	CAvo CBos CHar CPla ECha EMon MAsh NRar WCot WHal
¶ - 'Silver Lace'	CRDP
- x *sternii*	GKir
atrorubens Waldst. & Kit.	CBel CLCN ECha WAbe WStI
- WM 9028 from Slovenia	Last listed 1997
- WM 9101 from Slovenia	Last listed 1997
- WM 9216 from Slovenia	MPhe WCru
- WM 9317	MPhe
- WM 9319 from Slovenia	MPhe
- WM 9407	Last listed 1999
- WM 9617 from Slovenia	MPhe
- WM 9805 from Croatia	MPhe
x *ballardiae*	EOrc GKir LRHS MAsh MPhe WAbe WFar
- Anne Watson's strain	NRar
bocconei subsp. *bocconei*	See *H. multifidus* subsp. *bocconei*
colchicus	See *H. orientalis* Lamarck subsp. *abchasicus*
corsicus	See *H. argutifolius*
croaticus	CBel CLCN MAsh
- WM 9313	MPhe
- WM 9416	MPhe
- WM 9810 from Croatia	MPhe
cyclophyllus	EBee EPfP GBuc GKir LRHS MAsh MPhe NHol SPer SSpi WFar WPGP
- JCA 560.625	CLCN SSpi
* - WM 9412	Last listed 1998
dumetorum	CAvo CBel CLCN MAsh NHol WFar WLin WPGP
- WM 13.3	Last listed 1999
- WM 9025 from Croatia	MPhe
- WM 9209 from Hungary	MPhe
- WM 9301 from Slovenia	MPhe
- WM 9307 from Hungary	Last listed 1997
- WM 9413	WCru
- WM 9627 from Croatia	MPhe
§ x *ericsmithii*	CRDP EHrv GKir LRHS MAsh MBri NDov SBla WAbe WFar
foetidus ♀	More than 30 suppliers
- Bowles' form	CBro
- 'Chedglow'	CNat
* - 'Curio' (v)	CNat
- 'Geddington Mist'	MGed
- 'Green Giant'	CBel CSam MAsh MTho WCru
- Italian form	GBin MAsh NTow WCot WRus

- Kurt's Strain	Last listed 1998	
- 'Miss Jekyll's Scented'	Last listed 1999	
- 'Ruth'	CBel MAsh MPhe	
- scented	WFar	
- 'Sopron'	GBin MAsh MPhe WCru WFar WViv	
- Wester Flisk Group	More than 30 suppliers	
lividus ♀	CAvo CBot CBro CGle CLCN EBee EBrP EBre ELan EWes LBCl LBSe LBre LRHS MAsh MBBe MPhe NHar NHol NLar NPSI SBla SBre SWat WAbe WCru WFar	
- subsp. *corsicus*	See *H. argutifolius*	
multifidus	CLCN EBee EMar EPfP NBir NHol SPer WFar	
§ - subsp. *bocconei*	NDov WFar WPGP	
- - WM 9713 from Italy	MPhe	
- - WM 9719 from Italy	MPhe	
- - WM 9720 from Italy	MPhe	
- subsp. *hercegovinus*	CBel WFar	
- - WM 9105	MPhe	
- subsp. *istriacus*	CBro MAsh WFar	
- - WM 9222	Last listed 1997	
- - WM 9322	MPhe	
- - WM 9324	MPhe	
- - WM 9421	Last listed 1999	
- subsp. *multifidus*	MAsh	
- - WM 9104	MPhe	
- - WM 9529	MPhe	
- - WM 9748 from Croatia	MPhe	
- - WM 9833 from Croatia	MPhe	
- - WM 9225	WCru	
niger ♀	More than 30 suppliers	
- Ashwood strain	GKir MAsh	
- Blackthorn Group	EHrv GKir NCut SBla	
I - 'Crûg Hybrid'	WCru	
- Farmyard strain	WFar	
- from Austria	WByw	
- Harvington hybrids	COtt EHrv GKir LRHS MAsh	
- 'Louis Cobbett'	Last listed 1999	
§ - subsp. *macranthus*	WCot	
- - WM 9030	WCru	
- 'Madame Fourcade'	GKir	
- *major*	See *H. niger* subsp. *macranthus*	
- pink strain	Last listed 1999	
- 'Potter's Wheel'	CPMA CRDP EBee EBrP EBre ECot GBuc GKir LBCl LBSe LBre LRHS MBBe NPSI SBla SBre SRms SVil WCru WPyg	
- 'Saint Bridgid'	Last listed 1999	
- Sunrise Group WM 9519	CLCN MPhe	
- Sunset Group WM 9113	GBuc MPhe SPla	
- 'White Magic'	CB&S CBlo CPMA LRHS NDov WCru WWeb	
× *nigercors* ♀	CRDP EBrP EBre GKir LBCl LBSe LBre LPio LRHS MBBe MBri SBre WAbe WCru	
- 'Alabaster'	NBir	
× *nigristern*	See *H.* × *ericsmithii*	
odorus	CBel CLCN EBee EHrv NDov SBla SPer WCot WFar	
- subsp. *laxus*	CAvo	
- WM 9088 from Hungary	MPhe	
- WM 9103	Last listed 1998	
- WM 9202	MPhe WCru	
- WM 9310	GBuc	
- WM 9415	MPhe	
- WM 9728 from Hungary	MPhe	
N *orientalis* hort.	More than 30 suppliers	
¶ - double (d)	LCTD WFar	
¶ - anemone-centred	LCTD WFar	
- 'Agnes Brook'	WFib	

- 'Albin Otto'	GKir	
- Anderson's Red hybrids	CLCN	
- 'Angela Tandy'	WFib	
- 'Apple Blossom'	EBrP EBre LBCl LBSe LBre MBBe SBre WFar	
- 'Apricot'	LCTD WFar	
¶ - apricot 1	NRar	
¶ - apricot 2	NRar	
- Aquarius	CLCN	
- 'Ariel'	LCTD	
- Ashwood Garden hybrids	CCHP EHrv LRHS MAsh MBlu MRav SCoo WBod WSpi	
- Ashwood Garden hybrids, anemone-centred	MAsh	
- Ashwood Garden hybrids, double	MAsh	
- - 'Baby Black'	ECot	
- Ballard's Group	CFri EBrP EBre GKir LBCl LBSe LBre LRHS MBBe MBlu MBri NRar SBre SMad WCot WCru WFar	
- black	CBel CGle CLCN CRDP EPPr GBuc GDra NRar WCru WFar	
- blue-grey	GKir NPar WCot	
- 'Blue Wisp'	LCTD	
- 'Button'	LCTD	
- 'Carlton Hall'	WFib	
- 'Chartreuse'	Last listed 1997	
- 'Cheerful'	GKir LCTD NBir WCru	
- 'Citron'	LCTD	
- 'Compact Cream'	Last listed 1999	
- cream	CFri MCCP NHol NPSI WFar	
- 'Cygnus'	ECha	
- 'Dawn'	LCTD	
- deep red	ERav GKir WFar	
- 'Dick Crandon'	Last listed 1998	
- Draco strain	CLCN	
- 'Dusk'	LCTD WCru	
- 'Elizabeth Coburn'	WFib	
- 'Eric's Best'	ECha	
- 'Fred Whitsey'	WFib	
- Galaxy Group	NPar	
- 'Garnet'	LCTD WFar	
- 'Gertrude Raithby'	WFib	
- 'Gladys Burrow'	WFib	
- green	SAga WCru	
- green, spotted	CBel CRDP EBrP EBre LBCl LBSe LBre MBBe SBre WCru WFar	
- 'Greencups'	LCTD	
¶ - 'Günther Jürgl' (d)	LCTD	
- subsp. *guttatus*	CAvo CFri CLCN EBrP EBre GKir LBCl LBSe LBre LRHS MBBe MCCP NHol SAga SApp SBla SBre SMad WCot WCru	
- - cream	ECha	
- - light purple	Last listed 1997	
- - pink	NHol WCru	
- 'Hades' seedling	WCru	
- Hadspen hybrids	CHad	
- 'Harvington Pink'	GKir LRHS	
- 'Harvington Red'	GKir LRHS	
- 'Harvington Speckled'	GKir LRHS	
- 'Harvington White'	GKir LRHS MNaF	
- 'Harvington Yellow'	GKir LRHS	
- 'Helen Ballard'	LCTD	
¶ - Homelea hybrids, anemone-centred	CRDP	
¶ - Homelea hybrids, double (d)	CRDP	
- 'Ian Raithby'	WFib	
- 'Ingot'	LCTD	
- ivory	CLCN CRDP WFar	

- - WM 9723 from Italy   MPhe
¶ 'Winter Joy Bouquet'   EBrP EBre LBCl LBSe LBre MBBe
SBre

HELONIOPSIS (Melanthiaceae)
acutifolia B&SWJ 218   WCru
japonica   See *H. orientalis*
§ **orientalis**   CBro GBuc LRHS SIng SOkd
WCru
* - var. **albiflora**   Last listed 1999
- B&SWJ 956 from Korea   WCru
§ - var. **breviscapa**   CFil WCru WPGP
§ - var. **kawanoi**   CMea WCru
- var. **yakusimensis**   See *H. orientalis* var. *kawanoi*
umbellata B&SWJ 1839   WCru

HELWINGIA (Helwingiaceae)
chinensis   CPle WWat
japonica   CBot CPle EFEx WWat

HELXINE See SOLEIROLIA

HEMEROCALLIS ✿ (Hemerocallidaceae)
'Absolute Zero'   SApp SDay
'Adah'   SDay
'Addie Branch Smith'   EGol SDay
'Adoration'   SPer
'Aglow'   MTed
'Alan'   EBrP EBre LBCl LBSe LBre LRHS
MBBe SBre SCro WFar
'Albany'   Last listed 1999
'Alec Allen'   SDay SRos
'Alpine Mist'   SDay
altissima   EMon SDix
'Always Afternoon'   SApp
'Amadeus'   Last listed 1997
'Amazon'   LRHS
'Amazon Amethyst'   MCAu
'Ambassador'   Last listed 1998
'Amber Star'   LPBA
'Amen'   Last listed 1999
'American Revolution'   CPar LCaP MBNS SApp SDay SRos
'Amersham'   EGle GSki MNFA SMrm WLRN
¶ 'Angel Artistry'   SDay
'Angel Curls'   EGol
'Angel's Delight'   Last listed 1999
'Ann Kelley'   Last listed 1999
'Anna Warner'   SPer
'Annie Golightly'   Last listed 1998
¶ 'Annie Welch'   EBee ECGP ECle EPla MMil
¶ 'Antique Rose'   SDay
'Anzac'   EBrP EBre ECha ECtt EPla ERou
GAri GKir GMac LBCl LBSe LBre
LRHS MBBe MBri MNFA NHol
NMGW SAga SBre WFar
'Apple Court Champagne'   Last listed 1999
'Apple Court Damson'   CAbx
'Apple Tart'   Last listed 1999
'Apricot Angel'   Last listed 1999
'Apricot Beauty'   CBlo EBee LBuc NPri
'Apricot Surprise'   Last listed 1999
'Apricotta'   WBro WCot WPnP
'Arctic Snow'   SRos
'Arriba'   MNFA NBro WLRN
'Arthur Moore'   SDay
'Artistic Gold'   EGol
'Artist's Brush'   LBuc
'Aten'   CBlo MNFA SDay WAul
'Atlanta Bouquet'   SRos
'Atlanta Full House'   SDay
'Attention Please'   Last listed 1999
'Aurora Raspberry'   Last listed 1999

'Autumn Red'   CBlo EBee ERou NBir NCat NFai
NHaw NOak
'Ava Michelle'   SDay
'Aztec Furnace'   Last listed 1997
'Baby Betsy'   SDay
'Baby Darling'   SDay
'Baby Julia'   MTed
'Baby Talk'   CFir LRHS SVil
* 'Bailey Hay'   COIW LCaP LRHS MBNS
¶ 'Baja'   MNFA
'Bald Eagle'   EFou EGle
'Ballerina Girl'   SRos
'Ballet Dancer'   ERou
'Bangkok Belle'   Last listed 1999
'Barbara Mitchell'   SApp
'Baroni'   ECha
¶ 'Beat the Barons'   SRos
'Beauty Bright'   Last listed 1999
'Beauty to Behold'   SApp SDay SRos
'Bed of Roses'   MNFA
'Bedarra Island'   SDay
'Beijing'   Last listed 1999
'Bejewelled'   CBlo EBee EGol NMoo
'Beloved Country'   Last listed 1999
'Beloved Returns' ♀   MCAu
'Benchmark'   SRos
'Berlin Lemon' ♀   Last listed 1995
'Berlin Red' ♀   EBee ECGN EGle EMar EPla LBuc
LRHS MMil MNFA SChu
'Berlin Red Velvet' ♀   Last listed 1995
¶ 'Berlin Yellow'   EFou
'Berliner Premiere'   Last listed 1998
'Bernard Thompson'   SApp
'Bertie Ferris'   LBuc
'Bess Ross'   CMHG MCAu
'Bess Vestale'   ENot ERou MNFA MWat NHol
'Bette Davis Eyes'   SRos
'Betty Woods' (d)   CRDP SDay SRos
'Bibury'   SCro
'Big Bird'   EFou
'Big World'   LRHS MNFA
'Bitsy'   EBee EGle EGol MSte MTed WAul
¶ 'Black Eyed Stella'   LPan
I 'Black Eyed Susan'   MBNS
'Black Falcon'   Last listed 1999
'Black Knight'   SRms
'Black Magic'   CBlo CBro CHad CMGP CSev
EBee EGol ELan EPla ERou GMaP
LRHS MBro MNFA MRav NGdn
NHol SChu SPer WHer WMoo
WPnP
'Black Prince'   EWll SPer WAul WRus WViv
¶ 'Blessed Again'   SDay
¶ 'Blessing'   SRos
'Blonde Is Beautiful'   SRos
'Blue Sheen'   CFir CPou EFou EGle EGol LAst
LPan LRHS MBNS WMoo WWeb
'Blushing Angel'   Last listed 1997
'Blushing Belle'   CMil EBee EMar LRHS MBNS
MNFA WWin
'Bold Courtier'   Last listed 1998
'Bold One'   SRos
'Bonanza'   More than 30 suppliers
'Booger'   SRos
¶ 'Border Baby'   LFis
'Border Honey'   Last listed 1999
'Boulderbrook Serenity'   SDay
'Bourbon Kings'   EBee EGar EGol ERou MBel SDay
'Bowl of Roses'   MCAu
'Brand New Lover'   SApp
§ 'Brass Buckles'   CM&M EGol NHol SDay
¶ 'Bridget'   ELan

'Bright Spangles'   SApp SRos
'Brilliant Circle'   EFou SApp
'Brocaded Gown'   SRos
'Brunette'   SAga SApp
'Bruno Müller'   Last listed 1997
'Bubbly'   SDay
'Buffy's Doll'   SApp SDay SRos
'Bugs Ears'   Last listed 1998
'Bumble Bee'   LPan MBri WTin
'Buried Treasure'   LRHS MNFA
'Burlesque'   Last listed 1997
'Burning Daylight' ♀   CBos CMGP EBee EBrP EBre EGar
                          EMar EPla ERou GSki LBCl LBSe
                          LBre LRHS MBBe MBel MNFA
                          MNrw NHol NVic SBre SCob
                          SMrm SPer SRms WFar WViv
'Buttercurls'   WAul
'Butterfly Ballet'   SDay
'Butterfly Charm'   Last listed 1997
'Butterscotch Ruffles'   Last listed 1999
'Buttons'   Last listed 1997
'Buzz Bomb'   CRDP EBee EBrP EBre EGle GSki
                          LBCl LBSe LBre LRHS MBBe
                          MCAu MNFA SBre SPer SRos
                          WLRN WWal
'California Sunshine'   SRos
'Camden Gold Dollar'   SDay
¶ 'Cameroons'   SDay
'Canadian Goose'   EFou
'Canary Glow'   CTri EBrP EBre ERav LBCl LBSe
                          LBre MBBe SBre SRos SSpe WFar
'Candide'   SApp
'Cantique'   SApp
¶ 'Captive Audience'   SRos
'Caramea'   LAst NFai WFar WWal
'Carolipiecrust'   SApp
'Cartwheels' ♀   EBee EBrP EBre ECha EGra EMar
                          EPfP EPla LBCl LBSe LBre LRHS
                          MBBe MBel MCAu MCli MMil
                          MNFA SBre SPer WFar WMoo
'Casino Gold'   SRos
'Catherine Woodbery'   More than 30 suppliers
'Cedar Waxwing'   CBlo EBee EGol SCro
'Chantilly Lace'   CMHG
¶ 'Charbonier'   MNFA
'Charles Johnston'   SDay SRos
'Charlie Brown'   SDay
'Charlie Pierce Memorial' MBel SDay SRos
'Chartreuse Magic'   EGol SChu SPer
'Cherry Cheeks'   EBrP EBre EGol ELan EPfP ERav
                          ERou GKir LBCl LBSe LBre LRHS
                          MBBe MBNS MBri MCAu MRav
                          SBre SLod SRos SVil WCot WFar
'Cherry Kiss'   SRos
'Cherry Smoke'   SApp
'Chestnut Lane'   SDay
'Chic Bonnet'   SPer
'Chicago Apache'   COtt EGle EPfP LPan LRHS MBNS
                          MBel NCut SDay SRos SVil
'Chicago Arnie's Choice'   Last listed 1999
'Chicago Blackout'   CFir COtt EBee EFou EGol EPfP
                          SApp
'Chicago Cattleya'   CFir CPou EFou EGol MRav NCut
'Chicago Cherry'   NCut
'Chicago Coral'   Last listed 1999
'Chicago Fire'   EGol MBNS NCut
'Chicago Heirloom'   COtt EGol MCAu NCut SVil
'Chicago Jewel'   CFir EBee EGle SCro
'Chicago Knobby'   LPan
'Chicago Knockout'   CFir COtt EFou EGle EGol NCut
                          NPSI
'Chicago Peach'   EFou NCut

'Chicago Petite Lace'   Last listed 1999
'Chicago Petticoats'   EGol LRHS NCut
'Chicago Picotee Lace'   EGle EPfP GKir NCut SApp
'Chicago Picotee Memories' Last listed 1999
'Chicago Picotee Pride'   Last listed 1999
'Chicago Picotee Queen'   EBrP EBre LBCl LBSe LBre LRHS
                          MBBe MNFA SBre
'Chicago Plum Pudding'   Last listed 1999
'Chicago Princess'   EFou EGle EGol NCut
'Chicago Queen'   Last listed 1999
¶ 'Chicago Rainbow'   CFri NCut
'Chicago Rosy'   EFou EGol NCut
'Chicago Royal'   SDay
'Chicago Royal Crown'   LRHS MBri
'Chicago Royal Robe'   EBrP EBre EFou EGol GKir LBCl
                          LBSe LBre LLWP MBBe MBNS
                          MBel MNFA MRav MSte NBid
                          SBre SCro SPer WCot WWhi
                          WWin
'Chicago Silver'   CFir COtt EGle MCAu NCut
'Chicago Sugar Plum'   SDay
'Chicago Sunrise'   CHad EGol ENot EPla GMaP IBlr
                          LRHS MBNS MBri MChl MNFA
                          MSta NCut NHaw NHol NMoo
                          NOrc SApp SRos SVil WPer
'Chicago Violet'   MCAu
'Chief Sarcoxie' ♀   MCAu
'Children's Festival'   More than 30 suppliers
'Childscraft'   CLTr
'Chinese Autumn'   SRos
'Chinese Coral'   CKel WBcn
'Chinese Imp'   Last listed 1997
'Chloe's Child'   SCro
'Chocolate Dude'   Last listed 1999
'Choral Angel'   Last listed 1999
'Chorus Line'   MBel SDay SRos
'Chosen Love'   Last listed 1999
'Christmas Candles'   Last listed 1997
'Christmas Is'   EFou MBNS SApp
¶ 'Churchill Downs'   MNFA
'Ciao'   SApp
'Cinnamon Glow'   Last listed 1999
citrina   ELan EMon EWTr LRHS NGiC
                          SEas
'Civil Rights'   SRos
'Classic Simplicity'   LRHS
'Classy Lassie'   MTed
¶ 'Cleopatra'   SDay
'Colonial Dame'   CKel
'Colour Me Mellow'   Last listed 1998
'Comanche Eyes'   SDay
'Coming up Roses'   SRos
'Conspicua'   Last listed 1997
'Contessa'   CBro EHon SCro
'Cookie Monster'   LRHS
'Cool Jazz'   SRos
'Coral Mist'   EFou
'Coreana Yellow'   Last listed 1997
'Corky' ♀   More than 30 suppliers
'Corryton Pink'   SApp
'Corsican Bandit'   CM&M
'Cosmic Hummingbird'   SDay
'Countess Zora'   CMHG
'Country Club'   CBlo EBee EFou EGle LAst WWeb
'Court Magician'   SDay SRos
'Cranberry Baby'   EGle SRos
¶ 'Crazy Pierre'   CAbx
'Cream Cloud'   Last listed 1999
'Cream Drop'   CMGP EBee EBrP EBre ECtt EFou
                          EGle EGol EMar GMaP LBCl LBSe
                          LBre LRHS MBBe MBel MRav
                          MTis MWat NGiC NOrc NSti SBre

SChu SPer SSpe WCot WCra
WMoo WRus

'Crimson Icon'	MSte SDay
'Crimson Pirate'	EMil ERou GKir LRHS LRot MBNS MHer MNFA NBir NHol SPlb SRob
'Croesus'	NHol SCro SRms
'Croftway'	SCro
'Cupid's Bow'	EGol
'Cupid's Gold'	SDay SRos
'Custard Candy'	SRos
'Cynthia Mary'	EGle
'Dad's Best White'	EGol SCro
'Daily Bread'	Last listed 1998
'Daily Dollar'	GKir LRHS MBri
'Dainty Pink'	EGol
'Daisy MacCarthy'	LRHS
'Dallas Star'	Last listed 1999
'Dance Ballerina Dance'	SDay SRos
'Dancing Dwarf'	SDay
¶ 'Dancing Shiva'	SApp
'Dark Elf'	SDay
'Dawn Play'	CKel
'Decatur Imp'	EGol
'Decatur Piecrust'	MBel
'Delightsome'	SRos
'Demetrius'	MNFA SApp
'Designer Gown'	Last listed 1998
'Devon Cream'	SChu
'Devonshire'	SDay SRos
'Diamond Dust'	EBee EGle EMar EPla LRHS MBNS MTed NCat SChu SPer WLRN
'Dido'	CTri ERou GBuc MSte
'Display'	CKel
'Divertissment'	CAbx SApp
'Dominic'	SRos
'Dorethe Louise'	CRDP SDay SRos
'Dorothy McDade'	COlW EGol
'Double Coffee' (d)	Last listed 1998
'Double Cutie' (d)	EFou MBNS SDay
'Double Daffodil' (d)	Last listed 1999
'Double Delicious' (d)	WCot
'Double Firecracker' (d)	CB&S LRHS MBNS NLar
'Double Gardenia' (d)	Last listed 1999
'Double Honey' (d)	Last listed 1999
'Double Oh' (d)	MTed
'Double Oh Seven' (d)	SDay
'Double Pleasure' (d)	MBel
'Double Pompom' (d)	MCAu
'Double River Wye' (d)	CBlo CFir CFwr EGol LBuc LPan MChl MTed NCiC WCot WElm WHoo WWat WWye
¶ 'Dragon King'	SApp
'Dragon's Eye'	Last listed 1999
'Dresden Doll'	SPer
§ 'Dubloon'	CKel CMGP COlW ERou GAbr GBuc NHol SMer
dumortieri	More than 30 suppliers
'Dutch Beauty'	LRHS
'Dutch Gold'	MNrw NBro
'Ed Murray'	MCAu SRos
'Edelweiss'	EWTr SDay
'Edna Spalding'	SDay SRos
'Eenie Allegro'	CBro EGle EGol MBNS SPer SPla
'Eenie Fanfare'	COtt CSpe EFou EGle LRHS MNFA WCra
'Eenie Gold'	LRHS
'Eenie Weenie'	CBro CFee CKel ECtt EGle EGol EMil ERos GKir LRHS MBel MBri NBur SApp SChu SPer SRms WPer WWye
'Eenie Weenie Non-stop'	ECha SLod
¶ 'Egyptian Ibis'	MBNS
'Elaine Strutt'	MBNS SApp SDay WCot
'Elegant Greeting'	EBee LBuc MBNS NOak
'Elizabeth Ann Hudson'	Last listed 1997
'Elizabeth Salter'	SRos
'Emerald Dew'	SDay
¶ 'Emperor Butterfly'	SApp
¶ 'Enchanter's Spell'	SDay
'English Toffee'	SApp
'Entransette'	Last listed 1999
'Erica Nichole Gonzales'	Last listed 1997
'Erin Prairie'	SApp
'Esther Walker'	WBcn
'Evelyn Claar'	SCro
'Evening Gown'	Last listed 1999
'Fairy Charm'	Last listed 1999
'Fairy Frosting'	Last listed 1997
'Fairy Tale Pink'	MBel SDay SRos
'Faith Nabor'	SRos
'Fan Dancer'	EGol
'Fandango'	SPer
'Fashion Model'	SApp WPer
'Feather Down'	Last listed 1997
'Felicity'	CKel
'Femme Osage'	SRos
'Finlandia'	MNFA
'Fire Dance'	SCro
'First Formal'	SPer
'Flamboyant Show'	LBuc
'Flames of Fantasy'	MTed NCut SRos
'Flaming Sword'	CMGP GBuc LRHS NBlu NHol
flava	See *H. lilioasphodelus*
'Florissant Charm'	Last listed 1999
'Floyd Cove'	Last listed 1999
¶ 'Fly Catcher'	SRos
forrestii 'Perry's Variety'	EMon
¶ 'Forsyth Lemon Drop'	SDay
¶ 'Fragrant Pastel Cheer'	Last listed 1999
'Frances Fay'	SRos
'Francis Russell'	CKel
'Frans Hals'	EBrP EBre ECGN EMar EPla ERou GKir LBCl LBSe LBre LLWP LRHS LSpr MBBe MBri MBro MNrw MRav NFai SBre SEND SPer SPla SRos WFar WHoo WPer WPnP WPyg WWye
'French Porcelain'	SDay
'Frosted Encore'	Last listed 1998
fulva	CRow EGra IBlr LRHS MHar SRms STes WPnP WWin
N - 'Flore Pleno' (d)	CAvo CFee CKel CMHG CRow ECGN EGol EHon ELan IBlr LFis LHop MCAu MFir MRav NBro NFai SPer SRms STes SWat WEas WMoo WWin
N - 'Green Kwanso' (d)	CHar CRow CSWP IBlr MAvo MHer MMHG NTow SMad SPla WCot WFar WRha
§ - 'Kwanzo Variegata'	CBot CGle CRow CStr EBee EGle ELan EPPr IBlr LHop MRav MTed MTho SCob WBcn WCot WFar
- var. *littorea*	SSpi
¶ 'Gadsden Goliath'	SDay
'Gala Gown'	Last listed 1998
¶ 'Garden Plants'	SRos
'Garnet Garland'	CKel
'Gay Nineties'	Last listed 1998
'Gay Rapture'	SPer
'Gay Troubadour'	Last listed 1998
'Gemini'	SRos
'Gentle Country Breeze'	SRos
'Gentle Shepherd'	More than 30 suppliers
'George Cunningham'	CMGP CSev ECtt EGle EGol ELan

	ERou MBri MCAu MCli MRav NBir
	SChu SRos SUsu WFar
'Georgette Belden'	Last listed 1999
'Giant Moon'	CBre CMHG EBrP EBre EGol ELan
	EPla EPri ERou LBCl LBSe LBre
	LRHS MBBe MBri SBre SChu SMer
	WFar WRus
'Giddy Go Round'	Last listed 1997
'Gingerbread Man'	CRDP
¶ 'Girl Scout'	LPan
'Gold Crest'	LRHS MNFA
'Gold Imperial'	EWll NFla
'Golden Bell'	EGar LNor NGdn NHol
'Golden Chimes' ♀	More than 30 suppliers
'Golden Gate'	Last listed 1997
¶ 'Golden Ginkgo'	LRHS MBri MNFA
'Golden Orchid'	See H. 'Dubloon'
'Golden Peace'	SRos
'Golden Prize'	EBrP EBre EFou EPla LBCl LBSe
	LBre MBBe NGdn SBre SDay SRos
	WFar
'Golden Scroll'	SDay SRos
'Graceful Eye'	Last listed 1999
'Grand Palais'	Last listed 1998
'Grape Magic'	EGol
'Grape Velvet'	CBlo CSpe EGle LPan MCAu SAga
'Green Chartreuse'	Last listed 1999
'Green Drop'	WFar
'Green Eyed Giant'	Last listed 1998
'Green Flutter' ♀	CSev EBee EMar EWTr LGre LRHS
	MCLN NBir NGdn SAsh SDay
	SRos SVil WCot WSpi
'Green Glitter'	LRHS MNFA
'Green Gold'	CMHG LRHS MNFA
¶ 'Green Spider'	CAbx SApp
'Grumbly'	EBee ELan WPnP
'Guardian Angel'	WTin
'Halo Light'	Last listed 1998
'Happy Returns'	CB&S CMGP COtt ECha EGol
	ELan MBNS MBri SDay SRos
'Harbor Blue'	Last listed 1999
'Harvest Hue'	SDay
'Hawaian Punch'	EGol
'Hazel Monette'	EGol
'Heather Green'	Last listed 1997
'Heavenly Treasure'	SRos
'Heaven's Trophy'	Last listed 1999
'Heirloom Lace'	MCAu WFar
'Helios'	Last listed 1997
'Helle Berlinerin' ♀	Last listed 1995
¶ 'Helter Skelter'	CAbx
'Hemlock'	Last listed 1998
'Her Majesty'	Last listed 1998
'Hercules'	NFla
'Hermitage Newton'	Last listed 1998
'Heron'	Last listed 1999
'Hey There'	SDay SRos
'High Energy'	SApp
'High Tor'	GCal GQui
¶ 'Highland Lord' (d)	SDay
'Holiday Mood'	ELan ERou
'Honey Redhead'	CKel
'Hope Diamond'	CRDP
'Hornby Castle'	CBro LRHS NHol NVic WPer
'Hortensia'	CBlo
'Hot Ticket'	SRos
¶ 'Houdini'	NCut WAul
'Humdinger'	SRos
'Hyperion'	CSev EBee EBrP EBre ECGP ECha
	ECtt EGol GAri GKir LBCl LBSe LBre
	MBBe MGrG MNFA MRav NGdn
	NHol SApp SBre SChu SPer WWye

'Ice Cap'	LCaP MCli WPnP
'Ice Carnival'	EPfP LRHS MBNS MNFA WSpi
'Ice Castles'	Last listed 1998
'Icy Lemon'	SRos
¶ 'Ida Duke Miles'	SDay SRos
'Imperator'	EPla LPBA NHol WViv
'Imperial Blush'	Last listed 1998
'Indian Paintbrush'	EBee MBri MCAu NCut SVil WAul
'Inner View'	LPan NCut WAul
'Inspired Word'	SRos
'Invictus'	SRos
'Iridescent Jewel'	Last listed 1999
'Irish Elf'	LRot SApp
'Iron Gate Gnome'	Last listed 1997
'Iron Gate Iceberg'	Last listed 1998
'Jade Bowl'	Last listed 1999
'Jake Russell'	MNFA
'James Marsh'	EGle MNrw SRos WWye
'Janice Brown'	SRos
'Jedi Dot Pearce'	SRos
'Jenny Wren'	EMar GSki LRHS MBNS
'Jo Jo'	WWin
'Joan Senior'	CFri EBee ECGP EGle EGol EPfP
	LAst MBel MCAu MNFA MNrw
	NBur SApp SDay SRos WRus
	WWat WWin WWye
¶ 'Jock Randall'	MNFA SDay
'John Bierman'	SRos
'John Robert Biggs'	SApp
'Journey's End'	SDay
'Joylene Nichole'	SRos
'Judah'	SApp SRos
'Kate Carpenter'	SRos
'Katie'	NHaw NPri
'Katie Elizabeth Miller'	SRos
'Kazuq'	Last listed 1998
'Kecia'	MNFA
'Kelly's Girl'	Last listed 1997
¶ 'Kevin Michael Coyne'	CAbx
'Kindly Light'	SRos
'King Haiglar'	Last listed 1998
N 'Kwanso Flore Pleno'	See H. fulva 'Green Kwanso'
N 'Kwanso Flore Pleno Variegata'	See H. fulva 'Kwanzo Variegata'
'La Mer'	EFou
'La Peche'	Last listed 1998
'Lacy Marionette'	SApp
'Lady Cynthia'	Last listed 1998
'Lady Louise'	Last listed 1999
'Lady Mischief'	Last listed 1999
'Lady Neva'	CAbx SApp
'Lady of Leisure'	MBel
'Ladykin'	MBel
'Lark Song'	CKel EBrP EBre EGol EOrc LBCl
	LBSe LBre LRHS MBBe SBre WBcn
	WFar
'Late Cream'	Last listed 1999
'Lavender Aristocrat'	Last listed 1999
'Lavender Bonanza'	Last listed 1999
'Lavender Memories'	SApp
¶ 'Lavender Spider'	CAbx
'Lemon Bells' ♀	EBee EFou EGle EMar EPfP EPla
	EWll GSki LNor MBNS MCAu
	MNFA SChu SDay SRos
'Lemon Mint'	EGol MTed
'Lenox'	SRos
'Leonard Bernstein'	Last listed 1999
'Lilac Wine'	ECha EPla
§ lilioasphodelus ♀	More than 30 suppliers
'Lillian Frye'	EGol
¶ 'Lime Frost'	SRos
'Linda'	CMGP ERou EWll MRav NHol

'Lion Cub'	Last listed 1999
'Little Audrey'	EGle
'Little Bee'	EFou LPan MBNS
'Little Beige Magic'	EGol
'Little Big Man'	SDay
'Little Bugger'	LRHS MBNS
'Little Bumble Bee'	CFir EGle EGol MBNS MNFA WPGP
'Little Business'	EFou LRHS MBNS SApp SDay
¶ 'Little Cadet'	MNFA
'Little Cameo'	EGol
'Little Carnation'	SCro
'Little Cranberry Cove'	EGol
'Little Dandy'	EGol
'Little Dart'	ECha
'Little Deeke'	MNFA SDay SRos
'Little Dream Red'	Last listed 1998
'Little Fantastic'	EGol
'Little Fat Dazzler'	SDay
'Little Grapette'	CBos CHad CPlt EGle EGol LPan LRHS SApp SCro SRos SVil
'Little Gypsy Vagabond'	SDay SRos
'Little Heavenly Angel'	SApp
¶ 'Little Lassie'	MBNS
'Little Lavender Princess'	EGol
'Little Maggie'	MSte SDay
'Little Men'	CBlo
'Little Missy'	EMil
¶ 'Little Monica'	SDay
'Little Prince'	SDay
'Little Pumpkin Face'	EGol
'Little Rainbow'	EGol
'Little Red Hen'	LRHS MNFA SDay
¶ 'Little Sweet Sue'	MNFA
'Little Tawny'	Last listed 1999
'Little Violet Lace'	GSki SDay
'Little Wart'	EGol SDay
'Little Wine Cup'	More than 30 suppliers
'Little Woman'	SDay
'Little Zinger'	SDay
'Littlest Angel'	SDay
'Lochinvar'	EBee ENot
longituba B&SWJ 625	Last listed 1998
'Look'	Last listed 1997
'Lotus Land'	Last listed 1998
'Lullaby Baby'	EGol SDay SRos
luna	LNor NOak
'Lupine'	MTed
'Lusty Leland'	CBlo CPar EGle SCro SDay SRos
x *luteola*	SDay
'Luxury Lace'	More than 30 suppliers
'Lynn Hall'	EGol WViv
'Mabel Fuller'	SCro
¶ 'MacMillan Memorial'	SDay
¶ 'Mae Graham'	SApp
¶ 'Magic Carpet Ride'	CAbx
¶ 'Magic Filigree'	SDay
'Malaysian Monarch'	MBel
'Mallard'	EBrP EBre ECtt EFou EGol EMar LBCl LBSe LBre LRHS MBBe MBri MRav MTis SBre SRos SWal WBcn WCot WCra WPer
'Manchurian Apricot'	SRos
¶ 'Manhattan Night'	CAbx
¶ 'Marble Faun'	SRos
'Marion Moss'	Last listed 1998
'Marion Vaughn' ♀	CM&M CSev EBee EBrP EBre ECot EFou EGle EGol ELan EMan EPla GSki LBCl LBSe LBre LRHS MBBe MCAu MMil MNFA MWat NSti SBre SDix SSpi WCot WWat
'Mariska'	SRos

¶ 'Mark My Word'	SApp
'Mary Todd'	EGle EGol LPan MNFA NCut SCro
'Mary's Gold'	SRos
'Matador Orange'	Last listed 1997
'Matt'	SRos
'Mauna Loa'	EFou MBNS WCot
'Mavoureen Nesmith'	SCro
§ *maximum*	SMad
'May Colven'	EGol
'Meadow Gold'	Last listed 1998
'Meadow Mist'	EGle EGol
'Meadow Sprite'	SApp SDay SRos
'Mega Stella'	Last listed 1998
'Melody Lane'	EGol
'Meno'	EGol
'Metaphor'	Last listed 1997
'Mexican Way'	Last listed 1999
'Michele Coe'	EBee EGol EMar LBuc LRHS MBNS MCAu MNFA MTed NGdn SChu SDay SLod SRos WElm WLRN WMoo
middendorffii	CAvo EBee EMon EPPr GCal GMaP LRHS MCli NSti WPnP
- var. *esculenta*	EMon SMad
- 'Major'	CFee
'Mikado'	EBee EFou LRHS MWgw
'Millie Schlumpf'	SApp SDay SRos
'Ming Lo'	Last listed 1999
'Ming Porcelain'	SDay SRos
'Ming Snow'	Last listed 1999
'Mini Pearl'	EGol LRHS MBel MBri SApp SDay SRos WPer
'Mini Stella'	CBro EMil LRHS MBNS SDay WFar
Miniature hybrids	SRms WPer
minor	CBro EBee EGol EMon GCal SRms
'Missenden' ♀	MNrw NHaw
'Mission Moonlight'	COtt MCAu
'Missouri Beauty'	CPar CRos EBee LRHS MBNS
'Monica Marie'	SRos
'Moon Witch'	SDay SRos
'Moonlight Mist'	SRos
'Moonlit Crystal'	SApp
'Mormon Spider'	CAbx
'Morning Dawn'	CBlo EFou EGle
'Morocco Red'	CBro CTri ELan GSki MMil NGdn WWat
'Mosel'	Last listed 1997
'Mountain Laurel'	LRHS MBri MNFA WFar
'Mrs David Hall'	CMdw SCro SMrm
'Mrs Hugh Johnson'	CHad CMgP CSev EBee ECGN ECot EHon EOld LNor MSte NHol ERou
'Mrs John J.Tigert'	CKel SDay
'Mrs Lester'	EMon MNFA NHol
multiflora	EMon MNFA NHol
'My Belle'	Last listed 1998
'My Hope'	WCot
¶ 'My Melinda'	SDay
¶ *nana*	EPot
'Nanuq'	SDay
'Naomi Ruth'	CPou EGle EGol LAst MBNS
'Nashville'	CBro EBee EBrP EBre ELan ERou IBlr LBCl LBSe LBre MBBe MMil SBre
'Neal Berrey'	SRos
¶ 'Nefertiti'	LAst MChl NCut SApp
'Netsuke'	SApp
'Neyron Rose' ♀	CHea CMGP EGar EGol EMar ERou GSki MBNS MCAu MNFA NGdn SChu WMoo
'Night Beacon'	EFou EGol MBNS SApp SDay
'Night Raider'	SDay SRos
'Nigrette'	LPBA MTed MWat NHol

'Nile Plum'	SDay	
¶ 'Nivia Guest'	SDay	
'Nob Hill'	CLTr CMdw EGol MNFA SApp SRos	
'North Star'	GCal MTed	
'Norton Beauté'	MBel	
'Nova' ♀	Last listed 1996	
'Numinous Moments'	Last listed 1999	
'Ocean Rain'	SApp SDay SRos	
¶ x *ochroleuca*	SSpi	
¶ 'Old Tangiers'	CAbx	
'Olive Bailey Langdon'	EGol SApp SDay SRos	
'Oom-pa-pa'	ECha	
'Optic Elegance'	SAsh	
¶ 'Orange Velvet'	SRos	
'Orangeman' hort.	EBee GSki LRHS MBNS	
'Orchid Beauty'	ECha	
'Orchid Corsage'	Last listed 1999	
'Orford'	WWin	
'Oriental Ruby'	EGol MNFA	
'Outrageous'	SApp	
'Paige Parker'	EGol	
'Painted Lady'	Last listed 1998	
'Painted Trillium'	Last listed 1999	
'Pandora's Box'	EFou EGol ELan EPfP LGre MBri MChl NCut NPSI SDay SRos WAul	
¶ 'Pantherette'	CAbx	
'Paper Butterfly'	SRos	
'Paradise Pink'	EFou	
'Paradise Prince'	EGol	
'Pardon Me'	CMHG EGle EGol ELan LRHS MBNS MCAu SRos WAul WRus	
'Parian China'	Last listed 1999	
'Pastel Ballerina'	SRos	
'Pastel Classic'	SRos	
'Patchwork Puzzle'	SRos	
'Patricia Fay'	SApp	
'Patsy Bickers'	SApp	
'Peacock Maiden'	CAbx	
¶ 'Pearl Lewis'	SDay	
'Penelope Vestey'	EBee EGle EMar LRHS MBNS MNFA SPla SRos	
'Penny's Worth'	EGol EMil GKir MBri WAul	
'Permaquid Light'	CMHG	
'Persian Princess'	WBcn	
'Persian Shrine'	EGol	
'Petite Ballerina'	SDay	
'Phoebe'	Last listed 1999	
'Piccadilly Princess'	MBel SRos	
'Pink Attraction'	SApp	
'Pink Ballerina'	EBee EFou EGol	
'Pink Charm'	CMGP COIW EBee ENot LPBA LRHS MNFA MWat NGdn NHol NOrc SChu SEas SLod WCra WViv	
'Pink Cotton Candy'	SRos	
'Pink Damask' ♀	More than 30 suppliers	
'Pink Dream'	EBee EGar GChr LRHS MBNS MNFA NHol	
¶ 'Pink Glow'	CM&M	
'Pink Heaven'	EGol	
'Pink Interlude'	Last listed 1998	
'Pink Lady'	ERou MBrN MNrw MRav NBur SRms	
'Pink Lavender Appeal'	EGol	
'Pink Opal'	Last listed 1998	
'Pink Prelude'	CBlo EBee EWll LRHS MBNS MNFA SChu WWat	
'Pink Salute'	SRos	
'Pink Sundae'	ECha	
'Pink Super Spider'	SRos	
'Piquante'	EBee	
'Pixie Pipestone'	Last listed 1998	
plicata	Last listed 1999	
'Pojo'	Last listed 1998	
'Pompeian Purple'	EGol	
'Poneytail Pink'	EGol	
'Pony'	EGol	
'Pookie Bear'	SApp	
¶ 'Porcelain Pleasure'	SDay	
'Potter's Clay'	Last listed 1999	
'Prairie Bells'	CSWP EWTr MBro MCAu NCiC NFai STes WBar WFar WHoo WLRN WWhi	
'Prairie Blue Eyes'	EBee EGle EGol LRHS MNFA SApp SCro SPlb WBcn WHoo	
'Prairie Charmer'	SLod	
'Prairie Moonlight'	EWTr SApp	
'Prairie Sunset'	MCAu	
'Pretty Mist'	Last listed 1999	
'Pretty Peggy'	Last listed 1998	
'Prima Donna'	SCro	
'Primrose Mascotte'	MTed NBir WWin	
'Prince Redbird'	SDay	
'Princeton Grape'	SApp	
'Prize Picotee Deluxe'	Last listed 1999	
'Prize Picotee Elite'	WTin	
'Protocol'	Last listed 1998	
'Puddin'	See *H.* 'Brass Buckles'	
'Pumpkin Kid'	SRos	
¶ 'Puppet Lady'	SApp	
'Puppet Show'	SDay	
¶ 'Purple Pauper'	MCAu	
'Purple Rain'	EFou MBNS SApp	
'Purple Waters'	EPfP EWll LRHS MBNS MWgw WAul	
'Pursuit of Excellence'	SRos	
'Pyewacket'	SDay	
'Queen Beatrice'	EBee	
'Queen of May'	WCot	
'Queen's Gift'	SApp	
'Quick Results'	SRos	
'Quietness'	SRos	
'Quinn Buck'	SDay	
'Radiant'	Last listed 1997	
'Raindrop'	EGol	
'Rajah'	EGra LNor MBel MGed NBro NBus NCiC	
'Raspberry Pixie'	SDay	
'Raspberry Wine'	ECha SApp	
'Real Wind'	Last listed 1998	
'Red Cup'	WAul	
'Red Damask'	Last listed 1997	
'Red Joy'	Last listed 1997	
'Red Precious' ♀	EGol LRHS MBel MNFA MNrw SAsh	
'Red Rum'	EFou EMar EWTr EWll LBuc LPan MBNS MCli WPnP WRus	
'Red Torch'	Last listed 1998	
'Ricky Rose'	Last listed 1999	
¶ 'Riptide'	SApp	
¶ 'River Wye'	WTin	
¶ 'Robin Coleman'	MNFA	
¶ 'Rocket City'	ELan	
'Roger Grounds'	SApp	
'Romany'	LPBA	
'Ron Rousseau'	SApp	
'Root Beer'	MCAu WTin	
'Rose Emily'	SRos	
'Rose Festival'	MCAu	
'Rosella Sheridan'	SRos	
'Royal Charm'	SRos	
'Royal Corduroy'	MBel	
'Royal Crown'	MBri	
'Royal Heritage'	Last listed 1997	

'Royal Palace Prince'	Last listed 1999	
'Royal Prestige'	Last listed 1998	
'Royal Robe'	EFou EGar	
'Royal Saracen'	SDay	
'Royalty'	CKel WWpP	
¶ 'Rudolf Seyer'	MBNS	
'Ruffled Apricot'	LRHS SDay SRos WElm WHoo	
'Russell Prichard'	ERou	
'Russian Rhapsody'	Last listed 1997	
'Rutilans'	CFee	
'Sabie'	Last listed 1998	
'Sabra Salina'	SRos	
'Salmon Sheen'	Last listed 1998	
'Sammy Russell'	More than 30 suppliers	
'Sandra Walker'	EGol	
'Satin Clouds'	EGol	
'Satin Glow'	ECha	
'Satin Silk'	EBrP EBre LBCl LBSe LBre MBBe SBre	
'Scarlet Flame'	ECha	
* 'Scarlet Oak'	LRHS MBri MNFA	
'Scarlet Orbit'	SApp SDay SRos	
'Scarlet Romance'	Last listed 1999	
'Scarlet Royalty'	Last listed 1999	
'Scarlet Tanager'	LRHS	
'Schoolgirl'	EBrP EBre LBCl LBSe LBre MBBe SBre	
¶ 'Scotland'	SApp	
'Screech Owl'	LRHS	
'Searcy Marsh'	EGol	
'Sebastian'	SRos	
¶ 'Secret Splendor'	CAbx	
¶ 'Seminole Blood'	CAbx	
'Serena Sunburst'	MBel SRos	
¶ 'Shady Lady'	SDay	
'Shaman'	SApp SRos	
'Shooting Star'	SPla	
'Show Amber'	Last listed 1998	
'Silent Stars'	Last listed 1999	
'Silken Fairy'	EGol SDay	
'Siloam Angel Blush'	SDay	
'Siloam Baby Doll'	Last listed 1997	
'Siloam Baby Talk'	CRDP EFou EGle EGol LPan NBir SCro SRos	
'Siloam Bertie Ferris'	EFou	
'Siloam Bo Peep'	CRDP EGol	
'Siloam Brian Henke'	SRos	
'Siloam Button Box'	EGol	
'Siloam Byelo'	EGol SDay	
'Siloam Cinderella'	EGol SDay SRos	
'Siloam David Kirchhoff'	SRos	
'Siloam Doodlebug'	EGol SRos	
'Siloam Double Classic' (d)	MBel SRos	
'Siloam Edith Scholar'	EGol	
'Siloam Ethel Smith'	EGol SDay SRos	
'Siloam Fairy Tale'	CRDP EGol	
¶ 'Siloam French Doll'	SApp	
'Siloam Frosted Mint'	SApp	
'Siloam Gold Coin'	SDay	
'Siloam Grace Stamile'	SRos	
'Siloam Gumdrop'	Last listed 1999	
'Siloam Joan Senior'	EGol	
'Siloam June Bug'	EGle EGol ELan MNFA WPnP	
'Siloam Kewpie Doll'	EGol	
'Siloam Little Girl'	EGol SDay SRos	
'Siloam Merle Kent'	SRos	
'Siloam Nugget'	SApp	
'Siloam Orchid Jewel'	EGol SDay	
'Siloam Pee Wee'	EGol	
'Siloam Pink Glow'	EFou EGle EGol	
'Siloam Pink Petite'	EGol	
'Siloam Plum Tree'	EGol	

'Siloam Pocket Size'	EGol MSte SApp	
'Siloam Prissy'	EGol	
'Siloam Purple Plum'	EGol	
'Siloam Red Ruby'	EGol	
'Siloam Red Toy'	EGol MNFA	
'Siloam Red Velvet'	EGol	
'Siloam Ribbon Candy'	EGol SDay	
'Siloam Rose Dawn'	SDay SRos	
'Siloam Rose Queen'	SDay	
'Siloam Royal Prince'	CM&M EGle EPfP NHol SCro	
'Siloam Shocker'	EGol SApp	
'Siloam Show Girl'	EGol MBNS MBri	
'Siloam Sugar Time'	EGol	
'Siloam Tee Tiny'	EGle EGol	
'Siloam Tinker Toy'	EGol	
'Siloam Tiny Mite'	EGol SDay	
'Siloam Toddler'	EGol	
'Siloam Tom Thumb'	EGol	
'Siloam Ury Winniford'	CBro CRDP EBee EGol MBNS SDay SPer	
'Siloam Virginia Henson'	EGol MNFA NPSI SDay SRos WRus	
'Silver Ice'	MBel SRos	
'Silver Trumpet'	EFou EGle SCro	
'Silver Veil'	Last listed 1997	
'Sirius'	NHol	
'Sirocco'	CBlo EBee EFou WHoo	
¶ 'Slender Lady'	CAbx SRos	
'Smoky Mountain Autumn'	SApp	
'Snappy Rhythm'	MNFA	
'Snowfall'	EGol	
'Snowy Apparition'	EWTr EWll MBri MNFA MSte	
'Snowy Eyes'	EBee MBNS WWye	
'Sombrero Way'	Last listed 1999	
'Someone Special'	SRos	
'Song Sparrow'	LRHS MBri WPer WWye	
¶ 'Spanish Glow'	SApp	
'Sparkling Dawn'	MBel	
'Sparkling Stars'	Last listed 1999	
¶ 'Spider Breeder'	CAbx	
¶ 'Spider Miracle'	CAbx	
¶ 'Spider Web'	CAbx	
'Spiderman'	SRos	
¶ 'Spinneret'	CAbx	
'Spring Ballerina'	Last listed 1999	
'Stafford'	More than 30 suppliers	
'Staghorn Sumach'	MBri	
'Starling'	CFir CPar EFou EGle EGol SApp	
'Stars and Stripes'	MNFA	
'Stella de Oro' ♀	More than 30 suppliers	
'Stineette'	WCot	
'Stoke Poges' ♀	CSev EBee ECGP EGle EMar EPfP EPla LAst LRHS MMil MNFA SChu SDay SPer SRos	
'Strawberry Candy'	EFou LPan SDay SRos	
I 'Streaker' hort. (v)	WCot	
¶ 'Streaker' McKinney	MNFA	
'Strutter's Ball'	MNFA SApp SDay SRos SVil WAul	
'Sugar Cookie'	CRDP SDay SRos	
'Summer Air'	LRHS MBri	
'Summer Interlude'	WMoo	
'Summer Jubilee'	SDay	
'Summer Wine'	CHad CMGP CPar CRos ECha EFou EGle EGol EMar EPla EWTr LRHS MBNS MBro MCAu MMil NFai NPri NSti SChu SDay SMrm SPer WCot WCra WHoo WPyg WWat	
'Sun Pixie'	SCro	
'Sunday Gloves'	EGol	
¶ 'Sunday Morning'	SDay	
'Sunset Pea'	Last listed 1997	
'Superlative'	SRos	

'Suzie Wong' MNFA
'Sweet Pea' EGol
'Sweet Refrain' Last listed 1997
¶ 'Swirling Spider' CAbx
'Swirling Water' Last listed 1999
'Taj Mahal' SApp
'Tang' MBNS MNFA
¶ 'Tani' SDay
'Tasmania' SPer
'Techny Peach Lace' SRos
'Techny Spider' SRos
'Teenager' EGol
'Tejas' CEIw EMil LRHS MBNS
'Tender Sheperd' EGol
'Tetraploid Bubbles' MBri
'Tetraploid Stella de Oro' SDay
'Tetrina's Daughter' ♀ CMGP EPfP NHol
'Thousand Voices' Last listed 1999
'Thumbelina' ECha MNFA
§ **thunbergii** CAvo ECha EMon MNrw SMac
  SSpi
'Time Lord' SDay
'Timeless Fire' SApp SRos
'Tinker Bell' MSte SRos
'Tiny Temptress' SDay
¶ 'Tobacco Road' SApp
'Todd Munroe' Last listed 1999
'Tom Wise' SRos
'Tonia Gay' CRDP SRos
'Tootsie' SDay
'Tootsie Rose' SDay SRos
'Torpoint' LRHS MBNS MNFA
'Towhead' EGol ENot LRHS MRav MTed
  WCot
'Toyland' CMGP CSev EGar EGol GSki LRHS
  MBNS NGdn SSpe WLRN
'Triple Threat' SDay
'Tropical Toy' SDay
'True Glory' SApp
¶ 'Tuscawilla Tigress' CAbx
'Twenty Third Psalm' WTin
'Tylwyth Teg' SApp
'Upper Class Peach' Last listed 1999
'Varsity' EBee EBrP EBre EGol GMac LBCl
  LBSe LBre MBBe MCAu NBir SBre
  SRos
'Vera Biaglow' SDay
¶ 'Vespers' CPou WCra
vespertina See *H. thunbergii*
'Vicountess Byng' Last listed 1998
'Victoria Aden' CBro
'Video' SDay
'Vintage Bordeaux' Last listed 1999
'Virginia Henson' COtt EBee
'Virgin's Blush' Last listed 1997
* 'Vohann' Last listed 1998
'Walk Humbly' Last listed 1999
¶ 'Walking on Sunshine' SRos
'Wally Nance' LRHS SApp
'Water Witch' EGol SDay
'Waxwing' WPer
'Wayside Green Imp' EBee EFou EGol MChl SCro
'Wayside Green Lamp' EGle MNrw MSte
'Wayside Princess' Last listed 1999
'Wee Chalice' EGol
¶ 'Welchkins' SDay
'Whichford' ♀ CBro CHad CLTr CMea EBee EBrP
  EBre ECtt EGol ELan LBCl LBSe
  LBre LGre LRHS MBBe MNFA
  SBre SChu SPer WWal WWat
  WWin
'White Coral' LRHS

'White Dish' EGol
'White Temptation' CFir EBee EGol MBel SDay WAul
¶ 'White Tie Affair' MAvo SDay
'Whooperie' MBel
'Wild Welcome' Last listed 1997
'Wind Frills' SApp
'Wind Song' Last listed 1998
¶ 'Windmill Yellow' CAbx
'Window Dressing' EGol
'Windsor Tan' MCAu
'Wine Bubbles' EGol LRHS SApp
'Wine Delight' Last listed 1998
¶ 'Wings of Song' SApp
'Winnetka' MCAu
'Winnie the Pooh' SDay
'Winsome Lady' ECha
¶ 'Winter Olympics' SDay
'Wishing Well' SChu
* 'Witch Hazel' COtt MCAu
'Witches Coven' Last listed 1999
'Wood Duck' COtt EFou
'Woodbury' Last listed 1998
'Wren' COtt
'Wynn' MBel
¶ 'Yabba Dabba Doo' CAbx
¶ 'Yellow Explosion' SApp
'Yellow Lollipop' MNFA SRos
'Yellow Mantle' MNFA
'Yellow Petticoats' MTed
'Yellow Rain' SAsh WCot
'Yesterday Memories' SRos
'Zampa' SDay
'Zara' SPer

HEMIGRAPHIS (Acanthaceae)
§ **alternata** Last listed 1998
colorata See *H. alternata*

HEMIONITIS (Adiantaceae)
arifolia Last listed 1997

HEMIPHRAGMA (Scrophulariaceae)
heterophyllum CC 2428 MDCh

HEMIZYGIA (Lamiaceae)
transvaalensis Last listed 1997

HEPATICA ✿ (Ranunculaceae)
acutiloba CBro CLAP EBee GCrs GKir
  GMaP LAma MAsh MAvo WCru
americana CArn GBuc GCrs MAsh WCru
angulosa See *H. transsilvanica*
henryi EPot LAma NPSI WCru
maxima B&SWJ 4344 WCru
x **media** Last listed 1999
- 'Ballardii' ♀ GKir IBlr
- 'Harvington Beauty' CLAP MAsh WCot
§ **nobilis** ♀ More than 30 suppliers
¶ - var. **asiatica** MS&S
- blue CRDP GAbr LPio MAsh MS&S
  NHar NSla SBla WCru
- 'Cobalt' WHil
¶ - dark blue CLAP NHol
- double pink See *H. nobilis* 'Rubra Plena'
- dwarf white WHil
- grey/lilac semi-double CRDP
  (d)
- var. **japonica** CBro CRDP LAma MAsh SBla
  SMrm WCru
- lilac MTho SBla WHil
- mottled leaf MAsh MTho
¶ - Picos strain SBla

- pink   CRDP EPot GCrs MAsh MS&S NWCA SBla SIng SRms
* - 'Pyrenean Marbles'   CLAP
- red   GKir MAsh NNrd WAbe
- var. *rubra*   CLAP CRDP NMen NSla WHil
§ - 'Rubra Plena' (d)   WPnP
¶ - violet   SBla
- white   CRDP GAbr GCrs LPio MAsh MS&S NSla SBla SIng WCru WHil WIvy
§ *transsilvanica* ♀   CBro CLAP CRDP EBee ECha EPot EWTr GCrs GKir LAma LHop LRHS MBro MS&S MWat NHar NHol NMen SBla SPer WAbe WCru
- *alba*   Last listed 1997
¶ - 'Blue Jewel'   CFir
- 'De Buis'   CLAP EBee LPio MDun
- 'Eisvogel'   CBro NPar
- 'Elison Spence' (d)   IBlr NPar
- Jan/Feb flowering form   NPar
- 'Lilacina'   ECha NPar
- 'Loddon Blue'   NPar
- pink   SBla
triloba   See *H. nobilis*

x HEPPIMENES (Gesneriaceae)
I   'Purple Queen'   NMos

HEPTACODIUM (Caprifoliaceae)
miconioides   CB&S CBot CFil CPMA CPle CWSG ELan EPfP GQui IDee MBel MBlu MCCP MTis SMac SPan WCot WCwm WPGP WSHC WWat

HEPTAPLEURUM See SCHEFFLERA

HERACLEUM (Apiaceae)
candicans B&SWJ 2988   WCru
lanatum   See *Hemerocallis maximum*
- 'Washington Limes' (v)   WCot
lehmannianum   WCot
mantegazzianum   CRow EOas EPfP MFir NPSI WOak
minimum 'Roseum'   CInt WFar WPat
sphondylium   Last listed 1997
- *roseum*   CNat

HERBERTIA (Iridaceae)
§ *lahue*   LRHS

HERMANNIA (Sterculiaceae)
candicans   See *H. incana*
flammea   Last listed 1999
§ *incana*   CHal
sp. JCA 15523   CPBP
* *stricta*   WAbe

HERMODACTYLUS (Iridaceae)
§ *tuberosus*   CAvo CBro CMea CTri EBee EBrP EBre ECGP ECha EMan EPar LAma LBCl LBSe LBre LPio LRHS MBBe MNrw MRav NFai NRog SBre STes WCot WHil
- MS 976/762   Last listed 1998

HERNIARIA (Caryophyllaceae)
glabra   EOHP EWFC GBar GPoy MSal SIde WHer WOak WWye

HERTIA See OTHON

HESPERALOE (Agavaceae)
funifera   CTbNAh

parviflora   CTbh CTrC EOas LPio
- 'Rubra'   Last listed 1997

HESPERANTHA (Iridaceae)
§ *baurii*   CLAP CLyd CNic CStu GBuc GKir IMGH NMen SSpi WAbe WCot
bubrii   See *H. cucullata* 'Rubra'
* *cucullata* 'Rubra'   NWCA
* *geminata*   Last listed 1998
buttonii   EMan GBuc MFir WCot
mossii   See *H. baurii*
pauciflora   Last listed 1999
vaginata   Last listed 1999
woodii   CFir WCot

HESPERIS ❀ (Brassicaceae)
¶ *dinarica*   EBrP EBre LBCl LBSe LBre MBBe SBre
lutea   See *Sisymbrium luteum*
matronalis   More than 30 suppliers
- *alba*   See *H. matronalis* var. *albiflora*
§ - var. *albiflora*   EBee EFou EMar EPfP EWTr LRHS MBct MCAu MCLN NPSI NPri SMrm SPer SSvw WCot WFar WOve WPer WWat WWye
- - 'Alba Plena' (d)   CFri CGle CMea CRDP EBee ELan LRHS MCLN MNrw NPri SBla SIde WCot WFar
- double (d)   CHad CSev GKir MBri
- double pink (d)   Last listed 1999
- 'Lilacina'   Last listed 1999
- 'Lilacina Flore Pleno' (d)   CBos CGle CMil EBee GMaP GMac MBNS MCLN NBrk NHaw NPri SMrm SUsu WFar
- violet   LRHS
* *silviniana*   Last listed 1998
steveniana   EBee ECoo SMrm STes SWat
* *sylviniana*   NCat

HETEROCENTRON (Melastomataceae)
§ *elegans*   CInt CLTr CTre EMan

HETEROMELES See PHOTINIA

HETEROMORPHA (Apiaceae)
arborescens   SPlb

HETEROPAPPUS (Asteraceae)
altaicus   EBee GBin WPer

HETEROTHECA (Asteraceae)
horrida   Last listed 1998
mucronata   EBee
¶ *pumila*   NTow
§ *villosa*   CRDP LBuc WCot

HEUCHERA ❀ (Saxifragaceae)
§ *americana*   CHid CRDP CRow EBee ECha EOrc GBar MHar NBir NFai NSti SLod WWat
- Dale's Strain   EBee ECGN EMan EPPr GMaP LRHS MNrw MTed MWrn NCat NDov NLar WWoo
- 'Harry Hay'   LGre
- 'Picta'   EPPr WCot
'Amethyst Myst'   WCot
'Angel's Pink'   WCot
'Autumn Leaves'   Last listed 1999
'Beauty Colour'   CFee EBee EBrP EBre EMan EPfP GKir LBCl LBSe LBre MBBe MBct MBri SBre SPer
'Black Velvet'   EFou

'Blackbird'	NPro
bracteata	CHid
Bressingham hybrids	EBee EBrP EBre EWTr GKir LAst LBCl LBSe LBre LRHS MBBe NArg NBir NFla NMir NOak SBre SPer SRms SSca WMoo WPer WWin WWoo
x *brizoides* 'Gracillima'	CGle EPPr
¶ 'Brown-coral'	WCot
'Can-can'	CBos CHid CMHG COtt EBee EWTr LRHS MBri MCLN MDun MLLN MTis NDov NHol NPSI NPri SCob SUsu WCot
'Canyon Delight'	WCot
'Canyon Pink'	WCot
'Cappuccino'	WCDu WCot
'Cascade Dawn'	CHEx CHid CMHG EBee EMan EPPr EWTr LFis LHop LPio LRHS LRot MBct MBel MCLN MSCN NCut NHol NLar SCob SPer WCot
'Cathedral Windows'	WCot
'Chablo'	See *H.* Charles Bloom = 'Chablo'
'Champagne Bubbles'	WCot
§ Charles Bloom = 'Chablo'	EBrP EBre LBCl LBSe LBre MBBe SBre
'Cherries Jubilee'	WCot
'Cherry Red'	Last listed 1997
'Chiqui'	SUsu
chlorantha	GBin
'Chocolate Ruffles'PBR	More than 30 suppliers
coral bells	See *H. sanguinea*
'Coral Bouquet'	WCot
'Coral Cloud'	MRav
¶ 'Crispy Curly'	EWll
cylindrica	MBNS MBel MRav MSte SSca WPer
- var. *alpina*	Last listed 1998
- - NNS 96-116	Last listed 1999
- 'Chartreuse'	CGle LPio
- 'Greenfinch'	More than 30 suppliers
- 'Hyperion'	EPPr
'Dainty Bells'	WCot
'David'	Last listed 1997
'Dennis Davidson'	See *H.* 'Huntsman'
'Diana Clare'	WCot
* Dr Salter's hybrid	NCat
'Ebony and Ivory'	WCot
I 'Eco Magnififolia'	CLAP WCot
¶ 'Eden's Aurora'	NCut
'Eden's Joy'	EBee
'Eden's Mystery'	CFri EBee NCut SVil
'Eden's Shine'	EBee
'Edge Hill'	SRms
elegans NNS 95-289	Last listed 1999
'Emperor's Cloak'	ECtt MWll NFla NLar NPro STes WElm WMoo WSan WUnu
'Firebird'	CBlo EPPr NVic
Firefly	See *H.* 'Leuchtkäfer'
glabra	EBee
glauca	See *H. americana*
'Green Ivory'	CGle CHar EBee EBrP EBre EMan EOrc EPPr GMaP LBCl LBSe LBre LNor LRHS MBBe MBel MRav NBus NCat NGdn NSti SBre SPer SRCN
'Greenfinch'	GKir MHer SMad WElm WFar WGwG
grossulariifolia	EBee MBNS WCot WPer
'Hailstorm' (v)	Last listed 1999
hallii	NTow WCot
'Helen Dillon' (v)	CHid CLAP CMHG CMil EBee GBri GMaP LAst LFis LRHS MBri

	MCLN MGrG MLLN NCut NHol NLar NPri NSti SApp SCob SPer SPla SUsu WByw WCot WFar WPnP WSan
'Heuros'PBR	See *H.* Rosemary Bloom = 'Heuros'
'High Society'	WCot
hispida	EBee EMan MSte MWrn SAga WPer
§ 'Huntsman'	CGle EBee ECha EGar ELan EMan EWTr GBri GBuc MRav SMad WBcn WRus
'Jack Frost'	Last listed 1999
¶ 'Jubilee'	NCat
'Lady Romney'	GCal NCat
§ 'Leuchtkäfer'	CB&S CFee CFri COIW EBee ECtt ESis GChr LRHS MBro MCli MFir MRav MTis NBrk NFai NMir NOrc SCob SMac SPer SRms SWat WFar WGor WMoo WPer WPnP
'Magic Wand'	WCot
'Martha's Compact'	WCot
maxima	IHdy
mexicana	WCot
micans	See *H. rubescens*
micrantha	EBee ESis MWgw SRms WCFE WCot
- var. *diversifolia*	
Bressingham Bronze = 'Absi'PBR	EBee ECle EPla LRHS MBri NHol SPer SPla SVil WFar WWol
N - - 'Palace Purple' ♀	More than 30 suppliers
- JLS 86275CLOR	Last listed 1998
- 'Martha Roderick'	WCot
'Mint Frost'	CLAP CMHG COtt EBee EFou EMan EPPr EWTr GBin GBri GKir LRHS MBri MCAu MCLN MLLN MTis NDov NHol NPSI NPro SMad SWat WCot WFar WOVN WSpi
'Monet'	See *H. sanguinea* 'Monet'
'Morden Pink'	CLAP
'Mother of Pearl'	Last listed 1997
'Northern Fire'	CLAP EBee
'Oakington Jewel'	CHid EBee ELan EMan LRHS WCot
'Opal'	WCot
'Orphei'	NChi
'Painted Lady'	GBuc LFis LPio SCob
'Palace Passion'	WCot
parishii	Last listed 1999
¶ - NNS 93-384	NWCA
parvifolia	Last listed 1999
- var. *nivalis*	EBee
'Pearl Drops'	EBee EPPr NCat
'Persian Carpet'	CHid EBee GCal GKir LFis LRHS LRot MBel MDun MLLN MSCN NBir NCut NGdn NHol NSti SApp SPer SSpi SUsu WCot WFar WOve WRus WWeb
'Petite Marble Burg'	COtt LAst NDov NPSI WCot
'Petite Marble Burgundy'	EBee
'Petite Pearl Fairy'	COtt EBee MBri NDov NPSI WCot
'Pewter Moon'	CBro CHEx EBee EFou EHoe ELan EMil LFis LPio LRHS MBel MRav NBir NCat NHol SChu SCob SPer WCot WPar WPnP WWat
'Pewter Veil'	EBee EFou EMan EPfP EWTr SCob WCot WEas
pilosissima	ESis GBin GBuc NFai SMac
'Pink Spray'	EPPr
§ 'Pluie de Feu'	CFir EBee EMan EPfP GBri GCal MBNS MBel MCli MRav

¶ 'Plum Pudding'PBR — More than 30 suppliers
'Pretty Polly' — Last listed 1999
pringlei — See *H. rubescens*
* x *prubonicana* 'Dr. Sitar's
  Hybrids' — NArg NCat
pubescens — GBri
  - 'Alba' — NChi WCot
  - 'Hob' — WCot
pulchella — CPBP EBee ESis NFai NFla SSca
  WMoo
  - JCA 9508 — NMen NWoo
'Purple Petticoats' — EFou WCot
'Purple Sails' — WCot
¶ 'Quilter's Joy' — EFou
'Rachel' — More than 30 suppliers
Rain of Fire — See *H.* 'Pluie de Feu'
'Raspberry Regal' — CMHG EBee EFou EGle GMac
  LAst MCLN MLLN MRav MSph
  NCut NDov NHol NPSI NSti WCot
'Red Spangles' ♀ — CGle EBrP EBre LBCl LBSe LBre
  LRHS MBBe MBNS MCAu NBir
  SBre SCob
'Regal Robe' — WCot
'Regina' — EFou
richardsonii — GBin MNrw WUnu
'Ring of Fire' — CLAP COtt EBee EFou ELan EPfP
  EWTr GBri GCHN GMac IArd
  LAst LRHS MBri NHol NPri NSti
  SApp SPla WCot WFar
§ Rosemary Bloom = — EBrP EBre LBCl LBSe LBre LRHS
  'Heuros'PBR — MBBe SBre SPer
§ *rubescens* — EDAr ELan MTho NBro NHar
  NMen SIng WCot WPer WWin
rubra 'Redstart' — SUsu
'Ruby Ruffles' — WCot
'Ruby Veil' — EBee EBrP EBre EFou EWTr GKir
  LBCl LBSe LBre MBBe NHol SBre
  SCob WCot WGor
'Ruffles' — CRow ECha LRHS WCot
§ *sanguinea* — CAgr CGle LRHS MHer NBro
  NCat NFor SHFr SHel SMer SPer
  WByw WLin WPer
  - 'Alba' — EMon
§ - 'Monet' (v) — MBri
  - 'Sioux Falls' — EBee
§ - 'Snow Storm' (v) — EBrP EBre ELan GKir LBCl LBSe
  LBre MBBe MBar MBel MHer
  NCut SBre SPer SPlb WAbe WCot
  WFar
  - 'Splendens' — MWhi WOve
¶ - 'Splish Splash' (v) — WCot
  - 'Taff's Joy' (v) — CRow EWes MNrw NPro SMac
  WCot
  - 'White Cloud' (v) — EBee MWll NCut SRms WMoo
'Santa Anna Cardinal' — Last listed 1998
'Schneewittchen' (v) — EMan EPPr EPfP EWTr LRHS
  MRav NCat WCot
'Scintillation' ♀ — EBee EBrP EBre ECtt LBCl LBSe
  LBre LRHS MBBe NCat SBre SRms
'Shady Barbara' — EPPr WCot
'Shere Variety' — EBee
'Silver Streak' — See x *Heucherella* 'Silver Streak'
'Silver Veil' — CRow
'Sioux Falls' — EWes GBri
'Smokey Rose' — WCot
'Snow Storm' (v) — See *H. sanguinea* 'Snow Storm'
'Souvenir de Wolley-Dod' — MAvo WCot
'Stormy Seas' — CHid CMCo CMHG CSpe EBee
  ELan EPPr EPla GCHN GKir LFis
  LRHS MBel MCAu MCLN MLLN
  MMil MRav MSCN NBir NCut
  NHol NPri NSti SChu SCob SPer

  SUsu SWat WCot
'Strawberries and Cream' — EBee WCot
'Strawberry Swirl' — CFai CMHG EBee EMan GMaP
  GMac LAst LFis LRot MBct MBel
  MCAu MLLN MMil MRav NHol
  NLar NSti SPer SSpi SWat WCot
  WOVN
Super hybrids — WFar
'Velvet Cloak' — WCot
'Velvet Night' — WCot
versicolor — Last listed 1997
villosa — ECGN ECha EGar MRav
¶ - 'Biddulph Brown' — WCot
  - 'Royal Red' — ECha EGar MRav
'Wendy Hardy' — CLAP WCot
'Whirlwind' — WCot
'White Spires' — WCot
'Widar' — EPPr WCot
'Winter Red' — EBrP EBre EFou LBCl LBSe LBre
  MBBe SBre SRCN
'Yeti' — EFou
'Zabelliana' — GBri GCal NPro

x HEUCHERELLA (Saxifragaceae)

alba 'Bridget Bloom' — CB&S CElw CGle CSam EBee
  ECha ELan EMan EOld EPar EWTr
  GCHN GKir GMaP LGro LRHS
  MBro MRav NFai NHol NOrc
  SCob SPer SRms WBea WFar
  WHoo WPnP WRus
§ - 'Rosalie' — More than 30 suppliers
'Ninja' — See *Tiarella* 'Ninja'
'Pink Frost' — Last listed 1999
'Quicksilver' — CB&S CSpe EBee ECGN EMan
  EPPr GCHN GMaP GMac LAst
  MBri NCut NDov NPSI NPri NSti
  SCob SMad SPer SSpi WBea WCot
  WFar WLin
§ 'Silver Streak' — More than 30 suppliers
tiarelloides ♀ — CSev EBee EMan EPfP LRHS
  MWgw NCat NFai NFor SCob
  SPer WRus
¶ 'Viking Ship' — NSti
* 'White Blus' — Last listed 1999

HEXASTYLIS See ASARUM

x HIBANOBAMBUSA (Poaceae - Bambusoideae)
I *tranquillans* — CDDB EFul EPla IJus LPan NDov
  SDry WJun
I - f. *kimmei* — Last listed 1999
I - 'Shiroshima' (v) — CFil CPMA EBee EOas EPla ERod
  ISta LJus MBrN MCCP MWhi
  NDov NMoo NVic SDry WCru
  WJun WNor WPGP

HIBBERTIA (Dilleniaceae)
aspera — CGre CPle CRHN LHil SAga WWat
§ *cuneiformis* — CPle ERea
dentata — Last listed 1998
procumbens — ESis ITim WAbe
§ *scandens* ♀ — CGre CHEx CPIN CPle CRHN
  ECou ELan ERea GQui LChe LCns
  LRHS SOWG WMul
tetrandra — See *H. cuneiformis*
volubilis — See *H. scandens*

HIBISCUS ✿ (Malvaceae)
acetosella — Last listed 1998
biseptus — Last listed 1998
cannabinus — SIde
cardiophyllus — Last listed 1998

coccineus	MSte SOWG
bamabo	SSta
buegelii	See *Alyogyne buegelii*
leopoldii	IOrc SPer SRms
manibot	See *Abelmoschus manibot*
* *moesiana*	MBri
moscheutos	CArn CFir MSte
mutabilis	SOWG
- pink	Last listed 1999
- var. *versicolor*	Last listed 1999
paramutabilis	SMad
pedunculatus	Last listed 1999
purpureus 'Variegatus'	SLim
rosa-sinensis	EBak LRHS MBri SOWG
- 'Casablanca'	MBri
- 'Cooperi' (v)	CHal LChe SOWG
- 'Dainty Pink'	See *H. rosa-sinensis* 'Fantasia'
§ - 'Dainty White'	LChe
- 'El Capitolio'	SOWG
- 'El Capitolio' sport	LChe
§ - 'Fantasia'	LChe
- 'Full Moon' (d)	LChe
- 'Helene'	ELan
- 'Herm Geller'	LChe
- 'Holiday'	MBri
- 'Kardinal'	MBri
- 'Koeniger'	MBri
- 'La France'	See *H. rosa-sinensis* 'Fantasia'
- 'Lemon Chiffon' (d)	LChe
- 'Meteor'	LChe
- 'Pink la France'	See *H. rosa-sinensis* 'Fantasia'
- 'Swan Lake'	See *H. rosa-sinensis* 'Dainty White'
- 'Thelma Bennell'	SOWG
- 'Tivoli'	MBri
- 'Weekend'	LChe
- 'White la France'	See *H. rosa-sinensis* 'Dainty White'
rubis	Last listed 1999
sabdariffa	ECon
schizopetalus ♀	LChe SOWG
sinosyriacus	EPfP LRHS
- 'Autumn Surprise'	WWat
- 'Lilac Queen'	LRHS MBri WBcn
- 'Ruby Glow'	MGos
syriacus	WNor
- 'Admiral Dewey'	IOrc MGos SPla
- 'Ardens' (d)	CBlo CEnd EMui EPfP IOrc LRHS MGos MRav SLim SPer
- Blue Bird	See *H. syriacus* 'Oiseau Bleu'
- 'Coelestis'	EMil IOrc MGos SPer
¶ - 'Comte d'Hainault'	SLim
- 'Diana' ♀	CDoC EMil EPfP LRHS SLon WBcn
- 'Dorothy Crane'	CBlo CEnd EBee ENot LRHS MGos WWes
- 'Duc de Brabant' (d)	CDoC EMil EMui IOrc LRHS SPer
- 'Elegantissimus'	See *H. syriacus* 'Lady Stanley'
- 'Hamabo' ♀	EBee EMil ENot EPfP IOrc LPan LRHS MAsh MBri MGos MRav MWat SLim SPar SPer SPla SPlb WStI
- 'Helene'	CDoC LRHS MBri
- 'Jeanne d'Arc' (d)	IOrc SLon
§ - 'Lady Stanley' (d)	CMil IOrc LRHS MAsh SLim SPer SPla
- Lavender Chiffon = 'Notwoodone'	ENot EPfP LRHS MGos SMad
- 'Lenny'	EBee ENot MGos
- 'Meehanii' (v)	CBot CEnd EBee ELan ENot EPfP LRHS MAsh MBri MGos SCoo SLim SPer SPla SSta WBcn
- 'Monstrosus'	CBlo IOrc

§ - 'Oiseau Bleu' ♀	More than 30 suppliers
- Pink Giant™ = 'Flogi' ♀	CB&S CDoC CEnd EBrP EBre ELan EPfP IOrc LBCl LBSe LBre LPan LRHS MBBe MBri MGos SBre SLon SPer WDin
¶ - 'Purpureus Plenus' (d)	SLim
- 'Red Heart' ♀	CEnd EBee ELan EPfP GChr IOrc LRHS MAsh MBri SPer SPla SRms WDin WStI WWeb
- 'Rosalbane'	LRHS MBri
- 'Roseus Plenus' (d)	SLim WBcn
- Russian Violet = 'Floru'	CDoC CEnd COtt EBee ELan EMil IOrc LRHS MBri MGos MRav
- 'Speciosus'	EMui IOrc SLon SPer
- 'Totus Albus'	EMil IOrc WSHC
- 'Variegatus'	See *H. syriacus* 'Meehanii'
- White Chiffon = 'Notwoodtwo'	ENot LRHS MGos SPer
- 'William R. Smith'	CBlo EBee ELan ENot IOrc LPan LRHS MAsh MGos SPer SRPl SSta WWeb WWes
- 'Woodbridge' ♀	CB&S CDoC CEnd CTri EBee ELan EMil ENot EPfP GChr GOrc IOrc LPan LRHS MAsh MBri MGos MRav NFla SLim SPer SPla SPlb SReu SSpi SSta WDin WStI
tiliaceus	Last listed 1998
trionum	CArn CHad CInt SOWG WKif WSan
- 'Spirits Bay'	Last listed 1997
- 'Sunny Day'	ELan

HIERACIUM (Asteraceae)

argenteum	Last listed 1999
aurantiacum	See *Pilosella aurantiaca*
bombycinum	See *H. mixtum*
brunneocroceum	See *Pilosella aurantiaca* subsp. *carpathicola*
§ *glaucum*	LNor NHol WByw WEas WWin
§ *lanatum*	CGle EHol GBin NBir NBro NNrd WEas WPer WRos WWin
maculatum	CInt CRow EBee ECoo EHoe EMar EPar EPla GGar GKir LRHS MFir MPEx NBid NCat NCut NGdn NPer NSti NWCA WOak WPer WRos
- 'Blue Leaf'	WCot
§ *mixtum*	MDCh
murorum	CPea
pilosella	See *Pilosella officinarum*
praecox	See *H. glaucum*
x *rubrum*	EBrP EBre LBCl LBSe LBre MBBe SBre
scotostictum	Last listed 1998
variegatum	See *Hypochaeris variegata*
villosum	CInt EBee EHoe LRHS MDun NBro NFor WHer WPer WRos WWin
waldsteinii	EBee MBro NFor
welwitschii	See *H. lanatum*

HIEROCHLOE (Poaceae)

odorata	ELau EMon EPPr GPoy IIve
redolens	GAbr GAri GOrn

HIMALAYACALAMUS (Poaceae - Bambusoideae)

§ *falconeri*	CFil EFul EPla SDix SDys WPGP
§ - 'Damarapa'	EPVP EPla ISta LJus SCob SDix WJun
§ *bookerianus*	CFil ISta LJus WJun

HIMANTOGLOSSUM (Orchidaceae)
hircinum	EFEx

HIPPEASTRUM ✿ (Amaryllidaceae)
x *acramannii*	GCal
advenum	See *Rhodophiala advena*
- BCW 4764	Last listed 1998
'Ambiance'	Last listed 1999
'Apple Blossom'	LAma NRog
'Baby Star'	LRHS
'Beautiful Lady'	LAma
'Bestseller' ♀	LAma
bifidum	See *Rhodophiala bifida*
'Byjou'	NRog
¶ 'Calimero'	ETub
'Christmas Gift'	LRHS
¶ 'Clown'	ETub
'Double Record' (d)	Last listed 1998
'Dutch Belle'	LAma
elwesii	SBla
- BCW 4999	Last listed 1998
'Fantastica'	LAma
¶ 'Floris Hekker'	ETub
'Germa'	ETub
'Green Goddess'	LRHS
'Inca'	LAma
'Jewel'	ETub LRHS
'Lady Jane'	LRHS
'Lemon Lime'	ETub LAma LRHS
'Lima'	LAma
'Ludwig's Goliath'	LAma
'Mary Lou'	LAma
'Melusine'	Last listed 1999
'Orange Souvereign' ♀	Last listed 1991
'Oskar'	NRog
papilio	LAma LHil NRog
* - 'Butterfly'	ETub LRHS
'Papillon'	LAma
'Pasadena'	LRHS
¶ 'Philadelphia' (d)	ETub
'Picotee'	LAma LRHS
'President Johnson'	Last listed 1998
'Red Lion'	Last listed 1998
sp. BCW 5038	Last listed 1998
sp. BCW 5154	Last listed 1998
'Star of Holland' ♀	Last listed 1998
stylosum	Last listed 1998
¶ 'Unique' (d)	ETub
'United Nations'	LAma
'White Dazzler'	LAma
'Yellow Pioneer'	LAma

HIPPOBROMA See LAURENTIA

HIPPOCREPIS (Papilionaceae)
§ *comosa*	CKin EWFC SSpi
- 'E.R. Janes'	Last listed 1999
§ *emerus*	CB&S CMHG CPle CTri ELan EPfP
	ERea LHop NFla STre WHCG
	WPat WSHC WTro

HIPPOLYTIA (Asteraceae)
§ *herderi*	LHop LLWP

HIPPOPHAE (Elaeagnaceae)
rhamnoides ♀	More than 30 suppliers
- 'Askola' (f)	MGos
¶ - 'Hergo' (f)	CAgr
- 'Leikora' (f)	MBlu MGos SPer WMou WPat
- 'Pollmix' (m)	MBlu MGos SPer
salicifolia	CLnd WPGP

HIPPURIS (Hippuridaceae)
vulgaris	CBen CRDP EHon EMFW LGuA
	WMAq WWye

HIRPICIUM (Asteraceae)
armerioides	NWCA

HISTIOPTERIS (Dennstaedtiaceae)
incisa	CFil

HOHERIA ✿ (Malvaceae)
§ *angustifolia*	CFil CPMA ECou SMac WPGP
'Borde Hill'	EPfP SPer SSpi SSta WHCG
glabrata ♀	CB&S CFil ECou WPGP WSpi
- 'Silver Stars'	EPfP
'Glory of Amlwch' ♀	CFil CGre CMHG CPMA CSam
	CWit EPfP GCal LRHS MBel
	SMad SSpi SSta WCru WPGP
	WSHC
§ *lyallii* ♀	CB&S CDoC CPLG CPle CSam
	ECou ELan EPfP GGar IOrc SSta
	WBod WDin
microphylla	See *H. angustifolia*
populnea	CB&S CBot SVen
- 'Alba Variegata'	SMad
sexstylosa ♀	CAbb CBot CDoC CFee CHEx
	CHid ELan EPfP GKir IOrc ISea
	LRHS MBel MBlu MDun SLon SPer
	SSta WGer
- 'Pendula'	CB&S
- 'Stardust' ♀	CAbP CFil CMCN CPMA EPfP
	LRHS MBri SBrw SMad SPer SReu
	SSpi WPGP WSpi WWat
¶ - 'Starshine'	ERea

HOLBOELLIA (Lardizabalaceae)
coriacea	CB&S CBot CGre CHEx CPIN
	CSam EPfP LRHS MDun MGos
	SAPC SArc SBra SOWG WCru
fargesii DJHC 506	WCru
latifolia	CHEx COtt CPIN CSam CTrG CTri
	EBee SAPC SArc SLim SOWG SPer
	WCFE WCru WWat
- S&F 95134	ISea

HOLCUS (Poaceae)
lanatus	CKin
mollis 'Albovariegatus'	More than 30 suppliers
- 'White Fog'	CChe CCuc EBee EHul WLeb

HOLODISCUS (Rosaceae)
discolor	CFil CPle EBee ECtt ELan EPla
	EWes GKir GOrc IDee LRHS
	MBlu MBri MTis NSti SDys SLon
	SMad SPer SSpi SSta WHCG
	WPat WSHC
- var. *ariifolius*	EPfP EWTr GChr WPGP
- var. *discolor*	CB&S
- NJM 94044	WPGP
dumosus	Last listed 1998

HOMALOCLADIUM (Polygonaceae)
§ *platycladum*	CHal LEdu

HOMERIA (Iridaceae)
breyniana	See *H. collina*
- var. *aurantiaca*	See *H. flaccida*
§ *collina*	SMrm
§ *flaccida*	LAma LBow NRog
marlothii	Last listed 1998
ochroleuca	LAma LBow NRog

HOMOGLOSSUM See GLADIOLUS

HOMOGYNE (Asteraceae)
alpina Last listed 1997

HORDEUM (Poaceae)
jubatum CBrm CCuc CInt CSpe EGoo EHoe EMan EPGN EPPr EPla EWTr EWes LHop LIck LRHS MTis NChi NSti SIng SLod SUsu WElm WRos WWhi WWye

HORKELIA (Rosaceae)
fusca capitata EBee
rydbergii Last listed 1999

HORMINUM (Lamiaceae)
pyrenaicum CElw CMHG CNic ELan GDra LLWP MBro NMen SBla SHFr SRms SSmi WPer WPyg WWin
- pale blue MSte

HOSTA ✿ (Hostaceae)
'Abba Dabba Do' (v)	CBdn EGol EMic EPGN LHos LRHS SApp
'Abby'	CBdn EGol EMic EPGN LHos
'Abiqua Ariel'	CBdn SApp
¶ 'Abiqua Blue Crinkles'	CBdn
'Abiqua Drinking Gourd'	CBdn EFou EGol EMic EPGN GSki LRHS
'Abiqua Moonbeam' (v)	CBdn EPGN LHos
'Abiqua Recluse'	EGol LHos LRHS
'Abiqua Trumpet' (*tokudama*)	EGol
aequinoctiiantha	EGol LHos
'Aksarben'	EMic
albomarginata	See H. 'Paxton's Original' (*sieboldii*)
§ 'Albomarginata' (*fortunei*)	CB&S CBdn CHar EBee EGol EMic EPGN GKir LFis MBar MLov MNrw NBir NFai SPer WHoo WViv
'Allan P. McConnell' (v)	CBdn EGol EMic EPGN LHos NHar
'Alpine Aire'	EMic
'Alvatine Taylor'	CBdn
'Amanuma'	EGol EMic MHom
'Amber Maiden' (v)	EGol LHos
¶ 'American Dream'	LHos
'Anne Arett' (v)	EPGN
'Antioch' (*fortunei*) (v)	CBdn EGol EMic MBel MLov MMiN MRav MSte NCut WFar
'Aoki' (*fortunei*)	EBee EMic EPGN LHos NHol SCob
'Aphrodite' (*plantaginea*) (d)	CBlo CFir EGol EMic EMon EPGN LHos LRHS NCut
'Apple Green'	EMic
'Aqua Velva'	EGol LHos LRHS
'Argentea Variegata' (*undulata*)	See H. *undulata* var. *undulata*
'Aspen Gold' (*tokudama* hybrid)	EMic
'August Beauty'	CBdn
'August Moon'	More than 30 suppliers
I 'Aurea' (*nakaiana*)	Last listed 1998
aureafolia	See H. 'Starker Yellow Leaf'
'Aureoalba' (*fortunei*)	See H. 'Spinners' (*fortunei*)
'Aureomaculata' (*fortunei*)	See H. *fortunei* var. *albopicta*
* 'Aureomarginata'	CBlo GKir MLov
§ 'Aureomarginata' (*montana*)	CBdn EBrP EBre EGol EHoe EMic EPGN GCal LBCl LBSe LBre LSyl MBBe MMiN NHol NLar SApp
§ 'Aureomarginata' (*ventricosa*) ♀	SBre SCro SPla SSpi WRus WWoo CBdn CBro CHad EBee EBrP EBre ECha EGol EMic EPGN LBCl LBSe LBre LRHS MBBe MBro MMiN NVic SApp SBre SPer SRms WRus
'Aureostriata' (*tardiva*)	See H. 'Inaho'
'Aurora Borealis' (*sieboldiana*) (v)	EGol EPGN LHos
¶ 'Austin Dickinson'	EMic
'Azure Snow'	EGol LHos LRHS
'Babbling Brook'	EGol
¶ 'Baby Bunting'	EPGN
'Banyai's Dancing Girl'	EMic
'Barbara White'	EGol
¶ 'Barbara-Ann'	EPGN
'Beauty Substance'	CBdn EGol EPGN
'Bee's Colossus'	SApp
bella	See H. *fortunei* var. *obscura*
'Bennie McRae'	EGol
'Betcher's Blue'	EGol EMic
'Betsy King'	EBee EPGN LHos MRav NCut NHol WWoo
'Bette Davis Eyes'	EGol
'Betty'	EGol EPGN
'Big Boy' (*montana*)	EGol EPGN GKir
'Big Daddy' (*sieboldiana* hybrid)	More than 30 suppliers
'Big Mama' (*sieboldiana* hybrid)	EGol EMic EPGN LHos LRHS
'Bill Brincka' (v)	EGol
'Birchwood Elegance'	CBdn
§ 'Birchwood Parky's Gold'	CBdn CMHG EGol EMic EPGN EPfP EWTr LHos LRHS MBNS MLov MMiN MTed NHar NHol NOak SApp SCob SIng SRms SSpi WRus
'Birchwood Ruffled Queen'	EGol EMic
¶ 'Bitsy Gold'	EGol
¶ 'Bitsy Green'	EGol
'Black Beauty'	EGol EPGN
'Black Hills'	CBdn EGol EPGN LHos LRHS
§ 'Blonde Elf'	EGol EMic EPGN LHos SApp
'Blue Angel' misapplied	See H. *sieboldiana* var. *elegans*
'Blue Angel' (*sieboldiana*) ♀	CB&S CBdn EGol EHoe ELan EMic EOrc EPGN EPfP GMaP LHos LRHS MBel MBro MMiN MWat NOrc SMrm WCot
'Blue Arrow'	CBdn EGol EPGN LHos
'Blue Belle' (Tardiana Group)	CBdn ECha EGol EMic EPGN LHos MBro MMiN MSte NGdn WHoo WTin
'Blue Blazes'	LHos LRHS
'Blue Blush' (Tardiana Group)	EGol EPGN LHos
'Blue Boy'	CBdn CHad EGol EMic EPGN LCaP LHos MMiN NHol
'Blue Cadet'	CB&S CBdn CHad EGol EMic GCHN GSki LAst LHos MBar MBel MMiN NBee NCat NCut NFai NLar NOak WCra WFar WRus WWol WWoo
¶ 'Blue Cup'	CBdn EPGN
'Blue Danube' (Tardiana Group)	CBdn EGol EMic MMiN
'Blue Diamond' (Tardiana Group)	CBdn CHad CMHG EGol EMic EPGN MMiN WFar WShe
'Blue Dimples' (Tardiana Group)	CBdn EGol LHos LRHS MMiN
'Blue Edger'	CBdn ECha
'Blue Heart' (*sieboldiana* var. *elegans*)	ECha EMic LPio
'Blue Jay'	CBdn EGol

¶ 'Blue Lady' CBdn
'Blue Lake' Last listed 1997
'Blue Mammoth' CBdn EGol EMic EPGN LHos LRHS
(*sieboldiana*)
'Blue Moon' (Tardiana CBdn EBrP EBre EFou EGol EOrc
Group) EPGN ERos LBCl LBSe LBre LGre
LHos MBBe MBNS MLov NHol
SBre
'Blue Seer' (*sieboldiana*) CBdn EGol
'Blue Shadows' CBdn CBlo CWin EBee EPGN
(*tokudama*) (v) LHos LRHS NCut SApp WRus
WSan
'Blue Skies' (Tardiana CBdn CBlo EGol EPGN LHos
Group)
¶ 'Blue Umbrellas' MLov
'Blue Umbrellas' CBdn EGol ELan EMic EOrc EPGN
(*sieboldiana* hybrid) GGar GSki LHos LRHS MMiN
NGdn NHol WTin
'Blue Velvet' CBdn MMiN
'Blue Vision' EPGN LHos LRHS
'Blue Wedgwood' CBdn CBro CRow EGol ELan
(Tardiana Group) EOrc EPGN GKir LAst LHos MBel
MBri MLov MWat NDov NHol
SChu SPla WCFE WHil WRus
WWat
'Bold Edger' (v) EPGN LHos
'Bold Ribbons' (v) CBdn EGol EMic LHos MMiN
'Bold Ruffles' (*sieboldiana*) EGol LRHS
'Bonanza' (*fortunei*) EMic
'Border Bandit' (v) EGol LHos
'Borsch 1' CBdn
'Borwick Beauty' CBdn EPGN
(*sieboldiana*) (v)
'Bountiful' EGol EMic
'Bouquet' EGol
'Bressingham Blue' CBdn CWin EBee EBrP EBre ECtt
EGol EMic GGar LBCl LBSe LBre
LHos LRHS MBBe MRav NDea
SBre SPer SSea WFar WWpP
'Bright Glow' (Tardiana EGol EMic
Group)
'Bright Gold' LHos
'Bright Lights'
(*tokudama*) (v) CBdn EGol EMic EPGN LHos
'Brim Cup' (v) CBdn CWin EGol EMic EPGN
GKir LHos MBri SRCN WRus
'Brooke' EGol EMic EPGN
'Brother Ronald' (Tardiana CBdn EGol LRHS
Group)
'Bruce's Blue' EGol GSki
'Buckshaw Blue' CBdn CBos EFou EGol EPGN
MMiN MMoz NBir NGdn NTow
SSpi
'Butter Rim' (*sieboldii*) (v) EGol
* 'Caerula' (*ventricosa*) Last listed 1999
I 'Calypso' EPGN
'Camelot' (Tardiana Group) CBdn EGol LHos LRHS
'Camouflage' ECha
'Canada Blue' EFou
'Candy Hearts' CBdn CMHG EGle EGol EMic
EPGN LHos MHom MMiN
¶ *capitata* B&SWJ 588 WCru
- MSF 850 CFil WPGP
caput-avis See *H. kikutii* var. *caput-avis*
'Carnival' (v) CBdn EGol
'Carol' (*fortunei*) (v) CBdn CLAP EBee EGol EMic LHos
MMiN WHal
'Carrie Ann' See *H.* 'Carrie' (*sieboldii*)
§ 'Carrie' (*sieboldii*) (v) EGol EMic SApp
¶ 'Cavalcade' EMic
'Celebration' (v) EGol ELan EMic EPGN LHos LRHS
MMiN WRus

'Challenger' EMic MMiN
'Change of Tradition' (v) CBdn EMic
'Chantilly Lace' (v) EGol EPGN WTin
'Chartreuse Wiggles' EGol EPGN LHos LRHS
(*sieboldii*)
'Cheatin Heart' (v) EGol
'Chelsea Babe' (v) EGol LHos
'Chelsea Ore' CHad
(*plantaginea*) (v)
'Cherry Berry' CBdn CWin EBee EGol EMic
EPGN MBri MCLN NBro SVil
'Chinese Sunrise' CBdn EGol EMic EOrc EPGN
(*cathayana*) (v) MBel MMiN NHol SApp SCro
WHil
'Chiquita' EGol LHos
§ 'Chôkô Nishiki' CBdn CFir EBee EGle EGol EPGN
(*montana*) (v) MLov MMiN SChu
'Christmas Tree' (v) CBdn CWin EGle EGol EMic
EPGN GBri LHos LRHS MLov
MMiN SApp WRus
'Citation' (v) EGol LRHS
'Clarence' CBdn
'Claudia' MMiN
clausa EMic
- var. *normalis* CBdn EBrP EBre EGol GCal GQui
LBCl LBSe LBre LHos LRHS MBBe
MCli MGed NGdn NLar SBre
'Collectors Choice' EGol
'Color Glory' CBlo CWin EBee EGle EGol EPGN
(*sieboldiana*) (v) LHos NCut SApp WRus
'Colossal' EGol EMic LRHS
'Coquette' (v) CBdn
'County Park' EGol
'Cream Delight' (*undulata*) See *H. undulata* var. *undulata*
'Cream Edge' See *H.* 'Fisher Cream Edge'
(*fortunei*)
'Crepe Suzette' (v) CBdn EGol LHos LRHS
'Crested Reef' CBdn EBee EGol EMic LHos
¶ 'Crested Surf' (v) EGol
§ *crispula* (v) ♀ CBdn CHad CRow EGol EHon
EMic EPGN EPar EWTr GGar
GMac LGro LHos MBar NChi NFai
SChu SRms SSpi
'Crown Jewel' (v) EPGN LHos
'Crown Prince' CBdn EGol EMic EPGN
§ 'Crowned Imperial' CBdn EMic EPGN MMiN NHol
(*fortunei*) (v)
'Crumples' (*sieboldiana*) Last listed 1999
'Crusader' (v) CBdn EGol EPGN LHos LRHS
'Cupid's Dart' (v) EGol
'Curlew' (Tardiana Group) CBdn EGol EMic MMiN
'Dark Star' (v) EGol EPGN SApp
'Dartmoor Forest' CBdn
'Darwin's Standard' CBdn
'Dawn' CBdn EGol EPar LHos
'Daybreak' CBdn CWin EGol EMic EPGN
LHos LRHS NBro SVil
decorata CBdn EGol EMil LHos MBar MCli
MMiN
'Delia' EPGN
'Devon Blue' (Tardiana CBdn EGol EMic LCaP MMiN
Group)
'Devon Cream' EMic
'Devon Desire' CBdn
'Devon Discovery' CBdn
'Devon Giant' CBdn
'Devon Gold' CBdn
'Devon Green' CBdn CLAP EPGN GBri LHos
MLov MMiN NBro WFar WIvy
WRus
'Devon Mist' CBdn
'Devon Tor' CBdn EMic EPGN LHos

'Dew Drop' (v)	CBdn EGol
'Diamond Tiara' (v)	CBdn EGol EMic EPGN LHos LRHS SChu
'Dimple'	Last listed 1999
'Domaine de Courson'	GBin WFar
'Don Stevens' (v)	CBdn EGol
¶ 'Donahue Piecrust'	CBdn
'Dorothy'	Last listed 1999
'Dorset Blue' (Tardiana Group)	EGol EPGN GSki LRHS
'Dorset Charm' (Tardiana Group)	CBdn EGol EMic MMiN
'Dorset Flair' (Tardiana Group)	EGol EMic
'Doubloons'	EGol LHos LRHS
'Drummer Boy'	CBdn EGol EMic MGan
'Duchess'	LHos
'DuPage Delight' (sieboldiana) (v)	CBdn EGol EPGN LHos MMiN
¶ 'Edge of Night' (v)	CBdn
'El Capitan' (v)	CBdn EGol EMic EPGN LRHS
§ elata	EGol EGra EMic MCli MMiN WWat
'Elatior' (nigrescens)	CBdn EMic LHos
'Eldorado'	See H. 'Frances Williams' (sieboldiana)
'Elegans'	See H. sieboldiana var. elegans
§ 'Elegans Alba' (sieboldiana)	Last listed 1997
'Elfin Power' (sieboldii) (v)	EGol
'Elisabeth'	CBdn EBee EPGN LAst LBuc
'Elizabeth Campbell' (fortunei) (v)	CBdn CLAP EMic EPGN LHos MMiN MSte SSpi
'Ellen'	EMic
'Ellerbroek' (fortunei) (v)	EGol EMic GSki MMiN
'Elsley Runner'	EGol
'Elvis Lives'	CBdn EGol LRHS
'Emerald Carpet'	Last listed 1999
'Emerald Skies'	EGol
'Emerald Tiara' (v)	CBdn EGol EPGN LHos LRHS MMiN
'Emily Dickinson' (v)	CBdn EGol LHos LRHS SApp
'Eric Smith' (Tardiana Group)	CBdn EGol EMic EPGN LGre MHom SChu WFar
'Eric Smith Gold'	Last listed 1999
'Evelyn McCafferty' (tokudama hybrid)	EGol
'Evening Magic' (v)	EGol EPGN LHos
'Excitation'	CBdn EGol EMic LPio
'Fair Maiden' (v)	CBdn EGol EPGN
'Fall Bouquet' (longipes hypoglauca)	EGol
'Fall Emerald'	CBdn EMic
¶ 'Fan Dance'	EGol
'Fantastic' (sieboldiana hybrid)	EGol LRHS
'Feather Boa'	EMic EPGN LHos NHar
* 'Fenman's Fascination'	EMic
'Fire and Ice' (v)	CBdn CWin EBee EGol EPGN MBri
§ 'Fisher Cream Edge' (fortunei)	CBdn MMiN
'Floradora'	CBdn EGol EMic EPGN
'Flower Power'	CBdn EGol LHos LRHS
fluctuans	EMic
'Fond Hope' (sieboldiana)	MMiN
'Fool's Gold' (fortunei)	CBdn EMic
'Formal Attire' (sieboldiana hybrid) (v)	CBdn EGol LHos LRHS
'Forncett Frances' (v)	EGol LHos
'Fortis'	See H. undulata var. erromena
fortunei	CBdn CHad CRow EGol EMic
	NDea NHol SChu SPer WEas WWal
§ - var. albopicta ♀	More than 30 suppliers
§ - - f. aurea ♀	CBdn CHad CMGP CMHG CRow ECha EGol EHoe ELan EPGN EPla GMaP LHyd LRHS MBar MLov MMiN NLar SChu SCro SPer SPla SRms WFar WRus
- - - dwarf	Last listed 1997
- f. aurea	See H. fortunei var. albopicta f. aurea
§ - var. aureomarginata ♀	More than 30 suppliers
- var. gigantea	See H. montana
§ - var. hyacinthina ♀	CBdn CGle CHad EBee EGol EMic EOld EOrc EPGN GCal LHos LRHS MBar MMiN NBus NCut NDea NOrc SSpi WFar WWin
- - variegated	See H. 'Crowned Imperial' (fortunei)
§ - var. obscura	CBdn ECho EGol EMic LHos
- var. rugosa	EMic
'Fountain'	NHol
'Fragrant Blue'	CBdn EGol LHos LRHS
'Fragrant Bouquet' (v)	CBdn CBlo CWin EFou EGol EMic EPGN LHos LRHS MMiN SChu WRus
'Fragrant Gold'	EGol EPGN LHos MMiN
'Francee' (fortunei) (v) ♀	More than 30 suppliers
§ 'Frances Williams' (sieboldiana) (v) ♀	More than 30 suppliers
'Frances Williams Improved' (sieboldiana) (v)	EGol EWTr MMiN
'Frances Williams seedlings	NSti
'Freising' (fortunei)	EBee GCHN
'Fresh' (v)	EGol EPGN LHos
¶ 'Fried Bananas'	EMic
'Fried Green Tomatoes'	CBdn EPGN LRHS
'Fringe Benefit' (v)	CWin EBrP EBre EGol EMic EPGN GKir LBCl LBSe LBre LHos MBBe MMiN SBre
'Frosted Jade' (v)	CBdn EGol EMic EPGN LHos LRHS
'Gaiety' (v)	EGol EPGN
'Gaijin'	CBdn
'Gala' (v)	EPGN
'Gay Blade' (v)	EGol
¶ 'Gay Search' (v)	EPGN
'Geisha' (v)	CBdn EGol EPGN LHos MCCP
'Gene's Joy'	EPGN LHos
'Gigantea' (sieboldiana)	See H. elata
'Gilt Edge' (sieboldiana) (v)	EMic LCaP
'Ginko Craig' (v)	More than 30 suppliers
glauca	See H. sieboldiana var. elegans
* 'Glauca' (fortunei)	MMiN
I 'Gloriosa' (fortunei) (v)	EGol EMic EPGN LHos MMiN
'Glory'	CBdn
'Gold Drop'	CBdn ECho EGol EMic EOrc EPGN LGre ELHos LRHS NHol
'Gold Edger'	More than 30 suppliers
'Gold' (fluctuans)	See H. 'Ogon Sagae'
'Gold Flush' (ventricosa)	EMic
§ 'Gold Haze' (fortunei)	CBdn CHad EGol EMic EOrc EPGN MBel NBir NHol
'Gold Leaf' (fortunei)	EGol
'Gold Regal'	CBdn CWin EGol EMic EPGN LCaP LHos MMiN MSte
'Gold Splash'	MBro WHoo
'Gold Standard' (fortunei) (v)	More than 30 suppliers

'Goldbrook' (*fortunei*) (v)   EGol WBcn
'Goldbrook Genie'   EGol
¶ 'Goldbrook Girl'   EGol
'Goldbrook Glamour' (v)   EGol
'Goldbrook Glimmer'   EGol
   (Tardiana Group) (v)
'Goldbrook Gold'   EGol
'Goldbrook Grace'   EGol
'Goldbrook Gratis' (v)   EGol
'Goldbrook Grayling'   EGol
'Goldbrook Grebe'   EGol
'Golden Age'   See *H.* 'Gold Haze' (*fortunei*)
'Golden Anniversary'   CBdn EBee EMic EPGN LHos
   LRHS NHol
'Golden Bullion'   CBdn EGol EMic EPGN GBri LRHS
   (*tokudama*)
'Golden Circles'   See *H.* 'Frances Williams'
   (*sieboldiana*)
'Golden Decade'   EGol
¶ 'Golden Guernsey'   EMic
'Golden Isle'   EGol EMic
'Golden Mammoth'   LHos
   (*sieboldiana*)
'Golden Medallion'   CBro CMHG CTri EGol ELan EMic
   (*tokudama*)   EOrc EPGN LHos LPan LRHS
   MBNS MBel MMiN NFai NGdn
   NHol SSea WFar WWat
'Golden Nakaiana'   See *H.* 'Birchwood Parky's Gold'
'Golden' (*nakaiana*)   See *H.* 'Birchwood Parky's Gold'
'Golden Oriole'   CBdn LHos
'Golden Prayers'   CBdn CHad EGle EGol ELan EMic
   (*tokudama*)   ENot EOrc EPGN ERos GSki LGre
   LHos LRHS MBel MMiN MRav
   NBro NFai NGdn NHol NOrc
   SChu WAbe WRus
'Golden Scepter'   CBdn CMHG EGol EMic EPGN
   (*nakaiana*)   LHos MMiN NHol WFar
'Golden Sculpture'   CBdn EGol LHos LRHS
   (*sieboldiana*)
'Golden Spider'   EGol EMic LHos
'Golden Sunburst'   CBdn CHad EGol ELan EMic
   (*sieboldiana*)   EPGN GSki LHos MMiN NHol
   SMrm WFar
'Golden Tiara' (v) ♀   More than 30 suppliers
¶ 'Golden Waffles'   LHos
'Goldsmith'   EGol EMic
'Good as Gold'   EMic EPGN LHos
gracillima   CRow EBee EPGN EPar
'Granary Gold' (*fortunei*)   EGol EPGN LHos LRHS SChu
'Grand Master'   CBlo EGol EMic EPGN LCaP LHos
'Grand Tiara' (v)   CBdn EGol EPGN
¶ 'Gray Cole' (*sieboldiana*)   CBdn
'Great Expectations'   CBdn CLAP CWin EGle EGol EMic
   (*sieboldiana*) (v)   EPGN GBri LHos LRHS MBNS
   MBel MCLN MLov NBro SApp
   SChu WRus WWoo
'Green Acres' (*montana*)   EGle EMic EPGN LGre MMiN
   MSte SApp SChu WFar
'Green Angel'   EGol
'Green Formal'   MMiN
'Green Fountain' (*kikutii*)   CBdn EFou EGol EMic EPGN
   LHos LRHS MLov MMiN MSte
'Green Gold' (*fortunei*) (v)   CBdn MMiN
'Green Piecrust'   CBdn EGol EPGN LHos LRHS
'Green Ripples'   CHid
'Green Sheen'   EGol EPGN LHos
'Green Summer Fragrance'   CBdn
'Green Velveteen'   CBdn EGol
'Green with Envy' (v)   EGol
'Greenwood'   Last listed 1999
'Grey Beauty'   Last listed 1999
'Grey Piecrust'   EGol

'Ground Master' (v)   More than 30 suppliers
'Ground Sulphur'   EGol EPGN
'Guacamole' (v)   CBdn EGol EMic EPGN WTin
'Gum Drop'   CBdn EMic EPGN LHos
¶ 'Gun Metal Blue'   EGol
'Hadspen Blue' (Tardiana   More than 30 suppliers
   Group)
'Hadspen Blue Jay'   CHad
   (Tardiana Group)
'Hadspen Dolphin'   EMic
   (Tardiana Group)
'Hadspen Hawk' (Tardiana   EGol LGre LRHS
   Group)
. 'Hadspen Heron'   CBdn CHad EGol EMic EPGN
   (Tardiana Group)   LHos MHom NPar SChu
'Hadspen Samphire'   CBos CHad EGol EMic EPGN
   LRHS WRus
'Hadspen Seersucker'   CHad SLod
'Hadspen White' (*fortunei*)   EMic LHos
'Haku-chu-han'   CBdn
   (*sieboldii*) (v)
'Hakujima' (*sieboldii*)   EGol LGre
§ 'Halcyon' ♀ (Tardiana   More than 30 suppliers
   Group)
'Happiness' (Tardiana   CBdn CWin EGol EHoe EPGN
   Group)   LHos MHom MRav
'Happy Hearts'   EGol EMic MMiN
'Harmony' (Tardiana   CBdn EGol EMic EPGN LRHS
   Group)
'Harrison'   EMic
'Harvest Glow'   EGol
* 'Hazel'   EMic
'Heart Ache'   EGol
'Heartleaf'   EMic MMiN
¶ 'Heart's Content' (v)   CBdn
'Heartsong' (v)   EGol LHos
'Heide Eurm'   LHos
'Helen Doriot'   EGol EMic
   (*sieboldiana*)
'Helen Field Fischer'   Last listed 1999
   (*fortunei*)
belonioides hort.   See *H. rohdeifolia*
   f. *albopicta*
'Herifu' (v)   EGol EMic MMiN
'Hilda Wassman' (v)   EGol
'Hirao Majesty'   CBdn EGol
'Hirao Splendor'   EGol LHos
'Hirao Supreme'   EGol
'Hirao Tetra'   CBdn
'Hoarfrost'   EMic
'Holstein'   See *H.* (Tardiana Group) 'Halcyon'
¶ 'Honey'   MMiN
'Honey Moon'   CBdn EGol
§ 'Honeybells' ♀   More than 30 suppliers
'Honeysong' (v)   CBdn EPGN
'Hoosier Harmony' (v)   CBdn EGol EMic LRHS
'Hoosier Homecoming'   SApp
§ 'Hyacintha Variegata'   CMHG GBri MHer MMiN
   (*fortunei*)
'Hydon Gleam'   EMic EPGN LHos MMiN
'Hydon Sunset' (*nakaiana*)   CBdn CM&M CMHG EBrP EBre
   EGol EMic EOrc EPGN GGar LBCl
   LBSe LBre LHos LHyd MBBe MBel
   MBro MLov MMiN NFai NHol
   NOak NSti SBre SIng SMad WAbe
   WHoo WWat
hypoleuca   EGol
§ 'Inaho'   CBdn EGol EPGN LHos MMiN
¶ 'Inca Gold'   EGol
'Inniswood' (*montana*) (v)   CBdn CBlo CLAP EFou EGle EGol
   EPGN LHos LRHS MMiN NSti
   SApp

'Invincible'   CBdn CLAP EFou EGle EGol EMic
EPGN LGre LHos LRHS MBNS
MLov MMiN SVil WRus WTin
'Iona' (*fortunei*)   CBdn EGol EMic EPGN LHos
MMiN SSpi
'Irische See' (Tardiana   Last listed 1997
Group)
'Irish Breeze'   EPGN
'Iron Gate Delight' (v)   CBdn
'Iron Gate Glamor'   EGol EPGN LHos MMiN
¶ 'Iron Gate Special'   EMic
'Iron Gate Supreme' (v)   EMic EPGN MMiN
¶ 'Island Charm' (v)   CBdn EGol
'Iwa Soules'   EGol
'Jade Beauty'   CBdn
'Jade Cascade'   CB&S CBdn CLAP CMil EFou
EGol EMic LPan LRHS MSte NHol
NLar SApp SMrm SPla WCot
WOVN
'Jade Scepter' (*nakaiana*) EGol EMic LRHS
'Jadette' (v)   EGol EPGN NHar SChu
'Janet' (*fortunei*) (v)   CBdn CWin EGol EMic EOrc
GMaP LCaP LRHS MMiN NBus
WBar WSan WWoo
'Japan Boy'   See *H.* 'Montreal'
'Japan Girl'   See *H.* 'Mount Royal' (*sieboldii*)
'Joker' (*fortunei*) (v)   CBdn GKir
'Jolly Green Giant'   EMic
(*sieboldiana* hybrid)
'Journeyman'   EBrP EBre EGol LBCl LBSe LBre
LHos MBBe SBre
'Julie Morss'   CBdn CBlo EGol EMic EPGN LHos
MBel MMiN MMoz WRus
'Jumbo' (*sieboldiana*)   EMic LHos
'June' PBR (Tardiana   CBdn EBrP EBre EGol EMic ENot
Group) (v)   EPGN EPfP GBin GSki LBCl LBSe
LBre LHos MBBe MCLN MLov
MRav NHar SApp SBre SCob
SMrm SWal WHil WSan WWeb
'June Beauty' (*sieboldiana*) MMiN
'Just So' (v)   CBdn EGol EPGN LHos LRHS
'Kabitan'   See *H. sieboldii* f. *kabitan*
¶ 'Katherine Lewis'   CBdn
(Tardiana Group) (v)
'Kath's Gold'   SIng
'Kelly'   Last listed 1997
'Kelsey'   EMic
'Kifukurin' (*kikutii*) (v)   CBdn
¶ 'Kifukurin Ko Mame'   CBdn
(*gracillima*) (v)
I 'Kifukurin' (*pulchella*) (v) CBdn EGol EMic
'Kifukurin Ubatake'   EPGN
(*pulchella*)
kikutii   EGol EMic EOrc MMiN
§ - var. *caput-avis*   EBrP EBre EGol EMic LBCl LBSe
LBre MBBe SBre
- var. *polyneuron*   CLAP EGol SApp
- var. *tosana*   EGol
§ - var. *yakusimensis*   CBdn CRDP EGol EMic GDra
NTow SMad
§ 'Kirishima'   CBdn EMic EPGN MBel NHar SIng
kiyosumiensis   CRow NHol
'Klopping Variegated'   EGol EMic
(*fortunei*)
'Knave's Green'   EPGN
'Knockout' (v)   CWin EGol EPGN LAst LHos
'Krinkled Joy'   Last listed 1999
'Krossa Cream Edge'   EBee EPGN LHos
(*sieboldii*) (v)
'Krossa Regal' ♀   More than 30 suppliers
'Lacy Belle'   EGol LRHS
'Lady Helen'   EMic

'Lady Isobel Barnett' (v)   EPGN SApp
¶ 'Lakeport Blue'   LHos
'Lakeside Black Satin'   EPGN
'Lakeside Symphony' (v)   EGol LHos
§ *lancifolia* ♀   More than 30 suppliers
'Leather Sheen'   EGol EPGN LHos
'Lee Armiger' (*tokudama* EGol
hybrid)
'Lemon Delight'   CBdn EGol EPGN LHos
'Lemon Lime'   CBdn EGol EMic LHos LRHS
MMiN MNrw SIng WHil
'Lemon Twist'   LHos LRHS
'Leola Fraim' (v)   CBdn EGol EPGN LHos LRHS
MMiN
'Leviathan'   EMic
* *lilacina*   SCro WFar WMoo
¶ 'Limey Lisa'   LHos
'Little Aurora'   EGol EMic EPGN
(*tokudama* hybrid)
'Little Blue' (*ventricosa*)   EGol EMic SLod
¶ 'Little Bo Beep' (v)   EGol
¶ 'Little Caesan' (v)   EGol
'Little Fatty'   MMiN
'Little Razor'   EGol
'Little White Lines' (v)   CBdn EGol EMic EPGN LHos
LRHS
'Little Wonder' (v)   CBdn EGol LHos SChu
longipes   EGol LGre
longissima   CMHG EGol NDlv SRPl WCru
- var. *longissima*   Last listed 1998
§ 'Louisa' (*sieboldii*) (v)   ECha EGol LHos MSte NNrd
'Love Pat' (*tokudama*) ♀   CBdn CFir CWin EGol EMic
EPGN GSki LHos MLov MMiN
MRav SVil WWoo
'Lucky Charm'   EMic
'Lucy Vitals' (v)   CBdn EMic
'Lunar Eclipse' (v)   CWin EGol EMic EPGN LGre
MMiN
¶ 'Lunar Orbit' (v)   CBdn
'Maculata Aurea'   Last listed 1998
'Maekawa'   EGol
¶ 'Mama Mia' (v)   EGol EMic
'Maple Leaf'   Last listed 1999
(*sieboldiana*) (v)
N 'Marginata Alba' (*fortunei*) CBot CHad EBee ECha GKir LPBA
MMiN NDea WWin
'Marilyn'   EGol EPGN LHos LRHS
'Marquis' (*nakaiana*   EGol
hybrid)
'Maruba Iwa' (*longipes*   CBdn
var. *latifolia*)
'Maruba' (*longipes*   EGol
var. *latifolia*)
'Mary Jo'   EMic
'Mary Marie Ann'   EPGN LHos
(*fortunei*) (v)
§ 'Masquerade' (v)   CBdn EGol EPGN LHos NHar
WFar
'Mediovariegata'   See *H. undulata* var. *undulata*
(*undulata*)
¶ 'Medusa' (v)   EGol
'Mentor Gold'   EGol LHos
'Mesa Fringe' (*montana*)   CBdn MMiN
* 'Metallic Sheen'   CBdn LHos LRHS
* 'Metallica'   CBdn
'Midas Touch'   CBdn EGol EOrc EPGN LHos
(*tokudama* hybrid)   NBus NDov NHol NLar WRus
'Middle Ridge'   EMic NCut NHol
§ 'Midwest Gold'   MHom SApp
'Midwest Magic' (v)   CBdn EGol LHos LRHS MMiN
'Mildred Seaver'   CBdn CWin EGol EMic EPGN
LHos LRHS MMiN

'Millie's Memoirs' (v)	EGol
'Minnie Klopping'	EMic EPGN
§ *minor*	CBdn CBro EBrP EBre EGol ELan EMic EPGN ERos GDra GGar GSki LBCl LBSe LBre LHos MBBe MTho NHol SBre SSpi WFar
- hort. f. *alba*	See *H. sieboldii* var. *alba*
- Goldbrook form	EGol
'Minor' (*ventricosa*)	See *H. minor*
'Minuta' (*venusta*)	Last listed 1999
'Minuteman' (*fortunei*) (v)	CBdn CWin EBee EGle EPGN GBin LAst LRHS MBNS NCut SApp
'Misty Waters' (*sieboldiana*)	EMic
'Moerheim' (*fortunei*) (v)	CBdn EGol EMic EPGN EPar GBin LHos LRHS MBar MBri MLov MMiN NHol SChu WHal
N *montana*	CBdn CBlo CHad ECha EGol EMic EPGN GCHN GGar MMiN NHol
- 'Aureomarginata'	See *H.* 'Aureomarginata' (*montana*)
§ 'Montreal'	Last listed 1999
'Moon Glow' (v)	EGol EPGN LHos LRHS
'Moon River' (v)	CBdn EGol EPGN LHos LRHS
'Moon Shadow' (v)	EGol
'Moonbeam'	CBdn
'Moonlight' (*fortunei*) (v)	CBdn EGol EMic EPGN GCHN GMaP LRHS MMiN SApp WRus
'Moscow Blue'	EGol LRHS
'Mount Fuji' (*montana*)	MMiN
* 'Mount Hope' (v)	EGol
'Mount Kirishima' (*sieboldii*)	See *H.* 'Kirishima'
§ 'Mount Royal' (*sieboldii*)	NHol
'Mountain Snow' (*montana*) (v)	CBdn CWin EBee EGol EMic EPGN LHos LRHS
'Mountain Sunrise' (*montana*)	EGol
'Munchkin'	CBdn
nakaiana	GCal SRms WWat
'Nakaimo'	CBdn NHol
'Nameoki'	NHol SRPl
'Nana' (*ventricosa*)	See *H. minor*
§ 'Nancy Lindsay' (*fortunei*) (v)	CBdn EBee EGol EMic EPGN LHos MMiN NGdn SChu SMrm
'Neat Splash' (v)	CBdn EBee NBir NHol
'Neat Splash Rim' (v)	EPGN WWoo
'New Wave'	EGol LHos
¶ 'New Zealand Nugget'	SApp
'Nicola' (Tardiana Group)	EGol EMic EPGN MHom WRus
'Night before Christmas' (v)	CBdn CFir COtt CWin EBee EGle EGol EPGN GBin LAst LPan MBel MCLN MLov MSCN NBro NCut SApp WRus WWoo
nigrescens	CBdn EBee EGol EMic EPGN GCal LHos LRHS MTed
'Nokogiryama'	EGol EMic
'North Hills' (*fortunei*) (v)	CBdn EBee EGol EMic EPGN LHos LPio LRHS MMiN NBir NCut NGdn SChu SMrm WWat
¶ 'Northern Exposure' (v)	CFir CWin EGol LHos
'Northern Halo' (*sieboldiana*) (v)	EGol EMic LHos LRHS MMiN
'Northern Lights' (*sieboldiana*)	EGol LHos LRHS
'Northern Sunray' (*sieboldiana*) (v)	Last listed 1999
'Obscura Marginata' (*fortunei*)	See *H. fortunei* var. *aureomarginata*
¶ 'Obsession'	EGol
§ 'Ogon Sagae'	WFar
'Okazuki Special'	CBdn EGol

'Old Faithful'	EGol
'Olga's Shiny Leaf'	EGol EMic
'On Stage'	See *H.* 'Chôkô Nishiki' (*montana*)
'On Stage' (*montana*)	See *H.* 'Chôkô Nishiki' (*montana*)
'Oriana' (*fortunei*)	EGol EMic
'Osprey' (Tardiana Group)	CBdn EGol LRHS
'Oxheart'	EMic
pachyscapa	EMic
'Pacific Blue Edger'	CBdn CBlo CFir CWin EFou EGle EGol EPGN LHos MBri WHil
'Pandora's Box' (v)	CBdn EGol EPGN
'Paradigm' (v)	EGol EPGN
'Paradise Joyce'	CBdn EGol MLov
'Paradise Power'	CBdn EGol
'Paradise Puppet'	CBdn
'Paradise Red Delight'	CBdn
'Paradise Standard'	CBdn
'Pastures Green'	EGol
'Pastures New'	EFou EGol EMic EPGN LGre LHos MHom NCut NHol SApp
'Patrician' (v)	EPGN
'Patriot' (v)	More than 30 suppliers
'Paul's Glory' (v)	CBdn CWin EGle EGol EMic EPGN GBin LHos LRHS NCut NPri SVil WRus
§ 'Paxton's Original' (*sieboldii*) (v) ♀	CMGP ECha EGol EPGN GKir LHyd MBar MHer MRav NLar SRms WPer
'Peace' (v)	CBdn EGol EMic EPGN LHos
'Pearl Lake'	CBdn EBee EGol EMic EPGN LGre LHos LPan LRHS MBel MMiN NCut NHol SApp
'Peedee Gold Flash'	CBdn EPGN LHos NHar
'Pelham Blue Tump'	EGol EMic
¶ 'Permanent Wave'	EGol
'Perry's True Blue'	EMic MMiN
'Peter Pan'	CBdn EGol EMic
'Phoenix'	EGol GBin SApp
'Phyllis Campbell' (*fortunei*)	See *H.* 'Sharmon' (*fortunei*)
'Picta' (*fortunei*)	See *H. fortunei* var. *albopicta*
'Piecrust Power'	CBdn EGol
'Piedmont Gold'	CBdn EGol EMic EOrc EPGN LGre MMiN MSte
'Pineapple Poll'	CBdn EMic EPGN LHos LRHS MMiN
'Pizzazz' (v)	CBdn CWin EGle EGol EPGN LAst LHos MLov MMiN NCut NHol SApp
plantaginea	CBdn EGol EMic EPar LEdu LGre MHom MLov SSpi WCru
- var. *grandiflora*	See *H. plantaginea* var. *japonica*
§ - var. *japonica* ♀	CBot CGle CHad CLAP ECha EMic EPGN EPar GSki MCAu NBus SChu WWat
'Platinum Tiara' (*nakaiana*) (v)	CBdn EPGN LHos MMiN
'Pooh Bear' (v)	CBdn EGol
'Popo'	EGol
'Potomac Pride'	CBdn EPGN LHos LRHS
'Puck'	EGol
¶ 'Purple and Gold'	CBdn
'Purple Dwarf'	CBdn CBlo EGol GKir LHos LRHS NHol NLar WCra WWoo
'Purple Lady Finger'	Last listed 1999
'Purple Profusion'	EGol EMic
pycnophylla	EGol
'Queen Josephine' (v)	CBdn CWin EGol EMic EPGN LAst LHos MBri NCut SApp WRus
¶ 'Queen of Islip' (*sieboldiana*) (v)	CBdn
'Radiant Edger' (v)	CBdn CWin EBee EGol EPGN LHos LRHS

'Raleigh Remembrance' EGol LHos LRHS
'Rascal' (v) CBdn EGol LHos LRHS
'Raspberry Sorbet' CBdn EGol LHos LRHS
rectifolia LHos NHol WWat
'Regal Splendor' (v) CBdn CWin EBee EGol EMic
EPGN GSki LHos LRHS MMiN
NPSI SCob WRus
'Resonance' (v) EPGN LHos LRHS MBri MMiN
'Reversed' (v) CBdn CBlo CLAP CWin EGol
ELan EMic EPGN EPfP LHos
LRHS MLov NBro NCut NGdn
WRus
'Rhapsody' (*fortunei*) (v) EGol EMic
'Richland Gold' (*fortunei*) EGol EMic EPGN LRHS
'Rippling Waves' EGol EMic
'Robert Frost' (v) CBdn EGol
'Robusta' (*fortunei*) See *H. sieboldiana* var. *elegans*
§ *rohdeifolia* (v) CLAP EGol GGar LBuc WHal
§ - f. *albopicta* CBdn EGol ELan EPGN EPar NHol
SChu
'Rosemoor' EGol
'Rough Waters' MMiN
'Royal Sovereign' CHEx
§ 'Royal Standard' ♀ More than 30 suppliers
'Royalty' EGol LHos
'Ruffles' Last listed 1999
rupifraga EGol
'Russell's Form' EMic
(*ventricosa*)
'Ryan's Big One' Last listed 1999
§ 'Sagae' ♀ CBdn CLAP CWin EBee EBrP EBre
EGle EGol EMic EPGN EPfP LBCl
LBSe LBre LPan LRHS MBBe MBri
MLov MMiN MMoz MNrw NCut
NPSI SApp SBre SCob SMrm
WCot WFar
'Saint Elmo's Fire' EGol
§ 'Saishu Jima' (*sieboldii* EGol EMic EPla NHol WCru
spathulata)
'Salute' EGol
'Samual Blue' Last listed 1998
'Samurai' (*sieboldiana*) (v) CBdn CWin EBee EGol EMic LHos
MRav NBro SApp
¶ 'Sarah Kennedy' (v) EPGN
'Savannah' EGol LHos LRHS
'Sazanami' (*crispula*) See *H. crispula*
'Scooter' CBdn EPGN LHos
'Sea Bunny' EGol
'Sea Dream' (v) CBdn EGol EMic EPGN LHos MMiN
'Sea Drift' EGol EPGN
'Sea Fire' EGol LRHS
'Sea Gold Star' CBdn EGol EPGN LRHS
'Sea Lotus Leaf' CBdn EGol EMic EPGN LRHS
SApp
'Sea Mist' (v) CBdn
'Sea Monster' EGol LRHS
'Sea Octopus' EGol
'Sea Sapphire' EGol LHos LRHS
'Sea Sprite' (v) LBuc LHos LRHS MMiN
'Sea Thunder' (v) CBdn EGol EPGN
'Sea Yellow Sunrise' CBdn EGol EMic
'Second Wind' CBdn EPGN LHos LRHS
(*fortunei*) (v)
'See Saw' (*undulata*) EGol EMic MMiN WPnP
'Semperaurea' GSki
(*sieboldiana*)
'Sentinels' Last listed 1998
'September Sun' (v) CBdn EGol EMic EPGN LHos
LRHS MMiN
'Serena' (Tardiana Group) Last listed 1997
'Serendipity' CBdn EGol EMic EPGN LHos
MHom

'Shade Fanfare' (v) ♀ More than 30 suppliers
'Shade Master' CB&S CBdn CBlo EBrP EBre
EGol GBin GKir LAst LBCl LBSe
LBre MBBe NHol SBre SMer SVil
WHil
§ 'Sharmon' (*fortunei*) (v) CBdn EGol EMic EPGN MBel
MMiN NHol SChu
'Sheila West' CBdn
'Shelleys' (v) EGol
'Sherborne Profusion' CBdn EMic
(Tardiana Group)
'Sherborne Songbird' EMic
(Tardiana Group)
'Sherborne Swan' EMic
(Tardiana Group)
'Sherborne Swift' CBdn EGol EMic
'Shining Tot' CBdn EGol EPGN LHos
'Shogun' (v) EGol LHos
* 'Showboat' CBdn EGol EPGN LHos
sieboldiana CHad CMHG CRow EBee EFou
EGol ELan EMic EPar LFis LHos
LHyd MBNS MLov MRav NChi
NFor NHol SPer SPlb SRms WCru
WFar WPnP WWat
§ - var. *elegans* ♀ More than 30 suppliers
- var. *mira* Last listed 1997
§ *sieboldii* var. *alba* CHad CMGP EGol ELan SSpi
§ - f. *kabitan* (v) CBdn CLAP EBrP EBre EGol EMic
EPGN LBCl LBSe LBre LHos MBBe
MLov NHar SBre SChu
- f. *shiro-kabitan* (v) EGol EPGN
'Silver and Gold' MMiN
* 'Silver Chimes' Last listed 1998
'Silver Crown' See *H.* 'Albomarginata' (*fortunei*)
'Silver Lance' (v) EGol EMic EPGN
'Silvery Slugproof' CBdn MMiN SApp
(Tardiana Group)
'Sitting Pretty' (v) EGol EPGN LHos
¶ 'Slim Polly' CBdn
'Snow Cap' (v) CBdn CBlo CWin EGle EGol EMic
EPGN LHos SApp WWoo
'Snow Crust' (*elata*) (v) CBdn EGol EMic LRHS MMiN
'Snow Flakes' (*sieboldii*) CBdn CHEx EBee EGol EPGN
EPfP GCal GKir LHos LPio LRHS
MBar MBri MCli NBro NFla NHol
NPro SCob SLod SPer WFar WRHF
'Snow White' EGol
(*undulata*) (v)
'Snowden' More than 30 suppliers
'Snowstorm' (*sieboldii*) CBdn NHol
'So Sweet' CBdn CBlo CLAP EGol EMic
EPGN GSki LHos MBro MLov
SMrm WRus WWat WWoo
'Something Blue' CBdn LHos
¶ 'Something Different' EPGN
(*fortunei*) (v)
sp. from Japan Last listed 1998
'Sparkling Burgundy' EGol
'Special Gift' CBdn EBee EGol EMic LBuc LHos
LRHS
¶ 'Spilt Milk' CBdn EGol
(*tokudama*) (v)
'Spinners' EBrP EBre LBCl LBSe LBre LHos
MBBe SBre
§ 'Spinners' (*fortunei*) (v) CBdn CHad ECha EGol EMic
MMiN SChu SSpi
'Sprengeri' Last listed 1998
'Spritzer' (v) CBdn EGol EMic EPGN LHos
¶ 'Squash Casserole' EGol
'Squash Edge' EPGN
(*sieboldiana*) (v)
'Squiggles' (v) EGol LHos

§ 'Starker Yellow Leaf' — EMic
'Stenantha' (*fortunei*) — EMic
'Stenantha Variegated' (*fortunei*) (v) — NHol
'Stiletto' (v) — CBdn EGol EMic EPGN LHos NHar NPro
'Striptease' (*fortunei*) (v) — CBdn CWin EGol EMic EPGN GBin LHos MBri MLov SApp WRus
'Sugar and Cream' (v) — CM&M CWin EBee EGol EMic EOrc EPGN LAst LHos LPio LRHS MCLN MMiN NGdn SChu
'Sugar Plum Fairy' (*gracillima*) — EGol
'Sultana' (v) — CBdn
'Sum and Substance' ♀ — More than 30 suppliers
'Summer Fragrance' — CBdn EGol EMic EPGN LHos LRHS MMiN
'Summer Music' (v) — CBdn EGle EGol EPGN LAst LHos NCut SApp WRus
'Summer Snow' (*sieboldiana*) (v) — EPGN LHos
'Sun Glow' — EGol
'Sun Power' — CBdn CBro CWin EBrP EBre EGol EMic EOrc EPGN EPar LBCl LBSe LBre LHos LRHS MBBe MCLN MMiN MWat NBro NLar NSti SBre WRus
'Sundance' (*fortunei*) (v) — EGol EMic MMiN
* 'Sunflower' — NOak
¶ 'Sunset' — SIng
'Super Bowl' — EGol LRHS
'Super Nova' (v) — CBdn EGol LHos LRHS
'Susy' — MMiN
'Suzuki Thumbnail' — EMic
¶ 'Sweet Bo Beep' — EGol
¶ 'Sweet Marjorie' — EGol
'Sweet Standard' — Last listed 1997
'Sweet Susan' — CBlo EGol EMic EOrc LRHS MBNS MMiN SPer
'Sweet Tater Pie' — CBdn EPGN
'Sweetheart' — EMic
'Sweetie' (v) — CBdn EGol LHos LRHS
'Swirling Hearts' — EGol LHos LRHS
¶ *takabashii* 'Gosan' — EGol
'Tall Boy' — CBdn CSev EBee ECha EGol EPla GCal LHos MWgw SPer SSpi WWat
'Tall Twister' — Last listed 1999
'Tamborine' (v) — CBdn EGol EPGN LHos LRHS MMiN SApp
Tardiana Group — CBdn CBro CMGP EGol ELan MHom NGdn NHol SPer WKif
Tardiana Group pink-flowered — MMiN
tardiflora — CBdn CFil EGol EMic ERos SApp WCot WPGP
tardiva — EBrP EBre LBCl LBSe LBre LHos LRHS MBBe SBre
'Tea and Crumpets' — EPGN
'Temple Bells' — EGol LHos LRHS
'Tenryu' — EGol EPGN LHos
'The Twister' — EGol EMic MMiN
'Thomas Hogg' — See *H. undulata* var. *albomarginata*
'Thumb Nail' — CBdn ECha EGol GAri GSki
tibae — Last listed 1999
'Tiny Tears' (*venusta*) — EGol LRHS
tokudama — CHad EFou EGol EPGN LNor LRHS MBro MMiN NBir NFai NGdn NHol NSti SChu SCob WKif
§ - f. *aureonebulosa* — CWin EGol EPGN LGre LHos LRHS

- f. *flavocircinalis* (v) — CBdn CWin EBee ECha EGol EMic EPGN GCHN LHos LRHS MMiN MMoz NBro NCut SApp SMad WFar WWoo
'Torchlight' (v) — EGol EMic LRHS
'Tot Tot' — GAri
¶ 'Touchstone' — CBdn
'Trail's End' — EMic
'True Blue' — CBdn EGol EMic LHos MMiN SApp WWoo
'Tutu' — EGol
¶ 'Twiggy' — MMiN
'Twilight' (*fortunei*) (v) — CBdn EPGN LHos MBNS
'Twinkle Toes' — EGol EMic
'Twist of Lime' — CBdn EGol
¶ 'Ultraviolet Light' — EGol
undulata — LFis LRHS NDea SRms WFar
§ - var. *albomarginata* — More than 30 suppliers
§ - var. *erromena* ♀ — CBdn CMGP EHon EMic EPfP LFis LHos LPBA MBro MLov NBid NFla NHol SPer WWpP
§ - var. *undulata* (v) ♀ — CBdn CBot CBro CRow EBee EHoe EHon ELan ENot EPGN GChr LAst LGro LHos LPBA MMiN MTis NVic SChu SPer SSea WEas WFar WKif WRus WWin
- var. *univittata* (v) ♀ — CBro CRow ECha EGol EPGN EPfP GGar LHos MBel MMiN NDov NFai NPro SCob SPla WFar WKif
'Urajiro Hachijo' — EGol
'Urajiro' (*hypoleuca*) — EGol
'Valentine Lace' — CBdn EGol EMic EPGN LPan LRHS
¶ 'Van Wade' (v) — EPGN MMiN
'Vanilla Cream' (*cathayana*) — EGol EPGN LHos LRHS
'Variegata' (*gracillima*) — See *H.* 'Vera Verde'
'Variegata' (*tokudama*) — See *H. tokudama* f. *aureonebulosa*
'Variegata' (*undulata*) — See *H. undulata* var. *undulata*
'Variegata' (*ventricosa*) — See *H.* 'Aureomarginata' (*ventricosa*)
'Variegated' (*fluctuans*) — See *H.* 'Sagae'
ventricosa ♀ — More than 30 suppliers
- var. *aureomaculata* — CHad EGol EMic ENot EPGN LHos MMiN NBir NCut NSti SPer
- 'Aureomarginata' — See *H.* 'Aureomarginata' (*ventricosa*)
I 'Venucosa' — EGol EMic WFar
'Venus Star' — EPGN GSki LHos
venusta ♀ — More than 30 suppliers
- dwarf — CSWP LGre
- x *sieboldiana* — Last listed 1999
- *yakusimensis* — See *H. kikutii* var. *yakusimensis*
§ 'Vera Verde' (v) — CBdn EPGN ERos GQui NBir SIng
'Verna Jean' (v) — CBdn EGol
'Veronica Lake' (v) — CBdn EGol LRHS
'Viette's Yellow Edge' (*fortunei*) (v) — MMiN
'Vilmoriniana' — EGol EMic MMiN
'Viridis Marginata' — See *H. sieboldii* f. *kabitan*
'Wagtail' (Tardiana Group) — EMic
'Wahoo' (*tokudama*) (v) — EGol
¶ 'Warwick Curtsy' — EGol
'Warwick Essence' — EGol EMic
'Waving Winds' (v) — EGol LHos
¶ 'Waving Wuffles' — EMic
'Wayside Blue' — EMic MMiN
'Wayside Perfection' — See *H.* 'Royal Standard'
'Weihenstephan' (*sieboldii*) — EGol
'Wheaton Blue' — CBdn LHos LRHS
'Whirlwind' (*fortunei*) (v) — CBdn EBee EGol EPGN GBin

	LHos MCLN MLov NCut SVil WRus
¶ 'Whirlwind Tour' (v)	EGol
'White Christmas' (*undulata*) (v)	CBdn EGol EPGN LHos LRHS
'White Fairy' (*plantaginea*)	CBdn EPGN
'White Feather' (*undulata*)	Last listed 1999
'White Gold'	CBdn EGol EPGN LHos
'White Tacchi'	EMon
'White Triumphator'	CBdn
'Wide Brim' (v) ♀	More than 30 suppliers
'Wind River Gold'	EGol EMic
'Windsor Gold'	See *H.* 'Nancy Lindsay' (*fortunei*)
'Winfield Blue'	EGol LRHS
* 'Winfield Gold'	CBdn EGol EMic MMiN
'Winning Edge' (*tokudama*)	EGol
'Wogon Giboshi'	See *H.* 'Wogon' (*sieboldii*)
§ 'Wogon' (*sieboldii*)	CBdn CBro CM&M CRDP CRow EMic EPGN EPla GMaP NHar NHol NMen NSti
'Wogon's Boy'	CBdn EGol EMic EPGN
'Wrinkles and Crinkles'	EMic EPGN LRHS
'Yakushima-mizu' (*gracillima*)	EGol
* *yakushimana*	NHar
'Yellow Boa'	EMic
'Yellow Edge' (*fortunei*)	See *H. fortunei* var. *aureomarginata*
'Yellow Edge' (*sieboldiana*)	See *H.* 'Frances Williams' (*sieboldiana*)
'Yellow River' (*montana*) (v)	CBdn ECha EGol EMic EPGN LHos LRHS
'Yellow Splash' (v)	CBdn ECha EPGN LHos LRHS MBel EChu
'Yellow Splash Rim' (v)	EGol EMic LHos MBel MMiN WBcn
¶ 'Yellow Waves'	CBdn
yingeri	EGol WCot
- B&SWJ 546	WCru
'Zager Blue'	EMic
'Zager Green'	EMic
'Zager White Edge' (*fortunei*) (v)	CLAP EMic EPGN LHos
'Zounds'	More than 30 suppliers

HOTTONIA (Primulaceae)
palustris	CBen ECoo EHon ELan EMFW LPBA MSta NDea NVic SWat SWyc

HOUSTONIA (Rubiaceae)
caerulea L.	ECho SIng WWin
- hort.	See *H. michauxii*
- L. var. *alba*	CInt WPer
§ *michauxii*	GAri
- 'Fred Mullard'	EWes NPri

HOUTTUYNIA (Saururaceae)
cordata	CAgr EMar GBar IBlr MWgw NSti SWat WFar
§ - 'Boo-Boo' (v)	EMan EPfP EPla MCLN
§ - 'Chameleon' (v)	More than 30 suppliers
- 'Flame' (v)	LRHS
- 'Flore Pleno' (d)	CBen CGle CRow ECha EHon ELan EPla GBar LPBA MRav MSta NBir NBro NPer SIde SIng SLon SPer SRms SWat SWyc WFar WRus WWin
- 'Joker's Gold'	EBee EPPr
* - 'Pied Piper'	CDoC LRHS SAga WCot
- 'Terry Clarke' (v)	See *H. cordata* 'Boo-Boo'
- 'Tricolor'	See *H. cordata* 'Chameleon'

- Variegata Group	EPot GBar IBlr LPBA MAsh NBro NDea SIng SMac

HOVEA (Papilionaceae)
celsii	See *H. elliptica*
§ *elliptica*	Last listed 1997

HOVENIA (Rhamnaceae)
acerba	CFil WPGP
dulcis	CB&S CGre CMCN CPle ELan EPfP LEdu MNaF SCob

HOWEA (Arecaceae)
§ *belmoreana*	LPal
forsteriana ♀	EPVP LPal LRHS MBri

HOYA (Asclepiadaceae)
acuta	Last listed 1998
angustifolia	Last listed 1999
archboldiana	LChe
arnottiana	Last listed 1998
§ *australis*	LCns LRHS SOWG
bandaensis	Last listed 1998
bella	See *H. lanceolata* subsp. *bella*
bilobata	Last listed 1999
carnosa ♀	CB&S CPlN EBak ECon ELan EOHP GQui LCns LRHS NRog SRms
- 'Compacta'	CHal
* - *compacta* 'Hindu Rope'	NPer
- 'Exotica' ♀	Last listed 1998
* - 'Jungle Garden'	Last listed 1998
* - 'Krinkle'	NPer
- 'Krinkle Eight'	Last listed 1998
- 'Latifolia'	ECon
- 'Red Princess'	MBri
- 'Rubra'	Last listed 1998
- 'Tricolor'	NPer
- 'Variegata'	LCns MBri SRms
cinnamomifolia	LChe SOWG
* *compacta* 'Tricolor'	NPer
cumingiana	Last listed 1999
darwinii hort.	See *H. australis*
densifolia	LChe
eitapensis	Last listed 1999
engleriana	Last listed 1998
fusca 'Silver Knight'	Last listed 1997
globulosa	LChe
imperialis	LChe
inconspicua	Last listed 1999
kerrii	LChe
lacunosa	LChe LRHS
§ *lanceolata* subsp. *bella* ♀	CHal GQui LCns MBri NRog SRms
linearis	LChe
longifolia	Last listed 1999
macgillivrayi	LChe
magnifica	Last listed 1999
motoskei	LChe
multiflora	ECon LChe LCns MBri SOWG
- 'Variegata' (v)	LChe
neocaledonica	Last listed 1998
nicholsoniae	LChe
nummularioides	Last listed 1999
odorata	Last listed 1999
parviflora	Last listed 1999
pauciflora	Last listed 1999
polyneura	Last listed 1998
pubicalyx 'Red Buttons'	LChe
* - 'Silver Pink'	LChe
purpureofusca	Last listed 1998
shepherdii	Last listed 1999

'Shibata'　Last listed 1999

HUGUENINIA (Brassicaceae)
alpina　See *H. tanacetifolia*
§ *tanacetifolia*　Last listed 1999
　- subsp. *suffruticosa*　GOrP

HUMATA (Davalliaceae)
pyxidata　See *Davallia solida* var. *pyxidata*
tyermannii　NMar

HUMEA (Asteraceae)
elegans　See *Calomeria amaranthoides*

HUMULUS (Cannabaceae)
japonicus　ECoo MSal
lupulus　CArn CB&S CPlN ECoo ELau GAri
　　GBar GPoy ILis MHer MSal SIde
　　WHer WSel WStl WWye
　- 'Aureus' ♀　More than 30 suppliers
　- 'Aureus' (f)　CGdn GBar MAnH MCCP MSCN
　　SMad SSoC WCot WWat
　- 'Aureus' (m)　MCCP WWat
　- 'Cobbs'　GPoy SDea
　- 'First Gold'^PBR　SDea
　- 'Fuggle'　CAgr GPoy SDea
　- 'Hallertauer'　SDea
　- 'Hip-hop'　EMon
　- 'Mathon'　CAgr SDea
　- 'Northdown'　CAgr SDea
　- 'Taff's Variegated' (v)　EMon EWes GOrP WHil
　- 'Wye Challenger'　CAgr GPoy

HUNNEMANNIA (Papaveraceae)
fumariifolia 'Sunlite'　Last listed 1999

HUTCHINSIA See PRITZELAGO

HYACINTHELLA (Hyacinthaceae)
lineata M&T 5048　Last listed 1998
millingenii　Last listed 1999

HYACINTHOIDES (Hyacinthaceae)
§ *hispanica*　CAvo CBro CHid EWFC IBlr LRHS
　　MBri NBir NHol WWye
　- 'Alba'　Last listed 1998
　- *algeriensis* AB&S 4337　Last listed 1998
　- 'Excelsior'　LRHS
　- 'La Grandesse'　CBro
　- 'Rosabella'　CBro
　- 'Rose'　NCat
§ *italica*　WShi
§ - *vicentina*　Last listed 1998
　- - *alba*　Last listed 1997
§ *non-scripta*　CArn CAvo CBro CKin EOld EPar
　　EPot ETub EWFC IBlr LAma LFox
　　LRHS MHer MMal NMir NRog
　　SPlb WHer WShi
　- pink bell　Last listed 1998

HYACINTHUS ✿ (Hyacinthaceae)
amethystinus　See *Brimeura amethystina*
azureus　See *Muscari azureum*
comosus 'Plumosus'　See *Muscari comosum* 'Plumosum'
fastigiatus　See *Brimeura fastigiata*
¶ multiflowered blue　ETub
¶ multiflowered white　ETub
orientalis　GVer
　- 'Amethyst'　EWal LAma NRog
　- 'Amsterdam'　EWal LAma NRog
　- 'Anna Liza'　NRog

　- 'Anna Marie' ♀　CAvo CBro ETub EWal LAma MBri NRog
　- 'Ben Nevis' (d)　LAma MBri NRog
　- 'Bismarck'　LAma NRog
　- 'Blue Giant'　LAma NRog
　- 'Blue Jacket' ♀　CBro ETub LAma NRog
　- 'Blue Magic'　EWal LAma NRog
　- 'Blue Orchid' (d)　LAma
　- 'Blue Star'　LAma
　- 'Borah' ♀　EWal LAma NRog
　- 'Carnegie'　CBro ETub EWal LAma NRog
　- 'City of Haarlem' ♀　CBro ETub EWal LAma NRog
　- 'Colosseum'　LAma
　- 'Concorde'　Last listed 1998
　- 'Delft Blue' ♀　CAvo CBro EWal LAma MBri NRog
　- 'Distinction'　LAma
　- 'Edelweiss'　Last listed 1998
　- 'Fondant'　LAma
　- 'Gipsy Queen' ♀　CBro ETub EWal LAma MBri NRog
　- 'Hollyhock' (d)　EWal LAma MBri NRog
　- 'Jan Bos'　CAvo ETub EWal LAma NRog
　- 'King Codro' (d)　LAma MBri NRog
　- 'King of the Blues'　LAma NRog
　- 'La Victoire'　LAma NRog
　- 'Lady Derby'　EWal LAma
　- 'L'Innocence' ♀　CBro LAma NRog
　- 'Lord Balfour'　LAma
　- 'Madame Krüger'　Last listed 1998
　- 'Marconi' (d)　LAma NRog
　- 'Marie'　LAma NRog
　- 'Mont Blanc'　EWal
　- 'Mulberry Rose'　EWal LAma NRog
¶ - multiflowered　GVer
　- 'Myosotis'　LAma
§ - 'Oranje Boven'　LAma
　- 'Ostara' ♀　CBro EWal LAma MBri NRog
　- 'Paul Hermann'　ETub
　- 'Peter Stuyvesant'　ETub EWal LAma NRog
　- 'Pink Pearl' ♀　CBro LAma NRog
　- 'Pink Royal' (d)　LAma NRog
　- 'Princess Margaret'　LAma
　- 'Prins Hendrik'　Last listed 1998
　- 'Queen of the Pinks'　LAma NRog
　- 'Queen of the Violets'　NRog
　- 'Rosalie'　EWal
　- 'Rosette' (d)　LAma
　- 'Salmonetta'　See *H. orientalis* 'Oranje Boven'
§ - 'Sneeuwwitje'　LAma NRog
　- Snow White　See *H. orientalis* 'Sneeuwwitje'
　- 'Violet Pearl'　CBro LAma NRog
　- 'Vuurbaak'　LAma
　- 'White Pearl'　CAvo LAma NRog
✲ 'Woodstock'　ETub LAma

HYBANTHUS (Violaceae)
floribundus　Last listed 1998

HYDRANGEA ✿ (Hydrangeaceae)
angustipetala　CFil
　- B&SWJ 3454　WCru
　- B&SWJ 3814　WCru
anomala　Last listed 1997
　- subsp. *anomala*　SSpi
　- - B&SWJ 2411　WCru
　- from Taiwan　Last listed 1999
　　B&SWJ 3117
§ - subsp. *petiolaris* ♀　More than 30 suppliers
§ - - var. *cordifolia*　CFil EPla GKir MBNS
　- - dwarf　See *H. anomala* subsp. *petiolaris* var. *cordifolia*

- - *tiliifolia*	EPfP GCal MBlu SNut WFar WSHC WWat
- - 'Yakushima'	CFil WCru WPGP
§ *arborescens*	CArn CFil MRav NFor WPGP
- 'Annabelle' ♀	More than 30 suppliers
§ - subsp. *discolor*	WCru
- - 'Sterilis'	CFil SPla SSpi WCru WPGP
- 'Grandiflora' ♀	CB&S CBot CFil EWTr GOrc MRav SBod SPer WBod WCru WDin WHCG WSHC WWin
- 'Hills of Snow'	CMil
- subsp. *radiata*	CFil LRHS NHlc SNut SSpi WCru WPGP WWat
aspera	CBlo CFil CGre GKir GOrc IOrc SAga SSpi SSta WCru
¶ - 'Anthony Bullivant'	SSpi
- Kawakamii Group	CFil CMil SSta WCru WPGP
§ - 'Macrophylla' ♀	CBlo CFil CMil EPfP LRHS MBel MBri SPer SSpi WCru WGer WPGP WWat
- 'Mauvette'	CFil MBlu SPer SSpi SSta WBcn WCru WPGP
- 'Peter Chappell'	SSpi
§ - subsp. *robusta*	CFil GAri SNut WCru WPGP
- 'Rocklon'	CFil WCru WPGP
- 'Rosthornii'	See *H. aspera* subsp. *robusta*
- 'Sam Macdonald'	CFil SSpi WPGP
§ - subsp. *sargentiana* ♀	CB&S CBot CFil CHEx CHad COtt EBee ELan ERav LNet LRHS MBlu MBri MRav SMad SPer SSpi SSta WAbe WBod WCru WDin WPGP WWat
- - large-leaved	WPGP
- 'Spinners'	SSpi
- subsp. *strigosa*	CFil CMil EPfP GOrc WCru WPGP WWat
- 'Taiwan'	LRHS SSpi
§ - Villosa Group ♀	More than 30 suppliers
§ 'Blue Deckle' (L)	CFil CMHG MBNS MRav NHlc SNut SSpi WBcn WPGP
'Brilliant'	NHlc
cinerea	See *H. arborescens* subsp. *discolor*
'Diabolo'	Last listed 1998
§ 'Grant's Choice' (L)	NHlc
§ *heteromalla*	CFai CFil CMHG CMil CTrG SSpi WCru WPGP
- B&SWJ 2142	WCru
- Bretschneideri Group ♀	GAri GQui NHlc WBod WCru WWat
- DJHC 493	WCru
- HWJCM 148	WCru
- HWJCM 180	WCru
- 'Morrey's Form'	WCru
- S&F 338	ISea
- 'Snowcap'	GQui NHlc WBcn WCru WWat
- f.*xanthoneura*	CFil GAri SSpi
- - 'Wilsonii'	WCru WSHC
- 'Yalung Ridge'	NHlc WCru
hirta	CFil CMil
- B&SWJ 5000	WCru
integerrima	See *H. serratifolia*
integrifolia	CFil CPlN
- B&SWJ 022	WCru
involucrata	CFil EPfP LRHS NHlc SSpi SSta WCru
- dwarf	CFil WCru
- 'Hortensis' (d) ♀	CElw CFil CPle EPfP IOrc SBrw SSpi WAbe WCru WKif WPGP WSHC
* - 'Sterilis'	EPfP
'Korale Red'	WBcn

'Lavender Blue'	Last listed 1999
lobbii B&SWJ 3214	WCru
longipes	CFil ERav WCru WPGP WWat
luteovenosa	CFil WCru
macrophylla	LRHS
¶ - 'Adria Pink'	NBlu
- Alpen Glow	See *H. macrophylla* 'Alpenglühen'
§ - 'Alpenglühen' (H)	CB&S CFil ELan IOrc NHlc NPro SBod SRms WPGP
- 'Altona' (H) ♀	CB&S CFil GAri IOrc ISea LRHS MGos MRav NHlc NPri SBod SPer WLRN WPGP WStI
- 'Amethyst' (H/d)	CFil WPGP
- 'Ami Pasquier' (H) ♀	CB&S CBlo CDoC CFil EBee EPfP GKir IOrc LRHS MRav NHlc SLim SSpi WGer WPGP
* - 'Aureomarginata'	EPfP
- 'Aureovariegata'	CEnd CFil ELan LRHS SNut WBcn WPGP
- 'Ayesha' (H) ♀	More than 30 suppliers
- 'Ayesha Blue' (H)	MAsh
- 'Beauté Vendômoise' (L)	CFil CMil SSpi WPGP
- 'Belzonii' (L)	NHlc
- 'Benelux' (H)	CB&S CWSG WGwG WLRN WTro
* - 'Bicolour'	MAsh
§ - 'Blauer Prinz' (H)	CFil GCHN IOrc LRHS NHlc WLRN
§ - 'Blauling' (L)	CDoC CWSG NHlc
§ - 'Blaumeise' (L)	CFil MAsh NHlc SSpi WBod WGer WPGP
- 'Blue Bonnet' (H)	CFil COtt EPfP MAsh SPer WHen WLRN WPGP
- Blue Prince	See *H. macrophylla* 'Blauer Prinz'
- 'Blue Sky'	See *H. macrophylla* 'Blaumeise'
- Blue Tit	See *H. macrophylla* 'Blaumeise'
- 'Blue Wave'	See *H. macrophylla* 'Mariesii Perfecta'
- Bluebird	See *H. macrophylla* 'Blauling'
- 'Bodensee' (H)	CB&S GKir LRHS NFla SBod WStI
- 'Bouquet Rose' (H)	CBlo CCHP ECtt MRav NFla WBod WGwG
- 'Brunette' (H)	CFil CMil
- 'Buchfink' (L)	CFil WPGP
- 'Cordata'	See *H. arborescens*
- 'Covent Garden'	Last listed 1998
- 'Deutschland' (H)	CTri IOrc
- 'Domotoi' (H/d)	CFil SPan
- DragonflyPBR	See *H. macrophylla* Libelle = 'Hobella'
* - 'Dwaag Pink'	MRav
- 'Eldorado' (H)	EHol
§ - 'Enziandom' (H)	CB&S CFil SSpi WPGP
§ - 'Europa' (H) ♀	CB&S CTrw GChr GKir IOrc LRHS MAsh MGos NCut NHlc SBod SEND WBod WGwG WStI WWal
§ - Fasan™ (L)	CFil NHlc WPGP WSPU
- 'Firelight'	See *H. macrophylla* 'Leuchtfeuer'
¶ - 'Fireworks'	CMil
- 'Fischers Silberblau' (H)	CFil
- Forever Pink	EBrP EBre LBCl LBSe LBre MBBe SBre WGer
§ - 'Frau Katsuko'	ERav LRHS SPer
- 'Frillibet' (H)	CDoC CFil EPfP LRHS NHlc WPGP
- 'Gartenbaudirektor Kuhnert' (H)	SMer
§ - 'Générale Vicomtesse de Vibraye' (H) ♀	CB&S CDoC CEnd CFil CMHG CTri EBee EPfP GCHN GKir LRHS MBar MBri NFla NHlc SLim SNut SPer SSpi WBod WLRN WPGP WWin

- Gentian Dome — See *H. macrophylla* 'Enziandom'
- 'Geoffrey Chadbund' — See *H. macrophylla* 'Möwe'
- 'Gerda Steiniger' — CB&S CBlo
- 'Gertrud Glahn' (H) — CB&S CBlo NCut
- 'Glowing Embers' — CFil LRHS MBri SEND WPGP
- 'Gold Dust' (v) — CFil EPla WPGP
- 'Goliath' (H) — CBlo CFil EPfP LRHS WPGP
- 'Hamburg' (H) — CEnd CFil CTri EBee ECtt ENot EPfP IOrc LPVe LPan LRHS MGos MRav NCut NHlc SDix WFar WStl WWeb
- 'Harlequin' — CFil WPGP
- 'Harry's Pink Topper' (H) — MAsh
- 'Hatfield Rose' (H) — CB&S
- 'Heinrich Seidel' (H) — CB&S CFil NHlc WPGP
- 'Holstein' (H) — CFil MAsh WPGP
¶ - 'Homigo' PBR (H) — WBcn
§ - 'Hörnli' (H) — CFil LPan WPGP
- 'Intermezzo' — NHlc WLRN
- 'Izu-no-hana' (L/d) — CFil CMil
- 'James Grant' — See *H.* 'Grant's Choice'
§ - 'Joseph Banks' (H) — CB&S
- 'Kardinal' (L) — CFil WPGP
- 'King George' (H) — CB&S CDoC CFil CWSG EBee EBrP EBre EOld GKir IOrc LBCl LBSe LBre LRHS MBBe MBar MGos MRav NHlc SBre SLim SPer SRPl WBod WFar WPGP WStl WWal
- 'Kluis Superba' (H) — CB&S CBlo CFil CTri GOrc IOrc MRav NHlc WPGP
§ - 'Koningin Wilhelmina' (H) — CFil WBcn WPGP
§ - 'La France' (H) — CB&S CBlo COtt CTri CWSG EBee GChr LRHS MBar MRav SRPl WFar
- Lady Fujiyo® (H) — CPLG LRHS
- Lady Katsuko® (H) — See *H. macrophylla* 'Frau Katsuko'
- Lady Mariko® (H) — LRHS SPer
- Lady Nobuko® (H) — LRHS SPer
- Lady Taiko Blue® (H) — CB&S LRHS SPer
- Lady Taiko Pink® (H) — CB&S LRHS
- 'Lanarth White' (L) ♀ — CB&S CDoC CFil CTbh CTri EBee EPfP MRav NHlc SLim SPer SReu SRms SSpi WBod WCru WPGP WPnP WWat
§ - 'Leuchtfeuer' (H) — LRHS MBel MBri WGer
§ - Libelle = 'Hobella' PBR (L) — CB&S CBlo CDoC CFil CWSG EBee MAsh MBri NHlc SLim SNut SPer WKif WPGP WWat WWeb
- 'Lilacina' (L) — CFil EPfP MWhi NHlc SLPl SPer SSpi WBod WKif WPGP
§ - 'Maculata' (L) — EHol ELan GQui IOrc SEas WWat
§ - 'Madame A. Riverain' (H) — CFil COtt CWSG LRHS SBod WLRN WTro
§ - 'Madame Emile Mouillère' (H) ♀ — More than 30 suppliers
- 'Maréchal Foch' (H) — CFil CTri IOrc WPGP
- 'Mariesii' (L) — CFil CMHG CTri EBee ELan ENot EPla ISea LRHS NHlc SDix SPer WAbe WKif WLRN WPnP WStl WWat
§ - 'Mariesii Perfecta' (L) ♀ — More than 30 suppliers
- 'Mariesii Variegata' (L) — Last listed 1999
- 'Masja' (H) — CB&S COtt CWSG EBee EGra IOrc LRHS MBri MGos MRav NFla SVil
- 'Mathilda Gutges' (H) — CDoC CFil CWSG SSpi WPGP WStl
- 'Mini Hörnli' — See *H. macrophylla* 'Hörnli'
- misapplied 'Bluebird' — See *H. serrata* 'Bluebird'
- 'Miss Belgium' (H) — CFil CTri IOrc MBri NHlc SBod SEas

- 'Miss Hepburn' — COtt NHlc SPer
- 'Mousmée' — CFil
- 'Mousseline' (H) — LPan
§ - 'Möwe' (L) ♀ — CB&S CDoC CEnd CFil CMil EBee ECtt ENot LRHS MBri MRav NHlc SBod SChu SDix SMad SNut SPer SRms SSpi SSta WPGP WWeb
- 'Münster' (H) — NHlc
- 'Niedersachsen' (H) — CFil MRav NHlc SMer WPGP
- 'Nigra' (H) ♀ — CB&S CChe CFil CGre CTre ELan EPla IOrc MBel MGos SDix SNut SPer WCru WFar WGwG WPGP WStl WWal
- 'Nikko Blue' (H) — CB&S CBlo CFil EPfP MBri SEND WBod WPGP
- var. **normalis** — NHlc
§ - 'Nymphe' (H) — LRHS
- 'Oamacha' — NHlc
- 'Otaksa' (H) — CFil NHlc
- 'Parzifal' (H) ♀ — CB&S CFil CTrw EPfP NHlc WBod WLRN WPGP WWal
- 'Pax' — See *H. macrophylla* 'Nymphe'
- Pheasant — See *H. macrophylla* Fasan
- 'Pia' (H) — CB&S CDoC CFil CPla EBee ELan GKir IOrc MAsh MBNS MTho NHol SBod SLim SPer SPla SRms WAbe WCru WFar WPGP WPat WWat
- 'Pink Wave' (L) — Last listed 1998
- 'Prinses Beatrix' — CB&S CChe CFil WBcn WPGP
- 'Quadricolor' (L/v) — CAbb CFil CMil CTbh EBee EHoe EPla LRHS MBri MRav NSti SAga SDix SLim SNut SPer SPla SPlb SRPl SRms WCot WCru WHCG WPGP WSHC
- Queen Wilhelmina — See *H. macrophylla* 'Koningin Wilhelmina'
- 'R.F. Felton' — CB&S
- 'Red Emperor' (H) — Last listed 1997
- Redbreast — See *H. macrophylla* 'Rotkehlchen'
- 'Regula' (H) — CTrw
- 'Renate Steiniger' (H) — CFai LRHS WBod
- 'Rex' — NHlc
- 'Rosita' (H) — LPan LRHS MAsh
§ - 'Rotkehlchen' (L) — CFai CFil WPGP
- 'Rotschwanz' (L) — CFil CMil NHlc SSpi
- 'Saint Claire' — CB&S
¶ - 'Schwabenland' — NPri
- 'Sea Foam' (L) — EPla IOrc NHlc WSPU
- 'Seascape' — NHlc
* - 'Shower' — LRHS
- 'Sibylla' (H) — CB&S CFil NHlc WPGP
- Sister Therese — See *H. macrophylla* 'Soeur Thérèse'
§ - 'Soeur Thérèse' (H) — CBlo CFil GAri IOrc LPan LRHS MAsh MBri MGos WPGP WStl
- 'Souvenir du Président Paul Doumer' (H) — CBlo
- 'Taube' (L) — CB&S CFil GQui
N - Teller Blau (L) — CBlo CDoC COtt EBee MBri NHlc NMoo SCoo SLim SSta WDin WWeb
N - Teller Rosa (L) — CDoC MAsh NMoo SCoo SSta
N - Teller Rot (L) — CBlo CDoC MAsh MBri NMoo SCoo SPlb WDin
N - 'Teller Variegated' — See *H. macrophylla* 'Tricolor'
N - Teller Weiss PBR — See *H. macrophylla* 'Libelle'
- 'Thomas Hogg' (L) — Last listed 1997
- 'Tokyo Delight' (L) — CBlo CBrd CChe CDoC CEnd CFil EBee IOrc NHlc SSpi WPGP
- 'Tovelit' — GAri LRHS WWeb
N - 'Tricolor' (L/v) ♀ — CB&S CBot CDoC CFil CGre ERav

	GOrc LAst LRHS MAsh MBel
	MGos MTis SAga SBod SLon SPer
	SReu WCru WFar WKif WPGP
	WPnP WPyg WWal
- 'Universal' (H)	NHlc
- 'Ursula'	Last listed 1997
- 'Val de Loire'	CBlo CWSG
- 'Variegata'	See *H. macrophylla* 'Maculata'
- 'Veitchii' (L) ♀	CB&S CBot CFil CMHG CMil EBee
	ENot EPfP MBri MRav NHlc SBod
	SDix SPer SSpi WBod WPGP
	WWat
- 'Vicomte de Vibraye'	See *H. macrophylla* 'Générale
	Vicomtesse de Vibraye'
- 'Westfalen' (H) ♀	LRHS NCat NHlc SDix SPla WLRN
	WWal
- 'White Lace' (L)	ELan
- 'White Wave' (L) ♀	CBlo CFil EBee ENot EWTr GGar
	LRHS MBar NFla SBod SEND SNut
	SRms SSht SSpi WBod WDin
	WLRN WPGP WStI
paniculata	CFil CMCN CTrw GGar GKir
- 'Brussels Lace'	CAbP CFil LRHS MAsh SNut SSpi
- 'Burgundy Lace'	CB&S CMil CPMA MBel MBlu
- 'Everest'	LRHS SNut
- 'Floribunda' ♀	CFil CHad EPfP EWTr LRHS SNut
	SPer SSpi WPGP WRHF
- from Taiwan B&SWJ	WCru
3556	
- from Taiwan B&SWJ	WCru
3804	
- 'Grandiflora' ♀	More than 30 suppliers
- 'Greenspire'	LBuc LRHS MBlu WBcn
- 'Kyushu' ♀	More than 30 suppliers
- Pink Diamond	CAbP CBlo CDoC CMCN CTbh
= 'Interhydia'	EBee EBrP EBre ENot LBCl LBSe
	LBre LRHS MAsh MBBe MBlu
	MBri SBre SLim SMad SPla SSpi
	SSta WCru
- 'Praecox' ♀	SPer WCru WPat WWin
- 'Tardiva'	CB&S CBot CDoC LPan LRHS
	MAsh MGos MRav SDix SPer
	SRms WFar WHCG WLRN WPat
	WPyg
- 'Unique' ♀	CDoC CFil EPfP EPla GOrc LFis
	LHop LRHS MAsh MBri SNut SPer
	SPla SSpi WBod WCru WPGP
	WWat
- 'White Lace'	CB&S MBlu
- 'White Moth'	CB&S CFil CMil CPMA SNut
'Pink Showers'	NHlc
§ 'Preziosa' ♀	More than 30 suppliers
quelpartensis	CB&S CPlN CRHN CTre GQui
	SSpi WCru
quercifolia ♀	More than 30 suppliers
¶ - 'Burgundy'	EPfP
- 'Flore Pleno'	See *H. quercifolia* Snow Flake
- 'Harmony'	CEnd CFil CHad SSta WHCG
	WPGP
- 'Pee Wee'	EPfP GEil LRHS MAsh SPla
- 'Sike's Dwarf'	CEnd CFil LRHS SSpi WPGP
* - 'Snow'	CWSG
§ - Snow Flake™ (d)	CAbP CB&S CDoC CDul CEnd
	CFil CMil CPMA CSPN ELan EMil
	EPfP ERav GKir IOrc LRHS MAsh
	MBri SBrw SLon SMur SPer SSpi
	SSta WHCG WWat
- Snow Queen = 'Flemygea'	CB&S CDoC CPMA EPfP GOrc
	IOrc ISea MAsh MBri MGos MRav
	MSte SCob SLim SPer SPla SSta
	WCot WHCG WWat
- 'Stardust'	CRos

- 'Tennessee Clone'	CFil WPGP
robusta	SLPl
sargentiana	See *H. aspera* subsp. *sargentiana*
scandens	CFil CPle
- subsp. *chinensis*	WCru
B&SWJ 3420	
- subsp. *liukiuensis*	WCru
¶ - - B&SWJ 6022	WCru
seemannii	More than 30 suppliers
serrata	CCHP CTrw NHlc WCru
- 'Acuminata'	See *H. serrata* 'Bluebird'
- 'Aigaku'	WPGP
- 'Amacha'	CFil WPGP
- 'Amagyana'	CMil CPLG
- 'Belle Deckle'	See *H.* 'Blue Deckle'
- 'Beni-gaku'	CB&S CFil CMil NFla WLRN
	WPGP
- 'Blue Deckle' (L)	WPGP
§ - 'Bluebird' ♀	More than 30 suppliers
* - *chinensis*	NHlc
- 'Diadem'	CBlo CBrd CFil CMil NHlc NPro
	SBod SDix WCru WLRN WPGP
	WWat
- 'Grayswood' ♀	CB&S CEnd CFil CHig GEil GKir
	GQui LRHS MRav NHlc SDix SPer
	WKif WLRN WPGP WWat
- 'Intermedia'	CFil WPGP
- 'Jogasaki'	CFil
- 'Kiyosumi'	CFil CMil
- *koreana*	Last listed 1999
- 'Macrosepala'	Last listed 1999
- 'Miranda' (L)	CBrd CEnd CFil COtt NHlc SSpi
	WFar WLRN WPGP WWat
- 'Miyama-yae-murasaki'	CFil
(d)	
- 'Preziosa'	See *H.* 'Preziosa'
* - 'Pulchella'	SPla
* - 'Pulchra'	CEnd CMil SSpi
- 'Rosalba' ♀	CBrd CFil EPfP MRav SPer SPla
	WPGP WSHC
- 'Shichidanka-nishiki' (d/v)	CFil CMil
- 'Shirofugi'	CFil
- 'Shirotae' (d)	CFil
- var. *thunbergii*	CB&S CFil CMHG GQui WPGP
- 'Tiara'	CFil SSpi WBcn WPGP
- 'Uzu Azisai'	CFil
- subsp. *yezoensis*	CFil NHlc WPGP
'Wryneck' (H)	
§ *serratifolia*	CFil CGre CHEx CPlN EPfP EPla
	SAPC SArc SBra SLon SSpi SSta
	WCru WPGP WSHC
sikokiana B&SWJ 5035	WCru
'Silver Slipper'	Last listed 1999
tiliifolia	See *H. anomala* subsp. *petiolaris*
villosa	See *H. aspera* Villosa Group
xanthoneura	See *H. heteromalla*

HYDRASTIS (Ranunculaceae)
canadensis	CArn GBuc GPoy WCru

HYDROCHARIS (Hydrocharitaceae)
morsus-ranae	CBen CRDP CRow CWat EHon
	EMFW LPBA MSta NDea SWat

HYDROCOTYLE (Apiaceae)
asiatica	See *Centella asiatica*
moschata	CInt GAri WPer WWin
* *palustris*	Last listed 1998
¶ *ranunculoides*	NHol
* *sibthorpioides* 'Variegata'	EBee EMan EMon EPPr GCal
	WCHb WCot WPer
vulgaris	CRDP EMFW EWFC MSta WWeb

HYDROPHYLLUM (Hydrophyllaceae)

canadense	EBee EMar WCru
virginianum	CRDP MSal
- purple	EBee

HYLOMECON (Papaveraceae)

§ *japonica*	CRDP EBee EPar ERos GCrs GKir IMGH MSte NBir NHol NMGW NRya NTow NWCA WAbe WCot WCru WFar

HYLOTELEPHIUM See SEDUM

HYMENANTHERA See MELICYTUS

HYMENOCALLIS (Amaryllidaceae)

'Advance'	LAma LBow LRHS
§ *caroliniana*	LAma
x *festalis*	ERea LAma LBow MBri NRog SDeJ
- 'Zwanenburg'	Last listed 1998
barrisiana	LBow LRHS
littoralis	NRog
§ *longipetala*	LBow LRHS
narcissiflora	Last listed 1997
occidentalis	See *H. caroliniana*
'Sulphur Queen'	LBow LRHS NRog SDeJ

HYMENOSPORUM (Pittosporaceae)

flavum	CPLG LRHS SOWG

HYMENOXYS (Asteraceae)

grandiflora	See *Tetraneuris grandiflora*
subintegra	Last listed 1998

HYOPHORBE (Arecaceae)

¶ *indica*	CRoM
§ *lagenicaulis*	CRoM LPal
verschaffeltii	CRoM LPal

HYOSCYAMUS (Solanaceae)

albus	GBar MChe MSal
niger	CArn EMFP EWFC GPoy MChe MSal WHer WWye
* - 'Capel Ulo'	Last listed 1997

HYPERICUM ✿ (Clusiaceae)

acmosepalum	CFil GIBF WPGP
- SBEC 93	Last listed 1997
§ *addingtonii*	EPla SPan
adenotrichum	GCHN
aegypticum	CInt CLyd CPBP EDAr GCHN LBee LRHS MHer NHol NMen NWCA NWoo SIng SRot WFar WLin WPat WPer WPyg
¶ - long-styled	SIng
amblycalyx	Last listed 1999
androsaemum	CAgr CArn ECha EGoo ENot GKir GOrc ISea MHer MHew MSal NPer WDin
§ - 'Albury Purple'	CB&S CElw CPle GBuc GCHN GEil GKir MCCP MRav MTed WPat
- 'Autumn Blaze'	MGos
§ - 'Dart's Golden Penny'	SLPl SPer WBcn
- 'Excellent Flair'	NPro
- 'Orange Flair'	CBlo
§ - f. *variegatum*	CBlo CCHP EBee NSti SPer WCot
'Mrs Gladis Brabazon' (v)	WWeb
§ *annulatum*	EMon
ascyron	EBee IIve

atboum	CLyd GCHN MBro NBir NTow SIng WPat WPer
atomarium	EBee WPGP
augustinii	Last listed 1999
balearicum	CFil CLyd CPle MTho SDry SPan WAbe WPGP
§ *beanii*	LRHS
bellum	CPle EPfP GCal
cf. - ACE 2467	Last listed 1999
- subsp. *latisepalum*	Last listed 1997
buckleyi	GCHN SIng WPat
calycinum	CB&S CChe CLan EBee ELan ENot EPfP GChr GKir GOrc IIve LBuc LGro MBar MGos MRav MWat NWea SPer WDin WGwG
§ *cerastioides*	CCHP CMea EDAr ESis GCHN GKir LBee LRHS MHar SIng SRms WAbe WPer WWin
choisyanum B&L 12469	Last listed 1997
coris	CLyd ECha EWes LRHS MBro MHar MTho MWat NFla NTow SRms WHoo
crux-andreae	EBee
cuneatum	See *H. pallens*
x *cyatbiflorum* 'Gold Cup'	CDoC GOrc SPan
x *dummeri* 'Peter Dummer'	CBlo EMil GKir MBri NHol
'Eastleigh Gold'	SLon
elatum	See *H.* x *inodorum*
elodeoides	EBee MSta
elongatum	EMon
empetrifolium	CPle EWes
§ - subsp. *oligantbum*	GCHN
- 'Prostatum'	See *H. empetrifolium* subsp. *tortuosum*
§ - subsp. *tortuosum*	CLyd EDAr EWes
§ *forrestii* ♀	CFil CLan CPle EPfP LRHS MGos NWea WPGP WWat
¶ - Hird 54	WPGP
N *fragile* hort.	See *H. olympicum* f. *minus*
frondosum	SPer
- 'Buttercup'	CBlo
- Sunburst™	CBlo EBee EPfP EPla LRHS MBri MGos SPan
N 'Gemo'	EBee
'Gold Penny'	See *H. androsaemum* 'Dart's Golden Penny'
grandiflorum	See *H. kouytchense*
benryi L 753	SRms
'Hidcote' ♀	More than 30 suppliers
'Hidcote Variegated'	CCHP EBee GCHN MCCP SEas SHFr SLim SPer SRms WFar
bircinum	EOHP
- subsp. *albimontanum*	SPan
- subsp. *cambessedesii*	LRHS
- subsp. *majus*	EMon
birsutum	CKin
bookerianum	Last listed 1999
bumifusum	GAri
byssopifolium	CPle SHFr
§ x *inodorum*	GGar
- 'Albury Purple'	See *H. androsaemum* 'Albury Purple'
- 'Elstead'	ECtt ELan EWTr GKir MBar MGos MRav MWat NBid NFla SPer SRms WDin WHCG WWin
- 'Summergold' (v)	CBlo MCCP
- 'Ysella'	ECha EWes MRav NPro NSti SDry SPer
japonicum	EWes
kalmianum	CChe EWes
kamtscbaticum	EDAr MHar
kelleri	GCHN ITim

§ **kiusianum** | CInt GCHN MBar MTho NWCA
var. **yakusimense** | SIng
§ **kouytchense** ♀ | CB&S CPle CSam EMon EPfP
| EWes GQui LRHS MBri SDry SPan
| WKif WPat WPyg
lagarocladum | Last listed 1999
lancasteri | CBlo EBee ELan EPfP LRHS SPan
| WBcn
- L 750 | Last listed 1997
leschenaultii hort. | See *H. addingtonii*, *H.* 'Rowallane'
linarioides | CLyd GTou
'Locke' | LAst
maclarenii | WBod
- L 863 | Last listed 1998
'Milkmaid' | GEil
montanum | MSal
x **moserianum** ♀ | CLan EBee EBrP EBre ENot EPfP
| LBCl LBSe LBre MBBe MBar MBri
| MRav NPer SBre SPer SRms WStI
| More than 30 suppliers
§ - 'Tricolor' (v) | See *H.* x *moserianum* 'Tricolor'
- 'Variegatum' | See *H. androsaemum* f.
'Mrs Brabazon' | *variegatum* 'Mrs Gladis Brabazon'
nummularium | NBir
oblongifolium | CPle WLRN
- CC 1706 | GGar
olympicum ♀ | CAgr ECha EFer ELan EPot GCHN
| GDra GKir GLil LGro LRHS MBrN
| MFir MHer MWat NFor NMen
| SBla SEas SIng SPer SRms SSmi
| WHen
I - 'Calypso' | CBlo NPro
- 'Eden Star' | NPro
- 'Edith' | SAsh WPyg
- 'Grandiflorum' | See *H. olympicum* f. *uniflorum*
§ - f. **minus** | ECtt EGoo EMNN GCHN GCal
| GDra LRHS MOne SPlb SRms
| WPer WStI WWin
§ - - 'Sulphureum' | CBot ESis EWes MHar MLLN
| MRav MWhi SPer SRms WCFE
| WSHC WWin
§ - - 'Variegatum' | EWes LBee WPat WPyg
§ - f. **uniflorum** | CM&M EDAr GAri LIck MBar
| MBro NBro NPri NVic SEND
| WAbe
- - 'Citrinum' ♀ | CElw CLyd CMea ECha ECtt EDAr
| EPot CLyd LBee LHop LRHS
| MBro MWat NBro NHol SBla
| WAbe WEas WHoo WKif WPGP
| WPat WWat
orientale | EBee EWes GCHN MBro NMen
- JCA 3302 | NHol
§ **pallens** | ECho
patulum var. **forrestii** | See *H. forrestii*
- var. **henryi** Rehder | See *H. pseudohenryi*
et hort.
- - Veitch ex Bean | See *H. beanii*
perforatum | CAgr CArn CKin ELau EOHP EPfP
| EWFC GBar GPoy MChe MGas
| MHer MHew MPEx NHex NMir
| SIde WHer WJek WMoo WOak
| WSel WWye
- 'Crusader' (v) | WAlt
polyphyllum | See *H. olympicum* f. *minus*
- 'Citrinum' | See *H. olympicum* f. *minus*
| 'Sulphureum'
- 'Grandiflorum' | See *H. olympicum* f. *uniflorum*
- 'Sulphureum' | See *H. olympicum* f. *minus*
| 'Sulphureum'
- 'Variegatum' | See *H. olympicum* f. *minus*
| 'Variegatum'
prolificum | CFai CPle ECtt ENot EPla GCHN

| | MAsh MMHG SAga SPan
§ **pseudohenryi** | SPan
- B&L 12009 | Last listed 1997
- L 1029 | GBuc
pseudopetiolatum | GTou
I - **orientale** | Last listed 1998
- var. **yakusimense** | See *H. kiusianum* var.
| *yakusimense*
pulchrum | IIve NCut
quadrangulum L. | See *H. tetrapterum*
reptans hort. | See *H. olympicum* f. *minus*
- Dyer | CPBP ECha ESis EWes MHar
roeperianum | Last listed 1999
§ 'Rowallane' ♀ | CB&S CBot CLTr CLan CPle CTrw
| EPfP EPla GKir ISea SDix WAbe
scouleri subsp. **nortoniae** | Last listed 1997
sp. ACE 2321 | Last listed 1997
sp. ACE 2524 | Last listed 1997
sp. S&SH 381 | Last listed 1999
stellatum | CGre EMon EPla SLon WWat
subsessile B&L 12486 | EMon
'Sungold' | See *H. kouytchense*
tenuicaule KR 743 | ISea
§ **tetrapterum** | CArn CKin EWFC MHew MSal
tomentosum | GCHN
trichocaulon | CLyd ELan EWes GCHN MBro
| NHol WPat WPyg WWin
uralum | Last listed 1997
- CC 1225 | Last listed 1997
wilsonii | Last listed 1997
xylosteifolium | SLon
yakusimense | See *H. kiusianum* var.
| *yakusimense*
yezoense | Last listed 1998

HYPHAENE (Arecaceae)
¶ **petersiana** | LBlo

HYPOCALYMMA (Myrtaceae)
robustum | Last listed 1998

HYPOCHAERIS (Asteraceae)
radicata | CKin IIve NMir
uniflora | Last listed 1998
§ **variegata** | CLTr

HYPOCYRTA See NEMATANTHUS

HYPOESTES (Acanthaceae)
aristata | ERea
§ **phyllostachya** (v) ♀ | MBri
- 'Bettina' (v) | MBri
- 'Carmina' (v) | MBri
- 'Purpuriana' (v) | MBri
- 'Wit' (v) | MBri
sanguinolenta misapplied See *H. phyllostachya*

HYPOLEPIS (Dennstaedtiaceae)
* **distans** 'Compacta' | WRic
millefolium | GAri

HYPOXIS (Hypoxidaceae)
argentea | Last listed 1997
¶ **decumbens** | SIng
hirsuta | EWes
hygrometrica | CRDP CStu ECou EPot WAbe
parvula | SBla
- var. **albiflora** | EPot
§ - - 'Hebron Farm Biscuit' | CBro EWes SBla WAbe
- pink-flowered | EPot
setosa | Last listed 1997
villosa | Last listed 1997

HYPOXIS x RHODOHYPOXIS (Hypoxidaceae)
H. parvula x *R. baurii*   See x *Rhodoxis hybrida*

HYPSELA (Campanulaceae)
   longiflora   See *H. reniformis*
§ *reniformis*   EDAr ELan EMNN EMan GKir
                 LBee LRHS MRav NHar NMen
                 NNrd NOak NWCA SIng SSmi
                 WFar WWin
   - 'Greencourt White'   GBuc GGar
   sp. RB 94066   MNrw

HYPSEOCHARIS (Oxalidaceae)
   bilobata   Last listed 1999

HYSSOPUS (Lamiaceae)
   officinalis   CArn CGdn CSev ECha EGoo
                 ELan ELau EWTr GKir GPoy LBuc
                 LRHS MBNS MBar MBri MChe
                 MHer NFai SChu SIde SRob
                 WCHb WGwG WHbs WHer WOak
                 WOve WPer WWye
   - f. *albus*   ECha EGoo ELau EWTr GPoy
                 MChe MHer SChu SIde WBry
                 WCHb WCer WHer WJek WPer
                 WSel WWye
§ - subsp. *aristatus*   CArn EBee EBrP EBre EDAr ELau
                 ESis GPoy LBCl LBSe LBre LLWP
                 LRHS MBBe MChe NChi SBre SIde
                 WCHb WEas WJek WSel WWin
                 WWye
   - 'Roseus'   CM&M EBee ECha EGoo ELau
                 EWTr GPoy LLWP LRHS MBNS
                 MChe MHer NChi NFai
                 NFor SChu SIde SSca WCHb WCer
                 WGwG WHer WJek WKif WPer
                 WWye
§ - f. *ruber*   Last listed 1999
* *schugnanicus*   EBee LLWP
* - *albus*   EBee
¶ *seravschanicus*   IIve
   tianschanicus   LLWP

HYSTRIX (Poaceae)
   patula   CBrm CCuc CInt EBee ECGN
                 EHoe EMan EMon EPGN EPPr
                 GBin GBri GCal LLWP LRHS
                 MCCP MMoz MNrw MWhi NBro
                 NFai NSti SHFr SPlb SUsu WCot
                 WHal WLRN WPer WWye

I

IBERIS (Brassicaceae)
   amara   EWFC MSal
   candolleana   See *I. pruitii* Candolleana Group
   commutata   See *I. sempervirens*
   'Correvoniana'   WEas
   'Dick Self'   EBrP EBre GKir LBCl LBSe LBre
                 LRHS MBBe SBre
   gibraltarica   EMan MHer NFor NPri SIng SRms
                 SWal WGor
   jordanii   See *I. pruitii*
§ *pruitii*   CPBP EBur SBla
§ - Candolleana Group   Last listed 1998
   saxatilis   EDAr WPer
   - *candolleana*   See *I. pruitii* Candolleana Group
   semperflorens   WCot WSPU

§ *sempervirens* ♀   CB&S CTri ELan EMan LGro MHer
                 MWat NArg NBid NBro NFai NFla
                 NFor NOrc NVic SEND SRms STre
                 WCFE WPer WWal
   - 'Little Gem'   See *I. sempervirens* 'Weisser
                 Zwerg'
   - 'Pinky Perpetual'   Last listed 1998
   - 'Pygmaea'   MWat NHar NMen WHil
§ - 'Schneeflocke' ♀   ENot GKir LRHS MBro SPer SRCN
                 WHoo WPyg
   - Snowflake   See *I. sempervirens*
                 'Schneeflocke'
   - 'Starkers' (v)   Last listed 1997
§ - 'Weisser Zwerg'   CMea EBrP EBre ECha ECtt ELan
                 EMNN LBCl LBSe LBee LBre LRHS
                 MBBe MBro MHer NHar NMen
                 NTow SBla SBre SIng SRms WAbe
                 WHoo WWin
   spathulata   Last listed 1999

IDESIA (Flacourtiaceae)
   polycarpa   CB&S CFil CMCN CPle CTho EPfP
                 LRHS MBel SMad SSpi SSta WPat
                 WWat WWoo
   - Sich 848   WPGP

ILEX ✿ (Aquifoliaceae)
N x *altaclerensis*   SHHo
   - 'Atkinsonii' (m)   CRos SHHo
   - 'Balearica'   SRPl WWat
   - 'Barterberry' (f)   Last listed 1999
   - 'Belgica' (f)   SHHo
§ - 'Belgica Aurea' (f/v) ♀   CB&S CDoC CMHG CRos EPfP
                 GKir LNet LPan MBar MBri MWat
                 NWea SEND SHHo WBcn WWat
   - 'Camelliifolia' (f) ♀   CCHP CDul CMCN CMHG CRos
                 EBee GKir LPan MBlu MBri MRav
                 MWat NWea SBod SHHo SPer
                 WBcn WWat
   - 'Golden King' (f/v) ♀   More than 30 suppliers
   - 'Hendersonii' (f)   CBlo SBod SHHo WBcn
   - 'Hodginsii' (m) ♀   CBlo CCHP CMCN CRos ECot
                 IOrc MBar NWea SEND SHHo
   - 'Howick' (f/v)   SHHo WBcn
¶ - 'James G. Esson' (f)   SBir SHHo
   - 'Lady Valerie' (f/v)   SHHo
   - 'Lawsoniana' (f/v) ♀   More than 30 suppliers
   - 'Maderensis'   GKir NRib
   - 'Maderensis Variegata'   See *I. aquifolium* 'Maderensis
                 Variegata'
   - 'Marnockii' (f)   SHHo
¶ - 'Moorei' (m)   SHHo
   - 'Mundyi' (m)   CCHP SHHo
   - 'Nigrescens' (m)   Last listed 1997
   - 'Purple Shaft' (f)   CMCN EWTr MRav SHHo
   - 'Ripley Gold' (f/v)   CBlo CMHG GKir LPan MAsh
                 NHol SAga SHHo
   - 'Silver Sentinel'   See *I.* x *altaclerensis* 'Belgica
                 Aurea'
   - 'W.J. Bean' (f)   SHHo
   - 'Wilsonii' (f) ♀   IOrc LPan MWat NWea SBod
                 SHHo
   aquifolium ♀   CB&S CChe CKin CSam CTri
                 EBee ELau ENot EWTr GChr GKir
                 IOrc ISea LHyr LNet LRHS MBar
                 MBri MGos MWat NWea SHFr
                 SHHo WDin WMou WOrn WStI
   - 'Alaska' (f)   CBlo CDoC CEnd CMCN EBee
                 EBrP EBre EMil ENot GKir LBCl
                 LBSe LBre LBuc MAsh MBBe NHol
                 NSti SBir SBre SHHo WRHF
   - 'Alcicornis' (m)   CMCN

pringlei	CMCN
§ *purpurea*	CMCN
'Pyramidalis'	See *I. aquifolium* 'Pyramidalis'
rotunda	CMCN
rugosa	CMCN
'September Gem' (f)	CMCN
serrata	CMCN
'Sparkleberry' (f)	LPan LRHS
suaveolens	CMCN
verticillata	CAgr CDul CGre CMCN CPne
	EPla GKir IMGH LPan MBlu NWea
- (f)	EPfP GAri NWea SMur
- (m)	CDoC EPfP GAri SMur WLRN
	WWat
- 'Afterglow' (f)	MBlu
- f. *aurantiaca* (f)	CBlo MBlu SMur
- f. *chrysocarpa*	CMCN
- 'Compacta'	See *I. verticillata* 'Nana'
* - 'Fructu Albo' (f)	Last listed 1999
* - 'Golden Male' (m)	Last listed 1998
* - 'Golden Rain'	Last listed 1998
- 'Jim Dandy' (m)	MBlu
§ - 'Nana' (f)	MBlu
- 'Red Sprite'	See *I. verticillata* 'Nana'
- 'Southern Gentleman' (m)	MBlu
- 'Stop Light' (f)	MBlu
- 'Sunset' (f)	MBlu
- 'Winter Red' (f)	CDoC CMCN GKir MBlu MMHG
	WRHF WWat
vomitoria	CMCN
x *wandoensis*	CMCN SBir SHHo
'Washington' (f)	CPle SBir
yunnanensis	CMCN GAri

ILIAMNA See SPHAERALCEA

ILLICIUM (Illiciaceae)

anisatum	CArn CB&S CFil CPle EPfP SRPl
	SSpi WOTO WPGP WPat WPyg
	WSHC WWat
floridanum	CB&S CFil CPle EPfP SBrw SSpi
	WPGP WWat
henryi	CFil CMCN CPLG CPle WPGP
	WSHC

IMPATIENS (Balsaminaceae)

auricoma	EBak SHFr
balfourii	EBee WCot
'Ballerina'	CInt
'Blackberry Ice'	CHal
capensis	Last listed 1998
'Cardinal Red'	CHal CInt
congolensis	EPfP
cristata	Last listed 1999
'Dapper Dan' (v)	CHal
'Diamond Orange'	Last listed 1999
'Diamond Rose'	CHal
'Diamond Scarlet'	CHal
double flowered (d)	EBak
'Evening Blush'	CInt
¶ Fiesta Series	NPri
'Burgundy Rose' [PBR] (d)	
¶ - 'Fiesta White' [PBR] (d)	NPri
¶ - 'Lavender Orchid' [PBR] (d)	WWol
¶ - 'Pink Ruffle' [PBR] (d)	NPri
¶ - 'Salmon Sunrise' [PBR] (d)	NPri WWol
¶ - 'Salsa Red' [PBR] (d)	NPri
¶ - 'Sparkler Red' [PBR] (d)	NPri
¶ - 'Sparkler Rose' [PBR] (d)	NPri
- 'Sparkler Salmon' [PBR] (d)	Last listed 1999
glandulifera	MCCP MHer WHer
- 'Candida'	CBre EMon

'Golden Surprise'	Last listed 1997
hawkeri	EBak
hians	SHFr
'Madame Pompadour'	CHal
New Guinea Group	CHal EBak MBri WLRN
niamniamensis	EBak ERea LCns LHil SSte
- 'Congo Cockatoo'	CHal CInt ECon EOHP LIck SHFr
	SRms SVen
- 'Golden Cockatoo' (v)	EBak MCCP WSpi
I - 'Variegata'	ECon
omeiana	EBee MNrw WCot
¶ 'Orange Gem'	WWol
'Orange Surprise'	Last listed 1999
'Peach Ice' (v)	CHal
pseudoviola	LHil SHFr
* - 'Alba'	CSpe
- 'Woodcote'	CSpe LHil
'Purple Chico'	Last listed 1999
'Raspberry Ripple'	CHal
'Salmon Princess'	CHal CInt
¶ 'Seashells Apricot'	CHal
(Seashells Series)	
¶ 'Seashells Papaya'	CHal
(Seashells Series)	
¶ 'Seashells Tangerine'	CHal
(Seashells Series)	
¶ 'Seashells Yellow'	CHal
(Seashells Series)	
sodenii	CFee GCal LHil SDys SHFr WPGP
¶ sp. from China	GCal
sp. from Uganda	EMan GCal
sulcata	SHFr
sultani	See *I. walleriana*
sylvicola	CFir
§ Tagula = 'Kigula' [PBR]	Last listed 1999
(Paradise Series)	
tinctoria	CDoC CFil CFir CGre CHEx CTre
	CWit GCal LHil MNrw SVen WCot
	WCru WPGP
- subsp. *elegantissima*	CFee
- subsp. *tinctoria*	Last listed 1998
ugandensis	CFil WPGP
¶ Velvetea™ = 'Secret Love'	CInt
§ *walleriana*	EBak MBri
¶ - 'Cherry Ice' [PBR]	CHal
¶ - 'Orange Ice' [PBR]	CHal
* - 'Variegata'	CHal
zombensis	SHFr WCot

IMPERATA (Poaceae)

brevifolia	CBrm
cylindrica	CPla CSam EPar MSal WCot
- 'Red Baron'	See *I. cylindrica* 'Rubra'
§ - 'Rubra'	More than 30 suppliers

INCARVILLEA (Bignoniaceae)

§ *arguta*	CBot EBee GCal LGre LPio MHar
	WAbe WWin
brevipes	See *I. mairei*
compacta	NHar NSla
- ACE 1455	EBee
delavayi	More than 30 suppliers
- 'Bees' Pink'	EBee GBuc GCal
- 'Snowtop'	More than 30 suppliers
diffusa	Last listed 1999
forrestii	LPio NSla
- KGB 43	Last listed 1998
grandiflora	CLAP CRDP ELan NWoo SBla
himalayensis	GBuc GCrs NHar NSla SBla
'Frank Ludlow'	
- 'Nyoto Sama'	GBuc GDra
longiracemosa	Last listed 1999

lutea L. 1986 — EBee

§ *mairei* — EBee EGoo EWTr GDra GMaP LAst LRHS MHar MLLN NLar SLod SMrm SSca WPer WWin
- B&L 12602 — Last listed 1999
- var. *mairei* ACE 2233 — NHar
- - ACE 2420 — NHar
- - CLD 101 — GCrs
- - f. *multifoliata* — See *I. zhongdianensis*
- - - ACE 64 — See *I. zhongdianensis* ACE 2201

§ *olgae* — EBee ELan EMan EMon NPSI SBla

przewalskii — WAbe

¶ - J&JA 447850 — SBla

sinensis — Last listed 1999
- 'Alba' — Last listed 1999
- 'Cheron' — EBee
'Snowcap' — Last listed 1997

youngbusbandii — Last listed 1998

§ *zhongdianensis* — EBee GBuc GCrs NSla SBla SMrm WPGP
- ACE 1600 — Last listed 1998

§ - ACE 2201 — NHar
- ACE 2278 — NHar NWCA
- CLD 233 — Last listed 1999

INDIGOFERA (Papilionaceae)

amblyantha ♀ — CArn CB&S CEnd EMil EPfP GCal IDee MBel MBlu SDry SSpi WSHC WSpi

articulata — CFil
australis — SOWG
decora f. *alba* — EPfP IDee
dielsiana — CB&S EPfP
* *frigida* HWJCM 107 — Last listed 1999
¶ *frutescens* — WPGP
gerardiana — See *I. heterantha*
hebepetala — WAbe WCru WDin WSHC
§ *heterantha* ♀ — CB&S CBot CDul CMCN CPle EBee ELan EMil IDee IMGH IOrc LRHS MAsh MBlu SBrw SCob SLon SPer SReu SSpi SSta WAbe WBod WCot WFar WOve WPGP WSHC
- CC 1708 — Last listed 1999
kirilowii — CFil CGre EPfP SOWG WSHC
pendula — Last listed 1999
potaninii — WCru WHer
pseudotinctoria — CFil EPfP SRms WPGP WWat
tinctoria — CArn MSal

INDOCALAMUS (Poaceae - Bambusoideae)

hamadae — EPla ERod SDry WJun
latifolius — EOas EPla ISta LJus SDry WJun
- 'Hopei' — EPla
longiauritus — EPla SDry
solidus — CDDB EPVP EPla ERod ISta LJus LPal MMoz MWht SDry WJun WMul
§ *tessellatus* — CFil CMCo EBee EFul EPfP EPla ERod ISta LJus MCCP MWht NMoo WJun WPGP

INULA ✿ (Asteraceae)

acaulis — MBro SSca WCot
¶ *barbata* — EBrP EBre LBCl LBSe LBre LHop MBBe SBre
candida — Last listed 1999
conyzae — MHew MSal
crithmoides — WHer
dysenterica — See *Pulicaria dysenterica*
ensifolia — GKir IBlr LFis MLLN MRav MSte MTho NBro NDea NFai SBea

WBea WFar WHoo WPnP WPyg SUsu
- 'Compacta' — SUsu
- 'Gold Star' — CBlo CMGP EBee ECtt EPfP MHer MWgw NBir NFor NOak SUsu WFar WLRN WPer

glandulosa — See *I. orientalis*
'Golden Beauty' — See *Buphthalmum salicifolium* 'Golden Wonder'

helenium — CArn CSam CSev EBee ECGN ELau EWFC GBar GPoy ILis LRHS MChe MHer MHew MLLN MSal NArg NBid NMir SRCN SRms WByw WCer WHbs WHer WOak WPer WWye
¶ - 'Goliath' — ELau

helianthus-aquaticus — Last listed 1997
CLD 658

¶ *hirta* — WPer

hookeri — CBos CBre CMHG CMea CRDP CSam CSev ECha ELan ELau EMar GKir GMac IBlr MBel MCLN MFir MSte NChi NDea NHol NPer SDix SLod SRms WAbb WBea WByw WEas WLin

¶ *macrocephala* — EBee
magnifica — More than 30 suppliers
* 'Mediterranean Sun' — Last listed 1998
oculus-christi — EBee EWes
* 'Oriental Star' — Last listed 1997
§ *orientalis* — COIW CPea EBee EPfP EWTr LRHS MBri MBro MCAu NFai NFla NMir NSti SMac SPer WByw WFar WHoo WPGP WPer WPyg

racemosa — EBee EMon EPPr EPla GBin GCal IBlr MNrw MSte NBid NChi NSti SMrm SRms WFar
- CC&McK 620 — GCHN
- 'Sonnenspeer' — NLar WPer
rhizocephala — CSam MHer
royleana — GCal MNrw MRav MSte SSca
¶ 'Sonnestrahl' — LGre
verbascifolia — Last listed 1999

IOCHROMA (Solanaceae)

§ *australe* — CB&S CGre CPle EWTr LRHS SMad SOWG SVen WCDu WCot
§ - 'Andean Snow' — CBot LHil
§ - 'Bill Evans' — CPLG EWll
- large-flowered — Last listed 1998
§ *calycinum* — Last listed 1999
cyaneum — CGre CPLG CPle ERea SOWG SVen SYvo WMul
- dark — Last listed 1998
- large — LHil
§ - 'Trebah' — CB&S ERea LHil SYvo
§ - 'Woodcote White' — LHil
gesnerioides 'Coccineum' — WMul
§ *grandiflorum* — CHEx CSev LHil SOWG SVen SYvo WMul
macrocalyx — See *I. calycinum*
violaceum misapplied — See *I. cyaneum* 'Trebah'
warscewiczii — See *I. grandiflorum*

IPHEION (Alliaceae)

'Alberto Castillo' — CBro CLAP CMea EBee ELan EPot ERos EWes MTho SBla WCot WHoo WIvy
dialystemon — WAbe
§ 'Rolf Fiedler' ♀ — CAvo CBro CMea CSpe CStu EBee EBur ECho ELan EPar EPot ETub EWes LAma LRHS MRav MTho NMen NSla SBla WAbe WCot WFar

sellowianum   LBow SOkd
§ *uniflorum*   CBro CHal EBee ECha ETub LAma
     MBri MBro MNrw MRav NMen
     NRog NWCA NWoo SIng SRms
     WAbb WBea WFar WHoo WPer
- 'Album'   CAvo CBro CMea ECha ELan EPar
     EPot ERos EWes LPio LRHS MRav
     MTho NMGW SBla SIng
- 'Charlotte Bishop'   CAvo CPlt ECha SBla SDys SUsu
- 'Froyle Mill' ♀   CAvo CBro CHal CMea CPne
     CSWP EBee EBur ELan EPar EPot
     ERos EWes LPio LRHS MBro MRav
     MTho NMGW NMen SAga SBla
     SIng SUsu WHoo WWat
- 'Wisley Blue' ♀   CAvo CBro CMea CPlt EBee ECha
     ELan EPar EPot ERos ETub LAma
     LRHS MBro MRav MS&S MTho
     NMen NNrd NWCA SBla SIng
     SRms WBea WFar WHoo WPyg

IPOMOEA (Convolvulaceae)
acuminata   See *I. indica*
alba   CPlN
* *andersonii*   CPlN
batatas 'Blackie'   CPlN CSpe WMul
bonariensis   SVen
brasiliensis   See *I. pes-caprae* subsp.
     brasiliensis
carnea   LChe LRHS SOWG
- subsp. *fistulosa*   Last listed 1998
coccinea   Last listed 1998
—(L.) A. Gray   See *I. hederifolia*
     var. *hederifolia*
§ *hederifolia*   Last listed 1998
horsfalliae ♀   CPlN
§ *indica* ♀   CHEx CHal CLTr CPlN CSpe ERea
     LCns LRHS MGrG MWst SOWG
     SYvo WMul
* - 'Morning Face'   MGrG
learii   See *I. indica*
leptophylla   EBee
§ *lobata*   LIck LRHS SHFr SUsu SYvo
pennata 'Relli Valley'   Last listed 1998
§ *pes-caprae*   Last listed 1998
     subsp. *brasiliensis*
purpurea   SRCN WHer
- 'Kniola's Purple-black'   Last listed 1998
quamoclit   CPlN
'Quebra Plata'   Last listed 1998
'Scarlett O'Hara'   Last listed 1997
tuberosa   See *Merremia tuberosa*
versicolor   See *I. lobata*

IPOMOPSIS (Polemoniaceae)
§ *aggregata*   Last listed 1999
- subsp. *aggregata*   Last listed 1997
- subsp. *bridgesii*   Last listed 1999

IRESINE (Amaranthaceae)
herbstii   CHal EBak ERea IBlr LHil
- 'Aureoreticulata'   CHal LHil
- 'Brilliantissima'   CHal LHil
lindenii ♀   LHil

IRIS ✿ (Iridaceae)
'A.W. Tait' (Spuria)   GCal
'Abracadabra' (SDB)   Last listed 1999
'Abridged Version' (MTB)   NZep
'Acapulco Gold' (TB)   SCro
'Ace of Clubs' (SDB)   NZep
'Action Front' (TB)   CHad COtt ERou NCat NGdn
     WLRN

'Actress' (TB)   EFou
¶ 'Adobe Rose' (TB)   ESgl
'Adobe Sunset' (Spuria)   Last listed 1999
'Adrienne Taylor' (MDB) ♀   MCAu
afghanica   Last listed 1998
'Afternoon Delight' (TB)   ESgl MCAu
'Agnes James' (CH) ♀   CBro
'Ain't She Sweet' (IB)   SCro
'Alastor' (TB)   Last listed 1998
'Albatross' (TB)   CKel
albicans ♀   SCro WHal
'Alcazar' (TB)   EPfP EWTr NMoo SWat WEas
'Alenette' (TB)   MCAu
'Alice Goodman' (TB)   Last listed 1997
'Alien' (IB)   Last listed 1999
¶ 'Alien Mist' (TB)   LIri
'Alizes' (TB)   ESgl LIri
'All Right' (IB)   NZep SCro
'Allegiance' (TB)   MCAu WEas
'Alpine Lake' (MDB)   NZep
'Already' (MDB)   Last listed 1999
'Alsterquelle' (SDB)   WTin
'Altruist' (TB)   SCro
'Amadora' (TB)   CKel
'Amaranth Gem' (SDB)   Last listed 1999
'Ambassadeur' (TB)   ERou EWTr
'Amber Blaze' (SDB)   NZep
'Amber Queen' (DB)   CGle COtt EBee ECtt ELan EMan
     ERos MCCP NMen SCro SPer
     WGwG WLRN WWal
'Amber Tambour' (TB)   Last listed 1998
'American Sweetheart' (TB)   LIri
'America's Cup' (TB)   Last listed 1999
'Amethyst Crystal' (CH)   Last listed 1999
'Amethyst Flame' (TB)   CKel EBrP EBre ERou LBCl LBSe
     LBre MBBe NMGW SBre SRms
'Amethyst Sunset' (MTB)   Last listed 1999
'Amigo' (TB) ♀   SCro
'Amphora' (SDB)   CBro ERos
'Anastasia' (TB)   CKel
'Ancilla' (Aril)   Last listed 1999
¶ 'Andalou' (TB)   ESgl
'Angel Unawares' (TB)   MCAu
'Angelic' (SDB)   MCAu
'Angel's Tears'   See *I. bistrioides* 'Angel's Eye'
anglica   See *I. latifolia*
'Anna Belle Babson' (TB)   SCro
'Annabel Jane' (TB)   CKel MCAu SCro
'Anne Elizabeth' (SDB)   CBro ERos
'Annikins' (IB) ♀   Last listed 1996
'Apache Warrior' (IB)   Last listed 1999
aphylla   NOrc
'Aplomb' (TB)   LIri
'Apollodorus' (TB)   Last listed 1998
'Apollo's Touch' (IB)   NZep
* 'Apple Court'   SApp
'Appledore' (SDB)   CBro ERos MBro
¶ 'Appointer'   CRow
'Apricot Skies' (BB)   NZep
'April Ballet' (MDB)   Last listed 1998
'Arab Chief' (TB)   CKel
'Arabi Pasha' (TB)   EBee SCro WLRN
'Arabi Treasure' (IB)   CLTr
* 'Arabic Night' (IB)   MCAu
'Archie Owen' (Spuria)   Last listed 1999
'Arctic Fancy' (IB) ♀   MMil
'Arctic Snow'   MCAu
'Arctic Star' (TB)   CKel MFir
'Arctic Tern' (TB)   Last listed 1999
'Arden' (BB) ♀   Last listed 1999
arenaria   See *I. humilis*
'Argus Pheasant' (SDB)   MCAu

'Arnold Sunrise' (CH) ♀   WWst
'Arnold Velvet' (SDB)   Last listed 1999
'Around Midnight' (TB)   SCro
'Arpège' (TB)   EBee
¶ 'Art School Angel' (TB)   LIri
'Ask Alma' (IB)   CKel EFou NZep SCro
¶ 'Atala' (TB)   LIri
* 'Atlantique' (TB)   CKel
§ *atrofusca*   Last listed 1999
   - MS&CL 56   Last listed 1998
   - S&L 38   Last listed 1998
'Attention Please' (TB)   CKel
§ *attica*   CBro CPBP ERos GCrs LBee LRHS
   MBro MNrw NNrd WHal WLin
   - lemon   NNrd
   - S&L 486   Last listed 1998
§ *aucheri* ♀   CBro LAma
'Audacious' (BB)   NZep
'Aunt Martha' (BB)   MBri NMGW
'Austrian Sky' (SDB)   CMea CSam EBee EBrP EBre ENot
   LBCl LBSe LBre MBBe MBro MMil
   NSti SBre WPGP
'Autumn Leaves' (TB)   MMil
'Avanelle' (IB)   EFou ERou WBcn
'Az Ap' (IB)   LIri MCAu NZep SCro
'Aztec Star' (SDB)   Last listed 1999
'Azure Excho' (IB)   MMil
'Azurea' (MDB)   NFla
'Baboon Bottom' (BB)   LIri
'Babushka' (SDB)   Last listed 1999
'Baby Bengal' (BB)   Last listed 1998
'Baby Bibs' (MTB)   NZep
'Baby Blessed' (SDB)   CBro NZep
'Baby Face' (TB)   MMil
'Baccarat' (TB)   Last listed 1998
'Back in Black' (TB)   CKel
'Baked Alaska' (TB)   MMil
bakeriana   LAma LRHS
'Ballerina Blue' (TB)   ERou
'Ballyhoo' (TB)   LRHS
'Banbury Beauty' (CH) ♀   CLAP CPlt NSti
'Banbury Fair' (CH)   WWst
'Banbury Gem' (CH) ♀   Last listed 1999
'Banbury Melody' (CH) ♀   CFee WBcn
'Banbury Ruffles' (SDB)   EBee MCAu MMil NMGW NMen
   SCro
'Banbury Velvet' (CH) ♀   Last listed 1995
'Banbury Welcome' (CH)   IBlr
'Bang' (TB)   CKel
'Baria' (SDB)   Last listed 1998
'Barletta' (TB)   Last listed 1998
'Barnett Anley'   Last listed 1999
barnumae   Last listed 1999
   - *polakii*   See *I. polakii*
'Baroque Prelude' (TB)   CKel MMil
'Barrymore Charmer' (TB)   Last listed 1998
'Basso' (IB)   SCro
'Batik' (BB)   LIri SCro WCot
'Batsford' (SDB)   CBro NNrd
¶ 'Battle Hymn' (TB)   LIri
'Battle Shout' (IB)   Last listed 1999
'Bayberry Candle' (TB)   LIri
'Be Dazzled' (SDB)   EFou
'Be Happy' (SDB)   NZep
'Beauty Mark' (SDB)   NZep
'Beckon' (TB)   CKel
'Bedford Lilac' (SDB)   NZep
'Bee Wings' (MDB)   NZep WEas
'Before the Storm' (TB)   LIri SCro
'Belise' (Spuria) ♀   Last listed 1999
'Belissinado' (Spuria)   Last listed 1999
'Bellboy' (MTB)   NZep

'Belvi Queen' (TB)   MNrw
* 'Ben Hasel'   ECha
N 'Benton Arundel' (TB)   SCro
'Benton Cordelia' (TB)   Last listed 1997
'Benton Dierdre' (TB)   SCro SRms
'Benton Evora' (TB)   ENot EOld
N 'Benton Lorna' (TB)   SCro
'Benton Nigel' (TB)   Last listed 1998
'Benton Sheila' (TB)   SCro
'Berkeley Gold' (TB)   CBlo COtt EBrP EBre ECtt EPfP
   ERav EWes LBCl LBSe LBre LNor
   MBBe MCAu NGdn NMGW NOrc
   SBre SCob SPer WLRN
'Best Bet'   MCAu
'Betsey Boo' (SDB)   Last listed 1999
'Betty Chatten' (TB)   NMen WLRN
'Betty Cooper' (Spuria)   Last listed 1999
¶ 'Betty Frances' (TB)   ESgI
'Betty my Love' (Spuria)   Last listed 1997
'Betty Simon' (TB)   CKel
'Betty Wood' (SDB)   Last listed 1999
'Beverly Sills' (TB)   LIri MCAu SCro
'Bewdley' (IB) ♀   Last listed 1999
'Bewilderbeast' (TB)   LIri
'Beyond' (TB)   SCro
¶ 'Bianco'   MCAu
'Bibury' (SDB) ♀   EGle MCAu MMil SCro
N 'Big Day' (TB)   CKel WBcn
'Big Money' (TB) ♀   WWst
biglumis   See *I. lactea*
biliottii   CBro
'Black as Night' (TB)   Last listed 1998
'Black Dragon' (TB)   SCro
'Black Flag' (TB)   Last listed 1997
'Black Gamecock' (La)   Last listed 1999
'Black Hills' (TB)   EBee MCAu
'Black Hills Gold' (TB)   Last listed 1999
'Black Ink' (TB)   COIW
'Black Knight' (TB)   EBee MRav NGdn SLod
'Black Lady' (MTB)   Last listed 1997
'Black Swan' (TB)   CHad COtt EBee EBrP EBre ECha
   ECtt ELan EMan ERav LBCl LBSe
   LBre MBBe MCLN NGdn SBre
   WCot WWal
'Black Watch' (IB)   CKel
'Blackbeard' (BB) ♀   CKel
'Blazing Saddles' (TB)   NZep
'Blenheim Royal' (TB)   MCAu SCro
'Blitz' (SDB)   NZep
'Blood Covenant' (SDB)   NZep
bloudowii   CLAP
'Blue Admiral' (TB)   CKel
'Blue Ballerina' (CH) ♀   Last listed 1999
'Blue Denim' (SDB)   CBro CM&M EBee ECtt EGle ENot
   EWTr GMaP MBNS MRav NBir
   SIng WElm WHoo
'Blue Doll' (MDB)   NZep
'Blue Duchess' (TB)   CKel
'Blue Emperor'   SRPl
'Blue Eyed Blond' (IB)   SCro
'Blue Eyed Brunette' (TB) ♀   MBri MCAu
'Blue Hendred' (SDB)   MCAu NBir
'Blue Horizon'   ERos NMen
'Blue Icing' (IB)   EFou
'Blue Lassie' (Spuria)   Last listed 1999
'Blue Line' (SDB) ♀   NZep
'Blue Luster' (TB) ♀   CHar CKel SCro
'Blue Magic' (Dut)   NRog
'Blue Moss' (TB)   Last listed 1999
'Blue Pigmy' (SDB)   CBlo CGle CMil EBee ERos MCCP
   NCat NMen SCob SCro SPer
   WElm WGwG WLRN WWal

'Blue Pools' (SDB)	EFou EGle MBri NBir NZep SCro WPnP WTin
'Blue Reflection' (TB)	MMil
'Blue Rhythm' (TB)	CBlo CKel CM&M CMGP EBee EMan ERou EWTr MCAu MCli MWgw NFai NMoo SCro SMrm SPer WLRN
'Blue Sapphire' (TB)	CHad
'Blue Shimmer' (TB)	CBlo COtt EBee ELan EMan ENot EPfP MCAu MRav NFai NGdn SCro SPer SWat WGwG WWal
'Blue Smoke' (TB)	CKel
'Blue Staccato' (TB)	CKel SCro
¶ 'Blue Velvet' (TB)	WMoo
'Blue Zephyr' (Spuria)	Last listed 1999
'Bluebeard' (TB)	Last listed 1999
'Bluebird Wine' (TB)	MCAu
'Blushes' (IB)	SCro
'Blushing Pink' (TB)	SCro
¶ 'Bodacious' (TB)	ESgl
'Bodderlecker' (SDB)	EFou
'Bold Lassie' (SDB)	WHer
'Bold Print' (IB)	MCAu SCro WWin
¶ 'Bollinger' (TB)	MCAu
'Bonny' (MDB)	CBro
'Boo' (SDB)	CKel MCAu NZep
¶ 'Boss Tweed' (TB)	LIri
'Bourne Graceful'	CMGP EBee EPPr GCal SCob SSpi WElm WGwG WLRN WWal
¶ 'Bouzy Bouzy' (TB)	ESgl
bracteata	CFil EWoo WPGP WPer
- JCA 13427	CLAP
'Braithwaite' (TB)	CBlo CKel CMGP COtt EBee EBrP EBre ELan ENot ERou LBCl LBSe LBre MBBe SBre SCob SCro SMrm SRms SSpe SWat WElm WLRN
'Brannigan' (SDB)	CBro GKir MBri MCli MMil NBir NSti
¶ 'Brasilia'	NBir
'Brass Tacks' (SDB)	NZep
'Brassie' (SDB)	CBro CKel ERos MBNS MCli WHil
'Breakers' (TB) ♀	CKel
brevicaulis	GBin
'Bridal Crown' (TB)	SCro
§ 'Bride' (DB)	CCuc CM&M MBro
'Bride's Halo' (TB)	SCro
'Bright Button' (DB)	CKel
'Bright Moment' (SDB)	Last listed 1999
'Bright Vision' (SDB)	NZep
'Bright White' (MDB)	CBlo CBro CKel EPot ERos EWTr MBNS NMen NNrd
'Bright Yellow' (DB)	MRav
'Brighteyes' (IB)	EBee EBrP EBre ESis GKir LBCl LBSe LBre MBBe MBro SBre SCro SRms WPer
'Brilliant Excuse' (TB)	NZep
'Brindisi' (TB)	CKel SCro
'Bristo Magic' (TB)	SCro
'Bristol Gem' (TB)	SCro
'Broad Grin' (SDB)	Last listed 1999
'Broadleigh Ann' (CH)	CBro WWst
'Broadleigh Carolyn' (CH) ♀	CBro
'Broadleigh Charlotte'	CBro WWst
'Broadleigh Clare' (CH)	CBro LRHS
'Broadleigh Dorothy' (CH)	CBro GGar WWst
'Broadleigh Elizabeth' (CH)	CBro
N 'Broadleigh Emily' (CH)	CBro
N 'Broadleigh Florence' (CH)	CBro
'Broadleigh Jean'	CBro WWst
'Broadleigh Joan' (CH)	CBro
'Broadleigh Joyce' (CH)	CBro WWst
'Broadleigh Lavinia' (CH)	CBro LRHS MRav WWst

'Broadleigh Mitre' (CH)	CBro LRHS
'Broadleigh Nancy' (CH)	CBro LRHS
'Broadleigh Peacock' (CH)	CBro CHad CNic IBlr MMil MRav SUsu
N 'Broadleigh Rose' (CH)	CBos CBro CElw CHad CMdw CPlt EPPr GBuc GKir IBlr LRHS MRav SMrm
'Broadleigh Sybil' (CH)	CBro NHol
'Broadleigh Victoria' (CH)	CBro CFri GBuc
'Broadway' (TB)	NZep SCro
'Broadway Baby' (IB)	CKel
'Bromyard' (SDB) ♀	CBro MMil
'Bronzaire' (IB) ♀	MCAu
'Bronze Beauty' (*hoogiana* hybrid)	EPot
'Bronze Bird' (TB)	Last listed 1998
N 'Bronze Charm' (TB)	Last listed 1998
'Bronze Cloud' (TB)	CKel
'Bronze Queen' (Dut)	LRHS
'Broseley' (TB)	Last listed 1999
'Brown Lasso' (BB) ♀	EFou LIri SCro
'Brown Trout' (TB)	NBir
'Brownstone' (Spuria)	Last listed 1997
'Brummit's Mauve'	Last listed 1999
'Bryngwyn' (TB)	Last listed 1999
'Bubbling Over' (TB)	SCro
bucharica Foster ♀	CBro EPar EPot GIBF LAma NRog
- hort.	See *I. orchioides*
- 'Yellow Dushanbe'	EBee WWst
'Buckden Pike' (TB) ♀	Last listed 1995
bulleyana	EWoo GCrs MBro NWoo SRms
- ACE 1665	Last listed 1999
- ACE 2296	EBee GBuc
'Bumblebee Deelite' (MTB)	NZep
'Burford' (BB)	Last listed 1999
'Burgundy Brown' (TB)	NZep
¶ 'Burgundy Bubbles' (TB)	LIri
'Burmese Dawn' (TB)	Last listed 1997
'Butter Pecan' (IB)	LIri SCro
'Buttercup Bower' (TB)	MBri NMGW
'Buttercup Charm' (MDB)	NZep
'Buttermere' (TB)	SRms
'Butterpat' (IB)	NZep
'Butterscotch Kiss' (TB)	EBee EBrP EBre ELan EMan ERou LBCl LBSe LBre MBBe MMil MRav NCiC SBre SCro SMrm
'Button Box' (SDB)	NZep
'Bygone Era' (TB)	Last listed 1998
'Byword' (SDB)	Last listed 1999
'Cable Car' (TB)	CKel
'Caliente' (TB)	EPfP MCAu
'California Style' (IB)	NZep
§ Californian hybrids	CElw CGle CLTr ELan MAvo MRav SSpi WCFE WCot WWhi
'Calypso Mood' (TB)	SCro
'Cambridge Blue'	See *I.* 'Monspur Cambridge Blue'
'Camelot Rose' (TB)	Last listed 1999
'Camera Shy' (TB)	Last listed 1999
'Campbellii'	See *I. lutescens* 'Campbellii'
'Can Can Red' (TB)	Last listed 1997
canadensis	See *I. hookeri*
'Canary Bird' (TB)	Last listed 1999
'Cannington Bluebird' (TB)	Last listed 1999
'Cannington Ochre' (SDB)	CBro
'Cannington Skies' (IB) ♀	MMil
'Cannington Sweet Puff' (TB)	EFou
'Cannonball' (TB)	Last listed 1998
'Cantab' (Reticulata)	CAvo CBro EBrP EBre EPar EPot ETub LAma LBCl LBSe LBre MBBe NRog SBre
'Capricious' (TB)	SCro

		EBee GCal LHil NCiC NDov WCot WCru WFar WPGP WPer
	'Conjuration' (TB)	LIri MMil
	'Connoisseur' (Spuria)	WTin
	'Constant Wattez' (IB)	CKel EWTr LBuc
	'Consummation' (MTB)	NZep
	'Copper Classic' (TB)	NZep SCro
	'Cops' (SDB)	NZep
	'Coral Chalice' (TB)	ERou
	'Coral Joy' (TB)	Last listed 1999
	'Coral Strand' (TB)	MCAu
	'Coral Wings' (SDB)	NZep
	'Corn Harvest' (TB)	MMil NZep
	'Corrida' (TB)	LBuc
	'Côte d'Or' (TB)	SCro
	'Cotton Blossom' (SDB)	Last listed 1999
	'Cotton Plantation' (La)	Last listed 1999
	'Cozy Calico' (TB)	SCro
	'Cracklin Burgundy' (TB)	SCro
¶	'Cranapple' (BB)	LIri
	'Cranberry Ice' (TB)	SCro
	'Cream Cake' (SDB)	NZep
	'Cream Soda' (TB) ♀	CKel
	'Creative Stitchery' (TB)	SCro
	'Cregrina' (TB)	Last listed 1999
¶	'Creme d'Or' (TB)	ESgl LIri
	cretensis	See *I. unguicularis* subsp. *cretensis*
	'Cricket Lane' (SDB)	NZep
	'Crimson Fire' (TB)	SCro
¶	'Crimson Tiger' (TB)	LIri
	'Crinoline' (TB)	Last listed 1998
N	'Crispen Rouge' (TB)	Last listed 1998
	'Crispette' (TB)	MCAu
	cristata ♀	CPBP EPot GBuc LAma MDHE MOne SIng SRms WCru
	- 'Abbey's Violet'	Last listed 1999
	- 'Alba'	EBee EPot ERos GCrs LBee LRHS MDHE NHar SChu
	- x **gracilipes**	EPot
	- x **lacustris**	EPot NMen NTow
	crocea ♀	Last listed 1998
	'Croftway Lemon' (TB)	SCro
	'Cross Stitch' (TB)	MMil NZep
	'Crown Sterling' (TB)	SCro
	'Crushed Velvet' (TB)	Last listed 1999
	'Cruzin' (TB)	Last listed 1999
¶	'Crystal Glitters' (TB)	ESgl
	'Cum Laude' (IB)	SCro
	cuniculiformis ACE 2224	GBuc
	'Cup Race' (TB)	Last listed 1998
	'Curlew' (IB)	MCAu
	'Cutie' (IB)	NZep
	'Cyanea' (DB)	SIng
	cycloglossa	LRHS WWst
	- HW&E 7727	CLAP
	'Daisy Fresh' (MDB)	Last listed 1999
	'Dale Dennis' (DB)	Last listed 1999
	'Dame Judy' (TB)	Last listed 1997
	'Dancers Veil' (TB) ♀	CKel EBrP EBre ECtt EFou ELan ERou GKir LBCl LBSe LBre MBBe MRav NVic SBre SCoo SCro SMer
	'Dancin'' (IB)	NZep
	'Dancing Eyes' (SDB)	Last listed 1999
	'Dancing Gold' (MTB)	NZep
	danfordiae	CAvo CB&S CBro EBrP EBre ELan EPar EPot ETub GCrs LAma LBCl LBSe LBre LRHS MBBe MBNS MBri NRog SBre WCot WLin
	'Dante' (TB)	CKel
	'Dappled Pony' (MTB)	Last listed 1997
	'Dark Blizzard' (IB)	NZep

	'Dark Bury' (TB)	Last listed 1999
	'Dark Rosaleen' (TB) ♀	Last listed 1999
	'Dark Spark' (SDB)	MCAu
	'Dark Vader' (SDB)	Last listed 1999
	'Darkover' (SDB)	Last listed 1999
	'Darkside' (TB)	SCro
	'David Chapman' (TB)	CKel
	'Dawn Candle' (Spuria)	Last listed 1999
	'Dawn Favour' (SDB)	Last listed 1999
	'Dawn Glory' (TB)	SCro
	'Dawning' (TB)	LIri
	'Dazzling Gold' (TB)	SCro
§	**decora**	CBro EBee MNrw WLin WCru
	- B&SWJ 2122	CBlo CMGP COtt EBee EMan EOld EPfP ERav MWgw NOrc SCob SCro SPer SWat
	'Deep Black' (TB)	SCro
	'Deep Fire' (TB)	SCro
	'Deep Pacific' (TB)	LRHS MBri MCAu
	'Deft Touch' (TB)	Last listed 1999
	delavayi ♀	CKel GMaP IBlr LSyl WCot WViv
	'Delicate Air' (SDB)	Last listed 1999
	'Delphi' (TB)	SCro
	'Delta Blues' (TB)	Last listed 1999
	'Delta Butterfly' (La)	WMAq
	'Demelza' (TB)	Last listed 1999
	'Demon' (SDB)	CKel CLTr CPlt EFou LRHS MBri
	'Denys Humphries' (TB)	CKel
	'Depth of Field' (TB)	LRHS
	'Deputé Nomblot' (TB)	Last listed 1997
	'Derring Do' (SDB)	Last listed 1999
	'Derwentwater' (TB)	CBlo CKel MCAu MMil SRms
	'Desert Dream' (AB)	SWyc
	'Desert Dream' (Sino-Sib)	GDra
	'Desert Echo' (TB)	EFou
	'Desert Quail' (MTB)	Last listed 1999
	'Desert Song' (TB)	CKel EBee MCAu
	'Designer Gown' (TB)	ERou
	'Designer's Choice' (TB) ♀	Last listed 1999
	'Devilry' (SDB)	Last listed 1999
	'Dew Point' (IB)	SCro
¶	'Diabolique' (TB)	LIri
	'Die Braut'	See *I.* 'Bride'
	'Diligence' (SDB) ♀	Last listed 1996
	'Discretion' (TB)	SCro
	'Dixie Pixie' (SDB)	EGle WTin
	'Doctor Behenna' (TB)	Last listed 1999
	'Doll Dear' (SDB)	Last listed 1999
	'Doll House' (MDB)	CBlo
	'Doll Ribbons' (MTB)	NZep
	'Doll Type' (IB)	Last listed 1999
*	'Don Brownsay'	MMil
	'Dorothy Marquart' (TB)	Last listed 1999
	'Dorothy Robbins' (CH)	WWst
	'DoSiDo' (SDB)	SCro
	'Dot and Dash' (TB)	MBri
	'Dotted Doll' (MTB)	Last listed 1999
	'Double Lament' (SDB) ♀	CBro ERos MMil NNrd SCro SSte
	douglasiana ♀	CHad EBee EPar EPla IBlr SMac SSpi WAbe WFar
¶	- 'Amiguita'	CFir WWst
*	- Bandon strain	SSpi
	'Dovedale' (TB) ♀	Last listed 1999
	'Doxa' (IB)	SCro
	'Dream Builder' (TB)	NMGW
	'Dream Indigo' (IB)	CKel
	'Dreamcastle' (TB)	CKel
	'Dreamsicle' (TB)	SCro
	'Dresden Candleglow' (IB)	CKel
	'Driftwood' (Spuria)	Last listed 1999
	'Drive You Wild' (CH)	Last listed 1999
	'Dualtone' (TB)	CKel

'Dundee' (TB) SCro
'Dunlin' (MDB) CBro ERos MBri NBir NMen NNrd
NRar
'Dusky Challenger' (TB) ESgI LIri MCAu SCro
'Dusky Dancer' (TB) ♀ Last listed 1993
'Dutch Chocolate' (TB) MMil
dykesii CRow EBee
¶ 'Dynamite' (TB) LIri
'Eagle's Flight' (TB) NMGW
'Eardisland' (IB) ♀ MMil
'Earl' (TB) MMil
'Earl of Essex' (TB) MMil SCro
'Early Edition' (IB) EFou
'Early Frost' (IB) SCro
'Early Light' (TB) ♀ Last listed 1999
'East Indies' (TB) Last listed 1999
'Eastertime' (TB) Last listed 1999
'Easy Strolling' (SDB) Last listed 1999
'Echo de France' (TB) CKel ESgI
¶ 'Ecstatic Echo' (TB) LIri
'Edale' (TB) ♀ Last listed 1996
'Edge of Winter' (TB) CKel
'Edith Wolford' (TB) LIri MCAu SCro
¶ 'Ed's Blue' (DB) ELan
'Edward' (Reticulata) EPot LAma
'Edward of Windsor' (TB) CHad CMil EBee ELan ERou EWTr
NCiC NOrc WLRN
'Eirian' (TB) Last listed 1999
'Eleanor's Pride' (TB) CKel MMil
¶ 'Electrique' (TB) LIri
elegantissima See *I. iberica* subsp.
elegantissima
'Elixir' (Spuria) Last listed 1999
'Elizabeth Arden' (TB) CKel
'Elizabeth of England' (TB) LBmB
'Elizabeth Poldark' (TB) ESgI LIri
¶ *elizabethae* EHyt
'Ellen Manor' (TB) MCAu
'Elvinhall' CBro
'Ember Days' (TB) MMil
'Empress of India' (TB) EBee EWTr LBuc
'Enchanted Gold' (SDB) NZep
¶ 'Enfant Prodige' SWyc
(SpecHybrid)
'English Cottage' (TB) EGar GCal MCAu MMil MWat
SCro WIvy
'Ennerdale' (TB) MCAu SRms
§ *ensata* ♀ CBen CBlo CMHG COIW EBee
ECGP ELan EPfP EWTr GMac
LPBA LRHS LSyl MCAu MNrw
MSta NBro NGdn NLar SPlb SRms
SWat WFar WHil WPer WPyg
WWin
- 'Activity' CBlo CLAP CRow LRHS
- 'Agrippine' Last listed 1997
¶ - 'Aioi' CRow
¶ - 'Alba' CGle ECha
- 'Apollo' CBen CRow ETub SWyc
¶ - 'Artist' NBro
* - 'Asahi-no-sora' LBmB
¶ - 'Ashi-no-ukifune' SWyc
- 'Barnhawk Sybil' SSpi
¶ - 'Barr Purple East' ♀ CRow NBrk
- 'Bellender Blue' Last listed 1999
- 'Blue Embers' Last listed 1997
¶ - 'Blue Lagoon' SWyc
I - 'Blue Peter' CBen CRow SWyc
- 'Blue Skies' Last listed 1999
- 'Blush' NBro
¶ - 'Blushing Crimson' SWyc
- 'Butterflies in Flight' Last listed 1999
- 'Calamari' Last listed 1997

- 'Caprician Butterfly' ♀ SWyc
* - 'Carnival Prince' CFir CLAP
- 'Center of Attention' Last listed 1999
¶ - 'Charm' EBrP EBre LBCl LBSe LBre MBBe
SBre
- 'Chico Geisho' SWyc
- 'Chitose-no-tomo' CRow
¶ - 'Chiyodajo' SWyc
- 'Chiyo-no-haru' Last listed 1997
- 'Continuing Pleasure' ♀ Last listed 1995
* - 'Cry of Rejoice' EBee WAul WFar
- 'Crystal Halo' NBrk
- 'Dancing Waves' CRow NBrk
¶ - 'Dappled Dragon' SWyc
- 'Darling' CLAP CRow EBee IBlr LRHS NBrk
NBro WAul
- 'Dresden China' CRow NBrk
¶ - 'Eden's Blue Pearl' CHid
- 'Edens Charm' CMil MSCN NCat NHol SVil WAul
WWye
¶ - 'Eden's Harmony' NCat
¶ - 'Eden's Paintbrush' CMil ELan NPSI WAul
¶ - 'Eden's Picasso' CFir GBin NPSI
¶ - 'Eden's Purple Glory' CHid WHil
¶ - 'Electric Glow' SWyc
- 'Emotion' CLAP EWTr LRHS MChl WAul
- 'Enchanting Melody' Last listed 1999
¶ - 'Eternal Feminine' SWyc
- 'Fairy Carillon' Last listed 1999
- 'Flashing Koi' NBrk SWyc
- 'Flying Tiger' ♀ SWyc
- 'Freckled Geisha' SWyc
- 'Frilled Enchantment' Last listed 1997
- 'Fringed Cloud' ♀ SWyc
- 'Frosted Pyramid' NBrk
I - 'Galatea' Last listed 1999
* - 'Galathea' GCal
- 'Geisha Gown' SWyc
- 'Geisha Parasol' SWyc
- 'Gci-sho-mi' WWye
- 'Gipsy' CSpe LRHS WAul
¶ - 'Give-me-Patience' ♀ SWyc
¶ - 'Glebe Ghost' (v) CGle
- 'Glitter and Gayety' NBrk
¶ - 'Good Omen' SWyc
- 'Gracieuse' CLAP EBee EGle NBro WAul
WCDu WFar
- 'Hakug-yokuro' Last listed 1998
- 'Hakuro' See *I. ensata* 'Shiratsuyu'
- 'Hana-aoi' IBlr
- 'Happy Awakening' SWyc
¶ - 'Harlequinesque' SWyc
¶ - 'Haru-no-umi' SWyc
- 'Hatsu-shimo' CRow IBlr
- 'Hercule' CHad CRow EBee EGle NBrk
NGdn SMrm
- Higo hybrids CRow IBlr LPBA MSta SPer
¶ - Higo white SPer
N - 'Hokkaido' CGle CRow IBlr NBrk
¶ - 'Hue and Cry' ♀ SWyc
- 'Imperial Magic' ♀ SWyc
* - 'Innocence' CBlo LRHS MBri
- 'Iso-no-nami' CLAP MBri NBro WAul
N - 'Iso-no-ob' Last listed 1999
¶ - 'Izu-no-umi' SWyc
¶ - 'Jewelled Sea' SWyc
- 'Kalamazo' SWyc WFar
- 'Katy Mendez' ♀ SWyc
¶ - 'Knight in Armor' SWyc
¶ - 'Koh Dom' SPer
¶ - 'Koh Shan' SPer
- 'Komo-no-ibo' SWat

'Golden Ruby' (SDB) — Last listed 1999
'Golden Spice' (TB) — Last listed 1999
'Golden Starlet' (SDB) — Last listed 1999
N 'Golden Surprise' (TB) — CKel
'Golden Veil' (TB) — CKel
'Golden Waves' (Cal-Sib) ♀ — CBro
N 'Goldfinder' (TB) — CKel
I 'Goldilocks' (TB) — CKel
¶ 'Gondalier' (TB) — LBmB
'Good and True' (IB) — SCro
'Good Looking' (TB) — LIri
'Good Nature' (Spuria) — Last listed 1999
'Good Show' (TB) — SCro
'Gordon' (Reticulata) — EPot LAma LRHS WBea
'Goring Ace' (CH) ♀ — WWst
gormanii — See *I. tenax*
'Gosh' (SDB) — CKel
¶ 'Gossip' (DB) — CBro
gracilipes — Last listed 1999
- 'Alba' — Last listed 1998
¶ - x *lacustris* — EPot MNaF WAbe
graeberiana — CLAP EPot
- white fall — LRHS WWst
- yellow fall — LRHS WWst
graminea ♀ — CAvo CBro CHad CRow EBee
ECha EFou ELan EPar EPla ERos
IBlr LEdu LRHS MBel MBro NMen
NNrd NSti SCro SIng SMrm SOkh
WCot WFar WPnP WPyg WRus
WWat
- 'Hort's Variety' — EGar GCal NCat
- var. *pseudocyperus* — CRow LHop NSti SDys
graminifolia — See *I. kerneriana*
'Granada Gold' (TB) — ENot SRms
'Grand Baroque' (TB) — MMil
'Grand Waltz' (TB) — SCro
'Grandpa's Girl' (MTB) — Last listed 1999
'Grapelet' (MDB) — ERos NZep
'Grapesicle' (SDB) — NZep
'Graphic Arts' (TB) — Last listed 1999
'Grecian Skies' (TB) — SCro
'Green Halo' (DB) — EGle LGre
'Green Ice' (TB) — CKel
'Green Jungle' (TB) — Last listed 1999
N 'Green Little' (DB) — Last listed 1997
¶ 'Green Prophecy' (TB) — LIri
'Green Spot' (IB) ♀ — CBot CBro CHad EBee ECtt ELan
EPla ESis GKir LGre MMil MRav
MWat NBir NHol NMGW NMen
NSti SAga SChu SPer WCFE WEas
WElm WFar WHoo
¶ 'Green Streak' (TB) — LIri
'Greenstuff' (SDB) — LGre MMil
'Gringo' (TB) — MCAu
'Gudrun' (TB) — Last listed 1999
'Gypsy Boy' (SDB) — MMil NMGW NZep
'Gypsy Caravan' (TB) — CKel SCro
'Gypsy Jewels' (TB) — CKel
'Gypsy Romance' (TB) — LIri
'Gyro' (TB) — Last listed 1999
'H.C. van Vliet' (Dut) — NRog
'Hagar's Helmet' (IB) — Last listed 1999
'Hallowed Thought' (TB) — MMil MWat
¶ 'Halo in Rosewood' (TB) — LIri
balopbila — See *I. spuria* subsp. *balopbila*
'Handshake' (TB) — LIri
'Happening' (SDB) — NZep
* 'Happy Border' — Last listed 1998
'Happy Choice' (Spuria) — Last listed 1999
'Happy Mood' (IB) ♀ — MCAu
'Happy Song' (BB) — EFou
'Happy Thought' (IB) — Last listed 1997

'Harbor Blue' (TB) — CKel EWes MWat SCro
'Harleqinade' (BB) — Last listed 1999
'Harlow Gold' (IB) — NZep
'Harmony' (Reticulata) — CAvo CBro EBrP EBre EPot LAma
LBCl LBSe LBre LRHS MBBe MBri
NRog SBre
'Harriette Halloway' (TB) — CBlo CMGP SMrm WElm
bartwegii — Last listed 1998
subsp. *pinetorum*
¶ 'Harvest King' (TB) — ESgl
'Hazy Skies' (MTB) — Last listed 1999
'Headlines' (TB) — CKel
'Heather Hawk' (TB) — MCAu
'Heavenly Days' (TB) — Last listed 1999
'Helen Boehm' (TB) — SCro
'Helen McGregor' (TB) — CKel
'Helen Proctor' (IB) — NZep SCro
'Helen Traubel' (TB) — Last listed 1998
'Helge' (IB) — COlW EPfP NFai SCob SWat
'Hellcat' (IB) — NZep
'Hello Darkness' (TB) — LIri
'Hell's Fire' (TB) — SCro
'Hercules' (Reticulata) — GCal LAma WBea
'Hers' (IB) — SCro
¶ 'Hi' (IB) — LIri
'High Barbaree' (TB) — MBri
'High Command' (TB) — CKel SCro
'High Life' (TB) — SCro
'Highline Halo' (Spuria) — Last listed 1998
'Hills of Lafayette' (IB) — Last listed 1998
'Hindenburg' (TB) — Last listed 1997
'Hindu Magic' (TB) — Last listed 1999
'His' (IB) — SCro
bistrio — LAma
- subsp. *aintabensis* — EPot LAma
- subsp. *bistrio* — Last listed 1998
§ *bistrioides* 'Angel's Eye' — CLAP ERos
- 'Angel's Tears' — See *I. bistrioides* 'Angel's Eye'
¶ - 'Lady Beatrice Stanley' — CLAP
N - 'Major' ♀ — CBro CLAP LAma MBri
- 'Reine Immaculée' — ERos
- var. *sophenensis* — CLAP
'Hocus Pocus' (SDB) — EFou EPPr
'Holden Clough' ♀ — CBot CGle CHad CHar CKel EBee
EFou ELan EMFW EPla EPri GMaP
LRHS MCAu MFir MMil MRav
NChi NGdn NSti SBla SSvw SWyc
WEas WMaN WPnP WSan WWin
'Hollywood Blonde' (TB) — Last listed 1997
'Holy Night' (TB) — Last listed 1997
'Honey Behold' (SDB) — CKel
'Honey Crunch' (TB) — Last listed 1999
'Honey Glazed' (IB) — MCAu NZep WBcn
'Honey Mocha' (TB) — SCro
'Honey Pot' (MDB) — Last listed 1998
'Honington' (SDB) ♀ — MCAu MMil
'Honky Tonk Blues' (TB) — LIri
'Honorabile' (MTB) — CKel
boogiana ♀ — EPot LAma LRHS MMal
- 'Alba' — EPot
- 'Purpurea' — EPot LRHS
§ *bookeri* — EBee EDAr ELan GCHN MHar
NTow NWoo SOkd WAbe
bookeriana — WCot
'Hopscotch' (BB) — SCro
'Horatio' (TB) — Last listed 1999
'Hot Chocolate' (TB) — LIri
'Hot Fudge' (IB) — Last listed 1999
'Hot Spice' (IB) — MCAu NZep
'Howard Weed' (TB) — Last listed 1997
¶ 'Howdy Do' (TB) — LIri
'Hubbub' (IB) — SCro

'Hugh Miller' (TB)	MCAu
'Hula Doll' (MDB)	CBlo CMea EGle MBri NMen
§ *humilis*	NNrd
byrcana	CBro LAma LRHS
'I Do' (TB)	MMil NZep
§ *iberica*	Last listed 1999
§ - subsp. *elegantissima*	EPot
- subsp. *iberica*	Last listed 1997
'Ice Chip' (SDB)	Last listed 1999
'Ice Dancer' (TB) ♀	Last listed 1995
¶ 'Iced Tea' (TB)	LIri
'Ida' (Reticulata)	EPot LAma
'Ideal' (Dut)	Last listed 1999
'Ila Remembered' (Spuria)	Last listed 1999
illyrica	See *I. pallida*
imbricata	Last listed 1998
'Immortality' (TB)	MCAu SCro
'Imperator' (Dut)	CB&S MTis
* 'Imperator' (TB)	EBee
'Imperial Bronze' (Spuria)	EFou NFor
'Impetuous' (BB)	EFou
'Inaugural Ball' (TB)	Last listed 1997
'Indeed' (IB)	Last listed 1999
'Indian Chief' (TB)	CLTr CM&M EBee LRHS MBri
	MCAu
'Indian Jewel' (SDB)	EGle
'Indian Pow Wow' (SDB)	CRDP
N 'Indian Sunset' (TB)	CKel
'Indigo Flight' (IB)	EFou
'Indigo Princess' (TB)	Last listed 1999
¶ 'Infernal Fire' (TB)	LIri
'Infinite Grace' (TB)	SCro
'Ingenuity' (SDB)	Last listed 1999
'Innocent Heart' (IB) ♀	MCAu SCro
innominata	CFil CGle CHad CLon CRow EBee
	ECha ELan IBlr LBee MNrw
	MTho NBro NHar NMen SChr
	SRms WEas WGwG WPGP WWal
	WWat
- 'Alba'	SIng
- apricot	IBlr NWoo
- Ballyrogan hybrids	IBlr
- copper	IBlr
N - 'Doctor Riddle's Form'	CGle
- hybrids	SIng
- J&JA 12897	SSpi
- JCA 13225	CLAP SSpi
- JCA 13227	SSpi
- JCA 1460800	Last listed 1999
- rose	CNic ERos
N - 'Spinners'	SSpi
- yellow	NNrd NRya
'Inscription' (SDB)	EGle
'Interpol' (TB)	Last listed 1998
'Into the Night' (TB)	Last listed 1999
'Irish Doll' (MDB)	CMea EGle
* 'Irish Temper' (SDB)	MMil
'Irish Tune' (TB)	SCro
'Ishmael' (SDB)	EGle
¶ 'It's Magic' (TB)	LIri
J 437	Last listed 1999
'J.S. Dijt' (Reticulata)	CAvo CBro EBrP EBre EPar EPot
	LAma LBCl LBSe LBre LRHS MBBe
	MBri MMal NRog SBre WBea
'Jack o' Hearts' (SDB)	ERos
'Jade Mist' (SDB)	EGle GKir LRHS MBri
'Jaime Lynn' (TB)	Last listed 1998
'Jan Reagan' (SDB)	NZep
'Jane Phillips' (TB) ♀	CHad CKel EBrP EBre ECha ECtt
	EGle ELan ENot ERav ERou GKir
	LBCl LBSe LBre MBBe MCAu MMil
	MRav NGdn NOrc SBre SCro
	SMrm SPer SWat WPnP
'Jane Taylor' (SDB)	CBro EGle
'Janice Chesnik' (Spuria)	Last listed 1999
japonica ♀	NPer WFar WHil
- 'Aphrodite' (v)	WPnP
- L 638	SCro
N - 'Ledger's Variety'	CAvo CBro CGre CKel CRow
	CSpe ECha ELan EPar EPfP EPla
	EPri LHil MRav SChr WWat
- 'Variegata' ♀	CAvo CBot CHad CKel CLon
	CRow EBee ECha EPar EPla GGar
	LRHS NBro NFai NFla NOrc NPer
	SArc SCob SMad SSpi WBea WEas
	WFar WHer WHil WPic WViv
'Jasper Gem' (MDB)	EGle ERos MBri MMil NBir
'Java Charm' (TB)	MMil
'Jay Kenneth' (IB)	Last listed 1999
'Jazzamatazz' (SDB)	Last listed 1999
'Jazzebel' (TB)	SCro
'Jean Guymer' (TB)	CLTr MMil NBir WBcn
'Jeanne Price' (TB)	MCAu
'Jeannine' (Reticulata)	LAma
'Jeremy Brian' (SDB) ♀	MCAu MMil SUsu
'Jersey Lilli' (SDB)	NSti WViv
'Jesse's Song' (TB)	NZep SCro
¶ 'Jester' (TB)	LIri
'Jewel Baby' (SDB)	CBro NMGW NZep
'Jewel Bright' (SDB)	EFou MCAu
'Jiansada' (SDB)	CBro
'Jitterbug' (TB)	LIri
'Jo Jo' (TB)	Last listed 1997
'Joanna Taylor' (MDB)	ERos NMen NZep
N 'Joe Elliott' (CH)	EGle
'Joette' (MTB)	Last listed 1999
'John' (IB)	SCro
'John Taylor' (SDB)	CKel
'Jolly Fellow' (SDB)	SUsu
'Jolt' (TB)	Last listed 1998
jordana	See *I. atrofusca*
'Joyce' (Reticulata)	CAvo CBro EPar EPot LAma LRHS
	MBri MMal NRog WRHF
'Joyce Terry' (TB)	GKir LRHS MBri
'Joyful' (SDB)	SCro
'Joyous Isle' (SDB)	Last listed 1997
'Jubilee Gem' (TB)	CKel
'Juliet' (TB)	Last listed 1997
juncea	CArn
'June Prom' (IB)	SCro
'Juneau' (TB)	CKel
'Jungle Fires' (TB)	Last listed 1997
'Jungle Shadows' (BB)	LGre MCAu MRav
¶ 'Jurassic Park' (TB)	LIri
'Just Jennifer' (BB)	MCAu
'Just Magic' (SDB)	Last listed 1999
kaempferi	See *I. ensata*
'Karen Christine' (TB)	SCro
'Karen Maddock' (TB)	Last listed 1999
kashmiriana	CB&S
'Katharine Hodgkin' (Reticulata) ♀	CAvo CBro CLAP EBee EBrP EBre
	EPot ERos GAbr GCrs LAma LBCl
	LBSe LBre LRHS MBBe MRav
	MTho NHar NRog NSla SBre
	SMrm WAbe WCot WIvy
'Katie-Koo' (IB) ♀	CKel
'Katinka' (CH)	WWst
'Katy Petts' (SDB)	EFou NZep
'Kayleigh Jayne Louise' (TB)	CKel
'Kayo' (TB)	CHad EFou EGle MMil NZep
'Kelway Renaissance' (TB)	CKel
kemaonensis	GDra NHar
'Kent Pride' (TB)	CMGP CMil EBee EBrP EBre EFou
	EPPr ERou GKir LBCl LBSe LBre

		MBBe MMil MRav MWat SBre
		SCro SMrm SWat
	'Kentucky Bluegrass' (SDB)	EFou MMil SUsu WWin
	'Kentucky Derby' (TB)	SCro
	'Kermit' (IB)	SCro
§	*kerneriana* ♀	CBro EBee ELan EMon ERos GBuc LRHS MNrw SUsu WPGP WPen
	'Keyhaven' (SDB)	Last listed 1999
	'Kildonan' (TB)	MCAu
	'Kilt Lilt' (TB)	SCro
	'Kinetic' (SDB)	CKel
	'Kirkstone' (TB)	Last listed 1997
	kirkwoodii MS&CL 555	Last listed 1998
	'Kissing Circle' (TB)	Last listed 1999
	'Kista' (SDB)	Last listed 1998
	'Kiwi Capers' (SDB)	NZep
	'Kiwi Slices' (SDB)	NMGW
	klattii	See *I. spuria* subsp. *musulmanica*
	'Knick Knack' (MDB)	CBro CGle EGle ELan EMan ERos GMaP LGre LPio LRHS MRav NMGW NMen SCro SIng WGwG WHil WWal WWin
¶	'Kochii' (IB)	GCal
I	*kopetdagensis*	Last listed 1997
	korolkowii 'Violacea'	Last listed 1998
	kuschakewiczii	Last listed 1998
*	'Kuvatuib' (SDB)	Last listed 1998
	'La Nina Rosa' (BB)	Last listed 1998
	'La Senda' (Spuria)	WCot
	'Lace Artistry' (TB)	SCro
	'Laced Cotton' (TB)	SCro
	'Laced Lemonade' (SDB)	EFou LRHS MBri
§	*lactea* ♀	GBin NSla SCro
	- CC 220	Last listed 1999
	- SULE 1	Last listed 1997
	lacustris ♀	CBro CNic EPot ERos GCrs MBro NBro NCat NHar NMen NWCA SIng WAbe
	'Lady Belle' (MTB) ♀	Last listed 1999
	'Lady Friend' (TB)	ERou SCro
	'Lady Madonna' (TB)	SCro
	'Lady Mohr' (AB)	CKel
¶	'Lady of Fatima' (TB)	ESgl
	'Lady of Nepal' (IB)	Last listed 1999
§	*laevigata* ♀	CKel CRow CWat ECha EGle EGol EHon ELan LPBA MRav MSta NBrk NBro NDea NGdn SPer SWat SWyc WAbe WFar WMAq WShi
	- 'Alba'	CBen CRow ECha EGol EHon LEdu LPBA SSpi SWat SWyc WAbe
	- 'Albopurpurea'	EMFW
	- 'Atropurpurea'	CRow EGol IBlr LPBA
	- 'Colchesterensis'	CBen CRow CWat EGol EHon EMFW LPBA MSta SWat SWyc WMAq
I	- 'Dorothy'	LPBA MSta NGdn
*	- 'Dorothy Robinson'	SWat
	- 'Elegant'	See *I. laevigata* 'Weymouth Elegant'
I	- 'Elegante'	CRow SWat SWyc
¶	- 'Elgar'	WMAq
	- 'Goshobeni'	CRow
¶	- 'Liam Johns'	CRow
	- 'Midnight'	See *I. laevigata* 'Weymouth Midnight'
N	- 'Monstrosa'	SWyc
	- 'Mottled Beauty'	CRow CWat MSta SWyc
	- 'Murasama'	CRow
	- 'Odiham'	SWyc
	- 'Plena' (d)	SWyc
N	- 'Plum Purple'	EGle

	- 'Regal'	CBen SWyc
I	- 'Reveille'	EGle
	- 'Richard Greany'	CRow
	- 'Rose Queen'	See *I. ensata* 'Rose Queen'
	- 'Shirasagi'	CRow
I	- 'Snowdrift'	CBen CRow CWat EGol EHon EMFW EPla LPBA MCAu MSta NDea NGdn SCro SPer SWat SWyc WMAq
	- 'Surprise'	See *I. laevigata* 'Weymouth Surprise'
	- 'Tamagawa'	CRow
	- 'Variegata' ♀	CBen CBos CRow CWat ECha EGol EHoe EHon EMFW EPla EWTr LEdu LPBA LRHS MSta NBid NDea NGdn NOrc SCob SPer SSpi SWat SWyc WMAq WRus WWat
	- 'Violet Garth'	CRow
	- 'Weymouth'	See *I. laevigata* 'Weymouth Blue'
§	- 'Weymouth Blue'	CRow SWyc
§	- 'Weymouth Elegant'	CBen
§	- 'Weymouth Midnight'	CBen CRow CWat EGol EHon SWat SWyc
§	- 'Weymouth Surprise'	CWat
	'Lake Placid' (TB)	SCro
	'Land o' Lakes' (TB)	SCro
N	'Langport Chapter' (IB)	CKel
N	'Langport Chief' (IB)	CKel
N	'Langport Chimes' (IB)	CKel
N	'Langport Claret' (IB)	CKel
N	'Langport Curlew' (IB)	CKel
N	'Langport Duchess' (IB)	CKel
N	'Langport Duke' (IB)	Last listed 1997
N	'Langport Fairy' (IB)	CKel
N	'Langport Fashion' (IB)	Last listed 1997
N	'Langport Flame' (IB)	CKel EWTr MMil
N	'Langport Flush' (IB)	SCro
N	'Langport Haze' (IB)	CKel
N	'Langport Hero' (IB)	Last listed 1997
N	'Langport Honey' (IB)	CKel
N	'Langport Hope' (IB)	CKel
N	'Langport Jane' (IB)	CKel
N	'Langport Lord' (IB)	CKel
N	'Langport Magic' (IB)	MMil
N	'Langport Minstrel' (IB)	CKel
N	'Langport Myth' (IB)	CKel
N	'Langport Pagan' (IB)	WTin
N	'Langport Pearl' (IB)	Last listed 1998
	'Langport Phoebe' (IB)	CKel
	'Langport Phoenix' (IB)	CKel
N	'Langport Pinnacle' (IB)	CKel
N	'Langport Pleasure' (IB)	CKel
N	'Langport Prince' (IB)	MMil
N	'Langport Robe' (IB)	CKel
N	'Langport Robin' (IB)	CKel
N	'Langport Romance' (IB)	CKel
N	'Langport Smoke' (IB)	CKel
N	'Langport Song' (IB)	CKel MMil
N	'Langport Star' (IB)	CKel
N	'Langport Storm' (IB)	CKel EFou MMil WBcn
N	'Langport Sultan' (IB)	CKel
N	'Langport Sun' (IB)	CKel
N	'Langport Sunbeam' (IB)	CKel
N	'Langport Swift' (IB)	CKel
	'Langport Sylvia' (IB)	CKel
N	'Langport Tempest' (IB)	CKel
N	'Langport Vale' (IB)	CKel
N	'Langport Violet' (IB)	CKel EWTr
N	'Langport Vista' (IB)	CKel
N	'Langport Warrior' (IB)	CKel
N	'Langport Wren' (IB) ♀	CBro CKel CMil LGre MBel MBri MMil NBir

'Margrave' (TB) — MCAu
'Marhaba' (MDB) — CBro ERos MCAu
'Maria Tormena' (TB) — SCro
'Mariachi' (TB) — Last listed 1997
'Marilyn Holloway' (Spuria) — ECha
¶ 'Mariposa Skies' (TB) — LIri
'Marmalade Skies' (BB) — NZep
'Maroon Caper' (IB) — Last listed 1999
'Marshlander' (TB) — EFou SCro
'Marty' (IB) — Last listed 1998
'Martyn Rix' — See I. confusa 'Martyn Rix'
'Mary Frances' (TB) ♀ — SCro
'Mary McIlroy' (SDB) ♀ — CBro MMil WTin
'Mary Randall' (TB) — Last listed 1997
'Master Touch' (TB) — SCro
'Matchpoint' (TB) — Last listed 1999
'Matinata' (TB) — CKel EBee EBrP EBre LBCl LBSe
LBre MBBe SBre
'Maui Moonlight' (IB) ♀ — EFou LIri MMil NZep
'May Melody' (TB) — CKel MBri
'Meadow Court' (SDB) — CBro CKel EBee ERos LRot MCAu
NBro NZep WWin
'Media Luz' (Spuria) — Last listed 1999
'Meg's Mantle' (TB) ♀ — CKel
'Melbreak' (TB) — Last listed 1997
'Melissa Sue' (TB) — SCro
mellita — See I. suaveolens
 - var. *rubromarginata* — See I. suaveolens
'Melon Honey' (SDB) ♀ — CKel EGle MCAu MMil NZep
WWin
'Menton' (SDB) — Last listed 1997
I 'Merry Day' (IB) — Last listed 1997
'Merseyside' (SDB) — EGle
'Mesmerizer' (TB) — LIri
'Metaphor' (TB) — MMil
'Michael Paul' (SDB) ♀ — Last listed 1997
'Michele Taylor' (TB) — SCro
'Midday Blues' (IB) — NZep
'Midnight Fire' (TB) — ERou
'Midnight Madness' (SDB) — Last listed 1998
¶ 'Midnight Oil' (TB) — LIri
milesii ♀ — CPou MHar NBir SCro WPer WPic
 - CC&McK 741 — GCHN
 - CR 346 — WPer
'Mini Agnes' (DB) — CBro
'Minnesota Glitters' (TB) — SCro
'Minnie Colquitt' (TB) — CKel SCro
'Miss Carla' (IB) ♀ — MMil SCro
'Mission Ridge' (TB) — CKel
'Mission Sunset' (TB) — EBrP EBre LBCl LBSe LBre MBBe
MCAu SBre
'Missouri Gal' (Spuria) — Last listed 1999
missouriensis ♀ — CRow EWoo IBlr SSpi
 - var. *arizonica* — EBee
'Mister Roberts' (SDB) — NZep
'Moment' (SDB) — Last listed 1999
'Monaco' (TB) — EFou
'Money' (TB) — SCro
monnieri — IBlr NLar SDix STes
Monspur Group — EBee ECGP GCal SSpi WCot
WPGP WPic
§ 'Monspur Cambridge — WPic
Blue' (Spuria)
¶ 'Moon Pearl' (CH) — WWst
'Moon Shadows' (SDB) — WViv
'Moon Sparkle' (IB) — CKel
'Moonlight' (TB) — NFor WCot
'Moonlight Waves' — See I. ensata 'Moonlight Waves'
¶ 'Moonraker' (TB) — LIri
'Moon's Delight' (TB) — Last listed 1997
'Morning Hymn' (TB) — SCro
'Morning Show' (IB) — SCro

'Morocco' (TB) — SCro
'Morwenna' (TB) ♀ — MCAu
* 'Mount Stewart Black' — EBee EGar GCal
'Mrs Horace Darwin' (TB) — CFir SWat
¶ 'Mrs Nate Rudolph' (SDB) — EFou EGle LGre MBri
* 'Mrs Richmond' — Last listed 1999
'Mulberry Rose' (TB) — CKel
munzii — EWoo
'Muriel Neville' (TB) — MCAu
'Murmuring Morn' (TB) — Last listed 1997
'Music Box' (SDB) — NZep
'Mute Swan' (TB) — MCAu
'My Honeycomb' (TB) — Last listed 1999
'My Mary' (TB) — CKel
N 'My Seedling' (MDB) — CBro ERos NMen WIvy
'My Smoky' (TB) — CKel
¶ 'Mystic Warrior' (TB) — LIri
'Mystique' (TB) — SCro
'Naivasha' (TB) — CKel
'Nambe' (MTB) — Last listed 1999
'Nampara' (TB) — Last listed 1999
'Nancy Hardy' (MDB) — CBro ERos NMen
'Nancy Lindsay' — See I. lutescens 'Nancy Lindsay'
'Nashborough' (TB) — CKel
'Natascha' (Reticulata) — EPot LAma
'Navajo Blanket' (TB) — SCro
'Navajo Jewel' (TB) — Last listed 1999
'Navy Blues' (TB) — Last listed 1999
'Nectar' (TB) — CKel
nectarifera — Last listed 1999
'Needlecraft' (TB) — CKel MMil
'Needlepoint' (TB) — SCro
'Neil Diamond' (TB) — Last listed 1999
* 'Nel Jupe' (TB) — EOld
'Neon Pixie' (SDB) — NZep
'Neophyte' (Spuria) — Last listed 1999
nepalensis — See I. decora
nertschinskia — See I. sanguinea
'New Idea' (MTB) — CLTr MCAu
'New Snow' (TB) — CKel MCAu
'Nibelungen' (TB) — CKel EOld EPfP NFai
'Nice 'n' Nifty' (IB) — NZep WTin
nicolai — WWst
'Nigerian Raspberry' (TB) — Last listed 1999
¶ 'Night Attack' (TB) — LIri
¶ 'Night Game' (TB) — LIri
'Night Owl' (TB) — CKel MBct MMil SCro
'Night Ruler' (TB) — Last listed 1997
¶ 'Nights of Gladness' (TB) — ESgI
nigricans S&L 148 — Last listed 1998
'Nimble Toes' (SDB) — Last listed 1999
'Nineveh' (AB) — Last listed 1998
I 'No-Name' (CH) — Last listed 1997
¶ 'Noon Siesta' (TB) — ESgI
'Norton Sunlight' (Spuria) ♀ — Last listed 1995
'Nova' — WWst
'Nylon Ruffles' (SDB) — SUsu
'Ochraurea' (Spuria) — EBee GCal
ochroleuca — See I. orientalis
'Offenham' (TB) — Last listed 1999
'Oklahoma Bandit' (IB) — Last listed 1999
¶ 'Oklahoma Crude' (TB) — LIri
'Ola Kala' (TB) — CMGP EBee EBrP EBre ECle ERou
EWTr LBCl LBSe LBre MBBe
MCAu SBre SCob SCro SPer
WLRN
'Old Flame' (TB) — NMGW
'Oliver' (SDB) — Last listed 1999
'Olympiad' (TB) — Last listed 1999
'Olympic Challenger' (TB) — MCAu
'Olympic Torch' (TB) ♀ — Last listed 1999
'One Accord' (SDB) — SCro

'One Desire' (TB)	NZep	
'Open Sky' (SDB)	MMil NZep	
'Orange Blaze' (SDB)	CBro	
'Orange Caper' (SDB)	EBrP EBre EGoo LBCl LBSe LBre	
	MBBe MRav NZep SBre	
§ 'Orange Chariot' (TB)	MCAu	
'Orange Dawn' (TB) ♀	Last listed 1999	
'Orange Grove' (TB)	MBri	
'Orange Jewelius' (TB)	Last listed 1999	
'Orange Maid' (Spuria)	WBcn	
¶ 'Orange Order' (TB)	MCAu	
N 'Orange Plaza'	NMen	
'Orange Tiger' (SDB)	NZep	
'Orchardist' (TB)	Last listed 1999	
'Orchidarium' (TB)	CKel	
§ *orchioides*	CMea EBee ELan EPot ERos MMal	
	NMen NWCA	
- yellow	Last listed 1998	
'Oregold' (SDB)	NZep	
'Oregon Skies' (TB)	SCro	
'Oriental Baby' (IB)	CKel	
'Oriental Blush' (SDB)	WBcn	
'Oriental Glory' (TB)	MCAu	
'Oriental Touch'	CRow	
(SpecHybrid)		
§ *orientalis* Mill. ♀	CBot CMil CRow ECGP ELan EPPr	
	LPBA MNrw MWgw SChu SSpi	
	WPic WWin WWst	
- 'Alba'	See *I. sanguinea* 'Alba'	
'Orinoco Flow' (BB) ♀	CKel LIri	
'Oritam' (TB)	SCro	
'Ornament' (SDB)	Last listed 1999	
'Ouija' (BB) ♀	Last listed 1995	
'Out Yonder' (TB)	MCAu	
'Ovation' (TB)	SCro	
'Overnight Sensation' (TB)	SCro	
¶ 'Owyhee Desert' (TB)	LIri	
¶ 'Ozone Alert' (TB)	LIri	
'Pacer' (IB)	NZep	
Pacific Coast hybrids	See *I. Californian* hybrids	
'Pacific Gambler' (TB)	EFou	
'Pacific Mist' (TB)	SCro	
'Pagan Pink' (TB)	LIri	
'Pagan Princess' (TB)	MCAu	
'Paint It Black' (TB)	Last listed 1999	
'Pajaro Dunes' (CH) ♀	Last listed 1999	
'Palace Gossip' (TB)	Last listed 1997	
'Pale Primrose' (TB)	MCAu WBar WEas	
'Pale Shades' (IB) ♀	CBro CKel ERos	
'Pale Suede' (SDB)	Last listed 1999	
pale yellow (Sino-Sib)	NWoo	
§ *pallida*	CHad ECGN EFou ELau GGar	
	GKir GMaP MCAu MCCP MRav	
- 'Argentea Variegata'	More than 30 suppliers	
- 'Aurea'	See *I. pallida* 'Variegata'	
- 'Aurea Variegata'	See *I. pallida* 'Variegata'	
- subsp. *cengialtii* ♀	Last listed 1998	
- var. *dalmatica*	See *I. pallida* subsp. *pallida*	
§ - subsp. *pallida* ♀	CBot CKel EBee EBrP EBre ECha	
	ELan LBCl LBSe LBre LHil MBBe	
	MBri MCAu SBre SCob SCro SDix	
	SMrm SPer WCot WWal	
N - 'Variegata' ♀	More than 30 suppliers	
'Paltec'	CHad CPlt CPou EBee LGre	
'Pandora's Purple' (TB)	SCro	
'Panocha' (TB)	Last listed 1999	
'Paradise' (TB) ♀	EPfP LIri SCro STes	
'Paradise Bird' (TB) ♀	Last listed 1999	
paradoxa f. *choschab*	Last listed 1999	
'Paricutin' (SDB)	CBro EGle	
'Paris Lights' (TB)	SCro	
'Party Dress' (TB)	CM&M CMGP EBee ECtt ELan	

	ENot ERav ERou EWTr MRav	
	NGdn NOrc SCoo SMrm SPer	
	WWal	
'Pascoe' (TB) ♀	Last listed 1999	
'Pastel Charm' (SDB)	CFri CKel CM&M CMGP EBee	
	MCli MSCN	
'Pastel Delight' (SDB)	NZep	
'Path of Gold' (DB)	CBro MBri	
'Patterdale' (TB)	NBir NMGW NVic	
'Pauline' (Reticulata)	CAvo CBro EPot LAma LRHS	
	NRog	
'Peace and Harmony' (TB)	LIri	
'Peach Band' (TB)	ERou	
'Peach Bisque' (TB)	Last listed 1997	
'Peach Eyes' (SDB)	CBro NZep	
'Peach Float' (TB)	Last listed 1999	
'Peach Petals' (BB)	NZep	
. 'Peach Picotee' (TB)	ESgl LIri SCro	
'Peach Spot' (TB)	MMil	
'Peaches ala Mode' (BB)	Last listed 1999	
'Peaches 'n' Topping' (BB)	Last listed 1999	
'Peachy Face' (IB)	Last listed 1999	
'Pearly Dawn' (TB)	EBee ECha ECtt MWat NGdn SCro	
	SPer WLRN	
'Pegasus' (TB)	SCro	
'Peggy Chambers' (IB) ♀	EFou MMil	
'Peking Summer' (TB)	SCro	
'Pennies' (MDB)	NZep	
'Pennyworth' (IB)	SCro	
'Penrhyn' (TB)	Last listed 1999	
'People Pleaser' (SDB)	NZep SCro	
'Peppermint Twist' (SDB)	NZep	
'Perfect Interlude' (TB)	Last listed 1997	
'Persian Berry' (TB)	SCro	
'Persian Doll' (MDB)	NZep	
'Persian Romance' (TB)	Last listed 1998	
persica	Last listed 1998	
'Pet' (SDB)	MCAu NSti NZep	
¶ 'Pewter Treasure' (TB)	LIri	
'Phil Keen' (TB) ♀	CKel	
'Phillida' (CH) ♀	WWst	
'Pied Pretty' (SDB)	SCro	
'Pigeon' (SDB)	NZep	
'Pigmy Gold' (IB)	EBee ENot ERos	
'Pinewood Amethyst' (CH)	CPlt WWst	
'Pinewood Charmer' (CH)	Last listed 1999	
'Pinewood Poppet' (CH)	Last listed 1999	
'Pinewood Sunshine' (CH)	CPlt	
'Pink Angel' (TB)	SCro	
'Pink Bubbles' (BB)	EFou NZep	
'Pink Clover' (TB)	Last listed 1999	
'Pink Confetti' (TB)	SCro	
'Pink Divinity' (TB)	MMil	
'Pink Horizon' (TB)	SCro SGar	
'Pink Kitten' (IB)	NZep	
'Pink Lamb' (BB)	Last listed 1999	
N 'Pink Lavender' (TB)	SCro	
'Pink 'n' Mint' (TB)	SCro	
'Pink Pussycat'	MBri	
N 'Pink Randall' (TB)	SCro	
'Pink Ruffles' (IB)	CHar CKel WBcn	
¶ 'Pink Swan' (TB)	ESgl	
'Pink Taffeta' (TB)	CKel SCro	
'Pinnacle' (TB)	CKel SWat	
'Pipes of Pan' (TB)	MRav	
'Piquant Lass' (MTB)	NZep	
'Pirate's Quest' (TB)	Last listed 1999	
'Pixie' (Reticulata)	EPot	
'Pixie Flirt' (MDB)	ERos	
planifolia	WWst	
- AB&S 4609	Last listed 1998	
* - 'Alba'	Last listed 1998	

- S&L 301	Last listed 1998
'Planned Treasure' (TB)	Last listed 1998
'Playgirl' (TB)	SCro
'Pledge Allegiance' (TB)	MCAu MMil SCro
'Plickadee' (SDB)	CBro EPot
'Plum Perfect' (SDB)	SCro
* 'Plums 'n' Cream'	Last listed 1998
'Pogo' (SDB)	CMil EBee ECtt EGle ELan ENot
	EPot GKir GMaP MMil MRav
	NNrd SCro SRms
'Pogo Doll' (AB)	Last listed 1999
¶ 'Point Made' (TB)	LIri
§ polakii (Oncocyclus)	Last listed 1997
'Pony' (IB)	Last listed 1999
'Port of Call' (Spuria)	Last listed 1999
'Post Time' (TB)	SCro
'Pot Luck' (IB)	Last listed 1997
'Powder Pink' (TB)	CKel
'Prairie Sunset' (TB)	NBlu
'Praise the Lord' (TB)	Last listed 1999
'Prancing Pony' (TB)	CKel SCro
'Pretender' (TB)	LRHS MBri
'Prettie Print' (TB)	SCro
'Priceless Pearl' (TB)	SCro
'Pride of Ireland' (TB)	SCro
'Prince' (SDB)	EFou EGle
'Prince Indigo' (TB)	ENot
'Princess' (TB)	Last listed 1997
'Princess Beatrice'	See I. pallida subsp. pallida
prismatica	EPla NNrd WTin
- alba	GAbr
'Professor Blaauw' (Dut) ♀	ETub LRHS
'Prophetic Message' (AB)	EFou
'Prosper Laugier' (IB)	SCro
'Protégé' (Spuria) ♀	Last listed 1999
'Proud Tradition' (TB)	LIri SCro
'Provencal' (TB)	CKel MCau
pseudacorus ♀	More than 30 suppliers
- 'Alba'	CRow SSpi SWyc
- var. bastardii	CKel CRDP CRow CWat ECGP
	ECha EGol EMFP EMFW LPBA
	SLon SWyc WFar
- 'Beuron'	CRow
- cream	EGol MTed NBir NBrk
- dwarf	SWyc
N - 'Ecru'	CRow SWyc
- 'Esk'	GCal MTed
N - 'Flore Pleno' (d)	CAvo CBot CKel CRow EBee
	EMFW EPPr MCAu MInt SWyc
	WCot
- 'Golden Daggers'	CRow
I - 'Golden Fleece'	SPer
- 'Golden Queen'	CRow MSta SWyc
- 'Ilgengold'	CRow
N - 'Ivory'	CRow
- 'Lime Sorbet' (v)	WCot
* - nana	LPBA
- 'Roy Davidson'	CKel
- 'Sun Cascade'	CRow SWyc
- Tangarewa Cream Group	SWyc
- 'Tiggah'	CRow NSti
- 'Turnipseed'	CRow EBee
- 'Variegata' ♀	More than 30 suppliers
- x versicolor	SCro
- 'Wychwood Multifloral'	SWyc
pseudocaucasica	Last listed 1999
pseudopumila	Last listed 1997
- MS 986/975	Last listed 1998
pumila	EBee EPla EPot LRHS MBro MHer
	NFor MGW NMen NWCA SRPl
	WHil WWin
- atroviolacea	CKel MBro

- subsp. attica	See I. attica
- 'Aurea'	MBro
* - 'Gelber Mantel'	MSCN
- 'Goldcrest' (I)	Last listed 1998
¶ - 'Jackanapes'	WEas
- 'Lavendel Plicata'	CNic EBee EWTr MSCN NBro
	NNrd
- 'Purpurea'	Last listed 1999
- 'Violacea'	MBro SCro SRms
- yellow	NFla
'Pumpkin Center' (SDB)	NZep
'Puppet' (SDB)	EGle EPot
'Puppet Baby' (MDB)	NZep
'Puppy Love' (MTB)	NMGW NZep
purdyi	Last listed 1999
'Pure Allure' (SDB)	NZep
'Pure-as-the' (TB)	Last listed 1999
'Purgatory' (TB)	Last listed 1999
'Purple Gem' (Reticulata)	CBro EPot LAma
'Purple Landscape' (SDB) ♀	Last listed 1999
'Purple Sensation' (Dut)	CB&S EWTr
'Purple Song' (TB)	Last listed 1998
'Purple Streaker' (TB)	SCro
purpurea	See I. galatica
purpureobractea	Last listed 1999
'Pushy' (SDB)	Last listed 1999
'Quark' (SDB)	CBro CKel NZep
'Quechee' (TB)	CBlo EPfP ERou EWTr EWll GMaP
	LNor MRav MWat NGdn SCro
	WLRN
'Queen in Calico' (TB)	MCAu SCro
'Queen of Hearts' (TB)	SCro
'Queen's Ivory' (SDB)	Last listed 1998
'Queen's Pawn' (SDB)	NMGW NZep
'Quiet Lagoon' (SDB)	NZep
'Quiet Thought' (TB)	Last listed 1999
'Quintana' (CH)	WWst
'Rabelais' (TB)	CKel EBee
'Radiant Summer' (TB)	SCro
'Rain Dance' (SDB) ♀	NMGW NZep
'Rainbow Goddess' (TB)	Last listed 1999
'Rainbow Trout' (TB)	Last listed 1999
'Rajah' (TB)	EBee EPfP ERav ERou MRav
	NGdn NOrc SLod WWal
'Rancho Grande' (TB)	Last listed 1997
'Rancho Rose' (TB)	SCro
'Ranger' (TB)	Last listed 1997
'Rapture in Blue' (TB)	Last listed 1999
'Rare Edition' (IB)	CKel EBrP EBre EFou GKir LBCl
	LBSe LBre LIri MBBe MBri NZep
	SBre SCro
'Rare Treat' (TB)	NZep
'Raspberry Acres' (IB)	LRHS MBri MCAu
'Raspberry Blush' (IB) ♀	CKel EFou NZep SCro
'Raspberry Frills' (TB)	Last listed 1997
'Raspberry Fudge' (TB)	LIri
'Raspberry Jam' (SDB)	EGle MMil NZep SUsu
'Raspberry Sundae' (BB)	NZep
'Rathe Primrose' (IB)	SCro
'Raven Hill' (TB)	Last listed 1998
'Razoo' (SDB)	CKel
'Real Jazzy' (MTB)	CKel
I 'Red Flash' (TB)	CKel
'Red Hawk' (TB)	LIri SCro
'Red Heart' (SDB)	CBlo GMaP MRav WPer
'Red Lion' (TB)	EFou NZep
'Red Orchid' (IB)	EWTr MCli
'Red Revival' (TB)	MCAu MWat SCro
'Red Rufus' (TB)	EFou
N 'Red Rum' (TB)	CKel
'Red Tornado' (TB)	Last listed 1997
'Red Zinger' (IB)	EFou NZep SCro

'Redwing' (TB)   MWat WPer
'Redwood Supreme'   Last listed 1999
  (Spuria)
'Regal Surprise'   CRow
  (SpecHybrid)
'Regards' (SDB)   CBro EGle
§ **reichenbachii**   CPBP ERos LBee
  - Balkana Group   Last listed 1999
  - NS 700   CPou LRHS
'Repartee' (TB)   SCro
§ **reticulata** ♀   CB&S CBro EPar EPot ETub LRHS
                              MBNS NRog
* - 'Violet Queen'   EPot
'Riches' (SDB)   NZep
'Ride the Wind' (TB)   LIri SCro
'Right Royal' (TB)   ENot
'Rime Frost' (TB)   MCAu MMil
'Ring o' Roses' (CH) ♀   Last listed 1995
'Ringo' (TB)   CKel LIri MCAu NMGW SCro
'Rio del Mar' (CH) ♀   Last listed 1995
'Ripple Chip' (SDB)   NZep WTin
'Rippling Waters' (TB)   WBcn
'Rising Moon' (TB)   SCro
'Ritz' (SDB)   WGwG
'River Hawk' (TB)   SCro
'River Patrol' (TB)   EFou
'Roaring Camp' (CH) ♀   Last listed 1995
'Robert J. Graves' (TB)   Last listed 1997
§ x **robusta** 'Dark Aura'   CRDP
§ - 'Gerald Darby' ♀   CBro CElw CFee CHad CKel
                              CMGP CRDP CRow EBee ECha
                              EGol EMFW EMon EPar GMac IBlr
                              MBri MBro NSti SCro SUsu SWat
                              SWyc WEas WPen WRus WWhi
  - 'Mountain Brook'   CRow
  - 'Nutfield Blue'   NSti
§ 'Rocket' (TB)   CMGP EBee ERav EWTr GMaP
                              MBel MRav NBir NGdn SCro
                              SMrm WLRN
¶ 'Rogue' (TB)   LIri
* 'Rogue Orange' (TB)   CKel
'Role Model' (TB)   Last listed 1997
'Roman Emperor' (TB) ♀   EFou
'Romance' (TB)   ERou
¶ 'Romano' (Dut)   MNrw
'Romantic Mood' (TB)   LIri
'Romp' (IB)   Last listed 1999
'Ron' (TB)   SCro
'Rose Queen'   See *I. ensata* 'Rose Queen'
'Rose Violet' (TB) ♀   NMGW
'Roselene' (TB)   SCro
'Rosemary's Dream' (MTB)   CKel
rosenbachiana   Last listed 1997
'Roseplic' (TB)   CKel
¶ 'Rosette Wine' (TB)   LIri
'Rosy Air' (SDB)   Last listed 1999
'Rosy Wings' (TB)   Last listed 1999
'Roulette' (TB)   MBri
'Roustabout' (SDB)   EFou EGle
N 'Roy Elliott'   CBos CHad MBro NHol NMen
                              SIng WPer
'Royal Ascot' (TB)   Last listed 1999
'Royal Contrast' (SDB) ♀   MMil NZep
'Royal Fairy' (SDB)   Last listed 1999
'Royal Intrigue' (TB)   SCro
'Royal Magician' (SDB)   WHoo WTin
'Royal Midget' (SDB)   Last listed 1999
'Royal Regency' (TB)   SCro
N 'Royal Toss' (TB)   Last listed 1998
'Royal Touch' (TB)   EFou
'Royal Viking' (TB)   Last listed 1997
'Royal Yellow' (Dut)   NRog

'Royalist' (TB)   Last listed 1997
'Ruby Chimes' (IB)   LGre MCAu SCro
'Ruby Contrast' (TB)   Last listed 1999
'Ruby Gem' (TB)   CKel
'Ruby Locket' (SDB)   Last listed 1999
'Ruby Mine' (TB)   MCAu
rudskyi   See *I. variegata*
'Ruffled Ballet' (TB)   SCro
'Ruffled Revel' (SDB)   CKel
'Ruffled Surprise' (TB)   SCro
'Ruffles and Lace' (TB)   SCro
'Rushing Stream' (TB)   Last listed 1999
'Russian White' (Spuria)   Last listed 1999
'Rustam' (TB)   CKel
'Rustic Cedar' (TB)   EPfP ESgI
N 'Rustic Jewel' (TB)   CKel EWTr
'Rustler' (TB)   SCro
'Rusty Dusty' (SDB)   NZep
'Ruth Couffer' (BB)   Last listed 1999
'Ruth Knowles' (SDB)   Last listed 1999
'Ruth Margaret' (TB)   CKel
ruthenica   ERos GOrP NMen WPer
  - var. **nana** L 1280   SBla
'Sable' (TB)   EBee MCAu MCLN MRav MWat
                              MWgw NGdn NOrc SCro SMrm
                              SPer WLRN
'Sable Night' (TB)   CKel ERou
'Sager Cedric' (TB)   Last listed 1999
'Sahara Sands' (Spuria)   ECha
'Saint Crispin' (TB)   CM&M EBee ERou EWTr MRav
                              MWat SCob SCro SMrm SPer
                              WGwG WLRN WWal
'Sally Jane' (TB)   MCAu
'Salonique' (TB)   MCAu NFai
* 'Saltbox' (SDB)   WIvy
'Saltwood' (SDB) ♀   CBro
'Sam' (SDB)   NZep
'Sam Carne'   Last listed 1999
'Samurai Warrior' (TB)   Last listed 1999
'San Leandro' (TB)   Last listed 1999
'Sand and Sea' (TB)   Last listed 1999
'Sand Princess' (MTB)   EFou
'Sandy Caper' (IB)   MCAu
'Sangreal' (IB)   LBuc
§ **sanguinea** ♀   CAvo WCot
  - AGSJ 625   Last listed 1998
§ - 'Alba'   CRow GCHN IBlr
  - x **laevigata**   SCro
  - 'Nana Alba'   Last listed 1999
§ - 'Snow Queen'   More than 30 suppliers
'Santana' (TB)   SCro
'Sapphire Beauty' (Dut)   NRog
'Sapphire Gem' (SDB)   CKel MCAu
'Sapphire Hills' (TB)   MCAu SCro
'Sapphire Jewel' (SDB)   NZep
'Sarah Taylor' (SDB) ♀   CBro EFou SCro
sari   Last listed 1999
'Sass with Class' (SDB)   WTin
'Satin Gown' (TB)   EPri GKir MBri MCAu
'Saturnalia' (TB)   SCro
'Saucy Peach' (BB)   Last listed 1999
'Saxon Princess' (TB)   Last listed 1999
'Scarlet Ribbon' (TB)   Last listed 1997
¶ 'Scented Bubbles' (TB)   LIri
schachtii MS&CL 510   Last listed 1998
'Schortman's Garnet   SCro
  Ruffles' (TB)
'Scintilla' (IB) ♀   MMil SCro
'Scintillation' (TB)   SCro
'Scribe' (MDB)   CBro EBee EGle GKir LRHS MBri
                              NBir
'Scrimmage' (SDB)   NZep

¶ - 'Maggie Smith' — EFou
- 'Maranatha' — EFou
N - 'Marcus Perry' — CRow MSte
- 'Marilyn Holme's' — GGar NFor WCot
- 'Marlene Ahlburg' — CAbx
§ - 'Melton Red Flare' — EHon ELan SDys WCot WHer WWpP
- 'Mikiko' ♀ — Last listed 1999
* - 'Moonlight' — NWoo
- 'Mountain Lake' — SWat
- 'Mrs Rowe' — CFee CPou CRow EBee EFou EGar EGle LLWP MCAu MRav MSte SWat WLin WRus
- 'Mrs Saunders' — CAbx
- 'My Love' — Last listed 1999
- 'Navy Brass' — EGle GBuc WLin
- 'Nora Distin' — EGar MCAu WLin
- 'Nottingham Lace' — EGle NBrk WBcn
- 'Oban' ♀ — Last listed 1999
- 'Orville Fay' ♀ — EFou EGar EGle GMac SCro SLod WCot
- 'Ottawa' — CAbx CLTr CPou CRow EBee ELan ERou LRHS MBNS MBri SCro SDys SPer SWat WFar
- 'Outset' — SCro
- 'Papillon' — CLTr CMGP ECGN EGle ELan ERou GKir LRHS MCli MWat NBro NCat NFai NGdn NHol SChu SPer WFar WLin WPer WPnP WWat
N - 'Pearl Queen' — CBos MTPN
- 'Perry's Blue' — More than 30 suppliers
I - 'Perry's Favourite' — CFee CRow
I - 'Perry's Pigmy' — GBuc MSte
- 'Persimmon' — CFir CHid CRos EBee EGar EGle EMan EMou ERou GCHN GKir LRHS MArl MCli MWat NMoo
* - 'Phosphor Flame' — WViv
- 'Pink Haze' — CHar CKel CRow EFou EGar SCro
- 'Pirate Prince' — NPer
- 'Pirouette' — Last listed 1998
- 'Pontypool' — Last listed 1999
- 'Pounsley Purple' — CPou
§ - 'Primrose Cream' — CMea MTed WCot
- 'Purpeller' — Last listed 1999
- 'Purple Cloak' — MSte WBcn
- 'Purple Mere' — CAbx WLin
- 'Rebeboth Gem' — Last listed 1997
N - 'Red Flag' — NHol
- 'Reddy Maid' — NBrk
- 'Redflare' — See I. sibirica 'Melton Red Flare'
- 'Rejoice Always' — WTin
- 'Rimouski' — Last listed 1999
N - 'Roger Perry' — CFee CRow
I - 'Royal Blue' — ECha GBuc
- 'Ruffled Velvet' ♀ — CBlo CHar CHea CHid CKel EBee EFou EGle GKir GMac MBNS MChl MRav MSte NBrk NBro SCro SVil WFar WHil WHoo WPGP
- 'Ruffles Plus' — Last listed 1999
- 'Sally Kerlin' — SCro
- 'Savoir Faire' — CRDP ECha EGle
- 'Sea Horse' — NCat
- 'Sea Shadows' ♀ — EFou MBel NBir NSti SHel WCot WLin
- 'Shirley Pope' ♀ — EBee EBrP EBre EGar GKir LBCl LBSe LBre LGre LRHS MBBe MBri MCAu SBre
- 'Showdown' — EBee ECtt EGar EGle LRHS MCAu MChl NFai NHol SAga SCro WWat
N - 'Shrawley' — CAbx EGar
- 'Silver Edge' ♀ — More than 30 suppliers
- 'Sky Wings' — CRow EBee ECha EGle EMou

MArl
- 'Snow Queen' — See I. sanguinea 'Snow Queen'
- 'Snowcrest' — CBre EBee NBrk
- 'Soft Blue' ♀ — SCro
N - 'Southcombe White' — COIW CRow EGar GBuc GCal LPio MBel NGdn
- 'Sparkling Rosé' — More than 30 suppliers
- 'Splashdown' ♀ — SWat
- 'Steve' — EBrP EBre LBCl LBSe LBre MBBe SBre
- 'Summer Sky' — CAbx MCAu SWat WCot WLin WTin WViv
- 'Super Ego' — WCot WTin
- 'Superba' — WLin
- 'Swank' — CAbx
- 'Teal Velvet' — GMac
¶ - 'Tealwood' — WLin
- 'Temper Tantrum' — CKel
- 'The Gower' — Last listed 1998
- 'Thelma Perry' — WCot
- 'Towanda Redflare' — EGle SOkh
- 'Tropic Night' — CHad CHea EBee ECGP EFou ERou GMac LAst LGre LRHS MBel MBri MRav MSta NBrk NGdn NHol NRya NSti SPer SSoC SWat WFar WHal WRus WWat
- 'Tycoon' — CHid EBee IBlr LRHS NCat NChi NHol SPer WLRN WLin
- 'Velvet Night' — Last listed 1999
- 'Vi Luihn' — CB&S ECha EGle
- 'Violetmere' — WLin
- 'Weisse Etagen' ♀ — SCro
- 'Welcome Return' — Last listed 1997
- 'Welfenprinz' ♀ — Last listed 1995
- white — EGle
- 'White Magnificence' — Last listed 1998
I - 'White Queen' — SSvw
* - 'White Swan' — EBee SAga
- 'White Swirl' ♀ — More than 30 suppliers
- 'Wisley White' ♀ — EGle NFai SRms
¶ - 'Yellow Court' — CRow
- 'Zakopane' ♀ — Last listed 1995
§ 'Sibirica Alba' — CRow ECGP ECha EWTr GDra GGar LLWP LPio SRms WWye
§ 'Sibirica Baxteri' — CFee CRow
sieboldii — See I. sanguinea
'Sierra Grande' (TB) — LIri
'Sierra Nevada' (Spuria) — EFou WBcn
'Silent Strings' (IB) — MBri
'Silhouette' (TB) — Last listed 1999
'Silicon Prairie' (TB) — Last listed 1999
'Silkirim' (TB) — Last listed 1999
'Silver Down' (SDB) — MCAu
'Silver Tide' (TB) — WEas
'Silverado' (TB) — LIri MCAu MMil SCro
'Silvery Moon' (TB) — SCro
sindjarensis — See I. aucheri
'Sindpers' (Juno) ♀ — WWst
'Sing Again' (IB) — CBlo
sintenisii ♀ — CBro CHid SIng
'Sister Helen' (TB) — MMil
'Siva Siva' (TB) — EBrP EBre ENot ERou LBCl LBSe LBre MBBe MCAu MRav SBre WHer
'Skating Party' (TB) — Last listed 1999
'Skiers' Delight' (TB) — LIri MCAu SCro
'Skip Stitch' (SDB) — Last listed 1999
'Sky and Snow' (SDB) — Last listed 1997
'Sky Hooks' (TB) — LIri SCro
'Sky Search' (TB) — Last listed 1999
'Skyblaze' (TB) — Last listed 1999
'Skyfire' (TB) — Last listed 1997

¶ 'Skywalker' (TB)   LIri
'Slap Bang' (SDB)   NZep
'Sleepy Time' (MDB)   NZep
'Slim Jim' (MTB)   Last listed 1999
'Small Sky' (SDB)   CBro NCat
'Small Wonder' (SDB)   Last listed 1999
N 'Smart Girl' (TB)   CKel
'Smarty Pants' (MTB)   Last listed 1999
'Smell the Roses' (SDB)   NZep
'Smoke Rings' (TB)   SCro
'Smokey Dream' (TB)   CKel
'Smooth Orange'   See I. 'Orange Chariot'
'Sneak Preview' (TB)   Last listed 1998
'Sno Jo' (SDB)   SCro
'Snow Elf' (SDB)   Last listed 1999
'Snow Festival' (IB)   MMil NZep
'Snow Fiddler' (MTB)   NZep
'Snow Tracery' (TB)   ENot MBri
'Snow Tree' (SDB)   NZep
'Snow Troll' (SDB)   MCAu MMil WWin
'Snowbrook' (TB)   SCro
'Snowcone' (IB)   SCro
'Snowdrift' (*laevigata*)   See I. *laevigata* 'Snowdrift'
'Snowmound' (TB)   MCAu SCro
'Snowshill' (TB)   Last listed 1999
'Snowy Owl' (TB) ♀   Last listed 1999
'Snowy River' (MDB)   NZep
'Snowy Wonderland' (TB)   Last listed 1998
'Soaring Kite' (TB) ♀   Last listed 1999
'Social Event' (TB)   LIri
'Social Register' (TB)   Last listed 1998
'Soft Breeze' (SDB)   NZep
'Soft Caress' (TB)   Last listed 1999
'Solar Wind' (AB)   Last listed 1999
'Solid Gold' (TB)   Last listed 1997
'Solid Mahogany' (TB)   MCAu MMil MRav
'Somerset Blue' (TB)   CKel
'Somerset Girl' (TB)   CKel
N 'Somerset Vale' (TB)   CKel
* 'Somerton Brocade' (SDB)   CKel
* 'Somerton Gold' (SDB)   CKel
'Song of Norway' (TB) ♀   MCAu MMil NZep SCro WBcn
'Sonja's Selah' (BB)   LIri
'Sonoran Senorita' (Spuria)   Last listed 1999
'Sooner Serenade' (TB)   Last listed 1999
'Sostenique' (TB)   MCAu
'Soul Power' (TB)   ERou
'Southern Clipper' (SDB)   LRHS MBri
'Souvenir de Madame   Last listed 1999
   Gaudichau' (TB)
sp. AGSJ 431   EWoo
sp. CLD 1399   NHol
'Space Mist' (TB)   Last listed 1998
'Spanish Coins' (MTB)   NZep
'Spanish Lime' (Spuria)   Last listed 1999
'Sparkling Cloud' (SDB)   EGle WWin
¶ 'Sparkling Eyes' (DB)   EFou
'Spartan'   CKel
N 'Specify' (TB)   Last listed 1998
'Spiced Custard' (TB)   SCro
'Spin-off' (TB)   SCro
'Spirit of Memphis' (TB)   MMil
'Splash of Red' (SDB)   MMil NZep
'Split Decision' (SDB)   NZep
'Spring Bells' (SDB)   EFou
'Spring Dancer' (IB)   SCro
'Spring Festival' (TB)   CKel
'Spring Signal' (TB)   Last listed 1999
'Springtime' (Reticulata)   LAma LRHS NRog
spuria   CPou ECGP ELan MBct SWyc
   - subsp. *carthaliniae*   WPer
§   - subsp. *halophila*   MCAu

¶ - 'Lilacina'   WHal
   - subsp. *maritima*   Last listed 1999
§   - subsp. *musulmanica*   NTow
¶   - subsp. *notha*   MDCh
   - - CC 1550   WCot
   - subsp. *ochroleuca*   See I. orientalis
   - subsp. *sogdiana*   Last listed 1997
N 'Spuria Alba'   SWyc
'Spyglass Hill' (TB)   Last listed 1997
x *squalens*   Last listed 1999
'Squeaky Clean' (SDB)   Last listed 1997
'Stapleford' (SDB)   CBro EGle
'Star Sailor' (TB)   SCro
'Star Shine' (TB)   MCAu
'Starcrest' (TB)   LIri SCro
¶ 'Starheart' (IB)   MCAu
'Starry Eyed' (SDB)   EGle
¶ 'Starshadow'   MCAu
¶ 'Starship' (TB)   LIri
'Startler' (TB)   SCro
'Staten Island' (TB)   CKel ELan ENot MBri MCAu MMil
   SRms
'Status Seeker' (TB)   Last listed 1999
'Stella Polaris' (TB)   SCro
'Stellar Lights' (TB)   Last listed 1997
'Step by Step' (BB)   Last listed 1997
'Stepping Out' (TB) ♀   EBrP EBre EFou LBCl LBSe LBre
   LIri MBBe MBri SBre SCro
'Sterling Prince' (TB)   Last listed 1997
'Stitch in Time' (TB)   MCAu SCro
'Stockholm' (SDB)   CKel NZep
stolonifera   Last listed 1998
'Stop the Music' (TB)   SCro
N 'Storrington' (TB)   SCro
'Storybook' (TB)   SCro
'Strange Child' (SDB)   NZep
'Stratagem' (TB)   LIri
¶ 'Strawberry Ice' (IB)   EFou
'Strawberry Love' (IB) ♀   MMil
'Strawberry Sensation' (TB)   NZep
¶ 'Street Vendor' (TB)   LIri
'Stylish' (DB)   Last listed 1999
stylosa   See I. unguicularis
'Suave' (TB)   SCro
§ *suaveolens*   CBro CNic EPot LPio LRHS MBro
   NMen NNrd WIvy
*   - var. *flavescens*   WWst
   - 'Rubromarginata'   ERos
*   - var. *violacea*   EBee WWst
subbiflora   Last listed 1998
'Sudeley' (SDB)   SCro
'Sugar' (IB)   MCAu NSti
'Sugar Candy' (CH)   WWst
'Sultan's Palace' (TB)   CKel MTPN SCro
'Sultry Mood' (TB)   LIri
'Summer Luxury' (TB)   NMGW NZep
'Sumptuous' (TB)   SCro
'Sun Dappled' (TB)   ERou MMil
'Sun Doll' (SDB) ♀   NZep
'Sun King' (TB)   Last listed 1999
'Sun Miracle' (TB) ♀   Last listed 1993
'Sunday Chimes' (TB)   SCro
'Sundown Red' (IB)   NBir
'Sunlit Sea' (Spuria)   Last listed 1999
'Sunny Dawn' (IB) ♀   Last listed 1999
'Sunny Day' (Spuria) ♀   Last listed 1999
'Sunny Heart' (SDB)   Last listed 1997
'Sunny Honey' (IB)   NZep SCro
'Sunny Smile' (IB) ♀   Last listed 1995
'Sunset Sky' (TB)   Last listed 1997
'Sunshine Isle' (SDB)   MMil NZep
'Superlation' (TB)   SCro

'Superstition' (TB) ♀ — EFou MCAu MMil SCro
'Supreme Sultan' (TB) — SCro
'Surprise Orange' (MDB) — NZep
'Susan Bliss' (TB) — CKel EBee ELan EPfP GMaP NFai SMer
susiana — EBot LAma
'Swaledale' (TB) — MCAu
'Swazi Princess' (TB) — CKel SCro
'Sweertii' — Last listed 1997
'Sweet Kate' (SDB) ♀ — Last listed 1999
'Sweet Musette' (TB) — MCAu SCro
'Sweet 'n' Neat' (SDB) — SCro
'Sweeter than Wine' (TB) — SCro
'Swing and Sway' (TB) — Last listed 1999
'Swizzle' (IB) — Last listed 1999
'Sybil' — Last listed 1998
'Syllable' (SDB) — Last listed 1998
'Sylvia Murray' (TB) — MCAu
'Symphony' (Dut) — LRHS
'Syncopation' (TB) — Last listed 1999
'Tall Chief' (TB) — EBrP EBre LBCl LBSe LBre MBBe NBrk SBre SCro
'Tall Ships' (TB) — Last listed 1999
'Tan Tingo' (IB) — EFou
'Tangerine Sky' (TB) — MCAu SCro
'Tangerine Sunrise' (TB) ♀ — Last listed 1999
'Tantara' (SDB) — SCro WTin
taochia — Last listed 1998
* - *flava* — WWst
'Tarheel Elf' (SDB) — WTin
'Tarn Hows' (TB) — SRms
'Taupkin' (SDB) — Last listed 1999
'Tease' (SDB) — Last listed 1997
tectorum — CSWP ERos GSki MNrw WHil
- 'Alba' — CKel CPou SIng
- Burma form — Last listed 1997
- 'Variegata' — EPla MCCP MRav SVil
'Tell Fibs' (SDB) — CBro EGle
'Temple Gold' (TB) — CKel
'Temple Meads' (IB) — CKel
'Templecloud' (IB) ♀ — CKel LIri
'Ten' (SDB) — NZep SCro
§ *tenax* — CBlo CLAP CNic ECho GSki
- 'Alba' — SIng
'Tennessee Vol' (TB) — LIri
'Tennessee Woman' (TB) — Last listed 1999
tenuis — Last listed 1998
tenuissima — Last listed 1999
'The Bride' — See *I.* 'Bride'
'The Citadel' (TB) — CKel SCro
N 'The Monarch' (TB) — Last listed 1998
'The Rocket' — See *I.* 'Rocket'
'Theatre' (TB) — MMil SCro
'Theda Clark' (IB) — SCro
'Theseus' (Aril) — Last listed 1998
'Third Charm' (SDB) — CBro
'Third World' (SDB) — CBro
thompsonii — Last listed 1999
'Thornbird' (TB) — ESgl LIri
'Thousand Lakes' (SDB) — NZep
'Three Cherries' (MDB) — CBro EGle
'Thriller' (TB) — MMil
'Throb' (TB) — LIri
thunbergii — See *I. sanguinea*
'Thunder Mountain' (TB) — Last listed 1998
'Thundercloud' (TB) — MCAu
'Tide's In' (TB) — ERou SCro
'Tiger Butter' (TB) — Last listed 1997
'Tiger Honey' (TB) — LIri
'Tillamook' (TB) — Last listed 1999
'Time for Love' (TB) — NZep
'Timeless Moment' (TB) — SCro

'Timmie Too' (BB) — Last listed 1999
tingitana var. *fontanesii* — ELan
    AB&S 4452
- SB&L 218 — Last listed 1998
'Tinkerbell' (SDB) — COtt CPBP CStu EBee EGle EMan LGre SChu SCro WGwG WLRN WWal WWin
'Tinted Crystal' (TB) — Last listed 1997
'Tintinara' (TB) ♀ — CKel
'Tiny Freckles' (MDB) — NZep
'Tirra Lirra' (SDB) ♀ — MMil
'Titan's Glory' (TB) ♀ — CKel LIri MCAu MRav SCro WCot
Tol-Long — IHdy MSte
'Tom Tit' (TB) — Last listed 1998
'Tomingo' (SDB) — WViv
'Tomorrow's Child' (TB) — SCro
'Toni Lynn' (MDB) — Last listed 1998
'Toots' (SDB) — EGle WTin
'Top Flight' (TB) — ENot ERou SPer SRms WLRN
N 'Topolino' (TB) — CKel SAga WBcn
'Topsy Turvy' (MTB) — Last listed 1999
'Torchlight' (TB) — Last listed 1998
'Tornado Watcher' (AB) — Last listed 1999
'Total Eclipse' — SRms
'Touch of Spring' (TB) — MMil
'Toy Boat' (SDB) — NMGW
¶ 'Tracy Tyrene' (TB) — ESgl
'Treasure' (TB) — MCAu
'Trevaunance Cove' (TB) — Last listed 1999
'Triffid' (TB) — LIri
'Triplicate' (SDB) — LGre MBri
trojana — Last listed 1999
'Truly' (SDB) — MCAu SCro
'Trust' (TB) — LIri
'Tu Tu Turquoise' (SDB) — NZep
tuberosa — See *Hermodactylus tuberosus*
'Tumbleweeds' (SDB) — NZep
N 'Tuscan' (TB) — CKel WBcn
'Tut's Gold' (TB) — MCAu SCro
'Twice Thrilling' (TB) — Last listed 1999
'Twist of Fate' (TB) — SCro
'Two Rubies' (SDB) — NZep
'Tyke' (MTB) — NZep
typhifolia — Last listed 1997
'Ultimatum' (TB) — LIri
'Ultra Pretty' (TB) — SCoo
'Unfurled Flag' — Last listed 1997
§ *unguicularis* ♀ — More than 30 suppliers
- 'Abington Purple' — CAvo CBro
- 'Alba' — CAvo CBro ECha
N - 'Bob Thompson' — CAvo
- broken form — Last listed 1999
- subsp. *carica* — IBlr WCot
    var. *angustifolia*
§ - subsp. *cretensis* — EPot NMen WHil
- - MS 720 — Last listed 1998
- - S&L 478 — Last listed 1998
- - S&L 550 — Last listed 1998
¶ - - white — SBla
N - 'Francis Wormsley' — MRav
- L&R 65 — Last listed 1998
- var. *lazica* — See *I. lazica*
¶ - 'Marondera' — CAvo
- 'Mary Barnard' — CAvo CBro CFee CGle CHar CPou CSam CSev CSpe ECha LRHS MBro MRav NLar NMen SCob SIng WByw WGwG WRus
N - 'Oxford Dwarf' — CBro ECho
- 'Palette' — ELan
¶ - 'Peacock' — WWst
- 'Unguicularis Marginata' — Last listed 1999
§ - 'Walter Butt' — CAvo CGle ECha IHdy MRav NBir

xiphium	EBee SSpi
- 'Lusitanica'	EBee
'Yellow Girl' (SDB)	NMGW NZep
'Yellow Queen' (Dut)	Last listed 1999
'Yo-yo' (SDB)	NZep
'Yvonne Pelletier' (TB)	MCAu
'Zantha' (TB)	Last listed 1999
'Zeeland' (BB)	Last listed 1999
¶ 'Zen'	EBrP EBre LBCl LBSe LBre MBBe SBre
'Zink Pink' (BB)	LIri SCro
'Zowie' (SDB)	NZep
'Zua' (IB)	LGre MTed SCro
'Zulu Chief' (Spuria)	Last listed 1997

ISATIS (Brassicaceae)
tinctoria	CArn COld CSev EOHP EWFC GPoy ILis LRHS MChe MHer MHew MSal SIde WCHb WHer WJek WOak WPer WSel WWye

ISCHYROLEPIS (Restionaceae)
ocreata	LHil WNor
¶ *sieberi* var. *venustula*	CTrC
§ *subverticillata*	CHEx CTrC

ISMENE See HYMENOCALLIS

ISOLEPIS (Cyperaceae)
§ *cernua*	CHal EMFW MBri MCCP

ISOLOMA See KOHLERIA

ISOMERIS See CLEOME

ISOPLEXIS (Scrophulariaceae)
canariensis	CAbb CBot CFil CHEx CSpe EWll LEur SHFr SSoC SUsu WEas WHil WSPU
isabelliana	CFil WCot
sceptrum	CBot CFil CFir CHEx CSpe EWll GCal SAPC SArc SSoC WCot
¶ - pink	CSpe

ISOPOGON (Proteaceae)
anethifolius	Last listed 1998
dubius	Last listed 1997

ISOPYRUM (Ranunculaceae)
¶ *biternatum*	GBuc
§ *nipponicum*	Last listed 1997
var. *sarmentosum*	
obwianum	See *I. nipponicum* var. *sarmentosum*
thalictroides	CGle

ISOTOMA See LAURENTIA

ITEA (Escalloniaceae)
ilicifolia ♀	More than 30 suppliers
japonica 'Beppu'	MGos SLPl
virginica	CAbP CB&S CDoC CLTr CMCN CMHG CPle CWit ELan EWTr MBlu MGos MRav NArg SLon SPer WHCG WSHC WTro WWat
§ - 'Henry's Garnet'	CDoC CEnd CFai CMCN CPMA EBee EPfP EPla MBlu NLar SBrw SRPl WCwm WWes
¶ - 'Merlot'	CPMA
- 'Sarah Eve'	CMCN
- Swarthmore form	See *I. virginica* 'Henry's Garnet'
yunnanensis	IOrc

ITOA (Flacourtiaceae)
orientalis S&F 92300	ISea

IVESIA (Rosaceae)
gordonii	NWCA
pygmaea	Last listed 1998

IXIA (Iridaceae)
Bird of Paradise	See *I.* 'Paradijsvogel'
'Blue Bird'	LAma
'Castor'	Last listed 1998
¶ *dubia*	CGrW
flexuosa	CGrW NRog
'Hogarth'	LAma
hybrids	SDeJ
'Mabel'	NRog
maculata	NRog
'Marquette'	NRog
monadelpha	CGrW LBow
paniculata	LBow NRog
§ 'Paradijsvogel'	LAma
polystachya	LBow NRog
'Rose Emperor'	LAma NRog
thomasiae	WCot
'Venus'	LAma
viridiflora	WCot
¶ 'Yellow Emperor'	ETub WCot

IXIOLIRION (Amaryllidaceae)
pallasii	See *I. tataricum*
§ *tataricum*	CHar EBee LAma MBri MMal WViv
- Ledebourii Group	CAvo LAma

IXORA (Rubiaceae)
chinensis 'Apricot Queen'	SOWG
coccinea	Last listed 1999
'Golden Ball'	SOWG
'Pink Malay'	SOWG

J

JABOROSA (Solanaceae)
integrifolia	CFir CPLG EBee ELan GCal MNrw MTed WCot WCru WPGP
squarrosa F&W 7836	Last listed 1999

JACARANDA (Bignoniaceae)
acutifolia Kunth	MBri
- hort.	See *J. mimosifolia*
§ *mimosifolia*	CB&S ECon ERea GQui LCns LRHS SOWG

JACOBINIA See JUSTICIA

JAMESBRITTENIA (Scrophulariaceae)
breviflora JCA 3-810-200	Last listed 1999
§ *grandiflora*	Last listed 1999
§ *jurassica*	NMen

JAMESIA (Hydrangeaceae)
americana	CPle WAbe WWat WWin

JASIONE (Campanulaceae)
amethystina	EBee
§ *crispa*	Last listed 1998
§ *heldreichii*	GAbr MBro NNrd SAga SBla SRms WElm WPyg WWin

jankae	See *J. heldreichii*
§ *laevis*	ECot EHol LRHS SAga SRms
§ - 'Blaulicht'	CFwr EBee ECha EMan EMar EPfP
	ESis LRHS MBNS MBri MHer
	MWgw NBrk NLar SLod SMrm
	SPlb SSvw WMoo WOve WPer
	WRos WWal
- Blue Light	See *J. laevis* 'Blaulicht'
montana	EDAr EWFC GKir MChe SSca
	WHer
perennis	See *J. laevis*

JASMINUM (Oleaceae)

angulare	CGre CPlN EHol ERea LRHS
	SOWG
azoricum ♀	CGre CPlN CRHN ECon ELan
	EPfP ERea GQui LCns LPan LRHS
	WMul
beesianum	More than 30 suppliers
bignoniaceum	CPlN WSHC
floridum	EWes
fruticans	CMac CPle ELan EPla WBcn WCru
- HH&K 126	Last listed 1999
grandiflorum 'De Grasse'	CPlN ERea LRHS SOWG
humile	CBlo CPle GOrc GSki IMGH LPan
	MHer SHFr WBod WFar WKif
	WPic
- f. *farreri*	WCru
§ - 'Revolutum' ♀	More than 30 suppliers
- f. *wallichianum*	CPle
¶ - - B&SWJ 2559	WCru
- - B&SWJ 2987	Last listed 1999
§ *laurifolium* f. *nitidum*	CPlN ERea LChe
¶ *leratii*	CPlN
§ *mesnyi* ♀	CGre CMac CPle EBak EBee ECtt
	ELan ERea IOrc LPan NBea SAga
	SBra SLim SOWG SYvo WCot
	WSHC
multipartitum	Last listed 1999
¶ - bushy	CSpe
nitidum	See *J. laurifolium* f. *nitidum*
§ *nobile* subsp. *rex*	Last listed 1999
nudiflorum ♀	More than 30 suppliers
- 'Argenteum'	See *J. nudiflorum* 'Mystique'
- 'Aureum'	EBee ELan EPfP EPla GOrc GQui
	LRHS MAsh MCCP MRav NHol
	NSti SLim SPer SPla WCot WHCG
	WPat
* - 'Compactum'	Last listed 1999
§ - 'Mystique' (v)	CPMA ELan EPfP LRHS MAsh
	SLim SMur SPer SSta WCot WPat
- 'Nanum'	MBro NHol WPat
odoratissimum	ERea LRHS SOWG
officinale ♀	More than 30 suppliers
§ - f. *affine*	CB&S CRHN CSam CTri EBrP
	EBre ELan ENot EOrc EPla ERea
	IOrc LBCl LBSe LBre LPri MAsh
	MBBe MRav NHol SBre SDix SEas
	SLim SMad SRms WCru WWeb
§ - 'Argenteovariegatum' ♀	More than 30 suppliers
- 'Aureovariegatum'	See *J. officinale* 'Aureum'
§ - 'Aureum'	More than 30 suppliers
- CC 1709	WCot WHCr
- 'Devon Cream'PBR	SPar
- Fiona Sunrise	More than 30 suppliers
= 'Frojas'PBR	
- 'Grandiflorum'	See *J. officinale* f. *affine*
- 'Inverleith'	CDoC EBee ELan GCal GOrc LAst
	LHop LRHS MAsh MBNS MBri
	MCCP MRav NFai SBra SCoo SLim
	SMad SPan SPer SPla SSoC SVil
	WGwG WWal

- 'Variegatum'	See *J. officinale*
	'Argenteovariegatum'
parkeri	CB&S CBot CFee EPla ESis IMGH
	LHop MAsh MBNS MBlu MBro
	NHol SIde SIng SSta WAbe WCru
	WFar WPat WPyg WWat
polyanthum ♀	CArn CB&S CPlN CRHN CTri
	CTrw EBak EBee EPfP ERea ERom
	GQui ISea LPan LRHS MBri NBea
	NRog SLim SRms WBod WCFE
primulinum	See *J. mesnyi*
reevesii	See *J. humile* 'Revolutum'
rex	See *J. nobile* subsp. *rex*
sambac	CPlN CRHN ECon ELan EPfP
	LChe LCns LPan LPri LRHS SOWG
	SYvo WMul
- 'Grand Duke of	ERea LChe LRHS SOWG
Tuscany' (d)	
- 'Maid of Orleans' (d)	ERea LChe LRHS SOWG
§ *simplicifolium*	Last listed 1999
subsp. *australiense*	
§ - subsp. *suavissimum*	Last listed 1999
x *stephanense* ♀	More than 30 suppliers
suavissimum	See *J. simplicifolium* subsp.
	suavissimum
tortuosum	CPlN
volubile	See *J. simplicifolium* subsp.
	australiense

JATROPHA (Euphorbiaceae)

integerrima	ECon LRHS SOWG
multifida	Last listed 1997
podagrica	ECon LChe LRHS

JEFFERSONIA (Berberidaceae)

diphylla	CArn CBro CElw CGle CHid EBee
	EPar GKir IBlr LAma LRHS MDun
	MSal MTho NBir NHar NHol
	NRog WAbe WCru WFar WWat
	WWye
dubia	EWes GCrs IBlr LRHS NBir NHar
	NMen NRog SBla WCru
- 'Alba'	SBla

JOHANNESTEIJSMANNIA (Arecaceae)

lanceolata	Last listed 1999
magnifica	LPal

JOVELLANA (Scrophulariaceae)

¶ *procumbens*	CPne
punctata	CGre CPle CSpe LHil MBlu
repens	CFir IBlr WCot WCru
sinclairii	CGle CPLG CPne ECou IBlr SSpi
	SUsu WCot WCru
violacea ♀	CAbP CAbb CB&S CGle CHEx CPle
	CSpe CWit EMan EMil ERea GCal
	IBlr ISea ITim LHil SAPC SArc SDry
	WBod WBor WCru WPic WSHC

JOVIBARBA ✿ (Crassulaceae)

§ *allionii*	CMea CTri CWil EPot LBee LRHS
	MBro SIng SRms SSmi WAbe WPer
	WWin
- x *hirta*	CWil GAbr MBro MOne NHol
	NNrd SDys SIng SSmi WLRN
- 'Oki'	CWil MOne
- x *sobolifera*	SSmi
§ *arenaria*	CWil ESis GAbr GCHN MBro
	MDHE NMen SIng SSmi
- from Murtal	MDHE SSmi
- from Passo Monte	CWil
Crocecar Nico	

'Emerald Spring'	CWil
§ **heuffelii**	CWil LRHS NHol NMen NPri WPer
- 'Aga'	Last listed 1998
- 'Aiolos'	NHol
- 'Alemene'	Last listed 1998
- 'Almkroon'	Last listed 1998
- 'Angel Wings'	CWil NHol
- 'Apache'	Last listed 1998
- 'Aquarius'	CWil
- 'Artemis'	Last listed 1998
- 'Beacon Hill'	CWil MBro
- 'Belcore'	CWil
- 'Benjamin'	NHol
- 'Bermuda'	CWil
- 'Bermuda Sunset'	NHol
- 'Brandaris'	NHol
- 'Brocade'	NHol
- 'Bronze Ingot'	CWil
- 'Bros'	Last listed 1998
- 'Chocoleto'	CWil WTin
- 'Cleopatra'	Last listed 1998
- 'Copper King'	Last listed 1998
- 'Cythera'	Last listed 1998
¶ - 'Dunbar Red'	NHol
- 'Fandango'	CWil
- 'Gento'	CWil NHol
- 'Geronimo'	NHol
- 'Giuseppi Spiny'	CWil NHol
- var. **glabra**	Last listed 1998
- - from Anabakanak	CWil NHol WTin
- - from Anthoborio	CWil NMen WTin
- - from Backovo	NHol
- - from Bansko Vihren	Last listed 1998
- - from Galicica	Last listed 1998
- - from Haila	CWil NMen
- - from Jakupica, Macedonia	CWil
- - from Kapaenianum	WTin
- - from Koprovnik	CWil
- - from Kosovo, Yugoslavia	Last listed 1998
- - from Ljuboten	CWil NMen WTin
- - from Osljak	Last listed 1998
- - from Pasina Glava	CWil
- - from Pelister	Last listed 1998
- - from Rhodope	CWil MHom NHol
- - from Stogovo	Last listed 1998
- - from Treska Gorge, Macedonia	CWil MBro WTin
- - from Vitse	CWil
- 'Gold Rand'	NHol
- 'Goya'	Last listed 1998
- 'Grand Slam'	Last listed 1998
- 'Green Land'	CWil
- 'Greenstone'	CWil MBro NHol NMen WTin
- 'Harmony'	Last listed 1998
- 'Helena'	Last listed 1998
- 'Henry Correvon'	CWil
- 'Iason'	Last listed 1998
- 'Ikaros'	Last listed 1998
- 'Inferno'	CWil
- 'Iole'	Last listed 1998
- 'Iuno'	CWil
- 'Jade'	CWil NMen
- 'Kapo'	Last listed 1998
- var. **kopaonikensis**	CWil NMen
- 'Mary Ann'	MHom
- 'Miller's Violet'	CWil WTin
- 'Minuta'	CWil NHol NMen WTin
- 'Mont Rose'	Last listed 1998
- 'Mystique'	CWil MBro

- 'Nannette'	Last listed 1998
- 'Nobel'	Last listed 1998
- 'Opele'	NHol
- 'Orion'	CWil NMen
- 'Pampero'	Last listed 1998
- 'Passat'	Last listed 1998
- var. **patens**	Last listed 1999
- 'Pink Skies'	MBro
- 'Prisma'	CWil WTin
- 'Purple Haze'	MBro
- 'Pyrope'	Last listed 1998
- 'Red Rose'	Last listed 1998
- 'Rhodope'	Last listed 1998
- 'Springael's Choice'	Last listed 1998
- 'Suntan'	CWil
- 'Sylvan Memory'	CWil
- 'Tan'	CWil MBro
- 'Tancredi'	Last listed 1998
- 'Torrid Zone'	CWil WTin
- 'Tuxedo'	CWil
- 'Vesta'	Last listed 1998
- 'Violet'	CWil
- 'Vulcan'	Last listed 1998
§ **hirta**	CHal CWil GAbr GCrs MDHE MOne NHol NMen SBla SIng STre WPer
- subsp. **borealis**	CWil EGln MBro MOne NDlv NHol
- from Wintergraben	SIng SPlb
- subsp. **glabrescens**	ESis
- - from Belansky Tatra	CWil GCHN MDHE MOne NDlv SSmi
- - from High Tatra	CCuc MDHE
- - from Smeryouka	CCuc CWil MBro SIng SSmi
- - var. **neilreichii**	LRHS
- 'Lowe's 66'	MOne
¶ - var. **neilreichii**	MHom
- 'Preissiana'	CWil MBro MOne NDlv NHol NMen NNrd SIng
x **mitchellii** 'Sandy'	Last listed 1998
- 'Suzan'	Last listed 1998
x **nixonii** 'Jowan'	Last listed 1998
§ **sobolifera**	CHEx CWil ELau ESis GCHN MBro MOne NHol NMen SIng SPlb SSmi WPer
- 'August Cream'	CWil
- 'Green Globe'	CWil ELau MDHE NNrd SDys
* - 'Miss Lorainne'	CWil

JUANULLOA (Solanaceae)

aurantiaca	See *J. mexicana*
§ **mexicana**	SOWG

JUBAEA (Arecaceae)

§ **chilensis**	CBrP CHEx CRoM LPJP LPal WMul
spectabilis	See *J. chilensis*

JUGLANS ✿ (Juglandaceae)

§ **ailanthifolia**	CMCN EOas ESim WPGP
- var. **cordiformis**	CAgr
- - 'Fodermaier' seedling	Last listed 1999
§ x **bixbyi**	WGWT
californica (F)	WGWT
cathayensis (F)	WGWT
cinerea (F)	CDul CMCN WGWT
- x **ailanthifolia**	See *J.* x *bixbyi*
- 'Craxezy' (F)	CAgr
- 'Kenworthy' seedling	CAgr
§ **elaeopyren**	Last listed 1999
x **intermedia**	WGWT
mandschaurica	CMCN WGWT

microcarpa WGWT
- subsp. *major* See *J. elaeopyren*
nigra (F) ♀ CB&S CLnd CMCN EBee EWTr
GChr GKir GTwe IOrc LHyr
LNet LPan LRHS MAsh MGos
NBea NWea SDea SEND SKee
SLim SPer WDin WMou WPGP
WStI
- 'Emma Kay' (F) CAgr
- 'Laciniata' CMCN CTho GKir MBlu WGWT
- 'Purpurea' MBlu
¶ - 'Thomas' (F) ESim
regia (F) ♀ More than 30 suppliers
- 'Axel' (F) WGWT
- 'Broadview' (F) CBlo CDoC CDul CEnd CTho
EMui ERea ESim GTwe LRHS
MBlu MBri MCoo MGos SCoo
SDea SKee WGWT WMou
- 'Buccaneer' (F) CDul CTho ERea ESim GTwe
LRHS SDea SKee WGWT WMou
¶ - 'Cascade' (F) ESim
- 'China B' (F) WGWT
- 'Coenen' (F) WGWT WMou
- 'Franquette' CDoC CTho ENot GTwe LRHS
MCoo SKee
- 'Hansen' (F) WGWT
- 'Hartley' (F) SKee
- 'Laciniata' CMCN GKir MBlu WGWT WMou
- 'Lara' GTwe
- 'Mayette' (F) SKee
- 'Meylannaise' (F) SKee
- 'Northdown Clawnut' Last listed 1998
- Number 139 ESim
- Number 16 (F) WGWT
- Number 26 ESim
- 'Parisienne' (F) SKee
- 'Plovdivski' (F) WGWT WMou
- 'Proslavsk' (F) WGWT WMou
- 'Purpurea' CMCN WGWT
- 'Rita' WGWT WMou
- 'Ronde de Montignac' (F) SKee
- 'Soleze' (F) SKee WGWT
sieboldiana See *J. ailanthifolia*

JUNCUS (Juncaceae)

acutus WWye
articulatus CKin
* *balticus* 'Spiralis' ECho WCot
bulbosus CKin
compressus CKin
concinnus Last listed 1997
conglomeratus CKin EHoe
- 'Spiralis' GKir WCot
§ *decipiens* 'Curly-wurly' CCuc CFee CMea CMil CSpe EBee
EHoe EMan EMon EPGN EPla
EWes GCal LRHS MBrN MFir SVil
SWat WHal WLeb WPGP WWye
- 'Spiralis' See *J. decipiens* 'Curly-wurly'
effusus CKin EMFW LPBA NSti SWat
SWyc WMAq
- 'Cuckoo' (v) CNat WAlt
- 'Gold Strike' (v) LIck LLWG WCot
§ - f. *spiralis* More than 30 suppliers
ensifolius CCuc CInt CRow CWat EHoe LHil
LIck MSta SUsu WCot
filiformis 'Spiralis' CBrm GIBF WCot WRus
inflexus CAgr CKin EHon SWat SWyc
- 'Afro' CMea EMon EPGN LRHS MBrN
NBro WAlt
membranaceus HLMS NRya
94.0541
pallidus EBee GCal LIck WCot

¶ *patens* 'Carman's Gray' CCuc CFee CHar CInt EPPr EPla
GCal LPan LRHS MCCP MTed
NPSI SApp WCot WPGP
squarrosus CKin
tenuis Last listed 1998
xiphioides CCuc EHoe EPla LRHS NOGN
SWal
- JLS 86096LACA EMon EPPr

JUNELLIA (Verbenaceae)

wilczekii WFar
- F&W 7770 NWCA

JUNIPERUS ✿ (Cupressaceae)

chinensis SEND
- 'Aurea' ♀ CB&S CKen CMac EHul EOrn
EPla GChr LCon LNet MAsh MBar
MGos
§ - 'Blaauw' ♀ CDoC CMac EHul ENot EOrn
GAri GKir GPin LCon LLin MAsh
MBar MGos SLim STre WStI
- 'Blue Alps' CDoC CMHG CSli EBrP EBre EHul
EOrn GKir IMGH LBcl LBSe LBre
LCon LLin LNet LPan MAsh MBBe
MBar MBri MGos SBre SEND SLim
WFar WGwG
- 'Blue Point' MBar MGos
- 'Densa Spartan' See *J. chinensis* 'Spartan'
- 'Echiniformis' CKen CMac EOrn
- 'Expansa Aureospicata' (v) CBlo CDoC CKen CMac EBrP
EBre EHul EOrn EPfP LBcl LBSe
LBre LCon LLin MBBe MBar
MGos SBod SBre SLim SRms SSmi
§ - 'Expansa Variegata' (v) More than 30 suppliers
- 'Globosa Cinerea' MBar
- 'Japonica' EOrn MBar SMer
- 'Japonica Variegata' (v) EBrP EBre LBcl LBSe LBre MBBe
SBre SLim
- 'Kaizuka' ♀ CBlo CDoC EBrP EBre EHul EOrn
GKir LBcl LBSe LBee LBre LCon
LRHS MAsh MBBe MBar SBre
SLim SMer WLRN
- 'Kaizuka Variegata' See *J. chinensis* 'Variegated
Kaizuka'
- 'Keteleeri' LCon MBar WCwm
- 'Kuriwao Gold' See *J.* x *pfitzeriana* 'Kuriwao
Gold'
- 'Kuriwao Sunbeam' See *J.* x *pfitzeriana* 'Kuriwao
Sunbeam'
- 'Obelisk' ♀ CBlo EHul LBee LCon LRHS MBar
MGos SBod WLRN WShe
- 'Oblonga' EHul EPla LLin MAsh MBar SMer
STre
§ - 'Parsonsii' CMac MBar STre WCFE
- 'Plumosa' MBar
- 'Plumosa Albovariegata' EOrn MBar
- 'Plumosa Aurea' ♀ CBlo CDoC EHul ENot EOrn
LCon MBar SIng WDin WFar
- 'Plumosa Aureovariegata' CKen EOrn LCon MBar SLim
- 'Pyramidalis' ♀ CDoC EBrP EBre EHul ENot EPfP
GAri GChr GKir IMGH LBcl LBSe
LBre LCon LLin MAsh MBBe MGos
SBod SBre SRms WFar WWeb
- 'Pyramidalis Variegata' See *J. chinensis* 'Variegata'
- 'Robust Green' EOrn LCon MBar SLim
- 'San José' CDoC EHul EOrn LCon LLin
MAsh MBar SLim WLRN
§ - var. *sargentii* CBlo GAri STre
- - 'Glauca' GAri
- - 'Viridis' GAri
- 'Shimpaku' CKen EGra EOrn EPla LCon LLin
MBar

§ - 'Spartan'	EHul LBee
§ - 'Stricta'	CKen EHul GKir LBee LRHS MAsh MBar MGos NBee SLim SPla WDin WStI
- 'Stricta Variegata'	See *J. chinensis* 'Variegata'
- 'Sulphur Spray'	See *J.* x *pfitzeriana* 'Sulphur Spray'
§ - 'Variegata' (v)	MBar
§ - 'Variegated Kaizuka' (v)	EHul EOrn EPla LCon MAsh MBar NHol WWeb
- 'Wilson's Weeping'	WBcn
communis	CAgr CArn CKin CTrG EHul GAri GChr GPoy ITim MHer MSal NHex NWea SIde
- (f)	SIde
- 'Arnold'	LLin MBar MGos
- 'Arnold Sentinel'	CKen
- 'Atholl'	CKen GAbr
I - 'Aureopicta'	MBar
- 'Barton'	CBlo LLin MBar NHol
- 'Berkshire'	CKen EPot
- 'Brien'	CDoC CKen
¶ - 'Brynhyfryd Gold'	CKen WBcn
§ - var. **communis**	ECho MBar NDlv SRms
- 'Compressa' ♀	More than 30 suppliers
§ - 'Constance Franklin' (v)	ECho EHul MBar WBcn
- 'Corielagen'	CKen LCon MBar MGos MWat
- 'Cracovia'	CKen EHul
- var. **depressa**	GPoy MBar
- 'Depressa Aurea'	CKen CMac CSli EHul ENot GKir LBee LLin LPan LRHS MBar MGos NDlv SBod SMer WStI
- 'Depressed Star'	EHul GPin MBar
- 'Derrynane'	EHul
- 'Effusa'	CKen
- 'Gelb'	See *J. communis* 'Schneverdingen Goldmachangel'
§ - 'Gold Cone'	CKen CSli EBrP EBre EHul ESis GChr GKir LBCl LBSe LBee LBre LCon LLin LRHS MAsh MBBe MBar MBri MGos NDlv NHol SBre SLim SMer WAbe
- 'Golden Showers'	See *J. communis* 'Schneverdingen Goldmachangel'
- 'Green Carpet' ♀	CDoC CKen EBrP EBre EHul EOrn EPla GKir IMGH LBCl LBSe LBee LBre LCon LLin LRHS MAsh MBBe MBar MBri SBre SLim SMer SSmi WCFE WFar WWeb
- 'Greenmantle'	Last listed 1999
- 'Haverbeck'	CKen
- var. **hemispherica**	See *J. communis* var. *communis*
- 'Hibernica' ♀	CBrm CDoC CKen CMac CSam EHul EOrn GChr GKir IMGH LBee LCon LLin LRHS MBar MGos NWea SBod SLim SMer SPer SPla WCFE WDin WStI
- 'Hibernica Variegata'	See *J. communis* 'Constance Franklin'
- 'Hornibrookii' ♀	CDoC CMac EHul ENot EOrn LLin MBar MGos SBod SMer SPla STre WDin WWin
- 'Horstmann'	EPla GAri MBar SLim
I - 'Horstmann's Pendula'	LCon LLin WBcn
- 'Kemerton Priory'	Last listed 1998
¶ - 'Kenwith Castle'	CKen
§ - 'Minima'	SBod
- 'Prostrata'	ISea
- 'Pyramidalis'	WGor
- 'Repanda' ♀	CB&S CBrm CDoC CMac CSli EHul ENot EPfP GChr GKir LCon LLin MAsh MBar MGos NBid NDlv
	NWea SBod SLim SMer SPer WCFE WFar WGwG
§ - var. **saxatilis**	EHul
§ - 'Schneverdingen Goldmachangel'	CBlo EOrn GKir MAsh SLim SMer WWeb
- 'Sentinel'	CDoC CSli EBrP EBre EHul EPfP IOrc LBCl LBSe LBre LCon LPan LRHS MAsh MBBe MBar MBri NBee SBre SLim WCFE WDin
- 'Sieben Steinhauser'	CKen
- 'Silver Mist'	CKen
- 'Spotty Spreader' (v)	SCoo SLim
- Suecica Group	EHul ENot MBar NWea SRms
- 'Suecica Aurea'	CBlo EHul EOrn
- 'Zeal'	CKen
conferta	See *J. rigida* subsp. *conferta*
¶ - 'Blue Tosho'	GKir
- var. **maritima**	See *J. taxifolia*
davurica	EHul
- 'Expansa'	See *J. chinensis* 'Parsonsii'
- 'Expansa Albopicta'	See *J. chinensis* 'Expansa Variegata'
- 'Expansa Variegata'	See *J. chinensis* 'Expansa Variegata'
deppeana	GAri
var. **pachyphlaea**	
- 'Silver Spire'	EGra MBar MGos
x **gracilis** 'Blaauw'	See *J. chinensis* 'Blaauw'
horizontalis	NWea
- 'Alpina'	CKen
§ - 'Andorra Compact'	CKen MBar WMoo
- 'Bar Harbor'	CKen CMac EHul GKir LLin MBar MGos NWea SBod WGor
§ - 'Blue Chip'	CKen CMac EBrP EBre EHul ENot EOrn EPfP GKir LBCl LBSe LBee LBre LCon LLin LRHS MAsh MBBe MBar MBri MGos SBod SBre SLim SPer SPla SSmi
- 'Blue Moon'	See *J. horizontalis* 'Blue Chip'
- 'Blue Pygmy'	CKen EPot
- 'Blue Rug'	See *J. horizontalis* 'Wiltonii'
- 'Douglasii'	CKen CMac EHol EHul MBar WGor
- 'Emerald Spreader'	CKen EHul ENot GKir MBar MGos SLim
- 'Glacier'	CKen
- Glauca Group	CMac EHul ENot GOrc LLin MBar MGos SMer SPer WWin
- 'Glomerata'	CKen MBar
- 'Golden Carpet'	EOrn GKir IMGH LCon MBri NPro SLim SPer
- 'Golden Spreader'	CDoC GKir WBcn
- 'Grey Pearl'	CKen CSli EBrP EBre EHul LBCl LBSe LBre MAsh MBBe MBri SBod SBre SLim
- 'Hughes'	CKen CMac CSli EBrP EBre EHul ENot GKir LBCl LBSe LBee LBre LCon LLin LRHS MAsh MBBe MBar MBri MGos NDlv SBod SBre SLim SPla
- 'Jade River'	CKen EHul LBee LRHS MGos SLim WLRN
- 'Mother Lode'	CKen
- 'Neumänn'	CKen
- 'Petraea'	Last listed 1998
- 'Plumosa' ♀	NDlv
- 'Plumosa Compacta'	See *J. horizontalis* 'Andorra Compact'
- 'Prince of Wales'	CKen CSli EBrP EBre EHul GKir LBCl LBSe LBee LBre LCon LLin LRHS MAsh MBBe MGos SBre SLim WGor WLRN

- var. **saxatalis**	See *J. communis* var. *saxatilis*
- - E. Murray	See *J. communis* var. *communis*
- 'Turquoise Spreader'	CBlo CKen EHul MBar WWeb
- 'Variegata'	MBar
- 'Venusta'	See *J. virginiana* 'Venusta'
- 'Villa Marie'	CKen
- 'Webber'	MBar SLim
- 'Wilms'	Last listed 1998
§ - 'Wiltonii' ♀	CKen CSli EHul ENot EOrn LLin MGos
- 'Winter Blue'	LBee LRHS SLim
- 'Youngstown'	CBlo CMac CSWP EBrP EBre GKir LBCl LBSe LBre LCon LLin MAsh MBBe MBar MGos SBod SBre SPla WFar WGor
- 'Yukon Belle'	CKen
oxycedrus	GAri
x **pfitzeriana** 'Armstrongii'	EHul
- 'Blaauw'	See *J. chinensis* 'Blaauw'
- 'Blound'PBR	See *J. x pfitzeriana* Gold Sovereign = 'Blound'
- 'Blue and Gold' (v)	CKen EHul EOrn MBar SLim SPer
- 'Blue Cloud'	See *J. virginiana* 'Blue Cloud'
§ - 'Carbery Gold'	CDoC CMac CSam CSli EHul EOrn LBee LCon LRHS MAsh MBar MBri MGos NHol SAga SLim SSmi WLRN WWeb
- 'Gold Coast'	CDoC CKen CMac EBrP EBre EHul ENot EPfP GKir LBCl LBSe LBee LBre LCon LRHS MAsh MBBe MBar MBri MGos MWat SBre SLim
§ - Gold Sovereign = 'Blound'PBR	EBrP EBre EOrn GKir LBCl LBSe LBee LBre MAsh MBBe MGos NHol SBre SMer
- 'Gold Star'	EOrn WBcn
* - 'Golden Joy'	SLim
- 'Golden Saucer'	CSli MAsh MBar MBri SCoo
- 'Goldkissen'	MBri
§ - 'Kuriwao Gold'	CBlo CMac EBrP EBre EHul EPfP GKir LBCl LBSe LBee LBre LLin LNet MBBe MBar MGos NHol SBod SBre SLim SMer STre WStl
§ - 'Kuriwao Sunbeam'	NHol
- 'Milky Way' (v)	SLim
- 'Mint Julep'	CDoC CMac EBrP EBre EHul ENot GChr GKir IMGH LBCl LBSe LBee LBre LCon LLin LPan LRHS MAsh MBBe MBar MGos SBre SLim SPer WFar
- 'Mordigan Gold'	LPan
- 'Old Gold' ♀	CBrm CChe CDoC CKen CMac CSli EHul ENot EOrn EPfP GKir GOrc IMGH LBee LBuc LCon LLin LRHS MAsh MBar MGos NDlv NHol NWea SBod SLim SMer SPer WDin WFar
- 'Old Gold Carbery'	See *J. x pfitzeriana* 'Carbery Gold'
- 'Pfitzeriana Aurea'	CB&S CDoC CDul CMac EHul ENot EPfP GChr LCon LLin LRHS MBar MBri MGos MWat NFla NWea SBod SLim SRms WCFE WDin WFar WGwG
- 'Pfitzeriana Compacta' ♀	CMac ECho EHul MBar SLim SPer
- 'Pfitzeriana Glauca'	CSli EHul GChr IMGH LPan LRHS MBar SLim SPer WGor
- 'Richeson'	MBar
- 'Saybrook Gold'	LPan MBri
- 'Silver Cascade'	EHul
§ - 'Sulphur Spray' ♀	More than 30 suppliers
§ - 'Wilhelm Pfitzer' ♀	CMac EHul ENot EPfP LLin MBar NWea SBod SLim SRms WFar WStl
- 'Winter Surprise' (v)	CBlo MGos
§ **pingii** 'Glassell'	CDoC ECho MBar MGos
§ - 'Pygmaea'	CBlo CDoC EOrn ESis LCon MBar
§ - var. **wilsonii**	CBlo CDoC CKen ECho EHul EOrn LCon MBar
procumbens	Last listed 1998
- 'Bonin Isles'	LLin MGos SLim SPla
- 'Nana' ♀	CDoC CKen CMac EBrP EBre EHul EOrn GKir IMGH LBCl LBSe LBee LBre LCon LLin LRHS MAsh MBBe MBar MBri MGos MWat NHol SBre SIng SLim SPla SSmi WCFE WPyg
recurva 'Castlewellan'	EOrn LCon LLin MGos WCwm
- var. **coxii**	CMac EHul EOrn EPla GGGa GKir ISea LCon LLin MBar MBri MGos SLim SRms WCFE WCwm WPic
§ - 'Densa'	CKen EHul EOrn GAri LLin MBar NHol SPla
- 'Embley Park'	EHul MAsh MBar SLim
- 'Nana'	See *J. recurva* 'Densa'
rigida	EHul GCal LBee LCon LLin MBar MWat SBod SLim SPer SRms STre WFar
§ - subsp. **conferta**	LCon SPer
* - - 'Blue Ice'	CKen EOrn GPin LLin WGwG
¶ - - 'Blue Pacific'	CBlo CMac COtt EHul GAri GKir LCon MAsh MBar MBri SLim WCFE
¶ - - 'Emerald Sea'	EHul
sabina	GPoy NWea
- 'Arcadia'	SRms
§ - 'Blaue Donau'	CBlo EHul MBar MGos SRms
- Blue Danube	See *J. sabina* 'Blaue Donau'
- 'Broadmoor'	EHul
- 'Buffalo'	EHul
- Cupressifolia Group	MBar
- 'Hicksii'	CMac MBar NWea
- 'Knap Hill'	See *J. x pfitzeriana* 'Wilhelm Pfitzer'
- 'Mountaineer'	See *J. scopulorum* 'Mountaineer'
- 'Rockery Gem'	CBlo EHul EOrn MGos SLim SPla WGor
- 'Skandia'	CKen
- 'Tamariscifolia'	More than 30 suppliers
- 'Tripartita'	See *J. virginiana* 'Tripartita'
- 'Variegata' (v)	CMac EHul MAsh MBar NWea SLim WBcn WPyg
sargentii	See *J. chinensis* var. *sargentii*
scopulorum	CKen MBar
- 'Blue Arrow'	CKen COtt EOrn EPfP EPla GChr GKir IMGH LBee LCon LLin LPan LRHS MAsh MBar MBri MGos MWat NBee SCoo SLim SPer SPla
- 'Blue Banff'	CKen
- 'Blue Heaven' ♀	EHul LCon MAsh MBar SLim SPla
- 'Blue Pyramid'	EHul
- 'Boothman'	EHul
- 'Gray Gleam'	Last listed 1998
- 'Moonglow'	CSli EBrP EBre EHul LBCl LBSe LBre MAsh MBBe MBar SBre
§ - 'Mountaineer'	EHul
- 'Mrs Marriage'	CKen
- 'Repens'	MBar MGos
- 'Silver Star' (v)	CBlo EHul MBar MGos
- 'Skyrocket'	More than 30 suppliers
- 'Springbank'	CSli EHul LBee LCon LRHS MBar
- 'Tabletop'	MBar WBcn
- 'Tolleson's Blue Weeping'	LCon
- 'Wichita Blue'	CBlo EHul EPfP LPan SEND WGor
§ **squamata**	Last listed 1998
- 'Blue Carpet' ♀	More than 30 suppliers

- 'Blue Spider'	CKen LLin LRHS MBar SLim WGor WLRN
- 'Blue Star' ♀	More than 30 suppliers
- 'Blue Star Variegated'	See *J. squamata* 'Golden Flame'
- 'Blue Swede'	See *J. squamata* 'Hunnetorp'
- 'Chinese Silver'	EHul LCon MBar SLim WBcn WLRN
¶ - 'Dream Joy'	CKen SLim
- var. *fargesii*	See *J. squamata*
- 'Filborna'	CBlo CDoC CKen LBee MBar MWat SLim SMer
- 'Glassell'	See *J. pingii* 'Glassell'
§ - 'Golden Flame' (v)	CKen
- 'Holger' ♀	CBrm CDoC CKen CMac EBrP EBre EHul EOrn EPla GAri GKir LBCI LBSe LBee LBre LCon LLin LRHS MAsh MBBe MBar MBri MGos MWat SBod SBre SLim WCFE WStI WWeb
§ - 'Hunnetorp'	CBlo EOrn GKir LCon MBar MBri MGos
- 'Loderi'	See *J. pingii* var. *wilsonii*
- 'Meyeri'	EHul ENot EOrn GOrc IMGH MBar NBlu NWea SBod SLim SMer STre WDin WFar WStI WWin
- 'Pygmaea'	See *J. pingii* 'Pygmaea'
- 'Wilsonii'	See *J. pingii* var. *wilsonii*
§ *taxifolia*	EOrn GPin IMGH LBee LCon WWeb
virginiana	CAgr
§ - 'Blue Cloud'	CDoC EHul LCon MBar SLim WGor WLRN
- 'Burkii'	CDoC EHul LCon
- 'Frosty Morn'	CKen ECho EHul LCon MAsh MBar
- 'Glauca'	CSWP EHul NWea
- 'Golden Spring'	CKen
- 'Grey Owl' ♀	CMac CSli EHul ENot GKir LCon LLin MBar MGos NWea SLim SLon SMer SPla SRms STre WDin WGor WGwG WPyg
- 'Helle'	See *J. chinensis* 'Spartan'
- 'Hetzii'	CB&S CBlo CKen CMac ECho EHul MBar NWea SBod WLRN
- 'Hillii'	MBar
- 'Hillspire'	EHul
- 'Nana Compacta'	MBar
- 'Pendula'	Last listed 1997
- 'Silver Spreader'	CBlo EHul LCon MGos WBcn WGwG
- 'Staver'	EHul
- 'Sulphur Spray'	See *J.* x *pfitzeriana* 'Sulphur Spray'
§ - 'Tripartita'	MBar
§ - 'Venusta'	CKen

JURINEA (Asteraceae)

alata	EMan GOrP
ceratocarpa	See *Saussurea ceratocarpa*
mollis	GBuc

JURINELLA See JURINEA

JUSSIAEA See LUDWIGIA

JUSTICIA (Acanthaceae)

aurea	ERea
§ *brandegeeana* ♀	CHal MBri
- 'Lutea'	See *J. brandegeeana* 'Yellow Queen'
§ - 'Yellow Queen'	CHal
§ *carnea*	CHEx CHal CSev EBak EHol ERea

	GCal LCns LHil LRHS MBri SLdr SMad SOWG WMul
floribunda	See *J. rizzinii*
guttata	See *J. brandegeeana*
* 'Norgard's Favourite'	MBri
¶ *ovata*	SMad
pauciflora	See *J. rizzinii*
pectoralis	Last listed 1998
- Puerto Rican cultivar	Last listed 1998
* - var. *stenophylla*	Last listed 1998
peruviana	Last listed 1998
pobliana	See *J. carnea*
§ *rizzinii* ♀	CHal CInt CSev ERea IBlr LCns LHil SOWG
¶ sp.	EOHP
spicigera	ERea
suberecta	See *Dicliptera suberecta*

K

KADSURA (Schisandraceae)

japonica	CB&S CGre CPlN EMil
- B&SWJ 1027	WCru
- 'Shiromi'	CPlN EMil EPfP EPla SBra
- 'Variegata'	EPfP GOrc MCCP SBra WSHC
sp.	CMac

KAEMPFERIA (Zingiberaceae)

¶ *galanga*	LEur
¶ *pulchra*	LEur
rotunda	GPoy LAma LChe

KALANCHOE (Crassulaceae)

bebarensis	CHal MBri
blossfeldiana	EOHP LRHS
- 'Variegata'	CHal
daigremontiana	CHal SRms
§ *delagoensis*	CHal STre
fedtschenkoi	CHal
§ *lateritia*	Last listed 1999
manginii	EOHP
pumila ♀	CHal ERea EWoo IBlr LHil STre WEas
'Tessa' ♀	MBri MLan SPet
tomentosa ♀	CHal WEas
tubiflora	See *K. delagoensis*
'Wendy' ♀	Last listed 1999
zimbabwensis	See *K. lateritia*

KALIMERIS (Asteraceae)

§ *incisa*	EMon EWll GMac WCot
- 'Alba'	EFou EMon SHel SSvw
- 'Blue Star'	EFou
* - 'Variegata'	SCob SRCN
integrifolia	CPlt ECha GMac WTin
§ *mongolica*	EBee WPer
§ *pinnatifida*	EBee EPPr WCot
§ *yomena* 'Shogun' (v)	CRDP EBee ECha EFou EHoe ELan EMan EMar EMon GBri GBuc LFis MAvo MLLN NBid NBir NSti SCob SPer SPla SUsu WCot WFar WOve
- 'Variegata'	See *K. yomena* 'Shogun'

KALMIA ✿ (Ericaceae)

angustifolia ♀	MBar SPar SRms WDin
- var. *angustifolia* f. *candida*	WAbe
- var. *pumila*	SReu WAbe

- f.*rubra*	CB&S CDoC CMHG EBrP EBre ELan GChr ISea LBCl LBSe LBre LRHS MAsh MBBe MGos NDlv NHol SBre SBrw SPer SReu SSta WHar WPat WPyg WWat
cuneata	Last listed 1997
latifolia ♀	CB&S CTrG EBee ELan EMil ENot GGGa LNet MBar MGos MLan NBee NWea SBrw SPer SReu SSpi SSta WBod WBrE WDin WGer WHar WNor WPyg WStl WWat WWeb
- 'Alpine Pink'	CBrm SBrw SSht WBod
- 'Brilliant'	NHol
- 'Bullseye'	GGGa SBrw
- 'Carol'	Last listed 1999
- 'Carousel'	CAbP CB&S ELan EPfP GGGa GKir LRHS MGos SVil
- 'Clementine Churchill'	CBlo
- 'Elf'	LRHS MGos
- 'Freckles'	CB&S ELan EPfP GGGa GKir GOrc ISea LRHS MAsh MGos MLan NDlv SBrw SPer
- 'Fresca'	LRHS SVil
¶ - 'Galaxy'	GGGa
- 'Goodrich'	Last listed 1998
- 'Heart of Fire'	CAbP GGGa LRHS NDlv
- 'Heart's Desire'	Last listed 1999
¶ - 'Hotspur Red'	LPan
- 'Little Linda'	CBlo GGGa GKir GOrc IMGH LRHS MAsh MBri NDlv SBrw WBod
- 'Minuet'	CAbP CBlo CDoC EPfP GGGa GKir IMGH LRHS MAsh MBri MLan MMHG NDlv SBrw SSpi WBod
- 'Nipmuck'	MGos
- 'Olympic Fire'	CBrm ELan EPfP GGGa GKir LRHS MAsh MGos NDlv SBrw SPer SSpi
- 'Ostbo Red' ♀	CB&S CBlo CDoC EBee EMil GGGa GKir IMGH IOrc ISea LNet MBri MGos MLan NDlv SBrw SPer SReu SSht SSpi SSta WBod WLRN
- 'Peppermint'	GGGa MBri
- 'Pink Charm'	ELan GGGa ISea MAsh SBrw SMer WLRN
- 'Pink Frost'	CB&S GGGa LPan NDlv NHol SBrw WBod WWat
- 'Pink Star'	Last listed 1997
¶ - 'Pristine'	GGGa
- 'Quinnipiac'	LPan NHol
- 'Raspberry Glow'	MBri
- 'Richard Jaynes'	LRHS SVil
- 'Sarah'	GGGa MBri SSpi
- 'Silver Dollar'	GGGa LPan NHol
- 'Snowdrift'	LRHS SPer
§ *microphylla*	GGGa WAbe WPat
* - 'Mount Shasta'	Last listed 1998
- var.*occidentalis*	Last listed 1998
polifolia	CB&S MBar MBro MRav NHol WPat WPyg
- var.*compacta*	WAbe WSHC
- 'Glauca'	See *K. microphylla*
- f.*leucantha*	GGGa SSta WAbe
- 'Nana'	SSta

KALMIOPSIS (Ericaceae)

leachiana ♀	EPot GCrs GKir NHar SOkd SSta WAbe
- Cedar Park form	Last listed 1997
- 'Curry County'	Last listed 1999

- from Umpqua Valley	Last listed 1997
- 'Glendoick'	GGGa MAsh MBro MDun NHar NHol WPat WPyg
¶ - 'Hiawatha'	SReu
- 'Marcel le Piniec'	CPMA GGGa
* - 'Shooting Star'	NHol WAbe WPat

x KALMIOTHAMNUS (Ericaceae)

ornithomma	Last listed 1999
- 'Cosdon'	WAbe
- 'Haytor'	WAbe

KALOPANAX (Araliaceae)

pictus	See *K. septemlobus*
§ *septemlobus*	CB&S CFil CHEx ELan SCob SMac WOTO
- var.*maximowiczii*	CDoC EPfP MBlu NBee SMad

KECKIELLA (Scrophulariaceae)

§ *antirrhinoides*	NWCA
- *antirrhinoides*	EBee
§ *cordifolia*	EMan
corymbosa	CGra
- JCA 11618	NWCA
rothrockii	Last listed 1998

KELSEYA (Rosaceae)

uniflora	WAbe

KENNEDIA (Papilionaceae)

beckxiana	LChe LRHS SOWG
coccinea	CPIN GQui LPan LRHS
macrophylla	CPIN
nigricans	CPIN LChe SOWG
prostrata	SVen
rubicunda	CPIN CRHN

KENTIA (Arecaceae)

belmoreana	See *Howea belmoreana*

KENTRANTHUS See CENTRANTHUS

KERRIA (Rosaceae)

japonica (d)	See *K. japonica* 'Pleniflora'
- 'Albescens'	CBot CFai NPro WWat
- 'Golden Guinea' ♀	CChe EBee ECtt ELan EPfP GKir LRHS MAsh MGos MNrw NPro SCoo SLim SPer SSte WTro WWat WWeb
- misapplied (single)	See *K. japonica* 'Simplex'
§ - 'Picta' (v)	CB&S CDul EBee EBrP EBre EHoe ELan GOrc IOrc LAst LBCl LBSe LBre LRHS MBBe MBar MBri MGos MHar NBee SBre SHel SLim SLon SPer SRms WDin WSHC WWal WWat
§ - 'Pleniflora' (d) ♀	More than 30 suppliers
§ - 'Simplex'	CB&S CPle ELan GKir IOrc NFla NWea WDin WFar WOTO
- 'Variegata'	See *K. japonica* 'Picta'

KHADIA (Aizoaceae)

sp.	CTrC EOas

KICKXIA (Scrophulariaceae)

elatine	EWFC
spuria	EWFC

KIRENGESHOMA (Hydrangeaceae)

palmata ♀	More than 30 suppliers
- dwarf	WCot
§ - Koreana Group	CHid CLAP CRDP EBee ECha

	ELan EPar GKir LRHS MBel MBri MCli MRav NDov SCro SLod SPer WAbe WFar WOVN

KITAGAWIA (Apiaceae)
§ *litoralis* — IIve

KITAIBELA (Malvaceae)
vitifolia — CFee CGle CPea CSpe EBee ECoo ELan EMar EMon EWTr GCal GMac MNrw NBid NChi NSti SPlb SRCN WCer WCot WFar WHer WPer WPic WRos WWin

KITCHINGIA See KALANCHOE

KLEINIA (Asteraceae)
articulata	See *Senecio articulatus*
¶ *grantii*	ERea
repens	See *Senecio serpens*
senecioides	WEas

KNAUTIA (Dipsacaceae)
§ *arvensis*	CArn CKin ECoo EWFC MChe MGas MHer MHew MLLN NLan NMir WGwy WHer WJek
dipsacifolia	LFis LGre WCot
* *jankiae*	WHer
§ *macedonica*	More than 30 suppliers
- Melton Pastels	CMGP EBee EPfP GKir LBuc LHop SCob SRot SWat WBar WElm
- pink	CMil CSam SSpi
- 'Red Dress'	Last listed 1998
¶ *sarajevensis*	CMdw
§ *tatarica*	EBee

KNIGHTIA (Proteaceae)
excelsa — Last listed 1998

KNIPHOFIA ✿ (Asphodelaceae)
'Ada'	EBee ECGP ERou EWes GCHN MLLN MRav
'Alcazar'	EBee ECot EMan EPar EPfP GKir LRHS MCAu MRav NPri SPla WCFE WCot WFar WViv
* 'Amber'	IBlr
'Amsterdam'	LRHS MWat
'Apple Court'	NBir
'Apricot'	CHad CMdw EPla
'Apricot Sensation'	ECha
'Apricot Souffle'	ECha EMan GBri MLLN WCot
'Atlanta'	CFil GCal IBlr LRHS SHel WCot
baurii	EBee WCot WHil
'Bees' Flame'	EWTr SLod
'Bees' Lemon'	CAbb CCuc EBee EMan EMil IHdy LAst LPio WCot
'Bees' Sunset' ♀	EBee EGle EWTr GBri IHdy MRav MWgw SMrm WCot WHil WLRN WPGP
* *bicolor*	WCot
'Border Ballet'	ECtt EMan LRHS MFir MRav NBir NBro NFai NLar NMir SCob SMrm SWat WFar
brachystachya	CTrC GCal SPlb WCot
'Bressingham Comet'	CGle CLon CPea EBee EBrP EBre ECtt EGle EPfP GCal LBCl LBSe LBre LRHS MBBe MRav SBre SCob SDys WRus
'Bressingham Gleam'	WCot
Bressingham hybrids	EBrP EBre LBCl LBSe LBre LRHS MBBe NBir SBre

Bressingham Sunbeam = 'Bresun'	EGar
breviflora	EBee
Bridgemere hybrids	LRHS
'Brimstone' ♀	More than 30 suppliers
buchananii	EBee WCot
'Buttercup' ♀	CCuc CGle CMHG CMdw
'C.M. Prichard' hort.	See *K. rooperi*
'C.M. Prichard' Prichard	WCot
'Candlelight'	CPlt EBee SDys SUsu WCot WViv
* 'Candlemass'	LPio
'Catherine's Orange'	WCot
caulescens ♀	More than 30 suppliers
citrina	CBot CFir EBee ECGN EMan EPfP LAst NBus NChi NCut NLar WCot WPer WWat
'Cobra'	CRDP CStr EFou ERou GCHN LRHS MTed WCot WHil
'Corallina'	EWll LCaP NHaw NPri WPnP WViv
'David' ♀	Last listed 1987
'Dawn Sunkiss'	ECho
'Dorset Sentry'	GBuc WCot
'Dr E.M. Mills'	WViv
'Drummore Apricot'	CAbb EBee EMan MChl WCot
'Earliest of All'	COtt EBee EBrP EBre EWll LBCl LBSe LBre LCaP LRHS MBBe MBNS NHol SBre SPer
'Early Buttercup'	ECot GBri MMil NCat NHaw WFar WViv
* 'Early Yellow'	Last listed 1997
§ *ensifolia*	CMdw CPou EBee EGar WBcn
'Erecta'	IBlr WCot
'Ernest Mitchell'	EGle MRav WCot
Express hybrids	EBee NLar
'Fairyland'	MNrw NBus NCut WBro WCot WRHF WTin
* 'Fat Yellow'	MWgw
fibrosa	CFir CTrC EBee WCot WHil
'Fiery Fred'	EBee EGar EGle ELan EOld LRHS NHaw WCot WEas WPnP
foliosa	EBee EBrP EBre LBCl LBSe LBre LRHS MBBe SBre SChr
¶ 'Forncett Harvest'	EFou
'Frances Victoria'	WCot
galpinii hort.	See *K. triangularis* subsp. *triangularis*
- Baker ♀	CBot CGle CMGP EBee ENot GBri NBir NFla SAga SPer SRms WWat
¶ 'Gilt Bronze'	WCot
'Gladness'	GBin NSti WCot
'Goldelse'	CLon ECha EGle IBlr NBir WCot
'Goldfinch'	CMdw SMrm WViv
gracilis	EBee SApp WCot
'Green and Cream'	MNrw
'Green Jade'	CMdw COtt CRow EBee EBrP EBre ECha EGar EMan EPar GBri GKir IBlr LBCl LBSe LBre LGre MBBe MRav MTed NBir SBre SChu SEND WBro WCot WPGP
'H.E. Beale'	EBee GCal MRav NHaw WCot WPGP
hirsuta	EBee EBrP EBre EMan EMar LBCl LBSe LBre LPio MBBe SBre WCot WPGP
- H&B 16444	EMon
- JCA 346 900	SSpi WCot
'Hollard's Gold'	MRav WCot
'Ice Queen'	EBee EFou EGle EOrc GBri LGre LPio MCAu MRav SMad WCot
ichopensis	CFil EBee GBuc IBlr WCot WPGP
'Innocence'	WCot
isoetifolia	IBlr

'Jenny Bloom'	More than 30 suppliers
'John Benary'	COtt CPou EBee EGle EMan EPPr
	GBin IBlr LRHS MBri MMil NCut
	NPSI NSti WCot WKif WWol
'Johnathan'	WCot
'Kingston Flame'	Last listed 1998
late orange	Last listed 1998
laxiflora	CFil CPou EBee IHdy SSpi WCot
	WPGP
'Lemon Ice'	WCot
'Light of the World'	CAbb CBos CElw CFai CMil COtt
	CSpe EBee EMan EMar EPPr EWTr
	GCHN LAst LRHS MBel MCLN
	MLLN MMil NDov NLar NPSI NSti
	SMad WCot
'Limelight'	Last listed 1997
linearifolia	CFil EBee IBlr MNrw MWll SDix
	SMrm SPlb WCot
'Little Elf'	CLon LGre LPio SBla SDys
'Little Maid' ♀	More than 30 suppliers
littoralis	EBee
'Lord Roberts'	WCot
'Luna'	WCot
'Lye End'	Last listed 1998
macowanii	See *K. triangularis* subsp.
	triangularis
'Maid of Orleans'	CRow EBee GBri GKir IBlr NHaw
	WCot
'Mellow Yellow'	IBlr
'Mermaiden'	CMHG EBee EGar NPri WCot
'Minister Verschuur'	EBee EMar GBin WCot WViv
'Modesta'	EBee GBri IBlr WCot WPGP
	WSHC
'Mount Etna'	CGle WCot
multiflora	Last listed 1998
'Nancy's Red'	CAbb CMil COtt EBee EMan GBri
	LAst LGre LHop LPio MChl MMil
	MSph MSte NHaw NLar NPSI NSti
	SDys SMad SUsu WCot WGor
	WPGP
natalensis	EBee GBuc LPio WCot
nelsonii	See *K. triangularis* subsp.
	triangularis
'Nobilis'	See *K. uvaria* 'Nobilis'
northiae	CBot CFil CFir CHEx CPou EBee
	EOas GCal IBlr SAPC SArc SCob
	SPlb SSpi SWat WAbe WCot WPGP
'Notung'	IBlr
* 'Old Court Seedling'	WCot
'Painted Lady'	CTri GCal MBro MRav WCot
	WHoo WPGP
parviflora	CPou
pauciflora	CBro EMar GCal SDys WCot
'Percy's Pride'	More than 30 suppliers
'Pfitzeri'	SRms
porphyrantha	EBee WCot
praecox	CFil CTrC EBee WCFE WCot
	WPGP
'Primrose Beauty'	Last listed 1999
'Primulina' hort.	EBee EBrP EBre LBCl LBSe LBre
	LRHS MBBe SBre
'Prince Igor'	ECha EFou MTed SChu
pumila	EBee EGar MNrw
'Ranelagh Gardens'	SArc
ritualis	CFil GCal WCot WPGP
§ *rooperi*	CBot CFil CMdw GBri GCal IBlr
	LGre LPio MNrw NRib WCot
	WPic WViv
- 'Torchlight'	CPne WViv
'Ross Sunshine'	EOrc
'Royal Caste'	EBee MMil MRav NBir NCut NOrc
'Royal Standard' ♀	CB&S COtt EBee EBrP EBre ELan

	EMan ENot EPfP GBri IBlr LBCl
	LBSe LBre LRHS MBBe MNrw
	MRav SAga SBre SLon SMad SRms
	WCot WFar
rufa	CPou EBee WCot
'Safranvogel'	EGar IBlr
'Samuel's Sensation' ♀	EBee EBrP EBre EGar GBri IBlr
	LBCl LBSe LBre LRHS MBBe SBre
	WCot WPGP
sarmentosa	CFil EBee WCot WPGP WWoo
'September Sunshine'	MRav
'Shining Sceptre'	CSam EBee EBrP EBre ECha ECtt
	EFou EGar LBCl LBSe LBre LLck
	LPio LRHS MBBe MLLN MRav
	MWat NCut SBre SMad WCot
	WLRN
'Sir C.K. Butler'	EGar
sp. from Ethiopia	WCot
splendida	GCal
'Springtime'	WCot
'Star of Baden-Baden'	NBir SMad WCot
'Strawberries and Cream'	EBee EMan EPfP LGre LPio MGrG
	MSte SAga SUsu WCot WPnP
	WWye
stricta	WCot
'Sunbeam'	NBir
'Sunningdale Yellow' ♀	CMdw COIW CPou EBee ECha
	EGar EHrv EMan GCHN GMaP
	MFir MWat SChu SLod SRms
	WCot WEas
'Tawny King'	WCot
thomsonii var. *snowdenii*	CPou WCru WSHC
- var. *thomsonii*	CBot CFir ECha EOrc GBri IBlr
	LHil MNrw MSte NTow WCot
	WHal
- - triploid variety	Last listed 1998
'Timothy'	CAbb CElw CFai CPou EBee EFou
	EGle EMan LAst LGre MMil NDov
	NHaw NSti SAga SChu SUsu
	WCot WViv
'Toasted Corn'	Last listed 1997
'Toffee Nosed' ♀	EBee ECGP EFou EGar EMar EPfP
	ERou GBri GCal IBlr LPio MCAu
	MMil MRav NBir NTow SChu SPer
	SUsu WCot WSHC
'Torchbearer'	EGar IBlr WCot WTre
triangularis ♀	CBot CHad CInt CMHG EBee
	ECGN EPfP GCal LRHS SMrm
	WHil
§ - subsp. *triangularis*	CBot CBro CGle COIW EBee
	EMar GBuc IBlr LRHS MRav MTis
	NBro NHaw NPri SIng SMrm
	SRms SWat WViv
'Tubergeniana'	WCot
I 'Tuckii'	EBee EMan EWll MNrw
tuckii Baker	See *K. ensifolia*
typhoides	EBee WCot WHal
tysonii	Last listed 1999
'Underway'	Last listed 1997
uvaria	EBee LEdu LPio LRHS MCAu
	MHer NBir NVic SCob SPer SRms
	SSpi WByw WCot WHoo WPnP
	WPyg
* - Fairyland hybrids	LLck
- 'Flamenco'	EWll WHil
§ - 'Nobilis' ♀	GBri IBlr MLLN SAPC SArc SDix
	WCot
'Vanilla'	LPio MRav
'Vesta'	EGar
'Wrexham Buttercup'	EBee EGar EMan GBri IBlr MLLN
	WCot
'Yellow Hammer'	CBot ECha NCat WFar

'Zululandiae' | WCot

KNOWLTONIA (Ranunculaceae)
bracteata | Last listed 1997
transvaalensis | Last listed 1997

KOCHIA See BASSIA

KOELERIA (Poaceae)
cristata | See *K. macrantha, K. pyramidata*
glauca | More than 30 suppliers
§ *macrantha* | CBrm EBee EMan EPPr NCut NHol NNor NOGN
§ *pyramidata* | Last listed 1997
vallesiana | CCuc EHoe EMon EPPr ESis LRHS

KOELLIKERIA (Gesneriaceae)
'Red Satin' | NMos

KOELREUTERIA (Sapindaceae)
bipinnata | Last listed 1999
* - var. *integrifoliola* | CFil WPGP
paniculata ♀ | More than 30 suppliers
- var. *apiculata* | CMHG
- 'Fastigiata' | EBee EPfP MBlu SSpi

KOHLERIA (Gesneriaceae)
'Clytie' | MBri
'Dark Velvet' | CHal WDib
eriantha ♀ | CHal CPle CSpe MBri WDib
'Hanna Roberts' | WDib
hirsuta | Last listed 1999
* x *hybrida* | NMos
'Jester' | CHal WDib
* 'Linda' | CHal
'Strawberry Fields' ♀ | MBri NMos
§ *warscewiczii* ♀ | CHal LRHS WDib

KOLKWITZIA (Caprifoliaceae)
amabilis | CB&S CGre CTrw ELan EMil GOrc ISea LPan MGos MHar MWat NBee NFor NWea SEas SRms WCFE WDin WFar WFro WGwG WHCG WHar WNor WStI WWin
- 'Maradco' | EPfP LRHS MAsh NPro SPla
- 'Pink Cloud' ♀ | More than 30 suppliers

KOSTELETZKYA (Malvaceae)
virginica | EMan SPlb

KUNZEA (Myrtaceae)
ambigua | CGre ECou SOWG SPlb
baxteri | CTrC SOWG
capitata | SOWG
§ *ericoides* | ECou GAbr SOWG
- 'Blue Leaf' | CCpl
'Mauve Mist' | Last listed 1999
muelleri | Last listed 1998
parvifolia | CPLG CTrC SOWG
pomifera | Last listed 1998
recurva | Last listed 1998

L

+ LABURNOCYTISUS (Papilionaceae)
'Adamii' | CBlo CDoC CDul COtt CPMA ELan EPfP GAri GKir IOrc LBuc LPan MBlu MBri SMad SPer SSpi

LABURNUM ❁ (Papilionaceae)
alpinum | EPfP GChr
- 'Pendulum' | CB&S CBlo CDoC EBrP EBre ELan EPfP GKir IOrc LBCl LBSe LBre LNet LPan LRHS MAsh MBBe MBar MBri MGos MRav MWat NBee SBre SLim SPer WDin WOrn
§ *anagyroides* | CBlo ENot GAri GChr ISea NWea SEND SRms WDin
- 'Aureum' | Last listed 1999
- 'Pendulum' | CLnd EBee
vulgare | See *L. anagyroides*
x *watereri* 'Vossii' ♀ | More than 30 suppliers
I - 'Vossii Goldleaf' | LPan
* - 'Vossii Pendulum' | CBlo

LACHENALIA (Hyacinthaceae)
§ *aloides* | LBow LHil MBri SRob
- var. *aurea* ♀ | LBow LRHS MSte
- var. *luteola* | LBow
- 'Pearsonii' | LRHS
- var. *quadricolor* ♀ | LBow WCot
- var. *vanzyliae* | LBow
§ *bulbifera* | LBow LRHS MBri
- 'George' | LBow
contaminata | LBow
hybrid Lac. 213 | Last listed 1997
liliiflora | Last listed 1998
orchioides var. *glaucina* | WCot WHil
pallida | Last listed 1998
pendula | See *L. bulbifera*
purpureocoerulea | WCot
pustulata | LRHS
reflexa | WCot
rubida | Last listed 1998
tricolor | See *L. aloides*
unifolia | WCot

LACHNANTHES (Haemodoraceae)
§ *caroliana* | Last listed 1999
tinctoria | See *L. caroliana*

LACTUCA (Asteraceae)
alpina | See *Cicerbita alpina*
perennis | MAvo MTho NChi NMGW NPSI WCot WHer
virosa | CArn MSal

LAGAROSIPHON (Hydrocharitaceae)
§ *major* | CBen CRow EHon EMFW NDea SWyc WMAq

LAGAROSTROBOS (Podocarpaceae)
§ *franklinii* | CB&S CDoC CTrG IOrc LLin WPic

LAGERSTROEMIA (Lythraceae)
indica ♀ | LPan SEND SPlb SYvo
- 'Rosea' ♀ | CB&S LPan SEND
subcostata | CB&S

LAGUNARIA (Malvaceae)
patersonii | CFil CPLG WPGP
- 'Royal Purple' | ERea

LALLEMANTIA (Lamiaceae)
iberica | Last listed 1999
peltata | Last listed 1999

LAMBERTIA (Proteaceae)
formosa | Last listed 1998

LAMIASTRUM See LAMIUM

LAMIUM ✿ (Lamiaceae)

album	CKin EWFC SMrm
- 'Aureovariegatum'	See *L. album* 'Goldflake'
- 'Brightstone Gem'	EMon NBrk WCHb
- 'Friday' (v)	EGar EHoe EMan EMar EMon
	EPPr EWTr MSCN MTho SSte
	WCHb WHer WHil WRos
- 'Golden Halo'	Last listed 1998
§ - 'Goldflake' (v)	WCHb
- 'Pale Peril'	NBrk
armenum	Last listed 1999
eriocephalum	Last listed 1998
subsp. *eriocephalum*	
flexuosum	EPPr
§ *galeobdolon*	CArn CCHP CTri EWFC EWTr
	LGro MHar MHer MSal MWat NFai
	SRms WOak
- subsp. *galeobdolon*	EMon
- 'Hermann's Pride'	More than 30 suppliers
- 'Kirkcudbright Dwarf'	EBee EWes
- subsp. *montanum*	EMon WCHb
'Canfold Wood'	
§ - - 'Florentinum'	CHal CRow ECha EHoe ELan
	ENot EPPr EPar EPfP GKir MCAu
	MRav NVic SEas SHel WFar WPer
	WPnP
- 'Purple Heart'	EMon
§ - 'Silberteppich'	CRow ECha EFou ELan EMar
	EOrc LRHS MRav MTho NFor
	NVic SBla WCot WPer WWat
- 'Silver Angel'	EMon NSti
- Silver Carpet	See *L. galeobdolon* 'Silberteppich'
- 'Silver Spangled'	EGar
- 'Variegatum'	See *L. galeobdolon* subsp.
	montanum 'Florentinum'
garganicum	CGle EGar EPPr EWes MBct NChi
subsp. *garganicum*	WCot WHil WPer
- subsp. *garganicum*	Last listed 1998
LM&S 94023B	
- 'Laevigatum'	Last listed 1998
- subsp. *laevigatum*	Last listed 1999
HH&K 315	
- - HH&K 332	Last listed 1999
- subsp. *pictum*	See *L. garganicum* subsp.
	striatum
- subsp. *reniforme*	See *L. garganicum* subsp.
	striatum
§ - subsp. *striatum*	SBla SMrm
- - DS&T 89011T	EPPr
luteum	See *L. galeobdolon*
maculatum	CArn CRow EGoo EMon MMal
	NArg SEND SHFr SMac SRms
	WByw WGwG WRos WWye
- AL&JS 90226JU	EMon
- 'Album'	CGle CRow ELan EMon ENot
	EPPr LGro LRHS MWat NChi SHel
	SPer SRms WByw WRos WWat
- 'Anne Greenaway'	EPPr GBri MCAu MCLN MGrG
	NCat SMrm SUsu WCHb WCot
	WEas
- 'Annecy'	MInt
§ - 'Aureum'	More than 30 suppliers
- 'Beacon Silver'	More than 30 suppliers
- 'Beedham's White'	NBir NSti SCro
- 'Brightstone Pearl'	EGoo EMon EPPr WCer
- 'Cannon's Gold'	EBee ECtt EGar EHoe ELan EWes
	GBuc NSti SCob SPla
N - 'Chequers'	CDoC EBee LRHS SCob SPer SPla
	WCFE WPnP WWpP

- 'Chequers Board'	EPla
- 'Dingle Candy'	CMdw EMon
- 'Edinburgh Broadstripes'	EPla
- 'Elaine Franks'	CHid CSam NCat
- 'Elisabeth de Haas' (v)	CHal EBee EGar EMan EMon
	EWes GPin MMal SCob WCHb
	WCer WPer
- 'Gold Leaf'	See *L. maculatum* 'Aureum'
- Golden Anniversary	EBee LAst LEdu LRHS MCCP NArg
= 'Dellam' (v)	NBro NHol NPri SCob WFar
	WPnP WRHF WWeb
- 'Golden Nuggets'	See *L. maculatum* 'Aureum'
- 'Golden Wedding'	COtt
- 'Hatfield'	EMon GAbr GBuc
- 'Ickwell Beauty' (v)	EMon EWes GBri LFis WElm
	WRHF
- 'Immaculate'	EBee EPla
- 'James Boyd Parselle'	CLTr EBee EGle MCAu MLLN
	SCro WCFE WCHb WCot WRHF
	WWat
- 'Margery Fish'	SRms WEas
- 'Pink Nancy'	CBot EGoo GAbr GKir MTho
	WCer WFar
- 'Pink Pearls'	EGar EMan EPPr EWTr LHrt LRHS
	MMal NCiC SCob WMoo
- 'Pink Pewter'	More than 30 suppliers
- 'Purple Winter'	EPla LRHS
- 'Red Nancy'	CBlo EGar EMar EMon GCal WCer
§ - 'Roseum'	CGle CRow EBee EFer ELan EMar
	EPar EPla EWTr GKir LGro LHop
	LRHS MMal MRav MWat NArg
	NChi NFai NFor NSti SPer WPer
	WWat
- 'Shell Pink'	See *L. maculatum* 'Roseum'
- 'Sterling Silver'	EWes WPer
- 'White Nancy' ♀	More than 30 suppliers
- 'Wild White'	EPla
- 'Wootton Pink'	CBos CLTr EBee EGar GBuc GCal
	GMac LFis LRHS MBri MBro MHer
	NBir SSvw WBro WCra WEas
	WElm WHoo WPer
microphyllum	Last listed 1999
orvala	More than 30 suppliers
- 'Album'	CBot CBre CFri CPle EBrP EBre
	EGar ELan EOrc EPPr LBCl LBSe
	LBre LRHS MBBe MFir SAga SBre
	SEas SMrm WCot WHer
- 'Silva'	WCot
sandrasicum	Last listed 1999

LAMPRANTHUS (Aizoaceae)

aberdeenensis	See *Delosperma aberdeenense*
amoenus	Last listed 1999
aurantiacus	CB&S CHEx NBrk SPet
aureus	CTrC EOas
'Bagdad'	CHEx
blandus	CB&S CHEx
§ *brownii*	CB&S CHEx CHal ECho ELan
	EOas NBir SChr SEND WPat
'Carn Brea'	Last listed 1999
coccineus	Last listed 1998
coralliflorus	CTrC EOas
§ *deltoides*	CHEx CTrC MRav SPet WCot
	WEas
edulis	See *Carpobrotus edulis*
falcatus	EOas
glaucus	CHEx SEND
haworthii	CHal SVen
multiradiatus	CTrC EOas SEND
oscularis	See *L. deltoides*
roseus	SPet WEas
scaber	CTrC

spectabilis	CB&S EOas SAPC SArc SPet WBrE
- 'Tresco Apricot'	CB&S
- 'Tresco Brilliant'	CB&S CHEx
- 'Tresco Fire'	CHal
- 'Tresco Peach'	CHEx CStu
- 'Tresco Red'	CB&S
tegens	EOas
'Tresco Pearl'	CHEx

LANTANA (Verbenaceae)

'Aloha' (v)	WWol
camara	ELan EPfP ERea LRHS MBri SRms
	SYvo
- 'Brasier'	ERea
- 'Cocktail'	Last listed 1999
- 'Feston Rose'	ERea
- 'Firebrand'	SYvo
- forms	ERea
- 'Mine d'Or'	ERea
- 'Mr Bessieres'	ERea
¶ - red	WWol
- 'Snow White'	ERea
¶ - 'Sonja'	NPri
* 'Cocktail'	CLTr
'Gold Dust'	Last listed 1998
'Gold Mound'	Last listed 1999
§ *montevidensis*	CHal ERea LHil SYvo
* - alba	ERea LHil
§ - 'Boston Gold'	CHal
- 'Malans Gold'	ERea
- 'White Lightning'	Last listed 1998
- 'Whiteknights'	Last listed 1999
'Radiation'	ERea
sellowiana	See *L. montevidensis*
'Spreading Sunset'	SOWG

LAPAGERIA (Philesiaceae)

rosea ♀	CB&S CHEx CMac CPlN CRHN
	CWSG EPla ERea GKir GQui
	IMGH MDun NRib SOWG SPer
	SReu SSpi WNor WWat
- var. *albiflora*	CPlN
- - 'White Cloud'	Last listed 1999
- 'Flesh Pink' ♀	CPlN CRHN
- 'Nash Court' ♀	CPlN ECot EMil ERea

LAPEIROUSIA (Iridaceae)

cruenta	See *Anomatheca laxa*
laxa	See *Anomatheca laxa*

LAPIEDRA (Amaryllidaceae)

martinezii MS 423	Last listed 1998

LAPORTEA (Urticaceae)

* *bulbifera* 'Variegata' (v)	WCot

LAPSANA (Asteraceae)

communis	WJek
- 'Inky'	CNat
- 'Patchy' (v)	Last listed 1998

LARDIZABALA (Lardizabalaceae)

biternata	CPlN CTrG

LARIX (Pinaceae)

decidua ♀	CB&S CDoC CDul EMac ENot
	EWTr GChr GKir LCon LPan MBar
	NWea SMad SPar SPer WDin WFar
	WHar WMou WStI
- 'Corley'	CKen LCon LLin MBlu
- 'Croxby Broom'	CKen
- 'Globus'	NHol SLim

- 'Horstmann Recurved'	SLim
- 'Little Bogle'	CKen NHol
- 'Oberförster Karsten'	CKen
- 'Pendula'	CB&S GKir
¶ - 'Puli'	CEnd COtt GKir MBlu NHol SLim
	SPer
x *eurolepis*	See *L. x marschlinsii*
europaea	Lam. & DC. See *L. decidua*
gmelinii	GAri ISea
- var. *olgensis*	Last listed 1999
- 'Tharandt'	CKen
§ *kaempferi* ♀	CDoC CDul CLnd CTri ENot
	GChr GKir LBuc LCon LNet MBar
	MGos NWea SLim SPer STre WFro
	WMou WNor WStI
- 'Bambino'	CKen
- 'Blue Ball'	CKen LLin
- 'Blue Dwarf'	CEnd CKen COtt GKir IMGH
	LCon LNet MAsh MGos SLim
- 'Blue Haze'	CKen
- 'Blue Rabbit'	CKen
- 'Blue Rabbit Weeping'	CEnd COtt GKir LCon LLin LPan
	MGos NHol SLim WDin
- 'Cruwys Morchard'	CKen
- 'Cupido'	NHol
- 'Diane'	CBlo CEnd CKen GAri GKir
	LCon LLin MAsh MBlu MBri
	NHol SLim
- 'Elizabeth Rehder'	CKen
- 'Grant Haddow'	CKen
- 'Green Pearl'	CKen
- 'Grey Green Dwarf'	NHol
- 'Grey Pearl'	CKen
- 'Hobbit'	CKen
* - 'Jacobsen's Pyramid'	CEnd LLin NHol
¶ - 'Jakobsen'	LCon
- 'Little Blue Star'	Last listed 1997
- 'Nana'	CKen IMGH LLin WWes
I - 'Nana Prostrata'	CKen
- 'Pendula'	CBlo CDoC CEnd EPfP IOrc MBar
	MBlu MGos NHol SLim SPer
- 'Stiff Weeping'	SLim
- 'Swallow Falls'	CKen
- 'Varley'	CKen NHol
- 'Wehlen'	CKen
- 'Wolterdingen'	CKen MBlu
- 'Yanus Olieslagers'	CKen
laricina	GAri LCon SMad
- 'Arethusa Bog'	CKen MBlu
* - 'Bear Swamp'	CKen
- 'Newport Beauty'	CKen
leptolepis	See *L. kaempferi*
§ x *marschlinsii*	ENot GChr NWea WMou
- 'Domino'	CKen LLin
- 'Gail'	CKen
- 'Julie'	CKen
occidentalis	GAri
* x *pendula* 'Pendulina'	GAri
russica	See *L. sibirica*
§ *sibirica*	GAri ISea MBar
sukaczevii	See *L. sibirica*

LARREA (Zygophyllaceae)

tridentata	Last listed 1999

LASERPITIUM (Apiaceae)

siler	NLar

LASIAGROSTIS See STIPA

LASTREOPSIS (Dryopteridaceae)

microsora	Last listed 1999

LATANIA (Arecaceae)

loddigesii	LPal
verschaffeltii	LPal

LATHYRUS ✿ (Papilionaceae)

albus	CEnd
amphicarpos	EBee
angulatus	Last listed 1998
angustifolius	Last listed 1999
annuus	Last listed 1998
- red	Last listed 1998
aphaca	Last listed 1998
§ *articulatus*	Last listed 1999
aurantius	NHol WLRN
§ *aureus*	CElw CHEx CLTr EBee EMon
	GBuc GCal MAvo MGrG MTho
	NWCA SBla SUsu WCru WEas
	WHal WHil WPGP WPat WViv
azureus hort.	See *L. sativus*
belinensis	Last listed 1998
chilensis	Last listed 1998
chloranthus	EWll
cicera	Last listed 1998
cirrhosus	EMon
clymenum	Last listed 1998
- *articulatus*	See *L. articulatus*
cyaneus hort.	See *L. vernus*
- (Steven) K.Koch	Last listed 1998
* - 'Alboroseus'	CGle MTho
davidii	EMon WCot
filiformis	Last listed 1998
fremontii hort.	See *L. laxiflorus*
gloeospermus	Last listed 1998
§ *gmelinii*	NLar
- 'Aureus'	See *L. aureus*
gorgonii	Last listed 1998
grandiflorus	CGle CSev EBee ECha EMon
	EWTr LGre NLar SMad SMrm SSad
	SUsu SWat WCot
heterophyllus	EBee EMon MNrw WViv
hierosolymitanus	Last listed 1998
hirsutus	Last listed 1999
hirticarpus	Last listed 1998
aff. *hookeri*	EBee
inconspicuus	Last listed 1998
inermis	See *L. laxiflorus*
japonicus	SMad WViv
- subsp. *maritimus*	EBee LFis WMoo
laetiflorus var. *vestitus*	See *L. vestitus*
laevigatus	NLar
lanszwertii	Last listed 1998
latifolius ♀	More than 30 suppliers
- 'Albus' ♀	CBot ELan EMan EMon GChr
	GDra GKir LGre MNrw SHFr
	SRms SSpi SUsu WEas WHoo
- 'Blushing Bride'	Last listed 1999
- deep pink	Last listed 1999
- pale pink	Last listed 1999
- Pink Pearl	See *L. latifolius* 'Rosa Perle'
- 'Red Pearl'	CBlo CPIN ECtt EFou ELan MBri
	MHer NPri SIng SMrm SPer SPlb
	SSvw WPer WRus
§ - 'Rosa Perle' ♀	CBlo CChe COIW CTri ECtt EFou
	EMan GAbr GKir MAvo MBri
	MCAu MSte NFai NLar NPer SBra
	SMrm SPer SSvw STes WRus WViv
- 'Rose Queen'	CB&S
I - 'Rubra'	EPfP
- 'Splendens'	CB&S NFai WOak
- Weisse Perle	See *L. latifolius* 'White Pearl'
§ - 'White Pearl' ♀	CB&S CGle CHea CMea COIW

	ECha EFou EOrc EWTr GAbr
	LPVe MBNS MBri MCAu MHer
	MSte MTis NFai NLar NPer SBra
	SMad SPer SSoC SSvw WCra
	WOve WPer WRus WWat
§ *laxiflorus*	CFri CSpe EBee ECoo EMon
	MCCP MNrw MTho NLar SSca
	WWin
linifolius	EMon
- var. *montanus*	CKin EBee WGwy
luteus (L.) Peterm.	See *L. gmelinii*
- Munby	Last listed 1999
- 'Aureus'	See *L. aureus*
marmoratus	Last listed 1998
montanus	EBee
§ *nervosus*	CPIN CPou CSpe MFir MTho SBla
	SRCN SRms WPnP
neurolobus	CNic EWll MOne
niger	CHid EBee EMar EMon NLar SHFr
	SOkh WGwy WHil
nissolia	ELan
ochrus	EWll MTPN
odoratus ♀	CGle CHar EWll SAga SUsu
- 'America' ♀	Last listed 1996
- 'Bicolor'	ELan
- 'Matucana'	Last listed 1998
- 'Painted Lady'	CGle SMrm
- 'The Busby Pea'	Last listed 1998
palustris	MNrw NLar
pannonicus	MFir NCat
paranensis	Last listed 1998
polyphyllus	WCot
pratensis	CKin EWFC SHel SSca WViv
pubescens	CRHN EBee EMon GBuc
roseus	EMon
rotundifolius	CPIN EBee ECoo EMon EWTr
	GCal GDra LGre MNrw MTho
	SUsu WHoo WPyg
- hybrids	LGre
- 'Tillyperone'	EMon
§ *sativus*	CHad CSpe SRCN SSad
- var. *azureus*	See *L. sativus*
setifolius	Last listed 1998
sphaericus	Last listed 1998
sylvestris	CKin CNat EBee ELan EMon EWll
	MHer MLLN MNrw MSCN MSte
	NChi SHel SYvo WCot WGwy
	WPnP
- 'Wagneri'	Last listed 1999
tingitanus	CRHN
- 'Flame'	Last listed 1998
- *roseus*	Last listed 1998
- 'Roseus'	CRHN
- salmon pink	Last listed 1998
transsilvanicus	EMon
tuberosus	EBee EMon MNrw WCot
'Tubro'	EMon
undulatus	Last listed 1997
* *uniflorus*	MSCN
venetus	EMon MNrw WViv
§ *vernus* ♀	More than 30 suppliers
- 'Alboroseus' ♀	More than 30 suppliers
- var. *albus*	EWes
- *aurantiacus*	See *L. aureus*
- 'Caeruleus'	CRDP EBee EMon LGre SMrm
	WPGP
* - 'Cyaneus'	SAga SOkh SWat WRus WSan
- 'Flaccidus'	EMon WKif WSan WTin
- 'Rosenelfe'	CBot EMan WHil WSan WViv
- f. *roseus*	ECha MRav WCot
¶ - 'Spring Beauty'	WViv
- 'Spring Melody'	EBee LFis LPio SMrm SOkh WCot

		WPat WRHF WShe
§	*vestitus*	Last listed 1998
	- var. *alefeldii*	EBee
	- var. *vestitus*	EMon
	vinealis	Last listed 1998

LAURELIA (Monimiaceae)

§	*sempervirens*	CB&S CFil CGre CTrw WPGP
	serrata	See *L. sempervirens*

LAURENTIA (Campanulaceae)

§	*axillaris*	CGdn CLTr EBrP EBre EDAr LBCl
		LBSe LBre LHil LLck LRHS MBBe
		MBNS SBre SCoo SHFr WWin
¶	- pink	LLck
¶	- white	CLTr LLck
*	'Fairy Carpet'	CLTr EMan
¶	*fluviatilis*	CLTr ECou WCru
	minuta	Last listed 1997
	sp.	Last listed 1999

LAURUS (Lauraceae)

§	*azorica*	CB&S CGre WSPU WWat
	canariensis	See *L. azorica*
	nobilis ♀	More than 30 suppliers
	- f. *angustifolia*	CMCN CSWP EPla GQui MBlu
		MRav SAPC SArc SDry WCHb
		WOak WPGP WSel WWat
	- 'Aurea' ♀	CB&S CDul CGre CMHG EBee
		ELan ELau EMil EPVP EPla ERav
		ERea GQui IOrc LNet LRHS MAsh
		MBlu MChe SBrw SLim SLon
		SMad SPer WCHb WPat WPyg
		WSel WWat
	- 'Crispa'	MRav

LAVANDULA ✿ (Lamiaceae)

N	'Alba'	CArn CB&S CBot CSev ELan
		GCHN GOrc NYoL SIde SPer SWat
		WEas WOak WPer
§	x *allardii*	CArn CSev EMil ENor EOHP GBar
		MChe NHHG SDow SPan SRCN
		WJek WOut WPen WSel
	- 'African Pride'	GBar SDow
	- clone B	SDow
	- forms	WTus
§	*angustifolia*	CArn CLan EBee EDAr ELau ENot
		GOrc GPoy LBuc LRHS MBar
		MBri MChe MGos MHer MMal
		MWat NFla NFor NPer NYoL SAga
		SEas SMac SPlb SRPl WAbe WPyg
		WTus WWye
	- 'Alba'	CChe EBee EDAr EHoe ELau EPfP
		GChr GPoy LBuc LHop MBNS
		MChe MHer NFai NMen SLon
		WSel WWat
	- 'Alba Nana'	See *L. angustifolia* 'Nana Alba'
	- 'Arabian Knight'	LRHS MHer
	- 'Ashdown Forest'	CSev EBee ELau MChe MHer
		SDow SMrm SRPl WJek WLRN
		WTus
	- 'Beechwood Blue'	NYoL SDow WTus
	- 'Blue Mountain'	LRHS SDow
§	- 'Bowles' Early'	CSam ENor GBar MChe NGCt
		SDow WTus
	- 'Bowles' Grey'	See *L. angustifolia* 'Bowles' Early'
	- 'Bowles' Variety'	See *L. angustifolia* 'Bowles' Early'
	- 'Cedar Blue'	CSev EGoo ELau GBar NYoL
		SDow SHDw SIde SMrm SPla
		WBar WTus
	- 'Compacta'	NGCt WTus
	- 'Dwarf Blue'	EMil MHer MWhi WTus

I	- 'Eastgrove Nana'	WEas WTus
	- 'Folgate'	CArn CB&S ECGP ELau GBar LAst
		MChe MHer NGCt NHHG NYoL
		SDow SIde WGwG WSel WTus
	- 'Fring Favourite'	SDow WTus
	- 'Heacham Blue'	SDow
§	- 'Hidcote' ♀	More than 30 suppliers
	- 'Hidcote Pink'	CArn CGle EDAr EOld ESis GBar
		GKir MHer NFai NFor NMen NSti
		SDow SLim SPer SRPl SSoC
		WGwG WHen WPer WSel WStl
		WTus WWat
	- 'Imperial Gem'	CArn CRos EBee ELau ENor ESis
		GBar LRHS MAsh MBri MChe
		MHer NHHG SDow SEas SIde
		WHoo WSel WTus WWeb
§	- 'Jean Davis'	EBee GBar LHop NHHG SDow
		SIde WSel WTus WWat
	- 'Lady'	MChe MWat NOrc SDow SEND
		SHDw WLRN WTus
N	- 'Lavender Lady'	ELau EOHP LAst NYoL WPer
		WWeb
	- Little Lady = 'Batlad'[PBR]	ENor SDow WGwG WTus
	- Little Lottie = 'Clarmo'	CFai ECGP ENor EPfP LRHS MAsh
		NDov SCoo SDow SPer SVil WElm
		WTus
	- 'Loddon Blue'	CB&S CWSG ELau GBar MNaF
		NHHG NYoL SDow SIde WJek
		WTus
§	- 'Loddon Pink'	CWSG ECle ELan ENor ENot ERea
		GBar GCHN GKir LRHS MAsh
		MChe NYoL SDow SRPl WAbe
		WEas WGwG WHoo WJek WPGP
		WStl WTus WWal WWat
	- 'Maillette'	SDow
	- 'Miss Donnington'	See *L. angustifolia* 'Bowles' Early'
	- 'Miss Katherine'[PBR]	CFai ELan ENor EPfP LRHS SDow
		WTus
	- 'Munstead'	More than 30 suppliers
§	- 'Nana Alba'	CB&S CSev ECha EDAr ELan ELau
		ENor ENot GBar GPoy LHop
		LRHS MAsh MBar MBri MHer
		MMal NHHG SDow SPer WEas
		WGwG WHoo WKif WPat WSel
		WTus WWat
	- 'Nana Atropurpurea'	SDow WSel WTus
	- No. 9	SDow
	- 'Princess Blue'	EBee ELan ELau ENor GBar LFis
		LRHS MAsh MBNS NYoL SAga
		SDow SIde SRPl SSca WPer WSel
		WTus WWeb WWoo
§	- 'Rosea'	CArn CB&S CChe CDul CMea
		CPri EBee ECha EDAr EGoo EHoe
		EWTr GBar GChr GPoy LRHS
		MBar MBri MMal NHHG SDow
		SIde SPer WGwG WHer WTus
		WWeb
	- 'Royal Purple'	CArn ELau ENor EOld EWTr EWes
		GBar LFis LRHS MAsh MBNS
		MHer NGCt NHHG NYoL SDow
		SIde WTus WWye
N	- 'Twickel Purple' ♀	EBee EPfP GKir LHop LRHS
		MBNS MChe MHer MNDov NHHG
		NYoL SCoo SDow SIde SPer
		WGwG WSel WTus
¶	'Avonview'	CB&S MHer SDow
	'Blue Cushion'	EBrP EBre GBar LBCl LBSe LBre
		MAsh MBBe MBNS NPri SBre
*	'Blue Star'	Last listed 1999
	'Bowers Beauty'	NGCt WTus
	buchii var. *buchii*	SDow
	- var. *gracilis*	SDow WTus

N 'Cambridge Lady'	Last listed 1999
canariensis	CSev ENor EOHP ERea GBar
	MHer NHHG SDow SHDw SSad
	WCHb WJek WTus
x *christiana*	ELau GBar MHer SDow SHDw
	WJek WTus
'Cornard Blue'	See *L* 'Sawyers'
dentata	CArn CInt CSev ELan ELau ENor
	EPri ERea GBar LFis MChe MHer
	NBrk NHHG SDow SDry SPer
	WGwG WHer WOak WPat WTus
	WWye
§ - var. *candicans*	CGle CSev EBee ENor EOHP GBar
	LHil LHop MChe MHer MSCN
	NHHG SDow SMrm SSad WCHb
	WEas WPer WTus WWye
- 'Linda Ligon' (v)	GBar SDow WTus
- 'Ploughman's Blue'	NGCt SDow WTus
- 'Royal Crown'	CStr ENor GBar SDow WTus
- silver	See *L dentata* var. *candicans*
- 'Silver Queen'	MHer SHDw WTus
'Devantville Cuche'	ELau NSti SDow WJek WTus
'Dilly Dilly'	LRHS WTus
I 'Edelweiss'	NGCt
¶ 'Fathead'	CChe COtt ENor EPfP EWTr GBar
	LRHS MAsh MHer NGCt SDow
	WJek WTus WWol
* 'Fontwell'	SRPl
'Fragrant Memories'	EBee ELau ERea GBar LRHS MAsh
	SDow SSoC WTus
'Goodwin Creek Grey'	GBar MChe SDow WTus
¶ 'Helmsdale'	More than 30 suppliers
heterophylla hort.	See *L* x *allardii*
'Hidcote Blue'	See *L. angustifolia* 'Hidcote'
§ x *intermedia*	SRPl
- 'Abrialii'	SDow WTus
- 'Alba'	ECle ENor GBar NHHG SDow
	SRPl WLRN WTus
N - 'Arabian Night'	COtt LRHS MHer SDow WTus
- 'Bogong'	NGCt WTus
§ - Dutch Group ♀	CArn EDAr ELan ENot EOld EPfP
	EWTr GBar GKir MBar MBri MHer
	NYoL SCoo SDow SPer SWat
	WHen WJek WPer WSel WTus
§ - - Walberton's Silver	ENor LRHS WWeb
Edge™ = 'Walvera' (v)	
- 'Grappenhall'	CArn CEnd CSam EBee ELau EMil
	ENor GBar GKir LRHS MAsh
	MChe MHer MRav NFai NVic
	NYoL SDow SPer WGwG WPer
	WPnn WSel WTus WWat WWye
- 'Grey Hedge'	SDow WTus
- 'Grosso'	CChe COtt CPri CSev ELau ENor
	EPfP GBar LRHS MHer NDov NSti
	NYoL SDow WJek WLRN WSel
	WTus
- 'Hidcote Giant'	LRHS NPer SDow WSel WTus
	WWat
* - 'Hidcote White'	EGoo MHer WTus
¶ - 'Impress Purple'	SDow
- 'Lullingstone Castle'	CBod ELau NSti NYoL SDow SIde
	WJek WSPU WTus
- Old English Group	CArn CBod ELan ELau MMal NBrk
	NYoL SDow SIde WHoo WJek
	WOak WSel WTus WWat
- 'Seal'	CArn EBee ECle ELau GBar MChe
	MHer NGCt NHHG NSti NYoL
	SDow SIde SMrm WGwG WHCG
	WPer WSel WTus WWal WWat
- 'Super'	SDow
N - 'Twickel Purple'	CArn CMHG CSev ECGP ELau
	ENot EWes LFis NHHG SMrm

	SWat WGwG WJek WOak WPnn
	WWat
'Jean Davis'	See *L. angustifolia* 'Jean Davis'
lanata ♀	CArn CBot CGle CLon ECha ELan
	ENor GBar GPoy MBro MChe
	MWat NGCt NHHG NSti NWCA
	SDow SDry SHFr WEas WGwG
	WTus WWye
- x *angustifolia*	GBar NHHG WTus
§ *latifolia*	CArn SDow WTus
* - 'Alba'	Last listed 1997
'Loddon Pink'	See *L. angustifolia* 'Loddon Pink'
mairei x *intermedia*	WTus
¶ 'Marshwood'	CRos EBee EBrP EBre ENor EPfP
	IOrc LBCl LBSe LBre LBuc LRHS
	MAsh MBBe MBel MHer NYoL
	SBre SCoo SDow SLim SPer SPla
	SWat WTus WWat
minutolii	ENor MHer SDow WTus
multifida	CArn CSev ENor ERea EWTr
	MChe MHer SDow SSad WCHb
	WGwG WHer WOut WTus
	WWal
officinalis	See *L. angustifolia*
§ *pinnata*	CArn CSev ENor ERea GBar
	MChe MHer NHHG SDow SDry
	SPer SRob SSad SVen WCHb WEas
	WHal WTus
pterostoechas pinnata	See *L pinnata*
pubescens	SDow
'Richard Gray'	EMon GBar LRHS NBrk SDow
	WAbe WBcn WHen WTus
'Rosea'	See *L. angustifolia* 'Rosea'
rotundifolia	MHer SDow WTus
¶ 'Roxlea Park'	EWTr
'Saint Brelade'	GBar NGCt SDow WTus
§ 'Sawyers'	More than 30 suppliers
* 'Silber Dwarf'	Last listed 1999
'Silver Edge'	See *L* x *intermedia* (Dutch
	Group) Walberton's Silver Edge
	= 'Walvera'
N *spica* nom. rejic.	See *L. angustifolia*, *L. latifolia*, *L.*
	x *intermedia*
- 'Hidcote Purple'	See *L. angustifolia* 'Hidcote'
stoechas ♀	More than 30 suppliers
- var. *albiflora*	See *L. stoechas* f. *leucantha*
- subsp. *atlantica*	SDow WTus WWol
- subsp. *cariensis*	SDow
- dark	WTus
- 'Kew Red'	CFai CMea ELau EWll GBin LRHS
	MAsh MBel MHer NGCt NGHP
	NPro SAga SDow SEas SHDw
	SMad SPer SUsu WBcn WTus
	WWat WWol
§ - f. *leucantha*	CArn CBot CMHG CSev CTre
	ECha ELan ELau GBar LAst MBNS
	MBri MChe MHer NWoo SChu
	SDow SPer WAbe WCHb WEas
	WPer WTus WWat
- subsp. *luisieri*	GBar SDow WHer
- subsp. *lusitanica*	MHer SDow WTus
* - 'Nana'	Last listed 1999
- 'Papillon'	See *L. stoechas* subsp.
	pedunculata
§ - subsp. *pedunculata* ♀	More than 30 suppliers
- - 'James Compton'	CCHP EBee EMon ERea LRHS
	MAsh NDov SDow SLim SSoC
	SUsu WLin WTus
- 'Pippa'	WTus
- 'Pukehou'	LRHS WTus
- subsp. *sampaioana*	GBar SDow WTus
- 'Snowman'	ENor GKir IOrc LRHS MAsh

	MHer MWat NDov NYoL SDow SLim SRPl WFar WTus WWal
- 'Sugar Plum'	WTus
- 'Summerset Mist'	NGCt WTus
- 'Willow Vale'	CFai CMHG CMea COtt EBee ENor EPfP GBar LGre LRHS MHer MTis MWat NGCt SAga SDow SPan WEas WElm WHoo WJek WPGP WSPU WTus WWeb
* - 'Wine Red'	CFwr WTus
subnuda	WTus
vera hort.	See *L.* x *intermedia* Dutch Group
- DC.	See *L. angustifolia*
viridis	CArn CPla CSev EGoo ELan ENor ERav GBar GOrc LGre LRHS MChe MHer NHHG NPer SDow SPer SSad STes WCHb WGwG WHer WPer WPnn WTus WWat WWye

LAVATERA (Malvaceae)

¶ *acerifolia*	WEas
* 'Alba'	LFis
arborea	CArn GBar SChr WHer
- 'Rosea'	See *L.* 'Rosea'
- 'Variegata'	CInt ELan EMan GBar LHop NPer NSti SBod SDix SEND WCHb WCot WCru WEas WHer WWal
assurgentiflora	GBri
'Barnsley' ♀	More than 30 suppliers
'Barnsley Perry's Dwarf'	Last listed 1997
bicolor	See *L. maritima*
'Blushing Bride'	CBlo CDoC EBee EBrP EBre ELan EPfP LBCl LBSe LBre LFis LRHS MAsh MBBe MBri MLLN MSCN NPri SBod SBre SDix SMrm SPla WBcn WHar
'Bredon Springs' ♀	More than 30 suppliers
* 'Bressingham Pink'	SMad
'Burgundy Wine' ♀	More than 30 suppliers
cachemiriana	EBee ELan GBuc GCal MFir NBur NPer NSti
'Candy Floss' ♀	EBee ENot EPfP LRHS MAsh MBNS MBar MGos NPer SMrm SPer WDin WStI WWal WWol
'Chedglow' (v)	Last listed 1998
'Eye Catcher'	CElw CFai GKir LFis LRHS MAsh MBNS SPer
¶ 'Golden My Foot!' (v)	CNat
'Kew Rose'	CBlo CDoC EBee EMil EPfP LRHS MAsh NPer SLim SPla SSoC WGwG
'Lara Rose' (v)	MGos
'Lavender Lady'	GKir SMrm
'Lilac Lady'	CB&S CElw CFai ECha ELan LFis LRHS MAsh MAvo MBNS MCCP SLod SPer
'Linda'	WBcn
'Lisanne'	EBee EOrc LFis LRHS MCCP MHer MNrw NHol NPri NPro SMer SMrm
§ *maritima* ♀	CBot CDoC CGle CMHG CRHN EBee ELan EOld LHil LHop LHrt MAsh SDry SMrm SPer SUsu WCFE WCot WEas WFar WHCG WKif
- *bicolor*	See *L. maritima*
'Mary Hope'	CFai LRHS NPro
¶ Memories = 'Stelav'PBR	CChe ELan EPfP LRHS NPro
'Moonstone'	SMrm
oblongifolia	CBot

N *olbia*	CGle GKir MHer MSCN MWat NFai SPlb SRms
'Pavlova'	CDoC EBee EPfP LRHS MAsh MCCP NHol SMrm
'Peppermint Ice'	See *L. thuringiaca* 'Ice Cool'
'Pink Frills'	CBot EBrP EBre LBCl LBSe LBre LHop LRHS MAvo MBBe MBar MNrw MTis NBrk SBre SDry SSoC WCot WHar WPyg WRus WStI
plebeia	Last listed 1998
'Poynton Lady' (v)	MGos NEgg
§ 'Rosea' ♀	CB&S CChe EBee EBrP EBre ECha ELan ENot EWTr GChr LBCl LBSe LBre LRHS MAsh MBBe MBar MBri MGos NFor SBod SBre SLon SPer WBod WDin WFar WWin
'Shadyvale Star'	NPro
'Shorty'	NBrk WFar
'Snowcap'	CBlo
'Sweet Dreams'	MBri
N *thuringiaca*	EBot MWhi NBro NPri WFar
- AL&JS 90100YU	Last listed 1998
§ - 'Ice Cool'	CBot CElw ECha ECtt ELan EOrc ERav EWTr GCal LRHS MAsh MBar MGos MHer NBee NBrk NPer SMrm SPer SSoC WCFE WFar WHen
'Variegata'	See *L.* 'Wembdon Variegated'
§ 'Wembdon Variegated'	MCCP MLLN NPer
'White Angel'	MBri
¶ 'White Satin'	CFai MBri

LAWSONIA (Lythraceae)

| *inermis* | WGwG |

LEDEBOURIA (Hyacinthaceae)

adlamii	See *L. cooperi*
§ *cooperi*	CHal CRDP CStu EBee ELan EMan ERos ESis GCal GCrs IBlr LHil SCob SIng WAbe WCDu
* *pauciflora*	Last listed 1997
§ *socialis*	CHEx CHal CMdw CSWP CSev CSpe CStu EBot EOHP ERav ERos IBlr LHil MBro NChi NRog
violacea	See *L. socialis*

x LEDODENDRON (Ericaceae)

| § 'Arctic Tern' ♀ | CDoC GChr GGGa GKir LHyd LMil LRHS MAsh MBar MDun MGos MLea NHar NHol NLAp SLdr SPer SReu WAbe WPic |

LEDUM (Ericaceae)

glandulosum var. *columbianum*	
	Last listed 1999
groenlandicum	GEil MBar MGos WAbe WSHC
- 'Compactum'	LRHS MAsh
macrophyllum	CFir
palustre	EPot GGGa GPoy MGos SRPl WAbe
- subsp. *decumbens*	GCrs GGGa
'Teshio'	SSta

LEEA (Leeaceae)

| *coccinea* | See *L. guineensis* |
| § *guineensis* | MBri |

LEGOUSIA (Campanulaceae)

| ¶ 'Devon Sky' | EMan |
| *hybrida* | CFri EWFC |

LEIBNITZIA (Asteraceae)
anandria   NWCA

LEIOPHYLLUM (Ericaceae)
buxifolium ♀   CB&S EPfP EPot GCrs GKir LRHS
    MBro NHol SBrw SSpi SSta WPat
    WPyg
- var. *bugeri*   NHar WAbe

LEMBOTROPIS See CYTISUS

LEMNA (Lemnaceae)
gibba   CWat LPBA
minor   CWat EHon EMFW LPBA MSta
    SWat
minuscula   Last listed 1997
polyrhiza   See *Spirodela polyrhiza*
trisulca   CWat EHon EMFW LGuA LPBA
    MSta SWat

LEONOTIS (Lamiaceae)
dysophylla 'Pussytoes'   Last listed 1998
- 'Toastytoes'   Last listed 1999
leonitis   See *L. ocymifolia*
leonurus   EBee ERav LHil SMad
* *menthifolia*   Last listed 1999
nepetifolia   EMan WCFE WCot
§ *ocymifolia*   CFee CTbh EPPr WHer WWye
- var. *ocymifolia*   WCot
¶ - var. *raineriana*   WCot
'Staircase'   WRos WSan

LEONTICE (Berberidaceae)
albertii   See *Gymnospermium albertii*

LEONTODON (Asteraceae)
autumnalis   CKin
hispidus   CKin MGas NMir
§ *rigens*   EMan GAri GBri GBuc GKir NBid
    NSti NTow SDix SMrm WCot
- 'Girandole'   CInt EBee LIck MNrw NHol SUsu
    WPer WWal

LEONTOPODIUM (Asteraceae)
alpinum   EBot EBrP EBre EWTr GAbr
    GCHN GKir GTou LBCl LBSe LBre
    LRHS MBBe MBro NFla NFor
    NMen NNrd SBre SPlb SRms WPer
    WWin
- 'Mignon'   CMea ELan EMNN EWes GCrs
    GDra GTou MBro NMen NNrd
    SIng SSmi WHoo
- subsp. *nivale*   SBla WLin
hayachinense   Last listed 1998
    miyabeanum
himalayanum   Last listed 1998
kamtschaticum   Last listed 1999
linearifolium KS 2111   Last listed 1999
§ *ochroleucum*   WPer
    var. *campestre*
palibinianum   See *L. ochroleucum* var.
    campestre
wilsonii   ECha

LEONURUS (Lamiaceae)
artemisia   EOHP MSal WWye
cardiaca   CArn EBee EMan EMon EWFC
    GBar GPoy MChe MHer MHew
    MPEx MSal NHex SIde WHbs
    WHer WSel WWye
- 'Crispus'   EMon

macranthus   EFEx
- var. *alba*   EFEx
sibiricus   EPPr EWll IIve LEdu MMHG MSal
    WElm WSan

LEOPOLDIA (Hyacinthaceae)
comosa   See *Muscari comosum*
spreitzenhoferi   See *Muscari spreitzenhoferi*
tenuiflora   See *Muscari tenuiflorum*

LEPECHINIA (Lamiaceae)
calycina   Last listed 1998
§ *chamaedryoides*   CGre
floribunda   CPle

LEPIDIUM (Brassicaceae)
barnebyanum   Last listed 1997
- NNS 93-420   Last listed 1998
¶ *campestre*   CArn
nanum   Last listed 1999
¶ *ruderale*   MSal
¶ *virginicum*   MSal

LEPIDOTHAMNUS (Podocarpaceae)
§ *laxifolius*   CMHG

LEPIDOZAMIA (Zamiaceae)
hopei   LPal
peroffskyana   CBrP CRoM LPal

LEPTINELLA (Asteraceae)
§ *albida*   GCrs LGro WLin
§ *atrata*   Last listed 1999
- subsp. *luteola*   EWes GGar NWCA SChu SDys
    SSmi
§ *dendyi*   EWes MHer NLAp NMen WMAq
- 'Southley'   Last listed 1997
filicula   ECou
* *hispida*   Last listed 1998
maniototo   Last listed 1999
§ *minor*   ECou MOne SSmi
§ *pectinata*   Last listed 1999
- var. *sericea*   See *L. albida*
§ *potentillina*   CTri ECha EHoe ESis MBNS
    MWgw SChu SIng SRms WCru
    WPer WRHF WWin
§ *pusilla*   SDys SSmi
§ *pyrethrifolia*   CInt CSam NMen SIng
- var. *linearifolia*   ELan
- var. *pyrethrifolia*   NTow
reptans   See *L. scariosa*
§ *rotundata*   CInt ECou WPer
§ *scariosa*   Last listed 1998
§ *serrulata*   MBar WCru WLRN
* aff. *socialis* JJ&JH 9401641 Last listed 1998
§ *squalida*   CNic ECha GGar IBlr MBar NBro
    NRya NSti SIng SSmi WPer
§ - 'Platt's Black'   CInt EDAr GAri GCrs LRHS NSti
    SDys SIng SSmi

LEPTODACTYLON (Polemoniaceae)
§ *californicum*   CPBP EBee
- subsp. *glandulosum*   Last listed 1998
pungens pulchriflorum   Last listed 1998

LEPTOPTERIS (Osmundaceae)
hymenophylloides   Last listed 1997
* *laxa*   Last listed 1997
* *media*   Last listed 1997
moorei   Last listed 1997
superba   Last listed 1997
wilkesiana   Last listed 1997

LEPTOSPERMUM ✿ (Myrtaceae)

arachnoides	Last listed 1998
argenteum	CB&S
brachyandrum weeping, silver-leaved form	Last listed 1998
citratum	See *L. petersonii*
* *compactum*	CPLG
cunninghamii	See *L. myrtifolium*
epacridoideum	Last listed 1998
ericoides	See *Kunzea ericoides*
flavescens Sm.	See *L. polygalifolium*
- misapplied	See *L. glaucescens*
§ *glaucescens*	Last listed 1998
§ *grandiflorum*	CFil CTrG Elan GGar ISea LRHS SBrw SOWG WSHC
grandifolium	ECou SSpi
'Green Eyes' (*minutifolium* x *scoparium*)	ECou
humifusum	See *L. rupestre*
juniperinum	SPlb
laevigatum	Last listed 1997
- 'Yarrum'	ECou
§ *lanigerum* ♀	CB&S CMHG CTri ECou IOrc SLim SOWG WDCP WWin
- 'Cunninghamii'	See *L. myrtifolium*
- 'King William'	ECou
- 'Silver Sheen'	See *L. myrtifolium* 'Silver Sheen'
- 'Wellington'	ECou
liversidgei	ECou
macrocarpum	Last listed 1997
minutifolium	ECou
§ *myrtifolium*	CTri ECou Elan EPfP EPla EWes GGar SDry SOWG SPer SSta WPat WPic WPyg
- 'Newnes Forest'	ECou
- x *scoparium*	ECou
§ - 'Silver Sheen'	CPMA LRHS SBrw SLon WGer
nitidum	ECou
* - 'Cradle'	ECou
obovatum	CMHG
§ *petersonii*	CArn ECou EOHP
phylicoides	See *Kunzea ericoides*
'Pink Surprise' (*minutifolium* x *scoparium*)	ECou SOWG
polyanthum	Last listed 1998
§ *polygalifolium*	CTrC SRms
prostratum	See *L. rupestre*
pubescens	See *L. lanigerum*
riparium	Last listed 1998
rodwayanum	See *L. grandiflorum*
rotundifolium	CTrC ECou EOHP
- from Jervis Bay	Last listed 1998
§ *rupestre* ♀	CTri ECou EPot GTou MBar MGos NHar SDry SRms WLin WSHC WWat
- x *scoparium*	ECou
scoparium	CArn CMFo ECou ELau ERom GAri IOrc WDin
¶ - 'Adrianne'	MAsh
- 'Autumn Glory'	EHoe SLim SMrm SPer WStI
- 'Avocet'	ECou
- 'Black Robin'	LRHS SOWG
- 'Blossom'	CB&S ECou SOWG WGer
- 'Boscawenii'	LHil
- 'Bunting'	Last listed 1997
- 'Burgundy Queen'	CB&S ECou
- 'Chapmanii'	CMHG CTrG CTri
- 'Charmer'	Last listed 1998
- 'Cherry Brandy'	Last listed 1998
- 'Chiff Chaff'	Last listed 1997

- 'Coral Candy'	CB&S SOWG
- 'Elizabeth Jane'	GQui
- 'Fascination'	CGre
- 'Firecrest'	Last listed 1997
- 'Fred's Red'	EWes
- 'Gaiety Girl' (d)	CBrm
- 'Grandiflorum'	CTrw WGer
- var. *incanum* 'Keatleyi' ♀	CMHG ECou EPfP MGos SOWG WPyg
- - 'Wairere'	ECou
- 'Jubilee' (d)	CB&S ISea
¶ - 'Kerry'	MAsh
- 'Leonard Wilson' (d)	CTri ECou EWes
- 'Lyndon'	ECou
- 'Martini'	CDoC CTrC CTrG IOrc LHil LRHS MGos SOWG WCot WWeb
- 'McLean'	ECou
- Nanum Group 'Huia'	CB&S CDoC ENot IOrc
- - 'Kea'	ESis GQui MRav WGer WPyg
- - 'Kiwi' ♀	CB&S CBrm CDoC Elan ENot EPfP EWes GGar GQui IOrc ISea ITim LRHS MDun MGos NHol SBrw SLim WGer WLRN WPat WPyg WWat
- - 'Kompakt'	EPot
- - 'Nanum'	EPot NMen SBod SIng WDCP
- - 'Pipit'	EPot EWes
- - 'Tui'	CTrC
- 'Nichollsii' ♀	CB&S CGre CMHG CTri ENot GQui ITim SOWG WDCP WHar WSHC
- 'Nichollsii Nanum' ♀	CDoC CMea EPot ITim NHol SIng SRms WAbe WPat WPyg
- 'Pink Cascade'	CB&S CBlo CTri IMGH IOrc SAga SBrw SLim SPer
- 'Pink Champagne'	Last listed 1997
- 'Pink Damask'	SPer
- var. *prostratum*	See *L. rupestre*
- 'Red Damask' (d) ♀	CB&S CChe CDoC CGdn CGre CLan CTrC CTre EBee Elan GGar GQui IMGH IOrc LHil LRHS MGos MRav SAga SBod SBrw SIng SOWG SRms SSht WBod WSHC WWeb
- 'Red Ensign'	SBod
- 'Red Falls'	CDoC ECou SOWG
- 'Redpoll'	ECou
- 'Redstart'	Last listed 1997
- 'Robin'	Last listed 1998
- 'Rosy Morn'	ISea
- 'Ruby Glow' (d)	LRHS WBod
* - 'Ruby Wedding'	LRHS
* - 'Silver Spire'	SOWG
- 'Snow Flurry'	CB&S CTrC ENot IMGH ISea SLim SRPl SSte
- 'Sunraysia'	CTrw
- 'Winter Cheer'	Last listed 1998
- 'Wiri Joan'	Last listed 1999
- 'Wiri Linda'	Last listed 1999
sphaerocarpum	Last listed 1998
squarrosum	CTrC
trinervium	Last listed 1998

LESCHENAULTIA (Goodeniaceae)

biloba	ECou
¶ *formosa* red	ECou
¶ - yellow	ECou

LESPEDEZA (Papilionaceae)

bicolor	CAgr CB&S CWit GOrc SEND WFar
buergeri	CB&S LRHS SMur WSHC

floribunda	Last listed 1999
sp. from Yakushima	Last listed 1999
thunbergii ♀	CB&S CDul EBee ELan EMil EPfP
	EWTr LHop LRHS MAsh MBel
	MBlu MWhi NFla SLon SMad
	SOWG SPer SSpi SSta WCot WDin
	WFar WOTO WSHC
- 'Albiflora'	Last listed 1999
- 'Summer Beauty'	EPfP MGos
* - 'Variegata'	LRHS
tiliifolia	See *Desmodium elegans*

LESQUERELLA (Brassicaceae)

alpina	Last listed 1999
arctica var. *purshii*	WPat

LEUCADENDRON (Proteaceae)

argenteum	CBrP CHEx CTrC CTrF
comosum	Last listed 1998
discolor	Last listed 1997
eucalyptifolium	CTrC
galpinii	CTrC
laureolum	CTrC
nobile	Last listed 1999
'Safari Sunset'	CTrC
salicifolium	CTrC
salignum	Last listed 1999
- 'Early Yellow'	CTrC
- 'Fireglow'	CTrC
strobilinum	Last listed 1999
tinctum	CTrC
uliginosum	Last listed 1999

LEUCANTHEMELLA (Asteraceae)

§ *serotina* ♀	More than 30 suppliers

LEUCANTHEMOPSIS (Asteraceae)

§ *alpina*	GCrs LBee LRHS
bosmariensis	See *Rhodanthemum*
	bosmariense
§ *pectinata*	LBee WAbe
- JCA 627.801	CPBP
radicans	See *L. pectinata*

LEUCANTHEMUM ✿ (Asteraceae)

atlanticum	See *Rhodanthemum atlanticum*
catananche	See *Rhodanthemum catananche*
'Fringe Benefit'	EMon NPer
bosmariense	See *Rhodanthemum*
	bosmariense
mawii	See *Rhodanthemum gayanum*
§ *maximum* (Ramond) DC.	CBlo GAbr GCHN MWgw NBro
	NPer NSti NVic WBea WCer
	WOak
§ - hort.	See *L. × superbum*
- *uliginosum*	See *Leucanthemella serotina*
nipponicum	See *Nipponanthemum*
	nipponicum
§ × *superbum*	EWTr MHer MNrw WFar
- 'Aglaia' (d) ♀	More than 30 suppliers
- 'Alaska'	EBee EMan LRHS NFai NOak SPer
	SRCN WPer WViv WWal WWpP
- 'Amelia'	NCut
- 'Anita Allen'	CElw MAvo WCot WFar
- 'Annie House'	Last listed 1997
- 'Antwerp Star'	MFir NCat
- 'Beauté Nivelloise'	EBee ECha EMan LFis MAvo MBel
	SUsu WPer WRHF WRha
¶ - 'Becky'	LBmB
- 'Bishopstone'	CMGP CMil EBee ELan EMan
	MRav SCou WEas
- 'Christine Hagemann'	EFou LRHS MAvo MBri NHaw

	WHoo WWoo WWpP
- 'Cobham Gold' (d)	CBre CElw CMil EBee ECha EMan
	ERea GBuc NFla NOrc WWpP
- 'Coconut Ice'	EBee EWTr GAbr WPer
- 'Colwall'	LHil
- double cream	EBee
- 'Droitwich Beauty'	WSPU
- 'Esther Read' (d)	CBlo CElw CGle CM&M CMCo
	EBee ELan EMan ERea LAst LFis
	MFir NFla SHel SRms SWat WByw
	WCot WFar
- 'Everest'	EMan NOak SRms
- 'Fiona Coghill'	CElw EBee EFou GBri IBlr LFis
	MAvo MFir MLLN NBrk WCot
- 'H. Seibert'	CMil CSam MArl
- 'Highland White	LRHS
Dream'PBR	
- 'Horace Read' (d)	CElw CHea CMGP CMdw CMea
	CMil CRDP EBee ECha ELan
	EMan ERea LFis MGas NPer SAga
	WEas WPer
- 'Jennifer Read'	ERea
- 'John Murray'	WAbb
- 'Little Miss Muffet'	LRHS MBri
- 'Little Princess'	See *L. × superbum*
	'Silberprinzesschen'
- 'Manhattan'	EBee EBrP EBre GBuc LBCl LBSe
	LBre LRHS MBBe NCat SBre
- 'Mayfield Giant'	MWgw WPer
- 'Mount Everest'	CBlo EGar SRms WCot
- 'Phyllis Smith'	CGle CHea COlW CPlt ECha EGar
	EGle EMan GAbr LFis LRHS MAvo
	MBel MBri MCLN MTis NGiC NFai
	NGdn SAga SHel SMad SSvw
	WAbb WBea WFar WHil WLin
	WMoo
- 'Polaris'	LRHS NFai NOak WMoo
- 'Rheinblick'	NCut WLRN
- 'Rijnsburg Glory'	Last listed 1999
* - 'Schneehurken'	LCTD MAvo SAsh SMad
- 'Schwabengruss'	CStr
- 'Shaggy'	CBos GMaP LFis MLLN NFla SWat
§ - 'Silberprinzesschen'	CMea COlW EBee ECGP EWTr
	GAbr GKir LRHS MFir NMir NOak
	NPri SPlb SRms WBea WCot WFar
	WHen WMoo WPer
- 'Snow Lady'	CM&M GCHN LRHS NMir NPer
	SPet WFar WHen
- 'Snowcap'	CBlo EBee EBrP EBre ECha EGar
	EGle EMan ENot GAri LBCl LBSe
	LBre LRHS MBBe MBri MRav MTis
	NFla SBre SLon SMrm SPer SSpe
	SUsu WLRN
§ - 'Sonnenschein'	More than 30 suppliers
- 'Starburst' (d)	EFou EMan LRHS MBri SHel SRms
	WHen
- 'Summer Snowball'	CPar EBee EGle EMan EWes LRHS
	MAvo MBri SHel SUsu WCot WFar
- Sunshine	See *L. × superbum* 'Sonnenschein'
- 'Supra'	Last listed 1999
- 'T.E. Killin' (d) ♀	CElw CGle EBee ECGP ECha
	EMan EMar LAst LBuc LRHS
	MAvo MCLN NPSI SAsh WFar
	WCot WPer
- 'White Iceberg'	EBee LRHS
- 'White Knight'	NCut
- 'Wirral Pride'	CBlo CHea EBee EFou ELan
	EMan ENot EOrc GAbr GKir
	GMaP LAst LFis LRHS MBro
	MCAu MCLN MFir MRav MWat
	NFai NFla SPer SRms WBea
	WByw WEas WFar
§ - 'Wirral Supreme' (d) ♀	

'Tizi-n-Test'   See *Rhodanthemum gayanum*
                      'Tizi-n-Test'
§ *vulgare*   CArn CKin ECoo EPar EWFC
                      EWTr GBar LEdu MHer MHew
                      MMal NLan NMir WHen WHer
                      WJek WOak WShi WWye
- 'Avondale'   MCCP
- 'Hullavington' (v) CNat
§ - 'Maikönigin'   GCal NCut WRHF
- 'Maistern'   MBro
- May Queen   See *L. vulgare* 'Maikönigin'
- 'Sunny'   CBre WAlt
- 'Woodpecker's'   Last listed 1998

LEUCOCHRYSUM (Asteraceae)
§ *albicans*   EBee
§ - subsp. *albicans* Last listed 1997
  var. *incanum*

LEUCOCORYNE (Alliaceae)
'Andes'   Last listed 1997
'Caravelle'   Last listed 1997
coquimbensis   Last listed 1998
ixioides   ETub LBow WCot
* - *alba*   Last listed 1998
odorata   Last listed 1999
purpurea   LBow WCot

LEUCOGENES (Asteraceae)
acklandii   NHar NSla
grandiceps   EPot GCrs GNor GTou ITim NHar
                      NSla SIng WAbe
leontopodium   EPot GNor GTou ITim NHar
                      NMen NSla WAbe
tarabaoa   Last listed 1999

LEUCOJUM ✿ (Amaryllidaceae)
aestivum   CB&S CBlo CFee LAma LRHS
                      MAvo MBri NChi NEgg NMGW
                      NMen NRog SRms SYvo WAbe
                      WCot WCra WEas WFar WGwy
                      WHil WHoo WShi WWye
- 'Gravetye Giant' ♀ CAvo CBro CHad EBee ECha ELan
                      EMar EPar EPot ERav ETub LAma
                      LFox LGre LRHS MBro MCAu
                      MMal MNrw MRav NFla NRog
                      SIng WAbb WCot WPGP WPnP
                      WShi
autumnale ♀   More than 30 suppliers
- 'Cobb's Variety'   GCal WCot
- var. *oporanthum*   EPot MPEx NRog SIng
- var. *pulchellum*   CBro EPot
nicaeense ♀   CBro CGra CPBP CRDP CStu EBur
                      EPot GCrs LRHS MTho NMen
                      SSpi WCot WIvy
roseum   CBos CStu EBur EPot LAma NSla
tingitanum   Last listed 1998
trichophyllum   CBro ERos
- f. *purpurascens*   EPot
valentinum   CAvo CBro
vernum ♀   CBro EMon EPar ETub GCrs GDra
                      LAma LPio LRHS MBri MMal
                      MNrw MRav NMGW NMen SRms
                      WAbe WBod WCot WFar WHer
                      WHil WPGP WShi
- var. *carpathicum* CLAP ECha EPot LAma MRav
- 'Podpolozje'   NPar
- var. *vagneri*   CLAP ECha EMon LFox WTin

LEUCOPHYLLUM (Scrophulariaceae)
¶ *frutescens*   SOWG

LEUCOPHYTA (Asteraceae)
§ *brownii*   CInt ECou LHil MRav SVen

LEUCOPOGON (Epacridaceae)
ericoides   MBar WPat
§ *fasciculatus*   ECou
§ *fraseri*   ECou GCrs IMGH
parviflorus   See *Cyathodes parviflora*

x LEUCORAOULIA (Asteraceae)
§ hybrid (*Raoulia hectorii* EPot GTou NSla SIng WAbe WLin
  x *Leucogenes*
  grandiceps)
§ *loganii*   CPBP EPot GCrs GNor ITim NRya
                      NWCA WAbe

LEUCOSCEPTRUM (Lamiaceae)
canum   CTrG
stellipilum formosanum EBee WCru
B&SWJ 1804

LEUCOSIDEA (Rosaceae)
sericea   Last listed 1999

LEUCOSPERMUM (Proteaceae)
conocarpodendron   CTrF
cordifolium   Last listed 1997

LEUCOTHOE (Ericaceae)
axillaris 'Royal Red' WLRN
- 'Scarletta'   See *L.* Scarletta = 'Zeblid'
carinella   CB&S LRHS MBri MGos
catesbyi   Last listed 1999
davisiae   SSta
fontanesiana   See *L. walteri*
grayana   Last listed 1999
keiskei   EPfP LRHS
- 'Minor'   SReu
- 'Royal Ruby'   CEnd NHol SEas WDin WWeb
populifolia   See *Agarista populifolia*
¶ 'Red Lips'   MGos
§ Scarletta® = 'Zeblid' More than 30 suppliers
§ *walteri* ♀   LRHS SPer STre WStl WWat
- Lovita™   CEnd GCal LRHS MBri MRav SSta
- 'Nana'   LRHS MAsh
- 'Rainbow'   CB&S CLan CTrG EBee EMil ENot
                     GKir IOrc LNet LRHS MAsh MBar
                     MGos MRav NBee SBrw SLim
                     SPer SRPl SReu SRms SSta WDin
                     WFar WWal WWeb
* - 'Red Pimpernel' Last listed 1997
- 'Rollissonii' ♀   MBar MRav SPla SReu SRms SSta
                     WBod
'Zeblid'   See *L.* Scarletta = 'Zeblid'

LEUZEA (Asteraceae)
§ *centauroides*   CGle EBlw EBrP EBre ECGP ECha
                     EGle ELan EOld GCal LBCl LBSe
                     LBre LGre MBBe MBro NBid
                     NWoo SBre WByw WCot WHoo
                     WCA
conifera   NWCA
- *macrocephala*   WAbe
§ *rhapontica*   EMan

LEVISTICUM (Apiaceae)
officinale   CAgr CArn CSev ELau GBar GMaP
                     GPoy MBar MChe MHer MHew
                     NBid SDix SIde SWat WGwG
                     WHbs WHer WOak WPer WSel
                     WWye

LEWISIA ✿ (Portulacaceae)

'Archangel'	NRya
'Ashwood Carousel Hybrids'	GCrs MAsh
'Ashwood Pearl'	MAsh
'Ben Chace'	MAsh
Birch strain	CB&S ECho ELan
brachycalyx ♀	CGra EWes GTou ITim MAsh MTho NHar NNrd NWCA WLRN
cantelovii	CPBP MAsh
columbiana	GTou MAsh MDHE NHar SIng
- 'Alba'	GCHN GCrs MAsh
- 'Edithiae'	Last listed 1998
- 'Rosea'	CMea GCrs MAsh WGor
- subsp. *rupicola*	GCHN MAsh NNrd NWCA WGor
- subsp. *wallowensis*	CGra CPBP MAsh MDHE NMen WGor
congdonii	MAsh
cotyledon ♀	LRHS MAsh MNrw MOne NNrd NWCA WBrE WPat
- f. *alba*	CPBP EPot GDra GTou LHop MAsh MBro WHoo WPyg
- Ashwood Ruby Group	MAsh NHar
- Ashwood strain	CNic EBrP EBre ESis EWes LBCl LBSe LBee LBre LRHS MAsh MBBe MBri MOne NRya NSla SBre SRms WGor WHoo WPyg
¶ - 'Ballet Royale'	NArg
- Crags hybrids	Last listed 1999
¶ - 'Fransi'	ESis
- var. *beckneri* ♀	GDra MAsh WGor
- - JCA 11031	Last listed 1998
- var. *bowellii*	SRms WGor
- hybrids	CBrm CFee CNic EMNN EPot GDra GTou ITim LHop MBro NHar NMen SCob SIng WAbe WGor WLin WWin
- J&JA 12959	NWCA
- 'John's Special'	GCHN GCrs GDra
- magenta strain	MAsh WGor WPyg
¶ - 'Regenbogen'	ESis
- 'Rose Splendour'	EPar WGor
- 'Sundance'	Last listed 1998
- Sunset Group ♀	EOld GAbr GCHN GDra GKir MBri MHer NHar WPer
- 'White Splendour'	MAsh SIng WGor
'George Henley'	EBrP EBre EPot EWes LBCl LBSe LBre LHop MAsh MBBe NMen NRya SBre SIng SRms WAbe
* 'Holly'	MDHE
hybrids	EDAr WBod
'Joyce Halley'	GCrs
leana	MAsh
'Little Plum'	GCHN SIng
§ *longipetala*	GCHN GCrs GDra GTou MAsh MOne NRya NTow NWCA
- x *cotyledon*	GTou
* *longiscapa*	MAsh
'Margaret Williams'	Last listed 1997
§ *nevadensis*	CMea CNic EPot ERos ESis GCHN GDra GTou ITim MAsh MBri MBro MNrw MTho NMen NNrd NRya NWCA SRms SRot WLin WPer WPyg
- *bernardina*	See *L. nevadensis*
- 'Rosea'	CGra GCrs
oppositifolia	GCrs MAsh NNrd
- J&JA 13450	NWCA
- 'Richeyi'	MAsh
'Phyllellia'	MAsh
'Pinkie'	CPBP EDAr EPot GCrs MAsh MBro MDHE NMen NNrd

pygmaea	CGra ESis EWes GCHN GCrs GTou ITim LRHS MAsh MBri MDCh NBir NHar NMen NNrd NWCA WPer
- subsp. *longipetala*	See *L. longipetala*
- 'Whiskey Peak'	Last listed 1998
Rainbow mixture	WGor
rediviva	CGra EWes GCHN GCrs GTou ITim MAsh NHar NRya NSla NWCA SIng WAbe WLin
- Jolon strain	MAsh WGor
- subsp. *minor*	CGra EPot SIng WAbe
- var. *rediviva*	Last listed 1999
- white	MAsh NWCA
'Regensbergen'	WPer
serrata	MAsh
sierrae	MAsh MBro NMen NNrd
'Trevosia'	MAsh MDHE SIng
triphylla	CInt MAsh NNrd NWCA
tweedyi ♀	CPBP EBrP EBre GCrs GDra GTou LBCl LBSe LBre LHop LRHS MAsh MBBe MOne NHar NWCA SBre SIng WAbe WGor
- 'Alba'	GCrs LRHS MAsh NWCA WGor
- 'Elliott's Variety'	MAsh WGor
- 'Rosea'	GDra LRHS MAsh NWCA SIng WGor

LEYCESTERIA (Caprifoliaceae)

crocothyrsos	CBrm CGre CInt CPle GAri GQui MHer NCut NFla SGar SLon STes SWal WBod WLRN WWat
formosa	More than 30 suppliers

LEYMUS (Poaceae)

§ *arenarius*	More than 30 suppliers
hispidus	See *Elymus hispidus*
mollis	Last listed 1998
¶ 'Niveus'	EHul
§ *racemosus*	MMHG
¶ sp. from Falkland Islands	EPPr

LHOTZKYA See CALYTRIX

LIATRIS (Asteraceae)

aspera	EMan
cylindracea	IIve
elegans	Last listed 1998
* *ixioides*	CB&S
ligulistylis	EMan WMoo
¶ *punctata*	IIve
pycnostachya	CPea EMon MLLN SRms WMoo WPer
¶ *scariosa* 'Gracious'	EWll
- 'Magnifica'	CB&S
- 'September Glory'	Last listed 1999
§ *spicata*	More than 30 suppliers
- 'Alba'	CHor EBee ECha EFou ELan EPfP GGar LAma LAst LBow LPio MBel MNrw NFai SDeJ SLon SPer SPlb WHoo WPer
- *callilepis*	See *L. spicata*
- 'Floristan Violett'	CBlo CBrm CHar EBee EOld EPfP EWTr GAbr GCHN LAst LRHS MBct MHer MTis NPri SCoo SMer SPlb WBar WFar WLRN WMoo WPer
- 'Floristan Weiss'	More than 30 suppliers
- Goblin	See *L. spicata* 'Kobold'
§ - 'Kobold'	CB&S CBlo CHar COlW EBee ECtt ENot EPfP GKir GMac LRHS MBri MRav NGdn NLar SPla SRms

	SSca SSea WCot WHoo WMoo
	WPer
¶ *squarrosa*	IIve

LIBERTIA ✿ (Iridaceae)

'Amazing Grace'	CPne EBee EPPr IBlr SCob SLod
	SMrm
'Ballyrogan Blue'	IBlr
Ballyrogan hybrid	IBlr
* *breunioides*	CPLG IBlr
caerulescens	CAbb CLTr CPou EPPr GBin IBlr
	LPio MHar MWll NBir NLar WCot
	WFar WPGP WPic WSan WWhi
chilensis	See *L. formosa*
elegans	GBuc IBlr WCDu
§ *formosa*	More than 30 suppliers
- brown-stemmed	IBlr
grandiflora	More than 30 suppliers
ixioides	CAvo CElw CGle ECha ECou
	EMan GGar IBlr MFir NSti WLeb
	WPic WPyg WRHF
- 'Tricolor'	IBlr
'Nelson Dwarf'	IBlr
paniculata	IBlr
peregrinans	CAbb CElw CFee EBee EBrP EBre
	ECha EGoo EMan EPla ESis GCal
	IBlr LBCl LBSe LBre LPio LRHS
	MBBe MFir MRav SBre SUsu WAbe
	WHal WPrP WWye
- East Cape form	IBlr
- 'Gold Leaf'	CB&S GOrP IBlr LPio MRav SOkh
	WCot WPic
* *procera*	CFil EBee IBlr WPGP
pulchella	CGle EBrP EBre GBin IBlr LBCl
	LBSe LBre MBBe SBre
- Tasmanian form	Last listed 1997
sessiliflora	CFee EBee IBlr NBir WPic
- RB 94073	EPPr MNrw SMad
Shackleton hybrid	IBlr
sp. from New Zealand	EPla
tricolor	EBee GBuc
* *umbellata*	IBlr WCDu

LIBOCEDRUS (Cupressaceae)

¶ *bidwillii*	CDoC
chilensis	See *Austrocedrus chilensis*
decurrens	See *Calocedrus decurrens*
¶ *plumosa*	CDoC

LIBONIA See JUSTICIA

LICUALA (Arecaceae)

grandis	MBri
¶ *ramsayi*	CBrP
spinosa	LPal

LIGULARIA ✿ (Asteraceae)

alatipes	GBin
altaica	Last listed 1998
amplexicaulis	IBlr
calthifolia	CRow
clivorum	See *L. dentata*
§ *dentata*	CHEx CRow EGar EWTr GKir
	NBro NCut SPla SRms SWat WCru
	WFar
- 'Dark Beauty'	GSki
- 'Desdemona' ♀	More than 30 suppliers
- 'Orange Princess'	EBee NPer WPer
- 'Othello'	CBlo CRow EBee EBlw EGar EGle
	EMan GKir IBlr LAst LRHS MBel
	MBri MCAu MWgw NCut NLar
	SCro SLod SSpe SWat WCot WFar

	WHil WPnP
- 'Ox-eye'	WGer
- 'Rubrifolia'	GDra
- 'Sommergold'	ECha EGar IBlr SPer WFar
fischeri	EBee EGar MCCP MLLN NFor
	WCot
- B&SWJ 1158	WCru
- B&SWJ 2570	WCru
- B&SWJ 606a	Last listed 1999
glabrescens	CRow
§ 'Gregynog Gold' ♀	CBlo CHad CRow EBee ECha
	EGle EOld EWTr GKir GMaP IBlr
	LRHS MBri NBro NDea NOrc
	SChu SCro SMrm SPer WCru
	WElm WPyg
x *hessei*	CRow EBee EBrP EBre EGar GAri
	GKir GMaP LBCl LBSe LBre MBBe
	SBre SWat WFar
hodgsonii	EBrP EBre EGar GKir IBlr LBCl
	LBSe LBre LRHS MBBe MBri
	MNrw SBre WCru WFar WPer
intermedia B&SWJ 4383	WCru
- B&SWJ 606a	WCru
japonica	CRow EBee ECha EGar NLar WFar
- B&SWJ 2883	WCru
macrophylla	CRow MWhi WFar
x *palmatiloba*	CFai CFir EBee EBrP EBre EGar
	EGle EMan EPar GCal GKir IBlr
	LBCl LBSe LBre MBBe MCli MRav
	NDea NOak NSti SBla SBre SCro
	SLod SLon SWat WCot WCra WFar
§ *przewalskii*	More than 30 suppliers
- 'B-M's Lacerated'	Last listed 1999
¶ - *variegated*	EBlw
sachalinensis	GBin GCal WCot
sibirica	Last listed 1999
smithii	See *Senecio smithii*
sp. B&SWJ 2977	WCru
sp. HWJCM 211 from Nepal	WCru
* *speciosa*	ECha EGar
stenocephala	CBlo EBee EGar EMil GKir IBlr
	LFis MSCN NBro NDea SWat
	WCot WFar
- B&SWJ 283	WCru
* 'Sungold'	LRHS NDov WCot
tangutica	See *Sinacalia tangutica*
'The Rocket' ♀	More than 30 suppliers
tsangchanensis	Last listed 1999
tussilaginea	See *Farfugium japonicum*
veitchiana	CRow EBee EGar EMan EOas EPfP
	GCal GDra GKir IBlr LRHS MBri
	MSte NDea NSti SWat WCot WCru
	WFar
'Weihenstephan'	GKir IBlr LRHS MBri WGer
wilsoniana	CRow EBee EBrP EBre ECtt EGar
	LBCl LBSe LBre LRHS MBBe MCli
	MLLN MRav NCut SBre SWat
	WFar
'Zepter'	EGar GBuc GCal LRHS MBri MTed
	WCot

LIGUSTICUM (Apiaceae)

jeholense	EBee
lucidum	CDul CMCN EHol EPfP IIve MSal
	WCwm WGer
porteri	MSal
scoticum	EOHP GBar GPoy IIve ILis MSal

LIGUSTRUM ✿ (Oleaceae)

chenaultii	See *L. compactum*
§ *compactum*	CFai EPla WWat
§ *delavayanum*	CB&S EMon ERom GAri LHyr

chalcedonicum (IX) ♀	CLAP
'Charisma' (Ia)	MBri
'Chinook' (Ia)	NRog
Citronella Group (Ic)	CAvo ETub LAma LRHS NRog
'Colombo' (Ia)	Last listed 1999
columbianum (IX)	Last listed 1998
¶ 'Con Amore' (VIIb)	SCoo
concolor var.	Last listed 1997
partheneion (IX)	
'Concorde' (Ia)	SDeJ
'Connecticut King' (Ia)	ETub LAma LRHS NBrk NRog
	SDeJ
'Corina' (Ia)	MBNS MBri NOak SDeJ SGar
	WGor
'Corsage' (Ib)	NRog
'Côte d'Azur' (Ia)	CBro CHar EBrP EBre EPot ETub
	LAma LBCl LBSe LBre MBBe SBre
	SDeJ WGor
'Crimson Pixie' (Ia)	CBro
x *dalhansonii* (IX)	CLAP
§ – 'Marhan' (II) ♀	Last listed 1999
'Dame Blanche' (VII)	LAma
'Dandy' (Ia)	WWeb
'Darling' (VII)	Last listed 1998
§ *dauricum*	CPou GCrs
davidii (IX) ♀	LAma
§ – var. *willmottiae* (IX)	GIBF MWll WViv
'Denia' (Ib)	LRHS
'Destiny' (Ia)	NRog
'Devon Early Gems'	CLAP
'Dominique' (VII)	NRog
duchartrei	CBro CNic GCrs LAma SMac SSpi
	WAbe
§ 'Ed' (VII)	LAma LRHS
'Electric' (Ia)	LAma
'Elfin Sun'	LAma LRHS
'Ellen Willmott' (II)	CLAP
'Elvin's Son'	Last listed 1998
'Elysee'	Last listed 1998
'Enchantment' (Ia) ♀	CSut LAma MBNS MBri NRog
	SDeJ WLRN
'Eros'	CLAP
'Esperanto'	Last listed 1998
euxanthum ACE	Last listed 1997
1268 (IX)	
– KGB 492 (IX)	Last listed 1997
Everest Group (VIId)	Last listed 1999
'Exception' (Ib/d)	LAma
¶ *fargesii* (IX)	LAma
'Fata Morgana' (Ia)	ETub LRHS
'Festival' (Ia)	LAma
'Fire King' (Ib)	CBro CLAP LAma NBir NRog SDeJ
¶ 'Flower Carpet Sunshine'	SCoo
formosanum (IX)	EBrP EBre EPPr LBCl LBSe LBre
	MBBe MDCh NBro SBre SEND
	STes WCot WSan WViv
– B&SWJ 1589 (IX)	WCru
– var. *formosanum* (IX)	Last listed 1998
– var. *pricei* (IX) ♀	CGle CInt CSWP CSam EBee ELan
	ESis ITim LBee LHop LRHS LSyl
	MBri MHer MNrw MTho NChi
	NMen NNrd NWCA NWoo SRot
	WAbe WHer WPer WPyg
– 'Snow Queen' (IX)	CMil
– 'White Swan' (IX)	GCrs
'Fresco' (VII)	Last listed 1998
'Friendship' (VII)	Last listed 1998
'Furore' (VIIc)	Last listed 1998
'Garden Party' (VII)	ETub LRHS
'Geisha' (VII)	Last listed 1998
'Golden Melody' (Ia)	Last listed 1999
§ Golden® Pixie = 'Ceb	Last listed 1998

Golden' (Ia)	
Golden Splendor	ETub LAma MBNS NRog SWat
Group (VIa)	
'Golden Sunrise' (Ia)	Last listed 1997
'Gran Cru' (Ia)	EBrP EBre LBCl LBSe LBre MBBe
	SBre
'Gran Paradiso' (Ia)	LAma
'Grand Cru'	LAma NOak SDeJ
grayi (IX)	GCrs NSla SSpi
'Green Dragon' (VIa) ♀	Last listed 1995
Green Magic Group (VIa)	CHar
'Hannah North' (Ic)	Last listed 1997
hansonii (IX) ♀	IBlr LAma NRog
Harlequin Group (Ic)	SDeJ
henryi (IX) ♀	CAvo CHar CLAP CSWP EBee
	EPot LAma LBow LRHS MLLN
	MWll NRog SDeJ WCot
'Hit Parade' (VII)	LAma
humboldtii (IX)	WWst
Imperial Gold Group (VIIc)	Last listed 1997
Imperial Silver Group (VIIc)	LAma
japonicum (IX)	EFEx
– 'Albomarginatum' (IX)	Last listed 1999
'Jetfire' (Ia)	SDeJ
'John Dix' (Ib)	Last listed 1999
'Journey's End' (VIId)	CHar LAma LBre ETub LAma LBCl
	LBSe LBre LRHS MBBe MBNS
	MLLN NRog SBre SDeJ
§ 'Joy' (VIIb)	CHar LAma LRHS
'Karen North' (Ic) ♀	Last listed 1997
§ *kelleyanum* (IX)	CLAP GGGa
kelloggii (IX)	Last listed 1998
'King Pete' (Ib)	NOak SDeJ
'Kiss Proof' (VIIb)	LRHS
'Kiwi Fanfare'	CBrm
'Kyoto' (VIId)	LAma
'Lady Alice' (VI)	CLAP
'Lady Ann' (VIb)	SDeJ
'Ladykiller' (Ia)	NRog
§ *lancifolium* (IX)	CLTr EMFP LAma LBow SDeJ
	WCot
– B&SWJ 539 (IX)	WCru
– 'Flore Pleno' (IX/d)	CLAP CMil CSWP CSam EBrP
	EBre EMFP EMon GCal GSki IBlr
	LBCl LBSe LBre LRHS MBBe NSti
	SBre WCot WCru WFar
– Forrest's form (IX)	CLAP IBlr
– var. *fortunei* (IX)	Last listed 1997
§ – var. *splendens* (IX)	CBro EBee EBot ETub LAma
	LBow MLLN SDeJ WCot
lankongense (IX)	GCrs
– ACE 2210 (IX)	EPot
'Le Rêve'	See *L.* 'Joy'
leichtlinii 'Iwashimiza' (IX)	WCot
'Lemon Pixie' [PBR] (Ia)	GKir LAma LRHS
leucanthum (IX)	LAma WCru
¶ – var. *centifolium* (IX)	WWst
'Liberation' (I)	NBir
'Limelight' (VIa) ♀	Last listed 1999
'Little Kiss' (Ia/d)	ETub
'Little Snow White' (V)	Last listed 1998
'Lollypop' (Ia)	ETub LRHS MNrw SCoo
longiflorum (IX) ♀	CAvo EBee LAma LRHS NRog
	SCoo WCot
– 'Casa Rosa'	See *L.* 'Casa Rosa'
– 'Gelria' (IX)	SDeJ
§ – 'White American' (IX)	CBro CSWP ETub LRHS MBri
lophophorum (IX)	GCrs LAma WCru
– ACE 1767 (IX)	EPot
'Lovely Girl' (VIIb)	ETub
'Luxor' (Ib)	CSut LRHS NBir
mackliniae (IX) ♀	CLAP CNic GBuc GCrs GGGa

maculatum var. **davuricum**	GTou IBlr NHar SBla SSpi WAbe See *L. dauricum*
- Japanese double (IX)	EMon
- *monticola* (IX)	Last listed 1999
'Marco Polo' (Ia)	LAma LRHS SCoo
'Marhan'	See *L.* x *dalhansonii* 'Marhan'
'Marie North' (Ic)	CLAP
martagon (IX)	CArn CAvo CBro CGdn CMea CSWP EBee EBot ECha EFou ETub LAma LBow LRHS NBir NPSI NRog SDeJ WAbe WCot WGwy WShi WWat
- var. *album* (IX) ♀	CAvo CBro CLAP CMea CNic CPou CSWP EBee EBot ECGP EFou ELan ETub LAma LBow LPio LRHS MRav MTho MWll NBir SAga SDeJ WAbe WGwy WShi
- var. *cattaniae* (IX) ♀	Last listed 1998
- 'Inshriach' (IX)	WCot
- 'Netherhall Pink' (IX/d)	Last listed 1998
- 'Netherhall White' (IX/d)	Last listed 1998
- 'Plenum' (IX/d)	EMon
'Mecca'	Last listed 1998
'Medaillon' (Ia)	LAma NRog
medeoloides (IX)	EFEx GCrs GGGa SSpi
michiganense (IX)	CSWP GCrs
'Milano' (Ia)	Last listed 1998
'Miss America'	GKir LRHS
'Miss Burma' (VII)	LRHS
'Miss Rio' (VII)	LRHS SCoo
'Mona Lisa' (VIIb/d)	ETub LAma LRHS MBri
§ *monadelphum* (IX) ♀	CBro CCuc CLAP ETub GKir LAma LBow NRog SSpi
'Mont Blanc' (Ia)	LAma MLLN NBir SDeJ
'Monte Negro' (Ia)	ETub
'Monte Rosa' (Ic)	SDeJ
'Montreux' (Ia)	CSut LAma
'Moonflower' (Ia)	Last listed 1998
'Moulin Rouge' (Ib)	NRog
'Mr Ed'	See *L.* 'Ed'
'Mr Ruud'	See *L.* 'Ruud'
'Mrs R.O. Backhouse' (II) ♀	Last listed 1996
'Muscadet' PBR (VII)	CSut LRHS
§ *nanum* (IX)	GCrs GGGa LAma NRog WCru
- CH&M (IX)	Last listed 1997
- var. *flavidum* (IX)	EPot GCrs WCru
- from Bhutan (IX)	WCru
- Kirkpatrick 242 (IX)	GCrs
- 'Len's Lilac' (IX)	WCru
- McBeath's form (IX)	WCru
neilgherrense (IX)	CFil WPGP
nepalense (IX)	CBro CLAP CMil CSWP EBee EPot GCrs GKir LAma LRHS SBla SDeJ WCot WCru
- B&SWJ 2985	WCru
'New Yellow'	MBri
'Nippon' (VIId)	Last listed 1998
nobilissimum (IX)	EFEx
'Olivia' (Ia)	ETub LAma LRHS MLLN SDeJ
Olympic Group (VIa)	LAma SDeJ
'Omega' (VII)	LAma SDeJ
§ 'Orange Aristo' (Ia)	MBri
'Orange Delight'	WWeb
'Orange Pixie' (Ia)	EBrP EBre GKir LAma LBCl LBSe LBre LRHS MBBe MBri NMoo SBre SCoo WGor
'Orange Triumph' (Ia)	EPot LAma
'Orchid Beauty' (Ia)	MBri
'Orestes' (Ib)	CLAP
oxypetalum (IX)	GCrs GGGa

- var. *insigne* (IX)	CLAP GDra GGGa GIBF GNor LAma NHar NSla NTow SSpi WAbe WCru
'Pandora' PBR (Ia)	Last listed 1998
¶ *papilliferum*	LAma
pardalinum (IX)	CAvo CCuc CGle CMea ELan LRHS NSla WWhi
- var. *giganteum* (IX) ♀	CLAP MNrw
parryi (IX)	SSpi
parvum (IX)	Last listed 1997
'Peach Pixie' (Ia)	LAma NBir SCoo
'Peachblush' (Ia)	Last listed 1998
'Peggy North' (Ic)	CLAP
'Perugia' (VIId)	LAma
philadelphicum (IX)	Last listed 1998
philippinense (IX)	CBrm EGar NSla NTow
- B&SWJ 4000 (IX)	WCru
Pink Perfection Group (VIa) ♀	CAvo CBro CHar EBrP EBre LAma LBCl LBSe LBre MBBe MBNS NRog SBre SWat
'Pink Pixie' PBR (Ia)	Last listed 1999
I 'Pink Regale'	Last listed 1999
'Pink Sunburst' (VId)	SDeJ
'Pink Tiger' (Ib)	CBro CLAP ETub LRHS WGor
'Pirate' (Ia)	Last listed 1999
pitkinense (IX)	EMon SOkd
'Polka'	WWeb
pomponium (IX)	CLAP
¶ *primulinum* (IX)	WWst
§ *pumilum* (IX) ♀	CAvo CBro CLAP EPot LAma LRHS MLLN MTho NBir SDeJ WHil WVlv
pyrenaicum (IX) ♀	CAvo CBro CLAP CMea ELan LPio MWll WByw WCot WGwy WPGP WRha WShi WViv
§ - subsp. *carniolicum*	NSla
§ - - var. *albanicum* (IX)	SSpi
- subsp. *pyrenaicum* var. *rubrum* (IX)	Last listed 1998
'Red Carpet' (Ia)	LRHS MBri NBir WGor
Red Jewels Group (Ic)	LAma
Red Knight	See *L.* 'Roter Cardinal'
'Red Lion' (Ia)	SDeJ
'Red Night' (I)	EGoo LRHS NRog
¶ 'Red Tiger' (Ib)	CLAP
regale (IX) ♀	CArn CAvo CBro CHar CSam CSut EBee EBrP EBre ETub LAma LBCl LBSe LBow LBre LEdu LRHS MBBe MCLN MLLN NEgg NRog SBre SDeJ WCot WEas WFar WPyg WWat
- 'Album' (IX)	CAvo CSWP EBee EBrP EBre LAma LBCl LBSe LBow LBre LRHS MBBe NRog SBre SDeJ
§ - 'Royal Gold' (IX)	MBNS SDeJ
'Rodeo' (VIII)	Last listed 1999
'Roma' (Ia)	LAma LPio LRHS MBNS NBir
'Rosefire' (Ia)	NOak
'Rosemary North' (I) ♀	CLAP
'Rosita' (Ia)	MBri NRog
¶ *rosthornii*	WCru
'Royal Gold'	See *L. regale* 'Royal Gold'
'Royal Queen' (VIIb)	CSut
rubellum (IX)	EFEx
§ 'Ruud' (VII)	CBro LAma LRHS
'Sam' (VII)	LAma SCoo WGor
'Sancerre' (Ia)	Last listed 1998
'Sans Pareil' (Ia)	SDeJ
'Sans Souci' (VIId)	MBri
sargentiae	CLAP CPou
¶ *sempervivoideum* (IX)	EPot LAma
'Sensation'	Last listed 1998

shastense	See *L. kelleyanum*
'Shocking Pink'	Last listed 1999
'Showbiz' (VIII)	LAma
'Silly Girl' (Ia)	Last listed 1998
'Simoen' (Ia)	SDeJ
¶ 'Sinai' (Ia)	CSut
'Snow Princess'	LAma
'Snow Trumpet' (V)	CSam WLRN
souliei ACE 1192 (IX)	Last listed 1997
sp. from China (IX)	WCru
speciosum (IX) ♀	WCot
- var. *album* (IX)	CAvo CBro EBot EPot LAma LPio LRHS NBir SDeJ
¶ - 'Coral Queen' (IX)	CSut
¶ - var. *gloriosoides* (IX)	LAma
- 'Grand Commander' (IX)	SDeJ
- 'Ida Uchida' (IX)	LRHS
- var. *roseum* (IX)	SDeJ
- var. *rubrum* (IX)	CAvo CBro CHar CLAP EBot EPot ETub LAma LBow LRHS MLLN NBir NRog SDeJ
§ - 'Uchida' (IX)	SDeJ
'Sphinx' (Ia/d)	Last listed 1999
'Star Gazer' (VIIc)	CBro CSut EBrP EBre ECot LAma LBCl LBSe LBre LRHS LRot MBBe MBNS NRog SBre SCoo SDeJ WGor
* 'Sterling Silver'	NOak
'Sterling Star' (Ia)	CLAP CSut LAma NRog SDeJ
stewartianum (IX)	LAma
¶ *sulphureum*	LAma
'Sun Ray' (Ia)	CBro LRHS NRog
superbum (IX) ♀	LAma NRog
'Sweet Kiss' (Ia)	Last listed 1999
szovitsianum	See *L. monadelphum*
taliense (IX)	LAma WCru
'Tamara' (Ib)	MBNS MBri NRog
tenuifolium	See *L. pumilum*
x *testaceum* (IX) ♀	LAma NRog SDeJ
¶ 'Theseus' (Ic)	CLAP
tigrinum	See *L. lancifolium*
'Trance' (VIIb)	MBri
'Uchida Kanoka'	See *L. speciosum* 'Uchida'
vollmeri (IX)	WAbe
wallichianum	CPou EBee LAma NRog SDeJ
'Walter Bentley' (Ic)	Last listed 1999
¶ *wardii* (IX)	WWst
washingtonianum (IX)	Last listed 1998
- var. *purpurascens* (IX)	Last listed 1998
'White American'	See *L. longiflorum* 'White American'
'White Happiness' (Ia)	LAma
'White Henryi' (VId)	EFEx
'White Journey's End' (VIId)	Last listed 1998
'White Kiss' (Ia/d)	LAma LRHS
'White Mountain' (VIIc)	SDeJ
¶ 'White Paradise' (V)	SCoo
¶ 'White Tiger' (Ib)	CLAP
wigginsii (IX)	GCrs GGGa
willmottiae	See *L. davidii* var. *willmottiae*
Yellow Blaze Group (Ia)	LAma NRog
¶ 'Yellow Bunting' (I)	WWst
'Zephyr' (Ia)	Last listed 1998

LIMNANTHES (Limnanthaceae)

douglasii ♀	CFee CMGP CTrG CTri ELan IBlr NBus SIng WEas WElm WHer WWpP

LIMNOPHILA (Scrophulariaceae)

aromatica	EOHP MSal

LIMONIUM (Plumbaginaceae)

bellidifolium	ECha EDAr IMGH MBro MGed MHar NTow SBla SIng WEas WHoo WPer
cosyrense	CInt CMea MHer NMen SRms WPer WWin
aff. *delicatulum*	Last listed 1999
dumosum	See *Goniolimon tataricum* var. *angustifolium*
globulariifolium	See *L. ramosissimum*
gmelinii	SPlb WPer
- 'Perestrojka'	Last listed 1998
gougetianum	NTow
latifolium	See *L. platyphyllum*
* *maritimum*	CSpe
minutum	CNic WTin
otolepis	CLTr
paradoxum	Last listed 1999
peregrinum	CSpe EBee
perezii	CTrF EDAr WPer
§ *platyphyllum*	CGle COIW EBee EWTr LFis LRHS MCAu MHer MNrw MWat MWgw NArg NMir SCob SPer SPla SRCN SRms WBrE WCot WEas WGwG WHoo WPer WWal WWin
- 'Robert Butler'	EMan GCal GKir LBuc LRHS MRav NCat
- 'True Blue'	Last listed 1997
- 'Violetta'	CTri EBrP EBre ECGN ECGP ECha ELan EMan GKir LBCl LBSe LBre LRHS MBBe MBri MMHG MRav NLar SBre SPer WHoo
purpuratum	CSpe
§ *ramosissimum*	EBee
rumicifolium	Last listed 1997
speciosum 'Blue Diamond'	See *Goniolimon incanum* 'Blue Diamond'
tataricum	See *Goniolimon tataricum*
tomentellum	Last listed 1998
vulgare	EEls WHer

LINANTHASTRUM See LINANTHUS

LINANTHUS (Polemoniaceae)

nuttallii	Last listed 1997

LINARIA (Scrophulariaceae)

aeruginea	EBee
- subsp. *nevadensis*	EBee
alpina	CMea CSpe GTou LFis LPVe LRHS MTho NWCA SRms WPer
- 'Purpurea'	NMGW
- 'Rosea'	NMGW
'Anstey'	CElw EMan
anticaria	Last listed 1999
- 'Antique Silver'	EBee ECha EMan EWTr GBuc MBro WHoo WPGP
¶ 'Blue Lace'	NPri
cymbalaria	See *Cymbalaria muralis*
§ *dalmatica*	CGle EBee ECha ELan MFir MHar MInt NBid NBro NChi NSti SChu SOkh WBor WCot WKif WOut WPer
x *dominii* 'Carnforth'	CGle EBee EMar MBrN NBro NSti WBry WMaN
- 'Yuppie Surprise'	CHid EBee EMan EMon LAst LPio NBir NGdn SCob SPer WCra WLRN WPGP WSpi
genistifolia	MGed
- subsp. *dalmatica*	See *L. dalmatica*
'Globosa Alba'	See *Cymbalaria muralis* 'Globosa Alba'

hepaticifolia	See *Cymbalaria hepaticifolia*
* *lobata alba*	SPlb
'Natalie'	SAga
nevadensis	Last listed 1998
- 'Gemstones'	EWll LRHS
origanifolia	See *Chaenorhinum origanifolium*
pallida	See *Cymbalaria pallida*
§ *peloponnesiaca*	EBee
pilosa	See *Cymbalaria pilosa*
purpurea	CFri CGle CKin COlW EBee EFou ELan ERav EWFC EWTr MCAu MChe MFir NBro NCat NFai NFla NFor NPer SRms WCra WHen WOve WPer WWye
- 'Alba'	See *L. purpurea* 'Springside White'
- Anstey's form	CPou
- 'Canon Went'	More than 30 suppliers
- 'Radcliffe Innocence'	See *L. purpurea* 'Springside White'
§ - 'Springside White'	CElw CGle EBee ECha EMan ERav EWTr GBuc LGre MAvo MSte NBid SSvw WHer WLRN WMaN WPer WRha
- 'Thurgarton Beauty'	WCot
- 'Vainglorious'	CNat
- 'Winifrid's Delight'	CBlo CHea CMGP EBee ECGP EMan EMar EPfP LAst LRHS MMil MRav NBrk SPer SUsu WCot WLRN
repens	CKin EWFC MNrw WCot WHbs WHer
sibthorpiana	See *L. peloponnesiaca*
'Sue'	EBee EMan
supina	WWpP
'Tony Aldis'	CSpe WKif
triornithophora	CElw CFir CGle CPea CSpe EBee ECha GBin GBuc MBel MFir MSCN SRCN WBea WCot WFar WOve WRha WWye
- pink	CBot CGle CSpe EMan WPer
- purple	ELan STes WBea
tristis var. *lurida* 'Toubkal'	SBla
vulgaris	CArn CFri CKin ELau EWFC MChe MGas MMal NMir WHer WJek WPer
¶ - 'Peloria'	CNat CPBP EMon WAlt WCot

LINDELOFIA (Boraginaceae)

§ *anchusoides* (Lindl.) Lehm.	GBri GMac NBid
§ - hort.	See *L. longiflora*
§ *longiflora*	CFir CWit EBee ECGN EMan GBin GBuc GCal GDea LRHS MLLN MRav MTed WPGP WPer
- 'Alba'	Last listed 1999

LINDERA (Lauraceae)

aggregata	Last listed 1998
angustifolia	CFil
benzoin	CFil CMCN EPfP WPGP WWoo
erythrocarpa	CFil CMCN EPfP WPGP
megaphylla	Last listed 1999
obtusiloba ♀	CFil CMCN EPfP LRHS SSpi SSta WNor WPGP WWoo
praecox	CFil WPGP
praetermissa	CFil EPfP WPGP
sericea	CFil
¶ *strychnifolia*	EPfP
triloba	CFil WPGP
umbellata	CFil

LINDERNIA (Scrophulariaceae)

¶ *grandiflora* blue	ECou
¶ - pink	ECou

LINNAEA (Caprifoliaceae)

borealis	GAri GDra GKir ILis IMGH MHar WAbe
- var. *americana*	NHar NMen NWCA

LINUM ✿ (Linaceae)

alpinum subsp. *julicum*	Last listed 1998
altaicum	NChi
arboreum ♀	CLon MBro NHol NWCA SBla SIng SMrm WAbe WKif WPat WWat
aretioides	Last listed 1997
austriacum	Last listed 1999
bienne	CKin
bulgaricum	See *L. tauricum*
campanulatum	Last listed 1998
capitatum	CPBP EBee NSla
* *columbianum*	Last listed 1998
dolomiticum	Last listed 1998
flavum	CGle CTri EPfP GTou SHFr WHoo
- 'Compactum'	LHop MBro MHar MHer MNrw NWCA SBla SMer SMrm SRCN SRms WCot WWin
'Gemmell's Hybrid' ♀	CLyd CMea EPot LRHS MBro NBir NHar NHol NMen NWCA SBla SIng WAbe WLin WPat
kingii var. *sedoides*	Last listed 1998
leonii	EBee LRHS WKif
marginale	Last listed 1998
monogynum	EBee ECou EPPr NMen NTow NWCA WCot WPGP
§ - var. *diffusum*	ECou
- dwarf	GTou NWCA
- 'Nelson'	See *L. monogynum* var. *diffusum*
narbonense	CLon CSpe EMan LBee LGre LGro LRHS MBri MBro NFai NOak SMrm SRms WCra WHoo WKif WPyg
- 'Heavenly Blue' ♀	SUsu SVal WEas WHen
§ *perenne*	CArn ECha EFer ELan EOld EWFC GCal GKir GMaP LRHS MBri MCAu MChe MHer MWgw NFor NMir SIde SMad SPer SRCN SRms STes WHer WPer WWin WWye
- album	CGle ECha ELan EMan EPfP MCAu SPer SRms WHen WPer WRus
- subsp. *alpinum*	WPer
- - 'Alice Blue'	CPBP NHar NMen SBla WLin WWin
- subsp. *anglicum*	Last listed 1997
§ - 'Blau Saphir'	CFri CSam EGar GAbr LRHS MBct NOrc SMrm SRms WHen
- Blue Sapphire	See *L. perenne* 'Blau Saphir'
- 'Diamant'	CBod LPVe LRHS NCiC NPri
- subsp. *extra-axillare*	CLyd
- subsp. *lewisii*	EBee NBir NTow SMrm
- 'White Diamond'	WElm WHen
rubrum	CSpe MChe
sibiricum	See *L. perenne*
suffruticosum	CPBP
- subsp. *salsoloides* 'Nanum'	NHar NWCA SBla SIng WPat
- - 'Prostratum'	GBuc
§ *tauricum*	EBee
tenuifolium	Last listed 1998

* *tweedyi*   NBir
  viscosum   Last listed 1998

LIPARIS (Orchidaceae)
  coelogynoides   ECou
  cordifolia   EFEx
  fujisanensis   EFEx
  krameri var. *krameri* EFEx
  kumokiri   EFEx
  makinoana   EFEx
  nigra   EFEx
  sootenzanensis   EFEx

LIPPIA (Verbenaceae)
  alba   MSal
  canescens   See *Phyla canescens*
  chamaedrifolia   See *Verbena peruviana*
  citriodora   See *Aloysia triphylla*
  dulcis   CArn EOHP MSal
  graveolens   EOHP
  nodiflora   See *Phyla nodiflora*
  repens   See *Phyla nodiflora*
  scaberrima   EOHP

LIQUIDAMBAR ✿ (Hamamelidaceae)
  acalycina   LPan SSta WNor WPat
¶ 'Elstead Mill'   LPan
  formosana   CEnd CGre CLnd CMCN CPle
                           CTho EBee ELan EPfP GChr LPan
                           MAsh MBlu SFur SMad SPer SSta
                           WNor WPGP WWat
  - Monticola Group   EPfP SSta WPGP
  orientalis   CLnd CMCN CPMA EPfP LPan
                           SBir SSta
  styraciflua   More than 30 suppliers
  - 'Andrew Hewson'   CLnd CPMA LRHS MAsh SBir
                           SSta
  - 'Anja'   SBir SSta
  - 'Anneke'   LRHS SBir SSta
* - 'Argentea'   CLnd
  - 'Aurea'   CDul CLnd COtt CTho IOrc LNet
                           SMad SSta WPat
  - 'Aurea Variegata'   CDoC CPMA SBir
  - 'Aurora'   CPMA SLim
  - 'Burgundy'   CDul CLnd CPMA CTho MAsh
                           SBir SSta WPat WWes
¶ - 'Festeri'   CEnd SBir SSta
  - 'Festival'   SSta
  - 'Globe'   CPMA
  - 'Golden Treasure' (v) CPMA LNet LRHS SMad SSpi
                           WPat
  - 'Gumball'   CLnd CPMA EPfP SMad SSta
                           WPat
¶ - 'Jennifer Carol'   CPMA
  - 'Kia'   CEnd CPMA
¶ - 'Kirsten'   SSta
  - 'Lane Roberts' ♀   CDoC CDul CLnd CMCN CTho
                           EBee EPfP GKir IOrc LNet LPan
                           LRHS MAsh MBlu MBri SBir
                           SLim SMad SReu SSta WDin
                           WPat WPyg
  - 'Manon' (v)   CDoC CEnd CPMA SLim
  - 'Moonbeam' (v)   CDul CEnd CPMA CTho MAsh
                           SBir SLim SSta WPat
  - 'Naree'   CPMA
  - 'Palo Alto'   CPMA MAsh SSta WPat
  - 'Parasol'   CEnd CPMA SBir SMad SSta
  - 'Pendula'   CPMA LNet LRHS SBir SMad SSta
                           WBod WWes
¶ - 'Penwood'   SSta
  - 'Rotundiloba' (v)   CPMA SSta
  - 'Silver King' (v)   CDul CPMA EBee EPfP IMGH

                           LRHS SLim SPer SSta
  - 'Stared'   CLnd CPMA
¶ - 'Stella'   CDoC
  - 'Thea'   LNet LRHS SBir SSta
  - 'Variegata'   CB&S CBot CPMA ELan EPfP
                           LNet LPan LRHS MAsh MGos
                           NHol SLim SPer SSpi SSta WDin
                           WPat
  - 'Worplesdon' ♀   More than 30 suppliers

LIRIODENDRON ✿ (Magnoliaceae)
  chinense   CAbP CMCN EPfP MBlu WPGP
                           WWat
  tulipifera ♀   More than 30 suppliers
  - 'Ardis'   CMCN SSpi
  - 'Arnold'   CMCN
  - 'Aureomarginatum' ♀   More than 30 suppliers
  - 'Aureum'   CMCN
  - 'Crispum'   CMCN
  - 'Fastigiatum' ♀   CB&S CDoC CDul CMCN COtt
                           CTho EBee ELan ENot EPfP IMGH
                           LPan LRHS MAsh MBlu MBri SPer
                           WOrn
  - 'Glen Gold'   CEnd CMCN EBee MBlu SMad
  - 'Integrifolium'   CDul
  - 'Mediopictum'   CB&S CMCN CTho ELan LBuc
                           LNet MBlu

LIRIOPE ✿ (Convallariaceae)
  'Big Blue'   See *L. muscari* 'Big Blue'
§ *exiliflora*   CEnd EBee EBrP EBre EMan EPPr
                           EPar GCal LBCl LBSe LBre LRHS
                           MBBe NArg NLar SApp SBre
                           WRus
  - 'Ariaka-janshige' (v) CRDP EMan LHop SWat
  - 'Silvery Sunproof'   Last listed 1997
  - 'Silvery Sunproof'   See *L. spicata* 'Gin-ryu' , *L.*
    misapplied   *muscari* 'Variegata'
§ *gigantea*   LRHS SWat WWal
  graminifolia hort.   See *L. muscari*
  hyacinthifolia   See *Reineckea carnea*
¶ *kansuensis*   ERos
  koreana   GCal
  'Majestic'   ENot
§ *muscari* ♀   More than 30 suppliers
  - 'Alba'   See *L. muscari* 'Monroe White'
  - 'Aztec Gold'   WWal
  - B&SWJ 561   WCru
§ - 'Big Blue'   EBee EMan ENot EPfP EWll LRHS
                           MRav NArg NFla SApp SCob
                           WCFE WMoo
  - 'Christmas Tree'   WWal
  - 'Evergreen Giant'   See *L. gigantea*
  - 'Gold-banded'   CHea EMan EPfP GCal IOrc LRHS
                           NRib SCob SWat WFar WGwG
                           WRus WViv WWal
  - 'Ingwersen'   GBin NCut
  - 'John Burch' (v)   EBee EMan SUsu WPer
  - 'Lilac Beauty'   Last listed 1999
  - 'Majestic' misapplied See *L. exiliflora*
  - 'Mini Mondo'   WGwG WWal
§ - 'Monroe White'   More than 30 suppliers
  - 'Paul Aden'   CFil EPfP WPGP
  - 'Royal Purple'   EBee ENot NOrc WGwG WPer
                           WWal
  - 'Silver Ribbon'   EMan EPfP LHil NEgg SEas
                           WPrP
  - 'Silvery Midget' (v)   SUsu WMoo WWal
  - 'Superba'   Last listed 1997
§ - 'Variegata'   CAbb CFir CMil CWSG EBee ECot
                           ELan EMan EPPr EPar EPla ERav
                           EWes IOrc LAst LRHS MTho NArg

	NBir NSti SCob SMad SPer SPla SRms WPGP WRus
* - 'Variegated Alba'	CFir
- variegated white bloom	SAga
- 'Webster Wideleaf'	WPer
'New Wonder'	Last listed 1999
platyphylla	See *L. muscari*
'Samantha'	ECha LRHS
§ *spicata*	CBro CHor LPio NFai NOrc SSpi SWat WCot WHoo
- 'Alba'	CRow EPPr GCal MRav MTho SUsu WTin WWin
§ - 'Gin-ryu' (v)	CAvo CFir EPla EWes LEdu LHop LPio LRHS MBel MRav MSte SCob WCot WPGP WWal
- 'Silver Dragon'	See *L. spicata* 'Gin-ryu'

LISTERA (Orchidaceae)
ovata	WHer

LITHOCARPUS ✿ (Fagaceae)
densiflorus	CAgr CMCN
edulis	CHEx SArc
§ *glaber*	Last listed 1998
pachyphyllus	CB&S

LITHODORA (Boraginaceae)
* *buglossoides*	WFar
§ *diffusa*	MWat
- 'Alba'	EMil EPot EWTr GAri GKir IOrc LBee LRHS MBri MGos NHar SPer WPat
- 'Cambridge Blue'	EWTr LRHS NHol SAga SLdr SMer SPer
- 'Compacta'	CLyd EGle EPot EWes WCot
- 'Grace Farwell'	Last listed 1997
- 'Grace Ward' ♀	CGle EWes MBro MGos NHar NHol SBod SIng WAbe WPat
- 'Heavenly Blue' ♀	More than 30 suppliers
- 'Inverleith'	ELan EWes WFar
¶ - 'Pete's Favourite'	WAbe
- 'Picos'	CLyd EDAr EGle EPot GCrs GTou NHol NMen WAbe WPat
- 'Star'PBR	CLyd GKir LRHS MAsh SBod SCoo SIng SPer WBod
graminifolia	See *Moltkia suffruticosa*
hispidula	NMen SAga
x *intermedia*	See *Moltkia* x *intermedia*
§ *oleifolia* ♀	CLyd CMea EPot MBro MWat NBir NHol NMen NSla NTow SBla WPat
rosmarinifolia	CSpe GKir LRHS
zahnii	CMHG NMen NTow SSpi WLin WPat

LITHOPHRAGMA (Saxifragaceae)
parviflorum	CMea GDra MNrw MSte MTho NBir NMen NRya NWCA SSpi WCru

LITHOSPERMUM (Boraginaceae)
diffusum	See *Lithodora diffusa*
doerfleri	See *Moltkia doerfleri*
erythrorhizon	MSal WHer
officinale	ELau EWFC GBar GPoy MSal WHer
oleifolium	See *Lithodora oleifolia*
purpureocaeruleum	See *Buglossoides purpurocaerulea*

LITSEA (Lauraceae)
glauca	See *Neolitsea sericea*

japonica	CHEx

LITTONIA (Colchicaceae)
modesta	CGre CHal CRHN

LITTORELLA (Plantaginaceae)
§ *uniflora*	WCot

LIVISTONA (Arecaceae)
australis	CAbb CBrP CRoM CTrC EPVP LPal
chinensis ♀	CBrP LPJP LPal LRHS MWst WMul
decipiens	CRoM CTrC LPal
¶ *jenkinsiana*	CRoM WMul
mariae	LPal
saribus	EPVP

LLOYDIA (Liliaceae)
serotina	Last listed 1999

LOASA (Loasaceae)
lateritia	See *Caiophora lateritia*
triphylla var. *volcanica*	EWes GCal

LOBELIA (Campanulaceae)
'Alice'	WCot WFar
anatina	CFai CFir EWTr EWll LRHS WLRN
angulata	See *Pratia angulata*
'Bees' Flame'	CFir CLAP CRos CRow EBee MAnH SWat WLRN
* 'Bees Ridge'	Last listed 1997
bridgesii	CSpe CTbh GCal
'Brightness'	CCuc CRos CRow EBee ELan IHdy SPer
'Butterfly Blue'	CB&S EBee EBrP EBre EGle GBuc GGar LBCl LBSe LBre LRHS MAvo MBBe MBri MTis NCiC NHol SBre
'Butterfly Rose'	EBrP EBre EGle GBuc GMac LBCl LBSe LBre LFis MBBe SBre WCHb WHil
cardinalis ♀	CArn CRDP CRow CWat EFou EHon GCHN GCal GKir LPBA LRHS MSal MSta NArg NDea SChu SPer SPlb SRms SUsu SWyc WCot WFar WMAq WWye
- 'Alba'	WPyg
- subsp. *graminea* var. *multiflora*	CFir
- 'Rose Beacon'	WCot
- 'Shrimp Salad'	Last listed 1997
* 'Cherry Pie'	EMan
'Cherry Ripe'	CElw CLAP CM&M CRos CSev EBee ECoo ELan IHdy LRHS NCut NHlc NHol SMrm WCHb WEas WLRN
'Cinnabar Deep Red'	See *L.* 'Fan Tiefrot'
'Cinnabar Rose'	See *L.* 'Fan Zinnoberrosa'
'Complexion'	GCHN LRHS
Compliment Blue	See *L.* 'Kompliment Blau'
Compliment Deep Red	See *L.* 'Kompliment Tiefrot'
Compliment Purple	See *L.* 'Kompliment Purpur'
Compliment Scarlet	See *L.* 'Kompliment Scharlach'
'Dark Crusader'	CBos CElw CMHG CRos CRow EBee EFou ELan EMar LFis LRHS MBri MTis NDea NPro SAga SChu SMrm WCHb WCru WEas WRus WSan
deckenii subsp. *elgonensis*	Last listed 1999

dortmanna | EMFW
erinus 'Kathleen | WFoF
Mallard' (d)
- 'Richardii' | See *L. richardsonii*
'Eulalia Berridge' | CGle CLAP CMil CRos CSam EBee
EGle EMil GBuc LFis LRHS MBri
MMil SAga SMrm WCru WDyG
excelsa | CTbh WCot WPic
Fan Deep Red | See *L.* 'Fan Tiefrot'
'Fan Deep Rose' | See *L.* 'Fan Orchidrosa'
§ 'Fan Orchidrosa' ♀ | EBee EMan NCut SRot WHil
WLRN
'Fan Scharlach' ♀ | SRot WHil WWeb
§ 'Fan Tiefrot' ♀ | EBee GBuc GCHN GMac LAst
LRHS SHel SMad SRms SSpi SWat
WCHb WHil WLRN WPer
§ 'Fan Zinnoberrosa' ♀ | CB&S CFir CFwr CGle EBee EMan
EWTr GGar LAst LRHS NCut SAga
SRms SRot WCHb WHil WPer
WWin WWye
'Flamingo' | See *L.* 'Pink Flamingo'
'Frances' | Last listed 1999
fulgens | EPfP IBlr WByw WEas
- 'Elmfeuer' | CHar GMac SMrm WHil WPen
- 'Illumination' | GBuc
- 'Saint Elmo's Fire' | WGor
'Galen' | Last listed 1998
georgiana | EBee
x **gerardii** | CLAP CSam EWll SSte WBor
- 'Alba' | CRow
- 'Eastgrove Pink' | WEas
- 'Rosencavalier' | EBee LRHS MBri SMrm WFar
WHil
§ - 'Vedrariensis' | More than 30 suppliers
gibberoa | CHEx
inflata | CArn GPoy MSal WCHb WWye
'Jack McMaster' | SUsu
'Kimbridge Beet' ♀ | CMac
§ 'Kompliment Blau' | CBlo CFir CHor EMan LRHS NArg
NCut NHol WPer
§ 'Kompliment Purpur' | Last listed 1998
§ 'Kompliment Scharlach' ♀ | CBlo CHor CRos CSWP EBee
EBrP EBre EPfP GCHN LBCl LBSe
LBre LRHS MBBe MBNS NCut
NPer SBre SPer SSpi WCHb WFar
WPer
§ 'Kompliment Tiefrot' | CHor NArg WPer
laxiflora | CBot CInt EGra MTho SAga
- var. **angustifolia** | CGre CHEx CHea CPle CSam
CSpe CTbh EBee EMan ERea GCal
IBlr LHop MSte SHFr SMac SMrm
SRms WAbe WPer WWye
'Lena' | SWat
lindblomii | CLTr
linnaeoides | EWes GCHN SPlb WEas
¶ 'Lipstick' | WCra
§ **lutea** | CInt LRHS
pedunculata | See *Pratia pedunculata*
perpusilla | See *Pratia perpusilla*
'Pink Elephant' ♀ | CGle CLAP CMHG CMil CSWP
CSev EBee EPri NBrk NBur WFar
WHil WPGP
§ 'Pink Flamingo' | CRow EBee EBrP EBre EFou
EMFW EPar GCHN LAst LBCl
LBSe LBre LRHS MBBe NFai
NFor SAga SBre SMrm SPer
SWat WBor WCHb WFar WPyg
WWye
polyphylla | Last listed 1999
puberula | CFir EBee
'Purple Towers' | GBuc WCot
pyramidalis B&SWJ 316 | Last listed 1997

'Queen Victoria' ♀ | More than 30 suppliers
'Rachel's Pink' | IHdy
'Red Hugh' | IHdy
* **rediviva** | EBrP EBre LBCl LBSe LBre MBBe
SBre
regalis | WCHb WHal
repens | See *Pratia repens*
§ **richardsonii** ♀ | CInt LHil LIck LRHS WLRN
WWol
roughii | Last listed 1997
'Rowden Magenta' | CRow
'Royal Robe' | Last listed 1999
'Ruby Slippers' | WCot
N 'Russian Princess' | CGle CRDP CRos CRow CSam
EBlw IHdy LRHS MAnH MBri
NBrk SAga SMad SUsu WCHb
WCot WFar WHil WLRN WWeb
'Sandy's Pink' | Last listed 1999
sessilifolia | EBee EGle GBuc GCal LRHS NChi
SMrm WCot WLRN WPer WSan
WWye
- B&L 12396 | EMon
- B&SWJ 520 | Last listed 1998
siphilitica | More than 30 suppliers
- 'Alba' | CBlo CPea CPou CRow CSam
EBee EPfP EPri LHil LRHS MLLN
NChi SRms SSca WCHb WCra
WFar WHoo WPer WPyg WWye
- Blue selection | CFri NLar
- 'Rosea' | MNrw
'Sonia' | CGle
'Spark' | GBuc WCot
'Sparkle Divine' | WCot
x **speciosa** | CBrd CRow EBee MNrw WLRN
- dark | CMHG CRos CRow EGle SMrm
'Tania' | CFir CGle CHEx CRDP CRow
CSpe EBee EFou EGle EMan EMar
GBri GMac IBlr LRHS MBel MCLN
MLLN MMil NSti SAga SChu SMad
SMrm SUsu WCHb WCot WFar
WHil WRus
¶ 'Temptation White' | WWol
treadwellii | See *Pratia angulata*
'Treadwellii'
tupa | More than 30 suppliers
* - candelabra | NArg
- dark orange | SArc SMrm
- JCA 12527 | WCot
urens | SSpi WPGP
¶ - pale | CFil
valida | EMan GBuc GQui LRHS SUsu
WLRN WOut
- 'South Seas' | EWTr WBar
vedrariensis | See *L.* x **gerardii** 'Vedrariensis'
'Wildwood Splendour' | Last listed 1997
'Will Scarlet' | CCuc CLAP CRos EBee EBrP EBre
LBCl LBSe LBre MBBe SBre
'Zinnoberrosa' | See *L.* 'Fan Zinnoberrosa'

LOBELIA x PRATIA (Campanulaceae)
L. sp. x *P.* sp. | Last listed 1998

LOBOSTEMON (Boraginaceae)
montanus | Last listed 1997

LOESELIA (Polemoniaceae)
mexicana | ERea

LOISELEURIA (Ericaceae)
procumbens | Last listed 1999
- from Japan | GCrs WAbe
- 'Saint Anton' | Last listed 1997

LOMANDRA (Lomandraceae)
longifolia   EBee ECou GCal

LOMARIA See BLECHNUM

LOMATIA (Proteaceae)
dentata   CHEx
ferruginea   CAbb CB&S CDoC CFil CHEx
     CLan CTrG EPfP ISea SAPC SArc
     SBrw WCru WPGP
fraseri   SSpi
hirsuta   CFil
longifolia   See *L. myricoides*
§ **myricoides**   CAbb CDoC CFil CHEx CPLG
     CTrG CTrw EPfP LRHS SArc SSpi
     WBod WWat
silaifolia   CDoC EPfP
§ **tinctoria**   CB&S CCpl CDoC CHEx CTrw
     ELan EPfP LRHS SArc SSpi WBod

LOMATIUM (Apiaceae)
brandegeei   Last listed 1999
columbianum   Last listed 1999
dissectum var. **multifidum**   Last listed 1999
grayi   Last listed 1999
laevigatum   EBee
macrocarpum   Last listed 1999
martindalei   EBee
nudicaule   EBee
utriculatum   EBee MSal

LOMATOGONIUM (Gentianaceae)
sp. ACE 2331*   Last listed 1999

LONICERA ✿ (Caprifoliaceae)
§ **acuminata**   CPIN LRHS MAsh SLim WGwG
     WSHC
 - B&SWJ 2150   Last listed 1999
 - B&SWJ 3480   WCru
albertii   CFai MBNS MRav SPan WHCG
     WSHC
albiflora   WSHC
 - var. **albiflora**   SBra
alpigena   Last listed 1998
alseuosmoides   CPIN SBra SLon WBcn WCru
     WSHC WWeb
altmannii   Last listed 1999
§ x **americana** (Miller)   CBlo CHad CRHN CSPN EPfP
   K. Koch   LHop LRHS MAsh MBri MGos
     NBea SBra SEas SLim SReu SSta
     WBod WCru WWeb
§ - hort.   See *L.* x *italica*
 'Anna Landers'   WCFE
x **brownii**   CMac
§ - 'Dropmore Scarlet'   More than 30 suppliers
N - 'Fuchsioides'   EPfP MBro NBrk NSti WSHC
     WWat
caerulea   CPle MRav WHCG
 - var. **altaica**   Last listed 1998
 - var. **edulis**   CAgr ESim LEdu
 - f. **empbyllocalyx**   CPle
californica   See *L. hispidula* var. *vacillans*
§ **caprifolium** ♀   CDoC CRHN EBee ECtt ELan
     EOrc EPla LBuc LPri LRHS
     MAsh MBar MBri NBea NFai
     NMGW SBra SPer WCot WCru
     WWat
 - 'Anna Fletcher'   CRHN MBNS SBra SPan WCru
     WWat WWeb
 - 'Cornish Cream'   Last listed 1999
 - f. **pauciflora**   See *L.* x *italica*

chaetocarpa   CMHG CPle SPan WPat
§ **chrysantha**   CMCN CPle GBin NRya
ciliosa   CPIN NBea SBra
'Clavey's Dwarf'   IOrc MGos NBrk NHol
cyanocarpa KGB 438   Last listed 1998
deflexicalyx KGB 165   Last listed 1998
dioica   SBra
'Early Cream'   See *L. caprifolium*
etrusca   EPla LPri LRHS MRav WWeb
 - 'Donald Waterer' ♀   CBlo EBee LHop LRHS MAsh SBra
     WFar WGor
 - 'Michael Rosse'   EBee EBrP EBre ELan LBCl LBSe
     LBre LRHS MBBe MBNS MBel
     SBra SBre SRms WRHF WWat
 - 'Superba' ♀   CBlo CPIN CRHN EBee ECtt EPfP
     LRHS MAsh NBrk SBra SEND
     SLim SPan SPer WCru WPen
     WSHC WWat
ferdinandii   Last listed 1998
flexuosa   See *L. japonica* var. *repens*
fragrantissima   More than 30 suppliers
gibbiflora Maxim.   See *L. chrysantha*
 - Dippel   NRya
giraldii Rehder   CBot CPIN EBee EPfP LPri NHol
     SBra WCru
 - hort.   See *L. acuminata*
glabrata   SBra SLPl SLim WCru
gracilis   MBlu
grata   See *L.* x *americana* (Miller) K.
     Koch
x **beckrottii**   CB&S CBlo CDoC CMac CRHN
     CTri EBee ECtt EWTr GOrc LPri
     LRHS MBar NBea NBee WBod
     WCru WDin WLRN WStI WWeb
N - 'Gold Flame'   More than 30 suppliers
§ **henryi**   More than 30 suppliers
 - var. **subcoriacea**   See *L. henryi*
bildebrandiana   CGre CPIN LRHS SBra SOWG
     WPGP
hirsuta   NBea SBra
§ **hispidula** var. **vacillans**   WWat
'Honey Baby' PBR   MBlu MGos MRav NHol WPat
implexa   CPIN EHol EPla GCal LGre MBNS
     NPro SBra SEas WCot WCru
     WSHC
infundibulum var. **rockii**   EPfP SSpi
insularis   CMCN CPle MBlu MTPN SPan
involucrata   CMCN CMHG CPle EPla GBin
     GOrc LHil LHop MBNS MBar
     MBlu MRav NChi NHol SPan
     SPer WCFE WDin WFar WHCG
     WPyg
 - var. **ledebourii**   CPle EBee ELan EPfP EPla GChr
     GKir MBel MTis NHol SDys WOve
     WWin
§ x **italica** ♀   More than 30 suppliers
§ - Harlequin = 'Sherlite' PBR   (v) CBlo CBot EBee ECtt EMil
     ENot GKir LAst LRHS MAsh MBel
     MGos MRav MTis NBea NEgg
     NHol NSti SBra SLim SMad SPer
     SPla SPlb SVil WCru WLRN WPGP
     WWeb
 - 'Sherlite' PBR   See *L.* x *italica* Harlequin =
     'Sherlite'
§ **japonica** 'Aureoreticulata'   More than 30 suppliers
 - 'Cream Cascade'   MAsh WRHF
 - 'Dart's Acumen'   SLPl
 - 'Dart's World'   MBel NHol SBra SLPl SVil WLRN
 - 'Halliana' ♀   More than 30 suppliers
 - 'Hall's Prolific'   More than 30 suppliers
§ - 'Horwood Gem' (v)   EBee ECtt NHol NPro SBra SLim
     WBcn WWeb

– 'Peter Adams'	See *L. japonica* 'Horwood Gem'
¶ – 'Red World'	MTis
§ – var. *repens* ♀	More than 30 suppliers
– 'Variegata'	See *L. japonica* 'Aureoreticulata'
korolkowii	CBot CPle EBee EPfP LFis LRHS MBNS MWat NBir SPan SPla SSta SUsu WHCG WSHC WWat WWin
– var. *zabelii*	ELan SEas
lanceolata KGB 488	Last listed 1998
maackii	CMCN CPMA EPfP SPan WHCG WWat
– f. *podocarpa*	CPle
* *macgregorii*	CMCN
'Mandarin'PBR	CDoC GKir LRHS MAsh MBri NPri SCoo WWeb
microphylla	Last listed 1998
¶ *modesta* var. *lushenensis*	WWat
morrowii	Last listed 1998
x *muscaviensis*	Last listed 1999
myrtillus KGB 298	Last listed 1998
nigra	EPla
nitida	CB&S CChe CKin CTri EBee EPfP GChr GOrc LHyr LRHS MRav NWea SPer SRPl STre WDin WFar WHar WHen WStI
– 'Baggesen's Gold' ♀	More than 30 suppliers
– 'Eden Spring'	NPro
– 'Elegant'	IOrc LBuc
– 'Ernest Wilson'	MBar SRms
– 'Fertilis'	SPer SRms
– 'Hohenheimer Findling'	Last listed 1998
– 'Lemon Beauty' (v)	CDoC EBee EHoe EPla LRHS MBNS MBri MGos MTis NFai NFla NRib SPer WBcn WLeb
– 'Lemon Queen'	CCHP WLRN
§ – 'Maigrün'	CChe EBee EMil LRHS MBri NFai NFla NPro SPer WFar WGwG WTro
– Maygreen	See *L. nitida* 'Maigrün'
– 'Red Tips'	CWSG EBee EHoe EPla LRHS MBNS MBel MBri MGos MLLN NFai NHol WLRN WPnP
– 'Silver Beauty' (v)	More than 30 suppliers
* – 'Silver Cloud'	CWSG
– 'Silver Lining'	See *L. pileata* 'Silver Lining'
– 'Silver Queen'	WEas
– 'Twiggy' (v)	EWTr LRHS MBri MGos NFai NHol NPro WGer WLRN
nummulariifolia	Last listed 1998
periclymenum	CArn CKin CTri ELau EPla EWFC GChr GPoy MHer NBea NFor NMir NWea SHFr SPlb WDin WHCG WWye
§ – 'Belgica' ♀	More than 30 suppliers
– 'Belgica' misapplied	See *L.* x *italica*
* – 'Cream Cascade'	GKir NPri
– 'Florida'	See *L. periclymenum* 'Serotina'
– 'Graham Thomas' ♀	More than 30 suppliers
– 'Harlequin'PBR	See *L.* x *italica* Harlequin = 'Sherlite'
– 'Heaven Scent'	EMil SBra
– 'Honeybush'	EBee
– 'La Gasnaérie'	EBee EPla GAri NHol SBra SLim SPan
– 'Liden'	SBra
– 'Munster'	CB&S EBee EPla MBri NBrk SBra WBcn WSHC
– 'Purple Queen'	CBlo
– 'Red Gables'	CBlo CSam EBee MBNS MBri MRav NHol SBra SLim SPan SPla SVil WCot WGor WPat WWat
N – 'Serotina' ♀	More than 30 suppliers
– 'Serotina' EM '85	MBri WCru WWat
– 'Serpentine'	SBra
– *sulphurea*	EPla EWll NFai
– 'Sweet Sue'	ECtt ELan EPfP GCal LRHS MAsh MBNS MLan NFor SBra WBcn WFar
– 'Winchester'	ECtt
– yellow	Last listed 1997
pileata	More than 30 suppliers
– 'Moss Green'	CBlo CDoC EBee MGos SLon WHCG
– 'Pilot'	SLPl
§ – 'Silver Lining' (v)	CBlo EPla GBuc MLLN WCot
– 'Stockholm'	SLPl
pilosa Maxim.	See *L. strophiophora*
– Willd. CD&R 1216	SBra
praeflorens	Last listed 1997
prolifera	SBra
prostrata	Last listed 1998
x *purpusii*	CDoC CGdn CPle CSam ECle EWTr MBNS MBar MBel MGos MWat NBea SLim SPer SRms WBod WCFE WEas WFar WHCG WHar WPyg WSHC WWeb WWin
– 'Winter Beauty' ♀	More than 30 suppliers
pyrenaica	CPle SPan WPat
quinquelocularis	CPle
– f. *translucens*	MBlu
ramosissima	CMCN
§ *rupicola* var. *syringantha*	CBrm CDul CHar CMHG CPle CSam EBee ELan GEil GKir LAst LHop MBlu MGos MTis MWhi NBea SPan SPer SPla WCFE WCru WFar WHCG WSHC WWat WWin
– var. *syringantha* 'Grandiflora'	GQui WAbe WPyg
ruprechtiana	Last listed 1999
¶ *saccata*	EPfP
segreziensis	Last listed 1999
sempervirens ♀	CBot CPIN CRHN EBee ELan EPar EPfP GAri GOrc LPri LRHS MBNS MCCP NBea SBra SPer SSta WCru WLRN WLeb WSHC
– 'Dropmore Scarlet'	See *L.* x *brownii* 'Dropmore Scarlet'
N – f. *sulphurea*	CBlo CPIN EBee EPfP LRHS NBea SBra SPan SPer WSHC
serotina 'Honeybush'	CDoC CPle MAsh MBlu NHol SBra SLim
setifera	CBot EHol
– 'Daphnis'	EPfP
similis var. *delavayi*	CBot CDoC CLTr CPIN CSPN CSam EBee EPla GOrc LRHS MAsh MBel NBea NFai SBra SDix SLPl SPan SPla SUsu WCru WPGP WPen WSHC WWat
'Simonet'	SBra
sp. ACE 1413	Last listed 1998
sp. CLD 315	Last listed 1997
sp. from Sikkim B&SWJ 2654	WCru
sp. KBE 062	NHol
¶ sp. KR 291	EPla
sp. LS&H 17465	Last listed 1999
splendida	CBot SBra WCru
'Spring Romance'	SLon
standishii	CB&S EBee EHol MBel MGos MRav NFai SPer WCru WDin WFar WHCG WRha WWin
'Stone Green'	NPro SPla

§ *stropbiopbora*	WWat
syringantba	See *L. rupicola* var. *syringantba*
tangutica KGB 535	Last listed 1998
tatarica	CFai MRav MWhi NFla SLon WFar
	WHCG WWin
- 'Alba'	CFai CPMA MTed SPan
- 'Arnold's Red'	CB&S CBot CPle EBee ELan EPfP
	MBlu SPan
- 'Hack's Red'	CB&S CFai EBee EPfP MRav SCob
	SPan SPer WCot WHCG WPyg
- 'Rosea'	Last listed 1997
- f. *sibirica*	Last listed 1997
- 'Zabelii'	EPfP MGos
x *tellmanniana* ♀	More than 30 suppliers
- 'Joan Sayer'	EBrP EBre EPla GOrc LBCl LBSe
	LBre LHop MBBe MBNS MCCP
	MGos NBrk SBra SBre SPan WBcn
	WCFE WCru WLeb WWat
thibetica	CPle MBlu SPer WWat
tragopbylla ♀	CB&S CDoC CPlN CSam EBee
	ELan EPla GCal IOrc LHop LPri
	LRHS MAsh MBNS MBri NHol
	NSti SBra SLim SPar SPer SSpi SSta
	WCru WDin WSHC WWat
¶ - 'Pharoah's Trumpet'	ERea
trichosantba KGB 404	Last listed 1998
webbiana	ELan
x *xylosteoides*	MRav
- 'Clavey's Dwarf'	MBel MBlu MGos SLPl SPan
- 'Miniglobe'	ESis NPro
* *yunnanensis* 'Variegata'	Last listed 1998

LOPEZIA (Onagraceae)
racemosa	CPla MCCP SHFr WRos WSan

LOPHOMYRTUS (Myrtaceae)
§ *bullata*	CCHP CGre CTre ECou GQui
	IDee SPer WCHb
- 'Matai Bay'	CB&S CTrC
'Gloriosa' (v)	CB&S CPle LRHS WCHb
'Little Star'	CB&S LRHS
§ *obcordata*	CGre CPle
'Pinkalina'	WGer
§ x *ralpbii*	WCHb WPic WWat
- 'Andrea'	Last listed 1998
§ - 'Kathryn'	CB&S CDoC CPle CTre ERea
	WCHb WSHC WWat
¶ - 'Krinkly'	SVen
I - 'Multicolor' (v)	CTrC
¶ - 'Pixie'	Last listed 1999
¶ - 'Red Dragon'	CTrC
¶ - 'Sundae' (v)	CB&S
§ - 'Traversii' (v)	LRHS SMur
- 'Variegata'	EBrP EBre ERea LBCl LBSe LBre
	MBBe SBre
* - 'Wild Cherry'	Last listed 1999
'Tricolor'	CPle CTre
'Versicolor'	CB&S

LOPHOSORIA (Dicksoniaceae)
quadripinnata	Last listed 1999

LOPHOSPERMUM (Scrophulariaceae)
§ *erubescens* ♀	CBot CHEx CHal CRHN LFis MSte
	MTis
- 'Garnet'	Last listed 1997
§ 'Red Dragon'	CPla CSpe SUsu SYvo
§ *scandens*	CB&S CRHN ELan EWes
§ - 'Pink Ice'	LRHS SOWG

LOPHOSTEMON (Myrtaceae)
§ *confertus*	Last listed 1998

LOROPETALUM (Hamamelidaceae)
chinense	CFil CMCN SSpi
- f. *rubrum*	CFil SLon WPGP
- - 'Blush'	CFil WPGP
- - 'Fire Dance'	CDoC WCot
I - - 'Zhuzhou Fuchsia'	CMCN

LOTONONIS (Papilionaceae)
¶ *pulcbella*	SPlb

LOTUS (Papilionaceae)
bertbelotii ♀	CFee CGle CHEx CHal CSpe
	ECon EDAr ELan ERea LHil SChu
	SRms WEas WKif
- deep red	EDAr LIck
- Kew form	Last listed 1997
- x *maculatus*	CLTr CSpe EDAr LHil MSCN
	WIvy
corniculatus	CArn CKin CLTr EWFC MCoo
	MHer MHew MNaF NLan SIde
	WGwy WOak
- 'Plenus' (d)	CInt EPot LFis MTho NHol WAlt
	WCot WGwy WPer
'Gold Flash'	Last listed 1999
§ *hirsutus*	More than 30 suppliers
- 'Brimstone'	EBee GBin LHop LRHS NPro
	SBrw SPan SPer SVil
- dwarf	Last listed 1999
- 'Lois'	WSPU
- 'Silver Mist'	SCro
jacobaeus	CInt
maculatus ♀	CGle CSpe ECon LRHS SHFr
	SOWG SVen WIvy
maritimus	EWll LGre MWgw NNrd SHFr
	SRot SSvw WWin
mascaensis hort.	See *L. sessilifolius*
pedunculatus	See *L. uliginosus*
pentapbyllus	GCal
subsp. *herbaceus*	
§ - subsp. *pentapbyllus*	NBrk
§ *sessilifolius*	ERea LHil
suffruticosus	See *L. pentapbyllus* subsp.
	pentapbyllus
¶ *tetragonolobus*	SRot
§ *uliginosus*	EWFC MGas NMir

LOXOSTYLIS (Anacardiaceae)
alata	Last listed 1997

LUCULIA (Rubiaceae)
grandifolia	LRHS SOWG
gratissima ♀	CB&S CHEx
- 'Early Dawn'	Last listed 1999
- 'Rosea'	ECon LRHS SOWG
pinceana 'Fragrant Cloud'	CB&S

LUDWIGIA (Onagraceae)
grandiflora	CRow SWyc WMAq
palustris	Last listed 1997
uruguayensis	LPBA

LUETKEA (Rosaceae)
pectinata	EBee GCHN GDra NRya WAbe

LUMA (Myrtaceae)
§ *apiculata* ♀	More than 30 suppliers
§ - 'Glanleam Gold' (v)	More than 30 suppliers
- 'Variegata'	CMHG CTri ISea SAga WCru
	WWat WWye
§ *chequen*	CFee CGre GAri GGar IDee
	MHer NHex WCHb WCwm WJek
	WWat

LUNARIA (Brassicaceae)

§ *annua*	EBot GAbr MWgw NCat SIde SWat WByw WHer WOak
I - 'Alba Variegata'	CFri CSpe EMar EMon EPla MAnH MFir MHer WByw WCot
- var. *albiflora* ♀	EBot EWTr NBir NCat SIde SWat WCer WCot
- 'Ken Aslet'	Last listed 1997
- 'Munstead Purple'	Last listed 1999
* - 'Stella'	WHen
- 'Variegata'	CHar EBot IBlr MTho NBid NBir SWat WCot WEas WHer WSan
- violet	NBir WFar
biennis	See *L. annua*
rediviva	ECGP ECha EMon EPla GCHN GGar GLil IBlr LRHS MHer NBid NChi NPer NSti SSpi SUsu WCot WEas WFar WHen WHer

LUPINUS ✿ (Papilionaceae)

¶ 'African Sunset'	CWCL
'Alan Titchmarsh'	MWoo
albifrons	CSpe EBee
- var. *flumineus*	Last listed 1998
alopecuroides	Last listed 1998
¶ 'Amber Glow'	CWCL
angustifolius	Last listed 1998
'Anne Gregg' ♀	MWoo
arboreus ♀	More than 30 suppliers
- 'Barton on Sea'	CNat
- blue	CBrm CCHP CFri CHar CMea ECGP GChr MCCP MGrG MWll NCut NLar SPer WFar WShe
- cream	ECGP
- 'Golden Spire'	Last listed 1998
- 'Mauve Queen'	NBee SUsu
- mixed	Last listed 1999
- 'Snow Queen'	CBrm CInt MCCP NCut SMad
¶ - 'Sulphur Yellow'	NCut
arcticus	EBee
argenteus	Last listed 1998
- var. *depressus*	See *L. argenteus* var. *utahensis*
§ - var. *utahensis*	Last listed 1999
- var. *wyethii*	Last listed 1998
¶ 'Aston Villa'	CWCL
Band of Nobles Series ♀	ECtt GAbr WFar
'Barnsdale'	MWoo
benthamii	CFri
'Beryl, Viscountess Cowdray'	GBuc
bicolor	Last listed 1998
¶ 'Bishop's Tipple'	CWCL
¶ 'Blue Moon'	CWCL
breweri	EBee
caespitosus	See *L. lepidus* var. *utahensis*
¶ 'Candy Floss'	CWCL
chamissonis	CFri CHEx CPla CSpe EBrP EBre EGoo EMan EWes LBCl LBSe LBre LGre LHop LRHS MBBe MTho SBre SDry SDys SMrm SPer SSpi SUsu WPen WRus
'Chandelier'	More than 30 suppliers
'Chelsea Pensioner'	MWoo
¶ 'Copperlight'	CWCL
¶ 'Coral Reef'	CWCL
¶ 'Corngold'	CWCL
'Deborah Woodfield' ♀	MWoo
densiflorus var. *aureus*	See *L. microcarpus* var. *densiflorus*
¶ 'Desert Sun'	CWCL
¶ 'Devon Lace'	CWCL
¶ 'Dolly Mixture'	CWCL
Dwarf Gallery hybrids	GKir LIck
'Dwarf Lulu'	See *L.* 'Lulu'
'Esmerelder' ♀	MWoo
Gallery Series	COIW EBrP EBre LBCl LBSe LBre MBBe NCut NFai NPri SBre SCoo SPlb WLRN
'Gallery Blue' (Gallery Series)	ECtt EPfP LRHS NCut NLar NNor SCoo SPer WHil WViv
'Gallery Pink' (Gallery Series)	EPfP LRHS NLar SCoo SPer SPla WHil WViv
'Gallery Red' (Gallery Series)	ECtt LRHS NLar SCoo SPer SPla WHil WViv
'Gallery White' (Gallery Series)	EPfP EWTr LPVe LRHS NLar SCoo SPer SPla WHil WViv
'Gallery Yellow' (Gallery Series)	ECtt EWTr LRHS NCut NLar SCoo SPer SPla WHil WViv
'Garden Gnome'	WPer
'Helen Sharman' ♀	MWoo
'Household Brigade'	MWoo
'Judith Chalmers'	MWoo
'Kayleigh Ann Savage' ♀	MWoo
¶ 'Lady Penelope'	CWCL
latifolius	WAbe
- subsp. *parishii*	Last listed 1998
- var. *subalpinus*	Last listed 1999
lepidus	EMan
- var. *lobbii*	WAbe
- var. *sellulus*	Last listed 1999
§ - var. *utahensis*	Last listed 1998
leucophyllus	Last listed 1997
'Little Eugenie'	MWoo
littoralis	EMan GDra WHil WPer
§ 'Lulu'	COtt EBrP EBre ECtt ELan LBCl LBSe LBre LRHS MBBe MRav NMir SBre SPer SRPl WFar WHil WMoo
luteus	Last listed 1998
micranthus	Last listed 1998
microcarpus	Last listed 1997
§ - var. *densiflorus*	Last listed 1998
microphyllus	Last listed 1998
Minarette Group	CBlo ECtt LRHS MBri SRms WGor
Mirakel hybrids	CBlo
'Misty'	MWoo
montanus	Last listed 1998
'Mrs Perkins'	SMrm
mutabilis	Last listed 1998
var. *cruckshanksii*	
'My Castle'	More than 30 suppliers
nanus	Last listed 1998
'Nigel Colborn'	MWoo
'Noble Maiden'	More than 30 suppliers
nootkatensis	CPea
'Olive Tolley' ♀	MWoo
oreophilus F&W 7353	Last listed 1997
'Party Dress'	MWoo
perennis	CGle ECGN SCou
'Pink Fortune'	Last listed 1999
'Poached Salmon'	SMrm
'Polar Princess'	EWes MGrG SWat WLRN
polyphyllus	EBee
- var. *burkei*	Last listed 1998
'Pope John Paul' ♀	MWoo
propinquus	Last listed 1998
¶ 'Red Arrow'	CWCL
'Rising Sun'	Last listed 1999
'Rote Flamme'	ECGN EWes EWll LPVe
'Royal Parade' ♀	Last listed 1996
'Royal Wedding'	MWoo
Russell hybrids	CB&S ELan EWTr GChr GKir MHer NFla SPlb SRms SSea
¶ 'Sand Pink'	CWCL

sericatus — Last listed 1997
sericeus — Last listed 1999
- *fikerianus* — Last listed 1999
¶ 'Sherbert Dip' — CWCL
¶ 'Soft Kisses' — CWCL
sparsiflorus — Last listed 1998
¶ 'Storm' — CWCL
'Stuart Ogg V.M.H.' — MWoo
succulentus — Last listed 1998
'Sundown' — Last listed 1997
'Sunset' — MWoo
'Sunshine' — CGle
texensis — Last listed 1998
'The Chatelaine' — More than 30 suppliers
'The Governor' — More than 30 suppliers
'The Page' — EBee EBrP EBre ELan EMan EOld GAbr GAri LBCl LBSe LBre LNor LRHS MBBe MBri MRav NBrk NFai NMir SBre SMer SPer WFar WPer
'Thundercloud' — CHad CPlt SMrm
'Troop the Colour' ♀ — MWoo
variicolor — CSpe MBri SSpi WFar
- JJA 11167 — NChi
versicolor — CElw CFri CPea EBee EMan LGro MCCP MHer MLLN MSCN MWll SMad WBea WPGP
'Windermere' — MWoo
'Yellow Boy' — Last listed 1998

LUZULA (Juncaceae)

alpinopilosa — GBin
x *borreri* 'Botany Bay' (v) — CCuc EMon EPPr EPla GBin GDea MCCP WLeb
campestris — CKin
canariensis — WWye
forsteri — CBrm EPPr
lactea — EMon EPGN EPPr LRHS
leptophylla — NHar
luzuloides — WPer
- 'Schneehäschen' — CInt EGar EMon EPPr GBin GCal MWgw
maxima — See *L. sylvatica*
multiflora — EHoe
¶ *nivalis* — WByw
nivea — More than 30 suppliers
pilosa — EPla GCal GOrP IBlr
plumosa — Last listed 1997
pumila — ESis
purpureosplendens — CElw
rufa — ECou
sp. from New Guinea — EBee EWes GCal
§ *sylvatica* — CCuc CKin CRow CSWP EFou EPPr EPla GDea GKir GOrn LNor MFir MLLN MMoz MRav NBro NOrc SCob WHer WPGP WShi
- 'A. Rutherford' — See *L. sylvatica* 'Taggart's Cream'
- 'Aurea' — More than 30 suppliers
- 'Aureomarginata' — See *L. sylvatica* 'Marginata'
I - 'Auslese' — EBee EPPr GBin LRHS
- 'Hohe Tatra' — More than 30 suppliers
§ - 'Marginata' — More than 30 suppliers
* - f. *nova* — EPPr MMoz
- 'Select' — SLPl
§ - 'Taggart's Cream' (v) — CElw CRow EHoe EMar EMon LRHS SCob WBea WLeb
- 'Tauernpass' — EHoe EMon EPPr EPla GCal LRHS NBea
- 'Wäldler' — CCuc EHoe EMon EPPr LRHS
ulophylla — CBod CInt EBee ECou EGoo EMan GBin GBuc MAvo MDCh NHol NWCA WPat

LUZURIAGA (Philesiaceae)

radicans — CFee EBee IBlr WCot WCru WSHC
- MK 92 — SSpi

x LYCENE (Caryophyllaceae)

§ *kubotae* — EBee

LYCHNIS ✿ (Caryophyllaceae)

alpina — CMHG CTri EBee EPfP EWFC GDra GKir GTou NFla NPri NVic SBea SRPl WBea WPer WWal WWin
- 'Alba' — GTou NBir
- compact — GTou
- 'Rosea' — SRms
§ x *arkwrightii* — CGle EBee EBrP EBre ECha ELan LBCl LBSe LBee LBre MBBe NNor SBre SIng SRot WBea WWin
- 'Vesuvius' — CB&S CFri CGle ENot EOld EPla GKir LRHS MHer MMal MNrw MTis NBir NCut NFai NScob SPer SRms STes WOve WPer
* 'Blushing Bride' — Last listed 1999
chalcedonica ♀ — More than 30 suppliers
- var. *albiflora* — CM&M CSam EBee ECha IBlr LAst LFis LRHS MBri NBid NBro NChi NFai NOak NSti SPer WCer WCot WFar WHen WPer WWhi
- - 'Snow White' — EWTr EWll
- apricot — MBro NBid WPyg
- Beverley seedling — Last listed 1999
- 'Carnea' — GCal LRHS MFir NCat WCot
¶ - 'Dusky Salmon' — WElm
- 'Flore Pleno' (d) — CMil EBee ECha ECle ELan GBuc GCal GKir MCCP MCLN MLLN MMil MOne NChi NHaw NHol NLar NPri NSti WCot WFar WSan
- 'Morgenrot' — MCCP NCut NLar
- 'Rauhreif' — Last listed 1999
- 'Rosea' — CGle CHad CSam EBee EBrP EBre EMan EPfP GKir LBCl LBSe LBre LIck LRHS MBBe MBel NFai SBre STes WByw WCer WGwG WHen WPer
- 'Rosea Plena' (d) — Last listed 1999
* - 'Salmonea' — CM&M EBee ECle GBri LAst LPio LRHS MBNS MBri MTis NBir NCiC NCro SPer SRms WCot WLRN
- salmon-pink — SRms WWhi
¶ - 'Summer Sparkle' — SWal
- 'Valetta' — Last listed 1997
cognata — CGle EBee SMrm
§ *coronaria* — More than 30 suppliers
- 'Abbotswood Rose' — See *L. x walkeri* 'Abbotswood Rose'
- 'Alba' ♀ — CGle COlW CStr EBee ECha EFou EHoe ELan EWTr LPio LRHS MBNS MBri MBro MCAu MHew NBid NFai NOak NOrc NSti SPer SRms WCot WFar WHer WPGP WPer WWin
I - 'Alba Variegata' — MCCP
- 'Angel's Blush' — CSev EBee EMan LRHS MBNS MTis NBus SPer SRPl WPer WRHF WRha WRus WWal
- Atrosanguinea Group — CBre CInt EBee EFou EMan IBlr LPio LRHS MTis NCut NFai NPri SPer WPer

- 'Cerise'	MArl NBus WElm
- 'Dancing Ladies'	WRHF
- 'Eastgrove Pink'	Last listed 1999
- 'Flottbek'	MOne NCat NCut NLar
- Gardeners' World	GKir
= 'Blych' PBR (d)	
- 'Hutchinson's Cream' (v)	EMan EMon SYvo WCot
- Oculata Group	CGle CMHG CSpe EBee EGoo
	GKir IBlr LEdu LRHS MCLN MFir
	MTho NFai NOak NSti SPlb SSvw
	WCer WFar WHen WHer WPer
§ coronata var. sieboldii	EBee WBar WSan
dioica	See *Silene dioica*
flos-cuculi	More than 30 suppliers
- var. albiflora	CInt CSam ECoo EPar GDea NBro
	NBus NDea STes WCHb WHer
	WWhi
* - 'Little Robin'	Last listed 1998
- 'Nana'	CInt CNic EDAr GAbr NHol NRya
	SBea WBea WCot WPat WPer
	WPyg WWin
flos-jovis	CGle CTri EBee EMan EPfP EWTr
	LRHS MFir MHar MMal NCut NFla
	NOak SMer SRCN SRms WLRN
	WPer
- 'Alba'	EBee NFla WCot
- 'Hort's Variety'	CLTr GKir MAvo NSti SBla SCro
	SUsu WBea
- 'Minor'	See *L. flos-jovis* 'Nana'
§ - 'Nana'	CInt MHar MSCN NBid NFai NPro
	NWCA SSca WCot WPyg
- 'Peggy'	CM&M EBee EMan GCal MCCP
fulgens	EBee
x haageana	EBee LRHS NWCA SIng SRms
	SSca
- 'Burning Desire'	Last listed 1999
kubotae	See x *Lycene kubotae*
lagascae	See *Petrocoptis pyrenaica* subsp.
	glaucifolia
miqueliana	EBee EGar MBNS WMoo
- 'Variegated Lacy Red' (v)	WCot
'Molten Lava'	CBlo CFir CInt GMaP LRHS MCli
	NArg NOrc NPro SCob SRms
	WMoo WPer
nutans	MSal
preslii minor	EBee
* sikkimensis	EBee
sp. from Andes	Last listed 1997
'Terry's Pink'	EBee MLLN NCut NLar
§ viscaria	CArn CGle ECha EGar MSal NCiC
	NFor SCro SGar SMac SSca WBea
	WGwy WHer
- alba	EBee ECha EMan GCal MCCP
	MLLN NBro WWeb
- alpina	See *L. viscaria*
- subsp. atropurpurea	EBee SBea SRCN WBea WWhi
- 'Feuer'	NLar NPri WLRN WWhi
- 'Firebird'	EFou WWpP
- 'Plena' (d)	LFis MInt NPSI WHil WTin
- 'Schnee'	EWTr LBuc NPri
- 'Snowbird'	GMac NBur WGwG WWpP
- 'Splendens'	CBlo EPfP EWTr LRHS MChl NFla
* - 'Splendens Alba'	EPPr
- 'Splendens Plena' (d) ♀	CGle EBee ECha EGar GMac MArl
	MBri MWgw NBro WBea WCot
	WEas WFar WOve
§ x walkeri	GBuc
'Abbotswood Rose' ♀	
wilfordii	CFir CPou EBee MLLN MTis
§ yunnanensis	CSam EBee EGar GBin GBuc
	LLWP MFir MSte NBid NHol WBea
	WPer

- alba	See *L. yunnanensis*

LYCIANTHES (Solanaceae)
rantonnetii	See *Solanum rantonnetii*

LYCIUM (Solanaceae)
barbarum	ELan IIve SMad SPan WSHC
	WWye
chinense	CArn GPoy
europaeum	Last listed 1997

LYCOPODIUM (Lycopodiaceae)
clavatum	GPoy

LYCOPSIS See ANCHUSA

LYCOPUS (Lamiaceae)
americanus	EBee MSal
europaeus	CArn ELau EWFC GBar GPoy
	MChe MHew MSal WGwG WHer
	WJek WWye
exaltatus	Last listed 1998
sp. JLS 88040	Last listed 1997
virginicus	COld MSal WWye

LYCORIS (Amaryllidaceae)
albiflora	SDeJ WCot
aurea	LRHS
¶ longituba	WWat
radiata	EBot LRHS WWat
squamigera	WWat

LYGEUM (Poaceae)
spartum	EPPr

LYGODIUM (Schizaeaceae)
japonicum	WRic
§ microphyllum	NMar
palmatum	Last listed 1997
scandens	See *L. microphyllum*

LYONIA (Ericaceae)
ligustrina	LRHS SMur
ovalifolia var. elliptica	Last listed 1998
villosa B&SWJ 2161	Last listed 1999

LYONOTHAMNUS (Rosaceae)
floribundus	CAbb SAPC SArc SSpi WCru
	WWat
subsp. aspleniifolius	

LYSICHITON ✿ (Araceae)
americanus ♀	More than 30 suppliers
- NNS 96-155	Last listed 1999
camtschatcensis ♀	CBen CCuc CHEx CLAP CRow
	CWat ECha EHon ELan EMFW
	EPar EPfP GAbr GKir LPBA MSta
	NDea NOrc SPer SSpi SWat
	WCot
- x americanus	SSpi
'Devonshire Cream'	CCuc

LYSIMACHIA ✿ (Primulaceae)
¶ acroadenia	CPLG
§ atropurpurea	CHal CLTr CPle CSpe EBee ECGN
	EGar EGle ELan EMan EMar EWTr
	GBri LRHS MCCP MGrG MNrw
	NFai SBea SMad SRCN SUsu WCot
	WFar WPGP WPer WSpi
- 'Beaujolais'	CFri WViv WWpP
- 'Geronimo'	CBlo CSpe MTis
barystachys	CHea CRow EBee EBrP EBre EMar

	GCHN LBCl LBSe LBre MBBe MRav NCut SBre SMer WCot WOve
ciliata	More than 30 suppliers
§ - 'Firecracker' ♀	More than 30 suppliers
- 'Purpurea'	See *L. ciliata* 'Firecracker'
clethroides ♀	More than 30 suppliers
- from Guizhou, China	EWes
- 'Lady Jane'	CBlo
§ *congestiflora*	CLTr LHil LPVe NCut NPer SHFr WLRN
- Outback Sunset® (v)	CHal ECtt GPin LRHS NBir NPri WCDu WGwG WLRN
- 'Silver Bird'	Last listed 1997
- 'Sunbeam'	Last listed 1998
- 'Sunset Gold'	Last listed 1997
decurrens	EBee WPGP
- JCA 4.542.500	WCot
ephemerum	More than 30 suppliers
fortunei	EBee EBrP EBre LBCl LBSe LBre MBBe SBre SHel SMac WCot
henryi	CLTr EWes GBuc
japonica var. *minutissima*	CInt CRow CStu GBuc GCHN MDCh MTho NLar SIng WCru WPer
lanceolata	Last listed 1998
lichiangensis	CFir CSam EBee EBrP EBre EMFP EMan GKir GSki LBCl LBSe LBre MBBe MCCP MLLN NArg SAga SBre SHFr SMac WBor WPer WPnP WRus
- B&L 12317	CGle
- B&L 12464	Last listed 1999
lyssii	See *L. congestiflora*
mauritiana	EMan GMac NCut WCot WPnP
minoricensis	CPle EBee EEls EHrv ELan EMan EPla EPri EWTr LRHS NCut SCob SHFr SMac SSca STes SWat WByw WHer WLRN WOve WPer WRos WWin
nemorum	EFer EWFC WPer WRHF
- 'Little Sun'	WAlt
- 'Pale Star'	CBre WAlt WCot
nummularia	More than 30 suppliers
- 'Aurea' ♀	More than 30 suppliers
ovata	Last listed 1997
pseudohenryi	EBee
punctata L.	More than 30 suppliers
§ - 'Alexander' (v)	More than 30 suppliers
- dwarf	Last listed 1999
¶ - 'Golden Glory' (v)	WCot
- misapplied	See *L. verticillaris*
* - 'Snow Lady'	Last listed 1999
- 'Sunspot'	EBee
- 'Variegata'	See *L. punctata* 'Alexander'
- *verticillata*	See *L. verticillaris*
I 'Purpurea'	See *L. atropurpurea*
serpyllifolia	SHFr WCot
sertulata	WCot
thyrsiflora	EHon MSta NDea SWat WHer WMAq
§ *verticillaris*	WCot
vulgaris	CArn EHon EWFC LPBA MHew MMal SIde WCot WFar WGwy WPer WWye
- subsp. *davurica*	WCot

LYSIONOTUS (Gesneriaceae)

pauciflora	GCrs NTow
- B&SWJ 1679	WCru
- B&SWJ 189	WCru
- B&SWJ 303	WCru
- B&SWJ 335	WCru

LYTHRUM (Lythraceae)

'Croftway'	Last listed 1997
'Red Wings'	Last listed 1998
salicaria	More than 30 suppliers
- 'Blush'	More than 30 suppliers
- 'Brightness'	EBee NArg NCat NFla NHol
§ - 'Feuerkerze' ♀	More than 30 suppliers
- Firecandle	See *L. salicaria* 'Feuerkerze'
- 'Florarose'	NCat
- 'Happy'	SMrm
- 'Lady Sackville'	CBos GBuc GCal GGar GMaP LFis LRHS MBNS MCAu NCat SUsu
- 'Morden Pink'	LGre LRHS MBri SUsu
- 'Robert'	More than 30 suppliers
- 'Rose'	ELan MWgw
- 'Stichflamme'	EFou NCat
- 'The Beacon'	CRow EMan GCal SRms
- Ulverscroft form	MTed
- 'Zigeunerblut'	CPlt CRDP EGle LGre MRav SAga
virgatum	LGre NCat SMrm SPer WCot WWye
- 'Dropmore Purple'	CLTr CRDP EFou EWTr LRHS MBri MCAu MCLN MSte NCut WFar
- 'Rose Queen'	ECha EMan MRav SUsu WPer
- 'Rosy Gem'	CM&M CRow EBee ECtt EGar EPfP GKir GMac LSyl MBNS MFir MTis MWat NBid NBro NOak SBea SCob SMer SRms STes WBea WHoo WPer
- 'The Bride'	Last listed 1999
- 'The Rocket'	CRow CTri EBee EGle LAst LRHS NCat NHol NSti SMer SPer WElm WWin

LYTOCARYUM (Arecaceae)

§ *weddellianum* ♀	LPal MBri

M

MAACKIA (Papilionaceae)

amurensis	CB&S CMCN EBee ELan EPfP SFur WNor
- var. *buergeri*	Last listed 1999
chinensis	CMCN MBlu WShe
fauriei	CPle

MACBRIDEA (Lamiaceae)

caroliniana	EBee

MACFADYENA (Bignoniaceae)

§ *unguis-cati*	CPlN CRHN

MACHAERANTHERA (Asteraceae)

lagunensis	Last listed 1997
shastensis	EBee

MACHILUS See PERSEA

MACKAYA (Acanthaceae)

§ *bella* ♀	ERea SYvo

MACLEANIA (Ericaceae)

insignis	CPlN

MACLEAYA (Papaveraceae)

N *cordata* ♀	CArn CHEx CMCo COIW EBee ECoo ELan EMar EPar GKir LGre

- 'Flamingo'	LRHS MSCN MWat NOrc SAga SCob SPar SPer SPlb SRCN SRms WAbe WCot WEas WFar WPer WWhi WWin EBee ECha EOld GCHN GCal MCLN SMrm WWye	
x *kewensis*	MBro MTed WElm WHoo WPGP WPyg	
§ *microcarpa*	EPPr MAnH NPSI SWat WHer WSel	
- 'Kelway's Coral Plume' ♀	More than 30 suppliers	
'Spetchley Ruby'	WCot	

MACLURA (Moraceae)
pomifera	CB&S CCHP CFil CMCN CPle IDee SLon SMHT WDin WPGP WPic WWat

MACRODIERVILLA See WEIGELA

MACROPIPER (Piperaceae)
§ *excelsum*	CHEx ECou
- 'Aureopictum'	CHEx

MACROZAMIA (Zamiaceae)
communis	CBrP CRoM LPal WNor
diplomera	CBrP
dyeri	See *M. riedlei*
lucida	CBrP
miquelii	CBrP LPal
moorei	CBrP CRoM CTrC LPal
mountperiensis	CBrP
§ *riedlei*	CBrP LPal
spiralis	Last listed 1998

MADIA (Asteraceae)
¶ *elegans*	EMan

MAESA (Myrsinaceae)
¶ *montana*	CPLG

MAGNOLIA ✿ (Magnoliaceae)
acuminata	CB&S CFil CMCN EPfP
* - 'Kinju'	CFil
- 'Koban Dori'	CFil CPMA
- large yellow	Last listed 1999
§ - var. *subcordata*	CB&S WPGP
§ - - 'Miss Honeybee'	LRHS SSpi
'Albatross'	CPMA CTho SSpi
'Ann' ♀	COtt CTrh SSpi
'Anne Rosse' AM	CFil
'Apollo'	CB&S CFil CPMA CTho EMil LRHS SSpi
asbei	See *M. macrophylla* subsp. *asbei*
'Athene'	CMHG CPMA CTho LRHS
'Atlas'	CB&S CEnd CFil CMHG CPMA CTho SSpi
'Betty' ♀	CB&S CBlo CDoC CLAP IOrc LNet LPan MAsh MGos SSta WLRN WPyg
'Big Dude'	CFil SSpi WPGP
biondii	CFil SSpi WPGP
x *brooklynensis* 'Woodsman'	CPMA LBuc SBrw SSta
'Butterflies'	CDoC CFai CFil CPMA EPfP LRHS MAsh MDun SSpi SSta WPGP
'Caerhays Belle'	CB&S CPMA
'Caerhays Surprise'	CB&S CPMA
campbellii	CB&S CDul CFil CMCN CPMA CRos CSam CTho EBee ELan EPfP IOrc ISea LRHS MNes SSpi WPGP

¶ - Alba Group	CB&S CEnd CMHG CPMA CTho MGos SPer WBod WPGP
- - 'Strybing White'	CPMA
- 'Betty Jessel'	CMHG CTho
- 'Darjeeling'	CB&S CPMA
- subsp. *mollicomata*	CB&S CEnd CPMA CSam CTrw EPfP ISea LRHS WHCr WPGP
- - 'Lanarth'	CEnd WBod
- (Raffillii Group) 'Charles Raffill' ♀	CAbP CB&S CBlo CLnd CPMA ELan LRHS MDun MGos MLan SBrw SPer SRPl WBod WCwm WWat
- - 'Kew's Surprise'	CB&S CPMA
- x *sargentiana* var. *robusta*	WPic
'Cecil Nice'	CFil
Chameleon	See *M*. 'Chang Hua'
§ 'Chang Hua'	CPMA
'Charles Coates'	LRHS WGer
'Columbus'	CFil CPMA WPGP
cordata	See *M. acuminata* var. *subcordata*
- 'Miss Honeybee'	See *M. acuminata* var. *subcordata* 'Miss Honeybee'
'Cup Cake'	Last listed 1997
cylindrica hort.	See *M*. 'Pegasus'
- Wilson	CMCN LRHS SSpi
* 'Dan Quing'	CPMA
¶ 'Dark Shadow'	WPGP
'David Clulow'	CB&S CPMA SSpi
dawsoniana	CB&S CMCN CPMA
¶ - 'Chyverton Red'	SSpi
- 'Clarke'	LRHS
dealbata	See *M. macrophylla* subsp. *dealbata*
delavayi	CB&S CFil CHEx CMCN EPfP GGGa LRHS SAPC SArc WPGP
- S&F 432	Last listed 1998
§ *denudata* ♀	CB&S CMCN CTho CTrw EMac EMil EPfP IOrc LPan LRHS SMur SPer SReu SSpi SSta WBod WNor WWat
- 'Forrest's Pink'	CFil COtt CPMA
¶ - 'Gere'	CB&S
'Elisa Odenwald'	CFil WPGP
'Elizabeth' ♀	CDoC CFil CLAP CMCN CPMA CTho ELan EPfP GGGa LRHS MAsh MDun MGos MNes NHol SPer SSpi SSta WBod WPGP
Fragrant Cloud	See *M*. 'Dan Quing'
'Frank Gladney'	Last listed 1997
'Full Eclipse'	CFil WPGP
'Galaxy' ♀	CB&S CDoC CEnd CFil CLAP CPMA CTho EPfP IOrc ISea LPan LRHS MBar MBlu MGos SLdr SSpi SSta WBod WPGP
'George Henry Kern'	CB&S CBlo CDoC COtt EBee EMil IOrc ISea LPan LRHS MGos MSte SSpi SSta WBod
globosa	CFil GGGa WPGP WWat
¶ 'Gold Star'	CFil CPMA LRHS SSpi WPGP
grandiflora	CBlo CDul CHEx CMCN EBrP EBre EPfP LAst LBCl LBSe LBre LRHS MBBe MRav NBlu SAPC SArc SBre SRPl WDin WNor WWat
- 'Angustifolia'	Last listed 1999
- 'Edith Bogue'	EBee ENot
- 'Exmouth' ♀	More than 30 suppliers
- 'Ferruginea'	CB&S
- 'Galissonnière'	CBlo COtt GOrc IMGH IOrc LHyr LPan LRHS MGos SBrw SLim SSpi WBod

I - 'Galissonnière Nana' LPan
- 'Goliath' ♀ CB&S CBlo CEnd CFil CHEx ELan EPfP IOrc LNet SBrw SPla SSpi SSta WBod WPGP
- 'Little Gem' CBlo CDoC CPMA LRHS MAsh SSpi WBcn WStI
* - 'Nana Flore Pleno' CPMA
- 'Russet' CPMA LNet
- 'Saint Mary' CPMA
- 'Samuel Sommer' CHEx CPMA SAPC SArc WGer
- 'Silver Tip' Last listed 1999
- 'Undulata' IOrc
- 'Victoria' CDoC CFil EBee ELan EPfP LAst LHyd LRHS MAsh MBlu MBri SBrw SLim SReu SSpi SSta WCwm WPGP

'Hawk' CFil
'Heaven Scent' ♀ CAbP CB&S CBlo CDoC CMCN COtt CSam CTho CTrh CTrw EBee ELan EPfP GChr IOrc LPan LRHS MAsh MBar MBlu MGos MWat SBrw SPer SSpi SSta WDin WPGP WPyg
'Helen Fogg' CFil WPGP
heptapeta See M. denudata
§ 'Hong Yur' CPMA
'Hot Lips' CFil WPGP
hypoleuca See M. obovata Thunb.
'Iolanthe' ♀ CB&S CDoC CEnd CFil CMCN CMHG CPMA CTho GKir LRHS MAsh MGos NHol SPer SSpi SSta WBod WPGP
'Jane' ♀ CBlo CDoC COtt ELan GKir IOrc LRHS MAsh MBri MGos NHol SBrw SLdr SPer SSta
'Joe McDaniel' See M. x soulangeana 'Joe McDaniel'
'Jon Jon' Last listed 1999
'Judy' ♀ COtt
§ x *kewensis* 'Kew Clone' Last listed 1998
- 'Wada's Memory' ♀ CB&S CDoC CFil CLAP CMCN CMHG CPMA CTho CTri EBee ELan EPfP GKir LRHS MAsh MBri SPer SSpi SSta

kobus CB&S CBlo CDul CGre CMCN CPMA CTho ENot IOrc LHyd LPan NMoo SPer SSta WBod WDin WNor WSpi WWat
- var. *borealis* CPMA CTho
- 'Norman Gould' See M. stellata 'Norman Gould'
* 'Laura' Last listed 1999
'Lilenny' SSta
§ *liliiflora* CBlo CTrw MAsh MBar
§ - 'Nigra' ♀ More than 30 suppliers
* 'Limelight' CFil
x *loebneri* CB&S LRHS WNor WShe
- 'Ballerina' CDoC COtt SBrw SSta
¶ - 'Donna' SSpi
- 'Leonard Messel' ♀ More than 30 suppliers
- 'Merrill' ♀ More than 30 suppliers
- 'Neil McEacharn' IOrc
- 'Powder Puff' Last listed 1999
- 'Raspberry Fun' Last listed 1999
- 'Snowdrift' CMCN SSta
- 'Spring Joy' Last listed 1999
- 'Spring Snow' CMCN
- 'Star Bright' Last listed 1998
macrophylla CBrP CFil CHEx CMCN EPfP MBlu SAPC SArc SMad SSpi WMul WNor WPGP
§ - subsp. *ashei* WNor
§ - subsp. *dealbata* Last listed 1999

- 'Sara Gladney' Last listed 1998
'Manchu Fan' CB&S CPMA EMil IOrc SMur SSta WBod
'Mark Jury' CPMA
'Marwood Spring' CB&S CTho
'Maryland' ♀ CFil CPMA SBrw SSpi WPGP
'Milky Way' CFil CMHG COtt CPMA CTho MGos SMur WBod
'Nimbus' Last listed 1997
§ *obovata* Thunb. ♀ CFil CHEx CMCN CPMA CTho EPfP MLan SMad SPer SSpi SSta WCwm WWat
- Diels See M. officinalis
§ *officinalis* CFil WPGP
- var. *biloba* ♀ EPfP
§ 'Pegasus' ♀ IOrc ISea SSpi
'Peppermint Stick' ♀ CPMA MGos SSta
'Peter Smithers' CPMA IOrc
'Phelan Bright' CFil WPGP
'Pickard's Coral' Last listed 1999
'Pickard's Crystal' Last listed 1997
'Pickard's Opal' Last listed 1998
'Pickard's Pink Diamond' Last listed 1997
'Pickard's Ruby' CDoC COtt
§ 'Pickard's Schmetterling' CDoC SSta
'Pickard's Sundew' See M. 'Sundew'
'Pinkie' ♀ COtt IOrc LRHS MAsh MBri SSta
'Pirouette' SSpi
'Princess Margaret' CPMA SSpi
x *proctoriana* ♀ CAbP CDoC CFil EPfP IOrc LRHS SPer WPGP
- 'Proctoriana' LHyd
- 'Slavin's Snowy' LRHS
* 'Purple Glow' Last listed 1999
'Purple Prince' Last listed 1999
quinquepeta See M. liliiflora
'Randy' ♀ COtt
'Raspberry Ice' CDoC CLAP CMHG COtt CRos CTho CTrw IOrc LRHS SSta
'Ricki' ♀ COtt CPMA EMil IOrc MBri MGos SSta WWat
rostrata WWat
'Rouged Alabaster' LRHS
'Royal Crown' CDoC EMil SSta
'Ruby' CPMA MGos WBod
salicifolia ♀ CFil CMCN EBee EPfP ISea LRHS SPer SSpi SSta
- var. *concolor* SSpi
* - 'Rosea' Last listed 1999
- 'W.B. Clarke' See M. 'W.B. Clarke'
sargentiana CFil IOrc
- var. *robusta* CB&S CBrd CEnd CLnd CMCN ELan EPfP IMGH IOrc ISea MGos SPer SSpi SSta WBod WCwm WPGP WWat
- - *alba* Last listed 1998
- - 'Multipetal' CBrd
'Sayonara' ♀ COtt CPMA EPfP IOrc MBlu SBrw SSpi WDin
'Schmetterling' See M. 'Pickard's Schmetterling'
'Serene' CPMA SSpi SSta
* 'Seyu' Last listed 1998
sieboldii CB&S CBlo CGre CMCN CPMA EBee ELan EMil EPfP GKir IOrc LPan LRHS MBar MBri MDun MGos SLon SPer SSpi SSta WBod WNor WSpi WWat
¶ - B&SWJ 4127 WCru
- subsp. *sinensis* ♀ CB&S CBlo CDoC CMCN CSam ELan EPfP GGGa MDun SMad SPer SSpi SSta WBod WDin WLRN WWat

× *soulangeana*	More than 30 suppliers
§ - 'Alba'	CB&S CBlo CDul CEnd ENot IOrc LPan LRHS MAsh MGos SLim SPer SSpi WWat
- 'Alba Superba'	See *M.* × *soulangeana* 'Alba'
- 'Alexandrina' ♀	CB&S CBlo COtt IOrc LRHS MGos
- 'Alexandrina Alba'	Last listed 1999
- 'Amabilis'	COtt IOrc
- 'Brozzonii' ♀	CDoC CMHG EPfP IOrc LPan LRHS SSpi
¶ - 'Burgundy'	ISea
- 'Burgundy' Clarke	CB&S CBot CDoC LRHS SSta
§ - 'Joe McDaniel'	CDoC
- 'Lennei' ♀	CB&S CBlo CDoC CEnd CMCN CMHG EPfP IOrc LPan LRHS MAsh MGos NHol NPri SBrw SLim SPer SRms SSta WGer WNor WPGP WPyg WStI
- 'Lennei Alba' ♀	CMCN IOrc SLdr SSta
- 'Nigra'	See *M. liliiflora* 'Nigra'
- 'Pickard's Sundew'	See *M.* 'Sundew'
- 'Picture'	CBlo CDoC IOrc
- Red Lucky	See *M.* 'Hong Yur'
- 'Rubra' misapplied	See *M.* × *soulangeana* 'Rustica Rubra'
§ - 'Rustica Rubra' ♀	CB&S CDoC CEnd CMCN EBrP EBre ELan ENot EPfP IMGH IOrc LBCl LBSe LBre LNet LPan LRHS MAsh MBBe MBri SBre SPer SReu SRob SSpi SSta WPGP WWat
- 'San José'	CRos IOrc LRHS MAsh MBri SSpi SSta
- 'Verbanica'	LRHS MAsh SSpi
- 'White Giant'	SBrw WPGP
'Spectrum'	CB&S CFil CPMA MGos SSpi WBod WPGP
sprengeri	WNor WShe WWes
- var. *diva*	CB&S CFil CMCN SSpi
- - 'Burncoose'	CB&S
- - 'Claret Cup'	WPGP
- - 'Lanhydrock'	CFil SSpi
- var. *elongata*	COtt IOrc ISea
- 'Eric Savill'	CFil SSpi
'Star Wars'	CB&S CDoC CFil CPMA CTho EMil EPfP SBrw SSpi SSta
§ *stellata* ♀	More than 30 suppliers
- 'Centennial'	CDoC SBrw SSta
- 'Chrysanthemiflora'	LRHS SSpi
- 'Jane Platt'	SSpi
- f. *keiskei*	CEnd COtt
- 'King Rose'	CB&S CBlo COtt EPfP LRHS MAsh MBlu MBri SBrw SPer WBod
- 'Massey'	Last listed 1997
§ - 'Norman Gould'	CMCN COtt EPfP MBri SSta
- 'Rosea'	COtt ELan IOrc LRHS MDun MGos WPyg
- 'Royal Star'	CB&S CBlo CBrm CDoC CEnd CLAP CLan CMCN CSam EBee ECtt EMil ENot EPfP IOrc LPan LRHS MAsh MBri MGos NHol SBrw SPer SSpi SSta WHar WOrn WStI
- 'Waterlily' ♀	CB&S CBlo CEnd CMCN CRos CSam ELan EMil EPfP GOrc IOrc LRHS MAsh SPer SPla SSht SSpi SSta WPyg
'Summer Solstice'	SSpi
'Sundance'	CFil CPMA EMil MDun MGos WBod WPGP
§ 'Sundew'	CB&S CDoC CMCN EPfP IOrc MGos SBrw SMrm WBod WPGP
'Susan' ♀	More than 30 suppliers

× *thompsoniana*	CMCN
'Tiffany'	Last listed 1999
'Tina Durio'	CDoC
'Todd Gresham'	CPMA WPGP
tripetala	CB&S CHEx CLnd CMCN CPne EOas EPfP LPan MDun MLan NWea SMad SSpi SSta WBod WCwm WDin WPGP WWat
- 'Woodlawn'	EPfP
× *veitchii*	CDoC EPfP SSpi SSta WBod
- 'Isca'	CTho
- 'Peter Veitch'	CFil CGre CTho SSta
virginiana	CGre CMCN CPMA SSpi WPGP
- 'Havener'	Last listed 1999
'Vulcan'	CB&S CMHG COtt CPMA CTho
§ 'W.B. Clarke'	Last listed 1997
× *watsonii*	See *M.* × *wiesneri*
§ × *wiesneri*	CB&S CMCN CPMA ELan EPfP GKir ISea LRHS MAsh MBlu SPer SSpi SSta
wilsonii ♀	More than 30 suppliers
- 'Gwen Baker'	CEnd
'Winelight'	CFil
'Yellow Bird'	CFil COtt CPMA EPfP LRHS MBlu MDun MGos MNes SSpi SSta
'Yellow Fever'	CB&S CFil CPMA EMil MDun SMur SSta
'Yellow Lantern'	CFil EPfP GKir LRHS MAsh SSpi SSta WPGP

× MAHOBERBERIS (Berberidaceae)

aquisargentii	CAbP CPle EBee ENot EPfP EPla GBin GKir MRav NHol SLon WPat WPyg WWat
'Dart's Treasure'	EPla WFar
'Magic'	MGos
miethkeana	MBar SRms

MAHONIA ✿ (Berberidaceae)

§ *aquifolium*	CAgr CB&S CDul EBee ENot GCHN GChr GKir GOrc LAst MBar MBri MGos MRav MWat NFla NFor NWea SPer SPlb SReu WCFE WDin WFar WStI WWat
- 'Apollo' ♀	CMac ECtt ELan EMil ENot EOld EPfP EPla GKir IOrc LRHS MAsh MBar MBri MGos NBee SMer SReu SSta WPyg WWat
- 'Atropurpurea'	CDoC ELan ENot EPla EWTr GKir LRHS MAsh NBee SPer SPla
* - 'Cosmo Crawl'	MGos
- 'Fascicularis'	See *M.* × *wagneri* 'Pinnacle'
- 'Green Ripple'	EPfP EPla MBri MGos WBcn WFar
- 'Mirena'	MGos
- 'Orange Flame'	EPfP MBlu
- 'Smaragd'	CB&S CBlo CDoC CMac EBee ELan ENot EPfP EPla IOrc MBlu MGos SLPl WHCG WPyg
- 'Versicolor'	MBlu
bealei	See *M. japonica* Bealei Group
confusa	CDoC CFil EPla WCru WPGP WWat
eutriphylla	See *M. trifolia*
fortunei	EPla WBcn WSHC
fremontii	GCal
- × *haematocarpa*	Last listed 1998
gracilipes	MDun WSPU
'Gulf Tide'	Last listed 1997
haematocarpa	GCal
japonica ♀	More than 30 suppliers
§ - Bealei Group	CB&S CDul CLan EBee EBrP EBre ELan EPfP EPla GKir IOrc LAst

	LBCl LBSe LBre LRHS MAsh MBBe
	MBar MGos MRav NPer SBre SEas
	SLim SMer SRPl WDin WWeb
- 'Hiemalis'	See *M. japonica* 'Hivernant'
§ - 'Hivernant'	EPla MGos NBlu WPyg
lomariifolia ♀	CB&S CBot CHEx ENot EPfP IOrc
	LRHS SAPC SArc SDry SLon SPla
	SSpi WSHC WSpi
x *media* 'Arthur Menzies'	EPla
- 'Buckland' ♀	CAbP CB&S CDul CEnd CMac
	CSam CTrw EBee ECtt EPfP LRHS
	MAsh MBri SPer SRPl SRms WBod
	WPat WPyg WRHF WWat
- 'Charity' ♀	More than 30 suppliers
- 'Charity's Sister'	EPla MBri
- 'Faith'	EPla
- 'Lionel Fortescue' ♀	More than 30 suppliers
- 'Underway' ♀	CSam EPfP EPla LRHS MBri SMur
	SPla WWes
- 'Winter Sun' ♀	More than 30 suppliers
nervosa	CB&S CCtt EPfP EPla MBlu NBee
	NHol SBrw SPer SSta WPGP
pallida	CFil WPGP WWat
- T&K 553	Last listed 1997
N *pinnata*	EBee ELan ENot EPfP EPla IOrc
	MBar
piperiana	Last listed 1997
pumila	SSpi WCru
repens	EPla ERav MWhi WBod
- 'Rotundifolia'	EPla
russellii	CFil CGre
¶ x *savilliana*	EPla
siamensis	CGre
§ *trifolia*	EPla
trifoliolata	EPfP
- var. *glauca*	CEnd
x *wagneri* 'Fireflame'	EPla
- 'Moseri'	EMil SSpi WPat WSPU
§ - 'Pinnacle' ♀	EPfP EPla EWTr LRHS MAsh
	MGos NFor SBrw SMur SPer
- 'Sunset'	MBlu
- 'Undulata' ♀	ECtt ENot EPfP MBlu SDix SPer
	SRms WHCG

MAIANTHEMUM (Convallariaceae)

bifolium	CAvo CHid CRDP CRow EBee
	EMon EPot EWFC GBuc GKir
	MDun MNrw MTho NBro NMen
	SLod SRms WCru WGwy WLin
	WPGP WTin WWat WWye
§ - subsp. *kamtschaticum*	CAvo CLAP CRDP CRow EPar
	LSyl SUsu WCot
* - - 'Variegatum'	Last listed 1999
canadense	GCal MSal
dilatatum	See *M. bifolium* subsp.
	kamtschaticum
oleraceum	WCru WViv

MALACOTHAMNUS (Malvaceae)

fremontii	WLin

MALEPHORA (Aizoaceae)

lutea	CNic EOas

MALLOTUS (Euphorbiaceae)

japonicus	Last listed 1997

MALPIGHIA (Malpighiaceae)

coccigera	Last listed 1999

MALUS ✿ (Rosaceae)

'Adirondack'	EPfP MAsh MGos

x *adstringens* 'Hopa'	CBlo CLnd MAsh SCrf
- 'Simcoe'	CDoC CLnd EBee MGos
'Aldenhamensis'	See *M.* x *purpurea*
	'Aldenhamensis'
* *arborescens*	CTho
x *atrosanguinea*	Last listed 1999
§ - 'Gorgeous'	CBlo CDul COtt GChr GKir GTwe
	MAsh MBri MGos SCrf SLim WDin
	WJas
baccata	CFil CLnd CMCN CTho GTwe
	NWea SEND WNor
- 'Dolgo'	COtt
- 'Gracilis'	CSam
- 'Lady Northcliffe'	CLnd SFam
- var. *mandshurica*	EPfP
¶ - 'Street Parade'	MBri
aff. *baccata* MF 96038	SSpi
§ *bhutanica*	CDul CLnd CMCN CTho SPer
	SRPl WHCr WNor
brevipes	CTho
'Butterball'	CLnd GKir LRHS MBlu MBri WJas
* 'Cheal's Weeping'	NBea SPer WStI
coronaria var. *dasycalyx*	CBlo CDoC CEnd CLnd CSam
'Charlottae' (d)	ENot EPfP LRHS MAsh MBlu
	MBri SCrf SFam SMHT SPer
'Crittenden'	EBee ENot
* 'Directeur Moerlands'	CBlo CDoC CDul EPfP EWTr GKir
	LRHS MAsh MBri MGos WJas
domestica (F)	MGos
- 'Acklam Russet' (D)	Last listed 1997
- 'Acme' (D)	SDea SKee
- 'Adams's Pearmain' (D)	CCAT CTho GKir GTwe LBuc
	LRHS SDea SFam SKee WJas
- 'Admiral' (D)	Last listed 1997
- 'Advance' (D)	SKee
- 'Akane' (D)	SDea
§ - 'Alexander' (C)	SKee
- 'Alfriston' (C)	SKee
- 'Alkmene' (D) ♀	GTwe SDea SKee
- 'All Red Gravenstein' (D)	NRog
- 'Allen's Everlasting' (D)	GTwe SDea SKee
- 'Allington Pippin' (D)	CCAT CSam CTho CTri LRHS
	NRog SDea SKee WJas
- 'American Mother'	See *M. domestica* 'Mother'
- 'Anna Boelens' (D)	SDea
- 'Annie Elizabeth' (C)	CCAT CTho GKir GTwe LRHS
	MBri MCoo SDea SFam SKee WJas
- 'Anniversary'	SDea
- 'Api Noir' (D)	Last listed 1999
- 'Api Rose' (D)	WJas
- 'Ard Cairn Russet' (D)	GTwe SDea SKee
¶ - 'Arkansas' (D)	SKee
- 'Aromatic Russet' (D)	SKee
- 'Arthur Turner' (C) ♀	CDoC EBee EMui GChr GKir
	GTwe LBuc LRHS MGos NRog
	SCrf SDea SFam SKee WJas
- 'Arthur W. Barnes' (C)	SKee
- 'Ashmead's Kernel' (D) ♀	CCAT CSam CTho CTri EBrP EBre
	EMui ERea GKir GTwe LBCl LBSe
	LBre LBuc LRHS MBBe MWat
	NRog NWea SBre SCrf SDea SFam
	SKee WHar WJas
- 'Ashton Bitter' (Cider)	CCAT CEnd CTho GTwe SFam
- 'Ashton Brown	CCAT CTho
Jersey' (Cider)	
- 'Autumn Pearmain' (D)	CTho SDea WJas
- 'Baker's Delicious' (D)	SDea
- 'Ballarat Seedling' (D)	Last listed 1997
¶ - 'Ball's Bittersweet' (Cider)	CTho
- 'Balsam'	See *M. domestica* 'Green Balsam'
- 'Banns' (D)	SKee
- 'Barnack Beauty' (D)	CTho SKee

- 'Barnack Orange' (D) — SKee
- 'Bascombe Mystery' (D) — Last listed 1999
- 'Baumann's Reinette' (D) — SKee
- 'Baxter's Pearmain' (C/D) — SKee
- 'Beachamwell' (D) — Last listed 1997
- 'Beauty of Bath' (D) — CCAT CDoC CTho CTri GKir GTwe IOrc LBuc LRHS NRog SCrf SDea SFam SKee WJas
- 'Beauty of Hants' (D) — SKee
- 'Beauty of Kent' (C) — SDea SKee
- 'Beauty of Moray' (C) — SKee
- 'Bedwyn Beauty' (C) — CTho
- 'Beeley Pippin' (D) — GTwe SDea SKee
¶ - 'Belfleur Kitaika' (D) — SKee
¶ - 'Belfleur Krasnyi' (D) — SKee
- 'Bell Apple' (Cider/C) — CTho
- 'Belle de Boskoop' (C/D) ♀ — CCAT CTho GTwe NRog SDea SKee
¶ - 'Belle Flavoise' — SKee
- 'Bembridge Beauty' (F) — SDea
- 'Ben's Red' (D) — CEnd CTho SKee
- 'Bess Pool' (D) — SDea SFam SKee WJas
- 'Bewley Down Pippin' — See *M. domestica* 'Crimson King'
- 'Billy Down Pippin' (F) — CTho
- 'Bismarck' (C) — CTho NRog SKee
- 'Black Dabinette' (Cider) — CCAT CTho
- 'Black Tom Putt' (C/D) — CTho
- 'Blaze' (D) — Last listed 1999
- 'Blenheim Orange' (C/D) ♀ — CCAT CDoC CTho CTri EMui GBon GKir GTwe LBuc LRHS MBri MWat NRog SCrf SDea SFam SKee SPer WJas WWeb
- 'Blenheim Red' — See *M. domestica* 'Red Blenheim'
- 'Bloody Ploughman' (D) — SKee
- 'Blue Pearmain' (D) — SDea SKee
- 'Blue Sweet' (Cider) — CTho
- Bolero[PBR] — See *M. domestica* Bolero = 'Tuscan'
§ - Bolero = 'Tuscan' [PBR] (D/Ball) — LRHS MGos SDea
- 'Boston Russet' — See *M. domestica* 'Roxbury Russet'
- 'Bountiful' (C) — CCAT COtt EMui GKir GTwe LRHS MBri MGos SDea WHar WStI
- 'Bow Hill Pippin' (D) — Last listed 1999
- 'Box Apple' (D) — SKee
- 'Braddick Nonpareil' (D) — SKee
- 'Braeburn' (D) — SDea SKee
- 'Bramley's Seedling' (C) ♀ — More than 30 suppliers
- 'Bread Fruit' (C/D) — CEnd
- 'Breakwell's Seedling' (Cider) — CCAT CTho
- 'Bridgwater Pippin' (C) — CCAT CTho WJas
- 'Bringewood Pippin' (D) — WJas
- 'Broad-eyed Pippin' (C) — SKee
¶ - 'Brown Crofton' (D) — SKee
- 'Brown Snout' (Cider) — CCAT CTho
- 'Brown Thorn' (Cider) — CCAT
- 'Brownlees Russet' (D) — CTho EMui GTwe LRHS NRog NWea SDea SFam SKee
- 'Brown's Apple' (Cider) — CCAT GTwe
- 'Broxwood Foxwhelp' (Cider) — CCAT CTho
- 'Bulmer's Norman' (Cider) — CCAT
- 'Burn's Seedling' (D) — CTho
- 'Burr Knot' (C) — SKee
- 'Burrowhill Early' (Cider) — CTho
- 'Bushey Grove' (C) — SDea SKee
- 'Calville Blanc d'Hiver' (D) — SKee
- 'Calville des Femmes' (C) — Last listed 1997
- 'Cambusnethan Pippin' (D) — SKee

- 'Camelot' (Cider/C) — CCAT CTho
- 'Cap of Liberty' (Cider) — CCAT
- 'Captain Broad' (D/Cider) — CCAT CEnd CTho
- 'Captain Kidd' (D) — Last listed 1997
- 'Captain Smith' (F) — CEnd
- 'Carlisle Codlin' (C) — GKir GTwe
- 'Caroline' (D) — Last listed 1997
- 'Carswell's Orange' (D) — SKee
- 'Catherine' (C) — Last listed 1997
- 'Catshead' (C) — CCAT GQui SDea SKee WJas
- 'Cellini' (C/D) — SDea
- 'Charles Ross' (C/D) ♀ — CCAT CDoC CMac CSam CTho EBrP EBre EMui EWTr GBon GKir GTwe LBCl LBSe LBre LRHS MBBe MBri MWat NBea NRog NWea SBre SDea SFam SKee WHar WJas
- 'Charlotte' [PBR] (C/Ball) — LBuc LRHS MGos SDea
- 'Chaxhill Red' (Cider/D) — CTho
- 'Cheddar Cross' (D) — CTri SKee
- 'Chelmsford Wonder' (C) — SKee
- 'Chisel Jersey' (Cider) — CCAT CTho
- 'Chivers Delight' (D) — CCAT CSam EMui GTwe LRHS SCrf SDea SKee WJas
- 'Chorister Boy' (D) — CTho
- 'Christmas Pearmain' (D) — CTho GTwe SDea SFam SKee
- 'Cider Lady's Finger' (Cider) — CCAT CTho
¶ - 'Cistecké' (D) — SKee
- 'Claygate Pearmain' (D) ♀ — CCAT CTho GTwe SDea SFam SKee WJas
- 'Close' (D) — Last listed 1997
- 'Coat Jersey' (Cider) — CCAT
- 'Cockle Pippin' (D) — CTho GTwe SDea SKee
- 'Cockpit' (C) — Last listed 1997
- 'Coeur de Boeuf' (C/D) — SKee
- 'Coleman's Seedling' (Cider) — CTho
- 'Collogett Pippin' (C/Cider) — CEnd CTho
- 'Colonel Vaughan' (C/D) — CTho SKee
¶ - 'Cooper's Seedling' (C) — SCrf
- 'Cornish Aromatic' (D) — CCAT CDoC CSam CTho EMui GTwe LRHS SCrf SDea SFam SKee WJas
- 'Cornish Crimson Queen' (F) — GTwe
- 'Cornish Gilliflower' (D) — CCAT LRHS SDea SFam SKee WJas
- 'Cornish Honeypin' (D) — CTho
- 'Cornish Longstem' (D) — CEnd CTho
- 'Cornish Mother' (D) — CEnd
- 'Cornish Pine' (D) — CEnd CTho SDea SKee
- 'Coronation' (D) — SDea SKee
- 'Costard' (C) — GTwe SKee
- 'Cottenham Seedling' (C) — SKee
- 'Coul Blush' (D) — SKee
- 'Court of Wick' (D) — CCAT CTho SKee
- 'Court Pendu Plat' (D) — CCAT CTho LBuc MWat NRog NWea SDea SFam SKee WJas
§ - 'Court Royal' (Cider) — CCAT CTho
- 'Cox's Orange Pippin' (D) — CB&S CCAT CMac EBrP EBre EWTr GTwe LBCl LBSe LBre LBuc LRHS MBBe MBri MWat NRog NWea SBre SCrf SDea SFam SKee SPer WJas WWeb
- 'Cox's Pomona' (C/D) — CTho SDea SKee WJas
- 'Cox's Rouge de Flandres' (D) — SKee
- 'Cox's Selfing' (D) — CBlo CWSG ERea GTwe LBuc MBri MGos SCrf SKee WHar WJas WWeb

- 'Crawley Beauty' (C) — GTwe LRHS SDea SFam SKee WJas
- 'Crimson Bramley' (C) — CCAT SKee
- 'Crimson Cox' (D) — SDea
§ - 'Crimson King' (Cider/C) — CCAT CTho
- 'Crimson Peasgood' (C) — EBee
- 'Crimson Queening' (D) — SKee WJas
- 'Crimson Victoria' (Cider) — CTho
- Crispin — See *M. domestica* 'Mutsu'
§ - 'Crowngold' PBR (D) — CEnd EMui GBon GTwe LRHS
- 'Cummy Norman' (Cider) — CCAT
- 'Curl Tail' (D) — SKee
- 'Cutler Grieve' (D) — SDea
- 'Dabinett' (Cider) — CCAT CEnd CTho CTri EMui GTwe SCrf SDea SKee
- 'D'Arcy Spice' (D) — CCAT LRHS SDea SFam SKee
- 'Dawn' (D) — SKee
¶ - 'De Boutteville' (Cider) — CTho
- 'Deacon's Blushing Beauty' (C/D) — SDea
- 'Deacon's Millennium' — SDea
- 'Decio' (D) — SKee
- 'Delkid' (F) — GTwe
¶ - 'Delprim' (D) — SKee
- 'Devon Crimson Queen' (D) — CTho
- 'Devonshire Buckland' (C) — CEnd CTho WJas
- 'Devonshire Crimson Queen' (D) — SDea
- 'Devonshire Quarrenden' (D) — CCAT CEnd CSam CTho EMui LRHS SDea SFam SKee WJas
¶ - 'Devonshire Red' (D/C) — CTho
- 'Dewdney's Seedling' (C) — GTwe SKee
- 'Diamond Jubilee' (D) — SKee
- 'Discovery' (D) ♀ — CB&S CDoC CTri EBee EBrP EBre EMui EWTr GBon GKir GTwe IOrc LBCl LBSe LBre LBuc LRHS MBBe MBri MWat NBee NRog NWea SBre SDea SFam SKee SPer WJas WWeb
- 'Doctor Hare's' (C) — MCoo WJas
- 'Doctor Harvey' (C) — SFam
- 'Doctor Kidd's Orange Red' — See *M. domestica* 'Kidd's Orange Red'
- 'Dog's Snout' (C/D) — NRog
- 'Domino' (C) — SKee
- 'Don's Delight' (C) — CTho
- 'Doux Normandie' (Cider) — CCAT
- 'Dove' (Cider) — CTho
- 'Downton Pippin' (D) — SKee WJas
- 'Dredge's Fame' (D) — CTho
- 'Duchess of Oldenburg' (C/D) — SKee
- 'Duchess's Favourite' (D) — SKee
- 'Duck's Bill' (D) — Last listed 1997
- 'Dufflin' (Cider) — CCAT CTho
- 'Duke of Devonshire' (D) — CSam CTho SDea SFam SKee WJas
- 'Duke of Gloucester' (C) — WJas
N - 'Dumeller's Seedling' (C) — See *M. domestica* 'Dummellor's Seedling'
I - 'Dumelow's Seedling' — See *M. domestica* 'Dummellor's Seedling'
§ - 'Dummellor's Seedling' (C) ♀ — CCAT CTho SDea SKee
- 'Dunkerton Late Sweet' (Cider) — CCAT CTho
- 'Dunn's Seedling' (D) — SDea
- 'Dutch Codlin' (C) — CTho
§ - 'Dutch Mignonne' (D) — SKee
¶ - 'Eady's Magnum' (C) — SKee
- 'Early Blenheim' (D/C) — CEnd CTho
- 'Early Bower' (D) — CEnd
- 'Early Julyan' (C) — SKee WJas

- 'Early Victoria' — See *M. domestica* 'Emneth Early'
- 'Early Worcester' — See *M. domestica* 'Tydeman's Early Worcester'
- 'Easter Orange' (D) — GTwe SCrf SKee
- 'Ecklinville' (C) — SDea SKee WJas
- 'Edward VII' (C) ♀ — CDoC GTwe SCrf SDea SFam SKee WJas
- 'Egremont Russet' (D) ♀ — More than 30 suppliers
- 'Ellis' Bitter' (Cider) — CCAT CEnd CTho GTwe SFam
- 'Ellison's Orange' (D) ♀ — CCAT CSam CTri EBee GBon GKir GTwe LBuc LRHS MBri NRog NWea SDea SFam SKee WHar WJas WStI
¶ - 'Elmore Pippin' (D) — SKee
- 'Elstar' (D) ♀ — CCAT EMui GTwe IOrc SDea SKee
- 'Elton Beauty' (D) — SDea SKee
§ - 'Emneth Early' (C) ♀ — CTho GTwe NRog SDea SFam SKee WJas
- 'Emperor Alexander' — See *M. domestica* 'Alexander'
- 'Empire' (D) — SKee
- 'Encore' (C) — SDea
- 'English Codling' (C) — CTho
- 'Epicure' — See *M. domestica* 'Laxton's Epicure'
- 'Ernie's Russet' (D) — SDea
- 'Evening Gold' (C) — SDea
- 'Eve's Delight' (D) — SDea
- 'Exeter Cross' (D) — CCAT SDea SFam
- 'Eynsham Dumpling' (C) — Last listed 1997
- 'Fair Maid of Devon' (Cider) — CCAT
- 'Fair Maid of Taunton' (D) — CCAT WJas
- 'Fairfield' (D) — CTho
- 'Fall Pippin' (D) — Last listed 1997
- 'Fall Russet' (D) — GTwe
- 'Falstaff' PBR (D) ♀ — CCAT CDoC EMui EPfP GKir GTwe LRHS MBri MGos SDea SKee WJas
- 'Fameuse' (D) — SKee
- 'Fearn's Pippin' (D) — SKee
- 'Feuillemorte' (D) — SKee
- 'Fiesta' PBR (D) ♀ — CDoC CSam EBee EBrP EBre EMui GBon GChr GTwe LBCl LBSe LBre LBuc LRHS MBBe MBri MGos SBre SCrf SDea SFam SKee WHar WJas WWeb
- 'Fillbarrel' (Cider) — CCAT CTho
- 'Fillingham Pippin' (C) — Last listed 1997
- 'Fireside' (D) — Last listed 1998
- 'Firmgold' (D) — SDea
- 'Five Crowns' (D) — SKee
- 'Flamenco'™ (D) — MGos SDea
§ - 'Flower of Kent' (C) — CCAT SCrf SDea SKee
- 'Flower of the Town' (D) — SKee WJas
- 'Folkestone' (D) — Last listed 1997
- 'Forfar' — See *M. domestica* 'Dutch Mignonne'
- 'Forge' (D) — SDea SKee
- 'Formosa Nonpareil' (C) — WJas
- 'Fortune' — See *M. domestica* 'Laxton's Fortune'
- 'Foster's Seedling' (D) — SKee
- 'Foulden Pearmain' (D) — Last listed 1997
- 'Frederick' (Cider) — CCAT CTho
- 'French Crab' (C) — CTho SDea
- 'Freyberg' (D) — SKee
- 'Fuji' (D) — SDea SKee
- 'Gala' (D) — EBee GBon GTwe MBri SCrf SDea SFam SKee
§ - 'Gala Mondial' (F) — WJas
I - 'Gala Royal' — See *M. domestica* 'Royal Gala'

- 'Galloway Pippin' (C) GKir GTwe SKee
- 'Gascoyne's Scarlet' (D) SDea SFam SKee
- 'Gavin' (D) SDea SKee
- 'Genesis II' (D/C) SDea
- 'Genet Moyle' (C/Cider) CCAT CTho SKee WJas
- 'George Carpenter' (D) CTho SDea SKee
- 'George Cave' (D) CTho GTwe LBuc LRHS NBee NRog SCrf SDea SFam SKee WJas
- 'George Neal' (C) ♀ CTho SDea SFam
- 'Gilliflower of Gloucester' (D) CTho
- 'Gin' (Cider) Last listed 1997
- 'Gladstone' (D) CTho SKee WJas
§ - 'Glass Apple' (C/D) CEnd
- 'Gloria Mundi' (C) SDea SKee
- 'Glory of England' (C) WJas
- 'Gloster '69' (D) GTwe SDea SKee
- 'Gloucester Cross' (D) SKee
¶ - 'Gloucester Underleaf' CTho
¶ - 'Golden Ball' CTho
- 'Golden Bittersweet' (D) CCAT CTho
- 'Golden Delicious' (D) ♀ EBrP EBre GBon LBCl LBse LBre LRHS MBBe MBri NRog NWea SBre SCrf SDea SKee SPer WHar WStI WWeb
- 'Golden Glow' SDea
- 'Golden Harvey' (D) CCAT CTho
- 'Golden Knob' (D) CCAT CTho SKee
- 'Golden Noble' (C) ♀ CCAT CDoC CSam CTho EMui GTwe LRHS SDea SFam SKee
- 'Golden Nugget' (D) Last listed 1998
- 'Golden Pearmain' (D) Last listed 1998
- 'Golden Pippin' (C) CTho SKee
- 'Golden Reinette' (D) GTwe SKee
- 'Golden Russet' (D) GTwe SDea SKee WJas
- 'Golden Spire' (C) CTho NRog SDea SKee
- 'Golden Wonder' (C) CEnd
- 'Goldilocks' (D) GTwe
- 'Gooseberry' (C) SKee
- 'Goring' (Cider) CCAT CTho
- 'Grand Sultan' (D) CTho
- 'Granny Smith' (D) CLnd EBee GTwe SCrf SDea SKee SPer
- 'Gravenstein' (D) CCAT SDea SFam SKee
§ - 'Green Balsam' (C) NRog
- 'Greensleeves' PBR (D) ♀ CCAT CDoC CSam EBee EBrP EBre EMui GKir GTwe LBCl LBSe LBre LBuc LRHS MBBe MBri MGos NBee NRog NWea SBre SCrf SDea SKee WHar WJas WWeb
- 'Greenup's Pippin' (D) Last listed 1999
- 'Grenadier' (C) ♀ CCAT CDoC CTri GKir GTwe IOrc LRHS MBri MGos NBee NRog SCrf SDea SKee WJas WStI
¶ - 'Grvena Lepogvetka' (D) SKee
- 'Halstow Natural' (Cider) CTho
- 'Hambledon Deux Ans' (C) SDea SKee WJas
- 'Hambling's Seedling' (C) SKee
- 'Hangy Down' (Cider) CTho
- 'Haralson' (D) Last listed 1998
§ - 'Harry Master's Jersey' (Cider) CCAT CTho CTri SDea
- 'Harvey' (C) SDea SKee
- 'Hawthornden' (C) CTho SKee
- 'Hereford Cross' (D) SKee
- 'Herefordshire Beefing' (C) CEnd SKee WJas
¶ - 'Herefordshire Pippin' (D) CTho
- 'Herring's Pippin' (D) CTri GTwe SDea SKee
- 'Heusgen's Golden Reinette' (D) CCAT SKee
- 'High View Pippin' (D) SKee

- 'Hill's Seedling' (C) SKee
- 'Histon Favourite' (D) SKee
- 'Hoary Morning' (C) CCAT CTho SDea SKee
- 'Hocking's Green' (C/D) CEnd CTho
- 'Holland Pippin' (C) SKee
- 'Hollow Core' (C) CTho
- 'Holstein' (D) COtt CSam CTho GTwe SDea SKee
§ - 'Honeygold' (D) CEnd
- 'Hormead Pearmain' (C) SKee
- 'Horneburger Pfannkuchen' (C) SKee
- 'Houblon' (D) Last listed 1997
- 'Howgate Wonder' (C) CCAT CDoC EMui GBon GChr GKir GTwe IOrc LBuc LRHS MBri MGos NBee NRog SCrf SDea SFam SKee WJas
- 'Hubbard's Pearmain' (D) SKee
- 'Idared' (D) ♀ GBon GKir GTwe LRHS MGos SDea SKee
- 'Improved Cockpit' (D) NRog
- 'Improved Dove' (Cider) CCAT
- 'Improved Keswick' (C/D) CEnd
- 'Improved Lambrook Pippin' (Cider) CCAT CTho
- 'Improved Pound' (Cider) Last listed 1998
- 'Improved Redstreak' (Cider) CTho
- 'Improved Woodbine' (Cider) Last listed 1998
- 'Ingrid Marie' (D) SCrf SDea SKee WJas
- 'Irish Peach' (D) GTwe LBuc LRHS SDea SFam SKee WJas
- 'Isaac Newton's Tree' See M. domestica 'Flower of Kent'
- 'Isle of Wight Pippin' (D) SDea
- 'Isle of Wight Russet' (D) SDea
- 'Jackson's' (Cider) See M. domestica 'Crimson King'
¶ - 'Jacques Lebel' (C) SKee
- 'James Grieve' (D) ♀ CB&S CCAT CDoC CMac EBee EMui EWTr GBon GChr GKir GTwe IOrc LBuc LRHS MBri MWat NBea NBee NRog SDea SFam SKee SPer WHar WJas WWeb
¶ - 'Jersey Black' (D/Cider) SKee
- 'Jerseymac' (D) SDea
- 'Jester' (D) GTwe NRog SDea SKee
- 'John Apple' (C) SKee
- 'John Standish' (D) CCAT CTri GTwe SCrf SDea
- 'John Toucher's' See M. domestica 'Crimson King'
- 'Johnny Andrews' (Cider) CCAT CTho
- 'Johnny Voun' (D) CEnd CTho
- 'Jonagold' (D) ♀ EWTr GTwe LBuc MBri NWea SCrf SDea SFam SKee SPer WJas
- 'Jonagold Crowngold' PBR See M. domestica 'Crowngold'
§ - 'Jonagored' PBR (D) EBee NRog SDea
- 'Jonared' (D) GTwe LRHS
- 'Jonathan' (D) SDea SKee
- 'Jordan's Weeping' (C) GTwe SDea WJas
- 'Josephine' (D) SDea
- 'Joybells' (D) SKee
- 'Jubilee' See M. domestica 'Royal Jubilee'
- 'Jupiter' PBR (D) ♀ CCAT CDoC CTri EBee EWTr GBon GKir GTwe IOrc MGos MWat NBea NRog SCrf SDea SFam SKee WJas
- 'Kandil Sinap' (D) SKee
- 'Kapai Red Jonathan' (D) SDea
- 'Karmijn de Sonnaville' (D) SDea SKee
§ - 'Katja' (D) CCAT CDoC CSam EBee EMui EWTr GBon GChr GKir GTwe

	IOrc LBuc LRHS MBri NBee NRog
	SCrf SDea SKee SPer WHar WJas
- Katy	See *M. domestica* 'Katja'
- 'Kendall' (D)	Last listed 1999
- 'Kent' (D)	GTwe SCrf SDea SKee
- 'Kentish Fillbasket' (C)	SKee
- 'Kentish Pippin' (C/Cider/D)	SKee
- 'Kentish Quarrenden' (D)	SKee
- 'Kerry Pippin' (D)	SKee
- 'Keswick Codling' (C)	CTho EBee GKir GTwe LRHS MBri NRog NWea SDea SKee WJas
§ - 'Kidd's Orange Red' (D) ♀	CCAT COtt EBrP EBre EMui GTwe LBCl LBSe LBre LBuc LRHS MBBe SBre SCrf SDea SFam SKee WJas
- 'Kilkenny Pippin' (F)	GTwe
- 'Killerton Sharp' (Cider)	CTho
- 'Killerton Sweet' (Cider)	CTho
- 'King Byerd' (C/D)	CEnd CTho
- 'King Charles' Pearmain' (D)	CTho SKee
- 'King Coffee' (D)	Last listed 1999
- 'King George V' (D)	SKee
- 'King Luscious' (D)	SDea
§ - 'King of the Pippins' (D) ♀	CCAT CTho CTri GTwe SCrf SDea SFam SKee
- 'King of Tompkins County' (D)	SKee
- 'King Russet' (D) ♀	SDea
- 'King's Acre Bountiful' (C)	SKee WJas
- 'King's Acre Pippin' (D)	CTho SDea SFam SKee WJas
- 'Kingston Bitter' (Cider)	CTho
- 'Kingston Black' (Cider/C)	CCAT CTho SDea SKee
- 'Knobby Russet' (D)	GTwe SKee
¶ - 'Korobovka' (D)	SKee
- 'Lady Henniker' (D)	CCAT CTho GTwe NRog SDea SKee WJas
- 'Lady Lambourne' (C/D)	Last listed 1997
- 'Lady of the Wemyss' (C)	SKee
- 'Lady Stanley' (D)	Last listed 1997
- 'Lady Sudeley' (D)	CTho SDea SKee WJas
- 'Lady's Finger' (C/D)	CEnd
- 'Lady's Finger of Hereford' (D)	WJas
- 'Lady's Finger of Lancaster' (C/D)	NRog SKee
- 'Lady's Finger of Offaly' (D)	SDea
- 'Lamb Abbey Pearmain' (D)	SKee
- 'Landsberger Reinette' (D)	SKee
- 'Lane's Prince Albert' (C) ♀	CCAT CSam EMui GBon GKir GTwe LRHS MGos MWat NRog NWea SCrf SDea SFam SKee WJas
- 'Langley Pippin' (D)	SDea SKee
§ - 'Langworthy' (Cider)	CCAT CTho
§ - 'Lass o' Gowrie' (C)	SKee
§ - 'Laxton's Epicure' (D) ♀	CDoC CTho GBon GTwe IOrc LRHS NRog SCrf SDea SFam SKee WJas
§ - 'Laxton's Fortune' (D) ♀	CCAT CDoC CMac EMui GKir GTwe LRHS MGos NRog NWea SCrf SDea SFam SKee WHar WJas
- 'Laxton's Rearguard' (D)	SKee WJas
- 'Laxton's Royalty' (D)	SDea SFam
§ - 'Laxton's Superb' (D)	CB&S CCAT CDoC CSam CTri EMui GBon GChr GKir GTwe IOrc LBuc LRHS MBri NRog SCrf SDea SKee WHar WJas
- 'Leathercoat Russet' (D)	CTho SKee

- 'Lemon Pippin' (C)	CCAT CTho SDea SKee WJas
- 'Lewis's Incomparable' (C)	SKee
- 'Liberty' (D)	SDea
- 'Limberland' (C)	CTho
¶ - 'Limoncella' (D)	SKee
- 'Linda' (D)	SKee
- 'Listener' (Cider/D)	CCAT CTho
- 'Lobo' (D)	SCrf
§ - 'Loddington' (C)	SKee
- 'Lodi' (C)	SDea
- 'London Pearmain' (D)	Last listed 1999
- 'London Pippin' (C)	CTho
- 'Longkeeper' (D)	CEnd CTho
- 'Longstem' (Cider)	CTho
- 'Lord Burghley' (D)	GTwe SDea SKee
- 'Lord Derby' (C)	CCAT CMac CTho EMui GTwe MBri MWat NRog SCrf SDea SFam SKee WJas
- 'Lord Grosvenor' (C)	GTwe SKee
- 'Lord Hindlip' (D)	GTwe LRHS SDea SFam SKee WJas
- 'Lord Lambourne' (D) ♀	CCAT CDoC CTri EBrP EBre EMui GChr GKir GTwe IOrc LBCl LBSe LBre LRHS MBBe MWat NRog SBre SCrf SDea SFam SKee SPer WHar WJas
- 'Lord Stradbroke' (C)	SKee
- 'Lord Suffield' (C)	CTri SKee
- 'Loyal Drain' (Cider)	Last listed 1998
- 'Lucombe's Pine' (D)	CEnd CTho
- 'Lucombe's Seedling' (D)	CTho SKee
- 'Mabbott's Pearmain' (D)	SDea
- 'Madresfield Court' (D)	SDea SKee WJas
- 'Major' (Cider)	CCAT CTho
- 'Malling Kent' (D)	CSam EMui LRHS SDea SFam SKee WJas
- 'Maltster' (D)	SKee WJas
- 'Manaccan Primrose' (C/D)	CEnd
- 'Manks Codlin' (C)	CTho SKee
- 'Mannington's Pearmain' (D)	SKee
- 'Margil' (D)	CCAT CTho GTwe SDea SFam SKee
- 'May Queen' (D)	SDea SFam SKee WJas
- 'Maypole' PBR (D/Ball)	LRHS MGos SDea WJas
- 'McCutcheon' (F)	Last listed 1998
- 'McIntosh' (D)	SKee
- 'Médaille d'Or' (Cider)	CCAT
- 'Medina' (D)	GTwe
- 'Melba' (D)	SKee
- 'Melcombe Russet' (D)	CTho
- 'Melon' (D)	SDea
- 'Melrose' (D)	GTwe SKee
- 'Merchant Apple' (C)	CCAT
- 'Merchant Apple of Illminster' (D)	CCAT CTho
- 'Mère de Ménage' (C)	SFam
- 'Merton Beauty' (D)	SKee
- 'Merton Charm' (D) ♀	Last listed 1996
- 'Merton Knave' (D)	GTwe MGos SDea SFam
- 'Merton Russet' (D)	SDea
- 'Merton Worcester' (D)	SDea SKee
- 'Michaelmas Red' (D)	GTwe NRog SKee WJas
- 'Michelin' (Cider)	CCAT CEnd CTho EMui GTwe SDea
- Miel d'Or	See *M. domestica* 'Honeygold'
- 'Miller's Seedling' (D)	GTwe SKee WJas
- 'Millicent Barnes' (D)	SDea
- 'Mollie's Delicious' (D)	SKee
- 'Monarch' (C)	CCAT CTri GTwe NRog SDea SFam SKee WJas
I - 'Mondial Gala'	See *M. domestica* 'Gala Mondial'

- 'Morgan's Sweet' (C/Cider) — CCAT CTho CTri SDea SKee
- 'Moss's Seedling' (D) — SDea
§ - 'Mother' (D) ♀ — CDoC GTwe LRHS SCrf SDea SFam SKee WJas
- 'Mrs Phillimore' (D) — SKee
- 'Muscadet de Dieppe' (Cider) — CCAT
§ - 'Mutsu' (D) — CCAT EBee GTwe MBri NRog SCrf SDea SKee
- 'Neasdale Favorite' (F) — Last listed 1999
- 'Nettlestone Pippin' (D) — SDea
- 'Newton Wonder' (D/C) ♀ — CCAT CDoC CMac CSam CTho CTri GTwe LRHS NRog SCrf SDea SFam SKee WJas
- 'Newtown Pippin' (D) — SDea
¶ - 'Nine Square' (D) — CTho
- 'Nittany Red' (D) — SDea
- 'No Pip' (C) — CTho
- 'Nonpareil' (D) — CTho SFam SKee
- 'Norfolk Beauty' (C) — SKee
- 'Norfolk Beefing' (C) — SDea SFam SKee
- 'Norfolk Royal' (D) — CDoC GTwe LRHS SDea SKee
- 'Norfolk Summer Broadend' (C) — SKee
- 'Norfolk Winter Coleman' (C) — SKee
- 'Northcott Superb' (D) — CTho
- 'Northern Greening' (C) — GTwe SKee
§ - 'Northwood' (Cider) — CCAT CTho
- 'Nutmeg Pippin' (D) — SDea
- 'Oaken Pin' (C) — CTho
- 'Old Pearmain' (D) — CTho SDea SKee
- 'Old Somerset Russet' (D) — CTho
- 'Opalescent' (D) — SKee
- 'Orange Goff' (D) — SKee
¶ - 'Orangenburg' (D) — SKee
- 'Orin' (D) — SKee
- 'Orkney Apple' (F) — SKee
- 'Orleans Reinette' (D) — CCAT CTho EMui GTwe LRHS MWat SCrf SDea SFam SKee WJas
- 'Osier' (Cider) — CCAT
- 'Oslin' (D) — SKee
- 'Owen Thomas' (D) — CTri
- 'Paignton Marigold' (Cider) — CTho
- 'Paulared' (D) — Last listed 1999
- 'Payhembury' (C/Cider) — CTho
- 'Peacemaker' (D) — SKee
- 'Pear Apple' (D) — CEnd
- 'Pearl' (D) — CTho SDea
- 'Peasgood's Nonsuch' (C) ♀ — CCAT GKir GTwe LBuc LRHS SCrf SDea SFam SKee WJas
- 'Peck's Pleasant' (D) — SKee
- 'Pendragon' (D) — CTho
- 'Penhallow Pippin' (D) — CTho
- 'Pennard Bitter' (Cider) — CCAT
- 'Peter Lock' (C/D) — CCAT CEnd CTho
- 'Peter's Pippin' (D) — SDea
- 'Peter's Seedling' (D) — SDea
- 'Pickering's Seedling' (D) — SKee
¶ - 'Pigeonette de Rouen' (D) — SKee
- 'Pig's Nose Pippin' (D) — CEnd SKee
- 'Pig's Nose Pippin' Type III (D)
- 'Pig's Snout' (Cider/C/D) — CCAT CEnd CTho
- 'Pine Golden Pippin' (D) — SKee
- 'Pitmaston Pine Apple' (D) — CCAT CTho LRHS NRog SCrf SDea SFam SKee WJas
- 'Pitmaston Russet Nonpareil' (D) — SKee

- 'Pixie' (D) ♀ — CSam GTwe SDea SFam SKee WJas
- 'Plum Vite' (D) — CTho CTri
- 'Plympton Pippin' (C) — CEnd CTho
§ - 'Polka' = 'Trajan' PBR (D/Ball) — LRHS MGos SDea
- 'Polly' (C/D) — CEnd
- 'Polly Prosser' (D) — SKee
- 'Polly Whitehair' (C/D) — CTho SDea SKee
- 'Pomeroy' (D) — CCAT
- 'Pomeroy of Somerset' (D) — CTho
- 'Ponsford' (C) — CCAT CTho
- 'Port Wine' — See M. domestica 'Harry Master's Jersey'
- 'Porter's Perfection' (Cider) — CCAT CTho
- 'Pott's Seedling' (C) — SKee
¶ - 'Prima' (D) — ESim
¶ - 'Princesse' — SKee
- 'Priscilla' (D) — Last listed 1999
¶ - 'Purpurroter Cousinot' (D) — SKee
- 'Queen' (C) — CEnd CTho SKee
- 'Queen Cox' (D) — EMui GBon MRav SDea SKee
- 'Queens' (D) — CTho
- 'Racky Down' (F) — SKee
- 'Red Alkmene' (D) — MBri
- 'Red Astrachan' (D) — SKee
§ - 'Red Blenheim' (C/D) — SKee
- 'Red Charles Ross' (C/D) — SDea
¶ - 'Red Delicious' (D) — SCrf
- 'Red Devil' (D) — COtt CWSG EBee EMui EPfP GKir GTwe LBuc LRHS MBri NBee SDea SKee WJas
- 'Red Ellison' (D) — CCAT CTho CTri GTwe NRog SCrf SDea
¶ - 'Red Elstar' (D) — SCrf
- 'Red Falstaff' PBR (D) — GKir LRHS MBri MCoo SKee
- 'Red Fuji' (D) — SDea
- 'Red James Grieve' — See M. domestica 'Redcoat Grieve'
- 'Red Jersey' (Cider) — CCAT
- 'Red Joaneting' (D) — SKee
- 'Red Jonagold' PBR — See M. domestica 'Jonagored'
¶ - 'Red Jonathan' (D) — SDea
- 'Red Miller's Seedling' (D) — SCrf SDea
- 'Red Robin' (F) — CEnd
- 'Red Ruby' (F) — CTho
¶ - 'Red Sauce' (C) — SKee
- 'Red Victoria' (C) — GTwe WJas
§ - 'Redcoat Grieve' (D) — CDoC SDea SKee
- 'Redfree' (D) — Last listed 1999
- 'Redsleeves' (D) — GTwe SDea
- 'Redstrake' (Cider) — CCAT
- 'Reine de Pommes' (Cider) — CCAT
- 'Reine des Reinettes' — See M. domestica 'King of the Pippins'
- Reine des Reinettes — Last listed 1997
- 'Reinette d'Obry' (Cider) — CCAT
- 'Reinette Dorée de Boediker' (D) — GTwe
- 'Reinette du Canada' (D) — SKee
- 'Reinette Rouge Etoilée' (D) — CCAT SDea
- 'Reverend Greeves' (C) — SDea
- 'Reverend W. Wilks' (C) — CCAT CDoC COtt EMui GKir LBuc LRHS MBri MWat NRog SCrf SDea SFam SKee WJas
- 'Ribston Pippin' (D) ♀ — CCAT CTho CTri EMui GTwe LBuc LRHS MWat NRog SCrf SDea SFam SKee WJas

- 'Rival' (D) — SDea SKee WJas
- 'Rivers' Nonsuch' (D) — Last listed 1999
- 'Robin Pippin' (D) — GTwe
- 'Rome Beauty' (D) — SDea
- 'Rosemary Russet' (D) ♀ — CCAT CSam CTho GTwe NRog SCrf SDea SFam SKee WJas
- 'Ross Nonpareil' (D) — GTwe SDea SKee
- 'Rough Pippin' (D) — CEnd CTho
- 'Roundway Magnum Bonum' (D) — CCAT CTho SDea SFam SKee
§ - 'Roxbury Russet' (D) — SKee
§ - 'Royal Gala' (D) ♀ — EMui LBuc LRHS SDea SKee
§ - 'Royal Jubilee' (C) — SKee
- 'Royal Russet' (C) — SDea
- 'Royal Snow' (D) — SKee
- 'Royal Somerset' (C/Cider) — CCAT CTho
- 'Rubens' (D) — SKee
- 'Rubinette' (D) — CDoC COtt GTwe MBri MGos SCrf WJas
- 'S.T.Wright' (C) — Last listed 1997
- 'Saint Albans Pippin' (D) — SKee
- 'Saint Augustine's Orange' (D) — SKee
- 'Saint Cecilia' (D) — SDea WJas
§ - 'Saint Edmund's Pippin' (D) ♀ — CTho ERea GTwe LRHS SCrf SDea SFam SKee
- 'Saint Edmund's Russet' — See *M. domestica* 'Saint Edmund's Pippin'
- 'Saint Everard' (D) — SKee
- 'Saint Magdalen' (D) — SKee
- 'Saltcote Pippin' (D) — SKee
- 'Sam Young' (D) — SKee
- 'Sandlands' — SDea
- 'Sandringham' (C) — SKee
- 'Sanspareil' (D) — CTho SKee
- 'Saturn'^PBR — GTwe
- 'Saw Pits' (F) — CEnd
- 'Scarlet Nonpareil' (D) — SKee
- 'Scarlet Pimpernel' (D) — SCrf
¶ - 'Schoolmaster' (C) — SKee
- 'Scilly Pearl' (C) — WJas
- 'Scotch Bridget' (C) — GKir SKee WJas
- 'Scotch Dumpling' (C) — GKir GTwe LRHS MCoo
- 'Seaton House' (C) — SKee
- 'Sercombe's Natural' (Cider) — CCAT CTho
¶ - 'Severn Bank' (C) — SKee
- 'Shakespeare' (D) — WJas
- 'Sheep's Nose' (C) — CCAT SDea SKee
- 'Shenandoah' (C) — SKee
- 'Shoesmith' (C) — Last listed 1998
- 'Sidney Strake' (C) — CEnd
- 'Sir Isaac Newton's' — See *M. domestica* 'Flower of Kent'
- 'Sir John Thornycroft' (D) — SDea
- 'Sisson's Worksop Newtown' (D) — SKee
¶ - 'Skovfoged' (C) — SKee
- 'Slack Ma Girdle' (Cider) — CCAT CTho
- 'Smart's Prince Arthur' (C) — SDea
- 'Snell's Glass Apple' — See *M. domestica* 'Glass Apple'
- 'Somerset Lasting' (C) — CTho
- 'Somerset Redstreak' (Cider) — CCAT CTho
- 'Sops in Wine' (C/Cider) — CCAT CTho SKee
- 'Sour Bay' (Cider) — CTho
- 'Sour Natural' — See *M. domestica* 'Langworthy'
- 'Spartan' (D) — CDoC EBrP EBre EMui EWTr GBon GKir GTwe LBCl LBSe LBre LBuc LRHS MBBe MGos NBea NRog SBre SCrf SDea SFam SKee SPer WJas WStI

- 'Spencer' (D) — CTri SKee
- 'Spotted Dick' (Cider) — CTho
- 'Spur Mac' (D) — SDea
- 'Stable Jersey' (Cider) — CCAT
- 'Stamford Pippin' (D) — SDea SKee
- 'Star of Devon' (D) — CCAT CTho SDea
- 'Stark' (D) — SDea
- 'Starking' (D) — SKee
- 'Starkrimson' (D) — SKee
- 'Starkspur Golden Delicious' (D) — SKee
- 'Stembridge Cluster' (Cider) — CCAT
- 'Stembridge Jersey' (Cider) — CCAT
- 'Steyne Seedling' (D) — SDea
- 'Stirling Castle' (C) — GKir GTwe SKee
- 'Stobo Castle' (C) — SKee
- 'Stockbearer' (C) — CTho
- 'Stoke Edith Pippin' (D) — WJas
- 'Stoke Red' (Cider) — CCAT CTho
- 'Stone's' — See *M. domestica* 'Loddington'
- 'Stoup Leadington' (C) — SKee
- 'Strawberry Pippin' (D) — WJas
- 'Striped Beefing' (C) — SKee
- 'Stub Nose' (F) — SKee
- 'Sturmer Pippin' (D) — GTwe LRHS MWat SCrf SDea SFam SKee WJas
* - 'Sugar Apple' — CTho
- 'Sugar Bush' (C/D) — CTho
- 'Sugar Loaf' — See *M. domestica* 'Sugar Apple'
- 'Summer Golden Pippin' (D) — SKee
- 'Summer Granny' (D) — Last listed 1997
- 'Summer Stubbard' (D) — CTho
- 'Summerred' (D) — CWSG
- 'Sunburn' (D) — Last listed 1998
- 'Sunnydale' (D/C) — SDea
- 'Sunrise'^PBR (D) — EMui LRHS SKee
- 'Sunset' (D) ♀ — CCAT CDoC CMac CSam CTri EMui EPfP EWTr GKir GTwe LBuc LRHS MBri NBea NBee NRog NWea SCrf SDea SFam SKee SPer WHar WJas
- 'Suntan' (D) ♀ — CCAT CSam CTho EBee GBon GTwe LRHS MWat NBee SDea SKee
- 'Superb' — See *M. domestica* 'Laxton's Superb'
- 'Surprise' (D) — GTwe SKee
- 'Sweet Alford' (Cider) — CCAT CTho
- 'Sweet Bay' (Cider) — CTho
- 'Sweet Blenheim' (Cider) — Last listed 1998
- 'Sweet Cleave' (Cider) — CTho
- 'Sweet Coppin' — See *M. domestica* 'Court Royal'
- 'Tale Sweet' (Cider) — CCAT CTho
- 'Tamar Beauty' (F) — CEnd
- 'Tan Harvey' (Cider) — CCAT CEnd CTho
- 'Taunton Fair Maid' (Cider) — CCAT CTho
- 'Taylor's' (Cider) — CCAT SDea
- 'Taylor's Sweet' (Cider) — CCAT
- 'Telamon'^PBR — See *M. domestica* Waltz = 'Telamon'
- 'Ten Commandments' (D/Cider) — CCAT SDea SKee WJas
¶ - 'Téton de Demoiselle' (D) — SKee
- 'The Rattler' (F) — CEnd
- 'Thomas Rivers' (C) — CTho SDea SKee
- 'Thorle Pippin' (D) — SKee
- 'Tidicombe Seedling' — CTho
- 'Tillington Court' (C) — WJas

– 'Tom Putt' (C)	CCAT CSam CTho CTri GKir GTwe LBuc LRHS SDea SKee WJas
– 'Tommy Knight' (D)	CEnd CTho
– 'Tower of Glamis' (C)	GTwe SKee
– Town Farm Number 59 (Cider)	CTho
– 'Trajan'PBR	See *M. domestica* Polka = 'Trajan'
– 'Transparente de Croncels' (C)	CTho
– 'Tregoana King' (C/D)	CEnd CTho
– 'Tremlett's Bitter' (Cider)	CCAT CTho SDea
– 'Tuscan'PBR	See *M. domestica* Bolero = 'Tuscan'
– 'Twenty Ounce' (C)	CCAT GTwe SKee WJas
– 'Twinings Pippin' (D)	SKee
§ – 'Tydeman's Early Worcester' (D)	CLnd GTwe LRHS NBee NRog SDea SKee WJas
– 'Tydeman's Late Orange' (D)	GTwe NRog SDea SFam SKee
– 'Tyler's Kernel' (C)	SKee
– 'Underleaf' (D)	CCAT
– 'Upton Pyne' (D)	CCAT CSam CTho SCrf SDea SKee
– 'Veitch's Perfection' (C/D)	CTho
– 'Venus Pippin' (C/D)	CEnd
– 'Vickey's Delight' (D)	SDea
– 'Vilberie' (Cider)	CCAT
– 'Vista-bella' (D)	GTwe NBee SDea SKee WJas
¶ – 'Vitgylling' (D/C)	SKee
– 'Wagener' (D)	NRog SDea SKee
§ – Waltz = 'Telamon' PBR (D/Ball/C)	LRHS MGos SDea
– 'Wanstall Pippin' (D)	SKee
– 'Warner's King' (C) ♀	CCAT CTho CTri NRog SCrf SDea SKee WJas
¶ – 'Warrior'	CTho
– 'Wealthy' (D)	SDea SKee
– 'Wellington' (C)	See *M. domestica* 'Dummellor's Seedling'
* – 'Wellington' (Cider)	CTho
§ – 'Wellspur' (D)	GTwe
– 'Wellspur Red Delicious'	See *M. domestica* 'Wellspur'
– 'Welsh Russet' (D)	SDea
– 'Wheeler's Russet' (D)	Last listed 1997
– 'White Alphington' (Cider)	CTho
– 'White Close Pippin' (Cider)	CTho
– 'White Jersey' (Cider)	CCAT
– 'White Joaneting' (D)	CTho
– 'White Melrose' (C)	GTwe SDea SKee
– 'White Paradise' (C)	SKee
– 'White Transparent' (C/D)	SDea SKee
– 'William Crump' (D)	CCAT LRHS SDea SFam SKee WJas
– 'Winston' (D) ♀	CCAT CDoC CTri EBee GTwe LRHS NRog NWea SCrf SDea SFam SKee
– 'Winter Banana' (D)	NRog SDea SKee
– 'Winter Gem'	COtt EMui LRHS MBri MGos SKee
– 'Winter Majetin' (C)	Last listed 1997
– 'Winter Peach' (D/C)	CEnd CTho
– 'Winter Pearmain' (D)	SKee
– 'Winter Quarrenden' (D)	SDea
– 'Winter Queening' (D/C)	CTho SDea
– 'Winter Stubbard' (C)	CTho
¶ – 'Wolf River' (D/C)	SKee
– 'Woodbine'	See *M. domestica* 'Northwood'
– 'Woolbrook Pippin' (D)	CCAT CTho
– 'Woolbrook Russet' (C)	CCAT CTho SKee
– 'Worcester Pearmain' (D) ♀	CB&S CCAT CTho EBee EMui EWTr GBon GChr GKir GTwe LBuc LRHS MBri MWat NRog NWea SDea SFam SKee SPer WHar WJas WStI WWeb
– 'Wormsley Pippin' (D)	SKee WJas
– 'Wyatt's Seedling'	See *M. domestica* 'Langworthy'
– 'Wyken Pippin' (D)	GTwe SDea SFam SKee WJas
– 'Yarlington Mill' (Cider)	CCAT CTho CTri SDea SKee
– 'Yellow Ingestrie' (D)	SFam SKee WJas
– 'Yorkshire Greening' (C)	Last listed 1997
– 'Young America' (D)	SKee
– 'Zabergäu Renette' (D)	SKee
'Donald Wyman'	CBlo
'Echtermeyer'	See *M.* x *gloriosa* 'Oekonomierat Echtermeyer'
§ 'Evereste' ♀	CBlo CDoC CEnd CLnd EBee EMui EPfP GChr GKir GTwe LPan LRHS MAsh MBlu MBri MRav NPri SCrf SFam WDin WHar WJas
florentina	CMCN CTho WMou
floribunda ♀	More than 30 suppliers
'Gardener's Gold'	CEnd
§ x ***gloriosa*** 'Oekonomierat Echtermeyer'	CBlo EBee GKir GQui SCrf SDea SSta WDin WJas
'Golden Gem'	CBlo CEnd EPfP GTwe MDun
'Golden Hornet'	See *M.* x *zumi* 'Golden Hornet'
'Goldsworth Purple'	CTho
x ***hartwigii*** 'Katherine' ♀	Last listed 1995
x ***heterophylla*** 'Redflesh'	Last listed 1999
'Hillieri'	See *M.* x *schiedeckeri* 'Hillieri'
hupehensis ♀	CBlo CEnd CLnd CMCN CTho EBee ENot EPfP GKir GTwe LRHS MBri SCrf SFam SLPl SPer WMou WWat
'John Downie' (C) ♀	More than 30 suppliers
'Kaido'	See *M.* x *micromalus*
kansuensis	CLnd WMou
'Laura'PBR	CBlo COtt LRHS MAsh MGos SLim WGer WGor
¶ 'Louisa'	MAsh
x ***magdeburgensis***	CLnd MRav NWea
* 'Mamouth'	Last listed 1997
§ x ***micromalus***	CLnd GAri
x ***moerlandsii***	CLnd
– 'Liset'	CBlo CDul CEnd CLnd COtt EBee ENot GChr MAsh SFam SPer WFar WJas WStI
§ – 'Profusion'	More than 30 suppliers
– 'Profusion Improved'	CEnd COtt EWTr GKir SLim WOrn
orthocarpa	CLnd
Perpetu®	See *M.* 'Evereste'
'Pink Perfection'	CEnd CLnd EBee ENot GChr MAsh MBri MDun
Pom'Zaï® = 'Courtabri'	CDoC
prattii	CTho
'Profusion'	See *M.* x *moerlandsii* 'Profusion'
prunifolia 'Cheal's Crimson'	NRog
– 'Pendula'	Last listed 1999
pumila 'Cowichan'	CBlo GKir LRHS MBri
– 'Dartmouth'	CBlo CDul CLnd CSam CTho CTri NRog SFam
– 'Montreal Beauty'	GKir LRHS MAsh MBri WJas
– 'Niedzwetzkyana'	CLnd
§ x ***purpurea*** 'Aldenhamensis'	CBlo CLnd CTho SCrf SDea WDin WOrn
– 'Eleyi'	CBlo CDul CLnd ENot EPfP MAsh NWea SCrf
– 'Lemoinei'	IOrc LPan
– 'Neville Copeman' ♀	CDoC CDul CLnd EBee EPfP LPan MAsh MGos WJas WOrn
– 'Pendula'	See *M.* x *gloriosa* 'Oekonomierat Echtermeyer'

'Red Ace'	CDul
'Red Glow'	CBlo CDoC CLnd COtt EBee
	GChr GQui SCrf WJas WLRN
'Red Jade'	See *M.* x *schiedeckeri* 'Red Jade'
§ x *robusta*	CBlo CDoC CLnd CTri EBee
	GTwe LPan NWea SCrf SLon SRPl
- 'Red Sentinel' ♀	More than 30 suppliers
- 'Red Siberian' ♀	SDea SPer
- 'Yellow Siberian' ♀	CLnd
'Royal Beauty' ♀	CBlo CLnd EBee EBrP EBre EPfP
	GKir GTwe LBCl LBSe LBre LBuc
	LPan LRHS MAsh MBBe MBri
	MGos MRav SBre SCrf SMHT
	WDin WHar
'Royalty'	More than 30 suppliers
'Rudolph'	CDul EBee ENot LPan LRHS SLim
sargentii	See *M. toringo* subsp. *sargentii*
x *schiedeckeri*	Last listed 1998
'Exzellenz Thiel'	
§ - 'Hillieri'	CLnd EBee SCrf SFam
§ - 'Red Jade'	More than 30 suppliers
- 'Sun Rival'	WJas
Siberian crab	See *M.* x *robusta*
sieboldii	See *M. toringo*
sikkimensis	WHCr
- B&SWJ 2431	WCru
'Snowcloud'	CBlo CDul CEnd CLnd EBee ENot
	EPfP LRHS MBri SPer WShe
sp. CLD 417	Last listed 1997
spectabilis	CLnd
'Sun Rival'	CBlo CDul CEnd COtt EBee EMui
	EPfP GTwe LRHS MAsh MBri
	MDun MGos SCoo SFam SLim
	WHar WWeb
sylvestris	CDul CKin CLnd EPfP GAri GChr
	LBuc LHyr NBee NRog NWea
	WDin WLRN
§ *toringo*	SSpi WShe
§ - subsp. *sargentii*	CBlo CDul CMCN EBee ECtt ENot
	LPan LRHS MBri MGos NWea
	SFam SPer WNor WWat
- - 'Tina'	MAsh
toringoides	See *M. bhutanica*
transitoria ♀	CBlo CEnd CFil CLnd CTho EPfP
	GKir LRHS MAsh MBri SPer SSpi
	WWat
- 'R.J. Fulcher'	CLnd CTho
- 'Thornhayes Tansy'	CDul CLnd CTho
trilobata	CBlo CLnd CTho EPfP MGos
	WMou
tschonoskii ♀	More than 30 suppliers
- 'White Star'	See *M.* 'White Star'
'Van Eseltine'	CBlo CCHP CDoC CDul CLnd
	EBee GKir GTwe LRHS MBri SFam
	SPer WJas
'Veitch's Scarlet'	CDul CLnd CTho GQui GTwe
	NRog SFam
'White Candle' (d)	CBlo
§ 'White Star'	CBlo CBrm CDul CEnd EBee
	LRHS SLim
'Winter Gold'	CBlo CDoC CDul CLnd CSam
	LCaP MAsh WStI
¶ 'Wintergold'	SCrf
'Wisley Crab'	CLnd EBee GTwe SDea SFam
	SKee
yunnanensis	CMCN
- 'Veitchii'	CTho
¶ - var. *veitchii*	GIBF
x *zumi* var. *calocarpa*	CLnd
§ - 'Golden Hornet' ♀	More than 30 suppliers
- 'Professor Sprenger'	CLnd

MALVA (Malvaceae)

alcea	CAgr EPfP
- 'Alba'	NPro
- var. *fastigiata*	CArn CGle EMan EPPr GMac
	LRHS NBid NBro NCat NVic SAga
	SCob SPer SRCN SRms WEas
	WPer
bicolor	See *Lavatera maritima*
crispa	See *M. verticillata*
'Gibbortello'	EWTr MCLN NBro NCut
hispida	CNat
moschata	More than 30 suppliers
- f. *alba* ♀	More than 30 suppliers
- - 'Pirouette'	WHen WOve
¶ - 'Kirikee Sunrise'	Ilve
- 'Romney Marsh'	See *Althaea officinalis* 'Romney
	Marsh'
- *rosea*	ECha LFis NCut NPer WByw
	WPnP
§ *neglecta*	EWFC
sylvestris	CAgr CGle CKin EOld EWFC
	GCHN MChe NBro SMad SWat
	WFar WHer WJek WPer WRos
	WWin WWye
- 'Brave Heart'	CM&M GBri MWll NBro NCut
	NLar NPer SLod
- 'Highnam'	WAlt
- 'Inky Stripe'	Last listed 1998
I - 'Magic Hollyhock' (d)	SGar
- Marina® = 'Dema'PBR	LRHS MAsh MBri SUsu
- subsp. *mauritanica*	CSpe EBee ECoo ELan EMar EPfP
	GBri MHer NBro NFai NFor NPer
	NSti WMoo WRus
¶ - - 'Bibor Fehlo'	CSpe EWTr MWll NCut NGdn
- 'Perry's Blue'	NPer
- 'Primley Blue'	CB&S CBot CElw CGle ECha ELan
	EOld ERav EWTr GBri LFis LGre
	LHop LRot MTho MTis NBrk
	NGdn NPer NSti SAga SMad SPer
	WBea WFar WWin
- 'Richard Perry'	NPer
- 'Zebrina'	CM&M EBee EMar EWTr GBri
	LAst MCLN MHer MWll NBrk
	NFai NGdn NPer SAga SLod WElm
	WFar WHil WMoo WRha
§ *verticillata*	ELan
- 'Crispa'	MChe WRha

MALVASTRUM (Malvaceae)

x *hypomadarum*	See *Anisodontea* x *hypomadara*
	(Sprague) Bates
lateritium	More than 30 suppliers
¶ - 'Blossom Pink'	NArg
- 'Eastgrove Silver' (v)	Last listed 1997
* - 'Variegatum'	Last listed 1998

MALVAVISCUS (Malvaceae)

arboreus	Last listed 1999
- var. *mexicanus*	ERea SYvo

MANDEVILLA (Apocynaceae)

x *amabilis*	LRHS
x *amoena* 'Alice du Pont' ♀	CB&S CPIN ECon ELan EMil EPfP
	ERea GQui LCns LRHS SOWG
	WMul
boliviensis	CPIN ECon ELan EPfP LChe LRHS
	SOWG
§ *laxa*	CBot CHEx CPIN ECon ELan ERea
	LRHS SOWG SYvo WCot WCru
	WPic WSHC
sanderi	EPfP LCns MBri

- 'Rosea'	ERea
splendens	EBak LRHS SOWG SYvo
suaveolens	See *M. laxa*
yellow form	SOWG

MANDRAGORA (Solanaceae)
autumnalis	EEls GCal IIve MSal
§ *officinarum*	CBrd EBee EEls EMon GCal GPoy
	MHer MSal WWye

MANETTIA (Rubiaceae)
inflata	See *M. luteorubra*
§ *luteorubra*	CPIN ELan EPfP

MANFREDA See AGAVE

MANGLIETIA (Magnoliaceae)
insignis	CFil CHEx SSpi

MANILKARA (Sapotaceae)
zapota	LBlo

MANSOA (Bignoniaceae)
hymenaea	CPIN

MARANTA (Marantaceae)
leuconeura	MBri
var. *erythroneura*	
- var. *kerchoveana* ♀	CHal LBlo LRHS MBri

MARGYRICARPUS (Rosaceae)
§ *pinnatus*	CFee CPle ESis NChi NWCA
	WPer
setosus	See *M. pinnatus*

MARISCUS See CYPERUS

MARRUBIUM (Lamiaceae)
candidissimum	See *M. incanum*
catariifolium	ECha
cylleneum	ECha EGar EMFP EMar WPer
* - 'Velvetissimum'	EGle SBla SCro WCHb
'Gold Leaf'	ECha MBel
§ *incanum*	CGle EBee EMan IIve MBri NChi
	WEas
libanoticum	ECha EGar EMon MSte SCob
	WPer
pestalloziae	WCot
supinum	CArn NWoo
velutinum	CGle EGar
vulgare	CArn ELau GBar GPoy MChe
	MHer MHew NOrc SIde WCHb
	WCer WHer WOak WPer WSel
	WWye
- 'Green Pompon'	ELau IIve MCCP NLar

MARSDENIA (Asclepiadaceae)
erecta	See *Cionura erecta*

MARSHALLIA (Asteraceae)
caespitosa	Last listed 1999
grandiflora	EBee
trinerva	WCot

MARSILEA (Marsileaceae)
mutica	SWyc
quadrifolia	SWyc
* *schelpiana*	SWyc

MASCAGNIA (Malpighiaceae)
macroptera	CPIN

MASCARENA See HYOPHORBE

MASSONIA (Hyacinthaceae)
echinata	CStu
¶ *pustulata*	CStu

MATELEA (Asclepiadaceae)
obliqua	MNrw

MATRICARIA (Asteraceae)
chamomilla	See *M. recutita*
parthenium	See *Tanacetum parthenium*
§ *recutita*	GPoy MChe MHew

MATTEUCCIA (Woodsiaceae)
orientalis	CFil EBee MBri NHar NMar NOrc
	WRic
pensylvanica	CCuc EMon NHar WRic
struthiopteris ♀	More than 30 suppliers
¶ - 'Bedraggled Feathers'	EMon

MATTHIOLA (Brassicaceae)
* *arborescens alba*	NCut
§ *fruticulosa*	EBee
- 'Alba'	EBee
- subsp. *perennis*	CWes EBee MCCP NSti NWCA
incana	CFri MArl MCCP SIng STes WCot
	WPer WRHF WRha WRus
- *alba*	NBir WWhi
- hybrid	Last listed 1999
¶ *integrifolia*	EBee
pink perennial	Last listed 1998
scapifera	NTow
sinuata	EWFC
thessala	See *M. fruticulosa*
white perennial	CArn CGle CHad CMil CSev
	CSpe GVer LCot MBct NBrk
	NFai NPer NTow SEND WEas
	WHoo WPyg

MAURANDELLA (Scrophulariaceae)
§ *antirrhiniflora*	LRHS

MAURANDYA (Scrophulariaceae)
§ *barclayana*	CBot CPIN CRHN MBri MNrw
	SRCN SYvo
- *alba*	CBot
erubescens	See *Lophospermum erubescens*
lophantha	See *Lophospermum scandens*
lophospermum	See *Lophospermum scandens*
'Pink Ice'	See *Lophospermum scandens*
	'Pink Ice'
§ *purpusii*	Last listed 1999
'Red Dragon'	See *Lophospermum* 'Red
	Dragon'
scandens	See *Lophospermum scandens*
§ 'Victoria Falls'	LCns LRHS SLod SOWG SYvo

MAYTENUS (Celastraceae)
boaria	CGre CMCN CPle EPfP SAPC SArc
	WPic WWat
magellanica	CFil WWat

MAZUS (Scrophulariaceae)
alpinus B&SWJ 119	Last listed 1999
pumilio	ECou
radicans	EBee ECou WCru
reptans	CAgr CNic EMan EPar EWTr NFla
	NWCA WOut WPer WPyg
- 'Albus'	WCru WPer

MECONOPSIS ✿ (Papaveraceae)

aculeata	GGGa GTou
baileyi	See *M. betonicifolia*
x *beamisbii*	GBuc
§ betonicifolia ♀	More than 30 suppliers
- var. *alba*	EBee EDAr GAbr GBuc GCan
	GChr GCrs GGGa GGar GMac
	IBlr IMGH LSyl MBri NChi NHar
	NLar SRms WCru
- Harlow Carr strain	Last listed 1997
¶ - 'Hensol Violet'	GBuc GCal GCrs
- var. *pratensis*	Last listed 1999
- purple	IBlr WCru
- violet	Last listed 1998
cambrica	CGle CKin CMea EBrP EBre ELan
	EMar EWFC EWTr GTou LBCl
	LBSe LBre MBBe NCat NFla NHol
	SBre SChu SIng WAbe WBea
	WBod WCru WFar WHen WHer
	WOve WPer WWye
- var. *aurantiaca*	CTri NBir WAbe WHen
- *flore-pleno* (d)	CGle EPar GBuc MTho NBid NCat
	WAbe WFar
- - orange (d)	CCuc MGW WAbe WCot WCru
	WPnP
- - yellow (d)	WCot WCru
§ - 'Frances Perry'	CCuc GBuc GCal IBlr NTow
	WCot WCru WFar WPnP
- 'Muriel Brown' (d)	WCot WCru WPnP
- 'Rubra'	See *M. cambrica* 'Frances Perry'
chelidoniifolia	CFil GCal IBlr SSpi WCru WFar
	WPGP
¶ 'Dawyck'	GCrs
delavayi	GGGa
dhwojii	GBri GCan GGGa LRHS MNes
gracilipes	GFle
grandis ♀	CBrd CGle CPBP CPla CSam EDAr
	EGle GCan GFle GGGa GMac
	LRHS MNes NBrk NFla NHar NSla
	SBla WAbe WEas WHen WLin
	WOve WViv
- Balruddry form	GGGa
- 'Betty Sheriff's Dream Poppy'	GBuc
- GS 600	CLAP GBuc GCan GMac IBlr NBir
	NWCA
- Kessel's strain	Last listed 1999
- PS&W 5423	Last listed 1998
borridula	CPBP GCan GFle GGGa LRHS
	MTho
- var. *racemosa*	Last listed 1998
- Rudis Group	Last listed 1999
integrifolia	GCrs GGGa LSyl
- ACE 1798	GTou
§ - subsp. *integrifolia* 'Wolong'	GCrs
'James Cobb'	See *M. integrifolia* subsp. *integrifolia* 'Wolong'
¶ 'Jimmy Bayne'	GBuc GCrs GMaP
Kingsbarns hybrids	GCrs GGGa
lancifolia	GBuc
aff. *lancifolia* KGB 737	Last listed 1998
latifolia	Last listed 1999
* longifolia	Last listed 1999
¶ 'Mrs Jebb'	GCrs
§ napaulensis	CFil CSam EBee EDAr GAbr
	GCan GChr GCrs GDra GGar
	GGGa IBlr IMGH LHop LRHS
	MBri MCAu MNes NChi NLar
	NWCA SLon WEas WHer WHil
	WRos WViv WWin

- HWJCM 301	Last listed 1999
- pink	WLin
- red	EBee GBuc NBir WAbe WCru WPGP
- scarlet	Last listed 1998
§ - Wallich's form	GCan
nudicaulis	See *Papaver nudicaule*
paniculata	GFle GGGa IBlr IMGH LRHS NBir
	WAbe WLin
- BC 9314	Last listed 1998
- CC&McK 296	GTou
- compact	Last listed 1998
- Ghopte Group	WAbe
- Ghunsa Group	EGle MNes WAbe
- ginger foliage	Last listed 1998
pseudointegrifolia	GCrs GGGa WViv
- subsp. *robusta*	Last listed 1998
punicea	EGle GCan GCrs GGGa NHar
quintuplinervia ♀	CLAP CPBP GBri GCan GCrs
	GGGa GTou IBlr NBir NHar
	NMGW NRya NSla
* - 'Kay's Compact'	GBuc IBlr
regia	CPBP CSam EBee EDAr GAbr
	LRHS NLar WBar WOve WViv
- bicolour	EBee NLar
- x *grandis*	GBuc
- hybrids	CAbP
robusta	Last listed 1999
x *sarsonsii*	GCan
x *sbeldonii* ♀	CB&S CBrd EBee EDAr GBuc
	GCrs GGGa GMaP GMac LAst
	LRHS MBri MDun MFir NBir NCut
	NHar SPer SSpi WAbe WCru WLin
	WPGP WViv
- Ballyrogan form	IBlr
- 'Blue Ice'	GTou
- 'Branklyn'	CFil GBri GCrs GGar IBlr
- Crewdson hybrids	CLAP GBuc GDra GMaP MNes
	MOne NBrk
- 'Lingholm'	CLAP GBuc GCal GCan GCrs
	GFle GGar LHop
- 'Miss Jebb'	Last listed 1997
* - 'Mrs McMurtrie'	IBlr
- 'Ormswell'	GBuc IBlr
- 'Silver'	Last listed 1998
- 'Slieve Donard' ♀	CFil CLAP GBri GBuc GCrs GDra
	GGar IBlr MNes NHar SBla
- 'Springhill'	GBuc IBlr
simplicifolia	Last listed 1998
sp. CH&M 1013	Last listed 1998
superba	GBuc GCan GFle GGGa MNes
	WAbe
villosa	GBuc GCal GCan GGGa GTou
	IBlr NBir WAbe
wallicbii hort.	See *M. napaulensis* Wallich's form
- *alba* BC 9370	Last listed 1998
- BC 9361	Last listed 1998
¶ 'Willie Duncan'	GCrs

MEDEMIA (Arecaceae)

argun	Last listed 1999

MEDEOLA (Convallariaceae)

virginica	LAma WCru

MEDICAGO (Papilionaceae)

arborea	CPLG CPle ELan IBlr WHer
sativa	CKin EWFC IIve MPEx WHer
- subsp. *sativa*	IBlr

MEDINILLA (Melastomataceae)

magnifica	LCns LRHS MBri

myriantha 'Pink Pixie'   ECon

MEEHANIA (Lamiaceae)
cordata   Last listed 1997
* *garganica garganica*   Last listed 1998
    B&SWJ 1210
urticifolia   EMon MHar MSte
  - B&SWJ 1210   WCru
  - 'Wandering Minstrel' (v)   EMon

MEGACARPAEA (Brassicaceae)
polyandra   GDra

MELALEUCA (Myrtaceae)
acerosa   SOWG
acuminata   SPlb
alternifolia   CArn ECou ELau EOHP GPoy
    MSal SOWG SSte WDCP
armillaris   SOWG SPlb
bracteata   CTrC
brevifolia   Last listed 1998
calycina subsp. *dempta*   Last listed 1998
capitata   Last listed 1998
coccinea   SOWG
cuticularis   SPlb
decora   SOWG
decussata   CTrC ECou LRHS SOWG SPan
    SPlb SSte
densa   Last listed 1998
§ *diosmatifolia*   Last listed 1999
elliptica   CTrC SOWG SSte
ericifolia   CTri SOWG SPlb
  - *nana*   SPlb
erubescens   See *M. diosmatifolia*
filifolia   SOWG
fulgens   SOWG WDCP
gibbosa   CAbb IDee SBrw SOWG WSHC
    WTro
halmaturorum   Last listed 1999
holosericea hort.   See *M. smartiorum*
huegelii   SOWG
hypericifolia   ECou EPVP SOWG SPlb SSte
incana   CTrC SOWG SSte
lanceolata   Last listed 1998
lateritia   CTrC SSte
leucadendra   MSal SMrm
linariifolia   CTrC ECou LRHS SPlb SSte
nesophila   ECou SOWG SPlb SSte
platycalyx   SOWG
pulchella   SOWG
¶ *pungens*   SPlb
pustulata   ECou SOWG SSte
quinquenervia   See *M. viridiflora* var. *rubriflora*
radula   Last listed 1998
rhaphiophylla   Last listed 1998
* *rosmarinifolia*   SOWG
sieberi   Last listed 1998
§ *smartiorum*   SOWG
spathulata   SOWG
spicigera   Last listed 1998
squamea   ECou WPic
squarrosa   CAbb CGre CTrC ECou SOWG
    SPlb SSte
striata   Last listed 1998
styphelioides   Last listed 1999
suberosa   Last listed 1998
tenella   Last listed 1998
teretifolia   Last listed 1998
thymifolia   ECou SOWG SPlb SSte
thymoides   Last listed 1998
uncinata   Last listed 1999
undulata   Last listed 1998

viminea   Last listed 1998
viridiflora   GQui
§ - var. *rubriflora*   Last listed 1998
wilsonii   CTrC SOWG

MELAMPODIUM (Asteraceae)
¶ *paludosum*   SMrm

MELANDRIUM (Caryophyllaceae)
rubrum   See *Silene dioica*

MELANDRIUM See VACCARIA

MELANOSELINUM (Apiaceae)
§ *decipiens*   CHEx CTrF EOHP LGre WCot
    WHal
* *melanops*   IHdy

MELASPHAERULA (Iridaceae)
graminea   See *M. ramosa*
§ *ramosa*   CAvo CBre CPLG WCot
  - 'Lea'   WCot

MELASTOMA (Melastomataceae)
malabathricum   Last listed 1997

MELIA (Meliaceae)
azadirachta   GPoy
§ *azedarach*   CArn CB&S CPle ELau GPoy
    LPan
  - var. *japonica* See *M. azedarach*

MELIANTHUS (Melianthaceae)
comosus   EWes SSte
major ♀   More than 30 suppliers
minor   CFir
pectinatus   IHdy
sp. from Richtersveld, North Last listed 1999
    Cape, South Africa
villosus   CFir CFri CGdn SPlb

MELICA (Poaceae)
altissima   LRHS MWhi
  - 'Alba'   EHoe
  - 'Atropurpurea' More than 30 suppliers
ciliata   CCuc CFri COIW CPea CSam
    EBee ECGN EHoe EMon EPPr
    EPla EWsh GBin GCHN MMoz
    NChi NHol NNor WPer
  - bronze   Last listed 1997
  - subsp. *magnolii* Last listed 1997
* - 'Pearl Eyelash'   CInt
  - subsp. *taurica* Last listed 1997
macra   EBee EHoe EPPr WPGP
* *minima*   Last listed 1997
nutans   CBod CBrm CCuc EHoe EPPr
    EWsh GBin NHol SBea SUsu WHal
    WRos WWye
penicillaris   EPPr WPer
picta   Last listed 1997
subulata   Last listed 1997
transsilvanica   ECGN GBin NNor
  - 'Atropurpurea' EBee NCut NHol SMac
uniflora   CKin
  - f. *albida*   CCuc CFil EBee EHoe EMan EMon
    EPPr MAvo SUsu WCot WRHF
  - 'Variegata'   CBre CCuc CFil EHoe EMan EMon
    EPPr EPla GCal MBrN MBri WCot
    WWye

MELICOPE (Rutaceae)
ternata   ECou

MELICYTUS (Violaceae)

alpinus	ECou
angustifolius	CPle ECou
crassifolius	CPle ECou EPfP EPla STre WHCG WWat
obovatus	ECou
ramiflorus	ECou

MELILOTUS (Papilionaceae)

officinalis	CArn CKin GBar GPoy MChe SIde WHer WSel WWye
- subsp. *albus*	SIde WHer

MELINIS (Poaceae)

nerviglumis	EPPr

MELIOSMA (Meliosmaceae)

myriantha	Last listed 1999
simplicifolia	CB&S
subsp. *pungens*	
veitchiorum	Last listed 1999

MELISSA (Lamiaceae)

officinalis	CArn CChe CHal EDAr EFer ELau GPoy MBar MBri MChe MHer MHew MMal NArg NGCt SIde SPlb SSoC WBea WGwG WOak WPer WWye
- 'All Gold'	CArn CBre CHal CMGP CSev ECha EHoe ELan ELau GBar MBri MChe MHer NBid NFai NPri NSti NVic SPer WWye
* - subsp. *altissima* 'Atropurpurea'	NArg
§ - 'Aurea' (v)	More than 30 suppliers
* - 'Compacta'	ELau GPoy MHer
¶ - 'Quedlinburger Niederliegende'	CArn
- 'Small-Ness'	MNes
N - 'Variegata' misapplied	See *M. officinalis* 'Aurea'

MELITTIS (Lamiaceae)

melissophyllum	CFir CRDP EMan LPio MCAu MHew MRav SIng SRms SSpi WAbb WWye
- subsp. *albida*	SSpi
- pink	EMon GOrP MInt SOkh

MENISPERMUM (Menispermaceae)

canadense	CPlN GPoy MSal
davuricum	Last listed 1999

MENTHA ✿ (Lamiaceae)

aquatica	CArn CBen CKin CRow CWat ECoo EHon ELau EWFC GPoy LPBA MChe MHer MHew MSta NPer SIde SLon SPlb SWat SWyc WGwG WHer WMAq WOak
§ - var. *crispa*	IIve
- krause minze	See *M. aquatica* var. *crispa*
¶ - 'Mandeliensis'	IIve
arvensis	CArn ELau EOHP IIve MHer MSal SIde WHer WJek
¶ - 'Banana'	EOHP
- 'New Fancy' (v)	Last listed 1999
- var. *piperascens*	EOHP MSal SAga
§ - - 'Sayakaze'	ELau EOHP
asiatica	CStr ELau EOHP IIve NGCt SIde WHer
Bowles' mint	See *M.* x *villosa* var. *alopecuroides* Bowles' mint
* *brevifolia*	EOHP SIde WHer
§ *cervina*	CBen CWat EMFW EOHP LPBA MSta SWat WBar
- *alba*	EMFW EOHP MCCP WMAq
citrata	See *M.* x *piperita* f. *citrata*
cordifolia	See *M.* x *villosa*
corsica	See *M. requienii*
crispa L. (1753)	See *M. spicata* var. *crispa*
- L. (1763)	See *M. aquatica* var. *crispa*
- x *piperita*	EDAr GBar SRms
diemenica	EOHP
* - var. *koiscikoko*	Last listed 1997
¶ 'Dionysus'	IIve
'Eau de Cologne'	See *M.* x *piperita* f. *citrata*
Eucalyptus mint	ELau EOHP GBar WBea WGwG WOak WRha
gattefossei	CArn ELau EOHP
x *gentilis*	See *M.* x *gracilis*
§ x *gracilis*	CArn ELau EOHP GBar MChe MMal NDea NPri SIde WBea WJek WRHF WWye
- 'Aurea'	See *M.* x *gracilis* 'Variegata'
§ - 'Variegata'	CBrm CSev ECha ECoo EHoe EMar GPoy ILis MBar MHar MHer MRav NArg NGCt SHel WGwG WHer WOak WOve WPer WSel
haplocalyx	ELau EOHP MSal
* 'Hillary's Sweet Lemon'	ELau EOHP
* *lacerata*	SIde
I 'Lavender'	WBea WGwG
Lavender mint	CBod ELau EMan GBar GPoy IIve MHer MRav WBry WJek WRha
§ *longifolia*	CAgr CRDP ECha ECoo ELau EMar GBar GVer IIve LHop MMal MRav NSti SPlb WEas WGwG WHer WJek WOak WPer WSel WWye
- Buddleia Mint Group	CArn ELau EMan GAbr GGar MHer MPEx MRav NBus SIde WBea WBry WGwG WRha WSel
- silver	CArn ELau MHer WBea
* - 'Variegata'	CBod ELau NCat NSti WJek WOak
x *piperita*	CAgr CArn CSev ECha EDAr EHoe ELau GBar GPoy ILis MBri MChe MHer MHew MMal NArg NFor SPlb WBea WGwG WHbs WOak WPer WWye
* - alba	GBar
- 'Black Mitcham'	EOHP GBar
§ - f. *citrata*	More than 30 suppliers
* - - 'Basil'	CBod ELau EOHP GBar IIve LLWP MHer MRav SHDw SIde WBea WBry WGwG WJek WOak WRha
- - 'Chocolate'	CArn CBod ELau EMan EOHP GBar GKir MHer NArg NGCt SHDw SIde WBea WBry WGwG WJek WPer
¶ - - 'Grapefruit'	EOHP
- - 'Lemon'	ELau EMan EOHP GAbr GBar MBri MHer MMal SHDw SIde WBea WCHb WGwG WJek WOak WPer WRha WSel
- - 'Lime'	EMan EOHP LHrt MHer MTed NGCt SHDw SIde WBea WCHb WGwG WJek
- - orange	GBar MHer
¶ - - 'Swiss Ricola'	EOHP
- - 'Logee's' (v)	EBee EMan EOHP EWes MHer NWoo WBea WBry WCHb WHer WJek WRha
¶ - 'Murray Mitcham'	SIde
- f. *officinalis*	ELau SIde

¶ – 'Reine Rouge' · Ilve
– 'Reverchonii' · Last listed 1999
pulegium · CAgr CArn CSev EBot ECha EDAr
ELau EWFC GBar GPoy MChe
MHer MHew MPEx NArg NFla SIde
SPlb WCHb WGwG WHbs WHer
WJek WOak WPer WWye
– 'Upright' · CArn CBod EOHP GBar GPoy
MHer SHDw SIde WBry WCHb
WJek WPer WSel
pycantheum pilosum · Last listed 1997
§ **requienii** · CArn ELau EPot ESis GBar GKir
GPoy ILis LEdu MBar MBri MChe
MMal NLAp SDix SIde SIng SPlb
SRms WEas WGwG WOak WPat
WPer WSel WWye
rotundifolia hort. · See M. suaveolens
rubra var. **raripila** · See M. x smithiana
'Sayakarze' · See M. arvensis var. piperascens
'Sayakaze'
§ x **smithiana** · CArn EDAr ELau EOHP GAbr GBar
GPoy ILis MChe MHer NPri WBea
WBry WGwG WHer WOak WPer
WRha WWye
– 'Capel Ulo' (v) · ELau EOHP WHer
sp. Nile Valley mint · CArn CBod ELau EOHP SHDw
SIde WCHb
§ **spicata** · CAgr CArn CSev EDAr GBar GPoy
ILis MBar MBri MChe MHer MHew
MMal NFai NFor SRms WBea WGwG
WHer WJek WOak WPer WWye
¶ – Algerian fruity · Ilve
– 'Argentina' · SIde
* – 'Brundall' · ELau EOHP ILis MTed
¶ – 'Canaries' · Ilve
§ – var. **crispa** · CArn EDAr ELau EOHP GAbr
GBar LFis MHer NArg NFai NPri
NSti SIde WCHb WCer WCot
WGwG WPer WRha WSel WWye
¶ – – 'Moroccan' · CArn CInt CSev EDAr ELau EMan
EOHP GAbr GBar GKir GPoy Ilve
MHar MHer NArg SHDw SIde
WBea WBry WCHb WCer WGwG
WHer WJek WOak WSel WWye
¶ – 'Guernsey' · EOHP NGCt SHDw
– 'Newbourne' · ELau
– 'Spanish Furry' · EOHP
– 'Spanish Pointed' · ELau EOHP
– 'Tashkent' · CArn EDAr ELau EOHP MHer
MTed NGCt SHDw SIde WBea
WBry WCHb WGwG WJek
– subsp. **tomentosa** · Last listed 1999
¶ – 'Ukraine' · Ilve
* – 'Variegata' · SHDw WHer
¶ – 'Verte Blanche' · Ilve
¶ – 'Westmeath' · Ilve
§ **suaveolens** · CAgr CArn ELau GBar GPoy ILis
MBri MHew MMal SIde WBea
WGwG WHer WOak WPer
* – 'Grapefruit' · Ilve
* – 'Jukka' · Ilve
* – 'Mobillei' · EOHP SIde
* – 'Pineapple' · Ilve
– subsp. **timija** · ELau WJek
* – 'Variegata' · More than 30 suppliers
sylvestris L. · See M. longifolia
¶ x **thuringer** · EOHP
§ x **villosa** · CArn EOHP
– var. **alopecuroides** · CBre EDAr ELau EMan GBar GGar
Bowles' mint · GPoy Ilve ILis MChe MHer NFai
SIde SWat WGwG WHer WJek
WOak WWye

viridis · See M. spicata

MENYANTHES (Menyanthaceae)
trifoliata · CBen CNic CRow CWat ECoo
EHon ELau EMFW EWFC GBar
GPoy LPBA MHew MSta NDea NVic
SLon SWyc WMAq WShi WWye

MENZIESIA (Ericaceae)
alba · See Daboecia cantabrica f. alba
ciliicalyx · SSpi
– dwarf form · SReu SSta
– **lasiophylla** · See M. ciliicalyx var. purpurea
– var. **multiflora** · GGGa MDun SReu SSta
§ – var. **purpurea** · GGGa SSta
ferruginea · SReu SSta
polifolia · See Daboecia cantabrica
'Spring Morning' · Last listed 1999

MERCURIALIS (Euphorbiaceae)
perennis · GPoy WHer WShi
– 'Cae Rhos Lligwy' · WHer

MERENDERA (Colchicaceae)
attica · Last listed 1999
eichleri · See M. trigyna
filifolia AB&S 4665 · Last listed 1998
kurdica · LAma
§ **montana** · ERos WIvy
– MS 900/913 · Last listed 1998
– S&F 221 · Last listed 1998
pyrenaica · See M. montana
raddeana · See M. trigyna
sobolifera · EPot
§ **trigyna** · LAma

MERREMIA (Convolvulaceae)
§ **tuberosa** · CPIN

MERTENSIA (Boraginaceae)
ciliata · CMdw EBrP EBre GKir LBCl LBSe
LBre LRHS MArl MBBe MBri
MNrw NChi SBre SWat WRus
echioides · NTow
franciscana · EBee GCal WCru
maritima · GPoy MSal WCru WLin WRos
WWin
– subsp. **asiatica** · See M. simplicissima
primuloides · CPlt GCal WAbe
pterocarpa · See M. sibirica
§ **pulmonarioides** ♀ · More than 30 suppliers
§ **sibirica** · CLAP CSpe EBee GBri LGre NChi
NDlv NTow SPlb WByw WWin
§ **simplicissima** · CBot EBee ECho ELan EMan GKir
MNrw NBir NWCA SBla WByw
WCru WHoo WWhi
virginica · See M. pulmonarioides
viridis · Last listed 1998

MERXMUELLERA See RYTIDOSPERMA

MERYTA (Araliaceae)
sinclairii · CTrC

MESEMBRYANTHEMUM (Aizoaceae)
'Basutoland' · See Delosperma nubigenum
brownii · See Lampranthus brownii

MESPILUS (Rosaceae)
germanica (F) · CB&S CBlo CDul CLnd ELan IOrc
LPan MWat WDin WMou
– 'Bredase Reus' (F) · SKee

- 'Dutch' (F)	SDea SFam SKee
- 'Large Russian' (F)	ERea ESim GTwe
- 'Macrocarpa'	SKee
- 'Monstrous' (F)	SDea
- 'Nottingham' (F)	CAgr CEnd CSam CTho EBee
	EMui ENot EPfP ERea GKir GTwe
	LBuc LPan LRHS MBlu MLan NBee
	SDea SFam SKee SPer WJas WMou
- 'Royal' (F)	CAgr ESim SKee

METAPANAX See PSEUDOPANAX

METASEQUOIA (Taxodiaceae)
glyptostroboides ♀	More than 30 suppliers
- 'Fastigiata'	See M. glyptostroboides 'National'
- 'Gold Rush'	GKir LLin MBlu SLim
- 'Green Mantle'	EHul EWTr
§ - 'National'	MGos
- 'Sheridan Spire'	CEnd LNet

METROSIDEROS (Myrtaceae)
carmineus	CHEx
- 'Carousel' (v)	ERea
- 'Ferris Wheel'	ERea
diffusus	CPlN
§ excelsus	CAbb CHEx CTrC CTrG EBak
	ECou WDCP
- 'Aureus'	ECou
- 'Parnell'	CB&S CTrC
- 'Scarlet Pimpernel'	ERea SOWG
- 'Spring Fire'	CAbb CB&S GQui
- 'Upper Hut'	CTrC
fulgens	Last listed 1998
'Goldfinger' (v)	ERea
kermadecensis	ECou LHil
- 'Radiant' (v)	CPLG
- 'Variegatus'	CB&S CDoC ECou ERea GQui
	LHil SLon
lucidus	See M. umbellatus
'Moon Maiden'	ERea
'Pink Lady'	ERea
robustus	GQui
'Thomasii'	ECon EPfP LCns LRHS SOWG
tomentosus	See M. excelsus
§ umbellatus	CGre CHEx ECou
villosus	SOWG
- 'Tahiti'	CB&S GQui

MEUM (Apiaceae)
athamanticum	CGle CRDP CSev CSpe EBee EBrP
	EBre EFou EMan EPla GBri GCal
	GPoy LBCl LBSe LBre MBBe MHew
	MRav MSal MTho NBrk SBre SMrm
	SOkh WFar WPer WPrP

MICHAUXIA (Campanulaceae)
campanuloides	NChi WCot WPic WSan
laevigata	Last listed 1997
tchihatchewii	CBot CSpe LHop WLin WSan

MICHELIA (Magnoliaceae)
¶ chapensis	CFil WPGP
compressa	EPfP
crassipes	WPGP
doltsopa	CB&S CFil CGre CHEx GQui IDee
	LRHS SSpi
figo	CAbb CFil CGre ERea GQui SSpi
	WPGP
maudiae	CFil WPGP
§ sinensis	CFil CMCN
wilsonii	See M. sinensis
yunnanensis	CFil

MICRANTHUS (Iridaceae)
alopecuroides	Last listed 1998
plantagineus	LBow

MICROBIOTA (Cupressaceae)
decussata ♀	More than 30 suppliers
- 'Jakobsen'	CKen
- 'Trompenburg'	CKen

MICROCACHRYS (Podocarpaceae)
tetragona	CDoC ECho ECou EOrn EPla
	LCon MBri

MICROCOELUM See LYTOCARYUM

MICROGLOSSA (Asteraceae)
albescens	See Aster albescens

MICROLEPIA (Dennstaedtiaceae)
speluncae	MBri

MICROLOMA (Asclepiadaceae)
hereroense	Last listed 1998
sagittatum	Last listed 1998

MICROMERIA (Lamiaceae)
chamissonis	ELau
corsica	See Acinos corsicus
croatica	NTow
dalmatica	EBee
rupestris	See M. thymifolia
§ thymifolia	CPBP EBee EMan GPoy NMen
	SPlb
viminea	See Satureja viminea

MICROSERIS (Asteraceae)
ringens hort.	See Leontodon rigens

MICROSORUM (Polypodiaceae)
diversifolium	See Phymatosorus diversifolius
punctatum 'Grandiceps'	Last listed 1998

MICROSTROBOS (Podocarpaceae)
fitzgeraldii	CKen
niphophilus	ECou

MIKANIA (Asteraceae)
§ dentata	CPlN MBri
scandens	Last listed 1999
ternata	See M. dentata

MILIUM (Poaceae)
effusum	CKin COld
- 'Aureum'	More than 30 suppliers
- var. esthonicum	EBee EMon EPPr

MILLETTIA (Papilionaceae)
§ japonica	LNet
Murasaki-natsu-fuji	See M. reticulata
§ reticulata	LNet

MIMOSA (Mimosaceae)
hostilis	Last listed 1998
pudica	EAnd LPVe LRHS MLan
scabrella	Last listed 1998

MIMULUS (Scrophulariaceae)
'A.T. Johnson'	MSCN NVic
alatus	EBee
'Andean Nymph'	CM&M
* 'Andean Nymph'	CPBP
F & W 8384	

'Andean Nymph' forms	CGle CSpe GKir LRHS MNrw SPlb
§ 'Andean Nymph'	CLTr CMea CPlt EBrP EBre ELan
Mac&W 5257 ♀	EPot LBCl LBSe LBre MBBe MSCN
	NMGW SBre SRot SWat WRos
aridus	EBee
§ *aurantiacus* ♀	More than 30 suppliers
§ - var. *puniceus*	CBot CHal CLTr CSpe CTri EBee
	ELan LHil LHop MHar SAga SDry
	SMrm SUsu
¶ 'Aztec Trumpet'	EDAr
x *bartonianus*	EBee EMan EWes GMac
bifidus	CSpe EBee
¶ - 'Tapestry'	CSpe
- 'Verity Buff'	CSpe LHil LIck
- Verity hybrids	ERea LHil
§ - 'Verity Purple'	CSpe LIck
- 'Verity Rose'	CLTr LHil
- 'Wine'	See *M. bifidus* 'Verity Purple'
x *burnetii*	EMan LPBA SRms
californicus	Last listed 1998
Calypso Series	SRms
cardinalis ♀	EBee EHon ELan LPBA MFir
	MNrw MTho NDea NFai NFor
	NMGW SHFr SPer WBor WCot
	WFar WHer WOve WPGP WPer
	WWeb WWin
- 'Dark Throat'	Last listed 1997
cupreus	Last listed 1999
- 'Minor'	ECho
- 'Whitecroft Scarlet' ♀	ECha EDAr ELan GDra LPBA LRHS
	MNrw MOne NHar SRms WPer
	WWin
cusickii	Last listed 1998
'Eleanor'	SAga SMrm SUsu
glutinosus	See *M. aurantiacus*
- *atrosanguineus*	See *M. aurantiacus* var. *puniceus*
- *luteus*	See *M. aurantiacus*
§ *guttatus*	CBen CKin CRow EWFC GAbr
	GAri GMas NDea SRms WMAq
	WMoo WPer
§ - 'Richard Bish' (v)	CMea CRDP EBee EDAr EMan
	LHop MCCP NCat SAga SCob
	WByw WCot
- variegated	See *M. guttatus* 'Richard Bish'
'Highland Orange'	EDAr GKir LRHS MOne NHar
	SIng SPlb WGor WPer
'Highland Pink'	ECtt EDAr EMan EPfP EWTr GKir
	LRHS MOne NHar SIng SPlb
	WGor WPer
I 'Highland Pink Rose'	SWal
'Highland Red' ♀	ECtt EDAr EMFW EPfP EWTr
	GDra GKir LPBA LRHS MOne
	NArg NNrd SIng SPlb SRms WHen
	WPer WWin
'Highland Yellow'	ECtt EDAr GKir LRHS MNrw SIng
	SPlb WHen WPer
hose-in-hose	CLTr EBee ECha EMFW NChi
	WMAq
hose-in-hose orange	Last listed 1999
hose-in-hose yellow	EBee ECal
'Inca Sunset'	EDAr EWes
'Inshriach Crimson'	Last listed 1999
'June Gold'	Last listed 1999
langsdorffii	See *M. guttatus*
lewisii ♀	EBee EDAr GDra GTou MTho
	NWCA SLon SPer SRms WPGP
	WPer WRha
¶ - 'Albus'	SGar
longiflorus	CBot CLTr
- 'Santa Barbara'	CLTr LHil LIck SMrm SUsu
'Lothian Fire'	WMAq WWeb
luteus	CBen CRow CWat ECha EHon
	LPBA MHer MSta NDea NFai SHFr
	WByw WMAq
* - 'Variegatus'	CRow GMac MHer NGdn NPer
* 'Major Bees'	EPfP GCal
'Malibu Scarlet'	Last listed 1998
(Malibu Series)	
Malibu Series	NFor
'Mandarin'	EBrP EBre LBCl LBSe LBre MBBe
	SBre
moschatus	CRow NCat WCru
nanus	Last listed 1998
'Old Rose'	EBee
'Orange Glow'	EPfP WHal
'Orkney Gold'	GOrP
'Popacatapetl'	CHal CSpe EBee LHil LHop LIck
	MHar MSte SChu SMrm SUsu
primuloides	EDAr ELan EPot GCrs LRHS NHar
	NMen NNrd NWCA SPlb WFar
'Puck'	GKir GMac LRHS NPro
'Queen's Prize'	Last listed 1997
'Quetzalcoatl'	LIck SMrm
Red Emperor	See *M.* 'Roter Kaiser'
ringens	CBen CRow CWat EBee EHon
	EMFW EWTr GBri LPBA MSta
	NDea SPer SPlb SRms WFar WHil
	WMAq WPer WWeb
§ 'Roter Kaiser'	EDAr MNrw SRms WBar
'Royal Velvet'	Last listed 1997
sp. Mac&W 5257	See *M.* 'Andean Nymph' Mac&W
	5257
Threave variegated	EBee GBri GBuc GCal GKir NBir
'Tigrinus'	MWll
'Tigrinus Queen's Prize'	LIck
tilingii	CHal ECho GTou NNrd
'Western Hills'	MGrG
'Wine Red'	See *M. bifidus* 'Verity Purple'
'Wisley Red'	ECha ECot ELan SRms
'Yellow Velvet'	Last listed 1997

MINA See IPOMOEA

MINUARTIA (Caryophyllaceae)

capillacea	Last listed 1998
caucasica	See *M. circassica*
§ *circassica*	CLyd ESis MDHE NWCA WPer
dianthifolia	Last listed 1998
inamoena	Last listed 1999
juniperina	ESis
- NS 270	NWCA
laricifolia	CLyd LRHS
§ *obtusiloba*	Last listed 1999
parnassica	See *M. stellata*
§ *recurva*	Last listed 1997
rossii subsp. *rossii*	NWCA
§ *rubella*	NTow
§ *stellata*	EPot MNaF NDlv NMen NNrd
	NTow SIng
- NS 758	NWCA
§ *verna*	NHar NMen
- subsp. *caespitosa* 'Aurea'	See *Sagina subulata* var.
	glabrata 'Aurea'

MIRABILIS (Nyctaginaceae)

jalapa	CArn CGdn CSWP EBot ELan
	LAma LIck LRHS MBri MLLN MSal
	SEND SHFr SRms SYvo WCot

MISCANTHUS (Poaceae)

flavidus B&SWJ 3697	WCru
floridulus ♀	CFir CSev EBee EFou EHoe GCal
	LRHS MMoz NBea NPSl NVic SCob
	SDix SMad SSoC WCot WFar WWoo

nepalensis EHoe EWes LEdu SMrm
- CLD 1314 Last listed 1997
§ x *oligonensis* 'Juli' LPan LRHS
§ - 'Wetterfahne' EBrP EBre EGle EPPr LBCl LBSe
LBre MBBe SBre
oligostachyus EBee EPPr GCal
§ - 'Afrika' LGre
§ - 'Nanus Variegatus' CBrm CCuc CRow EBee EHoe
EMon EPPr EWes LRHS MMoz
WCot WPGP
- 'Purpurascens' SApp
* 'Purpurascens' EHul
sacchariflorus More than 30 suppliers
sinensis ♀ CHEx EBee EPla GBin LHrt MMoz
NFla NOak SLon WRos
- 'Adagio' EPPr LEdu WCot
- 'Afrika' See *M. oligostachyus* 'Afrika'
- 'Arabesque' EFou LPan LRHS MMoz
- 'Augustfeder' EBrP EBre LBCl LBSe LBre LPan
MBBe SBre
- 'Autumn Light' EPPr LRHS
- C&L 143a EPla
- 'China' CBrm CFir CHar EBee ECGN
EHoe EMan EPGN EPPr EPla EWes
EWsh GBin LRHS NHol SChu
SWat
- var. **condensatus** Last listed 1998
- - 'Cabaret' (v) EFou SRos WCot WHal
- - 'Cosmopolitan' (v) More than 30 suppliers
- - 'Emerald Giant' Last listed 1999
- 'Dixieland' (v) EGle EPPr LEdu LPan LRHS MMoz
- dwarf form Last listed 1997
¶ - 'Federriese' EBrP EBre LBCl LBSe LBre MBBe
SBre
- 'Ferne Osten' CCuc CHar CHid CWit EBee EBrP
EBre ECGN ECha EFou EPGN
EPPr EPla GKir LBCl LBSe LBre
LEdu LGre LRHS MBBe MBri
MChl MMoz MWgw NBea NHol
SBre SUsu WFar
- 'Flamingo' CCtw CCuc EBee EBrP EBre EGle
EHoe EPGN EPPr EPla LBCl LBSe
LBre LGre LPan LRHS MBBe MBri
MChl MMoz NBea NBee NHol
SBre WFar WViv
- 'Gearmella' EBee EBrP EBre EPPr GKir LBCl
LBSe LBre LEdu MBBe SBre
¶ - 'Gewitterwolke' LGre
¶ - 'Ghana' LGre
- 'Goldfeder' (v) EPla LRHS WBcn
- 'Goliath' LPan
- 'Gracillimus' More than 30 suppliers
- 'Graziella' CCuc CHar EBee EBrP EBre EGle
EHoe EMan EPGN EPPr EPla
LBCl LBSe LBre LGre LPan LRHS
MBBe MBri MMoz MSte NBus
NHol SBre SPer SUsu SVil WLRN
WPGP WPrP
- 'Grosse Fontäne' CBrm ECha EHoe EPGN EPla
EWsh GKir LEdu LRHS MMoz
SMad WCot
¶ - 'Haiku' LGre
- 'Hercules' LPan LRHS MAvo
¶ - 'Hermann Müssel' LGre
- 'Juli' See *M. x oligonensis* 'Juli'
- 'Kaskade' CKno EBee EBrP EBre EPGN EPla
GKir LBCl LBSe LBre LRHS MBBe
MBri NOGN SBre WBcn
- 'Kleine Fontäne' More than 30 suppliers
- 'Kleine Silberspinne' More than 30 suppliers
- 'Krater' LEdu WRHF
§ - 'Little Kitten' EPla EWsh LEdu MBar WCru

- 'Malepartus' More than 30 suppliers
- 'Morning Light' (v) More than 30 suppliers
- New Hybrids CCuc EHul MTis
- 'Nippon' CElw EBee EHoe EMan EPGN
EPPr EPla LEdu LHil LRHS MCAu
MCCP MCLN MMoz NHol SChu
SDys SMad WRus
- 'November Sunset' EPPr EWes LPan LRHS MMoz
- 'Overdam' MAvo
- 'Poseidon' EPPr SDys
- 'Positano' LPan LRHS MMoz
- 'Pünktchen' (v) CBrm ECha EFou EGle EPPr EPla
LGre LPan LRHS SMad
- var. **purpurascens** CBrm CInt CMea CWit EBee
ECGN ECha EGar EGol EHoe
EMan EPPr EPla EWsh GAri MBrN
MLLN SCob SSoC WWat
- - 'Roter Pfeil' LGre
¶ - 'Richard Nouson' LGre
- 'Roland' LGre SAga
- 'Rotfuchs' CLon GKir LGre
- 'Rotsilber' (v) CSpe EBee EBrP EBre ECha EFou
EGle EHoe EMan EOld EPGN
EPPr EPla EWTr EWsh GKir LBCl
LBSe LBre LEdu LPan LRHS MBBe
SBre SRCN STes WCot WPnP
WViv
- S&F 92302 Last listed 1999
- 'Sarabande' CBrm ECGN EFou EHoe EPla
LPan LRHS
§ - 'Silberfeder' More than 30 suppliers
- 'Silberpfeil' (v) EPla
- 'Silberspinne' CCuc CPou EBee EFou EGar EGle
EPla GKir LEdu LGre LHil LPan
LRHS SPlb SWal
- 'Silberturm' SVil
- Silver Feather See *M. sinensis* 'Silberfeder'
- 'Sioux' EBee EGle EPPr EPla GBin GKir
LRHS MMoz WBcn
- 'Sirene' EBee EBrP EBre EPGN EPPr EPla
GKir LBCl LBSe LBre LPan LRHS
MBBe MBel NHol SBre
- 'Slavopour' EPla
- 'Spatgrun' EPPr EPla
- 'Strictus' (v) CBrm CCtw CMea EBee ECha EFul
EGar EMan EPPr EPla GKir LEdu
LRHS MBri MChl MMoz NBea NBee
NOak SDix WCot WRus WViv
- 'Undine' More than 30 suppliers
- 'Variegatus' More than 30 suppliers
- 'Vorläufer' EBrP EBre EFou EHoe EPla GKir
LBCl LBSe LBre LGre MBBe SBre
- 'Wetterfahne' See *M. x oligonensis*
'Wetterfahne'
§ - 'Yaku-jima' EBee ECha EGle EPPr WPGP
- 'Yakushima Dwarf' More than 30 suppliers
- 'Zebrinus' (v) More than 30 suppliers
¶ - 'Zwergelefant' LPan MMoz
sp. from Yakushima EPla
tinctorius See *M. oligostachyus* 'Nanus
'Nanus Variegatus' Variegatus'
- 'Variegatus' Last listed 1998
transmorrisonensis CBod EHoe EMan EPPr EPla GBin
LEdu MMoz SMad
yakushimensis See *M. sinensis* 'Yaku-jima' , *M.*
sinensis 'Little Kitten'

MISOPATES (Scrophulariaceae)
orontium EWFC

MITCHELLA (Rubiaceae)
repens WCru WWat

MITELLA (Saxifragaceae)

breweri	CGle CHal CNic EBee ECha GBin LSyl MLLN MRav MSte NHol NSti SHFr SRms SSpi WByw WEas WFar WPer WWat WWye
caulescens	ECha GAbr LFis MLLN MRav NBro NHol WPer WPrP
diphylla	EBee
formosana B&SWJ 125	EBee WCru
ovalis	EBee
stauropetala	NCat NWoo

MITRARIA (Gesneriaceae)

coccinea	CAbb CB&S CHEx CMac CNic CPlN CPle CRHN CTrG CTrw CWit ELan EPot ERea GGGa GGar IDee IOrc MBlu NSti SArc SLon SPer SSpi WBod WBor WCot WGwG WSHC WWat
- Clark's form	MDun
- 'Lake Caburgua'	GCal
- Lake Puye form	CDoC CFee CGre ERea GQui LRHS MGos SBra SPan SSta SVen WCru WWal WWat

MOLINIA (Poaceae)

altissima	See *M. caerulea* subsp. *arundinacea*
caerulea	COtt EBee
§ - subsp. *arundinacea*	CBrm CCuc EBrP EBre ECGN ECha EFou EPla GBin LBCl LBSe LBre LHil MBBe SAga SBre SPer WPer
- - 'Bergfreund'	ECGN EHoe EMon EPPr EPla EWsh GCal SCou SDys SUsu WDyG WWye
- - 'Fontäne'	EFou EPPr EPla GBin LGre LPan MSte
- - 'Karl Foerster'	CCuc EBee ECGN EFou EHoe EMan EPPr EPfP EPla GBin GCal LBuc LEdu LGre LPan MMil MMoz SApp SVil WCot WFar WLRN WMoo
- - 'Skyracer'	EFou EPPr GBri LIck LPan MMoz WCot
- - 'Transparent'	CCuc CKno CLon CPlt EFou EGle EHoe EPPr EPla GBri GCal LGre LPan MMoz SCob SMad WCot WHal WPrP
- - 'Windspiel'	CCuc CInt CLTr CRow EBee ECGN ECha EFou EHoe EMil EMon EPPr EPla EWsh GCal LEdu LGre LPan MWgw NSti WCot WPGP
- - 'Zuneigung'	EHoe LGre LPan
- subsp. *caerulea*	CElw CNat EBee EMon EPPr
'Carmarthen' (v)	LRHS WCot WPrP
- - 'Claerwen' (v)	EMan EPPr GBuc GCal
- - 'Dauerstrahl'	GBin NHol WPrP
- - 'Edith Dudszus'	CBod CCuc CM&M EBee ECGN ECha EHoe EPPr EPla LGre LRHS MBrN MMoz MWgw NOGN SPer SUsu SVil WHal WPGP WPrP
- - 'Heidebraut'	CCuc CElw ECGN ECha EGle EHoe EMon EPPr EPla LGre LRHS MWgw SVil WFar
- - 'Moorflamme'	EPPr LPan
- - 'Moorhexe'	CInt CMil EBee ECGN ECha EHoe EMan EMon EPPr EPla EWsh GBri GCal GDea LEdu LRHS MAvo

	MCAu NOak NSti NVic SMad SSoC SVil WCot WPrP
- - 'Strahlenquelle'	CElw EBee EMan EMon EPGN EPPr EPla GCal LRHS MMoz NOGN WPGP WPrP
- - 'Variegata' ♀	More than 30 suppliers
litoralis	See *M. caerulea* subsp. *arundinacea*

MOLOPOSPERMUM (Apiaceae)

peloponnesiacum	EBee LGre NChi NLar SMrm WCot WCru

MOLTKIA (Boraginaceae)

§ *doerfleri*	CPle MBro NChi WWat
graminifolia	See *M. suffruticosa*
§ x *intermedia* ♀	CMea CNic LHil SOkd SRms WWin
petraea	EBee MWat
§ *suffruticosa*	LRHS

MOMORDICA (Cucurbitaceae)

balsamina	CPIN MSal
charantia	MSal

MONADENIUM (Euphorbiaceae)

lugardae	MBri
'Variegatum'	MBri

MONARDA ✿ (Lamiaceae)

'Adam'	GAbr GCal LRHS MLLN MSte WViv
'Aquarius'	CBlo CElw CGle CLTr EBee EFou EGle EMan EMon EWTr LRHS MCAu MSte NPro NSti SAga SChu SCro SMad SOkh WCHb WFar WOve WRus WWat WWeb WWhi
austromontana	CArn CBlo EBee ECoo EWes EWll SCro SIde SSvw WCot WPer
'Baby Spice'	LRHS
§ 'Balance'	CGle CSev EBee EGar EGle EMan EMon GCal LGre LRHS MSCN MSte NSti NVic SChu SCro SMrm WCHb WFar WHil WHoo WOve WPGP WPyg WRus WWat
'Beauty of Cobham' ♀	More than 30 suppliers
'Blaukranz'	EFou SChu
§ 'Blaustrumpf'	CElw GBri LFis MHer MSte NCiC NLar NOrc SPer WRus
Blue Stocking	See *M.* 'Blaustrumpf'
Bowman	See *M.* 'Sagittarius'
bradburyana	EMon WCHb
'Cambridge Scarlet' ♀	More than 30 suppliers
'Capricorn'	CBlo CGle CLTr CSev CStr EBee EFou EGar EGle EMan EMar GBuc LRHS MSte NCat NSti SChu SCro SOkh WCHb WCot WHoo WPyg WRus WWal
'Cherokee'	EGar EPPr GBri LGre MAvo MRav SAga WCHb WFar
citriodora	CAgr CArn GPoy LRHS MChe MHer MSal SIde SRms SWat WGwG WJek WPer WSel WWye
- PC&H 215	Last listed 1998
'Comanche'	CMea CStr EFou LGre SAga WCHb WFar WViv
'Croftway Pink' ♀	More than 30 suppliers
'Dark Ponticum'	EGar LRHS MGrG
didyma	CAgr CArn CBlo EDAr GKir LAst LRHS LSyl MChe MFir MSal

	NArg NBro SWat WHbs WJek WOak
- 'Alba'	CBot MHer MSCN
- 'Duddiscombe'	CSam
- 'Goldmelisse'	WBea WHil
- 'Red Explode'	Last listed 1997
'Donnerwolke'	SChu
'Elsie's Lavender'	CHal CLTr CStr EFou EGar EGle EMon GBri GBuc LPio LRHS NBro WCHb
§ 'Feuerschopf'	GMac MSte SAga
Firecrown	See *M.* 'Feuerschopf'
§ 'Fishes'	More than 30 suppliers
fistulosa	CArn CMea EBee EWTr GPoy LRot MChe MHew MMal MSal SIde WGwG WHer WJek WMoo WPer
'Forncett Bishop'	Last listed 1999
'Gardenview'	EWes GCal GMac MAnH NBrk NSti SMrm WRHF
'Gardenview Scarlet'	EBee EBrP EBre EFou EOrc GBri LBCl LBSe LBre LRHS MBBe NCat NChi SBre WCHb WPer
'Hartswood Wine'	MRav SMad
'Kardinal'	CGle EFou MSte
* 'Keureschol'	NCat
'Kruisbekje'	Last listed 1999
'Lambada'	LRHS
'Libra'	See *M.* 'Balance'
'Loddon Crown'	CBos CLTr EBee ECGP EFou EMar EMon LRHS MBri NChi NHol WCHb WFar WMaN
* 'Mahogany'	CElw CHid CSam CStr EBee EFou EGle EMan EMar EMon EWTr GAbr GBri GGar GMaP LRHS MBel MCLN MRav MTis NChi NCiC NHol NSti SPer WCHb WSan WWye
'Marshall's Delight'	EBee EBrP EBre EMar LBCl LBSe LBre LPio MBBe SBre SMrm WHil WRus
* 'Melissa'	CGle EFou EGle
menthifolia	CArn EBee EGar EWTr EWll LRHS SAga STes WHer
'Mohawk'	EBee EFou EGle EMan EMar EMon LFis LGre LRHS MAvo MCAu NCat NCiC SAga SMrm WCHb WLRN WRus
'Mrs Perry'	EFou EWes NHol
'Osage'	Last listed 1998
'Ou Charm'	CBos CElw CHad CHid CStr EBee ECGP EFou EMon EPPr EWes GBri LFis LRHS MLLN MMil NChi NCiC NDov SAga SCro SMad SMrm SUsu WCHb WFar WHil WSan
'Pale Ponticum'	EMon
'Panorama'	CBlo ECtt EOld MMal MSal SPlb WElm WMoo WPer
'Pawnee'	EFou SChu WCHb
pectinata	Last listed 1999
'Petite Delight'	LRHS NPro
'Pink Tourmaline'	LGre LRHS MBri SAga SMad SMrm WCHb WFar
'Pisces'	See *M.* 'Fishes'
Pisces	See *M.* 'Fishes'
'Poyntzfield Pink'	GPoy
Prairie Glow = 'Prärieglut'	MBri
Prairie Night	See *M.* 'Prärienacht'
'Präriebrand'	MBri
§ 'Prärienacht'	More than 30 suppliers
punctata	CArn CBot CGle ELan EMan GCal

	LHop LLWP LPio LRHS MLLN MSal SAga SIde SMrm SWat WCHb WMoo WWye
purple	Last listed 1998
'Purple Ann'	LGre SAga
'Ruby Glow'	CMGP EBee ECGN EMan LGre LRHS MArl MBri MChl MTis NCat NCiC NHol SUsu WCHb WFar WLRN
§ 'Sagittarius'	CGle EBee EGar EGle EMan EMon LRHS MBel MMil MSCN MWgw NCat NGdn SChu WCHb WHoo WLRN WPGP WRus WWal WWat
'Sahin's Mildew-free'	WCHb WCot
§ 'Schneewittchen'	CBlo CStr EBee ECha ECtt EGar ELan EMan EOrc EWTr LAst LRHS MLLN MMal MSCN NBro NLar NOrc NSti SChu SIde SPer WGwG WHil WRus
Scorpio	See *M.* 'Scorpion'
'Scorpio'	See *M.* 'Scorpion'
§ 'Scorpion'	CGle EFou EMan EMon LGre LRHS MBel MBro MCAu MMil MSte MTis NCat SAga SChu SMad SOkh WCHb WHil WHoo WOve WPyg WRHF WRus
'Sioux'	EFou EWes GBuc GKir GMac LRHS MAvo SAga SMrm WCHb WFar WHil WRha
'Snow Maiden'	See *M.* 'Schneewittchen'
'Snow Queen'	EBee EFou EPfP GKir LPio LRHS MTis SCoo SMrm SPla WSan WWat
Snow White	See *M.* 'Schneewittchen'
'Squaw'	More than 30 suppliers
stipitatoglandulosa	Last listed 1997
'Talud'	EGar EMon NCat SMrm
'Twins'	CBod CMil EBee EFou EMar LRHS MLLN NHaw NHol NPri SWat WCHb WHil WHoo WRus
'Vintage Wine'	CLTr ECtt EGar ELan NFai NFla SSca WCHb WHil WRus WWye
* *violacea*	WCHb
'Violet Queen'	EBee EBrP EBre EMar LBCl LBSe LBre LRHS MBBe MBel NCat NPro SBre

MONARDELLA (Lamiaceae)

cinerea	CPBP
linoides subsp. *stricta*	Last listed 1998
macrantha	CPBP
- var. *arida*	CPBP
¶ *nana* subsp. *tenuiflora*	NWCA
	NNS 95-352
§ *neglecta*	Last listed 1998
odoratissima	CArn CGle ECoo EMan LEdu SVen WPic
palmeri NNS 95354	Last listed 1999
§ *sheltonii*	EBee
villosa subsp. *neglecta*	See *M. neglecta*
- subsp. *sheltonii*	See *M. sheltonii*
viridis	Last listed 1997

MONOPSIS (Campanulaceae)

debilis	Last listed 1998
'Goldfinch'	Last listed 1999
lutea	See *Lobelia lutea*
'Midnight'	CSpe CWes
unidentata	CInt

MONSONIA ✿ (Geraniaceae)

emarginata	GCHN

speciosa — Last listed 1998

MONSTERA (Araceae)
deliciosa (F) ♀ — LBlo MBri SRms
- 'Variegata' ♀ — MBri SRms

MONTBRETIA See CROCOSMIA

MONTIA (Portulacaceae)
australasica — See *Neopaxia australasica*
californica — See *Claytonia nevadensis*
parvifolia — See *Naiocrene parvifolia*
perfoliata — See *Claytonia perfoliata*
sibirica — See *Claytonia sibirica*

MORAEA (Iridaceae)
alpina — Last listed 1998
alticola — Last listed 1999
- CDR 180 — Last listed 1999
§ *aristata* — LBow
§ *bellendenii* — LBow WCot
§ *fugax* — IBlr
gawleri — Last listed 1998
glaucopsis — See *M. aristata*
huttonii — CFir CGre EBee WCru
iridioides — See *Dietes iridioides*
longifolia Sweet — See *M. fugax*
loubseri — Last listed 1998
papilionacea — EBee
pavonia var. *lutea* — See *M. bellendenii*
polystachya — EBee
sp. S&SH 4 — Last listed 1999
sp. S&SH 47 — Last listed 1999
sp. S&SH 78 — Last listed 1998
spathacea — See *M. spathulata*
§ *spathulata* — CBro EBee ERos GCal MAvo MFir
SMad SVen WCot WPGP WSHC
thomsonii — LBow
¶ *tricuspidata* — EBee
villosa — LBow

MORICANDIA (Brassicaceae)
arvensis — EBee

MORINA (Morinaceae)
* *afghanica* — Last listed 1999
longifolia — More than 30 suppliers
nepalensis — Last listed 1999
persica — GBuc

MORISIA (Brassicaceae)
hypogaea — See *M. monanthos*
§ *monanthos* — CInt CPla MBar NTow NWCA
- 'Fred Hemingway' — CGra EBrP EBre EPot GCrs IMGH
ITim LBCl LBSe LBre LRHS MBBe
NHar NMen NSla SBla SBre SIng
WPat

MORUS (Moraceae)
§ *alba* — CArn CB&S CHEx CLnd CMCN
CTho CWSG ECrN ELan ERea
GChr GKir GTwe IOrc LBuc LPan
LRHS NWea SMHT SPer WDin
WMou WSpi WUnu WWat
- 'Black Tabor' — WShe
- var. *multicaulis* — ERea
- 'Pendula' — CDoC CEnd ELan EPfP ERea
GTwe IMGH LHyr LNet LPan
LRHS MAsh MBlu MBri MLan
MWat SPer WDin WOrn
- 'Platanifolia' — LPan MBlu
- var. *tatarica* — CAgr LEdu WOTO

'Illinois Everbearing' (F) — ESim
nigra (F) ♀ — More than 30 suppliers
§ - 'Chelsea' (F) — CEnd COtt CWSG EMui ERea
GTwe LRHS MBri MGos SLim SPer
- 'King James' — See *M. nigra* 'Chelsea'
- 'Large Black' (F) — EMui
- 'Wellington' (F) — CEnd WShe

MUCUNA (Papilionaceae)
bennettii — CPlN
macrocarpa — CPlN
pruriens var. *utilis* — Last listed 1999
¶ *sempervirens* — CPlN

MUEHLENBECKIA (Polygonaceae)
astonii — ECou SMac
australis — Last listed 1998
axillaris hort. — See *M. complexa*
- Walp. — CTri ECou EPla ESis GAri GCal
MHar NCat NTow SDry
§ *complexa* — CB&S CDoC CHEx CHal CPlN
CTrC EBee ECou EPla ESis GQui
IBlr LRHS MCCP NFai SAPC SArc
SBra SDry SLim SLon SMac WCFE
WSHC WWat
- 'Nana' — See *M. axillaris* Walp.
- var. *trilobata* — CPlN EPla IBlr WCru
ephedroides — ECou
- 'Clarence Pass' — ECou
- var. *muriculata* — ECou
gunnii — CPlN ECou
platyclados — See *Homalocladium*
platycladum

MUHLENBERGIA (Poaceae)
japonica — CBrm CCuc EHoe EMan EMon
'Cream Delight' (v) — EPPr LRHS MCCP MTed WCot
WLeb
lindheimeri — WCot
mexicana — CBrm
rigens — CBrm WCot

MUKDENIA (Saxifragaceae)
§ *rossii* — CLTr CRDP EMan EMon EPla GCal
NCat SMac SSpi WCot WCru

MURRAYA (Rutaceae)
* *elliptica* — SOWG
exotica — See *M. paniculata*
koenigii — EOHP GPoy LChe
§ *paniculata* — CArn ERea LChe SSte

MUSA (Musaceae)
§ *acuminata* (F) — MBri
§ - 'Dwarf Cavendish' (F) ♀ — ERea LBlo LCns LPJP WMul
¶ - subsp. *sumatrana* — WMul
x 'Grande Nair'
- 'Zebrina' — WMul
basjoo — CAbb CB&S CBrP CFil CHEx CTor
CTrC EBee ECon EOas EPVP EPfP
ERea LBlo LCns LPJP LPal LPan
LRHS MCCP NMoo SAPC SArc
SChr SLdr SPar SSoC WCot WMul
WPGP
- 'Sakhalin' — WMul
¶ 'Brazilian' — WMul
¶ 'Cardaba' — WMul
cavendishii — See *M. acuminata* 'Dwarf
Cavendish'
coccinea — See *M. uranoscopus*
¶ 'Double' — WMul
'Dwarf Red' (F) — LBlo

	ensete	See *Ensete ventricosum*
¶	'Grande Nain'	WMul
	bookeri	See *M. sikkimensis*
	'Kru' (F)	LBlo WMul
§	*lasiocarpa*	EOas LBlo WMul
¶	'Mysore'	WMul
	nana	See *M. acuminata*
	'Orinoco'	EOas WMul
	ornata ♀	LBlo LPal WMul
	x *paradisiaca*	Last listed 1997
	'Rajapuri'	EOas WMul
	'Red Iholena' (F)	LBlo WMul
§	*sikkimensis*	EOas WMul
§	*uranoscopus* ♀	LBlo WMul
	velutina	EOas LBlo WMul
*	*violacea*	LPal
¶	'Williams Hybrid'	WMul

MUSCARI ✿ (Hyacinthaceae)

	ambrosiacum	See *M. muscarimi*
	armeniacum ♀	CBro EPar EPfP ETub LRHS MBri NMGW NRog SRms WCot WPer WShi
	- 'Argaei Album'	LAma LRHS NEgg
	- 'Babies Breath'	See *M. neglectum* 'Baby's Breath'
	- 'Blue Pearl'	LRHS
	- 'Blue Spike' (d)	CBro EPar EPfP LAma LRHS MBri NEgg NRog WCot WPer
	- 'Cantab'	Last listed 1997
	- 'Early Giant'	LAma
	- 'Fantasy Creation'	ETub LRHS WCot
	- 'Heavenly Blue'	LAma
	- 'Saffier'	LAma LRHS
¶	- 'Valerie Finnis'	CBro
§	*aucheri* ♀	CAvo EPar LAma NRog
§	*azureum* ♀	CAvo CBro CNic EPar EPfP ERos LAma LRHS NMen NRog SRms
	- 'Album'	CBro EPar ERos ETub LAma LRHS NRog WCot
	botryoides	LAma NRog
	- 'Album'	CAvo CBro EPfP LAma LRHS MBri NRog SRms WShi
¶	- 'Superstar'	ETub
	chalusicum	See *M. pseudomuscari*
§	*comosum*	CBro EPar LRHS WPer
*	- 'Album'	Last listed 1997
	- 'Monstrosum'	See *M. comosum* 'Plumosum'
§	- 'Plumosum'	CAvo CBro CRDP EMan EMon EPar LAma LRHS MBri SMrm SUsu WCot
	grandifolium JCA 689.450	CMil WCot
	- var. *populeum* AB&S 5357	Last listed 1998
	inconstrictum S&L 19/20	Last listed 1998
	latifolium	CAvo CBro EPar LAma LRHS NRog WCot WPer
*	- 'Blue Angels'	NBir
§	*macrocarpum*	CAvo CBro LAma LRHS WAbe
	mirum	Last listed 1999
	moschatum	See *M. muscarimi*
§	*muscarimi*	CAvo CBro EPar ETub GVer LAma WCot
	- var. *flavum*	See *M. macrocarpum*
§	*neglectum*	CSWP LAma SEND WShi
	- B&S 349	Last listed 1998
§	- 'Baby's Breath'	CMil SAga WCot
	pallens	Last listed 1998
	paradoxum	See *Bellevalia paradoxa*
	parviflorum	WCot
§	*pseudomuscari* ♀	Last listed 1998

	- BSBE 842	Last listed 1999
	racemosum	See *M. neglectum*
	'Sky Blue'	Last listed 1997
§	*spreitzenhoferi*	Last listed 1997
	- MS 712	Last listed 1998
§	*tenuiflorum*	Last listed 1999
	- S&L 91	Last listed 1998
	tubergenianum	See *M. aucheri*
	'White Beauty'	Last listed 1997

MUSCARIMIA (Hyacinthaceae)

ambrosiacum	See *Muscari muscarimi*
macrocarpum	See *Muscari macrocarpum*

MUSELLA (Musaceae)

lasiocarpa	See *Musa lasiocarpa*

MUSSCHIA (Campanulaceae)

wollastonii	CHEx CTrF

MUTISIA (Asteraceae)

	brachyantha x *oligodon*	Last listed 1998
	clematis	CRHN
	coccinea	CPIN
	decurrens	CPIN IBlr
	ilicifolia	CPIN IBlr ISea LRHS WSHC
	latifolia	Last listed 1998
	microphylla	WCot
	oligodon	CPIN IBlr
	retrorsa	Last listed 1999
	- JCA 14345	Last listed 1998
	retusa	See *M. spinosa* var. *pulchella*
	sinuata JCA 14351	Last listed 1998
	spinosa	Last listed 1999
§	- var. *pulchella*	SSpi
	subulata	Last listed 1999

MYOPORUM (Myoporaceae)

	acuminatum	See *M. tenuifolium*
	debile	ECou
	insulare	Last listed 1998
	laetum	CDoC CHEx LHil SVen
§	*tenuifolium*	Last listed 1997

MYOSOTIDIUM (Boraginaceae)

§	*hortensia*	CB&S CFil CHEx CPla ECre EWes GBin GBuc GCal GOrP IBlr IDee IHdy NCiC SMrm SSpi WCot WCru WElm WKif WPGP
	- white	CPLG GBin
	nobile	See *M. hortensia*

MYOSOTIS (Boraginaceae)

§	*alpestris*	WPat
¶	- 'Gold 'n' Sapphires'	NSti
	- 'Ruth Fischer'	NBir NMen
	arvensis	EWFC
	australis	GCal MMHG NChi NWCA
	'Bill Baker'	Last listed 1999
	colensoi	ECou EDAr MTho NMen NNrd NWCA
	explanata	EBee NMen NNrd WEas
	palustris	See *M. scorpioides*
	'Popsy'	Last listed 1998
	pulvinaris	CPBP
	rakiura	GTou
	rebsteineri	LRHS SRot
	rupicola	See *M. alpestris*
§	*scorpioides*	CBen CRow ECoo EHon EMFW EPfP EWFC EWTr LPBA MMal MSta NDea SPlb SRms SWat SWyc WEas WMAq

- 'Blaqua' (v)	See *M. scorpioides* Maytime = 'Blaqua'
- 'John Beaty'	Last listed 1998
§ - Maytime = 'Blaqua' (v)	LPBA WWpP
- 'Mermaid'	CBen CMGP CRow CWat ECha EHon EPPr GMac LGuA LHop LPBA MFir MSta NBrk NCat SDix SRms SWat WFar WPer WRus
- 'Pinkie'	CRDP CRow CWat EMFW GMac SWat WElm
- 'Snowflakes'	CRow
secunda	CKin
sylvatica	EWFC
- *alba*	See *M. sylvatica* f. *lactea*
§ - f. *lactea*	CRow
¶ - 'Snowdrift' (v)	CRDP
traversii AGS 90	Last listed 1997
uniflora	CGra

MYRCEUGENIA (Myrtaceae)
chrysocarpa	CGre
¶ *ovata*	CTrG
¶ *planipes*	CTrG

MYRICA (Myricaceae)
californica	CFil CPle GAri
cerifera	CArn CPle
gale	GAri GPoy MGos SWat WDin WGwy WSel WWye
pensylvanica	IMGH

MYRIOPHYLLUM (Haloragaceae)
§ *aquaticum*	CBen CHEx CRow CWat EHon ELan EMFW LPBA MCCP MSta NDea SLon SWat SWyc WFar WMAq WWeb
brasiliense	See *M. aquaticum*
proserpinacoides	See *M. aquaticum*
* 'Red Stem'	LPBA
spicatum	CBen EHon EMFW SWyc
verticillatum	EHon

MYRRHIS (Apiaceae)
odorata	CArn CBre CKin CSev ECha EEls ELau EWFC GBar GMaP GPoy ILis MChe MHer MHew MMal MSal NBid SIde SPer WByw WCer WEas WHbs WHer WOak WPer WSel WWye
- 'Forncett Chevron'	EFou

MYRSINE (Myrsinaceae)
africana	CB&S CPle EPfP WHCr WWat
australis	Last listed 1998
¶ *divaricata*	CTrC
nummularia	Last listed 1999

MYRTEOLA (Myrtaceae)
§ *nummularia*	GAri GDra NMen

MYRTUS (Myrtaceae)
apiculata	See *Luma apiculata*
bullata	See *Lophomyrtus bullata*
chequen	See *Luma chequen*
communis ♀	More than 30 suppliers
- 'Flore Pleno' (d)	GQui
- 'Jenny Reitenbach'	See *M. communis* subsp. *tarentina*
- 'Microphylla'	See *M. communis* subsp. *tarentina*
- 'Nana'	See *M. communis* subsp. *tarentina*

§ - subsp. *tarentina* ♀	More than 30 suppliers
- - 'Compacta'	WWye
§ - - 'Microphylla Variegata'	CBlo CInt CPle SAPC SAga SPer WHal WJek WOak WSHC WWat
- 'Tricolor'	See *M. communis* 'Variegata'
§ - 'Variegata'	CArn CBot CBrm CMCN EBee ECtt ELau EMil EPfP EWTr GBar LEdu LHop LRHS MAsh MHer SDry SEas SPer STre WFar WOak WPGP WPnn WSel WStI WWat WWye
'Glanleam Gold'	See *Luma apiculata* 'Glanleam Gold'
lechleriana	See *Amomyrtus luma*
luma	See *Luma apiculata*
nummularia	See *Myrteola nummularia*
obcordata	See *Lophomyrtus obcordata*
x *ralphii*	See *Lophomyrtus* x *ralphii*
'Traversii'	See *Lophomyrtus* x *ralphii* 'Traversii'
ugni	See *Ugni molinae*
* *variegata* 'Penlee'	CTrG

N

NAIOCRENE (Portulacaceae)
§ *parvifolia*	CNic

NANDINA (Berberidaceae)
domestica ♀	CB&S CBot CDoC CHad ELan EWTr GOrc IOrc ISea LEdu LHop LPan LRHS MAsh NFla NRog SLon SPla SPlb SRPl SReu SRms SSpi SSta WBod WDin WGwG WStI WWat
¶ - B&SWJ 4923	WCru
- 'Fire Power'	More than 30 suppliers
- 'Harbor Dwarf'	LRHS WWat
- var. *leucocarpa*	Last listed 1999
- 'Nana'	See *N. domestica* 'Pygmaea'
- 'Nana Purpurea'	EPla
§ - 'Pygmaea'	GAri WBod WDin
- 'Richmond'	CB&S CBlo ELan EPfP GKir LRHS MAsh MBlu MGos MMea SBod SPer SPla WFar

NANNORRHOPS (Arecaceae)
ritchieana	CBrP EPVP LPal

NARCISSUS ✿ (Amaryllidaceae)
'Abalone' (2)	EWal
'Accent' (2) ♀	CQua ICar
'Accord' (2)	ICar
'Achduart' (3)	CQua EHof GEve ICar
'Achentoul' (4)	ICar
'Achnasheen' (3)	CQua ICar
'Acropolis' (4)	CQua ETub EWal ICar LAma LRHS
'Actaea' (9) ♀	ETub LRHS MBri NRog
'Admiration' (8)	CQua
'Advocat' (3)	CQua
'Affable' (4)	ICar
'Aflame' (3)	LAma MBri
'Ahwahnee' (2)	IDun
'Aintree' (3)	CQua
'Aircastle' (3)	CQua EWal ICar
'Akepa' (5)	ICar
I *albidus* subsp. *occidentalis* (13)	ERos
'Albus Plenus Odoratus'	See *N. poeticus* 'Plenus'

'Alley Inn' (4)	Last listed 1998	
'Alliance' (1)	EWal	
'Alpine Glow' (1)	Last listed 1998	
'Alston' (2)	IDun	
'Altruist' (3)	CQua EWal	
'Altun Ha' (2)	CQua EHof IDun	
'Amber Castle' (2)	CQua ICar	
'Amber Light' (2)	EWal	
'Ambergate' (2)	EWal GEve LAma LRHS	
'Amberglow' (2)	EWal LRHS	
'Amboseli' (3)	Last listed 1998	
'American Shores' (1)	IDun	
'Amor' (3)	EWal	
'Amstel' (4)	CQua	
'Andalusia' (6)	ERos ICar	
'Androcles' (4)	ICar	
'Angel' (3)	ICar	
'Angel Face' (3)	EHof	
'Angel Wings'	See *N.* 'Celtic Wings'	
Angel's Tears	See *N. triandrus* subsp. *triandrus*	
	var. *triandrus*	
'Angkor' (4)	CQua ICar	
'Ann Abbott' (2)	EWal	
'Annalong' (3)	IBal	
'Anniversary' (2)	EWal	
'Anthea' (2)	EWal	
'Apostle' (1)	ICar	
'Apotheose' (4)	EWal	
'Applins' (2)	IDun	
'Apricot' (1)	CBro	
'Apricot Sundae' (4)	ICar	
'April Charm' (2)	ICar	
'April Love' (1)	CQua EHof IBal ICar	
'April Snow' (2)	CBro CQua	
'April Tears' (5) ♀	EWal LAma NRog	
'Apropos' (2)	Last listed 1999	
'Aranjuez' (2)	Last listed 1999	
'Arbar' (2)	EWal	
'Arcady' (2)	EWal	
'Arctic Char' (2)	ICar	
'Arctic Gem' (3)	Last listed 1998	
'Arctic Gold' (1) ♀	CQua ICar	
'Ardglass' (3)	IBal ICar	
'Ardour' (3)	ICar	
'Ardress' (2)	CQua	
'Argosy' (1)	CQua	
'Arish Mell' (5)	CQua EWal ICar	
'Arizona Sunset' (3)	Last listed 1998	
'Arkle' (1)	CQua GEve ICar	
'Arleston' (2)	IDun	
'Armley Wood' (2)	ICar	
'Arpege' (2)	CQua	
'Arran Isle' (2)	IDun	
'Arthurian' (1)	IDun	
'Artillery' (3)	EWal	
'Asante' (1)	IDun	
'Ashmore' (2)	CQua EHof IDun	
'Ashton Wold' (2)	EHof	
'Asila' (2)	IDun	
'Aslan' (4)	ICar	
'Aspasia' (8)	CBro	
§ ***assoanus*** (13)	CBro CLAP EPar EPot LAma	
- MS 511 (13)	Last listed 1998	
- MS 581 (13)	Last listed 1998	
- MS 582 (13)	Last listed 1998	
- var. *praelongus*	Last listed 1998	
MS 656 (13)		
§ ***asturiensis*** (13) ♀	CBro CNic CSam EPar IBlr MNrw	
	MS&S	
- giant form	See *N. asturiensis* 'Wavertree'	
§ - 'Wavertree' (1)	EPot	
'Atholl Palace' (4)	IDun	

atlanticus (13)	CLAP	
- SB&L 78 (13)	Last listed 1998	
'Attrus' (2)	EWal	
'Audubon' (2)	CQua EWal	
* 'Aunt Betty' (1)	IDun	
'Auntie Eileen' (2)	CQua	
§ ***aureus*** (13)	CQua	
'Auspicious' (2)	IDun	
'Avalanche' (8) ♀	CQua EWal LRHS	
'Avalon' (2)	CQua	
'Ave' (2)	ICar	
'Avenger' (2)	ICar	
'Baby Doll' (6)	EWal ICar	
'Baby Moon' (7)	CFwr CQua EPar EPot ETub LAma	
	LRHS MBri NRog SRms	
'Baccarat' (11a)	ICar MBri	
'Badanloch' (3)	CQua	
'Badbury Rings' (3) ♀	IDun	
'Bailey' (2)	ICar	
'Balalaika' (2)	CQua	
'Baldock' (4)	CQua	
'Ballyarnett' (1)	ICar	
'Ballycastle' (3)	ICar	
'Ballyfrema' (1)	ICar	
'Ballygarvey' (1)	CQua EWal	
'Ballygowan' (3)	IBal	
'Ballykinler' (3)	IBal	
'Ballylig' (1)	ICar	
'Ballylough' (1)	ICar	
'Ballymorran' (1)	IBal	
'Ballynahinch' (3)	IBal	
'Ballynichol' (3)	IBal	
'Ballyrobert' (1)	EHof	
'Ballyvaddy' (2)	ICar	
'Ballyvoy' (1)	ICar	
'Baltic Shore' (3)	IBal	
'Balvenie' (2)	CQua	
'Bambi' (1)	CBro ERos NRog	
'Banbridge' (1)	IBal ICar	
'Bandesara' (3)	IDun	
'Bandleader' (2)	EWal	
'Banstead Village' (2)	CQua	
'Bantam' (2) ♀	CBro CQua ERos EWal	
'Barbizon' (4)	IDun	
'Barley Sugar' (3)	ICar	
'Barleygold' (2)	IBal	
'Barleythorpe' (1)	EWal	
'Barleywine' (2)	IBal	
'Barlow' (6)	CQua	
'Barnesgold' (1)	IDun	
'Barnum' (1) ♀	IDun	
'Baronscourt' (1)	ICar	
'Barrett Browning' (3)	ETub MBri NRog	
'Bartley' (6)	EWal	
'Bastion' (1)	Last listed 1997	
'Beach Party' (2)	Last listed 1998	
'Beauvallon' (4)	Last listed 1998	
'Bebop' (7)	CBro ICar	
'Bedgebury' (1)	ICar	
'Bedruthan' (2)	CQua	
'Beefeater' (2)	EWal	
'Beige Beauty' (3)	EWal ICar	
'Belbroughton' (2)	EHof	
'Belcanto' (11a)	CQua ICar	
'Belisana' (2)	LAma	
'Bell Song' (7)	CAvo CBro CQua ERos EWal	
	LRHS WShi	
'Beltrim' (2)	ICar	
'Ben Aligin' (1)	CQua	
¶ 'Ben Avon' (1)	GEve	
'Ben Hee' (2)	CQua	
'Ben Loyal' (2)	GEve	

'Ben Vorlich' (2)   ICar
'Berceuse' (2)   IDun
'Bere Ferrers' (4)   CQua
'Bergerac' (11a)   CQua
'Berkeley Court' (4)   Last listed 1998
'Berlin' (2)   EWal
bertolonii (13)   Last listed 1998
'Beryl' (6)   CBro CQua ERos EWal ICar LAma
     LRHS

'Best of Luck' (3)   IBal
¶ 'Best Seller' (1)   LHpC
'Bethany' (2)   EWal
'Betsy MacDonald' (6)   CQua
'Biffo' (4)   CQua
'Big John' (1)   GEve
'Bilbo' (6)   CQua
'Binkie' (2)   CBro EWal LAma LRHS MBri
'Birdsong' (3)   CQua
'Birma' (3)   EWal LAma
'Birthright' (1)   EWal
'Biscayne' (1) ♀   Last listed 1997
'Bishops Light' (2)   CQua
'Bishopstone' (1)   ICar
'Bittern' (12)   ICar
'Blarney' (3)   CQua EWal
'Blessing' (2)   EWal
'Blue Bird' (2)   EWal
'Blue Danube' (1)   IDun
'Blushing Maiden' (4)   CQua
'Bob Minor' (1)   CQua
'Bobbysoxer' (7)   CBro CQua ERos EWal ICar LAma
     MTho
'Bobolink' (2)   CQua
'Bodilly' (2)   EWal
'Bodwannick' (2)   CQua
'Bolton' (7)   CBro
'Bonamargy' (2)   ICar
'Border Beauty' (2)   IDun
'Border Chief' (2)   ICar
'Borrobol' (2)   EHof
'Bosbigal' (11a)   CQua
'Boscastle' (7)   CQua
'Boslowick' (11a)   CQua
'Bosmeor' (2)   CQua
'Bossa Nova' (3)   CQua
'Bossiney' (11a)   CQua
'Boudoir' (1)   ICar
'Boulder Bay' (2)   IDun
'Bouzouki' (2)   IDun
'Bowles' Early Sulphur' (1)   CRow
'Bracken Hill' (2)   ICar
'Braid Song' (9)   ICar
'Brandaris' (11a)   CQua GEve
'Brave Journey' (2)   ICar
'Bravoure' (1) ♀   CQua EWal
'Breakthrough' (2)   EWal
'Brentswood' (8)   CQua
'Bridal Crown' (4)   EPfP ETub EWal LAma LRHS
'Bridesmaid' (2)   IBal
'Bright Flame' (2)   CQua
'Brighton' (1)   LAma
'Brindle Pink' (2)   IDun
'Broadland' (2)   CQua
'Broadway Star' (11b)   ETub EWal LAma LRHS
'Brodick' (3)   GEve IDun
'Brookdale' (1)   Last listed 1998
'Broomhill' (2) ♀   CQua
broussonetii (13)   CFil
- S&F 269 (13)   Last listed 1998
'Brunswick' (2)   LHpC
'Bryanston' (2) ♀   Last listed 1998
'Bryher' (3)   ICar

'Budock Bells' (5)   CQua
'Buffawn' (7)   EWal
'Bugle Major' (2)   EHof
bujei   See *N. hispanicus* var. *bujei*
'Bulbarrow' (2)   Last listed 1998
bulbocodium (13) ♀   CBro CFil CMea CStu ETub LBee
     LBow LRHS NMGW NWCA SRms
     WPGP
§ - subsp. **bulbocodium** (13)   CBro
§ - - var. **citrinus** (13)   EPot SSpi
- - var. **conspicuus** (13)   CAvo CBro CQua CSam EPar EPot
     ERos GCrs LAma MBri MS&S
     NMen NRog NRya SIng WPyg
- - **filifolius** (13)   CBro
- - var. **genuinus** x   Last listed 1999
     cantabricus subsp.
     tananicus ACS 4656
     (13)
- - - x - var. **kesticus**   Last listed 1999
     S&F 72 (13)
- - - x 'Jessamy'   Last listed 1999
- - - S&F 177 (13)   Last listed 1998
§ - - var. **graellsii** (13)   Last listed 1999
- - - MS 408 (13)   Last listed 1998
- - - MS 567 (13)   Last listed 1998
- - var. **nivalis** (13)   LHpC LRHS
§ - - var. **tenuifolius** (13)   CAvo EPot MNrw SIng
- - - S&B 189 (13)   Last listed 1998
- - - x **triandrus** (13)   Last listed 1999
§ - 'Golden Bells' (10)   CBro EWal LRHS WWeb
- subsp. **mairei**   Last listed 1998
     S&F 181 (13)
- var. **mesatlanticus**   See *N. romieuxii* subsp.
     romieuxii var. *mesatlanticus*
* - 'Monserrat' (10)   Last listed 1999
- subsp. **praecox** var.   Last listed 1999
     paucinervis (13)
* - subsp. **viriditubus**   Last listed 1999
     MS 453 (13)
- subsp. **vulgaris**   See *N. bulbocodium* subsp.
     bulbocodium
'Bullseye' (3)   EWal
'Bunclody' (2)   CQua ICar
'Bunting' (7) ♀   CQua ICar
'Burma Star' (2)   ICar
'Burning Bush' (3)   IDun
'Burntollet' (1)   CQua IDun
'Bushmills' (3)   ICar
'Buster' (2)   EWal
'Buttercup' (7)   CBro
'Butterscotch' (2)   CQua ICar
'By Jove' (1)   EWal
'Cabernet' (2)   IDun
'Cabra' (1)   ICar
'Cadence' (3)   ICar
'Caedmon' (9)   CQua
'Cairndhu' (2)   ICar
'Cairngorm' (2)   ICar
'Cairntoul' (3)   CQua EHof
'Calabar' (2)   EWal
calcicola B&S 413 (13)   Last listed 1998
- MS 450 (13)   Last listed 1998
'California Rose' (4)   IDun
'Callaway' (3)   ICar
'Camelford' (2)   Last listed 1998
'Camellia' (4)   Last listed 1999
'Camelot' (2) ♀   EWal
'Campernelli Plenus'   See *N.* x *odorus* 'Double
     Campernelle'
'Campion' (9)   CQua IDun
'Canaliculatus' (8)   CBro CQua EPar LAma LBow
     LRHS MBri NMen

canaliculatus Gussone	See *N. tazetta* subsp. *lacticolor*
'Canarybird' (8)	CBro
'Canasta' (11a)	CQua ICar
'Candida' (4)	EWal
'Canisp' (2)	CQua ICar
'Cantabile' (9) ♀	CBro CQua IBal
cantabricus (13)	CFil LRHS SSpi WPGP
- subsp. *cantabricus* (13)	CLAP ERos
- - var. *foliosus* (13) ♀	EPot LRHS
- - - S&F 284/2 (13)	Last listed 1998
- - var. *petunioides* (13)	LAma
- - - S&F 365/2 (13)	Last listed 1998
- - S&F 396 (13)	Last listed 1998
* - subsp. *monophyllus*	Last listed 1999
var. *laciniatus* (13)	
- x *romieuxii* (13)	NHar
'Cantatrice' (1)	Last listed 1997
'Canticle' (9)	IBal
'Capax Plenus'	See *N.* 'Eystettensis'
'Cape Cool' (2)	ICar
'Cape Cornwall' (2)	CQua
'Cape Point' (2)	IDun
'Capisco' (3)	CQua IBal
'Caracas' (2)	Last listed 1999
'Caramba' (2)	CQua
'Carbineer' (2)	LAma
'Carclew' (6)	CQua
'Cardinham' (3)	CQua
'Cargreen' (9)	CQua
'Cariad' (5)	CQua
'Carib Gipsy' (2) ♀	CQua EHof IDun
'Caribbean Snow' (2)	EHof
'Carlingford' (2)	IBal
'Carlton' (2) ♀	ETub LAma MBri NRog
'Carnearny' (3)	GEve ICar
'Carnkeeran' (2)	ICar
'Carnkief' (2)	CQua
'Caro Nome' (2)	EWal
'Carrara' (3)	EWal
'Carrickbeg' (1)	CQua
'Carson Pass' (2)	Last listed 1998
'Cassata' (11)	CQua EWal LAma LRHS NBir NRog
'Casterbridge' (2)	IDun
'Castle Dobbs' (4)	ICar
'Castlehill' (3)	IBal
'Catistock' (2)	CQua
'Cauldron' (2)	CQua IDun
'Cavalryman' (3)	IDun
'Cavendish' (4)	IDun
'Cavoda' (1)	ICar
'Caye Chapel' (3)	EHof
'Cazique' (6)	CQua
x *cazorlanus* (13)	Last listed 1997
'Ceasefire' (2)	IDun
'Cedric Morris' (1)	CBro CElw CLAP ECha IBlr NPSI SIng SSpi WCot
'Celestial Fire' (2)	EHof
'Celtic Gold' (2)	CQua
'Centannées' (11b)	ETub LHpC
'Ceylon' (2) ♀	EWal
'Cha-cha' (6)	CBro CQua
'Changing Colors' (11a)	LHpC
'Chania' (1)	ICar
'Chanterelle' (11a)	EWal ICar LAma NRog
'Chapman's Peak' (2)	IDun
'Charity May' (6) ♀	CBro CQua EWal IBal ICar LAma MBri NRog
'Charleston' (2)	Last listed 1998
'Charter' (2) ♀	EWal
'Chaste' (1)	IDun
'Chat' (7)	CQua ICar

'Cheer Leader' (3)	CQua
'Cheerfulness' (4) ♀	CQua ETub EWal LAma LRHS MBri NRog
'Cheetah' (1)	IDun
¶ 'Chelsea Girl' (2)	GEve
'Chemeketa' (2)	IDun
'Chenoweth' (2)	CQua
'Chérie' (7)	CBro CQua
'Cherrygardens' (2)	CQua EHof IDun
'Chesterton' (9) ♀	CQua
'Chickadee' (6)	CBro CQua
'Chickerell' (3)	CQua IDun
'Chief Inspector' (1)	CQua IDun
'Chig' (2)	EWal
'Chilmark' (3)	IDun
'Chiloquin' (1)	CQua
'China Doll' (2)	EHof
'Chinchilla' (2)	IDun
'Chinese White' (3)	ICar
'Chinita' (8)	CBro CQua EWal
'Chit Chat' (7) ♀	CBro
'Chivalry' (1)	EWal
'Chobe River' (1)	IDun
'Churchfield' (2)	ICar
'Churchman' (2)	IBal ICar
'Churston Ferrers' (4)	CQua
citrinus	See *N. bulbocodium* subsp. *bulbocodium* var. *citrinus*
'Citronita' (3)	CQua EHof
'Clady Cottage' (2)	ICar
'Clare' (7)	CBro CQua ICar
'Claridges' (4)	Last listed 1998
'Claverley' (2)	IDun
'Clockface' (3)	EWal
'Cloneytrace' (1)	ICar
'Close Encounter' (2)	ICar
'Close Harmony' (4)	IDun
'Cloud Nine' (2)	CBro EWal
'Clouded Yellow' (2)	EHof
'Clouds Rest' (2)	IDun
'Codlins and Cream'	See *N.* 'Sulphur Phoenix'
'Colblanc' (11a)	ICar LRHS
'Collector's Choice' (2)	ICar
'Colorama' (11a)	CQua
'Colour Sergeant' (2)	IBal
'Colourful' (2)	IDun
'Columbus' (2)	ICar
'Colville' (9)	CQua
'Comal' (1)	CQua IDun
'Compressus'	See *N.* x *intermedius* 'Compressus'
concolor (Haworth) Link	See *N. triandrus* subsp. *triandrus* var. *concolor*
'Conestoga' (2)	IBal IDun
'Confuoco' (2)	Last listed 1999
'Congress' (11a)	CQua EWal
* 'Connie Number 1'	Last listed 1999
* 'Connie Number 2'	Last listed 1999
'Connor' (2)	ICar
'Conval' (2)	Last listed 1999
'Cool Autumn' (2)	CQua
'Cool Crystal' (3)	CQua EHof ICar IDun
'Cool Evening' (11a)	IDun
'Cool Shades' (2)	EHof
'Coolattin' (2)	ICar
'Cophetua' (1)	ICar
'Copper Nob' (2)	IBal
'Coppins' (4)	Last listed 1997
'Coquille' (2)	EWal
'Cora Ann' (7)	CBro
'Coral Light' (2)	ICar
'Corbiere' (1)	CQua EHof IDun

'Corbridge' (2)	EWal	
cordubensis (13)	SSpi	
- MS 434 (13)	Last listed 1998	
- MS 91-71 (13)	Last listed 1999	
'Cornerstone' (2)	EWal	
'Cornet' (6)	CQua	
'Corofin' (3)	CQua	
'Coromandel' (2)	IDun	
'Corozal' (3)	EHof	
'Cosmic Dance' (3)	IDun	
'Cotehele' (1)	Last listed 1998	
'Cotinga' (6)	CQua	
'Cotton Candy' (4)	IDun	
¶ 'Counsellor' (1)	LHpC	
'Country Morning' (3)	ICar	
'Crackington' (4) ♀	CQua IDun	
'Cragford' (8)	EWal LAma LRHS	
'Craig Stiel' (2)	CQua	
'Craigarusky' (2)	IBal	
'Craigdun' (2)	Last listed 1998	
'Craigywarren' (2)	EWal	
'Creag Dubh' (2)	CQua GEve ICar	
'Crenelet' (2)	Last listed 1998	
'Crimson Chalice' (3)	IDun	
'Crinoline' (2)	EWal	
'Cristobal' (1)	CQua	
'Crock of Gold' (1)	CQua EWal	
'Croila' (2)	CQua IDun	
'Crown Royalist' (2)	IBal	
'Cryptic' (1)	IDun	
'Crystal River' (3)	EWal	
'Cuan Gold' (4)	IBal	
cuatrecasasii (13)	Last listed 1998	
- MS 429 (13)	Last listed 1998	
- var. *segimonensis* MS 559 (13)	Last listed 1998	
'Cuesta' (2)	Last listed 1998	
'Cul Beag' (3)	CQua	
'Cupid's Eye' (3)	IDun	
'Curly' (2)	LRHS	
cyclamineus (13) ♀	CBro CFil CRDP EPar LAma LCTD MS&S NRog SBla SRms SSpi WAbe WCru WPGP
'Cyclataz' (8)	CQua	
'Cyclope' (1)	LHpC	
cypri (8)	CBro CQua	
'Cyros' (1)	CQua	
'Dailmanach' (2)	CQua EHof IDun	
'Dainty Miss' (7)	CQua	
'Daiquiri' (3)	ICar	
'Dallas' (3)	CQua	
'Dalliance' (2)	ICar	
'Dancer' (2)	Last listed 1997	
'Dancing Partner' (2)	EWal	
'Danes Balk' (2)	ICar	
'Dateline' (3)	CQua IDun	
'David Alexander' (1)	CQua	
'Daviot' (2)	ICar	
'Dawn' (5)	CBro	
'Dawn Chorus' (1)	Last listed 1998	
'Dawn Mist' (2)	EWal	
'Dawn Run' (2)	IDun	
'Daydream' (2) ♀	CQua ETub EWal ICar LAma	
'Debutante' (2)	CQua	
'Decoy' (2)	ICar IDun	
'Del Rey' (1)	Last listed 1999	
'Delabole' (2)	Last listed 1999	
'Delia' (6)	IDun	
'Delibes' (2)	LAma	
'Dell Chapel' (3)	ICar	
'Delnashaugh' (4)	CQua ICar	
'Delos' (3)	CQua	
'Delphin Hill' (4)	IBal	
'Delta Flight' (6)	IDun	
'Delta Wings' (6)	Last listed 1998	
'Demand' (2)	CQua ICar	
'Derryboy' (3)	IBal	
'Dervock' (4)	ICar	
'Desdemona' (2)	EWal NRog	
'Desert Bells' (7)	CQua	
'Desert Rose' (2)	ICar	
'Diane' (6)	EWal	
'Diatone' (4)	GEve IDun	
'Dick Wilden' (4)	EWal LAma	
'Dickcissel' (7)	CBro CQua ICar	
'Dimity' (3)	CQua	
'Dimple' (9)	Last listed 1998	
'Dinkie' (3)	CBro	
'Discovery' (4)	ICar	
'Dispatch Box' (1) ♀	Last listed 1998	
'Diversion' (3)	ICar	
'Divertimento' (7)	ICar	
'Doctor Alex Fleming' (2)	EWal	
'Doctor Hugh' (3)	CQua EHof EWal IDun	
'Doctor Jazz' (2)	EHof	
'Dolly Mollinger' (11b)	EWal ICar	
'Don Carlos' (2)	ICar	
'Dorchester' (4)	IDun	
'Double Blush' (4)	ICar	
I 'Double Campernella'	See *N.* x *odorus* 'Double Campernelle'
'Double Campernelle'	See *N.* x *odorus* 'Double Campernelle'
'Double Diamond' (4)	CQua	
'Double Event' (4) ♀	Last listed 1993	
'Double Fashion' (4)	EWal	
Double pheasant eye	See *N. poeticus* 'Plenus'
Double Roman	See *N.* 'Romanus'
'Doubleday' (4)	IDun	
'Doubtful' (3)	CQua ICar	
'Dove of Peace' (6)	Last listed 1998	
'Dove Wings' (6) ♀	CBro CQua EWal IBal ICar LAma	
'Dovekie' (12)	ICar	
'Dover Cliffs' (2)	CQua	
'Downpatrick' (1)	CQua ICar	
'Dream Castle' (3)	EWal	
'Drenagh' (2)	ICar	
'Drumadarragh' (1)	ICar	
'Drumawillan' (2)	ICar	
'Drumbeg' (2)	IBal	
'Drumboe' (2)	Last listed 1999	
'Drumlin' (1)	IBal	
'Drumnabreeze' (2)	ICar	
'Drumrunie' (2)	ICar	
¶ *dubius* (13)	CBro LHpC	
- var. *dubius* MS 512 (13)	Last listed 1998	
'Duet' (4)	EWal	
'Duke of Windsor' (2)	Last listed 1999	
'Dulcimer' (9)	CQua	
'Dunadry Inn' (4)	IDun	
'Dunkery' (4)	IDun	
'Dunley Hall' (3)	IDun	
'Dunmurry' (1)	Last listed 1999	
'Dunskey' (3)	CQua	
'Dutch Master' (1) ♀	CQua ETub EWal LAma MBri NRog	
'Dynamite' (2)	EWal	
'Earendil' (2)	IDun	
'Early Blossom' (1)	ICar	
¶ 'Early Bride' (2)	LHpC	
'Early Splendour' (8)	CQua LAma	
'Earthlight' (3)	EHof	
'East Wind' (1)	ICar	
'Easter Bonnet' (2)	LAma	
'Easter Moon' (2)	ICar	

'Eastern Dawn' (2) — EWal
'Eastertide' (4) — Last listed 1999
'Eaton Park' (3) — Last listed 1998
'Eaton Song' (12) — CBro CQua
'Eclat' (2) — ICar
'Eddy Canzony' (2) — CQua
'Edgbaston' (2) — EHof
'Edge Grove' (2) — ICar
'Edward Buxton' (3) — LAma MBri
'Egard' (11a) — CQua EWal
'Egg Nog' (4) — ICar
'Eland' (7) — CQua
'Elburton' (2) — CQua
elegans var. *elegans* — Last listed 1998
  S&F 316 (13)
'Elf' (2) — CBro CQua
'Elfin Gold' (6) — IDun
'Elizabeth Ann' (6) — CQua IDun
'Elka' (1) — CQua IBal ICar
'Elmley Castle' (1) — Last listed 1998
'Elphin' (4) — CQua GEve ICar
'Elrond' (2) — CQua
'Elven Lady' (2) — IDun
'Elvira' (8) — CBro CQua
'Elwing' (2) — Last listed 1998
'Elysian Fields' (2) — EWal
'Emily' (2) — CQua IBal ICar
'Eminent' (3) — CQua EWal
'Emperor's Waltz' (6) — CQua IDun
'Empress of Ireland' (1) ♀ — CQua EHof EWal IBal
'Englander' (6) — EPot
'English Caye' (1) — EHof
'Ensemble' (4) — CQua
'Entrancement' (1) — EWal
'Eribol' (2) — GEve
'Erlicheer' (4) — CQua
'Eskylane' (2) — ICar
'Estrella' (3) — CQua
'Estremadura' (2) — ICar
'Ethereal Beauty' (2) — IDun
'Ethos' (1) — IDun
'Etincelante' (11a) — ICar
'Euphony' (2) — Last listed 1998
'Euryalus' (1) — CQua
'Evelix' (2) — GEve
'Evendine' (2) — EWal
'Everglades' (4) — Last listed 1998
'Everpink' (2) — Last listed 1999
'Evesham' (3) — IDun
'Exalted' (2) — ICar
'Exception' (1) — LHpC
'Exemplar' (1) — EWal
'Eye Level' (9) — IBal
'Eyecatcher' (3) — ICar
§ 'Eystettensis' (4) — CBro CQua EBot ECha ERos IBlr
'Fair Head' (9) — CQua
'Fair Prospect' (2) — CQua ICar
'Fairgreen' (3) — CQua ICar
'Fairsel' (3) — IBal
'Fairy Chimes' (5) — CBro CQua
'Fairy Footsteps' (3) — IBal ICar
'Fairy Island' (3) — CQua ICar
'Fairy Spell' (3) — IBal
'Falconet' (8) ♀ — CBro CQua ERos EWal
'Falstaff' (2) — CQua ICar
'Fanad Head' (9) — IBal
'Far Country' (2) — GEve ICar
'Faro' (1) — IBal
'Farranfad' (2) — IBal
'Fastidious' (2) — CQua
'Favor Royal' (3) — IBal
'Favourite' (2) — EWal

'February Gold' (6) ♀ — CAvo CBro EPar ETub EWal IBal LAma LBow LRHS MBNS MBri NBir NMGW NRog SRms WPnP WShi
'February Silver' (6) — CBro EPar ETub EWal LAma LRHS NMGW NRog
'Feeling Lucky' (2) ♀ — EWal
'Felindre' (9) — CQua EWal IBal
'Feock' (3) — CQua
fernandesii (13) — CBro
'Ferndown' (3) — CQua EHof IDun
'Festivity' (2) — EWal
'ffitch's Ffolly' (2) — CQua
'Fieldfare' (3) — ICar
'Fiji' (4) — ICar
'Filly' (2) — EWal
'Filoli' (1) — IDun
'Fine Gold' (1) — CQua
'Fine Romance' (2) — CQua EHof
'Fiona MacKillop' (2) — IDun
'Fionn' (2) — ICar
'Fire Raiser' (2) — ICar
'Firebrand' (2) — CQua
'Firestorm' (2) — IBal
'First Hope' (6) — Last listed 1999
'Flaming Meteor' (2) — ICar
'Flashback' (6) — IDun
'Flirt' (6) — CQua ICar
'Flomay' (7) — CBro
'Florida Manor' (3) — IBal
'Flower Carpet' (1) — LAma LHpC
'Flower Drift' (4) — LAma LRHS
'Flower Record' (2) — LAma
'Fly Half' (2) — CQua
'Flycatcher' (7) — CQua
'Flying Saucer' (2) — EWal
'Focal Point' (2) — ICar
'Fool's Gold' (4) — ICar
'Foray' (2) — EWal
'Foresight' (1) — ICar LAma
'Forge Mill' (2) — CQua ICar
'Fort Knox' (1) — EWal
'Fortissimo' (2) — LHpC
'Fortune' (2) — EWal LAma NRog
'Foundling' (6) ♀ — CBro CQua EWal GEve IBal ICar
'Foxfire' (2) — ICar
'Fragrant Breeze' (2) — EWal
'Fragrant Rose' (2) — CQua EHof EWal ICar IDun
'Francolin' (1) — IDun
'Frank's Fancy' (9) — IBal
'Fresh Lime' (1) — EHof
'Fresh Season' (10) — Last listed 1999
'Fresno' (3) — IDun
'Frigid' (3) — IBal ICar
'Frolic' (2) — EWal
'Front Royal' (2) — CQua ICar
'Frostbite' (4) — IBal
'Frostkist' (6) — CBro CQua
'Frou-frou' (4) — CQua ICar
'Fruit Cup' (7) — CQua
'Fuego' (3) — ICar
'Full House' — EWal
'Fulwell' (4) — Last listed 1998
'Furnace Creek' (2) — IDun
'Fynbos' (3) — IDun
'Gabriël Kleiberg' (11a) — ICar
gaditanus (13) — CBro
 – MS 526 (13) — Last listed 1998
'Galway' (2) — EWal
'Garden News' (3) — IDun
'Garden Princess' (6) — CBro LAma
'Gay Cavalier' (4) — CQua
'Gay Kybo' (4) ♀ — CQua

'Gay Mood' (2) EWal
'Gay Song' (4) CQua ICar
'Gay Time' (4) EWal
§ *gayi* (13) CBro CQua
'Geevor' (4) CQua
'George Leak' (2) CQua
'George's Pink' (2) ICar
'Georgie Girl' (6) CQua IDun
'Geranium' (8) ♀ CBro CQua EWal LAma LRHS
  MBri NRog
'Gettysburg' (2) CQua
'Gigantic Star' (2) EWal LAma MBri
'Gilda' (2) IBal
'Gillan' (11a) CQua
'Gin and Lime' (1) ♀ CQua EHof ICar
'Gipsy Queen' (1) CQua
'Gironde' (11) CQua
'Glasnevin' (2) ICar
'Glaston' (2) ICar
'Glen Cassley' (3) GEve
'Glen Clova' (2) CQua LHpC
¶ 'Glen Lorne' (2) GEve
'Glenamoy' (1) ICar
'Glendermott' (2) ICar
'Glendun' (3) ICar
'Glenfarclas' (1) ♀ GEve ICar
'Glenganagh' (4) ICar
'Glenside' (2) CQua
'Glissando' (2) CQua
'Gloriosus' (8) CQua
'Glowing Red' (4) CQua
¶ 'Goblet' (1) LHpC
'Goff's Caye' (2) EHof IDun
'Gold Bond' (2) IDun
'Gold Bullion' (1) ICar
'Gold Convention' (2) ♀ CQua IDun
'Gold Ingot' (2) IDun
'Gold Medal' (1) EWal LAma
'Gold Mine' (2) IBal
'Gold Phantom' (1) ICar
'Gold Strike' (1) ICar
'Golden Amber' (2) CQua IBal ICar
'Golden Aura' (2) ♀ CQua EWal IBal ICar
'Golden Bear' (4) Last listed 1998
'Golden Bells' See *N. bulbocodium* 'Golden Bells'
'Golden Cheer' (2) CQua
'Golden Cycle' (6) CQua
'Golden Dawn' (8) ♀ CQua ETub EWal LRHS
'Golden Ducat' (4) EWal ICar LAma MBri NBir NRog
'Golden Girl' (1) ICar
'Golden Halo' (2) IBal ICar
'Golden Harvest' (1) LAma LRHS MBri NRog
'Golden Jewel' (2) ♀ CQua GEve ICar
'Golden Joy' (2) CQua ICar
'Golden Orchid' (11a) Last listed 1997
'Golden Perfection' (7) LAma
'Golden Quince' PBR (12) CBro
'Golden Radiance' (1) IBal
'Golden Rapture' (1) ♀ CQua
'Golden Riot' (1) EWal
'Golden Sceptre' (7) CBro
'Golden Sheen' (2) IDun
'Golden Sovereign' (1) IBal
'Golden Strand' (2) IBal
'Golden Topaz' (2) IBal
'Golden Vale' (1) ♀ CQua
'Golden Wings' (6) IBal
'Goldfinger' (1) IDun
'Goldhanger' (2) EHof
'Goldsithney' (2) CBro
'Golitha Falls' (2) CQua
'Golly' (4) EWal

'Good Measure' (2) EWal
'Goose Green' (3) IBal
'Gossamer' (3) EWal
'Gouache' EWal
'Gourmet' (2) Last listed 1997
'Grace Note' (3) CQua ICar
'Gracious Lady' (2) Last listed 1998
'Graduation' (2) Last listed 1998
graellsii See *N. bulbocodium* subsp.
  bulbocodium var. *graellsii*
'Grand Monarque' See *N. tazetta* subsp. *lacticolor*
  'Grand Monarque'
'Grand Primo CQua
  Citronière' (8)
'Grand Prospect' (2) CQua
'Grand Soleil d'Or' (8) CQua EPfP LAma NRog
'Gransha' (3) IBal
¶ 'Grasmere' (1) ♀ GEve
'Greatwood' (1) CQua
'Green Bridge' (3) ICar
'Green Chartreuse' (2) EHof
'Green Glens' (2) ICar
'Green Gold' (2) EWal
'Green Island' (2) EWal
'Green Lodge' (9) IBal
'Greenfinch' (3) ICar
'Greenlet' (6) CQua LHpC LRHS
'Greenodd' (3) CQua
'Greenpark' (9) IBal
'Greenstar' (4) EWal
'Gresham' (4) CQua IDun
'Grey Lady' (3) ICar
'Gribben Head' (4) CQua
'Grosvenor' (4) Last listed 1998
'Grullemans Senior' (2) Last listed 1999
'Guinevere' (2) ICar
'Gulliver' (3) CQua
'Gwennap' (1) CQua
'Gwinear' (2) CQua
'Halgarry' (3) ICar
'Halley's Comet' (3) CQua EHof
'Hallworthy' (2) Last listed 1998
'Halolight' (2) EWal
'Halstock' (2) Last listed 1998
'Halvose' (8) CBro
'Hambledon' (2) CQua EHof IDun
'Hammoon' (3) EWal
'Happy Face' (2) ICar
'Happy Fellow' (2) EHof IDun
'Harmony Bells' (5) CQua ICar
'Hartington' (2) CQua
'Hartlebury' (3) CQua
* 'Hat' (10) Last listed 1999
'Hawaii' (4) IBal
'Hawangi' (3) IDun
'Hawera' (5) ♀ CAvo CBro CQua EPar EPfP EPot
  ETub EWal ICar LAma LRHS MBri
  MBro NMGW NRog WHil
'Haye' (2) Last listed 1999
'Hazel Rutherford' (2) GEve
'Heamoor' (4) CQua
'Heart's Desire' (4) EWal
'Heat Haze' (2) ICar
bedraeantbus (13) Last listed 1999
– MS 419 (13) Last listed 1998
'Helen's Tower' (2) IBal
'Helford Dawn' (2) CQua
bellenicus See *N. poeticus* var. *bellenicus*
'Hembleton' (2) Last listed 1998
benriquesii See *N. jonquilla* var. *benriquesii*
'Hero' (1) CQua EWal
'Hesla' (7) CBro ICar

'Heslington' (3) — EHof
'Hessenford' (2) — Last listed 1998
'Hexameter' (9) — CQua
'Hexworthy' (3) — Last listed 1998
'High Note' (7) — EWal
'High Society' (2) — CQua EHof EWal ICar IDun
'Highfield Beauty' (8) ♀ — CQua EWal ICar
'Highland Wedding' (2) — ICar
'Highlite' (2) — CQua ICar
'Highway Song' (2) — ICar
'Hilford' (2) — IBal
'Hill Head' (9) — IBal
'Hillstar' (7) — CQua LHpC
'Hilltown' (2) — IBal
¶ *hispanicus* (13) — LHpC
'Holiday Fashion' (2) — EWal
'Holland Sensation' (1) — LAma
'Holly Berry' (2) — CQua
'Hollypark' (3) — IBal
'Holme Fen' (2) — EHof
'Homage' (2) — EWal
'Home Fires' (2) — LHpC
'Honey Guide' (5) — CQua
'Honeybird' (1) — CQua EWal ICar
'Honeyorange' (2) — IDun
'Honolulu' (4) — EWal LRHS
'Hoopoe' (8) — CBro CQua ICar
'Hope' (4) — EWal
'Horace' (9) — CQua ICar
'Horn of Plenty' (5) — CBro CQua
'Hors d'Oeuvre' (8) — CBro
'Hot Gossip' (2) — CQua EHof ICar IDun
'Hot Toddy' (4) — ICar
'Hotspur' (2) — CQua
* *humilis mauretanicus* — Last listed 1998
  S&F 260 (13)
'Hunting Caye' (2) — EHof
'Ice Dancer' (2) — IDun
'Ice Follies' (2) ♀ — CQua ETub EWal LAma LRHS MBri NBir NRog
'Ice King' (4) — EWal NBir
'Ice Wings' (5) — CAvo CBro CQua EPot EWal LRHS WShi
'Idless' (1) — CQua
'Immaculate' (2) — CQua ICar
'Impresario' (2) — Last listed 1998
'Inara' (4) — CQua
'Inca' (6) — CQua
'Indian Chief' (4) — Last listed 1999
'Indian Maid' (7) — CQua
'Indora' (4) — CQua
'Inglescombe' (4) — LAma
'Ingrid Evensen' (2) — Last listed 1999
'Initiation' (1) — ICar
'Innis Beg' (2) — ICar
'Inniswood' (1) — ICar
'Innovator' (4) — IDun
'Inny River' (1) — IDun
'Interim' (2) — CQua
'Interloper' (6) — IDun
§ x *intermedius* (13) — CBro
§ - 'Compressus' (8) — CQua
'Interval' (2) — IBal
'Intrigue' (7) — EWal ICar IDun
'Inverpolly' (2) — EHof GEve
¶ 'Investment' (1) — LHpC
'Ireland's Eye' (9) — IBal
'Irene Copeland' (4) — EWal LHpC
'Irish Coffee' (3) — Last listed 1998
'Irish Light' (2) — CQua ICar
'Irish Linen' (3) — CQua ICar
'Irish Luck' (1) — EWal LAma

'Irish Minstrel' (2) ♀ — Last listed 1997
'Irish Mist' (2) — CQua ICar
'Irish Nymph' (3) — ICar
'Irish Ranger' (3) — ICar
'Irish Rover' (2) — Last listed 1998
'Irish Splendour' (3) — ICar
'Irvington' (3) — IDun
'Islander' (4) — ICar
'Islandhill' (3) — IBal
'Ita' (2) — IDun
'It's True' (1) — EWal
'Itzim' (6) ♀ — CAvo CBro CQua ERos ETub
'Ivory Gull' (5) — CQua
jacetanus MS 580 (13) — Last listed 1998
'Jack Snipe' (6) ♀ — CAvo CBro CQua EPot ERos EWal LAma LBow LRHS MBNS MBri NRog WPnP WShi
'Jackadee' (2) — IDun
'Jacobin' (1) — IDun
'Jamage' (8) — CQua
'Jamaica Inn' (4) — CQua
'Jambo' (2) — IDun
'Jamboree' (2) — CQua
'Jamestown' (3) — IBal
'Jana' (6) — CQua ICar
'Jane MacLennan' (4) — GEve
'Janis Babson' (2) — ICar
'Jennie Tait' (2) — ICar
'Jenny' (6) ♀ — CAvo CBro CQua EPar EPot ERos ETub EWal IBal ICar LAma LRHS NBir NRog WPnP WShi
'Jessamy' (10) — Last listed 1999
'Jetage' (6) — CBro
'Jetfire' (6) ♀ — CBro CQua EPot ERos EWal ICar LAma LRHS
'Jewel Song' (2) — ICar
'Jezebel' (3) — CBro
¶ 'Johann Strauss' (2) — LHpC
'Johanna' (5) — CBro
'John Ballance' (1) — IBal
'John Daniel' (4) — CQua
'John of Salisbury' (2) — EWal
'John's Delight' (3) — CQua
§ 'Jolity' (2) — EWal
jonquilla (13) ♀ — CAvo CBro CQua ELau EPar EPot ERos LAma LBow LRHS NRog WPGP WShi
§ - var. *henriquesii* (13) — CBro CFil WPGP
- - MS 455 (13) — Last listed 1998
- var. *jonquilla* B&S — Last listed 1998
  420 (13)
- var. *stellaris* MS — Last listed 1998
  466 (13)
'Joppa' (7) — CQua
'Joseph Macleod' (1) — EWal
'Joy' — See *N.* 'Jolity'
'Joy Bishop' — See *N. romieuxii* 'Joy Bishop' ex JCA 805
'Joybell' (6) — CQua
¶ 'Juanita' (2) — LHpC
'Jubilation' (2) — EWal
'Jules Verne' (2) — LAma LHpC
'Julia Jane' — See *N. romieuxii* 'Julia Jane' ex JCA 805
'Jumblie' (12) ♀ — CBro CQua EPot ERos EWal LAma LRHS MBri NRog WShi
'Jumbo Gold' (1) — Last listed 1998
juncifolius — See *N. assoanus*
'June Lake' (2) — IDun
'Kamau' (9) — IDun
'Karachi' (2) — Last listed 1998
'Karamudli' (1) — Last listed 1999

'Kaydee' (6) ♀	CQua IDun	
'Kazuko' (3)	EWal	
'Kea' (6)	CQua	
'Keats' (9)	CBro CQua ICar	
'Kebaya' (2)	Last listed 1998	
'Kehelland' (4)	CBro	
'Kelanne' (2)	Last listed 1998	
'Kenbane Head' (9)	IBal	
'Kenellis' (10)	CBro CQua	
'Ken's Favourite' (2)	Last listed 1999	
'Kernow' (2)	CQua	
'Kidling' (7)	CQua	
'Kildrum' (3)	EWal ICar	
'Kilkenny' (1)	Last listed 1997	
'Killara' (8)	CQua	
'Killearnan' (9)	CQua EHof	
'Killeen' (2)	IBal	
'Killyleagh' (3)	IBal	
'Kilmood' (2)	IBal	
'Kiltonga' (2)	IBal	
'Kilworth' (2)	CQua EWal LAma	
'Kimmeridge' (3)	CQua	
'Kindled' (2)	ICar	
'King Alfred' (1)	EWal	
'King Size' (11a)	GEve ICar	
'Kinglet' (7)	ICar	
'King's Bridge' (1)	Last listed 1998	
'King's Grove' (1)	CQua IDun	
'Kings Pipe' (2)	CQua	
'King's Stag' (1)	ICar	
'Kingscourt' (1) ♀	CQua ICar	
'Kirkcubbin' (3)	IBal	
'Kirkinriola' (3)	ICar	
'Kirklington' (2)	Last listed 1999	
'Kissproof' (2)	EWal	
'Kit Hill' (7)	CQua	
'Kitty' (6)	CBro ERos	
'Klamath' (2)	EWal	
'Knockanure' (2)	ICar	
'Knocklayde' (3)	ICar	
'Krakatoa' (2)	EWal	
'La Argentina' (2)	Last listed 1999	
'La Riante' (3)	LHpC	
'La Vella' (2)	Last listed 1998	
'Ladies' Choice' (7)	IDun	
'Lady Ann' (2)	IDun	
'Lady Be Good' (2)	EHof	
'Lady Emily' (2)	IBal	
'Lady Serena' (9)	CQua	
'Lake Tahoe' (2)	IDun	
'Lamanva' (2)	CQua	
'Lamerton' (2)	Last listed 1999	
'L'Amour'	See N. 'Madelaine'	
'Lanarth' (7)	CBro	
'Lancaster' (3)	IBal	
'Landmark' (2)	EWal	
'Langford Grove' (3)	ICar	
'Lapwing' (5)	CBro EWal	
'Larkelly' (6)	CBro	
'Larkfield' (2)	ICar	
'Larkhill' (2)	CQua	
'Larkwhistle' (6) ♀	CBro LHpC	
¶ 'Las Vegas' (1)	LHpC	
'Last Promise' (1)	ICar	
'Last Word' (3)	EWal	
'Latchley' (2)	CQua	
'Late Call' (3)	IBal	
¶ 'Laurens Koster' (8)	LHpC	
'Lavender Lass' (6)	CQua	
'Lee Moor' (1)	CQua	
'Lemon Beauty' (11b)	CQua EWal LRHS	
'Lemon Cloud' (1)	EWal	

'Lemon Grey' (3)	IDun	
'Lemon Heart' (5)	CBro	
'Lemon Sails' (2)	IDun	
'Lemon Silk' (6)	CQua	
'Lemon Snow' (2)	Last listed 1998	
'Lemonade' (3)	CQua	
'Lennymore' (2)	IDun	
'Leonaine' (2)	EWal	
'Leslie Hill' (1)	ICar	
'Lewannick' (2)	CQua	
'Liberty Bells' (5)	CAvo CBro CQua EPot EWal LAma LRHS MBri NRog	
'Lichfield' (3)	EWal	
'Lighthouse' (3)	GEve	
'Lighthouse Reef' (1)	EHof	
'Lilac Charm' (6)	CQua IDun	
'Lilac Hue' (6)	CBro	
'Lillande' (4)	ICar	
'Limbo' (2)	CQua EWal IDun	
'Limegrove' (3)	Last listed 1998	
'Limehurst' (2)	CQua	
'Limelight' (1)	EWal	
'Limerick' (3)	EWal	
'Limpopo' (3)	IDun	
'Lingerie' (4)	NZep	
'Lintie' (7)	CBro CQua EWal LAma LRHS MBri NRog	
'Lionheart' (4)	EWal	
'Lisanore' (2)	Last listed 1998	
'Lisbarnett' (3)	IBal	
'Lisnamulligan' (3)	IBal	
'Lisnamurrican' (2)	ICar	
'Lisrenny' (1)	ICar	
'Little Beauty' (1)	CAvo CBro CQua EPot ERos LAma LRHS	
'Little Dancer' (1)	CBro	
'Little Gem' (1) ♀	CAvo CBro CQua EPot LAma LRHS NRog	
'Little Princess' (6)	ICar	
'Little Rusky' (7)	Last listed 1998	
'Little Sentry' (7)	CBro CQua	
'Little Soldier' (10)	CQua	
'Little Spell' (1)	CBro LHpC	
'Little Witch' (6)	CAvo CBro CQua EPot ERos EWal LAma LRHS MBri NRog	
'Liverpool Festival' (2)	CQua	
'Lizard Light' (2)	EWal	
lobularis	See *N. pseudonarcissus* 'Lobularis'	
'Loch Alsh' (3)	IDun	
'Loch Assynt' (3)	CQua ICar	
'Loch Brora' (2)	CQua GEve ICar	
'Loch Carron' (2)	ICar	
'Loch Fada' (2)	CQua	
'Loch Hope' (2)	CQua ICar	
¶ 'Loch Leven' (2)	GEve	
'Loch Loyal' (2)	ICar	
'Loch Lundie' (2)	CQua ICar	
'Loch Maberry' (2)	CQua ICar	
'Loch Naver' (2)	CQua	
'Loch Owskeich' (2) ♀	Last listed 1995	
¶ 'Loch Scridain' (2)	GEve	
'Loch Stac' (2)	CQua ICar	
'Logan Rock' (7)	CQua	
longispathus MS 546 (13)	SSpi	
'Lorikeet' (1)	CQua NZep	
'Lostwithiel' (2)	Last listed 1998	
'Lothario' (2)	LAma NRog	
'Lough Bawn' (2)	GEve ICar	
'Lough Cuan' (1)	IBal	
'Lough Gowna' (1)	IDun	
'Lough Ryan' (1)	IBal	
'Loughanisland' (1)	IBal	

'Loughanmore' (1) — ICar
'Lovable' (3) — EWal
'Loveny' (2) — CQua
'Ludgvan' (4) — Last listed 1999
'Lunar Sea' (1) — EWal
'Lundy Light' (2) — CQua
'Lurgain' (1) — EWal
'Lurig' (2) — ICar
'Lyrebird' (3) — CQua
'Lyric' (9) — CQua
'Lysander' (2) — CQua
§ 'Madelaine' (2) — EWal
* 'Madison' — EWal
'Magic Flute' (2) — ICar
'Magician' (2) — NZep
'Magna Carta' (2) — Last listed 1998
'Magnet' (1) — LAma MBri
'Magnificence' (1) — LAma
'Majarde' (2) — Last listed 1999
'Majestic Star' (1) — CQua IDun
'Makasa Sun' (2) — IDun
'Malin Head' (5) — IBal
'Manchu' (2) — EWal
'Manly' (4) — CQua EWal
'Manon Lescaut' (2) — EWal
'Marabou' (4) — Last listed 1998
'Maraval' (1) — EWal
'March Sunshine' (6) — CBro EWal LAma
¶ 'Margaret Mitchell' (3) — LHpC
'Marie-José' (11b) — Last listed 1999
'Marjorie Treveal' (4) — CQua
'Marlborough' (2) — CQua
'Martha Washington' (8) — CBro CQua
'Martinette' (7) — CQua LRHS
marvieri — See *N. rupicola* subsp. *marvieri*
'Mary Bohannon' (2) — EWal
'Mary Copeland' (4) — EWal LAma
'Mary Kate' (6) — CQua IDun
'Mary Lou' (6) — IDun
'Mary Robinson' (2) — ICar
'Mary Schouten' (2) — GEve
'Mary Sumner' (1) — ICar
'Mary Veronica' (3) — EHof
'Mary's Pink' (2) — ICar
'Marzo' (7) — IDun
'Masai Mara' (2) — Last listed 1998
'Matador' (8) — CQua
'Max' (11a) — CQua
'Maya Dynasty' (2) — CQua
'Mayan Gold' (1) — IBal
'Media Girl' (2) — IDun
x *medioluteus* (13) — CBro
'Medusa' (8) — CBro
'Megalith' (2) — Last listed 1998
'Melancholy' (1) — IDun
'Melbury' (2) — CQua
'Meldrum' (1) — Last listed 1998
'Mellon Park' (3) — Last listed 1998
'Melodious' (2) — Last listed 1999
'Menabilly' (4) — CQua
'Men-an-Tol' (2) — CQua
'Menehay' (11a) — CQua
'Mentor' (2) — Last listed 1998
'Menucha' (2) — ICar
'Mercato' (2) — LAma
'Meredith' (3) — ICar
'Merida' (2) — IBal
'Merlin' (3) ♀ — CQua EHof GEve
'Merlin's Castle' (3) — ICar
'Merry Bells' (5) — CQua ICar
'Merrymeet' (4) — CQua
'Mexico City' (2) — IBal

'Michaels Gold' (2) — EHof IDun
'Midas Touch' (1) — CQua ICar
'Midget' — CAvo CBro EPot ETub LRHS
'Milan' (9) — CQua ICar
'Milestone' (2) — ICar
'Millennium' (1) — CBro
'Millgreen' (1) — EWal
'Minicycla' (6) — CBro LRHS
minimus hort. — See *N. asturiensis*
'Minnow' (8) ♀ — CAvo CBro CQua EPot ERos ETub EWal LAma LRHS MBri NRog WShi
§ *minor* (13) ♀ — CBro CQua EBot LAma WShi
- var. *pumilus* 'Plenus' — See *N.* 'Rip van Winkle'
- Ulster form — IBlr
'Mint Cup' (3) — ICar
minutiflorus B&S 412 (13) — Last listed 1998
'Miss Kitty' (2) — ICar
'Miss Primm' (2) — IDun
'Mission Bells' (5) — CQua ICar
'Missouri' (2) — EWal
'Mistral' (11) — ICar
'Misty Dawn' (3) — IBal
'Misty Glen' (2) ♀ — CQua ICar
'Misty Moon' (3) — ICar
'Mite' (6) — CBro LHpC
'Mitylene' (2) — CQua
'Mockingbird' (7) — IDun
'Modern Art' (2) — EWal
'Mol's Hobby' (11a) — EWal
'Mona Lisa' (2) — EWal
'Mondragon' (11a) — CQua EWal
'Mongleath' (2) — CQua
'Monks Wood' (1) — EHof
'Montclair' (2) — CQua
'Montego' (3) — CQua
'Monza' (4) — IDun
'Moon Jade' (3) — Last listed 1997
'Moon Ranger' (3) — IBal
'Moon Rhythm' (4) — IBal ICar
'Moon Tide' (3) — IBal
'Moon Valley' (2) — GEve IDun
'Moonbird' (11a) — ICar
'Moonflight' (4) — ICar
'Moonshine' (5) — CBro
'Moonshot' (1) — EWal
'Moonspell' (2) — IBal ICar
'Moralee' (4) — IDun
§ *moschatus* (13) — CBro EPot
- 'Cernuus Plenus' (4) — ICar
'Mother Catherine Grullemans' (2) — LAma
'Mount Angel' (3) — Last listed 1998
'Mount Fuji' (2) — CQua
'Mount Hood' (1) ♀ — ETub EWal LAma MBri NBir
'Mount Oriel' (2) — IBal
'Mountjoy' (7) — EWal
'Mourneview' (1) — IBal
'Movie Star' (2) — IDun
'Mowana' (2) — Last listed 1998
'Moyarget' (3) — ICar
'Moyle' (9) — IBal
'Moyola' (2) — ICar
'Mrs Langtry' (3) — CQua WShi
'Mrs R.O. Backhouse' (2) — LAma MBri WShi
'Mrs William Copeland' (4) — EWal
'Mulatto' (1) — EWal
'Mullion' (3) — CQua
'Mulroy Bay' (1) — IDun
'Murlough' (9) — CQua IBal
'Murrayfield' (3) — Last listed 1998
'Muscadet' (2) — Last listed 1999

'Music Hall' (1) — LHpC
'My Lady' (2) — EWal
'My My' (2) — EWal
'My Word' (2) — ICar
'Naivasha' (2) — IDun
'Nampa' (1) — Last listed 1999
'Namraj' (2) — CQua
'Nancegollan' (7) — CBro CQua
'Nangiles' (4) — CQua
'Nansidwell' (2) — CQua
nanus — ICar LHpC
'Narok' (4) — Last listed 1998
'Neahkahnie' (1) — Last listed 1998
'Nether Barr' (2) — IDun
§ *nevadensis* (13) — SSpi
'New Penny' (3) — ICar
'New Song' (2) — EWal
'New Star' (2) — EWal
'New World' (2) — EWal
'New-baby' (7) — CQua EWal
'Newcastle' (1) — CQua EWal ICar
'Newton Ferrers' (4) — Last listed 1998
'Nick's Pink' (1) — ICar
'Night Music' (4) — CQua
'Nightcap' (1) — CQua
'Nile' (1) — ICar IDun
'Nirvana' (7) — CBro
'Niveth' (5) — CQua ICar
nobilis var. *nobilis* — Last listed 1998
  MS 486 (13)
- var. *primigenius* — Last listed 1998
  MS 593 (13)
'Nonchalant' (3) — IDun
'Nor-nor' (2) — CBro
'North Rim' (2) — Last listed 1998
'Northern Sceptre' (2) — IBal ICar
'Northwest' (1) — IDun
'Noss Mayo' (6) — CBro CQua
'Notable' (3) — Last listed 1997
'Notre Dame' (2) ♀ — IDun
'Nouvelle' (3) — IBal
'Nuage' (2) — EWal
'Numen Rose' (2) — IDun
Nylon Group (10) — CBro CLAP EPot SSpi
- yellow (10) — EPot
'Oadby' (1) — CQua
'Oakwood' (3) — EWal
'Obdam' (4) — EWal
'Obelisk' (11a) — CQua
obesus (13) — CLAP EPot ERos
- MS 451 (13) — Last listed 1998
'Obsession' (2) — Last listed 1998
obvallaris (13) ♀ — CAvo CBro EPot ERos LBow NRog
  WHer WShi
'Ocarino' (4) — CQua
'Ocean Blue' (2) — IDun
x *odorus* (13) — LHpC WCot WShi
§ - 'Double Campernelle' (4) — CQua EPar LAma WCot
'Odyssey' (4) — ICar IDun
'Oecumene' (11a) — CQua
'Ohio' (2) — Last listed 1998
Old Pheasant's Eye — See *N. poeticus* var. *recurvus*
'Olympic Gold' (1) — Last listed 1998
'Omaha' (3) — IBal
'Orange Beacon' (2) — ICar
'Orange Monarch' (2) — Last listed 1999
'Orange Queen' (3) — LHpC
'Orange Walk' (3) — EHof
'Orangery' (11a) — ICar LAma LRHS MBri NRog
'Oratorio' (2) — EWal
'Ormeau' (2) ♀ — CQua ICar
'Oryx' (7) ♀ — CQua IDun

'Osmington' (2) — CQua EHof
'Ottoman Gold' (2) — IBal
'Ouma' (1) — CQua
'Our Tempie' (3) — IDun
'Ouzel' (6) — CQua
'Owen Roe' (1) — Last listed 1997
'Owston Wood' (1) — Last listed 1998
'Oykel' (3) — CQua GEve ICar
'Oz' (12) — CQua
'Painted Desert' (3) — CQua ICar
'Pale Sunlight' (2) — CQua ICar
'Palette' (11a) — ICar
§ *pallidiflorus* (13) — ECha
'Palmares' (11a) — CQua EWal ICar
'Palmyra' (3) — ICar
'Panache' (1) — CQua EWal ICar
panizzianus (13) — Last listed 1998
'Pankot' (2) — ICar
'Paolo Veronese' (2) — EWal
'Paper White' — See *N. papyraceus*
¶ 'Paper White — LHpC
  Grandiflorus' (8)
'Papillon Blanc' (11b) — EWal LAma
'Papua' (4) ♀ — CQua
§ *papyraceus* (8) — CQua ETub EWal LAma LBow
  LRHS MBri NRog
- AB&S 4399 (13) — Last listed 1998
'Paradigm' (4) — IDun
'Parcpat' (7) — CBro
'Parfait' (4) — ICar
'Paricutin' (2) — EWal
'Parisienne' (11a) — EWal LAma NRog
'Park Avenue' (4) — Last listed 1998
'Park Gate' (2) — ICar
'Park Springs' (3) — CQua ICar
'Parkfields Beauty' (2) — ICar
'Parterre' (2) — Last listed 1998
'Parthenon' (4) — ICar
'Party Time' (2) — IDun
'Passionale' (2) ♀ — CQua EWal IBal LAma NBir
¶ 'Pasternak' (1) — LHpC
'Pastiche' (2) — CQua
'Pastorale' (2) — EWal
'Patabundy' (2) — CQua
'Patois' (9) — IDun
patulus (13) — Last listed 1998
'Paula Cottell' (3) — CBro
'Pawley's Island' (2) — Last listed 1998
'Pay Day' (1) — ICar
'Peach Prince' (4) — CQua
'Peacock' (2) — ICar
I 'Pearlax' — See *N. 'Perlax'*
'Pearlshell' (11a) — CQua GEve
'Peeping Tom' (6) ♀ — CBro EPar EWal LAma LRHS MBri
  NRog SRms
'Pelynt' (3) — Last listed 1998
'Pencrebar' (4) — CAvo CBro CQua EPot ERos LAma
  LRHS MBri WShi
'Pengarth' (2) — CQua
'Penkivel' (2) — CQua
'Pennance Mill' (2) — CQua
'Pennine Way' (1) — CQua
'Penpol' (7) — CBro CQua
'Penril' (6) — CQua
'Pentille' (1) — CQua
'Penvose' (2) — EWal
'Pepper' (2) — CBro
'Pequenita' (7) — CBro
'Percuil' (6) — CQua
perez-chiscanoi — Last listed 1999
  MS 560 (13)
'Perimeter' (3) — CQua EWal IBal ICar

'Red Hot' (2) — Last listed 1999
'Red Hugh' (9) — IBal
'Red Mission' (2) — Last listed 1998
'Red Rascal' (2) — ETub LHpC
'Red Spartan' (2) — Last listed 1998
'Redhill' (2) — EWal
'Redman' (2) — IBal
'Redstart' (3) — EWal
'Refrain' (2) — EHof
'Regal Bliss' (2) — CQua
'Reggae' (6) ♀ — ICar
'Rembrandt' (1) — LAma MBri
'Rendezvous Caye' (2) — EHof
'Replete' (4) — CQua ICar
'Reprieve' (3) — Last listed 1997
requienii — See *N. assoanus*
'Resplendent' (2) — ICar
'Revival' (4) — EWal
'Ridgecrest' (3) — IDun
'Riding Mill' (3) — EWal
'Riesling' (11a) — Last listed 1999
rifanus — See *N. romieuxii* subsp.
 — *romieuxii* var. *rifanus*
'Rijnveld's Early — CAvo CBro CQua EWal LRHS MBri
 Sensation' (1) ♀
'Rikki' (7) — CBro CQua ERos
'Rim Ride' (3) — ICar
'Rima' (1) — CQua
'Rimmon' (3) — CQua IDun
'Rimski' (2) — Last listed 1998
'Ring Fence' (3) — IDun
'Ringhaddy' (3) — IBal
'Ringing Bells' (5) — CQua
'Ringleader' (2) — CQua EWal
'Ringmaster' (2) — CQua ICar
'Ringwood' (3) — Last listed 1998
'Rio Bravo' (2) — IBal
'Rio Gusto' (2) — IBal
'Rio Lobo' (2) — IBal
'Rio Rondo' (2) — IBal
'Rio Rouge' (2) — IBal ICar
§ 'Rip van Winkle' (4) — CAvo CBro CSWP EPar EPot ERos
 — ETub LAma LBow LRHS MBri
 — NMGW NRog SLod WShi
'Rippling Waters' (5) ♀ — CBro CQua EPot ICar LAma LRHS
'Riptide' (1) — ICar
'Ristin' (1) — CQua
'Rival' (6) — CQua
'Rivendell' (3) — ICar IDun
'River Dance' (2) — IDun
'Rob Roy' (3) — EWal
'Rock Creek' (3) — IDun
'Rockall' (3) — CQua ICar
'Rockport' (2) — ICar
'Rococo' (2) — EWal
'Roger' (6) — CBro
'Romance' (2) ♀ — CQua EWal LAma
§ 'Romanus' (4) — CQua
'Romany Red' (3) — Last listed 1998
romieuxii (13) ♀ — CAvo CBro CFil CNic EPot ERos
 — LRHS SSpi WAbe WPGP
- AB&S 4384 (13) — NHar
- subsp. *albidus* (13) — Last listed 1998
- - S&F 110 (13) — Last listed 1998
- - S&F 256 (13) — Last listed 1999
§ - - var. *zaianicus* (13) — LHpC
§ - - - f. *albus* (13) — Last listed 1998
§ - - - f. *lutescens* (13) — Last listed 1999
§ - - - - S&F 374 (13) — NHar
- 'Atlas Gold' — Last listed 1999
- 'Atlas Gold' JCA 805Y (10) — EPot GCrs NHar
- JCA 805 (10) — EPot NHar

§ - 'Joy Bishop' ex — EPot
 JCA 805 (10)
§ - 'Julia Jane' ex — ERos GCrs NHar
 JCA 805 (10)
§ - subsp. *romieuxii* — Last listed 1999
 var. *mesatlanticus* (13)
§ - - var. *rifanus* — Last listed 1998
 SB&L 207 (13)
- S&F 370 (13) — Last listed 1998
- 'Treble Chance' ex — EPot
 JCA 805 (10)
'Rory's Glen' (2) — ICar
'Rosado' (11a) — EWal
'Roscarrick' (6) — CQua
'Rose Gold' (1) — IDun
'Rose of May' (4) — ICar
'Rose Royale' (2) — CQua IBal
'Roseate Tern' (2) — CQua
'Rosedown' (5) — CBro
'Roseworthy' (2) — ERos LAma
'Rossferry' (2) — IBal
'Rosy Sunrise' (2) — LAma LRHS
'Rosy Trumpet' (1) — CBro
'Rosy Wonder' (2) — EWal
'Round Robin' (2) — ICar
'Royal Ballet' (2) — CQua
'Royal Coachman' (2) — ICar
'Royal Command' — See *N.* 'Royal Decree'
§ 'Royal Decree' (2) — EWal
'Royal Orange' (2) — EWal
'Royal Princess' (3) — CQua EHof
'Royal Regiment' (2) — CQua ICar
'Royal Wedding' (2) — ICar
'Rubh Mor' (2) — CQua EHof
'Ruby Rose' (4) — IDun
'Ruby Tail' (2) — EWal
'Rubyat' (6) — IBal
'Rugulosus' (7) ♀ — CAvo CBro EBot EPar ERos LAma
 — LRHS NRog WCot
rupicola (13) — CAvo CBro CLAP ERos MS&S NSla
 — SSpi
§ - subsp. *marvieri* (13) ♀ — SSpi
- - AB&S 4414 (13) — NHar
- - S&F 126 (13) — Last listed 1998
- MS 567 (13) — Last listed 1998
§ - subsp. *watieri* (13) — CBro GCrs MTho
'Rushmore' (2) — IDun
'Rustom Pasha' (2) — CQua
'Ruth Haller' (5) — ICar
'Rutland Water' (2) — Last listed 1997
'Rytha' (2) — CQua
'Saberwing' (5) — CQua ICar
'Sabine Hay' (3) — CQua EWal ICar IDun
'Sacajawea' (2) — EWal
'Saint Dilpe' (2) — CQua
'Saint Duthus' (1) — GEve
'Saint Keverne' (2) ♀ — CQua EWal IBal LAma NRog
'Saint Keyne' (8) — CQua
'Saint Mawes' (2) — Last listed 1998
'Saint Patrick's Day' (2) — CQua EWal LAma
'Saint Piran' (7) — CQua
'Salmon Trout' (2) — CQua EWal LAma
'Salome' (2) — EWal LAma LRHS MBri NBir NRog
'Samantha' (4) — CQua
'Samaria' (3) — CBro
'Samba' (5) — ERos
'Samite' (1) — EWal
'Sancerre' (11a) — CQua
'Sandycove' (2) — IDun
'Sandymount' (2) — IBal
'Sarah' (2) — EWal
'Sarah Dear' (2) — Last listed 1999

'Sargeant's Caye' (1)	EHof	
'Sateen' (2)	EWal	
'Satellite' (6)	EWal ICar	
'Satin Pink' (2)	EWal MBri	
'Saturn' (3)	CQua ICar	
'Savoir Faire' (2)	IDun	
scaberulus (13)	CBro ERos	
'Scamp' (3)	ICar	
'Scarlet Elegance' (2)	LAma	
'Scarlet Gem' (8)	EWal LAma	
'Scarlett O'Hara' (2)	CQua LAma	
'Sea Dream' (3)	CQua EWal	
'Sea Gift' (7)	CBro	
'Sea Green' (9)	CQua	
'Sealing Wax' (2)	CQua EWal	
'Segovia' (3) ♀	CBro CQua ERos	
'Selma Lagerlöf' (2)	Last listed 1999	
'Sempre Avanti' (2)	LAma MBri NRog	
'Sennocke' (5)	CBro	
'Seraglio' (3)	CQua	
'Serena Beach' (4)	IDun	
'Serena Lodge' (4) ♀	IDun	
serotinus (13)	LHpC	
- S&F 285 (13)	Last listed 1998	
- S&F 298 (13)	Last listed 1998	
'Sextant' (6)	CQua EWal	
'Shanes Castle' (1)	ICar	
'Shangani' (2)	IDun	
'She' (2)	EWal	
'Sheelagh Rowan' (2)	EHof	
'Sheer Joy' (6)	IDun	
'Sheerline' (2)	Last listed 1998	
'Sherborne' (4)	IDun	
'Sherpa' (1)	CQua IDun	
'Sheviock' (2)	CQua	
'Shimna' (1)	IBal	
'Shining Light' (2)	CQua ICar	
'Shorecliffe' (2)	IDun	
'Shot Silk' (5)	Last listed 1999	
'Show Band' (2)	Last listed 1998	
'Siam' (2)	Last listed 1999	
'Sidley' (3)	CQua IDun	
'Sidney' (9)	Last listed 1998	
'Signorina' (2)	IDun	
'Silent Pink' (2)	IDun	
'Silent Valley' (1)	CQua EHof	
'Silk Cut' (2)	CQua	
'Silken Sails' (3)	ICar	
'Silken Wings' (2)	IDun	
'Silver Bells' (5)	CQua IDun	
'Silver Blaze' (2)	Last listed 1998	
'Silver Chimes' (8)	CBro CQua EWal LAma LRHS NBir NRog	
'Silver Crystal' (3)	IDun	
'Silver Plate' (11a)	CQua	
'Silver Princess' (3)	Last listed 1997	
'Silver Standard' (2)	CQua EWal	
'Silver Surf' (2)	CQua IDun	
'Silverwood' (3)	IDun	
'Simply Bloomfield' (2)	ICar	
'Singing Pub' (3)	IDun	
'Sir Watkin' (2)	CQua	
'Sir Winston Churchill' (4) ♀	CQua EWal LAma LRHS NRog	
'Skerry' (2)	ICar	
'Slaney' (3)	ICar	
'Sligachan' (1)	GEve	
'Small Fry' (1)	Last listed 1997	
'Small Talk' (1)	CQua	
'Smokey Bear' (4)	CQua	
'Snoopie' (6)	CQua	
'Snow Bunting' (7)	CBro	
'Snowcrest' (3)	CQua	

'Snowfire' (4)	ICar	
'Snowshill' (2)	CQua	
'Society Belle' (2)	Last listed 1998	
'Solar Tan' (3)	CQua IDun	
'Soldier Brave' (2)	EWal	
'Soledad' (2)	ICar	
'Soleil d'Or' (8)	EWal MBri	
¶ 'Solveig's Song'	EHyt	
'Sonata' (9)	CQua	
'Songket' (2)	Last listed 1998	
'Sophia' (2)	Last listed 1998	
'Soprano' (2)	IDun	
'Sorbet' (11b)	EWal LHpC	
'Sorcerer' (3)	CQua	
'South Street' (2)	CQua	
'Sovereign' (11a)	IDun	
'Spaniards Inn' (4)	CQua	
'Spanish Moon' (1)	EWal	
'Sparkling Eye' (8)	IBal	
'Spellbinder' (1) ♀	EWal LAma MBri	
'Sperrin Gold' (1)	IDun	
'Spirit of Rame' (3)	CQua	
'Split Image' (2)	IDun	
'Sportsman' (2)	CQua	
'Spring Dawn' (2)	EWal	
'Spring Morn' (2)	CQua IDun	
'Stadium' (2)	EWal	
'Stainless' (2)	ETub	
'Standard Value' (1)	LAma	
'Stanway' (3)	CQua	
'Star Glow' (2)	Last listed 1998	
'Star War' (2)	Last listed 1999	
'Starfire' (7)	CQua ICar	
'State Express' (2)	CQua EHof	
'Statue' (2)	EWal	
'Steenbok' (3)	IDun	
'Step Forward' (7)	ERos	
'Stilton' (9)	CQua	
'Stint' (5)	CBro CQua	
'Stocken' (7)	CBro	
* 'Stockens Gib'	Last listed 1997	
'Stoke Charity' (2)	EHof ICar	
'Stoke Doyle' (2)	EHof	
'Stormy Weather' (1)	CQua ICar IDun	
'Stourbridge' (2)	ICar	
'Stranocum' (3)	ICar	
'Strathkanaird' (1)	ICar	
'Stratosphere' (7)	CQua ICar	
'Stray' (6)	ICar	
'Strines' (2)	CQua EWal	
'Stromboli' (2)	EWal	
'Suave' (3)	CQua EHof	
'Suda Bay' (2)	ICar	
'Sugar and Spice' (3)	EHof	
'Sugar Bird' (2)	IDun	
'Sugar Loaf' (4)	CQua	
'Sugarbush' (7)	CBro MBri NRog	
'Suilven' (3)	GEve	
'Sumo Jewel' (6)	CQua	
'Sun Disc' (7) ♀	CBro CQua EPot ERos ETub EWal ICar LAma LRHS MBri	
'Sunapee' (3)	Last listed 1998	
'Sundial' (7)	CAvo CBro CMea CQua EPot ERos EWal ICar LAma LRHS	
'Suntory' (3)	CQua	
'Suntrap' (2)	IDun	
'Super Bowl' (2)	IDun	
'Surfside' (6) ♀	CBro CQua LRHS	
'Surrey' (2)	CQua	
'Susan Pearson' (7)	ICar	
'Suzie Dee' (6)	IDun	
'Suzie's Sister' (6)	IDun	

'Suzy' (7) ♀ — CBro EWal ICar LAma MBri NRog
'Swaledale' (2) — CQua
'Swallow Wing' (6) — IDun
'Swansdown' (4) — EWal ICar
'Sweet Blanche' (7) — CQua
'Sweet Charity' (2) — EWal LHpC
'Sweet Harmony' (2) — Last listed 1999
'Sweet Pepper' (7) — CBro
'Sweet Sue' (3) — EHof
'Sweetness' (7) ♀ — CAvo CBro CQua EWal IBal LAma NRog WShi
'Swing Wing' (6) — CQua
'Sydling' (5) — CQua
'Sylvan Hill' (1) — IBal
'Taffeta' (10) — CAvo CBro LRHS
'Tahiti' (4) ♀ — CQua EWal LAma LRHS MBri NRog
'Tain' (1) — GEve ICar
'Takoradi' (4) — ICar
'Talwyn' (1) — CQua
'Tamar Fire' (4) ♀ — CQua
'Tamar Lad' (2) — CQua
'Tamar Snow' (2) — CQua
'Tamara' (2) — CQua
tananicus S&F 44 — Last listed 1999
'Tangent' (2) — CQua EWal ICar
'Tara Rose' (2) — Last listed 1997
'Tardree' (1) — ICar
'Tarlatan' (10) — CBro
'Taslass' (4) — CQua
'Tater-Du' (5) — CQua
tazetta subsp. *aureus* — See *N. aureus*
§ - subsp. *lacticolor* (13) — CQua WPGP
§ - - 'Grand Monarque' (8) — CQua
- - MS 517 (13) — Last listed 1998
- - MS 519 (13) — Last listed 1998
- subsp. *papyraceus* — See *N. papyraceus*
'Teal' (1) — EHof
'Tedstone' (1) — EWal
'Tehidy' (3) — CQua
§ 'Telamonius Plenus' (4) — CBro LAma WShi
'Temple Cloud' (4) — IDun
tenuifolius — See *N. bulbocodium* subsp. *bulbocodium* var. *tenuifolius*
§ x *tenuior* (13) — Last listed 1999
'Terracotta' (2) — IDun
'Terrapin' (3) — IDun
'Testament' (2) — EWal
'Tête-à-tête' (12) ♀ — CAvo CBro CQua EPar EPot ERos ETub EWal LAma LBow LRHS MBNS MBri WHil WPnP
'Texas' (4) — LAma MBri
'Thalia' (5) — CAvo CBro CMea ERos ETub EWal ICar LAma LBow LRHS MBri NBir NRog WShi
'The Alliance' (6) — CQua
'The Knave' (6) — CQua
'The Little Gentleman' (6) — CBro
'Thoughtful' (5) — CBro CQua EWal
'Three Trees' (1) — ICar
'Thunderbolt' (1) — EWal
'Tibet' (2) — EWal LRHS
'Tiercel' (1) — CQua
'Tiffany' (10) — Last listed 1998
'Tiger Moth' (6) — Last listed 1998
'Timolin' (3) — CQua ICar
'Tinnell' (1) — Last listed 1997
'Tiritomba' (11a) — CQua EWal
'Titania' (6) — CQua
'Tittle-tattle' (7) — CBro CQua EWal IBal LAma
'Toby' (2) — EWal
'Toby the First' (6) — CQua

'Tonga' (4) — ICar
'Top Hit' (11a) — CQua
'Top of the Hill' (3) — IBal ICar
'Topkapi' (2) — IBal
'Topolino' (1) — CAvo CBro CQua EPot LAma LRHS NRog
'Torcross' (3) — Last listed 1998
'Torr Head' (9) — IBal
'Torridon' (2) — CQua EHof GEve ICar
'Toscanini' (2) — Last listed 1999
'Tracey' (6) — CBro CQua
'Tranquil Morn' (3) — EWal
'Trebah' (2) — CQua
'Treble Two' (7) — CQua
'Trefusis' (1) — CQua
'Tregarrick' (2) — CQua
'Trehane' (6) — CQua
'Trena' (6) — CBro CQua EWal
'Tresamble' (5) — CBro CQua EWal LAma
'Trevelmond' (2) — CQua
'Treverva' (6) — CQua
'Treviddo' (2) — CQua
'Trevithian' (7) ♀ — CBro CQua EWal IBal LAma LRHS NRog
'Trewidland' (2) — CQua
'Trewirgie' (6) — CBro CQua
triandrus (13) ♀ — NSla WPGP
- var. *albus* — See *N. triandrus* subsp. *triandrus* var. *triandrus*
§ - subsp. *triandrus* var. *concolor* (13) — CBro MS&S
§ - - var. *pulchellus* (13) — LAma
§ - - var. *triandrus* (13) — EBot
'Tricollet' (11a) — EWal
'Triller' (7) — ICar
'Tripartite' (11a) — CQua EWal GEve ICar NZep
'Triple Crown' (3) ♀ — CQua IDun
'Tristram' (2) — CQua EHof
'Tropic Isle' (4) — ICar
'Tropical Heat' (2) — IDun
'Trousseau' (1) — CQua EWal
'Troutbeck' (3) — CQua
'Trumpet Warrior' (1) — IDun
'Tudor Grove' (2) — Last listed 1998
'Tudor Minstrel' (2) — CQua EWal
'Tuesday's Child' (5) ♀ — CQua EWal ICar MBNS
'Tullybeg' (3) — LHpC
'Tullygirvan' (2) — ICar
'Tullynog' (4) — ICar
'Tullyroyal' (2) — IBal
'Turncoat' (6) — CQua
'Tutankhamun' (2) — CQua
'Tweeny' (2) — Last listed 1998
'Twicer' (2) — Last listed 1998
'Tyee' (2) — CQua
'Tykky-dew' (2) — EHof
'Tynan' (2) — ICar
'Tyneham' (3) — Last listed 1998
'Tyrian Rose' (2) — IDun
'Tyrone Gold' (1) ♀ — IDun
'Tywara' (1) — EHof
'Ufo' (3) — EWal
'Ulster Bank' (3) — Last listed 1998
'Ulster Bullion' (2) — IBal
'Ulster Prince' (1) ♀ — Last listed 1994
'Ultimus' (2) — EWal
'Uncle Duncan' (1) — CQua EHof IDun
'Uncle Remus' (1) — EWal
'Unique' (4) — CQua EWal ICar LAma
'Unsurpassable' (1) — LAma
'Vahu' (2) — IDun
'Val d'Incles' (3) — IDun

'Valdrome' (11a) | CQua ICar MBri
'Valediction' (3) | Last listed 1998
'Valinor' (2) | Last listed 1998
'Value' (2) | IDun
'Van Sion' | See *N.* 'Telamonius Plenus'
'Vandyke' (2) | IDun
'Verdin' (7) | CQua ICar
'Verger' (3) | LAma MBri
'Vernal Prince' (3) | CQua GEve
'Verona' (3) ♀ | CQua LHpC
'Vers Libre' (9) | CQua
'Verwood' (3) | Last listed 1998
'Vice-President' (2) | ICar
'Victorious' (2) | CQua
'Victory' (2) | EWal
'Vigil' (1) ♀ | CQua EWal ICar
'Vigilante' (1) | Last listed 1998
'Viking' (1) ♀ | CQua EHof GEve
'Vilna' (2) | EWal
'Violetta' (2) | CQua EWal ICar
'Vireo' (7) | ICar
viridiflorus (13) | WCot
- MS 500 (13) | Last listed 1998
- S&F 323 (13) | Last listed 1998
'Vivarino' (11?b) | EWal
'Volare' (2) | Last listed 1998
'Voltage' (2) | Last listed 1998
'Vulcan' (2) ♀ | CQua EWal
'W.P. Milner' (1) | CAvo CBro CMea EPot LAma LRHS MBri NRog
'Waif' (6) | CQua ICar
'Waldorf Astoria' (4) | CQua IDun
'Walesby' (2) | Last listed 1998
'War Dance' (3) | IDun
'Warbler' (6) | CQua
'Warleigh' (2) | Last listed 1998
'Warm Day' (2) | ICar
'Waterperry' (7) | CBro LAma NRog
watieri | See *N. rupicola* subsp. *watieri*
- AB&S 4518 (13) | SSpi
'Wavelength' (3) | IDun
'Waxwing' (5) | CQua
'Wee Bee' (1) | CQua
'Wendy Walsh' (2) | ICar
'Westbury' (4) | Last listed 1998
'Westward' (4) | CQua EWal
'Wetherby' (3) | Last listed 1998
'Whang-hi' (6) | CQua
'Wheal Jane' (2) | CQua
'Wheal Kitty' (7) | CQua
'Whetstone' (1) | CQua
'Whipcord' (7) | IDun
'Whisky Mac' (2) | EHof
'Whisper' (5) | EWal
'Whitbourne' (3) | EWal
'White Butterfly' (2) | EWal
'White Cross' (2) | Last listed 1998
'White Hill' (2) | IBal
'White Hunter' (1) | ICar
'White Lady' (3) | CQua WShi
'White Lion' (4) ♀ | CQua EWal LAma NRog
'White Marvel' (4) | CQua CSWP EWal LAma LRHS NRog
'White Mist' (2) | ICar
'White Phantom' (1) | ICar
'White Plume' (2) | EWal
'White Star' (1) | CQua EHof ICar IDun
'Whiteabbey' (2) | IBal
'Widgeon' (2) | EWal
willkommii (13) | CBro
'Winchester' (2) | EWal
'Wind Song' (2) | EHof

'Windjammer' (1) | EWal
'Winfrith' (2) | EWal
'Winged Victory' (6) | Last listed 1998
'Witch Doctor' (3) | IBal
'Witch Hunt' (4) | IBal
'Wodan' (2) | Last listed 1999
'Woodcock' (6) | CBro CQua
'Woodgreen' (2) | EWal
'Woodland Prince' (3) | CQua
'Woodland Star' (3) | CQua
'Woodvale' (2) | Last listed 1998
'Worcester' (2) | EWal
'Xit' (3) | CBro CQua
'Xunantunich' (2) | EHof IDun
'Yeats' (3) | ICar
'Yellow Cheerfulness' (4) ♀ | EWal LAma LRHS MBri NRog
'Yellow Standard' (2) | LAma LHpC
'Yellow Sun' (3) | LAma
'Yes Please' (2) | EWal
'York Minster' (1) | EHof IDun
'Yoshiko' (2) | Last listed 1998
'Young Blood' (2) | IDun
'Young Idea' (7) | EWal
'Your Grace' (2) | EHof
zaianicus | See *N. romieuxii* subsp. *albidus* var. *zaianicus*
- var. *albus* | See *N. romieuxii* subsp. *albidus* var. *zaianicus* f. *albus*
- *lutescens* S&F 374 | See *N. romieuxii* subsp. *albidus* var. *zaianicus* f. *lutescens* S&F 374
'Zelah' (1) | Last listed 1998
'Zion Canyon' (2) | Last listed 1998

NARDOPHYLLUM (Asteraceae)
bryoides | GTou

NARDOSTACHYS (Valerianaceae)
grandiflora | GPoy

NARTHECIUM (Melanthiaceae)
ossifragum | WShi

NASSAUVIA (Asteraceae)
gaudichaudii | Last listed 1998

NASSELLA (Poaceae)
trichotoma | CHar EBee EGar EHoe EMan EMon EPPr EPla GBin LHil LJus LRHS MCCP MCLN MGed SApp SMrm SPla WCot WDyG WElm WPGP WRos

NASTURTIUM (Brassicaceae)
officinale | SWat WHer

NAUTILOCALYX (Gesneriaceae)
pemphidius | WDib

NECTAROSCORDUM (Alliaceae)
bivalve | ERos
§ *siculum* | More than 30 suppliers
§ - subsp. *bulgaricum* | CBro CHad CHar CRDP EBee ECha EPar EPot ERos ETub IBlr LBow LEdu LPio LRHS MDun MNrw NBid NOrc SOkh SSpi WAbb WBrE WCot
tripedale | CLAP

NEILLIA (Rosaceae)
affinis | CPLG CPle EBee NBid NPro SBrw WHCG

tentaculata	WMEx
tobaica	WMEx
tomoriana	WMEx
truncata	WMEx
ventricosa	WMEx
- slim x *spectabilis*	WMEx
vieillardii	WMEx

NEPETA (Lamiaceae)

argolica	See *N. sibthorpii*
aff. *betonicifolia*	EMon
DS&T 89054T	
'Blue Beauty'	See *N. sibirica* 'Souvenir d'André Chaudron'
bucharica	GBuc WOut
* *buddlejifolium*	NLar
camphorata	CSam EMFP GAbr GBar GTou MLLN MNrw MSte SAga SCro SIde WOve
cataria	CAgr CArn COlW CSev EBee ELau GBar GPoy LRHS MChe MHer MMal MSal NBro SIde WHer WLin WMoo WOak WPer WSel WWye
§ - 'Citriodora'	CArn CBot CLTr CSam CStr EBee EFou ELau GBar GPoy IIve MHer MSal NFai NFla SChu SIde SSpe WBar WBea WCHb WHer WSel WWye
citriodora Dum.	See *N. cataria* 'Citriodora'
clarkei	CMHG CSam CStr EBee EFou EMan MHar MNrw MSte NCat SAga SBla SCro SSvw SWat WPer
dinphya	Last listed 1998
§ x *faassenii*	More than 30 suppliers
- 'Alba'	CStr EBee EPfP EWTr NLar
glechoma 'Variegata'	See *Glechoma hederacea* 'Variegata'
govaniana	More than 30 suppliers
grandiflora	CLTr EFou LFis MGrG MRav NFai NSti SIde SMrm WHer WWhi
- 'Bramdean'	CMea CRDP CSam CStr EBee ECha EGar LGre MBri NCat SAga SMrm SUsu WKif WOut
- 'Dawn to Dusk'	More than 30 suppliers
- 'Pool Bank'	CRDP CStr EFou EGoo MBel NCat NFai SAga SChu SDys SGar SMrm SUsu
hederacea 'Variegata'	See *Glechoma hederacea* 'Variegata'
* *kubabiana*	EBee
kubanica	EMan EMon
laevigata	Last listed 1999
lanceolata	See *N. nepetella*
latifolia	EBee LRHS MLLN
* *longipes*	CSam CStr EBee EMan EMar EMon GBri LAst MLLN MMil MSte NGdn NSti SAga SBla SChu SCro SHel SMrm SSvw WCot WFar WHal WOut WPer WPrP WRus WViv
macrantha	See *N. sibirica*
mariae JJH 948425	Last listed 1999
melissifolia	EBee WCHb WPer WWye
mussinii hort.	See *N. x faassenii*
§ *nepetella*	CFri CStr EBee EMon GBri NBir NChi WFar WPer WWhi
nervosa	More than 30 suppliers
- 'Forncett'	CSam
- 'Forncett Select'	EBee EFou EMan NDov SDys SMrm
§ *nuda*	CPlt CSam EBee ECha EMan MLLN WFar WMaN WPer

- subsp. *albiflora*	CStr EBee ECha EGar
* - 'Anne's Choice'	CStr EWTr WCot
* - 'Grandiflora'	WPic
- 'Nacre'	CStr
- subsp. *nuda*	CBre CStr EGar EMou
pannonica	See *N. nuda*
parnassica	CMea CPlt CSam CStr EBee EMan EMil EWTr GAri LRHS MBct MSCN MWll NFla NLar SAga SMad SMrm WElm WHer WPic WUnu WWhi
- CDB 13073	SCro
§ *phyllochlamys*	CBot CLTr CPBP MSte NTow SAga CLTr CStr EBee EFou EMan EMon MMil MSte SAga SVil WMaN
'Porzellan'	
§ *prattii*	CRDP EBee EPPr SMrm
- BQE 903	Last listed 1999
'Purple Blotch'	CStr
§ *racemosa*	CArn CBot COlW CSam CSev EBee EBrP EBre ECGN ELan ELau GBar GKir LBCl LBSe LBre LRHS MBBe MChe MFir MRav NFai NGCt SBre SIde WOak WWin WWye
- *alba*	GKir
- 'Blue Ice'	CStr GBuc WElm WHoo
- 'Grog'	EFou
- 'Karen's Blue'	EFou
- 'Little Titch'	CMea CStr EBee ECGP EFou EMan GCal LRHS SAga SChu SCro SMrm SSpe
- 'Snowflake'	CBlo CBot CGle CMea EBee EFou ELan EMil ERav GCal GKir LPio LRHS MCAu MSte MWat NBir NBrk NCat NSti SChu SEas SHel SPer SRPl SSpe STes WFar WSel
§ - 'Superba'	CBlo CLTr EFou EGoo ELan ELau EMon EPPr GBuc MBro SEas WHoo
- 'Walker's Low'	More than 30 suppliers
reichenbachiana	See *N. racemosa*
salviifolia	EBee
§ *sibirica*	CBlo CFri CGle CLTr EBee ECGN ECha EFou ELau EWTr GKir GMac LGre LRHS MBri MNrw MRav MSal NBro NPri NSti SChu SCro WCot WFar WHal WOve WPer WWye
§ - 'Souvenir d'André Chaudron'	More than 30 suppliers
§ *sibthorpii*	CSam EBee MNrw WPer
sintenisii	CSWP CStr EGar
'Six Hills Giant'	More than 30 suppliers
sp. DS&T 89048T	CStr EMon
sp. DS&T 89054T	Last listed 1998
stewartiana	CFri CHar CStr GBuc GCHN MBro MFir MLLN WElm WHoo WOut WSan
- ACE 1611	EBee GBuc SMrm WLRN
- CLD 551	EMan
subsessilis	More than 30 suppliers
- AGSJ 251	SDys
- pink	CSam CStr EBee EGle EMon GBri GBuc NChi SAga WPrP WViv
* - *sensibilis*	SWat WCot
- var. *yesoensis*	CPlt CStr
tenuifolia	MSal
teydea	MNrw
'Thornbury'	Last listed 1997
transcaucasica	CStr EBee LPio SRCN
¶ - 'Blue Infinity'	NArg
troodii	EMan

tuberosa	CPle CStr EBee ECha ECoo EMan
	GBri LRHS MAvo MRav SChu
	SCob SCro SSca STes WCot WOut
	WPen WPic WWhi WWye
ucranica	Last listed 1999

NEPHROLEPIS (Oleandraceae)

cordifolia	GQui MBri NMar
exaltata ♀	ERea LRHS
- 'Bostoniensis'	MBri
- 'Rooseveltii'	Last listed 1999
- 'Smithii'	MBri
- 'Smithii Linda'	MBri
- 'Teddy Junior'	MBri
- 'Todeoides'	NMar

NEPHROPHYLLIDIUM (Menyanthaceae)

cristagalli	IBlr

NERINE ✿ (Amaryllidaceae)

'Afterglow'	LAma MBNS SSpr
'Airies'	SSpr
'Amalfi'	SSpr
'Angelico'	SSpr
angustifolia	Last listed 1998
'Atlanta'	SSpr
'Baghdad'	SSpr
'Belladonna'	SSpr
'Berlioz'	SSpr
'Betty Hudson'	Last listed 1999
'Blanchefleur'	SSpr
* 'Borde Hill White'	SSpr
bowdenii ♀	More than 30 suppliers
- 'Alba'	CBro SCoo WCot
¶ - 'E.B.Anderson'	WCot
- Logan strain	GCal
- 'Manina'	WCot
- 'Mark Fenwick'	CB&S ECha EPot GCal WCot
§ - 'Mollie Cowie' (v)	EMon GOrP IBlr MTed WCot
	WCru
- 'Pink Triumph'	CB&S CBlo CLyd EBee GBuc IBlr
	LAma LNor LRHS NRog SDeJ SPer
	WCot
- 'Variegata'	See *N. bowdenii* 'Mollie Cowie'
- 'Wellsii'	CRDP WCot
'Brahms'	SSpr
'Brocade'	Last listed 1998
'Camellia'	Last listed 1997
'Canasta'	SSpr
'Cardinal'	SSpr
'Carnival'	SSpr
'Caroline'	SSpr
'Catherine'	SSpr
'Catkin'	Last listed 1997
'Christmas'	Last listed 1997
'Clarabel'	SSpr
'Clarissa'	SSpr
'Clent Charm'	SSpr
corusca 'Major'	See *N. sarniensis* var. *corusca*
crispa	See *N. undulata*
'Cynthia Chance'	SSpr
'Dame Alice Godman'	SSpr
'Darius'	SSpr
'Dorellia'	SSpr
'Dover'	Last listed 1997
'Drucilla'	SSpr
'Druid'	Last listed 1997
'Dunkirk'	SSpr
'Elspeth'	SSpr
'Enchantress'	Last listed 1997
'Eve'	SSpr
'Evening'	SSpr

'Ffiske'	SSpr
filamentosa	CAvo CBro WCDu
filifolia	CRDP EPot GCal MNrw WCot
flexuosa	MRav SSpr
- 'Alba'	CAvo CBro EBee LAma LGre
	LRHS MRav SDeJ SSpr
- pink	Last listed 1998
'Fortune'	SSpr
¶ from Lime Close	LGre
'Gaby Deslys'	SSpr
'Gaiety'	Last listed 1997
'Glensavage Gem'	SSpr
'Glensavage Spider'	SSpr
'Gloaming'	SSpr
'Goya'	SSpr
'Grilse'	Last listed 1998
'Hamlet'	SSpr
'Harlequin'	SSpr
'Harry Dalton'	SSpr
'Hawaii'	SSpr
'Helen Smith'	SSpr
'Helena'	SSpr
'Hera'	LGre
* ***hirsuta***	Last listed 1997
humilis	CStu WCot
- Breachiae Group	Last listed 1998
- Tulbaghensis Group	Last listed 1998
'Inchmery Kate'	SSpr
innominata	SSpr
'Janet'	SSpr
'Jenny Wren'	SSpr
'Jill'	SSpr
'Joan'	CAvo SSpr
'Judith'	SSpr
'Juliet Berkeley'	SSpr
'Kasmir'	SSpr
* 'Killi'	Last listed 1999
'Kilwa'	SSpr
'King Leopold'	SSpr
'King of the Belgians'	GAbr LAma SSpr WCot
'Kingship'	SSpr
'Kola'	SSpr
'Konak'	SSpr
'Koriba'	SSpr
krigei	Last listed 1998
'Kymina'	SSpr
'Kyoto'	SSpr
'Kyrie'	SSpr
'Lady Cynthia Colville'	SSpr
'Lady Eleanor Keane'	SSpr
'Lady Llewellyn'	Last listed 1998
'Lambourne'	SSpr
laticoma	Last listed 1998
'Latu'	SSpr
'Lawlord'	SSpr
'Leila Hughes'	SSpr
'Lindhurst'	Last listed 1997
'Locharber'	SSpr
'Lord Grenfell'	IBlr
'Lottery'	SSpr
'Lucinda'	SSpr
'Lyndhurst Salmon'	SSpr
'Mandarin'	SSpr
'Mansellii'	SSpr
'Maria'	SSpr WCot
'Marnie Rogerson'	CBro CGle WCot
masoniorum	CBro CLyd CStu LGre MTho WCot
'Meadowbankii'	SSpr
'Miss Edith Godman'	SSpr
'Monet'	SSpr
'Mrs Goldsmith'	SSpr
'Natasha'	SSpr

'Nena' — Last listed 1998
'Noreen' — SSpr
'Oberon' — SSpr
'Orange Queen' — SSpr
peersii — WCot
'Penelope' — SSpr
'Pink Galore' — SSpr
'Plain Jane' — SSpr
'Plymouth' — SSpr
pudica — WCot
¶ 'Quinton Wills' — LGre
* 'Red Pimpernel' — GAbr LAma MBNS
'Rembrandt' — SSpr
'Rose Camellia' — Last listed 1998
'Rushmere Star' — SSpr
'Salmonia' — SSpr
sarniensis — CBro EBot ECha LRHS NRog SYvo
* - 'Alba' — WCot
§ - var. *corusca* — LAma WCot
- - 'Major' — EBot LBow SSpr
- var. *curvifolia* — SSpr WCot
f. *fothergillii*
- - - 'Queen Mary' — Last listed 1998
Smee No. 11 — Last listed 1998
'Smokey Special' — SSpr
'Snowflake' — SSpr
'Solent Swan' — SSpr
'Stephanie' — LAma SSpr
'Stephanie' x 'Moscow' — SSpr
§ *undulata* — CBlo CBro EBee EBot ECha ERos
LAma LBow LGre LRHS MBri
WCot

* - 'Alba' — WCot
'Vestal' — SSpr
'Vicky' — Last listed 1999
'White Swan' — LAma MBNS SSpr
'Wolsey' — SSpr
'Zeal Giant' — CBro LGre SAga

NERIUM ✿ (Apocynaceae)

oleander — CBrP CHEx CMdw EBak EBee
EEls LPan LRHS SArc SRms
- 'Album' — EEls
- 'Album Plenum' (d) — EEls LPio
- 'Alsace' — EEls ERea
- 'Altini' — EEls
- 'Angiolo Pucci' — EEls
* - 'Avalanche' — CB&S
- 'Belle Hélène' — Last listed 1999
- 'Bousquet d'Orb' — EEls LPio
§ - 'Carneum Plenum' (d) — EEls
- 'Cavalaire' (d) — EEls
* - 'Clare' — ERea SOWG
- 'Cornouailles' — EEls LPio
- 'Docteur Golfin' — EEls
- 'Emile Sahut' — EEls
- 'Emilie' — EEls ERea
- 'Flavescens Plenum' (d) — CFee EEls ERea
- 'Framboise' — LPio
- 'Géant des Batailles' — EEls ERea SOWG
- 'Hardy Pink' — ERea LPio
- 'Hardy Red' — EEls ERea LPio
- 'Hawaii' — EEls
* - 'Isabelle' — EEls
- 'Isle of Capri' — EEls ERea SOWG
- 'Italia' — ERea
- 'J.R.' — EEls
- 'Jannoch' — EEls ERea
- 'Louis Pouget' (d) — EEls
- 'Madame Allen' (d) — EEls
- 'Madame Léon Blum' — Last listed 1999
- 'Madame Planchon' (d) — ERea

- 'Magaly' — ERea
- 'Maresciallo Graziani' — EEls
- 'Margaritha' — EEls ERea
- 'Marie Gambetta' — EEls
- subsp. *mascatense* — EEls
- 'Mont Blanc' — EEls LPio
- 'Mrs Roeding' — See *N. oleander* 'Carneum Plenum'
- 'Nana Rosso' — EEls
- 'Navajo' — LPio
- 'Oasis' — EEls
- subsp. *oleander* — EEls
- 'Papa Gambetta' — EEls
* - 'Peach Blossom' — ERea
- 'Petite Pink' — EEls
- 'Petite Red' — EEls
- 'Petite Salmon' — EEls
- 'Professeur Granel' (d) — EEls ERea LPio
- 'Provence' (d) — EEls ERea SOWG
- 'Rosario' (d) — ERea
- 'Rose des Borrels' — EEls
- 'Rosée du Ventoux' (d) — EEls ERea SOWG
- 'Roseum' — EEls
- 'Roseum Plenum' (d) — CB&S CRHN EEls
- 'Rosita' — EEls ERea
- 'Sealy Pink' — CB&S EEls
* - 'Snowflake' — EEls ERea SOWG
- 'Soeur Agnès' — EEls ERea
- 'Soleil Levant' — EEls ERea
- 'Souvenir d'Emma Schneider' — EEls
- 'Souvenir des Iles Canaries' — EEls
- 'Splendens' (d) — ERea SOWG
- 'Splendens Giganteum' (d) — EEls
- 'Splendens Giganteum Variegatum' (d/v) — EEls
- 'Tito Poggi' — EEls ERea SHFr
- 'Variegatum' — CBot CGre ERea
- 'Variegatum Plenum' (d) — WCot
- 'Villa Romaine' — EEls
- 'Ville de Carpentras' (d) — EEls ERea
* - 'Ville de la Londe' — Last listed 1999
* - 'Yellow Queen' — CB&S

NERTERA (Rubiaceae)

balfouriana — ECou
depressa — Last listed 1999
granadensis — MBri

NEVIUSIA (Rosaceae)

alabamensis — Last listed 1999

NICANDRA (Solanaceae)

physalodes — CArn EMan EWTr EWll MGed
NHex SSoC SYvo WRos
- *alba* — LCot
* - 'Blacky' — SMrm
¶ - 'Splash of Cream' (v) — CGdn EMan EWll
- 'Violacea' — SLod SRms

NICOTIANA (Solanaceae)

acuminata — Last listed 1998
alata — Last listed 1998
colossea — CTrG
glauca — CGle EMan EMar ERea MSte
WHer
knightiana — EBee
langsdorffii ♀ — CB&S CHad ELan EMan EMar
EMon GBri LPio SMrm SUsu WEas
WHer WMaN WOve WPer WRus

- 'Cream Splash' (v)   CPla EMar EMon WBar WHer
* **mutabilis**   CSpe
   noctiflora   Last listed 1998
   rustica   Last listed 1998
   suaveolens   WRus
   sylvestris ♀   CHEx CHad COIW CSpe CTrC
     EMan EMar EWTr LPVe MGed
     SEND SMrm WEas WHer WRus
     WWye
   tabacum   CArn WWye
¶ - Hungarian   Ilve

NIDULARIUM (Bromeliaceae)
   flandria   See *Neoregelia carolinae*
     (Meyendorffii Group) 'Flandria'

NIEREMBERGIA (Solanaceae)
§ **caerulea** ♀   ECha EHrv EMan EWTr IMGH
   frutescens   See *N. scoparia*
   hippomanica   See *N. caerulea*
§ **repens**   CFee CTri EDAr EPot GKir LRHS
     MBro NBus NLAp NNrd SSca
     WWat WWin
   rivularis   See *N. repens*
§ **scoparia**   CGle EBee MGrG WRus
   - 'Mont Blanc'   LRHS
   - 'Purple Robe'   LRHS

NIPHAEA (Gesneriaceae)
   oblonga   NMos

x NIPHIMENES (Gesneriaceae)
   'Lemonade'   NMos

NIPPONANTHEMUM (Asteraceae)
§ **nipponicum**   CNic CSam EBee GCal GMac LAst
     LPio NSti SRms WCot WPGP
   - roseum   CSam

NOCCAEA See THLASPI

NOLINA (Agavaceae)
   beldingii   Last listed 1999
   brevifolia   Last listed 1999
   durangensis   CTbh
   greenii   Last listed 1999
   longifolia   Last listed 1997
   palmeri   Last listed 1999
   parryi   WCot
§ **recurvata** ♀   CRoM LCns LPal MBri
   texana   NWCA

NOMOCHARIS (Liliaceae)
   aperta   EPot GBuc GCrs GDra GKir LAma
     MDun NDlv SSpi WAbe WCru
   - ACE 2271   Last listed 1998
   - CLD 229   GBuc GKir
   farreri   GCrs GKir WCru
   x **finlayorum**   GCrs WAbe
   mairei   See *N. pardanthina*
   meleagrina   EPot LAma
   nana   See *Lilium nanum*
§ **pardanthina**   GBuc LAma NHar NSla WAbe
     WCru
   - f. **punctulata**   GBuc GGGa GKir MDun WCru
   saluenensis   GTou WAbe WCru

NONEA (Boraginaceae)
   lutea   CMea MFir MLLN NOrc WAbb
     WByw WCHb WHal WWye

NOTELAEA (Oleaceae)
   ligustrina   Last listed 1997

NOTHOCHELONE See PENSTEMON

NOTHOFAGUS ✿ (Fagaceae)
   alessandrii   Last listed 1998
§ x **alpina**   CDul CLnd CMCN GAri IOrc
     NWea WMou WNor
   antarctica   CB&S CLnd CMCN CMHG CTho
     ECrN ELan ENot GChr GGar IOrc
     ISea LPan MBar MBlu MBri MGos
     NBee NHol SPer STre WDin WNor
     WSHC
   cunninghamii   GAri GGGa ISea STre WNor
   dombeyi   CB&S GAri IOrc LHyd SAPC SArc
     SBir WBod WNor
   fusca   CB&S CDoC
   menziesii   CB&S
   moorei   Last listed 1999
§ **nervosa**   LPan SBir
¶ **nitida**   ISea
   obliqua   CDoC CDul CGre CLnd CMCN
     CSam GAri IOrc ISea NWea WDin
     WMou WNor
   procera Oerst.   See *N. nervosa*
   - misapplied   See *N.* x *alpina*
   pumilio   CMCN GAri ISea
   solanderi   CMHG GGar
   - var. **cliffortioides**   CB&S CLnd WCwm

NOTHOLAENA See CHEILANTHES

NOTHOLIRION (Liliaceae)
   bulbuliferum   GKir WCot
   - C 5074   Last listed 1998
   campanulatum   MWll
   macrophyllum   GCrs
   thomsonianum   GCrs

NOTHOPANAX See POLYSCIAS

NOTHOSCORDUM (Alliaceae)
   gracile   CPLG
   inodorum   GBuc
   - **macrostemon** CL 7/76   Last listed 1998
   neriniflorum   See *Caloscordum neriniflorum*

NOTOBUXUS (Buxaceae)
   natalensis   SLan

NOTOSPARTIUM (Papilionaceae)
   carmichaeliae   ECou
   - 'Hodder'   ECou
   - 'Seymour'   ECou
   glabrescens   ECou
   - 'Ben More'   ECou
   - 'Woodside'   ECou
   'Joy'   ECou
   torulosum   ECou
   - 'Blue Butterfly'   ECou
   - x **glabrescens**   ECou
   - 'Malvern Hills'   ECou

NOTOTRICHE (Malvaceae)
   compacta   Last listed 1998

NUPHAR (Nymphaeaceae)
   advena   Last listed 1998
   japonica var. **variegata**   CRow
   lutea   CBen CRow EHon EMFW LPBA

	MSta SLon SWat
pumila	MSta
- variegata	MSta
'Shirley Bryne'	Last listed 1998

NUXIA (Buddlejaceae)
congesta	Last listed 1998

NYMPHAEA ✿ (Nymphaeaceae)
'Afterglow' (T/D)	Last listed 1999
alba	CBen CRow EHon EMFW LGuA
	LPBA MSta SWat SWyc WMAq
	WStl WWeb
§ - subsp. *occidentalis* (H)	MSta SWyc
- 'Plenissima' (H)	MSta SWyc
- var. *rubra* (H)	MSta
'Albatros' (H)	EHon LGuA LPBA MSta SWat
	SWyc WBcn
'Albatros' misapplied	See *N.* 'Hermine'
'Albert Greenberg' (T/D)	Last listed 1999
¶ 'Almost Black' (H)	SWyc
'Amabilis' (H)	CBen CRow EMFW LPBA MSta
	SWat SWyc WBcn WMAq
'American Star' (H)	CWat MSta SWat SWyc WMAq
'Andreana' (H)	CWat LPBA MSta SWat SWyc
'Anna Epple' (H)	SWyc
'Apple Blossom Pink'	See *N.* 'Marliacea Carnea'
'Apricot Pink' (T)	Last listed 1999
'Arc-en-ciel' (H)	LLWG MSta SWat SWyc WMAq
'Arethusa' (H)	MSta SWyc
'Atropurpurea' (H)	CBen EMFW LGuA LPBA MSta
	SWat SWyc WMAq
'Attraction' (H)	CBen CRow EHon EMFW LGuA
	LPBA MSta SWat SWyc WMAq
'Aurora' (H)	EMFW LGuA LPBA MSta SWat
	SWyc WMAq
'Ballerina'	SWyc
'Barbara Davies' (H)	MSta
'Barbara Dobbins'	MSta SWyc
'Baroness Orczy' (H)	MSta SWyc
'Bateau' (H)	MSta SWyc
'Berit Strawn'	SWyc
'Berthold' (H)	CBen MSta SWyc
'Betsy Sakata'	SWyc
'Black Princess'	SWyc
'Bleeding Heart'	SWyc
'Blue Beauty' (T/D)	CBen
'Bory de Saint-Vincent' (H)	MSta SWyc
'Brakeleyi Rosea' (H)	EMFW LPBA MSta SWyc
'Burgundy Princess'	SWyc
caerulea (T/D)	Last listed 1999
candida	CBen EHon EMFW LPBA MSta
	SWyc WMAq
- var. *biradiata* (H)	SWyc
- var. *neglecta* (H)	SWyc
- var. *rubra* (H)	MSta
'Candidissima' (H)	MSta SWyc
'Candidissima Rosea' (H)	MSta SWyc
'Cardinal' (H)	SWyc
'Carolina Sunset'	SWyc
'Caroliniana' (H)	CWat MSta SWyc
'Caroliniana Nivea' (H)	CBen CWat EMFW MSta SWyc
'Caroliniana Perfecta' (H)	CBen LPBA MSta SWat SWyc
'Caroliniana Rosea' (H)	MSta
'Celebration'	MSta SWyc
§ 'Charlene Strawn' (H)	EMFW MSta SWat SWyc WBcn
	WMAq
'Charles de Meurville' (H)	CBen CRow EMFW LPBA MSta
	SWyc WMAq
'Charles's Choice'	SWyc
'Château le Rouge' (H)	MSta SWyc
'Cherokee'	SWyc

'Chromelia'	SWyc
'Chrysantha' (H)	EMFW MSta SWyc
'Chubby'	MSta SWyc
'Citrus Star'	SWyc
'Clyde Itkins'	SWyc
'Colonel A.J. Welch' (H)	CBen CRow EHon EMFW LPBA
	MSta SWat SWyc WMAq
'Colonel Lindbergh' (T/D)	Last listed 1999
'Colorado'	SWyc
colorata	MSta
'Colossea' (H)	CBen EHon EMFW LPBA MSta
	SWyc
'Comanche' (H)	CBen EMFW MSta SWat SWyc
	WMAq
'Comte de Bouchaud' (H)	LLWG MSta
'Conqueror' (H)	EMFW IArd LPBA MSta SWat
	SWyc WWeb
cordata 'Pink Pons'	Last listed 1997
'Dallas'	LLWG SWyc
'Danieda'	SWat
§ 'Darwin' (H)	CBen MSta SWat SWyc WMAq
x *daubenyana* (T/D)	Last listed 1999
'David' (H)	MSta
'Denver'	SWyc
'Deva'	MSta
'Director George T. Moore'	LGuA
(T/D)	
'Doll House'	SWyc
'Dorothy Lamour' (H)	SWyc
'Ellisiana' (H)	CBen EMFW LPBA MSta SWat
	SWyc
'Elysée' (H)	MSta
'Ernst Epple Senior'	SWyc
'Escarboucle' (H) ♀	CBen CRow CWat EHon EMFW
	LPBA MSta SWat SWyc WBcn
	WMAq
'Esmeralda' (H)	MSta SWat
'Eucharis' (H)	MSta
'Evelyn Randig' (T/D)	MSta
'Evelyn Stetston'	SWyc
'Exquisita'	See *N.* 'Odorata Exquisita'
§ 'Fabiola' (H)	CBen CRow EHon EMFW LPBA
	MSta SWat SWyc WBcn WMAq
'Fantastic Pink'	SWyc
'Fenna Harder'	SWyc
'Fiesta'	SWyc
'Firecrest' (H)	CBen CWat EHon EMFW LPBA
	MSta SLon SWat SWyc WBcn
	WMAq
'Fishers Pink'	SWyc
'Florida Sunset'	SWyc
'Formosa' (H)	MSta SWyc
'France' (H)	MSta
'Fritz Junge' (H)	MSta SWyc
'Froebelii' (H)	CBen CRow CWat EHon EMFW
	LGuA LPBA MSta SWat SWyc
	WBcn WMAq
'Fulva' (H)	MSta SWyc
'Galatée' (H)	MSta SWyc
'General Pershing' (T/D)	Last listed 1999
gigantea	MSta
'Gladstoneana' (H) ♀	CBen CRow EHon EMFW LPBA
	MSta SWat SWyc WMAq
'Gloire du Temple-sur-Lot'	CBen EMFW MSta SWat SWyc
(H)	WMAq
'Gloriosa' (H)	CBen EMFW LPBA MSta SWat
	SWyc WWeb
'Gold Medal' (H)	CBen SWyc
'Golden West' (T/D)	Last listed 1999
'Goliath' (H)	MSta SWyc
'Gonnère' (H) ♀	CBen CRow CWat EHon
	EMFW LPBA MSta SWat SWyc

	WBcn WMAq
'Gracillima Alba' (H)	SWyc
'Granat'	SWyc
'Graziella' (H)	LPBA MSta SWat SWyc WBcn WMAq
'Green Smoke' (T/D)	Last listed 1999
'Grésilias' (H)	MSta
'Gypsy'	SWyc
'H.C. Haarstick' (T/D)	Last listed 1999
'Hal Miller' (H)	LLWG MSta SWyc
¶ 'Hassell'	LLWG
'Helen Fowler' (H)	EMFW MSta SLon SWat SWyc WMAq
¶ 'Helen Hariot'	LLWG
x *belvola*	See N. 'Pygmaea Helvola'
§ 'Hermine' (H)	CBen EMFW MSta SWat SWyc WMAq
'Hever White' (H)	MSta SWyc
'High Life'	SWyc
'Hollandia' Koster (H)	SWyc
'Hollandia' misapplied	See N. 'Darwin'
¶ 'Iga Erfurt Zwerg'	SWyc
'Improved Firecrest'	SWyc
'Indiana' (H)	CBen CWat EMFW LPBA MSta SWat SWyc WMAq
'Irene' (H)	SWyc
'Irene Heritage'	CBen SWyc
'J.C.N. Forrestier' (H)	MSta
'Jack Wood' (T)	Last listed 1999
'James Brydon' (H) ♀	CBen CRow CWat EHon EMFW LPBA MSta SWat SWyc WBcn WMAq
'James Hudson' (H)	MSta SWyc
'Jean de Lamarsalle' (H)	MSta
¶ 'Jean Forrestier'	SWyc
'Jean Laydeker' (H)	MSta
'Jean Marie'	SWyc
'Jim Saunders'	SWyc
'Joanne Pring' (H)	MSta SWat SWyc
¶ 'Joey Tomocik'	LGuA SWyc WMAq
'Julian Decelle'	Last listed 1999
'Juliana' (H)	CWat EMFW MSta SWyc
'Karl Epple'	SWyc
'Kiss of Fire' (H)	SWyc
'Labeaugere'	SWyc
'Lactea' (H)	MSta
'Laura Strawn'	SWyc
'Laydekeri Floribunda'	SWyc
'Laydekeri Fulgens' (H)	CBen EMFW LPBA MSta SWat SWyc WMAq
'Laydekeri Lilacea' (H)	CBen CRow EMFW LPBA MSta SWat SWyc WMAq
'Laydekeri Purpurata' (H)	EMFW LPBA MSta SLon SWat SWyc WBcn WMAq
'Laydekeri Rosea' Laydeker (H)	Last listed 1997
'Laydekeri Rosea' misapplied	See N. 'Laydekeri Rosea Prolifera'
§ 'Laydekeri Rosea Prolifera' (H)	CBen EMFW LPBA MSta SWyc
'Lemon Chiffon'	SWyc
'Leviathan' (H)	MSta
'Lily Pons'	SWyc
'Limelight'	SWat
'Liou'	SWyc
'Little Sue'	SWyc
'Livingstone' (H)	MSta SWyc
'Loose' (H)	SWyc
'Louise' (H)	SWyc
'Louise Villemarette'	SWyc
'Luciana'	See N. 'Odorata Luciana'
'Lucida' (H)	CBen CWat EMFW LPBA MSta

	SWat SWyc WMAq
'Lusitania' (H)	MSta SWyc
'Lustrous' (H)	SWyc
'Madame Bory Latour-Marliac' (H)	MSta SWyc
'Madame de Bonseigneur' (H)	MSta
'Madame Julien Chifflot' (H)	MSta
'Madame Maurice Laydeker' (H)	MSta SWyc
'Madame Wilfon Gonnère' (H)	CBen CWat EHon EMFW LPBA MSta SWat SWyc WBcn WMAq WWeb
¶ 'Marechal Petain'	SWyc
'Margaret Randig' (T/D)	Last listed 1999
'Marguerite Laplace' (H)	SWyc
'Marliacea Albida' (H)	CBen CWat EHon LPBA MSta SWat SWyc WMAq
§ 'Marliacea Carnea' (H)	CBen CRow EHon EMFW LPBA MSta SWat SWyc WBcn WMAq
§ 'Marliacea Chromatella' (H) ♀	CBen CRow EHon EMFW LPBA MSta SLon SWat SWyc WBcn WMAq
'Marliacea Flammea' (H)	MSta SWyc
'Marliacea Ignea' (H)	MSta SWyc
'Marliacea Rosea' (H)	EMFW MSta SWyc WMAq
'Marliacea Rubra Punctata' (H)	MSta SWyc
'Maroon Beauty' (T/N)	Last listed 1999
'Martha'	SWyc
'Mary'	SWyc
'Mary Exquisita' (H)	MSta
'Mary Patricia' (H)	MSta SWyc
'Masaniello' (H)	CBen CRow EHon EMFW LPBA MSta SWat SWyc WBcn WMAq
'Maurice Laydeker' (H)	EMFW LLWG MSta SWyc
'Maxima' (H)	WMAq
'Mayla'	LLWG SWyc
§ 'Météor' (H)	CBen CWat EMFW MSta SWyc WBcn WMAq
mexicana	LGuA MSta SWyc
'Moorei' (H)	CBen EHon EMFW LPBA MSta SLon SWat SWyc WMAq
'Mount Shasta'	SWyc
'Mrs C.W.Thomas' (H)	MSta SWyc
'Mrs C.W.Ward' (T/D)	Last listed 1999
'Mrs Richmond' misapplied	See N. 'Fabiola'
'Murillo' (H)	MSta SWyc
'Neptune' (H)	MSta SWyc
¶ 'Newchapel Beauty'	WMAq
'Newton' (H)	EMFW MSta SWat SWyc WMAq
'Nigel' (H)	MSta SWat SWyc
'Nobilissima' (H)	MSta SWyc
'Norma Gedye' (H)	CBen CWat MSta SWat SWyc WMAq
'Occidentalis'	See N. alba subsp. occidentalis
'Odalisque' (H)	CWat EMFW MSta SWyc
§ *odorata* (H)	CBen CRow EHon LGuA LPBA MSta SWyc WBcn WMAq
'Odorata Alba'	See N. odorata
'Odorata Eugénia de Land' (H)	MSta
§ 'Odorata Exquisita' (H)	MSta SWyc
odorata var. *gigantea* (H)	MSta
* - 'Jasmine'	SWyc
§ 'Odorata Luciana' (H)	EMFW MSta SWyc
odorata 'Maxima' (H)	SWyc
§ - var. *minor* (H)	CBen CRow EMFW LPBA MSta SWat SWyc WMAq
- 'Pumila'	See N. odorata var. minor
- var. *rosea* (H)	EMFW MSta SWyc

- 'Roswitha' (H)   SWyc
- f. *rubra* (H)   MSta
'Odorata Sulphurea' (H)   LGuA MSta SWat SWyc WBcn
§ 'Odorata Sulphurea   CBen CRow EMFW LPBA MSta
  Grandiflora' (H)   SWat SWyc
'Odorata Turicensis' (H)   LPBA MSta SWyc
'Odorata William B. Shaw'   See *N.* 'W.B. Shaw'
'Osceola'   SWyc
'Pam Bennett' (H)   CBen MSta
'Pamela' (T/D)   CBen
'Patio Joe'   SWyc
'Paul Hariot' (H)   CWat EHon EMFW LPBA MSta
                                   SWat SWyc WBcn WMAq
'Peach Blossom'   SWyc
'Peaches and Cream'   SWyc
Pearl of the Pool (H)   LLWG MSta SWat SWyc
'Pennsylvania' (T/D)   Last listed 1999
'Perry's Baby Red'   CBen SWyc
'Perry's Black Opal'   SWyc
'Perry's Cactus Pink'   SWyc
'Perry's Crinkled Pink'   SWyc
'Perry's Darkest Red'   SWyc
'Perry's Double White' (d)   CBen SWyc
'Perry's Dwarf Red'   SWyc
'Perry's Fire Opal'   SWyc
'Perry's Magnificent'   SWyc
'Perry's Pink' (H)   LGuA MSta SWat SWyc WMAq
'Perry's Pink Beauty'   SWyc
'Perry's Pink Bicolor'   SWyc
'Perry's Pink Delight'   SWyc
'Perry's Pink Heaven'   SWyc
'Perry's Red Beauty'   SWyc
'Perry's Red Bicolor'   SWyc
'Perry's Red Blaze'   SWyc
'Perry's Red Glow'   SWyc
'Perry's Red Sensation'   Last listed 1997
'Perry's Red Star'   SWyc
'Perry's Red Wonder'   SWyc
'Perry's Rich Rose'   SWyc
'Perry's Stellar Red'   SWyc
'Perry's Strawberry Pink'   SWyc
'Perry's Super Red'   SWyc
'Perry's Super Rose'   SWyc
'Perry's Vivid Rose'   SWyc
'Perry's Viviparous Pink'   CBen SWyc
'Perry's White Star'   SWyc
'Perry's White Wonder'   SWyc
'Perry's Wildfire'   SWyc
'Perry's Yellow Sensation'   CBen
'Peter Slocum' (H)   MSta SWat SWyc
'Philippe Laydeker' (H)   MSta
'Phoebus' (H)   MSta SWat SWyc WBcn
'Phoenix' (H)   MSta
'Picciola' (H)   MSta SWyc
'Pink Beauty'   SWyc
'Pink Cameo'   SWyc
'Pink Glory' (H)   SWyc
'Pink Grapefruit'   SWyc
'Pink Opal' (H)   CBen CWat EMFW LPBA MSta
                                   SLon SWyc
'Pink Peony'   SWyc
'Pink Platter' (T/D)   CBen
'Pink Pumpkin'   LLWG SWyc
'Pink Sensation' (H)   CBen CWat EMFW LGuA MSta
                                   SWat SWyc WMAq
'Pink Shadow'   SWyc
'Pink Sparkle'   SWyc
'Pink Starlet'   SWyc
'Pink Sunrise'   MSta SWyc
'Pöstlingberg' (H)   MSta SWyc
'Président Viger' (H)   MSta SWyc
'Pride of Palm Beach'   SWyc

'Princess Elizabeth' (H)   EHon EMFW LLWG LPBA MSta
                                   SWyc
'Pygmaea Alba'   See *N. tetragona*
§ 'Pygmaea Helvola' (H) ♀   CBen CRow EHon EMFW LGuA
                                   LPBA MSta SWat SWyc WMAq
                                   WWeb
'Pygmaea Rubis' (H)   CRow EHon LPBA MSta SWat
                                   SWyc WMAq
'Pygmaea Rubra' (H)   CBen CWat EMFW LGuA MSta
                                   SWyc WMAq
'Radiant Red' (T/D)   SWyc
'Ray Davies' (H)   MSta SWyc
'Red Beauty'   Last listed 1999
'Red Cup' (T)   Last listed 1999
'Red Flare' (T/N)   Last listed 1999
'Red Sensation'   SWyc
'Red Spider'   SWyc
'Reflected Flame'   SWyc
'Regann'   SWyc
'Rembrandt' Koster (H)   SWyc
'Rembrandt' misapplied   See *N.* 'Météor'
'René Gérard' (H)   CBen CWat EHon EMFW LPBA
                                   MSta SWat SWyc WBcn WMAq
'Rio'   Last listed 1997
'Robinsoniana' (H)   EMFW MSta SWyc
'Rosa Mundi'   SWyc
'Rosanna'   SWyc
'Rosanna Supreme' (H)   MSta SWat SWyc
'Rose Arey' (H)   CBen CRow EHon EMFW LPBA
                                   MSta SWat SWyc WBcn WMAq
'Rose Magnolia' (H)   EMFW MSta SLon SWat SWyc
§ 'Rosea' (H)   CBen EMFW LPBA MSta SWyc
                                   WMAq
'Rosea Minima'   SWyc
'Rosennymphe' (H)   CBen LPBA MSta SWat SWyc
                                   WMAq
'Rosette'   Last listed 1997
'Rosita' (H)   MSta
'Rosy Morn' (H)   EMFW MSta SWyc
'Saint Louis' (T/D)   Last listed 1999
'Saint Louis Gold' (T/D)   Last listed 1999
'Sanguinea' (H)   EMFW MSta SWyc
'Seignouretti' (H)   EMFW MSta SWyc WBcn WMAq
'Senegal' (H)   MSta SWyc
'Sioux' (H)   CBen CWat EHon EMFW LPBA
                                   MSta SWat SWyc WMAq
'Sir Galahad' (T/N)   Last listed 1999
'Sirius' (H)   CBen CWat EMFW MSta SWat
                                   SWyc
'Solfatare' (H)   EMFW MSta SWyc
'Somptuosa' (H)   EMFW MSta SWyc WMAq
'Souvenir de Fridolfing'   SWyc
  (H)
'Souvenir de Jules   MSta SWyc
  Jacquier' (H)
'Speciosa' (H)   MSta
'Spectabilis' (H)   MSta
'Splendida' (H)   MSta SWyc WMAq
'Stardust'   SWyc
'Steven Strawn'   SWyc
'Sturtevantii' (T/N)   Last listed 1999
'Suavissima' (H)   MSta
'Sultan' (H)   EMFW MSta SWyc
'Sunburst'   SWyc
'Sunny Pink'   SWyc
'Sunrise'   See *N.* 'Odorata Sulphurea
                                   Grandiflora'
'Superba' (H)   MSta
'Sylphida' (H)   MSta
'Temple Fire' (H)   MSta
§ *tetragona* (H)   CBen CRow EHon EMFW LGuA
                                   LPBA MSta SWyc WMAq

- 'Alba'	See *N. tetragona*
- 'Johann Pring' (H)	EMFW
§ - var. *rubra* (H)	MSta
'Texas Dawn' (H)	EMFW LGuA MSta SWyc WMAq
'Thomas O'Brian'	SWyc
tuberosa (H)	CBen LPBA MSta SWyc WMAq
'Tuberosa Flavescens'	See *N.* 'Marliacea Chromatella'
tuberosa 'Maxima' (H)	MSta
- 'Richardsonii' (H)	EHon EMFW MSta SWyc WWeb
- 'Rosea'	See *N.* 'Rosea'
'Tulipiformis' (H)	MSta
'Venus'	SWyc
'Venusta' (H)	MSta SWyc
'Vera Louise' (H)	MSta SWyc
'Vésuve' (H)	CWat EMFW MSta SWat SWyc
'Victoria Longwood' (T)	MSta
'Virginalis' (H)	MSta SWat SWyc
'Virginia' (H)	MSta SWyc
§ 'W.B. Shaw' (H)	CBen EHon EMFW LPBA MSta
	SWat SWyc WMAq
'Walter Pagels'	MSta SWyc WMAq
'Weymouth Red'	CBen
'White Cup'	SWyc
'White Sultan'	SWyc
'William Doogue' (H)	EMFW MSta SWyc WBcn
'William Falconer' (H)	CBen CWat EMFW LPBA MSta
	SLon SWat SWyc
'Wood's White Knight' (T/N)	Last listed 1999
'Wow'	SWyc
'Wucai'	SWyc
'Yellow Dazzler' (T/D)	Last listed 1999
'Yellow Princess'	SWyc
'Yellow Queen'	SWyc
'Yellow Sensation'	SWyc
'Yogi-gi'	SWyc
'Yul Ling'	EMFW LLWG SWat SWyc
'Ziyu'	SWyc

NYMPHOIDES (Menyanthaceae)

peltata	CRDP CWat ECoo EMFW LGuA
	MHew NDea SLon SWat SWyc
	WMAq
§ - 'Bennettii'	CBen EHon IBlr LPBA MSta

NYSSA (Cornaceae)

aquatica	CMCN CTho SSpi SSta
sinensis ♀	CAbP CB&S CDoC CEnd CGre
	CMCN CPMA CSam CTho ELan
	EPfP GKir LPan LRHS MBri
	NHol SBrw SRPl SReu SSpi SSta
	WBod WCwm WNor WPGP WPat
	WWat
sylvatica ♀	CB&S CDoC CDul CLnd CMCN
	CPMA CSam CTho ELan EMil
	GChr GKir LPan LRHS MBar MBri
	MGos MMea WNea SBrw SLim
	SPer SReu SSpi SSta WBod WDin
	WNor WPGP WWat
- 'Jermyns Flame'	SSpi
- 'Sheffield Park'	LRHS SSpi
- 'Windsor'	LRHS SSpi
- 'Wisley Bonfire'	LRHS SSpi

OAKESIELLA See UVULARIA

OCHAGAVIA (Bromeliaceae)
rosea	CHEx

OCHNA (Ochnaceae)
serrulata	Last listed 1999

OCIMUM (Lamiaceae)

'African Blue'	CArn EOHP GPoy WJek
§ *americanum*	WHer WPer
- 'Meng Luk'	See *O. americanum*
¶ - 'Spice'	MChe NGHP WPer
basilicum	CArn CSev EDAr EEls GPoy LRHS
	MBri MChe MMal SIde SWat
	WGwG WHer WPer WSel WWye
- 'Anise'	See *O. basilicum* 'Horapha'
- *campborata*	See *O. kilimandscharicum*
* - 'Cinnamon'	CSev LRHS MChe MHer MMal
	MSal NGHP SHDw WGwG WHer
	WJek WPer WSel
- 'Dark Opal'	CBod MHer NGHP SHDw WJek
	WSel
- 'Genovese'	ELau MHer WGwG
- 'Glycyrrhiza'	See *O. basilicum* 'Horapha'
- 'Green Globe'	MChe WGwG
- 'Green Ruffles'	LRHS MChe SWat WJek WSel
- 'Holy'	See *O. tenuiflorum*
§ - 'Horapha'	CArn CSev EDAr EOHP GPoy
	MChe MHer MMal MSal NGHP
	SIde WJek WPer
* - 'Horapha Nanum'	NGHP WJek
- 'Minette'	Last listed 1999
- 'Napolitano'	CBod MChe MHer MMal NGHP
	SIde SWat WJek WPer
- 'New Guinea'	EOHP
- 'Purple Ruffles'	EOHP MChe MMal SIde SWat
	WJek WPer WSel
- var. *purpurascens*	CArn CSev GPoy MBri MChe SIde
	WGwG WHer WPer
- 'Red Rubin'	EOHP MChe MHer NGHP WGwG
	WJek
- 'Thai'	See *O. basilicum* 'Horapha'
canum	See *O. americanum*
x *citriodorum*	CArn LRHS MChe MHer MMal
	MSal NGHP SHDw SIde SWat
	WGwG WJek WPer WSel
I - 'Lime'	WJek
- 'Siam Queen'	EDAr LRHS WJek
gratissimum	ELau
§ *kilimandscharicum*	Last listed 1999
- x *basilicum*	GPoy
var. *purpurascens*	
minimum	CArn CBod CSev ELau GPoy
	LRHS MBri MChe MHer SIde
	WHer WJek WPer WSel WWye
sanctum	See *O. tenuiflorum*
¶ 'Spicy Globe'	WJek
§ *tenuiflorum*	CArn CSev EDAr GPoy LRHS
	MChe MSal NGHP SHDw SIde
	SWat WHer WJek WPer

ODONTONEMA (Acanthaceae)
strictum	LHil WMul

OEMLERIA (Rosaceae)
§ *cerasiformis*	CB&S CPle EPfP MWat SSpi WCot
	WEas WHCG WPGP WSHC WWat
	WWin

OENANTHE (Apiaceae)
aquatica 'Variegata'	EMFW
crocata	Last listed 1998
fluviatilis	Last listed 1997
* *javanica* 'Atropurpurea'	EHoe
- 'Flamingo'	CBen CRow EBee ELan EMan

EMar EMon EPri EWTr GGar LFis
LRHS MBNS MBel MNrw MSCN
NBro NHol SAga SCoo SLod SLon
SUsu WCot WFar WHer WMAq
WOve WPer

pimpinelloides   Last listed 1997

OENOTHERA ✿ (Onagraceae)

§ **acaulis**   CBot CSpe EBee GCal GMac
IMGH MNrw WRos
- **alba**   CMea WCot
§ - **'Aurea'**   NEgg NTow NWCA SIng SRot
WPer
- BC&W 4110   Last listed 1997
affinis   Last listed 1999
'African Sun'[PBR]   EMan SBod SRot
* **alpina**   Last listed 1998
'Apricot Delight'   ECoo EMan EWTr LRHS MCCP
MDCh NCut NEgg WMoo
argillicola   WPer
'Beach'   SUsu
berlandieri   See *O. speciosa* 'Rosea'
§ **biennis**   CArn CKin CRow CSev EBrP EBre
EHoe ELau GPoy LBCl LBSe LBre
MBBe MChe MHer MHew MMal
MRav NBro SBre SIde WHer WJek
WOak WPer
brachycarpa   EBee
brevipes   Last listed 1997
caespitosa   CPBP EBee EMan MGed MTho
NRib WHer
¶ - subsp. **caespitosa**   NWCA
    NNS 93-505
- subsp. **marginata**   Last listed 1999
* **campylocalyx**   NBur WUnu
cheiranthifolia   WPer
childsii   See *O. speciosa* 'Rosea'
cinaeus   See *O. fruticosa* subsp. *glauca*
'Colin Porter'   CInt EBur EDAr LFis MNrw
NWCA WUnu
coryi   EBee
¶ 'Crown Imperial'   WWeb
deltoides   Last listed 1997
- var. **howellii**   SMrm
§ **elata** subsp. **bookeri**   EBee EMan WPer
erythrosepala   See *O. glaziouana*
flava   EBee
fremontii   Last listed 1997
§ **fruticosa**   EBrP EBre LBCl LBSe LBre MBBe
NBro SBre SPlb
- 'Camel' (v)   CPlt EBee EGle EMan EPPr LHop
SAga SUsu WCot WWeb
- Fireworks   See *O. fruticosa* 'Fyrverkeri'
- subsp. **fruticosa**   EBee
§ - 'Fyrverkeri' ♀   More than 30 suppliers
§ - subsp. **glauca** ♀   CBlo CElw COlW EBrP EBre EPfP
EWTr LBCl LBSe LBre MBBe MBct
MNrw MTho NBro SBre SPet
SRms WEas WPer
- - 'Erica Robin' (v)   CBos CElw CMGP CMea CMil
EBee EFou EGle EGra EMan EMar
EMon GBuc LAst LHop LRHS
MArl MAvo MGrG MRav NPro
SAga SCob SMrm SSpe SUsu WCot
WHil WPGP WSan
- - 'Frühlingsgold' (v)   EMon SUsu WCot
¶ - - 'Goudsberg'   SMrm
¶ - - narrow grey leaved   SUsu
- - Solstice   See *O. fruticosa* subsp. *glauca*
'Sonnenwende'
§ - - 'Sonnenwende'   CBre CElw EBee EBrP EBre EMon
EWTr LBCl LBSe LBre LRHS MBBe

MLLN NPro SBre SOkh
- - 'Sundrops'   CLTr
- - 'Sunspot' (v)   GBuc
- Highlight   See *O. fruticosa* 'Hoheslicht'
§ - 'Hoheslicht'   Last listed 1998
- 'Lady Brookeborough'   LHop MRav
- 'Michelle Ploeger'   EBee EBrP EBre EMan LBCl LBSe
LBre MBBe SBre
- var. **riparia**   SOkh WRus
- 'Silberblatt'   MAvo MMil
- 'Yellow River'   LRHS MHar WRHF
- 'Youngii'   EBee EPfP EWTr LFis LIck MCCP
MLLN SCob WPer
glabra hort.   ECha NSti SIng SUsu
- Miller   See *O. biennis*
§ **glaziouana**   CFri CSam ECoo EOHP IBlr IIve
NBir SIde WCot WOut WPer
WWye
heterantha   EBee
* 'Hollow Meadows'   Last listed 1998
bookeri   See *O. elata* subsp. *bookeri*
kunthiana   CStr EBee EDAr EGoo EMan GCal
LRHS NCut NWCA SCob SSvw
WPer
§ **laciniata**   Last listed 1997
lamarckiana   See *O. glaziouana*
lavandulifolia   Last listed 1998
'Lemon Sunset'   EBee ECoo LAst MCCP NCut
SWat WMoo
linearis   See *O. fruticosa*
'Longest Day'   EFou EPfP LRHS MArl MBrN NFai
WHil
§ **macrocarpa** ♀   More than 30 suppliers
- 'Greencourt Lemon'   Last listed 1998
macrosceles   EBee
mexicana   See *O. laciniata*
missouriensis   See *O. macrocarpa*
* **mollis**   EBee
'Moonlight'   Last listed 1999
muricata   EBee
nuttallii   NCut
oakesiana   EBee
odorata Jacquin   CArn CSpe GCal IBlr LHil NOrc
- Hook. & Arn.   See *O. biennis*
- hort.   See *O. stricta, O. glaziouana*
- cream   WHal
- 'Sulphurea'   See *O. stricta* 'Sulphurea'
organensis   EBee MLLN
pallida   EWTr IBlr NCut NFai SWat
- 'Innocence'   CBot ECtt LRHS MBNS SRot WHer
WPer
- subsp. **trichocalyx**   Last listed 1997
- 'Wedding Bells'   EBee NPer
'Penelope Hobhouse'   GBuc SAga SUsu SWat
§ **perennis**   EBrP EBee EMFP GKir LBCl LBSe
LBre LFis MBBe MTho NFai NNrd
SBre SIng SOkh SRms SWat WEas
WPer
WByw
'Pink Domino'   Last listed 1997
primiveris   See *O. perennis*
pumila   CMea CSam NPer WWye
rosea   EBee
serrulata   Last listed 1999
sp.   MTho
sp. from South America   CBlo CMea CSev EBee EMon
speciosa   EWTr MBel MRav SAga SEND
SPer STes SWat WCot WElm WHer
WHil WOut WPer WSan
- 'Ballerina'   EMan LHop WCFE
- var. **childsii**   See *O. speciosa* 'Rosea'
- 'Pink Petticoats'   CFri CM&M EBee ECha ECoo

	LAst MArl MCCP MWgw NCut NFai NPer SAga SIde SWat WBea WBro WSan
§ - 'Rosea'	CBot CFir CGle CRDP EBee ECoo ELan LIck LRHS MCCP MNrw SAga SWat WHer WPGP WPer WUnu WWin
- 'Siskiyou'	CHea CLTr COtt CRDP CSpe EBee EMan GMac LAco LHil LRHS MArl MCAu MCLN MTis NPri SBod SCob SCoo SHar SIng SLon SMrm SUsu SWat WCru WHer WMaN WRus WWeb
- 'Siskiyou' variegated	LRHS
- yellow leaved	EBee
§ *stricta*	CHad CKin CMea EBee ECGP EWFC MCAu NCut SIng SUsu WBry WPer WWye
* - 'Moonlight'	Last listed 1999
§ - 'Sulphurea'	CElw CHad CMil ECoo EGoo ELan EMan GCal IBlr MBel NPer SAga SChu SCro SMrm SUsu WAbb WBea WCot WHal WPGP WPer
'Summer Sun'	EBee EPla LBuc LRHS MCLN SMer SSpe
'Sunburst' (v)	EMan
taraxacifolia	See *O. acaulis*
tetragona	See *O. fruticosa* subsp. *glauca*
- var. *fraseri*	See *O. fruticosa* subsp. *glauca*
- 'Sonnenwende'	See *O. fruticosa* subsp. *glauca* 'Sonnenwende'
tetraptera	NWCA
texensis	SWat
- 'Early Rise'	EMan SAga
triloba	Last listed 1997
versicolor	Last listed 1999
- 'Sunset Boulevard'	CFwr CHar CM&M CMil CPou CRDP CSpe EBee ECoo ECtt EMan GBri LAst LCot MHer NBus NGHP SAga SPer SSvw WBar WBea WElm WHer WOve WPer WSan WWin
'Woodside White'	LRHS

OLEA (Oleaceae)

europaea (F) ♀	CArn CFil CSWP CTrC EEls EPVP EPfP ERea ERom GAri LCns LHyr LPan LRHS SAPC SArc SEND SHFr STre WJek WMul WNor
¶ - 'Aglandau' (F)	GVer
- 'Arbequina'	CGOG
¶ - 'Bouteillan'	MWst
- 'Cailletier' (F)	ERea
- 'Chelsea Physic Garden'	WPGP
§ - var. *europaea* 'Cipressino' (F)	ERea LPan
- - 'El Greco' (F)	CB&S CPLG ERea
¶ - - 'Manzanillo'	ERea
- 'Picholine' (F)	ERea
- - 'Pyramidalis'	See *O. europaea* var. *europaea* 'Cipressino'
- 'Picual'	CGOG

OLEARIA ✿ (Asteraceae)

albida Hook. f.	CB&S
- var. *angulata*	Last listed 1999
- × *paniculata*	Last listed 1998
algida	ECou
arborescens	GChr GEil GGar GSki
* - 'Variegata'	NPro
argophylla	ECou

avicenniifolia	CB&S CPle ECou EPla GGar GKir WGer WLRN WSHC
- 'White Confusion'	WPen WWat
canescens	Last listed 1999
capillaris	CChe CPle ECou GGar SDry SPan WTro WWat
chathamica	CDoC
§ *cheesemanii*	CDoC CMHG CPle EBee GGar SLon SPer WGer WSHC
coriacea	ECou
erubescens	CDoC CPle
- × *ilicifolia*	Last listed 1999
floribunda	CPle GGar
forsteri Tresco form	CDoC
fragrantissima	Last listed 1998
frostii	CPle WKif
furfuracea	CDoC CHEx CPle CPne
glandulosa	CPle ECou
gunniana	See *O. phlogopappa*
× *haastii*	More than 30 suppliers
- 'McKenzie'	ECou
hectorii	ECou
§ 'Henry Travers' ♀	CDoC CPle GGar GKir GQui IBlr ISea MDun SMrm
hookeri	EPot
§ *ilicifolia*	CDoC CFil CPle EBee GSki LRHS MDun SDry SPer SSht SSpi WCru WSHC
§ - × *moschata*	GCHN
insignis	Last listed 1999
- var. *minor*	WCru
lacunosa	MDun
lepidophylla	CPle ECou
- green	Last listed 1997
- silver	ECou
lirata	CDoC CPle ECou
macrodonta ♀	More than 30 suppliers
- 'Intermedia'	Last listed 1998
- 'Major'	EPfP GCHN GGar
- 'Minor'	CDoC ELan EPfP GEil GQui WPat WWat
microphylla	Last listed 1998
× *mollis* (Kirk) Cockayne	CPle GQui NFor SPer SSpi WSHC
- hort.	See *O. ilicifolia* × *moschata*
- (Kirk) Cockayne 'Zennorensis' ♀	CB&S CDoC CGre CLan CMHG CPle ISea MDun SDry SOWG WCru WWat
moschata	CPle GKir GSki
myrsinoides	CFai CMHG CPle
§ *nummulariifolia*	CDoC CMHG CPle CTri ECou EPfP EPla GKir ISea NFor SArc SDry SEND SPan SPer STre WAbe WBod WKif WSHC WWal WWat
- var. *cymbifolia*	ECou GGar
- hybrids	ECou
obcordata	Last listed 1998
odorata	CPle ECou WBod WHCG
oleifolia	See *O.* 'Waikariensis'
paniculata	CGre CHEx CMHG CPle CTri EPfP GGar GSki ISea SDry SPan SVen WAbe WGer WPic
§ *phlogopappa*	CPle EBee ECou GGar MTis SPan WBrE WCot WPic
- 'Comber's Blue'	CB&S CPle EPfP GCHN GChr IBlr LRHS NPer SPer SSta
§ - 'Comber's Pink'	CB&S CDoC CPle ELan EPfP GChr IBlr LRHS NPer SBrw SPan SPer WBod
- pink	CTrG SReu SSta
- 'Rosea'	See *O. phlogopappa* 'Comber's Pink'
- Splendens Group	CAbb

- var. *subrepanda*	CGre CPle LEdu SEND SPan WBod
§ *ramulosa*	CDoC CInt CPle LHil WGwG WKif WSHC WWal
- 'Blue Stars'	ECou LRHS WWat
- *ramulosa*	ECou
rani Druce	ISea
- hort.	See *O. cheesemanii*
x *scilloniensis* hort.	See *O. stellulata* DC.
- Dorrien-Smith ♀	GGar
- 'Master Michael'	CBlo CBot CDoC NFai SBrw SOWG SPan SPer SPla WBea WSHC
semidentata	See *O.* 'Henry Travers'
solandri	CDoC CPle CWSG ECou EPla GBin GGar GKir GOrc NFai SDix SDry SHFr SPan SPer WWat
- 'Aurea'	CB&S GQui
stellulata hort.	See *O. phlogopappa*
- DC.	CBot CChe CDoC CGre CTrG CWit ECou ELan ENot ISea LRHS MWat NSti NWea SDix SOWG SPer SPla SSta WAbe WEas WHCG WPic WSHC WStI WWeb
¶ - 'Michael's Pride'	CPLG
traversii	CAbb CB&S CDoC CFai CMHG CPle CTre IOrc SBrw SEND SVen WGer WLRN
§ - 'Tweedledum' (v)	CCHP CLyn ECou EHoe GOrP SLon SPan
- 'Variegata'	See *O. traversii* 'Tweedledum'
virgata	CPle ECou GGar GSki
- 'Laxifolia'	CTrC CTre SPan
- var. *lineata*	CPle ECou SEND WCru WDin WPic WSHC
- - - 'Dartonii'	CB&S ECou SLPl WGer
- var. *ramuliflora*	Last listed 1998
viscosa	CPle
§ 'Waikariensis'	CBlo CBot CMHG CPle CSam CTrC ECou EPla LHop LRHS MSCN SChu SEND SPan WBod WCFE WGer WWat

OLIGOSTACHYUM (Poaceae - Bambusoideae)

lubricum	See *Semiarundinaria lubrica*

OLSYNIUM (Iridaceae)

§ *douglasii* ♀	CBro EDAr ELan EPar EPot GCrs GDra GMaP NHar NMen NRya NTow SIng WAbe WLin
- 'Album'	EPar EPot GAbr GCrs GDra GMaP NHar NRya WAbe
- var. *inflatum*	EWes
- JCA 11132	SBla
§ *filifolium*	MHar MNrw
§ *junceum*	CFri EBee GAri SBla
- JCA 12289	MTho
- JCA 14211	CFir
scirpoideum F&W 776	EBee

OMPHALODES (Boraginaceae)

cappadocica ♀	More than 30 suppliers
- 'Alba'	GKir LLWP SRms WEas
- 'Anthea Bloom'	IBlr NTow
- 'Cherry Ingram' ♀	More than 30 suppliers
- 'Lilac Mist'	CBos CElw EBee EMan LPio MRav NDov NPSI WCot
- 'Starry Eyes'	More than 30 suppliers
§ *linifolia* ♀	CMea CRDP CSpe ECoo NTow WEas
- *alba*	See *O. linifolia*
lojkae	Last listed 1998

luciliae	NTow WHoo
nitida	CElw EMon GGar NRya WCot
verna	More than 30 suppliers
- 'Alba'	CBot CBre CGle EBee ECha EGle ELan EMon GAbr LAst LFis LHop MTho NChi NHol NLar SAga SCob SIng SPer SRPl SRms SSvw WBea WFar WHoo WOve WRus WWat
- 'Elfenauge'	CElw CMil EBee EMon EPPr SMrm SUsu WCot
- *grandiflora*	WCot

OMPHALOGRAMMA (Primulaceae)

delavayi	Last listed 1997

ONCOSTEMA See SCILLA

ONOBRYCHIS (Papilionaceae)

gracilis HH&K 185	Last listed 1999
montana HH&K 325	Last listed 1999
viciifolia	EMan EWFC MGed MSal WCot WWye

ONOCLEA (Woodsiaceae)

sensibilis ♀	More than 30 suppliers
- copper	CFil CRow WPGP

ONONIS (Papilionaceae)

repens	CArn CInt CKin MSal NMir WGwy
rotundifolia	CPle MSal SLon
spinosa	CKin EWFC EWll LFis MHer MSal WFar WPer
- 'Alba'	Last listed 1997

ONOPORDUM (Asteraceae)

acanthium	More than 30 suppliers
arabicum	See *O. nervosum*
bracteatum	WPer
§ *nervosum* ♀	CArn CSpe EBee EBot ERav LFis NBro SRCN SRms WFar WWhi

ONOSERIS (Asteraceae)

salicifolia	Last listed 1998

ONOSMA (Boraginaceae)

alborosea	CSev ECha EGoo EOrc GBri GCal MFir SBla SChu WEas WKif WPGP WPer
echioides	Last listed 1997
helvetica	MBro WPat
aff. *isaurica*	Last listed 1999
nana	NTow
- Mac&W 5785	Last listed 1997
- white	Last listed 1999
rutila	Last listed 1997
sericea	Last listed 1999
stellulata	CLyd NChi SSpi
taurica ♀	MOne NBir NChi SGar WWin

ONYCHIUM (Adiantaceae)

contiguum	EFer WAbe
japonicum	CBos CFil CRDP GQui NMar SBla SChu WAbe WCot
- 'Dali' L 1649	CBos SBla

OPHIOPOGON ✿ (Convallariaceae)

'Black Dragon'	See *O. planiscapus* 'Nigrescens'
bodinieri	ERos EWes SApp SMac
- B&L 12505	CHid CLAP EBee EPPr EPla MTed
chingii	GCal

- 'Chinese Whisper'   EMon
formosanus B&SWJ 3659   EBee WCru
'Fuku-ho-ryu'   Last listed 1998
'Gin-ryu'   See *Liriope spicata* 'Gin-ryu'
graminifolius   See *Liriope muscari*
* 'Haku-ryu'   EMon
intermedius   EPla ESis MSte WCot WPGP
- 'Argenteomarginatus'   EBee ERos EWes SAga WPGP
- *parviflorus*   NSti
- 'Variegatus'   See *O. intermedius* 'Argenteomarginatus'
§ *jaburan*   CHid CMGP EBee LAma LEdu MSte NHol WPnP WWat
- 'Variegatus'   See *O. jaburan* 'Vittatus'
§ - 'Vittatus' (v)   CMHG EBee EHoe EMan EPfP EWes LRHS NEgg NFla SCob SYvo WCot WFar WRus
japonicus   CBro CRow EPPr EPla NSti SSte
- 'Albus'   CLAP NHol
- B&SWJ 561   Last listed 1999
- 'Compactus'   CFil EBee LRHS SMac SPla SSpi WCot WPGP WWye
- 'Kigimafukiduma'   CMil CWSG EPPr EPla SCob WCot WGwG WRus
- 'Minor'   CCuc CInt EGar EPfP EPla NPSI WPGP
- 'Nanus Variegatus'   Last listed 1998
- 'Nippon'   EBee WWat
- 'Tama-ryu'   Last listed 1999
* - 'Tama-ryu Number Two'   ECho ESis NHar
* - 'Variegatus'   Last listed 1999
malcolmsonii B&SWJ 5264   WCru
planiscapus   CFee CMHG CPea CSWP CSev EBee EPar EPla GCal GOrn LHil MBel MRav MSte MTho NBro NHar SAga WPrP WWal
- *leucanthus*   EPPr WCot
- 'Little Tabby' (v)   CLAP EBee ESis MMoz NPro SAga SBla WCot WDyG WPGP
* - *minimus*   ERos
§ - 'Nigrescens' ♀   More than 30 suppliers
- 'Silver Ribbon'   SWat
'Rhyuko'   Last listed 1998
'Spring Gold'   EMon
'Tama-hime-nishiki'   EMon
wallichianus   SSpi WCot WPGP WWat

OPHRYS (Orchidaceae)
apifera   WCot WHer
- subsp. *trollii*   Last listed 1999

OPLISMENUS (Poaceae)
§ *africanus* 'Variegatus' ♀   CHal
¶ *undulatifolius*   MAvo

OPUNTIA ✿ (Cactaceae)
cantabrigiensis   SChr
compressa   EPVP SChr
engelmannii   CCpl SChr
¶ *erinacea*   EOas
ficus-indica   SAPC
grabamii   SChr
* *grandiflora*   SChr
* *haematocarpa*   CCpl
humifusa   ELau EOas SMad WCot
§ *lindheimeri*   CHEx EOas SAPC SArc SChr
linguiformis   See *O. lindheimeri*
phaeacantha   CHEx EOas SAPC SArc SChr
polyacantha   SChr
¶ *rhodantha*   EOas EPVP SChr
robusta   SChr

santa-rita   CCpl
tardospina   See *O. lindheimeri*
tuna   CCpl

ORCHIS (Orchidaceae)
elata   See *Dactylorhiza elata*
foliosa   See *Dactylorhiza foliosa*
fuchsii   See *Dactylorhiza fuchsii*
laxiflora   Last listed 1999
maculata   See *Dactylorhiza maculata*
maderensis   See *Dactylorhiza foliosa*
majalis   See *Dactylorhiza majalis*
§ *mascula*   CHdy WHer WShi
militaris   Last listed 1999
morio   CHdy EFEx LAma
spectabilis   EFEx

OREOPANAX (Araliaceae)
epremesnilianus   CHEx

OREOPTERIS (Thelypteridaceae)
§ *limbosperma*   CCuc EMon SRms

ORESITROPHE (Saxifragaceae)
¶ *rupifraga*   EBee

ORIGANUM ✿ (Lamiaceae)
acutidens   WCHb WLin WWye
amanum ♀   CPBP CRDP EGle ELan EWes LBee LRHS MBro NBir NTow SBla SChu SIng WAbe WElm WWye
- var. *album*   CPBP CRDP ECho EGle SBla SIng WAbe WPat
'Barbara Tingey'   CElw CPBP CRDP CSpe ECou EGle ELan EPot EWes LBee LEdu LHop LRHS MBro MHer MNrw MTho SAga SBla SChu SIng SUsu WAbe WCFE WCot WCru WHoo WPat WWye
I 'Bristol Cross'   CElw ECha NHex WPat
'Buckland'   CGle CRDP ESis LGre LRHS MSte NWCA SBla WPat WPyg WWye
caespitosum   See *O. vulgare* 'Nanum'
§ *calcaratum*   CMea ELan LRHS MTho NTow SBla SSad WAbe WPat WPyg
cordifolium   SBla
creticum   See *O. vulgare* subsp. *hirtum*
dictamnus   CArn CMea EBee EEls ELan EPot GPoy LRHS NMen SBla SHDw SSad WAbe WRus WWye
'Dingle Fairy'   CM&M EBee EGoo EMan EMar EWes GBar MHer MLLN MMHG MNrw NHex WBry WWye
'Erntedank'   Last listed 1998
'Frank Tingey'   CPBP ECho ELan SBla SUsu WAbe
'Gold Splash'   EDAr GBar
'Goudgeel'   CStr WLin
heracleoticum L.   See *O. vulgare* subsp. *hirtum*
§ x *hybridinum*   MBro SAga SBla WPat WPyg WWat WWin
'Ingolstadt'   EBee LGre SAga SCro WWye
'Kent Beauty'   CLTr CMea CRDP CSpe ECha EGle ELan EMan EPot GKir LGre LLWP LRHS MBro MCAu MSte NWCA SAga SBla SChu SCob SIng SUsu WAbe WCot WHoo WOVN WPat WWye
'Kent Beauty Variegated'   ELan
laevigatum ♀   CArn CGle CLyd CMHG CStr ELan EPot MBro MHar NBro NMir NPer NWCA SAga SBla SIng SMer SUsu WAbe WByw WEas WHoo WLin

	WPer WWin WWye
- *album*	EOHP
* - *aureum*	WJek
- 'Herrenhausen' ♀	More than 30 suppliers
- 'Hopleys'	More than 30 suppliers
- hybrids	Last listed 1997
- 'Springwood'	WCot WWye
libanoticum	EPot NTow
- hybrids	Last listed 1997
majorana	CArn CSev EDAr ELan ELau GPoy
	MChe MHer MMal MSal NHex
	SIde SWat WGwG WJek WPer
	WSel WWye
microphyllum	CArn CBot CFee CGle CMHG
	EDAr EGle ESis GBar ITim LGre
	LRHS MAvo MTho SAga SBla
	SChu WAbe WCot WCru WPat
	WPyg WWye
minutiflorum	ECho ELan MHer
'Norton Gold'	CBre CElw CLTr EBee EBrP EBre
	ECha EPot GBar GBuc LBCl LBSe
	LBre LRHS MBBe MBro MNaF
	NHex NPer SBre SIde WPyg
'Nymphenburg'	CFee ECha MSte SAga SDys SUsu
	WCru WWhi
onites	CArn EDAr EEls ELau GBar GPoy
	ILis MChe MHer MSal MWat SBla
	SIde WGwG WHer WJek WOak
	WPer WSel WWye
'Pink Cloud'	EDAr
* *prismaticum*	SIde
pulchellum	See *O.* x *hybridinum*
'Purple Cloud'	EBee EDAr
'Rosenkuppel'	More than 30 suppliers
* 'Rotkugel'	CElw EGle LGre NCat SAga WCot
	WCru
rotundifolium ♀	CArn CElw CGle CRDP CSev CStr
	ELan ESis LEdu LGre NBir NHex
	SBla SChu SMer WAbe WOve
	WRus WSan
scabrum	CArn NHex WWye
- subsp. *pulchrum*	Last listed 1999
sipyleum	EBee SBla WAbe WLin
sp. from Santa Cruz	CArn
sp. from Yunnan, China	NWoo
sp. Mac&W 5882	See *Nepeta phyllochlamys*
tournefortii	See *O. calcaratum*
villosum	See *Thymus villosus*
virens	CArn
vulgare	CArn CFri CKin CSev ECoo EDAr
	ELau EWFC GBar GKir GPoy
	MBar MChe MHer MHew MMal
	NBro NFai NHex NLan NMir SIde
	WByw WGwG WHer WOak WPer
	WWye
- 'Acorn Bank'	CArn CBod EBee ELau EWes
	MHer SIde WBry WCHb WHer
	WJek
- var. *album*	CElw LGre WHer WJek
- 'Aureum' ♀	More than 30 suppliers
- 'Aureum Album'	EMar MCLN WHer WWhi
- 'Aureum Crispum'	EDAr EGoo ELau EOrc ESis GAbr
	GBar ILis NBid NFai NHex SIde
	SWat WCer WJek WOak WRha
	WSel WWye
- 'Compactum'	CArn CRDP CSev ECha EDAr
	EGoo ELau EOHP GAbr GBar
	GCal GPoy ILis LEdu MHar NHex
	SAga SBla SIde SWat WCHb WOak
	WPer WSel WWye
- 'Compactum Album'	Last listed 1998
- 'Corinne Tremaine' (v)	SAga WHer

- 'Country Cream' (v)	CArn EBee EHoe ELau EMan EMar
	EWes GAbr LAst LEdu MBNS
	MLLN MMal MMil NArg NBir NFai
	NPri SAga SChu SHDw SIng SPer
	SWat WAbe WCot WWat
- *formosanum*	WCru
B&SWJ 3180	
§ - 'Gold Tip' (v)	CLTr CMea CSev CStr EDAr EHoe
	ELau EMar EOrc GAbr GBar ILis
	MHer NArg NFai NHex NHol NSti
	SIde SWat WCHb WHer WOak
	WWye
- 'Golden Shine'	CM&M EWes MWat NGHP SIde
	WRha
§ - subsp. *birtum*	CArn EOHP GPoy LEdu MSal
	NWoo SIde WJek WPer
- - 'Greek'	CBod ELau Ilve MHer MMal
	WGwG
- x *majorana*	EDAr ELau
§ - 'Nanum'	ESis GBar LRHS NCat WCot WJek
- 'Polyphant' (v)	CElw CHar CInt CLTr CMHG CMil
	CSev EBee EDAr EGle EMan
	EOHP ESis GBar LHop LPio MLLN
	NHex NPro NWoo WAbe WBea
	WCHb WCot WHer WJek WOve
	WSel WWye
- 'Thumble's Variety'	CBod CElw CFri EBee EBrP EBre
	ECGP ECha ECoo EGle EGoo
	EHoe EMan GBar GKir LBCl LBSe
	LBre LRHS MBBe MHer NHex
	NHol SBre SLon SSvw SWat WElm
	WWat
- 'Variegatum'	See *O. vulgare* 'Gold Tip'
- 'Webb's White'	SIde
'White Cloud'	EDAr

ORIXA (Rutaceae)

japonica	CBot EPfP SSpi WDin WPGP
	WWat

ORLAYA (Apiaceae)

grandiflora	CRDP WCot WHal

ORNITHOGALUM (Hyacinthaceae)

arabicum	CBro CGle CMea EBot ETub
	LAma LBow LRHS MBri MLLN
	WCot
arcuatum	Last listed 1998
balansae	See *O. oligophyllum*
caudatum	See *O. longibracteatum*
chionophilum	Last listed 1998
comosum	Last listed 1998
concinnum MS 452	Last listed 1998
dubium	CSut ETub LPio LRHS MMHG
	WCot WHil
exscapum	Last listed 1998
fimbriatum	EPot WCot
lanceolatum	CAvo LRHS WCot
§ *longibracteatum*	CGre CHEx CStu LHil SYvo WHer
magnum	CAvo CMea EBee ETub
montanum	LRHS WCot
- BSBE 2360	Last listed 1999
nanum	See *O. sigmoideum*
narbonense	CBro CHar EBee GBuc GVer
	LRHS WCot
nutans ♀	CAvo CBro CMea CRDP EBee
	EMan EMon EPar EPot ETub EWFC
	LAma LBow LRHS MLLN MNrw
	NMen NRog WBea WCot WPer
§ *oligophyllum*	CBro EBee EPot LRHS MNrw
orthophyllum	EPot
subsp. *kochii*	

ponticum	ERos
pyramidale	CAvo CHar EBee EBot MNrw
pyrenaicum	CAvo CMea ECha ERos WShi
- AB&S 4600	Last listed 1998
- Flavescens Group	Last listed 1998
reverchonii	CAvo CMea WCot
saundersiae	LBow
sessiliflorum AB&S 4619	Last listed 1998
sibthorpii	See *O. sigmoideum*
§ *sigmoideum*	EPot WAbe
spicatum MS 585	Last listed 1998
tenuifolium	Last listed 1998
thyrsoides	EBot LAma LRHS LSyl MBri
umbellatum	CBro CNic ELan EMon EPar ETub
	EWFC GPoy LAma LRHS MBri
	MHer MNrw NHol NRog SRms
	WBea WCot WFar WPer WShi
	WWye
unifolium MS 435	Last listed 1998

ORONTIUM ✿ (Araceae)

aquaticum	CBen CHEx CWat EHon EMFW
	LPBA MSta NDea SWat WMAq
	WWeb

OROSTACHYS (Crassulaceae)

§ *aggregata*	SChr
chanetii	Last listed 1997
furusei	EBee WCot
iwarenge	Last listed 1998
malacophylla	See *O. aggregata*
§ *spinosa*	NMen NTow NWCA WCot

ORPHIUM (Gentianaceae)

frutescens	CPLG WCot

ORTHROSANTHUS (Iridaceae)

chimboracensis	CFir WAbe WPGP WPer WPic
- JCA 13743	CPou
laxus	CPBP EBee ERos GBuc SMad
	WWin
multiflorus	Last listed 1999
polystachyus	CMdw CSpe EMan WElm

ORYZOPSIS (Poaceae)

lessoniana	See *Stipa arundinacea*
miliacea	CFri CInt CLTr ECha EHoe EMan
	EPPr LRHS WCot
paradoxa	EBee EPPr

OSCULARIA See LAMPRANTHUS

OSMANTHUS (Oleaceae)

armatus	CFil CTri EPfP LPan NHol WWat
§ x *burkwoodii* ♀	More than 30 suppliers
§ *decorus*	CB&S CTri ELan EPfP EPla GKir
	GOrc MGos MRav NWea SPer SSta
	WBod WDin WWat
delavayi ♀	More than 30 suppliers
- 'Latifolius'	GKir LRHS WBcn WWat
forrestii	See *O. yunnanensis*
x *fortunei*	CGre CPle EPfP LPan LRHS SLPl
	WWat
fragrans	LPan SAPC SArc
¶ - f.*thunbergii*	WWat
§ *heterophyllus*	CB&S CGre CLan EBee EMil ENot
	ERav GCHN GOrc LPan LRHS
	MBar NFor SBrw SCob SPer SRPl
	SReu SRms SSpi SSta WDin WStI
§ - all gold	CAbP CBlo EGra LAst MBlu SPer
	SPla WSHC

- 'Argenteomarginatus'	See *O. heterophyllus* 'Variegatus'
§ - 'Aureomarginatus'	CB&S CDoC CFil CMHG CPMA
	EBee EHoe EMil EPfP IOrc LHop
	LRHS SAga SLon SPer WLeb
- 'Aureus' misapplied	See *O. heterophyllus* all gold
- 'Aureus' Rehder	See *O. heterophyllus*
	'Aureomarginatus'
§ - 'Goshiki' (v)	More than 30 suppliers
N - 'Gulftide' ♀	CBlo CDoC EBee EMil EPfP LRHS
	MGos SCob SPla WFar WRHF WStI
	WWat
- 'Purple Shaft'	CAbP ELan EPfP LRHS WWat
- 'Purpureus'	CAbP CB&S CBot CDoC CMHG
	EHoe EPfP LRHS MAsh MBri
	MDun MGos MRav MSph NDlv
	SDry SLon SSpi WRHF WStI
- 'Rotundifolius'	CFil MBri
- Tricolor	See *O. heterophyllus* 'Goshiki'
§ - 'Variegatus' ♀	More than 30 suppliers
ilicifolius	See *O. heterophyllus*
serrulatus	CBot WPGP
suavis	GKir LRHS WWat
§ *yunnanensis*	CHEx CMHG EPfP MBlu SAPC
	SArc WPGP WWat

x OSMAREA (Oleaceae)

burkwoodii	See *Osmanthus* x *burkwoodii*

OSMARONIA See OEMLERIA

OSMORHIZA (Apiaceae)

aristata B&SWJ 1607	WCru
longistylis	Last listed 1998
occidentalis	ELau

OSMUNDA ✿ (Osmundaceae)

cinnamomea ♀	CFil CLAP NHar NMar SSpi WPGP
	WRic
claytoniana ♀	CFil CLAP EBee EPfP GCal LSyl
	NMar NOGN WCru WRic
japonica	WCru
regalis ♀	More than 30 suppliers
§ - 'Cristata' ♀	CFil CLAP CRDP ELan GCal LPBA
	MBri NHol SLon WFib WPGP
	WRic
✽ - 'Grandiceps'	NMar
- 'Purpurascens'	More than 30 suppliers
§ - 'Undulata'	ELan EMon GBin LRHS NHol
	NMar WFib WRic WWoo
schroderi 'Contorta'	Last listed 1999

OSTEOMELES (Rosaceae)

schweriniae B&L 12360	CPle SAga
subrotunda	Last listed 1999

OSTEOSPERMUM ✿ (Asteraceae)

'African Queen'	See *O.* 'Nairobi Purple'
'Anglia Yellow'	Last listed 1999
¶ 'Bamba'PBR	EWTr LIck
barberae hort.	See *O. jucundum*
'Beauty of Croftway'	SCro
¶ 'Beira'PBR	LIck
'Blackthorn Seedling'	See *O. jucundum* 'Blackthorn
	Seedling'
'Blue Streak'	ECtt ERav LPio SLon SMrm
'Bodegas Pink' (v)	Last listed 1999
'Brickell's Hybrid'	See *O.* 'Chris Brickell'
'Buttermilk' ♀	CB&S CGle CHEx CHal CLTr
	CSpe CTbh ELan LAst LHop LRHS
	MBri MLan NFai SLod SRms SUsu
	WEas WPer WRos
'Cannington John'	MArl

'Cannington Joyce'   Last listed 1998
'Cannington Katrina'   SRms
'Cannington Kira'   Last listed 1999
'Cannington Roy'   CGle CLTr CMHG CSam ECtt LFis
    LLWP LPio MBri NFai SIng SMrm
    SRms WAbe
'Cannington Vernon'   Last listed 1999
'Catriona'   Last listed 1999
caulescens hort.   See *O.* 'White Pim'
§ 'Chris Brickell'   CLTr CSev ECGP EWTr GCal MSte
    NBur WHen WPer
'Coconut Ice'   See *O.* 'Croftway Coconut-ice'
§ 'Croftway Coconut-ice'   Last listed 1997
'Dennis Weston'   Last listed 1998
'Durban'   Last listed 1999
ecklonis   CGle CHEx CTbh GMaP ISea
    MCLN NBro NFla NGdn SCro
    SMrm WBar WFar WMoo WPer
    WWin
* - deep pink   Last listed 1997
  - var. *prostratum*   See *O.* 'White Pim'
§ - 'Starshine' (v)   Last listed 1998
'Edna Bond'   MCLN WEas
'Giant'   CSpe
'Giles Gilbey' (v)   CHal CMHG CTbh LHop LRHS
    MBNS NBur NCiC SAga SVen
    WEas WLRN
¶ 'Giles Gilbey White'   LHop
'Glistener'   Last listed 1998
'Gold Sparkler' (v)   CB&S LRHS SMrm
'Gweek Variegated' (v)   CLTr NPer
'Hopleys' ♀   LHop MBNS
¶ 'Irish'   EPot
'James Elliman'   ECtt LLWP SRms
'Jewel'   COtt
§ *jucundum* ♀   CFri CMHG CMea ECha LRHS
    MCLN MMal MNrw MRav MTis
    MWat NBrk NChi NDov NFai
    NGdn NHol NPer SAga SDix
    SEND SIng SPlb SRms WCFE
    WHen WHil WPat
  - 'Ballyrogan Pink'   Last listed 1998
§ - 'Blackthorn Seedling' ♀   CPlt CSWP ECha GMac MBri
    NCiC NGdn SAga SUsu WWpP
  - var. *compactum*   CLyd CMea CPBP LHop MHer
    SMer WAbe WHen WLin
  - 'Elliott's Form'   WCot
  - 'Jackarandum' ♀   Last listed 1997
§ - 'Killerton Pink'   CBrm CMHG WPer
§ - 'Langtrees' ♀   ECtt EOrc GAbr LHop SMrm
§ - 'Merriments Joy' ♀   SMrm
'Kerdalo'   Last listed 1997
'Killerton Pink'   See *O. jucundum* 'Killerton Pink'
'Kirsty Louise'   Last listed 1999
'Kriti'   Last listed 1997
'La Mortola'   CHad CLTr
§ 'Lady Leitrim' ♀   CHEx CHea CLTr CTbh EBlw
    ECha EFou EOld EOrc GBri LHop
    LHrt LPio MArl MBNS MCLN
    MMal NBrk NBus SAga SChu
    SSvw WAbe WLin WRus
'Langtrees'   See *O. jucundum* 'Langtrees'
¶ 'Lusaka'ᴾᴮᴿ   LIck
'Mercury'   Last listed 1999
'Merriments Joy'   See *O. jucundum* 'Merriments Joy'
'Mira'   CHal
'Molly's Choice'   SMrm
¶ 'Nairobi'ᴾᴮᴿ   EWTr
§ 'Nairobi Purple'   CFee CHEx ELan GBuc NBur
    SAga WLRN WPer
¶ Nasinga® Series   LIck

¶ Nasinga® White = 'Aksillo'   EWTr
¶ *oppositifolium*   SPlb
'Painted Lady'   SCro
'Pale Face'   See *O.* 'Lady Leitrim'
'Peggyi'   See *O.* 'Nairobi Purple'
'Penny Pink'   ECtt LPio NFai
'Pink Whirls' ♀   CB&S CBot CHEx ERav LHop
    LRHS MBri NFai SRms SUsu WPer
¶ 'Pollux'   MBNS
'Port Wine'   See *O.* 'Nairobi Purple'
'Royal Purple'   Last listed 1998
¶ 'Saturn'ᴾᴮᴿ   WWol
'Seaspray'   COtt
'Silver Sparkler' (v) ♀   CBrm CMHG CSpe CTbh EBrP
    EBre ELan ERav LBCl LBSe LBre
    LHop LRHS MBBe MBNS MLan
    NBur NFai SBre SChu SRms WEas
'Snow White'   CHal SMrm
'Soler'   WWol
* 'Sophie'   CSpe
'Sparkler'   CHEx EBrP EBre LBCl LBSe LBre
    LHil MBBe MSte SBre SVen
'Stardust'ᴾᴮᴿ ♀   COtt LRHS MAsh NPer SCoo
'Starshine'   See *O. ecklonis* 'Starshine'
'Stringston Gemma'   CHal
Sunny® Alex   LRHS
Sunny® Boy   Last listed 1999
Sunny® Caroline   Last listed 1999
Sunny® Girl   ECtt
Sunny® Gustav   Last listed 1998
Sunny® Ingrid   Last listed 1999
Sunny® Lady   CTbh MLLN
Sunny® Martha   LRHS
Sunny® Sonja   Last listed 1999
* 'Superbum'   CHEx
'Tauranga'   See *O.* 'Whirlygig'
'Tiberias'   Last listed 1998
'Tresco Peggy'   See *O.* 'Nairobi Purple'
'Tresco Pink'   IBlr
'Tresco Purple'   See *O.* 'Nairobi Purple'
'Tresco Sally'   SMrm
¶ 'Volta'ᴾᴮᴿ   LIck
'Weetwood' ♀   CFri CMHG ECtt EOld GAbr GCal
    GMaP LHop MBNS MBri MHar
    MSte NBrk SMrm WAbe WEas
    CB&S EBrP EBre ERav LAst LBCl
§ 'Whirlygig' ♀   LBSe LBre LHop MBBe MBri MLan
    MSCN SBre SRms WCFE WPer
§ 'White Pim' ♀   CLTr CMHG ELan GMac IBlr
    LRHS NPer SChu SCro SDix SPer
    SUsu
'Wine Purple'   See *O.* 'Nairobi Purple'
Wisley hybrids   WEas WRus
'Zambesi'   LRHS
'Zimbar'   ELan LRHS
'Zulu'   CHal CMHG LRHS MBNS MLan

OSTRYA (Corylaceae)

carpinifolia   CB&S CDul CLnd CMCN GChr
    IOrc LRHS MAsh MBar MBlu
    WMou WNor WOrn
japonica   CFil CMCN
virginiana   CB&S CFil CMCN EPfP IMGH
    WFro WNor

OSTRYOPSIS (Betulaceae)

¶ *davidiana*   CMCN

OTACANTHUS (Scrophulariaceae)

caeruleus   Last listed 1999

OTHONNA (Asteraceae)

	capensis	CHal
§	*cheirifolia*	CBot CPle CSam CSev EBee ECha EGoo ELan NBir NFor SDry SMac SPer SRms WCot WEas WPer

OTHONNOPSIS See OTHONNA

OURISIA (Scrophulariaceae)

	caespitosa	GCrs IMGH NMen NRya NWCA
	- var. *gracilis*	GTou IBlr NMen
§	*coccinea*	CGle GBuc GGar IMGH LRHS MSCN NBir NTow SMac SSpi WWat
	crosbyi	IBlr
	elegans	See *O. coccinea*
	fragrans	Last listed 1998
	'Loch Ewe'	CPla GAbr GDra GGar IBlr MDun NHar WCot WCru WPGP
	macrophylla	CGdn GAbr GAri GBuc GDra GGar IBlr IMGH NHar WAbe
	microphylla	GCrs WAbe
*	- *alba*	CGra WAbe
	- JCA 2698501	CPBP
	modesta	Last listed 1997
	polyantha F & W 8487	CPBP WAbe
	'Snowflake' ♀	EBee EPot GAbr GCrs GDra GGar GMaP IBlr IMGH MDun MOne NBir NHar NMen NWCA WWin

OXALIS ✿ (Oxalidaceae)

	acetosella	CKin EWFC IIve LNor MHer MMal MSal NMir WCra WGwy WHer WShi
	- 'Dappled Shade' (v)	CNat
	- var. *subpurpurascens*	WCot
	adenophylla ♀	CBro CElw CMea EDAr EPot ETub GAbr GDra GGar GKir LAma LHop LRHS MBar MMal NEgg NHar NMen NNrd NRog NWCA SIng WAbe WBea WEas WPer
	- dark	GDra MTho
	anomala	WCot
§	*articulata*	LGro LRHS MTho NPer WCot WWin
	- 'Alba'	LRHS NTow
	- 'Aureoreticulata'	MTho
	- 'Festival'	EDAr
	- 'Foundation Pink'	Last listed 1999
	'Beatrice Anderson'	CPBP GCrs IMGH MBro MTho NHar NHol NMen NNrd SBla WAbe
	bowiei	CMea EPot
	'Bowles'White'	MTho
	brasiliensis	CNic CStu EPot GCrs MTho NMen
	chrysantha	SIng WAbe
	compacta F&W 8011	CPBP
	corniculata	MTho
	var. *atropurpurea*	
	debilis	CSpe LHil
	- 'Aureoreticulata'	WCot
	deppei	See *O. tetraphylla*
§	*depressa*	CNic EPot EWes MTho NBir NHol NMen NNrd NRya NSla SIng SRms
§	*drummondii*	SMrm
	enneaphylla ♀	EPot GCrs GGar LRHS MTho NMen NRya SIng
	- x *adenophylla*	See *O.* 'Matthew Forrest'
	- 'Alba'	CMea EPot ERos GGar MBro NHol

		NMen NNrd NTow WAbe WIvy
I	- 'Hythe Seedling'	Last listed 1999
	- 'Lady Elizabeth'	SBla
	- 'Minutifolia'	EPot ERos GCrs LRHS MBro MTho NHol NMen NRya SSmi WAbe WIvy
*	- 'Minutifolia Alba'	Last listed 1998
*	- 'Minutifolia Rosea'	CGra
*	- 'Patagonia'	EPot
	- 'Rosea'	CBro EPot ERos GDra MTho NHar NHol NMGW NRya SBla SIng
	- 'Rubra'	GDra NHar NHol
	- 'Ruth Tweedie'	NSla
	- 'Sheffield Swan'	NHol NMen SBla SOkd WAbe
	flava	LAma NNrd
	floribunda hort.	See *O. articulata*
	geminata	NBir
	glabra	CSpe
	'Gwen McBride'	GCrs
	hedysaroides	Last listed 1998
	'Hemswell Knight'	NHar NMen
	hirta	CBro LBow LHil MTho NNrd
	- 'Gothenburg'	CPBP ERos LBow MTho NMen
	imbricata	EPot
	incarnata	Last listed 1997
	inops	See *O. depressa*
	'Ione Hecker' ♀	CBro CLyd EPot ERos GGar GMaP GTou LBee MTho NHar NHol NMen NNrd NRya NSla NTow NWoo WAbe WIvy
§	*laciniata*	EPot ERos GCrs MTho NHar NHol NMen NSla SBla
	- dark	Last listed 1999
	- x *enneaphylla*	Last listed 1998
	- hybrid seedlings	NHar
	lactea double	See *O. magellanica* 'Nelson'
	lasiandra	CFwr EDAr EPot
	lobata	CBro ERos EWes IMGH LBow LHop LRHS MTho NNrd NTow WCot
	magellanica	CFee CHal CMHG CSpe CTri ESis GCHN GGar GMaP LBee LRHS MTho NHol SIng SPlb WBea WCru WPer
	- 'Flore Pleno'	See *O. magellanica* 'Nelson'
§	- 'Nelson' (d)	CElw CHal CRDP CRow CSpe EBee EDAr EPot EWes GCHN GCal GGar GMac LBee LRHS MTho NBir NBro NHar NHol NPer NWoo SSca WCru WLin WPer
	- 'Old Man Range'	Last listed 1998
§	'Matthew Forrest'	NNrd
	melanosticta	LBow
	nabuelbuapiensis F&W 8469	CPBP
	obtusa	CLyd CSpe ECha EPot MTho NCat NTow NWCA SSad
	- apricot	WCot
	oregana	CPBP CRDP CRow ECha GBuc IMGH NChi WCru WPGP
	- f. *smalliana*	EBee WCru WHal
	palmifrons	CPBP MTho
	patagonica	ERos GCrs NHar NHol
*	*perdicaria citrino*	EPot
	pes-caprae	CPLG
*	*pulchra*	CSpe
§	*purpurea*	CSpe LHop LRHS NHol WAbe
	- 'Ken Aslet'	CBro CFee CLyd CNic EDAr EPot NHol NNrd NTow SUsu WAbe WLin
	regnellii	See *O. triangularis* subsp. *papilionacea*

rosea hort.   See *O. rubra*
§ *rubra*   WCot
  semiloba   WCot
¶ sp. F&W 8673   CPBP
  speciosa   See *O. purpurea*
  squamata   CPBP WCot
  squamosoradicosa   See *O. laciniata*
  stipularis   CMea
  succulenta Barnéoud   CFee CSpe LHil
  'Superstar'   WAbe
§ *tetraphylla*   CM&M EBot EPot LAma LRHS
     MBri MTho NCat NOrc NPer
     NRog SSoC SWal WByw
  - *alba*   Last listed 1997
  - 'Iron Cross'   EBee EDAr EMan LAma MAvo
     MMHG NBir NHol SLod WBea
     WBro WHal WHil
  triangularis   CMea EDAr EMan LAma NBir
     NHol NPer SPar WFar WPyg
  - 'Cupido'   CRDP EBee WPer WWin
§ - subsp. *papilionacea*   EBee GGar LAma LRHS MMHG
     NRog WWin
  - - 'Atropurpurea'   EBee WCot
  - - *rosea*   Last listed 1998
  - subsp. *triangularis*   Last listed 1998
  tuberosa   GPoy LEdu WHer
  - 'Fat White'   IIve
  'Ute'   CGra
  valdiviensis   EWll GAri MDCh NTow WElm
     WSan
  versicolor   CStu EPot ERos MTho NMen SBla
     SIng SOkd SSad WAbe WCot
  vespertilionis Torr. &   See *O. drummondii*
  A. Gray
  vulcanicola   CFee CStu SDix WLRN
  zeckoevleyensis   WCot

OXERA (Verbenaceae)
  pulchella   CPIN

OXYCOCCUS See VACCINIUM

OXYDENDRUM (Ericaceae)
  arboreum   CAbP CB&S CDoC CEnd CMCN
     EPfP GKir GOrc IMGH LEdu LPan
     MBri MGos SBrw SRPl SSpi SSta
     WDin WNor WPGP WWat
  - 'Chameleon'   EPfP GKir LRHS MAsh SPer SSpi
     SSta

OXYLOBIUM (Papilionaceae)
  ellipticum   Last listed 1997

OXYPETALUM (Asclepiadaceae)
  caeruleum   See *Tweedia caerulea*

OXYRIA (Polygonaceae)
  digyna   GCHN GGar GKir NBro WGwy
     WHer

OXYTROPIS (Papilionaceae)
  campestris   Last listed 1998
  oreophila JCA 13585   CPBP
  - var. *jonesii* NNS 93-517   Last listed 1998
  podocarpa   Last listed 1999
  shokanbetsuensis   Last listed 1998
  splendens   CGra
  viscida   CGra

OZOTHAMNUS (Asteraceae)
  antennaria   CMHG WSHC
§ *coralloides* ♀   EPot GCrs NWCA SIng

§ 'County Park Silver'   ECou EDAr EPot ESis EWes NHar
     NSla NTow NWCA SBla SIng WPat
§ *hookeri*   CAbb CDoC ECou GGar NWCA
     SChu SPan SPer WPat
§ *ledifolius* ♀   CMHG CPle CSam EBee ECha
     ELan EMil GTou LHop LRHS MBri
     NBir NFor SChu SPan SPer SSpi
     WHCG WHar WPat WSHC WWat
  lycopodioides   ECou
§ *microphyllus*   ITim
§ *purpurascens*   Last listed 1999
  'Rose Dazzler'   Last listed 1998
§ *rosmarinifolius*   CB&S CDoC CMHG CTrG CWit
     EBee ELan EPla ERea GGar GOrc
     IOrc LRHS MBlu MNrw NFor
     SBrw SChu SPer WBod WBrE
     WEas WHCG WWat
  - 'Kiandra'   ECou
  - 'Purpureus'   Last listed 1998
  - 'Silver Jubilee' ♀   CB&S CBlo CDoC CEnd CHEx
     CSam CTrC EBee ELan GOrc LHil
     LRHS MAsh NFor NSti SLon SPer
     SRPl SSpi WCot WFar WHCG WTro
  scutellifolius   ECou
  secundiflorus   Last listed 1999
§ *selago*   EWes ITim
  - 'Minor'   GCrs NMen NWCA
§ - var. *tumidus*   SIng
  'Sussex Silver'   SBrw SPan WPyg WTro
  'Threave Seedling'   CSam SMrm SPan
§ *thyrsoideus*   CB&S CPLG CPle WWat

PACHYPHRAGMA (Brassicaceae)
§ *macrophyllum*   CSev EBee ECha EGle EHrv ELan
     EMon IBlr LRHS MRav NCiC NSti
     SSpi WCot WCru WEas WWin

PACHYPODIUM (Apocynaceae)
¶ *geayi*   CRoM
  lamerei   CRoM MBri
¶ *rutenbergianum*   CRoM
¶ - var. *meridionale*   CRoM

PACHYSANDRA (Buxaceae)
  procumbens   EPla WCot WCru
  stylosa   CDoC EPla MRav SMad
  terminalis ♀   More than 30 suppliers
  - 'Green Carpet'   CB&S CBlo CDoC CElw EBee
     EBrP EBre ECot EGol EPfP EPla
     GAri GKir LBCl LBSe LBre LRHS
     MAsh MBBe MBar MBri MGos
     NPro SBre SCoo SPla WRus WWat
  - 'Variegata' ♀   More than 30 suppliers

PACHYSTACHYS (Acanthaceae)
  lutea ♀   CHal ERea LRHS MBri

PACHYSTEGIA See OLEARIA

PACHYSTIMA See PAXISTIMA

PACKERA (Asteraceae)
§ *aurea*   EBee EMan MSal
  fendleri RMRP 96515   Last listed 1999

PAEDERIA (Rubiaceae)
  scandens   CPIN WCru WSHC

– var. *velutina*	WCru

PAEDEROTA (Scrophulariaceae)

§ *bonarota*	CLyd NWCA
lutea	Last listed 1998

PAEONIA ✿ (Paeoniaceae)

albiflora	See *P. lactiflora*
'America'	MCAu
'Angel Cobb Freeborn'	MCAu
anomala	CFil EPot MPhe SSpi
arietina	See *P. mascula* subsp. *arietina*
'Avant Garde'	ECha MCAu WKif
'B.G. Fahr'	MBri
'Ballerina'	CKel
banatica	See *P. officinalis* subsp. *banatica*
'Barbara'	MCAu
beresovskii	CFil MPhe
'Black Pirate'	CKel
broteroi	CLAP NTow SCou
brownii	EPot
'Buckeye Belle'	EBee EFou MBri MCAu
'Burma Midnight'	Last listed 1999
'Burma Ruby'	Last listed 1997
* 'Byzantine'	Last listed 1997
californica	CLAP
cambessedesii ♀	CBrd CBro CFil CKel CLAP EBee
	EGle EPot LRHS MHom MTho
	NBir NMen SAga SBla SSpi WAbe
	WCot WPGP
* 'Carl G.Klehm'	Last listed 1999
'Carol'	Last listed 1998
caucasica	See *P. mascula* subsp. *mascula*
chamaeleon	Last listed 1999
'Chinese Dragon'	CKel
'Chocolate Soldier'	Last listed 1997
'Claire de Lune'	MCAu MPhe
'Claudia'	Last listed 1998
clusii	LRHS
'Coral Fay'	Last listed 1999
corallina	See *P. mascula* subsp. *mascula*
¶ *coriacea* var. *atlantica*	CBro
– var. *maroccana*	Last listed 1998
'Crusader'	Last listed 1999
'Cytherea'	Last listed 1999
daurica	See *P. mascula* subsp. *triternata*
'Daystar'	CKel
decora	See *P. peregrina*
'Defender' ♀	Last listed 1998
delavayi ♀	More than 30 suppliers
– dark red	Last listed 1999
– x *delavayi* var. *lutea*	GKir WWat
– from China	MPhe
– hybrid	ENot
§ – var. *ludlowii* (S) ♀	CB&S CBlo CGle CGre CKel
	CSam EBee ELan EOrc EWTr
	GGGa ISea LRHS MPhe NBrk
	NPer SLPl SMad SPer SPlb SRPl
	SSpi WCot WEas WHoo WWat
	WWoo
§ – var. *lutea* (S)	CBlo GGChr LRHS MAsh MBro
	MWll SLon SRms STre SUsu WEas
	WHar WHil WPyg WTin WWat
– 'Mrs Sarson'	CBlo SLPl SWat
§ – Potaninii Group (S)	EBee SSpi
– Trollioides Group (S)	EBee
'Early Bird'	GKir SCou
'Eastgrove Ruby Lace'	WEas
'Ellen Cowley'	MCAu
emodi	CLAP LPio MPhe
'Fei Yan Hong Zhuang' (S)	MCAu
'Flame'	MCAu WCot

Gansu Mudan Group	CKel MPhe
'Hei Hua Kui'	See *P. suffruticosa* 'Hei Hua Kui'
'Heritage'	Last listed 1999
'High Noon'	CKel MCAu
'Honor'	MCAu
'Horizon'	Last listed 1999
'Huang Hua Kui' (S)	MPhe
humilis	See *P. officinalis* subsp.
	microcarpa
'Illini Belle'	Last listed 1999
'Illini Warrior'	MCAu
'Isani Gidui'	See *P. lactiflora* 'Isami-jishi'
japonica hort.	See *P. lactiflora*
'Jean E. Bockstoce'	Last listed 1999
'Jin Yu Jiao Zhang' (S)	MPhe
'Joseph Rock'	See *P. rockii*
kavachensis	Last listed 1997
kesrouanensis	MPhe
kevachensis	See *P. mascula* subsp. *mascula*
'Kinkaku'	See *P.* x *lemoinei* 'Souvenir de
	Maxime Cornu'
'Kinko'	See *P.* x *lemoinei* 'Alice Harding'
'Kinshi'	See *P.* x *lemoinei* 'Chromatella'
'Kintei'	See *P.* x *lemoinei* 'L'Espérance'
Kohlein's hybrid	CLAP
§ *lactiflora*	EBee ECha MPhe SSpi
– 'A.F.W. Hayward'	CKel
– 'Adolphe Rousseau'	CB&S CKel EBee LRHS MBri
* – 'Afterglow'	CKel
– 'Agida'	EBee GCHN LRHS MRav SMer
– 'Albâtre'	CKel
– 'Albert Crousse'	CB&S CKel GKir MCAu NBlu
– 'Alexander Fleming'	CKel EBee ECot GKir MCAu NBir
	SMrm
– 'Alice Harding'	WCGr
– 'Angel Cheeks'	MCAu
– 'Anna Pavlova'	CKel
– 'Antwerpen'	CKel
– 'Arabian Prince'	CKel
– 'Argentine'	CKel
– 'Armance Dessert'	CKel
– 'Artist'	CKel
– 'Asa Gray'	CKel
– 'Auguste Dessert'	CBlo CKel EBee MPhe
§ – 'Augustin d'Hour'	EBee
– 'Aureole'	CKel
– 'Avant Garde'	Last listed 1999
– 'Bahram'	Last listed 1997
– 'Ballerina'	CKel
– 'Banner of Purity'	Last listed 1998
– 'Baroness Schröder'	ELan LRHS
– 'Barrington Belle'	EBee GKir LRHS MBri NCut
– 'Barrymore'	CKel
– 'Beacon'	CKel
– 'Beatrice Kelway'	CKel
– 'Beau Geste'	CKel
– 'Beauty Spot'	CKel
– 'Beersheba'	CKel
– 'Belle Center'	MCAu
– 'Belle of Somerset'	CKel
– 'Bertha Gorst'	CKel
– 'Bethcar'	CKel
– 'Better Times'	Last listed 1999
– 'Blaze of Beauty'	CKel
– 'Blaze of Glory'	CKel
– 'Blenheim'	CKel
– 'Blithe Spirit'	CKel
– 'Bloodshot'	CKel
– 'Bloodstone'	CKel
– 'Blush Queen'	CKel ELan MBel MCAu
– 'Blush White'	CKel
– 'Border Gem'	GCHN GKir MRav SMer

- 'Bouchela'	CKel
- 'Boulanger'	CKel
- 'Bower of Roses'	CKel
- 'Bowl of Beauty' ♀	More than 30 suppliers
- 'Bowl of Cream'	EBee MBri MCAu NHol WCGr
- 'Boy Kelway'	CKel
- 'Break o' Day'	Last listed 1998
- 'Bridal Veil'	CKel
- 'Bridesmaid'	CKel
- 'Bright Knight'	Last listed 1999
- 'British Beauty'	CKel
- 'British Empire'	CKel
- 'Bunker Hill'	CBlo CKel EBee SLdr SMur SPer
	SRPl SVil
- 'Butch'	Last listed 1998
- 'Butter Bowl'	MCAu
- 'Calypso'	CKel
- 'Canarie'	LRHS MBri
- 'Candeur'	CKel
- 'Captain Alcock'	CKel
- 'Captivation'	CKel
- 'Carmen'	CKel
- 'Carnival'	CKel
- 'Cascade'	CKel
- 'Catherine Fontijn'	CKel EBee LBuc WCGr
- 'Charles' White'	WCGr
- 'Charm'	MCAu
- 'Cheddar Cheese'	Last listed 1999
- 'Cheddar Gold'	GKir LRHS
- 'Cherry Hill'	CKel
- 'Chestine Gowdy'	CKel
- 'Chocolate Soldier'	Last listed 1997
- 'Christine Kelway'	CKel
- 'Cincinnati'	Last listed 1999
- 'Claire Dubois'	GKir MCAu SMer WCGr
- 'Colonel Heneage'	Last listed 1998
- 'Cornelia Shaylor'	CKel ELan GKir
- 'Coronation'	CKel
- 'Countess of Altamont'	CKel
- 'Country Girl'	CKel
- 'Couronne d'Or'	Last listed 1999
- 'Crimson Banner'	CKel
- 'Crimson Glory'	CKel MPhe
- 'Crimson Velvet'	CKel
- 'Cringley White'	SBod
- 'Dandy Dan'	Last listed 1998
- 'Dark Lantern'	CKel
- 'Dark Song'	CKel
- 'Dark Vintage'	CKel
- 'David Kelway'	CKel
- 'Dawn Crest'	CKel
- 'Dayspring'	CKel
- 'Daystar'	CKel
- 'Denise'	CKel
- 'Desire'	CKel
- Diana Drinkwater	CKel SCou
- 'Dinner Plate'	LRHS MBri MCAu WCGr WCot
- 'Display'	CKel
- 'Do Tell'	EBee SVil
- 'Docteur H. Barnsby'	CKel
- 'Dominion'	CKel
- 'Doreen'	EBee MBel MCAu MRav
- 'Dorothy Welsh'	CKel
- 'Dragon'	Last listed 1997
- 'Dresden'	CKel
- 'Duchess of Bedford'	CKel
- 'Duchess of Somerset'	CKel
- 'Duchesse de Nemours' ♀	More than 30 suppliers
- 'Duke of Devonshire'	CKel
- 'Edith Cavell'	CKel
- 'Edmund Spencer'	CKel
- 'Edouard Doriat'	CKel

- 'Edulis Superba'	CBlo CKel EBee EBrP EBre ELan
	ENot GKir LBCl LBSe LBre LEdu
	LRHS MBBe MBNS MCAu SBre
	SPer SRPl
- 'Ella Christine Kelway'	CKel
- 'Elsa Sass'	WCGr
- 'Emma Klehm'	Last listed 1998
- 'Emperor of India'	CKel
- 'Empire State'	Last listed 1999
- 'Enchantment'	CKel
- 'English Princess'	CKel
- 'Ethelreda'	CKel
- 'Eugénie Verdier'	Last listed 1997
- 'Evening Glow'	CKel
- 'Evening World'	CKel
- 'Fantin-Latour'	CKel
- 'Félix Crousse' ♀	CBlo CKel CTri ELan EPfP GChr
	GKir GMaP LAst LRHS MBri
	MCAu SMer SMrm SPer SRms
	SWat
- 'Festiva Maxima' ♀	CBlo CKel CTri EBee EBrP EBre
	ECot ELan EPfP GKir LBCl LBSe
	LBre LRHS MBBe MBri MBro
	MCAu MTis NLar SBre SCob SMer
	SMrm SPer SRms WHoo WPyg
- 'Flag of War'	CKel
- 'Flamboyant'	CKel
- 'Flamingo'	CKel
- 'France'	CKel
- 'Gainsborough'	CKel
- 'Garden Beauty'	CKel
- 'Gay Ladye'	CKel
- 'Gay Paree'	MBri MCAu
- 'Gay Sister'	CKel
- 'Gayborder June'	CKel
- 'Gazelle'	CKel EBee
- 'Général Joffre'	CKel
- 'Général MacMahon'	See P. lactiflora 'Augustin d'Hour'
- 'General Wolfe'	CKel
- 'Germaine Bigot'	CKel MCAu
- 'Gertrude'	CKel
- 'Gilbert Barthelot'	MCAu WCGr
- 'Gleam of Light'	CKel
- 'Gloriana'	Last listed 1998
- 'Glory Hallelujah'	Last listed 1998
- 'Glory of June'	CKel
- 'Glory of Somerset'	CKel
- 'Gold Mine'	CKel
- 'Golly'	Last listed 1999
- 'Grace Loomis'	CKel
- 'Great Lady'	CKel
- 'Great Sport'	CKel
- 'Grover Cleveland'	CKel
- 'Gypsy Girl'	CKel
- 'Heartbeat'	CKel
- 'Heirloom'	CKel
- 'Helen Hayes'	Last listed 1998
- 'Henri Potin'	CKel
- 'Her Grace'	CKel
- 'Her Majesty'	CKel
- 'Herbert Oliver'	CKel
- 'Hit Parade'	MCAu
- 'Honey Gold'	EBee MCAu SVil
- 'Huge Delight'	CKel
- 'Hyperion'	CKel
- 'Immaculée'	CKel ETub
- 'Indian Pink'	CKel
- 'Ingenieur Doriat'	CKel
- 'Inspecteur Lavergne'	CKel EFou LRHS MBel MBri
	MCAu MRav SPer
- 'Instituteur Doriat'	CKel MPhe
§ - 'Isami-jishi'	Last listed 1998

- 'Jacques Doriat'   CKel
- 'James Kelway'   Last listed 1998
- 'James Pillow'   MCAu
- 'James R. Mann'   CKel
- 'Jan van Leeuwen'   CKel GKir LRHS
- 'Jappensha-Ikhu'   MBri
- 'Jeanne d'Arc'   CKel
- 'Joan Kelway'   CKel
- 'Joseph Plagne'   CKel
- 'Joy of Life'   Last listed 1998
- 'June Morning'   CKel
- 'June Rose'   MCAu
- 'Kansas'   CKel ELan LRHS MBri MCAu
                             WCGr
- 'Karen Gray'   MBri MCAu
- 'Karl Rosenfield'   CBlo CKel EBee EBrP EBre ECot
                             ENot EPfP LBCl LBSe LBre LRHS
                             MBBe MBri MBro NBee SBre
                             SCob SMrm SPer SPla SRms WFar
                             WHoo WLow WViv
- 'Katherine Havermeyer'   CKel
- 'Kathleen Mavoureen'   CKel EBee
- 'Kelway's Brilliant'   CKel
- 'Kelway's Fairy Queen'   CKel
- 'Kelway's Glorious'   CBlo EWTr GKir MBNS MBri
                             MCAu MTed WCGr
- 'Kelway's Gorgeous'   EBee
- 'Kelway's Lovely'   CKel
- 'Kelway's Majestic'   CKel
- 'Kelway's Malmaison'   Last listed 1998
- 'Kelway's Queen'   CKel
- 'Kelway's Scented Rose'   CKel
- 'Kelway's Supreme'   CKel SWat
- 'Kelway's Unique'   CKel
- 'Kestrel'   CKel
- 'King Arthur'   CKel
- 'King George VI'   Last listed 1998
- 'King of England'   CKel
- 'Knight of the Thistle'   CKel
- 'Knighthood'   CKel
- 'Krinkled White'   EBee EFou LRHS MBri MRav
                             WCGr
- 'La France'   CKel
- 'La Lorraine'   Last listed 1998
- 'Lady Alexandra Duff' ♀   CBlo CKel COtt EBee EPfP GKir
                             LRHS MBri MCAu MRav SRms
                             WCGr
- 'Lady Ley'   CKel
- 'Lady Mayoress'   CKel
- 'Lady Orchid'   Last listed 1999
- 'Langport Triumph'   CKel
- 'Largo'   Last listed 1998
- 'Laura Dessert' ♀   CKel EWTr EWll GKir LRHS
                             MCAu SPer WCGr
- 'Le Cygne'   SLdr
- 'Le Jour'   MBri
- 'L'Eclatante'   CKel MMil WViv
- 'Legion of Honor'   CKel
- 'Lemon Ice'   CKel
- 'Letitia'   CKel
- 'Lillian Wild'   Last listed 1999
- 'Lois Kelsey'   MBel
- 'Lora Dexheimer'   Last listed 1998
- 'Lord Avebury'   CKel
- 'Lord Cavan'   CKel
- 'Lord Kitchener'   CKel MPhe
- 'Lord Rosebery'   CKel
- 'Lorna Doone'   CKel
- 'Lottie Dawson Rea'   Last listed 1998
- 'Lotus Queen'   MCAu
- 'Louis Barthelot'   CKel
¶ - 'Louis Joliet'   NCut

- 'Louis van Houtte'   CKel LRHS MBri
- 'Lyric'   CKel
- 'Madame Calot'   CKel EBee LRHS MCAu MSph
                             SRms WCGr
- 'Madame Claude Tain'   LRHS WCot
- 'Madame Ducel'   CKel
- 'Madame Emile Debatène'   CKel MBNS
- 'Madame Jules Dessert'   CKel
- 'Madelon'   CKel EFou
- 'Magic Melody'   CKel
- 'Magic Orb'   CKel
- 'Major Loder'   CKel
- 'Margaret Truman'   CKel
- 'Marguérite Gerard'   CKel
- 'Marie Crousse'   MCAu
- 'Marie Lemoine'   CKel MCAu SMur WCot
- 'Marietta Sisson'   Last listed 1998
- 'Marquisite'   CKel
- 'Mary Brand'   CKel
- 'Matilda Lewis'   Last listed 1998
- 'Meteor Flight'   CKel
- 'Mikado'   Last listed 1998
- 'Minnie Shaylor'   Last listed 1999
- 'Mischief'   MCAu
- 'Miss America'   MCAu
- 'Miss Eckhart'   CKel WCGr
- 'Mister Ed'   MCAu
- 'Monsieur Jules Elie' ♀   CBot CKel EBee EBrP EBre EFou
                             EPfP EWTr GKir LBCl LBSe LBre
                             LRHS MBBe MBel MBri MCAu
                             MMil MPhe NCut SBre SPer SVil
                             WCGr
- 'Monsieur Martin   Last listed 1999
  Cahuzac'
- 'Mother's Choice'   EFou MCAu
- 'Mr G.F. Hemerik'   CKel GKir LRHS MBri
- 'Mrs Edward Harding'   LRHS WCGr
- 'Mrs F.J. Hemerik'   MCAu
- 'Mrs Franklin D.   Last listed 1998
  Roosevelt'
- 'Mrs J.V. Edlund'   Last listed 1998
- 'My Pal Rudy'   Last listed 1998
- 'Myrtle Gentry'   CKel
- 'Nancy Nicholls'   Last listed 1998
¶ - 'Nancy Nora'   SVil
- 'Nectar'   CKel
- 'Newfoundland'   Last listed 1998
- 'Nice Gal'   Last listed 1998
- 'Nick Shaylor'   MCAu
- 'Nobility'   CKel
- 'Noonday'   CKel
- 'Ornament'   CKel
- 'Orpen'   CKel
- 'Othello'   CKel
- 'Pageant'   CKel
- 'Paper White'   CKel
- 'Paul M. Wild'   MCAu
- 'Pauline Maunder'   CKel
- 'Peche'   EBee
- 'Peregrine'   CKel
- 'Peter Brand'   LRHS
- 'Peter Pan'   CKel
- 'Petticoat Flounce'   Last listed 1999
- 'Phedar White'   Last listed 1999
- 'Philippe Rivoire'   Last listed 1998
- 'Philomèle'   Last listed 1998
- 'Pillow Talk'   MCAu WCGr
- 'Pink Dawn'   CKel
- 'Pink Delight'   CKel
- 'Pink Giant'   LRHS MBri
- 'Pink Lemonade'   Last listed 1999
- 'Pink Parfait'   Last listed 1999

- 'Pink Princess'	LRHS MBri
- 'President Franklin D. Roosevelt'	CBlo EBrP EBre GCHN GKir LBCl LBSe LBre MBBe SBre SMer SWat
- 'Président Poincaré'	CBlo CKel EBrP EBre GKir LBCl LBSe LBre LRHS MBBe MRav SBre SMur SWat
- 'President Taft'	See P. lactiflora 'Reine Hortense'
- 'President Wilson'	Last listed 1998
- 'Pride of Huish'	CKel
- 'Pride of Somerset'	CKel
- 'Primevere'	EBee EWll LRHS
- 'Princess Beatrice'	CKel
- 'Pure Delight'	CKel
- 'Queen Elizabeth'	CKel
- 'Queen of the Belgians'	CKel
- 'Queen's Grace'	CKel
- 'Raspberry Sundae'	MCAu MRav WCot
- 'Red Dwarf'	CKel
- 'Red King'	CKel
- 'Red Warrior'	CKel
§ - 'Reine Hortense'	CKel MCAu MRav
- 'Rembrandt'	Last listed 1998
¶ - 'Renato'	EFou SVil
- 'Rose of Delight'	CKel
- 'Ruby Light'	CKel
- 'Ruth Cobb'	Last listed 1998
- 'Sainfoin'	CKel
- 'Sarah Bernhardt' ♀	More than 30 suppliers
- 'Shawnee Chief'	Last listed 1999
- 'Shimmering Velvet'	CKel
- 'Shirley Temple'	CBlo CKel EBee EFou ELan EWTr LRHS MBNS MBel MBri MCAu MMil NCut WCGr WHoo WPyg
- 'Silver Flare'	CKel
- 'Sir Edward Elgar'	CKel
- 'Smiling Morn'	CKel
- 'Solange'	CKel LRHS MCAu SPer
- 'Sorbet'	COtt EBee LRHS WCGr
- 'Souvenir de Louis Bigot'	CKel
- 'Spearmint'	CKel
- 'Strephon'	CKel
- 'Surugu'	SLdr
- 'Sweet Sixteen'	Last listed 1999
- 'Tamate-boko'	Last listed 1998
- 'Thérèse'	CKel
- 'Top Brass'	CBot MCAu MRav
- 'Toro-no-maki'	Last listed 1997
- 'Torpilleur'	CKel
- 'Tourangelle'	Last listed 1998
- 'Translucient'	CKel
- var. trichocarpa	Last listed 1998
- 'Utopia'	CKel
- 'Victoire de la Marne'	CKel EWTr SMur
- 'Vogue'	CBlo CKel EBee LRHS MCAu SMur
- 'Westerner'	Last listed 1999
- 'White Wings'	CB&S CBlo CKel COtt EBee ELan EPfP GKir LRHS MBri NBee SPer
- 'Whitleyi Major' ♀	CKel GKir LRHS
- 'Wiesbaden'	CKel MCAu
- 'Wilbur Wright'	CKel
- 'Windsor Lad'	CKel
- 'Wings of Love'	CKel
- 'Winston Churchill'	CKel
- 'Wladyslawa'	Last listed 1999
- 'Zus Braun'	CKel
- 'Zuzu'	Last listed 1999
'Late Windflower'	ECha
x lemoinei	WHal
§ - 'Alice Harding' (S)	CKel MCAu SPer
§ - 'Chromatella' (S)	CKel LAma
§ - 'L'Espérance'	LAma
§ - 'Souvenir de Maxime Cornu' (S)	CKel LAma LRHS MCAu SPer
lithophila	See P. tenuifolia subsp. lithophila
lobata 'Fire King'	See P. peregrina
'Lois Arleen'	Last listed 1998
ludlowii	See P. delavayi var. ludlowii
lutea	See P. delavayi var. lutea
- var. ludlowii	See P. delavayi var. ludlowii
macrophylla	MPhe
- from W Georgia	Last listed 1999
'Mai Fleuri'	LRHS MCAu WTin
mairei	MPhe
§ mascula	CAvo CBro EPfP LRHS NBir SCou
§ - subsp. arietina	EBee MHom SCou WKif
- - 'Northern Glory'	GKir LSpr WCot
§ - subsp. mascula	CBro EPot SBla WCot WWoo
- - from SE Georgia	WPGP
§ - subsp. russoi	SCou
* - - var. leiocarpa	SCou
§ - subsp. triternata	CLAP MPhe SBla SSpi
- - from Crimea	WPGP
mlokosewitschii ♀	More than 30 suppliers
- from E Georgia	Last listed 1998
mollis	See P. officinalis subsp. villosa
'Montezuma'	MCAu
'Moonrise'	Last listed 1998
'Nymphe'	CKel LRHS MCAu MRav SCou WCGr WHoo
obovata ♀	CLAP GKir SSpi
- var. alba ♀	GBin NWoo WAbe WEas
- - 'Grandiflora'	GKir MRav MWgw
officinalis	CBlo CFil NBrk SCou
- 'Alba Plena'	CBlo CKel CPou GMaP LRHS MBri MRav SPer
- 'Anemoniflora Rosea' ♀	GKir LRHS MBri MCAu
§ - subsp. banatica	SSpi
- - WM 9727	MPhe
- 'China Rose'	GKir LRHS
- subsp. humilis	See P. officinalis subsp. microcarpa
- 'James Crawford Weguelin'	WCot
- 'Lize van Veen'	GKir
§ - subsp. microcarpa	EBee SBla SCou SSpi
- 'Mutabilis Plena'	IBlr
- 'Rosea Plena' ♀	CBlo CKel EBee EPfP GAbr LRHS MCAu MRav NMGW SPer SWat WLRN
- 'Rosea Superba Plena'	CKel EFou SLdr
- 'Rubra Plena' ♀	CBlo CKel CPou EBee EFou EPfP GKir LRHS MBri MCAu SPer SRms SWat WCot WFar
§ - subsp. villosa	ELan LRHS MBri SCou
- WM 9821 from Slovenia	MPhe
ostii	CKel MPhe
¶ - dark-flowered (S)	CKel
papaveracea	See P. suffruticosa
paradoxa	See P. officinalis subsp. microcarpa
'Paula Fay'	MCAu MRav
'Peppermint Stick'	Last listed 1999
§ peregrina	CFil CLAP EBee ECho MPhe NWoo SBla SSpi
- from Macedonia	WPGP
§ - 'Otto Froebel' ♀	CBlo EBrP EBre GKir LBCl LBSe LBre LRHS MBBe MBri NLar SBre WCot
- 'Sunshine'	See P. peregrina 'Otto Froebel'
potaninii	See P. delavayi Potaninii Group
* 'Raspberry Ice'	Last listed 1999
'Red Charm'	EFou MCAu
'Reine Supreme'	Last listed 1999

'Requiem' Last listed 1999
rhodia MPhe
§ **rockii** (S) MPhe MWll SSpi
¶ – 'Fen He' (S) MPhe
¶ – 'He Ping Lian' MPhe
¶ – 'Hong Lian' (S) MPhe
romanica See *P. peregrina*
'Rose Garland' Last listed 1998
'Roselette' Last listed 1998
russoi See *P. mascula* subsp. *russoi*
'Scarlett O'Hara' Last listed 1999
sinensis See *P. lactiflora*
'Smouthii' GKir
steveniana CLAP MPhe
 – from SE Georgia Last listed 1999
§ **suffruticosa** CBlo CPMA EBee ELan GOrc LPan
 MGos MPhe SRPl SSpi WStI
¶ – 'Akashigata' (S) CKel
* – 'Alice Palmer' CKel
 – 'Bai Yu' (S) CKel MCAu MPhe
 – 'Bang Ning Zi' (S) MPhe
 – Bird of Rimpo See *P. suffruticosa* 'Rimpo'
 – Black Dragon Brocade See *P. suffruticosa* 'Kokuryû-
 nishiki'
 – Black Flower Chief See *P. suffruticosa* 'Hei Hua Kui'
 – Brocade of the Naniwa See *P. suffruticosa* 'Naniwa-
 nishiki'
 – 'Cai Die' (S) MPhe
* – 'Cai Jing Qui' (S) MPhe
 – 'Cang Zhi Hong' MPhe WViv
 – 'Cardinal Vaughan' (S) CKel
 – Charming Age See *P. suffruticosa* 'Howki'
 – 'Chen Hong' (S) MPhe
 – Chinese hybrids (S) Last listed 1999
 – 'Da Zong Zi' (S) MPhe
 – 'Dou Lu' (S) CKel MPhe
 – Double Cherry See *P. suffruticosa* 'Yae-zakura'
 – 'Duchess of Kent' (S) CKel
 – 'Duchess of Marlborough' CKel
 – 'Er Qiao' (S) CKel
 – Eternal Camellias See *P. suffruticosa* 'Yachiyo-
 tsubaki'
§ – 'Fei Yan Hong Zhuang' (S) MCAu
 – 'Fen Lan Zhu' (S) MPhe
 – 'Fen Qiao' (S) MPhe
 – 'Fen-dang-bai' WViv
 – 'Feng Dan Bai' CKel MCAu MPhe
 – 'Feng Zhong Guan' (S) CKel
 – Flight of Cranes See *P. suffruticosa* 'Renkaku'
 – Floral Rivalry See *P. suffruticosa* 'Hana-kisoi'
 – Flying Swallow See *P. suffruticosa* 'Fei Yan Hong
 Lady in Red Zhuang'
 – 'Ge Jin Zi' (S) MPhe
* – 'Glory of Huish' CKel
 – 'Godaishu' (S) LAma LRHS SPer
 – 'Guan Shi Mo Yu' (S) MPhe
§ – 'Hakuojisi' (S) EBee LRHS MCAu
§ – 'Hana-daijin' (S) LAma LRHS MCAu SPer
§ – 'Hana-kisoi' (S) LAma LRHS MCAu SPer
¶ – 'Haru-no-akebono' (S) CKel
§ – 'He Bai' (S) MPhe
§ – 'He Hua Lu' (S) MPhe
§ – 'Hei Hua Kui' (S) CKel MCAu
* – 'Hei Hue Kui' (S) MPhe
§ – 'Higurashi' (S) EBee
 – 'Hong Cai Qiu' (S) MPhe
 – 'Hou Lian Jin Dan' (S) Last listed 1999
§ – 'Howki' (S) LRHS MCAu
 – 'Hu Die Qun Wu' (S) MPhe
 – 'Hu Hong' (S) MPhe
 – Jewel in the Lotus See *P. suffruticosa* 'Tama-fuyo'
 – Jewelled Screen See *P. suffruticosa* 'Tama-sudare'

 – 'Jia Ge Jin Zi' (S) CKel MCAu WViv
 – 'Jiao Rong San Bian' (S) MPhe
 – 'Jin Pao Hong' (S) MPhe
¶ – 'Jitsugetsu-nishiki' (S) CKel
 – 'Joseph Rock' See *P. rockii*
 – Kamada Brocade See *P. suffruticosa* 'Kamada-
 nishiki'
§ – 'Kamada-fuji' (S) CKel LAma
§ – 'Kamada-nishiki' (S) Last listed 1999
§ – 'Kaow' (S) LRHS MCAu
 – King of Flowers See *P. suffruticosa* 'Kaow'
 – King of White Lions See *P. suffruticosa* 'Hakuojisi'
* – 'Kingdom of the Moon' LRHS
 – 'Kinkaku' See *P.* x *lemoinei* 'Souvenir de
 Maxime Cornu'
 – 'Kinshi' See *P.* x *lemoinei* 'Alice Harding'
§ – 'Kokuryû-nishiki' (S) LAma
 – 'Koshi-no-yuki' CKel
 – 'Lan Tian Yu' (S) CKel MCAu MPhe
* – 'Large Globe' Last listed 1997
 – 'Li Hua Xue' (S) MPhe
 – 'Ling Hua Zhan' (S) MPhe
 – 'Liu Li Guan Zhu' (S) MPhe
 – 'Lord Selbourne' (S) Last listed 1998
 – Lotus Green See *P. suffruticosa* 'He Hua Lu'
 – 'Lu He Hong' MCAu
 – 'Luo Han Hong' MPhe WViv
 – 'Luo Yang Hong' MPhe
 – Magnificent Flower See *P. suffruticosa* 'Hana-daijin'
 – 'Montrose' (S) CKel
* – 'Mrs Shirley Fry' CKel
 – 'Mrs William Kelway' (S) CKel
§ – 'Naniwa-nishiki' (S) Last listed 1998
¶ – 'Nigata Akashigata' (S) CKel
 – Palace of Gems See *P. suffruticosa* 'Shugyo-kuden'
 – Pride of Taisho See *P. suffruticosa* 'Taisho-no-
 hokori'
 – 'Qing Long Wo Mo CKel MCAu MPhe
 Chi' (S)
 – 'Qing Shan Guan Xue' (S) WViv
 – 'Raphael' (S) CKel
¶ – 'Reine Elizabeth' (S) CKel
§ – 'Renkaku' (S) CKel LRHS MCAu
§ – 'Rimpo' (S) CKel EBee LAma SPer
 – subsp. *rockii* (S) See *P. rockii*
 – 'Rou Fu Rong' (S) MCAu
 – 'Ruan-zhi-lan' MPhe WViv
 – 'San Bian Sai Yu' (S) MPhe WViv
 – Seven Gods of Fortune See *P. suffruticosa* 'Sitifukujin'
¶ – 'Shiguregumo' (S) CKel
 – 'Shimane-akashigata' Last listed 1999
 – 'Shimane-chojuraku' CKel
 – 'Shimane-hakugan' CKel
¶ – 'Shimane-seidai' (S) CKel
¶ – 'Shintoyen' (S) CKel
¶ – 'Shirotae' (S) CKel
 – 'Shou An Hong' (S) MCAu MPhe
 – 'Shugyo-kuden' (S) MCAu
§ – 'Si He Lian' (S) MPhe
§ – 'Sitifukujin' (S) MCAu
 – 'Sumi-no-ichi' CKel
 – 'Superb' (S) CKel
§ – 'Taisho-no-hokori' (S) LRHS MCAu
§ – 'Taiyo' (S) LAma LRHS SPer
§ – 'Tama-fuyo' (S) LAma
§ – 'Tama-sudare' (S) LRHS MCAu
 – 'Tao Hong Xian Mei' (S) Last listed 1999
 – The Sun See *P. suffruticosa* 'Taiyo'
 – Twilight See *P. suffruticosa* 'Higurashi'
 – 'Wen Gong Hong' (S) MPhe
 – Wisteria at Kamada See *P. suffruticosa* 'Kamada-fuji'
 – 'Wu Long Feng Sheng' (S) CKel MPhe

- 'Xue Gui' (S) — MPhe
- 'Xue Ta' (S) — CKel
§ - 'Yachiyo-tsubaki' (S) — CKel LAma LRHS MCAu
§ - 'Yae-zakura' (S) — LAma MCAu
- 'Yan Long Zi Zhu Pan' (S) — CKel
- 'Yin Fen Jin Lin' (S) — MCAu
- 'Yin Hong Qiao Dui' (S) — CKel MCAu MPhe
- 'Ying Luo Bao Zhu' (S) — WViv
- 'Yomo-zakura' (S) — LRHS
- 'Yoshinogawa' (S) — EBee LRHS
- 'Yu Hu Die' (S) — MPhe
- 'Yu Lu Dian Cui' (S) — WViv
- 'Yu Pan Zheng Yan' (S) — MPhe
- 'Yu Xi Ying Xue' (S) — CKel MPhe
- 'Zhao Fen' (S) — MPhe
- 'Zhi Hong' (S) — CKel
- 'Zhong Sheng Hong' (S) — MPhe
- 'Zhu Sha Lei' (S) — CKel MCAu MPhe
- 'Zi Ban Bai' (S) — CKel MPhe
- 'Zi Er Qiao' (S) — CKel
- 'Zi Jin Pan' (S) — WViv
- 'Zi Lan Kui' (S) — CKel MPhe
'Sunshine' — See *P. peregrina* 'Otto Froebel'
szechuanica — MPhe
tenuifolia — CBot CLAP GCal
- subsp. *biebersteiniana* — MPhe
- subsp. *carthalinica* — MPhe
- from E Georgia — WPGP
§ - subsp. *lithophila* — MPhe
- 'Plena' — CRDP GKir LRHS MBri MPhe WCot
- 'Rosea' — Last listed 1998
turcica — MPhe
veitchii — CKel CLAP MHom MTho SCou SDys SSpi WAbe WEas
- dwarf — MPhe
- from China — MPhe
- var. *leiocarpa* — Last listed 1999
- var. *woodwardii* — CLyd ERos GDra MBel MTho NHar NSla NWCA SSpi WHoo
'Windchimes' — Last listed 1999
wittmanniana — CBot CLAP NTow WSPU
'Yao Huang' (S) — CKel MCAu MPhe
'Yellow Crown' (S) — Last listed 1998
'Yellow Dream' (S) — WCot

PAESIA (Dennstaedtiaceae)
scaberula — CBos CFil GCal SSpi WAbe WRic

PALIURUS (Rhamnaceae)
spina-christi — CArn CPle SLon SMad WSPU

PANAX (Araliaceae)
ginseng — GPoy
japonicus — GPoy
pseudoginseng — Last listed 1998
quinquefolius — GPoy

PANCRATIUM (Amaryllidaceae)
canariense — Last listed 1997
foetidum S&L 354 — Last listed 1998
maritimum — EBee EBot LRHS

PANDANUS (Pandanaceae)
tectorius 'Veitchii' ♀ — Last listed 1990
¶ *utilis* — LPal

PANDOREA (Bignoniaceae)
jasminoides — CPIN CSpe EBak ECon ECot LRHS SLon SOWG
§ - 'Charisma' (v) — CB&S CPIN EHol EMil EPfP LPan LRHS SOWG WCot

§ - 'Lady Di' — CPIN ERea LRHS SOWG SYvo
- 'Rosea' — MCCP
- 'Rosea Superba' ♀ — CB&S CRHN EBee ECon EHol EMil ERea LRHS
- 'Variegata' — See *P. jasminoides* 'Charisma'
lindleyana — See *Clytostoma callistegioides*
pandorana — CPIN CSpe ERea SYvo WCot
- 'Golden Rain' — CB&S CPIN CRHN ECon ERea SOWG
- 'Ruby Heart' — CPIN
¶ - 'Snowbells' — CPIN

PANICUM (Poaceae)
bulbosum — EHoe EPla
clandestinum — CCuc EHoe EPPr EPla EWes LEdu MCCP NPro WHil
coloratum 'Bambatsi' — Last listed 1997
miliaceum — EGle MSal
virgatum — CCuc CTri MSte MWhi WBro WPer
¶ - 'Cloud Nine' — EFou LGre
- 'Hänse Herms' — CBrm CInt CMil EBee EHoe EPPr LGre MBri SCou
- 'Heavy Metal' — EBee EBlw EFou EGle EHoe EMan EPPr EPla LHrt LPan MBNS MMil NBea NSti SLod SPer SPla WCot WHil WPrP
- 'Pathfinder' — Last listed 1997
¶ - 'Prairie Sky' — LGre MAnH WCot
- 'Rehbraun' — EBee EBrP EBre ECGN EGle EHoe EPPr EWTr LBCl LBSe LBre LEdu LPan MBBe MCAu NOak SApp SBre SMad WPGP WRus
- 'Rotstrahlbusch' — CSpe EBee EBrP EBre ECGN EFou EHoe EPPr EPla LBCl LBSe LBre LRHS MBBe MChl NBea SBre SPla WCot WHil
- 'Rubrum' — More than 30 suppliers
- 'Squaw' — EFou EGle EHoe EPGN EPPr GKir LGre LPan NPro SApp WCot WFar WHil WPnP WPrP WWye
- 'Strictum' — CCuc EHoe EMil EWes LGre
- 'Warrior' — CBrm EBee EBrP EBre EFou EGle EHoe EMan EPPr GKir LBCl LBSe LBre LEdu LGre LPan MAnH MBBe MCCP MChl NCut NPSI NSti SApp SAsh SBre WPGP WPnP
'Wood's Variegated' — SApp

PAPAVER ✿ (Papaveraceae)
aculeatum — Last listed 1998
alboroseum — CInt CSam EBee EDAr GCHN GTou MSCN NHol WPat
¶ 'Alpha Centauri' — SWat
(Super Poppy Series)
§ *alpinum* L. — CSpe EDAr EMNN GCHN GDra GKir GTou LRHS MMHG SIng SRms WWin
- *album* — CMea
- cut petal — CInt
- subsp. *ernesti-mayeri* — Last listed 1998
- 'Flore Pleno' (d) — NBir
¶ *amurense* — EBee
anomalum — Last listed 1998
- *album* — CMil CSpe EBee EMon EWll MWgw NArg NFai STes WElm WSan
apokrinomenon — MWll
argemone — EWFC
§ *atlanticum* — CLTr CNic EBee ECoo EMar EOld GBuc GCHN MMal NBro NSti SPlb

- 'Flore Pleno' (d)	CM&M CSpe EBee LFis MCCP MWll NBro NFai WCot	
¶ 'Atlantis' (Super Poppy Series)	SWat	
¶ 'Aurora' (Super Poppy Series)	SWat	
bracteatum	See *P. orientale* var. *bracteatum*	
burseri	SRot	
¶ 'Cathay' (Super Poppy Series)	SWat	
¶ 'Celebration' (Super Poppy Series)	SWat	
commutatum ♀	CInt ELan MAvo MRav WCot WEas	
corona-sancti-stephani	Last listed 1998	
degenii	GCHN	
dubium	Last listed 1997	
fauriei	Last listed 1999	
§ 'Fireball'	CMHG CRow ECha EGle GCal LHop MTis MWat NCat NTow WCot WRHF	
¶ 'Harlequin' (Super Poppy Series)	SWat	
heldreichii	See *P. spicatum*	
x *hybridum* 'Flore Pleno' (d)	EBee EMon NBrk SWat WWal	
¶ 'Jacinth' (Super Poppy Series)	SWat	
julicum	Last listed 1997	
kluanense	CSam	
lapponicum	Last listed 1998	
- subsp. *occidentale*	Last listed 1998	
lateritium	CPou MLLN MMal SRms STes WPGP	
- 'Flore Pleno' (d)	EBee	
¶ *macounii* subsp. *discolor*	IIve	
¶ 'Medallion' (Super Poppy Series)	SWat	
microcarpum	Last listed 1998	
§ *miyabeanum*	CGle CSpe EDAr ELan GCHN GDra GKir GTou LHop LRHS NWCA WFar WGwG WPer WWin	
- *album*	ECho	
- 'Pacino'	EDAr EWll LRHS	
- *tatewakii*	See *P. miyabeanum*	
nanum 'Flore Pleno'	See *P.* 'Fireball'	
§ *nudicaule*	CBlo ELan LEdu WPer	
- Champagne Bubbles Group	EBrP EBre LBCl LBSe LBre LRHS MBBe SBre WFar WLRN	
- Constance Finnis Group	EMon GBuc LRHS WCot	
- var. *croceum*	EWTr	
¶ - - 'Flamenco'	LRHS NArg WViv	
- Garden Gnome Group	See *P. nudicaule* Gartenzwerg Series	
§ - Gartenzwerg Series	CBlo CSpe EMil GAbr LRHS MBri NArg NCut NFla NPri SPlb WGor WViv	
§ - Oregon Rainbow Group	Last listed 1998	
- 'Pacino'	CWes SRms WFar WLRN WWeb	
- 'Solar Fire Orange'	WViv	
- 'Wonderland Mixed'	EWll LPVe	
oreophilum	Last listed 1998	
orientale	CB&S EPfP EWTr LHrt LRHS MBro MMal NCut SCou SRms SWat WFar WPer	
- 'Abu Hassan'	SWat	
- 'Aglaja' ♀	CMil EBee LRHS MCAu NHaw SUsu SWat WCot	
- 'Aladin'	SWat	
- 'Ali Baba'	SWat	
- 'Allegro'	More than 30 suppliers	

- 'Arwide'	EFou SWat	
- 'Aslahan'	ECha SWat	
- 'Atrosanguineus'	NPSI SWat WCot WSpi	
- 'Avebury Crimson'	LGre MRav MWat SAga SWat	
- 'Ballkleid'	ECha	
- 'Beauty Queen'	CBlo EBee EBrP EBre ECot EGle GGar GMac LBCl LBSe LBre LRHS MBBe MBri MRav MWgw NBrk NCat NGdn SBre SDix SRPl SSoC SWat WLRN	
- 'Big Jim'	SWat	
- 'Black and White' ♀	More than 30 suppliers	
- 'Blackberry Queen'	SWat WCot	
¶ - 'Blickfang'	SWat	
- 'Blue Moon'	EFou GKir NBir SWat WLRN	
- 'Bonfire Red'	CStr EBee ELan LRHS SWat WBro	
§ - var. *bracteatum* ♀	CRDP CSam EBot ECha GCHN GDra NBir NFai SWat SYvo	
- - JCA 751202	WPGP	
- 'Brilliant'	EBee LRHS NFai WRHF	
* - 'Carneum'	CM&M EBee LRHS	
- 'Carnival'	EFou SWat	
- 'Catherina'	EBee LRHS SWat	
- 'Cedar Hill'	EBee EFou GMac LRHS MMil SWat WMaN	
- 'Cedric Morris' ♀	CGle CHad CMil EBee ECha EFou EGle ELan EMan EOld EPri GCal LAst MCAu MRav NSti SAga SChu SMrm SWat WCot WEas WElm WLRN WMaN WPGP	
- 'Charming'	CBos CHad CLon CMil CPar EBee LGre LRHS MMil SAga SWat	
- 'China Boy'	CMil SWat	
* - 'Choir Boy'	CM&M CRDP EBee EGle MBct NBrk STes WPrP WRHF	
¶ - 'Coral Reef'	MWll SWat	
¶ - 'Corrina'	SWat	
- 'Curlilocks'	CLon CMGP CPar EBee EBrP EBre ELan EMan GAbr LAst LBCl LBSe LBre LRHS LRot MBBe MCLN MRav NBrk NCut NPSI SAga SBre SPer SPla SRms SWat WWin WWoo	
- 'Derwisch'	SWat	
* - 'Diana'	CHad SMrm	
- 'Doppelte Freude'	Last listed 1999	
- double red shades (d)	SSvw	
- 'Doubloon'	EBrP EBre GKir LBCl LBSe LBre MBBe NBrk NGdn NHaw NSti SBre SWat	
- 'Dwarf Allegro'	GBuc MFir NFor NOak	
- 'Effendi' ♀	EFou MBct SUsu SWat	
- 'Elam Pink'	CLon CMil ECha LGre MTis SWat WCot WSpi	
- 'Erste Zuneigung'	EBee ECha EGle	
¶ - 'Eskimo Pie'	SWat	
- 'Fatima'	CBos CHad CMil SMrm SWat WWeb	
- 'Feuerriese'	SWat	
¶ - 'Feuerzwerg'	SWat	
¶ - 'Fiesta'	SWat	
- 'Flamenco'	SWat	
N - 'Flore Pleno' (d)	GLil SSvw	
- 'Forncett Summer'	CMGP EBee EFou LBuc LPio SWat WCot WElm	
- 'Garden Glory'	CPar CPlt CRDP EBee EFou LRHS MBri MCAu NCat SRPl SWat WLRN	
- 'Garden Gnome'	GKir	
- 'Glowing Embers'	EBrP EBre GKir LBCl LBSe LBre LRHS MBBe SBre SWat	
- 'Glowing Rose'	SWat	

*	- 'Goldie'	ELan
	- Goliath Group	CElw CGle CMil CSev EBee EMan LRHS MCLN NBrk NBro NOak NVic SCob SDix SPer SRPl SUsu SWat WCot WEas WFar WHoo WPyg
	- - 'Beauty of Livermere' ♀	CHad CLon CM&M CRDP CSam EMan MBro MCAu MCLN MRav MTis MWll NBro NGdn NLar NSti SAga SChu SLod SMrm SRms SSvw SWat WCot WElm WLRN WOve WPyg WSpi WWhi
	- 'Graue Witwe'	CLon CMil EBee EFou EGle GBuc NBrk SMrm SUsu SWat WCot WMaN WPGP WRha
	- 'Halima'	SWat
	- 'Harvest Moon'	EBee EBrP EBre EHol GKir LBCl LBSe LBre LPio LRHS MBBe MBri MRav NHaw SBre SWat WCot
	- 'Helen Elisabeth'	CBlo CSpe EBee EBrP EBre ECtt EFou EGle EMan GCal LAst LBCl LBSe LBre LPio MBBe MBel MCAu MCLN MLLN NBrk NFai NGdn SBre SWat WCra WFar
	- 'Hewitt's Old Rose'	WCot
	- 'Hula Hula'	SWat
	- 'Indian Chief'	CM&M CMil CPar CRDP EBee EBlw EGle EOld GBin LPio LRHS MSte NFai SAga WBar
	- 'Joanne'	NLar
	- 'John III' ♀	EBee EFou SWat WPGP
	- 'John Metcalf'	CMil CRDP EBee EFou EGle LPio LRHS MCAu SChu SUsu SWat WBro WCot
	- 'Juliane'	CLon EBee ECha EGle EPri GMac LGre LHop MBct MCAu SWat WCot WWhi
	- 'Karine' ♀	More than 30 suppliers
	- 'Khedive' ♀	SWat
	- 'King George'	GBuc MWat SWat
	- 'Kleine Tänzerin'	CLon CMil CPou EBee EFou EGle LGre LRHS MBct MCAu MCLN MLLN NGdn NPSI NSti SAga SUsu SWat WCot WLRN WPGP
	- 'Kollebloem'	SWat
	- 'Lady Frederick Moore'	LPio MTed SWat WCot WCra
	- 'Lady Roscoe'	SWat
	- 'Ladybird'	ELan LRHS MRav MSte NBrk NPSI SPla WCot
	- 'Lambada'	SWat
I	- 'Lauren's Lilac'	SWat
	- 'Leuchtfeuer' ♀	CMil EBee SWat
	- 'Lighthouse' ♀	SWat
	- 'Lilac Girl'	CLon ECha EGle LGre MCAu SWat WCot WMaN
¶	- 'Maiden's Blush'	SWat
	- 'Marcus Perry'	CBlo EBee ENot EPfP GChr GGar GMaP LRHS MRav NPri SCob SPer SWat WFar
¶	- 'Mary Finnan'	SWat
	- 'Master Richard'	LRHS SWat
	- 'May Queen' (d)	CM&M CMGP CPou EBee EWes GBuc IBlr LRHS WCot WElm WPen
	- 'May Sadler'	COIW ENot EOld SWat WSpi
	- 'Midnight'	Last listed 1997
	- 'Mrs H.G. Stobart'	CRDP SWat
	- 'Mrs Marrow's Plum'	See *P. orientale* 'Patty's Plum'
	- 'Mrs Perry' ♀	More than 30 suppliers
	- 'Nanum Flore Pleno'	See *P.* 'Fireball'
	- 'Noema'	SWat
	- 'Orange Glow'	EWTr

	- 'Orangeade Maison'	CPou CStr EBee SWat WBro WCot
	- 'Oriana'	EBee EHol LRHS MMil SWat WLRN
¶	- 'Oriental'	SWat
	- 'Pale Face'	SWat
	- pale pink	LRHS
§	- 'Patty's Plum'	More than 30 suppliers
	- 'Perry's White'	More than 30 suppliers
	- 'Peter Pan'	SWat
	- 'Petticoat'	SWat
	- 'Picotée'	More than 30 suppliers
	- 'Pink Lassie'	SWat
¶	- 'Pink Panda'	SWat
	- 'Pinnacle'	CMil CSWP EBee GAri GLil LRHS MAvo MSCN NCut NFai NHaw NPri SCob SWat WPGP WWoo
	- 'Pizzicato'	CBlo CHor CM&M CPar LGre LRHS MCli MGed MWll NArg NBur NPer SAga SSvw SWat WGwG WLRN WOve
	- 'Polka'	SWat
	- 'Prince of Orange'	EBee SWat
	- Princess Victoria Louise	See *P. orientale* 'Prinzessin Victoria Louise'
	- 'Prinz Eugen'	CRDP EFou SWat
§	- 'Prinzessin Victoria Louise'	CBlo CSWP EBee EMan EWTr GKir GLil GMaP LFis LRHS MBel MLLN MMil NBro SMad SMrm SSoC SSvw SWat WCer WPer
	- 'Prospero'	EBee
	- 'Queen Alexandra'	EBee GKir NChi NLar
	- 'Raspberry Queen'	CMil CPlt CPou EBee EGle ELan EMan GBin GMaP LAst LRHS MArl MAvo MBel MRav MTis NPri NSti SAga SWat WBro WCot WFar WHal WHoo WPGP WSpi WWoo
¶	- 'Raspberry Ruffles'	SWat
	- 'Redizelle'	Last listed 1997
	- 'Rembrandt'	CBlo ECot GMac LRHS MMil NFla NMoo NPri SWat WBar WPer WViv
	- 'Rose Queen'	WCot
	- 'Rosenpokal'	CM&M EBee SWat WBro
¶	- 'Roter Zwerg'	ECha
¶	- 'Royal Chocolate Distinction'	SWat
	- 'Royal Wedding'	CMil EBee EGle EMan GKir LAst LPio LRHS MHer MMil MRav MWll NChi NLar NPri SAga SChu SMrm SPla SSvw SWat WCot WLRN WMoo WOve
*	- 'Saffron'	CHad CMil SAga
	- 'Salmon Glow'	CB&S EBee GLil LAst LRHS MHer SCob SWat WFar WPer WViv
	- 'Salome'	SWat
	- scarlet	MWgw
	- 'Scarlet King'	CBlo EBee EWll LRHS MMil SAga SWat WLRN
	- 'Showgirl'	CRDP CSam SWat
	- 'Sindbad'	EBee EFou LRHS SLod SWat
¶	- 'Snow Goose'	SWat
	- 'Snow Queen'	MNrw
	- 'Spätzünder'	EFou GMac SWat
*	- *splendidissimum*	Last listed 1999
	- 'Springtime'	CMGP EBee EFou EGle LRHS MCAu MSCN SAga SWat WBro WElm WMoo WWoo
	- Stormtorch	See *P. orientale* 'Sturmfackel'
§	- 'Sturmfackel'	EBee SWat
	- 'Suleika'	EFou SWat
	- 'Sultana'	CPlt EBee ECha EGle EOld GMac LGre MWat SSoC SWat

- 'Türkenlouis'	COlW EBee EBrP EBre EFou EGle EMan GKir GLil GMaP GMac LAst LBCl LBSe LBre LCaP LRHS MBBe MCAu MSCN NCut SBre SPar STes SUsu SWat WCot WHoo
- 'Turkish Delight' ♀	CBlo EBee ELan GCHN GMaP GMac LRHS MMil MRav NBir NBro NCat SLod SMer SPer SSoC SUsu SWat WFar
- 'Tutu'	SWat
¶ - 'Victoria Dreyfuss'	SWat
¶ - 'Water Babies'	SWat
- 'Watermelon'	CMil COtt CRDP EBee EBrP EBre EFou EMan LAst LBCl LBSe LBre LCaP LRHS MAnH MAvo MBBe MBel MCAu SBre SWat WBro WWoo
- 'Wild Salmon'	STes
¶ - 'Wisley Beacon'	SWat
- 'Wunderkind'	EBee EGle SWat
paucifoliatum	Last listed 1999
- JCA 752300	WCot WPGP
pilosum	EMan GBuc GDea NCat SBea SRms SSvw SWat
¶ 'Pink Lightning' (Super Poppy Series)	SWat
radicatum	Last listed 1998
rhaeticum	Last listed 1999
rhoeas	CArn EWFC GPoy MHew MMal WElm WJek
- Angels' Choir	SWat WHer
- 'Mother of Pearl'	SWat
- Shirley	MMal
- 'Valerie Finnis'	Last listed 1999
¶ *rupifragrum* 'Tangerine Dream'	LFis MCCP
rupifragrum	CFir CGle CMCo ECha ESis EWTr GAbr GCHN LEur LHil LPio MFir MLLN WEas WFar WOve WPer WRha WWin
- 'Flore Pleno' (d)	CSWP CSpe EBee EMan LPio LRHS MWll NChi WCot WCru WHen WHer WWhi
sendtneri	EWTr MHer WLin
¶ 'Serena' (Super Poppy Series)	SWat
¶ 'Shasta' (Super Poppy Series)	SWat
¶ 'Sinbad'	SLod
somniferum ♀	CArn EWll GPoy SWat
- 'Black Beauty'	CSpe SWat
¶ - 'Chedglow Variegated' (v)	CPla EMan
- 'Pink Chiffon'	SWat WEas
¶ - 'White Cloud' (d)	CSpe
§ *spicatum*	CHea CSam ECGP ECha EGoo EMan EWTr GCal LHop MFir MHar NBir NFai SMrm WAbe WCot WEas WMoo
¶ 'Summer Breeze'	WHil
tauricola	MWll
triniifolium	CSpe
¶ 'Viva' (Super Poppy Series)	SWat
* 'Witchery'	WWeb

PARABENZOIN See LINDERA

PARACHAMPIONELLA See STROBILANTHES

PARADISEA (Asphodelaceae)

liliastrum ♀	CHid CMdw EBee EMan ERos GIBF LPio MTis NCat NChi NWoo SSpi WCFE WCot WWhi

- 'Major'	Last listed 1999
lusitanica	CAvo CGle CMHG CMil CRDP EBee ERos LPio NEgg NPSI SSpi WCot WMoo

PARAHEBE ❀ (Scrophulariaceae)

'Arabella'	LRHS
¶ 'Betty'	GGar
x *bidwillii*	ECou EMNN GAri LFis MHer MRav NDlv NWCA SRms SRot WWat
- 'Kea'	CFee ECou ECtt EMNN ESis GCHN NHar SBla SHel SRot WFar WPer
canescens	ECou
§ *catarractae* ♀	CMHG EBee ECou EMNN EMar EWTr GGar GKir MFir MNrw MWat NBee NBro NFor NMen NTow SAga SBrw SMer SOkh SUsu WBrE WCru WFar WHen WOve WPer WWhi
¶ - 'Baby Blue'	EPfP MAsh
- blue	CHar EMar EPfP GKir NBee SPan SPer SPla WWat
§ - 'Delight' ♀	CChe CLTr ECou ESis EWes GCHN GGar LFis LHop LRHS MBro MHer NBrk NPer SDix SHFr SMrm SRot WEas WFar WHen WHoo WPyg
- subsp. *diffusa*	ECou EMNN IOrc LRHS MHer MMil NHar NPer NVic
- - 'Annie'	ECou
- - 'Pinkie'	CLTr ECou
¶ - from Chatham Island	EWes
- garden form	ECha LLWP SBla WAbe
- subsp. *martinii*	ECou
- 'Miss Willmott'	EWTr MSCN NPri NVic SPer SPlb WPer
- 'Porlock Purple'	See *P. catarractae* 'Delight'
- 'Rosea'	CPri ESis WWat
- 'Tinycat'	Last listed 1998
- white	CBot ECha EMNN ESis GCHN IBlr LHop MBro MFir NCat NFla NMen SHel SOkh SUsu WEas WPer WWat WWhi
decora	ECou GAri GCHN NSla
densifolia	See *Chionobebe densifolia*
derwentiana	ECou EMon
§ *formosa*	CPle ECou WHCG WSPU
- erect	ECou
- lax	Last listed 1999
- white	ECou
'Gillian'	ECou ECtt GAri GGar LAco LFis MMil WFar WPer
'Greencourt'	See *P. catarractae* 'Delight'
guthrieana	SVen
§ *hookeriana*	GGar MHer NMen SAga SMrm WPyg WWat
'Joy'	ECou EWes
¶ 'Julia'	GGar
¶ 'June'	GGar
¶ 'Lesley'	GGar
linifolia	CTri EMNN EPot
- 'Blue Skies'	ECou EDAr
§ *lyallii*	CBot CPri ECou EDAr ESis LAst MBar MHer MWat NDlv NFor NHol NWCA SAga SBla SPlb SRms WAbe WTro WWin
¶ - 'Baby Pink'	EPfP GKir MAsh
- 'Clarence'	CLyd ECou
- 'Engel's Blue'	Last listed 1998
- 'Glacier'	CLTr ECou

- 'Julie-Anne'	CPri ECou EPfP ESis GCal LRHS MAsh SPan
- 'Rosea'	CTri GGar LFis WPer WPyg
* **martinii**	LRHS
'Mervyn'	CLyd ECou ECtt EDAr GCHN GGar LAco LFis NDlv WHen WPer
olsenii	ECou GGar
§ **perfoliata** ♀	More than 30 suppliers
- dark blue	GBuc GCal MBro SMad
- 'Pringle'	CAbP EPfP GKir LRHS MAsh SMrm
'Snowcap'	EPfP LRHS MAsh SPlb

PARAJUBAEA (Arecaceae)

cocoides	CBrP LPJP LPal

PARAQUILEGIA (Ranunculaceae)

adoxoides	See *Semiaquilegia adoxoides*
§ **anemonoides**	GCrs GGGa GKir GTou NHar SBla WAbe
- ACE 1370	Last listed 1998
grandiflora	See *P. anemonoides*

PARASERIANTHES (Mimosaceae)

distachya	See *P. lophantha*
§ **lophantha** ♀	CAbb CHEx CPle CRHN EBak ERea LHil SAPC SArc SOWG WMul

PARASYRINGA See LIGUSTRUM

x PARDANCANDA (Iridaceae)

norrisii	CArn CFir EBee EMan EWes GSki LIck LRHS NCut NPri WBea WFoF
- 'Dazzler'	WHil

PARDANTHOPSIS (Iridaceae)

dichotoma	EBee
- RMRP 95-0501	Last listed 1999

PARDOGLOSSUM (Boraginaceae)

cheirifolium	Last listed 1998

PARIETARIA (Urticaceae)

§ **judaica**	ELau EWFC GPoy MHew MSal WHer
- 'Corinne Tremaine'	Last listed 1997

PARIS ✿ (Trilliaceae)

¶ **bashanensis**	LEur
birmanica	Last listed 1999
bockiana	WCru
fargesii	EBee WCru
- var. **petiolata**	LEur WCru
incompleta	EPot
japonica	WCru
lancifolia	WCru
§ **polyphylla**	CFir EBee WCru
* - var. **appendiculata**	LEur
- var. **stenophylla**	LAma
- **yunnanensis alba**	Last listed 1999
pubescens	WCru
quadrifolia	CFil CFir CLAP CRDP GPoy LGre MSal SSpi WCru WHer WShi
- JMH 79	MDun
tetraphylla	WCru
thibetica	WCru
verticillata	LAma WCru
violacea	WCru

PARNASSIA (Parnassiaceae)

cabulica	Last listed 1998

nubicola	GDra NHar
palustris	WHer
- **palustris**	Last listed 1997

PAROCHETUS (Papilionaceae)

africanus ♀	CHid EWes GAri GBuc WCot
communis	CB&S CFee CGle CNic CPea GDra GMaP GMac MRav NBro NPer SRms SVen WBea WBor WCot WWhi
* - 'Blue Gem'	Last listed 1997
- dark	GCal
- Himalayan form	IBlr
- Himalayan form HWJCM 526	EBee WCru
- summer-flowering	Last listed 1999

PARONYCHIA (Illecebraceae)

argentea	CLyd MBro NHol WPat WPer
§ **capitata**	CHal CLyd CTri NNrd SRms WHoo WPat WPer WWin
§ **kapela**	EMan NTow SPlb SSmi WPer
- 'Binsted Gold' (v)	CInt CMGP EMon LRHS MBro
- subsp. **serpyllifolia**	Last listed 1999
nivea	See *P. capitata*
serpyllifolia	See *P. kapela* subsp. *serpyllifolia*

PARROTIA (Hamamelidaceae)

persica ♀	More than 30 suppliers
- 'Burgundy'	CPMA
- 'Globosa'	LPan
§ - 'Lamplighter' (v)	CPMA
- 'Pendula'	CPMA EPfP GKir IOrc
- 'Vanessa'	CMCN CPMA GKir LPan LRHS MBri SBrw SSpi SSta
- 'Variegata'	See *P. persica* 'Lamplighter'

PARROTIOPSIS (Hamamelidaceae)

jacquemontiana	CB&S CEnd CPMA LBuc

PARRYA (Brassicaceae)

eriocalyx	Last listed 1998
menziesii	See *Phoenicaulis cheiranthoides*

PARSONSIA (Apocynaceae)

capsularis	CPLG CPIN ECou
heterophylla	CPIN ECou ERea

PARTHENIUM (Asteraceae)

integrifolium	CArn EBrP EBre GPoy IIve LBCl LBSe LBre MBBe MSal SBre

PARTHENOCISSUS (Vitaceae)

§ **henryana** ♀	More than 30 suppliers
himalayana	ECtt
- 'Purpurea'	See *P. himalayana* var. *rubrifolia*
§ - var. **rubrifolia**	CBlo EBee EPfP GOrc LRHS MAsh MRav SLim WCru WWat
inserta	Last listed 1997
§ **quinquefolia** ♀	More than 30 suppliers
- var. **engelmannii**	EBee LBuc MGos NFla SPer WAbe WCFE
- 'Star Showers' (v)	Last listed 1999
striata	See *Cissus striata*
§ **tricuspidata** ♀	CCHP CHEx EBee ECtt EPfP GKir MGos NFor SMer SPer SReu SSoC WDin WHil
- B&SWJ 1162	Last listed 1999
- 'Beverley Brook'	CBlo CMac GOrc MBri SBra SPla SRms
- 'Green Spring'	CBlo IArd MBlu MBri MGos NBrk
- 'Lowii'	CBlo CMac EBee ECot EPfP EPla

	EWTr LRHS MBlu MGos MRav SLon SPer
- 'Minutifolia'	Last listed 1999
- 'Robusta'	CSam EBee LPan LRHS MBNS
§ - 'Veitchii'	More than 30 suppliers

PASITHEA (Anthericaceae)
| caerulea | EBee |

PASPALUM (Poaceae)
| glaucifolium | LEdu |
| quadrifarium | Last listed 1997 |

PASSIFLORA ✿ (Passifloraceae)
actinia	CPas CPIN CRHN LChe LPri SLim SSte
acuminata	Last listed 1999
adenopoda	CPas
'Adularia'	CPas LChe LPri SSte WHer
alata (F) ♀	CAbb CPas CPIN EBak ELan ERea LChe LCns LPri LRHS SSte
- 'Shannon' (F)	CPas SSte
x alatocaerulea	See P. x belotii
allantophylla	CPas
'Allardii'	CPas
¶ amalocarpa	CPas
ambigua	CPas
'Amethyst' ♀	CAbb CChe CPas CRHN CSPN ELan EMil EOrc LCns LHop LPri LRHS MCCP SAga SBra WPGP WPat
§ amethystina Mikan	CB&S CDoC CPas CPIN ECre EHol ERea LCns LRHS SSte
ampullacea (F)	CPas LPri
¶ 'Andy'	CPas
anfracta	CPas SSte
N antioquiensis Karst ♀	CB&S CGre CHEx CPIN CTbh EHol ELan ERea GQui LChe LPri LRHS MAsh MTis SAga SOWG WMul
apetala	CPas
¶ x atropurpurea	SSte
§ aurantia	CPas ERea LPri WHer
auriculata	CPas
banksii	See P. aurantia
¶ baubinifolia	CPas
§ x belotii	CPas ECre EHol ELan EMui ERea LChe LCns LPri LRHS MAsh SMrm SSte
- 'Impératrice Eugénie'	See P. x belotii
biflora Lamarck	CPas LPri
boenderi	CPas
brevipes	Last listed 1999
'Byron Beauty'	CPas LPri
§ caerulea ♀	More than 30 suppliers
- 'Constance Elliot' ♀	CB&S CBot CDoC CMac CPas CPIN CRHN CSPN EBee ELan EMil EMui EOrc LChe LPri LRHS MAsh NBea SBra SLim SOWG SPer SPla SReu SSta SSte
- rubra	CBlo ECtt LRHS SSte
I x caeruleoracemosa	See P. x violacea
x caponii	ERea
capsularis	CPas SSte SVen
¶ cerasina	CPas
chinensis	See P. caerulea
cincinnata	CPas
cinnabarina	CPas
cirrhiflora	CPas
citrina	CPas CPIN ECon ECtt ELan ERea LChe LCns LPri LRHS SOWG SSte
coccinea (F)	CPas CPIN LPri LRHS

colinvauxii	CPas
x colvillii	CPas CPIN
conzattiana	CPas
§ coriacea	CPas CPIN LChe LPri LRHS SSte
costaricensis	CPas
crenata	CPas
cumbalensis	CPas SSte
- var. cumbalensis	Last listed 1998
JCA 13988	
cuneata	CPas LPri
§ - 'Miguel Molinari'	CPas
cuprea	CPas SSte
I 'Curiosa'	CPas
cuspidifolia	CPas
§ cyanea	CPas
¶ 'Debby'	CPas
x decaisneana (F)	CPas CPIN LPri
§ - 'Innesii'	Last listed 1999
dioscoreifolia	Last listed 1997
discophora	CPas
edulis (F)	CAgr CPas CPIN EBak EMui LPri LRHS SSte WHer
- B&SWJ 3624	WCru
- 'Crackerjack' (F)	ERea
§ - f. edulis (F)	Last listed 1998
- f. flavicarpa (F)	CPas ECon ELan LChe LPri SSte
* - 'Golden Nuggett' (F)	CPas
- 'Norfolk' (F)	CPas
- 'Supreme'	Last listed 1998
'Elizabeth' (F)	CPas LChe
'Empress Eugenie'	See P. x belotii
* escorbariana	Last listed 1999
* 'Evatoria'	Last listed 1997
x exoniensis ♀	CBot CGre CPas CPIN CRHN ECre LPri MAsh SMrm SSte
* exura	CPas
filipes	CPas
foetida	CPas LPri LRHS SOWG SSte
- bibiscifolia	Last listed 1998
- var. birsuta (F)	CPas
- var. birsutissima	CPas
- var. orinocensis	CPas
* garayaglia	CPas
garckei	CPas
gibertii	CPas
gigantifolia	CPas
gilbertiana	CPas
glandulosa	CPas
gracilis	CPas
gracillima	CPas
guatemalensis	CPas
babnii	CPas
belleri	CPas CPIN
berbertiana (F)	CPas CPIN SSte SVen
¶ birtiflora	CPas
boloseicea	CPas
incana	See P. seemannii
incarnata (F)	CArn CBlo CPas EMui LChe LPri MSal NBrk SPlb SSte
	SSte
'Incense' (F) ♀	CBlo CPas CPIN EBak ECre EMui LChe LRHS MAsh SLim SSte
¶ indecora	CPas
* jalunsachensis	CPas
¶ 'Jeanette'	CPas
¶ 'Jelly Joker'	CPas
jilekii	Last listed 1999
jorullensis	CPas
juliana	CPas
kalbreyeri	CPas
karwinskii	CPas
x kewensis	CPas LChe LPri SSte

* *kirkii*	Last listed 1999
lancearia	CPas
¶ *lancetellesis*	CPas
laurifolia (F)	CPas
§ *ligularis* (F)	CPas LRHS SSte
'Lilac Lady'	See *P.* x *violacea* 'Tresederi'
lindeniana	CPas
lourdesae	See *P. cuneata* 'Miguel Molinari'
lowei	See *P. ligularis*
lutea	CPas
¶ *macrophylla*	CPas
maliformis (F)	CPas CPIN
manicata (F)	CPas CPIN CRHN NBrk SSte
matthewsii	Last listed 1997
'Mavis Mastics'	See *P.* x *violacea* 'Tresederi'
mayana	See *P. caerulea*
¶ *mayarum*	CPas
¶ *membranacea* (F)	CPas
menispermifolia	See *P. pilosa*
* *microstipula*	CPas
miersii	CPas
misera	CPas SSte
mixta (F)	CPIN ERea LChe
- x *antioquiensis*	CDoC SAga
* - var. *pinanga*	CPas
mollissima (F) ♀	CAbb CB&S CPas CPIN CRHN EBak ELan EPfP ERea LChe LRHS MAsh SMrm SOWG SSte SVen WHer WMul
morifolia	CPas CPIN SSte WMul
mucronata	CPas
multiflora	CPas
murucuja	CPas SSte
naviculata	CPas
nelsonii	Last listed 1999
nitida (F)	CPas
oblongata	CPas
obtusifolia	See *P. coriacea*
oerstedii	CPas
- var. *choconhiana*	CPas
onychina	See *P. amethystina*
organensis	CPas
pallens	CPas
palmeri	CPas SSte
penduliflora	CPas SSte
perfoliata	CPas SSte
* 'Perfume'	CPas
phoenicea	CPas LPri SMrm SSte
- 'Ruby Glow' (F)	Last listed 1999
§ *pilosa*	CPas
¶ *pilosicorona*	CPas
pinnatistipula (F)	CPas SVen
x *piresii*	CPas SSte
pittieri	CPas
platyloba	CPas CPIN
punctata	CPas
'Pura Vida'	CPas LPri SSte
'Purple Haze'	CPas CRHN LPri
'Purple Passion'	See *P. edulis* f. *edulis*
quadrangularis L. (F) ♀	CPas CPIN CTbh EBak ERea LChe LPan LPri LRHS WMul
* - *macrocarpa* (F)	CPas
quadrifaria	CPas
quadriflora	Last listed 1999
quinquangularis	CPas
racemosa ♀	CBlo CPas CPIN ELan ERea IBlr LChe LPri LRHS MAsh NBea SOWG
'Red Inca'	CPas
¶ *resticulata*	CPas
retipetala	See *P. cyanea*
rovirosae	CPas LRHS SSte

rubra	CBlo CPas EWes SLim WBod WStI
* *rufa*	CPas
'Saint Rule'	CPas LPri
sanguinolenta	CPas ELan ERea LChe LPri LRHS MAsh SSte
'Sapphire'	CPas LPri
§ *seemannii*	CPas SSte
serrata	See *P. serratodigitata*
serratifolia	CPas
§ *serratodigitata*	CPas SSte
serrulata	CPas
sexflora	CPas LRHS
'Smythiana'	CPas
standleyi	CPas
'Star of Bristol' ♀	CHEx CPas LPri SLim
'Star of Clevedon'	CPas
'Star of Kingston'	CPas
stipulata	CPas
suberosa	CPas LPri SSte
subpeltata	CPas SSte
'Sunburst'	CPas CPIN LPri LRHS SOWG SSte
talamancensis	CPas
tatei	Last listed 1999
tenuifila	CPas
§ *tetrandra*	CGre CPas ECou
tica	Last listed 1999
x *tresederi*	See *P.* x *violacea* 'Tresederi'
¶ *trialata*	CPas
tricuspis	CPas
tridactylites	CPas SSte
trifasciata	CPas CPIN SSte
tripartita	CPas
- JCA 13982	Last listed 1998
* *triphostemmatoides*	CPas
trisecta	CPas
tuberosa	CPas
tulae	CPas SSte
umbilicata	CPas CPIN WCru
urbaniana	CPas
vespertilio	CPas
§ x *violacea* ♀	CBlo CPas CPIN CRHN ECon ERea LCns LRHS MBri
- 'Dedorina'	Last listed 1999
- 'Eynsford Gem'	CPas
- 'Lilac Lady'	See *P.* x *violacea* 'Tresederi'
§ - 'Tresederi'	CPas EBee MAsh SAga
- 'Victoria'	CPas LPri SLim
viridiflora	CPas
vitifolia (F)	CHEx CPas CPIN ECon ELan ERea LChe LPri LRHS SOWG
- 'Scarlet Flame' (F)	CPas LPri
¶ *wurdackii*	CPas
xiikzodz	CPas
yucatanensis	CPas
zamorana	CPas

PASTINACA (Apiaceae)
sativa	CKin

PATERSONIA (Iridaceae)
occidentalis	Last listed 1998

PATRINIA (Valerianaceae)
gibbosa	CLyd CRDP EBee EWTr GCHN NFla SSca SWal WCru WPnP WRus
rupestris	EBee IIve
* *sambucifolia*	Last listed 1998
saniculifolia	EBee WCru
scabiosifolia	CBlo CMil EBee ECha ECoo EMan GBuc GOrP NBir NChi NLar SEND SMrm SSca SSvw SUsu

	WElm WPic WWin
- 'Nagoya'	MNrw
triloba	CLyd CPla CRDP EBrP EBre EDAr
	EPPr GKir LBCl LBSe LBre LRHS
	MBBe MRav NMen NWoo SBre
	SSpi SUsu
* - 'Minor'	ECho
- var. *palmata*	GCHN GKir NBus WFar
- var. *triloba*	CGle GCal GDea NTow WWin
villosa	Last listed 1999

PAULOWNIA (Scrophulariaceae)

fargesii Franchet	CLnd IMGH SLPl SMad
- Osborn	See *P. tomentosa* 'Lilacina'
fortunei	CGre CMCN WLRN WNor
¶ *kawakamii*	CFil WPGP
tomentosa ♀	More than 30 suppliers
- 'Coreana'	CGre
§ - 'Lilacina'	CB&S

PAVONIA (Malvaceae)

§ x *gledhillii*	Last listed 1998
multiflora Jussieu	ERea
praemorsa	CBot

PAXISTIMA (Celastraceae)

canbyi	MBro NPro SPan WAbe WPat
myrsinites	See *P. myrtifolia*
§ *myrtifolia*	EPla ESis WWat

PECTEILIS (Orchidaceae)

* *dentata*	EFEx
§ *radiata*	EFEx
* - 'Albomarginata'	EFEx
- 'Aureomarginata'	EFEx

PEDILANTHUS (Euphorbiaceae)

| *tithymaloides* 'Variegatus' LChe |

PEGANUM (Zygophyllaceae)

| *harmala* | CArn MSal WWye |

PELARGONIUM ✿ (Geraniaceae)

'A Happy Thought'	See *P.* 'Happy Thought'
'A.M. Mayne' (Z/d)	CWDa SPet
'Abba' (Z/d)	CWDa
'Abel Carrière' (I/d)	SKen WFib
abrotanifolium (Sc)	CSev MHer WEas WFib
- broad-leaved	Last listed 1998
'Acapulco'	LRHS NPri
acerifolium hort.	See *P. vitifolium*
acetosum	GCal MSte SHFr SMrm
* - 'Variegatum'	CSpe MSte
acraeum	WFib
Action (Z/d)	Last listed 1999
'Acushla by Brian' (Sc)	MWhe NFir
'Ada Sutterby' (Dw/d)	SKen WFib
'Adagio' (Dw)	ESul
'Adam's Quilt' (Z/C)	SKen WEas
'Adele' (Min/d)	ESul WFib
'Ade's Elf' (Z/St)	NFir SSea
'Aerosol' (Min)	ESul WFib
'African Belle' (R)	Last listed 1998
'Afterglow' (Z)	WFib
'Ailsa' (Min/d)	ESul SKen
'Ainsdale Angel' (A)	LDea
'Ainsdale Beauty' (Z)	Last listed 1998
'Ainsdale Claret' (Z)	NFir
'Ainsdale Eyeful' (Z)	LVER
'Akela' (Min)	ESul
'Alan West' (Z/St)	Last listed 1998
§ Alba = 'Fisalb' PBR (Z/d)	LRHS SKen

'Alberta' (Z)	SKen WFib
'Albert's Choice' (R)	WFib
album	CWDa
alchemilloides	CRHN WFib
'Alcyone' (Dw/d)	ESul SKen WFib
'Alde' (Min)	ESul LHil MWhe NFir SKen WEas
'Aldenham' (Z)	WFib
'Aldham' (Min)	ESul LVER WFib
'Aldwyck' (R)	EBSP LDea WFib
'Alex' (Z)	CWDa SKen
'Alex Mary' (R)	SSea WFib
'Alfred Wolfe'	Last listed 1997
'Algenon' (Min/d)	ESul WFib
'Alice Crousse' (I/d) ♀	WFib
'Alice Greenfield' (Z)	NFir
'Alison' (Dw)	ESul
'Alison Jill' (Z/d)	CWDa
'Alison Wheeler' (Min/d)	MWhe
'All My Love' (R)	LDea WFib
¶ 'Allicia' (R)	EBSP
'Alma' (Min/C)	ESul
'Almost Heaven' (Dw/Z/v)	MWhe
'Alpine Glow' (Z/d)	MWhe
'Alpine Orange' (Z/d)	CWDa
'Alta Bell' (R)	WFib
'Altair' (Min/d)	ESul WFib
alternans	CSev WEas
'Always' (Z/d)	WFib
'Alys Collins' (Z/d)	WFib
'Amarantha' (Z)	Last listed 1999
'Amari' (R)	LDea
'Ambrose' (Dw/d)	ESul WFib
'Amethyst' (R)	EBSP LDea LRHS SKen WFib
§ 'Amethyst' (I/d) ♀	ECtt LDea LVER MWhe NPri WFib
	WLRN
'Ami' (R)	WFib
'Anabell Stephenson'	WFib
(Dw/d)	
'Andersonii' (Sc)	EWoo MHer WFib
'Andrew Salvidge' (R)	LDea WFib
'Androcles' (A)	NFir
I 'Andromeda' (Min)	WFib
'Ange Davey' (Z/d)	WFib
'Angela Brook'	CWDa
'Angela Read' (Dw)	ESul
'Angela Woodberry' (I/d)	CWDa
'Angelique' (Dw/d)	ESul LVER NFir WFib
'Anglia' (Dw)	ESul
'Ann Hoystead' (R) ♀	WFib
'Ann Redington' (R)	LDea WFib
'Ann Sothern' (Z)	WFib
'Anna' (Dw)	ESul WFib
'Anna Scheen' (Dw)	ESul
'Anne Wilkie-Millar' (Z/d)	WFib
¶ 'Annsbrook Aquarius' (St)	ESul NFir
¶ 'Annsbrook Beauty' (A/C)	ESul LDea LVER
'Annsbrook Capricorn'	ESul
(St/d)	
¶ 'Annsbrook Hope' (Dw/C)	ESul
'Annsbrook Jupitor' (St)	ESul NFir
'Annsbrook Mars' (St)	ESul
'Annsbrook Pluto' (St)	ESul NFir
'Annsbrook Venus' (St)	ESul
antidysentericum	Last listed 1998
'Antigua' (R)	LDea WFib
'Antoine Crozy' (ZxI/d)	WFib
'Antoinette' (Min)	ESul
'Apache' (Z/d) ♀	CHal CWDa WFib
'Aphrodite' (Z)	CWDa ECtt WFib
'Apollo' (R)	CWDa
'Apple Betty' (Sc)	LDea WFib
'Apple Blossom	ECtt ESul LRHS LVER MBri MWhe

'Rosebud' (Z/d) ♀	NFir NSwl SKen SMrm SUsu WEas WFib
'Appledram' (R)	EBSP LDea WFib
'Apri Parmer' (Min)	ESul
'Apricot' (Z/St/d)	ESul NFir SKen
'Apricot Queen' (I/d)	LDea
'Apricot Star'	CSpe MSte MWhe
'April Hamilton' (I)	LDea WFib
'Aquarell' (R)	Last listed 1997
'Arctic Frost'	Last listed 1998
'Arctic Queen' (R)	Last listed 1997
§ 'Arctic Star' (Z/St/d)	CSpe ESul LRHS LVER NFir SKen SSea WEas WWol
'Arcturus' (Min)	WFib
'Ardens'	CSpe EWoo LHil NFir NSwl SAga SSad SSea SUsu WCot WEas
'Ardwick Cinnamon'	ESul LDea LVER NFir
aridum	Last listed 1998
'Aries' (Min/C)	ESul MWhe
'Arizona' (Min/d)	ESul SKen WFib
'Arnside Fringed Aztec' (R)	LDea
'Aroma' (Sc)	EWoo LIck WFib
'Arron Dixon' (A)	NFir
'Arthington Slam' (R)	LDea
'Arthur Biggin' (Z)	MWhe SKen
articulatum	Last listed 1998
'Ashby' (Sc)	LVER
'Ashby' (U)	Last listed 1998
'Ashfield Blaze' (Z/d)	LVER WFib
'Ashfield Jubilee' (Z/C)	NFir SKen
'Ashfield Monarch' (Z/d) ♀	LVER MWhe NFir WFib
'Ashfield Serenade' (Z) ♀	SKen WFib
'Ashley Stephenson' (R)	WFib
'Askham Fringed Aztec' (R) ♀	EBSP LDea LVER
'Askham Slam' (R)	LDea
asperum Ehr. ex Willd.	See P. 'Graveolens'
'Astrakan' (Z/d)	Last listed 1998
'Athabasca' (Min)	ESul
'Atomic Snowflake' (Sc/v)	CArn CHal CInt EDAr ERav ESul GBar LDea LVER MHer MSte MWhe NFir SKen SPet SSea WCHb WFib WJek
'Attar of Roses' (Sc) ♀	CArn CBrm CHal CInt CLTr CRHN EDAr EOHP ERav ESul GBar LDea LRHS LVER MHer MWhe NFir NHHG SIde SKen WCHb WFib WWye
'Attraction' (Z/St/d)	WFib
'Aubusson' (R)	WFib
'Audrey' (Z/d)	WFib
'Audrey Baghurst' (I)	CWDa
'Audrey Clifton' (I/d)	ECtt SKen WFib
'Augusta'	LHop SMrm
'Auralia' (Z/d)	Last listed 1998
auritum	Last listed 1998
'Aurora' (Z/d)	MWhe SKen
'Aurore'	See P. 'Unique Aurore'
australe	CFir ERav EWes EWoo SMrm SSpi SUsu WFib
'Australian Mystery' (R/Dec)	NFir NSwl
'Autumn' (Z/d)	MWhe WFib
'Autumn Colours' (Min)	ESul
'Autumn Festival' (R)	WFib
'Autumn Haze' (R)	EBSP WFib
'Autumn Mist' (R)	WFib
'Avril'	ESul
'Aztec' (R) ♀	EBSP LDea LVER MSte NFir WEas WFib
'Aztec Fimbriant'	SMrm
'Baby Birds Egg' (Min)	CSpe ESul NFir WFib
'Baby Brocade' (Min/d)	ESul LVER WFib

'Baby Face' (Dw)	EWoo
'Baby Helen' (Min)	ESul
'Baby James' (Min)	ESul
'Baby Snooks' (A)	LDea
'Babylon' (R)	EBSP NFir WFib
'Badley' (Dw)	ESul
Balcon Imperial	See P. 'Roi des Balcons Impérial'
'Balcon Lilas'	See P. 'Roi des Balcons Lilas'
'Balcon Rose'	See P. 'Hederinum'
'Balcon Rouge'	See P. 'Roi des Balcons Impérial'
'Balcon Royale'	See P. 'Roi des Balcons Impérial'
¶ 'Bali Sunrise' (St)	NFir
'Bali Surprise' (Z/St)	Last listed 1998
'Ballerina' (Dw/d)	ERav MWhe
'Ballerina' (R)	See P. 'Carisbrooke'
'Bandit' (Min)	ESul
'Bantam' (Min/d)	ESul WFib
§ 'Barbe Bleu' (I/d)	ECtt LDea LVER MWhe NFir SKen SSea SUsu WFib
'Barking' (Min)	ESul NFir
barklyi	Last listed 1998
'Barnston Dale' (Dw)	ESul NFir
'Barock '96'	NPri
§ Barock = 'Fisrock' PBR (I)	NSwl
'Baron de Layres' (Z/d)	WFib
'Baronne A. de Rothschild' (Z/d)	WFib
'Bashful' (Min)	Last listed 1997
'Bath Beauty' (Dw)	SKen WEas
'Baylham' (Min)	ESul
¶ Beach® = 'Fisbea' PBR (I/d)	NPri
'Beacon Hill' (Min)	ESul
'Beatrice Cottington' (I/d)	SKen WFib
'Beatrix' (Z/d)	LVER SKen WFib
'Beau Geste' (R)	EBSP
'Beauty' (Z)	WFib
'Beauty of Bath' (R)	WFib
'Beauty of Calderdale' (Z/C)	WFib
¶ 'Beauty of Diane' (I/d)	LDea
N 'Beauty of Eastbourne'	See P. 'Lachskönigin'
'Beauty of El Segundo' (Z/d)	SKen WFib
'Beauty of Jersey' (I/d)	WFib
'Beckwith's Pink' (Z)	EWoo SKen
'Belinda Adams' (Min/d) ♀	MWhe NFir WFib
§ 'Belladonna' (I/d)	ECtt NPri WWol
'Belstead' (Min)	NFir
'Belvedere' (R)	EBSP
'Bembridge'	SSea
'Ben Franklin' (Z/v) ♀	LVER MWhe NFir WFib
'Ben Matt' (R)	LDea WFib
'Ben Nevis' (Dw/d)	ESul
'Bentley' (Dw)	ESul
'Bergpalais' PBR (Z/d)	Last listed 1998
'Berliner Balkon' (I)	SKen
'Bern'	Last listed 1998
'Bernado'	WLRN
'Beromünster' (Dec)	ESul EWoo LDea LVER MSte NFir WEas WFib
'Bert Pearce' (R)	EBSP LDea WFib
'Beryl Gibbons' (Z/d)	LVER MWhe
'Beryl Read' (Dw)	ERea ESul
'Beryl Reid' (R)	EBSP LDea WFib
'Berylette' (Min/d)	ESul SKen WFib
'Bess' (Z/d)	ESul LVER SKen
'Beta' (Min/C)	ESul
'Bette Shellard' (Z/d)	LVER MWhe NFir
'Betty' (Z/d)	LVER
'Betty Dollery' (Z/d)	Last listed 1998
'Betty Hulsman' (A)	ESul LDea NFir
'Betty Read' (Dw)	ESul
'Betty West' (Min/d)	Last listed 1998
betulinum	EWoo WFib

'Betwixt' (Z/v) — NFir SKen SSea WFib
'Bev Foster' (d) — Last listed 1998
'Bewerley Park' (Z/C/d) — WFib
'Bianca' (Min/d) — ESul
'Bicester Gem' — Last listed 1998
'Bi-coloured Startel' (Z/St/d) — MWhe NFir
'Biedermeier' (R) — Last listed 1998
'Bildeston' (Z/C) — ESul NFir
'Bill West' (I) — Last listed 1998
'Billie Read' (Dw/d) — ERea ESul
'Bingo' (Min) — ESul
'Bird Dancer' (Dw/St) ♀ — CPlt CSpe ERav ESul LHil LVER MSte MWhe NFir SAga SHFr SKen SSea SUsu WEas WFib
'Birthday Girl' (R) — WFib
'Bitter Lemon' (Sc) — ESul
'Black Butterfly' — See P. 'Brown's Butterfly'
'Black Country Bugle' (Z/d) — CWDa
'Black Knight' (R) — CMdw CSpe ESul EWoo LDea LVER MSte NFir WFib
'Black Magic' (R) — WFib
'Black Night' (A) — ESul NFir
'Black Pearl' (Z/d) — WFib
'Black Prince' (R) — CElw NFir WEas
'Black Velvet' (R) — LDea
'Black Vesuvius' — See P. 'Red Black Vesuvius'
'Blackcurrant Sundae' — Last listed 1998
'Blakesdorf' (Dw) — ESul MWhe
'Blanca' (Z/d) — LVER
'Blanche Roche' — EWoo NPri SCoo WLRN
§ 'Blandfordianum' (Sc) — EWoo LDea SSad
§ 'Blauer Frühling' (I/d) — LVER SKen
'Blaze Away' — Last listed 1999
'Blazonry' (Z/v) — MWhe NFir SKen WFib
'Blendworth' (R) — LDea
'Bloomfield Abundance' — Last listed 1998
'Blooming Gem' (Min/I/d) — LDea
'Blue Beard' — See P. 'Barbe Bleu'
'Blue Blizzard' — NPri WWol
'Blue Fox' (Z) — CWDa
'Blue Orchid' (R) — LDea WFib
'Blue Peter' (I/d) — SKen
'Blue Spring' — See P. 'Blauer Frühling'
'Bluebeard' — ERav
§ 'Blues' PBR (Z/d) — CWDa
'Blush Kleine Liebling' (Min) — WFib
'Blush Mariquita' (R) — WFib
'Blush Petit Pierre' (Min) — ESul
'Blushing Bride' (I/d) — LDea SKen
'Blushing Emma' (Z) — ESul WFib
'Bob Legge' (Z/d) — WFib
'Bode's Trina' (I) — CWDa
'Bodey's Picotee' (R) ♀ — WFib
'Bold Candy' (R) — LDea
'Bold Carmine' (Dw) — NFir
'Bold Dawn' (Z) — NFir
'Bold Flame' (Z/d) — WFib
¶ 'Bold Gypsy' (R) — LDea
¶ 'Bold Moonlight' — EWoo
'Bold Queen' (Z) — NFir
'Bold Romance' (Z) — NSwl
'Bold Sunrise' (Z/d) — LVER NFir
'Bold Sunset' (Z/d) — LVER NFir WFib
'Bold White' (Z) — NFir
'Bolero' (U) ♀ — EWoo LVER MSte NFir NPri SSea WFib
'Bonito' (I/d) — LVER
'Boogy' — Last listed 1998
'Bosham' (R) — EBSP LDea WFib
'Botham's Surprise' (Z/d) — Last listed 1998
'Both's Snowflake' (Sc/d) — EWoo
'Botley Beauty' (R) — EBSP LDea WFib

'Boudoir' (Z/C/d) — ESul
'Bouldner' — Last listed 1998
bowkeri — Last listed 1998
'Brackenwood' (Min/d) ♀ — ESul LVER NFir WFib
'Bramford' (Dw) — ESul
'Braque' (R) — LDea WFib
'Brasil' — WLRN WWol
'Bravo' (Z/d) — MWhe WFib
'Break o' Day' (R) — LDea WEas
'Bredon' (R) ♀ — WFib
'Brenda' (Min/d) — ESul
'Brenda Hyatt' (Dw/d) — ESul WFib
'Brenda Kitson' (Z/d) — LVER MWhe
'Brialyn Beauty' (A) — LDea NFir
'Brialyn Moonlight' (A) — ESul LDea
¶ 'Briarlyn Beauty' — MWhe
'Briarlyn Moonglow' (A) — LVER
'Briarlyn Moonglow' (A) — LVER
'Bridal Veil' (Min/C) ♀ — Last listed 1995
'Bridesmaid' (Dw/C/d) — ESul NFir SKen WFib
'Brightstone' — Last listed 1998
'Brightwell' (Min/d) — ESul WFib
'Brilliant' (Dec) — MHer WFib
¶ 'Brilliantine' (Sc) — EWoo
¶ 'Brimham Rocks' (Z/C) — NFir
'Bristol' (Z/v) — SKen WFib
'Britannia' (R) — LDea
'Brixworth Boquet' (Min/C/d) — MWhe
'Brixworth Charmer' (Z/v) — MWhe
'Brixworth Melody' (Z/v) — MWhe
'Brixworth Pearl' (Z) — MWhe
'Brixworth Rhapsody' (Z/v) — MWhe
'Brixworth Starlight' (I/v) — MWhe
'Broadway' (Min) — WFib
'Brocade' (Z/d) — WFib
'Brockbury Scarlet' (Ca) — WFib
'Bronze Corinne' (Z/C/d) — SKen SPet
'Bronze Nuhulumby' (R) — WFib
'Bronze Queen' (Z/C) — MWhe
'Bronze Velvet' (R) — LDea WFib
'Brook' — Last listed 1999
'Brook's Purple' — See P. 'Royal Purple'
'Brookside Abigail' — Last listed 1998
'Brookside Astra' — Last listed 1998
'Brookside Betty' (Dw/C/d) — ESul
'Brookside Bolero' (Z) — ESul
'Brookside Candy' (Dw/d) — ESul WFib
'Brookside Champagne' (Min/d) — ESul
'Brookside Cinderella' (Z/C/d) — Last listed 1999
'Brookside Flamenco' (Min/d) — ESul MWhe WFib
'Brookside Primrose' (Min/C/d) — ESul MWhe NFir SKen WFib
'Brookside Rosita' (Min) — ESul
'Brookside Serenade' (Z) — ESul WFib
'Brookside Spitfire' (Dw/d) — ESul
§ 'Brown's Butterfly' (R) — EBSP LDea LHop NFir WEas WFib
§ 'Bruni' (Z) — CHal MWhe
§ 'Brunswick' (Sc) — ESul EWoo LDea LVER MHer MSte WFib
'Brutus' (Z) — CWDa
bubonifolium — Last listed 1998
'Bucklesham' (Dw) — ESul
'Budbridge' (St) — Last listed 1999
'Bumblebee' (Dw) — Last listed 1998
'Burgenlandmädel' (Z/d) — LVER SKen WFib
'Burgundy' (R) — LDea LVER WFib
'Burnaby' (Min) — WFib
'Burstall' (Min/d) — Last listed 1998
'Bushfire' (R) ♀ — EBSP LDea WFib

	'Butley' (Min)	ESul
	'Buttercup Don' (Z/d)	Last listed 1997
	'Butterfly' (Min/v)	ECtt NPri
§	'Butterfly' (I)	NFir WFib
§	Cabaret (Z/d)	Last listed 1999
	caffrum	Last listed 1998
	'Cal'	See *P.* 'Salmon Irene'
	'Caledonia' (Z)	SKen
	'Caledonian Maiden' (Z)	WFib
	'California Brilliant' (U)	NFir
	'Caligula' (Min/d)	WFib
	'Calypso' (Z)	WFib
	'Cameo' (Dw/d)	MWhe WFib
	'Camilla' (Dw)	Last listed 1998
	'Camphor Rose' (Sc)	CLTr ESul MHer NFir SSea
*	'Canadian Centennial'	Last listed 1999
	'Can-can' (I/d)	WFib
	candicans	WFib
	'Candy' (Min/d)	ESul
	'Candy Kisses' (D)	ESul
	canescens	See *P.* 'Blandfordianum'
	'Capel' (Dw/d)	ESul
	'Capella' (Min)	WFib
	Capen (Z/d)	Last listed 1998
	capitatum	CInt MHer WEas WFib
	'Capri' (Sc)	WFib
	'Caprice' (R)	EWoo WFib
	'Capricorn' (Min/d)	ESul
	'Captain Starlight' (A)	ESul EWoo LDea LHil LVER NFir
		NSwl SSea WEas WFib
¶	'Caravan' (A)	LDea
	'Cardinal'	See *P.* 'Kardinal'
	'Cardinal Pink' (Z/d)	CWDa
	'Carefree' (U)	EWoo MSte NFir WFib
	'Cariboo Gold' (Min/C) ♀	ESul NFir SKen
§	'Carisbrooke' (R) ♀	CLTr LDea SKen SSea WEas WFib
	'Carmel' (Z)	EWoo WFib
	'Carnival' (R)	See *P.* 'Marie Vogel'
	'Carnival' (Z)	WFib
	carnosum	Last listed 1998
	'Carol Ann' (Z)	Last listed 1997
	'Carol Gibbons' (Z/d)	LVER MWhe NFir
	'Carole' (R)	EBSP
	'Carole Munroe' (Z/d)	LVER
	'Caroline Plumridge' (Dw)	ESul WFib
	'Caroline Schmidt'	CHal LDea LRHS LVER MSte
	(Z/d/v) ♀	MWhe NFir NWoo SKen SSea
		SYvo WFib WWol
	'Carolyn' (Min)	ESul
	'Carousel' (Z/d)	CWDa
	'Casanova' (Z/d)	WLRN
*	'Cascade Lilac'	WFib
*	'Cascade Pink'	WFib
*	'Cascade Red'	WFib
§	Casino (Z/d)	Last listed 1998
	'Cassata' (R)	WFib
	'Catford Belle' (A) ♀	CSpe ESul LDea MWhe NFir SKen
		SSea WEas WFib
	'Cathay' (Z/St)	ESul MWhe NFir SSea
	'Cathy' (Z/St)	Last listed 1999
	'Cathy' (R)	NFir
	caucalifolium	Last listed 1998
	subsp. *caucalifolium*	
	- subsp. *convolvulifolium*	WFib
	caylae	Last listed 1998
	'Cayucas' (I/d)	SKen
	'Celebration' (Z/d)	ESul
	'Celia' (Min)	WFib
*	Century Series (Z) ♀	SSea
	ceratophyllum	Last listed 1998
	'Cézanne' (R)	ERav LDea LVER SMrm WFib
§	Champagne (Z)	CWDa

	'Chantilly Claret' (R)	EBSP LDea
	'Chantilly Lace' (R)	EBSP LDea
	'Charity' (Sc) ♀	CBrm EDAr ERav ESul EWoo LDea
		Llck LVER MSte MWhe NFir WFib
§	'Charles Gounod' (Z/d)	SKen
§	Charleston (Z)	Last listed 1998
	'Charlie Boy' (R)	LDea WFib
	'Charlotte Bidwell' (Min)	ESul NFir
	'Charlotte Brontë' (Z/C)	NFir
	'Charlotte Read' (Dw)	ERea
	'Charm' (Min)	ESul
	'Charmant'	CWDa
	'Charmer' (R)	LDea
	'Charmy Snowflake'	WFib WHer
	'Chattisham' (Min)	NFir
	'Cheerio' (seed raised)	Last listed 1995
	(Z) ♀	
	'Chelmondiston' (Min/d)	ESul MWhe
§	'Chelsea Gem' (Z/d/v) ♀	LRHS LVER SKen SSea WFib
	'Chelsea Morning' (Z/d)	WFib
	'Chelsworth' (Min/d)	ESul WFib
	'Chelvey' (R)	LDea WFib
	'Cherie' (Min)	WFib
	'Cherie' (R)	EBSP LDea WFib
	'Cherie' (Z) ♀	Last listed 1995
	'Cherie Bidwell' (Dw/d)	ESul NFir
	'Cherie Maid' (Z/v)	EWoo SSea WFib
	'Cherry' (Z/d)	WFib
	'Cherry' (Min)	LVER WFib
	'Cherry Baby' (Dec)	NFir
	'Cherry Cocktail' (Z/v)	MWhe
	'Cherry Galilee' (I/d)	SKen
	'Cherry Hazel Ruffled' (R)	LDea
	'Cherry Orchard' (R)	LDea LVER SKen SSea WFib
	'Cherry Sundae' (Z/d/v)	ESul LVER NFir WFib
	'Cherryade' (Dw)	Last listed 1998
	'Cheryldene' (R)	LDea
	'Chessington' (Z/C)	Last listed 1998
	'Chew Magna' (R)	WFib
	'Chic'	Last listed 1998
	'Chi-Chi' (Min)	ESul
	'Chieko' (Min/d)	ESul MWhe WFib
	'Chiltern Surprise' (Z/St)	NFir
	'Chime' (Min/d)	ESul
	'China Doll' (Dw/d)	WFib
	'Chinz' (R)	EWoo NFir
	'Chiquita' (R)	WFib
	'Chocolate Blotch' (Z/C)	Last listed 1999
§	'Chocolate Peppermint'	CHal CInt CLTr CSev ERav ESul
	(Sc) ♀	GBar LDea LHil LRHS LVER MHer
		MWhe NBur NFir NHHG NSwl
		SKen SSea SYvo WCHb WEas
		WFib WHer WJek
	'Chocolate Tomentosum'	See *P.* 'Chocolate Peppermint'
	'Choice Cerise' (R)	LDea
	'Chorus Girl' (R)	Last listed 1998
	'Chrissie' (R)	EBSP
	'Christie' (Z/d)	Last listed 1998
¶	'Christina Beere' (R)	LDea
	'Christopher Ley' (Z)	LVER SKen
¶	'Chusan'	EWoo
	'Cindy' (Dw/d)	ESul
	'Circus Day' (R)	LDea WFib
	'Citriodorum' (Sc) ♀	CArn CInt EOHP LDea LRHS
		MHer NHHG WCHb WFib WPer
	'Citronella' (Sc)	LDea LRHS MHer MSte WFib
	citronellum (Sc)	CInt WFib WPer
	'Clair' (Min)	WFib
	'Clara Read' (Dw)	ESul
	'Claret Cruz' (I)	CWDa
	'Claret Rock Unique' (U)	CLTr EWoo LDea MHer MSte NFir
		SKen SMrm WFib

'Clarissa' (Min) — ESul
'Clatterbridge' (Dw/d) — ESul LVER NFir WFib
'Claude Read' (Dw) — ERea ESul
'Claudette' (Min) — ESul
'Claudius' (Min) — ESul
'Claydon' (Dw/d) — ESul NFir
'Claydon Firebird' (R) — EBSP
'Cleopatra' (Z) — WFib
'Clorinda' (U/Sc) — CHal CSev ERea ESul EWoo GBar LVER MHer MSte NBur SKen SSea WFib WHer WJek
'Clorinda Variegated' — See *P.* 'Variegated Clorinda'
'Clown' (R) — WFib
¶ 'Coconut Ice' (Dw) — ESul
§ Coco-Rico (I) — SKen
'Coddenham' (Dw/d) — ESul LVER WFib
'Colette' (Min) — WFib
§ 'Colonel Baden-Powell' (I/d) — LDea
'Colonel Drabbe' (Z/d) — Last listed 1999
§ Columbia (Z/Sc) — Last listed 1998
columbinum — Last listed 1998
'Comedy' — NPri WLRN
'Concolor Lace' (Sc) — CLTr CRHN ESul MHer NFir SSea
'Conspicuous' (R) — EWoo WFib
'Contrast' (Z/d/C/v) — LRHS MBri MWhe NFir SKen SSea WEas WFib WWol
'Cook's Freckles' (I) — Last listed 1999
'Cook's Red Spider' (Ca) — WFib
'Copdock' (Min/d) — ESul
'Copthorne' (Sc) ♀ — CMdw LDea LVER MHer SKen WFib
'Coral Frills' (Dw) — ESul
'Coral Sunset' (d) — CWDa
'Coralglow' (Z/d) — Last listed 1998
cordifolium — EWoo WFib
'Coriand' (Z/d) — WFib
coriandrifolium — See *P. myrrhifolium* var. *coriandrifolium*
'Cornell' (I/d) — ECtt WFib
'Coronia' (Z/Ca) — CWDa
coronopifolium — Last listed 1998
'Corsair' (Z/d) ♀ — MWhe WFib
cortusifolium — Last listed 1998
'Cotswold Queen' (Z/d) — Last listed 1999
'Cotta Lilac Queen' (I/d) — LVER
'Cottenham Beauty' (A) — EWoo LDea NFir
'Cottenham Charm' (A) — ESul
'Cottenham Delight' (A) — ESul NFir
'Cottenham Gem' (A) — ESul
'Cottenham Pride' (A) — Last listed 1999
'Cottenham Surprise' (A) — ESul LDea NFir
'Cotton Candy' (Dw/d) — ESul
'Cottontail' (Min/d) — ESul LVER
cotyledonis — WFib
'Countess Mariza' — See *P.* 'Gräfin Mariza'
'Countess of Birkenhead' (Z) — Last listed 1999
'Countess of Scarborough' — See *P.* 'Lady Scarborough'
'Country Girl' (R) — NFir WFib
'Courbet' — Last listed 1997
'Cover Girl' (Z/d) — WFib
'Cramdon Red' (Dw) — SKen WFib
'Crampel's Crimson' — EWoo
'Crampel's Master' (Z) — LVER SKen
'Cranbrook Black' — EWoo
¶ 'Cranbrooks Unique' — EWoo
'Cransley Blends' (R) — EBSP LDea WFib
'Cransley Star' (A) — ESul LDea MWhe WFib
crassicaule — Last listed 1998
'Cream and Green' — NFir
'Creamery' (Z/d) — WFib

§ 'Creamy Nutmeg' (Sc/v) — CArn CHal CLTr EDAr EOHP ESul GBar LDea LRHS LVER MHer MWhe NBur NFir SRob SSea
'Creed's Seedling' (Z/C) — ERav
'Creeting St Mary' (Min) — ESul
'Creeting St Peter' (Min) — ESul
'Crescendo' (I/d) — ECtt
'Crimson Crampel' (Z) — CWDa
'Crimson Fire' (Z/d) — MBri MWhe SKen
'Crimson Unique' (U) ♀ — CSpe EWoo LHil MHer SAga SKen SSea WFib
§ *crispum* (Sc) — GBar GPoy LDea MHer NHHG WCHb WFib WJek WRha
– 'Major' (Sc) — ESul LRHS SKen WFib WPer
– 'Minor' — MHer
– 'Peach Cream' (Sc/v) — CHal LRHS MWhe WFib WJek
– 'Variegatum' (Sc/v) ♀ — CHal CRHN CSev EDAr GBar GPoy LDea LRHS LVER MHer MWhe NFir SKen SRob SSea WCHb WEas WFib
'Crock O Day' (I/d) — LVER
'Crocketta' (I/d/v) — LVER NFir SSea
'Crocodile' — See *P.* 'The Crocodile'
'Crowfield' (Min/d) — ESul LVER
¶ 'Crown Jewels' (R) — LDea
'Crystal Palace Gem' (Z/v) — LRHS LVER MWhe SKen SMrm SSea WFib
cucullatum — ERav EWoo SVen WFib
'Culpho' (Min/C/d) — ESul
'Cupid' (Min/Dw/d) — ESul WFib
'Cynthia' (Min) — Last listed 1997
'Cyril Read' (Dw) — ERea ESul
§ 'Czar' (Z/C) — WFib
'Dainty Lassie' (Dw/v) — ESul
'Dainty Maid' — ESul EWoo LVER NFir SSea SYvo
'Dale Queen' (Z) — WFib
'Dame Anna Neagle' (Dw/d) ♀ — WFib
'Dancer' (Dw) — ESul
'Dandee' (Z/d) — Last listed 1999
¶ 'Danielle Marie' (A) — LDea
'Danny West' — Last listed 1998
'Dark Lady' (Sc) — WFib
'Dark Red Irene' (Z/d) — LVER MWhe WFib
'Dark Secret' (R) — CSpe EBSP EWoo LDea MSte SKen WFib
'Dark Venus' (R) — LDea WFib
'Darmsden' (A) ♀ — ESul LDea NFir
dasyphyllum — Last listed 1998
'David John' (Dw/d) — ESul
'Davina' (Min/d) — ESul MWhe WFib
'Dawn' (Z/d) — Last listed 1999
'Dawn Star' (Z/St) — ESul NFir WFib
'Daybreak' (Z/v) — NFir
'Deacon Arlon' (Dw/d) — ESul LVER MWhe SKen
'Deacon Avalon' (Dw/d) — WFib
'Deacon Barbecue' (Z/d) — ESul MWhe SKen
'Deacon Birthday' (Z/d) — ESul LVER MWhe WFib
'Deacon Bonanza' (Z/d) — ESul MWhe SKen WFib
'Deacon Clarion' (Z/d) — ESul SKen
'Deacon Constancy' (Z/d) — ESul LVER MWhe
'Deacon Coral Reef' (Z/d) — ESul MWhe SKen WFib
'Deacon Delight' — EWoo
'Deacon Finale' (Z/d) — ESul LVER
'Deacon Finito' — See *P.* 'Finito'
'Deacon Fireball' (Z/d) — ESul LVER MWhe SKen WFib
'Deacon Flamingo' (Z/d) — ESul MWhe
'Deacon Gala' (Z/d) — ESul MWhe
'Deacon Golden Bonanza' (Z/C/d) — ESul WFib
'Deacon Golden Gala' (Z/C/d) — ESul SKen

I   'Deacon Golden Lilac   ESul SKen WFib
    Mist' (Z/C/d)
    'Deacon Golden Mist'   See *P.* 'Golden Mist'
    'Deacon Jubilant' (Z/d)   ESul MWhe SKen
    'Deacon Lilac Mist' (Z/d)   ESul LVER MWhe NFir SKen WFib
    'Deacon Mandarin' (Z/d)   ESul MWhe SKen
    'Deacon Minuet' (Z/d)   ESul LVER MWhe NFir SKen
    'Deacon Moonlight' (Z/d)   ESul LVER MWhe
    'Deacon Peacock' (Z/C/d)   ESul MWhe SKen
    'Deacon Picotee' (Z/d)   ESul LVER MWhe SKen
    'Deacon Regalia' (Z/d)   ESul MWhe SKen WFib
    'Deacon Romance' (Z/d)   ESul MWhe SKen WFib
    'Deacon Summertime' (Z/d)   ESul LVER MWhe NFir
    'Deacon Sunburst' (Z/d)   ESul LVER MWhe SKen
    'Deacon Suntan' (Z/d)   ESul LVER MWhe SKen WFib
    'Deacon Trousseau' (Z/d)   ESul MWhe SKen WFib
¶   'Deans Delight' (Sc)   LDea
¶   'Debbie' (A)   NFir
    'Debbie Parmer' (Dw/d)   ESul
    'Deborah Miliken' (Z/d)   Last listed 1998
    'Decora Impérial' (I)   LVER SKen
    'Decora Lavender' (I)   LVER
§   'Decora Lilas' (I)   ECtt SKen
    'Decora Mauve'   See *P.* 'Decora Lilas'
§   'Decora Rose' (I)   ECtt SKen
    'Decora Rouge' (I)   ECtt
    'Deerwood Lavender   EWoo LDea WFib
    Lad' (Sc)
¶   'Deerwood Lavender   LDea
    Lass'
    'Degas' (R)   WFib
    'Delhi' (R)   WFib
    'Delightful' (R)   WFib
    'Delilah' (R)   LDea
    'Delta' (Min/d)   ESul
    'Denebola' (Min/d)   ESul LVER WFib
    denticulatum   EWoo MHer NHHG SKen WCHb
         WFib WJek
§   - 'Filicifolium' (Sc)   CHal CInt ERav EWoo GBar MHer
         NHHG WFib WJek
    desertorum   Last listed 1998
    'Destiny' (R)   WFib
    'Devon Cream'   Last listed 1998
    'Diabolo'   WWol
    'Diadem' (R)   WFib
    'Diana Palmer' (Z/d)   SKen WFib
    'Diane' (Min/d)   ESul WFib
    'Diane Louise' (d)   Last listed 1998
    'Dibbinsdale' (Z)   ESul NFir
    dichondrifolium (S/c)   EWoo LVER NFir SSad WFib
    - × *reniforme* (Sc)   NFir
    'Diddi-Di' (Min/d)   ESul
    'Didi' (Min)   ESul SKen WFib
    'Dinky' (Min/d)   ESul
§   Disco (Z/d)   CWDa
    'Distinction' (Z)   CSpe MWhe NFir SAga SKen WFib
    'Doctor A. Chipault' (I/d)   LDea WFib
    'Doctor A. Vialettes' (Z/d)   CWDa
    'Doctor Margaret Sturgis'   WFib
    (Z/d)
    'Dodd's Super Double'   CHal WFib
    (Z/d)
    'Dolce Vita'   Last listed 1998
    'Dollar Bute' (R)   LDea NFir
    'Dollar Princess' (Z/C)   NFir SKen
    'Dolly Daydream' (C)   Last listed 1997
    'Dolly Moon' (C)   Last listed 1997
    'Dolly Read' (Dw)   ERea ESul WFib
    'Dolly Varden' (Z/v) ♀   LDea LVER MWhe NFir SKen
         WFib
    dolomiticum   WFib
    'Dolphin' (Min)   WFib

    'Don Quixote' (A)   LDea
¶   'Don's Barbra Leonard'   NFir
    (Dw/B)
    'Don's Carosel' (Z/v)   NFir
    'Don's Claire Pearson'   NFir
    (Z/C)
    'Don's Helen Bainbridge'   NFir
    (Z/C)
¶   'Don's Jubilee' (Dw/C)   NFir
    'Don's Judith Ann' (Z/v)   NFir
    'Don's Little Meg' (Z/C)   NFir
    'Don's Mona Noble' (Z/C/v)   NFir SKen
    'Don's Pateley Bridge' (Z/St)   NFir
    'Don's Richard A.   NFir
    Costain' (Z/C)
    'Don's Seagold'   NFir
    'Don's Silva Perle' (Dw/v)   NFir SKen
    'Don's Snowfire' (Z/C)   NFir
    'Don's Southport' (Z/C)   NFir
    'Don's Stokesley Gem'   NFir
    (Z/C)
    'Don's Sunkissed' (Dw/v)   NFir
    'Don's Whirlygig' (Z/C)   NFir
    'Dopey' (Min)   Last listed 1997
    'Doreen' (Z/d)   LVER
    'Doreen Featherby' (R)   WFib
*   'Doreen Maddison'   Last listed 1998
    'Doris Brook' (Z/d)   WFib
    'Doris Frith' (R)   LDea WFib
    'Doris Hancock' (R)   WFib
    'Doris Moore' (Z)   Last listed 1998
    'Doris Shaw' (R)   WFib
¶   'Dorothy May' (A)   LDea
    'Double Bird's Egg' (Z/d)   CWDa
    'Double Grace Wells'   ESul
    (Min/d)
    'Double Henry Jacoby'   See *P.* 'Double Jacoby'
§   'Double Jacoby' (Z/d)   WFib
    'Double Lilac White' (I/d)   SKen
    'Double New Life' (Z/d)   CHal CWDa
    'Double Orange' (Z/d)   SKen
    'Double Pink Bird's Egg'   SKen
    (Z/d)
    'Double White Lilac Eye'   Last listed 1998
    (I/d)
    'Dove' (Z)   WFib
    'Dovedale' (Dw/C)   ESul NFir
    'Downlands' (Z/d)   Last listed 1998
    'Dream' (Z)   CWDa EWoo WFib
    'Dresden China' (R)   LDea
    'Dresden Pink' (Dw)   LVER WFib
    'Dresden Pippa Rosa' (Z/S)   SKen
    'Dresden White' (Dw)   LVER
¶   Dresdner Coralit   LVER
    = 'Coralit' [PBR] (I/d)
¶   Dresdner Purpalit (I)   LVER
¶   Dresdner Rosalit   LVER
    = 'Rosalit' [PBR] (I/d)
    'Drummer Boy' (Z)   CWDa SKen
    'Dryden' (Z)   SKen WFib
    'Dubonnet' (R)   LDea SYvo WFib
    'Duchess of Devonshire' (Z)   Last listed 1999
    'Duke of Buckingham' (Z/d)   LVER
    'Duke of Devonshire' (Z/d)   LVER
    'Duke of Edinburgh'   See *P.* 'Hederinum Variegatum'
    'Dulcie' (Min)   ESul
    'Dunkery Beacon' (R)   LDea WFib
    'Dusty Rose' (Min)   ESul WFib
§   'Dwarf Miriam Baisey' (Min)   LVER WFib
    'Dwarf Miriam Read'   See *P.* 'Dwarf Miriam Baisey'
    'E. Dabner' (Z/d)   CWDa SKen WFib
    'Earl of Chester' (Min/d) ♀   WFib

'Earliana' (Dec)	CHal ESul LDea SKen
'Earlsfour' (R)	LDea MSte
'Earth Magic' (Z/v)	NFir
'Earth Summit' (Z/v)	Last listed 1999
'Eastbourne Beauty' (I/d)	WFib
'Easter Morn' (Z/St)	NFir WFib
echinatum	EWoo NSwl SAga
- 'Album'	SSad
- 'Miss Stapleton'	See *P.* 'Miss Stapleton'
¶ 'Eclipse' (Dw/d)	NFir
'Eclipse' (I)	ESul MWhe SKen WFib
'Eden Gem' (Min/d)	ESul WFib
* 'Eden Rose' (Sc)	Last listed 1997
'Edith Steane' (Dw/d)	ESul LVER
'Edmond Lachenal' (Z/d)	WFib
'Edna' (Z/d)	WFib
'Edward Hockey' (Z)	WFib
'Edward Humphris' (Z)	EWoo SKen
'Edwin Clarke' (Dw/Min)	ESul
'Eileen' (I)	LVER WFib
'Eileen Postle' (R) ♀	WFib
'Eileen Stanley' (R)	LDea
'Elaine' (R)	LDea
'Elbe Silver'	NFir NPri
'Eldorado'	WLRN
'Eleanor' (Z/d)	Last listed 1998
'Electra' (Z/d)	CWDa LVER SKen WFib
elegans	Last listed 1998
'Elfin Rapture' (R)	WFib
'Elgar' (R)	WFib
'Elizabeth Angus' (Z)	SKen WFib
'Elizabeth Cartwright' (Z)	WFib
'Elizabeth Read' (Dw)	ERea ESul WFib
'Elmsett' (Z/C/d)	ESul LVER NFir
'Elna' (Min)	ESul
elongatum	Last listed 1998
'Els' (Min/St)	ESul LVER SKen SYvo
'Els Variegated' (Min/St/v)	SMrm
'Elsi' (I/d/v)	LVER WFib
'Elsie Hickman' (R)	LDea WFib
'Elsie Portas' (Z/C/d)	ESul SKen
'Embassy' (Dw)	ESul WFib
'Emerald' (I)	SKen
'Emma Hössle'	See *P.* 'Frau Emma Hössle'
'Emma Jane Read' (Dw/d)	ERea ESul MWhe NFir WFib
'Emma Louise' (Z)	SKen
'Emmy Sensation' (R)	LDea
'Emperor Nicholas' (Z/d)	MWhe SKen
'Empress' (Z)	SKen
'Ena' (Min)	ESul
'Enchantress' (I)	SKen
'Encore' (Z/d/v)	LRHS LVER MWhe NFir
endlicherianum	EPot NWCA
'Endora' (Min)	ESul
'Endsleigh' (Sc)	Last listed 1998
englerianum	Last listed 1998
'Enid Blackaby' (R)	WFib
'Enid Read' (Dw)	ERea NFir WFib
'Eric Ellis' (Dw/d)	WFib
'Eric Hoskins' (Z/d)	WFib
* 'Eric Lee'	CWDa
'Erwarton' (Min/d)	ESul LVER NFir
'Escapade' (Dw/d)	ESul WFib
'Esteem' (Z/d)	WFib
'Etna' (Min)	WFib
'Evelyn'	ESul
'Evesham Wonder' (Z/d)	WFib
'Evka' PBR (I/v)	LVER NFir NPri
exhibens	Last listed 1998
'Explosive'	NPri WLRN WWol
exstipulatum	EWoo WEas WFib
'Fair Dinkum' (Z/v)	ESul MWhe NFir

§ 'Fair Ellen' (Sc)	CLTr ERav EWoo LDea MHer
	SKen WFib WPer
'Fairlee' (DwI)	Last listed 1998
¶ 'Fairy Lights' (Dw/St)	ESul
'Fairy Orchid' (A)	ESul LDea LVER NFir SSea
'Fairy Princess' (R)	LDea
'Fairy Queen'	LDea WEas
'Fairy Tales' (Dw)	WFib
'Falkland Brother' (Z/C/v)	WFib
'Falkland Hero' (Z/v)	MWhe NFir WFib
'Fandango' (Z/St/d)	ESul LVER MWhe NFir WFib
* 'Fanfare'	CWDa
'Fanny Eden' (R)	WEas WFib
'Fantasia' white (Dw/d) ♀	ESul MWhe WFib
'Fareham' (R) ♀	LDea MSte WFib
'Fascination' (Z/Ca)	WFib
'Feneela' (Dw/d)	ESul
'Fenton Farm' (Z/C)	ESul NFir
'Festal' (Min/d)	ESul
'Feuerriese' (Z)	LVER SKen
'Fiat' (Z/d)	CWDa SKen
'Fiat Queen' (Z/d)	SKen WFib
'Fiat Supreme' (Z/d)	SKen WFib
§ 'Fidelio' (Z/d)	Last listed 1998
'Fiery Sunrise' (R)	EBSP LDea
'Fiesta' (R)	WFib
'Fiesta' (I/d)	LDea
'Fifth Avenue' (R)	CSpe EWoo MSte WFib
'Filicifolium'	See *P. denticulatum* 'Filicifolium'
'Filigree' (Dw/v)	NFir
§ 'Finito' (Dw/d)	ERea
'Fir Trees All Gold' (R)	NFir
'Fir Trees Echoes of	NFir
Pink' (A)	
'Fir Trees Fire Star' (Z/St)	NFir
¶ 'Fir Trees Pink Fondant'	NFir
(Z/b/d)	
'Fir Trees Raggety' (Dw)	NFir
'Fir Trees Roseberry	NFir
Topping' (Dw)	
'Fir Trees Scarlet	NFir
Supreme' (Z)	
'Fire Cascade' (I)	Last listed 1998
'Fire Dragon' (Z/St/d)	SKen
'Fire Light' (Min/d)	WFib
'Firebrand' (Z/d)	LVER
'Firefly' (Min/d)	ESul WFib
'Fireglow' (Z/d)	Last listed 1997
'Firestone' (Dw)	ESul
'First Blush' (R)	WFib
'First Love' (Z)	LVER NFir
fissifolium	Last listed 1998
'Flair' (I)	NPri
'Flair' (R)	WFib
'Flair Greetings' (Z/C)	Last listed 1998
'Flakey' (I/d/v) ♀	CSpe ESul LDea MWhe NFir SKen
	WFib
'Flame' (Z)	WFib
'Flarepath' (Z/C/v)	NFir
'Flesh Pink' (Z/d)	CWDa
'Fleur d'Amour' (R)	WFib
'Fleurette' (Dw/d)	CHal ESul MWhe SKen WFib
§ 'Flirt' (Min)	ESul WFib
'Floral Cascade' (Fr/d)	WFib
'Florence Storey' (Z/C/d)	WFib
'Floria Moore' (Dec)	EWoo NFir
'Flower Basket' (R)	LAco LDea NFir
'Flower of Spring' (Z/v) ♀	CHal LVER MWhe SKen SPet SSea
	SYvo WFib
'Flowerfield' (Z)	WFib
'Flowton' (Dw/d)	ESul
* 'Forever' (d)	CWDa

'Fox' (Z/d) — CHal
'Foxhall' (Dw) — ESul
Fragrans Group (Sc) — CHal CLTr CRHN CSev ESul EWoo GPoy LRHS MHer MMal MWhe NHHG SKen WFib WHer WPer WWye
- 'Creamy Nutmeg' — See P. 'Creamy Nutmeg'
§ - 'Fragrans Variegatum' (Sc/v) — CInt CSev CSpe ERav ESul LIck MWhe NFir SKen WCHb WFib WJek
- 'Snowy Nutmeg' — See P. (Fragrans Group) 'Fragrans Variegatum'
'Fraiche Beauté' (Z/d) — CWDa WFib
'Francis James' (Z) — EWoo WFib
'Francis Parmenter' (MinI/v) — NPri
'Francis Parrett' (Min/d) ♀ — ESul LVER MWhe SKen WFib
'Francis Read' (Dw/d) — ERea ESul
'Frank Headley' (Z/v) ♀ — CHal CSpe ERav ESul LDea LHil LRHS LVER MMil MSte MWhe NFir NPer SKen SMrm SPet SSea WEas WFib
'Frank Parrett' (Min/d) — ESul
§ 'Frau Emma Hössle' (Dw/d) — MWhe WFib
'Frau Käthe Neubronner' (Z/d) — CWDa
'Freak of Nature' (Z/v) — MWhe NFir SKen SSea WFib
'Freckles' (Z/d) — WFib
'Frensham' (Sc) — ESul EWoo MHer SSea WFib
¶ 'Freshwater' (St/C) — ESul MWhe
'Freston' (Dw) — ESul
'Freya' (Min) — Last listed 1997
'Friary Wood' (Z/C/d) — ESul NFir WFib
'Friesdorf' (Dw) — ERav ESul LVER MWhe NFir SKen WEas WFib
'Frills' (Min/d) — ESul MWhe NFir WFib
'Fringed Angel' (A) — LDea
'Fringed Apple' (Sc) — LDea NBur
§ 'Fringed Aztec' (R) ♀ — EBSP LDea NFir NSwl WFib
'Fringed Rouletta' (I) — LDea
'Frosty' — See P. 'Variegated Kleine Liebling'
'Frosty Petit Pierre' — See P. 'Variegated Kleine Liebling'
'Frühlingszauber Lilac' (R) — EBSP
frutetorum — Last listed 1998
fruticosum — EWoo WFib
'Fuji' (R) — NFir
fulgidum — WFib
'Funny Girl' (R) — WFib
'Fynn' (Dw) — ESul
'Gabriel' (A) — EWoo LDea LVER
'Galilee' (I/d) ♀ — LDea LVER SKen WFib
'Galway Star' (Sc/v) ♀ — MHer WFib
'Garda' (I/d) — ECtt
'Garibaldi' (Z/d) — CWDa WFib
'Garland' (R) — ESul
'Garland' (Dw/d) — LVER
¶ 'Garnet' (Min) — NFir
'Garnet' (Z/d) — ESul LVER WFib
'Garnet Rosebud' (Min/d) — ESul LVER SAga
'Garnet Wings' (R) — WFib
'Gartendirektor Herman' (Dec) — ERav EWoo NFir SMrm WFib
'Gary Salvidge' (R) — LDea
'Gay Baby' (DwI) — ESul LDea MWhe
'Gay Baby Supreme' (DwI) — ESul
'Gazelle' (Z) — Last listed 1998
§ 'Gemini' (Z/St/d) — ESul MWhe NFir NSwl WFib
'Gemma' (R) — LDea LVER NFir
'Gemma' (Min/C) — LVER WFib
¶ 'Gemma Finito' (R) — LDea
'Gemma Jewel' (R) ♀ — EBSP
'Gemma Rose' (R) — LDea
¶ 'Gemma Sweetheart' (R) — LDea

'Gemstone' (Sc) ♀ — CBrm ESul EWoo LDea MHer NFir WFib
'Genetrix' (Z/d) — WFib
'Genie' (Z/d) — LVER MWhe SKen WFib
'Gentle Georgia' (R) — WFib
'Geoff May' (Dw) — ESul WFib
'Geoffrey Harvey' (Z/d) — WFib
'Geoffrey Horsman' (R) — WFib
'Georgia' (R) — WFib
'Georgia Peach' (R) — EBSP WFib
'Georgie' (R) — LDea
'Georgina Blythe' (R) ♀ — WFib
'Geo's Pink' (Z/v) — MWhe
'Gerald Caws' (d) — Last listed 1998
'Gerald Portas' (Dw/C) — ESul
'Gerald Wells' (Min) — ESul
'Geraldine' (Min) — ESul
'Geronimo' (R) — WFib
'Gess Portas' (Z/v) — ESul SKen
'Ghost Story' (Z/C) — NFir
'Giant Butterfly' (R) — LDea
'Giant Oak' (Sc) — MSte WFib
gibbosum — WFib
'Gilbert West' (Z) — SKen
'Gilda' (R) — EBSP LDea NFir
'Gill' (Min/Ca) — ESul
'Gillian Clifford' (Z/d) — Last listed 1998
¶ 'Ginger Rogers' (Z) — NFir
* 'Giro Fly' — Last listed 1998
'Glacier Claret' (Z) — Last listed 1998
'Glacier Crimson' (Z) — SKen
'Glacis' PBR (Z/d) — WFib
'Gladys Evelyn' (Z/d) — WFib
'Gladys Stevens' (Min/d) — ESul
x *glaucifolium* — Last listed 1998
glaucum — See P. *lanceolatum*
'Gleam' (Z/d) — LVER
'Glenn Barker' (Z/d) — WFib
'Glenshree' (R) — WFib
'Gloria Pearce' (R) — LDea WFib
'Glory' (Z/d) — WFib
'Glowing Embers' (R) — LDea WFib
§ *glutinosum* — Last listed 1997
'Goblin' (Min/d) — ESul SKen WFib
'Godshill' (R) — LDea
* 'Gold Medallion' — Last listed 1998
'Gold Star' (Z/St/C) — ESul
'Golden Baby' (DwI/C) — LDea MWhe NFir
'Golden Brilliantissimum' (Z/v) — LRHS LVER MWhe NFir SKen WFib
'Golden Butterfly' (Z/C) — ESul
'Golden Chalice' (Min/v) — ESul LVER MWhe NFir
'Golden Clorinda' (U/Sc/C) — CRHN EWoo LDea MHer NFir WEas
'Golden Crest' (Z/C) — SKen SMrm
'Golden Ears' (Dw/St/C) — ESul MWhe NFir NPer WFib
'Golden Everaarts' (Dw/C) — ESul
'Golden Fleece' (Min/C/d) — ESul
'Golden Gates' (Z/C) — ESul SKen
'Golden Harry Hieover' (Z/C) — ESul MBri SKen
'Golden Mirage' (Z/v) — NFir WFib
§ 'Golden Mist' (Dw/C/d) — LVER
'Golden Orange' (Dw/C) — ESul
'Golden Orfe' (Dw/C) — WFib
'Golden Petit Pierre' (Min/C) — ESul
'Golden Princess' (Min/C) — WFib
'Golden Princess' (R) — Last listed 1998
'Golden Roc' (Min/C) — ESul
'Golden Ruth' (Z) — WFib
'Golden Staphs' (Z/St/C) — ESul LVER NFir SSea WFib

'Golden Stardust' (Z/St)   LVER
'Golden Tears' (Minl/C/d)   Last listed 1999
'Golden Wedding' (Z/d/v)   LRHS LVER MWhe NFir
'Golden Well Sweep' (Sc)   NFir WFib
'Goldie' (R)   WFib
'Goldilocks' (A)   ESul LDea WFib
'Gooseberry Leaf'   See *P. grossularioides*
'Gordano Midnight' (R)   EWoo LDea WFib
¶ 'Gordano Midnight'   EWoo
'Gordino Pixie' (R)   Last listed 1998
'Gosbeck' (A)   ESul LDea SSea
'Gosport Girl' (R)   EBSP LDea
'Gothenburg'   EBSP
¶ 'Grace' (A)   LDea
'Grace Read' (Min)   Last listed 1997
'Grace Thomas' (Sc) ♀   LDea WFib
'Grace Wells' (Min)   ESul WFib
'Gracious Lady' (Z/d)   WFib
§ 'Gräfin Mariza' (Z/d)   SKen WFib
'Grand Slam' (R)   EBSP LDea LVER NFir SKen WFib
¶ 'Grandad Mac' (Dw/St)   ESul NFir
grandiflorum   WFib
'Grandma Fischer'   See *P.* 'Grossmutter Fischer'
'Grandma Ross' (R)   EBSP LDea
'Granny Hewitt' (Min/d)   ESul
§ 'Graveolens' (Sc)   CHal CLTr CSev ERav ESul EWoo GPoy LRHS LVER MHer MWhe NFir SSea WFib WJek
'Great Blakenham' (Min)   ESul
'Great Bricett' (Min/d)   ESul LVER
'Green Ears' (Z/St)   ESul NFir WFib
'Green Eyes' (I/d)   SKen
'Green Goddess' (I/d)   LDea SKen
'Green Gold Petit Pierre' (MiN)   ESul
'Green Lady' (Sc)   WFib
'Green Woodpecker' (R)   LDea LVER SSea
§ 'Greengold Kleine Liebling' (Min/C/v)   ESul SKen
'Greengold Petit Pierre'   See *P.* 'Greengold Kleine Liebling'
'Greetings' (Min/v)   ESul MBri NFir WFib
§ 'Grenadier' (Z/St/d) ♀   Last listed 1998
§ 'Grenadier' (Z)   CWDa
'Grey Lady Plymouth' (Sc/v)   ESul EWoo LDea MHer NFir SIde WFib
'Grey Monk' (Z)   Last listed 1997
'Grey Sprite' (Min/v)   ESul WFib
greytonense   Last listed 1998
griseum   WFib
* 'Groombridge Success' (d)   CWDa
§ 'Grossmutter Fischer' (R)   LDea WFib
§ *grossularioides*   CInt EOHP ESul MHer
'Grozser Garten' (Dw)   ESul
'Grozser Garten Weiss' (Dw)   ESul
'Guardsman' (Dw)   ESul
'Guido' (Z)   LRHS
'Gurnard'   Last listed 1998
'Gustav Emich' (Z/d)   SKen WFib
'Gwen' (Min/v)   MWhe WFib
'H. Guinier'   See *P.* 'Charles Gounod'
'H. Rigler' (Z)   SKen
'Hadleigh' (Dw)   ESul
'Hamble Lass' (R)   LDea
'Hanchen Anders' (Z)   WFib
§ 'Hannaford Star' (Z/St/d)   ESul NFir WFib
'Hannah' (A)   ESul
'Hans Rigler' (Z/d)   WFib
'Hanson Pixie' (R)   LDea
'Happy Appleblossom' (Z/v)   LVER NFir
§ 'Happy Thought' (Z/v) ♀   CHal LDea LRHS LVER MBri MWhe NFir SKen SSea
'Happy Valley' (R)   EBSP LVER WFib

'Harbour Lights' (R)   EBSP LDea WFib
'Harewood Slam' (R)   EBSP EWoo LDea MSte SMrm WEas WFib
'Harkstead' (Min)   ESul
'Harlequin' (Dw)   Last listed 1998
'Harlequin Alpine Glow' (I/d)   LVER MWhe WFib
'Harlequin Candy Floss' (I/d)   CWDa
'Harlequin Liverbird' (I)   WFib
'Harlequin Mahogany' (I/d)   LDea LVER MWhe SKen WFib
§ 'Harlequin Miss Liver Bird' (I)   SKen
'Harlequin My Love' (I)   Last listed 1997
'Harlequin Picotee' (I/d)   LDea LVER SKen
'Harlequin Pretty Girl' (I)   MWhe WFib
'Harlequin Rosie O'Day' (I)   LDea MWhe SKen WFib
'Harlequin Ted Day' (I/d)   LDea LVER
'Harmony' (R)   LVER
'Harold Bowie' (Z/d)   WFib
'Harold Headley' (Z/v)   Last listed 1998
'Harriet Le Hair' (Z)   SKen
'Harvard' (I/d)   LVER WFib
'Harvey' (Z)   MWhe
havlasae   Last listed 1998
'Hayley Charlotte' (Z/v)   MWhe
'Hay's Radiant' (Z/d)   WFib
'Hazel' (R)   LVER WFib
* 'Hazel Adair'   LDea
'Hazel Anson' (R)   LDea
'Hazel Barolo' (R)   LDea
'Hazel Beauty' (R)   Last listed 1998
'Hazel Birkby' (R)   EBSP LDea WFib
'Hazel Blake' (R)   WFib
'Hazel Burgundy' (R)   EBSP LDea
'Hazel Burtoff' (R)   EBSP LDea WFib
'Hazel Carey' (R)   LDea
¶ 'Hazel Cerise' (R)   LDea
'Hazel Cherry' (R)   LDea MSte WFib
'Hazel Chick' (R)   Last listed 1999
'Hazel Choice' (R)   EBSP LDea NFir WFib
'Hazel Dean' (R)   NFir
'Hazel Glory' (R)   LDea WFib
'Hazel Gowland' (R)   LDea
¶ 'Hazel Gypsy' (R)   EBSP LDea WFib
'Hazel Harmony' (R)   LDea
'Hazel Heather' (R)   LDea
'Hazel Henderson' (R)   LDea
'Hazel Herald' (R)   EBSP LDea
'Hazel Mistique' (R)   LDea
'Hazel Peach' (R)   Last listed 1998
'Hazel Perfection' (R)   LDea NFir
'Hazel Rose' (R)   LDea
'Hazel Saga' (R)   EBSP WFib
'Hazel Satin' (R)   LDea
'Hazel Shiraz' (R)   LDea
'Hazel Star' (R)   EBSP
'Hazel Stardust' (R)   EBSP LDea NFir
* 'Hazel Whitaker'   Last listed 1998
'Hazel Wright' (R)   LDea
§ 'Hederinum' (I)   SKen SSea
§ 'Hederinum Variegatum' (I/v)   CHal LDea NFir WFib
'Heidi' (Min/d)   ESul
* 'Helen Bowie'   CWDa
'Helen Christine' (Z/St)   ESul NFir WFib
'Helena' (I/d)   LDea MWhe SKen WFib
'Helter Skelter' (Z/v)   Last listed 1998
'Hemingstone' (A)   ESul LDea
'Hemley' (Sc)   LDea
'Henhurst Gleam' (Dw/C/d)   ESul WFib
'Hermione' (Z/d)   CHal MWhe WFib

'High Tor' (Dw/C/d)	SKen WFib	
'Highfields Always' (Z/d)	Last listed 1999	
'Highfields Appleblossom' (Z)	LVER NFir SKen	
'Highfields Attracta' (Z/d)	LVER SKen	
'Highfields Ballerina' (Z/d)	LVER WFib	
'Highfields Candy Floss' (Z/d)	LVER NFir	
'Highfields Charisma' (Z/d)	LVER	
'Highfields Choice' (Z)	LVER SKen	
'Highfields Comet' (Z)	SKen	
'Highfields Contessa' (Z/d)	LVER SKen WFib	
'Highfields Dazzler' (Z)	Last listed 1999	
'Highfields Delight' (Z)	LVER	
'Highfields Fancy' (Z/d)	LVER NFir SKen	
'Highfields Fantasy' (Z/d)	Last listed 1997	
'Highfields Festival' (Z/d)	LVER MWhe NFir SKen	
'Highfields Flair' (Z/d)	LVER	
'Highfields Joy' (Z/d)	Last listed 1998	
'Highfields Melody' (Z/d)	Last listed 1998	
'Highfields Orange' (Z)	LVER MWhe	
'Highfields Paramount' (Z)	SKen	
'Highfields Pearl' (Z)	Last listed 1998	
'Highfields Perfecta' (Z)	CWDa	
'Highfields Pink' (Z)	Last listed 1998	
'Highfields Prestige' (Z)	Last listed 1997	
'Highfields Pride' (Z)	LVER SKen	
'Highfields Prima Donna' (Z/d)	LVER MWhe SKen WFib	
'Highfields Promise' (Z)	SKen	
'Highfields Serenade' (Z)	LVER	
'Highfields Snowdrift' (Z)	LVER SKen	
'Highfields Sonata' (Z)	Last listed 1999	
'Highfields Sugar Candy' (Z/d)	ECtt SKen WFib	
'Highfields Supreme' (Z)	LVER	
'Highfields Symphony' (Z)	LVER WFib	
'Highfields Vogue' (Z)	LVER	
'Highscore' (Z/d)	Last listed 1999	
'Hi-jinks' (Z/v)	Last listed 1998	
'Hildegard' (Z/d)	CHal SKen WFib	
'Hills of Snow' (Z/v)	CHal LVER MBri SKen SSea WFib	
'Hillscheider Amethyst'	See P. 'Amethyst'	
'Hindoo' (RxU)	EWoo LVER NFir SSea WFib	
'Hintlesham' (Min)	ESul	
hirtum	Last listed 1998	
hispidum	Last listed 1998	
'Hitcham' (Min/d)	ESul WFib	
'Holbrook' (Min/C/d)	ESul NFir	
'Holly West'	Last listed 1998	
'Hollywood Star' (Z) ♀	Last listed 1994	
'Holmes Miller' (Z/d)	ESul	
'Honeywood Hannah' (R)	WFib	
'Honeywood Jonathan' (R)	EBSP WFib	
'Honeywood Lindy' (R)	EBSP	
'Honeywood Margaret' (R)	EBSP	
'Honeywood Matthew' (Dw)	ESul	
'Honeywood Suzanne' (Min/Fr)	ESul LVER NFir SKen WFib	
'Honne Früling' (Z)	SKen WFib	
'Honneas' (Min)	ESul	
'Honnestolz' (Min)	ESul SKen	
'Hope' (Z)	Last listed 1999	
'Hope Valley' (Dw/C/d) ♀	ESul MWhe NFir SKen	
'Horace Parsons' (R)	WFib	
'Horace Read' (Dw)	ERea ESul	
'Horning Ferry' (Dw)	ESul	
'House and Garden' (R)	NFir WFib	
'Howard Stanton' (R)	WFib	
'Howard's Orange' (R)	LDea	
'Hugo de Vries' (Dw/d)	CWDa WFib	

	'Hula' (U)	EWoo MHer NFir WFib
	'Hulda Conn' (Ca/d)	WFib
	'Hunter's Moon' (Z/C)	ESul NFir
	'Hurdy-gurdy' (Z/d/v)	ESul MWhe NFir WFib
	HWD Corelli	Last listed 1998
	HWD Gabrieli	Last listed 1998
	HWD Monteverdi	Last listed 1998
	HWD Onyx	Last listed 1998
	HWD Romanze	Last listed 1998
	HWD Vivaldi	Last listed 1998
	hypoleucum	Last listed 1998
	'Ian Read' (Min/d)	ERea ESul LVER WFib
	'Icecrystal'PBR	CWDa WLRN
	'Icing Sugar' (I/d)	ESul LDea SSea WFib
*	'Ilse Fisher'	CWDa
	'Immaculatum' (Z)	EWoo WFib
	'Imperial Butterfly' (A/Sc)	ERav ESul LDea LVER MSte MWhe NFir NSwl WFib
	'Improved Petit Pierre' (Min)	ESul
	'Improved Ricard' (Z/d)	WFib
	'Ina' PBR (Z/d)	WFib
	'Inca' (R)	LDea WFib
	incrassatum	NBur
	'Ingres' (I/d) ♀	ECtt
	inquinans	WFib
	iocastum	Last listed 1998
	ionidiflorum	CSpe LHil
	'Ipswich Town' (Dw/d)	Last listed 1999
	'Irene' (Z/d) ♀	WFib
	'Irene Cal' (Z/d)	Last listed 1998
	'Irene Collet' (R)	LDea
	'Irene Corsair' (Z/d)	Last listed 1997
	'Irene La Jolle' (Z/d)	Last listed 1997
	'Irene Toyon' (Z) ♀	Last listed 1996
*	'Iris Monroe'	CWDa
	'Isaac Middleton' (Z)	Last listed 1997
§	'Isabell' (Z/d)	WFib
	'Isidel' (I/d) ♀	SKen WFib
	'Isobel Gamble' (Z/d)	Last listed 1997
	'Italian Gem' (I)	SKen
	'Ivalo' (Z/d)	MWhe SKen WFib
	'Ivory Snow' (Z/d/v)	EWoo LVER MWhe NFir SKen
	'Jacey' (Z/d)	LVER SKen
	'Jack Read' (Dw)	ERea
	'Jack Wood' (Z/d)	NFir
§	'Jackie' (I/d)	LVER MBri NSwl SKen WFib
¶	'Jackie Davies' (R)	LDea
	'Jackie Gall'	See P. 'Jackie'
	'Jackie's Gem' (I/d)	MWhe
¶	'Jacko' (I/d)	EWoo
	'Jacqueline' (Z/d)	SKen
	'Jana' PBR (Z/d)	Last listed 1999
	'Jane Biggin' (Dw/C/d)	ESul MWhe SKen
	'Janet Hofman' (Z/d)	WFib
	'Janet James'	Last listed 1998
	'Janet Kerrigan' (Min/d)	ESul MWhe WEas WFib
	'Janet Scott' (Z)	CWDa
	'Janna Whelan' (Dw/d)	Last listed 1998
	'Jasmin' (R)	EBSP LDea
	'Jaunty' (Min/d)	ESul SSea WFib
	'Jayne' (Min/d)	ESul
	'Jayne Eyre' (Min/d)	CHal ESul MWhe NFir SKen WFib
§	'Jazz'	CWDa WWol
	'Jean Bart' (I)	CWDa
	'Jean Beatty' (Dw/d)	LVER
	'Jean Oberle' (Z/d)	SKen WFib
§	'Jeanne d'Arc' (I/d)	SKen WFib
	'Jenifer Read' (Dw)	ERea ESul
	'Jennifer' (Min)	ESul
	'Jer'Rey' (A)	LDea
	'Jessel's Unique' (U)	LDea LRHS MHer MSte NFir SPet

'Jessika' (Z/d) — Last listed 1998
* 'Jetfire' (d) — CWDa GEve
'Jewel' (R) — EBSP
'Jeweltone' (Z/d) — WFib
'Jill Portas' (Z/C) — ESul
'Jim Field' (R) — WFib
'Jimmy Read' (Min) — ERea
'Jinny Reeves' (R) — EBSP LDea WFib
'Joan Cashmore' (Z/d) — ESul WFib
'Joan Fairman' (R) — WFib
'Joan Fontaine' (Z) — WFib
'Joan Hayward' (Min) — ESul
'Joan Morf' (R) — EBSP LDea NFir SKen SSea WFib
'Joan of Arc' — See *P.* 'Jeanne d'Arc'
'Joan Sharman' (Min) — ESul
'Joanna Pearce' (R) — EBSP LDea SKen
'John Thorp' (R) — LDea
'John West' — Last listed 1997
'John's Angela' — LVER
'John's Chameleon' — Last listed 1998
'John's Pride' — MBri NFir
'Joseph Haydn' (R) — EBSP
'Joseph Haydon' (R) — LDea
'Joseph Paul' (R) — Last listed 1998
'Joseph Warren' (I/d) — Last listed 1999
'Joseph Wheeler' (A) — LDea MWhe
'Joy' (Z/d) — CSpe SKen
'Joy' (R) ♀ — EBSP LDea LRHS LVER NFir NSwl WFib
'Joy' (I) — Last listed 1998
'Joy Lucille' (Sc) — CSev ESul EWoo LDea MHer WFib
'Joyce Delamere' (Z/C/d) — WFib
'Joyden' — CWDa
'Joyful' (Min) — ESul
'Jubel Parr' (Z/d) — CWDa
'Judith Thorp' (R) — EBSP
'Judy Read' (Dw) — ESul
'Julia' PBR (R) ♀ — EBSP LDea
'Juliana' (R) — LDea
'Julie' (A) — ESul
¶ 'Julie Collie' (Dw) — NFir
'Julie Smith' (R) — LDea WFib
'June Patricia' (d) — Last listed 1998
'Jungle Night' (R) — EBSP WFib
'Juniper' (Sc) — MHer WFib
'Jupiter' (Min/d) — SKen WFib
'Jupiter' (R) — EBSP NFir
'Just Rita' (A) — SSea
'Just William' (Min/C/d) — ESul
'Kamahl' (R) — WFib
'Kandy Waterman' (d) — Last listed 1998
§ 'Kardinal' (Z/d) — Last listed 1998
'Kardino' — Last listed 1998
'Karl Hagele' (Z/d) — LVER SKen SYvo WFib
'Karmin Ball' — CWDa WFib
karooicum — Last listed 1998
'Kath Peat' (Z/d) — WFib
'Kathleen Gamble' (Z) — SKen
'Kathryn' (Min) — ESul
'Kathryn Portas' (Z/v) — ESul SKen
'Kayleigh West' (Min) — ESul
'Keepsake' (Dw/d) — ESul WFib
¶ 'Keith Vernon' (Z) — NFir
'Keith Vernon' (Fr/d) — Last listed 1998
'Kelvedon Beauty' (Min) — WEas
'Ken Salmon' (Dw/d) — ESul
'Kennard Castle' (Z) — CWDa
'Kenny's Double' (Z/d) — WFib
¶ 'Ken's Golden Stellar' (Dw/St/C) — NFir
'Kensington' (A) — LDea
'Kerensa' (Min/d) — ESul SKen

'Kershy' (Min) — Last listed 1999
'Kesgrave' (Min/d) — ESul LVER
'Kettle Baston' (A) ♀ — ESul LDea NFir WFib
'Kimono' (R) — EBSP EWoo LDea NFir
'Kinder Charm' (R) — Last listed 1997
'Kinder Gaisha' (R) — NFir
'King Edmund' (R) — LDea WFib
'King of Balcon' — See *P.* 'Hederinum'
'King of Denmark' (Z/d) — LVER SKen WFib
¶ 'King's Ransom' (R) — LDea
'Kingsmill' (R) — LDea
'Kingswood' (Z) — Last listed 1998
'Kirton' (Min/d) — ESul
'Kiwi' — Last listed 1999
§ 'Kleine Liebling' (Min) — ESul EWoo MWhe WFib
'Kosset' (Min/d) — Last listed 1998
'Krista' (Min/d) — ESul WFib
* 'Kristy' — Last listed 1998
'Kumuzura' (Z/C) — NFir
'Kyoto' (R) — NFir
'Kyra' (Min/d) — ESul WFib
'L.E. Wharton' (Z) — SKen
'La France' (I/d) ♀ — LDea LVER MWhe SKen WEas WFib
'La Jolla' (Z/d) — Last listed 1998
'La Paloma' (R) — LDea WEas WFib
'Laced Mini Cascade' — Last listed 1999
'Laced Mini Rose Cascade' (I) — NFir
'Laced Red Mini Cascade' (I) — NFir
Lachsball (Z/d) — SKen WFib
§ 'Lachskönigin' (I/d) — LVER SKen WEas WFib
'Lady Alice of Valencia' — See *P.* 'Grenadier' (Z)
'Lady Churchill' (Z/v) — WFib
'Lady Cullum' (Z/C/v) — MWhe
'Lady Ilchester' (Z/d) — EWoo SKen WFib
'Lady Love Song' (R) — EBSP LVER NFir
'Lady Mary' (Sc) — ESul EWoo LVER MHer WFib
'Lady Plymouth' (Sc/v) ♀ — CHal CInt CLTr CRHN CSpe EDAr ERav ESul GBar LDea LRHS LVER MHer MSte MWhe NFir NHHG SKen SSea SYvo WEas WFib WHer WWye
§ 'Lady Scarborough' (Sc) — EWoo LDea MHer WFib
laevigatum — WEas
'Lakeland' (I) — Last listed 1998
'Lakis' (R) — EDAr LDea
'Lambada' — NPri
'Lamorna' (R) — LDea SKen WFib
'Lancastrian' (Z/d) — WFib
lanceolatum — Last listed 1998
'Langley' (R) — LDea
'Lanham Lane' (I) — LDea MWhe NFir
'Lanham Royal' (Min/d) — ESul
'Lara Aladin' (A) — LDea WFib
'Lara Candy Dancer' (Sc) ♀ — CRHN EOHP ESul LDea WFib
'Lara Jester' (Sc) — EWoo WFib
'Lara Maid' (A) ♀ — ESul MWhe WEas WFib
'Lara Nomad' (Sc) — EWoo LDea
'Lara Starshine' (Sc) ♀ — ESul EWoo NFir SSea WFib
'Lark' (Min/d) — ESul
'Larkfield' (Z/v) — SSea
N 'Lass o' Gowrie' (Z/v) — LRHS LVER MSte MWhe NFir SKen WFib
'Lass o' Gowrie' (American) (Z/v) — WFib
'Laura' (Z/d) — Last listed 1998
'Laura Parmer' (Dw/St) — ESul
'Laura Wheeler' (A) — ESul LDea MWhe
* 'Laurel Heywood' (R) — WFib
'Lauripen' (Z/d) — Last listed 1999

'Lavender Feathers' (R)	Last listed 1998	
'Lavender Frills' (R)	Last listed 1997	
'Lavender Grand Slam' (R) ♀	EBSP LDea LVER NFir WFib	
'Lavender Harewood Slam' (R)	EBSP LDea	
'Lavender Mini Cascade'	See P. 'Lila Mini Cascade'	
'Lavender Sensation' (R)	WFib	
'Lavender Wings' (I)	LDea	
laxum	Last listed 1998	
'Layham' (Dw/d)	ESul	
'Layton's White' (Z/d)	CWDa SKen	
'Le Lutin' (Z/d)	CWDa WFib	
'L'Elégante' (I/v) ♀	CHal EWoo LAst LDea LVER MWhe NFir NSwl SKen SSea WEas WFib WLRN	
'Lemon Air' (Sc)	ESul	
'Lemon Crisp'	See P. crispum	
'Lemon Fancy' (Sc)	CInt LDea LVER MHer MWhe NFir WFib WJek	
'Lemonii'	Last listed 1997	
'Len Chandler' (Min)	ESul	
'L'Enfer'	See P. 'Mephistopheles'	
'Lenore' (Min)	ESul	
'Leo' (Min)	ESul	
'Leonie Holbrow' (Min)	ESul	
'Leopard' (I/d)	CWDa	
'Lerchenmuller' (Z/d)	Last listed 1998	
'Leslie Judd' (R)	WFib	
'Leslie Salmon' (Min/C)	ESul MWhe	
'Lethas' (R)	LDea	
¶ 'Letitia' (St)	NFir	
'Letitia' (A)	Last listed 1999	
§ Leucht-Cascade	WFib	
'Levington' (Min/d)	WFib	
Lila Compakt-Cascade	See P. 'Decora Lilas'	
§ 'Lila Mini Cascade' (I)	ESul MWhe	
'Lilac Cascade'	See P. 'Roi des Balcons Lilas'	
'Lilac Domino'	See P. 'Telston's Prima'	
'Lilac Elaine' (R)	LDea	
'Lilac Gem' (Min/I/d)	LDea LVER MWhe NFir SKen WFib	
'Lilac Jewel' (R)	EBSP	
'Lilac Mini Cascade' (I)	LDea LVER NFir	
'Lili Marlene' (I)	LVER SKen	
'Lilian' (Dw)	ESul	
'Lilian Pottinger' (Sc)	CArn CHal CInt CRHN ESul GBar LDea MHer MWhe NFir SKen SSea WEas WFib WHer	
'Limelight' (Z/v)	SSea	
'Limoneum' (Sc)	CSev LDea LRHS MHer NBur SKen WEas WFib	
'Lin Davis' (Z/C)	Last listed 1999	
'Linda' (R)	EBSP LDea WFib	
'Linda' (Z/d)	WFib	
'Lindsey' (Min)	ESul	
'Lindy Portas' (I/d)	SKen	
'Lisa' (Min/C)	ESul WFib	
'Little Alice' (Dw/d) ♀	ESul MWhe NFir WFib	
'Little Blakenham' (A)	ESul LDea	
'Little Fi-fine' (Dw)	ESul NFir WFib	
'Little Gem' (Sc)	EWoo LDea LVER MHer WFib	
'Little Jip' (Z/C)	LVER NFir	
'Little John' (Min/d)	WFib	
'Little Margaret' (Min/v)	ESul	
¶ 'Little Perky' (MinI)	ESul	
'Little Primular' (Min)	ESul	
'Little Trot' (Z/v)	WFib	
'Little Vectis' (D)	Last listed 1998	
'Lively Lady' (Dw/C)	ESul	
'Liverbird'	See P. 'Harlequin Miss Liver Bird'	
lobatum	Last listed 1998	
'Lolette' (Min)	ESul	
'Lollipop' (Z/d)	WFib	
'Longshot' (R)	WFib	
* 'Loraine Howarth'	ERav	
'Lord Baden-Powell'	See P. 'Colonel Baden-Powell'	
'Lord Bute' (R) ♀	CElw CSpe EBSP ERav EWoo LDea LHil LHop LIck LRHS LVER MSCN MSte NCiC NFir NPer NSwl SIde SKen SMer SMrm SUsu WEas WFib	
* 'Lord Constantine'	LDea	
'Lord de Ramsey'	See P. 'Tip Top Duet'	
'Lord Roberts' (Z)	EWoo WFib	
'Lorelei' (Z/d)	CWDa WFib	
'Loretta' (Dw)	ESul	
'Loripen' (Z/d)	Last listed 1999	
'Lorna' (Dw/d)	ESul	
* 'Lotus'	WLRN	
'Louise' (Min)	EBSP ESul LRHS	
'Love Song' (R/v)	EBSP EWoo LDea LVER NFir SSea	
'Love Story' (Z/v)	ESul	
* 'Loverly' (Min/d)	ESul	
'Lovesong' (Z/d)	Last listed 1998	
'Lowood' (R)	WFib	
'Lucilla' (Min)	ESul	
'Lucinda' (Min)	ESul	
'Lucy' (Min)	ESul	
'Lucy Gunnett' (Z/d/v)	ERav MWhe NFir WFib	
'Lucy Jane' (R)	LDea	
'Lulu' (I)	NPri	
'Luna'	NPri	
luridum	Last listed 1999	
'Lustre' (R)	EBSP WFib	
'Luz del Dio' (R)	WFib	
'Lyewood Bonanza' (R)	EBSP LDea LVER	
'Lyn West'	Last listed 1997	
'Lynne Valerie' (A)	LDea	
'Lyric' (Min/d)	ESul LVER WFib	
'M.J. Cole' (I/d)	LDea	
'Mabel Grey' (Sc) ♀	CHal CRHN CSev CSpe ERav ESul EWoo LIck LRHS LVER MHer MSte MWhe NBur NFir NHHG SKen WEas WFib WHer WJek	
§ 'Madame Auguste Nonin' (U/Sc)	CHal LVER MHer NFir NWoo SKen WFib	
'Madame Butterfly' (Z/C/d)	ESul MWhe NFir SKen	
'Madame Crousse' (I/d) ♀	WEas WFib	
'Madame Dubarry' (Z)	WFib	
'Madame Fournier' (Min/C)	ESul	
'Madame Guinier'	See P. 'Charles Gounod'	
'Madame Hibbault' (Z)	SKen	
'Madame Kingsbury' (U)	Last listed 1998	
'Madame Layal' (A)	ESul EWoo LDea LIck MSte NFir SKen WFib	
'Madame Margot'	See P. 'Hederinum Variegatum'	
'Madame Recamier' (Z/d)	WFib	
'Madame Salleron' (Min/v) ♀	LDea LRHS LVER MSte SKen	
'Madame Thibaut' (R)	LDea WFib	
'Madge Hill' (Min)	WFib	
'Madge Taylor' (R)	NFir	
'Magaluf' (I/C/d)	SSea WFib	
'Magda' (Z/d)	ESul LVER WFib	
magenteum	Last listed 1998	
'Magic'	WLRN WWol	
'Magic Lantern' (Z/C)	NFir SKen	
'Magic Moments' (R)	WFib	
'Magnum' (R)	WFib	
* 'Mahogany' (I/d)	ECtt	
'Maid of Honour' (Min)	ESul	
'Mairi' (A)	ESul LDea WFib	
'Maja' (R)	WFib	

'Maloja' (Z)	SKen WFib	
'Mamie' (Z/d)	SKen	
'Mandarin' (Z)	Last listed 1997	
'Mangles' Variegated' (Z/v)	SKen SPet SSea	
'Mantilla' (Min)	SKen	
'Manx Maid' (A)	ESul LDea NFir SKen WFib	
'Maple Leaf'	EWoo	
'Marble Sunset'	See *P.* 'Wood's Surprise'	
¶ 'Marbled Roger' (R)	LDea	
'Marchioness of Bute' (R)	LDea MSte NFir WFib	
'Maréchal MacMahon' (Z/C)	SKen WFib	
¶ 'Margaret Parmenter' (I/C)	ESul	
'Margaret Pearce' (R)	LDea	
'Margaret Salvidge' (R)	LDea WFib	
'Margaret Soley' (R) ♀	LDea	
'Margaret Stimpson' (R)	LDea	
'Margaret Thorp'	Last listed 1999	
'Margaret Waite' (R)	WFib	
'Margery Stimpson' (Min/d)	ESul LVER WFib	
'Maria Wilkes' (Z/d)	WFib	
'Marie Rober' (R)	SKen WFib	
'Marie Thomas' (Sc)	LDea	
'Marie Thomson' (Sc)	SSea	
§ 'Marie Vogel' (R)	MSte WFib	
'Marilyn' (Dw)	ESul	
'Marion' (Min)	ESul	
'Mariquita' (R)	WFib	
* 'Marja'	LDea	
'Marktbeherrscher' (Z/d)	WFib	
'Marmalade' (Dw/d)	ESul LVER MWhe SKen WFib	
§ 'Mars' (Z/d)	WLRN	
'Martha Parmer' (Min)	ESul	
'Martin Parrett' (Min/d)	WFib	
'Martin's Splendour' (Min)	ESul	
'Martlesham'	ESul	
'Mary Ellen Tanner' (Min/d)	Last listed 1997	
'Mary Read' (Min)	ERea ESul	
¶ 'Mary Rose' (R)	LDea	
'Mary Spink' (Z/C/d)	LVER NFir	
'Mary Webster' (Min)	ESul	
'Masquerade' (R)	ESul	
'Masterpiece' (Z/C/d)	ESul SKen	
'Mataranka' (Min/d/C/v)	MWhe NFir	
'Matisse' (I)	Last listed 1997	
'Matthew Salvidge' (R)	EBSP LDea WFib	
'Maureen' (Min)	Last listed 1999	
'Maureen Mew'	Last listed 1998	
'Mauve Beauty' (I/d)	SKen WFib	
'Mauve Duet' (A)	ESul	
'Maxime Kovalevski' (Z)	WFib	
'Maxine' (Z/C)	NFir	
'Maxine Colley' (Z/d/v)	LVER	
'May Day' (R)	LDea	
'May Magic' (R)	NFir WFib	
'May Rushbrook' (Z)	NFir	
* 'Maya'	NPri SCoo	
'Mayor of Seville' (Z/d)	WFib	
'Maytime' (Z/d)	WFib	
I 'Meadowside Dark and Dainty'	NFir	
'Meadowside Fancy' (Z/d/C)	LVER	
'Meadowside Harvest' (Z/St)	ESul NFir	
I 'Meadowside Mahogany' (Z/C)	LVER	
'Meadowside Midnight'	MWhe SHFr	
'Meadowside Orange' (Z/d)	LVER	
'Medallion' (Z/C)	WFib	
'Meditation' (Dw)	ESul	
'Medley' (Min/d)	ESul LVER MWhe WFib	
'Melanie' (R)	ESul LDea WFib	

* 'Melissa' (Min)	ESul	
Meloblue = 'Penblue'PBR	WLRN	
'Melody'PBR (Z/d)	Last listed 1998	
'Melva Bird' (Z/d)	WFib	
'Memento' (Min/d)	ESul LVER SKen WFib	
'Memories' (Z/d)	WFib	
'Mendip' (R)	WFib	
'Meon Maid' (R)	EBSP LDea WFib	
§ 'Mephistopheles' (Min/C)	Last listed 1997	
Mercutio (Z/d)	Last listed 1998	
'Mere Carribean' (R)	NFir	
'Mere Casino' (Z)	LVER	
* 'Mere Champagne'	Last listed 1998	
'Mere Cocktail' (R)	WFib	
'Mere Flamenco' (R)	WFib	
'Mere Greeting' (Z/d)	MWhe	
'Mere Iced Cocktail' (R)	WFib	
'Mere Meteor' (R)	WFib	
'Mere Sunglow' (R)	LDea WFib	
'Merle Seville' (Z/d)	SKen	
'Merry-go-round' (Z/C/v)	ESul LVER MWhe NFir WFib	
'Mexically Rose' (R)	WFib	
'Mexican Beauty' (I)	CHal MWhe SKen WEas WFib	
'Mexicanerin'	See *P.* 'Rouletta'	
'Michelle' (Min/C)	LDea WFib	
'Michelle West' (Min)	ESul	
'Midas Touch' (Dw/C/d)	ESul	
'Milden' (Z/C)	ESul NFir	
'Milkmaid' (Min)	WFib	
'Millbern Choice' (Z)	MWhe	
'Millbern Clover' (Min/d)	ESul MWhe	
'Millbern Engagement' (Min/d)	MWhe	
'Millbern Peach' (Z)	MWhe	
'Millbern Serenade'	MWhe	
'Millbern Sharna' (Min/d)	ESul MWhe	
¶ Millennium Dawn (Dw)	LVER	
'Miller's Valentine' (Z/v)	ESul LVER NFir WFib	
'Millfield Gem' (I/d)	LVER SKen WFib	
'Millfield Rival' (Z)	WFib	
'Millfield Rose' (I/d)	LVER MWhe SKen WEas	
'Millie' (Z/d)	CWDa WFib	
'Mimi' (Min/C/d)	ESul SSea	
'Mini-Czech' (Min/St)	ESul LVER	
minimum	Last listed 1998	
'Minnie' (Z/d/St)	LVER	
'Minnie Clifton'	Last listed 1997	
'Minstrel'	Last listed 1999	
'Minstrel Boy' (R)	EBSP LDea WFib	
'Minuet' (Z/d)	WFib	
'Minx' (Min/d)	ESul WFib	
* 'Mirage'	CWDa	
'Miranda' (Dw)	ESul	
'Miriam Basey'	See *P.* 'Dwarf Miriam Baisey'	
'Miss Australia' (R/v)	LDea NFir SKen WFib	
'Miss Burdett Coutts' (Z/v)	ESul LVER MWhe NFir SKen SPet WFib	
'Miss Farren' (Z/v)	SSea	
'Miss Flora' (I)	CWDa MWhe	
'Miss Liverbird' (I/d)	ECtt	
'Miss McKinsey' (Z/St)	NFir	
'Miss Muffett' (Min/d)	ESul	
§ 'Miss Stapleton'	Last listed 1998	
'Miss Wackles' (Min/d)	ESul SKen WFib	
'Mistress' (Z/C)	NFir	
'Misty' (Z)	ESul	
'Mitzou'	LVER	
'Modesty' (Z/d)	SKen WFib	
'Modigliani' (R)	Last listed 1997	
'Mohawk' (R)	EBSP LVER NFir NSwl WFib	
'Molina' (I)	NPri SCoo	
mollicomum	Last listed 1998	

'Mollie' (R) WFib
* 'Molly' NFir
'Mona Lisa'PBR EBSP
'Monarch' (Dw/v) ESul
'Monica Bennett' (Dw) ESul SKen WEas
'Monks Eleigh' ESul
'Monkwood Charm' (R) LDea
'Monkwood Delight' (R) Last listed 1998
'Monkwood Dream' (R) Last listed 1999
'Monkwood Rhapsody' (R) Last listed 1998
'Monkwood Rose' (A) LDea NFir
'Monkwood Sprite' (R) LDea
'Monsal Dale' (Dw/C/d) ESul SKen
'Monsieur Ninon' (U) CLTr CRHN EWoo MSte WFib
'Monsieur Ninon' hort. See *P.* 'Madame Auguste Nonin'
'Mont Blanc' (Z/v) EWoo LVER MWhe NFir SKen WFib
'Moon Maiden' (A) ESul NFir WFib
'Moonflight' (R) WFib
'Moonlight' Last listed 1998
'Moor' (Min/d) ESul
'Moppet' (Min/d) ESul
'Morello' PBR (R) WFib
'More's Victory' (U/Sc) SSea
'Morning Cloud' (Min/d) ESul
'Morning Star' (Z/St/d) WFib
'Morning Sunrise' (Min/v) Last listed 1997
'Morph Red' (R) WFib
'Morval' (Dw/C/d) ♀ ESul LVER MWhe NFir SKen WFib
'Morwenna' (R) CMdw EWoo LDea MSte NFir SKen WFib
'Mosaic Silky' (Z/C/d/v) LVER
'Mosaic Sugar Baby' (Dwl) Last listed 1998
'Mountie' (Dw) ESul
'Mr Everaarts' (Dw/d) ESul MWhe WFib
'Mr Henry Apps' (Dw/C/d) MWhe
'Mr Henry Cox' (Z/v) ♀ LDea LVER MWhe NFir NSwl SKen WFib
'Mr Pickwick' (Dw) Last listed 1998
'Mr Ritson' (Min) ESul
'Mr Wren' (Z) CHal EWoo LVER MWhe SKen SPet WFib
'Mrs A.M. Mayne' (Z) SKen
'Mrs Cannell' (Z) SKen
'Mrs Dumbrill' (A) ESul LDea LIck SKen
'Mrs E G Hill' (Z) CWDa
'Mrs Farren' (Z/v) MWhe SKen WFib
'Mrs G.H. Smith' (A) ESul EWoo LDea MSte MWhe NFir SSea WFib
'Mrs G. More' (R) SSea WFib
'Mrs J.C. Mappin' (Z/v) ♀ EWoo SKen SSea
¶ 'Mrs J.J. Knight' EWoo
'Mrs Kingsbury' (U) EWoo SKen WEas WFib
'Mrs Kingsley' (Z/v) Last listed 1997
'Mrs Langtry' (R) LDea
'Mrs Lawrence' (Z/d) SKen WFib
'Mrs Margaret Thorp' (R) EBSP WFib
'Mrs Martin' (I) WFib
'Mrs Mary Bard' (R) WFib
'Mrs McKenzie' (Z/St) WFib
'Mrs Morf' (R) EBSP LDea NFir
'Mrs Parker' (Z/d/v) LRHS LVER MWhe NFir SPet WFib
'Mrs Pat' (Min/St/C) ESul MWhe NFir
'Mrs Pollock' (Z/v) LDea LRHS LVER MWhe NFir SKen SSea WFib WWol
'Mrs Quilter' (Z/C) LDea LVER MBri MWhe SKen SMrm SSea WFib
'Mrs Reid's Pink' EWoo
'Mrs Salter Bevis' (Z/Ca/d) ESul LVER WFib
'Mrs Strang' (Z/d/v) LVER MWhe SKen SSea WEas
'Mrs Tarrant' (Z/d) CHal WFib
'Mrs W.A.R. Clifton' (I/d) ERav LDea SKen WFib

multibracteatum Last listed 1998
multicaule Last listed 1998
'Muriel' Last listed 1997
'Music Man' (R) WFib
mutans Last listed 1998
'Müttertag' (R) EBSP LDea MSte
§ 'Mutzel' (I/v) LDea LVER NFir
'My Choice' (R) LDea
'My Love' (I/d) Last listed 1999
§ *myrrhifolium* Last listed 1999
§ - var. *coriandrifolium* Last listed 1999
'Mystery' (U) ♀ LAco LVER WFib
'N.C. Fass' (R) LDea
'Nacton' (Min) ESul
'Nadine' (Dw/C/d) ESul
Nadja (Z/d) Last listed 1998
'Nan Greeves' (Z/v) Last listed 1997
'Nancy Grey' (Min) ESul NFir
'Nancy Hiden' (R) WFib
nanum Last listed 1998
'Naomi' (R) LDea
'Narina' (I) NPri
'Natalie' (Dw) ESul
'Naughton' (Min) ESul
'Naunton Velvet' (R) Last listed 1999
'Naunton Windmill' (R) Last listed 1999
'Navajo' (R) WFib
'Nedging Tye' (A) Last listed 1999
'Needham Market' (A) ESul LDea MSte NFir
'Neene' (Dw) ESul
'Neil Clemenson' (Sc) ESul EWoo WFib
'Neil Jameson' (Z/v) NFir SKen
'Nell Smith' (Z/d) WFib
'Nellie' (R) LDea
'Nellie Nuttall' (Z) WFib
'Nels Pierson' (I) WFib
'Neon Fiat' (Z/d) WFib
'Nervosum' (Sc) ESul
'Nervous Mabel' (Sc) ♀ ESul LDea MHer NFir WFib
'Nettlecombe' (Min/St) ESul
'Nettlestead' (I) ESul
'Nettlestead' (Dw/d) LVER WFib
'Neville West' (Z) SSea
'New Life' (Z) ESul MWhe NFir
'New Phlox' (Z) WFib
'Nicholas Purple' (R) Last listed 1998
* 'Nicky' Last listed 1999
'Nicola Buck' (R) LDea
'Nicola Gainford' Last listed 1997
'Nicor Star' (Min) ESul WFib
'Nikki' (A) LDea
'Nimrod' (R) LDea
'Noche' (R) LDea SKen SMrm WFib
nodosum WEas
'Noel' (Z/Ca/d) LVER WFib
'Noele Gordon' (Z/d) LVER WFib
'Noir' (R) Last listed 1999
'Nomad' (R) NFir
'Nono' (I) WFib
'North Star' (Dw) ESul
'Northern Lights' (R) LDea
* 'Norvic' (d) CWDa
'Notting Hill Beauty' (Z) SKen
'Nouvelle Aurore' (Z) Last listed 1999
'Nuhulumby' (R) Last listed 1999
'Oakfield' Last listed 1998
'Obergarten' (Z/d) WFib
'Occold Embers' (Dw/C/d) ESul NFir WFib
'Occold Lagoon' (Dw/d) ESul NFir SKen
'Occold Orange Tip' (Min/d) ESul
'Occold Profusion' (Min/d) ESul NFir
'Occold Ruby' (Dw/C) CWDa

'Occold Shield' (Dw/C/d) ESul LRHS NFir WFib
'Occold Surprise' (Min/d) ESul
'Occold Tangerine' (Dw) ESul
'Occold Volcano' (Dw/d) ESul
* 'Odessy' (Min) WFib
odoratissimum (Sc) CHal ESul GPoy LDea LRHS LVER
MHer NFir NHHG SKen WCHb
WFib WJek
- 'Variegatum' (Sc) WEas
oenothera Last listed 1998
'Offton' (Dw) ESul
'Old Orchard' (A) LDea
'Old Rose' (Z/d) WFib
'Old Spice' (Sc/v) ESul GBar MHer NFir WFib
'Oldbury Cascade' (I/v) EWoo NFir
'Olga' (R) LDea
'Olive West' Last listed 1997
'Olivia' (R) EBSP
'Olympia' (Z/d) CWDa WFib
'Onnalee' (Dw) ESul
'Opera House' (R) WFib
'Orange Fizz' (Z/d) Last listed 1997
'Orange Imp' (Dw/d) ESul
'Orange Parfait' (R) WFib
'Orange Puff' (Min) WFib
'Orange Ricard' (Z/d) MWhe SKen WFib
'Orange River' (Dw/d) ESul SKen WFib
'Orange Ruffy' (Min) ESul
'Orange Sal' (R) Last listed 1998
'Orange Splash' (Z) SKen
'Orangeade' (Dw/d) ESul LVER SKen WFib
'Orangesonne' (Z/d) LVER WFib
'Orchid Paloma' (Dw/d) ESul SKen
'Oregon Hostess' (Dw) ESul
oreophilum Last listed 1998
'Orion' (Min/d) ESul MWhe SKen WFib
'Orsett' (Sc) ♀ EWoo LDea LVER
* 'Oscar' CWDa
'Osna' (Z) SKen
otaviense Last listed 1998
'Otto's Red' (R) NFir
ovale subsp. **hyalinum** Last listed 1998
- subsp. **ovale** WFib
- subsp. **veronicifolium** Last listed 1998
'Oyster' (Dw) ESul
PAC cultivars See under cultivar name
'Paddie' (Min) ESul
'Pagoda' (Z/St/d) CSpe ESul LVER MSte MWhe
SKen WFib
'Paisley Red' (Z/d) NFir WFib
'Palais' (Z/d) LRHS SKen WFib
'Pam Craigie' (R) LDea
'Pamela Underwood' (R) WFib
panduriforme EWoo MHer WFib
papilionaceum CHEx CRHN CTbh EWoo LHil
MHer WEas
'Parasol' (R) WFib
'Parisienne' (R) EBSP LDea
'Parmenter Pink' (Min) ESul
'Partisan' (R) Last listed 1997
'Party Dress' (Z/d) MWhe SKen WFib
'Pascal' (Z) SKen
'Pat Thorpe' (R) WFib
'Patience' (Z/d) WFib
'Paton's Unique' (U/Sc) ♀ CHal CRHN CTbh ERav EWoo
LIck LVER MHer MSte NFir WEas
WFib
* 'Patricia' (I) CWDa
'Patricia Andrea' (T) LVER NFir NPer
'Patricia Read' (Min) ERea ESul
'Patsy 'Q'' (Z/C) SKen
patulum Last listed 1998

'Paul Crampel' (Z) CHal LVER WFib
'Paul Gotz' (Z) SKen
'Paul Gunnett' (Min) MWhe
'Paul Humphries' (Z/d) WFib
'Paul Sloan' (Z) WFib
'Paul West' (Min/d) ESul
'Paula Scott' (R) LDea
'Pauline' (Min/d) ESul MWhe WFib
'Pavilion' (Min) ♀ Last listed 1998
'Pax' (R) LDea WFib
'Peace' (Min/C) ESul WFib
'Peace Palace' (Dw) ESul
'Peach' (Z) Last listed 1999
'Peach Princess' (R) EBSP NFir
'Peaches and Cream' (R) EWoo MHer
'Pearl Brocade' (R) WFib
'Pearl Eclipse' (I) Last listed 1999
Pearl Necklace See P. 'Perlenkette'
'Pearly Queen' (Min/d) ESul
'Pegasus' (Min) Last listed 1998
'Peggy Sue' (R) EBSP LDea LVER
'Peggy West' (Min/C/d) Last listed 1998
PELFI cultivars See under cultivar name
peltatum WFib
- 'Lateripes' SKen
'Penny' (Z/d) MWhe SKen WFib
'Penny Lane' (Z) Last listed 1998
'Penny Serenade' (Dw/C) ESul SKen
'Pensby' (Dw) ESul NFir
'Penve' PBR (Z/d) Last listed 1998
¶ 'Peppermint Lace' (Sc) EWoo
'Peppermint Star' (Z/St) NFir
'Perchance' (R) SSea
'Percival' (Dw/d) Last listed 1997
'Perfect' (Z) SKen
* 'Perle Blanche' (I) CWDa
§ 'Perlenkette' (Z/d) Last listed 1997
§ Perlenkette Orange (Z/d) Last listed 1998
§ Perlenkette Weiss Last listed 1997
= 'Perlpenei'
'Persian King' (R) LDea
'Persimmon' (Z/St) WFib
'Petals' (Z/v) MSte SKen WWol
'Peter Godwin' (R) EBSP LDea WFib
'Peter Grieve' (Z/v) WFib
'Peter Read' (Dw/d) ERea ESul
'Peter's Choice' (R) EBSP LDea LVER
'Peter's Luck' (Sc) ♀ ESul
'Petit Pierre' See P. 'Kleine Liebling'
'Petite Blanche' (Dw/d) LVER WFib
'Petronella' (Z/d) ESul
'Phil Rose' (I) CWDa MWhe
'Philomel' (I/d) WFib
'Philomel Rose' (I/d) LDea
'Phlox New Life' (Z) ESul
'Phyllis' (U/v) EWoo LHil LVER MHer NFir NSwl
SSea
'Phyllis Mary' (R) WFib
'Phyllis Read' (Min) ERea ESul WFib
'Phyllis Richardson' (R/d) LDea WFib
'Phyllis Variegated' LHop
'Picardy' (Z/d) SKen
'Pickaninny' (Min) ESul
'Pier Head' (Z) NFir
'Pin Mill' (Min/d) ESul
'Pink Aura' ESul NFir
'Pink Aurore' (U) MHer MSte
'Pink Black Vesuvius' WFib
(Min/C)
'Pink Blizzard' NPri WLRN WWol
'Pink Boar' EWoo
'Pink Bonanza' (R) EBSP LDea WFib

'Pink Bouquet' (Z/d)	Last listed 1998
'Pink Bouquet' (R)	EBSP WFib
'Pink Capitatum'	See P. 'Pink Capricorn'
§ 'Pink Capricorn' (Sc)	EWoo WFib
'Pink Carnation' (I/d)	LDea
'Pink Cascade'	See P. 'Hederinum'
'Pink Champagne' (Sc)	CRHN ESul MHer WFib
'Pink Charm' (I)	Last listed 1997
'Pink Cloud' (Z/d)	WFib
'Pink Countess Mariza' (Z)	SKen
'Pink Crampel' (Z)	CWDa
'Pink Dolly Varden' (Z/v)	SSea
'Pink Eggshell' (Dw)	Last listed 1997
'Pink Flamingo' (R)	LDea
'Pink Fondant' (Min/d)	ESul
'Pink Gay Baby'	See P. 'Sugar Baby'
'Pink Golden Ears' (Dw/St/C)	SKen
'Pink Golden Harry Hieover' (Z/C)	ESul
'Pink Grace Wells' (Min)	Last listed 1998
'Pink Grozser Garten' (Dw)	Last listed 1998
'Pink Happy Thought' (Z/v)	LRHS LVER NFir WFib
'Pink Ice' (Min/d)	ESul LVER NFir
'Pink Kewense' (Min)	Last listed 1998
'Pink Lively Lady' (Dw/C)	Last listed 1997
'Pink Margaret Pearce' (R)	WFib
'Pink Mini Cascade'	See P. 'Rosa Mini-cascade'
'Pink Parfait' (Z)	Last listed 1997
'Pink Pearl' (Z/d)	WFib
'Pink Rambler' (Z/d)	MWhe SKen WFib
'Pink Raspail' (Z/d)	WFib
'Pink Rosebud' (Z/d)	NFir SKen WFib
'Pink Ruffles' (R)	EBSP
'Pink Satisfaction' (Z)	Last listed 1998
'Pink Snow' (Min/d)	ESul
'Pink Splash' (Min/d)	ESul
'Pink Star' (Z/St)	WFib
'Pink Tiny Tim' (Min)	ESul WFib
'Pinocchio' (R)	WFib
'Pixie' (Dw)	ESul
'Pixie Glow' (Z/St)	NFir
'Pixie Rose' (Z/St)	NFir WFib
'Platinum' (Z/v)	Last listed 1998
'Playmate' (Min/St)	ESul SKen WFib
'Plenty' (Z/d)	CWDa WFib
'Plum Rambler' (Z/d)	EWoo SKen WFib
'Poetesse' (A)	LDea
'Polka' (U)	EWoo LVER MHer NFir SSea WFib
'Pom Pom' (Z/d)	WFib
'Pompeii' (R)	LDea NFir WFib
¶ 'Porcelain' (Z)	SKen
¶ 'Porchfield' (Min/St)	ESul
'Portsmouth' (R)	Last listed 1997
'Potpourri' (Min)	SKen
'Potter Heigham' (Dw)	ESul
'Powder Puff' (Dw/d)	ESul
praemorsum	Last listed 1998
'Prairie Dawn' (Z/d)	WFib
'Presto' (Min)	ESul MWhe
¶ 'Presto' (St)	NFir
'Preston Park' (Z/C)	SKen SMrm SPet WFib
'Pretty Girl' (I)	LDea
'Pretty Polly' (Sc)	MHer WFib
¶ 'Pride of Exmouth'	CStu
'Pride of the West' (Z)	Last listed 1999
'Prim' (Min/d)	ESul
'Primavera' (R)	EBSP LDea
'Prince Consort' (R)	LVER
'Prince of Orange' (Sc)	CArn CInt CLTr CRHN CSev EDAr EOHP ESul EWoo GBar GPoy LDea LIck LRHS LVER MHer MSte
	MWhe NFir NHHG SSea WCHb WFib WHer
'Prince of Wales' (Z)	WFib
'Prince Regent' (R)	NFir
'Princeanum' (Sc) ♀	EWoo MHer WFib
'Princess Alexandra' (R)	LVER SSea
'Princess Alexandra' (Z/d/v)	MWhe NFir WFib
'Princess Anne' (Z)	MSte
'Princess Consort' (R)	LDea
'Princess Josephine' (Z)	EWoo LDea WFib
'Princess of Balcon'	See P. 'Roi des Balcons Lilas'
'Princess of Wales' (R)	EBSP ERav LDea WFib
'Princess Virginia' (R/v)	LDea LIck LVER WFib
'Professor Eckman' (R)	WFib
'Promenade' (Z/d)	WFib
'Prospect' (Z/d)	MWhe
pseudofumarioides	Last listed 1998
pseudoglutinosum	EWoo WFib
pulchellum	Last listed 1998
pulverulentum	Last listed 1998
'Purple Ball'	See P. Purpurball
'Purple Emperor' (R)	LDea WFib
'Purple Heart' (Dw/St)	ESul NFir
'Purple Orchard' (R)	LDea
'Purple Pride' (I/d)	CWDa
'Purple Rambler' (Z/d)	MWhe
'Purple Unique' (U/Sc)	EWoo MHer MSte NFir SKen WFib
Purple Wonder (Z/d)	Last listed 1998
§ Purpurball (Z/d)	SKen
'Pygmalion' (Z/d/v)	SSea WFib
'Quakeress' (R)	LDea WFib
'Quakermaid' (Min)	Last listed 1998
'Quantock' (R)	WFib
'Quantock Beaujolais' (A)	LDea
'Quantock Beauty' (A)	LDea MWhe NFir
¶ 'Quantock Marjorie' (A)	NFir
'Quantock Matty' (A)	EWoo NFir
¶ 'Quantock May' (A)	LDea
'Quantock Rita' (A)	NFir
'Quantock Rory' (A)	LDea
'Quantock Rose' (A)	LDea
'Quantock Sapphire' (A)	LDea
¶ 'Quantock Star' (A)	LDea
'Queen Esther' (Z/d/St)	LVER
'Queen Ingrid' (Z)	Last listed 1998
'Queen of Denmark' (Z/d)	LVER SKen WFib
'Queen of Hearts' (I/d)	LVER WFib
I 'Queen of the Lemons'	EWoo
quercetorum	Last listed 1999
N *quercifolium* (Sc)	CHal CRHN CSev EWoo GPoy MHer NFir NHHG SKen SSea SYvo WEas WFib WJek WWye
- 'Fair Ellen'	See P. 'Fair Ellen'
¶ - variegated	MHer
quinquelobatum	CSpe SGar
'R.A.Turner' (Z/d)	WFib
'Rachel' (Min)	ESul
'Rachel Fisher' (Z)	WFib
radens (Sc)	EPfP WFib
'Radiance' (Z/d)	WFib
'Radiant' (Z/d)	WFib
'Radio' (Z/d)	WFib
'Radior' (Min)	WFib
'Rads Star' (Z/St)	ESul NFir WFib
'Radula' (Sc) ♀	CSev ERav ESul GBar LDea LIck MHer MWhe SKen WCHb WFib
'Radula Roseum' (Sc)	SSea
radulifolium	Last listed 1998
'Ragamuffin' (Min/d)	ESul MWhe NFir WFib
'Rager's Pink' (Dw/d)	ESul
'Rager's Star' (Min)	ESul
¶ 'Ragers Veri-Star' (Min/C)	ESul

'Rakastani' (Z)	SKen	
ranunculophyllum	Last listed 1998	
rapaceum	Last listed 1998	
'Rapture' (R)	WFib	
'Raspberry Parfait' (R)	LDea	
'Raspberry Ripple' (A)	ESul LDea NFir	
'Raspberry Sundae' (R)	CLTr	
'Raspberry Sweet' (Z/St)	NFir WFib	
'Raviro' (I)	WFib	
'Ray Bidwell' (Min)	ESul MWhe NFir	
'Ray Coughlin' (Z/C/d)	WFib	
'Raydon' (Min)	ESul	
'Rebecca' (Min/d)	ESul WFib	
'Red Admiral' (Min/d/v)	ESul SKen	
§ 'Red Black Vesuvius'	CHal CSpe ESul LVER MWhe	
(Min/C)	SKen WEas WFib	
'Red Blizzard'	NPri WWol	
¶ 'Red Cactus' (St)	NFir	
'Red Cascade' (I) ♀	MWhe	
'Red Fox' (Min)	Last listed 1998	
'Red Gables'	WCFE	
'Red Galilee' (I/d)	MWhe SKen	
'Red Gem' (Min)	ESul	
'Red Glow' (Min)	ESul	
'Red Ice' (Min/d)	ESul MWhe NFir	
* 'Red Irene' (Z/d)	CWDa	
* 'Red Kewense'	ESul	
'Red Light' (Z/d)	WFib	
'Red Magic Lantern' (Z/C)	SKen	
'Red Mini Cascade'	See *P.* 'Rote Mini-cascade'	
'Red Pandora' (T)	LVER	
'Red Rambler' (Z/d)	CHal LVER MWhe SKen WFib	
'Red Satisfaction' (Z)	Last listed 1998	
'Red Silver Cascade'	See *P.* 'Mutzel'	
'Red Spangles' (R)	WFib	
'Red Spider' (Min/Ca/d)	ESul WFib	
'Red Startel' (Z/St/d)	MWhe SKen WFib	
'Red Susan Pearce' (R)	EBSP LDea	
'Red Tiny Tim' (Min)	WFib	
'Red Velvet' (R)	WFib	
'Red Witch' (Dw/St/d)	ESul LVER NFir WFib	
'Redondo' (Min/d)	ESul LVER MWhe WEas WFib	
'Reflections' (Z/d)	WFib	
'Reg 'Q'' (Z/C)	NFir	
'Regal Perchance'	Last listed 1998	
'Regina' (Z/d)	LVER NFir SKen SPet WEas WFib	
'Reifi Vanderlea'	EWoo	
'Rembrandt' (R)	LDea LVER SKen SSea SYvo WEas WFib	
'Remo' (Z/d)	Last listed 1998	
'Renate Parsley'	LHil NFir WFib	
'Rene Roué' (Dw)	ESul NFir	
'Renee Ross' (I/d) ♀	CWDa LVER WFib	
reniforme	GBar MHer SAga WEas WFib	
'Retah's Crystal' (Z/v)	ESul LRHS LVER MWhe NFir	
'Rhineland' (I)	SKen	
'Rhodamant' (I/d)	WFib	
'Rhodamine' (R)	Last listed 1999	
'Rhodo' (R)	WFib	
ribifolium	Last listed 1998	
Rica (Z/d)	Last listed 1998	
'Richard Gibbs'	EWoo MHer	
'Richard Key' (Z/d/v)	WFib	
'Richard West' (I/d)	CWDa	
'Rietje van der Lee' (A)	ESul WFib	
'Rigel' (Min/d)	ESul MWhe NFir SKen WFib	
'Rigi' (I)	ECtt MBri SKen WFib	
'Rigoletto' (I)	EWoo LDea NFir	
'Rimey' (St)	NFir	
'Rimfire' (R)	EBSP LDea LVER NFir WFib	
'Rio' (Z)	Last listed 1998	
'Rio Grande' (I/d)	LDea LVER MWhe NFir NSwl	
	NWoo SKen WEas WFib	
'Rising Sun'	NFir	
'Rita Brook' (Z/d)	WFib	
'Rita Coughlin' (R)	WFib	
'Rita Scheen' (A)	ESul LDea MWhe SSea WFib	
'Rita Thomas' (Z)	WFib	
'Ritchie'	EBSP	
'Robbie Hare' (R)	WFib	
'Robe' [PBR] (Z/d)	LRHS LVER	
'Rober's Lavender' (Dw)	ESul	
'Rober's Lemon Rose' (Sc)	CInt CRHN ERav ESul EWoo GBar MHer SKen WCHb WEas WFib WHer WJek WWye	
'Rober's Salmon Coral' (Dw/d)	ESul	
'Robert Fish' (Z/C)	ESul LRHS	
'Robert McElwain'	WFib	
'Robin' (Sc)	LDea LVER	
'Robin' (R)	EWoo LDea WEas	
¶ Rocky Mountain White® = 'Fisrowi' [PBR] (Z/d)	WWol	
rodneyanum	Last listed 1998	
'Roger's Delight' (R)	EWoo LDea	
rogersianum	See *P. worcesterae*	
'Rogue' (R)	EBSP EWoo LDea MSte WFib	
'Roi des Balcons'	See *P.* 'Hederinum'	
§ 'Roi des Balcons Impérial' (I) ♀	MWhe SSea	
§ 'Roi des Balcons Lilas' (I) ♀	MWhe SKen SSea	
'Roi des Balcons Rose'	See *P.* 'Hederinum'	
§ Rokoko (Z)	CWDa	
§ 'Roller's David' (I/d)	CWDa	
'Roller's Echo' (A)	ESul LDea LIck MWhe NFir	
¶ 'Roller's Gabriella' (A)	LDea	
'Roller's Pathfinder' (I/d/v)	LDea LVER	
'Roller's Pioneer' (I/v)	EWoo LDea SAga SKen	
'Roller's Satinique' (U) ♀	EWoo LIck MHer WFib	
'Rollisson's Unique' (U)	ERav MHer MSte NBur NFir WFib	
'Romeo' (R)	LVER	
§ Romy (I)	LDea	
§ 'Rosa Mini-cascade' (I)	ESul LVER MWhe NFir WLRN	
§ Rosais (I/d) ♀	Last listed 1995	
'Rosaleen' (Min)	ESul	
'Rosalie' (Min)	Last listed 1999	
'Rosamunda' (Z/d)	WFib	
'Roscobie' (Z/d)	Last listed 1999	
'Rose Bengal' (A)	CRHN ESul LDea MWhe WEas WFib	
¶ 'Rose Evka' (Dw/I/v)	NFir	
'Rose Irene' (Z/d)	MWhe WFib	
'Rose Jewel'	EBSP	
'Rose of Amsterdam' (Min/d)	ESul	
'Rose Rambler' (Z/d)	WEas	
'Rose Silver Cascade' (I)	LDea LVER	
'Rose Slam' (R)	WFib	
'Rose Startel' (Z/St)	Last listed 1997	
'Rose Unique' (Z)	Last listed 1998	
'Rosebud Supreme' (Z/d)	Last listed 1997	
'Rosecrystal' [PBR] (Z/d)	LVER	
'Rosee Normande' (Z/d)	WFib	
* 'Roselo'	CWDa	
'Rosemarie' (Z/d)	MWhe	
'Rosemine' (Z/d)	WFib	
'Rose's Orange'	Last listed 1999	
'Rosette' (Dw)	SKen WFib	
'Rosina Read' (Dw)	ERea ESul LVER WFib	
'Rosita' (Dw/d) ♀	Last listed 1997	
'Rosmaroy' (R)	EBSP LDea LVER NFir	
§ 'Rospen' (Z/d)	LVER SKen SYvo WFib	
* 'Rosseau' (Min)	WFib	
'Rosy Dawn' (Min/d)	WFib	

¶	'Rosy Morn' (R)	NFir
§	'Rote Mini-cascade' (I)	LDea LVER MWhe SKen WFib
	'Rotherfield' (I/d)	LDea
	'Rotlieb' (Z/d)	WFib
§	'Rouletta' (I/d)	ECtt LDea LVER MWhe NPri SKen SSea WFib WLRN
	'Rousillon' (R)	LDea WFib
	'Rousseau' (Dw/C)	ESul
	'Royal Ascot' (R)	CHal ERav ESul EWoo LDea MSte NFir NSwl SMrm
	'Royal Blaze' (Z/v)	Last listed 1997
	'Royal Carpet' (Min/d)	ESul
	'Royal Claret' (I/d)	WEas
	'Royal Fiat' (Z/d)	Last listed 1998
	'Royal Norfolk' (Min/d)	ESul LVER MWhe NFir SKen
	'Royal Oak' (Sc) ♀	CBrm CElw CInt CSev EWoo GBar LDea MHer MWhe NBur WEas WFib WHer WPer WRha
*	'Royal Princess' (R) ♀	Last listed 1998
§	'Royal Purple' (Z/d)	CHal LVER SKen WFib
*	'Royal Salmon'	CWDa
	'Royal Sovereign' (Z/C/d)	LDea LVER
	'Royal Star' (R)	LDea
	'Royal Surprise' (R)	LDea NFir
	'Royal Wedding' (R)	LDea
	'Rubella' (Z/d)	WFib
*	'Rubican'	CWDa
	'Rubin Improved' (Z/d)	SKen WFib
	'Ruby' (Min/d)	ESul WFib
	'Ruby Orchid' (A)	LDea NFir
¶	'Ruby Wedding' (Z)	NFir
	'Ruffled Velvet' (R)	EWoo SSea
	'Rushmere' (Dw/d)	ESul WFib
	'Russet Wings' (R)	WFib
	'Rustler' (Min)	WFib
	'Rusty' (Dw/C/d)	ESul
	'Ruth Bessley'	Last listed 1997
	'Ruth Karmen' (I/d)	Last listed 1999
	'Ryan Dollery' (Z)	Last listed 1997
	'Ryecroft Pride' (Z/d)	WFib
	'Ryecroft White' (Z/d)	WFib
	'Sabine' PBR (Z/d)	LVER
	'Saint Malo'	NFir
	'Sally Anne' (R)	Last listed 1999
	'Sally Munro' (R)	LDea
	'Sally Read' (Dw/d)	ERea ESul
	'Salmon Beauty' (Min/d)	WFib
	'Salmon Black Vesuvius' (Min/C)	ESul
	'Salmon Comet' (Min)	Last listed 1997
§	'Salmon Irene' (Z/d)	WFib
	'Salmon Queen'	See P. 'Lachskönigin'
	'Salmon Slam' (R)	WFib
	'Salmon Startel' (Z/St/d)	ESul MWhe
	salmoneum	Last listed 1998
	'Saltford' (R)	WFib
	'Samantha' (R)	EBSP LDea WFib
	'Samantha Stamp' (Dw)	WFib
	'Samba' (R)	WFib
	'Sancho Panza' (Dec) ♀	CSpe ESul EWoo LDea LVER MSte NFir NSwl SKen SSea WEas WFib
	'Sandra Haynes' (R)	Last listed 1998
	'Sanguineum'	CSpe
	'Santa Maria' (Z/d)	LVER SKen WFib
	'Santa Marie' (R)	LDea
	'Santa Paula' (I/d)	ECtt LDea LVER MWhe SKen
	'Sante Fe' (Z/C)	Last listed 1997
	'Sasha' (Min)	WFib
	'Sassa' PBR (Z/d)	CWDa
§	'Satellite' (Z/St)	WFib
	'Satsuki' (R)	EBSP LDea NFir
	'Saturn' (Z)	NFir
	'Saxifragoides'	SSea
§	scabrum	WFib
	'Scandens'	Last listed 1998
*	'Scarlet Kewense'	Last listed 1998
	'Scarlet Nosegay'	CHal
	'Scarlet Pet' (U)	CLTr CRHN ESul NFir
	'Scarlet Pimpernel' (Z/C/d)	ESul WFib
	'Scarlet Queen' (Z)	Last listed 1998
	'Scarlet Rambler' (Z/d)	EWoo LVER SKen SMrm WEas WFib
	'Scarlet Unique' (U)	CRHN EWoo LDea MHer MSte NFir SKen SSea WCHb WFib
	'Scatterbrain' (Z)	CWDa
	schizopetalum	Last listed 1998
§	'Schneekönigin' (I/d)	ECtt LDea LVER MSte SKen WEas
§	'Schöne Helena' PBR (Z/d)	CWDa
*	'Schone von Grenchen (I)'	Last listed 1999
	'Seale Orchid' (A)	SSea
	'Seale Rose Pink' (Z/v)	SSea
	'Seaview Star' (Z/St)	Last listed 1997
	'Secret Love' (Sc)	WFib
	'Seeley's Pansy' (A)	CSpe ESul LDea WFib
	'Sefton' (R) ♀	EBSP LDea WFib
	'Selby' (Z/C/d)	WFib
	'Selina'	ESul
	'Semer' (Min)	ESul LVER SKen
	senecioides	Last listed 1998
	'Senorita' (R)	LDea
	'Sensation' (Z)	Last listed 1999
	'Serena' PBR (Min)	Last listed 1999
	sericifolium	Last listed 1998
*	'Serre de la Madone' (Sc)	WEas
	'Shalimar' (St)	CSpe MSte NFir WFib
¶	'Shanklin' (Dw/St)	ESul
	'Shanks' (Z)	NFir
	'Sharon' (Min/d)	ESul WFib
	'Sharon Louise' (Min)	Last listed 1998
	'Sharon West' (Dw)	Last listed 1999
	'Shaun Jacobs' (Min/d)	Last listed 1998
	'Shaunough' (Min)	Last listed 1997
	'Sheila' (Dw)	ESul
	'Shelley' (Dw)	ESul SKen
	'Shenandoah' (Min)	WFib
	'Sheraton' (Min/d)	MWhe
	'Shimmer' (Z/d)	LVER MWhe WFib
	'Shirley Anne' (Dw/d)	Last listed 1998
	'Shirley Ash' (A)	ESul LDea SKen WFib
	'Shirley Maureen' (R)	LDea WFib
	'Shiva'	Last listed 1999
	'Shocking' (Z/d)	Last listed 1997
	'Shogan' (R)	NFir
	'Shotley' (Min)	ESul
	'Shottesham Pet' (Sc)	EWoo MHer SKen
	'Shrubland Pet' (U/Sc)	EWoo MHer SKen
	'Shrubland Rose' (Sc)	WFib
	sidoides	CSpe LHil NFir WCot WEas
¶	- black	CSpe
	'Sienna' (R)	LDea NFir
	'Silberlachs' (Z/d)	WFib
	'Silky'	ESul
	'Silpen' (Z/d)	WFib
*	'Sils'	CWDa
	'Silver Anne' (R)	NFir WFib
*	'Silver Cascade'	ERav
	'Silver Kewense' (Dw/v)	ESul NFir SKen WFib
*	'Silver Lights'	CWDa
	'Silver Monarch'	ESul
	'Silver Wings' (Z/v)	ESul EWoo LRHS LVER MWhe NFir SSea WFib
	'Silvia' (R)	EBSP
	'Simon Portas' (I/d)	SKen
	'Simon Read' (Dw)	ERea ESul

'Simplicity' (Z)   LVER
'Single New Life' (Z)   Last listed 1997
'Sir Arthur Hort' (I)   WFib
'Sister Henry' (Z/d)   WFib
'Sister Teresa' (Z/d)   Last listed 1998
'Skelly's Pride' (Z)   LVER SKen WEas
'Skies of Italy' (Z/C/d)   CHal MBri NFir SKen SSea WFib
'Sleuring's Robin' (Min/d)   WFib
'Small Fortune' (Dw)   ESul SKen
'Smuggler' (R)   LDea
'Snape'   ESul
'Sneezy' (Min)   NFir
Snow Queen   See *P.* 'Schneekönigin'
'Snow White' (Min)   ESul
'Snowbaby' (Min/d)   ESul
'Snowball' (Z/d)   Last listed 1998
'Snowberry' (R)   EBSP
'Snowdon' (Min)   WFib
'Snowdrift' (I/d)   LVER WFib
'Snowmass' (Z/d)   CHal MWhe SKen
'Snowstorm' (Z)   EWoo WFib
'Snowy Baby' (Min/d)   WFib
'Sofie'   See *P.* 'Decora Rose'
'Solano' (R)   Last listed 1999
'Solent Star'   NFir
'Solent Waves' (R)   EBSP LDea WFib
'Solferino' (A)   ESul LDea SKen
§ Solidor (I/d) ♀   LDea NFir WFib
Solo = 'Guillio' (Z/I)   EWoo LVER
'Sombrero' (R)   WFib
'Somersham' (Min)   ESul
'Something Special' (Z/d)   LVER MWhe NFir WFib
'Sonata' (Dw/d)   ESul
'Sonnesport' (Z)   WFib
'Sophie Cascade'   CWDa
'Sophie Dumaresque' (Z/v)   LVER MBri MWhe NFir SKen
   WFib
'Sophie Koniger' (Z/d)   WFib
'Sorcery' (Dw/C)   ESul MWhe SKen
¶ 'Sound Appeal' (A)   ESul
'South American Bronze'   LDea SKen SMrm WFib
   (R) ♀
'South American Delight'   LVER
   (R)
¶ 'South Walsham Broad'   ESul
   (Dw)
'Southern Belle' (A)   LDea
'Southern Belle' (Z/d)   WFib
'Southern Charm' (Z/v)   LVER NFir
'Southern Cherub' (A)   LDea
¶ 'Southern Gem' (Min/d)   ESul
¶ 'Southern Peach' (d)   ESul
'Souvenir' (R)   CHal LDea SSea
'Spanish Angel' (A) ♀   ESul LDea NFir SSea
'Sparkler' (Z)   LVER
'Special Moment' (R)   WFib
'Speckles' (Z)   Last listed 1998
'Spellbound' (R)   WFib
'Spital Dam'   ESul NFir
'Spitfire' (Z/Ca/v)   ESul LVER NFir WFib
'Spithead Cherry' (R)   EBSP LDea WFib
'Splash Down'   Last listed 1998
§ 'Splendide'   CInt CMdw CRDP CSpe LHil
   LHop NFir NSwl SAga SMrm SSad
   SSea WEas WWol
'Splendour' (R) ♀   Last listed 1996
¶ 'Spotlite Hotline' (I)   LDea
¶ 'Spotlite Winner' (I)   LDea
'Spot-on-Bonanza' (R)   EBSP LDea NFir WFib
'Spring Bride' (R)   LDea
'Spring Park' (A)   ESul MHer WFib
'Springfield Ann' (R)   EBSP

'Springfield Betty' (R)   EBSP
'Springfield Black' (R)   EBSP LDea LVER NSwl
'Springfield Charm' (R)   EBSP
'Springfield Kate' (R)   EBSP
'Springfield Mary Parfitt' (R)   EBSP
¶ 'Springfield Moonbeam' (R)   EBSP
'Springfield Pearl' (R)   LDea
'Springfield Purple' (R)   EBSP
'Springfield Stripey' (R)   EBSP
'Springfield Unique' (R)   EBSP LDea
'Springtime' (Z/d)   MWhe WFib
'Sprite' (Min/v)   MWhe
'Sproughton' (Dw)   ESul
'St Helen's Favourite' (Min)   ESul
'Stacey' (R)   LDea
'Stadt Bern' (Z/C)   LRHS LVER MBri MSte MWhe
   NFir SKen WEas WFib
'Stanton Drew' (Z/d)   WFib
'Staplegrove Fancy' (Z)   EWoo
× *stapletoniae*   See *P.* 'Miss Stapleton'
'Star Flecks'   NFir
'Star Glitter'   Last listed 1998
'Star of Persia' (Z/Ca)   WFib
'Starbust'   NFir
¶ 'Starflecks' (St)   LVER
'Starlet' (Ca)   WFib
'Starlight' (R)   WFib
'Starlight Magic' (A) ♀   ESul LDea WEas
'Starry Eyed' (Dw)   ESul
'Startel Salmon' (Z/St)   WFib
'Stella Ballerina'   ERav
'Stella Read' (Dw/d)   ERea ESul WFib
'Stellar Apricot' (Z/St)   ERav NFir
'Stellar Arctic Star'   See *P.* 'Arctic Star'
'Stellar Cathay' (Z/St/d)   ERav LRHS NFir WFib
'Stellar Dawn Star' (Z/St)   NFir WEas WFib
'Stellar Grenadier'   See *P.* 'Grenadier'
'Stellar Hannaford Star'   See *P.* 'Hannaford Star'
'Stellar Orange' (Z/St)   Last listed 1997
* 'Stellar Orange Pixie' (d)   CWDa
'Stellar Pixie Rose' (St)   NFir
'Stellar Ragtime' (Z/St/d)   Last listed 1998
'Stellar Snowflake' (Z/St)   NFir
'Stellar Telstar' (Z/St/d)   Last listed 1997
stenopetalum   Last listed 1998
'Stephen Read' (Min)   ERea ESul
'Stewart Read' (Dw)   ERea
stipulaceum   Last listed 1998
'Stirling Stent' (Z)   CWDa
* 'Strasbourg'   Last listed 1997
'Strawberries and Cream'   NFir
   (Z/St)
'Strawberry Fayre' [PBR]   LVER
'Strawberry Sundae' (R)   EBSP LDea LVER MSte NFir WEas
   WFib
'Stringer's Delight'   ESul
'Stringer's Souvenir'   ESul LVER
   (Dw/d/v)
'Stuart Mark' (R)   LDea
'Stutton' (Min)   ESul
sublignosum   Last listed 1998
suburbanum subsp.   Last listed 1998
   bipinnatifidum
¶ 'Suffolk Amethyst' (A)   ESul
'Suffolk Gold' (Min/C)   Last listed 1998
§ 'Sugar Baby' (DwI)   ECtt ESul LDea MBri SKen WEas
   WFib
'Summer Cloud' (Z/d)   SKen WFib
'Summertime' (R)   Last listed 1998
'Sun Kissed' (Min)   ESul
'Sun Rocket' (Dw)   MWhe WFib
'Sunbeam' (Dw/d)   Last listed 1999

* 'Sundance Orange Scarlet' Last listed 1995
  (seed raised) (Z) ♀
'Sundridge Moonlight'   WFib
  (Z/C)
'Sunraysia' (Z/St)   NFir WFib
¶ 'Sunridge Moonlight' (Dw) NFir
'Sunrise' (R)   EBSP LDea LVER SKen WEas WFib
'Sunset' (Z)   WFib
'Sunset Snow' (R)   LDea LVER NFir WFib
'Sunshine Mistress' (Z/C)   NFir
¶ 'Sunspot' (Min/C)   NFir
'Sunspot Petit Pierre'   ESul
  (Min/v)
'Sunstar' (Min/d)   ESul WFib
'Super Rose' (I)   MWhe SKen
'Super Spot on Bonanza' (R) LVER
'Supernova' (Min/d)   Last listed 1997
'Supernova' (Z/St/d)   CWDa ESul MWhe NFir SKen
                            WFib
'Surcouf' (I)   WFib
'Susan Payne' (Dw/d)   ESul
'Susan Pearce' (R)   LDea LVER SKen WFib
'Susan Read' (Dw)   ERea ESul
* 'Susan Screen'   CWDa
'Susie 'Q'' (Z/C)   ESul LVER MWhe NFir SKen SPet
                            SSea
'Sussex Beauty' (Dw/C/d)   CWDa
'Sussex Delight' (Min)   CWDa NFir SKen
'Sussex Gem' (Min/d)   SKen
'Sussex Jewel' (Min)   SKen
'Sussex Lace'   See P. 'White Mesh'
'Swanland Lace' (I/d/v)   LVER WFib
'Swedish Angel' (A)   ESul EWoo LDea LVER MWhe
                            NFir SSea
'Sweet Charlotte' (R)   Last listed 1997
* 'Sweet Lady Mary' (Sc)   WFib
'Sweet Mimosa' (Sc) ♀   CBrm CHal CLTr CRHN EWoo
                            LDea LIck LVER MHer MSte NFir
                            SKen SSea WEas WFib
'Sweet Miriam' (Sc)   LDea
'Sweet Sue' (Min)   ESul WFib
I 'Sweet William' (St)   LVER
'Swilland' (A)   ESul LDea MWhe
'Sybil Bradshaw' (R)   LDea WFib
'Sybil Holmes' (I/d)   ECtt LVER MBri MWhe SKen WFib
'Sylvia Gale' (R)   WFib
'Sylvia Marie' (Dw/d)   MWhe NFir SKen
'Sylvia Mariza'   Last listed 1998
* 'Tamara'   CWDa
'Tami' (Min)   Last listed 1997
'Tamie' (Dw/d)   ESul MWhe NFir NSwl
'Tamie D' (Min)   Last listed 1997
'Tammy' (Dw/d)   ESul LVER MWhe WFib
'Tangerine' (Min/Ca/d)   ESul WFib
§ 'Tango' PBR (Z/d)   Last listed 1998
'Tanzy' (Min)   ESul
'Tapestry' (R)   LDea
'Tapestry' (Min/v)   NFir WEas
'Tashmal' (R)   EBSP
'Tattingstone' (Min)   ESul
'Tavira' (I/d)   LVER WFib
'Ted Brooke' (Z/d)   WFib
'Ted Dutton' (R)   WFib
'Teddy Roosevelt' (Z/d)   WFib
'Telstar' (Min/d)   ESul SKen WFib
§ 'Telston's Prima' (R)   LDea
'Tenderly' (Dw/d)   ESul
'Tenerife Magic' (MinI/d)   ESul
tenuicaule   WFib
'Terence Read' (Min)   ERea
ternatum   Last listed 1998
tetragonum   CInt SSea SVen WFib

'The Axe' (A)   ESul
'The Barle' (A) ♀   LDea LVER
'The Boar' (Fr) ♀   CSpe EWoo LDea LVER MSte NFir
                            SRms WPer
'The Bray' (A)   LDea
'The Creedy' (A)   LDea
§ 'The Crocodile' (I/C/d)   ECtt LDea LVER MWhe NFir SKen
                            SSea WEas WFib
'The Culm' (A)   ESul EWoo LDea MSte
'The Czar'   See P. 'Czar'
'The Dart' (A)   LDea
'The Duchess' (I/d)   WFib
¶ 'The Heddon' (A)   LDea
'The Joker' (I)   WFib
'The Kenn-Lad' (A)   LDea NFir
'The Lowman' (A)   LDea
'The Lyn' (A)   LDea
'The Mole' (A)   LDea LVER SKen
'The Okement' (A)   LDea
'The Otter' (A)   LDea
'The Prince' (Min)   Last listed 1997
'The Speaker' (Z/d)   SKen WFib
'The Tamar' (A)   LDea
'The Tone' (A) ♀   LDea
'Thomas Earle' (Z)   WFib
'Thomas Gerald' (Min/C)   ESul SKen
'Thorley'   Last listed 1997
'Tiberias' (I/d)   Last listed 1998
'Tiffany' (Min/d)   Last listed 1998
'Tilly' (Min)   CHal NFir SAga
'Tim' (Min)   ESul
'Timothy Clifford' (Min/d) ESul MWhe NFir WFib
'Tinkerbell' (A)   LDea NFir
§ 'Tip Top Duet' (A) ♀   ESul EWoo LDea LIck LRHS LVER
                            MWhe NFir NWoo SLod SSea
                            WEas WFib
'Token' (Z)   Last listed 1998
¶ 'Tollemache Blush'   EWoo
'Tom Portas' (Dw/d)   ESul
'Tom Tit' (Dw)   SPet
'Tomcat' PBR (Z/d)   LVER NSwl
tomentosum (Sc) ♀   CArn CHEx CHal CRHN CSev
                            CSpe CTbh EWoo GBar GPoy
                            LDea MHer MMal MSCN MWhe
                            NFir NHHG SKen WEas WFib
                            WWye
 - 'Chocolate'   See P. 'Chocolate Peppermint'
'Tommay's Delight' (R)   EBSP LDea WFib
tongaense   WFib
'Tony' (Min)   ESul
'Topscore' (Z/d)   WFib
'Toreador' (Z/d)   WFib
'Torento' (Sc)   ESul EWoo LDea MHer SKen WFib
'Tornado' (R)   EBSP LDea NFir WFib
'Tortoise Shell' (R)   WFib
'Toyon' (Z/d)   SKen WFib
'Tracy' (Min/d)   ESul NFir
tragacanthoides   Last listed 1998
transvaalense   WFib
'Traute Hausler' (A)   LDea
'Trautlieb' (Z/d)   CWDa WFib
'Treasure' (Z/d)   Last listed 1998
'Treasure Chest' (Z)   Last listed 1998
'Treasure Trove' (Z/v)   NFir
'Trésor' (Dw/d)   CWDa
tricolor hort.   See P. 'Splendide'
 - Curt.   CPla SSad
trifidum   NSwl SSad SSea WEas WFib
'Trimley' (Dw/d)   ESul
'Trinket' (Min/d)   SKen
'Triomphe de Nancy' (Z/d)   WFib
triste   SSad WFib

'Trudie' (Dw) — ESul LVER SKen WFib
'Trulls Hatch' (Z/d) — MWhe SKen
'Tu Tone' (Dw/d) — ESul
'Tuddenham' (Min/d) — WFib
'Tuesday's Child' (Dw/C) — SKen
'Tunias Perfecta' (R) — WFib
'Turkish Coffee' (R) — EBSP NFir NSwl WFib
'Turkish Delight' (Dw/C) — ESul LVER MWhe NFir WFib
'Turtle's Surprise' (Z/d/v) — SKen
'Turtle's White' (R) — LDea
'Tuyo' (R) — WFib
'Tweedle-Dum' (Dw) — MWhe
'Twinkle' (Min/d) — ESul WFib
'Tyabb Princess' (R) — LDea WFib
'Ullswater' (Dw/C) — ESul
§ 'Unique Aurore' (U) — EWoo LVER MHer MSte NFir SKen WEas WFib
'Unique Mons Ninon' — EWoo
'Unity' (Dw) — LVER
'Urchin' (Min) — ESul MWhe NFir SHFr WFib
'Ursula Key' (Z/v) — SKen WFib
'Valanza' (A) — ESul
'Valcandia' (Dw) — Last listed 1997
'Valencia' (R) — EBSP
'Valenciana' (R) — WFib
'Valentin' (R) — Last listed 1998
'Valentina' (Min/d) — ESul WFib
'Valentine' — EBSP
'Vancouver Centennial' (Dw/St/C) ♀ — CSpe ERav ESul LAco LDea LRHS LVER MBri MWhe NFir NSwl SKen WFib
'Vandersea' — EWoo
§ 'Variegated Clorinda' (Sc/v) — EWoo WCHb WFib
'Variegated Fragrans' — See P. (Fragrans Group) 'Fragrans Variegatum'
§ 'Variegated Kleine Liebling' (Min/v) — ESul NFir SSea WFib
'Variegated La France' (I) — WFib
'Variegated Lorelei' (Z/d/v) — Last listed 1997
'Variegated Madame Layal' (A/v) ♀ — ESul EWoo WFib
* 'Variegated Peppermint' — Last listed 1998
'Variegated Petit Pierre' — See P. 'Variegated Kleine Liebling'
'Vasco da Gama' (Dw/d) — ESul WFib
¶ 'Vectis Blaze' (I) — EWoo
'Vectis Cascade' — Last listed 1998
'Vectis Glitter' (Z/St) — LVER MWhe NFir
'Vectis Gold' (Z/St/C) — NFir
'Vectis Star' — Last listed 1997
'Velvet' (Z) — CWDa LVER
'Velvet Duet' (A) ♀ — CHal ESul EWoo LDea LIck LRHS LVER NFir SKen SSea
'Venus' (Dw/d) — ESul LRHS
'Vera Dillon' (Z) — SKen WFib
'Verdale' (A) — LDea WFib
'Verity Palace' (R) — EWoo LDea WFib
'Verona' (Z/C) — CHal MBri SKen
'Verona Contreras' (A) — ESul LDea MWhe WFib
* 'Veronica' (Z) — MWhe SKen
'Vibrant' — Last listed 1997
'Vicki Town' (R) — WFib
'Vicky Claire' (R) — EBSP LDea NFir SKen SMrm WFib
'Victoria' (Z/d) — SKen
'Victoria Regina' (R) — LDea WFib
'Video Blush' (Min) — Last listed 1998
'Viking' (Min/d) — SKen
'Viking Red' (Z) — MWhe
'Village Hill Oak' (Sc) — ESul LDea LVER MHer
* 'Ville de Dresden' (I) — Last listed 1998
'Ville de Paris' — See P. 'Hederinum'
'Vina' (Dw/C/d) — ESul LVER MWhe NFir SKen WFib
'Vincent Gerris' (A) — ESul LDea MWhe

Vinco = 'Guivin' [PBR] (I/d) — CWDa
violareum hort. — See P. 'Splendide'
'Violet Lambton' (Z/v) — NFir WFib
'Violetta' (R) — LDea WFib
'Virginia' (R) — LDea WFib
'Virginia Ley' (Z) — SKen
'Viscossisimum' — ERav MHer SKen
viscosum — See P. glutinosum
§ *vitifolium* — MHer
'Vivat Regina' (Z/d) — WFib
'Voodoo' (U) ♀ — CBrm CSpe EWoo LVER MSte NCiC NFir NSwl WFib
§ Vulcan (Z/d) — WLRN
'W.H. Heytman' (R) — WFib
'Wallace Fairman' (R) — LDea
'Wallis Friesdorf' (Dw/C/d) — ESul MWhe
'Wantirna' (Z/v) — ECtt EWoo LVER NFir
'Warrior' (Z/C) — LVER WFib
'Washbrook' (Min/d) — ESul NFir
'Watersmeet' (R) — LDea
'Wattisham' (Dec) — LDea WEas
'Waveney' (Min) — ESul
'Wayward Angel' (A) ♀ — ESul LDea LVER SKen WFib
'Wedding Gown' (R) — Last listed 1998
'Wedding Lace' (I) — Last listed 1999
'Wedding Royale' (Dw/d) — ESul LVER
Weisse Perle (Z/d) — Last listed 1998
'Welcome' (Z/d) — WFib
'Welling' (Sc) — LDea LVER NFir
'Wellington' (R) — LDea WFib
'Wendy' (Min) — Last listed 1997
'Wendy Anne' — SKen
'Wendy Hawley' (R) — Last listed 1998
'Wendy Read' (Dw/d) — ERea ESul MWhe WFib
'Wensum' (Min/d) — ESul WFib
'West Priory' — Last listed 1997
'Westdale Appleblossom' (Z/C) — ESul LVER SAga
* 'Westdale Beauty' (d) — CWDa
'Western Zoyland' (R) — WFib
'Weston Triumph' (Z/C/v) — NFir
'Whisper' (R) — WFib
'White Birds Egg' (Z) — WFib
'White Blizzard' — NPri WWol
'White Boar' (Fr) — EWoo MSte
'White Bonanza' (R) — EBSP WFib
'White Butterfly' (Z/C) — LVER
'White Charm' (R) — EBSP LDea
'White Chiffon' (R) — EBSP LVER
¶ 'White Duet' (A) — LDea
'White Eggshell' (Min) — ESul LVER
'White Feather' (Z/St) — WFib
'White Frills' (Z/d) — WFib
'White Gem' (Min) — Last listed 1999
'White Glory' (R) ♀ — EBSP LDea WFib
'White Lively Lady' (Dw/C) — ESul
§ 'White Mesh' (I/v) — ECtt LVER MBri MWhe SKen WFib
White Pearl Necklace — See P. Perlenkette Weiss = 'Perlpenei'
'White Queen' (Z/d) — CWDa
'White Unique' (U) — CHal EWoo LDea MHer MSte NBur WFib
whytei — Last listed 1998
'Wickham Lad' (R) — LDea
Wico = 'Guimongol' [PBR] (I/d) — NPri WLRN
* 'Wild Spice' — LDea LVER
'Wilf Vernon' (Min/d) — ESul
'Wilhelm Kolle' (Z) — WFib
'William Sutton' (R) — WFib
'Winford Festival' — LVER
'Winford Winnie' — Last listed 1998

'Winnie Read' (Dw/d)   ERea ESul
'Winston Churchill' (R)   LDea
'Wirral Big Bang' (Z/C)   NFir
'Wirral Look Alike' (Z/C)   SKen
'Wirral Moonglow'   NFir
'Wirral Moonraker' (Z/C)   NFir
'Wirral New Look' (Z/C)   Last listed 1999
'Wirral Sunlight' (Z/C)   NFir
'Wirral Target' (Z/d)   ESul MWhe NFir
'Wishing Star'   ESul
'Wispey' (St)   NFir
¶ 'Wispy' (Dw/St/C)   ESul
'Witnesham' (Min/d)   ESul
§ 'Wood's Surprise'   ESul LDea LVER MWhe NFir SKen
   (MinI/d/v)   WFib
'Wookey' (R)   WFib
§ worcesterae   Last listed 1998
'Wrington' (R)   WFib
'Wroxham' (Dw)   ESul
* 'Wychwood'   EWoo LDea
'Wyck Beacon' (I/d)   SKen
'Wycombe Maid' (Min/d)   WFib
'Wydcombe' (d)   Last listed 1998
'Xenia Field' (Z)   Last listed 1998
xerophyton   Last listed 1998
'Yale' (I/d) ♀   CHal LDea LVER MBri MSte
   MWhe SKen WFib
'Yarrabee Jane' (R)   WFib
'Yhu' (R)   EBSP LDea WFib
'Yolanda' (Min/C)   ESul
'York Florist' (Z/d/v)   LVER
'York Minster' (Dw/v)   SKen
'Yours Truly' (Z)   Last listed 1997
'Yvonne' (Z)   WFib
'Zamma' (R)   LDea NFir
¶ 'Zemmies' (MinI)   ESul
'Zena' (Dw)   ESul NSwl
'Zinc' (Z/d)   WFib
'Zoe' (D)   LDea
zonale   EWoo WFib
'Zulu King' (R)   WFib
'Zulu Warrior' (R)   WFib

PELLAEA (Adiantaceae)

atropurpurea   EFer
boivinii var. viridis   Last listed 1998
§ calomelanos   Last listed 1999
cordifolia   WRic
falcata   MBri
hastata   See P. calomelanos
ovata   WRic
paradoxa   Last listed 1997
rotundifolia ♀   CHal MBri NMar
sagittata   NMar

PELLIONIA See ELATOSTEMA

PELTANDRA (Araceae)

alba   See P. saggitifolia
§ saggitifolia   SWyc
§ undulata   CRow LPBA MSta SWat SWyc
virginica Schott   See P. undulata
- Rafinesque   EMFW SLon SWyc

PELTARIA (Brassicaceae)

alliacea   LEdu

PELTIPHYLLUM See DARMERA

PELTOBOYKINIA (Saxifragaceae)

§ tellimoides   CLAP GOrP NHol SMac WCru
   WFar WMoo

watanabei   EBee GCHN GTou LFis SMac
   WFar

PENNANTIA (Icacinaceae)

corymbosa   ECou

PENNELLIANTHUS See PENSTEMON

PENNISETUM (Poaceae)

§ alopecuroides   More than 30 suppliers
¶ - 'Bruno Ears'   EHoe
¶ - 'Cassian's Choice'   CBrm EBee EFou EHoe SLod SUsu
- 'Hameln'   More than 30 suppliers
- 'Herbstzauber'   LPan LRHS
- 'Little Bunny'   CBrm CCuc CInt CWes EBee
   EBrP EBre EHoe EPGN EPPr GCal
   GKir LBCl LBSe LBre LPan LRHS
   MBBe NPSI NPro SBre SLod WHil
¶ - 'Little Honey' (v)   LPan
- 'Moudry'   CBrm EFou EHoe LEdu
¶ - 'National Arboretum'   LPan
¶ - var. purpurascens   WCru
   B&SWJ 5822
- f. viridescens   CBrm CCtw CCuc ECha EFou
   EHoe ELan EMan EWsh GGar
   LPan LRHS MAvo MLLN MMoz
   MTis NSti SCob SPla SSoC WBea
   WWat
- 'Weserbergland'   CFir EBee EPPr LPan LRHS
- 'Woodside'   CCuc CMea CWes EBee EHoe
   EMan EPPr EPla SApp
compressum   See P. alopecuroides
flaccidum   CBod EBee EMan EMon EPPr
   LRHS
incomptum   CCuc CInt EBrP EBre EHoe LBCl
   LBSe LBre LRHS MBBe SBre SLod
- purple   EBee WPGP
longistylum hort.   See P. villosum
macrourum   CBrm CCuc CElw CFil CHea CInt
   CKno CRDP EBee EHoe EPGN
   EPPr EPla EWsh MAnH SUsu
   WPGP
orientale ♀   More than 30 suppliers
purpureum   Last listed 1999
rueppellii   See P. setaceum
§ setaceum ♀   CBrm CCuc CElw CInt EPPr
   MAnH MBrN MNrw MWat SWal
   WLRN WMoo
- 'Burgundy Blaze'   LPan
- 'Rubrum'   CInt
sp. B&SWJ 3854   WCru
speciosum B&SWJ 3503   Last listed 1999
§ villosum   More than 30 suppliers

PENSTEMON ✿ (Scrophulariaceae)

'Abberley'   SAga WPer
¶ 'Abbeydale Blue'   MGed
'Abbotsmerry'   CAxe CFwr EBee LGre MLLN
   WSPU
'Agnes Laing'   LPen LRHS MBNS
albertinus   See P. humilis
albidus   Last listed 1999
§ 'Alice Hindley' ♀   More than 30 suppliers
alpinus   CLyd EWes GAbr GTou MHar
   NOak SAga SYvo
§ 'Andenken an Friedrich   More than 30 suppliers
   Hahn' ♀
§ angustifolius   MNrw MWgw SRms WPer
antirrhinoides   See Keckiella antirrhinoides
'Apple Blossom' ♀   More than 30 suppliers
'Apple Blossom' misapplied   See P. 'Thorn'
aridus   CPBP

arizonicus   See *P. whippleanus*

arkansanus   MNrw

¶ 'Ashton'   MGed MLLN WSPU

'Astley'   Last listed 1999

attenuatus   WPer

auriberbis   EBee

azureus   CLyd EBee WPer WRha

baccharifolius   LGre

'Barbara Barker'   See *P.* 'Beech Park'

§ *barbatus*   CBot CGle EBee EBrP EBre ECha EHrv ELan EMan EWTr GCHN LBCl LBSe LBre LGre MAsh MBBe MBro MWat SBre SChu SMrm SPer SRms SSea WHCG WHer WWin

- 'Cambridge Mixed'   EWTr EWll LRHS

- subsp. *coccineus*   LRHS MCAu MCCP MHer MTis NChi NDlv NLar WMoo

- 'Jingle Bells'   EBee GKir LPen

- K 92.319   NHar

- Limoges form   GCal

- orange   LRHS SAga

- var. *praecox*   SCob WPer WShe

- - f. *nanus*   CBot EMil GCHN LRHS MSte SCob SRms

- - - 'Rondo'   NBro NLar

* - 'Roseocampanulatus'   WSPU

barrettiae   GCHN

'Beckford'   CAxe EBee MGed WSPU

§ 'Beech Park' ♀   CInt EBee ELan EWes IHdy LHil LHop LPen LRHS MBNS MBel MLLN NHaw SAga WHCG WRus WSPU

§ *berryi*   EPot SMrm

'Bisham Seedling'   See *P.* 'White Bedder'

'Blackbird'   More than 30 suppliers

'Blue Spring' misapplied   See *P. heterophyllus* 'Blue Springs'

'Bodnant'   EBee MBel WPer

bradburii   See *P. grandiflorus*

¶ 'Bredon'   CFwr WSPU

'Breitenbush Blue'   SAga

bridgesii   See *P. rostriflorus*

'Bridget's White'   Last listed 1997

'Burford Purple'   See *P.* 'Burgundy'

'Burford Seedling'   See *P.* 'Burgundy'

'Burford White'   See *P.* 'White Bedder'

§ 'Burgundy'   CAxe CLTr CMHG CSam EBee EOrc GCHN GKir GMac LAst LHrt LLWP LPen LRHS NFai NPer SChu SMac SMrm SPer WHCG WHil WHoo WMaN WPer WRus WWye

caeruleus   See *P. angustifolius*

caespitosus   EBrP EBre LBCl LBSe LBre MBBe NWCA SBre

- *albus*   Last listed 1997

- misapplied 'Claude Barr' (purple-flowered)   See *P. procumbens* 'Claude Barr'

- subsp. *suffruticosus*   See *P. tusharensis*

- white   Last listed 1998

calycosus   Last listed 1999

§ *campanulatus*   CMHG EBee EWes GCal LPen MAsh MLLN NHar NHol NMen NNrd NTow SAga SHFr SLon SRms WAbe WBea WGwG WHCG WPer WSPU WWal

- CD&R 1355   Last listed 1999

- subsp. *chihuahuensis*   SAga

- *pulchellus*   See *P. campanulatus*

- *roseus* misapplied   See *P. kunthii*

'Candy Pink'   See *P.* 'Old Candy Pink'

cardinalis   Last listed 1999

- subsp. *regalis*   Last listed 1998

cardwellii   CMea CPBP EPot EWes GTou NHar SAga SRms

- x *davidsonii*   CGra WAbe

- K 92.321   Last listed 1997

¶ 'Carolyn Orr' (v)   WCot

'Castle Forbes'   CAxe MHar MLLN NBur WEas WHCG WPer WWoo

'Catherine de la Mare'   See *P. heterophyllus* 'Catherine de la Mare'

* 'Centra'   EBee GCHN MLLN

centranthifolius   Last listed 1999

JJA 13106

'Charles Rudd'   CAxe CBlo CBod CGle GEil LPen LRHS MHar MLLN NCut NFai SAga SChu SUsu WEll WHCG WMaN WOve

§ 'Cherry' ♀   CBlo EBee EOrc GMac LPen LRHS MBNS MHer MLLN NBur NCiC SCro SMrm SPla SPlb SSte WHCG WPer WPyg WRus WSPU WWoo

'Cherry Ripe' misapplied   See *P.* 'Cherry'

* orange   LRHS SAga

* 'Chester Scarlet' ♀   CMCo EOrc GBri GCHN LHop LPen LRHS MBel MCLN MNrw MRav NBrk NFai SAga SDix SLon WEas WEll WHCG WMaN WPer WRus WSPU WWhi WWye

clevelandii   NWCA

   subsp. *connatus*

clutei   EBee EPPr EWTr WElm

¶ *cobaea*   CNic

comarrhenus cyaneus   See *P. cyaneus*

'Comberton'   EBee WSPU

confertus   CGra CMHG CNic CTri EBee EMNN EWTr LPen LPio MBNS MHer NChi NMen NWCA SRms WHCG WPer WRHF WSPU

'Connie's Pink' ♀   CAxe EBee EMar ENot LHop LPen MLLN MSte NBur NCiC WEll WHCG WLin WSPU

* 'Coral Pink'   CStr GMac

¶ 'Coral Sea'   MGed

cordifolius   See *Keckiella cordifolia*

'Cottage Garden Red'   See *P.* 'Windsor Red'

§ 'Countess of Dalkeith'   CBlo CHea CLTr EBee EOrc EWTr EWes GBri LHil LHop LLWP LPen LRHS MLLN MNes MNrw NHaw SAga SOkh SPer SPlb SUsu WHCG WSPU WWhi

'Craigieburn Chenille'   Last listed 1998

'Craigieburn Taffeta'   Last listed 1998

crandallii   CPBP

- subsp. *glabrescens*   SAga SUsu WHCG

- subsp. *taosensis*   NDov NWCA

cristatus   See *P. eriantherus*

§ *cyaneus*   Last listed 1999

davidsonii   EWes SRms WAbe

- var. *davidsonii*   CGra

§ - var. *menziesii* ♀   EBee GTou MFir NBus NHar NWCA SRms WSPU

¶ - - 'Broken Top Mountain'   CLyd

- - 'Microphyllus'   EPot NBus NHar NMen NSla WAbe WLin

- - 'Tolmie Peak'   CGra

- var. *praeteritus*   NHar WLin

'Dazzler'   CBlo CBod CM&M EBee NChi SEas WPer WSPU

§ *deaveri*   EBee MGed WSPU

deustus   SRms

'Devonshire Cream'   CAxe CElw LPen LRHS WHCG

'Diane'   Last listed 1999

diffusus   See *P. serrulatus*

digitalis   CNic EBee EBrP EBre ECha EGar

	EMan LBCl LBSe LBre LGre LPen
	MBBe MBNS SBre WAbb WEas
	WHCG WPer
§ - 'Husker Red'	More than 30 suppliers
- pink	Last listed 1997
- 'Purpureus'	See *P. digitalis* 'Husker Red'
discolor	CMea SMrm
- pale lavender	WFar
§ 'Drinkstone'	CGle EHol LHop LPen LRHS
	MLLN NChi NCiC SAga SDix
	SMrm WEll WHCG WPer WSPU
'Drinkwater Red'	See *P.* 'Drinkstone'
eatonii	SRms
- subsp. *undosus*	NWCA
* *edgeworthii*	Last listed 1999
'Edithiae'	EOrc MBro SChu SRms WEas
	WHCG WIvy WKif
¶ 'Elmley'	MLLN WEll WSPU
§ *eriantherus*	CGra WHCG
'Etna'	CAxe GKir LRHS MBri MMil
euglaucus	EBee
§ 'Evelyn' ♀	More than 30 suppliers
'Fanny's Blush'	Last listed 1997
'Firebird'	See *P.* 'Schoenholzeri'
'Flame'	CGle EMan LHop LPen LRHS
	MAnH WHCG WPer WSPU
'Flamingo'	CBrm CMea EBee EPfP EWes LAst
	LPen LRHS MBNS MBro MCLN
	MWrn NHaw NHol SAga SMrm
	WHoo WLRN WLin WMaN WSPU
	WWoo
frutescens	GTou WSPU
fruticosus	LFis MNrw NHar NWCA SRms
	WAbe WLin
§ - var. *scouleri* ♀	MAsh MBro MHar MOne SBla
	SRms WCFE WIvy WSPU
- - f. *albus* ♀	CMea LGre LHop LPen NWCA
	SAga SBla SChu SIng WAbe WCFE
	WEas WIvy WKif WSPU
- - 'Amethyst'	WAbe WLin
- - 'Hopleys'	Last listed 1998
- var. *serratus*	Last listed 1999
- - 'Holly'	LAco LGre NMen SAga SBla SMrm
'Fujiyama'	CAxe GKir LRHS MBri MGed
'Gaff's Pink'	SChu
'Gaiety'	CM&M
gairdneri	CGra
'Garden Red'	See *P.* 'Windsor Red'
'Garnet'	See *P.* 'Andenken an Friedrich
	Hahn'
'Garnet Variegated'	Last listed 1999
gentianoides	MNrw MWhi NBro WRus WSPU
'Geoff Hamilton'	LHop MBNS
'George Elrick'	LPen MBNS
§ 'George Home' ♀	CGle CLTr ECGP ECtt EWes GAbr
	LHil LPen LRHS MBNS MLLN
	MNrw NBur NHaw SChu SMrm
	WByw WHCG WMaN WRus WWoo
glaber	CElw CMHG EBee GMac LGre
	LHop LLWP LPen LRHS MBNS
	MBro MLLN MRav NBro NGdn
	SAga SHFr SHel SPer WEas WEll
	WHCG WHoo WKif WPer WRus
	WSPU
gormanii	EBee MLLN
gracilis	EBee GCHN GCal WPer WSPU
§ *grandiflorus*	EBee
hallii	CGra CPBP EPot EWes GKir GTou
	LRHS SIng WSPU
hartwegii ♀	EBee GMac LHop LPen SAga
	SChu WAbe WHCG WPer WRus
	WSPU

- 'Albus'	CAxe EBee LGre LHop LPen
	LRHS MSte NFor SAga WHCG
	WSPU
bavardii	Last listed 1998
¶ 'Hergest Croft'	MGed
heterodoxus	EBee SGar
¶ - NNS 93-564	NWCA
§ *heterophyllus*	More than 30 suppliers
- 'Blue Eye'	WMaN WSPU
- 'Blue Fountain'	LPen WSPU
- 'Blue Gem'	CBod CElw CTri EBrP EBre EOrc
	LBCl LBSe LBre LRHS MBBe MBro
	SBre SIng SMrm SPla WHoo
	WPGP WSPU
§ - 'Blue Springs'	CBlo CBot CGle CLon EBrP EBre
	EWTr LBCl LBSe LBre LFis LPen
	LRHS MAnH MBBe MBri MCLN
	MLLN MSte NBir NFla SBla SBre
	WAbe WRus
§ - 'Catherine de la Mare' ♀	More than 30 suppliers
- 'Heavenly Blue'	CBlo EBrP EBre ECtt LBCl LBSe
	LBre LFis LRHS MBBe MBNS
	MCLN NHaw SBre SWat WCFE
	WEll WLRN WOve WRus WWal
	WWhi
* - 'John D.'	Last listed 1997
- subsp. *purdyi*	WHCG
- 'True Blue'	See *P. heterophyllus*
- 'Züriblau'	LRHS MBro SMrm WWat
'Hewell Pink Bedder' ♀	CBlo CGle EBee EBrP EBre EGra
	ENot GBri GCHN LBCl LBSe LBre
	LPen LRHS MBBe MBNS MBel
	MCLN SAga SBre SChu SEas SPar
	WHCG WPer WSPU WWol
'Hewitt's Pink'	WEll
§ 'Hidcote Pink' ♀	More than 30 suppliers
'Hidcote Purple'	CElw CM&M LFis LHil NBrk NCiC
	SChu
* 'Hidcote White'	CM&M EBee EOrc MHer NHol
	WAbe WRus
'Hillview Pink'	WHil
'Hillview Red'	Last listed 1998
§ *hirsutus*	CGle CNic EBee EPPr LGre MNrw
	NChi SOkh WPer WSan
- f. *albiflorus*	CMea CNic EBee
- bronze-leaved	Last listed 1999
- var. *minimus*	MLLN SGar
- var. *pygmaeus*	CLyd CMea CNic CRDP EBee
	EDAr EWTr GTou LFis MBro
	MHar MHer NHar NMen NWCA
	SBla SPlb SRms SRot WHoo WLin
	WPer WWin
- - f. *albus*	CMea WPer
- - 'Purpureus'	WLin
'Hopleys Pink'	NDov
'Hopleys Variegated'	EBee EGar EMan EMar EOrc LFis
	LHop MBel MHer MNrw NBir
	SLod WCot WEll WHer WSPU
	WSan WWeb
'Hower Park'	Last listed 1997
§ *humilis*	CNic EBee MLLN SRms WBar
	WShe
- Mckay's form	Last listed 1998
- 'Pulchellus'	NWCA
'Hyacinth-flowered' seed mixture from Burpee, USA	Last listed 1998
isophyllus ♀	CStr EGra EPfP LPen LRHS MAsh
	MMil SChu WFar WHCG WHoo
	WPer WWin
jamesii	EOrc NChi SVen
janisbiae	Last listed 1998

'Jill Lucas'	SCro	
¶ 'Jingle Bells'	EWll	
'John Booth'	CFwr WEas WEll	
'John Nash'	CSWP MDCh MHer SHFr SMrm WEll	
'John Nash' misapplied	See *P.* 'Alice Hindley'	
'Joy'	CBlo EBee MBro MGed MLLN MSte NCiC WCFE WOve WPer WPyg WWoo	
¶ 'Juggler'	CFwr LPen NCut	
'June'	See *P.* 'Pennington Gem'	
¶ 'Kilimanjaro'	MGed	
'King George V'	More than 30 suppliers	
'Knight's Purple'	LPen MGed WHCG	
'Knightwick'	CAxe LPen MGed SAga WEll WPer WSPU	
'Kummel'	ELan	
§ *kunthii*	CPBP LPen WAbe WSPU	
labrosus	LHop	
laetus subsp. *laetus*	Last listed 1998	
§ – subsp. *roezlii*	CSam GChr GCrs GDra LRHS MLLN MLan MTis NHar NMen NWCA SIng SRms WAbe WWin	
laricifolius	Last listed 1998	
§ 'Le Phare'	CBod EBee LLWP LPen LRHS MBNS WHCG WPer WSPU	
leiophyllus	MBro	
leonensis	Last listed 1999	
'Lilac and Burgundy'	LPen LRHS MBNS WEll	
linarioides	CPBP EBee EWes LPen MBro NHol WPat	
– subsp. *coloradoensis*	Last listed 1998	
– JCA 9694	WLin	
'Little Witley'	CAxe LPen MBNS SAga WHCG WPer	
* 'Logan Pink'	GMac	
'Lord Home'	See *P.* 'George Home'	
lyallii	CGdn CHar CMea EBee EHrv ELan EMan EMar ESis ITim LFis LPen LRHS MCCP MGrG MLLN MNrw MSCN SAga SSte WByw WSPU WSan WWeb	
'Lynette'	CAxe LFis LPen LRHS MBNS WHCG WHil WPer	
'Macpenny's Pink'	SChu WWoo	
'Madame Golding'	CGle CSWP EBee LFis LGre LPen LRHS MBNS MLLN MNrw SAga SMrm SPlb WHCG WPer WSPU	
¶ 'Maiden's Blush'	MGed	
'Margery Fish' ♀	CElw CPou ESis LRHS MAvo MMil MNrw MSte NFai WPer WRha WSPU	
'Maurice Gibbs' ♀	CBlo ECoo LPen MBNS MLLN SAga SWal WFoF WHCG WSPU WWol	
mensarum	Last listed 1999	
menziesii	See *P. davidsonii* var. *menziesii*	
'Merlin'	Last listed 1998	
Mexicali hybrids	EBee	
mexicanus	SAga	
'Midnight'	CBrm CElw CGle CLTr CSam EBee GBri LFis LLWP LPen MBel MBro MRav NBrk SAga SChu SMrm SUsu WCFE WCot WHCG WPer WRus WSPU WWat WWin	
'Modesty'	CAxe CBlo EBee LLWP LPen LRHS MBNS NCiC WEll WHCG WSPU	
'Molly Margaret'	GCHN	
montanus	CNic EBee GCHN	
'Mother of Pearl'	More than 30 suppliers	
* 'Mountain Wine'	LRHS	

I 'Mrs Golding'	Last listed 1997	
'Mrs Miller'	LPen MBNS NBur	
'Mrs Morse'	See *P.* 'Chester Scarlet'	
multiflorus	EBee LPen	
§ 'Myddelton Gem'	CGle CLTr ECGP LPen LRHS MBNS MNrw MWat NCiC WFoF WHCG WSPU	
'Myddelton Red'	See *P.* 'Myddelton Gem'	
nemorosus	EBee	
neomexicanus	EBee	
neotericus	Last listed 1999	
newberryi ♀	CMea EPot GKir LGre LRHS MHer NBir NMen WKif WSPU WWin	
– subsp. *berryi*	See *P. berryi*	
– f. *humilior*	EPot GEil SMrm	
§ – subsp. *sonomensis*	NHar NMen NWCA WAbe	
§ *nitidus*	MNrw	
'Oaklea Red'	CFwr ECtt LRHS MBri MLLN SWat WEll	
§ 'Old Candy Pink'	EBee LLWP LPen MSte SAga WEas WEll WPer WRus WSPU WWhi	
'Old Silk'	MGed	
oliganthus	Last listed 1998	
ophianthus	Last listed 1998	
'Osprey' ♀	More than 30 suppliers	
ovatus	CBrm EBee GCHN GCal LPen LPio LRHS MBro MHer MLLN NDlv SRms WHCG WKif WLin WSan	
'Overbury'	WSPU	
pachyphyllus	CNic	
palmeri	EBee	
'Papal Purple'	CMHG GMac LLWP LPen LRHS MBNS MBro MLLN MSte NBrk NChi SAga SChu SMrm SRms STes WEll WElm WFar WHCG WHoo WRus WSPU WWhi WWye	
'Papal Purple' x 'Evelyn'	CAxe	
parvulus	Last listed 1999	
'Patio Coral'	GKir LRHS MLLN	
'Patio Pink'	GKir LLWP LRHS MBri MLLN WEll	
¶ 'Patio Red'	MGed	
'Patio Shell'	GKir LRHS MBri	
'Patio Swirl'	Last listed 1998	
'Patio Wine'	GKir LLWP LRHS MBri MLLN	
'Peace'	CLTr CRos LHop LPen LRHS MBNS NCiC SAga SSca WHCG WMaN WRus WSPU	
¶ 'Pearl'	MGed	
peckii	Last listed 1998	
§ 'Pennington Gem' ♀	More than 30 suppliers	
¶ 'Pensham Capricorn Moon'	MGed	
¶ 'Pensham Just Jayne'	MGed	
¶ 'Pensham Plum Jerkin'	MGed	
'Pershore Carnival'	CAxe CFwr LRHS MGed MLLN NPro WSPU	
'Pershore Fanfare'	CAxe LRHS MGed MLLN WSPU	
'Pershore Pink Necklace'	LPen LRHS MLLN SChu WCot WEas WEll WHCG WMaN WSPU WSan	
¶ 'Pershore Twilight'	MGed	
'Phare'	See *P.* 'Le Phare'	
'Phyllis'	See *P.* 'Evelyn'	
pinifolius ♀	CGra CLTr CMHG CMea EDAr EPot ESis GCHN GDra GKir ITim LFis LRHS MBro NFor NHar SAga SBla SRms SSmi WFar WHoo WLin WPat WRus WSPU WWat WWin	
– 'Mersea Yellow'	More than 30 suppliers	
– 'Wisley Flame' ♀	CMea EPfP ESis LRHS	
'Pink Dragon'	CLyd GCHN GDra MSCN NDov	

	NHar SAga SChu SOkh WHCG WSPU
'Pink Endurance'	CMea CStr EBrP EBre ELan LBCl LBSe LBre LPen LRHS MBBe MBro MCLN MLLN NHaw SAga SBre SEas SIng WCot WEas WEll WHCG WHal WHoo WMaN WPer WSPU
'Pink Ice'	NCiC WHil
'Pink Profusion'	SMrm SUsu
'Port Wine' ♀	CAxe CBlo CGle CHar CLTr CRDP CSam EBee ERav GCHN LHil LPen LRHS MBel MLLN NChi NCiC SAga SPer WCot WHCG WHoo WMaN WPer WSPU
'Powis Castle'	EBee EWes WPer WWye
'Prairie Dusk'	LPen
'Prairie Fire'	EBee LPen SAga WSPU
* 'Prairie Pride'	LPen
'Primrose Thomas'	MBel NHaw
'Priory Purple'	WHCG WPer
procerus	EBee GBri LPen MDHE MHer MLLN SRms WPer
- var. *brachyanthus*	Last listed 1998
§ - var. *formosus*	EPot
- var. *procerus*	Last listed 1999
§ - 'Roy Davidson' ♀	CMea CPBP LBee LRHS NHol SAga SBla SOkd WAbe WFar WLin
- var. *tolmiei*	EPot GCHN GCal LPen MNaF NChi NHol NWCA SGar
- - white	CGra
§ *procumbens* 'Claude Barr'	CPBP
pruinosus	CGra EBee
pubescens	See *P. hirsutus*
pulchellus Greene	See *P. procerus* var. *formosus*
- Lindley	See *P. campanulatus*
* *pulcherrimus*	NBro
pumilus	Last listed 1998
'Purple and White'	See *P.* 'Countess of Dalkeith'
'Purple Bedder'	CGle CHea COIW EBee EPfP GAbr LAst LHrt LPen LRHS MAsh MCLN MLLN MNrw MWat NCiC NHaw SAga SWat WEll WFar WGor WHCG WSPU WWal
'Purple Dragon'	Last listed 1999
'Purple Gem'	GDra
'Purple Passion'	EBee EBrP EBre EPfP EWes LBCl LBSe LBre LRHS MBBe MLLN SBre SCro WLRN
¶ 'Purple Sea'	MGed
'Purpureus Albus'	See *P.* 'Countess of Dalkeith'
purpusii	Last listed 1999
§ *putus*	WLin
'Rajah'	EBee WLin
'Raspberry Ripple'	Last listed 1997
rattanii	Last listed 1997
'Raven' ♀	CLon EBee EOrc GBri LLWP LPen LRHS MBel MBro MCAu MCLN MTis NBrk NBro NHaw SAga SChu WCot WEas WHCG WHal WHoo WMaN WPer WPyg WRus WSPU WWin WWol
'Razzle Dazzle'	LRHS MBNS SPlb WEll WPer
'Red Ace'	MLLN MNrw
'Red Emperor'	CMHG CStr ECtt MBNS MBel MLLN NFai NHaw SPlb WEas WEll WHCG WPer WSPU
'Red Knight'	LPen LRHS MBNS
¶ 'Red Sea'	MGed
'Rich Purple'	LLWP LRHS MBNS NDov SPlb WMaN
'Rich Ruby'	More than 30 suppliers
richardsonii	MLLN MNrw MSCN SRms WGwG
'Ridgeway Red'	WSPU
roezlii Regel	See *P. laetus* subsp. *roezlii*
roseocampanulatus	See *P. barbatus* 'Roseocampanulatus'
§ *rostriflorus*	SAga WLin
- JJA 9548	Last listed 1998
'Rosy Blush'	CAxe EBee LPen LRHS MBNS WHCG
'Roundhay'	CFee
'Roy Davidson'	See *P. procerus* 'Roy Davidson'
'Royal White'	See *P.* 'White Bedder'
'Rubicundus' ♀	CGle EBee ECtt EGra ELan LFis LHop LPen LRHS MAsh MBNS SAga SMrm WAbe WCot WHCG WRus WSPU WWal WWeb WWol
'Ruby'	See *P.* 'Schoenholzeri'
'Ruby Field'	EBee GAbr NCiC WHCG WWoo
'Ruby Gem'	LPen LRHS MBNS
* 'Ruby Wine'	GKir SRPl
rupicola ♀	CMea EBee GDra GTou LHop LRHS MBro NSla NWCA SAga SBla SRms WAbe WWin
- 'Albus'	LGre NSla WAbe
- 'Diamond Lake'	CMea MBro NHar WPat
- lilac	Last listed 1999
- mauve hybrid	GDra LGre
'Russian River'	CLTr CSWP EBee EWes LAst LHrt LLWP LPen LRHS MBel MBro MCLN NHaw SMrm SOkh SPlb WHCG WPer WPyg WSPU WWat
rydbergii	EPot
'Sapphire'	Last listed 1999
* Saskatoon hybrids	Last listed 1999
* *scariosus* var. *garrettii*	Last listed 1998
Scarlet Queen	See *P.* 'Scharlachkönigin'
§ 'Scharlachkönigin'	CSWP LRHS MGed
§ 'Schoenholzeri' ♀	More than 30 suppliers
scouleri	See *P. fruticosus* var. *scouleri*
secundiflorus	CPBP CWes EBee WCot
§ *serrulatus*	EBee ECha EWes GTou LPen MBel MSte SGar SHFr SRms WSPU
- 'Albus'	EBee LPen MSte WSPU WWin
'Shell Pink'	LPen WPer
* 'Sherbourne Blue'	WEll WPer
* 'Shrawley'	WPer
'Sissinghurst Pink'	See *P.* 'Evelyn'
'Six Hills'	CPBP NHar SAga SDys SRms WAbe WHCG WLin WSPU
'Skyline'	EPfP EWTr WWeb
smallii	EBee EMan LGre LPen SIng
'Snow Storm'	See *P.* 'White Bedder'
'Snowflake'	See *P.* 'White Bedder'
'Snowstorm'	CB&S CSam EBee ELan EWTr GKir MBNS MRav NBir WEas WHCG
sonomensis	See *P. newberryi* subsp. *sonomensis*
'Sour Grapes' hort.	See *P.* 'Stapleford Gem'
§ 'Sour Grapes' M. Fish	More than 30 suppliers
'Southcombe Pink'	MLLN WEll WHCG
'Southgate Gem'	GChr GDea GKir LPen LRHS MNrw MWat SCro WEll WHCG
'Souvenir d'Adrian Regnier'	GCHN
'Souvenir d'André Torres'	LLWP
'Souvenir d'André Torres' misapplied	See *P.* 'Chester Scarlet'
sp. P&C 150	CFee
sp. PCHA 148	EBee SHFr WHoo WLin
speciosus	Last listed 1998
- subsp. *kennedyi*	Last listed 1998
§ 'Stapleford Gem' ♀	More than 30 suppliers
strictus	CBlo EBee EWTr GCHN LGre

	LPio MBNS MLLN MWgw NChi SRms SSvw WLin WPer WSPU
- 'Bandera'	Last listed 1999
¶ 'Stromboli'	MGed MMil
subglaber	EBee
'Sutton's Pink Bedder'	EBee LRHS MBNS SPlb WSPU
'Sylvia Buss'	LPen
tall pink	See *P.* 'Welsh Dawn'
N 'Taoensis'	EWes SSea
taosensis	See *P. crandallii* subsp. *taosensis*
ternatus	See *Keckiella ternata*
teucrioides	EPot NWCA WLin
- JCA 1717050	CPBP
§ 'Thorn'	CBod CGle CLTr CLon CSWP
	CSpe ELan EOrc EWTr LAst LHop
	LPen LRHS MBel MLLN MNrw
	MTis NBrk NFai NGdn SAga SCro
	SMrm SOkh SPla WHCG WHoo
	WRus WSPU WWal
I 'Thorn Cross'	GMac NEgg
'Threave Pink'	LLWP
* 'Threave White'	WPen
'Torquay Gem'	GBuc LPen SDys WHCG WPer
tracyi	Last listed 1999
'True Sour Grapes'	See *P.* 'Sour Grapes' M. Fish
tubaeflorus	EBee
§ **tusharensis**	CPBP
uintahensis	Last listed 1998
§ **unilateralis**	Last listed 1999
utahensis	CBot EBrP EBre EWes GBri LBCl
	LBSe LBre MBBe SAga SBre WPer
- white	Last listed 1998
venustus	CFir EBee GBuc MHar MHer
	MLLN MNrw SRms WHCG WWye
'Vesuvius'	CAxe GKir MBri MGed
virens	EBee MHer NTow NWCA WLin
	WPat
* - **albus**	GCHN WWin
- R/Mr 7890	WPer
virgatus subsp.	See *P. deaveri*
arizonicus	
- subsp. **asa-grayi**	See *P. unilateralis*
- subsp. **putus**	See *P. putus*
washingtonensis	CGra
watsonii	EBee EMan MLLN SRms WHCG
	WPer
§ 'Welsh Dawn'	LPen WEll WSPU
§ **whippleanus**	CGle CLon CRDP EBee LPen MSte
	WAbb WPer
- dark form	MBro
§ 'White Bedder' ♀	More than 30 suppliers
'Whitethroat'	EBee LPen LRHS MBNS MLLN
	SOkh SRCN WCot WEll WHCG
	WMaN WPer WSPU WWin
wilcoxii	Last listed 1998
§ 'Windsor Red'	CBlo CBod CFwr EBee EPfP EWTr
	LPen LRHS MAsh MBNS MSte
	NCiC SUsu WGor WHCG WSPU
	WWoo
§ **wislizeni**	EBee EBrP EBre EPfP LBCl LBSe
	LBre MBBe MLLN MLan MNrw
	MOne NOak SBre SRms WMaN
	WWal
wrightii	Last listed 1999

PENTAGLOTTIS (Boraginaceae)

§ **sempervirens**	CArn CKin EPfP GPoy MHer
	MHew MSal WBea WHen WOak
	WWye

PENTAPTERYGIUM See AGAPETES

PENTAS (Rubiaceae)

lanceolata	CHal LRHS MBri
- 'Candy Stripe'	Last listed 1999
- 'New Look Pink'	LPVe
- 'New Look Red'	LPVe
- 'Red Star'	Last listed 1999

PEPEROMIA (Piperaceae)

§ **argyreia** ♀	MBri
arifolia	CHal
caperata	LRHS MBri
- 'Little Fantasy' ♀	CHal
- 'Variegata' ♀	Last listed 1993
clusiifolia	CHal
- 'Variegata'	CHal
glabella	CHal
¶ - 'Variegata'	CHal
griseoargentea	CHal
magnoliifolia	See *P. obtusifolia* Magnoliifolia Group
obtusifolia 'Jamaica'	MBri
§ - Magnoliifolia Group	Last listed 1999
- - 'Golden Gate' (v)	MBri
- - 'Greengold'	CHal MBri
- - 'USA'	MBri
- 'Tricolor' (v)	MBri
orba 'Pixie'	MBri
I - 'Pixie Variegata'	MBri
pulchella	See *P. verticillata*
sandersii	See *P. argyreia*
scandens ♀	MBri
- 'Variegata'	CHal MBri
§ **verticillata**	CHal

PERESKIA (Cactaceae)

aculeata f. **rubescens**	WCot
corrugata	LRHS

PERESKIOPSIS (Cactaceae)

§ **diguetii**	CHal
spathulata	See *P. diguetii*

PEREZIA (Asteraceae)

linearis	GBuc
recurvata	GCrs GTou NWCA

PERICALLIS (Asteraceae)

§ **lanata** (L'Hér.) B. Nord.	ELan LHil LHop MBlu SAga WEas
- Kew form	CRHN CSpe SMrm
multiflora	SAga

PERILLA (Lamiaceae)

* 'Acuta Kudo'	EOHP
§ **frutescens** var. **crispa** ♀	CArn LRHS MChe WJek
- green	EOHP
- var. **nankinensis**	See *P. frutescens* var. *crispa*
- var. **purpurascens**	CArn CFri EOHP MChe WJek

PERIPLOCA (Asclepiadaceae)

graeca	CArn CB&S CCHP CMac CPIN
	CPle CRHN EWTr GQui NBea
	NFla SBra SYvo WCot WSHC
sepium	CPLG CPIN CPle

PERISTROPHE (Acanthaceae)

speciosa	ERea SYvo

PERNETTYA See GAULTHERIA

PEROVSKIA (Lamiaceae)
atriplicifolia	CArn CBot CDul CPle ERav GPoy LGre MBri MHer MSCN SIde SLod WHCG
- 'Little Spire'	MBri
'Blue Haze'	GCal
'Blue Spire' ♀	More than 30 suppliers
'Filigran'	CMGP ECGP EFou GCal MBel SChu
'Hybrida'	WWeb
scrophulariifolia	Last listed 1998

PERSEA (Lauraceae)
americana 'Hass' (F)	CGOG
thunbergii	CGre

PERSICARIA (Polygonaceae)
§ *affinis*	CB&S CBlo CTri ECha GCrs GKir MBar MTho MWhi NBro NVic SMer SWat WCFE WFar WMoo WOve
- 'Darjeeling Red' ♀	CB&S CBlo CRow EBee ELan ENot EPla GCal GChr GKir LGro LHil LRHS MBri MRav NBid NBir NChi NFla NHol SMrm WBea WFar WHen WHer WPnP
- 'Dimity'	See *P. affinis* 'Superba'
- 'Donald Lowndes' ♀	More than 30 suppliers
¶ - 'Kabouter'	LBuc
- 'Ron McBeath'	CRow
§ - 'Superba' ♀	More than 30 suppliers
alata	See *P. nepalensis*
alpina	CRow
amphibia	CRow
§ *amplexicaulis*	CBre COld CRow ELan EMar GMaP LGro MBro MHer MSCN MWat NChi NDea NFor NOrc SChu SEND WFar WHoo WMoo WPyg WRHF
- 'Alba'	CRow ECha EFou EGar EMan EPla LGre LRHS MBri WBea WCot WFar
- 'Arun Gem'	See *P. amplexicaulis* var. *pendula*
- 'Atrosanguinea'	CBlo CNic CRow EBee ECha EGra EMan EPla GGar LAst LFis LRHS MFir NBir NDea NFai NFla NHol NTow NVic SPer SRms WFar WWin WWoo
- 'Blotau'	See *P. amplexicaulis* Taurus = 'Blotau'
¶ - 'Clent Charm'	WSPU
- 'Cottesbrooke Gold'	CRow WCot
- 'Firedance'	LGre SMrm
- 'Firetail' ♀	CRow EBrP EBre ECha ECtt EFou EMan EPla LBCl LBSe LBre LLWP LRHS MBBe MBel MCAu MRav MTis NHol NLar NSti SAga SBre SUsu WBea WElm WFar WRus WWhi
- 'Inverleith'	CBre CRow EBee EBrP EBre ECha ECtt EGar EPla LBCl LBSe LBre MBBe NCat SBre SCob SDys SMrm WMoo WPGP WWye
* - var. *pendula*	CRow ECha GAri MBri NBir WBea WCot WFar
- 'Rosea'	CRow EBee ECha ELan EMan EPla LGre LRHS MBri MRav NSti SDys SUsu WBea WMoo WPGP
- 'Rowden Gem'	CRow

- 'Rowden Jewel'	CRow
- 'Rowden Rose Quartz'	CRow
¶ - 'Summer Dance'	EFou
§ - Taurus = 'Blotau'	CElw CRow EGar EPla GBin LRHS MLLN WFar
§ *bistorta*	CArn CBlo CKin CRow ELau GBar GPoy MChe MHer MHew MSal MWhi SWat WGwG WSel WWye
- subsp. *carnea*	CRow EBee ECha EGar ELan EMan NBir WFar
- 'Hohe Tatra'	CRow EBee EMan GKir LGre MTed
- 'Superba' ♀	More than 30 suppliers
bistortoides	MSal
* 'Blush Clent'	WSPU WTin
campanulata	CElw CRow ECha EMar EWTr GBuc GCal GGar LHop MHar MSCN MWat NBid NBro NFai NFor NGdn SPer WBcn WBea WFar WOve WWat WWin WWye
- Alba Group	CRow EWTr GCal GGar MWgw NBro NSti WHer WWat WWye
¶ - 'Madame Figard'	CRow
- 'Rosenrot'	CBre CRow EBee EBrP EBre EMan EPla GBuc GCal LBCl LBSe LBre LFis MBBe NHol NLar SBre SSpi SWat WBea WCot
- 'Southcombe White'	CRow EBrP EBre EPla GAri GBri LBCl LBSe LBre MBBe SBre WBea WRos
capitata	CHal CInt CLTr CRow SCro SHFr SIng SMac SRms WBea WMoo WOut
- from Afghanistan	WBea
conspicua	EBee
coriacea	CRow
elata	CHor EBrP EBre EMar EMon GAri GBuc GGar GOrP LBCl LBSe LBre MBBe SBre SLod
emodi	CRow EBee WWat
§ *longiseta*	MSal
§ *macrophylla*	CRow EBrP EBre LBCl LBSe LBre MBBe MTed NFla SBre
microcephala	CRow EWes SAga SCro SMac WCot
¶ - 'Red Dragon'	CRow
¶ - var. *wallichii*	CRow
milletii	CRDP CRow EBee EBrP EBre EPla EWes GAri GBuc LBCl LBSe LBre LFis LGre LRHS MBBe MBri MTho NOak NSti SBre WCot WCru WMoo WWat
§ *mollis*	CRow
§ *nepalensis*	CRow EPPr NHol SMad
§ *odorata*	CArn EBlw ELau EOHP Iive MSal WJek
orientalis	MSal SMrm
polymorpha	CRow EBee EBrP EBre ECha EFou EMan EMon LBCl LBSe LBre LGre MBBe MTed SBre SCob SMrm
polystachya	See *P. wallichii*
* *regeliana*	LRHS
§ *runcinata*	CLTr CRow EBee EMar GCHN GGar NLar WBar WFar WHer WOut WPer WWin
¶ - Needham's form	CRow
* *rupestris*	Last listed 1998
scoparia	See *Polygonum scoparium*
sphaerostachya Meissner	See *P. macrophylla*
tenuicaulis	CBlo CLyd CRow EBee EMon EPar EPla GGar MFir NChi NDea

	NHol SIng WCot WCru WFar WMoo
§ *tinctoria*	EOHP
vacciniifolia ♀	More than 30 suppliers
- 'Ron McBeath'	CRow
§ *virginiana*	CMHG CRow EPla MFir NLar
- Compton's form	CRow EBee MTed NCat WCot
- 'Lance Corporal'	CRow EBee EFou
§ - 'Painter's Palette' (v)	More than 30 suppliers
- Variegata Group	CBot CRow EBee ECha GCal NLar WCot
vivipara	CRow WCot
§ *wallichii*	CRow ECha GBri NSti SDix
§ *weyrichii*	EMan GCal MTed NBir NBro NLar WBea WCot

PETALOSTEMON See DALEA

PETAMENES See GLADIOLUS

PETASITES (Asteraceae)

albus	CRow EMon GGar GPoy MHer
fragrans	CHEx CNat EGra ELan EMon EPar MGas MHer MSta SWat WFar WHer WOak
hybridus	CKin EMFW LEdu MCli WHer
* - 'Variegatus'	Last listed 1997
japonicus var. *giganteus*	CArn CHEx CRow ECha EGol ELan EMon EOld EPar EPfP LEdu MSCN NCut NVic WCra WCru
§ - var. *giganteus* 'Nishiki-buki' (v)	CHEx CRow EBee ECoo EEls EGar EMon EPla IBlr MSCN WCDu WCHb WCru WFar WHil WPGP
- - 'Variegatus'	See *P.japonicus* var. *giganteus* 'Nishiki-buki'
- f. *purpureus*	WCot WCru
palmatus	CRow EBee GCal NSti WCru WFar
¶ - 'Golden Palms'	NSti
- JLS 86317CLOR	EMon SMad WCot
paradoxus	EBee EGar EMon EPPr MRav MSCN WCot WPGP

PETREA (Verbenaceae)

volubilis	CPIN LChe LRHS SOWG WMul

PETROCALLIS (Brassicaceae)

lagascae	See *P.pyrenaica*
§ *pyrenaica*	GCrs NWCA WPer
- *alba*	GCrs

PETROCOPTIS (Caryophyllaceae)

¶ *pseudoviscosa*	EHyt
pyrenaica	EBur SBla SRms
§ - subsp. *glaucifolia*	CNic EDAr ESis GTou MNrw NBir WAbe WPer
- - 'Alba'	Last listed 1999

PETROCOSMEA (Gesneriaceae)

kerrii	NTow

PETROMARULA (Campanulaceae)

pinnata	CPou EBee GBin NChi WCot

PETROPHYTUM (Rosaceae)

caespitosum	CGra GTou NHar NWCA WAbe
cinerascens	NWCA SIng
§ *hendersonii*	NHol NWCA WAbe

PETRORHAGIA (Caryophyllaceae)

¶ *illyrica* subsp. *haynaldiana*	NArg
nanteuilii	CNat EWFC

§ *saxifraga* ♀	EBur MBNS MMal MNrw MPEx NPri SRms WBea WGwG WMoo WPat WPer WWhi
§ - 'Rosette'	MTho WWin

PETROSELINUM (Apiaceae)

§ *crispum*	CArn CSev EDAr GKir GPoy ILis LRHS MBar MChe NPri SIde WPer WSel WWye
- 'Bravour' ♀	ELau MHer MMal
- 'Champion Moss Curled'	EDAr
- var. *crispum*	Last listed 1997
- 'Darki'	CSev
- French	CArn CBod EDAr ELau IIve MHer MMal WJek WWye
- 'Greek'	ELau
¶ - 'Green River'	EOHP
- 'Italian'	See *P. crispum* var. *neapolitanum*
§ - var. *neapolitanum*	CBod EDAr ELau IIve MHer NGCt
§ - var. *tuberosum*	CBod MHer SIde WHer
hortense	See *P.crispum*
tuberosum	See *P.crispum* var. *tuberosum*

PETTERIA (Papilionaceae)

ramentacea	CFil EPfP SLPl

PETUNIA (Solanaceae)

¶ Lavender Star = 'Harstar'	WWol
Surfinia Pink Vein = 'Suntosol'[PBR]	GKir WWol
Surfinia White = 'Kesupite'	GKir

PEUCEDANUM (Apiaceae)

formosanum B&SWJ 3647	EBee WCru
litorale	See *Kitagawia litoralis*
officinale	Last listed 1997
ostruthium	GPoy
- 'Daphnis' (v)	EBee EMan EMon EPPr MTed NChi NPro WPGP
palustre	Last listed 1997
verticillare	CRDP EBee EMan SMad SMrm SSca

PEUMUS (Monimiaceae)

boldus	CGre

PHACELIA (Hydrophyllaceae)

bolanderi	CPBP EBee
sericea subsp. *ciliosa*	Last listed 1998
- subsp. *sericea*	EPot
tanacetifolia	Last listed 1997

PHACOCAPNOS See CYSTICAPNOS

PHAEDRANASSA (Amaryllidaceae)

dubia	Last listed 1998
tunguraguae	WCot
viridiflora	Last listed 1998

PHAEDRANTHUS See DISTICTIS

PHAENOCOMA (Asteraceae)

prolifera	Last listed 1997

PHAENOSPERMA (Poaceae)

globosa	CHar EBee EGar EHoe EPPr EPla EWes LEdu LHil LRHS NHol SCob

PHAGNALON (Asteraceae)

helichrysoides	Last listed 1999

PHAIOPHLEPS (Iridaceae)
nigricans   See *Sisyrinchium striatum*

PHAIUS (Orchidaceae)
minor   EFEx

PHALARIS (Poaceae)
§ *aquatica*   Last listed 1997
- 'Austalia'   Last listed 1998
- 'Uneta'   Last listed 1998
arundinacea   CKin EPla MBNS MLan SPlb SWat
- 'Elegantissima'   See *P. arundinacea* var. *picta* 'Picta'
- 'Luteovariegata'   EMon
- var. *picta*   CCHP GKir LRHS LSyl NBid NCut SLon
- - 'Aureovariegata'   CB&S CRow CSWP MRav NPer SAga SWat
- - 'Feesey' (v)   More than 30 suppliers
- - 'Luteopicta' (v)   EBee EHoe EPla LRHS
§ - - 'Picta' (v) ♀   More than 30 suppliers
- - 'Tricolor' (v)   EHoe EMon EPla GAri GOrn SSoC WBea
- 'Streamlined' (v)   EMon EPla EWsh LRHS SLPl WLeb
- 'Turkey Red'   Last listed 1998
- 'Yugoslavian'   Last listed 1998
tuberosa stenoptera   See *P. aquatica*

PHALOCALLIS (Iridaceae)
coelestis   Last listed 1999

PHANEROPHLEBIA (Dryopteridaceae)
caryotidea   See *Cyrtomium caryotideum*
falcata   See *Cyrtomium falcatum*
fortunei   See *Cyrtomium fortunei*

PHARBITIS See IPOMOEA

PHASEOLUS (Papilionaceae)
caracalla   See *Vigna caracalla*

PHEGOPTERIS (Thelypteridaceae)
§ *connectilis*   CCuc EFer EMon LSyl NMar NVic SRms
decursive-pinnata   CCuc EMon NHol NMar WRic
¶ *hexagonoptera*   WRic

PHELLODENDRON (Rutaceae)
amurense   CB&S CFil CGre CMCN ELan EPfP LEdu LPan SSpi WDin WNor
- var. *sachalinense*   MAsh WPGP
chinense   Last listed 1999
lavalleei   WPGP

PHILADELPHUS ✿ (Hydrangeaceae)
ACE 1907   WHCr
'Albâtre' (d)   LRHS MBri
'Atlas' (v)   Last listed 1999
'Avalanche'   CMHG EBrP EBre LBCl LBSe LBre LRHS MBBe NPro SBre SEas SPer SRms WDin WHCG WWat
'Beauclerk' ♀   More than 30 suppliers
'Belle Etoile' ♀   More than 30 suppliers
'Boule d'Argent' (d)   CMHG
'Bouquet Blanc'   GKir GQui SEas SPer SRms WKif
brachybotrys   CFil EPfP MRav NHol WHCG WPGP
'Buckley's Quill' (d)   MRav WBcn
'Burfordensis'   MAsh SPer WWat
'Burkwoodii'   Last listed 1999
¶ *caucasicus*   GEil

coronarius   CTri EBee LBuc LRHS MWat NFor SPer SRPl
- 'Aureus' ♀   More than 30 suppliers
- 'Bowles' Variety'   See *P. coronarius* 'Variegatus'
- 'Gold Mound'   MGos MRav
§ - 'Variegatus' (v) ♀   More than 30 suppliers
coulteri   Last listed 1998
'Coupe d'Argent'   MRav
'Dame Blanche' (d)   EBee EWTr LRHS MBri NPro
delavayi   CFil CPle EPfP WCru WHCG WPGP
- ACE   WHCr
- var. *calvescens*   See *P. purpurascens*
- - ACE 2206   SSpi
¶ - EDHCH 97170   EPPr
'Enchantement' (d)   MRav SDix WLRN
§ 'Erectus'   CBlo CCHP EBee EHol ENot EPfP EWTr MRav NWea SLon SPer WHCG WWat
'Etoile Rose'   Last listed 1999
fragrans   CFil WPGP
'Frosty Morn'   CB&S EBee GOrc LRHS MGos SPer SPla WRHF
'Glacier'   Last listed 1999
§ 'Innocence' (v)   CBot CEnd CHar CPMA CPle ECtt EHoe ELan EPla GChr GKir LHop LRHS MBri MGos MRav NPro SEas SPer SReu SSta WFar WHCG
'Innocence Variegatus'   See *P.* 'Innocence'
inodorus var. *grandiflorus*   CPle
§ *insignis*   MRav
intectus   GKir ISea
x *lemoinei*   CBlo CTri EBee GEil GKir MGos NFor SEas SRPl WFar WGwG WStl WWal
- 'Erectus'   See *P.* 'Erectus'
- 'Lemoinei'   EWTr
'Lemon Hill'   WBcn
lewisii   CAgr GKir WUnu
- L 1896   CFil WPGP
madrensis   LHop WPGP
- CD&R 1226   WWat
'Manteau d'Hermine' (d) ♀   More than 30 suppliers
'Marjorie'   CHar
mexicanus   CFil WPGP
¶ - 'Rose Syringa'   WPGP
microphyllus   CBlo CBot CDul CMHG ELan EPfP ESis GKir GOrc LGre LRHS MAsh MBro MHar MRav NHol SLon SPer SReu SSpi WHCG WPat WSHC WWat
¶ - var. *occidentalis*   SPer
'Minnesota Snowflake' (d)   EBee ECtt EWes IOrc LRHS MBel MRav NPro WBcn
x *monstrosus* 'Monster'   Last listed 1998
'Mont Blanc'   CB&S
'Mrs E.L. Robinson' (d)   CBlo ECtt EPla LAst
'Natchez' (d)   ECtt GKir MBNS SPan SVil
'Oeil de Pourpre'   MBri
¶ *palmeri*   CFil WPGP
'Perryhill'   SPer
pubescens   Last listed 1998
§ *purpurascens*   LBuc MRav SMrm
x *purpureomaculatus*   Last listed 1998
schrenkii   CFil WPGP
§ 'Silberregen'   CBlo CDoC CPle EBee ECtt EWTr GOrc IOrc LRHS MAsh MBar MGos MRav NBee NPro SEas SPan SRms WDin WPat WWat
Silver Showers   See *P.* 'Silberregen'
'Snowflake'   EMil NMoo WLRN

'Souvenir de Billiard' — See *P. insignis*
subcanus — GOrc MRav
'Sybille' ♀ — CBlo CMHG ENot EPfP GKir GOrc LRHS MBri MRav NFla NHlc SPer SRms SSpi WHCG WKif WPat WSHC
tenuifolius — CMCN
tomentosus — CFil WHCG WPGP
– B&SWJ 2707 — WCru
'Velléda' — CFil
'Virginal' (d) ♀ — More than 30 suppliers
'Virginal' LA '82 — CDul NWea
'Voie Lactée' — GEil MRav
White Rock — CDoC COtt EBee LRHS MAsh NMoo SPer WBcn WLRN

PHILESIA (Philesiaceae)
buxifolia — See *P. magellanica*
§ *magellanica* — EMil GGGa GSki SSpi WCru

PHILIBERTIA (Asclepiadaceae)
gilliesii — Last listed 1999

PHILLYREA (Oleaceae)
angustifolia — CDoC CFil CMCN COtt CPle EPfP ERom MGos SEND SLPl SPer SSpi WAbe WPGP WWat
– f. *rosmarinifolia* — CB&S CFil WPGP
decora — See *Osmanthus decorus*
§ *latifolia* — CFil CHEx CPle EPfP LRHS SAPC SArc SLPl SSpi WPGP WWat
media — See *P. latifolia*

PHILODENDRON (Araceae)
§ *angustisectum* ♀ — MBri
elegans — See *P. angustisectum*
'Emerald Queen' — MBri
epipremnum — See *Epipremnum pinnatum*
erubescens ♀ — MBri
– 'Burgundy' ♀ — LRHS MBri
– 'Imperial Red' — Last listed 1999
– 'Red Emerald' — CHal EBak MBri
melanochrysum — MBri
'New Red' — MBri
pedatum — MBri
'Purple Queen' — MBri
radiatum — MBri
scandens ♀ — CHal LBlo
selloum — WMul
tuxtlanum 'Royal Queen' — MBri
– 'Tuxtla' — MBri

PHILOTHECA (Rutaceae)
§ *myoporoides* — ECon LCns

PHLEUM (Poaceae)
. *hirsutum* — Last listed 1997
pratense — EHoe EPla
– subsp. *bertolonii* — CKin

PHLOMIS ✿ (Lamiaceae)
alpina — Last listed 1997
* *anatolica* — LRHS
* – 'Lloyd's Variety' — CAbP EBee ELan EPla GCal LHop LRHS MBri MSte SPan SPer WEas WPen WWat
angustifolia — Last listed 1999
aff. *anisodonta* — WPhl
¶ – white — WPhl
armeniaca — WPhl
atropurpurea — EMon GBin WPhl
betonicoides — EMon WPhl

– B&L 12600 — Last listed 1998
bourgaei JMT 260 — WPhl
– 'Whirling Dervish' JMT 271 — WPhl
bovei subsp. *maroccana* — CBot EPla GCal LFis LPio SPan WCot WPhl
breviflora — WPhl
cancellata — Last listed 1999
cashmeriana — CArn CBot CGle CPle ECha NLar WCFE WPhl
– CC&MR 31 — Last listed 1997
chrysophylla ♀ — CAbP CBot CPle CSam EBee ELan EPfP LAst LRHS MDun SBla SDix SDry SPer WCFE WCot WPGP WPhl WWat
¶ *cretica* — WPhl
crinita — Last listed 1999
cypria — Last listed 1999
¶ – var. *occidentalis* — WPhl
§ 'Edward Bowles' — SDry SLPl SLon SPan WCot WPhl
* 'Elliot's Variety' — CPLG
fruticosa ♀ — More than 30 suppliers
– SCH 3149 — WHCr
grandiflora — CBot SEND
– JMT 256 — WPhl
italica — CB&S CBot CDoC CHad CPle CSam EBee ELan EMil EWTr LFis LHil LHop MBel MLLN MRav NBir SBrw SChu SPer WCFE WCot WEas WFar WHer WPhl WSHC WWat WWin WWye
¶ – 'Pink Glory' — WPhl
lanata — CAbP CFee CMil EBee ELan EPfP LHop LRHS SBrw SDry SPan SPer WCot WEas WGer WPhl WWat WWye
¶ – 'Pygmy' — WPhl
leucophracta — LRHS
– 'Golden Janissary' JMT 255 — WPhl
– 'Silver Janissary' — WPhl
linearis var. *plumosa* JMT 416 — Last listed 1999
longifolia — CBot CHad LHop LRHS SPer
– var. *bailanica* — CPle LRHS WFar WSPU WWat
– var. *longifolia* — WPhl
lunariifolia JMT 258 — WPhl
lychnitis — WPhl
lycia — CAbP LRHS WPhl
macrophylla HWJCM 250 — WCru
monocephala — WPhl
nissolei JMT 268 — WPhl
platystegia — WPhl
purpurea — CPle CSam EBee ELan EPfP LRHS NBir SBrw SPan SRCN WCot WOut WPhl WSHC WWat
– *alba* — CBot EPfP LHop
– subsp. *almeriensis* — WPhl
¶ – 'Compact' — WPhl
– 'Green Leaf' JMT 499 — Last listed 1999
rigida — EBee WCru
§ *russeliana* ♀ — More than 30 suppliers
samia Boissier — See *P. russeliana*
– L. 'Green Cap' JMT 285 — WPhl
– 'Green Glory' — WPhl
– JMT 285 — LRHS WPhl
sp. B&SWJ 2210 — Last listed 1997
tuberosa — CBot CFir CPou EBee EGar EMan EMar EPPr GCal MCAu NChi NLar NSti SMad SOkh SSvw WCru WHil WPGP WPhl
– 'Amazone' — CFir CWit ECha EFou LAst LFis

LGre SAga WFar

viscosa hort. See *P. russeliana*
- Poiret WPhl

PHLOX ✿ (Polemoniaceae)

adsurgens ♀ EDAr ITim WAbe
- 'Alba' SBla WAbe
- 'Red Buttes' CGle CLyd EPot LPio SBla SCro
- 'Wagon Wheel' CLyd EBrP EBre EDAr EPot EWes
  LBCl LBSe LBre LHop LRHS MBBe
  MBro NFla NHar NSla SBre SIng
  SMrm SUsu WCot WFar WPat
  WRus WWin
albomarginata Last listed 1999
x **arendsii** 'Anja' MTed WCot WRus
- 'Cathelijne' Last listed 1999
- 'Hilda' CStr MTed
- 'Lisbeth' WCot
§ - 'Luc's Lilac' Last listed 1999
- 'Suzanne' WCot
austromontana EPot NWCA
bifida ITim NHol
- 'Alba' WAbe
- blue CStr ELan LRHS SUsu
- 'Colvin's White' CLyd EDAr LRHS SAga SBla
- 'Minima Colvin' ECtt EPot
- 'Petticoat' CLyd CMea LRHS NCat SBla SUsu
  WAbe
- 'Ralph Haywood' CLyd WAbe
- 'Starbrite' CLyd ITim LRHS MOne SBla WFar
- 'Sunset' Last listed 1998
* - 'The Fi' EWes WAbe WIvy
'Black Buttes' CLyd MNaF NNrd NTow WAbe
'Bleeklila' WCot
borealis EDAr ELan EWes GDra ITim
* - **arctica** EPot
bryoides See *P. muscoides*
caespitosa CMea EWes GCHN ITim NDlv
  NMen
- subsp. **condensata** See *P. condensata*
canadensis See *P. divaricata*
carolina 'Bill Baker' More than 30 suppliers
- 'Magnificence' CFri CM&M EGle EMon EWes
  GBuc LAst MSte SCro SMrm SOkh
  SSvw SUsu WHil
- 'Miss Lingard' ♀ More than 30 suppliers
* 'Casablanca' Last listed 1998
* 'Chanel' MLan
'Charles Ricardo' CPlt EBee EGle GBuc MBro NTow
  SAga SHel SUsu WHoo WPyg
  WRus
'Chattahoochee' See *P. divaricata* subsp. *laphamii*
  'Chattahoochee'
* **chonela** 'Nana' CMea
§ **condensata** GCrs IMGH ITim NWCA WAbe
covillei See *P. condensata*
'Daniel's Cushion' See *P. subulata* 'McDaniel's
  Cushion'
diffusa Last listed 1998
- NNS 95-46 Last listed 1998
§ **divaricata** ♀ EHol GKir MRav MSte NPri SBod
  SHel SPlb WCot WPer WRus
  WWin
- f. **albiflora** ELan
- 'Blue Dreams' More than 30 suppliers
- 'Blue Perfume' EFou EMil NBrk
- 'Clouds of Perfume' CHea CM&M EBee EFou EMan
  EWTr GBri GMaP LRHS MChl
  MWgw NCat NFla NHol NSti SBla
  SBod SCro SMrm SWat WFar
  WRus WSan
- 'Dirigo Ice' CLyd EGle EMan ERav LAco LFis

- 'Eco Regal' Last listed 1998
- 'Eco Texas Purple' CLAP EBee EMan GMac MAvo
  NBrk NHar SAga SUsu WPGP
  WRus
- 'Fuller's White' CLyd MAvo
§ - subsp. **laphamii** CLyd CSam EDAr EGle EWes
  NDov NSti SBod WCru WFar
  WFoF WHil WRus
§ - - 'Chattahoochee' ♀ CBot CSpe EBee EDAr ELan
  EMNN EMan EPot EWes GCrs
  GMac LHop LRHS MBro NHol
  SAga SBla SBod SIng SLod SMrm
  SUsu WAbe WCFE WMaN WPat
  WSHC WWin
- - 'Chattahoochee EDAr EWes LHop LRHS WCot
  Variegated'
- 'Louisiana Purple' EBee EGle
- 'May Breeze' More than 30 suppliers
* - 'White Perfume' CM&M EMil MBrN
douglasii NHol NWCA SRms
- 'Apollo' CLyd CPBP EDAr EPot GDra LRHS
  NHol NLAp NMen SAga WWin
- 'Boothman's Variety' ♀ CGle CLyd CNic ECha EDAr ELan
  EPar EPot GKir LRHS MWat NMen
  SIng SRms WEas WHoo WWin
- 'Concorde' GDra
- 'Crackerjack' ♀ CLyd CNic EDAr ELan EMNN
  EPot GAbr GDra GKir ITim LRHS
  MHar MHer MWat NHar NLAp
  NMen SAga SBod SIng WAbe
  WLin
- 'Eva' CLyd CM&M EBrP EBre EDAr
  ELan EMNN GTou LBCl LBSe LBre
  LRHS MBBe MOne NBir NHar
  NHol NMen SBre SIng SMrm
  WPer WWin
- 'Galaxy' CLyd EWes GDra NHar
- 'Holden Variety' Last listed 1998
- 'Ice Mountain' CPBP ECho EDAr ELan NPri SAga
  SMrm SRot
- 'Iceberg' ♀ CLyd EPot GDra GMaP ITim NHar
  NMen WWin
- 'J.A. Hibberson' CLyd EPot
- Lilac Queen See *P. douglasii* 'Lilakönigin'
§ - 'Lilakönigin' CLyd EDAr
- x **multiflora** Last listed 1997
  var. **depressa**
¶ - 'Napoleon' CPBP
- 'Ochsenblut' MDHE MHer
- 'Red Admiral' ♀ EBrP EBre EMNN EPot ESis EWes
  GCHN GCrs GDra GKir LBCl
  LBSe LBre LRHS MBBe NHar
  NHol NMen SBod SBre SMrm
  WFar
- 'Rose Cushion' EDAr EWes GDra LRHS MDHE
  MHer NMen
- 'Rose Queen' CLyd CStr GDra
- 'Rosea' EBrP EBre EDAr ELan EMNN EPar
  ESis LBCl LBSe LBre LRHS MBBe
  NMen NWCA SBod SBre SIng
  SMer SMrm WFar
- 'Silver Rose' GCrs GTou
- 'Sprite' SRms
- 'Tycoon' See *P. subulata* 'Tamaongalei'
- 'Violet Queen' ELan EWes GDra NHar NHol
  WFar
- 'Waterloo' CLyd CPBP EPot LRHS NHar NHol
  NMen SAga SChu SIng
drummondii SAga
'Geddington Cross' MAvo MGed MWgw

* 'Herfstsering'	Last listed 1998
* 'Hesperis'	LGre MAnH SUsu
hirsuta	Last listed 1999
boodii	CLyd ECho WAbe
* 'Hortensia'	Last listed 1998
'Kelly's Eye' ♀	CLyd CM&M CPBP CSam ECha ECtt EDAr ELan EMNN EPot GAbr LHop LRHS MMil NMen SIng WFar WPer
kelseyi	GCrs NWCA
- 'Lemhi Purple'	CGra CPBP
- 'Rosette'	CLyd EPot LRHS NMen SIng WPer
longifolia	Last listed 1998
'Louisiana'	WHil
maculata	NOrc WPer
- 'Alba'	GKir
- 'Alpha' ♀	More than 30 suppliers
- Avalanche	See *P. maculata* 'Schneelawine'
- 'Delta'	CHea EBee EMan GMac LRot MLLN NHol NPri NSti SCro SPer SPla WFar WHil WMaN WRus
- 'Good White'	SMrm
- 'Natascha'	More than 30 suppliers
- 'Omega' ♀	CHea CMHG EBee EFou EMan GCHN GKir GMaP LRHS LRot MBNS MCAu MRav NBid NBrk NHol NLar NSti SChu SMrm SPer SSpi WFar WMaN WRus WSHC WWye
- 'Princess Sturdza'	Last listed 1998
- 'Reine du Jour'	LGre SAga SMrm SOkh SUsu
- 'Rosalinde'	EFou EMan MBel MCAu MRav MSte NCat NHol SChu SCro WLin
§ - 'Schneelawine'	EBee NCat WRus
* *matineus*	LGre
mesoleuca	See *P. nana* subsp. *ensifolia*
'Millstream'	See *P.* x *procumbens* 'Millstream'
'Millstream Jupiter'	Last listed 1999
missoulensis	SIng
§ *muscoides*	EWes
§ *nana* subsp. *ensifolia*	Last listed 1997
- 'Mary Maslin'	SBla
- 'Vanilla Cream'	SBla
nivalis	NMen
- 'Camlaensis'	CLyd EPot ITim WPat
- 'Jill Alexander'	Last listed 1997
- 'Nivea'	LRHS NTow WLRN
ovata	EMan MNrw WRus
paniculata	CBos CHad EWTr LGre NBid NFor SDix WCot
- 'A.E.Amos'	CTri ERou
- 'Aida'	CB&S EGar ERou MWat WRus
- var. *alba*	GCal MCAu SDix WCot
- 'Alba Grandiflora' ♀	WEas
- 'Albert Leo Schlageter' ♀	ERou SRms
- 'Alexander'	Last listed 1998
- 'Amethyst'	CCHP CFir CSam EBee EGar EGle EPfP ERou GKir LFis MBNS MBel MCAu NBir SMer WWye
- 'Annie Laurie'	Last listed 1997
- 'Anthony Six'	Last listed 1997
- 'Balmoral'	CGle CM&M ECtt EOld GChr GKir LLWP LRHS MLLN MRav MSte NSti SMer SPla SWat WHil WLRN
- 'Barnwell'	EFou ELan GMac
- 'Betty Symons-Jeune'	ERou
- 'Bill Green'	LRHS SMrm
- 'Blue Boy'	CM&M EBee EFou EGle ERou EWTr LRHS MBel NPSI WHoo WSan
- 'Blue Evening'	LGre

- 'Blue Ice' ♀	CSev EBee EFou LRHS MWat SMrm WLRN
- 'Blue Moon'	Last listed 1999
- 'Blue Paradise'	CRDP EBee EBrP EBre EFou EGle LBCl LBSe LBre LGre MBBe MBNS MBri MRav MSte NPSI SAga SBla SBre SMrm STes SVil WFar WHil WPGP WRus WWye
- 'Blushing Bride'	SRms
- 'Bonny Maid'	CBla
- 'Border Gem'	CB&S EBee EBrP EBre EFou EMon GKir LBCl LBSe LBre MBBe MSte NCut SBre SMer SWat WCot
- 'Branklyn'	EBrP EBre GKir LBCl LBSe LBre LGre LRHS MBBe MRav SBre SMer WFar
- 'Bressingham White'	NBrk
- 'Brigadier' ♀	CBla CSam CTri EBee EBrP EBre ELan GKir GMaP LBCl LBSe LBre LRHS MBBe MFir MWat SBre SPer SRms
- 'Bright Eyes' ♀	CBla CBlo COtt CRDP EBee EBrP EBre ENot GKir LBCl LBSe LBre LRHS MArl MBBe MBel SBre SMer
- 'Caroline van den Berg'	CTri EGar ERou GKir SMer SRms WCot
- 'Cecil Hanbury'	CBlo ERou NBlu SRms
- 'Charmaine'	CBla
- 'Chintz'	MRav SRms
- 'Cinderella'	ERou MBel NLar NPri
- 'Cool of the Evening'	CBla MRav
- 'Count Zeppelin'	See *P. paniculata* 'Graf Zeppelin'
- 'Darwin's Joyce'	See *P. paniculata* 'Norah Leigh'
- 'David'	CStr EBrP EBre LBCl LBSe LBre MBBe SBre WCot WHil
- 'Discovery'	EBee LBuc
- 'Dodo Hanbury Forbes' ♀	CBla EGar EHol
- 'Dresden China'	ERou SWat
- 'Düsterlohe'	CSam CStr GBuc SMrm
- 'Eclaireur'	SWat
¶ - 'Eden's Crush'	CM&M LRot NCat NCut SVil
- 'Elie'	EBee LFis NFai WFar
- 'Elizabeth Arden'	EFou ERou MSte SWat WMaN
- 'Endurance'	ERou
- 'Etoile de Paris'	LGre SYvo
- 'Europe'	CB&S CGle EBee EFou ELan EOld ERou LRHS MBri MCAu MFir MWat NFai SPer WFar
- 'Eva Cullum'	CM&M CTri EBrP EBre ECGP EFou EGle GKir LBCl LBSe LBre LHop LRHS MArl MBBe MLLN MRav NFai SBre SMer SPer WCot
- 'Eventide' ♀	EBee EBrP EBre ECtt EFou EGar EPfP ERou EWTr GKir LBCl LBSe LBre LRHS MArl MBBe MCAu MCLN NChi NLar SBre SMer SPer SWat WCot WViv
- 'Excelsior'	CBlo MRav
- 'Fairy's Petticoat'	MWat WCot
- 'Firefly'	Last listed 1997
- 'Flamingo'	EBrP EBre EFou LBCl LBSe LBre LRHS MBBe MBNS NLar SBre
- 'Franz Schubert'	CHea CTri EBee EBrP EBre ECGP EFou EGar EGle GKir GMac LBCl LBSe LBre LRHS MBBe MTis NLar NSti SBre SMer STes SWat WCot WMaN WSan
§ - 'Frau A. von Mauthner'	LBuc
- 'Frosted Elegance'	CFwr EFou
§ - 'Fujiyama' ♀	More than 30 suppliers
- 'Glamis'	CBla MWat
§ - 'Graf Zeppelin'	CBla EWll LRHS MWat SRms

- 'Hampton Court'	NBrk
- 'Harewood'	ERou
- 'Harlequin' (v)	EBrP EBre ECha GBuc GKir LBCl LBSe LBre MBBe MRav NBid SBre SPla WCot WFar
- 'Iceberg'	MFir
- 'Iris'	GBuc LGre LPio SMrm SRms
¶ - 'Judy'	LBuc
- 'Jules Sandeau'	EBrP EBre LBCl LBSe LBre MAvo MBBe SBre
§ - 'Juliglut'	MWat SWat WCot
- July Glow	See *P. paniculata* 'Juliglut'
- 'Kirchenfuerst'	EFou
- 'Kirmesländler'	CB&S EBee ERou LRHS MLLN SRPl
- 'Lady Clare'	SRms
- 'Latest Red'	See *P. paniculata* 'Spätrot'
* - 'Laura'	CM&M COtt EBee EGle LFis LRot NCut SAga SCob WFar WHil WHoo
§ - 'Lavendelwolke'	LGre SWat
- Lavender Cloud	See *P. paniculata* 'Lavendelwolke'
- 'Le Mahdi' ♀	EBrP EBre LBCl LBSe LBre MBBe MRav MWat SBre SRms WCot
- 'Lichtspiel'	EFou LGre
- 'Lilac Time'	CBla EBee EWll MBel NCat
- 'Little Boy'	CFri EBee EGle STes WFar WHoo WRus
- 'Little Laura'	EFou
- 'Little Lovely'	Last listed 1998
- 'Lizzy'PBR	MBri
- 'Look Again'	ERou
- 'Mary Christine'	EBee
- 'Mary Fox'	CSam ERou MRav
- 'Mia Ruys'	EFou ERou GMac MArl MLLN
- 'Mies Copijn'	GMaP
* - 'Miss Elie'	CHea CMGP EFou EGle SVil WHil WHoo
- 'Miss Holland'	EGle LCaP WHoo
- 'Miss Jill'	CBos CHea EBee EFou EGle GMaP NCut SUsu SVil WCot WHil WRus
- 'Miss Jo-Ellen'	EBee EFou EGle GBri NPSI WHil
- 'Miss Karen'	EGle
- 'Miss Kelly'	CCHP CMGP COtt EBee EFou LRot WHil
- 'Miss Margie'	EBee EFou EGle GBri GMaP NPSI WHil
- 'Miss Mary'	CM&M EBee EFou EGle GBri WRus
* - 'Miss Pepper'	EBrP EBre EFou EMil EWll LBCl LBSe LBre LFis MBBe NFai SBre SVil WFar WHil
- 'Miss Universe'	EBee EGle LCaP MCCP WHil WHoo
¶ - 'Miss Wilma'	EBee GMaP NPSI WBar
* - 'Monica Lynden-Bell'	NCat WCot
- 'Mother of Pearl' ♀	CBla CGle CHad EBee EBrP EBre ECGP ELan GMac LBCl LBSe LBre LRHS MBBe MWat NVic SBre SPer WCot
- 'Mount Fujiyama'	See *P. paniculata* 'Fujiyama'
- 'Mrs A.E. Jeans'	SRms
- 'Mrs Fincham'	LFis
- 'Newbird'	ERou SRms
* - 'Nicky'	EFou EGle LCaP LFis MRav NBir NCat NLar SPer WFar WHil
§ - 'Norah Leigh' (v)	More than 30 suppliers
- 'Orange Perfection'	CB&S CBlo CM&M EBee EBrP EBre EPfP EWTr LBCl LBSe LBre LRHS MBBe MBNS MCCP MCli NPri SBre SCob WHil WViv

- 'Othello'	CBla
- 'Otley Choice'	CBlo CM&M EBee LAst LFis LRHS MSte MWat NLar NSti SCoo WLRN
- 'P.D. Williams'	WCot
- 'Pastorale'	MWat NCat WCot
- 'Pat Coleman'	EFou
- 'Pax'	LGre WViv
- 'Pike'	WCot
- 'Pink Posie' PBR (v)	MAsh MBri SPer WCot WWeb
- 'Popeye'	EFou MBri WHil
- 'Prime Minister'	CStr
- 'Prince of Orange' ♀	CBla CBlo CElw CGle CMGP CSam EBee EBrP EBre EFou EGle ELan ERou GKir LBCl LBSe LBre LRHS MBBe MRav MWat NPri SAga SBre SPer WCot
- 'Prospero' ♀	CBla CSam EOrc LFis MBel MCAu MRav NBid SAga SMer SMrm SPer WCot
- 'Rapture'	MWat
- 'Red Indian'	ERou MWat
- 'Rembrandt'	EBrP EBre ERou LBCl LBSe LBre MBBe SBla SBre WCot
- 'Rheinländer'	Last listed 1997
- 'Rijnstroom'	CB&S EBee EBrP EBre ECot ERou GMac LBCl LBSe LBre LFis LRHS MBBe MBel NCat NFai SBre WViv
- 'Rosa Pastell'	LGre SAga
- 'Rosa Spier'	Last listed 1999
- 'Rougham Supreme'	ERou
- 'Russian Violet'	MRav MWat
- 'San Antonio'	EBrP EBre LBCl LBSe LBre MBBe MBel MRav SBre
- 'Sandringham'	CBlo CSam CTri EBee EBrP EBre GKir LBCl LBSe LBre LRHS MArl MBBe MNrw MRav MSte NBir SBre SMer SPer SRPl
- 'Schneerausch'	LGre
- 'Septemberglut'	EBee
- 'Silver Salmon'	Last listed 1999
- 'Sir John Falstaff'	Last listed 1997
- 'Sir Malcolm Campbell'	ERou
- 'Skylight'	EBee MWat NVic SMrm WLRN
¶ - 'Snow White'	NCut SVil
- 'Snowball'	Last listed 1997
- 'Snowdrift'	ERou GKir
§ - 'Spätrot'	Last listed 1998
- 'Spitfire'	See *P. paniculata* 'Frau A. von Mauthner'
- 'Starfire'	More than 30 suppliers
* - 'Steeple Bumpstead'	CMil WCot
- 'Sternhimmel'	ERou LGre
- 'Sweetheart'	Last listed 1998
- 'Tenor'	CBlo CFir CM&M CTri EBee ECGP EFou GChr GKir LRHS LRot MBel MCAu MSte NFai NPri SAga SMrm WFar
- 'The King'	EBee LRHS SWat WViv
- 'Toits de Paris'	MWat
* - 'Úspech'	EBee EFou LBuc MSte MTis SPer
- 'Utopia'	LGre
- 'Vintage Wine'	CTri MCli
- 'Violetta Gloriosa'	LGre
- 'Visions'	EBee WHil
- 'White Admiral' ♀	More than 30 suppliers
- 'William Ramsay'	CTri EOld
- 'Windsor' ♀	CBla CBlo EBee EFou EPfP ERou EWTr GKir LFis LRHS MBel MCAu MLLN MTis SCoo SMrm SRms
pilosa	EBrP EBre ECha EFou EMan GMac LBCl LBSe LBre MBBe NPro SBre

SMrm SUsu WFar WRus

§ x **procumbens** 'Millstream' ♀
EDAr NTow SAga SBla WWin
- 'Variegata' ECha EDAr EMNN ESis LRHS
MHer MRav NHol NWCA SBla
SPlb WAbe WFar WLin WPat
WWin
pulchra 'Eco Pale Moon' Last listed 1999
- 'Eco Place' Last listed 1999
x **rugellii** Last listed 1999
'Scented Pillow' LRHS
stansburyi CPBP
stolonifera EPar GKir GMaP LRHS MHar
MNrw NPri WCot
- 'Ariane' ECha EDAr EPar MBro MNrw
NHar SBla SCro SMrm WAbe WFar
WViv WWin
- 'Blue Ridge' ♀ CFir CPea EBee ECha EDAr EGle
EMan EPar GBuc GCHN GKir
GMaP IMGH LFis NHar NLar
SMrm SRms SSca SUsu WFar WSan
WWin
* - 'Bob's Motley' (v) WCot
- 'Bruce's White' Last listed 1997
- compact Last listed 1998
- 'Compact Pink' NCat WFar
- 'Fran's Purple' CLAP CLyd EMan GMac NHar
SCro WAbe WFar
- 'Home Fires' EBee EDAr MNrw NBro NHar
SCro SMrm
- 'Mary Belle Frey' EBrP EBre EMan LBCl LBSe LBre
MBBe MSte NSti SAga SBre SCro
SMrm WAbe WFar WWin
- 'Pink Ridge' CLAP GBuc MNrw NHar NLar
- 'Purpurea' NHar
- variegated MNrw MRav WAbe WCot
- 'Violet Vere' CLAP CLyd CSpe CStr EBee EDAr
EGle GBuc LHop MBro MNrw
NHar SAga SLod SMrm WFar
WPyg
subulata EPar GKir NWCA
- 'Alexander's Surprise' CGle CMHG CMea ECtt EDAr
EPot GAbr GCHN LBee LRHS
NBir NFla SChu SPlb
- 'Amazing Grace' CTri EDAr ELan ESis EWes GKir
LBee LHop LRHS MHer MOne
NMen NSla SChu WPer WWin
- 'Apple Blossom' EDAr GAbr GDra NPri SAga
WLRN WRHF
- 'Atropurpurea' EBrP EBre EDAr GCHN LBCl LBSe
LBre LRHS MBBe MRav NFor SBre
WWin
- 'Beauty of Ronsdorf' See *P. subulata* 'Ronsdorfer
Schöne'
- 'Betty' CTri ECtt EMNN MBNS MDHE
NCat WPer
- 'Blue Eyes' See *P. subulata* 'Oakington Blue
Eyes'
- 'Blue Saucer' MDHE
- 'Bonita' CStr EMNN GKir LBee LRHS
MHar NPri SMer SMrm WWin
- 'Bressingham Blue Eyes' See *P. subulata* 'Oakington Blue
Eyes'
- 'Brightness' CNic CTri GCHN GKir GTou
LRHS
- subsp. **brittonii** 'Rosea' CPBP NHol WPer
- 'Candy Stripe' EPfP LRHS NHol
- 'Cavaldes White' NCat
- 'Christine Bishop' LRHS SAga
- 'Coral Eye' EPfP
- 'Daisy Hill' Last listed 1998
- 'Drumm' See *P. subulata* 'Tamaongalei'

- 'Eco Pale Moon' Last listed 1998
- 'Emerald Cushion' CSam EDAr EMan EWTr MHer
MMal NFor SAga SCob
- 'Emerald Cushion Blue' CLyd CNic EBrP EBre ELan EPfP
GKir GTou LBCl LBSe LBre MBBe
NMen SBre SMrm WPer
- 'Fairy' SAga WPer
- 'G.F. Wilson' See *P. subulata* 'Lilacina'
- 'Greencourt Purple' EDAr NCat
* - 'Holly' EPot MDHE NMen
- 'Jupiter' SChu
- 'Kimono' See *P. subulata* 'Tamaongalei'
§ - 'Lilacina' CLyd CMea ECha ECtt EDAr ELan
EWTr GTou LGro LRHS MWat
NFor SChu WAbe WPer WWin
§ - 'Maischnee' CLyd EBrP EBre ECtt EDAr EMNN
EPot EWTr GAbr GKir LBCl LBSe
LBre LGro LHop LRHS MBBe
MHer MOne MWat NFor NHol
SBre SMrm WEas WWin
- 'Marjorie' CLyd CMHG ECtt ELan EMNN
LBee LRHS MBro MHar MMal
NMen NPri WLRN
- 'Mauve Queen' MWat
- May Snow See *P. subulata* 'Maischnee'
§ - 'McDaniel's Cushion' ♀ CLyd EBrP EBre ECha EDAr ELan
EMNN EPot GKir GTou ITim LBCl
LBSe LBee LBre LRHS MBBe MMil
NFor NHol NMen SBre SPlb WFar
WPer WWin
- 'Mikado' See *P. subulata* 'Tamaongalei'
- 'Model' LGro NSla
- 'Moonlight' CLyd ECtt MBro SAga SLod WPer
- 'Nelsonii' Last listed 1997
- 'Nettleton Variation' (v) CMea CMil CPBP EDAr ELan EPot
ESis EWes GKir LBee LHop LRHS
MBro MHer NHol SAga SIng SPlb
WAbe WPat
§ - 'Oakington Blue Eyes' CNic EBrP EBre ECGP EPar
GCHN GDra GKir LBCl LBSe LBre
LRHS MBBe SBre SMrm SRms
WPer
- 'Pink Buttons' NCat
- 'Pink Pearl' EWes
- 'Red Wings' ♀ CGra EBrP EBre ECtt GCHN GKir
LBCl LBSe LBre LRHS MBBe
MWgw NFor NMen SAga SBre
SRms WFar
§ - 'Ronsdorfer Schöne' EPot LBee LRHS NNrd SAga
- 'Rose Mabel' EDAr
- 'Samson' ELan GTou LRHS MHar SMer
WPer WWin
- 'Scarlet Flame' CMea CSam EBrP EBre ECha ECtt
EDAr ELan EMNN LBCl LBSe LBre
LGro MBBe MHer MWat NHol
SAga SBre SMrm WPer WWin
- 'Schneewittchen' CLyd
- 'Sensation' GTou SRms
- 'Snow Queen' See *P. subulata* 'Maischnee'
- 'Southcroft' Last listed 1997
- 'Starglow' GTou SIng WPer
§ - 'Tamaongalei' CLyd CMea CMil CPBP EDAr
EMan EWes GDra GKir GMac
IMGH LHop LRHS MBel MNrw
NCat NHar SAga SBla SChu SCoo
SLod SMrm SRms SUsu WAbe
WHoo WLin WWin
- 'Temiskaming' ECha EDAr ELan EMNN ENot
EWes GCHN GDra LBee LGro
LRHS MHar NMen SChu SRms
WAbe
- violet seedling CLyd NHol

- 'White Delight'	CLyd EBrP EBre ECtt EDAr ELan EMNN GCHN GTou LBCl LBSe LBee LBre LRHS MBBe NMen SBre SRms WPer
- 'White Swan'	Last listed 1997
* 'Sweet William'	Last listed 1998
'Tiny Bugles'	CGra
'Vivid'	EDAr MDHE

PHOENICAULIS (Brassicaceae)
§ *cheirantboides* NWCA

PHOENIX (Arecaceae)
canariensis ♀	CB&S CBrP CGre CHEx CTbh CTrC EBlw EGln EPVP LCns LPJP LPal LRHS MBri MCCP MWst NMoo NRib SAPC SArc SEND WMul
dactylifera (F)	CHEx CRoM LCns LPal
paludosa	Last listed 1999
reclinata	CRoM CTrC EPVP LPJP WMul
roebelenii ♀	CBrP CRoM EGln EPVP EPfP LCns LPal MBri WMul
rupicola	CRoM LPal
sylvestris	LPal
theophrasti	LPJP LPal WMul

PHORMIUM ✿ (Agavaceae)
'Amazing Red'	Last listed 1999
'Apricot Queen' (v)	CAbb CB&S EBee EPVP GQui IBlr IOrc LRHS MDun NMoo NPri SPer WBod WCot WHil
Ballyrogan variegated	IBlr
* 'Black Edge'	IBlr MRav NPri
'Bronze Baby'	More than 30 suppliers
colensoi	See *P. cookianum*
§ *cookianum* ♀	CB&S CHEx CTrC ECre EMil IBlr IOrc MGos NPSI SAPC SArc SLPl WHil WMul WWat
- 'Alpinum Purpureum'	See *P. tenax* 'Nanum Purpureum'
* - 'Flamingo'	CSpe ECre IOrc WHil
- subsp. *bookeri*	CAbb CB&S CEnd CTrC EBee
'Cream Delight' (v) ♀	EHoe ELan ENot EPfP EWTr IOrc LRHS MBlu MDun MGos NArg NFla SAga SPer SRPl WCFE WLRN WLeb
- - 'Tricolor' ♀	CDoC CFil CHEx CTrC EBee ELan ENot EPla IBlr IOrc LRHS SArc SHFr SLim SPer SRms SSpi WCot WDin WHil WLeb WPGP
* 'Copper Beauty'	CBlo COtt EGln NMoo WLRN
'Dark Delight'	IBlr IOrc
'Dazzler' (v)	IBlr MGos WCot
'Duet' (v) ♀	CB&S CDoC COtt CTrC EBee EHoe EPfP IBlr IOrc LRHS WBcn
'Dusky Chief'	LRHS WLeb
* 'Emerald Pink'	COtt WGer
'Evening Glow'	CSpe ECle EPVP EPfP IBlr IOrc LRHS MAsh MDun SPla
'Firebird'	CB&S
'Flamingo'	LRHS MDun WPat
'Gold Sword' (v)	CB&S COtt EBee IBlr LRHS WHil CHEx IBlr
'Guardsman' (v)	CB&S COtt ECou EHoe IBlr IOrc LRHS MBrN NPSI WLeb
'Jack Spratt' (v)	
'Jester'	CB&S CDoC CFir CGdn CHEx COtt CSpe CTrC EHoe ELan ENot EWll GKir GQui IBlr IOrc LEdu LRHS MAsh MCCP MDun NPSI NPri SPla WBcn WBod WCot WLeb

¶ 'Limelight'	CB&S
§ 'Maori Chief' (v)	CFil EPfP GQui IBlr IOrc LRHS NFor NMoo WCot WLRN WPGP
'Maori Eclipse'	CBlo
§ 'Maori Maiden' (v)	CB&S CTrC EBee ECre EHoe GQui IOrc LRHS MGos MSCN SMad WBod WCot WHil WLeb
§ 'Maori Queen' (v)	CB&S CDoC EPfP GQui IBlr IOrc LRHS MAsh MGos NMoo WLRN
§ 'Maori Sunrise' (v)	CB&S CBlo CDoC EBee EPfP IArd IBlr IOrc LRHS MCCP MDun MGos MSte NPri SAga SLim WHil WLRN WLeb
'Pink Panther' (v)	CAbb CB&S CBlo CDoC ELan EPfP EWll GKir GQui IBlr IOrc LEdu LRHS MAsh MDun MGos NPri SPla WBod WDin WLeb
* 'Pink Stripe'	CSpe ECle IBlr IOrc LRHS MAsh MDun WCot
'Platt's Black'	CB&S EPfP GKir LJus LRHS MAsh SMad SPla WLeb WPat
'Rainbow Chief'	See *P.* 'Maori Chief'
Rainbow hybrids	CSpe
'Rainbow Maiden'	See *P.* 'Maori Maiden'
'Rainbow Queen'	See *P.* 'Maori Queen'
'Rainbow Sunrise'	See *P.* 'Maori Sunrise'
'Sea Jade'	IBlr
'Stormy Dawn'	WCot
'Sundowner' (v) ♀	CB&S CDoC CSpe CTrC EBee ELan EMil ENot EOld GQui IBlr IOrc LRHS MDun MGos SLdr SLim SMad SPer SSoC WCot WFar WLeb WStI
'Sunset' (v)	IBlr IOrc
'Surfer' (v)	COtt ECle EHoe IBlr IOrc LPan MCCP SMad WBcn WLeb WWat
tenax ♀	More than 30 suppliers
- 'Co-ordination'	CAbb ECle IBlr IOrc LRHS WBcn
- 'Dark Edge'	ERav
* - dwarf	EMil IBlr
- *lineatum*	SEND
§ - 'Nanum Purpureum' ♀	CHad CRDP IBlr MSte SEND WCot
- Purpureum Group ♀	More than 30 suppliers
- 'Radiance' (v)	IBlr
- 'Rainbow Queen'	See *P.* 'Maori Queen'
- 'Rainbow Sunrise'	See *P.* 'Maori Sunrise'
- 'Variegatum' ♀	CFil CHEx EPfP IBlr LPal LPan LRHS NMoo SAPC SArc SEND SPlb SRms WBrE WMul WPGP WPat
- 'Veitchianum' (v)	IBlr LRHS SPer WPGP
- 'Yellow Queen'	Last listed 1997
'Thumbelina'	CB&S EHoe IOrc LRHS MSte WLeb
'Tom Thumb'	IOrc LPan WDin
'Yellow Wave' (v) ♀	More than 30 suppliers

PHOTINIA ✿ (Rosaceae)
§ *arbutifolia*	CPle
beauverdiana ♀	CPle CTho SRms WWat
¶ - var. *notabilis*	EPfP
§ *davidiana*	CDul CSam EBee ELan EPfP GChr GKir IOrc ISea LRHS MBar MRav SEas SPer SRPl SRms WFar WNor WWat
- 'Palette' (v)	More than 30 suppliers
- var. *undulata*	CMHG LRHS MRav WBcn
- - 'Fructu Luteo'	CBlo CMHG CSam CTrG EPfP EPla GKir LRHS MBri MRav SPer WFar WWat
- - 'Prostrata'	ELan EPfP MBar MRav NLar SPer

		WFar WWat
x	*fraseri*	CMCN
	- 'Birmingham'	CBlo CLan EHoe GKir LPan LRHS SCob SLim SRms SSht WLRN WPyg WSHC
	- 'Red Robin' ♀	More than 30 suppliers
	- 'Robusta' ♀	CBlo WShe
§	- 'Rubens'	ELan EPfP LRHS MAsh MBri SDry SPer SPla SSta WPat WPyg
§	*glabra* 'Parfait' (v)	CAbP ELan LRHS MAsh MRav SDry SPer SPla WBcn WFar WPat WPyg
	- 'Pink Lady'	See *P. glabra* 'Parfait'
	- 'Rubens'	See *P.* x *fraseri* 'Rubens'
	- 'Variegata'	See *P. glabra* 'Parfait'
	glomerata	CHEx
	lasiogyna	CMCN
	lindleyana	Last listed 1999
	microphylla S&F 92307	Last listed 1999
¶	*niitakayamensis*	GIBF
§	*nussia*	CDoC
§	'Redstart' ♀	CBlo CEnd CPle EPfP GKir LRHS MGos SLon SPer SSta WWat
§	*serratifolia*	CBlo CBot CHEx CMHG CPle EPfP LRHS SAPC SArc SDry SPer SSta WBod WPGP WPat WPyg WSHC WWat
	serrulata	See *P. serratifolia*
	villosa ♀	CAbP CDul CPle CTho GAri IOrc MBar SSpi
	- var. *laevis*	EWTr LBuc LPan

PHRAGMITES (Poaceae)

§	*australis*	EMFW GBin NDea SWat WMAq
	- subsp. *pseudodonax*	EMon EPPr LRHS SMad
	- var. *striatopictus*	EMon EPPr
	- 'Variegatus'	CCuc CHEx CInt CNat CRDP CWat ECGP EHoe EMFW EMan EMon EPPr EPar EPla IBlr LRHS MMoz MRav MTed NSti SMad SMer SSoC SWyc WRus
	communis	See *P. australis*
¶	*karka* 'Candy Stripe' (v)	LLWG
	- 'Variegatus'	Last listed 1998
¶	sp. from Sichuan, China	EPPr

PHUOPSIS (Rubiaceae)

§	*stylosa*	More than 30 suppliers
	- 'Purpurea'	CElw ELan MNrw MRav NBrk NCat NChi SChu WByw WFar WGwy WHal

PHYGELIUS ✿ (Scrophulariaceae)

	aequalis	CBlo CBot CFee CGle CKno CSev LFis LRHS MNrw MWgw SChu SDix SMac WCFE WPer WSHC WSan WWat WWhi
	- *albus*	See *P. aequalis* 'Yellow Trumpet'
	- 'Apricot Trumpet'	GKir
	- 'Aureus'	See *P. aequalis* 'Yellow Trumpet'
	- Cedric Morris form	CKno
	- 'Cream Trumpet'	See *P. aequalis* 'Yellow Trumpet'
	- 'Indian Chief'	See *P.* x *rectus* 'African Queen'
*	- 'Pink Trumpet'	CDoC CLTr EFou GCal LRHS NFor SCoo SLon SMac SMrm SOkh WRha
	- Sensation = 'Sani Pass'[PBR]	CKno CSpe ECtt EPla GBri LRHS MAsh SBla SCoo SPer WHil
§	- 'Yellow Trumpet' ♀	More than 30 suppliers
¶	'Bridgetown Beauty'	CKno
§	*capensis* ♀	More than 30 suppliers
	- x *aequalis*	See *P.* x *rectus*
	- 'Caborn Flame' (v)	EBee
¶	- CD&R	EWes
	- *coccineus*	See *P. capensis*
	- 'Janet's Jewel' (v)	CKno
	- orange	CKno EGar LHop
	- pink	Last listed 1999
	- *roseus*	CTrw
	- S&SH 50	SMac
	'Golden Gate'	See *P. aequalis* 'Yellow Trumpet'
¶	Logan form	EBee
§	x *rectus*	EPla SYvo
§	- 'African Queen' ♀	More than 30 suppliers
	- 'Devil's Tears' ♀	More than 30 suppliers
	- 'Moonraker'	CChe CDoC CKno CLTr ECtt ELan EMil ESis EWTr GMac GOrc LFis LRHS MAsh MBNS MBro MHer MRav NFai NLar SMac SMad SPlb SRms SUsu WBea WHoo WPGP WWat
	- 'Pink Elf'	CKno ELan ERav ESis GOrc SLon SMac
	- 'Salmon Leap' ♀	CDoC CKno CM&M ELan EOrc GChr GKir LAst LHil LHop LRHS MAsh MBNS MBel MBri NFai SHFr SLim SMac WFar WHal WHil WOve WPer WWeb WWol
	- 'Sunshine'	CKno COtt LRHS MAsh WGwG WWeb WWol
§	- 'Winchester Fanfare'	More than 30 suppliers
	- 'Winton Fanfare'	See *P.* x *rectus* 'Winchester Fanfare'
	'Trewidden Pink'	CBrm CCHP CChe CElw CKno CM&M CPar EMan EPri EWTr LFis LHop MAvo MBro MHer MMil NChi NCiC NFai NFla SHFr SMac SSvw WGwG WHal WHoo WPGP WRus WSan WWat

PHYLA (Verbenaceae)

§	*canescens*	WCru WHal
§	*nodiflora*	CFri CNic ECha EEls GKir NWCA SEND SIng WPer
	- 'Alba'	CNic NFla

PHYLICA (Rhamnaceae)

	arborea 'Superba'	CB&S CPLG
	ericoides	CPLG

x PHYLLIOPSIS (Ericaceae)

	'Coppelia' ♀	EPot GCrs GGGa MAsh MDun NHar NHol SReu SSta WAbe WPat WPyg
	hillieri 'Askival'	GCrs GGGa WAbe
	- 'Pinocchio'	CMHG EPot GCrs GGGa GTou LRHS MAsh MDun NHar NHol WAbe WPat WPyg
	'Hobgoblin'	EPot NHol SReu WPat
	'Mermaid'	GGGa SReu SSta WAbe
	'Puck'	WAbe
	'Sprite'	GCrs NHol SReu SSta WAbe WPat
	'Sugar Plum'	CWSG MDun SBrw WAbe

PHYLLITIS See ASPLENIUM

PHYLLOCLADUS (Phyllocladaceae)

¶	*trichomanoides* var. *alpinus*	CDoC

PHYLLODOCE (Ericaceae)

	aleutica	EPot GChr GCrs GGGa GKir MBar NDlv NHar WAbe

¶ - x *caerulea*	GCrs
§ - subsp. *glanduliflora*	EPot GDra NHol
§ - - 'Flora Slack'	CMHG GGGa
- - white	See *P. aleutica* subsp. *glanduliflora* 'Flora Slack'
x *alpina*	GDra
breweri	GGGa GKir
caerulea ♀	GDra GGGa GKir NDlv NHar WAbe
- *japonica*	See *P. nipponica*
¶ - 'Viking'	GCrs
empetriformis	GChr GDra GGGa MBar MBri NHar NSla SRms WAbe
glanduliflora	See *P. aleutica* subsp. *glanduliflora*
x *intermedia*	GDra
- 'Drummondii'	CMHG GKir
- 'Fred Stoker'	CMHG
§ *nipponica* ♀	GCrs WAbe
- var. *oblongo-ovata*	GKir WAbe
tsugifolia	GCrs

PHYLLOSTACHYS ✿ (Poaceae - Bambusoideae)

angusta	CFil EPla SDry WJun
arcana	EPla ISta SDry WJun
- 'Luteosulcata'	EPla GKir SDry WJun WNor
§ *atrovaginata*	EPla SDry WJun
aurea ♀	More than 30 suppliers
- 'Albovariegata'	EFul EPla SDry
- 'Flavescens Inversa'	EPla ERod ISta SDry WJun
- 'Holochrysa'	EFul EPla ERod ISta SDry WJun
- 'Koi'	EPla ERod MMoz NMoo SDry
aureocaulis	See *P. vivax* 'Aureocaulis' , *P. aureosulcata* 'Aureocaulis'
aureosulcata	EBee EFul EPfP EPla ERod ISta LBlo LRHS MMoz NDov SDry WJun
- f. *alata*	EPla SDry
¶ - 'Argus'	EPla
§ - 'Aureocaulis'	CDoC CFil EFul EPVP EPfP EPla GKir ISta LJus LPan MMoz MNes MWst NMoo SDry SPla WJun WMul WNor WPGP
- 'Harbin'	EPla SDry
¶ - 'Harbin Inversa'	EPla ERod
- 'Lama Temple'	EPla
- 'Spectabilis'	CDDB CDoC CFil EBee EFul ELan EOas EPVP EPfP EPla ISta LJus LNet LPal LPan LRHS MBrN MCCP MMoz MWhi MWht SArc SDry WJun WMul WNor WPGP
bambusoides	CB&S CDDB EPla ISta SDix SDry WJun
§ - 'Allgold'	CFil EPla ERod GKir GOrc LJus NMoo SDry WJun
- 'Castillonis' ♀	CAbb CB&S CDDB CFil EFul EPla ERod ISta LEdu LJus LNet MMoz NDov NMoo SDix SDry WJun WPGP
- 'Castillonis Inversa'	CFil EPla ERod LJus SDry WJun WPGP
- Holochrysa	See *P. bambusoides* 'Allgold'
- 'Katashibo'	EPla
- 'Kawadana'	EPla SDry
- 'Marliacea'	EPla WJun
- f. *subvariegata*	CFil EPla SDry WPGP
- 'Sulphurea'	See *P. bambusoides* 'Allgold'
- 'Tanakae'	CDDB LJus SDry
bissetii	CDDB CDoC CFil EBee EFul EOas EPfP EPla ERod ISta LJus LPal LPan MBrN MCCP MMoz MWgw MWht NDov SDry SPla WJun

	WNor WPGP
¶ *circumpilis*	EPla
congesta hort.	See *P. atrovaginata*
decora	EPla ISta LJus MWht NMoo SDry WJun
dulcis	EPVP EPfP EPla ERod LEdu LJus LPJP WJun
§ *edulis*	CAbb CGre EFul EHoe EPla ISta SDry WJun
- 'Bicolor'	SDry
§ - var. *heterocycla*	SDry
- f. *pubescens*	See *P. edulis*
- *subconvexa*	See *P. viridiglaucescens*
flexuosa	CFil CHEx EFul EPla ISta LNet MDun SCob SDry WJun WPGP
glauca	CAbb EBee EPla ERod
- 'Yunzhu'	EPla LJus SDry WJun
§ *heteroclada*	SDry WJun
- 'Solid Stem' misapplied	See *P. heteroclada* 'Straight Stem'
§ - 'Straight Stem'	EPla SDry
heterocycla	See *P. edulis* var. *heterocycla*
- f. *pubescens*	See *P. edulis*
humilis	EBee EPla ERod LPan MCCP MMoz SDry WJun
iridescens	EPla SDry WJun
linearis	EBee
lithophila	Last listed 1999
lofushanensis	CFil EPla WPGP
makinoi	EPla WJun
mannii	EPla SDry WJun
meyeri	EPla ISta SDry WJun
nidularia	EBee EPla ISta LJus SDry WJun
- smooth sheath	EPla
¶ *nigella*	EPla
nigra ♀	More than 30 suppliers
- 'Boryana'	CFil EBee EFul EPla ISta LJus NDov SArc SDix SDry WJun WPGP
- 'Fulva'	EPla
- 'Hale'	EPla
- var. *henonis* ♀	EFul EPla ERod ISta LJus MWht SDry WJun
- 'Megurochiku'	EPla SDry WJun
- f. *nigra*	EPla
- f. *punctata*	CFil EPVP EPfP EPla ISta LJus MWht SDry WJun WPGP
- 'Tosaensis'	EPla
¶ - 'Wisley'	EPla
nuda	CDDB EPla ISta SDry WJun
- f. *localis*	MWht SDry
parvifolia	EPla ERod WJun
platyglossa	CFil WPGP
praecox	EPla WJun
propinqua	CDDB CDoC EOas EPla ISta LJus MCCP MMoz SArc WJun WMul
- 'Bicolor'	EPla WJun
- 'Li Yu Gai'	CFil EPla WPGP
¶ *pubescens* 'Mazel'	NMoo
purpurata	See *P. heteroclada*
rubicunda	CFil EPla WJun
rubromarginata	EPla SDry WJun
stimulosa	EPla LJus WJun
sulphurea	See *P. bambusoides* 'Allgold'
- 'Houzeau'	EPla ERod SDry
- 'Robert Young'	EPla SDry
- 'Sulphurea'	See *P. bambusoides* 'Allgold'
§ - var. *viridis*	CDDB EPla ERod GKir ISta LPal LPan NMoo SDry
- - 'Mitis'	See *P. sulphurea* var. *viridis*
violascens	CB&S CFil EFul EPla ISta LJus SDry WJun WPGP
virella	CFil EPla WPGP

§ *viridiglaucescens* ♀ CB&S CDDB CFil CHEx EBee EFul
EGln ELan EPfP EPla GKir ISta
LJus LPan MBrN MMoz MWht
SArc SCob SDry SEND WCot
WJun
viridis See *P. sulphurea* var. *viridis*
vivax EFul EPla ERod GOrc ISta
LJus MMoz SDry WJun WMul
WNor
§ - 'Aureocaulis' CAbb CDDB CDoC CFil EFul
EOas EPVP EPfP EPla ERod ISta
LJus LPJP LRHS MMoz MWht
SDry WJun WMul WNor WPGP
- 'Huanvenzhu' EPla ISta WJun
¶ - 'Katrin' CAbb

x PHYLLOTHAMNUS (Ericaceae)
erectus GCrs GGGa NHar NHol SReu
WAbe WPat WPyg

PHYMATOSORUS (Polypodiaceae)
§ *diversifolius* CFil WRic

PHYMOSIA (Malvaceae)
§ *umbellata* CBot CGre LCns LRHS SOWG

PHYODINA See CALLISIA

PHYSALIS (Solanaceae)
alkekengi ♀ ERav EWTr GKir MLan
- var. *franchetii* CArn CB&S COIW EBee ELan
ENot GAbr GChr GLil LRHS MBri
MCAu MHer NBir NBro NFai NFla
NMir SAga SEas SHel SLon SMad
SPer SRPl SRms WFar WOve WPer
WWin
- - dwarf NCut SIng WHil
- - 'Gigantea' ECGP GBuc NFor
- - 'Variegata' CRDP EBee EMan EPla ERav EWes
IBlr MTed NPro
edulis (F) EWll LPVe SRCN
peruviana (F) EOHP
pubescens (F) Last listed 1997

PHYSARIA (Brassicaceae)
alpina NWCA
didymocarpa MDCh

PHYSOCARPUS (Rosaceae)
opulifolius MSal WUnu
- 'Dart's Gold' ♀ More than 30 suppliers
- 'Diabolo'ᴾᴮᴿ More than 30 suppliers
- var. *intermedius* EPla
§ - 'Luteus' CBot CDoC CMHG CPle EBee
EPfP ESis GEil GKir IMGH ISea
MBar MGos MRav MWhi NFor
SPer SRms WBod WDin WFar
WMoo
ribesifolius 'Aureus' See *P. opulifolius* 'Luteus'

PHYSOCHLAINA (Solanaceae)
orientalis CRDP EBee EMan MSal NChi

PHYSOPLEXIS (Campanulaceae)
§ *comosa* ♀ EPot LRHS MBro WHoo WPyg

PHYSOSTEGIA (Lamiaceae)
angustifolia CElw CSam EBee
§ *virginiana* CTri EBee EWTr GBar GCHN
GKir GMaP LAst MBNS MHew
SRms SWat SYvo WByw WFar
WRHF

- 'Alba' CBot CGle ECGN EPfP GBar GBri
GMaP LNor LRHS MSte MTis NLar
NOrc SHel SPlb SUsu WEas WRHF
WRha
§ - 'Crown of Snow' CFir CMdw EBee ECoo ECtt EWTr
GKir LPVe LRHS MBNS MCLN
MHer MMal MSCN NArg NCiC
NMir STes WHil WPer WRos
- dwarf Last listed 1998
- 'Galadriel' Last listed 1998
- 'Grandiflora' CFir SIde WLRN
- 'Grandiflora Rose' NArg SWal
- pale pink EFou SUsu SWat
- 'Red Beauty' CFir LRHS SMrm SPla WPyg WWin
- 'Rosea' CB&S CBot CHar ECGN GKir
LNor MBel SRPl STes WOve WPer
- Schneekrone See *P. virginiana* 'Crown of
Snow'
- 'Snow Queen' See *P. virginiana* 'Summer Snow'
- subsp. *speciosa* EMon
§ - - 'Bouquet Rose' EBee ECha EMan EMar ENot EOld
LFis LLWP LRHS MBri MCAu MFir
MRav MSte NCat NFla NMir NPri
SChu SPer SSea WElm WFar WPyg
WRos WRus
- - Rose Bouquet See *P. virginiana* subsp. *speciosa*
'Bouquet Rose'
§ - - 'Variegata' CB&S CGle CRDP EBee ECha
EFou EGra EHoe ELan EMan
EWTr GKir LFis LHop LRHS MBel
MBri MHer MRav NOak SAga
SOkh SRms WEas WFar WPer
WWhi WWin
§ - 'Summer Snow' ♀ CB&S EBee ECha EFou ELan ENot
LAst LHop LRHS MBel MBri
MCAu MFir MWat NFla NHol SPer
SRms WBea WFar WHoo WOve
WRus WWin
- 'Summer Spire' ECha ELan EMan EWTr MSte
NHol SPer WBea WFar
- 'Van Wassenhove' EBee EMon
- 'Vivid' ♀ CGle CMGP CRDP EBee ECha
EFou ELan EMan EMon LRHS
MBro MCLN MMal MRav MWat
NHol NOak SAga SDix SMac SPer
SPlb SRms WCot WHoo WPyg
WWin

PHYTEUMA (Campanulaceae)
balbisii See *P. cordatum*
betonicifolium Last listed 1998
charmelii CPea
comosum See *Physoplexis comosa*
§ *cordatum* SSca
globulariifolium Last listed 1997
halleri See *P. ovatum*
hemisphaericum MHer WPat WRHF
humile EDAr
japonicum Last listed 1997
nigrum CElw GCal LBee LRHS MNrw
NBid SSca WMoo WPyg
orbiculare EBee ECGN WPyg
§ *ovatum* Last listed 1999
scheuchzeri CNic CPea CRDP EBee ECha
EMan EWTr GTou LFis MBro
NOrc NPri SBla SRms SRot SSca
WMoo WWin
sieberi CElw GDra NBir
spicatum CRDP NBro WWye
- subsp. *coeruleum* GBin
tenerum CKin
zahlbruckneri Last listed 1999

PHYTOLACCA (Phytolaccaceae)

acinosa	CArn EBee EOas IBlr MHew MSal NLar SWat WHer
§ *americana*	CArn CHEx CSev EBee ECha ELan ELau EMar EOas GKir GPoy IBlr LRHS MBNS MChe MHer MSal NLar SEND SIde SPer SRms SWat WByw WEas WFar WHer WJek WPer WWye
¶ - B&SWJ 1000	WCru
clavigera	See *P. polyandra*
decandra	See *P. americana*
dioica	CPLG
esculenta	CHid CPLG EBee GBin NLar
§ *polyandra*	EBee ECGP ECha GBin GBuc GCHN NBid NBro NHex SRms WFar WWye
tibetica	GPoy MSal

PICEA ✿ (Pinaceae)

§ *abies*	CDul CTri EHul ENot GChr GKir LBuc LCon LRHS MBar MBri MGos NBee NWea WDin WMou
- 'Acrocona'	CDoC ECho EHul EOrn GKir LCon LRHS MAsh MBar MBri MGos
- 'Archer'	CKen
- 'Argenteospica' (v)	LCon MAsh NHol
- 'Aurea'	ECho EOrn IMGH LLin
- 'Aurea Magnifica'	Last listed 1999
- 'Capitata'	CBlo CKen GAri MBar
- 'Cinderella'	MAsh
- 'Clanbrassiliana'	CBlo CDoC CKen IMGH LCon MAsh MBar
¶ - Columnaris Group	GAri
¶ - Compacta Group	LBee LRHS
I - 'Congesta'	CKen
- 'Crippsii'	CKen
I - 'Cruenta'	CKen
- 'Cupressina'	CKen
- 'Diffusa'	CBlo CKen LCon MBar
- 'Elegans'	MBar
- 'Ellwangeriana'	LCon
- 'Excelsa'	See *P. abies*
- 'Fahndrich'	CKen
- 'Finedonensis'	LCon
- 'Formanek'	CKen LCon LLin
- 'Four Winds'	CAbP CKen
- 'Frohburg'	CDoC COtt GAri GKir LCon LRHS MBar MBri MGos
- 'Globosa'	CBlo MBar WStl
- 'Globosa Nana'	MGos
- 'Gregoryana'	CKen CMac IMGH LCon MBar NDlv WAbe
- 'Humilis'	LCon
- 'Hystrix'	LCon NLar
- 'Inversa'	EHul EOrn GAri GKir IOrc LCon LLin LPan MBar MGos
- 'J.W. Daisy's White'	See *P. glauca* 'J.W. Daisy's White'
- 'Little Gem' ♀	CBlo CDoC CKen CMac CNic EBrP EBre EHul EOrn GKir IMGH LBCl LBSe LBee LBre LCon LLin LRHS MAsh MBBe MBar MBri MGos NBee SAga SBre SLim SPer WAbe
- 'Mariae Orffiae'	CKen
- 'Maxwellii'	EHul MBar MGos
- 'Merkii'	GAri
- 'Nana'	MBar
- 'Nana Compacta'	CKen EHul IMGH LBee LLin MBar MOne

- 'Nidiformis' ♀	CDoC CKen CMac EBrP EBre EHul ENot EOrn GKir IOrc LBCl LBSe LBre LCon LLin LPan LRHS MBBe MBar MBri MGos NWea SAga SBre SLim SRms WDin WGwG WStl
- 'Norrkoping'	CKen
- 'Ohlendorffii'	CKen EHul LCon LPan MAsh MBar WStl
- 'Pachyphylla'	CKen
- 'Pendula Major'	Last listed 1998
- 'Procumbens'	MBar
- 'Pseudomaxwellii'	CBlo LCon
- 'Pumila'	EOrn
- 'Pumila Nigra'	CMac EHul LCon LLin MBar MGos NHar SLim
- 'Pusch'	CKen
- 'Pygmaea'	CKen MAsh MBar MGos
- 'Reflexa'	EHul IMGH LCon LLin MAsh
- 'Repens'	LRHS MBar MGos NBee
- 'Rydal'	LCon
- 'Saint James'	CKen
- 'Tabuliformis'	MBar
- 'Tufty'	EOrn
- 'Walter Bron'	CKen
- 'Waugh'	MBar
- Will's Dwarf	See *P. abies* 'Wills Zwerg'
§ - 'Wills Zwerg'	LCon LPan LRHS MAsh
¶ *alcoquiana*	CDoC
I - 'Prostrata'	LCon MBar
asperata	Last listed 1999
brachytyla	Last listed 1999
breweriana ♀	More than 30 suppliers
* - 'Frühlingsgold'	Last listed 1998
engelmannii	CBlo MBar
¶ - subsp. *engelmannii*	EHul LCon LPan MBar NWea
glauca	CDoC CKen EOrn GKir LCon LLin LPan LRHS SCoo SLim SSmi WGor WWeb
- 'Alberta Blue'	CBlo CDoC CNic EBrP EBre EHul EOrn EPot GChr GKir IMGH LBCl LBSe LBee LBre LCon LLin MAsh MBBe MBar MBri MGos NBee NDlv SAga SBre SLim SSmi WFar
- var. *albertiana* 'Alberta Globe' ♀	
- - 'Conica' ♀	More than 30 suppliers
- - 'Gnome'	CKen
- - 'Laurin'	CDoC CKen EBrP EBre EOrn GPin LBCl LBSe LBee LBre LCon LRHS MAsh MBBe MBar MBri SBre SSmi SSta
- - 'Tiny'	CKen EHul EOrn EPot LCon LLin MBar
¶ - 'Arneson's Blue Variegated'	CKen LCon MBri SLim
- 'Blue Planet'	CKen
- 'Coerulea'	LCon MBar
¶ - 'Cy's Wonder'	CKen
- 'Densata'	Last listed 1998
- 'Echiniformis' ♀	CKen EHul EPot GAri GKir LBee LCon LRHS MBar MBri
- 'Goldilocks'	CKen
§ - 'J.W. Daisy's White'	CDoC CKen EOrn GKir LCon LLin LRHS MAsh MGos NPro SCoo SLim SMur SPer SPla WGor EHul EOrn EPot LCon MBar MGos
- 'Lilliput'	CKen
- 'Nana'	CKen
- 'Piccolo'	CKen GKir LRHS MBri SLim
- 'Rainbow's End' (v)	CKen
- 'Sander's Blue'	CKen EOrn MBri
- 'Zucherhut'	LRHS MAsh MBar MBri

glebnii — LCon
- 'Sasanosei' — CKen
- 'Shimezusei' — CKen
jezoensis — GAri MGos
- subsp. *bondoensis* — WNor
kosteri 'Glauca' — See *P. pungens* 'Koster'
§ *koyamae* — CBlo
likiangensis — CMCN LCon
- var. *balfouriana* — See *P. likiangensis* var. *rubescens*
- var. *purpurea* — See *P. purpurea*
§ - var. *rubescens* — CDoC GKir LCon NHol WWes
mariana — GChr NWea
- 'Aureovariegata' — LCon
- 'Doumetii' — EOrn
- 'Ericoides' — GAri
- 'Fastigiata' — CKen EOrn
- 'Nana' ♀ — More than 30 suppliers
x *mariorika* — MBar
¶ *obovata* var. *coerulea* — GIBF
I - 'Glauca' — LCon
omorika ♀ — CB&S CDoC CDul CMCN ENot
GChr GKir LBuc LCon LNet MBar
MGos NBee NWea SPer WCFE
WDin WMou WPGP WWat
¶ - 'Frohnleiten' — CKen
- 'Karel' — CKen
- 'Nana' ♀ — CMac GAri LBee LCon LNet LPan
LRHS MBar NBee SLim
- 'Pendula' ♀ — CBlo CDoC GKir IOrc LCon LPan
LRHS MBar SSta
- 'Pimoko' — CKen GKir LCon LRHS MAsh
- 'Schneverdingen' — CKen
- 'Treblitsch' — CDoC CKen
orientalis ♀ — CLnd GChr LCon LPan NWea
WTro
§ - 'Aurea' (v) ♀ — CMac EBrP EBre EHul ELan GKir
IOrc LBCl LBSe LBre LCon LLin
LPan LRHS MBBe MBar MBri
NHol SBre SLim SMad
- 'Aureospicata' — CDoC CTho ECho MAsh
- 'Bergman's Gem' — CKen
- 'Early Gold' (v) — LPan
- 'Gowdy' — MBar
- 'Kenwith' — CKen
¶ - Pendula Group — MGos
- 'Professor Langer' — CKen
- 'Reynolds' — CKen
- 'Skylands' — CBlo CDoC CKen LCon MAsh
MGos SLim
* - 'Wittbold Compact' — LBee
pungens — GChr MBar NWea WDin WNor
- 'Blaukissen' — CKen
- 'Corbet' — Last listed 1999
- 'Drayer' — Last listed 1997
- 'Erich Frahm' — CDoC EBrP EBre GAri GKir LBCl
LBSe LBre LCon LNet LPan LRHS
MAsh MBBe MBar MBri MGos
SBre SCoo SLim WWeb
- 'Fat Albert' — EBrP EBre GKir LBCl LBSe LBre
LNet LPan MBBe MBri SBre
¶ - Glauca Group — EHul EWTr GChr LBee MBar
NBee NWea WDin WMou WStI
- 'Glauca Globosa' — See *P. pungens* 'Globosa'
- 'Glauca Procumbens' — LNet
§ - 'Glauca Prostrata' — EHul GKir MBar SLim
- 'Globe' — CKen LCon
I - 'Globosa' ♀ — CB&S CDoC CKen EBrP EBre
EHul ELan EOrn IOrc LBCl LBSe
LBee LBre LCon LLin LPan MAsh
MBBe MBar MBri MGos MWat
NBee NHol SBre SLim SRms WPyg
WStI

I - 'Globosa Viridis' — EHul
- 'Gloria' — CKen LCon
- 'Hoopsii' ♀ — More than 30 suppliers
- 'Hoto' — CDoC EHul EOrn IOrc LCon
MBar WPyg WWeb
- 'Hunnewelliana' — EOrn
- 'Iseli Fastigiate' — CDoC COtt EBrP EBre GKir LBCl
LBSe LBre LCon LNet MAsh MBBe
SBre
§ - 'Koster' ♀ — CDoC CMac EHul EOrn GKir IOrc
LCon LLin LNet LPan MAsh MBar
MGos NBee NWea SLim SMad
SPer SRms WDin WStI
- 'Koster Fastigiata' — LPan
- 'Koster Prostrate' — Last listed 1999
- 'Lucky Strike' — CKen LCon LLin MAsh MGos
- 'Maigold' (v) — CKen
- 'Moerheimii' — EHul EOrn LCon LNet MBar
MGos
- 'Montgomery' — CBlo CKen LCon MBar NHol
- 'Mrs Cesarini' — CKen
- 'Procumbens' ♀ — CKen
- 'Prostrata' — See *P. pungens* 'Glauca Prostrata'
- 'Saint Mary's Broom' — CKen
- 'Schovenhorst' — EHul EOrn LPan
- 'Thomsen' — CKen EHul EOrn GKir LCon
MAsh
- 'Thuem' — EHul EOrn LCon MGos
- 'Wendy' — CKen
§ *purpurea* ♀ — GKir LCon
rubens — GAri LCon NWea
schrenkiana — LCon
sitchensis — CDul GChr GKir LBuc LCon
NWea WMou
- 'Nana' — CDoC NHol
- 'Papoose' — See *P. sitchensis* 'Tenas'
- 'Silberzwerg' — CKen
- 'Strypemonde' — CKen
§ - 'Tenas' — CDoC GKir LCon NHol
smithiana ♀ — GAri LCon SBir SLim WFro
¶ sp. from Japan — WHCr
spinulosa — WWat

PICRASMA (Simaroubaceae)
ailanthoides — See *P. quassioides*
§ *quassioides* — CMCN WPGP

PICRIS (Asteraceae)
echioides — CKin EWFC WHer

PICRORHIZA (Scrophulariaceae)
kurrooa — GPoy

PIERIS ✿ (Ericaceae)
'Bert Chandler' — CHig ELan GKir LRHS SPer SSpi
'Flaming Silver' (v) ♀ — More than 30 suppliers
'Flamingo' — CHig CTrh CTrw GKir LRHS
MAsh MBar MGos NDlv NHol
WAbe WBod WFar WPat WPyg
floribunda — IOrc
'Forest Flame' ♀ — More than 30 suppliers
formosa — CHig
- B&SWJ 2257 — WCru
- var. *forrestii* — CCHP CDoC CTre CTrw ISea
NWea SBrw
- - 'Fota Pink' — WHar
- - 'Jermyns' ♀ — CHig IOrc
- - 'Wakehurst' ♀ — CB&S CHig CLan CTrG EPfP GGar
IOrc LHyd LRHS MAsh MRav
NWea SBrw SRPl SReu SSta WBod
WFar WWal
§ Havila® = 'Mouwsvila' (v) — CDoC GOrc IOrc MAsh MBri

	MGos NHol SBrw WLRN
japonica	CB&S CHEx CHig CLan CTrw
	MBar MGos NWea SArc SReu
	WDin
- 'Balls of Fire'	CTrh
- 'Bisbee Dwarf'	MBar MBro NHar NHol NLAp
	SReu WPat WPyg
- 'Blush' ♀	CHig GKir LRHS MAsh MBri NHol
	SBod SEas WSHC
- 'Brookside Miniature'	NHol WPat
¶ - 'Buchanan's Dwarf'	SReu SSta
- 'Cavatine' ♀	CMHG GKir LRHS SBod
§ - 'Christmas Cheer'	CLan GKir IOrc MGos NHol SBrw
	WLRN
- 'Coleman'	Last listed 1998
- 'Compact Crimson'	Last listed 1999
- 'Compacta'	NHol WAbe
- 'Crispa'	CHig MDun
- 'Cupido'	CBlo CDoC EMil LRHS MAsh
	MBar MBri MGos WLRN
- 'Daisen'	CHig CLan CTrw
§ - 'Debutante' ♀	CDoC CHig ENot EPfP GKir LRHS
	MAsh MBri NHol SBrw SRPl SSpi
	WLRN WStI WWat
- 'Don'	See *P. japonica* 'Pygmaea'
- 'Dorothy Wyckoff'	CB&S CLan CMHG CTrG GKir
	LRHS MAsh MBri NDlv NHol
	SBrw SPer SSta WCwm
- 'Firecrest' ♀	CB&S CHig CMHG CTrG CTrh
	ENot IOrc MBri NDlv SBrw SSht
	SSpi WBod WPat
- 'Flaming Star'	ECot
- 'Geisha'	NHol WPat
- 'Glenroy Pink Plenty'	Last listed 1999
- 'Grayswood' ♀	CHig CMHG CSam EPfP GKir
	IOrc LRHS MBri NHol
- 'Little Heath' (v) ♀	More than 30 suppliers
- 'Little Heath Green' ♀	CChe CDoC CHig CMHG CTrG
	GAri GKir LHyd LRHS MAsh MBar
	MBri MGos NDlv SBrw SPer SSta
	WBrE WFar WOTO WPic WWat
	WWeb
- 'Minor'	MBar NHar NHol WPat WPyg
- 'Mountain Fire' ♀	More than 30 suppliers
- 'Pink Delight' ♀	CAbP CB&S CDoC CHig EBee
	GKir LRHS MBar MGos MRav
	SBrw SPer SRms WPat
- 'Prelude' ♀	CChe CTrG CWSG GCHN LRHS
	MAsh MBri MRav NHol WPat
- 'Purity' ♀	CB&S CBlo CDoC CHig CMHG
	EPfP GKir IOrc LRHS MAsh MBar
	MGos MLan NHol SBrw SEas
	SMer SRPl SReu SSta WBod WDin
	WFar WLRN WStI
§ - 'Pygmaea'	CMHG EPla GDra MBro NHar
	NHol WPat WPyg
- red	CHig
- 'Red Mill'	CAbP CBlo CEnd CHig CMHG
	EPfP GKir LRHS MAsh NHol SBod
	SPer SSpi WFar WLRN WPat
- 'Robinswood'	WBcn
¶ - 'Rokujo's Dwarf'	SReu SSta
- 'Rosalinda'	WFar
- 'Rosea'	LHyd
- 'Rowallane'	IBlr
- 'Sarabande' ♀	CHig COtt GKir LRHS MAsh MBri
	MGos NHol SBrw WGwG WPat
	WPyg
- 'Scarlett O'Hara'	GKir MGos
- 'Select'	MGos
- 'Snowdrift'	GCHN LRHS MSta SSta
- 'Spring Candy'	MGos

- 'Spring Snow'	LRHS
- Taiwanensis Group	CGre CHig CMHG CTre CTrh
	EPfP GCHN GGar IOrc LHyd
	LRHS MBar MRav NHol NWea
	SRPl SRms SSta WFar WPat WWat
- 'Temple Bells'	CHig ENot SMer SPar
- 'Tickled Pink'	CHig NHol
- 'Tilford'	CDoC CHig LRHS MBri NHol SSta
	WPat
- 'Valley Fire'	CTrh
- 'Valley Rose'	CChe CHig COtt CSam CTrh
	ENot EPfP GCHN MAsh MBel
	MGos NBee SPer SSpi WGwG
	WStI
- 'Valley Valentine' ♀	CDoC CLan COtt CTrh ENot EPfP
	GKir LRHS MAsh MBri MGos
	NDlv NHol SBod SBrw SPer SReu
	SSta WAbe WBod WCwm WPat
	WStI WWeb
§ - 'Variegata' (Carrière)	CHig CMHG EPot IOrc LHyd
Bean	MBar MGos NBee NDlv NHol
	SLdr SPer SReu SSta WAbe
	WBod WDin WHar WPat WSHC
	WWat
- 'Variegata' hort.	See *P. japonica* 'White Rim'
- 'Wada's Pink'	See *P. japonica* 'Christmas Cheer'
- 'White Cascade'	CHig SBrw
- 'White Pearl' ♀	CAbP MAsh MBri MGos NBee
	SBrw SPer
§ - 'White Rim' (v) ♀	CB&S CDoC GKir LRHS MAsh
	MGos SBrw SLim WFar
- 'Whitecaps'	Last listed 1999
- 'William Buchanan'	GCrs MBar MBro NHar NHol
	WPat WPyg
- var. *yakushimensis*	CBlo WBod WSHC
¶ *koidzumiana*	SSta
'Mouwsvila'	See *P. Havila* = 'Mouwsvila'
nana	GAri MBar NHar
- 'Redshank'	SOkd

PILEA (Urticaceae)

* 'Anette'	MBri
cadierei ♀	CHal MBri
- 'Minima' ♀	Last listed 1995
involucrata	Last listed 1992
'Moon Valley' ♀	
- 'Norfolk' ♀	CHal
§ *microphylla*	CHal EBak
muscosa	See *P. microphylla*
nummulariifolia	CHal
peperomioides ♀	CHal CSev
repens	MBri

PILEOSTEGIA (Hydrangeaceae)

viburnoides ♀	More than 30 suppliers
- B&SWJ 3565	WCru

PILOSELLA (Asteraceae)

§ *aurantiaca*	CLTr CMCo CNic ElAn EWFC
	LNor MBNS MFir MHer MHew
	MMal NArg NBid NLAp NOrc
	NSti SBea SIde SIng SSmi WCer
	WElm WHer WOak WWye
§ - subsp. *carpathicola*	GGar
§ *officinarum*	CKin EWFC MGas NRya WGwy
§ x *stoloniflora*	Last listed 1999

PILULARIA (Marsileaceae)

globulifera	CNat

PIMELEA (Thymelaeaceae)

arenaria	ECou

coarctata	See *P. prostrata*
drupacea	ECou
filiformis	ECou
physodes	Last listed 1998
§ *prostrata*	CLyd CTri ECou EPot GCrs GNor IMGH MBar NHar NHol NWoo SRot WAbe WPat WPer
- f. *parvifolia*	ECou
- Tennyson's form	SBla
sericeovillosa	Last listed 1997
suteri	Last listed 1997

PIMPINELLA (Apiaceae)

anisum	CArn MSal SIde WHer WSel
bicknellii	WCot
brachycarpa B&SWJ 863	Last listed 1998
flabaultii	CElw EBee
major 'Rosea'	CRDP EBee EMan EMon LHop SMrm WCot WFar WHal WPGP
saxifraga	CAgr EBee EWFC

PINANGA (Arecaceae)

¶ *coronata*	CBrP

PINELLIA ✿ (Araceae)

cordata	CRDP EPot WCot WCru
pedatisecta	CRDP CRow EBee MRav SSoC WCot WCru
pinnatisecta	See *P. tripartita*
ternata	CRDP CRow CStu EPar EPot MSal WCru WWye
- B&SWJ 3532	WCru
§ *tripartita*	CStu EBee WCru
- B&SWJ 1102	WCru
- 'Purple Face' B&SWJ 4850	WCru

PINGUICULA ✿ (Lentibulariaceae)

acuminata	WMEx
agnata	WMEx
cyclosecta	SHmp
eblersiae	EFEx WMEx
emarginata	WMEx
esseriana	EFEx WMEx
¶ *gigantea*	SHmp
gracilis	WMEx
grandiflora	CRDP CSWC EAnd EFEx EPot GCrs LRHS NHar NMen NRya WAbe WHer WMEx WPGP
- subsp. *coenocantabrica* NS 307	NWCA
gypsicola	WMEx
hemiepiphytica	WMEx
¶ *heterophylla*	SHmp
'Kewensis'	WMEx
laueana	SHmp WMEx
longifolia subsp. *longifolia*	EFEx WPGP
macrophylla	SHmp WMEx
¶ *moctezumae*	SHmp
moranensis alba	Last listed 1998
- var. *caudata*	CSWC EFEx WMEx
- *flos-mulionis*	Last listed 1998
- 'Kirkbright'	Last listed 1998
- var. *mexicana*	WMEx
- *moreana*	EFEx
- *morelia*	Last listed 1997
- *superba*	EFEx
potosiensis	WMEx
primuliflora	EAnd WMEx
reticulata	WMEx
rotundifolia	SHmp WMEx

'Sethos'	WMEx
vulgaris	EFEx WMEx
'Weser'	WMEx
zecheri	WMEx

PINUS ✿ (Pinaceae)

	albicaulis	WNor
	- 'Flinck'	CKen
	- 'Nana'	See *P. albicaulis* 'Noble's Dwarf'
§	- 'Noble's Dwarf'	CKen
	aristata	CAbP CBlo CDoC CFil CMCN EBrP EBre EHul EOrn GChr GKir LBCl LBSe LBre LCon LLin MBBe MBar MGos NHol SBre SReu SSta STre WFro
	- 'Cecilia'	CKen
	- 'Sherwood Compact'	CKen
	armandii	CB&S CDul CGre CMCN CSWP LCon SFur
	- S&F 313	Last listed 1999
	- TW 415	Last listed 1997
	attenuata	STre
	austriaca	See *P. nigra* subsp. *nigra*
N	*ayacahuite*	GChr LCon
	banksiana	CDul CLnd CSam EHul LCon
	- 'Chippewa'	CKen
I	- 'Compacta'	CKen
	- 'H.J. Welch'	CKen
	- 'Manomet'	CKen
	- 'Neponset'	CKen LCon
	- 'Wisconsin'	CKen
	bungeana	CAbP CDoC CLnd EHul EPfP LCon LLin MBlu SFur SIng SLPl SMad WFro WNor
	- 'Diamant'	CKen
	canariensis ♀	EHul ISea
	cembra ♀	CDul EHul GChr GKir LCon LPan MBar NWea STre
	- 'Aurea'	See *P. cembra* 'Aureovariegata'
§	- 'Aureovariegata'	CKen LLin
	- 'Barnhourie'	CKen
	- 'Blue Mound'	CKen
	- 'Chalet'	CKen
	- 'Compacta Glauca'	CDoC LRHS MBri
¶	- 'Glauca Group'	GKir
*	- 'Griffithii'	WDin
	- 'Inverleith'	CKen
	- 'Jermyns'	CKen
	- 'King's Dwarf'	CKen
	- 'Nana'	See *P. pumila* 'Nana'
	- 'Roughills'	CKen
	- 'Stricta'	CKen
	- witches' broom	CKen
	contorta	CB&S CBlo CDoC GChr GKir Ilve LCon MBar MGos NWea STre WDin WMou
	- 'Asher'	CKen
	- 'Frisian Gold'	CKen
	- var. *latifolia*	CLnd WTro
	- 'Spaan's Dwarf'	CBlo CDoC CKen GKir LCon LLin MAsh MBar MBri MGos SLim
	coulteri ♀	CMCN LCon LLin WNor WPGP
	densiflora	CDul CMCN EHul ISea LCon LEdu SPla STre WFro WNor
	- 'Alice Verkade'	CBlo CDoC EHul GKir LBee LCon LLin LNet LRHS MAsh MBri SLim
	- 'Aurea'	EHul LCon MBar MGos SLim
	- 'Jane Kluis'	CDoC CKen COtt EHul GKir LBee LCon LNet LRHS MAsh MBri
	- 'Oculus-draconis' (v)	GKir MAsh MBar MBri MGos SLim
	- 'Pendula'	CDoC CKen GKir LLin MBri SLim
	- 'Pygmy'	CDoC

* - 'Pyramidalis'	ECho
- 'Umbraculifera'	CDoC GKir IMGH IOrc LCon LLin
	LPan LRHS MAsh MBar MBri
	MGos MOne SLim SSta
§ *devoniana*	CGre
edulis	LCon
flexilis	CBlo CDul LCon
- 'Firmament'	CDoC LCon LLin MAsh
- 'Glenmore Dwarf'	CKen
- 'Nana'	CKen
- 'Pendula'	LLin
- WB No. 1	CKen
- WB No. 2	CKen
gerardiana	Last listed 1999
greggii	Last listed 1998
griffithii	See *P. wallichiana*
halepensis	CLnd
hartwegii	Last listed 1999
§ *heldreichii* ♀	CDul CMac LCon LNet MBar
	SCoo WNor
- 'Aureospicata'	LCon LLin MBar
- 'Groen'	CKen
- var. *leucodermis*	See *P. heldreichii*
- - 'Compact Gem'	CDoC CKen EBrP EBre GKir IOrc
	LBCl LBSe LBre LCon LLin LNet
	LPan MBBe MBar MBri MGos SBre
	SCoo SLim SSta WPyg
- 'Malink'	CKen
- 'Pygmy'	CKen
- 'Satellit'	CDoC EHul EOrn GKir IOrc LBee
	LLin LPan LRHS MAsh MGos SLim
- 'Schmidtii'	See *P. heldreichii* 'Smidtii'
§ - 'Smidtii' ♀	CDoC CKen LCon LLin MAsh
	MBar MBri SLim
- 'Zwerg Schneverdingen'	CKen
jeffreyi ♀	CAgr CDul CLnd CMCN LCon
	MBar NWea WFro
- 'Joppi'	CKen
koraiensis	LCon NWea WNor
- 'Bergman'	CKen
- 'Dragon Eye'	CKen
- 'Jack Corbit'	CKen
- 'Shibamichi' (v)	CKen
- 'Silver Lining'	MAsh
- 'Silveray'	CDoC GKir MBri
- 'Silvergrey'	CKen
- 'Winton'	CKen
lambertiana	LCon
leucodermis	See *P. heldreichii*
longaeva	CLnd EPfP
magnifica	See *P. devoniana*
massoniana	WNor
monophylla	GChr LLin
N *montezumae*	CGre CLnd CMCN IOrc ISea LLin
	SAPC SArc WNor
monticola	CLnd
- 'Pendula'	MBar
- 'Pygmy'	See *P. monticola* 'Raraflora'
§ - 'Raraflora'	CKen
- 'Skyline'	LPan MBar
- 'Windsor Dwarf'	CKen
mugo	CB&S CBlo CDul CTri EHul ENot
	LEdu MAsh MBar MGos NWea
	SRms WDin WFar WStI
* - 'Benjamin'	CKen
- 'Bisley Green'	LLin
- 'Brownie'	CKen
- 'Carsten'	CKen LLin SLim
- 'Carsten's Wintergold'	See *P. mugo* 'Winter Gold'
I - 'Columnaris'	Last listed 1998
- 'Corley's Mat'	CKen EBrP EBre GKir LBCl
	LBSe LBre LLin MAsh MBBe SBre

	SLim WWeb
- 'Gnom'	CBlo CDoC CFee CKen CMac
	EHul EOrn GKir IMGH LCon LLin
	LPan LRHS MBar MBri MGos
	MOne NBee WDin WFar
- 'Hoersholm'	CKen
- 'Humpy'	CFee CKen EBrP EBre EOrn GAri
	GKir IMGH LBCl LBSe LBee LBre
	LCon LLin LRHS MAsh MBBe
	MBar MBri MGos MOne SBre
	SLim WAbe
- 'Jacobsen'	CKen
¶ - 'Janovsky'	CKen
- 'Kissen'	CBlo CKen LCon MAsh MGos
- 'Klosterkotter'	MGos
- 'Knapenburg'	NHol
- 'Kobold'	CBlo NHol
- 'Krauskopf'	CKen
- 'Laarheide'	GKir MAsh MBri
- 'Laurin'	CKen
- 'March'	CKen
- 'Mini Mops'	CKen
- 'Minikin'	CKen
- 'Mops' ♀	CBlo CDoC EBrP EBre EHul EPla
	GChr GKir LBCl LBSe LBee LBre
	LCon LLin LPan LRHS MAsh
	MBBe MBar MBri MGos NBee
	SBre SLim SPer SSta WDin WPyg
- 'Mops Midget'	LBee LLin MAsh MBri SLim
- var. *mughus*	See *P. mugo* subsp. *mugo*
§ - subsp. *mugo*	CMCN EOrn LPan MBar NWea
- 'Mumpitz'	CKen
- 'Ophir'	CDoC CKen EBrP EBre EHul
	EOrn EPla GKir IMGH IOrc LBCl
	LBSe LBee LBre LCon LLin LNet
	LRHS MAsh MBBe MBar MBri
	MGos SBre SLim SPer SSta WDin
- 'Pal Maleter' (v)	CDoC GKir LCon LLin MBri SLim
- 'Piggelmee'	CKen
- Pumilio Group ♀	CBlo CDoC CDul CMac EHul
	ENot EOrn IOrc LBee LCon LLin
	LPan MBar MBro MGos NBlu NFla
	NWea STre WNor
- var. *rostrata*	See *P. mugo* subsp. *uncinata*
¶ - 'Rushmore'	CKen
- 'Spaan'	CKen
- 'Sunshine' (v)	CKen SLim
§ - subsp. *uncinata*	NWea
- - 'Grüne Welle'	CKen
- - 'Paradekissen'	CKen
- 'White Tip'	CKen
§ - 'Winter Gold'	CKen EBrP EBre EHul EOrn EPfP
	GKir IOrc LBCl LBSe LBre LCon
	LLin LPan MAsh MBBe SBre SSta
- 'Winzig'	CKen
- 'Zundert'	CBlo CDoC CKen GKir LLin LNet
	LRHS MAsh MBar MBri MGos
- 'Zwergkugel'	CKen
muricata ♀	CAbP CDoC CDul CLnd GChr
	LCon MGos
nigra ♀	CB&S CBlo CDoC CDul ECrN
	LCon LNet LRHS MBar MGos
	WDin WMou
* - 'Asterix'	Last listed 1998
- var. *austriaca*	See *P. nigra* subsp. *nigra*
- 'Black Prince'	CBlo CDoC CKen EOrn GKir
	IMGH LBee LCon LLin LRHS
	MAsh MBri SCoo SLim WGor
N - 'Cebennensis Nana'	CKen
- var. *corsicana*	See *P. nigra* subsp. *laricio*
- 'Frank'	CKen
- 'Géant de Suisse'	Last listed 1997

- 'Hornibrookiana'	CKen LLin LPan
§ - subsp. *laricio* ♀	CDoC CDul CKen ENot GChr LBuc LCon MBar MGos NWea SMad WMou
- - 'Bobby McGregor'	CKen LLin SLim
- - 'Globosa Viridis'	GAri LLin NHol SLim
- - 'Goldfingers'	CKen LLin
§ - - 'Moseri' ♀	CKen GAri LCon LLin SLim SSta
- - 'Pygmaea'	CKen ECho
- - 'Spingarn'	CKen
- - 'Talland Bay'	CKen
- - 'Wurstle'	CKen
- subsp. *maritima*	See *P. nigra* subsp. *laricio*
- 'Molette'	Last listed 1998
- 'Nana'	CDoC LPan LRHS
§ - subsp. *nigra*	CDoC CLnd EWTr GChr LBuc LPan MGos NWea WStI
- - 'Bright Eyes'	CKen ECho EHul EOrn IMGH LBee LCon LLin LRHS MAsh
- - 'Helga'	CKen
- - 'Schovenhorst'	CKen
- - 'Strypemonde'	CKen
- - 'Yaffle Hill'	CKen
- 'Obelisk'	CKen
- subsp. *pallasiana*	LCon
* - *serotina*	Last listed 1998
- 'Uelzen'	CKen
palustris	LCon LLin MAsh
parviflora ♀	CMCN GAri LCon LPan NWea STre WDin WNor
- 'Adcock's Dwarf' ♀	CDoC CKen GKir LLin MBar MGos SLim
¶ - Aizu-goyo Group	CKen
- 'Al Fordham'	CKen
- 'Aoi'	CKen
- 'Ara-kawa'	CKen
¶ - Azuma-goyo Group	CKen
I - 'Baasch's Form'	CKen
- 'Bergman'	CBlo CDoC LCon MAsh MBar
- 'Blue Giant'	ECho
- 'Bonnie Bergman'	CKen LLin
- 'Brevifolia'	GAri LPan
- 'Dai-ho'	CKen
- 'Daisetsusan'	CKen
- 'Draijer's Dwarf'	GKir MBri
¶ - 'Fukai' (v)	CKen
- 'Fukiju'	CKen
¶ - Fukushima-goyo Group	CKen
¶ - 'Fuku-zu-mi'	LLin
- 'Fu-shiro'	CKen
¶ - Glauca Group	CDoC CMac EHul GAri GChr IOrc LCon LLin LPan MBar MBri MGos NFla
I - 'Glauca Nana'	CKen
- 'Gyok-kan'	CKen
- 'Gyok-ke-sen'	CKen
- 'Gyo-ko-haku'	CKen
- 'Gyokuei'	CKen
¶ - 'Gyokusen Sämling'	CKen
- 'Gyo-ku-sui'	CKen
- 'Hagaromo Seedling'	CKen
- 'Hakko'	CKen
- 'Hatchichi'	CKen
- 'Hatsumi'	Last listed 1998
- 'Ibo-can'	CKen
- 'Ichi-no-se'	CKen
- 'Iri-fune'	CKen
¶ - Ishizuchi-goyo Group	CKen
- 'Jyu-roko-ra-kan'	CKen
- 'Ka-ho'	CKen
- 'Kanzan'	CKen
- 'Kiyomatsu'	CKen
- 'Kobe'	CKen LLin
- 'Kokonde'	Last listed 1999
- 'Kokonoe'	CBlo CKen LCon
- 'Kokuho'	CKen
- 'Koraku'	CKen
- 'Kusu-dama'	CKen
- 'Meiko'	CKen
¶ - 'Michinoku'	CKen
- 'Myo-jo'	CKen
- Nasu-goyo Group	CKen
- 'Negishi'	CDoC CKen GAri LCon LLin LPan LRHS MAsh MBri
¶ - 'Ogon-janome'	CKen
- 'Ossorio Dwarf'	CKen
- var. *pentaphylla*	LPan
¶ - 'Richard Lee'	CKen
¶ - 'Ryo-ku-ho'	CKen
¶ - 'Ryu-ju'	CKen
¶ - 'San-bo'	CDoC CKen MBar
§ - 'Saphir'	CKen ECho LCon
- 'Seiryoden'	CKen
- 'Setsugekka'	CKen
¶ - 'Shika-shima'	CKen
¶ - Shiobara-goyo Group	CKen
- 'Shizukagoten'	CKen
¶ - 'Shu-re'	CKen
¶ - 'Tani-mano-uki'	CKen
- 'Tempelhof'	COtt CTho GAri GKir LNet LPan MBar SLim
¶ - 'Tenysu-kazu'	CKen
I - 'Zelkova'	LLin
- 'Zui-sho'	CKen
patula ♀	CAbb CB&S CDoC CDul CGre CLnd ECre LCon LLin LPan MBlu SAPC SArc SBir SCoo SLim WWat
peuce	MBar NWea STre WFro
- 'Arnold Dwarf'	CKen
pinaster ♀	CBlo CDoC CDul CLnd EHul GChr LCon
pinea ♀	CAgr CDoC CHEx CKen CMac EPfP GChr GVer IOrc LCon LEdu LLin LPan MGos SAPC SArc SEND WNor
- 'Queensway'	CKen
ponderosa ♀	CLnd ISea LCon LLin NWea
pseudostrobus	Last listed 1999
pumila	CAgr
- 'Buchanan'	CKen
- 'Draijer's Dwarf'	CDoC EOrn LLin SLim
§ - 'Glauca' ♀	CBlo CKen LCon LLin LNet LRHS MBar MBri
- 'Globe'	GKir LCon LLin LNet MAsh MBri
- 'Jeddeloh'	CKen
- 'Knightshayes'	CKen
§ - 'Nana'	SRms
- 'Säntis'	CKen MAsh
- 'Saphir'	See *P. parviflora* 'Saphir'
radiata ♀	CB&S CDoC CDul CHEx CTrC CTrw ENot GChr IOrc LCon LRHS NWea SAPC SArc STre WDin
¶ - Aurea Group	CBlo CDoC CKen GKir LBee LCon LLin LPan LRHS MAsh MBri SLim SMur
- 'Bodnant'	CKen
- 'Isca'	CKen
- 'Marshwood' (v)	CKen
resinosa 'Don Smith'	CKen
- 'Joel's Broom'	CKen
- 'Nobska'	CKen
- 'Quinobequin'	CKen
- 'Watnong'	CKen

rigida	EHul LCon STre
roxburghii	Last listed 1999
sabineana	CAgr LCon
x *schwerinii*	CDoC LRHS
¶ - 'Wiethorst'	CKen
strobiformis	Last listed 1999
- 'Fox Tail'	EPfP
strobus	CB&S CDoC CDul CGre CTho EHul GAri GChr GKir IOrc ISea LCon LPan MBar NWea SEND STre WNor
§ - 'Alba'	LCon MGos
- 'Amelia's Dwarf'	CKen
- 'Anna Fiele'	CKen
¶ - 'Aurea'	LCon
- 'Bergman's Mini'	CKen
- 'Bergman's Pendula Broom'	CKen
I - 'Bergman's Sport of Prostrata'	CKen
- 'Bloomer's Dark Globe'	CKen
- 'Blue Shag'	CBlo CDoC CKen COtt GKir LLin MBri MGos SLim WPyg
- 'Densa'	CKen LCon MAsh
- 'Dove's Dwarf'	CKen
¶ - 'Ed's Broom'	CKen
- 'Fastigiata'	CKen GKir LLin LPan LRHS
- 'Hillside Gem'	CKen
- 'Horsford'	CKen
- 'Jericho'	CKen
- 'Krügers Lilliput'	LCon LLin LRHS MBri SLim
- 'Macopin'	MGos
- 'Merrimack'	CKen
- 'Minima'	CDoC CKen LCon LLin LRHS MAsh MBar MBlu MBri SLim
- 'Minuta'	CKen
- 'Nana'	See *P. strobus* 'Radiata'
- 'Nivea'	See *P. strobus* 'Alba'
- 'Northway Broom'	CKen LLin
- 'Pendula'	CKen GKir LCon SMad
§ - 'Radiata'	CDoC EHul EPla GKir IOrc LNet LRHS MBar NBee SLim
- 'Reinshaus'	CKen LCon LLin
- 'Sayville'	CKen
- 'Sea Urchin'	CKen
- 'Uncatena'	CKen
- 'Verkade's Broom'	CKen
sylvestris ♀	CB&S CDoC CDul CGre CKin ECrN EHul ENot EOrn GChr GKir LBuc LCon LHyr LLin MBar MGos NBee NWea SPer SReu STre WDin WMou WNor WStI
- 'Abergeldie'	CKen
- 'Andorra'	CKen
§ - 'Argentea'	LNet
§ - 'Aurea Group' ♀	CBlo CDoC CKen CMac EBrP EBre EHul GKir IMGH IOrc LBCl LBSe LBee LBre LCon LLin LNet LRHS MAsh MBBe MBar SBre SLim SPer SSta WLRN
- 'Aurea'	See *P. sylvestris* Aurea Group
- 'Avondene'	CKen
- 'Beuvronensis' ♀	CDoC CKen CLnd CMac EOrn GAri GKir IMGH LBee LCon LLin LNet LRHS MAsh MGos NHol SLim SSta
- 'Bonna'	GKir LCon
- 'Brevifolia'	CBlo MBar
- 'Buchanan's Gold'	CKen
- 'Burghfield'	CBlo CKen LCon LLin
- 'Chantry Blue'	CBlo CDoC EHul EOrn GKir IMGH LBee LCon LLin LRHS MAsh MBar MGos SLim
- 'Clumber Blue'	CKen
- 'Compressa'	GAri
- 'Corley'	LLin
- 'Dereham'	CKen LLin
- 'Doone Valley'	CKen LLin
- 'Edwin Hillier'	See *P. sylvestris* 'Argentea'
¶ - 'Fastigiata Group'	CDoC CEnd CKen EOrn IMGH LBee LCon LLin LPan LRHS MAsh MBar MGos SLim
- 'Frensham'	CBlo CDoC CKen EOrn IMGH LCon LLin MAsh MGos MOne
- 'Globosa'	GAri LRHS MBri
- 'Gold Coin' ♀	CBlo CDoC CKen EOrn LBee LCon LLin LRHS MAsh MBri MGos NHol SLim WPyg
- 'Gold Medal'	CKen LCon LLin
- 'Grand Rapids'	CKen
- 'Green Flare'	Last listed 1999
- 'Hibernia'	Last listed 1997
- 'Hillside Creeper'	CKen LCon LLin SLim
- 'Inverleith' (v)	EHul GAri LCon LLin MBar MGos NHol SLim
- 'Jeremy'	CKen LCon LLin SLim WAbe
- 'Kelpie'	Last listed 1999
- 'Kenwith'	CKen
- 'Lakeside Dwarf'	LLin
- 'Little Brolly'	Last listed 1999
- 'Lodge Hill'	CBlo CDoC CKen EBrP EBre EOrn IMGH LBCl LBSe LBre LCon LLin LRHS MAsh MBBe MOne SBre SLim WAbe
- 'Longmoor'	CKen
- 'Martham'	CKen LLin
- var. *mongolica*	GIBF
- 'Moseri'	CDoC ECho GKir LBee LRHS MAsh MBri
- 'Nana Compacta'	LLin
- 'Nana' misapplied	See *P. sylvestris* 'Watereri'
§ - 'Nisbet's Gem'	CKen LLin
- 'Padworth'	CKen
- 'Pixie'	CKen LCon
¶ - 'Pulham'	LLin
- 'Pygmaea'	SLim
- 'Pyramidalis Compacta'	Last listed 1999
- 'Reedham'	LLin
- 'Repens'	CKen
- 'Sandringham'	CBlo LCon LLin
- 'Saxatilis'	CBlo CKen EOrn LCon LLin
¶ - subsp. *scotica*	GIBF GTre
- 'Scott's Dwarf'	See *P. sylvestris* 'Nisbet's Gem'
- 'Scrubby'	LLin
- 'Sentinel'	CKen
- 'Skjak I'	CKen
- 'Skjak II'	CKen
- 'Spaan's Slow Column'	CKen
- 'Tage'	CKen LLin
- 'Tanya'	CKen
¶ - 'Tilhead'	CKen
- 'Treasure'	CKen LLin
- 'Variegata'	Last listed 1998
§ - 'Watereri'	CDoC CMac EHul ENot GKir IOrc LBee LCon LLin LNet LPan LRHS MAsh MBar MBri MGos NHol SLim WDin WWeb
- 'Westonbirt'	CKen EHul MAsh
- 'Wishmoor'	LLin
* - 'Wolf Gold'	CKen
* - 'Yaff Hill'	LLin
tabuliformis	CMCN LCon MBlu SFur
- S&F 96040	ISea
taeda	Last listed 1997

taiwanensis	ISea
thunbergii	CDul CLnd EHul LCon LLin MGos SEND SPla STre WFro WNor
- 'Akame'	CKen
- 'Akame Yatsabusa'	Last listed 1999
- 'Aocha-matsu' (v)	CKen
- 'Banshosho'	CKen
- 'Compacta'	CKen
- 'Dainagon'	CKen
- 'Iwai'	CKen
- 'Kotobuki'	CKen
I - 'Ko-yo-sho'	Last listed 1998
- 'Kujaku'	CKen
- 'Kyushu'	CKen
- 'Miyajuna'	CKen
- 'Nishiki-ne'	CKen
¶ - 'Oculus-draconis' (v)	LLin
- 'Ogon'	CKen
§ - 'Sayonara'	CBlo CDoC CKen GAri LCon LLin NHol
- 'Senryu'	CKen
- 'Shio-guro'	CKen
- 'Suchiro Yatabusa'	CKen
- 'Sunsho'	CKen
- 'Taihei'	CKen
I - 'Thunderhead'	CKen
- 'Yatsubusa'	See *P. thunbergii* 'Sayonara'
¶ - 'Yumaki'	CKen
uncinata	See *P. mugo* subsp. *uncinata*
virginiana	Last listed 1999
- 'Wate's Golden'	CKen
§ *wallichiana* ♀	CAbP CBlo CDoC CDul CKen CMCN CTho EHul EPfP GChr IOrc LCon LLin LPan LRHS MBar MGos NBee NWea SBir SLim WGer WNor WTro
- CC 1740	WHCr
¶ - CC 2045	WHCr
- 'Densa'	LCon MAsh MBri
- 'Nana'	CKen EHul LCon MBar SLim
- 'Umbraculifera'	LRHS MBri
- 'Zebrina' (v)	CBlo CDoC GKir LCon MBar MGos
yunnanensis	CDoC WNor WShe
- S&F 96250	ISea

PIPER (Piperaceae)

auritum	MSal
betle	MSal
excelsum	See *Macropiper excelsum*
methysticum	Last listed 1998
nigrum	MSal

PIPTANTHUS (Papilionaceae)

forrestii	See *P. nepalensis*
laburnifolius	See *P. nepalensis*
§ *nepalensis*	More than 30 suppliers
- B&SWJ 2241	WCru
- S&F 95180	ISea
tomentosus	CFil SDry WPGP

PISONIA (Nyctaginaceae)

brunoniana	See *P. umbellifera*
§ *umbellifera*	Last listed 1998
- 'Variegata'	Last listed 1998

PISTACIA (Anacardiaceae)

chinensis	CB&S CMCN CPMA ELan EWes
lentiscus	CB&S
terebinthus	CFil

PISTIA (Araceae)

stratiotes	MSta

PITTOSPORUM ✿ (Pittosporaceae)

anomalum	ECou SDry
- (f)	ECou
- (m)	ECou
- 'Falcon'	ECou
- 'Raven' (f)	ECou
- 'Starling' (m)	ECou
* *argyrophyllum*	IOrc
'Arundel Green'	CBlo CDoC LRHS MBri MTed SDry
bicolor	CFil CPle ECou GQui SAPC SArc WPGP
buchananii	CPle SVen
¶ aff. *buchananii*	GGar
colensoi	ECou
- 'Cobb' (f)	ECou
- 'Wanaka'	ECou
crassifolium	CB&S CFil CPle ECou ERea IOrc WPGP
- 'Havering Dwarf'	ECou
- 'Napier'	ECou
- x *tenuifolium*	CCHP ECou
- 'Variegatum'	CGre LHil WSPU
'Craxten' (f)	CPne ECou
cuneatum	LHop
dallii	Last listed 1998
daphniphylloides var. *adaphniphylloides*	CFil CGre CPne
- ETE 275	WPGP
divaricatum	ECou
'Essex' (v)	ECou
eugenioides	CB&S CMHG CTrG GGar SLon WLRN
- 'Platinum'	Last listed 1999
- 'Variegatum' ♀	CB&S CDoC CGre EBee EPfP GQui IOrc LRHS NPSI SAga WSHC WSPU
'Garnettii' (v) ♀	More than 30 suppliers
heterophyllum	CPle ECou IArd
- variegated	ECou
buttonianum	SVen
'Limelight' (v)	CB&S CBlo CGre EMil LRHS WWes
lineare	ECou
§ 'Margaret Turnbull' (v)	CB&S ECou EMil LHop LRHS MGos WBcn
michiei	ECou
- (f)	ECou
- (m)	ECou
- 'Jack' (m)	ECou
- 'Jill' (f)	ECou
'Nanum Variegatum'	See *P. tobira* 'Variegatum'
obcordatum	ECou
- var. *kaitaiaense*	ECou
omeiense	CFil CGre CPne WPGP
phillyreoides	CFil
pimeleoides var. *reflexum* (m)	ECou
¶ *podocarpum*	CDoC
ralphii	ECou
- 'Green Globe'	ECou
- 'Variegatum'	SSpi
revolutum	Last listed 1998
rhombifolium	Last listed 1998
'Saundersii' (v)	CBlo EMil
tenuifolium ♀	More than 30 suppliers
- 'Abbotsbury Gold' (v)	CAbb CChe CDoC CSam CTri CWSG EBee ECou ELan EMil

EWes GOrc LRHS SDry SLim SPer
SRPl WAbe WSHC
- 'Atropurpureum' CB&S WBcn
- 'County Park Dwarf' ECou WCru
- 'Deborah' (v) ECou EHol LRHS
- 'Dixie' CMHG ECou
§ - 'Eila Keightley' (v) CBlo CMHG IOrc
- 'Elizabeth' CDoC ECou LRHS NPSI
* - 'French Lace' ECou
- 'Gold Star' CB&S CDoC ECou EMil LRHS
- 'Golden King' CDoC CMHG LRHS MRav SLim
SRPl SRms
- 'Golden Princess' (f) ECou
* - 'Green Elf' ECou
* - 'Green Thumb' LRHS SPla
- 'Irene Paterson' (v) ♀ CAbb CB&S CDoC CGre CMHG
CSam EBee ECou ELan GKir
GOrc IOrc LHop LRHS MBri
MGos SAga SDry SLim SLon SPer
SPla SRms SSht SSpi SSta WAbe
WCFE WSHC
- 'James Stirling' ECou IOrc LRHS WSHC
- 'John Flanagan' See P. 'Margaret Turnbull'
- 'Katie' CB&S
- 'Loxhill Gold' CDoC EBee LRHS SEas
- 'Marjory Channon' (v) CB&S LRHS NPer SRPl
- 'Mellow Yellow' CAbP LRHS WBcn
- 'Moonlight' NPSI
- 'Nigricans' CB&S CLan
- 'Princess' (f) Last listed 1998
- 'Purpureum' CPle CSam CTri CTrw ECou EPfP
IOrc LRHS LSpr SDry SPer SPla
SRms
* - 'Silver Dollar' MBri
- 'Silver Magic' CB&S EMil
- 'Silver 'n' Gold' LRHS
- 'Silver Princess' (f) ECou
- 'Silver Queen' (f/v) ♀ More than 30 suppliers
- 'Silver Sheen' LRHS
- 'Stirling Gold' (v) ECou EPfP EWes EWll
- 'Sunburst' See P. tenuifolium 'Eila Keightley'
¶ - 'Tandara Gold' CTrC SPla
- 'Tiki' CB&S ECou
- 'Tom Thumb' ♀ More than 30 suppliers
- 'Tresederi' (f/m) CGdn CTrw ECou LRHS
- 'Variegata' CB&S CDoC ECou EMil LRHS
- 'Victoria' CDoC EMil
- 'Warnham Gold' ♀ CB&S CDoC CMHG COtt CTrw
EBee ECou ELan EPfP IOrc LRHS
MCCP SDry SEas SLim SSpi WAbe
WDin WWat
- 'Wendle Channon' (v) CB&S CDoC CEnd CMHG CSam
CWSG EBee ECot ECou EPfP GKir
LRHS SLim SPla SRPl WSHC WWat
- 'Winter Sunshine' LRHS SSta
tobira ♀ CB&S CBot CDoC CFil CHEx
CLTr CPle CTrC EBee ECou IOrc
LHil LRHS MGos SAPC SArc SPar
SPer SSpi SSta WAbe WBrE WEas
WPen WPic WPyg WSHC WStI
WWat
- B&SWJ 4362 WCru
- 'Nanum' CB&S CDoC EBee ECou EPla
ERea IOrc LPan SAPC SArc SLim
§ - 'Variegatum' ♀ CB&S CBot CGre CPle ECou EPfP
ERea GQui LHop LRHS MBri SAga
SLon SPer SSta WCru WPGP
* - 'Variegatum Last listed 1998
Linearifolium' (v)
undulatum CHEx ECou
- 'Variegatum' CGre
¶ viridiflorum ECou

PITYROGRAMMA (Adiantaceae)
triangularis CFil

PLAGIANTHUS (Malvaceae)
betulinus See P. regius
divaricatus CFil CPLG WPGP
lyallii See Hoheria lyallii
§ regius CPLG ECou GGar GQui LRHS

PLAGIORHEGMA See JEFFERSONIA

PLANTAGO (Plantaginaceae)
alpina Last listed 1997
argentea WPic
asiatica MSal
- 'Variegata' CRow EBee EGoo ELau EMan
GBri GBuc MBNS NBro NEgg
NLar NSti WElm WHer WRos
WWye
coronopus CKin EWFC IIve
cynops EMon LRHS MTho
* gaudichaudii Last listed 1997
lanceolata EWFC MHew
- 'Ballydowling CNat
Variegated' (v)
- 'Burren Rose' CNat CRow
- 'Freaky' Last listed 1998
- 'Martin's Freaky' WAlt
- 'Streaker' (v) CRow WCot WHal WHer
major EWFC WHbs
- 'Atropurpurea' See P. major 'Rubrifolia'
- 'Bowles' Variety' See P. major 'Rosularis'
- 'Bract Act' WAlt
- 'Frills' CNat CRow WCot WHer
* - 'Karmozijn' EMan
§ - 'Rosularis' CArn CInt CRow CSpe EBee
ECha ILis MFir MHar MHer MTho
NBro NChi NEgg NLar NSti WBea
WHal WHer WPer WWye
§ - 'Rubrifolia' CArn CHid CRow CSpe EBee
ECha ECoo EPla LFis MCAu MFir
MHar MHer MNrw NBid NBro
NChi NEgg NHar NSti WBar WBea
WCer WHer WPer WRos WWye
- 'Subtle Streak' (v) WAlt
- 'Variegata' Last listed 1998
maritima CKin WHer
media CKin EWFC MHew
nivalis EBee MBro NNrd NTow WWin
psyllium CArn GPoy MSal
raoulii EPPr WCot WHer
rosea See P. major 'Rosularis'
sempervirens Last listed 1998
sp. RCB/Eq N-3 WCot
uniflora See Littorella uniflora

PLATANTHERA (Orchidaceae)
bologlottis EFEx
metabifolia EFEx

PLATANUS ✿ (Platanaceae)
x acerifolia See P. x hispanica
§ x hispanica ♀ CB&S CBlo CDul CKin CLnd
CMCN CTho EBee ECrN EMil
ENot EWTr GChr IOrc LBuc LHyr
LPan MAsh MGos NWea SEND
SMHT SPer WDin WFar WMou
- 'Liberty' Last listed 1999
- 'Pyramidalis' CTho
- 'Suttneri' (v) CBlo CDoC CEnd CLnd CTho
LNet SMad

- 'Tremonia' | LRHS
occidentalis | CDul
orientalis ♀ | CLnd CMCN EPfP IOrc LPan SMad WDin WMou
- 'Cuneata' | GKir LRHS MBri
§ - f. **digitata** | CLnd CTho ERod SLPl
- var. **insularis** | CEnd
- 'Laciniata' | See *P. orientalis* f. *digitata*
- 'Mirkovec' | CDoC GKir LRHS MBri SMad SPer

PLATYCARYA (Juglandaceae)
strobilacea | CMCN IDee

PLATYCERIUM (Polypodiaceae)
alcicorne hort. | See *P. bifurcatum*
§ **bifurcatum** ♀ | LCns LRHS MBri
grande hort. | See *P. superbum*
§ **superbum** ♀ | LCns

PLATYCLADUS See THUJA

PLATYCODON ✿ (Campanulaceae)
grandiflorus ♀ | CArn CGle CNic COIW EBee EBrP EBre ECha ELau LBCl LBSe LBre LFis LHop LRHS MBBe MFir MHer MNrw MPEx MSal NFai NOrc SBre SCob SIng WHoo WWye
- **albus** | CBro CRDP EBee EOld LAst LHop MBri MBro MMal NFai NOak SCob SPer SPla SSca SYvo WHoo WLow WOve WPer
- 'Apoyama' ♀ | CLyd EBee ESis GMac LBee LRHS MBro MHar WHoo WPer WWin
- **apoyama albus** | MBro WCFE WEas WHoo WPyg
- - 'Fairy Snow' | WLin
¶ - 'Astra Blue' (Astra Series) | CMGP
¶ - Astra Series | EDAr
- 'Baby Blue' | SRms
- 'Blue Haze' | EBee NCat WElm WLRN
- 'Blue Pearl' | WHoo
- 'Blue Pygmy' | Last listed 1997
- 'Blue Surf' | Last listed 1998
- 'Florist Blue' | CMdw WMoo
- 'Florist Rose' | NOak SSca WMoo WWye
- 'Florist Snow' | CMdw NOak WMoo WWye
- 'Fuji Blue' | CBlo EWll LIck NLar
- 'Fuji Pink' | CBlo CBro CRDP EBee EBrP EBre EPfP ESis EWTr LAst LBCl LBSe LBre MBBe MRav MTis NLar SBre SCob SMrm SPer SPla SRPl WGwG WLin
- 'Fuji White' | CBlo CMil NLar SMrm SPla
- 'Hakone' | CRDP EBee EMan LHop MBro MRav NCat SMrm WHoo WPyg WWal
- 'Hakone Blue' | NLar
* - 'Hakone Double Blue' | CBro EBee ECGP LRHS MCAu MTis SLod WCot WLRN
- 'Hakone White' | EBee MBro NLar NMen WHoo
- 'Mammoth Blue' | Last listed 1998
- 'Mammoth White' | Last listed 1998
- 'Mariesii' ♀ | CBro CGle CNic EBee EBrP EBre ECtt ENot EWTr GKir GMaP LBCl LBSe LBre LFis LRHS MBBe MRav NBir NMen SBre SPer SRms WEas WHoo WLow WPer WWin
- **mariesii albus** | EBee ESis MBro WHoo WPyg
- 'Misato Purple' | EBee
- Mother of Pearl | See *P. grandiflorus* 'Perlmutterschale'
- 'Park's Double Blue' (d) | MLLN NOak SSca WHoo WMoo WPyg

§ - 'Perlmutterschale' | CGle CMGP CMil EBee EPfP GMac MBri SRCN WHoo WPyg
- **pumilus** | EBee MBro MHar NChi NWCA WCFE WHoo WPyg
- 'Purple Dwarf' | Last listed 1997
- Purple Princess = 'Hime-murasaki' | Last listed 1997
- **roseus** | CNic MNrw WHoo
- 'Sentimental Blue' | EBee EDAr NLar SMrm WHil WLRN
- 'Shell Pink' | See *P. grandiflorus* 'Perlmutterschale'
- 'Zwerg' | EBee LGre

PLATYCRATER (Hydrangeaceae)
arguta | WCru
¶ - B&SWJ 6266 | WCru

PLECOSTACHYS (Asteraceae)
§ **serpyllifolia** | CHal CLTr

PLECTRANTHUS (Lamiaceae)
amboinicus | EOHP LHil
* - 'Tansania' | EOHP
* - 'Variegatus' | EOHP
argentatus | CHad CMdw CSev CSpe EBee EMan LHil MSte SAga SDix SMrm SRCN SUsu SVen WKif
¶ - 'Hill House' (v) | EMan LHil
australis misapplied | See *P. verticillatus*
bebrii | See *P. fruticosus*
ciliatus | LHil
coleoides 'Marginatus' | See *P. forsteri* 'Marginatus'
- 'Variegatus' | See *P. madagascariensis* 'Variegated Mintleaf'
excisus | EMon
§ **forsteri** | LHil
§ - 'Marginatus' | CHal ERea LHil NFai SVen
§ **fruticosus** | CHal GBri LHil
birtellus gold | Last listed 1999
'Jan Jaas Veldia' | Last listed 1999
§ **madagascariensis** 'Variegated Mintleaf' | CHal LHil MRav SHFr SRms
§ **oertendablii** ♀ | EBak LHil
ornatus | Last listed 1999
purpuratus | EOHP
* **purpureus** | SVen
¶ **sinensis** | EBrP EBre LBCl LBSe LBre MBBe SBre
sp. podena | CArn
Swedish ivy | See *P. verticillatus*, *P. oertendablii*
§ **thyrsoideus** | CHal SVen
§ **verticillatus** | CHal EOHP WEas
zatarbendii | EMan LHil
zuluensis | CFee CFwr CMdw LHil

PLEIOBLASTUS ✿ (Poaceae - Bambusoideae)
akebono | EPla SDry
§ **auricomus** ♀ | More than 30 suppliers
- 'Bracken Hill' | EPla SDry
- f. **chrysophyllus** | CPMA EPla MMoz SDry WJun
- 'Vagans' | EBee
- **variegatus** | CHar SAga
§ **chino** | CHEx EPVP EPla ISta MDun SDry
§ - f. **angustifolius** | LHil MMoz SDry
- var. **argenteostriatus** | EPla WViv
- f. **aureostriatus** (v) | EPla ISta LJus NDov SDry WCru
- f. **elegantissimus** | CEnd CFir COtt EBee EGln EPla ISta LJus LRHS MMoz MWhi NDov SDry WJun
- var. **bisauchii** | EPla
- 'Kimmei' | SDry

- 'Murakamianus'	EPla SDry
fortunei	See *P. variegatus*
'Gauntlettii'	See *P. humilis* var. *pumilus*
glaber 'Albostriatus'	See *Sasaella masamuneana* f. *albostriata*
gramineus	EPla ISta SDry WJun
§ *hindsii* hort.	EPla LJus LPan SArc SDry
§ *humilis*	CBlo ELan LPan
§ - var. *pumilus*	CCuc CDDB CDoC CRow CSam CTrC EBee EHoe EPar EPfP EPla GKir ISta LJus LPan LRHS MBlu MBri NHol SDry SPlb WFar WJun WNor WPat WPer
kongosanensis	EPla SDry
'Aureostriatus' (v)	
linearis	CFir EBee EFul EPla ISta LRHS MMoz NMoo SDry WJun
longifimbriatus	EPla WJun
oleosus	EPla SDry WJun
§ *pygmaeus*	More than 30 suppliers
§ - var. *distichus*	CDDB EFul EPPr EPla GBin LHil LJus LRHS MMoz SDry WJun WWin
* - - 'Mini'	WCot
§ - 'Mirrezuzume'	EPla GBin WWat
shibuyanus 'Tsuboi' (v)	CDoC CEnd COtt EBee EPPr EPla ERod ISta LJus LPJP LRHS MBrN MMoz MWhi MWht NDov NMoo SDry WCru WJun
§ *simonii*	CHEx EBee EBrP EBre EFul EPla GBin GCal ISta LBCl LBSe LBre LJus LRHS MBBe MDun MMoz MWhi SArc SBre SDry
- var. *heterophyllus*	See *P. simonii* f. *variegatus*
§ - f. *variegatus*	CFil EPla ISta MBar MBlu SDry SPer WJun WPGP
§ *variegatus* ♀	More than 30 suppliers
- var. *viridis*	SDry
viridistriatus	See *P. auricomus*

PLEIONE ✿ (Orchidaceae)

§ *albiflora*	Last listed 1999
§ - 'Pinchbeck Diamond'	EPot GCrs
Alishan g.	CNic EPot GCrs LBut NSpr
- 'Foxhill'	NSpr
- 'Merlin'	NSpr
- 'Mount Fuji'	LBut
- 'Soldier Blue'	LBut
Asama g.	LBut
§ *aurita*	EFEx GCrs LAma NSpr
Bandai-san g.	LBut
Barcena g.	LBut
Beerenberg g.	LBut
Berapi g.	EPot LBut
Brigadoon g.	LBut NSpr
- 'Stonechat'	LBut
Britannia g.	LBut
- 'Doreen'	LBut NSpr
§ *bulbocodioides*	EPot ERos IBlr LBut MBro NNrd NSpr WFar
- 'Lapwing'	LBut
- (Limprichtii Group) 'Primrose Peach'	Last listed 1997
- Pricei Group	See *P. formosana* Pricei Group
§ - 'Yunnan'	EPot LBut NSpr
Captain Hook g.	LBut NSpr
chunii	See *P. aurita*
x *confusa*	EFEx EPot GCrs
Cotopaxi g.	LBut
Danan g.	LBut
Deriba g.	LBut
Eiger g.	EPot ERos LBut NSpr

- cream	EPot ERos GCrs LBut
El Pico g.	GCrs LBut NSpr
- 'Goldcrest'	GCrs LBut
- 'Kestrel'	GCrs LBut
- 'Pheasant'	LBut
- 'Starling'	LBut
Erebus g.	LBut
- 'Quail'	LBut
Erh Hai g.	NSpr
Etna g.	CNic EPot GCrs LBut
- 'Bullfinch'	GCrs
formosana ♀	EFEx EPot ETub GCrs IBlr LAma NTow SCob SDeJ SIng
- 'Achievement'	LBut
I - 'Alba'	CNic EPot GCrs IBlr SIng
- Arline g.	Last listed 1999
- 'Avalanche'	EPot LBut NSpr
- 'Ben Nevis'	LBut
- 'Blush of Dawn'	EPot GCrs LBut NSpr
- C.P. Diamond g.	Last listed 1999
- 'Cairngorm'	NSpr
- 'Christine Anne'	NSpr
- 'Clare'	EPot ERos GCrs LBut NSpr
- Eugene g.	EPot
- 'Greenhill'	LBut
I - 'Iris'	LBut NSpr
- Kate g.	EPot
- 'Lilac Beauty'	Last listed 1999
- 'Little Winnie'	EPot
- 'Lucy Diamond'	EPot GCrs LBut
- Lulu g.	EPot
- 'Oriental Grace'	EPot LBut MFir
- 'Oriental Jewel'	Last listed 1999
- 'Oriental Splendour'	EPot LBut NSpr
- 'Pitlochry'	LBut
- 'Polar Sun'	EPot GCrs NSpr
§ - Pricei Group	EPot ERos NTow
- 'Red Spot'	Last listed 1999
- 'Serenity'	LBut
¶ - 'Snow Bunting'	LBut
- 'Snow Cap'	Last listed 1999
- 'Snow White'	GCrs LBut
- 'Snowy Owl'	LBut
forrestii	EFEx EPot GCrs LAma
Fuego g.	LBut NSpr
- 'Wren'	LBut
Fujiyama g.	LBut
Gerry Mundey g.	LBut
grandiflora	Last listed 1999
'Hallmark'	GCrs
Hekla g.	EPot GCrs LBut NSpr
- 'Partridge'	LBut
¶ Helgafell g.	LBut
hookeriana	GCrs
humilis	SDeJ
- 'Frank Kingdon Ward'	GCrs
Irazu g.	GCrs LBut NSpr
- 'Irazu Violet'	GCrs
Jorullo g.	LBut NSpr
- 'Long-tailed Tit'	LBut
Katla g.	LBut NSpr
Katmai g.	LBut
Keith Rattray g.	LBut
Kilauea g.	EPot LBut
¶ - 'Curlew'	LBut
Kituro g.	LBut
Krakatoa g.	Last listed 1998
Lascar g.	LBut
¶ *limprichtii* ♀	EFEx EPot LBut NTow
- mauve	GCrs
- pink	GCrs
Lipari g.	LBut

maculata	EFEx
Marco Polo g.	LBut NSpr
Matupi g.	LBut NSpr
'Mayfield'	GCrs
Mayon g.	LBut
Mazama g.	LBut
Myojin g.	LBut
Novarupta g.	LBut
Orinoco g.	LBut
- 'Gemini'	LBut
Orizaba g.	LBut
Paricutin g.	LBut
Pavlof g.	LBut
pinkepankii	See *P. albiflora*
Piton g.	EPot GCrs LAma LBut
pogonioides (Rolfe) Rolfe	See *P. bulbocodioides*
- hort.	See *P. speciosa*
praecox	Last listed 1999
Rainier g.	LBut
Rakata g.	LBut
¶ - 'Blackbird'	LBut
- 'Shot Silk'	LBut
¶ - 'Skylark'	LBut
San Pedro g.	LBut
¶ San Salvador g.	LBut
scopulorum	EFEx
Shantung g.	EPot GCrs LAma LBut NSpr
- 'Candyfloss'	NSpr
- 'Ducat'	EPot GCrs LAma LBut NSpr
- 'Gerry Mundey'	LBut NSpr
- 'Golden Jubilee'	NSpr
- 'Golden Plover'	LBut
¶ - 'Gwen'	EPot
- 'Mikki'	NSpr
- 'Muriel Harberd' ♀	CRDP EPot GCrs NSpr
- 'R6.7'	NSpr
- 'Ridgeway'	EPot GCrs LBut NSpr
- 'Stephanie Rose'	Last listed 1998
Sorea g.	LBut
Soufrière g.	LBut NSpr
§ *speciosa*	EPot GCrs LBut
- 'Blakeway Phillips'	NSpr
Stromboli g.	EPot GCrs LBut NSpr
- 'Fireball'	GCrs LBut NSpr
- 'Robin'	LBut
Surtsey g.	LBut
- 'Stephanie Rose'	NSpr
Taal g.	LBut
Tacana g.	LBut
¶ x *taliensis*	LBut
Tambora g.	LBut
Tarawera g.	LBut
Tolima g.	CNic EPot LBut NSpr
- 'Moorhen'	GCrs
Tongariro g.	EPot ERos GCrs LBut NSpr
- 'Jackdaw'	LBut
Versailles g.	EFEx EPot LAma LBut NSpr
- 'Bucklebury' ♀	CNic EPot GCrs LBut NSpr
- 'Heron'	LBut
- 'Muriel Turner'	EPot LAma LBut NSpr
Vesuvius g.	EPot LBut NSpr
- 'Aphrodite'	EPot
- 'Leopard'	LBut
* - 'Phoenix'	GCrs LBut NSpr
Volcanello g.	GCrs LBut NSpr
Wunzen g.	LBut
yunnanensis hort.	See *P. bulbocodioides* 'Yunnan'
—(Rolfe) Rolfe	LAma LBut
Zeus Weinstein g.	LBut NSpr
- 'Desert Sands'	LBut

PLEOMELE See DRACAENA

PLEUROSPERMUM (Apiaceae)
brunonis	EBee EDAr WHal

PLEXIPUS (Verbenaceae)
namaquanus	Last listed 1999

PLUMBAGO (Plumbaginaceae)
§ *auriculata* ♀	CB&S CDoC CEnd CHEx CLTr CPIN CPle CRHN CSpe EBak EBee ELan ERav ERea LRHS MBri MLan MRav MTis NEgg NRog SIde SOWG SPer SRms SYvo WBod
- var. *alba*	CB&S CBot CRHN CSev CSpe EBak ELan EMil EPfP ERav ERea LCns LRHS MLan SEND SOWG SPer SYvo
* - *aurea*	LIck
¶ - dark blue	CSpe
- Royal Cape = 'Monott'	ERav
capensis	See *P. auriculata*
§ *indica*	CHal LCns LRHS SOWG
- *rosea*	See *P. indica*
larpentiae	See *Ceratostigma plumbaginoides*
zeylanica	Last listed 1997

PLUMERIA (Apocynaceae)
§ *obtusa*	LChe
rubra	ECon LBlo LChe LRHS SOWG
- f. *acutifolia*	LChe LRHS SOWG
- f. *lutea*	Last listed 1998
'Singapore'	See *P. obtusa*

PNEUMATOPTERIS See CYCLOSORUS

POA (Poaceae)
abyssinica	Last listed 1997
acicularifolia	Last listed 1998
alpina nodosa	CInt GBin NFor
araratica	Last listed 1997
badensis 'Ingelkissen'	Last listed 1997
buchananii	Last listed 1998
bulbosa	EPPr
chaixii	CBod CCuc EBee EHoe EMan EMon EPPr GBin LRHS NHol NNor SLPl WFoF
cita	EPPr
colensoi	CBod CCtw CCuc EBee EHoe GChr LPan MCCP MWhi NFor SPla
eminens	Last listed 1998
- from Magadan, Siberia	EPPr
fawcettiae	Last listed 1997
glauca	Last listed 1997
bothamensis	Last listed 1998
imbecilla	Last listed 1998
x *jemtlandica*	EHoe NHol
labillardierei	CBrm CKno EBee ECGP ECha EHoe EMan EPPr WDyG
nemoralis	Last listed 1997

PODALYRIA (Papilionaceae)
biflora	Last listed 1997
calyptrata	Last listed 1997
¶ *canescens*	SPlb
sericea	Last listed 1999

PODANTHUS (Asteraceae)
ovatifolius G&K 4386	CGre CPLG

PODOCARPUS (Podocarpaceae)

acutifolius	CB&S CDoC ECou EPla MBar STre
- (f)	ECou
- (m)	ECou
andinus	See *Prumnopitys andina*
'Autumn Shades' (m)	CDoC ECou
'Blaze' (f)	ECou LLin SIng SLim
chilinus	See *P. salignus*
'Chocolate Box' (f)	ECou
'County Park Fire' PBR (f)	CDoC CKen CWSG ECou EOrn
	LCon LLin MGos SCoo SIng SLim
	WGor
cunninghamii	CB&S ECou WCwm
- 'Kiwi' (f)	ECou
- x *nivalis* (f)	ECou
- 'Roro' (m)	ECou
dacrydioides	See *Dacrycarpus dacrydioides*
elongatus	Last listed 1998
ferrugineus	See *Prumnopitys ferruginea*
'Golden Dwarf'	See *Prumnopitys ferruginea*
	'Golden Dwarf'
'Havering' (f)	Last listed 1999
henkelii	CGre CTrC WMul
latifolius	CTrC ECou
lawrencei	CBlo ECho EHul GAri IOrc
- (f)	ECou MBar SSmi
- 'Alpine Lass' (f)	ECou
- 'Blue Gem' (f)	CBlo CDoC ECou EOrn EPla
	LCon LLin MAsh MBar MBri
	MGos MOne SLim WBcn WLRN
	WWat
- 'Kiandra'	ECou
macrophyllus (m)	ECou
–	CDoC CGre EOrn LPan SAPC
	SArc SMad WWat
- 'Angustifolius'	CHEx SLon
- 'Aureus'	CB&S
'Maori Prince' (m)	Last listed 1999
nivalis	CMHG CMac EBrP EBre ECou
	EOrn EPla LBCl LBSe LBre LLin
	MBBe MBar SBre SIng SPla SRms
	SSmi WWat
- 'Arthur' (m)	ECou
- 'Bronze'	EPla
- 'Clarence' (m)	ECou LLin
- 'Green Queen' (f)	ECou
- 'Jack's Pass' (m)	ECou
- 'Kaweka' (m)	ECou SIng
- 'Little Lady' (f)	ECou SIng
- 'Livingstone' (f)	ECou SIng
- 'Lodestone' (m)	ECou
- 'Moffatt' (f)	ECou LLin SIng
- 'Otari' (m)	ECou LLin
- 'Park Cover'	ECou SIng
- 'Princess' (f)	ECou
- 'Ruapehu'	ECou EPla SIng
* 'Redtip'	SLim
¶ 'Rough Creek'	LLin
§ *salignus* ♀	CB&S CDoC CGre CHEx EPla
	IDee IOrc ISea SAPC WSHC
¶ - (f)	ECou
- (m)	ECou
spicatus	See *Prumnopitys taxifolia*
'Spring Sunshine'	ECou LLin SIng
totara	CGre CHEx CMHG ECou LEdu
	STre WPic
¶ - 'Albany Gold'	CTrC
- 'Aureus'	CB&S CDoC ECou EPla LLin MBar
	WLRN
- 'Pendulus'	CDoC ECou
'Young Rusty'	ECou SIng

PODOPHYLLUM (Berberidaceae)

delavayi	WCru
difforme	WCru
emodi	See *P. hexandrum*
- var. *chinense*	See *P. hexandrum* var. *chinense*
§ *hexandrum*	CBos CBro CElw CHEx CRDP
	CRow EOld EPar ERos GCal GCrs
	GGar GKir GPoy LAma LRHS
	MBri MSal NBid NChi NHar
	NWCA SSpi WFar WPGP WWye
§ - var. *chinense*	CRow GBuc IBlr SMad WCru
	WWat
- 'Majus'	EBee WCot
mairei	WCru
peltatum	CArn CBro CRow EBee GCal
	GPoy IBlr LAma LGre MSal NHar
	NSti SSpi WCru WViv WWat
pleianthum	WCru
versipelle	SSpi WCru

PODRANEA (Bignoniaceae)

¶ *brycei*	CPIN
§ *ricasoliana*	CPIN ERea LChe LRHS SOWG
	WMul

POGONATHERUM (Poaceae)

§ *paniceum*	LRHS MBri
saccharoideum	See *P. paniceum*

POGONIA (Orchidaceae)

japonica alba	Last listed 1999
ophioglossoides	SSpi

POGOSTEMON (Lamiaceae)

§ *cablin*	CArn GPoy MSal
heyneanus	MSal
patchouly	See *P. cablin*
sp. from An Veleniki Herb Farm, Pennsylvania	
	CArn

POLEMONIUM ✿ (Polemoniaceae)

acutiflorum	See *P. caeruleum* subsp. *villosum*
- var. *nipponicum*	See *P. caeruleum* subsp.
	nipponicum
'Apricot Beauty'	See *P. carneum* 'Apricot Delight'
N *archibaldiae*	MBro NFai SRms SYvo
§ *boreale*	EBee EBrP EBre EMan GCal GGar
	LBCl LBSe LBre LRHS MBBe
	MNrw MOne SBre SEas WMoo
	WOut
* - *album*	NChi
¶ - 'Heavenly Habit'	NCut
brandegeei Greene	EBee NArg NBro STes WByw
	WPer
§ - subsp. *mellitum*	GCHN LCot
§ *caeruleum*	More than 30 suppliers
- var. *album*	See *P. caeruleum* subsp.
	caeruleum f. *album*
§ - subsp. *amygdalinum*	EBee
- 'Bambino Blue'	EBee LRHS WPer WWpP
- 'Blue Bell'	ELau MAvo
- Brise d'Anjou =	COtt EBrP EBre EMan EOrc EWes
'Blanjou' PBR (v)	GKir LBCl LBSe LBre LRHS MBBe
	MCLN MRav SBre SCoo SPer
	WWeb
§ - subsp. *caeruleum*	More than 30 suppliers
f. *album*	
- subsp. *dissectum*	Last listed 1999
- 'Golden Showers' (v)	CStr MCCP NPro
- var. *grandiflorum*	See *P. caeruleum* subsp.
	himalayanum

§ - subsp. **himalayanum** | EBee WPer
* - - 'Album' | IIve
- 'Humile' | See P. 'Northern Lights'
- 'Idylle' | EMan GMac
¶ - 'Iverna Jewel' | IIve
- 'Larch Cottage Variegated' (v) | NLar
- misapplied, Himalayan | See P. cashmerianum
- 'Newark Park' | EPPr
§ - subsp. **nipponicum** | EBee GBin WPer
¶ - 'Sky Blue' | MTis
§ - subsp. **villosum** | CStr EBee IIve
carneum | CGle CMea EBee ECha EGle EMan EOrc GKir LAst MCAu MCCP MFir MNrw MTho NCut NHar SIng SPer SSpi STes WBea WFar WPer WSan WWin

§ - 'Apricot Delight' | CBot ECoo EMar EWTr GAbr GBri GMac LAst MCCP MCLN MNrw MSCN NBir NCut NFai SAga SIde STes SUsu WCot WHer WLin WOve WPer WPnP WSpi WWhi WWin

§ **cashmerianum** | CLTr CMdw EBee ECGN GAbr GBuc GCHN LRHS MBro MHar NBur NOak SPer WBea WFar WHen WHoo WPyg

- **album** | Last listed 1997
chartaceum | NWCA
- NNS 93-650 | Last listed 1999
'Churchills' | CBre CLAP EBee NFai WBro WPGP WPrP
¶ 'Cottage Dream' | CStr
§ 'Dawn Flight' | WFar
'Daydawn' | Last listed 1997
delicatum | See P. pulcherrimum subsp. delicatum
'Eastbury Purple' | CElw CStr
elegans | Last listed 1998
'Elworthy Amethyst' | CElw EBee MAvo NCot SUsu WCot
eximium | Last listed 1998
flavum | See P. foliosissimum var. flavum
foliosissimum A Gray | CGle EPPr MNrw WHoo WPer
- hort. | See P. archibaldiae
- var. **albiflorum** | See P. foliosissimum var. alpinum
§ - var. **alpinum** | EBee NBir
§ - var. **flavum** | Last listed 1999
'Glebe Cottage Lilac' | CElw CGle CHar CMil CStr EBee LPio WBea WPGP
'Glebe Cottage Violet' | Last listed 1999
'Hannah Billcliffe' | CLAP LCot
'Hidako White' | Last listed 1998
§ 'Hopleys' | CLAP CStr EMan GBar GBri GCal GMac LFis LHop NBrk NCot NGdn SUsu WByw WCot WFar
x **jacobaea** | EPPr WBea WCot
'Katie Daley' | See P. 'Hopleys'
kiushianum | EBee
§ 'Lambrook Mauve' ♀ | More than 30 suppliers
liniflorum | EBee
'Mary Mottram' | EBee
mellitum | See P. brandegeei subsp. mellitum
'North Tyne' | NChi
§ 'Northern Lights' | CBos CStr EBee ELan EMan EMon EPPr EWes GBri GMaP LGre MBri MCCP MNrw MTed SAga WFar WMoo
'Norwell Mauve' | MNrw
occidentale | See P. caeruleum subsp. amygdalinum
pauciflorum | CGle CMea EBee ECGN EOrc GKir GTou LAst LHop LPio LRHS MCAu MNrw MTho NBid NBir NMir NOak SHFr SPer SRms WBea WElm WHer WPer WWhi WWin

- form | Last listed 1998
- subsp. **binckleyi** | Last listed 1999
- silver-leaved | LRHS STes WOve WSan
§ 'Pink Beauty' | CBre CMGP EBee EFou ELan LRHS NCat SCro SUsu WCer
'Pink Pearl' | Last listed 1999
pulchellum Salisbury | See P. reptans
- Willdenow | Last listed 1997
- Turczaninow | See P. caeruleum
pulcherrimum Hooker | EBee GAbr GCal GTou LHop NBro NHar WBea WHen WPer WWye
- hort. | See P. boreale
- **album** | Last listed 1998
§ - Hooker subsp. **delicatum** | MTho NHar NWCA
- Hooker var. **pulcherrimum** | STes SVal
- Hooker 'Tricolor' | NArg NBus
- hort. 'Tricolor' | See P. boreale
§ **reptans** | CAgr CArn CHea CLTr ECoo ELau GBar GBri GPoy MHer MSal NBro SIng WBea WFar WPer WWye
- 'Album' | See P. reptans 'Virginia White'
- 'Blue Pearl' | CElw CGle CMea COIW EBee EMan EPPr EPar GAri LFis LRHS MBel MLLN MNrw NBro NChi NFla NGdn NHol SCro SHel SOkh SPer SUsu WBea WFar WHen WOve WPGP
- 'Dawn Flight' | See P. 'Dawn Flight'
- 'Firmament' | EMon
- 'Lambrook Manor' | See P. 'Lambrook Mauve'
- 'Pink Beauty' | See P. 'Pink Beauty'
¶ - 'Pink Dawn' | WElm
* - 'Sky Blue' | NBro NCut
§ - 'Virginia White' | CBre CStr EBee LRHS NChi NPri COIW
- 'White Pearl' | COIW
richardsonii Graham | See P. boreale
- hort. | See P. 'Northern Lights'
'Sapphire' | CStr EBee EMan GMac MBel MBrN NFai WBea
scopulinum | See P. pulcherrimum subsp. delicatum
'Sonia's Bluebell' | CElw CGle CLAP CMil CStr EBee EWes LGre MAvo MNrw MSte SUsu WMaN WPrP
'Southern Skies' | CBre
'Theddingworth' | MAvo MTed SUsu WBar
viscosum | EPot GBuc GCHN WHen
- NNS 93-658 | Last listed 1999
yezoense | CBre CM&M CStr GBri GCal MNrw WFar WWhi
- **hidakanum** | Last listed 1999
- 'Purple Rain' | CBre CHar CPea CStr EMan EWes GBuc MAvo MBct MCCP MCLN MLLN MNrw MTis MWhi NFla SPer WCot WFar WHer WPrP WRha WSan

POLIANTHES (Agavaceae)

§ **geminiflora** | LAma
nelsonii | CFir
tuberosa ♀ | CB&S CSpe EBot GVer LRHS NRog
* - 'Marginata' (v) | Last listed 1997
- 'The Pearl' (d) | LAma

POLIOMINTHA (Lamiaceae)

bustamanta	CLon EBee ELan LGre NBir SAga WCot
incana	EBee

POLIOTHYRSIS (Flacourtiaceae)

sinensis	CAbP CFil GKir LRHS MAsh MBri WWes

POLLIA (Commelinaceae)

japonica	EBee EMan

POLYGALA (Polygalaceae)

¶ *alpicola*	SOkd
calcarea	CLyd MBro MDun NHar NHol NWCA WAbe WPat
- Bulley's form	LBee LRHS SIng
- 'Lillet' ♀	CLyd EPot GCrs LRHS MBro NHar NMen NTow SBla SIng SSte WAbe WFar WPat WWin
chamaebuxus ♀	GCrs GDra GKir IMGH MDun NHar NWoo SIng SRms WLin WWin
- *alba*	LBee LRHS WAbe
§ - var. *grandiflora* ♀	CB&S CNic EPot EWTr GChr GDra GGar GKir IMGH LBee LHop LRHS MAsh MBar MBro MDun MGos NHar NHol NLAp NMen NWCA SBla SChu SSmi WAbe WFar WPat WSHC WWin
- 'Kamniski'	CMHG EPot NHar NMen
- 'Loibl'	EPot SBla
- 'Purpurea'	See *P. chamaebuxus* var. *grandiflora*
- 'Rhodoptera'	See *P. chamaebuxus* var. *grandiflora*
§ x *dalmaisiana* ♀	CAbb CLTr CRHN CSpe ERea GQui IDee LHop MSCN SBla SMur SUsu SVen WCFE
'Dolomite'	NHar
myrtifolia	LCns LRHS SHFr SMrm WWye
- 'Grandiflora'	See *P. x dalmaisiana*
¶ 'Rosengarten'	SBla
vayredae	WPat
virgata	ECon EPfP ERea LRHS
vulgaris	EWFC IOrc

POLYGONATUM (Convallariaceae)

acuminatifolium	LEur
alte-lobatum B&SWJ 286	WCru
§ *biflorum*	CArn CBro CHid CPou EBee EBrP EBre EGar EGle EGol ELan EMan EOrc EPot GCHN IBlr LBCl LBSe LBre LRHS MBBe MSal NCat NLar SBre SSpi WCot WCru WFar WPnP
- dwarf	EPla IBlr WCot
canaliculatum	See *P. biflorum*
¶ *cathcartii*	LEur
cirrhifolium	CLAP EBee MDun NPar WCru WPGP
commutatum	See *P. biflorum*
cryptanthum	WCru
curvistylum	CLAP EBee ECha IBlr LGre WCDu WFar WViv
cyrtonema hort.	See *Disporopsis pernyi*
- B&SWJ 271	WCru
§ *falcatum*	CLyd EBee EGle EPla ERav IBlr MDun NOak SIng WHer WWat WWin
* - *nanum*	CAvo
§ - 'Variegatum'	More than 30 suppliers

'Falcon'	See *P. humile*
geminiflorum	EBee IBlr WFar
giganteum	See *P. biflorum*
§ *graminifolium*	CLAP CMGP CPBP EPot ERos LGre MSte WCot WCru
- GW 803	Last listed 1999
§ *hirtum*	CHid CLAP EMon EPla EPot IBlr NDov WCru WFar
- BM 7012	EBee
hookeri	CBro EBee EDAr EGle EPot ERos GGar IBlr LBee LGre LRHS MTho NHar NHol NMen NNrd NRya NSla NWCA SIng SMac SRot WAbe WCru WHal WHil WLin
§ *humile*	CGle CLAP CRDP EBee ELan EPla ERos GBri IBlr MBel NHar NMen SBla SSpi SUsu WAbe WCot WCru WFar WHal WRus
§ x *hybridum* ♀	More than 30 suppliers
- 'Bethberg'	CRow EBee
* - 'Bittenberg'	WCot
- 'Flore Pleno' (d)	Last listed 1998
- 'Nanum'	CNic
§ - 'Striatum' (v)	More than 30 suppliers
- 'Variegatum'	See *P. x hybridum* 'Striatum'
inflatum	WCru
involucratum	WCru
¶ *kingianum*	LEur
¶ - yellow-flowered B&SWJ 6562	WCru
'Langthorns Variegated' (v)	ELan
lasianthum	WCru
latifolium	See *P. hirtum*
multiflorum L.	CRow EBee EGar EPla EWTr GKir LRHS NVic SAga SPlb SRms
- hort.	See *P. x hybridum*
- *giganteum*	See *P. biflorum*
* *nanum* 'Variegatum'	ELau
nodosum	WCru
* 'Nymans Variety'	NRar
¶ *obtusifolium*	EBee
§ *odoratum*	CAvo CBro CRow CSWP EBee ELau EPar EPfP EPla EPot EWFC EWTr IBlr MSal NLar NRya SAga SMac SSpi WCru WShi
- dwarf	IBlr
- 'Flore Pleno' (d) ♀	CLAP CMGP CRow EHrv IBlr NRar SBla WCot WHoo
- 'Grace Barker'	See *P. x hybridum* 'Striatum'
- Kew form	EPot
- var. *pluriflorum*	GBuc IBlr SSpi
- - 'Variegatum'	CBro EGle EGol EPla IBlr LGre LRHS MBro MCli MRav NLar WCot WCru WRus WWat WWin
- - 'Variegatum' misapplied	See *P. falcatum* 'Variegatum'
- 'Silver Wings'	CLAP ECha
officinale	See *P. odoratum*
oppositifolium B&SWJ 2537	EBee WCru
§ *orientale*	CHid EBee
pluriflorum	See *P. graminifolium*
polyanthemum	See *P. orientale*
prattii	LEur
pubescens	WCru
pumilum	See *P. falcatum*
punctatum	EBee
- B&SWJ 2395	WCru
racemosum	SIng
roseum	WHer
¶ *sewerzowii*	EPla
sibiricum	IBlr WCru
sp. Himalaya	Last listed 1999

stenophyllum	CAvo
stewartianum	CLAP EPar IBlr NDov
verticillatum	CAvo CBro CHid CLyd CMCo
	CRow EBee EBrP EBre ECha EPla
	EPot IBlr LBCl LBSe LBre MBBe
	MTho NDov NHol SBre SMad
	WCot WCru WFar WWat
- CC 1324	CPLG
- 'Himalayan Giant'	CHid EBee
* - *rubrum*	CArn CHid CRow EGar EHrv EPPr
	EPar IBlr LGre MSte MTho WCot
- 'Serbian Dwarf'	CHid EBee
aff. *verticillatum* CLD 1308 EMon

POLYGONUM ✿ (Polygonaceae)

affine	See *Persicaria affinis*
amplexicaule	See *Persicaria amplexicaulis*
aubertii	See *Fallopia baldschuanica*
aviculare	CArn
baldschuanicum	See *Fallopia baldschuanica*
bistorta	See *Persicaria bistorta*
compactum	See *Fallopia japonica* var.
	compacta
cuspidatum	See *Fallopia japonica*
equisetiforme hort.	See *P. scoparium*
filiforme	See *Persicaria virginiana*
longisetum	See *Persicaria longiseta*
molle	See *Persicaria mollis*
multiflorum	See *Fallopia multiflora*
odoratum	See *Persicaria odorata*
polystachyum	See *Persicaria wallichii*
reynoutria	See *Fallopia japonica*
runciforme	See *Persicaria runcinata*
§ *scoparium*	CRow EMan EPPr EPla MFir NFai
	SDry SDys SIng WCot WWat
tinctorium	See *Persicaria tinctoria*
weyrichii	See *Persicaria weyrichii*

POLYLEPIS (Rosaceae)

australis	CPle LEdu

POLYMNIA (Asteraceae)

sonchifolia	LEdu

POLYPODIUM ✿ (Polypodiaceae)

§ *aureum* ♀	Last listed 1994
- ruffled	Last listed 1997
australe	See *P. cambricum*
§ *cambricum*	EFer NHar NMar WCot WRic
§ - 'Barrowii'	NMar WRic
- 'Cambricum' ♀	WRic WWye
- 'Cristatum'	WRic
- (Cristatum Group)	WRic
'Diadem'	
- - 'Grandiceps Forster'	CCuc WRic
- - 'Grandiceps Fox' ♀	WRic
- 'Hornet'	WRic
¶ - 'Oakleyae'	WAbe WPGP
- Omnilacerum Group	Last listed 1998
- 'Omnilacerum Oxford'	CLAP WRic
- Plumosum Group	Last listed 1998
- 'Prestonii'	WRic
- Pulcherrimum Group	CCuc EGol NHar
- 'Pulcherrimum Addison'	WRic
- Pulcherrimum Group	WRic
bifid	
- 'Richard Keyse'	WRic
- Semilacerum Group	NMar WRic
- - 'Carew Lane'	WRic
- - 'Falcatum O'Kelly'	WRic
- - 'Jubilee'	NMar WRic
- - 'Robustum'	NMar WRic

- 'Whilharris' ♀	CCuc CFil CLAP WPGP WRic
x *coughlinii*	WRic
'Bifidograndiceps'	
glycyrrhiza	WRic
- Grandiceps Group	WRic
- 'Longicaudatum' ♀	CCuc EMon NMar WFib WRic
	WWye
¶ - 'Malahatense'	NMar
- 'Malahatense' (fertile)	WRic
- 'Malahatense' (sterile)	WRic
interjectum	CCuc CLAP EFer EMon EPVP
	NMar NOrc NVic WFib WRic
¶ - 'Acutum'	NMar
- 'Bifidograndiceps'	WPGP WRic
- 'Cornubiense' ♀	CFil CLAP CRDP ECha EFer EMon
	GCal NBir NBro NHar NHol NMar
	NVic SSpi WAbe WPGP WRic
- 'Ramosum Hillman'	WRic
x *mantoniae*	Last listed 1999
scouleri	NBro
vulgare	More than 30 suppliers
- 'Bifidomultifidum'	CBos CLAP EMon GBin MBri
	NBus NHar NHol NMar SLon
	WCot WFib WWat
* - 'Congestum Cristatum'	Last listed 1997
- 'Cornubiense Grandiceps'	CCuc SRms WFib WRic
* - 'Cornubiense Multifidum'	CCuc NHar WCot
- Ramosum Group	NMar

POLYPOGON (Poaceae)

monspeliensis	SWal

POLYSCIAS (Araliaceae)

'Elegans'	MBri
fruticosa	MBri
sambucifolia	Last listed 1999
scutellaria 'Pennockii' (v)	MBri

POLYSTICHUM ✿ (Dryopteridaceae)

acrostichoides	CLAP GCal GQui IOrc NHar SNut
	SSpi WRic
aculeatum ♀	More than 30 suppliers
- Grandiceps Group	EFer NMar
andersonii	CLAP NHar NHol
braunii	CB&S EBrP EBre EGol GGar LBCl
	LBSe LBre MBBe MLan NMar
	NOGN SBre
- x *proliferum*	NWoo
californicum	Last listed 1999
caryotideum	See *Cyrtomium caryotideum*
falcatum	See *Cyrtomium falcatum*
falcinellum	CFil
fortunei	See *Cyrtomium fortunei*
* *fructuosum*	Last listed 1999
imbricans	CLAP NHar SArc
lonchitis	NWoo
makinoi	CCuc CLAP NHol NMar WFib
mehrae	Last listed 1999
mobrioides	NMar
munitum ♀	CBlo CFil CLAP CMil EBee EFer
	GKir IOrc LRHS LRot MBri MTed
	NBus NFla NHar NHol NOrc
	NWoo SAPC SArc SNut SRms SSpi
	WFib WPGP WRic WWoo
- 'Incisum'	GCal
neolobatum	WRic
polyblepharum ♀	More than 30 suppliers
proliferum (R. Br.) C. Presl	WRic
* - *plumosum*	NOak
retrorsopaleaceum	NMar WRic
richardii	Last listed 1999
rigens	CLAP EBee EFer GCal LHil NBus

§ **setiferum** ♀
§ - Acutilobum Group

- Congestum Group

- 'Congestum'

- 'Congestum Cristatum'
§ - 'Cristatogracile'
- 'Cristatopinnulum'
- Cristatum Group
- Cruciatum Group
- Dahlem Group

- Divisilobum Group
- - 'Herrenhausen'

- - 'Madame Patti'
- - 'Mrs Goffey'
- - 'Ray Smith'
- 'Divisilobum Densum' ♀

- 'Divisilobum
Iveryanum' ♀
* - 'Divisilobum Latipes'
- 'Divisilobum Laxum'
- Foliosum Group
- 'Gracile'
¶ - 'Grandiceps'
- 'Grandidens'
- 'Hirondelle'
- Lineare Group
- Multilobum Group
- Percristatum Group
- Perserratum Group
- 'Plumo-Densum'

- 'Plumosodensum'

- Plumosodivisilobum
Group

§ - 'Plumosomultilobum'

- Plumosum Group

* - **plumosum grande**
'Moly'
- Proliferum Group

* - 'Proliferum Wollaston'
- 'Pulcherrimum Bevis' ♀

* - 'Ramopinnatum'
* - **ramulosum**
- Revolvens Group
- Rotundatum Group
- - 'Cristatum'
- 'Wakeleyanum'
N - 'Wollaston'

NDlv NHar NHol NMar NOGN
SNut SRms WFib WRic
More than 30 suppliers
CB&S CFil CLAP CMHG CRDP
ECha EPot GAri LHil NCat NHar
NHol NVic SDix SMad SSpi STes
WAbe WCot WPGP WWol
CMil CRDP IOrc MBri NHar NHol
NMar SChu SPer SPla SRms WFib
WRic
GCal LRHS NBir SNut WGor
WWat
EFer
NHar NMar
CFil EMon NHar NMar WPGP
SRms
Last listed 1998
CCuc CDoC CLAP EBrP EBre
ECha EFer ELan LBCl LBSe LBre
LHil MBBe MBri MSte NBus SBre
SMac SNut SPer SRCN WAbe WRic
More than 30 suppliers
EBee EBrP EBre ECha EFer ELan
EMar EPfP GKir LBCl LBSe LBre
LRHS MBBe MBri MCCP NMar
NOGN NOrc SBre SPer WAbe
WRic
Last listed 1998
Last listed 1999
Last listed 1998
CLAP EPfP NMar NOrc SNut SSoC
SSpi WCot
NHol SRms

NMar
EPar SChu
EFer
MBri MDun WRic
CLAP
WRic
SRms
CFil WFib
WRic
See P. setiferum 'Cristatogracile'
NMar
See P. setiferum
'Plumosomultilobum'
See P. setiferum
'Plumosomultilobum'
CCuc CMil CRow ECha EGol
NBid NHar SPla WAbe WCru WFib
WWat
CDoC EBee EMon LRHS MBri
NBus NFla SNut SPer SRms WRic
CBos CCuc CLAP CSam CSpe
MBri NOrc SArc SChu SSoC WFib
WStI
WFib

See P. setiferum Acutilobum
Group
LSyl NRib SNut
CLAP EMon SDix WFib WPGP
WRic
NMar
NMar
CCuc EFer
CRDP NMar WFib
Last listed 1998
SRms
CCuc CLAP GBin MDun NCiC
WAbe WWoo

silvaticum
stenophyllum
triangulum
tsussimense ♀

xiphophyllum

Last listed 1999
WRic
NMar
CCuc CDoC CLAP CRDP EBee
EFou GQui LRHS MBri MSte NBir
NBus NHol NMar SEas SNut SPer
SPlb SRms WFib WRic
WRic

POLYXENA (Hyacinthaceae)
§ **ensifolia**
odorata
pygmaea

ERos LBow
CLyd WAbe
See P. ensifolia

POMADERRIS (Rhamnaceae)
apetala
elliptica

Last listed 1998
ECou

PONCIRUS (Rutaceae)
§ **trifoliata**

- 'Flying Dragon'

CAgr CB&S CDoC CFil ELan ENot
EPfP EREa LRHS MBlu MCCP
NWea SAPC SArc SLon SMad SPar
WDin WFar WPGP WPat WSHC
WWat
CAgr

PONERORCHIS (Orchidaceae)
taiwanensis   Last listed 1997

PONTEDERIA (Pontederiaceae)
cordata ♀

- **alba**
¶ - dark blue
§ - var. **lancifolia**

¶ - light blue
- 'Pink Pons'
dilatata
lanceolata

CBen CHEx CRow CWat ECha
ECtt EHon EMFW EPfP LGuA
LPBA MCCP MSta NDea NPer
SCoo SLon SPlb SWat SWyc
WMAq
CRow EMFW LGuA SWyc
SWyc
CRow EMFW LGuA MSta SWat
SWyc
SWyc
CRow LLWG SWyc
EMFW SWyc
See P. cordata var. lancifolia

POPULUS ✿ (Salicaceae)
x **acuminata**
alba

- 'Bolleana'
§ - f. **pyramidalis**
§ - 'Raket'

- 'Richardii' ♀

- Rocket
§ 'Balsam Spire' (f) ♀

§ **balsamifera**

x **berolinensis**
x **canadensis** 'Aurea' ♀

¶ - 'Aurea' x **jackii** 'Aurora'
- 'Eugenei' (m)
- 'Robusta' (m)

WMou
CBlo CDoC CDul CKin CLnd CTri
ECrN ENot EWTr GChr GKir
GVer IOrc LBuc MBar NBee
NWea SPer WDin WMou WStI
See P. alba f. pyramidalis
CB&S NBee SRms WMou
CBlo CLnd CTho ELan ENot EPfP
IOrc MGos NWea SPer
CDul CLnd CTho EBee ECtt GChr
IOrc LPan MBar SPer SRPl WFar
WMou
See P. alba 'Raket'
CDoC CDul CLnd CTho ENot
GKir IOrc LBuc NWea WMou
CBlo CDoC CTho CTri ENot GKir
MGos NWea SMHT SPer SRms
WCot WDin WHer
CDoC
CDoC CLnd CTho EBee EMil
ENot LPan MDun MRav SPer
WDin WGer WMou
MRav
CTho WMou
CDoC CDul CKin CLnd CTri EBee
EMil ENot IOrc LBuc NWea WDin
WMou

- 'Serotina' (m)	CDoC MAsh WDin WMou
x **candicans**	See *P.* x *jackii*
x **canescens**	CDoC ELan GChr GKir MBri
	WDin WMou
- 'De Moffatt' (m)	ENot
- 'Tower'	WMou
¶ x **generosa** 'Beaupré'	CTho WMou
§ x **jackii** (f)	WDin
¶ - 'Aurora' (f/v)	CB&S CBlo CDul CKin CMHG
	CTrw EBee ELan ENot EWTr
	GChr GKir GOrc IOrc LBuc LRHS
	MAsh MBar MBri MGos MWat
	NBee NWea SPer SRms WDin
	WFar WHar WJas
lasiocarpa ♀	CDoC CHEx CLnd CMCN CTho
	EPfP MBlu MRav SLPl SMad
	WMou WPGP
§ - var. **tibetica**	WMou
maximowiczii	WMou
nigra	CDul EBee EWTr GChr NWea
	SPer WDin
- (f)	EBee SLPl
- (m)	SLPl
- subsp. **betulifolia** ♀	CBlo CDul CKin CTho GChr LBuc
	MGos NWea WMou
- - (f)	WMou
- - (m)	WMou
N - 'Italica' (m) ♀	CBlo CDoC CDul CLnd CTho
	CTri EBee ELan EMac ENot EPfP
	GChr IOrc LBuc LRHS MBri MGos
	NBee NWea SPer SRms WDin
- 'Italica Aurea'	See *P. nigra* 'Lombardy Gold'
§ - 'Lombardy Gold' (m)	CCHP CEnd CTho EBee SMad
	SPer SRPl WMou
- 'Pyramidalis'	See *P. nigra* 'Italica'
simonii	Last listed 1997
- 'Fastigiata'	CB&S NSti WMou
- 'Obtusata'	WMou
szechuanica	WMou
¶ - var. **tibetica**	WPGP
tacamahaca	See *P. balsamifera*
'Tacatricho 32'	See *P.* 'Balsam Spire'
tomentosa	WMou
tremula ♀	CBlo CDul CKin CLnd CTho EBee
	ELan ENot GChr GKir GTre IOrc
	LBuc LHyr LRHS NBee NWea SPer
	WDin WMou
§ - 'Erecta'	CDul CEnd CLnd CTho EBee LPan
	LRHS MBri SMad WMou
- 'Fastigiata'	See *P. tremula* 'Erecta'
- 'Pendula' (m)	CEnd CLnd CTho EBee SRPl
	WCFE WDin WMou
trichocarpa	CBlo CDul CTho SPer
- 'Fritzi Pauley' (f)	CDul CTho WMou
violascens	See *P. lasiocarpa* var. *tibetica*
wilsonii	WMou
yunnanensis	CFil CMHG WMou WPGP

PORTULACA (Portulacaceae)

grandiflora	MBri
oleracea	CArn ELau MChe MHer SIde
	WHer WJek
- var. **aurea**	ELau MChe MHer WJek

POTAMOGETON (Potamogetonaceae)

crispus	EHon EMFW WMAq
pectinatus	EHon

POTENTILLA ♣ (Rosaceae)

alba	CGle CSev ECha EFou ELan EMar
	GCHN LGro MHar MRav MTho
	NChi NFai SCro SPer SUsu WByw

	WCot WPer
alchemilloides	EBrP EBre LBCl LBSe LBre MBBe
	MNrw SBre SMer SOkh WPer
alpicola	WPer
ambigua	See *P. cuneata*
andicola	EBee
anserina	CArn CKin EEls EWFC GBar MGas
	MHer MHew WHbs WHer
- 'Golden Treasure' (v)	MLLN WCot WHer
- 'Shine'	WAlt
anserinoides	EBee EMan GCal MBel WCot
	WMoo WPer WWat
arbuscula hort.	See *P. fruticosa* 'Elizabeth'
'Arc-en-ciel'	CFri CHid EMan NCat
argentea	CBlo CSWP CSev LIck LPVe
	MBNS MRav NFai NHol NNor
	SPlb SSte WBea WCru WPer WWat
- 'Calabre'	Last listed 1997
- **glabra**	Last listed 1997
arguta	EBee
argyrophylla	See *P. atrosanguinea* var.
	argyrophylla
* - **insignis rubra**	NChi
atrosanguinea	More than 30 suppliers
§ - var. **argyrophylla**	CGle EBee ECha ELan GCHN
	GCal GTou LRHS MBel MCLN
	MRav MWat NBir NBro NFai NMir
	NNrd NOak SCro SRms WByw
	WFar WPGP WPer WWhi WWin
- - SS&W 7768	GDra MSte NMGW SRms
- CC 1384	CPou
- var. **leucochroa**	See *P. atrosanguinea* var.
	argyrophylla
aurea	CPea EBee ECtt EDAr EMNN EPfP
	LRHS MBri MTho NArg NFla
	NMen NMir NOrc SHFr SRms
	SSmi WRHF
- 'Aurantiaca'	CElw EDAr GCHN LRHS NNrd
	SRot
§ - subsp. **chrysocraspeda**	NHol NMen
§ - 'Goldklumpen'	EDAr EGar MChl MRav NPro SCro
- - 'Plena' (d)	GCHN GDra GTou LRHS MBro
	NHar SRot WWin
'Blazeaway'	EBee EPPr LRHS MBel MBri NCat
	NHol WElm WFar WLRN
brevifolia	NWCA
- NNS 94-25	Last listed 1998
* **bulleyana**	WWeb
calabra	ECha EDAr EMan EPPr SIng SMer
	WByw WHer WWin
§ **cinerea**	CTri LBee LRHS NHar NMen SBla
	SSmi
clusiana	Last listed 1997
collina	CNic
concinna bicrenata	Last listed 1999
§ 'Craigieburn Cochineal'	Last listed 1998
§ **crantzii**	CBrm CMea CTri EBee EWFC
	GCHN GCrs GTou LBee MBar
	MSte SIng SRms
- 'Nana'	See *P. crantzii* 'Pygmaea'
§ - 'Pygmaea'	ECtt EPfP MOne MTPN NMen
§ **cuneata** ♀	CLyd CNic EDAr ESis GDra GTou
	MTho NHar NMen NRya NWCA
	SDys SSmi WPer WWin
aff. **cuneata** CC 1461	Last listed 1999
delavayi	EBrP EBre LBCl LBSe LBre MBBe
	MBro MNrw NBus SBre
detommasii	MHar WPer
dickinsii	NTow SOkd
dombeyi	GCHN
* 'Emilie'	CMea EFou GCal MBNS MBri
	NLar WFar

§ *erecta*	CAgr CArn CKin EOHP GBar
	GPoy LFis MChe MHer MHew
	MSal WHbs WOak WWye
eriocarpa	CLyd EMNN GCHN GDra IMGH
	MBro MHar MWat NHar NHol
	NMen WAbe
¶ – CC 2633	MDCh
'Etna'	CBlo CElw CFri CLon CStr EBee
	ECtt ELan GAbr GCal GKir GTou
	LFis MCAu MNrw NCat NFai NFor
	SAga WBro WByw WCru WHen
	WLin WPGP WPer WWhi
'Everest'	See *P. fruticosa* 'Mount Everest'
'Fireflame'	EBee ECha NLar
fissa	EBee MNrw MSte NBir NRya
	WBar WUnu
'Flambeau'	CHad EBee MRav NDov NLar
	WRha
'Flamenco'	CBre CSam CTri EBee EFou ELan
	MArl MBri MNrw MRav NFor
	SUsu WAbb WByw WFar
fragariformis	See *P. megalantha*
fruticosa	LBuc NWea
– 'Abbotswood' ♀	More than 30 suppliers
– 'Abbotswood Silver' (v)	CBlo CLTr CLyd ECtt LAst MAsh
	MBNS MRav SLim SLon SPla WFar
	WHar WWal
– 'Annette'	CBlo LRHS MBri NPro WBod
	WHCG WWeb
– var. *arbuscula* hort.	See *P. fruticosa* 'Elizabeth'
– var. *arbuscula* (D. Don)	Last listed 1997
Maxim. KW 5774	
– 'Argentea Nana'	See *P. fruticosa* 'Beesii'
– 'Beanii'	NHol SPer WWeb
§ – 'Beesii' ♀	ELan EPfP ESis GKir IMGH LRHS
	MAsh MBar MBlu NHol SPer SPla
	WAbe WHCG WLRN WSHC WWeb
	WWin
– 'Beverley Surprise'	EHol NPro WHCG WWeb
– 'Blink' [PBR]	See *P. fruticosa* Princess = 'Blink'
– 'Buttercup'	Last listed 1999
– 'Cascade'	WBcn WHCG
* – 'Chelsea Star'	WHCG
* – 'Chilo' (v)	MGos WBcn
– 'Clotted Cream'	MBar
– var. *dahurica*	WHCG
– – 'Farrer's White'	WWat
– – 'Hersii'	See *P. fruticosa* 'Snowflake'
– – 'Rhodocalyx'	CPle WHCG WWat
– 'Dart's Cream'	LRHS MBri MRav
– 'Dart's Golddigger'	CTri EBee ECtt ENot SLPl
§ – 'Dart's Nugget'	Last listed 1999
– 'Daydawn' ♀	More than 30 suppliers
– 'Eastleigh Cream'	Last listed 1998
* – 'Eden Lemonlight'	Last listed 1998
§ – 'Elizabeth' ♀	CB&S CDoC CLan EBee ENot
	GDra GKir LGro LRHS MBar MBri
	MGos MWat NFor NWea SPer
	SRms WBod WCFE WDin WFar
	WMoo
– 'Farreri'	See *P. fruticosa* 'Gold Drop'
– 'Floppy Disc'	CBlo CCHP EPfP GKir LRHS
	MGos NCut NHol NWoo SPer SPla
	SSta
– 'Frances Lady Daresbury'	GKir
– 'Friedrichsenii'	Last listed 1999
¶ – 'Funny Face'	MBri
– 'Glenroy Pinkie'	CSam EBee EPfP LRHS MRav MTis
	NPro SAga SEas SLon WAbe
	WHCG WWeb
– 'Glenroy Seashell'	Last listed 1999
§ – 'Gold Drop'	NFor WHCG WWat WWeb
– 'Golden Dwarf'	LRHS MBri MGos
* – 'Golden Nugget'	WLRN
– 'Golden Spreader'	EBrP EBre GKir LBCl LBSe LBre
	MBBe NPro SBre
– 'Goldfinger' ♀	CChe CDoC EBee ELan ENot EPfP
	EWTr GChr GKir GOrc IOrc
	LRHS MAsh MBri MGos MRav
	SEas SLim SMer SPer SPlb SRPl
	WAbe WDin WHCG WHar WStl
	WWeb
– Goldkugel	See *P. fruticosa* 'Gold Drop'
– 'Goldstar'	CMHG EBee EBrP EBre ENot GAri
	GCHN GKir IOrc LBCl LBSe LBre
	LRHS MBBe MBri SBre WFar
	WHCG
– 'Goldteppich'	LBuc MBar
– 'Goscote'	MGos
– 'Hachmann's Gigant'	Last listed 1997
– 'Hopleys Little Joker'	WPat WPyg
– 'Hopleys Orange'	CChe CDoC CMHG EPfP EWes
	GAri GCHN GKir LHop LRHS
	MBri MWat SAga WBod WFar
	WGor WHCG WWin
¶ – 'Hopleys Pink'	LHop
– 'Hurstbourne'	NPro
– 'Jackman's Variety'	CCHP CSam ECtt ENot SPer SRms
	WBod WStl WWeb
– 'Judith'	Last listed 1997
– 'Katherine Dykes' ♀	CChe CDoC EBee ENot EPfP
	GChr GDra GKir LRHS MAsh
	MBar MRav SLim SLon SPer SRPl
	SRms WBod WDin WFar WGwG
	WHar WMoo WStl WWeb
* – 'King Cup'	WWeb
– 'Klondike' ♀	CB&S CLan EBee EPfP GKir MAsh
	NFor NWea
§ – 'Knap Hill'	EBee ENot GDra GEil NFor WWeb
– 'Knap Hill Buttercup'	See *P. fruticosa* 'Knap Hill'
– 'Kobold'	CBlo GEil MBar WTro
* – 'Lemon and Lime'	MBlu NPro
– 'Limelight'	EBee GKir LRHS MBri WFar
– 'Logan'	Last listed 1997
– 'London Town'	CMHG
– 'Longacre Variety' ♀	CTri GDra GKir MBar NHol NWea
	WBod WWat WWeb
§ – 'Maanelys' ♀	CTrw ECtt ELan MWat NFla NWea
	SPer SRms WDin WHCG WMoo
	WWeb
– 'Macpenny's Cream'	WHCG
§ – 'Manchu'	ENot GDra MBar MBri MRav NFla
	NFor SChu SPer SRms WCFE
	WWat WWin
§ – Marian Red Robin =	CDoC EBee EBrP EBre ELan ENot
'Marrob' [PBR]	EPfP GCHN GChr GKir LAst LBCl
	LBSe LBre LRHS MAsh MBBe MBri
	MGos MRav MTis MWat SBre
	SCoo SLim SPer WDin WStl
	WWeb
– 'Marrob' [PBR]	See *P. fruticosa* Marian Red
	Robin = 'Marrob'
– 'Medicine Wheel	ELan EWes LRHS MAsh MBri
Mountain'	MRav NPro NTow SLim SPer
	WHCG WWeb
– 'Milkmaid'	Last listed 1999
– Moonlight	See *P. fruticosa* 'Maanelys'
§ – 'Mount Everest'	CChe MBar NCut NHol NWea
	SLon SRms WHCG WWeb
– 'Nana Argentea'	See *P. fruticosa* 'Beesii'
– 'New Dawn'	CDoC ECle GKir LRHS MAsh
	MBri SPer WFar
– 'Northman'	Last listed 1997
– 'Nugget'	See *P. fruticosa* 'Dart's Nugget'

- 'Ochroleuca' — Last listed 1997
- 'Orange Star' — CBlo CCHP WHCG
- 'Orange Stripe' — Last listed 1999
- 'Orangeade' — CBlo LRHS MAsh SMur SReu SSta WWeb
- 'Peaches and Cream' — WHCG
* - 'Peachy Proud' — NPro
- 'Perryhill' — SPer
* - 'Pierce Ogon' — Last listed 1998
- 'Pink Beauty' — ENot LRHS NPri SCoo SPer
- 'Pink Glow' — GDra
- 'Pink Pearl' — EBrP EBre GKir LBCl LBSe LBre MBBe SBre WBcn WMoo WWin
- 'Pink Queen' — MBri WRHF
- 'Pretty Polly' — CChe EBee ENot EPfP GKir IOrc LAst LRHS MAsh MBar MBri MGos NHol SPer SSta WAbe WBod WDin WFar WHCG WHar WStI WWal
- 'Primrose Beauty' ♀ — CDoC CLan EBee ELan ENot GKir LAst LRHS MBar MGos MRav NFla NFor SLim SMer SPlb WAbe WDin WFar WGwG WHar WMoo WStI WWat WWeb
§ - Princess = 'Blink'PBR — CDoC EBee EBrP EBre ELan ENot GChr GKir LBCl LBSe LBre LRHS MBBe MBNS MBar MGos MWgw SBre SIng SLim SPer SReu SRms WDin WFar WHar WStI WWeb
- 'Prostrate Copper' — NPro
- var. pumila — MBro WPat
§ - var. pyrenaica — Last listed 1999
- 'Red Ace' — CDoC EBee EBrP EBre ECtt ELan ENot GChr GKir GOrc LBCl LBSe LBre LHop LRHS MBBe MBar MBri MGos NWea SBre SLim SPer SRms WDin WFar WHCG WHar WWal WWeb
- Red Robin PBR — See P.fruticosa Marian Red Robin = 'Marrob'
- 'Royal Flush' — GAri MBar MBri SAga WHCG WStI
- 'Ruth' — Last listed 1997
- 'Sandved' — Last listed 1997
- 'Silver Schilling' — LHop NPro
- 'Snowbird' — EBrP EBre EPfP LBCl LBSe LBre LRHS MBBe MBNS MBlu MBri MGos NPro SBre SLim WWeb
§ - 'Snowflake' — CB&S WHCG WLRN WMoo
- 'Sommerflor' — ENot
- 'Sophie's Blush' — CChe EBee LAst MRav NHol WDin WSHC WWeb
- 'Sunset' — CB&S CBrm CChe CSam EBee ELan ENot GChr GDra GKir GOrc LRHS MAsh MBar MBri MGos MTis NFor NWea SLim SPer SReu SRms SSta WBod WFar WGwG WStI WWal
- 'Tangerine' ♀ — More than 30 suppliers
- 'Tilford Cream' ♀ — More than 30 suppliers
- 'Tom Conway' — WHCG WWeb
§ - var. veitchii — SPer WStI
- 'Vilmoriniana' — CBot CHad CHar CTri ELan EPfP LRHS MAsh MRav NFor SLon SMac SPer SSpi WAbe WCFE WGwG WHCG WSHC WWat
- 'Walton Park' — Last listed 1999
- 'Wessex Silver' — CFai WHCG
- 'Whirligig' — CFai WHCG
- 'White Rain' — CLTr GDra GKir NFor WWeb
- 'Wickwar Trailer' — CLyd EPot ESis MBro WHCG WHoo
- 'William Purdom' — WHCG

- 'Yellow Bird' — LRHS MGos
- 'Yellow Carpet' — WHCG
- 'Yellow Giant' — WWeb
'Gibson's Scarlet' ♀ — More than 30 suppliers
glandulosa — EBee MNrw
'Gloire de Nancy' — CLAP CSpe EBee EBrP EBre ELan GAri GCal LBCl LBSe LBre LRHS MBBe MRav NBir SBre WCot WElm
'Gold Clogs' — See P.aurea 'Goldklumpen'
'Grace Darling' — CWit ECle GChr GGar GKir NEgg NHol WBod WGor WGwG WWeb CBrm EBee NChi NNrd
gracilis
§ - var. glabrata — EBee EPPr
- subsp. nuttallii — See P.gracilis var. glabrata
'Harlow Cream' — NBid
'Helen Jane' — CGle EBee EBrP EBre GKir LBCl LBSe LBre LPio LRHS MBBe MBel MBri MBro MCLN MRav NBir NGdn NLar SBre SLod WElm WFar WPer
'Herzblut' — EBee EPfP GBuc MNrw NLar
x hopwoodiana — CGle CHad CPlt CPou EBee EPPr LGre LRHS MBri MCLN MNrw MTis NBir SAga SUsu WAbb WByw WLin WPGP
* x hybrida 'Jean Jabber' — EBee EWll GBuc MRav
¶ hyparctica — MDCh
- nana — CLyd GCrs LBee LRHS MBro NHol SRms WPat WPyg
* 'Limelight' — ELan EPla MAsh MRav SPla SRPl SSta WFar WHCG
* lutea — EPPr
'Mandshurica' — See P.fruticosa 'Manchu'
§ megalantha ♀ — More than 30 suppliers
'Melton' — EBee ECoo LAst MNrw NBir NChi NOak SAga SIng WHen
* 'Melton Fire' — ECtt GKir LRHS NArg STes SVen WBea WBro WCot WElm
miyabei — Last listed 1998
'Monarch's Velvet' — See P.thurberi 'Monarch's Velvet'
'Monsieur Rouillard' — CGle CLon CSam EBrP EBre EPPr GKir LBCl LBSe LBre LFis MBBe MBel MHer MNrw MSCN MWat NDov NFor SBre SUsu WByw WCot WCru WElm WHoo WSan
'Mont d'Or' — LRHS MBri MRav
montana — GCHN MBel NHol WHer WPer
nepalensis — CSam EBee ECha EDAr GAbr GKir IMGH LAst LHop LLWP MFir NBro NChi NFor NPro NSti SAga SHFr SHel SMac
- 'Craigieburn' — Last listed 1998
- 'Kirsten' — Last listed 1998
¶ - 'Master Floris' — SAga WFar WHer
§ - 'Miss Willmott' ♀ — More than 30 suppliers
- red — WLin
¶ - 'Ron McBeath' — EFou GBin
- 'Roxana' — CGle EBee ECGP ELan GBuc GKir MBNS MBel MRav NBro NFai SHel WAbb WBea WByw WFar WPer
- 'Shogran' — CPne EBee NBur WBea
§ neumanniana — EWFC SHel
- aurea — Last listed 1999
- 'Goldrausch' — ECha MRav
§ - 'Nana' — CInt CSev EMNN EPot LBee LRHS MBro MHer MNaF MWat NHar NMen NNrd SPlb SRms SSmi WEas WWin
nevadensis — CLyd CTri ECho SRms WPer
nitida — NHar NMen SRms
- 'Alannah' — Last listed 1998

- 'Alba'	EPot
- 'Lissadell'	CPBP
- 'Rubra'	CMea CNic EDAr GCrs GTou
	IMGH MBro MHer MWat NBir
	NHol NMGW NTow NWCA SBla
	SRms SSmi WAbe WPat
nivea	GTou SRot
'Nunk'	CBlo MBar WWeb
* 'Olympic Mountains'	WPer
ovina	WPer
palustris	EBee LGuA MSta NLar WGwy
	WUnu
pamirica	WUnu
pedata	LLWP NChi
peduncularis	WCot
- CC&McK 532	GCHN
'Pink Panther'^{PBR}	See *P.fruticosa* Princess = 'Blink'
¶ *pyrenaica* Ramond	SIng
ex DC.	
recta	CBlo CBrm ELau EMan EWFC
	GTou MCAu MHew
- 'Alba'	CBlo CPea EGoo GMaP NDov
	NFai NPri WPer WWhi
- 'Citrina'	See *P.recta* var. *sulphurea*
- HH&K 205	Last listed 1999
- 'Macrantha'	See *P.recta* 'Warrenii'
§ - var. *sulphurea* ♀	CGle CHad CLon CMil CPea
	CSam EBee EGoo GCal GMac
	MBel MFir MNrw MTis NCat NFai
	SAga SIng SUsu WCra WFar WHal
	WHer WHoo WLin WPer WPyg
§ - 'Warrenii'	CHea CPea EBee EFou GMaP
	LRHS MBNS MCAu MCLN MFir
	MRav MTis MWat NFai NMir
	NOrc SCro SHel SIng SPer SRms
	WFar WHal WMoo WOve WPer
	WPyg
reptans	CKin EWFC
- 'Pleniflora' (d)	MInt WAlt
rupestris	CAgr CGle CHea CInt CLTr
	CM&M CTri ECha EMan EWFC
	LFis MCLN MFir MLLN MNrw
	NChi NDlv NSti WByw WFar
	WHal WPer WUnu WWin
schillingii	Last listed 1997
sp. CC 1767	Last listed 1999
speciosa	EMan NChi
* - var. *discolor*	Last listed 1997
- var. *speciosa*	Last listed 1998
- - NS 765	Last listed 1999
sterilis	CHid EWFC
- 'Turncoat' (v)	Last listed 1998
'Sungold'	ECho ESis WHCG
tabernaemontani	See *P.neumanniana*
ternata	See *P.aurea* subsp.
	chrysocraspeda
thurberi	CGle CHid EBee EMan EWes GCal
	LGre LPio MHar MNrw MRav
	NChi NLar
§ - 'Monarch's Velvet'	CBot CHar CLTr CMdw CPou
	CSpe EBee ECGP ECtt EWTr GKir
	LRHS MBri MCli MRav MTis NArg
	NDov SBea SRot SSvw SUsu WBro
	WFar WGor WHoo WLRN
- 'White Queen'	See *P.* 'White Queen'
tommasiniana	See *P.cinerea*
x *tonguei* ♀	CFee CHea CPar EBee ECha ECtt
	EFou EWTr GCHN GDra GKir
	LHop LRHS MBel MBri MCLN
	MNrw MRav NChi NFai NGdn
	NHar SAga SBla SIng SRms SSmi
	WFar WPer WWat

tormentilla	See *P.erecta*
tridentata	See *Sibbaldiopsis tridentata*
verna	See *P.neumanniana*
- 'Pygmaea'	See *P.neumanniana* 'Nana'
'Versicolor Plena' (d)	CMea
villosa	See *P.crantzii*
'Volcan'	CMil EBee EPPr EWes GCal LGre
	MBNS MBri SAga WAbb WFar
	WWeb
wallichiana 'Cream	Last listed 1998
Cracker'	
* 'White Beauty'	Last listed 1997
§ 'White Queen'	CMea EWTr EWll GKir LRHS
	MNrw SBea SRot WElm
'William Rollison' ♀	More than 30 suppliers
willmottiae	See *P.nepalensis* 'Miss Willmott'
'Yellow Queen'	CB&S CTri EMil EPfP LLWP
	MNrw MRav NFai NVic SCro
	SMer SPer SWat WFar WWeb

POTERIUM See SANGUISORBA

PRATIA (Campanulaceae)

§ *angulata*	CLTr EWll GGar NHar
- 'Jack's Pass'	GAri NHar
- 'Messenger'	ECou
- 'Ohau'	Last listed 1997
¶ - x *pedunculata*	GGar
- 'Tim Rees'	EDAr
§ - 'Treadwellii'	ECha EDAr ELan LBee LRHS
	MBNS SIng SLod SPlb SRPl WHal
	WHen
- 'Woodside'	ECou
¶ 'Celestial Spice'	ECou
macrodon	NNrd WCru
§ *pedunculata*	CMHG CMea ECha ECou EDAr
	ELan ESis GCHN GGar GKir
	GMac GTou LBee LRHS MBar
	NFla NRya NVic SHFr SIng SPlb
	SRms SSmi SUsu WFar WHen
	WHoo WPer WWhi WWin
- 'Blue Stars'	WCru
- 'Clear Skies'	Last listed 1997
- 'County Park'	CInt CMea CSpe ECha ECou EDAr
	ELan EPot ESis GGar GMac MBar
	NFla NHar NNrd NWCA SBla SIng
	SPlb SRms SSmi WFar WHal
	WHoo WPat WPer WPyg WWin
- 'Kiandra'	ECou
- 'Kinsey'	Last listed 1997
- 'Tom Stone'	CLTr EPot MBNS NHar NNrd
	SYvo
§ *perpusilla*	ECou
- 'Fragrant Carpet'	ECou WFar
- 'Summer Meadows'	ECou WPer
§ *repens*	Last listed 1999

PRESLIA See MENTHA

PRIMULA ✿ (Primulaceae)

acaulis	See *P.vulgaris*
'Adrian Jones' (2)	NHol NNrd SIng WAbe
'Aire Mist' (*allionii* hybrid)	CGra EPot GNor MFie NHar NHol
(2)	WLin
'Alan Robb' (dPrim)(30)	EBee MBNS MBri MBro NHol SPer
'Alexina' (*allionii* hybrid)	NHar NHo
(2)	l
algida (11)	CPla ECho
* *algida algonis* (11)	WHil
§ *allionii* (2)	EMNN EPot GTou ITim MBro
	MFie NCra NHar NHol NNrd
	NWCA WAbe

– 'A.K. Wells' (2) — EPot WAbe
¶ – 'Agnes' (2) — EHyt
– 'Aire Waves' — See *P.* 'Aire Waves'
– var. *alba* (2) — EMNN NHol
¶ – 'Allen Queen' (2) — NHar
* – 'Alexander' (2) — Last listed 1998
– 'Anna Griffith' (2) — CGra EPot GCHN ITim LRHS MFie NHol NNrd NWCA SIng WAbe
– 'Anne' (2) — EPot ITim
§ – 'Apple Blossom' (2) — CGra EPot GAbr MDHE NNrd NTow
– 'Archer' (2) — EMNN NMen WLin
– x *auricula* 'Blairside Yellow' (2) — CPBP GNor
– x – 'Old Red Dusty Miller' hort. (2) — MDHE MFie NHar NHol NNrd
– 'Austen' (2) — EPot NHol NMen NNrd SIng WAbe
– 'Avalanche' (2) — GNor ITim NHar NMen NTow SIng WAbe
– 'Bill Martin' (2) — CStu EPot
– 'Brilliant' KRW 448/69 (2) — Last listed 1999
– Burnley form (2) — NHol
¶ – 'Candy' (2) — EHyt
– CH 1989 (2) — Last listed 1999
– 'Chris Norton' CCN/03 (2) — ITim
– 'Clarence Elliott' — See *P.* 'Clarence Elliott' (2)
– 'Claude Flight' (2) — NHar
– x *clusiana* (2) — Last listed 1999
¶ – 'Confection' (2) — EHyt
– 'Crowsley Variety' (2) — CNic CPBP EPot LRHS NMen NSla NTow NWCA SBla SIng WAbe WLin
– 'Crowsley Variety' x *pubescens* 'The General' (2) — EPot
– 'Crusader' (2) — Last listed 1999
– 'Crystal' KRW 425/69 (2) — EHyt
* – 'E.G. Watson' — Last listed 1999
§ – 'Edinburgh' (2) — EMNN EPot ITim MFie NHol NNrd
– 'Edrom' (2) — ITim SIng
– 'Elizabeth Baker' (2) — EMNN GNor MFie WAbe
¶ – 'Elizabeth Burrow' (2) — EHyt
– 'Elizabeth Earle' (2) — EPot NHol NMen WAbe
– 'Elliott's Large' — See *P. allionii* 'Edinburgh'
– 'Elliott's Variety' — See *P. allionii* 'Edinburgh'
– 'Fanfare' (2) — CGra EPot LRHS WGwG
¶ – 'Flute' (2) — EHyt
– 'Frank Barker' (2) — EPot NHol
– 'Gavin Brown' (2) — EPot
– GFS 1984 (2) — CGra
§ – 'Gilderdale Glow' (2) — MFie NHar
– 'Giuseppi's Form' — See *P. allionii* 'Mrs Dyas'
– 'Grandiflora' (2) — Last listed 1998
– Hartside 383/12 — See *P. allionii* 'Gilderdale Glow'
– Hartside 383/3 (2) — EPot NHol NMen NNrd
– Hartside 383/6 — Last listed 1998
– 'Hemswell' (2) — Last listed 1998
– 'Hemswell Blush' — See *P.* 'Hemswell Blush'
– 'Hemswell Ember' — See *P.* 'Hemswell Ember'
– x *hirsuta* (2) — MFie
– 'Hocker Edge' (2) — NHol NNrd
– 'Horwood' KD/KRW 397/60 (2) — WAbe
– 'Huntsman' — MFie
– Ingwersen's form (2) — GTou NHol
– JCA 4161/16 (2) — EPot
– JCA 4161/21 — See *P. allionii* 'Travellers' JCA 4161/21
– JCA 4161/22 — See *P. allionii* 'Jenny' JCA 4161/22
– JCA 4161/23 — CGra EPot

§ – 'Jenny' JCA 4161/22 (2) — CGra EPot
– 'Julia' JCA 4161/31 — EPot
– K R W — See *P. allionii* 'Ken's Seedling'
§ – 'Kath Dryden' (2) — WHil
§ – 'Ken's Seedling' (2) — EPot NHol NNrd WAbe
– KRW 1971 (2) — Last listed 1997
– KRW 392/56 (2) — Last listed 1999
– KRW 455/70 (2) — Last listed 1999
– KRW 461/71 (2) — Last listed 1999
– KRW 525/76 (thrum, white) (2) — Last listed 1999
– 'Lindisfarne' (2) — EHyt
– Lismore 79/7 (2) — Last listed 1999
– Lismore 81/19/3 — MFie
– Lismore P85/16xx (2) — Last listed 1999
– x 'Lismore Treasure' (2) — CPBP NWCA WLin
¶ – 'Louise' (2) — EHyt
– 'Margaret Earle' (2) — NHol WAbe
– 'Marion' (2) — EMNN EPot GNor ITim NDlv NHol
– 'Marjorie Wooster' KRW 331/52 (2) — NWCA WAbe
– 'Martin' (2) — EPot NHol NNrd
– 'Mary Berry' (2) — EMNN EPot MFie WAbe
¶ – 'Maurice Dryden' (2) — EHyt
§ – 'Mrs Dyas' (2) — EMNN ITim NHar NHol NNrd WAbe
– Nettleton 8824 (2) — EPot
¶ – 'New Dawn' (2) — EHyt
– pale (2) — WLin
I – 'Paula' (2) — EHyt
– x *pedemontana* — See *P.* x *sendtneri*
– 'Peggy Wilson' (2) — EPot EWes NHol
– 'Pennine Pink' Hartside 383/7 (2) — EPot NHol
– 'Perkie' — Last listed 1997
– 'Perkie' JCA 4161/12 (2) — NNrd
– 'Phobos' (2) — Last listed 1997
– 'Picton's Variety' (2) — EPot NDlv
– 'Pink Aire' (2) — See *P.* 'Pink Aire'
– 'Pink Beauty' (2) — EPot
– 'Pinkie' KRW 271/51 (2) — CGra
– 'Praecox' (2) — EPot MFie NHol NNrd NSla
– x *pubescens* 'Harlow Car' (2) — CLyd GMac NHar
– 'Raymond Wooster' KRW 321/52 (2) — LRHS NHol
– 'Roger Bevan' (2) — Last listed 1999
I – 'Roy' (2) — EHyt
– x *rubra* (2) — MBro NHol
– 'Saint Dalmas' (2) — EPot
– 'Scimitar' (2) — EMNN NHar NHol
– 'Serendipity' (2) — Last listed 1998
– 'Snowflake' KRW 367/56 (2) — CGra CPBP EMNN EPot LRHS NHar NTow NWCA WAbe
– 'Stanton House' (2) — NDlv NHol
– 'Stephen' JCA 4161/6 (2) — EMNN EPot
– 'Sylvia Martinelli' — Last listed 1998
– 'Tranquillity' Hartside 383/1 (2) — MFie NHar NHol NMen NNrd WLin
§ – 'Travellers' JCA 4161/21 (2) — CGra EPot
– 'Viscountess Byng' (2) — EMNN EPot WLin
– W 1971 (2) — Last listed 1999
– x 'White Linda Pope' (2) — MFie NHol
– 'William Earle' (2) — EMNN EPot LRHS MFie NDlv NHar NHol NMen NWCA SIng WAbe

alpicola (26) — CFee CRow CSWP EBrP EBre GAbr GDra GFle GGar GKir GMac LBCI LBSe LBre LPBA LRHS MBBe MFie NBid NBro NCra NDlv SBre

	SPer WAbe WRus
- var. *alba* (26)	CPla CRow CSWP EBrP EBre
	GBuc GGar LBCl LBSe LBre LSyl
	MBBe MMal MNrw SBre SPer
	SWat
§ - var. *alpicola*	EBee GBuc GFle LSyl MNrw
	WAbe
- var. *luna*	See *P. alpicola* var. *alpicola*
- var. *violacea* (26)	CPla CRow GAbr GDra GGar
	LRHS LSyl MBri MFie MNrw NHar
	SPer SWat WAbe WWhi
'Altaica'	See *P. elatior* subsp. *meyeri*
altaica grandiflora	See *P. elatior* subsp. *meyeri*
* 'Amaranth'	WHil
amoena	See *P. elatior* subsp. *meyeri*
anisodora	See *P. wilsonii* var. *anisodora*
'April Rose' (dPrim)(30)	CMea MRav NBid
x *arctotis*	See *P.* x *pubescens*
atrodentata (9)	GCrs
aurantiaca (4)	CPla GAri GBar GFle LSyl MSta
	SIng SRms
aureata (21)	GGGa GGar NCra WAbe
- subsp. *fimbriata* (21)	GCrs
§ *auricula* L. (2) ♀	CFri EDAr ELan GCrs GKir GNor
	GTou LRHS MHer NBro NCra
	NSla NWCA SPer SPlb SSmi WAbe
	WMAq
- var. *albocincta* (2)	NWCA
- subsp. *auricula* (2)	GTou
- subsp. *balbisii*	See *P. auricula* subsp. *ciliata*
- subsp. *baubinii* (2)	MBro
§ - subsp. *ciliata* (2)	GFle NNrd
auricula hort. (B)	WLin
- 'Admiral'	MCre
- 'Adrian' (A)	MCre MFie NCra NNrd SHya SPop
- 'Aga Khan'	SHya
- 'Agamemnon'	MCre NCra
- 'Alamo'	MCre NCra SPop
- 'Alan Ravenscroft' (A)	MFie
- 'Albert Bailey' (S/d)	MCre
- 'Albury' (d)	Last listed 1998
- 'Alfred Niblett' (S)	EMNN NNrd
- 'Alice Haysom' (S)	ELan MCre MFie NNrd SHya WHil
	WLin
- 'Alicia' (A)	ECGP SHya SPop
- 'Alien' (S)	SHya
- 'Alison Jane' (A)	CLyd MCre MFie NCra NOak
	SHya
- 'Allansford'	EMNN
¶ - 'Allensford' (A)	MCre
- 'Almondbury' (S)	NCra SHya
- alpine mixed (A)	CNic MMal NCra SRms
- 'Amicable' (A)	MCre NCra SHya
- 'Andrea Julie' (A)	EMNN MCre MFie MOne NCra
	NHar NHol NNrd SHya SPop WHil
	WLin
- 'Ann Taylor' (A)	MCre NCra SHya
- 'Antoc' (S)	EMNN MFie
- 'Anwar Sadat' (A)	EMNN MCre MFie
- 'Applecross' (A)	EMNN MCre MFie NCra NHar
	NNrd SHya WLin
- 'Arctic Fox'	NCra
- 'Argus' (A)	CLyd GAbr MCre MFie NBir NCra
	NHar NNrd SHya SPop SUsu WLin
- 'Arthur Delbridge' (A)	MCre MFie
- 'Arundel Star'	Last listed 1998
- 'Arundell' (S/St)	EMNN GAbr MCre NHar NNrd
	SHya SPop WHil WLin
- 'Astolat' (S)	EMNN MCre MFie NCra NNrd
	NOak SHya SPop SUsu WLin
- 'Atlantean'	NCra
- 'Aurora' (A)	MFie SHya

- 'Austin'	NCra
- 'Aviemore' (A)	Last listed 1997
- 'Avril Hunter' (A)	MCre MFie SHya
- 'Aye Aye'	NCra
- 'Bacchus' (A)	MCre MFie
- 'Ballet' (S)	MFie
- 'Barbara Mason'	NCra
- 'Barbarella' (S)	EMNN MCre MFie SPop
- Barnhaven doubles	CSWP GAbr MCCP
- 'Basuto' (A)	EMNN MCre MFie SHya SPop
- 'Beatrice' (A)	CLyd EMNN GAbr MCre MFie
	NCra NNrd SHya WLin
¶ - 'Beckminster' (A)	MCre
- 'Bedford Lad' (A)	MCre SHya
- 'Beechen Green' (S)	EMNN GNor NCra NNrd SHya
- 'Bellezana'	MFie
- 'Ben Lawers' (S)	SHya
- 'Ben Wyves' (S)	MCre SHya
- 'Bendigo' (S)	SHya WHil
- 'Bilton' (S)	CLyd NCra
- 'Blackfield' (S)	MFie
- 'Blackhill' (S)	EMNN
¶ - 'Blackpool Rock' (St)	SHya
- 'Blairside Yellow' (B)	EWes NHar NHol
- 'Blakeney' (d)	MCre
- 'Blossom' (S)	EMNN MFie NCra NNrd SHya
	WLin
- 'Blue Bonnet' (A)	GAbr GNor MCre SPop
- 'Blue Heaven'	NCra
- 'Blue Jean' (S)	EMNN MFie NCra
- 'Blue Mist' (B)	GAbr GNor
- 'Blue Nile' (S)	EMNN MFie
- 'Blue Steel' (S)	SHya
- 'Blue Velvet' (B)	EMNN GNor MFie NBro SHya
	SPop WLin
- 'Blue Wave' (d)	Last listed 1999
¶ - 'Bob Dingley' (A)	MCre
- 'Bob Lancashire' (S)	EMNN GNor MCre MFie NCra
	NHar NNrd SHya SPop WHil
- 'Bolero' (A)	MCre SHya SPop
¶ - 'Bollin Tiger' (St)	SHya
- 'Bookham Firefly' (A)	EMNN GNor MBro MCre MFie
	NCra NHar NHol NNrd SHya
	SPop WLin
- 'Boy Blue' (S)	SHya
¶ - 'Bradford City' (A)	NCra
- 'Bravura'	NCra
- 'Brazil' (S)	EMNN GAbr GNor LRHS MCre
	MFie NCra NHol NNrd NOak
	WLin
- 'Bredon Hill' (S)	Last listed 1997
- 'Brenda's Choice' (A)	MCre MFie SHya
- 'Bright Eyes' (A)	MCre MFie NCra SHya
- 'Broad Gold' (A)	MCre SHya
- 'Broadwell Gold' (B)	CLyd GAbr SHya
- 'Brookfield' (S)	EMNN GCrs MCre MFie NCra
	NNrd SHya SPop
- 'Broughton' (S)	MFie
- 'Brown Bess' (A)	GNor MCre MFie NCra NNrd
	SHya SPop WLin
- 'Brownie' (d)	NBir NCra
- 'Buccaneer'	NCra
- 'Bucks Green'	SPop
- 'Bunty' (A)	MFie
- 'Butterwick' (A)	ECGP LRHS MCre MFie NCra
	NHar NHol NPri SHya SPop WHil
	WLin
- 'C.F. Hill' (A)	EMNN SHya
- 'C.G. Haysom' (S)	EMNN MCre MFie NCra NHar
	SHya SPop WLin
- 'C.W. Needham' (A)	EMNN MCre MFie NCra NHol
	NNrd SHya SPop WHil WLin

I	– 'Calypso' (A)	MCre
*	– 'Cambodumun'	MCre NCra SPop
	– 'Camelot' (d)	CLyd ELan EMNN GCrs MCre
		MFie MOne NBro NChi NCra
		NHar NHol NNrd NPri SHya SPop
		SUsu WFar
¶	– 'Cameo' (A)	MCre
	– 'Camilla' (A)	Last listed 1997
	– 'Candida' (d)	MCre SHya SPop
	– 'Carole' (A)	MFie WLin
	– 'Carreras'	MCre NCra
	– 'Catherine' (d)	MCre NCra
	– 'Chaffinch' (S)	GNor SHya
	– 'Chamois' (B)	Last listed 1997
	– 'Chantilly Cream' (d)	MCre
	– 'Chelsea Bridge'	EMNN MCre
¶	– 'Chelsea Girl' (d)	NCra
	– 'Cherry' (S)	EMNN GAbr NCra SHya
	– 'Cherry Picker' (A)	MCre
	– 'Cherrypicker' (A)	Last listed 1997
	– 'Cheyenne' (S)	EMNN GAbr MCre MFie
	– 'Chloë' (S)	NCra SHya
	– 'Chloris' (S)	NBir SHya
¶	– 'Chocolate Soldier' (A)	MCre
	– 'Chorister' (S)	CLyd ECGP ELan EMNN GAbr
		GNor MBro MCre MFie MOne
		NCra NHol NNrd NOak NPri
		SHya SUsu WLRN WLin
	– 'Cicero' (A)	Last listed 1998
	– 'Cindy' (A)	Last listed 1999
*	– 'Cinnamon' (d)	MCre WHil
*	– 'Cinnamon' (S)	SHya
	– 'Clare' (S)	MCre NCra SHya
	– 'Clatter-Ha'	GCrs
	– 'Claudia Taylor'	NHar SHya WLin
	– 'Clunie' (S)	GNor MCre WHil
	– 'Clunie II' (S)	GCrs SHya WLin
	– 'Coffee' (S)	MCre MFie NCra SHya SUsu
	– 'Colbury' (S)	CStu MCre MFie NCra NHar SHya
		WLin
	– 'Colonel Champney' (S)	GNor MFie NNrd SHya SPop SUsu
		WLin
	– 'Comet' (S)	MFie NNrd
	– 'Connaught Court' (A)	SPop
	– 'Connie' (S)	Last listed 1999
	– 'Conservative' (S)	MFie SHya SUsu
	– 'Consett' (S)	EMNN MFie NCra NNrd
	– 'Coppernob' (S)	Last listed 1998
	– 'Coral' (S)	MFie NCra
	– 'Corona' (S)	Last listed 1998
	– 'Corrie Files' (d)	Last listed 1998
	– 'Cortina' (S)	EMNN GNor MCre MOne NCra
		NHar NHol NNrd NOak SPop
		SUsu WLin
	– 'County Park Red' (B)	ECou
	– 'Craig Vaughan' (A)	LAco MCre MFie NCra NNrd SHya
¶	– 'Cranbourne' (A)	MCre
¶	– 'Creecy' (A)	MCre
	– 'Creenagh Stripe' (A)	Last listed 1997
	– 'Crimple'	SHya
	– 'Cuckoo Fair'	SPop
	– 'Curry Blend'	GAbr
	– 'D.S.J.' (S)	SHya
	– 'Daftie Green' (S)	EMNN NNrd
	– 'Dakota' (S)	EMNN NCra
	– 'Dales Red' (B)	NCra NNrd
	– 'Daphnis' (S)	Last listed 1997
	– 'Dark Tiger' (St)	Last listed 1999
¶	– 'Dawn' (A)	NCra
	– 'Deep Wilson'	Last listed 1999
	– 'Delilah' (d)	GNor MCre MFie WLin
	– 'Denna Snuffer'	EMNN GNor

	– 'Devon Cream' (d)	GNor MCre MFie NCra NHol
		WFar WLin
	– 'Diane'	EMNN MFie
	– 'Divint Dunch' (A)	MCre SHya SPop
	– 'Doctor B. Sharma' (S)	Last listed 1998
	– 'Doctor Duthie' (S)	Last listed 1998
	– 'Doctor Lennon's	MFie
	White' (B)	
	– 'Donhead' (A)	MCre MFie SHya WHil
	– 'Donna Clancy' (S)	MFie SHya
	– 'Doris Jean' (A)	SHya
	– 'Dorothy' (S)	Last listed 1997
	– double maroon (d)	Last listed 1998
	– double yellow (d)	Last listed 1998
	– 'Doublet' (d)	CLyd EMNN GAbr GNor MCre
		MFie NCra NHol NNrd NOak NSla
		SHya SPop WHil WLin
	– 'Doubloon' (d)	Last listed 1998
	– 'Doublure' (d)	GAbr GNor MCre SHya
¶	– 'Douglas Bader' (A)	MCre
	– 'Douglas Black' (S)	SHya
	– 'Douglas Green' (S)	MFie SHya
	– 'Douglas Red' (A)	WLin
	– 'Douglas White' (S)	EMNN MFie SHya
	– 'Dovedale' (S)	SHya
¶	– 'Dovey Tiger' (St)	SHya
	– 'Dowager' (A)	MCre MFie
	– 'Dubarii' (A)	NCra
*	– 'Dusky'	WLin
	– 'Dusky Maiden' (A)	EMNN GNor MCre NCra SHya
		WLin
	– 'Dusky Yellow' (B)	MBro
	– 'Dusty Lemon' (d)	Last listed 1998
	– 'Dusty Miller' (B)	EBrP EBre LBCl LBSe LBre MBBe
		NBid SBre
	– 'E'	Last listed 1997
	– E82 (S)	Last listed 1997
	– 'Ed Spivey' (A)	MCre
¶	– 'Edith Allen' (A)	MCre
¶	– 'Edith Allen' (A)	Last listed 1998
	– 'Eglinton'	NCra
	– 'Eileen K' (S)	SHya
	– 'Elegance' (S)	SHya
	– 'Elizabeth Ann' (A)	EMNN MCre MFie NCra SHya
	– 'Ellen Thompson' (A)	MCre MFie NNrd SHya WLin
	– 'Elmor Vete' (S)	Last listed 1998
	– 'Elsie' (A)	EMNN GNor MCre MFie
	– 'Elsie May' (A)	EMNN GNor MCre MFie NCra
		NNrd SHya SPop WLin
	– 'Elsinore' (S)	MCre
	– 'Embley' (S)	CLyd GNor NCra SHya
	– 'Emery Down' (S)	MFie SHya SPop
	– 'Enlightened' (A)	NCra SHya
I	– 'Erica' (A)	EMNN MCre MFie NHar WLin
	– 'Error' (S)	SHya
	– 'Ethel'	Last listed 1997
	– 'Ettrick' (S)	Last listed 1998
	– 'Eve Guest' (A)	Last listed 1998
	– 'Everest Blue' (S)	SHya SPop SUsu
¶	– 'Exhibition Blau'	MFie
	(Exhibition Series) (B)	
¶	– 'Exhibition Gelb'	MFie
	(Exhibition Series) (B)	
¶	– 'Exhibition Rot'	MFie
	(Exhibition Series) (B)	
	– 'Eyeopener'	MCre SPop
	– 'Fairy' (A)	Last listed 1998
	– 'Falcon' (S)	SHya
	– 'Falsefields' (S)	SHya
	– 'Fanciful' (S)	CLyd MFie SHya WLin
	– 'Fancy Pin'	NNrd
¶	– 'Fandancer' (A)	MCre

- 'Fanfare' (S) — SHya
- 'Fanny Meerbeck' (S) — EMNN GNor MFie NCra NHol NNrd NOak SUsu WHil WLin
- 'Favorite' — EMNN NNrd SHya
- 'Favourite' (S) — MCre SPop
- 'Figaro' (S) — NCra SHya
- 'Finavon' — GCrs
- 'Finchfield' (A) — EMNN MCre MFie SHya SUsu
- 'Firenze' — NCra SPop
- 'Flamingo' (S) — Last listed 1998
- 'Fleminghouse' (S) — MCre NCra SHya
- 'Forsinard' (S) — Last listed 1998
- 'Fradley' (A) — SHya
- 'Frank Crosland' (A) — MFie NCra SHya WHil
- 'Frank Faulkner' (A) — Last listed 1998
- 'Frank Taylor' (S) — SHya
- 'Frittenden Yellow' (B) — WLin
- 'Frosty' (S) — SHya
- 'Fuller's Red' (S) — CLyd MFie
- 'Gaia' (d) — NHol SHya
- 'Galen' (A) — MCre MFie NCra NNrd
- 'Gay Crusader' (A) — EMNN MCre MFie SHya
- 'Gee Cross' (A) — EMNN MCre MFie
§ - 'Geldersome Green' (S) — EMNN GNor MCre MFie SHya SPop WHil
- 'Generosity' (A) — MCre SPop
- 'George Harrison' (B) — GAbr
- 'George Rudd' (S) — SHya
- 'George Swinford's Leathercoat' (B) — SHya
- 'Geronimo' (S) — EMNN GNor MFie SPop
- 'Gizabroon' (S) — CLyd EMNN MCre MFie NCra NNrd WLin
- 'Gleam' (S) — EMNN GCrs GNor MFie NNrd SHya SPop WLin
- 'Glencoe' (S) — Last listed 1998
- 'Gleneagles' (S) — MCre SHya
- 'Glenelg' (S) — GAbr MCre MFie SHya SPop
- 'Glenluce' (S) — SHya
- 'Gnome' (B) — NHol
- 'Goldcrest' (S) — Last listed 1997
- 'Golden Chartreuse' (d) — MCre
- 'Golden Eagle' — NCra
- 'Golden Fleece' (S) — GNor
- 'Golden Hind' (S) — SPop
- 'Golden Splendour' (d) — MCre MFie SHya
- 'Goldthorn' (A) — MCre
¶ - 'Goldwin' (A) — MCre
- 'Good Report' — NCra SPop
- 'Gordon Douglas' (A) — MCre MFie NCra SHya SUsu
- 'Gorey' — NCra
- 'Grace Ellen' (S) — SHya
¶ - 'Green Bottle' — SHya
- 'Green Isle' (S) — EMNN GAbr MCre MFie NBir NNrd SHya WHil WLin
- 'Green Jacket' (S) — GNor MCre NNrd SHya
- 'Green Mansions' (S) — Last listed 1999
- 'Green Mouse' (S) — MFie NCra SHya
- 'Green Parrot' (S) — CLyd EMNN GNor MCre NCra
- 'Green Shank' (S) — GNor MFie NHar NNrd SHya WLin
- 'Greenfinger' (S) — Last listed 1997
- 'Greenheart' (S) — EMNN GNor SHya
- 'Greenpeace' (S) — LRHS NCra NHar SHya
- 'Greensleeves' (S) — GNor
- 'Greta' (S) — ELan EMNN GNor MCre NHar NNrd NOak SHya SPop WHil WLin
- 'Gretna Green' (S) — GNor MFie NCra SHya
- 'Grey Bonnet' (S) — SHya
- 'Grey Edge' — SUsu
- 'Grey Friar' (S) — SHya

- 'Grey Hawk' (S) — NCra SHya
- 'Grey Lag' — EMNN GNor MFie SHya
- 'Grey Monarch' (S) — GNor MCre MFie SHya
- 'Grey Shrike' (S) — SHya
- 'Grey Tarquin' (S) — Last listed 1998
- 'Grizedale' (S) — Last listed 1999
- 'Guildersome Green' — See *P. auricula* 'Geldersome Green'
- 'Guinea' (S) — EMNN GAbr MCre MFie NCra NNrd SHya SPop WLin
- 'Gwen' (A) — MCre SHya
- 'Gwen Baker' (d) — NCra
¶ - 'Gypsy' (A) — MCre
- 'Habanera' — NCra SPop
- 'Haffner' (S) — NCra
- 'Harmony' (B) — MCre MFie
- 'Harrison Weir' (S) — Last listed 1998
- 'Harry Hotspur' (A) — SPop
- 'Harry "O"' (S) — MCre SHya
- 'Harvest Moon' (S) — Last listed 1997
- 'Haughmond' (A) — EMNN MCre MFie
- 'Hawkwood' (S) — EMNN GNor MCre NCra NHar NNrd SPop
- 'Hawkwood Fancy' (S) — MFie SHya WLin
* - 'Hazel' (A) — MCre MFie NCra SHya
- 'Hazel's Fancy' (S) — SHya
- 'Headdress' (S) — MCre MFie SPop
- 'Heady' — NCra
- 'Hebers' — NCra
- 'Helen' (S) — SHya
- 'Helen Barter' (S) — SHya
- 'Helena' (S) — EMNN GNor MCre MFie NNrd NOak SHya
- 'Helena Brown' (S) — SHya
- 'Hetty Woolf' — EMNN GNor MCre NNrd
- 'Hew Dalrymple' (S) — NCra SHya
¶ - 'Hillhouse' (A) — MCre
- 'Hinton Admiral' (S) — SHya WLin
- 'Hinton Fields' (S) — GNor MCre MFie NCra SHya
- 'Hoghton Gem' (d) — Last listed 1998
- 'Holyrood' (S) — MFie
- 'Hopleys Coffee' — GNor
- 'Hopleys Double Mauve' (d) — Last listed 1998
¶ - 'Howard Telford' (A) — MCre
- 'Humphrey' (S) — SHya
- 'Hurstwood Midnight' — MBro MFie NHol WLin
* - 'Hyacinth' (S) — LRHS NWCA
- 'Ibis' (S) — MCre MFie SHya
- 'Ice Maiden' — NCra
- 'Idmiston' (S) — MCre SHya SPop WLin
- 'Imber' (S) — Last listed 1997
- 'Immaculate' — SPop
- 'Impassioned' (A) — NCra SPop
- 'Impeccable' — NCra
- 'Indian Love Call' — MCre NCra WHil
- 'Jack Dean' (A) — MCre MFie SHya SPop WHil
- 'Jack Stant' (S) — SHya
- 'James Arnot' (S) — GNor MFie NCra NHar NOak SHya
- 'Jane Myers' (d) — MFie
- 'Janet' — Last listed 1998
- 'Janie Hill' (A) — MCre SHya
- 'Jeanne' (A) — SHya
- 'Jeannie Telford' (A) — MCre NCra
- 'Jenny' (A) — EMNN GAbr MCre MFie NNrd WHil
- 'Jessie' (d) — SHya
- 'Jezebel' (B) — SHya
¶ - 'Joan Butler' — SHya
- 'Joan Elliott' (A) — CLyd GAbr MFie
- 'Joanne' (A) — MCre SHya

- 'Joe Perks'   NCra
¶ - 'Joe Perry' (A)   MCre
- 'Joel'   MFie
- 'Johann Bach' (B)   MFie
- 'John Gledhill' (A)   MCre
- 'John Stewart' (A)   EMNN MCre MFie
- 'John Wayne' (A)   MCre MFie
- 'John Woolf' (S)   Last listed 1998
- 'Joy' (A)   CLyd EMNN GNor MCre MFie
                                 NCra NHol NNrd SHya SPop WLin
- 'Joyce'   GAbr MCre MFie NBir SHya SPop
                                 WLin
- 'Julia' (S)   SHya
- 'July Sky' (A)   MCre SHya
- 'Jupiter' (S)   MCre SHya
- 'K.H.B.' (S)   Last listed 1999
- 'Karen Cordrey' (S)   CStu GNor WHil WLin
- 'Kath Dryden'   See *P. allionii* 'Kath Dryden'
- 'Kathy' (A)   Last listed 1998
- 'Kelso' (A)   MFie
- 'Kens Green' (S)   Last listed 1998
- 'Kercup' (A)   MFie NCra NNrd
¶ - 'Kevin Keegan' (A)   MCre
- 'Khachaturian'   NCra
- 'Kim' (A)   EMNN MCre MFie NNrd SHya
                                 WLin
- 'Kincraig' (S)   Last listed 1998
- 'Kingcup' (A)   MCre MFie NCra SHya SPop
¶ - 'Kintail' (A)   MCre
- 'Kiowa' (S)   MFie
- 'Kirklands' (d)   MFie NNrd SPop
- 'Königin der Nacht' (St)   SHya
- 'Lady Croft' (S)   Last listed 1997
- 'Lady Daresbury' (A)   EMNN MCre MFie NCra
- 'Lady Emma Monson' (S)   SHya
- 'Lady Joyful' (S)   MCre SHya
- 'Lady Zoë' (S)   MFie NCra
- 'Lamplugh'   NNrd
- 'Landy' (A)   GCrs MCre
- 'Langley Park' (A)   MCre MFie WHil
- 'Larkhill' (A)   Last listed 1997
¶ - 'Larry' (A)   MCre SPop
- 'Lavender Lady' (B)   NCra
- 'Laverock' (S)   MCre NBro SHya
- 'Laverock Fancy' (S)   EMNN GNor MFie WLin
- 'Leather Jacket'   GAbr NHol
- 'Lechistan' (S)   EMNN MCre MFie NHar NHol
                                 NNrd WHil WLin
- 'Lee' (A)   MCre
¶ - 'Lee Clark' (A)   MCre
- 'Lee Paul' (A)   CStu EMNN GNor MCre MFie
                                 NCra SHya SPop WHil WLin
- 'Lee Sharpe' (A)   MCre SHya
- 'Lemon Drop' (S)   MCre SHya
- 'Lemon Sherbet' (B)   MFie
- 'Lewis Telford' (A)   Last listed 1998
- 'Lich'   EMNN
- 'Lichfield' (A)   MCre SHya
- 'Light Hearted'   NCra
- 'Lilac Domino' (S)   MCre MFie NCra SHya SPop WLin
- 'Lillian Hill' (A)   SHya
- 'Lincoln Green' (S)   Last listed 1999
- 'Lindley' (S)   EMNN NHar
- 'Lindsey Moreno' (S)   Last listed 1998
- 'Ling' (A)   EMNN MCre MFie NCra SPop
- 'Lingen seedling No. 1   Last listed 1998
- 'Lisa' (A)   CLyd MCre MFie NCra NHar
                                 NNrd WLin
- 'Lisa Clara' (S)   EMNN GNor SHya
- 'Lisa's Smile' (S)   MFie NCra
- 'Little Rosetta' (d)   Last listed 1999
- 'Lord Saye and Sele' (St)   GAbr GCrs GNor MCre MFie

SHya SPop WLin
- 'Louisa' (d)   MFie
- 'Louisa Woolhead' (d)   SPop
- 'Lovebird' (S)   EMNN GAbr GNor MCre MFie
                                 NCra NHar NNrd SHya SUsu WLin
- 'Lucy Locket' (B)   NCra
¶ - 'Lynn Cooper'   SHya
- 'Madame Gina' (S)   MFie
- 'Maggie' (S)   EMNN GNor NNrd SHya
- 'Magnolia' (B)   MFie
- 'Maid Marion' (d)   MCre
- 'Mandarin'   MCre SPop
- 'Manka' (S)   NCra SHya
- 'Mansell's Green'   MFie NNrd SHya
- 'Margaret' (S)   SHya
- 'Margaret Faulkner' (A)   EMNN GNor MCre MFie NCra
                                 SHya
- 'Margaret Martin' (S)   SHya WLin
- 'Margot Fonteyn'   NCra SPop
¶ - 'Marie Crousse' (d)   MFie SHya
- 'Marigold' (d)   CLyd NCra WFar
¶ - 'Marion Howard   MCre MFie
  Spring' (A)
- 'Mark' (A)   EMNN MCre MFie NBro NCra
                                 NHol SPop
- 'Marmion' (S)   SHya
- 'Martin Luther King' (S)   MFie
- 'Mary' (d)   GNor MCre SHya
- 'Mary of Dunoon' (S)   Last listed 1999
- 'Mary Taylor' (S)   SHya
- 'Mary Zac'   NNrd
- 'Matthew Yates' (d)   CHad MCre MFie MOne NChi
                                 NCra NHol NPri SPop SUsu WCot
                                 WLin WRha
- 'Maureen Millward'   EMNN MCre MFie NNrd SPop
¶ - 'May' (A)   MCre
- 'May Tiger' (S)   SHya
- 'Mazetta Stripe' (S/St)   WLin
- 'McWatt's Blue' (B)   GAbr
- 'Meadow Lark'   MCre NCra
- 'Mellifluous'   MCre NCra
- 'Merlin' (A)   Last listed 1998
- 'Merlin Stripe' (St)   MCre SHya
- 'Mermaid'   GAbr MCre NCra SHya
- 'Merridale' (A)   EMNN MCre MFie NCra SHya
- 'Mersey Tiger' (S)   GAbr SHya
- 'Metha'   NCra
- 'Mick' (A)   NCra
- 'Midnight' (S)   CLyd EMNN NCra NHar NNrd
- 'Mikado' (S)   MCre MFie SHya SPop WLin
- 'Millicent' (A)   MFie
- 'Mink' (A)   MFie WHil
- 'Minley' (S)   EMNN GCrs GNor ITim MCre
                                 MFie NBro NCra NHar NNrd SHya
                                 SPop WLin
- 'Minstrel' (S)   SHya
- 'Mipsie Miranda' (d)   SHya
- 'Mirabella Bay'   NCra
¶ - 'Mirandinha' (A)   MCre
- 'Miriam' (A)   Last listed 1998
- 'Mish Mish' (d)   NNrd SHya
¶ - 'Mohawk' (S)   MCre
- 'Mojave' (S)   EMNN GNor MBro MCre MFie
                                 NCra NHar NHol SPop WLin
- 'Mollie Langford'   MCre SPop
- 'Moneymoon' (S)   MFie
- 'Monica' (A)   MFie
- 'Monk' (A)   MCre MFie NNrd SHya WHil
¶ - 'Monmouth Tabby'   SHya
- 'Moonglow' (S)   EMNN MFie NCra
- 'Moonlight' (S)   EHyt
- 'Moonrise' (S)   EMNN MFie

	- 'Roxburgh' (A)	EMNN MCre SHya SPop
	- 'Royal Purple' (S)	Last listed 1997
	- 'Royal Velvet' (A)	GAbr NNrd
	- 'Royalty' (S)	Last listed 1997
	- 'Ruby Hyde' (B)	GAbr
	- 'Rusty Dusty'	GAbr
	- 'Sailor Boy' (S)	MFie SHya
	- 'Saint Boswells' (S)	MCre MFie NCra SHya
	- 'Saint Elmo' (d)	MFie
	- 'Saint Gerrans'White' (B)	MFie
	- 'Saint Quentin' (S)	Last listed 1998
	- 'Salad' (S)	MFie SHya
	- 'Sale Green' (A)	SHya
	- 'Sally'	MCre WHil
	- 'Salome' (A)	Last listed 1997
	- 'Sam Hunter'	NCra
	- 'Sandhills' (A)	MCre
	- 'Sandmartin' (S)	MFie
	- 'Sandra' (A)	ELan EMNN GAbr MCre MFie SHya SPop WHil WLin
	- 'Sandwood Bay' (A)	CLyd EMNN GAbr GNor LRHS MCre MFie NBro NCra NHar NNrd SHya SPop WHil
	- 'Sarah Lodge' (d)	EMNN GAbr MFie
	- 'Satchmo'	EMNN
	- 'Scipio' (S)	SHya
	- 'Seaton Burn' (S)	Last listed 1998
	- 'Serenity' (S)	EMNN GNor MCre MFie SHya
¶	- 'Sergeant Wilson'	SHya
	- 'Shalford' (d)	MFie NHol SPop WLin
	- 'Sharman's Cross' (S)	NCra SHya
	- 'Sharon Louise' (S)	MCre
	- 'Sheila' (S)	MCre MFie NHar NNrd SHya SPop WLin
	- 'Shere' (S)	EMNN MCre MFie NCra SHya SPop WLin
	- 'Shergold' (A)	MCre
	- 'Sherwood'	EMNN MCre MFie NHar SHya WHil WLin
	- 'Shirley Hibberd' (S)	Last listed 1998
	- 'Shotley' (A)	EMNN MCre
	- 'Shrewton' (S)	Last listed 1998
	- 'Sibsey' (d)	SPop
¶	- 'Silas' (B)	NCra
	- 'Silverway' (S)	MCre NCra SHya
	- 'Sir Hardy Amies' (A)	SHya
	- 'Sir John Hall'	NCra
	- 'Sirbol' (A)	MCre
	- 'Sirius' (A)	CLyd GAbr LAco LRHS MCre MFie MOne NCra NHar NHol SHya SPop WHil WLin
¶	- 'Skylark' (A)	MCre
	- 'Slioch' (S)	EMNN GNor MFie NNrd SHya SPop
	- 'Snooty Fox' (A)	EMNN MFie NNrd WLin
	- 'Snooty Fox II' (A)	MCre SHya
	- 'Snowy Owl'	GNor MCre MFie SHya
	- 'Soncy Face'	NCra
	- 'Sonya' (A)	WLin
	- 'South Barrow' (d)	EMNN GAbr MCre SUsu WHil
¶	- 'Southease Jane'	SHya
	- 'Space Age' (S)	Last listed 1997
	- 'Splendour' (S)	Last listed 1998
	- 'Spring Meadows' (S)	ECGP MCre MFie MOne NChi NCra NHol NPri SHya SPop
	- 'Springtime'	NCra SPop
	- SS TY 72 (S)	Last listed 1999
	- 'Standish' (d)	GAbr NCra NHol SHya
	- 'Stant's Blue' (S)	EMNN GNor MCre MFie NBro NHol SHya
	- 'Star Wars' (S)	SHya
	- 'Starry' (S)	NHar NHol NNrd WLin

	- 'Stella' (S)	MFie
	- 'Stoke Poges' (A)	Last listed 1998
	- 'Stonnal' (A)	MCre MFie NHar
	- 'Streamlet' (S)	Last listed 1999
	- 'Stripey' (d)	Last listed 1997
¶	- 'Stuart West' (A)	MCre
	- 'Stubb's Tartan' (S)	NHar WHil
¶	- 'Subliminal' (A)	MCre
	- 'Sue' (A)	MCre MFie
	- 'Sue Douglas' (A)	Last listed 1998
	- 'Sugar Plum Fairy'	NNrd
	- 'Summer Sky' (A)	MCre
	- 'Sumo'	MCre NCra SPop
	- 'Sunburst' (S)	GCrs
I	- 'Sunflower' (S)	MCre MFie NHar NHol WLin
	- 'Sunsal' (S)	MFie
	- 'Sunstar' (S)	EMNN MFie
	- 'Super Para' (S)	EMNN GCrs GNor MCre MFie NNrd SHya
	- 'Superb' (S)	NCra SHya
	- 'Susan' (A)	MCre MFie
	- 'Susannah' (d)	GAbr LRHS MFie MOne NChi NHol NPri SHya SPop WLRN WLin
	- 'Sweet Pastures' (S)	EMNN GNor MFie NCra NHol SHya SPop
	- 'Swift' (S)	MFie
	- 'Swinley' (S)	Last listed 1998
	- 'Sword'	CStu GNor MCre NNrd SHya
	- 'Symphony' (A)	SUsu WHil
	- 'Tall Purple Dusty Miller' (B)	MFie SPop
	- 'Tally-ho' (A)	SHya
	- 'Tarantella' (A)	EMNN GNor MCre MFie NCra NNrd SHya WLin
	- 'Tawny Owl'	GAbr NBro
	- 'Ted Gibbs' (A)	MCre
	- 'Ted Roberts' (A)	EMNN MCre MFie NCra SPop WLin
	- 'Teem' (S)	EMNN GNor MCre MFie NCra SHya WLin
	- 'Tenby Grey' (S)	MFie
	- 'The Baron' (S)	GNor MCre MFie MOne NHar NHol SPop WHil WLin
	- 'The Bishop' (S)	MFie NCra
	- 'The Bride' (S)	EMNN NCra
	- 'The Cardinal' (d)	SUsu
	- 'The Czar' (A)	MCre SHya
	- 'The Maverick' (S)	SHya
	- 'The Raven' (S)	EMNN MFie
	- 'The Sneeps'	MCre NCra WHil
	- 'The Snods' (S)	EMNN MFie NCra WHil
	- 'Thebes'	NCra
	- 'Thetis' (A)	MCre MFie NCra SHya WHil WLin
	- 'Thirlmere' (d)	SHya
	- 'Three Way Stripe'	MCre SHya
	- 'Tinkerbell' (S)	MCre MFie NCra SHya WLin
	- 'Tomato'	WLin
	- 'Tomboy' (S)	MFie
	- 'Tomma'	NCra
	- 'Tosca' (S)	EMNN GCrs GNor MCre NNrd SHya SPop WLin
¶	- 'Trish' (S)	GAbr
	- 'Trojan' (S)	SHya
	- 'Trouble' (d)	CHad EBee EMNN LPio LRHS MCre MFie MOne NChi NCra NHar SHya SMrm SPop WLin
	- 'Trudy' (S)	EMNN GAbr GCrs GNor MCre MFie NCra NNrd
	- 'True Briton' (S)	MCre MFie SHya
	- 'Trumpet Blue' (S)	MFie
	- 'Tumbledown' (A)	MFie
	- 'Tummel'	NCra

- 'Tuthmoses'	NCra
- 'Two Tone' mauve (d)	WHil
- 'Tye Lea' (S)	MFie SHya
¶ - 'Tye Lea Green' (S)	MCre
- 'Typhoon' (A)	MCre MFie WHil
- 'Unforgetable'	MCre NCra
- 'Upton Belle' (S)	Last listed 1997
- 'V.I. Hinney'	MCre
- 'Valerie' (A)	MCre MFie NCra NNrd SHya WHil
- 'Valerie Clare'	NCra
- 'Vee Too' (A)	MCre MFie SHya SPop
- 'Velvet Moon'	NCra
- 'Venetian'	NCra
- 'Vera' (A)	MFie
- 'Verdi' (A)	EMNN MCre MFie NCra SHya
- 'Victoria' (S)	SHya
- 'Victoria de Wemyss' (A)	MCre MFie WHil
- 'Vulcan' (A)	MFie NBro NCra SHya SPop
- 'Waincliffe Fancy' (S)	Last listed 1997
- 'Waincliffe Red' (S)	MFie
- 'Walhampton' (S)	EMNN SHya
- 'Walton' (A)	MCre MFie SHya
- 'Walton Heath' (d)	EMNN GAbr MCre MFie SHya SPop WHil WLin
- 'Warwick' (S)	NCra SHya
- 'Watt's Purple' (d)	Last listed 1997
- 'Wedding Day' (S)	MFie
- 'Wendy'	SIng WLin
- 'White Ensign' (S)	EMNN GAbr GNor MCre MFie NCra NNrd NOak SHya SPop WLin
- 'White Water'	NCra
- 'White Wings' (S)	EMNN GNor MCre MFie NCra NNrd SHya WLin
- 'Wide Awake' (A)	MCre MFie
- 'Wincha' (S)	GCrs MFie SHya WLin
- 'Windways Mystery' (B)	MFie
- 'Winifrid' (A)	CLyd EMNN LRHS MCre MFie NCra NHar NHol SHya SPop WHil
- 'Woodmill' (A)	MCre SHya
- 'Woodstock' (S)	Last listed 1997
- 'Wor Jackie' (S)	EMNN NHar
- 'Wycliffe Midnight'	GAbr GNor
- 'Y.I. Hinney' (A)	EMNN MFie
- 'Yelverton' (S)	MFie
- 'Yorkshire Grey' (S)	MFie NBro NNrd SHya
- 'Zambia' (d)	CLyd GAbr MFie SHya SPop SUsu WHil WLin
¶ - 'Zona' (A)	MCre
auriculata (11)	SBla
- 'Duchess of York' (2)	CLAP CLTr GBuc WBro
'Barbara Midwinter' (6x30)	CMea NDov WAbe
Barnhaven Blues Group (Prim)(30) ♀	GAbr
Barnhaven doubles (dPoly)(30)	CSWP
Barnhaven Gold-laced Group	See *P.* Gold-laced Group Barnhaven
¶ Barnhaven hybrids	NCot
Barnhaven Traditional Group	CSWP
'Beamish Foam' (Poly)(30)	NDov
'Beatrice Wooster' (2)	CLyd EPot LRHS MBro MFie NDlv NHar NHol NNrd NWCA SIng WAbe
'Beeches' Pink'	GAbr
beesiana (4)	More than 30 suppliers
¶ 'Belinda'	EHyt
'Belinda Red Shades' (Belinda Series) ♀	Last listed 1995
'Bellamy's Pride'	CLyd
bellidifolia (17)	CPla

§ - subsp. ***byacinthina*** (17)	Last listed 1998
beluensis	See *P.* x *pubescens* 'Freedom'
Bergfrühling Julianas Group (Prim)(30)	MFie
§ x ***berninae*** 'Windrush' (2)	CLyd NHar NNrd WAbe
'Betty Green' (Prim)(30)	Last listed 1998
'Bewerley White'	See *P.* x *pubescens* 'Bewerley White'
bbutanica	See *P. whitei* 'Sherriff's Variety'
x ***biflora*** (2)	Last listed 1998
'Big Red Giant' (dPrim)(30)	CBlo EBee LFis MBNS MOne NHar WWol
bileckii	See *P.* x *forsteri* 'Bileckii'
'Blue Riband' (Prim)(30)	CGle EDAr EPfP LSur MRav WAbe WFar
'Blue Sapphire' (dPrim)(30)	CBlo CElw GAbr LRHS MOne NChi SIng SLod SPer SUsu WWol
Blue Striped Victorians Group (Poly)(30)	GAbr
'Blutenkissen' (Prim)(30)	GAbr GMaP
'Bon Accord Purple' (dPoly)(30)	CGle WFar WRus
'Bonfire' (4)	GDra GGar
'Bootheosa' (21)	Last listed 1999
boothii alba (21)	GCrs GGGa WAbe
- subsp. ***autumnalis*** (21)	GCrs WAbe
- subsp. ***repens*** (21)	MNrw
'Boothman's Ruby'	See *P.* x *pubescens* 'Boothman's Variety'
boveana (12)	MFie SBla
§ ***bracteosa*** (21)	GCrs GFle ITim NHar WAbe
'Brimstone' (Poly)(30)	CGle
'Broadwell Pink' (2)	Last listed 1999
'Broadwell Ruby' (2)	Last listed 1998
'Bronwyn' (Prim)(30)	WCot
'Broxbourne'	CLyd NHar
'Buckland Wine' (Prim)(30)	Last listed 1999
x ***bulleesiana*** (4)	CM&M CMGP EBee LFis NBro NLAp SMrm SPer SRms STes SWat WFar WHil WPer
- Moerheim hybrids (4)	WFar
bulleyana (4) ♀	More than 30 suppliers
- ACE 2484 (4)	EPot WAbe
burmanica (4)	CInt CPla EBee GAbr GBuc GDra GFle GGar MSta NCra NDea NHar SRms
'Butterscotch' (Prim)(30)	CGle CSWP
'Caerulea Plena' (dPrim)(30)	GCal
calderiana (21)	GDra GFle NHar
- subsp. ***strumosa*** BC 9347 (21)	Last listed 1998
candelabra hybrids (4)	CBro EMNN EPot GGar NCra WRos
Candy Pinks Group (Prim)(30)	GAbr
capitata (5)	CGle CInt CPla CSpe EBee EDAr GDra GFle GTou LRHS LSyl MBri MFie NCra NHar WAbe WBea WFar WPer
- subsp. ***capitata*** (5)	GGar
- subsp. ***crispata*** AGS/ES 407 (5)	Last listed 1998
- dark (5)	Last listed 1999
- ex CC 2368 (5)	Last listed 1999
- KEKE 274 (5)	Last listed 1998
- subsp. ***mooreana*** (5)	CFir EDAr EWTr GCan GFle LPBA MCli NDlv SPlb WHil
- subsp. ***spbaerocephala*** (5)	Last listed 1999
- - ACE 2092 (5)	EPot
capitellata (11)	Last listed 1999
'Captain Blood' (dPrim)(30)	CBos NSti SIng SUsu WRha WWol

'Carmen' (Prim)(30)   CLyd
Carnation Victorians   CSWP GAbr MFie
    Group (Poly)(30)
'Casquet'   CSWP
cernua (17)   GDra GFle MFie NHar WLin
'Charlen' (dPrim)(30)   NHar
Chartreuse Group   CGle CSWP GAbr MFie NDov
    (Poly)(30)   WRha
'Cherry' (Prim)(30)   Last listed 1999
'Chevithorne Pink' (Poly)   GAbr
    (30)
§ *chionantha* (18) ♀   CGle CMHG CPla EBee EDAr
    EWTr GDra GFle GGGa GKir
    GMaP GTou LAst LRHS LSyl MBri
    MFie MNrw NChi NCra NDea
    NFor NHar SPer WFar WGwG
    WHil WLin WWat
- subsp. *brevicaula*   Last listed 1997
    ACE 1689 (18)
§ - subsp. *melanops* (18)   CGle CPla EBee GCan GFle LRHS
    NHar
§ - subsp.   CPla WRha
    sinoplantaginea (18)
§ - subsp. *sinopurpurea*   CGle CPla EBee GAbr GDra GFle
    (18)   GGGa GTou LSyl MLLN NCra SPer
    WAbe WFar WHil WLin WPer
    WWhi
- - ACE 1421 (18)   EPot
'Chocolate Soldier'   GGar
    (dPrim)(30)
chungensis (4)   CGle EDAr GFle GGar GKir
    GTou MBri MLLN NHar SRms
    WAbe
§ - x *pulverulenta* (4)   EBee EBrP EBre GBuc LBCl LBSe
    LBre MBBe MFie NLar NPri
    SBre SMrm WAbe WElm WFar
    WHil
x *chunglenta*   See *P. chungensis* x *pulverulenta*
§ 'Clarence Elliott' (2)   CGra CLyd CStu NHar WLin
clarkei (11)   CLyd GCrs GFle GTou NWCA
clusiana (2)   EBee GDra NHol NSla
- 'Murray-Lyon' (2)   Last listed 1999
cockburniana (4)   CInt CRow EBee GDra GFle GGar
    GMac GTou LRHS MBri MFie
    NCra NHar NWCA SRms WAbe
    WFar WHil
concholoba (17)   CPla GAbr GFle GGar GTou MFie
    NHar WAbe
'Corporal Baxter'   EPfP MBNS MBri MOne NChi
    (dPrim)(30)   SLod SMrm SPer SUsu WRha
    WWol
cortusoides (7)   CPla EBee GFle MNrw NCra SRms
    WHil WOve
Cowichan (Poly)(30)   CInt GAbr NCra NSti
Cowichan Amethyst Group CSWP GAbr SPer
    (Poly)(30)
Cowichan Blue Group   CSWP EWoo GAbr SPer
    (Poly)(30)
Cowichan Garnet Group   CSWP EWoo GAbr GCan MFie
    (Poly)(30)   NDov SPer
Cowichan Red Group   WFar
    (Poly)(30)
Cowichan Venetian Group CSWP GAbr NDov
    (Poly)(30)
Cowichan Yellow Group   GAbr NDov SPer WCot
    (Poly)(30)
¶ 'Craddock White' (Prim)   CBos
    (30)
'Craven Gem' (Poly)(30)   GAbr LSur
Crescendo Series (Poly)(30) GAbr
'Crimson Cushion'   Last listed 1998
'Crimson Queen' (Prim)(30) Last listed 1999

'Crimson Velvet' (2)   EMNN GAbr GNor MBro NHol
    NNrd SIng SRms
crispa   See *P. glomerata*
x *crucis* (2)   Last listed 1997
* *cuneata*   GTou
cuneifolia (8)   GFle GNor
* - *alba* (8)   Last listed 1998
¶ - subsp. *heterodonta* (8)   GFle
daonensis (2)   GFle
darialica (11)   CGle CPla ELan GFle NCra WHil
'David Green' (Prim)(30)   SIng
'David Valentine'   GAbr LSur
'Dawn Ansell' (dPrim)(30)   CElw CGle CRow CSpe EPri GGar
    LFis LRHS MBNS MBri MCAu
    MCLN MOne MRav NEgg NHar
    NHol NSti SIng SLod SPer SSte
    SUsu WCot WHer WHil WWol
Daybreak Group (Poly)(30) CSWP MFie
deflexa (17)   GCrs GFle LRHS LSyl WLin
- ACE 2283 (17)   EPot
denticulata (9) ♀   More than 30 suppliers
- var. *alba* (9)   More than 30 suppliers
- blue (9)   GKir NLar
- 'Bressingham Beauty' (9) EBrP EBre LBCl LBSe LBre MBBe
    SBre
- var. *cachemiriana* (9)   EPfP LRHS
- CC 2660 (9)   Last listed 1999
- 'Glenroy Crimson' (9)   CLAP CRDP EBee SRms
- 'Inshriach Carmine' (9)   Last listed 1998
- 'Karryann' (9/v)   WCot
- lilac (9)   EHon GKir GTou MFie NPri
- purple (9)   GAbr GKir IBlr
- red (9)   CRow EMNN EPar GGar GKir
    NOrc SIng
- 'Robinson's Red' (9)   EPot GBuc
- 'Ronsdorf' (9)   LRHS
- rose (9)   NHar
- 'Rubinball' (9)   EBrP EBre EPfP GAri GKir LBCl
    LBSe LBre LRHS MBBe NHol SBre
    WCot
- ruby (9)   CInt EBee EHon GAbr GTou LNor
    MBri MCLN MFie NBro NOak
    SRms WHen WPer WPyg
- 'Snowball' (9)   MCLN MFir NOak WHen WPyg
deorum (2)   CGra
x *deschmannii*   See *P.* x *vochinensis*
'Desert Sunset' (Poly)(30) CSWP MFie
deuteronana alba (21)   Last listed 1997
'Devon Cream' (Prim)(30)   ECha GBuc WFar
'Dianne'   See *P.* x *forsteri* 'Dianne'
'Doctor Mary' (Prim)(30)   GAbr
'Dora'   Last listed 1998
'Dorothy' (Poly)(30)   LSur MRav
'Double Lilac'   See *P. vulgaris* 'Lilacina Plena'
drummondiana (21)   Last listed 1998
'Duckyls Red' (Prim)(30)   EDAr GBuc MBct NChi
'Dusky Lady'   WBar WFar
'Early Irish Yellow'   Last listed 1998
    (Prim)(30)
'Easter Bonnet' (dPrim)(30) CBlo EPot LRHS MCLN MOne
    NDov NHol SPer
edelbergii (12)   GFle MFie
edgeworthii   See *P. nana*
elatior (30) ♀   CGle CKin CPla CRow CSev EBee
    EDAr ELau GFle GLil LFox LRHS
    LSur LSyl MHar MNrw MSal NChi
    NCra NFla NMen NOrc NSti SIng
    SPer SRms WFar WHil
- hose in hose (30)   NBid
- hybrids (30)   SIng
- subsp. *intricata* (30)   Last listed 1998
* - 'Katy McSporran' (30)   SPer

- subsp. *leucophylla* (30) EBee ECho
§ - subsp. *meyeri* (30) Last listed 1997
- subsp. *pallasii* (30) Last listed 1997
elliptica (11) Last listed 1997
ellisiae (21) NSla SOkd
'Erin's Gem' (Poly)(30) CGle
§ *erythra* (26) Last listed 1998
'Ethel Barker' (2) CNic ITim LFox LRHS MBro NDlv
NHar NHol NNrd SIng WAbe
'Ethel M. Dell' (dPrim)(30) Last listed 1997
'Eugénie' (dPrim)(30) CGle CHid CSpe ECle MBNS
MOne NChi NDov NHar NHol
SIng WCot WLRN
'Fairy Rose' KRW EPot WAbe
180/48 (2)
farinosa (11) CLyd CPla EBee EWFC GFle MBri
MFie MSal NCra NHar NMen
WPer
- JCA 786.500 (11) Last listed 1998
fasciculata (11) EDAr NSla SBla
- CLD 345 (11) IMGH NHar WAbe
'Fife Yellow' (dPoly)(30) GBuc
'Fire Dance' (Poly)(30) MFie
Firefly Group (Poly)(30) GAbr LFox NDov
firmipes (26) EBee NTow WLRN
§ *flaccida* (28) ♀ GDra GFle GGGa NCra NHar
WAbe
Flamingo Group (Poly)(30) CSWP GAbr MFie
§ x *floerkeana* (2) Last listed 1999
- f. *biflora alba* (2) SBla
florida (29) GGGa
florindae (26) ♀ More than 30 suppliers
- bronze (26) MFie
- hybrids (26) GAbr GGar LFox MFie MSCN
WHil WLin
- orange (26) CSam GMac IBlr LSyl MNrw NChi
WCru WFar
- 'Ray's Ruby' (26) GBuc MCLN MNrw NBir SPer
WCot WOve WWhi
- red (26) EBee GCal GGar LSyl MFie MSta
NBid WFar
Footlight Parade Group CSWP NDov
(Prim)(30)
forrestii (3) GCrs GGGa MFie NHar WAbe
¶ - ACE 2474 GFle
- C&Cu 9431 (3) Last listed 1998
§ x *forsteri* (2) EMNN WAbe
§ - 'Bileckii' (2) EPar EPot GCrs LBee LRHS MBro
NBro NHar NWCA SRms SSmi
WAbe
- 'Dianne' (2) GAbr GBuc MBro NBro NHar
NHol NNrd SIng WAbe WGwG
- 'Dianne' hybrids (2) MFie
'Freckles' (dPrim)(30) CSpe EBee ECle GGar MBNS
MOne NHar NHol SIng SPer WHil
WLRN
'Freedom' See *P.* x *pubescens* 'Freedom'
¶ 'Fritz Kummert' (2) EHyt
frondosa ♀ CGle CInt CLyd CPla CSam EBee
GCrs GFle LFox LRHS MBri MBro
MFie NCra NHar NMen NWCA
SMrm WAbe WHoo
'Frühlingszauber' (Prim) Last listed 1997
(30)
Fuchsia Victorians Group CSWP MFie
(Poly)(30)
Galligaskins Group (Poly) Last listed 1997
(30)
'Garnet' (*allionii* hybrid) MFie
'Garryard Guinevere' See *P.* 'Guinevere'
'Gartenmeister Bartens' Last listed 1997
(Prim)(30)

gaubana (12) GFle MFie
gemmifera (11) GFle GGGa NHar
- ACE 1375 (11) Last listed 1998
- ACE 1427 (11) NWCA WAbe
- ACE 1541 (11) Last listed 1999
- var. *zambalensis* (11) WAbe
geraniifolia (7) SIng WHil
- CC 2295 (7) Last listed 1999
§ 'Gigha' (Prim)(30) CSpe
glaucescens (2) CLyd CNic GFle MBro MFie NFla
NHar NSla SIng
- subsp. *calycina* See *P. glaucescens* subsp.
glaucescens
§ - subsp. *glaucescens* (2) Last listed 1999
- JCA 786.900 (2) Last listed 1998
'Glebe Grey' (Prim)(30) CGle
§ *glomerata* (5) CSWP GBuc GCrs GGGa WAbe
'Gloria' (Prim)(30) Last listed 1999
'Gloriosa' (Prim)(30) LSur
'Glowing Embers' (4) CGle EBee LRHS MFie NBir
glutinosa Allioni See *P. allionii*
- Lapeyrouse (2) Last listed 1998
Gold-laced Group (Poly) CBre CElw CGle CM&M CPla
(30) CRDP CSWP EBee ELan ERav
EWoo GAbr GGar GMac LFox
MBri MBro NBid NCra NHar
NWCA SPer SUsu WFar WHer
WHil
§ - Barnhaven CFri CLAP GAbr LPio MFie
- Beeches strain (Poly) LSur
(30) ♀
'Gordon' ♀ Last listed 1997
gracilipes (21) CGle GFle GGGa GGar MOne
NHar NWCA SRms WAbe
- early (21) NHar WAbe
- L&S 1 (21) NHar WAbe
- L&S 1166 (21) NHar
- late (21) NHar WAbe
- 'Major' See *P. bracteosa*
- 'Masterton' (21) Last listed 1997
- 'Minor' See *P. petiolaris*
- 'Winter Jewel' (21) Last listed 1998
'Graham' Last listed 1997
Grand Canyon Group MFie
(Poly)(30)
'Granny Graham' (Prim) Last listed 1999
(30)
griffithii (21) GFle GGGa
'Groeneken's Glory' CGle CInt EDAr ELan GAbr LRHS
(Prim)(30) LSur MBri MRav NBro NCra NFla
SIng SPer WFar
§ 'Guinevere' (Poly)(30) ♀ More than 30 suppliers
'Hall Barn Blue' GAbr LSur
§ *halleri* (11) CPla EBee EDAr GCHN GCan
GFle GTou MFie NCra NHar
NMen NWCA WAbe
- 'Longiflora' See *P. halleri*
Harbinger Group CGle NDov
(Prim)(30)
'Harbour Lights' CSWP MFie
Harlow Carr hybrids (4) GFle MLLN NDea NDlv WEas
WHil
Harvest Yellows Group MFie NDov
(Poly)(30)
x *heeri* (2) Last listed 1999
'Helge' (Prim)(30) GAbr LSur
helodoxa See *P. prolifera*
§ 'Hemswell Blush' (2) GNor NHol WLin
§ 'Hemswell Ember' (2) EMNN MFie NDlv NHar
heucherifolia (7) CPla GCan LFox LSyl MSCN
hidakana (24) SOkd
hirsuta (2) CNic GCrs GFle GTou LRHS MFie

¶ - var. *exscapa* (2) — GFle
- from Switzerland (2) — MFie
- 'Lismore Snow' (2) — NHar
hose in hose (Poly)(30) — CGle CSWP MNrw NCra
'Husky' ♀ — Last listed 1999
§ 'Hyacinthia' (2) — CLyd EMNN EPot
byacinthina — See *P. bellidifolia* subsp. *byacinthina*

iantbina — See *P. prolifera*
Indian Reds Group (Poly)(30) — MFie
'Ingram's Blue' (Prim)(30) — CRos LRHS WPGP
Inshriach hybrids (4) — CMHG EBrP EBre GAbr GCan GDra LBCl LBSe LBre LHop MBBe MBri MFie MSCN NLar SBre SPer WFar WWal

integrifolia (2) — GCrs GFle IMGH WAbe WHil WShe
x *intermedia* (2) — Last listed 1998
§ 'Inverewe' (4) ♀ — EBee GAbr GAri GCal GGar NHar WPGP

involucrata (11) — See *P. munroi*
- *alba* CC 1422 (11) — Last listed 1999
ioessa (26) — CPla EWes GGGa MBri NWCA WAbe
- HWJCM 300 (26) — WCru
- hybrids (26) — Last listed 1997
'Iris Mainwaring' (Prim) (30) — GAbr LSur MDHE NCra NDov SIng
irregularis — GCrs GGGa
Jack in the Green Group (Poly)(30) — CGle CMGP CSWP LSur MNrw MRav MWgw NChi NCot NCra WFar WHer WRha WRus
Jackanapes Group (Poly) (30) — Last listed 1998
Jackanapes on Horseback Group (Poly)(30) — Last listed 1997
'Jackaroo' (4) — GGar
'Jackie Richards' (2) — WLin
¶ *jaffreyana* (11) — GCrs
japonica (4) ♀ — CGle CMHG CRow CSam ECha GFle GGar GKir GTou LPBA LRHS MFir NBid NBro NChi NCra NFor NHar NHol SWat WAbe WCru WFar WPer
- 'Alba' (4) — EBee EWTr GBin MCAu WAbe WHil WShe
- 'Apple Blossom' (4) — EBee SCob
* - 'Atropurpurea' (4) — SIng
* - 'Carminea' — NBro WHil
- 'Fromfield Pink' (4) — Last listed 1998
- 'Fuji' (4) — CSWP GCan GDra GFle GMac MBri MSta NBro
- 'Fuji' hybrids (4) — NLar
¶ - 'Merve's Red' — WPGP
- 'Miller's Crimson' (4) — More than 30 suppliers
- 'Oriental Sunrise' (4) — CMil CSWP SPer
- 'Postford White' (4) — More than 30 suppliers
- red (4) — WAbe
- 'Valley Red' (4) — GBin GBuc GFle GMac LSyl WHil
jesoana (7) — EBee
- B&SWJ 618 (7) — WCru
Jewel Group — LSur
'Jill' — LSur
'Joan Hughes' (*allionii* hybrid) (2) — CLyd EHyt NHar WAbe
¶ 'Joanna' — ECou
'Johanna' (11) — CGle GFle GGar LSyl NBro NHar NWCA WAbe
'John Fielding' (6x30) — WCot
'Jo-Jo' (2) — CLyd WAbe

juliae (30) — CGle CPla CRDP GFle LRHS SPlb WAbe WCot
- white (30) — CGle
x *juribella* (2) — Last listed 1998
'Kate Haywood' — CLyd
'Ken Dearman' (dPrim)(30) — CSpe EBee EPfP EPot MBNS MCLN MOne MRav NBid NEgg NHol NSti SIng SMrm SPer WWol
kewensis (12) ♀ — EBee GFle MFie NWCA WAbe
'Kinlough Beauty' (Poly) (30) — EBrP EBre EPar GAbr LBCl LBSe LBre LFox LRHS LSur MBBe NCra NSti NWCA SBre WEas
kisoana (7) — CPla MTho WCru
- *alba* (7) — CLAP CPla GGGa MTho
'Lady Greer' (Poly)(30) ♀ — CGle CInt CPla CSam ECGN EDAr ELan GAbr ITim LFox LSur MRav NBir NChi NCra NHar NRya NSti NWCA SIng SLod SMac SSmi SUsu WCot WEas WWat
'Lambrook Lilac' (Poly)(30) — Last listed 1999
§ *latifolia* (2) — NCra WLRN
- cream (2) — Last listed 1998
latisecta (7) — GGar
§ *laurentiana* (11) — EBee GFle NWCA
'Lea Gardens' (*allionii* hybrid) (2) — MFie NHol
'Lee Myers' (*allionii* hybrid) (2) — GNor MFie NDlv NHar NNrd
¶ 'Lemon Punch' — NArg
'Lilac Fairy' — NHar
'Lilac Time' — SIng
'Lilian Harvey' (dPrim)(30) — CElw CGle EBee GDea LRHS MOne MRav NBir NDov NHol SIng SPer WWol
Limelight Group (Poly)(30) — EWoo MFie
'Lingwood Beauty' (Prim) (30) — GAbr LSur
'Linnet' (21) — ITim
'Lismore' (2) — NHol
¶ 'Lismore Jewel' (2) — EHyt
'Lismore Pink Ice' — Last listed 1998
'Lismore Yellow' (2) — EPot GTou NHar NNrd SBla SIng WAbe
Lissadel hybrids (4) — GMac
'Little Egypt' (Poly)(30) — EWoo
* 'Little Poppet' — GAbr
littoniana — See *P. vialii*
§ x *loiseleurii* (2) — EBrP EBre LBCl LBSe LBre MBBe MBro SBre WHil
§ - 'Aire Waves' (2) — GNor
longiflora — See *P. halleri*
luteola (11) — GFle GGar MFie MHer MNrw NHol NPri WFar
macrophylla (18) — GFle GTou
- H 78 (18) — Last listed 1998
magellanica (11) — CGra WAbe
malacoides (3) — MBri
marginata (2) ♀ — EBrP EBre EMNN EPot GAbr GCrs GDra GFle LBCl LBSe LBre LFox LHop LRHS MBBe MBro NCra NDlv NHar NHol SBre SIng SSmi WAbe WFar
- *alba* (2) — EPot LRHS MBro NBro NCra NDlv NHar NHol NNrd SIng SSmi
- 'Amethyst' (2) — EPot
- 'Arthur Branch' (2) — EPot
- 'Baldock's Mauve' (2) — Last listed 1997
- 'Barbara Clough' (2) — CLyd MFie SBla WAbe
- 'Beamish' (2) ♀ — CLyd EPot NBro NRya
- 'Beatrice Lascaris' (2) — EPot ITim MBro MFie NHar NHol SIng WAbe
- 'Beverley Reid' (2) — Last listed 1998

- 'Caerulea' (2) — CLyd EPot LBee WAbe
- 'Clear's Variety' (2) — EMNN EPot NHar NNrd
- 'Correvon's Variety' (2) — CLyd NCra
- cut-leaved (2) — NHol
- 'Doctor Jenkins' (2) — NHar NHol
- 'Drake's Form' (2) — EPot ITim NHol SOkd
- dwarf (2) — LRHS MFie
- 'Earl L. Bolton' (2) — EPot NHol NNrd WAbe
- 'Elizabeth Fry' (2) — CLyd LFox MBro NNrd
- 'F.W. Millard' (2) — MBro NHar
- 'Grandiflora' (2) — MBro NHar NHol NNrd SIng
- 'Highland Twilight' (2) — CPBP NNrd
- 'Holden Clough' — Last listed 1999
- 'Holden Variety' (2) — EMNN MBro NDlv NHar NHol NNrd SIng WAbe
- 'Hyacinthia' — See P. 'Hyacinthia'
- 'Ivy Agee' (2) — CLyd EPot
- 'Janet' (2) — CLyd EMNN EPot
- 'Jenkins Variety' (2) — CLyd EPot SIng
- 'Kesselring's Variety' (2) — CLyd CM&M CStu ELan EPot GNor MBro NDlv NHar NNrd SIng SSmi WAbe WWin
- 'Laciniata' — Last listed 1999
* - 'Lilac' (2) — LFox NHar NNrd
- 'Lilac Domino' — Last listed 1998
- lilac — MFie
- 'Linda Pope' (2) ♀ — CLyd CPBP EMNN EPot ITim NCra NHar NHol SUsu WAbe
- maritime form (2) — NNrd
- 'Messingham' (2) — EPot
- 'Millard's Variety' (2) — CLyd
- 'Mrs Carter Walmsley' (2) — Last listed 1997
- 'Nancy Lucy' (2) — WAbe
- 'Napoleon' (2) — ITim NHar NHol NNrd
- 'Prichard's Variety' (2) ♀ — CLyd ELan EMNN EPot ITim LBee LFox LRHS MBro MFie NCra NDlv NHar NRya SIng SSmi WAbe WEas
- 'Rheniana' (2) — EPot SIng
- 'Rosea' (2) — EPot NHol SIng
- 'Rubra' — Last listed 1999
- 'Sheila Denby' (2) — EMNN NNrd
- small flowered (2) — Last listed 1997
- 'Snowhite' (2) — WAbe
¶ - 'The President' (2) — EHyt
- violet form (2) — EMNN MBro NHar
- 'Waithman's Variety' (2) — EPot GTou
- wild collected — MFie
'Maria Talbot' (allionii hybrid) (2) — NNrd
'Marianne Davey' (dPrim) (30) — CGle EPri MRav NMGW
'Marie Crousse' (dPrim) (30) — CGle EBee GAbr LRHS MBNS MBro MOne MRav MWgw NHar NHol SIng SMrm SPer SUsu WHil WLin WRha
Marine Blues Group (Poly) (30) — CSWP MFie
'Mars' (allionii hybrid) (2) — EPot GNor MBro NDlv NHar NHol NNrd WLin
'Marven' (2) — CLyd MBro NCra NHol NNrd NWoo
'Mary Anne' — GAbr LSur
'Mauve Jack in the Green' — Last listed 1999
'Mauve Queen' (Prim)(30) — LSur
Mauve Victorians Group — CSWP MFie
'Mauvekissen' — Last listed 1997
'McWatt's Claret' (Poly) (30) — GAbr NCra
'McWatt's Cream' (Poly) (30) — CBos CSWP EDAr GAbr GFle GGar LHop LRHS LSur NBro NChi NCra NHol NMen WLin

megaseifolia (6) — Last listed 1997
melanops — See P. chionantha subsp. melanops
x **meridiana** (2) — EBrP EBre EPot LBCl LBSe LBre MBBe MFie NHar SBre WLin
§ - 'Miniera' (2) — CLyd CPBP EPot
'Mexico' — MFie
Midnight Group — CSWP MFie
'Miniera' — See P. x meridiana 'Miniera'
minima (2) — CGra CLyd GFle GTou IMGH MFie NBro NHar NWCA WAbe
- var. alba (2) — CMea GCrs GGGa NSla
- x hirsuta (2) — See P. x forsteri
- x wulfeniana (2) — See P. x vochinensis
'Miss Indigo' (dPrim)(30) — CElw CGle LFis LRHS MBNS MBri MCAu MCLN MOne MRav NHar NHol NSti SIng SLod SMrm SPer WCot WEas WHil WWol
'Miss Luck' — Last listed 1999
mistassinica alba (11) — Last listed 1997
- var. **macropoda** — See P. laurentiana
miyabeana (4) — GCrs GFle
- B&SWJ 3407 (4) — WCru
modesta (11) — SIng
- alba (11) — GFle SUsu
- var. **faurieae** (11) — MFie
- 'Flore Pleno' (d) — Last listed 1999
- var. **samanimontana** (11) — Last listed 1998
mollis (7) — WHil
'Morton' — Last listed 1998
moupinensis (21) — GKir WAbe
- C&H 7038 (21) — GFle GGGa
* 'Mrs Eagland' — GAbr
'Mrs McGillivray' (Prim) (30) — GAbr LSur
§ **munroi** (11) — GCan GFle NBro NHar NWCA SIng SWat WAbe
¶ - CD&R 2409 (11) — WAbe
§ - subsp. **yargongensis** (11) — CGle CLyd CPla EBee GAbr GCHN GCrs GFle GGar GTou LRHS MBri MFie NBro NCra NHar NWCA SBod SWat WAbe WFar WHil
Munstead strain (Poly)(30) — LSur
x **murettiana** (2) — Last listed 1999
muscarioides (17) — CGle CPla GCan GFle GTou MFie NHar WAbe
Muted Victorians Group (Poly)(30) — CSWP MFie NDov
§ **nana** (21) — WAbe
nepalensis — See P. tanneri subsp. nepalensis
'Netta Dennis' — GCrs
New Pinks Group (Poly) (30) — CFri CSWP GAbr MFie NDov
'Nightingale' — WAbe
nivalis Pallas — See P. chionantha
§ **nutans** Georgi (25) — Last listed 1998
- Delavay ex Franch. — See P. flaccida
obconica (19) — LRHS MBri MFie
'Old Port' (Poly)(30) — CElw GBin LSur MBro WPat
Old Rose Victorians Group (Poly)(30) — CSWP MFie
'Olive Wyatt' (dPrim)(30) — EPri
'Oriental Sunrise' (4) — MBri MFie NDov
Osiered Amber Group (Prim)(30) — CSWP GAbr NDov
'Our Pat' (dPoly)(30) — GAbr IBlr WPnP WRus
* 'Page' — EHyt
Pagoda hybrids (4) — MBri
palinuri (2) — MFie
palmata (7) — GFle GGGa NHar WAbe

Pantaloons Group (Poly) (30) — Last listed 1997

'Paris '90' (Poly)(30) — CFri CSWP EWoo GAbr MFie NDov

parryi (20) — GCrs MLLN NCra NHar NWCA WFar WHil

¶ 'Pat Cottle' (d) (Poly) (30) — CBos

'Peardrop' (2) — CGra GAbr NHol WLin

pedemontana (2) — GFle MSte NHar NWCA

- 'Alba' (2) — Last listed 1999

'Perle von Bottrop' (Prim) (30) — CLTr GAbr

'Peter Klein' (11) — CNic CStu GAbr GDra GFle ITim NHar WAbe WPyg WTin

§ *petiolaris* (21) — EPar GCHN GCrs GFle GGGa GNor ITim MDun MOne NCra NHar WAbe

- LS&H 19856 — See *P.* 'Redpoll'

'Petticoat' — Last listed 1999

§ 'Pink Aire' (2) — ITim MFie

'Pink Fairy' — Last listed 1999

'Pink Gem' (dPrim)(30) — Last listed 1999

'Pink Ice' (*allionii* hybrid) (2) — CGra CLyd CPBP EPot MDHE MFie NHol NNrd SIng WLin

'Pink Profusion' (Prim)(30) — Last listed 1998

pinnatifida (17) — GGGa

poissonii (4) — CGle CHar CMHG CNic CPla GCan GFle GGar GMac IBlr LPBA MFie MSCN WAbe

- ACE 1946 (4) — NWCA WCot WCru

- ACE 2407 (4) — EPot WCot

- CLD 193 (4) — LSyl

polyanthus (30) — NCra WFar

polyneura (7) — CNic CPla ECha EDAr GFle GGar LSyl MFie MNes MNrw NBid NDea SRms WHil

- ACE 1429 (7) — EPot

'Port Wine' — GAbr

praenitens — See *P.sinensis*

prenantha (4) — GCrs GGGa WAbe

'Prince Silverwings' (dPoly)(30) — WEas

§ *prolifera* (4) ♀ — CMHG CTbh CTrw EBee ECha EHon GFle GGar GMac LPBA LRHS LSyl MFir MLLN MNrw MRav MSCN SPer SRms SSpi SWat WAbe WFar WGwy WPer WWat

§ x *pubescens* (2) ♀ — CInt EMan EPot EWTr GAbr LFox MBro SMrm SSmi WLRN WPer

- 'Alba' (2) — NHar WAbe

- 'Alison Gibbs' (2) — Last listed 1998

- x *allionii* (2) — CFri NNrd

- 'Apple Blossom' (2) — CLyd EMNN EPot MFie SIng

- 'Balfouriana' (2) — CNic LFox MBro

§ - 'Bewerley White' (2) — EBee EDAr MBro NCra NDlv NNrd WWin

- 'Blue Wave' (2) — LAco MFie NNrd

§ - 'Boothman's Variety' (2) — CInt CLyd CStu EMNN ITim LRHS MBro MFie NCra NDlv NHar NHol NNrd NWCA SBla SIng SSmi SUsu WWin

- 'Carmen' — See *P.* x *pubescens* 'Boothman's Variety'

- 'Chamois' (2) — MFie

- 'Christine' (2) — CLyd EMNN LBee MBro MFie NCra NDlv NHar NHol NNrd

- 'Cream Viscosa' (2) — EMNN MBro MFie NDlv NHol NMGW NNrd

- 'Deep Mrs Wilson' (2) — SUsu

- 'Ellen Page' (2) — MFie

- 'Elphenor' (2) — NNrd

- 'Faldonside' (2) — CInt CLTr CLyd EDAr EMNN EPot GCHN MBro NCra NDlv NHol NMGW NNrd WWin

§ - 'Freedom' (2) — CLyd CStu ELan EMNN EPot GTou ITim LRHS MBro MFie NCra NDlv NHar NHol NNrd SBod SIng SRms WEas WWin

- 'George Harrison' (2) — GAbr MFie

- 'Greenslacks Yellow' — Last listed 1998

- 'Harlow Car' (2) — CLyd EMNN GMac ITim LFox MBro MFie NDlv NHar NNrd WFar

- 'Henry Hall' (2) — CLyd CStu EDAr EWes

- 'Herbert Beresford' (2) — Last listed 1998

- 'Hurstwood Red Admiral' (2) — Last listed 1998

- 'Joan Danger' (2) — CLyd MFie NHol NNrd

- 'Joan Gibbs' (2) — CLyd ELan LBee LRHS MBro MFie NCra NHar NNrd SIng

- 'Kath Dryden' (2) — MFie

- 'Lilac Fairy' (2) — NDlv

- mixed (2) — Last listed 1997

- 'Mrs J.H. Wilson' (2) — CLyd ITim LRHS MBro MFie NCra NDlv NHol WLRN

- 'Pat Barwick' (2) — EMNN LFox MBro MFie NDlv NHol

- 'Peggy Fell' (2) — GCrs MDHE MFie

- 'Pink Freedom' (2) — NDlv

- 'Roseille' (2) — Last listed 1998

- 'Rufus' (2) — CLyd GCrs ITim NCra NHol NNrd WTin

- 'S.E. Matthews' (2) — Last listed 1999

- 'Sid Skelton' (2) — EMNN SIng

- 'Snowcap' — CGra EPot GCrs

- 'Sonya' (2) — NNrd

- 'The General' (2) — CLyd GNor MBro NCra NNrd SPop WWin

- 'Victoria' (2) — EMNN

§ - 'Wedgwood' (2) — EMNN GNor

- white (2) — Last listed 1997

- x 'White Linda Pope' — Last listed 1998

- 'Winifred' — NDlv NHol

pulchra (21) — GCrs GKir

pulverulenta (4) ♀ — More than 30 suppliers

- Bartley hybrids (4) ♀ — CBot CGle EBee GBuc GMac SMur

- 'Bartley Pink' (4) — CPla CPlt GBuc GCan LSyl WEas

'Purple Splendour' — Last listed 1999

'Purpurkissen' (Prim)(30) — NHol

'Quaker's Bonnet' — See *P. vulgaris* 'Lilacina Plena'

'Rachael Kinnon' (2) — WLin

'Rachel Kinnen' (2) — MFie SIng

'Ramona' (Poly)(30) — MFie

'Raven' — Last listed 1997

'Ravenglass Vermilion' — See *P.* 'Inverewe'

'Red Sunset' (4) — GDra

'Red Velvet' (dPrim)(30) — EBee MOne SMrm

§ - 'Redpoll' (21) — EPar GCrs GGar NHar WAbe

reidii (28) — GFle MBri NCra

- var. *williamsii* (28) — EBrP EBre GDra GGGa GNor GTou LBCl LBSe LBre MBBe MBri NHar SBre WLin

- - *alba* (28) — GDra GFle MBri

reptans (16) — GGGa

'Reverie' (Poly)(30) — EWoo MFie

'Rhubarb and Custard' (Poly)(30) — CGle

'Romeo' (Prim)(30) — LSur NCra

'Rose O'Day' (dPrim)(30) — MCLN MOne NHol

rosea ♀ — CBot CPla CRow EBee EDAr EPar GDra GFle GGGa GKir GTou LHop LRHS MFie MHer NBid

	NCra NDea NFla NHar NSti SIng
	SSpi WFar
- CC&McK 367 (11)	GCHN
- 'Delight'	See *P. rosea* 'Micia Visser-de Geer'
- 'Gigas' (11)	EBrP EBre LBCl LBSe LBre MBBe
	MSta NHol SBre WFar
- 'Grandiflora' (11)	CGle COIW CPea EHon ELan
	EMNN ENot EPar EWTr GBar
	GCrs GFle LPBA LSyl MBri MRav
	NDlv NMen SBea SIng SRms WPer
§ - 'Micia Visser-de Geer'	LRHS
(11)	
* - *splendens* (11)	Last listed 1997
rotundifolia	See *P. roxburghii*
'Rowallane Rose' (4)	CBro GBuc MTed SSpi WRus
§ *roxburghii* (25)	Last listed 1998
'Roy Cope' (dPrim)(30)	CLTr MBro MOne MRav NBid
	NBir
'Roydon Ruby'	WCot
rubra	See *P. erythra*
rusbyi (20)	Last listed 1999
Rustic Reds Group (Poly)	CSWP MFie NDov
(30)	
'Sandy' (21)	Last listed 1999
'Sapphire'	Last listed 1999
saxatilis (7)	MFie
scandinavica (11)	MFie WHil
x *scapeosa* (21)	NHar
§ 'Schneekissen' (Prim)(30)	CHid CNic GAbr MBri MCLN
	NBro NChi SBla WHil WRus WViv
'Schneekissen Improved'	EBrP EBre LBCl LBSe LBre MBBe
(Prim)(30)	SBre
scotica (11)	EBee GCrs GFle GTou LFox MFie
	NCra NWCA WAbe
secundiflora (26)	CGle CInt CLTr CPla EBee ELan
	GAbr GDra GFle GGGa GGar
	GKir GTou LRHS LSyl MBro
	MNrw MTis NChi NCra NWoo
	SPer SPlb SRms SUsu WAbe WCru
	WHil WHoo
§ x *sendtneri* (2)	MFie
septemloba (7)	GFle WAbe
x *serrata*	See *P. x vochinensis*
serratifolia (4)	GGGa
¶ 'Shizuko Hara'	EHyt
sibthorpii	See *P. vulgaris* subsp. *sibthorpii*
sieboldii (7) ♀	CBre CGle CRow EMNN EPar
	GFle LFox MBri MNrw NCra
	NHar NMen NRya NWCA SIng
	SMac SRms SSpi SUsu WAbe WEas
	WFar WLin
- *alba* (7)	CLAP NBro NDov NMen SRot
	WCru WFar
- blue (7)	NMen
- 'Carefree' (7)	NBro NMen
- 'Cherubim' (7)	EBee ECtt GCHN GMac
- 'Dancing Ladies' (7)	CGle
- 'Galaxy' (7)	Last listed 1999
- 'Geisha Girl' (7)	CFir CLAP ECtt GCHN MRav
	WAbe WFar
- 'Lilac Sunbonnet' (7)	CGle EPfP NHol
- 'Manakoora' (7)	CGle MFie
- 'Mikado' (7)	CFir EBee ECtt GCHN MFie MRav
	NNrd
- 'Pago-Pago' (7)	CGle CInt CLAP CMea MFie NBro
- 'Seraphim' (7)	GMac
- 'Snowflake' (7)	CGle CMea GCHN NSla WAbe
- 'Tah-ni' (7)	CFri NBro
- 'Winter Dreams' (7)	CGle CInt CLAP MFie NBid NBro
§ *sikkimensis* (26)	More than 30 suppliers
- ACE 1422 (26)	GBuc WCru
- ACE 1822 (26)	Last listed 1998

- B&SWJ 2471 (26)	WCru
- CC&McK 1022 (26)	GTou
- crimson and gold (26)	MBro
- var. *hopeana* (26)	GCrs GFle
¶ - MECC 051 (26)	GGar
- MECC 82 (26)	GGar
- 'Tilman Number 2' (26)	GAbr GDra
aff. *sikkimensis*	GBuc
ACE 2176 (26)	
Silver-laced Group (Poly)	CGle EPar
(30)	
- 'Silver Lining' (Poly)(30)	LRHS
§ *sinensis* (27)	MBri
- 'Fanfare Mixed' (27)	MFie
sinoplantaginea	See *P. chionantha* subsp.
	sinoplantaginea
sinopurpurea	See *P. chionantha* subsp.
	sinopurpurea
'Sir Bedivere' (Prim)(30)	GAbr
smithiana	See *P. prolifera*
'Snow Carpet'	See *P.* 'Schneekissen'
'Snow Cushion'	See *P.* 'Schneekissen'
'Snow Queen'	Last listed 1998
'Snow White' (Poly)(30)	MRav
Snowcushion	See *P.* 'Schneekissen'
'Snowruffles'	Last listed 1997
sonchifolia (21)	GGGa MDun
- from Tibet (21)	MDun
sorachiana	See *P. yuparensis*
sp. ACE 1867	NWCA
sp. B&SWJ 2165	WCru
sp. BC 9331	Last listed 1998
spectabilis (2)	GFle NHar
- JCA 789.400 (2)	MFie
- JCA 789.401 (2)	Last listed 1999
specuicola J&JA	NWCA
1.768.600 (11)	
Spice Shades Group	CSWP EWoo GAbr MFie NDov
(Poly)(30)	
* 'Squire'	EHyt
¶ 'Starlight'	EHyt
x *steinii*	See *P. x forsteri*
'Stradbrook Dainty' (2)	EHyt EPot MFie NHol
'Stradbrook Dream' (2)	EHyt EPot MFie NHol
'Stradbrook Gem' (2)	WAbe
'Stradbrook Lilac Lustre'	MFie
(2)	
'Stradbrook Lucy' (2)	ITim NHol
¶ 'Stradbrook Mauve Magic'	MFie
(2)	
stricta (11)	CPBP GFle
Striped Victorians Group	CMil CSWP GAbr MFie NChi
	NDov
'Sue Jervis' (dPrim)(30)	CElw GAbr LFis MBro NHar NSti
	SBla WBar WHal WRha WWol
suffrutescens	NWCA WAbe
'Sunshine Susie' (dPrim)	CGle EBee EPri GAbr LRHS MBNS
(30)	MBri MCAu MCLN MOne MRav
	NDov NHol SIng SMrm SPer SUsu
	WCot WHil WLRN WWol
'Sylvia' (Prim)(30)	Last listed 1997
takedana (24)	GGGa
tanneri (21)	Last listed 1999
§ - subsp. *nepalensis* (21)	ITim
- subsp. *tsariensis* var.	GGGa
alba (21)	
'Tantallon' (21)	GCrs GGar GNor NHar
'Tawny Port' (Poly)(30)	CGle CLTr CMea GAbr NBro NCra
	SRms
'The Grail' (Prim)(30)	Last listed 1998
tibetica (11)	GFle GGGa
'Tie Dye' (Prim)(30)	WCot

'Tinney's Jewel' — Last listed 1998
'Tinney's Moonlight' — Last listed 1999
'Tipperary Purple' (Prim) (30) — GAbr WPnP
'Tomato Red' (Prim)(30) — CFee GAbr LBee NCra
'Tony' — ITim NHar WLin
'Torchlight' (dPrim)(30) — Last listed 1998
tosaensis (24) — Last listed 1998
¶ - var. *brachycarpa* — GFle
'Tournaig Pink' (4) — GGar
tschuktschorum (18) — Last listed 1997
'Val Horncastle' (dPrim) (30) — CBos CHad LRHS MBNS MCAu MCLN MOne MWgw NBid NDov NHar SIng SMrm SPer SPla WWol
Valentine Victorians (Poly) (30) — CSWP MFie
veris (30) ♀ — More than 30 suppliers
* - *alba* — Last listed 1998
- subsp. *canescens* JCA 789.600 (30) — Last listed 1997
- hybrids (30) — WWal
- red (30) — CM&M GFle
* - 'Rhandirmwyn Red' — WRha
- 'Sunset Shades' — GOrP NLar WBea
vernalis — See *P. vulgaris*
verticillata (12) — GFle MFie
§ *vialii* (17) ♀ — More than 30 suppliers
§ *villosa* (2) — GCrs GFle GTou
- var. *cottica* — See *P. villosa*
Violet Victorians Group (Poly)(30) — CSWP MFie NDov
viscosa Allioni — See *P. latifolia*
§ x *vochinensis* (2) — CFee CLyd MBro NHar NHol NNrd NWCA SIng
§ *vulgaris* (Prim)(30) — More than 30 suppliers
- *alba* (30) — CGle CRow WAbe WLin
- 'Alba Plena' (Prim)(30) — CGle CHad CRow CSWP GAbr GBuc GGar IBlr NChi WRus
- Ballyrogan cream edge (Prim)(30) — IBlr
- Barnhaven Gold — NDov
- 'Double Sulphur' (dPrim)(30) — Last listed 1997
- green-flowered — See *P. vulgaris* 'Viridis'
§ - 'Lilacina Plena' (dPrim) (30) — CBot CGle GAbr IBlr LFis LSur MBNS MCAu MCLN MRav NDov SMrm SPer WHil WWol
§ - subsp. *sibthorpii* (Prim)(30) ♀ — CGle CMHG CSam GAbr GTou LFox LRHS LSur MBro MRav NBro NChi NCra NWCA SBla SRms WAbe WEas WHil WLin WPyg
- - *alba* from Lebanon — MFie
- - HH&K 265 (Prim)(30) — Last listed 1997
- - HH&K 337 (30) — GFle
- - JCA 790.401 (Prim)(30) — Last listed 1997
§ - 'Viridis' (Prim)(30) — CRow CSWP IBlr
- 'Viridis' semi-double (Prim)(30) — Last listed 1997
- white hose-in-hose (Prim) (30) — Last listed 1998
waltonii (26) — CPla EBee GCrs GFle MNrw MSCN NChi SIng
- hybrids (26) — GGar
'Wanda' (Prim)(30) ♀ — CGle CRow EDAr ELan ENot GAbr LRHS LSur NBid NSti NVic SBla SIng SMer SPer SRms WCFE WFar WHoo
Wanda Group (Prim)(30) — CNic SIng
- pale mauve (30) — Last listed 1999
'Wanda Hose in Hose' (Prim)(30) — CGle GAbr LSur MMHG NChi WCot WHer WHil

'Wanda Jack in the Green' (Prim)(30) — CRow MBro MLLN WFar
wardii — See *P. munroi*
warshenewskiana — CNic MFie NHol NRya
watsonii (17) — GCan GCrs GGGa GTou MFie NHar SIng WAbe
'Wedgwood' — See *P. x pubescens* 'Wedgwood'
¶ 'Wharfedale Ballerina' (2) — EHyt
'Wharfedale Bluebell' (2) — CLyd NHar WGwG
'Wharfedale Butterfly' (2) — NHar NHol NNrd
'Wharfedale Crusader' (2) — NHol NNrd
'Wharfedale Gem' (*allionii* hybrid) (2) — GNor MFie NHar NHol NNrd WAbe
'Wharfedale Ling' (*allionii* hybrid) (2) — CGra CPBP CStu EPot MFie NHar NHol WAbe WLin
¶ 'Wharfedale Sunshine' (2) — EHyt
'Wharfedale Superb' (*allionii* hybrid) (2) — MFie NHar NHol NNrd
'Wharfedale Village' (2) — CLyd NHar NHol WGwG
'White Linda Pope' (2) — CLyd NHar
'White Linda Pope' seedlings (2) — SIng
'White Wanda' (Prim)(30) — CGle CRow GAbr LSur NDov WCru
whitei (21) — CBrd GCrs MDun WAbe
§ - 'Sherriff's Variety' (21) — IBlr
wigramiana (28) — WAbe
'William Genders' (Poly) (30) — GAbr LSur
wilsonii (4) — CPla GBuc GFle GMac LSyl MBro MNes MNrw NDlv SLon SWat WAbe WHer WHil WHoo WOve WPyg
§ - var. *anisodora* (4) — CPla EBee GCan GFle MFie
'Windrush' — See *P. x berninae* 'Windrush'
'Windward Blue' — SBla
'Winter White' — See *P. 'Gigha'*
'Wisley Crimson' — See *P. 'Wisley Red'*
§ 'Wisley Red' (Prim)(30) — Last listed 1999
wollastonii (28) — WAbe
'Woodland Blue' — NWoo
wulfeniana (2) — CGra MBro MFie WAbe
yargongensis — See *P. munroi* subsp. *yargongensis*
§ *yuparensis* (11) — EBee GFle NMen WAbe
'Zenobia' — Last listed 1997

PRINSEPIA (Rosaceae)

sinensis — CFee CMCN CPle GBin GEil MBlu WBcn
uniflora — CB&S CPLG
utilis — CTrG

PRITCHARDIA (Arecaceae)

¶ *affinis* — LBlo

PRITZELAGO (Brassicaceae)

alpina — CNic

PROBOSCIDEA (Pedaliaceae)

louisianica — EFEx
parviflora — EFEx

PROSTANTHERA (Lamiaceae)

aspalathoides — ECou LGre SOWG WCot WWye
cuneata ♀ — More than 30 suppliers
- 'Alpine Gold' — CMHG CPle CWSG SBod SLim
- 'Fastigiata' — SPan
- Kew form — Last listed 1999
'Eddington Blue' — SBod
incisa — CTrw EPPr SHDw
- 'Rosea' — WSHC

lasianthos	CB&S CDoC CRHN CSev ECou EWes LGre LRHS SBod SBrw SHDw SOWG WWye
- var. *subcoriacea*	CPle
melissifolia	ECon ECre LCns LRHS SAga SBrw SLod WSel
- var. *parvifolia*	CTrw ECre GCHN GGar WAbe WSHC
nivea	CPle ECou LGre
ovalifolia	ECou LHil MMil SBod
'Poorinda Ballerina'	CAbb CDoC CLyn CSev ECon EMan EOrc GKir LHil LHop LRHS MGos SAga SBod SMur SOWG SPer
rotundifolia ♀	CAbb CB&S CInt CPle CSam CSev CTrG CTri EOHP ERea ISea SAga SBod SBrw SEND SOWG SPer WBod WWye
- *alba*	EBee
- 'Chelsea Girl'	See *P. rotundifolia* 'Rosea'
§ - 'Rosea'	CGdn CTrC CTrG EOHP ERea MLan SBod SHDw SLon WWye
saxicola var. *montana*	Last listed 1998
walteri	CAbb CDoC ECou LGre WHCG

PROTEA (Proteaceae)

acaulos	Last listed 1999
aristata	CTrC
aurea	CTrC
burchellii	CCpl
compacta	CTrF
coronata	CTrF
cynaroides	CB&S CCpl CCtw CHEx CTrC CTrF
¶ - 'Imperial Monarch'	CTrC
eximia	CCtw CTrC
grandiceps	CTrC
lacticolor	CGre
laurifolia	CTrC
magnifica	Last listed 1998
nana	Last listed 1999
neriifolia	Last listed 1999
repens	CTrC
simplex	CFil
¶ *speciosa*	CTrF
subvestita	CCpl CTrC CTrF
susannae	CTrF
venusta	Last listed 1997

PRUMNOPITYS (Podocarpaceae)

§ *andina*	CGre SLon WWat
elegans	See *P. andina*
§ *ferruginea*	Last listed 1998
§ - 'Golden Dwarf'	CLTr
§ *taxifolia*	ECou

PRUNELLA (Lamiaceae)

§ *grandiflora*	CAgr EBee EBot ECha EFer EWTr GBar GKir MNrw MWat SRms SWat WCHb WOve WRos WWye
- 'Alba'	EBee ECha EPfP EWTr GKir LPio MCAu NBid NCut NLar NOrc SBea SPer SPla WCHb WOve WWhi
- 'Blue Loveliness'	EBee EMan GAbr GTou SPla WCHb
- 'Carminea'	SPer
- 'Little Red Riding Hood'	See *P. grandiflora* 'Rotkäppchen'
- 'Loveliness' ♀	CDoC EBee EBrP EBre ECha ECtt EPar EWTr GKir LAst LBCl LBSe LBre MBBe MBel MCAu MRav

	NBro NGdn NSti NVic SBod SBre SPer SPla SPlb WFar WWin
- 'Pagoda'	LAst LIck NBrk NLar NOak WCHb WElm WMoo
- 'Pink Loveliness'	CMCo EBee EBrP EBre EPar GCHN GTou LBCl LBSe LBre LRHS MBBe MWgw NArg SBre SRms WByw WCHb WFar WWin WWye
- purplish blue	Last listed 1997
- *rosea*	CBlo EPfP MWat WByw WHil WWhi
§ - 'Rotkäppchen'	CPea ECtt GCHN WMoo
- 'Rubra'	NCut WPer
- 'White Loveliness'	EBee EBrP EBre EPar GCHN LBCl LBSe LBre LRHS MBBe NBrk SBre WByw WFar WPer WRus WWin WWye
hyssopifolia	EBee
incisa	See *P. vulgaris*
* 'Inshriach Ruby'	NBir SPla WCHb
laciniata	CMCo SSvw WCHb
- pink	Last listed 1999
- white	Last listed 1999
§ *vulgaris*	CArn CKin EWFC GAbr GBar GPoy MChe MHer MHew MSal NLan NMir NSti SIde WCHb WHbs WHer WOak WWye
- *alba*	WAlt WHer
- 'Gleam' (v)	WAlt
- 'Inner Glow' (v)	WAlt
¶ - 'Marbled White' (v)	WAlt
- 'Ruth Wainwright' (v)	CNat WCHb
- 'Saintlow'	Last listed 1998
- 'Voile'	Last listed 1998
x *webbiana*	See *P. grandiflora*

PRUNUS ✿ (Rosaceae)

'Accolade' ♀	CAbP CBlo CDoC CDul CLnd COtt CSam CTho EBee ECrN ECtt ENot EWTr GKir IOrc LPan LRHS MAsh MBri MRav NBea NWea SEND SLim SPer SSta WDin WJas WStI
§ 'Amanogawa' ♀	More than 30 suppliers
¶ x *amygdalopersica*	ESim
'Ingrid' (F)	
- 'Pollardii'	CBlo CLnd ENot MAsh WJas
- 'Spring Glow'	CDoC CDul LRHS MBri WJas
amygdalus	See *P. dulcis*
¶ 'Aratama'	MBri
armeniaca 'Alfred' (F)	CTho EMui ERea GTwe MBri SDea SPer
- 'Blenheim' (F)	ERea
- 'Bredase' (F)	SDea
- 'De Nancy'	See *P. armeniaca* 'Gros Pêche'
- 'Early Moorpark' (F)	ERea GBon GTwe LRHS SDea SFam WWeb
- 'Farmingdale' (F)	ERea SDea
- 'Goldcot' (F)	ERea SDea
- 'Golden Glow' (F)	GTwe LRHS MCoo
§ - 'Gros Pêche' (F)	Last listed 1999
- 'Hemskirke' (F)	ERea
- 'Hongaarse' (F)	SDea
- 'Moniqui' (F)	CGOG
- 'Moorpark' (F) ♀	CEnd EMui ERea EWTr GKir GTwe LBuc MGos NRog SDea SKee SPer WStI
- 'New Large Early' (F)	ERea GTwe SDea SEND SKee
- 'Royale' (F)	Last listed 1999
- 'Tross Orange' (F)	SDea
'Asano'	See *P.* 'Geraldinae'

avium ♀ | CB&S CBlo CDul CKin CLnd CSam EBee ECrN ENot EWTr GChr GKir LBuc LHyr LPan MBar MBri MGos MRav NBee NWea SFam SKee SPer SRPl WDin WHar WMou WOrn
- 'Amber Heart' (F) | SDea SKee
- 'August Heart' (F) | Last listed 1997
- 'Bigarreau Gaucher' (F) | SKee
§ - 'Bigarreau Napoléon' (F) | GTwe LRHS MGos SDea SFam SKee
- 'Birchenhayes' | See *P. avium* 'Early Birchenhayes'
- 'Black Eagle' (F) | CTho
- 'Black Elton' (F) | Last listed 1997
- 'Black Glory' (F) | Last listed 1997
- 'Black Tartarian' (F) | SKee
- 'Bottlers' | See *P. avium* 'Preserving'
- 'Bradbourne Black' (F) | SKee
- 'Bullion' (F) | CEnd CTho
- 'Burcombe' (F) | CEnd CTho
- 'Celeste' (D) | COtt EMui GTwe LRHS
- 'Cherokee' | See *P. avium* 'Lapins'
- 'Circassian' (F) | SKee
- 'Colney' (F) | GTwe SFam WJas
- 'Dun' (F) | CTho
§ - 'Early Birchenhayes' (F) | CEnd CTho
- 'Early Rivers' (F) | GTwe LRHS SDea SKee
- 'Elton Heart' (F) | CTho
- 'Fastigiata' | Last listed 1999
- 'Fice' (F) | CEnd CTho
- 'Florence' (F) | SKee
- 'Governor Wood' (F) | GTwe SKee
- 'Grandiflora' | See *P. avium* 'Plena'
- 'Greenstem Black' (F) | CTho
- 'Hertford' (F) | SFam SKee
- 'Inga' (F) | SFam SKee
- 'Ironsides' (F) | Last listed 1999
- 'Kassins Frühe Herz' (F) | Last listed 1999
- 'Kentish Red' (F) | CTho
§ - 'Lapins' (F) | EMui GTwe LRHS SDea SFam SKee WHar WJas
- 'May Duke' | See *P.* x *gondouinii* 'May Duke'
- 'Merchant' (F) ♀ | GTwe SKee
- 'Mermat' (F) | GTwe
- 'Merpet' (F) | GTwe
- 'Merton Bigarreau' (F) | Last listed 1997
- 'Merton Crane' (F) | SKee
- 'Merton Favourite' (F) | Last listed 1999
- 'Merton Glory' (F) | CDoC GTwe LRHS MGos SFam
- 'Merton Heart' (F) | Last listed 1997
- 'Merton Late' (F) | Last listed 1997
- 'Merton Marvel' (F) | Last listed 1997
- 'Merton Premier' (F) | Last listed 1999
- 'Merton Reward' | See *P.* x *gondouinii* 'Merton Reward'
- 'Nabella' (F) | WJas
- 'Napoléon' | See *P. avium* 'Bigarreau Napoléon'
- 'Newstar' (F) | EMui
- 'Noble' (F) | Last listed 1997
- 'Noir de Guben' (F) | GTwe SKee
¶ - 'Noir de Meched' (D) | SKee
- 'Nutberry Black' (F) | Last listed 1999
- 'Old Black Heart' (F) | Last listed 1999
§ - 'Plena' (d) ♀ | CB&S CBlo CLnd CSam CTho EBee ECrN ELan ENot EPfP GChr GKir IOrc LBuc LHyr LPan LRHS MGos MNaF NBee NWea SFam SPer WDin WHar WJas WOrn
§ - 'Preserving' (F) | CTho
- 'Ronald's Heart' (F) | Last listed 1997
- 'Roundel Heart' (F) | SKee

- 'Sasha' (F) | GTwe
- 'Small Black' (F) | CTho
- 'Smoky Dun' (F) | Last listed 1997
- 'Starking Hardy Giant' (F) | Last listed 1997
- 'Starkrimson' (F) | GTwe
- 'Stella' (F) ♀ | CEnd CMac CSam EMui ERea EWTr GBon GChr GKir GTwe LBuc LRHS MBri MGos NBee NRog SDea SFam SKee SPer WHar WJas WWeb
- 'Stella Compact' (F) | COtt MBri SDea SKee WHar
- 'Summer Sun' (D) | EMui GTwe MCoo
- 'Summit' (F) | SKee
- 'Sunburst' (F) | CEnd EMui EWTr GTwe LBuc LRHS MBri SCrf SDea SFam SKee WJas WWeb
- 'Turkish Black' (F) | SKee
* - 'Upright' | CTho
- 'Van' (F) | GTwe SKee
- 'Vega' (F) | GTwe SFam WJas
- 'Waterloo' (F) | CTho SKee
- 'White Heart' (F) | CTho SKee
'Benden' | Last listed 1999
* 'Beni-no-dora' | SMur
* 'Beni-yutaka' | CBlo CEnd LBuc LRHS MBri SLim
* 'Birch Bark' | Last listed 1997
'Blaze' | See *P. cerasifera* 'Nigra'
x *blireana* ♀ | CBlo CEnd LBuc CDul CLnd EBee ENot GChr LPan LRHS MAsh MBri MRav MWat SMHT SPer SRPl SSta WHar

'Blushing Bride' | See *P.* 'Shôgetsu'
bucharica JJH 98807 | Last listed 1999
campanulata | Last listed 1999
cerasifera | CAgr CBlo CTri GAri GChr GKir GTre LBuc NWea SKee WDin WMou
- 'Cherry Plum' (F) | EMui SKee
- 'Crimson Dwarf' | CDoC GKir LPan
* - 'Green Glow' | CBlo
- 'Hessei' (v) | CBlo CEnd LRHS MAsh MBri MGos SLim
- 'Kentish Red' (F) | Last listed 1999
§ - Myrobalan Group (F) | CBlo CKin SDea SKee
§ - 'Nigra' ♀ | CBlo CDoC CDul CLnd CTri EBee ECrN ELan EWTr GChr IOrc LBuc LNet LPan LRHS MAsh MBri MGos MRav NBea NBee NWea SDea SPer SRms WDin WHar WOrn WStI
- 'Pendula' | CTho
§ - 'Pissardii' | CBlo EBrP EBre GKir LBCl LBSe LBre LPan MAsh MBBe MBar NBea NFor NWea SBre SFam SLim WFar WJas
* - 'Princess' | CBlo EMui MAsh SLim
- 'Rosea' | LRHS MBri
- 'Spring Glow' | CEnd EBee LRHS
- 'Vesuvius' | SRPl
cerasus 'Montmorency' (F) | SKee
- 'Morello' (F) ♀ | CMac CTho EBee EBrP EBre EMui EWTr GBon GChr GKir GTwe LBCl LBSe LBre LBuc LRHS MBBe MBri MGos NBee NRog SBre SDea SFam SKee SPer WJas WWeb
- 'Nabella' (F) | SKee
- 'Rhexii' (d) | CBlo CDul MAsh MGos SPer
- 'Wye Morello' (F) | Last listed 1999
'Cheal's Weeping' | See *P.* 'Kiku-shidare-zakura'
§ 'Chôshû-hizakura' | CBlo CLnd GChr GKir IOrc LNet MBri SPer

§ x *cistena* ♀ — CB&S CBlo EBrP EBre ELan EPfP GChr IOrc LBCl LBSe LBre LRHS MBBe MBar MBri MDun MGos MWat NBee SBre SEas SPer SPla WDin

- 'Crimson Dwarf' — See *P.* x *cistena*
'Collingwood Ingram' — GKir LRHS MBri
'Comet' PBR — See *P.* Easter Bonnet = 'Comet'
conradinae — See *P. hirtipes*
davidiana — CTho
domestica 'Allgroves Superb' (D) — ERea
- 'Angelina Burdett' (D) — ERea GTwe NRog SKee
- 'Anna Späth' (C/D) — SKee
- 'Ariel' (C/D) — SDea SKee
- 'Autumn Compote' (C) — Last listed 1997
- 'Avalon' PBR (D) — GTwe LRHS SDea SKee
- 'Belgian Purple' (C) — SKee
- 'Belle de Louvain' (C) — CTho ERea GTwe NRog SDea SKee
- 'Birchenhayes' (F) — CEnd
- 'Black Diamond' — See *P. salicina* 'Black Diamond'
- 'Blue Imperatrice' (C/D) — Last listed 1997
- 'Blue Tit' (C/D) ♀ — EMui ERea GTwe SDea SKee
- 'Bonne de Bry' (D) — SKee
§ - 'Bountiful' (C) — ERea
- 'Brandy Gage' (C/D) — SKee
- 'Bryanston Gage' (D) — CTho SKee
- 'Burbank' (C/D) — SDea
- 'Burcombe' — CEnd
- 'Bush' (C) — SKee
- 'Cambridge Gage' (D) ♀ — More than 30 suppliers
- 'Chrislin' (F) — CTho
- 'Coe's Golden Drop' (D) — CTho EMui ERea GKir GTwe LRHS MGos SCoo SDea SFam SKee
- 'Count Althann's Gage' (D) — ERea GTwe NRog SDea SFam SKee
- 'Cox's Emperor' (C) — SKee
- 'Crimson Drop' (D) — ERea SKee
- 'Cropper' — See *P. domestica* 'Laxton's Cropper'
- 'Curlew' (C) — SDea
- 'Czar' (C) ♀ — CDoC CSam CTri EBrP EBre EMui EWTr GChr GKir GTwe IOrc LBCl LBSe LBre LBuc LRHS MBBe MGos NBea NRog NWea SBre SDea SFam SKee WWeb
- 'Delicious' — See *P. domestica* 'Laxton's Delicious'
- 'Denniston's Superb' — See *P. domestica* 'Imperial Gage'
- 'Diamond' (C) — SKee
- 'Dittisham Black' (C) — CTho
- 'Dittisham Ploughman' (C) — CSam CTho SKee
- 'Dunster Plum' (F) — CTho
- 'Early Laxton' (C/D) ♀ — ERea GTwe SDea SFam SKee
- 'Early Orleans' — See *P. domestica* 'Monsieur Hâtif'
- 'Early Prolific' — See *P. domestica* 'Rivers's Early Prolific'
- 'Early Rivers' — See *P. domestica* 'Rivers's Early Prolific'
- 'Early Transparent Gage' (C/D) — CTho CTri EMui ERea GTwe LBuc SDea SFam
- 'Early Victoria' (C/D) — SDea
- 'Edwards' (C/D) ♀ — GTwe LBuc NRog SDea SFam SKee
- 'Excalibur' PBR (D) — GTwe LRHS SDea
§ - 'German Prune Group' (C) — SKee
- 'Giant Prune' (C) — GTwe LRHS NRog SKee
I - 'Godshill Big Sloe' (F) — SDea

- 'Godshill Blue' (C) — SDea
¶ - 'Godshill Minigage' (F) — SDea
- 'Golden Transparent' (D) — CTho ERea GTwe NRog SFam SKee
- 'Goldfinch' (D) — GTwe NRog SKee
- Green Gage Group — See *P. domestica* Reine-Claude Group
- - 'Old Green Gage' — See *P. domestica* (Reine-Claude Group) 'Reine-Claude Vraie'
- 'Grey Plum' (F) — CTho
- 'Grove's Late Victoria' (C) — SKee
- 'Guthrie's Late Green' (D) — SKee
- 'Herman' (C/D) — CSam GTwe LRHS MBri SDea SKee
- 'Heron' (F) — GTwe
- 'Impérial Epineuse' (D) — SKee
§ - 'Imperial Gage' (C/D) ♀ — CTho EMui ERea GTwe LBuc SDea SFam SKee
- 'Jan James' (F) — CEnd
- 'Jefferson' (D) ♀ — EMui ERea GTwe NRog SDea SFam SKee
* - 'Jubilaeum' (C/D) — GTwe SKee
- 'Kea' (C) — CTho SKee
- 'Kirke's' (D) — CTho CWSG ERea GTwe SDea SFam SKee
- 'Landkey Yellow' (F) — CTho
- 'Late Muscatelle' (D) — ERea SKee
- 'Laxton's Bountiful' — See *P. domestica* 'Bountiful'
§ - 'Laxton's Cropper' (C) — GTwe NRog SKee
§ - 'Laxton's Delicious' (D) — GTwe SKee
- 'Laxton's Delight' (D) ♀ — GTwe
- 'Laxton's Gage' (D) — SDea SKee
- 'Manaccan' (C) — CTho
- 'Marjorie's Seedling' (C) ♀ — CDoC CTho EBrP EBre ECrN EMui ERea EWTr GBon GTwe LBCl LBSe LBre LBuc LRHS MBBe MGos MWat SBre SCrf SDea SEND SFam SKee WJas
- 'McLaughlin' (D) — SKee
- 'Merton Gem' (C/D) — GTwe SFam SKee
- 'Monarch' (C) — GTwe SKee
§ - 'Monsieur Hâtif' (C) — SKee
- 'Ontario' (C/D) — GTwe SKee
- 'Opal' (D) ♀ — CDoC EMui EPfP ERea EWTr GTwe IOrc LBuc MBri MGos MLan MWat NWea SDea SEND SFam SKee WWeb
- 'Orleans' (C) — SKee
- 'Oullins Gage' (C/D) ♀ — CDoC ECrN EMui EPfP ERea GBon GChr GKir GTwe LBuc MBri MWat NRog SDea SFam SKee SPer WJas WWeb
- 'Pershore' (C) ♀ — CTho ERea GTwe NRog SDea SFam SKee WStI
- 'Pond's Seedling' (C) — SDea SKee
- 'President' (C/D) — GTwe LPan SDea SKee
- 'Prince Englebert' (C) — SKee
- 'Priory Plum' (D) — SDea
- 'Purple Pershore' (C) — CTri CWSG ERea GTwe NRog SDea SFam SKee
- 'Quetsche d'Alsace' — See *P. domestica* German Prune Group
- 'Reeves' (C) ♀ — GTwe SFam SKee
§ - Reine-Claude Group (C/D) — EMui GTwe NRog SDea SFam SKee SPer
¶ - - 'Reine Claude de Brahy' (D) — SKee
- - 'Reine-Claude de Bavais' (D) — CTho CTri ERea GTwe NRog SDea SFam SKee
§ - - 'Reine-Claude Vraie' (C/D) — EPfP ERea WCFE WJas

§ - - 'Willingham Gage'   ERea GTwe LRHS MLan
     (C/D)
   - 'Reine-Claude Dorée'   See *P. domestica* Reine-Claude
                             Group
   - 'Reine-Claude Violette'   CTho ERea SKee
     (D)
§ - 'Rivers's Early Prolific'   CTho ECrN ERea GTwe MCoo
     (C)   MWat NRog NWea SCoo SDea
                                  SKee
   - 'Royale de Vilvoorde' (D)   ERea SKee
   - 'Sanctus Hubertus' (D) ♀   GTwe LCaP SDea SKee
   - 'Severn Cross' (D)   GTwe SKee
¶ - 'Stanley' (C/D)   LPan
¶ - 'Stella'   LPan
   - 'Stint' (C/D)   SKee
   - 'Swan' (C)   GTwe
   - 'Transparent Gage' (D)   ERea SKee
   - 'Upright' (F)   CEnd
   - 'Utility' (D)   SKee
¶ - 'Valor' (C/D) ♀   MCoo SKee
   - 'Victoria' (C/D) ♀   More than 30 suppliers
* - 'Violetta' (C/D)   ERea SKee
   - 'Warwickshire Drooper'   CSam CTho ERea GBon GTwe
     (C)   SDea SFam SKee
   - 'Washington' (D)   CTho ERea SDea SKee
   - 'White Magnum Bonum'   CTho SDea
     (C)
   - 'Willingham'   See *P. domestica* (Reine-Claude
                                 Group) 'Willingham Gage'
   - 'Wyedale' (C)   GTwe
§ *dulcis*   CDul CLnd CTri EMui EWTr LHyr
                                 LPan MAsh MWat NBea NWea
                                 SCrf SDea SFam SRPl WDin
                                 WOrn
   - 'Balatoni' (F)   LRHS MBri
   - 'Macrocarpa' (F)   ESim
* - 'Phoebe' (F)   ESim
   - 'Roseoplena'   CBlo MBri
¶ - 'Titan' (F)   ESim
§ Easter Bonnet =   LRHS
     'Comet'[PBR]
   Fragrant Cloud = 'Shizuka'   CEnd CWSG EPfP GKir LRHS
                                 MAsh MBri SLim SPer
   fruticosa 'Globosa'   CBlo CWSG LPan LRHS
   'Fugenzô'   CBlo
¶ 'Fuki'   MBri
§ 'Geraldinae'   CLnd GKir LRHS MAsh MBri
                                 WPyg
   glandulosa 'Alba Plena'   CB&S CEnd CPle CSam EBee ECtt
     (d) ♀   ESis GChr LRHS MGos MWat
                                 NBea NBee NHol SPer SPla
                                 SReu SRms SSpi WCFE WDin
                                 WSHC
   - 'Rosea Plena'   See *P. glandulosa* 'Sinensis'
§ - 'Sinensis' (d) ♀   CEnd CPle ESis LRHS MGos MRav
                                 NWea SPer SPla SRPl SReu SRms
                                 SSpi WSHC
§ x *gondouinii* 'May Duke'   CTho SKee
     (F)
§ - 'Merton Reward' (F)   SKee
   'Gyoikô'   CTho
   'Hakanagoto'   Last listed 1999
   'Hally Jolivette'   CEnd COtt ELan GKir LRHS MAsh
                                 MBri SPla WBcn
¶ 'Hanagasa'   MBri
¶ 'Hana-kagoto'   MBri
   'Hillieri'   ECrN MBar MGos
   'Hillieri Spire'   See *P.* 'Spire'
   'Hilling's Weeping'   GKir LRHS MBri
§ *hirtipes*   CTho SFam
   'Hisakura'   See *P.* 'Chôshû-hizakura'
   Hollywood   See *P.* 'Trailblazer'

   incisa   CTri GAri IOrc NBea SLPl SPer
                                 SSpi
   - 'Beniomi'   GAri MRav
   - 'February Pink'   CAbP CBlo CPMA LRHS MBri
                                 MRav NPro
   - 'Fujima'   NHol SMur WPat WPyg WWat
   - 'Kojo-no-mai'   More than 30 suppliers
   - 'Mikinori'   CB&S LRHS MBri MGos
   - 'Oshidori'   LRHS MBri MGos MRav NHol
                                 WFar WPyg WShe
* - 'Otome'   MBri WFar
   - 'Pendula'   LRHS MBri
   - 'Praecox' ♀   CTho EPfP LRHS MAsh MBri
   - 'The Bride'   CEnd GKir MAsh MBri
§ - f. *yamadae*   CB&S CEnd LBuc LRHS
   insititia 'Blue Violet   SKee
     Damson' (F)
§ - 'Bradley's King Damson'   GTwe SKee
     (F)
   - bullace (C)   SDea
   - 'Dittisham Damson' (C)   CTho
   - 'Farleigh Damson' (C)   ERea EWTr GTwe SDea SFam
                                 SKee WJas
   - 'Godshill Damson' (C)   SDea
   - 'Golden Bullace'   See *P. insititia* 'White Bullace'
   - 'King of Damsons'   See *P. insititia* 'Bradley's King
                                 Damson'
   - 'Langley Bullace' (C)   CTho ERea SKee
   - 'Merryweather Damson'   CDoC CMac CTho EBrP EBre
     (C)   EMui ERea GBon GChr GKir
                                 GTwe LBCl LBSe LBre LBuc MBBe
                                 MBri NBee NRog SBre SDea
                                 SFam SKee SPer WHar WJas WStI
                                 WWeb
   - 'Mirabelle de Nancy' (C)   CTho GTwe SDea SFam SKee
   - 'Mirabelle de Nancy   SDea
     (Red)' (C)
§ - 'Prune Damson' (C) ♀   CSam CTho CTri EMui EPfP ERea
                                 GBon GTwe LBuc MBri MGos
                                 MWat NRog SDea SFam SKee
                                 WHar WJas
   - 'Shepherd's Bullace' (C)   CTho ERea SKee
   - 'Shropshire Damson'   See *P. insititia* 'Prune Damson'
   - 'Small Bullace' (C)   SKee
§ - 'White Bullace' (C)   ERea SKee
   - 'Yellow Apricot' (C)   ERea SKee
§ *jamasakura*   CTho
   'Jô-nioi'   CEnd CLnd CTho SMHT
§ 'Kanzan' ♀   More than 30 suppliers
§ 'Kiku-shidare-zakura' ♀   More than 30 suppliers
   Korean hill cherry   See *P. x verecunda*
   kurilensis   See *P. nipponica* var. *kurilensis*
   'Kursar' ♀   CBlo CDul COtt CTho EBee EMui
                                 EPfP GKir IOrc LNet LRHS MAsh
                                 MBri SFam SLim
   laurocerasus ♀   CB&S CChe CDul CKin EBee
                                 ELan EPfP GChr GKir GTre LHyr
                                 LNet LPan MRav MWat NBea
                                 NFor NWea SEND SPer SRPl SReu
                                 WFar WMou WStI
   - 'Aureovariegata'   See *P. laurocerasus* 'Taff's Golden
                                 Gleam'
   - 'Camelliifolia'   CTri EPla MBlu SMad WCFE WDin
                                 WHCG WPGP WPyg
N - 'Castlewellan' (v)   CBot CDoC CDul CLTr CTrw EPfP
                                 EPla IOrc ISea LAst MBar MGos
                                 MTis NBea NHol SDix SEND SPer
                                 SPla SSta WGwG WHar WLeb
                                 WWat
   - 'Caucasica'   MGos
   - 'Cherry Brandy'   EGra ENot NPro SPer WCot
                                 WLRN WStI

- Dart's Lowgreen™	See *P. laurocerasus* Low 'n' Green = 'Interlo'
- 'Etna'	CDoC EBee LRHS MGos
- 'Golden Splash'	WBcn
- Green Carpet	See *P. laurocerasus* 'Grünerteppich'
- 'Green Marble' (v)	CTri EBee WSHC
- 'Interlo'	See *P. laurocerasus* Low 'n' Green = 'Interlo'
§ - 'Latifolia'	CHEx EPla GKir SAPC SArc SLPl SMad
§ - Low 'n' Green = 'Interlo'	ENot
- 'Magnoliifolia'	See *P. laurocerasus* 'Latifolia'
- 'Mano'	EMil MGos
- 'Marbled White'	See *P. laurocerasus* 'Castlewellan'
- 'Mischeana'	MBri SLPl
- 'Mount Vernon'	EBee MBar MBri MGos NBee WDin
- 'Otinii'	CHEx
- 'Otto Luyken' ♀	More than 30 suppliers
- Renault Ace = 'Renlau'PBR	EBee
- 'Reynvaanii'	EPla LRHS MBri WBcn
- 'Rotundifolia'	CDoC CTri EMil ENot GKir LBuc LPan LRHS MBNS MBar MBri MGos NBea NFla NWea SRms WDin WHar WStI
- 'Rudolf Billeter'	EPla
- 'Schipkaensis'	NFor SPer
§ - 'Taff's Golden Gleam' (v)	CEnd MGos WCot WWes
N - 'Variegata'	CCHP MBNS MGos SRms
- 'Zabeliana'	CDoC CLan EBee ENot EPfP EPla GChr GKir MBar NWea SPer SRms WDin WPyg WWin
* *longipedunculata*	GKir LRHS MBri
lusitanica ♀	More than 30 suppliers
- subsp. *azorica* ♀	EPla SMad WPGP WWat
- 'Myrtifolia'	EBee EPfP EPla GKir LRHS MBri MRav SMad WCFE WShe WWat
- 'Variegata'	More than 30 suppliers
maackii	CTho EPfP NBea SEND SSpi WDin WWat
- 'Amber Beauty'	CDul CPMA EBee GChr LPan LRHS MBri NBee SLPl WPyg
mahaleb	CAgr CTho
* 'Mahogany Lustre'	MBlu
¶ 'Matsumae-akatsukinokane'	MBri
¶ 'Matsumae-usugasanesomei'	MBri
'Mount Fuji'	See *P.* 'Shirotae'
mume	NBea WNor WOTO
- 'Alboplena'	CChe
§ - 'Beni-chidori'	CB&S CBlo CCHP CEnd CPMA EBee EPfP LRHS MBlu MBri MGos NBea SLim SSpi SSta WJas WPGP
- 'Beni-shidori'	See *P. mume* 'Beni-chidori'
* - 'Ken Kyo'	LRHS
* - 'Kyo Koh'	LRHS SPla
§ - 'Omoi-no-mama' (d)	CEnd CPMA LRHS MBri MMHG
- 'Omoi-no-wac'	See *P. mume* 'Omoi-no-mama'
- 'Pendula'	CLnd LRHS MBri
- 'Yae-kankobane' (d)	LRHS
myrobalana	See *P. cerasifera* Myrobalan Group
§ *nipponica* var. *kurilensis*	CB&S MAsh
- var. *kurilensis* 'Brilliant'	EBee GKir LPan MBri MGos

- - 'Ruby'	CDul CEnd GChr GKir LRHS MBri MGos NBee NEgg SMur
- - 'Spring Joy'	LRHS MBri
'Okame' ♀	CBlo CLnd CSam CTho EBee EBrP EBre EPfP GKir LBCl LBSe LBre LRHS MAsh MBBe MBri MGos MRav NWea SBre SLim SPer SRPl
§ 'Okumiyako'	CBlo CEnd LRHS SFam WDin
padus	CBlo CDul CKin CLnd ECrN EMac GChr GKir GTre IOrc LBuc LHyr LNet MGos NBea NBee NWea SSpi WDin WMou WOrn
- 'Albertii'	CTho LPan SLPl WJas
- 'Colorata' ♀	CBlo CDoC CDul CEnd CMHG CSam CTho ECrN ELan GChr IOrc LBuc LNet LPan MGos NBee SMHT SPer SSpi WDin WJas
- 'Dropmore'	Last listed 1997
- 'Grandiflora'	See *P. padus* 'Watereri'
- 'Plena' (d)	CTho
- 'Purple Queen'	CBlo CEnd CTho ENot WStI
§ - 'Watereri' ♀	CB&S CBlo CDoC CDul CLnd CTho EBee ECrN ELan ENot EPfP GChr IOrc LPan MGos NWea SPer SRPl WDin WJas WOrn
'Pandora' ♀	CB&S CBlo CLnd EBee ECrN ENot EPfP GChr GKir LHyr LPan LRHS MAsh MBri MRav MWat NBea NBee NBlu NWea SCrf SEND SPer SRPl
§ *pendula* var. *ascendens* 'Rosea'	CBlo CBlo
§ - 'Pendula Rosea' ♀	CBlo CEnd EBee ENot LPan LRHS MAsh SPer WJas
§ - 'Pendula Rubra' ♀	CBlo CDoC CCit CTri EBee ENot EPfP LNet LRHS MAsh MBri MGos SFam SLim SPer
§ - 'Stellata'	LRHS
persica 'Amsden June' (F)	ERea GTwe SDea SFam
- 'Bellegarde' (F)	ERea GTwe SDea SFam SKee
- 'Bonanza' (F)	EMil EMui ERea
- 'Doctor Hogg' (F)	SDea
- 'Duke of York' (F) ♀	CTri ERea GTwe LRHS SDea SFam SKee WWeb
- 'Dymond' (F)	ERea
- 'Flat China' (F)	ERea
- 'Francis' (F)	SKee
- 'Garden Anny' (F)	EMil ERea LRHS
- 'Garden Lady' (F)	EMui ERea GTwe LRHS WWeb
- 'Garden Silver'	Last listed 1997
- 'Hale's Early' (F)	ERea GTwe SEND SFam SKee SPer
- 'Hylands' (F)	SDea
- 'Kestrel' (F)	Last listed 1998
- 'Klara Mayer' (d/F)	CBlo GKir
- 'Melred'	Last listed 1997
- 'Merrill O'Henry'	See *P. persica* 'O'Henry'
- 'Natalia' (F)	SDea
- var. *nectarina* Crimson Gold (F)	SDea
- - 'Early Gem' (F)	ERea SDea
- - 'Early Rivers' (F) ♀	CMac EMui ERea GTwe NRog SDea SFam
- - 'Elruge' (F)	ERea GTwe SDea SEND SFam
- - 'Fantasia' (F)	CGOG ERea SDea
- - 'Fire Gold' (F)	SDea
- - 'Garden Beauty' (F/d)	WWeb
- - 'Humboldt' (F)	ERea GTwe SDea
- - 'John Rivers' (F)	ERea GTwe SFam

- - 'Lord Napier' (F) ♀	CDoC CWSG EMui ERea EWTr GKir LBuc LRHS MGos SDea SEND SFam SKee SPer WStI WWeb
- - 'Nectared' (F)	EWTr GTwe LCaP
- - 'Nectarella' (F)	EMui ERea GTwe LRHS
- - 'Pineapple' (F)	CTri ERea GTwe LRHS SCrf SDea SFam WWeb
- - 'Red Haven' (F)	GTwe SDea SKee
- - 'Rivers Prolific' (F)	Last listed 1997
- - 'Ruby Gold' (F)	SDea
- - 'Terrace Ruby' (F)	LRHS WWeb
§ - 'O'Henry' (F)	CGOG
- 'Peregrine' (F) ♀	CMac CTri CWSG EMui ERea EWTr GBon GKir GTwe LBuc LRHS MBri MGos NRog SCrf SDea SFam SKee SPer WJas WStI WWeb
- 'Purpurea'	EBee
- 'Reliance' (F)	SDea
- 'Robin Redbreast' (F)	SDea
- 'Rochester' (F) ♀	CWSG EMui ERea EWTr GBon GKir GTwe LRHS MBri SDea SFam SPer WStI
- 'Royal George' (F)	GTwe NRog SFam
- 'Rubira' (F)	Last listed 1998
- 'Sagami-shidare'	LRHS MBri
- 'Saturne' (F)	EMui LRHS
- 'Springtime' (F)	ERea SDea
- 'Terrace Amber'	LRHS WWeb
- 'Terrace Diamond'	LRHS WWeb
- 'Terrace Garnet'	ENot LRHS WWeb
- 'Terrace Pearl'	WWeb
- 'Weeping Flame' (F)	LRHS
- 'White Cascade'	LRHS MBri
'Pink Perfection' ♀	CB&S CBlo CDul CLnd EBee EBrP EBre ENot GChr LBCl LBSe LBre LHyr LPan LRHS MAsh MBBe MBri NBee SBre SFam SLon SPer SRPl SSta WFar WJas WOrn
'Pink Shell' ♀	CBlo CLnd CTho EBee GKir LRHS MBri SFam WStI
pissardii	See *P. cerasifera* 'Pissardii'
'Pissardii Nigra'	See *P. cerasifera* 'Nigra'
prostrata	SBla WPat
* - 'Anita Kistler'	ECho
* - var. *discolor*	WNor
* - 'Pygmaea'	Last listed 1999
pumila	SEas
- var. *depressa*	CPMA CPle GAri IHar MBar MBlu MRav NPro
'Red Cascade'	SDea
'Royal Burgundy'	CEnd CWSG GKir IMGH LRHS MAsh MBri SLim SPer
rufa	CTho
- FK 40	Last listed 1997
§ *salicina* 'Black Diamond' (F)	SDea
¶ - 'Methley' (D)	ESim
- 'Satsuma' (F)	ERea
¶ - 'Shiro' (D)	ESim
sargentii ♀	CB&S CBlo CDoC CDul CLnd CSam CTho EBee ECrN ELan ENot GChr GKir IOrc LBuc LHyr LPan LRHS MAsh MBri MGos NBea NWea SFam SPer WDin WJas
¶ - 'Charles Sargent'	MBri
- 'Columnaris'	GKir LRHS MBri
- Rancho™	CLnd CMCN ENot SLPl SSta WOrn
x *schmittii*	CLnd ENot MAsh SPer WJas
'Sekiyama'	See *P.* 'Kanzan'

serotina	CDul
§ *serrula* ♀	More than 30 suppliers
¶ - Branklyn form	GKir MBri
¶ - Dorothy Clive form	GKir
- x *serrulata*	CTho
- var. *tibetica*	See *P. serrula*
serrulata 'Erecta'	See *P.* 'Amanogawa'
- 'Grandiflora'	See *P.* 'Ukon'
- var. *hupehensis*	SLPl
- 'Longipes'	See *P.* 'Okumiyako'
- 'Miyak'	See *P.* 'Okumiyako'
N - var. *pubescens*	See *P.* x *verecunda*
- 'Rosea'	See *P.* 'Kiku-shidare-zakura'
- var. *spontanea*	See *P. jamasakura*
'Shidare-zakura'	See *P.* 'Kiku-shidare-zakura'
'Shimizu-zakura'	See *P.* 'Okumiyako'
'Shirofugen' ♀	CB&S CBlo CDoC CLnd CTho EBee EMil EPfP GChr GKir IOrc LBuc LPan LRHS MAsh MBri MWat SCrf SFam SPer SSta WDin WJas WOrn
§ 'Shirotae' ♀	CBlo CDoC CEnd CLnd CSam CTho CTri EBee ECrN ELan ENot GKir IOrc LBuc LHyr LPan LRHS MAsh MDun MGos MRav NBee NWea SFam SPer SRPl SSta WOrn WWeb
§ 'Shôgetsu' ♀	CLnd CTho EBee ELan EPfP GKir IOrc LPan LRHS MBri SFam SLim SPer WDin
'Shosar'	CBlo CEnd CLnd GKir LRHS MBri SPer
'Snow Goose'	EBee GKir LRHS MBri MDun
¶ 'Snow Showers'	MDun
spinosa	CDoC CDul CKin CSam CTri ECrN EPfP GChr GTre LBuc LHyr LRHS MBri NBee NWea SPer STre WDin WHer WMou WNor
- 'Plena' (d)	CEnd CTho SRPl
- 'Purpurea'	MBlu WHCG WMou WPat
§ 'Spire' ♀	CBlo CDoC CLnd CTho EBee ENot EPfP EWTr GKir IOrc LBuc LHyr LPan LRHS MGos MRav NBlu NWea SPer WFar WJas WNor
x *subhirtella*	
- var. *ascendens*	See *P. pendula* var. *ascendens*
- 'Autumnalis' ♀	More than 30 suppliers
- 'Autumnalis Rosea' ♀	More than 30 suppliers
§ - 'Dahlem'	LRHS
- 'Fukubana' ♀	CBlo CLnd CTho GChr GKir LPan LRHS MAsh MBri SCoo
- 'Pendula' hort.	See *P. pendula* 'Pendula Rosea'
- 'Pendula Rubra'	See *P. pendula* 'Pendula Rubra'
- 'Plena'	See *P.* x *subhirtella* 'Dahlem'
N - 'Rosea'	CLnd GKir MRav SMad
- 'Stellata'	See *P. pendula* 'Stellata'
'Sunset Boulevard'	GKir LRHS MBri
'Taihaku' ♀	More than 30 suppliers
* *takesimensis*	Last listed 1999
'Taki-nioi'	EBee NWea
'Taoyame'	CLnd GKir LRHS MBri WPyg
tenella	CB&S CDul CEnd ELan SIng WCot WHCG WMou
- 'Fire Hill' ♀	CEnd CPMA ELan EPfP GKir LNet LRHS MBar MGos NBee SBod SPer SRPl SSpi WCot WDin WJas WOrn WPat WPyg
tibetica	See *P. serrula*
tomentosa	CAgr SBod
§ 'Trailblazer' (C/D)	CBlo CEnd CLnd CTho EBee IOrc LPan MGos NWea SKee SSta WStI

triloba	CB&S CBlo LBuc LPan LRHS NBee WDin
- 'Multiplex' (d) ♀	EBrP EBre ENot GChr LBCl LBSe LBre LRHS MBBe MGos MRav SBre SPer SRms WJas
- Rosemund	LRHS MBri MGos
§ 'Ukon' ♀	CB&S CBlo CDoC CDul CLnd CTho CTri EBee ENot GChr GKir IOrc LBuc LNet LRHS MBar MBri MGos MRav NBee NWea SFam SPer SRPl SSta WDin WHar WOrn WPyg WStI
'Umineko'	CBlo CDoC CLnd EBee ENot GChr GKir IOrc MGos SPer
§ x *verecunda*	CBlo CDoC CLnd EBee GChr NWea SPer WJas
- 'Autumn Glory'	CTho NBea SMHT
virginiana 'Schubert'	CBlo CDoC CLnd CTho EBee ENot EPla GChr IOrc LPan WJas
yamadae	See *P. incisa* f. *yamadae*
§ x *yedoensis* ♀	CLnd CSam CTho EBee ENot NWea SFam SLim SPer SRPl WDin WJas WOrn WWat
- 'Ivensii'	CB&S CBlo CDoC CDul GKir LRHS MAsh MBri MGos SFam SPer WStI
- 'Pendula'	See *P.* x *yedoensis* 'Shidare-yoshino'
- 'Perpendens'	See *P.* x *yedoensis* 'Shidare-yoshino'
§ - 'Shidare-yoshino'	CBlo CDoC CEnd CLnd CTho EBee ECrN EPfP GChr GKir LNet LRHS MBar MBri MGos MRav MWat NBee NWea SLim SPer WOrn WPyg
- 'Tsubame'	LRHS MBri
'Yoshino'	See *P.* x *yedoensis*
'Yoshino Pendula'	See *P.* x *yedoensis* 'Shidare-yoshino'

PSEUDERANTHEMUM (Acanthaceae)
reticulatum 'Eldorado'	LChe
seticalyx	ECon

PSEUDOCYDONIA (Rosaceae)
§ *sinensis*	CB&S LNet

PSEUDOFUMARIA See CORYDALIS

PSEUDOLARIX (Pinaceae)
§ *amabilis* ♀	CDoC CEnd CFil CGre CMCN CTho EHul EPfP GKir ISea LCon LNet LRHS MBar MBlu MBri SFur STre WBod WNor WWat
kaempferi	See *P. amabilis*

PSEUDOMUSCARI See MUSCARI

PSEUDOPANAX ✿ (Araliaceae)
(Adiantifolius Group) 'Adiantifolius'	CHEx CTrC GQui
- 'Cyril Watson' ♀	CHEx SVen
arboreus	CAbb CB&S CHEx
chathamicus	CHEx SAPC SArc
crassifolius	CAbb CB&S CBot CHEx CTrC LPan SAPC SArc SMad SVen
davidii	SLon
delavayi	Last listed 1997
discolor	ECou
ferox	CAbb CB&S CHEx LEdu SAPC SArc SMad
laetus	CAbb CHEx ECou SAPC

lessonii	CB&S CHEx ECou
- 'Gold Splash' (v) ♀	CB&S SVen
- hybrids	CHEx
'Linearifolius'	CTrC
'Purpureus' ♀	CAbb CHEx
'Sabre'	Last listed 1998
¶ *simplex*	LEdu
'Trident'	CTrC SVen
valdiviensis	Last listed 1998

PSEUDOPHEGOPTERIS (Thelypteridaceae)
levingei	CCuc EMon

PSEUDOPHOENIX (Arecaceae)
* *nativo*	MBri

PSEUDOSASA (Poaceae - Bambusoideae)
§ *amabilis*	SDry
§ - hort.	See *Arundinaria tecta*
§ *japonica* ♀	CB&S CBlo CHEx EBee EFul EOas EPfP EPla GKir ISta LBlo LEdu LJus LRHS MBrN MWht NBee NMoo NVic SAPC SDry SMad SPer WCFE WCru WDin WJun
§ - 'Akebonosuji' (v)	CHEx EFul EPVP EPla ISta LJus MMoz SDry WJun WNor
- 'Tsutsumiana'	CDoC CHEx EBee EPla ERod ISta LJus MMoz SDry WJun
- 'Variegata'	See *P. japonica* 'Akebonosuji'
owatarii	SDry
pleioblastoides	EPla SDry
usawai	EPla WJun

PSEUDOTSUGA (Pinaceae)
§ *menziesii* ♀	CB&S CDoC CDul GChr GKir IOrc LBuc LCon LLin LRHS MBar MBlu NWea WMou
- 'Bhiela Lhota'	CKen
- 'Blue Wonder'	CKen
- 'Densa'	CKen
- 'Fastigiata'	CKen
- 'Fletcheri'	CKen MBar SLim
- var. *glauca*	LCon MBar STre
- 'Glauca Pendula' ♀	LCon MBar MBlu MGos SMad
I - 'Gotelli's Pendula'	CKen
- 'Graceful Grace'	CKen
- 'Julie'	CKen
- 'Little Jamie'	CKen MBar
- 'Little Jon'	SLim
- 'Lohbrunner'	CKen
- 'McKenzie'	CKen
- 'Nana'	CKen
- 'Stairii'	CKen
- 'Tempelhof Compact'	SLim
taxifolia	See *P. menziesii*

PSEUDOWINTERA (Winteraceae)
§ *colorata*	CB&S CCHP CDoC CMCN CPla CTrw IOrc ISea SLon WBod WCru WFoF WPat WPic WPyg WWat
- 'Mount Congreve'	LRHS WGer

PSIDIUM (Myrtaceae)
cattleyanum	See *P. littorale* var. *longipes*
guajava (F)	GPoy
littorale (F)	ERea
¶ - var. *littorale*	ESim
§ - var. *longipes* (F)	LBlo

PSORALEA (Papilionaceae)
affinis	CHEx
bituminosa HH&K 174	Last listed 1999

glandulosa	WPGP
pinnata	CTrC CTrG LHil
¶ *tenuiflora*	EBee

PSYCHOTRIA (Rubiaceae)

capensis	Last listed 1998
viridis	Last listed 1998

PTELEA (Rutaceae)

trifoliata ♀	CB&S CFil CLnd CMCN CPMA
	EBee EPfP MAsh SPer SRms
	SSpi WDin WFar WHCG WNor
	WOrn
– 'Aurea' ♀	CAbP CB&S CBot CDul CEnd
	CLnd CPMA CPle ELan EPfP GKir
	LRHS MBlu MBri MGos SMur SPer
	SSpi SSta WHCG WPGP WPat
	WPyg

PTERACANTHUS See STROBILANTHES

PTERIDIUM (Dennstaedtiaceae)

aquilinum Percristatum	IOrc
Group	

PTERIDOPHYLLUM (Papaveraceae)

racemosum	EFEx EPot WCru

PTERIS (Pteridaceae)

argyraea	MBri NMar
bulbifera	Last listed 1997
cretica ♀	MBri SAPC SArc
– var. *albolineata* ♀	GQui MBri SRms
– 'Cristata'	MBri
– 'Gautheri'	MBri
– 'Parkeri'	MBri
– 'Rivertoniana'	MBri
– 'Rowei'	MBri
– 'Wimsettii'	MBri
ensiformis	MBri NMar
* – 'Arguta'	MBri
– 'Victoriae'	MBri
¶ *gallinopes*	EMon
longifolia	NMar
tremula	GQui MBri NMar SRms
umbrosa	MBri WRic
vittata	SRms

PTEROCARYA (Juglandaceae)

fraxinifolia ♀	CAgr CB&S CDoC CDul CLnd
	CMCN CTho CTrG ECrN ENot
	EPfP EWTr IOrc MAsh MBlu WDin
	WMou WPGP
– var. *dumosa*	Last listed 1998
x *rehderiana*	CTho WMou
rhoifolia	Last listed 1998
stenoptera	CB&S CFil CLnd CMCN CTho
	SLPl SMad WMou WPGP
– 'Fern Leaf'	WMou

PTEROCELTIS (Ulmaceae)

tatarinowii	CMCN WHCr

PTEROCEPHALUS (Dipsacaceae)

depressus	WPat
hookeri	Last listed 1998
parnassi	See *P.perennis*
§ *perennis*	EDAr ESis GCHN LBee LRHS
	MBro MHer NBir NHar NMen
	NTow NWCA SBla SMer SRms
	WAbe WEas WHoo WPat WPyg
	WWin

– subsp. *perennis*	Last listed 1999
pinardii	Last listed 1997

PTEROSTYLIS (Orchidaceae)

abrupta	Last listed 1999
alata	Last listed 1999
Bantam g.	Last listed 1999
coccinea	SSpi WIvy
– red	Last listed 1999
concinna	Last listed 1999
– yellow	Last listed 1999
curta	CStu WIvy
Cutie g. 'Harold's Pride'	Last listed 1999
Dunkle g.	Last listed 1999
erecta	Last listed 1999
fischii	Last listed 1999
Hookwink g.	Last listed 1999
x *ingens*	Last listed 1999
Joseph Arthur g.	Last listed 1999
Marelba g.	Last listed 1999
Mary Eleanor g.	Last listed 1999
Nodding Grace g.	Last listed 1999
nutans white	Last listed 1999
obtusa	Last listed 1999
ophioglossa	Last listed 1999
pedunculata	Last listed 1999
procera	Last listed 1999
robusta	Last listed 1999
russellii	Last listed 1999
Sentinel g.	Last listed 1999
stricta	Last listed 1999
Talhood g.	Last listed 1999
taurus	Last listed 1998
x *toveyana*	Last listed 1999
truncata	SSpi
Trunkfish g.	Last listed 1999

PTEROSTYRAX ✿ (Styracaceae)

corymbosa	CB&S CMCN CPMA SSpi WWat
hispida ♀	CB&S CBrd CCHP CFil CHEx
	CLnd CMCN CPMA CPle CSam
	EPfP EPla GKir LRHS MBel MBlu
	MRav SFur SSpi WBod WOTO
	WPGP WWat
psilophylla	CMCN CPle

PTILIMNIUM (Apiaceae)

capillaceum	Last listed 1999

PTILOSTEMON (Asteraceae)

afer	EHrv EMan MWgw
casabonae	Last listed 1998
§ *diacantha*	Last listed 1998

PTILOTRICHUM See ALYSSUM

PUERARIA (Papilionaceae)

montana var. *lobata*	CAgr CArn CPIN
thunbergiana	Last listed 1998

PULICARIA (Asteraceae)

§ *dysenterica*	CArn CKin EWFC MChe MHer
	MSal NMir SIde WCHb WJek
	WOak WWye

PULMONARIA ✿ (Boraginaceae)

'Abbey Dore Pink'	WAbb
affinis	CElw CLAP EMon LRHS
– 'Margaret'	Last listed 1999
angustifolia ♀	CRow CSam EWTr GDra GGar
	GKir LRHS MBro MHew MSal
	NBrk NFla NHol NOrc SChu SIng

	SMer SRms WByw WEas WFar WHil WWat WWin
* - *alba*	EMon NSti
- subsp. *azurea*	CBro CElw CFri COlW CRow EBee EFou ELan EMon EPla ERav GMac LAst LNor LRHS MBNS MBri MCLN MRav NBro NTow SMer SPer SPla SRms WFar WPnP WWye
- 'Blaues Meer'	CBos CFir CSam EBee EGle GBuc GKir LPio MBNS SPla WCru
- 'Munstead Blue'	CElw CGle CHea CLAP COlW CWit EBee ECha EFou EGle EHrv EPar LFis LLWP LPio LSpr MTho MWgw NBrk NHol NRya NSti SAga SRms WCru WRus
- 'Rubra'	See *P. rubra*
'Apple Frost'	NSti
'Barfield Regalia'	CGle CLAP CMHG EMon MBro NCat NChi NSti SDys WByw WCer
'Benediction'	NSti
'Berries and Cream'	NSti
'Beth's Blue'	ECha EMon LRHS MBri MGrG WByw WCru
'Beth's Pink'	CElw ECha ERav MBel NCat WCru WFar
'Blauer Hügel'	CBel CElw EMon LRHS NSti
§ 'Blauhimmel'	CLAP EMon LRHS MBro WCru WElm WFar
¶ 'Blue Buttons'	EPla
'Blue Crown'	CElw CGle CLAP CSev EMon EWes LRHS MBri NSti SAga SSpe WCot WEas WHal WPGP
'Blue Ensign'	More than 30 suppliers
'Blue Moon'	See *P. officinalis* 'Blue Mist'
¶ 'Blue Pearl'	EBee EMon MBel NHaw NSti
'Blue Star'	Last listed 1999
'Botanic Hybrid'	Last listed 1997
'British Sterling'	CLAP
'Buckland'	Last listed 1997
Cally hybrid	CLAP EBee EMon GCal NSti WCot
'Cedric Morris'	CElw NSti
'Chintz'	CLAP CPlt EBee EPPr GBuc MAvo NHol NSti WCru WHal
'Cleeton Red'	EMon NCat NSti SDys WCru
'Coral Springs'	EBee EBrP EBre GKir LBCl LBSe LBre MBBe NSti SBre
'Corsage'	CElw EBee EGle
¶ 'Cotton Cool'	CBel CElw CFil EBee EGar EMon EPla MAvo NSti SSpi WCot WCru WMoo WPGP
'Crawshay Chance'	Last listed 1999
¶ 'Dark Vader'	NSti
'De Vroomen's Pride'	CFir CHid CLAP EBee EGle EMan LAst MSCN NCut WPnP WWat
'Diana Clare'	CLAP WCot
'Duke's Silver'	CElw CLAP
'Elworthy Rubies'	CElw MAvo
¶ 'Emerald Isles'	NSti
'Esther'	CElw NSti SDys WRus
'Excalibur'	CBos CElw CHid CLAP EBee EBrP EBre ECha EMan EPPr GBin GBuc GKir LAst LBCl LBSe LBre MBBe MChl MMil NSti SBre SMad SPla SUsu WCot WRus
'Fiona'	NHaw
'Glacier'	CElw CGle CMea CMil CStr EBee ECGP EMan EMon EOrc EPPr LPio LRHS MArl MBel NCat NChi NHaw NSti SAga STes SVil WCer WCot WCru WHal WWhi

¶ 'Golden Haze'	NSti
'Hazel Kaye's Red'	CBel CElw LPio NSti
'Highdown'	See *P.* 'Lewis Palmer'
'Joan's Red'	CElw WCot
§ 'Lewis Palmer' ♀	More than 30 suppliers
¶ 'Lime Close'	LGre
'Little Star'	EBee EMon GBuc GOrP LRHS MTed
longifolia	More than 30 suppliers
§ - 'Ankum'	CBos CElw CGle CLAP CSpe EBee EGle EMan EPla GBuc LPio LRHS MBel MBrN MBri MChl MRav NSti SCob SSpe SUsu WByw WCot WLin WPGP WRus
- 'Ballyrogan Blue'	IBlr
- 'Bertram Anderson'	More than 30 suppliers
- subsp. *cevennensis*	EBee EBrP EBre EMan GKir LBCl LBSe LBre MBBe MBri SBre SSpi
- 'Coen Jansen'	See *P. longifolia* 'Ankum'
- 'Coral Spring'	EMan MBNS
- 'Dordogne'	CGle CLAP EBee EBrP EBre EFou EGle GBuc GKir LBCl LBSe LBre LEdu LRHS MBBe MGrG MRav SBla SBre SUsu WCru WPGP
- from France	EPPr
¶ - 'Howard Eggins'	WSPU
- wild-collected	WCot
'Lovell Blue'	CElw WRus
'Majesté'	CBos CElw CFil CHid CLAP EBee EFou EGle EHoe EMan EWes LAst LRot MAvo MBri MCLN MChl NSti SMad SUsu WBar WCot WHil WHoo WPGP WWat WWhi WWye
§ 'Margery Fish' ♀	CBro CGle CLAP COtt EBee EMan EPla GKir LFis LPio LRHS MBri MLLN NBro NChi NSti SHFr SMer SPer WByw WCru WEas WHil WWat WWye
'Mary Mottram'	CElw CLAP EFou EMan LAst MBel MBri MCLN MChl MLLN MMil NBir NCut NSti SAga WByw WCer WCot WCru WHal WMaN WMoo WWhi
'Mawson's Blue'	More than 30 suppliers
¶ 'May Bouquet'	NSti
'Merlin'	CLAP EBee EMon LRHS NSti SSpi
¶ 'Middleton Red'	CElw
§ 'Milchstrasse'	CLAP
Milky Way	See *P.* 'Milchstrasse'
mollis	CBel CBot CLAP CSWP EBee EMon EOrc GCal LRHS MBri NBrk NCat NSti NWoo SMrm WByw WCot WCru
- 'Royal Blue'	EWll GCHN MRav SLod
- 'Samobor'	CLAP SCob WCot
mollissima	Last listed 1997
'Monksilver'	CBel EMon NSti
'Moonstone'	CElw CLAP LAst LGre LPio WRus
'Mournful Purple'	CElw CGle CLAP CRow EGle ERav NBrk SWat WCru
'Mrs Kittle'	CElw EBee EMan GBri MBro MCLN MChl MGrG MRav NCut NHaw NSti SDys SSpi WByw WCot WCru WHal WRus
'Netta Statham'	EBee ECha
'Nürnberg'	CElw EFou EMon EPPr LFis LRHS MAvo MBel MBro NHaw WCru WHal
obscura	EGar EMon LRHS MBel
'Ocupol'[PBR]	See *P.* Opal = 'Ocupol'

officinalis | CAgr CArn CBro CGle CHar
CRow EHon EMon EOrc EPar
EWFC GBar GPoy LLWP LRHS
MChe MFir MHer MHew NBrk
NChi NVic SIde WCru WFar WHal
WHbs WWye
- 'Alba' | NCat WByw
§ - 'Blue Mist' | More than 30 suppliers
- 'Bowles' Blue' | See *P. officinalis* 'Blue Mist'
- Cambridge Blue Group | EBee ECGN EFou EGar EMon
ERav LAst LRHS NFai NHol NLar
NSti WByw WCru WEas WHal
WRus
- 'Marjorie Lawley' | NPar
- 'Plas Merdyn' | IBlr
- **rubra** | See *P. rubra*
- 'Stillingfleet Gran' | EBee LPio NSti
- 'White Wings' | CElw CHea CLAP CMil EBee
EMan EMon EPPr EPla EPri GKir
GMac LPio LRHS MBNS MBro
MCLN NCut NDov NPri NSti STes
WEas WFar WMaN WMoo
'Oliver Wyatt's White' | EBee EMon WPGP
§ Opal = 'Ocupol'^PBR | More than 30 suppliers
'Patrick Bates' | MBel WCru
'Paul Aden' | CLAP
'Pewter' | LPio
¶ 'Polar Splash' | NSti
'Purple Haze' | NSti
¶ 'Raspberry Ice' | NSti
'Raspberry Splash' | Last listed 1999
* 'Rowlatt Choules' | SSpi
'Roy Davidson' | More than 30 suppliers
§ **rubra** ♀ | CElw CGle COlW CSWP CStr
ECha ELan EMar EOrc EWTr GKir
LFis LLWP MCAu MFir MSCN
NBid NHol NOrc NSti SChu SEas
SIng SRms WByw WCru WElm
WFar WRha
- var. **alba** | See *P. rubra* var. *albocorollata*
§ - var. **albocorollata** | CBel CBre CElw CFil CFri CGle
CMHG EBee ECha EGle EHrv
EMar EMon GKir LAst LRHS MBel
MBro MCLN MFir MSte NCat NSti
WByw WCru WFar WRus WWat
- 'Ann' | CBel CElw CLAP EBee ECGP
EMon EPPr IBlr LPio LRHS MBro
MTed MWrn NSti WByw WCru
WFar
* - **argentea** | SCob
- 'Barfield Pink' | CElw CRow EBee ECtt EGle ELan
EMon GBar GCal GKir LAst LRHS
MBel MBro MCLN MMil NBro
NLar SAga SChu SMrm WCer
WCru WHal WLin WPnP WRus
- 'Barfield Ruby' | CLAP EMon GBuc LRHS
- 'Bowles' Red' | CBel CBot CElw CMea CWit EBee
EBrP EBre ECtt EHrv ENot ERav
EWTr GAbr GGar GKir LBCl
LBSe LBre LRHS MBBe MWgw
SBre SCro SMrm SPer WCra WFar
WHal
- 'David Ward' (v) | More than 30 suppliers
- 'Prestbury Pink' | EMon LLWP LRHS
- 'Redstart' | More than 30 suppliers
- 'Warburg's Red' | CElw EMon
§ **saccharata** | CFri CHEx CRow EBee ECha ELan
EWTr LGro MBro MCAu MFir
NHol SChu SIng SRms WCru
WPyg WWat WWin
- 'Alba' | CBro CElw CRow ECha EGar
GBuc MBel NOak SRms

- Argentea Group ♀ | CBro CElw CGle CRow CSev
EBee ECha ECoo EFou ELan EMar
EOld EOrc GAbr GMaP LAst LRHS
MCLN MRav MTho NBro NChi
NFla NSti SPer SSpi WCot WCru
WSan WWat
- 'Blauhimmel' | See *P.* 'Blauhimmel'
- 'Bofar Red' | Last listed 1997
- 'Brentor' | CElw CRow
¶ - 'Clent Skysilver' | WSPU
- 'Diana Chappell' | CElw MBel MSCN NCat SSpi
- 'Dora Bielefeld' | More than 30 suppliers
- 'Frühlingshimmel' | CBel CBro CElw CGle EBee ECha
EFou EGle GKir LGre LPio MAvo
MBel MRav NDov NTow SMrm
WFar WHal WLin WPrP WRus
- 'Glebe Cottage Blue' | CElw ECGP LPio NSti WWpP
- 'Jill Richardson' | EGar ELan
- 'Lady Lou's Pink' | LFis WCru
- 'Leopard' | CBos CElw CGle CLAP CMea
CSam EBee ECtt GBuc GMaP LAst
LFis LRHS MBel NSti SBla SMrm
WCot WCru WHoo WRus WWol
- 'Mrs Moon' | CWit EBee EBlw ECtt EFou ENot
EWTr GChr GKir GMaP LRHS
MBNS MCAu MWgw NBrk NBro
NFla NHol NOrc SChu SPer WCru
WHen WHil WPnP WPyg WWal
- 'Old Rectory Silver' | CLAP MWrn
- 'Picta' | See *P. saccharata*
- 'Pink Dawn' | CMHG EMan EOrc LFis LRHS
MBri NBus NPri NSti WCru
- 'Reginald Kaye' | CElw CRow ECha EMFP ERav
EWes MBro NBrk NDov NSti
* - **rubra** ♀ | WByw
- 'Snow Queen' | Last listed 1997
- 'South Hayes' | CLAP
- 'White Leaf' | WRus
'Saint Ann's' | CElw CLTr EMon LRHS NSti
¶ 'Silver Maid' | WCot
'Silver Mist' | MAvo NPar
'Silver Spring' | Last listed 1998
¶ 'Silver Streamers' | NSti
¶ 'Sissinghurst White' ♀ | More than 30 suppliers
'Skylight' | CElw MAvo
'Smoky Blue' | CBlo CFri CLAP EBee EBlw EFou
EMon EPfP LAst LRHS MBro
MCLN NPri NSti SCob SMer SWat
WByw WFar WHal WWat WWoo
'Snowy Owl' | Last listed 1999
'Spilled Milk' | NLar NSti
'Tim's Silver' | ECha NBrk NPar WBcn
¶ 'Trevi Fountain' | NSti
'Ultramarine' | CElw EMon
vallarsae | LAst
- 'Margery Fish' | See *P.* 'Margery Fish'
'Victorian Brooch' | CLAP LRHS NSti
'Weetwood Blue' | CBre CElw CLAP EBee MSte
'Wendy Perry' | CElw CFil CLAP
'Wisley White' | CElw

PULSATILLA (Ranunculaceae)

alba | CBro
albana | CBro GCrs LRHS WLin
- 'Lutea' | Last listed 1999
- white | SOkd
alpina | CBot SRms WHil
§ - subsp. **apiifolia** ♀ | ELan GTou MHer NHar NMen
WLin
- subsp. **sulphurea** | See *P. alpina* subsp. *apiifolia*
ambigua | EBee
aurea | GCrs

bungeana	Last listed 1998
campanella	Last listed 1998
caucasica	CBro LRHS
cernua	EBrP EBre GBuc LBCl LBSe LBre LRHS MBBe NDov SBre
chinensis	Last listed 1998
* *czerna*	Last listed 1998
daburica	Last listed 1998
x *gayeri*	NBir
georgica	Last listed 1999
halleri ♀	EBrP EBre ECGP EMan GKir LBCl LBSe LBre MBBe MMil NDlv NSla SBre
- *alba*	Last listed 1997
- subsp. *slavica* ♀	CBro CLyd GCrs LRHS NNrd NWCA WWin
- subsp. *taurica*	MSte
koreana	CBro LRHS
* *lutea*	Last listed 1998
montana	Last listed 1999
- var. *australis*	Last listed 1998
¶ *multifida*	Ilve
occidentalis	CGra EBee
§ *patens*	Last listed 1999
- subsp. *flavescens*	Last listed 1999
- var. *multifida* NNS 96221	EPot
- subsp. *trisecta*	Last listed 1997
* *pinnata*	Last listed 1998
pratensis	GPoy GTou
- subsp. *nigricans*	CBro LRHS
rubra	CHar
* *serotina*	Last listed 1998
turczaninovii	EBee
* *ucrainica*	Last listed 1998
§ *vernalis* ♀	EPot GCrs GDra GTou NHar NSla NTow WAbe
§ *vulgaris* ♀	More than 30 suppliers
- 'Alba' ♀	More than 30 suppliers
- 'Barton's Pink'	CMil EWes EWll GKir LRHS SBla WRus
- Czech fringed hybrids	CNic
- 'Eva Constance'	CBro CRDP EBrP EBre ESis GKir LBCl LBSe LBre LHop LRHS MBBe SBre SIng WAbe
- 'Flore Pleno' (d)	CLyd CNic
- 'Gotlandica'	CLyd GDra NHol
- subsp. *grandis*	CLAP
- - 'Budapest'	SIng
- - f. *dissecta*	Last listed 1999
- - ex 'Budapest'	GCrs NMen
- Heiler hybrids	EMan LBuc SIng WElm
- 'Miss Beveridge'	NOak
- pale pink	GKir
- 'Papageno'	CBot CGle CMGP CSpe EDAr EMan GCrs LGre LRHS NLar NSla SAga SMrm SUsu WHil WViv
- Red Clock	See *P. vulgaris* 'Röde Klokke'
§ - 'Röde Klokke'	EWTr LGre LRHS MBro NHol WHil
- *rosea*	SCob SUsu
- Rote Glocke	See *P. vulgaris* 'Röde Klokke'
- var. *rubra*	CB&S CGle CSpe EDAr EFou ELan EOrc GAbr LRHS MBri MBro MTis NBid NHar NHol SPer SRms STes WCot WHoo WPer WRus WSel
- violet blue	SCob
§ - 'Weisse Schwan'	CBlo CFwr EOld LFis MCLN NMen
- White Swan	See *P. vulgaris* 'Weisse Schwan'
* *wisetonensis*	Last listed 1998

PULTENAEA (Papilionaceae)
daphnoides	Last listed 1998

PUNICA (Punicaceae)
granatum	ECon ERea GAri GVer LPan LRHS MPEx SOWG STre WSHC
¶ - 'Fina Tendral'	ERea
¶ - 'Legrelleae' (d)	CPLG
- var. *nana*	CArn CHal CPle EOHP EPfP ERea GAri LPan LRHS SBrw SLon SMrm SRCN SRms WPat WWat
- f. *plena* (d)	CB&S MRav WCFE
- - 'Flore Pleno Luteo' (d)	Last listed 1997
- - 'Rubrum Flore Pleno' (d) ♀	LPan WPat
* - 'Striata'	SOWG
¶ - 'Wonderful' (F)	ESim

PUSCHKINIA (Hyacinthaceae)
scilloides	LRHS
§ - var. *libanotica*	CBro ELan EPar EPot ETub LAma LRHS NRog WPer WShi
- - 'Alba'	EPar EPot LAma LRHS NRog
- Polunin 5238	Last listed 1998

PUTORIA (Rubiaceae)
calabrica	CLyd NWCA

PUYA (Bromeliaceae)
alpestris	CFil CHEx CTbh CTrC SAPC SSpi WPGP
berteroniana	CHEx WPic
chilensis	CAbb CB&S CBrd CDoC CHEx CTbh CTrC EBee ECre EOas EPVP SAPC SArc
coerulea	CFir CHEx GBin SPlb
- var. *coerulea*	SCob
- F&W 8411	WLRN
- JCA 14371	Last listed 1999
- RB 94100	Last listed 1999
§ - var. *violacea*	CHEx
- - F&W 7911	WLRN
conquimbensis	Last listed 1997
laxa	CHEx
mirabilis	CHEx CTrC WPGP
raimondii	Last listed 1998
venusta	CHEx WPic
- JCA 14369	Last listed 1999
violacea	See *P. coerulea* var. *violacea*
weberbaueri	CHEx

PYCNANTHEMUM (Lamiaceae)
californicum	WCot
montanum	WCot
muticum	EBee MRav
pilosum	CArn CHal CSev EBee ELau EMan GPoy MHer MSal NLar NPri SIde WGwG WHer WPer WPic WWye
tenuifolium	EBee EMan SOkh WCot

PYCNOSTACHYS (Lamiaceae)
urticifolia	Last listed 1998

PYGMAEA See CHIONOHEBE

PYRACANTHA ✿ (Rosaceae)
Alexander Pendula	CBlo EBee EHol ENot GAri LHop MRav SEas SRms WHar WWat
angustifolia	CBlo WCFE WUnu
§ *atalantioides*	CBlo CMac CSam SPlb WCFE
§ - 'Aurea'	CBlo WWin

'Brilliant'	EBee EPfP
'Buttercup'	EPla GAri WBcn
'Cadange'PBR	See *P.* Saphyr Orange = 'Cadange'
'Cadaune'PBR	See *P.* Saphyr Jaune = 'Cadaune'
'Cadrou'PBR	See *P.* Saphyr Rouge = 'Cadrou'
coccinea	Last listed 1999
§ - 'Lalandei'	CBlo CMac CSam EBee NFor SMer SPer WGwG
- 'Red Column'	CBlo CChe CMac EBee ECtt ELan GChr GKir LBuc LRHS MBNS MBar MGos MRav MWat NBee NFla NWea SAga SCoo SEas WBod WDin WGwG WHar
- 'Red Cushion'	CBlo EBee ENot LBuc LRHS MGos MRav SRms
- 'Rutgers'	SLPl
- 'Telstar'	Last listed 1998
crenulata	WCFE
- S&SH 385	Last listed 1999
Dart's Red	CBlo EBee GKir LRHS MBri WBod WLRN
gibbsii	See *P. atalantioides*
- 'Flava'	See *P. atalantioides* 'Aurea'
'Gold Rush'	WSPU
'Golden Charmer'	CBlo EBee EBrP EBre ECtt ENot EPfP LBCl LBSe LBre LRHS MBBe MGos NWea SBre SPer SRms WBod WDin WFar WGwG WHar
'Golden Dome'	LRHS SEas
'Golden Glow'	CBlo LRHS
'Golden Sun'	See *P.* 'Soleil d'Or'
'Harlequin' (v)	CB&S CBlo ECtt EHol NPro SReu WCot WLeb WSHC WWeb
'John Stedman'	See *P.* 'Stedman's'
'Knap Hill Lemon'	CChe MBlu WSPU
'Mohave'	CB&S CBlo CChe CMac EBee EBrP EBre ELan GKir LBCl LBSe LBre LRHS MBBe MBar MGos MWat NDlv NWea SBre SPer SReu SRms WDin WStI
'Mohave Silver' (v)	CBlo EBee EGra LAst LRHS MBNS MGos MWat SEas WGwG
'Monrovia'	See *P. coccinea* 'Lalandei'
'Mozart'	WWeb
'Navaho'	CBlo EPfP GKir MAsh MRav WBcn
'Orange Charmer'	CB&S CBlo CChe CTri EBee ELan ENot GKir MAsh MGos MWat NBee NWea SMer SPer SPlb WStI WWeb
'Orange Glow' ♀	More than 30 suppliers
* 'Red Pillar'	CBlo GKir SRPl
'Renault d'Or'	LRHS SLPl
rogersiana ♀	CBlo EBee ENot EPfP LRHS MRav
- 'Flava' ♀	CBlo CTri EBee EHol ENot EPfP MAsh MBar MRav MWhi NFla NFor NWea SMer SRPl WGwG
§ Saphyr® Jaune = 'Cadaune'PBR	CBlo CDoC CEnd EBee EPfP IOrc LRHS MAsh MBNS MGos MRav SPer WLRN WWeb
§ Saphyr® Orange = 'Cadange'PBR	CBlo CDoC CEnd COtt EBee EPfP GKir IOrc LRHS MAsh MBri MGos MRav NPri SPer WLRN WWeb
§ Saphyr® Rouge = 'Cadrou'PBR	CBlo CDoC CEnd COtt EBee EPfP IOrc LRHS MBri MGos MRav SPer WLRN WWeb
'Shawnee'	CBlo CMac EBee ECot EPfP LRHS MAsh MRav MWat NDlv
§ 'Soleil d'Or'	More than 30 suppliers

'Sparkler' (v)	CBlo CDoC CMac CPMA EHoe LHop LRHS MAsh MGos NHol SPer WFar WHar
§ 'Stedman's'	MBri
'Teton'	CMHG CMac EBee ELan ENot EPla ESis GKir LHop LRHS MAsh MBar MBri MGos MRav NDlv SPla SRms WDin WFar WLRN WStI
'Watereri' ♀	CBlo SLPl SPer
'Yellow Sun'	See *P.* 'Soleil d'Or'

PYRENARIA (Theaceae)
* *spectabilis*	EPfP

PYRETHROPSIS See RHODANTHEMUM

PYRETHRUM See TANACETUM

+ PYROCYDONIA (Rosaceae)
'Danielii' (F)	WMou

PYROLA (Ericaceae)
rotundifolia	SSpi WHer

PYROSTEGIA (Bignoniaceae)
venusta	CPiN LChe LCns LRHS SOWG WMul

PYRROCOMA (Asteraceae)
clementis	EBee
§ *lanceolata*	EBee

PYRROSIA (Polypodiaceae)
* *heterophylla*	NMar
lingua 'Variegata' (v)	EMon

PYRUS ✿ (Rosaceae)
amygdaliformis	CTho
- var. *cuneifolia*	CTho
betulifolia	CMCN MAsh WJas
calleryana	CAgr
- 'Bradford'	CLnd
- 'Chanticleer' ♀	CB&S CBlo CDoC CDul CEnd CLnd CTho EBee ENot GKir IArd IOrc LHyr LPan LRHS MAsh MBlu MGos MRav NBee NWea SLim SPer SSta WDin WJas WOrn WWat
- 'Redspire'	WGer
x *canescens*	CTho
communis (F)	CKin GChr GIBF LBuc MBlu NRog SKee SPer STre WMou
- 'Autumn Bergamot' (D)	CTho SKee
- 'Barland' (Perry)	Last listed 1998
- 'Barnet' (Perry)	CTho
- 'Baronne de Mello' (D)	CTho SFam SKee
- 'Beech Hill' (F)	CDul CLnd CTho EBee EMil ENot EPfP
- 'Belle Guérandaise' (D)	SKee
- 'Belle Julie' (D)	SKee
- 'Bergamotte d'Automne' (D)	SKee
- 'Bergamotte Esperen' (D)	SKee
- 'Beth' (D) ♀	CDoC CWSG EMui EPfP GBon GTwe LBuc LRHS MBri MGos NBee NRog SDea SFam SKee SPer WHar
- 'Beurré Alexandre Lucas' (D)	SKee
- 'Beurré Bedford' (D)	Last listed 1998
- 'Beurré Bosc' (D)	SKee

- 'Beurré Clairgeau' (C/D) SKee
- 'Beurré d'Amanlis' (D) SKee
- 'Beurré d'Avalon' (D) CTho
- 'Beurré de Beugny' (D) Last listed 1999
- 'Beurré de Naghin' (C/D) SKee
- 'Beurré Dumont' (D) SFam
- 'Beurré Gris d'Hiver' (D) Last listed 1997
- 'Beurré Hardy' (D) ♀ CDoC CTho EMui ERea
EWTr GKir GTwe LRHS MBri
MWat NBea NRog SDea SFam
SKee
- 'Beurré Mortillet' (D) SKee
- 'Beurré Six' (D) SKee
- 'Beurré Superfin' (D) ERea GTwe SFam SKee
- 'Bianchettone' (D) SKee
- 'Bishop's Thumb' (D) SDea
- 'Black Worcester' (C) GTwe SDea SFam SKee WJas
WSPU
- 'Blakeney Red' (Perry) CTho SDea
- 'Blickling' (D) SKee
- 'Brandy' (Perry) CTho SDea
- 'Bristol Cross' (D) GTwe
- 'Brown Bess' (Perry) Last listed 1998
§ - 'Butirra Precoce
Morettini' (D) SDea
- 'Catillac' (C) ♀ CTho GTwe NRog SFam SKee
- 'Chalk' See *P. communis* 'Crawford'
- 'Chaumontel' (D) SKee
- 'Clapp's Favourite' (D) CTho GTwe IOrc SKee
- 'Colmar d'Eté' (D) CTho
- 'Comte de Lamy' (D) SKee
- 'Concorde' PBR (D) ♀ CDoC CSam CTho CWSG
EMui EPfP ERea EWTr GTwe
LBuc LRHS MBri MGos MLan
NBee NRog NWea SDea
SFam SKee WHar WJas
WWeb
- 'Conference' (D) ♀ More than 30 suppliers
- 'Craig's Favourite' (D) Last listed 1999
- 'Crassane' CTho
§ - 'Crawford' (D) SKee
- 'Deacon's Pear' (D) SDea
- 'Devoe' (D) SDea
- 'Docteur Jules Guyot' (D) SDea SKee
- 'Double de Guerre' (C/D) SKee
- 'Doyenné Boussoch' (D) SKee
- 'Doyenné d'Eté' (D) ERea SFam SKee
- 'Doyenné du Comice' More than 30 suppliers
(D) ♀
- 'Doyenné Georges SKee
Boucher' (D)
- 'Duchesse d' SKee
Angoulême' (D)
- 'Durondeau' (D) CTho GTwe NRog SDea SFam
SKee
- 'Easter Beurré' (D) SKee
- 'Emile d'Heyst' (D) CTho GTwe
- 'English Caillot Rosat' (D) Last listed 1997
- 'Eva Baltet' (D) SKee
- 'Fair Maid' (D) Last listed 1997
- 'Fertility Improved' See *P. communis* 'Improved
Fertility'
- 'Fondante d'Automne' CTho SKee
(D)
- 'Forelle' (D) ERea SKee
- 'Gansel's Bergamot' (D) Last listed 1999
- 'Gin' (Perry) CTho
- 'Glou Morceau' (D) CTho EMui GTwe LRHS MWat
NRog SDea SFam SKee
- 'Glow Red Williams' (D) SFam
- 'Gorham' (D) CTho GTwe LRHS MCoo SFam
SKee

- 'Gratiole de Jersey' (D) CTho
- 'Green Horse' (Perry) CTho
- 'Green Pear of Yair' (D) SKee
- 'Hacon's Imcomparable' SKee
(D)
- 'Harrow Delight' (D) SDea
- 'Harvest Queen' (D/C) SDea
- 'Hendre Huffcap' (Perry) Last listed 1998
- 'Hessle' (D) GTwe NRog SDea SFam SKee
- 'Highland' (D) SKee
¶ - 'Holme Lacy' MCoo
§ - 'Improved Fertility' (D) CDoC GBon GTwe SDea SKee
¶ - 'Jack Green' CTho
- 'Jargonelle' (D) CTho GTwe NRog SDea SFam
SKee
- 'Joséphine de Malines' CTho GTwe LRHS SDea SFam
(D) ♀ SKee
- 'Judge Amphlett' (Perry) Last listed 1998
- 'Laxton's Foremost' (D) SKee
- 'Laxton's Satisfaction' (D) SFam
- 'Le Lectier' (D) SKee
- 'Louise Bonne of CDoC CTho CTri EMui GTwe
Jersey' (D) LRHS MBri MGos NRog SDea
SFam SKee
- 'Madame Treyve' (D) Last listed 1997
- 'Maggie Duncan' (F) Last listed 1999
- 'Marguérite Marillat' (D) SDea
- 'Marie-Louise' (D) Last listed 1999
- 'Martin Sec' (C/D) Last listed 1997
¶ - 'Max Red Bartlett' MCoo
- 'Merton Pride' (D) CTho GTwe MWat SDea SFam
SKee
- 'Merton Star' (D) SKee
- 'Monarch' (D) CLnd
- 'Moonglow' (D/C) MCoo SDea
- 'Moorcroft' (Perry) Last listed 1998
- 'Morettini' See *P. communis* 'Butirra Precoce
Morettini'
- 'Nouveau Poiteau' (C/D) CTho GTwe LRHS SKee
- 'Oldfield' (Perry) Last listed 1998
- 'Olivier de Serres' (D) SFam SKee
- 'Onward' (D) ♀ CLnd EMui GTwe LBuc LRHS
MGos NRog NWea SDea SFam
SKee WHar
§ - 'Packham's Triumph' (D) CDoC GTwe LRHS NRog SDea
SKee
- 'Passe Colmar' (D) CTho
- 'Passe Crassane' (D) SKee
- 'Pear Apple' (D) SDea
- 'Pitmaston Duchess' CWSG GTwe SDea SKee
(C/D) ♀
- 'Red Comice' (D/C) GTwe SKee
- 'Robin' (C/D) ERea SDea SKee
- 'Roosevelt' (D) SKee
- 'Santa Claus' (D) SDea SFam SKee
- 'Seckle' (D) SFam SKee
- 'Soleil d'Automne' (F) SKee
- 'Souvenir du Congrès' Last listed 1998
(D)
- 'Sucrée de Montluçon' Last listed 1997
(D)
- 'Swan's Egg' (D) CTho
- 'Thompson's' (D) GTwe SFam
- 'Thorn' (Perry) CTho
- 'Triomphe de Vienne'
(D) SFam
- 'Triumph' See *P. communis* 'Packham's
Triumph'
- 'Uvedale's St Germain' CTho SKee
(C)
- 'Vicar of Winkfield' GTwe SDea SKee
(C/D)

- 'Williams' Bon Chrétien' (D/C) ♀ — More than 30 suppliers
- 'Williams Red' (D/C) — GTwe SKee
- 'Winnal's Longdon' (Perry) — CTho
- 'Winter Christie' (F) — Last listed 1999
- 'Winter Nelis' (D) — CTho GTwe LRHS SDea SFam SKee
- 'Zéphirin Grégoire' (D) — Last listed 1997
cordata — CTho SKee
cossonii — CTho
elaeagnifolia — CTho WWat
- var. **kotschyana** — CBlo CEnd GKir LRHS MAsh MRav SLim
nivalis — CLnd CTho ENot EPfP SLPl SMHT SPer
pashia CLD 114 — Last listed 1999
pyraster — Last listed 1998
pyrifolia '20th Century' — See *P. pyrifolia* 'Nijisseiki'
- 'Chojura' (F) — ESim IOrc
- 'Kumoi' (F) — LBuc SDea
* - 'Nashi Kumoi' — LPan
§ - 'Nijisseiki' (F) — ESim
- 'Shinseiki' (F) — EMui LRHS SDea SKee SLim
- 'Shinsui' (F) — SDea SKee
salicifolia 'Pendula' ♀ — More than 30 suppliers
ussuriensis — CBlo CMCN

Q

QUERCUS ✿ (Fagaceae)
§ **acuta** — CB&S CHEx CMCN
¶ **acutifolia** — CMCN
§ **acutissima** — CLnd CMCN SBir WNor WShe
aegilops — See *Q. ithaburensis* subsp. *macrolepis*
affinis — CMCN
agrifolia — CB&S CMCN LEdu SBir
alba — CMCN NWea
- f. **elongata** — LRHS
aliena — CMCN SBir
- var. **acutiserrata** — CMCN
almifolia — CDul
arkansana — CMCN SBir
austrina — CMCN
baloot — Last listed 1997
x **beadlei** — See *Q. × saulii*
bicolor — CMCN LRHS SBir WDin WNor
borealis — See *Q. rubra*
brantii — CMCN
breweri — See *Q. garryana* var. *fruticosa*
x **bushii** — CMCN GKir MBlu
canariensis ♀ — CFil CLnd CMCN CTho CTrG EPfP IDee LRHS WMou WTro
canbyi — Last listed 1998
castaneifolia — CB&S CLnd CMCN EPfP LPan LRHS WMou
- 'Green Spire' ♀ — CDoC CDul CLnd CMCN EBee EPfP GKir LRHS MAsh MBlu MBri SMad SPer
cerris ♀ — CB&S CBlo CDoC CDul CKin CLnd CMCN EBee ECrN EMil ENot GChr GKir IOrc LPan LRHS MGos NWea SEND SMHT SPer SSta WDin WFro WMou WTro
§ - 'Argenteovariegata' — CDul CMCN CTho EPfP GKir LRHS MBlu MBri SMad WMou
* - 'Marmorata' — CLyn

- 'Variegata' — See *Q. cerris* 'Argenteovariegata'
- 'Wodan' — CMCN GKir LRHS MBlu
chapmanii — CMCN
chrysolepis — CMCN SBir
coccifera — CDul CFil CMCN IDee WPGP WWes
- subsp. **calliprinos** — CMCN
coccinea — CAbP CB&S CDul CLnd CMCN CWSG EPfP EWTr GChr GIBF GKir IOrc LRHS MAsh NBea NWea SBir SPer SSta STre WNor WOrn
- 'Splendens' ♀ — CDoC CDul CEnd CFil CMCN COtt CTho EBee ELan EPfP GKir IOrc LPan LRHS MBlu MBri NBee SPer SSpi WDin WPGP
x **comptoniae** — CMCN
crassipes — CMCN
dentata — CMCN EPfP GKir LRHS
¶ - 'Adelaide' — MBlu
- 'Carl Ferris Miller' — CFil CMCN LRHS MBlu SMad WPGP
- 'Pinnatifida' — CMCN GKir LRHS MBlu SMad
- 'Sir Harold Hillier' — LRHS MBlu
douglasii — CLnd CMCN
dumosa — CMCN WNor
durandii — See *Q. sinuata* var. *sinuata*
durata — Last listed 1997
ellipsoidalis — CAbP CDul CMCN GKir LRHS SBir WNor WWat WWes
- 'Hemelrijk' — CDoC CFil GKir LRHS MBlu WPGP
engelmannii — CMCN
fabrei — SBir
faginea — CMCN SBir
falcata — CDul CLnd CMCN
- var. **pagodifolia** — See *Q. pagoda*
x **fernaldii** — CMCN
frainetto — CDoC CDul CLnd CMCN CTho EBee EPfP GChr GGar GKir IOrc ISea LPan LRHS MBlu MBri SEND SMad SPer WDin WMou WNor
- 'Hungarian Crown' ♀ — CMCN LRHS
- 'Trump' — GKir MBlu SMad WPGP
fruticosa — See *Q. lusitanica* Lamarck
gambelii — CMCN
- x **macrocarpa** — Last listed 1998
garryana — CMCN
§ - var. **fruticosa** — CMCN
- x **turbinella** — Last listed 1998
geminata — Last listed 1997
georgiana — CMCN
gilva — Last listed 1997
glabra — See *Lithocarpus glaber*
glabrescens — Last listed 1999
glandulifera — See *Q. serrata*
§ **glauca** — CFai CMCN EPfP SAPC SArc SBir WNor
hartwissiana — CMCN
x **hastingsii** — CMCN
hemisphaerica — CMCN SBir
x **heterophylla** — CDul CMCN SBir
x **hickelii** — CMCN
hinckleyi — WDin
¶ **hintonii** — CMCN
x **hispanica** — CLnd WPic
- 'Ambrozyana' — CMCN GKir LRHS SMad
- 'Diversifolia' — CMCN GKir MBlu WMou
- 'Fulhamensis' — CMCN
§ - 'Lucombeana' ♀ — CDul CMCN CTho EPfP MBlu SPer WMou

- 'Suberosa'	CTho
- 'Wageningen'	CMCN EPfP WMou
ilex ♀	More than 30 suppliers
ilicifolia	CDul CMCN LRHS MBlu WNor WShe WWat
imbricaria	CDul CMCN LRHS MBlu SBir WWes
incana Bartram	CMCN IOrc
- Roxburgh	See *Q. leucotrichophora*
infectoria	CDul
- subsp. *veneris*	CMCN
ithaburensis	CMCN
§ - subsp. *macrolepis*	CMCN GKir MBlu
kelloggii	CMCN GIBF LRHS WWes
x *kewensis*	CMCN WMou
laevigata	See *Q. acuta*
laevis	CMCN EPfP MBlu
§ *laurifolia*	CDul CMCN MBlu SBir
¶ *laurina*	CMCN
§ *leucotrichophora*	CMCN
liaotungensis	See *Q. wutaishanica*
x *libanerris*	SBir
- 'Rotterdam'	CMCN
libani	CDul CMCN EPfP
lobata	CAgr CMCN
x *lucombeana*	See *Q.* x *hispanica*
- 'William Lucombe'	See *Q.* x *hispanica* 'Lucombeana'
x *ludoviciana*	CMCN EPfP
§ *lusitanica* Lamarck	CDul CMCN
lyrata	CMCN SBir
* Macon	GKir LRHS
macranthera	CMCN EPfP GKir
macrocarpa	CLnd CMCN LRHS SMad WDin WNor
- x *robur*	Last listed 1998
macrolepis	See *Q. ithaburensis* subsp. *macrolepis*
marilandica	CDul CEnd CMCN EPfP LRHS SBir WWes
'Maurii'	LPan
mexicana	CMCN
michauxii	CMCN LRHS
mongolica subsp.	CMCN
crispula var.	
grosseserrata	
§ *montana*	CMCN MBlu
muehlenbergii	CAgr CDul CMCN CTho EPfP LRHS NWea SBir
myrsinifolia	See *Q. glauca*
nigra	CMCN CMHG MBlu SBir WNor
nuttallii	See *Q. texana*
obtusa	See *Q. laurifolia*
§ *pagoda*	CMCN MBlu SBir
palustris ♀	CDoC CDul CLnd CMCN CTho EPfP GChr GKir LPan LRHS MBlu MBri NRib NWea SBir SPer WDin WNor WOrn
* - 'Compacta'	LRHS
¶ - 'Green Dwarf'	CMCN
- 'Pendula'	CEnd CMCN
* - 'Swamp Pygmy'	CMCN GKir MBlu
pedunculata	See *Q. robur*
pedunculiflora	See *Q. robur* subsp. *pedunculiflora*
§ *petraea* ♀	CDoC CDul CKin CLnd GChr GKir IOrc LBuc MBlu NBee NWea SPer WDin WFro WMou WTro
- 'Columna'	Last listed 1997
§ - 'Insecata'	CDoC CEnd CMCN GKir LRHS WPGP
- 'Laciniata'	See *Q. petraea* 'Insecata'
- 'Mespilifolia'	CTho

§ - 'Purpurea'	CMCN GKir LRHS MBlu
- 'Rubicunda'	See *Q. petraea* 'Purpurea'
§ *phellos* ♀	CDul CLnd CMCN CTho EPfP GChr LRHS MAsh MBlu SLPl SLdr WDin WNor WWat WWes
phillyreoides	CB&S CDul CMCN EPfP SBir SLPl WNor WWat
planipocula	CMCN
'Pondaim'	CMCN LRHS
pontica	CMCN EPfP LRHS MBlu NWea
prinoides	Last listed 1998
prinus L.	CAgr CMCN MBlu
- Engelm.	See *Q. montana*
pubescens	CDul CMCN GKir
pumila Michaux	See *Q. montana*
- Walt.	See *Q. phellos*
pyrenaica	CLnd CMCN CTho
- 'Pendula'	CMCN MBlu
¶ *rhysophylla*	EPfP MBlu
§ *robur* ♀	More than 30 suppliers
- 'Argenteomarginata'	CDul CMCN MBlu SMad SSta
- 'Atropurpurea'	GKir
* - 'Compacta'	MBlu
- 'Concordia'	CB&S CBlo CEnd CFil CMCN COtt ELan EPfP GChr GKir LRHS MBlu SMad
- 'Contorta'	CMCN GKir LRHS
- 'Cristata'	CDul CMCN MBlu
- 'Cucullata'	CMCN
* - *dissecta*	CMCN
- 'Facrist'	CBlo CDul CEnd
- f. *fastigiata*	CBlo CDoC CDul CLnd CTho EBee ENot GChr IOrc LHyr LPan LRHS MBar MGos MWat NBee NWea SCoo SLPl SPer WDin WOrn
- 'Fastigiata Koster' ♀	CDoC CDul CMCN COtt EMil EPfP GKir LPan MCoo SSta
- 'Fastigiata Purpurea'	Last listed 1997
- 'Fennessii'	CMCN LRHS MBlu SMad
- 'Filicifolia'	See *Q.* x *rosacea* 'Filicifolia'
- 'Fürst Schwarzenburg' (v)	CMCN MBlu
- 'Hentzei'	CMCN
- 'Hungaria'	LRHS MBlu
- 'Irtha'	EPfP MBlu
- x *lobata*	Last listed 1998
- X *macrocarpa* X *muehlenbergii*	Last listed 1997
- X *macrocarpa* X *virginiana*	Last listed 1997
- 'Pectinata'	CTho MBlu
§ - subsp. *pedunculiflora*	CMCN
- f. *pendula*	CDul CEnd CMCN CTho
- 'Purpurascens'	CEnd CMCN GKir MBlu
- 'Raba'	CMCN
¶ - 'Salfast'	MBlu
- 'Strypemonde'	CMCN
- x *turbinella*	CMCN
- f. *variegata*	LRHS
§ x *rosacea* 'Filicifolia'	CEnd CLnd NBea WMou
§ *rubra* ♀	More than 30 suppliers
- 'Aurea'	CDul CEnd CFil CMCN CTho EPfP GKir LRHS MAsh MBlu SMad SSpi WPGP
¶ - 'Magic Fire'	MBlu
* - 'Sunshine'	CMCN LRHS MBlu
rugosa	CMCN
sadleriana	CMCN
sartorii	Last listed 1998

§ × *saulii*	CMCN SBir
× *schochiana*	CMCN
schottkyana	SBir
× *schuettei*	Last listed 1997
semecarpifolia	ISea
§ *serrata*	CMCN SBir
sessiliflora	See *Q. petraea*
shumardii	CB&S CMCN EPfP LRHS SBir
	WDin WNor WWes
stellata	CMCN
suber	CB&S CDoC CDul CLnd CMCN
	CTho EPfP GAri GChr IDee ISea
	LRHS SAPC SArc SEND SSpi STre
	WDin WPGP
§ *texana*	CMCN EPfP SBir WWes
trojana	CMCN
turbinella	CMCN
× *turneri*	CDoC CDul CLnd CMCN CTho
	WMou
- 'Pseudoturneri'	CB&S GChr LPan LRHS MBlu
vacciniifolia	CMCN
variabilis	CMCN EPfP MBlu NWea WWes
velutina	CDul CGre CLnd CMCN CTho
	LRHS SBir WWat
- 'Albertsii'	MBlu
- 'Rubrifolia'	CMCN EPfP
virgiliana	See *Q. pubescens* subsp.
	pubescens
virginiana	CMCN
'Warburgii'	CMCN EPfP
wislizeni	CMCN IOrc
§ *wutaishanica*	CMCN

QUILLAJA (Rosaceae)

saponaria	CGre CPLG CPle CTrG

QUIONGZHUEA (Poaceae - Bambusoideae)

tumidinoda	See *Chimonobambusa*
	tumidissinoda

QUISQUALIS (Combretaceae)

indica	LChe

R

RACOSPERMA See ACACIA

RAMONDA (Gesneriaceae)

§ *myconi* ♀	CLAP CPBP MBro NHar NMen
	NSla NTow NWCA NWoo SBla
	SIng SRms
- var. *alba*	SIng
- 'Rosea'	CLAP SBla
nathaliae ♀	CLAP CPBP NHar
- 'Alba'	SBla SOkd
pyrenaica	See *R. myconi*
serbica	GCrs

RANUNCULUS ✿ (Ranunculaceae)

abnormis	GCrs NRya
aconitifolius	CGle EBee ECha EMFP EPar NSti
	SMrm WCot
- 'Flore Pleno' (d) ♀	CBos CHea CRow EPar EPri GBuc
	GKir IBlr LGre MBri NBir NPar
	NTow SBla SMac WByw WHer
	WHil
acris	EWFC NLan
* - citrinus	CBos CElw EBrP EBre ECoo EGle
	EPar EPri EWoo LBCl LBSe LBre

	MBBe MCAu NRya SBre SMrm
	WAlt WElm WFar WPrP WRha
	WSan
- 'Cricket' (v)	WAlt
- 'Farrer's Yellow'	CRow
- 'Flore Pleno' (d)	CElw CFee CFir CGle CRow EBee
	ECha EGle ELan EMan EPar GAbr
	GKir LPio MCAu MInt NBid NBro
	NChi NFai NHex NRya NSti SMac
	SRms WAlt WByw WHal WLin
	WSan
- 'Hedgehog'	EMon EPPr WCot
- 'Stevenii'	CFee CRow EPPr SDix WCot
- 'Sulphureus'	CElw CGle MSte NCat NSti SMrm
	WEas WHal
alpestris	NMen NRya
amplexicaulis	EPot ERos GCrs GDra GTou MRav
	NHar NMen NSla SBla WAbe
	WCot
aquatilis	CBen EHon EMFW NDea SWat
	SWyc
× *arendsii* 'Moonlight'	CElw SAga
asiaticus	Last listed 1999
- Accolade	SCoo WStI
¶ - var. *albus*	SBla
¶ - var. *flavus*	SBla
- red	Last listed 1997
- Tecolote hybrids	LAma
auricomus	CKin
baurii	Last listed 1998
bilobus	Last listed 1999
bulbosus	CKin EWFC
§ - 'F.M. Burton'	CBos CRDP EBee EGar EGle
	EMon GCal NRya NSti NTow SCro
	SUsu WAlt WCot WHal WRus
	WWin
- *farreri*	See *R. bulbosus* 'F.M. Burton'
- 'Speciosus Plenus'	See *R. constantinopolitanus*
	'Plenus'
calandrinioides ♀	SBla SVal WAbe WCot
- dwarf	Last listed 1998
- S&F 37	WCot
§ *constantinopolitanus*	CElw CGle CRDP CRow EBee
'Plenus' (d)	ECha GCal GKir IHdy LRHS MBri
	MBro MInt MLLN MRav NBid
	NBro NRya WCot WEas WFar
	WHil
cortusifolius	CFir CRDP EBee EMan EMar
	MTed NPSl WCot WCru WSpi
crenatus	CLyd CStu EBee GTou ITim LRHS
	NHar NMen NRya NSla SBla WHal
	WHil
creticus	EMon WCot
eschscholtzii	IMGH
extorris 'Flore Pleno'	EMon
ficaria	CArn CKin CNat CRow ELau
	EWFC GBar MChe MGas
	MHer MHew MMal MNaF
	MSal WFar WHbs WHer WShi
	WWye
- 'Aglow in the Dark'	CNat EBee
- var. *albus*	CElw CGle CRow EMon ERos
	LRHS NRya SIng WByw
- anemone centred	See *R. ficaria* 'Collarette'
- 'Ashen Primrose'	CRow EBee
§ - var. *aurantiacus*	CMea CNic CRow EBee ECha
	EMon EPar GDra LRHS MBro
	MRav NMen NNrd NRya SIng
	SRms WAbe WFar
¶ - 'Bantam Egg'	CRow
- 'Blackadder'	CRow
- 'Bosvigo'	CHid

- 'Bowles' Double'	See *R. ficaria* 'Double Bronze', 'Picton's Double'
- 'Brambling'	CBre CHea CLAP CRow EBee EMon LRHS MRav NRya WCot
- 'Brazen Child'	CRow EBee
- 'Brazen Daughter'	CRow
- 'Brazen Hussy'	More than 30 suppliers
- 'Bregover White'	CRow EBee
¶ - 'Budgerigar'	CRow
- 'Bunch' (d)	CRow
- 'Button Eye'	Last listed 1998
¶ - 'Cartwheel' (d)	CRow
- 'Champernowne Giant'	CRow
- 'Chedglow'	CRow
- 'Chocolate Cream'	CRow
§ - subsp. *chrysocephalus*	CRow ECha EMon NRya SIng SSvw WCot WFar WHer
¶ - 'Clouded Yellow' (v)	CRow
- 'Coffee Cream'	CRow EBee
¶ - 'Coker Cream'	CRow
§ - 'Collarette' (d)	CGle CInt CRDP CRow CStu EBee EMon EPar EPot ERos GAbr GBar GCal GGar LRHS MRav MTho NMGW NMen NNrd NRya SBla SMac WAbe WCot WFar WHil
- 'Coppernob'	CBre CElw CHid CRDP CRow LPio WCot WFar WPnP
¶ - 'Corinne Tremaine'	WHer
- 'Coy Hussy' (v)	CNat
- 'Crawshay Cream'	CElw CRow
- 'Cupreus'	See *R. ficaria* var. *aurantiacus*
- 'Damerham' (d)	CRow EMon LRHS
¶ - 'Deborah Jope'	CRow
¶ - 'Diane Rowe'	EMon
¶ - 'Dimpsey'	CRow
§ - 'Double Bronze' (d)	CRow EBee EMon EMou EPar ERos LRHS MTho NRya SIng WCot
- double cream	See *R. ficaria* 'Double Mud'
- double green eye (d)	CRow
§ - 'Double Mud' (d)	CLAP CRow EMon ERos LRHS MBro MTho NNrd NRya NWoo SBla SIng WBro WCot WFar WHal
- double yellow	See *R. ficaria flore-pleno*
- 'Dusky Maiden'	CRow EMon LRHS WFar
- 'E.A. Bowles'	See *R. ficaria* 'Collarette'
- 'Elan' (d)	CRow
- subsp. *ficariiformis*	EMon
§ - *flore-pleno* (d)	CFee CGle CInt CRow EBee ECha ELan EMar EMon EPar ERos GAbr GDra IMGH LRHS NDea NNrd NRya NSti SIng SRms WCot WFar WHil WWin
- 'Fried Egg'	CRow
- 'Green Petal'	CAvo CElw CMea CRow CStu EBee EMon EPar LRHS MRav MS&S MTho NNrd NRya SSvw WCot WHal
¶ - 'Green Wheel'	WCot
¶ - 'Greencourt Gold' (d)	CRow
- 'Holly'	See *R. ficaria* 'Holly Green'
¶ - 'Holly Bronze'	CRow
§ - 'Holly Green'	CRow
- 'Hoskin's Miniature'	CRow
¶ - 'Hoskin's Variegated' (v)	CRow
- 'Hyde Hall'	EMon LRHS WFar
- 'Inky'	CNat
¶ - 'Jake Perry'	CBos
- 'Jane's Dress'	CHid CNat CRow
¶ - 'Ken Aslet Double' (d)	CRow EMon LRHS WHal
¶ - 'Lambrook Black'	WHer
¶ - 'Laysh On' (d)	CRow

- 'Lemon Queen'	WCot
¶ - 'Leo'	EMon
- 'Limelight'	CRow
- 'Little Southey'	CRow EBee
- subsp. *major*	See *R. ficaria* subsp. *chrysocephalus*
- 'Martin Gibbs'	CNat
- 'Mimsey' (d)	CRow
- 'Mobled Jade'	CNat CRow EBee
- 'Newton Abbot'	CBre CRow
- 'Norton'	Last listed 1998
¶ - 'Oakenden Cream'	CRow
¶ - 'Old Master'	WCot
- 'Orange Sorbet'	CRow EMon
- 'Palest Cream'	CNic CSam
§ - 'Picton's Double' (d)	CGle CRow EBee EMou GBar GCal MTho NNrd NRya WAbe
- 'Primrose'	CRow EMon GGar LRHS MRav MTho NCat NRya WCot
¶ - 'Primrose Elf'	CRow
- 'Quillet' (d)	CRow
¶ - 'Ragamuffin' (d)	CRow
- 'Randall's White'	CGle CRDP CRow CSWP EBee ECha LSyl MRav MTho NTow WCot WFar
- 'Rowden Magna'	CRow
- 'Ruby Baker'	Last listed 1998
- 'Salad Bowl' (d)	CRow
- 'Salmon's White'	CAvo CBre CFee CRow EBee ELan EMar EPPr EPar EPot MRav NNrd NRya SSvw WAbe WFar WHal WHil
¶ - 'Samidor'	CRow
- 'Sheldon'	CNat CRow
¶ - 'Sheldon Night'	CNat
- 'Sheldon Silver'	CNat CRow
- single cream	EMon
¶ - 'South Downs'	CNat
- 'Suffusion'	CNat CRow
- 'Sutherland's Double' (d)	CRow
- 'Sweet Chocolate'	CRow
¶ - 'Torquay Elf'	CRow
- 'Tortoiseshell'	CHid CRow EBee MAvo MRav WBro WCot WFar
- 'Trenwheal' (d)	CRow
¶ - 'Undercurrent' (v)	WAlt
- 'Winkworth'	EMon
- 'Wisley White'	NSti
- 'Yaffle'	CBre CRow EBee EMon EMou LRHS MRav SIng WCot
x *flabaultii*	GGar
flammula	CArn CBen CKin CRow EHon EMFW LPBA MSta NDea SWat SWyc
- subsp. *minimus*	CRow
gouanii	NRya NTow
gramineus ♀	More than 30 suppliers
- 'Pardal'	SBla WFar
- 'Granby Cream'	MGrG
¶ *graniticola*	GGar
hederaceus	EMFW SWyc
illyricus	ECha NRya SRot WCru
insignis	CRDP GNor
kochii	Last listed 1999
lanuginosus	EPPr WCot
- AL&JS 89066YU	Last listed 1999
lingua	CFir CKin COld ECoo EMFW EWFC MCCP SLon SPlb
- 'Grandiflorus'	CBen CRow EHon LPBA MSta NDea NRya SWat SWyc WMAq WWye

lyallii	CPla GCal GGar GNor SBla WSan
macauleyi	GCrs
macrophyllus	WCru
millefoliatus	EBee ERos MTho NMen NRya WCot WHil
montanus	Last listed 1999
- double	EBee SBla
- 'Molten Gold' ♀	CStu EPot GCrs MRav MTho NBro NHar NHol NMen NRya NTow SBla SIng SRot WLin
muelleri var. *brevicaulis*	Last listed 1997
nivicola	EBee
ophioglossifolius	Last listed 1998
parnassiifolius	GCrs GTou NHar NMen NTow SBla WAbe
platanifolius	EBee LGre
pyrenaeus	NSla
repens	CKin EWFC
- 'Boraston O.S.' (v)	WCHb
¶ - 'Buttered Popcorn'	EPPr
- 'Cat's Eyes' (v)	CNat WAlt
¶ - 'Creeping Beauty'	WAlt
- 'Dinah Myte' (v)	Last listed 1998
¶ - 'Gathering Gloom' (v)	WAlt
- 'Gloria Spale'	CBre WAlt
- 'In Vein' (v)	WAlt
- 'Joe's Golden'	EHoe NSti WAlt WCer
- 'Justin Time' (v)	WAlt
¶ - 'Little Creep'	WAlt
- var. *pleniflorus* (d)	CBre CInt CNic CRow ECha GCal GGar GKir NSti WAlt WEas WFar
- semi-double (d)	WAlt
- 'Timothy Clark' (d)	EMon MInt WAlt
rupestris	See *R. spicatus*
sceleratus	WHer
serbicus	EBee GCal
sp. from Morocco	Last listed 1997
sp. from NE China	Last listed 1998
speciosus 'Flore Pleno'	See *R. constantinopolitanus* 'Plenus'
§ *spicatus*	CRDP WHil

RANZANIA (Berberidaceae)

japonica	Last listed 1999

RAOULIA (Asteraceae)

australis Hooker	CLTr CLyd EDAr EHoe EMNN EPot GAbr ITim MBar MWat NBro NNrd NWCA SIng WAbe WHoo WPyg
- hort.	See *R. hookeri*
- 'Calf'	ITim
§ - Lutescens Group	ECha EPot GAri ITim
- 'Saxon's Pass'	Last listed 1999
glabra	GAbr
grandiflora	SOkd WAbe
haastii	CLyd ECou
§ *hookeri*	CLyd ECha ECou EDAr EPot GKir IMGH ITim LBee LRHS MHer NNrd NWCA SBla SIng SPlb SRms WAbe WFar WLin
- var. *apice-nigra*	WAbe
- var. *laxa*	EPot EWes
x *loganii*	See x *Leucoraoulia loganii*
lutescens	See *R. australis* Lutescens Group
monroi	ITim
* *nova*	ITim
petriensis	GCrs
x *petrimia* 'Margaret Pringle'	ITim NHar WAbe

subsericea	CLyd ECou GCrs NMen
tenuicaulis	ECha ECou GAbr GAri SPlb

RAOULIA x LEUCOGENES
See x LEUCORAOULIA

RATIBIDA (Asteraceae)

columnifera	CFri EBee EMan Ilve WMoo
- f. *pulcherrima*	EBee ECGN EGoo LEur
pinnata	EBee EBrP EBre EGar LBCl LBSe LBre LRHS MBBe SBre SCro WCot

RAUVOLFIA (Apocynaceae)

serpentina	Last listed 1997

RAVENALA (Strelitziaceae)

madagascariensis	CRoM LBlo LPal WMul

RAVENEA (Arecaceae)

rivularis	CRoM LCns LPal

RECHSTEINERIA See SINNINGIA

REGELIA (Myrtaceae)

ciliata	SOWG
velutina	SOWG

REHDERODENDRON (Styracaceae)

macrocarpum	CB&S EPfP

REHMANNIA (Scrophulariaceae)

angulata hort.	See *R. elata*
§ *elata*	CBot CFri CGle CSev CSpe EBee ELan EMan GKir LAst LPio LRHS MCLN MHer MNrw MPEx SCob SLon SMrm SRPl SSoC WCru WFar WPer WWin WWye
- 'Popstar'	WElm
glutinosa ♀	CSpe LGre WWye
¶ *piasezkii*	LHop

REICHARDIA (Asteraceae)

¶ *picroides*	CAgr

REINECKEA (Convallariaceae)

§ *carnea*	More than 30 suppliers
- 'Variegata'	WCot WCru

REINWARDTIA (Linaceae)

§ *indica*	CGre CPle LChe LRHS
- S&SH 106	Last listed 1999
trigyna	See *R. indica*

RESEDA (Resedaceae)

alba	MHer
lutea	CKin EWFC MSal SIde
luteola	CKin EWFC GBar GPoy MChe MHer MHew MSal SIde WCHb WHer WOak WWye

RESTIO (Restionaceae)

¶ *festuciformis*	CTrC
pachystachyus	CCpl CTrC
quadratus	WNor
subverticillatus	See *Ischrolepis subverticillata*
tetraphyllus	CStu WCot

RETAMA (Papilionaceae)

§ *monosperma*	Last listed 1997

REYNOUTRIA See FALLOPIA

RHABDOTHAMNUS (Gesneriaceae)
solandri   Last listed 1998

RHAGODIA (Chenopodiaceae)
baccata   CCpl
triandra   CPLG ECou

RHAMNUS (Rhamnaceae)
alaternus   CFil
- var. *angustifolia*   CFil WHCr WPGP WWat
§ - 'Argenteovariegata' ♀   More than 30 suppliers
- 'Variegata'   See *R. alaternus*
                            'Argenteovariegata'
cathartica   CKin GChr LBuc MPEx NWea
                            WDin WGwy WMou
dahurica   IIve
frangula   CArn CKin CSam ENot GChr
                            LBuc MBlu NWea STre WDin
                            WGwy WMou
- 'Aspleniifolia'   EBee ENot EPfP EPla GChr LBuc
                            MBlu MBri SMur SPan
- 'Columnaris'   EMil SLPl
x *hybrida* 'Billardii'   Last listed 1999
japonica   Last listed 1999
libanotica   WLin
pallasii   WLin
prinoides   Last listed 1997

RHAPHIOLEPIS (Rosaceae)
x *delacourii*   CCHP CMHG EPfP GQui IMGH
                            LRHS SBrw SMur WBcn WBod
                            WHCG WLRN WWat
- 'Coates' Crimson'   CDoC EMil EPfP GQui MBlu
                            SBra SBrw SLon SOWG SPer
                            WSHC
- 'Enchantress'   CMHG EBrP EBre ENot LBCl LBSe
                            LBre MBBe SBre SMur
- 'Spring Song'   EBee
- 'Spring Time'   SPer
indica   CGre ERom SEND WWat
§ *umbellata* ♀   CAbb CB&S CBot CCHP CHEx
                            CSam CTri EBee EPfP GQui
                            LHop LRHS MBlu MRav SBra
                            SBrw SOWG WHCG WPic WSHC
                            WWat
- f. *ovata* B&SWJ 4706   WCru

RHAPHITHAMNUS (Verbenaceae)
cyanocarpus   See *R. spinosus*
§ *spinosus*   CGre CPle ERea WAbe WBod
                            WPic

RHAPIDOPHYLLUM (Arecaceae)
hystrix   CBrP CRoM EPVP LPal

RHAPIS (Arecaceae)
§ *excelsa* ♀   CBrP CTrC LBlo LPal WMul
multifida   LPal

RHAZYA (Apocynaceae)
orientalis   See *Amsonia orientalis*

RHEKTOPHYLLUM See CERCESTIS

RHEUM ✿ (Polygonaceae)
§ 'Ace of Hearts'   More than 30 suppliers
'Ace of Spades'   See *R.* 'Ace of Hearts'
acuminatum   CRow EBee GBin WViv
- HWJCM 252   WCru

alexandrae   EBee GAri GCal IBlr
altaicum   IIve
¶ 'Andrew's Red'   GTwe
§ *australe*   CArn CRow EBee LRHS MBro
                            MLLN MSal NBro NLar WCot
                            WFar WHoo WPyg
N x *cultorum*   See *R.* x *hybridum*
emodi   See *R. australe*
forrestii   CAgr
- ACE 2286   Last listed 1997
§ x *hybridum*   CAgr
- 'Appleton's Forcing'   GTwe
- 'Baker's All Season'   GTwe
- 'Canada Red'   GTwe
- 'Cawood Delight'   GTwe LRHS SEND
- 'Champagne'   GTwe WSpi
- 'Daw's Champion'   GTwe
- 'Early Champagne'   GTwe
- 'Early Cherry'   GTwe
- 'Fenton's Special'   GTwe
- 'Fulton's Strawberry   Last listed 1999
  Surprise'
- 'German Wine'   GTwe
- 'Goliath'   GTwe
- 'Grandad's Favorite'   EBrP EBre LBCl LBSe LBre MBBe
                            SBre
- 'Greengage'   GTwe
- 'Hammond's Early'   GTwe LRHS SEND
- 'Harbinger'   GTwe
- 'Hawke's Champagne'   GTwe
- 'Mac Red'   GTwe
- 'Prince Albert'   GTwe
- 'Red Prolific'   GTwe
- 'Reed's Early Superb'   GTwe
- 'Saint Kevin'   IIve
- 'Stein's Champagne'   GTwe
- 'Stockbridge Arrow'   CSut GTwe LRHS
- 'Stockbridge Bingo'   GTwe
- 'Stockbridge Emerald'   GTwe
- 'Stockbridge Guardsman'   GTwe
* - 'Strawberry'   EMui GTwe
- 'Sutton's Cherry Red'   GTwe
- 'The Sutton'   GTwe LBuc
- 'Timperley Early'   CDoC CMac CSam CTri EMui
                            GChr GTwe LBuc LRHS NFai
                            SDea SPer
- 'Tingley Cherry'   GTwe
- 'Valentine'   GTwe
- 'Victoria'   GKir GTwe LRHS MHer
- 'Zwolle Seedling'   GTwe
kialense   EBee EGle GCal NSti
* *maximum*   Last listed 1998
nobile   Last listed 1999
¶ - CC 2807   CPou
- HWJCM 307   Last listed 1998
- S&F 95170   Last listed 1998
officinale   CAgr CHEx GCal GKir LRHS MBri
                            SWat
palmatum ♀   CArn CB&S CBlo CHEx
                            EBee ECha ELan EWTr GKir
                            LPBA LRHS MRav MSal NCut
                            NDea NFla NGdn SPer SSpi
                            SWat WCot WFar WMul WPyg
                            WStI
- 'Atropurpureum'   See *R. palmatum*
                            'Atrosanguineum'
§ - 'Atrosanguineum'   CBot CHEx CRow EBrP EBre
                            ECha EGar ELan EOld EPar EPla
                            GBuc GKir LBCl LBSe LBre LRHS
                            MBBe MBri MWgw NBid NBro
                            NFor SBre SCob SSoC SWat WCru
                            WWin

- 'Bowles' Crimson' CHad GKir LRHS MBri SAga
- 'Hadspen Crimson' CHad GOrP NPSI WCot
- var. *palmatum* WHil
- 'Red Herald' LRHS MBri
- *rubrum* COtt EBrP EBre GCHN GKir LBCl
  LBSe LBre LRHS MBBe MCCP
  SBre
- 'Saville' GKir LRHS MBri MLLN
- var. *tanguticum* CHEx CRow EBee ECha EGar
  GKir LRHS MAvo MBri MCCP
  MSCN MSal MSta NCat NCut NSti
  SPer SRCN SRms SSoC SWat WCot
  WHoo
I - - 'Rosa Auslese' WViv
   rhaponticum CAgr EBee NLar
* *robertianum* Last listed 1997
  spiciforme Last listed 1997
  tataricum EBee EGar GCal LEdu
  tibeticum WWoo
  - SEP 20 Last listed 1999
  undulatum CRow

RHEXIA (Melastomataceae)
mariana Last listed 1997
- var. *purpurea* Last listed 1997

RHINEPHYLLUM (Aizoaceae)
broomii Last listed 1998

RHODANTHE (Asteraceae)
§ *anthemoides* ECou

RHODANTHEMUM (Asteraceae)
§ *atlanticum* ECho EWes
§ *catananche* CPBP ECho EPot EWes NTow
  SIng WAbe
§ *gayanum* EBee EDAr EMFP LRHS SAga SCro
  WEas WHen WKif
- 'Flamingo' See *R. gayanum*
§ - 'Tizi-n-Test' LBee LRHS SBla
- 'Tizi-n-Tichka' CInt CPBP EWes LBee LRHS
  NBir NTow SBla SIng SLod
  SUsu
§ *hosmariense* ♀ CMHG ECha EDAr ELan EPot LFis
  LHop LRHS NNrd SAga SBla SCoo
  SCro SPer SRms SSmi SYvo WAbe
  WCot WEas
sp. from High Atlas, SIng
  Morocco

RHODIOLA (Crassulaceae)
alsia Last listed 1998
angusta NSla
arctica Last listed 1998
bupleuroides CLD 1196 EMon
crassipes See *R. wallichiana*
§ *fastigiata* EMon GCal NMen
- x *kirilovii* Last listed 1998
gelida Last listed 1998
§ *heterodonta* ECha EGle ELan LPio MRav
himalensis See *R. 'Keston'*
§ *ishidae* Last listed 1998
§ 'Keston' SSmi
§ *kirilovii* GBin GKir GTou
- var. *rubra* EBee EBrP EBre LBCl LBSe LBre
  MBBe SBre SSmi WFar
pachyclados See *Sedum pachyclados*
pamiroalaica Last listed 1998
§ *primuloides* NMen
§ *quadrifida* Last listed 1998
recticaulis EBee
rhodantha EBee

§ *rosea* EBee EBrP EBre ECha EHoe ELan
  EMan LBCl LBSe LBre MBBe MFir
  MHer NBid NFor NHol NSla NSti
  SBre SCro SPer SRms SSmi STre
  WAbb WCDu WCot WEas WFar
  WWhi
§ - subsp. *integrifolia* Last listed 1999
semenowii EBee GAri MHar
sp. CC&McK 158 GCHN
sp. EMAK 0516 Last listed 1998
§ *trollii* CNic GCrs
§ *wallichiana* GAri GCrs WCot
§ *yunnanensis* Last listed 1997

RHODOCHITON (Scrophulariaceae)
§ *atrosanguineus* ♀ CArn CB&S CEnd CGle CHEx
  CMac CPlN CRHN CSpe ELan
  EPfP ERea LRHS MAsh MNes NFai
  SHFr SOWG SUsu SYvo
volubilis See *R. atrosanguineus*

RHODOCOMA (Restionaceae)
arida CTrC LHil
¶ *capensis* CTrC
fruticosa CTrC
gigantea CTrC LHil WNor

RHODODENDRON ✿ (Ericaceae)
'A.J. Ivens' See *R. 'Arthur J. Ivens'*
'Abbot' (EA) WBod
'Abegail' NMun SLdr
'Abendrot' LRHS MBri
aberconwayi IOrc LMil MDun NMun SLdr SReu
- 'His Lordship' GGGa LHyd
- pink NMun
'Accomplishment' CWri
'Achilles' Last listed 1998
* *acpunctum* S&F 313 Last listed 1997
acrophilum Argent GGGa
  2768 (V)
'Actress' IOrc LHyd NMun
'Addy Wery' (EA) ♀ CDoC ENot IOrc LKna MBar
  MGos NMun SBod SBrw SCam
  SLdr SReu WBod WStI
adenogynum GGGa MDun NMun SLdr
§ - Adenophorum Group EMui SLdr
- - F 20444 SLdr
- - 'Kirsty' NMun SLdr
- - R 11471 NMun
- CLD 795 LMil
- PA Cox 6502 GGGa
- white NMun SLdr
adenophorum See *R. adenogynum*
  Adenophorum Group
adenopodum GGGa MDun NMun SLdr SReu
- A.M. form SLdr
adenosum LMil MDun NHol NMun SLdr
- Kuluense Group NMun SLdr
- R 18228 GGGa
'Admiral Piet Hein' SReu
'Adonis' (EA/d) CMac IOrc MBar SCam
§ 'Adorable' (EA) IOrc
'Adriaan Koster' IOrc SLdr
adroserum See *R. lukiangense* R 11275
  USDAPI 52910
'Advance' (O) LRHS NMun SLdr
aeruginosum See *R. campanulatum* subsp.
  aeruginosum
aganniphum GGGa NMun SLdr WBod
§ - var. *aganniphum* GGGa NMun SLdr
  Doshongense Group
- - - C&V 9541 GGGa

– – – KW 5863	NMun SLdr
– – F 16472	NMun
– – Glaucopeplum Group	GGGa LHyd
– – Schizopeplum Group	GGGa
– – SSNY 138	Last listed 1999
– CNW 1174	LMil
– EGM 284	LMil
– var. *flavorufum*	GGGa MDun NMun SLdr
– – EGM 160	LMil
– – PA Cox 5070*	GGGa
– – SSNY 143	GGGa
– PA Cox 6003	Last listed 1999
– 'Rusty'	NMun
– SSNY 320a	Last listed 1999
agapetum	See *R. kyawii* Agapetum Group
x *agastum*	NMun SLdr
– PW 98	LMil
'Ahren's Favourite'	SBrw
'Aida' (R/d)	SReu
'Aksel Olsen'	ECho GKir MBar MDun NHol
'Aladdin' (EA)	CDoC ECho GGGa IOrc SLdr
	WFar
Aladdin Group & cl.	CWri SReu
Albatross Group & cl.	CWri LHyd LKna LMil SBrw SLdr
	SReu SSta
'Albatross Townhill Pink'	LMil
'Albert Schweitzer'	CWri EMil GGGa LMil MBar SBrw
	SLdr SReu
albertsenianum	Last listed 1998
albiflorum (A)	GGGa SReu
albrechtii (A) ♀	GGGa LHyd LMil MDun SReu
¶ – Whitney form (A)	LMil
'Alena'	GGGa
'Alex Hill'	Last listed 1997
'Alexander' (EA)	CTrh GQui IOrc LMil MAsh MBri
	MGos SBod SReu
'Alfred'	LRHS
'Alice' (EA)	LHyd LKna WBod
'Alice' (hybrid) ♀	IOrc LHyd LKna MDun NMun
	SBrw SLdr SReu
'Alice Street'	Last listed 1998
'Alisa Nicole' (V)	Last listed 1998
Alison Johnstone	CB&S GGGa MAsh MBri MDun
Group & cl.	MLea NMun SLdr SReu WBod
	WPic
(Alix Group) 'Alix'	SLdr
'Aloha'	MBar NDlv SReu
'Alpine Dew'	Last listed 1997
Alpine Gem Group	GQui NHol
'Alpine Glow' ♀	NMun SLdr
alutaceum	NMun
– var. *alutaceum*	GGGa
§ – – Globigerum Group	LMil
– – – R 11100	GGGa NMun
§ – var. *iodes*	GGGa LMil NMun SLdr
§ – var. *russotinctum*	GGGa SLdr
– – R 158	SLdr
§ – – Triplonaevium Group	Last listed 1997
– – – USDAPI 59442/	GGGa
R10923	
§ – – Tritifolium Group	Last listed 1998
– – – R 158*	Last listed 1997
amagianum (A)	LMil
Amaura Group	WBod
ambiguum	CHig LMil LRHS SLdr SReu WAbe
– 'Jane Banks'	LMil
* – KR 185 select*	GGGa
'America'	CB&S IOrc MBar MGos SBrw SLdr
	WFar
amesiae	GGGa NMun SLdr
'Amethyst'	LHyd
§ 'Amethystinum' (EA)	LKna

'Amity'	CDoC CWri ECho MAsh MLea
§ 'Amoenum' (EA/d)	CDoC CMac CTrG CTrh CTrw
	IOrc LHyd LKna LRHS MBar
	MGos NMun SLdr SPer WBod
	WFar WPic
'Amoenum Coccineum'	SReu
(EA/d)	
Amor Group & cl.	LHyd SLdr
'Analin'	See *R.* 'Anuschka'
'Anatta Gold' (V)	Last listed 1998
'Anchorite' (EA)	GQui LMil SLdr
'Andre'	NMun SLdr SReu
* 'Andrea'	NMun
Angelo Group & cl.	CWri LHyd LMil MDun SReu
Anita Group	SLdr
'Anita Dunstan'	LMil MLea MNaF
'Ann Lindsay'	SBrw SReu
'Anna Baldsiefen' ♀	ENot LMil LRHS MBri NHol SBrw
	SReu SSta WAbe
'Anna H. Hall'	IOrc MAsh MDun
'Anna Rose Whitney' ♀	CB&S GChr GGGa GKir IOrc
	LHyd LKna LMil LPan LRHS MAsh
	MBar MBri MDun MGos MLea
	NMun SBrw SLdr SPer SReu SSta
'Annabella' (K) ♀	LRHS MBri MDun SLdr SReu
annae	GGGa LMil LRHS MDun NMun
	SLdr
§ – Hardingii Group	NMun
aff. *annae* C&H 7185	LMil
'Anne Frank' (EA)	COtt MGos SReu WBod
'Anne George'	LHyd
'Anne Rothwell'	LHyd
'Anne Teese'	LMil
'Anneke' (K)	MBar MBri SLdr SReu SSta WBod
'Anniversary Gold'	Last listed 1999
'Anny' (EA)	IOrc LKna
anthopogon	LMil SLdr
– subsp. *anthopogon*	Last listed 1998
BL&M 332	
– – Sch 2259	Last listed 1998
– 'Betty Graham'	GGGa LMil
– CH&M 2052	Last listed 1998
¶ – from Marpha Meadow,	WAbe
Nepal	
§ – subsp. *hypenanthum*	LMil LRHS MDun
– – 'Annapurna'	GGGa NHol
§ *anthosphaerum*	GGGa NMun SLdr SReu
– F 17943	Last listed 1997
– F 26432	SLdr
– F 5848	SLdr
– Gymnogynum Group	NMun
§ – Heptamerum Group	NMun
– – KW 5684	NMun
§ 'Antilope' (Vs)	LMil SPer SReu SSta
'Antje'	MAsh
¶ 'Antonio'	LMil
Antonio Group & cl.	Last listed 1997
'Antoon van Welie'	SBrw
§ 'Anuschka'	GKir LRHS SBrw
§ *anwheiense* ♀	LHyd LMil MDun NMun SLdr
	SReu
aperantum	GGGa MDun
– F 26933	SLdr
– F 27022	GGGa
– JN 498	GGGa
'Aphrodite' (EA)	GQui
apodectum	See *R. dichroanthum* subsp.
	apodectum
'Apotheose' (EA)	Last listed 1997
'Apotrophia'	SLdr
'Apple Blossom'	CMac CTrh LRHS SLdr SReu
N 'Appleblossom'	See *R.* 'Ho-o'

	'Apricot Fantasy'	LMil SMur
	'Apricot Surprise'	GKir LRHS
	'Apricot Top Garden'	SLdr
	'April Dawn'	GGGa
	'April Gem'	MBri
§	'April Glow'	LHyd SLdr
	'April Rose'	MBri
	'April Showers'	ENot
	'April Snow' (d)	Last listed 1998
	'April White'	MBri
I	'Arabella'	MAsh
	'Arabesque'	MBri SLdr
	araiophyllum	GGGa
¶	- KR 4029	LMil
	Arbcalo Group	Last listed 1998
§	*arborescens* (A)	GGGa LHyd LKna LMil LRHS NMun SLdr SReu
¶	- pink (A)	LMil
	arboreum	CB&S GGGa IOrc ISea LMil MDun NMun SLdr SReu
	- subsp. *arboreum* KR 966	NMun
	- B 708	Last listed 1999
	- B&SWJ 2244	WCru
	- 'Blood Red'	NMun
	- C&S 1651	NMun
	- C&S 1695	NMun
	- subsp. *cinnamomeum*	GGGa NMun SLdr SReu
	- - var. *album*	SLdr SReu
	- - var. *cinnamomeum* BM&W 172	Last listed 1999
	- - - Campbelliae Group	NMun SLdr
	- - var. *roseum*	CWri GGGa NMun
	- - - BB 151*	NMun
*	- - - *crispum*	SLdr
	- - - 'Tony Schilling' ♀	LHyd LMil NMun SLdr
§	- subsp. *delavayi*	GGGa ISea NMun SLdr WBod
	- - C&H 7178	GGGa
	- - C&S 1515	NMun
	- - CNW 994	LMil
¶	- - EGM 360	LMil
	- - KW 21796	NMun
	- 'Heligan'	CWri SReu
	- mid-pink	SLdr
*	- *nigrescens*	Last listed 1998
§	- subsp. *nilagiricum*	GGGa SLdr
	- var. *roseum*	SLdr
	- TSS 26	Last listed 1997
§	- subsp. *zeylanicum*	ISea NMun SLdr
	- - 'Rubaiyat'	NMun
	'Arborfield'	Last listed 1998
	Arbsutch Group	Last listed 1998
§	Arbutifolium Group	SLdr
	x *arbutifolium*	See *R.* Arbutifolium Group
	'Arcadia' (EA)	LKna
¶	'Arctic Fox' (EA)	GGGa
§	'Arctic Glow'	MNaF
	'Arctic Regent' (K)	GQui
	'Arctic Tern'	See x *Ledodendron* 'Arctic Tern'
§	*argipeplum*	CWri NMun SLdr
	- from Bhutan	MDun
	- Cave 6714	Last listed 1998
	- KR 1231	Last listed 1997
	- SEH 581	GGGa
	'Argosy' ♀	LMil NMun SReu
	argyrophyllum	MDun NMun SLdr
	- subsp. *argyrophyllum* var. *cupulare*	SLdr
	- - KW 772711*	SLdr
	- - pink	SLdr
	- - W/A 1210	SLdr
§	- subsp. *hypoglaucum*	NMun SLdr

§	- - 'Heane Wood'	GGGa
	- subsp. *nankingense*	GGGa IOrc LMil NMun
	- - 'Chinese Silver' ♀	LHyd LMil LRHS MDun NMun SLdr SReu
	Ariel Group	SLdr
§	*arizelum*	GGGa LMil LRHS MDun NMun SLdr
	- 'Brodick'	Last listed 1997
	- F 21861	Last listed 1997
	- KW 20922	Last listed 1997
	- R 25	GGGa
	- Rubicosum Group	NMun SLdr
	- - USDAPI 59550/ R 11207	SLdr
	'Arkle'	Last listed 1997
	'Armantine'	LKna
	armitii Woods 2518 (v)	GGGa
	'Arneson Gem' (M)	CDoC GGGa LMil MDun
	'Arneson Ruby' (K)	CDoC MDun
§	'Arpege' (Vs)	SReu
	'Arthur Bedford'	CWri LHyd LKna SBrw SLdr SReu
§	'Arthur J. Ivens'	SLdr
	'Arthur Osborn'	CHig GGGa LRHS SLdr
	'Arthur Stevens' ♀	SLdr
	'Arthur Warren'	LKna
	'Asa-gasumi' (EA)	LHyd SLdr
	'Ascot Brilliant'	SBrw SLdr
¶	*asterochnoum*	LMil
	- C&H 7051	GGGa
	Asteroid Group	SLdr
	'Astrid'	ENot
	atlanticum (A)	GAri GGGa LMil NMun SSpi WWat
	- 'Seaboard' (A)	LMil SLdr SPer
	'Atlantis'	Last listed 1998
	'Audrey Wynniatt' (EA)	MAsh
	Aufgast Group	CB&S CTrw IOrc SBod WBod
	'August Lamken'	MAsh MBri
	augustinii	CB&S CHig CSam CTrG CTrw CWri GGGa IOrc LHyd LMil MLea NMun SLdr SSpi SSta WAbe WBod WGer
	- subsp. *augustinii* C 7008	GGGa
	- - C&H 7048	GGGa
	- - 'Smoke'	CGre
	- - W/A 1207	Last listed 1997
§	- subsp. *chasmanthum*	GGGa LMil SLdr
	- - C&Cu 9407 white	GGGa
	- - C&Cu 9418 pale pink	Last listed 1998
§	- Electra Group & cl.	GGGa LHyd LMil MDun NMun SLdr
	- EN 3527	Last listed 1998
	- Exbury best form	SReu
§	- subsp. *hardyi*	GGGa SLdr
§	- subsp. *rubrum*	GGGa
	- - 'Papillon'	NMun
*	- 'Trewithen'	LMil
I	- 'Werrington'	SReu
§	*aureum*	GGGa GPoy LMil MDun NMun SLdr
	auriculatum	CWri GGGa LMil MDun NHol NMun SLdr SReu SSta
	- x *degronianum*	Last listed 1997
	- hybrid	SLdr
	- PW 50	GGGa
	- Reuthe's form	SReu
	auritum	GGGa NMun WPic
	'Aurora' (K)	LRHS NMun SLdr
§	*austrinum* (A) ♀	LMil
¶	- yellow (A)	LMil
	'Autumn Gold'	COtt LMil LRHS SBrw SLdr

'Avalanche' ♀	LMil SReu	
Avalanche Group & cl.	Last listed 1999	
'Award'	LMil	
'Ayah'	SReu	
'Aya-kammuri' (EA)	LHyd	
¶ Azamia Group	LHyd	
Azor Group & cl.	CHig LHyd NMun SLdr SReu	
'Azorazie'	NMun	
'Azuma-kagami' (EA) ♀	CDoC LHyd LKna LMil WBod	
'Azuray'	Last listed 1999	
'Azurika'	NHol	
'Azurro'	GGGa LMil MDun	
'Azurwolke'	Last listed 1997	
'Babette'	MAsh MBri	
'Babuschka'	GGGa	
'Baby Scarlet'	SSta	
'Babylon'	Last listed 1998	
'Bad Eilsen'	SBrw	
'Baden-Baden'	CDoC GCHN GCrs LKna LRHS	
	MAsh MBar MDun MGos NHol	
	NMun NWea SBod SLdr SSta WFar	
'Bagshot Ruby' ♀	ENot LKna MDun NWea	
baileyi	GGGa LMil NMun SLdr	
– LS&H 17359	NMun	
bainbridgeanum hybrid	LMil	
– USDAPI 59184/ R11190	NMun SLdr	
bakeri	See *R. cumberlandense*	
balangense EN 3530	GGGa	
balfourianum	GGGa LMil MDun NMun SLdr	
¶ – AC 1575	LMil	
– var. *aganniphoides*	NMun SLdr	
– F 16811	Last listed 1997	
– F 29256*	SLdr	
– SSNY 224	GGGa	
'Ballerina' (K)	SReu	
'Balsaminiflorum'	See *R. indicum* 'Balsaminiflorum'	
'Balzac' (K)	IOrc MBri MGos SBrw SLdr	
'Bambi'	LHyd NMun SBrw SLdr SReu	
'Bambino'	CAbP COtt LNet MAsh	
'Bandoola'	SReu	
'Banzai' (EA)	Last listed 1998	
'Barbara Coates' (EA)	LHyd SLdr	
'Barbara Reuthe'	SReu	
barbatum	GGGa ISea LHyd LMil MDun	
	NMun SLdr SReu	
– B 235*	Last listed 1997	
– BB 152	Last listed 1999	
– BL&M 325	NMun	
– DF 525	Last listed 1999	
– KW 5659*	Last listed 1997	
– LS&H 17512	Last listed 1997	
– TSS 30	Last listed 1997	
'Barbecue' (K)	LMil	
Barclayi Group	LHyd	
'Barclayi Helen Fox'	NMun SLdr	
'Barclayi Robert Fox'	NMun SLdr	
'Barmstedt'	CWri	
'Barnaby Sunset'	GAri GGGa GKir LRHS NHol	
¶ 'Barry Rodgers'	GGGa	
'Bashful' ♀	EMui EPfP GKir IOrc LHyd LRHS	
	MGos NMun SLdr SReu	
§ *basilicum*	GGGa IDee LMil LRHS NMun	
	SLdr	
– AC 616	NMun SBla	
– S&F 381	ISea	
– TW 368	Last listed 1997	
x *bathyphyllum*	NMun SLdr	
– PA Cox 6542	GGGa	
bauhiniiflorum	See *R. triflorum* var.	
	bauhiniiflorum	
beanianum	GGGa LMil NMun SLdr	
– compact	See *R. piercei*	

– KW 6805	NMun	
'Beatrice Keir' ♀	LHyd LMil NMun SLdr SReu	
'Beattie' (EA)	SLdr	
Beau Brummel Group & cl.	LMil	
'Beaulieu Manor'	GQui	
'Beauty of Littleworth' ♀	LHyd LKna LMil NMun SLdr SPer	
	SReu	
'Beaver' (EA)	Last listed 1999	
beesianum	GGGa LMil NMun SLdr	
– F 10195	NMun	
– F 16375	SLdr	
– R 176	Last listed 1997	
– red bud	SLdr	
– SSNY 250	GGGa	
– SSNY 303	GGGa	
'Beethoven' (EA) ♀	CTrG CTrh LHyd LRHS NMun	
	SBod SLdr SReu WGor WPic	
'Belkanto'PBR	ENot	
'Belle Heller'	MBri SLdr WGwG WLRN	
'Belle of Tremeer'	Last listed 1997	
Bellerophon Group	NMun	
'Ben Morrison' (EA)	SReu	
'Bengal' (Rh)	GKir LRHS MAsh MBar MBri	
	MDun NHol SReu	
'Bengal Beauty' (EA)	GQui LMil	
'Bengal Fire' (EA)	CMac SLdr	
'Beni Glasso' (A)	SLdr	
§ 'Benifude' (EA)	WBod	
'Beni-giri' (EA)	CMac	
I 'Benjamen'	GGGa	
'Bergie Larson'	CB&S CDoC CWri LMil MAsh	
	MDun MLea	
bergii	See *R. augustinii* subsp. *rubrum*	
'Berg's Yellow'	CWri MBri MDun	
'Bernard Shaw'	SReu	
'Bernstein'	NBlu	
'Berryrose' (K) ♀	CB&S CTri ENot EPfP GKir IOrc	
	LHyd LKna LMil MAsh MBar MBri	
	MDun NMun SBrw SLdr SPer	
	SReu WBod WLRN	
§ 'Beryl Taylor'	GGGa NMun	
'Better Half'	Last listed 1998	
'Betty' (EA) ♀	CTrG LHyd SLdr WBod	
'Betty Anne Voss' (EA)	CDoC GKir LHyd SCoo SReu	
'Betty Stewart'	Last listed 1998	
'Betty Wormald' ♀	CDoC CHig CWri GKir LKna LMil	
	LRHS MAsh MBri MGos MLea	
	NMun SBrw SLdr SReu SSta WGer	
beyerinckianum (V)	CEqu	
bhutanense	MDun SLdr	
– AC 119	NMun	
– AC 124	NMun	
– EGM 077	GGGa	
– KR 1753	Last listed 1997	
'Big Punkin'	LMil	
'Bijou de Ledeberg' (EA)	Last listed 1999	
'Billy Budd'	LHyd	
'Binfield'	SLdr	
'Birthday Girl'	COtt LMil	
'Birthday Greeting'	NMun SLdr	
'Biscuit Box'	NMun SLdr	
Biskra Group & cl.	GGGa NMun	
'Blaauw's Pink' (EA) ♀	CChe CDoC CHig CMac CTrh	
	EBee ENot GKir GQui IOrc LHyd	
	LKna LMil LRHS MAsh MBar MBri	
	MGos NMun SBod SBrw SLdr	
	SPer SReu SRms WBod WFar	
'Black Hawk' (EA)	CB&S COtt CTrG	
'Black Knight' (A)	SLdr	
'Black Magic'	COtt CWri LMil	
'Black Satin'	COtt LMil	
'Black Sport'	MLea	

¶ 'Blatgold'	GGGa
Blaue Donau	See R. 'Blue Danube'
'Blazecheck'	GKir LRHS MGos SCoo
'Blewbury' ♀	CDoC LHyd LMil MDun NMun SLdr SReu SSta
'Blitz'	Last listed 1998
'Blizzard' (EA)	Last listed 1999
'Blue Bell'	LKna
'Blue Boy'	LMil LRHS SMur
'Blue Carpet'	Last listed 1998
'Blue Chip'	LHyd NMun SLdr
§ 'Blue Danube' (EA) ♀	CChe CDoC CMac CTrG CTrh CTri EBee ENot GKir IOrc LHyd LKna LMil LRHS MAsh MBar MBri NMun SBod SBrw SLdr SPer SReu SSta WBod WFar WGwG WStI
Blue Diamond Group & cl.	CB&S CBrm CChe CMHG CTrh CWri EBee ENot GChr LHyd LKna LRHS MBar MDun MGos NHol NMun NWea SBod SBrw SLdr SReu SRms WBod WGwG WPic
'Blue Ensign'	LRHS
'Blue Gown'	LKna
'Blue Haze'	LHyd
'Blue Monday'	SLdr WBod
'Blue Moon'	MBar
'Blue Mountain'	GDra NWea
'Blue Pacific'	Last listed 1999
'Blue Peter' ♀	CDoC CHig CWri ENot GGGa IOrc LHyd LKna MAsh MBar MBri MGos NMun SBrw SLdr SReu SSta WStI
'Blue Pool'	LMil LRHS MBar WBod
Blue Ribbon Group	CMHG CTrw ISea
'Blue River'	Last listed 1997
'Blue Silver'	GGGa NHol
'Blue Star'	GKir LHyd LRHS MBri MDun MLea SBrw SReu WAbe
'Blue Steel'	See R. fastigiatum 'Blue Steel'
Blue Tit Group	CB&S CSam CTrG CTre GDra GKir LHyd LKna LRHS MAsh MBar NHol NMun SBrw SLdr SReu SSta STre WBod
Bluebird Group & cl.	ECho ENot IOrc LKna MBar MDun MGos NDlv SLdr SRms WBod
Bluestone Group	WBod
'Bluette'	ISea MDun MLea NDlv WAbe
'Blumiria'	GGGa
'Blurettia'	CWri
'Blushing Belle' (V)	CEqu
'Bobbie'	SReu
'Bob's Blue'	Last listed 1999
'Bob's Choice' (V)	Last listed 1998
'Boddaertianum' ♀	LHyd SReu
bodinieri USDAPI 59585/ R11281	NMun
'Bodnant Yellow'	CSam
'Bonfire'	SReu
Bonito Group & cl.	Last listed 1997
'Bonnie Babe'	Last listed 1997
¶ 'Bo-peep' ♀	LHyd SReu
Bo-peep Group & cl.	CB&S CHig CSam LMil MLea NMun SLdr
'Borderer'	Last listed 1998
'Boskoop Ostara'	GGGa
'Boule de Neige'	MDun SLdr
'Boulodes'	Last listed 1997
'Bounty'	Last listed 1997
'Bouquet de Flore' (G) ♀	LMil MBar MBri SLdr SPer SReu WGer

'Bow Bells' ♀	GChr GKir NMun SBrw SLdr WFar WWat
Bow Bells Group & cl.	CSam CWri EBrP EBre IOrc ISea LBCl LBSe LBre LHyd LKna LMil MAsh MBBe MBar MBri MDun MGos MLea SBod SBre
'Bow Street'	LHyd
brachyanthum	GGGa NMun SLdr
- subsp. *hypolepidotum*	GGGa LMil MDun NMun SLdr
§ - - KW 7038	NMun
- L&S 2764	See R. glaucophyllum var. glaucophyllum L&S 2764
brachycarpum	GGGa NMun SLdr
- subsp. *brachycarpum* Tigerstedtii Group	SLdr SReu
§ - subsp. *fauriei*	NMun SLdr
* - - *nemota*	SLdr
- pink	NMun SLdr
- 'Roseum Dwarf'	GGGa NMun
brachysiphon	See R. maddenii subsp. maddenii
bracteatum CH&M 2586	Last listed 1997
'Brazier' (EA)	CTrh LHyd LRHS NMun SLdr
'Brazil' (K)	LKna SBrw SReu
Break of Day Group & cl.	Last listed 1998
'Bremen'	MOne
'Brentor'	SLdr
'Breslau' (EA)	SBrw
'Brets Own'	NMun SLdr
¶ 'Bric-a-brac' ♀	LHyd SReu
Bric-a-brac Group & cl.	CB&S CTrw MDun NMun SLdr
'Bride's Bouquet' (EA/d)	SReu
'Bridesmaid' (O)	ENot SLdr
'Brigadoon'	GGGa
'Bright Forecast' (K)	MDun SLdr WGor
'Brigitte'	CWri GGGa LRHS MAsh MBri
'Brilliant' (EA)	MGos
'Brilliant' (hybrid)	MGos NHol
'Brilliant Blue'	Last listed 1999
'Brilliant Crimson'	Last listed 1999
'Brilliant Pink'	Last listed 1999
'Britannia' ♀	CB&S CSam CWri GKir IOrc ISea LHyd LKna LNet LRHS MAsh MBar MBri MGos NMun NWea SBrw SLdr SPer SReu SSta WFar
'Britannia' x *griersonianum*	SLdr
'Brocade' ♀	CSam LHyd LKna LMil MAsh MBri NMun SLdr
'Bronze Fire' (A)	SReu
'Broughtonii'	CWri GGGa NMun SLdr
'Brown Eyes'	CWri
'Bruce Brechtbill'	CDoC GGGa GKir LMil LRHS MAsh MBri MLea NHol SBrw SLdr SReu SSta
'Bruce Hancock' (Ad)	Last listed 1998
bryophilum (V)	SLdr
'Buccaneer' (EA)	CTrh IOrc LHyd SBod
'Bud Flanagan'	LMil NMun
'Buketta'	GGGa
bullatum	See R. edgeworthii
bulu C&V 9503	GGGa
'Bungo-nishiki' (EA/d)	CMac
bureaui ♀	CAbP GGGa IOrc LHyd LMil MDun NMun SLdr SReu SSta
- 'Ardrishaig'	GGGa
- C&H 7158	GGGa
- CNW 1039	GGGa
- CNW 957	GGGa
- CNW 965	GGGa
- CNW 969	GGGa
* - *cruentum* CNW 922	Last listed 1999

- EGM 141	Last listed 1997
- x Elizabeth Group	SReu
- F 15609	NMun
I - 'Lem's Variety'	LMil WAbe
- x *prattii* PA Cox 5066	Last listed 1998
- R 25439	NMun
- S&F 510	ISea
- S&F 517	ISea
bureauoides	MDun NMun SReu
- PA Cox 5039	GGGa
- PA Cox 5076	GGGa
'Burma Road'	SLdr
burmanicum ♀	GGGa LMil MDun NMun SLdr
Bustard Group	Last listed 1998
'Butter Brickle'	Last listed 1997
'Butter Yellow'	ECho MBri
'Buttercup' (K)	MBar
'Buttered Popcorn'	Last listed 1998
'Butterfly'	LKna MDun NMun SBrw SLdr
'Buttermint'	CTrh GAri LRHS MAsh MBri MLea NMun SLdr SReu
'Buttersteep'	Last listed 1998
'Buttons and Bows' (K)	GGGa LMil
'Buzzard' (K)	LKna LMil
'C.B. van Nes' ♀	Last listed 1996
'C.I.S.'	MDun NMun SLdr
'Caerhays Lavender'	CB&S IOrc
caesium	GGGa
calendulaceum (A)	LHyd LMil SReu
¶ - red (A)	LMil
- yellow	LMil
Calfort Group & cl.	NMun SLdr
caliginis (V)	CEqu
callimorphum	GGGa LMil NMun SLdr
- var. *myiagrum* F 21821a	NMun SLdr
- - KW 6962	NMun
calophytum ♀	CHEx CWri GGGa LHyd LMil MDun NMun SLdr
- var. *calophytum* W/A 4279	SLdr
- Grieg's form	SLdr
- Knott 151	NMun
- var. *openshawianum* C&H 7055	GGGa
- - EGM 318	LMil
- W 1523	SLdr
- W/V 1523	Last listed 1997
calostrotum	CHig LMil LRHS WAbe
- 'Gigha' ♀	CDoC GGGa GKir LMil LRHS MAsh MBri MDun MOne NHar WAbe
§ - subsp. *keleticum* ♀	CTrG GAri GChr GDra LHyd MAsh MBar MDun MGos NHol SBod SBrw SRms WGer
- - F 19915	NHol
- - F 21756	NMun SLdr
- - R 58	LMil
§ - - Radicans Group	GCrs LHyd LMil MAsh MBar MBri MBro MDun MLea NHol SRms WAbe WPat WPyg
- - - mound form	NHol
- - - USDAPI 59182/R 11188	MLea
- subsp. *riparium*	LMil
- - Calciphilum Group	GGGa MDun WBod
- - - Yu 19754	Last listed 1998
§ - - Nitens Group	CDoC GGGa LMil MDun NDlv WAbe
- - PA Cox 6157	Last listed 1998
§ - - Rock's form R 178	GGGa NHol
¶ - - S&F 95089	ISea
- S&F 357	ISea

caloxanthum	See R. *campylocarpum* subsp. *caloxanthum*
'Calsap'	GGGa
Calstocker Group	Last listed 1998
Calsutch Group	SLdr
calvescens var. *duseimatum*	NMun
camelliiflorum	GGGa LMil MDun SLdr
- Rump 5696A	Last listed 1997
'Cameronian' (Ad)	LKna
campanulatum	COtt IOrc LHyd LKna MDun NMun SLdr SReu WAbe
§ - subsp. *aeruginosum*	GGGa LMil MDun NMun SLdr SReu
- - Airth 10	GGGa
- - EGM 068	Last listed 1999
- *album*	NMun SLdr
- - SS&W	Last listed 1997
- B&SWJ 2633	Last listed 1998
- Bu 249	Last listed 1999
- Bu 258	Last listed 1999
- subsp. *campanulatum* B 643	Last listed 1999
- - BL&M 283	NMun
- - 'Roland Cooper'	NMun SLdr
- DF 563	Last listed 1999
- HWJCM 195	WCru
- 'Knap Hill' ♀	LHyd NMun SReu
- SMM 41	SLdr
- SS&W 9107	SLdr
- TSS 11	NMun SLdr
- TSS 7	SLdr
- 'Waxen Bell'	LHyd NMun SLdr
§ 'Campfire' (EA)	SLdr
Campirr Group	LHyd
campylocarpum	CHig GGGa LHyd LMil MDun NMun SLdr SReu
- BM&W 150	Last listed 1999
§ - subsp. *caloxanthum*	GGGa IOrc
- - forms	NMun SLdr
- - KR 3516	LMil
§ - - Telopeum Group	NMun
§ - - - KW 5718B	NMun SLdr
- subsp. *campylocarpum* Elatum Group	MDun NMun
- - TSS 12	NMun
- x *decorum*	SLdr
- DF 558	Last listed 1999
- East Nepal	MDun
- var. *elatum*	SLdr
- x *fortunei*	SLdr
- LS&H 16495*	NMun
- TW 31*	Last listed 1997
campylogynum	GCrs MGos MLea SLdr SSpi
- 'Album'	See R. 'Leucanthum'
- apricot	Last listed 1998
- 'Beryl Taylor'	See R. 'Beryl Taylor'
I - 'Bramble'	WWeb
- Brodick form	SLdr
- Castle Hill form	LMil SReu
- Charoopoeum Group	GCrs GGGa LMil MBar MDun MGos NHar NHol WAbe
- - 'Patricia'	ECho MAsh MBri MDun WAbe
- claret	ECho GGGa LMil MDun WAbe
§ - Cremastum Group	CTrG GGGa LHyd LMil NHol NMun WAbe
- - 'Bodnant Red'	CHig GGGa LHyd MDun NMun SLdr WBod
* - - 'Cerise'	Last listed 1999
- KW 21481	Last listed 1998
- var. *leucanthum*	See R. 'Leucanthum'

- Myrtilloides Group   CB&S CDoC CTrh CTrw GAri GGGa GQui IOrc LHyd LMil MDun MLan NMun SLdr SReu WAbe
- - - Farrer 1046   GGGa
- - PA Cox 6051*   GGGa
- - PA Cox 6096   GGGa
- - pink   CTrh MBar WAbe
- - plum   GGGa WAbe
- - S&F 95181   ISea
- - salmon pink   ECho EPot MAsh MBri MDun NHar NHol WBod
camtschaticum   GGGa MLea SLdr
- var. *albiflorum*   GGGa
¶ - from Hokkaido, Japan   GCrs
- - red   GGGa
canadense (A)   GGGa NHol SLdr SReu
- f. *albiflorum* (A)   GGGa LMil
¶ - dark-flowered (A)   LMil
- - 'Deer Lake' (A)   SReu
'Canary'   LKna SLdr SReu
'Canby' (K)   MLea
§ × *candelabrum*   NMun
canescens (A)   LMil
'Cannon's Double' (K/d)   GGGa LMil MNaF
'Canzonetta' (EA)   GGGa MGos
capitatum   GGGa
'Caprice' (EA)   SReu
'Captain Jack'   CWri GGGa SLdr
'Caractacus'   EMil IOrc MBar SBrw WFar
'Carat'   SLdr SReu
cardiobasis   See *R. orbiculare* subsp. *cardiobasis*
Carex Group & cl.   Last listed 1997
'Carillon Bells'   CEqu
Carita Group   LKna SReu
'Carita Golden Dream' ♀   LKna LMil NMun SLdr
'Carita Inchmery' ♀   LHyd LKna NMun SBrw SLdr
'Carmen' ♀   CSam GChr GDra GGGa GKir ISea LHyd LKna LMil LRHS MAsh MBar MBri MDun MLea NHar NHol NMun NWea SBod SBrw SLdr SReu SRms WBod
carneum   GGGa LMil
'Caroline Allbrook' ♀   CDoC CSam CWri EMui GGGa LHyd LMil MAsh MBri MGos MLea MOne NDlv NHol NMun SBrw SLdr SReu
'Caroline de Zoete'   LHyd
carolinianum   See *R. minus* var. *minus*
'Cary Ann'   CB&S CSam CWri GCHN GChr GKir ISea LRHS MLea NMun SLdr SReu
'Cassley' (Vs)   LMil LRHS SLdr
'Castle of Mey'   SLdr
catacosmum   GGGa SLdr
- R 11185   SLdr
§ 'Catalode'   SBrw
catawbiense   CHig GGGa LHyd NMun SLdr
'Catawbiense Album'   CWri GKir IOrc NWea
'Catawbiense Boursault'   CWri IOrc
'Catawbiense Grandiflorum'   GKir IOrc LRHS SBrw
'Catherine Hopwood'   NMun SLdr
caucasicum   LHyd
§ - 'Cunningham's Sulphur'   LRHS MDun
- ex AC&H   GGGa NMun
'Caucasicum Pictum'   GGGa LHyd LMil MAsh MBar MBri SBrw SLdr
'Cayenne' (EA)   SLdr
'Cecile' (K) ♀   CB&S GChr GKir LHyd LKna LMil LRHS MAsh MBar MBri MDun

    MGos NMun SLdr SPer SReu
'Celestial' (EA)   CMac
I 'Celtic Cross'   CB&S
'Centennial'   See *R.* 'Washington State Centennial'
'Centennial Celebration'   IOrc
cephalanthum   GGGa LMil
- subsp. *cephalanthum*   Last listed 1999
- - Crebreflorum Group   GAri GGGa LMil LRHS
- - - Week's form   Last listed 1997
- - Nmaiense Group   GGGa
  C&V 9513
- - SBEC 0751   GGGa
- subsp. *platyphyllum*   GGGa
- - CNW 835   Last listed 1999
cerasinum   GGGa ISea LMil MDun NMun SLdr
- C&V 9504   GGGa
- 'Cherry Brandy'   LHyd NMun
- 'Coals of Fire'   NMun SLdr
- deep pink   NMun SLdr
- × *forrestii* subsp. *forrestii*   Last listed 1999
- KW 11011   NMun SLdr
- KW 5830   SLdr
- KW 6923   Last listed 1997
- KW 8258   Last listed 1997
- red form   SLdr
¶ - S&F 95067   ISea
'Cetewayo'   SBrw SLdr SReu
chaetomallum   See *R. haematodes* subsp. *chaetomallum*
'Chaffinch' (K)   LKna
chamaethomsonii   GGGa LMil NHar NMun SLdr
- CCH&H 8195   GGGa
- var. *chamaedoron*   Last listed 1999
  F 21768
- var. *chamaethauma*   LMil
  KW 5847
- var. *chamaethomsonii*   GGGa
  Exbury form L&S
§ - - F 21723   NMun
- - pink forms L&S   GGGa
- - Rock form   Last listed 1998
'Chameleon' (EA)   IOrc
chameunum   See *R. saluenense* subsp. *chameunum*
§ 'Champagne' ♀   GKir IOrc LHyd LKna LMil LRHS MDun MGos MLea NMun SBrw SLdr SPer SReu
championiae   GGGa
'Chanel' (Vs)   SReu SSta
'Chanticleer' (EA)   CTrh SBrw SLdr SReu
chapaense   See *R. maddenii* subsp. *crassum*
¶ 'Chapeau'   LMil
charitopes   GGGa LMil NMun SLdr
- subsp. *charitopes*   SReu
  F 25570
§ - subsp. *tsangpoense*   GGGa GQui LMil NHol
- - C&V 9575*   GGGa
* 'Charles Puddle'   WBod
'Charlotte Currie'   SLdr
* 'Charlotte de Rothschild' (A)   Last listed 1998
'Charlotte de Rothschild' (hybrid) ♀   LMil NMun SLdr
Charmaine Group & cl.   GGGa MDun NHol WBod
'Charme La'   GGGa
'Charming Valentino' (V)   CEqu
chasmanthum   See *R. augustinii* subsp. *chasmanthum*
§ (PJM Group) 'Checkmate'   Last listed 1997

'Cheer'   COtt CWri IOrc LMil LPan
                                LRHS MAsh MBar MBri SBrw SLdr
                                WGor
'Cheerful Giant' (K)   CDoC GKir LMil LRHS MLea
'Chelsea Reach' (K/d)   LKna
'Chelsea Seventy'   COtt ENot GKir LRHS NMun SLdr
                                SReu
'Chenille' (K/d)   LKna
'Cherokee'   SCam SLdr
'Chetco' (K)   CDoC LMil
'Chevalier Félix de   CWri EMil LMil MGos NMun
   Sauvage' ♀   SBrw SReu
'Cheyenne'   SLdr
'Chicago' (M)   LKna
'Chiffchaff'   LHyd NMen SLdr WAbe
chibsinianum C&H 7189   GGGa
'Chikor'   CTrG GGGa GKir LKna LRHS
                                MAsh MBar MBri MDun MGos
                                MLea NFla NHar NHol NMun
                                SBrw SLdr SReu SRms WBod WFar
                                WSHC
China Group & cl.   LKna SBrw SReu
'China A'   LKna SBrw SLdr
'Chinchilla' (EA)   GQui WGor
'Chink'   CB&S CGre ENot MBar MDun
                                NMun SLdr WBod
¶ 'Chintz'   WBod
'Chionoides'   GGGa IOrc LKna SLdr
'Chipmunk' (E/d)   LRHS
'Chippewa' (EA)   CTri GGGa GKir LMil LRHS MBri
chlorops   SLdr
'Chocolate Ice' (K/d)   LKna
'Chopin' (EA)   WBod
'Choremia' ♀   MLea NMun SLdr SReu
'Chorister' (K)   LKna
'Chris' (EA)   SLdr
'Chris Bagley'   SBrw
christi (V)   Last listed 1998
- Sandham 61/86 (V)   GGGa
'Christina' (EA/d)   CMac CTrh SLdr SReu WBod
                                WGor
'Christmas Cheer' (EA/d)   See *R.* 'Ima-shojo'
'Christmas Cheer' (hybrid)   CB&S CHig CMac CWri GGGa
                                IOrc ISea LHyd LKna LMil LRHS
                                MGos MLea NMun SBrw SLdr
                                SPer SReu WPic
'Christobel Maude'   LHyd
§ 'Christopher Wren' (K)   SLdr
chrysanthum   See *R. aureum*
chryseum   See *R. rupicola* var. *chryseum*
chrysodoron   GGGa LMil NMun
¶ 'Chrysomanicum' ♀   NMun
ciliatum ♀   CB&S CSam GGGa IOrc LHyd
                                NMun SLdr
- 'Multiflorum'   See *R.* 'Multiflorum'
ciliicalyx subsp. *lyi*   See *R. lyi*
- S&F 535   ISea
¶ - 'Walter Maynard'   LMil
¶ 'Cilpinense' ♀   GGGa LHyd SReu
Cilpinense Group & cl.   CB&S CHig CWri ENot GKir
                                IOrc LKna LMil LRHS MAsh
                                MBar MDun NFla NHol
                                NMun SBrw SLdr WAbe WBod
                                WFar
cinnabarinum   LMil MDun NMun SLdr
- B&SWJ 2633   WCru
- Bu 268   Last listed 1998
- 'Caerhays Lawrence'   NMun SLdr
- 'Caerhays Philip'   Last listed 1999
- subsp. *cinnabarinum*   SLdr
- - 'Aestivale'   LMil MDun
- - B 652   Last listed 1999

- - BL&M 234   LMil
- - Blandfordiiflorum   GGGa MDun NMun SLdr
   Group
§ - - 'Conroy' ♀   GGGa LMil MDun SReu
- - Ghunsa Nepal   MDun
- - LS&H 21283   Last listed 1997
I - - 'Mount Everest'   SLdr
- - 'Nepal' ex LS&M 21283   LMil MDun SLdr
- - Roylei Group   GGGa LMil MDun MLea NMun
                                SLdr SReu
- - 'Vin Rosé'   LMil MDun
- SHE 638   Last listed 1997
§ - subsp. *tamaense*   GGGa NMun
- - KW 21003   NMun
- - KW 21021   GGGa NMun
§ - subsp. *xanthocodon* ♀   CHig LSea LMil MDun MLea
                                NMun SLdr SReu WBod
§ - - Concatenans Group   CB&S CSam CWri GGGa MDun
                                NMun SLdr
- - - 'Amber'   LMil MDun MLea
- - - C&V 9523   GGGa
- - - KW 5874   LHyd LMil
- - - LS&T 6560   NMun
- - - mustard form   NMun
- - 'Daffodilly'   LHyd
- - EGM 88   LMil
- - forms   NMun
- - KW 8239   NMun
- - Purpurellum Group   GGGa MDun NMun SLdr
Cinnkeys Group & cl.   CPMA GGGa LMil MDun SLdr
Cinzan Group   SReu
citriniflorum   NMun
- CCH&H 8177   GGGa
- var. *citriniflorum*   LMil
- var. *boraeum*   NMun
- - F 21850*   GGGa
- - F 25901   NMun SLdr
- R 108   GGGa
'Clarissa' (EA/d)   IOrc
'Claydian Variegated'   GGGa
clementinae   GGGa LHyd MDun NMun SLdr
                                SReu
- F 25705   LMil NMun SLdr
- F 25917   Last listed 1997
- x *pronum*   GGGa
- R 25401   SLdr
'Cliff Garland'   GQui LMil MDun
Clio Group   NMun SLdr
'Coccineum Speciosum'   GGGa IOrc LHyd LMil MBar MBri
   (G) ♀   SReu SSta
'Cockade' (EA)   LKna
'Cockatoo' (K)   LKna
coelicum F 21830   See *R. pocophorum* var.
                                pocophorum F 21830
- F 25625   GGGa
§ - KW 21075   NMun
§ - KW 21077   NMun SLdr
coeloneuron   GGGa LMil MDun
- EGM 108   Last listed 1997
'Colin Kenrick' (K/d)   LKna
collettianum H&W 8975   GGGa
'Colonel Coen'   CWri GGGa MLea
Colonel Rogers Group   LHyd NMun SLdr SReu
'Colyer' (EA)   LHyd SLdr
Comely Group   NMun SLdr
- 'Golden Orfe'   SLdr
complexum F 15392   GGGa
- SSNY 296   Last listed 1998
'Comte de Gomer' (hybrid)   CB&S
concatenans   See *R. cinnabarinum* subsp.
                                xanthocodon Concatenans
                                Group

concinnum — CHig CTrw CWri LHyd LMil MDun MLea NMun SLdr
- Benthamianum Group — Last listed 1997
- PA Cox 5011 — Last listed 1998
- PA Cox 5085 — Last listed 1998
- Pseudoyanthinum Group ♀ — GGGa GQui LMil MDun NMun SLdr WPic
'Concorde' — LHyd LRHS
'Conroy' — See *R. cinnabarinum* subsp. *cinnabarinum* 'Conroy'
'Consolini's Windmill' — LMil
'Constable' — LHyd NMun SLdr
'Constant Nymph' — LKna
'Contina' — GGGa
Conyan Group — LHyd
cookeanum — See *R. sikangense* Cookeanum Group
'Cora Grant' (EA) — Last listed 1998
'Coral Beauty' — Last listed 1997
¶ 'Coral Mist' — GGGa LMil
'Coral Redwing' (EA) — MAsh
'Coral Reef' — NMun SLdr SReu
'Coral Sea' (EA) — SReu
'Coral Velvet' — COtt
'Corany' (A) — SLdr
coriaceum — GGGa LMil NMun SLdr
¶ - AC 1921 — LMil
- F 16364 — Last listed 1997
- F 21843 — Last listed 1997
- PA Cox 6531 — GGGa
- R 120 — NMun
- S&F 348 — Last listed 1998
'Corneille' (G/d) ♀ — LKna LMil SPer SReu
'Cornish Cracker' — NMun SLdr
Cornish Cross Group — LHyd NMun SLdr SReu
Cornish Early Red Group — See *R.* Smithii Group
'Cornish Red' — See *R.* Smithii Group
Cornubia Group — NMun SLdr
'Corona' ♀ — LKna
'Coronation Day' — SLdr SReu
'Coronation Lady' (K) — ENot LKna MBri
'Corringe' (K) ♀ — LMil
'Corry Koster' — LKna SBrw
coryanum — GGGa NMun SLdr
- 'Chelsea Chimes' ex KW 6311 — GGGa LMil
'Cosmopolitan' — CWri GChr GGGa IOrc LMil LPan LRHS MAsh MBar MDun MGos SBrw
'Costa del Sol' — NMun SLdr
¶ Cote Group no. 10 (G) — LMil
'Cotton Candy' — LMil NMun
'Countess of Athlone' — IOrc LKna SBrw SLdr
'Countess of Derby' — IOrc SBrw SLdr SReu
'Countess of Haddington' ♀ — CB&S CWri LMil MDun NMun SLdr
¶ 'Countess of Stair' — WPic
'County of York' — See *R.* 'Catalode'
cowanianum — GGGa
Cowslip Group — CSam CWri GKir LHyd LKna LMil LRHS MBar MDun MGos NHol NMun SLdr SReu
coxianum C&H 475B — GGGa
'Craig Faragher' (V) — CEqu
'Cranbourne' — SReu
'Crane' — GGGa GKir GQui LMil LRHS MDun WAbe
crassum — See *R. maddenii* subsp. *crassum*
'Cream Crest' — GQui ISea MDun WAbe
'Cream Glory' — LHyd SReu

'Creamy Chiffon' — CDoC CWri GCHN GGGa LHyd MGos MLea SLdr WGwG
§ 'Creeping Jenny' ♀ — GGGa LHyd LRHS MBar MDun MLea NHol SLdr
cremastum — See *R. campylogynum* Cremastum Group
§ 'Crest' ♀ — CSam CWri GGGa IOrc ISea LHyd LKna LMil MDun MGos MLea SLdr SReu
'Crete' — COtt LMil LRHS MDun SReu
'Crimson Pippin' — GGGa LMil
crinigerum — GGGa LMil LRHS MDun NMun SLdr
- bicolored — SLdr
- var. crinigerum KW 7123 — NMun
- - KW 8164 — NMun
- - R 100 — NMun
- - R 38 — NMun
- var. euadenium — NMun
'Crinoline' (K) — LRHS SBrw SLdr SReu
'Crooksbury Gold' — SLdr
Crossbill Group — CB&S CGre SLdr WPic
* crossium — SReu
'Crosswater Red' (K) — LMil
'Crowthorne' — Last listed 1997
cruttwellii (V) — GGGa
cubittii — See *R. veitchianum* Cubittii Group
cucullatum — See *R. roxieanum* var. *cucullatum*
cultivar FH 8 — LMil
§ cumberlandense (A) — GGGa LMil LRHS
¶ - 'Camp's Red' (A) — LMil
- 'Sunlight' (A) — LMil
cuneatum — GGGa LMil NMun
- F 27119* — NMun
- R 11392 — NMun
§ - Ravum Group — CHig WPic
'Cunningham's Blush' — GAri GGGa LRHS
'Cunningham's Sulphur' — See *R. caucasicum* 'Cunningham's Sulphur'
'Cunningham's White' — CB&S CHig CSam CWri GChr GGGa GKir IOrc LKna LMil LRHS MAsh MBar MBri MDun MGos NMun NWea SBrw SLdr SPer SReu WFar WStl WWeb
'Cupcake' — GGGa
'Curlew' ♀ — More than 30 suppliers
'Cutie' — Last listed 1998
cyanocarpum — GGGa LMil MDun NMun SLdr
- AC 676 — NMun
- Bu 294 — GGGa
- EN 2458 — Last listed 1998
'Cynthia' ♀ — CWri ENot GGGa IOrc LHyd LKna LMil MBar MBri MDun MGos MLan NMun NWea SBod SBrw SLdr SReu SSta WFar
'Dagmar' — Last listed 1997
'Daimio' (EA) — Last listed 1999
'Dainty Drops' (V) — CEqu
'Dairymaid' — LHyd LKna NMun SBrw SLdr SReu
dalhousieae — GGGa SLdr
§ - var. rhabdotum ♀ — GGGa SLdr
Damaris Group — NMun SLdr
'Damaris Logan' — See *R.* 'Logan Damaris'
Damozel Group & cl. — WStl
'Dandy' (hybrid) — LKna
Dante Group — SLdr
'Daphne' (hybrid) — SLdr
'Daphne Jewiss' — SReu

'Doc' ♀	CB&S EBee ENot EPfP GKir IOrc LHyd LMil LRHS MAsh MBar MDun MGos NDlv NMun SBrw SLdr SReu WStI	
'Doctor Arnold W. Endtz'	CWri IOrc NMun SBrw	
'Doctor Ernst Schäle'	GGGa MAsh	
'Doctor H.C. Dresselhuys'	IOrc MBar SBrw	
'Doctor Herman Sleumer' (V)	GGGa	
'Doctor M. Oosthoek' (M) ♀	MAsh SReu	
'Doctor Stocker'	NMun SLdr	
'Doctor Tjebbes'	ISea SBrw	
'Doctor V.H. Rutgers'	IOrc MBar SBrw WFar	
'Donald Waterer'	SBrw	
'Doncaster'	ENot GKir IOrc LKna LRHS MBar MGos NMun NWea SBrw SLdr WFar	
'Dopey' ♀	CDoC CWri EBee EMui ENot GGGa GKir IOrc LHyd LMil LRHS MAsh MBar MBri MDun MGos MLea NDlv NHol NMun SBrw SLdr SReu WGwG WWeb	
'Dora Amateis' ♀	CB&S COtt GGGa GKir ISea LHyd LMil LRHS MAsh MBar MBri MGos NHol NMun SBrw SLdr SPer SReu WBod WGwG WPic	
Dormouse Group	GGGa LMil SBrw SLdr	
'Dorothea'	SLdr	
'Dorothy Amateis'	Last listed 1997	
'Dorothy Corston' (K)	LKna	
'Dorothy Hayden' (EA)	LHyd SLdr	
doshongense	See *R. aganniphum* var. *aganniphum* Doshongense Group	
'Double Beauty' (EA/d)	IOrc LKna LRHS SBod SReu SSta	
'Double Damask' (K/d) ♀	LHyd LKna SReu	
'Double Date' (d)	GGGa	
'Double Delight' (K/d)	GGGa MLea	
'Doubloons'	NMun SLdr	
Dragonfly Group	MDun SReu	
- × *serotinum*	SLdr	
'Drake's Mountain'	ECho MAsh MBar MBri MDun	
'Dreamland'	COtt CWri ENot LHyd LMil LRHS MAsh MGos MLea MNaF SBrw SLdr SReu	
'Driven Snow' (EA)	ENot SBod	
drumonium	See *R. telmateium*	
'Drury Lane' (K)	GQui SLdr	
dryophyllum hort.	See *R. phaeochrysum* var. *levistratum*	
'Duchess of Portland'	SReu	
'Duchess of Rothesay'	NMun	
'Duchess of Teck'	SReu	
'Dusky Dawn'	NMun SLdr	
'Dusky Orange'	SReu	
'Dusty Miller'	CAbP CDoC COtt EBee GKir ISea LHyd LRHS MAsh MBar MGos NBlu NDlv SLdr WAbe	
'Earl of Athlone'	LHyd SReu	
'Earl of Donoughmore' ♀	LHyd LKna SBrw SReu SSta	
'Early Beni' (EA)	LHyd	
Early Brilliant Group	LKna	
'Early Gem'	Last listed 1999	
early red hybrid	SLdr	
'Ebony Pearl'	CDoC CWri GGGa MDun MLan	
eclecteum	LMil MDun NMun SLdr	
- var. *bellatulum*	Last listed 1997	
- - R 110*	Last listed 1997	
- var. *eclecteum*	Last listed 1997	
'Kingdon Come' ex KW 6869		

- - R 23512	Last listed 1997	
- PA Cox 6054	GGGa	
- 'Rowallane Yellow'	NMun	
'Eddy' (EA)	LKna NMun	
× *edgarianum*	LMil	
§ *edgeworthii* ♀	GGGa LHyd LMil NMun WAbe WBod	
- AC 666	NMun	
- forms	CWri GGGa	
- × *leucaspis*	CB&S	
- × *moupinense*	GGGa	
- S&F 607	Last listed 1998	
- Yu 17431	Last listed 1997	
'Edith Bosley'	GGGa	
'Edith Mackworth Praed'	SReu	
Edmondii Group	Last listed 1997	
'Edna Bee' (EA)	GQui LMil	
'Egret' ♀	GAri GGGa GKir ITim LHyd LRHS MAsh MBar MBri MDun MGos MLea NHar NHol SLdr WAbe WGer	
'Ehrengold'	Last listed 1998	
'Eider'	COtt GCHN GGGa ISea LRHS NMun SReu WFar	
'Eileen'	SReu	
'Eisprinzessin' (EA)	GGGa	
'El Alamein'	Last listed 1998	
'El Camino'	COtt CWri MBri MLea NMun SLdr	
'El Greco'	NMun SLdr	
Eldorado Group	GQui	
¶ 'Eleanor' (EA)	WBod	
'Eleanor Habgood'	SLdr	
Eleanore Group & cl.	IOrc	
Electra Group & cl.	See *R. augustinii* Electra Group & cl.	
elegantulum	GGGa LHyd LMil LRHS MDun NMun SLdr	
'Elfenbein'	Last listed 1997	
'Elfin Gold'	GGGa SReu	
'Elisabeth Hobbie' ♀	GDra GGGa LKna LMil MBar MDun MGos SLdr	
Elizabeth Group & cl.	CB&S CDoC CSam CTrh CTrw CWri EBee GDra GGGa IMGH IOrc LHyd LKna LMil MAsh MBar MGos NHol NMun NWea SBod SBrw SLdr SPer SReu WBod WFar	
N 'Elizabeth' (EA)	ENot GKir GOrc IOrc MGos	
'Elizabeth de Rothschild'	LMil MDun NMun	
'Elizabeth Gable' (EA)	Last listed 1997	
'Elizabeth Jenny'	See *R. 'Creeping Jenny'*	
'Elizabeth Lockhart'	CGre GChr GGGa GKir GQui MBar MDun MGos MLea WAbe	
'Elizabeth of Glamis'	GGGa	
'Elizabeth Red Foliage'	GChr GGGa GKir LMil LRHS MDun NHol SBrw SPer	
elliottii	GGGa NMun SLdr SReu	
- KW 7725	NMun	
Elsae Group & cl.	NMun SLdr SReu	
'Else Frye'	GGGa	
'Elsie Lee' (EA)	CDoC CGre CTrh GGGa LMil LRHS MAsh SBod SBrw SReu SSta	
'Elsie Pratt' (K)	MBar MBri SReu SSta	
'Elsie Straver'	LRHS NHol SBrw SLdr SReu	
'Elsie Watson'	GGGa LMil	
'Elspeth'	LHyd LKna	
'Emanuela'	LMil	
§ 'Emasculum' ♀	CGre COtt CSam LKna SReu	
'Ember Glow'	NMun	
Emerald Isle Group	SReu	
'Emma Williams'	CPne	
'Empire Day'	LKna SLdr	
'Ems'	Last listed 1998	

'Enborne'	LHyd NMun SLdr
'Endre Ostbo'	Last listed 1998
'English Roseum'	IOrc SLdr
'Erato'PBR	ENot GGGa LMil
eriogynum	See *R. facetum*
eritimum	See *R. anthosphaerum*
'Ernest Inman'	LHyd NMun SLdr
erosum	GGGa NMun SLdr
erubescens	See *R. oreodoxa* var. *fargesii*
	Erubescens Group
§ x *erythrocalyx*	NMun
Panteumorphum	
Group	
N 'Esmeralda'	CMac CTrG SBod
Ethel Group & cl.	SLdr WBod
'Etna'	SLdr
'Etoile de Sleidinge'	SBrw
'Etta Burrows'	CWri GGGa MDun MLea
'Euan Cox'	GGGa NHar NHol WAbe
euchaites	See *R. neriiflorum* subsp.
	neriiflorum Euchaites Group
euchroum	NMun SLdr
eudoxum	GGGa MDun NMun
- var. *eudoxum* PA Cox	GGGa
6036	
- - R 10950	See *R. temenium* var.
	mesopolium R 10950
- - R 6c	NMun
- KW 5879*	NMun
'Eunice Updike' (EA)	LHyd
'Europa'	SReu
eurysiphon	NMun SLdr
- Arduaine form	GGGa
- KW 21557*	NMun
'Eva Goude' (K)	LKna
'Evelyn Hyde' (EA)	SLdr
'Evening Fragrance' (A)	SReu
'Evening Glow'	NHol
'Evensong' (EA)	LKna
'Everbloom' (EA)	NMun SLdr
'Everest' (EA)	ENot LHyd MAsh WBod
'Everestianum'	GGGa IOrc LKna MBar SBrw SLdr
exasperatum	NMun SLdr
- KW 8250	GGGa
'Exbury Albatross'	LKna
'Exbury Calstocker'	LMil
'Exbury Fabia'	SReu
'Exbury May Day'	SReu
'Exbury Naomi'	LHyd LKna LMil NMun SLdr
'Exbury White' (K)	EPfP GQui
excellens AC 146	GGGa
- S&F 92074	ISea
- S&F 92079	ISea
- S&F 92303	ISea
eximium	See *R. falconeri* subsp. *eximium*
'Exotic'	Last listed 1999
'Exquisitum' (O) ♀	CDoC EPfP GGGa LMil LRHS
	MBri MLea SLdr SSpi
exquisitum	See *R. oreotrephes* Exquisitum
	Group
F.C. Puddle Group & cl.	SLdr
§ *faberi*	GGGa MDun NMun SLdr
- EGM 111	Last listed 1999
- subsp. *prattii*	See *R. prattii*
¶ 'Fabia' ♀	GGGa LHyd LMil SReu
Fabia Group & cl.	GCHN IOrc LKna MDun NMun
	SBrw SLdr
'Fabia' x *bureaui*	SLdr
'Fabia Roman Pottery'	MDun
§ 'Fabia Tangerine'	COtt MDun MLea SReu SRms
	WBod
§ *facetum*	GGGa LMil NMun SLdr WBod

¶ - AC 3049	LMil
- CLD 1522*	Last listed 1998
- Farrer 1022	NMun
- S&F 315	ISea
¶ - S&F 612	ISea
- TW 360	Last listed 1997
'Faggetter's Favourite' ♀	LKna LMil MDun NMun SLdr
	SReu SSta
Fairy Light Group	LMil MAsh MBri MDun SLdr
'Fairy Mary'	Last listed 1999
'Falcon'	See *R.* (Hawk Group) 'Hawk
	Falcon'
falconeri ♀	CDoC CHEx COtt GGGa IOrc
	ISea LHyd LMil LRHS MDun
	NMun SLdr SPer SReu
- B&SWJ 2437	WCru
* - Cox's species	SReu
- DF 526	Last listed 1999
§ - subsp. *eximium*	GGGa LMil LRHS MDun
- subsp. *falconeri*	Last listed 1999
BM&W 66	
- - EGM 55	Last listed 1997
'Faltho'	SLdr
'Fanal' (K)	SLdr
'Fanny'	See *R.* 'Pucella'
'Fantastica'	GGGa LHyd LMil LRHS MBri
	MDun SReu
fargesii	See *R. oreodoxa* var. *fargesii*
'Fashion'	CChe CTrG SLdr
fastigiatum ♀	GCrs GDra LMil MBar MBri MDun
	NMen NMun SLdr
§ - 'Blue Steel'	CB&S COtt CTri CWSG CWri
	GChr GGGa GKir IMGH LMil
	LRHS MAsh MBri MBro MDun
	NHar NHol NMun SBrw SReu
	WAbe WPat WPyg
- C&H 7159	GGGa
§ - 'Harry White'	SReu
- pink	Last listed 1999
- S&F#518	ISea
- SBEC 804/4869	GGGa MDun NHol
'Fastuosum Flore Pleno'	CWri GGGa GKir IOrc ISea LHyd
(d) ♀	LKna LMil LRHS MBar MBri MGos
	MLea NMun NWea SBrw SLdr
	SReu SSta WFar
faucium	GGGa NMun SLdr
- C&V 9508	GGGa
- K&R 5024	GGGa
¶ - KR 3465	LMil
§ - KW 6401	NMun
aff. *faucium* KW 5732	NMun
'Faulk Lemon'	Last listed 1998
fauriei	See *R. brachycarpum* subsp.
	fauriei
'Favorite' (EA)	CMac CTrw IOrc LHyd LKna
	MBri NMun SLdr
'Fedora' (EA) ♀	CB&S LHyd LKna SLdr
'Fernanda Sarmento' (A)	SReu
ferrugineum	GGGa LKna LMil MBar MGos
	NMen NMun SLdr SReu WAbe
- Ascreavie form	NHol
* - *compactum*	ECho
- Glenarn form	NHol
* - 'Hill of Tarvit'	NHol
- 'Plenum' (d)	MDun
'Festive'	LHyd
'Feuerwerk' (K)	SLdr
fictolacteum	See *R. rex* subsp. *fictolacteum*
'Fidelio' (EA)	Last listed 1997
Fine Feathers Group	WBod
Fire Bird Group	LHyd SLdr
¶ 'Fire Rim'	GGGa

'Fireball' (K) | CB&S CDoC CTri GGGa LHyd
 | LMil MLea SBrw SPer WWeb
'Fireball' (hybrid) | GKir LRHS SLdr WLRN WWal
Firedrake Group | SReu
'Firefly' (K) | ENot
'Firefly' (EA) | See *R*. 'Hexe'
'Fireglow' | LRHS SLdr WFar
'Fireman Jeff' | Last listed 1999
'Flamenco Dancer' (V) | ERea
'Flaming Bronze' | SReu
'Flaming June' (K) | LKna
§ *flammeum* (A) | LMil
¶ 'Flanagan's Daughter' | GKir
Flashlight Group | Last listed 1998
§ Flava Group & cl. | CDoC CWri LMil LRHS MBar
 | MGos NDlv SReu SSta
'Flava Glendoick' | Last listed 1997
'Flava Lackblatt' | CDoC MAsh MBri MLea
flavidum | GGGa MDun
 - 'Album' | LHyd LMil LRHS MDun SBod
 - PA Cox 5064 | MDun
 - PA Cox 6143 | GGGa
§ 'Flavour' | LKna
fletcherianum | NMun SLdr WAbe
 - R 22302 | NMun SLdr
 - 'Yellow Bunting' | GGGa
fleuryi | LMil
 - KR 3286 | GGGa
§ *flinckii* | GGGa LMil MDun NMun
 - CH&M 3080 | GGGa
floccigerum | GGGa LMil NMun SLdr WBod
 - bicolored | NMun
 - R 10 | Last listed 1997
 - USDAPQ 3966/ R18465 | Last listed 1997
aff.*floccigerum* F 20305 | SLdr
'Floradora' (M) | SReu
'Flora's Garden' | Last listed 1997
'Flora's Green' | Last listed 1997
'Florence Archer' | Last listed 1997
'Floriade' | LHyd LKna
floribundum | LMil NMun SLdr
¶ - EGM 294 | LMil
 - PA Cox 5090 | Last listed 1997
 - 'Swinhoe' | SLdr
'Florida' (EA/d) ♀ | CMac CTrh LKna LMil LRHS
 | MAsh SBrw SReu SSta WBod WFar
formosanum | GGGa
formosum ♀ | CB&S CGre ERea GGGa GQui
 | NMun
§ - var.*formosum* | GGGa SLdr WAbe
 Iteaphyllum Group |
 - - 'Khasia' C&H 320 | GGGa
 - var.*inaequale* C&H 301 | GGGa
forrestii | GGGa LMil NMun
 - subsp.*forrestii* F 21723 | See *R. chamaethomsonii* var.
 | *chamaethomsonii* F 21723
 - - LS&T 5582 | NMun
 - Repens Group | GGGa LMil NMun SLdr
¶ - - - 'Seinghku' ♀ | GGGa LHyd
 - Tumescens Group | GGGa NHol NMun SLdr
 - - C&V 9517 | GGGa
Fortorb Group | NMun
Fortune Group & cl. | NMun SLdr
fortunei | CB&S COtt CWri GGGa IOrc ISea
 | LHyd LKna LMil MDun NMun
 | SLdr SReu WBod
§ - subsp.*discolor* ♀ | GGGa LMil LRHS NMun SLdr
 - - 'Hilliers Best' | SLdr
§ - Houlstonii Group | LMil LRHS NMun SLdr
¶ - - - 'John R. Elcock' | LMil
 - 'Foxy' | NMun SLdr
 - 'Lu-Shan' | MDun

 - 'Mrs Butler' | See *R. fortunei* 'Sir Charles Butler'
§ - 'Sir Charles Butler' | LMil
'Fox Hunter' | LKna
fragariiflorum C&V 9519 GGGa
 - hybrid LS&E 15828 | Last listed 1999
¶ - LS&E 15828 | GGGa
'Fragrantissimum' ♀ | CB&S CDoC CGre CHad CTrG
 | CTre CTrw CWri Elan GGGa IOrc
 | ISea LHyd LMil MDun MRav
 | NMun WAbe
'Francis B. Hayes' | IOrc
Francis Hanger | NMun SLdr SReu
 (Reuthe's) Group |
'Frank Baum' | CWri NMun SReu
'Frank Galsworthy' ♀ | LKna LMil SBrw SReu
'Frans van der Bom' (M) | MBri SLdr
'Fraseri' (M) | GGGa
'Fred Harris' | SLdr
'Fred Nutbeam' (EA) | MGos
'Fred Peste' | GGGa IOrc LMil MAsh MDun
 | SReu
'Fred Rose' | Last listed 1998
'Fred Wynniatt' ♀ | CWri LHyd LMil MDun NMun
 | SLdr SReu
'Fred Wynniatt Stanway' | See *R*. 'Stanway'
'Freya' (R/d) | LMil
'Fridoline' (EA) | GGGa
'Frieda' (EA) | SLdr
'Frigate' | WLRN
'Frilled Petticoats' | NMun SLdr SReu
'Frills' (K/d) | LHyd
'Frilly Lemon' (K/d) | LMil MDun SLdr
'Frome' (K) | LKna
'Frontier' | Last listed 1999
'Frosted Orange' (EA) | LMil
'Frosthexe' | GGGa
'Fudetsukasi' | Last listed 1998
'Fuju-kaku-no-matsu' (EA) | MGos
'Fuko-hiko' (EA) | NMun
'Fulbrook' | NMun SLdr
'Fulgarb' | SLdr
fulgens | GGGa LHyd LMil MDun NMun
 | SLdr SReu
 - DF 543 | Last listed 1999
fulvum ♀ | CDoC GGGa IOrc LHyd LMil
 | LRHS MDun NMun SLdr SReu
 | SSta
¶ - AC 3083 | LMil
 - subsp.*fulvoides* | NMun SLdr
 - - PA Cox 6026 | GGGa
 - - PA Cox 6532 | GGGa
 - - R 143 | NMun
 - - R 180 | NMun
 - subsp.*fulvum* F 24110 | SLdr
 - - Farrer 874 | SLdr
 - TW 379 | Last listed 1997
'Furnivall's Daughter' ♀ | CWri ENot GChr GGGa IOrc LHyd
 | LKna LMil LRHS MBar MBri MGos
 | NMun SBrw SLdr SReu SSta WFar
'Fusilier' ♀ | LHyd SLdr SReu
Fusilier Group & cl. | Last listed 1999
'Gabriele' (EA) | GQui SSpi
'Gabrielle Hill' (EA) | CDoC COtt
'Gaiety' (EA) | IOrc LMil SBrw SReu
'Galactic' | NMun SLdr
galactinum | NMun SLdr
 - CC&H 4023 | Last listed 1997
 - EN 3537 | GGGa
 - W/A 4254 | NMun
'Galathea' (EA) | CDoC LMil
'Gallipoli' (K) | Last listed 1998
'Gandy Dancer' | CDoC CWri MDun

'Garden State Glow' (EA/d) SBod SReu
'Gartendirektor Glocker' CDoC CWri GGGa LMil MDun
MLan MLea MOne SBrw SSta
'Gartendirektor Rieger' CWri GGGa LMil LRHS MBri
MDun NHol SBrw SReu
'Gauche' (A) GQui MAsh SLdr
'Gaugin' GQui
'Gauntlettii' x *thomsonii* SLdr
'Geisha' (EA) MBar
'Geisha Lilac' (EA) CDoC COtt EcHo GKir LRHS
MBar MBri NBlu WLRN
'Geisha Orange' (EA) CDoC COtt CTrh GGGa GKir
LRHS MBar MBri MGos NDlv SLdr
WLRN WWeb
'Geisha Purple' (EA) COtt MBar MOne WFar
'Geisha Red' (EA) COtt EBee EPfP MBar MBri STre
WAbe WFar
'Gekkeikan' (EA) CB&S
'Gena Mae' (A/d) GGGa LMil
'General Eisenhower' SBrw SReu
'General Eric Harrison' LHyd NMun SLdr
'General Practitioner' ENot NMun SLdr
'General Sir John du Cane' NMun
'General Wavell' (EA) CMac COtt LKna SLdr
'Gene's Favourite' SReu
genestierianum GGGa
CC&H 8080
'Genghis Khan' NMun
'Geoffroy Millais' LMil
'Georg Arends' GKir LRHS SLdr
'George Hardy' CWri
'George Hyde' (EA) LMil
'George Johnstone' (EA) ♀ Last listed 1999
'George Reynolds' (K) GKir LRHS
'George's Delight' CWri GGGa MLea
'Georgette' LHyd NMun SLdr
§ x *geraldii* SLdr
'Germania' LRHS MBar
Gertrud Schäle Group CTri LRHS MBar MDun NHol
SReu
'Getsutoku' (EA) GAri SReu
'Gibraltar' (K) ♀ CB&S CSam EBrP EBre ENot
GChr GGGa GKir IOrc LBCl LBSe
LBre LKna LMil LRHS MAsh MBBe
MBar MBri MGos MLea SBre SBrw
SLdr SPer SReu SSta WBod WWal
giganteum See *R. protistum* var. *giganteum*
'Gigi' Last listed 1997
'Gilbert Mullier' MBri
'Ginger' (K) CDoC EPfP LMil NMun SBrw SLdr
'Ginny Gee' ♀ CBrm CDoC COtt CSam CTrh
CWri GChr GGGa GKir LHyd
LMil LRHS MAsh MBar MBri
MDun MGos MLea NHar NHol
NMun SBrw SPer SReu SSta WAbe
WFar WGwG
§ 'Girard's Hot Shot' (EA) CTrh EcHo GGGa GQui LMil
SBod SBrw SReu SVil
'Glacier' (EA) SLdr
'Glad Tidings' Last listed 1998
Gladys Group & cl. Last listed 1998
'Glamora' (EA) LHyd SLdr
glanduliferum C&H 7131 GGGa
- EGM 347 LMil
¶ - PW 044 LMil
glaucophyllum GGGa LHyd LMil MDun NMun
SLdr
- var. *album* GGGa
- BH form LMil
* - 'Branklyn' Last listed 1998
§ - var. *glaucophyllum* Last listed 1999
L&S 2764

- 'Glenarn' Last listed 1998
§ - subsp. *tubiforme* NMun SLdr WBod
'Glencora' (EA) LHyd
'Glenn Dale Adorable' See *R.* 'Adorable'
¶ 'Glenroy Carpet' SReu
'Glen's Orange' CWri
glischroides GGGa
glischrum GGGa NMun SLdr SReu
- C&Cu 9316 GGGa
- CNW 398 ISea
- subsp. *glischroides* LMil NMun SLdr
- subsp. *glischrum* GGGa
§ - subsp. *rude* GGGa LMil MDun NMun SLdr
- - C&V 9524 GGGa
globigerum See *R. alutaceum* var. *alutaceum*
Globigerum Group
'Glockenspiel' (K/d) LKna
'Gloria' LMil
'Gloria Mundi' (G) SLdr SReu
'Glory of Leonardslee' SLdr
'Glory of Penjerrick' NMun SLdr
'Glowing Embers' (K) EBee GChr GKir LRHS MAsh MBri
MDun MLea SBrw SLdr SPer SReu
WBod WFar WWeb
'Gloxineum' Last listed 1999
Goblin Group & cl. SLdr
'Gog' (K) LHyd LKna SLdr WLRN
'Gold Crest' (K) LKna
'Gold Dust' (K) Last listed 1998
'Gold Mohur' SBrw SLdr SReu
'Goldball' See *R.* 'Christopher Wren'
'Goldbukett' LHyd SBrw
'Golden Bee' GGGa NHol
'Golden Belle' CWri LMil MDun SMur
'Golden Coach' COtt MDun MLea NMun SLdr
'Golden Eagle' (K) CDoC COtt GKir MDun MGos
SCoo SLdr
'Golden Eye' (K) LKna
'Golden Flare' (K) CB&S CDoC LHyd LRHS MAsh
SLdr SReu
'Golden Fleece' LKna SReu
'Golden Gate' CDoC LMil MDun NMun SLdr
WGor
'Golden Horn' (K) GQui SLdr WGor
Golden Horn Group & cl. IOrc NMun SLdr
'Golden Horn Persimmon' See *R.* 'Persimmon'
'Golden Lights' (A) GChr GKir LHyd LMil LRHS
'Golden Orfe' ♀ Last listed 1997
'Golden Oriole' ♀ LKna SReu
Golden Oriole Group & cl. CB&S NHol NMun
§ - 'Talavera' ♀ CB&S
'Golden Princess' COtt LMil MDun NHol
'Golden Ruby' Last listed 1999
'Golden Splendour' LMil
'Golden Star' Last listed 1998
'Golden Sunset' (K) COtt EBee LRHS MAsh MBar MBri
MGos SBrw
'Golden Torch' ♀ CAbP CB&S COtt CWri EBee
ENot GChr GGGa GKir IOrc ISea
LHyd LMil LNet LRHS MAsh MBri
MDun MGos MLea NDlv NMun
SLdr SReu SSht SSta WWeb
'Golden Wedding' CB&S CWri LMil LRHS MDun
MLea
'Golden Wit' EcHo SBrw SLdr
'Goldfee' LHyd WWeb
'Goldfinch' (K) LKna
'Goldfinger' Last listed 1999
'Goldflimmer' (v) EMil ENot GGGa GKir LRHS
MAsh MGos NHol SBrw SPer
SReu WWeb
'Goldfort' CWri LKna SBrw SReu

'Goldika' LMil
'Goldilocks' Last listed 1997
'Goldkrone' CDoC CSam CWri ENot GGGa
ISea LHyd LMil MAsh MBri MDun
MGos MLea NMun SBrw SLdr
SReu
'Goldprinz' GGGa
'Goldstrike' SLdr
'Goldsworth Crimson' LHyd SBrw
'Goldsworth Orange' GGGa LHyd LKna LRHS MGos
NMun SBrw SLdr SPer SReu
'Goldsworth Pink' LKna SBrw SReu
'Goldsworth Yellow' CSam LKna MGos SLdr SReu
'Golfer' GGGa
'Gomer Waterer' ♀ CB&S CDoC CHig CWri GChr
GGGa GKir IOrc LHyd LKna LMil
LRHS MAsh MBar MBri MDun
MGos MLea NMun NWea SBod
SBrw SLdr SPer SReu SSta WFar
'Good News' SLdr
'Goosander' LHyd
'Gordon Jones' GGGa
'Govenianum' (Ad) LKna
'Grace Seabrook' CDoC COtt CSam CWri GGGa
GKir LHyd LRHS MAsh MDun
MLea SLdr SReu

gracilentum (V) Last listed 1997
'Graciosum' (O) LKna SReu
'Graf Zeppelin' Last listed 1998
'Graham Thomas' LMil SReu
'Graham Vivian' SLdr
'Grand Slam' MDun
grande GGGa IOrc LMil NMun SLdr
 - DF 524 Last listed 1999
 - EGM 58 Last listed 1997
 - pink NMun
 - TSS 37 NMun
§ aff. *grande* KR 13649 NMun
'Grandeur Triomphante' SReu
 (G)
gratum See *R. basilicum*
'Grayswood Pink' Last listed 1999
'Graziella' GGGa
'Greensleeves' LKna LMil
'Greenway' (EA) CB&S CGre CTre IOrc SLdr
Grenadier Group & cl. SBrw
'Greta' (EA) LHyd
'Gretzel' NMun SReu
'Grierdal' Last listed 1997
Grierocaster Group Last listed 1997
griersonianum GGGa IOrc ISea LHyd MDun
NMun SLdr
 - F 24116 NMun
griffithianum GGGa LMil MDun NMun SLdr
WPic
 - EGM 101 Last listed 1997
. 'Grisette' SLdr
'Gristede' CDoC COtt GGGa LMil LRHS
MDun MOne NHol SBrw SReu
groenlandicum GGGa
¶ 'Grosclaude' ♀ NMun SLdr
'Grouse' MLea NHar
'Grouse' x *keiskei* var. ECho MDun
 ozawae 'Yaku Fairy'
'Grumpy' CDoC EBee EMui ENot GGGa
GKir IOrc LHyd LMil LNet LRHS
MAsh MBar MBri MGos MLea NBlu
NDlv NMun SAga SBrw SLdr SReu
Guardsman Group SLdr
§ 'Gumpo' (EA) CMac SLdr
'Gumpo Pink' (EA) SLdr WBod
'Gumpo White' (EA) SBod WAbe

'Gwenda' (EA) LHyd
'Gwillt-king' Last listed 1998
'Gyokushin' (EA) Last listed 1999
'H.H. Hume' (EA) CDoC IMGH SLdr SSht
'H.O. Carre' (EA) CMac
'H.Whitner' NMun SLdr
habrotrichum GGGa LMil NMun
 - F 15778 NMun
'Hachmann's Bananaflip' LHyd
'Hachmann's Brasilia' CWri SBrw
'Hachmann's Charmant' GGGa LMil
'Hachmann's Feuerschein' ENot LMil
'Hachmann's Juanita' (K) MBri
'Hachmann's Marlis' ENot LHyd LMil SBrw SReu
'Hachmann's Polaris' LMil MBri
'Hachmann's Porzellan' LHyd
§ 'Hachmann's Rokoko' (EA) ECho GGGa
'Hachmann's Rosita' Last listed 1999
haematodes GGGa MDun NMun SLdr SRms
 - AC 710 NMun
 - Bu 290 GGGa
 - C&Cu 9445 Last listed 1998
§ - subsp. *chaetomallum* GGGa LMil NMun
 - - F 25601 NMun
¶ - - JN 493 GGGa
 - - KW 21077 See *R. coelicum* KW 21077
 - - R 18359 NMun SLdr
 - - R 41 NMun
 - CLD 1283 LMil
 - ex Hobbie Last listed 1997
 - subsp. *haemotodes*
 F 6773 NMun SLdr
 - - McLaren S124A NMun SLdr
 - - SBEC 585 GGGa
 aff. *haematodes* KW 6955 SLdr
'Haida Gold' ISea MGos MLea NMun SLdr SReu
SSta
'Hakurakuten' (EA) Last listed 1997
Halcyone Group SLdr
'Halfdan Lem' CAbP CSam GGGa LHyd LMil
MAsh MBri MGos MLea NMun
SBrw SLdr SPer SReu SSta
'Hallelujah' CWri SMur
'Halopeanum' WBod
'Halton' NMun
'Hamlet' (M) LMil
'Hammondii' (Ad) LKna
'Hana-asobi' (EA) CB&S LHyd LRHS SLdr
hanceanum CHig NMun SLdr WBod
 - 'Canton Consul' GGGa LHyd
 - EN 2104 GGGa
 - x *lutescens* WBod
 - Nanum Group CB&S GGGa WBod
hancockii S&F 464 ISea
'Handsworth Scarlet' SLdr
'Hansel' CDoC MAsh MDun
§ *baofui* Guiz 75 GGGa
Happy Group IOrc
'Harbinger' (EA) SLdr
§ 'Hardijzer Beauty' (Ad) ♀ IOrc LKna LRHS SReu
hardingii See *R. annae* Hardingii Group
'Hardy Gardenia' (EA/d) SBrw SReu
hardyi See *R. augustinii* subsp. *hardyi*
'Harkwood Friendship' Last listed 1998
'Harkwood Moonlight' Last listed 1999
'Harkwood Premiere'[PBR] GGGa LMil LPan MGos
'Harkwood Red' (EA) CTrh GQui LMil SCam SLdr
'Harmony' (EA/d) SLdr
'Harry Tagg' CTrG GGGa SLdr
'Harumiji' (EA) Last listed 1998
'Harvest Moon' (K) CSam GKir LRHS MAsh SCoo
SReu

'Harvest Moon' (hybrid)	LHyd LRHS MBar MDun MGos SBrw SLdr SReu
'Hatsugiri' (EA) ♀	CHig CMac EBee ENot EPfP IOrc LHyd LKna LMil MBar SBod SLdr SReu
(Hawk Group) 'Crest'	See R. 'Crest'
- 'Hawk Buzzard'	SLdr
§ - 'Hawk Falcon'	SReu
§ - 'Hawk Merlin'	Last listed 1999
- 'Jervis Bay'	See R. 'Jervis Bay'
'Haze'	SLdr
'Hazel Fisher'	LMil
'Heather Macleod' (EA)	LHyd SLdr
heftii	NMun
'Heidelberg' (K/d)	Last listed 1999
'Heiwa' (EA)	Last listed 1997
'Heiwa-no-kagami' (EA)	GAri
'Helen Close' (EA)	CTrh SLdr
'Helen Curtis' (EA)	SReu
'Helene Schiffner' ♀	CWri GGGa NMun SLdr SReu
§ *heliolepis*	GGGa IOrc LMil LRHS SLdr WBod
- AC 759	NMun
- Bu 292	Last listed 1998
- C&Cu 9313	Last listed 1998
- var. *fumidum*	See R. *heliolepis* var. *heliolepis*
§ - var. *heliolepis*	LRHS SLdr
- - CNW 1038	ISea
- - CNW 944	LMil
§ - - F 6762	NMun
- - SSNY 66	NMun
- S&F 489	ISea
- S&F 516	ISea
- SSNY 314	Last listed 1998
- Yu 7933*	Last listed 1997
hemidartum	See R. *pocophorum* var. *hemidartum*
x *hemigynum*	NMun SLdr
hemitrichotum	NMun
§ - F 30940	NMun
- KW 4050	NMun
hemsleyanum	GGGa IOrc MDun NMun SLdr
- EN 2097	GGGa
- x *ungernii*	GGGa
aff. *hemsleyanum* C&H 7189	LMil
'Henry Street'	Last listed 1998
heptamerum	See R. *degronianum* subsp. *heptamerum*
'Herbert' (EA)	CMac
§ 'Hexe' (EA)	WBod
hidakanum	SReu
'Higasa' (EA)	CHig GAri
'High Gold'	Last listed 1999
'High Summer'	LMil
'Hilda Margaret'	SReu
himantodes (V)	Last listed 1998
'Hino-crimson' (EA) ♀	CDoC CGre CMac CTrG CTrh CTri EBee IOrc LKna LMil LRHS MAsh MBar MBri MGos SBrw SLdr SPer SReu SSta WFar WLRN WStI WWeb
'Hinode-giri' (EA) ♀	CB&S CDoC CHig CMac CTrw ENot LHyd LKna NMun SBod SCam SLdr SReu WPic
'Hinode-no-kumo' (EA)	NMun SLdr
'Hinomayo' (EA) ♀	CB&S CMac CTrG CTre GQui IOrc LHyd LKna LMil LRHS MAsh MBar NMun SLdr SPer SReu SSta WBod WPic WStI
'Hino-scarlet'	See R. 'Campfire'
'Hino-tsukasa' (EA)	NMun SLdr
hippophaeoides	CB&S CDoC CHig EPfP LMil LRHS MDun NMen NMun SLdr WAbe WFar
- 'Bei-ma-shan'	See R. *hippophaeoides* 'Haba Shan'
- F 22197A	SLdr
§ - 'Haba Shan' ♀	GGGa LMil MBri MDun MOne
- 'Inshriach'	WBod
- var. *occidentale*	GGGa
- C&Cu 9314	
- Yu 13845	CDoC GGGa MDun
hirsutum	GGGa LHyd LMil SLdr SReu WPyg
- f. *albiflorum*	GGGa
- 'Flore Pleno' (d)	ECho GCrs GGGa MBar MDun MLea WAbe WBod
hirtipes	GGGa
- C&V 9546	GGGa
¶ - KR 5059	LMil
- KW 10616	Last listed 1999
- KW 5659	Last listed 1999
- KW 6223	NMun
- LS&E 15765	Last listed 1999
- LS&T 3624	NMun
x *hodconeri*	NMun
- LS&H 21296	See R. *hodgsonii* LS&H 21296
- 'pink'	NMun
- TSS 9	See R. *hodgsonii* TSS 9
hodgsonii	GGGa IOrc LMil LRHS MDun NMun SLdr SReu
- B 653	Last listed 1999
- B&SWJ 2656	WCru
- BL&M 232	Last listed 1997
- DF 532	Last listed 1999
§ - LS&H 21296	NMun
- 'Poet's Lawn'	NMun
- SU 323	Last listed 1997
- TSS 42A	NMun SLdr
§ - TSS 9	NMun SLdr
aff. *bodgsonii* EGM 81	Last listed 1997
'Hojo-no-odorikarako' (EA)	NMun SLdr
'Holden'	CWri
'Hollandia' (hybrid)	IOrc SBrw
'Homebush' (K/d) ♀	CB&S CDoC CMHG ENot EPfP GChr GGGa GKir IOrc LHyd LKna LMil LRHS MBar MBri MDun MLea MNaF SLdr SPer SReu SSta
'Honey'	LKna NMun SBrw
'Honey Bee'	Last listed 1999
'Honeymoon'	NMun SLdr WLRN
'Honeysuckle' (K)	IOrc MBar SLdr SReu WBod
'Hong Kong'	COtt MDun
hongkongense	GGGa NMun
'Honourable John Boscawen'	SBrw
§ 'Ho-o' (EA)	CB&S CGre SLdr
bookeri	NMun SLdr SReu
- KW 13859	NMun
- KW 8238	SLdr
- Tigh-na-Rudha form	GGGa
'Hope Findlay'	LHyd
'Hoppy'	CWri EBee ENot GChr GKir LMil LRHS MAsh MDun MLea NMun SLdr SReu WGwG
'Horizon Dawn'	Last listed 1997
'Horizon Lakeside'	GGGa LMil
'Horizon Monarch'	GGGa LMil MDun
'Horizon Snowbird'	Last listed 1997
borlickianum	GGGa NMun
- KW 9403	NMun
'Hortulanus H. Witte' (M)	MBri SLdr SReu WFar
'Hot Shot'	See R. 'Girard's Hot Shot'

'Hotei' ♀	CB&S CSam CWri GCHN GChr GGGa GKir ISea LHyd LMil LRHS MBar MBri MDun MGos NMun SLdr SReu SSta WGer
Hotspur Group (K)	GGGa SCoo WLRN
'Hotspur' ♀	GKir SLdr
'Hotspur Red' (K) ♀	CDoC CSam GKir LKna LMil LRHS MBri SBrw SReu
'Hotspur Yellow' (K)	SReu
boulstonii	See *R. fortunei* subsp. *discolor* Houlstonii Group
buanum	LMil
– C&H 7073	GGGa
– EGM 330	Last listed 1999
– EN 4028	Last listed 1997
'Hugh Koster'	IOrc LKna MGos NMun SBrw SLdr
Humming Bird Group	CB&S CMHG CSam GGGa ISea LHyd LKna LRHS MBar MBri MDun MGos MLea NHol NMun SLdr SReu SRms WBod
bunnewellianum	GGGa SLdr
'Hurricane'	COtt LRHS SBrw SLdr
'Huzzar'	MDun
'Hyde and Seek'	GQui SBrw
'Hydie' (EA/d)	MGos
'Hydon Ball'	LHyd LRHS
'Hydon Ben'	LHyd
'Hydon Comet'	LHyd
'Hydon Dawn' ♀	CDoC COtt CWri GGGa GKir ISea LHyd LMil LRHS MBri MGos MLea NDlv NMun SBrw SLdr SReu SSta
'Hydon Glow'	LHyd NMun SLdr
'Hydon Gold'	LHyd
'Hydon Haley'	LHyd
'Hydon Hunter' ♀	CB&S COtt GGGa IOrc LHyd LMil LNet LRHS MAsh MBri NDlv NMun SBrw SLdr SPer SReu SSta
'Hydon Juliet'	LHyd
* 'Hydon Magic'	NBlu
'Hydon Mist'	LHyd
'Hydon Pearl'	LHyd
'Hydon Pink'	LHyd
'Hydon Primrose'	LHyd
'Hydon Rodney'	LHyd
'Hydon Salmon'	LHyd NMun
'Hydon Velvet'	LHyd SReu
bylaeum	NMun
– KW 6401	See *R. faucium* KW 6401
– KW 6833	NMun
bypenanthum	See *R. anthopogon* subsp. *hypenanthum*
Hyperion Group	LKna LMil SBrw SReu SSta
byperythrum	GGGa MDun NHol NMun SLdr
* – *album*	NMun
– ETOT 183	ISea
– subsp. *fauriei*	Last listed 1997
– pink	NMun SLdr
bypoglaucum	See *R. argyrophyllum* subsp. *hypoglaucum*
– 'Heane Wood'	See *R. argyrophyllum* subsp. *hypoglaucum* 'Heane Wood'
Ibex Group & cl.	NMun
'Ice Cream'	LHyd LKna
'Ice Cube'	MDun MLea
'Ice Maiden'	SReu
'Iceberg'	See *R. 'Lodauric Iceberg'*
'Icecream Flavour'	See *R. 'Flavour'*
'Icecream Vanilla'	See *R. 'Vanilla'*
¶ 'Idealist' ♀	LHyd SReu
Idealist Group & cl.	CWri NMun SLdr
'Ightham Gold'	SReu
'Ightham Peach'	SReu
'Ightham Purple'	SReu
'Ightham Yellow'	NMun SLdr SReu
'Igneum Novum' (G)	MBri SReu
'Il Tasso' (R/d)	LKna
'Ilam Louie Williams' (A)	SReu
§ 'Ilam Melford Lemon' (A)	LMil
§ 'Ilam Ming' (A)	LMil
§ 'Ilam Red Velvet'	SLdr
'Ilam Violet'	LKna WBod
'Imago' (K/d)	LKna
§ 'Ima-shojo' (EA/d) ♀	GAri LHyd LMil WBod
'Impala' (K)	LKna
impeditum ♀	CB&S CHig EBee ENot GGGa ISea LHyd LKna MAsh MBar MDun MGos MLea NHar NHol NMun NWea SBrw SLdr SReu SSta WBod WFar
– 'Blue Steel'	See *R. fastigiatum* 'Blue Steel'
* – 'Compactum'	Last listed 1997
– dark compact form	LKna
– F 20454	Last listed 1997
§ – F 29268	GGGa NMun
– 'Harry White's Purple'	See *R. fastigiatum* 'Harry White'
– 'Indigo'	CMHG LRHS MAsh MBri MDun NHar WAbe
– 'Johnston's Impeditum'	LKna
– 'Moerheim'	See *R.* 'Moerheim'
– 'Pygmaeum'	MBro NHol WPat
– Reuthe's form	SReu
– 'Russell's Blue'	SBrw SReu
– 'Williams'	SLdr
imperator	See *R. uniflorum* var. *imperator*
Impi Group & cl.	LKna NMun SBrw SLdr
'Ina Hair'	Last listed 1998
inconspicuum (V)	Last listed 1997
'Independence Day'	GGGa
§ *indicum* (EA)	WBod
§ – 'Balsaminiflorum' (EA/d)	CMac WAbe
– 'Crispiflorum' (EA)	Last listed 1997
– var. *eriocarpum* 'Gumpo'	See *R.* 'Gumpo'
x *inopinum*	GGGa NMun
insigne ♀	GGGa IOrc LHyd LMil LRHS MDun NMun SLdr
– hybrid	SLdr
– Reuthe's form	SReu
– x *yakushimanum*	SReu
Intermedium Group	Last listed 1999
x *intermedium* white	GGGa
Intrepid Group	SReu
intricatum	GGGa WAbe
– KW 4184	NMun
– PA Cox 5060	Last listed 1998
Intrifast Group	GAri GGGa LHyd LRHS MAsh NHar NHol SLdr WAbe
iodes	See *R. alutaceum* var. *iodes*
'Irene'	SBrw
'Irene Koster' (O) ♀	CMHG GGGa LHyd LKna LMil MAsh MBri MLea SLdr SPer SReu WWeb
'Irohayama' (EA) ♀	CDoC CHig CMac CTrw GQui LHyd LKna LMil SLdr SPer SReu SSta
irroratum	CWri LMil NMun SLdr
– C&H 7185	GGGa
– subsp. *irroratum* C&H 7100	GGGa
– subsp. *kontumense* var. *ningyuenense* EGM 339	LMil
– 'Langbianense' KR 3295	LMil

'Kathleen' pale pink (EA) LHyd
'Kathleen' rosy red (EA) LKna WBod
'Kathleen' salmon pink (EA) IOrc
* 'Katinka' (hybrid) GGGa
'Katinka' (EA) GGGa
'Katisha' (EA) LHyd SLdr
'Katrina' SLdr
'Katy Watson' SReu
kawakamii (V) GGGa
'Keija' SReu
'Keinohana' (EA) NMun
keiskei CHig LHyd NMun SLdr
¶ – compact SLdr
– 'Cordifolium' NHol WAbe
– 'Ebino' GGGa NHol
– var. *ozawae* EPot GGGa LMil LRHS MDun
    'Yaku Fairy' ♀ NHar SReu WAbe
– – 'Yaku Fairy' x Last listed 1997
    campylogynum
– – 'Yaku Fairy' x NHol
    campylogynum
    var. *leucanthum*
– – 'Yaku Fairy' x EPot
    lowndesii
– – 'Yaku Fairy' x Last listed 1998
    spinuliferum
keleticum See *R. calostrotum* subsp.
    keleticum
§ 'Ken Janeck' GGGa LRHS SLdr
§ *kendrickii* GGGa MDun NMun
– MH 62 GGGa
¶ 'Kenneth' WBod
'Kentucky Colonel' SLdr
'Kermesinum' (EA) COtt GGGa LRHS MBar SLdr SPlb
    SReu WPat
'Kermesinum Album' (EA) GGGa MBar MGos
I 'Kermesinum Rose' (EA) GChr LRHS MBar MBri SLdr SReu
* 'Kermesinum Wit' SReu
kesangiae AC 110 NMun
– CH&M 3058 GGGa
– CH&M 3099 GGGa
– EGM 061 Last listed 1999
– var. *kesangiae* KR 1136 NMun
aff. *kesangiae* KR 1640 GGGa MDun NMun
Kewense Group See *R.* Loderi Group
keysii CB&S GGGa LMil MDun NMun
    SLdr
– KR 974 NMun
– KW 8101* NMun
– 'Unicolor' NMun SLdr
'Kijei' Last listed 1998
¶ 'Kilimanjaro' ♀ GGGa SReu
Kilimanjaro Group & cl. LMil NMun SBrw SLdr SSta
'Kimberly' GGGa
'Kimbeth' GGGa
'Kimigayo' (EA) LHyd
'King Fisher' NMun
'King George' Loder See *R.* 'Loderi King George'
'King George' Van Nes SReu
'King of Shrubs' SLdr
kingianum See *R. arboreum* subsp.
    zeylanicum
'Kingston' MAsh MDun
§ 'Kirin' (EA/d) ♀ CGre CHig CMac CTrw IOrc
    LHyd LKna LMil LRHS SBod SLdr
    WBod
'Kirishima' (EA) LKna SRms
'Kiritsubo' (EA) GAri IOrc LHyd
'Kitty Cole' SLdr
kiusianum (EA) ♀ GGGa LHyd NMun SReu SRms
– 'Album' (EA) GAri LHyd LMil SReu WAbe
– 'Amoenum' See *R.* 'Amoenum'

– 'Ekubo' (EA) SReu
– 'Hillier's Pink' (EA) LMil
– var. *kiusianum* CTrh
    'Mountain Gem' (EA)
* – 'Mount Fuji' (EA) LMil WAbe
– var. *sataense* (EA) Last listed 1997
'Kiwi Majic' GGGa LMil
'Klondyke' (K) ♀ CB&S CTri EBee ENot EPfP GChr
    GGGa GKir IOrc LMil LRHS MAsh
    MBri MGos MLea SBrw SLdr SReu
'Kluis Sensation' ♀ CB&S ENot IOrc LHyd LKna
    MDun MGos NMun NWea SBrw
    SLdr SReu
'Kluis Triumph' LKna SBrw SReu
'Knap Hill Apricot' (K) LKna
'Knap Hill Red' (K) LKna LMil SLdr SMur
'Kobold' (EA) NMun SLdr
'Koichiro Wada' See *R. yakushimanum* 'Koichiro
    Wada'
'Kokardia' LRHS SLdr
'Komurasaki' (EA) NMun
kongboense GGGa
– C&V 9540 GGGa
aff. *kongboense* KR 3725 LMil
§ 'Koningin Emma' (M) LMil MBri
§ 'Koningin Wilhelmina' (M) IOrc SMer WBod
konori M Black (V) Last listed 1998
– var. *phaeopeplum* (V) GGGa
'Koster's Brilliant Red' (M) ENot LRHS SLdr SReu
kotschyi See *R. myrtifolium*
'Kozan' (EA) Last listed 1999
'Kupferberg' GGGa
§ 'Kure-no-yuki' (EA/d) ♀ CMac CTrG LHyd LKna LMil LRHS
    MAsh SBod
'Kusudama' (EA) GAri
kyawii NMun SLdr WPic
§ – Agapetum Group NMun
'Lacs' Last listed 1998
lacteum LMil LRHS MDun NMun SLdr
– bright yellow NMun
– C 7164 GGGa
– CNW 930 GGGa
– CNW 936 GGGa
– CNW 966 NMun
– forms NMun
– KR 2760 GGGa
– S&F 374 ISea
– SBEC 345 GGGa
'Ladt Decis' Last listed 1997
'Lady Adam Gordon' LHyd SLdr
'Lady Alice Fitzwilliam' ♀ CB&S CDoC CGre CMHG CTrG
    GGGa ISea LHyd LMil NMun SLdr
    WWat
'Lady Annette de Trafford' LKna
'Lady Armstrong' CWri
Lady Bessborough Group SLdr
    & cl.
'Lady Bessborough See *R.* 'Roberte'
    Roberte'
'Lady Bowes Lyon' LHyd NMun SLdr
Lady Chamberlain Group GGGa LMil NMun SLdr
    & cl.
'Lady Chamberlain See *R.* 'Salmon Trout'
    Salmon Trout'
'Lady Clairmont' SBrw
'Lady Clementine CWri GGGa LHyd LKna LMil
    Mitford' ♀ MDun MGos MLea NMun NWea
    SBrw SLdr SPer SRPl SReu
'Lady Decies' SReu
'Lady Eleanor Cathcart' ♀ CHig EPfP GGGa IOrc LKna
    NMun SBrw SLdr
'Lady Elphinstone' (EA) LHyd SLdr

'Lady Grey Egerton'	LKna
Lady Linlithgow Group	Last listed 1998
'Lady Longman'	LHyd SBrw SSta
'Lady Louise' (EA)	LHyd SLdr
'Lady Primrose'	SLdr SReu
'Lady Robin' (EA)	LMil
'Lady Romsey'	LMil
'Lady Rosebery' (K)	MAsh MBri
Lady Rosebery Group & cl.	MLea NMun SLdr
Ladybird Group & cl.	LMil SReu
laetum (V)	CEqu GGGa
Lamellen Group	LHyd SLdr
'Lampion'	ENot GGGa LHyd
'Lamplighter' ♀	LMil SReu
lanatoides	NMun
- C&C 7548	GGGa
- C&C 7574	GGGa
- C&C 7577	GGGa
- KW 5971	NMun
lanatum	LMil NMun SLdr
- 716652	Last listed 1997
¶ - B&SWJ 2464	WCru
- BB 185b	NMun
- C 2148	Last listed 1997
- Cooper 2148	SLdr
- DF 538	Last listed 1999
- dwarf cream	GGGa
- Flinckii Group	See *R. flinckii*
- KR 873	Last listed 1998
'Langmans'	LKna
'Langworth'	CWri ECho LKna LMil SBrw SLdr SReu
lanigerum	MDun NMun SLdr SReu
- C&V 9530	GGGa
- 'Chapel Wood'	SLdr
- KW 6258	Last listed 1997
- KW 8251	GGGa
- pink	NMun
- red	NMun
- 'Round Wood' ex KW 6258	Last listed 1998
subsection Lapponica ACE 1787	Last listed 1998
lapponicum	LMil
- Confertissimum Group	GGGa
- Japanese	GGGa
- Parvifolium Group from Siberia	GGGa WBod
'Lapwing' (K)	LKna MAsh MBri
'Lascaux'	SReu
lasiostylum ETOT 135	Last listed 1998
- ETOT 136	Last listed 1998
'Late Love' (EA)	CDoC MGos SSpi
late pink Inverewe	WBod
§ *latoucheae* (EA)	Last listed 1999
- PW 86 (EA)	GGGa
laudandum var. *temoense*	GGGa LMil MDun
Laura Aberconway Group & cl.	SLdr WBod
'Laura Morland' (EA)	LHyd
'Lava Flow'	LHyd NHol
'Lavender Brilliant'	CTrh
'Lavender Girl' ♀	CWri GGGa LHyd LKna LMil LRHS MGos NMun SBrw SLdr SReu SSta
'Lavender Lady' (EA)	CTrG
'Lavender Princess'	Last listed 1998
'Lavender Queen'	CWri NMun
'Lavendula'	GGGa LMil MNaF
'Le Progrès'	SReu
'Lea Rainbow'	MLea

'Ledifolium'	See *R.* x *mucronatum*
'Ledifolium Album'	See *R.* x *mucronatum*
'Lee's Dark Purple'	CDoC CWri LMil MBar NMun NWea SBrw SPer WFar WGwG
'Lee's Scarlet'	LKna LMil SLdr
'Lemon Cloud'	GGGa
* 'Lemon Drop' (A)	GGGa
'Lemon Grove'	SReu
'Lemon Ice'	Last listed 1997
'Lemon Lodge'	CB&S
'Lemon Minuet' (V)	CEqu
'Lemonora' (M)	LRHS MBri SLdr
'Lem's 121'	CWri
'Lem's Cameo' ♀	GGGa LHyd LMil NMun SReu SSta
'Lem's Monarch' ♀	CDoC CWri GGGa LMil LRHS MDun MGos MLea SReu SSta
'Lem's Stormcloud'	LRHS
'Lem's Tangerine'	LMil
'Lemur' (EA)	CTrh GChr GGGa LRHS MBri NHol SReu WAbe WPat
'Leni'	GKir LRHS
'Leny' (EA)	NHol
'Leo' (EA)	GQui LHyd LKna LMil NMun SLdr SReu
'Leo' (hybrid)	EPfP LRHS NMun
'Leonardslee Brilliant'	SLdr
'Leonardslee Giles'	SLdr
'Leonardslee Hybrid'	SLdr
'Leonardslee Pink Bride'	SLdr
'Leonardslee Primrose'	SLdr
Leonore Group & cl.	NMun SReu
lepidostylum ♀	CWri GGGa LHyd LMil MAsh MBar MBri MDun NHar NMun SLdr SReu WSHC
lepidotum	GGGa LHyd LMil MDun NMun WAbe
- var. *album*	Last listed 1999
- Elaeagnoides Group	GGGa
- FMB 279	Last listed 1999
- x *lowndesii*	Last listed 1998
- M Black 602	GGGa
- 'Reuthe's Purple'	See *R.* 'Reuthe's Purple'
- TW 40	Last listed 1997
- yellow	NMun
leptanthum (V)	CEqu
§ *leptocarpum*	GGGa LMil
- C&H 420	NMun
leptothrium	GGGa NMun
Letty Edwards Group & cl.	LKna NMun SLdr SReu
§ 'Leucanthum'	CHig GGGa LMil
leucaspis ♀	CGre CHig ERea GGGa IOrc LHyd MDun NMun SLdr SReu
- KW 7171	NMun SLdr
'Leverett Richards'	LHyd SReu
levinei	GGGa
'Lila Pedigo'	CDoC COtt CWri GGGa MAsh MLea
'Lilac Time' (EA)	MBar SLdr
'Lilacinum' (EA)	WPic
'Lilacinum' (hybrid)	Last listed 1997
liliiflorum Guiz 163	GGGa
'Lillie Maude' (EA)	Last listed 1999
'Lilliput' (EA)	LRHS MAsh SBod
'Lily Marleen' (EA)	CTri SCoo SLdr SReu WGwG
'Linda'	CSam CTri EBee GGGa LRHS MAsh MBar MBri MDun MGos SReu WWeb
'Linda Lee'	SLdr
'Linda R' (EA)	Last listed 1997
lindleyi ♀	GQui LMil NMun
- 'Dame Edith Sitwell'	GGGa LMil
- L&S	GGGa

'Linearifolium' See *R. stenopetalum* 'Linearifolium'
'Linnet' (K/d) LKna
'Linwood Salmon' (EA/d) SReu
Lionel's Triumph Group LMil NMun SLdr
& cl.
'Lissabon Rosa' Last listed 1998
litiense See *R. wardii* var. *wardii* Litiense Group
'Little Beauty' (EA) SCam SLdr
'Little Ben' ECho MAsh MBar MDun WAbe WBod
'Little Bert' Last listed 1998
'Little Grace' (V) CEqu
'Little Jessica' Last listed 1997
'Little Jock' Last listed 1999
'Little One' (V) CEqu
'Loch Earn' GGGa
'Loch o' the Lowes' CDoC GGGa LMil MBri MDun MOne
'Loch Rannoch' GChr GGGa GKir LRHS
'Loch Tummel' GGGa
lochiae (V) CEqu GGGa
'Lochinch Spinbur' GQui
Lodauric Group SReu
§ 'Lodauric Iceberg' ♀ GGGa LKna LMil SBrw SReu
'Lodbrit' SReu
§ Loderi Group CB&S SLdr
'Loderi Fairy Queen' NMun SLdr
'Loderi Fairyland' LHyd MDun NMun SLdr
§ 'Loderi Game Chick' CB&S CWri LHyd LMil MLea NMun SLdr SReu SSta
'Loderi Georgette' NMun SLdr
'Loderi Helen' NMun SLdr
§ 'Loderi Julie' NMun SLdr SReu
§ 'Loderi King George' ♀ CB&S CSam CWri GGGa ISea LHyd LKna LMil MDun MLea NMun SLdr SReu SSta
'Loderi Patience' LHyd NMun SLdr
'Loderi Pink Diamond' ♀ CWri LMil
'Loderi Pink Topaz' LHyd LMil MDun NMun SLdr
'Loderi Pretty Polly' CWri NMun
'Loderi Princess Marina' NMun SLdr
'Loderi Sir Edmund' LHyd NMun SLdr
'Loderi Sir Joseph Hooker' LHyd NMun SLdr
'Loderi Titan' SReu
§ 'Loderi Venus' ♀ CDoC CWri GGGa IOrc LHyd LKna LMil MDun MLea NMun SLdr SReu SSta
'Loderi White Diamond' LHyd NMun SLdr
'Loder's White' ♀ CWri ENot GGGa LHyd LKna LMil MLea NMun SBrw SLdr SReu SSta
'Lodestar' Last listed 1997
§ 'Logan Damaris' LHyd NMun SLdr SReu
'Loki' SLdr
'Lollipop' MLea
longesquamatum GGGa LMil NMun SLdr
longipes var. GGGa
    chienianum EN 4074
¶ - EGM 336 LMil
- EGM 337 LMil
- var. *longipes* C&H 7072 GGGa
- - C&H 7113 GGGa
longistylum GGGa NMun
'Longworth' NMun
'Looking Glass' Last listed 1998
lopsangianum See *R. thomsonii* subsp. *lopsangianum*
- LS&T 5651 NMun
loranthiflorum (V) Last listed 1997
'Lord Roberts' CB&S CHig CSam CTri CWri EBee ENot GChr GGGa GKir IOrc LKna

LMil LRHS MBar MBri MGos MLea NMun SBrw SLdr SReu WFar WWeb
'Lord Swaythling' LHyd SLdr
'Lori Eichelser' CSam LMil MAsh MDun MLea NDlv NHar
'Lorna' (EA) ENot GQui LMil
'Louis Pasteur' SBrw SReu
'Louisa' (EA) SSpi
'Louise Dowdle' (EA) GChr LMil
'Lovely William' SLdr
lowndesii WAbe
'Lucy Lou' CSam GGGa NHol
ludlowii GGGa
- x *viridescens* NHol
ludwigianum GGGa
lukiangense MDun NMun
§ - R 11275 NMun
§ - R 72 NMun
'Lullaby' (EA) LKna SLdr
'Lunar Queen' LHyd NMun SLdr
Luscombei Group SLdr
'Luscombei Splendens' SLdr
luteiflorum LMil
- KW 21040 GGGa NMun
- KW 21556 GGGa
- TW 390 Last listed 1997
lutescens CB&S CGre CHig CTre IOrc LMil LRHS MDun NMun SLdr SReu SSta WAbe WBod WWat
- 'Bagshot Sands' ♀ GGGa LHyd LMil LRHS SReu
- C&H 7124 GGGa
- PA Cox 5092 NHol
- PA Cox 5100 NHol
§ *luteum* (A) ♀ CB&S CDoC CMHG CPMA CTrG CTre CTri CWri GChr GGGa ISea LKna LMil LRHS MAsh MBar MBri MGos MLea NMun SBrw SLdr SReu SRms SSta WBod WPic WWat
¶ - 'Golden Comet' GGGa
§ *lyi* NMun
- KR 2861 GGGa
- KR 2962 GGGa
x *lysolepis* KW 4456 Last listed 1997
* 'Mac Ovata' CMac
macabeanum ♀ CB&S CDoC CHEx GGGa GKir LMil LRHS MDun NMun SLdr SPer SReu SSpi SSta WGer WHer
- deep cream CWri SLdr
- DT 10 GGGa
- KW 7724 NMun
- Reuthe's form SReu
- x *sinogrande* MDun SReu
macgregoriae (V) CEqu ERea
- P Woods 2646 (V) GGGa
macranthum See *R. indicum*
'Macranthum Roseum' (EA) SBod SReu
macrophyllum GGGa
macrosmithii See *R. argipeplum*
'Macrostemon' See *R.* (Obtusum Group) 'Macrostemon'
maculiferum NMun SLdr
- subsp. *anwheiense* See *R. anwheiense*
- Guiz 120* GGGa
- Guiz 121 GGGa
- Guiz 148 Last listed 1997
'Madame Albert Moser' LKna
'Madame de Bruin' LKna SBrw SLdr
'Madame F.V. Chauvin' Last listed 1998
'Madame Ida Rubenstein' SBrw
'Madame Knutz' Last listed 1998

'Madame Masson'	CHig CSam CWri GChr GGGa GKir LMil LRHS MAsh MGos MLea NMun SLdr SPer SReu SSta
'Madame van Hecke' (EA)	COtt EPfP GChr GKir MAsh MBri SBrw SLdr SReu WFar WGor
maddenii ♀	CGre LHyd LMil NMun SLdr
§ - subsp. *crassum* ♀	CTrw GGGa LMil NMun SLdr SReu WBod WPic
- - AC 708	NMun
§ - - Obtusifolium Group	NMun SLdr
§ - subsp. *maddenii*	NMun WAbe
§ - - Polyandrum Group	CB&S GQui ISea NMun SLdr
'Madeline's Yellow'	SLdr
'Mademoiselle Masson'	SBrw WFar
'Maestro'	LHyd
N 'Magnificum' (A)	Last listed 1998
magnificum	LMil NMun SLdr SReu
'Maharani'	GGGa
§ *makinoi* ♀	CEqu CHig GGGa LHyd LMil LRHS MDun NMun SLdr SReu SSta
mallotum	GGGa LHyd LMil MDun NMun SLdr SReu
- F 17853	Last listed 1997
- Farrer 815	Last listed 1997
'Malvaticum' (EA)	Last listed 1998
'Manda Sue'	LRHS MAsh WGor
Mandalay Group	LRHS SLdr
'Manderley'	MDun SBrw
manipurense	See *R. maddenii* subsp. *crassum* Obtusifolium Group
'Manor Hill'	SLdr
'Marcel Ménard'	SBrw SReu
'Marchioness of Lansdowne'	SBrw
'Marcia'	LHyd SLdr
'Mardi Gras'	GGGa
Margaret Dunn Group & cl.	CWri
'Margaret Falmouth'	SReu
'Margaret George' (EA)	LHyd SLdr
'Maria Elena' (EA/d)	Last listed 1998
'Marianne' (EA/d)	Last listed 1998
'Maricee'	GGGa MBri SLdr WAbe WGer
'Marie' (EA)	CMac
'Marie Curie'	SReu
'Marilee' (EA)	CDoC GKir LRHS MGos MOne
Mariloo Group	NMun SLdr
'Marinus Koster' ♀	LKna MAsh MBri SLdr
'Marion'	LMil
'Marion Merriman' (K)	LKna
'Marion Street' ♀	LHyd LMil NMun SLdr SReu
'Mark Turner'	SReu
'Markeeta's Flame'	Last listed 1999
'Markeeta's Prize' ♀	CDoC CSam CWri EBee GAri GGGa LMil LRHS MAsh MBri MGos MLan MLea NMun
'Marlene Peste'	Last listed 1999
'Marley Hedges'	GGGa
'Marlies' (K)	SLdr
'Marmot' (EA)	Last listed 1999
'Mars'	SBrw SLdr SReu
'Martha Hitchcock' (EA)	LKna SRms
'Martha Isaacson' (Ad)	MBri MGos SReu
'Martine' (Ad)	LKna MBri MGos SLdr WBod
martinianum	MDun NMun SLdr
aff. *martinianum* KW 21557	GGGa
'Maruschka' (EA)	GGGa
'Mary Drennen'	LMil
'Mary Fleming'	MDun NMun SBod SLdr WLRN
'Mary Forte'	SBrw
'Mary Helen' (EA)	CDoC GKir LHyd LRHS SCoo SReu WBod WPat
'Mary Meredith' (EA)	LHyd
'Mary Poppins'	EBee GKir LRHS MAsh SCoo
'Maryke'	LMil
'Master Mariner'	Last listed 1997
'Master of Elphinstone' (EA)	Last listed 1998
¶ 'Matador' ♀	LHyd
Matador Group & cl.	NMun SReu WBod
'Mauna Loa' (K)	LKna
'Maurice Skipworth'	CB&S
'Mavis Davis'	GGGa
maximum	GGGa NMun SLdr
- 'Weeldon's Red'	GGGa
'Maxine Childers'	LMil
§ 'Maxwellii' (EA)	CMac SLdr WBod
'May Day' ♀	CPne LHyd LRHS SReu
May Day Group & cl.	CB&S CSam CTrw CWri ISea LKna MBri MDun MGos NMun SLdr SSta WBod
'May Glow'	MGos
May Morn Group & cl.	SReu
'Mayor Johnstone'	GKir LRHS
'Mazurka' (K)	LKna
meddianum	GGGa NMun SLdr
- var. *atrokermesinum*	NMun SLdr
- - F 26476	NMun
- - KW 21006a	GGGa
- var. *meddianum* F 24219	SLdr
Medea Group	SLdr
Medusa Group	GGGa SReu
megacalyx	GGGa ISea
'Megan' (EA)	GGGa IOrc MAsh SLdr SReu
megaphyllum	See *R. basilicum*
megeratum	GGGa NMun SReu
- 'Bodnant'	WAbe WBod
- R 18861	SLdr
'Meicho' (EA)	GAri
mekongense	GGGa
- var. *mekongense*	SReu
§ - - KW 21079	Last listed 1997
§ - - KW 5829	NMun SLdr
- - Rubroluteum Group	See *R. viridescens* Rubroluteum Group
- - Viridescens Group	See *R. viridescens*
§ - var. *melinanthum*	NMun
- var. *rubrolineatum*	LRHS NMun
'Melford Lemon'	See *R.* 'Ilam Melford Lemon'
'Melina' (EA/d)	GGGa
melinanthum	See *R. mekongense* var. *melinanthum*
'Merganser' ♀	GGGa LMil LRHS MDun MLea NHol SReu WAbe
'Merlin' (EA)	LRHS SLdr
'Merlin' misapplied	See *R.* (Hawk Group) 'Hawk Merlin'
Metis Group	WBod
metternichii	See *R. degronianum* subsp. *heptamerum*
- var. *pentamerum*	See *R. degronianum* subsp. *degronianum*
'Mi Amor'	LMil
'Michael Hill' (EA)	CB&S COtt CTrh LHyd MAsh MNaF SSpi
'Michael Waterer' ♀	MDun NMun SLdr
'Michael's Pride' ♀	CB&S GQui NMun
micranthum	CGre GGGa MDun NMun SLdr
microgynum	NMun SLdr
- F 14242	GGGa NMun SLdr
microleucum	See *R. orthocladum* var. *microleucum*

micromeres	See *R. leptocarpum*
microphyton	Last listed 1997
'Midnight Mystique'	GGGa
'Midori' (EA)	Last listed 1998
'Midsummer'	SLdr
'Mikado' (EA)	See *R. kaempferi* 'Mikado'
'Mikado' (hybrid)	LRHS
mimetes	NMun SLdr
§ - var. *simulans*	NMun SLdr
- - F 20428	GGGa NMun SLdr
'Mimi' (EA)	CMac LHyd
'Mimra'	SLdr
'Ming'	See *R.* 'Ilam Ming'
¶ *miniatum*	GGGa
'Minterne Cinnkeys'	MDun
minus	GQui
§ - var. *minus*	SLdr
§ - - Carolinianum Group	LMil
§ - - Punctatum Group	MBar
'Misomogiri'	CHig
'Miss Muffet' (EA)	SLdr
'Mizu-no-yamabuki' (EA)	Last listed 1998
§ 'Moerheim' ♀	GKir LRHS MAsh MBar MDun
	MOne NHol SLdr SReu SSta WStI
§ 'Moerheim's Pink'	LHyd LKna LMil MDun NHol SLdr
	SPer
'Moerheim's Scarlet'	LKna
'Moffat'	SReu
'Moidart' (Vs)	LMil SPer
'Moira' (EA)	LRHS
'Moira Salmon' (EA)	LHyd SLdr
'Molalla Red' (K)	LMil
§ *molle* subsp. *japonicum*	GGGa LHyd
(A)	
- subsp. *japonicum*	GGGa
JR 871 (A)	
- subsp. *molle* C&H	GGGa
7181 (A)	
mollicomum	NMun
- F 10347	NMun
- F 30940	See *R. hemitrichotum* F 30940
Mollis orange (M)	MBar NBlu SRms
Mollis pink (M)	GGGa MBar SRms
Mollis red (M)	MBar SRms
Mollis salmon (M)	GGGa GQui
Mollis yellow (M)	GQui MBar NBlu SRms
'Molly Ann'	CDoC GGGa LRHS MDun SReu
	WGor
'Molly Miller'	LRHS
'Monaco'	CWri SLdr
monanthum CCH&H 8133	GGGa
'Monica'	Last listed 1998
monosematum	See *R. pachytrichum* var.
	monosematum
montiganum	ISea
¶ - AC 2060	LMil
montroseanum	LMil MDun NMun SLdr WCru
* - 'Baravalla'	CWri GGGa
- 'Benmore'	NMun SLdr
'Moon Maiden' (EA)	CDoC GQui LMil SLdr SVil
Moonbeam Group	LKna
Moonshine Group & cl.	SReu
'Moonshine Bright'	LHyd MDun SLdr SReu
'Moonshine Crescent'	SReu
'Moonshine Supreme'	LKna SReu
Moonstone Group (hybrid)	CB&S GAri MAsh MBar MDun
	MLea NMun SLdr
- pink-tipped	NHol
'Moonstone Yellow'	GGGa
'Moonwax'	CB&S CSam CWri SMur
§ 'Morgenrot' ♀	EMui GChr GGGa LMil LRHS MBri
	MGos SReu

morii ♀	CWri GGGa LHyd LMil MDun
	NMun SLdr
- ETOT 90	ISea
- W/A 10955	SLdr
'Morning Cloud' ♀	CABP GKir IOrc LHyd LMil LRHS
	MBar MBri MNaF NDlv NMun
	SBrw SLdr SReu
'Morning Magic'	CWri LHyd NMun SBrw SLdr
Morning Red	See *R.* 'Morgenrot'
'Morvah'	SLdr
'Moser's Maroon'	CWri LHyd LKna LMil LRHS
	MGos NMun SBrw SLdr WGwG
'Moser's Strawberry'	LKna
'Motet' (K/d)	LKna
'Moth'	GGGa NHol
'Mother Greer'	GGGa
'Mother of Pearl'	LKna SBrw SLdr SReu
'Mother Theresa'	LKna
'Mother's Day' (EA) ♀	More than 30 suppliers
§ *moulmainense*	Last listed 1999
'Mount Everest'	GGGa LHyd LMil SBrw SLdr SReu
	SSta
'Mount Rainier' (K)	LMil SReu
'Mount Saint Helens'	GGGa LMil MLea
'Mount Seven Star'	See *R. nakaharae* 'Mount Seven
	Star'
'Mountain Star'	SLdr
moupinense ♀	CB&S CHig ERea GGGa IDee
	LHyd NMun SLdr SReu
- C&K 140	GGGa
- pink	GGGa MDun WAbe
'Mozart' (EA)	SBod WBod
'Mrs A.T. de la Mare' ♀	CWri ENot GGGa IOrc LHyd
	LKna LMil MBri NMun SBrw SLdr
	SReu SSta
'Mrs Anthony Waterer' (O)	LKna
'Mrs Anthony Waterer'	LKna SBrw
(hybrid)	
'Mrs Ashley Slocock'	SReu
'Mrs Betty Robertson'	CHig EBee MAsh MLea SReu
'Mrs C.B. van Nes'	SReu
Mrs C. Whitner Group	NMun SLdr
'Mrs Charles E. Pearson' ♀	CB&S CWri ENot LHyd LKna LMil
	MLea NMun SBrw SLdr SPer SReu
'Mrs Davies Evans' ♀	LHyd LKna MBar SBrw SReu SSta
'Mrs Dick Thompson'	SReu
'Mrs Donald Graham'	SReu
'Mrs Doorenbos'	CMac
'Mrs E.C. Stirling'	LHyd LKna SRms
'Mrs Emil Hager' (EA)	LHyd
'Mrs Furnivall' ♀	CB&S CDoC CWri EPfP GGGa
	LHyd LKna LMil LRHS MBri MGos
	MLea SLdr SReu WGer
'Mrs G.W. Leak'	CB&S CSam ENot EPfP GGGa ISea
	LHyd LKna LMil MAsh MBri MLea
	NMun SBrw SLdr SPer SReu
'Mrs Helen Koster'	LKna
'Mrs Henry Agnew'	NMun SLdr
'Mrs J.C. Williams'	LKna LMil NMun SLdr
'Mrs J.G. Millais'	LKna LMil NMun SLdr
'Mrs James Horlick'	NMun SLdr
'Mrs John Waterer'	SBrw
'Mrs Kingsmill'	SLdr
'Mrs Lindsay Smith'	LKna SBrw
'Mrs Lionel de	MDun NMun SReu
Rothschild' ♀	
Mrs Lionel de Rothschild	LKna
Group & cl.	
'Mrs P.D. Williams' ♀	LKna SBrw SReu
'Mrs Peter Koster' (M)	SLdr
'Mrs Philip Martineau'	LKna
'Mrs R.S. Holford' ♀	LKna NMun SBrw SLdr

'Mrs T.H. Lowinsky' ♀	CHig EPfP GCHN GGGa LKna LMil MBri MDun MGos NMun NWea SBrw SLdr SPer SReu SSta
'Mrs W.C. Slocock'	LKna MAsh MBri MDun NMun SBrw SLdr SPer SReu SSta
'Mrs William Agnew'	LKna SLdr
'Mucronatum'	See *R.* x *mucronatum*
§ x *mucronatum* (EA)	CHig LRHS NMun SLdr SRms WPic
'Mucronatum Amethystinum'	See *R.* 'Amethystinum'
mucronulatum	GGGa LHyd LMil NMun SLdr WAbe
- B&SWJ 786	WCru
- var. *chejuense*	See *R. mucronulatum* var. *taquetii*
- 'Cornell Pink' ♀	GGGa LHyd LMil
- 'Mahogany Red'	GGGa
§ - var. *taquetii*	GGGa
- 'Winter Brightness' ♀	Last listed 1996
multicolor (V)	CEqu
§ 'Multiflorum'	SReu
'Muncaster Bells'	NMun
'Muncaster Hybrid'	NMun
'Muncaster Mist'	NMun SLdr
'Muriel'	SLdr
'My Lady'	GGGa
§ *myrtifolium*	LHyd LMil SLdr
nakaharae (EA)	NMun SLdr SReu
§ - 'Mariko' (EA)	EPot GGGa LHyd LMil MBar MBro MGos NHol SLdr WPat WPyg
§ - 'Mount Seven Star' (EA)	CHig ECho GGGa LHyd LMil MAsh MBri MBro NHol SLdr SReu WAbe WPat
§ - orange (EA)	GKir LMil LRHS MAsh MNaF MOne SBrw SReu SSta
- pink (EA)	CHig GKir LHyd LMil LRHS SBrw SLdr SPer SReu SSta
- red (EA)	SLdr
- 'Scree' (EA)	SReu
'Nakahari Orange'	See *R. nakaharae* orange
'Nakahari-mariko'	See *R. nakaharae* 'Mariko'
nakotiltum	NMun SLdr
'Nancy Evans'	CDoC COtt CWri GGGa GKir ISea LMil LRHS MAsh MDun MLea MNaF SBrw SPer SReu SSpi
'Nancy of Robinhill' (EA)	LHyd
'Nancy Waterer' (G) ♀	MBri SLdr SReu
'Nanki Poo' (EA)	LHyd SLdr
'Naomi' (EA)	GQui IOrc LKna LMil LRHS SLdr
Naomi Group & cl.	CSam CWri ISea LKna MLea SReu
- 'Paris'	See *R.* 'Paris'
'Naomi Astarte'	LKna MDun SLdr
'Naomi Early Dawn'	NMun
'Naomi Glow'	Last listed 1997
'Narcissiflorum' (G/d) ♀	CDoC ENot IOrc LHyd LKna LMil SPer SReu
'Naselle'	GGGa LMil
'Nassau' (EA/d)	Last listed 1998
'Nelly de Bruin'	SBrw
neriiflorum	GGGa ISea LMil MDun NMun SLdr SReu SSpi
- Bu 287	GGGa
§ - subsp. *neriiflorum* Euchaites Group	NMun SLdr
- - L&S 1352	GGGa
- - Phoenicodum Group	Last listed 1997
- - - Farrer 877	GGGa NMun
§ - subsp. *phaedropum*	NMun SLdr
- - C&H 422	NMun
- - CCH&H 8125	GGGa
- - KR 1778	Last listed 1997

¶ - - KR 5593	LMil
- - KW 6845*	NMun
- - KW 8521	Last listed 1998
- S&F 366	ISea
- S&F 375	ISea
Neriihaem Group	NMun
nervulosum Sleumer (V)	GGGa
'Nestor'	SReu
'Nettie' (EA)	Last listed 1998
'Netty Koster'	MBri SBrw
'New Comet'	LHyd LMil NMun SLdr SReu
'New Moon'	SLdr SReu
'Newcomb's Sweetheart'	LMil MDun SMur
'Niagara' (EA) ♀	CTrh ENot EPfP GQui LHyd LMil WBod
'Nichola' (EA)	SBod SBrw SReu
'Nico' (EA)	CMac GKir LRHS MAsh MBri WBod WPat
'Nicoletta'	GGGa LMil MAsh
'Night Light' (K)	GKir
'Night Sky'	CDoC COtt GGGa LHyd LMil MBri MDun MLea MOne NHol
'Nightingale'	SReu
nigroglandulosum	GGGa
¶ 'Nihon-no-hasa' (A)	CHig
x *nikomontanum*	LMil
nilagiricum	See *R. arboreum* subsp. *nilagiricum*
'Nimbus'	LKna LMil SLdr
Nimrod Group	CWri NMun SLdr
'Nishiki' (EA)	CMac
nitens	See *R. calostrotum* subsp. *riparium* Nitens Group
nitidulum	NMun WAbe
- var. *nitidulum* C 5059	Last listed 1998
- - C 5107	Last listed 1998
- var. *omeiense* KR 185	GGGa LMil NHol
nivale subsp. *boreale* Ramosissimum Group	GGGa
§ - - Stictophyllum Group	GGGa LMil
- subsp. *nivale* Sch 2269	Last listed 1997
niveum ♀	GGGa LMil LRHS MDun NMun SLdr SReu
- 'Clyne Castle'	SLdr
- 'Nepal'	LHyd
- 'Tower Court'	SLdr
'Noble Mountain'	LMil
nobleanum	See *R.* Nobleanum Group
§ Nobleanum Group	GGGa LHyd LKna LMil NMun SLdr SSta WBod
'Nobleanum Album'	LHyd LKna LMil NMun SLdr SReu SSta WBod
'Nobleanum Coccineum'	ISea LMil NMun SLdr SReu
'Nobleanum Lamellen'	SLdr
'Nobleanum Venustum'	CWri ISea LHyd LKna LMil SBrw SReu SSta WBod
'Nofretete'	GGGa
¶ 'Nora'	WPic
'Nordlicht' (EA)	SLdr
N 'Norma' (R/d) ♀	ENot LMil MBri SReu
Norman Shaw Group & cl.	LHyd
'Northern Hi-Lights' (A)	GKir LRHS SLdr
'Northern Lights'	See *R.* 'Arctic Glow'
'Northern Star'	GKir SLdr
¶ 'Northern Starburst'	LMil
'Northlight'	MBri
notiale (V)	Last listed 1998
'Nova Zembla'	EPfP GChr GGGa LRHS MBar MGos SBrw SLdr SReu SSta WGwG WStI
¶ 'Nuccio's Spring Charm' (EA)	MAsh

nudiflorum	See *R. periclymenoides*
* ***nummularia*** L&S 17294	Last listed 1998
nuttallii ♀	GGGa ISea LMil SLdr
'Oban'	GGGa LMil MDun MLea NHol
	WAbe
Obtusum Group (EA)	LHyd
§ - 'Macrostemon' (EA)	WBod
obtusum f.*amoenum*	See *R.* 'Amoenum'
occidentale (A) ♀	CGre GGGa LMil SLdr SReu
- forms (A)	GGGa
¶ ***ochraceum***	LMil
- C&H 7052	GGGa
'Odee Wright' ♀	CWri GChr GGGa LRHS MDun
	MLea NMun SLdr SReu
¶ 'Odoratum' (Ad)	MLea
'Oh-Too'	SBrw
'Oi-no-mezame' (EA)	LHyd
'Old Copper'	CWri LNet MBri SBrw WGer
'Old Gold' (K)	SReu
'Old Port'	LHyd SBrw SReu SSta
¶ 'Old Sensation'	MAsh
Oldenburgh Group	SLdr
oldhamii (EA)	CTre NMun
- ETOT 60 (EA)	Last listed 1998
- ETOT 601 (A)	GGGa
'Olga'	LHyd LKna LMil NMun SBrw SLdr
	SReu SSta
'Olga Mezitt'	GGGa LHyd NHol
¶ ***oligocarpum*** Guiz 148*	GGGa
'Olin O. Dobbs'	Last listed 1998
'Olive'	LHyd LKna LMil WBod
'Olive Judson'	Last listed 1998
'Oliver Cromwell'	SReu
Olympic Lady Group	LHyd SLdr
'Olympic Sunrise'	LMil
Omar Group	MBar
§ 'One Thousand Butterflies'	COtt CWri GGGa MAsh MDun
	MLea
N 'Ophelia'	SCam SLdr
'Oporto'	SLdr
'Optima' (EA)	Last listed 1997
'Orange Beauty' (EA) ♀	CDoC CMac CTrh GGGa LHyd
	LKna MAsh MBar MGos NMun
	SBod SLdr SReu SSta WBod WFar
	WPic
'Orange King' (EA)	WLRN
'Orange Scout'	SLdr WGor WWal
'Orangengold'	GGGa
orbiculare	CWri GGGa IDee LHyd LMil LRHS
	MDun NMun SLdr SSta
- C&K 230	GGGa
§ - subsp.*cardiobasis*	NMun SLdr
- subsp.*orbiculare* W/V 1519	
	NMun
- Sandling Park form	SReu
'Orchid Lights'	GKir LRHS SLdr
'Oregon Trail'	Last listed 1997
Oreocinn Group	Last listed 1999
oreodoxa	LMil NMun SLdr SReu
§ - var.*fargesii* ♀	GGGa IOrc LMil NMun SLdr
§ - - Erubescens Group	NMun SLdr
- Knott 348	NMun
- var.*oreodoxa* EN 4212	GGGa
- - W/A 4245	NMun
- var.*shensiense*	GGGa
oreotrephes	CB&S IOrc LHyd LMil MDun
	NMun SLdr SReu
- C&Cu 9449	Last listed 1999
- 'Davidian's Favourite'	Last listed 1997
§ - Exquisitum Group	ISea SReu
- F 20489	NMun
- F 20629	NMun

- KW 9509	NMun SLdr
- R 96	Last listed 1997
- S&F 640	ISea
- Timeteum Group	SReu
aff.***oreotrephes*** C&V	GGGa
9557	
Orestes Group	SLdr
orthocladum	LHyd LMil MDun
§ - var.*microleucum* ♀	GGGa ISea LMil NMun WAbe
	WPat
- var.*orthocladum*	GGGa NHol
F 20488	
'Oryx' (O)	LKna
'Osmar'	CB&S GGGa MDun MGos
'Ostara'	CB&S COtt GGGa MBri MGos
'Ostbo's Low Yellow'	SLdr
'Ostfriesland'	Last listed 1999
'Ouchiyama'	LKna
'Oudijk's Favorite'	Last listed 1999
'Oudijk's Sensation'	CDoC CTrh GCHN GGGa LKna
	MGos MOne
(Our Kate Group)	SLdr
'Our Kate'	
'Ovation'	NHol
ovatum (A)	CB&S NMun WBod
- CNW 548	ISea
- red CNW 557	LMil
- W/A 1391 (A)	NMun
- white CNW 548	LMil
Oxlip Group	Last listed 1998
'Oxydol' (K) ♀	MAsh
'P. den Ouden'	SBrw
x *williamsianum*	
§ ***pachypodum***	GGGa LMil
pachysanthum ♀	CDoC LHyd LMil MDun NMun
	SLdr SMur SReu SSpi
- 'Crosswater'	LMil
- x *morii*	Last listed 1997
- x *proteoides*	GGGa
- RV 72/001	GGGa NMun SLdr
pachytrichum	GGGa LRHS NMun SLdr
- C&K 229	Last listed 1998
§ - var.*monosematum*	ISea SLdr
- - CNW 953	LMil
- - CNW 956	GGGa
- - W/V 1522	NMun
- var.*pachytrichum*	LMil
'Sesame'	
- - W/A 1203	NMun
'Palestrina' (EA) ♀	CB&S CBrm CChe CHig CMac
	CTrh EPfP IOrc LHyd LKna LRHS
	MGos NMun SBod SBrw SLdr SPer
	SReu SSta WBod WFar
'Pallas' (G)	MBri SReu
'Palma'	See *R. parmulatum* 'Palma'
'Pamela Miles' (EA)	LHyd
'Pamela-Louise'	Last listed 1997
'Pancake'	CMac
'Panda' (EA)	CDoC CMac GGGa LHyd LMil
	LRHS MBar MBri MDun NDlv
	SBrw SCoo SLdr SPer SReu WAbe
panteumorphum	See *R. x erythrocalyx*
	Panteumorphum Group
'Papaya Punch'	LMil MDun
papillatum	NMun SLdr
'Paprika Spiced'	CDoC COtt CWri LMil MAsh MBri
	MDun MLea MNaF SLdr
'Parade' (A)	LMil
'Paradise' (EA)	CTrh
'Paradise Pink' (EA)	ENot
paradoxum	SLdr
- C&K 228	GGGa

– CC&H 3906	GGGa
'Paramount' (K/d)	LKna
§ 'Paris'	LHyd
'Parisienne'	Last listed 1997
parmulatum	LMil MDun NMun SLdr
¶ – C&C 7538	GGGa
– KW 5875	NMun
– mauve	NMun SLdr
– 'Ocelot'	GGGa LHyd MDun NMun SLdr
	WBod
§ – 'Palma'	Last listed 1998
– pink	GGGa NMun
parryae ♀	GGGa
'Party Pink'	CWri LMil SPer
'Patricia's Day'	Last listed 1998
'Patty Bee' ♀	CB&S CDoC CSam CTrh CWri EPot
	GChr GGGa GKir IMGH LHyd LMil
	LRHS MAsh MBar MBri MDun
	MGos MLea MNaF NHar NHol
	SBod SReu SSpi SSta WAbe WFar
patulum	See *R. pemakoense* Patulum
	Group
'Pavane' (K)	LKna
'Peace'	GGGa NMun
'Peach Blossom'	See *R*. 'Saotome'
'Peach Lady'	SLdr
'Pearl Diver'	Last listed 1997
'Peep-bo' (EA)	LHyd SLdr
'Peeping Tom'	CDoC GKir LMil LRHS MAsh
	MDun MNaF NMun SReu
'Peggy Bannier'	SBrw
'Pelopidas'	SBrw
pemakoense	CTrG GGGa LHyd MBar MGos
	NHol NMun SLdr SReu WAbe
§ – Patulum Group	GGGa MAsh MBar MBri NHol
	NMun SLdr WPat WPyg
¶ 'Pemakofairy'	WAbe
'Pematit Cambridge'	SBod
pendulum	LMil
– CH&M 3094	GGGa
– LS&T 6660	GGGa
Penelope Group	SReu
'Penheale Blue' ♀	CDoC CTre CTrh GGGa GOrc
	LMil LRHS MAsh NDlv NHol SLdr
	WGer
Penjerrick Group & cl.	Last listed 1997
'Penjerrick Cream'	LHyd NMun SLdr
'Penjerrick Pink'	LHyd NMun SLdr
pennivenium	See *R. tanastylum* var.
	pennivenium
'Pennywhistle' (V)	Last listed 1999
'Penrose'	Last listed 1999
'Percy Wiseman' ♀	CB&S CDoC CSam CWri EBee
	GChr GGGa GKir IOrc LHyd LMil
	LNet LRHS MAsh MBar MBri
	MDun MGos MLea NDlv NHol
	NMun SBrw SLdr SReu SSta
peregrinum	NMun SLdr
'Perfect'	Last listed 1999
'Perfect Lady'	LMil LRHS
§ **periclymenoides** (A)	GGGa LMil SLdr
I 'Periwinkle' (V)	CEqu
'Persil' (K) ♀	CB&S CSam ENot EPfP GChr
	GGGa LHyd LKna LRHS MAsh
	MBar MBri MDun MGos SBrw
	SCoo SLdr SPer SReu WBod
§ 'Persimmon'	LKna NMun SLdr
¶ 'Peste's Fire Light'	GGGa
'Peter Alan'	Last listed 1998
'Peter Berg'	MGos
'Peter John Mezitt'	See *R*. (PJM Group) 'Peter John
	Mezitt'

'Peter Koster' (hybrid) ♀	CWri NMun SBrw SLdr WStI
'Petrouchka' (K)	LKna MBri
phaedropum	See *R. neriiflorum* subsp.
	phaedropum
phaeochrysum	GGGa MDun NMun SLdr
– var. *agglutinatum*	GGGa MDun NMun
– – EGM 134	LMil
§ – var. *levistratum*	NMun SLdr SReu
– – EGM 143	LMil
– McLaren cup winner	NMun
– var. *phaeochrysum*	LMil
EGM 129	
– – 'Greenmantle'	NMun SLdr
– USDAPI 59029/ R11323	NMun
'Phalarope'	GGGa LRHS MBar MDun MGos
	NHol SReu WAbe WBod
'Pheasant Tail'	NMun SLdr
'Phoebe' (R/d)	SReu
phoenicodum	See *R. neriiflorum* subsp.
	neriiflorum Phoenicodum Group
pholidotum	See *R. heliolepis* var. *heliolepis* F
	6762
'Phyllis Korn'	CWri LHyd LMil MAsh MDun
	MLea NLar SBrw SLdr SPer
'Piccolo' (K/d)	LKna
§ **piercei**	GGGa LMil MDun NMun SLdr
– KW 11040	GGGa NMun
Pilgrim Group & cl.	LKna NMun
pingianum	NMun SLdr
– EGM 304	LMil
– KR 150	NMun SLdr
– KR 184	GGGa
'Pink and Sweet' (A)	CDoC LMil MLea
'Pink Bedspread'	SReu
'Pink Bountiful'	LKna
'Pink Bride'	SLdr
'Pink Cherub' ♀	CWri EBee EMui ENot LHyd LRHS
	MBar MOne NMun SLdr SReu
N 'Pink Delight'	ERea LKna LRHS MAsh SLdr
	WBod
'Pink Drift'	ENot GChr ISea LKna MAsh MBar
	MDun MGos NHar NHol NMun
	NWea SBod SLdr WAbe WGwG
'Pink Frills'	Last listed 1998
'Pink Ghost'	NMun SLdr
'Pink Gin'	LMil
'Pink Glory'	NMun SLdr
'Pink Leopard'	ISea LMil MDun MLea NMun
'Pink Pancake' (EA)	CB&S CTrh GQui LMil LRHS
	MGos MOne SReu SSpi SVil
'Pink Pearl' (hybrid)	CB&S CTri ENot GChr GGGa
	GKir ISea LHyd LKna LMil LRHS
	MAsh MBar MDun MGos NHol
	NMun NWea SBod SBrw SLdr
	SPer SReu SSta WBod WFar
'Pink Pebble' ♀	CTrw LHyd NMun SLdr SReu
'Pink Perfection'	MBar MGos NMun SBrw SLdr
	SReu WFar
'Pink Pillow'	SReu
'Pink Poppet' (V)	CEqu
'Pink Rosette'	LKna
N 'Pink Ruffles'	ENot WBod
'Pink Sensation'	LRHS MBri MDun
'Pinkerton'	LHyd LKna
'Pintail'	GGGa LMil WAbe
'Pipaluk'	NMun
'Pipit'	GGGa WAbe
'Pippa' (EA) ♀	CMac CTrG
PJM Group	CWri MAsh MBri MLea SSta
§ – 'Peter John Mezitt' ♀	LHyd LMil NMun SLdr SReu
	WBod WGer WLRN
'PJM Elite'	GGGa

x *planecostatum* (V) — Last listed 1997
planetum — Last listed 1998
pleistanthum — Last listed 1997
- F 15002 — Last listed 1998
- R 11288 — See *R. rigidum* R 11288
pocophorum — GGGa NMun SLdr
- forms — NMun
§ - var. *hemidartum* — GGGa NMun SLdr
- KW 21075 — See *R. coelicum* KW 21075
§ - var. *pocophorum* — SLdr
F 21830
- - USDAPI 59190/R11201 — NMun
pogonostylum — See *R. irroratum* subsp. *pogonostylum*
'Point Defiance' — CWri GGGa LMil MDun SLdr
'Polar Bear' (EA) — LRHS MBar MDun MGos SLdr
¶ 'Polar Bear' ♀ — LHyd SReu SSpi
Polar Bear Group & cl. — CDoC COtt CSam CWri GAri GGGa GKir ISea LMil MAsh MLea NMun SLdr WGer
'Polar Haven' (EA) — LKna
'Polar Sea' — Last listed 1999
'Polaris' — ENot LMil LRHS MBri MGos MNaF SReu
'Polgrain' — Last listed 1998
§ *poluninii* — GGGa
polyandrum — See *R. maddenii* subsp. *maddenii* Polyandrum Group
'Polycinn' — Last listed 1997
§ *polycladum* — GGGa LHyd LMil LRHS MAsh MDun MLea SBrw
§ - Scintillans Group — GDra MBar MBri MLea NHol NMun SLdr WPic
¶ - - 'Policy' ♀ — GGGa SReu
polylepis — GGGa NMun
- C&K 284 — GGGa
- EGM 351 — LMil
- EN 3619 — Last listed 1998
§ *ponticum* — CDoC CWri GChr GGGa LHyd LMil MBar MGos MLea NWea SBrw SLdr SPer WFar
- AC&H 205 — GGGa
- 'Aureomarginatum' — SBrw
- 'Cheiranthifolium' — NMun SLdr
- 'Foliis Purpureis' — CWri SReu
- 'Roseum' — SBrw
§ - 'Silver Edge' (v) — LMil SBrw SLdr SMur
- 'Variegatum' (v) — CB&S CHig EBee EBrP EBre ENot GGGa GKir IOrc ISea LBCl LBSe LBre LRHS MAsh MBBe MBar MBri MGos NBlu NMun SBre SReu SRms SSta WGer WWeb
'Pooh-Bah' (EA) — LHyd
'Pook' — LHyd
'Popacatapetl' — SLdr SReu
¶ 'Popcorn' (V) — GGGa
'Port Knap' (EA) — LKna
'Port Wine' (EA) — LKna
'Potlatch' — GGGa
poukhanense — See *R. yedoense* var. *poukhanense*
'Powder Puff' — Last listed 1998
§ 'Praecox' ♀ — CB&S CTrw EBee ENot GChr GGGa LHyd LKna LMil LRHS MAsh MBar MBri MGos NHol NMun SBod SBrw SLdr SPer SReu SSta WBod WFar WGwG
praecox — See *R.* 'Praecox'
- 'Emasculum' — See *R.* 'Emasculum'
praestans — GGGa LMil MDun NMun SLdr
- KW 13369 — NMun
- PA Cox 6025A — GGGa
praeteritum — Last listed 1998

praevernum — GGGa LMil NMun SLdr SReu
§ *prattii* — CWri LMil MDun NMun SLdr
- EGM 147 — LMil
'Prawn' — LKna SReu
Prelude Group & cl. — SLdr
preptum — GGGa SLdr
'President Roosevelt' (v) — GChr GKir IOrc LKna LNet LRHS MAsh MDun MGos NMun SBrw SLdr SReu SSta WWeb
'Pretty Girl' — LKna
'Pretty Woman' — GGGa
'Pride of Leonardslee' — SLdr
'Pridenjoy' — LMil
'Prima Donna' — LMil SReu
primuliflorum — GGGa LMil LRHS MDun WAbe
- 'Doker-La' — LMil LRHS MDun WAbe
- KW 4160 — NMun
- PA Cox 6136 white — GGGa
'Prince Camille de Rohan' — LMil SBrw
'Prince of Wales' (EA) — SBrw
'Princess Alice' ♀ — CB&S CGre CHig LHyd NMun SLdr WAbe WPic
'Princess Anne' ♀ — CMHG CSam ENot GDra GGGa GKir LHyd LMil LRHS MAsh MBar MDun MGos MLea NMun SBod SBrw SLdr SPer SReu SSta WAbe
'Princess Ida' (EA) — LHyd SLdr
'Princess Juliana' — WBod WGor
'Princess Margaret of Windsor' (K) — GQui
'Princess Margaret Toth' — Last listed 1999
principis — LMil MDun NMun SLdr
- C&V 9547 — GGGa
¶ - 'Lost Horizon' KW 5656 — LMil
- LS&E 15831 — NMun
§ - Vellereum Group — NMun SLdr
- - 'Far Horizon' KW 5656 — SLdr
- - KW 5656 — NMun
§ *prinophyllum* (A) — LMil
'Prins Bernhard' (EA) — IOrc LKna MAsh SLdr
'Prinses Juliana' (EA) — SLdr SReu WFar
'Professor Hugo de Vries' ♀ — LKna MGos SBrw SReu
'Professor J.H. Zaayer' — MGos SBrw
pronum — GGGa
- x *proteoides* — GGGa
- R 151* — NMun
- R.B. Cooke form — GGGa
- Towercourt form — GGGa
§ 'Prostigiatum' — MGos
prostigiatum — See *R.* 'Prostigiatum'
prostratum — See *R. saluenense* subsp. *chameunum* Prostratum Group
proteoides — GGGa
* - 'Ascreavie' — GGGa
- C 6542a — GGGa
- EGM 281 — LMil
- KGB 700 — GGGa
- R 151 — NMun
protistum — LMil NMun SLdr
§ - var. *giganteum* — LMil NMun SLdr SReu
- KR 1986 — GGGa
- KW 8069 — NMun
pruniflorum — GGGa NMun SLdr
- KW 7038 — See *R. brachyanthum* subsp. *hypolepidotum* KW 7038
prunifolium (A) — LMil SLdr
- 'Summer Sunset' (A) — NMun
przewalskii — GGGa NMun SLdr
- C&K 370 — GGGa
- CH&M 2545 — Last listed 1999
- subsp. *dabanshanense* — GGGa
- PA Cox 5073 — GGGa

pseudochrysanthum ♀	GGGa LHyd LMil MDun NMun SLdr SReu SSta
- dwarf	WAbe
- ETE 442	GGGa
- ETE 443	GGGa
- ETOT 162	Last listed 1997
- ETOT 164	Last listed 1997
- ETOT 167	ISea
Psyche Group	See *R.* Wega Group
'Psyche' (EA)	MDun
'Ptarmigan' ♀	CB&S CDoC GChr GGGa LHyd LMil MBar MDun MGos MLea NHar NHol NMun SBod SBrw SLdr SPer SReu SSta WBod WFar WPat
pubescens	LMil SLdr
- KW 3953	GGGa
pubicostatum	LMil
- CNW 906	ISea
- CNW 927	GGGa
§ 'Pucella' (G) ♀	MAsh SLdr SReu
pudorosum	NMun SLdr
- L&S 2752	GGGa
'Puget Sound'	SLdr
'Pulchrum Maxwellii'	See *R.* 'Maxwellii'
pumilum	GCrs GDra GGGa MDun NMun WAbe
'Puncta'	GGGa NHol
punctatum	See *R. minus* var. *minus* Punctatum Group
purdomii	GGGa SLdr
'Purple Diamond'	See *R.* Diamant Group purple
'Purple Emperor'	LKna
'Purple Gem'	NHar NHol
purple Glenn Dale	Last listed 1997
'Purple Heart'	ENot
'Purple Peterli'	GGGa
'Purple Queen' (EA/d)	Last listed 1999
'Purple Splendor' (EA)	CMac CTrh EBee IOrc LKna MGos SLdr
'Purple Splendour' ♀	CB&S CHig CWri EBee ENot GChr GGGa LHyd LKna LMil LRHS MAsh MBar MBri MDun MGos MLea NMun NWea SBrw SLdr SReu SSta WFar
'Purple Triumph' (EA)	CB&S IOrc LKna LMil NMun SCam SLdr SReu SSta WBod
'Purpur Geisha'	GGGa
'Purpurtraum' (A)	GGGa
Quaver Group	SRms
'Queen Alice'	GKir LRHS MDun
'Queen Anne's'	LMil
'Queen Elizabeth II' ♀	LHyd LMil SLdr SPer SReu SSta
Queen Emma	See *R.* 'Koningin Emma'
'Queen Mary'	MBar SBrw
'Queen Mother'	See *R.* 'The Queen Mother'
¶ 'Queen of Hearts' ♀	LHyd
Queen of Hearts Group & cl.	CWri NMun SLdr
'Queen Souriya'	SReu
Queen Wilhelmina	See *R.* 'Koningin Wilhelmina'
quinquefolium (A) ♀	LMil NMun SLdr
racemosum	CB&S CGre LMil MBar MDun NMun SLdr SReu SSpi
- AC 719	NMun
- ACE 1367	WAbe
- 'Glendoick'	GGGa
- 'Rock Rose' ex R 11265 ♀	CWri EPfP GGGa LHyd LMil MBri NMun
- S&F 365	ISea
- SSNY 47	GGGa
- x ***tephropeplum***	MBar
- x ***trichocladum*** SBEC	NHol
- TW 385	Last listed 1997
- 'White Lace'	LHyd SReu
'Racil'	LHyd LKna MBar MDun MGos MLea
'Racoon' (EA)	GGGa
radicans	See *R. calostrotum* subsp. *keleticum* Radicans Group
'Radistrotum'	SLdr
'Rainbow'	LKna NMun SLdr
'Ramapo' ♀	GChr GGGa GKir LMil LRHS MBar MDun MGos MLea MNaF MOne NHar NHol NLAp NMen SBrw SPer SReu SSta WAbe WBod
ramsdenianum	GGGa NMun SLdr
¶ - KR 5619	LMil
'Rangoon'	Last listed 1998
'Raphael de Smet' (G/d)	SReu
rarum (V)	CEqu
'Rashomon' (EA)	LHyd SLdr SReu WBod
'Raspberry Delight' (K/d)	Last listed 1999
'Raspberry Ripple'	LKna SReu
ravum	See *R. cuneatum* Ravum Group
'Razorbill' ♀	CDoC GGGa LHyd LMil MAsh MBri MDun MGos MLea NHar WAbe
recurvoides	GGGa LHyd LMil MDun NMun SReu
- Keillour form	GGGa
- KW 7184	NMun SLdr
recurvum	See *R. roxieanum* var. *roxieanum*
Red Admiral Group	NMun
Red Argenteum Group	NMun
'Red Bird' (EA)	CMac
'Red Carpet' ♀	LMil LRHS NMun SLdr
'Red Delicious'	LMil
'Red Diamond'	See *R.* Diamant Group red
'Red Dragon'	Last listed 1998
'Red Fountain' (EA)	LMil LRHS MOne WLRN
'Red Glow'	LHyd NMun SLdr
'Red Jack'	Last listed 1997
'Red Poll'	Last listed 1997
'Red Red'	Last listed 1998
'Red Riding Hood'	CWri LKna
'Red Rum'	Last listed 1997
'Red Sunset' (EA/d)	GKir LRHS
'Red Velour'	CAbP
'Red Velvet'	See *R.* 'Ilam Red Velvet'
'Red Wood'	GGGa
'Redmond' (EA)	LHyd
'Redshank' (K)	MAsh MBri
'Redwing' (EA)	CDoC SLdr SPer
'Reich's Schneewittchen'	GGGa
Remo Group	SLdr
'Rendezvous'	ENot LMil SReu
'Renoir' ♀	LHyd LMil SLdr SReu
Repose Group & cl.	Last listed 1998
reticulatum (A) ♀	GGGa LMil NMun SLdr SReu
* - *leucanthum* (A)	GGGa
- 'Sea King' (A)	LHyd
retusum (V)	GGGa
§ 'Reuthe's Purple' ♀	GGGa NHol NMun SReu
'Rêve d'Amour' (Vs)	SReu SSta
Rêve Rose Group & cl.	Last listed 1997
'Revlon'	LHyd
'Rex' (EA)	LRHS SLdr
rex	COtt GGGa IDee IOrc LHyd LMil MDun NMun SLdr
- subsp. ***arizelum***	See *R. arizelum*
- EGM 295	LMil
§ - subsp. ***fictolacteum***	GGGa LHyd LMil MDun NMun

	SLdr SReu
– – 'Cherry Tip' R 11385	NMun SLdr
¶ – – Hird 120	WPGP
¶ – – Miniforme Group	MDun
¶ – – – F 25512	GGGa
– – S&F 649	ISea
– – TW 407	Last listed 1997
– – USDAPI 59104/ R11043	NMun
¶ – subsp. *gratum*	LMil
– subsp. *rex* 'Quartz' ♀	Last listed 1995
– Sich 1037	Last listed 1998
– Sich 1134	Last listed 1998
– Sich 1154	Last listed 1998
– Sich 1159	Last listed 1998
– Sich 1236	Last listed 1998
– x Sincerity Group	NMun SLdr
rhabdotum	See *R. dalhousieae* var. *rhabdotum*
'Ria Hardijzer'	LKna MBri
Rickshaw Group	SLdr
rigidum	ISea LHyd LMil NMun
* – *album*	CHig NMun WBod
§ – R 11288	Last listed 1997
'Ring of Fire'	CDoC CWri LMil MDun MLea SReu
'Rio Grande'	SLdr
'Ripe Corn'	LKna NMun SLdr SReu
¶ 'Riplet' ♀	GAri GGGa MDun MLea NHar WAbe
'Ripples' (EA)	CTrh
ririei	GGGa LHyd NMun SLdr
¶ – AC 2036	LMil
– Guiz 75	See *R. haofui* Guiz 75
– W/V 1808	NMun
– W/V 5139	NMun SLdr
¶ 'Robert Croux'	SLdr
'Robert Keir' ♀	NMun SLdr
'Robert Korn'	LMil MDun
'Robert Seleger'	GGGa LMil LRHS NHar WAbe
'Robert Whelan' (A)	SReu
§ 'Roberte'	SBrw
'Robin Hill Frosty' (EA)	LHyd SLdr
'Robin Hill Gillie' (EA)	LHyd
Robin Hood Group	NMun
'Robin Redbreast'	NMun
'Robinette'	CWri
'Rocket'	CAbP GKir LMil LRHS MBri MDun NMun SLdr WGwG
'Rokoko'	See *R.* 'Hachmann's Rokoko'
Romany Chai Group	LHyd SLdr SPer
'Romarez'	SLdr
'Romy'	NMun SLdr
'Rosa Marie'	SLdr
'Rosa Mundi'	ENot
* 'Rosabelle'	CEqu
Rosalind Group & cl.	SLdr
'Rosata' (Vs)	MBri MDun SLdr SReu SSta
'Rose Bud'	MDun
'Rose Elf'	ECho MDun NHar NHol
'Rose Glow' (A)	SReu
'Rose Gown'	SReu
'Rose Greeley' (EA)	CDoC CHig CTrh GQui IOrc MNaF SBod SPer SReu WFar WLRN
'Rose Haze' (A)	SReu
'Rose Ruffles' (K)	Last listed 1999
'Rose Torch' (A)	SReu
* *roseatum* F 17227	GGGa
'Rosebud' (EA/d) ♀	CB&S CDoC CGre CHig CMac CTrh CTrw ECho GGGa IOrc LHyd LKna MAsh MBar MGos

	NMun SBod SLdr SReu WBod WLRN
'Rosemary Hyde' (EA)	SLdr
roseotinctum	See *R. sanguineum* subsp. *sanguineum* var. *didymoides* Roseotinctum Group
roseum	See *R. prinophyllum*
'Roseum Elegans'	ECho GChr LRHS MBar NMun SBrw SLdr
* 'Rosie Posie' (V)	CEqu
'Rosiflorum'	See *R. indicum* 'Balsaminiflorum'
'Rosy Bell'	LKna
'Rosy Cream'	Last listed 1999
'Rosy Dream'	CAbP COtt CWri LMil LRHS MAsh MBri MLea
'Rosy Fire' (A)	SReu
'Rosy Lea'	MLea
'Rosy Lights'	CTri GChr LMil LRHS
'Rothenburg'	CSam LHyd SLdr SReu
rothschildii	GGGa LMil LRHS MDun NMun SLdr
– C&Cu 9312	GGGa
roxieanum	LHyd LMil NMun SLdr SReu
§ – var. *cucullatum*	ISea MDun NMun
– – CNW 680	GGGa
– – CNW 690	LMil
– – dwarf Dawyck	GGGa
– – R 10920	NMun
– – SBEC 0345	NMun SLdr
§ – – SBEC 350	GGGa
– var. *oreonastes* ♀	CDoC GGGa LHyd LMil LRHS MDun NMun SLdr SSta
– – CNW 307	GGGa
– – CNW 723	GGGa
– – CNW 740	GGGa
– – CNW 743	GGGa
– – Nymans form	SReu
– – USDAPI 59222/ R11312	GGGa NMun
– var. *parvum*	GGGa
– R 25422	NMun SLdr
– var. *recurvum* CNW 727	Last listed 1999
§ – var. *roxieanum*	NMun
– – CNW 727	GGGa
– – F 16508	NMun
– USDAPI 59159/ R11141	NMun SLdr
'Royal Blood'	SLdr
'Royal Command' (K)	COtt GKir LMil LRHS MBar SBrw SLdr
Royal Flush Group	ISea
'Royal Lodge' (K) ♀	Last listed 1999
'Royal Pink'	Last listed 1999
'Royal Purple'	WBod
'Royal Ruby' (K)	LRHS MBri
'Roza Stevenson' ♀	LHyd NMun SBrw SLdr
'Rozanne Waterer' (K)/d	LKna
'Rubicon'	CWri MLea
rubiginosum	GGGa IOrc LHyd LMil NMun SLdr SReu
§ – Desquamatum Group	CB&S LHyd NMun SLdr
– – EGM 272	LMil
– pink	LMil
– S&F 368	ISea
– S&F 404	Last listed 1998
– white	LMil
Rubina Group	Last listed 1998
'Rubinetta' (EA)	LRHS WFar
rubroluteum	See *R. viridescens* Rubroluteum Group
'Ruby F. Bowman'	CWri MDun MGos NMun SBrw SLdr SReu

'Ruby Hart'	CB&S GGGa MAsh MDun NHol SBrw SReu	
¶ Ruddigore Group	WBod	
rude	See *R. glischrum* subsp. *rude*	
'Ruffles and Frills'	CDoC ECho MDun MOne	
rufum	GGGa NMun SLdr	
- subsp. *hammel*	SLdr	
- Hummel 31	Last listed 1997	
- Sich 155	GGGa	
- W/V 1808*	Last listed 1998	
rugosum Sinclair 240 (V)	GGGa	
'Rumba' (K)	LKna	
'Rumpelstilzchen'	GGGa	
rupicola	CHig GDra NMun	
§ - var. *chryseum*	GGGa LHyd LMil NMun	
- var. *muliense*	NMun	
- - Yu 14042	GGGa	
russatum ♀	CSam EBee ENot EPot GDra GGGa LMil MDun NMun SLdr WPic	
- blue-black	LMil	
- C&Cu 9315	GGGa	
- 'Purple Pillow'	MDun NHar WWeb	
* - 'Tower Court'	NMun	
- Waterer form	Last listed 1997	
russotinctum	See *R. alutaceum* var. *russotinctum*	
'Sabina'	CTrh	
'Sacko'	CDoC CHig ECho GGGa LMil MAsh MBri MDun MOne NHol	
¶ 'Saffrano'	NBlu	
'Saffron Queen'	CB&S CGre CTrG CTrw WBod	
'Sahara' (K)	LKna	
'Saint Breward'	CB&S CTrG GGGa LHyd LRHS MAsh MDun MLea NHol SBod SLdr SPer WAbe WGer	
'Saint Keverne'	SLdr	
'Saint Merryn' ♀	CTrG EBee ENot GAri GGGa LHyd LRHS MAsh MBri MDun MOne NHol NMun SLdr WBod WGer WWeb	
'Saint Michael'	SReu	
'Saint Minver' ♀	LHyd SLdr	
'Saint Tudy' ♀	EPfP LHyd LKna MDun NMun SLdr	
'Sakata Red' (EA)	CGre IOrc WBod	
'Sakon' (EA)	NMun SLdr	
'Salmon Bedspread'	SReu	
'Salmon Sander' (EA)	SLdr	
§ 'Salmon Trout'	LMil	
'Salmon's Leap' (EA/v)	CB&S CChe COtt GQui LMil LRHS SBrw SCoo SLdr SPer SReu WAbe WFar	
saluenense	GGGa LHyd LMil NMun SLdr WAbe	
§ - subsp. *chameunum* ♀	GGGa LMil NMun SLdr WGer	
- - PA Cox 6112	GGGa	
§ - - Prostratum Group	GGGa WAbe	
- JN 260	GGGa	
- subsp. *riparioides* R 178	See *R. calostrotum* subsp. *riparium* Rock's form R 178	
- subsp. *saluenense*	LMil	
Exbury form R 11005		
- - F 19479	NMun	
'Sammetglut'	CWri SReu	
'Samuel Taylor Coleridge' (M)	MBri	
sanctum	Last listed 1999	
'Sandling'	Last listed 1997	
'Sandy' (DA)	SLdr	
'Sang de Gentbrugge' (G)	SReu	
sanguineum	GGGa LMil MDun NMun SLdr SReu	

§ - subsp. *didymum*	GGGa MDun NMun SLdr	
- var. *hlmertum*	SLdr	
- PA Cox 6056	GGGa	
- subsp. *sanguineum* var. *cloiophorum* R 10899	NMun	
- - - USDAPI 59553/ R11212	NMun SLdr	
- - var. *didymoides* Consanguineum Group	NMun SLdr	
- - - - KW 6831	LMil	
§ - - - Roseotinctum Group	LMil	
- - - - USDAPI 59038/ R10903	GGGa LMil NMun SLdr	
- - var. *haemaleum*	CWri GGGa LMil NMun SLdr	
- - - F 21732	NMun	
- - - F 21735	GGGa NMun	
- - - R 31	GGGa	
- - - USDAPI 59303/ R10895	NMun	
- - - USDAPI 59453/ R10938	NMun	
- - var. *sanguineum* F 25521	LMil	
- - - R 10893	NMun SLdr	
- - - USDAPI 59096/R11029	NMun SLdr	
'Santa Maria'	CDoC COtt LRHS SLdr SReu SSta	
santapaui (V)	Last listed 1998	
§ 'Saotome' (EA)	LHyd	
'Sapphire' ♀	CTrG EBee LKna LRHS MAsh MBar MDun SLdr SRms	
'Sappho' ♀	CB&S CWri EBee ENot GGGa IOrc LHyd LKna LMil LRHS MBar MGos MLea NMun SBrw SLdr SPer SReu SSta WFar WGer WGwG	
'Sapporo'	GGGa MAsh	
'Sarah Boscawen'	SReu	
sargentianum ♀	LMil MLea NMun SLdr WAbe	
- 'Whitebait'	GGGa MBro NMun WAbe	
Sarita Loder Group & cl.	SLdr	
¶ 'Sarled' ♀	GGGa LHyd LMil SReu	
Sarled Group & cl.	CB&S GDra NHar NMun SLdr SPer SRms WAbe WBod WWat	
'Saroi' (EA)	NMun SLdr	
'Saskia' (K)	LKna	
'Satan' (K) ♀	COtt GGGa LKna LRHS MBri SReu	
'Satsuki' (EA)	CGre ECho LNet	
'Saturnus' (M)	GKir SLdr	
scabrifolium	NMun SLdr	
§ - var. *spiciferum*	GGGa NMun SLdr WPic	
- - S&F 502	ISea	
- - S&F 534	ISea	
'Scarlet Wonder' ♀	CDoC CMHG CTrh CWri EPot GGGa GKir IMGH ISea LKna LMil LRHS MAsh MBar MBri MGos MLea NHol NMun NWea SBod SBrw SLdr SPer SReu SSht SSta WBod WFar	
Scarlett O'Hara Group	Last listed 1997	
schistocalyx	SLdr	
schlippenbachii (A) ♀	CB&S CGre GGGa LHyd LMil NMun SLdr SReu SSta WWat	
- 'Sid's Royal Pink' (A)	LMil MDun	
'Schneeflöckchen'	GGGa	
'Schneekrone'	GGGa LMil MAsh MBri NHol	
'Schneeperle' (EA)	GGGa	
'Schneespiegel' [PBR]	ENot	
'Schneewolke'	LMil	

'Schubert' (EA)	MBar MGos SLdr WBod	
scintillans	See *R. polycladum* Scintillans Group	
'Scintillation'	CDoC CWri EBee GGGa LMil LRHS MAsh MBar MLea NMun SBrw SLdr	
scopulorum	SLdr	
- KW 6354	GGGa	
scottianum	See *R. pachypodum*	
'Scout' (EA)	SLdr	
scyphocalyx	See *R. dichroanthum* subsp. *scyphocalyx*	
Seagull Group & cl.	NMun SLdr	
searsiae	NMun SLdr	
- W/A 1343	Last listed 1997	
'Sea-shell'	SLdr	
'Sea-Tac'	Last listed 1999	
'Seb'	SLdr	
'Second Honeymoon'	CDoC CWri MAsh MLea SBrw SReu	
'Seikai' (EA)	SLdr	
seinghkuense	EBee	
¶ - CCH&H 8106	GGGa	
- KW 9254	GGGa	
selense	GGGa LMil NMun SLdr	
- CNW 690	Last listed 1998	
§ - subsp. *dasycladum*	MDun NMun SLdr	
- - F 11312	NMun	
- - KW 7189	NMun	
- - R 11269	NMun	
- subsp. *jucundum*	GGGa LMil MDun NMun SLdr	
¶ - - KR 4051B	LMil	
- - S&F 660	ISea	
- PA Cox 6041	GGGa	
- subsp. *selense* F 14458	NMun SLdr	
- - PA Cox 6024	GGGa	
§ - subsp. *setiferum*	NMun	
semnoides	GGGa NMun SLdr	
- F 21870	NMun	
- F 25639	NMun	
- R 25388	NMun	
'Senator Henry Jackson'	GGGa LMil	
'Sennocke' ⚲	GGGa LHyd	
'September Morn'	Last listed 1999	
'September Song'	CDoC COtt CWri GGGa LHyd LMil LRHS MAsh MBri MDun MLea	
'Serendipity'	GGGa	
serotinum	LMil NMun SLdr SReu	
¶ - SEH 242	LMil	
serpyllifolium (A)	CB&S GGGa NMun SLdr	
- var. *albiflorum* (A)	GAri	
'Sesterianum'	CMHG SLdr	
¶ 'Seta' ⚲	LHyd LMil	
Seta Group & cl.	CB&S CHig NMun SLdr SReu	
setiferum	See *R. selense* subsp. *setiferum*	
setosum	GGGa LMil MDun NMun	
- TW 30	Last listed 1997	
'Seven Stars' ⚲	MDun NMun SLdr SReu WPyg	
'Shamrock'	CB&S CDoC CSam EPfP GCrs GKir ISea LRHS MAsh MBar MDun MLea NHar NHol SBrw SLdr SReu WAbe WBod WFar WGwG	
'Sham's Candy'	ERea	
'Shanty' (K/d)	LKna	
'Sheila' (EA)	CDoC LRHS	
x *sheilae* (V)	CEqu	
shepherdii	See *R. kendrickii*	
Shepherd's Delight Group	SLdr	
sherriffii	GGGa MDun NMun SLdr	
- L&S 2751	NMun	

I 'Shiko Lavender' (A)	LMil	
Shilsonii Group	NMun SLdr SReu	
'Shinimiagagino' (EA)	NMun	
'Shinnyo-no-hikari' (EA)	GAri	
'Shi-no-noe' (EA)	NMun SBod SLdr	
'Shinsei' (EA)	GAri	
'Shin-seikai' (EA/d)	CB&S	
'Shintoki-no-hagasane' (EA)	LHyd	
'Shintsune' (EA)	NMun SLdr	
Shot Silk Group	NMun SLdr	
'Shrimp Girl'	ENot LHyd LRHS MAsh MGos NMun SLdr SReu	
'Shukishima' (EA)	NMun SLdr	
'Shuku-fuku' (EA)	GAri	
shweliense	GGGa SReu	
¶ *sichotense*	GGGa	
sidereum	GGGa LMil NMun SLdr	
- KR 2710*	GGGa	
- KW 13649	See *R. aff. grande* KR 13649	
- KW 6792	NMun SLdr	
- S&F 314	ISea	
- S&F 318	ISea	
- TW 345	Last listed 1997	
- TW 350	Last listed 1997	
siderophyllum	SLdr	
- EGM 346	LMil	
sikangense	LRHS MDun NMun SLdr	
- C&K 246	GGGa	
§ - Cookeanum Group	NMun	
- - CNW 1060	LMil	
- EGM 108	LMil	
- var. *exquisitum* CNW 958	LMil LRHS	
- R 18042	NMun	
- var. *sikangense* PA Cox 5012	GGGa	
- - PA Cox 5105	GGGa NHol	
* *sikkimense* SD 1108	GGGa	
§ 'Silberwolke'	COtt ENot LRHS SBrw SReu	
'Silkcap'	Last listed 1999	
'Silky'	Last listed 1999	
Silver Cloud	See *R.* 'Silberwolke'	
Silver Edge	See *R. ponticum* 'Silver Edge'	
¶ 'Silver Fountain' (EA)	LMil	
'Silver Glow' (EA)	CMac	
‹ 'Silver Jubilee'	GGGa LHyd LMil SLdr	
'Silver Moon' (EA)	IOrc LRHS NMun SLdr SPer	
'Silver Queen'	ECho	
'Silver Sixpence' ⚲	EBee ENot EPfP GKir IOrc LRHS MAsh MBar MDun MLea NMun NWea SLdr SReu	
'Silver Skies'	LMil	
'Silver Slipper' (K) ⚲	CDoC CGre GKir LHyd LKna LMil LRHS MBar MBri SLdr SPer SReu SSta WGor	
'Silverwood' (K)	LMil	
'Silvester' (EA)	COtt MBri SLdr WPat	
simiarum	GGGa	
'Simona'	CWri LRHS SReu	
simsii (EA)	CMac LMil LRHS SLdr	
- S&F 431 (EA)	ISea	
simulans	See *R. mimetes* var. *simulans*	
'Sinbad'	Last listed 1998	
sinofalconeri C&H 7183	GGGa WBod	
- S&F 92142	ISea	
- SEH 229	LMil	
sinogrande ⚲	CB&S CHEx GGGa IOrc LMil MDun NMun SLdr SPer WBod WPic	
¶ - KR 4027	LMil	
- KW 21111	NMun SLdr	
- S&F 327	Last listed 1999	

- S&F 329	Last listed 1999
- S&F 350	ISea
- TW 341	Last listed 1997
- TW 383	Last listed 1997
'Sir Charles Lemon' ♀	CDoC CWri LMil MDun NMun
	SLdr SReu
Sir Frederick Moore	Last listed 1997
Group & cl.	
* 'Sir G.E. Simpson'	NMun
'Sir George Sansom'	SLdr
'Sir William Lawrence' (EA)	LKna SReu
Siren Group & cl.	Last listed 1999
'Skookum'	ECho LMil MBri MGos
'Sleeping Beauty'	WAbe
'Sleepy'	ENot IOrc MAsh NDlv NMun SLdr
	SPer SReu WGwG WLRN
smirnowii	GGGa LMil NMun SLdr SReu
smithii	See *R. argipeplum*
§ Smithii Group	CWri SReu
smithii Argipeplum Group	See *R. argipeplum*
'Sneezy'	CB&S EBee ENot GChr GGGa
	GKir LHyd LMil LRHS MAsh MBar
	MGos NHol NMun SLdr SReu SSta
	WGwG
'Snipe' ♀	CDoC EBee ENot GGGa GKir
	LHyd LMil LRHS MAsh MBar MBri
	MDun MGos MNaF MOne NHar
	NHol NWea SPer SReu
'Snow' (EA)	CMac LRHS MBar SCam SLdr
'Snow Crown'	Last listed 1998
'Snow Hill' (EA)	GQui LHyd LMil
'Snow Lady' ♀	ENot EPfP GCrs LMil MAsh MBar
	MGos MLea NHar NHol SLdr
'Snow Queen' ♀	SLdr
Snow Queen Group & cl.	LKna LMil SReu
'Snowbird'	GGGa LMil LRHS
'Snowflake'	See *R.* 'Kure-no-yuki'
'Snowstorm'	CWri ECho MAsh MDun
'Soho' (EA)	GAri GQui LNet
'Soir de Paris' (Vs)	CDoC GGGa MAsh MBar MBri
	MDun MLea NMun SLdr SReu
	SSta WBod
'Soldier Sam'	SBrw SReu SSta
'Solidarity'	ECho MAsh MLea WLRN
'Solway' (Vs)	LMil
'Sonata'	CWri GAri GGGa MDun SReu
¶ 'Sonatine'	LMil
'Songbird'	GCHN GChr GDra LHyd LKna
	LMil LRHS MBar MBri NMun SLdr
	SReu WBod
'Songster'	Last listed 1998
'Sophie Hedges' (K/d)	LKna
sororium KR 3080 (V)	GGGa
- KR 3085	LMil
- var. *wumengense*	LMil
CNW 990	
Souldis Group	LMil MDun SLdr SMur
souliei	IOrc LMil NMun SLdr
- C&K 371	Last listed 1998
- deep pink	GGGa
- PA Cox 5056	Last listed 1998
- white	GGGa
'Southern Cross'	CSam CWri MDun MLea NMun
'Souvenir de Congo'	SBrw
'Souvenir de D.A. Koster'	SLdr
'Souvenir de Doctor	CWri LKna MBar SBrw SLdr
S. Endtz' ♀	
'Souvenir du Président	LKna
Carnot' (G/d)	
'Souvenir of Anthony	LKna SBrw SReu
Waterer' ♀	
'Souvenir of W.C. Slocock'	CSam LKna NMun SBrw SLdr

	SReu SSta
sp. ACE 2256	Last listed 1998
sp. ACE 2384	Last listed 1998
'Sparkler' (Vs)	GGGa
'Sparkler' (hybrid)	LRHS MGos MLea
speciosum	See *R. flammeum*
'Spek's Brilliant' (M)	SReu
'Spek's Orange' (M) ♀	MGos SReu
sperabile	NMun
- var. *sperabile* F 26446	Last listed 1998
- var. *weihsiense*	GGGa LMil NMun SLdr
- - CNW 564	ISea
- - F 26453	SLdr
sperabiloides	GGGa NMun
- R 125	NMun
sphaeranthum	See *R. trichostomum*
sphaeroblastum	GGGa LMil NMun SLdr
- F 20416	SLdr
- KR 1481*	NMun
- var. *wumengense*	ISea
CNW 510	
- - CNW 942	GGGa
- - CNW 963	GGGa
- - CNW 968	GGGa
- - S&F 515	ISea
spiciferum	See *R. scabrifolium* var.
	spiciferum
'Spicy Lights'	LMil
spilotum	GGGa NMun SLdr
spinuliferum	GGGa NMun SLdr
- S&F 247	ISea
'Spinulosum'	Last listed 1997
'Spitfire'	MGos SBrw SReu
'Spoonbill' (K)	LKna
'Spring Beauty' (EA)	CMac SReu
'Spring Magic'	LMil NMun SLdr SPer
'Spring Pearl'	See *R.* 'Moerheim's Pink'
'Spring Rose'	MAsh NMun SLdr
'Spring Sunshine'	LMil
'Springbok'	LHyd
'Squirrel' (EA)	CDoC COtt GGGa GKir LHyd
	LMil LRHS MAsh MBri MGos
	NDlv SLdr SPer SReu WBod
'Squirrel' tall form (EA)	SLdr
'Staccato'	GGGa
Stadt Essen Group & cl.	GGGa LMil
stamineum	NMun
- S&F 417	ISea
- W/V 887	NMun
'Standishii'	SLdr
'Stanley Rivlin'	LHyd SLdr
§ 'Stanway'	LMil NMun
'Starcross'	Last listed 1997
'Starfish'	SReu
'Stella'	NMun
stenaulum	See *R. moulmainense*
§ *stenopetalum*	CMac ISea LMil NMun SLdr SReu
'Linearifolium' (A)	WAbe WBod WPic
stenophyllum	See *R. makinoi*
stewartianum	GGGa MDun NMun SLdr
- CCH&H 8137	GGGa
- CLD 1300*	Last listed 1999
- F 26921	NMun
- S&F 370	ISea
'Stewartstonian' (EA) ♀	CMac IOrc LHyd LMil MBar MBri
	SBod SReu SSta WBod WFar
stictophyllum	See *R. nivale* subsp. *boreale*
	Stictophyllum Group
'Stoat' (EA)	GQui
'Stranraer'	MAsh MBri
'Strawberry Cream'	GGGa NHol
'Strawberry Ice' (K) ♀	CB&S CMHG ENot EPfP GGGa

	GKir IOrc LKna LMil LRHS MAsh
	MBar MBri MDun MGos SPer
	SReu
'Streatley' ♀	SLdr
strigillosum	GGGa MDun NMun SLdr
- C&H 7035	GGGa
- C&H 7047	GGGa
- EGM 338	LMil
- Reuthe's form	SReu
'Striped Beauty'	Last listed 1999
'Suave'	WBod
subansiriense C&H 418	GGGa NMun SLdr
suberosum	See *R. yunnanense* Suberosum
	Group
subsection *Fortunea*	Last listed 1999
sp. PW 099*	
subsection *Triflora*	Last listed 1999
PW 020*	
subsection *Triflora*	LMil
PW 097	
succothii	GGGa LHyd MDun NMun SLdr
- BB 185A	NMun
- CH&M 3079	Last listed 1997
- CH&M 3105	Last listed 1997
- CH&M 3109	NHol
- CH&M 3125	Last listed 1997
- EGM 086	LMil
- KW 13666	SLdr
- LS&H 19850	Last listed 1997
- LS&H 21295	NMun SLdr
'Suede'	MDun
'Sugar Pink'	LMil LRHS
'Sugared Almond' (K) ♀	Last listed 1999
sulfureum	CHig NMun
- SBEC 249	GGGa
'Sumatra'	Last listed 1997
'Summer Blaze' (A)	SReu
'Summer Flame'	SLdr SReu
'Summer Fragrance' (O) ♀	SReu SSta
'Sun Chariot' (K) ♀	CB&S LHyd LKna LRHS MAsh
	MBri MMHG SLdr SReu
'Sunbeam' (EA)	See *R.* 'Benifude'
'Sunbeam' (hybrid)	LKna SReu
I 'Sundance'	Last listed 1997
'Sunny' (V)	GGGa
'Sunny Day'	SLdr
'Sunny Splendour' (V)	ERea
(Sunrise Group) 'Sunrise'	SLdr
'Sunset over Harkwood'	Last listed 1997
'Sunset Pink' (K)	LHyd LMil LRHS
'Sunstruck'	GGGa
'Sunte Nectarine' (K) ♀	GQui LHyd LMil MBri SCoo
superbum (V)	GGGa
'Superbum' (O)	SReu
'Surprise' (EA)	CDoC CTrh CTri LRHS MAsh
	NMun SCoo SLdr
'Surrey Heath' ♀	CB&S CMHG COtt CWri EBee
	ENot GGGa GKir LMil LNet LRHS
	MAsh MBar MBri MDun MGos
	MLea NDlv NMun SBrw SLdr
	SReu
'Susan' ♀	CB&S CDoC CSam CWri GGGa
	LHyd LKna LMil LRHS MAsh MBri
	MDun MLea NMun SBrw SLdr
	SPer SReu
'Susannah Hill' (EA)	CDoC CTrh LMil MGos SBod
	SReu
'Sussex Bonfire'	NMun SLdr
sutchuenense	CHig CWri GGGa IDee LMil LRHS
	MDun NMun SLdr
- var. *geraldii*	See *R.* x *geraldii*
'Swamp Beauty'	GGGa LMil MDun

'Swansdown'	MDun
'Swansong' (EA)	CMac
'Sweet Mac' (V)	CEqu
'Sweet Seraphim' (V)	Last listed 1997
'Sweet Simplicity' ♀	LKna SBrw
'Sweet Sixteen'	CWri NMun SLdr
'Sweet Sue'	EBee LRHS NMun SLdr SReu
	WLRN
'Swift'	CDoC GGGa GQui MBri MOne
	WAbe WGer
'Sword of State' (K)	Last listed 1998
'Sylphides' (K)	LKna MAsh MBri
'Sylvester'	CDoC LRHS MGos SReu
'Sylvia' (EA/d)	Last listed 1997
taggianum 'Cliff Hanger'	LMil
ex KW 8546	
'Taka' (A)	SLdr
'Takasago' (EA/d)	LHyd LMil
'Talavera'	See *R.* (Golden Oriole Group)
	'Talavera'
taliense	GGGa LHyd MDun NMun SLdr
- F 6772	NMun SLdr
- KR 2765*	GGGa
- S&F 92069	Last listed 1998
- SBEC 350	See *R. roxieanum* var. *cucullatum*
	SBEC 350
- SSNY 352	GGGa
subsection *Taliensia*	LMil
CNW 256	
'Tally Ho'	SLdr
Tally Ho Group & cl.	NMun SLdr SReu
tamaense	See *R. cinnabarinum* subsp.
	tamaense
¶ 'Tamafuyo' (EA)	WBod
'Tama-no-utena' (EA)	LHyd SLdr
'Tan Crossing'	SReu
'Tanager' (EA)	CDoC CTrh LKna
tanastylum	SLdr
§ - var. *pennivenium*	NMun SLdr
- - S&F 593	ISea
'Tangerine'	See *R.* 'Fabia Tangerine'
'Tangiers' (K)	Last listed 1998
tapetiforme	GGGa
'Tara' (hybrid)	SLdr
Taranto Group	SLdr
¶ 'Tarentella'	CDoC ENot
Tasco Group	SLdr
tashiroi (EA)	NMun
'Tatjana'	ENot LMil
tatsienense	GGGa
- EGM 321	LMil
'Taurus' ♀	COtt CWri GGGa LMil MGos
	MLea
'Tay' (K)	Last listed 1997
'Teal' ♀	CTri GGGa LRHS MBar MBri
	MDun MGos MLea NHol NMun
	SLdr SReu
'Teddy Bear'	CDoC GGGa LMil LRHS MDun
	SLdr SMur
§ *telmateium*	NMun
telopeum	See *R. campylocarpum* subsp.
	caloxanthum Telopeum Group
temenium	MDun
- var. *dealbatum*	LMil
- - EGM 275	LMil
- - Glaphyrum Group	NMun
F 21902	
- EGM 274	LMil
- var. *gilvum* 'Cruachan'	GGGa LMil NMun
R 22272	
- - R 101	NMun
- - R 22271	NMun

§ – var. *mesopolium*	NMun	
R 10950		
– P Cox 6037B	GGGa	
– R 10909	NMun	
– var. *temenium* F 21734	NMun	
– – F 21809	NMun	
'Temple Belle' ♀	LRHS MDun	
Temple Belle Group	CSam LHyd LKna MLea NDlv NMun SLdr	
'Tensing'	SLdr	
§ *tephropeplum* ♀	GGGa MDun NMun SLdr	
– Deleiense Group	See *R. tephropeplum*	
– KW 6303	NMun	
– S&F 92069	ISea	
– USDAPQ 3914/R 18408	GGGa	
'Tequila Sunrise'	NMun SLdr	
'Terra-cotta'	LKna LMil	
'Terra-cotta Beauty' (EA)	CTrG WPat	
Tessa Group & cl.	CDoC LKna LMil LRHS MGos MOne	
'Tessa Bianca'	GGGa	
'Tessa Roza' ♀	GGGa GQui LHyd MAsh	
thayerianum	GGGa NMun SLdr	
'The Dowager'	SLdr	
§ 'The Hon. Jean Marie de Montague' ♀	CAbP CWri EPfP IOrc LKna LMil LRHS MBri MDun MLea NMun SBrw SLdr	
'The Master' ♀	LKna NMun SBrw SLdr SReu	
§ 'The Queen Mother'	LHyd	
'The Warrior'	MDun	
'Theme Song'	Last listed 1998	
thomsonii	GGGa LHyd LMil MDun NHol NMun SLdr SReu	
– AC 113	NMun	
– B&SWJ 2638	WCru	
– BL&M 153*	Last listed 1999	
– Bu 270	GGGa	
– var. *candelabrum*	See *R.* x *candelabrum*	
– 'Davidian'	SLdr	
– DF 540	Last listed 1999	
§ – subsp. *lopsangianum*	GGGa MDun SLdr	
§ – – LS&T 6561	NMun	
– LS&H 1949*	NMun	
– MH 70	GGGa	
– subsp. *thomsonii* BL&M 228	NMun	
– – L&S 2847	GGGa NMun	
Thomwilliams Group	Last listed 1999	
Thor Group & cl.	GGGa SBrw SReu	
'Thousand Butterflies'	See *R.* 'One Thousand Butterflies'	
'Thunderstorm' ♀	LHyd LKna SReu	
thymifolium	GGGa	
'Tiana'	GGGa	
'Tibet'	GQui LMil MBar MDun NHar	
'Tidbit'	GGGa LHyd LKna LMil MGos MLea NMun SLdr WGer	
'Tilford Seedling'	LKna	
I 'Tilgates Peach'	CWri	
'Timothy James'	GKir LRHS SReu	
'Tinkerbird'	GGGa	
'Tiny' (EA/d)	Last listed 1997	
'Tit Willow' (EA)	GKir LHyd LRHS SCoo WGwG	
'Titian Beauty' ♀	CB&S CDoC COtt CWri EBee GChr GGGa GKir IOrc LMil LNet LRHS MAsh MBri MDun MGos MLea NDlv NMun SBrw SLdr SPer SReu SSht	
'Titipu' (EA)	LHyd SLdr	
'Toff' (V)	Last listed 1997	
'Tolkien'	SReu SSta	
'Tom Williams'	NMun SLdr	
'Tomba'	Last listed 1997	

'Tonkonatsu' (EA)	SLdr	
'Too Bee'	GGGa NHol WAbe	
'Top Banana'	LRHS MDun MLea	
'Top Hat'	Last listed 1998	
'Topsvoort Pearl'	SReu	
'Torch'	LKna MGos	
'Toreador' (EA)	CTrG SLdr	
'Torero'	GGGa	
'Torridon' (Vs)	LMil SLdr	
'Tortoiseshell Champagne'	See *R.* 'Champagne'	
'Tortoiseshell Orange' ♀	LHyd LKna LMil LRHS MAsh MBri MDun SBrw SPer SReu SSta WGer	
'Tortoiseshell Pale Orange'	Last listed 1999	
'Tortoiseshell Salome'	LKna SBrw SReu	
'Tortoiseshell Scarlet'	MAsh SReu	
'Tortoiseshell Wonder' ♀	LHyd LKna LMil LRHS MAsh MGos NMun SLdr SPer SReu	
tosaense (EA)	Last listed 1997	
– 'Ralph Clarke' (EA)	Last listed 1998	
'Totally Awesome' (K)	GGGa	
'Tottenham' (hybrid)	Last listed 1999	
'Tower Beauty' (A)	LHyd	
'Tower Dainty' (A)	LHyd	
'Tower Daring' (A)	LHyd	
'Tower Dexter' (A)	LHyd	
'Tower Dragon' (A)	LHyd	
'Trail Blazer'	GGGa	
traillianum	GGGa LMil NMun SLdr	
– CNW 746	ISea	
§ – var. *dictyotum*	NMun SLdr	
– – 'Kathmandu'	NMun	
– F 5881*	NMun SLdr	
aff. *traillianum*	LMil	
aberrans CNW 747		
'Travis L'	Last listed 1999	
Treasure Group	GDra IOrc LHyd SLdr	
'Trebah Gem'	NMun SLdr	
'Tregedna'	NMun SLdr	
'Tregedna Red'	SReu	
'Tretawn'	SLdr	
'Trewithen Orange'	CDoC CTrw MBar NMun SLdr	
'Trewithen Purple'	CTrw	
'Trianon'	NMun	
trichanthum	CHig GGGa IOrc LMil NMun SLdr	
– 'Honey Wood'	LHyd LMil SLdr	
trichocladum	LMil NMun SLdr	
– CNW 880	ISea	
– KW 21079	See *R. mekongense* var. *mekongense* KW 21079	
– S&F 661	ISea	
– S&F 96179	ISea	
§ *trichostomum* ♀	GGGa MDun NMun SSpi WAbe	
– KW 4465	NMun	
– Ledoides Group	LMil NMun SLdr SReu	
– – 'Collingwood Ingram'	LMil LRHS SReu	
– Radinum Group	SSta	
triflorum	CWri GGGa IOrc ISea LMil MDun NMun SLdr	
§ – var. *bauhiniiflorum*	CB&S LMil MDun NMun SLdr	
– C&V 9573	GGGa	
– S&F 95149	ISea	
– var. *triflorum* Mahogani Group	NMun SLdr	
'Trilby'	SReu	
triplonaevium	See *R. alutaceum* var. *russotinctum* Triplonaevium Group	
tritifolium	See *R. alutaceum* var. *russotinctum* Tritifolium Group	
'Troll' (EA)	SLdr SReu	
'Troupial' (K)	LKna	
'Trude Webster'	CHig CSam GGGa MBri MLea SReu	

aff. *tsaii* C&H 7022	Last listed 1999	
- H&M 1490	GGGa	
tsangpoense	See *R. charitopes* subsp. *tsangpoense*	
tsariense	GGGa LMil NHol NMun SLdr	
- var. *magnum*	NMun	
- Poluninii Group	See *R. poluninii*	
- x *proteoides*	GGGa	
- var. *trimoense*	GGGa NMun	
- var. *tsariense* L&S 2766	Last listed 1997	
- 'Yum Yum'	CWri GGGa NMun SLdr	
aff. *tsariense*	LMil	
§ *tsusiophyllum*	GAri GGGa WAbe	
'Tsuta-momiji' (EA)	LHyd	
tubiforme	See *R. glaucophyllum* subsp. *tubiforme*	
'Tuffet'	SReu	
'Tulyar'	LKna	
'Tunis' (K)	ECho MAsh	
'Turkish Delight'	Last listed 1998	
N 'Twilight' (EA)	MBri	
'Twilight Pink'	MAsh NMun	
'Twilight Sky' (A)	ENot SBrw SLdr	
'Tyermannii' ♀	LMil	
'Ukamuse' (EA/d)	LHyd	
'Uki Funei' (EA/v)	Last listed 1999	
'Umpqua Queen' (K)	MLea	
Ungerio Group	NMun SLdr	
ungernii	CWri GGGa NMun SLdr	
uniflorum	LMil MDun NHol NMun WAbe	
§ - var. *imperator*	LMil	
- - KW 6884	GGGa	
- var. *uniflorum* KW 5876	NMun SLdr	
'Unique' (G)	LKna	
'Unique' (hybrid) ♀	CB&S CDoC CHig CSam CWri GChr GGGa GKir LHyd LKna LMil LNet LRHS MAsh MBri MDun MLea NMun SBrw SLdr SReu SSta WGwG WWeb	
'Unique Marmalade'	LMil MAsh	
'Unknown Warrior'	SBrw SReu	
uvariifolium	GGGa NMun SLdr	
- CNW 127	ISea	
- CNW 1275	ISea	
¶ - CNW 382	CWri	
- var. *griseum* KR 3423	LMil	
¶ - - KR 3428	LMil	
¶ - - KR 3782	LMil	
- LS&E 15817	Last listed 1998	
- PA Cox 6519	GGGa	
- 'Reginald Childs'	LMil	
- var. *uvariifolium* USDAPI 59623/ R11391	NMun	
- 'Yangtze Bend'	GGGa	
vaccinioides CCH&H 8051 (V)	GGGa	
Valaspis Group & cl.	SLdr	
'Valentine' (EA)	GGGa	
valentinianum	CB&S CSam GGGa NMun SLdr WAbe WGer	
- F 24347	NMun	
- var. *oblongilobatum* C&H 7186	LMil	
Valpinense Group & cl.	WBod	
'Van'	LMil	
'Van Nes Sensation'	LMil	
'Van Weerden Poelman'	EMil SBrw	
Vanessa Group & cl.	LMil SReu WBod	
'Vanessa Pastel' ♀	CHig GGGa LHyd LMil MDun MLea NMun SLdr SReu	
§ 'Vanilla'	LKna	
¶ Vanity Fair Group	WBod	

vaseyi (A) ♀	GGGa LHyd LMil	
- white (A)	LMil	
'Vayo' (A)	SLdr	
veitchianum ♀	GGGa	
§ - Cubittii Group ♀	GGGa NMun SLdr	
- - 'Ashcombe'	LHyd	
- KNE Cox 9001	GGGa	
- 'Veldtstar'	Last listed 1997	
vellereum	See *R. principis* Vellereum Group	
'Velvet Gown' (EA)	ENot IOrc SReu	
venator	GGGa MDun NMun SLdr	
'Venetia' (K)	MBri	
'Venetian Chimes'	EBee ENot IOrc ISea NMun SLdr SReu	
vernicosum	GGGa LMil NMun SLdr	
- C&H 7009	Last listed 1998	
- Euanthum Group F 5880	NMun	
- F 5881	NMun	
- JN 180	GGGa	
- McLaren T 71	NMun SLdr	
- S&F 411	ISea	
- Yu 13961	SLdr	
- Yu 14694	Last listed 1997	
aff. *vernicosum* C&H 7150	Last listed 1998	
x *verruculosum*	Last listed 1998	
'Veryan Bay' ♀	CB&S LMil	
vesiculiferum	NMun SLdr	
'Vespers' (EA)	CTrh	
'Victoria Hallett'	SLdr SReu	
'Vida Brown' (EA/d)	CMac ENot LKna LMil MBri SBod SReu SSta WPat	
'Viking' (EA)	LHyd WBod	
'Vincent van Gogh'	GGGa LMil MAsh	
'Vinecourt Duke' (R/d)	ECho GKir LRHS MDun	
'Vinecourt Troubador' (K/d)	CDoC ECho MDun	
'Vineland Dream' (K/d)	ECho	
'Vineland Fragrance'	CDoC CWri GGGa MDun MLea	
I 'Vinestar' AM/T	LHyd LMil	
'Vintage Rosé' ♀	LMil LRHS MLea NMun SLdr SReu	
'Violet Longhurst' (EA)	LHyd SLdr	
'Violetta' (EA)	GGGa LRHS NMen WGwG	
virgatum	Last listed 1997	
- subsp. *oleifolium* KW 6279	Last listed 1998	
Virginia Richards Group & cl.	CHig GAri GChr GGGa GKir LHyd LRHS MDun MGos NMun SLdr SReu SSta WGer	
§ *viridescens*	LMil MDun	
- 'Doshong La'	LMil WAbe	
- KW 5829	See *R. mekongense* var. *mekongense* KW 5829	
§ - Rubroluteum Group	GGGa LMil	
viscidifolium	GGGa NMun	
viscosum (A) ♀	GGGa GQui LHyd LKna LMil LRHS SReu	
* - *aemulans* (A)	Last listed 1997	
- 'Antilope'	See *R.* 'Antilope'	
- 'Arpege'	See *R.* 'Arpege'	
- 'Grey Leaf' (Vs)	LMil	
- var. *montanum* (A)	IBlr	
- f. *rhodanthum* (A)	LMil	
- 'Roseum' (Vs)	LMil	
'Viscount Powerscourt'	ENot SLdr	
'Viscy'	CDoC CWri EBee ECho GGGa GQui LHyd LMil LRHS MAsh MDun WGer	
'Vital Spark'	Last listed 1998	
'Vivacious'	MDun	
Volker Group	See *R.* Flava Group & cl.	
'Vulcan' ♀	CB&S ENot EPfP GGGa LMil MLea SBrw SLdr	

'Vulcan' x *yakushimanum* MAsh SReu
'Vulcan's Flame' Last listed 1997
'Vuyk's Rosyred' (EA) ♀ CDoC CHig CMac CTri ENot GChr GQui IOrc LHyd LKna LMil LRHS MAsh MBar MBri MGos SBod SBrw SLdr SPer SReu WBod WFar WStI WWeb
'Vuyk's Scarlet' (EA) ♀ CB&S CChe CDoC CMac CTrh GChr GGGa GKir GQui IOrc LHyd LKna LMil LRHS MAsh MBar MBri MGos NMun SBrw SLdr SPer SReu SSta WBod WFar WWeb
'W.E. Gumbleton' (M) SReu
¶ 'W.F.H.' ♀ CWri LMil NMun SLdr
'W. Leith' SLdr
wadanum LMil
  var. *leucanthum*
'Wagtail' GGGa LRHS NHol WAbe
wallichii GGGa MDun SLdr
- B&SWJ 2633 WCru
- Bu 249 Last listed 1998
- Bu 262 Last listed 1998
- Bu 290 Last listed 1998
- DM 21 LMil
- KR 813* Last listed 1997
- KR 882 Last listed 1997
- LS&H 17527 NMun
- TW 32 Last listed 1997
Walloper Group NMun SLdr SReu
'Wallowa Red' (K) ECho LMil MLea
'Wally Miller' MBri SReu SSta
walongense NMun
aff. *walongense* C&H 373 GGGa
wardii IDee IOrc ISea LHyd LMil LRHS MDun NMun SLdr WBod
- C&V 9558 GGGa
- C&V 9606 GGGa
- L&S form* GGGa SReu
- P Cox 6119 Last listed 1999
- var. *puralbum* GGGa NMun
- - F 10616 NMun
- - Yu 14757 Last listed 1997
- SHEG 5672 NMun
¶ - var. *wardii* CSam
- - C&V 9548 GGGa
- - F 21551 NMun
- - KW 4170 Last listed 1997
- - KW 5736 NMun
§ - - Litiense Group NMun SLdr
¶ - - - CNW 1079 ISea
- - LS&E 15764 NMun
- - LS&T 5679 NMun
- - LS&T 5686 NMun
- - LS&T 6591 NMun
- - R 18333 Last listed 1997
- - R 25391 Last listed 1997
- - SSNY 99 Last listed 1997
- yellow GGGa
'Ward's Ruby' (EA) CTrh CTrw
'Warrior' (EA) SBrw
§ 'Washington State Centennial' (A) GGGa
wasonii GGGa LHyd LMil MDun NMun
- McLaren AD 106 Last listed 1997
- f. *rhododactylum* NMun SLdr SReu
- - KW 1876 GGGa
- var. *wenchuanense* NHol
  C 5046
- white SLdr SReu
- yellow Last listed 1999
'Waterfall' WBod

watsonii GGGa MDun NMun SLdr SReu
- CC&H 3939 Last listed 1998
- EGM 109 Last listed 1999
- PA Cox 5075 GGGa
¶ 'Waxbill' GGGa
'Waxwing' LKna
websterianum EGM 146 LMil
- PA Cox 5123 GGGa
- PA Cox 5123a Last listed 1998
'Wee Annie' (V) CEqu
'Wee Bee' CDoC EPot GCrs GGGa GKir LMil LRHS MAsh MBri MDun MLea MNaF NDlv NHar NHol SPer SReu SSpi WAbe
§ Wega Group LHyd
¶ 'Welkin' WBod
'Wellesleyanum' Last listed 1998
'Werei' NMun
'Werrington' CGre
'Westminster' (O) LKna LMil
'Weston's Innocence' Last listed 1998
'Weston's Pink Diamond' GGGa LMil NHol
'Weybridge' NMun SLdr
weyrichii (A) GGGa
'Wheatear' GGGa
'Whidbey Island' LMil
'Whisperingrose' LMil LRHS MBri MLea
'White Cloud' MAsh
'White Frills' (EA) LMil
White Glory Group & cl. NMun SLdr
'White Gold' MDun
'White Grandeur' (EA) CTrh
'White Jade' (EA) SLdr
'White Lady' (EA) LKna MBar SBrw SLdr WGor
'White Lights' (A) GChr LMil LRHS MLea MNaF
'White Olympic Lady' LKna
'White Perfume' SReu
¶ 'White Peter' GGGa
'White Sport' (A) SLdr
'White Swan' (hybrid) ♀ ENot LKna LMil SBrw SReu
'White Wings' GQui SLdr WPic
'Whitethroat' (K/d) ♀ EPfP GKir GQui IOrc LKna LMil LRHS MAsh MBri SLdr
'Whitney's Dwarf Red' SLdr
'Wigeon' GGGa GKir LMil LRHS NHol
wightii GGGa MDun NMun SLdr
- BM&W 153* Last listed 1999
- DF 542 Last listed 1999
- KR 877 Last listed 1997
'Wilbrit Rose' SBod
'Wild Affair' Last listed 1997
'Wilgen's Ruby' ♀ LKna LRHS MAsh MBar MGos NWea SBrw WStI
'Willbrit' CDoC CWri ECho LHyd MAsh MDun MGos MOne WGor
williamsianum ♀ CB&S CDoC CSam CTrG CWri GChr GGGa ISea LHyd LMil LRHS MAsh MBar MDun MGos MLea NMun NWea SBrw SLdr SReu SRms SSpi WBod WPic WSHC
- Caerhays form LMil MDun
- pink WWat
- 'Special' GGGa
- white CPMA NMun WWat
'Willy' (EA) CTrh LRHS SCam SLdr
wilsoniae See *R. latoucheae*
Wilsonii Group CTrG
'Wilsonii' (Ad) LKna
wiltonii GGGa LMil MDun NMun SLdr
- CC&H 3906 GGGa
'Windbeam' SBod
'Windlesham Scarlet' ♀ EBee ENot LHyd SBrw

'Windsor Hawk' CWri
'Windsor Lad' LKna SBrw SReu
¶ 'Winsome' (hybrid) ♀ GGGa LHyd
Winsome Group & cl. CB&S CHig CSam CTrw CWri
 GCHN GKir IOrc LKna LRHS
 MBar MDun MLea NMun SBrw
 SLdr SSta WBod
'Winston Churchill' (M) MBar SReu
I 'Winter Green' (EA) Last listed 1997
I 'Wintergreen' (EA) COtt CTrh
'Wishmoor' ♀ LMil NMun SLdr SReu
'Witch Doctor' CDoC ECho LMil MAsh SBod
 SBrw
'Witchery' GGGa
'Wojnar's Purple' LMil
'Wombat' (EA) CDoC COtt CTrh CTri GChr
 GGGa GKir LHyd LMil LRHS MBar
 MGos NHol SLdr SReu WAbe
'Wonderland' LKna
wongii CSam GGGa GQui LMil NMun
'Woodcock' GGGa WBod
'Woodside' Last listed 1998
¶ 'Woody's Friggin' Riggin'' MAsh
'Wren' CSam GChr GCrs GGGa LRHS
 MAsh MBar MBri MDun MLea
 MOne NHar NHol SReu WAbe
'Wryneck' (K) ♀ LHyd LMil MAsh MBri SReu
¶ x *xanthanthum* MLea
xanthocodon See *R. cinnabarinum* subsp.
 xanthocodon
xanthostephanum NMun
 – CCH&H 8070 GGGa
 – KR 3095 LMil
'Yachiyo Red' Last listed 1997
'Yaku Angel' MDun
'Yaku Incense' MAsh MBri MDun
'Yaku Prince' CAbP IOrc MBri
'Yaku Princess' CAbP IOrc
'Yaku Queen' Last listed 1998
yakushimanum CB&S CDoC CMHG CSam CWri
 EPfP GGGa IOrc LHyd LKna LMil
 LRHS MAsh MBar MBri MDun
 MGos MLea NHol NMun NWea
 SBrw SLdr SPer SReu SSta WAbe
 WGer
I – 'Angel' Last listed 1999
I – 'Beefeater' SLdr
 – 'Berg' MDun
 – x *bureaui* MLea SReu
 – x *campanulatum* GGGa
 'Roland Cooper'
 – x 'Coronation Day' SLdr
 – x *decorum* GGGa SLdr SReu
 – 'Edelweiss' GGGa
 – x 'Elizabeth' GGGa
 – Exbury form SReu
 – x 'Floriade' SLdr
 – x *griersonianum* SLdr
§ – 'Koichiro Wada' ♀ CPMA EBee GGGa LHyd MGos
 NMun SBrw SLdr SReu WWat
 – x *lanatum* GGGa
 – subsp. *makinoi* See *R. makinoi*
 – 'Mist Maiden' MLea
 – x *pachysanthum* GGGa SLdr SReu
 – x *ponticum* GGGa
 – x *proteoides* GGGa
 – x *rex* SReu
 – x 'Sappho' Last listed 1998
 – 'Snow Mountain' SReu
I – 'Torch' Last listed 1997
 – x *tsariense* GGGa
 – subsp. *yakushimanum* See *R.* 'Ken Janeck'
 'Ken Janeck'

* 'Yaya' Last listed 1997
'Yaye' (EA) CDoC
§ *yedoense* SLdr SReu
 var. *poukhanense*
'Yellow Cloud' (K) CDoC ECho
'Yellow Dane' GGGa
'Yellow Hammer' ♀ CTrG EPfP LRHS MDun NWea
 SBrw
Yellow Hammer Group CB&S CHig CSam CWri GGGa
 LKna LMil MBar MGos NMun
 SBod SLdr SReu SRms SSta WAbe
 WBod
'Yellow Petticoats' MAsh MBri MLea
'Yellow Pippin' CWri
'Yellow Rolls Royce' MDun
'Yoga' (K) LKna
'Yol' SLdr
I 'Yolanta' WAbe
'Youthful Sin' Last listed 1999
'Yo-zakura' (EA) NMun
yungningense LMil NMun
 – F 29268 See *R. impeditum* F 29268
yunnanense CB&S CHig GGGa IOrc ISea LHyd
 LMil LRHS MDun NMun SLdr
 WPic
 – AC 751 MDun NMun
 – C&H 7145 GGGa
 – KGB 551 SReu
 – KGB 559 SReu
 – 'Openwood' ♀ GGGa LMil
 – pink GGGa
 – 'Red Throat' SLdr
 – S&F 379 ISea
 – S&F 400 ISea
 – S&F 96102 ISea
§ – Suberosum Group NMun
 – TW 400 Last listed 1997
 – white GGGa WAbe
aff. *yunnanense* ACE 2097 Last listed 1998
'Yvonne Dawn' NMun
zaleucum MDun
 – AC 685 MDun NMun
 – F 15688 GGGa
 – F 27603 NMun
 – Flaviflorum Group NMun
 KW 20837
 – S&F 347 ISea
 – S&F 578 ISea
 – TW 373 Last listed 1997
Zelia Plumecocq Group NMun
 & cl.
zeylanicum See *R. arboreum* subsp.
 zeylanicum
zoelleri (V) CEqu
Zuiderzee Group SBrw SLdr

RHODOHYPOXIS (Hypoxidaceae)

'Albrighton' CRDP ELan EPot ERos EWes
 LAma NMen SBla SIng WAbe WPat
'Appleblossom' CAvo EPot ERos EWes GCrs MNaf
 NMen SIng WAbe
baurii ♀ CAvo CElw CHea CInt CRDP ELan
 EPot GCrs IMGH LRHS MBro
 MTho NNrd NSla NTow SRms
 WPyg WWin WWye
 – 'Alba' CRDP CTri EDAr WWye
 – var. *baurii* EPot EWes GCrs LBee SIng
 – var. *confecta* EPot EWes SIng
 – 'Dulcie' EDAr EPot EWes NTow SOkd
 WAbe
 – forms Last listed 1997
* – x *parousia* EWes

- pink	NLAp WCru
- 'Pinkeen'	EPot WAbe
- var. *platypetala*	CRDP EPot EWes NHol NMen WAbe
- - x *milloides* , Burtt 6981	EWes
- red	SPlb WCru
- 'Susan Garnett-Botfield'	EPot EWes SIng WAbe
- white	WCru
'Betsy Carmine'	Last listed 1997
'Confusion'	EWes WAbe
'Dawn'	CAvo EWes EPot EWes LAma NHol NMen SBla WAbe
deflexa	CGra CLyd CRDP CStu EWes GCrs IMGH SIng SMrm WAbe
'Donald Mann'	EWes NMen
'Douglas'	CRDP EPot LAma NHol NMen NNrd SBla SIng WAbe WLRN WPat WPyg
'Dusky'	EPot
'E.A. Bowles'	EWes GCrs NMen SIng WAbe
'Emily Peel'	EPot EWes WAbe
'Eva-Kate'	EPot ERos EWes LAma SBla SIng WAbe WPat
'Fred Broome'	ELan EPot EWes GCrs LAma NHol NMen NTow SBla SIng WAbe WFar WPat WPyg
'Garnett'	EDAr EPot EWes GCrs SBla WAbe WPat
'Great Scott'	ECho EPot ERos EWes SIng WAbe
'Harlequin'	CAvo ELan EPot EWes LAma NHol NMen SIng WAbe
'Hebron Farm Biscuit'	See *Hypoxis parvula* var. *albiflora* 'Hebron Farm Biscuit'
'Hebron Farm Cerise'	See x *Rhodoxis* 'Hebron Farm Cerise'
'Hebron Farm Pink'	See x *Rhodoxis hybrida* 'Hebron Farm Pink'
§ 'Helen'	EPot EWes NHol SBla SIng WAbe
hybrids	ELan
'Knockdolian Red'	NHol
'Margaret Rose'	EPot EWes GCrs NMen WAbe
milloides	CPla CRDP EPot EWes IMGH LBee LRHS NHol NMen NWCA SBla SIng SSpi WAbe
- 'Claret'	CRDP EWes SBla WAbe
- 'Damask'	CRDP EWes SBla
- giant	SMrm
'Monty'	EPot EWes SIng WAbe
'New Look'	ERos EWes NMen SIng WAbe
'Perle'	EPot ERos EWes NMen NNrd WAbe
'Picta'	CAvo CRDP EPot EWes GCrs LAma NHol NNrd SBla SSpi WAbe WPat
'Pink Pearl'	EPot EWes NHol
'Pinkeen'	EWes GCrs SIng
'Ruth'	EPot EWes LAma NHol SBla WAbe
'Shell Pink'	EWes
'Starry Eyes' (d)	CRDP
'Stella'	EPot ERos EWes GCrs NHol NMen SBla SIng WAbe
'Tetra Pink'	EWes SIng WAbe
'Tetra Red'	EPot EWes NHol NMen SIng WAbe WWin
'Tetra White'	See *R.* 'Helen'
thodiana	CAvo CRDP EPot ERos EWes SBla SIng SSpi WAbe

RHODOHYPOXIS x HYPOXIS See x RHODOXIS

RHODOMYRTUS (Myrtaceae)

tomentosa	Last listed 1997

RHODOPHIALA (Amaryllidaceae)

§ *advena*	Last listed 1999
- yellow	Last listed 1997
bakeri F&W 7196	Last listed 1997
§ *bifida*	LBow
- *spathacea*	LBow
chilensis	CLAP
elwesii	Last listed 1999
montana	NWoo
- JCA 14366	SBla
- JCA 14422	SBla

RHODORA See RHODODENDRON

RHODOTHAMNUS (Ericaceae)

chamaecistus	GCrs WAbe

RHODOTYPOS (Rosaceae)

kerrioides	See *R. scandens*
§ *scandens*	CB&S CBot CDul CGdn CPle EPfP EWTr GBin IMGH LRHS SLon SMac SSpi WBod WCru WSHC WSPU WWin

x RHODOXIS (Hypoxidaceae)

¶ 'Aurora'	EWes
§ 'Hebron Farm Cerise'	EWes
§ *hybrida*	CRDP EWes SBla SIng SMrm WAbe
§ - 'Hebron Farm Pink'	CBro EWes GCrs NMen SBla SIng WAbe
- 'Hebron Farm Red Eye'	EWes SBla SIng WAbe

RHOEO See TRADESCANTIA

RHOICISSUS (Vitaceae)

capensis ♀	Last listed 1990

RHOPALOSTYLIS (Arecaceae)

baueri	CBrP LPal
cheesemanii	CBrP
sapida	CBrP CHEx CRoM CTrC ECou LPal MWst
- 'Chatham Island'	CBrP

RHUS (Anacardiaceae)

ambigua B&SWJ 3656	WCru
§ *aromatica*	CAgr CArn CFil ELau EPfP WPGP
chinensis	CDoC EPfP
copallina	EPfP LRHS SMur
¶ *coriaria*	EPfP
cotinus	See *Cotinus coggygria*
glabra	CAgr CArn CB&S CDoC NFla SPer
- 'Laciniata'	See *R.* x *pulvinata* Autumn Lace Group
- 'Laciniata' Carrière	Last listed 1997
N *hirta*	See *R. typhina*
incisa	Last listed 1997
integrifolia	CArn
leptodictya	Last listed 1997
pendulina	Last listed 1999
potaninii	EPfP WWat
§ x *pulvinata* Autumn Lace Group	CDoC EPfP GKir MGos SDix
- - 'Red Autumn Lace' ♀	GKir LRHS MBlu MBri SPer
punjabensis	Last listed 1997
§ *radicans*	CArn COld CPIN GPoy

succedanea	Last listed 1999
¶ *sylvestris*	EPfP
toxicodendron	See *R. radicans*
trichocarpa	SLPl SSpi
trilobata	See *R. aromatica*
N *typhina* ♀	More than 30 suppliers
§ - 'Dissecta' ♀	CB&S CDoC CDul CLnd EBee ELan ENot EPfP GChr GKir IOrc MBar MBri MGos MWat SEND SPer WCFE WDin WTro
- 'Laciniata' hort.	See *R. typhina* 'Dissecta'
§ *verniciflua*	CFil CLnd GIBF SSpi

RHYNCHELYTRUM See MELINIS

RHYNCHOSIA (Papilionaceae)
sordida	Last listed 1999

RHYNCHOSPORA (Cyperaceae)
§ *colorata*	CInt CRow LLWG MCCP

RIBES ✿ (Grossulariaceae)
alpinum	CAgr ELan ENot GOrc IOrc LBuc NSti NWea SPer SRms WDin WTro
- 'Aureum'	CMHG EBee EHoe ELan EPla NFor NPro WCot WDin WSHC WTro
- 'Schmidt'	MBar NFla
amarum	Last listed 1998
americanum	EPla
- 'Variegatum'	EBee EHoe ELan EPla EWTr NHol SPan WPat WPyg
aureum hort.	See *R. odoratum*
* - 'Roxby Red'	MCoo
'Black Velvet' (F)	CBlo CMac COtt LRHS MBri MCoo SPer
bracteosum	CPle
californicum	Last listed 1998
x *culverwellii*	CAgr EMui GTwe LBuc LRHS SDea
Jostaberry (F)	
diacanthum	CFil
¶ *dikuscha*	IIve
divaricatum	CAgr
- 'Worcesterberry' (F)	CAgr CMac EMui LRHS MBri MGos NRog SDea SPer
¶ *fragans*	IIve
gayanum	CGre CPle SLPl SPan WHCG
x *gordonianum*	CDoC CGre CMHG CMil CPle EBee EPfP EPla GBin GEil LHop LRHS MBel MRav NSti SEND SLim SLon SMRm SPan WFar WHCG WPyg WWat
'Kathleen'	Last listed 1999
laurifolium	CB&S CBot CFil CPla CPle CSam EBee ELan IOrc MBel MRav SEND SLim SPer SSpi SSta WCot WCru WDin WHCG WPGP WPyg WSHC WWal WWat WWin
- (f)	CPMA
- (m)	CPMA WCFE
- 'Mrs Amy Doncaster'	EPla
¶ - Rosemoor form	WHCG
lobbii	CPle
nigrum 'Amos Black' (B)	GTwe
- 'Baldwin' (B)	CMac GBon LRHS SDea SPer WStI WWeb
* - 'Barchatnaja' (F)	CAgr
- 'Ben Alder' PBR (B)	CBlo LRHS SDea
- 'Ben Connan' PBR (B) ♀	COtt EMui EPfP GTwe LRHS MGos SCoo SDea WLRN
- 'Ben Lomond' PBR (B) ♀	CBlo CTri EBee EMui GBon GChr GKir GTwe LBuc LRHS MBri

	MGos NBee NRog SDea WStI
- 'Ben Loyal' (B)	GTwe
- 'Ben More' (B)	CBlo GKir GTwe LRHS MBri NBee SDea SPer WStI
- 'Ben Nevis' (B)	CBlo CTri EBee GTwe SDea
- 'Ben Sarek' PBR (B) ♀	CBlo CSam CSut EBee EBrP EBre EMui ERea GChr GKir GTwe LBCl LBSe LBre LBuc LRHS MBBe MBri MGos NRog SBre SDea SPer WWeb
- 'Ben Tirran' PBR (B)	CBlo CDoC LBuc LRHS MGos
- 'Black Reward' (B)	CAgr LRHS
- 'Blackdown' (B)	Last listed 1997
- 'Blacksmith' (B)	Last listed 1999
- 'Boskoop Giant' (B)	CMac GTwe LRHS NRog SPer
* - 'Byelorussian Sweet' (B)	CAgr
* - 'Cascade' (F)	Last listed 1997
* - 'Cherry' (F)	Last listed 1997
- 'Consort' (B)	CAgr
- 'Daniel's September' (B)	GTwe
- 'Farleigh' (B)	EMui
- 'Foxendown' (B)	EMui
* - 'Hystawneznaya' (F)	CAgr
* - 'Jet' (B)	CBlo GTwe LRHS NRog SPer
* - 'Kosmicheskaya' (F)	CAgr
¶ - 'Laciniatum'	EMon
- 'Laxton's Giant' (B)	GTwe
- 'Mendip Cross' (B)	CBlo GTwe
- 'Pilot Alexander Mamkin' (B)	Last listed 1998
- 'Seabrook's' (B)	Last listed 1997
- 'Wellington XXX' (B)	CBlo ERea GTwe LBuc LRHS MBri NBee NRog WStI WWeb
- 'Westwick Choice' (B)	GTwe
§ *odoratum*	More than 30 suppliers
- 'Crandall'	ESim
praecox	CB&S MBlu SEND
propinquum	Last listed 1999
roezlii	CPle
rubrum 'Blanka' (W)	CSut
- 'Cascade' (R)	Last listed 1998
¶ - 'Cherry' (R)	CAgr
- 'Fay's New Prolific' (R)	GTwe
- 'Hollande Rose' (P)	GTwe
- 'Jonkheer van Tets' (R) ♀	CAgr EMui GTwe IArd LRHS MCoo SDea WTro
- 'Junifer' (R)	CAgr EMui GTwe
- 'Laxton's Number One' (R)	CAgr CBlo CSam CTri EBrP EBre EMui GBon GChr GTwe LBCl LBSe LBre LRHS MBBe MBri NRog SBre SDea SPer WWeb
- 'Laxton's Perfection' (R)	MCoo
- 'October Currant' (P)	GTwe
- 'Raby Castle' (R)	GTwe
- 'Red Lake' (R) ♀	CAgr CBlo CMac CSam EBrP EBre ERea GBon GChr GKir GTwe LBCl LBSe LBre LBuc LRHS MBBe MBri MGos NBee NRog SBre SDea SPer WStI
- 'Redstart' PBR (R)	CBlo COtt GTwe LBuc LRHS MBri SDea WWeb
- 'Rondom' (R)	SDea
- 'Rovada' (R)	CSut EMui GTwe
- 'Stanza' (R) ♀	GTwe SDea
§ - 'Versailles Blanche' (W)	CBlo CDoC CMac CSam CTri EMui EPfP GChr GKir GTwe LBuc MBri MGos SDea SPer WWeb
- 'White Dutch' (W)	MCoo
- 'White Grape' (W) ♀	CBlo CTri GTwe NRog
- 'White Pearl' (W)	CB&S
- 'White Transparent' (W)	GTwe
- White Versailles	See *R. rubrum* 'Versailles Blanche'

- 'Wilson's Long Bunch' (R)	GTwe
sanguineum	CBlo CLTr CPle CSam GChr GKir MBar NCut NFor WStI
- 'Albescens'	SLon SPer WBcn
- 'Brocklebankii' ♀	CAbP CBlo EBee EPar EPfP EPla GKir LHop LRHS MGos MWat NPri SBrw SLim SPer WAbe WGwG WSHC
- double	See *R. sanguineum* 'Plenum'
- 'Elk River Red'	GKir LRHS
- 'Flore Pleno'	See *R. sanguineum* 'Plenum'
- 'Giant White'	EPla
- var. *glutinosum* 'Albidum'	SChu
- 'King Edward VII'	CBlo CDoC EBee ECtt GChr GKir LBuc LRHS MBar MGos MWat NBee NFor NWea SLim SLon SMer SPer SPla SRPl SReu SRms WCFE WDin WFar WGwG WMoo WStI WTro WWeb
- 'Koja'	LRHS MBri NPro
- 'Lombartsii'	CBlo MRav
§ - 'Plenum' (d)	CBot MTed WCot
¶ - 'Poky's Pink'	CLyn EBrP EBre GKir GSki LBCl LBSe LBre LRHS MAsh MBBe MBri MGos MRav SBre
- 'Pulborough Scarlet' ♀	CB&S CBlo CChe CDoC CLTr EBee ELan ENot EWTr GChr GKir GOrc LRHS MAsh MGos MRav MWat NBee NBir NFla SLim SMer SPer SPla SRms WFar WWeb
- 'Red Pimpernel'	CDoC LAst LRHS MBNS MBri WBcn WFar
- 'Splendens'	Last listed 1997
- 'Taff's Kim' (v)	CBlo CPMA EPla
- 'Tydeman's White' ♀	CBlo CChe CPle ECtt ELan EPfP EPla LAst MBar MBlu SSpi WStI
§ - White Icicle = 'Ubric'[PBR]	CBlo CBot CWSG EBee EBrP EBre GKir GSki LBCl LBSe LBre LRHS MAsh MBBe MBri MGos NBir NFla SBre SLim SPer SPla WWat
speciosum ♀	More than 30 suppliers
tenue	EPla
uva-crispa	GTwe
var. *reclinatum*	
'Achilles' (C/D)	
- - 'Admiral Beattie' (F)	GTwe NRog
- - 'Alma' (D)	NRog
- - 'Annelii' (F)	CAgr SDea
- - 'Aston Red'	See *R. uva-crispa* var. *reclinatum* 'Warrington'
- - 'Australia' (F)	NRog
- - 'Bedford Red' (D)	GTwe NRog
- - 'Bedford Yellow' (D)	GTwe
- - 'Beech Tree Nestling' (F)	GTwe
- - 'Bellona' (C)	NRog
- - 'Blucher' (F)	GTwe NRog
- - 'Bright Venus' (D)	GTwe
- - 'Broom Girl' (D)	GTwe NRog
- - 'Captivator' (F)	GTwe
- - 'Careless' (C) ♀	CBlo CMac CSam CTri EBee EMui ERea GBon GKir GTwe IOrc LRHS MBri MGos NBee NRog SDea SPer WStI WWeb
- - 'Catherina' (C/D)	Last listed 1997
- - 'Champagne Red' (F)	GTwe
- - 'Clayton' (F)	NRog
- - 'Cook's Eagle' (C)	GTwe
- - 'Cousen's Seedling' (F)	GTwe
- - 'Criterion' (C)	GTwe NRog
- - 'Crown Bob' (C/D)	GTwe LRHS NRog
- - 'Dan's Mistake' (D)	GTwe LRHS NRog

- - 'Drill' (F)	GTwe
- - 'Early Sulphur' (D/C)	CBlo GTwe LRHS NRog SDea WStI
- - 'Edith Cavell' (F)	GTwe
- - 'Firbob' (D)	GTwe NRog
- - 'Forester' (D)	GTwe
- - 'Freedom' (C)	GTwe LRHS NRog
- - 'Gipsey Queen' (F)	GTwe
- - 'Glenton Green' (F)	GTwe
- - 'Golden Ball' (D)	SDea
- - 'Golden Drop' (D)	GTwe LRHS
- - 'Green Gem' (C/D)	GTwe NRog
- - 'Green Ocean' (F)	GTwe
- - 'Greenfinch' [PBR] (F) ♀	CWSG EBee EMui GTwe LRHS MGos SDea
- - 'Greengage' (D)	NRog
- - 'Gretna Green' (F)	GTwe
- - 'Guido' (F)	GTwe NRog
- - 'Gunner' (D)	CTri GTwe NRog
- - 'Heart of Oak' (F)	GTwe NRog
- - 'Hebburn Prolific' (D)	GTwe
- - 'Hedgehog' (D)	GTwe
- - 'Hero of the Nile' (C)	GTwe NRog
- - 'High Sheriff' (D)	GTwe LRHS NRog
- - 'Hinnonmäki'	CAgr
- - 'Hinnonmäki Gul'	SDea
- - 'Hinnonmäki Röd' (F)	GTwe MCoo SDea
- - 'Howard's Lancer' (C/D)	GTwe NRog SDea
- - 'Invicta' [PBR] (C) ♀	CBlo CDoC CMac CSut CTri CWSG EBee EBrP EBre EMui GBon GChr GKir LBCl LBSe LBre LBuc LRHS MBBe MBri MGos SBre SDea SPer WStI WWeb
- - 'Ironmonger' (F)	CBlo GTwe LRHS NRog
- - 'Jubilee' (C/D)	COtt CTri LBuc MBri MGos NRog WStI
- - 'Keen's Seedling' (D)	GTwe
- - 'Keepsake' (C/D)	CBlo GTwe LRHS NRog SDea
- - 'King of Trumps' (F)	GTwe LRHS NRog
- - 'Lancashire Lad' (C/D)	GTwe LRHS NRog
- - 'Langley Gage' (D)	GTwe LRHS NRog
- - 'Laxton's Amber' (F)	GTwe
- - 'Leveller' (C/D) ♀	CBlo CMac CTri EBrP EBre EMui GBon GChr GKir GTwe LBCl LBSe LBre LBuc LRHS MBBe MBri MGos NRog SBre SDea SPer WStI WWeb
- - 'London' (C/D)	GTwe LRHS NRog
- - 'Lord Derby' (C/D)	CBlo GTwe MBri NRog
- - 'Lord Kitchener' (F)	NRog
- - 'Macherauch's Seedling' (F)	NRog
- - 'Marigold' (F)	NRog
¶ - - 'Martlet' [PBR] (F)	GTwe
- - 'Matchless' (D)	NRog
- - 'May Duke' (C/D)	LRHS NRog SDea
- - 'Mitre' (C)	GTwe
- - 'Pax' [PBR]	CDoC CWSG EMui GTwe LBuc SDea WLRN
- - 'Peru'	GTwe NRog
- - 'Pitmaston Green Gage' (F)	GTwe
- - 'Plunder' (F)	GTwe NRog
- - 'Prince Charles' (F)	GTwe
- - 'Queen of Hearts' (F)	NRog
- - 'Queen of Trumps' (C)	GTwe NRog
- - 'Rifleman' (D)	GTwe
- - 'Rokula' [PBR]	CDoC EMui GTwe
- - 'Rosebery' (D)	GTwe
- - 'Scotch Red Rough' (D)	GTwe
- - 'Scottish Chieftan' (D)	GTwe
- - 'Sir George Brown' (D)	NRog

- - 'Snowdrop' (C) — GTwe
- - 'Speedwell' (F) — NRog
- - 'Spinefree' (F) — GTwe
- - 'Sultan Juror' (F) — NRog
- - 'Surprise' (C) — GTwe NRog
- - 'Suter Johnny' (F) — NRog
- - 'Telegraph' (F) — GTwe
- - 'The Leader' (F) — NRog
- - 'Tom Joiner' (F) — GTwe
- - 'Trumpeter' (C) — NRog
- - 'Victoria' (F) — GTwe LRHS NRog
§ - - 'Warrington' (D) — GTwe NRog
- - 'Whinham's Industry' — CBlo CMac CSam CSut EMui ERea
  (C/D) ♀ — GBon GChr GKir GTwe IOrc
  — LBuc MBri MGos NBee NRog
  — SDea SPer WStI
- - 'White Eagle' (C) — NRog
- - 'White Lion' (C/D) — GTwe LRHS
- - 'White Transparent' (C) — GTwe
- - 'Whitesmith' (C/D) — CTri GTwe LRHS NRog SDea WStI
- - 'Woodpecker' (F) — GTwe LRHS NRog
- - 'Yellow Champagne' (F) — GTwe LRHS NRog
¶ valdivianum — EPla
viburnifolium — CPle EBee LEdu LRHS SPan SSta
  — SVen WPGP WWat

RICHEA (Epacridaceae)
dracophylla — SAPC
milliganii — Last listed 1999
scoparia — Last listed 1999

RICINUS (Euphorbiaceae)
communis — CHEx
- 'Carmencita' ♀ — LBlo
- 'Gibsonii' — EOas LBlo
- 'Impala' — LBlo MLan SSoC
- 'Niger' — WMul
- 'Zanzibariensis' — EOas LBlo WMul

RIGIDELLA (Iridaceae)
orthantha — CPLG

RIOCREUXIA (Asclepiadaceae)
¶ torulosa — SPlb

RIVINA (Phytolaccaceae)
humilis — Last listed 1997

ROBINIA (Papilionaceae)
¶ x ambigua — SSpi
boyntonii — CTho MGos
fertilis — SSpi WShe
hispida ♀ — CCHP CEnd CLnd CTho EBee
  — ELan EPfP GKir LNet LRHS MBlu
  — SPer SSpi SSta WJas WPyg WSHC
  — WSPU
- 'Macrophylla' — CBlo CEnd SSpi
N - 'Rosea' — CB&S CBlo CBot EBee ENot LRHS
  — MGos WPGP
kelseyi — CBlo CDul IOrc SPer WPyg
x margaretta — See R. x margaretta 'Pink
  Casque Rouge — Cascade'
§ - 'Pink Cascade' — CBlo CDoC CEnd CTho EBee EPfP
  — LNet LPan LRHS MAsh MBri MGos
  — MMea SPer SRPl SSpi WDin WPyg
neomexicana — CLnd
pseudoacacia ♀ — CBlo CCHP CLnd ELan ENot GAri
  — GKir LBuc LPan MCoo SMHT
  — WFar WNor
- 'Bessoniana' — CBlo CLnd CTho EBee ENot
- 'Fastigiata' — See R. pseudoacacia 'Pyramidalis'
- 'Frisia' ♀ — More than 30 suppliers

- 'Inermis' hort. — See R. pseudoacacia
  — 'Umbraculifera'
- 'Lace Lady'ᴾᴮᴿ — EBee ELan ENot LPan LRHS MAsh
  — MBri MGos MRav SCoo WWes
* - 'Mimosifolia' — MBri
§ - 'Pyramidalis' — CTho ENot
- 'Rozynskiana' — CTho SFam
- 'Sandraudiga' — SMad
- 'Tortuosa' — CBlo CDul CEnd CLnd CTho
  — EBee ELan EMil EPfP LPan LRHS
  — MAsh MBri MGos MMea SLdr SPar
  — SPer SRPl WPGP
§ - 'Umbraculifera' — CLnd EMil ENot LPan MGos SFam
- 'Unifoliola' — CTho
x slavinii 'Hillieri' ♀ — CBlo CDul CEnd CLnd CTho
  — EBee ECrN ELan EPfP EWTr IOrc
  — LPan LRHS SFam SPer SSpi WWat
* 'Twisty Baby' — EPfP

ROCHEA See CRASSULA

RODGERSIA ✿ (Saxifragaceae)
aesculifolia ♀ — More than 30 suppliers
- green bud — IBlr
- 'Irish Bronze' — EBrP EBre IBlr LBCl LBSe LBre
  — LPio MBBe SBre
- pink — IBlr
aff. aesculifolia petaloid — IBlr
'Blickfang' — IBlr
'Die Anmutige' — CRow
¶ 'Die Schöne' — CLAP
'Elfenbeinturm' — IBlr
henrici — CRow IBlr MCCP MCli SPer SWat
  — WLin WPnP WRus
¶ - 'Buckshaw White' — IBlr
- hybrid — EBee GAri NHol NLar SCob WCru
'Koriata' — IBlr
'Kupfermond' — CRow IBlr
'Maigrün' — IBlr
nepalensis — CFil IBlr WCot
new hybrids — WHil
¶ 'Panache' — IBlr
'Parasol' — CFil CHad CLAP ELan GBuc IBlr
  — NHol SSpi WPGP WPnP
pinnata — More than 30 suppliers
- 'Alba' — GKir IBlr LRHS MBri NHol WPnP
- 'Buckland Beauty' — IBlr SSpi
- 'Cally Salmon' — GCal
- 'Elegans' — CHEx CHad EBrP EBre ELan EMan
  — ENot EPar EPla GKir GMaP IBlr
  — LAst LBCl LBSe LBre LRHS MBBe
  — MBel MRav NHol NOrc SBre
  — SMrm SSoC WGer WHil WWat
  — WWin
- I. 1670 — CLAP SSpi
¶ - Mount Stewart form — IBlr
- 'Perthshire Bronze' — IBlr
- 'Rosea' — IBlr
- 'Superba' ♀ — More than 30 suppliers
- white — GCal
podophylla ♀ — More than 30 suppliers
- 'Bronceblad' — IBlr
- Donard form — CFil IBlr WCot
- 'Rotlaub' — CRow EGle GCal IBlr LRHS MBri
  — WCot
- 'Smaragd' — CLAP CRow EBee GCal IBlr LRHS
purdomii hort. — GCal IBlr LRHS SSpi WCDu
§ 'Reinecke Fuchs' — IBlr
'Rosenlicht' — CRow MTed
'Rosenzipfel' — IBlr
sambucifolia — More than 30 suppliers
- dwarf pink-flowered — GKir IBlr

- dwarf white-flowered IBlr
- large green-stemmed IBlr
- large red-stemmed IBlr
- x *pinnata* IBlr
sp. ACE 2303 GBuc WAbe
sp. CLD 1329 NHol
sp. CLD 1432 NHol
sp. from Castlewellan IBlr
tabularis See *Astilboides tabularis*

ROELLA (Campanulaceae)
ciliata Last listed 1998
maculata Last listed 1998

ROHDEA ✿ (Convallariaceae)
japonica CFil WCot WPGP
- 'Gunjaku' (v) EMon
- 'Lance Leaf' EPla SApp
- long-leaved WCru
- 'Talbot Manor' (v) CFil EPla SApp WCot WPGP
- 'Tama-jishi' (v) WCot
- 'Tuneshige Rokujo' WCot
- variegated WCot
watanabei B&SWJ 1911 WCru

ROMANZOFFIA (Hydrophyllaceae)
§ *sitchensis* CLyd CTri
suksdorfii E. Greene See *R. sitchensis*
tracyi Last listed 1997
unalaschcensis CNic GGar GTou NWCA SRms
SSca WPer WWin

ROMNEYA (Papaveraceae)
coulteri ♀ More than 30 suppliers
§ - var. *trichocalyx* IBlr SBra SBrw SCro SPer SSpi
§ - 'White Cloud' ENot ERea IBlr MRav SMad WSpi
- 'White Sails' IBlr
x *hybrida* See *R. coulteri* 'White Cloud'
trichocalyx See *R. coulteri* var. *trichocalyx*

ROMULEA (Iridaceae)
¶ *atrandra* EHyt
battandieri AB&S 4659 Last listed 1998
bifrons AB&S 4359/4360 Last listed 1998
bulbocodium CBro CNic CPLG
- var. *clusiana* Last listed 1999
- - MS 239 Last listed 1999
- - S&F 237 Last listed 1998
- - Serotina Group Last listed 1999
* - 'Knightshayes' CLAP
- var. *leichtliniana* CNic
- - MS 784 Last listed 1999
¶ - WM 9908 MPhe
campanuloides Last listed 1998
columnae AB&S 4659 Last listed 1998
engleri S&F 3 Last listed 1998
hirta Last listed 1998
ligustica var. *rouyana* Last listed 1998
S&F 360
linaresii CNic
- var. *graeca* Last listed 1997
- - CE&H 620 Last listed 1998
longituba See *R. macowanii*
§ *macowanii* CPBP NMen
- var. *alticola* Last listed 1999
minutiflora NRog
monticola Last listed 1998
nivalis LBow
pratensis Last listed 1997
ramiflora Last listed 1998
¶ - subsp. *gaditana* EHyt
- S&F 63 Last listed 1998

requienii CStu
- L65 Last listed 1999
rosea NRog
sabulosa Last listed 1998
saldanhensis Last listed 1998
sp. S&F 367 Last listed 1998
tabularis Last listed 1997
tempskyana EPot
* *zahnii* CNic WCot

RONDELETIA (Rubiaceae)
amoena LChe

RORIPPA (Brassicaceae)
nasturtium-aquaticum MHew WMAq

ROSA ✿ (Rosaceae)
A Shropshire Lad CSam LRHS MAus MJon SWCr
= 'Ausled' PBR (S)
Aalsmeer Gold® Last listed 1998
= 'Bekola' (HT)
Abbeyfield Rose ENot GCoc GGre MMat SJus SPer
= 'Cocbrose' PBR (HT) ♀ SWCr
§ 'Abbotswood' EBls MAus
(*canina* hybrid)
Aberdeen Celebration GCoc
= 'Cocmystery' (F)
Abigaile® = 'Tanelaigib' MJon NBat
PBR (F)
'Abington Park Last listed 1998
Northampton' (HT)
Abraham Darby® CGro CSam EBee EBrP EBre GGre
= 'Auscot' PBR (S) GKir IHar LBCl LBSe LBre LRHS
LStr MAus MBBe MDun MFry
MGan MJon NPri SBre SPer SRPl
SSea SWCr WAct WHCG WStI
Acapulco = EBee IDic MFry MJon
'Dicblender' PBR (HT)
§ Ace of Hearts MBur
= 'Korred' (HT)
acicularis EPla
- var. *nipponensis* EBls
'Adam' (ClT) EBls MAus
'Adam Messerich' (Bb) EBee EBls MAus SWCr WHCG
'Adélaïde d'Orléans' (Ra) ♀ CRHN EBls LRHS MAus MBri
SFam SPer SWCr WAct WHCG
Admirable = 'Searodney' MBur
(Min)
'Admiral Rodney' (HT) MGan MJon NBat NRog
Adolf Horstmann® (HT) MGan SWCr
Adriana = 'Frydesire' (HT) MFry
'Adrienne Berman' (HT) Last listed 1998
'Agatha' (G) EBls
Agatha Christie = CGre MBri MJon MMat SApu SJus
'Kormeita' PBR (ClF) SWCr
'Agathe Incarnata' (DxG) SWCr
'Aglaia' (Ra) WHCG
'Agnes' (Ru) EBee EBls ENot EPfP GCoc LRHS
MAus MGan MMat SJus SPer SSea
SWCr WAct WHCG WOVN
'Aimée Vibert' (Ra) EBee EBls IHar MAus SFam SPer
SRPl SWCr WAct WHCG
Air France = 'Meifinaro' Last listed 1997
(Min)
'Alain Blanchard' (G) EBls MAus WHCG
x *alba* (A) EBls NRog
§ - 'Alba Maxima' (A) ♀ CHad EBls EMFP ENot GChr
GCoc LRHS MAus MDun MMat
SFam SPer SRPl SSea SWCr WAct
WHCG
§ - 'Alba Semiplena' (A) ♀ CHad EBls LRHS MAus SJus SPer
SWCr WAct WGer WHCG

- Celestial	See *R.* 'Céleste'	EBrP EBre GKir ISea LBCl LBSe
- 'Maxima'	See *R.* x *alba* 'Alba Maxima'	LBre LRHS LStr MAus MBBe MGan
Alba Meidiland®	WOVN	MMat NFla NRog SApu SBre SPer
= 'Meiflopan' PBR		SSea SWCr WAct WHCG
(S/GC)		'Améthyste' (Ra)	Last listed 1998
'Albéric Barbier' (Ra) ♀	CHad CRHN CSam EBee EBls	Amorette	See *R.* Snowdrop = 'Amoru'
	ENot EWTr GKir LRHS LStr MAus	'Amy Robsart' (RH)	EBls MAus SJus SWCr
	MBNS MBri MFry MGan MJon	Anabell = 'Korbell' (F)	MGan
	MMat NRog NWea SApu SJus SPer	'Anaïs Ségalas' (G)	MAus
	SRPl SSea SWCr WAct WHCG	§ 'Andersonii'	EBls MAus SWCr WAct
	WOVN	(*canina* hybrid)	
Albert Weedall	Last listed 1997	§ 'Anemone' (Cl)	EBls MAus
= 'Scriveo' (HT)		anemoniflora	See *R.* x *beanii*
'Albertine' (Ra) ♀	More than 30 suppliers	anemonoides	See *R.* 'Anemone'
'Alchymist' (S/Cl)	CHad CPou EBee EBls ENot IHar	- 'Ramona'	See *R.* 'Ramona'
	LRHS MAus MBri MGan MJon	Angela Rippon®	MDun MFry MGan MJon SRPl
	MMat SFam SPer SPla SWCr WAct	= 'Ocaru' (Min)	SSea SWCr WGer
	WHCG	'Angela's Choice' (F)	MGan SWCr
Alec's Red® = 'Cored' (HT)	CB&S CGro EBls GCoc GGre GKir	'Angèle Pernet' (HT)	EBls
	IHar LPlm LRHS LStr MAus MBri	'Angelina' (S)	EBls SWCr
	MGan MJon MMat NRog SPer	§ Anisley Dickson®	IDic LGod MGan NBat SApu SPer
	SWCr WWeb	= 'Dickimono' PBR (F) ♀	SWCr
§ Alex C. Collie	Last listed 1999	'Ann Aberconway' (F)	MJon SWCr
= 'Cococrust' (F)		§ Ann = 'Ausfete' PBR	LRHS MAus SWCr
Alexander®	CGro EBls ENot GChr GCoc GGre	'Anna de Diesbach' (HP)	EBls
= 'Harlex' (HT) ♀	LGod LPlm LRHS LStr MFry MGan	Anna Ford® = 'Harpiccolo'	GGre IHar LGod LPlm LRHS LStr
	MJon MMat NRog SApu SPer SSea	PBR (Min/Patio) ♀	MAus MGan MJon SApu SWCr
	SWCr	Anna Livia = 'Kormetter'	ENot MGan MJon MMat SJus SWCr
'Alexander Hill Gray' (T)	EBls	PBR (F) ♀	
'Alexander von	MGan	'Anna Olivier' (T)	EBls
Humboldt' (Cl)		'Anna Pavlova' (HT)	EBls SSea
'Alexandre Girault' (Ra)	CRHN EBee EBls EMFP LRHS	§ Anna Zinkeisen	SWCr WAct WOVN
	MAus MBri SPer SWCr WAct	= 'Harquhling' (S)	
	WHCG	Anne Cocker® (F)	GCoc MGan SWCr
§ 'Alfred Colomb' (HP)	EBls	'Anne Dakin' (ClHT)	MAus
'Alfred de Dalmas'	See *R.* 'Mousseline'	Anne Harkness®	MAus MGan MJon NRog SSea SWCr
misapplied		= 'Harkaramel' PBR (F)	
'Alida Lovett' (Ra)	EBls MAus	¶ Anne Marie Laing	EBls
§ Alison = 'Coclibee' PBR (F)	GCoc SApu SWCr	= 'Jospink' (F)	
§ 'Alister Stella Gray' (N) ♀	EBee EBls EMFP EWTr IHar LRHS	Anne Moore	Last listed 1997
	MAus MGan NHaw SPer SSea	= 'Morberg' (Min)	
	SWCr WAct WHCG	'Anne of Geierstein' (RH)	EBls MAus MGan SWCr
All in One PBR	See *R.* Exploit = 'Meilider'	'Anne Watkins' (HT)	EBls
'Allen Chandler' (ClHT)	EBls MAus	Antique PBR	See *R.* Antique '89 = 'Kordalen'
Allgold® (F)	CB&S CGro EBls GCoc GKir LStr	§ Antique '89®	EBee EBls MBri MJon MMat SJus
	MAus MGan MJon SSea WStI	= 'Kordalen' PBR (ClF)	SWCr WGer
'Aloha' (ClHT)	More than 30 suppliers	'Antoine Rivoire' (HT)	EBls
alpina	See *R.* pendulina	'Antonia d'Ormois' (G)	EBls
Alpine Sunset® (HT)	CTri EBls GGre GKir MGan SPer	Anusheh = 'Payable' (F)	Last listed 1997
	SWCr	Anvil Sparks®	See *R.* 'Ambossfunken'
altaica hort.	See *R.* pimpinellifolia	apothecary's rose	See *R.* gallica var. officinalis
	'Grandiflora'	'Apple Blossom' (Ra)	EBls SWCr WHCG
Altissimo®	CHad EBls EMFP LRHS MAus	'Applejack' (S)	EBls
= 'Delmur' (Cl) ♀	MGan MJon MMat SPer SSea	'Apricot Garnet'	See *R.* 'Garnette Apricot'
	SWCr WAct WGer	'Apricot Nectar' (F)	LStr MAus MGan SPer SWCr
'Amadis' (Bs)	EBls MAus SWCr WHCG	'Apricot Silk' (HT)	CB&S CTri EBls GKir IHar MAus
Amanda = 'Beesian' PBR (F)	LStr MBri MJon SApu SWCr		MGan NRog SPer SWCr WWeb
'Amatsu-otome' (HT)	Last listed 1997	Apricot Summer®	ENot MBri MJon MMat WGer
'Amazing Grace' (HT)	GCoc GGre SWCr	= 'Korpapiro' PBR (Patio)	
Amber Nectar	LStr MJon SWCr	Apricot Sunblaze®	EBls MJon SJus SWCr
= 'Mehamber' PBR (F)		= 'Savamark' PBR (Min)	
Amber Queen®	CGro EBls ELan GCoc GGre	'Apricot Wine' (F)	IHar
	GKir	¶ April Fools Day	SWCr
= 'Harroony' PBR (F) ♀	LGod LPlm LStr MAus MBri MBur	= 'Gregsil' (HT)	
	MFry MGan MJon NRog SApu	'April Hamer' (HT)	NBat
	SJus SPer SRPl SSea SWCr	§ Arc Angel = 'Fryorst' (HT)	MFry
§ 'Ambossfunken' (HT)	MGan SWCr	§ Arcadian = 'Macnewye'	MJon
§ Ambridge Rose	LRHS MAus MBri SWCr	PBR (F)	
= 'Auswonder' (S)		'Archiduc Joseph'	See *R.* 'Général Schablikine'
'Amélia'	See *R.* 'Celsiana'	misapplied	
'Amelia Louise' (Min)	Last listed 1997	'Archiduchesse Elisabeth	EBls
'American Pillar' (Ra)	CGro CRHN CSam EBee EBls	d'Autriche' (HP)	

Arctic Sunrise | Last listed 1997
= 'Bararcsun' (Min/GC)
'Ardoisée de Lyon' (HP) | EBls
Ards Beauty | IDic MGan SApu SPer SWCr
= 'Dicjoy' PBR (F)
'Ards Rover' (ClHP) | EBls
'Arethusa' (Ch) | EBls EMFP SWCr
'Arizona Sunset' (Min) | NBat
§ **arkansana** var. **suffulta** | EBls WHCG
Armada® = 'Haruseful' | GCoc SApu SWCr
PBR (S)
'Arrillaga' (HP) | MAus
Artful Dodger | MBur
= 'Sabbelief' (Patio)
'Arthur Bell' (F) ♀ | EBls EBrP EBre GChr GCoc GGre
| GKir IHar LBCl LBSe LBre LPlm
| LStr MAus MBBe MBur MGan
| MMat NRog SApu SBre SPer SRPl
| SSea SWCr WWeb
'Arthur de Sansal' (DPo) | EBls MAus WHCG
'Arthur Scargill' (Min) | Last listed 1997
arvensis | CKin EBls LBuc MAus NWea WAct
§ 'Aschermittwoch' (Cl) | EBls
¶ Ascot Bonnet | LStr
= 'Helbonnet' (F)
Ash Wednesday | See R. 'Aschermittwoch'
'Assemblage des | EBls MAus
Beautés' (G)
'Astrid Späth Striped' (F) | EBls
Atco Royale | MFry
= 'Frywinner' PBR (F)
Atlantic Star | MFry MJon SWCr
= 'Fryworld' PBR (F)
§ Audrey Gardner | SWCr
= 'Peaspecial'
(Min/Patio)
Audrey Wilcox® | MFry
= 'Frywilrey' (HT)
'August Seebauer' (F) | EBls MAus
'Auguste Gervais' (Ra) | EBls IHar LRHS MAus SPer SWCr
| WHCG
Auguste Renoir® | GGre
= 'Meitoifar' PBR (HT)
'Augustine Guinoisseau' | EBls MAus
(HT)
'Augustine Halem' (HT) | EBls
'Aunty Dora' (F) | SWCr
'Ausspry' (1984) | See R. Belle Story = 'Auselle'
'Ausspry' (1985) | See R. Sir Walter Raleigh =
| 'Ausspry'
Austrian Copper | See R. foetida 'Bicolor'
Austrian Yellow | See R. foetida
'Ausvariety'PBR | See R. Kathryn Morley =
| 'Ausclub'
'Autumn' (HT) | NRog
'Autumn Bouquet' (S) | EBls
'Autumn Delight' (HM) | EBls MAus WHCG
Autumn Fire | See R. 'Herbstfeuer'
'Autumn Sunlight' (ClF) | MGan SPer SWCr
'Autumn Sunset' (S) | EBls
'Autumnalis' | See R. 'Princesse de Nassau'
'Aviateur Blériot' (Ra) | EBls MAus
'Avignon' (F) | Last listed 1999
Avocet = 'Harpluto' (F) | GGre SWCr
Avon = 'Poulmulti' PBR (GC) | EBee ELan ENot GCoc LGod LStr
| MAus MGan MJon SApu SPer SSea
| SWCr WHCG WOVN
Awakening | EBls WHCG
= 'Probuzini' (Cl)
Awareness = 'Frybingo' | MFry SWCr
PBR (HT)
'Ayrshire Splendens' | See R. 'Splendens'

'Baby Bio' (F/Patio) | CB&S MBri MGan NRog SWCr
'Baby Darling' (Min) | MAus MGan SSea
'Baby Faurax' (Poly) | MAus
Baby Gold Star (Min) | See R. 'Estrellita de Oro'
'Baby Katie' (Min) | NBat
Baby Love = 'Scrivluv' PBR | MAus MJon SWCr
(yellow) (Min/Patio)
§ Baby Masquerade® | ELan GCoc LGod LPlm MBur
= 'Tanba' (Min) | MGan MJon MMat NRog SWCr
| WStI
Baby Sunrise | MJon SJus
= 'Macparlez' (Min)
'Bad Neuenahr' (Cl) | MGan
'Ballerina' (HM/Poly) ♀ | More than 30 suppliers
Ballindalloch Castle | GCoc
= 'Cocneel' PBR (F)
'Baltimore Belle' (Ra) | CRHN EBls MAus WHCG
Bangor Cathedral | MJon
= 'Kirmelody' (HT)
banksiae (Ra) | CCHP CGre GQui LPan SRms
- **alba** | See R. banksiae var. banksiae
§ - var. **banksiae** (Ra/d) | CBot EPfP ERea LRHS LStr MAus
| SBra SPer SPla SSea WWat
- 'Lutea' (Ra/d) ♀ | More than 30 suppliers
- var. **normalis** (Ra) | CBot CGre MAus SWCr WHer
| WOut
- S&F 96051 (Ra) | ISea
Bantry Bay® (ClHT) | EBls LStr MGan MMat SJus SPer
| SPla SSea SWCr
Barbara Austin | LRHS MAus
= 'Austop' PBR (S)
'Barbara Carrera' (F) | EBls
§ Barkarole® | LStr MJon SApu SJus SSea SWCr
= 'Tanelorak' PBR (HT)
'Baron de Bonstetten' (HP) | EBls
'Baron de Wassenaer' | EBls MGan SWCr
(CeMo)
'Baron Girod de l'Ain' (HP) | EBee EBls LRHS MAus SPer SPla
| SSea SWCr WAct WHCG
'Baroness Rothschild' (HP) | See R. 'Baronne Adolph de
| Rothschild'
'Baroness Rothschild' (HT) | See R. Baronne Edmond de
| Rothschild = 'Meigriso'
§ 'Baronne Adolph de | EBee EMFP IOrc LRHS MDun
Rothschild' (HP) | MGan SWCr WHCG
§ Baronne Edmond de | MAus SSea SWCr WAct
Rothschild® =
'Meigriso' (HT)
'Baronne Henriette de | EBls
Snoy' (T)
'Baronne Prévost' (HP) ♀ | EBls MAus SFam WAct WHCG
¶ Baroque = 'Harbaroque' | SWCr
PBR (GC/F/S)
§ Barry Fearn = | MMat
'Korschwama' PBR (HT)
'Bashful' (Poly) | MGan
Basildon Bond | IHar
= 'Harjosine' (HT)
Battersby Beauty | NBat
= 'Horbatbeauty' (HT)
§ x **beanii** (Ra) | EPla
'Beau Narcisse' (G) | MAus
'Beauté' (HT) | EBls MAus MGan SWCr
Beautiful Britain | EBls GGre IDic LStr MAus MBri
= 'Dicfire' PBR (F) | MGan MJon NRog SJus SWCr
'Beauty of Rosemawr' (ClT) | EBls
Beauty Star®PBR | See R. Liverpool Remembers =
| 'Frystar'
Behold = 'Savahold' (Min) | NBat
'Bel Ange' (HT) | MGan SWCr
Belfast Belle | Last listed 1998
= 'Dicrobot' (HT)

bella — Last listed 1999
§ Bella = 'Pouljill' PBR (S) — EBee GGre SWCr
'Belle Amour' (AxD) — EBls MAus SWCr WHCG
'Belle Blonde' (HT) — MGan SPer SWCr
'Belle de Crécy' (G) ♀ — EBls GCoc GKir IOrc LRHS LStr MAus MMat SFam SJus SPer SWCr WAct WHCG
'Belle des Jardins' misapplied — See *R.* 'Centifolia Variegata'
Belle Epoque = 'Fryyaboo' PBR (HT) — GCoc LStr MBur MFry MGan MJon MMat SApu SJus SWCr
'Belle Isis' (G) — EBls MAus SPer SWCr
'Belle Lyonnaise' (ClT) — EBls
'Belle Poitevine' (Ru) ♀ — EBls MAus
'Belle Portugaise' (ClT) — EBls MAus
§ Belle Story® = 'Auselle' (S) — MAus SPer
Belle Sunblaze = 'Meidanego' (Min) — IHar
Bellevue® = 'Poulena' (HT) — Last listed 1998
§ 'Belvedere' (Ra) — EBls MAus MBri SWCr WHCG
* 'Bengal Beauty' — WCot WWat
Benita® = 'Dicquarrel' PBR (HT) — IDic LGod MJon
'Bennett's Seedling' (Ra) — MAus
Benson and Hedges Gold® = 'Macgem' PBR (HT) — Last listed 1997
Benson and Hedges Special = 'Macshana' PBR (Min) — ELan GGre MAus MBri MJon SWCr
§ Berkshire = 'Korpinka' PBR (GC) — ENot LStr MGan MJon MMat SRum SSea SWCr WOVN WWeb
§ Best Wishes = 'Chessnut' PBR (Cl/v) — COtt GCoc GGre LStr MBri MJon SSea SWCr
Bettina® = 'Mepal' (HT) — MAus MGan SWCr
Betty Driver = 'Gandri' PBR (F) — MBri MGan SPer SWCr
Betty Harkness = 'Harette' PBR (F) — GCoc SApu
'Betty Prior' (F) — GCoc MGan SWCr
'Betty Uprichard' (HT) — EBls
¶ Bewitched = 'Poulbella' PBR (F) — SWCr
'Beyreuth' (S) — MGan
Bianco = 'Cocblanco' PBR (Patio/Min) — GCoc MAus SJus
§ Bibi Maizoon® = 'Ausdimindo' PBR (S) — IHar LRHS MAus SPer
Biddulph Grange = 'Frydarkeye' (S) — MFry
Biddy = 'Benbid' (Min) — Last listed 1997
§ *biebersteinii* — EBls
'Big Chief' (HT) — MJon NRog
Big Purple® = 'Stebigpu' PBR (HT) — EBee MJon SApu SWCr
Birthday Girl = 'Meilasso' PBR (F) — GGre MJon NPri SApu SWCr
Birthday Wishes = 'Guesdelay' (HT) — LPlm
'Bishop Darlington' (HM) — Last listed 1999
Bishop Elphinstone = 'Cocjolly' (F) — GCoc
'Bit o' Sunshine' (Min) — MDun MGan SWCr
'Black Beauty' (HT) — MAus MJon
'Black Ice' (F) — MGan SWCr
'Black Jack' (Ce) — See *R.* 'Tour de Malakoff'
Black Jack™ = 'Minkco' (Min/Patio) — NBat
Black Jade™ = 'Benblack' (Min/Patio) — Last listed 1997
'Black Prince' (HP) — EBls
'Blairii Number One' (Bb) — EBls

'Blairii Number Two' (ClBb) ♀ — EBee EBls EWTr LRHS MAus MBri SFam SPer SWCr WAct WHCG
'Blanche de Vibert' (DPo) — EBls MAus WHCG
'Blanche Double de Coubert' (Ru) ♀ — CHad CSam EBee EBls ELan ENot GCoc IOrc LBuc LRHS LStr MAus MFry MGan MJon MMat NRog SApu SFam SJus SPer SRPl SRum SWCr WAct WHCG WOVN
'Blanche Moreau' (CeMo) — EBls IHar MAus MGan SPer SWCr WAct
'Blanchefleur' (CexG) — EBls MAus SSea SWCr
blanda — EBls
'Blaydon Races' (F) — Last listed 1998
§ Blenheim = 'Tanmurse' PBR (GC) — ECle MBur MGan MJon SApu SWCr WOVN
Blessings® (HT) ♀ — CB&S CGro EBee EBls EBrP EBre EWTr GGre LBCl LBSe LBre LGod LPlm LStr MAus MBBe MBri MBur MFry MGan MJon NRog SApu SBre SPer SRPl SSea SWCr WWeb
'Bleu Magenta' (Ra) ♀ — EBee EBls MAus SWCr WHCG
¶ 'Bliss' (S) — EBls
'Bloomfield Abundance' (Poly) — CPou EBls MAus SPer SWCr WHCG WHer
'Bloomfield Dainty' (HM) — EBls
'Blossomtime' (Cl) — NRog SMad SPer
'Blue Diamond' (HT) — MGan SWCr
§ Blue Moon® = 'Tannacht' (HT) — CGro EBls EBrP EBre ELan GChr GCoc GGre GKir LBCl LBSe LBre LGod LPlm MAus MBBe MBur MGan MJon NPri NRog SApu SBre SPer SWCr WWeb
Blue Parfum® = 'Tanfifum' PBR — MAus MJon SWCr
Blue Peter = 'Ruiblun' PBR (Min) — MFry MJon SApu SSea SWCr WWeb
'Blush Boursault' (Bs) — EBls MAus
'Blush Damask' (D) — EBls SSea SWCr WHCG
'Blush Noisette' — See *R.* 'Noisette Carnée'
'Blush Rambler' (Ra) — EBee EBls MAus SPer SPla SWCr WHCG
'Blushing Lucy' (Ra) — LRHS MAus MTPN SMrm SPer WAct WHCG WSHC
'Bob Collard' (F) — Last listed 1998
§ Bob Greaves = 'Fryzippy' (F) — MFry
'Bob Woolley' (HT) — NBat
'Bobbie James' (Ra) ♀ — CHad EBee EBls EBrP EBre LBCl LBSe LBre LRHS LStr MAus MBBe MBri MFry MGan MJon MMat NBat SBre SFam SJus SPer SSea SWCr WAct WHCG
'Bobby Charlton' (HT) — MFry MGan NRog SWCr
'Bobolink' (Min) — MGan
'Bon Silène' (T) — EBls
Bonfire Night® (F) — CGro ENot MBur MGan MMat SWCr
Bonica 82®PBR — See *R.* Bonica = 'Meidomonac'
§ Bonica® = 'Meidomonac' PBR (GC) ♀ — More than 30 suppliers
'Bonn' (HM/S) — CB&S LRHS MAus MGan NRog
¶ 'Bonne Nouvelle' (F) — SWCr
'Bonnie Scotland' (HT) — MGan SWCr
Bonsoir = 'Dicbo' (HT) — MGan
'Border Coral' (F) — Last listed 1998
'Bospeabay'PBR — See *R.* 'Tender Loving Care'
'Botzaris' (D) — EBls SFam
'Boule de Nanteuil' (G) — EBls
'Boule de Neige' (Bb) — CPou EBls ENot EWTr GCoc IHar LGod LRHS LStr MAus MDun MMat NFla SFam SJus SPer SPla SWCr WAct WHCG WOVN

'Bouquet d'Or' (N)   EBls MAus SWCr WHCG
¶ 'Bouquet Tout Fait' (N)   WHCG
'Bouquet Tout Fait' misapplied   See *R.* 'Nastarana' (N)
'Bourbon Queen' (Bb)   EBls EMFP MAus SSea SWCr WHCG
Bow Bells = 'Ausbells' (S)   LRHS MAus
Boy O Boy = 'Dicuniform' [PBR] (GC)   IDic
Boys' Brigade® = 'Cocdinkum' [PBR] (Patio)   GCoc MGan SApu SWCr
§ *bracteata*   CRHN EHol GQui MAus WHCG WWat
¶ 'Brandysnap' (F)   GKir
§ Brass Ring = 'Dicgrow' [PBR] (Min/Patio)   ELan ENot IDic IHar MFry MGan SApu SPer SWCr WStl
Brave Heart = 'Horbondsmile' (F)   GGre NBat SWCr
Breath of Life = 'Harquanne' [PBR] (ClHT)   CGro CSam EBls ELan EPfP GGre GKir IHar LGod LRHS LStr MAus MBri MFry MGan MJon NBat SApu SJus SPer SSea SWCr
Bredon® = 'Ausbred' (S)   MAus MBri
'Breeze Hill' (Ra)   EBls MAus
§ 'Brenda Colvin' (Ra)   ISea MAus
'Brennus' (China hybrid)   EBls
'Briarcliff' (HT)   EBls
Bridal Pink™ = 'Jacbri' (F)   MJon SWCr
Bride = 'Fryyearn' [PBR] (HT)   GCoc LStr MFry MJon SApu SWCr
Bright Fire = 'Peaxi' [PBR] (Cl)   MBri MJon SApu SWCr
Bright Smile® = 'Dicdance' [PBR] (F/Patio)   GCoc IDic IHar LStr MAus MFry MGan SPer SSea SWCr
Bright Spark = 'Rubrispa' (Min)   Last listed 1998
'Brindis' (ClF)   MGan
Britannia = 'Frycalm' [PBR] (HT)   MFry
Broadlands = 'Tanmirson' (GC)   CSam EBee ECle LGod MAus MBur MGan MJon SApu SChu SRPl SWCr WGer
Brother Cadfael™ = 'Ausglobe' [PBR] (S)   IHar LRHS MAus MBNS MBri MJon SPer SWCr WOVN WWeb
§ Brown Velvet = 'Maccultra' [PBR] (F)   MJon SApu SWCr
'Brownie' (F)   SWCr
'Browsholme Rose' (Ra)   Last listed 1998
§ *brunonii* (Ra)   CDoC EBls EWes MAus WLRN
- 'Betty Sherriff' (Ra)   CDoC SSpi
- CC 1235 (Ra)   Last listed 1997
- CC&McK 362 (Ra)   Last listed 1997
§ - 'La Mortola' (Ra)   MAus SPer SWCr
Bubbles = 'Frybubbly' [PBR] (GC)   MFry
'Buccaneer' (HT)   LRHS
Buck's Fizz = 'Poulgar' (F)   GGre MGan SApu SJus SWCr
'Buff Beauty' (HM) ♀   More than 30 suppliers
'Bullata'   See *R.* x *centifolia* 'Bullata'
§ 'Burgundiaca' (G)   EBee EBls LFis LRHS MAus SSea SWCr WAct
Burgundian rose   See *R.* 'Burgundiaca'
'Burma Star' (F)   GCoc SWCr
burnet, double pink   See *R. pimpinellifolia* double pink
burnet, double white   See *R. pimpinellifolia* double white
Bush Baby = 'Peanob' [PBR] (Min)   LGod LStr MJon SApu SPer SSea SWCr WStl
Buttercup = 'Ausband' [PBR] (S)   LRHS
Buttons = 'Dicmickey' [PBR] (Min/Patio)   IDic

By Appointment = 'Harvolute' [PBR] (F)   GGre SWCr
'C.F. Meyer'   See *R.* 'Conrad Ferdinand Meyer'
§ *caesia* subsp. *glauca*   Last listed 1998
'Café' (F)   SWCr WBcn
'Cairngorm' (F)   Last listed 1999
'Caledonian' (HT)   NBat
californica (S)   MAus SSea
- 'Plena'   See *R. nutkana* 'Plena'
'Callisto' (HM)   EMFP MAus SWCr WHCG
Calypso = 'Poulclimb' [PBR] (Cl)   ECle SApu SWCr
'Camaïeux' (G)   CPou EBee EBls LRHS MAus SPer SSea SWCr WAct WHCG
Cambridgeshire = 'Korhaugen' [PBR] (GC)   EBee ENot LGod LRHS LStr MAus MMat NPri SPer SSea SWCr WWeb
'Camélia Rose' (Ch)   EBls WHCG
'Cameo' (Poly)   EBls MAus MGan
Camille Pissaro = 'Destricol' (F)   WWeb
'Canary Bird'   See *R. xanthina* 'Canary Bird'
§ Can-can = 'Legglow' (HT)   SWCr
Candy Rose® = 'Meiranovi' [PBR] (S)   CKin EPfP EWFC GChr GIBF GKir
canina (S)   LBuc LHyr MAus MHew NWea SRPl WMou
- 'Abbotswood'   See *R.* 'Abbotswood' (*canina* hybrid)
- 'Andersonii'   See *R.* 'Andersonii' (*canina* hybrid)
- deep pink (S)   MAus
- 'Inermis' (S)   Last listed 1998
'Cantabrigiensis' (S) ♀   EBee EBls ENot GChr LRHS MAus NBus NRog SFam SPer SSea SWCr WAct WHCG WOVN WWat
Canterbury = 'Ausbury' (S)   MAus
'Capitaine Basroger' (CeMo)   EBls MAus
'Capitaine John Ingram' (CeMo) ♀   EBee EBls MAus SPer SSea SWCr
'Captain Christy'   See *R.* 'Climbing Captain Christy'
Captain Cook = 'Macal' (F)   Last listed 1998
'Captain Hayward' (HP)   EBls
'Captain Scarlet' (ClMin)   WWeb
'Cardiff Bay' (HT)   Last listed 1997
'Cardinal de Richelieu' (G) ♀   CHad CPou EBee EBls EPfP EWTr GCoc IOrc LRHS LStr MAus MFry MMat SApu SFam SPer SWCr WAct WHCG
Cardinal Hume® = 'Harregale' (S)   EBls MGan SPer SWCr
'Care 2000' (S)   EBls
Carefree Beauty™ = 'Bucbi' (S)   SWCr
§ Carefree Wonder™ = 'Meipitac' (S)   SWCr
Caring for You = 'Coclust' (HT)   GCoc
'Carmen' (Ru)   EBls MAus
§ 'Carmenetta' (S)   EBls MAus SWCr
'Carol' (Gn)   See *R.* 'Carol Amling'
§ 'Carol Amling' (Gn)   MJon SWCr
carolina   CGre LHop WHCG
Caroline de Monaco® = 'Meipierar' (HT)   MJon
'Caroline Testout'   See *R.* 'Madame Caroline Testout'
§ Casino® = 'Macca' (ClHT)   CGro CSam EBls GKir LPlm MBur MFry MGan MJon SPer SWCr WStl
§ Castle Howard Tercentenary = 'Tantasch' [PBR] (F)   LStr

§ Castle of Mey = 'Coclucid' GCoc MJon
PBR (F)
Catherine Cookson =   NBat
'Noscook' (HT)
'Catherine Mermet' (T)   EBls MAus
'Catherine Seyton' (RH)   EBls
§ 'Cécile Brünner' (Poly) ♀   CHad EBee EBls ELan EMFP ENot
GCoc LStr MAus MGan MMat
NRog SJus SMad SPer SPla SRum
SSea SWCr WAct WHCG WOVN
WWat
'Cécile Brünner, White'   See R. 'White Cécile Brünner'
Cecily Gibson =   MJon
'Evebright' (F)
¶ 'Celebration' (F)   SWCr
¶ Celebration 2000 =   LBow
'Horcoffitup' PBR (S)
§ 'Céleste' (A) ♀   EBee EBls EMFP ENot EWTr GCoc
IHar LGod LRHS LStr MAus MDun
MFry MMat NFla SApu SFam SJus
SPer SWCr WAct WGer WHCG
WOVN
'Célina' (CeMo)   EBls MGan
'Céline Forestier' (N) ♀   EBls EMFP MAus SFam SPer SWCr
WAct WHCG
§ 'Celsiana' (D)   EBls IHar LRHS MAus SFam
SPer SRPl SSea SWCr WAct
WHCG
Centenaire de Lourdes®   EBls
= 'Delge' (F)
Centenary = 'Koreledas'   ENot MMat SPer SWCr
PBR (F)
§ x centifolia (Ce)   CTri EBls IOrc MAus NRog SJus
SSea SWCr WAct WHCG
§ - 'Bullata' (Ce)   EBls MAus SWCr
§ - 'Cristata' (Ce) ♀   EBls EMFP ENot EPfP LRHS LStr
MAus MMat NBus NFla NRog
SFam SJus SPer SWCr WAct
WHCG
§ - 'Muscosa' (CeMo) ♀   CTri EBls ENot GCoc IOrc
LRHS MAus MGan MMat NFla
NRog SFam SJus SSea SWCr
WAct
- 'Parvifolia'   See R. 'Burgundiaca'
§ 'Centifolia Variegata' (Ce)   EBls MAus MGan
Century Sunset =   SApu
'Tansas' (HT)
'Cerise Bouquet' (S) ♀   EBls IHar LRHS MAus SJus SPer
SWCr WAct WHCG WKif
Cha Cha = 'Cocarum'   SApu
(Patio/Min)
Champagne® =   MJon
'Korampa' PBR (F)
'Champion' (HT)   MAus
'Champneys' Pink Cluster'   EBls MAus SFam
(China hybrid)
§ Champs Elysées® =   MGan SWCr
'Meicarl' (HT)
'Chanelle' (F)   EBls GCoc MAus MGan NRog
SPer SSea SWCr
Chapeau de Napoléon   See R. x centifolia 'Cristata'
'Chaplin's Pink Climber'   EBls MBri MGan NHaw SWCr
(Cl)
Chardonnay = 'Macrealea'   MJon
(HT)
Charisma = 'Peatrophy' (F) Last listed 1997
Charity = 'Auschar' (S)   LRHS MAus MJon SWCr WWeb
Charles Austin® = 'Ausles' IHar MAus MBri SJus WAct WHCG
(S)
Charles Aznavour® =   SWCr
'Meibeausai' (F)
'Charles de Mills' (G) ♀   CHad EBee EBls ELan EMFP ENot

EWTr GCoc IHar LGod LRHS LStr
MAus MFry MJon MMat NFla
SFam SJus SPer SRum SWCr WAct
WHCG
'Charles Gater' (HP)   EBls
'Charles Lefèbvre' (HP)   EBls
'Charles Mallerin' (HT)   EBls
Charles Notcutt =   ENot MMat SWCr
'Korhassi' PBR (S)
Charles Rennie   LRHS MAus MJon SWCr WGer
Mackintosh® =   WWeb
'Ausren' PBR (S)
Charleston '88 =   SWCr
'Meiresty' (HT)
Charleston = 'Meiridge'   MGan SWCr
(F)
Charlotte = 'Auspoly' PBR   CAbP IHar LRHS MAus MJon
(S)   SApu SPer SWCr WAct
§ Charmian® = 'Ausmian'   MAus
(S)
'Charter 700' (F)   MFry
Chartreuse de Parme =   WWeb
'Delviola' (S)
'Château de Clos-Vougeot' Last listed 1999
(HT)
§ Chatsworth = 'Tanotax'   MBri MFry MGan MJon SApu
PBR (Patio/F)   SCoo SPer SSea SWCr
§ Chaucer® = 'Auscer' (S)   MAus MBri
Chelsea Belle =   NBat
'Talchelsea' (Min)
Chelsea Pensioner =   LPlm SApu
'Mattche' (Min)
§ Cherry Brandy '85® =   MBur MFry MGan MJon SWCr
'Tanryrandy' PBR (HT)
'Cherryade' (S)   MGan
Cheshire = 'Fryelise' (HT)   MFry
'Cheshire Life' (HT)   MAus MBur MFry MGan MJon
NPri SWCr WStI
Chester Cathedral =   MJon
'Franshine' (HT)
Chianti = 'Auswine' (S)   EBls MAus MBri MDun SWCr
WHCG
Chicago Peace® =   EBls GGre GKir LGod LPlm MAus
'Johnago' (HT)   MGan MJon NRog SWCr WStI
Child of Achievement PBR   See R. Bella = 'Pouljill'
Childhood Memories =   MBri SWCr
'Ferho' (HM/Cl)
Child's Play™ =   Last listed 1997
'Savachild' (Min)
Chilterns = 'Kortemma'   ENot MMat SWCr
PBR (GC)
Chinatown® (F/S) ♀   CB&S CGro EBls EBrP EBre ELan
EWTr GGre GKir LBCl LBSe LBre
LPlm LStr MAus MBBe MGan
MJon NRog SApu SBre SJus
SPer SSea SWCr
chinensis 'Minima' sensu   See R. 'Pompon de Paris' (MinCh)
stricto hort.
- 'Mutabilis'   See R. x odorata 'Mutabilis'
- 'Old Blush'   See R. x odorata 'Pallida'
'Chloris' (A)   EBls EMFP SWCr
'Chorus Girl' (F)   MGan SWCr
Chris = 'Kirsan' PBR (Cl)   EBee LStr MJon MMat SApu SSea
SWCr
Christian Dior = 'Meilie'   EBls
(HT)
'Christine Gandy' (F)   MGan SWCr
Christopher = 'Cocopher'   GCoc
PBR (HT)
Christopher Columbus®   MBri MJon MMat SApu SWCr
= 'Meinronsse' (HT)
§ 'Chromatella' (N)   EBls MAus

'Chrysler Imperial' (HT)   EBls MAus
Cider Cup = 'Dicladida'   GChr GCoc GGre GKir IDic LGod
  PBR (Min/Patio) ♀   LStr MAus MBri MDun MFry MJon
    NBat SApu SWCr
'Cinderella' (Min)   EWTr MGan
cinnamomea   See *R. majalis*
'Circus' (F)   MGan SWCr
City Lights = 'Poulgan'   LGod MMat
  PBR (Patio)
City of Belfast® =   EBls MAus SWCr
  'Macci' (F)
City of Birmingham =   Last listed 1999
  'Korholst' (S/HT)
'City of Cardiff' (HT)   Last listed 1997
'City of Leeds' (F)   ENot GGre GKir MGan NRog SPer
    SWCr WStI
City of London® =   EBls GKir MBur MJon SApu SJus
  'Harukfore' PBR (F) ♀   SPer SRPl SWCr
'City of Newcastle' (HT)   Last listed 1998
'City of Portsmouth' (F)   CB&S MGan
'City of Worcester' (HT)   Last listed 1997
City of York = 'Direktör   EBls
  Benschop' (Cl)
Clair Matin® = 'Meimont'   CHad EBee EBls MAus SPer SWCr
  (ClS)   WAct
'Claire Jacquier' (N)   EBls MAus SFam SPer SWCr WAct
    WHCG
Claire Rayner =
  'Macpandem' PBR   LPlm LStr MJon WGer
  (F/Patio)
Claire Rose® =   CGro CSam EBee GKir LRHS
  'Auslight' PBR (S)   MAus MBNS MJon SPer SWCr
Claire Scotland =   Last listed 1997
  'Cocdimity' (Min/Patio)
Clarissa® =   MAus
  'Harprocrustes' (Min)
'Clementina Carbonieri'   EBls
  (T)
Cleo = 'Beebop' (HT)   MJon
§ Cleopatra = 'Korverpea'   EBee ENot MBur MMat SWCr
  PBR (HT)
'Cliff Richard' (F)   SWCr
Climbing Alec's Red®   SPer SWCr
  (ClHT)
'Climbing Allgold' (ClF)   EBls GGre MGan SSea SWCr
'Climbing Arthur Bell' PBR   CSam CTri LPlm NRog SApu SPer
  (ClF)   SWCr
'Climbing Ballerina' (Ra)   MBri MGan SWCr
Climbing Bettina® =   EBls MAus
  'Mepalsar' (ClHT)
Climbing Blessings®   EBls SWCr
  (ClHT)
'Climbing Blue Moon'   MGan SWCr
  (ClHT)
§ 'Climbing Captain   EBls MAus
  Christy' (ClHT)
'Climbing Cécile   CHad EBee EBls EPfP LGod LRHS
  Brünner' (ClPoly) ♀   LStr MAus NFla SApu SFam SJus
    SPer SSea SWCr WAct WHCG
    WSHC WWat
'Climbing Château de   EBls MAus
  Clos-Vougeot' (ClHT)
'Climbing Cherryade'   MGan
  (ClHT)
'Climbing Christine'   MAus
  (ClHT)
§ 'Climbing Columbia'   ERav ERea NRog SPer WHCG
  (ClHT)
'Climbing Comtesse   EBls MAus
  Vandal' (ClHT)
'Climbing Crimson Glory'   EBls EMFP GCoc MAus MGan
  (ClHT)   NRog SMad SWCr WStI

§ 'Climbing Devoniensis'   CPou EBls MAus
  (ClT)
'Climbing Ena Harkness'   CB&S CSam CTri EBls GCoc GGre
  (ClHT)   MAus MBNS MBri MBur MGan
    NRog SPer SPla SWCr WStI WWeb
'Climbing Ernest H.   MGan
  Morse' (ClHT)
'Climbing Etoile de   More than 30 suppliers
  Hollande' (ClHT) ♀
'Climbing Fashion' (ClF)   EBls
Climbing Fragrant Cloud   CB&S ELan MGan SWCr
  = 'Colfragrasar' (ClHT)
§ 'Climbing Frau Karl   EBls NRog
  Druschki' (ClHP)
'Climbing General   EBls MAus
  MacArthur' (ClHT)
§ Climbing Gold Bunny =
  'Meigro-Nurisar' PBR   MJon WGer
  (ClF)
§ 'Climbing Golden Dawn'   MAus
  (ClHT)
'Climbing Grand-mère   EBls
  Jenny' (ClHT)
'Climbing Home Sweet   MAus
  Home' (ClHT)
'Climbing Iceberg' (ClF) ♀   More than 30 suppliers
'Climbing Irish Fireflame'   MAus
  (ClHT)
'Climbing Jazz' PBR (Cl/F)   See *R.* That's Jazz = 'Poulnorm'
'Climbing Josephine   LRHS MAus MGan
  Bruce' (ClHT)
'Climbing la France' (ClHT)CPou MAus SWCr
§ 'Climbing Lady Hillingdon' EBee EBls EBrP EBre EMFP EPfP
  (ClT) ♀   LBCl LBSe LBre LRHS MAus MBBe
    MGan SApu SBre SFam SPer SRPl
    SWCr WAct WHCG WSHC
'Climbing Lady Sylvia'   CPou EBls EPfP LRHS MAus MGan
  (ClHT)   NRog SPer SWCr
'Climbing Little White Pet'   See *R.* 'Félicité Perpétue'
'Climbing Madame Abel   EBls MAus
  Chatenay' (ClHT)
'Climbing Madame   EBls EBrP EBre EPfP LBCl LBSe
  Butterfly' (ClHT)   LBre LRHS MAus MBBe MGan
    SBre SJus SPer SWCr
'Climbing Madame   CPou EBls MAus NRog SPer SWCr
  Caroline Testout' (ClHT)WBcn WSHC
§ 'Climbing Madame   EBls MAus MGan SPer SWCr
  Edouard Herriot' (ClHT)
'Climbing Madame Henri   EBls MAus
  Guillot' (ClHT)
'Climbing Maman Cochet'   EBls MAus
  (ClT)
'Climbing Masquerade'   EBls GGre GKir LPlm LRHS MAus
  (ClF)   MGan MJon NRog SSea SWCr
    WStI WWeb
'Climbing McGredy's   MGan
  Yellow' (ClHT)
§ 'Climbing Mevrouw G.A.   EBls MAus
  van Rossem' (ClHT)
'Climbing Mrs Aaron Ward' EBls MAus
  (ClHT)
'Climbing Mrs G.A. van   See *R.* 'Climbing Mevrouw G.A.
  Rossem'   van Rossem'
'Climbing Mrs Herbert   CPou EBee EBls LRHS MAus NRog
  Stevens' (ClHT)   SPer SWCr WHCG
'Climbing Mrs Sam   CGro EBls LPlm MAus MBri MGan
  McGredy' (ClHT) ♀   MJon NRog SWCr
'Climbing My Love' (ClHT)   Last listed 1999
'Climbing Niphetos' (ClT)   EBls MAus
'Climbing Ophelia' (ClHT)   EBee EBls MAus SPer SWCr
§ Climbing Orange   MBri MJon SApu SPer SWCr
  Sunblaze = 'Meiji
  Katarsar' PBR (ClMin)

'Climbing Pascali' (ClHT) CB&S MGan

§ 'Climbing Paul Lédé' (ClT) CPou EBee EBls EBrP EBre LBcl LBSe LBre LRHS MAus MBBe SBre SWCr WHCG

¶ 'Climbing Peace' (ClHT) SWCr

'Climbing Picture' (ClHT) EBls MAus MGan

§ 'Climbing Pompon de Paris' (ClMinCh) CBot CRHN EBls LHop LRHS MAus MGan MRav SPer SRPl SWCr WHCG WSHC

'Climbing Richmond' (ClHT) EBls MAus

'Climbing Roundelay' (Cl) EBls

¶ Climbing Rumba® (ClF) SWCr

'Climbing Shot Silk' (ClHT) ♀ EBee EBls MAus MGan SPer SWCr

§ 'Climbing Souvenir de la Malmaison' (ClBb) CPou EBls MAus SPer SWCr WAct WHCG

'Climbing Spartan' (ClF) Last listed 1997

'Climbing Spek's Yellow' (ClHT) MAus

'Climbing Summer Sunshine' (ClHT) MBri

Climbing Super Star = 'Tangostar' (ClHT) MAus SWCr

'Climbing Sutter's Gold' (ClHT) MAus MGan SWCr

'Climbing Talisman' (ClHT) EBls

'Climbing the Doctor' (ClHT) MGan

'Climbing the Queen Elizabeth' (ClF) EBls MGan SWCr

'Climbing White Cloud'PBR See R. White Cloud = 'Korstacha'

'Cloth of Gold' See R. 'Chromatella'

Cocktail® = 'Meimick' (S) EBls MGan WAct

Colchester Beauty = 'Cansend' (F) Last listed 1999

§ Colibre '79 = 'Meidanover' PBR (Min) ELan LStr SWCr

Colibre '80PBR See R. Colibre '79 = 'Meidanover'

§ Colibri = 'Meimal' (Min) LGod MGan SPer

§ 'Colonel Fabvier' (S) EBee EBls MAus SWCr

colonial white See R. 'Sombreuil'

Colorama = 'Meirigalu' (HT) Last listed 1998

Colour Wonder = 'Korbico' (HT) SWCr

'Columbian' (ClHT) See R. 'Climbing Columbia'

§ Colwyn Bay (F) MJon

§ 'Commandant Beaurepaire' (Bb) EBls LRHS MAus SWCr

common moss See R. × centifolia 'Muscosa'

Commonwealth Glory = 'Harclue' PBR (HT) GGre SWCr

Compassion® (ClHT) ♀ More than 30 suppliers

§ 'Complicata' (G) ♀ EBls EPfP IHar LEdu LRHS LStr MAus MBri MGan MRav NRog SApu SFam SJus SPer SSea SSpi SWCr WAct WHCG WOVN

N 'Comte de Chambord' misapplied See R. 'Madame Knorr'

'Comtesse Cécile de Chabrillant' (HP) EBls MAus

'Comtesse de Lacépède' misapplied See R. 'Du Maître d'Ecole'

§ 'Comtesse de Murinais' (DMo) EBls IHar MAus SFam SWCr

Comtesse de Ségur = 'Deltendre' (S) WWeb

§ 'Comtesse du Caÿla' (Ch) MAus SSea

'Comtesse Vandal' (HT) MAus

'Condesa de Sástago' (HT) EBls

§ 'Conditorum' (G) EBls SFam SSea

Congratulations = 'Korlift' PBR (HT) EBee ENot GCoc GGre LGod LPlm LStr MFry MGan MJon MMat NPri SApu SJus SPer SSea SWCr

Conquest = 'Harbrill' PBR (F) SWCr

§ 'Conrad Ferdinand Meyer' (Ru) EBls EWTr MAus MGan SPer SRum SWCr WAct

Conservation = 'Cocdimple' PBR (Min/Patio) GCoc GGre LStr MBri MJon SApu SSea SWCr

Constance Fettes = 'Cocnest' (F) Last listed 1997

Constance Spry = 'Austance' (ClS) ♀ More than 30 suppliers

§ 'Cooperi' (Ra) CCHP EBls MAus SLon SPer SSea WAct WSHC

Cooper's Burmese See R. 'Cooperi'

'Copenhagen' (ClHT) EBls LRHS MAus MBri

'Copper Delight' (F) NRog

Copper Pot = 'Dicpe' (F) MGan SPer SWCr

'Coral Cluster' (Poly) EBls MAus MGan

'Coral Creeper' (ClHT) EBls

Coral Dawn® (ClHT) EBls IHar MFry MJon

Coral Reef = 'Cocdarlee' PBR (Min/Patio) GCoc GGre LStr MBri SWCr

'Coral Satin' (Cl) EBls MGan

'Coralie' (D) EBls

'Coralin' (Min) MGan

Cordon Bleu = 'Harubasil' PBR (HT) MBur

'Cornelia' (HM) ♀ CB&S CHad CSam EBee EBls ENot EWTr GCoc GKir LRHS LStr MAus MBri MFry MJon MMat NRog SApu SFam SJus SPer SRPl SSea SWCr WAct WHCG WOVN WWeb

'Coronation Gold' (F) Last listed 1999

'Coronet' (F) WHCG

'Coryana' EBls

corymbifera EBls

corymbulosa EBls

'Cosimo Ridolfi' (G) EBls

Cottage Garden = 'Haryamber PBR (Patio/Min) Last listed 1998

cottage maid See R. 'Centifolia Variegata'

Cottage Rose™ = 'Ausglisten' PBR (S) MAus MBri MJon SJus SWCr

Country Lady = 'Hartsam' PBR (HT) MBur SApu SJus SWCr

Country Living™ = 'Auscountry' PBR (S) EBls LRHS MAus SWCr

'Country Maid' (F) Last listed 1997

'Coupe d'Hébé' (Bb) EBls MAus MBri

§ Courage = 'Poulduf' PBR (HT) GGre NEgg SWCr

'Cramoisi Picotée' (G) EBls MAus

'Cramoisi Supérieur' (Ch) EBls MAus WHCG

Crathes Castle = 'Cocathes' GCoc

Crazy for You = 'Wekroalt' PBR (F) GCoc LGod MJon

Crème de la Crème = 'Gancre' (Cl) MGan SWCr

'Crépuscule' (N) EBls SSea WHCG

Cressida = 'Auscress' (S) MAus

crested moss See R. × centifolia 'Cristata'

Cricri = 'Meicri' (Min) MAus MGan SWCr

Crimson Cascade = 'Fryclimbdown' PBR (Cl) GKir MAus MBri MFry NBat SApu SJus SWCr

'Crimson Conquest' (ClHT) — EBls
crimson damask — See *R. gallica* var. *officinalis*
'Crimson Descant' (Cl) — Last listed 1999
'Crimson Gem' (Min) — MGan
'Crimson Globe' (Mo) — MGan SWCr
'Crimson Glory' (HT) — EBls MBur MGan SWCr WAct
'Crimson Rambler' (Ra) — MAus WBcn
'Crimson Shower' (Ra) ♀ — EBee EBrP EBre EMFP LBCl LBSe LBre LPlm LRHS MAus MBBe MGan MJon NRog SBre SPer SWCr WGer WHCG WHer WStI
'Cristata' — See *R.* x *centifolia* 'Cristata'
Crown Princess Margareta™ = 'Auswinter' (S) — SCoo
Crystal Palace® = 'Poulrek' PBR (Patio) — EBee MJon MMat SWCr
cuisse de nymphe — See *R.* 'Great Maiden's Blush'
'Cupid' (ClHT) — EBee EBls EMFP LRHS MAus SPer SWCr WAct
¶ 'Cupid's Heart' (HT) — SWCr
Curiosity = 'Cocty' (HT/v) — GGre MJon SWCr
§ Cymbeline = 'Auslean' (S) — MAus SPer SWCr
'Cynthia Brooke' (HT) — EBls
'D'Aguesseau' (G) — EBls MAus
Daily Express = 'Frychambi' (HT) — Last listed 1998
'Daily Mail' — See *R.* 'Climbing Madame Edouard Herriot'
§ Daily Post = 'Frytrooper' (F) — MFry
Daily Sketch = 'Macai' (F) — MGan SWCr
'Dainty Bess' (HT) — EBls MAus MRav SSea
Dainty Dinah = 'Cocamond' PBR (Min/Patio) — LStr SApu SWCr
'Dainty Maid' (F) — EBls MAus
'Dairy Maid' (F) — MAus
'Daisy Hill' ('Macrantha' hybrid) — EBls
Dalli Dalli® = 'Tanlilida' (F) — Last listed 1998
x *damascena* var. *bifera* — See *R.* x *damascena* var. *semperflorens*
§ - var. *semperflorens* (D) — EBls EMFP LRHS MAus SSea SWCr WAct WHCG
N - 'Trigintipetala' misapplied — See *R.* 'Professeur Emile Perrot'
§ - var. *versicolor* (D) — EBls ENot LRHS MAus MGan SFam SPer SSea SWCr WAct WHCG
'Dame Edith Helen' (HT) — EBls
'Dame of Sark' (F) — Last listed 1997
Dame Wendy = 'Canson' PBR (F) — EBee MAus MGan MJon SWCr
'Danaë' (HM) — CPou EBee EBls EMFP MAus SWCr WHCG
Dancing Pink = 'Hendan' (F) — NBat
'Danny Boy' (ClHT) — IDic
Danny Boy = 'Dicxcon' PBR (Patio) — GCoc
§ Danse des Sylphes® = 'Malcair' (Cl) — EBls SWCr
Danse du Feu® (Cl) — CB&S CGro EBee EBls ELan ENot EWTr GChr GCoc GGre GKir LGod LPlm LRHS LStr MAus MBri MFry MGan MJon MMat NRog SApu SMad SPer SSea SWCr WWeb
'Daphne Gandy' (F) — MGan SWCr
Dapple Dawn = 'Ausapple' (S) — LRHS MAus SPer SWCr
Darling Flame = 'Meilucca' (Min) — ELan MGan SApu SWCr

'Dart's Defender' — SLPl
Dave Hessayon = 'Driscobruce' (HT) — Last listed 1997
David Whitfield = 'Gana' PBR (F) — MGan SWCr
davidii — EBls MAus SWCr
Dawn Chorus = 'Dicquasar' PBR (HT) — CGro EBrP EBre GCoc GGre IDic IHar LBCl LBSe LBre LGod LPlm LStr MBBe MBri MFry MGan MJon MMat SApu SBre SJus SPer SRPl SSea SWCr WWeb
'Daybreak' (HM) — EBls MAus NRog SWCr WAct WHCG
Daylight = 'Interlight' (F) — Last listed 1999
Dazzler = 'Genpat' PBR (Patio) — MJon
§ 'De Meaux' (Ce) — EBls ENot LFis LRHS MAus MMat SPer SPla SRPl SSea SWCr WHCG
'De Meaux, White' — See *R.* 'White de Meaux'
§ 'De Rescht' (DPo) ♀ — CBos CPou EBee EBls ENot EPfP IHar LRHS MAus MBri MDun MGan MJon MMat SPer SWCr WAct WGer WHCG
'Dearest' (F) — CB&S GGre MGan MJon NRog SPer SRPl SWCr WStI
'Debbie Thomas' (HT) — Last listed 1997
§ Deborah Devonshire = 'Boscherrydrift' PBR (F) — SWCr
Deb's Delight = 'Legsweet' PBR (F) — ELan MJon SWCr
'Debutante' (Ra) — EBls LRHS MAus SFam SWCr
'Deep Secret' (HT) — CGro CTri EBee EBrP EBre EPfP GCoc GGre GKir LBCl LBSe LBre LPlm MBBe MBur MFry MGan MJon NRog SApu SBre SJus SPer SRum SSea SWCr WWeb
'Delambre' (DPo) — EBls MAus MRav
'Delicata' (Ru) — MAus
'Dembrowski' (HP) — EBls
Denman = 'Landen' (HT) — MJon SApu
'Dentelle de Malines' (S) — EBls LRHS MAus WAct
'Deschamps' (N) — EBls
'Desprez à Fleurs Jaunes' (N) ♀ — CPou EBee EBls EMFP IHar LRHS MAus NPri SFam SPer SPla SWCr WHCG WSHC
'Deuil de Paul Fontaine' (Mo) — EBls
'Devon Maid' (Cl) — SWCr
'Devoniensis' (ClT) — See *R.* 'Climbing Devoniensis'
Diadem® = 'Tanmeda' PBR (F) — SRPl SWCr
'Diamond Jubilee' (HT) — EBls SWCr
Diana, Princess of Wales = 'Jacshaq' (HT) — IDic
Diana's Crowning Glory = 'Dicyardstick' — IDic
Dick's Delight = 'Dicwhistle' PBR (GC) — IDic SWCr
'Dickson's Flame' (F) — MGan SWCr
Die Welt® = 'Diekor' (HT) — NBat
'Diorama' (HT) — MAus MGan SWCr
'Directeur Alphand' (HP) — EBls WHCG
Disco Dancer® = 'Dicinfra' PBR (F) — IDic
Dixieland Linda = 'Beadix' (ClHT) — EBls
Dizzy Heights = 'Fryblissful' (Cl) — GCoc MFry
Doc = 'Degenhard' (Poly) — MGan
'Docteur Andry' (HP) — EBls
'Docteur Grill' (T) — EBls MAus

'Doctor A.J. Verhage' (HT) MGan
'Doctor Abrahams' (HT) Last listed 1999
Doctor Dick NBat NRog
= 'Cocbaden' (HT)
'Doctor Edward EBls
Deacon' (HT)
§ Doctor Goldberg MGan SWCr
= 'Gandol' (HT)
Doctor Jackson™ MAus
= 'Ausdoctor' (S)
'Doctor John Snow' (HT) MGan
Doctor McAlpine MBri MJon SWCr
= 'Peafirst' PBR (F/Patio)
'Doctor W. Van Fleet' (Ra/Cl) EBls MAus WSHC
'Doktor Eckener' EBls MGan
'Don Charlton' (HT) NBat
'Don Juan' (Cl) MGan
Donald Davis Last listed 1999
= 'Chewbeaut' (F)
§ 'Doncasteri' EBls MAus
'Dopey' (Poly) MGan
'Doreen' (HT) NRog SWCr
Doris Tysterman® (HT) CGro EBls EBrP EBre GGre GKir
LBCl LBSe LBre LPlm LStr MAus
MBBe MGan MJon NRog SBre
SPer SWCr
'Dorothy Perkins' (Ra) CGro CRHN CTri EBee EBls GChr
GCoc GGre GOrc LFis LPlm LRHS
LStr MAus MGan MJon NPer
NRog SApu SPer SRPl SSea SWCr
WHCG
'Dorothy Wheatcroft' (F) MGan SWCr
'Dorothy Whitney Last listed 1999
Wood' (HT)
'Dorothy Wilson' (F) EBls
Dortmund® (ClHScB) EBee EBls LGod LPlm LRHS MAus
MGan SPer SWCr WAct WHCG
Double Delight® CGro ELan GCoc GGre LPlm LStr
= 'Andeli' (HT) MBri MGan MJon NRog SApu
SPer SWCr
Dove® = 'Ausdove' (S) EBee
§ Dr. Jo = 'Fryatlanta' (F) MFry
'Dream Girl' (Cl) ♀ MAus MBri SFam
Dream Lover GCoc SWCr
= 'Peayetti' PBR (Patio)
'Dream Time' (HT) Last listed 1997
'Dream Waltz' (F) Last listed 1997
'Dreamglo' (Min) Last listed 1998
'Dreaming Spires' (Cl) MBri MJon MMat SApu SJus SPer
SRum SWCr
Dreamland MFry MGan SWCr
= 'Träumland' (F)
'Dresden Doll' (MinMo) EBls MAus SApu SPer
Drummer Boy SJus SWCr
= 'Harvacity' PBR
(F/Patio)
§ 'Du Maître d'Ecole' (G) ♀ EBls MAus SWCr WHCG
Dublin Bay® More than 30 suppliers
= 'Macdub' (Cl) ♀
'Duc de Fitzjames' (G) EBls SWCr
'Duc de Guiche' (G) ♀ CPou EBls MAus SFam SPer SSea
SWCr WAct WHCG
'Duchess of Portland' See R. 'Portlandica'
Duchess of York PBR See R. Sunseeker = 'Dicracer'
'Duchesse d'Albe' (T) EBls
'Duchesse d'Angoulême' (G) EBls MAus SFam SSea SWCr
'Duchesse d'Auerstädt' (N) EBls
'Duchesse de Buccleugh' (G) EBls MAus SWCr
§ 'Duchesse de CBos EBee EBls LRHS MAus SFam
Montebello' (G) ♀ SPer SWCr WHCG
'Duchesse de Rohan' EBls
(CexHP)

'Duchesse de Verneuil' EBls MAus SFam
(CeMo)
§ Duke Meillandina MBri SApu
= 'Meipinjid' PBR (Min)
'Duke of Edinburgh' (HP) EBls MAus
'Duke of Wellington' (HP) EBls SWCr WHCG
'Duke of Windsor' (HT) IHar MGan SPer
'Duke of York' (Ch) SWCr
Duke Sunblaze® PBR See R. Duke Meillandina =
'Meipinjid'
'Dundee Rambler' (Ra) EBls MAus
'Dupontii' (S) EBee EBls LRHS MAus SFam SPer
SWCr WAct WHCG WOVN
'Dupuy Jamain' (HP) EBls WHCG
'Durham Prince Bishop' Last listed 1998
(HT)
Dusky Dancer See R. Daily Post = 'Frytrooper'
'Dusky Maiden' (F) EBls MAus WHCG
'Düsterlohe' (Ra) Last listed 1998
Dutch Gold® (HT) CGro CTri MAus MGan NRog SPer
SRPl SSea SWCr
Dwarf King See R. Zwergkönig '78 =
(introduced 1978) 'Korkönig'
'E.H. Morse' See R. 'Ernest H. Morse'
'Easlea's Golden EBee EBls LRHS MAus SWCr WAct
Rambler' (Ra) WHCG
'Easter Morning' (Min) ELan MAus MDun MGan MJon
SApu SPer SWCr
Easy Going GCoc SWCr
= 'Harflow' PBR (F)
'Eblouissant' (Poly) MGan
ecae EBls LRHS MAus
- 'Helen Knight' See R. 'Helen Knight' (ecae
hybrid)
'Eclair' (HP) EBls WHCG
'Eddie's Jewel' EBls MAus MGan
(moyesii hybrid)
Eden Rose® (HT) EBls MGan SWCr
Eden Rose '88 MJon SApu SJus SPer SWCr
= 'Meiviolin' PBR (ClHT)
'Edith Bellenden' (RH) EBls
Edith Holden LGod MAus MJon SApu SJus
= 'Chewlegacy' PBR (F)
eglanteria See R. rubiginosa
Eglantyne = 'Ausmark' (S) CAbP CSam EBrP EBre IHar LBCl
LBSe LBre LRHS LStr MAus MBBe
MJon MMat SBre SJus SPer SWCr
WWeb
'Elegance' (ClHT) EBls MAus MGan SWCr
§ elegantula 'Persetosa' (S) EBls ENot MAus SPer SWCr WAct
WHCG
§ Elina® = 'Dicjana' GGre IDic LGod LStr MAus MBur
PBR (HT)¿ MFry MGan MJon MMat NBat
NRog SApu SJus SPer SWCr
'Eliza Boëlle' (HP) WHCG
Elizabeth Harkness® (HT) EBls MAus MBur MGan SPer
SWCr
Elizabeth Heather
Grierson = 'Mattnot' MMat SWCr
(ClHT)
Elizabeth of Glamis® CGro EBls EWTr GChr GCoc IHar
= 'Macel' (F) MBri MGan NRog SPer SWCr
'Elizabeth Philp' (F) LPlm SWCr
Ellen® = 'Auscup' (S) MAus
'Ellen Poulsen' (Poly) MGan
'Ellen Willmott' (HT) CHad EBls MAus SWCr
'Elmshorn' (S) CB&S MGan SWCr WHCG
Elsie Warren NBat
= 'Milsweet' (F)
Emanuel® = 'Ausuel' (S) MAus SPer
Emily = 'Ausburton' PBR (S) MAus SApu
'Emily Gray' (Ra) CGro CPou EBls EBrP EBre ENot

Emily Louise = 'Harwilla' (Patio) GKir LBCl LBSe LBre LRHS LStr MAus MBBe MBur MGan MJon MMat NFla NPri NRog SBre SPer SSea SWCr WAct WHCG Last listed 1998

Emma Kate = 'Jayemm' (F) Last listed 1997

'Emma May' (HT) Last listed 1997

Emma Mitchell = 'Horharpdos' (Patio) Last listed 1998

'Emma Wright' (HT) MAus

'Emmerdale' (F) WStI

'Empereur du Maroc' (HP) EBls EMFP MAus SWCr WAct WHCG

'Empress Josephine' See R. x francofurtana

Empress Michiko = 'Dicnifty' PBR (HT) GCoc IDic SApu SWCr

Ena Baxter = 'Cocbonne' (HT) GCoc

'Ena Harkness' (HT) CGro EBls ELan GChr GGre LRHS MBur MGan NRog SWCr WStI

§ 'Enfant de France' (HP) EBls

x engelmannii EBls

English Elegance® = 'Ausleaf' (S) MAus

English Garden® = 'Ausbuff' PBR (S) EBee EBrP EBre EMFP ENot EPfP IHar LBCl LBSe LBre LRHS LStr MAus MBBe MBNS MBri MMat NLar SApu SBre SPer SSea SWCr WAct WWeb

'English Miss' (F) EBee EBls EWTr GKir LPlm LStr MAus MFry MGan MJon SApu SJus SPer SSea SWCr WStI WWeb

'Eos' (moyesii hybrid) EBls MAus SSea

'Erfurt' (HM) EBls EMFP MAus MGan SPla SWCr WHCG

§ 'Erinnerung an Brod' (S) WHCG

§ 'Ernest H. Morse' (HT) CTri EBls EWTr GChr GCoc GGre GKir IHar MAus MBur MGan MJon NRog SApu SPer SSea SWCr SSea

¶ 'Ernest May' (HT)

Eroica = 'Erotika' (HT) Last listed 1998

Escapade® = 'Harpade' (F) ♀ EBls EWTr MAus MGan SWCr

Especially for You = 'Fryworthy' PBR (HT) EBee GCoc LGod LStr MBur MFry NPri SApu SJus SSea SWCr

Essex = 'Poulnoz' PBR (GC) EBee EBrP EBre ENot LBCl LBSe LBre MBBe MGan MMat SApu SBre SPer SWCr WHCG WOVN

Esther Ofarim® = 'Korfarim' (F) Last listed 1997

§ 'Estrellita de Oro' (Min) LPlm MAus MGan SPer

'Etain' (Ra) EBee

§ 'Etendard' SWCr WAct

§ Eternally Yours = 'Macspeego' PBR (HT) MJon

'Ethel' (Ra) EBee EMFP SWCr

Ethel Austin = 'Frymestin' (F) Last listed 1999

'Etoile de Hollande' (HT) CHad EBee GKir LRHS MDun SFam SSea

'Etoile de Lyon' (T) EBls

'Eugène Fürst' (HP) EBls WHCG

'Eugénie Guinoisseau' (Mo) EBls SWCr WHCG

Euphoria = 'Intereup' PBR (GC/S) ECle GCoc IDic MJon MMat SApu SWCr

Euphrates = 'Harunique' (persica hybrid) MAus MGan SWCr WAct

Europeana® (F) MAus MGan SWCr

Eurostar = 'Poulreb' PBR (F) ENot MMat SApu SWCr

'Eva' (HM) EBls

'Evangeline' (Ra) EBls EWTr MAus WAct

Evelyn® = 'Aussaucer' PBR (S) CAbP CSam EBee EBrP EBre EMFP EPfP GCoc IHar LBCl LBSe LBre LGod LRHS LStr MAus MBBe MFry MJon MMat SApu SBre SChu SPer SWCr

§ Evelyn Fison = 'Macev' (F) ELan ENot EPfP GChr GGre GKir MAus MGan MJon NRog SApu SPer SWCr

Evelyn Grace = 'Horavme' (F) NBat

Evening Star® = 'Jacven' (HT) MAus

'Evening Telegraph' (HT) Last listed 1997

'Everest Double Fragrance' (F) EBls

'Excelsa' (Ra) CTri EBls EPfP GChr GGre GKir LGod LStr MAus MGan MJon NBus NRog NWea SRum SSea WAct WStI

Exception (Ru) WLRN

§ Exploit® = 'Meilider' PBR (Cl) GGre SWCr

§ Eye Paint = 'Maceye' (F) MAus MGan MJon SMrm SWCr

'Eyecatcher' (F) Last listed 1997

Eyeopener = 'Interop' PBR (S/GC) CGro EBls IDic MGan MJon

'F.E. Lester' See R. 'Francis E. Lester'

§ 'F.J. Grootendorst' (Ru) EBls GOrc IOrc LGod LRHS LStr MAus MGan NRog SSea WAct

'Fabvier' See R. 'Colonel Fabvier'

§ Fair Bianca® = 'Ausca' (S) IOrc MAus MBri

Fairhope = 'Talfairhope' (Min) NBat

Fairy Changeling = 'Harnumerous' (Poly) MAus

§ Fairy Damsel = 'Harneatly' (Poly/GC) EBls MAus MBur

Fairy Queen = 'Sperien' (Poly/GC) IDic MBri SSea SWCr

'Fairy Rose' See R. 'The Fairy'

§ Fairy Snow = 'Holfairy' (S) Last listed 1998

§ Fairygold = 'Frygoldie' PBR (Patio) MBri MFry SWCr

Fairyland® = 'Harlayalong' (Poly) EBls MAus MBur SApu SWCr

Fancy Pants™ = 'Kinfancy' (Min) Last listed 1997

'Fantin-Latour' (centifolia hybrid) ♀ CHad CSam EBee EBls ELan ENot GCoc IHar LGod LRHS LStr MAus MBri MDun MGan MMat NHaw NRog SApu SFam SJus SPer SRPl SSea SWCr WAct WGer WHCG WSHC

fargesii hort. See R. moyesii var. fargesii

farreri var. persetosa See R. elegantula 'Persetosa'

Fascination = 'Jacoyel' (HT) ECle GKir LStr MBri SCoo

§ Fascination = 'Poulmax' PBR (F) EBee EPfP GCoc LGod LPlm LRHS MFry MGan MMat SApu SPer SRum SSea SWCr SRum

'Fashion Flame' (Min) SRum

Favorite Rosamini = 'Ruifaro' (Min) Last listed 1998

fedtschenkoana hort. EBls LRHS MAus MGan SPer SWCr WAct WHCG

Fée des Neiges® See R. Iceberg = 'Korbin'

'Felicia' (HM) ♀ CHad CSam EBee EBls ELan ENot EWTr GChr GCoc IHar LGod LStr MAus MBri MFry MJon MMat NFla NRog SApu SFam SJus SPer SSea SWCr WAct WHCG WOVN

'Félicité Parmentier' (AxD) ♀ — EBls LRHS MAus MDun SFam SJus SPer SWCr WAct WHCG

§ 'Félicité Perpétue' (Ra) ♀ — CB&S EBee EBls ELan EWTr GCoc GKir IHar ISea LRHS LStr MAus MBri MGan MMat SApu SFam SJus SPer SRPl SSea SWCr WAct WHCG WSHC

Felicity Kendal = 'Lanken' PBR (HT) — MBri MJon SWCr

'Fellenberg' (Ch) — EBls LRHS MAus SWCr WHCG

Fellowship = 'Harwelcome' PBR (F) — EBee GCoc IHar LGod LPlm LStr MAus MBur MFry MGan MJon MMat SJus SSea SWCr WGer

'Femina' (HT) — MGan SWCr

'Ferdinand Pichard' (Bb) ♀ — CPou EBee EBls EMFP ENot EPfP IHar LFis LRHS MAus MBri MDun MGan MJon MMat NFla SJus SPer SSea SWCr WAct WFoF WGer WHCG WOVN

§ Ferdy® = 'Keitoli' PBR (GC) — EBls ELan ENot MAus SApu SPer SWCr WOVN

Fergie = 'Ganfer' PBR (F/Patio) — MGan SWCr

Festival = 'Kordialo' PBR (Patio) — CGro ENot IHar LGod LStr MAus MBri MDun MGan MJon MMat SApu SPer SSea SWCr WGer WOVN

§ 'Feuermeer' (F) — Last listed 1999

Fiesta = 'Macfirinlin' PBR (Patio) — LStr MJon NBat SWCr

Fifi = 'Hanfif' (F) — NBat

Figurine™ = 'Benfig' (Min) — Last listed 1997

filipes 'Brenda Colvin' — See R. 'Brenda Colvin'

§ - 'Kiftsgate' (Ra) ♀ — More than 30 suppliers

§ 'Fimbriata' (Ru) — CPou EBls LRHS MAus MBri SPer SWCr WAct WHCG

Financial Times Centenary = 'Ausfin' (S) — MAus SWCr

§ Fine Gold = 'Weegold' (HT) — Last listed 1997

§ Fiona® = 'Meibeluxen' PBR (S/GC) — EBls GGre SWCr WHCG WOVN

'Fire Princess' (Min) — Last listed 1997

'Firecracker' (F) — EBls

Firefly® = 'Macfrabro' PBR (Min) — MJon SWCr

'First Love' (HT) — EBls MGan SWCr

'Fisher and Holmes' (HP) — EBls MAus WAct WHCG

Fisherman's Friend® = 'Auschild' PBR (S) — MAus SPer SWCr

Flair = 'Dicrelax' PBR (F) — IDic LStr MJon SWCr

Flamenco = 'Poultika' PBR (Cl) — SWCr

Flamingo PBR — See R. Margaret Thatcher = 'Korflüg'

Flamingo Meidiland = 'Meisolroz' PBR — WOVN

'Fleur Cowles' (F) — MBur SWCr

'Flora' (Ra) — CRHN EBls MAus SFam

'Flora McIvor' (RH) — EBls MAus MGan

Florence Nightingale = 'Ganflor' PBR (F) — MBur MGan SApu SPer SWCr

Flower Carpet™ PBR — See R. Pink Flower Carpet = 'Noatraum'

Flower Carpet Sunshine = 'Noasun' (GC) — WWeb

'Flower Carpet Twilight — See R. Twilight = 'Noatwi'

Flower Child = 'Harchild' (Patio) — SWCr

Flower Power = 'Frycassia' PBR (Patio) — GCoc GKir LStr MFry

§ foetida (S) — EBls MAus

§ - 'Bicolor' (S) — EBls ENot IHar LRHS MAus MGan MMat NRog SPer WAct

§ - 'Persiana' (S) — EBls MAus MGan SPer

foliolosa — EBls SLPl SWCr WHCG

Fond Memories = 'Kirfelix' PBR (Patio) — GCoc LStr

'Forgotten Dreams' (HT) — MJon

forrestiana — EBls MAus SWCr WHCG

x fortuneana (Ra) — EBls

fortune's double yellow — See R. x odorata 'Pseudindica'

'Fountain' (HT/S) — EBls LStr MAus MGan SApu SPer SWCr

Fragrant Cloud = 'Tanellis' (HT) — CGro EBls EBrP EBre GChr GCoc GGre GKir IHar LBCl LBSe LBre LStr MAus MBBe MBri MBur MFry MJon MMat NBat NRog SApu SBre SPer SSea SWCr WWeb

'Fragrant Delight' (F) ♀ — CTri GCoc GKir LPlm LStr MFry MGan MJon SApu SPer SRPl SWCr WWeb

Fragrant Dream = 'Dicodour' PBR (HT) — GGre IDic LStr MBri SApu SWCr

Fragrant Gold = 'Tanduft' (HT) — GCoc LStr SWCr

'Fragrant Hour' (HT) — MGan SWCr

Frances Perry = 'Bosrexcity' PBR (F) — SWCr

'Francesca' (HM) — EBls LFis LRHS MAus MGan SFam SPer SWCr WAct WHCG

Francine Austin® = 'Ausram' PBR (S/GC) — LRHS MAus SPer SWCr WAct

'Francis Dubreuil' (T) — EBls

§ 'Francis E. Lester' (HM/Ra) ♀ — CHad CRHN CSam EBee EBls EBrP EBre LBCl LBSe LBre LRHS MAus MBBe MBri SBre SFam SPer SSea SWCr WAct WHCG

§ x francofurtana ♀ — CPou EBls LRHS MAus MRav SFam SSea SWCr WAct WHCG

'François Juranville' (Ra) ♀ — CPou CRHN EBee EBls GChr LRHS LStr MAus MBri MGan MMat NBus NRog SApu SMad SPer SRPl SWCr WAct

'Frank MacMillan' (HT) — Last listed 1997

'Frank Naylor' (S) — SWCr

'Frau Astrid Späth' (F) — NRog

§ 'Frau Karl Druschki' (HP) — EBls MAus SWCr WAct

'Fräulein Octavia Hesse' (Ra) EBls

'Fred Gibson' (HT) — Last listed 1997

'Fred Loads' (F/S) ♀ — EBls MAus MGan SApu SWCr

Freddie Mercury = 'Batmercury' (HT) — MJon NBat

Free as Air = 'Mehbronze' PBR (Patio) — MBri

Freedom® = 'Dicjem' PBR (HT) ♀ — ENot GCoc GGre IDic IHar LGod LPlm LStr MAus MBur MFry MGan MMat NBat NRog SApu SJus SPer SSea SWCr WWeb

'Freiherr von Marschall' (T) — EBls

'Frensham' (F) — CB&S EBls LStr MGan SSea SWCr

Fresh Pink (Min/Poly) — MGan

Friday's Child = 'Horabi' (HT) — Last listed 1997

Friend for Life = 'Cocnanne' PBR (F) — GCoc GGre MJon SWCr

'Fringette' (Min) — MGan

'Fritz Nobis' (S) ♀ — EBee EBls ENot GCoc IHar LRHS LStr MAus MGan MRav NFla NHaw SJus SPer SWCr WAct WHCG

Frothy = 'Macfrothy' PBR (Min) — MJon SWCr

'Fru Dagmar Hastrup' (Ru) ♀ — More than 30 suppliers

'Frühlingsanfang' (PiH)   EBls MAus MBri SWCr WAct WHCG
'Frühlingsduft' (PiH)   EBee EBls NRog SWCr
'Frühlingsgold' (PiH) ♀   More than 30 suppliers
'Frühlingsmorgen' (PiH)   EBee EBls EBrP EBre ENot GCoc GKir LBCl LBSe LBre LFis LRHS LStr MAus MBBe MBri MGan MMat NRog SApu SBre SJus SPer SWCr WAct WHCG WOVN
'Frühlingsschnee' (PiH)   EBls
'Frühlingszauber' (PiH)   EBls
¶ 'Frybizzy' (Cl)   MFry
¶ 'Fryescape' (HT)   MFry
'Fulgens'   See *R.* 'Malton' (China hybrid)
Fulton Mackay = 'Cocdana' PBR (HT)   GCoc MFry MGan SApu SWCr
Fyvie Castle = 'Cocbamber' PBR (HT)   GCoc GGre MGan
'Gail Borden' (HT)   MAus MGan SWCr
§ *gallica* (G)   EBls SSea
  - 'Complicata'   See *R.* 'Complicata'
  - 'Conditorum'   See *R.* 'Conditorum'
§ - var. *officinalis* (G) ♀   EBls GCoc GKir GPoy LRHS MAus MBri MJon MMat NRog SApu SFam SJus SPer SSea SWCr WAct WHCG
  - 'Velutiniflora' (G)   EBls
§ - 'Versicolor' (G) ♀   CHad CSam EBee EBls ELan ENot EWTr GChr GCoc GGre GKir LGod LStr MAus MBri MDun MFry MGan MJon NHaw NRog SApu SJus SPer SPla SRPl SSea SWCr WHCG WWeb
Galway Bay® = 'Macba' (ClHT)   CSam EBrP EBre GKir LBCl LBSe LBre LRHS MBBe MGan MMat SBre SPer SWCr
¶ 'Garden Beauty' (F)   SWCr
§ Garden News = 'Poulrim' PBR (HT)   GGre SWCr
Garden Party™ = 'Kormollis' PBR (F)   ENot MMat SWCr
¶ 'Gardener's Pink' (Ra)   WHCG
'Gardenia' (Ra)   EBee SPer SWCr WHCG
§ 'Garnette' (Gn)   SWCr
§ 'Garnette Apricot' (Gn)   SPla
'Garnette Carol'   See *R.* 'Carol Amling'
'Garnette Golden'   See *R.* 'Golden Garnette'
'Garnette Pink'   See *R.* 'Carol Amling'
'Garnette Red'   See *R.* 'Garnette'
Gary Lineker = 'Pearobin' (F)   Last listed 1999
'Gary Player' (HT)   NBat
'Gateshead Festival' (HT)   Last listed 1998
'Gaujard'   See *R.* Rose Gaujard = 'Gaumo'
'Gavotte' (HT)   Last listed 1997
Gee Gee™ = 'Benjee' (Min)   Last listed 1997
'Gelbe Dagmar Hastrup' PBR   See *R.* Yellow Dagmar Hastrup = 'Moryelrug'
'Général Galliéni' (T)   EBls
'Général Jacqueminot' (HP)   EBls MAus WAct
'Général Kléber' (CeMo)   EBls LRHS MAus SFam SPer SSea SWCr WAct WHCG
§ 'Général Schablikine' (T)   EBls MAus SWCr
N *gentiliana* (Ra)   EBls LRHS MAus WHCG
Gentle Touch = 'Diclulu' PBR (Min/Patio) ♀   CGro EBls GGre IDic IHar MBri MDun MFry MJon MMat NRog SApu SPer SWCr
'Geoff Boycott' (F)   Last listed 1997
Geoff Hamilton™ = 'Ausham' PBR (S)   ENot IHar LRHS MAus MBNS MJon MMat SCoo SPer SWCr WWeb

§ Geordie Lad = 'Horkorblush' (HT)   NBat
'Georg Arends' (HP)   EBls MAus
'George Dickson' (HT)   EBls MAus
'George R. Hill' (HT)   NBat
'Georges Vibert' (G)   EBls MAus WHCG
Geraldine = 'Peahaze' PBR (F)   MGan SWCr
§ 'Geranium' (*moyesii* hybrid) ♀   More than 30 suppliers
Gerbe d'Or   See *R.* Casino = 'Macca'
'Gerbe Rose' (Ra)   EBls MAus WAct
Gertrude Jekyll® = 'Ausbord' PBR (S)¿   More than 30 suppliers
'Ghislaine de Féligonde' (Ra/S)   EBls EMFP EWTr LStr SWCr WHCG WWat
gigantea   EBls ISea
  - 'Cooperi'   See *R.* 'Cooperi'
Giggles = 'Kingig' (Min)   Last listed 1999
Gilda PBR   See *R.* The Daily Telegraph = 'Peahigh'
§ Gingernut = 'Coccrazy' PBR (Patio)   GCoc GGre MBri SApu SWCr
Ginny-Lou = 'Trobinka' (Min)   SJus
Gipsy Boy   See *R.* 'Zigeunerknabe'
Glad Tidings = 'Tantide' PBR (F)   CGro LPlm MAus MBri MBur MGan MJon NRog SApu SJus SPer SWCr WWeb
Glamis Castle = 'Auslevel' PBR (S)   CBlo EBls EBrP EBre GKir IHar LBCl LBSe LBre LRHS LStr MAus MBBe MBri MJon SBre SJus SPer SWCr WHCG WWeb
§ *glauca* Pourr. (S) ♀   More than 30 suppliers
'Glenfiddich' (F)   CGro EWTr GChr GCoc GGre LPlm LStr MAus MBri MGan MJon NRog NWea SPer SSea SWCr WStl WWeb
'Glenn Dale' (Cl)   EBee SWCr
Glenshane = 'Dicvood' PBR (GC/S)   IDic SWCr
'Gloire de Bruxelles' (HP)   EBls
'Gloire de Dijon' (ClT) ♀   More than 30 suppliers
'Gloire de Ducher' (HP)   CPou MAus MDun MGan SWCr WAct WHCG
'Gloire de France' (G)   EBee EBls MAus SWCr
'Gloire de Guilan' (D)   EBls MAus SWCr WAct
'Gloire des Mousseuses' (CeMo)   EBls MAus SFam SWCr WAct WHCG
'Gloire du Midi' (Poly)   MAus
'Gloire Lyonnaise' (HP)   EBee EBls SWCr WHCG
'Gloria Mundi' (Poly)   EBls MGan SWCr
Gloriana = 'Chewpope' PBR (ClMin)   ECle MBri MJon SWCr
Glowing Amber = 'Manglow' PBR (Min)   NBat
glutinosa   See *R. pulverulenta*
'Goethe' (CeMo)   EBls
§ Gold Bunny = 'Meifronuri' (F)   MBri MGan MJon SWCr
Gold Crown   See *R.* 'Goldkrone'
'Goldbusch' (RH)   EBls MAus MGan SSea WAct
'Golden Anniversary' (Patio)   GCoc GGre GKir NEgg SPer SWCr
§ Golden Beryl = 'Manberyl' (Min)   NBat
Golden Celebration™ = 'Ausgold' PBR (S)   CTri EBrP EBre ENot GGre GKir IHar LBCl LBSe LBre LRHS LStr MAus MBBe MBri MGan MJon MMat NPri SApu SBre SJus SPer SWCr WGer
Golden Chersonese = 'Hilgold' (S)   EBls MAus NRog

'Golden Dawn' (ClHT) See *R*. 'Climbing Golden Dawn'
§ Golden Days = 'Rugolda' MBri
  PBR (HT)
Golden Future = SWCr
  'Horanymoll' (Cl)
'Golden Garnette' (Gn) Last listed 1998
'Golden Glow' (Cl) EBls MGan SWCr
Golden Halo™ = Last listed 1997
  'Savahalo' (Min)
Golden Hands = GGre
  'Chessupremo' PBR
  (Min/Patio)
Golden Handshake = MBri
  'Chewsunford' PBR
  (ClMin/ClPatio)
Golden Hope = 'Mehac' (F) LStr SWCr
§ Golden Jewel = GCoc NBat SApu SWCr
  'Tanledolg' PBR (Patio)
Golden Jubilee = ELan GCoc GGre LPlm LStr
   MAus
  'Cocagold' (HT) SWCr
Golden Melody = 'Irene EBls
  Churruca' (HT)
Golden Moments = MFry SWCr
  'Frytranquil' PBR (HT)
'Golden Moss' (Mo) EBls
'Golden Ophelia' (HT) EBls
§ Golden Penny = 'Rugul' EWTr MFry MGan MJon WGer
  (Min)
Golden Quill = Last listed 1999
  'Tanellelog' (F)
'Golden Rambler' See *R*. 'Alister Stella Gray'
§ Golden Rosamini = Last listed 1998
  'Intergol' (Min/Patio)
'Golden Salmon' (Poly) MGan
'Golden Salmon EBls
  Supérieur' (Poly)
'Golden Shot' (F) MGan SWCr
Golden Showers® (Cl) ♀ More than 30 suppliers
'Golden Slippers' (F) CB&S MGan SWCr
'Golden Sunblaze' See *R*. 'Rise 'n' Shine'
§ Golden Symphonie = MBri MJon SWCr
  'Meitoleil' PBR
  (Min/Patio)
Golden TimesPBR See *R*. Kordes' Golden Times =
   'Kortime'
Golden Wedding = More than 30 suppliers
  'Arokris' PBR (F/HT)
'Golden Wings' (S) ♀ CHad EBee EBls ENot EWTr GCoc
   IHar LFis LRHS LStr MAus MBri
   MFry MGan MJon MMat NFla
   SApu SJus SPer SSea SWCr WAct
   WHCG WOVN
Golden Years® = MAus MJon SWCr
  'Harween' PBR (F)
'Goldfinch' (Ra) CHad EBee EBls EMFP GGre IHar
   LRHS LStr MAus MBri SApu SFam
   SPer SWCr WAct WHCG
Goldfinger = 'Pearoyal' (F) Last listed 1999
'Goldilocks' (F) NRog
§ 'Goldkrone' (HT) Last listed 1997
Goldschatz®PBR See *R*. Castle Howard
   Tercentenary = 'Tantasch'
§ Goldstar = 'Candide' MGan SApu SWCr
  PBR (HT)
Good as Gold = LStr MBri MFry MJon NPri SApu
  'Chewsunbeam' PBR SWCr WGer
  (ClMin)
Good Life = 'Cococircus' GCoc
  (HT)
Good Luck = 'Burspec' MJon SPer SWCr
  PBR (F/Patio)

Good Morning = 'Fryyat' (F) Last listed 1997
§ Gordon Snell = 'Dicwriter' IDic
Gordon's College = GCoc SApu
  'Cocjabby' PBR (F)
'Grace Abounding' (F) SWCr
'Grace Darling' (T) EBls
Grace de Monaco® = EBls MAus MGan SWCr
  'Meimit' (HT)
§ Grace Donnelly = SWCr
  'Horlexstrip' (HT/F)
Graceland = 'Kirscot' MJon
  (Min/Patio)
Graham Thomas = More than 30 suppliers
  'Ausmas' PBR (S)¿
Granada (HT) EBls
Grand Hotel® = 'Mactel' ENot MJon MMat SPer SWCr
  (ClHT)
Grand-mère Jenny = EBls MGan SWCr
  'Grem' (HT)
'Grandpa Dickson' (HT) EBls EBrP EBre GGre GKir IHar
   LBCl LBSe LBre LGod LPlm MAus
   MBBe MBur MGan MJon NBat
   NRog SApu SBre SPer SWCr WWeb
¶ Granny's Favourite (F) GGre SWCr
¶ Great Expectations = LBow LStr
  'Mackalves'
§ 'Great Maiden's Blush' (A) EBls GCoc GOrc MDun MFry
   MMat SFam SRPl WAct
'Great News' (F) MAus SWCr
'Great Ormond Street' (F) EBls
'Great Western' (Bb) EBls
'Green Diamond' (Min) EWTr MAus MJon
Greenall's Glory = MAus MJon SSea SWCr
  'Kirmac' PBR (F/Patio)
'Greenmantle' (RH) EBls MAus MGan
Greensleeves® = EBls LStr MAus SPer SWCr
  'Harlenten' (F)
Greer Garson = Last listed 1999
  'Cocoddy' (HT)
Greetings = 'Jacdreco' GCoc IDic LPlm SWCr
  PBR (F)
'Grey Dawn' (F) SWCr
'Grimpant Cramoisi EBls WHCG
  Supérieur' (ClCh)
'Grootendorst' See *R*. 'F.J. Grootendorst'
'Grootendorst Supreme' MAus SPer SWCr
  (Ru)
N 'Gros Choux de Hollande' EBls WHCG
  (Bb)
Grouse = 'Korimro' PBR EBls ENot GCoc IHar MAus MJon
  (S/GC) MMat SApu SWCr WAct WOVN
§ Grumpy = 'Burkhardt' (Poly) MGan
'Gruss an Aachen' (Poly) CBos EBls EPfP EWTr LStr MAus
   MBri MGan SPer SWCr WAct
   WHCG
'Gruss an Teplitz' CPou EBls EMFP LFis LRHS MAus
  (China hybrid) SPer SRPl SWCr WHCG
Guernsey Love = SJus
  'Troblove' (Min)
'Guinée' (ClHT) CBos CHad CSam EBls EBrP EBre
   ELan GKir IHar LBCl LBSe LBre
   LRHS LStr MAus MBBe MBri MBur
   MGan MMat SBre SChu SPer SSea
   SWCr WHCG
Guletta® See *R*. Golden Penny = 'Rugul'
'Gustav Grünerwald' (HT) EBls MAus
Gwen Mayor = 'Cocover' GCoc
  PBR (HT)
Gwent = 'Poulurt' PBR (GC) EBee EBrP EBre ELan ENot GCoc
   LBCl LBSe LBre LGod LPlm LStr
   MBBe MFry MGan MMat NPri
   SApu SBre SPer SSea SWCr WOVN

§ *gymnocarpa* — EBls ENot MAus MDun MGan
var. *willmottiae* — MMat SPer SWCr WAct WHCG
Gypsy Boy — See *R.* 'Zigeunerknabe'
'Hadangel'^{PBR} — See *R.* 'Smooth Angel'
'Hadvelvet'^{PBR} — See *R.* 'Smooth Velvet'
'Hakuun' (F/Patio) — GChr MAus MGan SWCr
Hamburger Phönix® (Ra) — CGro EBls MGan SPer SWCr WAct
Hampshire = 'Korhamp' ^{PBR} (GC) — ENot MAus MGan MMat SApu SWCr
Hand in Hand = 'Haraztec' ^{PBR} (Patio/Min) — GCoc MBri MJon SWCr
Handel® = 'Macha' (Cl) ♀ — More than 30 suppliers
Hannah Gordon = 'Korweiso' ^{PBR} (F) — EBee ENot LStr MBur MGan MJon MMat NBat NRog SPer SSea SWCr
'Hannah Hauxwell' (Patio/F) — NBat NRog SWCr
'Hanne' (HT) — NRog
'Hansa' (Ru) — EBee EBls ENot LBuc MAus MGan MMat SPer SWCr WHCG WOVN
'Happy' (Poly) — MGan
Happy Anniversary = 'Bedfranc'^{PBR} — LBow
Happy Anniversary = 'Delpre' (F) — CTri GChr GGre GKir LStr MJon NEgg SWCr WWeb
'Happy Birthday' (Min/Patio) — GGre LStr NEgg SWCr
Happy Child = 'Auscomp' ^{PBR} (S) — EBrP EBre IHar LBCl LBSe LBre LRHS MAus MBBe MJon SBre SJus SPer SWCr WGer
Happy Ever After = 'Dicvanilla' ^{PBR} (F) — IDic SWCr
'Happy Thought' (Min) — Last listed 1999
Happy Times = 'Bedone' ^{PBR} (Patio/Min) — GGre SWCr
Happy Wanderer® (F) — Last listed 1997
Harewood = 'Taninaso' ^{PBR} (Patio/F) — MJon SApu SWCr

¶ x *barisonii* — MMat
§ - 'Harison's Yellow' (PiH) ♀ — EBls MAus NFla SPer SWCr WAct
§ - 'Lutea Maxima' (PiH) — EBls MAus
§ - 'Williams' Double Yellow' (PiH) — EBls GChr GCoc MAus SWCr
Harlow Carr = 'Kirlyl' (F) — MJon
'Harry Edland' (F) — SSea
'Harry Maasz' (GC/Cl) — EBls
'Harry Wheatcroft' (HT) — CB&S CGro EBls GGre MAus MBur MGan MJon NRog SWCr
Harvest Fayre = 'Dicnorth' ^{PBR} (F) — CGro IDic LGod MAus MGan MMat NRog SApu SPer SWCr
¶ 'Harvest Festival' ^{PBR} (HT) — SWCr
'Hazel Rose' (HT) — Last listed 1997.
'Headleyensis' — EBls MAus SWCr WHCG
'Heart of England' (F) — MBur
§ Heartbeat '97 = 'Cocorona' ^{PBR} (F) — GCoc NBat SWCr
Heartbreaker = 'Weksibyl' (Min) — Last listed 1997
Heather Austin = 'Auscook' ^{PBR} (S) — IHar LRHS MAus NPri
Heather Honey = 'Horsilbee' (HT) — SWCr
§ 'Heather Muir' (*sericea* hybrid) (S) — EBls EHol MAus
'Heaven Scent' (F) — MJon NBat
Heavenly Rosalind = 'Ausmash' ^{PBR} (S) — LRHS MAus SWCr
§ 'Hebe's Lip' (DxSwB) — EBls MAus WAct
'Hector Deane' (HT) — EBls MGan
'Heidi Jayne' (HT) — MBur
'Heinrich Schultheis' (HP) — EBls
§ 'Helen Knight' (*ecae* hybrid) (S) ♀ — EBls MAus MBri SSea SWCr WHCG
¶ Helen Margaret = 'Horblush' (F) — NBat

'Helen Traubel' (HT) — EBls MGan SWCr
Helena = 'Poulna' ^{PBR} (S) — ECle LPlm
helenae — EBls GCal MAus SPer SWCr
- hybrid — WHCG
Helga® = 'Helgrui' (HT/F) — SRPl
'Helhein'^{PBR} — See *R.* Super Sparkle = 'Helfels'
Hello = 'Cochello' (Min/Patio) — Last listed 1998
hemisphaerica (S) — EBls MAus SWCr WAct
hemsleyana — CHid
'Henri Fouquier' (G) — EBls
§ 'Henri Martin' (CeMo) ♀ — CTri EBls IOrc LRHS MAus NBus NRog SPer SWCr WAct WHCG
Henri Matisse = 'Delstrobla' (HT) — WWeb
'Henry Nevard' (HP) — EBls MAus
'Her Majesty' (HP) — EBls
§ 'Herbstfeuer' (RH) — EBls MAus SWCr
Heritage® = 'Ausblush' ^{PBR} (S) — More than 30 suppliers
'Hermosa' (Ch) — CBos EBee EBls ECre EMFP LFis LRHS MAus NBus SWCr WAct WHCG
Hero® = 'Aushero' (S) — MAus
Hertfordshire = 'Kortenay' ^{PBR} (GC) — EBrP EBre ENot GCoc LBCl LBSe LBre LPlm LRHS MBBe MMat SBre SPer SWCr WOVN
Hi Society = 'Cocquation' (Patio) — GCoc
'Hiawatha' (Ra) — EBls MAus SWCr
x *hibernica* — MAus
'Hidcote Gold' (S) — EBls MAus
High Hopes = 'Haryup' ^{PBR} (Cl) — EBee GGre LGod LRHS LStr MBri MBur MFry MGan MJon SApu SJus SWCr WHCG WWeb
High Sheriff = 'Harwellington' ^{PBR} (HT) — SWCr
§ 'Highdownensis' (*moyesii* hybrid) (S) ♀ — EBls ELan LRHS MAus SFam SPer SWCr
Highfield® = 'Harcomp' ^{PBR} (Cl) — IHar LGod MAus MBri MJon SApu SJus SPer SWCr
Highland Laddie = 'Cocflag' (F) — GCoc
Hilda Murrell® = 'Ausmurr' (S) — MAus
§ 'Hillieri' (S) — EBls MAus
'Hippolyte' (G) — EBls MAus WSHC
Hole-in-one = 'Horeagle' (F) — Last listed 1998
holodonta — See *R. moyesii* f. *rosea*
holy rose — See *R.* x *richardii*
Home on Time = 'Cocquamber' (HT) — GCoc GGre SWCr
'Home Sweet Home' (HT) — EBls MAus
Home Sweet Home = 'Mailoeur' (Cl/G) — LStr SSea
'Homère' (T) — EBls MAus
Honey Bunch® = 'Cocglen' ^{PBR} (F) — GCoc LGod LStr MBri MJon NBat SApu SPer SWCr
'Honey Favorite' (HT) — MAus
Honeymoon — See *R.* 'Honigmond'
§ 'Honigmond' (F) — GGre NPri SWCr
'Honorine de Brabant' (Bb) — CHad CPou EBls IHar LFis LRHS MAus MBri SFam SPer SPla SWCr WHCG
§ Hope '98 = 'Coclament' ^{PBR} (F/Patio) — GCoc GGre NEgg SWCr
'Horace Vernet' (HP) — EBls
horrida — See *R. biebersteinii*
'Horstmanns Rosenresli' (F) — EBls
Hot Gossip = 'Jacati' (Patio/Min) — GGre MBri SWCr
House Beautiful = 'Harbingo' ^{PBR} (Patio) — SJus SWCr

Johnnie Walker =	MFry
'Frygran' PBR (HT)	
'Josephine Bruce' (HT)	CB&S EBls LGod MAus MBur
	MGan NRog SWCr WStI
'Josephine Wheatcroft'	See R. 'Rosina'
'Joseph's Coat' (S/Cl)	IArd LGod LStr MBri MFry MGan
	MMat SSea SWCr
'Journey's End' (HT)	MGan SWCr
'Jubilee Celebration' (F)	Last listed 1999
Jude the Obscure =	CAbP IHar LRHS MAus MJon
'Ausjo' PBR (S)	
§ Judi Dench = 'Peahunder'	MBri
(F)	
'Judy Fischer' (Min)	LGod SWCr
Judy Garland = 'Harking'	SJus SWCr
(F)	
'Julia Mannering' (RH)	MAus
'Julia's Rose' PBR (HT)	CGro LStr MAus MBur MGan
	MJon SApu SPer SWCr
Julie Andrews =	Last listed 1998
'Fryvivacious' PBR (F)	
Julie Cussons =	Last listed 1999
'Fryprincess' (F)	
'Juliet' (HP)	EBls
¶ jundzillii	CFee
June Laver™ = 'Lavjune'	Last listed 1998
(Min)	
'Juno' (Ce)	EBls MAus SWCr WAct WHCG
'Just Jenny' (Min)	NBat
Just Joey® (HT) ♀	CGro EBee EBls ELan GCoc GGre
	GKir LGod LPlm LStr MAus MBri
	MBur MFry MGan MJon MMat
	NRog SApu SJus SPer SSea SWCr
	WWeb
Just Magic = 'Trobic' (Min)	MJon
'Karl Foerster' (PiH)	EBls MAus
Karla	See R. Daily Post = 'Frytrooper'
'Kassel' (S/Cl)	EBls MAus WAct
'Katharina Zeimet' (Poly)	EBls MAus MGan NRog WAct
	WHCG
'Kathleen' (HM)	EBls
'Kathleen Ferrier' (F)	EBls MGan SWCr
'Kathleen Harrop' (Bb)	EBls ENot IHar LRHS LStr MAus
	MBri MBur MMat SFam SPer SRPl
	SWCr WAct WHCG WSHC
Kathleen Jane =	SWCr
'Horcoed' (S/F)	
'Kathleen O'Rourke' (HT)	Last listed 1997
Kathleen's Rose =	MJon
'Kirkitt' (F)	
§ Kathryn McGredy® =	MJon SWCr
'Macauclad' PBR (HT)	
§ Kathryn Morley =	CAbP EBrP EBre IHar LBCl LBSe
'Ausclub' PBR (F)	LBre LRHS MAus MBBe MBri
	MJon NPri SBre SWCr
'Katie' (ClF)	MGan SWCr
Katie Crocker =	MBur
'Burbrindley' (F)	
'Kazanlik' misapplied	See R. 'Professeur Emile Perrot'
Keep in Touch™ =	GCoc
'Hardrama' (F)	
Keepsake = 'Kormalda'	ENot LPlm MGan MMat SWCr
PBR (HT)	
Kent® = 'Poulcov' PBR	EBee ELan ENot EPfP GGre LStr
(S/GC)	MJon MMat SPer SPla SRPl SSea
	SWCr WHCG WOVN
'Kerryman' (F)	SWCr
'Kew Rambler' (Ra)	CRHN EBee EBls MAus MRav
	SFam SPer SWCr WHCG
'Kiese' (canina hybrid)	MJon
'Kiftsgate'	See R. filipes 'Kiftsgate'
'Kilworth Gold' (HT)	MGan

'Kim' (Patio)	NRog
Kind Regards =	SWCr WWeb
'Pentiger' (F)	
King Henry = 'Genwine'	SWCr
PBR (S)	
King William = 'Genpink'	SWCr
PBR (S)	
King's Ransom® (HT)	CB&S EBls GGre MGan MJon
	MMat SPer SWCr
'Kirsten Poulsen' (Poly)	EBls
Kiss 'n' Tell = 'Seakis' (Min)	MBur
'Kitty Hawk' (Min)	NBat
x kochiana	EBls
'Köln am Rhein' (Cl)	MGan
§ 'Königin von Dänemark'	CHad EBee EBls EMFP ENot EPfP
(A) ♀	GCoc IHar LRHS MAus MBri
	MDun MMat NFla SApu SJus SPer
	SRum SSea SWCr WAct WHCG
§ Kordes' Golden Times =	Last listed 1999
'Kortime' PBR (F)	
'Kordes' Robusta' PBR	See R. Robusta = 'Korgosa'
Korona® = 'Kornita' (F)	MGan NRog SWCr
I 'Korred' (1983)	See R. Ace of Hearts = 'Korred'
'Korresia' (F)	EBee EBls EPfP GCoc GGre GKir
	IHar LGod LStr MAus MBri MFry
	MGan MJon MMat NRog SJus SPer
	SWCr
I 'Korstegli'PBR	See R. Lancashire = 'Korstegli'
§ Kristin™ = 'Benmagic' (Min)	NBat
Kronenbourg® = 'Macbo'	EBls LPlm MAus
(HT)	
'Kronprinzessin Viktoria'	EBee EBls MAus SWCr WHCG
(Bb)	
L.D. Braithwaite® =	CSam EBrP EBre ELan ENot IHar
'Auscrim' PBR (S)	LBCl LBSe LBre LGod LPlm LRHS
	LStr MAus MBBe MFry MGan
	MJon MMat SApu SBre SJus SPer
	SRPl SSea SWCr WAct WHCG
	WWeb
'La Belle Distinguée' (RH)	EBls MAus WHCG
'La Belle Sultane'	See R. 'Violacea'
'La Follette' (Cl)	EBls
'La France' (HT)	EBls MAus
'La Mortola'	See R. brunonii 'La Mortola'
'La Noblesse' (Ce)	EBls
'La Perle' (Ra)	CRHN MAus
'La Reine' (HP)	EBls
'La Reine Victoria'	See R. 'Reine Victoria'
'La Rubanée'	See R. 'Centifolia Variegata'
La Sévillana =	EBls NHaw SApu SPer SWCr
'Meigekanu' PBR (F/GC)	WOVN
'La Ville de Bruxelles' (D) ♀	EBls MAus MRav SFam SPer SWCr
	WAct WHCG
'Lady Alice Stanley' (HT)	EBls
'Lady Barnby' (HT)	EBls
'Lady Belper' (HT)	EBls
'Lady Curzon' (Ru)	EBls MAus SWCr
Lady Diana = 'Dicxotic'PBR	IDic
'Lady Elgin'	See R. Thaïs = 'Memaj'
'Lady Forteviot' (HT)	EBls
'Lady Gay' (Ra)	EBee MAus SWCr WHCG
'Lady Godiva' (Ra)	MAus
'Lady Hillingdon' (ClT)	See R. 'Climbing Lady Hillingdon'
'Lady Hillingdon' (T)	LRHS MAus
'Lady Iliffe' (HT)	MGan SWCr
Lady in Red = 'Sealady'	MBur
(Min)	
'Lady Jane' (HT)	Last listed 1997
'Lady Love '95' (Patio)	GGre SWCr
Lady MacRobert =	GCoc
'Coclent' (F)	
'Lady Mary Fitzwilliam' (HT)	EBls

Lady Mavis Pilkington = SWCr
'Kortlitze' (HT)
§ Lady Meillandina® = Last listed 1999
'Meilarco' PBR (Min)
Lady Mitchell = SWCr
'Haryearn' (HT)
'Lady of Stifford' (F) Last listed 1997
'Lady Penelope' (MinCl) WWeb
§ 'Lady Penzance' (RH) CB&S EBls LRHS MAus MFry
MGan SApu SPer SWCr WAct
§ Lady Rachel = EBee
'Candoodle' (F)
'Lady Romsey' (F) EBls
Lady Rose® = 'Korlady' MJon
(HT)
'Lady Seton' (HT) SPer
'Lady Stuart' (Ch) Last listed 1998
Lady Sunblaze PBR See R. Lady Meillandina =
'Meilarco'
'Lady Sylvia' (HT) EBee EBls MAus MGan NRog SPer
WStI
Lady Taylor = 'Smitling' MBur
(F/Patio)
'Lady Waterlow' (ClHT) EBls MAus SPer SWCr WHCG
laevigata (Ra) EBls MAus SWCr
- 'Anemonoides' See R. 'Anemone'
- 'Cooperi' See R. 'Cooperi'
'Lafter' (S) EBls
'Lagoon' (F) EBls
L'Aimant = 'Harzola' PBR (F) ECle GCoc LGod LStr MFry MGan
MJon MMat SApu SJus SWCr
'Lakeland' (HT) MAus
'Lamarque' (N) MAus
Laminuette® (F) MJon
§ Lancashire = 'Korstesgli' ENot GCoc LStr MMat NPri SSea
PBR (GC) SWCr
Lancashire Life = MBri
'Ruilanca' PBR (F)
§ 'Lanei' (CeMo) EBls
Langdale Chase = Last listed 1999
'Fryrhapsody' (F)
Langford Light = 'Lannie' Last listed 1997
(Min/GC)
Laughter Lines = IDic MGan SWCr
'Dickerry' (F)
Laura Anne = GCoc
'Cocclarion' (HT)
§ Laura Ashley = MAus SWCr
'Chewharla' PBR
(GC/ClMin)
Laura Ford® = CGro CTri EBrP EBre GGre GKir
'Chewarvel' PBR IHar LBCl LBSe LBre LStr MAus
(ClMin) ♀ MBBe MBri MGan MJon MMat
NBat NPri NRog SApu SBre SJus
SWCr WWeb
'Laura Jane' (HT) MGan
'Laura Louisa' (Cl) EBls EWTr
Laura = 'Meidragelac' (HT) SWCr
Laurence Olivier® = Last listed 1998
'Meinagre' (F)
'Lavender Jewel' (Min) IHar MAus MBur
'Lavender Lassie' (HM) ♀ CHad CPou EBee EMFP IOrc
LRHS MAus MFry MGan SPer
SWCr WHCG
'Lavender Pinocchio' (F) MAus WAct
Lavinia PBR See R. Lawinia = 'Tanklewi'
§ Lawinia = 'Tanklewi' PBR CTri EBee GKir LRHS LStr MBri
(ClHT) ♀ SApu SJus SPer SWCr
'Lawrence Johnston' (Cl) EBls LRHS MAus NPri SFam SPer
SWCr WAct
'Le Havre' (HP) EBls
'Le Rêve' (Cl) EBls MAus SWCr

'Le Vésuve' (Ch) EBls MAus
Leander® = 'Auslea' (S) MAus
Leaping Salmon = CGro EBee ELan GCoc IOrc LGod
'Peamight' PBR (ClHT) LStr MAus MBri MGan MJon SApu
SChu SPer SPla SWCr WOVN WStI
'Leda' (D) EBee EBls EMFP MAus SFam SPer
SWCr WAct
'Lemon Pillar' See R. 'Paul's Lemon Pillar'
Len Turner = 'Dicjeep' IDic SApu
PBR (F)
¶ Léonardo de Vinci = SApu
'Meideauri' PBR (F)
Leonidas = 'Meicofum' Last listed 1999
PBR (HT)
'Léonie Lamesch' (Poly) EBls
'Léontine Gervais' (Ra) CAbP CRHN LRHS MAus SWCr
WAct WHCG
Leslie's Dream = IDic
'Dicjoon' PBR (HT)
'Leuchtstern' (Ra) EBls
'Leverkusen' (Cl) CHad EBls EWTr LRHS MAus
MDun MGan MJon SPer SPla SRPl
SSea SWCr WAct WHCG WSHC
'Leveson-Gower' (Bb) EBls
'Ley's Perpetual' (ClT) CPou EBee EBls SWCr WBcn
x Iheritieriana (Bs) EBee SWCr
'Lilac Charm' (F) EBls MAus
§ Lilac Rose™ = 'Auslilac' (S) MAus
Lilian Austin® = 'Ausli' (S) MAus MBri SWCr
Liliana = 'Poulsyng' PBR (S) EBee ECle LPlm
§ Lilli Marlene = 'Korlima' (F) CTri EBls GCoc LStr MAus MGan
MMat NRog SPer SWCr
'Lily the Pink' (HT) Last listed 1997
'Lime Kiln' (Ra) Last listed 1998
Lincoln Cathedral = MGan MJon SPer SWCr
'Glanlin' PBR (HT)
Lincolnshire Poacher = NBat
'Glareabit' (HT)
Lions International = MFry
'Frycharm' (HT)
§ Little Artist® = MJon
'Macmanly' (Min)
Little Bo-peep = 'Poullen' ENot MJon MMat
PBR (Min/Patio)
'Little Buckaroo' (Min) CBrm ELan LGod MGan SPer
SWCr WStI
'Little Dorrit' (Poly) NRog WAct
'Little Flirt' (Min) MAus MGan SWCr
'Little Gem' (DPMo) EBls MAus MGan
Little Jackie™ = 'Savor' NBat
(Min)
Little Jewel = 'Cocabel' Last listed 1997
(Patio)
'Little Len' (Min/Patio) Last listed 1999
Little Marvel = 'Ruigerdan' MBri
(Min)
¶ Little Muff = 'Horluisbond' NBat
(Min)
Little Prince = 'Coccord' Last listed 1997
(F/Patio)
Little Rambler = MJon MMat SApu SWCr
'Chewramb' PBR
(MinRa)
§ Little Rascal = 'Peaalamo' GGre SWCr
PBR (Patio/Min)
Little Russell = 'Trobric' MJon
(Min)
* 'Little White' Last listed 1998
'Little White Pet' See R. 'White Pet'
Little Woman = 'Diclittle' IDic LStr SApu SSea SWCr
PBR (Patio)
'Liverpool Echo' (F) LPlm MJon

§ Liverpool Remembers = 'Frystar' PBR (HT) — LGod MBri MBur MFry SWCr
'Living Fire' (F) — MBur MGan NRog SWCr
Lloyds of London = 'Canlloyd' (F) — SWCr
'Lollipop' (Min) — MGan
'Long John Silver' (Cl) — EBls
longicuspis hort. — See *R. mulliganii*
- Bertoloni (Ra) — EBls
§ - var. *sinowilsonii* (Ra) — EBls GCal MAus
Longleat = 'Macinca' (Min) — Last listed 1997
§ Lord Byron = 'Meitosier' PBR (ClHT) — LStr MBri MJon SApu SWCr
'Lord Penzance' (RH) — EBee EBls LRHS MAus MGan SPer SWCr WAct
L'Oréal Trophy = 'Harlexis' PBR (HT) — MAus MJon
'Lorraine Lee' (T) — EBls
'Los Angeles' (HT) — EBls
'L'Ouche' misapplied — See *R.* 'Louise Odier'
'Louis Gimard' (CeMo) — EBls LRHS MAus SPer WAct WHCG
'Louis Philippe' (Ch) — EBls
'Louis XIV' (Ch) — CHad EBls WHCG
Louisa Stone = 'Harbadge' (S) — SWCr
§ 'Louise Odier' (Bb) — EBee EBls EBrP EBre EMFP IHar LBCl LBSe LBre LFis LRHS LStr MAus MBBe MBri MDun SApu SBre SFam SJus SPer SPla SRPl SRum SSea SWCr WAct WHCG WOVN
¶ Love Knot = 'Chewglorious' ECle
'Love Token' (F) — MBur
Lovely Fairy® = 'Spevu' PBR (Poly/GC) — IDic MJon WAct
Lovely Lady™ = 'Dicjubell' PBR (HT) ♀ — CTri EBee IDic LPlm LStr MGan MJon SApu SJus SWCr
'Lovers' Meeting' PBR (HT) — GGre GKir LPlm MBur MGan MJon NBat NRog SPer SSea SWCr WStI
Loving Memory = 'Korgund' PBR (HT) — EBee ENot GCoc GGre LPlm LStr MFry MGan MMat NPri SPer SRum SSea SWCr
Loving Touch™ (Min) — Last listed 1997
LU 87 — Last listed 1998
Lucetta = 'Ausemi' (S) — MAus SPer WAct
luciae — EBls
- var. *onoei* — CLyd EPot NMen
'Lucilla' (Patio) — NBat
Lucky Duck = 'Diczest' PBR — IDic
'Lucy Ashton' (RH) — MAus
Luis Desamero = 'Tinluis' (Min) — NBat
'Lutea Maxima' — See *R.* x *harisonii* 'Lutea Maxima'
'Lykkefund' (Ra) — EBls MAus
'Lyon Rose' (HT) — EBls
'Ma Perkins' (F) — EBls SSea
'Ma Ponctuée' (DPMo) — EBls
'Mabel Morrison' (HP) — EBls MAus
Macartney rose — See *R. bracteata*
Macmillan Nurse = 'Beamac' (S) — EBls
'Macrantha' (Gallica hybrid) — EBls LRHS MAus SPer WAct
x *macrantha* 'Raubritter' — See *R.* 'Raubritter' ('Macrantha' hybrid)
macrophylla — MAus SWCr
- B&SWJ 2603 — WCru
- 'Doncasteri' — See *R.* 'Doncasteri'
§ - 'Master Hugh' ex SS&W 7822 ♀ — EBls MAus

'Macyou'PBR — See *R.* Regensberg = 'Macyoumis'
Madam Speaker = 'Meizuzes' PBR (HT) — SApu SWCr
'Madame Abel Chatenay' (HT) — EBls MAus
'Madame Alfred Carrière' (N) ♀ — More than 30 suppliers
'Madame Alice Garnier' (Ra) — EBee EBls SPer SWCr
'Madame Antoine Mari' (T) — EBls
'Madame Berkeley' (T) — EBls
'Madame Bravy' (T) — EBls MAus
'Madame Butterfly' (HT) — EBls MAus MBur MGan SApu SFam SPer SSea SWCr
§ 'Madame Caroline Testout' (HT) — EBee GKir LRHS NLar SFam WAct
'Madame Charles' (T) — EBls
'Madame d'Arblay' (Ra) — EBls
'Madame de Sancy de Parabère' (Bs) — EBls MAus SFam SWCr WHCG
'Madame de Watteville' (T) — EBls
'Madame Delaroche-Lambert' (DPMo) ♀ — EBls MAus WAct WHCG
'Madame Driout' (ClT) — EBls WHCG
'Madame Eliza de Vilmorin' (HT) — EBls
'Madame Ernest Calvat' (Bb) — EBls MAus
'Madame Eugène Résal' misapplied — See *R.* 'Comtesse du Cayla'
'Madame Gabriel Luizet' (HP) — EBls
'Madame Georges Bruant' (Ru) — EBls MAus
§ 'Madame Grégoire Staechelin' (ClHT) ♀ — More than 30 suppliers
'Madame Hardy' (ClD) ♀ — CPou CSam EBee EBls ENot GCoc IHar LGod LRHS LStr MAus MBri MGan MJon MMat NFla SApu SFam SJus SPer SSea SWCr WAct WHCG WOVN
'Madame Isaac Pereire' (ClBb) ♀ — More than 30 suppliers
'Madame Jules Gravereaux' (ClT) — EBls MAus
'Madame Jules Thibaud' (Poly) — MAus SWCr
§ 'Madame Knorr' (DPo) ♀ — CPou EBls EMFP EPfP LRHS MAus MMat SJus SPer SSea SWCr WAct WOVN
'Madame Laurette Messimy' (Ch) — EBls MAus WHCG WSHC
'Madame Lauriol de Barny' (Bb) — CBos EBls MAus MGan SFam SWCr WHCG
'Madame Legras de Saint Germain' (AxN) — EBls IHar LRHS MAus SFam SJus SPer SWCr WAct WHCG
'Madame Lombard' (T) — EBls
'Madame Louis Laperrière' (HT) — EBls MAus MGan SPer SWCr
'Madame Louis Lévêque' (DPMo) ♀ — EBls SWCr WHCG
'Madame Pierre Oger' (Bb) — EBee EBls ENot LRHS LStr MAus MMat SApu SPer SRum SSea SWCr WAct WHCG
'Madame Plantier' (AxN) — CBos EBls IHar LRHS MAus MDun SPer SSea SWCr WHCG WOVN
'Madame Scipion Cochet' (T) — EBls WHCG
'Madame Victor Verdier' (HP) — EBls
'Madame Wagram, Comtesse de Turenne' (T) — EBls

'Madame William Paul' EBls
(PoMo)
'Madame Zöetmans' (D) EBls MAus
'Madeleine Selzer' (Ra) EBls MAus MGan
'Madge' (HM) SDix
Maestro® = 'Mackinja' (HT) MAus
'Magenta' (S/HT) EBls MAus SPer SWCr WAct
Magic Carpet = 'Jaclover' EPfP GCoc GGre IDic LGod LPlm
PBR (S/GC) LRHS LStr MAus MFry MGan
MJon MMat SApu SCoo SJus SPer
SRPl SSea SWCr
§ Magic Carrousel® = LPlm MAus WStI
'Moorcar' (Min)
Magic Fire® = SWCr
'Lapjaminal' (F)
'Magna Charta' (HP) EBls
'Magnifica' (RH) EBls MAus MGan
Maid of Kent = 'Rum 1 SPer SRum SWCr
Cookson' PBR (Cl)
N 'Maiden's Blush' (A) CSam EBee EBls EBrP EBre ELan
EMFP ENot GKir IHar LBCl LBSe
LBre LRHS MAus MBBe MGan
SApu SBre SChu SFam SJus SPer
SRum SSea SWCr WHCG WWeb
'Maiden's Blush, Great' See R. 'Great Maiden's Blush'
'Maigold' (ClPiH) ♀ More than 30 suppliers
§ majalis Last listed 1998
Make a Wish = 'Mehpat' LStr MBri SWCr
PBR (Min/Patio)
'Malaga' (ClHT) MMat
§ Malcolm Sargent = SPer SWCr
'Harwharry' PBR (HT)
Maltese rose See R. 'Cécile Brünner'
§ 'Malton' (China hybrid) EBls
Malverns = 'Kordehei' (GC) ENot MMat SWCr
Mandarin® = 'Korcelin' LStr MJon MMat SSea SWCr
PBR (Min)
'Manettii' (N) EBls
'Manning's Blush' (RH) EBls MAus SWCr WAct WHCG
Manou Meilland® = SWCr
'Meitulimon' (HT)
Manuela® (HT) MGan
'Manx Queen' (F) MGan MJon SWCr
Many Happy Returns = EBee EBrP EBre ENot GCoc GKir
'Harwanted' PBR (S/F) ♀ LBCl LBSe LBre LGod LPlm LStr
MAus MBBe MBri MBur MFry
MGan MJon MMat SApu SBre SJus
SPer SWCr WOVN WWeb
'Marbrée' (DPo) EBls MAus
'Marcel Bourgouin' (G) EBls SWCr
'Märchenland' (F/S) EBls MAus
§ 'Marchesa Boccella' CPou EBee EBls EMFP EPfP GKir
(DPo) ♀ MAus MGan MMat NFla SJus SPer
SPla SSea SWCr WAct WWeb
'Marcie Gandy' (HT) MGan SWCr
'Maréchal Davoust' (CeMo) EBls MAus SFam
'Maréchal Niel' (N) EBls ERea MAus MGan SPer SWCr
WHCG
'Margaret' (HT) MBur MGan SWCr
Margaret Merril = More than 30 suppliers
'Harkuly' (F/HT) ♀
§ Margaret Thatcher = MJon
'Korflüg' PBR (HT)
Margaret's World = MJon
'Kirbill' (F)
'Margo Koster' (Poly) EBls MAus NRog SWCr WAct
Marguerite Anne = GCoc NBat SApu
'Cocredward' PBR (F)
'Marguérite Guillard' (HP) EBls
'Marguerite Hilling' (S) ♀ EBee EBls ENot GCoc GGre LRHS
MAus MBri MGan MJon MMat
NRog SApu SMad SPer SRPl SWCr

WAct WHCG WOVN
Maria Theresa® (HT) Last listed 1998
x mariae-graebnerae WHCG
Marianne Tudor = Last listed 1998
'Frymartor' (HT)
'Marie de Blois' (CeMo) EBls
'Marie Louise' (D) EBee EBls IHar LRHS MAus SFam
SWCr WAct WHCG
'Marie Pavič' (Poly) EBls MAus WHCG
'Marie van Houtte' (T) EBls MAus
'Marie-Jeanne' (Poly) EBls MAus
'Marijke Koopman' (HT) MFry
Marinette = 'Auscam' PBR (S) LRHS MAus MBri MJon NPri
SWCr
Marjorie Fair® = EBls LPlm MAus MGan SApu
'Harhero' (Poly/S) SWCr WAct WOVN
Marjorie May = MJon SWCr
'Horsunpegy' (HT)
'Marlena' (F/Patio) GCoc MAus MGan SWCr
Marry Me = 'Dicwonder' ECle IDic MBri MJon SApu SWCr
PBR (Patio)
'Martha' (Bb) EBls MAus
'Martian Glow' (F/S) MGan
'Martin Frobisher' (Ru) EBls MAus
'Mary' (Poly) LStr SWCr
Mary Donaldson = MGan SWCr
'Canana' (HT)
§ Mary Gammon = MFry
'Fryssweetie' (Min/Patio)
Mary Hayley Bell = SWCr
'Korporalt' (S)
'Mary Manners' (Ru) EBls SPer SWCr
Mary Pope = 'Korlasche' ENot MMat SWCr
PBR (HT)
Mary Rose® = 'Ausmary' More than 30 suppliers
PBR (S)
Mary Sumner = 'Macstra' SWCr
(F)
'Mary Wallace' (Cl) EBls MAus
Mary Webb® = MAus MBri
'Auswebb' (S)
'Masquerade' (F) CB&S CGro EBls LGod LStr MAus
MDun MGan MJon MMat NRog
SSea SWCr WStI
'Master Hugh' See R. macrophylla 'Master Hugh'
ex SS&W 7822
Matangi® = 'Macman' (F) LGod MGan NRog SWCr
Matthias Meilland® = SWCr
'Meifolio' (F)
'Maurice Bernardin' (HP) EBls
'Max Graf' See R. x jacksonii 'Max Graf'
'Maxima' See R. x alba 'Alba Maxima'
maximowicziana CC 541 WHCr
'May Queen' (Ra) CPou CRHN EBee EBls EMFP
LRHS MAus NLar SFam SPer SWCr
Mayor of Casterbridge = IHar LRHS MAus MBNS MJon
'Ausbrid' PBR (S)
'McCartney Rose' PBR (HT) See R. The McCartney Rose =
'Meizeli'
'McGredy's Sunset' (HT) NRog
'McGredy's Yellow' (HT) EBls MBur MGan
'Meg' (ClHT) CHad EBee EBls EWTr LRHS
MAus MBri MGan NHaw SPer
SWCr WAct WHCG
'Meg Merrilies' (RH) EBls MAus MGan SSea SWCr WAct
'Megiddo' (F) MGan SWCr
'Meicobius' PBR See R. Terracotta = 'Meicobuis'
Meillandina® = 'Meirov' MGan
(Min)
Melina® See R. Sir Harry Pilkington =
'Tanema'

'Melinda' (HT)	Last listed 1998
Melody Maker =	IDic MAus MBur MGan MJon
'Dicqueen' PBR (F)	SWCr
Memento® = 'Dicbar' PBR	IDic MGan SWCr
(F)	
'Memoriam' (HT)	MGan SWCr
Memory Lane =	GGre SWCr
'Peavoodoo' PBR (F)	
Mercedes = 'Merkor' (F)	MJon
'Mermaid' (Cl) ♀	CB&S CGro EBls ENot EWTr GCoc
	GKir IHar LHop LRHS LStr MAus
	MGan MJon MMat NRog SApu
	SBra SJus SLPl SMad SPer SSea
	SSoC SWCr WAct WHCG WWat
'Merveille de Lyon' (HP)	EBls
§ Message = 'Meban' (HT)	MGan SWCr
Meteor® (F/Patio)	MGan SWCr
§ 'Mevrouw Nathalie	CHad EBls LRHS LStr MAus SPer
Nypels' (Poly) ♀	SWCr WAct WKif WOVN
'Mexico' (Min)	LPlm
§ Michael Crawford =	LGod
'Poulvue' PBR (HT)	
'Michèle Meilland' (HT)	EBls MAus MGan
micrantha	Last listed 1998
x *micrugosa*	EBls MAus
- 'Alba'	EBls MAus
Middlesborough Football	NBat
Club = 'Horflame' (HT)	
Middlesex County =	NBat
'Bosanne' (F)	
Mike Thompson =	NBat
'Sherired' (HT)	
¶ 'Millennium Memories' (F)	SWCr
'Millennium Rose 2000'PBR	See *R.* Rose 2000 =
	'Cocquetrum'
Millionaire = 'Peazara'	GGre SApu
PBR (F)	
Mimi = 'Meidesi' (Min)	MGan
Mini Metro = 'Rufin'	MFry
PBR (Min)	
Minijet® = 'Meirutego'	Last listed 1997
(Min)	
Minilights = 'Dicmoppet'	IDic SApu SWCr
PBR (Patio)	
'Minnehaha' (Ra)	EBls EMFP LGod MAus SWCr
Minnie Pearl® =	Last listed 1997
'Savahowdy' (Min)	
mirifica stellata	See *R. stellata* var. *mirifica*
Mischief = 'Macmi' (HT)	EBls GGre MAus MGan NRog SPer
	SWCr
§ Miss Dior = 'Harencens'	SWCr
PBR (S)	
'Miss Edith Cavell' (Poly)	EBls
Miss Harp = 'Tanolg' (HT)	MGan NRog
Miss Ireland = 'Macir' (HT)	Last listed 1998
'Miss Lowe' (Ch)	EBls
§ Miss Pam Ayres =	MMat SWCr
'Kormarie' (S)	
§ Mister Lincoln® (HT)	EBls LGod MAus MBri MGan SPer
	SWCr
Mistress Quickly =	LRHS LStr MAus MJon NPri SWCr
'Ausky' PBR (S)	WWeb
'Modern Times' (HT)	IDic
'Mojave' (HT)	MAus MGan SWCr
Moje Hammarberg® (Ru)	ENot MJon WAct
§ Molineux = 'Ausmol' PBR (S)	EBrP EBre ENot GCoc GKir IHar
	LBCl LBSe LBre LGod LRHS MAus
	MBBe MBri MJon MMat NPri SBre
	SWCr WWeb
§ *mollis*	Last listed 1998
Molly McGredy =	SWCr
'Macmo' (F)	

'Mona Ruth' (Min)	MGan
'Monique' (HT)	EBls MGan
'Monsieur Tillier' (T)	EBls
'Moon Maiden' (F)	Last listed 1998
Moonbeam = 'Ausbeam' (S)	MAus
'Moonlight' (HM)	CHad CTri EBls EWTr IHar LRHS
	MAus MGan NBus NRog SJus SPer
	SWCr WAct WHCG
'Morgengruss' (Cl)	MGan SPer
Moriah = 'Ganhol' PBR (HT)	MGan
'Morlettii' (Bs)	EBls EHol MRav SWCr WHCG
Morning Jewel® (ClF) ♀	GCoc LPlm MAus MFry MGan
	MJon NRog SPer SWCr
Morning Mist = 'Ausfire' (S)	LRHS MAus
moschata (Ra)	EBls EMFP MAus MRav SSea
	SWCr
- 'Autumnalis'	See *R.* 'Princesse de Nassau'
- var. *nepalensis*	See *R. brunonii*
Mother's Day =	ELan GKir LStr MJon NEgg NPri
'Moersdag' (Poly/F)	SWCr
Mother's Love =	Last listed 1997
'Tinlove' (Min)	
Mountain Snow =	LRHS MAus MBri
'Aussnow' (Ra)	
Mountbatten® =	CGro EBls EBrP EBre ELan ENot
'Harmantelle' PBR (F) ♀	EWTr GGre GKir LBCl LBSe
	LBre LGod LPlm LStr MAus MBBe
	MFry MGan MJon MMat SApu
	SBre SJus SPer SRPl SSea SWCr
	WWeb
§ 'Mousseline' (DPoMo)	EBls EMFP LRHS MAus SPer SSea
	SWCr WAct WHCG
'Mousseuse du Japon'	See *R.* 'Japonica'
moyesii (S)	CPne CSam EBls ELan ENot IHar
	IOrc ISea LEdu MAus MFry MGan
	MJon MMat NRog NWea SPer
	SWCr WAct WOVN
- 'Evesbatch' (S)	WAct
§ - var. *fargesii* (S)	EBls
- 'Geranium'	See *R.* 'Geranium' (*moyesii*
	hybrid)
- 'Highdownensis'	See *R.* 'Highdownensis' (*moyesii*
	hybrid)
- 'Hillieri'	See *R.* 'Hillieri'
- *holodonta*	See *R. moyesii* f. *rosea*
§ - f. *rosea* (S)	EBls GCal MMat
- 'Sealing Wax'	See *R.* 'Sealing Wax' (*moyesii*
	hybrid)
'Mozart' (HM)	MJon NLar SWCr WHCG
'Mr Bluebird' (MinCh)	MAus MGan SWCr WStI
'Mr Chips' (HT)	MBur
Mr J.C.B. = 'Dicsun' PBR (S)	IDic
'Mr Lincoln'	See *R.* Mister Lincoln
'Mrs Anthony Waterer' (Ru)	EBls MAus MDun SPer SWCr
	WAct WHCG
'Mrs Arthur Curtiss James'	EBee SWCr
(ClHT)	
'Mrs B.R. Cant' (T)	EBls
Mrs Doreen Pike =	LRHS MAus NHaw WAct
'Ausdor' PBR (Ru)	
'Mrs Eveline Gandy' (HT)	MGan
'Mrs Foley Hobbs' (T)	EBls
'Mrs Honey Dyson' (Ra)	CHad
'Mrs John Laing' (HP)	EBls LRHS MAus SJus SPer SWCr
	WHCG
'Mrs Oakley Fisher' (HT) ♀	CHad EBee EBls MAus SPer WAct
	WCot
'Mrs Paul' (Bb)	EBls MAus
'Mrs Pierre S. duPont' (HT)	EBls
'Mrs Sam McGredy' (HT)	MAus MGan
'Mrs Walter Burns' (F/Patio)	MGan SWCr
'Mullard Jubilee' (HT)	IHar MGan SWCr

§ *mulliganii* (Ra) ♀ — CDoC EBee EBls EPfP IHar MAus MJon SJus SPer SPla SWCr WHCG
multibracteata (S) ♀ — EBls MAus WHCG
multiflora (Ra) — EBls GIBF LBuc MAus SWCr WPic
- 'Carnea' (Ra) — EBls
- var. *cathayensis* (Ra) — EBls
§ - 'Grevillei' (Ra) — EBee EBls MAus SPer SWCr
- 'Platyphylla' — See *R. multiflora* 'Grevillei'
- var. *watsoniana* — See *R. watsoniana*
Mummy = 'Dicwhynot' — IDic
'München' (HM) — MAus
mundi — See *R. gallica* 'Versicolor'
- 'Versicolor' — See *R. gallica* 'Versicolor'
'Mutabilis' — See *R.* x *odorata* 'Mutabilis'
'My Choice' (HT) — MGan SWCr
'My Joy' (HT) — NBat SWCr
'My Little Boy' (Min) — MBur
My Love = 'Cogamo' (HT) — MAus MBur MJon SWCr
My Valentine® = 'Mormyval' (Min) — Last listed 1998
Myra = 'Battoo' (HT) — NBat
Myriam® = 'Cocgrand' (HT) — GCoc MJon SApu
'Nancy's Keepsake' (HT) — NBat
nanothamnus — Last listed 1997
'Narrow Water' (Ra) — CBos EBee EBls LFis SWCr WAct WHCG
§ 'Nastarana' (N) — EBls WHCG
'Nathalie Nypels' — See *R.* 'Mevrouw Nathalie Nypels'
'National Trust' (HT) — EBls GGre GKir IHar MGan MJon NRog SPer SWCr WStI
'Nestor' (G) — EBls MAus
'Nevada' (S) ♀ — More than 30 suppliers
Never Forgotten = 'Gregart' (HT) — SWCr
'New Arrival' (Patio/Min) — GGre SWCr
New Daily Mail = 'Pussta' (F) — Last listed 1997
§ 'New Dawn' (Cl) ♀ — More than 30 suppliers
New Fashion = 'Poulholm' PBR (Patio) — ENot SWCr
New Horizon = 'Dicplay' (F) — IDic
'New Look' (F) — MGan SWCr
'New Penny' (Min) — IHar MGan SWCr
New Zealand = 'Macgenev' PBR (HT) — LPlm MJon NBat SApu SWCr
News® = 'Legnews' (F) — MAus MGan SWCr
Nice Day = 'Chewsea' PBR (ClMin) — CGro EBrr EBre ENot GGre GKir LBCl LBSe LBre LStr MBBe MBri MBur MFry MJon MMat NBat SApu SBre SJus SWCr WWeb
'Nicola' (F) — MGan SWCr
Nigel Hawthorne = 'Harquibbler' (S) — WAct
Night Light® = 'Poullight' PBR (Cl) — EBee LPlm MBri MBur MFry MGan MJon SApu SJus SWCr
Nimbus = 'Leggrey' (F) — SWCr
Nina Weibull® (F) — Last listed 1999
nitida — EBls ELan ENot EPla GChr LRHS MAus NWea SPer SRPl SWCr WAct WHCG WHer WOVN
- 'Defender' — Last listed 1997
Noble Antony = 'Ausway' PBR (S) — ENot LRHS MAus MJon MMat SCoo SWCr WWeb
§ 'Noisette Carnée' (N) — CBos CHad EBee EBls EPfP EWTr GChr LRHS MAus MBNS MBri SLPl SPer SSea SWCr WAct WHCG WSHC
Norfolk = 'Poulfolk' PBR (GC) — EBls EBrP EBre ENot GCoc LBCl LBSe LBre MBBe MGan MMat SApu SBre SPer SPla SSea SWCr WHCG WOVN

'Norma Major' (HT) — Last listed 1997
Northamptonshire = 'Mattdor' PBR (GC) — ENot LGod MGan MMat SWCr
Northern Lights® (HT) — GCoc
'Northumberland WI' (HT) — Last listed 1998
'Norwich Castle' (F) — EBls EWTr MBri
Norwich Cathedral = 'Beacath' (HT) — EBls
'Norwich Pink' (Cl) — MAus
'Norwich Salmon' (Cl) — MAus
'Norwich Union' (F) — EBls
Nostalgie® = 'Taneiglat' PBR (HT) — LStr
'Nova Zembla' (Ru) — EBls MAus
'Nozomi' (ClMin/GC) ♀ — CGro CLyd EBls ELan ENot EWTr GCoc GGre LPlm LRHS LStr MAus MFry MGan MJon SApu SJus SPer SSea SWCr WAct WHCG WOVN
'Nuits de Young' (CeMo) — EBls GCoc IHar MAus MMat SFam SWCr WHCG
'Nur Mahal' (HM) — EBls MAus SWCr WHCG
nutkana (S) — EBls MAus
§ - var. *hispida* (S) — EBls
§ - 'Plena' (S) ♀ — EBls ENot EPfP MAus NFla SFam SRPl SWCr WGer WHCG
'Nymphenburg' (HM) — EBls MAus SPer SWCr
'Nypels' Perfection' (Poly) — MAus
'Nyveldt's White' (Ru) — EBls MAus
'Oakington Ruby' (MinCh) — Last listed 1997
Octavia Hill = 'Harzeal' PBR (F/S) — EBee LStr MFry MJon SApu SJus SPer SRum SWCr WAct WHCG
Oddball = 'Horodd' (F) — GGre
x *odorata* 'Fortune's Double Yellow' — See *R.* x *odorata* 'Pseudindica'
§ - 'Mutabilis' (Ch) ♀ — CGre CRHN EBls ECre EHol EMFP MAus MMat SJus SMrm SWCr WAct WCFE WCot WHCG WOVN WWat
§ - 'Ochroleuca' (Ch) — EBls
§ - 'Odorata' (Ch) — EBls
- Old Crimson China (Ch) — EBls WAct
§ - 'Pallida' (Ch) — EBls EMFP EPfP GCoc LRHS MAus MMat NFla SPla SSea SWCr WHCG
§ - 'Pseudindica' (ClCh) — EBls MAus WSHC
§ - Sanguinea Group (Ch) — EBls WHCG
§ - 'Viridiflora' (Ch) — EBls GChr LRHS MAus MBur MMat SPer SSea SSoC SWCr WAct WHCG
'Oeillet Flamand' — See *R.* 'Oeillet Parfait'
'Oeillet Panaché' (Mo) — WAct
§ 'Oeillet Parfait' (G) — EBls MAus
officinalis — See *R. gallica* var. *officinalis*
'Oh La La' (F) — SWCr
'Ohl' (G) — EBls SWCr
§ Ohshima Rose = 'Cochunter' (HT) — GCoc
'Oklahoma' (HT) — MGan SWCr
old blush China — See *R.* x *odorata* 'Pallida'
old cabbage — See *R.* x *centifolia*
Old John = 'Dicwillynily' PBR (F) — ECle IDic MJon
Old Master = 'Macesp' (F) — MAus MGan SWCr
old pink moss rose — See *R.* x *centifolia* 'Muscosa'
Old Port = 'Mackati' PBR (F) — MJon SApu
old red moss — See *R.* 'Henri Martin' , R.'Lanei'
old velvet moss — See *R.* 'William Lobb'
old yellow scotch (PiH) — See *R.* x *harisonii* 'Williams' Double Yellow'
Olde Romeo = 'Hadromeo' PBR (HT) — SApu SWCr
Oliver Twist = 'Sabbyron' (Patio) — MBur

	'Omar Khayyám' (D)	EBls ENot MAus SWCr
§	'Ombrée Parfaite' (G)	EBls SWCr
	Open Arms = 'Chewpixcel' PBR (ClMin)	LGod MFry MJon SWCr WGer
	'Ophelia' (HT)	EBls MAus MBur MGan SWCr
	'Orange Honey' (Min)	MBur
§	Orange Sensation® (F)	EBls ENot GChr MAus MGan NRog SWCr
§	Orange Sunblaze® = 'Meijikatar' PBR (Min)	EBls GGre MGan MJon MMat SJus SSea SWCr
	Orange Triumph® (Poly)	EBls
	Orangeade (F)	MGan SWCr
§	Oranges and Lemons™ = 'Macoranlem' PBR (S/F)	CGro EBee ENot GCoc GGre LGod LPlm LStr MBri MBur MFry MGan MJon MMat SApu SJus SSea SWCr WGer WWeb
	'Oriana' (HT)	SWCr
	'Orient Express' (HT)	MJon
	'Orpheline de Juillet'	See R. 'Ombrée Parfaite'
	Othello® = 'Auslo' PBR (S)	MAus SApu SPer WAct
	Our George = 'Kirrush' (Patio)	MJon
§	Our Jubilee = 'Coccages' (HT)	SWCr
	Our Love = 'Andour' (HT)	GGre SWCr
	Our Molly = 'Dicreason' PBR (GC/S)	IDic MGan SApu
	'Over the Rainbow' (Min)	EWTr
	Owen's Pride = 'Kirpink' (F)	MJon
	Oxfordshire = 'Korfullwind' PBR (GC)	ENot LStr MMat SJus SSea SWCr
	Paddy McGredy = 'Macpa' (F)	CGro MAus MGan MJon NRog SWCr
	Paddy Stephens = 'Macclack' PBR (HT)	GCoc MFry MJon
	'Paint Box' (F/Min)	SWCr
	Painted Moon = 'Dicpaint' PBR (HT)	GCoc IDic
	Pallas = 'Harvestal' (Min)	SWCr
	'Pam Ayres'	See R. Miss Pam Ayres = 'Kormarie'
	Panache = 'Poultop' PBR (Patio)	LStr SWCr WGer
	'Panorama Holiday' (F/HT)	MBur
	'Papa Gontier' (T)	EBls MAus
	'Papa Hémeray' (Ch)	EBls
	Papa Meilland® = 'Meisar' (HT)	EBls MAus MGan MJon NRog SApu SPer SWCr
	'Papillon' (ClT)	EBls
	Paprika™ = 'Meiriental' (F)	MAus SWCr
	'Pâquerette' (Poly)	EBls
	'Parade' (Cl) ♀	MAus MFry MGan SJus SWCr WHCG
	Paradise® = 'Weizeip' (HT)	MGan SWCr
	Parkdirektor Riggers® (Cl)	CRHN CSam EBee EBls LStr MAus MBri MGan SPer SWCr WHCG
	Parks's yellow China	See R. x odorata 'Ochroleuca'
	'Parkzierde' (Bb)	EBls
	Parson's pink China	See R. x odorata 'Pallida'
	Partridge = 'Korweirim' PBR (GC)	EBls MAus MGan MJon MMat SApu SJus SPer SWCr WAct WOVN
	Party Girl® (Min)	NBat
	Party Trick = 'Dicparty' PBR (F)	IDic MBri
	parvifolia	See R. 'Burgundiaca'
	Pascali® = 'Lenip' (HT)	EBls EBrP EBre ELan ENot EWTr GCoc GGre GKir LBCl LBSe LBre LStr MAus MBBe MBur MGan MJon MMat NRog SBre SPer SRPl SSea SWCr

	Passion (Ru)	WLRN
§	Pat Austin = 'Ausmum' PBR (S)	CSam ENot LRHS MAus MBri MJon MMat NBus SWCr WFoF WWeb
	Pathfinder = 'Chewpobey' PBR (GC)	CBrm MJon MMat SWCr
	Patricia = 'Korpatri' (F)	SRum SWCr
	'Paul Crampel' (Poly)	EBls MAus MGan NRog WAct
	'Paul Lédé' (ClT)	See R. 'Climbing Paul Lédé'
	Paul McCartney PBR (HT)	See R. The McCartney Rose = 'Meizeli'
	'Paul Neyron' (HP)	EBls EMFP MAus MMat SPer SWCr WAct WHCG
	'Paul Ricault' (CexHP)	EBls MAus
	Paul Shirville = 'Harqueterwife' PBR (HT) ♀	ENot GGre IHar LPlm MAus MFry MGan MMat NRog SApu SJus SPer SSea SWCr
	'Paul Transon' (Ra) ♀	CHad CRHN EBee EBls EMFP IHar LRHS MAus MBri SJus SPer SWCr WOVN
	'Paul Verdier' (Bb)	EBls
§	'Paulii' (Ru)	EBls ELan ENot LFis MAus MMat SWCr WAct WHCG WOVN
	'Paulii Alba'	See R. 'Paulii'
	'Paulii Rosea' (Ru/Cl)	EBls MAus SWCr WAct WHCG
	'Paul's Early Blush' (HP)	EBls
	'Paul's Himalayan Musk' (Ra) ♀	More than 30 suppliers
§	'Paul's Lemon Pillar' (ClHT)	CHad EBee EBls EBrP EBre LBCl LBSe LBre LRHS MAus MBBe MBNS NRog SBre SMad SPer SSea SWCr
	'Paul's Perpetual White' (Ra)	EBls SWCr WHCG
	'Paul's Scarlet Climber' (Cl/Ra)	CGro EBee EBls ELan ENot EPfP GChr GGre GKir LGod LRHS LStr MAus MGan MJon MMat SApu SPer SSea SWCr WWeb
¶	'Paws' (S)	EBls
	'Pax' (HM)	CPou EBls EMFP MAus SPer SRPl SWCr WHCG WKif
	Peace = 'Madame A. Meilland' (HT) ♀	CB&S CGro EBls ELan EWTr GChr GCoc GGre GKir LGod LPlm LStr MAus MBri MBur MFry MGan MJon NRog SApu SPer SRPl SSea SWCr WWeb
	Peace Sunblaze PBR (Min)	See R. Lady Meillandina = 'Meilarco'
§	Peacekeeper = 'Harbella' PBR (F)	GGre SJus SWCr
	Peach Blossom = 'Ausblossom' PBR (S)	LRHS MAus SWCr
§	Peach Sunblaze = 'Meixerul' PBR (Min)	MBri SApu SJus SRum
	'Peachy White' (Min)	MAus
§	Pearl Anniversary = 'Whitston' PBR (Min/Patio)	GGre LStr MBri SSea SWCr
	Pearl Drift® = 'Leggab' PBR (S)	EBls LStr MAus MJon SPer SWCr WHCG
	Peaudouce PBR	See R. Elina = 'Dicjana'
§	Peer Gynt® = 'Korol' (HT)	LPlm MGan MMat SWCr
	Pegasus = 'Ausmoon' PBR (S)	IHar LRHS LStr MAus MJon SWCr
	'Peggy Netherthorpe' (HT)	Last listed 1997
	'Pélisson' (CeMo)	EBls
§	pendulina	EBls MAus WHCG
	'Penelope' (HM) ♀	More than 30 suppliers
	Penelope Keith = 'Macfreego' PBR (Min/Patio)	MJon SApu
	'Penelope Plummer' (F)	EBls

Penny Lane = 'Hardwell' PBR (Cl) — CGro EBee ECle ENot EPfP GCoc GKir LGod LPlm LRHS LStr MBri MFry MGan MJon MMat NBat SApu SCoo SJus SPer SRum SSea SWCr

Pensioner's Voice = 'Fryrelax' PBR (F) — MFry SWCr

§ Penthouse = 'Macngauru' (HT) — MJon SWCr

x penzanceana — See R. 'Lady Penzance'

Peppermint Ice = 'Bosgreen' PBR (F) — MJon SApu SWCr

Perception™ = 'Harzippee' PBR (HT) — SApu SJus

Perdita® = 'Ausperd' (S) — IOrc LRHS MAus MJon SPer SRPl SWCr WAct WHCG

§ Perestroika = 'Korhitom' PBR (F/Min) — ENot LStr MDun MJon MMat SApu SJus SWCr WGer

§ Perfecta = 'Koralu' (HT) — EBls MGan SWCr

'Perla de Montserrat' (Min) — Last listed 1997

'Perle des Jardins' (T) — EBls MAus

'Perle des Panachées' (G) — EBls

§ 'Perle d'Or' (Poly) ♀ — CHad EMFP ENot EWTr GCoc LRHS MAus MMat NRog SChu SPer SPla SWCr WAct WHCG WWat

'Perle von Hohenstein' (Poly) — EBls

Pernille Poulsen® (F) — EBls

Perpetually Yours™ = 'Harfable' (Cl) — GCoc LGod

Persian yellow — See R. foetida 'Persiana'

persica — MAus

Peter Pan = 'Chewpan' PBR (Min) — GKir SSea

Peter Pan = 'Sunpete' (Patio) — MJon

Petit Four® = 'Interfour' (Min/Patio) — SApu

'Petite de Hollande' (Ce) — EBee EBls LRHS MAus SPer SWCr WAct WHCG

Petite Folie® = 'Meiherode' (Min) — SWCr

'Petite Lisette' (CexD) — EBls MAus SPer WHCG

'Petite Orléannaise' (Ce) — EBls

Phab Gold = 'Frybountiful' PBR (F) — MFry

§ Phantom = 'Maccatsan' (S/GC) — MBur MJon WGer

'Pharisäer' (HT) — EBls

§ Pheasant = 'Kordapt' PBR (GC) — ELan ENot GCoc MAus MJon MMat SJus SPer SWCr WAct WHCG WOVN

Philippa = 'Poulheart' PBR (S) — EBee EBls

phoenicia — EBls

'Phyllis Bide' (Ra) ♀ — EBee EBls EMFP EPfP IHar LRHS LStr MAus MGan NHaw SApu SJus SPer SRPl SSea SWCr WHCG

Picasso = 'Macpic' (F) — EBls MAus MGan SWCr

Piccadilly® = 'Macar' (HT) — CB&S CGro EBls GGre GKir IHar LPlm MAus MGan MJon MMat NRog SApu SPer SSea SWCr

Piccolo = 'Tanolokip' PBR (F/Patio) — GGre LStr MBri MFry MJon SApu SSea SWCr WGer

'Picture' (HT) — EBls MAus MGan NRog SPer

'Pierre Notting' (HP) — EBls

Pierrine™ = 'Micpie' (Min) — Last listed 1997

Pigalle '84 = 'Meicloux' (F) — SWCr

'Pilgrim' PBR — See R. The Pilgrim = 'Auswalker'

Pillar Box = 'Chewaze' PBR (F) — MGan SWCr

Pimlico® = 'Meidujuran' (F) — SWCr

§ pimpinellifolia — CKin EBls ECha ENot GChr LBuc MAus MDun MGan NWea SPer SWCr WHCG WOVN

- 'Altaica' — See R. pimpinellifolia 'Grandiflora'

§ - 'Andrewsii' ♀ — MAus WAct

- 'Bakewell Scots Briar' — Last listed 1998

§ - double pink — EBls SWCr

§ - double white — CNat EBls GCoc MAus SWCr WAct WBcn

- double yellow — See R. x harisonii 'Williams' Double Yellow'

§ - 'Dunwich Rose' — EBee EBls EBrP EBre ENot EPfP LBCl LBSe LBre LRHS MAus MBBe MBri MGan SBre SPer SWCr WAct WHCG

- 'Falkland' — EBls ECha MAus

§ - 'Glory of Edzell' — EBls MAus

§ - 'Grandiflora' — EBls MAus SJus SWCr

- 'Harisonii' — See R. x harisonii 'Harison's Yellow'

- HH&K 328 — Last listed 1999

- var. hispida — MAus

- 'Irish Marbled' — EBls

- 'Lutea' — See R. x harisonii 'Lutea Maxima'

- 'Marbled Pink' — EBls MAus

- 'Mary, Queen of Scots' — EBls MAus SRms SWCr WAct

- 'Mrs Colville' — EBls MAus

- 'Ormiston Roy' — MAus

- x pendulina — See R. x reversa

§ - 'Robbie' — MAus WAct

- 'Single Cherry' — EBls MAus

- 'Stanwell Perpetual' — See R. 'Stanwell Perpetual'

- 'Variegata' — CArn

- 'William III' — EBls MAus SLPl

'Pineapple Poll' (F) — SWCr

Pink Bells® = 'Poulbells' PBR (GC) — CGro EBls ENot GCoc MAus MMat SApu SPer SWCr WAct WHCG WOVN

'Pink Bouquet' (Ra) — CRHN MAus

Pink Chimo = 'Interchimp' (S/GC) — IDic

Pink Drift = 'Poulcat' PBR (Min/GC) — ENot SWCr

'Pink Elizabeth Arden' (F) — Last listed 1997

'Pink Favorite' (HT) — MGan NRog SPer SWCr

§ Pink Flower Carpet™ = 'Noatraum' PBR (GC) ♀ — CTri EBrP EBre ELan GGre GKir IHar LBCl LBSe LBre LRHS MAus MBBe MFry MGan MJon MMat SBre SCoo SJus SPer SPla SWCr WWeb

'Pink Garnette' — See R. 'Carol Amling'

'Pink Grootendorst' (Ru) ♀ — CB&S EBls ENot EPfP IOrc LRHS LStr MAus MGan MJon MMat NFla NRog SPer SSea SWCr WAct WHCG

'Pink Hedgerose' PBR — See R. Romantic Hedgerose = 'Korworm'

§ Pink Hit® = 'Poutype' PBR (Min/Patio) — ENot MMat

Pink La Sevillana® = 'Meigeroka' PBR (F/GC) — SWCr

Pink Meidiland® = 'Meipoque' PBR (GC) — MGan WOVN

pink moss — See R. x centifolia 'Muscosa'

Pink Panther® = 'Meicapinal' (HT) — SWCr

'Pink Parfait' (F) — EBls GCoc GGre MAus MGan NRog SPer SSea SWCr

Pink Peace = 'Meibil' (HT) — CB&S GGre SWCr

Pink Pearl = 'Kormasyl' PBR (HT) — SApu SWCr

'Pink Perpétué' (Cl) — More than 30 suppliers

Pink Posy = 'Cocanelia' (Min/Patio) — MAus

'Pink Prosperity' (HM) — EBls MAus

'Pink Showers' (ClHT) — WAct

§ Pink Sunblaze® = 'Meijidiro' PBR (Min/Patio) — SWCr

Pink Surprise = 'Lenbrac' (Ru) — MAus

Pink Wave = 'Mattgro' PBR (GC) — SWCr

Pinocchio = 'Rosenmärchen' (F) — EBls

'Pinta' (HT) — EBls

Piroschka® = 'Tanpika' (HT) — Last listed 1999

'Pixie Rose' (Min) — EWTr

Playgroup Rose = 'Horsun' (F) — NBat SWCr

Pleine de Grâce = 'Lengra' (S) — EBls LRHS MAus WAct

'Plentiful' (F) — EBls

Poetry in Motion = 'Harelan' PBR (HT) — GCoc MBri NBat SApu SWCr

Polar Star = 'Tanlarpost' PBR (HT) — EBee EBls GGre LGod LPlm LStr MFry MGan MJon NRog SApu SPer SRPl SWCr

x *polliniana* — SLPl

'Polly' (HT) — EBls MGan NRog SWCr

polyantha grandiflora — See R. *gentiliana*

pomifera — See R. *villosa*

– 'Duplex' — See R. 'Wolley-Dod'

Pomona = 'Fryyeh' PBR (F) — MFry

'Pompon Blanc Parfait' (A) — EBls MAus SFam

'Pompon de Bourgogne' — See R. 'Burgundiaca'

§ 'Pompon de Paris' (MinCh) — EBls MAus

'Pompon de Paris' (ClMinCh) — See R. 'Climbing Pompon de Paris'

'Pompon Panaché' (G) — EBls MAus

Porcelain PBR — See R. Margaret Thatcher = 'Korflüg'

'Porcellina' (F) — MJon

Portland Dawn = 'Seatip' (Min) — Last listed 1997

portland rose — See R. 'Portlandica'

§ 'Portlandica' — EBls LRHS MAus SPer SSea SWCr WAct WHCG

Portmeirion™ = 'Ausgard' (S) — SCoo

Pot o' Gold = 'Dicdivine' PBR (HT) — IDic LStr MAus MFry MGan MJon SApu SPer SWCr

I 'Poulduff' PBR — See R. Courage = 'Poulduf'

'Poulink' PBR — See R. Pink Hit = 'Poutipe'

'Poullack' PBR — See R. Lakeland Princess = 'Poullak'

Pour Toi = 'Para Ti' (Min) — ENot LPlm MAus MGan MJon MMat SPer SWCr

¶ Powder Puff (F) — GGre SWCr

prairie rose — See R. *setigera*

'Precious Platinum' (HT) — IHar LGod MJon SJus SPer SWCr

Preservation = 'Bosijurika' (S/F) — GGre SWCr

§ 'Président de Sèze' (G) ♀ — EBls LRHS MAus SFam SPer SWCr WAct WHCG

President Heidar Aliyev 'Cocosimber' PBR (HT) — GCoc

'President Herbert Hoover' (HT) — EBls

Press and Journal = 'Coclion' (HT) — GCoc

'Prestige' (S) — NRog

Pretty in Pink = 'Dicumpteen' PBR (GC) — IDic MJon SWCr

Pretty Jessica = 'Ausjess' (S) — GKir LRHS MAus MJon SPer

Pretty Lady = 'Scrivo' PBR (F) — ECle LStr MJon SWCr

Pretty Polly® = 'Meitonje' PBR (Min) — CGro CTri EPfP GGre GKir LStr MBri MFry MGan MJon MMat SApu SJus SWCr WWeb

Pride Meidiland™ = 'Meirumour' PBR (GC) — WMoo

Pride of England = 'Harencore' PBR (HT) — GCoc GGre SWCr

'Prima Ballerina' (HT) — CGro EBls GCoc GGre GKir LPlm LStr MAus MGan MJon MMat NBat NRog SPer SSea SWCr

primula (S) ♀ — CHad EBls EMFP ENot MAus MJon MMat SPer SSea SWCr WAct WHCG

'Prince Camille de Rohan' (HP) — EBls MAus WHCG

'Prince Charles' (Bb) — EBls MAus SWCr WHCG

Prince Sunblaze® PBR (Min) — See R. Red Sunblaze = 'Meirutral'

Princess Alexandra = 'Pouldra' PBR (S) — ECle SWCr

Princess Alice = 'Hartanna' PBR (F) — LGod MGan SApu SWCr

'Princess Chichibu' (F) — SWCr

§ Princess Margaret of England = 'Meilista' (HT) — SWCr

Princess Michael of Kent® = 'Harlightly' (F) — MGan SWCr

§ Princess of Monaco = 'Meimagarmic' (S) — SWCr

¶ 'Princess of Wales' (HP) — MMat

Princess of Wales = 'Hardinkum' PBR (F) — CTri ECle ENot EWTr GCoc LStr MBri MGan SApu SCoo SPer SWCr

Princess Royal = 'Dicroyal' PBR (HT) — EBee GCoc GGre IDic MBri

'Princesse Adélaïde' (Mo) — EBls

§ 'Princesse de Nassau' (Ra) — EBls MAus SWCr WAct WHCG

'Princesse Louise' (Ra) — CRHN MAus SFam

'Princesse Marie' misapplied — See R. 'Belvedere'

Priscilla Burton® = 'Macrat' (F) — MAus

§ 'Pristine' PBR (HT) — IDic MAus MGan MJon SPer SRum SWCr

N 'Professeur Emile Perrot' (D) — EBls MAus SWCr

'Prolifera de Redouté' misapplied — See R. 'Duchesse de Montebello'

Prominent® = 'Korp' (F) — SWCr

'Prosperity' (HM) ♀ — CB&S EBee EBls EMFP ENot GCoc GOrc IOrc LRHS MAus MFry MGan MJon MMat NRog SJus SPer SWCr WAct WHCG WOVN

Prospero® = 'Auspero' (S) — MAus MBri WAct

'Prudhoe Peach' (F) — Last listed 1998

x *pruhoniciana* 'Hillieri' — See R. 'Hillieri'

Pudsey Bear PBR (HT) — See R. The Pudsey Bear = 'Bedchild'

§ *pulverulenta* — EBls

Pure Bliss = 'Dictator' PBR (HT) — GCoc IDic MJon

'Purity' (Cl) — SWCr

'Purple Beauty' (HT) — MGan SWCr

'Purple Splendour' (F) | MAus

§ Purple Tiger = 'Jacpurr' PBR (F) | IDic MBri MBur MJon SApu SWCr

'Purpurtraum' (Ru) | WHCG

Pzazz = 'Poulzazz' PBR (Min/Patio) | LStr MJon SWCr

Quaker Star = 'Dicperhaps' (F) | IDic

quatre saisons | See *R.* x *damascena* var. *semperflorens*

'Quatre Saisons Blanche Mousseuse' (DMo) | EBee EBls IHar SWCr

Queen Charlotte = 'Harubondee' PBR (HT) | Last listed 1998

Queen Elizabeth | See *R.* 'The Queen Elizabeth'

Queen Mother = 'Korquemu' PBR (Patio) ♀ | CTri EBls ELan ENot EPfP LGod LRHS LStr MAus MBri MFry MGan MJon MMat NPri SApu SPer SSea SWCr

Queen Nefertiti® = 'Ausap' (S) | Last listed 1997

'Queen of Bedders' (Bb) | EBls

Queen of Denmark | See *R.* 'Königin von Dänemark'

Queen of the Belgians | See *R.* 'Reine des Belges'

Racy Lady = 'Dicwaffle' PBR | IDic NBat

Radiant™ = 'Benrad' (Min) | Last listed 1997

Radio Times = 'Aussal' PBR (S) | LRHS MAus MJon NPri

Radox Bouquet = 'Harmusky' (F) | GCoc GGre SWCr

'Radway Sunrise' (S) | Last listed 1997

Ragtime = 'Poultime' (Cl) | EBee

'Rainbow' (T) | Last listed 1998

Rainbow Magic = 'Dicxplosion' PBR | IDic MBri SWCr

'Ralph Tizzard' (F) | SSea

'Rambling Rector' (Ra) ♀ | More than 30 suppliers

§ 'Ramona' | EBls MAus SWCr WHCG WSHC

§ 'Raubritter' | EBee EBls LRHS MAus MBri SPer

('Macrantha' hybrid) | SRPl SWCr WAct WHCG

Raven | See *R.* Daily Post = 'Frytrooper'

'Ravenswood Village' (HT) | Last listed 1997

Ray of Hope = 'Cocnilly' PBR (F) | GCoc GGre NEgg SWCr

Ray of Sunshine = 'Cocclare' PBR (Patio) | GCoc LStr MBri MFry SWCr

¶ 'Raymond Carver' (S) | EBls

'Raymond Chenault' (Cl) | MGan

Razzle Dazzle = 'Frybright' PBR (F) | MFry

'Rebecca Claire' (HT) | MJon

Reconciliation™ = 'Hartillery' PBR (HT) | GGre SJus SWCr

Red Ace = 'Amruda' PBR (Min) | MJon SWCr

Red Bells® = 'Poulred' PBR (Min/GC) | CGro EBls ENot MAus MMat SPer SWCr WHCG WOVN

Red Blanket® = 'Intercell' PBR (S/GC) ♀ | CGro EBls ENot EWTr GCoc IDic MAus MGan MMat SPer SWCr WAct WOVN

§ Red Coat = 'Auscoat' (F) | LRHS MAus SWCr

Red Dagmar = 'Speruge' PBR (S) | IDic LBuc

'Red Dandy' (F) | MGan

Red Devil® = 'Dicam' (HT) | GGre LPlm MAus MGan MJon NBat NRog SWCr

Red Dot® = 'Intermunder' PBR (S/GC) | IDic WOVN

'Red Elf' (Min) | Last listed 1997

'Red Garnette' | See *R.* 'Garnette'

'Red Grootendorst' | See *R.* 'F.J. Grootendorst'

'Red Max Graf' PBR | See *R.* Rote Max Graf = 'Kormax'

Red Meidiland® = 'Meineble' PBR (GC) | SWCr WOVN

red moss | See *R.* 'Henri Martin'

Red New Dawn | See *R.* 'Etendard'

Red Rascal = 'Jacbed' PBR (S/Patio) | IDic MBri MFry MJon SApu SWCr

red rose of Lancaster | See *R. gallica* var. *officinalis*

Red Splendour = 'Davona' (F) | NRog

§ Red Sunblaze = 'Meirutral' PBR (Min) | MJon WWeb

Red Trail = 'Interim' PBR (S/GC) | IDic MJon WOVN

Red Velvet | See *R.* Judi Dench = 'Peahunder'

§ 'Red Wing' (S) | EBls LRHS MAus WAct

§ Redgold = 'Dicor' (F) | GGre MGan SWCr

Redouté = 'Auspale' PBR (S) | CAbP EBrP EBre LBCl LBSe LBre LRHS MAus MBBe SBre SJus SPer SWCr WWeb

Regal Red = 'Cocfoster' (S) | Last listed 1999

§ Regensberg® = 'Macyoumis' PBR (F/Patio) | CTri ENot LPlm MAus MBri MFry MGan MJon MMat NRog SApu SPer SSea SWCr

§ 'Reine des Belges' (Cl) | EBls

'Reine des Centifeuilles' (Ce) | EBls SFam

'Reine des Violettes' (HP) | CHad CPou EBee EBls IHar LGod LRHS LStr MAus MDun SApu SChu SJus SPer SWCr WAct WHCG

'Reine Marie Henriette' (ClHT) | EBls

§ 'Reine Victoria' (Bb) | EBls EBrP EBre EMFP EPfP IHar LBCl LBSe LBre LRHS LStr MAus MBBe MGan NHaw SBre SJus SPer SPla SWCr WAct

Remember Me® = 'Cocdestin' PBR (HT) ♀ | EBrP EBre GCoc GGre LBCl LBSe LBre LGod LPlm LStr MBBe MBri MFry MGan MJon MMat NBat NRog SApu SBre SJus SPer SSea SWCr

Remembrance = 'Harxampton' PBR (F) | LStr MBri SApu SPer SSea SWCr

§ Rémy Martin® = 'Starqueli' (HT) | SWCr

Renaissance = 'Harzart' PBR (HT) | ECle GCoc GGre LStr MBur MFry MJon SJus SSea SWCr

'René André' (Ra) | CRHN EBee EBls EMFP MAus SWCr

'René d'Anjou' (CeMo) | EBls MAus

Repens Meidiland® = 'Meilontig' PBR (S) | WOVN

'Rescht' | See *R.* 'De Rescht'

Rest in Peace = 'Bedswap' (Patio/F) | GGre SWCr

'Rêve d'Or' (N) | EBee EBls MAus SPer SWCr WSHC

'Réveil Dijonnais' (ClHT) | EBls MAus

'Reverend F. Page-Roberts' (HT) | EBls

'Rhodes Rose' (S) | Last listed 1998

Richard Buckley = 'Smitshort' (F) | MBur

§ x *richardii* | EBls MAus SWCr WAct WHCG

§ 'Rise 'n Shine' (Min) | LGod MGan SWCr

Rising Star™ = 'Hareast' PBR (F) | SJus

'Ritter von Barmstede' (Cl) | MGan SWCr

'Rival de Paestum' (T) | EBls MAus

'River Gardens' | NPer

Road to Freedom = 'Franlac' (F) | SWCr

Rob Roy® = 'Cocrob' (F) — GCoc GGre MBur MGan SPer SWCr

'Robert le Diable' (Ce) — EBls MAus SPer SWCr WAct WHCG

'Robert Léopold' (Mo) — EBls

'Robin Hood' (HM) — EBls SWCr

Robin Redbreast® = 'Interrob' PBR (Min/GC) — EBls IDic IHar MJon SApu SRPl SWCr WWeb

§ Robusta® = 'Korgosa' PBR (Ru) — EBls MAus MJon SWCr

Roche Centenary = 'Dicvintage' PBR (Patio) — IDic

'Roger Lambelin' (HP) — EBls ENot MAus MMat SPer SWCr

Romance® = 'Tanezamor' PBR (S) — GGre MJon MRav SWCr WWeb

§ Romantic Hedgerose = 'Korworm' PBR (F/S) — ENot MMat

§ Rosabell® = 'Cocceleste' PBR (F/Patio) — GCoc GGre MFry SApu

Rosalie Coral = 'Chewallop' PBR (ClMin) — CGro MJon SApu

'Rosamini Gold' — See R. Golden Rosamini = 'Intergol'

§ Rosarium Uetersen® = 'Kortersen' (ClHT) — MJon

§ Rose 2000 = 'Cocquetrum' PBR (F) — CTri GCoc GKir NEgg SWCr

'Rose à Parfum de l'Haÿ' (Ru) — EBls

§ 'Rose d'Amour' (S) ♀ — EBls ISea MAus SJus SWCr WHCG

'Rose de Meaux' — See R. 'De Meaux'

'Rose de Meaux White' — See R. 'White de Meaux'

'Rose de Rescht' — See R. 'De Rescht'

'Rose des Maures' misapplied — See R. 'Sissinghurst Castle'

'Rose d'Hivers' (D) — EBls

'Rose d'Orsay' (S) — EBls

'Rose du Maître d'Ecole' — See R. 'Du Maître d'Ecole'

'Rose du Roi' (HP/DPo) — EBls MAus WAct WHCG

'Rose du Roi à Fleurs Pourpres' (HP) — EBls MAus

'Rose Edouard' (Bb) — EBls

§ Rose Gaujard® = 'Gaumo' (HT) — EBls GGre GKir LGod LPlm MAus MBur MGan MMat SWCr

¶ 'Rose Hannes' (HT) — SWCr

'Rosecarpe' (HT) — Last listed 1998

§ Roselina = 'Korsaku' PBR (GC) — ENot MMat SWCr

§ 'Rose-Marie Viaud' (Ra) — CFee EBee MAus SWCr WHCG

'Rosemary Foster' — SSpi

'Rosemary Gandy' (F) — MGan SWCr

Rosemary Harkness = 'Harrowbond' PBR (HT) — LStr MJon SApu SPer SWCr

'Rosemary Rose' (F) — EBls NRog SPer

'Rosenelfe' (F) — EBls

'Roseraie de l'Haÿ' (Ru) ♀ — More than 30 suppliers

'Rosette Delizy' (T) — EBls

Rosie Larkin = 'Fryyippee' (S) — MFry

§ 'Rosina' (Min) — CBrm MGan

'Rosy Cheeks' (HT) — LPlm MBur MGan SWCr

Rosy Cushion® = 'Interall' PBR (S/GC) ♀ — ENot GCoc IDic IHar MAus MGan SApu SPer SRPl SWCr WAct WHCG WOVN

Rosy Future = 'Harwaderox' PBR (F/Patio) — MBri SApu SJus SWCr

¶ 'Rosy Glow' (F) — NBat

'Rosy Mantle' (Cl) — CB&S GCoc LPlm MGan SPer SWCr

§ Rote Max Graf® = 'Kormax' PBR (GC/Ru) — EBls ENot SWCr WAct

Rouge Meilland® = — SWCr

'Meimalyna' (HT)

'Roundelay' (HT) — EBls MAus

§ Roxburghe Rose = 'Cocember' PBR (HT) — GCoc

roxburghii (S) — LRHS SMad SRPl SWCr WAct WHCG

- f. normalis (S) — CFee EBls MAus

- 'Plena' — See R. roxburghii f. roxburghii

§ - f. roxburghii (d/S) — MAus

'Royal Albert Hall' (HT) — EBls GCoc

Royal Baby = 'Delbrad' (F/Min) — Last listed 1998

§ Royal Brompton Rose = 'Meivildo' (HT) — SWCr

'Royal Conquest' (HT) — SJus

Royal Flush = 'Peapatio' (F/Patio) — MBri SWCr

'Royal Gold' (ClHT) — EBls ENot LPlm LStr MBri MFry MGan MMat NRog SSea SWCr WStI

'Royal Highness' (HT) — EBls MGan NRog

'Royal Occasion' (F) — SPer SWCr

Royal Romance® = 'Rulis' PBR (HT) — SJus SWCr

Royal Salute = 'Macros' (Min) — ENot MJon MMat NRog SWCr

'Royal Smile' (HT) — EBls

Royal Volunteer = 'Cocdandy' (HT) — Last listed 1998

Royal William = 'Korzaun' PBR (HT) ♀ — CGro CTri ELan GGre GKir LGod LPlm LStr MAus MBur MGan MJon MMat NRog SApu SJus SPer SRPl SWCr

Royal Worcester = 'Trobroy' PBR (S) — MJon WGer

'Rubens' (HP) — EBls

§ rubiginosa ♀ — CB&S CKin EBee EBls ENot EWFC GChr GPoy ILis LBuc MAus MHer MMat NFla SFam SPer SWCr WAct WMou

rubra — See R. gallica

rubrifolia — See R. glauca

- 'Carmenetta' — See R. 'Carmenetta'

'Rubrotincta' — See R. 'Hebe's Lip'

rubus (Ra) — CRHN MAus MBNS

- S&F 579 (Ra) — ISea

Ruby Anniversary = 'Harbonny' PBR (Patio) — CTri LRHS LStr MBri MFry SJus SWCr

Ruby Celebration = 'Peawinner' PBR (F) — GGre LRHS MBri MJon SWCr

'Ruby Pendant' (Min) — Last listed 1997

¶ Ruby Rambler = 'Chewrubyramb' — WWeb

'Ruby Wedding' (HT) — More than 30 suppliers

'Ruga' (Ra) — CCHP EBls MAus

rugosa (Ru) — CAgr EBee EPfP EWTr GChr GKir LBuc LHyr MAus MBri MHer NWea SPlb SWCr WStI

- 'Alba' (Ru) ♀ — CB&S CHad EBee EBls ECGP ELan EMFP ENot GChr GGre LBuc LRHS LStr MAus MBri MMat NWea SJus SPer SWCr WAct WHen WOVN

- 'Rubra' (Ru) ♀ — CB&S CCHP CTri EPfP GGre LBuc LRHS MFry MMat SPer SRum SWCr WAct WHen

- 'Scabrosa' — See R. 'Scabrosa'

'Rugosa Atropurpurea' (Ru) — NRog

'Rugspin' (Ru) — WAct

'Ruhm von Steinfurth' (HP) — EBls

Running Maid® = 'Lenramp' (S/GC) — MAus WAct

Rush® = 'Lenmobri' (S)　　MAus
Rushing Stream = 　　MAus
　'Austream' PBR (GC)
'Ruskin' (HPxRu)　　EBls MAus SWCr
'Russelliana' (Ra)　　CRHN EBee EBls EMFP MAus
　　　　　SFam SSea SWCr WAct WHCG
　　　　　WRha
Rutland = 'Poulshine' PBR　　ENot MMat SRPl SWCr WOVN
　(Min/GC)
'Sadler's Wells' (S)　　EBls
'Safrano' (T)　　EBls
Saint Boniface = 　　ENot MMat
　'Kormatt' PBR (F/Patio)
'Saint Catherine' (Ra)　　CFee
'Saint Cecilia® = 'Ausmit'　　CSam ELan LRHS MAus MBNS
　PBR (S)　　MJon SJus SWCr
Saint Christopher = 　　SJus
　'Harcogent' PBR (HT)
Saint Dunstan's Rose = 　　MBri MJon SApu SPer
　'Kirshru' PBR (S)
Saint Helena = 'Canlish' (F)　EBee
Saint John™ = 'Harbilbo'　　SWCr WHCG
　PBR (F)
Saint John's rose　　See R. x richardii
Saint Mark's rose　　See R. 'Rose d'Amour'
'Saint Nicholas' (D)　　EBls MAus WHCG
'Saint Prist de Breuze' (Ch)　EBls
Saint Swithun = 'Auswith'　　EMFP GKir GQui LRHS MAus
　PBR (S)　　MJon SWCr
'Salet' (DPMo)　　EBee EBls MAus WHCG
Salita® = 'Kormorlet' (Cl)　　MJon
'Sally Holmes' PBR (S) ♀　　CHad EBls ENot GCoc IHar
　　　　　MAus MBri MFry MGan MJon
　　　　　MMat SApu SPer SWCr WAct
　　　　　WHCG
Sally's Rose = 'Canrem'　　EBee SApu SJus SWCr
　PBR (HT)
Salmo = 'Poulnoev' PBR　　MBri MJon MMat
　(Patio)
'Salmon' (ClMin)　　Last listed 1997
§ Samaritan = 'Harverag'　　MAus SApu SJus SWCr
　PBR (HT)
sancta　　See R. x richardii
'Sander's White Rambler'.　　CHad CRHN EBee EBls EBrP EBre
　(Ra) ♀　　EMFP LBCl LBSe LBre LRHS MAus
　　　　　MBBe MGan MJon NRog SBre
　　　　　SMad SPer SRPl SWCr WAct
　　　　　WHCG WWeb
'Sandringham Centenary'　　EBls
　PBR (HT)
'Sanguinea'　　See R. x odorata Sanguinea
　　　　　Group
§ Sarabande = 'Meihand' (F)　MGan SWCr
Sarah® PBR (HT)　　See R. Jardins de Bagatelle =
　　　　　'Meimafris'
Sarah Jo = 'Mehrex' (HT)　　Last listed 1997
Sarah Robinson = 　　Last listed 1998
　'Trobinette' (Min)
'Sarah van Fleet' (Ru)　　CGro EBls EBrP EBre ENot GCoc
　　　　　LBCl LBSe LBre LBuc LRHS LStr
　　　　　MAus MBBe MFry MGan MMat
　　　　　NFla NRog SApu SBre SFam SPer
　　　　　SPla SRum SWCr WAct WOVN
Sarah, Duchess of York PBR　See R. Sunseeker = 'Dicracer'
Satchmo® (F)　　SWCr
Savoy Hotel = 　　CTri EPfP GCoc GGre LGod LStr
　'Harvintage' PBR (HT) ♀　MAus MFry MGan MJon SApu
　　　　　SJus SPer SWCr
§ 'Scabrosa' (Ru) ♀　　EBls EMFP GCoc LRHS MAus
　　　　　MGan MJon SPer SWCr WAct
　　　　　WHCG WOVN
Scarlet Fire　　See R. 'Scharlachglut'

§ Scarlet Gem® = 'Meido'　　ELan MGan SWCr
　(Min)
Scarlet Glow　　See R. 'Scharlachglut'
Scarlet Meidiland® = 　　MGan SWCr WOVN
　'Meikrotal' PBR (S/GC)
Scarlet Patio = 'Kortingle'　ENot MMat
　PBR (Patio)
'Scarlet Pimpernel'　　See R. Scarlet Gem = 'Meido'
Scarlet Queen　　CB&S CGro EBls GGre GKir MBur
　Elizabeth® = 'Dicel' (F)　SWCr WStI
'Scarlet Showers' (Cl)　　MGan
Scarletta (Min)　　Last listed 1998
'Scented Air' (F)　　MGan SPer SWCr
§ Scent-sation = 'Fryromeo'　GCoc GKir MFry SApu
　(HT)
Sceptre'd Isle™ = 　　CAbP ENot IHar LRHS MAus
　'Ausland' PBR (S)　　MMat SPer SWCr WWeb
§ 'Scharlachglut' (ClS) ♀　　EBls ELan ENot LRHS MAus MGan
　　　　　MMat NFla SApu SPer SWCr WAct
　　　　　WHCG WOVN
* schmidtiana　　CFee
'Schneelicht' (Ru)　　EBls MAus
Schneewittchen　　See R. Iceberg = 'Korbin'
§ 'Schneezwerg' (Ru) ♀　　EBls ELan ENot GCoc IHar IOrc
　　　　　MAus MBri MGan MJon MMat
　　　　　SApu SPer SPla SRPl SSea SWCr
　　　　　WAct WHCG WOVN
'Schoolgirl' (Cl)　　CB&S CGro EBls EBrP EBre ELan
　　　　　ENot GChr GGre GKir LBCl LBSe
　　　　　LBre LPlm LStr MBBe MBri MFry
　　　　　MGan MJon MMat NRog SApu
　　　　　SBre SPer SSea SWCr WWeb
'Scintillation' (S/GC)　　EBls MAus
Scotch rose　　See R. pimpinellifolia
Scotch yellow (PiH)　　See R. x harisonii 'Williams'
　　　　　Double Yellow'
'Scotch Yellow' (HT)　　MJon
Scotland's Trust = 　　Last listed 1998
　'Coclands' (HT)
Scottish Special = 　　GCoc MBri
　'Cocdapple' (Min/Patio)
Sea of Fire　　See R. 'Feuermeer'
'Sea Pearl' (F)　　ENot MGan MMat SWCr
'Seagull' (Ra) ♀　　EBee EBls ELan EMFP GGre LGod
　　　　　LRHS LStr MAus MGan MJon
　　　　　NBus NPri NRog NWea SPer SRPl
　　　　　SSea SWCr WAct WGer WHCG
§ 'Sealing Wax'　　EBls LRHS MAus MJon SWCr
　(moyesii hybrid)　　WAct
Searle Peach (Patio)　　SSea
Selfridges = 'Korpriwa'　　MMat NBat NRog SWCr
　PBR (HT)
'Semiplena'　　See R. x alba 'Alba Semiplena'
'Sénateur Amic' (Cl)　　EBls
'Senator Burda'　　See R. Spirit of Youth =
　　　　　'Meivestal'
§ serafinoi　　Last listed 1997
sericea (S)　　CFee MAus WHCG
　- BC 9355 (S)　　Last listed 1998
　- 'Heather Muir'　　See R. 'Heather Muir' (sericea
　　　　　hybrid)
* - var. morrisonensis　　Last listed 1998
　B&SWJ 1549
　- subsp. omeiensis　　CHad EBee EBls ELan EMFP ENot
　f. pteracantha (S)　　EPfP MAus MGan MMat NRog
　　　　　NWea SApu SMad SPer SSea SWCr
　　　　　WAct WOVN
　- 'Red Wing'　　See R. 'Red Wing'
　- S&F 505　　ISea
* - S&F 95043　　ISea
¶ sertata　　GIBF
§ setigera　　EBls MAus

setipoda | EBls MAus WAct WHCG WWat
'Seven Seas' (F) | MBur
Seven Sisters rose | See *R. multiflora* 'Grevillei'
Sexy Rexy® = 'Macrexy' | CGro EBrP EBre ELan GCoc GGre
  PBR (F) ♀ | GKir IHar LBCl LBSe LBre LStr
  | MAus MBBe MBri MFry MGan
  | MJon NBat NRog SBre SJus SPer
  | SSea SWCr WWeb
§ 'Shailer's White Moss' | EBls EMFP LRHS MAus MGan
  (CeMo) ♀ | NRog SFam SJus SWCr WHCG
Sharifa Asma® = | EBee EBrP EBre ENot GCoc IHar
  'Ausreef' PBR (S) | LBCl LBSe LBre LRHS LStr MAus
  | MBBe MJon MMat NPri SBre SJus
  | SPer SWCr WAct
'Sheelagh Baird' (S/Poly) | SWCr
Sheer Delight = | SWCr
  'Harwazzle' (Patio)
Sheila's Perfume = | EBee GCoc GGre LPlm LStr MGan
  'Harsherry' PBR (HT/F) | MJon SApu SJus SPer SWCr
'Shepherd's Delight' (F) | MGan SWCr
sherardii | Last listed 1998
Sheri Anne = 'Morsheri' | MAus
  (Min)
Shine On = 'Dictalent' PBR | COtt GCoc IDic MBri MFry MJon
  (Patio) | SJus SWCr WWeb
Shining Light = | GCoc
  'Cocshimmer' PBR (Patio)
Shirley Spain = | GCoc
  'Cocharod' (F)
Shocking Blue® = | ENot LPlm MGan MJon MMat
  'Korblue' PBR (F) | SPer SWCr
Shona = 'Dicdrum' PBR (F) | IDic SWCr
Short 'n' Sweet = | SWCr
  'Tinshort' (Min)
'Shot Silk' (HT) | EBls GCoc MAus MBur MGan
  | SWCr
Shrewsbury Show = | Last listed 1998
  'Fryshrewby' (HT)
'Shropshire Lass' (S) | LRHS MAus SPer SWCr
Sightsaver = 'Fryaffair' | MFry SWCr
  PBR (HT)
§ Silver Anniversary = | EBee ELan EPfP GCoc GGre GKir
  'Poulari' PBR (HT) | LGod LRHS LStr MAus MFry
  | MGan MJon MMat NEgg SApu
  | SCoo SJus SPer SSea SWCr
Silver Jubilee® (HT) ♀ | More than 30 suppliers
'Silver Lining' (HT) | EBls MAus MBur SWCr
'Silver Moon' (Cl) | CRHN EBls MAus
'Silver Tips' (Min) | MAus
'Silver Wedding' (HT) | EBls EBrP EBre GChr GCoc GGre
  | IHar LBCl LBSe LBre LPlm LRHS
  | MAus MBBe MBri MBur MFry
  | MGan MJon NRog SApu SBre SPer
  | SRPl SRum SWCr
¶ Silver Wedding | GGre SWCr
  Celebration (F)
§ Simba = 'Korbelma' PBR | EBee MGan MMat SApu SJus
  (HT) | SWCr
Simon Robinson = | MJon
  'Trobwich' PBR (Min/GC)
§ Singin' in the Rain = | MJon SApu SWCr
  'Macivy' PBR (F)
sinowilsonii | See *R. longicuspis* var.
  | *sinowilsonii*
'Sir Cedric Morris' (Ra) | EBls ELan SSea
Sir Clough = 'Ausclough' (S) | MAus
Sir Edward Elgar = | EBls EBrP EBre LBCl LBSe LBre
  'Ausprima' PBR (S) | LRHS LStr MAus MBBe MJon NPri
  | SBre SWCr
'Sir Frederick Ashton' (HT) | EBls
'Sir Joseph Paxton' (Bb) | MAus
'Sir Lancelot' (F) | Last listed 1999

Sir Neville Marriner = | NBat
  'Glanmusic' (F)
§ Sir Walter Raleigh® = | MAus MBri
  'Ausspry' (S)
Sir William Leech = | NBat
  'Hortropic' (HT)
§ 'Sissinghurst Castle' (G) | EBls SWCr
'Sleepy' (Poly) | MGan
Smarty® = 'Intersmart' | EBls IDic IHar MAus MGan MJon
  PBR (S/GC) | SApu SPer SWCr WAct WOVN
§ 'Smooth Angel' PBR (HT) | ELan LGod LStr MGan NPri SApu
  | SWCr
Smooth Lady = 'Hadlady' | ELan GGre LGod LStr MGan
  (HT) | SWCr
Smooth Melody = | SPer
  'Hadmelody' PBR (HT)
Smooth Perfume = | Last listed 1999
  'Hadperfume' (HT)
Smooth Prince = | ELan LGod LStr MGan SWCr
  'Hadprince' PBR (HT)
Smooth Romance = | LStr MGan SWCr
  'Hadromance' PBR (HT)
Smooth Satin = 'Hadsatin' | Last listed 1998
  PBR (HT)
§ 'Smooth Velvet' PBR (HT) | GGre LGod MGan SPer
'Sneezy' (Poly) | MGan
Snow Carpet® = | CBrm EBls ENot GCoc MAus
  'Maccarpe' PBR | MFry MJon SWCr WAct
  (Min/GC) ♀
'Snow Dwarf' | See *R.* 'Schneezwerg'
Snow Goose = 'Auspom' | LRHS MJon SPer
  PBR (Cl/S)
'Snow Queen' | See *R.* 'Frau Karl Druschki'
§ Snow Sunblaze™ = | SPer SWCr
  'Meigovin' PBR (Min)
Snow White = 'Landisney' | MJon
  (HT)
Snowball = 'Macangeli' | MJon
  PBR (Min/GC)
'Snowdon' (Ru) | EBls LRHS MAus
'Snowdrift' | WHCG
§ Snowdrop = 'Amoru' | MFry
  (Min/Patio)
'Snowflake' (Ra) | WHCG
§ Snowgoose = 'Barshifle' | MAus
  (F)
'Snowline' (F) | SPer
'Soldier Boy' (Cl) | WHCG
§ Solitaire® = 'Macyefre' | MBri MJon SWCr
  PBR (HT)
§ 'Sombreuil' (ClT) | CHad EBee EBls EMFP EPfP LRHS
  | MAus MRav SChu SFam SJus SPer
  | SPla SWCr WAct WHCG
¶ Someday Soon = | NBat
  'Seasoon' (Min)
Sonia | See *R.* Sweet Promise =
  | 'Meihelvet'
'Sophie's Perpetual' (ClCh) | EBls ENot LRHS MAus MGan
  | NHaw SJus SPer SWCr WAct
  | WHCG
Sophy's Rose = 'Auslot' | MAus WWeb
  PBR (S)
soulieana (Ra/S) ♀ | EBls MAus SWCr WAct WKif
'Soupert et Notting' | EBls LRHS MAus SPer SWCr
  (DPoMo)
'Southampton' (F) ♀ | EBls EWTr GChr GGre LStr MAus
  | MGan NRog SApu SPer SSea SWCr
'Souvenir d'Alphonse | EBls WHCG
  Lavallée' (ClHP)
'Souvenir de Brod' | See *R.* 'Erinnerung an Brod'
'Souvenir de Claudius | EBee EBls LRHS MAus NRog SPer
  Denoyel' (ClHT) ♀ | SWCr

'Souvenir de François   EBls
Gaulain' (T)

'Souvenir de Jeanne   EBls WHCG
Balandreau' (HP)

'Souvenir de la   See *R.* 'Climbing Souvenir de la
Malmaison' (ClBb)   Malmaison'

'Souvenir de la   EBls ENot EWTr GCoc IHar IOrc
Malmaison' (Bb)   LRHS MAus MDun MGan MMat
   SJus SPer SWCr WAct

'Souvenir de Madame   CPou EBls EHol MAus SWCr
Léonie Viennot' (ClT)

'Souvenir de Philémon   EBls MAus
Cochet' (Ru)

'Souvenir de Pierre   EBls
Vibert' (DPMo)

'Souvenir de Saint Anne's'   CHad EBee EBls EMFP EWTr IHar
(Bb) ♀   LRHS MAus SWCr WAct WHCG

'Souvenir d'Elise Vardon' (T) EBls

'Souvenir di Castagneto'   MRav
(HP)

'Souvenir du Docteur   CBos CHad CPou EBee EBls LRHS
Jamain' (ClHP)   LStr MAus MMat SFam SJus SPer
   SSea SWCr WAct WHCG

'Souvenir du Président   EBls MAus
Carnot' (HT)

'Souvenir d'un Ami' (T)   EBls

spaldingii   See *R. nutkana* var. *hispida*

Spangles = 'Ganspa' PBR (F) MBri MGan SWCr

'Spanish Beauty'   See *R.* 'Madame Grégoire
   Staechelin'

Sparkling Scarlet =   EBrP EBre ELan LBCl LBSe LBre
'Meihati' (ClF)   LPlm MBBe MGan SBre SWCr

'Sparrieshoop' (ClS)   SWCr

§ Special Friend =   GCoc LStr
   'Kirspec' PBR (Patio)

Special Occasion =   GCoc MFry SApu SWCr
   'Fryyoung' PBR (HT)

'Spectabilis' (Ra)   EBls EWTr MAus SFam WHCG

Spek's Centennial PBR (F)   See *R.* Singin' in the Rain =
   'Macivy' (F)

'Spek's Yellow' (HT)   EBls

Spellbound PBR   See *R.* Garden News = 'Poulrim'

'Spencer' misapplied   See *R.* 'Enfant de France'

spinosissima   See *R. pimpinellifolia*

§ Spirit of Youth =   SApu
   'Meivestal' (HT)

§ 'Splendens' (Ra)   CHad EBee EBls ELan MAus SLPl
   SSea SWCr WAct

'Spong' (G)   EBls MAus SWCr WAct

¶ 'Spring Bride' (Ra)   SWCr

§ St Tiggywinkle =   ENot LGod MMat SWCr
   'Korbasren' PBR (GC)

¶ 'St Wilfred's Hospice'   SApu

'Stacey Sue' (Min) ♀   EWTr

Stacey's Star =   NBat
   'Horstacey' (Patio)

§ 'Stanwell Perpetual' (PiH)   EBee EBls EMFP ENot GCoc LStr
   MAus MBri MDun MMat SApu
   SPer SSea SWCr WAct WHCG
   WOVN WWeb

Star Child® =   Last listed 1997
   'Dicmadder' (F)

'Star of Waltham' (HP)   WHCG

Stardust® =   GGre MJon SWCr
   'Peavandyke' PBR
   (Patio/F)

Starina® = 'Megabi' (Min) MGan SWCr

Starlight Express =   GKir SCoo SPer SWCr
   'Trobstar' PBR (Cl)

'Stars 'n' Stripes' (Min)   LGod LPlm MAus MFry SSea

Stella (HT)   EBls MGan

stellata   MAus

§ - var. *mirifica*   EBls MAus MGan SWCr

'Stephanie Diane' (HT)   LPlm

Sterling Silver™ (HT)   EBls LStr MAus MGan SWCr

Strawberry Fayre =   COtt EBrP EBre GCoc GKir LBCl
'Arowillip' PBR   LBSe LBre MBBe MBri MFry SBre
(Min/Patio)   SWCr WWeb

'Strawberry Ice' (F)   MJon

'Stromboli' (F)   SWCr

subcanina   Last listed 1998

subcollina   Last listed 1998

§ Sue Hipkin =   SWCr
   'Harzazz' PBR (HT)

§ Sue Lawley =   MGan MJon SWCr
   'Macspash' (F)

Sue Ryder® = 'Harlino' (F) Last listed 1997

§ Suffolk =   EBee EBrP EBre ELan ENot
   GCoc

   'Kormixal' PBR (S/GC)   LBCl LBSe LBre LPlm LStr MAus
   MBBe MGan MMat NPri SApu
   SBre SJus SPer SSea SWCr WAct
   WLRN WOVN WWeb

suffulta   See *R. arkansana* var. *suffulta*

Suma = 'Harsuma' PBR   PfP GCoc GGre LGod MJon
(GC) ♀   ESApu SJus SRum SWCr WAct
   WOVN

Summer Breeze =   ENot MMat SWCr
'Korelasting' PBR (Cl)

Summer Dream =   LStr MAus MFry SApu SJus SWCr
'Frymaxicot' PBR (F)

§ Summer Fragrance =   GCoc GGre MGan SWCr
'Tanfudermos' PBR (HT)

Summer Holiday® (HT)   MBur SPer SWCr

Summer Lady® =   MBri MBur MJon SApu
'Tanydal' PBR (HT)

Summer Love =   IHar MJon
'Franluv' (F)

¶ 'Summer Magic' (Patio)   SWCr

Summer Palace =   EBee ECle
'Poulcape' PBR (F/Patio)

Summer Sérénade® =   Last listed 1998
'Smitfirst' (F)

Summer Snow =   MJon
'Weopop' (Patio)

'Summer Sunrise' (GC)   EBls

'Summer Sunset' (GC)   EBls

Summer Wine =   EBee ENot MBri MGan MJon
'Korizont' PBR (Cl) ♀   MMat SApu SJus SPer SWCr

§ Sun Hit™ =   ENot GGre LGod MMat MRav
'Poulsun' PBR (Patio)   SApu SWCr

'Sunblaze' PBR   See *R.* Orange Sunblaze =
   'Meijikatar'

Sunblest = 'Landora' (HT)   CGro CTri GGre LPlm MBur MFry
   NRog SWCr

Sunderland Supreme =   NBat
'Nossun' (HT)

Sunmaid® (Min)   Last listed 1999

§ Sunny Sunblaze™ =   SJus
'Meiponal' PBR (Min)

Sunrise =   GCoc MBri MBur MFry MJon
'Kormarter' PBR (Cl)   MMat SApu SWCr WGer

§ Sunseeker =   EPfP GGre IDic LGod MJon SWCr
'Dicracer' PBR (F/Patio)

§ Sunset Boulevard =   ENot GCoc GGre GKir LGod
'Harbabble' PBR (F)   LPlm LStr MAus MBri MDun MFry
   MJon NBat SApu SCoo SJus SPer
   SSea SWCr WWeb

Sunset Celebration PBR   See *R.* Warm Wishes =
   'Fryxotic'

Sunset Song =   GCoc
'Cocasun' (HT)

'Sunshine' (Poly)   MGan SPer

'Sunsilk' (F)   Last listed 1998

Super Elfin = 'Helkleger' PBR (Ra) — LStr MGan MMat SPer SSea SWCr

Super Excelsa® = 'Helexa' (Ra) — LStr MGan SSea SWCr

Super Fairy = 'Helsufair' PBR (Ra) — EBee LStr MGan MMat SPer SSea SWCr

§ Super Sparkle = 'Helfels' PBR (Ra) — LStr MGan SApu SWCr

§ Super Star® = 'Tanorstar' (HT) — CGro EBls EBrP EBre ENot GKir IHar LBCl LBСl LBSe LBre LPlm LStr MAus MBBe MGan MJon SBre SWCr WWeb

'Super Sun' (HT) — SWCr

'Surf Rider' (S) — Last listed 1997

'Surpasse Tout' (G) — EBls MAus WHCG

§ 'Surpassing Beauty of Woolverstone' (ClHP) — EBls WHCG

§ Surrey = 'Korlanum' PBR (GC) ♀ — EBee EBrP EBre ELan ENot GCoc LBCl LBSe LBre LFis LGod LPlm LStr MAus MBBe MFry MGan MJon MMat SApu SBre SJus SPer SPla SSea SWCr WAct WOVN WStl

Susan Hampshire = 'Meinatac' (HT) — EBls MGan SWCr

¶ 'Susan Jellicoe' PBR (HT) — SWCr

Susan = 'Poulsue' (S) — EBee SWCr

Sussex = 'Poulave' PBR (GC) — EBrP EBre ENot GCoc LBCl LBSe LBre LPlm LStr MBBe MBur MFry MGan MJon MMat SApu SBre SJus SPer SPla SSea SWCr WOVN

'Sutter's Gold' (HT) — EBls MAus MBur MGan SWCr

Swan® = 'Auswhite' (S) — MAus MJon

Swan Lake = 'Macmed' (Cl) — EBee EBls EBrP EBre ELan ENot GGre GKir LBCl LBSe LBre LGod LRHS MAus MBBe MBur MFry MGan MMat SBre SPer SRPl SWCr WWeb

'Swanland Gem' (F) — Last listed 1997

Swany® = 'Meiburenac' (Min/GC) ♀ — EBls ELan MAus MGan SApu SPer SRPl SWCr WAct WHCG WOVN

Sweet Bouquet = 'Sabchurchill' (HT) — MBur

¶ 'Sweet Charity' (S) — SWCr

Sweet Dream = 'Fryminicot' PBR (Patio) ♀ — More than 30 suppliers

'Sweet Fairy' (Min) — LPlm

Sweet Juliet® = 'Ausleap' PBR (S) — CAbP EBee EBls EBrP EBre GKir IHar LBCl LBSe LBre LGod LPlm LRHS MAus MBBe MBri MJon NBat SApu SBre SJus SPer SWCr WAct WOVN

Sweet Magic = 'Dicmagic' PBR (Min/Patio) ♀ — CGro EBrP EBre ENot GGre IDic IHar LBCl LBSe LBre LGod LPlm LStr MBBe MBri MDun MFry MGan MJon MMat NBat SApu SBre SJus SWCr WWeb

Sweet Memories = 'Whamemo' (Patio) — COtt CTri EBrP EBre EPfP GCoc GKir LBCl LBSe LBre LStr MBBe MJon SBre SCoo SPer SPla SSea SWCr WGer

Sweet Nell = 'Cocavoter' (F) — Last listed 1997

Sweet Petite = 'Fryxquisite' (Patio) — Last listed 1999

§ Sweet Promise = 'Meihelvet' (GC) — MGan SWCr

'Sweet Repose' (F) — MAus MGan SWCr

'Sweet Revelation' PBR — See R. Sue Hipkin = 'Harzazz'

§ Sweet Symphonie = 'Meibarke' PBR (Patio) — EBrP EBre ENot LBCl LBSe LBre MBBe MBri MJon MMat SBre SWCr SWat

'Sweet Thoughts' (Patio) — LPlm

'Sweet Velvet' (F) — MGan SWCr

'Sweet Wonder' (Patio) — COtt GKir SWCr

N Sweetheart = 'Cocapeer' PBR (HT) — GCoc MGan SWCr

sweginzowii — GCal MAus MMat SWCr

- 'Macrocarpa' — EBls

'Sydonie' (HP) — EBls

Sympathie® (ClHT) — IHar LPlm MFry MGan MJon MMat SJus SPer SWCr

Symphony® = 'Auslett' (S) — MJon WAct

taiwanensis — CFil

taiwanianus ETE 77 — Last listed 1999

'Talisman' (HT) — EBls

Tall Story® = 'Dickooky' PBR (F) ♀ — EBls IDic MJon SApu SWCr WHCG WOVN

'Tallyho' (HT) — EBls

Tambourine = 'Hardolly' PBR (F) — GCoc

Tamora = 'Austamora' (S) — MAus

§ Tango = 'Macfirwal' PBR (F) ♀ — LPlm MBri MJon NRog SWCr

Tapis Jaune® — See R. Golden Penny = 'Rugul'

Tatton Park = 'Fryentice' (F) — MFry

§ 'Tausendschön' (Ra) — EBls

'Tea Rambler' (Ra) — EBls

§ Tear Drop = 'Dicomo' PBR (Min/Patio) — IDic LStr MFry MGan MJon SApu SPer SWCr

§ Teasing Georgia = 'Ausbaker' PBR (S) — IHar LRHS

Ted Gore = 'Hormislac' (F) — NBat

§ Teeny Weeny = 'Teeny' PBR (Min) — MJon

'Telstar' (F) — MGan SWCr

'Temple Bells' (ClMin/GC) — EBls MAus NRog

§ Tender Loving Care' PBR (F) — SWCr

'Tenerife' (HT) — WStl

Tequila Sunrise = 'Dicobey' PBR (HT) ♀ — CTri GGre GKir IDic IHar LPlm LStr MBri MBur MFry MGan MJon NRog SApu SJus SPer SSea SWCr

§ Terracotta = 'Meicobuis' PBR (HT) — Last listed 1999

'Texas Centennial' (HT) — EBls

§ Thaïs = 'Memaj' (HT) — EBls

'Thalia' (Ra) — MAus

Thank You = 'Chesdeep' PBR (Patio) — GGre MJon SWCr

¶ Thanks a Million (HT) — GGre SWCr

§ That's Jazz = 'Poulnorm' PBR (CIF) — LPlm SApu

§ The Alexandra Rose = 'Ausday' PBR (S) — CSam LRHS MAus SWCr

'The Bishop' (CexG) — EBls MAus

'The Bride' (T) — EBls

The Cheshire Regiment = 'Fryzebedee' (HT) — MFry

§ The Children's Rose = 'Meilivar' PBR (F) — SApu

'The Colwyn Rose' — See R. Colwyn Bay

The Compass Rose = 'Korwisco' PBR (S) — ENot MMat NFla SApu SPer SWCr

The Compassionate Friends = 'Harzodiac' PBR (F) — GGre SJus SWCr

§ The Countryman® = 'Ausman' PBR (S) — CAbP EBrP EBre LBCl LBSe LBre LRHS MAus MBBe MBNS MFry SBre SJus SWCr

The Coxswain = 'Cocadilly' (HT) — GCoc

§ The Daily Telegraph = 'Peahigh' PBR (F) — SWCr

The Dark Lady = 'Ausbloom' PBR (S) — CSam EBrP EBre IHar LBCl LBSe LBre LRHS MAus MBBe MBri MJon NBus SBre SJus SWCr WWeb

'The Doctor' (HT) — EBls MAus MGan SSea
§ The Dove = 'Tanamola' PBR (F) — MGan SWCr
'The Ednaston Rose' (Cl) — SRPl SWCr WHCG
§ 'The Fairy' (Poly) ♀ — More than 30 suppliers
The Fisherman's Cot = 'Harwicklow' (F) — SWCr
The Flower Arranger = 'Fryjam' (F) — MJon
'The Garland' (Ra) ♀ — CRHN EBee EBls EMFP LRHS MAus SFam SPer SPla SWCr WAct WHCG
The Herbalist™ = 'Aussemi' (S) — LRHS MAus
The Holt = 'Mehsherry' PBR (F/S) — Last listed 1997
'The Honorable Lady Lindsay' (S) — Last listed 1998
'The Knight' (S) — Last listed 1998
The Lady = 'Fryjingo' PBR (S) ♀ — LPlm MAus MBur MFry MJon
¶ The Maidstone Rose = 'Kordauerpa' — ENot
'The Margaret Coppola Rose'PBR — See R. White Gold = 'Cocquiriam'
§ The McCartney Rose = 'Meizeli' PBR (HT) — LStr MJon SApu SPer SWCr
'The New Dawn' — See R. 'New Dawn'
The Nun = 'Ausnun' (S) — MAus
The Observer = 'Frytango' (HT) — Last listed 1997
The Painter = 'Mactemaik' PBR (F) — GCoc LStr MBur MFry MJon SApu SSea SWCr
§ The Pilgrim = 'Auswalker' PBR (S) — CAbP CHad EBee EBrP EBre GKir IHar LBCl LBSe LBre LFis LRHS MAus MBBe MBri MDun MJon SBre SChu SJus SPer SWCr WHCG
The Prince® = 'Ausvelvet' PBR (S) — EBrP EBre LBCl LBSe LBre LRHS LStr MAus MBBe MBNS MBri MJon NPri SBre SPer SWCr WWeb
'The Prioress' (S) — MAus
§ The Pudsey Bear = 'Bedchild' PBR (HT) — GGre SWCr
§ 'The Queen Elizabeth' (F) ♀ — More than 30 suppliers
The Reeve® = 'Ausreeve' (S) — MAus
'The Royal Brompton Rose' — See R. Royal Brompton Rose = 'Meivildo'
The Scotsman = 'Poulscot' (HT) — GCoc
The Seckford Rose = 'Korpinrob' (S) — ENot MJon MMat NFla SWCr
§ The Squire® = 'Ausquire' (S) — MAus WAct
§ The Times Rose = 'Korpeahn' PBR (F) ♀ — EBee ENot LGod LStr MGan MJon MMat SJus SPer SRPl SSea SWCr
§ The Valois Rose = 'Kordadel' PBR (Min/Patio) — MMat
§ The Wife of Bath = 'Ausbath' (S) — LRHS MAus MBri
'Thelma' (Ra) — EBls MAus
'Thérèse Bugnet' (Ru) — EBls
Thinking of You = 'Frydandy' (HT) — ECle GCoc LGod MFry
'Thisbe' (HM) — EBls MAus SPer SWCr WAct WHCG
§ Thomas Barton® = 'Meihirvin' PBR (HT) — LStr SApu SWCr
Thora Hird = 'Tonybrac' (F) — MAus
'Thoresbyana' — See R. 'Bennett's Seedling'

¶ 'Thoughts of You' (HT) — SWCr
Thousand Beauties — See R. 'Tausendschön'
threepenny bit rose — See R. elegantula 'Persetosa'
'Tiara' (RH) — SWCr
Tiger Cub = 'Poulcub' PBR (Patio) — MMat
Tigris® = 'Harprier' (persica hybrid) (S) — WAct
'Till Uhlenspiegel' (RH) — EBls
'Tina Turner' (HT) — MBur MJon NBat SWCr
Tintinara = 'Dicuptight' PBR (HT) — IDic MFry SWCr
Tip Top® = 'Tanope' (F/Patio) — CB&S CTri EBee ELan EWTr GCoc GKir MBri MGan NRog SPer SWCr WStI
'Tipo Ideale' — See R. X odorata 'Mutabilis'
'Tipsy Imperial Concubine' (T) — EBls
Titanic = 'Macdako' (F) — GCoc LPlm
Tivoli = 'Poulduce' PBR (HT) — MAus SWCr
'Toby Tristam' (Ra) — CRHN WWat
'Tom Foster' (HT) — NBat
tomentosa — Last listed 1998
Too Hot to Handle = 'Macloupri' PBR (S/Cl) — LStr MJon SApu SSea WGer
Top Marks = 'Fryministar' PBR (Min/Patio) — EBrP EBre GCoc LBCl LBSe LBre / God LPlm LStr MBBe MBri MBur LMDun MFry MGan MJon MMat NRog SApu SBre SCoo SPer SSea SWCr WStI WWeb
Topaz Jewel PBR — See R. Yellow Dagmar Hastrup = 'Moryelrug'
'Topeka' (F) — SWCr
§ Toprose = 'Cocgold' PBR (F) — EBee EBrP EBre GCoc GGre GKir LBCl LBSe LBre MBBe SBre SJus SWCr
Topsi® (F/Patio) — NRog SPer
Torvill and Dean = 'Lantor' (HT) — MJon
§ Toulouse-Lautrec® = 'Meirevolt' PBR (S) — SApu
§ 'Tour de Malakoff' (Ce) — EBls IHar LRHS MAus SFam SPer SRPl SWCr WAct WHCG
Tournament of Roses = 'Jacient' PBR (HT) — IDic MAus MJon
Tower Bridge = 'Haravis' (HT) — SWCr
§ Toynbee Hall = 'Korwonder' PBR (F) — ENot MMat SWCr
'Trade Winds' (HT) — MGan SWCr
Tradescant™ = 'Ausdir' PBR (S) — EBrP EBre IHar LBCl LBSe LBre LRHS MAus MBBe MGan SBre SWCr
Tradition PBR — See R. Tradition '95 = 'Korkeltin'
§ Tradition '95® = 'Korkeltin' PBR (Cl) — MBri MMat SJus SWCr
Tranquility = 'Barout' (HT) — MBur
transmorrisonensis ETE 214 — Last listed 1999
'Treasure Trove' (Ra) — CRHN EBls EMFP IHar LRHS MAus MBur SWCr WAct
Trevor Griffiths = 'Ausold' PBR (S) — LRHS MAus SWCr
'Tricolore de Flandre' (G) — EBls LRHS MAus
Trier® (Ra) — CPou EBee EBls MAus MMat SWCr WHCG
'Trigintipetala' misapplied — See R. 'Professeur Emile Perrot'
'Triomphe de l'Exposition' (HP) — MAus
'Triomphe du Luxembourg' (T) — EBls MAus
tripbylla — See R. X beanii

Troika® = 'Poumidor' (HT) ♀ — CTri ENot GKir IHar LStr MAus MBur MFry MGan MJon MMat SPer SWCr

Troilus = 'Ausoil' (S) — MAus

'Tropicana' — See *R.* Super Star = 'Tanorstar'

§ Tropico Sunblaze = 'Meiglassol' PBR (Min) — Last listed 1998

Trumpeter® = 'Mactru' (F) ♀ — EBee ENot GCoc IArd IHar LGod LPlm LStr MAus MBri MFry MGan MJon MMat NBat SPer SSea SWCr

Tumbling Waters = 'Poultumb' PBR (F/S) — ENot NFla SWCr

'Tuner Bridge' (S) — Last listed 1999

Turn of the Century = 'Gregeliz' (F) — SWCr

'Tuscany' (G) — GCoc MAus SJus SPer WAct WHCG

'Tuscany Superb' (G) ♀ — CHad CPou EBee EBls EMFP ENot IHar LRHS MAus MDun MMat NFla SPer SSea SWCr WAct WHCG WKif

tuschetica — Last listed 1998

Twenty-fifth = 'Beatwe' (F) — EBls

§ Twenty-one Again! = 'Meinimo' PBR (HT) — MBri MJon MRav SApu SWCr

§ Twilight = 'Noatwi' (GC) — IHar LRHS SCoo SWCr WWeb

Tynwald = 'Mattwyt' PBR (HT) — LStr MJon MMat SWCr

'Typhoon' (HT) — IHar MBur MJon

'Tzigane' (HT) — SWCr

'Ulrich Brünner Fils' (HP) — EBls MAus

'Uncle Bill' (HT) — EBls

Uncle Walter = 'Macon' (HT) — EBls SWCr WStI

UNICEF = 'Cocjojo' PBR (F) — GCoc SWCr

§ 'Unique Blanche' (Ce) — EBee EBls MAus SSea SWCr

Valencia® = 'Koreklia' PBR (HT) — ENot LGod MBur MJon MMat NBat SWCr

§ Valentine Heart = 'Dicogle' PBR (F) — EBee IDic LGod MFry MJon SApu SJus SWCr

Valerie Sykes = 'Horflashrob' (F) — GChr GGre MJon NBat SApu SPer SRum SWCr

'Vanguard' (Ru) — EBls

'Vanity' (HM) — EBls MAus SPer

'Variegata di Bologna' (Bb) — CHad EBee EBls EMFP GOrc LFis LRHS MAus MMat SSea SWCr WAct MJon SWCr

Vatertag® —

'Veilchenblau' (Ra) ♀ — CHad CRHN EBee EBls ELan LFis LGod LRHS LStr MAus MBur MGan SApu SJus SPer SSea SWCr WAct WHCG WKif WSHC

Velvet Fragrance = 'Fryperdee' PBR (HT) — GCoc LStr MAus MBri MFry MJon NBat SApu SWCr

¶ 'Velvet Hit' — MMat

'Venusta Pendula' (Ra) — EBls MAus

¶ 'Vera Dalton' (F) — SWCr

'Verschuren' (HT/v) — ELan

versicolor — See *R. gallica* 'Versicolor'

'Vesper' (F) — SWCr

'Vick's Caprice' (HP) — EBls MAus

'Vicomtesse Pierre du Fou' (ClHT) — EBls MAus

Victor Hugo® (HT) — See *R.* Spirit of Youth = 'Meivestal'

'Victoriana' (F) — MAus SWCr

Vidal Sassoon = 'Macjuliat' PBR (HT) — MBur MGan MJon MMat SApu SWCr

'Village Maid' — See *R.* 'Centifolia Variegata'

villosa auct. — See *R. mollis*

- L. — EBls MAus MMat WAct

- 'Duplex' — See *R.* 'Wolley-Dod'

§ 'Violacea' (G) — EBee EBls SWCr WHCG

Violet Carson = 'Macio' (F) — MAus MGan SWCr

'Violette' (Ra) — EBee EBls GOrc MAus SPer SWCr WAct WHCG WHer

'Violinista Costa' (HT) — EBls

virginiana ♀ — EBls ENot GCal GChr MAus MGan MSte NWea SPer SRPl SWCr WAct WHCG WHen WOVN

- 'Plena' — See *R.* 'Rose d'Amour'

'Virgo' (HT) — EBls

'Viridiflora' — See *R.* X *odorata* 'Viridiflora'

Vital Spark = 'Cocacert' (F) — MGan SWCr

'Vivid' (Bourbon hybrid) — EBls

Voice of Thousands = 'Horsunsmile' (F) — NBat

vosagiaca — See *R. caesia* subsp. *glauca*

'W.E. Lippiat' (HT) — EBls

Wandering Minstrel = 'Harquince' (F) — SWCr

wardii var. *culta* — MAus

'Warley Jubilee' (F) — Last listed 1997

Warm Welcome = 'Chewizz' PBR (ClMin) ♀ — EBrP EBre GCoc GGre GKir LBCl LBSe LBre LGod LStr MAus MBBe MBri MFry MJon MMat NBat NRog SBre SJus SMad SPer SSea SWCr WWeb

§ Warm Wishes = 'Fryxotic' PBR (HT) — EBee GCoc GGre GKir LGod LPlm LStr MAus MBri MBur MFry MGan MJon SApu SJus SWCr WWeb

'Warrior' (F) — MGan SPer SWCr

Warwick Castle® = 'Auslian' PBR (S) — MAus MBNS NBus SPer

Warwickshire = 'Korkandel' PBR (GC) — ENot MMat SJus SPer SWCr WOVN

§ *watsoniana* (Ra) — EBls

webbiana — EBls MAus SWCr WHCG

'Wedding Day' (Ra) — More than 30 suppliers

§ 'Wee Barbie' PBR (Min) — SSea

Wee Cracker = 'Cocmarris' PBR (Patio) — GCoc GGre SWCr

Wee Jock = 'Cocabest' PBR (F/Patio) — GChr GCoc GGre GKir LStr MBri SSea SWCr

'Weetwood' (Ra) — CRHN MAus SPer

'Weisse aus Sparrieshoop' (S) — MGan

Weisse Wolcke®*PBR* — See *R.* White Cloud = 'Korstacha'

'Well Done' (Patio/Min) — GGre SWCr

Welwyn Garden Glory™ = 'Harzumber' (HT) — SJus

'Wembley Stadium' (F/HT) — MGan SWCr

'Wendy Cussons' (HT) — CB&S CGro EBls GChr GCoc GKir LPlm MAus MBur MGan MJon NRog SApu SPer SWCr

Wenlock® = 'Auswen' (S) — EBrP EBre GGre IHar LBCl LBSe LBre LRHS MAus MBBe MBNS SBre SPer SWCr

§ Westerland™ = 'Korwest' (F/S) ♀ — EWTr MGan MJon MMat SWCr WGer

'Westfield Star' (HT) — MAus

Wheelhorse Classic™ = 'Harélite' (F) — SWCr

'Whisky Gill' (HT) — MGan SWCr

Whisky Mac = 'Tanky' (HT) — CB&S CGro EBls EBrP EBre ELan GChr GCoc GGre LBCl LBSe LBre LGod LPlm MAus MBBe MBri MBur MFry MGan MJon NRog SApu SBre SPer SSea SWCr WWeb

'White Bath' — See *R.* 'Shailer's White Moss'

White Bells® = 'Poulwhite' PBR (Min/GC) — EBls ENot MAus MMat SPer SRPl SWCr WAct WHCG WOVN

§ 'White Cécile Brünner' (Poly) — EBls MAus WHCG

'Yolande d'Aragon' (HP) EBls
York and Lancaster See *R.* x *damascena* var. *versicolor*
Yorkshire Bank = MFry SWCr
'Rutrulo' PBR (HT)
Yorkshire = 'Korbarkeit' ENot GCoc LStr MMat NPri SSea
(GC) SWCr
'Yorkshire Lady' (HT) NBat
§ Yorkshire Sunblaze® = Last listed 1997
'Meiblam' (Min)
Young Quinn® = MBur SWCr
'Macbern' (HT)
Young Venturer = Last listed 1997
'Mattsun' (F)
Yves Piaget® See *R.* Royal Brompton Rose =
'Meivildo'
'Yvonne Rabier' (Poly) ♀ EBls LStr MAus SPer SSea SWCr
WAct WHCG
Zambra® = 'Meicurbos' (F) CB&S
'Zenobia' (Mo) Last listed 1997
'Zéphirine Drouhin' (Bb) ♀ More than 30 suppliers
§ 'Zigeunerknabe' (S) ♀ EBee EBls EMFP GOrc MAus SPer
SSea SWCr WAct WHCG
Zitronenfalter® (S) MGan
'Zweibrücken' (Cl) MGan
§ Zwergkönig® '78 = MAus MDun
'Korkönig' (Min)

ROSCOEA ✿ (Zingiberaceae)

alpina CBro CMea CPBP EBee EBrP EBre
EPot ERos GDra GKir IBlr LBCl
LBSe LBre MBBe MTho NWCA
SBea SBre SRms WAbe WCot
WCru WSan
- CC 1820 WCot
- pink MSCN
auriculata CAvo CBro CFir CLAP CRDP EBee
EMar ETub IBlr LEur MLLN MTho
NHar SBla SCro WCot WCru WPyg
WViv
australis CFir IBlr
'Beesiana' CAvo CBro CFir CHEx CLAP
CRDP EBee ECha EMan ERos IBlr
LAma LEur MBel MTho NHar
NHol WAbe WCru WPyg
¶ 'Beesiana' pale-flowered LEur
'Beesiana' white CLAP EBee MBNS NHol WAbe
cautleyoides ♀ More than 30 suppliers
- Blackthorn strain SBla
- 'Grandiflora' Last listed 1998
- x *humeana* IBlr
- hybrid MLLN
¶ - 'Jeffrey Thomas' CLAP WCot
- 'Kew Beauty' CLAP CRDP EBee EBrP EBre GKir
LBCl LBSe LBre MBBe MTho SBla
SBre
- 'Kew Beauty' seedlings GCal
humeana ♀ CBro CLAP GCrs LAma LRHS
NHar SBla WCru
¶ - 'Purple Streaker' EBee WPGP
procera See *R. purpurea*
§ *purpurea* More than 30 suppliers
- var. *gigantea* CC 1757 WCot
- lilac LEur
¶ - 'Polaris' LEur
- var. *procera* See *R. purpurea*
¶ - short CLAP
¶ - tall CLAP
§ *scillifolia* CBro CFir CFwr CRDP EBee EBrP
EBre ERos GCal LAma LBCl LBSe
LBre LEur LRHS MBBe MTho NBir
NHar NMen NRog NTow SBre
WCot WCru

- pink IBlr WCDu WViv
tibetica EBrP EBre LBCl LBSe LBre MBBe
SBre WCru

ROSMARINUS ✿ (Lamiaceae)
* 'Boule' WCHb
* *calabriensis* Last listed 1999
corsicus 'Prostratus' See *R. officinalis* Prostratus
Group
'Green Ginger' CFri GBin MChe NCut NHex
NPer SDow WElm WShe WWoo
lavandulaceus hort. See *R. officinalis* Prostratus
Group
- Noë See *R. eriocalyx*
'Loddon Pink' ERav
officinalis More than 30 suppliers
- var. *albiflorus* CArn CSev EBee ELau ESis GAbr
GBar GPoy LRHS MBar MChe
MHer NChi NHHG NSti SChu
SDow SEas SHDw SLim SMac
SPer SRms WCHb WEas WOak
WWye
- 'Alderney' MHer NGCt SDow
§ - var. *angustissimus* CGle CMHG CSev EBee
ECha
'Benenden Blue' EGoo ELau GBar GPoy LHop
LRHS MAsh MChe MGos MHer
MWgw NHHG SChu SDix SDow
SIde SLim SMer SPer STre WEas
WGwG WWat WWye
§ - - 'Corsican Blue' CArn GBar GPoy SCro SDow
SHDw SIde WPer
- - 'Corsicus Prostratus' CB&S ELau SMac
- 'Aureovariegatus' See *R. officinalis* 'Aureus'
§ - 'Aureus' (v) CMil CPla GBar IBlr LRHS
MAsh MHar NHHG SDry SEas
SMad WByw WCHb WEas
WHer
¶ - 'Capernaille' NGCt
- 'Collingwood Ingram' See *R. officinalis* var.
angustissimus 'Benenden Blue'
- dwarf blue ELau GBar
- 'Fastigiatus' See *R. officinalis* 'Miss Jessopp's
Upright'
- 'Fota Blue' CArn CBod CSev ELau EOHP
GBar MHer NHHG NSti SAga
SCro SDow SHDw SIde SPan
WCHb WJek WWye
- 'Frimley Blue' See *R. officinalis* 'Primley Blue'
* - 'Ginger-scented' WCHb WRus
¶ - 'Golden Rain' NGCt SDow
- 'Guilded' See *R. officinalis* 'Aureus'
- 'Gunnel's Upright' GBar WRha
- 'Iden Blue' SIde
- 'Iden Blue Boy' SIde
- 'Iden Pillar' SIde
- Israeli NGCt
- 'Jackman's Prostrate' CB&S ECtt
- 'Lady in White' ELan EPfP LAst LRHS SDow SPer
WGwG WWat
- *lavandulaceus* See *R. officinalis* Prostratus
Group
- 'Lilies Blue' GPoy
- 'Lockwood Variety' GBar SDow WPer
- 'Majorca Pink' CB&S CChe CSam EGoo ELau
GBar LRHS MHer MMal NSti
SDow SIde SLon SPer SRms SSht
SSoC WCHb WGwG WPer WWat
WWye
- 'McConnell's Blue' More than 30 suppliers
* - 'Miss Jessopp's Prostrate' Last listed 1998
§ - 'Miss Jessopp's Upright' ♀ More than 30 suppliers

- 'Mrs Harding' — CBod MHer SDow
§ - 'Primley Blue' — CArn CSam CSev CWSG EDAr ELau GBar LRHS MChe MRav NHHG NSti SChu SDow SIde SMer WCHb WHer WPer WWye
§ - Prostratus Group ♀ — More than 30 suppliers
- - 'Gethsemane' — SIde
- - 'Trewithen' — Last listed 1998
¶ - - white — WWat
- f. *pyramidalis* — See *R. officinalis* 'Miss Jessopp's Upright'
¶ - 'Rampant Boule' — SDow
- *repens* — See *R. officinalis* Prostratus Group
- 'Roscus' — CArn CMHG CWit EBee ELan ELau EMil GChr GPoy LHop LRHS MChe MHer NHHG NSti SAga SChu SDow SEas SLim SRPl SSoC WAbe WEas WGwG WHer WOak WPer WWye
- 'Russell's Blue' — WHer WWat
- 'Severn Sea' ♀ — More than 30 suppliers
- Silver Spires® = 'Wolros' — SIde WFar
- 'Sissinghurst Blue' ♀ — CArn CB&S CMGP CSev EBee ECha ELan ELau EMil EPfP ERav GBar LRHS MAsh MMal MTis SAga SDow SIde SPer SRms WCHb WGwG WRHF WSel WWat WWye
- 'Sissinghurst White' — WGwG
- 'Sudbury Blue' — EDAr ELau GBar MChe MHer NHHG NSti SDow SHDw WEas WJek
- 'Trusty' — ECtt ELan LHop LRHS SDow WPer
- 'Tuscan Blue' — CDoC CSWP CSev EBee ECGP ECot ECtt ELau EMil EPri LRHS MHer MWat MWgw NFla NHex NSti SDow SDry SIde SMer WCHb WGwG WHer WJek WPGP WPer WRha WWat WWye
- 'Variegatus' — See *R. officinalis* 'Aureus'
- 'Vicomte de Noailles' — ERea
repens — See *R. officinalis* Prostratus Group AGM

ROSTRINUCULA (Lamiaceae)
dependens Guiz 18 — CBot

ROSULARIA ✿ (Crassulaceae)
acuminata — See *R. alpestris* subsp. *alpestris*
§ *aizoon* — ESis
alba — See *R. sedoides*
alpestris — MSte
§ - subsp. *alpestris* — Last listed 1998
§ *chrysantha* — EBur ESis MBro MHer NMen NNrd SIng SPlb WFar WLow
- Number 1 — CWil
crassipes — See *Rhodiola wallichiana*
hissarica K 92.380 — Last listed 1997
§ *muratdaghensis* — EBur MBro NNrd SChr SIng
pallida A. Berger — See *R. chrysantha*
- Stapf — See *R. aizoon*
platyphylla hort. — See *R. muratdaghensis*
rechingeri — CWil
§ *sedoides* — CWil GCHN LRHS MBar SChu SIng WPer WWin
§ - var. *alba* — CWil EDAr GCHN MBar NFla SChu WPyg WWin
sempervivum — CWil EWes NMen
§ - subsp. *glaucophylla* — CWil NTow
serpentinica — CWil
spatulata hort. — See *R. sempervivum* subsp. *glaucophylla*

turkestanica — CWil

ROTHMANNIA (Rubiaceae)
capensis — LRHS SOWG
§ *globosa* — Last listed 1997

RUBIA (Rubiaceae)
manjith — Last listed 1999
peregrina — CArn EWFC GBar GPoy MHew MSal
tinctorum — CArn ELau EOHP GBar GPoy MHew MSal NHex SIde SWat WCHb WHer WWye

RUBUS ✿ (Rosaceae)
'Adrienne' (F) — EMui
alceifolius — CGle CInt CStr SMac
arcticus — CGle CInt EPPr GGar MBro MCCP NHar SRms SRot WBea WCot WCru WPat
- subsp. *stellarcticus* (F) — Last listed 1998
- - 'Anna' (F) — ESim
- - 'Beata' (F) — ESim
- - 'Linda' (F) — ESim
- - 'Sofia' (F) — ESim
australis — Last listed 1999
x *barkeri* — ECou
§ 'Benenden' ♀ — More than 30 suppliers
'Betty Ashburner' — CAgr CBlo CDoC CWit EPfP EPla GCal GKir GQui LBuc MGos MRav MWhi NArg NFla SPer WHCG WTro WWat
biflorus — CB&S CDoC CFil EBee EMon EPfP EPla ERav EWes LRHS MBlu SMac WWat
'Boysenberry, Thornless' (F) — EBee EMui GTwe LBuc LRHS SDea SPer
* *buergeri* 'Variegatus' — WCot WMoo
caesius 'Sidings' — CNat
calophyllus — WCot
calycinoides Hayata — See *R. pentalobus*
chamaemorus — GPoy
cissoides — WCot
cockburnianus (F) ♀ — More than 30 suppliers
¶ - 'Goldenvale' PBR — More than 30 suppliers
coreanus — CFil CPle EPla
crataegifolius — MBro SMac SPan WPat
'Emerald Spreader' — GKir LRHS MBri SBod WMoo
flagelliflorus — MBar WHCG
fockeanus hort. — See *R. pentalobus*
formosensis B&SWJ 1798 — WCru
x *fraseri* — EPla
fruticosus — CKin
- 'Adrienne' (F) — EMui
- 'Ashton Cross' (F) — CSam EMui GTwe LBuc LRHS SDea
- 'Bedford Giant' (F) — CBlo EBee GChr GTwe LRHS MGos SPer WWeb
- 'Black Satin' (F) — CBlo LRHS MBri SDea SPer WWeb
¶ - 'Cottenham Green' — EMon
- 'Dart's Ambassador' — EPla
- 'Dart's Robertville' — Last listed 1997
- 'Denver Thornless' (F) — Last listed 1997
- 'Fantasia' PBR (F)¿ — EMui LBuc
- 'Godshill Goliath' (F) — SDea
- 'Helen' — CSut EMui SDea
- 'Himalayan Giant' (F) — CBlo GTwe LRHS NRog SDea SPer
- 'John Innes' (F) — CTri NRog
- 'Loch Ness' PBR (F)¿ — CBlo COtt CSam EMui GChr GKir GTwe IArd LBuc LRHS MBri MGos SDea SPer

Tayberry Group (F) ♀ — CSam CTri EMui GChr GKir GTwe MBri MGos NRog SPer SRms WWeb

- 'Buckingham' (F) — CSut EMui LBuc LRHS WLRN
- 'Medana Tayberry' (F) — LRHS SDea

§ *thibetanus* ♀ — More than 30 suppliers
- 'Silver Fern' — See *R. thibetanus*
treutleri — Last listed 1997
tricolor — CAgr CB&S CChe CGle CHEx ELan ENot GBri GKir LGro MRav NFor NHol SDix SLon SPer WBod WDin WEas WHCG WOak WWat WWin WWye

- 'Dart's Evergreen' — SLPl
- 'Ness' — SLPl
tridel 'Benenden' — See *R.* 'Benenden'
'Tummelberry' (F) — GTwe LRHS
ulmifolius — CBot CSev EBee ELan ENot EPla
'Bellidiflorus' (d) — EWTr MBlu MRav NFor NSti SChu SMac SPer WAbb WHal

¶ *ursinus* — LEdu
'Veitchberry' (F) — EMui GTwe
§ Walberton Red™ = 'Odel' — MBel SPer
'Youngberry' (F) — SDea

RUDBECKIA ✿ (Asteraceae)

Autumn Sun — See *R.* 'Herbstsonne'
californica — CSam MNrw SSca WPer
deamii — See *R. fulgida* var. *deamii*
echinacea purpurea — See *Echinacea purpurea*
§ *fulgida* var. *deamii* ♀ — More than 30 suppliers
§ - var. *speciosa* — CFri CM&M CMGP CSam EBee ECha ELan EPfP LRHS MBel NCut SHel SPer SPlb SRms WCot WFar WPer WRus
- var. *sullivantii* — More than 30 suppliers
'Goldsturm' ♀
- 'Viette's Little Suzy' — EBee GKir LRHS
gloriosa — See *R. hirta*
'Goldquelle' ♀ — EBee ECha EFou EGar ELan EMan EPfP GMaP LRHS MBel MLLN NCut NGdn NOrc NPri SAga SCro SMad SMrm SPer SRms WCot WCra WFar WHil WWin
§ 'Herbstsonne' — More than 30 suppliers
§ *hirta* — IIve
- 'Irish Eyes' — LRHS
- var. *pulcherrima* — EBee EFou
§ 'Juligold' — CMGP EBee EFou LRHS NCat NGdn NHlc NTow SCro SMrm SSpe WFar WWoo
July Gold — See *R.* 'Juligold'
laciniata — CSam CStr EBee ECGN ELan EMan EMon EPPr EPfP GCal LFis MArl MFir NOrc NSti SMrm WByw WCot WLRN
- 'Golden Glow' — See *R. laciniata* 'Hortensia'
§ - 'Hortensia' — EMon LRHS MFir WCot
maxima — CGle EBee ECGN ECha EGar EMan EMon GBin LGre LRHS MBri MBro MCCP NChi NLar NSti SAga SDix SMrm SSoC SSvw WCot WRus
- 'Brilliant' — NCut
missouriensis — EBee
mollis — EBee
newmannii — See *R. fulgida* var. *speciosa*
nitida — WWoo
occidentalis — ECGN LFis MLLN NChi NCut NLar WFar WPer

- 'Green Wizard' — CM&M CMil EBee EFou EGar ELan EMan EWTr GCal GKir NBro NChi NLar SLon SMad SPer SRCN SSca WElm WHer WSan WWhi WWoo WWye
purpurea — See *Echinacea purpurea*
speciosa — See *R. fulgida* var. *speciosa*
subtomentosa — CHor CPou EBee EFou EGar EMan EMon GCal LRHS MNrw NSti
triloba — EBee ECGN EFou EMan GBri NCut SMad SSvw WBea WCot WSan

RUELLIA (Acanthaceae)

amoena — See *R. graecizans*
¶ *brittoniana* 'Chi Chi' — WCot
¶ - 'Katie' — WCot
caroliniensis — WCot
ciliata — WCot
devosiana — Last listed 1998
§ *graecizans* — Last listed 1997
humilis — EBee EMan GOrP WCot WHil WLRN
¶ *macrantha* — ERea
makoyana ♀ — CHal CSev IBlr MBri SYvo
¶ 'Mr Foster' — CHal
strepens — Last listed 1999

RUMEX (Polygonaceae)

§ *acetosa* — CArn CKin CSev ECha EDAr ELau GAbr GBar GPoy LRHS MChe MHer MHew NBir SIde WGwG WHer WSel WWye
- 'Crocodile' (v) — Last listed 1998
¶ - 'Saucy' (v) — WAlt
¶ - subsp. *vinealis* — WCot
acetosella — IIve MSal WSel
alpinus — WCot
flexuosus — CElw CRow EHoe EPPr IBlr
hydrolapathum — CArn CHEx EMFW EWFC LPBA MSta NDea SPlb
maritimus — EWFC
rubrifolius — SIde
rugosus — Last listed 1997
sanguineus — EMFW EMan GGar LPBA MSCN WCer WFar WGwG WMAq WWal
- var. *sanguineus* — CArn CElw CRow CSev EHoe ELan EPar EPla LRHS MHer MNrw MTho NBro NHol NSti WHer WOak WPer WSel WWye
scutatus — CArn CSev ELau GAbr GPoy MChe MHer MHew SIde WCer WHbs WHer WJek WWye
- 'Silver Shield' — CRDP CRow ELau EMar EPPr IBlr NSti WCHb WCot WJek WOak WWye
venosus — MSal
¶ *woodii* — WCot

RUMOHRA (Davalliaceae)

adiantiformis ♀ — WRic

RUPICAPNOS (Papaveraceae)

africana — NWCA SBla

RUSCHIA (Aizoaceae)

karrooica — SChr
macowanii — EOas
misera — EOas
putterillii S&SH 64 — Last listed 1999
rubricaulis — CTrC
uncinata — CTrC SChr

RUSCUS ✿ (Ruscaceae)

aculeatus	CArn CTri EBee ENot EPfP GKir
	GPoy LRHS MFir MRav NWea
	SAPC SArc SBrw SMac SRCN
	SRms SSta WBod WByw WDin
	WHer WPGP WRHF WSpi WStI
	WWye
- (f)	WMou
- hermaphrodite	EPla EWes GCal SPer WWat
- (m)	WMou
¶ - var. *angustifolius*	EPla MTed
- - (f)	EPla
¶ - var. *platyphyllus*	WWat
* - 'Wheeler's Variety' (f/m)	CPMA MRav WWat
hypoglossum	EPla GOrc LRHS MTed SAPC
	SEND WRHF
- WM 9804	MPhe
hypophyllum	MTed
x microglossum	GCal
racemosus	See *Danae racemosa*

RUSPOLIA (Acanthaceae)

pseuderanthemoides	Last listed 1997

RUSSELIA (Scrophulariaceae)

§ **equisetiformis** ♀	ERea SOWG
juncea	See *R. equisetiformis*

RUTA (Rutaceae)

chalepensis	CArn
§ - 'Dimension Two'	WHer
- prostrate	See *R. chalepensis* 'Dimension Two'
corsica	CArn
graveolens	CArn CFri CGle CWSG EFer GBar
	GPoy GVer LRHS MChe NOak
	SIde SPar WGwG WHer WJek
	WOak WPer WWye
- 'Harlequin'	Last listed 1999
- 'Jackman's Blue' ♀	More than 30 suppliers
- 'Variegata'	CArn CBot ECha ELan GBar GEil
	LRHS MChe NFor NGdn NPer
	SPer WBry WHer WJek WOak
	WCot
montana	WCot
prostrata	See *R. chalepensis* 'Dimension Two'

RUTTYA (Acanthaceae)

¶ **fruticosa** 'Scholesii'	ERea

x RUTTYRUSPOLIA (Acanthaceae)

'Phyllis van Heerden'	Last listed 1998

RYTIDOSPERMA (Poaceae)

arundinaceum	EBee

S

SABAL (Arecaceae)

§ **bermudana**	CRoM LPal
¶ **causiarum**	CRoM
etonia	LPal
mauritiiformis	Last listed 1997
§ **mexicana**	CRoM CTrC
minor	CBrP CHEx CRoM CTrC EPVP
	LPal WMul
palmetto	CArn CRoM CTrC LPal WMul
	WNor

princeps	See *S. bermudana*
rosei	CRoM LPal
texana	See *S. mexicana*
uresana	LPal

SABATIA (Gentianaceae)

kennedyana	Last listed 1999

SACCHARUM (Poaceae)

¶ **officinarum**	CInt
ravennae	CCtw EBee EHoe EMan EMon
	EWes GBin MSte NChi NSti SMad
	SPlb WWat

SADLERIA (Blechnaceae)

cyatheoides	Last listed 1999

SAGERETIA (Rhamnaceae)

§ **thea**	STre
theezans	See *S. thea*

SAGINA (Caryophyllaceae)

boydii	EMNN EWes ITim NDlv
japonica 'Flore Pleno'	EMon
subulata	NBlu
§ - var. *glabrata* 'Aurea'	ECha EDAr EFer ELan GKir LGro
	MBNS MOne MRav MWhi SIng
	SRms WEas WHal WPer WWin

SAGITTARIA (Alismataceae)

¶ **graminea** 'Crushed Ice' (v)	CRow LLWG
japonica	See *S. sagittifolia*
latifolia	CHEx COld EMFW LPBA NDea
	SWyc
* - 'Flore Pleno'	SWyc
¶ **montevidensis**	LLWG
§ **sagittifolia**	CBen CHEx CRow EHon EMFW
	EPfP LPBA MSta SLon SWat SWyc
	WMAq WShi
* - 'Bloomin Baby'	CRow LLWG
- 'Flore Pleno' (d)	CRow CWat EMFW LPBA MSta
	SWat SWyc WMAq
- var. *leucopetala*	WMAq
subulata	CRow

SAINTPAULIA (Gesneriaceae)

'Bright Eyes' ♀	Last listed 1992
'Colorado' ♀	Last listed 1992
'Delft' ♀	Last listed 1992
'Fancy Trail' ♀	Last listed 1995
'Garden News' ♀	Last listed 1992
'Granger's Wonderland' ♀	Last listed 1995
'Gredi' ♀	Last listed 1992
'Ice Maiden' ♀	Last listed 1992
'Maria' ♀	Last listed 1992
'Midget Valentine' ♀	Last listed 1995
'Moon Kissed' ♀	Last listed 1995
'Phoenix' ♀	Last listed 1992
'Rococo Pink' ♀	Last listed 1992
'Starry Trail' ♀	Last listed 1992
'Tomahawk' ♀	Last listed 1995

SALIX ✿ (Salicaceae)

acutifolia	ELan EPla GChr GIBF IOrc NSti
	SMrm SPer SPla
- 'Blue Streak' (m) ♀	CEnd CMHG CWiW EPfP EPla EWes
	IOrc MAsh MBlu MRav NBir SWat
- 'Pendulifolia' (m)	IOrc
aegyptiaca	CDoC CLnd GChr MBlu NWea
	WMou
alba	CKin CLnd CWiW GChr GKir
	GVer LBuc NWea WDin WMou

- f. *argentea*	See *S. alba* var. *sericea*
- 'Aurea'	CLnd CTho MRav WMou
- var. *caerulea*	CLnd ENot GChr LBuc NWea WMou
¶ - - 'Wantage Hall'	CWiW
- 'Cardinalis' (f)	CWiW
- 'Chermesina' hort.	See *S. alba* subsp. *vitellina* 'Britzensis'
- 'Dart's Snake'	CBlo CEnd CTho EBee ELan ENot EPfP LRHS MRav SCoo SPer WBcn
- 'Hutchinson's Yellow'	EPla GChr MBri MGos
- 'Liempde' (m)	ENot MRav
- 'Orange Spire'	Last listed 1997
¶ - 'Raesfeld'	CWiW
§ - var. *sericea* ♀	CB&S CLnd CMHG CTho ENot GChr GKir MBlu MRav NFor NWea SMad SPer WDin WGer WMou WTro WWat
- 'Splendens'	See *S. alba* var. *sericea*
N - 'Tristis'	CDul CLnd CTri ELan GChr GKir LRHS MAsh MBri MGos NWea SRms WDin WFar WHar
- subsp. *vitellina* ♀	CBlo CKin ELan EPla GChr GKir LBuc MBNS MBrN NWea SWat WDin WJas WOrn WPGP
§ - - 'Britzensis' (m) ♀	More than 30 suppliers
- 'Vitellina Pendula'	See *S. alba* 'Tristis'
- 'Vitellina Tristis'	See *S. alba* 'Tristis'
§ *alpina*	CLyd GAri GIBF NHol NWoo
¶ 'Americana'	CWiW
¶ *amplexicaulis* 'Pescara'	CWiW
¶ *amygdaloides*	CWiW
¶ 'Aokautere'	CWiW
apoda (m)	CLyd ESis EWes GIBF NHar NHol WPer
§ *arbuscula*	CB&S CBlo MBNS NHar NWCA SPan
arctica var. *petraea*	MBro WPat
arenaria	See *S. repens* var. *argentea*
aurita	CDul GChr
babylonica	CBlo CDul CTrG NBee WMou
- 'Annularis'	See *S. babylonica* 'Crispa'
§ - 'Crispa'	ELan EPla ERav LHop MRav SMad SPla WLRN
- 'Pan Chih-kang'	CWiW
- var. *pekinensis* 'Pendula'	Last listed 1999
§ - - 'Tortuosa' ♀	CArn CDoC CLnd CTho EBee ECrN ELan ENot EWTr GChr GKir IOrc LPan LRHS MAsh MBar MGos MWat NBea NFor NPer NWea SLon SPer SPlb SRms WCFE WHar WWat
¶ x *basaltica* (m)	GIBF
¶ *bicolor* (f)	GIBF
¶ - (m)	GIBF
¶ 'Blackskin'	CWiW
bockii	CBlo EBee GKir MBar NWCA WCFE WPer WWat
§ 'Bowles' Hybrid'	CAgr GChr LBuc MRav WMou
'Boydii' (f) ♀	CFee ELan EPot GCrs GDra GKir GTou MAsh MBri MBro MDun MGos NFor NHar NHol NMen SBla SIng SPer SRms SSmi WPat
§ 'Boyd's Pendulous' (m)	CFee CLyd GAri MBar SIng
breviserrata	CLyd GDra GIBF NWCA
caesia	GIBF SRPl
calyculata	Last listed 1998
candida	GIBF
caprea	CB&S CKin CLnd CTri ECrN ENot GChr GKir GTre LBuc LHyr NWea WDin WMou WTro

- 'Black Stem'	CNat
- 'Curlilocks'	CBlo COtt EBee MBar MBlu
§ - 'Kilmarnock' (m) ♀	More than 30 suppliers
- var. *pendula* (f)	See *S. caprea* 'Weeping Sally'
- - (m)	See *S. caprea* 'Kilmarnock' (m)
- var. *variegata*	Last listed 1997
§ - 'Weeping Sally' (f)	Last listed 1999
capusii	Last listed 1997
cascadensis	GIBF
cashmiriana	CFai CLyd MBro NHol WPat
* *caspica rubra nana*	SWat
¶ x *cepusiensis* (f)	GIBF
x *cernua*	NWCA
'Chrysocoma'	See *S.* x *sepulcralis* var. *chrysocoma*
cinerea	CB&S CDoC CDul CKin ENot GChr GKir GTre LBuc NWea WDin
- subsp. *oleifolia*	GChr
- 'Tricolor'	CArn CDoC GCHN SLim
¶ *commutata*	GIBF
x *cottetii*	CBlo GIBF MBar
daphnoides	CDoC CDul CLnd CSam EBee ELan ENot EPla GKir IOrc LNor MBrN NSti NWea SPer SPla SRms STre WDin WJas WMou WWat
- 'Aglaia' (m) ♀	CB&S CTri EPla WPGP
- 'Meikle'	CAgr CWiW
¶ - 'Netta Statham'	CWiW
¶ - 'Ovaro Udine'	CWiW
- 'Oxford Violet'	CWiW
¶ - 'Stewartstown'	CWiW
'E.A. Bowles'	See *S.* 'Bowles' Hybrid'
x *ebrhartiana*	CNat
§ *elaeagnos* ♀	CDoC CPle CTho EBee ENot EPfP GChr GKir LRHS MBNS MBlu MBrN MRav SPan SPer SWat WDin WMou
§ - subsp. *angustifolia*	CDul CLnd ELan IOrc LBuc LHop MRav MTis NWea SRms STre WWat WWin
elbrusensis	EPla
'Elegantissima'	See *S.* x *pendulina* var. *elegantissima*
x *erdingeri*	EPla
eriocephala	CWiW
'American Mackay'	
¶ - 'Kerksii' (m)	CWiW
¶ - 'Mawdesley'	CWiW
¶ - 'Russelliana' (f)	CWiW
§ 'Erythroflexuosa'	More than 30 suppliers
exigua	CB&S CDul CTho EBee ELan ENot EWTr EWes GChr IOrc MBar MBlu MBrN MBri MGos MRav NWea SDry SMad SPer SRPl WMou WWat
fargesii	CBot CDoC CEnd CFee CFil EBee ELan GKir GOrc LHop LRHS MBlu MDun MGos MRav NHar SBrw SDix SIng SLim SSpi WCot WCru WPGP WPat WWat
x *finnmarchica*	GIBF MBro
¶ *foetida* (f)	GIBF
formosa	See *S. arbuscula*
fragilis	CDul CKin CLnd LBuc MRav NWea WDin WMou WTro
¶ x *fruticosa* 'McElroy'	CWiW
§ *fruticulosa*	CGle CInt GAri GCrs GDra GKir GTou NMen NWCA SMrm WLin WWat
'Fuiri-koriyanagi'	See *S. integra* 'Hakuro-nishiki'

furcata — See *S. fruticulosa*
glauca — CNat
¶ - subsp. *callicarpaea* (f) — GIBF
glaucosericea — EBee WLRN WWat
'Golden Curls' — See *S.* 'Erythroflexuosa'
gracilistyla — CTho EPla WMou WWat
§ - 'Melanostachys' (m) ♀ — CB&S CBot CDul CMHG CSWP
EBee ECtt ELan EPla ERav GChr
GKir LHop MBNS MBar MBlu
MBrN MRav NBea NEgg SPer
SRms STre WCwm WFar WMou
WOak WPat WWat WWin
x *grahamii* (f) — GIBF
- 'Moorei' (f) — NWCA
x *greyi* — NPro
¶ *hastata* (f) — GIBF
- 'Wehrhahnii' (m) ♀ — More than 30 suppliers
helvetica ♀ — More than 30 suppliers
herbacea — ESis GAri GIBF GTou NMen WPer
hibernica — See *S. phylicifolia*
x *hirtei* 'Reifenweide' (f) — GChr
hookeriana — CMHG CTho ELan EPla MBlu
MRav NHol SLPl SSpi WMou
WWat
humilis var. *microphylla* — CBlo
incana — See *S. elaeagnos*
integra 'Albomaculata' — See *S. integra* 'Hakuro-nishiki'
§ - 'Hakuro-nishiki' (v) — More than 30 suppliers
- 'Pendula' (f) — LRHS WGer
irrorata — CDul CLnd IOrc NSti WMou
'Jacquinii' — See *S. alpina*
japonica hort. — See *S. babylonica* 'Lavalleei'
kinuyanagi (m) — ELan EPla SMrm
§ *koriyanagi* — CWiW
¶ 'Kumeti' — CWiW
'Kuro-me' — See *S. gracilistyla* 'Melanostachys'
¶ 'Lady Aldenham No.2' — ERav
¶ x *laestadiana* — GIBF
lanata ♀ — More than 30 suppliers
- hybrid — MBro NHol WPat
- Kew form — Last listed 1997
- 'Mark Postill' — See *S.* 'Mark Postill'
- 'Stuartii' — See *S.* 'Stuartii'
lapponum — GAri GChr GIBF MBro NWCA
SRms WPat
¶ - (m) — GIBF
¶ - var. *daphneola* (f) — GIBF
¶ - - (m) — GIBF
liliputa — See *S. turczaninowii*
§ *lindleyana* — CNic GAri NMen NOak NSti
WWat
'Maerd Brno' (f) — MBlu
magnifica ♀ — CEnd CFil CLnd CMCN CPle EBee
EPar EPfP EPla IDee MSte SDry
SLim SMad SSpi SWat WCru WHer
WMou
§ 'Mark Postill' (f) — CDoC LFis MBNS SPla
matsudana 'Tortuosa' — See *S. babylonica* var. *pekinensis*
'Tortuosa'
- 'Tortuosa Aureopendula' — See *S.* 'Erythroflexuosa'
'Melanostachys' — See *S. gracilistyla* 'Melanostachys'
¶ x *meyeriana* 'Lumley' (f) — CWiW
¶ x *mollissima* var. — CWiW
hippophaifolia
'Jeffries'
¶ - - 'Notts Spaniard' (f) — CWiW
¶ - - 'Trustworthy' (f) — CWiW
¶ - var. *undulata* — CWiW
'Kottenheider Weide'
moupinensis — IOrc WMou
§ *myrsinifolia* — EPla GChr MBlu MRav
§ *myrsinites* — GIBF

- var. *jacquiniana* — See *S. alpina*
myrtilloides — CLyd
- 'Pink Tassels' (m) — MBlu NWCA SIng WPat
- x *repens* — See *S.* x *finnmarchica*
nakamurana — CFai CFee GAri GIBF LRHS MAsh
var. *yezoalpina* — MBro MRav NHol NPro SRms
WPat WPyg WWat
nepalensis — See *S. lindleyana*
nigricans — See *S. myrsinifolia*
nivalis — See *S. reticulata* subsp. *nivalis*
¶ x *obtusifolia* — GIBF
* 'Onoga' — Last listed 1998
'Onusta' (m) — Last listed 1997
¶ *onychiophylla* (f) — GIBF
x *ovata* — CLyd GCrs NMen
§ x *pendulina* — CTho
var. *elegantissima*
pentandra — CBot CDul CKin GChr IOrc
NWea WDin WMou WWat
¶ - 'Patent Lumley' — CWiW
¶ 'Philip's Fancy' — NWCA
§ *phylicifolia* — CNat GChr WMou
¶ - 'Malham' — CWiW
polaris — CLyd GAri GIBF
§ x *punctata* — GIBF
§ *purpurea* — CB&S CDul GChr IOrc MBrN
NWea SRms WDin WMou
¶ - 'Brittany Green' (f) — CWiW
¶ - 'Continental Reeks' — CWiW
¶ - 'Dark Dicks' (f) — CWiW
- 'Dicky Meadows' — CAgr CWiW
* - 'Elegantissima' — CWiW
- 'Goldstones' — CAgr CWiW
- f. *gracilis* — See *S. purpurea* 'Nana'
- 'Green Dicks' — CAgr CWiW
- 'Helix' — See *S. purpurea*
- 'Howki' — WMou
¶ - 'Irette' (m) — CWiW
¶ - 'Jagiellonka' (f) — CWiW
- var. *japonica* — See *S. koriyanagi*
¶ - subsp. *lambertiana* — CWiW
¶ - 'Lancashire Dicks' (m) — CWiW
¶ - 'Leicestershire Dicks' (m) — CWiW
¶ - 'Light Dicks' — CWiW
¶ - 'Lincolnshire Dutch' — CWiW
§ - 'Nana' — CLTr CLyd CPle ELan EPfP EPla
GKir MWhi SChu SLPl SPan STre
WTro WWat
- 'Nancy Saunders' (f) — CSpe CTho CWiW EHoe EPPr
EPla GBuc MBNS MBlu MRav
MSte MWhi NPro NSti SUsu WCot
WSHC
- 'Pendula' ♀ — CBlo CEnd CTho EBee ENot
GOrc LRHS MAsh MBar MBri
MRav NWCA NWea WDin WStI
¶ - 'Read' — CWiW
¶ - 'Reeks' — CWiW
- 'Richartii' (f) — CWiW NSti WLRN
¶ - 'Uralensis' (f) — CWiW
pyrenaica — CLyd EWes GIBF NWCA
repens — GAri GIBF MBar SRms STre SWat
WDin
§ - var. *argentea* ♀ — CGle EBee ENot EPfP GDra GIBF
IOrc MBar MRav MWhi SPer
WDin WWat WWin
- from Saint Kilda — GCrs GKir MBro
- 'Iona' (m) — CBlo CLyd SIng WStI
- *pendula* — See *S.* 'Boyd's Pendulous' (m)
- 'Voorthuizen' (f) — EBee ESis MBar WGer WPyg WStI
reticulata ♀ — GCrs GDra GIBF GKir GTou NHar
NMen NRya NWoo WPat
§ - subsp. *nivalis* — EPot GIBF NWCA

retusa	CTri GAri GDra GGar GIBF GKir GTou MBro NHar NMen WPat WPyg
- x *pyrenaica*	ECho
rosmarinifolia hort.	See *S. elaeagnos* subsp. *angustifolia*
x *rubens* 'Basfordiana' (m) ♀	CDoC CLnd CTho CWiW EPla EWes GChr LNor MBNS MRav NWea SLon WLRN WMou
¶ - 'Bouton Aigu'	CWiW
¶ - 'Farndon'	CWiW
¶ - 'Flanders Red'	CWiW
¶ - 'Fransgeel Rood'	CWiW
¶ - 'Glaucescens'	CWiW
¶ - 'Golden Willow'	CWiW
¶ - 'Jaune de Falaise'	CWiW
¶ - 'Jaune Hâtive'	CWiW
¶ - 'Laurina'	CWiW
¶ - 'Natural Red'	CWiW
¶ - 'Parsons'	CWiW
¶ - 'Rouge Ardennais'	CWiW
¶ - 'Rouge Folle'	CWiW
¶ - 'Russet'	CWiW
¶ x *rubra*	CWiW
¶ - 'Abbey's Harrison'	CWiW
¶ - 'Continental Osier'	CWiW
- 'Eugenei' (m)	CDul EPla GChr GQui MBlu SWat WBcn WMou WWat WWin
¶ - 'Fidkin'	CWiW
¶ - 'Harrison's'	CWiW
¶ - 'Harrison's Seedling A' (f)	CWiW
¶ - 'Mawdesley'	CWiW
¶ - 'Mawdesley Seedling A' (f)	CWiW
¶ - 'Pyramidalis'	CWiW
schwerinii	CWiW
'Carin Ehrenberg'	
x *sepulcralis*	CDul NWea
—'Caradoc'	CWiW
§ - var. *chrysocoma* ♀	CDoC EBee ENot EPfP GAri GKir LBuc LHyr LPan LRHS MAsh MGos MWat NBee SCoo SLim SPer SRPl WLRN
serpyllifolia	CLyd CTri ESis MBro NHol NMen WPat WPyg
¶ - (f)	GIBF
- x *retusa*	NWCA
serpyllum	See *S. fruticulosa*
'Setsuka'	See *S. udensis* 'Sekka'
x *simulatrix*	CLyd GAri GIBF MBar NWCA WWat
¶ x *sobrina*	GIBF
x *stipularis* (f)	CLnd CMHG EPla GChr NWea
§ 'Stuartii'	GIBF GOrc MBar NMen NWCA SRms
subopposita	CDul EBee ELan EWes GOrc MBNS MBar MBlu NPro SIng WWat
¶ x *tetrapla*	GIBF
- 'Hutchinson's Nigricans'	Last listed 1998
thomasii	GIBF
triandra	WMou
¶ - 'Black German'	CWiW
- 'Black Hollander'	CAgr CWiW
- 'Black Maul'	CAgr CWiW
¶ - 'Grisette de Falaise'	CWiW
¶ - 'Grisette Droda'	CWiW
¶ - 'Long Bud'	CWiW
¶ - 'Noir de Challans'	CWiW
¶ - 'Noir de Touraine'	CWiW
¶ - 'Noir de Villaines'	CWiW
¶ - 'Sarda d'Anjou'	CWiW
- 'Semperflorens'	CNat

- 'Whissander'	CAgr CWiW
x *tsugaluensis* 'Ginme' (f)	CDul CMHG SLPl WTro WWat
§ *turczaninowii* (m)	GIBF
§ *udensis* 'Sekka' (m)	CB&S CLnd CMHG CTho ECtt ELan EPar EPla GChr IOrc NHol NWea STre SWat WMou WPyg
uva-ursi	CLyd GAri GIBF SLim
viminalis	CAgr CDul CKin CLnd ENot GChr LBuc NWea WDin WMou
- 'Bowles' Hybrid'	See *S.* 'Bowles' Hybrid'
- 'Brown Merrin'	CAgr
¶ - 'Green Gotz'	CWiW
- 'Reader's Red' (m)	CAgr
- 'Yellow Osier'	CAgr
violescens	Last listed 1997
vitellina 'Pendula'	See *S. alba* 'Tristis'
§ *waldsteiniana*	GIBF MBar
x *wimmeriana*	SRms
'Yelverton'	EPla LRHS MBri MRav SWat

SALVIA ✿ (Lamiaceae)

acetabulosa	See *S. multicaulis*
aethiopis	CPle CSev EOld LGre MLLN MSte WPer WWye
afghanica	CPle MRav
§ *africana*	CPle LPio WDyG WWye
africana-caerulea	See *S. africana*
africana-lutea	See *S. aurea*
agnes	CPle
albimaculata	SBla
algeriensis	CPle
amarissima	CPle CStr
ambigens	See *S. guaranitica* 'Blue Enigma'
§ *amplexicaulis*	CPle WPer WWye
angustifolia Michaux	See *S. azurea*
- Cavanilles	See *S. reptans*
apiana	EOHP SAga WCot
argentea ♀	More than 30 suppliers
arizonica	CPle CStr EBee GCal LIck MLLN MRod
atrocyanea	CPle CStr GBri LHil MLLN MRod SLod SSoC
aucheri	CPle EGar GBar GBuc GCal
§ *aurea*	CHal CPle CSev CStr EBee EGar ELan LHil LPio MHar MHer MMil SAga WCot WDyG WPer
¶ - 'Kirstenbosch'	CPle CStr MLLN MRav WCot WPer WWye
austriaca	CPle EBee GBri MBel SHFr WPer
§ *azurea*	CArn CPle EBee LGre LPio MNrw MSte SMrm
¶ - var. *grandiflora*	CPle CStr
bacheriana	See *S. buchananii*
§ *barrelieri*	CPle CStr EMan MRod NChi SHFr SLod
'Belhaven'	Last listed 1998
bertolonii	See *S. pratensis* Bertolonii Group
bicolor Desfontaines	See *S. barrelieri*
blancoana	CArn CBot CPle CStr EBee ECha ELau EMan GBar LEdu LHop MHer MLLN MSCN MSte MWgw NChi SAga SCro
blepharophylla	CPle CSev CSpe CStr EBee EOrc GBri LHil LHop LIck MHer MSte MWat SAga SOkh SSoC WGwG WPen WWoo WWye
'Blue Bird'	Last listed 1997
brachyantha	CPle EGar
broussonetii	Last listed 1998
§ *buchananii* ♀	CHad CHal CLon CPle CSWP CSam CStr ELan EOrc ERea GBri GQui LHop LIck MHer SAga SCro

Name	Suppliers / Notes
	SMrm SRCN SSoC SUsu WPnn WWol
¶ *bulleyana*	EMan MHer WCru
- misapplied	See *S. flava* var. *megalantha*
cacaliifolia ♀	CLTr CLon CPle CRHN CSpe CStr EBlw EEls EOrc GBri LHil MHar MHer MLLN MNrw MSte MWat SAga SHFr SPer SSoC SUsu WCot WEas WSHC WWye
caerulea hort.	See *S. guaranitica* 'Black and Blue'
- L.	See *S. africana*
caespitosa	CPle NWCA SBla SIng WLin
campanulata	CPle EBee
- CC&McK 1071	CFir
aff. *campanulata* ACE 2379	Last listed 1997
canariensis	CPle CStr LHil MLLN MSte SAga SHFr WSPU WSan WWye
* - f. *alba*	Last listed 1999
- f. *candidissima*	Last listed 1999
candelabrum ♀	CArn CLon CMea CMil CPle EMan EOrc GBri LGre MHer MRod MWgw SDix SHFr SSoC WCHb WCot WHer WKif WSHC WWye
candidissima	Last listed 1998
canescens	Last listed 1998
cardinalis	See *S. fulgens*
carduacea	Last listed 1998
castanea	CPle EBee EBrP EBre GBri LBCl LBSe LBre MBBe SBre SSoC
§ *chamaedryoides*	CPle CStr MHer SAga WWye
- silver	CSpe LGre LHil MRod MSte
chapalensis	CPle SAga
chiapensis	CPle EOrc
chinensis	See *S. japonica*
'Christine Yeo'	CPle EBee GBri Llck MRod SDys
cinnabarina	CPle CStr
cleistogama DeBarry & Paul	MHer
- misapplied	See *S. glutinosa*
clevelandii	CArn CPle MHer MRod
coabuilensis	LGre SAga SMrm SUsu WSHC WWye
coccinea	CBot CGle CPle EWTr GBri MHer MSte NBus SHFr WPer
- 'Coral Nymph'	CPle ELan EMan EOrc Llck LRHS SDys SLod SSoC SWat
- 'Desert Blaze' (v)	NDov
* - 'Indigo'	CMGP EGar ELan EPfP GBri MTis WSan
- 'Lactea'	CBot
- 'Lady in Red' ♀	EOrc Llck MRod SMrm SWat
- pink	Last listed 1998
* - 'Snow Nymph'	Llck
columbariae	Last listed 1998
compacta	Last listed 1998
concolor Lamb.	CPle CStr GCal LHil WDyG WSHC
- hort.	See *S. guaranitica*
confertiflora	CAbb CHal CPle CSam CSev CStr CTbh CWit ELan EOrc EWTr GBri LHil Llck MLLN MSCN MSte SAga SDys SLod SMrm SSoC WElm WWye
corrugata	CPle CSpe CStr EBee EPri GBri LGre LHil MTis SAga SCro SDys SVen WDyG WSPU WWye
cryptantha	CPle CStr
cyanescens	CPle EBee EPot
darcyi	CPle EBee LGre MRod SVen WPen WWye
davidsonii	Last listed 1999
'Dear Anja'	EFou LGre
digitaloides	CPle GBin WCot
discolor ♀	CBot CHad CPle CSev CSpe CStr EBee ELan ERea GQui LEdu LHil LHop Llck LPio MBNS MHer MLLN MSCN MTho MTis SRCN SSoC WCHb WWol WWye
* - *nigra*	CMdw
disermas	CPle CStr SPlb WHil
divinorum	EOHP GPoy
- palatable strain	Last listed 1998
dolichantha	Last listed 1999
dolomitica	Last listed 1999
dombeyi	CFir MRod
dominica	Last listed 1999
dorisiana	CPle CPne CSev CStr ELan EOHP MSte SVen WJek
dorrii var. *dorrii*	Last listed 1999
eigii	Last listed 1998
§ *elegans*	CMHG CPle CSev CStr ELau EPri EWes Llck MHar MSCN MSte SCro SLon SSoC WCer WCot WWye
- 'Frieda Dixon'	CPle EOHP
- prostrate	Last listed 1999
§ - 'Scarlet Pineapple'	More than 30 suppliers
* - 'Tangerine Sage'	CArn ELau EOHP GBar MHer MMal SRCN WBry WGwG WOak
eremostachya	CStr
fallax	Last listed 1999
farinacea	Last listed 1999
- 'Alba'	Last listed 1998
- 'Blue Victory' ♀	Last listed 1995
¶ - 'Cirrus'	NArg
- 'Rhea'	Llck LRHS
- 'Silver'	MRod
- 'Strata'	CPle LRHS
- 'Victoria' ♀	CPle ELau LPVe MHer
- 'White Victory' ♀	Last listed 1995
§ *flava* var. *megalantha*	CFai CGle CHea CPle CSev EBee ELan EOrc GBin LRHS MFir MNrw NChi NGdn NSti SHFr SSoC SSte WFar WOve WPer WWin WWye
¶ *forreri*	WOut
- CD&R 1269	CPle CStr GBri
§ *forsskaolii*	More than 30 suppliers
frigida	Last listed 1998
§ *fruticosa*	CArn CPle CStr ELau EOHP LRHS SIde
§ *fulgens* ♀	CGle CPle CSev CStr CWit ILis LHil MHer NBro SAga SHFr SSoC WCHb WCot WEas WKif WWhi WWye
* x *geradit*	NBir
gesneriiflora	CAbb CPle CSev MHer MSCN MSte SMrm WGwG WPer WWye
§ *glutinosa*	CArn CHad CPle CSam EBee ELan EOrc EPPr GCal MBel MCAu MNrw NBro NCat NHex NSti SAga SSoC WOut WPer WWye
- HH&K 294	Last listed 1999
grahamii	See *S. microphylla* var. *microphylla*
greggii	CPle EWes LPio MHer MSCN MSte SAga SPer SWat WOve WPer WWin
- 'Alba'	CHal CPle LHop Llck NGHP WHil
- 'Blush Pink'	See *S. microphylla* 'Pink Blush'
- CD&R 1148	CPle LHop Llck SDys
- 'Devon Cream'	See *S. greggii* 'Sungold'
- 'Keter's Red'	CPle MRod
§ - x *lycioides*	CPle CSev LHil LHop LPio SAga SSoC SUsu WDyG WSHC

- 'Peach' ♀	CPle CSpe EBee ELau EPfP EWes LHil LPio MHer MLLN MSte NBrk NPri SAga SOkh STes WAbe WPnn WSHC WWol WWye
- 'Peach' misapplied	See *S.* x *jamensis* 'Pat Vlasto'
- 'Raspberry Royal'	See *S.* 'Raspberry Royale'
¶ - 'Sparkler Cream'	LHil
¶ - 'Sundown'	NGHP
§ - 'Sungold'	CAbP CFai CPle CStr LIck LRHS SDys WWol
- yellow	LPio LRHS
§ *guaranitica* ♀	CAbb CBot CGle CPle CSpe EBrP EBre LBCl LBSe LBre LPio MBBe MHer MRav SAga SBre SPer SRCN SRPl SUsu WCHb WEas WSan
- 'Argentine Skies'	CLon CPle CSpe CStr EBee LHil LPio SDys SMrm SOkh WSHC WWye
§ - 'Black and Blue'	CGle CLTr CPle CRHN CSWP CSev CStr EPPr GBri LIck MSCN MSte MWat SGar SMrm SSoC SVen WPer WPnn WWye
§ - 'Blue Enigma' ♀	More than 30 suppliers
haematodes	See *S. pratensis* Haematodes Group
beldreichiana	Last listed 1999
henryi	CPle CStr
bians	CFir CFri CGle CHal CPle EBee ECoo EOrc GBri MBro MNrw NWoo SAga SRms SSoC SSte WBor WCer WCot WHoo WOve WPer WPyg WWye
bierosolymitana	CPle CStr SHFr SUsu
birtella	Last listed 1999
bispanica hort.	See *S. lavandulifolia*
- L.	CPle
borminum	See *S. viridis*
bypargeia	CPle EBee ECGN
indica	CPle SRms
'Indigo Spires' ♀	CLon CMdw CPle CStr EBee EPPr GBri LGre LHil MLLN MRod SAga SMrm SOkh SUsu WDyG WPen WSHC WWye
interrupta	CPle ECha EHol EMan EOHP EWes LFis SAga SChu WPen
involucrata ♀	CFir CPle CSev EBee EOrc GCal GQui LHil MHer NBro SCob SCro SMrm SRCN WSHC WSpi
- 'Bethellii'	More than 30 suppliers
- 'Boutin' ♀	CPle GBri MLLN
- dark-flowered	MSte
§ - 'Hadspen'	CBot CHad CSam CStr LIck MRod
- 'Mrs Pope'	See *S. involucrata* 'Hadspen'
I - var. *puberula*	CPle
- - 'El Butano'	Last listed 1999
iodantha	CPle WWye
x *jamensis*	LHil
- 'Cherry Queen'	CPle CStr SAga WWye
- 'Devantville'	CPle CSam CSev EPri LGre LHil LHop LPio MSCN MSte SAga SLod WPen WPnn WSHC WSpi WWye
- 'El Duranzo'	CPle LGre LPio
- 'Fuego'	CPle
- 'James Compton'	EBee LHil LPio MSte SHFr
- 'La Luna'	CLon CPle CSam CSev EPri LGre LHil LHop LPio MSCN MSte SAga SLod WPen WPnn WSHC WSpi WWye
- 'La Siesta'	CPle CSev LPio SAga WPnn
- 'La Tarde'	CLon CPle EBee LPio MRod MSte SAga
- 'Los Lirios' ♀	CMea CPle GBri LIck SLod SMrm
- 'Moonlight Serenade'	CPle CSev CStr GBri MRod
§ - 'Pat Vlasto'	CLon CPle GBri LGre LIck MSte SAga SMrm WEas WPen WSHC WWye
- pink seedling	Last listed 1997
- 'Pleasant Pink'	CPle EBee LHil
§ *japonica*	CPle WWye
judaica	CPle CStr EBee MLLN NChi
jurisicii	CFir CPle CStr EBee EOrc EWll MBro MLLN SHFr SMrm SSca SUsu WPyg WSHC WWye
karwinskyi	Last listed 1998
keerlii	Last listed 1998
koyamae	Last listed 1998
kuznetzovii	EBee
lanceolata	See *S. reflexa*
§ *lavandulifolia*	More than 30 suppliers
- pink	Last listed 1997
lemmonii	See *S. microphylla* var. *wislizenii*
leptophylla	See *S. reptans*
leucantha ♀	More than 30 suppliers
- 'Purple Velvet'	CPle GBri SDys
leucophylla	CStr MHer MRod SLon
longispicata	CPle
lycioides hort.	See *S. greggii* x *lycioides*
- A. Gray	CPle SDys
lyrata	CFri CPle EBee EMan EOHP GBri MSal MSph SHFr STes SUsu WOut WWye
¶ - 'Purple Knockout'	EMar EPPr SMrm WHil WPer
¶ *macellaria*	CSam
- misapplied	See *S. microphylla*
- yellow form	Last listed 1998
¶ *macrosiphon*	WWye
madrensis	CPle
'Maraschino'	WCot
marocana	Last listed 1999
mellifera	CArn CPle
merjamie	CPle EBee
- 'Mint-sauce'	CElw CFri CPla ECGP EMan MCCP MNrw MWrn NChi NPro SHFr WBea WPer WPrP
mexicana	CPle GBri LHil
- var. *minor*	CPle GBri LHop WPer
- T&K 550	CBot
§ *microphylla*	CArn CGle CLTr CMHG CPle CWit ELau EOHP EOrc EWes GBar LHil MChe MMal MSCN NFai SHFr SOkh SYvo WCru WHCG WPer
- 'Cerro Potosi'	CLon CMdw CPle CSev CStr EBee GBri LHil MRod SAga SHFr SMrm WPen
* - 'Huntingdon Red'	ELau EOHP
- 'Kew Red' ♀	CPle CStr SAga
- 'La Foux'	CHea CPle LGre LHil SDys SMrm
- 'Maraschino'	See *S.* 'Maraschino'
§ - var. *microphylla*	CFee CGle CHal CPle CRHN CSev CStr EBee ELan GCHN LGre LRHS MNrw MTho NTow SAga SDry SHFr SMrm SOWG SPer WCHb WCru WEas WPer WPnn WSHC WWat WWye
¶ - - 'La Foux'	MRod
- - 'Newby Hall' ♀	CBrm CPle CStr EBee LHil MBel MSte WPGP WPer
- var. *neurepia*	See *S. microphylla* var. *microphylla*
- 'Oregon Peach'	LRHS MAsh
- 'Oxford'	CPle CStr LFis
§ - 'Pink Blush' ♀	CAbP CBot CPle EBee ELan EMan EOrc EPri GBri LHil LRHS MAsh

	MLLN MMil MRod MSte NGHP
	SMrm SSpi WOve WSHC
- 'Pleasant View' ♀	CPle GBri
- purple	EBee GCal
* - 'Raspberry Ice'	LRHS
§ - 'Ruth Stungo' (v)	CPle SAga
- 'Trebah'	CTbh MMil MRod SGar
- 'Trelissick'	MMil MRod WWoo
- 'Trenance'	WWoo
- 'Trewithen'	Last listed 1999
- 'Variegata' splashed	See S. microphylla 'Ruth Stungo'
§ - var. wislizenii	CPle CStr SCro WPer
microstegia	Last listed 1998
miltiorbiza	CArn EOHP
miniata	CPle CStr SUsu
moorcroftiana	CFri CPle WPer
muelleri	CSpe MRod MSCN
§ multicaulis ♀	CPle CStr ECha EMan GCal MRav
	MSCN NTow WPer WSHC
munzii	CStr
* murrayi	WCot
napifolia	CStr EBee LGre SUsu
nemorosa	EBee EBrP EBre LBCl LBSe LBre
	MBBe NLar SBre SHFr SRms
- 'Amethyst' ♀	CElw CHal CLon CPle CPlt CStr
	EFou EGle GBri LGre LRHS MBel
	MBri MLLN MRod SAga SChu
	SDys SHel SMrm WCot
- 'Brightness'	Last listed 1999
- East Friesland	See S. nemorosa 'Ostfriesland'
- HH&K 246	Last listed 1999
- 'Lubecca' ♀	CPle EBee EBrP EBre EFou EGle
	EMan EPfP LBCl LBSe LBre LRHS
	MBBe MLLN MMil NCat SBre SMrm
	SOkh SPer SUsu WLRN WRus
§ - 'Ostfriesland' ♀	More than 30 suppliers
- 'Plumosa'	See S. nemorosa 'Pusztaflamme'
¶ - 'Porzellan' ♀	SHel
§ - 'Pusztaflamme' ♀	CHad CStr EBee ECha EMan LGre
	LRHS MBri MBro MCLN MLLN
	MMil SBla SCro SHel SMrm WCot
	WHoo WWye
- 'Rose Queen'	GKir SAga
- 'Rosenwein'	EBee GBuc LGre SMrm
§ - subsp. tesquicola	ECha EGle
- 'Wesuwe'	CPle ECha EGle
neurepia	See S. microphylla var.
	microphylla
nilotica	CPle EBee EWll SHFr WHer WOut
nipponica	CPle WPer
- 'Fuji Snow' (v)	EFou EWes GBri NPro WCot WHil
nubicola	CPle CStr GPoy SLod WWye
nutans	Last listed 1998
officinalis	CAgr CArn CChe CHal EBee EDAr
	ELau EWTr GBar GPoy LRHS
	MBar MBri MChe MGos MHer
	MMal MWat NFor NPri SHFr SPlb
	SRCN SRPl WDin WGwG WOak
	WPer WWat WWye
- 'Alba'	See S. officinalis 'Albiflora'
§ - 'Albiflora'	CBot COIW CPle ECha EOHP
	GBar LLWP MHer MLLN SIde
	WPer
N - 'Aurea'	CCHH EDAr EPar GPoy MBar MFir
	NFla NPri SUsu
- 'Berggarten'	CArn ECha EFou EGar ELau EMan
	EOHP EPPr EPri GBar GCal LGre
	LHop LPio MRav SAga SSvw WBry
	WCFE WHer WLin
	NPri WGwG
I - 'Blackcurrant'	CBot CSWP ELau MHer MLLN
§ - broad-leaved	SIde SWat WGwG WJek WWye

- 'Cedric'	Last listed 1998
¶ - 'Extrakta'	EOHP
* - 'Giant'	Last listed 1999
I - 'Ginger'	Last listed 1998
- 'Grandiflora'	Last listed 1998
- 'Grete Stolze'	Last listed 1999
- 'Herrenhausen'	CPle MSte WPen
§ - 'Icterina' (v) ♀	More than 30 suppliers
- 'Kew Gold' ♀	EGar ELau EMon GBar MRav
	WJek
- latifolia	See S. officinalis broad-leaved
- 'Minor'	EGoo MHar WHer
* - 'Minor Alba'	WHil
- narrow-leaved	See S. lavandulifolia
* - 'Pink Splash' (v)	WCHb
- prostrata	See S. lavandulifolia
¶ - 'Purpurascens' ♀	More than 30 suppliers
- 'Purpurascens Variegata'	CStr GBar NSti WEas WJek
- 'Robin Hill'	CBod GBar
- 'Rosea'	CPle CStr GBar IIve
- 'Selsley Splash'	Last listed 1998
* - tangerine	EDAr NPri
- Tomentosa Group	CArn
- 'Tricolor' (v) ♀	More than 30 suppliers
- 'Variegata'	See S. officinalis 'Icterina'
oppositiflora ♀	CPle MLLN MRod
oresbia	Last listed 1997
pachyphylla	Last listed 1999
patens ♀	More than 30 suppliers
- 'Alba' misapplied	See S. patens 'White Trophy'
- 'Blue Trophy'	LIck
- 'Cambridge Blue' ♀	More than 30 suppliers
- 'Chilcombe'	CPle CSam CStr EBlw GBri
	LHil LHop LIck MBel MSCN
	SAga SChu SCro SDys SHFr SSoC
	SUsu WHoo WPer WPnn
	WSHC
- 'Guanajuato'	CPle CSam CStr LGre LHil MHar
	MRod SMrm WHil WSHC
- 'Oxford Blue'	See S. patens
- 'Royal Blue'	See S. patens
§ - 'White Trophy'	CLon CPle CStr ELan EOrc EPri
	LHop LIck LRHS SAga SCro SLod
	SPer WRus WSHC WWol WWye
'Peaches and Cream'	Last listed 1997
penstemonoides	Last listed 1998
polystachya	CPle MRod WWye
populifolia	Last listed 1997
pratensis	CArn CKin CLon CPle ECoo ELan
	EMon LPio LRHS MNaF MSal
	NChi WPer WWye
- 'Albiflora'	EBee EMon LRHS SSvw
§ - Bertolonii Group	CPle MBel SEND
§ - Haematodes Group ♀	CHad COIW CPle EBee EBrP EBre
	ECha ELan LBCl LBSe LBre MBBe
	MBel MBro MNrw NBro NBus
	NLar SBre SRms WHoo WOve
	WPer WPyg WWye
- 'Indigo' ♀	EBrP EBre EFou EWll LBCl LBSe
	LBre LRHS MBBe MRav NLar SBre
- 'Lapis Lazuli'	CPle CPlt CStr EBee LGre WPGP
- 'Rosea'	CPle EBrP EBre LBCl LBSe LBre
	LRHS MBBe SBre WWye
	WPer
- 'Tenorei'	Last listed 1997
prostrata	CBel CPle CStr EGar MNrw MSal
przewalskii	NChi SHFr SSoC SUsu WOut WPer
	WWye
- ACE 1157	EBee WCot WCru
- CLD 247	Last listed 1998
¶ - DJH 210524	EPPr
pulchella	Last listed 1998

'Purple Majesty' — CLon CPle CStr GBri LPio SDys WWye

purpurea — CM&M CPle WShe

§ 'Raspberry Royale' ♀ — CLon CPle CSev ELan EPfP EPri EWoo LHil LHop LIck LRHS MAsh MBel MHer MSte NGHP SAga SGar SMrm SUsu SWal SWat WPen WRus WSHC WWol WWoo WWye

recognita — CBot CPle EBee GCal LGre

§ *reflexa* — Last listed 1998

regeliana hort. — See *S. virgata* Jacq.

- Trautv. — CHar CPle EGar MLLN NBir NChi WPer WRha

regla — CPle CStr

repens — CPle CStr WWye

- var. *repens* — WHil

§ *reptans* — CPle CSam CSpe LIck MHar SAga SLod SUsu WDyG WPer

ringens — CPle GCHN

§ *riparia* — CPle CStr MLLN MRod SUsu

roborowskii — Last listed 1999

roemeriana ♀ — CPle EBee EOrc NWCA WCru

¶ *rugosa* — CStr

rutilans — See *S. elegans* 'Scarlet Pineapple'

'San Antonio' — Last listed 1997

scabiosifolia — MRod

scabra — CFir CPle CStr WOut

sclarea — CArn CGle CPle EBee EBrP EBre EGoo ELau EWTr GPoy LBCl LBSe LBre LRHS MBBe MChe MHer MWat NChi NFai SBre SIde SRCN WCHb WHer WHoo WOak WPer WWye

* - 'Alba' — ECoo EOHP SUsu

§ - var. *sclarea* — More than 30 suppliers

N - var. *turkestanica* — See *S. sclarea* var. *sclarea*

§ - 'Vatican White' — CPle EBee EBrP EBre EMar GKir LBCl LBSe LBre MBBe SBre

- white-bracted — WSHC

scutellarioides — Last listed 1999

semiatrata Zucc. — CPle CSpe SUsu WWye

- hort. — See *S. chamaedryoides*

sinaloensis — CFai CPle MSte NCut

somalensis — CPle CStr EOHP

sonomensis — CPle

sp. ACE 2172 — Last listed 1997

sp. CC&McK 77 — GTou

sp. from Iran — Last listed 1998

spathacea ♀ — CPle LGre WWye

spinosa — Last listed 1998

splendens — Last listed 1998

§ - 'Van-Houttei' ♀ — CPle CStr MLLN MRod SDys SUsu SMrm

sprucei — Last listed 1998

squalens — Last listed 1998

§ *staminea* — CPle EBee EWTr MNrw NCut SHFr STes WPer WWye

stenophylla — CPle EBee WGwG WPer

stepposa — CPle EBee

x *superba* ♀ — CBot CGle CPle EBee EBrP EBre ELan EOrc LBCl LBSe LBre LEdu LRHS MBBe MBri MBro MWat SBre SCro SDix SMrm SPer SRCN SRms SSpe SSvw WCot WHoo WWhi WWye

- 'Adrian' — EFou SChu

- 'Forncett Dawn' — CStr EBee EFou EGle SChu

- 'Rubin' ♀ — CBos CStr EBee EFou SChu SMrm

- 'Superba' — CSev ECha EFou EHrv LGre SCro

x *sylvestris* 'Blauhügel' ♀ — More than 30 suppliers

§ - 'Blaukönigin' — CGle EBee EWTr GCHN GChr GKir LFis LNor LRHS MBro MWat NArg NCat NLar NMir NOak SCob SPar SPlb WBea WHil WPer WPyg

- Blue Queen — See *S.* x *sylvestris* 'Blaukönigin'

- 'Lye End' — ECtt GCal MRav WCot

§ - 'Mainacht' ♀ — More than 30 suppliers

- May Night — See *S.* x *sylvestris* 'Mainacht'

- 'Rose Queen' — CLon CPle EBee ECGN ECha ECoo ECtt EFou ELan EPfP GCHN GChr GKir LFis LRHS MCLN MSte NFla NOak NOrc SCoo SUsu WBea WHoo WPer WPyg WRus

- 'Rügen' — CStr EBee LBuc LRHS MBri WRus

- 'Schneehügel' (v) — EBee ECha EGle EMan EPfP GMaP MBNS MCAu MMil SAga SCro SHel SPer SUsu WLRN WWat WWye

- 'Tänzerin' ♀ — EFou EGle LGre NChi SChu SDys SMrm WCot

- 'Viola Klose' — CMGP CMil CStr EBee EFou EGle EMan EMar GKir LGre LRHS MBri SUsu

- 'Wissalink' — SMad SUsu

tachiei hort. — See *S. forsskaolii*

taraxacifolia — CPle CStr MRod

tarayensis — Last listed 1998

tesquicola — See *S. nemorosa* subsp. *tesquicola*

tiliifolia — CPle EBee SHFr SRms

tingitana — Last listed 1999

tomentosa — CPle EBee WCot

§ - HH&K 210 — Last listed 1999

transcaucasica — See *S. staminea*

transsylvanica — CArn CBel CHea CPle EBee EOrc EPPr EWll LRHS MBct MCAu MWgw NChi STes SWat WCFE WCot WPer

'Trelawney' — Last listed 1999

trijuga — Last listed 1999

triloba — See *S. fruticosa*

uliginosa ♀ — More than 30 suppliers

- 'African Skies' — NBrk WDyG

urica — CStr

'Van-Houttei' — See *S. splendens* 'Van-Houttei'

'Vatican City' — See *S. sclarea* 'Vatican White'

verbenaca — CArn CKin CPle EGar EWFC GCHN MHer MHew MNrw MSal NMir SWal WOut WPer WWye

- pink — Last listed 1998

verticillata — CArn CPle CStr EBee ECha EGoo EOld EPri LRHS MBro NFor SDys WOve WPer WWye

- 'Alba' — CLTr CMGP CPle CSev EBee ECGN ECha EGle EOrc EPfP LRHS MBel MCAu MGed NGdn NSti SCob SRPl WHer WPer WRus

- subsp. *amasiaca* — Last listed 1999

- HH&K 253 — Last listed 1997

- HH&K 267 — Last listed 1999

- HH&K 342 — Last listed 1997

- 'Purple Rain' — More than 30 suppliers

- 'White Rain' — EFou

¶ 'Vicki Romo' — MRod

villicaulis — See *S. amplexicaulis*

§ *virgata* Jacq. — CFri CPle LCot MBro MNrw WOut WPer WWye

§ *viridis* — CArn CPle EMar MChe SIde WJek

- var. *alba* — Last listed 1998

viscosa Sesse & Moc. — See *S. riparia*

- Jacquin — CPle CStr WSan WWye

wagneriana — Last listed 1998

xalapensis — Last listed 1999

SALVINIA (Salviniaceae)
* **braziliensis** LGuA

SAMBUCUS ✿ (Caprifoliaceae)
adnata B&SWJ 2252 WCru
- L 864 Last listed 1998
alba 'Variegata' WLRN
caerulea EPfP
canadensis NWea
- 'Adams' (F) Last listed 1998
- 'Aurea' CCHP ERav IOrc MBar NWea
WHar
- 'John's' CAgr
- 'Maxima' EPfP ERav GCal LGre SMad SMrm
- 'York' (F) CAgr
¶ **chinensis** B&SWJ 6542 WCru
coraensis See *S. williamsii* subsp. *coreana*
ebulus CKin CRow GKir SMad
formosana B&SWJ 1543 WCru
§ **javanica** EBee
- B&SWJ 4047 WCru
¶ **miquelii** SMad
nigra CDul CKin ENot GChr GKir GPoy
GTre LBuc MBri MHer NWea SIde
SMrm WMou
- 'Albomarginata' See *S. nigra* 'Marginata'
- 'Albovariegata' (v) CDul SSte WLRN WWeb
* - 'Ardwall' GCal
N - 'Aurea' ♀ CB&S CDul CInt CLnd CRow
EBee ELan EMon ENot EPfP ERav
MBar MRav NFla NWea SPer
WDin WFar WSHC
- 'Aureomarginata' CInt ELan GAri GChr MRav NFor
NSti WCFE WFar
- Black Beauty = 'Gerda' CChe CDoC CMFo CTri CWSG
ELan EMil EMui EPfP GChr GKir
LHop LRHS MBNS MBri MDun·
MGos NEgg NGHP NPro SBrw
SLim SMad SPer SPla WBod WCru
WGer WRHF WWeb
¶ - 'Bradet' CAgr
- 'Cae Rhos Lligwy' WAlt WHer
- 'Cannop' WAlt
- 'Castledean' WAlt
- 'Cool Head' WAlt
- 'Din Dryfol' (v) Last listed 1998
- 'Flex' (v) Last listed 1998
* - 'Frances' CNat WBcn WCot
- 'Godshill' CAgr SDea
- 'Golden Locks' GKir
- 'Greener Later' (v) Last listed 1998
§ - 'Guincho Purple' ♀ More than 30 suppliers
- 'Hadspen' Last listed 1999
- 'Heterophylla' See *S. nigra* 'Linearis'
- 'Ina' CAgr
- f.**laciniata** ♀ CB&S CDul CMHG CRow ELan
EMon EMui EWTr GChr MBlu
MLLN NFor NSti SChu SDix SEas
SLon SPer SSpi SSta WCFE WCot
WSHC
§ - 'Linearis' CFai ELan EPla SPer WWat
- 'Long Tooth' CNat
- 'Luteovariegata' WBcn
- 'Madonna' (v) CMHG EBee EPla EWTr GKir
LRHS MGos MRav MSph NHol
SEas SLim SMad SPer WCot
§ - 'Marginata' (v) CMHG CRow EHoe GChr GEil
IOrc LRHS MBar MBri MGos
MHer MLLN MRav NBid SDix
SLon SPer SRPl WBod WCot WDin
WFar WHar WSHC WWat WWin

- mosaic virus Last listed 1997
- 'Nana' EMon
- 'Pendula' EPla ERav
- 'Plena' (d) EMon EPla MInt WCot
- 'Pulverulenta' (v) CDoC CRow EPar EPla GCal GKir
LHop LRHS MAsh MLLN MRav
NSti SEas SPer WCot WSHC
- 'Purple Pete' CNat
- 'Purpurea' See *S. nigra* 'Guincho Purple'
- 'Pygmy' EPla
- 'Pyramidalis' CPMA EMon EPla MBlu WCot
- 'Sambu' (F) CAgr
- 'Samdal' (F) CAgr
- 'Samidan' (F) CAgr
- 'Samnor' (F) Last listed 1999
- 'Sampo' (F) CAgr
- 'Samyl' (F) CAgr
* - 'Tenuifolia' Last listed 1997
- 'Thundercloud' GKir LRHS MBri MTis NDov NPro
WCot WPat WWhi
- 'Variegata' See *S. nigra* 'Marginata'
- f.**viridis** CAgr CNat
- 'Witches Broom' EMon
racemosa CAgr CDul EPfP GChr NWea
WRha
- 'Aurea' CLnd CTri EHoe GKir
- 'Goldenlocks' MGos NHol NPro SPer WBcn
WPyg
- 'Moerheimii' EPla
- 'Plumosa Aurea' More than 30 suppliers
§ - var. **sieboldiana** EMon
- 'Sutherland Gold' ♀ More than 30 suppliers
- 'Tenuifolia' ♀ CMHG CSWP CWSG ELan EPfP
GSki LRHS MBro NSti SPer WCru
WHCG WPat WPyg
sieboldiana See *S. racemosa* var. *sieboldiana*
tigrina MBlu WWat
wightiana See *S. javanica*
§ **williamsii** subsp. **coreana** CMCN WFar

SAMOLUS (Primulaceae)
repens ECou

SANCHEZIA (Acanthaceae)
nobilis hort. See *S. speciosa*
§ **speciosa** CHal

SANDERSONIA (Colchicaceae)
aurantiaca CFwr LAma LBow LRHS NRog

SANGUINARIA (Papaveraceae)
canadensis CArn CBro CGle CSpe EPot ERos
EWTr GGar GPoy IBlr IMGH
LAma LRHS LSyl NRya SLon SMad
SPer WAbe WCru WShi WWat
WWin
- f.**multiplex** (d) CLAP CRDP EPPr EPot GKir LRHS
SAga
- - 'Paint Creek Double' SSpi
- - 'Plena' (d) ♀ CBro CEnd CLyd CRDP CStu EPar
EPot IMGH LAma MTis NHar
NHol NMen NPar NRya SBla SIng
SSpi WAbe WEas WHil WLin WSan
- 'Peter Harrison' LGre
- pink SAga

SANGUISORBA (Rosaceae)
§ **albiflora** CBlo CRow EBee EBrP EBre EFou
ELan GBuc LBCl LBSe LBre MBBe
MCLN MRav MTis NLar NPro
SBre WBea WCot WFar WPGP
WWin

armena	SSvw
benthamiana	CHEx
canadensis	CRow EBee ECha EGar GAbr
	GCal GPoy MFir MSte NHex SPer
	WCot WFar WWye
* *caucasica*	EBee WWye
hakusanensis	EBee ECha MNrw NBir NBro
	NChi NPro WWhi
magnifica alba	See *S. albiflora*
menziesii	EBee LGre SUsu WCot WPGP
§ *minor*	CAgr CArn CFri CKin EEls
	ELau EWFC GBar GPoy MBar
	MChe MGas MHer MHew
	NArg NBro NMir SIde WCHb
	WHbs WHer WOak WPer
	WWye
– subsp. *muricata*	WGwG
– – HH&K 289	Last listed 1999
obtusa	CInt CRow EBee ECha EFou ELan
	EPar GBuc GCal LFis LGre LHil
	MCAu MCLN MLLN MRav MTis
	NBro NFla NHex NHol NLar NSti
	SChu SPer SRPl SSoC WBea WCot
	WFar
– var. *albiflora*	See *S. albiflora*
officinalis	CArn CInt ECGN EPfP EWFC
	GBar MBel MCAu MHer NMir
	SSca SWat WMoo WWin WWye
– 'Arnhem'	LGre
– 'Tanna'	CBos CPlt EBee EMon EPPr GBri
	GCal LGre NBir NPro SLod SMrm
	SOkh WCot WMaN WPrP
parviflora	See *S. tenuifolia* var. *parviflora*
pimpinella	See *S. minor*
sitchensis	See *S. stipulata*
§ *stipulata*	CPlt GCal IBlr
tenuifolia	NLar WMoo WWhi
– 'Alba'	CBlo EBee GBuc WCot WPGP
§ – var. *parviflora*	EBee
– 'Purpurea'	WCot

SANICULA (Apiaceae)

elata B&SWJ 2250	Last listed 1999
europaea	EBee EWFC GBar GPoy MSal
	WHer WWye

SANIELLA (Hypoxidaceae)

verna	Last listed 1999

SANSEVIERIA ✿ (Agavaceae)

trifasciata 'Bantel's Sensation' ♀	Last listed 1995
– 'Craigii' ♀	Last listed 1995
– 'Golden Hahnii' (v) ♀	MBri
– 'Hahnii' ♀	Last listed 1995
– 'Laurentii' (v) ♀	MBri
– 'Moonshine' ♀	Last listed 1993

SANTOLINA ✿ (Asteraceae)

§ *chamaecyparissus* ♀	More than 30 suppliers
– var. *corsica*	See *S. chamaecyparissus* var. *nana*
– 'Double Lemon'	EPfP LFis SPla
– 'Lambrook Silver'	CDoC EBee ECtt EOHP EPPr EPfP
	ESis GKir LFis LRHS NHol SAga
	SCoo SEas SLim SPla
– 'Lemon Queen'	CArn CB&S CDoC EGoo ELau
	GBar GKir GOrc LAst LRHS MAsh
	MBel MGos MMal MHer NFla NSti
	SAga SEas SIde SPla SWat WCHb
	WFar WPer
– subsp. *magonica*	Last listed 1998

§ – var. *nana* ♀	CB&S EBee ECha ENot EPfP GKir
	LHop LRHS MBar MDun MHer
	NFai NFor SPer SRms SWat WPer
– – 'Weston'	Last listed 1999
– 'Pretty Carol'	CAbP EBee EBrP EBre EDAr ELan
	EMil EPfP GBar GKir GOrc LBCl
	LBSe LBre LRHS MAsh MBBe
	NBrk NFai SAga SBre SEas SIde
	SLim WWeb
– 'Small-Ness'	CDoC CLyd EBee EDAr EGoo
	EMon EPPr ESis EWes GBar GKir
	GOrc LRHS MAsh MBri MBro
	MHer MSte NHol NMen SIng
	SMrm SPer WAbe WFar WPat
	WPyg
– subsp. *squarrosa*	Last listed 1997
dentata	Last listed 1998
elegans	SOkd
incana	See *S. chamaecyparissus*
'Oldfield Hybrid'	MBel MLan WCot
pectinata	See *S. rosmarinifolia* subsp. *canescens*
§ *pinnata*	CArn CSev CTri MHer WPer
§ – subsp. *neapolitana* ♀	CArn CSev EBee ECha ELan ENot
	GBar LHop LRHS MBri NFor SDix
	SIde WEas WHCG WOak WSel
	WWye
– – cream	See *S. pinnata* subsp. *neapolitana* 'Edward Bowles'
§ – – 'Edward Bowles'	CGle CMil EBee ELan EMil GCal
	GOrc LHop MBNS MCLN MHer
	MRav MSCN MWgw NBid NBir
	NHol NPer NSti SChu SLim SPla
	WAbe WBea WCFE WHen WHer
	WPGP WSHC
– – 'Sulphurea'	CMea EGoo EPfP LGre LRHS MBel
	SPer WKif WPer WTro WWhi
	WWpP
rosmarinifolia	CArn CDoC CHad CMil ELau ESis
	EWTr GChr MBel MRav MWhi
	SLon SPan SRms WCHb WSel
	WWye
§ – subsp. *canescens*	EPfP LRHS MRav WPer WRHF
	WWye
§ – subsp. *rosmarinifolia*	CChe CSev EBee ECha EGoo ELan
	ENot EOHP GBar GCHN GKir
	LRHS MBri MHer NFai NSti SDix
	SPer WCHb WEas WHoo WSHC
	WTro WWin WWye
– – cream	NWoo
– – 'Primrose Gem' ♀	CB&S CDoC CHar EBee ECha
	EDAr ELau EMil EPfP ESis GBar
	GKir LHop LRHS NChi NSti SBod
	SEas SPer SPla SRPl WCot WPer
	WWal WWye
tomentosa	See *S. pinnata* subsp. *neapolitana*
virens	See *S. rosmarinifolia* subsp. *rosmarinifolia*
viridis	See *S. rosmarinifolia* subsp. *rosmarinifolia*

SANVITALIA (Asteraceae)

'Little Sun'	CSpe LRHS WWol

SAPIUM (Euphorbiaceae)

japonicum	CFil CMCN SMac WPGP

SAPONARIA (Caryophyllaceae)

x *boissieri*	SIng
'Bressingham' ♀	EBrP EBre EDAr EPot LBCl LBSe
	LBee LBre LRHS MBBe MTho

	NHar NHol SBla SBod SBre SIng
	WAbe WPat WPyg WWin
caespitosa	EPot EWes GTou NMen WLin
x *lempergii* 'Max Frei'	EBee GBuc LFis LGre LRHS SAga
	SBla SDix SOkh SUsu WCot
	WOVN
* 'Lilac Double'	MRav
lutea	NWCA WGor
ocymoides ♀	CB&S CLTr EBee ECha ECtt EDAr
	EHon ELau EMNN ENot ESis GAbr
	GBar GCHN GKir GTou LGro
	LRHS MHer MWgw NBid NFla
	NVic SRms WBea WFar WHoo
	WPer WStI WWin
- 'Alba'	ECha WAbe WFar
- 'Rubra Compacta' ♀	LRHS MTho WPyg
- 'Snow Tip'	EDAr ESis NDlv
officinalis	CAgr CArn CBre CKin CRow
	ELau EWFC GAbr GBar GMac
	GPoy LEdu MChe MHer MHew
	MSal NFai SIde SRCN SSea WFar
	WGwG WHer WOak WPer WWal
	WWye
- 'Alba Plena' (d)	CGle CRDP CSam EBee EBrP EBre
	ECha ECoo EMon GBar GMac
	LBCl LBSe LBre MBBe MSCN
	NBrk NSti SBre WCHb WElm WFar
	WHer WPer WRha WWin
§ - 'Dazzler' (v)	CRow ELau GBar MRav NBir
	NBrk NFai WCHb WHer
- 'Rosea Plena' (d)	CBre CFee CRDP CRow CSam
	EBee ECoo EEls ELan EMon GKir
	LLWP LRHS MBel MBri MCAu
	MSCN NArg NCat NFla NGdn
	NOrc SMrm SPer STes WBea
	WCHb WFar WOve WPer
- 'Rubra Plena' (d)	CBre CGle CHad CRDP ECha
	ELan EMon LFis MSCN NSti
	WCHb WHer WRha
- 'Variegata'	See *S. officinalis* 'Dazzler'
x *olivana* ♀	EDAr EPot ESis LFis MNaF MTho
	NHol NMen NTow SBla SIng
	WAbe WPat WPyg WWin
pamphylica	EBee MNrw
pulvinaris	See *S. pumilio*
§ *pumilio*	GCHN GTou WLin
'Rosenteppich'	NHol WLin WPat WPyg
sicula	Last listed 1999
zawadskii	See *Silene zawadskii*

SARACHA (Solanaceae)
¶ *punctata*	CGre

SARCOCAPNOS (Papaveraceae)
baetica	NWCA
enneaphylla	Last listed 1997

SARCOCOCCA ✿ (Buxaceae)
confusa ♀	More than 30 suppliers
hookeriana ♀	CBlo CTrG ECot EPfP ERav GSki
	IOrc WPGP
- B&SWJ 2585	WCru
- var. *digyna* ♀	More than 30 suppliers
- - 'Purple Stem'	EHol EPla ERav MGos MRav SCob
	WCru WDin WPGP
- var. *hookeriana*	CDoC GKir
- var. *humilis*	More than 30 suppliers
- HWJCM 92	WCru
- Sch 2396	EPla
orientalis	CFil CMCN CPMA ELan EPfP EPla
	LRHS MAsh MGos SMac SPla SSpi
	WPGP WSpi WWat WWeb

'Roy Lancaster'	See *S. ruscifolia* 'Dragon Gate'
ruscifolia	CB&S CPMA CPle CWSG EBee
	ELan ENot EPla GKir IOrc LEdu
	LFis LHop LRHS MAsh MBel
	MGos SCob SLon SPer SRms SSpi
	WAbe WCru WPGP WWat
- var. *chinensis* ♀	CFil CPMA CSam EPfP EPla MRav
	NHol WCru
- - L 713	EPla
§ - 'Dragon Gate'	CFil ELan EPla LRHS MAsh WPGP
saligna	CB&S CFil CPMA EPla WBod
	WCru WPGP WWat

SARMIENTA (Gesneriaceae)
repens ♀	WAbe WCru

SARRACENIA ✿ (Sarraceniaceae)
x *ablesii* (*rubra* X	WMEx
alata 'Red Lid')	
alata	CSWC GTro WMEx
- 'Citronelle'	WMEx
- copper lid	GTro
- x *flava* 'Maxima'	CSWC WMEx
- 'Nicolson'	WMEx
- pubescent	CSWC WMEx
- purple lid	GTro
- 'Red Lid'	CSWC
- 'Red Lid' x *flava*	WMEx
red pitcher	
- red x *purpurea*	WMEx
subsp. *venosa*	
- x *willisii*	WMEx
x *areolata*	CSWC GTro WMEx
- X (x *areolata* x	WMEx
alata red throat)	
x *catesbyi* ♀	CFil CSWC GTro WMEx
- x *excellens*	WMEx
x *chelsonii* ♀	WMEx
x *courtii*	Last listed 1998
x *excellens* ♀	CSWC GTro WMEx
x *exornata*	WMEx
x *farnhamii*	See *S.* x *readii* 'Farnhamii'
flava ♀	CFil CRDP CSWC EAnd GTro
	WMEx WPGP
- all green giant	WMEx
- 'Burgundy'	CSWC GTro WMEx
- var. *cuprea*	GTro
- 'Maxima'	CSWC WMEx WNor
- 'Maxima' x *purpurea*	Last listed 1998
subsp. *venosa*	
- 'Maxima' x *rubra*	Last listed 1998
subsp. *jonesii*	
- var. *ornata*	WMEx
- 'Prince George County'	WMEx
- purple tube	WMEx
¶ - veinless	CSWC
x *formosa*	Last listed 1997
x *harperi*	CSWC WMEx
'Judy'	GTro
leucophylla ♀	CSWC GTro WMEx
- x *excellens*	Last listed 1998
- white pitchers	WMEx
x *melanorhoda*	GTro WMEx
x *miniata*	WMEx
minor	CSWC GTro WMEx
- 'Okefenokee Giant'	CSWC WMEx
- tall	WMEx
x *mitchelliana* ♀	GTro WMEx
x *moorei*	GTro WMEx
- 'Brook's Hybrid'	GTro WMEx
- X (*leucophylla*	WMEx
X *moorei*)	

oreophila CSWC GTro WMEx
¶ - heavy-veined CSWC
- x *leucophylla* CSWC
- x *minor* CSWC
- x *purpurea* Last listed 1998
x *popei* CSWC WMEx
- x (x *popei* x *flava giant*) WMEx
psittacina CSWC EAnd GTro WMEx
purpurea CFil CSWC
- subsp. *purpurea* CSWC GTro LEdu WMEx
- - f. *heterophylla* CSWC WMEx
- subsp. *venosa* CSWC GTro WMEx
¶ - - var. *burkii* CSWC
- - x *oreophila* CSWC WMEx
§ x *readii* GTro WMEx
§ - 'Farnhamii' CSWC
- x (*leucophylla* x *readii*) WMEx
x *rehderi* WMEx
rubra CSWC GTro WMEx
- subsp. *alabamensis* CSWC WMEx
- subsp. *gulfensis* CSWC WMEx
* - - f. *heterophylla* CSWC
- - - strong green pitcher WMEx
- subsp. *jonesii* CSWC WMEx
* - - f. *heterophylla* CSWC
¶ - subsp. *rubra* CSWC
- subsp. *wherryi* CSWC
¶ - - yellow flower CSWC
x *swaniana* GTro WMEx
- x *popei* WMEx
x *wrigleyana* ♀ GTro

SARUMA (Aristolochiaceae)
henryi WCot

SASA ✿ (Poaceae - Bambusoideae)
chrysantha hort. See *Pleioblastus chino*
disticha 'Mirrezuzume' See *Pleioblastus pygmaeus* 'Mirrezuzume'
glabra f. *albostriata* See *Sasaella masamuneana* f. *albostriata*
kurilensis EPla ISta LJus NMoo SDry WJun WViv
- 'Shimofuri' (v) EPla ERod ISta LJus SDry WJun
- short EPla
megalophylla 'Nobilis' SDry
nana See *S. veitchii* f. *minor*
nipponica CEnd EPla SDry WJun
- 'Aureostriata' SDry
oshidensis EPla
§ *palmata* ♀ CB&S CHad COld EBee ENot EPVP GAri GOrc MCCP SMad WHer
- f. *nebulosa* CFir CHEx EBee EFul EOas EPla ISta LJus MBrN MMoz MWht NMoo SAPC SArc SDry WJun
- 'Warley Place' (v) SDry
quelpaertensis EPla GAri ISta SDry
senanensis EPla SDry
tessellata See *Indocalamus tessellatus*
tsuboiana CB&S CDoC EBee EPla ISta MMoz SDry WFar
§ *veitchii* More than 30 suppliers
§ - f. *minor* EBee EPla MCCP

SASAELLA (Poaceae - Bambusoideae)
bitchuensis hort. SDry
glabra See *S. masamuneana*
§ *masamuneana* EPla SMad

§ - f. *albostriata* (v) CDoC CFil COtt CPMA EBee EPPr EPla ERod EWsh ISta LEdu LJus MCCP MMoz MWht SDry WJun WPGP WViv
- f. *aureostriata* (v) COtt EPla GCal LJus MMoz SDry
§ *ramosa* EBee EPla GAri GBin GOrc ISta LEdu LJus MCCP MMoz MWht NRya SDry

SASAMORPHA (Poaceae - Bambusoideae)
§ *borealis* Last listed 1997

SASSAFRAS (Lauraceae)
albidum CArn CB&S CMCN CTho EPfP SSpi WPGP WWat
tzumu SSpi

SATUREJA (Lamiaceae)
biflora CArn
§ *coerulea* ♀ EWes NBir SIde WFar
douglasii EOHP SHDw WJek
hortensis CBod GPoy ILis MChe MHer MHew MLan WGwG WHbs WHer WJek WSel
montana CArn EDAr EEls ELau EWFC GPoy ILis LEdu LLWP MBri MChe MHer NMen SDix SIde SRms SRob WCHb WCer WHbs WHer WOak WPer WWye
* - *citriodora* GPoy IIve
- 'Coerulea' See *S. coerulea*
§ - subsp. *illyrica* LLWP
- prostrate white CRDP
- 'Purple Mountain' GPoy IIve LLWP
- *subspicata* See *S. montana* subsp. *illyrica*
parnassica LLWP WPer
repanda See *S. spicigera*
seleriana CInt NMen
spicata Last listed 1999
§ *spicigera* CArn CLyd CPBP EDAr ELau EPot GBar LFis LLWP MHar MHer NBir NPri WCHb WSel WWin WWye
thymbra CArn EOHP LLWP SHDw WJek
§ *viminea* EOHP

SAURAUIA (Actinidiaceae)
subspinosa CHEx

SAUROMATUM (Araceae)
guttatum See *S. venosum*
§ *venosum* EBee LAma LRHS MBri WCot WCru

SAURURUS (Saururaceae)
cernuus CBen CHEx CRow CWat EBrP EBre EHon ELan EMFW LBCl LBSe LBre LPBA MBBe MSta NDea SBre SWat WMAq
chinensis CRow EBee WCru

SAUSSUREA (Asteraceae)
albescens WCot
auriculata HWJCM 490 WCru
§ *ceratocarpa* Last listed 1998
- var. *depressa* Last listed 1998
grandiflora EBee
hypoleuca MNrw
pulchella EBee

SAXEGOTHAEA (Podocarpaceae)
conspicua CB&S CDoC CMCN ECou EPla LCon LLin SLon SMad WCwm

SAXIFRAGA ✿ (Saxifragaceae)

'Aemula' (x *borisii*) (7) NMen
§ 'Afrodite' (*sempervivum*) CLyd EPot
(7)
aizoides var. MBro
atrorubens (9)
aizoon See *S. paniculata*
'Aladdin' (x *borisii*) (7) NHol
¶ 'Alan Martin' (x EPot
boydilacina) (7)
'Alba' (x *apiculata*) (7) ELan EMNN GTou LFox LRHS
MBro MHer NHol NMen NSla SBla
SChu SIng SPlb SSmi WHoo WPat
WWin
'Alba' (x *arco-valleyi*) See *S*. 'Ophelia' (x *arco-valleyi*)
'Alba' (*oppositifolia*) (7) CLyd ELan EMNN EWes GKir
GTou NHar NMen WWin
'Albert Einstein' NMen NNrd
(x *apiculata*) (7)
* 'Albert Hawkins' Last listed 1999
'Albertii' (*callosa*) (8) GTou LRHS SIng SSmi WWin
'Albida' (*callosa*) (8) NFla
'Aldebaran' (x *borisii*) (7) EMNN NHar NMen
'Alfons Mucha' (7) CLyd EPot MWat NMen
¶ 'Allendale Acclaim' (7) EHyt
'Allendale Accord' NDlv
(*diapensioides* x
lilacina) (7)
¶ 'Allendale Betty' EHyt
¶ 'Allendale Celt' EHyt
'Allendale Joy' NMen
(x *wendelacina*) (7)
'Allendale Pearl' (x CLyd NDlv NMen
novacastelensis) (7)
'Alpenglow' (7) MWat NMen
alpigena (7) NSla
'Amitie' (x *gloriana*) (7) NMen
andersonii (7) CLyd EMNN ITim MDHE MWat
NMen NNrd NRya NTow
- McB 1475 (7) NHol
x *andrewsii* (8x11) MDHE MTho SSmi
x *anglica* 'Peggy Last listed 1998
Eastwood' (7)
angustifolia Haw. See *S. hypnoides*
'Anne Beddall' (x CLyd MWat NMen WAbe
goringiana) (7)
'Aphrodite' See *S*. 'Afrodite' (sempervivum)
(*sempervivum*) (7)
x *apiculata* sensu See *S*. 'Gregor Mendel' (x
stricto hort. *apiculata*)
'Apple Blossom' (15) GTou MDHE MOne NBro NFla
WGor
'Archfield White' NNrd
(*callosa*) (8)
§ 'Arco' (x *arco-valleyi*) (7) EPot MWat NMen
x *arco-valleyi* sensu See *S*. 'Arco' (x *arco-valleyi*)
stricto hort.
x *arendsii* (15) MDHE WEas
§ 'Aretiastrum' (x *boydii*) (7) CLyd EPot LFox NDlv NMen SIng
aretioides (7) GCHN NMen
'Ariel' (x *bornibrookii*) (7) LFox
'Assimilis' (x *petraschii*) (7) WAbe
'August Hayek' MBro MWat NMen NNrd
(x *leyboldii*) (7)
'Aurea Maculata' See *S*. 'Aureopunctata' (x *urbium*)
(*cuneifolia*)
§ 'Aureopunctata' CPri EBee EBrP EBre ECha ELan
(x *urbium*) (11/v) GBuc GCal LBCl LBSe LBre MBBe
MHer MWgw NHol SBre SIng
SMrm SPer SPlb SRms WHen
'Backhousei' (15) Last listed 1999

'Balcana' See *S. paniculata* var. *orientalis*
'Baldensis' See *S. paniculata* var. *baldensis*
'Ballawley Guardsman' (15) ECho LFox MBNS MDHE SIng
§ 'Beatrix Stanley' CLyd EMNN LFox MBro MHer
(x *anglica*) (7) NHar NMen
'Becky Foster' (x *borisii*) MWat
(7)
'Beechcroft White' (15) LRHS MDHE
'Bellisant' CLyd
(x *bornibrookii*) (7)
'Berenika' (x *bertolonii*) NMen
(7)
'Bettina' (x *paulinae*) (7) GCHN
x *biasolettoi* sensu See *S*. 'Phoenix' (x *biasolettoi*)
stricto hort.
biflora (7) Last listed 1999
x *bilekii* (7) CLyd
'Birch Baby' (15) SIng
'Birch Yellow' See *S*. 'Pseudoborisii' (x *borisii*)
'Black Beauty' (15) ECho LRHS MBro MDHE MHer
SSmi
¶ 'Black Forest Gateaux' CLAP
(*fortunei*) (5)
'Black Ruby' (*fortunei*) (5) CAbb CBos CFai CLAP CMil CSpe
EBee EMan GBin LAst LHop LPan
LRHS MBri MDun MSCN MTPN
MTis NCut NPSI SMad SPer SPla
WCot WCra WGor
'Blackberry and Apple Pie' CBos CFai CLAP EBee GBri NCut
(*fortunei*) (5) NDov NHol NPSI WCot WFar
* 'Blackhouse White' (8) Last listed 1998
'Blanik' (x *borisii*) (7) CLyd NMen
'Blanka' (x *borisii*) (7) NMen
'Blütenteppich' (15) WPer
'Bob Hawkins' (15/v) CLyd ELan GCHN GDra LFox
LRHS MDHE MHer NHar SMer
WWin
§ 'Bodensee' WPat
(x *hofmannii*) (7)
¶ 'Bohdalec' (7) NMen
'Bohemia' (7) CLyd EPot ITim NMen SBla WAbe
x *borisii* sensu stricto hort. See *S*. 'Sofia' (x *borisii*)
'Bornmuelleri' (7) NMen
'Boston Spa' CLyd EMNN GCHN LRHS MBro
(x *elisabethae*) (7) MHer NDlv NHol NMen NNrd
SChu SPlb WPat
'Brendan' Last listed 1999
'Bridget' (x *edithiae*) (7) CMea CPBP ESis ITim LFox LRHS
NDlv NMen WWin
'Brno' (x *elisabethae*) (7) NHol
broncbialis (10) CLyd
- var. *vespertina* See *S. vespertina*
'Brookside' (*burseriana*) CLyd EPot NMen
(7)
brunoniana See *S. brunonis*
§ *brunonis* (1) LFox WCru
- CC&McK 108 (1) NWCA
bryoides (10) GCrs GTou
x *burnatii* (8) CLyd LFox LRHS MBro NDlv
NMen NPro SIng WGor
burseriana (7) GCHN MBro NRya WGor WPyg
'Buttercup' (x *kayei*) (7) CLyd CPBP EPot GTou MBro
MWat NDlv NHol NMen NNrd
NWCA WHoo WPat WPyg
caesia (8) SRms
§ *callosa* (8) ♀ GCHN GTou MBro MWat NHar
NHol SBla WPat WTin
- var. *bellardii* See *S. callosa*
§ - subsp. *callosa* EPot MBro MDHE NBro NHol
var. *australis* (8) NMen NNrd WAbe
§ - subsp. *catalaunica* (8) MBro
§ - x *cochlearis* (8) NDlv NNrd

- var. *lantoscana*   See *S. callosa* subsp. *callosa* var. *australis*
- *lingulata*   See *S. callosa*
'Cambria Jewel' (15)   NMen NNrd
'Cambridge Seedling' (7)   MWat NMen
§ *camposii* (15)   GAbr SIng
'Camyra' (7)   MWat NDlv NNrd
canaliculata (15)   MDHE NMen NNrd
x *canis-dalmatica*   See *S.* x *gaudinii*
§ 'Carmen' (x *elisabethae*)   EMNN GKir ITim LRHS MBro
   (7)   MOne NDlv NMen NNrd NRya
'Carniolica' (*paniculata*)   CLyd LFox LRHS MBar MDHE
   (8)   NBro NMen NWCA SBla
¶ 'Carniolica' (x *pectinata*)   MDHE
   (8)
'Carnival' (15)   CPri
carolinica   See *S.* 'Carnolica' (*paniculata*)
'Castor' (x *bilekii*) (7)   MWat NHol SIng
catalaunica   See *S. callosa* subsp. *catalaunica*
'Caterhamensis'   WEas
   (*cotyledon*) (8)
caucasica var. *desoulavyi*   See *S. desoulavyi*
cebennensis (15) ♀   CLyd GCrs LFox NMen NRya
   NTow SIng
- dwarf (15)   NMen WAbe
¶ 'Cecilia' (7)   EHyt
¶ 'Cereus' (7)   NMen
cespitosa   GKir MDHE NWCA WAbe
'Chambers' Pink Pride'   See *S.* 'Miss Chambers' (x *urbium*)
'Cheap Confections'   CAbb CLAP CMil CSpe EBee
   (*fortunei*) (4)   MTPN MTis NCut NHol WCot
   WWhi
§ *cherlerioides* (10)   MBNS NRya NVic
'Cherrytrees' (x *boydii*) (7)   MBro
'Chetwynd' (*marginata*)   MWat WAbe
   (7)
'Chez Nous' (x *gloriana*)   CLyd NMen
   (7/v)
'Christine' (x *anglica*) (7)   LFox MWat NMen NNrd
cinerea (7)   WAbe
'Clare' (x *anglica*) (7)   Last listed 1999
'Clare Island' (15)   MDHE SIng
§ 'Clarence Elliott'   CLyd CNic EWes GCal LRHS MBro
   (*umbrosa*) (11) ♀   MHar MHer NHol NRya NVic
   WAbe WHoo WPat WWin
'Cleo' (x *boydii*) (7)   NMen
x *clibranii* (15)   MDHE
cliveorum McB1476 (7)   Last listed 1999
§ 'Cloth of Gold' (*exarata*   CLyd CMea ECha ELan GDra
   subsp. *moschata*) (15)   GTou LAst LBee LRHS MBar MHer
   MWhi NMen NRya NWCA SIng
   SPlb SRms SSmi WAbe WFar
   WWin
cochlearis (8)   CMea ESis LBee LRHS MOne
   MWat NBro NDlv NMen SSmi
   WPer WPyg WWin
'Cockscomb'   MDHE NMen SIng
   (*paniculata*) (8)
columnaris (7)   NSla
'Compacta' (*exarata*   MBro
   subsp. *moschata*) (15)
'Corona' (x *boydii*) (7)   LFox MWat NHol NMen
'Corrennie Claret' (15)   GTou
'Correvoniana'   ECtt ESis GCHN LRHS MBro
   (*paniculata*) (8)   MHer MOne NBus NDlv NRya
   SIng WGor WWin
§ 'Corrie Fee'   GCrs GKir GTou NHar NHol SIng
   (*oppositifolia*) (7)
corsica subsp.   Last listed 1998
   cossoniana (15)
§ *cortusifolia* (5)   CHEx CHid NHar SSpi

- dwarf (5)   Last listed 1997
- var. *fortunei*   See *S. fortunei*
§ *corymbosa* (7)   NMen
cotyledon (8)   GDra LBee LRHS NFor NHol SIng
   WEas WPer
§ 'Cranbourne' (x *anglica*)   CLyd CMea EBrP EBre EMNN
   (7) ♀   EPot LBCl LBSe LBre LFox LRHS
   MBBe MBro MWat NHar NHol
   NMen SBla SBre SSmi WPat
'Cream' (*paniculata*) (8)   SSmi
'Cream Seedling'   EBrP EBre ESis LBCl LBSe LBre
   (x *elisabethae*) (7)   MBBe MWat NDlv NMen SBre
'Crenata' (*burseriana*) (7)   CLyd EPot GCHN LFox LRHS
   MBro MWat NDlv NHar NMen
   NNrd WHoo
'Crimson Rose'   MBro NNrd
   (*paniculata*) (8)
crispa (4)   SIng
§ *crustata* (8)   GCHN MDHE NMen NWCA SIng
   WAbe
- var. *vochinensis*   See *S. crustata*
¶ 'Crystal Pink' (*fortunei*)   CMil LHop
   (5)
'Crystalie' (x *biasolettoi*)   EPot LRHS MBro NMen WPat
   (7)
'Cultrata' (*paniculata*) (8)   NBro
'Cumulus' (*iranica*   CLyd CPBP NMen SBla WAbe
   hybrid) (7) ♀
cuneata (15)   NHol
§ *cuneifolia* (11)   CHEx CNic GDra GGar LBee
   LRHS MHer MWat NDlv NFla NSti
   SSmi WRos
- var. *capillipes*   See *S. cuneifolia* subsp. *cuneifolia*
§ - subsp. *cuneifolia* (11)   Last listed 1999
* - var. *subintegra* (3)   ECho
cuscutiformis (5)   See *S.* 'Cuscutiformis' (*stolonifera*)
§ 'Cuscutiformis'   CInt EBee GCal MRav NTow
   (*stolonifera*) (5)   SRms WAbe WCru WOve
cymbalaria (2)   EBur
- var. *huetiana* (2)   CNic
daburica   See *S. cuneifolia*
'Dainty Dame'   CLyd LFox LRHS MWat NDlv
   (x *arco-valleyi*) (7)   NMen
'Dana' (x *megaseiflora*)   CLyd EMNN MWat NHol NMen
   (7)
'Dartington Double' (15/d)   CTri EBrP EBre EWes GCHN
   GDra GKir GTou LBCl LBSe LBre
   LRHS MBBe MDHE NHar NNrd
   SBre
'Dartington Double White'   MDHE
   (15/d)
'Dawn' (7)   NNrd
'Dawn Frost' (7)   Last listed 1999
'Delia' (x *hornibrookii*)   CLyd CNic NMen
   (7)
§ 'Denisa'   NMen
   (x *pseudokotschyi*) (7)
densa   See *S. cherlerioides*
'Dentata' (x *geum*)   See *S.* 'Dentata' (x *polita*)
§ 'Dentata' (x *polita*) (11)   ECha EPla GAbr GGar NVic SUsu
   WMoo
'Dentata' (x *urbium*)   See *S.* 'Dentata' (x *polita*)
§ *desoulavyi* (7)   GTou
diapensioides (7)   CLyd NMen
'Doctor Clay' (8)   LRHS MDHE NMen
'Doctor Ramsey' (8)   ESis EWes GTou ITim LBee LRHS
   MBro NDlv NNrd SIng SSmi
   WGor WHoo
'Donald Mann' (15)   EWes
aff. *doyalana* SEP 45 (7)   CGra

'Drakula' (*ferdinandi-*   CLyd LRHS MWat NDlv NMen
  coburgi) (7)
'Dubarry' (15)   ECho EWes LRHS MDHE SIng
'Duncan Lowe'   GCrs
  (*andersonii*) (7) ♀
'Dwight Ripley' (7)   LFox
'Edgar Irmscher' (7)   CLyd LFox MWat NMen
'Edie Campbell' (15)   MDHE
'Edith' (x *edithiae*) (7)   LRHS MBro NNrd
'Edward Elgar'   MWat NHol NMen
  (x *megaseiflora*) (7)
§ 'Egemmulosa' (*hypnoides*) Last listed 1999
  (15)
¶ 'Egmont' (7)   NMen
'Eleanora Francini Corti' (7) SBla
x *elegantissima* (15)   See S. x *clibranii*
'Elf' (7)   See S. 'Beatrix Stanley' (x *anglica*)
'Elf' (15)   ELan EMNN LRHS NMen NNrd
   SIng SRms SSmi WGor
'Eliot Hodgkin'   LFox NNrd
  (x *millstreamiana*) (7)
x *elisabethae*   See S. 'Carmen' (x *elisabethae*)
'Elizabeth Sinclair'   EPot NMen NNrd
  (x *elisabethae*) (7)
'Ellie Brinckerhoff'   Last listed 1999
  (x *hornibrookii*) (7)
§ 'Ernst Heinrich'   NMen NRya
  (x *heinrichii*) (7)
'Esther' (x *burnatii*) (8)   CMea EBrP EBre ELan ESis LBCl
   LBSe LBee LBre LRHS MBBe
   NMen SBla SBre SMer SSmi WHoo
§ 'Eulenspiegel' (x *geuderi*) CLyd EPot MBro NMen NNrd SIng
  (7)
exarata (15)   ITim LBee LFox LRHS NMen
§ - subsp. *moschata* (15)   MDHE
fair maids of France   See S. 'Flore Pleno' (*granulata*)
'Fairy' (*exarata*   ELan EPot NFla
  subsp. *moschata*) (15)
'Faldonside' (x *boydii*)   CLyd LFox MBro MWat NDlv
  (7) ♀   NHol NMen SBla WHoo WPat WPyg
'Falstaff' (*burseriana*) (7) CLyd EPot LFox MWat SBla SIng
x *farreri* hort. (8)   See S. *callosa* x *cochlearis*
§ 'Faust' (x *borisii*) (7)   EMNN NMen SBla SIng
federici-augusti   See S. *frederici-augusti*
'Ferdinand'   NMen
  (x *hofmannii*) (7)
ferdinandi-coburgi (7) ♀ CLyd EPot LFox LRHS NDlv
   NWCA
- var. *pravislavii*   See S. *ferdinandi-coburgi* var.
   rhodopea
- var. *radoslavoffii*   See S. *ferdinandi-coburgi* var.
   rhodopea
* - var. *rhodopea* (7)   CLyd EPot LRHS NDlv NMen
ferruginea (4)   Last listed 1997
'Findling' (15)   EPot GCHN LGro LRHS MBro
   MOne NMen NNrd SIng WAbe
   WWin
§ *flagellaris* (1)   WAbe
'Flamingo'   Last listed 1999
'Flavescens' (*paniculata*)   NBro
  (8)
x *fleischeri* (7)   Last listed 1999
§ 'Flore Pleno' (*granulata*)   CFir CRDP EBee EWes GAbr GBri
  (15/d)   LFox NBir NHar NPro NRya
   NWoo SUsu WCot WFar WHil
'Florissa' (*oppositifolia*) (7) CLyd GCHN LRHS
florulenta   See S. *callosa*
'Flowers of Sulphur'   See S. 'Schwefelblüte'
§ *fortunei* (5) ♀   CHEx CLTr CMea EBee EBrP EBre
   GMaP LBCl LBSe LBre MBBe MRav
   NBir NHol SBre SCob SIng SPer
   SRms SSpi WAbe WCru WMoo

- double-flowered(5/d)   EBee NCut NPSI SPer WFar
- var. *incisolobata* (5)   SSpi
- pink (5)   NPSI WAbe WFar
* - variegated (5)   EMan LAst MSCN NCut NPSI
   WFar
'Foster's Gold'   NMen
  (x *elisabethae*) (7)
'Four Winds' (15)   EWes LRHS NMen SBla SIng SSmi
   WGwG WMoo
fragosa   See S. *nidifica*
'Francesco Redi' (7)   Last listed 1999
'Francis Cade' (8)   ITim
'Franzii' (x *paulinae*) (7)   NDlv NMen
§ *frederici-augusti* (7)   SBla
§ - subsp. *grisebachii* (7) ♀ CLyd GTou NSla
'Friar Tuck' (x *boydii*) (7)   MWat NMen
'Friesei' (x *salmonica*) (7)   CLyd EMNN EPot NDlv NHar
   NMen
x *fritschiana* (8)   See S. x *pectinata*
'Funkii' (x *petraschii*) (7)   MWat NMen
'Gaertneri' (*mariae-*   NMen
  theresiae) (7)
'Gaiety' (15)   ECho ELan GDra MDHE NFla
   SIng
'Galaxie' (x *megaseiflora*) CLyd LFox NHol NMen
  (7)
'Ganymede' (*burseriana*)   Last listed 1997
  (7)
§ x *gaudinii* (8)   CLyd ECtt EMNN ESis GGar GTou
   LBee LRHS MBro NDlv NHar
   NHol NMen SIng SOkd WGor
   WPer
'Gelber Findling' (7)   EPot LRHS MDHE
'Gem' (x *irvingii*) (7)   CLyd EMNN MBro NHar NMen
   WAbe
'General Joffre' (15)   See S. 'Maréchal Joffre' (15)
georgei (7)   EPot NMen NWCA
- ENF 5 (7)   Last listed 1999
¶ - hybrid   GCrs
- McB 1379 (7)   NHol
geranioides (15)   GCHN
'Gertie Pritchard'   See S. 'Mrs Gertie Prichard'
  (x *megaseiflora*)
x *geuderi* sensu   See S. 'Eulenspiegel' (x *geuderi*)
  stricto hort.
§ x *geum* (11)   CHid EBee MRav NWoo SDys
   WFar
- Dixter form (11)   ECha WFar
'Gladys' (15)   Last listed 1998
'Gleborg' (15)   EWes LRHS MDHE
'Gloria' (*burseriana*) (7) ♀ CLyd LFox LRHS MBro NHol
   NMen NSla SBla WPat
x *gloriana* (7)   See S. 'Godiva' (x *gloriana*)
'Gloriosa' (x *gloriana*) (7)   See S. 'Godiva' (x *gloriana*)
§ 'Godiva' (x *gloriana*) (7)   CLyd EMNN ITim MWat NMen
'Goeblii' (7)   Last listed 1999
'Gold Dust'   CLyd CNic EMNN GTou LFox
  (x *eudoxiana*) (7)   MOne MWat NHar NMen NNrd
   NRya WWin
'Gold Leaf' (15)   Last listed 1997
'Golden Falls' (15/v)   CMea EWTr EWes GKir GTou
   LRHS MBNS MBro NMen SPlb
   WPat
Golden Prague   See S. 'Zlatá Praha' (x *pragensis*)
  (x *pragensis*)
'Gothenburg' (7)   CLyd NMen WAbe
'Grace' (x *arendsii*) (15/v)   See S. 'Seaspray' (x *arendsii*)
'Grace Farwell'   CLyd CNic EMNN GCHN
   ITim
  (x *anglica*) (7)   LRHS MBar MBro NDlv NHol
   NMen NRya NWCA SBla WHoo
   WPyg

'Gracilis' (x *geum*)   See *S.* 'Gracilis' (x *polita*)
§ 'Gracilis' (x *polita*) (11)   CNic
granulata (15)   CNic EWFC MHew NMen NRya
'Gratoides' (x *grata*) (7)   NMen
'Greenslacks Claire'   Last listed 1998
  (*oppositifolia*) (7)
'Greenslacks Heather'   Last listed 1998
  (*oppositifolia*) (7)
'Greenslacks Valerie'   Last listed 1998
  (*oppositifolia*) (7)
§ 'Gregor Mendel'   CMea ELan EMNN GDra GTou
  (x *apiculata*) (7) ♀   LRHS MBro NDlv NHol NLAp
                                       NMen SBla SIng SRms SSmi WAbe
                                       WHoo WPyg
grisebachii   See *S. frederici-augusti* subsp.
                                       grisebachii
- subsp. **montenegrina**   See *S. frederici-augusti*
'Gustav Hegi'   Last listed 1998
  (x *anormalis*) (7)
'Haagii' (x *eudoxiana*) (7)   ELan EMNN GCHN GCrs GTou
                                       MBro MOne NDlv NMen NNrd
                                       SSmi WWin
hallii   See *S. marshallii*
'Harlow Car' (7)   CLyd LFox NMen
'Harlow Car' x   CPBP
  (*poluniniana*) (7)
'Harold Bevington'   MDHE
  (*paniculata*) (8)
'Harry Marshall'   CLyd NMen
  (x *irvingii*) (7)
'Hartside Pink' (*umbrosa*)   NWoo
  (11)
'Hartswood White' (15)   EWTr MDHE MWat SIng
'Hedwig' (x *malbyana*) (7)   MWat
x **heinreichii** sensu   See *S.* 'Ernst Heinrich' (x
  stricto hort.   *heinrichii*)
'Herbert Cuerden'   NNrd
  (x *elisabethae*) (7)
'Hi-Ace' (15/v)   CLyd ELan GTou LFox LRHS MBro
                                       MHer NWCA SBla SPlb SSmi WFar
'Highdownensis' (8)   MDHE
'Hindhead Seedling'   CLyd EMNN LRHS MWat NDlv
  (x *boydii*) (7)   NHar NMen SIng
hirsuta (11)   EBrP EBre EMar LBCl LBSe LBre
                                       MBBe MDHE SBre WCru
'Hirsuta' (x *geum*)   See *S.* x *geum*
'Hirtella' (*paniculata*) (8)   MDHE
'His Majesty' (x *irvingii*)   EMNN LFox NHar NMen WAbe
  (7)
'Hocker Edge' (x   CLyd ITim LFox MWat NDlv
  arco-valleyi) (7)   NMen WAbe
'Holden Seedling' (15)   EMNN EPot EWes MDHE
x **hornibrookii** (7)   WPat
hostii (8)   CLyd GTou ITim LBee LRHS SIng
                                       WTin
§ - subsp. **hostii** (8)   MDHE
- - var. **altissima** (8)   STre
- subsp. **rhaetica** (8)   MDHE NBro NMen WAbe
'Hsitou Silver' B&SWJ 1980   WCru
  (*stolonifera*) (5)
hybrid JB 11   NMen
§ **hypnoides** (15)   EWFC GAbr GKir MOne NHar SSmi
hypostoma (7)   CLyd
'Icelandica' (*cotyledon*) (8)   NHol
'Icicle' (x *elisabethae*) (7)   MWat NMen
'Ingeborg' (15)   ECha LBee LRHS MDHE SIng
iranica (7)   CLyd EMNN GCHN GCrs MWat
                                       NMen
¶ - pink   CGra
'Irene Bacci' (x *baccii*) (7)   CLyd MWat NMen
'Iris Prichard'   CLyd ESis MBro NMen SIng WHoo
  (x *hardingii*) (7)   WPyg

'Irish' (15)   EPot MDHE
irrigua (15)   Last listed 1999
x **irvingii** sensu   See *S.* 'Walter Irving' (x *irvingii*)
  stricto hort.
'Ivana' (x *caroliquarti*) (7)   MWat
'James Bremner' (15)   LRHS MDHE NBur NFla SIng
'Jason' (x *elisabethae*) (7)   MWat
JB 14/89   Last listed 1999
'Jenkinsiae' (x *irvingii*)   More than 30 suppliers
  (7) ♀
§ 'Johann Kellerer'   CLyd GCrs LFox NDlv NSla SBla
  (x *kellereri*) (7)
'John Tomlinson'   CLyd NSla
  (*burseriana*) (7)
'Josef Čapek' (x   CLyd EPot NMen
  megaseiflora) (7)
'Josef Mánes' (x *borisii*)   NMen
  (7)
'Joy'   See *S.* 'Kaspar Maria Sternberg' (x
                                       petraschii)
'Judith Shackleton'   CLyd MWat NMen WAbe
  (x *abingdonensis*) (7)
'Juliet'   See *S.* 'Riverslea' (x *hornibrookii*)
§ **juniperifolia** (7)   CLyd EMNN GCHN GKir GTou
                                       ITim LRHS MHer MOne MWat
                                       NDlv NHar NNrd NWCA SChu
                                       SMer SRms SSmi
- var. **macedonica**   See *S. juniperifolia*
'Jupiter' (x *megaseiflora*)   CLyd EMNN LRHS MWat NHar
  (7)   NMen NNrd WAbe
§ **karadzicensis** (7)   EMNN NMen
'Karasin' (7)   CLyd NNrd
'Karel Čapek' (x   CLyd CMea CNic EPot MWat
  megaseiflora) (7)   NDlv NHol NMen NNrd
                                       NRya
'Karel Stivín' (x *edithae*)   CLyd EMNN MWat NMen
  (7)
'Karlstejn' (x *borisii*) (7)   Last listed 1999
§ 'Kaspar Maria Sternberg'   CLyd EMNN GCHN ITim LFox
  (x *petraschii*) (7)   LRHS MBro NHar NHol NMen
                                       NNrd WPat
'Kath Dryden' (x *anglica*)   CLyd NHol WAbe
  (7)
'Kathleen Pinsent' (8) ♀   CLyd EPot MBro MDHE NHar
                                       NVic NWCA SIng
'Kathleen' (x *polulacina*)   NHol
  (7)
x **kellereri** sensu   See *S.* 'Johann Kellerer' (x
  stricto hort.   *kellereri*)
'Kestoniensis' (x   MWat NNrd
  salmonica) (7)
'Kew Gem' (7)   NMen
'Kewensis' (x *kellereri*) (7)   MWat NMen SIng WAbe
¶ 'Kineton'   EHyt
'King Lear'   LFox LRHS MWat NMen SBla
  (x *bursiculata*) (7)
'Kingscote White' (15)   MDHE SIng
'Kinki Purple' B&SWJ 4972   WCru WHil
  (*stolonifera*) (7)
'Klondike' (x *boydii*) (7)   Last listed 1999
'Knapton Pink' (15)   EWTr MDHE NRya SIng SSmi
                                       WAbe
'Knapton White' (15)   EWTr MDHE NBro SIng
§ x **kochii** (7)   NHar NTow
§ 'Kolbiana' (x *paulinae*) (7)   CLyd MWat
'Koprvvnik' (*paniculata*) (8)   SIng WAbe
'Krasava'   CPBP EMNN NHar NHol NMen
  (x *megaseiflora*) (7)   WAbe
'Kyrillii' (x *borisii*) (7)   CLyd NMen
'Labe' (x *arco-valleyi*) (7)   CLyd CNic EPot LRHS NMen SBla
                                       SIng WAbe
'Labradorica' (*paniculata*)   See *S. paniculata* subsp. *neogaea*

'Lady Beatrix Stanley' — See *S.* 'Beatrix Stanley' (x *anglica*)
'Lagraveana' (*paniculata*) (8) — ELan NDlv WWin
x *landaueri* sensu stricto hort. — See *S.* 'Leonore' (x *landaueri*)
¶ 'Latina' (*oppostifolia*) (7) — CLyd ELan EMNN GCrs GDra GGar GTou MHer NHar SOkh
¶ 'Lemon Hybrid' (7) — NMen
'Lemon Spires' (7) — NMen
'Lenka' (x *byamgroundsii*) (7) — EMNN ITim NHar NMen NNrd NSla WAbe
'Leo Gordon Godseff' (x *elisabethae*) (7) — LRHS MOne NMen SBla
§ 'Leonore' (x *landaueri*) (7) — LRHS MWat
'Letchworth Gem' (x *urbium*) (11) — GCal
x *leyboldii* (7) — GTou NMen
'Lidice' (7) — CLyd EMNN NHar NMen NNrd WAbe WHoo
lilacina (7) — CLyd EMNN NHar NHol NMen NNrd WPat
'Limelight' (*callosa*) (8) — MDHE
'Lindau' (7) — MWat
lingulata — See *S. callosa*
'Lismore Carmine' (x *lismorensis*) (7) — CLyd MWat NMen
¶ 'Lismore Cherry' (7) — CLyd EHyt
* 'Lismore Gem' (7) — NMen
'Lismore Mist' (7) — Last listed 1999
'Lismore Pink' (x *lismorensis*) (7) — CLyd EPot MWat NMen NWCA
'Lohengrin' (x *boerhammeri*) (7) — MWat NNrd
'Lohmuelleri' (x *biasolettoi*) (7) — MWat
longifolia (8) — ELan GCrs NMen NSla NWCA
- JJA 861600 (8) — Last listed 1999
Love Me — See *S.* 'Miluj Mne' (x *poluanglica*)
'Lowndes' (*andersonii*) (7) — Last listed 1999
lowndesii (7) — Last listed 1999
'Ludmila Šubrová' (x *bertolonii*) (7) — CLyd
'Luna' (x *millstreamiana*) (7) — Last listed 1998
'Lusanna' (x *irvingii*) (7) — NHol
'Luschtinetz' (15) — MDHE
'Lutea' (*diapensioides*) — See *S.* 'Wilhelm Tell' (x *malbyana*), 'Primulina' (x *malbyana*)
'Lutea' (*marginata*) — See *S.* 'Faust' (x *borisii*)
'Lutea' (*paniculata*) (8) ♀ — CNic ESis GDra GTou LBee LRHS MBro NBro NDlv NMen NNrd SChu SIng SSmi
'Lutea' (x *stuartii*) (7) — Last listed 1999
§ 'Luteola' (x *boydii*) (7) ♀ — Last listed 1999
luteoviridis — See *S. corymbosa*
'Lužnice' (x *poluluteopurpurea*) (7) — MWat NDlv NMen
macedonica — See *S. juniperifolia*
'Magna' (*burseriana*) (7) — Last listed 1999
'Major' (*cochlearis*) (8) ♀ — LRHS MBro NMen WGor
'Major Lutea' — See *S.* 'Luteola' (x *boydii*)
mansburiensis (4) — Last listed 1998
§ 'Maréchal Joffre' (15) — LBuc MDHE
¶ 'Margaret Webster' (*trifurcata*) (15) — MDHE
'Margarete' (x *borisii*) (7) — CLyd MWat NDlv
marginata (7) — CLyd LFox
- var. *balcanica* — See *S. marginata* var. *rocheliana*
- var. *boryi* (7) — CLyd EPot LRHS MWat NMen SIng
- var. *coriophylla* (7) — EPot NWCA

- var. *karadzicensis* — See *S. karadzicensis*
§ - var. *rocheliana* (7) — CLyd CPBP EPot LRHS NMen
'Maria Callas' (x *poluanglica*) (7) — CLyd
'Maria Luisa' (x *salmonica*) (7) — CNic CPBP GCrs LFox MBro MWat NDlv NMen WAbe
'Marianna' (x *borisii*) (7) — CLyd NDlv NMen NNrd
'Marie Stivínová' (x *borisii*) (7) — MWat
'Maroon Beauty' (*stolonifera*) (5) — EMar WCot
'Mars' (x *elisabethae*) (7) — MWat
'Marshal Joffre' (15) — See *S.* 'Maréchal Joffre'
§ *marsballii* (4) — GCHN WWin
§ 'Martha' (x *semmleri*) (7) — CLyd EMNN NMen NNrd
matta-florida (7) — MWat
'May Queen' (7) — MWat NHol
media (7) — CLyd MWat
x *megaseiflora* sensu stricto hort. — See *S.* 'Robin Hood' (x *megaseiflora*)
'Melrose' (x *salmonica*) (7) — NMen
mertensiana (6) — CLyd GTou NBir WCru
- var. *bulbifera* (6) — CNic
'Meteor' (7) — NNrd
micranthidifolia (4) — EBee WPGP
'Millstream Cream' (x *elisabethae*) (7) — CGra CLyd EPot MWat NMen NNrd
§ 'Miluj Mne' (x *poluanglica*) (7) — LFox NHar NNrd
'Minnehaha' (x *elisabethae*) (7) — WAbe
'Minor' (*cochlearis*) (8) ♀ — EMNN ESis GTou LBee LFox LRHS MBro NHol NMen NVic NWCA SChu SIng WHoo WPat
'Minor Glauca' (*paniculata*) — See *S. paniculata* subsp. *neogaea*
'Minor' (*paniculata*) — See *S. paniculata* var. *brevifolia*
'Minutifolia' (*paniculata*) (8) — EPot LFox LRHS MBro MDHE NDlv NWCA SIng WAbe
§ 'Miss Chambers' (x *urbium*) (11) — CMea EBee EMon SUsu WCot WPen
'Mona Lisa' (x *borisii*) (7) — CLyd MBro MWat NHol WPat
§ 'Mondscheinsonate' (x *boydii*) (7) — NHol
'Moonlight' — See *S.* 'Sulphurea' (x *boydii*)
'Moonlight Sonata' (x *boydii*) — See *S.* 'Mondscheinsonate' (x *boydii*)
moschata — See *S. exarata* subsp. *moschata*
'Mother of Pearl' (x *irvingii*) (7) — CLyd EMNN NHar NMen WAbe
'Mother Queen' (x *irvingii*) (7) — MBro NHol WHoo WPat WPyg
'Mount Nachi' (*fortunei*) (5) — CLyd EBee EWes GCal LRHS NHar NMen NPSI SIng SMad SPla SSpi WAbe WCot WFar WPer
'Mrs E. Piper' (15) — LBuc MDHE SRms
§ 'Mrs Gertie Prichard' (x *megaseiflora*) (7) — LFox MWat NHol NMen
'Mrs Helen Terry' (x *salmonica*) (7) — CLyd EPot LRHS NDlv NMen
'Mrs Leng' (x *elisabethae*) (7) — NMen
mutata (8) — SIng
'Myra' (x *anglica*) (7) — EMNN LFox LRHS MBro MWat NHol NMen NWCA WHoo WPat WPyg
'Myra Cambria' (x *anglica*) (7) — GCHN MWat NHol NMen NNrd WAbe
'Nancye' (x *goringiana*) (7) — CGra CLyd CPBP NMen
§ *nelsoniana* (4) — NHol NNrd

'Neptun' (7) — Last listed 1999
¶ 'Nimbus' (7) — EHyt SOkh
'Niobe' (7) — NMen
nishidae (10) — MDHE
nivalis (4) — NHol NWCA
'Norvegica' (*cotyledon*) (8) — GTou MDHE WWin
'Notata' (*paniculata*) (8) — NMen
'Nottingham Gold' — CLyd EPot MWat NHol NMen
(x *boydii*) (7)
'Nugget' (7) — Last listed 1999
'Obristii' (x *salmonica*) (7) — ITim NHol NMen NNrd NRya
§ *obtusa* (7) — NMen
'Obtusocuneata' — ECho NHar SBla WAbe
(*fortunei*) (5)
'Ochroleuca' — CLyd EMNN ITim NMen
(x *elisabethae*) (7)
'Odysseus' (*sancta*) (7) — NMen
'Olymp' (*scardica*) (7) — NMen
'Opalescent' (7) — CLyd LFox MWat NMen NNrd
§ 'Ophelia' (x *arco-valleyi*) — MWat NHol
(7)
oppositifolia (7) — GKir GTou ITim MBNS MHer
MOne NSla SIng SPlb SRms
WWin
- var. *asiatica* (7) — Last listed 1998
- x *biflora* — See S. x *kochii*
- 'Corrie Fee' — See S. 'Corrie Fee' (*oppositifolia*)
- from Iceland (7) — SOkh
'Oriole' (x *boydii*) (7) — NMen
'Orjen' (*paniculata* — NNrd
var. *orientalis*) (8)
¶ 'Oxhill' — EHyt NMen
'Pandora' (*burseriana*) (7) — Last listed 1997
§ *paniculata* (8) — CNic ELan ESis GTou LPVe LRHS
MBro MHer MWat NDlv NMen
NSla NVic SPlb SRms WHoo WPyg
§ - var. *baldensis* (8) — CLyd ELan GDra GTou ITim LRHS
MBar MBro MWat NBro NDlv
NHol NMen NRya SBla SPlb SSmi
WAbe WWin
§ - var. *brevifolia* (8) — CNic SIng
§ - subsp. *cartilaginea* (8) — NHol SBla
§ - subsp. *kolenatiana* — See S. *paniculata* subsp.
cartilaginea
§ - subsp. *neogaea* (8) — MDHE
§ - var. *orientalis* (8) — MBro SSmi
paradoxa (15) — EPot LRHS SBla WCot WGor
'Parcevalis' (x *finnisiae*)
(7x9)
parnassifolia (1) — GCrs
'Parsee' — NMen NRya
(x *margoxiana*) (7)
x *patens* (8x9) — Last listed 1999
'Paula' (x *paulinae*) (7) — Last listed 1998
'Peach Blossom' (7) — CLyd EPot GCrs LRHS MWat
NMen NRya SBla
'Pearl Rose' (x *anglica*) (7) — LFox
'Pearly Gates' — CLyd MWat NMen NSla
(x *irvingii*) (7)
'Pearly Gold' (15) — CMea LRHS NRya SSmi
'Pearly King' (15) — CLyd ECho ELan LBee LRHS MHer
NMen NVic WAbe WFar
§ x *pectinata* (8) — NHol NNrd SIng
pedemontana (15) — MDHE
- subsp. *cervicornis* (15) — Last listed 1999
'Penelope' — CLyd EPot GCrs ITim LRHS MBro
(x *boydilacina*) (7) — NHol NMen SBla SIng WAbe
WHoo WPat WPyg
¶ *pensylvanica* — GCal
¶ 'Perikles' (7) — NMen
'Peter Burrow' — CLyd CPBP NHar NMen NNrd
(x *poluanglica*) (7) ♀

'Peter Pan' (15) — EMNN EPot EWTr GDra GKir
GTou LFox LGro LRHS MBro MHer
NFla NMen NNrd SSmi WPat
'Petra' (7) — CLyd EPot MBro NHol NMen
NNrd WAbe
x *petraschii* (7) — ITim
§ 'Phoenix' — CLyd LRHS NMen
(x *biasolettoi*) (7)
'Pilatus' (x *boydii*) (7) — MWat NMen SIng
'Pink Pearl' (7) — CMea
'Pixie' (15) — EBrP EBre EMNN GKir LBCl LBSe
LBee LBre LRHS MBBe MWat NFla
NMen NNrd SBre SIng SRms SSmi
'Pixie Alba' — See S. 'White Pixie'
'Plena' (*granulata*) — See S. 'Flore Pleno' (*granulata*)
'Pluto' (x *megaseiflora*) — Last listed 1999
'Pollux' (x *boydii*) (7) — EPot NHol
¶ x *poluanglica* (7) — NLAp
poluniniana (7) — CLyd EMNN ITim LFox NHar
NHol NWCA
'Pompadour' (15) — LRHS MDHE
'Popelka' (*marginata*) (7) — CLyd
porophylla (7) — GDra
- var. *thessalica* — See S. *sempervivum* f.
stenophylla
aff. *porophylla* (7) — NWCA
¶ 'Portae' (x *pectinata*) (8) — NNrd SIng
'Primrose Bee' — EPot
(x *apiculata*) (7)
'Primrose Dame' — EMNN ESis ITim MWat NHol
(x *elisabethae*) (7) — NMen WFar
¶ 'Primulaize' (9x11) — CLyd MBro NMen SRot
'Primulaize Salmon' (9x11) — LBee NDlv NWoo WPer
§ 'Primulina' — LFox NDlv
(x *malbyana*) (7)
primuloides — See S. 'Primuloides' (*umbrosa*)
§ 'Primuloides' — CGle GCHN LFox MBro NPri
(*umbrosa*) (11) ♀ — SRms WEas
'Prince Hal' — CLyd EMNN EPot ESis GCrs ITim
(*burseriana*) (7) — LRHS NDlv NHar NMen NNrd SIng
'Princess' (*burseriana*) (7) — CLyd LRHS NMen
'Probynii' (*cochlearis*) (8) — EPot MDHE MWat NMen
'Prometheus' — CLyd NNrd
(x *prossenii*) (7)
'Prospero' — MWat NMen
(x *petraschii*) (7)
x *prossenii* sensu — See S. 'Regina' (x *prossenii*)
stricto hort.
§ 'Pseudoborisii' — EPot ITim
(x *borisii*) (7)
'Pseudofranzii' — NWCA
(x *paulinae*) (7)
x *pseudokotschyi* — See S. 'Denisa' (x *pseudokotschyi*)
sensu stricto hort.
'Pseudosalomonii' — Last listed 1997
(x *salmonica*) (7)
'Pseudoscardica' — MWat
(x *wehrhahnii*) (7)
'Pseudovaldensis' — CNic MDHE
(*cochlearis*) (8)
pubescens subsp. — Last listed 1999
iratiana (15)
punctata Sternbo. (4) — See S. *nelsoniana*
'Pungens' (x *apiculata*) (7) — NDlv NHol NMen
'Purpurea' (*fortunei*) — See S. 'Rubrifolia' (*fortunei*)
'Purpurteppich' (15) — MDHE WPer
§ 'Pygmalion' (x *webrii*) (7) — CLyd ESis NHol NMen WPat
'Pyramidalis' — EPfP SRms
(*cotyledon*) (8)
'Pyrenaica' — EMNN NHar NMen
(*oppositifolia*) (7)
quadrifaria (7) — NHol

'Quarry Wood' CLyd ITim NMen
  (x *anglica*) (7)
'Rainsley Seedling' MDHE NBro NMen
  (*paniculata*) (8)
ramulosa (7) NMen
¶ 'Red Pixie' CPri
'Red Poll' CLyd MWat NMen NRya
  (x *poluanglica*) (7)
§ 'Regina' (x *prossenii*) (7) GCHN ITim NNrd SIng
retusa (7) CLyd EMNN NMen NSla NWCA
'Rex' (*paniculata*) (8) GCHN LBuc NHol NMen
rhodopetala (7) Last listed 1999
§ 'Riverslea' CGle CPBP LFox LRHS MBro
  (x *hornibrookii*) (7) ♀ MWat NHar NHol NMen WAbe
  WPat
¶ *rivularis* (14) MDCh
§ 'Robin Hood' CLyd EMNN ITim LFox LRHS MWat
  (x *megaseiflora*) (7) NHar NHol NMen SBla SIng
  WPat
'Rokujô' (*fortunei*) (5) GKir LRHS MBri WCot WFar
'Romeo' CLyd
  (x *hornibrookii*) (7)
rosacea subsp. *hartii* (15) Last listed 1998
'Rosea' (*cortusifolia*) (5) CLAP NHar
'Rosea' (*paniculata*) (8) ♀ GDra GTou LBee LRHS MBro
  NBro NDlv NHol NSla SBla SRms
  SSmi STre WPyg WWin
'Rosea' (x *stuartii*) (7) NDlv NMen
'Rosemarie' (x *anglica*) (7) CLyd ITim NHol NMen
'Rosenzwerg' (15) LRHS
'Rosina Sündermann' NDlv NSla
  (x *rosinae*) (7)
rotundifolia (12) CLyd EBee GBin NHol SSpi
§ - subsp. WCru WPer
  chrysospleniifolia
  var. *rhodopea* (12)
- subsp. *rotundifolia* SIng
  var. *heucherifolia* (12)
'Rubella' (x *irvingii*) (7) CLyd MWat
§ 'Rubrifolia' (*fortunei*) (5) CLAP EBee EBrP EBre ECha LBCl
  LBSe LBre LPan MBBe NBus NHar
  SBre SMad SSpi WAbe WCot WCru
  WFar WGer WSan
* 'Ruby Red' NPro
¶ 'Rusalka' (x *borisii*) (7) NMen SOkh
'Russell Vincent Prichard' NHol
  (x *irvingii*) (7)
'Ruth Draper' EMNN GCHN NHar NLAp NWCA
  (*oppositifolia*) (7) SBla
'Ruth McConnell' (15) CMea EWTr LBuc LRHS MDHE
'Sabrina' CLyd MWat
  (x *fallsvillagensis*) (7)
¶ 'Saint John's' EBur MBro MDHE NNrd WWin
  (x *pectinata*) (8)
'Saint Kilda' GCrs GTou
  (*oppositifolia*) (7)
x *salmonica* sensu See S. 'Salomonii' (x *salmonica*)
  stricto hort.
§ 'Salomonii' CLyd ITim MBro MOne NDlv
  (x *salmonica*) (7) NMen NNrd SIng SRms
¶ 'Samo' (x *bertolonii*) (7) CLyd
sancta (7) CLyd EPot GCHN LFox LRHS
  NMen SRms SSmi
- subsp. *pseudosancta* See S. *juniperifolia*
  var. *macedonica*
sanguinea (1) MDHE
'Sanguinea Superba' GDra MDHE SIng
  (x *arendsii*) (15) ♀
'Sara Sinclair' Last listed 1998
  x *arco-valleyi* (7)
sarmentosa See S. *stolonifera*
'Sartorii' See S. 'Pygmalion' (x *webrii*)

'Saturn' (x *megaseiflora*) MBro MWat NHol NMen WAbe
  (7)
'Sázava' ITim MWat NDlv NMen SOkh WAbe
  (x *poluluteopurpurea*)
  (7)
scardica (7) CPBP EMNN MBro MWat NBro
  NMen
- var. *dalmatica* See S. *obtusa*
- f. *erythrantha* (7) CLyd NNrd
¶ - JJ105 (7) EHyt
- var. *obtusa* See S. *obtusa*
§ 'Schelleri' (x *petraschii*) NNrd
  (7)
§ 'Schleicheri' Last listed 1998
  (x *landaueri*) (7)
'Schneeteppich' (15) WPer
§ 'Schwefelblüte' (15) GKir GTou LBee LRHS SIng SSmi
  WPat
scleropoda (7) Last listed 1999
§ 'Seaspray' (x *arendsii*) EWes
  (15/v)
'Seissera' (*burseriana*) (7) EPot NHol
x *semmleri* sensu See S. 'Martha' (x *semmleri*)
  stricto hort.
sempervivum (7) CLyd EPot LFox MBro NMen NSla
  NWCA WTin
- JCA 864.003 (7) CPBP MBro
§ - f. *stenophylla* GCHN GTou MHer
sibirica (14) GTou
¶ 'Silver Cushion' (15/v) CMea ELan EPfP EPot GTou LAst
  LRHS MBar MBro SIng SMer SPlb
  SSmi WAbe WMoo
'Silver Edge' NMen WAbe
  (x *arco-valleyi*) (7)
'Silver Mound' See S. 'Silver Cushion'
'Sir Douglas Haig' (15) MDHE NNrd SIng
'Snowcap' (*pubescens*) (15) GCrs LBee NDlv NMen NNrd
  NWCA
'Snowdon' (*burseriana*) MWat NMen
  (7)
'Snowflake' (8) MDHE NDlv
§ 'Sofia' (x *borisii*) (7) EPot LFox NNrd
'Somerset Seedling' (8) MDHE
§ 'Southside Seedling' (8) ♀ CLyd CPri ELan EPot ESis GTou
  LHop LRHS MBar MBro NBro
  NHar NHol NMen SIng SRms
  SSmi WAbe WCot WHil WHoo
  WLin WPat WPyg WWin
sp. BM&W 118 GDra
¶ sp. from Nepal, McB 1397 CLyd
sp. SEP 22 CLyd MWat
'Spartakus' Last listed 1998
  (x *apiculata*) (7)
spathularis (11) MHar WCot WEas WWin
'Speciosa' (*burseriana*) (7) NDlv
¶ 'Spinners Snow-storm' SSpi
  (*fortunei*) (5)
'Splendens' ELan EMNN ITim LFox NDlv
  (*oppositifolia*) (7) ♀ NHol NMen SMer SRms WGor
  WPat
'Sprite' (15) GCHN LRHS MDHE
spruneri (7) LRHS NMen
- var. *deorum* (7) Last listed 1998
'Stansfieldii' (15) EBrP EBre EMNN LBCl LBSe LBre
  LRHS MBBe MDHE NMen NNrd
  SBre SSmi
I 'Stansfieldii Rosea' MDHE
§ 'Stella' (x *stormonthii*) (7) SBla
stellaris (4) GTou
stenophylla See S. *flagellaris*
  ubsp. *stenophylla*
stolitzkae (7) EMNN GCrs NDlv NMen

§ ***stolonifera*** (5) ♀ — CArn CHEx CHal ECho GAri
MHar NBro SDix SIng WEas WFar

  - B&SWJ 1980 (5) — Last listed 1998

'Stormonth's Variety' — See *S.* 'Stella' (x *stormonthii*)

stribrnyi (7) — MWat

  - JCA 861-400 (7) — NWCA

'Sturmiana' (*paniculata*) (8) — MBro NMen SRms

'Suendermannii' (x *kellereri*) (7) — LRHS MWat NDlv NWCA

'Suendermannii Major' (x *kellereri*) (7) — CLyd LRHS NSla

'Suendermannii Purpurea' (x *kellereri*) (7) — GCHN

¶ 'Sugar Plum Fairy' (*fortunei*) (5) — CLAP

§ 'Sulphurea' (x *boydii*) (7) — CMea CPBP EMNN ESis LFox
LRHS MBro NDlv NHar NHol
NMen NNrd NWCA SChu SIng
WAbe WHoo WPat WPyg

'Sun Dance' (x *boydii*) (7) — NHol

'Superba' (*callosa* var. *australis*) (8) — GDra GTou MBro MDHE SSmi

'Sylva' (x *elisabethae*) (7) — MWat NMen

'Symons-Jeunei' (8) — MDHE

taygetea (12) — NTow

x ***tazetta*** (?11x12) — Last listed 1999

'Theoden' (*oppositifolia*) (7) ♀ — CLyd CPBP EMNN EWes GCrs
GTou MBro NHar NHol NPro
NWCA SBla WSan

'Thorpei' (7) — GCrs ITim NMen

'Timbalii' (x *gaudinii*) (8) — SIng

'Timmy Foster' (x *irvingii*) (7) — CLyd NHol NSla

x ***tiroliensis*** (8) — Last listed 1998

'Tom Thumb' (15) — MBro NMen NNrd

tombeanensis (7) — CLyd NMen

'Tricolor' (*stolonifera*) (5) ♀ — EBak LRHS SYvo WCru WFar

'Triumph' (x *arendsii*) (15) — ECtt EMNN GCHN GDra GTou
LRHS NMen NPri NVic

'Tully' (x *elisabethae*) (7) — ESis NHol WPat

'Tumbling Waters' (8) ♀ — GAbr LHop LRHS MBro NMen SIng
SRms WAbe WGor WPat WWin

§ 'Tvůj Den' (x *poluanglica*) (7) — NDlv NMen WAbe

§ 'Tvůj Píseň' x *poluanglica*) (7) — CLyd NDlv NHar WAbe

§ 'Tvůj Polibek' (x *poluanglica*) (7) — NDlv NHar NMen

§ 'Tvůj Přítel' (x *poluanglica*) (7) — NDlv NHar

§ 'Tvůj Úsměv' (x *poluanglica*) (7) — CPBP MWat NDlv NHar NMen

§ 'Tvůj Úspěch' (x *poluanglica*) (7) — NDlv NMen SBla SOkd WAbe

'Tycho Brahe' (x *doerfleri*) (7) — CLyd NMen

¶ 'Tysoe' — NMen

umbrosa (11) — COlW EBee EBrP EBre EMon LBCl
LBSe LBre LRHS MBBe MCAu
MRav SBre SMac SPer SPlb SRms
WHen WMoo WWat WWin

  - 'Aurea' — See *S.* 'Aureopunctata' (x *urbium*)

  - var. ***primuloides*** — See *S.* 'Primuloides' (*umbrosa*)

*   - ***subinteger*** — Last listed 1999

'Unique' — See *S.* 'Bodensee' (x *hofmannii*)

x ***urbium*** (11) ♀ — EBee ELan EPfP GDra LAst LEdu
LGro NDov NSti SIng WCFE WFar
WPer

  - ***primuloides*** — See *S.* 'Clarence Elliott' (*umbrosa*)

    'Elliott's Variety'

'Vaccariana' (*oppositifolia*) (7) — ECho WAbe

'Václav Hollar' (x *gusmusii*) (7) — MWat NMen

'Vahlii' (x *smithii*) (7) — NMen WAbe

'Valborg' — See *S.* 'Cranbourne' (x *anglica*)

'Valentine' — See *S.* 'Cranbourne' (x *anglica*)

'Valerie Finnis' — See *S.* 'Aretiastrum' (x *boydii*)

I 'Variegata' (*cuneifolia*) (3) — ECho ECtt EPfP ESis GCHN MBar
MBro NPri NVic SHFr SSmi WMoo
WPer

'Variegata' (*umbrosa*) — See *S.* 'Aureopunctata' (x *urbium*)

I 'Variegata' (x *urbium*) (3) — EBee EPar EPfP GDra GGar LAst
LGro LRHS MRav NCat NFor NLar
NSti NVic SRms SSmi WEas WWal
WWat WWin

vayredana (15) — CLyd WAbe

veitchiana (5) — EBee EPla NBro NCat NNrd WCru

'Venetia' (*paniculata*) (8) — MDHE NNrd SSmi

'Vesna' (x *borisii*) (7) — CLyd EMNN GCHN MOne MWat
NMen NNrd WWin

§ ***vespertina*** (10) — CGra

'Vincent van Gogh' (x *borisii*) (7) — CLyd ITim NHol NMen NNrd NRya

'Vladana' (x *megaseiflora*) (7) — CLyd EMNN EPot NHar NHol NMen

'Vlasta' (7) — CLyd MWat

'Vltava' (7) — Last listed 1998

'Volgeri' (x *hofmannii*) (7) — CLyd

'W.A. Clark' (*oppositifolia*) (7) — Last listed 1999

'Wada' (*fortunei*) (5) — CGle CLAP CWit EBee EPar GAbr
GCHN LAst MDun NBir NCut
NHar SPer SSpi WAbe WBea WCot
WFar

'Waithman's Variety' (8) — NNrd

§ 'Wallacei' (15) — ECho MDHE

'Walpole's Variety' (*longifolia*) (8) — CBrm NHar NNrd WPer

§ 'Walter Ingwersen' (*umbrosa*) (11) — SIng SRms

'Walter Ingwersen' (*umbrosa* var. *primuloides*) — See *S.* 'Walter Ingwersen' (*umbrosa*)

§ 'Walter Irving' (x *irvingii*) (7) — CLyd EMNN EPot LRHS NHar
NHol NMen

¶ 'Walton' — EHyt

¶ 'Weisser Zwerg' (15) — MDHE

'Welsh Dragon' (15) — MDHE WAbe

'Welsh Red' (15) — WAbe

'Welsh Rose' (15) — WAbe

wendelboi (7) — CLyd EMNN LFox MWat
NMen

'Wendrush' (x *wendelacina*) (7) — CLyd NMen

'Wendy' (x *wendelacina*) (7) — CNic NMen

'Wetterhorn' (*oppositifolia*) (7) — CLyd

'Wheatley Lion' (x *borisii*) (7) — NMen

'Wheatley Rose' (7) — CLyd LRHS NHol

'White Cap' (x *boydii*) (7) — NHol

'White Imp' (7) — CLyd

§ 'White Pixie' (15) — CLyd EMNN EPfP GKir LBee LFox
LGro LRHS MHer NNrd NPri
NRya SBla SIng SRms SSmi

'White Spire' (15) — MBro

'White Star' (x *petraschii*) — See *S.* 'Schelleri' (x *petraschii*)

'Whitehill' (8) — CLyd EBrP EBre EGoo ELan ESis
GCHN GTou LBCl LBSe LBee LBre
LFox LRHS MBBe MBro NBro

'Whitlavei Compacta' (*hypnoides*) (15) | NEgg NHol NMen SBre SIng SSmi WAbe WHoo WPat WPer WPyg WTin WWin MTPN NWoo

§ 'Wilhelm Tell' (x *malbyana*) (7) | Last listed 1999

'William Boyd' (x *boydii*) (7) | MWat

'Winifred' (x *anglica*) (7) | CLyd GCrs LFox MWat NMen WFar

'Winifred Bevington' (8x11) | More than 30 suppliers
'Winston Churchill' (15) | EPfP LRHS MBNS MDHE SIng
Winter Fire | See S. 'Winterfeuer' (*callosa*)
§ 'Winterfeuer' (*callosa*) (8) | Last listed 1997
'Winton' (x *paulinae*) (7) | Last listed 1999
'Wisley' (*frederici-augusti* subsp. *grisebachii*) (7) ♀ | GCHN MBro NHar NMen WFar WHoo WPat WPyg

'Wisley Primrose' | See S. 'Kolbiana' (x *paulinae*)
'Woodside Ross' (15) | MOne
'Yellow Rock' (7) | NRya
Your Day | See S. 'Tvuj Den' (x *poluanglica*)
Your Friend | See S. 'Tvuj Prítel' (x *poluanglica*)
Your Good Fortune | See S. 'Tvuj Uspech' (x *poluanglica*)
Your Kiss | See S. 'Tvuj Polibek' (x *poluanglica*)
Your Smile | See S. 'Tvuj Usmev' (x *poluanglica*)
Your Song | See S. 'Tvuj Písen' (x *poluanglica*)
Your Success | See S. 'Tvuj Uspech' (x *poluanglica*)
x *zimmeteri* (8x11) | EWes NNrd SSmi
§ 'Zlatá Praha' (x *pragensis*) (7) | CLyd NMen NRya
¶ 'Zlin' | NMen
* *zoblenschaferi* | Last listed 1997

SCABIOSA ✿ (Dipsacaceae)

africana | CElw WCot
alpina L. | See *Cephalaria alpina*
anthemifolia | Last listed 1999
atropurpurea | CLTr EBee EGoo MTis SMrm SUsu
- 'Ace of Spades' | CHad CSpe CWes GBri LFis NDov NSti SMad WCot WHil
- dark-flowered | CSpe
- 'Peter Ray' | EWes LRHS MBri
banatica | See S. *columbaria*
* 'Black Prince' | Last listed 1998
§ Butterfly Blue® | EPfP GKir LRHS MBNS MBri MRav MWgw SCoo SPer WWeb
caucasica | CSam ECha EPfP EWTr GChr LAst LRHS MBro NCat NChi NCut SBla WHoo WPyg WWin
- var. *alba* | CBot CPlt EPfP LRHS MBri WHoo
- 'Blue Lace' | MBri
- Blue Seal = 'Blausiegel' | EBee EBrP EBre LBCl LBSe LBre LRHS MBBe SBre
- 'Bressingham White' | SAsh
- 'Challenger' | MBri SAsh
- 'Clive Greaves' ♀ | CB&S CMGP EBee ECha ENot EOld GKir LAst LHop LRHS LRot MBri MBro MCAu NFor NMir SMer SPer SRms WCot WEas
- 'Fama' | CFai COIW EMan EWTr MBNS MHer NBir NLar SMrm SPlb SRms SSca WBar WFar WHoo WPyg
- 'Floral Queen' | Last listed 1997
- 'Goldingensis' | EBee EOld GKir GMac MBNS NCut NPri WFar WPer

- House's hybrids | NBro NVic SMac SRms WElm WFar WHil WMoo
- 'Isaac House' | Last listed 1999
- 'Kompliment' | ENot NChi NLar WShe
- 'Lavender Blue' | MTis NCut WFar
- 'Miss Willmott' ♀ | CGle CHad CM&M CSev EBee ECha EFou EWTr GKir LAst LHop LRHS MBel MBri MBro MCAu MHer MTis NFla SPer SRms SUsu WCot WFar WRus
- 'Moerheim Blue' | ECha MBri NFla
- 'Moonstone' | LRHS
- 'Mount Cook' | SAsh
- 'Nachtfalter' | LRHS MBri
- 'Penelope Harrison' | Last listed 1997
- 'Perfecta' | CSpe EBee EOrc GMaP LPio LRHS MTis NCut NLar SMrm SSca SWat WWhi
- 'Perfecta Alba' | COIW CSpe EBee EMan EWTr GKir GMaP LFis LPio MBro NCut NLar NOrc NPri SCob SMrm SSca SWat WOve WPyg WWhi
- 'Stäfa' | CM&M EBee GKir LHop LRHS MBel MBri MMHG SAsh SMrm SPer
'Chile Black' | CMea CSam CWes EBee ELan EMan EWes GCal LGre LRHS MAnH MCAu MSte NGdn NSti SAga SUsu WCot WHoo WPGP WRus
* 'Chile Red' | EBee ECoo GCal
cinerea | EBee WMoo WWin
§ *columbaria* | CKin EBee EWFC EWTr MChe MHew MLLN MNaF NLan NMir NWCA WHer WHoo WJek WPyg
* - *alba* | Last listed 1998
- 'Nana' | NBir NMen NPri SIng SSmi SUsu WPyg
§ - var. *ochroleuca* | CBot CFri CGle CMea CRDP EBee ECha LLWP LRHS MBNS MBro MCAu MCLN MLLN MRav NArg NBir NChi NCiC NLar NPri NSti SMrm SRms SSca WCot WHoo WPGP WWin
- subsp. *portae* | EBee
- var. *webbiana* | WLin
cretica | EBee
'Crimson Cushion' | CElw CFai
drakensbergensis | EBee
farinosa | CBot CElw EBee MHar SAga SGar SMrm WPGP WPer
- 'Schofield's Variegated' | Last listed 1998
gigantea | See *Cephalaria gigantea*
graminifolia | EBee EBrP EBre EDAr EMan GBuc LBCl LBSe LBre LPio LRHS MBBe NBir NMen NTow NWCA SBre SUsu
- 'Pinkushion' | CStr
- *rosea* | EWes
holosericea | Last listed 1998
incisa 'Pink Cheer' | Last listed 1999
¶ 'Irish Perpetual Flowering' | NDov
japonica | WPer
- var. *alpina* | CFri CHar CInt CLTr EBee ECoo ESis GTou LIck MBel MBro SRot WBea WCot WHoo WLin WRha WSan
lachnophylla | Last listed 1999
lucida | CGle EBee EMan EPar GDra GTou LRHS MBro MRav NPri SBla SMrm SSpe WCot WEas WPat WPer
mansenensis | EMon
maritima | EBee

'Midnight' CMea
minoana Last listed 1998
montana Mill. See *Knautia arvensis*
—(Bieb.) DC. See *Knautia tatarica*
ochroleuca See *S. columbaria* var. *ochroleuca*
parnassi See *Pterocephalus perennis*
* 'Perfecta Lilac Blue' CSev
'Perpetual Flowering' See *S.* Butterfly Blue
'Pink Buttons' EBee ECoo
'Pink Mist'[PBR] CGle ECha GKir LPio LRHS MCAu
NBir SCoo SPer SRms WWeb
pterocephala See *Pterocephalus perennis*
rhodopensis Last listed 1998
'Rosie's Pink' EMan
rumelica See *Knautia macedonica*
* 'Satchmo' Last listed 1997
silenifolia Last listed 1999
stellata Last listed 1999
succisa See *Succisa pratensis*
tatarica See *Cephalaria gigantea*
triandra EBee

SCABIOSA x CEPHALARIA (Dipsacaceae)
S. cinerea x *C. alpina* LRHS

SCADOXUS (Amaryllidaceae)
membranaceus Last listed 1997
multiflorus LAma LRHS MBri NRog
§ – subsp. *katherinae* ♀ Last listed 1995
– – 'King Albert' Last listed 1997
natalensis See *S. puniceus*
§ *puniceus* ERea NRog

SCAEVOLA (Goodeniaceae)
aemula 'Alba' Last listed 1997
– 'Blue Fan'[PBR] See *S. aemula* 'Blue Wonder'
§ – 'Blue Wonder'[PBR] CHal CSpe EMan LHil LHop SHFr
– 'New Wonder' WLRN
– 'Petite' CHal CLTr LHil
crassifolia Last listed 1998
hookeri Last listed 1999
¶ 'Saphira'[PBR] CGdn

SCANDIX (Apiaceae)
pecten-veneris EWFC

SCHEFFLERA (Araliaceae)
actinophylla ♀ EBak MBri SRms
arboricola ♀ CTrC LBlo MBri SEND
– 'Compacta' MBri
– 'Gold Capella' ♀ LRHS MBri
– 'Jacqueline' Last listed 1999
– 'Trinetta' MBri
digitata Last listed 1998
elegantissima ♀ Last listed 1997
microphylla B&SWJ 3872 WCru

SCHIMA (Theaceae)
argentea See *S. wallichii* subsp. *noronhae*
var. *superba*
¶ *wallichii* CFil
subsp. *liukiuensis*
§ – subsp. *noronhae* CHEx WBod WWat
var. *superba*
– subsp. *wallichii* ISea
var. *khasiana*
* *yunnanensis* GGGa

SCHINUS (Anacardiaceae)
molle Last listed 1999
patagonicus Last listed 1998
polygamus CGre

terebinthifolius SMad

SCHISANDRA (Schisandraceae)
arisanensis B&SWJ 3050 WCru
chinensis CArn CPlN WNor WSHC
– B&SWJ 4204 WCru
grandiflora CDoC EBee ECot ELan EPfP GCal
LRHS MBlu SSta
– B&SWJ 2245 WCru
– var. *cathayensis* See *S. sphaerandra*
henryi CPlN
propinqua var. *sinensis* CBot MBlu WCru
rubriflora CCHP CPLG CRHN CWSG EBee
EPfP GOrc IDee LRHS MAsh MBlu
MDun MGos MTis SBrw SLon
SPan SPer SSpi WBod
– (f) CB&S CPlN ELan MBlu MGos SBra
WSHC WWat
– (m) CPlN EMil NHol
§ *sphaerandra* CPlN
sphenanthera EBee ELan EMil EPfP LRHS MDun
SRPl WSHC

SCHIVERECKIA (Brassicaceae)
doerfleri Last listed 1997

SCHIZACHYRIUM (Poaceae)
§ *scoparium* CBrm EBee EBrP EBre EHoe
EMon EWes GBin LBCl LBSe LBre
MBBe NHol SApp SBre SCob
¶ – 'The Blues' LPan

SCHIZANTHUS (Solanaceae)
candidus Last listed 1997
– RB 94104 Last listed 1998
gilliesii Last listed 1998
grahamii JCA 12365 Last listed 1998
hookeri Last listed 1998

SCHIZOCENTRON See HETEROCENTRON

SCHIZOCODON See SHORTIA

SCHIZOLOBIUM (Papilionaceae)
parahybum LBlo

SCHIZOPHRAGMA (Hydrangeaceae)
corylifolium WCru
hydrangeoides More than 30 suppliers
¶ – B&SWJ 5954 WCru
– 'Brookside Littleleaf' WCru
– 'Moonlight' (v) CFil ELan EPfP GKir IMGH LRHS
MAsh MBlu MBri NSti SBla SBra
SBrw SMur SPer SPla SSpi SSta
WCot WCru WPGP WPat WSHC
* – f. *quelpartensis* WCru
B&SWJ 1160
– 'Roseum' CDoC CFil EBee EPfP GKir LRHS
MBlu SBla SLim SSpi WCru WSHC
integrifolium ♀ CB&S CFil CHEx CMac CPlN EPfP
LRHS MBel MGos SDix SSpi
WPGP WSHC WWat
– var. *fauriei* B&SWJ 1701 WCru
– var. *molle* CPlN
¶ *intergerrima* MBlu
'Properinque'

SCHIZOSTACHYUM (Poaceae - Bambusoideae)
§ *funghomii* EPla SDry WJun

SCHIZOSTYLIS ✿ (Iridaceae)
coccinea More than 30 suppliers

- f. *alba* — More than 30 suppliers
- 'Ballyrogan Giant' — CFir CLAP CMil EBee EGle IBlr WPGP
- 'Cardinal' — CPea NCiC WFar
- 'Elburton Glow' — WFar
- 'Fenland Daybreak' — More than 30 suppliers
- 'Gigantea' — See *S. coccinea* 'Major'
- 'Grandiflora' — See *S. coccinea* 'Major'
- 'Hilary Gould' — CLAP CRDP GBuc IBlr MAvo NBrk SUsu WBea WBro WFar WHal WHil
¶ - 'Hint of Pink' — MAvo
- 'Jennifer' ♀ — CAvo CBro CGle CGrW CLAP CRDP CTri EFou ERos IBlr MBri MRav NHol SApp SCro SRms STes SUsu WBro WFar WWat
¶ - late-flowering — SIng
- 'Maiden's Blush' — EBee ECGP EFou EGle EHrv EWll GKir LIck LPio LRHS MAvo MBel NFla NHol NLar WBro WByw WFar WMoo
§ - 'Major' ♀ — More than 30 suppliers
* - 'Marietta' — CHid
- 'Molly Gould' — EBee EGle MAvo SLod WBro WHil WPGP
- 'Mrs Hegarty' — More than 30 suppliers
- 'November Cheer' — CGrW EBee EBrP EBre ECot IBlr LBCl LBSe LBre LIck LRHS MBBe MSte NFor NLar SBre SSpe WBro WFar
¶ - 'Oregon Sunset' — SLod
- 'Pallida' — CMil CSam EBee ECha EGar EHrv ELan EMan EOld GBuc IBlr MBct WBor WFar
- 'Professor Barnard' — CFee CGle CSpe EBee GCal GMac IBlr MBri MSte NBrk WBro WFar WPnn WPyg WWat
¶ - 'Red Dragon' — WFar
- 'Salmon Charm' — CLAP EBee EBrP EBre EFou IBlr LBCl LBSe LBre LRHS MBBe SBre WBro WFar
- seedling — Last listed 1998
- 'Snow Maiden' — CFai CLAP CRDP EBee LCaP LIck LRHS MBNS WBro WLRN
§ - 'Sunrise' ♀ — More than 30 suppliers
- 'Sunset' — See *S. coccinea* 'Sunrise'
- 'Tambara' — CGrW CLAP CMHG CPou EBee EGar EMan GMac IBlr LRHS SApp WElm WFar WHil WPGP WPnP
- 'The Bride' — EBee
- 'Viscountess Byng' — CBro CGle CHea EBee EGar EGle EPot GCal LRHS MAvo NRog SRms WBea WBro WCot WFar WHal WPer
* - 'Zeal Blush' — IBlr
- 'Zeal Salmon' — CBro CFee CFir CLAP CPou EBee ECha EGar EGle GMac IBlr NBrk SApp SCro SSpi WFar WHil WMoo

SCHOENOPLECTUS (Cyperaceae)
§ *lacustris* — EMFW MMoz
- subsp. *tabernaemontani* — CBen EBrP EBre EHon EMFW
- 'Albescens' (v) — LBCl LBSe LBre LPBA MBBe MSta MTed SBre SWat SWyc WCot
§ - - 'Golden Spear' — Last listed 1999
- - 'Zebrinus' (v) — CBen CBot CInt EBrP EBre EHon ELan EMFW EPfP GBin LBCl LBSe LBre LPBA MBBe MSta NDea SBre SLon SPlb SWat SWyc WCot WMAq WPrP WWeb
pungens — MSta

SCHOENUS (Cyperaceae)
pauciflorus — CCuc CFil ECou EHoe EMan GOrn NChi WDyG WHal WPGP

SCHOTIA (Caesalpiniaceae)
brachypetala — SOWG

SCIADOPITYS (Sciadopityaceae)
verticillata ♀ — CB&S CDoC CDul CKen CTho EHul GKir IOrc ISea LBee LCon LLin LNet LPan LRHS MBar MBlu MBri MDun MGos NWea SLim SSpi WCwm WDin WNor
- 'Firework' — CKen
- 'Globe' — CKen
- 'Gold Star' — CKen
- 'Jeddeloh Compact' — CKen
- 'Picola' — CKen
- 'Pygmy' — CKen
- 'Shorty' — CKen
- 'Stenschnuffe' — CKen

SCILLA ✿ (Hyacinthaceae)
adlamii — See *Ledebouria cooperi*
amethystina — See *S. litardierei*
amoena — LAma LRHS
autumnalis — CAvo CNic EWFC LAma LRHS WShi
- subsp. *fallax* AB&S 4345 — Last listed 1998
baurii — Last listed 1997
bifolia ♀ — CAvo CBro EPar EPot LAma LRHS NRog WShi
- 'Alba' — EPot LRHS
- 'Rosea' — EPar EPot LAma LRHS NRog WPer
bithynica — SSpi WShi WWat
campanulata — See *Hyacinthoides hispanica*
chinensis — See *S. scilloides*
cilicica — CBro LAma
greilhuberi — WAbe
hanburyi S&L 78 — Last listed 1998
hohenackeri — Last listed 1999
- BSBE 811 — Last listed 1998
hyacinthoides — Last listed 1999
italica — See *Hyacinthoides italica*
japonica — See *S. scilloides*
libanotica S&L 113 — Last listed 1998
liliohyacinthus — CAvo CBre CBro CRDP CRow IBlr MMHG SSpi
- 'Alba' — Last listed 1997
lingulata var. *ciliolata* — CBro
- MS 320 — Last listed 1998
- S&F 288 — Last listed 1998
- S&L 253 — Last listed 1998
§ *litardierei* — CAvo EPot ERos LAma LRHS WCot
- *hoogiana* — Last listed 1997
mauretanica alba — Last listed 1998
- S&F 65 — Last listed 1998
messeniaca — SHel
¶ - 'Grecian Sky' — SUsu
§ *mischtschenkoana* — CAvo CBro EBrP EBre EPar EPot ETub LAma LBCl LBSe LBow LBre LRHS MBBe MBri NRog SBre
- 'Tubergeniana' ♀ — WCot
§ - 'Zwanenburg' — Last listed 1999
monophyllos — CFil LAma
- SB 184 — Last listed 1998
morrisii M 4015 — Last listed 1998
non-scripta — See *Hyacinthoides non-scripta*
numidica MS&CL 288 — Last listed 1998
nutans — See *Hyacinthoides non-scripta*

obtusifolia AB&S 4410 — Last listed 1998
paucifolia — Last listed 1998
persica — CAvo LRHS
 - BSBE 1054 — Last listed 1998
peruviana — CAvo CBro CFee CHEx CHad CMil CSWP CSpe CStu EPar EPot ERos LAma LRHS MTho NRog SMrm SSpi WAbe WCot WWhi
 - 'Alba' — CAvo CSWP LAma LPio MTho NRog
 - var. *elegans* — Last listed 1998
 - var. *venusta* — Last listed 1998
pratensis — See *S. litardierei*
puschkinioides — LAma
ramburei — LAma
 - B&S 406 — Last listed 1998
 - MS 417 — Last listed 1998
reverchonii — ERos
 - MS 418 — Last listed 1998
rosenii — GCrs LRHS
§ *scilloides* — CBro EPot ERos WCot
 - MSF 782 — SSpi
siberica ♀ — CAvo EPfP ETub LAma LRHS NEgg NMen NRog WPer WShi
 - 'Alba' — CBro EPar EPfP EPot LAma LRHS NEgg NRog WPer
 - subsp. *armena* — CHEx
 - 'Spring Beauty' — CBro EPar EPot LAma LRHS MBri NRog SRms
 - var. *taurica* — ERos
 - - M&T 4148 — Last listed 1998
tubergeniana — See *S. mischtschenkoana*
verna — ERos WHer WShi
 - JCA 878.000 — Last listed 1998
 - MS 483 — Last listed 1998
vicentina — See *Hyacinthoides italica vicentina*
violacea — See *Ledebouria socialis*

SCINDAPSUS (Araceae)
aureus — See *Epipremnum aureum*
pictus (v) — LRHS MBri
 - 'Argyraeus' ♀ — Last listed 1990

SCIRPOIDES (Poaceae)
§ *holoschoenus* — Last listed 1997

SCIRPUS (Cyperaceae)
cernuus — See *Isolepis cernua*
cespitosus — See *Trichophorum cespitosum*
¶ *cyperinus* — CBrm
holoschoenus — See *Scirpoides holoschoenus*
lacustris — See *Schoenoplectus lacustris*
 - 'Spiralis' — See *Juncus effusus* f. *spiralis*
maritimus — See *Bolboschoenus maritimus*
sylvaticus — CKin MTed SWyc
tabernaemontani — See *Schoenoplectus lacustris* subsp. *tabernaemontani*

SCLERANTHUS (Caryophyllaceae)
baldensis — Last listed 1999
biflorus — EGle ESis EWes LJus MBro SPlb WPer
perennis — CNat
singuliflorus — NHol WPat WPyg
uniflorus — CLyd EWes GAbr GAri NWCA SPlb
 - CC 466 — NWCA
 - CC 556 — Last listed 1999

SCOLIOPUS (Trilliaceae)
bigelowii — EBee GCrs WFar

hallii — Last listed 1999

SCOLOPENDRIUM See ASPLENIUM

SCOLYMUS See CYNARA

SCOPOLIA (Solanaceae)
carniolica — CAvo CFir COld ECGN EGle ELan EMon EPar GCal GDra GPoy MBel MBlu MHar MSal NLar NSti SPlb WCru WPGP
 - forms — EBee ECha IBlr NChi
 - subsp. *bladnikiana* — CAvo EBee EBrP EBre EPPr GOrP LBCI LBSe LBre LSpr MBBe SBre SDys WBcn WTin
 - - WM 9811 — MPhe
 - *podolica* — CMea
 - yellow — MHar
 - 'Zwanenburg' — CAvo EBee EPar WCot
lurida — MNrw MSal WWye
physaloides — MSal
sinensis — See *Atropanthe sinensis*

SCORZONERA (Asteraceae)
hispanica — WCot
humilis — GPoy
¶ *radiata* — EBee
suberosa subsp. *cariensis* — EBee EWes NTow SMad

SCROPHULARIA (Scrophulariaceae)
aquatica — See *S. auriculata*
§ *auriculata* — ELau EWFC MHer MSal NDea NOrc WHer WWye
 - 'Burdung' (v) — Last listed 1998
§ - 'Variegata' (v) — More than 30 suppliers
buergeriana 'Lemon and Lime' (v) — EBee EMan EMon EPPr WCot WPrP
canina subsp. *bicolor* — Last listed 1998
grandiflora — NArg WSan
macrantha — EBee WCot
nodosa — CArn CKin EBee ELau EWFC MChe MSal NMir WHbs WHer
 - *trachelioides* — CNat
 - *variegata* — See *S. auriculata* 'Variegata'
sambucifolia — GBin MNrw
scopolii — EBee
scorodonia — SRms
umbrosa — MSal
vernalis — EBee EWFC

SCUTELLARIA (Lamiaceae)
albida — EBee GDea
§ *alpina* — CLyd CPlt EBrP EBre GCHN GCrs LBCI LBSe LBee LBre LRHS MBBe NWCA SBla SBre SPlb SRms WGor WPer WWye
 - 'Arcobaleno' — WHil
 - 'Greencourt' — EBee
 - subsp. *supina* — Last listed 1999
altissima — CArn CGle EBee EGar ELan EMan EMar EPPr GBuc LFis MRav MSal NBro SPlb SSca SSvw STes WBar WBea WCHb WHoo WPer WWin WWye
baicalensis — CArn EBee GPoy IBlr MSal NCut SBla SOkh WPer WWye
barbata — MNrw
brevibracteata — SHFr
brittonii — Last listed 1998
canescens — See *S. incana*
columnae — Last listed 1998
diffusa — CPBP EBee WPer WWye

formosana	Last listed 1999
galericulata	CKin EWFC GPoy MHer MHew
	MSal WCHb WGwy WHer WJek
	WWye
- 'Corinne Tremaine' (v)	WHer
* *glandulosissima*	Last listed 1997
bastata	See *S. bastifolia*
§ *bastifolia*	CTri ECot ECtt EDAr EMNN EMar
	NFor NSti WPer
§ *incana*	CGle EBee ECGN EFou EHrv ELan
	EMan EPPr EWTr LFis LGre LRHS
	MNrw NSti SAga SMrm SUsu
	WCot WWoo WWye
indica var. *japonica*	See *S. indica* var. *parvifolia*
§ - var. *parvifolia*	CLyd CPBP EBee EBur EMan EWes
	LBee LRHS MTho NMen NTow
	NWCA SBla SSca SUsu WCot
	WCru
- - 'Alba'	CLyd CPBP LBee LRHS SBla
integrifolia	Last listed 1998
lateriflora	CArn CBod EBee ELau EOHP
	GBar GPoy MChe MHew MSal
	NSti SIde WCHb WCer WHbs
	WJek WPer WSel WWye
minor	CKin EWFC WGwy WWye
nana var. *sappbirina*	CPBP
- - JJA 1840650	NWCA
novae-zelandiae	ECou LRHS MTho SSca WCot
	WWye
orientalis	EBee LBee LRHS SBla WCot WCru
	WPat WWin
- subsp. *bicolor*	Last listed 1999
- subsp. *carica*	CStu WWye
¶ - 'Eastern Star'	NArg
- subsp. *pinnatifida*	NWCA WLin
pontica	WLin
prostrata	CMHG SSca WWin
resinosa	EBee
scordiifolia	CLyd CMea CMil ECha EPot GKir
	LFis MBro MNrw NMen NNrd
	NRya NWCA SBla SIng SRms SUsu
	WCot WFar WHal WHoo WPyg
	WRus WWin WWye
- 'Seoul Sapphire'	GDea WCot
serrata	Last listed 1997
supina	See *S. alpina*
tournefortii	LLWP WBor

SEBAEA (Gentianaceae)

¶ *thomasii*	SBla

SECURIGERA See CORONILLA

SECURINEGA (Euphorbiaceae)

ramiflora	CPLG

SEDASTRUM See SEDUM

SEDUM ✿ (Crassulaceae)

§ 'Abbeydore'	EBee EBrP EBre EGle EGoo EMan
	EMon LBCl LBSe LBre LRHS
	MAnH MBBe SBre SUsu
acre	CTri ECot EFer GPoy MBar MHer
	SPlb WLRN
- 'Aureum'	CInt EDAr EPfP LRHS MBar MOne
	MWat NHol NVic SRms WHoo
	WPat WPyg
- 'Elegans'	ECtt EDAr GDra GTou
§ - var. *majus*	CChe SSmi
- 'Minus'	SSmi WFar
aggregatum	See *Orostachys aggregata*
§ *aizoon*	EPfP SChu SIde WOve WWal

- 'Aurantiacum'	See *S. aizoon* 'Euphorbioides'
§ - 'Euphorbioides'	EBee EBrP EBre ECha ECtt EGoo
	ELan EMon ESis LBCl LBSe LBre
	LRHS MBBe MBel MHer MRav
	NFai NPro SBre SPer WCot WFar
albescens	See *S. rupestre* f. *purpureum*
§ *alboroseum*	EBee MTho
- 'Frosty Morn' (v)	More than 30 suppliers
§ - 'Mediovariegatum'	More than 30 suppliers
§ *album*	CHal EWFC MBNS NBro WPer
- 'Chloroticum'	EDAr SSmi
- 'Coral Carpet'	CNic EDAr EMan EPfP EPot GDra
	MBar MWat SChu SSmi
- var. *micranthum*	See *S. album* 'Chloroticum'
§ - subsp. *teretifolium*	CTri MBar
'Murale'	
algidum	See *S. alsium*
alpestre	Last listed 1998
§ *alsium*	Last listed 1998
altissimum	See *S. sediforme*
altum	EMon EPPr LGre WFar WPer
amplexicaule	See *S. tenuifolium*
§ *anacampseros*	CHEx CNic EGoo GCHN NDov
	NHol SSmi WPer
anglicum	SChr
athoum	See *S. album*
atlanticum	See *S. dasyphyllum* subsp.
	dasyphyllum var. *mesatlanticum*
atuntsuense	Last listed 1998
Autumn Joy	See *S.* 'Herbstfreude'
§ 'Bertram Anderson' ♀	More than 30 suppliers
beyrichianum hort.	See *S. glaucophyllum*
bithynicum 'Aureum'	See *S. hispanicum* var. *minus*
	'Aureum'
bodinieri	EBee EFou
brevifolium	MDHE
* - *potsii*	Last listed 1998
§ - var. *quinquefarium*	Last listed 1998
bronze-leaved	WHil
caeruleum	CInt SIng WUnu
'Carl'	EBee EGle EGoo EMan EMon
	LRHS NCat NSti SMad SUsu WCot
§ *caucasicum*	SUsu WAbb WEas
- DS&T 89001T	EMon
cauticola ♀	CLyd CNic CPri EDAr GCal MBrN
	MBro MHer MRav SRms SRot SSca
	SSmi WElm WWin
- from Lida	ECho
§ - 'Lidakense'	CMea CSam EBrP EBre EGle ELan
	EMan GKir LBCl LBSe LBre LRHS
	MBBe MBNS MBar MBri MBro
	MCLN MTis NFai NHar NSla NVic
	SBla SBre SChu SIng SRot SUsu
	WLin
- 'Robustum'	EBee EMon EWll
- x *tatarinowii*	EWes
'Cavalier'	EFou
confusum	SChr
crassipes	See *Rhodiola wallicbiana*
crassularia	See *Crassula milfordiae*
cryptomerioides	WCru
B&SWJ 054	
§ *cyaneum* Rudolph	GCHN NMen NWCA
- hort.	See *S. ewersii* var. *homophyllum*
dasyphyllum	CNic ESis GTou MBar MHer
	MOne MWat NHol NWCA SRms
	SSmi WRHF
- subsp. *dasyphyllum*	CHEx CHal
var. *glanduliferum*	
- - 'Lilac Mound'	MDHE
- - var. *macropbyllum*	MDHE SSmi
§ - - var. *mesatlanticum*	CNic MDHE NBir

- mucronatis	See *S. dasyphyllum* subsp. *dasyphyllum* var. *mesatlanticum*
- subsp. oblongifolium	Last listed 1998
debile	Last listed 1998
divergens	Last listed 1998
- large	Last listed 1998
douglasii	See *S. stenopetalum* 'Douglasii'
'Dudley Field'	GCHN
'Eleanor Fisher'	See *S. telephium* subsp. *ruprechtii*
ellacombeanum	See *S. kamtschaticum* var. *ellacombeanum*
erythrostichum	See *S. alboroseum*
§ *ewersii*	CHEx CNic EBee EBrP EBre EDAr EMNN EMon GCHN GDea GTou LBCl LBSe LBre LRHS MBBe MHer NBro SBre SPlb SSmi WFar
§ *- var. homophyllum*	CLyd MTPN SSmi
§ *fabaria*	MCLN WCot WEas
farinosum	Last listed 1998
fastigiatum	See *Rhodiola fastigiata*
floriferum	See *S. kamtschaticum*
forsterianum	EMFP LGro SPlb
subsp. *elegans*	
frutescens	STre
furfuraceum	NMen
gracile	SSmi
* 'Green Expectations'	CMil EBee
gypsicola	CHEx WPer
'Harvest Moon'	EBur
§ 'Herbstfreude' ♀	More than 30 suppliers
§ *heterodontum*	See *Rhodiola heterodonta*
hidakanum	CLyd EBee EMFP GCrs GTou MBro NBro NHol NMen WHoo WPat
himalense	See *Rhodiola* 'Keston'
§ *hispanicum*	CTri ECho SPlb
- 'Albescens'	CNic
- var. bithynicum	Last listed 1998
- glaucum	See *S. hispanicum* var. *minus*
§ *- var. minus*	ECtt GAri GTou MBar NNrd NPri NRya SChu SIng SPlb SSmi STre WMoo
§ *- - 'Aureum'*	ECha EDAr MBar SIng WMoo
humifusum	CPBP EBur NHol NMen NTow SSmi
hybridum	Last listed 1998
- 'Immergrünchen'	CPri
hyperaizoon	Last listed 1998
integrifolium	See *Rhodiola rosea* subsp. *integrifolia*
ishidae	See *Rhodiola ishidae*
japonicum	EGle
'Joyce Henderson'	EBee EFou EGle EMan ERav LPio MGrG MSCN NDov SBla SUsu WCot WEas
§ *kamtschaticum* ♀	EHol ESis MBar MHer
§ *- var. ellacombeanum* ♀	CNic EDAr EGoo ELan ESis MHer NMen
§ *- var. floriferum*	More than 30 suppliers
'Weihenstephaner Gold'	
- var. kamtschaticum	CBrm CHEx CLyd CPri CTri EDAr
'Variegatum' ♀	ELan ESis GCHN LBee MHer MWat NFla SBla SIng SRms SRot SSmi WCot WEas WFar WPyg
- var. middendorffianum	See *S. middendorffianum*
- 'Takahira Dake'	Last listed 1998
¶ *kimnachii*	EOas
kirilovii	See *Rhodiola kirilovii*
lanceolatum	Last listed 1998
laxum	Last listed 1998
- subsp. beckneri	Last listed 1998
- subsp. laxum	WCot

lineare	Last listed 1999
- 'Variegatum'	MBri
litorale	EBee
§ *lydium*	CTri EMNN GTou MBar MOne SPlb SSmi
- 'Aureum'	See *S. hispanicum* var. *minus* 'Aureum'
- 'Bronze Queen'	See *S. lydium*
'Lynda Windsor'	CRDP SAga
makinoi 'Variegatum' (v)	EBrP EBre LBCl LBSe LBre MBBe SBre
maweanum	See *S. acre* var. *majus*
maximowiczii	See *S. aizoon*
mexicanum	MBri
§ *middendorffianum*	CLyd ECho EDAr EGoo EMon GTou MBrN MDHE MHer MWat NMen SRms SRot WHoo WWin
- var. diffusum	SSmi
- 'Striatum'	Last listed 1999
monregalense	EDAr
'Moonglow'	NMen
moranense	CHal CNic NTow SSmi
morganianum ♀	CHal EBak LCns MBri
morrisonense	Last listed 1998
multiceps	SSmi
murale	See *S. album* subsp. *teretifolium* 'Murale'
N *nevii*	EGle SPlb
nicaeense	See *S. sediforme*
obcordatum	NMen
§ *obtusatum*	CPri EDAr EGle MBro NBro NFla NNrd NSla SSmi
§ *- subsp. retusum*	Last listed 1998
obtusifolium	CGra
* *- 'Variegatum'* (v)	Last listed 1997
ochroleucum	SSmi
'Green Spreader'	
§ *- subsp. ochroleucum glaucum*	Last listed 1998
oppositifolium	See *S. spurium* var. *album*
§ *oreganum*	CInt ECha EDAr EMNN ESis GTou MBar MWat NMen SHel SPlb SRms SRot SSmi WPer WPyg WWin
- 'Procumbens'	See *S. oreganum* subsp. *tenue*
§ *- subsp. tenue*	CNic ESis MBro NHol NRya WPat
§ *oregonense*	CLyd EBur GTou NMen NNrd
oryzifolium	Last listed 1998
- 'Minor'	EBur
oxypetalum	STre
§ *pachyclados*	More than 30 suppliers
pallidum	Last listed 1998
palmeri	CNic EOas NBir NTow SChr SSmi WCot WWhi
pilosum	EBur NMen NWCA SBla
§ *pluricaule*	GCHN GDra MBro NMen SChu SRms SRot
populifolium	CMHG CNic ECha GCHN GCal MBel MHar MHer SDry SSmi STre SUsu WPer
praealtum	EOas SChr SEND SPar
primuloides	See *Rhodiola primuloides*
pruinatum	Last listed 1998
pruinosum	See *S. spathulifolium* subsp. *pruinosum*
pulchellum	Last listed 1998
purdyi	NMen
'Purple Emperor'	CRDP EFou EGle EMan EMon EPPr SUsu WCot
quadrifidum	See *Rhodiola quadrifida*
quinquefarium	See *S. brevifolium* var. *quinquefarium*

'Red Bead'	Last listed 1998
reflexum L.	See *S. rupestre* L.
reptans	Last listed 1998
var. *carinatifolium*	
retusum	See *S. obtusatum* subsp. *retusum*
rhodiola	See *Rhodiola rosea*
¶ 'Ringmore Ruby'	CPou
rosea	See *Rhodiola rosea*
rubroglaucum hort.	See *S. oregonense*
- Praeger	See *S. obtusatum*
x *rubrotinctum*	CHEx CHal
§ 'Ruby Glow' ♀	More than 30 suppliers
§ *rupestre* L.	CAgr CNic EBot EPfP EWFC
	MBNS MBar MWhi SChu SIng
	SPlb SSmi WHer
- 'Minus'	CNic
- 'Monstrosum Cristatum'	NBir SMad
§ - f.*purpureum*	Last listed 1997
ruprechtii	See *S. telephium* subsp. *ruprechtii*
sarcocaule	See *Crassula sarcocaulis*
sarmentosum	SSmi
§ *sediforme*	EDAr MBro
- *nicaeense*	See *S. sediforme*
selskianum	CPri EBee GDra GTou MOne NPri
sempervivoides	EBur
sexangulare	EMNN GDra MBar MHer MOne
	NMen SPlb SRms SSmi WFar
sibiricum	WEas
sichotense	Last listed 1998
§ *sieboldii*	CSam LCns LGro MBri MBro SSmi
- 'Mediovariegatum' ♀	EBrP EBre EMan LBCl LBSe LBre
	MBBe MHer SBre SSmi WPer
'Silver Moon'	EBur ESis GCHN MDHE SSmi
¶ sp B&SWJ 737	EGoo
spathulifolium	CAgr ECha ESis GTou MOne NBus
	SChu SRCN WEas
- 'Aureum'	EBur ECtt GKir GTou MBar MWat
	SBod
- 'Cape Blanco' ♀	More than 30 suppliers
§ - subsp.*pruinosum*	MDHE
- 'Purpureum' ♀	More than 30 suppliers
- 'Roseum'	SSmi
§ *spectabile* ♀	CArn CFri EBee ELan EPfP GMaP
	LRHS MCAu MHer MRav NBee
	NCiC SGar SHFr SPer SPlb SRms
	WBea WFar WWin
- 'Abendrot'	EMon LRHS
- 'Album'	CCHP CHEx WMoo WTin
- 'Brilliant' ♀	More than 30 suppliers
- 'Brilliant Variegated' (v)	SCob
- 'Carmen'	WGwG WMoo
- 'Iceberg'	More than 30 suppliers
- 'Indian Chief'	CM&M EBee ECGN EGle GKir
	LRHS SAsh SCro SVil WCot WElm
	WFar WLRN WRus
- 'Lisa'	EMon MTPN
- 'Meteor'	CStr MBNS MChl MLLN MRav
	MWat NFai SCro WAbe WCot
	WPer
* - 'Mini'	ELan MRav NCat
- 'Pink Fairy'	WHil
- 'Rosenteller'	EBee EFou EGle EMon LRHS SMrm
- September Glow	See *S. spectabile* 'Septemberglut'
§ - 'Septemberglut'	EBrP EBre EMan EMon GKir LBCl
	LBSe LBre LRHS MBBe NDov SBre
	CBlo EBee EGle EGoo EMil EMon
	EPfP EWTr GLil GMaP LPio LRHS
	MBNS MHer MLLN MTis SCob
	SMrm SPer SPla WCot WFar WGor
	WViv WWeb
- 'Variegatum'	See *S. alboroseum*
	'Mediovariegatum'

spinosum	See *Orostachys spinosa*
spurium	CAgr CHEx EGoo LGro MBNS
	SBod SRms STre
§ - var.*album*	EGoo ESis MHar
* - 'Atropurpureum'	ECha NFor
- 'Coccineum'	MBar MHer WUnu
- Dragon's Blood	See *S. spurium* 'Schorbuser Blut'
- 'Erdblut'	CTri EBrP EBre GKir LBCl LBSe
	LBre LRHS MBBe NFla NMen SBre
- 'Fuldaglut'	CHal CNic CPri EBee EBrP EBre
	EDAr EHoe EMan LBCl LBSe LBre
	MBBe MBel MWat NHar SBre SChu
	SIng WCDu WMoo WPer WWin
- 'Glow'	CTri STre
- 'Green Mantle'	CBlo ECha SMer
- Purple Carpet	See *S. spurium* 'Purpurteppich'
- 'Purpureum'	CInt EGoo GDra SIng SRms
§ - 'Purpurteppich'	CPri EBrP EBre ESis GKir LBCl
	LBSe LBre LGro LRHS MBBe
	MRav NBro NHol SBre SHel SRms
	SRms
- 'Roseum'	CBlo NPro
- 'Ruby Mantle'	
§ - 'Schorbuser Blut' ♀	CMea EBee EPfP EPot GKir LRHS
	MBNS MBro MWat NBro NVic
	SHel SPlb SRms WEas WFar WHoo
	WPat WPyg WRHF
- 'Splendens Roseum'	LGro
- 'Tricolor'	See *S. spurium* 'Variegatum'
§ - 'Variegatum'	CNic ECha EDAr EGoo EHoe ESis
	LRHS MBar MHer MRav SBod
	SHel SIng SPla SPlb SSmi STre
	WBea WCot WEas WFar WOve
	WPat WPyg WWin
stenopetalum	NMen SPlb
§ - 'Douglasii'	CNic MOne NNrd SRms
stephanii	See *Rhodiola crassipes* var.
	stephanii
'Stewed Rhubarb Mountain'	CElw CLon CMGP CMil EBee
	EGle EMan EMon GAri MRav
	NDov WCot WPGP
stoloniferum	SSmi
'Strawberries and Cream'	EBee EGle EMon GBin GKir LGre
	LPio LRHS MBri MRav NCat NFai
stribrnyi	See *S. urvillei* Stribrnyi Group
'Sunset Cloud'	CMHG CSam EBee EGle EMon
	EWes EGcal LRHS MRav
takesimense	Last listed 1998
§ *tatarinowii*	CLyd EDAr NTow WViv
- K 92.405	Last listed 1997
§ *telephioides*	WCot
§ *telephium*	CAgr CArn EMon EWFC MBNS
	NBir NSti SRms WByw WCot
	WWye
- 'Abbeydore'	See *S.* 'Abbeydore'
- 'Arthur Branch'	CElw EMon EPPr GBuc MNrw
	MSte MTho WCot
- var. *borderi*	CElw EGle EMan EMon LRHS
- subsp.*fabaria*	See *S. fabaria*
* - 'Hester'	CWes EFou EMan SCob
* - 'Leonore Zuntz'	WCot
- 'Matrona'	More than 30 suppliers
§ - subsp. *maximum*	CBrm ECha MBel SChu
- - 'Atropurpureum' ♀	CBot CGle CHad CMea CSpe
	EBee ECha ECoo EGle ELan EMan
	EMar EWTr LRHS MFir MRav
	SChu WCot WMoo WWhi WWin
- - 'Gooseberry Fool'	CLon EGle EGoo EMon EWTr
	LGre LPio LRHS SUsu
- 'Mohrchen'	CHad CLon CRDP EBee ECGP
	EFou EGle EMan LPio LRHS MBri
	MLLN MTed NDov NGdn NSti
	SBla SChu SMrm WCot WHoo

– 'Munstead Red'	COIW EBee ECha EFou EGoo EMan EMon LFis LHop LRHS MBct MBel MCAu MChl MHer MRav NLar SLon SPer SPla SSpe SUsu WCot
– 'Roseovariegatum' (v)	EMon
– 'Roseum'	LHop
§ – subsp. *ruprechtii*	CMHG EBee ECha ECoo EGle EGoo EMan EMon EOld EOrc GCal GMaP LGre LRHS MBct MBri MFir MRav NSti SBla SPer SUsu WCot WEas WFar WPer WViv WWhi
– subsp. *telephium* 'Lynda et Rodney'	CRDP EGle EGoo EMan EMon
– 'Variegatum' (v)	CMea COtt ECoo LFis LRHS MBel SPar WHal WWin
– 'Veluwe se Wakel'	Last listed 1999
* – Washfield purple selection	EBee EMan EWes
§ *tenuifolium*	EBur
§ – subsp. *ibericum*	Last listed 1998
– subsp. *tenuifolium*	EBur
ternatum	Last listed 1998
trollii	See *Rhodiola trollii*
§ *urvillei* Stribrnyi Group	CLyd
¶ *ussuriense*	GCal
§ 'Vera Jameson' ♀	CLon CLyd EBee ECha EGle EHoe EMan EMar ENot LRHS MBrN MBri MFir MRav MTis NHol NSti SBla SChu SUsu WEas WMoo WPer WWhi
verticillatum	Last listed 1998
¶ 'Washfield Purple'	NSti
'Weihenstephaner Gold'	See *S. kamtschaticum* var. *floriferum* 'Weihenstephaner Gold'
weinbergii	See *Graptopetalum paraguayayense*
yezoense	See *S. pluricaule*
yunnanense	See *Rhodiola yunnanensis*

SEEMANNIA See GLOXINIA

SELAGINELLA ✿ (Selaginellaceae)

apoda	MBri
braunii	NMar WCot
douglasii	NMar
emmeliana	See *S. pallescens*
helvetica	CStu NHol
involvens	Last listed 1999
kraussiana ♀	CHal MBri NMar NRya WRic
– 'Aurea' ♀	CHal GGar MBri NMar SMad
– 'Brownii' ♀	MBri NMar NVic
– 'Variegata' ♀	MBri
martensii ♀	Last listed 1995
– 'Watsoniana'	NMar
§ *pallescens*	NMar
– 'Aurea'	NMar
sanguinolenta	SIng
tamariscina	Last listed 1998
uncinata ♀	Last listed 1995
vogelii	NMar

SELAGO (Scrophulariaceae)

flanaganii	Last listed 1998

SELINUM (Apiaceae)

carvifolium	Last listed 1997
¶ *striatum*	GCan
tenuifolium	See *S. wallichianum*

§ *wallichianum*	CHad CHid CRow EGoo EMan EWTr GKir LRHS SPer SSpi WPGP WWhi
§ – EMAK 886	CGle CMil CPou EBee GPoy MBri NSti SDix SMrm WEas

SELLIERA (Goodeniaceae)

radicans	SSca
– forms	ECou
– 'Lake Ellerman'	Last listed 1998

SEMELE (Ruscaceae)

androgyna	CHEx CPlN CRHN

SEMIAQUILEGIA ✿ (Ranunculaceae)

* *adnata* B&SWJ 1190	WCru
§ *adoxoides*	WPer WPrP WViv
'Early Dwarf'	Last listed 1999
§ *ecalcarata*	CBot CGle CMCo CMil CPlt EBrP EBre GBin GGar GKir LBCl LBSe LBre LEur MBBe MNrw NHar NHol NLar NOak SBre SIng SRms WCru WLin WPGP WPer WPrP WWhi WWin
– 'Flore Pleno' (d)	SPla WPrP WRha
simulatrix	See *S. ecalcarata*

SEMIARUNDINARIA (Poaceae - Bambusoideae)

§ *fastuosa* ♀	CDDB CDoC CHEx EBee EFul EGln EOas EPfP EPla ERod GOrc ISta LJus LPal MMoz NMoo NVic SAPC SArc SDry SPlb WJun WMul
– var. *viridis*	EPla ERod ISta LPJP SDry WCru WJun
kagamiana	CDoC EPla ISta LJus MMoz NMoo SDry WJun
§ *lubrica*	CFil ISta WPGP
makinoi	CDDB EPla WJun
nitida	See *Fargesia nitida*
§ *okuboi*	EPla ERod WJun
sinica	ISta
villosa	See *S. okuboi*
yamadorii	EPla ERod ISta SDry WJun
– 'Brimscombe'	EPla SDry
yashadake	EPla ISta SDry WJun
– *kimmei*	CAbb CDDB CDoC CFil EBee EPla ERod ISta LJus MMoz NMoo SDry WJun WPGP

SEMNANTHE (Aizoaceae)

lacera	Last listed 1999

SEMPERVIVELLA See ROSULARIA

SEMPERVIVUM ✿ (Crassulaceae)

¶ 'Aalrika'	CWil
'Abba'	MOne WHal WPer
acuminatum	See *S. tectorum* var. *glaucum*
'Aglow'	CWil MOne SSmi
¶ 'Aladdin'	CWil
'Albertnellii'	NHol
'Alcithoë'	CWil MOne
'Aldo Moro'	CWil MOne NMen SSmi
allionii	See *Jovibarba allionii*
¶ 'Allison'	CWil
'Alluring'	GAbr
'Alpha'	CWil ESis LBee LRHS MOne NHol SIng SRms SSmi STre WHal
altum	CWil NMen SSmi
'Amanda'	CWil MBro NMen SSmi WHoo WPer

	'Ambergreen'	CWil ELau NMen
	'Andorra'	NHol
	andreanum	CWil ESis NBro NHol SIng SSmi
	'Apache'	CWil NNrd SSmi
	'Apollo'	NHol
	'Apple Blossom'	CWil NBus SIng
	arachnoideum ♀	CMea CTri CWil EGoo ELan ELau EPot ESis GAbr LBee LRHS MBar MBro MWat NDlv NHol NNrd NWCA SBla SIng SPlb SSmi WAbe WEas WFar WHal WHoo WLow WPyg WWin
	- 'Abruzzii'	SIng
	- var. *bryoides*	CWil ESis GCHN MBro NMen SIng
	- x *calcareum*	CWil MBro NMen SSmi WTin
	- 'Clairchen'	CWil MBro NHol NMen
	- cristate	CWil
*	- *densum*	ESis
	- subsp. *doellianum*	See S. arachnoideum var. glabrescens
	- form no. 1	SSmi
¶	- from Fondo Majella, Italy	CWil
	- from Gorges du Valais	SIng
§	- var. *glabrescens*	NMen SSmi
	- - 'Album'	Last listed 1998
	- x *grandiflorum*	SIng
	- 'Gusseri'	SIng
	- 'Kappa'	See S. 'Kappa'
	- 'Laggeri'	See S. arachnoideum subsp. tomentosum
	- 'Mole Harbord'	LRHS
	- x *montanum*	SIng
	- x *nevadense*	CWil SDys SIng SSmi
	- 'Peña Prieta'	NHol
	- x *pittonii*	CWil MBro NHol NMen SSmi
	- 'Red Variety'	NMen
	- 'Rubrum'	LRHS MOne
	- 'Sultan'	MOne
§	- subsp. *tomentosum* ♀	CTri CWil EBrP EBre ECGP EMNN GCHN GKir LBCl LBSe LBre LRHS MBBe MBro MHer NHol NMen NPer NWCA SBre SChu SIng SMer SRms SSmi WPer WWin
	- - 'Minor'	NHol SIng
	- - misapplied	See S. x barbulatum 'Hookeri'
§	- - 'Stansfieldii'	GAbr STre WHal
	arenarium	See Jovibarba arenaria
	armenum	NMen
	'Aross'	CLyd GAbr NMen SSmi
	'Arrowheads Red'	SSmi
¶	'Artist'	CWil
	arvernense	See S. tectorum
	'Ashes of Roses'	CWil EGoo ELau EPot ESis MBro MOne NMen SSmi WAbe
	'Asteroid'	CWil NMen
	atlanticum	CWil NMen NNrd SSmi
	- 'Edward Balls'	CWil MOne SDys SIng
¶	- from Atlas Mts, Morocco	CWil
	- from Oukaimaden	CWil MBro MOne NHol NMen WTin
	'Atlantis'	NHol
	'Atropurpureum'	CWil ELau GAbr MBro MOne WGor WIvy
	'Aureum'	See Greenovia aurea
	balcanicum	MBro NMen
	ballsii	CWil GCHN NMen
	- from Smólikas	CWil MOne SSmi
	- from Tschumba Petzi	CWil SDys SIng SSmi
	'Banderi'	CWil MOne
§	x *barbulatum*	GCHN NMen SDys SIng SSmi WHoo WPer WPyg

§	- 'Hookeri'	CWil ESis MOne SSmi WAbe WPer
	'Bascour Zilver'	CWil GAbr SIng WHal
	'Bayan'	MTPN
*	'Beaute'	CWil
	'Bedazzled'	CWil
	'Bedivere'	CLyd CWil MOne NMen SSmi
*	'Bedivere Cristate'	CWil
¶	'Bedley Hi'	MHom
	'Bella Meade'	CHEx CWil ELau MOne SSmi
I	'Belladonna'	CWil MDHE NHol NMen NTow WPer
	'Bellotts Pourpre'	CWil NHol
	'Bennerbroek'	MDHE
	'Bernstein'	CWil MBro MHer SIng WHal
	'Beta'	NHol NMen SSmi WAbe
	'Bethany'	CWil NMen WHal
	'Bicolor'	EPfP NPSI
	'Big Mal'	NHol
	'Big Slipper'	NHol SSmi
	'Binstead'	NHol
	'Birchmaier'	NPSI
	'Black Claret'	NHol
	'Black Knight'	COIW ESis LBee LRHS SBla SRms WHal
	'Black Mini'	CWil ESis MOne NBir NDlv NMen
	'Black Mountain'	CWil MOne
	'Black Prince'	CLyd CMil
	'Black Velvet'	CWil MBro SSmi
	'Bladon'	WPer
	'Blari'	SSmi
	'Blood Tip'	CHEx CHal CLyd CWil EGln ELau ESis GAbr GCHN GDea LBee LRHS MBro MHer NHar NMen SChu SRms SSmi WGor WHal WHoo WLow
	'Blue Boy'	CWil ESis GAbr MOne NHol SIng WHoo
	'Blue Moon'	CLyd ELau MOne
	'Blue Time'	MOne WTin
	'Blush'	Last listed 1999
	'Boissieri'	See S. tectorum subsp. tectorum 'Boissieri'
	'Bold Chick'	SSmi
	'Booth's Red'	CHEx CLyd ELau MOne SIng WGor
	borisii	See S. ciliosum var. borisii
	borissovae	CWil NMen SSmi
	'Boromir'	CWil MOne SSmi
*	'Bowles' Variety'	WPer
¶	'Britta'	MOne
	'Brock'	CWil MHer NHol
	'Bronco'	CWil ELan MOne NMen NPSI SSmi
	'Bronze Pastel'	CLyd CWil MBro MOne NMen SSmi WTin
	'Bronze Tower'	NHol
	'Brown Owl'	CWil MOne NHol
	'Brownii'	COIW GAbr MOne NMen SBla WPer
*	'Brunette'	GAbr
	'Burgundy'	ELau MOne
¶	'Burgundy Velvet'	MOne
	'Burnatii'	CWil MOne
	'Butterbur'	CWil
	'Café'	CWil EGoo MBro NHol NMen NNrd SIng SSmi WPer
	x *calcaratum*	SIng SRms
	calcareum	CNic CWil ELau MBro MOne NBro SPlb SRms SSmi WPer
*	- 'Atropurpureum'	MBro
	- 'Benz'	SDys
	- 'Extra'	CWil

- from Alps, France	CWil MOne
- from Benz, Germany	Last listed 1997
¶ - from Calde la Vanoise, Francel	CWi
- from Ceuze	CWil
- from Col Bayard, France	CWil
- from Colle St Michael	CWil MOne
- from Gleize	CWil MOne NMen
- from Gorges du Cains	CWil MOne SSmi
- from Guillaumes, Mont Ventoux, France	CWil GAbr MOne NMen
- from Mont Ventoux, France	CWil MOne SSmi
- from Queyras	CWil MOne SSmi
- from Route d'Annôt	CWil MOne SSmi
- from Triora	CWil MBro MOne NHol NMen
- 'Greenii'	CWil ESis MOne NDlv NHol NMen NPSI SSmi
§ - 'Grigg's Surprise'	CInt CWil MHer MOne NMen
- 'Limelight'	CWil ESis MBro NMen SIng SSmi WHal
- 'Monstrosum'	See *S. calcareum* 'Grigg's Surprise'
- 'Mrs Giuseppi'	CWil ESis GAbr GCHN GDea LBee LRHS MBro MOne NOak SBla SChu SIng SRms SSmi STre WAbe WPer
- 'Pink Pearl'	CWil MOne NMen WTin
- 'Sir William Lawrence'	CPBP CWil EGln ELau ESis SChu WHal
'Caldera'	CWil
californicum	NDlv
'Caliph's Hat'	CWil
'Canada Kate'	CWil MOne WPer
'Cancer'	Last listed 1999
'Candy Floss'	CWil MOne SIng
cantabricum	CWil MDHE SSmi
- subsp. *cantabricum* from Leitariegos	CWil MOne NMen
- from Navafria	CWil NHol SIng
- from Peña Prieta	NMen SSmi
- from Piedrafita, Spain	SSmi
- from Riaño, Spain	CWil GAbr
- from San Glorio	CWil GAbr MBro NMen
- from Santander, Spain	SSmi
¶ - from Sierra del Cadi, Spain	CLyd
- from Ticeros	CWil MOne NMen
- from Valvernera	CWil
- subsp. *guadarramense* from Lobo No. 1	CWil MBro MOne SSmi
- - from Lobo No. 2	MOne SSmi
- - from Navafria No. 1	SSmi WTin
- - from Valvanera No. 1	NMen SSmi
- × *montanum* subsp. *stiriacum*	CWil SSmi WEas WTin
- subsp. *urbionense*	CLyd CWil SIng
- - from Picos de Urbión, Spain	MBro MOne NMen
'Canth'	CWil NHol
'Caramel'	Last listed 1999
* 'Carinal'	NBir
'Carluke'	MOne
'Carmen'	CHal CWil GAbr MBro MOne
'Carneus'	MOne NHol
'Carnival'	CHal MBro SSmi WPer
caucasicum	CWil MOne NMen SIng SSmi
'Cavo Doro'	CWil GAbr MDHE
¶ 'Centennial'	MOne
charadzeae	CWil NHol
'Cherry Frost'	CLyd MOne NNrd WLRN
'Cherry Tart'	CWil

'Chocolate'	NHol SSmi
× *christii*	MOne NHol SSmi
'Christmas Time'	NHol
chrysanthum	Last listed 1999
* *chyodi*	ELau
ciliosum	CPBP EGln ESis NMen SIng WLow
§ - var. *borisii*	CNic CTri ESis GCal GTou MBro NDlv NMen NNrd NPSI SChr WHal
- × *ciliosum* var. *borisii*	CHal CWil WTin
* - from Gallica	CLyd
- from Ochrid	CWil NMen
- var. *galicicum* 'Mali Hat'	CWil NMen
- × *marmoreum*	CWil MBro NMen SSmi
'Cindy'	CWil
'Circlet'	CWil NMen
* *cistaceum*	WEas
'Clara Noyes'	ELau WPer
'Clare'	CLyd MHer MOne NNrd SSmi
'Cleveland Morgan'	CWil LRHS NBro NHar
'Climax'	Last listed 1999
'Cobweb Capers'	MOne
'Cobweb Centre'	MOne
'Collage'	CWil NHol
'Collecteur Anchisi'	CWil MOne SDys SSmi
'Commander Hay' ♀	CHEx CLyd ESis EWes LHop NMen NPer NTow SRms SSmi WEas WFar WHal WLow
¶ 'Comte de Congae'	MOne NMen
'Congo'	CWil MOne
'Cornstone'	CWil NHol
'Corona'	MOne NHol SRms WPer
'Coronet'	Last listed 1999
'Corsair'	CWil ESis LEdu MBro MOne NMen SIng WGor WPer
'Cresta'	SSmi
'Crimson Velvet'	CHEx CWil MDHE MOne SSmi WPer
§ 'Crispyn'	CLyd CWil MBro MOne NHol NMen SSmi WEas
'Croky'	Last listed 1999
'Croton'	SIng WPer
'Cupream'	CWil MDHE NDlv
'Dakota'	CWil
'Dallas'	CLyd CWil MOne NHol SSmi
'Damask'	CWil GAbr MBro MDHE SSmi
'Dark Beauty'	CLyd CWil MBro MOne NMen SSmi WAbe WHal WLow
'Dark Cloud'	CWil GAbr MOne WTin
'Dark Point'	CWil MOne NMen SSmi
'Darkie'	CWil
davisii	CWil
'Deep Fire'	CWil GBin MOne NHol
× *degenianum*	GAbr MBro
'Delta'	WTin
densum	See *S. tectorum*
¶ 'Diane'	CWil
'Director Jacobs'	CWil GAbr GCHN MOne NHol NMen SIng SSmi WEas WWin
'Disco Dancer'	Last listed 1999
'Doctor Roberts'	NHol
dolomiticum	ELau
- from Rif Sennes	Last listed 1999
- × *montanum*	CWil MOne NBro NMen SSmi
'Donarrose'	NHol SIng
'Downland Queen'	CWil NHol
'Dragoness'	MOne
'Duke of Windsor'	CWil MOne NMen SSmi
'Dusky'	CWil SSmi
'Dyke'	CTri CWil GAbr MBro NHol NMen WHal
dzhavachischvilii	CWil MOne

'Edge of Night'	CWil NHol
¶ 'Eefje'	CWil
'El Greco'	CWil
'El Toro'	CWil ELau
'Elgar'	CWil MOne SIng
'Elizabeth'	WPer
'Elvis'	CLyd CWil GAbr MBro NMen
	SSmi
'Emerald Giant'	CWil MOne NHol
'Emerson's Giant'	CWil MOne NMen
'Emma Jane'	MOne
¶ 'Emmchen'	CWil
'Engle's'	CLyd CTri LRHS MHer MOne
	SRms WHal
'Engle's 13-2'	CWil MOne NBro NHar NHol
	SChu SSmi
'Engle's No. 1'	MBro
'Engle's Rubrum'	CPBP ESis GAbr GTou LBee NHol
	NMen
erythraeum	CLyd CWil NMen SIng WAbe
	WHal
– from Pirin, Bulgaria	NMen
'Excalibur'	CLyd CWil MBro NMen
'Exhibita'	CWil MBro SDys SSmi
'Exorna'	CWil ELau MOne NMen SSmi
	WEas
'Fair Lady'	CWil MOne NMen SSmi
'Fame'	CWil MDHE MOne NHol
× *fauconnettii*	CWil MBro NHol SIng SSmi
– 'Thompsonii'	CWil MOne NHol SIng SSmi
'Feldmaier'	MOne
'Festival'	CWil NMen
'Feu de Printemps'	MOne
'Fiesta'	CWil WHal
fimbriatum	See *S.* × *barbulatum*
'Finerpointe'	MBro MOne SSmi
'Fire Glint'	CWil GAbr MOne NHol
'Firebird'	CWil NMen
'First Try'	CWil
'Flaming Heart'	CWil MOne NMen SSmi WPer
¶ 'Flamingo'	MOne
'Flander's Passion'	ELau LBee LRHS SRms SSmi WPer
'Flasher'	CWil MBro WEas WPer
'Fluweel'	CWil
'Fontanae'	MOne
'Forden'	CHEx MOne WGor
'Ford's Amability'	CWil ESis SSmi
'Ford's Giant'	CWil
'Ford's Shadows'	SDys SSmi
'Ford's Spring'	CLyd CWil MOne NHol SSmi
	WPer WWin
'Freckles'	MOne
'Freeland'	WPer
'Frigidum'	NDlv
¶ 'Frolic'	SIng
'Frost and Flame'	NHol
'Frosty'	CWil MOne
'Fuego'	CWil MOne
× *funckii*	CWil EGln ELau MBrN MBro NHol
	NMen NPSI SDys SIng WPer
'Fuzzy Wuzzy'	CWil SSmi
'Galahad'	CWil GAbr
'Gambol'	NHol
'Gamma'	CHEx LBee LRHS NHol NMen
	SChu SDys SIng SRms WEas
'Garnet'	Last listed 1998
'Gay Jester'	CTri CWil GAbr MBro MOne SSmi
	WHoo WTin
'Gazelle'	Last listed 1999
'Georgette'	CWil MBro
'Ginnie's Delight'	CWil SSmi
'Gipsy'	CWil MBro

giuseppii	CWil MBro NHol NMen SIng SSmi
– from Peña Espigüete,	CWil MOne NMen SSmi
Spain	
– from Peña Prieta, Spain	CWil MOne NMen
'Gizmo'	CWil
'Gleam'	Last listed 1997
'Gloriosum'	ELau GAbr MBro NBus SSmi
'Glowing Embers'	CWil MBro MOne SSmi WHal
'Gollum'	MOne SSmi
'Granada'	GAbr MBro
'Granat'	CLyd CWil GCal MHer NPSI SRms
	WPer
'Granby'	MOne NMen SSmi
grandiflorum	CWil GCHN MBro NMen NPSI
	SIng SSmi WPer
– × *ciliosum*	CWil MOne NMen
– 'Fasciatum'	CWil MOne NMen SSmi
¶ – from Valpine	MOne
– 'Keston'	SSmi
– × *montanum*	SIng
'Grape Idol'	CWil
'Grapetone'	CWil SDys SSmi WHal
¶ 'Gratan'	MOne
'Graupurpur'	CWil
'Gray Dawn'	CWil MHom MOne
'Green Apple'	CWil GAbr SSmi
'Green Gables'	CWil MBro SSmi
'Green Giant'	MTPN
'Greenwich Time'	CWil NMen SSmi
* *greigii*	NNrd
'Grey Ghost'	CWil
'Grey Green'	CWil NHol
'Grey Lady'	CWil SSmi
'Greyfriars'	CLyd CWil MBro NMen SSmi
	WPer
'Greyolla'	CLyd CWil WPer
¶ 'Grunspan'	CWil
'Grunspecht'	MOne
¶ 'Gulle Dame'	CWil
'Hades'	CWil
¶ 'Hale Maumau'	MOne
'Hall's Hybrid'	GAbr NBro NHar NNrd
'Hall's Seedling'	Last listed 1998
'Happy'	CWil MBro MOne
'Hart'	CWil NHol
'Haullauer's Seedling'	Last listed 1997
'Havana'	CWil NMen
'Hayling'	CWil ELau LRHS MOne NHol
	NMen SSmi
'Heigham Red'	CWil ESis MOne NHol SSmi
'Heliotroop'	MOne SDys
helveticum	See *S. montanum*
'Hester'	CLyd CWil ELau ESis GAbr MBrN
	MBro MDHE NBro NHar NMen
	SIng SSmi
'Hey-Hey'	CLyd ELau LBee LEdu LRHS MBro
	NMen NPSI SPlb SRms WAbe
	WLow WPer
'Hidde'	CWil
'Hiddes Roosje'	MOne SSmi
¶ 'Hirsuta'	MOne
hirtum	See *Jovibarba hirta*
'Hookeri'	See *S.* × *barbulatum* 'Hookeri'
'Hopi'	CWil MOne NHol
'Hortulanus Smit'	Last listed 1999
'Hot Peppermint'	Last listed 1999
'Hot Shot'	CLyd
'Hullabaloo'	MOne
'Hurricane'	MOne
'Icicle'	CWil ELau LRHS NBro NHol
	NMen SIng SRms SSmi WGor
imbricatum	See *S.* × *barbulatum*

'Imperial'	CLyd CWil SSmi
¶ 'Inge'	CWil
ingwersenii	MOne SIng SSmi WLow
'Interlace'	CWil SSmi
'Iophon'	SSmi
'Irazu'	CWil GAbr MBro MOne NMen SDys
ispartae	CWil
italicum	CWil
¶ - 'Ricci'	MHom
'Itchen'	MOne NMen SIng SSmi
'IWO'	CWil GAbr NMen
'Jack Frost'	CWil MOne NBro NMen SChu SSmi
'Jane'	MOne
'Jasper'	MOne
'Jaspis'	CWil
'Jelly Bean'	CWil ESis MOne NMen SSmi
'Jet Stream'	CWil GAbr NMen SDys SSmi
'Jewel Case'	CWil ELau GAbr LRHS SIng SRms SSmi
'John T.'	MOne
'Jolly Green Giant'	CWil MOne
'Jo's Spark'	CWil
'Jubilee'	CLyd ELan GAbr NHol NMen SRms SSmi WEas WGor WLow WPer WWin
'Jubilee Tricolor'	MBro
'Jungle Fires'	CWil
'Jupiter'	ESis
'Justine's Choice'	CWil
'Kalinda'	CLyd NMen
§ 'Kappa'	CTri CWil MBro MOne NBro NHol SDys SIng SSmi
'Katmai'	CWil NHol
'Kelly Jo'	CLyd CWil NBro NHar NMen SIng SSmi
'Kermit'	Last listed 1999
'Kibo'	CWil
'Kilt'	Last listed 1999
'Kimble'	CWil WPer
kindingeri	CLyd CWil GTou MHer NMen NWCA SSmi
'King George'	CHal CLyd CTri CWil EGln ESis GAbr GBin LBee LRHS MBro MOne NMen NPer SChu SRms SSmi WGor WHal WHoo WPer WPyg
'Kip'	CWil NMen SSmi
'Kismet'	CWil MOne SSmi
¶ 'Koko Flanel'	CWil
'Kolibri'	GAbr MDHE
kosaninii	CWil ELau LRHS MBro MOne NMen SIng SSmi WPer
- from Koprivnik	CLyd MOne NMen SDys SSmi WAbe
- from Visitor	CWil MOne
'Krakeling'	CWil
'Kramers Purpur'	CWil
'Kramers Spinrad'	CHEx CLyd CWil ESis GAbr LEdu MBro MOne NMen SDys SIng SSmi WEas WHoo
'Lady Kelly'	CLyd CWil ESis MOne
'Launcelot'	WPer
'Lavender and Old Lace'	CLyd CWil ELau GAbr LRHS MOne NMen SChu SMer WCot
'Laysan'	CWil
Le Clair's hybrid No. 4	MOne
'Leneca'	SSmi
'Lennik's Glory'	See *S.* 'Crispyn'
* 'Lennik's Glory No. 1'	CWil MBro
'Lennik's Time'	MBro SSmi

'Lentevur'	CWil
'Lentezon'	CWil MOne
'Leocadia's Nephew'	CWil MOne
'Lilac Time'	CLyd CWil ELau GAbr LRHS MBro MHer MOne NMen NNrd SChu SRms SSmi WHal
I 'Linaria'	MTPN
'Lipari'	CWil SRms
'Lipstick'	CLyd ELau
'Lively Bug'	CWil MBro NNrd SDys SSmi WPer
'Lloyd Praeger'	See *S. montanum* subsp. *stiriacum* 'Lloyd Praeger'
'Lonzo'	CWil
'Lou Bastidou'	MOne
'Lowe's Rubicundum'	Last listed 1998
'Lynne's Choice'	CWil MOne SIng WHal
macedonicum	CWil MBro NDlv SSmi
- from Ljuboten	MOne NMen SSmi
¶ 'Madeleine'	CWil
'Magic Spell'	CWil MOne
'Magical'	CWil SSmi
'Magnificum'	CWil NMen
I 'Mahogany'	CHEx CLyd CTri CWil ELau GBin LBee LRHS MBro MOne NHol NMen SBla SRms WGor WHal
'Maigret'	CWil MOne
'Majestic'	CWil NMen SSmi
'Malabron'	Last listed 1999
'Malby's Hybrid'	See *S.* 'Reginald Malby'
'Marella'	CWil WPer
¶ 'Maria Laach'	CWil SIng
'Marijntje'	CWil NHol SSmi
'Marjorie Newton'	CWil
'Marmalade'	WTin
§ **marmoreum**	CLyd CMea CWil ELau LBee LRHS NMen NPSI SRms STre WEas WHal WPer
- 'Brunneifolium'	CLyd CWil EGoo ESis MBro MOne NHol NMen SChu SIng SSmi WPer
- from Kanzas Gorge	ELau MOne NHol SSmi
- from Monte Tirone	CWil SDys SSmi
- from Okol	CWil MOne NMen SSmi
- from Sveta Peta	Last listed 1998
- subsp. **marmoreum** var. **dinaricum**	MBro NMen
§ - - 'Rubrifolium'	GCal
§ - 'Ornatum'	SRms
'Marshall'	MBro
'Mary Ente'	Last listed 1999
'Matador'	Last listed 1999
'Mate'	NMen SSmi
'Maubi'	CPri CWil
'Mauna Kea'	SSmi
'Mauvine'	MOne
'Mavbi'	NNrd
'Medallion'	CWil MOne
'Meisse'	MOne
'Melanie'	CWil MBrN WIvy
'Mercury'	CWil ELau LRHS MDHE MOne NBro NHol SRms SSmi
'Merkur'	MOne
'Merlin'	CWil ESis SSmi
'Midas'	CWil
'Mila'	CLyd CWil
'Mini Frost'	CLyd CWil GAbr MOne NMen SIng
'Minuet'	CWil
'Moerkerk's Merit'	CWil GAbr SSmi
¶ 'Mohair'	MOne
'Mondstein'	CWil MOne NPSI
'Montage'	CWil MOne
I 'Montague'	Last listed 1999

§	*montanum*	CLyd CWil ESis LEdu LRHS SMer WPer
	- subsp. *burnatii*	SIng SSmi
¶	- subsp. *carpathicum*	CWil
	- *carpaticum*	MBro MOne NMen
	'Cmiral's Yellow'	
*	- Fragell form	SChr
	- from Anchisis	MBro MOne
	- from Arbizion	CWil MBro MOne
	- from Windachtal	CWil MBro
¶	- subsp. *montanum*	CWil
	- - var. *braunii*	WLow
	- 'Rubrum'	See S. 'Red Mountain'
§	- subsp. *stiriacum*	CWil ELau MBro MOne NMen SIng
	- - from Mauterndorf, Austria	SSmi
§	- - 'Lloyd Praeger'	CWil MOne SDys SSmi
	'More Honey'	CWil MOne
	'Morning Glow'	MOne WGor WHal
	'Mount Hood'	CWil LRHS MOne SRms SSmi WHal
	'Mrs Elliott'	MOne
	'Mulberry Wine'	CLyd CWil
	'Myrrhine'	CWil
	'Mystic'	CLyd CWil MBro NMen NNrd WPer
	'Nell'	MOne
	'Neptune'	CWil
	nevadense	CWil ELau MBro MOne NMen SRms SSmi
	- from Puerto de San Francisco	MOne
	- var. *birtellum*	CWil NMen SIng SSmi
	'Nico'	CWil
	'Night Raven'	CLyd CWil SIng SSmi
	'Nigrum'	See S. tectorum 'Nigrum'
	'Niobe'	CWil MOne
	'Nixes 27'	MOne
	'Noir'	CWil MOne NBro NMen SSmi
	'Norbert'	CWil MOne
	'Nortofts Beauty'	MOne
	'Nouveau Pastel'	CWil MBro MOne WHal
	'Octet'	MOne NMen SIng
	octopodes	CLyd ESis MDHE NBir
	- var. *apetalum*	CWil GAbr MOne NMen SIng SRms SSmi
	'Oddity'	CPBP CWil ELau MHer NMen WBea WCot WPer
	'Ohio'	ELau
	'Ohio Burgundy'	CWil ELau MDHE MOne NDlv NMen WAbe WPer
¶	'Old Rose'	MOne
	'Olivette'	MDHE SSmi WPer WTin
	'Omega'	MBro MOne SSmi WPer
	'Opitz'	CLyd CWil WPer
	'Ornatum'	MHer MOne SSmi WAbe WEas WHal
	ossetiense	CWil GAbr MOne NMen SIng SSmi
	'Othello'	CHEx CHal CMil CTri EBrP EBre ESis GAbr LBCl LBSe LBre MBBe NBir NPSI NVic SBre WCot
	'Packardian'	CWil ELau MOne NMen SSmi
	'Painted Lady'	CWil SSmi
	'Palissander'	CWil MBro MOne SSmi
	'Pam Wain'	MHom
	'Paricutin'	CWil SDys
	'Pastel'	CWil ELau MOne NMen SIng SSmi
	patens	See Jovibarba heuffelii
	'Patrician'	CWil EBrP EBre ESis LBCl LBSe LBee LBre LRHS MBBe SBre SRms

	'Peach Blossom'	CWil
	'Pekinese'	CLyd CWil ESis MBro NBro NMen NNrd SIng SRms SSmi WEas WPer WWin
	'Peterson's Ornatum'	MOne
	'Petsy'	CWil
*	'Pilatus'	CWil MOne NPSI SRms WTin
	'Pilosella'	Last listed 1999
	'Pink Cloud'	CWil MBro MOne SBla SSmi
	'Pink Dawn'	CWil MOne
	'Pink Delight'	CWil
	'Pink Flamingoes'	SSmi
	'Pink Lemonade'	MHom
*	'Pink Mist'	WPer
	'Pink Puff'	CLyd CWil MOne SSmi
	'Pippin'	CWil GAbr MBro WPer
	'Piran'	CWil MOne
	pittonii	CMea CWil ESis GAbr GCrs NMen SSmi WHal
	'Pixie'	CLyd CWil MOne NDlv NMen
	'Plumb Rose'	CWil MBro MOne NMen SChu
	'Pluto'	CWil SSmi
	'Poke Eat'	MOne SSmi
	'Polaris'	CLyd CWil SSmi
	'Poldark'	MOne
	'Pottsii'	CWil GAbr MOne
	'Powellii'	Last listed 1998
	'Prairie Sunset'	CWil MOne
	'Precious'	CWil SSmi
	'President Arsac'	Last listed 1999
¶	'Procton'	MOne
	'Proud Zelda'	CWil GAbr MOne NMen SSmi
	'Pruhonice'	CWil MOne
	'Pseudo-ornatum'	EPfP LBee LRHS NPSI SChu SRms
	'Pumaros'	CWil NMen SDys SSmi
	pumilum	CWil MBar NMen
	- from Adyl Su No. 1	CWil SSmi
	- from Adyl Su No. 2	SSmi
	- from Armchi	CWil SDys SIng SSmi
	- from Armchi x *ingwersenii*	MOne NMen
	- from El'brus No. 1	CWil SIng SSmi
	- from El'brus No. 2	SSmi
	- from Techensis	CWil NMen
	- x *ingwersenii*	CWil MBro WLow
	'Purdy'	WAbe
	'Purdy's 50-6'	CWil
	'Purdy's 90-1'	MOne
	'Purple Beauty'	CLyd CWil MOne
	'Purple King'	CWil
	'Purple Passion'	MBro
	'Purpurriese'	CWil GAbr
	'Queen Amalia'	See S. reginae-amaliae
	'Query'	Last listed 1997
	'Quintessence'	CWil NHol
	'R.H.I.'	Last listed 1998
	'Racy'	CWil
	'Radiant'	CWil
	'Ragtime'	MOne
	'Ramses'	MOne
	'Raspberry Ice'	CLyd CWil MBro NBro NHol NMen WPer
	'Red Ace'	CWil GAbr NBro NMen NPSI SSmi
	'Red Beam'	CWil MDHE MOne SSmi
	'Red Delta'	CWil MOne NBir SSmi
	'Red Devil'	CLyd CWil ELau MBro MOne NMen SSmi
	'Red Giant'	MOne MTPN
	'Red Indian'	CWil MOne
	'Red King'	Last listed 1999
¶	'Red Knight'	SSmi

§	'Red Mountain'	CHal CWil ELau LRHS MBro MOne MWat SRms SSmi WLRN
	'Red Prince'	CWil
¶	'Red Robin'	MOne
	'Red Rum'	WPer
	'Red Shadows'	CWil ESis WPer
	'Red Skin'	CWil
	'Red Spider'	NBro
	'Red Wings'	MOne SRms
	'Regal'	MOne
	'Regina'	Last listed 1999
	reginae	See *S. reginae-amaliae*
§	*reginae-amaliae*	NHol SSmi STre
	– from Kambeecho No. 1	Last listed 1999
	– from Kambeecho No. 2	MDHE NMen SDys SSmi
	– from Mavri Petri	CLyd CWil MBro MOne SDys SIng SSmi
	– from Peristéri, Greece	MBro SSmi
	– from Sarpun	CWil MOne NMen SSmi
	– from Vardusa	SDys
§	'Reginald Malby'	CTri CWil ITim LRHS MDHE SRms
¶	*regis-fernandii*	WTin
	'Reinhard'	CWil GAbr ITim MBrN MOne NMen NNrd SIng SRms SSmi WHal WPer
	'Remus'	CWil MBro MOne NMen NNrd SDys SIng WGor
	'Rex'	MOne NMen
	'Rhone'	CWil GAbr MBro MOne
*	*richardii*	MBar NBus
	'Risque'	CWil WPer
	'Rita Jane'	CLyd CWil MOne NMen SSmi
	'Robin'	CLyd CWil NBro NHol SRms
	'Ronny'	CWil
	'Roosemaryn'	MBro
	'Rose Splendour'	CWil MOne
x	*roseum* 'Fimbriatum'	CWil MBro NDlv NHol SSmi WEas
	'Rosie'	CLyd CMea CWil GAbr MBro MOne NBus NHol NMen SIng SRms SSmi WHal WHoo WPer WPyg
	'Rotkopf'	CWil MOne
	'Rotmantel'	SSmi WTin
	'Rotund'	CWil
	'Rouge'	CWil NMen
	'Royal Flush'	CWil
	'Royal Mail'	Last listed 1997
	'Royal Opera'	CWil MOne NMen
	'Royal Ruby'	CWil GCHN LBee LRHS MOne SChu SRms SSmi
	'Rubellum'	MOne
	'Rubikon Improved'	Last listed 1997
	'Rubin'	EGoo EPfP ESis GAbr MBro NBir NMen NNrd SRms SSmi WAbe WEas WHoo WPer WPyg
	'Rubrifolium'	See *S. marmoreum* subsp. *marmoreum* 'Rubrifolium'
	'Rubrum Ash'	CWil GAbr MBro MOne NMen WAbe
	'Rubrum Ornatum'	MHom
	'Rubrum Ray'	CWil MOne SSmi
*	'Ruby Glow'	ESis
	'Ruby Heart'	SSmi
¶	'Russian River'	WHoo
	'Rusty'	CWil WFar
	'Ruth'	Last listed 1999
	ruthenicum	LRHS MHom
	'Sabanum'	CLyd MOne
	'Safara'	CWil
	'Saffron'	CWil MOne
	'Saga'	CWil ELau MOne

	'Sanford's Hybrid'	MOne
	'Santis'	MBro
¶	'Sarah'	MOne
	'Sassy Frass'	CLyd MOne
	'Saturn'	CWil GAbr MOne NMen SSmi
	schlebanii	See *S. marmoreum*
	'Seminole'	CWil MOne
¶	'Shadri'	MOne
	'Sharon's Pencil'	CWil
	'Shawnee'	CWil
	'Sheila'	GAbr
	'Shenoua Koula'	SIng
¶	'Shirley Moore'	MOne
	'Shirley's Joy'	CHal CWil GAbr NMen WEas
	'Sideshow'	CWil MOne
	'Sigma'	MOne
	'Silberkarneol'	See *S.* 'Silver Jubilee'
	'Silberspitz'	CWil MHer NBro NMen WPer
§	'Silver Jubilee'	CWil GAbr MDHE NBro NDlv NPSI SRms SSmi
	'Silver Spring'	MOne
	'Silver Thaw'	CWil NMen SIng
	'Simonkaianum'	See *Jovibarba hirta*
	'Sioux'	CLyd CWil ESis GAbr MOne NMen SIng SSmi WPer
¶	'Skrocki's Beauty'	CWil
	'Skrocki's Bronze'	SSmi WPer
	'Skrocki's Purple Rose'	CWil
	'Slabber's Seedling'	CWil
	'Smokey Jet'	CWil
	'Snowberger'	CLyd CWil EGln ELau ESis GAbr LRHS MOne NHar NMen WHal WPer
	soboliferum	See *Jovibarba sobolifera*
	'Soothsayer'	CWil MOne
	'Sopa'	CWil MOne
	sosnowskyi	CWil MOne NMen SSmi
	sp. from Figaua Dhag	Last listed 1998
	sp. from San Glorio	Last listed 1999
	sp. from Sierra del Cadi	MOne NHol
	sp. from Sierra Nova	NDlv
	'Spanish Dancer'	CWil
	'Spherette'	CWil MBro NMen SSmi WPer
	'Spice'	CWil SSmi
	'Spinnelli'	MBro MOne
	'Spiver's Velvet'	MOne
	'Spode'	SSmi
	'Spring Mist'	CWil GCHN LRHS MBro MOne NHar SRms WGor WPer
	'Sprite'	CWil GAbr MOne NMen SDys SSmi
	stansfieldii	See *S. arachnoideum* subsp. *tomentosum* 'Stansfieldii'
¶	'Starburst'	CWil
	'Starion'	CWil MOne SSmi
	'Starshine'	CWil MBro MHer MOne NMen SSmi
	'State Fair'	CWil MBro SIng SSmi WPer
	'Strawberry Fields'	CWil MOne
	'Strider'	GAbr MBro WTin
	'Stuffed Olive'	CWil MOne SDys
	'Sun Waves'	CWil SSmi
¶	'Sunrise'	MOne
	'Super Dome'	CWil
	'Superama'	CWil
	'Supernova'	CWil
	'Syston Flame'	MOne
	'Tamberlane'	CWil
	'Tambimuttu'	CWil MOne
	'Tambora'	CWil
	'Tarn Hows'	Last listed 1999
	'Teck'	CWil

§ *tectorum* ♀	CArn CLyd CPri CSam CWil ELan
	EWFC GAbr GPoy GTou LRHS
	MBar MDHE MHer SIde SIng STre
	WAbe WJek WWye
* – 'Alp Gasson'	Last listed 1998
– subsp. *alpinum*	CWil MBro NMen SIng SSmi
– 'Atropurpureum'	ELan WTin
– 'Atroviolaceum'	CWil ESis GCal NHol NPSI WFar
¶ – from Eporn	MOne
– from Sierra del Cadi	SSmi
§ – var. *glaucum*	CWil ESis NDlv SSmi
§ – 'Nigrum'	CWil ESis LBee LRHS MBro MHer
	MOne NBro NHol NMen SIng
	SRms SSmi
– 'Red Flush'	CWil NHar NMen SDys SSmi
	WGor
– 'Robustum'	Last listed 1999
– 'Royanum'	ESis GAbr WEas
– 'Sunset'	CWil ESis NMen SIng SSmi WEas
	WHal
– subsp. *tectorum*	MOne
§ – – 'Atropurpureum'	CWil SSmi
§ – – 'Boissieri'	CWil MBro SSmi
– – 'Triste'	CWil ELau ESis LBee LRHS MBro
	MOne SIng SRms SSmi WAbe
– 'Violaceum'	CLyd SIng SRms WAbe
'Telfan'	MOne NMen
'Thayne'	NMen
thompsonianum	CWil ESis NDlv NHol NMen SSmi
'Tiffany'	MOne NHol WPer
'Tiger Bay'	Last listed 1998
'Tina'	WPer
¶ 'Tip Top'	CWil
'Titania'	CWil MBro NBro NHar NMen
	WHal
'Tombago'	CWil MOne
'Topaz'	CWil GAbr LBee LRHS MOne SBla
	SChu SRms
'Tordeur's Memory'	CWil MOne NMen SSmi
'Traci Sue'	ELau SSmi
'Trail Walker'	CWil MOne
transcaucasicum	CWil MOne SSmi
* 'Tree Beard'	CWil
'Tristesse'	CLyd CWil MOne NMen WGor
	WGwG
'Tristram'	Last listed 1999
'Truva'	CWil MOne NMen
'Twilight Blues'	CWil
'Unicorn'	CWil
x *vaccarii*	CWil NMen SSmi
'Vanbaelen'	CWil SDys SSmi
'Vaughelen'	CWil MBro MOne
* 'Velvet Prince'	CWil
x *versicolor*	NHol
vicentei	CWil MBro NDlv NMen
– from Gaton	MOne
'Victorian'	Last listed 1999
'Video'	CWil GAbr NMen
'Violet Queen'	CWil
'Virgil'	CWil GAbr MBro NMen SDys SIng
	SSmi WPer
'Virginus'	CLyd CWil MBro
¶ 'Vorgo' No. 1	WTin
'Vulcano'	CWil GAbr
'Watermelon Rind'	MOne
webbianum	See *S. arachnoideum* subsp.
	tomentosum
'Webby Flame'	CWil
'Webby Ola'	SSmi
'Weirdo'	CWil
'Wendy'	CLyd CWil MOne NMen
'Westerlin'	CLyd CWil GAbr MOne SSmi

¶ 'White Eyes'	SOkd
'Whitening'	CWil GAbr NMen SSmi
x *widderi*	SIng SSmi
'Wollcott's Variety'	ELau GAbr LRHS MOne NBir
	NHar WPer
wulfenii	CWil NMen
'Zaza'	CWil
zeleborii	CHal ELau WHal
'Zenith'	CWil GAbr
I 'Zenobia'	MHom
'Zenocrate'	CWil WHal
'Zeppelin'	CWil MBro
'Zinaler Rothorn'	Last listed 1997
'Zircon'	NMen
'Zone'	CWil NMen SSmi
'Zulu'	CWil

SENECIO (Asteraceae)

§ *abrotanifolius*	EBee
– var. *tiroliensis*	See *S. abrotanifolius*
aquaticus	Last listed 1998
§ *articulatus*	CHal LHil
aschenbornianus	GCal
aureus	See *Packera aurea*
bicolor subsp. *cineraria*	See *S. cineraria*
bidwillii	See *Brachyglottis bidwillii*
buchananii	See *Brachyglottis buchananii*
candicans	See *S. cineraria*
cannabifolius	EBee GCal
canus	Last listed 1998
chionophila	Last listed 1998
chrysanthemoides	See *Euryops chrysanthemoides*
§ *cineraria*	IBlr MBri NBlu
– 'Alice'	Last listed 1997
– 'Ramparts'	WEas
– Sch 3129	Last listed 1997
– 'Silver Dust' ♀	ENot EPfP EWTr GKir LRHS
– 'White Diamond' ♀	CLTr ECha LGro
compactus	See *Brachyglottis compacta*
confusus	CPln ECon ERea LCns SOWG
	WMul
doria	EBee EPPr LRHS SAga SCro WCot
	WFar WLRN
doronicum	Last listed 1999
elaeagnifolius	See *Brachyglottis elaeagnifolia*
elegans	LHil
eminens	Last listed 1997
erucifolius	Last listed 1999
fuchsii HH&K 293	Last listed 1997
– HH&K 318	Last listed 1998
glastifolius	EBee ERea LHil
grandiflorus	Last listed 1997
'Gregynog Gold'	See *Ligularia* 'Gregynog Gold'
greyi Hooker	See *Brachyglottis greyi*
– hort.	See *Brachyglottis* (Dunedin
	Group) 'Sunshine'
harbourii RMRP 96596	Last listed 1999
heritieri DC.	See *Pericallis lanata*
herreanus	MBri
¶ *hoffmannii*	CPln
incanus	SMrm
jacquemontianus	Last listed 1998
kirkii	See *Brachyglottis kirkii*
laciniatus	Last listed 1998
laxifolius Buchanan	See *Brachyglottis laxifolia*
– hort.	See *Brachyglottis* (Dunedin
	Group) 'Sunshine'
'Leonard Cockayne'	See *Brachyglottis* 'Leonard
	Cockayne'
leucophyllus	LHil WLin
leucostachys	See *S. viravira*
macroglossus	Last listed 1999

- 'Variegatus' ♀   CHal CPlN ERea
macrospermus   Last listed 1999
maritimus   See *S. cineraria*
mikanioides   See *Delairea odorata*
monroi   See *Brachyglottis monroi*
¶ **ovatus**   EMan
petasitis   CHEx LHil
polyodon   CInt EWes GBri MCCP MNrw
   SCro SUsu WFar
¶ - subsp. **subglaber**   EMon
- S&SH 29   CFir CRDP EBee SAga WCru
przewalskii   See *Ligularia przewalskii*
pulcher   CFil CGle CSam GBri MAvo MMil
   MNrw MTho NTow SMrm SUsu
   WCru WPGP
reinboldii   See *Brachyglottis rotundifolia*
rodriguezii   Last listed 1997
rowleyanus   EBak
scandens   CMac CPlN CPle ELan ERea
   MCCP MNrw MTho WCwm WHer
   WPGP
seminiveus   EBee
§ **serpens**   CHal LHil MBri
§ **smithii**   CRDP CRow ELan GOrP NChi
   WBcn WCot WCru WFar
speciosus   NBir NTow
spedenii   See *Brachyglottis spedenii*
squalidus   Last listed 1997
'Sunshine'   See *Brachyglottis* (Dunedin
   Group) 'Sunshine'
tamoides 'Variegatus'   ERea WPyg
tanguticus   See *Sinacalia tangutica*
§ **viravira** ♀   CGle CPle CSam EHol EMFP EMar
   ERea GBri LIck MBel MLLN MRav
   MWgw SLim SMac SMrm SPer
   SRPl WCot WEas WOve WSHC
   WWat

SENNA (Caesalpiniaceae)
alexandrina   MSal
artemisioides ♀   SOWG
§ **candolleana**   SPan
§ **corymbosa**   CBot CHEx CRHN ERea LChe
   LCns LHil LRHS SOWG SYvo
didymobotrya   SOWG
x **floribunda** ♀   Last listed 1995
hebecarpa   EBee MSal
§ **marilandica**   EBee ELau MSal
obtusa (Roxb.) Wight   CGre
- Clos   See *S. candolleana*
§ **obtusifolia**   MSal
§ **siamea**   Last listed 1999

SEQUOIA (Taxodiaceae)
sempervirens ♀   CB&S CDoC CDul CGre CMCN
   CTho CTrG EHul EPfP GChr GKir
   IOrc LCon LPan SLon SMad WDin
   WMou WNor
- 'Adpressa'   CDoC CMac CSli EBrP EBre EHul
   EOrn EPla GKir LBCl LBSe LBre
   LCon LLin MAsh MBBe MBar MBri
   MGos NWea SBre SLim WPyg
- 'Prostrata'   CSli EBrP EBre EOrn EPla LBCl
   LBSe LBre LCon LLin MBBe MBar
   MBri SBre

SEQUOIADENDRON (Taxodiaceae)
giganteum ♀   More than 30 suppliers
- 'Barabits Requiem'   LRHS MBlu MBri SMad
- 'Glaucum'   CBlo CDoC LCon LPan MBlu MBri
   NLar SMad
* - 'Glaucum Compactum'   MBri

- 'Hazel Smith'   MBlu SMad
- 'Pendulum'   CBlo CDoC LCon LPan MBlu
- 'Variegatum' (v)   CDoC WBcn

SERAPIAS (Orchidaceae)
lingua   CHdy LAma SBla SSpi

SERENOA (Arecaceae)
repens   CRoM EPVP LPal

SERIPHIDIUM (Asteraceae)
caerulescens   EEls
   subsp. **gallicum**
§ **canum**   EEls IIve
§ **ferganense**   EEls
§ **fragrans**   EEls
§ **maritimum** ♀   CArn EWFC GBar GGar GPoy ILis
   NSti
- var. **maritimum**   EEls
§ **novum**   EEls
§ **nutans**   EBee EEls MWat WAbe
§ **tridentatum**   CArn MWgw
- subsp. **tridentatum**   EEls
- subsp. **wyomingense**   EEls
tripartitum var. **rupicola**   EEls
§ **vallesiacum** ♀   EEls SAga WEas
vaseyanaum   EEls

SERISSA (Rubiaceae)
foetida   See *S. japonica*
§ **japonica**   STre
- **rosea**   STre
- 'Variegata'   CHal ECon STre

SERRATULA (Asteraceae)
coronata   EBrP EBre LBCl LBSe LBre MBBe
   SBre
§ **seoanei**   CBos CMea CNic CPla CRDP
   CSev CTri EBee ECha EDAr EMan
   EMon LGre LHop MBri MHer
   MWat SAga SDix SIng SRms SUsu
   WByw WCot WPGP WPat WWin
shawii   See *S. seoanei*
tinctoria   CArn CKin ELau EMan GBar
   MHew MSal
- subsp. **macrocephala**   EBee MTPN
wolffii   EBee

SESAMUM (Pedaliaceae)
indicum   CArn

SESBANIA (Papilionaceae)
punicea   SOWG

SESELI (Apiaceae)
dichotomum   Last listed 1998
elatum subsp. **osseum**   CFil EBee WCot
globiferum   LGre
gummiferum   CArn CBot CGle CSpe EBee EMon
   EWes LGre SAga SMrm WCot
hippomarathrum   CGle
libanotis   SAga
pallasii   EBee
rigidum   EBee
varium   Last listed 1999

SESLERIA (Poaceae)
§ **albicans**   EPPr
§ **argentea**   CBrm
§ **autumnalis**   LGre
caerulea   CCuc CElw CSam EGar EHoe
   ELan EMon LBuc LNor LPan LRHS

	MBel MLLN MMoz MWgw MWhi NBea SCob WCot
- subsp. *calcarea*	See *S. albicans*
cylindrica	See *S. argentea*
glauca	CInt EHoe LPan MAvo MSCN NLar NOak NPro NSti SChu WPer
beufleriana	CElw ECGN EHoe EMan EMon EPPr EPla LRHS MAvo
insularis	CSWP EMon EPPr LRHS MAvo
nitida	CCuc EGar EHoe EMar EMon EPPr LRHS MAvo MMoz NBea WPGP
sadleriana	EBee EPPr EWes

SETARIA (Poaceae)

palmifolia	CHEx CRoM EPPr WDyG WHal WMul
sphacelata	EBee LHil
¶ *viridis*	NSti WCot

SETCREASEA See TRADESCANTIA

SEVERINIA (Rutaceae)

buxifolia	SCit

SHEPHERDIA (Elaeagnaceae)

argentea	CAgr CB&S CPle EBee
canadensis	Last listed 1999

SHERARDIA (Rubiaceae)

arvensis	EWFC MSal

SHIBATAEA (Poaceae - Bambusoideae)

chinensis	EPla
kumasasa	CB&S CCuc CDoC CPCWit EBee EHoe EPla ERod al lOrc ISta LEdu LJus LNet MRMCCP MGos MMoz MWhi NV\Dry SPla WJun WNor
¶ - f. *aureostriata*	EPla ISta SDry
lancifolia	EPla SDry WJun

SHORTIA (Diapensiaceae)

galacifolia	IBlr
soldanelloides	IBlr SSpi
- f. *alpina*	IBlr
- var. *ilicifolia*	IBlr SSpi
- - 'Askival'	IBlr
- var. *magna*	GCrs IBlr
uniflora	IBlr
- var. *kantoensis*	SOkd
- var. *orbicularis*	GCrs IBlr SSpi
'Grandiflora'	

SIBBALDIA (Rosaceae)

parviflora NS 668	Last listed 1997
procumbens	GKir

SIBBALDIOPSIS (Rosaceae)

§ *tridentata*	Last listed 1999
- 'Lemon Mac'	SIng
- 'Nuuk'	GAri MGos NFla SMac SRPl

SIBIRAEA (Rosaceae)

altaiensis	See *S. laevigata*
§ *laevigata*	CFil

SIBTHORPIA (Scrophulariaceae)

¶ *europaea*	CHEx

SIDA (Malvaceae)

hermaphrodita	EMon WCot

petrophila	Last listed 1998

SIDALCEA (Malvaceae)

'Brilliant'	CFai CM&M EBee EPfP LCaP LRHS MMil NFai SPer WFar WViv
candida	More than 30 suppliers
- 'Bianca'	CBot CPea EBee LAst LCaP LFis MBel MSte MTis SMrm WFar WPer WWhi
'Crimson King'	MAvo WFar
'Croftway Red'	CB&S CMGP EBee ELan EMan EWTr GKir LRHS MFir SAga SChu SCro SHel SPer SSca WMaN WSan
Crown hybrids	CTri
cusickii	EBee
'Elsie Heugh'	More than 30 suppliers
hendersonii	EBee
hickmanii	Last listed 1999
subsp. *anomala*	
- - NNS 95462	WCot
hirtipes	EBee
* *integrifolia*	LGre
'Interlaken'	EBrP EBre LBCl LBSe LBre MBBe NFla NOrc SBre
¶ 'Little Princess'PBR	WWeb
'Loveliness'	CGle CRDP ELan EMan NCat NLar SAga SUsu WCot WViv
malviflora	MFir NSti SChu SRms
- 'Alba'	WFar
- dark-flowered	Last listed 1999
¶ 'Mary Martin'	EMan
'Monarch'	Last listed 1999
¶ 'Moorland Rose Coronet'	WMoo
'Mr Lindbergh'	EBee EMan LRHS SPer WCot WFar WRus
'Mrs Borrodaile'	CBos CM&M CMGP EBee ECGN EMan GBuc LRHS MBNS MCLN MMil MTis NGdn NHaw WCot WElm WFar WPGP WRus
'Mrs Galloway'	WFar
'Mrs T. Alderson'	EMan WFar WMoo
'My Love'	LGre LHop
neomexicana	EBee EMan GCal SSvw WBea WHil
'Oberon'	GBuc LPio SPer WEas WFar WMoo
oregana	CSam NBid
- subsp. *spicata*	Last listed 1998
'Party Girl'	CM&M EBee EBrP EBre ECot ECtt EFou EOld EWTr GKir LBCl LBSe LBre LPio LRHS MBBe MMal MPEx NCat NLar NOrc NPri NVic SBre SCob SHel SPlb WFar WOve WPer
'Präriebrand'	LGre
'Purpetta'	EWTr NChi NCut STes WBea
'Reverend Page Roberts'	CMCo LFis MMHG MRav SMrm WFar WMaN
'Rosaly'	CFri WShe
'Rosanna'	EWTr NCut WBea
'Rose Bouquet'	Last listed 1999
'Rose Bud'	CStr
'Rose Queen'	CGle EBee ECha ENot EWTr GChr LHop LRHS MBel MCAu MCLN MRav MTis NFla SAga SChu SPer SRms WFar
'Rosy Gem'	CBlo CFwr EBrP EBre LBCl LBSe LBre LCaP LRHS MBBe MBNS NCat NCut SBre WFar WShe
Stark's hybrids	LRHS SRms WBea
'Sussex Beauty'	CMCo CRDP EFou LFis MArl MCLN MLLN MRav NCat NCiC NGdn SChu SPer WCot WFar

'Sweet Joy'　EFou
'The Duchess'　MAvo WFar
'Twixt'　Last listed 1999
'William Smith' ♀　COtt CRDP CSam EBee EBrP EBre
　EMan EPfP EWes LAst LBcl LBSe
　LBre LRHS MBBe MCLN MLLN
　NCat NCiC NFla NGdn NOrc
　SAga SBre SLon SPer WCot
　MTis

¶ 'Wine Red'

SIDERITIS (Lamiaceae)

candicans　Last listed 1998
clandestina　Last listed 1999
glacialis　Last listed 1998
byssopifolia　LHil
macrostachys　WLin
scardica　Last listed 1999
scordioides　CBot EBee EBot ECha EMan
syriaca　EOHP SHFr
- subsp. syriaca　EBee NDov SRCN

SIEVERSIA (Rosaceae)

§ reptans　NSla

SILAUM (Apiaceae)

silaus　CKin EWFC

SILENE (Caryophyllaceae)

acaulis　EDAr ESis GCHN GTou ITim LBee
　LFis LRHS MBro MTho NMen
　NWCA SBla SRms SSmi WAbe
§ - subsp. acaulis　CGra EPot GDra NCat SPlb SRms
　EPot EWes GDra LRHS NHar NLan
- 'Alba'　WAbe
　Last listed 1997
§ - subsp. bryoides　See S. acaulis subsp. acaulis
- subsp. elongata　See S. acaulis subsp. bryoides
- subsp. exscapa　EPot GAbr GCHN GCrs GTou
- 'Frances'　IMGH ITim NHar NMen NRya
　NSla NWCA WAbe
　ECho ELan
- 'Francis Copeland'　CLyd EPot MBro WAbe
- 'Helen's Double' (d)　CLyd EPot MNaF
* - minima　CInt EBrP EBre EDAr ELan ESis
- 'Mount Snowdon'　EWes IMGH LBcl LBSe LBee LBre
　LRHS MBBe MTho NBus NHar
　NHol NMen NRya NWCA SBre
　WAbe WPat
　See S. acaulis subsp. acaulis
- 'Pedunculata'　NBrk
- 'Plena' (d)　CGra
- 'White Rabbit'　See S. latifolia subsp. latifolia
alba　CM&M CMea EBee EPfP ESis LFis
alpestris　MBar MHer MNrw MTho NNrd
　SRms SRot SSca WBea WFar WOut
　ESis EWes LBee LRHS NFor WWin
- 'Flore Pleno' (d) ♀　Last listed 1997
* andina　CPBP
argaea　See Lychnis × arkwrightii
× arkwrightii　WHer
armeria　CElw CSam GBuc MBNS MBel
asterias　MNrw NBid NBrk NBro NSti STes
　WPer WWin
　Last listed 1999
- NS 657　EBee
bellidioides　CGra
californica　Last listed 1998
campanula　Last listed 1999
caroliniana　Last listed 1998
- subsp. pensylvanica　Last listed 1997
caryophylloides
　subsp. echinus

chungtienensis　EBee
ciliata　Last listed 1998
§ compacta　MAvo NLar WCot
conica　EWFC
delavayi　Last listed 1998
- ACE 2449　Last listed 1999
aff. delavayi ACE 2466　EBee
densiflora HH&K 326　Last listed 1999
dinarica　Last listed 1998
§ dioica　CArn CKin EOld EPfP EWFC
　EWTr GDea MChe MHer MHew
　NFai NLan NLar SRms SWat WHen
　WHer WJek WRos WShi
- alba　Last listed 1997
- 'Clifford Moor' PBR (v)　EHoe LRHS MSCN NSti SCob
　SCoo WCHb WRus
- 'Compacta'　See S. dioica 'Minikin'
- 'Dorset'　Last listed 1998
§ - 'Flore Pleno' (d)　EBee ECha GMac LFis LLWP LRHS
　MBct MNrw MRav MTho NBid
　NBro NGdn SMrm WByw WEas
　WFar WHoo WPer WWin
§ - 'Graham's Delight' (v)　EMon GBri WCHb WCot WHer
- 'Ine'　CNat EMar MAvo WAlt WBea
　WRHF
¶ - lutea　GDea MHer
§ - 'Minikin'　Clyd ECha EMon LRHS MAvo
　NBrk NCat NDov SPer WAlt WBea
　WCot WTin
- 'Hissold' (v)　EMon WCHb
- 'Pembrokeshire Pastel' (v)　WAlt
- 'Richmond' (d)　EBee GBuc MAvo MInt
§ - 'Rosea Plena' (d)　CBre CGle CM&M EMan EMon
　MTho SChu SMrm WByw WCot
　WHer WPer
- 'Rubra Plena'　See S. dioica 'Flore Pleno'
- 'Thelma Kay' (d/v)　CMil CPlt CSev EBee EMan EMon
　GBuc GMac MAvo WAlt WCHb
　WHer WMoo WPGP
- 'variegata'　See S. dioica 'Graham's Delight'
elizabethae　LRHS NWCA
- alba　Last listed 1999
§ fimbriata　CBrd CHad EBee EEls ELan EPPr
　GCal MHer MRav MWat NSti SAga
　SHel SMrm WAbb WCot WElm
　WKif WRHF
- 'Marianne'　EMon MNrw
flavescens var.　Last listed 1998
　kirninsularis
　B&SWJ 296
fortunei HH&K 214　LFis
gallica　EWFC
bifacensis　LFis
hookeri　MTho NWCA
- Ingramii Group　CGra
- JCA 1855400　Last listed 1999
ingramii　CPBP
italica　EWFC
keiskei　ECha NTow WPer
- var. minor　EWes LRHS MDCh MTho NWCA
　SSca WAbe WWin
§ latifolia subsp. latifolia　CArn EWFC MGas NMir WHen
　WHer WJek
lerchenfeldiana　Last listed 1997
maritima　See S. uniflora
¶ mexicana　NArg
moorcroftiana　Last listed 1997
morrisonmontana　Last listed 1997
- B&SWJ 3149　EBee WCru
multifida　See S. fimbriata
noctiflora　EWFC
nutans　CArn EWFC MNrw SRms WHer

* - var. *salmoniana*	Last listed 1998
- var. *smithiana*	Last listed 1998
orientalis	See *S. compacta*
parishii var. *viscida*	Last listed 1999
NNS 95-474	
parnassica	Last listed 1997
pendula	LLWP
- 'Compacta'	Last listed 1999
petersonii	NWCA
pusilla	CHal CNic
regia	MNrw
rubra 'Flore Pleno'	See *S. dioica* 'Flore Pleno'
saxatilis	Last listed 1998
schafta ♀	CHal ECha EDAr EMNN EPfP
	GCHN GKir LRHS MBro MFir
	MHer MMal MWat NBid NWCA
	SIng SRms WFar WHoo WPer
	WWin
- 'Abbotswood'	See *Lychnis* x *walkeri*
	'Abbotswood Rose'
- 'Robusta'	LRHS
§ - 'Shell Pink'	CInt EPot EWes LRHS NWCA
	WAbe
sieboldii	See *Lychnis coronata* var.
	sieboldii
¶ 'Snowflake'	CPri
sp. ACE 1573	Last listed 1999
suksdorfii	CLyd EPot MBro WHoo WPyg
* *surortii*	WPer
tenuis ACE 2429	GBuc
thessalonica	EBee ELan MBro MCCP NCut
	SBea
undulata	Last listed 1998
§ *uniflora*	EGoo EMNN EMar EWFC GCHN
	MFir MWat NBid NBro NOak
	NWCA NWoo SRms WBar WHen
	WHer
- 'Alba Plena'	See *S. uniflora* 'Robin
	Whitebreast'
§ - 'Druett's Variegated' (v)	More than 30 suppliers
- 'Flore Pleno'	See *S. uniflora* 'Robin
	Whitebreast'
§ - 'Robin Whitebreast' (d)	CPBP ECha ECtt GCal GKir GMac
	MBar MHer MTho MWat MWgw
	NBid NBro NHol NOak SRPl SRms
	SRot WCot WHoo WMoo WOve
	WPer WPyg WWin
- 'Rosea'	CGle CNic ECtt EMNN EMar
	LRHS MRav NFor SMrm SRot SSca
	SUsu WPer
- 'Silver Lining' (v)	ELan GBuc
- 'Variegata'	See *S. uniflora* 'Druett's
	Variegated'
- Weisskehlchen	See *S. uniflora* 'Robin
	Whitebreast'
- 'White Bells'	CMea CTri EBee WBea WHoo
	WPyg WSHC
vallesia	WPer
virginica	Last listed 1999
§ *vulgaris*	CKin EWFC MChe MGas MHer
	NLan NMir
- subsp. *maritima*	See *S. uniflora*
wallichiana	See *S. vulgaris*
'Wisley Pink'	CHal
§ *zawadskii*	GBuc MNrw SSca WPer

SILPHIUM (Asteraceae)

¶ *integrifolium*	IIve
laciniatum	CArn EBee ELau SMad WCot
perfoliatum	CArn GPoy LRHS NSti WCot
	WFar
terebinthinaceum	LGre SMad WCot

SILYBUM (Asteraceae)

marianum	CAgr CArn CGle CInt CSpe
	ECoo EFer ELan EMan EPar
	EWFC GPoy MSal MWgw NArg
	NChi NFai NFla SIde SRCN
	WCer WEas WHer WHil WOak
	WWye
- 'Adriana'	CGdn ECoo MSph NArg
- white	CSpe EMar

SIMMONDSIA (Simmondsiaceae)

chinensis	ELau EOHP

SINACALIA (Asteraceae)

§ *tangutica*	CGle CHEx CRow EBee EMan
	GGar MBNS MNrw NBro NDea
	NSti SDix SMrm WAbb WCot
	WCru WFar WHil

SINARUNDINARIA (Poaceae - Bambusoideae)

anceps	See *Yushania anceps*
jaunsarensis	See *Yushania anceps*
maling	See *Yushania maling*
murieliae	See *Fargesia murieliae*
nitida	See *Fargesia nitida*

SINNINGIA (Gesneriaceae)

'Arion'	NMos
'Blanche de Méru'	NMos SDeJ
'Blue Wonder'	MBri
'Boonwood Yellow Bird'	NMos
canescens ♀	CHal
§ *cardinalis*	CHal EBak MLan WDib
§ x *cardosa*	MBri
'Cherry Belle'	NMos
'Diego Rose'	MBri
'Duchess of York'	CSut
'Duke of York'	CSut
'Etoile de Feu'	LAma MBri NMos
'Hollywood'	LAma NMos SDeJ
'Island Sunset'	NMos
'Kaiser Friedrich'	LAma MBri NMos
'Kaiser Wilhelm'	LAma MBri NMos
leucotricha	ERea
'Medusa'	NMos
'Mont Blanc'	CSut LAma MBri NMos SDeJ
'Pegasus'	NMos
'Princess Elizabeth'	SDeJ
'Red Tiger'	CSut
'Reine Wilhelmine'	SDeJ
'Royal Crimson'	CSut
Royal Pink Group	CSut
'Royal Tiger'	CSut
Tigrina Group	NMos SDeJ
tubiflora	Last listed 1998
¶ *verticillata*	CSpe
'Violacea'	MBri NMos
'Waterloo'	NMos

SINOBAMBUSA (Poaceae - Bambusoideae)

intermedia	EPla IJus
orthotropa	CFil EPla WPGP
rubroligula	CFil EPla WPGP
tootsik	EPla SDry WJun
§ - f. *albostriata*	SDry
- 'Variegata'	See *S. tootsik* f. *albostriata*

SINOCALYCANTHUS (Calycanthaceae)

chinensis	CB&S CEnd CGre CMCN CPMA
	EPfP IDee LNet LRHS SMad SRPl
	SSpi WPGP WWat WWoo

SINOFRANCHETIA (Lardizabalaceae)
chinensis   CPIN GCal WCru

SINOJACKIA ✿ (Styracaceae)
xylocarpa   EPfP MBel WWat

SINOWILSONIA (Hamamelidaceae)
henryi   CB&S CMCN

SISON (Apiaceae)
¶ *amomum*   CArn

SISYMBRIUM (Brassicaceae)
§ *luteum*   WHer

SISYRINCHIUM ✿ (Iridaceae)
x *anceps*	See *S. angustifolium*
§ *angustifolium*	CGrW CMHG EBot EBur ECha EWTr GBin GCHN GKir MBNS MBar MBel MSal MWat NChi NDea NFla NLAp NNrd SPlb SRms SSmi WBod WPer WWin
- *album*	GKir GMaP MSCN NChi NCut NLar WRHF
§ *arenarium*	CPBP EBur MDHE NMen
atlanticum	ESis MDHE NBro SUsu WPer
bellum hort.	See *S. idaboense* var. *bellum*
bermudianum	See *S. angustifolium*
- 'Album'	See *S. graminoides* 'Album'
birameum	See *S. graminoides*
'Biscutella'	CGrW CHad CLyd EBur ECtt EDAr LAst LHop NDea NMen SChu SLod SOkh SPlb SSmi SUsu WEas WGwG WHal WLRN WMoo
* 'Blue Ice'	CCuc CMea CPBP CSpe EBur EDAr EGar LAco LNor MBro MDHE NCat NHol SMrm WAbb WAbe WBea WFar WHal WHoo WPat WPer WPyg
boreale	See *S. californicum*
brachypus	See *S. californicum* Brachypus Group
brevipes F&W 7946	Last listed 1998
'Californian Skies'	More than 30 suppliers
§ *californicum*	CBen CGrW CInt CLon EBur EHon LPBA MBar MBct MFir MSta MWat NBid NBro NNrd SIng SSmi SWyc WMAq WPer WWin WWye
§ - Brachypus Group	CBro CGrW CMea ECtt EDAr EPot GCHN GGar GTou LAst LPVe MBNS MBct MHer MNrw MOne NDea NLar NVic SPlb SWat WBea WBrE WCer WElm WMoo
§ *chilense*	SIng
coeleste	EBur MDHE
coeruleum	See *Gelasine coerulea*
commutatum	CMil EDAr ERos GBuc MNrw MWgw SRot WBro WElm
convolutum	NDov
cuspidatum	See *S. arenarium*
demissum	CLyd CNic EBur
depauperatum	CLyd EBur EMar ESis NWCA WBea WHer WPer
'Devon Blue'	WFar
'Devon Skies'	CHid CMCo CMHG EBur MNrw WAbe WFar WSan WWin
douglasii	See *Olsynium douglasii*
'Dragon's Eye'	EBee SAsh SDys SIng SSca SSvw SUsu
'E.K. Balls'	CInt CLyd EBur ElAn LAst LBee LNor LRHS MBro MTho MWgw

	NBro NCat NFai NHol NMen NRya SBla SSmi SSvw SUsu WAbe WBea WHen WMoo WPat WWin
elmeri	EBur
filifolium	See *Olsynium filifolium*
§ *graminoides*	EBur NBro WPer
§ - 'Album'	CGrW EBur GAri GGar NBro WPer
- sterile	Last listed 1999
grandiflorum	See *Olsynium douglasii*
'Hemswell Sky'	CLyd EBur EHoe LAst MDHE MMil WBea WWye
'Iceberg'	CRDP NCat SDys SMrm SUsu WCDu
idahoense	CCuc EDAr GGar LRHS MHer SPlb SRms
§ - 'Album'	CGle EBur ECha EDAr ElAn EPot ERos EWTr GTou LAst LBee LRHS MNrw MTho MWat NDea NEgg NHol NMen SAga SBla SPlb SSmi SUsu WAbe WFar WPat WPer WWin WWye
§ - var. *bellum*	CBro CMHG EBrP EBre EBur ECha ElAn EPfP GCHN GTou LBCl LBSe LBre LEur LRHS MBBe MBNS MHer MNrw NMen NRya NWCA SBre SIng SRms WBea WHen WMAq WPat WPer
- - 'Rocky Point'	CLyd EBur LRHS WBea WPat WWeb
- blue	EGra
iridifolium	See *S. micranthum*
junceum	See *Olsynium junceum*
littorale	EBur NLar WBea WPer
macrocarpon ♀	CGra CInt CLyd CPBP EBur EPot ERos ESis GTou ITim LBee LRHS MHer NMen NWCA WBea WHal WPer WWye
'Marie'	EBur MDHE
'Marion'	CMil CRDP MSph NCat NHar SAsh SBla SDys SUsu WWye
'May Snow'	See *S. idaboense* 'Album'
§ *micranthum*	CBro EBur EWes
montanum	EBur ERos
- var. *crebrum*	CInt
- var. *montanum*	Last listed 1998
'Mrs Spivey'	EBur ECtt EMNN MBar MHer NMen NOak WElm WRHF
mucronatum	EBur
'North Star'	See *S.* 'Pole Star'
nudicaule	EBur
- x *montanum*	CFee CMHG EBur EMNN ITim MDHE MNrw NHar NHol NNrd NRya SRot SUsu WPer
patagonicum	EBur EDAr ERos GBuc NCat NNrd WBea WLRN WPer
pearcei	Last listed 1998
§ 'Pole Star'	CFee CLyd CNic CSpe EBur EMar GTou IBlr MFir NHar NHol SRPl SSvw SWal WBea WHal WPer
'Quaint and Queer'	CGrW CHea CInt CM&M CMil EBur ECha EMar ERav LNor MBel MBrN MRav MTho NBro NChi SSmi WBea WCra WLin WPer WRus WWhi WWin WWye
I 'Raspberry'	CMea EBur LAco NHol WAbe
scabrum	See *S. chilense*
'Sisland Blue'	EBur EWes MDHE
¶ sp. from Andes Mts	EWes
sp. from Tierra del Fuego	CRow
'Stars and Stripes'	LPBA
§ *striatum*	More than 30 suppliers

§ - 'Aunt May' (v)   More than 30 suppliers
  - 'Variegatum'   See *S. striatum* 'Aunt May'

SIUM (Apiaceae)
sisarum   ELau GBar GPoy MHer MSal SIde
                              WOak

SKIMMIA ✿ (Rutaceae)
anquetilia   MBar WBod WWat
x **confusa**   EHol
  - 'Isabella'   SLim
  - 'Kew Green' (m) ♀   CB&S CGre CMHG CTrG EBee
                              ELan ENot EPfP EPla GKir IOrc
                              LHop LRHS MAsh MBar MBri
                              MGos MRav NHol SCob SMac
                              SPer SPla SReu SSta WBod WCot
                              WFoF WPyg WWat
dulcamara   Last listed 1998
§ **japonica**   CLan CMHG CTrw EBrP EBre
                              EMil ENot EWTr GKir GQui LBCl
                              LBSe LBre MBBe MGos SBre SCob
                              SRPl SReu SSta WFar WGwG
                              WHCG WStI
  - (f)   CTrG CTri ELan SPer SRms
  - 'Alba'   See *S. japonica* 'Wakehurst White'
  - B&SWJ 5053   WCru
  - 'Bowles' Dwarf Female' (f) CHig CMHG EBee EPla LRHS
                              MBar MBri MGos MRav NHol
                              SCob SLim SPer WWat
  - 'Bowles' Dwarf Male' (m) CMHG EBee EPla LRHS MBar MBri
                              MHar SCob SLim WBod WWat
* - 'Bronze Beauty'   MBri
  - 'Bronze Knight' (m)   EBee ENot EPla GBin LRHS MAsh
                              MBar MBri MGos MRav NHol SEas
                              SLim SPan SSta WWat
  - 'Cecilia Brown' (f)   EPla WWat
  - 'Chameleon'   Last listed 1999
  - 'Claries Repens'   CDoC EPla LRHS MAsh MBri
  - 'Emerald King' (m)   LRHS MAsh MBar MBri WBcn
N - 'Foremanii'   See *S. japonica* 'Veitchii'
  - 'Fragrans' (m) ♀   CDoC CHig CSam CTrw EBee
                              ENot EPla GChr GKir IOrc LRHS
                              MAsh MBar MBel MBlu MGos
                              MRav NHol SCob SEas SLim SPer
                              SReu SSta WBod WFar WWat
  - 'Fragrantissima' (m)   EPla LRHS MBri WBod
  - 'Fructu Albo'   See *S. japonica* 'Wakehurst White'
  - 'Highgrove Redbud' (f)   EBee LRHS MBar MBri MGos SLim
                              SSta WBod
  - 'Keessen' (f)   Last listed 1998
  - 'Kew White' (f)   CAbP CB&S CBlo CDoC CSam
                              EBee EBrP EBre EPfP GKir LBCl
                              LBSe LBre MBBe MBel MBri MGos
                              NHol SBre SLon WHCG WLRN
                              WPnP WWat
  - 'Luwain'   LRHS NHol NPro WFar WLRN
¶ - 'Marlot'   EPfP
  - 'Nymans' (f) ♀   More than 30 suppliers
  - 'Oblata'   MBar SMer
  - 'Obovata' (f)   EPla
¶ - 'Red Dragon'   MBri
  - 'Red Princess' (f)   EPla LRHS MAsh MBri SCob
* - 'Red Riding Hood'   CLyn LRHS MBri NHol SPan
  - 'Redruth' (f)   CB&S CDoC CLan CSam EBee
                              EPla GKir IOrc LRHS MAsh MBar
                              MBri MGos NHol SLim SSta WBcn
                              WWat
§ - subsp. **reevesiana**   More than 30 suppliers
  - - B&SWJ 3763   WCru
  - - B&SWJ 3895   WCru
  - - 'Chilan Choice'   GKir LRHS MAsh SAga SLim SPla
                              SSta

  - - ETOT 182   WPGP
¶ - - 'Fata Morgana' (m)   MGos
¶ - - var. **reevesiana**   WCru
      B&SWJ 3544
  - - 'Robert Fortune' ♀   MBar SCoo WWat
§ - Rogersii Group   CTri IOrc MBar MWat
  - - 'Dunwood'   MBar
  - - 'George Gardner'   MBar
  - - 'Helen Goodall' (f)   MBar
§ - - 'Nana Femina' (f)   Last listed 1998
§ - - 'Nana Mascula' (m)   CTri
  - - 'Rockyfield Green'   MBar
  - - 'Snow Dwarf' (m)   EPla LRHS MBar MBri
  - - 'Rubella' (m) ♀   More than 30 suppliers
  - - 'Rubinetta' (m)   CChe EBee GKir IOrc LRHS
                              MAsh MBar MGos NHol SLim
                              WWeb
  - 'Ruby Dome' (m)   LRHS MBar MBri WBcn WWat
  - 'Ruby King' (m)   GKir LRHS MAsh MBar MBri
                              MGos NHol SSta WBod WStI
  - 'Scarlet Dwarf' (f)   LRHS MBar MBri
  - 'Stoneham Red'   LRHS MBri
  - 'Tansley Gem' (f)   EPfP LRHS MAsh MBar MBri
  - 'Thelma King'   GKir LRHS MBri
§ - 'Veitchii' (f)   CB&S CTri EBee ENot EPfP EPla
                              GChr GKir IMGH LRHS MAsh
                              MBar MGos MRav NHol SCob
                              SEND SLim SPer WBod WDin
                              WPnP WStI WWal WWeb
§ - 'Wakehurst White' (f)   CMHG CPle CTrw EPfP GKir
                              LRHS MBar MBri MRav SLim SLon
                              SPer SPla SReu SSpi SSta WBod
                              WCru WWat
  - 'White Gerpa'[PBR]   MGos
  - 'Winifred Crook' (f)   EPla GKir LRHS MBar MBri
                              WWat
  - 'Winnie's Dwarf'   CHig
  - 'Wisley Female' (f)   CDoC CTri ECtt EPla NHol SEas
                              SPan WWat
laureola   CDoC CSam EBee ECot ENot
                              MRav NHol SCob SRms WFar
                              WHCG WSHC
¶ - 'Borde Hill' (f)   NPri
  - HWJCM 544   WCru
¶ - subsp. **multinervia**   WPGP
      Schl 2154
  - T 132   WWat
  'Olympic Flame'   LRHS NHol NPro WLRN
reevesiana   See *S. japonica* subsp. *reevesiana*
rogersii   See *S. japonica* Rogersii Group

SMELOWSKIA (Brassicaceae)
calycina   Last listed 1998
  - NNS 94-137   Last listed 1999

SMILACINA (Convallariaceae)
atropurpurea   WCru
formosana B&SWJ 349   WCru
forrestii   WCru
fusca   WCru
henryi   WCru
japonica   LEur WCru
paniculata   WCru
racemosa ♀   More than 30 suppliers
  - var. **amplexicaulis**   GCal MTed
  - dwarf   Last listed 1997
  - 'Emily Moody'   SSpi
stellata   CAvo CRDP CRow EBee EMou
                              EPar EPla LHop SIng SLod SUsu
                              WCot WCru
  - BH 319   MDun
¶ **szechuanica**   LEur

SMILAX (Smilacaceae)

asparagoides 'Nanus'　　See *Asparagus asparagoides*
　　　　　　　　　　　　　'Myrtifolius'
aspera　　CFil CPlN EPla LEdu WCru WPGP
discotis　　CB&S CPlN CPle
excelsa　　Last listed 1999
glaucophylla B&SWJ 2971　WCru
rotundifolia　　LEdu
sagittifolia　　Last listed 1999
sieboldii　　CPlN MRav
　– B&SWJ 744　　WCru

SMITHIANTHA (Gesneriaceae)

'Calder Girl'　　NMos
'Carmel'　　NMos
'Carmello'　　NMos
'Castle Croft'　　NMos
'Cinna Barino'　　NMos
'Corney Fell'　　NMos
'Dent View'　　NMos
'Ehenside Lady'　　NMos
'Harecroft'　　NMos
'Little One'　　NMos WDib
'Matins'　　NMos
'Meadowcroft'　　NMos
'Multiflora'　　NMos
'New Yellow Hybrid'　　NMos
'Orange King'　　NMos
'Orangeade'　　NMos
'Pink Lady'　　NMos
'Sandybank'　　NMos
'Santa Clara'　　NMos
'Starling Castle'　　NMos
'Summer Sunshine'　　NMos
'Vespers'　　NMos
'Zebrina Hybrid'　　NMos

x SMITHICODONIA (Gesneriaceae)

§ 'Cerulean Mink'　　NMos

SMYRNIUM (Apiaceae)

olusatrum　　CArn CGle CSev EBee EBot GBar
　　　　　　　MChe MGas MHer MHew MSal
　　　　　　　SIde SWat SYvo WCer WHbs
　　　　　　　WHer WOak WWye
perfoliatum　　CGle CRDP CSpe EBee ELan EMar
　　　　　　　EOrc EPar GBuc MFir NSti SDix
　　　　　　　WCot

SOCRATEA (Arecaceae)

montana　　LPal

SOLANDRA (Solanaceae)

grandiflora　　CPlN ERea WMul
hartwegii　　See *S. maxima*
longiflora　　ERea
§ **maxima**　　CB&S ERea LChe WMul

SOLANUM (Solanaceae)

aviculare G.Forst.　　ERea WCot
* **conchifolium**　　LHil WCot WEas WSPU
crispum　　EHol WDin WStl
　– 'Autumnale'　　See *S. crispum* 'Glasnevin'
§　– 'Glasnevin' ♀　　More than 30 suppliers
　– 'Variegatum' (v)　　CCHP
dulcamara　　CArn EWFC GPoy
　– 'Hullavington' (v)　　CNat
　– 'Variegatum' (v)　　CB&S CMac CTrw EBee EHoe
　　　　　　　GOrc IBlr IOrc LRHS MAsh MBNS
　　　　　　　MBri NEgg NSti SBra SLon SRms
　　　　　　　WCot WWeb

'Gentianoides'　　LHil
jasminoides　　See *S. laxum*
laciniatum　　CArn CDoC CGle CInt CLTr CSev
　　　　　　　CSpe EMan ERea EWes IBlr LHil
　　　　　　　LHop LRHS MBlu MFir MHar
　　　　　　　MLLN MSCN MTis SAPC SArc
　　　　　　　SSoC SVen SYvo WCot WHer
§ **laxum**　　CB&S CPlN EBee EPfP LPan
　　　　　　　LRHS NSti SBra SPer SRms WDin
　　　　　　　WSHC
¶ – 'Album' ♀　　More than 30 suppliers
¶ – 'Album Variegatum' (v)　　ELan EPfP GQui LAst LHop LRHS
　　　　　　　MBNS SBra WSHC
* – 'Aureovariegatum' (v)　　CSam EBee EPfP LRHS MAsh SLim
　　　　　　　SPer SPla SPlb WBod
linearifolium　　Last listed 1998
¶ **marginatum**　　WRos
mauritianum　　Last listed 1999
muricatum (F)　　ECon
　– 'Lima' (F)　　ESim
　– 'Otavalo' (F)　　ESim
　– 'Quito' (F)　　ESim SSte
pseudocapsicum　　MBri
　– 'Ballon'　　MBri
quitoense (F)　　LBlo MPEx WMul
§ **rantonnetii**　　CPle ELan ERea LHil LIck LRHS
　　　　　　　SDix SMrm SOWG
　– 'Royal Robe'　　CB&S CRHN GQui
* – 'Variegatum' (v)　　ECon
seaforthianum　　CPlN ECon SOWG
sessiliflorum (F)　　LBlo
sisymbriifolium　　CPLG CSev WKif
wendlandii　　CPlN ERea SSte

SOLDANELLA (Primulaceae)

alpina　　EBee GTou MRav MTho MWat
　　　　　　　NHar NHol NMen SBla SIng SRms
　　　　　　　WAbe
austriaca　　GCrs NLAp WAbe
carpatica ♀　　GTou NCat NNrd NRya NTow
　　　　　　　SBla WAbe
　– 'Alba'　　EDAr NHar SBla WAbe
¶ – x **villosa**　　SBla
cyanaster　　NBir NRya SBla WAbe
dimoniei　　CFee EPot ITim NMen SBla WAbe
§ **hungarica**　　CLyd MTho NWCA WAbe WLin
minima　　CLyd GGar NBro NDlv NHar
　　　　　　　NRya NSla SBla WAbe
　– 'Alba'　　Last listed 1998
montana　　CLAP CLyd GCrs GTou IMGH
　　　　　　　MTho NMen NNrd SIng SSca
　　　　　　　WAbe WRHF WRha
　– subsp. **hungarica**　　See *S. hungarica*
pindicola　　EWes LBee MBro MOne NHar
　　　　　　　NHol NMen NNrd NWCA SIng
　　　　　　　SSmi WAbe
pusilla　　CNic GDra GGar ITim NRya NSla
　　　　　　　WAbe
villosa　　CLAP CRDP CTri EBee GGar
　　　　　　　LRHS MTho NHar NNrd NRya
　　　　　　　NSla NTow SBla WAbe WFar
　　　　　　　WRHF WRus

SOLEIROLIA (Urticaceae)

soleirolii　　CHEx CHal EPot LPBA LRHS MBri
　　　　　　　MCCP SHFr SIng STre WHer
　　　　　　　WOak
　– 'Argenta'　　See *S. soleirolii* 'Variegata'
§ – 'Aurea'　　CHal EPot STre WOak
　– 'Golden Queen'　　See *S. soleirolii* 'Aurea'
　– 'Silver Queen'　　See *S. soleirolii* 'Variegata'
§ – 'Variegata' (v)　　CHal WOak

SOLENANTHUS (Boraginaceae)
scardicus	Last listed 1999

SOLENOMELUS (Iridaceae)
chilensis	See *S. pedunculatus*
§ *pedunculatus*	CFee
segethii	EBee
sisyrinchium	CPBP
sp. RB 94117	Last listed 1997

SOLENOPSIS (Campanulaceae)
I *axillaris*	See *Laurentia axillaris*
'Fairy Carpet'	Last listed 1998

SOLENOPSIS See LAURENTIA

SOLENOSTEMON ✿ (Lamiaceae)
'Annie'	Last listed 1999
aromaticus	CHal CInt NHor
'Autumn'	CHal NHor
'Barnum'	Last listed 1999
'Beauty' (v)	CHal NHor
'Beauty of Lyons'	CHal NHor
'Beckwith's Gem'	CHal NHor
'Bizarre Croton'	NHor
'Black Dragon'	NHor
'Black Prince'	CHal NHor WDib
'Blackheart'	NHor
'Brightness' (v)	NHor
'Brilliant' (v)	NHor WDib
'Bronze Gloriosus'	NHor
'Buttercup'	CHal NHor WDib
'Buttermilk' (v) ♀	CHal NHor
'Carnival' (v)	CHal NHor
'Carousel'	Last listed 1999
'Chamaeleon' (v)	NHor WDib
'City of Liverpool'	NHor
'Copper Sprite'	NHor
'Coppersmith'	NHor
'Cream Pennant' (v)	Last listed 1999
'Crimson Ruffles' (v) ♀	CHal NHor WDib
'Crimson Velvet'	CHal NHor
'Crinkly Bottom'	NHor
'Dairy Maid' (v)	NHor
'Dazzler' (v)	CHal NHor
'Display'	CHal NHor
'Dolly'	Last listed 1999
'Dracula'	NHor
'Etna' (v)	CHal NHor
'Firebrand' (v) ♀	CHal NHor
'Firedance'	NHor
'Freckles' (v)	CHal NHor
'Funfair' (v)	CHal NHor
'Gloriosus'	CHal NHor
'Glory of Luxembourg' (v) ♀	CHal NHor
'Goldie'	CHal NHor
'Harvest Time'	NHor
* 'Holly' (v)	Last listed 1999
'Inky Fingers' (v)	NHor
'Jean' (v)	Last listed 1999
'Joseph's Coat' (v)	NHor
'Juliet Quartermain'	NHor WDib
'Jupiter'	CHal NHor
'Kentish Fire'	NHor
'Kiwi Fern' (v)	CHal NHor WDib
'Klondike'	CHal NHor
'Laing's Croton' (v)	CHal NHor
'Lemon Dash'	SSte
'Lemondrop'	CHal NHor
'Leopard' (v)	NHor
'Lord Falmouth' ♀	CHal NHor WDib

'Luminous'	NHor
'Melody'	NHor
'Midas'	CHal NHor
'Midnight'	NHor
'Mission Gem' (v)	CHal NHor
¶ 'Molten Lava'	NHor
'Mrs Pilkington' (v)	NHor
'Muriel Pedley'	NHor
'Nettie' (v)	NHor
'Ottoman'	CHal NHor
'Paisley Shawl' (v) ♀	CHal NHor WDib
¶ 'Palisandra'	CSpe
pentheri	CHal NHor
'Percy Roots'	Last listed 1999
'Petunia Gem'	Last listed 1997
'Phantom'	Last listed 1999
'Picturatus' (v) ♀	CHal NHor WDib
'Pineapple Beauty' (v) ♀	CHal NHor WDib
'Pineapplette' ♀	CHal NHor WDib
'Pink Shawl'	NHor
'Pink Showers'	Last listed 1999
'Primrose Cloud'	NHor
'Primrose Spray' (v)	Last listed 1999
'Purple Prowes'	NHor
'Raspberry Ripple'	NHor
'Red Croton'	NHor
'Red Heart'	Last listed 1999
'Red Mars'	WDib
'Red Nettie' (v)	CHal NHor
'Red Paisley Shawl' (v)	NHor
¶ 'Red Rosie'	NHor
'Red Stinger'	CHal NHor
'Red Velvet'	NHor
¶ 'Rose Blush' (v)	CHal NHor WDib
'Rosie'	NHor
'Roy Pedley'	NHor
'Royal Scot' (v) ♀	CHal NHor WDib
'Salmon Plumes' (v)	CHal NHor
'Saturn'	NHor
'Scarlet Ribbons'	CHal NHor
scutellarioides	MBri
'Speckles'	CHal NHor
'Spire'	NHor
'Strawberry Blush'	Last listed 1998
'Surprise'	Last listed 1999
thyrsoideus	See *Plectranthus thyrsoideus*
'Treales' (v)	CHal NHor
'Vesuvius'	CHal NHor
'Walter Turner' (v) ♀	CHal NHor WDib WWol
'White Gem' (v)	NHor
'White Pheasant' (v)	NHor
'Winsome' (v)	CHal NHor WDib
'Winter Sun' (v)	CHal NHor
'Wisley Flame'	NHor
'Wisley Tapestry' (v) ♀	NHor WDib
'Yellow Croton'	NHor

SOLIDAGO (Asteraceae)
Babygold	See *S.* 'Goldkind'
brachystachys	See *S. cutleri*
caesia	EBee ECha EGar EMan EMon EWes LRHS MFir WCot
canadensis	CTri ELan NCut NNor SPlb WByw WFar WHer
'Cloth of Gold'	CB&S COtt GKir LRHS MBri NPro NSti SMer WCot WLRN WOve
§ 'Crown of Rays'	CLyd EBrP EBre ECtt EFou LBCl LBSe LBre LRHS MArl MBBe MRav NArg SBre SMer WFar WWin
§ *cutleri*	CLyd EBee ELan EMon MBar MTho MWat NHol NNrd SBla SPlb SRms WHoo WPat WPer WPyg WWin

§ – *nana* — EPPr EWes
¶ 'Dzintra' — LBuc
'Early Bird' — EFou
'Early Sunrise'^{PBR} — EFou
§ *flexicaulis* — GMaP
– 'All Gold' — WCot
§ – 'Variegata' — CM&M EBee EBrP EBre ECoo
EGar ELan EMan EMar EMon ERav
GBin GMaP LBCl LBSe LBre LFis
LHop LRHS MBBe MHar NLar
NSti SBre SEas SMad SUsu WCot
WHer WPer
'Gardone' — WFar
gigantea — EMon EWTr LRHS WPer
glomerata — WHil WPer
Golden Baby — See *S.* 'Goldkind'
§ 'Golden Dwarf' — EFou LRHS MCAu SLon
'Golden Fleece' — See *S. sphacelata* 'Golden Fleece'
'Golden Rays' — See *S.* 'Goldstrahl'
'Golden Shower' — CSam MWat
'Golden Thumb' — See *S.* 'Queenie'
'Golden Wings' — CBre MWat
'Goldenmosa' ♀ — EBrP EBre ECGN EMan ENot EPfP
EWTr GMaP LBCl LBSe LBre LRHS
MBBe MBel MRav MWat SBre
SChu SPer WCot WFar
'Goldilocks' — LRHS NPri SRms
§ 'Goldkind' — CLTr CM&M CTri ECtt EGar EMan
GAbr GChr GKir LNor MBri MFir
MMal NArg NCut NFai NOak
NOrc SCob SMer WBea WByw
WFar WRHF
§ 'Goldstrahl' — LRHS WLRN
Goldzwerg — See *S.* 'Golden Dwarf'
graminifolia — EMon
hispida — EMon
hybrida — See x *Solidaster luteus*
latifolia — See *S. flexicaulis*
'Laurin' — EPfP NHol WHoo WPyg
'Ledsham' — CMGP EBee EMFP MMil WLRN
'Lemore' — See x *Solidaster luteus* 'Lemore'
'Leraft' — LBuc
* *leuvalis* — CStr
¶ 'Linner Gold' — EFou
microcephala — Last listed 1998
¶ Monte Solo® — WViv
= 'Dansolmonte'
multiradiata — ESis
odora — MSal
§ *ohioensis* — IIve
* 'Peter Pan' — WFar
§ 'Queenie' — CPea EBee ECha ESis GCHN
LRHS MHer MWat NPro NVic
SEas SLon SPer SRms WGwG
WLRN
randii — Last listed 1998
rigida — EBrP EBre LBCl LBSe LBre LRHS
MBBe MFir MRav SBre WCot
WPer
– subsp. *humilis* — EBee
– JLS 88002WI — EMon LFis
rugosa — ECha LGre MWgw
– var. *aspera* — EMon
– 'Fireworks' — CBre CPou CStr EFou EPPr GAri
NCat WCot WOve
sempervirens — CBlo EBrP EBre EMon LBCl LBSe
LBre MBBe SBre WCot
shortii — NSti
simplex var. *nana* — WPer
'Spätgold' — EFou
¶ *speciosa* — IIve WPer
§ *sphacelata* 'Golden Fleece' — EBee LRHS WLRN WWoo

Strahlenkrone — See *S.* 'Crown of Rays'
'Tom Thumb' — EGle MRav SRms WEas WRHF
ulmifolia — EBee IIve LRHS
virgaurea — CArn CBod CKin EWFC GPoy IIve
MHer SIde WGwG WHer WJek
WPer WSel WWye
– subsp. *alpestris* — CLyd CNic MTPN NHol WPat
var. *minutissima*
– var. *cambrica* — See *S. virgaurea* var. *minuta*
§ – var. *minuta* — GAri
¶ – 'Paleface' — EMon
– 'Praecox' — CM&M NHol WLRN
§ – 'Variegata' — EHoe NPro WAlt
vulgaris 'Variegata' (v) — See *S. virgaurea* 'Variegata'

x SOLIDASTER (Asteraceae)
hybridus — See x *S. luteus*
§ *luteus* — CMil CTri EFou EWTr GBri MBri
NFla SPla SRms WEas WHil
§ – 'Lemore' ♀ — CElw EBee EBrP EBre ECGN ECha
EFou ELan EMan EMon GMac
LBCl LBSe LBre LFis LRHS MBBe
MCLN MRav MWat NBus NVic
SBre SEas SPer WCot WFar
'Super' — EFou LGre WCot

SOLLYA (Pittosporaceae)
fusiformis — See *S. heterophylla*
§ *heterophylla* ♀ — More than 30 suppliers
– 'Alba' — LGre SMrm
– mauve — ECou
– pink — CPIN
– 'Pink Charmer' — EBee ERea LRHS SBra SMrm SMur
SPer WSHC
parviflora — Last listed 1999

SONCHUS (Asteraceae)
palustris — EMon NBur
platylepsis — Last listed 1998

SOPHORA (Papilionaceae)
§ *davidii* — ECou SOWG WPGP
flavescens — Last listed 1998
japonica ♀ — CAbP CB&S CDul CLnd EBee
ELan EMil ENot EPfP IOrc MBlu
MPEx MWhi NBee SMad SPer
WBod WDin WNor WOrn WPGP
– 'Pendula' — LRHS SMHT
– 'Regent' — LPan
§ 'Little Baby' — CB&S CCHP EPfP ERea MBlu
MGos SBod SHFr SMur WBod
macrocarpa — CFil GQui ISea SBra
microphylla — CCtw CHEx CPle CTrC ECou
LHop MBel MBlu SAPC SArc SPar
SRCN WBod WCru WHer WOTO
WPat WWat
– 'Dragon's Gold' — CDoC ECou ELan EPfP LRHS
MAsh
– 'Early Gold' — CB&S ERea GQui WPGP
– var. *fulvida* — ECou
– var. *longicarinata* — ECou
– Sun King = 'Hilsop'^{PBR} — LRHS MGos SCoo WWeb
prostrata Buch. — CBot ECou
– misapplied — See *S.* 'Little Baby'
– Pukaki form — ECou
secundiflora — Last listed 1999
tetraptera ♀ — CAbP CB&S CCtw CHEx CLnd
CMac CTrC CWit EBee ECou ECre
GQui IOrc ISea MBel MBlu MLan
NPSI SEND SRPl SRms WAbe
WPGP WWat
– 'Gnome' — Last listed 1998

- 'Goughensis'	WBod WCru
viciifolia	See *S. davidii*

SORBARIA (Rosaceae)

aitchisonii	See *S. tomentosa* var. *angustifolia*
arborea	See *S. kirilowii*
§ *kirilowii*	IOrc NFor SMad SPer
* - 'Glauca'	Last listed 1999
lindleyana	See *S. tomentosa*
¶ *rhoifolia*	EPfP
S&F 95205	ISea
sorbifolia	CAbP CB&S EBee EMil EPla GKir MBar MDun MTis MWhi NPro SEND SLPl SPan SPer WCot WDin WFar WHil
- var. *stellipila*	CFil SLPl WPGP
- - B&SWJ 776	WCru
§ *tomentosa*	CAbP EBrP EBre LBCl LBSe LBre MBBe SBre WCru WHCG
§ - var. *angustifolia* ♀	CDul CTri EBee ELan ENot EPfP EPla GKir IMGH LRHS MDun MGos MRav SEND SLon SPan SPer SSta WEas WHer WWat

SORBOPYRUS (Rosaceae)

¶ *auricularis* 'Shipova' (F)	ESim

SORBUS ❀ (Rosaceae)

§ *alnifolia*	CLnd CMCN EPfP SLPl WWat
americana	CLnd GIBF NWea
- 'Belmonte'	LRHS LSyl
- *erecta*	See *S. decora*
anglica	CMCN WMou
'Apricot Lady'	GKir LRHS LSyl MBri SSta WJas WWat
arachnoidea	LSyl
aria	CBlo CDul CKin CLnd CTri EBrP EBre EMac GChr GKir GTre LBCl LBSe LBre LBuc LHyr MBBe MBar NWea SBre WDin WMou WOrn WStI
- 'Aurea'	CLnd EBee MBlu
- 'Chrysophylla'	CDul CLnd CWSG GKir IMGH LRHS LSyl MBri MGos NWea SLim SPer SRPl
- 'Decaisneana'	See *S. aria* 'Majestica'
- 'Gigantea'	CDul
- 'Lutescens' ♀	More than 30 suppliers
- 'Magnifica'	CDoC CDul CTho ELan ENot GTre LPan MAsh SMHT WDin WJas
§ - 'Majestica' ♀	CDoC CDul CLnd CTho EBee ELan GTre LPan LSyl MAsh MGos NWea SLim SPer WJas WOrn
- 'Mitchellii'	See *S. thibetica* 'John Mitchell'
- var. *salicifolia*	See *S. rupicola*
x *arnoldiana*	CDul EBee GKir MAsh
'Apricot Queen'	
- 'Brilliant Yellow'	MBlu
- 'Chamois Glow'	WJas
aronioides	LSyl
arranensis	WMou
aucuparia	More than 30 suppliers
- 'Aspleniifolia'	CB&S CDul CLnd CTho EBee EBrP ECrN ENot GKir GTre LBCl LBSe LBre LHyr LPan LRHS MBBe MGos NBea NWea SBre SPer WDin WFar WJas WOrn
§ - 'Beissneri'	CLnd CTho GKir LSyl MGos
- 'Cardinal Royal'	CBlo EBee GQui LRHS WJas
- 'Dirkenii'	CBlo CDul CLnd COtt GKir LSyl MAsh MDun WJas

- 'Edulis' (F)	CDul CLnd CTho IOrc LBuc MGos NBea SMHT WDin
§ - 'Fastigiata'	CBlo CDoC CDul CEnd CSam CTho CTri ECrN EPfP EPla GKir GTre IOrc LRHS LSyl MAsh MBri MGos MWat NBee NWea WDin WFar WStI
§ - 'Fructu Luteo' ♀	CBlo ENot GTre LSyl MGos NBea NBee
- 'Hilling's Spire'	CBlo CTho GKir LRHS MAsh MBri MLan NBea SLPl
- 'Pendula'	CDul EBee
- *pluripinnata*	See *S. scalaris*
¶ - 'Rabina'	ESim
- 'Red Copper Glow'	MBlu
¶ - 'Rosina'	ESim
- 'Rossica'	Last listed 1997
- 'Rossica Major'	CDoC CDul CTho EBee GQui LSyl
- 'Rowancroft Coral Pink'	CTho LSyl MBar MGos
- 'Scarlet King'	MBlu
- 'Sheerwater Seedling' ♀	More than 30 suppliers
- 'Winterdown'	CNat
- 'Xanthocarpa'	See *S. aucuparia* 'Fructu Luteo'
bristoliensis	LSyl WMou
caloneura	CFil EPla LSyl WHCr WPGP WWat
'Carpet of Gold'	CBlo CLnd LSyl NBea WBod
cashmiriana ♀	More than 30 suppliers
- 'Rosea'	LSyl SSpi
- 'Rosiness'	GKir LRHS MBri MDun WPGP
chamaemespilus	GDra LSyl WPat
'Chinese Lace'	CDul CEnd CLnd CTho EBee ECot ECrN EPfP GKir LRHS LSyl MAsh MBlu MBri MDun MGos MLan NBea SFam SLim SMad SRPl SSpi WGor WJas WOrn WPyg
§ *commixta*	CB&S CDul CEnd CLnd CMCN CTho EBee ECrN EPfP GKir GTre IOrc LRHS LSyl MBar MBri MGos MLan MRav NBea SPer WDin WJas WOrn WStI
* - 'Creamlace'	CBlo EBee
- 'Embley' ♀	CB&S CBlo CDul CLnd CMCN CSam CTho EBee ECrN ELan ENot EPfP GKir LRHS LSyl MBar MBri MGos MLan MRav NBea NBee SSpi SSta WOrn
¶ - 'Jermyns'	MBri
- var. *rufoferruginea*	GChr GKir GQui LSyl MBlu WHCr
* - 'Serotina'	LSyl
conradinae hort.	See *S. pohuashanensis* (Hance) Hedlund
- Koehne	See *S. esserteauana*
¶ 'Copper Kettle'	MBri
'Coral Beauty'	CLnd
croceocarpa	CNat
cuspidata	See *S. vestita*
decipiens	Last listed 1998
§ *decora*	CDul CLnd CTho GIBF LSyl SPer
* - 'Grootendorst'	CDul
- var. *nana*	See *S. aucuparia* 'Fastigiata'
devoniensis	CDul CNat CTho LSyl WMou
discolor hort.	See *S. commixta*
- Hedlund	CLnd EBee LSyl MGos MWat NWea WJas
domestica	CDul CMCN CTho ENot EPfP GTre LBuc MAsh MWat NWea SLPl SPer WMou
- 'Maliformis'	See *S. domestica* var. *pomifera*
§ - var. *pomifera*	EHol WMou
§ - var. *pyrifera*	WMou
- 'Pyriformis'	See *S. domestica* var. *pyrifera*

'Eastern Promise' CBlo CDul EBee GChr GKir LRHS
LSyl MAsh MBri MWat SMHT SSta
WJas

'Edwin Hillier' LSyl

* *ellypsoidalis* LSyl
McLaren C 288

eminens WMou

epidendron LSyl

§ *esserteauana* CDoC CDul CSam CTho ENot
LSyl

- 'Flava' CTho EBee GKir GTre LRHS LSyl
- x *scalaris* LSyl

'Ethel's Gold' LSyl

folgneri CDoC CEnd CPMA CTho LSyl

- 'Lemon Drop' CBlo CDoC CEnd CLnd CPMA
GKir LRHS LSyl MBlu SMad SSpi

foliolosa CAbP CLnd CTho LSyl MBri

* - KR 3518 LSyl

forrestii CDul EBrP EBre EPfP GKir LBCl
LBSe LBre LSyl MBBe MBlu NBea
SBre SLPl SSpi

§ *fruticosa* CEnd CLnd COtt EBee EPfP GKir
MBri MMea NHol NWea SSpi SSta
WJas WPGP WPat

* - 'Koehneana' ♀ GChr GKir LRHS LSyl MDun SHFr
WTin

- R 13268 LSyl

'Ghose' CLnd CTho GKir LRHS MBri SPer
SSpi

* *glabrescens* 'Roseoalba' Last listed 1997

'Golden Wonder' CLnd EBee GKir LSyl MBlu NBea

* *gonggashanica* GKir

- L 1008 LSyl

* *gorrodini* CLnd

gracilis LSyl

§ *graeca* CDul CMCN LSyl SEND

barrowiana 'Bellona' LSyl

'Harvest Moon' GKir GQui LRHS MBri

bedlundii IBlr LSyl NBea WWes

belenae GGGa

bemsleyi CLnd LSyl MDun

x *bostii* CLnd ENot LRHS MRav SPer

§ *bupebensis* CB&S CDul CEnd CLnd CMCN
C.K.Schneid. ♀ CSam CTho EBee ECrN ISea LHyr
LSyl MAsh MBar NBee NWea SLPl
SRPl SSpi SSta WDin WJas WNor
WOrn WWat

* - 'Apricot' CBlo CEnd

§ - var. *obtusa* ♀ CDoC CMCN CSam EPfP GAri
GKir MBlu MDun MRav SFam
SMad SSpi SSta

- 'Pink Pagoda' CBlo CDoC CDul CLnd EBee
EMui EPfP EWTr GChr GKir IArd
IMGH LRHS LSyl MAsh MBri
MGos MLan MWat NWea SCoo
SLim SLon SPer WDin WGer WJas
WPyg WWat

- 'Rosea' See *S. bupebensis* var. *obtusa*

* - *roseoalba* B&L 12545 LSyl

- S&F 96268 ISea

bybrida L. NWea

- hort. See *S.* x *thuringiaca*

- 'Gibbsii' ♀ CBlo CDoC CLnd CTho EBee
ELan EPfP GKir LPan LRHS LSyl
MAsh NBlu

insignis CDoC

- S&F 96227 ISea

intermedia CAgr CB&S CDul CKin CLnd
EBee EMac ENot GChr GIBF GKir
GTre LSyl MGos NBee NWea
WDin WMou WStI

- 'Brouwers' ♀ ELan NBee WMoo

'Joseph Rock' ♀ More than 30 suppliers

§ x *kewensis* ♀ CDul CLnd CSam EBee GKir LSyl
SMHT SPer WBod

'Kirsten Pink' CBlo CCHP CLnd EBee GKir LSyl
MBlu MGos NEgg

koebneana hort. See *S. fruticosa*

aff. *koebneana* Schneider EPfP GKir LSyl MBri
Harry Smith 12799

kurzii LSyl

lanata hort. See *S. vestita*

lancastriensis CNat CTho LSyl WMou

latifolia CAgr CLnd CTho ENot NWea
WDin WMou

laxiflora Last listed 1998

- S&F 96126 ISea

'Leonard Messel' CTho LRHS LSyl MBri NBea

'Leonard Springer' ENot EPfP GQui NWea SSta

leyana WMou

lingsbiensis LSyl

'Lombart's Golden Wonder' CB&S CBlo CDoC CTho LBuc
LPan NWea WJas

longii LSyl

'Lowndes' CLnd

matsumurana hort. See *S. commixta*

—(Makino) Koehne Last listed 1997

megalocarpa CBlo CDoC CFil CPMA CSam
GKir LSyl WNor WPGP

meliosmifolia CSam LSyl WPGP

microphylla Yu 13815 LSyl

minima LSyl WMou

* 'Molly Sanderson' IBlr SSta

¶ *monbeigii* GIBF

- CLD 311 GKir LSyl

- McLaren D 84 LSyl

moravica 'Laciniata' See *S. aucuparia* 'Beissneri'

mougeotii GKir LSyl

multijuga Sch 1132 LSyl

'November Pink' CBlo CEnd EBee EPfP IOrc MAsh

pallescens LSyl

parva L 937 LSyl

'Peachiness' LSyl

'Pearly King' CB&S CSam CTho GKir LRHS LSyl
MBri NBea WJas

pekinensis See *S. reticulata* subsp.
pekinensis

§ 'Pink Pearl' GKir LRHS LSyl

'Pink-Ness' GKir LRHS MBri

pogonopetala Yu 14299 LSyl

pobuasbanensis hort. See *S.* x *kewensis*

—(Hance) Hedlund CSam CTho GKir LSyl NWea
WOTO

porrigentiformis CNat CTho LSyl

poteriifolia GCrs LSyl MFir NHar

§ *prattii* CMCN GAri GKir LSyl NBea
WWat

- var. *subarachnoidea* GBin

- var. *tatsienensis* See *S. prattii*

pseudofennica LSyl WMou

pseudovilmorinii EMon GKir LSyl

- MF 93044 SSpi

randaiensis LSyl

- B&SWJ 3202 NHol SSpi WCru

¶ 'Ravensbill' GKir MBri

'Red Marbles' LSyl

'Red Tip' CDoC CDul CLnd LSyl MBar MBlu
NEgg

reducta ♀ CB&S CEnd CLyd CMCN CSWP
EBee EPfP GAbr GChr GCrs GDra
GKir ISea ITim LRHS LSyl MBri
MBro MFir NHar NHol NWea SIng
SMad SPer SSpi SSta WNor WPat
WWat

reflexipetala	See *S. commixta*
rebderiana	CLnd GKir WNor
- 'Pink Pearl'	GKir LRHS LSyl
§ *reticulata*	LSyl
subsp. *pekinensis*	
rhamnoides S&F 96227	ISea
rinzenii	LSyl
rufopilosa	LSyl
§ *rupicola*	CNat CTho LSyl WMou
'Salmon Queen'	CLnd LSyl
sargentiana ♀	More than 30 suppliers
'Savill Orange'	LSyl
§ *scalaris* ♀	CB&S CBlo CDul CEnd CTho CTri
	EPfP GKir GTre IOrc LRHS LSyl
	MAsh MBri SPer SSpi WJas WOrn
	WWat
'Schouten'	ENot LRHS MBlu NBee
scopulina hort.	See *S. aucuparia* 'Fastigiata'
semi-incisa	LSyl
setschwanensis	GAri GGGa
'Signalman'	LRHS MBri
sp. CLD 237	LSyl
sp. Ghose	GKir LRHS LSyl
sp. Harry Smith 12732	GKir LRHS LSyl
sp. KR 3595	LSyl
sp. KR 3733	LSyl
sp. nova	LSyl
'Sunshine'	CDoC EBee LRHS LSyl MAsh MBri
	WJas
thibetica	LSyl
§ - 'John Mitchell' ♀	CDul CLnd CMCN CSam CTho
	ECrN ENot EPfP GChr GKir GQui
	IMGH LPan LRHS LSyl MAsh MBlu
	MBri MGos MRav NBea NWea
	SLim WJas WOrn WWat
§ x *thuringiaca*	LSyl NBea WMou
§ - 'Fastigiata'	CB&S CDoC CDul CLnd EBee
	ENot GKir MGos NBee WDin
	WJas
torminalis	CAgr CDul CKin CLnd CSam
	CTho CTri EPfP GKir GTre LBuc
	LRHS MBri MNaF NWea SPer
	WDin WGwy WMou
¶ *umbellata*	CMCN
- var. *cretica*	See *S. graeca*
x *vagensis*	CLnd WMou
§ *vestita*	CLnd CMCN CTho LSyl WWat
vexans	CNat
vilmorinii ♀	More than 30 suppliers
- 'Robusta'	See *S.* 'Pink Pearl'
wardii	CB&S CLnd CTho GKir LRHS LSyl
	MBri
'White Wax'	CBlo CDul EBee EMui MDun
	MGos MLan NEgg WDin
'Wilfrid Fox'	CLnd LSyl SLPl
willmottiana	WMou
wilsoniana	LSyl SLon
'Winter Cheer'	LSyl
¶ *zahlbruckneri*	LSyl
C.K. Schneid.	

SORGHASTRUM (Poaceae)

§ *avenaceum*	CBod ECGN ECha EHoe EMan
- 'Indian Steel'	CBrm EMan LPan MAnH MSte
nutans	See *S. avenaceum*

SORGHUM (Poaceae)

halepense	MSte
nigrum	Last listed 1998

SPARAXIS (Iridaceae)

bulbifera	CGrW NRog

elegans	CGrW NRog
- 'Coccinea'	LBow WCot
fragrans subsp. *acutiloba*	NRog
- subsp. *fimbriata*	LBow
- subsp. *grandiflora*	CGrW WCot
hybrids	CGrW LAma
tricolor	EPar GSki MBri MDun NRog
	WCot
§ *variegata*	LBow NRog
¶ *villosa*	CPLG

SPARGANIUM (Sparganiaceae)

§ *erectum*	CRow ECoo EHon EMFW EMan
	LPBA MSta NDea SWat SWyc
	WHer WMAq
ramosum	See *S. erectum*

SPARRMANNIA (Tiliaceae)

africana ♀	CAbb CHEx CPle ERea GQui
	LCns LHil MBri SAPC SArc SYvo
	WOak
- 'Variegata'	ERea LCns
palmata	See *S. ricinicarpa*
§ *ricinicarpa*	Last listed 1998

SPARTINA (Poaceae)

patens	EHoe
pectinata	CBod GBin WFar
- 'Aureomarginata'	More than 30 suppliers

SPARTIUM (Papilionaceae)

junceum ♀	CB&S CDoC EBee ELan EMil ENot
	EWTr LRHS MBel MBri MGos
	MWat NSti SArc SDix SLon SMad
	SPer SRCN SRms WBod WGwG
	WKif WStI

SPARTOCYTISUS See CYTISUS

SPATHANTHEUM (Araceae)

orbignyanum	WCot

SPATHIPAPPUS See TANACETUM

SPATHIPHYLLUM (Araceae)

'Mauna Loa' ♀	Last listed 1990
'Viscount'	MBri
wallisii	CHal EOHP LRHS MBri

SPATHODEA (Bignoniaceae)

campanulata	Last listed 1999

SPEIRANTHA (Convallariaceae)

§ *convallarioides*	CFil CLAP CRDP EBee ERos WCot
	WCru WPGP
gardenii	See *S. convallarioides*

SPERGULARIA (Caryophyllaceae)

purpurea	Last listed 1997
rupicola	CKin EWFC MNrw

SPHACELE See LEPECHINIA

SPHAERALCEA (Malvaceae)

ambigua	ELan
coccinea	EMan
fendleri	CB&S CBot CLTr CMHG CSam
	EOrc WWye
- subsp. *venusta*	Last listed 1998
grossulariifolia	Last listed 1997
'Hopleys Lavender'	EMan LHil LHop SAga
'Hyde Hall'	MCCP MLLN SMrm WWeb

incana	CM&M CPne CSev EBee MCCP SMrm SRCN WElm
malviflora	WPer
miniata	CMHG ELan LGre LHil MLLN SAga SLon WCot
munroana	CBot CMHG CSev EBee ELan LHil LHop MCCP SMrm WEas WSHC
- 'Dixieland Pink'	WEas
- pale pink	CSpe ECtt EMan LGre SAga SMrm
* - 'Shell Pink'	ECGP
'Newleaze Coral'	LHop LLWP SAga
'Newleaze Pink'	LHop
parvifolia	EBee
remota	EMan MNrw SPlb
rivularis	EBee EMan WMoo
umbellata	See *Phymosia umbellata*

SPHAEROMERIA (Asteraceae)
§ *capitata*	NWCA
compacta	CPBP

SPHENOMERIS (Dennstaedtiaceae)
chinensis	Last listed 1999

SPIGELIA (Loganiaceae)
marilandica	CRDP

SPILANTHES (Asteraceae)
acmella	EOHP MSal

SPIRAEA ✿ (Rosaceae)
'Abigail'	CDoC
albiflora	See *S. japonica* var. *albiflora*
arborea	See *Sorbaria kirilowii*
arcuata	Last listed 1998
§ 'Arguta'	More than 30 suppliers
x *arguta* 'Bridal Wreath'	See *S.* 'Arguta'
- 'Compacta'	See *S.* x *cinerea*
- 'Nana'	See *S.* x *cinerea*
bella	CPle WHCG
betulifolia	EBee GEil MRav SMac WHCG WPat WPyg
- var. *aemiliana*	CBot CMHG CPle EBrP EBre ECtt EPla ESis GKir LBCl LBSe LBre LHop MBBe MGos NHol SBre SLPl SPan SSta WWat
x *bumalda*	See *S. japonica* 'Bumalda'
- 'Wulfenii'	See *S. japonica* 'Walluf'
callosa 'Alba'	See *S. japonica* var. *albiflora*
canescens	Last listed 1997
cantoniensis	Last listed 1998
§ - 'Flore Pleno' (d)	CPle EMon MBlu MTed
- 'Lanceata'	See *S. cantoniensis* 'Flore Pleno'
chamaedryfolia	Last listed 1999
§ x *cinerea*	EPfP SSta WShe
- 'Grefsheim' ♀	CB&S CBlo CDoC COtt EBee ECtt ENot GKir GOrc LRHS MBri MGos SLim SPer SPla SSta WCFE WTro
- 'Variegata' (v)	Last listed 1999
crispifolia	See *S. japonica* 'Bullata'
decumbens	CPle
densiflora	EPot
douglasii	MBar
- subsp. *menziesii*	Last listed 1999
x *fontenaysii* 'Rosea'	Last listed 1999
formosana	Last listed 1999
- CC 1597	Last listed 1999
§ x *foxii*	SLPl
fritschiana	SLPl SLon WHCG
hendersonii	See *Petrophytum hendersonii*
henryi	CPle

§ *japonica*	CPle SBod
- 'Alba'	See *S. japonica* var. *albiflora*
§ - var. *albiflora*	CB&S CEnd CPle ESis LRHS MBar MWat SPer SRms WHCG
- 'Allgold'	NBee
- 'Alpina'	See *S. japonica* 'Nana'
- 'Alpine Gold'	CFai NHol NPro SPan
- 'Anthony Waterer' (v) ♀	More than 30 suppliers
- 'Blenheim'	SRms
§ - 'Bullata'	CFee CMHG EPfP ESis LRHS MBar NFla NWCA SPan SRms WAbe WHCG
§ - 'Bumalda'	CCuc GKir WFar
- 'Candle Light'	CAbP CB&S CBlo CWSG EBee EBrP EBre ECle EGra EPfP GChr GKir LAst LBCl LBSe LBre LRHS MAsh MBBe MGos NHol SBre SCoo SLim SPer SPla
- 'Country Red'	CBlo GChr
§ - 'Crispa'	CCuc EPfP LRHS MBar MBlu MBri NPro WFar
- 'Dart's Red'	CBlo GCHN GKir IOrc LRHS MBlu MBri SEas SSta WWeb
- 'Fire Light'	CAbP CB&S CBlo CChe EBee EBrP EBre ELan EPfP GKir LBCl LBSe LBre LRHS MAsh MBBe MBri MGos MTis NHol SBre SCoo SLim SPer SPla SSta WLRN WStI
- var. *fortunei* 'Atrosanguinea'	WHCG
- 'Froebelii'	CCuc EWTr LBuc
- 'Glenroy Gold'	SLon WHen
- 'Gold Mound' ♀	CMHG EBee ELan GChr GKir GOrc LRHS MBar MBel MBlu MBri MGos MHer MRav NBee NFor SEas SHFr SPer SPlb SRms WHar WSHC WTro
- 'Gold Rush'	CMHG MBNS WHCG WRus
- 'Golden Dome'	WHCG
- Golden Princess = 'Lisp'[PBR]	CTri EBrP EBre GKir IOrc LAst LBCl LBSe LBre LBuc LRHS MAsh MBBe MBar MGos MTis NHol SBre SEas SLon SPer SRPl SReu SRms SSta WCFE WFar WStI WWeb
- 'Goldflame' ♀	More than 30 suppliers
- 'Little Maid'	Last listed 1997
- 'Little Princess'	CB&S CBrm EBee EMil ENot EWTr GChr GKir LRHS MAsh MBar MBri MRav MWat NBee NHol SLim SPer SRms SSht SSta WAbe WDin WFar WHar WWal
¶ - 'Macrophylla'	SPan
- Magic Carpet = 'Walbuma'[PBR]	LRHS MAsh SCoo
- 'Magnifica'	WHCG WPat
- 'Manon Red Princess'	EBee
§ - 'Nana' ♀	CMHG EBee ENot ESis LRHS MBar MBri MRav MTho NHar SReu SRms WEas WHCG WPat WPer WPyg
- 'Nyewoods'	See *S. japonica* 'Nana'
- 'Pamela Harper'	Last listed 1999
N - 'Shirobana' ♀	More than 30 suppliers
§ - 'Walluf'	CCHP CFai COtt CPle GEil NFor SPan WHCG
latifolia	Last listed 1997
'Margaritae'	NPro SPer
mollifolia	Last listed 1998
myrtilloides	Last listed 1999
nipponica	CB&S GKir MBar
- 'Halward's Silver'	CBlo CFai LRHS MBri MRav NHol NPro SLPl WBcn WBod

- 'June Bride' — CBlo
§ - 'Snowmound' ♀ — More than 30 suppliers
- var. *tosaensis* hort. — See *S. nipponica* 'Snowmound'
- **var. *tosaensis*** — LHop MWat SReu
(Yatabe) Makino
¶ x *pachystachys* — GEil
palmata 'Elegans' — See *Filipendula purpurea* 'Elegans'
§ *prunifolia* (d) — CFai CPle ELan ENot EPla LHop MBlu SEas SLon SPer WHCG WWin
- 'Plena' — See *S. prunifolia*
x *pseudosalicifolia* — CBlo ENot GChr SHFr WWin
'Triumphans'
salicifolia — CPLG WFar
sp. CLD 138 — EMon
sp. CLD 1389 — Last listed 1997
stevenii — GAri SPer
'Summersnow' — SLPl
'Superba' — See *S. x foxii*
tarokoensis — Last listed 1998
thunbergii ♀ — CChe CPle CTri EBee ENot IOrc LHop MRav NFla NFor NWea SCoo SLim SMer SPer SRms WDin WGwG WHCG WWal
* - 'Mellow Yellow' — WWat
- 'Mount Fuji' — CAbP CCHP EBrP EBre EHoe EPfP EPla GSki LBCl LBSe LBre LRHS MBBe MBri MGos NPro SBre SCoo SLim WFar WTro
* - *rosea* — WBcn
- 'Tickled Pink' — CAbP LRHS MAsh NPro SPla
* - 'Variegata' (v) — Last listed 1999
tomentosa — Last listed 1999
trichocarpa — Last listed 1998
trilobata — WLRN
ulmaria — See *Filipendula ulmaria*
x *vanhouttei* ♀ — CB&S CTri EBee ENot EPfP IOrc MBar MRav NFla NFor SHFr SPer SRms WDin WFar WWal WWat
¶ - 'Gold Fountain' — WBcn
- Pink Ice = 'Catpan' (v) — CAbP CB&S CDoC CMHG COtt CWit EBee ECle EHoe ELan EMil GChr LAst LHop LRHS MAsh MGos MLLN MTis SEas SPer SPla SPlb SRPl WDin WFar WHar
veitchii — MRav
venusta 'Magnifica' — See *Filipendula rubra* 'Venusta'
wilsonii — Last listed 1999
'Wyndbrook Gold' — Last listed 1998

SPIRANTHES (Orchidaceae)
aestivalis — SSpi
cernua — Last listed 1999
- f. *odorata* 'Chadd's Ford' — EBee LEur LRHS WCot WSpi
ochroleuca — Last listed 1999
spiralis — SSpi

SPIRODELA (Lemnaceae)
§ *polyrhiza* — MSta

SPODIOPOGON (Poaceae)
sibiricus — ECGN ECha EMan EMon EPPr LEdu LRHS MAnH MSte NFor WCot

SPOROBOLUS (Poaceae)
fertilis — Last listed 1997
heterolepis — ECGN EPPr
wrightii — Last listed 1997

SPRAGUEA (Portulacaceae)
'Powder Puff' — LRHS
§ *umbellata* — Last listed 1998
§ - *glandulifera* — Last listed 1998

SPREKELIA (Amaryllidaceae)
formosissima ♀ — CSpe EBot LAma LBow LRHS NRog

STACHYS (Lamiaceae)
§ *affinis* — CArn CFir ELau GPoy LEdu
§ *albotomentosa* — LHop WCHb
alopecuros — WWin
alpina — CNat EBee
x *ambigua* — EWFC NSti
atherocalyx — EBee
balansae — NSti
betonica — See *S. officinalis*
§ *byzantina* — More than 30 suppliers
§ - 'Big Ears' — CMGP EBee ECha EGoo EMan EMon EWTr LHop MAnH MBct MCAu MCLN MWat SAga SCob SMrm WCot
§ - 'Cotton Boll' — CMGP COIW ECha EFou GCal LRHS MCLN MHar MTho MWat SPer WCot WGwG WWal WWat
- 'Countess Helen von Stein' — See *S. byzantina* 'Big Ears'
- gold-leaved[PBR] — See *S. byzantina* 'Primrose Heron'
- large-leaved — See *S. byzantina* 'Big Ears'
- 'Limelight' — EBee GKir SAga WCot
§ - 'Primrose Heron'[PBR] — COtt EBee ECha ECot EMan EPfP GKir GMaP LRHS MAnH MCAu MFir NLar NOrc NPSI NSti SMer SPer WBry
- 'Sheila McQueen' — See *S. byzantina* 'Cotton Boll'
- 'Silver Carpet' — More than 30 suppliers
§ - 'Striped Phantom' (v) — MCAu SAga WCHb WCot WEas
- 'Variegata' — See *S. byzantina* 'Striped Phantom'
candida — EBee NMen
chrysantha — LGre
citrina — CMea GCal LBee LRHS WCot
coccinea — CGle CHar CInt CPla EOrc LGre LLWP LRHS MFir MHer MTis NBir NFai NFla SHFr SMac SSca STes WCHb WOut WOve WRos WSan WWin
- apricot — Last listed 1999
I - 'Avondale Peach' — MAvo
- 'Axminster Lemon' — Last listed 1999
- 'Axminster Variegated' (v) — Last listed 1999
- 'El Salto' CDR 1384 — LHil
corsica — EBee
cretica — EBee EMan EOrc LEdu SRCN
densiflora — See *S. monieri*
§ *discolor* — GBri MBri MBro MLLN WCot WCru WHil WPer
germanica — CNat EBee EMan NArg WGwy WOut
¶ - subsp. *bithynica* — SBla
grandiflora — See *S. macrantha*
heraclea — EBee
'Hidalgo' — See *S. albotomentosa*
iva — EBee ESis LGre NTow
lanata — See *S. byzantina*
lavandulifolia — EBee WLin
§ *macrantha* — CArn CHea EBee ECha ECoo EOld GKir LAst LRHS LSpr MBel MBro MRav NOak NOrc NSti

		SMrm SRms WBea WCHb WEas WFar WLin WOve WPyg WWin
¶	- 'Alba'	ECha
*	- 'Hummelo'	EFou EMan EMil LAst SUsu
	- 'Nivea'	CElw EBee ECha EHrv ELan EMan EMar GCal NHol WPat WWal WWye
§	- 'Robusta' ♀	CGle ELan EPPr GKir MBri NBro NGdn SCro SHel SVal WCot WRHF WWye
	- 'Rosea'	CElw EBee EFou ELan GMaP MArl MCLN MGed SCro SHel SPlb WEas WRha WWye
	- 'Superba'	CGle CRDP EBee EGar GCHN LRHS MBel MBri MCAu MMHG NFai NFla SMrm SPer SPla WByw WCHb WCot WFar WPGP
	- 'Violacea'	CStr EBee MAvo WPGP
	marrubiifolia	EBee
§	monieri	CM&M CRDP EBee EMan LFis LRHS MCLN NLar SLon SMrm WCot WLin WPer
	- 'Hummelo'	EBee LGre SAga
	nivea	See S. discolor
§	officinalis	CArn CKin CSev CStr EBee EWFC EWTr GBar GPoy MChe MGas MHer MHew MPEx MSal NLan NMir SIde WBea WGwG WHbs WHer WOak WWye
	- 'Alba'	CArn CGle CMGP CRDP EBee MCLN NBro NHol WAlt WCHb WFar WRha WWye
	- 'Rosea'	WCot WPrP
	- 'Rosea Superba'	CGle ECha EPPr MBel MCLN SDix SIng WCot WFar WGwy
	olympica	See S. byzantina
	palustris	CKin ECoo EWFC LGuA LPBA MGas MSta NLan WGwy
	plumosa	Last listed 1998
	saxicola	Last listed 1997
	subsp. villosissima	
	setifera	EBee
	spicata	See S. macrantha
	sylvatica	CArn CKin EMan EWFC GPoy MHew NLan WGwy WHer
	- 'Hoskin's Variegated' (v)	WAlt WCHb
¶	- 'Huskers' (v)	EBee EPPr MCCP
	- 'Shade of Pale'	WAlt
	thirkei	EBee EOrc SSca
	tuberifera	See S. affinis

STACHYTARPHETA (Verbenaceae)
	mutabilis	SOWG

STACHYURUS (Stachyuraceae)
	chinensis	CB&S CMCN CPMA CRos LRHS MBri
¶	- 'Celina'	CEnd SSta
¶	- 'Joy Forever'	CEnd CPMA SSta
	himalaicus	CFil WPGP
	- HWJCM 009	WCru
	lancifolius	See S. praecox var. matsuzakii
	leucotrichus	CPMA
	'Magpie' (v)	CFil CPMA EPfP LRHS SSpi WCru WPGP WSpi
	praecox ♀	More than 30 suppliers
§	- var. matsuzakii	CFil CPMA WPGP
	- - B&SWJ 2817	WCru
*	- 'Rubriflora'	CPMA ELan EPfP LRHS MAsh
¶	szechuanensis	CB&S
	yunnanensis	CFil WPGP

STANLEYA (Brassicaceae)
albescens	Last listed 1998
elata	Last listed 1998
integrifolia	Last listed 1999
pinnata	EBee

STAPHYLEA (Staphyleaceae)
	bumalda	CB&S CMCN EPfP
	colchica ♀	CB&S EPfP IOrc SPer SRPl WDin WSHC WWat
	emodi	Last listed 1999
	holocarpa	CB&S CPle SSpi WWat
N	- var. rosea	CPMA ENot EPfP
N	- 'Rosea' ♀	MBlu MGos SSpi WSHC
	pinnata	CB&S CCHP EPfP LEdu WHCr WNor
	trifolia	CAgr CB&S

STATICE See LIMONIUM

STAUNTONIA (Lardizabalaceae)
	hexaphylla	CB&S CDoC CHEx CPIN CSam EBee EHol EMan EMil EPfP GQui LRHS MDun SBra SLon SPer SReu SSpi SSta WPGP WSHC
	- B&SWJ 4858	WCru
	purpurea B&SWJ 3690	WCru

STEGNOGRAMMA (Thelypteridaceae)
pozoi	EFer EMon

STEIRODISCUS (Asteraceae)
*	euryopoides	Last listed 1998

STELLARIA (Caryophyllaceae)
graminea	CKin EWFC NBid
holostea	CKin EWFC MChe NMir WHer

STEMODIA (Scrophulariaceae)
tomentosa	Last listed 1997

STENANTHIUM (Melanthiaceae)
occidentale	Last listed 1999
robustum	CRDP WPGP

STENOCARPUS (Proteaceae)
sinuatus	Last listed 1998

STENOCHLAENA (Blechnaceae)
palustris	MBri

STENOCOELIUM (Apiaceae)
divaricatum	Last listed 1999

STENOGLOTTIS (Orchidaceae)
fimbriata	GCrs
longifolia ♀	GCrs
woodii	GCrs

STENOMESSON (Amaryllidaceae)
§	miniatum	Last listed 1999
	variegatum	Last listed 1998

STENOTAPHRUM (Poaceae)
secundatum	CHEx CHal CInt IBlr WDyG
'Variegatum' (v) ♀	

STENOTUS (Asteraceae)
§	acaulis	Last listed 1997

STEPHANANDRA (Rosaceae)

incisa	CB&S CBlo CGle CPle GChr IOrc SPla WHCG WWal
§ - 'Crispa'	CDoC CGle CPle CWSG EBee ELan EMil ENot EWTr GKir GOrc LHop LRHS MBar MBlu MRav MWat MWhi NFla NFor NHol SHel SPer WCFE WDin WFar WHCG WWat
- 'Dart's Horizon'	SLPl
- 'Prostrata'	See *S. incisa* 'Crispa'
tanakae	CB&S CDoC CGle CMFo CPle ELan GOrc IMGH IOrc LRHS MBar MBlu MRav MWat NFla NFor SLPl SLon SMac SMad SPer SPla SRPl WDin WFar WHCG WPat

STEPHANIA (Menispermaceae)

glandulifera	CPlN

STEPHANOTIS (Asclepiadaceae)

floribunda ♀	CB&S CPlN EBak GQui LCns LRHS MBri SOWG SRCN
- *variegata* (v)	LCns

STERNBERGIA (Amaryllidaceae)

candida	CBro GCrs LAma
- JCA 933000	SSpi
§ *clusiana*	LAma
colchiciflora	Last listed 1999
fischeriana	CBro
greuteriana	SOkd
lutea	CAvo CBro CTri EBrP EBre EPot EWes LAma LBCl LBSe LBre LRHS MBBe MBri MWat NMen NRog NWCA SBre SDix SSpi WEas
- Angustifolia Group	CAvo CBro CMea EMon WCot
- var. *lutea* MS 971	Last listed 1998
macrantha	See *S. clusiana*
sicula	CBro ETub WCot
- from Dodona	Last listed 1997
- var. *graeca*	EPot
- MS 796	Last listed 1998

STEVIA (Asteraceae)

rebaudiana	EOHP GPoy

STEWARTIA ✿ (Theaceae)

gemmata	WNor WPGP WWat
'Korean Splendor'	See *S. pseudocamellia* Koreana Group
koreana	See *S. pseudocamellia* Koreana Group
malacodendron	ELan EPfP LRHS MBri SSpi SSta WBod
monadelpha	CMCN SSpi WNor WWat
ovata	CGre SPer SSpi SSta WWat
N - var. *grandiflora*	GKir LRHS
pseudocamellia ♀	More than 30 suppliers
- var. *koreana*	See *S. pseudocamellia* Koreana Group
§ - Koreana Group ♀	CB&S CBlo CEnd CGre CMCN CTho EPfP MBri MDun SBrw SPer SReu SSpi WDin WNor WPGP WWat
pteropetiolata	CB&S CWSG
- var. *koreana*	LRHS
rostrata	CB&S CFil WNor WPGP WWat
serrata	CGre GOrc LRHS SSpi
sinensis ♀	CB&S CPMA EPfP SSpi WNor WPGP

STICTOCARDIA (Convolvulaceae)

beraviensis	CPlN

STIGMAPHYLLON (Malpighiaceae)

ciliatum	CPlN

STIPA (Poaceae)

§ *arundinacea*	CChe ECoo EHul EWTr MMHG NBea NNor WFoF
- 'Gold Hue'	EPla WPnP
barbata	CBrm CSpe EBee EBrP EBre ECGN EGar EGle EMan EPPr EWes LBCl LBSe LBre LGre MBBe NOGN SBre SMrm SUsu WCot WHal
- 'Silver Feather'	EWsh SWal
boysterica	CFee
brachytricha	See *Calamagrostis brachytricha*
§ *calamagrostis*	More than 30 suppliers
- 'Lemperg'	EMan EPPr
capillata	More than 30 suppliers
¶ - 'Brautschleier'	GCal
comata	Last listed 1997
elegantissima	CCuc CInt LHil
extremiorientalis	ECha EGle EPPr GIBF LGre NDov NOGN SMad SUsu
gigantea ♀	More than 30 suppliers
- 'Gold Fontaene'	EBee EMon EPPr EWes SMad WCot WPGP WPrP
- 'Variegata' (v)	CHEx
grandis	CBrm ECha GBin WPer
joannis	EBee GCal
lasiagrostis	See *S. calamagrostis*
lessingiana	CPLG EPla GBin
mollis	Last listed 1997
offneri	CElw EWes LGre NDov SBla
papposa	CInt
patens	CCuc
pennata	CB&S CCuc EBee ECGN EMan EPPr GBin GCal GKir MAvo MFir NBid NChi NOak NPSI WLRN
pulcherrima	EPPr GCal
- 'Windfeder'	CFir ECGN SMrm
pulchra	GBin MCCP
robusta	EPPr
¶ sp. from Sikkim B&SWJ 2302	WCru
spartea	CBrm
§ *splendens*	CCuc ECoo EFou EHoe EMan EPPr LEdu MBrN SLod WFoF
stenophylla	See *S. tirsa*
tenacissima	CCuc ECha EFou EHoe EHul EMon EOld EPPr EPla WBro
tenuifolia	More than 30 suppliers
tenuissima	More than 30 suppliers
¶ - 'Pony Tails'	MLan
§ *tirsa*	LRHS
turkestanica	CCuc EBee LGre MMoz NDov SUsu WPGP
ucrainica	GBin LGre NDov

STOEBE (Asteraceae)

plumosa	CTrC

STOKESIA (Asteraceae)

cyanea	See *S. laevis*
§ *laevis*	CHea EBee ECGP ECha EGle EOld GKir LAst LFis LRHS MBro NBro NFor NLar SAga WBrE WFar WPGP WPer

– 'Alba'	CHea CM&M CMGP COIW CRDP	
	EBee ECGP ECha EGle EMan EPar	
	GKir GMac LAst LGre LRHS MBri	
	MCLN MRav NBrk NHol SAga SChu	
	SEas SPer STes SUsu SVil WRus	
– 'Blue Star'	CB&S CElw CGle CRDP CSam	
	EBee EFou ELan EMan EMar GKir	
	LGre LHop LRHS MBri MCLN	
	MFir MWgw NCut NFla NOak	
	SChu SEas SPer WRus WWin	
– 'Mary Gregory'	CElw CFai CFir CHea CPar EBee	
	EMan EMar GCal LAst LHop LRHS	
	MCAu MCLN MLLN MTed NDov	
	NHaw NHol NLar NPSl NPri NSti	
	SAsh SOkh SPer WCot WWhi	
– mixed	CPou	
– 'Omega Skyrocket'	CFai EBee EMan MLLN WCot	
	WRus	
– 'Purple Parasols'	CFai COtt EBee EMan EWll LFis	
	MSph NDov NSti SAsh SOkh SUsu	
	WCot	
– 'Silver Moon'	EBee EMan EMil LAst NDov	
	NHaw WCot	
– 'Träumerei'	CRDP EBee EMan EMar GMac	
	LAst LFis LRHS MBro MGrG MTis	
	NHol SLon SOkh WLRN WWal	
– 'Wyoming'	Last listed 1997	

STRANVAESIA See PHOTINIA

x STRANVINIA See PHOTINIA

STRATIOTES (Hydrocharitaceae)

aloides	CBen CWat ECoo EHon EMFW
	LGuA LPBA MSta NDea SWat
	SWyc

STRELITZIA (Strelitziaceae)

alba	LBlo WMul
caudata	LBlo
nicolai	CAbb CRoM ECon LBlo LPal
	WMul
reginae ♀	CAbb CB&S CBrP CHEx CTrC
	ECon ELan ERea GQui IBlr LCns
	LPal LPan LRHS SAPC SArc SRms
	WMul
– 'Humilis'	LBlo
– 'Kirstenbosch Gold'	LBlo

STREPTOCARPELLA See STREPTOCARPUS

STREPTOCARPUS ✿ (Gesneriaceae)

'Albatross' ♀	NHor WDib
'Amanda'	NHor WDib
'Anne'	NHor WDib
'Athena'	NHor WDib
baudertii	WDib
'Beryl'	WDib
'Bethan'	NHor WDib
'Black Panther'	NHor WDib
'Blue Angel' ♀	Last listed 1995
'Blue Gem'	NHor WDib
'Blue Heaven'	NHor WDib
'Blue Moon'	WDib
'Blue Nymph'	NHor WDib
'Blue Pencil'	Last listed 1999
'Blue Trumpets'	Last listed 1997
'Blue Upstart'	Last listed 1999
* 'Blushing Bride'	NHor WDib
* 'Boysenberry Delight'	WDib
'Branwen'	NHor WDib
candidus	NHor WDib

'Carol'	MBri WDib
¶ 'Carys'	WDib
'Catrin'	WDib
caulescens	CHal LHil WDib
– var. pallescens	WDib
'Chorus Line'	NHor WDib
'Clouds'	CSpe
'Cobalt Nymph'	MBri
'Concord Blue'	MBri WDib
'Constant Nymph'	NHor WDib
¶ 'Crystal Ice'	WDib
cyaneus	WDib
'Cynthia' ♀	MBri NHor WDib
'Diana' ♀	NHor WDib
dunnii	CFir WDib
'Eira'	NHor
'Elsi'	NHor WDib
'Emma'	WDib
'Falling Stars' ♀	CSpe MBri NHor WDib
'Festival Wales'	NHor WDib
'Fiona'	NHor WDib
¶ floribundus	WDib
gardenii	WDib
– JCA 3790400	Last listed 1999
glandulosissimus	CHal LCns LHil SSte SVen WDib
'Gloria' ♀	CSpe NHor WDib
'Good Hope'	ERea
¶ 'Grape Slush'	WDib
'Happy Snappy'	NHor WDib
'Heidi' ♀	MBri NHor WDib
'Helen' ♀	NHor WDib
'Holiday Blue' ♀	Last listed 1995
holstii	CHal LHil
'Huge White'	CSpe
'Jennifer'	NHor WDib
'Joanna'	MBri NHor WDib
johannis ♀	WDib
'Julie'	WDib
* 'Karen'	NHor WDib
kentaniensis	WDib
'Kim' ♀	CSpe NHor WDib
kirkii	WDib
'Laura'	NHor WDib
'Lisa' ♀	MBri NHor WDib
'Little Gem'	CSpe
* 'Louise'	NHor WDib
'Lynette'	WDib
'Lynne'	NHor WDib
'Maassen's White'	ERea NHor WDib
'Mandy'	NHor WDib
'Margaret'	NHor WDib
'Marie'	NHor WDib
* 'Maureen'	Last listed 1999
'Megan'	NHor WDib
¶ 'Melanie'	WDib
'Mini Nymph'	NHor WDib
'Myba'	Last listed 1999
'Neptune'	MBri WDib
'Nicola'	MBri NHor WDib
'Olga'	NHor WDib
'Party Doll'	NHor WDib
'Paula' ♀	MBri NHor WDib
pentherianus	SBla WDib
'Pink Fondant'	CSpe
'Pink Souffle'	NHor WDib
'Pink Upstart'	Last listed 1999
'Plum Crazy'	Last listed 1999
polyanthus	WDib
subsp. dracomontanus	
primulifolius	WDib
– subsp. formosus	WDib
* 'Purple Passion'	CSpe

rexii	WDib
* 'Rhiannon'	NHor WDib
'Rosebud'	NHor WDib
'Rosemary'	WDib
'Royal Mixed' ♀	Last listed 1995
'Ruby' ♀	MBri NHor WDib
'Ruffled Lilac'	CSpe
'Sally'	NHor WDib
'Sandra'	MBri NHor WDib
'Sarah' ♀	NHor WDib
saxorum ♀	CHal CInt EMan LCns LHil LIck
	MBri NHor NTow SEND SRms
	WDib
- compact	LCns WDib
'Sian'	WDib
'Snow White' ♀	CSpe NHor WDib
* 'Something Special'	NHor WDib
¶ 'Sophie'	WDib
'Stella' ♀	NHor WDib
stomandrus	WDib
* 'Sugar Almond'	CSpe
'Susan' ♀	NHor WDib
* 'Sweet Violet'	CSpe
'Tina' ♀	MBri NHor WDib
'Tracey'	NHor WDib
'Upstart'	Last listed 1998
'Violet Lace'	CSpe
'Wendy'	NHor WDib
'Wiesmoor Red'	MBri NHor WDib
'Winifred'	NHor WDib

STREPTOLIRION (Commelinaceae)
volubile	CPlN

STREPTOPUS (Convallariaceae)
amplexifolius	WCru
roseus	LAma

STREPTOSOLEN (Solanaceae)
jamesonii ♀	CHal CPlN CPle CSev EBak ELan
	EPfP ERea IBlr LCns LHil NRog
	SYvo WBod
- yellow	ERea

STROBILANTHES (Acanthaceae)
anisophylla	CSpe WCot
atropurpurea	CBot CGle CGre CHea CPle
	ECGN ECha ELan GCal GKir LHil
	LLWP LRHS MFir MHar NSti SMad
	SUsu WCot WCru WFar WHer
	WPer WPic WPnP WWin WWye
attenuata	SDys WCot WCru WFar WMoo
	WWin
- subsp. *nepalensis*	WWye
- - TSS	CGle EBee EMar WRHF
dyeriana ♀	CHal EBak
rankanensis	Last listed 1999
violacea	ERea LFis LHop SMac WPer

STROMANTHE (Marantaceae)
amabilis	See *Ctenanthe amabilis*
'Freddy'	MBri
sanguinea	CHal MBri
- var. *spectabilis* ♀	Last listed 1995
'Stripestar'	MBri

STRONGYLODON (Papilionaceae)
¶ *macrobotrys*	SOWG

STROPHANTHUS (Apocynaceae)
divaricatus	CPlN
kombe	CPlN MSal

preussii	CPlN
speciosus	CPlN MSal

STRUTHIOPTERIS (Blechnaceae)
niponica	See *Blechnum niponicum*

STRYCHNOS (Loganiaceae)
cocculoides	Last listed 1999
madagascariensis	Last listed 1999
spinosa	Last listed 1999

STUARTIA See STEWARTIA

STYLIDIUM (Stylidiaceae)
crassifolium ♀	Last listed 1995
macranthum	Last listed 1998

STYLOMECON (Papaveraceae)
heterophylla	WBor

STYLOPHORUM (Papaveraceae)
diphyllum	CPBP CPou EBee ECGN ECha
	EMar EPar LAma MBel MRav MSal
	WCru WWhi
lasiocarpum	EBee EMan EMar EWTr GMac
	MBel MCCP NCat NDlv SSca
	WBor WCot WCru WRos

STYPHELIA (Epacridaceae)
colensoi	See *Cyathodes colensoi*

STYRAX ✿ (Styracaceae)
americanus	CB&S SPlb
formosanus	WPGP
- var. *formosanus*	WCru
B&SWJ 3803	
hemsleyanus ♀	CAbP CB&S CFil CPMA CTho
	EPfP LRHS MBlu SMad SPer SSpi
	SSta WNor WPGP WWat
japonicus ♀	More than 30 suppliers
§ - Benibana Group	SReu SSta
- - 'Pink Chimes'	CAbP CEnd CMCN CPMA ELan
	EPfP LRHS MAsh MBlu MBri NPro
	SPer SSta WWes
- 'Carillon'	CEnd LRHS MAsh
- 'Fargesii'	CDoC EPfP GKir LRHS MAsh
	MBri SSpi SSta WFar
- 'Pendulus'	Last listed 1997
- 'Roseus'	See *S. japonicus* Benibana Group
obassia ♀	CArn CB&S CGre CMCN CTho
	CWSG EPfP IMGH LPan LRHS
	SReu SSpi SSta WBod WNor
	WPGP WWat
odoratissimus	CArn

SUCCISA (Dipsacaceae)
§ *pratensis*	CArn CKin CRDP EBee ECoo
	EMon EWFC MChe MFir MHer
	MHew NLan NLar SSpi WGwy
	WHer WJek
- *alba*	EBee SSpi
- 'Corinne Tremaine' (v)	WHer
- dwarf	CLyd NRya
- 'Peddar's Pink'	EWes
- *rosea*	SSpi

SUTERA (Scrophulariaceae)
African Sunset = 'Rarosil'	Last listed 1999
¶ 'Candy Floss'	LIck
cordata	LHop
- Knysna Hills®	Last listed 1999
- 'Lilac Pearls'	Last listed 1998

- mauve | Last listed 1997
- pale pink | Last listed 1997
- 'Pink Domino' | Last listed 1998
§ - 'Snowflake' | CSpe EDAr LHil LPVe MLan NPri SCoo SMer WLRN
grandiflora | See *Jamesbrittenia grandiflora*
halimifolia JCA 3-812 | EBee
jurassica | See *Jamesbrittenia jurassica*
- H&B 19148 | CPBP
¶ *neglecta* | SPlb
¶ Olympic Gold | NPri WWol
= 'Prosutv' (v) |
* *rosea* 'Plena' | Last listed 1997
¶ Sea Mist = 'Yagemil'^PBR | NPri

SUTHERLANDIA (Papilionaceae)

frutescens | CAbb CArn CSpe LRHS
- Edinburgh form | Last listed 1999
- 'Prostrata' | Last listed 1999
microphylla | Last listed 1998
- S&SH 56/61 | Last listed 1999
montana | CFir

SWAINSONA (Papilionaceae)

formosa | Last listed 1998
galegifolia 'Albiflora' | CPne CSpe SCro SOWG
tephrotricha | Last listed 1998

SWERTIA (Gentianaceae)

kingii | Last listed 1999
¶ *perennis* | EMan

SYAGRUS (Arecaceae)

§ *romanzoffiana* | CBrP CRoM LPJP LPal WMul

x SYCOPARROTIA (Hamamelidaceae)

semidecidua | CB&S CFil CPMA GKir LRHS MAsh SSta WPGP WWat

SYCOPSIS (Hamamelidaceae)

heterophylla | Last listed 1999
sinensis | CPLG EPfP LRHS SSpi SSta WSHC WWat

SYMPHORICARPOS (Caprifoliaceae)

albus | CChe CDul CKin ENot GChr NWea WDin
- 'Constance Spry' | MTed SRms
§ - var. *laevigatus* | CB&S ENot LBuc MBar
§ - 'Taff's White' (v) | WMoo
- 'Variegatus' | See *S. albus* 'Taff's White'
x *chenaultii* 'Hancock' | EBee ELan ENot EPfP GChr MBar MGos MRav MWat NPro SPer WDin WFar
x *doorenbosii* | CBlo EBee ENot GKir LBuc LRHS
'Magic Berry' | MBar NWea
- 'Mother of Pearl' | CBlo CDul EBee ECha ELan ENot EPfP GKir LBuc LRHS MBar MGos MRav NWea SPer WTro
- 'White Hedge' | EBee ELan ENot LBuc LRHS NWea SPer
orbiculatus | CBrm IMGH LRHS WGwG
- 'Albovariegatus' | See *S. orbiculatus* 'Taff's Silver Edge'
- 'Argenteovariegatus' | See *S. orbiculatus* 'Taff's Silver Edge'
- 'Bowles' Golden Variegated' | See *S. orbiculatus* 'Foliis Variegatis'
§ - 'Foliis Variegatis' (v) | CTri EHoe ELan ENot GChr GEil LRHS MGos MRav NSti SEas SMac SPer WEas WGwG WHCG WSHC WWal WWat WWin

§ - 'Taff's Silver Edge' (v) | CB&S CBrm EBee EHoe IOrc LRHS MBar NSti
- 'Variegatus' | See *S. orbiculatus* 'Foliis Variegatis'
rivularis | See *S. albus* var. *laevigatus*

SYMPHYANDRA ✿ (Campanulaceae)

armena | CLTr CPea EBee EBur EWTr GBuc MAvo NCut WPen
asiatica | WWat
cretica | CPBP EBee NTow
- *alba* | Last listed 1997
hofmannii | CGle COIW EBee EBur ELan MBro MTho NBrk NFai NLar SRms WElm WOve WPer WRha WSan WWin
§ *ossetica* | CElw CGle ELan EMan NCiC NWoo SSvw WElm WSan
§ *pendula* | CFir COIW EBee EWTr EWes GBuc GGar MBNS NLar SCro SRot WBar WPer
- *alba* | See *S. pendula*
* *tianschanica* | Last listed 1997
wanneri | EBee EBur EMan EPfP LRHS MCCP NMen WCot WWin
zangezura | CNic EBee EBur EEls LCot

SYMPHYTUM (Boraginaceae)

asperum | EBee ECha EGar ELan EMon MHew MRav MSal MTed NLar WCHb WCer WOak
* *azureum* | LAst LRHS MBri MCAu MSte SRPl WCHb WFar WGwy
'Belsay' | GBuc WHil
caucasicum | CBre CElw CMHG CSam ECha ELau EPar GBar GPoy LEdu LRHS MBri MHar NChi NFai NSti SIde SSvw WCHb WHer WHil WOak WRha WWye
- 'Eminence' | CGle CMdw CRDP EGoo WCHb WOve
- 'Norwich Sky' | CInt EBee NMir WCHb WPGP
'Denford Variegated' (v) | CRow MInt WBry
'Empire' | SDys
§ 'Goldsmith' (v) | More than 30 suppliers
'Hidcote Blue' | CBre CMGP CTri EBee ECha ELan ELau EPla GBar ILis LRHS MBri MCAu MCLN MSte NArg NBro NHol NSti SIde SLPl SMer WCru WElm WWin
§ 'Hidcote Pink' | CGle COIW EBee ECha ELau ENot EPla LAst LRHS MMal MRav MSte MWgw NFla NSti SLPl SRPl WCer WFar WMoo
'Hidcote Variegated' (v) | CGle SIng WCHb
¶ *ibericum* | CAgr CArn CGle CMHG COIW CSam EBee EBlw ECha ELau EPla GBar GPoy LGro LRHS MDun MFir MNrw MTis MWgw NSti SIde SIng SMer SRms WCHb WOve WWat WWye
- 'All Gold' | ECha ELau EMon MBri SLon WCru WMoo
- 'Blaueglocken' | CBod CSev EBee ECha NCat WSan
- dwarf | Last listed 1999
- 'Gold in Spring' | EBee EGoo EMon WCHb WCer WFar WRha
- 'Jubilee' | See *S.* 'Goldsmith'
- 'Langthorns Pink' | Last listed 1998
- 'Lilacinum' | EBee MBro SAga WCer WHer WWat
- 'Pink Robins' | EMon WCHb
- 'Variegatum' | See *S.* 'Goldsmith'

- 'Wisley Blue'	ELan EPfP EWTr LRHS NCat WCer WFar WWoo
'Lambrook Silver'	SRPl
'Lambrook Sunrise'	CLAP EBee EPla LRHS MRav NBus SCob WCot WLRN WPnP WSan
'Langthorns Pink'	ELan EMar GBar GBri GBuc GCal WCHb WCer
'Mereworth' (v)	EBee EMon WCHb WPGP
officinale	CArn CKin COld CSev EPla GBar GPoy MChe MHer MHew MNrw MSal NFai NHex NMir NPer SIde SRms WGwG WHer WOak WWye
¶ — 'Boraston White'	WCHb
* - blue	WWat
- *ochroleucum*	WHer
orientale	CElw CGle EMon WCHb
peregrinum	See *S.* x *uplandicum*
'Roseum'	See *S.* 'Hidcote Pink'
'Rubrum'	EBee ECot ELan EOrc EPfP EWes LAst LRHS MAnH MCAu MCLN MChl MSte NOrc SMrm SPer WCot WCru WOve
tuberosum	CArn CBre CElw CMHG COld CRDP EGar ELau EOHP GPoy MFir MHer MMal NCat NHol NSti WCHb WFar WHer WRha WWat WWye
- JMH 8106	MDun
§ x *uplandicum*	CSev ELan ELau EMar GBar MHew MSal SIde WCHb WCer WGwG WHbs WJek WOak WWye
- 'Axminster Gold' (v)	CLAP CPlt CRDP CRow EMan IBlr LHop SAga WCot
- 'Bocking 14'	CAgr CBod GBar GAbr
- 'Jenny Swales'	Last listed 1998
¶ - 'Lugh Samhoildánach'	IIve
- 'Variegatum' (v) ♀	CBot CGle CLAP CPlt ELau EMan EOrc EWTr EWes GBar GCal GKir GPoy MCLN MTho NGdn SCob WBea WCHb WCot WEas WFar WSpi WWat WWin

SYMPLOCARPUS ❀ (Araceae)
foetidus	Last listed 1997

SYMPLOCOS (Symplocaceae)
paniculata	MBlu WBcn
pyrifolia	CFil WPGP

SYNEILESIS (Asteraceae)
aconitifolia B&SWJ 879	WCru
palmata B&SWJ 1003	WCru
¶ *subglabrata* B&SWJ 298	WCru

SYNGONIUM (Araceae)
'Maya Red'	MBri
podophyllum ♀	LBlo
- 'Emerald Gem'	CHal
- 'Silver Knight'	MBri
- 'Variegatum' (v)	MBri
'White Butterfly'	CHal LRHS MBri

SYNNOTIA See SPARAXIS

SYNTHYRIS (Scrophulariaceae)
missurica	EBee NRya
pinnatifida	NWCA
- var. *canescens*	Last listed 1998
- var. *lanuginosa*	Last listed 1998
- var. *pinnatifida*	Last listed 1998
reniformis	IBlr WHil

stellata	CLAP CRDP EBrP EBre GCal GGar LBCl LBSe LBre LFis MBBe SBla SBre WPGP

SYRINGA ❀ (Oleaceae)
afghanica	See *S. protolaciniata*
amurensis	See *S. reticulata* subsp. *amurensis*
x *chinensis*	CTho WWat
- 'Saugeana'	SPer WPyg
'Correlata' (graft-chimaera)	IOrc
debelderorum	SSta
subsp. *patula*	
emodi	CBot WHCG
- 'Aurea'	IHar
- 'Aureovariegata'	CEnd CPMA LRHS WDin
'Fountain'	EPla
x *henryi* 'Alba'	WBcn
x *hyacinthiflora*	WStI
- 'Esther Staley' ♀	ENot MRav SFam WAbe
- 'Laurentian'	Last listed 1999
- 'Maiden's Blush'	MBri
- 'Pocohontas'	Last listed 1997
- 'Sunset' (d)	Last listed 1998
- 'The Bride'	Last listed 1998
'Josee'	EBee WPat
x *josiflexa* 'Bellicent' ♀	CEnd CPle CTho EBee ELan ENot GKir ISea MAsh MBar MGos MRav NFla NSti SMur SPer SPla SPlb SRms SSta WHCG WPat
¶ - 'James MacFarlane'	NRib
- 'Lynette'	CTho EPla WBcn
§ - 'Royalty'	COtt
josikaea	CBlo CPle CTho LBuc MBar MTis SPer WHCG
komarovii L 490	GGGa
§ - subsp. *reflexa* ♀	CDul CTho EPfP LBuc MBar MGos MRav WWat
§ x *laciniata* Mill.	CBot CPMA EBee EHol EPfP GChr GEil GKir LRHS MBri MRav SMrm SMur SSpi WGor WHCG WPGP WSHC WWat
§ *meyeri* var. *spontanea* 'Palibin' ♀	More than 30 suppliers
microphylla	See *S. pubescens* subsp. *microphylla*
- 'Superba'	See *S. pubescens* subsp. *microphylla* 'Superba'
'Minuet'	MGos
oblata	WWoo
- var. *donaldii*	SSta
palibiniana	See *S. meyeri* var. *spontanea* 'Palibin'
patula (Palibin) Nakai	See *S. pubescens* subsp. *patula*
- hort.	See *S. meyeri* var. *spontanea* 'Palibin'
pekinensis	See *S. reticulata* subsp. *pekinensis*
x *persica* ♀	CBlo CTri EPfP ERav GKir ISea MGos MWat SLon SPer SPla WPyg WSpi WWat
- 'Alba' ♀	CBot CTri GQui SPla WHCG WSHC WWat
- var. *laciniata*	See *S.* x *laciniata*
¶ - 'Taff's Treasure'	EMon
pinnatifolia	CBot GKir WHCG WPGP
x *prestoniae* 'Agnes Smith'	MGos
- 'Audrey'	MGos
- 'Coral'	COtt MBri WFar
- 'Desdemona'	SSpi
- 'Elinor' ♀	CBlo CMHG CPle ENot MRav NSti SPer

- 'Hiawatha'	MGos
- 'Isabella'	MGos SLdr
- 'Nocturne'	LRHS MGos WFar
- 'Redwine'	COtt LRHS MBri MGos
- 'Royalty'	See *S.* x *josiflexa* 'Royalty'
§ **protolaciniata**	CMHG EPla IDee MBlu SSta WAbe WFar
§ **pubescens**	GKir
subsp. **microphylla**	
§ - subsp. **microphylla**	More than 30 suppliers
§ 'Superba' ♀	
§ - subsp. **patula**	ELan EPfP IOrc LAst LNet LRHS MRav MWat NBee NWea SPla WAbe WStI
¶ - - 'Goscote Purity'	MGos
§ - - 'Miss Kim' ♀	CBlo CDoC EBee EBrP EBre ECle GKir GOrc LBCl LBSe LBre LRHS MAsh MBBe MBel MBri MGos MRav NPro SBre SLim SSta WDin WGwG WHCG WPat WPyg
reflexa	See *S. komarovii* subsp. *reflexa*
reticulata	Last listed 1997
§ - subsp. **amurensis**	Last listed 1999
- 'Ivory Silk'	EPfP
- var. **mandschurica**	See *S. reticulata* subsp. *amurensis*
§ - subsp. **pekinensis**	CBot CMCN
x **swegiflexa**	CPLG
sweginzowii	CSam CTho LBuc SPer WWat
tomentella	CDul CWSG LBuc NWea SRms
velutina	See *S. pubescens* subsp. *patula*
villosa	MWhi
vulgaris	GOrc LBuc MBar NWea
- 'Adelaide Dunbar' (d)	Last listed 1997
- 'Agincourt Beauty'	MBri
- var. **alba**	MBar
- 'Albert F. Holden'	Last listed 1999
§ - 'Andenken an Ludwig Späth' ♀	CB&S CBot CDoC CDul CTho CTri ENot EPfP GKir IOrc LPan LRHS MBar MBri MGos MRav NBlu NWea SEas SLim SLon SPer WFar WPyg WWeb
- 'Arthur William Paul' (d)	MRav
- 'Aurea'	EPla MRav WBcn
- 'Avalanche'	Last listed 1999
- 'Beauty of Moscow'	GKir LRHS MBri
- 'Belle de Nancy' (d)	EBee ELan MAsh MBri SLim WDin WLRN WPyg
- 'Charles Joly' (d) ♀	CB&S CBlo CDoC CDul CTho EBee ELan ENot EPfP GChr GKir IOrc LNet LRHS MAsh MBar MBri MGos MRav NBee NWea SEas SLim SPer SRPl WDin WFar WStI
- 'Charm'	Last listed 1997
- 'Condorcet' (d)	LNet
- 'Congo'	EBee ENot GKir NMoo SCoo SPer
- 'Edward J. Gardner' (d)	ENot LRHS MBri
- 'Ellen Willmott' (d)	MRav
- 'Firmament' ♀	ELan ENot SCoo SPer
- 'Glory'	MBri
- 'Katherine Havemeyer' (d) ♀	CB&S CBot CChe CDoC CDul CSam CTri EBee ELan ENot EPfP GChr GKir LBuc LRHS MAsh MBri MGos MRav SEas SFam SLim SPer SReu WDin WStI
- 'Krasavitsa Moskvy'	Last listed 1998
- 'Lucie Baltet'	MBri
- 'Madame Antoine Buchner' (d) ♀	ENot GKir
- 'Madame Florent Stepman'	CBlo LCaP
- 'Madame Lemoine' (d) ♀	More than 30 suppliers

- 'Masséna'	ENot MRav SCoo SPer
- 'Maud Notcutt'	ENot SCoo SPer WLRN
- 'Michel Buchner' (d)	CB&S EBee ENot IOrc MAsh MBar MBri MWat SLim SPer
- 'Miss Ellen Willmott' (d)	MBri
- 'Mrs Edward Harding' (d) ♀	EBee ENot GKir LBuc LNet MBri MGos NPri NWea SLim SPer WLRN
- 'Olivier de Serres'	MBri
- 'Paul Deschanel' (d)	MBri
- 'Paul Thirion' (d)	Last listed 1997
- 'Président Grévy' (d)	CDoC ECle MBri
- 'Primrose'	CBlo CBot CDoC CTho EBee ELan ENot EPfP GChr GKir IMGH LRHS MDun MRav SEas SPer SSta WDin WLRN
- 'Rochester'	MBri
- 'Romance'	Last listed 1999
- 'Sensation'	CBlo CDoC CPle EBee ENot EPfP GChr GKir LRHS MDun MRav SCoo SLdr SPer SSta
- 'Silver King'	Last listed 1999
- 'Souvenir d'Alice Harding' (d)	GKir LRHS
- 'Souvenir de Louis Spaeth'	See *S. vulgaris* 'Andenken an Ludwig Späth'
¶ - variegated	SLim
- variegated double (d)	MTed WBcn
- 'Vestale' ♀	CBlo EBee ENot SCoo SDix
wolfii	CPle LBuc MCCP
yunnanensis	CTho
- 'Rosea'	Last listed 1998

SYZYGIUM (Myrtaceae)

paniculatum	CTrC
wilsonii	ECon

T

TABERNAEMONTANA (Apocynaceae)

coronaria	See *T. divaricata*
§ **divaricata**	SOWG

TACCA (Taccaceae)

* **nivea**	Last listed 1999

TACITUS See GRAPTOPETALUM

TAGETES (Asteraceae)

lemmonii	SMac
lucida	EOHP MSal

TALBOTIA (Velloziaceae)

elegans	WCot

TALINUM (Portulacaceae)

calycinum	Last listed 1998
okanoganense	CGra NTow NWCA
rugospermum	Last listed 1998
teretifolium	Last listed 1999
'Zoe'	CGra WFar

TAMARINDUS (Caesalpiniaceae)

indica (F)	ELau LBlo SPlb

TAMARIX (Tamaricaceae)

africana	WWin
gallica	CBlo ENot GCHN NWea SAPC SArc WSHC

§ *parviflora* — CBlo EMil IOrc LRHS MGos
pentandra — See *T. ramosissima*
§ *ramosissima* — EBrP EBre ELan GVer LBCl LBSe LBre MBBe MBar SBre SEND SMrm SRms SSta WDin WSHC WTro WWeb
- 'Pink Cascade' — EBee EMil ENot EPfP GChr GKir LRHS MBri MGos MRav SEas SPer WDin WGwG WStl WWal
§ - 'Rubra' ♀ — CBlo CChe CDoC EBee EMil ENot EPfP IOrc LRHS MBlu MGos MMHG SLon WPyg
- 'Summer Glow' — See *T. ramosissima* 'Rubra'
tetrandra ♀ — More than 30 suppliers
- var. *purpurea* — See *T. parviflora*

TAMUS (Dioscoreaceae)
communis — CArn

TANACETUM ✿ (Asteraceae)
§ *argenteum* — MRav MTho SIng
- subsp. *canum* — EWes LRHS MAsh
§ *balsamita* — CArn COld ELan ELau EOHP ERav GPoy MBri MHer MSal WHbs WHer WJek WOak WPer WSel WWye
§ - subsp. *balsametoides* — CBod ELau GBar MChe MHer MRav NPri SIde WJek WWye
§ - subsp. *balsamita* — GPoy MRav MSal SIde
- var. *tanacetoides* — See *T. balsamita* subsp. *balsamita*
- *tomentosum* — See *T. balsamita* subsp. *balsametoides*
capitatum — See *Sphaeromeria capitata*
§ *cinerariifolium* — CArn CBod CInt EOHP GBar GPoy WPer
§ *coccineum* — GPoy MSal SRms WWin
I - 'Andromeda' — Last listed 1997
- 'Aphrodite' — Last listed 1998
- 'Bees' Pink Delight' — Last listed 1997
- 'Brenda' ♀ — Last listed 1998
* - 'Duplex' — Last listed 1998
- 'Duro' — GBuc NCut
- 'Eileen May Robinson' ♀ — ECot EPfP NCut SMrm
- 'Evenglow' — MRav SMrm
- 'H.M. Pike' — Last listed 1998
- 'James Kelway' ♀ — EBee ECot EPfP EWll GChr LRHS MBri MCAu MRav NBir NFai SMrm SRms
- 'K.M. Price' — Last listed 1998
- 'Kelway's Glorious' — NCut
- 'King Size' — MTis NMir WFar
- 'Laurin' — GKir
- 'Madeleine' (d) — Last listed 1999
- 'Phillipa' — Last listed 1997
- 'Pink Petite' — Last listed 1997
- 'Queen Mary' — Last listed 1999
- Robinson's giant flowered — SRms WMoo WRHF
- 'Robinson's Pink' — EBee GKir GMaP LAst NCiC NCut NOrc NPri SMer SMrm SRms
- 'Robinson's Red' — EBee GKir GMaP LAst LIck MTis NCiC NCut NOrc NPri SMer SMrm WRus
- 'Salmon Beauty' — Last listed 1998
- 'Scarlet Glow' — Last listed 1998
- 'Snow Cloud' — EBee LRHS MCAu SMrm
- 'Vanessa' — SMrm
§ *corymbosum* — CGle EBee GCal LFis NCat WCot
§ - subsp. *clusii* — EBee
- 'Festafel' — MRav
densum — ECho EPot WCFE

- subsp. *amani* — EBee ECha EMFP ESis GBar GTou LBee LGro LRHS MHer MWat NWCA SEND SPer SRms SSmi WAbe WWin
§ *baradjanii* — CGle ELan EMNN GCHN MBro MHar NFor SBla SChu WByw WEas WHer WHoo WSHC
berderi — See *Hippolytia berderi*
buronense — EBee
'Jackpot' — EWes LRHS NCat NPSI
§ *macrophyllum* — EMon GCal LGre WCot WPer
niveum — CArn CHad EBee EGar EOHP MSal WBea WBry WCot
§ *parthenium* — CAgr CArn CHEx CKin EEls ELau EWFC GBar GPoy MChe MHer MHew MMal NFai NHex NPer SGar SIde SRms WGwG WHer WOak WWye
- 'Aureum' — CHid CRow ECha EEls ELan ELau EOld GBar GPoy LGro MBri MChe MMal NFai NHex SIng SPer SRms WCot WEas WHer WOak WOve WPer WWin
- 'Ball's Double White' (d) — SRms
- double white (d) — CSWP GBar GPoy NPer SEND SRms
- 'Golden Ball' — NTow WCot
¶ - 'Malmesbury' — CNat
¶ - 'Minety' — CNat
- 'Plenum' (d) — EHrv
§ - 'Rowallane' (d) — EHol ELan GBuc GKir GMac MAvo MBri SUsu WCot
- 'Silver Ball' — LPVe
- 'Sissinghurst White' — See *T. parthenium* 'Rowallane'
- 'Snowball' (d) — Last listed 1999
- 'White Bonnet' (d) — CGle NBrk WEas
poteriifolium — LFis
§ *praeteritum* — LGre
- subsp. *massicyticum* — Last listed 1999
MP 95277
pseudacbillea — Last listed 1997
§ *ptarmiciflorum* — SMer
- 'Silver Feather' — EPPr
sp. CC&McK 460 — GTou
vulgare — CAgr CArn CKin CSev ECtt EEls ELau EWFC GPoy LRHS MChe MHar MHer MHew MMal MSal SIde WCot WWye
- var. *crispum* — CStr EBot ELan ELau EOHP EPla GBar GCal GPoy LFis MBri MHer MRav NHex NVic SIde WBea WCot WFar WHer WJek WOak WRha WSel
- 'Isla Gold' — CBod CBos CElw EBee EMon EWes GCal LFis MHar MMil SMad SUsu WBry WCHb WCot WFar WMoo WRha WWye
- 'Silver Lace' (v) — CElw EMon GBri LFis NBrk NHex NSti SEND WBea WCHb WCot WFar WHer

TANAKAEA (Saxifragaceae)
radicans — WCru

TAPISCIA (Staphyleaceae)
sinensis — CLyn

TARASA (Malvaceae)
bumilis — CPBP

TARAXACUM (Asteraceae)
¶ *albidum* — EBee

	– B&SWJ 509	Last listed 1999
	– DJH 452	CHid WCot
	carneocoloratum	Last listed 1998
I	*officinale*	MHew SIde
	– *sativum*	IIve
	– white-flowered	Last listed 1999
	pamiricum JJH 395	Last listed 1999

TARCHONANTHUS (Asteraceae)

¶	*camphoratus*	CTrC

TASMANNIA See DRIMYS

TAXODIUM (Taxodiaceae)

§	*distichum* ♀	More than 30 suppliers
	– var. *imbricatum*	CB&S CEnd IOrc LPan MBlu MBri
	'Nutans' ♀	SMad SMur
¶	– 'Secrest'	SMad
	mucronatum	WFro

TAXUS ✿ (Taxaceae)

	baccata ♀	More than 30 suppliers
	– 'Adpressa Aurea' (v)	CKen EPla GAri GKir
	– 'Adpressa Variegata'	EHul LCon MAsh SLim
	(m/v) ♀	
	– 'Aldenham Gold'	CKen
	– 'Amersfoort'	CDoC EOrn EPla LCon
	– 'Argentea Minor'	See *T. baccata* 'Dwarf White'
§	– Aurea Group	CBlo SRms WShe
I	– 'Aurea Pendula'	EBrP EBre EOrn LBCl LBSe LBre
		MBBe SBre
I	– 'Aureomarginata'	CB&S EOrn GKir WStI
¶	– 'Autumn Shades'	CB&S
	– 'Cavendishii' (f)	ECho
	– 'Compacta'	EOrn EPla
	– 'Corleys Coppertip'	CBlo CFee CKen CSam EHul EOrn
		GKir GPin LCon LLin LRHS MAsh
		MBar MBri MOne WGwG WLRN
	– 'Cristata'	Last listed 1998
	– 'David'	Last listed 1999
	– 'Dovastoniana' (f) ♀	CMac EHul LCon MBar NWea
	– 'Dovastonii Aurea'	CMac EHul EOrn EPla GChr GKir
	(m/v) ♀	LBee LCon LPan LRHS MBar MBlu
		MBri NWea SLim WDin
	– 'Drinkstone Gold' (v)	EHul EPla WBcn
§	– 'Dwarf White' (v)	EOrn EPla LCon
	– 'Elegantissima' (f/v) ♀	EHul EPfP NWea
§	– 'Erecta' (f)	EHul
§	– 'Fastigiata' (f) ♀	More than 30 suppliers
¶	– Fastigiata Aurea Group	CKen CLnd EHul ELan EPfP LAst
		LBuc LLin LPan MGos NBee NPer
		NRar SRms WBrE WFar WHar
		WLRN
	– 'Fastigiata	More than 30 suppliers
	Aureomarginata' (m) ♀	
	– 'Fastigiata Robusta' (f)	EBrP EBre EPfP EPla GKir LBCl
		LBSe LBre LRHS MAsh MBBe
		MBar MBri SBre WGer WPyg
	– 'Gemers Gold'	LPan
	– 'Glenroy New Penny'	Last listed 1999
	– 'Goud Elsje'	CKen EOrn GPin WLRN
	– 'Green Column'	CKen MBlu
	– 'Green Diamond'	CKen WBcn
	– 'Hibernica'	See *T. baccata* 'Fastigiata'
	– 'Icicle'	CB&S EPla LCon LLin MGos
	– 'Ivory Tower'	CB&S LCon LLin MGos
	– 'Melfard'	EHul
	– 'Nutans'	CKen CNic EHul EOrn ESis IMGH
		LCon LLin MBar MOne WLRN
	– 'Overeynderi'	EHul
	– 'Pendula'	MRav
	– 'Prostrata'	CMac

	– 'Pumila Aurea'	ELan
	– 'Pygmaea'	CKen IOrc
	– 'Repandens' (f) ♀	CDoC EHul LCon LPan MBar
		WCFE WFar WGer
I	– 'Repens Aurea' (v) ♀	CDoC CKen EHul ELan EOrn
		GCHN LCon LLin LRHS MAsh
		MBar MBri MGos NFla NHol
		SAga
	– 'Rushmore'	Last listed 1997
	– 'Semperaurea' (m) ♀	More than 30 suppliers
	– 'Silver Spire' (v)	CKen
	– 'Standishii' (f) ♀	More than 30 suppliers
	– 'Summergold' (v)	CSli EBrP EBre EHul ELan ENot
		GCHN GChr GKir IOrc LBCl LBSe
		LBre LCon MAsh MBBe MBar
		MGos NHol SBre SLim WBod
		WDin WPyg WStI
	– 'Washingtonii' (v)	Last listed 1998
	– 'White Icicle'	EOrn
	brevifolia	EPla LCon
	cuspidata	Last listed 1999
	– 'Aurescens' (v)	CKen EPla SRms
¶	– var. *nana*	EHul EOrn GAri LCon MBar SIng
		WGwG WLRN WWal
	– 'Robusta'	EHul LLin
	– 'Straight Hedge'	CDoC EHul GPin IMGH WLRN
¶	– 'Thayerae'	GIBF
	x *media* 'Brownii'	EHul LBuc
	– 'Hicksii' (f) ♀	CLnd EHul GKir IMGH LBuc LNet
		MBar NWea SLim WLRN
	– 'Hillii'	CBlo MBar
	– 'Lodi'	LBee
	– 'Viridis'	MGos

TECOMA (Bignoniaceae)

	x *alata*	Last listed 1999
	capensis ♀	CHEx CPIN CSev EBak ERea LHil
		LRHS SHFr SOWG SYvo
	– 'Apricot'	Last listed 1999
	– 'Aurea'	CSev ERea SOWG
§	– 'Coccinea'	Last listed 1999
	– 'Lutea'	LRHS WMul
	– subsp. *nyassae*	ERea
§	– 'Salmonea'	Last listed 1999
	garrocha	Last listed 1999
	'Orange Glow'	SOWG
	ricasoliana	See *Podranea ricasoliana*
	stans	Last listed 1999

TECOMANTHE (Bignoniaceae)

	dendrophila	CPIN
	speciosa	CPIN ECou

TECOMARIA See TECOMA

TECOPHILAEA (Tecophilaeaceae)

	cyanocrocus ♀	CAvo CBro EPot GCrs LAma LRHS
		SBla WCot
	– 'Leichtlinii' ♀	CAvo CBro EPot LAma LRHS SSpi
	– 'Purpurea'	See *T. cyanocrocus* 'Violacea'
	– Storm Cloud Group	GCrs
§	– 'Violacea'	CAvo CBro EPot GCrs LRHS
	violiflora	LAma

TECTARIA (Dryopteridaceae)

	gemmifera	GQui NMar

TECTONA (Verbenaceae)

	grandis	Last listed 1999

TELANTHOPHORA (Asteraceae)

	grandifolia	SAPC SArc

TELEKIA (Asteraceae)
§ *speciosa* — CNic COIW CSam EBee EBrP EBre ELan EPfP LBCl LBSe LBre LFis MBBe MCCP MCLN MFir MRav NBro NBus NPSI SBre SChr SDix WBor WFar WHer WPer WPrP WRHF

TELEPHIUM (Molluginaceae)
imperati — Last listed 1999

TELESONIX See BOYKINIA

TELINE See GENISTA

TELLIMA (Saxifragaceae)
grandiflora — More than 30 suppliers
- 'Delphine' — Last listed 1999
- 'Forest Frost' (v) — WCDu WCot
- Odorata Group — CBre ECha EGoo IHdy MRav NBrk NCat NSti WGwG WHen WPrP WWal WWat WWye
- 'Purpurea' — See *T. grandiflora* Rubra Group
- 'Purpurteppich' — CGle EBee EBrP EBre ECha EGoo EMan EPPr GKir LBCl LBSe LBre LPio LRHS MBBe MRav NDov SBre WWat
§ - Rubra Group — More than 30 suppliers

TELOPEA (Proteaceae)
mongaensis — Last listed 1997
speciosissima — CTrC
truncata — CCpl CDoC CFil ISea SSpi WCru WPGP
¶ - 'Forest Fire' — CPLG

TEMPLETONIA (Papilionaceae)
retusa — ECou

TEPHROSERIS (Asteraceae)
integrifolia — EBee WHer

TERMINALIA (Combretaceae)
¶ *catappa* (F) — LBlo

TERNSTROEMIA (Theaceae)
gymnanthera — See *T. japonica*
§ *japonica* — EPfP SAga

TETRACENTRON (Tetracentraceae)
sinense — CFil CGre CWSG EPfP GQui LRHS SFur SLon WWat

TETRADIUM (Rutaceae)
§ *daniellii* — CFil CMCN EPfP GKir SSpi WPGP WWat
§ - Hupehense Group — CB&S CMCN EBee GGGa GKir LRHS MBri SSpi WDin
glabrifolium B&SWJ 3541 — WCru
velutinum — CMCN

TETRAGONOLOBUS See LOTUS

TETRANEURIS (Asteraceae)
§ *grandiflora* — Last listed 1999
- JCA 11422 — Last listed 1998
§ *scaposa* — EPot LRHS

TETRAPANAX (Araliaceae)
§ *papyrifer* ♀ — CHEx SAPC SArc

TETRAPATHAEA See PASSIFLORA

TETRASTIGMA (Vitaceae)
voinierianum ♀ — CHEx CPlN ECon LCns MBri SAPC SArc

TEUCRIDIUM (Lamiaceae)
parvifolium — Last listed 1998

TEUCRIUM (Lamiaceae)
* *ackermannii* — CLyd EGoo LBee LHop LRHS MBro NMen SBla SCro SIng SMac WAbe WHoo WPat
* *arabii* — Last listed 1998
arduinoi — Last listed 1999
aroanium — CLyd CMea CPBP EGle EPot LBee LRHS MBro MWat NMen SBla SHFr
asiaticum — CSam EGoo SSca
bicolor — CPle SSta WWye
botrys — EGoo MHer MHew MSal
canadense — Last listed 1998
chamaedrys L. — CHal CSam EGoo ESis GBar LFis LRHS NGHP NHol NWCA SLim SRms SVen WCer WHbs WHoo WSel WTro WWat
- hort. — See *T.* x *lucidrys*
- 'Nanum' — CLyd MBro WPat WPyg WWye
- 'Rose Carpet' — CMGP EGoo EOrc
- subsp. *tauricola* — Last listed 1999
- 'Variegatum' — EGoo EMan GBar LLWP MHar WCHb WCot WOve WPer WRha
§ *creticum* — WLin
cyprium — Last listed 1998
* *discolor* — Last listed 1997
flavum — SRCN WCHb WPGP
- 'Album' — Last listed 1999
- 'Azureum' ♀ — CB&S CBot CHar CM&M CPle CSpe EBee ERav LRHS MBro MWhi SAga SBra SPer WBod WPat WPyg WSpi
- 'Collingwood Ingram' — EBee SLim
- 'Compactum' — CDoC EMan ESis LFis LHop SLon SPer SPla WAbe WWat
- dark — SMrm
halacysanum — Last listed 1998
hircanicum — More than 30 suppliers
§ x *lucidrys* — CAgr CArn CChe CFri CMea CSev EBee ECha EGoo ELan ELau ERea GAbr GPoy IOrc LAst MChe MHer MRav MTis NFla NGHP SIde SPer SRCN SRms WEas WGwG WOak WWin
lucidum — GBin WOak
marum — CArn EOHP MSal NMen SVen WJek
massiliense L. — EGoo EOrc WHer
- hort. — See *T.* x *lucidrys*
montanum — CMea
musimonum — CLyd NNrd
polium — CArn CLyd ESis MBro MWat WPat NWCA SBla SIng
- *aureum* — CHal CMea EMan GCrs LBee MBro NSla NWCA SBla WPat WPyg WWin WWye
pyrenaicum — CHal CMea EMan GCrs LBee MBro NSla NWCA SBla WPat WPyg WWin WWye
rosmarinifolium — See *T. creticum*
¶ *rotundifolium* — EBee
scordium — CNat WGwy WWhi
scorodonia — CArn CKin COld CSev EGoo ELau EWFC GBar GDea GPoy MChe MHer MHew MNaF MSal NMir WHer WJek WOak WSel WWye

¶ - 'Binsted Gold' — EGoo EMon WAlt
- 'Crispum' — CB&S CInt ELau EMar EOrc GBar MFir MHar MHer MLLN MSCN MWat MWgw NBid NBro NFai SMrm WBod WCHb WKif WOak WPer WSel WWat
* - 'Crispum Aureomarginatum' — MLLN
§ - 'Crispum Marginatum' (v) — More than 30 suppliers
- 'Winterdown' (v) — CMea CNat EMan EPPr LHop MSCN WAlt WCHb WCot WHer WHoo WLin
subspinosum — CLyd CMea ITim LBee LRHS MBro NHol NMen SBla WPat WPyg
webbianum — ECho

THALIA (Marantaceae)
dealbata — CHEx LEdu LGuA LLWG MSta WMAq WMul
¶ - broad-leaved — LLWG
¶ ***geniculata*** — LGuA

THALICTRUM ✿ (Ranunculaceae)
actaeifolium — EBee
adiantifolium — See *T. minus adiantifolium*
alpinum — EBee
angustifolium — See *T. lucidum*
aquilegiifolium — More than 30 suppliers
- var. ***album*** — CBot CMil ECGN ECha EFou EGle ELan EPla EWTr GGar LRHS MBri MBro MCAu MCLN MNrw MTis MWgw NBid NPSI NSti SCro SPer SSpi WHoo WPer
- dwarf — Last listed 1998
* - 'Hybridum' — CHad EBlw WFar WMoo WPer
- Purple Cloud — See *T. aquilegiifolium* 'Thundercloud'
- 'Purpureum' — CHid CSev EBee ECGN GGar LFis LPio MBro MTis NLar NPSI SPla WCru WHoo
§ - 'Thundercloud' ♀ — CBro CFir EBee EBrP EBre ECtt EMan GCal GKir LBCl LBSe LBre LRHS MBBe MBel MBri MCLN NHol SBre WPrP WSpi
baicalense — EBee
bulgaricum — See *T. flavidum*
calabricum — Last listed 1998
§ ***chelidonii*** — EBee EBrP EBre GMaP GMac LBCl LBSe LBre MBBe SBre
- B&SWJ 2520 — WCru
- dwarf — WPrP
clavatum — EBee
coreanum — See *T. ichangense*
coriaceum — EBee
cultratum HWJCM 367 — CFri EBee LFis SSpi STes WCru
dasycarpum — EMan LFis MLLN
* ***decorum*** — WCru
§ ***delavayi*** ♀ — More than 30 suppliers
- 'Album' — CGle CRDP CSpe EBee EBrP EBre ECha EFou LAst LBCl LBSe LBre LGre LPio LRHS MBBe MBro NOak SBre WHoo WWhi
- 'Hewitt's Double' (d) ♀ — More than 30 suppliers
- 'Sternhimmel' — Last listed 1997
diffusiflorum — GBri NHar SBla WSHC
dipterocarpum hort. — See *T. delavayi*
¶ 'Elin' — LGre
fendleri — GBuc
- NNS 93-738 — Last listed 1999
filamentosum — EMon

- B&SWJ 777 — WCru
finetii — Last listed 1998
§ ***flavidum*** — EBee
flavum — CGle EBee EFou EOld NBro NDea SSpi
- 'Chollerton' — See *T.* sp. from Afghanistan
I - 'Glauca' — CElw LSyl WTin
§ - subsp. ***glaucum*** ♀ — More than 30 suppliers
- 'Illuminator' — CHad CHid CSam EBee EBrP EBre ECle EMan EPPr GBri GKir LBCl LBSe LBre LRHS MArl MBBe MBel MBri MCLN MMil MOne NHol NPri SBre SMad STes SUsu WCot
flexuosum — See *T. minus* subsp. *minus*
foetidum — Last listed 1998
foliolosum B&SWJ 2705 — WCru
- S&SH 382 — GBri
§ ***ichangense*** — CBos GBri SAga SMrm
isopyroides — CLTr CLon CPBP CSev EBee EBrP EBre EMan EMon EPla GBin LAst LBCl LBSe LBre LPio LRHS MBBe MRav MWgw NGdn SBre SLon SMrm SRot WCot WCru WLRN WLin
javanicum B&L 12327 — Last listed 1998
kiusianum — More than 30 suppliers
- Kew form — CRDP WPat
koreanum — See *T. ichangense*
§ ***lucidum*** — CPou EBee ELan EMan LGre MRav NLar SSca
minus — CAgr CBos CMHG EBee ELan EMan EMon GAbr GBuc MBel MBri MNrw NHol NOak NSti WCDu WHil WPat WPrP WWye
§ - ***adiantifolium*** — CMGP EBee LAst LRHS MRav NOak SCob SMrm SRms WFar WPer WWat
§ - subsp. ***minus*** — EBee
§ - subsp. ***olympicum*** — WPer
- subsp. ***saxatile*** — See *T. minus* subsp. *olympicum*
morisonii — EBee
occidentale JLS 86255 — EMon MNrw
orientale — SBla WCot WPat
pauciflorum — Last listed 1997
polycarpum — NHol
polygamum — CBos EBee EBrP EBre GBri LBCl LBSe LBre LFis LGre MBBe MSal SBre WCot
punctatum B&SWJ 1272 — EBee EMan GBin GGar LGre LRHS MBri MTis NSti STes WCru WGwy
ramosum — Last listed 1998
reniforme B&SWJ 2159 — EMan WCru
- B&SWJ 2610 — EBee WCru
rhynchocarpum — Last listed 1998
rochebruneanum — More than 30 suppliers
* ***rugosum*** — GBuc
simplex — NHol
sp. ACE 1612 — EPPr
sp. B&SWJ 2520 — Last listed 1997
sp. B&SWJ 2622 — Last listed 1998
sp. CLD 564 — Last listed 1998
§ sp. from Afghanistan — EBee ELan EPot GBuc GKir GTou
sparsiflorum — EBee WPrP
speciosissimum — See *T. flavum* subsp. *glaucum*
sphaerostachyum — CElw GKir LRHS MBri WGer
squarrosum — EBee MTed
tuberosum — CAvo CElw CMea CRDP EBee EPot LGre SBla WCot
uchiyamae — EBee EBrP EBre GBri LBCl LBSe LBre MBBe SBre
venulosum — EBee
virgatum B&SWJ 2964 — WCru

THAMNOCALAMUS (Poaceae - Bambusoideae)

aristatus	EPfP EPla ISta LJus
crassinodus	EPla SDry
- dwarf	EPla
- 'Kew Beauty'	EFul EPfP EPla ERod EWes ISta
	LJus MMoz SDry WJun WPGP
- 'Lang Tang'	EPla WJun WPGP
- 'Merlyn'	CHEx EPla ERod SDry WJun WPGP
¶ *denudatus* I.1575	CFil
falcatus	See *Drepanostachyum falcatum*
falconeri	See *Himalayacalamus falconeri*
funghomii	See *Schizostachyum funghomii*
khasianus	See *Drepanostachyum khasianum*
maling	See *Yushania maling*
spathaceus hort.	See *Fargesia murieliae*
§ *spathiflorus*	CFil EFul EPla ISta SDry WJun
- subsp. *nepalensis*	EPla
§ *tessellatus*	EFul EOas EPla ISta LJus MMoz
	SDix SDry WJun

THAMNOCHORTUS (Restionaceae)

cinereus	LHil
insignis	CTrC WNor
lucens	CTrC
rigidus	CTrC LHil
spicigerus	CTrC LHil

THAPSIA (Apiaceae)

decipiens	See *Melanoselinum decipiens*
garganica	EBee EMan WCot

THEA See CAMELLIA

THELYMITRA (Orchidaceae)

'Goldfingers' 410	Last listed 1999
'Kay Nesbit'	Last listed 1999
luteocilium	Last listed 1999
'Melon Glow'	Last listed 1999
nuda	Last listed 1999
rubra	Last listed 1999
'Spring Delight' 458	Last listed 1998

THELYPTERIS ✿ (Thelypteridaceae)

limbosperma	See *Oreopteris limbosperma*
palustris	EBee EFer EMon MLan NHol
	SRms WFib WRic
phegopteris	See *Phegopteris connectilis*

THEMEDA (Poaceae)

triandra subsp. *australis*	Last listed 1997
from Adaminaby	
- subsp. *australis*	Last listed 1997
from Cooma	
- subsp. *japonica*	CBrm EHoe EPPr

THERMOPSIS (Papilionaceae)

barbata	Last listed 1997
caroliniana	See *T. villosa*
fabacea	See *T. lupinoides*
lanceolata	CFri CHad CTri EBee ECGP EMan
	EMar GBin LRHS LSpr MBel MBri
	MCAu MLLN MMil MTis SAga
	SLon SMac SMrm SOkh WFar
	WLin WPat WWye
§ *lupinoides*	EBee ECha EWTr NOrc SLod
	WCot WCru WFar WPer
mollis	EBee NBid
rhombifolia var. *montana*	CFri CMGP CRDP EBee EFou
	ELan EPfP ERav EWTr GAbr
	MGed MNrw NOrc NSti SGar SPer

§ *villosa*	SUsu WAbb WByw WGwG WLRN WOve WPer WRus WWal WWat CGle EBee EMan MLLN MRav MSte NFai NLar SBla SDix SPer WCot WPGP WRus

THEVETIA (Apocynaceae)

peruviana	LRHS MSal SOWG

THLADIANTHA (Cucurbitaceae)

dubia	CPIN EBee SDix
oliveri (f)	MSCN

THLASPI (Brassicaceae)

alpinum	EPot MWat
arvense	Last listed 1997
bellidifolium	NBir
biebersteinii	See *Pachyphragma macrophyllum*
bulbosum	GTou NWCA
§ *cepaeifolium*	CCuc GTou
subsp. *rotundifolium*	
- subsp. *rotundifolium*	Last listed 1997
var. *limosellifolium*	
fendleri	MNrw
rotundifolium	See *T. cepaeifolium* subsp. *rotundifolium*
stylosum	CNic

THRINAX (Arecaceae)

radiata	Last listed 1999

THRYPTOMENE (Myrtaceae)

saxicola 'F.C. Payne'	CPLG

THUJA ✿ (Cupressaceae)

'Extra Gold'	See *T. plicata* 'Irish Gold'
§ *koraiensis*	LCon MBar WCwm WHCr
occidentalis	NWea
¶ - Aurea Group	MBar
- 'Aureospicata'	EHul
- 'Autumn Glow'	Last listed 1999
- 'Beau Fleur'	LLin
- 'Beaufort' (v)	CKen EHul LLin MAsh MBar
- 'Caespitosa'	CBlo CKen CNic CSli LLin LRHS MOne NHol
- 'Cristata Aurea'	CKen
- 'Danica' ♀	CMac CSli EBrP EBre EHul ENot EOrn GKir IOrc LBCl LBSe LBre LCon LLin MAsh MBBe MBar MGos NWea SBod SBre SLim SMer SRms WCFE WFar WGwG WStI WWeb
- 'Dicksonii'	EHul
- 'Douglasii Aurea' (v)	CKen
- 'Ellwangeriana Aurea'	LBee MGos
- 'Emerald'	See *T. occidentalis* 'Smaragd'
- 'Ericoides'	CDoC CTri EHul LCon LRHS MAsh MBar SRms SSmi WStI
- 'Europa Gold'	CDoC EHul GKir IOrc LBee MAsh MBar MGos SLim WLRN
- 'Fastigiata'	CDul MBar
- 'Filiformis'	CKen EPla
- 'Froebelii'	Last listed 1997
- 'Globosa'	CBlo CMac MBar SBod WGor WGwG
I - 'Globosa Variegata'	CBlo CKen MBar
- 'Golden Gem'	Last listed 1997
- 'Golden Globe'	CBlo CDoC CSli EHul ENot EOrn LCon LNet LPan MBar MGos NBlu SBod SLim SPla WDin WLRN
- 'Golden Minaret'	EHul

	SBod SBre SLim SMer SPer SRms SSmi WCFE
- 'Sunshine'	CKen
* - 'Windsor Gold'	EHul
- 'Winter Pink' (v)	CBlo CKen
- 'Zebrina' (v)	CB&S CBrm CDoC CDul CMHG CMac CSli EHul EOrn GKir LCon LLin MAsh MBar MGos MWat NBee NEgg NWea SBod SLim SPer SRPl WCFE WFar WHar WWin
- 'Zebrina' Bedgebury form	Last listed 1999
standishii	WCwm

THUJOPSIS (Cupressaceae)

dolabrata ♀	CB&S CGre CTrG EHul GChr GKir IOrc LBee MBar MMHG NDlv NWea SPer WBrE WCwm WFar WTro WWat
- 'Aurea' (v)	CDoC CKen EHul EOrn LCon LLin MBar MGos SLim
- 'Laetevirens'	See *T. dolabrata* 'Nana'
§ - 'Nana'	CDoC CKen CMac EGra EHul EOrn LCon LLin MBar SLim SLon SRms STre WFar
- 'Variegata' (v)	CDoC EHul EOrn LCon LLin MBar NDlv SHFr SLim WLRN
koraiensis	See *Thuja koraiensis*

THUNBERGIA (Acanthaceae)

alata	CPIN MBri SYvo
coccinea	CPIN LRHS SOWG
erecta	CPIN ELan ERea LChe LCns LRHS SOWG
- 'Alba'	Last listed 1998
fragrans	CPIN ERea LRHS SOWG
grandiflora ♀	CPIN ECon ELan EPfP ERea LChe LCns LRHS SOWG WMul
- 'Alba'	CPIN LChe WMul
gregorii	CPIN CSpe LChe LCns LRHS SOWG
laurifolia	CPIN
¶ 'Lemon Star'	CSpe
¶ 'Molly'	CPIN
mysorensis ♀	CPIN ECon ERea LCns LRHS SOWG WMul
natalensis	LChe
petersiana	Last listed 1999

THYMUS ✿ (Lamiaceae)

'Anderson's Gold'	See *T. pulegioides* 'Bertram Anderson'
azoricus	See *T. caespititius*
'Belle Orchard'	Last listed 1997
'Caborn Lilac Gem'	LLWP
§ *caespititius*	CArn CLyd EDAr ELau EPot GAbr GBar GPoy ILis LLWP MBro MHer NHex NMen NRya SPlb SRot SSmi WAbe WCHb WPer
caespitosus	EDAr GKir LLWP
campboratus	CArn CBod ELau EOHP EWes GBar LLWP MHer MWat NHex SHDw WAbe WJek
- 'Derry'	LLWP SHDw
carnosus Boiss.	GBar SSmi
- misapplied	See *T. vulgaris* 'Erectus'
'Carol Ann' (v)	CBod ELau EWes LLWP MBNS
cephalotos	CMea WAbe
ciliatus	CArn CMea LLWP WPer
cilicicus	EDAr EWes GCHN LBee LRHS MChe SBla WAbe WCHb WJek WWye

x *citriodorus*	CArn EDAr ELau GAbr GBar GCHN GPoy LGro LLWP MBrN MChe MHer MMal NHex NMen NOak SRms WHen WJek WOak WPer WWye
- 'Archer's Gold'	See *T. pulegioides* 'Archer's Gold'
- 'Argenteus' (v)	LLWP MBro
- 'Aureus'	See *T. pulegioides* 'Aureus'
- 'Bertram Anderson'	See *T. pulegioides* 'Bertram Anderson'
§ - 'Golden King' (v)	CLyd EBrP EBre ECha EDAr ELan LBCl LBSe LBre LHop LLWP LRHS MBBe MBar MBri MBro MChe MHer NHex NSti SAga SBre WCHb WHoo WLin WPer WSel WStI
§ - 'Golden Lemon' (v)	CArn GPoy LLWP WJek WWye
- 'Golden Lemon' misapplied	See *T. pulegioides* 'Aureus'
- 'Golden Queen' (v)	CLTr CMea EDAr EOHP EPot ESis GBar MHer MMal NFla NPri NSla SRms WRHF WWin
- 'Nyewoods' (v)	GAbr
- *repandus*	SIde
- 'Silver King' (v)	LLWP
- 'Silver Posie'	See *T. vulgaris* 'Silver Posie'
- 'Silver Queen' (v) ♀	CB&S CHar CLyd CSam ECha EDAr ELan EOHP GPoy LRHS MBar MBro MChe MHer NHex SPlb SSmi WHoo WPyg WStI
* - 'Variegatus'	LHop MBri MBro MChe NMen WEas WFar WOak WWin
- 'Variegatus' misapplied	See *T. x citriodorus* 'Golden King'
- 'Villa Nova' (v)	LLWP
'Coccineus' ♀	CArn ECha EDAr ELan ELau EMNN ESis GDra GKir GTou LGro LLWP LRHS MBar MBri MBro MChe MHer MWat NHol SBla SIng SRot WHen WHoo WOak WPat WWin
comosus	CFri EDAr LLWP MChe NTow WAbe WPat WPer
'Creeping Lemon'	EDAr ELau LLWP MHer
'Creeping Orange'	EDAr LLWP
'Dartmoor'	GCal LLWP SIng
'Desboro'	EOHP GAbr LLWP MBNS MHer NHex
doerfleri	CLyd ECha EOHP GBar LLWP SIde WSel
- 'Bressingham'	More than 30 suppliers
'Doone Valley' (v)	More than 30 suppliers
drucei	See *T. polytrichus* subsp. *britannicus*
'E.B. Anderson'	See *T. pulegioides* 'Bertram Anderson'
'Elf'	MTPN
'Emma's Pink'	LLWP NHex
erectus	See *T. vulgaris* 'Erectus'
* *ericoides*	MHer
'Fragrantissimus'	CArn ELau EOHP ESis GAbr GBar GPoy LLWP MChe MHer MWat NHex NPri SIde WHen WJek WOak WPer WWye
* 'Golden Icing'	Last listed 1998
'Hardstoft Red' (v)	GBar LLWP MChe
§ 'Hartington Silver' (v)	More than 30 suppliers
herba-barona	CArn CFri CNic CTri EBot ECha EDAr ELau EOHP ESis GBar GPoy LEdu LLWP MHer NFor NHex SIde SRms SSmi STre WOak WPer WWye
- *citrata*	See *T. herba-barona* 'Lemon-scented'

§ - 'Lemon-scented'   CArn ECha ELau GBar GPoy
                                LLWP MHer MOne NHex SHDw
                                SIde WCHb WGwG
'Highland Cream'   See T. 'Hartington Silver'
I *hirsutus minus*   Last listed 1998
   hyemalis   LLWP
   integer   SBla
   lanuginosus hort.   See T. *pseudolanuginosus*
§ 'Lavender Sea'   ELau EWes LLWP
'Lemon Caraway'   See T. *herba-barona* 'Lemon-
                                scented'
* 'Lemon Variegated'   EDAr ELau
   leucotrichus   ILis MBro WPat
'Lilac Time'   EWes LLWP MHer WCHb
   longicaulis   CArn CLyd ECha EGoo ELau
                                GBar LLWP MBNS NHex WJek
                                WWye
¶ *longiflorus*   IIve
   marschallianus   See T. *pannonicus*
   mastichina   CArn EBee GBar MChe SBla SChu
                                SMac SSca WWye
   - 'Didi'   CArn LLWP MHer NHex
   membranaceus   CLyd CPBP WAbe
   micans   See T. *caespititius*
   minus   See *Calamintha nepeta*
   montanus Waldst. & Kit.   See T. *pulegioides*
   neiceffii   CArn CLyd ECha EGoo ELau GBar
                                LLWP MHer NHex NMen NTow
* *nummularius*   ELau LGro SSca
   odoratissimus   See T. *pallasianus* subsp.
                                pallasianus
'Onyx'   NHex
   pallasianus   ELau LLWP
§ - subsp. *pallasianus*   CBod GBar MHer MNaF SIde
§ *pannonicus*   LLWP MHer NHex WPer
'Peter Davis'   CArn CBod CFri EDAr EOHP ESis
                                LHop LLWP MBNS MChe MHer
                                NHex SBla SChu SIde SIng WJek
                                WRHF
§ 'Pink Ripple'   CBod ELau EWes LLWP MChe
                                MHer WCHb
'Pinkushion'   LLWP
§ *polytrichus*   CKin EEls EPot EWFC GPoy LLWP
   subsp. *britannicus*   MHew NSti WJek WPer
   - - 'Minor'   EPot LLWP MHer SIde WPer
§ - - 'Thomas's White' ♀   LLWP MHer
   - - variegated   WLin
'Porlock'   CMea CSev EDAr ELau ESis GBar
                                GPoy LLWP MChe MHer NHex
                                SIde SRms STre WHoo WJek
                                WOak WPer WPyg
   praecox   GBar LLWP MHer NLan NMir
   - subsp. *arcticus*   See T. *polytrichus* subsp.
                                britannicus
'Provence'   LLWP
§ *pseudolanuginosus*   More than 30 suppliers
   - 'Hall's Variety'   CHal ELau
§ *pulegioides*   CArn CBod ELau GBar GPoy
                                LLWP MBri MHer MMal NHex
                                NPri SHDw SIde WGwG WJek
                                WOak WPer WWye
§ - 'Archer's Gold'   More than 30 suppliers
§ - 'Aureus' ♀   EBrP EBre EDAr EMNN GBar
                                GDra GTou LBCl LBSe LBre LLWP
                                LRHS MBBe MBar MBri MBro
                                MHer MMal NFla NMen NWCA
                                SBla SBre SPlb SRms WHen WHoo
                                WPyg
§ - 'Bertram Anderson' ♀   More than 30 suppliers
   - 'Foxley' (v)   CBod ELau LLWP MChe SPlb
                                WCHb WJek WWpP
¶ - 'Golden Dwarf'   LLWP

§ - 'Goldentime'   EDAr GBar GKir LGro LLWP LRHS
                                MChe MHer WJek WSel
   - 'Sir John Lawes'   LLWP
¶ - 'Tabor'   WJek
¶ - variegated   GBar
'Redstart'   CBod CLyd ELau EOHP GBar LBee
                                LLWP LRHS MChe WCHb WOak
   richardii subsp. *nitidus* MHer STre WWye
   - subsp. *nitidus*   See T. *vulgaris* 'Snow White'
   'Compactus Albus'
¶ 'Rosedrift'   LLWP
   rotundifolius   ELau LLWP MHer SIde
§ 'Ruby Glow'   CFri EBrP EBre ELau EWes LBCl
                                LBSe LBre LLWP MBBe MChe
                                NHex NWoo SBre WJek
   serpyllum   CArn ELau GAbr GCHN LLWP
                                MBri MChe MWat NOak SIde SIng
                                SPlb SRms WJek WPer
   - var. *albus*   CHal ECha ELau EMNN ENot ESis
                                GDra GPoy GTou LLWP MBro
                                MHar MMal NNrd NVic SBla SChu
                                SIde SRms WHoo WOak WWye
   - 'Albus Variegatus'   See T. 'Hartington Silver'
   - 'Annie Hall'   CHal EBrP EBre EDAr ELau EMNN
                                EPot GAbr GBar LBCl LBSe LBee
                                LBre LGro LLWP LRHS MBBe
                                MBro MChe MHer NFor NHex
                                SBre SIde SIng SSmi WPer WWye
* - 'Atropurpureus'   LLWP
* - *coccineus* 'Major'   CMea EDAr GDra GKir LRHS
                                MHer SIde WAbe WJek
* - - 'Minor'   EBrP EBre EDAr ELau GAri GTou
                                LBCl LBSe LBre LLWP MBBe
                                MChe MHer SBre SIde SRms
* - - x *zygis sylvestris*   Last listed 1997
   - 'East Lodge'   LLWP
   - 'Elfin'   CArn CLyd CMea EDAr EOHP ESis
                                EWes GTou LBee LRHS MBri
                                MBro MHar MHer NMen NNrd
                                SBla SIng SPlb WAbe WBea WHoo
                                LLWP NNrd
   - 'Flossy'   LLWP NNrd
   - 'Fulney Red'   EWes LLWP
   - 'Goldstream' (v)   CLyd CMea ELau EMNN ESis
                                GAbr GBar LBuc LHop LLWP
                                LRHS MBar MBri MChe MHer
                                NNrd NSti SIde SPlb SRms WByw
                                WCHb WPer
   - 'Iden'   SIde
   - subsp. *lanuginosus*   See T. *pseudolanuginosus*
   - 'Lavender Sea'   See T. 'Lavender Sea'
   - 'Lemon Curd'   CBod CBrm CFri ELau EOHP GAbr
                                GBar LLWP MChe MHer NSti SIde
                                WCHb WJek WRha WSel WWye
   - 'Minimus'   CArn CBrm CHal CLyd ECha ELau
                                ESis GAbr GBar LLWP LRHS MBri
                                MChe MHer MMal NSti NTow
                                SIde SRot WCHb WOak WPat
                                WPer WRHF WSel WWye
§ - 'Minor'   CArn EMNN GBar GDra LBee
                                MBro MChe NHol NMen NSla
                                SBla SIde SIng SSmi WAbe WGwG
                                WHoo WLin WPyg WWin
* - 'Minor Albus'   GBar
   - 'Minus'   See T. *serpyllum* 'Minor'
   - 'Petite'   EOHP EWes LLWP
   - 'Pink Chintz' ♀   More than 30 suppliers
   - 'Pink Ripple'   See T. 'Pink Ripple'
   - subsp. *pulchellus*   LLWP
¶ - 'Purpurteppich'   LLWP
   - 'Rainbow Falls' (v)   CBod CFri EWes GAbr GBar LLWP
                                MChe MHer NCat NHex SHDw
                                SIde WBry

- 'Roseus'	EOHP SIde WOak
- 'Ruby Glow'	See *T.* 'Ruby Glow'
- 'Russetings'	CHal CLyd EDAr ELau EMNN
	EPot GBar LLWP MBar MBro
	MChe MHer NHex NHol NMen
	SIde SRms WOak WWin WWye
- 'September'	LLWP MHer
- 'Snowdrift'	CArn CHal CMea EDAr EGar
	ELau GBar LEdu MBar MBro
	MChe NHex NHol NSti SIde
	SSmi WAbe WJek WPat WPer
	WRHF
- 'Splendens'	GMaP LLWP
- 'Variegatus'	See *T.* 'Hartington Silver'
- 'Vey'	EWes GBar LLWP MChe MHer
	NHex SIng SSmi SUsu WCHb
sibthorpii	CArn
N 'Silver Posie'	See *T. vulgaris* 'Silver Posie'
sp. from Turkey	EWes LLWP
* *taeniensis*	CArn
* *valesiacus*	LLWP
§ *villosus*	Last listed 1998
vulgaris	CArn CChe CSam CSev ECha
	EDAr ELau GPoy LLWP LRHS
	MBar MBri MChe MHer MMal
	NFla NHex NVic SDix SPlb WJek
	WOak WPer
- *albus*	GBar LLWP NHex SIde WHen
- 'Aureus' hort.	See *T. pulegioides* 'Goldentime'
* - 'Compactus'	LLWP
- 'Dorcas White'	LLWP WPer
- 'English Winter'	Last listed 1998
§ - 'Erectus'	CArn CLyd GBar LLWP MHer
	NTow WEas WPer WWye
- French	ELau LLWP MHer
- 'French Summer'	SIde
- 'German Winter'	CArn
- 'Golden Pins'	CArn EGar GBar SBla
- 'Lemon Queen'	ELau
- 'Lucy'	EOHP GBar LLWP SIde WJek
- 'Pinewood'	GPoy LLWP MHer
- pink	LLWP
- 'Silver Pearl' (v)	EWes LLWP
§ - 'Silver Posie'	More than 30 suppliers
§ - 'Snow White'	ELau EWes LLWP NBus SHDw
	WJek
'Widecombe' (v)	LLWP
zygis	CArn

TIARELLA (Saxifragaceae)

¶ 'Black Ruby'	CHid
'Bronze Baby'	SCob
collina	See *T. wherryi*
cordifolia ♀	More than 30 suppliers
- 'Eco Red Heart'	Last listed 1998
- 'Glossy'	EBee GBuc GCal NDov SSpi WCot
	WPGP
- 'Oakleaf'	CLAP EBee EMan GCal NSti
	NWoo WPnP
- 'Rosalie'	See x *Heucherella alba* 'Rosalie'
- 'Running Tapestry'	CLAP WPnP WPrP
- 'Slick Rock'	EBee ECha EPPr
'Cygnet'	WCot
'Dark Eyes'	NCat WCot WHil
'Dark Star'	WCot
'Elizabeth Oliver'	CLAP WPnP WPrP
'Filigree Lace'	Last listed 1999
'Freckles'	WCot
'Inkblot'	WCot
* 'Laciniate Runner'	CLAP
'Martha Oliver'	CLAP EBee WAbe WCot WHal
	WPGP WPnP WTin

'Mint Chocolate'	CLAP EMan GBin LAst LRHS MBri
	MLLN MMil MTis NDov NPSI NSti
	SAsh WCot WFar WWhi
§ 'Ninja'	More than 30 suppliers
'Pinwheel'	EBee EBrP EBre LBCl LBSe LBre
	MBBe MRav NCat SBre WCot
polyphylla	EBee EPPr EPar GAbr GBin GMac
	LGro MLLN MRav MWrn NFla
	NOrc NSti SMac WBea WCru
	WFar WWhi WWye
- 'Filigran'	NLar SCob
- 'Moorgrün'	GCal MBel WWat
- pink	CGle CLAP CLTr EBee EPPr EPar
	MBel NDov
'Skeleton Key'	WCot
'Tiger Stripe'	CHid CLAP COtt EBee EMan EPfP
	LRHS NCut SCob SPer WCot
trifoliata	EBee ELan MRav NVic SBla WFar
- 'Incarnadine'	Last listed 1998
unifoliata	CMCo NCat
I 'Vivid Selection'	WTin
§ *wherryi* ♀	More than 30 suppliers
- 'Bronze Beauty'	CBos CLAP CMea COtt CPlt CRDP
	EBee ECha EMan EPar GBuc GCHN
	LAst MCLN MChl MRav NPro SAga
	SCob SUsu SWat WAbe WCot WFar
	WLin WPGP WPnP WWhi
- fig-leaved	Last listed 1999
- 'George Schenk'	Last listed 1999
¶ - 'Green Velvet'	WCDu
- 'Montrose'	CLAP EBee WPGP
- 'Pink Foam'	Last listed 1998

TIBOUCHINA (Melastomataceae)

grandifolia	LHil
granulosa	Last listed 1997
graveolens	ERea
* *holosericea* 'Elsa'	ERea
'Jules'	ECon ERea LChe
laxa 'Noelene'	Last listed 1998
* - 'Skylab'	Last listed 1997
organensis	CB&S ERea GQui LHil
paratropica	CLTr CPle CSev ERea LChe LHil
semidecandra hort.	See *T. urvilleana*
§ *urvilleana* ♀	CAbb CB&S CDoC CGre CHEx
	CRHN CSpe CTbh CWit EBak
	ECon ECre ELan ERea IOrc ISea
	LCns LHop LPan LRHS MTis SAPC
	SArc SLon SOWG SPer SRms SYvo
	WMul
- 'Edwardsii'	CSev LChe MLan NPSI
- 'Nana'	Last listed 1999

TIGRIDIA ♣ (Iridaceae)

hybrids	SDeJ
lutea	SDeJ
¶ *multiflora*	CFir
pavonia	CGre CMdw CPne EBot ERea
	GMac LAma LBow MBri NRog

TILIA ♣ (Tiliaceae)

americana	CLnd CMCN ENot LPan WMou
- 'Dentata'	Last listed 1998
- 'Fastigiata'	WMou
- 'Nova'	CDoC CTho
- 'Redmond'	CTho
amurensis	CMCN WMou
argentea	See *T. tomentosa*
begoniifolia	See *T. dasystyla*
'Chelsea Sentinel'	WMou
chenmoui	MBlu WMou
chinensis	CMCN WMou

chingiana	CMCN GKir SSta WMou
cordata ♀	CDul CKin CLnd EBee ECrN ELan
	ENot EWTr GChr GKir IOrc LBuc
	LHyr NBee NWea SPer WDin
	WMou WStl WWye
¶ - 'Böhlje'	CDul GChr SLPl
- 'Greenspire' ♀	CDoC CDul CLnd CTho EBee ENot
	IOrc LPan LRHS NBee WMou WOrn
- 'Len Parvin'	Last listed 1998
- 'Lico'	WMou
- 'Morden'	WMou
- 'Plymtree Gold'	CEnd CTho WMou
- 'Rancho'	Last listed 1998
- 'Roelvo'	Last listed 1998
- 'Swedish Upright'	CTho WMou
- 'Umbrella'	Last listed 1998
- 'Westonbirt Dainty Leaf'	WMou
- 'Winter Orange'	LRHS MBlu SBir WMou
§ *dasystyla*	CLnd MBlu WMou
- subsp. *caucasica*	WMou
x *euchlora* ♀	CDoC CDul CLnd EBee ECrN
	ENot EPfP GChr GKir LPan LRHS
	MBri MGos MWat NWea SPer SSta
	WDin WFar WMou WOrn
x *europaea*	CDul CLnd ELan NWea WMou
- 'Pallida'	CDul CTho WMou
- 'Pendula'	WMou
- 'Wratislaviensis' ♀	CBlo CDoC CDul CLnd CTho
	EPfP LBuc MBlu NWea SMad
	WMou
- 'Zwarte Linde'	Last listed 1998
x *flavescens* 'Glenleven'	Last listed 1998
§ 'Harold Hillier'	WMou
henryana	CDoC CDul CEnd CLnd CMCN
	CTho EBee EPfP ERod GKir LRHS
	MBlu SMad WMou
- var. *subglabra*	WMou WPGP
§ *heterophylla*	CTho WMou
- var. *michauxii*	CLnd SSta
'Hillieri'	See T. 'Harold Hillier'
insularis	MBlu WMou
intonsa	WMou
japonica	CMCN WMou
kiusiana	CMCN GKir WMou
koreana	WMou
laetevirens	SSta
ledebourii	WMou
mandshurica	CMCN
maximowicziana	SSta WMou WPGP
mexicana	WMou
miqueliana	CMCN WMou
'Moltkei'	CMCN WMou WPGP
mongolica ♀	CDoC CDul CLnd CMCN EBee
	ENot EPfP SMHT WMou
monticola	See T. *heterophylla*
neglecta	WMou
oliveri	CDul CMCN MBlu WMou WPGP
'Orbicularis'	WMou
paucicostata	Last listed 1998
'Petiolaris' ♀	CDoC CDul CEnd CLnd CMCN
	EBee ELan ENot EPfP EWTr IOrc
	LHyr LRHS MBri NBee NWea SPer
	SSta WDin WMou
platyphyllos	CDoC CDul CKin CMCN EMac
	ENot EPfP GChr GKir LBuc NWea
	SPer WDin WMou
- 'Aurea'	CDul CTho MAsh MBlu WMou
- 'Corallina'	See T. *platyphyllos* 'Rubra'
- 'Delft'	Last listed 1998
- 'Erecta'	See T. *platyphyllos* 'Fastigiata'
§ - 'Fastigiata'	CDul CTho EBee ENot SLPl
	WMou

- 'Grandiflora'	Last listed 1998
- 'Laciniata'	CEnd CMCN CTho GKir WMou
- 'Orebro'	SLPl
- 'Pannonia'	Last listed 1998
* - 'Pendula'	CTho
- 'Prince's Street'	WMou
§ - 'Rubra' ♀	CBlo CDoC CDul CLnd CTho
	EBee ECrN ENot EPfP GChr
	IOrc LBuc LHyr LRHS MBri
	MGos NBee NWea SLPl WFar
	WMou
- 'Tortuosa'	CBlo CDoC WMou
- 'Vitifolia'	WMou
taquetii	WMou
§ *tomentosa*	CAgr CDul CLnd CMCN CTho
	EBee ELan ENot GKir MNaF
	NWea SEND WDin WMou
- 'Brabant' ♀	CDoC ENot EPfP GChr IOrc NBee
	WMou
- 'Erecta'	Last listed 1998
- 'Silver Globe'	Last listed 1998
- 'Szeleste'	Last listed 1998
- 'Van Koolwijk'	MBlu
tuan	CMCN SSta WMou

TILLAEA See CRASSULA

TILLANDSIA (Bromeliaceae)

abdita	Last listed 1999
acostae	Last listed 1999
argentea	MBri
baileyi	Last listed 1999
balbisiana	Last listed 1999
brachycaulos	Last listed 1999
- var. *multiflora*	Last listed 1999
bulbosa	Last listed 1999
butzii	Last listed 1999
caput-medusae	Last listed 1999
circinnatoides	Last listed 1999
cyanea	LRHS MBri
x *erographica*	Last listed 1999
* *fasciculata* 'Tricolor' (v)	Last listed 1999
filifolia	Last listed 1999
flabellata	Last listed 1999
ionantha	Last listed 1999
- var. *scaposa*	See T. *kolbii*
juncea	Last listed 1999
§ *kolbii*	Last listed 1999
lindenii ♀	Last listed 1995
magnusiana	Last listed 1999
§ *matudae*	Last listed 1999
oaxacana	Last listed 1999
polystachia	Last listed 1999
punctulata	Last listed 1999
seleriana	Last listed 1999
sphaerocephala	Last listed 1999
tricolor var. *melanocrater*	Last listed 1999
usneoides	CHal SHmp
velickiana	See T. *matudae*
vicentina	Last listed 1999
wagneriana	Last listed 1999
xerographica	Last listed 1999

TITHONIA (Asteraceae)

rotundifolia 'Torch'	SMrm

TODEA (Osmundaceae)

barbara	Last listed 1999

TOFIELDIA (Melanthiaceae)

calyculata	NHol
pusilla	ERos

TOLMIEA (Saxifragaceae)

menziesii ♀	CGle ECha GAri LGro LRHS MBNS MBri MWgw NHol NOrc WByw
- 'Goldsplash'	See *T. menziesii* 'Taff's Gold'
- JLS 86284CLOR	Last listed 1998
- 'Maculata'	See *T. menziesii* 'Taff's Gold'
§ - 'Taff's Gold' (v) ♀	CGle CMHG CRow EBee ECha EHoe EMar EOHP EPar GMac MBri MHer NBid NFor NHol NMir NSti NVic SCob SHel SPlb WBea WByw WEas WHoo WOve WPyg WWye
- 'Variegata'	See *T. menziesii* 'Taff's Gold'

TOLPIS (Asteraceae)

barbata	Last listed 1997

TONESTUS (Asteraceae)

§ **lyallii**	CNic MHar WPer WWin

TOONA (Meliaceae)

§ **sinensis**	CHEx CMCN CTho EPfP GKir ISea SMac WPGP
- 'Flamingo' (v)	CB&S

TORENIA (Scrophulariaceae)

concolor formosana B&SWJ 124	WCru
¶ 'Summer Wave Large Blue'	CGdn
* 'Summerwave'	SCoo

TOVARA See PERSICARIA

TOWNSENDIA (Asteraceae)

condensata	Last listed 1998
exscapa	Last listed 1998
- NNS 93-74	Last listed 1999
florifera	Last listed 1999
formosa	CInt CMea NBir NMen NNrd WWin
hookeri	CGra NWCA
incana	CGra WLin
jonesii var. **tumulosa**	NTow
leptotes	CGra
mensana	NMen
montana	CGra
nuttallii	CGra NTow
parryi	Last listed 1998
§ **rothrockii**	CPBP NMen NWCA
sp. from California	CGra
spathulata	CGra
wilcoxiana hort.	See *T. rothrockii*

TOXICODENDRON (Anacardiaceae)

vernicifluum	See *Rhus verniciflua*

TRACHELIUM (Campanulaceae)

§ **asperuloides**	Last listed 1999
caeruleum ♀	CLTr EHol ERea WBrE WCot WFar
- 'Purple Umbrella'	CSam EMan
- 'White Umbrella'	CLTr EMan
jacquinii	Last listed 1997
- subsp. **rumelianum**	MBro NWCA WCot WHoo WPat WPyg

TRACHELOSPERMUM ✿ (Apocynaceae)

§ **asiaticum** ♀	More than 30 suppliers
* - 'Aureum'	LRHS
- 'Goshiki'	GQui MGos SPer SSpi
- var. **intermedium**	CFil WPGP
* **bodinieri** 'Cathayense'	GCal
jasminoides ♀	More than 30 suppliers
- 'Chamaeleon'	Last listed 1999
§ - 'Japonicum'	CRHN EPla GCal LRHS SBra SLPl SLon SSpi WWat
- 'Major'	CSPN CTrG SSpi
* - 'Oblanceolatum'	GCal
- 'Tricolor' (v)	CRHN ERav GCal LRHS SMur SSta
- 'Variegatum' ♀	More than 30 suppliers
- 'Waterwheel'	WWat
- 'Wilsonii' W 776	More than 30 suppliers
majus hort.	See *T. jasminoides* 'Japonicum'
- Nakai	See *T. asiaticum*
sp. from Nanking, China	Last listed 1998

TRACHYCARPUS (Arecaceae)

§ **fortunei** ♀	More than 30 suppliers
¶ - 'Nanus'	MGos
latisectus	CBrP EOas LPJP LPal WMul
martianus	LPJP LPal WMul
nanus	LPal
oreophilus	LPal
sikkimensis	Last listed 1999
takil	CRoM EOas EPVP LPJP LPal WMul
wagnerianus	CBrP EGln EOas EPVP LPJP LPal MWst SDry WMul WPGP

TRACHYSTEMON (Boraginaceae)

orientalis	CBre CGle CHEx CHid CRDP CSev EBee ECha EGol ELan EPar ERav MFir MRav MSCN NBid NPSI SCob SLon WByw WCru WFar WHer WWal WWat WWin WWye

TRADESCANTIA (Commelinaceae)

albiflora	See *T. fluminensis*
x **andersoniana** W. Ludwig & Rohw. nom. inval.	See *T. Andersoniana Group*
- 'Caerulea Plena'	See *T. virginiana* 'Caerulea Plena'
§ Andersoniana Group	CAgr MBro MFir MSal NFor WEas WPer WWin
¶ - 'Baby Doll'	GCHN
- 'Bilberry Ice'	CM&M CMGP CStr EBee EFou EMan EPla GKir LFis LRHS MBri MOne MWhi NBro NGdn NHaw NLar NTow SSpe WElm WHil WHoo WMaN WRus
- 'Blue and Gold'	EBee EBrP EBre EMan EPfP EPla LAst LBCl LBSe LBre LHop LRHS MBBe MBNS MBel MCAu MCLN MMHG NPro NSti SBre SPer SPla WCot WElm
- 'Blue Stone'	CMGP CMea ECha EFou NFai NPri NRya SRms WFar
¶ - 'Blushing Bride'	EFou
- Carmine Glow	See *T. (Andersoniana Group)* 'Karminglut'
- 'Charlotte'	CMGP EBee GCHN LCaP LRHS MAvo MGrG MOne NBro NGdn WHil
- 'Chedglow'	LHop SUsu WHil
- 'Concord Grape'	CFri EBrP EBre EFou EMan GKir LBCl LBSe LBre LFis LRHS MBBe MCAu MLLN MTed NSti SBre SUsu WHil WMaN WWhi
- 'Croftway Blue'	SCro
- 'Danielle'	WHil
- 'David's Blaby Blue'	MTed
- 'Domaine de Courson'	EBee LPio

- 'Double Grape' (d)	WCot
- 'Double Trouble' (d)	WCot
- 'Innocence'	More than 30 suppliers
- 'Iris Prichard'	CM&M CMGP EBee ELan EPar
	EPfP EPla GMaP LHop LRHS NLar
	NWoo SChu SCro SEas WPnP
	WWal
- 'Isis' ♀	CB&S CHar CMHG EBee ECtt
	EFou ELan EPar EPla GCHN GChr
	GGar LRHS MBel MRav MTis
	MWgw NFai NGdn NOrc SChu
	SPer SSoC WCer WCot WRus
	WWin
- 'J.C. Weguelin' ♀	CBlo EBee EMil EPfP GKir LCaP
	LRHS MBri NDlv NFai SRms
	WHoo WMaN WPnP WPyg
§ - 'Karminglut'	EBlw ELan EOld EPar EPfP GCHN
	GMaP LLWP MNrw NFla NHol
	NOrc NVic SVil WCer WHil WHoo
	WOve WRus WWye
- 'Leonora'	COIW ENot EPfP LRHS NCut NFai
	SRPl WPnP
- 'Little Doll'	CElw CFri EBee EFou EMan EWTr
	GKir LAst MAvo MChl MLLN
	MSph MTed SUsu WCot WMaN
	WWhi
¶ - 'Little White Doll'	WCot
- 'Osprey' ♀	More than 30 suppliers
- 'Pauline'	EBee ECtt EFou EMan EPla GCHN
	GGar GKir LRHS MBel MNrw
	MRav NBir NFai NLar SChu SMer
	WCer WHil WHoo WPyg WWal
	WWin
- 'Purewell Giant'	CTri EBee ECot NBro NCat NDlv
	SChu SPer WGor WKif WPyg
- 'Purple Dome'	CHar CMGP CRDP CStr EBee ECtt
	EFou EOld EPla GCHN GKir
	GMaP LRHS MRav NBir NCat NFai
	NGdn NMir SAga SPla WCer WPyg
	WWye
* - 'Red Grape'	EBrP EBre EFou GKir LBCl LBSe
	LBre MBBe SBre
- 'Rubra'	CMea EBee EPfP LFis MBel MOne
	MWgw NDea NDlv NFai NOrc
	NPri SChu SCro SLod SRPl SRms
	WBar WViv
- 'Valour'	CBlo EBee LRHS WHil WPnP
	WRHF
- 'Zwanenburg Blue'	CM&M CMGP ECha EFou EMan
	GCHN GKir LFis LRHS NBro NFai
	SEas WLow WWye
bracteata	NTow
- alba	SEas
brevicaulis	EBee ECha EFou EMFP EPar EPla
	ERos GBuc GDra LRHS MAvo
	MBel MTho NBro NLar
canaliculata	See *T. obiensis*
cerinthoides	CHal
- 'Variegata' ♀	Last listed 1995
fluminensis 'Albovittata'	CHal
- 'Aurea' ♀	CHal MBri
- 'Laekenensis' (v)	CHal MBri
- 'Maiden's Blush' (v)	CHal CSpe SVen WEas WFoF
- 'Quicksilver' (v) ♀	CHal MBri
- 'Rosea'	Last listed 1999
- 'Tricolor Minima' ♀	CHal
longipes	Last listed 1999
multiflora	See *Tripogandra multiflora*
navicularis	See *Callisia navicularis*
§ *obiensis*	EMan LPBA WPnP
§ *pallida*	CHal IBlr
- 'Purpurea' ♀	WCot

pendula	See *T. zebrina*
sillamontana ♀	CHal LChe MBri
spathacea	CHEx
- 'Vittata' ♀	CHal
'Tracey'	CM&M
tricolor	See *T. zebrina*
virginiana	CM&M MWhi SMrm
- 'Alba'	EWTr GCal WPer
§ - 'Caerulea Plena' (d)	CM&M CMGP EBee EFou ELan
	EMan EPla LRHS NHol NLar SChu
	SLod SRms WCot WFar WWal
- 'Rubra'	CM&M LAst NCut SPlb
* 'White Domino'	Last listed 1997
§ *zebrina* ♀	CHal
- *discolor*	CHal
- *pendula*	See *T. zebrina*
- 'Purpusii' ♀	CHal
- 'Quadricolor' (v) ♀	CHal

TRAGOPOGON (Asteraceae)

crocifolius	WCot
porrifolius	ILis
pratensis	CArn CKin CPou EWFC NMir

TRAPA (Trapaceae)

natans	Last listed 1999

TRAUTVETTERIA (Ranunculaceae)

carolinensis var. *japonica*	
	WCru
¶ - var. *occidentalis*	GKir

TRICHOCEREUS (Cactaceae)

pachanoi	ELau

TRICHOPETALUM (Anthericaceae)

§ *plumosum*	CBro

TRICHOPHORUM (Cyperaceae)

§ *cespitosum*	Last listed 1999

TRICHOSANTHES (Cucurbitaceae)

cucumerina	CPlN

TRICHOSTEMA (Lamiaceae)

lanatum	Last listed 1998

TRICUSPIDARIA See CRINODENDRON

TRICYRTIS ✿ (Convallariaceae)

'Adbane'	CLAP ELan EMan EWTr GKir LEur
	LRHS MBri MMHG NLar WCru
	WFar
affinis	GBuc LEur
- B&SWJ 2804	LEur WCru
- 'Variegata'	See *T.* 'Variegata' (*affinis* hybrid)
'Amanagowa'	CLAP WFar
bakeri	See *T. latifolia*
'Citronella'	Last listed 1997
dilatata	See *T. macropoda*
'Emily'	Last listed 1997
flava	WCru
formosana ♀	More than 30 suppliers
- B&SWJ 306	LEur WCot WCru WFar
- B&SWJ 355	LEur WCru WFar
¶ - B&SWJ 3635	WFar
- B&SWJ 3712	LEur WCru WFar
* - 'Dark Beauty'	EBee GSki LEur LRHS MBri MCLN
	SUsu WFar
- dark	LEur WFar
- 'Gates of Heaven'	LEur
- pale	LRHS WFar

- 'Samurai' (v)	LEur WCot
- 'Seiryu'	LEur WCot
- 'Shelley's'	CLAP GCal LEur NBro NTow
§ - Stolonifera Group	CAvo CB&S CBro CM&M CMHG EBee ELan EMan EMar EOld LEur LHop LRHS MRav NDea NFai SCro SPer WFar WPnP WWat WWin
- 'Variegata'	LEur MLLN WCru WFar
'Harlequin'	LEur
§ *birta*	More than 30 suppliers
§ - *alba*	CPea CSam EHrv ELan GBri LEur LRHS MBel MBro MRav NNrd WCru WFar WHil WWat WWin
* - 'Albomarginata'	EMar LEur
- B&SWJ 2827	WCru
- 'Golden Gleam' (v)	CBos CHea LEur WCot WFar
- hybrids	CM&M WCru WFar
- 'Kinkazan'	LEur WFar
- 'Makinoi Gold'	LEur WCru WFar
- var. *masamunei*	LEur WCru
- 'Matsukaze'	EBee LEur WFar
- 'Miyazaki'	CFir CHea CHid EFou EGar EGle ELan EMan EOld EPar GBuc LEur LRHS MBel MBro MHer NLar SCro WBea WCot WCru WFar
- 'Miyazaki Gold'	LEur
* - 'Nana'	ELan WFar
¶ - 'Taiwan Atrianne'	EWes
- 'Variegata'	CLAP CLon EFou EMan EMon EWes GBuc LEur SCob SMad SUsu WCot WCru WFar WHil WPnP
- 'White Flame' (v)	WCot
N Hototogisu	CBro CLAP CMea EBee EGle ELan EMan EMar EMon EOld EPar MTho SUsu WCot WCru WFar WHil
ishiiana	EBee LEur WCru WFar WPGP
- var. *surugensis*	LEur WCru WFar
Japanese hybrids	WHil
japonica	See *T. birta*
- 'Kinkazan'	WFar
'Kohaku'	CLAP LEur WCot WCru WFar WPGP
lasiocarpa B&SWJ 3635	WCru WFar
§ *latifolia*	CGle CHad EBee ELan EMar GGar GMaP LEur MBel MNrw NLar WCot WCru WFar WHil WPnP WWin
'Lemon Lime'	EBee LEur LRHS MLLN NPSI WCru WFar
'Lilac Towers'	EBee EBrP EBre EPar LBCl LBSe LBre LEur MBBe SBre WCru WFar WKif
macrantha	WWin
§ - subsp. *macranthopsis*	CLAP LEur WCot WCru WFar
macranthopsis	See *T. macrantha* subsp. *macranthopsis*
* *macrocarpa*	WFar
N *macropoda*	CGle CHid CLon CPea CSam EBee EGar ELan EMan EPar EPfP GBuc GMaP LEur LRot MGrG NBus WFar WWat
- B&SWJ 1271	LEur WCru
- variegated	WCru
maculata HWJCM 470	WCru
nana	LEur WCot WCru
obsumiensis	CGle CLAP ELan EMan EPot GBri LEur MTho SUsu WCot WCru WFar
perfoliata	LEur WCru WFar
'Shimone'	CHid CLAP ELan GBri GBuc LEur LRHS MBri WCru WFar WHil WKif

stolonifera	See *T. formosana* Stolonifera Group
¶ T&M hybrids	NArg
'Tojen'	CBro CLAP EBlw EGar ELan EOld EWes GBri GBuc GKir LEur LRHS MBri NBro SUsu WCru WFar
'Toki-no-mai'	LEur
'Tresahor White'	LEur
'Tresahor Yellow'	LEur
§ 'Variegata' (*affinis* hybrid)	GBri LEur WCru WFar
'White Towers'	CFee CHid CLAP EBee ECha EMan EPfP EWTr GKir GMac LEur LRHS MBel MBri MCAu NBus SCob WCru WFar WPnP WSan
'White Towers' spotted	ECha LEur SDys

TRIENTALIS (Primulaceae)

europaea rosea	CNat

TRIFOLIUM (Papilionaceae)

africanum	EBee
alpinum	GDra
arvense	EWFC
¶ *badium*	CInt
campestre	CKin
eximeum	Last listed 1999
incarnatum	MHer SIde WHer
macrocephalum	Last listed 1999
medium	Last listed 1997
nanum	CGra
ochroleucon	EWFC GBri GLil LBuc
pannonicum	EBee EMon EPPr GCal LGre MBel MLLN MSte SEND SMrm SOkh SUsu WCot WPGP WRus WSHC
pratense	EWFC MHer
- 'Dolly North'	See *T. pratense* 'Susan Smith'
- 'Ice Cool'	See *T. repens* 'Green Ice'
- 'Nina'	CBre WAlt WCHb
- 'Speech House' (v)	WAlt
- 'Sprite' (v)	Last listed 1998
§ - 'Susan Smith' (v)	CElw CRow EBee ECha EMan EMar EMon EWes IBlr LHop LRHS MCLN MHer MLLN MNrw MSCN MTho NFla NSti SIng WAlt WCHb WHer WHil WPic WRos
repens	COld EWFC EWTr NCat
- 'Arthur's Folly' (v)	WAlt
- 'Aureum'	Last listed 1999
- 'Douglas Dawson'	CNat
- 'Gold Net'	See *T. pratense* 'Susan Smith'
- 'Good Luck'	CRow MTho
§ - 'Green Ice'	CBre CInt CMea CRow CSev EBee EMan EMar LHop MTho NBir NSti WAlt WBea WByw WCHb WCot WHer WWye
- 'Harlequin' (v)	CBre EBee WAlt WBea WDyG WPer
- 'Hiccups' (v)	WAlt
¶ - 'Mrs Minnie Jones'	WHer
* - 'Pale Centre'	WAlt
- 'Pentaphyllum'	See *T. repens* 'Quinquefolium'
- 'Purp'	WAlt
- 'Purple Velvet'	EPPr
- 'Purpurascens'	CArn CBre CInt CRow GCal GDra GGar GMac ILis LNor LRHS MBNS MBel MHer NHlc NSti SSea WBea WHen WKif WMoo WOak WWhi
§ - 'Purpurascens Quadrifolium'	CNic ECha EDAr EMar EWes LAst MBel NBid NMir NNrd NPer SIde SIng SPer SPlb WAlt WCHb WFar WOve WPic WRHF WRus WWin WWye

- 'Quadrifolium'	EHoe EPar
§ - 'Quinquefolium'	WPer
- 'Shannel Pinnate'	Last listed 1998
- 'Tetraphyllum Purpureum'	See *T. repens* 'Purpurascens Quadrifolium'
* - 'Velvet and Baize' (v)	CNat
- 'Wheatfen'	CBre CPlt CRow EMan MTho NCat NPer SUsu WAlt WBea WCHb WCot WRHF
rubens	EBee ECGN EGoo EMan EMar EMon GBri LGre MAvo MMHG MSte SAga SMad SMrm SSca SSvw STes SUsu WBea WCot WHil WRus
- 'Peach Pink'	EMon EPPr LGre MAvo NCat STes SUsu WCot WRus WShe
subterraneum	EWFC
uniflorum	NWCA

TRIGONELLA (Papilionaceae)

foenum-graecum	CArn MSal SIde

TRIGONOTIS (Boraginaceae)

rotundifolia	EBee

TRILLIUM ✿ (Trilliaceae)

albidum	CBro GCrs GKir SSpi WCru
angustipetalum	CLAP
apetalon	LAma WCru
camschatcense	CAvo GCrs GKir LAma SSpi WCru
§ *catesbyi*	CBro EBee EPot GCrs LAma SSpi WCru
cernuum	CLAP EPot GCrs LAma WCru
chloropetalum	CBro CStu EBee EBrP EBre EPar GDra GKir LBCl LBSe LBre MBBe SBla SBre SSpi WAbb WCru
§ - var. *giganteum* ♀	SSpi
- var. *rubrum*	See *T. chloropetalum* var. *giganteum*
¶ - 'Volcano'	SSpi
- white	ECha
cuneatum	CBro EBee ECha ELan EPar EPfP EPot GAbr GGar ITim LAma LRHS MDun MTho NMen SCob SDeJ SPer SSpi WAbe WCru
¶ - x *luteum*	LEur
- red	GCrs
erectum ♀	More than 30 suppliers
§ - f. *albiflorum*	CBro CRDP EBrP EBre EPot GKir LAma LBCl LBSe LBre MBBe MSal SBre SSpi WCru
- 'Beige'	Last listed 1997
- f. *luteum*	GCrs LAma SSpi
flexipes	EPot GCrs GKir WCru
govanianum	LAma WCru
grandiflorum ♀	More than 30 suppliers
- 'Flore Pleno' (d) ♀	CBos EBrP EBre EPar GBuc GKir LBCl LBSe LBre MBBe NHar SBre
- 'Snowbunting' (d)	Last listed 1997
kurabayashii	CFil CLAP EPfP SSpi WPGP
§ *luteum* ♀	CB&S CBro CCuc CHid CLAP EBee EPar EPot EWTr GAbr GBuc GCrs GKir IMGH LAma LBow MDun NHar SCob SLod SPer SSpi WCru WFar
nivale	CGra GCrs
ovatum	GCrs GDra GNor LAma
- var. *hibbersonii*	CBro GBin GBuc GCrs GDra GMaP GNor NHar NMen NTow NBir
- 'Roy Elliott'	NBir
- 'Wayne Roberts'	Last listed 1997
parviflorum	GCrs SSpi

pusillum	EPot SSpi
- var. *pusillum*	GCrs NHar SBla
- var. *virginianum*	CBro LAma WCru
recurvatum	CB&S EBee EPar EPfP EPot GCrs GKir LAma NMen SPer WCru
rivale ♀	CBos CBro CElw CLAP GCrs LAma SBla SOkd WAbe
- 'Purple Heart'	Last listed 1997
rugelii	CLAP EPot GCrs GKir GMaP LAma SSpi WCru
¶ - x *vaseyi*	GCrs
sessile	CCuc CHid CLAP EBee EPot EWTr GBuc GKir IMGH LAma LBow MCCP NBir NHar NMen SCob SPer WCru WFar WLin WSHC WShi
- var. *luteum*	See *T. luteum*
- purple	Last listed 1999
smallii	LAma WCru
stylosum	See *T. catesbyi*
sulcatum	CAvo CBro CLAP EPar EPot GBuc GCrs GDra GKir MDun SSpi WCru
tschonoskii	LAma WCru
undulatum	EBee GCrs LAma WCru
vaseyi	CBro CLAP EPot GBuc GCrs GKir LAma SSpi WCru
viride	WCru WLin
viridescens	LAma

TRINIA (Apiaceae)

* *grandiflora*	Last listed 1997

TRIOSTEUM (Caprifoliaceae)

himalayanum	EBee
pinnatifidum	EMon WCot

TRIPETALEIA (Ericaceae)

§ *bracteata*	GKir

TRIPOGANDRA (Commelinaceae)

§ *multiflora*	CHal

TRIPTEROSPERMUM (Gentianaceae)

cordifolium B&SWJ 081	EBee WCru
japonicum B&SWJ 1168	WCru
lanceolatum B&SWJ 085	EBee WCru
taiwanense B&SWJ 1205	WCru

TRIPTERYGIUM (Celastraceae)

regelii	CFil CPlN WPGP
¶ *wilfordii*	CPlN

TRISETUM (Poaceae)

distichophyllum	EHoe
flavescens	CKin
¶ - 'Peter Hall' (v)	EPPr

TRISTAGMA (Alliaceae)

'Rolf Fiedler'	See *Ipheion* 'Rolf Fiedler'
uniflorum	See *Ipheion uniflorum*

TRISTANIA (Myrtaceae)

conferta	See *Lophostemon confertus*
laurina	See *Tristaniopsis laurina*

TRISTANIOPSIS (Myrtaceae)

§ *laurina*	CTrC

TRISTELLATEIA (Malpighiaceae)

australasiae	Last listed 1999

TRITELEIA (Alliaceae)

californica	See *Brodiaea californica*
§ 'Corrina'	CAvo EBee MNrw WCot
grandiflora	Last listed 1999
¶ *hyacinthina*	EBee ERos ETub LAma LRHS WBea
ixioides	CMea EBee ERos
- subsp. *ixioides*	Last listed 1997
- var. *scabra*	Last listed 1997
- 'Splendens'	WCot
- 'Starlight'	CAvo EBee EPot WCDu WCot
§ *laxa*	CAvo CMea EBee ELan LAma NRog WCot
§ - 'Koningin Fabiola'	CFwr CTri EBee ETub LAma MBri NBir NRog WBea WCot
- PJC 951	Last listed 1997
- Queen Fabiola	See *T. laxa* 'Koningin Fabiola'
¶ - 'Sierra Giant'	WCot
§ *peduncularis*	EBee LAma WCot
x *tubergenii*	EBee LAma
uniflora	See *Ipheion uniflorum*

TRITHRINAX (Arecaceae)

acanthocoma	CRoM EPVP LPal
campestris	LPal

TRITOMA See KNIPHOFIA

TRITONIA (Iridaceae)

crispa	LBow
crocata	CPou LBow NRog WHer
- 'Baby Doll'	Last listed 1999
- 'Bridal Veil'	Last listed 1999
- *hyalina*	Last listed 1998
- 'Pink Sensation'	Last listed 1999
- 'Prince of Orange'	CPou
- 'Princess Beatrix'	EBee
§ *disticha*	CAvo CBro CElw CFil CPou CSam
subsp. *rubrolucens*	CSev EBee ECha EGra EMan GCHN GGar GMac LRHS MBel MBri STes SUsu WCot WGer WHil WLin WPGP WPen WRHF WWhi WWin
lineata	Last listed 1997
'Orange Delight'	Last listed 1998
rosea	See *T. disticha* subsp. *rubrolucens*
securigera	Last listed 1998
squalida	LBow

TROCHETIOPSIS (Sterculiaceae)

§ *ebenus*	Last listed 1999
melanoxylon hort.	See *T. ebenus*

TROCHOCARPA (Epacridaceae)

thymifolia	SReu WAbe

TROCHODENDRON (Trochodendraceae)

aralioides	CB&S CDoC CFil CGre CMCN CTho EBee EPfP LRHS MBlu MGos SAPC SArc SLon SPer SReu SSpi SSta WCot WCru WSHC WWat

TROLLIUS (Ranunculaceae)

acaulis	EBee EGle EPPr EWes GDra MTho SMrm WPat WPyg
asiaticus	CRDP GBuc GKir
§ *chinensis*	CGle EBee ECha GCal LSyl NChi SRms SWat WBar
- 'Golden Queen' ♀	More than 30 suppliers
- 'Imperial Orange'	CGle WWal WWin

'Cressida'	EBee
x *cultorum* 'Alabaster'	CBos CHea CLAP CLon CRDP CRow EBee ECha GBuc GKir MRav MTed NLar NPar WFar WPGP WSan WTin WViv
- 'Baudirektor Linne'	ECtt GCHN MRav WFar
- 'Bressingham hybrids'	EBrP EBre LBCl LBSe LBre MBBe SBre
- 'Bunce'	Last listed 1999
- 'Byrne's Giant'	WFar
- 'Canary Bird'	CHea ELan EMil GBri NFla SMur SRms WRus
- 'Cheddar'	COtt EBee EFou EGle EMan GBin LRHS MBri MCAu MRav MTis NBro NPro WCot WCra WHil
- 'Commander-in-chief'	EMan NHol
- 'Earliest of All'	CGle CSam EGle EWTr GKir LRHS MBri NGdn SPer SPla SRms WGor
- 'Etna'	EBee EGle GKir LRHS MBri
§ - 'Feuertroll'	CMGP ECha EMar LRHS MBNS MBri NCut NPro SMur
- Fireglobe	See *T.* x *cultorum* 'Feuertroll'
- 'Golden Cup'	ECot NGdn
- 'Golden Monarch'	CBlo EPar
- 'Goldquelle' ♀	EHon SMur
- 'Goliath'	CGle WFar
- 'Helios'	CGle CHea CSam ECha
- 'Lemon Queen'	EBee EMan EPar EPfP EWTr GCal GKir LRHS LSyl MBri NFor SCro SPer SWat WFar WPnP WRus WSpi WWin
- 'Maigold'	MBri
- new hybrids	WFar WHil
- 'Orange Crest'	GCal
- 'Orange Globe'	NLar NPri WHil
- 'Orange Princess' ♀	EBee ENot EPfP GCHN GKir LRHS LSyl MBel NBro NDea NHol SPer SRms WPnP
- 'Prichard's Giant'	EGle ELan NBro NHol WCot
- 'Salamander'	SMur
§ - 'Superbus' ♀	CM&M CMGP CMHG CRDP EBee EFou EGle ELan EPar EPfP MBNS MBri NHol SLon SPer SSpi WFar WPnP
- 'T. Smith'	EGle LBuc MTis NBro NCut WCot WHil
europaeus	CBot CRow EBee ECha EPot EWFC EWTr LHop LRHS LSyl MBro MHer MNrw NDea NMir NSti SAga SRms SRot SUsu SWat WFar WHil WHoo WPer WPyg
- 'Superbus'	See *T.* x *cultorum* 'Superbus'
hondoensis	EBee EBrP EBre EPPr GBin LBCl LBSe LBre MBBe NLar SBre WElm WSan
¶ *laxus*	EWes
ledebourii hort.	See *T. chinensis*
¶ *pulcher*	NTow
pumilus	CGle EBrP EBre ECha ELan LBCl LBSe LBee LBre LRHS MBBe MBro MHer NNrd NWCA SBre SIng SPer SUsu WFar WPer WViv
- ACE 1818	GBuc WCot
* - *albidus*	Last listed 1998
- 'Wargrave'	EPot NMen
riederianus	EBee EBrP EBre LBCl LBSe LBre MBBe SBre
stenopetalus	EBee ECha EWes
yunnanensis	CGle EBrP EBre GBuc GKir LBCl LBSe LBre MBBe NBid NSti NWoo SBre SMac

– CD&R 2097   WCru

TROPAEOLUM ✿ (Tropaeolaceae)

azureum   CPla
brachyceras   NLar WCot
ciliatum ♀   More than 30 suppliers
incisum   SOkd
majus   CHEx EMFW WSel
 – 'Alaska' (v)   CBod SIde WJek WSel
 – 'Apricot Trifle'   Last listed 1999
* – 'Clive Innes'   ERea
 – 'Crimson Beauty'   CSpe MLLN
§ – 'Darjeeling Double' (d)   CSpe LHil LRHS WCot WCru
 – 'Darjeeling Gold' (d)   See *T. majus* 'Darjeeling Double'
 – 'Darjeeling Red'   Last listed 1999
 – 'Empress of India'   LRHS WEas WJek
 – 'Forest Flame'   LRHS
 – 'Hermine Grashoff' (d) ♀   CMHG CSWP CSpe ECtt ERea
     LHil LHop LRHS MLLN NPer SLod
     WEas WLRN
 – 'Margaret Long' (d)   CSpe LHil LRHS MLLN WEas
     WLRN
* – 'Peaches and Cream'   WJek
 – 'Red Wonder'   CHad CSWP CSpe LHil LRHS NPri
 – Tom Thumb mixed   WJek
 – 'Variegatum'   Last listed 1997
¶ – 'Wina'   WJek
peltophorum   Last listed 1998
pentaphyllum   CAvo CFil CLAP ECha ELan GCal
     IBlr MTho WCot
peregrinum   LRHS
polyphyllum   CFil CLAP CPlN EBee ECha GBuc
     GCrs WCot WPGP WTre
sessilifolium   Last listed 1999
speciosum ♀   More than 30 suppliers
sylvestre   WCru
¶ *tricolor* ♀   CAvo CFil CLAP CPlN EBee EPot
     MTho WCot
tuberosum   CB&S CGle CMHG GPoy LRHS
     NPSI SAga
 – var. *lineamaculatum*   More than 30 suppliers
   'Ken Aslet' ♀
 – P.J. Christian's form   Last listed 1998
 – var. *piliferum* 'Sidney'   CFil CGle IBlr IHdy WCru WPGP

TSUGA (Pinaceae)

canadensis   EHul GAri LCon LPan MBar NWea
     WDin
¶ – 'Abbott's Dwarf'   CKen MGos
§ – 'Abbott's Pygmy'   CKen
 – 'Albospica' (v)   EOrn LCon LRHS WGor
 – 'Aurea' (v)   LCon MBar WAbe
 – 'Baldwin Dwarf Pyramid'   MBar
 – 'Bennett'   EHul MBar
¶ – 'Betty Rose' (v)   CKen
 – 'Brandley'   CKen
§ – 'Branklyn'   CKen WBcn
 – 'Cinnamonea'   CKen
 – 'Coffin'   CKen
 – 'Cole's Prostrate'   CKen EOrn LCon LLin MAsh
     MBar NHol NLar
¶ – 'Creamcy' (v)   CKen
 – 'Curley'   CKen
 – 'Curtis Ideal'   CKen
 – 'Dwarf Whitetip'   LCon
* – 'Everitt's Dense Leaf'   CKen
¶ – 'Everitt's Golden'   CKen
 – 'Fantana'   CDoC EHul LBee LCon LLin LRHS
     MAsh MBar SBod SLim WAbe
     WLRN
 – 'Gentsch White' (v)   MGos
 – 'Golden Splendor'   Last listed 1997

 – 'Greenwood Lake'   Last listed 1998
 – 'Horsford'   CKen
 – 'Hussii'   CKen
 – 'Jacqueline Verkade'   CKen
 – 'Jeddeloh' ♀   CDoC CMac CSli EBrP EBre EHul
     ENot EOrn GChr GKir IMGH
     LBCl LBSe LBre LCon LLin LRHS
     MAsh MBBe MBar MBri MGos
     NBee SBre SLim WPyg WStI WWat
 – 'Jervis'   CKen LCon
¶ – 'Julianne'   CKen
 – 'Kingsville Spreader'   CKen
I – 'Lutea'   CKen
¶ – 'Many Cones'   CKen
 – 'Minima'   CKen
 – 'Minuta'   CDoC CKen EHul EOrn LBee
     LCon LLin LRHS MAsh MBar
     MGos SLon
 – 'Nana'   CMac EHul IOrc WLRN
 – 'Palomino'   CDoC CKen MBar
 – 'Pendula' ♀   CDoC CKen EHul ENot EOrn
     LBee LCon LRHS MBar MBri
     MOne NHol SLim WCwm WDin
 – 'Pincushion'   CKen
 – 'Prostrata'   See *T. canadensis* 'Branklyn'
 – 'Pygmaea'   See *T. canadensis* 'Abbott's
     Pygmy'
¶ – 'Rugg's Washington   CKen
   Dwarf'
¶ – 'Snowflake'   CKen EPla MGos
¶ – 'Stewart's Gem'   CKen
 – 'Verkade Petite'   CKen
 – 'Verkade Recurved'   CKen LCon MBar WBcn
¶ – 'Von Helms' Dwarf'   CKen
 – 'Warnham'   CKen ECho EOrn LBee LCon
     LRHS MAsh MBri
caroliniana   CKen
 'La Bar Weeping'
diversifolia   Last listed 1999
 – 'Gotelli'   CKen
heterophylla ♀   CDul ENot GAri GChr GKir IOrc
     LBuc LCon LRHS MBar NWea
     SMad SPer STre WDin
 – 'Iron Springs'   CKen EOrn
 – 'Laursen's Column'   CKen
menziesii   See *Pseudotsuga menziesii*
mertensiana   WCwm
 – 'Blue Star'   CKen MAsh MGos
 – 'Elizabeth'   CKen
I – 'Glauca Nana'   CKen
 – 'Quartz Mountain'   CKen
sieboldii 'Nana'   CKen

TSUSIOPHYLLUM (Ericaceae)

tanakae   See *Rhododendron*
     tsusiophyllum

TUBERARIA (Cistaceae)

guttata   WCru
lignosa   CInt CMHG NLAp NMen SGar
     SSpi WAbe

TULBAGHIA ✿ (Alliaceae)

acutiloba   CAvo EBee ERos
alliacea   CAvo CFee ERos WCot
capensis   CFee LGre LHil
cepacea   LHil NBir
§ – var. *maritima*   ERos WCot
coddii   CAvo CFee LGre
 – × *violacea*   CPne
cominsii   EBee LGre
 – × *violacea*   CAvo ERos LHil

dregeana	Last listed 1999
'Fairy Star'	ERos WCot
fragrans	See *T. simmleri*
fragrantissima	WCot
galpinii	EBee ERos WCDu WCot
- 'John Rider'	CAbb
* 'John May's Special'	WCot
'John Rider'	WPer
leucantha	CAvo EBee ERos LHil SAga
ludwigiana	EBee WCot
maritima	See *T. cepacea* var. *maritima*
¶ Marwood seedling	MTPN
natalensis	CAvo CPou EBee LGre
- pink	WCot
§ *simmleri*	CAvo EBee EWes LAma LHil LPio
	MSph WCot
violacea	CB&S CBro CMHG CPea CPou
	CSev EBee ECha EHrv ERav ETub
	IBlr LAma LHil LPan MTho SBea
	SCob SMrm SSpi SWat WCFE
	WCot WPGP
* - 'Alba'	CPea LPio WFar
- *pallida*	CAvo CPou CRDP LGre LHil SLod
	SMrm WCot
§ - 'Silver Lace' (v)	CAvo CBos CBro CFee CFri CGle
	CRDP CSWP CSpe EBee ELan
	EMon ERav ERea EWes LGre LPio
	MTho NBir SAga SCob SSpi SUsu
	WCot WFar WPGP
- *tricolor*	Last listed 1998
- 'Variegata'	See *T. violacea* 'Silver Lace'

TULIPA ✿ (Liliaceae)

'Abba' (2)	NRog
'Abu Hassan' (3)	LAma
acuminata (15)	CBro EBot LRHS
'Ad Rem' (4)	LAma NRog
'Addis' (14) ♀	LAma
'African Queen' (3)	LAma
aitchisonii	See *T. clusiana*
'Aladdin' (6)	EWal LAma LRHS NRog
'Alaska' (6)	Last listed 1999
albertii (15)	EBot LAma
'Albino' (3)	LAma
aleppensis (15)	LAma
'Aleppo' (7)	Last listed 1999
'Alfred Cortot' (12) ♀	LAma
'Ali Baba' (14) ♀	MBri
'Alice Leclercq' (2)	Last listed 1999
'All Bright' (5)	Last listed 1999
'Allegretto' (11)	LAma NRog
altaica (15) ♀	EPot LAma
amabilis PF 8955	See *T. hoogiana* PF 8955
'Ancilla' (12) ♀	CBro LAma NRog
'Angélique' (11) ♀	CAvo ETub EWal LAma LRHS
	MBri NBir NRog
anisophylla (15)	Last listed 1998
'Anne Claire' (3)	LAma
'Antwerp' (3)	Last listed 1999
'Apeldoorn' (4)	ETub EWal LAma LRHS MBri
	NRog
'Apeldoorn's Elite' (4) ♀	EWal LAma LRHS NRog
'Apricot Beauty' (1) ♀	CAvo CHid ETub EWal LAma
	LRHS MBri NBir NRog
'Apricot Jewel'	See *T. linifolia* (Batalinii Group)
	'Apricot Jewel'
'Apricot Parrot' (10) ♀	LAma NRog
'Arabian Mystery' (3)	CAvo LAma NBir
'Aristocrat' (5) ♀	LAma
'Arma' (7) ♀	Last listed 1999
'Artist' (8) ♀	CAvo LAma NBir
'Astarte' (3) ♀	Last listed 1991

'Athleet' (3)	LAma LRHS
'Attila' (3)	ETub LAma LRHS NRog
aucheriana (15) ♀	CBro EPot ERos LAma LBow
	LRHS
'Aurea'	See *T. greigii* 'Aurea'
'Aureola' (5)	Last listed 1999
australis (15)	EBot
'Baby Doll' (2) ♀	Last listed 1991
bakeri	See *T. saxatilis* Bakeri Group
'Balalaika' (5)	Last listed 1998
'Ballade' (6) ♀	LAma NRog
'Ballerina' (6) ♀	CAvo LAma
batalinii	See *T. linifolia* Batalinii Group
'Beauty of Apeldoorn' (4)	LAma NRog
Beauty Queen (1)	NRog
'Belcanto' (3)	Last listed 1999
'Bellflower' (7)	LAma
'Bellona' (3)	LAma NRog
'Berlioz' (12)	LAma
'Bestseller' (1)	NRog
biebersteiniana (15)	LAma
§ *biflora* (15)	CBro EBot LAma LRHS NRog
· *bifloriformis* (15)	LRHS
'Big Chief' (4) ♀	LAma MBri NRog
'Bing Crosby' (3)	ETub LAma
'Black Diamond' (5) ♀	Last listed 1991
'Black Parrot' (10) ♀	CAvo ETub LAma LRHS NRog
'Black Swan' (5)	LBmB
'Blenda' (3)	ETub
'Bleu Aimable' (5)	CAvo ETub LAma LRHS
'Blue Heron' (7) ♀	LAma NRog
'Blue Parrot' (10)	CSWP ETub EWal LAma LRHS
	NRog
¶ 'Blue Ribbon' (3)	CAvo
'Blushing Beauty' (5)	LBmB
'Blushing Bride' (5)	LBmB
'Blushing Lady' (5)	LAma
'Bonanza' (11)	LAma LRHS
'Boule de Neige' (2)	LAma
'Bravissimo' (2)	MBri
'Brilliant Star' (1)	LAma LRHS MBri NRog
'Burgundy' (6)	ETub LAma
'Burgundy Lace' (7)	LAma LRHS NRog
'Burns' (7)	LAma
butkovii (15)	LAma
I 'Calypso' (14) ♀	ETub
'Candela' (13) ♀	LAma NRog
¶ 'Candy Club' (5)	LBmB
'Cantata' (13)	CBro LAma
'Cantor' (5)	LAma
¶ 'Cap d'Or' (14)	LBmB
'Cape Cod' (14)	LAma LRHS NRog
'Capri' (4) ♀	Last listed 1995
'Caprice' (10)	LAma
'Captain Fryatt' (6)	Last listed 1999
carinata (15)	LAma
'Carlton' (2)	LAma NRog
'Carnaval de Nice' (11/v) ♀	ETub LAma MBri NRog
'Cassini' (3)	LAma
§ *celsiana* (15)	EBot LAma LRHS
'César Franck' (12)	LAma
'Charles' (3)	LAma NRog
'China Lady' (14) ♀	Last listed 1991
'China Pink' (6) ♀	CAvo CMea ETub LAma NRog
'Chopin' (12)	LAma LRHS NRog
'Christmas Dream' (1)	NRog
'Christmas Marvel' (1)	ETub LAma LRHS NRog
chrysantha Boiss.	See *T. montana*
- Boiss. ex Baker	See *T. clusiana* var. *chrysantha*
'Clara Butt' (5)	LAma NRog
§ *clusiana* (15)	CBro LAma
§ - var. *chrysantha* (15) ♀	CAvo LAma LBow LRHS NRog

– – 'Tubergen's Gem' (15)	CSWP LAma LRHS MBri
– 'Cynthia' (15) ♀	CAvo CSWP EPot LAma LRHS NRog
§ – var. *stellata* (15)	LAma
¶ 'Colour Spectacle' PBR (5)	LBmB
'Concerto' (13)	CBro ETub LAma
'Cordell Hull' (5)	NRog
'Corona' (12)	ETub LAma NRog
'Corsage' (14) ♀	LAma
'Couleur Cardinal' (3)	EBot ETub EWal LAma NRog
cretica (15)	Last listed 1998
'Crystal Beauty' (7) ♀	NRog
'Dancing Show' (8)	CAvo CMea LAma
dasystemon (15)	LAma
'Daydream' (4) ♀	LBmB
'Daylight' (12)	NRog
'Demeter' (3) ♀	Last listed 1989
'Diana' (1)	LAma NRog
'Diantha' (14)	Last listed 1999
didieri	See *T. passeriniana*
'Dillenburg' (5)	LAma
'Diplomate' (4)	NRog
'Dix' Favourite' (3)	Last listed 1999
'Doctor Plesman' (3)	LAma
'Doll's Minuet' (8)	LAma
'Don Quichotte' (3) ♀	LAma
'Donna Bella' (14) ♀	LAma
'Douglas Bader' (5)	CAvo LAma LRHS NRog
'Dover' (4) ♀	Last listed 1995
'Dreaming Maid' (3)	LAma
'Dreamland' (5) ♀	NRog
'Dutch Gold' (3)	LAma
'Dyanito' (6)	EWal NRog
'Early Harvest' (12) ♀	LAma NRog
'Easter Parade' (13)	EWal LAma
'Easter Surprise' (14) ♀	LAma
§ *edulis* (15)	LAma LRHS
eichleri	See *T. undulatifolia*
'Electra' (5)	EWal LAma MBri NRog
'Elegant Lady' (6)	ETub
'Elizabeth Arden' (4)	NRog
'Elmus' (5)	Last listed 1998
'Engadin' (14) ♀	Last listed 1995
¶ 'Erfurt' (11)	LBmB
'Esperanto' (8/v) ♀	LAma NRog
'Estella Rijnveld' (10)	ETub LAma LRHS NBir NRog
'Etude' (3) ♀	Last listed 1994
'Fair Lady' (12)	LAma
'Fancy Frills' (7) ♀	LAma
'Fantasy' (10) ♀	LAma LRHS
'Fashion' (12)	LAma NRog
ferganica (15)	LAma
'Feu Superbe' (13)	Last listed 1998
'Fidelio' (3) ♀	Last listed 1993
'Fire Queen' (3) ♀	Last listed 1991
'Fireside'	See *T.* 'Vlammenspel'
'First Lady' (3) ♀	LAma
'Flair' (1)	LAma NRog
'Flaming Parrot' (10)	LAma NRog
* 'Flowerdale'	CAvo
'Flying Dutchman' (5)	Last listed 1999
fosteriana (13)	GVer MBri
'Franz Léhar' (12)	LAma
'Frasquita' (5)	Last listed 1998
'Fresco' (14)	LAma
Fringed Group (7)	Last listed 1999
'Fringed Apeldoorn' (7)	NRog
'Fringed Beauty' (7) ♀	ETub MBri
'Fringed Elegance' (7) ♀	LAma
'Fritz Kreisler' (12)	LAma LRHS
'Fulgens' (6)	LAma
'Gaiety' (12)	LAma LRHS

'Galata' (13)	LAma
galatica (15)	LAma
'Garden Party' (3) ♀	LAma
¶ 'Gavota' (3)	LAma LBmB
'Generaal de Wet' (1)	ETub LAma MBri NRog
'General Eisenhower' (4)	LAma
'Georgette' (5)	EWal LAma MBri NRog
'Gerbrand Kieft' (11) ♀	NRog
'Giuseppe Verdi' (12)	EWal LAma LBow LRHS MBri NRog
'Glück' (12) ♀	EWal LAma NRog
'Gold Medal' (11)	LAma MBri
'Golden Age' (5)	LAma
'Golden Apeldoorn' (4)	EWal LAma LRHS MBri NRog
'Golden Artist' (8)	LAma MBri NRog
'Golden Emperor' (13)	LAma LRHS
'Golden Harvest' (5)	Last listed 1999
'Golden Melody' (3)	ETub LAma NRog
'Golden Oxford' (4)	LAma NRog
'Golden Parade' (4)	LAma NRog
'Golden Springtime' (4)	LAma
¶ 'Goldwest' (14)	ETub
'Gordon Cooper' (4)	EWal LAma NRog
'Goudstuk' (12)	LAma
'Grand Prix' (13)	LAma
'Green Eyes' (8)	LAma
'Green Spot' (8)	LRHS
¶ 'Green Wave' (10)	LBmB
greigii (14)	CBro LRHS
§ – 'Aurea' (14)	Last listed 1998
grengiolensis (15)	EPot LAma LRHS
'Greuze' (5)	LAma LRHS
'Grével' (3)	Last listed 1999
'Groenland' (8)	LAma NRog
'Gudoshnik' (4)	LAma NRog
hageri (15)	LAma
– 'Splendens' (15)	ETub LAma LRHS
'Halcro' (5) ♀	ETub LAma
'Hamilton' (7) ♀	LAma
'Hans Mayer' (4)	NRog
'Happy Family' (3)	LAma
¶ 'Happy Generation' (3)	LBmB
¶ 'Havran'	LAma
'Heart's Delight' (12)	CBro ETub EWal LAma LBow LRHS NRog
'Hibernia' (3)	Last listed 1999
'Hit Parade' (13)	LAma
'Hoangho' (2)	LAma NRog
'Hocus Pocus' (5)	LBmB
'Hollands Glorie' (4) ♀	LAma
'Hollywood' (8)	LAma NRog
hoogiana (15)	LAma
§ – PF 8955 (15)	Last listed 1998
§ *humilis* (15)	CAvo CBro EPar EPot ETub LAma LBow LRHS MBri WShi
– 'Eastern Star' (15)	LAma LRHS MBri
§ – 'Lilliput' (15)	CBro EPot LRHS
– 'Odalisque' (15)	EPot LAma LRHS
– 'Pallida' (15)	LRHS
– 'Persian Pearl' (15)	EPot LAma LRHS MBri NRog
§ – var. *pulchella* Albo caerulea Oculata Group (15)	EPot LAma
§ – Violacea Group (15)	CAvo CMea EPar ETub EWal LAma MBri
§ – – black base (15)	CBro LRHS
– – yellow base (15)	CBro LAma LBow LRHS
'Humming Bird' (8)	LAma NRog
'Hytuna' (11)	LAma NRog
'Ibis' (1)	LAma
¶ 'Ice Follies' (3)	LBmB
'Ile de France' (5)	LAma

'Inferno'	NBir
ingens (15)	LAma
'Inzell' (3)	ETub LAma
'Ivory Floradale' (4) ♀	LBmB
'Jacqueline' (6)	NRog
'Jeantine' (12) ♀	LRHS
'Jewel of Spring' (4) ♀	LAma
'Jimmy' (3)	NRog
'Jockey Cap' (14)	LAma
'Joffre' (1)	LAma MBri NRog
'Johann Strauss' (12)	CBro EWal LAma MBri NRog
'Johanna' (3)	Last listed 1998
'Juan' (13) ♀	LAma MBri
'Kansas' (3)	LAma
'Karel Doorman' (10)	LAma
'Kareol' (2)	NRog
kaufmanniana (12)	CAvo CBro EPot LBow NRog SRms
§ 'Kees Nelis' (3)	LAma MBri NRog
'Keizerskroon' (1) ♀	EBot EWal LAma NRog
'Kingsblood' (5) ♀	Last listed 1999
'Kleurenpracht'	See *T.* 'Princess Margaret Rose'
kolpakowskiana (15) ♀	LAma LRHS MBri NRog
§ 'Koningin Wilhelmina' (4) ♀	Last listed 1993
kurdica (15)	LAma LRHS
'La Tulipe Noire' (5)	LAma
* 'Lady Diana' (14)	MBri
lanata (15)	Last listed 1999
'Landseadel's Supreme' (5) ♀	Last listed 1997
'Large Copper' (14)	Last listed 1998
'Leen van der Mark' (3)	LAma
'Lefeber's Favourite' (4)	LAma
¶ 'Libretto Parrot' (10)	LAma
'Lilac Perfection' (11)	LBmB
'Lilac Time' (6)	LAma
'Lilac Wonder'	See *T. saxatilis* (Bakeri Group) 'Lilac Wonder'
'Lilliput'	See *T. humilis* 'Lilliput'
linifolia (15) ♀	CAvo EPar EPot ETub LAma LBow LRHS NRog
§ - Batalinii Group (15) ♀	CBro LAma NRog
§ - - 'Apricot Jewel' (15)	CAvo CBro
- - 'Bright Gem' (15) ♀	CAvo CBro EPot LAma LBow LRHS MBro NRog WHoo WPyg
- - 'Bronze Charm' (15)	CAvo CBro CMea EPot LAma
- - 'Red Gem' (15)	CBro LAma
- - 'Red Jewel' (15)	Last listed 1998
- - 'Yellow Jewel' (15)	EPot LAma
§ - Maximowiczii Group	CBro EPot LAma LBow
'London' (4)	LAma
'Longfellow' (14) ♀	Last listed 1994
'Love Song' (12)	Last listed 1997
¶ 'Lovely Surprise' (14)	ETub
'Lucifer' (5)	EWal
'Lucky Strike' (3)	LAma
§ 'Lustige Witwe' (3)	EWal LAma LRHS
¶ 'Lydia' (3)	LAma
§ 'Madame Lefeber' (13)	CBro EWal LBow LRHS MBri NRog
'Madame Spoor' (3)	Last listed 1997
'Magier' (5)	LAma
'Maja' (7)	LAma
¶ 'Make-Up' (3)	LBmB
'Mamasa' (5)	LAma
'March of Time' (14)	MBri
'Maréchal Niel' (2)	LAma
'Mariette' (6)	LAma LRHS
'Marilyn' (6)	ETub LAma LRHS NRog
'Marjolein' (6) ♀	NRog
marjolletii (15)	CBro LAma NRog
'Mary Ann' (14)	LAma
'Maureen' (5) ♀	ETub LAma
mauritiana (15)	LAma
maximowiczii	See *T. linifolia* Maximowiczii Group
'Maytime' (6)	LAma NRog
'Maywonder' (11) ♀	LAma
'Meissner Porzellan' (3)	LBmB
'Melody d'Amour' (5)	Last listed 1998
'Menton' (5)	ETub
'Merry Christmas' (1)	NRog
Merry Widow	See *T.* 'Lustige Witwe'
'Mickey Mouse' (1)	NRog
'Minerva' (3)	NRog
'Mirella' (3) ♀	Last listed 1993
'Miss Holland' (3)	MBri
'Mona Lisa' (6)	LAma NRog
¶ 'Monsella' (2)	LBmB
§ **montana** (15)	CBro EPot LAma LRHS
'Monte Carlo' (2) ♀	EWal LAma LRHS NRog
'Moonshine' (6)	NRog
'Most Miles' (3) ♀	Last listed 1994
'Mount Tacoma' (11)	CAvo ETub EWal LAma MBri NRog
'Mr Van der Hoef' (2)	LAma MBri NRog
'Mrs John T. Scheepers' (5) ♀	Last listed 1996
'Murillo' (2)	LAma
'Musical' (3) ♀	Last listed 1989
'My Lady' (4) ♀	LAma
'Negrita' (3)	LAma
neustruevae (15)	CBro EPot ETub
'New Design' (3/v)	ETub EWal LAma LRHS MBri NRog
'New Look' (7)	Last listed 1999
¶ 'Ollioules' (4) ♀	LBmB
'Olympic Flame' (4) ♀	Last listed 1993
'Orange Bouquet' (3) ♀	LAma LRHS NRog
'Orange Elite' (14)	LAma MBri
'Orange Emperor' (13) ♀	LAma LRHS MBri NRog
'Orange Favourite' (10)	LAma LRHS
¶ 'Orange Princess' (11) ♀	LBmB
'Orange Sun'	See *T.* 'Oranjezon'
'Orange Triumph' (11)	MBri
'Oranje Nassau' (2) ♀	LAma MBri NRog
§ 'Oranjezon' (4) ♀	LAma
'Oratorio' (14) ♀	LAma LRHS MBri
'Oriental Beauty' (14) ♀	LAma LRHS NRog
'Oriental Splendour' (14) ♀	EWal LAma
orphanidea (15)	EPot LAma LBow LRHS
- 'Flava' (15)	CBro ETub LAma
§ - Whittallii Group (15) ♀	CAvo CBro CMea LAma NRog
'Oscar' (3)	LBmB
ostrowskiana (15)	LAma
'Oxford' (4) ♀	LAma NRog
'Oxford's Elite' (4)	LAma
'Page Polka' (3)	LAma
'Palestrina' (3)	LAma
'Pandour' (14)	LAma MBri
'Parade' (4) ♀	LAma MBri
'Paris' (3)	Last listed 1997
§ **passeriniana** (15)	LAma
'Paul Richter' (3)	LAma
'Pax' (3)	LAma
'Peach Blossom' (2)	CAvo ETub LAma LRHS MBri NRog
'Peerless Pink' (3)	LAma
¶ 'Perestroyka' [PBR] (5)	LBmB
'Perlina' (14)	LAma
persica	See *T. celsiana*
'Philippe de Comines' (5)	LAma
'Picture' (5) ♀	LAma
'Pimpernel' (8/v)	LAma
'Pink Beauty' (1)	LAma

'Pink Impression' (4) ♀	LAma
'Pink Trophy' (1)	Last listed 1998
'Pinkeen' (13)	LAma
'Pinocchio' (14)	EWal LRHS NRog
'Plaisir' (14) ♀	LAma MBri
platystigma (15)	LAma
polychroma	See *T. biflora*
praestans (15)	LAma
- 'Fusilier' (15) ♀	CBro EPot ETub EWal LAma LBow LRHS MBri NBir NRog
- 'Unicum' (15/v)	EWal LAma LRHS MBri NRog
- 'Van Tubergen's Variety' (15)	LAma LRHS NRog WShi
'Preludium' (3)	LAma
'President Kennedy' (4) ♀	LAma
primulina (15)	Last listed 1998
'Prince Charles' (3) ♀	Last listed 1989
'Prince Karl Philip' (3)	NRog
'Prince of Austria' (1)	LAma
'Princeps' (13)	CBro EWal LAma MBri
§ 'Princess Margaret Rose' (5)	EWal
'Princesse Charmante' (14) ♀	Last listed 1999
'Prins Carnaval' (1) ♀	Last listed 1997
'Prinses Irene' (3) ♀	CMea ETub LAma MBri NBir NRog
'Professor Röntgen' (10)	LAma
'Prominence' (3)	Last listed 1997
pulchella humilis	See *T. humilis*
§ 'Purissima' (13) ♀	CAvo CBro ETub EWal LAma LBow LRHS NRog
'Queen' (4)	Last listed 1999
'Queen Ingrid' (14)	LAma LRHS
'Queen of Bartigons' (5) ♀	LAma NRog
'Queen of Marvel' (2)	NRog
'Queen of Night' (5)	CAvo CMea ETub EWal LAma LRHS MBri NRog
'Queen of Sheba' (6) ♀	CAvo LAma NRog
¶ 'Rajka' (6)	LAma
'Recreado' (5)	ETub
'Red Champion' (10)	LAma
'Red Emperor'	See *T.* 'Madame Lefeber'
'Red Georgette' (5) ♀	LRHS MBri
'Red Matador' (4)	LAma
'Red Parrot' (10)	LAma NRog
'Red Riding Hood' (14) ♀	CBro ETub EWal LAma LBow LRHS MBri NBir NRog
'Red Sensation' (10)	Last listed 1997
'Red Shine' (6) ♀	LAma
'Red Surprise' (14) ♀	Last listed 1995
'Red Wing' (7) ♀	LAma
'Reforma' (3)	Last listed 1997
Rembrandt Mix	ETub MBri
'Renown' (5)	Last listed 1997
rhodopea	See *T. urumoffii*
'Rijnland' (3)	Last listed 1997
'Ringo'	See *T.* 'Kees Nelis'
'Rockery Beauty' (13)	Last listed 1997
'Rockery Master' (14)	ETub
'Rockery Wonder' (14)	Last listed 1997
'Rococo' (10)	LBmB
'Rosanna' (14) ♀	Last listed 1991
'Rosario' (3)	Last listed 1998
* 'Rose Emperor' (13)	Last listed 1999
'Rosy Wings' (3)	LAma
'Ruby Red' (1)	NRog
'Safari' (14)	ETub
¶ 'Salmon Pearl' (3)	LBmB
¶ 'Sapporro' (6)	LAma
saxatilis (15)	CBro EBot EPfP LAma LRHS MBri NRog

§ - Bakeri Group (15)	CPou LAma
§ - - 'Lilac Wonder' (15) ♀	CAvo CBro EPot ETub LAma LRHS MBri NRog
- MS 769 (15)	Last listed 1998
'Scarlet Baby' (12)	LRHS NRog
'Scarlet Cardinal' (2)	Last listed 1997
'Scarlett O'Hara' (5)	LAma
'Schoonoord' (2)	ETub LAma MBri NRog
schrenkii (15)	LAma LRHS
'Scotch Lassie' (5)	LAma
'Shakespeare' (12)	CBro LAma LBow LRHS NRog
'Shirley' (3)	CAvo ETub EWal LAma LRHS MBri NRog
'Showwinner' (12) ♀	CBro ETub LAma MBri NRog
'Sigrid Undset' (5)	LAma
'Silentia' (3)	LAma
'Smiling Queen' (5)	Last listed 1999
'Smyrna' (14) ♀	Last listed 1991
¶ 'Snow Parrot' (10)	LBmB
'Snowflake' (3)	LAma
'Snowpeak' (5)	LAma
sogdiana (15)	LAma
'Sorbet' (5) ♀	LAma
'Sparkling Fire' (14)	LAma
sprengeri (15) ♀	CAvo CBro CFil CLAP CRDP EPar GCrs LAma MRav SSpi WIvy
- Trotter's form (15)	WCot
'Spring Green' (8) ♀	CAvo CMea ETub EWal LAma LRHS MBri NRog
'Spring Pearl' (13)	LAma
'Spring Song' (4)	LAma
stellata	See *T. clusiana* var. *stellata*
'Stockholm' (2) ♀	LAma NRog
'Stresa' (12) ♀	CBro LAma LRHS NRog
'Striped Apeldoorn' (4)	LAma NRog
'Striped Bellona' (3)	NRog
subpraestans (15)	EPot LAma
'Success' (3)	Last listed 1997
'Summit' (13)	Last listed 1999
'Sundew' (7)	NRog
'Sunray' (3)	LAma
'Susan Oliver' (8)	LAma
'Swan Wings' (7)	LAma
'Sweet Harmony' (5) ♀	LAma LRHS MBri NRog
'Sweet Lady' (14)	LAma NRog
'Sweetheart' (13)	CBro LAma LRHS NRog
sylvestris (15)	CAvo CBro CMea EPar EWFC LAma LBow LRHS NRog WCot WHer WShi
'Tamara' (3)	Last listed 1997
'Tango' (14)	LAma
tarda (15) ♀	CAvo CBro CMea EPar EPfP EPot ETub EWal LAma LBow LRHS MBri MBro NMGW NMen NRog WPyg WShi
'Teenager' (14)	Last listed 1997
'Temple of Beauty' (5) ♀	Last listed 1999
'Tender Beauty' (4) ♀	Last listed 1999
tetraphylla (15)	LAma
'Texas Flame' (10)	LAma LRHS NRog
'Texas Gold' (10)	LAma NRog
'The First' (12)	CBro LAma
¶ 'Tinka' (15)	LBmB
'Toronto' (14) ♀	LAma LRHS MBri
'Toulon' (13) ♀	MBri
'Towa' (14)	LAma
¶ 'Toyota' (5)	LBmB
'Trance' (4)	Last listed 1997
'Trinket' (14) ♀	LAma
'Triumphator' (2)	LAma
tschimganica (15)	LAma
tubergeniana (15)	LAma

- 'Keukenhof' (15)	LAma
turkestanica (15) ♀	CAvo CBro CSWP EPar EPfP EPot ETub LAma LBow LRHS MBri MBro NMen NRog SUsu WBea WHoo
'Uncle Tom' (11)	LAma MBri
§ **_undulatifolia_** (15)	CBro EBot LAma
'Union Jack' (5) ♀	EWal LAma
urumiensis (15) ♀	CAvo CBro EPot LAma LRHS MBri MBro NRog WHoo WPyg WShi
§ **_urumoffii_** (15)	LAma
'Valentine' (3) ♀	LAma
'Van der Neer' (1)	LAma
'Varinas' (3)	LAma
violacea	See _T. humilis_ Violacea Group
'Viridiflora' (8)	ETub
'Vivaldi' (12)	LAma
'Vivex' (4) ♀	LAma
§ 'Vlammenspel' (1)	LAma
'Vuurbaak' (2)	LAma
vvedenskyi (15)	CBro LAma NRog
- 'Blanka' (15)	Last listed 1999
- 'Hanka' (15)	EPot
- 'Lenka' (15)	Last listed 1999
- 'Tangerine Beauty' (15) ♀	LRHS MBri
¶ 'Weber's Parrot' (10)	LBmB
'West Point' (6) ♀	CAvo ETub EWal LAma LRHS NRog
* 'White Bouquet' (5)	NRog
'White Dream' (3)	ETub EWal LAma LRHS
¶ 'White Elegance' (6)	LBmB
'White Emperor'	See _T._ 'Purissima'
'White Parrot' (10)	CAvo ETub LAma LRHS NRog
'White Swallow' (3)	NRog
'White Triumphator' (6) ♀	CAvo CMea ETub EWal LAma LRHS NBir NRog
'White Virgin' (3)	LAma
whittallii	See _T. orphanidea_ Whittallii Group
'Willem van Oranje' (2)	LAma NRog
'Willemsoord' (2)	LAma LRHS MBri NRog
wilsoniana	See _T. montana_
'Wirosa' (11) ♀	Last listed 1991
¶ 'World Expression' PBR (5)⅄	LBmB
'Yellow Dawn' (14)	LAma LRHS
'Yellow Dover' (4) ♀	Last listed 1997
'Yellow Emperor' (5)	MBri
'Yellow Empress' (13)	LAma
¶ 'Yellow Flight' (3)	LAma
'Yellow Present' (3)	LAma
'Yellow Purissima' (13) ♀	NRog
'Yokohama' (3)	ETub LAma NRog
'Zampa' (14) ♀	EWal LAma
zenaidae (15)	Last listed 1998
'Zombie' (13)	LAma
'Zomerschoon' (5)	EBot ETub
'Zwanenburg' (5)	Last listed 1997

TUNICA See PETRORHAGIA

TUPISTRA (Convallariaceae)
aurantiaca B&SWJ 2267	WCru

TURBINA (Convolvulaceae)
corymbosa	Last listed 1998

TURNERA (Turneraceae)
ulmifolia	MSal

TURRAEA (Meliaceae)
obtusifolia	Last listed 1999

TUSSILAGO (Asteraceae)
farfara	CArn ELau EWFC GBar GPoy MHer MHew MSal SIde WHer WOak

TWEEDIA (Asclepiadaceae)
§ **_caerulea_** ♀	CFri CGle CInt CM&M CRHN CSev CSpe EMan ERea IBlr LGre LLWP SBra SHFr SLon SPer SYvo WEas WPic
¶ - pink	GCal

TYLOPHORA (Asclepiadaceae)
ovata	CPlN

TYPHA (Typhaceae)
angustifolia	CAgr CBen CKin CRow CWat EHon EMFW GBin LPBA MSta NPer SPlb SWat SWyc WWye
latifolia	CAgr CBen CRow CWat EHon EMFW LPBA MSta NPer SWal SWat SWyc WHer WMAq WWye
- 'Variegata'	CBen CRow CWat ELan EMFW LLWG LPBA MSta SWyc WCot WMAq
§ **_laxmannii_**	CBen CRow EHon EMFW LPBA MSta
minima	CBen CMHG CRDP CRow EHoe EHon EMFW EPfP GBin LEdu LPBA MSta NDea NPer SCoo SMad SWat SWyc WFar WMAq
shuttleworthii	CRow
stenophylla	See _T. laxmannii_

U

UGNI (Myrtaceae)
§ **_molinae_**	CGre CPle CTrC GAri IDee ISea LEdu MBel MDun SHFr SOWG WCHb WGwG WJek WPic WSHC WWal WWat WWye

ULEX (Papilionaceae)
europaeus	CDoC EGoo ENot EWFC EWTr GChr LBuc MCoo NWea WDin WHar WMou
- 'Aureus'	Last listed 1998
§ - 'Flore Pleno' (d) ♀	CB&S CDoC CInt CNic CTri EMon ENot EPla GChr GKir MGos NWea SPer WBcn WCot
- 'Plenus'	See _U. europaeus_ 'Flore Pleno'
- 'Prostratus'	MBar
gallii	IIve
- 'Mizen Head'	ESis GCal GGGa GSki LRHS MWhi NHar SLon SMad WBcn
§ **_minor_**	EPla
nanus	See _U. minor_

ULLUCUS (Basellaceae)
tuberosus	Last listed 1999

ULMUS ✿ (Ulmaceae)
davidiana 'Nire Keyaki'	Last listed 1999
'Dodoens'	IArd LBuc MGos NBee
§ **_glabra_**	CDul GChr GKir GTre NWea WDin
- 'Camperdownii'	CTho EBee ELan EWTr LPan NBee SPer

- 'Exoniensis'   CDul CTho SRPl
- 'Gittisham'   CTho
- 'Horizontalis'   See *U. glabra* 'Pendula'
- 'Lutescens'   CTri LRHS
- 'Nana'   WPat
§ - 'Pendula'   LPan
x *bollandica* 'Commelin' Last listed 1999
- 'Groeneveld'   Last listed 1999
- 'Jacqueline Hillier' CInt CTre EBrP EBre ELan EPla
                        GEil IMGH LBCl LBSe LBre
                        MBBe MBar MBro NHar NHol
                        NWea SBre SHFr SLon
                        SMad SPer SRms STre WCFE
                        WFar WHCG WPGP WPat
                        WPyg
- 'Lobel'   CDul MGos
- 'Wredei'   See *U. minor* 'Dampieri Aurea'
minor 'Cornubiensis'   CBlo
§ - 'Dampieri Aurea'   CBot CDul CEnd CLnd ELan
                        GKir LBuc LNet LPan LRHS
                        MAsh MBar MBlu MGos NBee
                        SLim SMad SPer SSta WDin
                        WPat
- 'Variegata'   EPot SCoo
montana   See *U. glabra*
parvifolia   CTho GAri NWea SMHT SMad
                        STre WFro WHCr WNor
- 'Frosty' (v)   ECho EPot
- 'Geisha' (v)   CBlo ELan MGos SBla WCot
                        WPat WPyg
§ - 'Hokkaido'   LBee MBro NHar NHol SBla
                        WAbe WPat WPyg
- 'Pygmaea'   See *U. parvifolia* 'Hokkaido'
- 'Seiju'   SMad
- 'Yatsubusa'   CLyd EPot ESis EWes MBro SIng
                        SPan STre WPat WPyg
'Plantijn'   Last listed 1997
procera   CDul CTho LBuc
- 'Argenteovariegata'   CDul CTho SMad
pumila   CAgr WNor WOTO
'Sapporo Autumn Gold'[PBR] MBlu

UMBELLULARIA (Lauraceae)
californica   CAgr CArn CB&S SAPC SArc
                        WSHC

UMBILICUS (Crassulaceae)
¶ *luteus*   CRDP
rupestris   EWFC GAri IIve NWCA SChr
                        WCot WCru WHer WShi
                        WWye

UNCINIA (Cyperaceae)
clavata   EPla
egmontiana   CElw EMan
N *rubra*   More than 30 suppliers
* - 'Dunn Valley'   Last listed 1999
sp. from Chile   EPla EWes GCal
uncinata   CFil CM&M EBee ECha
                        EHoe EMan GChr GGar
                        NHol NWCA SDix SUsu
* - *rubra*   CFir CFri CHar EBee ECot
                        EPGN LRHS MCLN MMHG
                        SCob SLim SMac STes

UNIOLA (Poaceae)
latifolia   See *Chasmanthium latifolium*

URCEOLINA (Amaryllidaceae)
miniata   See *Stenomesson miniatum*
peruviana   See *Stenomesson miniatum*
urceolata   Last listed 1997

URECHITES See PENTALINON

URGINEA (Hyacinthaceae)
fugax S&F 62   Last listed 1998
maritima   EBee EBot ELau GPoy LAma
                        MNrw MSal
- S&F 275   Last listed 1998
ollivieri MS&CL 281   Last listed 1998
undulata S&F 2   Last listed 1998

UROSPERMUM (Asteraceae)
delachampii   CGle COtt EBee EBrP EBre LBCl
                        LBSe LBre MBBe SAga SBre
                        WCot
¶ 'Sunbeam'   LHop

URSINIA (Asteraceae)
montana   NWCA
pilifera   WCot

URTICA (Urticaceae)
dioica   Last listed 1997
- 'Bradfield Purpler'   CNat
- 'Brightstone Bitch' (v) WAlt WCHb
- 'Chedglow' (v)   CNat WAlt
- 'Danae Johnston' (v)   CNat EMon GOrP WAlt WCHb
- 'Dusting' (v)   WAlt WCHb
- 'Dying for Attention' WAlt
- 'Good as Gold' (v)   CNat WAlt
- 'Ingdust' (v)   WAlt
- OBG mutant   CNat
- 'Spring Fever'   WAlt
galeopsifolia   CNat

UTRICULARIA (Lentibulariaceae)
alpina   CSWC WMEx
australis   EFEx
biloba   GTro
bisquamata   CSWC GTro SHmp WMEx
blancheti   CSWC
calcyfida   GTro WMEx
¶ *calycifida*   SHmp
capensis   WMEx
dichotoma   CSWC EFEx GTro WMEx
exoleta   See *U. gibba*
§ *gibba*   EFEx
intermedia   EFEx
laterifolia   EFEx GTro WMEx
livida   CSWC EFEx GTro WMEx
longifolia   CSWC GTro WMEx
menziesii   EFEx GTro
monanthos   EFEx
nephrophylla   GTro
novae-zelandiae   GTro
ochroleuca   EFEx
praelonga   GTro SHmp
prehensilis   GTro WMEx
pubescens   WMEx
reniformis   EFEx GTro SHmp WMEx
- *nana*   EFEx
sandersonii   GTro SHmp WMEx
- blue   GTro
subulata   EFEx WMEx
tricolor   GTro SHmp WMEx
vulgaris   CSWC EFEx LGuA WMEx

UVULARIA (Convallariaceae)
§ *caroliniana*   IBlr
disporum   LAma
grandiflora ♀   More than 30 suppliers
- dwarf form   IBlr

- var. *pallida* — CBos CPlt CRDP EBee ECha EMan EPPr EPar GBuc IBlr LGre MRav WCDu WCru
perfoliata — CStu EBee ECha EDAr EMan EPar EPfP EPla EPot GCrs LAma MBro MRav SIng WAbe WCru WIvy WPGP WWat
pudica — See *U. caroliniana*
sessilifolia — CRDP CStu EBee EPar EPot GCrs IBlr LAma WCru WIvy

V

VACCARIA (Caryophyllaceae)
§ *hispanica* — MSal
segetalis — See *V. hispanica*
* *violescens* — EBee

VACCINIUM ✿ (Ericaceae)
* *alpinum* — Last listed 1997
arctostaphylos — SReu SSta
caespitosum — GDra SOkd
'Cinderella' — SSta
consanguineum — LRHS SReu
corymbosum ♀ — CB&S CBlo EPfP MBar MGos NBee SReu SSta WDin WGer
- 'Berkeley' (F) — CTrh GTwe LBuc LRHS NBee SDea
- 'Blue Ray' (F) — GKir
- 'Bluecrop' (F) — CDoC CTrh EBee EMui EPfP GAri GChr GKir GTwe LBuc LRHS MBri MGos SDea SPer WStI WWeb
- 'Bluegold' — CTrh LRHS MAsh
- 'Bluejay' (F) — CTrh GKir LRHS
- 'Bluetta' (F) — GTwe LRHS
¶ - 'Collins' (F) — CTrh
- 'Concord' (F) — EBee ENot
- 'Coville' (F) — EMui
- 'Duke' (F) — CTrh EPfP GKir LRHS
- 'Earliblue' (F) — EMui GKir LRHS MGos SDea
- 'Elliott' (F) — Last listed 1999
- 'Goldtraube' (F) — CDoC LRHS MBlu MBri MGos SDea WStI
- 'Herbert' (F) — CTrh EMui GTwe MGos
- 'Ivanhoe' (F) — CTrh
- 'Jersey' (F) — GKir LRHS MGos SDea
- 'Nelson' (F) — CTrh
- 'Northland' (F) — GAri GTwe SDea
- 'Patriot' (F) — CTrh GAri GTwe LRHS MGos
- 'Pioneer' (F) — MBar
- 'Spartan' (F) — GAri GTwe LRHS
- 'Sunrise' (F) — GTwe
- 'Toro' (F) — GTwe LRHS
- 'Trovor' (F) — Last listed 1998
- 'Weymouth' (F) — SDea
crassifolium — GKir LRHS MAsh SSta
subsp. *sempervirens* 'Well's Delight' (F)
cylindraceum ♀ — EPfP MBro NHol SSta WAbe WPat WPyg
¶ - 'Tinkerbelle' — WAbe
- 'Tom Thumb' — WAbe
delavayi — GCHN GGar GKir LRHS MAsh MBar MDun NNrd SReu SSpi SSta WAbe WWat
donianum — See *V. sprengelii*
dunalianum — CB&S
- var. *caudatifolium* — WCru
B&SWJ 1716
emarginatum — SSta

floribundum — CDoC CFil CMHG EPfP GDra GGar GKir GSki GTou LRHS MAsh SBrw SPer SRPl SSpi SSta WAbe WPGP WPic
glaucoalbum ♀ — CAbP CDoC EPfP GGGa GKir LRHS MAsh MBar MBlu MRav SMad SPer SReu SSpi SSta WBod WDin
- B 173 — Last listed 1999
* *grandiflorum* — NLAp
griffithianum — SReu
§ *macrocarpon* (F) — ELan GKir GTwe LRHS MAsh MBar MBri SRms
- 'CN' (F) — ESim MGos
- 'Early Black' (F) — CB&S MGos SLdr
- 'Franklin' (F) — EPot ESim
- 'Hamilton' (F) — EPot GCrs NHol WAbe WPat WPyg
- 'McFarlin' (F) — EMui
¶ - 'Olson's Honkers' (F) — ESim
- 'Pilgrim' (F) — ESim
* 'McMinn' — GAri
moupinense — CDoC GKir IMGH ITim LRHS MAsh MBlu MGos WAbe
- small-leaved — Last listed 1999
- 'Variegatum' — WPyg
myrtillus — GPoy IIve WDin
'Nimo Pink' — MBar
nummularia — CNic EPot GDra GKir LRHS NHar SReu SSpi WAbe WPic
- LS&H 17294 — Last listed 1997
ovalifolium — GKir
ovatum — CB&S CMHG GSki LRHS MBar MDun SPer SSta WPic
§ *oxycoccos* (F) — CArn
* - *rubrum* — LRHS
padifolium — CFil CGre WPGP
pallidum — IBlr
palustre — See *V. oxycoccos*
parvifolium — SReu
praestans — GAri NHol
retusum — CGre CTrw LRHS WBod WPic
sikkimense — GGGa
§ *sprengelii* — CB&S
vitis-idaea — CAgr CNic EWTr GPoy MBar MGos SReu SRot WPyg
- 'Compactum' — EWes NHar
- Koralle Group ♀ — EPfP GChr MAsh MBar MBri MGos MRav NHol SPer SSta WPat WPyg
- var. *minus* — GAri MAsh NMen SOkd SSta SVil
- 'Red Pearl' — LRHS MAsh MGos SPer
* - 'Variegatum' — EWes WPat
wrightii var. *formosanum* — Last listed 1999
B&SWJ 1542

VAGARIA (Amaryllidaceae)
ollivieri S&F 266 — Last listed 1998

VALERIANA (Valerianaceae)
'Alba' — See *Centranthus ruber* 'Albus'
alliariifolia — EMon GCal NBro NSti WCot
arizonica — CLyd EDAr LFis MSte MTho NCat
'Coccinea' — See *Centranthus ruber*
dioica — CRDP
¶ *hardwickii* — GPoy
- CC 2227 — CPLG
jatamansi — GPoy
montana — GTou MBro NBro NRya SRms SWat

officinalis	CAgr CArn CFri CKin CRDP
	CSev EBee ECha ELau EWFC
	GBar GPoy ILis LRHS MChe MHer
	MHew MMal NBro NLar SAga
	SIde SRms SWat WHer WOak
	WPer WShi WWye
- subsp. *sambucifolia*	MCAu SHel WHil
* - 'Variegata'	WCHb
phu 'Aurea'	More than 30 suppliers
* - 'Purpurea'	ECoo
pyrenaica	ECha WCot WEas
saxatilis	NRya SRms
supina	CGra NWCA
tatamana	WEas
wallrothii	WCot

VALERIANELLA (Valerianaceae)
eriocarpa	Last listed 1997
§ *locusta*	GPoy
olitoria	See *V. locusta*

VALLEA (Elaeocarpaceae)
stipularis	CDoC
- var. *pyrifolia*	CGre CPLG CPle

VALLOTA See CYRTANTHUS

VANCOUVERIA (Berberidaceae)
chrysantha	CElw CFil EBee ECha EMan EOld
	GBuc IBlr MRav NWCA SLod SSpi
	WCru WSHC
hexandra	CFil EBee ECGN ECha EMan
	EMon EPar EPla ERos GBuc
	GCal GKir IBlr LHop NRya
	NSti SSca SSpi WBea WCru
	WMoo WWin
planipetala	IBlr WCru

VANIA (Brassicaceae)
campylophylla	Last listed 1997

VEITCHIA (Arecaceae)
merrillii	LBlo LPal

VELTHEIMIA (Hyacinthaceae)
§ *bracteata* ♀	CHal EBak ETub IBlr LBow LHil
	NRog SYvo WCot
¶ - 'Yellow Flame'	CPne
§ *capensis* ♀	CSev MTPN
viridifolia Jacquin	See *V. bracteata*
- hort.	See *V. capensis*

x VENIDIOARCTOTIS See ARCTOTIS

VENIDIUM See ARCTOTIS

VERATRUM (Melanthiaceae)
album	CFil CFir ECha LRHS NLar NPSI
	SBla WCot WCru WFar
- var. *flavum*	LGre WCot
- var. *oxysepalum*	WCru
californicum	ECha IBlr WCot
caudatum	Last listed 1997
formosanum	WCru
B&SWJ 1575	
nigrum ♀	CBos CBot CBro CFil CFir EWTr
	GCal LGre MNrw SChu SMad
	SMrm WCot WFar WTin
stamineum	WCru
viride	EBrP EBre ECha GKir IBlr
	LBCl LBSe LBre MBBe SBla
	SBre SSpi

VERBASCUM ✿ (Scrophulariaceae)
acaule	NMen NWCA
* - 'Album'	WCru
adzharicum	EBee EWll MBro WElm WHoo
	WOve WSan
Allstree hybrids	CFee EHol EHrv EMar
¶ 'Anglesey Sunshine'	MAvo NDov
'Arctic Summer'	See *V. bombyciferum*
	'Polarsommer'
arcturus	EBee NSti WPer
* *bakerianum*	WEas WMoo
'Bill Bishop'	SIng
blattaria	CGle CHid CPou EBee EBot EHrv
	ELan EMan EPPr EWFC LFis LIck
	LRHS MGed MHew NBir SCob
	SWat WEas WFar WHer WPer
	WUnu
- f. *albiflorum*	CLon CNic CSpe ECGN EMar
	LGre LLWP LRHS MBro MHer
	NCut NSti SGar SUsu WHer WKif
	WPer WPyg WRus WUnu
- pink	CFri CLTr EGoo EWll GAbr STes
	WOve
- yellow	EMan EPPr EWll NCut SWat WSan
§ *bombyciferum* ♀	CBre CSWP CSev IIve LHrt NCut
	NPSI NSti SRms WByw WCot
	WEas WHer
- BSSS 232	WCru
§ - 'Polarsommer'	COIW CSam EBee EBrP EBre
	EMan EWTr GAbr GKir LBCl LBSe
	LBre LRHS MBBe MBri MRav NBir
	SBre SPer SRms SWat WLow
- 'Silver Lining'	NFla NPer SRCN
'Broussa'	See *V. bombyciferum*
'Butterscotch'	MAnH
chaixii	CGdn CHea CSam EBee ECha
	EHrv GBuc GMac LRHS LRot
	MMHG NBir NCut WFar WMoo
	WPer WPyg
- 'Album'	More than 30 suppliers
- subsp. *austriacum*	EBee
- 'Clent Sunrise'	Last listed 1999
Cotswold Group 'Boadicea'	Last listed 1997
- 'Cotswold Beauty' ♀	CHad CLon COtt CPar CSpe EBee
	EMan EMar GKir GMaP LAst LFis
	LRHS MBel MMil MTis MWat
	NGdn NLar SChu SLod SSpe SUsu
	WLRN WPGP
- 'Cotswold Gem'	Last listed 1997
- 'Cotswold King'	CGle LPio WCot WSan
- 'Cotswold Queen'	More than 30 suppliers
- 'Gainsborough' ♀	More than 30 suppliers
- 'Mont Blanc'	CGle CMil EBee EBrP EBre ECot
	EFou EHrv EMan EMar GMaP LAst
	LBCl LBSe LBre LPio LRHS MBBe
	MLLN SBre SPer SWat WCot WRus
	WSan
- 'Pink Domino' ♀	More than 30 suppliers
- 'Royal Highland'	CGle CHad CLon COIW EBee
	ECot EFou EHrv ELan EMan GBri
	GKir LAst LPio LRHS MAvo MCLN
	MTis MWat NGdn NLar NSti SChu
	SMrm SWat WCot WRus
- 'White Domino'	EBee EFou LCaP LRHS MBNS
	MCAu NPri SPer WHil WRus WViv
creticum	ECoo EPri WPer
§ *densiflorum*	CArn EBee ECoo LAst LRHS NCut
	SIde SPer WHil WPer WRHF
dumulosum ♀	EDAr GCal MHar NWCA SBla
	WAbe WSan
'Ellenbank Rose'	Last listed 1998

	'Frosted Gold'	Last listed 1999
	'Golden Wings' ♀	CPBP CPla EPot ITim NMen NTow WAbe WPat
	'Helen Johnson' ♀	More than 30 suppliers
¶	hybrid	NWCA
	x *hybridum* 'Snow Maiden'	ECoo MAnH
	'Jackie'	CFri CHar CHea CSpe EBee EBrP EBre EMan EPPr GKir LAst LBCl LBSe LBre LRHS MBBe MBri MMil NPSI SBla SBre SCoo SPer STes WCDu WCot WRus WSpi WWol
¶	'Jolly Eyes'	GBin WRus
¶	'Lemon Queen'	MBel
	'Letitia' ♀	CPla EBrP EBre ELan EMan EPot EWes GCal IMGH LBCl LBSe LBee LBre LRHS MBBe MHar MTho NTow NWCA SBla SBre SIng SSmi WAbe WHoo WKif WPyg WRus WWin
	longifolium	EBee LRHS
	- var. *pannosum*	See V. *olympicum*
	lychnitis	CArn CLTr EBee LGre WHer
	macrurum	EBee
¶	'Megan's Mauve'	CFai CM&M CMGP CSpe ECot EMan EMar EWll GBin LAst LBuc LPio MAvo MCLN MMil NDov NGdn NPSI NSti SPer SUsu WElm WRus
	nigrum	CArn CFri CGle COlW EBee EPfP EWFC EWTr LRHS MBNS MCAu MChe MHew NChi SEND SMer SRCN SRob WHer WPer
	- var. *album*	COlW EBee GMac LPio MBct MBel MBri WWhi
§	*olympicum*	CGle CLTr CSam EBee ECha ECtt EGoo ELan ENot EPfP EWTr GKir LRHS MBNS MCAu MWgw NBid NOak SCob SDix SEND SRob WBry WCot WPer
	oreophilum	EBee
	phlomoides	Last listed 1999
	phoeniceum	CArn CFri CGle EBee ECGN ECoo ELan GMac LRHS MSCN MWgw NBro NCut NDov NMir NOak SCob SMer SPlb SRms SUsu WBro WEas WHen WHil WOve WPer WWin
*	- 'Album'	CSpe GMac LIck NSti SCob SUsu
	- 'Candy Spires'	Last listed 1998
¶	- 'Flush of Pink'	CM&M
	- 'Flush of White'	CBot CM&M EBee ECGN EMan EWll LAst LRHS MLLN NChi NCut SMrm SRob WGor WHen WHil WLin WWhi
	- hybrids	CBot COlW CSpe EGoo EMan EWTr MHer MMal NBid NChi NVic SRms SSea SWat WFar WGor WPer
¶	- 'Violetta'	EWll NChi SSvw
¶	'Pink Ice'	MAvo
	pulverulentum	CKin EWFC
	pyramidatum	EBee
¶	'Raspberry Ripple'	EMan EMar NPSI SPer
¶	'Raspberry Sorbet'	CPou
	rorippifolium	EGoo EMan EWll WHil
	'Silberkandelaber'	SMrm SSvw
	sinuatum	WCot
	'Southern Charm'	EBee ECoo ECtt EMan EWTr EWll LRHS MMrm SRot STes WGor WHil
*	'Spica'	CGle NCut SSvw WCot
	spicatum	CBot GMac WRus
	spinosum	CGle SBla
¶	'Summer Sorbet'	SPer
*	Sunset shades	Last listed 1999
	thapsiforme	See V. *densiflorum*
	thapsus	COld CSev EBot EOld EWFC GPoy MChe MHer MHew MMal NCut NFor NMir SRob WOak WSel WWye
	undulatum	CArn
	'Vernale'	CBot
	wiedemannianum	CSpe EWll GAbr SRCN WHer WLin

VERBENA ✿ (Verbenaceae)

I	'Adonis'	Last listed 1999
	'Adonis Light Blue'	CAsh LRHS
	'Adonis Mango'	CAsh
	'Aphrodite'	CAsh GPin
	'Apple Blossom'	CAsh LRHS
	'Artemis'	Last listed 1997
	'Aveyron'	CAsh SChu
¶	'Aztec Deep Lavender'	CAsh
¶	'Aztec Pink Magic'	CAsh
¶	'Aztec Rose Pink'	CAsh
	'Babylon Blue'	CAsh
	Babylon Pink	CAsh
	= 'Morena'PBR	
*	'Batesville Rose'	CAsh WCot
	'Blue Cascade'	CAsh LPVe
	'Blue Knight'	CAsh
	'Blue Lagoon'	CAsh
	'Blue Moon'	CAsh
	'Blue Prince'	CAsh CSpe NFai
¶	'Blue Royal'	CAsh
§	*bonariensis*	More than 30 suppliers
	'Boon'	CAsh SVil
	'Booty'	CAsh
	'Boughton House'	CAsh CSpe MSte
	'Bramley'	SChu
	brasiliensis	EBee EMan
*	'Calcutta Cream'	Last listed 1997
¶	'Calvado Pink'	CAsh
¶	'Calvado Scarlet'	CAsh
	canadensis	CAsh
	- 'Perfecta'	CAsh
	'Candy Carousel'	CAsh CElw CSev MBNS NPri SCro SUsu
	'Carousel'	CAsh NPri
	chamaedrifolia	See V. *peruviana*
	'Claret'	CAsh
	'Cleopatra Pink'	CAsh
	'Cleopatra White'	CAsh
	corymbosa	CAsh CM&M EBee ECGP ECha EMan LLWP MCLN SMrm WCot WPer WRHF
	- 'Gravetye'	CAsh CElw CHad GBuc GCal NChi NCiC WFar
	'Crimson Star'	CAsh
	'Cupido'	Last listed 1998
¶	'Diamond Butterfly'	CAsh MBNS
¶	'Diamond Carouselle'	CAsh MBNS NPri
¶	'Diamond Merci'	CAsh
¶	'Diamond Rhodonit'	CAsh MBNS
¶	'Diamond Topaz'	CAsh
	'Edith Eddleman'	CAsh COtt EBee ECtt LRHS MGrG MNrw NFai WCot
*	*exaltata*	Last listed 1999
*	'Fiesta'	CAsh WCot
¶	'Firecracker'	CAsh
*	'Foxhunter'	CAsh EMan
	'Freefall'	GBri
¶	'Freefall Burgundy'	CAsh
¶	'Freefall Light Lavender'	CAsh

¶ 'Freefall Purple'	CAsh
bastata	CAsh CFri CSev EBee EBot ECot EMan EOrc GBar GCal LRHS MChe MNrw NSti WCot WFar WHoo WPer WPic
- 'Alba'	CAsh EBee EMan EMon GBar GBuc MBel SSte WPer
- JLS 88010WI	Last listed 1999
- 'Rosea'	CAsh CPlt ECGN EFou EPPr GBuc SChu SUsu
'Hecktor'	EMan
'Hidcote Purple'	CAsh MBNS MSte WHoo
bispida	EBee
'Homestead Purple'	CAsh CSev EBee EBrP EBre ECGP EMan GMac LBCl LBSe LBre LFis LLWP LPio LRHS MBBe MBel MFir MLLN MMil NFai NFla SAga SBre SCob SCoo SUsu WCot WOve WWeb
'Huntsman'	CAsh GBuc MSte WEas
'Imagination'	CAsh LRHS
'Jenny's Wine'	LHil
'Jugend'	Last listed 1998
N 'Kemerton'	CAsh EMan
'Kurpfalz'	Last listed 1998
* 'La France'	CAsh CElw CSam ECha EMan MRav NDov SAga SChu SDix SMrm SUsu WHoo
'Lawrence Johnston' ♀	CAsh LRHS SYvo WEas WHen
¶ 'Lilla'	CAsh
litoralis	EBee
'Loveliness'	CAsh EMan IBlr LRHS SMer SMrm
macdougalii	EBee EMan
x *maonettii*	CAsh
'Nero'	CAsh NPri
officinalis	CArn CAsh EWFC GBar GPoy MChe MHer MHew MNaF MSal Slde WHer WJek WOak WPer WSel WWye
'Ophelia'	Last listed 1999
'Paradiso'	CAsh
patagonica	See *V. bonariensis*
* 'Peach Blossom'	CAsh WCot
'Peaches and Cream'	CAsh EMan LIck LRHS
§ *peruviana*	CAsh EBrP EBre EPfP LBCl LBSe LBre LRHS MAsh MBBe MRav SBre SChu SCro SDix SIng SRms
- 'Alba'	SCro
pblogiflora	Last listed 1999
'Piccolo'	CAsh
'Pink Bouquet'	See *V.* 'Silver Anne'
¶ 'Pink Cascade'	CAsh
'Pink Parfait'	CAsh CHal CSpe ELan EMan EOrc LHop MBNS MGrG MRav SCro SMer
'Pink Pearl'	ECtt
* 'Pink Perfection'	Last listed 1998
pulchella	See *V. tenera*
'Purple Kleopat'	Last listed 1999
'Purple Sissinghurst'	CAsh CSam MBNS
'Quartz Blue'	CAsh
'Quartz Burgundy'	CAsh
'Quartz Scarlet'	CAsh
'Raspberry Crush'	CAsh LRHS
'Red Cascade'	CAsh
'Red Sissinghurst'	CAsh NPri
§ *rigida* ♀	CAsh CBrm CFir CFri CHea COlW CSpe EBee ECGP ECha EGra LRHS MGrG NCut SAga SRms SUsu SYvo WCot WFar WOve

- 'Lilacina'	Last listed 1999
- 'Polaris'	CAsh CStr EBee SMrm SUsu
* 'Royal Purple'	CAsh EMan
Sandy Series ♀	Last listed 1995
scabridoglandulosa	CAsh
§ 'Silver Anne' ♀	CAsh CSam EBee ECtt EMan LFis LHrt LRHS MRav NFai NPri NTow SChu SCro SDix SMer SRms SUsu WEas WHen WHoo
§ 'Sissinghurst' ♀	CArn CAsh CGle CSam ECtt EMan LFis NFai NPri SCro SIng SRms WEas WHen WHoo WPyg WWin WWol
* 'Snow Flurry'	CAsh EWll WCot
* *spicata* 'Pam' (v)	Last listed 1999
¶ 'Splash Deep Rose'	CAsh
¶ 'Splash Light Violet'	CAsh
¶ 'Splash Purple'	CAsh
¶ 'Splash Rose'	CAsh
¶ 'Splash Violet'	CAsh
¶ 'Strawberry Parfait'	CAsh
stricta	CAsh EMan
'Sunmariba'PBR	See *V.* Temari Violet = 'Sunmariba'
'Sunvat'PBR	See *V.* Tapien Pearl = 'Sunvat'
'Sunver'PBR	See *V.* Tapien Pink = 'Sunver'
'Sunvop'PBR	See *V.* Tapien Violet = 'Sunvop'
supina	CAsh
Tapien® Lilac = 'Sunvil'PBR	CAsh
§ Tapien® Pearl = 'Sunvat'PBR	CAsh GPin
§ Tapien® Pink = 'Sunver'PBR	CAsh GPin LIck
¶ Tapien® Salmon	CAsh
§ Tapien® Violet = 'Sunvop'PBR	CAsh LIck NPri
Temari® Coral Pink = 'Sunmariripi'	CAsh
¶ Temari® Lilac	CAsh
¶ Temari® Patio Blue	CAsh
¶ Temari® Patio Pink	CAsh
¶ Temari® Patio Rose	CAsh
Temari® Pink = 'Sunmaripi'PBR	CAsh GPin
Temari® Scarlet = 'Sunmarisu'PBR	CAsh GPin MBNS NPri
¶ Temari Violet Star	CAsh NPri WWol
§ Temari® Violet = 'Sunmariba'PBR	CAsh GPin
Temari® White = 'Sunmaririho'	CAsh
§ *tenera*	CAsh
'Tenerife'	See *V.* 'Sissinghurst'
tenuisecta	CAsh WPer
- f. *alba*	Last listed 1999
- 'Edith'	CAsh
* 'Texas Appleblossom'	Last listed 1997
¶ 'Tortuga Hot Pink'	CAsh
¶ 'Tortuga Peach'	CAsh
¶ 'Tortuga White'	CAsh
¶ *urticifolia*	IIve
venosa	See *V. rigida*
'Violet Profusion'	CAsh
¶ 'Waterfall Blue'	CAsh
'White Cascade'	CAsh ECtt
¶ 'White Hecktor'	CAsh
* 'White Knight'	CAsh NPri
'White Sissinghurst'	CAsh

VERBESINA (Asteraceae)

alternifolia	EMan

VERNONIA (Asteraceae)

crinita	ECha GCal LFis SDix SMad
- 'Mammuth'	LGre
fasciculata	EBee EMan GCal
noveboracensis	EBee ECGN SMrm WCot WPer WRHF
- 'Albiflora'	WCot WPer

VERONICA (Scrophulariaceae)

amethystina	See *V. spuria*
armena	CLyd EWes LBee MBro MHer MSte MWat NMen SBla SRot
§ *austriaca*	MLLN SMrm SRPl WMoo
- Corfu form	CLyd CMea CNic EBee EMan EOrc EWes LGre LHop MSCN NBrk SLod SSvw WPer
- var. *dubia*	See *V. prostrata*
- 'Ionian Skies'	CLon CLyd CPBP CRDP CSpe ESis GBuc LBee LRHS MBel MNrw MRav SAga SBla SChu SHel SPer SUsu WCot WCru WFar WKif
§ - subsp. *teucrium*	CArn EBee LPVe MLLN MWgw NWCA SRms WFar WPer
- - 'Blue Blazer'	SCro
- - 'Blue Fountain'	LLWP
- - 'Crater Lake Blue' ♀	CHea CLon CRDP ECha ECtt EFou ENot EOrc IMGH LGre LRHS MCAu MFir MRav NBid NFai NFor SAga SMac SMrm SPlb SRms SUsu SByw WCot WEas WPat WPer WWin
- - 'Kapitän'	EBee ECha EGar GBuc MFir SMrm WFar WPer
- - 'Knallblau'	EBee EFou EMil GMac LRHS MBri SSvw WLRN
- - 'Königsblau'	WBea
- - 'Royal Blue' ♀	CLTr EBee ECot EFou EMan EPfP EWTr GBuc LPio LRHS MArl NOak NSti SPer WBea WMoo WPyg
- - 'Shirley Blue'	See *V.* 'Shirley Blue'
beccabunga	CArn CBen CKin CWat EHon ELan EMFW EWFC GPoy LPBA MGas MHew MSta NDea NMir SWat SWyc WHer WMAq
- 'Don's Dyke' (v)	Last listed 1998
bellidioides	GTou
Blue Bouquet	See *V. longifolia* 'Blaubündel'
'Blue Spire'	SWat WPer
bombycina	EPot NMen NTow NWCA WAbe
- subsp. *bolkardaghensis*	CPBP NMen
- subsp. *froediniana*	Last listed 1999
- Mac&W 5840	Last listed 1999
bonarota	See *Paederota bonarota*
caespitosa	MDHE
- subsp. *caespitosa*	CLyd NMen
- Mac&W 5849	NTow
candida	See *V. spicata* subsp. *incana*
x *cantiana* 'Kentish Pink'	CFri GBuc MBel MBro MHer SHel SIng SPla SSca WPer WSpi
* 'Catforth Border Guard'	NCat
caucasica	CRDP EMon LGre MSCN SAga WCru
chamaedrys	CKin IIve NMir
§ - 'Miffy Brute' (v)	EBee LFis MHar MLLN MRav NHol NPro WHer WLRN WRus
- 'Pam' (v)	WAlt WCHb WCot WWpP
- 'Variegata'	See *V. chamaedrys* 'Miffy Brute'
- 'Waterrow'	EMon WAlt
- 'Yorkley Wood'	WAlt
cinerea ♀	CLyd ECha MBro NTow WEas WPat

coreana	CLon
dichrus	EGoo
'Ellen Mae'	MCAu
exaltata	CBrd EBee ECGN EMFP EMan EMon GBuc LFis LGre LRHS MBct MLLN MNrw MSte NChi SAga WCot WOve WPer
- white	CBrd
filifolia	Last listed 1999
filiformis	MWhi
- 'Fairyland' (v)	EMon EWes WAlt WCHb
formosa	See *Parahebe formosa*
§ *fruticans*	GKir GTou
fruticulosa	NWCA
* *galactites*	Last listed 1998
gentianoides ♀	More than 30 suppliers
- 'Alba'	CMea CRDP EOrc GCal NBid NChi NSti
- 'Barbara Sherwood'	EBee EBrP EBre GKir GMac LBCl LBSe LBre MBBe MFir MLLN MTed NCiC SBre WCDu WCot
- 'Lilacina'	EBee EFou LRHS
- 'Nana'	EOrc MMil
- 'Pallida'	EBee EMan EPfP LCaP LRHS MBrN MRav NPri SSvw WRHF
- 'Robusta'	CMGP EBee ECha GMac LRHS MSph NDov NPSI SPet
- 'Tissington White'	CBos CLon EBee EBlw EFou EMar EOld EWTr GMaP LRHS LRot MCLN MLLN MTis NCut SAga SBla SHel SOkh SUsu SWat WAbb WBea WBro WFar WLin WOve WWin
- 'Variegata'	More than 30 suppliers
'Goodness Grows'	CMGP EBee EMan LAst LBuc LRHS NChi SChu SPla SSpe
grandis	EBee EWll
x *guthrieana*	CNic NMen SRms SRot WCru WFar WPer
hendersonii	See *V. subsessilis hendersonii*
incana	See *V. spicata* subsp. *incana*
* - 'Candidissima'	Last listed 1997
'Inspiration'	EFou LGre
* *keiskei* pink	Last listed 1999
kellereri	See *V. spicata*
kiusiana	CRDP CStr EBee EBrP EBre LBCl LBSe LBre MBBe MBel MTis SBre
kotschyana	Last listed 1998
- ES 309	Last listed 1999
'Lila Karina'	Last listed 1999
liwanensis	EDAr GCHN NMen NTow SMrm EPot
- Mac&W 5936	EPot
longifolia	EBee EGar ELan EOld EPfP EWTr MBel MCLN MFir MHar SAga STes WBea WEas WLRN
- 'Alba'	CHea EBee EGar ELan EMan EPfP EWTr LFis MBel SIde SSca WBea WMoo
§ - 'Blaubündel'	EBee EFou NFai
- 'Blauer Sommer'	CMGP EBee EFou EGar EMan LRHS NFla NGdn NHol SPer WRHF
§ - 'Blauriesin'	CM&M CTri ECtt EMil GMaP GMac MBri NSti SCob SMad SPer WRHF
- Blue Giantess	See *V. longifolia* 'Blauriesin'
- 'Fascination'	SMrm
- 'Foerster's Blue'	See *V. longifolia* 'Blauriesin'
- 'Joseph's Coat' (v)	EBee EMon NBrk WCot
- 'Lila Karina'	WPer
- 'Oxford Blue'	EBee LRHS WRHF
- pink	Last listed 1999

- 'Rose Tone'　EBee ECha MRav MTis SMrm WMoo
- 'Rosea'　CTri EBee EWTr MBel STes WCru WPer
- 'Schneeriesin'　EBee ECha ECtt EHrv GMaP LRHS MBri NWoo SCro SPer SSvw
lyallii　See *Parahebe lyallii*
macrostachya　Last listed 1999
　RMRP 95188
'Martje'　SMrm
montana　CKin
- 'Corinne Tremaine' (v)　EMan EMar EMon LHop MAvo MChl MLLN SAga SUsu WCot WHer
morrisonicola　Last listed 1998
　B&SWJ 086
nipponica　NChi WPer
* *nivalis nivea*　Last listed 1997
'Noah Williams' (v)　WCot
nummularia　WPer
officinalis　CArn CKin EWFC IIve WHbs
oltensis　CLyd CPBP ESis EWes NHol NMen WAbe WLin WPat WWin
- JCA 984.150　CNic NTow
¶ *orchidea*　EBrP EBre LBCl LBSe LBre MBBe SBre
orientalis　EBee
- subsp. *carduchorum*　Last listed 1997
- subsp. *orientalis*　EPot NMen
ornata　WCot WPer
pectinata　ESis GDra MBel
- 'Rosea'　CMea EWes GDra GKir NBus SHel WPer WWin
pedunncularis　CNic EOrc LBee LRHS SBla WEas
- 'Alba'　MHar WPer
§ - 'Georgia Blue'　More than 30 suppliers
- 'Oxford Blue'　See *V. peduncularis* 'Georgia Blue'
perfoliata　See *Parahebe perfoliata*
Pershore Gold　WLRN
　= 'Perglow'[PBR]
petraea 'Madame Mercier'　LRHS MMil SMrm
'Pink Damask'　CElw CHad CLon CSpe EBee EFou EMan EMil LFis LGre LRHS MBri MTis SCob SCro SMad SOkh SSvw WElm WRus
pinnata 'Blue Eyes'　ESis LBee LHop
prenja　See *V. austriaca*
§ *prostrata* ♀　CAgr CLyd CSam CSpe EMNN EPot ESis GDra GKir LBee LRHS MWat NFla NNrd SHFr SRms SSmi WCru WEas WFar WHoo WMoo WWin
- 'Alba'　CSpe MBro MWat WFar WHoo WPyg
§ - 'Blauspiegel'　CLon CPBP ECGP SBla WCru
- 'Blue Ice'　GKir SSmi
- Blue Mirror　See *V. prostrata* 'Blauspiegel'
- 'Blue Sheen'　ECtt ESis GKir LGre LRHS MBNS NBus SChu SIng WLin WPer WWin
- 'Loddon Blue'　GKir LRHS NVic SBla WPer
- 'Miss Willmott'　See *V. prostrata* 'Warley Blue'
- 'Mrs Holt'　CLyd CMea CSam CSpe CStr EBrP EBre EMNN ESis GKir LBCl LBSe LBre LGre LRHS MBBe NFla NFor NMen SAga SBla SBre SIng SRms SSmi WAbe WCru WWin
- 'Nana'　EMNN EPot ESis EWes MWat NHol NMen
- 'Rosea'　ESis MWat WFar WKif WPer
* - 'Shirley Holt'　CHar
- 'Silver Queen'　SRms

- 'Spode Blue' ♀　CLTr CMea LHop LRHS MHar MMil NWCA SAga SBla SCob SRms WLin WOut
- 'Trehane'　More than 30 suppliers
§ - 'Warley Blue'　CMGP
* 'Red Georgia'　LFis
repens　EWTr LNor LRHS MOne NNor WPer
'Rosalinde'　CBot GBuc LFis NCat SPla WPer
rupestris　See *V. prostrata*
saturejoides　CPBP MBro SRms WPer
saxatilis　See *V. fruticans*
schmidtiana　GTou WPer
- 'Nana'　EWTr MBro NHol WPat WRHF
- 'Nana Rosea'　Last listed 1997
selleri　See *V. wormskjoldii*
serpyllifolia　IIve
§ 'Shirley Blue' ♀　More than 30 suppliers
sieboldiana　WCot
§ *spicata*　EBee ELan EWTr LEdu LNor LRHS MBNS MBro MCAu NBid NFor SCob SMer SRms SSea WCot WOve WPer WWye
- 'Alba'　EBee EMan EMil MBNS MRav SCob SRPl WBea WFar WHil WOut WPer
- 'Barcarolle'　ELan LBuc MLLN
§ - 'Blaufuchs'　CBlo CMHG CSam MBel
- Blue Fox　See *V. spicata* 'Blaufuchs'
* - 'Corali'　Last listed 1997
§ - 'Erika'　ECha ECtt GBuc GMac IMGH MBro MLLN NArg NOak SCob SIde SPer SSca SSte SUsu WHil
- 'Heidekind'　CGle CLon CMea CSam ECha EDAr EFou ELan EOrc ESis IMGH LHop MBel MCLN MHer MTis NFor NHar NVic NWCA SBla SHel SIng SUsu SWat WCot WEas WFar WOve WWin
- subsp. *hybrida*　WHer
- hybrids　Last listed 1997
§ - 'Icicle'　CHad CLon CM&M EBee EFou EOrc LRHS MBri SLod SUsu WCot WPGP
§ - subsp. *incana* ♀　CGle CLon CSpe ECGN EHoe ELan ENot EWTr GKir GMaP LFis MBro MPEx MWat NFor NMir SBla SCob SPlb SRms SWat WBea WLin WMoo WPer WPyg
- - 'Mrs Underwood'　ECha
- - 'Nana'　ECha ESis SRms
- - 'Saraband'　WPer
- - 'Silver Carpet'　CMil EBee EFou LRHS MRav NDov NSti SCoo SPer
- - 'Wendy' ♀　GCal
- 'Minuet'　Last listed 1998
- 'Nana Blauteppich'　EMan MBNS SCob WBar WBea
- 'Pavane'　Last listed 1997
- red　WBea
- Red Fox　See *V. spicata* 'Rotfuchs'
- 'Romiley Purple'　ECGP EFou MBrN MBro MCAu MLLN MRav MSte NSti SChu SHel SLod SPer WHoo WPyg WSpi
- 'Rosalind'　EFou NLar
- *rosea*　See *V. spicata* 'Erika'
- 'Rosenrot'　EMan
§ - 'Rotfuchs'　CGle CStr EBee ECtt EFou ELan EOld EPar GKir LAst MRav NSti SCro SMrm SPer WBro WEas WHoo WOve WPer WWin
- 'Sahin's Early'　WCot
- 'Sightseeing'　NArg NBus

- subsp. *spicata* 'Nana'	SSmi
- *variegata*	MLLN NBir SRob
§ *spuria* L.	CStr EMon GGar NBur WPer
stelleri	See *V. wormskjoldii*
subsessilis	NCat
'Blaue Pyramide'	
* - *bendersonii*	MTed
'Sunny Border Blue'	EBee EPfP GMac LCaP SCob WCot
surculosa	Last listed 1998
tauricola	MDHE NTow
- JJH 92101536	LGre
- Mac&W 5835	Last listed 1999
- MP 93236	Last listed 1999
telephiifolia	EGoo EMNN EMan EWes NMen NTow NWCA WPyg WWin
teucrium	See *V. austriaca* subsp. *teucrium*
thessalica	EDAr NTow
thessalonica	EDAr MTPN
thymoides subsp. *pseudocinerea*	NWCA
- subsp. *thymoides*	ESis
'Ulster Blue Dwarf'	WCot
virginica	See *Veronicastrum virginicum*
waldsteiniana	Last listed 1999
'Waterperry Blue'	GKir LRHS MBel MRav NWoo WPer
wherryi	WPer
'White Icicle'	See *V. spicata* 'Icicle'
'White Spire'	CBot
whitleyi	CLyd CNic CTri MHar WWin
§ *wormskjoldii*	CMea EDAr ESis MBrN MBro MHar NFla NMen SBla SHel SRms WPer WWin
- 'Alba'	MDHE WPer

VERONICASTRUM (Scrophulariaceae)

§ *virginicum*	CArn CHea CRow EBee ECha EFou EMon GKir MBel MFir NSti SCob WMoo WPer WWhi WWin
- 'Alboroseum'	ECGN EMan
- *album*	More than 30 suppliers
- 'Apollo'	EFou LGre LRHS MBri
- 'Diane'	EBee LGre
- 'Fascination'	CLon EBee EFou GCal GMac LGre LRHS MBri SOkh SUsu WHil
§ - var. *incarnatum*	CLon ECGN EMan GKir GMaP LRHS MBel NFla SCro SPer SUsu
- 'Lavendelturm'	CLon CPlt CRDP EBee EMil LGre SOkh
* - 'Lila Karina'	Last listed 1998
- 'Pink Glow'	EBee EBrP EBre EFou ELan EMan EMil EPfP LBCl LBSe LBre LGre LRHS MBBe MCAu NSti SAga SBre SMrm SOkh WCDu
- 'Pointed Finger'	EFou SOkh
- *roseum*	See *V. virginicum* var. *incarnatum*
¶ - 'Ruby Glow'	LCaP
- var. *sibiricum*	EMon SCob SVal WMoo
- 'Spring Dew'	EFou LRHS MBri SOkh WHil
- 'Temptation'	EFou LGre MBri

VERSCHAFFELTIA (Arecaceae)

¶ *splendida*	LBlo

VESTIA (Solanaceae)

§ *foetida* ♀	CB&S CCHP CDoC CGre CPle EBee EMan EMar EPfP EPla EREa IBlr MNrw NChi SBrw SHFr SLod SOWG WEas WPGP WPat WPer WSHC WWye

lycioides	See *V. foetida*

VETIVERIA (Poaceae)

zizanioides	GPoy MSal

VIBURNUM ✿ (Caprifoliaceae)

acerifolium	CFil CPle WHCG WWat
'Allegheny'	WWat
alnifolium	See *V. lantanoides*
atrocyaneum	CFil CPle WHCG WPGP WPat WWal WWat
awabuki	CFil EPfP
betulifolium	CBrd CFil CMCN CPle CTrw EPfP EPla MBlu SMad SPer WHCG WPGP WWat
bitchiuense	CPMA CPle ELan WWes
x *bodnantense*	CBot CTri CTrw ENot MRav MWat NDlv NFor WHar WStl WWat WWin
- 'Charles Lamont' ♀	CBot CDoC CSam EBee ECtt ELan EMil EPfP GKir IBlr LPan LRHS MAsh MBri MGos MRav NHol SBrw SEND SLim SPan SPer SSpi SSta SVil WBod WPGP WPat WPyg WWat
- 'Dawn' ♀	More than 30 suppliers
- 'Deben' ♀	CDoC ENot EPfP GKir LRHS MBri MRav SPer SSta WBod WCru WDin WFar WWat
bracteatum	CFil CPle EPfP SLon
buddlejifolium	CEnd CPle GKir WHCG WWat
burejaeticum	Last listed 1999
x *burkwoodii*	More than 30 suppliers
- 'Anne Russell' ♀	CB&S CPMA CTri EBee EBrP EBre ELan EPfP EWTr EWes GKir IOrc LBCl LBSe LBre LRHS MAsh MBBe MGos MRav NBee NHol NSti SBod SBre SLon SPer SPlb WAbe WFar
- 'Chenaultii'	ELan EPfP SRPl WCru
¶ - 'Compact Beauty'	EPfP
- 'Fulbrook' ♀	CMHG EPfP LRHS MBri SLim WWat
- 'Mohawk'	CAbP CEnd CRos ELan LRHS MAsh MBri SCoo SMur SPla SSpi WBcn WPat
- 'Park Farm Hybrid' ♀	CBlo CDoC CPMA CSam CTri EBee EBrP EBre ELan ENot EPfP EPla GKir IOrc LBCl LBSe LBre LRHS MAsh MBBe MRav SBre SEas SLPl SPan SPer SRms WCru WPat WWat
x *carlcephalum* ♀	More than 30 suppliers
* - 'Variegatum'	CPMA
carlesii	CB&S ENot EPfP GKir IOrc LRHS MBlu NBee SCoo SPer SRPl SReu WStl
- 'Aurora' ♀	More than 30 suppliers
- 'Charis'	CMHG CPMA LRHS MBri WBod
- 'Compactum'	CPMA
- 'Diana'	CBlo CEnd CMHG CPMA CRos EPfP GKir LRHS SSpi SSta WPat WWat
cassinoides	CPle EPfP GKir WPat WWat
'Chesapeake'	CBrm CMHG CPMA CPle EWes LRHS NPro SEND WBcn WWes
chingii	CFil CPle EMon GGGa WPGP WWat
cinnamomifolium ♀	CB&S CBlo CFil CHEx CPle EPfP GKir ISea LNet LRHS MAsh NRib SAPC SArc SLon SPer SSpi WBod WHCG WLRN WPGP WSHC WWat

congestum	CPle EMon
¶ 'Conoy'	CPMA
cotinifolium	Last listed 1999
cylindricum	CBot CFil CGre CPle ELan EPfP WCru WPGP WWat
dasyanthum	CPle
davidii ♀	More than 30 suppliers
- (f)	CB&S CBot CDoC ELan EPfP GKir MAsh MGos SPer SPla SReu SRms SSta WBod WPat WWat
- (m)	CB&S CBot CDoC ELan EPfP GKir MGos MRav SPer SPla SReu SRms SSta WBod WPat WWat
dentatum	CPle EPfP WPGP
§ - var. *pubescens*	CPle SLon
dilatatum	LRHS SSpi WWes
- 'Eric'	EPfP
erosum	Last listed 1999
erubescens	WWat
- var. *gracilipes*	CPle EPfP WWat
'Eskimo'	CBlo CEnd CPMA EBee EPfP LRHS MAsh MBlu MBro MGos MRav NBlu NMoo SLim SSpi WPat WPyg WWes
§ *farreri* ♀	CB&S CDoC CDul CPle EBee ECtt ELan ENot EOld EPfP GKir LAst LBuc LRHS MBNS MBar MBri MGos MRav NHol NWea SPer WCFE WDin WGwG WHCG WHar WStI WWat
- 'Album'	See *V. farreri* 'Candidissimum'
§ - 'Candidissimum'	CBot CFil ELan EPfP GKir IMGH LHop LRHS MBri MMHG SPer SSpi WBcn WPyg WWat
- 'Farrer's Pink'	CPMA WWat
- 'Nanum'	CBlo CFil CPMA CPle EPfP MAsh MBar MRav NHol SChu SSta WHCG WPat WPyg WWat
foetidum	CPle LBuc
- var. *ceanothoides*	Last listed 1998
- var. *rectangulatum* B&SWJ 3637	CPle WCru
fragrans Bunge	See *V. farreri*
¶ 'Fragrant Cloud'	MGos
furcatum ♀	EPfP SSpi WHCG WWat
x *globosum* 'Jermyns Globe'	CB&S CBlo CDoC CFil CMHG CPle EPla MBar MGos MRav SBrw SEas SLon WBod WCru WHCG WWat
grandiflorum f. *foetens*	EPfP
¶ - 'Snow White'	ERea
harryanum	CFil CMHG CPle EBee EPfP EPla IOrc LRHS SOWG SPan WCru WPGP WSHC WWat
henryi	CFil CPle EPfP LRHS WHCG WPat WWat
x *hillieri*	CAbP CFil CPle MRav MWhi NRib WBcn WHCG WKif WPGP WWat
- 'Winton' ♀	CAbP CDoC CGre EPfP EPla GKir ISea LRHS MAsh MBri NPro SLim SOWG WBod WCru WFar WWat
japonicum	CFil CHEx CPle CSam EPfP WPGP WWat
x *juddii* ♀	More than 30 suppliers
koreanum	WBod
¶ - B&SWJ 4231	WCru
lantana	CKin CTri ENot GChr GKir IOrc LBuc LHyr MHer NWea SPer WDin WMou WStI WTro
- 'Aureum'	EHoe EPla GChr MBlu WBcn

- 'Mohican'	EBee NPro WWat
- 'Variefolium' (v)	CPMA
- 'Xanthocarpum'	Last listed 1999
§ *lantanoides*	EPfP GKir SSpi
lentago	CAbP CPle
lobophyllum	CPle EPfP
luzonicum B&SWJ 3930	WCru
macrocephalum	CPMA
- f. *keteleeri*	CPMA WWat WWes
mariesii	See *V. plicatum* 'Mariesii'
mullaba	CPle
- CC 1241	Last listed 1997
nervosum B&SWJ 2251a	WCru
nudum	CPle EPfP GIBF
- 'Pink Beauty'	CPMA LRHS MRav WPGP WShe WWat
odoratissimum	CB&S CFil CGre CHEx CPle CSam EBee SMad SSpi WPGP WSHC WWat
opulus	CB&S CKin CSam EBee ECtt ELan ENot EWTr GChr GKir GPoy IOrc LBuc LHyr MBar MBlu MBri MHer MRav MWat NBee NFor NWea SHFr SMac SPer WDin WFar WHar WMou
- 'Aureum'	More than 30 suppliers
- 'Compactum' ♀	More than 30 suppliers
N - 'Fructu Luteo'	ELan GKir SPan
- 'Harvest Gold'	SLim SPla
- 'Nanum'	CAbP CBlo CPle ELan EPla ESis GKir LRHS MBar MBri MRav NHol NMen NPro WDin WHCG WPGP WPat WWat
- 'Notcutt's Variety' ♀	CChe EBee ENot EPfP MGos SHFr SMac SMur SRms
- 'Park Harvest'	CRos EPla GKir LRHS MBri NSti SAga SLPl SMac
§ - 'Roseum' ♀	More than 30 suppliers
- 'Sterile'	See *V. opulus* 'Roseum'
* - 'Sterile Compactum'	IMGH
N - 'Xanthocarpum' ♀	More than 30 suppliers
¶ - 'Xanthocarpum Compactum'	EMon
N *plicatum*	ENot MBar WDin
- 'Cascade'	EWTr SSpi WPnP
- 'Dart's Red Robin'	ECtt GKir LRHS MBri MGos NHol WBcn
- 'Grandiflorum' ♀	CBlo CPle EPfP GKir LRHS MBar MBri SSta WBcn WHCG
- 'Lanarth'	CB&S CDoC CSam CTre EBee ECtt EMil ENot EPfP EWTr GKir IOrc LHop LRHS MGos NFla NHol NSti SPer SPla SRPl SSht SSta WBod WDin WHCG WPat WWat
- 'Magician'	Last listed 1999
§ - 'Mariesii' ♀	More than 30 suppliers
- 'Nanum'	See *V. plicatum* 'Nanum Semperflorens'
§ - 'Nanum Semperflorens'	CDoC EBee ECtt ESis IOrc MAsh MBlu MGos WCot WFar WHCG WPat WSHC WWal WWat
- 'Pink Beauty' ♀	CAbP CB&S CDoC CEnd CPle ECtt ELan EPfP GKir LHop LRHS MAsh MBlu MBri MGos MRav NBee NHol SPer SSpi SSta WBod WEas WFar WHCG WPat WSHC WWat WWeb
- 'Popcorn'	CAbP GKir LRHS MAsh SPan SSpi SSta
* - 'Prostratum'	ESis
- 'Rotundifolium'	IArd MBri NHol SRPl
- 'Rowallane' ♀	EPfP MBel WWat

N	- 'Saint Keverne'	SRob
	- 'Sterile'	CPle GKir GOrc
	- 'Summer Snowflake'	CDoC EBee ENot EPfP GKir IOrc
		LRHS MAsh MBri NHol SPer
		WBod WDin WHCG WWat WWeb
	- f. *tomentosum*	CLan ELan EWTr WDin WHCG
		WStl
	- 'Watanabe'	See *V. plicatum* 'Nanum
		Semperflorens'
	'Pragense' ♀	CB&S CMCN CPle EBee EPfP EPla
		GKir MBar MGos NHol NRib SLon
		SPer WBod WHCG WLRN WPat
		WPnP WPyg WRHF WWat
	propinquum	WWat
	- B&SWJ 4009	WCru
	pubescens	See *V. dentatum* var. *pubescens*
	recognitum	Last listed 1999
	x *rhytidophylloides*	CPle GKir NFor WWat
	- 'Dart's Duke'	ENot GKir LRHS MBri SLPl
	rhytidophyllum	More than 30 suppliers
	- 'Holland'	EPla
	- 'Roseum'	CBot MRav SLPl
	- 'Variegatum'	CPMA WBcn
	- 'Willowwood'	EBee LRHS MAsh SPer SSta WPat
		WWat
*	*ribesifolium*	Last listed 1997
	rigidum	CFil CPle
	sargentii	CBlo GBin IOrc WWat
	- 'Onondaga' ♀	More than 30 suppliers
	- 'Susquehanna'	EPfP
	semperflorens	See *V. plicatum* 'Nanum
		Semperflorens'
§	*setigerum*	CPle EPfP SLPl SMad SSpi
	'Shasta'	CBlo CDoC CMCN COtt CRos
		EPfP GKir LRHS MBri NHol NPro
		SSpi SSta
	sieboldii	CB&S CPle
	- B&SWJ 2837	WCru
	suspensum	SVen
	taiwanianum	WCru
	B&SWJ 3009	
	theiferum	See *V. setigerum*
	tinus	More than 30 suppliers
	- 'Bewley's Variegated'	CB&S CDoC EBee EMil MGos
		MRav SCoo
	- 'Compactum'	Last listed 1999
	- 'Eve Price' ♀	More than 30 suppliers
	- 'French White'	CBlo CDoC CMFo EBee EPfP EPla
		LRHS MBri MRav SCoo SEas SRms
		WGwG WPGP WWal WWat
	- 'Gwenllian' ♀	More than 30 suppliers
	- L. f. *hirtum*	CTre
	- 'Israel'	EMil SEas SPan SPer SPla WWat
	- 'Little Bognor'	LRHS MGos NPro SEas
	- 'Lucidum'	CB&S CBlo CPle CSam MGos SPla
		WCFE WWat
	- 'Lucidum Variegatum'	CFil CLan CPMA EHol SDry SLim
		WPGP
*	- 'Macrophyllum'	LPan
¶	- 'Magraf'	WBcn
*	- 'Pink Parfait'	MRav
	- 'Pink Prelude'	EBee ENot SEas
	- 'Purpureum'	CB&S CMFo EBee EHoe EPfP EPla
		GChr LRHS MAsh MRav SEas SLPl
		SLim SMac SPer SPla WFar WGwG
		WWal
	- 'Sappho'	Last listed 1998
¶	- 'Spring Bouquet'	NBee
	- subsp. *subcordatum*	GGGa
	C 2002	
	- 'Variegatum'	More than 30 suppliers
	tomentosum	See *V. plicatum*

	utile	CPle EPfP WHCG WPGP WWat
	wrightii	CPle EPfP MBro NHol SPan
		WHCG WPat WPyg
	- var. *bessei*	LRHS

VICIA (Papilionaceae)

	angustifolia	See *V. sativa* subsp. *nigra*
	cracca	CKin EWFC NLan
	narbonensis	CAgr
	orobus	MSCN WGwy
§	*sativa* subsp. *nigra*	CKin
	sepium	CKin EWFC
	sylvatica	EWFC WGwy

VIGNA (Papilionaceae)

§	*caracalla*	CPIN

VIGUIERA (Asteraceae)

	multiflora	Last listed 1998

VILLARESIA See CITRONELLA

VILLARSIA (Menyanthaceae)

	bennettii	See *Nymphoides peltata*
		'Bennettii'

VIMINARIA (Papilionaceae)

	juncea	Last listed 1998

VINCA ✿ (Apocynaceae)

	difformis	CGle CHad CHar CLTr COIW CTri
		EBee ECha EPla LHop LLWP LRHS
		NCat SDix SMac WCru
		WHer WOak WPic WWat
	- subsp. *bicolor* 'Alba'	EPla
	- - 'Jenny Pym'	EBee EMon EPPr LHop SCoo
		SMac SPan SRms WWat
	- - 'Ruby Baker'	EMon
	- subsp. *difformis*	EMon
	- Greystone form	CLTr EPPr EPla LHop MBNS SCoo
		SEND WPnP WRus
	- 'Oxford'	SLPl
	- 'Snowmound'	MRav WWat
	herbacea	Last listed 1997
	'Hidcote Purple'	See *V. major* var. *oxyloba*
	major	CB&S CChe EBee ELan ENot
		EOrc EWFC EWTr GChr GKir
		GPoy LBuc LRHS MBri MFir MGos
		MHer MWat NWea SBod SIde
		SPer WDin WGwG WStl
	- var. *alba*	CCHP GBuc IBlr
	- 'Caucasian Blue'	CFil WPGP
	- 'Elegantissima'	See *V. major* 'Variegata'
§	- subsp. *hirsuta* (Boiss.)	EMon WWye
	Stearn	
	- var. *hirsuta*	See *V. major* var. *oxyloba*
	- 'Honeydew' (v)	EMon
	- 'Jason Hill'	EMon MBel
§	- 'Maculata' (v)	CDoC EBee EMar EMon ENot
		EPla LHop LRHS MBar MBri
		MSCN NCiC NFai NHol SDry
		SLim SPar SPer WCru WMoo
		WWeb
§	- var. *oxyloba*	CNic COld ECtt ELan EMon
		EOrc EPla GSki LHop MRav SLPl
		SLim SMac SRms WHen WPic
		WWat
	- var. *pubescens*	See *V. major* subsp. *hirsuta*
		(Boiss.) Stearn
	- 'Reticulata'	ELan EMon MBel MSCN NSti
	- 'Surrey Marble'	See *V. major* 'Maculata'
§	- 'Variegata' ♀	More than 30 suppliers

minor	CAgr CDoC CKin ELan ENot EPar EWFC EWTr GCHN GChr GPoy MBar MBro MFir MHer MSCN MWat NSti NWea SIde WDin WOak WStI WWye
- f. *alba*	CB&S CBot CDoC ECha EGoo LAst LHop LRHS MAsh MBar MBri MGos NOak SEas SPer STre WCot WCru WStI WWat WWye
- 'Alba Aureavariegata'	See *V. minor* 'Alba Variegata'
§ - 'Alba Variegata'	CGle EBot EBrP EBre EGoo EHoe EPPr EPla GKir LAst LBCl LBSe LBre MBBe MBar MFir MGos NHol NPro SBre SPer SRms STre WBod WEas WFar WHer WWat
§ - 'Argenteovariegata' ♀	More than 30 suppliers
§ - 'Atropurpurea' ♀	More than 30 suppliers
- 'Aurea'	SPla WRHF
§ - 'Aureovariegata'	CB&S CBot CChe EBee EPla GChr GKir GPoy LAst LRHS MAsh MBar MFir MGos MRav NFor NHol SPer WHen WWye
- 'Azurea'	CHid
§ - 'Azurea Flore Pleno' (d) ♀	More than 30 suppliers
* - 'Blue and Gold'	EGoo EMon
- 'Blue Cloud'	MLLN NHol SBod
- 'Blue Drift'	CBlo EMon MBNS MLLN NHol SBod
- 'Blue Moon'	EBee ECtt NHol SPla WRHF
- 'Bowles' Blue'	See *V. minor* 'La Grave'
- 'Bowles' Variety'	See *V. minor* 'La Grave'
- 'Burgundy'	EPar LLWP SMac SRms WWye
- 'Caerulea Plena'	See *V. minor* 'Azurea Flore Pleno'
- 'Dartington Star'	See *V. major* var. *oxyloba*
- 'Dart's Blue'	Last listed 1998
- 'Double Burgundy'	See *V. minor* 'Multiplex'
¶ - 'Garnet'	EWTr
- 'Gertrude Jekyll' ♀	CDoC CLTr EBee ELan EMon ENot EOld EPla EWTr GChr GKir ILis LRHS MAsh MBri MRav NHol NSti SBod SChu SCoo SEND SLim SPer SVil WElm WHer WWat
- Green Carpet	See *V. minor* 'Grüner Teppich'
§ - 'Grüner Teppich'	EMon
§ - 'La Grave' ♀	CChe CDoC CSev EBee EBlw ECGP ECha ELan ENot EPla EWTr GAbr GKir LRHS MBro MRav NHol SBod SLim SPer SRms SSvw STre WBod WElm WPyg WWat
- 'Maculata' (v)	EGoo ELan EPPr SCoo WBcn
- 'Marion Cran'	CEnd GSki
§ - 'Multiplex' (d)	EBee ECtt EMon EOrc EPPr EPar EPla MAsh MBar MInt NHol SRms WCFE WCru WRHF WWat
- 'Oland Blue'	Last listed 1999
- 'Persian Carpet'	EMon
- 'Purpurea'	See *V. minor* 'Atropurpurea'
- 'Rubra'	See *V. minor* 'Atropurpurea'
- 'Sabinka'	CHid EGoo EMon EPla
- 'Silver Service' (v/d)	CHid EMon EPPr EPla GBuc MBel MInt MRav NHol WCot
- 'Variegata'	See *V. minor* 'Argenteovariegata'
- 'Variegata Aurea'	See *V. minor* 'Aureovariegata'
- 'White Gold'	CChe EBee NHol NPro WRHF

VINCETOXICUM (Asclepiadaceae)

forrestii ACE 1615	Last listed 1999
§ *hirundinaria*	EEls GPoy
nigrum	EMon NChi WCru WTin
officinale	See *V. hirundinaria*
sp. HH&K 142	Last listed 1999

VIOLA ✿ (Violaceae)

'Abigail' (Vtta)	LPVe
'Achilles' (Va)	LPVe
¶ 'Ada Jackson' (ExVa)	WOFF
'Adelina' (Va)	LPVe
* 'Admiral'	GMac
'Admiral Avellan'	See *V.* 'Amiral Avellan'
'Admiration' (Va)	GMac LPVe WBou
adunca	NWCA
- 'Alba'	WLRN
- var. *minor*	See *V. labradorica* Schrank.
aetolica	CInt
'Agnes Cochrane' (ExVa)	Last listed 1999
'Agneta' (Va)	LPVe
'Alanta' (Va)	LPVe SAga WWhi
§ *alba*	EWes NHol NMen SCro WWin
albanica	See *V. magellensis*
I 'Alcea' (Va)	LPVe
'Alethia' (Va)	LPVe
'Alexander Rayfield' (Va)	LPVe
'Alexia' (Va)	LPVe
'Alice Witter' (Vt)	CDev CGro
'Alice Wood' (ExVa)	Last listed 1999
'Alice Woodall' (Va)	LPVe
* 'Alison' (Va)	GMaP GMac WBou WOut WWhi
'Alison Lofts' (Va)	WCot
'Alma' (Va)	Last listed 1999
altaica	LPVe
'Alwyn' (Va)	LPVe
'Amelia' (Va)	GMac LPVe WBou WWhi
'Amethyst' (C)	Last listed 1998
§ 'Amiral Avellan' (Vt)	CDev CGro NBro WRus
'Andrena' (Va)	LPVe
'Angela' (Va)	LPVe
'Anita' (Va)	LPVe
'Ann' (SP)	WOFF
'Ann Kean' (Vtta)	LPVe
'Anna' (Va)	LPVe
'Anna Leyns' (Va)	LPVe
'Annabelle' (Va)	LPVe
'Annaliese' (C)	LPVe
'Anne Mott' (Va)	LPVe
'Annette Ross' (Va)	LPVe
I 'Annona' (Va)	LPVe
'Anthea' (Va)	LPVe
'Antique Lace' (Va)	GMac MHer NBrk
'Aphrodite' (Va)	LPVe
'Apollo' (Va)	LPVe
'Apricotta'	NHaw
'Arabella' (Va)	EBee LBee LPVe LRHS SChu SLod SMrm WBou WFar WLRN
arborescens	Last listed 1999
'Ardross Gem' (Va)	CGle CMHG CSam EBee EDAr GCHN GKir GMac LBee LHop LPVe LRHS NChi NSti WBou WEas WFar WIvy WKif WPer WWat WWhi WWin
arenaria	See *V. rupestris*
'Arkwright's Ruby' (Va)	LPVe NChi SGar SRms WWhi
'Artemis' (Va)	LPVe
arvensis	Last listed 1997
'Aspasia' (Va) ♀	EBee GMac LBee LPVe LRHS WBou
'Astrid' (Va)	LPVe
'Atalanta' (Vtta)	LPVe LRHS
'Athena' (Va)	LPVe
athois	LPVe
'Aurelia' (Va)	LPVe
'Aurora' (Va)	LPVe
'Avril' (Va)	LPVe
'Avril Lawson' (Va)	GMac MGrG NNrd WBou

'Baby Blue'	Last listed 1998	
'Baby Franjo'	COIW EDAr	
'Baby Lucia' (Va)	CElw COIW EDAr NCat	
'Barbara' (Va)	LPVe WBou	
'Barbara Cawthorne' (C)	LPVe	
'Barnsdale Gem'	MBNS NDov	
'Baronne Alice de Rothschild' (Vt)	CDev EDAr WLRN	
'Beatrice' (Vtta)	MAnH WBou	
'Becka' (Va)	LPVe	
* bella	EBee EWll LPVe WEas	
§ 'Belmont Blue' (C)	More than 30 suppliers	
§ bertolonii	EBee LPVe WBou	
'Beshlie' (Va) ♀	CElw CMea EBee GMaP GMac LPVe LRHS MBNS SChu WBou WEas WKif WOut	
'Bessie Cawthorne' (C)	LPVe SChu	
'Bessie Knight' (Va)	LPVe	
betonicifolia	LPVe	
* - albescens	NHar	
'Bettina' (Va)	LPVe	
'Betty' (Va)	LPVe	
'Bianca' (Vtta)	LPVe	
biflora	CMHG CPla EOld EPar MTho NChi NRya SIng	
'Bishop's Belle' (FP)	Last listed 1999	
'Bishop's Gold' (FP)	Last listed 1999	
'Black Ace' (Va)	LPVe	
* 'Black Beauty'	Last listed 1998	
¶ 'Black from Black'	WCot	
'Blue Butterfly' (C)	GMac	
'Blue Carpet' (Va)	GMac	
'Blue Cloud' (Va)	LPVe NChi	
'Blue Diamond'	EFou	
'Blue Moon' (C)	LRHS MCLN SChu SDys SMrm WBou WWat	
'Blue Moonlight' (C)	CElw GBuc GMac LRHS NChi SMrm WWat	
'Blue Perfection' (Va)	LRHS	
'Blue Tit' (Va)	SChu	
'Bonna Cawthorne' (Va)	LPVe	
bosniaca	See V. elegantula bosniaca	
'Boughton Blue'	See V. 'Belmont Blue'	
'Bournemouth Gem' (Vt)	CDev CGro	
§ 'Bowles' Black' (T)	CArn CDev CSWP ECha EDAr ELan EWTr GAbr LPVe LRHS MHer NBro SBla SRPl SRms WBea WBou WEas WOve WWat	
'Boy Blue' (Vtta)	LPVe	
'Brenda Hall' (Va)	LPVe	
'Bronwen' (Va)	LPVe	
'Bruneau' (dVt)	Last listed 1999	
* 'Bryony' (Vtta)	LPVe WBou	
'Bullion' (Va)	LPVe	
'Burnock Yellow' (Va)	Last listed 1999	
'Buttercup' (Vtta)	CInt GMac LBee LPVe LRHS NHar SChu SIng WBou WLRN WOut WWhi WWin	
'Butterpat' (C)	GMac MHer NBrk NHaw	
'Buxton Blue' (Va)	LPVe	
calaminaria	LPVe	
'Calantha' (Vtta)	LPVe	
calcarata	ELan LPVe	
§ - subsp. zoysii	GCHN	
'California' (Vt)	CDev EDAr	
'Callia' (Va)	LPVe	
I 'Calliandra' (Vtta)	LPVe	
I 'Calypso' (Va)	LPVe	
§ canadensis var. rugulosa	CRDP	
'Candida' (Vtta)	LPVe	
canina	CKin NBro	
* - alba	CBre	

'Carberry Seedling' (Va)	LPVe	
'Carina' (Vtta)	LPVe	
'Carnival' (Va)	NBrk	
'Carola' (Va)	LPVe	
'Caroline' (Va)	SMrm	
I 'Cassandra' (Vtta)	LPVe	
'Catforth Blue Ribbon'	NCat	
* 'Catforth Gold'	NCat	
* 'Catforth Suzanne'	NCat	
'Catherine Williams' (ExVa)	Last listed 1999	
'Cat's Whiskers'	CElw GBri GMac NBrk NChi WCru	
cazorlensis	SBla	
'Chandler's Glory' (Va)	LPVe	
'Chantal' (Vtta)	LPVe	
'Chantreyland' (Va)	NBir SRms	
'Charity' (Va)	LPVe	
* 'Charlotte'	CFri CSam WBou	
'Charlotte Mott' (Va)	LPVe	
'Chelsea Girl' (Va)	SMrm	
¶ 'Cherub'	GMac	
'Chloe' (Vtta)	LPVe	
* 'Christina'	WLRN	
'Christmas' (Vt)	CDev CGro EBee LCaP	
'Christobel' (Va)	LPVe	
'Cinderella' (Va)	Last listed 1999	
'Citrina' (Va)	LPVe	
'Claire' (Va)	LPVe	
'Clare Harrison' (Va)	LPVe	
'Clementina' (Va) ♀	CElw GCHN LPVe MRav NSti	
'Cleo' (Va)	GMac WBou	
'Clive Groves' (Vt)	CDev CGro	
'Clodagh' (Va)	LPVe	
'Clover' (Va)	LPVe	
'Coeur d'Alsace' (Vt)	CBre CDev CNic CPBP EBee EDAr EFou EPar GMac LPVe NBro WCot WEas WRus WWhi	
'Colette' (Va)	LPVe	
'Colleen' (Vtta)	LPVe	
'Columbine' (Va)	More than 30 suppliers	
§ 'Comte de Brazza' (dPVt)	CDev CTri GBar GMac WRha	
'Comte de Chambord' (dVt)	WRha	
'Connie' (Va)	LPVe	
'Connigar'	CSam	
'Coralie' (Vtta)	LPVe	
'Cordelia' (Va)	EBee LPVe NBro	
'Cornetto'	EBee MHer MMal	
Cornish indigenous mauve	EDAr	
* 'Cornish White'	CDev EDAr	
cornuta ♀	CElw CGle CHad CMea CPla EOrc EPot GGar IMGH LPVe MBro MFir MWat NBro NChi NSti NWCA SIng SMrm SPer SRms SUsu WBea WBou WFar WHen WHoo WPyg WRos WSpi	
- Alba Group ♀	More than 30 suppliers	
§ - 'Alba Minor'	EWes GMac LPVe MBNS MBro MCLN MFir NBro SChu WAbe WCot WFar WHoo WPyg WWat	
- blue	LPVe MHer WWat	
* - 'Bluestone Gold'	WCot	
¶ - 'Brimstone'	GMac	
¶ - 'Clouded Yellow'	GMac	
- 'Eastgrove Blue Scented' (C)	CLTr EBee GMac MCLN WBou WCot WEas WIvy WOut WRHF	
* - 'Gypsy Moth'	GMac	
- Lilacina Group (C)	CGle ECha GMac LPVe MBro MRav NCat NChi NFla SChu SMrm SWat WFar WHoo	
- 'Maiden's Blush'	EMan GMac NChi	
- 'Minor' ♀	CInt CPla CSam GMac LPVe LRHS MCLN MFir NBro SBla WAbe WBou WWat	

	– 'Minor Alba'	See *V. cornuta* 'Alba Minor'
	– pale blue	LRHS
*	– 'Paris White'	EBee EPfP
	– 'Purple Gem'	GMac
	– Purpurea Group	CElw CMea ECha GBuc SRPl WRus
	– 'Rosea'	LPVe
	– 'Seymour Pink'	Last listed 1999
¶	– 'Spider'	GMac
	– 'Variegata'	LPVe
*	– 'Victoria's Blush'	GMac MOne NHar NSti SMrm SUsu WBou WWhi
	– 'Violacea'	GMac LRHS
	– 'Yellow King'	EFou SSvw
	corsica	CInt EBee LPVe SDys
*	'Cottage Garden' (Va)	LRHS NHaw WFar
	'Countess of Shaftsbury' (dVt)	CDev
	'Cox's Moseley' (ExVa)	WOFF
	'Cream Princess'	Last listed 1999
	'Crepuscule'	Last listed 1999
	'Cressida' (Va)	LPVe
§	*cucullata* ♀	CGro SChu SRms WPrP
§	– 'Alba'	CBro ECGP EPar LFis LLWP NChi WEas
	– *rosea*	EWes
*	– 'Striata Alba'	LRHS MWgw
	cunninghamii	Last listed 1998
	– CC 463	Last listed 1999
	curtisii	See *V. tricolor* subsp. *curtisii*
	'Cuty' (Va)	LRHS
	'Cyril Bell' (Va)	LPVe
§	'Czar' (Vt)	CBre GVer ILis
§	'Czar Bleu' (Vt)	CDev CGro
	'Daena' (Vtta)	EBee LPVe
	'Daisy Smith' (Va)	GMac NChi SChu WBou
	'Dancing Geisha' (Vt)	WCot
	'Dartington Hybrid' (Va)	LPVe
	'Daveron' (C)	LPVe
	'David Rhodes' (FP)	Last listed 1999
	'David Wheldon' (Va)	LPVe
	'Davina' (Va)	LPVe SChu SDys
	'Dawn' (Vtta)	CBos LPVe WBou
	'Deanna' (Va)	LPVe
	'Decima' (Va)	LPVe
	declinata	NChi WOut
	'Delia' (Va)	GMac LPVe WBou
	'Delicia' (Vtta)	CBos LPVe MCLN NChi WBou
	'Delmonden' (Va)	CRDP SBla
	'Delphine' (Va)	LPVe NCiC SChu
	'Demeter' (Va)	LPVe
	'Desdemona' (Va)	EBee GMac LBee WBou
	'Desmonda' (Va)	LPVe SChu
	'Devon Cream' (Va)	GMac WBou
	diffusa glabella	Last listed 1999
	'Dimity' (Va)	LPVe
	'Dione' (Vtta)	LPVe
I	'Diosma' (Va)	LPVe
§	*dissecta*	GBin WCot WPer
§	– var. *chaerophylloides* f. *eizanensis*	EBee MTho NLar NWCA
	– var. *sieboldiana*	CRDP
	'Dobbie's Bronze' (Va)	Last listed 1999
	'Dobbie's Buff' (Va)	Last listed 1999
	'Dobbie's Red' (Va)	Last listed 1999
	'Doctor Smart' (C)	LPVe
	doerfleri	LPVe
	'Dominique' (Va)	LPVe
	'Dominy' (Vtta)	LPVe
	'Donau' (Vt)	CDev EDAr
	'Double White' (dVt)	CGle
	dubyana	EBee GBuc SSca
	'Duchesse de Parme' (dPVt)	CDev CGle CGro EDAr GMac
	'D'Udine' (dVt)	CDev CGro GMac WHer
	'Dusk'	WBou
	'E.A. Bowles'	See *V.* 'Bowles' Black'
	'Eastgrove Elizabeth' (C)	Last listed 1998
	'Eastgrove Elizabeth Booth'	WEas
	'Eastgrove Ice Blue' (C)	WEas
	'Eastgrove Twinkle' (C)	NCat WEas
	eizanensis	See *V. dissecta* var. *chaerophylloides* f. *eizanensis*
	'Elaine Cawthorne' (C)	LPVe
*	'Elaine Quin'	EBee NCiC SChu WBou
§	*elatior*	CElw CMea CPla CSWP CStu EBee EMon EPar EPla GBri LPVe LRHS MAvo MBel MHar MNrw NChi NHol SChu SSca SUsu WCot WFar WLin WPer WWye
§	*elegantula*	GCrs LPVe SSca
§	– *bosniaca*	LPVe
	'Elisha' (Va)	LPVe
	'Elizabeth' (Va)	EBee LPVe SChu SMrm SRms WBou WLRN
	'Elizabeth Cawthorne' (C)	LPVe
¶	'Elizabeth Christie' (FP)	WOFF
	'Elizabeth Lee'	Last listed 1998
	'Elizabeth McCallum' (FP)	Last listed 1999
	'Elliot Adam' (Va)	EBee WBou WOut
	'Elsie Coombs' (Vt)	CDev WPer
	'Emily Mott' (Va)	LPVe
	'Emma' (Va)	CMea LPVe NHar
	'Emma Cawthorne' (C)	CLTr LPVe
	'Enterea' (Va)	LPVe
	erecta	See *V. elatior*
	'Eris' (Va)	LPVe
	'Eros' (Va)	LPVe
	'Etain' (Va)	CBos ECha ELan EMan EWes GMaP GMac LGre LPVe MMil MOne NBrk NCiC NHaw SAga SBla WBou WFar WLRN WWhi
	'Ethena' (Va)	LPVe
	'Etienne' (Va)	LPVe
	'Evelyn' (ExVa)	Last listed 1997
	'Evelyn Cawthorne' (C)	LPVe
	'Fabiola' (Vtta)	GMac LBee LPVe LRHS NBir
¶	'Fantasy' (Va)	CBos WBou
	'Felicity' (Va)	LPVe
	'Felix'	MAnH
	'Finola Galway' (Va)	LPVe
	'Fiona' (Va)	CLon GMac LPVe MCLN NBrk NCat SChu WBou WOut
	'Fiona Lawrenson' (Va)	LPVe
	flettii	NChi SIng
	'Florence' (Va)	LPVe
	'Foxbrook Cream' (C)	CMea GBuc GMac LPVe MBel MHer NBrk NCiC SAga WBou WCot WHoo WSpi WWhi
	'Frances' (Va)	LPVe
¶	'Frances Perry'	NSti WWhi
	'Francesca' (Va)	LPVe
	'Freckles'	See *V. sororia* 'Freckles'
	'Gatina' (Va)	LPVe
I	'Gazania' (Va)	CMea LPVe WBou
	'Gazelle' (Vtta)	LPVe
	'Genesta Gambier' (Va)	CSam
	'George Lee'	Last listed 1998
	'Georgina' (Va)	LPVe
	'Geraldine' (Vtta)	LPVe
	'Geraldine Cawthorne' (C)	LPVe NCat
	'Giant Elk' (Vt)	Last listed 1999
¶	'Gill Elwell'	WBou
	'Gina' (Vtta)	LPVe

'Giselle' (Va)	LPVe
glabella	CLTr
'Gladys Findlay' (Va)	GMac LPVe WBou
¶ 'Gladys Hughes' (FP)	WOFF
* 'Glenda'	WBou
'Glenroyd Fancy' (ExVa)	Last listed 1999
'Gloire de Verdon' (PVt)	CGro
'Governor Herrick' (Vt)	CDev CGro NSti WPer WSpi
'Grace' (Va)	Last listed 1999
§ *gracilis*	CElw ECha LPVe WFar
- x *cornuta*	LPVe
- 'Lutea'	CLon CSam SMrm
* - 'Magic'	CElw SMrm
- 'Major'	WBou
'Green Jade' (v)	CPla EMan MBNS
'Grey Owl' (Va)	CLon CMea EBee LBee LGre LPVe LRHS NBrk SChu SLod SMrm WBou WKif WPGP
grisebachiana	Last listed 1998
* - *alba*	Last listed 1998
'Griselda' (Vtta)	LPVe
'Grovemount Blue' (C)	CMea
§ *grypoceras* var. *exilis*	CInt CNic EMan EMar GAri GBri NBus SBla SChu SMad
- 'Variegata'	EHoe NBir
'Gustav Wermig' (C)	GAbr LPVe MBel NHaw WBou
'Gwen Cawthorne' (C)	LPVe
'H.H. Hodge' (ExVa)	WOFF
'Hackpen'	CSam
'Hadria Cawthorne' (C)	LPVe
'Hansa' (C)	CHid NChi
'Haslemere'	See *V.* 'Nellie Britton'
'Hazeldene Blue'	Last listed 1999
* 'Heaselands'	CBos SMrm
I 'Hebe' (Vtta)	LPVe
§ *hederacea*	CDev CGro CMHG ECou GCHN GQui LPVe MNrw NBro NHar NNrd NOak SAga SIng SRms SUsu WOve WSpi WWhi WWye
- blue	CFee CInt CLTr WPer
- 'Putty'	ECou EWes
'Helen W. Cochrane' (ExVa)	WOFF
'Helena' (Va)	LPVe SChu
'Hera' (Va)	LPVe
'Hespera' (Va)	LPVe
I 'Hesperis' (Va)	LPVe
heterophylla	See *V. bertolonii*
subsp. *epirota*	
¶ 'Hetty Gattenby'	WBou
'Hextable' (C)	LPVe
hirta	CKin MHew
hispida	EBee LPVe
'Hopleys White'	CGro WHer
'Hudsons Blue'	CElw WEas
'Hugh Campbell' (ExVa)	Last listed 1999
'Huntercombe Purple' (Va) ♀	CElw CGle EDAr LBee LPVe LRHS MWat SAga SBla SChu SRms SUsu WBou WKif
'Hunter's Pride'	SMrm
'Hyperion' (Va)	LPVe
'I.G. Sherwood'	Last listed 1999
'Iantha' (Vtta)	LPVe
'Iden Gem' (Va)	LPVe WBou
'Inkie' (Va)	Last listed 1999
'Inverurie Beauty' (Va) ♀	CBos GKir GMaP LPVe MCLN MFir NBrk NCat SChu WBou WKif
'Inverurie Mauve' (Va)	LPVe
'Iona' (Va)	EBee LPVe
'Irina' (Va)	LPVe
'Irish Elegance' (Vt)	CDev NBro SChu
'Irish Mary' (Va)	LPVe SChu

'Irish Molly' (Va)	CBot CElw CFri CLon CSam CSpe EBee ECha ELan GKir GMac LPVe LRHS MCLN MHer NChi SBla SChu SIng SMrm SPer SRms WBou WEas WHer WRus WSHC WWhi WWin
'Isata' (Vtta)	EDAr LPVe
'Isla' (Vtta)	LPVe
'Isobel'	EWes
'Ita' (Va)	LPVe
'Iver Grove' (Va)	LPVe
'Ivory Queen' (Va)	CBos GMac LPVe NBrk WBou
'Ivory White' (Va)	CDev LPVe
* 'Jack Sampson'	CDev
'Jack Simpson'	EDAr
'Jackanapes' (Va) ♀	CElw CSam ECha ECtt ELan GKir GMac LPVe LRHS NBrk NChi SChu SIng SMrm SPer SRms WBou WFar WSpi WWhi WWin WWol
¶ 'Jacqueline Snocken' (ExVa)	WOFF
'James'	Last listed 1999
'James Pilling' (Va)	Last listed 1999
'Jane Askew' (Va)	LPVe
'Jane Mott' (Va)	LPVe
'Janet' (Va)	LPVe SMrm WLRN
'Janine' (Vtta)	LPVe
'Janna' (Va)	LPVe
japonica	Last listed 1998
- 'Rodney Davey'	MCCP
'Jean Arnot'	CGro
'Jeannie Bellew' (Va)	GMac LPVe NHar SChu SPer WBou WLRN WSpi WWol
'Jemma' (Va)	LPVe
'Jenelle' (Vtta)	LPVe
'Jenny' (Vtta)	LPVe
'Jersey Gem' (Va)	GMac LPVe
'Jessica' (Va)	LPVe
'Jessie East'	WEas
'Jessie Taylor' (FP)	Last listed 1999
'Jimmie's Dark' (ExVa)	Last listed 1999
'Joanna' (Va)	WBou
I 'Jocunda' (Va)	LPVe
'Joella' (Va)	LPVe
¶ 'John Goddard' (FP)	WOFF
'John Raddenbury' (Vt)	EDAr
'John Rodger' (SP)	WOFF
'John Wallmark' (c)	Last listed 1999
'John Yelmark' (Va)	LPVe
'John Zanini' (Vtta)	LPVe
'Johnny Jump Up' (T)	EWll
Joker Series (P) ♀	Last listed 1995
jooi	CInt GTou NBir NBro NMen SBla SIng SRms SSca WRha
jordanii	LPVe
'Jordieland Gem' (c)	EMan GMac NDov
'Josie' (Va)	LPVe
'Joyce Gray' (Va)	GMac WBou
'Judy Goring' (Va)	LPVe
'Julia' (Va)	LPVe MAnH WBou
'Julian' (Va)	CElw CLTr GMac SBla SRms WBou WIvy WWat
'Juno' (Va)	GMac LPVe
'Jupiter' (Va)	EBee LPVe SMrm
'Kate' (Va)	CElw SAga
'Katerina' (Va)	LPVe
'Kathy' (Vtta)	LPVe
'Katie Grayson' (C)	LPVe
'Katinka' (Va)	LPVe
keiskei	GCHN
'Kerrie' (Va)	LPVe
* 'Kerry Girl'	CDev
'Kiki McDonough' (C)	LPVe NBrk SChu

'Kilruna' (Va)	LPVe
* 'King of the Blacks'	Last listed 1999
'King of the Blues' (Va)	LPVe
'Kinvarna' (Va)	LPVe
'Kirsty' (Va)	LPVe
'Kitten'	EBee GMac LRHS NCat NSti SChu
	WBou
'Kitty White' (Va)	LPVe
koraiensis	NWCA
koreana	See *V. grypoceras* var. *exilis*
kusanoana	Last listed 1997
N *labradorica* hort.	See *V. riviniana* Purpurea Group
N – Schrank.	CGro CHar EBlw EMil EOld EWTr
	GLil LRHS LSyl MRav NPri SHFr
	SMer STre WCra WFar WSpi
N – *purpurea* misapplied	See *V. riviniana* Purpurea Group
lactea	Last listed 1997
'Lady Hulme Campbell'	Last listed 1999
(PVt)	
'Lady Saville'	See *V.* 'Sissinghurst'
'Lady Tennyson' (Va)	GMac LPVe SBla
'Lamorna' (Vtta)	LPVe
lanceolata	Last listed 1998
'Larissa' (Va)	LPVe
'Latona' (Va)	LPVe
'Laura' (C)	GBuc NBrk
'Laura Cawthorne'	EBee NDov
'Lavender Lady'	CGro
'Laverna' (Va)	LPVe
'Lavinia' (Va)	EBee GCrs LBee LPVe LRHS WBou
'Lawrence' (c)	Last listed 1999
'Leander' (Va)	LPVe
'Leda' (Va)	LPVe
'Lemon Sorbet'	CElw GKir MOne
'Leora' (Vtta)	LPVe
'Leora Hamilton' (C)	LPVe NCiC
'Lerosa' (Vtta)	LPVe
¶ 'Lesley Keay' (ExVa)	WOFF
'Leta' (Vtta)	LPVe
'Letitia' (Va)	CBos EFou GMac LPVe MMil
	SMrm SPer WBou WLRN WSpi
'Leto' (Va)	LPVe
'Lewisa' (Va)	LPVe
'Lianne' (Vt)	CDev WPer
'Lilac Rose' (Va)	GMac SAga WBou
'Liliana' (Va)	LPVe
'Liriopa' (Va)	LPVe
'Lisa Cawthorne' (C)	LPVe
'Little David' (Vtta) ♀	CBos CInt CSam EBee GMac LBee
	LPVe LRHS MHer WBou WEas
	WOut WPGP
'Little Johnny' (Va)	Last listed 1997
'Little Liz' (Va)	Last listed 1999
'Livia' (Vtta)	LPVe
'Lola' (Va)	LPVe
'Lord Nelson' (Va)	EWll LPVe
'Lord Plunket' (Va)	LPVe WBou
'Lorna' (Va) ♀	LPVe
'Lorna Cawthorne' (C)	CElw LPVe NCat WOut
'Lorna Moakes' (Va)	LPVe SAga
'Louisa' (Va)	LPVe
'Louise Gemmell' (Va)	LPVe NBrk NHaw SChu
'Luca' (Va)	LPVe
'Lucinda' (Va)	LPVe
'Lucy' (Va)	LPVe
'Ludy May' (Va)	LPVe
'Luna' (Vtta)	LPVe
§ *lutea*	EBot LPVe WBou WGwy
– subsp. *elegans*	See *V. lutea*
'Luxonne' (Vt)	CBre WLRN
lyallii	Last listed 1997
'Lydia' (Va)	LPVe SChu WBou

'Lydia Groves'	CDev CGro
'Lynn' (Va)	LPVe
'Lysander' (Va)	LPVe
macedonica	See *V. tricolor* subsp.
	macedonica
macloskeyi var. *pallens*	WLRN
'Madame Armandine	CDev EBee EDAr
Pagès' (Vt)	
'Madelaine' (Va)	LPVe
'Madge' (Va)	LPVe
'Maera' (Vtta)	LPVe
magellanica	NWoo
§ *magellensis*	NChi
'Magenta Maid' (Va)	MArl
'Maggie' (Va)	LPVe
'Maggie Mott' (Va) ♀	More than 30 suppliers
'Magic'	GMac LBee LRHS MArl SChu
	WBou WCru
'Maid Marion'	SRms
'Majella' (Vtta)	LPVe
'Malise' (Va)	LPVe
'Malvena' (Vtta)	LPVe
mandshurica	LPVe
¶ – 'Fuji Dawn' (v)	EMan MCCP WOut
* – *triangularis bicolor*	CInt
'Margaret' (Va)	WBou
'Margaret Cawthorne' (C)	LPVe
'Marian' (Va)	LPVe
'Marie-Louise' (dPVt)	CDev CGro CTri EPar
'Marika' (Va)	LPVe
'Mark Talbot' (Va)	Last listed 1999
'Maroon Picotee'	Last listed 1999
'Mars' (Va)	CLon LPVe
'Marsland's Yellow' (Vtta)	LPVe
'Martin' (Va) ♀	CInt CMHG CSam EBee ECha
	EWes GCHN GMac LBee LPVe
	LRHS MRav NBrk SAga SChu SDys
	SUsu WBou WFar WIvy WKif
	WPGP WWin
'Mary Cawthorne' (C)	LPVe
'Mary Ellen' (Va)	Last listed 1999
'Mary Wyllie'	Last listed 1999
'Mauve Beauty' (Va)	LPVe
'Mauve Haze' (Va)	GMac WBou WEas WWat
'Mauve Radiance' (Va)	GMac LPVe NVic WBou
'Mavis Tuck'	CSam
'May Mott' (Va)	GMaP GMac NBrk WBou
'Mayfly' (Va)	GMac NBrk WBou
'Meena' (Vtta)	LPVe
'Megumi' (Va)	LPVe
'Melinda' (Vtta)	LPVe WBou
* 'Melissa' (Va)	LPVe SChu
'Mercury' (Va)	LPVe WBou
'Merry Cheer' (C)	Last listed 1997
meryame	Last listed 1999
'Midnight Turk' (Va)	GBuc NSti WCot
'Milkmaid' (Va)	CFri CGle ECha EFou EWll
	GCrs LBee LRHS MCLN NBir
	NFla NHaw SIng WFar WKif
	WWhi
'Mina Walker' (ExVa)	Last listed 1999
'Minerva' (Va)	LPVe
* *minor* subsp. *calcarea*	Last listed 1998
'Miranda' (Vtta)	LPVe
'Miss Brookes' (Va)	LPVe WBou
'Miss Helen Mount'	Last listed 1998
'Mistral' (Va)	LPVe
'Misty Guy' (Vtta)	NChi WBou
'Mitzel' (Vtta)	LPVe
'Molly Sanderson' (Va) ♀	More than 30 suppliers
I 'Mona' (Va)	LPVe
'Monica' (Va)	LPVe SChu

'Putty'	WCru
'Queen Charlotte' (Vt)	CDev CGro CM&M EBee EDAr GCHN GMac ILis MHer NBro NFai NHar NMen NWCA WCot WGwG WPnP WSpi
'Queen Disa' (Vtta)	LPVe
'Queen Victoria'	See V. 'Victoria Regina'
'Quink' (Va)	Last listed 1999
'R.N. Denby' (ExVa)	Last listed 1999
'Ramona' (Va)	LPVe
'Rave' (Vtta)	Last listed 1999
* 'Raven'	GMac NCat NHar SAga SChu WBou WWat
'Ravenna' (Va)	LPVe
'Rebecca' (Vtta)	More than 30 suppliers
'Rebecca Cawthorne' (C)	LPVe
'Red Charm' (Vt)	CM&M EBee MWgw NBro NCat WElm WLRN
'Red Lion'	CDev CGro
'Red Queen' (Vt)	NSti
reichenbachiana	EPar EWFC
'Reine des Blanches' (dVt)	EFou WSpi
'Reliance' (Va)	Last listed 1999
'Remora' (Vtta)	LPVe
reniforme	See V. hederacea
'Rhoda' (Va)	LPVe
'Richard Vivian' (Va)	LPVe
'Richard's Yellow' (Va)	LPVe
riviniana	CArn CKin EWFC MCAu MGas MHer MMal WHer WJek WOak WShi
- 'Ed's Variegated' (v)	WCot
§ - Purpurea Group	More than 30 suppliers
- - x *verecunda* var. *yakusimana*	Last listed 1999
- white	EWes NWoo
¶ 'Rob Roy'	GMac
'Rodney Davey' (Vt/v)	CPla EBee EGar MDCh NBro NFai WElm WLRN
'Rodney Marsh'	NBir
'Romilly' (Va)	LPVe
'Rosalie' (Va)	LPVe
* 'Rosanna'	CDev
'Roscastle Black'	CPlt EBee GMaP GMac NCiC WBou WCot WPGP WWhi
'Rosemary Cawthorne' (C)	LPVe
'Rosine' (Vt)	EDAr GMac
'Rowan Hood' (ExVa)	Last listed 1999
'Rowena' (Va)	LPVe
'Royal Delft'	GCHN
¶ 'Royal Elk'	CGro
'Royal Picotee'	CElw
'Royal Robe' (VT)	CDev CGro
'Rubra' (Vt)	WPer
rugulosa	See V. canadensis var. rugulosa
§ *rupestris*	CGro WOak
§ - *rosea*	CDev CInt CLTr CNic CPla EDAr LLWP MBct MHer MNrw NCat NSti NWCA STre WEas WPrP
'Russian Superb' (Vt)	WLRN
'Ruth Blackall' (Va)	LPVe
'Ruth Elkans' (Va)	GMac LPVe NBrk
* 'Ruth Elkins'	WBou
'Saint Helena' (Vt)	CDev
'Saint Maur' (Va)	Last listed 1998
'Sally' (Vtta)	LPVe
'Samantha' (Vtta)	LPVe
'Sammy Jo' (Va)	Last listed 1999
'Sandra Louise' (C)	LPVe
'Sandra Louise' (Va)	Last listed 1997
'Sarah' (Va)	Last listed 1999
'Saughton Blue' (Va)	LPVe

selkirkii	CInt CNic CPla LPVe MDCh NBro NBus NWCA WOut
- 'Variegata'	GBri GBuc NBir
sempervirens	CInt
¶ *septemloba*	WOut
septentrionalis	CRDP ECha ELau EMan MNrw MOne MRav NBro NRya SSmi WWat
- *alba*	CHid CM&M CMHG CSWP EBee MRav MWgw NCiC WFar WLRN WPer WWat
'Septima' (Va)	LPVe
'Serena' (Va)	LPVe WBou
'Sheila' (Va)	WBou
'Sidborough Poppet'	CInt CMdw CNic CPBP EWes NHar SSca WPer
§ *sieberiana*	Last listed 1997
¶ *sieboldii*	NTow
'Sigrid' (Va)	LPVe
'Sir Fred Warner' (Va)	LPVe
§ 'Sissinghurst' (Va)	GMac LPVe NBir
'Sky Blue' (Va)	LPVe
'Smugglers' Moon'	SChu
'Snow Queen'	WWhi
'Sophie' (Vtta)	LPVe SChu
§ *sororia*	EBee EPPr GCHN GSki LPVe LRHS MSCN MWgw WLRN WWal
- 'Albiflora'	CSpe EDAr EMil EPPr EPar EPfP GMaP GSki LRHS MBNS MSph NHar NPro WLin WPer WRus
§ - 'Freckles'	More than 30 suppliers
- 'Priceana'	CBre CElw CM&M CNic EBee EMan EOrc EWTr MAvo NCat NCiC SLod SMrm WElm WLRN WPer WWal WWat
- 'Speckles' (v)	EMon
'Soula' (Vtta)	LPVe
¶ 'Spencer's Cottage'	WBou
* 'Stacey Proud' (v)	NPro
'Steyning' (Va)	LPVe WBou
stojanovii	CMea SBla WEas
striata	CInt
¶ 'Sugar Mouse'	GMac
'Sugar Plum'	GMac
§ 'Sulphurea' (Vt)	CDev CPBP CSWP EPar LPVe MHar MMHG MRav SIng SUsu WCot WHil WPer WWhi
'Susanah' (Vtta)	LPVe NCiC
'Susie' (Va)	WBou
'Swanley White'	See V. 'Comte de Brazza'
'Sybil' (SP)	Last listed 1999
'Sylvia Hart'	CPBP EWes MTho
* *takedana* 'Variegata'	Last listed 1997
'Talitha' (Va)	GMac LPVe
'Tamsin' (Va)	LPVe
* 'Tanith' (Vt)	CBre CDev EBee EDAr
'Tara' (Va)	LPVe
'Thalia' (Vtta)	LPVe WBou
'The Czar'	See V. 'Czar'
* 'The le Gresley Violet' (Vt)	CGro
'Thea' (Va)	LPVe
'Thelma' (Va)	LPVe
'Thetis' (Va)	LPVe
'Thierry' (Va)	LPVe
'Tiffany' (Va)	LPVe
'Tina' (Va)	LPVe
'Titania' (Va)	CGro LPVe
'Tom' (SP)	WOFF
'Tom Tit' (Va)	LPVe WBou
'Tomose' (Va)	Last listed 1998
'Tony Venison' (C/v)	CElw EDAr EHoe EMan LHop MBel MTho NBus NHaw WBou WBro WCot

'Toulouse' — EDAr WHer
tricolor — CKin EFer EWFC GBar GPoy MHer MHew MMal SIde WHer WJek WOak WSel
§ - subsp. *curtisii* — LPVe
§ - subsp. *macedonica* — LPVe
- 'Sawyer's Blue' — WPer
- subsp. *saxatilis* — See *V. tricolor* subsp. *macedonica*
'Tullia' (Vtta) — LPVe
Ultima Series ♀ — Last listed 1995
'Una' (Va) — LPVe
'Unity' (Vtta) — LPVe
'Valerie Proud' — NBrk
'Velleda' (Vtta) — LPVe
velutina — See *V. gracilis*
'Venetia' (Va) — LPVe
'Venus' (Va) — LPVe
verecunda B&SWJ 604a — WCru
- var. *semilunaris* — Last listed 1999
§ - var. *yakusimana* — CRDP ESis EWes
'Victoria' — See *V.* 'Czar Bleu'
'Victoria Cawthorne' (C) — CElw CMea CPBP EBee EMan GBuc GMac LPVe LRHS MAnH MBel MBro MHer MOne NChi NCiC SBla SChu WBou WEas WHoo WPGP WPyg WWat WWhi
§ 'Victoria Regina' (Vt) — CDev CRow EMon
'Victoria's Blush' (C) — CElw EBee MHer NChi
'Violacea' (C) — LPVe
'Virginia' (Va) — GMac LPVe SChu WBou
'Virgo' (Va) — LPVe
'Vita' (Va) — CLTr GBuc GMac LBee LPVe LRHS MBNS SAga SBla SChu SRms WBou WIvy WOut WSpi WWhi
vourinensis — LPVe
'Wanda' (Va) — LPVe
'Wasp' — GMac
'Wendy' (SP) — LPVe
'Westacre' (Va) — Last listed 1999
'White Gem' (Va) — Last listed 1999
'White Ladies' — See *V. cucullata* 'Alba'
'White Pearl' (Va) — GBuc GMac LGre WBou
'White Perfection' — LRHS MBNS
'White Superior' — CB&S
'White Swan' (Va) — CBos GMac LPVe NChi
'William Fife' (ExVa) — WOFF
'William Wallace' (Va) — LPVe
'Windward' (Vt) — NCat
'Winifred Jones' (Va) — Last listed 1999
* 'Winifred Warden' (Va) — MBNS WSpi
'Winifred Wargent' (Va) — LPVe SAga WLRN
'Winona' (Vtta) — LPVe
'Winona Cawthorne' (C) — GMac LPVe NChi NHaw SChu WBou WWhi
¶ 'Wisley White' — LBmB
'Woodlands Cream' (Va) — GMac NBrk NCiC WBou
'Woodlands Lilac' (Va) — LPVe SChu WBou
'Woodlands White' (Va) — LPVe WBou
'Xantha' (Va) — LPVe
yakusimana — See *V. verecunda* var. *yakusimana*
yezoensis — Last listed 1998
'Zalea' (Va) — LPVe
'Zara' (Va) — GMaP WBou
'Zenobia' (Vtta) — LPVe
'Zepherine' (Va) — LPVe
'Zeta' (Va) — LPVe
'Ziglana' (Va) — LPVe
'Zoe' (Vtta) — GMac LPVe LRHS NPri SChu SDys SMrm WBou WFar WLRN
'Zona' (Va) — LPVe
zoysii — See *V. calcarata* subsp. *zoysii*

VISCARIA (Caryophyllaceae)

vulgaris — See *Lychnis viscaria*

VITALIANA (Primulaceae)

§ *primuliflora* — CLyd GCrs GKir GTou MBro NSla WHoo WPyg
- subsp. *canescens* — Last listed 1998
- subsp. *praetutiana* — EPot MBro NHar NHol NMen NNrd NWCA SBla WAbe WFar WLin WPat WPyg
- - *chionantha* — Last listed 1999
- subsp. *tridentata* — NMen NNrd

VITEX (Verbenaceae)

agnus-castus — CAgr CArn CB&S CPLG EBee EEls ELan ELau GPoy LEdu LRHS MHer SLon SMad SPer SRPl WFar WWye
- 'Chaste Tree' — MCCP
- var. *latifolia* — LRHS MBri
- 'Silver Spire' — Last listed 1999
lucens — Last listed 1998
mombassae — Last listed 1999
negundo — CArn EOHP IIve

VITIS ✿ (Vitaceae)

'Abundante' (F) — WSuF
amurensis — CPIN EPfP EPla LRHS MBlu WWat
- B&SWJ 4138 — WCru
'Aurore' Seibel 5279 (W) — WSuF
'Baco' (R) — SDea
'Baco Noir' (O/B) — GTwe WSuF
Black Hamburg — See *V. vinifera* 'Schiava Grossa'
'Black Strawberry' (B) — WSuF
§ 'Boskoop Glory' (F) — CMac GTwe LBuc NBlu SCoo SDea WSuF
'Brant' (O/B) ♀ — More than 30 suppliers
californica (F) — ERea
'Canadice' — SDea
'Cascade' (O/B) — See *V.* Seibel 13053
Castel 19637 (W) — WSuF
'Cayuga' (W) — WSuF
'Chambourcin' (B) — WSuF
coignetiae ♀ — More than 30 suppliers
- B&SWJ 4744 — WCru
§ - Claret Cloak = 'Frovit'[PBR] — ELan EPfP GGar LRHS MAsh MCCP MTis NEgg SBrw SMur SPer SPla SSpi SVil WPGP WWat
- 'Frovit'[PBR] — See *V. coignetiae* Claret Cloak = 'Frovit'
* - 'Rubescens' — CPIN
'Dalkauer' (W) — WSuF
¶ 'Dusty Miller' — EWTr
ficifolia — See *V. thunbergii*
'Fiesta' — WSuF
flexuosa var. *choii* B&SWJ 4101 — WCru
§ - 'Fragola' (O/R) — CAgr CMac CPIN EBee EBrP EBre EPfP EPla ERea GTwe GVer LBCl LBSe LBre LRHS MAsh MBBe SBre SDea SEND SPer SRms WSuF WWat
henryana — See *Parthenocissus henryana*
'Himrod' (O/W) — ERea GTwe SDea WSuF
inconstans — See *Parthenocissus tricuspidata*
'Kemsey Black' (B) — WSuF
'Kuibishevski' (O/R) — WSuF
¶ *labrusca* — CPIN
- 'Concord' (O/B) — ERea
Landot 244 (O/B) — WSuF
'Léon Millot' (O/G/B) — CAgr EMui ERea LRHS MAsh SDea WSuF

'Maréchal Foch' (O/B)	WSuF	
'Maréchal Joffre' (O/B)	GTwe WSuF	
Oberlin 595 (O/B)	WSuF	
'Orion'	WSuF	
palmata	WCru	
parsley leaved	See *V. vinifera* 'Ciotat'	
parvifolia	CPlN WPat WShe	
'Phönix' (O/W)	WSuF	
piasezkii	WCru	
- B&SWJ 5236	WCru	
* 'Pink Strawberry' (O)	WSuF	
'Pirovano 14' (O/B)	ERea GTwe SDea WSuF	
§ 'Plantet' (O/B)	WSuF	
* 'Polaske Muscat' (W)	WSuF	
pseudoreticulata	CFil CPlN WPGP	
'Pulchra'	Last listed 1999	
quinquefolia	See *Parthenocissus quinquefolia*	
Ravat 51 (O/W)	WSuF	
¶ 'Regent'^PBR	MCoo	
¶ 'Rembrant' (R)	WSuF	
riparia	CPlN WCru	
'Rondo New Red'	Last listed 1999	
rotundifolia B&SWJ 4707	Last listed 1999	
'Schuyler' (O/B)	WSuF	
Seibel (F)	EMui GTwe SDea	
§ Seibel 13053 (O/B)	ERea LRHS MAsh SDea WSuF	
¶ Seibel 138315 (R)	WSuF	
¶ Seibel 5409 (W)	WSuF	
Seibel 5455	See *V.* 'Plantet'	
Seibel 7053	WSuF	
Seibel 9549	WSuF	
'Seneca' (W)	WSuF	
§ 'Seyval Blanc' (O/W)	CAgr ERea GTwe SDea WSuF	
Seyve Villard 12.375	See *V.* 'Villard Blanc'	
¶ Seyve Villard 20.473 (F)	MAsh WSuF	
Seyve Villard 5276	See *V.* 'Seyval Blanc'	
'Tereshkova' (O/B)	ERea SDea WSuF	
'Thornton'	WSuF	
§ *thunbergii*	WCru	
- B&SWJ 4702	WCru	
'Triomphe d'Alsace' (O/B)	CAgr LRHS MAsh NPer SDea WSuF	
'Trollinger'	See *V. vinifera* 'Schiava Grossa'	
'Vanessa'	ERea	
§ 'Villard Blanc' (O/W)	LRHS WSuF	
vinifera 'Abouriou' (O/B)	WSuF	
- 'Albalonga' (W)	WSuF	
§ - 'Alicante' (G/B)	ERea GTwe SDea WSuF	
- 'Apiifolia'	See *V. vinifera* 'Ciotat'	
- 'Appley Towers' (G/B)	ERea	
- 'Auxerrois' (O/W)	WSuF	
- 'Bacchus' (O/W)	SDea WSuF	
- 'Black Alicante'	See *V. vinifera* 'Alicante'	
- 'Black Corinth' (G/B)	ERea	
- 'Black Frontignan' (G/O/B)	ERea WSuF	
- Black Hamburgh	See *V. vinifera* 'Schiava Grossa'	
- 'Black Monukka' (G/B)	ERea WSuF	
- 'Blauburger' (O/B)	WCru	
- 'Blue Portuguese'	See *V. vinifera* 'Portugieser'	
- 'Buckland Sweetwater' (G/W)	ERea GTwe LRHS MBri SDea WSuF	
- 'Cabernet Sauvignon' (O/B)	SDea WSuF	
¶ - 'Canners'	ERea	
- 'Canon Hall Muscat' (G/W)	ERea	
- 'Cardinal' (O/R)	ERea	
- 'Chaouch' (G/W)	ERea	
- 'Chardonnay' (O/W)	LRHS MAsh NPer SDea WSuF	
§ - 'Chasselas' (G/O/W)	EMui ERea LRHS MAsh SDea WSuF WWeb	
- 'Chasselas d'Or'	See *V. vinifera* 'Chasselas'	
- 'Chasselas Rosé' (G/R)	ERea WSuF	
- 'Chasselas Vibert' (G/W)	ERea WSuF	
- 'Chenin Blanc' (O/W)	WSuF	
§ - 'Ciotat' (F)	EPla ERea SDea WCru WSuF WWat	
§ - 'Cot' (O/B)	WSuF	
¶ - 'Crimson Seedless'	ERea	
- 'Csabyongye' (W)	WSuF	
- 'Daitier de Beyrouth' (W)	WSuF	
- 'Dornfelder' (O/R)	CWSG EBee SLim WSuF	
- 'Dunkelfelder' (O/R)	WSuF	
- 'Early Van der Laan' (F)	Last listed 1999	
- 'Ehrenfelser' (O/W)	WSuF	
- 'Elbling' (O/W)	WSuF	
- EM 323158B	WSuF	
- 'Excelsior' (W)	WSuF	
- 'Faber' (O/W)	WSuF	
¶ - 'Ferdinand de Lessops'	ERea	
- 'Findling' (W)	WSuF	
- 'Forta' (O/W)	WSuF	
- 'Foster's Seedling' (G/W)	CBlo ERea GTwe SDea WSuF	
- 'Gagarin Blue' (O/B)	CAgr ERea GTwe NPer SDea WSuF	
- 'Gamay Hatif' (O/B)	ERea	
- 'Gamay Hatif des Vosges'	WSuF	
- 'Gamay Noir' (O/B)	WSuF	
- Gamay Teinturier Group (O/B)	WSuF	
- 'Gewürztraminer' (O/R)	LRHS MAsh SDea WSuF	
- 'Glory of Boskoop'	See *V.* 'Boskoop Glory'	
- 'Golden Chasselas'	See *V. vinifera* 'Chasselas'	
- 'Golden Queen' (G/W)	ERea	
- 'Goldriesling' (O/W)	WSuF	
- 'Gros Colmar' (G/B)	ERea	
- 'Gros Maroc' (G/B)	ERea	
- 'Grüner Veltliner' (O/W)	WSuF	
- 'Gutenborner' (O/W)	WSuF	
- 'Helfensteiner' (O/R)	WSuF	
- 'Huxelrebe' (O/W)	WSuF	
- 'Incana' (O/B)	CPlN EPla MRav WCFE WCot WCru WPen WSHC	
- 'Interlaken' (F)	ERea	
- 'Jubiläumsrebe' (O/W)	WSuF	
- 'Kanzler' (O/W)	WSuF	
- 'Kerner' (O/W)	WSuF	
- 'Kernling' (F)	WSuF	
- 'King's Ruby' (F)	ERea	
- 'Lady Downe's Seedling' (G/B)	ERea	
- 'Lady Hastings' (G/B)	ERea	
- 'Lady Hutt' (G/W)	ERea	
¶ - 'Lakemont'	ERea	
- 'Lucombe' (F)	Last listed 1997	
- 'Madeleine Angevine' (O/W)	EBee EMui ERea GTwe LRHS MAsh SDea SLim WSuF WWeb	
- 'Madeleine Royale' (G/W)	ERea WSuF	
- 'Madeleine Silvaner' (O/W)	EMui ERea GTwe LRHS MAsh MGos NPer SDea SPer WSuF	
- 'Madresfield Court' (G/B)	ERea GTwe WSuF	
- 'Malbec'	See *V. vinifera* 'Cot'	
¶ - 'Merlot' (G/B)	SDea	
- 'Mireille' (F)	GTwe SDea WSuF	
- 'Morio Muscat' (O/W)	WSuF	
- 'Mrs Pearson' (G/W)	ERea	
- 'Mrs Pince's Black Muscat' (G/B)	ERea	
§ - 'Müller-Thurgau' (O/W)	CBlo EBee EMui ERea GKir GTwe LRHS MAsh MBri MGos SDea SLim SPer WSuF WWeb	
- 'Muscat Blanc à Petits Grains' (O/W)	WSuF	

- 'Muscat Bleu' (O/B)   ERea
- 'Muscat Champion' (G/R)   ERea
- 'Muscat de Saumur'   WSuF
  (O/W)
- 'Muscat Hamburg' (G/B)   EMui ERea MAsh MGos SDea
                               WSuF
- 'Muscat of Alexandria'   CB&S CMac CRHN CSam
                               EHol
  (G/W)   EMui ERea SDea SLim SRPl
- 'Muscat of Hungary'   ERea
  (G/W)
- 'Muscat Ottonel' (O/W)   WSuF
- 'New York Muscat' (O/B)   ERea
- 'No. 69' (W)   WSuF
- 'Noir Hatif de Marseilles'   ERea WSuF
  (O/B)
- 'Oliver Irsay' (O/W)   ERea WSuF
- 'Optima' (O/W)   WSuF
- 'Ortega' (O/W)   WSuF
- 'Perle' (O/W)   WSuF
- 'Perle de Czaba' (G/O/W)   ERea
- 'Perlette' (O/W)   ERea WSuF
- 'Pinot Blanc' (O/W)   LRHS MAsh WSuF
- 'Pinot Gris' (O/B)   SDea WSuF
- 'Pinot Noir' (O/B)   WSuF
- 'Plavač Mali' (B)   WSuF
§ - 'Portugieser' (O/B)   WSuF
- 'Précoce de Bousquet'   WSuF
  (O/W)
- 'Précoce de Malingre'   ERea SDea
  (O/W)
- 'Primavis Frontignan'   WSuF
  (G/W)
- 'Prince of Wales' (G/B)   ERea
- 'Purpurea' (O/B) ♀   More than 30 suppliers
- 'Reichensteiner' (O/G/W)   SDea WSuF
- 'Reine Olga' (O/R)   ERea
¶ - 'Reliance'   ERea
- 'Riesling' (O/W)   LRHS MAsh WSuF
- Riesling-Silvaner   See V. vinifera 'Müller-Thurgau'
¶ - 'Rish Baba'   ERea
- 'Rondo' EM 6494-5 (O/B)   EMui WSuF
- 'Royal Muscadine'   WSuF
  (G/O/W)
- 'Saint Laurent' (G/O/W)   ERea WSuF
- 'Sauvignon Blanc' (O/W)   WSuF
- 'Scheurebe' (O/W)   WSuF
§ - 'Schiava Grossa' (G/B)   CMac CRHN CSam EBee ELan
                               EMui ERea GChr GKir GTwe
                               LBuc LRHS MAsh MBlu MBri
                               MGos MWat NBea NPer NRog
                               SDea SLim SPer SSht WDin WStI
                               WSuF
- 'Schönburger' (O/W)   SDea WSuF
- 'Septimer' (O/W)   WSuF
- 'Shiraz' (B)   WSuF
- 'Siegerrebe' (O/W)   EMui ERea GTwe LRHS SDea
                               WSuF WWeb
- 'Silvaner' (O/W)   WSuF
- 'Spetchley Red'   WCru WSPU
- Strawberry Grape   See V. 'Fragola'
¶ - 'Suffolk Red'   ERea
§ - 'Sultana'   EMui ERea GTwe SDea WSuF
- 'Syrian' (G/W)   ERea
- Teinturier Group (F)   ERea
- 'Thompson Seedless'   See V. vinifera 'Sultana'
- 'Trebbiano' (G/W)   ERea
* - 'Triomphe' (O/B)   EMui
- 'Wrotham Pinot' (O/B)   SDea WSuF
- 'Würzer' (O/W)   WSuF
- 'Zweigeltrebe' (O/B)   WSuF
* 'White Strawberry' (O/W)   WSuF

VRIESEA (Bromeliaceae)
carinata	MBri
duvaliana ♀	Last listed 1995
fosteriana ♀	Last listed 1990
hieroglyphica	MBri
x poelmanii	MBri
x polonia	MBri
psittacina ♀	Last listed 1995
saundersii ♀	MBri
splendens ♀	MBri
'Vulkana'	MBri

W

WACHENDORFIA (Haemodoraceae)
paniculata	Last listed 1997
thyrsiflora	CFir CHEx EBee IBlr WCot WPGP
- Trengwainton Form	Last listed 1998

WAHLENBERGIA (Campanulaceae)
albomarginata	ECou EMan GTou LRHS NHar
	NWCA
- 'Blue Mist'	ECou
- white form	Last listed 1997
* albosericea	Last listed 1997
cartilaginea	Last listed 1997
ceracea	Last listed 1997
congesta	CPBP LBee LRHS WPat
gloriosa	CSpe GCrs LBee LRHS MBro WFar
	WPat WPyg WWin
matthewsii	CPBP
pumilio	See Edraianthus pumilio
pygmaea	MBro WHoo WUnu
§ saxicola	CLyd CRow GTou NWCA SSca
	WPer
serpyllifolia	See Edraianthus serpyllifolius
simpsonii	GTou
sp. ECou	
stricta	Last listed 1997
tasmanica	See W. saxicola
trichogyna	Last listed 1997
undulata	CSpe

WALDSTEINIA (Rosaceae)
fragarioides	NWoo SIng WPer
geoides	EBee EMan EPPr EPfP LRHS NPro
	SPer WLRN
ternata	More than 30 suppliers
* - 'Variegata'	GKir IBlr NPro

WALLICHIA (Arecaceae)
densiflora	CBrP LPal
disticha	LPal

WASABIA (Brassicaceae)
japonica	GPoy

WASHINGTONIA (Arecaceae)
filifera ♀	CAbb CBrP CHEx CRoM CTbh
	CTrC CBlo LPal MBri SAPC SArc
	SPlb WMul
robusta	CRoM CTrC EPVP LPal WMul

WATSONIA (Iridaceae)
aletroides	CCtw WCot WHil
angusta	IBlr
ardernei	See W. borbonica subsp. ardernei
beatricis	See W. pillansii

I 'Best Red'	GCal
§ *borbonica*	CCtw CPne GGar IBlr SAga SWat
§ - subsp. *ardernei*	CLAP EBee GCal IBlr MSte SWat
	WHil WPGP
- subsp. *borbonica*	CLAP EBee WPGP
- pink form	CPou
brevifolia	See *W. laccata*
coccinea Baker	See *W. spectabilis*
- Herbert ex Baker	WHil
- dwarf form	Last listed 1997
densiflora	CB&S CFil CPou MSte WCot
distans	Last listed 1999
fourcadei	EBee WPGP
- S&SH 89	Last listed 1999
fulgens	MSte WHil
galpinii	CFir IBlr
gladioloides	CFil
§ *humilis*	CFil WPGP
¶ hybrid 674/76	WHil
hysterantha	IBlr
§ *laccata*	CPou SWat
lepida	CFil WHil
- JCA 3.192.800	SSpi
marginata	CPou EBee SWat WHil
marlothii	CFil
merianiae	CFil CPou GCal IBlr WCot WHil
* 'Mount Congreve'	Last listed 1998
§ *pillansii*	CCtw CFil CLAP CPou CTrC EBee
	IBlr SBla SMrm SWat WHil
pyramidata	See *W. borbonica*
roseoalba	See *W. humilis*
§ *spectabilis*	Last listed 1997
'Stanford Scarlet'	CLAP CPou EBee IBlr SBla SChr
	SUsu WPGP WSHC
stenosiphon	CPou EBee
tabularis	IBlr SWat
'Tresco Dwarf Pink'	CLAP CPou EBee GCal WCot
	WPGP
vanderspuyae	CCtw IBlr WHil
versfeldii	Last listed 1999
watsonioides	Last listed 1998
'White Dazzler'	Last listed 1997
wilmaniae	CFil CPou IBlr
- JCA 3.955.200	SSpi
wordsworthiana	Last listed 1997

WATTAKAKA See DREGEA

WEIGELA ✿ (Caprifoliaceae)

'Abel Carrière' ♀	CTri ECtt ENot EPfP NFla NWea
	SEND WCFE WLRN
'Avalanche' hort.	See *W.* 'Candida'
'Avalanche' Lemoine	See *W. praecox* 'Avalanche'
'Boskoop Glory'	GQui SPer
§ Briant Rubidor	CDoC EBee ECtt EHoe ENot GChr
= 'Olympiade' (v)	GKir IOrc LRHS MAsh MBNS
	MBar MBel MBri MGos MRav
	MWhi NFla NFor SEND SEas SLim
	SPer SPlb WBod WHCG WStI
	WWeb
'Bristol Ruby'	CChe CDul CHar EBee ELan ENot
	EWTr GChr GKir LRHS MBar
	MGos MHer MWhi NBee NFor
	NWea SLon SMer SPer SRms
	WDin WFar WGwG WStI WWal
	WWin
§ 'Candida'	CTri ELan EWes GEil GSki LRHS
	MBar MBel MBri NHol SEas SPer
Carnaval = 'Courtalor'PBR	CBlo CCHP COtt EBee GAri GKir
	LPan LRHS MBri WLRN WStI
'Centennial'	Last listed 1999
'Conquête'	GEil GKir

coraeensis	IDee MBlu SPan
- 'Alba'	GEil
'Davnik'	MTPN
decora	CPle GQui
'Eva Rathke'	CBlo CTri GKir NWea SCoo
* 'Eva Supreme'	Last listed 1999
'Evita'	GChr IOrc MBar MGos SEas SPer
Feline = 'Courtamon'PBR	SPer
'Fiesta' ♀	Last listed 1995
florida	CTrw EPfP EWTr MBar MWat
	SMer
- f. *alba*	CB&S MBar
- 'Bicolor'	CB&S SPan
- 'Bristol Snowflake'	CSWP EPfP GKir MAsh MBNS
	MBar MGos MHer NLar SPla
	WLRN
- 'Foliis Purpureis' ♀	More than 30 suppliers
- 'Java Red'	LRHS MBri
- 'Pink Princess'	WWeb
- Rubigold	See *W.* Briant Rubidor =
	'Olympiade'
- 'Samabor'	WFar
- 'Sunny Princess'	NHol
- 'Suzanne' (v)	CB&S LRHS MBri MGos NPro
- 'Tango'	CPMA ECtt LRHS MAsh MBri
	NPro WBcn
'Florida Variegata' ♀	More than 30 suppliers
florida 'Versicolor'	CCHP CMHG GQui MBel SLon
'Gold Rush'	CBlo
'Gustave Malet'	GQui
¶ *hortensis*	GIBF
- 'Nivea'	CPle MBri NPro
japonica	Last listed 1998
¶ - 'Dart's Colourdream'	EBee ECtt EPla EWes GOrc IOrc
	MBel MCCP MGos MRav SCoo
	SEas SLPl SLim
'Jean's Gold'	ELan MGos MRav NPri SBod
'Kosteriana Variegata'	CBlo EBee LRHS NHol WFar
	WLRN
'Looymansii Aurea'	CMHG CPle CTri ELan GEil GKir
	LAst LRHS MRav SEas SMac SPer
	SPla WBod WDin WHar WWal
	WWat WWin
Lucifer = 'Courtared'PBR	CDoC NHol WLRN
'Marjorie'	IMGH WLRN
maximowiczii	CPle GQui GSki WHCG WLRN
§ *middendorffiana*	More than 30 suppliers
'Minuet'	CBlo EPfP GSki MBar MGos MRav
	NPro SEas SPla
'Mont Blanc' ♀	CBot CDul MMHG
Nain Rouge =	CB&S CBlo LRHS NHol WLRN
'Courtanin'PBR	
'Nana Variegata'	GChr LRHS MBar MBri NBee
	NHol
'Newport Red'	CBlo EBee ENot GChr GKir LRHS
	MBNS MRav MWat NBee NWea
	SMer WGwG WLRN WStI WWal
'Olympiade' (v)	See *W.* Briant Rubidor =
	'Olympiade'
§ *praecox* 'Avalanche'	ECtt MRav WStI
- 'Espérance'	Last listed 1999
'Praecox Variegata' ♀	CChe CTri ELan EPfP GKir LRHS
	MAsh MBri MRav SMac SPer SPla
	SRPl SReu SRms SSta WCFE WCru
	WHCG WSHC WWat
'Red Prince'	CBlo EBee ELan LRHS MAsh MBri
	MGos SEas SLon WBod
* 'Rosabella'	Last listed 1998
Rubidor	See *W.* Briant Rubidor =
	'Olympiade'
Rubidor Variegata	See *W.* Briant Rubidor =
	'Olympiade'

Rubigold	See *W.* Briant Rubidor = 'Olympiade'
'Ruby Queen'^{PBR}	CDoC EPfP LRHS
'Rumba'	EMil GSki MBri MMHG MRav NPro
'Samba'	LRHS MBri
'Snowflake'	EBee ECtt EPla EWTr GKir NPro SEas SRms WDin
sp. CC 1279	Last listed 1998
subsessilis B&SWJ 1056	WCru
- CC 1289	Last listed 1998
'Victoria'	CBlo CDoC CLTr CMHG CSWP EBrP EBre ECtt ELan LBre LRHS MAsh MBBe MBel MBri SBre SCoo SPer WGor WHar WLRN WWeb
* 'Wessex Gold'	CFai WHCG

WEINMANNIA (Cunoniaceae)
¶ *racemosa* 'Kamahi'	CTrC
trichosperma	CGre CHEx CPLG IBlr ISea SAPC SArc

WELDENIA (Commelinaceae)
candida	NHar WAbe

WERNERIA (Asteraceae)
crassifolia	WCot

WESTRINGIA (Lamiaceae)
angustifolia	ECou
brevifolia	ECou
- Raleighii Group	ECou
§ *fruticosa* ♀	CB&S CInt CPle LHil SPan WJek
- 'Variegata'	CPle GQui LRHS WJek WSHC
- 'Wynyabbie Gem'	EMan LHop
longifolia	Last listed 1997
* *rigida* 'Variegata'	WCot
rosmariniformis	See *W. fruticosa*

WETTINIA (Arecaceae)
kalbreyeri	Last listed 1999
maynensis	LPal
quinaria	Last listed 1999

WIDDRINGTONIA (Cupressaceae)
cedarbergensis	Last listed 1999
cupressoides	See *W. nodiflora*
§ *nodiflora*	MBri
schwarzii	CTrC

WIGANDIA (Hydrophyllaceae)
urens	Last listed 1998

WIKSTROEMIA (Thymelaeaceae)
gemmata	SSta
nutans B&SWJ 4081	WCru

WISTERIA (Papilionaceae)
§ *brachybotrys*	CMCN SLim
§ - Murasaki-kapitan	CEnd LNet
- 'Okayama'	LNet
§ - 'Shiro-kapitan'	CB&S CEnd CPMA CTri EBee ELan ENot EPfP EWTr LNet LRHS MAsh MBri MGos MMea MRav NHol SBra SLim SLon SMad SPer WPGP WWat
* - 'White Silk'	CEnd CMMel
§ 'Burford'	CBlo CEnd CTri EBee EMui LNet LRHS MAsh MBri MMea MWat NBea NHol SLim WHar

'Caroline'	CB&S CDoC CEnd CMCN CPMA CSam EBee EPfP ERea GChr GKir GOrc LNet LRHS MBlu MGos MMea MRav NBea SPer SSpi
floribunda	CB&S CRHN ELan LPan LRHS MAsh SBra WDin WNor
§ - 'Alba' ♀	More than 30 suppliers
§ - 'Asagi'	LNet MMea
- 'Black Dragon'	See *W.* x *formosa* 'Yae-kokuryû' (d)
* - 'Blue Pacific'	LNet
- 'Burford'	See *W.* 'Burford'
* - 'Cascade'	CTrC LNet
§ - 'Domino'	CB&S CBlo CEnd CPMA CTri EBee EPfP GKir LNet LRHS MAsh MBar MGos MMea MRav MTis NBea NEgg NHol NSti SBra SLim SPer SSta WSHC WWat WWeb
- 'Fragrantissima'	See *W. sinensis* 'Jako'
¶ - 'Geisha'	LNet
* - 'Harlequin'	CB&S EBee LNet LRHS MGos MRav
- 'Hichirimen'	See *W. floribunda* 'Asagi'
- 'Hon-beni'	See *W. floribunda* 'Rosea'
- 'Honey Bee Pink'	See *W. floribunda* 'Rosea'
- 'Honko'	See *W. floribunda* 'Rosea'
- 'Jakohn-fuji'	See *W. sinensis* 'Jako'
§ - 'Kuchi-beni'	CB&S CPMA CTrC EBee ELan EPfP GKir LNet LRHS MGos MMea MRav SBra SLim WBod WWeb
- 'Lavender Lace'	See *W.* 'Lavender Lace'
- 'Lawrence'	LNet LRHS MGos
- 'Lipstick'	See *W. floribunda* 'Kuchi-beni'
- 'Longissima'	See *W. floribunda* 'Multijuga'
- 'Longissima Alba'	See *W. floribunda* 'Alba'
- 'Macrobotrys'	See *W. floribunda* 'Multijuga'
- 'Magenta'	LNet LRHS
§ - 'Multijuga' ♀	More than 30 suppliers
- Murasaki-naga	See *W. floribunda* 'Purple Patches'
- 'Murasaki-noda'	MGos
- 'Nana Richin's Purple'	CEnd LNet LRHS
- 'Peaches and Cream'	See *W. floribunda* 'Kuchi-beni'
- 'Pink Ice'	See *W. floribunda* 'Rosea'
§ - 'Purple Patches'	CPMA EBee GKir LNet LRHS MGos MMea MWat NPri SLim SPer
* - 'Purple Tassle'	LNet
- Reindeer	See *W. sinensis* 'Jako'
§ - 'Rosea' ♀	CB&S CEnd CPMA EBee ELan ENot EPfP IMGH IOrc LBuc LNet LRHS MAsh MBar MBri MGos MMea MWat NBea NHol SBra SLim SPer WFar WStI WWat WWeb
- 'Royal Purple'	CBlo EBee ERea LNet LRHS MMea WGor
¶ - 'Russelliana'	EBee
- 'Shiro-naga'	See *W. floribunda* 'Alba'
I - 'Shiro-nagi'	See *W. floribunda* 'Alba'
- 'Shiro-noda'	See *W. floribunda* 'Alba'
- 'Snow Showers'	See *W. floribunda* 'Alba'
- 'Variegata'	CPMA
- 'Violacea Plena' (d)	CBlo CDoC EBee LNet LPan LRHS MBri MGos MMea NPri SLon SPar SPer WDin
x *formosa*	CPMA LNet SLim WFro WWat
- 'Black Dragon' (d)	See *W.* x *formosa* 'Yae-kokuryû' (d)
- 'Domino'	See *W. floribunda* 'Domino'
- 'Issai' Wada pro parte	See *W. floribunda* 'Domino'

- 'Kokuryû' (d) — See *W.* x *formosa* 'Yae-kokuryû' (d)
§ - 'Yae-kokuryû' (d) — CB&S CEnd CPMA EBee EPfP EWTr GChr GKir IOrc LNet LRHS MAsh MGos MMea NHol SBra SLim SMad SPer SPla SReu SSpi SSta WGor WPyg WWat WWeb
frutescens — WNor WShe
- 'Alba' — See *W. frutescens* 'Nivea'
¶ - 'Amethyst Falls' — LNet
- 'Magnifica' — See *W. macrostachya* 'Magnifica'
§ - 'Nivea' — CMCN LNet
¶ - 'Swartley Purple' — LNet
Kapitan-fuji — See *W. brachybotrys*
'Kofuji' — See *Millettia japonica*
§ 'Lavender Lace' — CPMA EPfP LNet LRHS MRav WBod
macrostachya — LNet
'Bayou Two o'Clock'
- 'Clara Mack' — LNet
§ - 'Magnifica' — LNet
- 'Pondside Blue' — LNet
multijuga 'Alba' — See *W. floribunda* 'Alba'
'Showa-beni' — CEnd LNet LRHS SLim
sinensis ♀ — More than 30 suppliers
- 'Alba' ♀ — CB&S CBlo CDoC EBee ELan ENot EPfP IOrc ISea LBuc LNet LPan LRHS MBar MMea MWat NBlu SBra SLim SPer WDin WFar
- 'Amethyst' — CPMA EBee EPfP EREa LRHS MGos SBra SLon SPla
- 'Blue Sapphire' — CHad CPMA LRHS WBod
- 'Cooke's Special' — LNet
✳ - 'Imp' — Last listed 1997
§ - 'Jako' — CBlo CEnd LNet NHol SBra
- 'Larry's White' — LNet
- 'Plena' (d) — CPMA
- 'Prematura' — See *W. floribunda* 'Domino'
- 'Prematura Alba' — See *W. brachybotrys* 'Shiro-kapitan'
- 'Prolific' — CB&S CPMA CPlN CTri EBee ELan EPfP LBuc LPan LRHS MBri MGos MMea SBra SPer SSpi WPat
- 'Rosea' — LPan
I - 'Shiro-capital' — See *W. brachybotrys* 'Shiro-kapitan'
venusta — See *W. brachybotrys* 'Shiro-kapitan'
- var. *violacea* — See *W. brachybotrys* Murasaki-kapitan
villosa — WNor

WITHANIA (Solanaceae)
somnifera — CArn EOHP GPoy

WITTSTEINIA (Alseuosmiaceae)
vacciniacea — EBee WCru

WODYETIA (Arecaceae)
bifurcata — LPal

WOODSIA (Woodsiaceae)
fragilis — Last listed 1998
intermedia — NBro
obtusa — CLAP EBee EFer GBin LRHS NHar NHol WRic
polystichoides ♀ — GQui NHar SRms

WOODWARDIA ✿ (Blechnaceae)
fimbriata — NHol
martinezii — CFil

orientalis — WPic
- var. *formosana* — NMar
radicans ♀ — CAbb CFil CGre CHEx GQui ISea NMar SAPC SArc SMad WAbe WPic
unigemmata — SSpi WAbe WHal

WULFENIA (Scrophulariaceae)
amberstiana — SOkd
carinthiaca — CNic GAbr MOne NBir NMen SLod WMoo

WYETHIA (Asteraceae)
beliantboides — EBee EMan

X

XANTHIUM (Asteraceae)
¶ *sibiricum* — CArn

XANTHOCERAS (Sapindaceae)
sorbifolium ♀ — CAgr CB&S CBlo CBot CFil CLnd CMCN CTho EBee ELan IDee MBel MRav MWhi SMad SPan SSpi WDin WLRN WNor WPGP WWat

XANTHOPHTHALMUM (Asteraceae)
coronarium — CArn EEls WJek
§ *segetum* — EWFC MHew MMal WHer

XANTHORHIZA (Ranunculaceae)
simplicissima — CB&S CFil CRow EPfP GCal SDys SSpi WWat

XANTHORRHOEA (Xanthorrhoeaceae)
australis — CPLG NMoo WGer
johnsonii — NRog SHmp
preisii — LPan

XANTHOSOMA (Araceae)
lindenii — See *Caladium lindenii*
sagittifolium — CHEx WMul
violaceum — CHEx LHil WMul

XERODRABA (Brassicaceae)
mendocinensis — Last listed 1998

XERONEMA (Phormiaceae)
callistemon — ECou

XEROPHYLLUM (Melanthiaceae)
tenax — SSpi

XYLORHIZA See MACHAERANTHERA

XYLOSMA (Flacourtiaceae)
quichensis — Last listed 1999

XYSMALOBIUM (Asclepiadaceae)
stockenstroemense — EBee

YPSILANDRA (Melanthiaceae)
tbibetica — EBee WCru

YUCCA ✿ (Agavaceae)

aloifolia	CHEx CTrC LRHS MGos SAPC SArc SPlb WMul
¶ - 'Marginata'	EPVP MWst
¶ - 'Tricolor'	MWst
- 'Variegata'	LPal LPan SAPC SArc
angustifolia	See *Y. glauca*
angustissima	Last listed 1998
- var. *toftiae* JCA 1993500	EMon
arizonica	GCal
baccata	EOas GCal
brevifolia	CBrP CRoM
¶ - 'Jaegeriana'	CFir
carnerosana	Last listed 1999
desmetiana	Last listed 1999
elata	Last listed 1999
§ *elephantipes* ♀	CHEx LRHS MBri
faxoniana	Last listed 1998
- x *glauca*	Last listed 1998
filamentosa ♀	More than 30 suppliers
- 'Bright Edge' (v) ♀	More than 30 suppliers
- 'Variegata' ♀	CB&S CBlo CBot EPfP IOrc LHop LRHS MAsh MGos SAga SPer SPla SRms WDin WFar WGer
flaccida	EWTr MAsh NBee NFla SDix SEND SPar WShe
- 'Golden Sword' (v) ♀	CAbb CDoC CMHG CTrC EBrP EBre ELan GChr GKir IOrc LBCl LBSe LBre LHop LPio LRHS MAsh MBBe MBri MCCP MSCN NCut NMoo SBre SCoo SLim SPer WAbe WCot
- 'Ivory' ♀	More than 30 suppliers
x *floribunda*	SAPC SArc
'Garland's Gold' (v)	CB&S CDoC CHEx ELan GQui LEdu LRHS MAsh MBri MDun MGos WBod
§ *glauca*	CB&S CBrP CMHG CTrC EPfP GCal LRHS MBri NCut SAPC WBod WPGP
gloriosa ♀	CB&S CDoC CHEx ENot EOas EPla EWTr LNet LPan LRHS SAPC SArc SMad SPer SSpi WBrE WStI
- 'Aureovariegata'	See *Y. gloriosa* 'Variegata'
- 'Nobilis'	SDix
- 'Tricolor'	Last listed 1997
§ - 'Variegata' ♀	More than 30 suppliers
guatemalensis	See *Y. elephantipes*
harrimaniae	Last listed 1999
- var. *neomexicana*	Last listed 1999
kanabensis	GCal
navajoa	Last listed 1997
¶ *pendula* 'Tito Branca' (v)	EMon
recurvifolia ♀	CHEx EPfP SAPC SArc
rigida	CBrP
rostrata	CAbb CBrP CHEx EOas LPal SAPC SArc WMul
schidigera	GCal
schottii	CAbb CBrP
thompsoniana	Last listed 1998
* *torcelli*	Last listed 1999
torreyi	CTrC GCal WCot
valida	Last listed 1997
'Vittorio Emanuele II'	Last listed 1998
whipplei	CAbb CBot CBrP CCtw CDoC CFil CHEx CRoM CTrC EPVP GCal LEdu LRHS SAPC SRCN SSpi WPGP
- subsp. *cespitosa* JCA 1993600	Last listed 1999
- subsp. *parishii*	Last listed 1999

YUSHANIA (Poaceae - Bambusoideae)

§ *anceps* ♀	CDoC CFil CHEx CHad EFul EPla GAri IOrc ISta IJus MBri MDun MGos MMoz NBee NVic SAPC SArc SDry SPer SPla WCru WPGP
- 'Pitt White'	CFil EPla SDry WJun
¶ - 'Pitt White Rejuvenated'	ERod
chungii	CFil EPla WPGP
maculata	EPla ERod ISta IJus SDry WJun
§ *maling*	EPla ISta SDry WJun

Z

ZALUZIANSKYA (Scrophulariaceae)

capensis	Last listed 1999
¶ - 'Midnight Candy'	EMan
'Katherine'	MTPN SIng SRot
ovata	CPBP EBee EPot EWes GBri LPio LSpr MTho NBir NWCA SAga SBla SMrm SUsu WAbe WOve
* cf. *rostrata* DBG 219	NTow
sp. from Lesotho	CMdw GCal
sp. JCA 15665	WAbe
sp. JCA 15758	Last listed 1998
sp. PK 66 from USA	SSpi

ZAMIA (Zamiaceae)

floridana	LPal
furfuracea	CBrP LPal
muricata	LPal
pumila	CBrP
skinneri	LPal
standleyi	CBrP
vazquezii	CBrP

ZANTEDESCHIA (Araceae)

§ *aethiopica* ♀	CBen CHEx COIW CTbh CTrC CWat EHon EWes LAma LCns LPBA MNrw MSta NDea NOrc NPer NRog SDix SSoC SSpi SWat SYvo WBrE WEas WFar WMul WPic WWal
- 'Apple Court Babe'	CRow SApp
- 'Childsiana'	EBee
- 'Crowborough' ♀	More than 30 suppliers
- 'Gigantea'	Last listed 1998
- 'Green Goddess' ♀	More than 30 suppliers
- 'Little Gem'	ECha LPio
¶ - 'Mr Sam'	CLAP
- 'Pershore Fantasia' (v)	MAvo WFar WSPU
- pink	Last listed 1997
- 'Snow White'	Last listed 1998
¶ - 'White Gnome'	WFar
- 'White Sail'	CLAP GCal MTed WFib
albomaculata	CTrC EBee LAma LCaP NPSI NRog
- S&SH 35	Last listed 1999
'Apricot'	WViv
'Aztec Gold'	CHEx
'Best Gold'	LAma NRog
'Black Eyed Beauty'	LAma NRog
'Black Magic'	CHEx LAma WViv
'Bridal Blush'	LAma
'Cameo'	CSut LAma WViv
'Carmine Red'	CSut
¶ 'Celeste'	WViv
elliottiana ♀	CFir CHal CSut EOas GQui LAma NRog SYvo WPnn WViv

'Galaxy'   WViv
'Golden Sun'   WViv
'Harvest Moon'   CWit LAma
'Helen O'Connor'   SYvo
'Kiwi Blush'   CAbP CB&S CFir CLAP CRow EBee
                             ELan EMan EWll LRHS MBri MCCP
                             NPSI SEND SMad SPla SSpi STes
                             SUsu SVil WCot WFar WPnn WSan
'Lavender Petite'   LAma NRog
'Lime Lady'   EBee ECha
* 'Little Suzy'   WViv
'Majestic Red'   Last listed 1999
'Mango'   WPnn WViv
'Maroon Dainty'   LAma NRog
'Moonglow'   WViv
¶ 'Mr Martin'   NCut
'Pacific Pink'   LAma
'Pink Persuasion'   Last listed 1999
rebmannii ♀   CB&S CStu GQui LAma LCaP
                             MCCP SRms SYvo WHil WViv
- 'Alba'   Last listed 1998
- 'Little Dream'   WViv
- 'Superba'   Last listed 1998
* 'Romeo'   SYvo
'Ruby'   Last listed 1999
'Shell Pink'   LAma NRog
'Solfatare'   LAma LCaP WHil
* 'Sweet Suzie'   Last listed 1998
'Treasure'   Last listed 1999

ZANTHORHIZA See XANTHORHIZA

ZANTHOXYLUM (Rutaceae)
ailanthoides   CFil EPfP
- from Japan   WPGP
americanum   CFil CLnd GKir
armatum   CFil WPGP
¶ *bungeanum*   WPGP
coreanum   CFil WPGP
oxyphyllum   CDoC CFil EPla WPGP
piperitum   CFil LEdu WWat
¶ - purple-leaved   CFil
planispinum   MRav
schinifolium   CB&S LEdu
- B&SWJ 1245   WCru
simulans   CB&S CPLG

ZAUSCHNERIA (Onagraceae)
arizonica   See *Z. californica* subsp. *latifolia*
§ *californica*   CGdn CMHG EBee EPfP GQui
                             MCCP SLon WPnn
- 'Albiflora'   EPot
§ - subsp. *cana*   CLTr CSam ECGP ECha ELan IOrc
                             MHar SAga SChu
- - 'Sir Cedric Morris'   ELan EPfP LRHS MAsh SMur WWat
- 'Clover Dale'   EWes
§ - 'Dublin' ♀   ECha ELan EPot ERea LHop LRHS
                             MAsh MBro MHar MHer MRav
                             MSCN MWat SAga SBla SChu SHFr
                             SIng SRot SUsu WAbe WCot WCru
                             WEas WHer WHil WHoo WPat
                             WSHC WWin
§ - subsp. *garrettii*   NWCA SDys
- 'Glasnevin'   See *Z. californica* 'Dublin'
§ - subsp. *latifolia*   MBro NMen NWCA SAga WHoo
                             WPnn
- - 'Sally Walker'   EWes
§ - subsp. *mexicana*   EPot MHer NCat SRms WAbe
- 'Olbrich Silver'   EBee ECha EWes LHop MSCN
                             NLap NWCA SDys SOkh SUsu
                             WAbe WCot WCru WHil WPat
                             WWin

- 'Sierra Salmon'   LGre SDys
- 'Solidarity Pink'   CLTr MTho WKif WPat
- 'Western Hills'   CFir EBee LGre LHop MRav
                             NWCA SBla SIng SUsu WAbe
                             WPGP
cana villosa   See *Z. californica* subsp.
                             mexicana
* *septentrionalis*   NTow SAga SBla SMad

ZEBRINA See TRADESCANTIA

ZELKOVA ✿ (Ulmaceae)
abelicea   Last listed 1998
carpinifolia   CDul CLnd CMCN CTho GAri
                             LRHS MAsh STre WNor WWoo
byrcana   SBir
schneideriana   CMCN WWoo
serrata ♀   CB&S CBlo CDul CLnd CMCN
                             CTho ECrN ELan GChr IArd IOrc
                             LRHS MBar MBel NBea NWea SBir
                             SPer SRPl STre WBod WDin WFro
                             WMou WNor WPGP WWat
- 'Goblin'   CPMA MBro NHol SSta WPat
- 'Green Vase'   LPan LRHS
- 'Nira'   Last listed 1999
- 'Variegata'   CB&S CPMA MBlu MGos MNaF
                             SSta WBcn
- 'Yatsubusa'   STre
- 'Yrban Ruby'   MGos SSta
sinica   CB&S CLnd CMCN WNor
x *verschaffeltii*   GAri

ZENOBIA (Ericaceae)
pulverulenta   More than 30 suppliers
- f. *nitida*   SSta

ZEPHYRANTHES (Amaryllidaceae)
atamasca   CStu
candida   CAvo CBro CStu EBee EMan
                             EMon ERea ERos ITim LAma
                             LHop LRHS NMen NRog SDeJ
                             SDix WCot
'Capricorn'   Last listed 1997
chlorosolen   Last listed 1997
citrina   ERos LAma NMen NRog
drummondii   WCot
flavissima   CBro WCot
grandiflora   Last listed 1997
'Grandjax'   WCot
'La Buffa Rose'   WCot
x *lancasterae*   Last listed 1998
macrosiphon   Last listed 1997
morrisclintii   Last listed 1997
'Prairie Sunset'   Last listed 1997
primulina   Last listed 1997
puertoricensis   Last listed 1997
pulchella   Last listed 1997
reginae   Last listed 1997
robusta   See *Habranthus robustus*
rosea   LAma
smallii   Last listed 1997
sulphurea   LAma
verecunda   SIng

ZIGADENUS (Melanthiaceae)
elegans   EBee EBrP EBre ECha EMan
                             EPar ERos GCrs LBCl LBSe LBre
                             LGre LRHS MBBe MBro NDov
                             NHol NWCA SBre SSpi WPyg
                             WWin
fremontii   EBee
glaberrimus   SSpi

nuttallii	EBee EMan ERos LGre LRHS NHol WCDu
venenosus	EBee

ZINGIBER (Zingiberaceae)
¶ *chrysanthum*	WMul
¶ *clarkei*	WMul
mioga	GPoy WMul
* *neglectum*	LEur
officinale	GPoy MSal NHex
zerumbet	GPoy WMul
¶ - 'Darceyi' (v)	LEur

ZIZANIA (Poaceae)
aquatica	Last listed 1997
caducifolia	See Z. *latifolia*
§ *latifolia*	MSta

ZIZIA (Apiaceae)
aptera	EBrP EBre LBCl LBSe LBre MBBe SBre
aurea	EBee

ZIZIPHUS (Rhamnaceae)
§ *jujuba* (F)	LEdu LPan
- 'Lang' (F)	CB&S
- 'Li' (F)	LPan
sativa	See Z. *jujuba*

SUPPLEMENTARY KEYS TO THE DIRECTORY

NOMENCLATURE NOTES

These notes refer to plants in the main Plant Directory that are marked with a 'N'. 'Bean Supplement' refers to W.J. Bean *Trees & Shrubs Hardy in the British Isles* (Supplement to the 8th edition) edited by D L Clarke 1988.

Acer palmatum var. *coreanum*
  This includes, but is not synonymous with, the plant sold by Hilliers as *A. palmatum* 'Koreanum', now named *A. palmatum* var. *coreanum* 'Korean Gem'.
Acer palmatum 'Sango-kaku'/ 'Senkaki'
  Two or more clones are offered under these names. *A. palmatum* 'Eddisbury' is similar with brighter coral stems.
Acer pseudoplatanus 'Leopoldii'
  True 'Leopoldii' has leaves stained with yellowish pink and purple. Plants are often *A. pseudoplatanus* f. *variegatum*.
Acer pseudoplatanus 'Spaethii'
  The true cultivar has large leaves with light yellow specks.
Aconitum autumnale
  A synonym of *A. napellus* and *A. carmichaelii* Wilsonii Group.
Achillea ptarmica The Pearl Group/ *A. ptarmica* (The Pearl Group) 'Boule de Neige'/ *A. ptarmica* (The Pearl Group) 'The Pearl'
  In the recent trial of achilleas at Wisley, only one of the several stocks submitted as 'The Pearl' matched the original appearance of this plant according to Graham Stuart Thomas, this being from Wisley's own stock. At rather less than 60cm./2ft, this needed little support, being the shortest of the plants bearing this name, with slightly grey, not glossy dark green, leaves and a non-invasive habit. This has been designated as the type for this cultivar and only this clone should bear the cultivar name 'The Pearl'. The Pearl Group covers all other double-flowered clones of this species, including seed-raised plants which are markedly inferior, sometimes scarcely double, often invasive and usually needing careful staking. It has been claimed that

'The Pearl' was a re-naming of Lemoine's 'Boule de Neige' but not all authorities agree: all plants submitted to the Wisley trial as 'Boule de Neige' were different from each other, not the same clone as Wisley's 'The Pearl' and referrable to The Pearl Group.
Acorus gramineus 'Oborozuki' & 'Ogon'
  Although these seem to be the same clone in British gardens, 'Oborozuki' is a distinct brighter yellow cultivar in the USA.
Alchemilla alpina
  The true species is very rare in cultivation. Plants under this name are usually *A. plicatula* or *A. conjuncta*.
Alchemilla splendens
  The true species is probably not in cultivation in the British Isles.
Alopecurus pratensis 'Aureus'
  Name applies only to plants with all gold leaves, not to green and gold striped forms.
Anemone magellanica
  According to *European Garden Flora*, this is a variant of the very variable *A. multifida*.
Anemone nemorosa 'Alba Plena'
  This name is used for several double white forms including *A. nemorosa* 'Flore Pleno' and *A. nemorosa* 'Vestal'.
Anthemis 'Beauty of Grallagh'/'Grallagh Gold'
  The true 'Grallagh Gold' has golden yellow flowers. Plants with orange yellow flowers are *A.* 'Beauty of Grallagh'.
Artemisia granatensis hort.
  Possibly a variant of *A. absinthium*.
Artemisia ludoviciana var. *latiloba* / *A. ludoviciana* 'Valerie Finnis'
  Leaves of the former are glabrous at maturity, those of the latter are not.
Artemisia stelleriana 'Boughton Silver'
  This was thought to be the first validly published name for this plant, 'Silver Brocade' having been published earlier but invalidly in an undated publication. However, an earlier valid publication for the cultivar name 'Mori' has subsequently been found for the same plant. A proposal to conserve

'Boughton Silver' has been tabled because of its more widespread use.

Aster amellus Violet Queen
It is probable that more than one cultivar is sold under this name.

Aster dumosus
Many of the asters listed under *A. novi-belgii* contain varying amounts of *A. dumosus* blood in their parentage. It is not possible to allocate these to one species or the other and they are therefore listed under *A. novi-belgii*.

Aster x *frikartii* 'Mönch'
The true plant is very rare in British gardens. Most plants are another form of *A.* x *frikartii*, usually 'Wunder von Stäfa'.

Aster novi-belgii
See note under *A. dumosus*. *A. laevis* is also involved in the parentage of most cultivars.

Azara paraguayensis
This is an unpublished name for what seems to be a hybrid between *A. serrata* and *A. lanceolata*.

Berberis aristata
Plants so named may be either *B. chitria* or *B. floribunda*.

Berberis buxifolia 'Nana'/ 'Pygmaea'
See explanation in Bean Supplement.

Berberis stenophylla 'Lemon Queen'
This sport from 'Pink Pearl' was first named in 1982. The same mutation occurred again and was named 'Cream Showers'. The older name has priority.

Bergenia Ballawley hybrids
The name 'Ballawley' refers only to plants vegetatively propagated from the original clone. Seed-raised plants, which may differ considerably, should be called Ballawley hybrids.

Betula pendula 'Dalecarlica'
The true plant of this name is rare in cultivation in the British Isles and is probably not available from nurseries.

Betula utilis var. *jacquemontii*
Plants are often the clones *B. utilis* var. *jacquemontii* 'Inverleith' or *B. utilis* var. *jacquemontii* 'Doorenbos'

Blechnum chilense/B. tabulare
The true *B. tabulare* has an AGM and is grown in the British Isles but is probably not presently offered by nurseries. This name is often misapplied to *B. chilense*.

Brachyscome
Originally published as *Brachyscome* by Cassini who later revised his spelling to *Brachycome*. The original spelling has been internationally adopted.

Brachyglottis greyi and *laxifolia*
Both these species are extremely rare in cultivation, plants under these names usually being *B.* 'Sunshine'.

Calamagrostis x *acutiflora* 'Karl Foerster'
C. x *acutiflora* 'Stricta' differs in being 15cm taller,

10-15 days earlier flowering with a less fluffy inflorescence.

Caltha polypetala
This name is often applied to a large-flowered variant of *C. palustris*. The true species has more (7-10) petals.

Camassia leichtlinii 'Alba'
The true cultivar has blueish-white, not cream flowers.

Camassia leichtlinii 'Plena'
This has starry, transparent green-white flowers; creamy-white 'Semiplena' is sometimes offered under this name.

Camellia japonica 'Campbellii'
This name is used for five cultivars including 'Margherita Coleoni' but applies correctly to Guichard's 1894 cultivar, single to semi-double full rose pink.

Campanula lactiflora 'Alba'
This refers to the pure white flowered clone, not to blueish- or greyish-white flowered plants, nor to seed-raised plants.

Campanula persicifolia
Plants under "cup and saucer white" are not definitely ascribed to a particular cultivar. 'White Cup and Saucer' is a cultivar named by Margery Fish.

Carex morrowii 'Variegata'
C. oshimensis 'Evergold' is sometimes sold under this name.

Carya illinoinensis
The correct spelling of this name is discussed in *Baileya*, **10**(1) (1962).

Cassinia retorta
Now included within *C. leptophylla*. A valid infra-specific epithet has yet to be published.

Ceanothus 'Italian Skies'
Many plants under this name are not true to name.

Chamaecyparis lawsoniana 'Columnaris Glauca'
Plants under this name might be *C. lawsoniana* 'Columnaris' or a new invalidly named cultivar.

Chamaecyparis lawsoniana 'Elegantissima'
This name has been applied to two cultivars, 'Elegantissima' of Schelle and subsequently (invalidly) 'Elegantissima' of Hillier.

Chamaecyparis pisifera 'Squarrosa Argentea'
There are two plants of this name, one (valid) with variegated foliage, the other (invalid) with silvery foliage.

Chrysanthemum 'Anastasia Variegated'
Despite its name, this seems to be derived from 'Mei-kyo', not 'Anastasia'.

Cistus 'Silver Pink'
Plants under this name are not usually true to type. *C.* 'Grayswood Pink' (most commonly), *C.* 'Peggy Sammons' and *C.* x *skanbergii* are often offered under this name.

Clematis chrysocoma
The true *C. chrysocoma* is a non-climbing erect plant with dense yellow down on the young growth, still uncommon in cultivation.

Clematis heracleifolia 'Campanile'
Might be *C.* x *bonstedtii* 'Campanile' .

Clematis heracleifolia 'Côte d'Azur'
Might be *C.* x *bonstedtii* 'Côte d'Azur'

Clematis 'Jackmanii Superba'
Plants under this name are usually *C.* 'Gipsy Queen'.

Clematis montana
This name should be used for the typical white-flowered variety only. Pink-flowered variants are referable to *C. montana* var. *rubens*.

Clematis 'Victoria'
There is also a Latvian cultivar of this name with petals with a central white bar.

Colchicum 'Autumn Queen'
Entries here might refer to the slightly different *C.* 'Prinses Astrid'.

Cornus 'Norman Hadden'
See note in Bean Supplement, p.184.

Cotoneaster bullatus 'Firebird'
Considered by National Collection Holder, Jeannette Fryer, to be a new species. To be published as *C. ignescens* in 2000.

Cotoneaster dammeri
Plants sold under this name are usually *C. dammeri* 'Major'.

Cotoneaster frigidus 'Cornubia'
According to Hylmø this cultivar, like all other variants of this species, is fully deciduous. Several evergreen cotoneasters are also grown under this name, most are clones of *C.* x *watereri* or *C. salicifolius*.

Crataegus coccinea
C. intricata, *C. pedicellata* and *C. biltmoreana* are occasionally supplied under this name.

Crocus cartwrightianus 'Albus'
The plant offered is the true cultivar and not *C. hadriaticus*.

Dianthus fringed pink
D. 'Old Fringed Pink' and D. 'Old Fringed White' are also sometimes sold under this name.

Dianthus 'Musgrave's Pink' (p)
This is the registered name of this white-flowered cultivar.

Elymus magellanicus
Although this is a valid name, Roger Grounds has suggested that many plants might belong to a different, perhaps unnamed species.

Epilobium glabellum hort.
Plants under this name are not *E. glabellum* but are close to *E. wilsonii* Petrie or perhaps a hybrid of it.

Erodium glandulosum
Plants under this name are often hybrids.

Erodium guttatum
Doubtfully in commerce; plants under this name are usually *E. heteradenum*, *E. cheilanthifolium* or hybrids.

Erysimum cheiri 'Baden-Powell'
Plant of uncertain origin differing from *E. cheiri* 'Harpur Crewe' only in its shorter stature.

Erysimum 'Variegatum'
This name might refer to any of the variegated cultivars of *Erysimum*.

Eucryphia 'Penwith'
The cultivar name 'Penwith' was originally given to a hybrid of *E. cordifolia* x *E. lucida*, not *E.* x *hillieri*.

Fagus sylvatica Cuprea Group/Atropurpurea Group
It is desirable to provide a name, Cuprea Group, for less richly coloured forms, used in historic landscapes before the purple clones appeared.

Fagus sylvatica 'Pendula'
This name refers to the Knap Hill clone, the most common weeping form in English gardens. Other clones occur, particularly in Cornwall and Ireland.

Forsythia 'Beatrix Farrand'
The true plant might not be in cultivation.

Fragaria chiloensis 'Variegata', *F. vesca* 'Variegata'
Most, possibly all, plants under these names are *F.* x *ananassa* 'Variegata'.

Fuchsia
All names marked 'N', except the following, refer to more than one cultivar.

Fuchsia decussata
A hybrid of *F. magellanica* is also offered under this name.

Fuchsia loxensis
For a comparison of the true species with the hybrids 'Speciosa' and 'Loxensis' commonly grown under this name, see Boullemier's Check List (2nd ed.) p.268.

Fuchsia minimiflora
Some plants under this name might be *F.* x *bacillaris*.

Fuchsia 'Pumila'
Plants under this name might be *F. magellanica* var. *pumila*.

Gentiana cachemirica
Most plants sold are not true to type.

Geum 'Borisii'
This name refers to cultivars of *G. coccineum* Sibthorp & Smith, especially *G.* 'Werner Arends' and not to *G.* x *borisii* Kelleper.

Halimium alyssoides and *H. halimifolium*
Plants under these names are sometimes *H.* x *pauanum* or *H.* x *santae*.

Hebe 'C.P. Raffill'
See note in Bean Supplement, p.265.

Hebe 'Carl Teschner'
See note in Bean Supplement, p.264.

Hebe glaucophylla
A green reversion of the hybrid *H.* 'Glaucophylla Variegata' is often sold under this name.

Hedera helix 'Caenwoodiana'/ 'Pedata'
Some authorities consider these to be distinct cultivars while others think them different morphological forms of the same unstable clone.

Hedera helix 'Oro di Bogliasco'
Priority between this name and 'Jubiläum Goldherz' and 'Goldheart' has yet to be finally resolved.

Helleborus hybridus/ H. orientalis hort.
The name *H. hybridus* for acaulescent hellebore hybrids does not follow the International Code of Botanical Nomenclature Article Article H.3.2 requiring one of the parent species to be designated and does not seem to have been typified, contrary to Article 7 of the Code. However, the RHS Advisory Panel on Nomenclature and Taxonomy considers it to be a more meaningful and less invalid name than any of the alternatives and avoids the confusion that results from using *H. orientalis* hort. Though there has not been time to change entries this year, entries under the latter name will be changed to *H. hybridus* in our next edition. The Panel considers that the omission of the hybrid sign (×) from *H. hybridus* makes the name more acceptable under the rules of the Code.

Hemerocallis fulva 'Kwanso', 'Kwanso Variegata', 'Flore Pleno' and 'Green Kwanso'
For a discussion of these plants see *The Plantsman*, 7(2).

Heuchera micrantha var. diversifolia 'Palace Purple'
This cultivar name refers only to plants with deep purple-red foliage. Seed-raised plants of inferior colouring should not be offered under this name.

Hosta 'Marginata Alba'
This name is wrongly used both for *H. crispula* and, more commonly, for *H. fortunei* 'Albomarginata'.

Hosta montana
This name refers only to plants long grown in Europe, which differ from *H. elata*.

Hydrangea macrophylla Teller Series
This is used both as a descriptive common name for Lacecap hydrangeas (German *teller* = plate, referring to the more or less flat inflorescence) and for the series of hybrids raised by Wädenswill in Switzerland bearing German names of birds. It is not generally possible to link a hydrangea described by the series name plus a colour description (e.g. Teller Blau, Teller Rosa, Teller Rot) to a single cultivar.

Hypericum fragile
The true *H. fragile* is probably not available from British nurseries.

Hypericum 'Gemo'
Either a selection of *H. prolificum* or *H. prolificum* × *H. densiflorum*.

Ilex × altaclerensis
The argument for this spelling is given by Susyn Andrews, *The Plantsman*, 5(2) and is not superceded by the more recent comments in the Supplement to Bean's Trees and Shrubs.

Iris
Apart from those noted below, cultivar names marked 'N' are not registered. The majority of those marked 'I' have been previously used for a different cultivar.

Iris histrioides 'Major'
Two clones are offered under this name, the true one pale blue with darker spotting on the falls, the incorrect one violet-blue with almost horizontal falls.

Iris pallida 'Variegata'
The white-variegated *I. pallida* 'Argentea Variegata' is sometimes wrongly supplied under this name, which refers only to the gold-variegated cultivar.

Lamium maculatum 'Chequers'
This name refers to two plants; the first, validly named, is a large and vigorous form of *L. maculatum* with a stripe down the centre of the leaf; the second is silver-leaved and very similar to *L. maculatum* 'Beacon Silver'.

Lavandula 'Alba'
Might be either *L. angustifolia* 'Alba' or *L. × intermedia* 'Alba'

Lavandula angustifolia 'Lavender Lady'/ L. 'Cambridge Lady'
Might be synonyms of *L. angustifolia* 'Lady'.

Lavandula × intermedia 'Arabian Night'
Plants under this name might be *L. × intermedia* 'Impress Purple'.

Lavandula spica
This name is classed as a name to be rejected (*nomen rejiciendum*) by the *International Code of Botanical Nomenclature*.

Lavandula 'Twickel Purple'
Two cultivars are sold under this name, one a form of *L. × intermedia*, the other of *L. angustifolia*.

Lavatera olbia and L. thuringiaca
Although *L. olbia* is usually shrubby and *L. thuringiaca* usually herbaceous, both species are very variable. Cultivars formally ascribed to one species or the other have been shown to be hybrids and are listed by cultivar name alone.

Lobelia 'Russian Princess'
This has green, not purple, leaves and rich pink, not purple, flowers.

Lonicera × *americana*
Most plants offered by nurseries under this name
are correctly *L.* × *italica*. The true *L.* × *americana* is
still widely grown but is slow to propagate. See *The
Plantsman*, 12(2).

Lonicera × *brownii* 'Fuchsioides'
Plants under this name are usually *L.* × *brownii*
'Dropmore Scarlet'.

Lonicera × *heckrotii* 'Gold Flame'
This name applies to the original clone. Many
plants under this name are a different clone for
which the name 'American Beauty' has been
proposed.

Lonicera periclymenum 'Serotina'
See note in Bean Supplement, p.315.

Lonicera sempervirens f. *sulphurea*
Plants in the British Isles usually a yellow-flowered
form of *L. periclymenum*.

Macleaya cordata
Most, if not all, plants offered are *M.* × *kewensis*.

Magnolia × *highdownensis*.
Believed to fall within the range of variation of
M. wilsonii.

Mahonia pinnata
Most plants in cultivation under this name are
believed to be *M.* × *wagneri* 'Pinnacle'.

Malus domestica 'Dummellor's Seedling'
The phonetic spelling 'Dumelow's Seedling'
contravenes the ICBN ruling on orthography,
i.e. that, except for intentional latinizations,
commemorative names should be based on
the original spelling of the person's name
(Article 60.11). The spelling adopted here is
that used on the gravestone of the raiser in
Leicestershire.

Melissa officinalis 'Variegata'
The true cultivar of this name was striped with
white.

Narcissus poeticus 'Plenus'
A name of uncertain application used for *N.
poeticus* 'Spalding Double White' and *N. poeticus*
'Tamar Double White'.

Nemesia caerulea
The lavender blue clone 'Joan Wilder', described
and illustrated in *The Hardy Plant*, 14(1), 11-14,
does not come true from seed; it may only be
propagated from cuttings.

Osmanthus heterophyllus 'Gulftide'
Probably correctly *O.* × *fortunei* 'Gulftide'.

Papaver orientale 'Flore Pleno'
P. 'Fireball' is sometimes offered under this name
and possibly also *P. orientale* 'May Queen' and *P.
orientale* 'Olympia'.

Passiflora antioquiensis
According to National Colection holder John
Vanderplank, the true species is not in cultivation
in the British Isles. Plants under this name are
likely to be clones of *P.* × *exoniensis*.

Pelargonium 'Beauty of Eastbourne'
This should not be confused with *P.* 'Eastbourne
Beauty', a different cultivar.

Pelargonium 'Lass o' Gowrie'
The American plant of this name has pointed, not
rounded leaf lobes.

Pelargonium quercifolium
Plants under this name are mainly hybrids. The
true species has pointed, not rounded leaf lobes.

Penstemon 'Taoensis'
This name for a small-flowered cultivar or hybrid
of *P. isophyllus* originally appeared as 'Taoense' but
must be corrected to agree in gender with
Penstemon (masculine). Presumably an invalid
name (published in Latin form since 1958), it is
not synonymous with *P. crandallii* subsp.
glabrescens var. *taosensis*.

Pernettya
Botanists now consider that *Pernettya* (fruit a
berry) is not separable from *Gaultheria* (fruit a
capsule) because in some species the fruit is
intermediate between a berry and a capsule. For a
fuller explanation see D. Middleton, *The
Plantsman*, 12(3).

Picea pungens 'Glauca Pendula'
This name is used for several different glaucous
cultivars.

Pinus ayacahuite
P. ayacahuite var. *veitchii* (syn. *P. veitchii)* is
occasionally sold under this name.

Pinus montezumae
Plants propagated from mature trees in British
gardens are mostly an unnamed long-needled
variety of *P. rudis*.

Pinus nigra 'Cebennensis Nana'
A doubtful name, possibly a synonym for *P. nigra*
'Nana'.

Polemonium archibaldiae
Usually sterile with lavender-blue flowers. A self-
fertile white-flowered plant is sometimes sold
under this name.

Polystichum setiferum 'Wollaston'
Incomplete name which may refer to either of two
cultivars.

Populus nigra 'Italica'
See note in Bean Supplement, p.393.

Prunus laurocerasus 'Castlewellan'
We are grateful to Dr Charles Nelson for
informing us that the name 'Marbled White' is not
valid because although it has priority of
publication it does not have the approval of the
originator who asked for it to be called
'Castlewellan'.

Prunus laurocerasus 'Variegata'
The true 'Variegata', (marginal variegation), dates
from 1811 but this name is also used for the
relatively recent cultivar *P. laurocerasus*
'Castlewellan'.

Prunus serrulata* var. *pubescens
See note in Bean Supplement, p.398.
***Prunus* × *subhirtella* 'Rosea'**
Might be *P. pendula* var. *ascendens* 'Rosea',
P. pendula 'Pendula Rosea', or *P.* × *subhirtella*
'Autumnalis Rosea'.
Rheum* × *cultorum
The name *R.* × *cultorum* was published
without adequate description and must be
abandoned in favour of the validly published
R. × *hybridum*.
***Rhododendron* (azaleas)**
All names marked 'N', except for the following,
refer to more than one cultivar.
***Rhododendron* 'Hino-mayo'**
This name is based on a faulty transliteration
(should be 'Hinamoyo') but the spelling
'Hino-mayo' is retained in the interests of
stability.
Rhus typhina
Linnaeus published both *R. typhina* and *R. hirta* as
names for the same species. Though *R. hirta* has
priority, it has been proposed that the name *R.*
typhina should be conserved.
***Robinia hispida* 'Rosea'**
This name is applied to *R. hispida* (young shoots
with bristles), *R. elliottii* (young shoots with
grey down) and *R. boyntonii* (young shoots
smooth).
***Rosa* × *damascena* 'Trigintipetala'**
The true cultivar of this name is probably not in
cultivation in the Britsh Isles.
Rosa gentiliana
Plants under this name are usually the cultivar
'Polyantha Grandiflora' but might otherwise be
R. multiflora 'Wilsonii', *R. multiflora* var.
cathayensis, *R. henryi* or another hybrid.
***Rosa* 'Gros Choux de Hollande' (Bb)**
It is doubtful if this name is correctly applied.
***Rosa* 'Maiden's Blush'**
R. 'Great Maiden's Blush' may be supplied under
this name.
***Rosa* Jacques Cartier**
For a discussion on the correct identity of this rose
see *Heritage Rose Foundation News*, Oct. 1989 &
Jan. 1990.
***Rosa* 'Professeur Emile Perrot'**
For a discussion on the correct identity of this rose
see *Heritage Roses*, Nov. 1991.
***Rosa* Sweetheart**
This is not the same as the Sweetheart Rose, a
common name for *R.* 'Cécile Brünner'.
Rosa wichurana
This is the correct spelling according to the
ICBN 1994 Article 60.11 (which enforces
Recommendation 60C.1c) and not
wichuraiana for this rose commemorating Max
Wichura.

***Salix alba* 'Tristis'**
This cultivar should not be confused with *S. tristis*,
which is now correctly *S. humilis*. Although this
cultivar is distinct in European gardens, most
plants under this name in the British Isles are
S. × *sepulcralis* var. *chrysocoma*.
Salvia microphylla* var. *neurepia
The type of this variety is referable to the typical
variety, *S. microphylla* var. *microphylla*.
***Salvia officinalis* 'Aurea'**
S. officinalis var. *aurea* is a rare variant of the com-
mon sage with leaves entirely of gold. It is rep-
resented in cultivation by the cultivar 'Kew Gold'.
The plant usually offered as *S. officinalis* 'Aurea' is
the gold variegated sage *S. officinalis* 'Icterina'.
Salvia sclarea* var. *turkestanica
This invalid name is used for plants of *S. sclarea*
var. *sclarea* with particularly showy bracts. Plants
under this name are not *S. sclarea* var.
turkistaniana of Mottet.
***Sambucus nigra* 'Aurea'**
Plants under this name are usually not *S. nigra*.
Sedum nevii
The true species is not in cultivation. Plants under
this name are usually either *S. glaucophyllum* or
occasionally *S. beyrichianum*.
Senna corymbosa
Some plants sold as *S. corymbosa* are
S. × *floribunda*.
***Skimmia japonica* 'Foremanii'**
The true cultivar, which belongs to *S. japonica*
Rogersii Group, is believed to be lost to
cultivation. Plants offered under this name are
usually *S. japonica* 'Veitchii'.
***Spiraea japonica* 'Shirobana'**
Shirobana-shimotsuke is the common name for *S.*
japonica var. *albiflora*. Shirobana means white-
flowered and does not apply to the two-coloured
form.
Staphylea holocarpa* var. *rosea
This botanical variety has woolly leaves. The
cultivar 'Rosea', with which it is often confused,
does not.
Stewartia ovata* var. *grandiflora.
Most, possibly all, plants available from British
nurseries under this name are not true to name but
are derived from the improved Nymans form.
***Thymus serpyllum* cultivars**
Most cultivars are probably correctly cultivars
of *T. polytrichus* or hybrids though they will remain
listed under *T. serpyllum* pending
further research.
***Thymus* 'Silver Posie'**
The cultivar name 'Silver Posie' is applied to
several different plants, not all of them *T. vulgaris*.
***Tricyrtis* Hototogisu**
This is the common name applied generally to all
Japanese *Tricyrtis* and specifically to *T. hirta*.

Tricyrtis macropoda
This name has been used for at least five different species.
Uncinia rubra
This name is also misapplied to *U. egmontiana* and *U. uncinata.*
Verbena 'Kemerton'
Origin unknown, not from Kemerton.
Viburnum opulus 'Fructu Luteo'

See note below.
Viburnum opulus 'Xanthocarpum'
Some entries under this name might be the less compact *V. opulus* 'Fructu Luteo'.
Viburnum plicatum
Entries may include the 'snowball' form, *V. plicatum* 'Sterile'.
Viola labradorica
See Note in *The Garden*, **110**(2): 96.

COLLECTORS' REFERENCES

Abbreviations following a plant name, refer to the collector(s) of the plant. These abbreviations are expanded below, with a collector's name or expedition title. For a fuller explanation, turn to p.15.

A&JW	A. & J. Watson, S America
A&L	Ala & Lancaster expedition, N Iran, 1972
AB&S	Archibald, Blanchard & Salmon, Morocco 1980s
AC	Alan Clark, Kaiyuan/Kunming Yunnan Expedition, China, 1995
AC&H	Apold, Cox & Hutchinson, NE Turkey, 1962
AC&W	Albury, Cheese & Watson
ACE	Alpine Garden Society expedition, China, 1994
ACL	A.C. Leslie
AGS/ES	Alpine Garden Society expedition, Sikkim, 1983
AGSJ	Alpine Garden Society expedition, Japan, 1988
Airth	Murray Airth
Akagi	Akagi Botanical Garden
AL&JS	Leslie & Sharman, Yugoslavia, 1990
B L.	Beer, Nepal, 1975
B&L	Brickell & Leslie, China
B&M	C.D. Brickell & B. Mathew
B&S	P. Bird & M. Salmon
B&SWJ	B. & S. Wynn-Jones
BB	B. Bartholomew, Bhutan, 1974
BC	B. Chudziak, Kanchenjunga, Nepal, 1993
BC&W	Beckett, Cheese & Watson
BL&M	Beer, Lancaster & Morris, E Nepal, 1971
BM	B. Mathew
BM&W	Binns, Mason & Wright, Nepal, 1978
BS	Basil Smith
BSBE	Bowles Scholarship Botanical Expedition
BSSS	Crûg Expedition, Jordan, 1991
Bu	S. Bubert
C&C	P.A. & K.N.E. Cox, SE Tibet, 1996
C&Cu	K.N.E. Cox & J. Cubey
C&H	P.A. Cox & P.C. Hutchison, Assam, NE

	Frontier & N Bengal, 1965; Sichuan & Yunnan, China, 1995
C&K	Chamberlain & Knott
C&R	Christian & Roderick, California, Oregon, Washington
C&S	A. Clark & I. Sinclair, Bhutan, 1994
C&V	K.N.E. Cox & S. Vergera, SE Tibet, China, 1995
C&W	M. Cheese & J. Watson
CC	C. Chadwell
CC&H	D.F. Chamberlain, P.A. Cox & P.C. Hutchison, Sichuan, China, 1989
CC&McK	Chadwell & McKelvie, Nepal, West Himalaya, 1990-92
CC&MR	C. Chadwell & M. Ramsey, Kashmir, 1985; Himachal Pradesh & W Himalaya, 1989
CCH&H	Chamberlain, Cox, Hootman & Hutchison
CD&R	J. Compton, J. D'Arcy & E.M. Rix, China, Drakensburg, Mexico & Korea
CDB	C.D. Brickell
CDC&C	Compton, D'Arcy, Christopher & Coke
CE&H	Christian, Elliott & Hoog, Yugoslavia & Greece, 1982
CEE	Chengdu Edinburgh Expedition, Sichuan, China, 1991
CGW	C. Grey-Wilson
CH&M	P.A. Cox, P.C. Hutchison & D.M. McDonald, Sichuan & Yunnan, China, 1986; Bhutan, 1988
CHP&W	Chadwell, Howard, Powell & Wright, Kashmir, 1983
CL	C. Lovell
CLD	Kew, Edinburgh & RHS Expedition, Zhongdian (Chungtien), Lijiang & Dali, China, 1990
CM&W	M. Cheese, J. Mitchel & J. Watson
CN&W	A. Clark, J. Nielson & R. J Wilson, W. China
Cooper	R.E. Cooper (1890-1962), Bhutan, 1914 & '15; Punjab, India, 1916; NE Burma

CSE	Cyclamen Society Expedition	HWEL	J.M. Hirst & D. Webster, Lesotho
CT	Carla Teune	HWJCM	Crûg Heronswood expedition, E Nepal,
DBG	Denver Botanic Garden, Colorado		1995
DF	Derek Fox	HZ	Henrik Zetterlund
DJH	Dan Hinkley	J&JA	J.C. & J. Archibald
DJHC	Dan Hinkley, China	JCA	J.C. Archibald
DM	David Millais	JE	Jack Elliott
DS&T	Drake, Sharman & Thompson, Turkey,	JJ	John Jackson
	1989	JJ&JH	Josef J. & Jarmila Halda
ECN	E. Charles Nelson	JJH	Josef J. Halda
EDHCH	Eric D. Hammond (for Heronswood	JLS	J.L. Sharman, USA, 1988
	Nursery) China, 1997	JMT	J. Mann Taylor
EGM	E.G. Millais, Bhutan, 1988 (with others);	JN	Jens Nielson
	Sichuan & Yunnan, China, 1995	JR	J. Russell
EKB	E.K. Balls	JRM	J.R. Marr, Greece & Turkey, 1975
EM	East Malling Research Station clonal	JW	J. Watson
	selection scheme	K	G. Kirkpatrick
EMAK	Edinburgh Makalu Expedition, Nepal,	K&E	Kew & Edinburgh Expedition, China,
	1991		1989
EMR	E.M. Rix	K&LG	K.D. & L.M. Gillanders, Ecuador, 1994;
EN	Edward Needham		Yunnan, China, 1993, '94, '96; Vietnam,
ENF	E. Nigel Fuller		1992; Tibet, 1995
ES	Euroseeds (Mojmir Pavelka), Nový Jičin,	K&Mc	G. Kirkpatrick & R. McBeath.
	Czech Republic	KEKE	Kew/Edinburgh Kanchenjunga
ETE	Edinburgh Expedition, Taiwan, 1993		Expedition, NE Nepal, 1989
ETOT	M. Flanagan & T. Kirkham, Taiwan,1992	KGB	Kunming-Gothenburg Expedition,
F	George Forrest (1873-1932)		NW Yunnan, China, 1993
F&W	A. Flores & J. Watson, Chile, 1992	KR	K. Rushforth
Farrer	Reginald Farrer (1880-1920)	KRW	K.R. Wooster, breeder's number
FK	Fergus W. Kinmonth, China; Nepal;	KW	Frank Kingdon-Ward (1885-1958)
	Bhutan, 1990; Vietnam, 1991	L	Roy Lancaster
FMB	F.M. Bailey	L&S	F. Ludlow (1885-1972) & G. Sherriff
G	M.F. Gardner		(1898-1967)
G&K	M.F. Gardner & S.G. Knees	LA	Long Ashton Research Station clonal
G&P	M.F. Gardner & C. Page, Chile, 1992		selection scheme.
GG	George Gusman	Lismore	Lismore Nursery, breeder's number
G-W&P	Grey-Wilson & Phillips	LM&S	Leslie, Mattern & Sharman, Bulgaria,
GS	George Sherriff (1898-1967)		1994
Guitt	G.G. Guittonneau	LP	Hon. W.J.L. Palmer (1894-1971)
Guiz	J.B. Simmons, H. Fliegner & J. Russell,	LS&E	F. Ludlow, G. Sherriff & H. Elliot
	Guizhou, China, 1985	LS&H	F. Ludlow, G. Sherriff & Hicks, Bhutan,
H	Paul Huggins. Oxford University		1949
	Expedition, Tehri Garhwal, C Himalaya	LS&T	F. Ludlow, G. Sherriff & G. Taylor, SE
H&B	O. Hilliard & B.L. Burtt		Tibet, 1938
H&M	Howick & McNamara	M&PS	Mike and Polly Stone, Gravelly Range
H&W	Hedge & Wendelbo, Afghanistan, 1969		MT 1993
Harry Smith	Karl August Harald Smith	M&T	B. Mathew & J. Tomlinson
	(1889-1971)	Mac&W	MacPhail & Watson
Hartside	Hartside Nursery, breeder's number	McB	Ron McBeath, Nepal, 1981,
HCM	Heronswood Expedition to Chile, 1998		'83 & '90
HH&K	S. & S. Hannay & N. Kingsbury,	McLaren	Henry McLaren, 2nd Baron Aberconway
	Bulgaria, 1995		(1879-1953)
HLMS	L.S. Springate on Reading/Islamabad	MF	Maurice Foster, Yunnan, China, 1993 &
	Expedition, NE Pakistan, 1994		'96
HM&S	B. Halliwell, M. Mason & P. Smallcombe	MH	M. Heasman, Bhutan, 1992
Hummel	D. Hummel, China, 1950	MK	Michael Kammerlander
HW&E	Hedge, Wendelbo & Ekberg, Afghanistan,	MP	Mojmir Pavelka, Euroseeds, Czech
	1982		Republic

MPF	M.P. Frankis		SBEC	Sino-British Expedition, Cangshan, SW China, 1981
MS	M. Salmon			
MSF	M.S. Fillan, Tenerife, 1988; S Korea, 1989		SBEL	Sino-British Expedition, Lijiang, Yunnan, China, 1987
MS&CL	M. Salmon & C. Lovell		SBQE	Sino-British Qinghai Expedition, Royal Botanic Garden, Edinburgh, 1998
NJM	N.J. Macer, Mallorca, 1993; W Canada, 1994			
			SD	Sashal Dayal
NNS	Northwest Native Seeds (R. Ratko), Seattle.		Sch	A.D. Schilling, Nepal, 1975, '76, '77, '78, '83; Bhutan, 1988
NS	Nick Turland (Northside Seeds)		SEH	Steve Hootman
Og	Mikinori Ogisu		SEP	Swedish Expedition to Pakistan
P&C	D.S. Paterson & S. Clarke, Western USA, 1991		SF	P. Forde (Seaforde Gardens), Bhutan, 1990
P&W	Polastri & Watson, Chile		SH	Spencer Hannay
PB	Peter Bird		Sich	Simmons, Erskine, Howick & McNamara, Sichuan, China, 1988
PC&H	G. Pattison, P. Catt & M. Hickson, Mexico, 1994		SS&W	Stainton, Sykes & Williams, C Nepal, 1954
PD	Peter Davis			
PF	Paul Furse		SSNY	Sino-Scottish Expedition, NW Yunnan, China, 1992
PJC	P.J. Christian			
PJC&AH	P.J. Christian & A. Hoog, Greece & Yugoslavia, 1985		T	Nigel P. Taylor
			T&K	N.P. Taylor & S. Knees
Pras	Milan Prasil		TS&BC	T. Smythe & B. Cherry, Yunnan, China, 1994
PS&W	Polunin, Sykes & Williams, W Nepal, 1952			
			TSS	T. Spring-Smyth, E Nepal, 1961-62, '70
PW	Peter Wharton, Guizhou, China, 1994		TW	Tony Weston (with A.D. Schilling), Nepal, 1985; (with K. Rushforth) SW Yunnan, China 1993
R	J.F.C. Rock (1884-1962)			
RB	Ray Brown (Plant World, Devon), Chile, 1994			
			USDAPI	US Dept of Agriculture Plant Index Number
RCB/Eq	Robert Brown, Ecuador, 1998			
RH	R. Hancock		USDAPQ	US Dept of Agriculture Plant Quarantine Number
RMRP	Rocky Mountain Rare Plants, Denver, Colorado		USNA	United States National Arboretum
RS	Reinhart Suckow		VHH	Vernon H. Heywood
RV	Richard Valder		W	E.H. Wilson (1876-1930)
S&B	M. Salmon & J. Blanchard		W/A	E.H. Wilson, for Arnold Arboretum, 1906-19
S&F	Salmon & Fillan, Spain & Morocco			
S&L	I. Sinclair & D. Long, Bhutan, 1984		W/V	E.H. Wilson, for Veitch, 1899-1905
S&SH	Sheilah & Spencer Hannay, Lesotho, NE Cape Province, 1989 & '91; C Nepal, 1993		WM	Will McLewin
			Woods	Paddy Woods
			Wr	David & Anke Wraight
SB&L	Salmon, Bird & Lovell, Jordan & Morocco		Yu	Tse Tsun Yu (1908-86)

CLASSIFICATION OF GENERA

Genera including a large number of species or with many cultivars are often subdivided into groups. Please turn to p.15 for a fuller explanation.

ACTINIDIA

(s-p)   Self-pollinating

BEGONIA

(C)	Cane
(R)	Rex
(S)	Semperflorens Cultorum
(T)	x *tuberhybrida* (Tuberous)

CHRYSANTHEMUM

(By the National Chrysanthemum Society)
(1)	Indoor Large (Exhibition)
(2)	Indoor Medium (Exhibition)
(3a)	Indoor Incurved: Large-flowered
(3b)	Indoor Incurved: Medium-flowered
(3c)	Indoor Incurved: Small-flowered
(4a)	Indoor Reflexed: Large-flowered
(4b)	Indoor Reflexed: Medium-flowered
(4c)	Indoor Reflexed: Small-flowered
(5a)	Indoor Intermediate: Large-flowered
(5b)	Indoor Intermediate: Medium-flowered
(5c)	Indoor Intermediate: Small-flowered
(6a)	Indoor Anemone: Large-flowered
(6b)	Indoor Anemone: Medium-flowered
(6c)	Indoor Anemone: Small-flowered
(7a)	Indoor Single: Large-flowered
(7b)	Indoor Single: Medium-flowered
(7c)	Indoor Single: Small-flowered
(8a)	Indoor True Pompon
(8b)	Indoor Semi-pompon
(9a)	Indoor Spray: Anemone
(9b)	Indoor Spray: Pompon
(9c)	Indoor Spray: Reflexed
(9d)	Indoor Spray: Single
(9e)	Indoor Spray: Intermediate
(9f)	Indoor Spray: Spider, Quill, Spoon or Any Other Type
(10a)	Indoor, Spider
(10b)	Indoor, Quill
(10c)	Indoor, Spoon
(11)	Any Other Indoor Type
(12a)	Indoor, Charm
(12b)	Indoor, Cascade
(13a)	October-flowering Incurved: Large-flowered
(13b)	October-flowering Incurved: Medium-flowered
(13c)	October-flowering Incurved: Small-flowered
(14a)	October-flowering Reflexed: Large-flowered
(14b)	October-flowering Reflexed: Medium-flowered
(14c)	October-flowering Reflexed: Small-flowered
(15a)	October-flowering Intermediate: Large-flowered
(15b)	October-flowering Intermediate: Medium-flowered
(15c)	October-flowered Intermediate: Small-flowered
(16)	October-flowering Large
(17a)	October-flowering Single: Large-flowered
(17b)	October-flowering Single: Medium-flowered
(17c)	October-flowering Single: Small-flowered
(18a)	October-flowering Pompon: True Pompon
(18b)	October-flowering Pompon: Semi-pompon
(19a)	October-flowering Spray: Anemone
(19b)	October-flowering Spray: Pompon
(19c)	October-flowering Spray: Reflexed
(19d)	October-flowering Spray: Single
(19e)	October-flowering Spray: Intermediate
(19f)	October-flowering Spray: Spider, Quill, Spoon or Any Other Type
(20)	Any Other October-flowering Type
(22a)	Charm: Anemone
(22b)	Charm: Pompon
(22c)	Charm: Reflexed
(22d)	Charm: Single
(22e)	Charm: Intermediate
(22f)	Charm: Spider, Quill, Spoon or Any Other Type
(23a)	Early-flowering Outdoor Incurved: Large-flowered
(23b)	Early-flowering Outdoor Incurved: Medium-flowered
(23c)	Early-flowering Outdoor Incurved: Small-flowered
(24a)	Early-flowering Outdoor Reflexed: Large-flowered
(24b)	Early-flowering Outdoor Reflexed: Medium-flowered
(24c)	Early-flowering Outdoor Reflexed: Small-flowered
(25a)	Early-flowering Outdoor Intermediate: Large-flowered

(25b)	Early-flowering Outdoor Intermediate: Medium-flowered
(25c)	Early-flowering Outdoor Intermediate: Small-flowered
(26a)	Early-flowering Outdoor Anemone: Large-flowered
(26b)	Early-flowering Outdoor Anemone: Medium-flowered
(27a)	Early-flowering Outdoor Single: Large-flowered
(27b)	Early-flowering Outdoor Single: Medium-flowered
(28a)	Early-flowering Outdoor Pompon: True Pompon
(28b)	Early-flowering Outdoor Pompon: Semi-pompon
(29a)	Early-flowering Outdoor Spray: Anemone
(29b)	Early-flowering Outdoor Spray: Pompon
(29c)	Early-flowering Outdoor Spray: Reflexed
(29d)	Early-flowering Outdoor Spray: Single
(29e)	Early-flowering Outdoor Spray: Intermediate
(29f)	Early-flowering Outdoor Spray: Spider, Quill, Spoon or Any Other Type
(29K)	Early-flowering Outdoor Spray: Korean
(29Rub)	Early-flowering Outdoor Spray: Rubellum
(30)	Any Other Early-flowering Outdoor Type

CLEMATIS

(A)	Alpina Group (Section Atragene)
(D)	Diversifolia Group
(Fl)	Florida Group (double-flowered)
(Fo)	Forsteri Group
(H)	Heracleifolia Group
(I)	Integrifolia Group
(J)	Jackmanii Group
(L)	Lanuginosa Group
(P)	Patens Group
(T)	Texensis Group
(Ta)	Tangutica Group
(Vt)	Viticella Group

DAHLIA

(By the National Dahlia Society with corresponding numerical classification according to the Royal Horticultural Society's International Register)

(Sin)	1 Single
(Anem)	2 Anemone-flowered
(Col)	3 Collerette
(WL)	4 Waterlily (unassigned)
(LWL)	4B Waterlily, Large

(MWL)	4C Waterlily, Medium
(SWL)	4D Waterlily, Small
(MinWL)	4E Waterlily, Miniature
(GD)	5A Decorative, Giant
(LD)	5B Decorative, Large
(MD)	5C Decorative, Medium
(SD)	5D Decorative, Small
(MinD)	5E Decorative, Miniature
(SBa)	6A Small Ball
(MinBa)	6B Miniature Ball
(Pom)	7 Pompon
(GC)	8A Cactus, Giant
(LC)	8B Cactus, Large
(MC)	8C Cactus, Medium
(SC)	8D Cactus, Small
(MinC)	8E Cactus, Miniature
(S-c)	9 Semi-cactus (unassigned)
(GS-c)	9A Semi-cactus, Giant
(LS-c)	9B Semi-cactus, Large
(MS-c)	9C Semi-cactus, Medium
(SS-c)	9D Semi-cactus, Small
(MinS-c)	9E Semi-cactus, Miniature
(Misc)	10 Miscellaneous
(O)	Orchid-flowering (in combination)
(B)	Botanical (in combination)
(DwB)	Dwarf Bedding (in combination)
(Fim)	Fimbriated (in combination)
(Lil)	Lilliput (in combination)

DIANTHUS

(By the Royal Horticultural Society)

(p)	Pink
(p,a)	Annual Pink
(pf)	Perpetual-flowering Carnation
(b)	Border Carnation
(M)	Malmaison Carnation

FRUIT

(B)	Black (*Vitis*), Blackcurrant (*Ribes*)
(Ball)	Ballerina (*Malus*)
(C)	Culinary (*Malus, Prunus, Pyrus, Ribes*)
(Cider)	Cider (*Malus*)
(D)	Dessert (*Malus, Prunus, Pyrus, Ribes*)
(F)	Fruit
(G)	Glasshouse (*Vitis*)
(O)	Outdoor (*Vitis*)
(P)	Pinkcurrant (*Ribes*)
(Perry)	Perry (*Pyrus*)
(R)	Red (*Vitis*), Redcurrant (*Ribes*)
(W)	White (*Vitis*), Whitecurrant (*Ribes*)

GLADIOLUS

(B)	Butterfly
(G)	Giant

(L)	Large
(M)	Medium
(Min)	Miniature
(N)	Nanus
(P)	Primulinus
(S)	Small
(Tub)	Tubergenii

HYDRANGEA MACROPHYLLA

(H)	Hortensia
(L)	Lacecap

IRIS

(By the American Iris Society)

(AB)	Arilbred
(BB)	Border Bearded
(Cal-Sib)	Series *Californicae* × Series *Sibiricae*
(CH)	Californian Hybrid
(DB)	Dwarf Bearded (not assigned)
(Dut)	Dutch
(IB)	Intermediate Bearded
(La)	Louisiana Hybrid
(MDB)	Miniature Dwarf Bearded
(MTB)	Miniature Tall Bearded
(SDB)	Standard Dwarf Bearded
(Sino-Sib)	Series *Sibiricae*, chromosome number 2n=40
(Spuria)	Spuria
(TB)	Tall Bearded

LILIUM

(Classification according to *The International Lily Register* (ed. 3, 1982) with amendments from Supp. 10 (1992), Royal Horticultural Society)

(I)	Early-flowering Asiatic Hybrids derived from *L. amabile, L. bulbiferum, L. cernuum, L. concolor, L. davidii, L.* × *hollandicum, L. lancifolium, L. leichtlinii, L.* × *maculatum* and *L. pumilum*
(Ia)	Upright flowers, borne singly or in an umbel
(Ib)	Outward-facing flowers
(Ic)	Pendant flowers
(II)	Hybrids of Martagon type, one parent having been a form of *L. hansonii* or *L. martagon*
(III)	Hybrids from *L. candidum, L. chalcedonicum* and other related European species (excluding *L. martagon*)
(IV)	Hybrids of American species
(V)	Hybrids derived from *L. formosanum* and *L. longiflorum*
(VI)	Hybrid Trumpet Lilies and Aurelian

hybrids from Asiatic species, including *L. henryi* but excluding those from *L. auratum, L. japonicum, L. rubellum* and *L. speciosum.*

(VIa)	Plants with trumpet-shaped flowers
(VIb)	Plants with bowl-shaped flowers
(VIc)	Plants with flat flowers (or only the tips recurved)
(VId)	Plants with recurved flowers
(VII)	Hybrids of Far Eastern species as *L auratum, L. japonicum, L. rubellum* and *L. speciosum* (Oriental Hybrids)
(VIIa)	Plants with trumpet-shaped flowers
(VIIb)	Plants with bowl-shaped flowers
(VIIc)	Plants with flat flowers
(VIId)	Plants with recurved flowers
(VIII)	All hybrids not in another division
(IX)	All species and their varieties and forms

MALUS *SEE* FRUIT

NARCISSUS

(By the Royal Horticultural Society, revised 1998)

(1)	Trumpet
(2)	Large-cupped
(3)	Small-cupped
(4)	Double
(5)	Triandrus
(6)	Cyclamineus
(7)	Jonquilla and Apodanthus
(8)	Tazetta
(9)	Poeticus
(10)	Bulbocodium
(11a)	Split-corona: Collar
(11b)	Split-corona: Papillon
(12)	Miscellaneous
(13)	Species

NYMPHAEA

(H)	Hardy
(D)	Day-blooming
(N)	Night-blooming
(T)	Tropical

PAEONIA

(S)	Shrubby

PELARGONIUM

(A)	Angel
(C)	Coloured Foliage (in combination)
(Ca)	Cactus (in combination)
(d)	Double (in combination)

(Dec)	Decorative
(Dw)	Dwarf
(DwI)	Dwarf Ivy-leaved
(Fr)	Frutetorum
(I)	Ivy-leaved
(Min)	Miniature
(MinI)	Miniature Ivy-leaved
(R)	Regal
(Sc)	Scented-leaved
(St)	Stellar (in combination)
(T)	Tulip (in combination)
(U)	Unique
(Z)	Zonal

PRIMULA

(Classification as per W.W. Smith & Forrest (1928) and W.W. Smith & Fletcher (1941-49))

(1)	Amethystina
(2)	Auricula
(3)	Bullatae
(4)	Candelabra
(5)	Capitatae
(6)	Carolinella
(7)	Cortusoides
(8)	Cuneifolia
(9)	Denticulata
(10)	Dryadifolia
(11)	Farinosae
(12)	Floribundae
(13)	Grandis
(14)	Malacoides
(15)	Malvacea
(16)	Minutissimae
(17)	Muscarioides
(18)	Nivales
(19)	Obconica
(20)	Parryi
(21)	Petiolares
(22)	Pinnatae
(23)	Pycnoloba
(24)	Reinii
(25)	Rotundifolia
(26)	Sikkimensis
(27)	Sinenses
(28)	Soldanelloideae
(29)	Souliei
(30)	Vernales
(A)	Alpine Auricula
(B)	Border Auricula
(Poly)	Polyanthus
(Prim)	Primrose
(S)	Show Auricula

PRUNUS SEE FRUIT

PYRUS SEE FRUIT

RHODODENDRON

(A)	Azalea (deciduous, species or unclassified hybrid)
(Ad)	Azaleodendron
(EA)	Evergreen azalea
(G)	Ghent azalea (deciduous)
(K)	Knap Hill or Exbury azalea (deciduous)
(M)	Mollis azalea (deciduous)
(O)	Occidentalis azalea (deciduous)
(R)	Rustica azalea (deciduous)
(V)	Vireya rhododendron
(Vs)	Viscosa azalea (deciduous)

RIBES SEE FRUIT

ROSA

(A)	Alba
(Bb)	Bourbon
(Bs)	Boursault
(Ce)	Centifolia
(Ch)	China
(Cl)	Climbing (in combination)
(D)	Damask
(DPo)	Damask Portland
(F)	Floribunda or Cluster-flowered
(G)	Gallica
(Ga)	Garnette
(GC)	Ground Cover
(HM)	Hybrid Musk
(HP)	Hybrid Perpetual
(HT)	Hybrid Tea or Large-flowered
(Min)	Miniature
(Mo)	Moss (in combination)
(N)	Noisette
(Patio)	Patio, Miniature Floribunda or Dwarf Cluster-flowered
(Poly)	Polyantha
(PiH)	Pimpinellifolia hybrid (Hybrid Scots Briar)
(Ra)	Rambler
(RH)	Rubiginosa hybrid (Hybrid Sweet Briar)
(Ru)	Rugosa
(S)	Shrub
(T)	Tea

SAXIFRAGA

(Classification from Gornall, R.D. (1987). *Botanical Journal of the Linnean Society,* **95**(4).)

(1)	Ciliatae
(2)	Cymbalaria
(3)	Merkianae
(4)	Micranthes
(5)	Irregulares
(6)	Heterisia

(7)	Porphyrion
(8)	Ligulatae
(9)	Xanthizoon
(10)	Trachyphyllum
(11)	Gymnopera
(12)	Cotylea
(13)	Odontophyllae
(14)	Mesogyne
(15)	Saxifraga

TULIPA

(Classification from *Classified List and International Register of Tulip Names* by Koninklijke Algemeene Vereening voor Bloembollenculture 1996)

(1)	Single Early Group
(2)	Double Early Group
(3)	Triumph Group
(4)	Darwinhybrid Group
(5)	Single Late Group (including Darwin Group and Cottage Group)
(6)	Lily-flowered Group
(7)	Fringed Group

(8)	Viridiflora Group
(9)	Rembrandt Group
(10)	Parrot Group
(11)	Double Late Group
(12)	Kaufmanniana Group
(13)	Fosteriana Group
(14)	Greigii Group
(15)	Miscellaneous

VIOLA

(C)	Cornuta Hybrid
(dVt)	Double Violet
(ExVa)	Exhibition Viola
(FP)	Fancy Pansy
(PVt)	Parma Violet
(SP)	Show Pansy
(T)	Tricolor
(Va)	Viola
(Vt)	Violet
(Vtta)	Violetta

VITIS *SEE* FRUIT

REVERSE SYNONYMS

The following list of reverse synonyms is intended to help users find from which genus an unfamiliar plant name has been cross-referred. For a fuller explanation see p.15

Acacia – Racosperma
Acanthocalyx – Morina
Acca – Feijoa
x Achicodonia – Eucodonia
Achillea – Anthemis
Acinos – Calamintha
Acinos – Micromeria
Aethionema – Eunomia
Agapetes – Pentapterygium
Agarista – Leucothoe
Agastache – Cedronella
Aichryson – Aeonium
Ajania – Chrysanthemum
Ajania – Eupatorium
Albizia – Acacia
Alcea – Althaea
Allardia – Waldheimia
Allocasuarina – Casuarina
Aloysia – Lippia
Althaea – Malva
Alyogyne – Hibiscus
Alyssum – Ptilotrichum

x Amarygia – Amaryllis
Amaryllis – Brunsvigia
Amomyrtus – Myrtus
Amsonia – Rhazya
Anaphalis – Gnaphalium
Anchusa – Lycopsis
Androsace – Douglasia
Anemone – Eriocapitella
Anisodontea – Malvastrum
Anomatheca – Lapeirousia
Anredera – Boussingaultia
Antirrhinum – Asarina
Aphanes – Alchemilla
Arctanthemum –
 Chrysanthemum
Arctostaphylos – Arbutus
Arctotis – x Venidioarctotis
Arctotis – Venidium
Arenga – Didymosperma
Argyranthemum – Anthemis
Argyranthemum –
 Chrysanthemum
Armoracia – Cochlearia
Arundinaria – Pseudosasa
Asarina – Antirrhinum
Asarum – Hexastylis
Asclepias – Gomphocarpus
Asparagus – Smilax
Asperula – Galium

Asphodeline – Asphodelus
Asplenium – Camptosorus
Asplenium – Ceterach
Asplenium – Phyllitis
Asplenium – Scolopendrium
Aster – Crinitaria
Aster – Microglossa
Asteriscus – Pallenis
Astilboides – Rodgersia
Atropanthe – Scopolia
Aurinia – Alyssum
Austrocedrus – Libocedrus
Azorella – Bolax
Azorina – Campanula

Bambusa – Arundinaria
Bashania – Arundinaria
Bellevalia – Muscari
Bellis – Erigeron
Besseya – Veronica
Blechnum – Lomaria
Bolax – Azorella
Bolboschoenus – Scirpus
Borago – Anchusa
Borinda – Fargesia
Bothriochloa – Andropogon
Boykinia – Telesonix
Brachyglottis – Senecio
Bracteantha – Helichrysum

Brimeura – Hyacinthus
Brugmansia – Datura
Brunnera – Anchusa
Buglossoides – Lithospermum
Bulbine – Bulbinopsis
Buphthalmum – Inula

Cacalia – Adenostyles
Caiophora – Loasa
Caladium – Xanthosoma
Calamagrostis – Agrostis
Calamagrostis – Stipa
Calamintha – Clinopodium
Calliergon – Acrocladium
Callisia – Phyodina
Callisia – Tradescantia
Calocedrus – Libocedrus
Calocephalus – Leucophyta
Calomeria – Humea
Caloscordum – Nothoscordum
Calytrix – Lhotzkya
Camellia – Thea
Cardamine – Dentaria
Carpobrotus – Lampranthus
Cassiope – Harrimanella
Catapodium – Desmazeria
Cayratia – Parthenocissus
Centaurium – Erythraea
Centella – Hydrocotyle
Centranthus – Kentranthus
Centranthus – Valeriana
Cephalaria – Scabiosa
Ceratostigma – Plumbago
Cercestis – Rhektophyllum
Cestrum – Iochroma
Chaenomeles – Cydonia
Chaenorhinum – Linaria
Chamaecyparis – Cupressus
Chamaecytisus – Cytisus
Chamaedaphne – Cassandra
Chamaemelum – Anthemis
Chasmanthium – Uniola
Cheilanthes – Notholaena
Chiastophyllum – Cotyledon
Chimonobambusa – Arundinaria
Chimonobambusa – Gelidocalamus
Chimonobambusa – Quiongzhuea
Chionohebe – Pygmea
× Chionoscilla – Scilla
Chlorophytum – Diuranthera
Chondrosum – Bouteloua
Chrysanthemum – Dendranthema
Cicerbita – Lactuca
Cionura – Marsdenia
Cissus – Ampelopsis
Cissus – Parthenocissus
× Citrofortunella – Citrus
Citronella – Villaresia

Clarkia – Eucharidium
Clarkia – Godetia
Clavinodum – Arundinaria
Claytonia – Calandrinia
Claytonia – Montia
Clematis – Atragene
Cleyera – Eurya
Clinopodium – Acinos
Clinopodium – Calamintha
Clytostoma – Bignonia
Clytostoma – Pandorea
Cnicus – Carduus
Codonopsis – Campanumoea
Colobanthus – Arenaria
Consolida – Delphinium
× Coralia – Carmichaelia ×
   Corallospartium
Cordyline – Dracaena
Cornus – Chamaepericlymenum
Cornus – Dendrobenthamia
Coronilla – Securigera
Cortaderia – Gynerium
Corydalis – Fumaria
Corydalis – Pseudofumaria
Cosmos – Bidens
Cotinus – Rhus
Cotula – Leptinella
Crassula – Rochea
Crassula – Sedum
Crassula – Tillaea
Cremanthodium – Ligularia
Crinodendron – Tricuspidaria
Crocosmia – Antholyza
Crocosmia – Curtonus
Crocosmia – Montbretia
Cruciata – Galium
Ctenanthe – Calathea
Ctenanthe – Stromanthe
× Cupressocyparis – Chamaecyparis
Cyathodes – Leucopogon
Cyathodes – Styphelia
Cyclosorus – Pneumatopteris
Cymbalaria – Linaria
Cynara – Scolymus
Cyperus – Mariscus
Cypripedium – Criogenes
Cyrtanthus – Anoiganthus
Cyrtanthus – Vallota
Cyrtomium – Phanarophlebia
Cyrtomium – Polystichum
Cytisus – Argyrocytisus
Cytisus – Genista
Cytisus – Lembotropis
Cytisus – Spartocytisus

Daboecia – Menziesia
Dacrycarpus – Podocarpus
Dactylorhiza – Orchis

Danae – Ruscus
Darmera – Peltiphyllum
Dasypyrum – Haynaldia
Datura – Brugmansia
Datura – Datura
Davallia – Humata
Delairea – Senecio
Delosperma – Lampranthus
Delosperma – Mesembryanthemum
Dendrocalamus – Bambusa
Derwentia – Hebe
Desmodium – Lespedeza
Dichelostemma – Brodiaea
Dicliptera – Barleria
Dicliptera – Justicia
Diervilla – Weigela
Dietes – Moraea
Diplazium – Athyrium
Disporopsis – Polygonatum
Distictis – Phaedranthus
Distylium – Sycopsis
Dolichothrix – Helichrysum
Dracaena – Pleomele
Dracunculus – Arum
Dregea – Wattakaka
Drepanostachyum – Arundinaria
Drepanostachyum –
   Thamnocalamus
Drepanostachyum –
   Chimonobambusa
Drimys – Tasmannia
Duchesnea – Fragaria
Dunalia – Acnistus
Dypsis – Chrysalidocarpus
Dypsis – Neodypsis

Echeveria – Cotyledon
Echinacea – Rudbeckia
Edraianthus – Wahlenbergia
Egeria – Elodea
Elatostema – Pellionia
Eleutherococcus – Acanthopanax
Elliottia – Botryostege
Elliottia – Cladothamnus
Elymus – Agropyron
Elymus – Leymus
Ensete – Musa
Epilobium – Chamaenerion
Epipremnum – Philodendron
Epipremnum – Scindapsus
Episcia – Alsobia
Eranthis – Aconitum
Erigeron – Aster
Erigeron – Haplopappus
Erysimum – Cheiranthus
Eucodonia – Achimenes
Eupatorium – Ageratina
Eupatorium – Ajania

Eupatorium – Ayapana
Eupatorium – Bartlettina
Euphorbia – Poinsettia
Euryops – Senecio

Fallopia – Bilderdykia
Fallopia – Polygonum
Fallopia – Reynoutria
Farfugium – Ligularia
Fargesia – Arundinaria
Fargesia – Sinarundinaria
Fargesia – Thamnocalamus
Fatsia – Aralia
Felicia – Agathaea
Felicia – Aster
Fibigia – Farsetia
Filipendula – Spiraea
Foeniculum – Ferula
Fortunella – Citrus
Furcraea – Agave

Galium – Asperula
Galtonia – Hyacinthus
Gaultheria – Chiogenes
Gaultheria – x Gaulnettya
Gaultheria – Pernettya
Gelasine – Sisyrinchium
Genista – Chamaespartium
Genista – Cytisus
Genista – Echinospartum
Genista – Teline
Gentianopsis – Gentiana
Gladiolus – Acidanthera
Gladiolus – Anomalesia
Gladiolus – Homoglossum
Gladiolus – Petamenes
Glechoma – Nepeta
Gloxinia – Seemannia
Gomphocarpus – Asclepias
Goniolimon – Limonium
Graptopetalum – Sedum
Graptopetalum – Tacitus
Greenovia – Sempervivum
Gymnospermium – Leontice

Habranthus – Zephyranthes
Hacquetia – Dondia
x Halimiocistus – Cistus
x Halimiocistus – Halimium
Halimione – Atriplex
Halimium – Cistus
Halimium – x Halimiocistus
Halimium – Helianthemum
Halocarpus – Dacrydium
Haplopappus – Aster
Hechtia – Dyckia
Hedychium – Brachychilum
Hedyscepe – Kentia

Helianthella – Helianthus
Helianthemum – Cistus
Helianthus – Heliopsis
Helichrysum – Gnaphalium
Helictotrichon – Avena
Helictotrichon – Avenula
Heliopsis – Helianthus
Hepatica – Anemone
Herbertia – Alophia
Hermodactylus – Iris
Heterocentron – Schizocentron
Heterotheca – Chrysopsis
Hibbertia – Candollea
Hieracium – Andryala
Himalayacalamus –
    Arundinaria
Himalayacalamus –
    Drepanostachyum
Hippocrepis – Coronilla
Hippolytia – Achillea
Hippolytia – Tanacetum
Hoheria – Plagianthus
Homalocladium –
    Muehlenbeckia
Howea – Kentia
Hyacinthoides – Endymion
Hyacinthoides – Scilla
Hymenocallis – Elisena
Hymenocallis – Ismene
Hyophorbe – Mascarena
Hypochaeris – Hieracium
Hypoxis – Rhodohypoxis

Incarvillea – Amphicome
Indocalamus – Sasa
Iochroma – Acnistus
Iochroma – Cestrum
Iochroma – Dunalia
Ipheion – Tristagma
Ipheion – Triteleia
Ipomoea – Mina
Ipomoea – Pharbitis
Ipomopsis – Gilia
Ischyrolepis – Restio
Ismelia – Chrysanthemum
Isolepis – Scirpus

Jamesbrittenia – Sutera
Jeffersonia – Plagiorhegma
Jovibarba – Sempervivum
Juncus – Scirpus
Jurinea – Jurinella
Justicia – Beloperone
Justicia – Jacobinia
Justicia – Libonia

Kalanchoe – Bryophyllum
Kalanchoe – Kitchingia

Kalimeris – Aster
Kalimeris – Asteromoea
Kalimeris – Boltonia
Kalopanax – Eleutherococcus
Keckiella – Penstemon
Knautia – Scabiosa
Kniphofia – Tritoma
Kohleria – Isoloma
Kunzea – Leptospermum

Lablab – Dolichos
Lagarosiphon – Elodea
Lagarostrobos – Dacrydium
Lallemantia – Dracocephalum
Lamium – Galeobdolon
Lamium – Lamiastrum
Lampranthus –
    Mesembryanthemum
Lampranthus – Oscularia
Laurentia – Hippobroma
Lavatera – Malva
Ledebouria – Scilla
x Ledodendron – Rhododendron
Lepechinia – Sphacele
Lepidothamnus – Dacrydium
Leptinella – Cotula
Leptodactylon – Gilia
Leucanthemella –
    Chrysanthemum
Leucanthemella – Leucanthemum
Leucanthemopsis –
    Chrysanthemum
Leucanthemopsis – Tanacetum
Leucanthemum –
    Chrysanthemum
Leucochrysum – Helipterum
Leucophyta – Calocephalus
Leucopogon – Cyathodes
x Leucoraoulia – Raoulia
Leuzea – Centaurea
Leymus – Elymus
Ligularia – Senecio
Ligustrum – Parasyringa
Lilium – Nomocharis
Limonium – Statice
Linanthus – Linanthastrum
Lindelofia – Adelocaryum
Lindera – Parabenzoin
Liriope – Ophiopogon
Lithocarpus – Quercus
Lithodora – Lithospermum
Littorella – Plantago
Lophomyrtus – Myrtus
Lophomyrtus – Myrtus
Lophospermum – Asarina
Lophospermum – Maurandya
Lophostemon – Tristania
Lotus – Dorycnium

Lotus – Tetragonolobus
Ludwigia – Jussiaea
Luma – Myrtus
× Lycene – Lychnis
Lychnis – Agrostemma
Lychnis – Silene
Lychnis – Viscaria
Lycianthes – Solanum
Lytocaryum – Cocos
Lytocaryum – Microcoelum

Macfadyena – Bignonia
Macfadyena – Doxantha
Machaeranthera – Xylorhiza
Mackaya – Asystasia
Macleaya – Bocconia
Mahonia – Berberis
Mandevilla – Dipladenia
Mandragora – Atropa
Marrubium – Ballota
Matricaria – Chamomilla
Matricaria –
　　Tripleurospermum
Maurandella – Asarina
Maurandella – Maurandya
Maurandya – Asarina
Melicytus – Hymenanthera
Melinis – Rhynchelytrum
Mentha – Preslia
Merremia – Ipomoea
Millettia – Wisteria
Mimulus – Diplacus
Minuartia – Arenaria
Modiolastrum – Malvastrum
Moltkia – Lithodora
Moltkia – Lithospermum
Morina – Acanthocalyx
Mukdenia – Aceriphyllum
Muscari – Hyacinthus
Muscari – Leopoldia
Muscari – Leopoldia
Muscari – Muscarimia
Muscari – Pseudomuscari
Myricaria – Tamarix
Myrteola – Myrtus

Naiocrene – Claytonia
Naiocrene – Montia
Nectaroscordum – Allium
Nematanthus – Hypocyrta
Nemesia – Diascia
Neopaxia – Claytonia
Neopaxia – Montia
Neoregelia – Guzmania
Neoregelia – Nidularium
Nepeta – Dracocephalum
Nepeta – Origanum
Nephrophyllidium – Fauria

Nertera – Coprosma
Nipponanthemum –
　　Chrysanthemum
Nipponanthemum –
　　Leucanthemum
Nymphoides – Villarsia

Oemleria – Osmaronia
Oenothera – Chamissonia
Olearia – Pachystegia
Olsynium – Phaiophleps
Olsynium – Sisyrinchium
Onixotis – Dipidax
Ophiopogon – Convallaria
Orchis – Dactylorhiza
Oreopteris – Thelypteris
Orostachys – Sedum
Osmanthus – × Osmarea
Osmanthus – Phillyrea
Osteospermum – Dimorphotheca
Othonna – Hertia
Othonna – Othonnopsis
Ozothamnus – Helichrysum

Pachyphragma – Cardamine
Packera – Senecio
Paederota – Veronica
Papaver – Meconopsis
Parahebe – Derwentia
Parahebe – Hebe
Parahebe – Veronica
Paraserianthes – Albizia
Paris – Daiswa
Parthenocissus – Ampelopsis
Parthenocissus – Vitis
Passiflora – Tetrapathaea
Paxistima – Pachystema
Pecteilis – Habenaria
Pelargonium – Geranium
Peltoboykinia – Boykinia
Penstemon – Chelone
Pentaglottis – Anchusa
Pentalinon – Urechites
Pericallis – Senecio
Persea – Machilus
Persicaria – Aconogonon
Persicaria – Bistorta
Persicaria – Polygonum
Persicaria – Tovara
Petrocoptis – Lychnis
Petrophytum – Spiraea
Petrorhagia – Tunica
Petroselinum – Carum
Phegopteris – Thelypteris
Phoenicaulis – Parrya
Photinia – Heteromeles
Photinia – Stransvaesia
Photinia – × Stravinia

Phuopsis – Crucianella
Phyla – Lippia
Phymosia – Sphaeralcea
Physoplexis – Phyteuma
Physostegia – Dracocephalum
Pieris – Arcterica
Pilosella – Hieracium
Piper – Macropiper
Pisonia – Heimerliodendron
Plagiomnium – Mnium
Plecostachys – Helichrysum
Plectranthus – Solenostemon
Pleioblastus – Arundinaria
Pleioblastus – Sasa
Podranea – Tecoma
Polianthes – Bravoa
Polygonum – Persicaria
Polypodium – Phlebodium
Polystichum – Phanerophlebia
Poncirus – Aegle
Potentilla – Comarum
Pratia – Lobelia
Prumnopitys – Podocarpus
Prunus – Amygdalus
Pseudocydonia – Chaenomeles
Pseudopanax – Metapanax
Pseudopanax – Neopanax
Pseudopanax – Nothopanax
Pseudosasa – Arundinaria
Pseudotsuga – Tsuga
Pseudowintera – Drimys
Pterocephalus – Scabiosa
Ptilostemon – Cirsium
Pulicaria – Inula
Pulsatilla – Anemone
Pushkinia – Scilla
Pyrethropsis – Argyranthemum
Pyrethropsis – Chrysanthemum
Pyrethropsis – Leucanthemopsis
Pyrethropsis – Leucanthemum
Pyrrocoma – Haplopappus

Reineckea – Liriope
Retama – Genista
Rhapis – Chamaerops
Rhodanthe – Helipterum
Rhodanthemum –
　　Chrysanthemopsis
Rhodanthemum –
　　Chrysanthemum
Rhodanthemum –
　　Leucanthemopsis
Rhodanthemum – Leucanthemum
Rhodanthemum – Pyrethropsis
Rhodiola – Clementsia
Rhodiola – Rosularia
Rhodiola – Sedum
Rhododendron – Azalea

Rhododendron – Azaleodendron
Rhododendron – Rhodora
Rhodophiala – Hippeastrum
× Rhodoxis – Hypoxis ×
  Rhodohypoxis
× Rhodoxis – Rhodohypoxis
Rosularia – Cotyledon
Rosularia – Sempervivella
Rothmannia – Gardenia
Ruellia – Dipteracanthus
Ruschia – Mesembryanthemum
Rytidosperma – Merxmuellera

Saccharum – Erianthus
Sagina – Minuartia
Salvia – Salvia
Sanguisorba – Dendriopoterium
Sanguisorba – Poterium
Sasa – Arundinaria
Sasa – Pleioblastus
Sasaella – Arundinaria
Sasaella – Pleioblastus
Sasaella – Sasa
Sasamorpha – Sasa
Satureja – Micromeria
Sauromatum – Arum
Saussurea – Jurinea
Scadoxus – Haemanthus
Schefflera – Brassaia
Schefflera – Dizygotheca
Schefflera – Heptapleurum
Schizachyrium – Andropogon
Schizostachyum – Arundinaria
Schizostachyum – Thamnocalamus
Schoenoplectus – Scirpus
Scirpoides – Scirpus
Scirpus – Eriophorum
Sedum – Hylotelephium
Sedum – Rhodiola
Sedum – Sedastrum
Sedum – Villadia
Semiaquilegia – Aquilegia
Semiaquilegia – Paraquilegia
Semiarundinaria – Arundinaria
Semiarundinaria – Oligostachyum
Senecio – Cineraria
Senecio – Kleinia
Senecio – Ligularia
Senna – Cassia
Seriphidium – Artemisia
Shortia – Schizocodon
Sibbaldiopsis – Potentilla
Sieversia – Geum
Silene – Lychnis
Silene – Melandrium
Silene – Saponaria
Sinacalia – Ligularia
Sinacalia – Senecio

Sinarundinaria – Semiarundinaria
Sinningia – Gesneria
Sinningia – Rechsteineria
Sisymbrium – Hesperis
Sisyrinchium – Phaiophleps
× Smithicodonia –
  × Achimenantha
Solanum – Lycianthes
Soleirolia – Helxine
Solenopsis, – Isotoma
Solenostemon, – Coleus
× Solidaster – Aster
× Solidaster – Solidago
Sorbaria – Spiraea
Sparaxis – Synnotia
Sphaeralcea – Iliamna
Sphaeromeria – Tanacetum
Spirodela – Lemna
Spraguea – Calyptridium
Stachys – Betonica
Steirodiscus – Gamolepis
Stenomesson – Urceolina
Stenotus – Haplopappus
Steptocarpus – Streptocarpella
Stewartia – Stuartia
Stipa – Achnatherum
Stipa – Lasiagrostis
Stipa – Oryzopsis
Strobilanthes – Pteracanthus
Succisa – Scabiosa
Sutera – Bacopa
Syagrus – Arecastrum
Syagrus – Cocos

Tanacetum – Achillea
Tanacetum – Balsamita
Tanacetum – Chrysanthemum
Tanacetum – Matricaria
Tanacetum – Pyrethrum
Tanacetum – Spathipappus
Tanacetum – Sphaeromeria
Tecoma – Tecomaria
Tecomaria – Tecoma
Telekia – Buphthalmum
Tephroseris – Senecio
Tetradium – Euodia
Tetraneuris – Actinella
Tetraneuris – Hymenoxys
Tetrapanax – Fatsia
Thamnocalamus – Arundinaria
Thamnocalamus –
  Sinarundinaria
Thlaspi – Hutchinsia
Thlaspi – Noccaea
Thuja – Platycladus
Thuja – Thujopsis
Thymus – Origanum
Tiarella – × Heucherella

Tonestus – Haplopappus
Toona – Cedrela
Trachelium – Diosphaera
Trachycarpus – Chamaerops
Tradescantia – Rhoeo
Tradescantia – Setcreasea
Tradescantia – Tradescantia
Tradescantia – Zebrina
Trichopetalum – Anthericum
Trichophorum – Scirpus
Tripetaleia – Elliottia
Tripleurospermum – Matricaria
Tripogandra – Tradescantia
Tristagma – Beauverdia
Tristaniopsis – Tristania
Triteleia – Brodiaea
Tritonia – Crocosmia
Tropaeolum – Nasturtium hort.
Tuberaria – Helianthemum
Tulipa – Amana
Tweedia – Oxypetalum

Ugni – Myrtus
Ullucus – Anredera
Ursinia – Euryops
Uvularia – Oakesiella

Vaccinium – Oxycoccus
Verbascum – Celsia
Verbascum –
  × Celsioverbascum
Verbena – Glandularia
Verbena – Lippia
Veronicastrum – Veronica
Vigna – Phaseolus
Villadia – Sedum
Viola – Erpetion
Vitaliana – Androsace
Vitaliana – Douglasia

Weigela – Diervilla
Weigela – Macrodiervilla

Xanthophthalmum –
  Chrysanthemum
Xanthorhiza – Zanthorhiza

Yushania – Arundinaria
Yushania – Sinarundinaria
Yushania – Thamnocalamus

Zantedeschia – Calla
Zauschneria – Epilobium
Zephyranthes –
  × Cooperanthes
Zephyranthes – Cooperia
Zephyranthes – Habranthus

THE NAMING OF PLANTS

'The question of nomenclature is always a vexed one. The only thing certain is, that it is impossible to please everyone.'

W.J. BEAN - PREFACE TO FIRST EDITION OF *Trees & Shrubs Hardy in the British Isles.*

Following the acquisition of *The Plant Finder* by the Royal Horticultural Society, the Society's Advisory Panel on Nomenclature and Taxonomy was set up to try to establish the agreed list of plant names now held on the RHS horticultural database and used in this and other RHS publications. The panel looks at all recent and current proposals to change or correct names and strives for a balance between the stability of well-known names and botanical and taxonomic correctness according to the codes of nomenclature.

The Panel reports to the Society's Science and Horticultural Advice Committee. Unlike the independent Horticultural Taxonomy Group (Hortax), its aim is to consider individual problems of plant nomenclature rather than general principles. Chaired by Chris Brickell, the panel includes Susyn Andrews (Kew), Dr James Compton (University of Reading), Dr Stephen Jury (University of Reading), Sabina Knees (Edinburgh), Dr Alan Leslie (RHS), Tony Lord, Dr Simon Thornton-Wood (RHS), Piers Trehane (Index Hortensis) and Adrian Whiteley (RHS).

Many name changes proposed by nurseries and users of the *RHS Plant Finder* over the past year have been adopted but others have yet to be considered and approved by the Panel. We hope that all those who have generously told us about wrong names will be patient if the corrections they suggest are not immediately made. All such opinions are much valued but the volume of information is great and must be thoroughly checked before we make changes.

Families and genera used in the *RHS Plant Finder* are almost always those given in Brummitt's *Vascular Plant Families and Genera*. Thus, for the sixth year, there are no major changes to genera in this edition. For spellings and genders of generic names, Greuter's *Names in Current Use for Extant Plant Genera* is being followed. There are rare cases in which this disagrees with some prominent recent publications such as its use of the spelling *Diplarrhena* as opposed to *Diplarrena* in the current *Flora of Australia*. However, the general effect will be to keep names in exactly the same form as they are already known to gardeners.

In some cases the Panel feels that the conflicting views about the naming of some groups of plants will not be easily resolved. Our policy is to wait until an absolutely clear consensus is reached, not to rush to rename plants only to have to change names a second time when opinions have shifted yet again.

As in last year's, this edition contains few major changes to plant names. Among the most significant are changes to *Wisteria* following Peter Valder's recent book. However, we retain *W. floribunda* 'Alba' and *W. floribunda* 'Rosea' rather than Valder's preferred 'Shiro-noda' and 'Honbeni': the argument that 'Alba' and 'Rosea' should be rejected because they duplicate names of *W. sinensis* cultivars is not supported by the *International Code of Nomenclatue of Cultivated Plants*, which allows such duplicates provided the species name is always included. Nor are we willing to 'sink' cultivars that Valder considers might not be distinct without proof that they are indeed synonymous. There have been a number of corrections in *Androsace*, though we have yet to resolve difficulties involving *A. carnea* and its closest allies. We have adopted the spelling 'Solfatare' for the well-known *Crocosmia* × *crocosmiiflora* cultivar following the article by Dr Charles Nelson (*New Plantsman* 6(2): 75-77). Other proposals, for instance the 'sinking' of *Fortunella* in *Citrus* and of *Cimicifuga* in *Actaea*, the 'splitting' of *Platycladus* from *Thuja* and the adoption of *Helleborus hybridus* as the best name for acaulescent hellebore hybrids, remain under review and may well be adopted in future editions.

If nomenclatural arguments are finely balanced, we will retain old names in the interests of stability. This does not alter the fact that all involved in the publication of the *RHS Plant Finder* remain committed to the use of plant names that are as correct as possible. As before, gardeners and nurserymen may still choose to differ and use what names they want, many preferring a more conservative and a few a more radical approach to naming. Except for those names in which we have made corrections of a couple of letters to bring them in line with the codes of nomenclature, we are responsible for none of the name changes in this or any other edition of the *RHS Plant Finder*.

Of all the published works used in the preparation of this edition, it is perhaps those that can be consulted via the Internet that have been the greatest revelation to me, the most useful of them included in our Bibliography for the first time this year. Many, such as the *Flora of China Checklist*, aim to give a coherent taxonomic treatment of the flora of a country. Others, often created by amateurs, deal with the cultivars of a single genus. One gasps with amazement at some, such as Martin Miklánek's checklist of 3,200 *Sempervivum* and *Jovibarba* cultivars; the *Giboshi.com Hosta* and *HelpMeFind - Roses* databases are also outstanding, including photographs that make them perhaps even more inspiring and informative. I long for the day when every genus-based specialist plant society and every International Registrar has such a site. Websites are also invaluable for plant breeders who can use them to show and promote the plants they have raised, with photographs and names styled accurately according to whether they are cultivar names, trade designations or trademarks. It is paradoxical that the more commercial and popular potential new plants have, the harder it seems to be to find such information. Some such sites already exist but it seems a shame that some of the most successful and prolific plant breeders, perhaps especially of roses, seem to be slow to exploit such new technology. Many more retail nurseries seem to have excellent websites this year and it has been a great help and a particular pleasure to see pictures and read about so many of this year's new cultivars, whether they originated in the United States, continental Europe or the British Isles. May their enterprise bring them sales and prosperity and long may they continue to produce first-rate new garden plants.

RULES OF NOMENCLATURE

Throughout the *RHS Plant Finder* we try to follow the rules of nomenclature set out in the *International Code of Botanical Nomenclature 1994*

(ICBN) and the *International Code of Nomenclature for Cultivated Plants 1995* (ICNCP). Cultivar names which are clearly not permissible under the latter and for which there seems to be no valid alternative are marked **I** (for invalid), even if they have been accepted by the appropriate International Registrar. The commonest sorts of invalid names seem to be those that are wholly or partly in Latin (not permissible since 1959, e.g. 'Pixie Alba', 'Superba', 'Variegata') and those which use a Latin generic name as a cultivar name (e.g. *Rosa* 'Corylus', *Viola* 'Gazania').

Apart from being discourteous to the plants' originators and their countries, the translating of foreign plant names into English is a bad and insular practice that is likely to cause confusion, it is also contrary to Article 28 of the 1995 ICNCP. In this edition, as in the previous one, this and other Articles of the new Code are applied strictly. The Code requires that such translations be considered trade designations and not cultivar names and so should be presented in a different font (here sans serif) and not in quotes. It may be years yet before we make sense of the host of German names and apparent English translations for a genus such as *Coreopsis*, many of which must be synonyms. Throughout the *RHS Plant Finder*, we have tried to give preference to the original name in every case, although English translations are also given as trade designations where they are in general use.

The substitution of slick selling names by nurseries which do not like, or have not bothered to find out, the correct names of the plants they sell is sharp practice not expected of any reputable nursery. It is also a probable breach of the Trades Description Act.

The publication of the ICNCP has done a great deal to clarify nomenclature without generally introducing rules that cause destabilising name changes. However, it significantly alters the sort of plant names that have been allowed since 1 January 1996. Nurseries who name plants are strongly urged to check that the names they want to use are acceptable under the new Code.

One Article of the 1995 Code that affects names published since 1995 is Art. 17.13, dealing in part with the use of botanical or common generic names within a cultivar or group name. This bans names in which the last word of the cultivar name is the common or botanical name of a genus or species. Two sorts of such names are commonly found: those based on colours (ending Lilac, Lavender, Rose, Rosa, Apricot, Peach, Mauve (French for *Malva*)) and those based on personal names (Rosemary, Hazel). These will be marked **I** in the *RHS Plant Finder* if known to have been published after 1995 or marked with an asterisk if their date of publication is unknown. This rule does not preclude cultivar epithets ending with common names which apply to only part of a genus such as Cerise, Cherry, Lemon, Lime, Orange, Pink, or Violet, each of which refers to more than one species and/or their hybrids.

An Article of the new Code which the Panel has agreed it cannot implement is Art. 17.11, banning cultivar names consisting of solely adjectival words in a modern language, unless one of these words may be considered a substantive or unless the epithet is the recognized name of a colour. As this rule is retroactive, applying to all cultivar names whenever they were published, if applied strictly it could require rejection of several hundred cultivar names in the *RHS Plant Finder*, many of them very well known and widely used. Furthermore, it is difficult to apply. Many adjectives also have substantive meanings, albeit sometimes obscure ones, that might or might not justify acceptance of the names. It is not easy to decide which names of colours are accepted and which are not. Our Panel's judgement is that, as currently worded, this Article is unintentionally restrictive and potentially destabilizing. A future edition of the Code is unlikely to be so proscriptive. So for the time being we will not use this Article as a basis for making changes, nor for declaring already established names unacceptable.

ORTHOGRAPHY

The ruling on orthography (i.e. correct spelling) of commemorative names, re-stated in the 1994 *International Code of Botanical Nomenclature*, has aroused a great deal of debate at Panel meetings. This subject is discussed in the supplement to Bean's *Trees and Shrubs Hardy in the British Isles* (1988) and is given in ICBN Article 60 and the subsequent recommendations 60C.I. The meaning of Article 60.7 Example 10 (which tells us that the epithet *billardierii*, derived from the part-Latinization Billardierius, is unacceptable and must be corrected to *billardierei*) is not absolutely clear. However, my reading of it has been that except for full-scale Latinizations of names (e.g. *brunonius* for Brown, thus *Rosa brunonii*), the name of the person commemorated should remain in its original form. Names ending in -er (e.g. Solander, Faber) may become *solandri* (as in pure Latin, because -er is a usual Latin termination) or *solanderi*, if the specific name was originally spelt in this way. If this interpretation is correct, names such as *backhousiana, catesbaei, glazoviana, manescavii* and *bureavii* are not allowed and must be corrected to *backhouseana, catesbyi, glaziouana, manescaui* and bureaui respectively. However, not all of the several authors of the Code share the same

interpretation. The forthcoming new edition of the Code is expected to clarify what constitutes a Latinization and what does not. This may require a change of policy and of spelling of some names in our next edition.

If my reading of the Code's rulings on orthography is correct, botanical epithets commemorating someone whose name has been transliterated from script other than Roman (e.g. Cyrillic or Japanese) present problems. Though ICNCP tells us which system of transliteration should be used, it is sometimes difficult to apply orthographic corrections to these. Botanists whose names were originally in Cyrillic often had a preferred transliteration of their own name, often based on old French systems in the case of pre-Revolutionary Russian names, and it is hard to justify rejecting these. It is therefore difficult to be dogmatic about their orthography. However, implementation of this rule has been assisted by another new publication from Kew, *Authors of Plant Names,* which is particularly helpful in giving acceptable transliterations of names that were originally in Cyrillic.

VERIFICATION OF NAMES

Although we find that many nurseries have greatly improved the accuracy of their plant names, plants which are new entries often appear in their catalogues under a bewildering variety of wrong names and misspellings. This is partly a reflection on the rarity of the plants and nurserymen and women are not to be blamed for not finding correct names for plants that do not appear in recent authoritative garden literature. Some plants are simply too new for valid names and descriptions yet to have appeared in print.

Although we try to verify every name which appears in these pages, the amount of time which can be allotted to checking each of over 70,000 entries must be limited. There is always a proportion which do not appear in any of the reference sources used and those unverified names for which there may be scope for error are marked with an asterisk. Such errors may occur with species we cannot find listed (possibly synonyms for more recent and better known names) or may include misspellings (particularly of names transliterated from Japanese or Chinese, or commemorating a person). We are especially circumspect about names not known to the International Registrar for a particular genus. We are always grateful to receive information about the naming and origin of any asterisked plant and once we feel reassured about the plant's pedigree, the asterisk will be removed. Of course, many such names will prove to be absolutely correct and buyers can be reassured if they know that the selling nursery takes great care with the naming of its plants. However, although we are able to check that names are valid, correctly styled and spelt, we have no means of checking that nurseries are applying them to the right plant – *caveat emptor!*

We have great sympathy for gardeners who want to find a particular cultivar but are not sure to which species it belongs. The problem is acute for genera such as *Juniperus* and readers must search through all the entries to find their plants. Even nurseries seem uncertain of the species of 'Skyrocket'. Because gardeners generally do not know (or disagree) to which species cultivars of hostas and saxifrages should be ascribed, these have been listed by cultivar first, giving the species in parentheses.

ADJECTIVAL NAMES

Latin adjectival names, whether for species, subspecies, cultivar etc., must agree in gender with the genus, not with the specific name if the latter is a noun (as for *Styrax obassia, Lonicera caprifolium* etc.). Thus azaleas have to agree with *Rhododendron*, their true genus (neuter), rather than *Azalea* (feminine). For French cultivar names, adjectives should agree with whatever is being described. For roses, this is almost always *la rose* (feminine) but on rare occasions *le rosier* (when describing vegetative characteristics such as climbing forms), *l'oeillet* or *le pompon* (all masculine).

It is often the case that gardeners consider two plants to be distinct but botanists, who know of a whole range of intermediates linking the two, consider them to be the same species. The most notable example is for the rhododendrons, many species of which were 'sunk' in Cullen and Chamberlain's revision. In such cases we have always tried to provide names that retain important horticultural entities, even if not botanically distinct, often by calling the sunk species by a Group name, such as *Rhododendron rubiginosum* Desquamatum Group. Group names are also used for swarms of hybrids with the same parentage. These were formerly treated as grex names, a term now only used for orchids, thus grex names for lilies, bromeliads and begonias are now styled as Groups. A single clone from the Group may be given the same cultivar name, e.g. 'Polar Bear'. In many cases nursery catalogues do not specify whether the named clone is being offered or other selections from the hybrid swarm and entries are therefore given as e.g. *Rhododendron* Polar Bear Group & cl.

One requirement of the new ICNCP is that cultivar-group names used after 1 January 1996 must have been validly published with a description or reference to a previously published description. Such publication is beyond the scope and purpose of the *RHS Plant Finder*. As editor, I may not style the more variable taxa that appear in this and subsequent editions as cultivar-groups unless they have been published elsewhere as Groups. Nevertheless, I still feel it is helpful to gardeners and other plant users to use cultivar names only for those plants that fulfil the Code's requirement that a cultivar be distinct, uniform and stable in its narrow sense. This applies particularly to mixtures and races of seed-raised plants that embrace significant variation, are often not distinct from similar named selections and may be changed in character from year to year: Any new entries that are of this nature are here styled neither as cultivars nor as cultivar-groups but simply as epithets or descriptions, without quotation marks and thus beyond the scope of the new Code. This applies especially to plants described as 'strains' or 'hybrids', though the latter term is sometimes merely a provenance rather than a sign of common parentage. Thus plants here appearing as cultivars with their names in quotes have, as far as I can tell, uniform and predictable characteristics. There are a few cases in which it is difficult to tell whether a 'sunk' species remains horticulturally distinct enough to merit a group name, as for many of the rhododendrons. We would be grateful if users would let us know of any plants that we have 'sunk' in synonymy but which still need to be distinguished by a separate name. In many cases, the plants gardeners grow will be the most extreme variants of a species. Although one 'end' of the species will seem to be quite a different plant from the other 'end' to the gardener, the botanist will see them as the outer limits of a continuous range of variation and will give them the same species name. We often hear gardeners complain 'How can these two plants have the same name? They are different!' In such cases, although the botanist may have to 'lump' them under the same name, we will always try to provide an acceptable name to distinguish an important horticultural entity, even if it is not botanically distinct.

TAXONOMIC RANK

In this edition, subspecies, varietas and forma are shown as subsp., var. and f. respectively. Each of these ranks indicates a successively less significant change in the characteristics of the plant from the original type on which the species was based. In general terms, a subspecies may be expected to be more markedly different from the type of a species than a forma which may differ in only one characteristic such as flower colour, hairiness of leaf or habit.

The ICBN requires the rank of each infraspecific botanical epithet to be given. In many cases, it is not at all clear whether a colour form shown as, say, *alba* is a true botanical forma or a cultivar of garden origin. Our inclination here is not to treat such plants as cultivars if they are recorded as being naturally occurring, nor if they embrace considerable variation: forma *alba* would be preferred if a valid publication is recorded, otherwise a previously-published Group name or a simple description. In the absence of conclusive evidence we will leave such names styled as they are at present and so some ranks remain to be added in future editions. In many cases, *alba* is assumed without any proof to be the correct name for a white-flowered variant though research often shows that the validly published name is something quite different such as *albiflora, leucantha* or *nivea*.

AUTHOR CITATIONS

In many cases the same species name has been used by two or more authors for quite different plants. Thus *Bloomingthingia grandiflora* of Linnaeus might be an altogether different species from *B. grandiflora* of gardeners (*B. grandiflora* hort.). In such circumstances it becomes necessary to define whose *Bloomingthingia* we are considering by quoting the author of the name directly after the species name. Generally the more recent name will be invalid and may be cross-referenced to the plant's first validly published name. Authors' names appear directly after the species name and if abbreviated follow Brummitt and Powell's *Authors of Plant Names*. Abbreviations are also listed in e.g. Mabberley's *The Plant-Book*. Such names appear in a smaller typeface and neither in quotes nor in sans serif font so should not be confused with cultivar names or trade designations. In this edition we have uncovered yet more muddles resulting from two or more plants being known by the same name. We have, we hoped, resolved these by clearer cross-referencing.

HYPHENATION

Some items of the ICBN have been 'more honour'd in the breach than in the observance'. One such is the ruling on hyphenation (Article 60.9) which

forbids the use of hyphens after a 'compounding form' (i.e. *albo, pseudo, aureo, neo*). Hyphens are still permitted to divide separate words such as *novae-angliae* or *uva-crispa* and, following the Tokyo Congress, after a vowel terminating a compounding form when followed by the same vowel (e.g. *Gaultheria semi-infera, Gentiana sino-ornata*).

TERMINATIONS OF COMMEMORATIVE NAMES

Another item of the code which is often ignored is that covering terminations of commemorative names (Article 60.11, referring to Recommendation 60C). A botanical epithet commemorating Helena must be styled *helenae* whereas one commemorating Helen may be styled either *heleniae* or, following Helena as an established Latin form of the same name or, quite frequently, of Ellen, *helenae*; in such cases when either spelling could be legitimate, the original is followed. When there is no accepted Latin alternative, the *-iae* ending is used and this seems to be more correct for *murieliae* and *edithiae*. The genitive form of commemorative names ending in *-a* is always *-ae*, even if a man is being commemorated (as for *Picea koyamae*). It is this same article which requires that the well known *Crocosmia* be spelt *masoniorum* and not *masonorum* and that *Rosa wichurana* be spelt thus and not *wichuraiana*.

The *RHS Plant Finder* is useful not only as a directory of plant sources but as a 'menu' of plants grown by British gardeners. Such a list is of great value to private gardeners; landscapers can use it to check the range of plants they can incorporate in designs; gardeners in countries of the European Union can check which plants they can import by Mail Order; botanists can discover the species grown in Britain, some of them from recorded natural sources; nurserymen can use it to select for propagation first-rate plants that are still not readily available; horticultural authors, who often only want to write about plants the public are able to buy, will find it invaluable. For all such users, the *RHS Plant Finder* can be recommended as a source of standard, up-to-date and reliable nomenclature.

Tony Lord
March 2000

BIBLIOGRAPHY

The following list of bibliographic sources and references is by no means exhaustive but lists some of the more useful and available works used in the preparation of the *RHS Plant Finder*. Included for the first time this year are some of the most useful websites used to check Plant Finder entries. All of these were available on line in February and March 2000 and are dated according to their last update before being consulted. Their addresses should not be relied on indefinitely; some will probably change address or be taken off line even before the publication of our next edition. The websites of the raisers of new plants (not listed here) are also an invaluable source of information. For plants with PBR, the raiser will be found on the appropriate PBR database listed below.

GENERAL

The New Plantsman and *The Garden* are published regularly by the Royal Horticultural Society, Vincent Square, London SW1P 2PE.

Altwegg, A., Fortgens, G. & Siebler, E. (eds). (1996). *ISU Yearbook 1965-95.* Internationale Stauden-Union, Windisch, Germany.

Armitage, A.M. (1989). *Herbaceous Perennial Plants.* Varsity Press, Athens, Georgia.

Australian Plant Breeders' Rights List. (March 2000). Department of Agriculture and Forestry, Australia @ http://netenergy.dpie.gov.au/agfor/pbr/forms/accept.xls.

Australian Plant Names Index. (March 2000). Australian National Botanic Gardens @ http://www.anbg.gov.au/cgi-bin/apni

Bailey, L.H., Bailey, E.Z. *et al.* (1976). *Hortus Third.* Macmillan, New York.

Bean, W.J. (1970-1988). *Trees and Shrubs Hardy in the British Isles.* (8th ed. edited Sir George Taylor & D.L. Clarke & Supp. ed. D.L. Clarke). John Murray, London.

Beckett, K.A. (ed.) (1993-94). *Encyclopaedia of Alpines,* **1 & 2.** Alpine Garden Society, Pershore, Worcs.

Beckett, K.A. (1987). *The RHS Encyclopaedia of House Plants.* Century Hutchinson, London.

A Synonymized Checklist of the Vascular Flora of the United States, Puerto Rico and the Virgin Isles. (1998). BIOTA of North America Program @ http://www/csdl.tamu.edu/FLORA/b98/check98.htm.

Blundell, M. (1992). *Wild Flowers of East Africa.* Collins, London.

Bond, P. & Goldblatt, P. (1984). Plants of the Cape Flora. *Journal of South African Botany,* supp. vol. **13.** Kirstenbosch.

Bramwell, D.& Z. (1974). *Wild Flowers of the Canary Islands.* Stanley Thomas, London.

Brickell, C.D. (ed.). (1989). *RHS Gardeners' Encyclopedia of Plants and Flowers.* Dorling Kindersley, London.

Brickell, C.D. (ed.). (1996). *RHS A-Z Encyclopedia of Garden Plants.* Dorling Kindersley, London.

Brummitt, R.K. & Powell, C.E. (1992). *Authors of Plant Names.* Royal Botanic Gardens, Kew.

Brummitt, R.K. (1992). *Vascular Plant Families and Genera.* Royal Botanic Gardens, Kew.

Castroviejo, C. *et al.* (eds). (1987-98). *Flora Iberica: Plantas vasculares de la Península Ibérica e Islas Baleares,* vols **1-6, 8.** Real Jardín Botánico, CSIC, Madrid.

Catalogue of Cultivars in the United Kingdom National Fruit Collection. (1998). Wye College and Brogdale Horticultural Trust, Faversham, Kent.

Chittenden, F.J. (ed.). (2nd ed. 1965). *The Royal Horticultural Society Dictionary of Gardening.* Oxford University Press.

Clausen, R.R. & Ekstrom, N.H. (1989). *Perennials for American Gardens.* Random House, New York.

Clement, E.J. & Foster, M.C. (1994). *Alien Plants of the British Isles.* Botanical Society of the British Isles, London.

Community Plant Variety Office List of Grants and Applications for Plant variety Rights. (March 2000). CPVO, ANGERS Cedex-02, France @ http://www.cpvo.fr/en/default.html.

Cooke, I. (1998). *The Plantfinder's Guide to Tender Perennials.* David & Charles, Newton Abbot, Devon.

Cronquist, A. *et al.* (eds. (Vols **1, 3-6,** 1986-97). *Intermountain Flora: Vascular Plants of the Intermountain West, USA.* New York Botanical Garden.

Davis, B.& Knapp, B. (1992). *Know Your Common Plant Names.* MDA Publications, Newbury, Berks.

Davis, P.H. *et al.* (ed.). (1965-1988). *Flora of Turkey,* vols **1-10.** University Press, Edinburgh.

Fabian, A. & Germishuizen, G. (1997). *Wild Flowers of Northern South Africa.* Fernwood Press, Vlaeberg, South Africa.

Flora of China Checklist. (September 1998). Hosted by Missouri Botanical Garden @ http://mobot.mobot.org/Pick/Search/foctM.html.

Flora of New Zealand, vols **1-3.** (1961-80). Wellington, New Zealand.

Flora Mesoamericana Internet Version (W ³FM). (November 1999). Missouri Botanical Garden et al. @http://mobot.mobot.org/Pick/Search/index/mesoa.html.

Eggli, U. & Taylor, N. (1994). *List of Names of Succulent Plants other than Cacti Published 1950-92.* Royal Botanic Gardens, Kew.

Forrest, M. (ed. Nelson, E.C.). (1985). *Trees and Shrubs Cultivated in Ireland*. Boethius Press for An Taisce, Dublin.

Galbraith, J. (1977). *Field Guide to the Wild Flowers of South-East Australia*. Collins, London.

Gillett, H.J. & Walter, K.S. (1998). *1997 IUCN Red List of Threatened Plants*. IUCN, Gland, Switzerland & Cambridge, England.

Graf, A.B. (2nd ed. 1981). *Tropica*. Roehrs, New Jersey.

Greuter, W. *et al.* (ed.). (1994). *International Code of Botanical Nomenclature (Tokyo Code)*. Koeltz Scientific Books, Königstein, Germany.

Greuter, W., Brummitt, R.K., Farr, E. *et al.* (1993). *N.C.U.3 Names in Current Use for Extant Plant Genera*. Koeltz Scientific Books, Königstein, Germany.

Grierson, A.J.C & Long, D.G. (1983-91) vol. 1(1-3) & vol. 2(1); Noltie, H.J. (1994) vol. 3(1). *Flora of Bhutan*. Royal Botanic Garden Edinburgh.

Griffiths, M. (ed.) (1994). *RHS Index of Garden Plants*. Macmillan, London.

Harkness, M.G. (2nd ed. 1993). *The Bernard E. Harkness Seedlist Handbook*. Batsford, London.

Hatch, L.C. (comp.). (March 2000). *New Ornamentals Database* @ http://members.tripod.com/~Hatch-L/genera.html.

Heath, R.E. (1981). *Collectors Alpines*. Collingridge, Twickenham, London.

Hickman, J.C. (ed.). (1993). *The Jepson Manual: Higher Plants of California*. University of California Press, Berkeley & Los Angeles.

Hillier Manual of Trees and Shrubs. (6th ed. 1991). David & Charles, Newton Abbot, Devon.

Hirose, Y. & Yokoi, M. (1998). *Variegated Plants in Colour*. Varie Nine, Yamate-cho, Iwakuni, Japan.

Hogg, R. (5th ed. 1884). *The Fruit Manual*. Journal of Horticulture Office, London.

Huxley, A. (ed.). (1992). *The New Royal Horticultural Society Dictionary of Gardening*. Macmillan, London.

Index Kewensis on Compact Disc (Version 2 1997). Oxford University Press.

International Plant Name Index. (October 1999). Harvard University et al. @http://tc.huh.harvard.edu/searches/query-ipni.shtml.

IOPI Provisional Global Plant Checklist. (April 1999). International Organization for Plant Information, Berlin, Germany @ http://www.bgbm.fu-berlin.de/IOPI/GPC/query.htm.

Jacobsen, H. (1973). *Lexicon of Succulent Plants*. Blandford, London.

Jellitto, L. & Schacht, W. (3rd ed. 1990). Schacht, W. & Fessler, A. *Hardy Herbaceous Perennials*. Timber Press, Portland, Oregon.

Kelly, J. (ed.). (1995). *The Hillier Gardener's Guide to Trees and Shrubs*. David & Charles, Newton Abbot, Devon.

Krüssmann, G. (English ed. trans. Epp, M.E.). (1984-86). *Manual of Cultivated Broadleaved Trees & Shrubs*, vols. 1-3. Batsford, London.

Laar, H.J. van de. (1989). *Naamlijst van Houtige Gewassen*. Proefstation voor de Boomteelt en het Stedelijk Groen, Boskoop, Holland.

Laar, H.J. van de & Fortgens, Ing. G (1988). *Naamlijst van Vaste Planten*. Proefstation voor de Boomkwekerij, Boskoop, Holland.

Leslie, A.C. (1993). *New Cultivars of Herbaceous Perennial Plants* 1985-1990. Hardy Plant Society.

Mabberley, D.J. (1987). *The Plant-Book*. Cambridge University Press.

McGregor, R.L., Barkley, T.M. *et al.* (1986). *Flora of the Great Plains*. University Press of Kansas.

Metcalf, L.J. (1987). *The Cultivation of New Zealand Trees and Shrubs*. Reed Methuen, Auckland, New Zealand.

Morin, N.R. *et al.* (eds). (Vols 1-3 1993-97). *Flora of North America*. Oxford University Press, New York.

Ohwi, J. (ed. Meyer, F.G. & Walker, E.). (1965). *Flora of Japan*. Smithsonian Institution, Washington.

Phillips, R. & Rix, E.M. (1997). *Conservatory and Indoor Plants*, vols 1 & 2. Macmillan, London.

Phillips, R. & Rix, E.M. (1989). *Shrubs*. Pan Books, London.

Phillips, R. & Rix, E.M. (1991/2). *Perennials*. Pan Books, London.

Phillips, R. & Rix, E.M. (1993). *Vegetables*. Pan Books Ltd, London.

The New Plantsman. Royal Horticultural Society, London.

Polunin, O. & Stainton, A. (1984). *Flowers of the Himalaya*. Oxford University Press.

Posthumus, F. (comp.). (1998). *List of Registered Australian Native Cultivars*. Australian Cultivar Registration Authority Inc. @ http://www.anbg.gov.au/acra/acra.list.98.html.

Press, J.R. & Short, M.J. (1994). *Flora of Madeira*. HMSO, London.

Rehder, R. (2nd ed. 1940). *Manual of Cultivated Trees & Shrubs Hardy in North America*. Macmillan, New York.

Schlauer, J. (comp.) (March 2000). *Carnivorous Plant Database*. Hosted by Walker, R., HP Labs, Palo Alto, California, USA @ http://www.hpl.hp.com/bot/cp-home

Stace, C.A. (2nd ed. 1997). *New Flora of the British Isles*. Cambridge University Press.

Stainton, A. (1988). *Flowers of the Himalaya: A Supplement*. Oxford University Press.

Stearn, W.T. (2nd ed. 1973). *Botanical Latin*. David & Charles. Newton Abbot, England.

Stearn, W.T. (1992). *Stearn's Dictionary of Plant Names for Gardeners*. Cassell, London.

Taffler, S. (1988-99). *The Sport*, vols 1-22. Hardy Plant Society Variegated Plant Group, South Petherton, Somerset.

Thomas, G.S. (3rd ed. 1990). *Perennial Garden Plants*. J M Dent & Sons, London.

Trehane, R.P. (1989). *Index Hortensis* (Vol. 1: Perennials). Quarterjack Publishing, Wimborne, Dorset.

Trehane, R.P. (1995). *International Code of Nomenclature for Cultivated Plants - 1995*. Quarterjack Publishing, Wimborne, Dorset.

Tutin, T.G. (1964-1980). *Flora Europaea*, vols 1-5. Cambridge University Press.

Tutin, T.G. *et al.* (2nd ed. 1993). *Flora Europaea*, vol 1. Cambridge University Press.

US Patent Full-Text Database. (March 2000). US Patent and Trademark Office @ http://164.195.100.11/netahtml/search-bool.html.

Van der Werff, D. (ed.). (1995-99). *New, Rare and Unusual Plants*, vols 1-4. Aquilegia Publishing, Hartlepool, Co. Durham.

Walters, S.M. (ed.). *et al.* (1984-97). *The European Garden Flora*, vols 1-5. Cambridge University Press.

Warden, I.K. (1999). *The Sport*, vol. 23. Hardy Plant Society Variegated Plant Group, Martin, Lincs.

Willis, J.C. (8th ed. 1973). Revised Airy Shaw, H.K. *A Dictionary of the Flowering Plants and Ferns*. Cambridge University Press.

Wilson, H.D. (1978). *Wild Plants of Mount Cook National Park*. Christchurch, New Zealand.

W³TROPICOS Nomenclatural Database. (March 2000). Missouri Botanical Garden @ http://mobot.mobot.org/Pick/Search/pick.html.

Zander, R. (1993). *Handwörterbuch der Pflanzennamen*. Ulmer, Stuttgart, Germany.

GENERA

Acacia
Beckett, K.A. (1993). *The Plantsman*, 15(3):131-47.
Simmons, M.H. (2nd ed. 1987). *Acacias of Australia*. Nelson, Melbourne, Australia.

Acaena
Yeo, P.F. (1972). The species of *Acaena* with Spherical Heads Cultivated and Naturalized in the British Isles. Green, P. S. (ed.). *Plants Wild and Cultivated* Botanical Society of the British Isles, Middlesex.

Acer
De Jong, P.C. *et al. International Dendrology Society Year Book 1990*: 6-50. London.
Gelderen, C.J. van & Gelderen, D.M. van. (1999). *Maples for Gardens: A Color Encyclopedia*. Timber Press, Portland, Oregon.
Harris, J.G.S. (1983). *The Plantsman*, 5(1): 35-58.
Vertrees, J.D. (1978). *Japanese Maples*. Timber Press, Oregon.

Achillea
Thornton-Wood, S. (1999). *The Garden*, 124(6): 442-47.

Adiantum
Goudry, C.J. (1985). *Maidenhair Ferns in Cultivation*. Lothian, Melbourne, Australia.

Aeschynanthus
Dates, J.D. *The Gesneriad Register 1990: Check List of Aeschynanthus*. American Gloxinia and Gesneriad Society, Galesburg, Illinois.

Aesculus
Wright, D. (1985). *The Plantsman*, 6(4): 228-47.

Agapanthus
Snoeijer, W. (1998). Agapanthus: *A Review*. Snoeijer, Gouda, Netherlands.

Agapetes
Argent, G.C.G. & Woods, P.J.B. (1988). *The Plantsman*, 8(2): 65-85.

Ajuga
Adam, C.G. (1982). *Alpine Garden Society Bulletin*, 50(1): 82-84.

Allium
Dadd, R. (1997). *The Garden*, 122(9): 658-61.
Davies, D. (1992). *Alliums*. Batsford, London.
Mathew, B. (1996). *A Review of* Allium section Allium. Royal Botanic Gardens, Kew.

Alnus
Ashburner, K. (1986). *The Plantsman*, 8(3): 170-88.

Androsace
Smith, G.F. & Lowe, D.B. (1997). *The Genus Androsace*. Alpine Garden Society, Pershore, Worcs.

Anemone, Japanese
McKendrick, M. (1990). *The Plantsman*, 12(3): 140-51.
McKendrick, M. (1998). *The Garden*, 123(9): 628-33.

Anemone nemorosa
Toubøl, U. (1981). *The Plantsman*, 3(3): 167-74.

Anthemis tinctoria
Leslie, A.C. (1997). *The Garden*, 122(8): 552-55.

Apiaceae (Umbelliferae)
Ingram, T. (1993). *Umbellifers*. Hardy Plant Society, Pershore, Worcs.
Pimenov, M.G. & Leonov, M.V. (1993). *The Genera of the* Umbelliferae. Royal Botanic Gardens, Kew.

Aquilegia
Munz, P.A. (1946). *Aquilegia*: The Cultivated and Wild Columbines. *Gentes Herbarum*, 7(1). Bailey Hortorium, New York.

Araceae
Bown, D. (1988). *Aroids*. Century Hutchinson, London.

Arecaceae (Palmae - palms)
Jones, D.L. (1997). *Palms Throughout the World*. Reed Books, Chatswood, NSW, Australia.
Uhl, N.J. & Dransfield, J. (1987). *Genera Palmarum*. Alan Press, Lawrence, Kansas.

Argyranthemum
Cheek, R. (1993). *The Garden*, 118(8): 350-55.
Humphries, C.J. (1976). A Revision of the Macaronesian Genus *Argyranthemum. The Bulletin of the British Museum (Natural History)*, Botany, 5(4).

Arisaema
Gusman, G. (1997). *Alpine Garden Society Bulletin*, 65(1): 105-08 & 65(2): 195-200.

Mayo, J.J. (1982). *The Plantsman*, 3(4): 193-209.
Pradhan, U.C. (2nd ed. 1997). *Himalayan Cobra-lilies* (Arisaema): *Their Botany and Culture*. Primulaceae Books, Kalimpong, West Bengal, India.
Arum
Boyce, P. (1993). *The Genus* Arum. HMSO,London.
Asplenium
Rickard, M. (1997). *The Garden*, 122(2): 86-92.
Aster
Picton, P. (199?). *A Guide to the Asters Grown By Old Court Nurseries*. Old Court Nurseries, Colwall, Worcs.
Ranson, E.R. (1947). *Michaelmas Daisies*. Garden Book Club.
Aubrieta
International Registration Authority Checklist. (1975, unpublished). Weihenstephan, Germany.
Begonia
Ingles, J. (1990). *American Begonia Society Listing of Begonia Cultivars*. (Revised Edition Buxton Checklist).
Wall, B. (1989). *The Plantsman*, 11(1): 4-14.
Thompson, M.L. & Thompson, E.J. (1981). *Begonias: The Complete Reference Guide*. Times Books, New York.
Betula
Ashburner, K. (1980). *The Plantsman*, 2(1): 31-53.
Ashburner, K. & Schilling, A.D. (1985). *The Plantsman*, 7(2): 116-25.
Hunt, D. (ed.) (1993). Betula: *Proceedings of the IDS Betula Symposium*. International Dendrology Society, Richmond, Surrey.
Bougainvillea
Bor, N.L. & Raizada, M.B. (2nd ed. 1982). *Some Beautiful Indian Climbers and Shrubs*: 291-304. Bombay Natural History Society.
Choudhury, B. & Singh, B. (1981). *The International Bougainvillea Check List*. Indian Agricultural Research Institute, New Delhi.
Gillis, W.T. (1976). Bougainvilleas of Cultivation. *Baileya* 20(1): 34-41. New York.
Iredell, J. (1990). *The Bougainvillea Grower's Handbook*. Simon & Schuster, Brookvale, Australia.
Iredell, J. (1994). *Growing Bougainvilleas*. Cassell, London.
MacDaniels, L.H. (1981). A Study of Cultivars in *Bougainvillea*. *Baileya* 21(2): 77-100. New York.
Swithinbank, A. (1995). *The Garden*, 120(10): 634-37.
Bromeliaceae
Beadle, D.A. (1991). *A Preliminary Listing of all the Known Cultivar and Grex Names for the* Bromeliaceae. Bromeliad Society, Corpus Christi, Texas.
Luther, H.E. & Sieff, E. (1991). *An Alphabetical List of Bromeliad Binomials*. Bromeliad Society, Orlando, Florida.
Rauh, W. (1979). *Bromeliads*. Blandford Press, Dorset.
Brugmansia
Shaw, J.M.H. (1998). *The New Plantsman*, 5(1): 48-60 & 5(3): 192.

Buddleja
Maunder, M. (1987). *The Plantsman*, 9(2): 65-80.
Bulbs
Bryan, J.E. (1989). *Bulbs*, vols 1 & 2. Christopher Helm, Bromley, Kent.
Du Plessis, N. and Duncan, G. (1989). *Bulbous Plants of Southern Africa*. Tafelberg, Cape Town, South Africa.
Grey-Wilson, C. & Matthew, B. (1981). *Bulbs*. Collins, London.
Rix, M. & Phillips, R. (1981). *The Bulb Book*. Pan Books, London.
Scheepen, J. van (ed.). (1991). *International Checklist for Hyacinths and Miscellaneous Bulbs*. KAVB, Hillegom, Netherlands.
Buxus
Batdorf, L.R. (1989). *Checklist of Buxus*. American Boxwood Society.
Braimbridge, E. (1994). *The Plantsman*, 15(4): 236-54.
Callistemon
Mitchem, C.M. (1993). *The Plantsman*, 15(1): 29-41.
Calluna see Heathers
Calochortus
Martinelli, S. (1995). *Alpine Garden Society Bulletin*, 63(1 & 2): 71-92, 180-99. Pershore, Worcestershire.
Camellia
Gonos, A.A. (ed.) (23rd revd ed. 1999). *Camellia Nomenclature*. Southern California Camellia Society.
Savige, T.J. (1993, corrected 1994). *The International Camellia Register*. The International Camellia Society, Wirlinga, Australia.
Campanula
Lewis, P. & Lynch, M. (2nd ed. 1998). *Campanulas*. Batsford, London
Canna
Cooke, I. (1999). *The Garden*, 124(5): 364-69.
Carnivorous Plants
Pietropaulo, J. & Pietropaulo, P. (1986). *Carnivorous Plants of the World*. Timber Press, Oregon.
Slack, A. (Revd ed. 1988). *Carnivorous Plants*. Alphabooks, Sherborne, Dorset.
Carpinus
Rushforth, K. (1986). *The Plantsman*, 7(3 & 4): 173-91 & 212-16.
Caryopteris
Pattison, G. (1989). *The Plantsman*, 11(1): 15-18.
Cassiope
Blake, F.S. (1985). *Alpine Garden Society Bulletin*, 53(1): 61-65.
Starling, B. (1989). *The Plantsman*, 11(2): 106-16.
Stone, M. (1998). *Alpine Garden Society Bulletin*, 66(4): 484-92.
Ceanothus
Gardiner, J. (1997). *The Garden*, 122(5): 308-11.
Cercidiphyllum
Lancaster, C.R. (1997). *The Garden*, 122(10): 720-21.

Cestrum
Beckett, K.A. (1987). *The Plantsman*, **9**(3): 129-32.
Chaenomeles
Jewell, D. (1998). *The Garden*, **123**(2): 90-93.
Weber, C. (1963). Cultivars in the Genus *Chaenomeles*. *Arnoldia*, **23**(3): 17-75. Arnold Arboretum, Harvard, Massachusetts.
Chrysanthemum (Dendranthema)
Brummitt, R.K. (1997). The Garden, **122**(9): 662-63.
Gosling, S.G. (ed.). (1964). *British National Register of names of Chrysanthemums 1964*. National Chrysanthemum Society, Whetstone, London.
McDougall, A. (comp.) (1997). *British National Register of Names of Chrysanthemums: Amalgamated Edition 1964-96* and Supplementary Lists for 1996, '97 and '98. National Chrysanthemum Society, Amington, Staffs.
Cimicifuga
Compton, J.A. (1992). *The Plantsman*, **14**(2): 99-115.
Compton, J.A. (1997). *Botanical Journal of the Linnean Society*, **123**(1): 1-23.
Compton, J.A. & Culham, A. (2000). *The Garden*, **125**(1): 48-52.
Cistus
Page, R.G. (1991). *The Plantsman*, **13**(3): 143-56.
Page, R.G. (1996). *The New Plantsman*, **3**(3): 184-89.
Page, R.G. (1998). *The New Plantsman*, **5**(4): 219-30.
Citrus
Davies, F.S. & Albrigo, L.G. (1994). *Citrus*. CAB International, Wallingford, Oxon.
Saunt, J. (1990). *Citrus Varieties of the World*. Sinclair International Ltd., Norwich, England.
Cladrastis
Ma, J. & Spongberg, S.A. (1997). *International Dendrology Society Yearbook 1996*: 27-34.
Clematis
Evison, R.J. (1998). *The Gardener's Guide to Growing Clematis*. David & Charles, Newton Abbot, Devon.
Evison, R.J. & Matthews, V. (1994). *The New Plantsman*, **1**(2): 95-101.
Fisk, J. (1989). *Clematis, the Queen of Climbers*. Cassell, London.
Fretwell, B. (1989). *Clematis*. Collins, London.
Grey-Wilson, C. (1986). *The Plantsman*, **7**(4): 193-204.
Hutchins, G. (1990). *The Plantsman*, **11**(4): 193-208.
Lloyd, C. & Bennett, T.H. (1989). *Clematis*. Viking, London.
Oviatt-Ham, M. (1996). *The Garden*, **121**(3): 140-45.
Snoeijer, W. (1991). *Clematis Index*. Fopma, Boskoop, Netherlands.
Snoeijer, W. (1996). *Checklist of Clematis Grown in Holland*. Fopma, Boskoop, Netherlands.

Codonopsis
Matthews, Y.S. (1980). *Alpine Garden Society Bulletin*, **48**(2): 96-108.
Grey-Wilson, C. (1990). *The Plantsman*, **12**(2): 65-99.
Grey-Wilson, C. (1995). *The New Plantsman*, **2**(4): 213-25.
Conifers
Farjon, A. (1998). *World Checklist and Bibliography of Conifers*. Royal Botanic Gardens, Kew.
Krüssmann, G. (English trans. Epp, M.E.). (1985). *Manual of Cultivated Conifers*. Batsford, London.
Lewis, J. (comp.) & Leslie, A.C. (ed.) (1987, '89 & '92). *The International Conifer Register*, pt 1 (*Abies* to *Austrotaxus*), pt 2 (*Belis* to *Pherosphaera* (excluding Cypresses and Junipers) & pt 3 (Cypresses). Royal Horticultural Society, London.
Ouden, P. den & Boom, B.K. (1965). *Manual of Cultivated Conifers*. Martinus Nijhorff, The Hague, Netherlands.
Welch, H.J. (1979). *Manual of Dwarf Conifers*. Theophrastus, New York.
Welch, H.J. (1990). *The Conifer Manual*, 1. Kluwer Academic Publishers, Dordrecht, Holland.
Welch, H.J. (1993). *The World Checklist of Conifers*. Landsman's Bookshops Ltd, Bromyard, Herefordshire.
Coprosma
Hutchins, G. (1995). *The New Plantsman*, **2**(1): 12-37.
Cornus
Flanagan, M. (1997). *The Garden*, **123**(1): 16-19.
Howard, R.A. (1961). Registration Lists of Cultivar Names in *Cornus* L., *Arnoldia*, **21**(2): 9-18. Arnold Arboretum, Harvard, Massachusetts.
Corokia
Hutchins, G. (1994). *The Plantsman*, **15**(4):225-35.
Corydalis
Lidén, M. and Zetterlund, H. (1988). *Alpine Garden Society Bulletin*, **56**(2): 146-69.
Lidén, M. and Zetterlund, H. (1997). *Corydalis*. Alpine Garden Society, Pershore, Worcestershire.
Rix, E.M. (1993). *The Plantsman*, **15**(3): 129-30.
Corylopsis
Wright, D. (1982). *The Plantsman*, **4**(1): 29-53.
Corylus
Crawford, M. (1995). *Hazelnuts: Production and Culture*. Agroforestry Research Trust, Dartington, Devon.
Game, M. (1995). *The Garden*, **120**(11): 674-77.
Cotoneaster
Fryer, J. (1996). *The Garden*, **121**(11): 709-15.
Fryer, J. & Hylmö, B. (1998). *The New Plantsman*, **5**(3): 132-44.
Crassulaceae
Eggli, U. & 't Hart, H. (1995). *Evolution and Systematics of the* Crassulaceae. Backhuys Publishers, Leiden, Netherlands.
Crocosmia
Dunlop, G. (1999). *The Garden*, **124**(8): 599-605.

Kostelijk, P.J. (1984). *The Plantsman*, 5(4): 246-53.
Crocus
Jacobsen, N., Ørgaard, M. & Scheepen, J. van.
(1997). *The New Plantsman*, 4(1): 6-38.
Kerdorff, H. & Pasche, E. (1996). *Alpine Garden Society
Bulletin*, 64(3): 296-312.
Kerdorff, H. & Pasche, E. (1996). *Alpine Garden Society
Bulletin*, 64(4): 459-67.
Mathew, B. (1982). *The Crocus*. Batsford, London
Cyclamen
Grey-Wilson, C. (1988). *The Genus* Cyclamen.
Christopher Helm, Bromley, Kent.
Grey-Wilson, C. (1991). *The Plantsman*, 13(1):
1-20.
Grey-Wilson, C. (1997). *Cyclamen*. Batsford,
London.
Cypripedium
Cribb, P. (1997). *The Genus* Cypripedium.
Timber Press, Portland, Oregon.
Cynara
Wiklund, A. (1992). *The Genus* Cynara. Botanical
Journal of the Linnean Society, 109(1): 75-123.
Cyrtanthus
Holford, F. (1989). *The Plantsman*, 11(3): 170-75.
Dahlia
National Dahlia Society Classified Directory of Dahlias.
(25th ed. 1999). National Dahlia Society, Marlow,
Bucks.
Pycraft, D. (1969-95) & Hedge, R. (1996-'99).
International Register of Dahlia Names 1969 &
supps 1-10. Royal Horticultural Society, London.
Daphne
Brickell, C.D. & Mathew, B. (1976). *Daphne*.
Alpine Garden Society.
Daphniphyllum
Boyce, P. (1999). *Curtis's Botanical Magazine*, 16(4):
267-71. Blackwell, Oxford
Delphinium
Leslie, A.C. (1996). *The International* Delphinium
Register Cumulative Supplement 1970-1995. Royal
Horticultural Society, London.
Dendranthema see Chrysanthemum
Deutzia
Taylor, J. (1990). *The Plantsman*, 11(4): 225-40.
Dianthus
Leslie, A.C. (2nd ed. & supps 1-15, 1983-98).
The International Dianthus Register. Royal
Horticultural Society, London.
Diascia
Benham, S. (1987). *The Plantsman*, 9(1): 1-17.
Harrison, H. (1996). *The Hardy Plant*, 18(1):
41-48. Hardy Plant Society.
Lord, W.A. (1996). *The Garden*, 121(4):
192-94.
Dierama
Hilliard, O.M. & Burtt, B.L. (1990). *The Plantsman*,
12(2): 106-12.
Hilliard, O.M. & Burtt, B.L. (1991). *Dierama*. Acorn
Books CC. Johannesburg, South Africa.

Dionysia
Grey-Wilson, C. (1988). *The Plantsman*, 10(2):
65-84.
Grey-Wilson, C. (1989). *The Genus* Dionysia. Alpine
Garden Society, Woking, Surrey.
Dodecatheon
Mitchem, C.M. (1991). *The Plantsman*, 13(3):
157-70.
Douglasia
Mitchell, B. (1999). *The New Plantsman*, 6(2):
101-08.
Dracaena
Bos, J.J., Graven, P., Hetterscheid, W.L.A. & van de
Wege, J.J. (1992). *Edinburgh Journal of Botany*,
10(3): 311-31.
Drosera
Cheek, M. (1993). *Kew Magazine*, 10(3): 138-44.
Blackwell, Oxford.
Echinacea
Vernon, J. (1999). *The Garden*, 124(8): 588-91.
Epimedium
Barker, D.G. (1996). *Epimediums and Other Herbaceous
Berberidaceae*. Hardy Plant Society, Pershore, Worcs.
Stearn, W.T. (1995). *Curtis's Botanical Magazine*, 12(1):
15-25. Royal Botanic Gardens, Kew.
White, R. (1996). *The Garden*, 121(4): 208-14.
Episcia
Arnold, P. *The Gesneriad Register 1977*: Episcia.
American Gloxinia and Gesneriad Society,
Binghamton, New York.
Erica see also Heathers
Baker, H.A. & Oliver, E.G.H. (1967). *Heathers in
Southern Africa*. Purnell, Cape Town, South Africa.
Kirsten, G. & Schuman, D. (1992). *Ericas of
South Africa*. Fernwood Press, Vlaeberg, South Africa.
Eriogonum
Elliott, J. (1993). *Alpine Garden Society Bulletin*, 61(2):
200-14.
Erodium
Addyman, M. & Clifton, R. (1992). *Erodiums in
Cultivation*. NCCPG, Wisley, Surrey.
Bacon, L. (1990). *Alpine Garden Society Bulletin*, 58(1):
65-83.
Clifton, R.T.F. (4th ed., Issue 2, 1994). *The
Geraniaceae Group* Geranium *Family Species Check
List, Pt 1:* Erodium. The *Geraniaceae* Group,
Dover, Kent.
Leslie, A.C. (1980). *The Plantsman*, 2(2): 117-26.
Victor, D.X. (Unpublished Database, as at 26.2.99).
Tentative Checklist of Erodium *Cultivars*.
Erythronium
Mathew, B. (1992). A Taxonomic and Horticultural
Review of *Erythronium*. *Botanical Journal of the
Linnean Society*, 109(4): 453-71.
Mathew, B. (1998). *Alpine Garden Society Bulletin*,
66(3): 308-22.
Eucalyptus
Kelly, S. (3rd ed. 1989, 2 vols). Eucalyptus. Viking
O'Neil, South Yarra, Victoria, Australia.

Eucomis
Compton, J.A. (1990). *The Plantsman,* **12**(3): 129-39.

Eucryphia
Wright, D. (1983). *The Plantsman,* **5**(3): 167-85.

Euonymus
Brown, N. (1996). *The New Plantsman,* **3**(4): 238-43.
Lancaster, C.R. (1981). *The Plantsman,* **3**(3): 133-66.

Euphorbia
Turner, R. (1995). *Euphorbias.* Batsford, London.

Fagales
Frodin, D.G. & Govaerts, R. (1998). *World Checklist and Bibliography of* Fagales. Royal Botanic Gardens, Kew.

Fagus
Wyman, D. (1964). Registration List of Cultivar Names of *Fagus* L., *Arnoldia,* **24**(1): 1-8. Arnold Arboretum, Harvard, Massachusetts.

Fascicularia
Nelson, E.C. & Zizka, G. (1997). *The New Plantsman,* **4**(4): 232-39.
Zizka, G., Horres, R., Nelson, E.C. & Weising, K. (1999). *Botanical Journal of the Linnean Society,* **129**(4): 315-32.

Ferns
Goudey, C.J. (1988). *A Handbook of Ferns for Australia and New Zealand.* Lothian, Port Melbourne, Victoria, Australia.
Johns, R.J. (1996). *Index Filicum: Supplementum Sextum pro Annis 1976-90.* Royal Botanic Gardens, Kew.
Johns, R.J. (1997). *Index Filicum: Supplementum Septimum pro Annis 1991-95.* Royal Botanic Gardens, Kew.
Kaye, R. (1968). *Hardy Ferns.* Faber & Faber, London.
Johns, R.J. (1991). *Pteridophytes of Tropical East Africa.* Royal Botanic Gardens, Kew.
Jones, D.L. (1987). *Encyclopaedia of Ferns.* Lothian, Melbourne, Australia.
Rush, R. (1984). *A Guide to Hardy Ferns.* The British Pteridological Society, London.

Festuca
Wilkinson, M.J. & Stace, C.A. (1991). A new taxonomic treatment of the *Festuca ovina* aggregate in the British Isles. *Botanical Journal of the Linnean Society,* **106**(4): 347-97.

Ficus carica
Hendy, J. (1997). *The Garden,* **122**(9): 636-40.

Filipendula
Barnes, P.G. (1998). *The New Plantsman,* **5**(3): 145-53.

Fragaria
Day, D. (ed.). (1988, revd 1993). *Grower Digest 3: Strawberries.* Nexus Business Communications, London.

Fremontodendron
McMillan Browse, P. (1992). *The Plantsman,* **14**(1): 41-44.

Fritillaria
Jefferson-Brown, M. & Pratt, K. (1997). *The Gardener's Guide to Growing Fritillaries.* David & Charles, Newton Abbot, Devon.
Turrill, W.B. & Seely, J.R. (1980). Studies in the Genus *Fritillaria. Hooker's Icones Plantarum,* **39**(1 & 2). Royal Botanic Gardens, Kew.

Fuchsia
Bartlett, G. (1996). *Fuchsias - A Colour Guide.* Crowood Press, Marlborough, Wiltshire.
Boullemier, L.B. (2nd ed. 1991). *The Checklist of Species, Hybrids & Cultivars of the Genus* Fuchsia. Blandford Press, Dorset.
Goulding, E. (1995). *Fuchsias: The Complete Guide.* Batsford, London.
Johns, E.A. (1997). *Fuchsias of the 19th and Early 20th Century.* British Fuchsia Society, Summerfield, Worcs.
Nijhuis, M. (1994). *1000 Fuchsias.* Batsford, London.
Nijhuis, M. (1996). *500 More Fuchsias.* Batsford, London.

Galanthus
Davis, A.P. (1999). *The Genus* Galanthus. Timber Press, Portland, Oregon.

Gaultheria (inc. Pernettya).
Middleton, D.J. (1990/91). *The Plantsman,* **12**(3): 167-77 & **13**(3): 188-89.
Middleton, D.J. (1991). Infrageneric Classification of the Genus *Gaultheria. Botanical Journal of the Linnean Society,* **106**(3): 229-58.

Gentiana
Bartlett, M. (1975). *Gentians.* Blandford Press, Dorset.
Wilkie, D. (2nd ed. 1950). *Gentians.* Country Life, London.

Geranium
Abbott, P. (1994). *A Guide to Scented* Geraniaceae. Hill Publicity Services, Angmering, West Sussex.
Bath, T., & Jones, J. (1994). *The Gardener's Guide to Growing Hardy Geraniums.* David & Charles, Newton Abbot, Devon.
Clifton, R.T.F. (4th ed., Issue 2 1995). *Geranium Family Species Checklist, Pt2*: Geranium. The *Geraniaceae* Group of the British Pelargonium and Geranium Society, Dover, Kent.
Jones, J. *et al.* (1992). *Hardy Geraniums for the Garden.* Hardy Plant Society, Pershore, Worcs.
Victor, D.X. (Unpublished Database, as at 26.2.99). *Tentative Checklist of* Geranium *Cultivars.*
Yeo, P.F. (2nd ed. 1992). *Hardy Geraniums.* Croom Helm, London.

Gesneriaceae
Dates, J.D. *The Gesneriad Register 1986: Check List of Intergeneric Hybrids in the tribe* Gloxinieae. American Gloxinia and Gesneriad Society, Sugar Grove, Illinois.
Dates, J.D. *The Gesneriad Register 1987: Check List of Bucinellina, Columnea, Dalbergaria, Pentadenia, Trichantha and Intergeneric Hybrids.* American Gloxinia and Gesneriad Society, Galesburg, Illinois.

Dates, J.D. *The Gesneriad Register 1990: Appendix C: Registered Gesneriads 1957-90.* American Gloxinia and Gesneriad Society, Galesburg, Illinois.

Gladiolus

British Gladiolus Society List of Cultivars Classified for Show Purposes 1994. British Gladiolus Society, Mayfield, Derbyshire.

British Gladiolus Society List of European Cultivars Classified for Exhibition Purposes 1997. British Gladiolus Society, Mayfield, Derbyshire.

British Gladiolus Society List of European Cultivars Classified for Exhibition Purposes 1998. British Gladiolus Society, Mayfield, Derbyshire.

British Gladiolus Society List of New Zealand Cultivars Classified for Exhibition Purposes 1997. British Gladiolus Society, Mayfield, Derbyshire.

British Gladiolus Society List of New Zealand Cultivars Classified for Exhibition Purposes 1998. British Gladiolus Society, Mayfield, Derbyshire.

British Gladiolus Society List of North American Cultivars Classified for Exhibition Purposes 1997. British Gladiolus Society, Mayfield, Derbyshire.

British Gladiolus Society List of North American Cultivars Classified for Exhibition Purposes 1998. British Gladiolus Society, Mayfield, Derbyshire.

Goldblatt, P. & Manning, J. (1998). Gladiolus *in Southern Africa.* Fernwood Press, Vlaeberg, South Africa.

Lewis, G.J., Obermeyer, A.A. & Barnard, T.T. (1972). A Revision of the South African Species of *Gladiolus. Journal of South African Botany,* supp. vol. **10**. Purnell, Cape Town.

Gleditsia triacanthos

Santamour, F.S.Jr. & McArdle, A.J. (198?). *Checklist of Cultivars of Honeylocust.* USA.

Gramineae See *Poaceae*

Grevillea

Olde, P. & Marriott, N. (1995). *The Grevillea Book (3).* Kangaroo Press, Kenthurst, NSW, Australia.

Haemanthus

Snijman, D. (1984). A Revision of the Genus *Haemanthus. Journal of South African Botany,* supp. vol. **12**. National Botanic Gardens, Kirstenbosch, South Africa.

Halimium

Page, R.G. (1998). *The New Plantsman,* **5**(4): 219-30.

Hamamelidaceae

Wright, D. (1982). *The Plantsman,* **4**(1): 29-53.

Hamamelis

Coombes, A.J. (1996). *The Garden,* **121**(1): 28-33.

Lane, C. (1998). *The Garden,* **123**(1): 38-41.

Strand, C. (1998). *The New Plantsman,* **5**(4): 231-45.

Heathers

Small, D. & Small, A. (1992). *Handy Guide to Heathers.* Denbeigh Heather Nurseries, Suffolk.

Underhill, T. (1990). *Heaths and Heathers.* David & Charles, Newton Abbot, Devon.

Hebe

Hayter, T. (ed.). (1986-99). *Hebe News.* 20 Beech Farm Drive, Macclesfield, Cheshire.

Hutchins, G. (1979). *Hebe and Parahebe Species in Cultivation.* County Park Nursery, Essex.

Hutchins, G. (1997). *Hebes Here and There.* Hutchins & Davies, Caversham, Berks.

Chalk, D. (1988). *Hebes and Parahebes.* Christopher Helm, London.

Hedera

McAllister, H.A. (1988). *The Plantsman,* **10**(1): 27-29.

McAllister, H.A. & Rutherford, A. (1990). *Hedera helix* & *H. hibernica* in the British Isles. *Watsonia,* **18**. 7-15

Rose, P.Q. (1980). *Ivies.* Blandford Press, Dorset.

Rose, P.Q. (1996). *The Gardener's Guide to Growing Ivies.* David & Charles, Newton Abbot, Devon.

Rutherford, A., McAllister, H.A. & Rill, R.R. (1993). *The Plantsman,* **15**(2): 115-28.

Hedychium

Schilling, A.D. (1982). *The Plantsman,* **4**(3): 129-49.

Spencer-Mills, L. (1996). *The Garden,* **121**(12): 754-59.

Helichrysum

Hilliard, O.M. & Burtt, B.L. (1987). *The Garden,* **112**(6): 276-77.

Heliconia

Berry, F. & Kress, W.J. (1991). Heliconia: *An Identification Guide.* Smithsonian Institution Press, Washington.

Helleborus

Mathew, B. (1981). *The Plantsman,* **3**(1): 1-10.

Mathew, B. (1989). *Hellebores.* Alpine Garden Society, Woking, Surrey.

McLewin, W. & Mathew, B. (1995). *The New Plantsman,* **2**(2): 112-22.

McLewin, W. & Mathew, B. (1996). *The New Plantsman,* **3**(1): 50-60.

McLewin, W. & Mathew, B. (1996). *The New Plantsman,* **3**(3): 170-77.

Rice, G. & Strangman, E. (1993). *The Gardener's Guide to Growing Hellebores.* David & Charles, Newton Abbot, Devon.

Hemerocallis

Erhardt, W. (1988). Hemerocallis *Daylilies.* Batsford, London.

Grenfell, D. (1998). *The Gardener's Guide to Growing Daylilies.* David & Charles, Newton Abbot, Devon

Kitchingman, R.M. (1985). *The Plantsman,* **7**(2): 68-89.

Munson, R.W. (1989). Hemerocallis, *The Daylily.* Timber Press, Portland, Oregon.

Webber, S. (ed.). (1988). *Daylily Encyclopaedia.* Webber Gardens, Damascus, Maryland.

Hibiscus

Beers, L. & Howie, J. (2nd ed. 1990). *Growing Hibiscus.* Kangaroo Press, Kenthurst, Australia.

Chin H.F. (1986). *The Hibiscus: Queen of Tropical Flowers*. Tropical Press Sdn. Bhd., Kuala Lumpur, Malaysia

Dickings, I. (1995). *The Garden*, 120(8): 487-91.

Walker, J. (1999). *Hibiscus*. Cassell, London.

Hippeastrum

Alfabetische Lijst van de in Nederland in cultuur zijnde Amaryllis (Hippeastrum) Cultivars. (1980). Koninklijke Algemeene Vereeniging voor Bloembollencultur, Hillegom, Netherlands.

Read, R. (1998). *The Garden*, 123(10): 734-37.

Hosta

Grenfell, D. (1985). *The Plantsman*, 7(4): 251-54.

Grenfell, D. (1990). *Hosta*. Batsford, London.

Grenfell, D. (1993). *Hostas*. The Hardy Plant Society, Pershore, Worcs.

Grenfell, D. (1996). *The Gardener's Guide to Growing Hostas*. David & Charles, Newton Abbot, Devon.

Grenfell, D. (1993). *The Plantsman*, 15(3): 168-84.

Hammelman, T. (March 2000). *Giboshi.com Hosta Database*. T. & G. Hammelman, Shade Serenade, Omaha, Nebraska @ http://www.giboshi.com.

Hensen, K.J.W. (1985). *The Plantsman*, 7(1):1-35.

Schmid, W.G. (1991). *The Genus Hosta*. Timber Press, Oregon.

Hoya

Innes, C. (1988). *The Plantsman*, 10(3): 129-40.

Hyacinthus orientalis

Stebbings, G. (1996). *The Garden*, 121(2): 68-72.

Hydrangea

Haworth-Booth, M. (1975). *The Hydrangeas*. Garden Book Club, London.

Lawson-Hall, T. & Rothera, B. (1995). *Hydrangeas*. Batsford, London.

Mallet, C. (1992 & 1994). *Hydrangeas*, 1 & 2. Centre d'Art Floral, Varengeville-sur-Mer, France

Hypericum

Lancaster, C.R. & Robson, N.K.B. (1997). *The Garden*, 122(8): 566-71.

Robson, N.K.B. (1980). *The Plantsman*, 1(4): 193-200.

Ilex

Andrews, S. (1983). *The Plantsman*, 5(2): 65-81.

Andrews, S. (1984). *The Plantsman*, 6(3): 157-66.

Andrews, S. (1985). *The Garden*, 110(11): 518-22.

Andrews, S. (1994). *The Garden*, 119(12): 580-83.

Dudley, T.R. & Eisenbeiss, G.K. 1973 & (1992). *International Checklist of Cultivated* Ilex 1: *Ilex opaca*; 2: *Ilex crenata*. USDA, Washington.

Galle, F.C. (1997). *Hollies: the Genus* Ilex. Timber Press, Portland, Oregon.

Impatiens

Grey-Wilson, C. (1983). *The Plantsman*, 5(2): 65-81.

Grey-Wilson, C. (1997). *The Garden*, 122(8): 583-87.

Incarvillea

Grey-Wilson, C. (1994). *The New Plantsman*, 1(1): 36-52.

Grey-Wilson, C. (1998). *The New Plantsman*, 5(2): 76-98.

Iochroma

Shaw, J.M.H. (1998). *The New Plantsman*, 5(3):154-91.

Iridaceae

Innes, C. (1985). *The World of* Iridaceae. Holly Gate International, Sussex.

Iris

British Iris Society Species Group. (1997). *A Guide to Species Irises*. Cambridge University Press.

Hoog, M.H. (1980). *The Plantsman*, 2(3): 141-64.

Mathew, B. (1981). *The Iris*. Batsford, London.

Mathew, B. (1993). *The Plantsman*, 15(1): 14-25.

Stebbings, G. (1997). *The Gardener's Guide to Growing Irises*. David & Charles, Newton Abbot, Devon.

Iris (series Unguiculares)

Service, N. (1990). *The Plantsman*, 12(1): 1-9.

Juniperus

Lewis, J. (ed. Leslie, A.C.). (1998). *The International Conifer Register Part 4:* Juniperus. Royal Horticultural Society, London.

Kalmia

Jaynes, R.A. (1997). *Kalmia: Mountain Laurel and Related Species*. Timber Press, Portland, Oregon.

Pullen, A. (1997). *The Garden*, 122(6): 400-03.

Kniphofia

Grant-Downton, R. (1997). *The New Plantsman*, 4(3): 148-56.

Taylor, J. (1985). *The Plantsman*, 7(3): 129-60.

Kohleria

Dates, J.D. (ed.). *The Gesneriad Register 1985: Check List of* Kohleria. American Gloxinia and Gesneriad Society, Lincoln Acres, California.

Lachenalia

Duncan, G.D. (1988). *The Lachenalia* Handbook. *Annals of Kirstenbosch Botanic Gardens*, 17. South Africa.

Lantana

Howard, R.A. (1969). A Check List of Cultivar Names used in the Genus *Lantana*. *Arnoldia* 29(11): 73-109. Arnold Arboretum, Harvard, Massachusetts.

Larix

Horsman, J. (1988). *The Plantsman*, 10(1): 37-62.

Lathyrus

Norton, S. (1994). *The Garden*, 119(5): 216-21.

Norton, S. (1994). *The New Plantsman*, 1(2): 78-83.

Norton, S. (1996). *Lathyrus*. NCCPG, Wisley, Surrey.

Lavandula

Tucker, A.O. & Hensen, K.J.W. (1985). The Cultivars of Lavender and Lavandin. *Baileya*, 22(4): 168-177. New York.

Upson, T. (1999). *The Garden*, 124(7): 524-29.

Lavatera

Miller, D. (1999). *The Garden*, 124(9): 676-79.

Leguminosae (Caesalpiniaceae, Mimosaceae & Papilionaceae)

ILDIS Legume Web (World Database of Legumes). (March 2000). International Legume Database and Information Service via server at BIOSIS UK, York, England @ http://www.ildis.org/LegumeWeb/.

Lewis, G.P. (1987). *Legumes of Bahia*. Royal Botanic Gardens, Kew.

Lock, J.M. (1989). *Legumes of Africa*. Royal Botanic Gardens, Kew.

Lock, J.M. & Heald, J. (1994). *Legumes of Indo-China*. Royal Botanic Gardens, Kew.

Lock, J.M. & Simpson, K. (1991). *Legumes of West Asia*. Royal Botanic Gardens, Kew.

Roskov, Yu.R., Sytin, A.K. & Yakovlev, G.P. (1996). *Legumes of Northern Eurasia*. Royal Botanic Gardens, Kew.

Leptospermum

Dawson, M. (1997). *The New Plantsman*, 4(1): 51-59 & 4(2): 67-78.

Nomenclature Committee of the Royal New Zealand Institute of Horticulture. (1963). Check List of *Leptospermum* Cultivars. *Journal of the Royal New Zealand Institute of Horticulture*, 5(5): 224-30. Wellington, New Zealand.

Leucojum

Elliott, J. (1992). *The Plantsman*, 14(2): 70-79.

Lewisia

Elliott, R. (1978). *Lewisias*. Alpine Garden Society, Woking.

Mathew, B. (1989). *The Genus* Lewisia. Christopher Helm, Bromley, Kent.

Liliaceae sensu lato

Mathew, B. (1989). *The Plantsman*, 11(2): 89-105.

Lilium

Leslie, A.C. (3rd ed. & supps 1-15 1982-97). *The International Lily Register*. Royal Horticultural Society, London.

Liriodendron

Andrews, S. (1993). *IDS Yearbook 1992*: 15-19. London.

Lonicera

Bradshaw, D. (1991). *The Plantsman*, 13(2): 106-10.

Bradshaw, D. (1995). *The Garden*, 120(7): 406-11. Royal Horticultural Society, London.

Wright, D. (1983). *The Plantsman*, 4(4): 236-55.

Magnolia

Callaway, D.J. (1994). *Magnolias*. Batsford, London.

Frodin, D.G. & Govaerts, R. (1998). *World Checklist and Bibliography of* Magnoliaceae. Royal Botanic Gardens, Kew.

Holman, N. (1979). *The Plantsman*, 7(1): 36-39.

Hunt, D. (ed.). (1998). *Magnolias and their Allies*. International Magnolia Society & International Dendrology Society, Sherborne, Dorset.

Treseder, N.G. (1978). *Magnolias*. Faber & Faber, London.

Malus

Crawford, M. (1994). *Directory of Apple Cultivars*. Agroforestry Research Trust, Dartington, Devon.

Fiala, Fr J.L. (1994). *Flowering Crabapples*. Timber Press, Portland, Oregon.

Morgan, J. & Richards, A. (1993). *The Book of Apples*. Ebury Press, London.

Parfitt, B. (1965). *Index of the Apple Collection at the National Fruit Trials*. Ministry of Agriculture, Fisheries and Food, Faversham, Kent.

Rouèche, A. (March 2000). *Les Crets Fruits et Pomologie*. Les Croqueurs de Pommes et de Fruits Oubliés, Haute-Savoie, France @ http://le-village.ifrance.com/lescrets/datapom/ergp.htm.

Spiers, V. (1996). *Burcombes, Queenies and Colloggetts*. West Brendon, St Dominic, Cornwall.

Taylor, H.V. (1948). *The Apples of England*. Crosby Lockwood, London.

Meconopsis

Cobb, J.L.S. (1989). *Meconopsis*. Christopher Helm, Bromley, Kent.

Cox, P.A. (1996). *The New Plantsman*, 3(2): 80-83.

Grey-Wilson, C. (1992). *The Plantsman*, 14(1): 1-33.

Grey-Wilson, C. (1996). *The New Plantsman*, 3(1): 22-39.

Mimulus

Silverside, A.J. (1994). *Mimulus*: 180 Years of Confusion. *The Common Ground of Wild and Cultivated Plants* (eds Perry, A.R. & Ellis, R.G.). National Museum of Wales, Cardiff.

Moraea

Goldblatt, P. (1986). *The Moraeas of Southern Africa*. National Botanic Gardens of South Africa.

Narcissus

Blanchard, J.W. (1990). *Narcissus*. Alpine Garden Society, Woking, Surrey.

Kington, S. (3rd ed. & supp. 1, 1998). *The International Daffodil Register and Classified List 1998*. Royal Horticultural Society, London.

Throckmorton, T.D. (ed.). (1985). *Daffodils to Show & Grow and Abridged Classified List of Daffodil Names*. Royal Horticultural Society and American Daffodil Society, Hernando, Mississippi.

Nematanthus

Arnold, P. *The Gesneriad Register 1978: Check List of* Nematanthus. American Gloxinia and Gesneriad Society.

Nerium

Pagen, F.J.J. (1987). *Oleanders*. Agricultural University, Wageningen, Holland.

Toogood, A. (1997). *The Garden*, 122(7): 488-91.

Nothofagus

Hill, R.S. & Read, J. (1991). *Botanical Journal of the Linnean Society*, 105(1): 37-72.

Nymphaea

Davies, R. (1993). *Identification of Hardy Nymphaea*. Stapeley Water Gardens Ltd (for the International Water Lily Society), Cheshire.

Swindells, P. (1983). *Waterlilies*. Croom Helm, London.

Olearia

Heads, M. (1998). *Botanical Journal of the Linnean Society*, 127(3): 239-85.

Orchidaceae

Cribb, P. & Bailes, C. (1989). *Hardy Orchids*. Christopher Helm, Bromley, Kent.

Hunt, P.F. & Hunt, D.B. (1996). *Sander's List of Orchid Hybrids: Addendum 1991-1995*. Royal Horticultural Society, London.

Rittershausen, W. (ed.). (Quarterly). *The Orchid Review*. Royal Horticultural Society, London.

Origanum

Paton, A. (1994). *Kew Magazine*, 11(3): 109-17.

White, S. (1998). *Origanum: The Herb Marjoram and its Relatives*. NCCPG, Wisley, Surrey.

Osteospermum

Cheek, R.V. (1997). *The Garden*, 122(7): 506-11.

Ostrya

Rushforth, K. (1986). *The Plantsman*, 7(3 & 4): 173-91 & 212-16.

Oxalis

Erskine, P. (1998). *Alpine Garden Society Bulletin*, 66(3): 345-52.

Paeonia

Harding, A. & Klehm, R.G. (1993). *The Peony*. Batsford, London.

Haw, S.G. (1991). *The Plantsman*, 13(2): 94-97.

Haworth-Booth, M. (1963). *The Moutan or Tree Peony*. Garden Book Club, London.

Kessenich, G.M. (1976). *Peonies*. (Variety Check List, pts 1-3). American Peony Society.

Osti, G.L. (1999). *The Book of Tree Peonies*. Umberto Allemandi & C., Turin, Italy.

Rogers, A. (1995). *Peonies*. Timber Press, Portland, Oregon.

Wang L. *et al.*, (1998). *Chinese Tree Peony*. China Forestry Publishing House, Beijing, China.

Palmae *see Arecaceae*

Papaveraceae

Grey-Wilson, C. (1993). *Poppies*. Batsford, London.

Papaver orientale

Grey-Wilson, C. (1998). *The Garden*, 123(5): 320-25.

Parahebe

Heads, M. (1994). *Botanical Journal of the Linnean Society*, 115(1): 65-89.

Passiflora

Vanderplank, J. (2nd ed. 1996). *Passion Flowers*. Cassell, London.

Pelargonium

Abbott, P.G. (1994). *A Guide to Scented Geraniaceae*. Hill Publicity Services, Angmering, W. Sussex.

Baggust, H. (1988). *Miniature and Dwarf Geraniums*. Christopher Helm, Bromley, Kent.

A Checklist and Register of Pelargonium Cultivar Names, pt 1 (1978) & pt 2 (1985). Australian Geranium Society, Sydney.

Clifford, D. (1958). *Pelargoniums*. Blandford Press, London.

Complete Copy of the Spalding Pelargonium Checklist. Unpublished. USA.

Miller, D. (1996). *Pelargoniums*. Batsford, London.

Van der Walt, J.J.A. *et al.* (1977-88). *Pelargoniums of South Africa*, 1-3. National Botanic Gardens, Kirstenbosch, South Africa.

Penstemon

Charlesworth, G. (1994). *Alpine Garden Society Bulletin*, 62(2 & 4): 158-80 & 465-75.

Elliott, J. & Thornton-Wood, S. *The Garden*, 122(9): 652-55.

James, P. & Way, D. (1998). *The Gardener's Guide to Growing Penstemons*. David & Charles, Newton Abbot, Devon.

Lindgren, D.T. (1992). *List and Description of Named Cultivars in the Genus* Penstemon. University of Nebraska.

Lord, W.A. (1994). *The Garden*, 119(7): 304-09.

Nold, R. (1999). *Penstemons*. Timber Press, Portland, Oregon.

Philadelphus

Taylor, J. (1990). *The Plantsman*, 11(4): 225-40.

Wright, D. (1980). *The Plantsman*, 2(2): 104-16.

Phlomis

Mann Taylor, J. (1998). Phlomis: *The Neglected Genus*. NCCPG, Wisley, Surrey.

Phlox

Wherry, E.T. (1955). *The Genus* Phlox. Morris Arboretum Monographs III, Philadelphia, Penn.

Phlox paniculata

Stebbings, G. (1999). *The Garden*, 124(7): 518-21.

Phormium

Heenan, P.B. (1991). *Checklist of* Phormium *Cultivars*. Royal New Zealand Institute of Horticulture, Canterbury, New Zealand.

McBride-Whitehead, V. (1998). *The Garden*, 123(1): 42-45.

Phygelius

Coombes, A.J. (1988). *The Plantsman*, 9(4): 233-46.

Phyllostachys

Renvoize, S. (1995). *Curtis's Botanical Magazine*, 12(1): 8-15. Royal Botanic Gardens, Kew.

Pieris

Bond, J. (1982). *The Plantsman*, 4(2): 65-75.

Wagenknecht, B.L. (1961). Registration List of Names in the Genus Pieris. *Arnoldia*, 21(8). Arnold Arboretum, Harvard, Massachusetts.

Pinus

Muir, N. (1992). *The Plantsman*, 14(2): 80-98.

Plectranthus

Shaw, J.M.H. (1999). *The New Plantsman*, 6(2): 71-73.

Poaceae (Gramineae - Grasses)

Clayton, W.D. & Renvoize, S.A. (1986). *Genera Graminum*. HMSO, London.

Grounds, R. (1998). *The Plantfinder's Guide to Ornamental Grasses*. David & Charles, Newton Abbot, Devon.

Grounds, R. (1998). *Grasses*. Hardy Plant Society, Pershore, Worcestershire.

Podocarpus

Hutchins, G. (1991). *The Plantsman*, 13(2): 98-105.

Podophyllum

Shaw, J.M.H. (1999). *The New Plantsman*, 6(3): 158-65.

Polemonium
Nichol-Brown, D. (3rd ed. 1997). Polemonium. Nichol-Brown, Trimdon, Co. Durham.

Polypodium
Leslie, A.C. (1993). *The Garden*, 118(10): 450-52. Royal Horticultural Society, London.

Potentilla
Brearley, C. (1991). *The Plantsman*, 13(1): 42-53.
Brearley, C. (1992). *Alpine Garden Society Bulletin*, 60(3 & 4): 321-28 & 428-35.

Potentilla (shrubby).
Brearley, C. (1987). *The Plantsman*, 9(2): 90-109.
Davidson, C.G., Enns, R.J. & Gobin, S. (1994). *A Checklist of* Potentilla fruticosa: *The Shrubby Potentillas*. Agriculture and Agri-Food Canada Research Centre, Morden, Manitoba, Canada.
Davidson, C.G. & Lenz, L.M. (1989). Experimental Taxonony of *Potentilla fruticosa*. *Canadian Journal of Botany*, 67(12): 3520-28.

Primula
Fenderson, G.K. (1986). *A Synoptic Guide to the Genus* Primula. Allen Press, Lawrence, Kansas.
Green, R. (1976). *Asiatic Primulas*. The Alpine Garden Society, Woking.
Halda, J.J. (1992). *The Genus* Primula. Tethys Books, Colorado.
Hecker, W.R. (1971). *Auriculas & Primroses*. Batsford, London.
Richards, J. (1993). Primula. Batsford, London.
Smith, G.F., Burrow, B. & Lowe, D.B. (1984). *Primulas of Europe and America*. The Alpine Garden Society, Woking.
Wemyss-Cooke, T.J. (1986). *Primulas Old and New*. David & Charles, Newton Abbot.

Primula allionii
Archdale, B. & Richards, D. (1997). Primula allionii *Forms and Hybrids*. National Auricula and Primula Society, Midland and West Section.
Marcham, A.J. (1992). *Alpine Garden Society Bulletin*, 60(3): 255-67.

Primula auricula hort.
Baker, G. & Ward, P. (1995). *Auriculas*. Batsford, London.
Baker, G. (199?). *Double Auriculas*. National Auricula and Primula Society, Midland and West Section.
Baker, G. & Ward, P. (1995). *Auriculas*. Batsford, London.
Hawkes, A. (1995). *Striped Auriculas*. National Auricula and Primula Society, Midland and West Section.
Nicolle, G. (1996). *Border Auriculas*. National Auricula and Primula Society, Midland and West Section.
Telford, D. (1993). *Alpine Auriculas*. National Auricula and Primula Society, Midland and West Section.
Ward, P. (1991). *Show Auriculas*. National Auricula and Primula Society, Midland and West Section.

Proteaceae
Rebelo, T. (1995). *Proteas: A Field Guide to the Proteas of Southern Africa*. Fernwood Press, Vlaeberg, South Africa.

Prunus
Bultitude, J. *Index of the Plum Collection at the National Fruit Trials*. Ministry of Agriculture, Fisheries & Food, Faversham, Kent.
Crawford, M. (1996). *Plums*. Agroforestry Research Trust, Dartington, Devon.
Crawford, M. (1997). *Cherries: Production and Culture*. Agroforestry Research Trust, Dartington, Devon.
Grubb, N.H. (1949). *Cherries*. Crosby Lockwood, London.
Index of the Cherry Collection at the National Fruit Trials. 1986. Ministry of Agriculture, Fisheries & Food, Faversham, Kent.
Jacobsen, A.L. (1992). *Purpleleaf Plums*. Timber Press, Portland, Oregon.
Jefferson, R.M. & Wain, K.K. (1984). *The Nomenclature of Cultivated Flowering Cherries* (Prunus): *The Sato-zakura Group*. USDA, Washington
Smith, M.W.G. (1978). *Catalogue of the Plums at the National Fruit Trials*. Ministry of Agriculture, Fisheries & Food, Faversham, Kent.
Taylor, H.V. (1949). *The Plums of England*. Crosby Lockwood, London.

Pulmonaria
Hewitt, J. (1994). *Pulmonarias*. The Hardy Plant Society, Pershore, Worcs.
Hewitt, J. (1999). *The Garden*, 124(2): 98-105.
Mathew, B. (1982). *The Plantsman*, 4(2): 100-11.

Pyracantha
Egolf, D.R. & Andrick, A.O. (1995). *A Checklist of* Pyracantha *cultivars*. USDA, Washington

Pyrus
Crawford, M. (1996). *Directory of Pear Cultivars*. Agroforestry Research Trust, Dartington, Devon.
Parfitt, B. (1981). *Index of the Pear Collection at the National Fruit Trials*. Ministry of Agriculture, Fisheries & Food, Faversham, Kent.
Smith, M.W.G. (1976). *Catalogue of the British Pears*. Ministry of Agriculture, Fisheries & Food, Faversham, Kent

Quercus
Ávalos, S.V. (1995). *Contribución al concimiento del género* Quercus (Fagaceae) *en el estado de Guerrero, Mexico*. Facultad de Ciencias, UNAM, Ciudad Universitaria, Mexico.
Miller, H.A.& Lamb, S.H. (1985). *Oaks of North America*. Naturegraph Publishers, Happy Camp, California.
Mitchell, A. (1994). *The Plantsman*, 15(4): 216-24.
Muir, N. (1996). *The New Plantsman*, 3(4): 216-36.

Ranunculus ficaria
Carter, J.R.L. (1996). *The Garden*, 121(2): 90-95.

Raoulia
Hutchins, G. (1980). *The Plantsman*, 2(2): 100-03.

Rhododendron
Argent, G., Bond, J.D., Chamberlain, D.F., Cox, P.A. & Hardy, G.A. *The Rhododendron Handbook 1998*. Royal Horticultural Society, London.

Argent, G., Fairweather, G. & Walker, K. *Accepted Names in* Rhododendron *section* Vireya. Royal Botanic Garden, Edinburgh.

Chamberlain, D.F. (1982). *Notes from the Royal Botanic Garden, Edinburgh*, **39**(2). HMSO, Edinburgh.

Chamberlain, D.F. & Rae, S.J. (1990). A Revision of Rhododendron IV Subgenus *Tsutsusi. Edinburgh Journal of Botany*, **47**(2). HMSO, Edinburgh.

Cox, P.A. & Cox, K.N.E. (1988). *Encyclopaedia of* Rhododendron *Hybrids*. Batsford, London.

Cullen, J. (1980). *Notes from the Royal Botanic Garden, Edinburgh*, **39**(1). HMSO, Edinburgh.

Davidian, H.H. (1982, 1989, 1992 & 1995). *The* Rhododendron *Species*, 1-4. Batsford, London.

Galle, F.C. (1987). *Azaleas*. Timber Press, Portland, Oregon.

Lee, F.P. (1958). *The Azalea Book*. D. Van Nostrand, New York.

Leslie, A.C. (comp.). (1980). *The Rhododendron Handbook*. Royal Horticultural Society, London.

Leslie, A.C. (1989). *The International Rhododendron Register: Checklist of Rhododendron Names Registered 1989-1994* & supps 28-36. Royal Horticultural Society, London.

Salley, H.E. & Greer, H.E. (1986). Rhododendron *Hybrids*. Batsford, London.

Tamura, T. (ed.). (1989). *Azaleas in Kurume*. International Azalea Festival '89, Kurume, Japan.

Rhus

Coombes, A.J. (1994). *The New Plantsman*, **1**(2): 107-113.

Ribes

Crawford, M. (1997). *Currants and Gooseberries: Production and Culture*. Agroforestry Research Trust, Dartington, Devon.

Index of the Bush Fruit Collection at the National Fruit Trials. 1987. Ministry of Agriculture, Fisheries & Food, Faversham, Kent.

Romneya

McMillan Browse, P. (1989). *The Plantsman*, **11**(2): 121-24.

Rosa

Austin, D. (1988). *The Heritage of the Rose*. Antique Collectors' Club, Woodbridge, Suffolk.

Austin, D. (2nd ed. 1996). *English Roses*. Conran Octopus, London.

Beales, P. (1992). *Roses*. Harvill, London.

Beales, P., Cairns, T., Duncan, W. *et al.* (1998). *Botanica's Roses*. Grange Books, Hoo, Kent.

Bean, W.J. (1900-1988). 8th ed. rev. D.L. Clarke & G.S. Thomas. *Rosa* in *Trees and Shrubs Hardy in the British Isles*, 4 & supp.

Dickerson, B.C. (1992). *The Old Rose Advisor*. Timber Press, Portland, Oregon.

Haw, S.G. (1996). *The New Plantsman*, **3**(3): 143-46.

HelpMeFind - Roses Database (March 2000). HelpMeFind.com/Roses, Pipersville, Pennsylvania, USA @ http://www.helpmefind.com/sites/rrr/rsSearch.html.

McCann, S. (1985). *Miniature Roses*. David & Charles, Newton Abbot, Devon.

Pawsey, A. (17th ed. 1999). *Find That Rose!* British Rose Growers' Association, Colchester, Essex.

Phillips, R. & Rix, M. (1988). *Roses*. Macmillan, London.

Phillips, R. & Rix, M. (1993). *The Quest for the Rose*. BBC Books, London.

Thomas, G.S. (1995). *The Graham Stuart Thomas Rose Book*. John Murray, London

Verrier, S. (1996). Rosa gallica. *Florilegium*, Balmain, NSW, Australia.

Roscoea

Wilford, R. (1999). *Alpine Garden Society Bulletin*, **67**(1): 93-101.

Rosularia

Eggli, U. (1988). *A monograph study of the genus* Rosularia. Bradleya, 6 suppl. British Cactus & Succulent Society, Bury, Lancs.

Salix

Newsholme, C. (1992). *Willows*. Batsford, London.

Salvia

Clebsch, B. (1997). *A Book of Salvias*. Timber Press, Portland, Oregon.

Compton, J.A. (1994). *The Plantsman*, **15**(4): 193-215.

Saxifraga

Horn´y, R., Webr, K.M. & Byam-Grounds, J. (1986). Porophyllum *Saxifrages*. Byam-Grounds Publications, Stamford, Lincs.

Kohlein, F. (1984). *Saxifrages and Related Genera*. Batsford, London.

McGregor, M. (1995). *Saxifrages: The Complete Cultivars and Hybrids (International Register of Saxifrages*, 1st ed.). The Saxifrage Society.

McGregor, M. & Harding, W. (1998). *Saxifrages: The Complete List of Species*. The Saxifrage Society, Driffield, East Yorkshire.

McGregor, M. (October 1999). *The Saxifrage Society Website*. The Saxifrage Society @ http://www.skydancer.demon.co.uk/saxifrage/index.html.

Webb, D.A.& Cornell, R.J. (1989). *Saxifrages of Europe*. Christopher Helm, Bromley, Kent.

Saxifraga section Irregulares

McClintock, D.C. (1999). *The New Plantsman*, **6**(4): 208-13.

Saxifragaceae

Stocks, A. (1995). *Saxifragaceae*. Hardy Plant Society.

Schisandra

Whiteley, A. (1997). *The New Plantsman*, **4**(2): 88-97.

Sedum

Evans, R.L. (1983). *Handbook of Cultivated Sedums*. Ivory Head Press Motcombe, Dorset.

Hensen, K.J.W. & Groendijk-Wilders, N. (1986). *The Plantsman*, **8**(1): 1-20.

Stephenson, R. (1994). Sedum. Timber Press, Portland Oregon.

Sempervivum
Miklánek, M. (November 1998). *The List of Cultivars: Sempervivum and Jovibarba.* M. Miklánek, Piestany, Slovakia @ http://members.tripod.com/~miklanek/MCS/cv. html.
Mitchell, P.J. (1985). *International Cultivar Register for Jovibarba, Rosularia, Sempervivum.* The Sempervivum Society, W. Sussex.
Shortia
Barnes, P.G. (1990). *The Plantsman,* 12(1): 23-34.
Sinningia
Dates, J.D. *The Gesneriad Register 1988: Check List of Sinningia.* American Gloxinia and Gesneriad Society, Galesburg, Illinois.
Skimmia
Brown, P.D. (1980). *The Plantsman,* 1(4): 224-59.
Solenostemon
Pedley, W.K. & Pedley, R. (1974). *Coleus - A Guide to Cultivation and Identification.* Bartholemew, Edinburgh.
Sophora
Hutchins, G. (1993). *The Plantsman,* 15(1): 1-13.
Sorbus
McAllister, H.A. (1985). *The Plantsman,* 6(4): 248-55.
McAllister, H.A. (1996). *The Garden,* 121(9): 561-67.
Rushforth, K. (1991). *The Plantsman,* 13(2): 111-24.
Rushforth, K. (1992). *The Plantsman,* 13(4): 226-42 & 14(1): 54-62.
Wright, D. (1981). *The Plantsman,* 3(2): 65-98.
Streptocalyx
Innes, C. (1993). *The Plantsman,* 15(2): 73-81.
Streptocarpus
Arnold, P. *The Gesneriad Register 1979: Check List of Streptocarpus.* American Gloxinia and Gesneriad Society, Binghamton, New York.
Sutherlandia
Schrire, B.D & Andrews, S. (1992). *The Plantsman,* 14(2): 65-69.
Syringa
Fiala, Fr J.L. (1988). *Lilacs.* Christopher Helm, Bromley, Kent.
Rogers, O.M. (1976). *Tentative International Register of Cultivar Names in the Genus Syringa.* University of New Hampshire.
Taylor, J. (1990). *The Plantsman,* 11(4): 225-40.
Vrugtman, F. (1976-83). *Bulletin of the American Association of Botanical Gardens and Arboreta.*
Tilia
Muir, N. (1984). *The Plantsman,* 5(4): 206-42.
Muir, N. (1988). *The Plantsman,* 10(2): 104-27.
Tillandsia
Kiff, L.F. (1991). *A Distributional Checklist of the Genus Tillandsia.* Botanical Diversions, Encino, California.
Tricyrtis
Chesters, J. & Lanyon, J. (1996). *The Garden,* 121(9): 536-9.
Matthew, B. (1985). *The Plantsman,* 6(4): 193-224.
Trillium
Case, F.W. & Case, R.B. (1997). *Trilliums.* Timber Press, Portland, Oregon.

Jacobs, D.L. & Jacobs, R.L. (1997). *American Treasures.* Eco-Gardens, Decatur, Georgia.
Mitchell, R.J. (1989-92). *The Plantsman,* 10(4): 216-31, 11(2 & 3): 67-79 & 132-51, 12(1): 44-60, 13(4): 219-25.
Tulbaghia
Benham, S. (1993). *The Plantsman,* 15(2): 89-110.
Tulipa
Classified List and International Register of Tulip Names. (1987). Royal General Bulbgrowers' Association, Hillegom, Holland.
Ulmus
Green, P.S. (1964). Registration of the Cultivar Names in *Ulmus. Arnoldia,* 24(608). Arnold Arboretum, Harvard, Massachusetts.
Umbelliferae see Apiaceae
Veratrum
Mathew, B. (1989). *The Plantsman,* 11(1): 34-61.
Viola
Coombs, R.E. 1981 *Violets.* Croom Helm, London.
Farrar, E. (1989). *Pansies, Violas & Sweet Violets.* Hurst Village Publishing, Reading.
Fuller, R. (1990). *Pansies, Violas & Violettas.* Crowood Press, Marlborough, Wiltshire.
Perfect, E.G. (1996). *Armand Millet and his Violets.* Park Farm Press, High Wycombe, Bucks.
Zambra, G.L. (2nd ed. 1950). *Violets for Garden and Market.* Collingridge, London.
Vitis
Pearkes, G. (1989). *Vine Growing in Britain.* Dent, London.
Robinson, J. (1986). *Vines, Grapes and Wines.* Mitchell Beazley, London.
Watsonia
Goldblatt, P. (1989). *The Genus* Watsonia. National Botanic Gardens, South Africa.
Weigela
Howard, R.A. (1965). A Check-list of Cultivar Names in *Weigela. Arnoldia,* 25(9-11). Arnold Arboretum, Harvard, Massachusetts.
Taylor, J. (1990). *The Plantsman,* 11(4): 225-40.
Wisteria
McMillan-Browse, P. (1984). *The Plantsman,* 6(2): 109-22.
Valder, P. (1995). *Wisterias.* Florilegium, Balmain, N.S.W., Australia.
Zantedeschia
Toogood, A. & Mattin, A. (1998). *The Garden,* 123(3): 176-79.
Zauschneria (Epilobium).
Raven, P.H. (1976). *Annals of the Missouri Botanic Garden,* 63 326-340.
Zelkova
Ainsworth, P. (1989). *The Plantsman,* 11(2): 80-86.
Hunt, D. (1994). *I.D.S. Yearbook 1993,* 33-41. International Dendrology Society, Sherborne, Dorset.
Muir, N. (1991). *The Plantsman,* 13(2): 125-26.

INTERNATIONAL PLANT FINDERS

AUSTRALIA

Hibbert, Margaret (comp.). (2nd ed. 1998) *The Aussie Plant Finder 1998/99.* ISBN 1-876314-04-4. Lists around 30,000 plants available from almost 500 specialist nurseries throughout Australia. Orders: Florilegium, PO Box 644, Rozelle, NSW 2041, Australia. T +61 (0)2 9555 8589 F +61 (0)2 9818 4409. Website www.florilegium.com.au

CANADA

Ashley, A. & P. (comp.). (1996/97). *The Canadian Plant Source Book.* ISBN 0-9694566-2-X. 21,000 hardy plants available at retail and wholesale nurseries across Canada, including those who ship to US. English common names & English & French cross-indexes. Orders: 93 Fentiman Avenue, Ottawa, ON, Canada, K1S OT7. T +1 613 730-0755. F +1 613 730-2095. E-mail apashley@cyberus.ca $20 (Canadian or US) inc. p&p. Add $5 for airmail.

GERMANY

Erhardt, A. & W. (comp.). (3rd ed. 1997). *PPP-Index, The European Plant Finder.* ISBN-3-8001-6621-6. 80,000 plants and seeds available from 1,200 European retail and wholesale nurseries. CD-ROM included. Orders: The Plant Press, 10 Market Street, Lewes, East Sussex, BN7 2NB, UK. T (01273) 476151. E-mail john@plantpress.com. £25. Or Verlag Eugen Ulmer, PO Box 70 05 61, D-70574 Stuttgart. T +49 711-4507-121. E-mail info@ulmer.de DM 58,00. Website: www.flora-garten.de/daten/ppp/ppp.html

ITALY

Feroni, F. C., & Volta, T. (comp.) & Mondadori, G. (ed.). (1996). *Il Cercapiante.* ISBN 88-374-1366-1. 15,000 plants from 400 nurseries including 100 specialist suppliers; 100 European nurseries; all Italian botanical and professional Associations, all Italian Garden Clubs, wide Bibliography. Orders: Via Andrea Ponti 10, 20143 Milano. T +39 (0)2 89166367. E-mail edgmonga@tin.it L. 25,000.

NETHERLANDS

Terra (2000/2001). *Plantenvinder voor de lage landen.* ISBN 90-6255-936-0. Approx. 50,000 plants and 150 nurseries. Orders: Uitgeverij Terra, POB 188, 7200 AD Zutphen, Netherlands. T +31 575 525222. F +31 575 525242. Dfl. 24.50.

NEW ZEALAND

Gaddum, Meg (comp). (1999). *Gaddum's Plant Finder 2000.* ISBN 0 473 06210 0. 30,000 plants and seeds from 2000 nurseries with retail outlets. Common names included and indexed. NZ$ 39.95 plus postage overseas.

Gaddum Meg (comp.) (1999). *The Trade Plant Finder 1999-2000.* No ISBN. 33,000 plants and seeds from 235 nurseries. Wholesale nurseries easily identified. Includes separate supplement containing 3,700 new plants. NZ$ 85.00 + postage overseas.

Gaddum, Meg (comp.). (est. 1998) www.plantfinder.co.nz. Updated monthly, this searchable database contains plant finder data. Public access free. Trade access by subscription.

Orders: New Zealand Plant Finder, PO Box 2237, Gisborne, NZ, or email meg@plantfinder.co.nz or fax +64 6 862 3111.

UNITED KINGDOM

Pawsey, A (ed). (18th ed 2000-2001) *Find that Rose!* Covers Autumn 2000-Spring 2001 lists over 3,000 varieties with basic type, colour and fragrance codes together with essential details of approx 65 UK growers. Includes other helpful information such as how to find a rose with a particular Christian name or to celebrate a special event and where to see roses in bloom. Incorporating rose discount voucher and details of growers able to take (HTA) National Garden Tokens. Orders: The Editor, 303 Mile End Road, Colchester, Essex CO4 5EA. SAE for info. or send a cheque for £2.75 made out to *Find That Rose!* for a copy

USA

Isaacson, R. (comp.). (4th ed. 1996). *The Andersen Horticultural Library's Source List of Plants and Seeds.* Approx. 59,000 plants and seeds from 450 retail & wholesale outlets in the US & Canada. All are prepared to ship interstate. Does not include Orchids, Cacti or Succulents.

Facciola, S. (ed.). (1998). *Cornucopia II - A Source Book of Edible Plants.* ISBN 0-9628087-2-5. A very substantial and comprehensive volume (713 pages) which documents 3,000 species of edible plants & 7,000 cultivars available in the US and abroad.

Orders: Kampong Publications, 1870 Sunrise Drive, Vista, California 92084. T +1 760 726-0990. US$40.00.

Barton, B. (comp.). (5th ed. 1997). *Gardening by Mail.* ISBN 0-395-87770-9. A directory of mail order resources for gardeners in the USA and Canada, including seed companies, nurseries, suppliers of all garden necessaries and ornaments, horticultural and plant societies, magazines, libraries and books. E-mail & web addresses included. For up-to-date version (2000) see website: www.virtualgarden.com and click on 'Find a source'. Orders: Houghton Miffin Co., 222 Berkeley Street, Boston, MA 02116. T +1 800 726-0600. E-mail tusker@ap.net US$24.

Shank, D. (ed.). (Vol 9, Issues 1&2, 1998). *Hortus West: A Western North America Native Plant Directory & Journal.* Issn 1085 7095. Directory lists 2,500 western native species commercially available through 200 native plant vendors in eleven Western United States and two Canadian provinces.

Hill, Susan & Narizny, Susan (comp.) (2000) *The Pacific North West Plant Locator 2000/2001.* ISBN 0-967 4907-1-5. To be published spring 2000, will cover Oregon, Washington and Idaho, complete nursery information, how to contact nurseries and purchase plants and will add a common name/botanical name index. Plant listings only (no seeds). Orders: Black-Eyed Susans Press, PMB 227, 6327-C, SW Capitol Highway, Portland, OR 97201-1937, USA. Email bespress@aol.com. Price US$19.95 plus $4.00 p+p (USA) or $10.00 (outside USA). Website www.blackeyedsusanspress.com

Burch, Derek (comp.) & Galletta, Kay (ed.) *PlantFinder.* A monthly magazine produced for the wholesale nursery and landscape industry to provide current listings of plants and plant-related materials in the southern United States. Orders: Betrock Information Systems Inc., 7770 Davie Road Extension, Hollywood, Florida 33024-2516. Subscription cost US $59.95. Email betrock@betrock.com. Website www.hortworld.com

New England Wild Flower Society. (1999). *Sources of Propagated Native Plants and Wildflowers.* Source list of US nurseries selling nursery propagated, North American native plants and seeds. 75 nurseries listed. US $3.50 plus $1 postage. *New England Wild Flower Society Seed & Book Catalogue,* lists for sale 225-250 North American wildflower seeds. US $2.50 plus $1.75 postage. Orders: New England Wild Flower Society, Garden in the Woods, 180 Hemenway Road, Framingham, MA 01701-2699. E-mail newfs.org Website: http://www.newfs.org

Nurseries

The following nurseries stock between them
an unrivalled choice of plants but before making
a visit, please remember to check with the nursery
that the plant you seek is currently available.

NURSERIES CODES AND SYMBOLS

GEOGRAPHICAL KEY TO CODES

The first letter of each nursery code represents the area of the country in which the nursery is situated.

C SOUTH WEST

Bath & NE Somerset, Bournemouth, Channel Islands, City of Bristol, City of Plymouth, Cornwall, Devon, Dorset, Isles of Scilly, Poole, North Somerset, Somerset, South Gloucestershire, Swindon,Torbay, Wiltshire.

E EASTERN ENGLAND

Cambridgeshire, City of Peterborough, Essex, Lincolnshire, Norfolk, North Lincolnshire, NE Lincolnshire, Southend-on-Sea, Suffolk, Thurrock.

G SCOTLAND

All Scottish counties plus Orkney, Shetland.

I IRELAND

Northern Ireland & the Republic of Ireland.

L LONDON AREA

Nedfordshire, Bracknell Forest, Buckinghamshire, Hertfordshire, London, Luton, Middlesex, Milton Keynes, Reading, Slough, Surrey, West Berkshire, Windsor & Maidenhead, Wokingham.

M MIDLANDS

Birmingham, Cheshire, City of Derby, City of Leicester, City of Nottingham, City of Stoke-on-Trent, Coventry, Derbyshire, Dudley, Isle of Man, Leicestershire, Northamptonshire, Nottinghamshire, Oxfordshire, Rutland, Sandwell, Solihull, Staffordshire, Walsall, Warwickshire, Wirral, Wolverhampton.

N NORTHERN

Barnsley, Blackburn with Darwen, Bolton, Bradford, Bury,Calderdale, City of Kingston-upon-Hull, Cumbria, Darlington, Doncaster, Durham, East Riding of Yorkshire, Gateshead, Halton, Hartlepool, Kirklees, Knowlsley, Lancashire, Leeds, Liverpool, Manchester, Middlesborough, Newcastle-upon-Tyne, North Tyneside, North Yorkshire, Northumberland, Oldham, Redcar & Cleveland, Rochdale, Rotherham, St Helens, Salford, Sheffield, South Tyneside, Stockport, Stockton-on-Tees, Sunderland, Tameside, Trafford, Wakefield, Warrington, Wigan,York.

S SOUTHERN

Brighton & Hove, City of Portsmouth, City of Southampton, East Sussex, Hampshire, Isle of Wight, Kent, Medway, West Sussex.

W WALES AND THE WEST

All Welsh counties plus Gloucestershire (but not South Gloucestershire), Herefordshire, Shropshire, Telford & Wrekin, Worcestershire.

X ABROAD

KEY TO NURSERY SYMBOLS

⊠   Mail Order to UK or EU

✈   Exports beyond EU

Ⓐ   Also supplies Wholesale

◆   See Display advertisement

€   Euro accepted

Please, never use an old edition

HOW TO USE THE NURSERY LISTINGS

NURSERY DETAILS BY CODE (*page 796*)

The details given for each nursery have been compiled from information supplied to us in answer to a questionnaire. In some cases, because of constraints of space, the entries have been slightly abbreviated and blanks have been left where no information has been provided.

Each nursery is allocated a code, for example SLan. The first letter of each code indicates the main area of the country in which the nursery is situated. In this example, S=Southern England. The remaining three letters reflect the nursery's name, in this case Langley Boxwood Nursery in Hampshire.

In this main listing the nurseries are given in alphabetical order of codes for quick reference from the Plant Directory. All of the nurseries' details, such as address, opening times, mail order service etc., will be found here. If you wish to visit any of these nurseries you can find its location on the relevant map (following p.921), unless the nursery has requested this is not shown (this usually applies to mail order only nurseries).

OPENING TIMES

The word 'daily' implies every day including Sunday and Bank Holidays. Although opening times have been published as submitted and where applicable, it is always advisable, especially if travelling a long distance, to check with the nursery first. The initials NGS indicate that the nursery is open under the National Gardens Scheme.

MAIL ORDER - UK & EU

Many nurseries provide a mail order service which, in many cases, now extends to all members of the European Union. Where it is shown that there is 'No minimum charge' (Nmc) it should be realised that to send even one plant may involve the nursery in substantial postage and packing costs. Even so, some nurseries may not be prepared to send tender or bulky plants.

EXPORT

Export refers to mail order beyond the European Union. Nurseries that are prepared to consider exporting are indicated. However, there is usually a substantial minimum charge and, in addition, all the costs of Phytosanitary Certificates and Customs have to be met by the purchaser.

CATALOGUE COST

Some nurseries offer their catalogue free, or for a few stamps (the odd value quoted can usually be made up from a combination of first or second class stamps), but a large (at least A5) stamped addressed envelope is always appreciated as well. Overseas customers should use an equivalent number of International Reply Coupons (IRCs) in place of stamps.

WHOLESALE OR RETAIL

All nurseries listed in the *RHS Plant Finder* provide a retail service. Many retailers also have a wholesale trade and would frequently be prepared to offer discounts for large single orders.

SPECIALIST NURSERIES (*page 911*)

This list of nurseries has been introduced to help those with an interest in finding specialist categories of plant. Nurseries have been asked to classify themselves under one or more headings where this represents the type of plant they *predominantly* or *exclusively* have in stock. For example, if you wish to find a nursery specialising in ornamental grasses, look up 'Grasses' in the listing where you will find a list of nursery codes. Then turn to the Nursery Details by Code, for details of the nurseries.

Please note that not all nurseries shown here will have plants listed in the Plant Directory. This may be their choice or because the *RHS Plant Finder* does not list seeds or annuals and only terrestrial orchids and hardy cacti. For space reasons, it is rare to find a nursery's full catalogue listed in the Plant Directory.

In all cases, please ensure you ring to confirm the range available before embarking on a journey to the nursery.

The specialist plant groups listed in this edition are:

Acid loving	Fruit
Alpines/rock	Grasses
Aquatics	Hedging
Bamboos	Herbs
Bulbous plants	Orchids
Cacti & succulents	Ornamental trees
Carnivorous	Seed
Climbers	Specimen-sized plants
Conifers	Topiary
Conservatory	Wild flowers
Ferns	

Perennials and shrubs have been omitted as these are considered to be too general and serviced by a great proportion of the nurseries.

Nursery Index by Name

For convenience, an alphabetical index of nurseries is included on p.913. This gives the names of all nurseries listed in the book in alphabetical order of nursery name together with their code.

Deleted Nurseries

Every year a few nurseries ask to be deleted. This may be because they are about to move or close, or they are changing the way in which they trade. A small number do not reply and, as we have no current information concerning them, they are deleted.

Please, never use an old edition

USING THE THREE NURSERY LISTINGS

Your first reference from the Plant Directory is the Nursery Details by Code listing, which includes all relevant information for each nursery in order of nursery code. The Specialist Nurseries index is to aid those searching for a particular group of plants. The Nursery Index by Name is an alphabetical list for those who know a nursery's name but not its code and wish to check its details in the main list.

1 NURSERY DETAILS BY CODE

Once you have found your plant in the Plant Directory, turn to this list to find out the name, address, opening times and other details of the nurseries whose codes accompany the plant.

K E Y		
⊠ Mail order to UK or EU		
☒ Exports beyond EU	€ Euro accepted	
☒ Also supplies Wholesale	◆ See Display advertisement	

LLin

A geographical code is followed by three letters reflecting the nursery's name

LINCLUDEN NURSERY ⊠ EU ☒ ☒

Bisley Green, Bisley, Woking, Surrey GU24 9EN

☎ (01483) 797005   **Fax:** (01483) 474015

Contact: Mr & Mrs J A Tilbury

Opening Times: 0930-1630 Mon-Sat all year excl. B/hols.

Min. Mail Order UK: No minimum charge

Min. Mail Order EU: Nmc

Cat. Cost: 3 x 1st class

Credit Cards: Visa, MasterCard

Specialities: Dwarf, slow-growing & unusual conifers.

Map Ref: L, C3

Refer to the box at the base of alternate right-hand pages for a key to the symbols

A brief summary of the plants available plus any other special characteristics of the nursery

The map number is followed by the nursery's grid reference on the map

2 SPECIALIST NURSERIES

A list of 21categories under which nurseries have classified themselves if they exclusively, or predominantly, supply this range of plants.

CONIFERS

CKen CLnd CSli CTho
ECho EHul EMac EOrn
EPot GChr GPin GTre
LBee LCon LLin MAsh
MBar MGos NAsh NMoo
NOGN SCoo SCrf SLim
SRum WGor

3 NURSERY INDEX BY NAME

If you seek a particular nursery, look it up in this alphabetical index. Note its code and turn to the Nursery Details by Code list for more information.

NURSERY DETAILS BY CODE

Please note that all these nurseries are listed in alphabetical order by their code. All nurseries are listed in alphabetical order by their name in the **Nursery Index by Name** on page 913.

SOUTH WEST

CAbb   **ABBOTSBURY SUB-TROPICAL GARDENS** ⊠ EU
Abbotsbury, Nr Weymouth, Dorset DT3 4LA
☎ (01305) 871344
Fax: (01305) 871344
E-mail: gardens@abbotsbury.co.uk
Contact: David Sutton
Opening Times: 1000-1800 daily mid Mar-1st Nov. 1000-1500 Nov-mid Mar.
Min. Mail Order UK: £10.00 + p&p
Min. Mail Order EU: £20.00 + p&p
Cat. Cost: £2 + A4 Sae + 42p stamp
Credit Cards: Access, Visa, MasterCard, Switch.
Specialities: Less common & tender shrubs incl. palms, tree ferns, bamboos & plants from Australia, New Zealand & South Africa.
Map Ref: C, C5

CAbP   **ABBEY PLANTS**
Chaffeymoor, Bourton, Gillingham, Dorset SP8 5BY
☎ (01747) 840841
Contact: K Potts
Opening Times: 1000-1300 & 1400-1700 Tue-Sat Mar-Nov. Dec-Feb by appt.
Mail Order: None
Cat. Cost: 2 x 2nd class
Credit Cards: None
Specialities: Flowering trees & shrubs. Shrub roses incl. many unusual varieties.
Map Ref: C, B5

CAbx   **ABRAXAS GARDENS** ⊠ EU
7 Little Keyford Lane, Frome, Somerset BA11 5BB
☎ (01373) 472879
Contact: Duncan Skene
Opening Times: Daylight hours by appt.

Fri, Sat & Sun Apr-Jul 2000, Mar-Oct 2001.
Min. Mail Order UK: No minimum charge
Min. Mail Order EU: Nmc
Cat. Cost: Free
Credit Cards: None
Specialities: *Aster, Crocosmia, Iris sibirica, Hemerocallis* (spiders, spider variants & unusual forms). Many recent introductions available only in small numbers.
Map Ref: C, B5

CAgr   **AGROFORESTRY RESEARCH TRUST** ⊠ UK
46 Hunters Moon, Dartington, Totnes, Devon TQ9 6JT
E-mail: agrorestr@aol.com
Web Site: http://members.aol.com/-agrorestr/homepage.html
Contact: Martin Crawford
Opening Times: Not open. Mail order only.
Min. Mail Order UK: No minimum charge
Cat. Cost: 3 x 1st class
Credit Cards: None
Specialities: Mostly trees, shrubs & perennials. *Alnus, Berberis, Amelanchier, Carya, Elaeagnus, Juglans, Pinus, Quercus & Salix.* Also seeds.

CArn   **ARNE HERBS** ⊠ EU ☒ ☒
Limeburn Nurseries, Limeburn Hill, Chew Magna, Avon BS40 8QW
☎ (01275) 333399   Fax: (01275) 333399
E-mail: lyman@lymandixon.freeserve.co.uk
Contact: A Lyman-Dixon & Jenny Thomas
Opening Times: Most times, please check first.
Min. Mail Order UK: No minimum charge
Min. Mail Order EU: Nmc
Cat. Cost: £2.00 UK, 6 x IRC refundable on first order.
Credit Cards: None
Specialities: Herbs, wild flowers & cottage flowers.
Map Ref: C, A5

CAsh   **ASHFIELD COURT NURSERIES** ⊠ EU ☒ €
Farringdon, North Petherton, Somerset TA6 6PF

☎ (01278) 663438   **Fax:** (01278) 663438
E-mail: michael@michieli.fsnet.co.uk
Contact: Michael Michieli
Opening Times: 1000-1400 Wed, 1430-
1700 Sun Apr-Oct. Other times by appt.
Min. Mail Order UK: No minimum charge
Min. Mail Order EU: Nmc
Cat. Cost: 2 x 1st class
Credit Cards: None
Specialities: National Collection of *Verbena*.
Map Ref: C, B4

CAvo   AVON BULBS ✉ EU ◪
Burnt House Farm, Mid-Lambrook, South
Petherton, Somerset TA13 5HE
☎ (01460) 242177
Web Site: www.avonbulbs.com
Contact: C Ireland-Jones
Opening Times: Thu, Fri, Sat mid Sep-end
Oct & mid Feb-end Mar for collection of
pre-booked orders.
Min. Mail Order UK: £10.00 + p&p
Min. Mail Order EU: £20.00 + p&p
Cat. Cost: 4 x 2nd class
Credit Cards: Visa, Access
Specialities: Smaller & unusual bulbs.
Map Ref: C, B5

CAxe   AXE VALLEY PENSTEMONS
Blue Firs, Wessiters, Seaton, Devon EX12 2PJ
☎ (01297) 625342   **Fax:** (01297) 24085
E-mail: Sher.Bluefirs@btinternet.com
Contact: Mrs S K Reynolds
Opening Times: 1400-1700 Thu Jun-Aug.
Other times by appt.
Mail Order: None
Cat. Cost: Free plant list
Credit Cards: None
Specialities: *Penstemon*. National Collection
of *Penstemon* cultivars.
Map Ref: C, C4

CB&S   BURNCOOSE & SOUTH DOWN
NURSERIES ✉ EU ◪ ◪
Gwennap, Redruth, Cornwall TR16 6BJ
☎ (01209) 860316   **Fax:** (01209) 860011
E-mail: burncoose@eclipse.co.uk
Web Site: www.eclipse.co.uk/burncoose
Contact: C H Williams
Opening Times: 0830-1700 Mon-Sat &
1100-1700 Sun.
Min. Mail Order UK: No minimum charge
Min. Mail Order EU: Nmc*
Cat. Cost: £1.50 incl. p&p
Credit Cards: Visa, Access, Switch
Specialities: Extensive range of over 3000
ornamental trees & shrubs and herbaceous.
Rare & unusual *Magnolia, Rhododendron*.
Conservatory plants. 30 acre garden.

*Note: individual quotations for EU sales.
Map Ref: C, D1

CBdn   ANN & ROGER BOWDEN ✉ EU ◆ ◪
Cleave House, Sticklepath, Okehampton,
Devon EX20 2NL
☎ (01837) 840481   **Fax:** (01837) 840482
E-mail: bowdenshosta@eclipse.co.uk
Web Site: www.hostas-uk.com
Contact: Ann & Roger Bowden
Opening Times: By appt. only.
Min. Mail Order UK: No minimum charge
Min. Mail Order EU: Nmc
Cat. Cost: 3 x 1st class
Credit Cards: Visa, Access, EuroCard, Switch
Specialities: *Hosta* only. National Collection
of modern hybrid hostas.
Map Ref: C, C3

CBel   BELMONT HOUSE NURSERY
Little Horton, Devizes, Wiltshire SN10 3LJ
☎ (01380) 860510
Contact: Gordon Cottis
Opening Times: By appt. Please phone.
Mail Order: None
Cat. Cost: 2 x 2nd class
Credit Cards: None
Specialities: *Helleborus* hybrids & true
species, *Galanthus, Digitalis, Geranium,
Pulmonaria*, other hardy perennials.
Map Ref: C, A6

CBen   BENNETT'S WATER LILY FARM ✉ EU ◪
Putton Lane, Chickerell, Weymouth,
Dorset DT3 4AF
☎ (01305) 785150   **Fax:** (01305) 781619
E-mail: JB@waterlily.co.uk
Web Site: www.waterlily.co.uk
Contact: J Bennett
Opening Times: Tue-Sun Apr-Aug, Tue-Sat
Sept & Mar.
Min. Mail Order UK: £25.00 + p&p*
Min. Mail Order EU: £25.00 + p&p
Cat. Cost: Sae for price list
Credit Cards: Visa, Access, MasterCard, Switch
Specialities: Aquatic plants. National
Collection of water lilies.
*Note: mail order Apr-Sep only.
Map Ref: C, C5

CBla   BLACKMORE & LANGDON LTD ✉ EU ◪
Pensford, Bristol, Avon BS39 4JL
☎ (01275) 332300   **Fax:** (01275) 332300/

C

(01275) 331207
Contact: J S Langdon
Opening Times: 0900-1700 Mon-Sat,
1000-1600 Sun.
Min. Mail Order UK: No minimum charge
Min. Mail Order EU: Nmc
Cat. Cost: Sae
Credit Cards: MasterCard, Visa, Switch
Specialities: *Phlox, Delphinium* & *Begonia*.
Also seeds.
Map Ref: C, A5

CBlo   **BLOUNTS COURT NURSERIES**
Studley, Calne, Wiltshire SN11 9NH
☎ (01249) 812103   **Fax:** (01249) 812103
Contact: Mrs P E Rendell
Opening Times: 0900-1700 Mon, Tues, Fri
& Sat Nov-Feb, 0900-1800 Apr-Jul, 0900-
1730 Aug-Oct. 1030-1630 Sun all year.
Mail Order: None
Cat. Cost: None available.
Credit Cards: Visa, Access, Switch
Specialities: Wide range of shrubs, fruit &
ornamental trees, conifers, roses, container &
open ground. *Clematis,* climbers, herbaceous
incl. unusual varieties.
Map Ref: C, A6

CBod   **BODMIN PLANT AND HERB NURSERY**
Laveddon Mill, Laninval Hill, Bodmin,
Cornwall PL30 5JU
☎ (01208) 72837   **Fax:** (01208) 76491
Contact: Sarah Wilks
Opening Times: 0900-1800 (or dusk) 7 days.
Mail Order: None
Cat. Cost: 2 x 1st class for herb and/or hardy
Geranium list.
Credit Cards: MasterCard, Visa, Switch, Solo
Specialities: Herbs, herbaceous & grasses,
aquatic, marginal & bog plants, plus
interesting range of shrubs.
Map Ref: C, C2

CBos   **BOSVIGO PLANTS**
Bosvigo House, Bosvigo Lane, Truro,
Cornwall TR1 3NH
☎ (01872) 275774   **Fax:** (01872) 275774
Contact: Wendy Perry
Opening Times: 1100-1800 Thu-Sat
Mar-end Sep.
Mail Order: None
Cat. Cost: 4 x 1st class
Credit Cards: None
Specialities: Rare & unusual herbaceous.
Map Ref: C, D1

CBot   **THE BOTANIC NURSERY** ✉ UK ▣
(Office) Bath Road, Atworth, Nr Melksham,
Wiltshire SN12 8NU

☎ (01225) 706597, mobile 07850 328756
Fax: (01225) 700953
E-mail: info at the Botanic Nursery com.
Web Site: www.The Botanic Nursery.com
Contact: T & M Baker
Opening Times: 1000-1700 Fri & Sat plus
themed openings - send for details. Closed Jan.
Min. Mail Order UK: 30p Sae for mail order
lists.
Cat. Cost: £1.00 coin
Credit Cards: Visa, Access
Specialities: Rare hardy shrubs & perennials
for lime soils. *Eryngium, Papavera orientale*
cultivars, *Delphinium*. National Collection of
Digitalis. Note: nursery & plant sales address
Cottles Lane, Nr Stonar School, Atworth, Nr
Melksham, Wilts.
Map Ref: C, A5

CBrd   **BROADLEAS GARDENS LTD**
Broadleas, Devizes, Wiltshire SN10 5JQ
☎ (01380) 722035   **Fax:** (01380) 722035
Contact: Lady Anne Cowdray
Opening Times: 1400-1800 Wed, Thu &
Sun Apr-Oct.
Mail Order: None
Cat. Cost: 1 x 1st class
Credit Cards: None
Specialities: General range.
Map Ref: C, A6

CBre   **BREGOVER PLANTS** ✉ EU
Hillbrooke, Middlewood, North Hill, Nr
Launceston, Cornwall PL15 7NN
☎ (01566) 782661
Contact: Jennifer Bousfield
Opening Times: 1100-1700 Wed-Fri Mar-
mid Oct and by appt.
Min. Mail Order UK: No minimum charge*
Min. Mail Order EU: Nmc
Cat. Cost: 2 x 1st class
Credit Cards: None
Specialities: Unusual hardy perennials grown
in small garden nursery.
*Note: mail order Oct-Mar only.
Map Ref: C, C2

CBrm   **BRAMLEY LODGE GARDEN NURSERY**
Beech Tree Lane, Ipplepen, Newton Abbot,
Devon TQ12 5TW
☎ (01803) 813265
E-mail: bramleylodge@btinternet.com
Web Site:
www.btinternet.com/~bramleylodge.nursery
Contact: Susan Young
Opening Times: 1000-1600 Thu-Sun Mar-
Oct, 1000-1600 Sun Nov-Feb.
Mail Order: None
Cat. Cost: 3 x 1st class

Credit Cards: None
Speciality: Grasses. Also trees, shrubs &
perennials. Several small model themed
gardens.
Map Ref: C, C3

CBro   BROADLEIGH GARDENS ✉ EU
Bishops Hull, Taunton, Somerset TA4 1AE
☎ (01823) 286231   Fax: (01823) 323646
E-mail: cats@broadleighbulbs.co.uk
Web Site: www.broadleighbulbs.co.uk
Contact: Lady Skelmersdale
Opening Times: 0900-1600 Mon-Fri for
viewing only. Orders collected if prior notice
given.
Min. Mail Order UK: No minimum charge
Min. Mail Order EU: Nmc
Cat. Cost: 2 x 1st class
Credit Cards: Visa, MasterCard
Speciality: Jan catalogue: bulbs in growth
(*Galanthus, Cyclamen* etc.) & herbaceous.
June catalogue: dwarf & unusual bulbs.
National Collection of Alec Grey hybrid
daffodils.
Map Ref: C, B4

CBrP   BROOKLANDS PLANTS ✉ EU 🅱
25 Treves Road, Dorchester, Dorset
DT1 2HE
☎ (01305) 265846
E-mail: IanWatt@quicklink.freeserve.co.uk
Contact: Ian Watt
Opening Times: By appt. for collection of
plants only.
Min. Mail Order UK: £25.00 + p&p
Min. Mail Order EU: £25.00 + p&p
Cat. Cost: 2 x 2nd class
Credit Cards: None
Speciality: Palm & cycad seedlings &
young plants. Over 100 of the more hardy
species grown. Some specimen sized plants &
other distinctive foliage plants also available.
Hardy & half-hardy for the conservatory &
for indoors.
Map Ref: C, C5

CBur   BURNHAM NURSERIES ✉ EU 🅱🅱
Forches Cross, Newton Abbot,
Devon TQ12 6PZ
☎ (01626) 352233   Fax: (01626) 362167
E-mail: burnhamorchids@eclipse.co.uk
Web Site: www.eclipse.co.uk/burnhamorchids
Contact: Sara Rittershausen
Opening Times: 1000-1600 Mon-Sun.
Min. Mail Order UK: No minimum charge
Min. Mail Order EU: £100.00 + p&p
Cat. Cost: Large Sae + 40p stamp
Credit Cards: Visa, Switch, American
Express, MasterCard

Speciality: All types of orchid. Note: please
ask for details on export beyond EU.
Map Ref: C, C3

CCAT   CIDER APPLE TREES ✉ EU 🅱 €
(Office) 12 Tallowood, Shepton Mallet,
Somerset BA4 5QN
☎ (01749) 343368
Contact: Mr J Dennis
Opening Times: By appt. only.
Min. Mail Order UK: £6.00 + p&p
Min. Mail Order EU: £6.00 + p&p
Cat. Cost: Free
Credit Cards: None
Speciality: *Malus* (speciality standard trees).
Note: nursery is at Corkscrew Lane, Woolston.
Map Ref: C, B5

CCha   CHAPEL FARM HOUSE NURSERY
Halwill Junction, Beaworthy, Devon
EX21 5UF
☎ (01409) 221594
Contact: Robin or Toshie Hull
Opening Times: 0900-1700 Tue-Sat, 1000-
1600 Sun & B/hol Mons.
Mail Order: None
Cat. Cost: None issued.
Credit Cards: None
Speciality: Plants from Japan. Also
herbaceous. Japanese garden design service
offered.
Map Ref: C, C3

CChe   CHERRY TREE NURSERY 🅱
(Sheltered Work Opportunities), off New
Road Roundabout, Northbourne,
Bournemouth, Dorset BH10 7DA
☎ (01202) 593537 (01202) 590840
Fax: (01202) 590626
Contact: Stephen Jailler
Opening Times: 0830-1530 Mon-Fri,
0900-1200 most Sats.
Mail Order: None
Cat. Cost: A4 Sae + 2 x 2nd class
Credit Cards: None
Speciality: Hardy shrubs.
Map Ref: C, C6

**CCHP   COTSWOLD HARDY PLANTS LTD
✉ EU 🅱🅱**
Wibble Farm, West Quantoxhead, Nr
Taunton, Somerset TA4 4DD
☎ (01984) 632303   Fax: (01984) 633168
Contact: Mrs M L Francis
Opening Times: 0800-1700 Mon-Fri, 1000-
1600 Sat. All year excl. B/hols.
Min. Mail Order UK: No minimum charge
Min. Mail Order EU: Nmc
Cat. Cost: 2 x 1st class

C

Credit Cards: MasterCard, Switch, Visa
Specialities: Growers of a wide range of
hardy plants, many rare & unusual.
Map Ref: C, B4

CCol   COLD HARBOUR NURSERY ✉ UK
(Office) 19 Hilary Road, Poole, Dorset
BH17 7LZ
☎ (01202) 696875 evenings
E-mail: coldharbour@hilaryroad.freeserve.co.uk
Contact: Steve Saunders
Opening Times: 1000-1730 Tue-Fri & most
w/ends 1st Mar-end Oct.
Min. Mail Order UK: £6.00 + p&p
Cat. Cost: 3 x 2nd class
Credit Cards: None
Specialities: Unusual herbaceous perennials
incl. hardy *Geranium* & grasses. Note:
nursery is at Bere Road (opp. Silent Woman
Inn), Wareham, Dorset (no postal address).
Map Ref: C, B5

CCpl   CHAPEL-UNY NURSERY ✉ EU
Brane, Sancreed, Penzance,
Cornwall TR20 8RD
☎ (01736) 810649
Contact: Mr Charles Tricker
Opening Times: Not open.
Min. Mail Order UK: £20.00 + p&p
Min. Mail Order EU: £20.00 + p&p
Cat. Cost: 2 x 1st class
Credit Cards: None
Specialities: *Banksia, Protea* & other
Proteaceae, Agave, Aloe, Restio.
Map Ref: C, D1

CCtw   CHURCHTOWN NURSERIES ✉ UK
Gulval, Penzance, Cornwall TR18 3BE
☎ (01736) 362626   Fax: (01736) 362626
Contact: C Osborne
Opening Times: 1000-1700 Apr-Sep, 1000-
1600 Oct-Mar.
Min. Mail Order UK: No minimum charge
Cat. Cost: 1 x 1st class SAE for list.
Credit Cards: None
Specialities: Good, ever-increasing, range of
shrubs, herbaceous & tender perennials &
ornamental grasses incl. some of the more
unusual.
Map Ref: C, D1

CCuc   CUCKOO MILL NURSERY
Rose Ash, South Molton, Devon EX36 4RQ
☎ (01769) 550530
Contact: Peter Woollard
Opening Times: Most Sun & Wed Apr-Sep
but please phone first.
Mail Order: None
Cat. Cost: 3 x 1st class

Credit Cards: None
Specialities: Hardy ferns, grasses & *Astilbe*.
Shade & moisture loving plants.
Map Ref: C, B3

CCVT   CHEW VALLEY TREES ✉ UK ▣
Winford Road, Chew Magna,
Bristol BS40 8QE
☎ (01275) 333752   Fax: (01275) 333746
Contact: J Scarth
Opening Times: 0800-1700 Mon-Fri all
year. 0900-1600 Sat 2nd Sep-31st May.
Other times by appt.
Min. Mail Order UK: £5.00 + p&p*
Cat. Cost: Free
Credit Cards: Visa, MasterCard
Specialities: Native British trees & shrubs,
apple trees & hedging. *Note: max. plant
height for mail order 2.7m.
Map Ref: C, A5

**CDDB   DEVON & DORSET BAMBOO ✉ UK
▣ ◆**
(Office) 13 Morley Road, Exeter,
Devon EX4 7BD
☎ (01392) 422853   Fax: (01392) 422853
E-mail: tomgard@compuserve.com
Contact: Tom Gard
Opening Times: 1000-1730 Mon-Sat.
Phone first to ensure someone at nursery.
Min. Mail Order UK:
Cat. Cost: 1 x 1st or 2nd stamp.*
Credit Cards: None
Specialities: *Bamboo*. *Note: colour card
index available spring 2000, please phone for
details. Nursery located at Teign Valley
Nursery, Bridford, near Exeter EX6 7LB.
Map Ref: C, C3

CDev   DEVON VIOLET NURSERY ✉ EU ▣ ▣
Rattery, South Brent, Devon TQ10 9LG
☎ (01364) 643033   Fax: (01364) 643033
E-mail: devon.violets@virgin.net
Web Site: sweetviolets.co.uk
Contact: Joan & Michael Yardley
Opening Times: Oct 2000-June 2001.
Please ring first.
Min. Mail Order UK: 6 plants
Min. Mail Order EU: 6 plants
Cat. Cost: 2 x 2nd class
Credit Cards: Visa
Specialities: Violets & Parma violets.
National Collection of *Viola odorata*.
Map Ref: C, C3

CDob   SAMUEL DOBIE & SON ✉ UK
Long Road, Paignton, Devon TQ4 7SX
☎ (01803) 696411   Fax: (01803) 696450
Web Site: www.dobies.co.uk

Contact: Customer Services
Opening Times: 0830-1700 Mon-Fri
(office). Also answerphone.
Min. Mail Order UK: No minimum charge*
Cat. Cost: Free
Credit Cards: Visa, MasterCard, Switch,
Delta
Specialities: Wide selection of popular flower
& vegetable seeds. Also includes young
plants, summer flowering bulbs & garden
sundries. *Note: mail order to UK & Rep. of
Ireland only.

CDoC DUCHY OF CORNWALL ⊠ UK ◆
Penlyne Nursery, Cott Road, Lostwithiel,
Cornwall PL22 0HW
☎ (01208) 872668 Fax: (01208) 872835
E-mail: nursery@duchyofcornwall.gov.uk
Contact: Tracy Wilson
Opening Times: 0900-1700 Mon-Sat,
1000-1700 Sun. Closed B/hols.
Min. Mail Order UK: No minimum charge
Cat. Cost: Cat £2.00 (stamps or cheque)
Credit Cards: Visa, American Express,
Access, Switch, Delta
Specialities: Very wide range of all garden
plants incl. trees, shrubs, conifers, roses,
perennials, fruit & half-hardy exotics.
Map Ref: C, C2

CDul DULFORD NURSERIES ⊠ UK 🔲
Cullompton, Devon EX15 2DG
☎ (01884) 266361 Fax: (01884) 266663
Contact: David & Mary Barrow
Opening Times: 0730-1630 Mon-Fri.
Min. Mail Order UK: £20.00 + min £17.50
for carrier.
Cat. Cost: Free
Credit Cards: None
Specialities: Native, ornamental & unusual
trees & shrubs incl. oaks, maples, beech,
birch, chestnut, ash, lime, *Sorbus* & pines.
Map Ref: C, C4

CEgg EGGESFORD GARDENS ⊠ EU
Eggesford, Chulmleigh, Devon EX18 7QU
☎ (01769) 580250 Fax: (01769) 581041
Contact: Jonathon Parish, Peter Burks
Opening Times: 0900-1700 7 days excl.
Xmas, Boxing & New Year's Day.
Min. Mail Order UK: £15.00 + p&p
Min. Mail Order EU: £20.00 + p&p
Cat. Cost: £3.00 in stamps
Credit Cards: MasterCard, Visa, Switch,
Delta, American Express
Specialities: Wide general range. Strong in
shrubs, herbaceous, roses, *Clematis* & ivy.
Map Ref: C, B3

CElm ELM TREE NURSERY ⊠ UK
Court Farm, Sidbury, Sidmouth, Devon
EX10 0QG
☎ (01395) 597790 Fax: (01395) 597790
Contact: M Saunders
Opening Times: Not open to the public.
Min. Mail Order UK: £7.50 + p&p
Cat. Cost: 1 x 1st class
Credit Cards: None
Specialities: Hardy *Cyclamen*.

CElw ELWORTHY COTTAGE PLANTS
Elworthy Cottage, Elworthy, Lydeard St
Lawrence, Taunton, Somerset TA4 3PX
☎ (01984) 656427 Fax: (01984) 656427
E-mail: elworthycottage@care4free.net.uk
Web Site:
www.elworthycottage@care4free.net.uk
Contact: Mrs J M Spiller
Opening Times: 1000-1600 Tue, Thu & Fri
mid Mar-mid Oct & by appt.
Mail Order: None
Cat. Cost: 3 x 2nd class
Credit Cards: None
Specialities: *Clematis* & unusual herbaceous
plants esp. hardy *Geranium, Geum,* grasses,
*Campanula, Erysimum, Pulmonaria,
Origanum, Astrantia* & *Viola.* Note: nursery
on B3188, 5 miles north of Wiveliscombe.
Map Ref: C, B4

CEnd ENDSLEIGH GARDENS ⊠ UK 🔲 ◆
Milton Abbot, Tavistock, Devon PL19 0PG
☎ (01822) 870235 Fax: (01822) 870513
E-mail: Treemail@endsleigh-gardens.com
Contact: Michael Taylor
Opening Times: 0800-1700 Mon-Sat.
1400-1700 Sun excl. Dec & Jan.
Min. Mail Order UK: £12.00 + p&p
Cat. Cost: 2 x 1st class
Credit Cards: Visa, Access, Switch,
MasterCard
Specialities: Choice & unusual trees &
shrubs incl. *Acer* & *Cornus* cvs. Old apples &
cherries. Grafting service.
Map Ref: C, C3

CEqu EQUATORIAL PLANT CO. (VIREYAS) ⊠ EU
The White Cottage, Three Gates, Leigh, Nr
Sherborne, Dorset DT9 6JQ
☎ (01963) 210309 Fax: (01833) 690519
Contact: Blair & Jackie Sibun
Opening Times: By appt.
Min. Mail Order UK: No minimum charge

C

Min. Mail Order EU: Nmc
Cat. Cost: Free
Credit Cards: Visa, Access
Specialities: Vireya rhododendrons.

CFai   FAIRHAVEN NURSERY ✉ EU
Clapworthy Cross, Chittlehampton,
Umberleigh, Devon EX37 9QT
☎ (01769) 540528
Contact: Derek & Pauline Burdett
Opening Times: 1000-1600 all year, but
please check first.
Min. Mail Order UK: £10.00 + p&p
Min. Mail Order EU: £20.00 + p&p
Cat. Cost: 2 x 1st class
Credit Cards: None
Specialities: Propagate & grow a wide
selection of the more unusual varieties of
hardy trees, shrubs & perennials. Many
grown in small batches that may not be ready
to despatch at time of request. Orders will be
taken for delivery when available.
Map Ref: C, B3

CFee   FEEBERS HARDY PLANTS ✉ UK ◆
1 Feeber Cottage, Westwood, Broadclyst,
Nr Exeter, Devon EX5 3DQ
☎ (01404) 822118
Contact: Mrs E Squires
Opening Times: By prior appt. only during
2000.
Min. Mail Order UK: Limited mail order
Cat. Cost: Sae + 36p stamp
Credit Cards: None
Specialities: Plants for wet clay soils, alpines
& hardy perennials incl. those raised by
Amos Perry.
Map Ref: C, C4

CFil   FILLAN'S PLANTS ✉ EU ▣ ▣
Tuckermarsh Gardens, Tamar Lane, Bere
Alston, Devon PL20 7HN
☎ (01822) 855050   Fax: (01822) 841551
Contact: Mark Fillan
Opening Times: By appt. only.
Min. Mail Order UK: £20.00 + p&p
Min. Mail Order EU: £50.00 + p&p
Cat. Cost: 3 x 1st class
Credit Cards: None
Specialities: Ferns & *Hydrangea.*
Map Ref: C, C3

CFir   FIR TREE FARM NURSERY ✉ EU
Tresahor, Constantine, Falmouth, Cornwall
TR11 5PL
☎ (01326) 340593   Fax: (01326) 340593
E-mail: ftfnur@aol.com
Web Site: http://members.aol.com/ftfnur
Contact: Jim Cave

Opening Times: 1000-1700 Thu-Sun 1st
Mar-30th Sep.
Min. Mail Order UK: £25.00 + p&p
Min. Mail Order EU: £40.00 + p&p
Cat. Cost: 6 x 1st class
Credit Cards: Visa, Access, Delta, Switch
Specialities: Over 3000 varieties of cottage
garden & rare perennials & 140 types of
Clematis.
Map Ref: C, D1

CFri   FRIARS WAY NURSERY
Friars Way Nursery, Church Street, Upwey,
Weymouth, Dorset DT3 5QE
☎ (01305) 813243
Fax: (01305) 813243
E-mail: Friars@madasafish.com
Contact: Christina Scott
Opening Times: 1100-1700 Thu Apr-end
Aug & by prior appt.
Mail Order: None
Cat. Cost: 3 x 1st class
Credit Cards: None
Specialities: Hardy perennials, including
hardy geraniums.
Map Ref: C, C5

CFul   RODNEY FULLER ✉ UK
Coachman's Cottage, Higher Bratton
Seymour, Wincanton, Somerset BA9 8DA
Contact: Rodney Fuller
Opening Times: Not open.
Min. Mail Order UK: £25.00
Cat. Cost: 2 x 1st class
Credit Cards: None
Specialities: *Helianthemum.*

CFwr   THE FLOWER BOWER
Woodlands, Shurton, Stogursey, Nr
Bridgwater, Somerset TA5 1QE
☎ (01278) 732134   Fax: (01278) 732134
Contact: Sheila Tucker
Opening Times: Open most days, please
telephone first.
Mail Order: None
Cat. Cost: 4 x 2nd class
Credit Cards: None
Specialities: Unusual perennials. *Asters,* hardy
geraniums, penstemons, pot grown bulbs &
Phlox.
Map Ref: C, B4

CGdn   GODOLPHIN NURSERIES ▣
Godolphin Cross, Helston, Cornwall TR13 9RE
☎ (01736) 762598   Fax: (01736) 762983
E-mail: godolphin.nurseries@cwcom.net
Web Site: www.godolphinnurseries.cwc.net
Contact: Steven & Carey Kaack
Opening Times: 1000-1700 Tue, Thu-Sun

25th Mar-31st Oct. 1000-1700 Thu-Sat 1st
Nov-24th Mar. Open B/hols.
Mail Order: None
Cat. Cost: 2 x 2nd class A4 sae
Credit Cards: None
Specialities: Ferns, tender perennials, unusual
shrubs, herbs, grasses, bulbs, herbaceous
perennials & climbers.
Map Ref: C, D1

CGGs GRANNY GREENS LTD ⊠ EU 🖾 €
Merrymorn Court, Lynton, Devon EX35 6NX
E-mail: granny@grannygreens.co.uk
Web Site: www.grannygreens.co.uk
Opening Times: Not open to the public.
Min. Mail Order UK: No minimum charge
Min. Mail Order EU: Nmc
Cat. Cost: 4 x 2nd class
Credit Cards: None
Specialities: Organic herb & vegetable seed,
heirloom vegetable seed, untreated vegetable
& herb seed.

CGle GLEBE COTTAGE PLANTS
Pixie Lane, Warkleigh, Umberleigh, Devon
EX37 9DH
Fax: (01769) 540554
Contact: Carol Klein
Opening Times: 1000-1700 Wed-Fri.
Mail Order: None
Cat. Cost: £1.50
Credit Cards: None
Specialities: Extensive range of hard-to-find
perennials.
Map Ref: C, B3

CGOG GLOBAL ORANGE GROVES UK
⊠ EU 🖾 🖾
Horton Road, Horton Heath, Wimborne,
Dorset BH21 7JN
☎ (01202) 826244 **Fax:** (01202) 814651
Contact: P K Oliver
Opening Times: 1030-1700 7 days, unless
exhibiting.
Min. Mail Order UK: No minimum charge
Min. Mail Order EU: Nmc
Cat. Cost: Sae
Credit Cards: None
Specialities: *Citrus* trees, citrus fertiliser &
book "Success with Citrus". Peaches,
apricots, nectarines, mangoes, avocados.
Map Ref: C, C6

CGra GRAHAM'S HARDY PLANTS ⊠ EU
Southcroft, North Road, Timsbury, Bath,
Avon BA3 1JN
☎ (01761) 472187
E-mail: graplant@aol.com
Web Site: http://members.aol.com/graplant

Contact: Graham Nicholls
Opening Times: Not open to the public for
the near future.
Min. Mail Order UK: £1.50 + p&p
Min. Mail Order EU: £1.50 + p&p
Cat. Cost: 2 x 1st class or 2 x IRC
Credit Cards: None
Specialities: North American alpines esp.
*Lewisia, Eriogonum, Penstemon, Campanula,
Kelseya, Phlox.*
Map Ref: C, B5

CGre GREENWAY GARDENS ⊠ UK
Churston Ferrers, Brixham, Devon TQ5 0ES
☎ (01803) 842382 **Fax:** (01803) 842383
Contact: Roger Clark (Manager)
Opening Times: 1400-1700 (1630 Nov-
Feb) Mon-Fri, 1000-1200 Sat, excl. B/hols.
Also by appt.
Min. Mail Order UK: No minimum charge*
Cat. Cost: 3 x 1st class
Credit Cards: None
Specialities: Unusual trees & shrubs
particularly from temperate southern
hemisphere. *Note: mail order by carrier only.
Map Ref: C, D4

CGro C W GROVES & SON ⊠ EU 🖾
West Bay Road, Bridport, Dorset DT6 4BA
☎ (01308) 422654 **Fax:** (01308) 420888
E-mail: c.w.grovesandson@zetnet.co.uk
Contact: C W Groves
Opening Times: 0830-1700 Mon-Sat,
1030-1630 Sun.
Min. Mail Order UK: No minimum charge*
Min. Mail Order EU: £10.00 + p&p
Cat. Cost: 1 x 1st class
Credit Cards: Access, Visa, Switch, Delta,
MasterCard
Specialities: Nursery & garden centre
specialising in Parma & hardy *Viola*.
*Note: mainly violets by mail order.
Map Ref: C, C5

CGrW THE GREAT WESTERN GLADIOLUS
NURSERY ⊠ EU 🖾 ◆
Moor's Edge, Athelney, Bridgwater,
Somerset TA7 0SE
☎ (01823) 698996 **Fax:** (01823) 698090
E-mail: gladioli@aol.com
Contact: Frank Hartnell
Opening Times: By appt. only.
Min. Mail Order UK: No minimum charge
Min. Mail Order EU: Nmc
Cat. Cost: 2 x 1st class (2 catalogues)
Credit Cards: None
Specialities: *Gladiolus* species & hybrids,
corms & seeds.
Map Ref: C, B4

C

CHad　**Hadspen Garden & Nursery** €
Hadspen House, Castle Cary, Somerset
BA7 7NG
☎ (01749) 813707　**Fax:** (01749) 813707
E-mail: pope@hadspengarden.freeserve.co.uk
Contact: N & S Pope
Opening Times: 1000-1700 Thu-Sun &
B/hols. 1st Mar-1st Oct. Garden open at the
same time.
Mail Order: None
Cat. Cost: 3 x 1st class
Credit Cards: None
Specialities: Large leaved herbaceous.
Old fashioned and shrub roses.
Map Ref: C, B5

CHal　**Halsway Nursery** ✉ UK
Halsway, Nr Crowcombe, Taunton, Somerset
TA4 4BB
☎ (01984) 618243
Contact: T A & D J Bushen
Opening Times: Most days, please phone
first.
Min. Mail Order UK: £2.00 + p&p
Cat. Cost: 2 x 1st class*
Credit Cards: None
Specialities: *Coleus* & *Begonia* (excl. tuberous
& winter flowering). Also good range of
greenhouse & garden plants. *Note: list for
Coleus & *Begonia* only, no nursery list.
Map Ref: C, B4

CHar　**West Harptree Nursery** ✉ EU ⛏ 🌱
Bristol Road, West Harptree, Bath & North
East Somerset BS40 6HG
☎ (01761) 221370　**Fax:** (01761) 221989
E-mail: harptreenursery@netlineuk.net
Contact: Bryn & Helene Bowles
Opening Times: From 1000 Tue-Sun 1st
Mar-30th Nov.
Min. Mail Order UK: No minimum charge*
Min. Mail Order EU: Nmc
Cat. Cost: Large SAE for free names list.
Credit Cards: MasterCard, Delta, Switch,
Solo, JCB, Visa
Specialities: Unusual herbaceous perennials
& shrubs. Lilies, bulbs & grasses. *Note:
mail order Oct-Feb only.
Map Ref: C, B5

CHdy　**Hardy Orchids** ✉ EU ⛏ 🌱
New Gate Farm, Scotchey Lane, Stour
Provost, Gillingham, Dorset SP8 5LT
☎ (01747) 838368　**Fax:** (01747) 838308
Contact: N J Heywood
Opening Times: By appt. only.
Min. Mail Order UK: £10.00 + p&p
Min. Mail Order EU: £10.00 + p&p
Cat. Cost: 2 x 1st class

Credit Cards: None
Specialities: Hardy orchids - *Cypripedium* &
Dactylorhiza.
Map Ref: C, B5

CHea　**Heather Bank Nursery** ✉ UK
Woodlands, 1 High Street, Littleton Panell,
Devizes, Wiltshire SN10 4EL
☎ (01380) 812739
Contact: Mrs B Mullan
Opening Times: 1000-1500 Mon Wed &
Thu. Other times by appt.
Min. Mail Order UK: £10.00 + p&p
Cat. Cost: 3 x 1st class
Credit Cards: None
Specialities: *Campanula, Polemonium* &
cottage garden plants.
Map Ref: C, B6

CHEx　**Hardy Exotics** ✉ UK
Gilly Lane, Whitecross, Penzance,
Cornwall TR20 8BZ
☎ (01736) 740660　**Fax:** (01736) 741101
Contact: C Shilton/J Smith
Opening Times: 1000-1700 Mon-Sat 1100-
1700 Sun Mar-Oct, 1000-1700 Mon-Sat
closed Sun Nov-Feb. Please phone first in
winter months if travelling a long way.
Min. Mail Order UK: £30.00 + carriage
Cat. Cost: £1.00 postal order or 4 x 1st class
(no cheques)
Credit Cards: Visa, Access, MasterCard,
Connect, Delta
Specialities: We have the largest collection in
the UK of trees, shrubs & herbaceous plants
to create tropical & desert effects. Hardy &
half-hardy plants for gardens, patios &
conservatories.
Map Ref: C, C1

CHid　**Hidden Valley Nursery** ✉ UK
Umberleigh, Devon EX37 9BU
☎ (01769) 560567, mobile 07899 056168
Fax: (01769) 560567
E-mail: hiddenvalley.1@email.com
Web Site: www.hiddenvalleynursery.com
Contact: Linda & Peter Lindley
Opening Times: By appt. only.
Min. Mail Order UK: No minimum charge*
Cat. Cost: 2 x 1st class
Credit Cards: None
Specialities: Hardy perennials esp. shade
lovers. *Note: mail order during Mar only.

CHig　**The High Garden** ✉ EU 🌱
Courtwood, Newton Ferrers, South Devon
PL8 1BW
☎ (01752) 872528
Contact: F Bennett

Opening Times: By appt.
Min. Mail Order UK: £20.00 +p&p
Min. Mail Order EU: £40.00 + p&p
Cat. Cost: 60p
Credit Cards: None
Specialities: *Pieris* & *Rhododendron.*
Map Ref: C, D3

CHil **HILLSIDE COTTAGE PLANTS** ⊠ UK
Hillside, Gibbet Lane, Whitchurch,
North East Somerset BS14 0BX
☎ (01275) 837505
Contact: Josephine Pike
Opening Times: Normally here but please phone first in case at show, Mar-Oct.
Min. Mail Order UK: £15.00 + p&p
Cat. Cost: 3 x 1st class
Credit Cards: None
Specialities: Hardy *Geranium* (300+ varieties) & wide range of hardy perennials.
Map Ref: C, A5

CHor **HORTON VALE NURSERY**
Horton Heath, Wimborne, Dorset BH21 7JN
☎ (01202) 813473
Contact: David Wright
Opening Times: 0900-1700 Thu-Tue Feb-Nov.
Mail Order: None
Cat. Cost: None issued
Credit Cards: None
Specialities: Perennials.
Map Ref: C, C6

CInt **INTERNATIONAL ANIMAL RESCUE NURSERY**
Animal Tracks, Ash Mill, South Molton,
Devon EX36 4QW
☎ (01769) 550277 **Fax:** (01769) 550917
E-mail: i.a.r@eclipse.co.uk
Contact: Jo Hicks
Opening Times: 1000-1730 or dusk 365 days a year.
Mail Order: None
Cat. Cost: 3 x 1st class
Credit Cards: None
Specialities: Alpines, grasses, hardy perennials, cacti & succulents.
Map Ref: C, B3

CJas **JASMINE COTTAGE GARDENS**
26 Channel Road, Walton St Mary,
Clevedon, Somerset BS21 7BY
☎ (01275) 871850
E-mail: baron@bologrew.demon.co.uk
Web Site:
http://wkweb5.cableinet.co.uk/bologrew
Contact: Mr & Mrs M Redgrave
Opening Times: Wed & Thurs. Daily by appt.
Mail Order: None
Cat. Cost: None issued
Credit Cards: None
Specialities: *Rhodochiton, Asarina, Maurandya, Salvia, Solenopsis, Isotoma, Laurentia.*
Map Ref: C, A4

CKel **KELWAYS LTD** ⊠ EU ✈ 🏭
Langport, Somerset TA10 9EZ
☎ (01458) 250521 **Fax:** (01458) 253351
Contact: Mr David Root
Opening Times: 0900-1700 Mon-Fri, 1000-1700 Sat, 1000-1600 Sun.
Min. Mail Order UK: £4.00 + p&p*
Min. Mail Order EU: £8.00 + p&p
Cat. Cost: Free
Credit Cards: Visa, Access
Specialities: *Paeonia, Iris, Hemerocallis* & herbaceous perennials. *Note: mail order for *Paeonia, Iris* & *Hemerocallis* only.
Map Ref: C, B5

CKen **KENWITH NURSERY (GORDON HADDOW)** ⊠ EU ◆ ✈
Blinsham, Nr Torrington, Beaford,
Winkleigh, Devon EX19 8NT
☎ (01805) 603274 **Fax:** (01805) 603663
E-mail: conifers@kenwith63.freeserve.co.uk
Contact: Gordon Haddow
Opening Times: 1000-1630 Wed-Sat
Nov-Feb & by appt.
1000-1630 7 days Mar-Oct.
Min. Mail Order UK: £10.00 + p&p
Min. Mail Order EU: £50.00 + p&p
Cat. Cost: 3 x 1st class
Credit Cards: Visa, MasterCard, EuroCard
Specialities: All conifer genera.
Grafting a speciality. Many new introductions to UK. National Collection of dwarf conifers.
Map Ref: C, B3

CKin **KINGSFIELD CONSERVATION NURSERY** ⊠ UK 🏭
Broadenham Lane, Winsham, Chard,
Somerset TA20 4JF
☎ (01460) 30070 **Fax:** (01460) 30070
Contact: Simon Maccormack
Opening Times: Please phone for details.
Min. Mail Order UK: No minimum charge
Cat. Cost: 31p stamps
Credit Cards: None
Specialities: Native trees, shrubs, wild flowers & wild flower seeds.
Map Ref: C, C4

KEY
⊠ Mail order to UK or EU
✈ Exports beyond EU | € Euro accepted
🏭 Also supplies Wholesale | ◆ See Display advertisement

C

CKno **KNOLL GARDENS** ⊠ UK
Hampreston, Stapehill, Nr Wimborne,
Dorset BH21 7ND
☎ (01202) 873931 **Fax:** (01202) 870842
E-mail: enquiries@knollgardens.co.uk
Web Site: www.knollgardens.co.uk
Contact: N R Lucas
Opening Times: 1000-1700 7 days
Apr-Sep.
1000-1630 Wed-Sun Mar, Oct & Nov.
Min. Mail Order UK: £10.00*
Cat. Cost: available online only
Credit Cards: Visa, MasterCard
Specialities: National Collections of
deciduous *Ceanothus* & *Phygelius* (list
available). Grasses (main specialism), hardy
perennials, tender perennials.
*Note: mail order through web site only.
Map Ref: C, C6

CLan **THE LANHYDROCK GARDENS (NT)** ▣
Lanhydrock, Bodmin, Cornwall PL30 5AD
☎ (01208) 72220 **Fax:** (01208) 72220
Contact: Mr N.R. Teagle
Opening Times: Easter (or 1st Apr)-31st
Oct.
Mail Order: None
Cat. Cost: Free
Credit Cards: None
Specialities: Shrubs esp. *Camellia,*
rhododendrons & azaleas, *Magnolia* &
Ceanothus.
Map Ref: C, C2

CLAP **LONG ACRE PLANTS** ⊠ EU ▣
South Marsh, Charlton Musgrove, Nr
Wincanton, Somerset BA9 8EX
☎ (01963) 32802 **Fax:** (01963) 32802
Contact: Nigel Rowland
Opening Times: By appt. only.
Min. Mail Order UK: £10.00 + p&p
Min. Mail Order EU: £20.00 + p&p
Cat. Cost: 3 x 1st class
Credit Cards: None
Specialities: Ferns, lilies, woodland bulbs &
perennials. National Collection of *Asarum.*
Map Ref: C, B5

CLCN **LITTLE CREEK NURSERY** ⊠ EU ▣
39 Moor Road, Banwell, Weston-super-
Mare, North Somerset BS29 6EF
☎ (01934) 823739 **Fax:** (01934) 823739
Contact: Rhys & Julie Adams
Opening Times: 1000-1630 Thu-Fri Mar-
Apr. Other times by appt. Please phone first.
Min. Mail Order UK: No minimum charge
Min. Mail Order EU: Nmc
Cat. Cost: 3 x 1st class
Credit Cards: None

Specialities: Species *Cyclamen* (from seed)
& *Helleborus.*
Map Ref: C, B4

CLnd **LANDFORD TREES** ▣ €
Landford Lodge, Landford, Salisbury,
Wiltshire SP5 2EH
☎ (01794) 390808 **Fax:** (01794) 390037
E-mail: mo@landford-trees.demon.co.uk
Web Site: www.landford-trees.demon.co.uk
Contact: C D Pilkington
Opening Times: 0800-1700 Mon-Fri.
Mail Order: None
Cat. Cost: Free
Credit Cards: None
Specialities: Deciduous ornamental trees.
Map Ref: C, B6

CLoc **C S LOCKYER** ⊠ EU ▣ ◆
Lansbury, 70 Henfield Road, Coalpit Heath,
Bristol BS36 2UZ
☎ (01454) 772219 **Fax:** (01454) 772219
E-mail: sales@lockyerfuchsias.co.uk
Web Site: lockyerfuchsias.co.uk
Contact: C S Lockyer
Opening Times: By appt. only. (Many open
days & coach parties).
Min. Mail Order UK: 6 plants + p&p
Min. Mail Order EU: £12.00 + p&p
Cat. Cost: 4 x 1st class
Credit Cards: None
Specialities: *Fuchsia.*
Map Ref: C, A5

CLon **LONGHALL NURSERY** ⊠ EU ▣
Stockton, Nr Warminster,
Wiltshire BA12 0SE
☎ (01980) 621638 **Fax:** (01980) 621638
E-mail: www.designbywire.com
Contact: H V & J E Dooley
Opening Times: 0930-1700 Fri & Sat 3rd
Fri in Mar-last Sat in Sep.
Min. Mail Order UK: 10 plants + p&p
Min. Mail Order EU: 10 plants + p&p
Cat. Cost: 3 x 1st class
Credit Cards: None
Specialities: Many chalk tolerant plants esp.
Digitalis, Eryngium, Euphorbia & *Salvia.*
Map Ref: C, B6

CLTr **LITTLE TREASURES** ⊠ EU
Wheal Treasure, Horsedowns, Cornwall
TR14 0NL
☎ (01209) 831978 **Fax:** (01209) 831978
Contact: Bernadette Jackson
Opening Times: 1000-1600 Thurs & Fri.
Sat by appt only. Mid-Mar to end Sept.
Min. Mail Order UK: £15.00 + p&p
Min. Mail Order EU: £25.00 + p&p

Cat. Cost: 4 x 1st class
Credit Cards: None
Specialities: Cottage garden plants, shrubs &
tender perennials.
Map Ref: C, D1

CLyd LYDFORD ALPINE NURSERY ⊠ UK
2 Southern Cottages, Lydford, Okehampton,
Devon EX20 4BL
☎ (01822) 820398
Contact: Julie & David Hatchett
Opening Times: 1000-1700 Tue & Thu
Apr-Oct & by appt. Nov-Mar by appt. only.
Closed 20th Jun-2nd Jul 2000.
Min. Mail Order UK: £10.00 + p&p*
Cat. Cost: 2 x 1st class sae *Saxifraga* list only.
Credit Cards: None
Specialities: *Dianthus, Primula* & *Saxifraga.*
Very wide range of choice & unusual alpines
in small quantities. *Note: mail order
Saxifraga only.
Map Ref: C, C3

CLyn LYNASH NURSERIES ⊠ EU
Culhaven, Wall Ditch Lane, Boozer Pit,
Merriott, Somerset TA16 5PW
☎ (01460) 76643, (01460) 77764
Fax: (01460) 76643
E-mail: info@lynash.co.uk
Web Site: www.lynash.co.uk
Contact: Lynn Wallis & Ashley Wallis
Opening Times: 0900-1700 Thu-Sat, 1000-
1600 Sun.
Min. Mail Order UK: No minimum charge
Min. Mail Order EU: £20.00 + p&p
Cat. Cost: 4 x 1st class
Credit Cards: MasterCard, Visa, Solo,
Switch
Specialities: *Hebe.*
Map Ref: C, B5

CM&M M & M PLANTS
Lloret, Chittlehamholt, Umbesleigh, Devon
EX37 9PD
☎ (01769) 540448
Contact: Mr M Thorne
Opening Times: 0930-1730 Tue-Sat Apr-
Oct & 1000-1600 Tue-Sat Nov-Mar.
Mail Order: None
Cat. Cost: 4 x 1st class
Credit Cards: None
Specialities: Perennials. We also carry a
reasonable range of alpines, shrubs, trees &
roses.
Map Ref: C, B3

CMac MACPENNYS NURSERIES ⊠ UK
154 Burley Road, Bransgore, Christchurch,
Dorset BH23 8DB

☎ (01425) 672348
Contact: T & V Lowndes
Opening Times: 0800-1700 Mon-Fri, 0900-
1700 Sat 1400-1700 Sun.
Min. Mail Order UK: No minimum charge
Cat. Cost: A4 Sae with 4 x 1st class
Credit Cards: Access, American Express,
Delta, Access, EuroCard, MasterCard, Visa,
Switch, Solo
Specialities: General.
Map Ref: C, C6

CMCN MALLET COURT NURSERY ⊠ EU 🗑 🗑
Curry Mallet, Taunton, Somerset TA3 6SY
☎ (01823) 480748   Fax: (01823) 481009
E-mail: malcourt@currantbun.com
Web Site: www.malletcourt.co.uk
Contact: J G S & P M E Harris F.L.S.
Opening Times: 0900-1300 & 1400-1700
Mon-Fri. Sat & Sun by appt.
Min. Mail Order UK: No minimum charge
Min. Mail Order EU: Nmc
Cat. Cost: 31p Sae
Credit Cards: MasterCard, Visa
Specialities: Maples, oaks, *Magnolia,* hollies
& other rare and unusual plants including
those from China & South Korea.
Map Ref: C, B4

CMCo MEADOW COTTAGE PLANTS 🗑
Pitt Hill, Ivybridge, Devon PL21 0JJ
☎ (01752) 894532
Contact: Mrs L P Hunt
Opening Times: By appt. only.
Mail Order: None
Cat. Cost: 2 x 2nd class
Credit Cards: None
Specialities: Hardy *Geranium* & other hardy
perennials.
Map Ref: C, C3

CMdw MEADOWS NURSERY
5 Rectory Cottages, Mells, Frome, Somerset
BA11 3PA
☎ (01373) 813025
Contact: Sue Lees
Opening Times: 1000-1800 Tue-Sun 1st
Feb-31st Oct & B/hols.
Mail Order: None
Cat. Cost: 3 x 1st class
Credit Cards: None
Specialities: Hardy perennials, shrubs &
some conservatory plants.
Map Ref: C, B5

CMea THE MEAD NURSERY
Brokerswood, Nr Westbury, Wiltshire BA13
4EG
☎ (01373) 859990

C

Contact: Steve Lewis-Dale
Opening Times: 0900-1700 Wed-Sat &
B/hols, 1300-1700 Sun 1st Feb-10th Oct.
Closed Easter Sun.
Mail Order: None
Cat. Cost: 5 x 1st class
Credit Cards: None
Specialities: Perennials & alpines incl. pot
grown bulbs.
Map Ref: C, B5

CMFo   MAC FOLIAGE ✉ EU 🖾 ◆ €
Mac Foliage Plantation & Nursery,
Dartmoor National Park, Knapmore Hill,
Lounston, Nr Liverton, Newton Abbot,
Devon TQ12 6LB
☎ (01626) 821006   Fax: (01626) 330293
E-mail: paul.macpherson@ukmax.com
Web Site:
www.alexandermacpherson.freeserve.co.uk/
Contact: Paul Macpherson
Opening Times: Sat only, by appt.
Min. Mail Order UK: £50.00 + p&p
Min. Mail Order EU: £250.00 + p&p
Cat. Cost: 4 x 1st class
Credit Cards: None
Specialities: *Eucalyptus, Stephanandra,
Dodonea.*
Map Ref: C, C3

CMGP   MILTON GARDEN PLANTS ✉ EU
Milton-on-Stour, Gillingham, Dorset SP8 5PX
☎ (01747) 822484   Fax: (01747) 822484
E-mail: r.w.r.cumming@btinternet.co
Contact: Sue Hardy & Richard Cumming
Opening Times: 0900-1700 Tue-Sat &
B/hol Mons, 1000-1630 Sun. Closed Jan.
Min. Mail Order UK: No minimum charge
Min. Mail Order EU: £30.00 + p&p
Cat. Cost: £1.50 or 6 x 1st class
Credit Cards: Visa, Access, Switch, Delta
Specialities: Very wide range of perennials.
Ever changing selection of trees, shrubs,
conifers, alpines & herbs. Emphasis on good
information with display gardens alongside.
Map Ref: C, B5

CMHG   MARWOOD HILL GARDENS
Barnstaple, Devon EX31 4EB
☎ (01271) 342528
Contact: Dr Smart
Opening Times: 1100-1700 7 days.
Mail Order: None
Cat. Cost: 5 x 2nd class
Credit Cards: None
Specialities: Large range of unusual trees &
shrubs. *Eucalyptus,* alpines, *Camellia, Astilbe*
& bog plants.
Map Ref: C, B3

CMil   MILL COTTAGE PLANTS ✉ EU
The Mill, Henley Lane, Wookey, Somerset
BA5 1AP
☎ (01749) 676966
Contact: Sally Gregson
Opening Times: 1000-1800 Wed Mar-Sep
or by appt. Phone for directions.
Min. Mail Order UK: £5.00 + p&p
Min. Mail Order EU: £10.00 + p&p
Cat. Cost: 4 x 1st class
Credit Cards: None
Specialities: Unusual & period cottage plants
esp. *Campanula, Papaver orientale,* hardy
Geranium, Euphorbia, ferns, *Pulmonaria* &
grasses. Also *Hydrangea aspera* &
H. serrata cvs.
Map Ref: C, B5

CNat   NATURAL SELECTION ✉ UK €
1 Station Cottages, Hullavington,
Chippenham, Wiltshire SN14 6ET
☎ (01666) 837369
E-mail: martin@worldmutation.demon.co.uk
Web Site: www.worldmutation.demon.co.uk
Contact: Martin Cragg-Barber
Opening Times: Please phone first.
Min. Mail Order UK: £8.00 + p&p
Cat. Cost: 2 x 1st class
Credit Cards: None
Specialities: Unusual British natives &
others. Also seed.
Map Ref: C, A5

CNic   NICKY'S ROCK GARDEN NURSERY
Broadhayes, Stockland, Honiton, Devon
EX14 9EH
☎ (01404) 881213   Fax: (01404) 881213
E-mail: Dianabob.Dark@nickys.sagehost.co.uk
Contact: Diana & Bob Dark
Opening Times: 0900-dusk 7 days. Please
phone first to check & for directions.
Mail Order: None
Cat. Cost: 3 x 1st class
Credit Cards: None
Specialities: Plants for rock gardens, alpine
house, scree, troughs, banks, walls & front of
border & dwarf shrubs. Many unusual.
Map Ref: C, C4

COld   THE OLD MILL HERBARY
Helland Bridge, Bodmin,
Cornwall PL30 4QR
☎ (01208) 841206   Fax: (01208) 841206
Contact: Mrs B Whurr
Opening Times: 1000-1700 Thu-Tue
Apr-30th Sept.
Mail Order: None
Cat. Cost: 6 x 1st class
Credit Cards: None

C

Specialities: Culinary, medicinal & aromatic herbs, shrubs, climbing & herbaceous plants.
Map Ref: C, C2

COlW   THE OLD WITHY GARDEN NURSERY ⊠ UK
Cury Cross Lanes, Helston, Cornwall TR12 7AY
☎ (01326) 240817
Contact: S M Chandler or N D Chandler
Opening Times: 1000-1700 Wed-Mon mid Feb-end Oct.
Min. Mail Order UK: No minimum charge
Cat. Cost: 4 x 1st class
Credit Cards: MasterCard, Visa, Delta, Switch, American Express
Specialities: Cottage garden plants - perennials, biennials & grasses.
Map Ref: C, D1

COtt   OTTER NURSERIES LTD
Gosford Road, Ottery St Mary, Devon EX11 1LZ
☎ (01404) 815815   Fax: (01404) 815816
Contact: Mrs Pam Poole
Opening Times: 0800-1730 Mon-Sat, 1030-1630 Sun. Closed Xmas, Boxing Day & Easter Sun.
Mail Order: None
Cat. Cost: None issued
Credit Cards: Visa, Access, American Express, Diners, Switch
Specialities: Large garden centre & nursery with extensive range of trees, shrubs, conifers, climbers, roses, fruit & hardy perennials.
Map Ref: C, C4

CPar   PARKS PERENNIALS
242 Wallisdown Road, Wallisdown, Bournemouth, Dorset BH10 4HZ
☎ (01202) 524464
Contact: S Parks
Opening Times: Apr-Oct most days, please phone first.
Mail Order: None
Cat. Cost: None issued.
Credit Cards: None
Specialities: Hardy herbaceous perennials.
Map Ref: C, C6

CPas   PASSIFLORA (NATIONAL COLLECTION) ⊠ EU 🖪 🖾 €
Lampley Road, Kingston Seymour, Clevedon, North Somerset BS21 6XS
☎ (01934) 833350   Fax: (01934) 877255
Web Site: passion@3wa.co.uk
Contact: John Vanderplank or Jane Lindsay
Opening Times: 0900-1300 & 1400-1700 Mon-Sat.

Min. Mail Order UK: £20.00 + p&p
Min. Mail Order EU: £30.00 + p&p
Cat. Cost: 3 x 1st class
Credit Cards: Visa, Access, EuroCard, MasterCard
Specialities: *Passiflora.* National Collection of over 200 species & varieties. Note: retail nursery now at Kingston Seymour.
Map Ref: C, A4

CPBP   PARHAM BUNGALOW PLANTS ⊠ EU €
Parham Lane, Market Lavington, Devizes, Wiltshire SN10 4QA
☎ (01380) 812605
E-mail: jjs@pbplants.freeserve.co.uk
Contact: Mrs D E Sample
Opening Times: Please ring first.
Min. Mail Order UK: No minimum charge
Min. Mail Order EU: Nmc
Cat. Cost: Sae
Credit Cards: None
Specialities: Alpines & dwarf shrubs.
Map Ref: C, B6

CPea   PEAR TREE COTTAGE PLANTS ⊠ EU 🖾
Pear Tree Cottage, Prestleigh, Shepton Mallet, Somerset BA4 4NL
☎ (01749) 831487
Contact: PJ & PM Starr
Opening Times: 0900-1900 Tue-Sun 1st Mar-31st Oct.
Min. Mail Order UK: £17.50 p&p free
Min. Mail Order EU: £20.00 + p&p
Cat. Cost: 3 x 1st class
Credit Cards: None
Specialities: Wide general range with many unusual plants.
Map Ref: C, B5

CPev   PEVERIL CLEMATIS NURSERY €
Christow, Exeter, Devon EX6 7NG
☎ (01647) 252937
Contact: Barry Fretwell
Opening Times: 1000-1300 & 1400-1730 Fri-Wed, 1000-1300 Sun. Dec-Mar by appt.
Mail Order: None
Cat. Cost: 2 x 1st class
Credit Cards: None
Specialities: *Clematis.*
Map Ref: C, C3

CPhi   ALAN PHIPPS CACTI ⊠ EU
62 Samuel White Road, Hanham, Bristol BS15 3LX

KEY		
⊠ Mail order to UK or EU		
🖾 Exports beyond EU	€ Euro accepted	
🖪 Also supplies Wholesale	◆ See Display advertisement	

C

☎ (0117) 9607591
Contact: A Phipps
Opening Times: All times, but prior phone call essential to ensure a greeting.
Min. Mail Order UK: £5.00 + p&p
Min. Mail Order EU: £20.00 + p&p
Cat. Cost: Sae or 2 x IRC (EC countries only)
Credit Cards: None
Specialities: *Mammillaria, Astrophytum* & *Ariocarpus*. Species and varieties will change with times. Ample quantities exist in spring.
Map Ref: C, A5

CPla Plant World Botanic Gardens
⊠ UK 🆔 ◆
St Marychurch Road, Newton Abbot, South Devon TQ12 4SE
☎ (01803) 872939 **Fax:** (01803) 872939
Contact: Ray Brown
Opening Times: 0930-1700 7 days a week, Easter-end Sep.
Min. Mail Order UK: *
Cat. Cost: 3 x 1st class or $2
Credit Cards: Visa, Access, EuroCard, MasterCard
Specialities: Alpines & unusual herbaceous plants. 4 acre world botanic map. National Collections of *Primula*.
*Note: mail order for seed only.
Map Ref: C, C3

CPle Pleasant View Nursery ⊠ EU
Two Mile Oak, Nr Denbury, Newton Abbot, Devon TQ12 6DG
☎ (01803) 813388 answerphone
Contact: Mrs B D Yeo
Opening Times: Nursery open 1000-1700 Wed-Fri mid Mar-end Sep (closed for lunch 1245-1330). Garden open 1400-1700 Wed & Fri May-Sep.
Min. Mail Order UK: £20.00 + p&p
Min. Mail Order EU: £20.00 + p&p (Salvias only)
Cat. Cost: 5 x 2nd class or 2 x IRC
Credit Cards: None
Specialities: *Salvia* & unusual shrubs for garden & conservatory incl. *Buddleja, Viburnum, Ceanothus, Berberis, Lonicera, Spiraea*. National Collections of *Salvia* & *Abelia*. Off A381 at T.M. Oak Cross towards Denbury.
Map Ref: C, C3

CPLG Pine Lodge Gardens
Cuddra, St Austell, Cornwall PL25 3RQ
☎ (01726) 73500/77363
Fax: (01726) 73500
E-mail: sclemo@talk21.com
Web Site: www.thin-end.co.uk/pinehome.html

Contact: Ray & Shirley Clemo
Opening Times: 1400-1700 Wed-Sun Apr-Sep & B/hols.
Mail Order: None
Cat. Cost: 4 x 2nd class
Credit Cards: None
Specialities: Rare & unusual shrubs & herbaceous, some from seed collected on plant expeditions each year. National Collection of *Grevillea*.
Map Ref: C, D2

CPlN The Plantsman Nursery ⊠ EU ◆ 🆔
North Wonson Farm, Throwleigh, Okehampton, Devon EX20 2JA
☎ (01647) 231699 office/231618 nursery
Fax: (01647) 231157
E-mail: pnursery@aol.com
Web Site: www.plantsman.com
Contact: Guy & Emma Sisson
Opening Times: Mail order & strictly by appt.
Min. Mail Order UK: £25.00 + p&p
Min. Mail Order EU: £45.00 + p&p
Cat. Cost: £2.00
Credit Cards: MasterCard, Access, American Express, Delta, Diners, EuroCard, Switch, Visa
Specialities: Unusual hardy & tender climbers. Also seeds for non-EU countries. Note: seed list available for non-EU countries.
Map Ref: C, C3

CPlt Plantaholics
Hillside, Coombe Street, Pen Selwood, Wincanton, Somerset BA9 8NF
☎ (01747) 840852
Contact: Jane Edmonds
Opening Times: Usually 1000-1600 Fri & Sat, 17 Mar-23 Sept, but please phone first.
Mail Order: None
Cat. Cost: 2 x 2nd class
Credit Cards: None
Specialities: Small nursery concentrating mainly on high performance perennials for various situations. Many unusual & all propagated on the nursery.
Map Ref: C, B5

CPMA P M A Plant Specialities ⊠ EU 🆔 🆔
Lower Mead, West Hatch, Taunton, Somerset TA3 5RN
☎ (01823) 480774 **Fax:** (01823) 481046
E-mail: k@junker.net
Web Site: www.junker.net
Contact: Karan or Nick Junker
Opening Times: Strictly by appt. only.
Min. Mail Order UK: No minimum charge
Min. Mail Order EU: Nmc
Cat. Cost: 5 x 2nd class
Credit Cards: None

Specialities: Choice & unusual shrubs incl. grafted *Acer palmatum* cvs, *Cornus* cvs, *Magnolia* cvs. and a wide range of *Daphne.*
Map Ref: C, B4

CPne PINE COTTAGE PLANTS ⊠ EU ▣
Pine Cottage, Fourways, Eggesford, Chulmleigh, Devon EX18 7QZ
☎ (01769) 580076 Fax: (01769) 581427
E-mail: pcplants@mycabin.com
Contact: Dick Fulcher
Opening Times: By appt. only, also special open week for *Agapanthus* 31st July-6th Aug.
Min. Mail Order UK: £15.00 + p&p
Min. Mail Order EU: £20.00 + p&p
Cat. Cost: 3 x 1st class
Credit Cards: None
Specialities: National Collection of *Agapanthus.*
Map Ref: C, B3

CPou POUNSLEY PLANTS ⊠ EU ▣ €
Poundsley Combe, Spriddlestone, Brixton, Plymouth, Devon PL9 0DW
☎ (01752) 402873 Fax: (01752) 402873
E-mail: pou.599@aol.co.uk
Contact: Mrs Jane Hollow
Opening Times: Normally 1000-1700 Mon-Sat but please phone first.
Min. Mail Order UK: £10.00 + p&p*
Min. Mail Order EU: £20.00 + p&p
Cat. Cost: 2 x 1st class
Credit Cards: None
Specialities: Unusual herbaceous perennials & cottage plants. Selection of *Clematis* & old roses. Large selection of South African monocots. *Note: mail order Nov-Feb only.
Map Ref: C, D3

CPri DAVID PRICE ⊠ UK
24 Crantock Drive, Almondsbury, Bristol BS12 4HG
☎ (01454) 615578, mobile 0378 959285
Contact: David Price
Opening Times: Not open.
Min. Mail Order UK: £10.00 +p&p
Cat. Cost: 2 x 1st class
Credit Cards: None
Specialities: Wide range of rock & herbaceous plants, some unusual, incl. *Dianthus, Helianthemum, Lavendula, Hebe* & *Saxifraga.*
Map Ref: C, A5

CQua QUALITY DAFFODILS ⊠ EU ▣ ▣ €
14 Roscarrack Close, Falmouth, Cornwall TR11 4PJ
☎ (01326) 317959
Contact: R A Scamp
Opening Times: Mail order only.
Min. Mail Order UK: No minimum charge

Min. Mail Order EU: Nmc
Cat. Cost: 3 x 1st class
Credit Cards: None
Specialities: *Narcissus* hybrids & species.
Map Ref: C, D1

CRde ROWDE MILL NURSERY
Rowde, Devizes, Wiltshire SN10 1SZ
☎ (01380) 723016 Fax: (01380) 723016
Contact: Mrs J Cholmeley
Opening Times: 1000-1700 Thu-Sun & B/hol Mon Apr-Sep.
Mail Order: None
Cat. Cost: None issued
Credit Cards: None
Specialities: Wide range of hardy perennials, all grown on the nursery.
Map Ref: C, A6

CRDP R D PLANTS
Homelea Farm, Chard Road, Tytherleigh, Axminster, East Devon EX13 7BG
☎ (01460) 220206 only between 0830-0930
Contact: Rodney Davey & Lynda Windsor
Opening Times: 0900-1300 & 1400-1700 Mon-Fri & most w/ends, Mar-end Aug. Please check first. Feb by appt. for hellebores.
Mail Order: None
Cat. Cost: 4 x loose 2nd class
Credit Cards: None
Specialities: Choice & unusual herbaceous, retentive shade & woodland plants, *Helleborus,* plus rarities.
Map Ref: C, C4

CRHN ROSELAND HOUSE NURSERY ⊠ UK
Chacewater, Truro, Cornwall TR4 8QB
☎ (01872) 560451
E-mail: clematis@dialstart.net
Web Site: users.dialstart.net/~clematis
Contact: C R Pridham
Opening Times: 1200-1800 Mon & Tue Mar-Aug.
Min. Mail Order UK: £10.00 + p&p
Cat. Cost: 2 x 1st class
Credit Cards: None
Specialities: Climbing & conservatory plants.
Map Ref: C, D1

CRoM ROSEDOWN MILL PALMS AND EXOTICS ⊠ EU
Hartland, Bideford, Devon EX39 6AH
☎ (01237) 441527
E-mail: huwcol@aol.com
Web Site: www.rosedownmill.co.uk
Contact: Huw Collingbourne
Opening Times: 1200-1700 Sat, Sun & B/hols 1 May-31 Oct. Other times by appt.

C

Min. Mail Order UK: £25.00
Min. Mail Order EU: £25.00
Cat. Cost: Sae for list
Credit Cards: None
Specialities: Palms, cycads, pachypodiums.
Map Ref: C, B2

CRos   ROSEMOOR GARDEN (RHS)
Royal Horticultural Society Garden, Rosemoor,
Great Torrington, Devon EX38 8PH
☎ (01805) 624067   Fax: (01805) 622422
Contact: Jack Gingell
Opening Times: 1000-1800 Apr-Sep, 1000-
1700 Oct-Mar.
Mail Order: None
Cat. Cost: None issued
Credit Cards: Visa, Access, American Express
Specialities: National Collections of *Cornus*
and part *Ilex.* Many rare & unusual plants.
Map Ref: C, B3

CRow   ROWDEN GARDENS ⊠ EU ⊠ ⊠
Brentor, Nr Tavistock, Devon PL19 0NG
☎ (01822) 810275   Fax: (01822) 810275
Contact: John R L Carter
Opening Times: 1000-1700 Sat, Sun &
B/hols 26th Mar-end Sep. Other times by
appt.
Min. Mail Order UK: No minimum charge
Min. Mail Order EU: Nmc
Cat. Cost: £1.50
Credit Cards: None
Specialities: Aquatics, damp loving &
associated plants incl. rare & unusual
varieties. National Collections of *Polygonum*
& *Ranunculus ficaria.*
Map Ref: C, C3

CRsw   ROSEWARNE COLLECTIONS ⊠ UK
Duchy College, Rosewarne, Camborne,
Cornwall TR14 0AB
☎ (01209) 722100   Fax: (01209) 722159
E-mail: r.smith@cornwall.ac.uk
Contact: Ros Smith or Marshall Hutchens
Opening Times: By appt. only.
Min. Mail Order UK: £10.00 + p&p
Cat. Cost: 2 x 1st class
Credit Cards: None
Specialities: *Escallonia* species & hybrids.
National Collection of *Escallonia.*
Map Ref: C, D1

CSam   SAMPFORD SHRUBS ⊠ UK
Sampford Peverell, Tiverton, Devon
EX16 7EN
☎ (01884) 821164
E-mail: martin.h@virgin.net
Web Site: http://freespace.virgin.net/martin.h
and www.sampford.swest.co.uk

Contact: M Hughes-Jones & S Proud
Opening Times: 0900-1700 7 days Mar-
Jun. 0900-1700 Thu-Sat Feb & Jul-Nov,
1000-1600 Sun. Mail order Oct-mid Mar.
Min. Mail Order UK: £15.00 + p&p
Cat. Cost: Sae
Credit Cards: MasterCard, Switch, Solo,
Delta, Electron, Maestro, Visa
Specialities: Extensive range of good common
& uncommon plants, incl. herbaceous,
shrubs & trees. herbaceous, shrubs & trees.
Map Ref: C, B4

CSev   LOWER SEVERALLS NURSERY
Crewkerne, Somerset TA18 7NX
☎ (01460) 73234   Fax: (01460) 76105
Contact: Mary R Cooper
Opening Times: 1000-1700 Fri-Wed 1st
Mar-20th Oct & Sun 1400-1700 May & Jun.
Mail Order: None
Cat. Cost: 4 x 1st class
Credit Cards: None
Specialities: Herbs, herbaceous &
conservatory plants.
Map Ref: C, B5

CSil   SILVER DALE NURSERIES ⊠ EU ◆
Shute Lane, Combe Martin, Devon EX34
0HT
☎ (01271) 882539
E-mail: silverdale.nurseries@virgin.net
Contact: Roger Gilbert
Opening Times: 1000-1800 7 days.
Min. Mail Order UK: No minimum charge
Min. Mail Order EU: Nmc
Cat. Cost: 4 x 1st class
Credit Cards: Visa, MasterCard, EuroCard
Specialities: National Collection of *Fuchsia.*
Hardy fuchsias (cultivars and species).
Map Ref: C, B3

CSli   SLIPPS GARDEN CENTRE
Butts Hill, Frome, Somerset BA11 1HR
☎ (01373) 467013   Fax: (01373) 467013
Contact: James Hall
Opening Times: 0900-1730 Mon-Sat,
1000-1630 Sun.
Mail Order: None
Cat. Cost: None issued
Credit Cards: Visa, Access, MasterCard,
Delta, Switch
Specialities: Conifers. *Achillea.*
Map Ref: C, B5

CSpe   SPECIAL PLANTS ⊠ EU
Hill Farm Barn, Greenways Lane, Cold
Ashton, Chippenham, Wiltshire SN14 8LA
☎ (01225) 891686
E-mail: specialplants@bigfoot.com

C

Web Site: www.bigfoot.com/~specialplants
Contact: Derry Watkins
Opening Times: 1030-1600 7 days Mar-Sept. Other times please ring first to check.
Min. Mail Order UK: £10.00 + p&p*
Min. Mail Order EU: £10.00 + p&p
Cat. Cost: 4 x 2nd class
Credit Cards: None
Specialities: Tender perennials, *Felicia, Diascia, Lotus, Mimulus, Pelargonium, Salvia, Streptocarpus,* hardy geraniums etc. New introductions of South African plants. *Note: mail order Sep-Mar only.
Map Ref: C, A5

CSPN **SHERSTON PARVA NURSERY LTD** ⊠ EU ▣
Malmesbury Road, Sherston, Wiltshire
SN16 0NX
☎ (01666) 841066   **Fax:** (01666) 841132
E-mail: clematis@sherston-parva.prestel.co.uk
Contact: Martin Rea
Opening Times: 1000-1700 7 days 1 Feb-31 Dec. Closed Jan.
Min. Mail Order UK: No minimum charge
Min. Mail Order EU: Nmc
Cat. Cost: 4 x 1st class
Credit Cards: MasterCard, Delta, Visa
Specialities: *Clematis,* wall shrubs & climbers.
Map Ref: C, A5

CSto **STONE LANE GARDENS** ⊠ EU ▣
Stone Farm, Chagford, Devon TQ13 8JU
☎ (01647) 231311   **Fax:** (01647) 231311
Contact: Kenneth Ashburner
Opening Times: By appt. only.
Min. Mail Order UK: No minimum charge
Min. Mail Order EU: Nmc
Cat. Cost: £3.00 for descriptive catalogue
Credit Cards: None
Specialities: Wide range of wild provenance *Betula* and *Alnus.* Also interesting varieties of *Rubus, Sorbus* etc.
Map Ref: C, C3

CStr **SUE STRICKLAND PLANTS** ⊠ UK
The Poplars, Isle Brewers, Taunton, Somerset
TA3 6QN
☎ (01460) 281454   **Fax:** (01460) 281808
Contact: Sue Strickland
Opening Times: 0930-1430 Mon-Wed Apr-Jul & Sep. Other times by appt.
Min. Mail Order UK: No minimum charge*
Cat. Cost: 2 x 1st class
Credit Cards: None
Specialities: *Salvia* & unusual herbaceous perennials incl. *Nepeta, Helianthus, Origanum* & *Monarda.*
*Note: mail order for salvias only.
Map Ref: C, B4

CStu **STUCKEY'S ALPINES**
38 Phillipps Avenue, Exmouth, Devon
EX8 3HZ
☎ (01395) 273636
Contact: Roger Stuckey
Opening Times: As NGS dates or by appt.
Mail Order: None
Cat. Cost: None issued
Credit Cards: None
Specialities: National Collection of dwarf *Helichrysum.* Alpines in general. *Primula* especially *allionii* forms and show auriculas.
Map Ref: C, C4

CSut **SUTTONS SEEDS** ⊠ UK
Woodview Road, Paignton, Devon TQ4 7NG
☎ (01803) 696321   **Fax:** (01803) 696345
Contact: Customer Services
Opening Times: (Office) 0830-1700 Mon-Fri. Answerphone also.
Min. Mail Order UK: No minimum charge
Cat. Cost: Free
Credit Cards: Visa, MasterCard, Switch, Delta
Specialities: Over 1,000 varieties of flower & vegetable seed, bulbs, plants & sundries.

CSWC **SOUTH WEST CARNIVOROUS PLANTS** ⊠ EU ▣
2 Rose Cottages, Culmstock, Cullompton, Devon EX15 3JJ
☎ (01884) 841549   **Fax:** (01884) 841549
E-mail: flytraps@littleshopofhorrors.co.uk
Web Site: www.littleshopofhorrors.co.uk
Contact: Jenny Pearce & Alistair Pearce
Opening Times: By appt.
Min. Mail Order UK: £10.00 + p&p
Min. Mail Order EU: £20.00 + p&p
Cat. Cost: 3 x 2nd class
Credit Cards: MasterCard, Visa
Specialities: *Cephalotus, Nepenthes, Dionea, Drosera, Darlingtonia, Sarracenia, Pinguicula* & *Utricularia.* Specialists in hardy carnivorous plants & *Dionea muscipula* cvs.
Map Ref: C, B4

CSWP **SONIA WRIGHT PLANTS** ⊠ EU ▣
Grove Farm, Stitchcombe, Marlborough, Wiltshire SN8 2NG
☎ (01672) 514003   **Fax:** (01672) 541047
Contact: Anyas Simon
Opening Times: 1000-1800 Tues-Sat Mar-Oct. 1000-1600 Fri & Sat Nov-Feb.
Min. Mail Order UK: £15 Primulas only*
Min. Mail Order EU: £15 Primulas only

K E Y	⊠ Mail order to UK or EU	
	▣ Exports beyond EU	€ Euro accepted
	▣ Also supplies Wholesale	◆ See Display advertisement

C

Cat. Cost: 4 x 1st class
Credit Cards: None
Specialities: Barnhaven polyanthus & primroses. Grasses, grey-leaved plants, *Iris, Euphorbia, Penstemon,* old roses. *Note: mail order primroses only despatched autumn.
Map Ref: C, A6

CTbh TREBAH ENTERPRISES LTD
Trebah, Mawnan Smith, Falmouth,
Cornwall TR11 5JZ
☎ (01326) 250448 **Fax:** (01326) 250781
E-mail: mail@trebah-garden.co.uk
Web Site: www.trebah-garden.co.uk
Contact: Plant Sales Staff
Opening Times: 1030-1700 all year.
Mail Order: None
Cat. Cost: None issued
Credit Cards: Visa, Access, EuroCard,
American Express, Switch, Delta, Electron,
MasterCard, Solo
Specialities: Agave, tree ferns, palms,
Camellia, Gunnera & conservatory climbers.
Map Ref: C, D1

CTho THORNHAYES NURSERY ✉ EU 🔲
St Andrews Wood, Dulford, Cullompton,
Devon EX15 2DF
☎ (01884) 266746 **Fax:** (01884) 266739
E-mail: trees@thornhayes.demon.co.uk
Contact: K D Croucher
Opening Times: By appt. only.
Min. Mail Order UK: No minimum charge
Min. Mail Order EU: Nmc
Cat. Cost: 5 x 1st class
Credit Cards: None
Specialities: A broad range of forms of
ornamental, amenity & fruit trees incl.
West Country apple varieties.
Map Ref: C, A5

CThr THREE COUNTIES NURSERIES ✉ UK 🔲
Marshwood, Bridport, Dorset DT6 5QJ
☎ (01297) 678257 **Fax:** (01297) 678257
Contact: A & D Hitchcock
Opening Times: Not open.
Min. Mail Order UK: No minimum charge
Cat. Cost: 2 x 2nd class
Credit Cards: Visa, MasterCard
Specialities: Pinks & *Dianthus.*

CTor THE TORBAY PALM FARM ✉ EU 🔲 🔲
St Marychurch Road, Coffinswell,
Nr Newton Abbot, South Devon TQ12 4SE
☎ (01803) 872800 **Fax:** (01803) 322533
Contact: T A Eley
Opening Times: 0900-1730 Mon-Fri.
Min. Mail Order UK: £3.99 + p&p
Min. Mail Order EU: Poa

Cat. Cost: Free
Credit Cards: None
Specialities: *Cordyline australis, Trachycarpus fortuneii* & new varieties of *Cordyline.*
Map Ref: C, C4

CTrC TREVENA CROSS NURSERIES ✉ EU 🔲
Breage, Helston, Cornwall TR13 9PS
☎ (01736) 763880 **Fax:** (01736) 762828
E-mail: sales@trevenacrossnurseries.co.uk
Web Site: www.trevenacrossnurseries.co.uk
Contact: Graham Jeffery, John Eddy
Opening Times: 0900-1700 Mon-Sat,
1030-1630 Sun.
Min. Mail Order UK: No minimum charge
Min. Mail Order EU: Nmc*
Cat. Cost: A5 Sae with 2 x 1st class
Credit Cards: Access, Visa, Switch
Specialities: Specialist growers of South
African, Australian & New Zealand plants,
incl. *Aloe, Protea,* tree ferns, palms, *Restio,*
hardy succulents & a wide range of other
exotics. *Note: mail order to EU by
negotiation.
Map Ref: C, D1

CTre TREWIDDEN ESTATE NURSERY ✉ EU 🔲
Trereife, Penzance, Cornwall TR20 8TT
☎ (01736) 362087 **Fax:** (01736) 3331470
E-mail: bolitho@ckd.co.uk
Web Site: www.trewidden-nursery.co.uk
Contact: Bill Johnson
Opening Times: By appt. only.
Min. Mail Order UK: No minimum charge
Min. Mail Order EU: Nmc
Cat. Cost: 2 x 1st class
Credit Cards: None
Specialities: *Camellia* & unusual shrubs.
Map Ref: C, D1

CTrF TRESIDDER FARM PLANTS ✉ EU 🔲 🔲
Tresidder Farm, St Buryan, Penzance,
Cornwall TR19 6EZ
☎ (01736) 810656
Contact: N Milligan
Opening Times: By appt. Please phone.
Min. Mail Order UK: £15.00 + p&p
Min. Mail Order EU: £15.00 + p&p
Cat. Cost: Plant & seed lists available
Credit Cards: None
Specialities: *Proteaceae, Aloeaceae,* large *Aloe*
collection, unusual succulents.
Map Ref: C, D1

CTrG TREGOTHNAN NURSERY ✉ EU 🔲 🔲 €
Estate Office, Tregothnan, Truro,
Cornwall TR2 4AN
☎ (01872) 520325 **Fax:** (01872) 520291
E-mail: bigplants@tregothnan.co.uk

Web Site: www.tregothnan.com
Contact: Jonathon Jones
Opening Times: By appt. for collection only.
Min. Mail Order UK: No minimum charge
Min. Mail Order EU: Nmc
Cat. Cost: Printout from web site
Credit Cards: MasterCard, Visa, Delta,
EuroCard
Specialities: Unusual & rare plants from
own stock. Extra large specimens available
for instant effect. Known wild origin
plants.
Map Ref: C, D2

CTrh TREHANE CAMELLIA NURSERY
⊠ EU 🄰 🄼 €
J Trehane & Sons Ltd, Stapehill Road,
Hampreston, Wimborne, Dorset BH21 7ND
☎ (01202) 873490 Fax: (01202) 873490
Contact: Lorraine or Jeanette
Opening Times: 0900-1630 Mon-Fri all
year (excl. Xmas & New Year). 1000-1600
Sat-Sun in spring & by special appt.
Min. Mail Order UK: No minimum charge
Min. Mail Order EU: Nmc
Cat. Cost: Cat/Book £1.70
Credit Cards: Visa, Access, MasterCard
Specialities: Extensive range of *Camellia*
species, cultivars & hybrids. Many new
introductions. Evergreen azaleas, *Pieris,
Magnolia* & blueberries.
Map Ref: C, C6

CTri TRISCOMBE NURSERIES ◆
West Bagborough, Nr Taunton, Somerset
TA4 3HG
☎ (01984) 618267
Contact: S Parkman
Opening Times: 0900-1300 & 1400-1730
Mon-Sat. 1400-1730 Sun & B/hols.
Mail Order: None
Cat. Cost: None issued
Credit Cards: None
Specialities: Trees, shrubs, roses, fruit,
Clematis, herbaceous & rock plants.
Map Ref: C, B4

CTrw TREWITHEN NURSERIES ⊠ UK 🄰
Grampound Road, Truro, Cornwall
TR2 4DD
☎ (01726) 882764 Fax: (01726) 882301
Contact: M Taylor
Opening Times: 0800-1630 Mon-Fri.
Min. Mail Order UK: No minimum charge
Cat. Cost: £1.25
Credit Cards: None
Specialities: Shrubs, especially *Camellia* &
Rhododendron.
Map Ref: C, D2

CTuc EDWIN TUCKER & SONS ⊠ EU
Brewery Meadow, Stonepark, Ashburton,
Newton Abbot, Devon TQ13 7DG
☎ (01364) 652403 Fax: (01364) 654300
Contact: Geoff Penton
Opening Times: 0800-1700 Mon-Fri,
0800-1600 Sat.
Min. Mail Order UK: No minimum charge
Min. Mail Order EU: Nmc
Cat. Cost: Free
Credit Cards: Visa, MasterCard, Switch
Specialities: Over 90 varieties of seed potatoes.
Wide range of vegetables, flowers, green
manures & sprouting seeds in packets. All not
treated. Over 100 varieties of organically
produced seeds.
Map Ref: C, C3

CWat THE WATER GARDEN ⊠ UK
Hinton Parva, Swindon, Wiltshire
SN4 0DH
☎ (01793) 790558 Fax: (01793) 791298
E-mail: waterg@dircon.co.uk
Contact: Mike & Anne Newman
Opening Times: 1000-1700 Wed-Sun.
Min. Mail Order UK: £10.00 + p&p
Cat. Cost: 4 x 1st class
Credit Cards: Visa, Access, Switch
Specialities: Water lilies, marginal & moisture
plants, oxygenators & alpines.
Map Ref: C, A6

CWCL WESTCOUNTRY LUPINS ⊠ EU 🄰 🄼 ◆ €
Ford Hill Forge, Hartland, Bideford, Devon
EX39 6EE
☎ (01237) 441208 Fax: (01237) 441208
E-mail: SarahConibear@westcountrylupins.-
freeserve.co.uk
Contact: Sarah Conibear
Opening Times: Visitors by appt. only.
Min. Mail Order UK: No minimum charge
Min. Mail Order EU: Nmc
Cat. Cost: 2 x 1st class stamps
Credit Cards: None
Specialities: Lupins

CWDa WESTDALE NURSERIES ⊠ EU 🄼 🄰
Holt Road, Bradford-on-Avon, Wiltshire
BA15 1TS
☎ (01225) 863258
Fax: (01225) 863258
E-mail: westdale.nurseries@talk21.com
Contact: Louisa Bernal
Opening Times: 0900-1800 7 days.
Min. Mail Order UK: £10.00 + p&p
Min. Mail Order EU: £10.00 + p&p
Cat. Cost: 4 x 1st class
Credit Cards: MasterCard, Visa
Specialities: *Bougainvillea, Geranium,*

C

conservatory plants.
Note: export beyond EU by arrangement.
Map Ref: C, A5

CWdb **WOODBOROUGH GARDEN CENTRE**
Nursery Farm, Woodborough, Nr Pewsey,
Wiltshire SN9 5PF
☎ (01672) 851249   Fax: (01672) 851249
Contact: Els M Brewin
Opening Times: 0900-1700 Mon-Sat,
1100-1700 Sun.
Mail Order: None
Cat. Cost: None issued
Credit Cards: Access, Diners, EuroCard,
MasterCard, Switch, Visa
Specialities: Wide range of shrubs, trees,
herbaceous, alpines & herbs. Large
selection of climbers esp. *Clematis,* &
spring bulbs.
Map Ref: C, A6

CWes **WEST KINGTON NURSERIES LTD.** 🅶
Pound Hill, West Kington, Nr Chippenham,
Wiltshire SN14 7JG
☎ (01249) 782822   Fax: (01249) 782953
E-mail: Wkn.ltd@virgin.net
Contact: Jenny Hughes/Phil Walker
Opening Times: 0830-1700 Mon-Fri
(wholesale). 1000-1700 daily, incl.
B/hols (retail).
Mail Order: None
Cat. Cost: Free
Credit Cards: None
Specialities: Herbaceous, alpines, *Buxus* &
topiary. Herbaceous liners.
Map Ref: C, A5

CWhi **WHITEHOUSE IVIES** ⊠ EU
Eggesford Gardens, Chulmleigh, Devon
EX18 7QU
☎ (01769) 580250   Fax: (01769) 581041
Contact: Joan Burks
Opening Times: 0900-1700 7 days excl.
Xmas, Boxing & New Year's Day.
Min. Mail Order UK: £17.70 + p&p
Min. Mail Order EU: £17.70 + p&p
Cat. Cost: £1.50 or 6 x 1st class
Credit Cards: Visa, MasterCard, Switch, Delta
Specialities: Ivy, over 350 varieties.
Map Ref: C, B3

CWil **FERNWOOD NURSERY** ⊠ EU 🅶
Peters Marland, Torrington, Devon
EX38 8QG
☎ (01805) 601446   Fax: (01805) 601446
E-mail: hw@fernwood-nursery.co.uk
Web Site: www.fernwood-nursery.co.uk
Contact: Howard Wills & Sally Wills
Opening Times: Any time by appt. Please

phone first.
Min. Mail Order UK: No minimum charge
Min. Mail Order EU: Nmc
Cat. Cost: 3 x 1st class
Credit Cards: None
Specialities: National Collections of
Sempervivum, Jovibarba & *Rosularia.*
Map Ref: C, B3

CWin **WINFRITH HOSTAS** ⊠ UK 🅶
5 Knoll Park, Gatemore Road, Winfrith
Newburgh, Dorchester, Dorset DT2 8LD
☎ (01305) 852935
Contact: John Ledbury
Opening Times: By appt.
Min. Mail Order UK: No minimum charge
Cat. Cost: 2 x 1st class
Credit Cards: None
Specialities: *Hosta.*
Map Ref: C, C5

CWit **WITHLEIGH NURSERIES**
Quirkhill, Withleigh, Tiverton,
Devon EX16 8JG
☎ (01884) 253351
E-mail: withleigh.nurseries@ukf.net
Contact: Chris Britton
Opening Times: 0900-1730 Mon-Sat Mar-
Jun, Tue-Sat Jul-Feb.
Mail Order: None
Cat. Cost: None issued
Credit Cards: None
Specialities: Shrubs & herbaceous.
Map Ref: C, B4

CWiW **WINDRUSH WILLOW** ⊠ EU 🅶 🅶 €
Higher Barn, Sidmouth Road, Aylesbeare,
Exeter, Devon EX5 2JJ
☎ (01395) 233669   Fax: (01395) 233669
E-mail: windrushw@aol.com
Web Site: www.windrushwillow.com
Contact: Richard Kerwood
Opening Times: By appt.
Min. Mail Order UK: No minimum charge
Min. Mail Order EU: Nmc
Cat. Cost: 1 x 1st class
Credit Cards: None
Specialities: *Salix.* Unrooted cuttings
available Dec-Mar.

CWoo **IAN AND ROSEMARY WOOD** ⊠ UK
Newlands, 28 Furland Road, Crewkerne,
Somerset TA18 8DD
☎ (01460) 74630
Contact: Ian and Rosemary Wood
Opening Times: By appt. only. Primarily
mail order service.
Min. Mail Order UK: No minimum charge
Cat. Cost: 1 x 1st class

Credit Cards: None
Specialities: *Erythronium.*
Map Ref: C, B5

CWri NIGEL WRIGHT RHODODENDRONS ▣
The Old Glebe, Eggesford, Chumleigh,
Devon EX18 7QU
☎ (01769) 580632
Contact: Nigel Wright
Opening Times: By appt. only.
Mail Order: None
Cat. Cost: 2 x 1st class
Credit Cards: None
Specialities: *Rhododendron* only. 200 varieties
field grown. Root-balled, not potted. For
collection only. Specialist grower.
Map Ref: C, C3

CWSG WEST SOMERSET GARDEN
CENTRE ▣ EU
Mart Road, Minehead, Somerset TA24 5BJ
☎ (01643) 703812 **Fax:** (01643) 706470
E-mail:
westsomersetgardencentre@compuserve.com
Contact: Mrs J K Shoulders
Opening Times: 0800-1700 Mon-Sat, 1000-
1600 Sun. Winter times vary, please phone.
Min. Mail Order UK: No minimum charge
Min. Mail Order EU: Nmc
Cat. Cost: Please phone for availability.
Credit Cards: Access, Visa
Specialities: Wide general range. *Ceanothus.*
Map Ref: C, B4

CWtG THE WATER GARDENS
Highcroft, Moorend, Wembworthy,
Chumleigh, Devon EX18 7SG
☎ (01837) 83566
Contact: J M Smith
Opening Times: Garden open 1000-1700
Fri, Sun & Mon incl. B/hols Apr-Sep.
Mail Order: None
Cat. Cost: None issued
Credit Cards: None
Specialities: Water, bog, perennials, ferns for
sale in the garden. Entrance fee £2.00.
(Nursery closed.)
Map Ref: C, B3

EASTERN

EAnd ANDERS NURSERY ▣ UK
20 East Hall, Lodge Road, Feltwell,
Thetford, Norfolk IP26 4DP
☎ (01842) 827676
E-mail: timothy.anders@virgin.net
Contact: Timothy Anders
Opening Times: Please phone for appt.
Min. Mail Order UK: £10.00 + p&p

Cat. Cost: Sae
Credit Cards: None
Specialities: Carnivorous plants.
Map Ref: E, C5

EBak B & H M BAKER ▣
Bourne Brook Nurseries, Greenstead Green,
Halstead, Essex CO9 1RJ
☎ (01787) 472900/476369
Contact: B, HM and C Baker
Opening Times: 0800-1630 Mon-Fri,
0900-1200 & 1400-1630 Sat & Sun.
Mail Order: None
Cat. Cost: 20p + stamp
Credit Cards: MasterCard, Delta, Visa, Switch
Specialities: *Fuchsia* & conservatory plants.
Map Ref: E, C5

EBee BEECHES NURSERY ▣ EU
Village Centre, Ashdon, Saffron Walden,
Essex CB10 2HB
☎ (01799) 584362 **Fax:** (01799) 584362
E-mail: sales@beechesnursery.co.uk
Web Site: www.beechesnursery.co.uk
Contact: Alan Bidwell/Kevin Marsh
Opening Times: 0830-1700 Mon-Sat,
1000-1700 Sun & B/hols.
Min. Mail Order UK: No minimum charge
Min. Mail Order EU: Nmc
Cat. Cost: £3.50 fully descriptive or 2 x 1st
class for lists (herbaceous or shrubs)
Credit Cards: Visa, Access, MasterCard,
EuroCard, Switch
Specialities: Herbaceous specialists &
extensive range of other garden plants.
Map Ref: E, C5

EBls PETER BEALES ROSES ▣ EU ▣
London Road, Attleborough, Norfolk
NR17 1AY
☎ (01953) 454707 **Fax:** (01953) 456845
E-mail: sales@classicroses.co.uk
Web Site: www.classicroses.co.uk
Contact: Customer advisors
Opening Times: 0900-1700 Mon-Fri, 0900-
1630 Sat, 1000-1600 Sun. Jan closed Sun.
Min. Mail Order UK: No minimum charge
Min. Mail Order EU: Nmc
Cat. Cost: £2.00 reedemable with order
Credit Cards: Visa, MasterCard, Access,
Switch, Solo, Delta, JCB
Specialities: Old fashioned roses & classic
roses. National Collection of species roses.
Map Ref: E, C6

K E Y		
▣ Mail order to UK or EU		
▣ Exports beyond EU	€ Euro accepted	
▣ Also supplies Wholesale	◆ See Display advertisement	

E

EBlw   **BLACKWATER PLANTS** ✉ UK
Knowles Farm, Wycke Hill (A414), Maldon,
Essex CM9 6SH
☎ (01376) 517158, mobile 07931 311108
E-mail: blackwaterplants@ukonline.co.uk
Contact: Kirsty Bishop & Fiona Mildren
Opening Times: 1000-1700 (dusk in
winter) Wed-Sat, Mar-Oct & by appt.
Min. Mail Order UK: £10.00*
Cat. Cost: 2 x 1st class
Credit Cards: None
Specialities: Plants for shade & moist soils.
All plants grown in peat-free compost using
organic fertiliers, no chemicals. National
Collection of astrantias applied for.
*Note: mail order from Sep 2000 in autumn
& spring to Apr.
Map Ref: E, D2

EBot   **BOTANICUS** ✉ EU
The Nurseries, Ringland Lane, Old
Costessey, Norwich NR8 5BG
☎ (01603) 742063
Contact: Anthony Murphy
Opening Times: 1000-1700 Fri-Sun & B/hol
Mons Apr-Oct. 1000-1600 Sat Nov & Mar.
Min. Mail Order UK: £15.00 + p&p*
Min. Mail Order EU: £50.00 + p&p
Cat. Cost: £2.50
Credit Cards: None
Specialities: Historic garden plants grown in
Britain from Roman times to 1850,
particularly bulbs, herbaceous perennials &
shrubs. *Note: mail order for bulbs, corms,
tubers & rhizomes only.
Map Ref: E, B6

EBre   **BRESSINGHAM PLANT CENTRE (DISS)** ◆
Bressingham, Diss, Norfolk IP22 2AB
☎ (01379) 687464/688133
Fax: (01379) 688061
Contact: Russel Winteridge
Opening Times: 0900-1700 1st Nov-31st
Mar, 0900-1800 1st Apr-31st Oct, 7 days.
Mail Order: None
Cat. Cost: None issued
Credit Cards: Visa, Delta, Switch, MasterCard
Specialities: Very wide general range. Many
own varieties. Focus on hardy ornamental
plants & grasses. Perennials.
Map Ref: E, C6

EBrP   **BRESSINGHAM PLANT CENTRE
(ELTON)** ◆
Elton, Peterborough PE8 6SH
☎ (01832) 280058   Fax: (01832) 280081
Contact: Tom Green
Opening Times: 0900-1700 1st Nov-31st
Mar, 0900-1800 1st Apr-31st Oct, 7 days.

Mail Order: None
Cat. Cost: None issued
Credit Cards: Delta, Switch, MasterCard, Visa
Specialities: Very wide general range. Many
own varieties. Focus on hardy ornamental
plants & grasses. Perennials.
Map Ref: E, C4

EBSP   **BRIAN SULMAN** ✉ EU
54 Kingsway, Mildenhall, Bury St Edmunds,
Suffolk IP28 7HR
☎ (01638) 712297   Fax: (01638) 515052
Contact: Brian Sulman
Opening Times: Mail order only. Special
open w/end 10th/11th Jun 2000.
Min. Mail Order UK: £20.00
Min. Mail Order EU: £20.00
Cat. Cost: 2 x 1st class
Credit Cards: None
Specialities: Regal pelargoniums.
Map Ref: E, C5

EBur   **JENNY BURGESS** ✉ EU 🔟
Alpine Nursery, Sisland, Norwich, Norfolk
NR14 6EF
☎ (01508) 520724
Contact: Jenny Burgess
Opening Times: Any time by appt.
Min. Mail Order UK: £5.00 + p&p*
Min. Mail Order EU: £10.00 + p&p
Cat. Cost: 3 x 1st class
Credit Cards: None
Specialities: Alpines, *Sisyrinchium* &
Campanula. National Collection of
Sisyrinchium. *Note: only *Sisyrinchium* by
mail order.
Map Ref: E, B6

ECGN   **THE CONTENTED GARDENER
NURSERY** ✉ UK
The Garden House, 42 Wragby Road,
Bardney, Lincolnshire LN3 5XL
☎ (01526) 397307   Fax: (01526) 397280
E-mail: maryleeheykoop@aol.com
Contact: Lee Heykoop
Opening Times: Please phone to arrange a
visit.
Min. Mail Order UK: £15.00
Cat. Cost: A4 Sae + 2 x 1st class
Credit Cards: None
Specialities: Perennials & grasses for
naturalistic planting in dry and damp and
woodland edge.
Map Ref: E, B4

ECGP   **CAMBRIDGE GARDEN PLANTS**
The Lodge, Clayhithe Road, Horningsea,
Cambridgeshire CB5 9JD
☎ (01223) 861370

Contact: Mrs Nancy Buchdahl
Opening Times: 1100-1730 Thu-Sun mid Mar-31st Oct. Other times by appt.
Mail Order: None
Cat. Cost: 4 x 1st class
Credit Cards: None
Specialities: Hardy perennials incl. wide range of *Geranium, Allium, Euphorbia, Penstemon, Digitalis.* Some shrubs, roses & *Clematis.*
Map Ref: E, C5

ECha   THE BETH CHATTO GARDENS LTD ⊠ EU
Elmstead Market, Colchester, Essex CO7 7DB
☎ (01206) 822007   **Fax:** (01206) 825933
Contact: Beth Chatto
Opening Times: 0900-1700 Mon-Sat 1st Mar-31st Oct. 0900-1600 Mon-Fri 1st Nov-1st Mar. Closed Sun & B/hols.
Min. Mail Order UK: £20.00
Min. Mail Order EU: Ask for details
Cat. Cost: £3.00 incl. p&p
Credit Cards: Visa, Access, Switch
Specialities: Predominantly herbaceous. Many unusual for special situations.
Map Ref: E, D6

ECho   CHOICE LANDSCAPES ⊠ EU ▣ €
Priory Farm, 101 Salts Road, West Walton, Wisbech, Cambs PE14 7EF
☎ (01945) 585051   **Fax:** (01945) 580053
Contact: Michael Agg & Jillian Agg
Opening Times: 1000-1700 Tue-Sat, 1400-1700 Sun, closed Mon 1st Mar-31st Oct 2000 & 1st Feb-31st Nov 2001. Other times by appt.
Min. Mail Order UK: No minimum charge
Min. Mail Order EU: £10.00 + p&p
Cat. Cost: 4 x 1st class or 4 IRC
Credit Cards: Visa, MasterCard, Switch, Solo
Specialities: Dwarf conifers, heathers, alpines, acers, rhododendrons, hostas & lilies.
Map Ref: E, B5

EChP   CHOICE PLANTS ⊠ UK ◆
83 Halton Road, Spilsby, Lincs PE23 5LD
☎ (01790) 752361 mobile 0788 7913704
Contact: Joan Gunson, Jack Gunson
Opening Times: 1000-1700 Wed-Sun & B/hol Mon late Mar-mid Oct.
Min. Mail Order UK: £20.00
Cat. Cost: 2 x 1st
Credit Cards: None
Specialities: Hardy *Geranium, Crocosmia, Hemerocallis, Iris* & a good selection of unusual hardy perennials.
Map Ref: E, B5

ECle   CLEY NURSERIES LTD ⊠ UK
Holt Road, Cley-Next-the-Sea, Holt, Norfolk NR25 7TX
☎ (01263) 740892   **Fax:** (01263) 741138
Contact: Alec or Gill Mellor
Opening Times: 1000-1600 7 days.
Min. Mail Order UK: £10.00 + p&p
Cat. Cost: List 2 x 1st class
Credit Cards: Visa, Access, Switch
Specialities: Roses.
Map Ref: E, B6

ECon   CONSERVATORY PLANTLINE ⊠ EU ▣ ▣ €
Nayland Road, West Bergholt, Colchester, Essex CO6 3DH
☎ (01206) 242533   **Fax:** (01206) 242530
E-mail: info@scarletts.co.uk
Web Site: www.scarletts.org
Contact: Jane Wells
Opening Times: By appt. only.
Min. Mail Order UK: No minimum charge
Min. Mail Order EU: Nmc
Cat. Cost: £2.00
Credit Cards: MasterCard, EuroCard, Visa, Delta
Specialities: Conservatory plants. *Citrus.*
Map Ref: E, C5

ECoo   PATRICIA COOPER
Magpies, Green Lane, Mundford, Norfolk IP26 5HS
☎ (01842) 878496
Contact: Patricia Cooper
Opening Times: 0900-1700 Mon Tue Thu & Fri 1200-1700 Sat & Sun.
Mail Order: None
Cat. Cost: Free
Credit Cards: None
Specialities: Unusual hardy perennials, grasses, wild flowers, bog, aquatic & foliage plants.
Map Ref: E, C5

ECot   COTTAGE GARDENS
Langham Road, Boxted, Colchester, Essex CO4 5HU
☎ (01206) 272269
Contact: Alison Smith
Opening Times: 0800-1730 7 days spring & summer. 0800-1730 Thu-Mon Sep-Feb.
Mail Order: None
Cat. Cost: Free leaflet
Credit Cards: Visa, Access, Connect
Specialities: 400 varieties of shrubs, 390 varieties of herbaceous. Huge range of trees, alpines, herbs, hedging, all home grown. Garden antiques.
Map Ref: E, C6

E

ECou   COUNTY PARK NURSERY
Essex Gardens, Hornchurch, Essex
RM11 3BU
☎ (01708) 445205
Contact: G Hutchins
Opening Times: 0900-dusk Mon-Sat excl.
Wed, 1000-1700 Sun Mar-Oct. Nov-Feb by
appt. only.
Mail Order: None
Cat. Cost: 3 x 1st class
Credit Cards: None
Specialities: Alpines & rare and unusual
plants from New Zealand, Tasmania &
Falklands. National Collection of *Coprosma*
& *Parahebe*.
Map Ref: E, D5

ECre   CREAKE PLANT CENTRE
Nursery View, Leicester Road, South Creake,
Fakenham, Norfolk NR21 9PW
☎ (01328) 823018
Contact: Mr T Harrison
Opening Times: 1000-1300 & 1400-1730,
7 days excl. Xmas.
Mail Order: None
Cat. Cost: None issued
Credit Cards: None
Specialities: Unusual shrubs, herbaceous,
conservatory plants. Huge selection of hardy
Geranium.
Map Ref: E, B5

ECrN   CROWN NURSERY ⊠ EU 🔲
High Street, Ufford, Woodbridge, Suffolk
IP13 6EL
☎ (01394) 460755   Fax: (01394) 460142
Contact: Jill Proctor
Opening Times: 0900-1700 Mon-Sat.
Min. Mail Order UK: No minimum charge
Min. Mail Order EU: Nmc
Cat. Cost: 2 x 1st class
Credit Cards: Visa, Delta, MasterCard,
EuroCard, JCB, Switch
Specialities: Mature & semi-mature native &
ornamental trees.
Map Ref: E, C6

ECtt   COTTAGE NURSERIES ⊠ UK 🔲
Thoresthorpe, Alford, Lincolnshire
LN13 0HX
☎ (01507) 466968   Fax: (01507) 463409
Contact: W H Denbigh
Opening Times: 0900-1700 7 days 1st Mar-
31st Oct, 1000-1600 Thu-Sun Nov-Feb.
Min. Mail Order UK: £5.00 + p&p
Cat. Cost: 3 x 1st class
Credit Cards: None
Specialities: Wide general range.
Map Ref: E, A5

EDAr   D'ARCY & EVEREST ⊠ EU 🔲 €
(Office) 86 High Street, Needingworth, St
Ives, Huntingdon, Cambridgeshire
PE17 3SB
☎ (01480) 497672 (mobile) 07715 374440
Fax: (01480) 466042
E-mail: richard@darcyeverest.fsnet.co.uk
Contact: Angela Whiting
Opening Times: By appt. only.
Min. Mail Order UK: £10.00 + p&p
Min. Mail Order EU: £50.00 + p&p
Cat. Cost: 5 x 1st class
Credit Cards: None
Specialities: Alpines & herbs. Note: nursery
is at Pidley Sheep Lane (B1040),
Somersham, Huntingdon, Cambs PE17 3E
Map Ref: E, C2

EDrk   JOHN DRAKE ⊠ EU 🔲
Hardwicke House, Fen Ditton,
Cambridgeshire CB5 8TF
☎ (01223) 292246   Fax: (01223) 292246
Contact: John Drake
Min. Mail Order UK: £12.50
Min. Mail Order EU: £12.50
Cat. Cost: 3 x 1st class stamps*
Credit Cards: None
Specialities: National Collection of *Aquilegia*.
Seed only. *Note: seed catalogue available Aug.

EElm   ELM HOUSE NURSERY ⊠ UK 🔲
Freepost, PO Box 25, Wisbech,
Cambridgeshire PE13 2BR
☎ (01945) 581511 (24 hours)
Fax: (01945) 588235
Contact: Customer Services
Min. Mail Order UK: No minimum charge
Cat. Cost: Free
Credit Cards: Access, Visa, Switch
Specialities: *Chrysanthemum* & cutting-raised
plants.

EEls   ELSWORTH HERBS ⊠ EU
Avenue Farm Cottage,
31 Smith Street, Elsworth,
Cambridgeshire CB3 8HY
☎ (01954) 267414   Fax: (01954) 267414
Contact: Drs J D & J M Twibell
Opening Times: Advertised w/ends & by
appt. only.
Min. Mail Order UK: £10.00 + p&p
Min. Mail Order EU: £10.00 + p&p
Cat. Cost: 3 x 1st class
Credit Cards: None
Specialities: Herbs. National Collections of
Artemisia & *Nerium oleander*. Cottage garden
plants. Wide range of *Artemisia* &
Seriphidium, Nerium oleander.
Map Ref: E, C5

E

EFer THE FERN NURSERY ✉EU ▣
Grimsby Road, Binbrook, Lincolnshire
LN8 6DH
☎ (01472) 398092
Contact: R N Timm
Opening Times: 0900-1700 Sat & Sun Apr-
Oct or by appt.
Min. Mail Order UK: No minimum charge
Min. Mail Order EU: Nmc
Cat. Cost: 2 x 1st class
Credit Cards: None
Specialities: Ferns & hardy perennials.
Map Ref: E, A4

EFEx FLORA EXOTICA ✉EU ▣
Pasadena, South-Green, Fingringhoe,
Colchester, Essex CO5 7DR
☎ (01206) 729414
Contact: J Beddoes
Opening Times: Not open to the public.
Min. Mail Order UK: No minimum charge
Min. Mail Order EU: Nmc
Cat. Cost: 4 x 1st class
Credit Cards: None
Specialities: Exotica flora incl. orchids.

EFou FOUR SEASONS ✉EU €
Forncett St Mary, Norwich, Norfolk
NR16 1JT
☎ (01508) 488344 **Fax:** (01508) 488478
E-mail: mail@fsperennials.co.uk
Web Site: www.fsperennials.co.uk
Contact: J P Metcalf & R W Ball
Opening Times: Not open to the public.
Min. Mail Order UK: £15.00 + p&p
Min. Mail Order EU: £15.00 + p&p
Cat. Cost: Free
Credit Cards: Visa, MasterCard, Switch
Specialities: Herbaceous perennials.
Aconitum, Anemone, Aster, Campanula,
Chrysanthemum, Digitalis, Erigeron,
Geranium, Helenium, Iris, Salvia &
grasses.

EFul FULBROOKE NURSERY ✉EU
Home Farm, Westley Waterless, Newmarket,
Suffolk CB8 0RG
☎ (01638) 507124 **Fax:** (01638) 507124
E-mail: fulbrook@clara.net
Web Site: www.fulbrook.clara.net
Contact: Paul Lazard
Opening Times: By appt. most times incl.
w/ends.
Min. Mail Order UK: £6.00 + p&p
Min. Mail Order EU: £6.00 + p&p
Cat. Cost: 3 x 1st class
Credit Cards: None
Specialities: Bamboos & grasses.
Map Ref: E, C5

EGar GARDINER'S HALL PLANTS ✉EU ▣ €
Braiseworth, Eye, Suffolk IP23 7DZ
☎ (01379) 678285 **Fax:** (01379) 678192
Contact: Raymond Mayes or Joe Stuart
Opening Times: 1000-1800 Wed-Sat 1st
Apr-31st Oct.
Min. Mail Order UK: £20.00 + p&p
Min. Mail Order EU: £20.00 + p&p
Cat. Cost: 5 x 1st class
Credit Cards: None
Specialities: Herbaceous perennials incl.
Crocosmia, Euphorbia, Kniphofia, Monarda &
grasses.
Map Ref: E, C6

EGle GLEN CHANTRY
Ishams Chase, Wickham Bishops, Essex
CM8 3LG
☎ (01621) 891342 **Fax:** (01621) 891342
Contact: Sue Staines & Wol Staines
Opening Times: 1000-1600 Fri & Sat from
24 Mar-7 Oct. Also Sun & Mon on NGS
open days.
Mail Order: None
Cat. Cost: 4 x 1st class
Credit Cards: None
Specialities: A wide & increasing range of
perennials & alpines, many unusual.
Map Ref: E, D5

EGln GLENHIRST CACTUS NURSERY ✉EU
Station Road, Swineshead, Nr Boston,
Lincolnshire PE20 3NX
☎ (01205) 820314 **Fax:** (01205) 820614
E-mail: sabell@glenhirstcactiandpalms.co.uk
Web Site: www.glenhirstcact:andpalms.co.uk
Contact: N C & S A Bell
Opening Times: 1000-1700 Thu-Sat &
B/hols 1st Apr-30th Sep, other times
please phone first to check. Mail order all
year.
Min. Mail Order UK: No minimum charge
Min. Mail Order EU: Nmc
Cat. Cost: 2 x 1st class
Credit Cards: Visa, MasterCard, Switch,
Solo, Electron
Specialities: Extensive range of cacti &
succulent plants & seeds, incl.
Christmas cacti & orchid cacti. Hardy &
half-hardy desert plants. Display gardens.
Palms, *Cordyline, Bamboo,* treeferns,
Phormium & other hardy architectural
plants.
Map Ref: E, B4

E

EGol   GOLDBROOK PLANTS ✉ EU ⚙
Hoxne, Eye, Suffolk IP21 5AN
☎ (01379) 668770   Fax: (01379) 668770
Contact: Sandra Bond
Opening Times: 1000-1700 or dusk if
earlier, Thu-Sun Apr-Sep, Sat & Sun Oct-
Mar or by appt. Closed during Jan, Chelsea
& Hampton Court Shows.
Min. Mail Order UK: £15.00 + p&p
Min. Mail Order EU: £100.00 + p&p
Cat. Cost: 4 x 1st class
Credit Cards: None
Specialities: Very large range of *Hosta* (over
700), *Hemerocallis* & bog *Iris*.
Map Ref: E, C6

**EGoo   ELISABETH GOODWIN
NURSERIES ✉ UK**
Elm Tree Farm, 1 Beeches Road, West Row,
Bury St Edmunds, Suffolk IP28 8NP
☎ (01638) 713050
Contact: Elisabeth Goodwin
Opening Times: Open days 1000-1700 1st
Sun monthly Apr-Oct, or any time by prior
arrangement.
Min. Mail Order UK: No minimum charge
Cat. Cost: £1 coin or 4 x 1st class*
Credit Cards: None
Specialities: Drought tolerant plants for both
sun & shade esp. *Dianthus, Helianthemum,
Sedum, Teucrium* & *Vinca*. *Note: new mail
order catalogue each autumn.
Map Ref: E, C5

EGou   GOULDINGS FUCHSIAS ✉ EU ⚙ €
West View, Link Lane, Bentley, Nr Ipswich,
Suffolk IP9 2DP
☎ (01473) 310058   Fax: (01473) 310058
Contact: Mr E J Goulding
Opening Times: 12 Feb-11Jun 2000
1000-1700, excluding Tuesdays.
Min. Mail Order UK: See cat. for details
Min. Mail Order EU: See cat. for details.
Cat. Cost: 4 x 1st class
Credit Cards: None
Specialities: *Fuchsia* - new introductions,
basket, hardy, upright, terminal flowering
(triphylla), species, encliandras & paniculates.
Map Ref: E, C6

EGra   GRASMERE PLANTS ✉ UK
Grasmere, School Road, Terrington St John,
Wisbech, Cambs PE14 7SE
☎ (01945) 880514
E-mail: fleming@tstjohn.freeserve.co.uk
Contact: Angela Fleming
Opening Times: 1000-1700 Thu-Tue Apr-Jul
& Sep. 1000-1700 Sat & Sun Oct, Nov, Feb
& Mar. Other times by appt. Garden open.

Min. Mail Order UK: £10.00 + p&p*
Cat. Cost: 2 x 2nd class
Credit Cards: None
Specialities: Hardy perennials incl. *Geranium*
& grasses, shrubs & dwarf conifers.
*Note: mail order perennials only.
Map Ref: E, B5

EHan   HANGING GARDENS NURSERIES LTD
(Office) 15 Further Meadow, Writtle,
Chelmsford, Essex CM1 3LE
☎ (01245) 421020   Fax: (01245) 422293
E-mail: @hanginggardens.co.uk
Web Site: www. hanningardens.co.uk
Contact: Jim Drake & Louisa Drake
Opening Times: 0900-1800 Apr-Nov,
0900-1700 Dec-Mar, 7 days.
Mail Order: None
Cat. Cost: None issued
Credit Cards: Access, American Express,
Delta, EuroCard, MasterCard, Switch, Visa
Specialities: *Clematis*, David Austin roses,
basket & patio plants, excellent range of
hardy nursery stock. Note: nursery is at
Ongar Road West, (A414) Writtle bypass,
Writtle, Chelmsford.
Map Ref: E, D5

EHoe   HOECROFT PLANTS ✉ EU ◆
Severals Grange, Holt Road, Wood Norton,
Dereham, Norfolk NR20 5BL
☎ (01362) 684206   Fax: (01362) 684206
Contact: M Lister
Opening Times: 1000-1600 Thu-Sun 1st
Apr-1st Oct.
Min. Mail Order UK: No minimum charge
Min. Mail Order EU: Nmc
Cat. Cost: 5 x 2nd class/£1coin
Credit Cards: None
Specialities: 240 varieties of variegated and
300 varieties of coloured-leaved plants in all
species. 220 grasses.
Map Ref: E, B6

EHof   HOFFLANDS DAFFODILS ✉ EU ⚙
Bakers Green, Little Totham, Maldon, Essex
CM9 8LT
☎ (01621) 788678
Fax: (01621) 788445
E-mail: sales@hoffdaff.kemc.co.uk
Contact: John Pearson
Opening Times: By appt. only. Normally
mail order only.
Min. Mail Order UK: No minimum
charge
Min. Mail Order EU: Nmc
Cat. Cost: Free
Credit Cards: MasterCard, Visa
Specialities: *Narcissus*.

EHol HOLKHAM GARDENS
Holkham Park, Wells-next-the-Sea, Norfolk
NR23 1AB
☎ (01328) 711636 **Fax:** (01328) 711117
Contact: Tim Leese
Opening Times: 1000-1700 (or dusk) 7
days. Closed Xmas & Boxing Day.
Mail Order: None
Cat. Cost: 3 x 1st class
Credit Cards: Access, Visa, Switch
Specialities: Wide range of shrubs,
herbaceous perennials, alpines, wall plants,
climbers, roses, conservatory plants and
herbs, both common & unusual.
Map Ref: E, B5

EHon HONEYSOME AQUATIC
NURSERY ✉ UK ▣
The Row, Sutton, Nr Ely, Cambridgeshire
CB6 2PF
☎ (01353) 778889
Contact: D B Barker & D B Littlefield
Opening Times: At all times by
appointment only.
Min. Mail Order UK: No minimum charge
Cat. Cost: 2 x 1st class
Credit Cards: None
Specialities: Hardy aquatic, bog & marginal.
Map Ref: E, C5

EHrv HARVEYS GARDEN PLANTS ✉ EU ▣
Mulberry Cottage, Bradfield St George,
Bury St Edmunds, Suffolk IP30 0AY
☎ (01284) 386777
Fax: (01284) 386777 & answerphone
E-mail: roger@harveysgardenplants
Web Site: www.harveysgardenplants.co.uk
and www.hellebore.co.uk
Contact: Roger Harvey
Opening Times: 15th Jan-30th Jun & 1st
Sep-31st Oct.
Min. Mail Order UK: £15.00 + p&p
Min. Mail Order EU: Please enquire
Cat. Cost: 5 x 1st class
Credit Cards: None
Specialities: *Helleborus, Anemone,
Epimedium, Euphorbia, Eryngium, Astrantia,
Pulmonaria* & other herbaceous perennials.
Map Ref: E, C5

EHul HULL FARM ✉ UK ▣
Spring Valley Lane, Ardleigh, Colchester,
Essex CO7 7SA
☎ (01206) 230045 **Fax:** (01206) 230820
Contact: J Fryer & Sons
Opening Times: 1000-1600 7 days excl.
Xmas.
Min. Mail Order UK: £30.00 + p&p
Cat. Cost: 5 x 2nd class

Credit Cards: MasterCard, Visa
Specialities: Conifers.
Map Ref: E, C6

EHyt HYTHE ALPINES ✉ EU ▣
Methwold Hythe, Thetford, Norfolk
IP26 4QH
☎ (01366) 728543 **Fax:** (01366) 728543
Contact: Mike Smith
Opening Times: 1000-1700 Tue & Wed
Mar-Oct.
Min. Mail Order UK: No minimum charge
Min. Mail Order EU: Nmc*
Cat. Cost: 6 x 1st class, 4 x IRCs
Credit Cards: None
Specialities: Rare & unusual alpines, rock
garden plants & bulbs for enthusiasts &
exhibitors. *Note: export of dry bulbs only.
Map Ref: E, C5

EJWh JILL WHITE ✉ UK ▣
St Davids', Recreation Way, Brightlingsea,
Essex CO7 ONJ
☎ (01206) 303547
Contact: Jill White
Opening Times: By appt. only.
Min. Mail Order UK: No minimum charge
Cat. Cost: Sae
Credit Cards: None
Specialities: *Cyclamen* species esp. *Cyclamen
parviflorum.* Also seed.
Map Ref: E, D6

EKMF KATHLEEN MUNCASTER FUCHSIAS
✉ EU ▣
18 Field Lane, Morton, Gainsborough,
Lincolnshire DN21 3BY
☎ (01427) 612329
E-mail: jim@smuncaster.freeserve.co.uk
Web Site:
www.kathleenmuncasterfuchsias.co.uk
Contact: Kathleen Muncaster
Opening Times: 1000-dusk Thu-Mon. After
mid-Jul please phone to check.
Min. Mail Order UK: See cat. for details*
Min. Mail Order EU: See cat.
Cat. Cost: 2 x 1st class
Credit Cards: None
Specialities: *Fuchsia.* National Collection of
hardy fuchsias (full status). *Note: mail
orders to be received before 1st April.
Map Ref: E, A5

ELan LANGTHORNS PLANTERY
High Cross Lane West, Little Canfield,
Dunmow, Essex CM6 1TD
☎ (01371) 872611 **Fax:** (01371) 872611
Contact: P & D Cannon, P Seymour
Opening Times: 1000-1700 or dusk (if earlier)

E

7 days excl. Xmas fortnight & Easter Sun.
Mail Order: None
Cat. Cost: £1.50
Credit Cards: Visa, Access, Switch,
MasterCard, Delta
Specialities: Wide general range with many
unusual plants.
Map Ref: E, D5

ELau   LAUREL FARM HERBS ⊠ UK
Main Road, Kelsale, Saxmundham, Suffolk
IP13 2RG
☎ (01728) 668223
Contact: Chris Seagon
Opening Times: 1000-1700 Wed-Mon 1st
Mar-31st Oct. 1000-1500 Wed-Fri 1st Nov-
28th Feb.
Min. Mail Order UK: Please phone for
details.*
Cat. Cost: 4 x 1st class.
Credit Cards: None
Specialities: Herbs esp. rosemary, thyme,
lavender, mint, comfrey & sage. *Note: mail
order from May.
Map Ref: E, C6

EMac   FIRECREST (TREES & SHRUBS
NURSERY) ⊠ UK 🖼 €
Hall Road, Little Bealings, Woodbridge,
Suffolk IP13 6LU
☎ (01473) 625937   **Fax:** (01473) 625937
E-mail: mac@firecrest.org.uk
Web Site: www.firecrest.org.uk
Contact: Mac McGregor
Opening Times: 0830-1700 Mon-Fri,
1000 Sat.
Min. Mail Order UK: No minimum charge
Cat. Cost: 2 x 1st class
Credit Cards: None
Specialities: Trees & shrubs.
Map Ref: E, C3

EMan   MANOR NURSERY ⊠ EU
Thaxted Road, Wimbish, Saffron Walden,
Essex CB10 2UT
☎ (01799) 513481
Fax: (01799) 513481
E-mail: flora@gardenplants.co.uk
Web Site: www.gardenplants.co.uk
Contact: William Lyall
Opening Times: 0900-1700 summer. 0900-
1600 winter. Closed Xmas.
Min. Mail Order UK: 10 plants
Min. Mail Order EU: 10 plants
Cat. Cost: 4 x 2nd class
Credit Cards: Visa, Access, Switch,
EuroCard, MasterCard
Specialities: Uncommon perennials,
grasses, *Fuchsia*, hardy *Geranium*,

Pulmonaria, *Sedum* & cottage garden plants.
Variegated & coloured foliage plants.
Map Ref: E, C5

EMar   LESLEY MARSHALL ⊠ UK
Islington Lodge Cottage, Tilney All Saints,
King's Lynn, Norfolk PE34 4SF
☎ (01553) 765103
E-mail: lesley.marshall@talk21.com
Contact: Lesley & Peter Marshall
Opening Times: 0930-1800 Mon, Wed, Fri-
Sun Mar-Oct.
Min. Mail Order UK: 6 plants
Cat. Cost: £1 refundable. £1 coin/4 x 1st
class
Credit Cards: None
Specialities: Uncommon garden plants,
hardy perennials & plants for foliage effect.
Choice seed list. Some plants available in
limited quantities.
Map Ref: E, B5

EMcA   S M McARD (SEEDS) ⊠ EU 🖼
39 West Road, Pointon, Sleaford,
Lincolnshire NG34 0NA
☎ (01529) 240765   **Fax:** (01529) 240765
E-mail: s.mcard.seeds@ndirect.co.uk
Contact: Susan McArd
Opening Times: Not open.
Min. Mail Order UK: No minimum charge
Min. Mail Order EU: Nmc
Cat. Cost: 2 x 2nd class
Credit Cards: None
Specialities: Unusual & giant vegetables.
Seeds & plants.

EMFP   MILLS' FARM PLANTS
& GARDENS ⊠ EU 🖼
Norwich Road, Mendlesham, Suffolk IP14
5NQ
☎ (01449) 766425   **Fax:** (01449) 766425
Contact: Peter & Susan Russell
Opening Times: 0900-1730 Wed-Mon
Feb-Dec.
Min. Mail Order UK: No minimum charge*
Min. Mail Order EU: Nmc
Cat. Cost: 5 x 2nd class
Credit Cards: Access, Visa, Switch
Specialities: Pinks, old roses, wide general
range. *Note: mail order for pinks & roses only.
Map Ref: E, C6

EMFW   MICKFIELD FISH & WATERGARDEN
CENTRE ⊠ EU 🖼 🖼
Debenham Road, Mickfield, Stowmarket,
Suffolk IP14 5LP
☎ (01449) 711336   **Fax:** (01449) 711018
E-mail: mike@mickfield.co.uk
Web Site: www.mickfield.co.uk

Contact: Mike & Yvonne Burch
Opening Times: 0930-1700 7 days.
Min. Mail Order UK: No minimum charge
Min. Mail Order EU: £25.00 + p&p
Cat. Cost: £1.00
Credit Cards: Visa, Access, MasterCard, Switch
Specialities: Hardy aquatics, *Nymphaea* & moisture lovers.
Map Ref: E, C6

EMic   MICKFIELD HOSTAS ⊠ EU
The Poplars, Mickfield, Stowmarket, Suffolk
IP14 5LH
☎ (01449) 711576
Fax: (01449) 711576
E-mail: robinmilton@btconnect.com
Web Site: www.mickfieldhostas.co.uk
Contact: Mr & Mrs R L C Milton
Opening Times: By appt. only. See catalogue.
Min. Mail Order UK: See cat. for details
Min. Mail Order EU: See cat.
Cat. Cost: 4 x 1st class refundable with order
Credit Cards: See catalogue for details
Specialities: *Hosta,* over 450 varieties (subject to availability) mostly from USA. New varieties become available during the season.
Map Ref: E, C6

EMil   MILL RACE NURSERY ▣ €
New Road, Aldham, Colchester, Essex
CO6 3QT
☎ (01206) 242521   Fax: (01206) 241616
Contact: Bill Mathews
Opening Times: 0900-1730 7 days.
Mail Order: None
Cat. Cost: Sae + 2 x 1st class
Credit Cards: Access, Visa, Diners, Switch
Specialities: Over 400 varieties of herbaceous & many unusual trees, shrubs & climbers.
Map Ref: E, C5

EMNN   MARTIN NEST NURSERIES ⊠ EU ▣ ▣
Grange Cottage, Harpswell Lane,
Hemswell, Gainsborough, Lincolnshire
DN21 5UP
☎ (01427) 668369   Fax: (01427) 668080
Contact: M Robinson and J Shardlow
Opening Times: 1000-1600 7 days.
Min. Mail Order UK: No minimum charge
Min. Mail Order EU: £30.00 + p&p
Cat. Cost: 3 x 2nd class
Credit Cards: Visa, Access, Switch, MasterCard, American Express
Specialities: Alpines esp. *Primula,* auriculas & *Saxifraga*. National Collection of show & alpine auriculas.
Map Ref: E, A5

EMon   MONKSILVER NURSERY ⊠ EU
Oakington Road, Cottenham,
Cambridgeshire CB4 8TW
☎ (01954) 251555   Fax: (01223) 502887
E-mail: plants@monksilver.com
Web Site: www.monksilver.com
Contact: Joe Sharman & Alan Leslie
Opening Times: 1000-1600 Fri & Sat 1 Mar-30 Jun, 17 Sept & Fri & Sat Oct 2000.
Min. Mail Order UK: £15.00 + p&p
Min. Mail Order EU: £30.00 + p&p
Cat. Cost: 8 x 1st class
Credit Cards: None
Specialities: Herbaceous plants, grasses, *Anthemis, Arum, Helianthus, Lamium, Nepeta, Monarda, Salvia, Vinca,* sedges & variegated plants. Many NCCPG 'Pink Sheet' plants. Ferns.
Map Ref: E, C5

EMor   JOHN MORLEY ⊠ EU
North Green Only, Stoven, Beccles, Suffolk
NR34 8DG
E-mail: snowdrops@compuserve.com
Contact: John Morley
Opening Times: By appt. only.
Min. Mail Order UK: Details in cat.
Min. Mail Order EU: Details in cat.
Cat. Cost: 6 x 1st class
Credit Cards: None
Specialities: *Galanthus,* a comprehensive range of cultivars. Also seed.

EMou   FRANCES MOUNT PERENNIAL PLANTS ⊠ EU
1 Steps Farm, Polstead, Colchester, Essex
CO6 5AE
☎ (01206) 262811
Contact: Frances Mount
Opening Times: 1000-1700 Tue Wed & Sat. 1400-1800 Fri. Check w/ends & hols.
Min. Mail Order UK: £5.00 + p&p
Min. Mail Order EU: £5.00 + p&p
Cat. Cost: 3 x 1st class
Credit Cards: None
Specialities: Hardy *Geranium*.
Map Ref: E, C6

EMsh   S E MARSHALL & CO LTD. ⊠ EU ▣
Regal Road, Wisbech, Cambridgeshire
PE13 2RF
☎ (01945) 583407 (24 hours)
Fax: (01945) 588235
Contact: Customer Services

E

Min. Mail Order UK: No minimum charge
Min. Mail Order EU: £15.00 + p&p
Cat. Cost: Free
Credit Cards: Access, Visa, Switch
Specialities: Vegetables.

EMui   KEN MUIR ⊠ UK ▣
Honeypot Farm, Rectory Road, Weeley
Heath, Essex CO16 9BJ
☎ (01255) 830181   Fax: (01255) 831534
E-mail: kenmuir.fruit@virgin.net
Contact: Ken Muir
Opening Times: 1000-1600.
Min. Mail Order UK: No minimum charge
Cat. Cost: 3 x 1st class
Credit Cards: Visa, Access, Switch
Specialities: Fruit.
Map Ref: E, D6

ENor   NORFOLK LAVENDER ⊠ EU ▣
Caley Mill, Heacham, King's Lynn, Norfolk
PE31 7JE
☎ (01485) 570384   Fax: (01485) 571176
E-mail: admin@norfolk-lavender.co.uk
Web Site: www.norfolk-lavender.co.uk
Contact: Henry Head
Opening Times: 0930-1700 7 days.
Min. Mail Order UK: £15.00 + p&p
Min. Mail Order EU: £15.00 + p&p
Cat. Cost: 2 x 1st class
Credit Cards: Visa, Access, Switch
Specialities: National Collection of *Lavandula*.
Map Ref: E, B5

ENot   NOTCUTTS NURSERIES ⊠ EU ▣ ▣
Woodbridge, Suffolk IP12 4AF
☎ (01394) 383344   Fax: (01394) 445440
E-mail: sales@notcutts.co.uk
Web Site: www.notcutts.co.uk
Contact: Plant Adviser
Opening Times: Garden centres vary between
0830-1800 Mon-Sat & 1030-1630 Sun.
Min. Mail Order UK: £150.00 + p&p
Min. Mail Order EU: £300.00 + p&p
Cat. Cost: £4.00 + £1.00 postage
Credit Cards: Visa, Access, Switch, Connect
Specialities: Wide general range. Specialist
list of *Syringa*. National Collection of *Hibiscus*.
Map Ref: E, C6

EOas   OASIS ⊠ EU
42 Greenwood Avenue, South Benfleet,
Essex SS7 1LD
☎ (01268) 757666   Fax: (01268) 795646
E-mail: paul@oasisdesigns.co.uk
Web Site: www.oasisdesigns.co.uk
Contact: Paul Spracklin
Opening Times: Strictly by appt. only.
Min. Mail Order UK: No minimum charge

Min. Mail Order EU: £75
Cat. Cost: 2 x 1st class
Credit Cards: None
Specialities: Small nursery offering a range
of hardy & half-hardy exotic plants esp.
bamboos, palms, tree ferns, bananas &
unusual xerophytes.
Map Ref: E, D5

EOHP   OLD HALL PLANTS ⊠ UK
1 The Old Hall, Barsham, Beccles, Suffolk
NR34 8HB
☎ (01502) 717475
Contact: Janet Elliott
Opening Times: By appt. most days, please
phone first.
Min. Mail Order UK: No minimum charge*
Cat. Cost: 4 x 1st class
Credit Cards: None
Specialities: Herbs, over 600 varieties grown.
*Note: mail order of rare herbs only.
Map Ref: E, C6

EOld   OLD MILL HOUSE GARDEN NURSERY
Guithavon Valley, Witham, Essex CM8 1HF
☎ (01376) 512396   Fax: (01376) 512396
Contact: Kirsty Bishop & Sheila Bates
Opening Times: 1000-1730 (dusk in
winter) all year excl. 25th Dec-31st Jan.
Garden open as nursery.
Mail Order: None
Cat. Cost: 2 x 1st class
Credit Cards: None
Specialities: Herbaceous perennials, plus
large range of shrubs, alpines, herbs, bog &
water plants; also seasonal bedding.
Map Ref: E, D5

EOrc   ORCHARD NURSERIES ⊠ UK
Tow Lane, Foston, Grantham, Lincolnshire
NG32 2LE
☎ (01400) 281354   Fax: (01400) 281354
E-mail: orchnurs@lineone.net
Contact: Margaret Rose
Opening Times: 1000-1800 Wed-Mon 1st
Feb-30th Sept. Other times by appt.
Min. Mail Order UK: nmc
Cat. Cost: 5 x 2nd class
Credit Cards: None
Specialities: Small flowered *Clematis*, unusual
herbaceous esp. *Geranium, Helleborus, Hosta,
Salvia*. Sae for seed list, mainly *Helleborus*.
Map Ref: E, B4

EOrn   ORNAMENTAL CONIFERS ⊠ UK ◆
22 Chapel Road, Terrington St Clement,
Kings Lynn, Norfolk PE34 4ND
☎ (01553) 828874   Fax: (01553) 828874
Contact: Peter Rotchell

Opening Times: 0930-1700 7 days 1st Feb-
20th Dec.
Min. Mail Order UK: Cost of 4 plants + p&p*
Cat. Cost: New A4 colour cat. £2.50,
refundable with first order + 2 x 1st class.
Credit Cards: None
Specialities: Conifers & heathers. *Note:
mail order conifers only Oct-Nov, Mar-May.
Map Ref: E, B5

EPar   PARADISE CENTRE ⊠ EU ▥ €
Twinstead Road, Lamarsh, Bures, Suffolk
CO8 5EX
☎ (01787) 269449 **Fax:** (01787) 269449
E-mail: hedy@paradisecentre.com
Web Site: www.paradisecentre.com
Contact: Cees & Hedy Stapel-Valk
Opening Times: 1000-1700 Sat-Sun &
B/hols or by appt. Easter-1st Nov.
Min. Mail Order UK: £7.50 + p&p
Min. Mail Order EU: £25.00 + p&p
Cat. Cost: 5 x 1st class
Credit Cards: Visa, Access, Diners
Specialities: Unusual bulbous & tuberous
plants including shade & bog varieties. Also
some seeds.
Map Ref: E, C5

EPfP   THE PLACE FOR PLANTS
East Bergholt Place, East Bergholt, Suffolk
CO7 6UP
☎ (01206) 299224 **Fax:** (01206) 299224
E-mail: placeforplants@martex.net
Contact: Rupert & Sara Eley
Opening Times: 1000-1700 (or dusk) 7
days. Closed Xmas fortnight. Garden open
Mar-Oct.
Mail Order: None
Cat. Cost: Free list
Credit Cards: Visa, Access, MasterCard,
EuroCard, Delta, Switch
Specialities: Wide range of specialist &
popular plants. 15 acre mature garden.
Map Ref: E, C6

EPGN   PARK GREEN NURSERIES ⊠ EU ▥
Wetheringsett, Stowmarket, Suffolk IP14 5QH
☎ (01728) 860139 **Fax:** (01728) 861277
E-mail: nurseries@parkgreen-fsnet.co.uk
Web Site: www.parkgreen.co.uk
Contact: Richard & Mary Ford
Opening Times: 1000-1700 7 days Mar-Sep.
Min. Mail Order UK: No minimum charge
Min. Mail Order EU: Nmc
Cat. Cost: 4 x 1st class
Credit Cards: Visa, MasterCard, Delta, Switch
Specialities: *Hosta, Astilbe,* ornamental
grasses & herbaceous.
Map Ref: E, C6

EPla   P W PLANTS ⊠ EU ◆
Sunnyside, Heath Road, Kenninghall,
Norfolk NR16 2DS
☎ (01953) 888212 **Fax:** (01953) 888212
E-mail: pw.plants@paston.co.uk
Web Site: www.pw-plants.co.uk
Contact: Paul Whittaker
Opening Times: Every Fri & last Sat in
every month.
Min. Mail Order UK: No minimum charge
Min. Mail Order EU: Nmc
Cat. Cost: 5 x 1st class
Credit Cards: Visa, MasterCard, Switch,
JCB, Solo
Specialities: Bamboos, grasses, choice shrubs
& perennials, climbers (incl. wide selection
of *Hedera*).
Map Ref: E, C6

EPln   THE PLANT LOVERS ▣
Candlesby House, Candlesby, Spilsby,
Lincolnshire PE23 5RU
☎ (01754) 890256 **Fax:** (01754) 890594
Contact: Tim Wilson
Opening Times: Daily but please phone first.
Mail Order: None
Cat. Cost: None issued
Credit Cards: None
Specialities: *Sempervivum* (houseleeks) &
wide range of cacti & other succulents.
Brochure available.
Map Ref: E, B2

EPot   POTTERTON & MARTIN ⊠ EU ▣ ▥ €
Moortown Road, Nettleton, Caistor,
Lincolnshire LN7 6HX
☎ (01472) 851714 **Fax:** (01472) 852580
E-mail: pottin01@globalnet.co.uk
Web Site: www.users.globalnet.co.uk/~pottin01
Contact: Robert or Jackie Potterton
Opening Times: 0900-1630 7 days.
Min. Mail Order UK: No minimum charge
Min. Mail Order EU: Nmc
Cat. Cost: £1 in stamps only
Credit Cards: Electron, MasterCard, Delta,
Switch, Solo, JCB, Maestro, Visa
Specialities: Alpines, dwarf bulbs, conifers &
shrubs. Hardy orchids & *Pleione*. Seed list
sent out in Nov.
Map Ref: E, A5

EPPr   THE PLANTSMAN'S PREFERENCE ⊠ EU
Lynwood, Hopton Road, Garboldisham,
Diss, Norfolk IP22 2QN
☎ (01953) 681439
E-mail: plantpref@aol.com
Contact: Jenny & Tim Fuller
Opening Times: 0900-1700 Fri & Sun
Mar-Oct. Other times by appt.

E

Min. Mail Order UK: No minimum charge
Min. Mail Order EU: Nmc
Cat. Cost: 4 x 1st class
Credit Cards: None
Specialities: Hardy *Geranium* (362), grasses &
sedges (420). Unusual & interesting perennials.
Map Ref: E, C6

EPri   PRIORY PLANTS ⊠ UK
1 Covey Cottage, Hintlesham, Nr Ipswich,
Suffolk IP8 3NY
☎ (01473) 652656   Fax: (01473) 652656
Contact: Sue Mann
Opening Times: By appt. only. Please ring
first to avoid disappointment.
Min. Mail Order UK: £10.00 + p&p
Cat. Cost: 3 x 1st class
Credit Cards: None
Specialities: *Penstemon,* hardy *Geranium,*
Euphorbia, Campanula, Salvia & grasses.
Cottage garden perennials.
Map Ref: E, C6

EPts   POTASH NURSERY ⊠ UK
Cow Green, Bacton, Stowmarket, Suffolk
IP14 4HJ
☎ (01449) 781671
Contact: M W Clare
Opening Times: 1000-1700 Fri-Sun &
B/hol Mons mid Feb-end Jun.
Min. Mail Order UK: No minimum charge
Cat. Cost: 3 x 1st class
Credit Cards: None
Specialities: *Fuchsia.*
Map Ref: E, C6

EPVP   PALM VIEW PLANTS ⊠ EU
10 Milden Road, Ipswich, Suffolk IP2 0LB
☎ (01473) 402747   Fax: (01473) 424034
Contact: Robert Gooding
Opening Times: By appt. only.
Min. Mail Order UK: No minimum charge
Min. Mail Order EU: £50.00
Cat. Cost: Sae
Credit Cards: None
Specialities: Cold hardy exotics. *Bamboo,*
palms, succulents, tree ferns and many
unusual looking foliage plants.
Map Ref: E, C3

ER&R   RHODES & ROCKLIFFE ⊠ EU ⊠
2 Nursery Road, Nazeing, Essex EN9 2JE
☎ (01992) 463693   Fax: (01992) 440673
E-mail: R&RBegonias@aol.com
Contact: David Rhodes or John Rockliffe
Opening Times: By appt.
Min. Mail Order UK: £2.50 + p&p
Min. Mail Order EU: £5.00 + p&p
Cat. Cost: 2 x 1st class

Credit Cards: None
Specialities: *Begonia* species & hybrids.
National Collection of begonias.
Map Ref: E, D5

ERav   RAVENINGHAM GARDENS ⊠ EU ◆ ⊠
Norwich, Norfolk NR14 6NS
☎ (01508) 548222
Fax: (01508) 548958/548149
E-mail: raveningham@freenet.co.uk
Contact: Carol Clutten
Opening Times: Mail order only. Plants for
sale when gardens open, Sun & B/hol Mon,
Easter to end-Jul.
Min. Mail Order UK: No minimum charge
Min. Mail Order EU: Nmc
Cat. Cost: 4 x 1st class
Credit Cards: None
Specialities: Plants noted for foliage.
Variegated & coloured leaf plants,
herbaceous, snowdrops, *Pulmonaria* & hardy
Agapanthus. Note: Please ring for details of
wholesale & retail.
Map Ref: E, B6

ERea   READS NURSERY ⊠ EU ⊠
Hales Hall, Loddon, Norfolk NR14 6QW
☎ (01508) 548395   Fax: (01508) 548040
E-mail: plants@readsnursery.co.uk
Web Site: www.readsnursery.co.uk
Contact: Stephen Read
Opening Times: 1000-1700 (dusk if earlier)
Tue-Sat, 1100-1600 Sun & B/hols Easter-
end Sep & by appt.
Min. Mail Order UK: £10.00 + p&p
Min. Mail Order EU: £10.00 + p&p
Cat. Cost: 4 x 1st class
Credit Cards: Visa, Access, Diners, Switch
Specialities: Conservatory plants, vines,
Citrus, figs & unusual fruits & nuts. Wall
shrubs & climbers. Scented & aromatic
hardy plants. Box & yew hedging & topiary.
UK grown. National Collections of *Citrus,*
figs, vines.
Map Ref: E, B6

**ERob   ROBIN SAVILL CLEMATIS
         SPECIALIST ⊠ EU ⊠ ▣**
(Office) 2 Bury Cottages, Bury Road,
Pleshey, Chelmsford, Essex CM3 1HB
☎ (01245) 237380   Fax: (01245) 603882
E-mail: clematis@madasafish.com
Contact: Robin Savill
Opening Times: Mail order only. Visitors by
appt. only.
Min. Mail Order UK: 1 plant + p&p
Min. Mail Order EU: 1 plant + p&p
Cat. Cost: £2.00 or 8 x 1st class
Credit Cards: None

Specialities: Over 700 varieties of *Clematis* incl. many unusual species & cvs from around the world. National Collection of *Clematis viticella*.

ERod   THE RODINGS PLANTERY ⊠ EU ⊠
Anchor Lane, Abbess Roding, Essex CM5 0JW
☎ (01279) 876421
Contact: Jane & Andy Mogridge
Opening Times: By appt. only. Occasional open days, please phone for details.
Min. Mail Order UK: £15.00 + p&p
Min. Mail Order EU: £500.00 + p&p
Cat. Cost: 3 x 1st class
Credit Cards: None
Specialities: *Bamboo*. Rare & unusual trees.
Map Ref: E, D5

ERom   THE ROMANTIC GARDEN
⊠ EU ⊠ ⊠ ◆ €
Swannington, Norwich, Norfolk NR9 5NW
☎ (01603) 261488
Fax: (01603) 864231
E-mail: enquiries@romantic-garden.demon.co.uk
Web Site: www.romantic-garden.demon.co.uk
Contact: John Powles
Opening Times: 1000-1700 Wed Fri & Sat all year.
Min. Mail Order UK: £5.00 + p&p
Min. Mail Order EU: £30.00 + p&p
Cat. Cost: 4 x 1st class
Specialities: Half-hardy & conservatory. *Buxus* topiary, ornamental standards, large specimens.
Map Ref: E, B6

ERos   ROSEHOLME NURSERY ⊠ EU ⊠ ⊠
Roseholme Farm, Howsham, Market Rasen, Lincolnshire LN7 6JZ
☎ (01652) 678661   **Fax:** (01472) 852450
Contact: P B Clayton
Opening Times: By appt. for collection of orders.
Min. Mail Order UK: No minimum charge
Min. Mail Order EU: Nmc
Cat. Cost: 2 x 2nd class
Credit Cards: None
Specialities: Underground lines - bulbs, corms, rhizomes & tubers (esp. *Crocus, Iris*).
Map Ref: E, A5

ERou   ROUGHAM HALL NURSERIES ⊠ EU ⊠ ⊠
Ipswich Road, Rougham, Bury St. Edmunds, Suffolk IP30 9LZ
☎ (01359) 270577   **Fax:** (01359) 271149
E-mail: hardy-perennials@aol.com
Web Site: www.roughamhallnurseries.co.uk
Contact: A A & K G Harbutt

Opening Times: 1000-1600 Thu-Mon Easter-31st Oct.
Min. Mail Order UK: No minimum charge
Min. Mail Order EU: Nmc
Cat. Cost: 5 x 1st class
Credit Cards: MasterCard, Visa
Specialities: Hardy perennials esp. *Aster* (n-a, n-b & species), *Delphinium, Hemerocallis, Iris, Kniphofia, Papaver* & *Phlox*. National Collections of *Delphinium* & gooseberry. Please note delphiniums for collection only - no mail order.
Map Ref: E, C5

ERsn   SUE ROBINSON
21 Bederic Close, Bury St Edmunds, Suffolk IP32 7DN
☎ (01284) 764310   **Fax:** (01284) 764310
Contact: Sue Robinson
Opening Times: By appt. only.
Mail Order: None
Cat. Cost: None issued
Credit Cards: None
Specialities: Variegated & foliage plants. Garden open. Lectures at clubs & societies, group bookings welcome.

ESCh   SHEILA CHAPMAN CLEMATIS
Crowther Nurseries, Ongar Road, Abridge, Romford, Essex RM4 1AA
☎ (01708) 688090   **Fax:** (01708) 688677
Contact: Sheila Chapman
Opening Times: 0930-1700 (or dusk) all year excl. Xmas week.
Mail Order: None
Cat. Cost: 4 x 1st class
Credit Cards: Visa, Access, Switch, Connect, Delta, Discover, EuroCard, Electron, JCB, Laser, MasterCard
Specialities: Over 500 varieties of *Clematis*.
Map Ref: E, D5

ESgl   SEAGATE IRISES ⊠ EU €
(Office) Browse Partners, 36 Market Street, Long Sutton, Lincolnshire PE12 9DF
☎ (01406) 363189   **Fax:** (01406) 365447
E-mail: Sales@irises.co.uk
Web Site: www.irises.co.uk
Contact: Julian Browse or Wendy Browse
Opening Times: 1000-1800 daily Apr-Sep. Please ring for appt. Oct-Mar.
Min. Mail Order UK: No minimum charge
Min. Mail Order EU: Nmc carriage at cost
Cat. Cost: 2 x 1st class

KEY		
⊠ Mail order to UK or EU		
⊠ Exports beyond EU	€ Euro accepted	
⊠ Also supplies Wholesale	◆ See Display advertisement	

E

Credit Cards: Visa, Access
Specialities: Bearded *Iris,* mainly tall
bearded, 200 modern (1980s/90s) & over 50
historic (pre-1970) all in a display garden.
Some container grown available. Other
choice perennials. Note: nursery is on A17
Long Sutton Bypass, Long Sutton, Lincs
PE12 9RX.
Map Ref: E, B2

EShb   SHRUBLAND PARK NURSERIES
Coddenham, Ipswich, Suffolk IP6 9QJ
☎ (01473) 833187   Fax: (01473) 833187
Contact: Gill Stitt
Opening Times: By appt. only.
Mail Order: None
Cat. Cost: None issued
Credit Cards: None
Specialities: A new nursery offering an
increasing range of plants for the
conservatory & sheltered outdoor locations.
Map Ref: E, C3

ESim   CLIVE SIMMS ⊠ UK
Woodhurst, Essendine, Stamford,
Lincolnshire PE9 4LQ
☎ (01780) 755615
Contact: Clive & Kathryn Simms
Opening Times: By appt. for collection only
Min. Mail Order UK: No minimum charge
Cat. Cost: 2 x 1st class
Credit Cards: None
Specialities: Uncommon nut trees & unusual
fruiting plants.

ESis   SISKIN PLANTS ⊠ EU
April House, Davey Lane, Charsfield,
Woodbridge, Suffolk IP13 7QG
☎ (01473) 737567   Fax: (01473) 737567
E-mail: info@siskinplants.co.uk
Web Site: www.siskinplants.co.uk
Contact: Chris & Valerie Wheeler
Opening Times: 1000-1700 Tue-Sat Mar-Oct.
Min. Mail Order UK: No minimum charge
Min. Mail Order EU: Nmc
Cat. Cost: 4 x 1st class
Credit Cards: Visa, MasterCard
Specialities: Alpines, small perennials, grasses
& dwarf shrubs esp. plants for troughs.
National Collection of dwarf *Hebe.*
Map Ref: E, C6

ESou   SOUTHFIELD NURSERIES ⊠ EU ▣
Bourne Road, Morton, Nr Bourne,
Lincolnshire PE10 0RH
☎ (01778) 570168
Contact: Mr & Mrs B Goodey
Opening Times: 1000-1230 & 1330-1600 7
days. Nov-Jan by appt. only.

Min. Mail Order UK: No minimum charge
Min. Mail Order EU: Nmc
Cat. Cost: 1 x 1st class
Credit Cards: None
Specialities: A wide range of cacti &
succulents incl. some of the rarer varieties, all
grown on our own nursery.
Map Ref: E, B4

ESul   PEARL SULMAN ⊠ EU
54 Kingsway, Mildenhall, Bury St Edmunds,
Suffolk IP28 7HR
☎ (01638) 712297   Fax: (01638) 515052
Contact: Pearl Sulman
Opening Times: Not open. Mail order only.
Open w/end 10th/11th Jun 2000.
Min. Mail Order UK: £12.00 + p&p
Min. Mail Order EU: £12.00 + p&p
Cat. Cost: 4 x 1st class
Credit Cards: Visa, MasterCard
Map Ref: E, C5

**ET&M   THOMPSON & MORGAN
(UK) LTD ⊠ EU ▣ ▣**
Poplar Lane, Ipswich, Suffolk IP8 3BU
☎ (01473) 688821   Fax: (01473) 680199
E-mail: tm@thompson-morgan.com
Web Site: www.thompson-morgan.com
Contact: Michael Perry
Opening Times: W/end of 5th-6th Aug 2000.
Min. Mail Order UK: No minimum charge
Min. Mail Order EU: Nmc
Cat. Cost: Free
Credit Cards: Visa, Switch, MasterCard
Specialities: Largest illustrated seed catalogue
in the world.
Map Ref: E, C6

**ETho   THORNCROFT CLEMATIS
NURSERY ⊠ EU ▣ €**
The Lings, Reymerston, Norwich, Norfolk
NR9 4QG
☎ (01953) 850407   Fax: (01953) 851788
E-mail: sales@thorncroft.co.uk
Web Site: www.thorncroft.co.uk
Contact: Ruth P Gooch
Opening Times: 1000-1630 Thu-Tue 1st
Mar-31st Oct.
Min. Mail Order UK: No minimum charge
Min. Mail Order EU: Nmc
Cat. Cost: 5 x 2nd class
Credit Cards: MasterCard, Solo, Visa, Delta,
Switch
Specialities: *Clematis.*
Map Ref: E, B6

ETub   VAN TUBERGEN UK LTD ⊠ EU ▣
Bressingham, Diss, Norfolk IP22 2AB
☎ (01379) 688282   Fax: (01379) 687227

E-mail: van.tubergen@tesco.net
Web Site: www.vantubergen.co.uk
Contact: General Manager
Opening Times: Not open to the public.
Min. Mail Order UK: No minimum charge
Min. Mail Order EU: Nmc*
Cat. Cost: Free
Credit Cards: Visa, Access, MasterCard, Switch
Specialities: Bulbs. *Note: retail & wholesale
sales by mail order only (wholesale bulbs not
listed in RHS Plant Finder).

ETWh TREVOR WHITE OLD FASHIONED
ROSES ✉ EU 🄳
Bennetts Brier, The Street, Felthorpe,
Norwich, Norfolk NR10 4AB
☎ (01603) 755135   **Fax:** (01603) 755135
Contact: Mr T A & Mrs V J White.
Opening Times: 0900-1700 by appt only.
Min. Mail Order UK: No minimum charge
Min. Mail Order EU: £100 + p&p
Cat. Cost: Free
Credit Cards: None
Specialities: Old-fashioned, shrub, climbing
& rambling roses
Map Ref: E, B3

EWal J WALKERS BULBS ✉ EU 🄳
Washway House Farm, Holbeach, Spalding,
Lincolnshire PE12 7PP
☎ (01406) 426216   **Fax:** (01406) 425468
E-mail: walkers@taylors-bulbs.com
Contact: J W Walkers
Opening Times: Not open to the public.
Min. Mail Order UK: See cat. for details
Min. Mail Order EU: See cat.
Cat. Cost: 2 x 1st class
Credit Cards: Visa, Access
Specialities: Daffodils & *Fritillaria.*

EWes WEST ACRE GARDENS ✉ UK
West Acre, Kings Lynn, Norfolk PE32 1UJ
☎ (01760) 755562/755989
Fax: (01760) 755989
Contact: J J Tuite
Opening Times: 1000-1700 7 days 15th
Feb-15th Nov. Other times by appt.
Min. Mail Order UK: No minimum charge
Cat. Cost: 4 x 1st class
Credit Cards: None
Specialities: Unusual shrubs, herbaceous &
alpines. Large selection of *Rhodohypoxis* &
grasses.
Map Ref: E, B5

EWFC THE WILD FLOWER CENTRE ✉ UK
Church Farm, Sisland, Loddon, Norwich,
Norfolk NR14 6EF
☎ (01508) 520235   **Fax:** (01508) 528294

Contact: D G Corne
Opening Times: By appt. please.
Min. Mail Order UK: £3.80 + p&p
Cat. Cost: 2 x 2nd class
Credit Cards: None
Specialities: British native & naturalised wild
flower plants. 283+ varieties.
Map Ref: E, B6

EWll THE WALLED GARDEN
Park Road, Benhall, Saxmundham, Suffolk
IP17 1JB
☎ (01728) 602510   **Fax:** (01728) 602510
E-mail: jim@thewalledgarden.co.uk
Contact: J R Mountain
Opening Times: 0930-1700 Tue-Sun Mar-
Oct, Tue-Sat Nov-Feb.
Mail Order: None
Cat. Cost: 2 x 1st class
Credit Cards: Visa, MasterCard, Switch
Specialities: Tender & hardy perennials &
wall shrubs.
Map Ref: E, C6

EWoo WOOTTEN'S PLANTS
Wenhaston, Blackheath, Halesworth, Suffolk
IP19 9HD
☎ (01502) 478258   **Fax:** (01502) 478258
E-mail: woottens-plants@hotmail.com
Contact: M Loftus
Opening Times: 0930-1700 7 days.
Mail Order: None
Cat. Cost: £2.50 illus.
Credit Cards: Access, Visa, American
Express, Switch
Specialities: *Pelargonium, Penstemon, Salvia,*
auriculas & grasses.
Map Ref: E, C6

EWsh WESTSHORES NURSERIES
82 West Street, Winterton, North Lincs
DN15 9QF
☎ (01724) 733940   **Fax:** (01724) 733940
E-mail: westshnur@aol.com
Contact: Gail & John Summerfield
Opening Times: 0930-1830 (or dusk) Wed-
Mon 1st Mar-mid Nov.
Mail Order: None
Cat. Cost: 2 x 1st class
Credit Cards: None
Specialities: Ornamental grasses &
herbaceous perennials.
Map Ref: E, A5

EWTr WALNUT TREE GARDEN
NURSERY ✉ UK €
Flymoor Lane, Rocklands, Attleborough,
Norfolk NR17 1BP
☎ (01953) 488163   **Fax:** (01953) 483187

G

E-mail: jimnclare@aol.com
Web Site: www.walnut-tree-garden-nursery.co.uk
Contact: Jim Paine & Clare Billington
Opening Times: 0900-1800 Tue-Sun Feb-Nov & B/hols.
Min. Mail Order UK: £10.00
Cat. Cost: 2 x 1st class
Credit Cards: Visa, MasterCard, Switch, Solo
Map Ref: E, B5

EYou   ROY YOUNG SEEDS ⊠ EU ⊠ ▣
23 Westland Chase, West Winch, King's Lynn, Norfolk PE33 0QH
☎ (01553) 840867   **Fax:** (01553) 840867
Contact: Mr Roy Young
Opening Times: Not open.
Min. Mail Order UK: £3.00 + p&p
Min. Mail Order EU: £3.00 + p&p*
Cat. Cost: 1 x 1st class or 3 x IRCs
Credit Cards: None
Specialities: Cacti & succulent seeds only, for wholesale and retail purchase. 24pg catalogue listing approx. 2000 species, varieties & forms (retail). 18pg A5 listing (w/sale). *Note: £25 min. w/sale order charge.

SCOTLAND

GAbr   ABRIACHAN NURSERIES ⊠ EU
Loch Ness Side, Inverness, Inverness-shire, Scotland IV3 8LA
☎ (01463) 861232
Fax: (01463) 861232
Contact: Mr & Mrs D Davidson
Opening Times: 0900-1900 daily (dusk if earlier) Feb-Nov.
Min. Mail Order UK: No minimum charge
Min. Mail Order EU: Nmc
Cat. Cost: 4 x 1st class
Credit Cards: None
Specialities: Herbaceous, *Primula, Helianthemum,* hardy *Geranium* & *Sempervivum.*
Map Ref: G, B2

GAri   ARIVEGAIG NURSERY ⊠ UK ▣
Aultbea, Acharacle, Argyll, Scotland PH36 4LE
☎ (01967) 431331
E-mail: arivegaignursery@btinternet.com
Contact: E Stewart
Opening Times: 0900-1700 7 days Easter-end Oct.
Min. Mail Order UK: £10.00 + p&p*
Cat. Cost: 4 x 1st class
Credit Cards: None
Specialities: A wide range of unusual plants incl. those suited for the milder parts of the

country. *Note: mail order despatch late Jan-Mar & Oct-Nov only.
Map Ref: G, C1

GAul   AULTAN NURSERY
Newton of Cairnhill, Cuminestown, Turriff, Aberdeenshire, Scotland AB53 5TN
☎ (01888) 544702   **Fax:** (01888) 544702
E-mail: rlking@globalnet.co.uk
Contact: Richard King
Opening Times: 1330-1800 Sun Apr-Oct. Other times please phone first.
Mail Order: None
Cat. Cost: 2 x 1st class
Credit Cards: None
Specialities: Herbaceous perennials & shrubs, mostly grown in peat-free composts. A very wide range incl. many unusual items.
Map Ref: G, B3

GBal   BALLAGAN NURSERY
Gartocharn Road, Nr Balloch, Alexandria, Strathclyde G83 8NB
☎ (01389) 752947   **Fax:** (01389) 711288
E-mail: ballagan20freeserve.co.uk
Contact: Mr G Stephenson
Opening Times: 0900-1700 7 days.
Mail Order: None
Cat. Cost: None issued
Credit Cards: Visa, Access, Switch
Specialities: Home grown bedding and general nursery stock.
Map Ref: G, C2

GBar   BARWINNOCK HERBS ⊠ EU €
Barrhill, by Girvan, Ayrshire, Scotland KA26 0RB
☎ (01465) 821338   **Fax:** (01465) 821338
E-mail: herbs.scotland@barwinnock.com
Web Site: www.barwinnock.com
Contact: Dave & Mon Holtom
Opening Times: 1000-1800 7 days 1st Apr-31st Oct.
Min. Mail Order UK: No minimum charge
Min. Mail Order EU: Nmc
Cat. Cost: 3 x 1st class
Credit Cards: None
Specialities: Culinary, medicinal & fragrant leaved plants organically grown.
Map Ref: G, D2

GBin   BINNY PLANTS ⊠ EU €
West Lodge, Binny Estate, Ecclesmachen Road, Nr Broxbourn, West Lothian, Scotland EH52 6NL
☎ (01506) 858931   **Fax:** (01506) 858931
E-mail: binnycrag@aol.com
Contact: Billy Carruthers
Opening Times: 1000-1700 Thu-Mon

16 Mar-31 Oct.
Min. Mail Order UK: No minimum charge*
Min. Mail Order EU: £25.00
Cat. Cost: 3 x 1st class
Credit Cards: Visa, MasterCard, EuroCard
Specialities: Perennials incl. *Euphorbia,*
Geranium, Hosta. Plus large selection of grasses
& ferns.
*Note: mail order Oct-Mar only.
Map Ref: G, C3

GBon   BONHARD NURSERY
Murrayshall Road, Scone, Perth, Tayside,
Scotland PH2 7PQ
☎ (01738) 552791
Fax: (01738) 552791
Contact: Mr & Mrs Hickman
Opening Times: 1000-1800, or dusk if
earlier, 7 days.
Mail Order: None
Cat. Cost: Free (fruit trees & roses)
Credit Cards: Access, American Express,
EuroCard, MasterCard, Switch, Visa
Specialities: Herbaceous, conifers & alpines.
Fruit & ornamental trees. Shrub & species
roses.
Map Ref: G, C3

GBri   BRIDGE END NURSERIES
Gretna Green, Dumfries & Galloway,
Scotland DG16 5HN
☎ (01461) 800612   **Fax:** (01461) 800612
Contact: R Bird
Opening Times: 0930-1700 all year.
Evenings by appt.
Mail Order: None
Cat. Cost: None issued
Credit Cards: None
Specialities: Hardy cottage garden
perennials. Many unusual & interesting
varieties.
Map Ref: G,·D3

GBuc   BUCKLAND PLANTS ⊠ EU
Whinnieliggate, Kirkcudbright, Scotland
DG6 4XP
☎ (01557) 331323   **Fax:** (01557) 331323
Contact: Rob or Dina Asbridge
Opening Times: 1000-1700 Thu-Sun
Mar-Nov.
Min. Mail Order UK: £15.00 + p&p
Min. Mail Order EU: £50.00 + p&p
Cat. Cost: 3 x 1st class
Credit Cards: None
Specialities: A very wide range of scarce
herbaceous & woodland plants incl. *Anemone,*
Cardamine, Crocosmia, Erythronium,
Helleborus, Meconopsis, Tricyrtis & *Trillium.*
Map Ref: G, D2

GCal   CALLY GARDENS ⊠ EU 𝗚
Gatehouse of Fleet, Castle Douglas, Scotland
DG7 2DJ
Fax: (01557) 815029. Also information line.
Contact: Michael Wickenden
Opening Times: 1000-1730 Sat-Sun, 1400-
1730 Tue-Fri. Easter Sat-last Sun in Sept.
Min. Mail Order UK: £15.00 + p&p
Min. Mail Order EU: £50.00 + p&p
Cat. Cost: 3 x 1st class
Credit Cards: None
Specialities: Unusual perennials. *Agapanthus,*
Crocosmia, Eryngium, Euphorbia, hardy
Geranium & grasses. Some rare shrubs,
climbers & conservatory plants.
Map Ref: G, D2

GCan   CANDACRAIG GARDENS ⊠ UK
Strathdon, Aberdeenshire, Scotland AB3 8XT
☎ (01975) 651226   **Fax:** (01975) 651391
E-mail: candacraig@buchanan.co.uk
Web Site: www.buchanan.co.uk/the gardens
Contact: Mrs E M Young
Opening Times: 1000-1700 Mon-Fri &
1000-1800 Sat & Sun May-Sep or by appt.
Min. Mail Order UK: No minimum charge*
Cat. Cost: Sae or 1st class for list
Credit Cards: None
Specialities: A wide variety of hardy
perennials, *Meconopsis* & *Primula.* Also seeds.
*Note: offers mail order seeds only to EU.
Map Ref: G, B3

GCHN   CHARTER HOUSE NURSERY ⊠ EU
2 Nunwood, Dumfries, Dumfries &
Galloway, Scotland DG2 0HX
☎ (01387) 720363   **Fax:** (01387) 720363
E-mail: jross@chplants.fsnet.co.uk
Contact: John Ross
Opening Times: 0900-1700 Tue-Sat Mar-
Sep. Other times by appt.
Min. Mail Order UK: No minimum charge
Min. Mail Order EU: Nmc
Cat. Cost: 3 x 1st class
Credit Cards: None
Specialities: *Aquilegia, Geranium, Erodium,*
Saxifraga and *Campanula.* National
Collection of *Erodium.*
Map Ref: G, D2

GChr   CHRISTIE ELITE NURSERIES ⊠ UK 𝗚
The Nurseries, Forres, Moray, Scotland
IV36 3TW
☎ (01309) 672633   **Fax:** (01309) 676846

G

E-mail: celite@globalnet.co.uk
Contact: Dr S Thompson
Opening Times: 0800-1700 7 days.
Min. Mail Order UK: No minimum charge
Cat. Cost: Free
Credit Cards: Visa, Access
Specialities: Hedging & screening plants.
Woodland & less common trees, shrubs &
fruit.
Map Ref: G, B2

GCoc JAMES COCKER & SONS ⊠ EU ▣ €
Whitemyres, Lang Stracht, Aberdeen,
Scotland AB15 6XH
☎ (01224) 313261   Fax: (01224) 312531
E-mail: cockers@lineone.net
Web Site: www.roses.uk.com
Contact: Alec Cocker
Opening Times: 0900-1730 7 days.
Min. Mail Order UK: No minimum charge
Min. Mail Order EU: £4.55 + p&p
Cat. Cost: Free
Credit Cards: Visa, MasterCard
Specialities: Roses.
Map Ref: G, B3

GCrs CHRISTIE'S NURSERY ⊠ EU ♦ ▣
Downfield, Westmuir, Kirriemuir, Angus,
Scotland DD8 5LP
☎ (01575) 572977   Fax: (01575) 572977
E-mail: christiealpines@btinternet.com
Web Site: www.christies-nursery.co.uk
Contact: Ian & Ann Christie
Opening Times: 1000-1700 Wed-Sat &
Mon, 1300-1700 Sun 1st Mar-31st Oct.
Closed Sun from Jan.
Min. Mail Order UK: 5 plants + p&p
Min. Mail Order EU: On request
Cat. Cost: 2 x 1st class
Credit Cards: Access, Delta, EuroCard, JCB,
MasterCard, Switch, Visa
Specialities: Alpines, esp. gentians, *Cassiope,
Primula, Lewisia,* orchids, *Trillium* &
ericaceous.
Map Ref: G, C3

GDea DEANSTON NURSERY ⊠ EU ▣
Deanston Farm, Lochfoot, Dumfries,
Scotland DG2 8QX
☎ (01556) 690519   Fax: (01566) 690519
E-mail: smcc@appleonline.net
Contact: Susan McClelland
Opening Times: 1000-1800 (closed Tue &
Wed) 1st Apr-1st Oct. Other times by appt.
Min. Mail Order UK: No minimum charge
Min. Mail Order EU: Nmc
Cat. Cost: 2 x 1st class
Credit Cards: None
Specialities: A rapidly growing selection of

choice & unusual hardy plants, especially
herbaceous perennials, grasses & herbs.
Map Ref: G, D2

GDra MESSRS. JACK DRAKE ⊠ EU ▣
Inshriach Alpine Nursery, Aviemore,
Invernesshire, Scotland PH22 1QS
☎ (01540) 651287   Fax: (01540) 651656
E-mail: drakes.alpines@virgin.net
Web Site: www.kincraig.com/drakesalpines
Contact: John Borrowman
Opening Times: 0900-1700 Mon-Fri, 1000-
1600 Sat & B/hol Sun mid Feb-mid Nov.
Min. Mail Order UK: £10.00 + p&p
Min. Mail Order EU: £50.00 + p&p
Cat. Cost: £1.50
Credit Cards: Visa, MasterCard, Switch, JCB
Specialities: Rare and unusual alpines & rock
plants. Especially P*rimula, Meconopsis,
Gentian,* heathers etc.
Map Ref: G, B2

GEil EILDON PLANTS ⊠ EU ▣
Lowood Nurseries, Melrose, Roxburghshire,
Scotland TD6 9BJ
☎ (01896) 755530   Fax: (01896) 755530
Contact: R Sinclair
Opening Times: 1000-1700 7 days Mar-Jun.
Min. Mail Order UK: No minimum charge
Min. Mail Order EU: Nmc
Cat. Cost: 1 x 1st class
Credit Cards: None
Specialities: Specialist propagators of a wide
range of shrubs for sale as pot liners or
finished plants.
Map Ref: G, D3

GEve EVELIX DAFFODILS ⊠ EU €
Aird Asaig, Evelix, Dornoch, Sutherland,
Highland, Scotland IV25 3NG
☎ (01862) 810715
Contact: D C MacArthur
Opening Times: By appt. only.
Min. Mail Order UK: No minimum charge
Min. Mail Order EU: Nmc
Cat. Cost: 3 x 1st class available July.
Credit Cards: None
Specialities: New *Narcissus* cultivars for
garden display & exhibition.
Map Ref: G, B2

GFle FLEURS PLANTS ⊠ EU
2 Castlehill Lane, Abington Road,
Symington, Biggar, Scotland ML12 6SJ
☎ (01899) 308528
Contact: Jim Elliott
Opening Times: Please phone to arrange a
visit.
Min. Mail Order UK: £8.00 + p&p

Min. Mail Order EU: £20.00 + p&p
Cat. Cost: Sae
Credit Cards: None
Specialities: *Primula, Meconopsis.*
Map Ref: G ,D3

GGar   GARDEN COTTAGE NURSERY ⊠ UK
Tournaig, Poolewe, Achnasheen, Highland,
Scotland IV22 2LH
☎ (01445) 781777   Fax: (01445) 781777
E-mail: rrushbrooke@easynet.co.uk
Web Site: www.gcnursery.co.uk
Contact: R & L Rushbrooke
Opening Times: 1030-1800 Mon-Sat mid
Mar-mid Oct or by appt.
Min. Mail Order UK: £10.00 + p&p
Cat. Cost: 4 x 2nd class
Credit Cards: None
Specialities: Large range of herbaceous &
alpines esp. *Primula,* hardy *Geranium* &
moisture lovers. Expanding range of southern
hemisphere plants.
Map Ref: G, B2

GGGa   GLENDOICK GARDENS LTD ⊠ EU ☒ ▣
Glencarse, Perth, Scotland PH2 7NS
☎ (01738) 860205   Fax: (01738) 860630
E-mail: sales@glendoick.com
Web Site: www.glendoick.com
Contact: P A, E P & K N E Cox
Opening Times: By appt. only. Garden
centre open 7 days.
Min. Mail Order UK: £35.00 + p&p
Min. Mail Order EU: £100.00 + p&p
Cat. Cost: £1.50 or £1 stamps
Credit Cards: Visa, MasterCard, Delta,
Switch, JCB
Specialities: Rhododendrons, azaleas and
ericaceous, *Primula* & *Meconopsis.* Many
catalogue plants available at garden centre.
Map Ref: G, B2

GGre   GREENHEAD ROSES ⊠ EU ▣
Greenhead Nursery, Old Greenock Road,
Inchinnan, Renfrew, Strathclyde PA4 9PH
☎ (0141) 812 0121   Fax: (0141) 812 0121
Contact: C N Urquhart
Opening Times: 1000-1700 7 days.
Min. Mail Order UK: No minimum charge*
Min. Mail Order EU: Nmc
Cat. Cost: Sae
Credit Cards: Visa, Switch
Specialities: Roses. Wide general range,
dwarf conifers, trees, heathers,
rhododendrons & azaleas, shrubs, alpines,
fruit, hardy herbaceous & spring & summer
bedding.
*Note: mail order for bush roses only, Oct-Mar.
Map Ref: G, C2

GIBF   IAIN BRODIE OF FALSYDE ⊠ EU
(Office) Cuilalunn, Kinchurdy Road, Boat of
Garten, Inverness-shire, Scotland PH24 3BP
☎ (01479) 831464   Fax: (01479) 831672
E-mail: plants&seeds@falsyde.sol.co.uk
Contact: Iain Brodie of Falsyde
Opening Times: Please phone first.
Min. Mail Order UK: £20
Min. Mail Order EU: £30
Cat. Cost: 3 x 1st class
Credit Cards: None
Specialities: *Betulaceae, Rosaceae* & *Ericaceae.*
Note: nursery at Auchgourish Gardens, Boat
of Garten.
Map Ref: G, B2

GKir   KIRKDALE NURSERY
Daviot, Nr Inverurie, Aberdeenshire,
Scotland AB51 0JL
☎ (01467) 671264   Fax: (01467) 671282
E-mail: info@kirkdalenursery.co.uk
Web Site: www.kirkdalenursery.co.uk
Contact: Geoff or Alistair
Opening Times: 1000-1700 7 days
(summer), 1000-1600 7 days (winter)
Mail Order: None
Credit Cards: Visa, Access, Switch
Specialities: Trees, herbaceous, grasses.
Map Ref: G, B3

GLil   LILLIESLEAF NURSERY ⊠ EU ▣ €
Garden Cottage, Linthill, Melrose,
Roxburghshire, Scotland TD6 9HU
☎ (01835) 870415   Fax: (01835) 870415
Contact: Teyl de Bordes
Opening Times: 0900-1700 Mon-Sat,
1000-1600 Sun. Dec-Feb, please phone first.
Min. Mail Order UK: No minimum charge*
Min. Mail Order EU: Nmc
Cat. Cost: 2 x 1st class
Credit Cards: Visa, Access
Specialities: *Epimedium* & wide range of
common & uncommon plants. National
Collection of *Epimedium.* *Note: mail order
of *Epimedium* only.
Map Ref: G, D3

GMac   ELIZABETH MACGREGOR ⊠ EU ▣
Ellenbank, Tongland Road, Kirkcudbright,
Dumfries & Galloway, Scotland DG6 4UU
☎ (01557) 330620   Fax: (01557) 330620
E-mail: elizabeth@violas.abel.co.uk
Contact: Elizabeth MacGregor
Opening Times: Please phone.
Min. Mail Order UK: 6 plants £12.00 + p&p
Min. Mail Order EU: £50.00 + p&p
Cat. Cost: 4 x 1st class or 5 x 2nd class
Credit Cards: Visa, MasterCard
Specialities: Violets, violas & violettas, old

G

G

and new varieties. *Campanula, Geranium, Penstemon, Aster, Primula, Iris* & other unusual herbaceous.
Map Ref: G, D2

GMaP MACPLANTS ◳
Berrybank Nursery, 5 Boggs Holdings, Pencaitland, E Lothian, Scotland EH34 5BA
☎ (01875) 341179   Fax: (01875) 340842
E-mail: sales.macplants@virgin.net
Contact: Claire McNaughton
Opening Times: 1030-1700 7 days mid Mar-end Sept.
Mail Order: None
Cat. Cost: 4 x 2nd class
Credit Cards: None
Specialities: Herbaceous perennials, alpines, hardy ferns, violas & grasses.
Map Ref: G, C3

GNor SHEILA NORTHWAY AURICULAS ⊠ EU
Balmaclellan, Castle Douglas, Kirkcudbrightshire, Scotland DG7 3QR
☎ (01644) 420661
Contact: Sheila Northway
Opening Times: Mail order & by appt. only.
Min. Mail Order UK: £10.00 + p&p
Min. Mail Order EU: £10.00 + p&p
(normally 48 hr priority rate).
Cat. Cost: A4 Sae
Credit Cards: None
Specialities: *Primula allionii, P. auricula* & a limited range of alpines largely grown from wild seed, esp. New Zealand plants.
Map Ref: G, D2

GOrc ORCHARDTON NURSERIES
Gardeners Cottage, Orchardton House, Auchencairn, Castle Douglas, Kirkcudbrightshire DG7 1QL
☎ (01556) 640366
Contact: Fred Coleman
Opening Times: 1200-1800 Sun-Tue Apr-end Oct.
Mail Order: None
Cat. Cost: Basic plant list 2 x 1st class
Credit Cards: None
Specialities: Unusual shrubs, climbers and bamboos.
Map Ref: G, D2

GOrn ORNAMENTAL GRASSES ⊠ EU
14 Meadowside of Craigmyle, Kemnay, Inverurie, Aberdeenshire, Scotland AB51 5LZ
☎ (01467) 643544
Contact: John & Lois Frew
Opening Times: By appt.
Min. Mail Order UK: No minimum charge
Min. Mail Order EU: Nmc

Cat. Cost: 3 x 1st class
Credit Cards: None
Specialities: Ornamental grasses.
Map Ref: G, B3

GOrP ORKNEY PERENNIALS ⊠ EU ◳
5 Islands View Road, Kirkwall, Orkney KW15 1YP
☎ (0788) 0881893
Contact: Mr R Rendall
Opening Times: Mail order only.
Min. Mail Order UK: £10.00 + p&p
Min. Mail Order EU: £50.00 + p&p
Cat. Cost: £1.50 refundable with order.
Credit Cards: None
Specialities: Extensive range of hardy perennials, many rare, incl. *Geranium, Hosta,* grasses, ferns & seed. Britain's most northerly mail order nursery where the weather tests plants to their limits.

GPin PINEGROVE NURSERY
Oakley Road, Cairneyhill, Dunfermline, Fife, Scotland KY12 8HE
☎ (01383) 881493   Fax: (01383) 880784
Contact: Peter Millican
Opening Times: 1000-1700 7 days.
Mail Order: None
Cat. Cost: None issued
Credit Cards: MasterCard, Access, Visa, Switch
Specialities: Wide range of conifers, patio & basket plants, bedding plants.
Map Ref: G, C3

GPlc PLANTIECRUB GROWERS LTD ⊠ EU ◳
Gott, Shetland ZE2 9SH
☎ (01595) 840600   Fax: (01595) 840600
Contact: Olaf Isbister
Opening Times: 0830-1700 7 days a week.
Min. Mail Order UK: No minimum charge
Min. Mail Order EU: Nmc
Cat. Cost: 1 x 1st class
Credit Cards: Visa, Delta, MasterCard, Switch
Specialities: Bedding, perennials, basket & patio plants, indoor plants, glasshouse fruits & salads. Nurserymen & landscape contractors.
Map Ref: G, B3

GPoy POYNTZFIELD HERB NURSERY ⊠ EU ◳
Nr Balblair, Black Isle, Dingwall, Ross & Cromarty, Highland, Scotland IV7 8LX
☎ (01381) 610352*   Fax: (01381) 610352
Contact: Duncan Ross
Opening Times: 1300-1700 Mon-Sat 1st Mar-30th Sep, 1300-1700 Sun Jun-Aug.
Min. Mail Order UK: £5.00 + p&p
Min. Mail Order EU: £10.00 + p&p
Cat. Cost: 4 x 1st class

G

Credit Cards: None
Specialities: Over 350 popular, unusual & rare herbs esp. medicinal. Also seeds. *Note: phone only 1200-1300 & 1800-1900.
Map Ref: G, B2

GQui   QUINISH GARDEN NURSERY ✉ EU ▣
Dervaig, Isle of Mull, Argyll, Scotland
PA75 6QL
☎ (01688) 400344   **Fax:** (01688) 400344
Contact: Nicholas Reed
Opening Times: By appt. only.
Min. Mail Order UK: No minimum charge
Min. Mail Order EU: Nmc
Cat. Cost: 2 x 1st class
Credit Cards: None
Specialities: Specialist garden shrubs & conservatory plants.
Map Ref: G, C1

GSki   SKIPNESS PLANTS ✉ EU ▣
The Gardens, Skipness, Nr Tarbert, Argyll,
Scotland PA29 6XU
☎ (01880) 760201   **Fax:** (01880) 760201
E-mail: bill@skipnessplants.freeserve.co.uk
Web Site: www.geocities.com/eureka/7627/
Contact: Bill & Joan McHugh
Opening Times: 0900-1800 Mon-Fri, 0900-1600 Sat-Sun Feb-Nov.
Min. Mail Order UK: No minimum charge
Min. Mail Order EU: Nmc
Cat. Cost: £1.00*
Credit Cards: None
Specialities: Unusual herbaceous perennials, shrubs, climbers & grasses. *Note: catalogue cost refundable on first order.
Map Ref: G, C2

GTou   TOUGH ALPINE NURSERY ✉ EU ▣ ▣
Westhaybogs, Tough, Alford, Aberdeenshire,
Scotland AB33 8DU
☎ (01975) 562783 · **Fax:** (01975) 563561
E-mail: fred@alpines.co.uk
Web Site: www.alpines.co.uk
Contact: Fred & Monika Carrie
Opening Times: 1st Mar-31st Oct. Please check first.
Min. Mail Order UK: £15.00 + p&p
Min. Mail Order EU: £15.00 + p&p
Cat. Cost: 3 x 2nd class
Credit Cards: MasterCard, Access, Switch
Specialities: Alpines.
Map Ref: G, B3

GTre   TREEPAC ✉ EU ▣ ▣ €
(office) PO Box 11440, Ellon, Scotland
AB41 7YD
☎ (01358) 761473   **Fax:** (01358) 761473
E-mail: info@treepac.fsnet.co.uk

Web Site: www.treepac.fsnet.co.uk
Contact: Mrs Eleanor Tate
Opening Times: Please telephone for appt. or to place an order.
Min. Mail Order UK: £4.95
Min. Mail Order EU: £24.95
Cat. Cost: 2 x 1st class
Credit Cards: Visa
Specialities: Scottish native species & their cultivars, eg *Sorbus, Prunus*. Note: nursery is at Tanglandford, Triangle, Methlink, Aberdeen AB41 7EN.
Map Ref: G, B3

GTro   TROPIC HOUSE ✉ EU ▣
Langford Nursery, Carty Port, Newton
Stewart, Wigtownshire, Scotland DG8 6AY
☎ (01671) 402485, (01671) 404050
E-mail: bookcorner@wigtown.fsnet.co.uk
Contact: Mrs A F Langford
Opening Times: 1000-1700 7 days Easter-end Sep. Other times by appt.
Min. Mail Order UK: No minimum charge
Min. Mail Order EU: £20.00 + p&p
Cat. Cost: Sae
Credit Cards: None
Specialities: Carnivorous.
Map Ref: G, D2

GTwe   J TWEEDIE FRUIT TREES ✉ UK ◆
Maryfield Road Nursery, Nr Terregles,
Dumfries, Dumfrieshire, Scotland DG2 9TH
☎ (01387) 720880
Contact: John Tweedie
Opening Times: Please ring for times. Collections by appt.
Min. Mail Order UK: No minimum charge
Cat. Cost: Sae
Credit Cards: None
Specialities: Fruit trees & bushes. A wide range of old & new varieties.
Map Ref: G, D2

GUzu   UZUMARA ORCHIDS ✉ EU ▣ €
9 Port Henderson, Gairloch, Rosshire,
Scotland IV21 2AS
☎ (01445) 741228
Fax: (01445) 741228
E-mail: i.la_croix@virgin.net
Web Site: http://freespace.virgin.net/i.la_croix
Contact: Mrs I F La Croix
Opening Times: By appt only.
Min. Mail Order UK: No minimum charge
Min. Mail Order EU: Nmc

K E Y
✉ Mail order to UK or EU
▣ Exports beyond EU   € Euro accepted
▣ Also supplies Wholesale   ◆ See Display advertisement

Cat. Cost: Sae
Credit Cards: None
Specialities: African & Madagascan orchids.

GVer   VERITAS NURSERY ⊠ EU ▣ €
22 The Avenue, Girvan, Ayrshire, Scotland
KA26 9DS
☎ (01465) 713388   Fax: (01465) 713388
E-mail: info@fragrantgarden.co.uk
Web Site: www.fragrantgarden.co.uk
Contact: Craig Jamieson
Opening Times: Easter-end August 1100-
1700.
Min. Mail Order UK: No minimum charge
Min. Mail Order EU: Nmᴄ
Cat. Cost: 4 x 1st class
Credit Cards: Visa, MasterCard
Specialities: Fragrant plants.
Map Ref: G, D1

N. IRELAND & REPUBLIC

IArd   ARDCARNE GARDEN CENTRE
Ardcarne, Boyle, Co. Roscommon, Ireland
☎ 00 353 (0)79 67091
Fax: 00 353 (0)79 67341
E-mail: ardcane@indigo.ie
Contact: James Wickham, Mary Frances
Dwyer, Kirsty Ainge
Opening Times: 0900-1800 Mon-Sat,
1400-1800 Sun & B/hols.
Mail Order: None
Credit Cards: Access, Visa, American Express
Specialities: Coastal plants, native & unusual
trees, specimen plants & semi-mature trees.
Wide general range.
Map Ref: I, B2

IBal   BALLYDORN BULB FARM ⊠ EU ▣
Killinchy, Newtownards, Co. Down,
N. Ireland BT23 6QB
☎ (028) 9754 1250   Fax: (028) 9754 2276
E-mail: ringdaff@nireland.com
Contact: Sir Frank Harrison
Opening Times: Not open.
Min. Mail Order UK: £20.00 + p&p
Min. Mail Order EU: £30.00 + p&p
Cat. Cost: 4 x 1st class
Credit Cards: None
Specialities: New daffodil varieties for
exhibitors and hybridisers.

IBlr   BALLYROGAN NURSERIES ⊠ EU ▣▣
The Grange, Ballyrogan, Newtownards,
Co. Down, N. Ireland BT23 4SD
☎ (028) 9181 0451 (evenings)
Contact: Gary Dunlop
Opening Times: Only open by appt. for
viewing of National Collections.

Min. Mail Order UK: £10.00 + p&p
Min. Mail Order EU: £20.00 + p&p
Cat. Cost: 2 x 1st class
Credit Cards: None
Specialities: Choice herbaceous. *Agapanthus,
Celmisia, Crocosmia, Euphorbia, Meconopsis,
Rodgersia, Iris, Dierama* & *Phormium.* National
Collections of *Crocosmia, Celmisia* &
Euphorbia. Note: limited exports beyond EC.
Map Ref: I, B3

IBro   BROOKWOOD NURSERIES ⊠ EU
18 Tonlegee Road, Coolock, Dublin 5, Ireland
☎ 00 353 (0)18 473298
Contact: Jim Maher
Opening Times: For collection only. 1st
Feb-30th Apr.
Min. Mail Order UK: £5.00 + p&p
Min. Mail Order EU: £5.00 + p&p
Cat. Cost: 2 x 1st class
Credit Cards: None
Specialities: Hybrid *Crocosmia* rarities &
hardy *Cyclamen.*
Map Ref: I, C3

ICar   CARNCAIRN DAFFODILS ⊠ EU ▣▣
Broughshane, Ballymena, Co. Antrim,
N. Ireland BT43 7HF
☎ (028) 2586 1216   Fax: (028) 2586 2842
Contact: Mr & Mrs R H Reade
Opening Times: 1000-1700 Mon-Fri. Please
phone in advance.
Min. Mail Order UK: No minimum charge
Min. Mail Order EU: Nmc
Cat. Cost: Free
Credit Cards: None
Specialities: Old & new *Narcissus* cultivars,
mainly for show.
Map Ref: I, A3

IClo   CLONMEL GARDEN CENTRE ▣ €
Glenconnor House, Clonmel, Co. Tipperary,
Ireland
☎ 00 353 (0)52 23294
Fax: 00 353 (0)52 29196
E-mail: clonmelgc@eircom.net
Contact: Beth, Terry or Chris Hanna
Opening Times: 0900-1800 Mon-Sat,
1200-1800 Sun, 1000-1800 B/hols.
Mail Order: None
Credit Cards: Visa, Access, MasterCard, Laser
Specialities: Wide range of plants incl. many
less common varieties. The garden centre is
situated in the grounds of a Georgian
country house with extensive gardens.
Map Ref: I, D2

ICro   CROCKNAFEOLA NURSERY ▣ €
Killybegs, Co. Donegal, Ireland

☎ 00 353 (0)73 51018
Fax: 00 353 (0)73 51018
Contact: Andy McKenna
Opening Times: 0900-1900 Mon-Sat &
1200-1800 Sun in summer, until dusk in
winter. Closed Dec-Feb.
Mail Order: None
Cat. Cost: None issued
Credit Cards: None
Specialities: Hardy shrubs, trees & hedging
suitable for exposed areas.
Map Ref: I, B2

IDee   **DEELISH GARDEN CENTRE** ☒ EU
Skibbereen, Co. Cork, Ireland
☎ 00 353 (0)28 21374
Fax: 00 353 (0)28 21374
Contact: Bill & Rain Chase
Opening Times: 1000-1300 & 1400-1800
Mon-Sat, 1400-1800 Sun.
Min. Mail Order UK: IR£50.00 + p&p
Min. Mail Order EU: IR£100.00 + p&p
Cat. Cost: Sae
Credit Cards: Visa, Access
Specialities: Unusual plants for the mild
coastal climate of Ireland. Conservatory plants.
Sole Irish agents for Chase Organic Seeds.
Map Ref: I, D1

IDic   **DICKSON NURSERIES LTD** ☒ EU ☒ ☒
Milecross Road, Newtownards, Co. Down,
N. Ireland BT23 4SS
☎ (028) 9181 2206
Fax: (028) 9181 3366
E-mail: mail@dickson-roses.co.uk
Contact: A P C Dickson OBE, Linda Stewart
Opening Times: 0800-1230 & 1300-1700
Mon-Thu. 0800-1230 Fri.
Min. Mail Order UK: One plant
Min. Mail Order EU: £25.00 + p&p
Cat. Cost: Free
Credit Cards: None
Specialities: Roses esp. modern Dickson
varieties.
Map Ref: I, B3

IDun   **BRIAN DUNCAN** ☒ EU ☒ ☒
Novelty & Exhibition Daffodils,
15 Ballynahatty Road, Omagh, Co. Tyrone,
N. Ireland BT78 1PN
☎ (028) 8224 2931
Fax: (028) 8224 2931
E-mail: 113125.1005@compuserve.com
Contact: Brian Duncan
Opening Times: By appt. only.
Min. Mail Order UK: £20.00 + p&p
Min. Mail Order EU: £20.00 + p&p
Cat. Cost: £1.00 inc p&p
Credit Cards: None

Specialities: New hybrid & exhibition
daffodils & *Narcissus.*
Map Ref: I, B2

IHar   **HARRY BYRNE'S GARDEN CENTRE**
☒ EU €
Castlepark Road, Sandycove, Dublin,
Ireland
☎ 00 353 (0)12 803887
Fax: 00 353 (0)12 801077
E-mail: byrnesgc@connect.ie
Contact: H Byrne
Opening Times: 0900-1730 Mon-Sat 1200-
1730 Sun & B/hols.
Min. Mail Order UK: £20.00 + p&p
Min. Mail Order EU: £30.00
Cat. Cost: £1.00 Roses & *Clematis* only.
Credit Cards: Visa, MasterCard
Specialities: Roses, *Clematis,* patio & basket
plants. Wide variety of trees, shrubs,
herbaceous, alpines. .
Map Ref: I, C3

IHdy   **HARDY PLANT NURSERY** ☒ UK €
Ridge House, Ballybrack, Co. Dublin,
Ireland
☎ 00 353 (0)12 826973
Contact: Declan Hooke & Paul Cox
Opening Times: 0900-1700 Sat Apr-May &
Sep-Oct. Wed-Fri by appt.
Min. Mail Order UK: £30.00 + p&p*
Cat. Cost: 2 IRCs
Credit Cards: None
Specialities: Wide range of herbaceous
plants, some grown from wild collected seed.
*Note: mail order to UK & Ireland only.
Map Ref: I, C3

IIve   **IVERNA HERBS** ☒ EU ☒ €
Glenmalure, Rathdrum, Co. Wicklow,
Ireland
Contact: Peter O'Neill
Opening Times: Mail order, or write for appt.
Min. Mail Order UK: No minimum charge
Min. Mail Order EU: Nmc
Cat. Cost: £2.00 cheque
Credit Cards: None
Specialities: A rapidly growing selection of
herbs, wild flowers & unusual vegetables.
Rare medicinal plants from east & west. Free
delivery to UK.
Map Ref: I, C3

ILis   **LISDOONAN HERBS** ☒ EU ☒
98 Belfast Road, Saintfield, Co. Down,
N. Ireland BT24 7HF
☎ (028) 9081 3624
E-mail: b.pilcher@pop.dial.pipex.com
Contact: Barbara Pilcher

Opening Times: Most days - please phone to check.
Min. Mail Order UK: No minimum charge
Min. Mail Order EU: Nmc
Cat. Cost: 2 x 1st class
Credit Cards: None
Specialities: Aromatics, herbs, kitchen garden plants, some native species. Freshly cut herbs & salads.
Map Ref: I, B3

ILsc   LISCAHANE NURSERY €
Ardfert, Tralee, Co. Kerry, Ireland
☎ 00 353 (0)667 134222
Fax: 00 353 (0)667 134600
Contact: Dan Nolan/Bill Cooley
Opening Times: 0900-1800 Tue-Sat & 1400-1800 Sun summer. 0900-1700 Thu-Sat & Sun afternoon winter. Closed Mon.
Mail Order: None
Cat. Cost: None issued
Credit Cards: Visa, Access, Laser
Specialities: Coastal shelter plants, *Eucalyptus.*
Map Ref: I, D1

IMGH   M G H NURSERIES €
50 Tullyhenan Road, Banbridge, Co. Down, N. Ireland BT32 4EY
☎ (028) 4062 2795
Fax: (028) 4062 2795
Contact: Miss M G Heslip
Opening Times: 1000-2000 Tue-Fri & 1000-1700 Sat Apr-Sep, 1230-dusk Oct-Mar.
Mail Order: None
Cat. Cost: 3 x 1st class
Credit Cards: None
Specialities: Grafted conifers, holly, Japanese maples, box, ornamental trees & flowering shrubs.
Map Ref: I, B3

IOrc   ORCHARDSTOWN NURSERIES ✉ EU ⊠
4 Miles Out, Cork Road, Waterford, Ireland
☎ 00 353 (0)513 84273
Fax: 00 353 (0)513 84422
Contact: Ron Dool
Opening Times: 0900-1800 Mon-Sat, 1400-1800 Sun.
Min. Mail Order UK: No minimum charge*
Min. Mail Order EU: Nmc
Cat. Cost: List £2.00
Credit Cards: Visa, MasterCard
Specialities: Unusual hardy plants incl. shrubs, shrub roses, trees, climbers, *Rhododendron* species & water plants.
*Note: only some plants mail order.
Map Ref: I, D2

IRya   RYANS NURSERIES €
Lissivigeen, Killarney, Co. Kerry, Ireland
☎ 00 353 (0)64 33507
Fax: 00 353 (0)64 37520
E-mail: tlryan@eircom.net
Contact: Mr T Ryan
Opening Times: 0900-1800 Mon-Sat 1400-1800 Sun.
Mail Order: None
Cat. Cost: None issued
Credit Cards: Visa
Specialities: *Camellia, Pieris, Acacia, Eucalyptus, Dicksonia,* azaleas & many tender and rare plants.
Map Ref: I, D1

ISea   SEAFORDE GARDENS ✉ EU ⊠ ▣
Seaforde, Co. Down, N. Ireland BT30 8PG
☎ (028) 4481 1225
Fax: (028) 4481 1370
Contact: P Forde
Opening Times: 1000-1700 Mon-Fri all year. 1000-1700 Sat & 1300-1800 Sun mid Feb-end Oct.
Min. Mail Order UK: No minimum charge
Min. Mail Order EU: Nmc
Cat. Cost: Free
Credit Cards: None
Specialities: Over 700 varieties of self-propagated trees & shrubs. National Collection of *Eucryphia.*
Map Ref: I, B3

ISsi   SEASIDE NURSERY ✉ EU ⊠
Claddaghduff, Co. Galway, Ireland
☎ 00 353 (0)95 44687
Fax: 00 353 (0)95 44761
E-mail: seaside@anu.ie
Web Site: www.anu.ie/seaside/
Contact: Tom Dyck
Opening Times: 0900-1300 & 1400-1800 Mon-Sat, 1400-1800 Sun.
Min. Mail Order UK: No minimum charge
Min. Mail Order EU: Nmc
Cat. Cost: £3.00
Credit Cards: Visa
Specialities: Plants & hedging suitable for seaside locations. Rare plants originating from Australia & New Zealand esp. *Phormium, Astelia.*
Map Ref: I, B1

ISta   STAM'S BAMBOO NURSERY LTD. ▣ ⊠ €
The Garden House, Cappoquin, Co. Waterford, Ireland
☎ 00 353 (0)58 54787
Fax: 00 353 (0)58 52083
E-mail: stam@iol.ie
Web Site: www.se-growers.ie/stam.bamboo

Contact: Peter Stam
Opening Times: By appt. only.
Mail Order: None
Cat. Cost: Sae
Credit Cards: None
Specialities: Bamboos. Rare & architectural plants. *Note: export for large orders only.
Map Ref: I, D2

ITim TIMPANY NURSERIES
& GARDENS ⊠ EU ▣
77 Magheratimpany Road, Ballynahinch,
Co. Down, N. Ireland BT24 8PA
☎ (028) 9756 2812 Fax: (028) 9756 2812
E-mail: timpany@alpines.freeserve.co.uk
Web Site: www.alpines.freeserve.co.uk
Contact: Susan Tindall
Opening Times: 1030-1730 Tue-Sat, 1400-1700 Sun summer. Closed Mon excl. B/hols.
Min. Mail Order UK: No minimum charge
Min. Mail Order EU: £30.00 + p&p
Cat. Cost: £1.00 in stamps
Credit Cards: Visa, Access, MasterCard
Specialities: *Celmisia, Androsace, Primula, Saxifraga, Helichrysum, Dianthus Meconopsis & Cassiope.*
Map Ref: I, B3

LONDON AREA

LAco ACORN NURSERIES ⊠ UK
Quainton, Aylesbury, Buckinghamshire
HP22 4BX
☎ (01296) 655305 Fax: (01296) 655305
E-mail: robertstalloaks@aol.com
Contact: Alun Roberts
Opening Times: 0900-1700 Mar-Oct closed Sun.
Min. Mail Order UK: No minimum charge
Cat. Cost: 4 x 1st class
Credit Cards: MasterCard, Visa
Specialities: Hardy perennials, *Fuchsia, Dianthus.*
Map Ref: L, A3

LAma JACQUES AMAND ⊠ EU ▣ ▣
The Nurseries, 145 Clamp Hill, Stanmore,
Middlesex HA7 3JS
☎ (020) 8420 7110 Fax: (020) 8954 6784
E-mail: john.amand@btinternet.com
Contact: Stuart Chapman, John Amand or Martine de Groot
Opening Times: 0900-1700 Mon-Fri, 0900-1400 Sat-Sun. Limited Sun opening in Dec & Jan.
Min. Mail Order UK: No minimum charge
Min. Mail Order EU: Nmc
Cat. Cost: 1 x 1st class
Credit Cards: Visa, Access

Specialities: Rare and unusual species bulbs esp. *Arisaema, Trillium, Fritillaria,* tulips.
Map Ref: L, B3

LAst ASTERBY & CHALKCROFT
NURSERIES ◆
The Ridgeway, Blunham, Nr Sandy,
Bedfordshire MK44 3PH
☎ (01767) 640148 Fax: (01767) 640217
E-mail: nursery@asterby.freeserve.co.uk
Web Site: www.asterby.freeserve.co.uk
Contact: Elizabeth Aldridge
Opening Times: 1000-1700 Tues-Sun. Closed Mons (except B/hols).
Mail Order: None
Cat. Cost: 2 x 1st class
Credit Cards: Visa, MasterCard, Switch
Specialities: Hardy shrubs & herbaceous. *Clematis* & trees.
Map Ref: L, A3

LAyl AYLETT NURSERIES LTD ▣
North Orbital Road, London Colney,
St Albans, Hertfordshire AL2 1DH
☎ (01727) 822255 Fax: (01727) 823024
E-mail: Aylett Nurseries@compuserve.com
Web Site: www.martex.co.uk/hta/aylett
Contact: Roger S Aylett
Opening Times: 0830-1730 Mon-Fri, 0830-1700 Sat, 1030-1600 Sun.
Mail Order: None
Cat. Cost: Free
Credit Cards: MasterCard, Switch, Visa, Connect
Specialities: Dahlias.
Map Ref: L, B3

LBCI BRESSINGHAM PLANT CENTRE
(CLANDON) ◆
Clandon Park, West Clandon, Guildford,
Surrey GU4 7RQ
☎ (01483) 222925
Fax: (01483) 211903
Contact: Norma Moore
Opening Times: 0900-1700 1st Nov-31st Mar, 0900-1800 1st Apr-31st Oct 7 days.
Mail Order: None
Cat. Cost: None issued.
Credit Cards: Visa, Delta, Switch, MasterCard
Specialities: Very wide general range. Many own varieties. Focus on hardy ornamental plants & grasses. Perennials.
Map Ref: L, C3

L

LBee **BEECHCROFT NURSERY** 📧
127 Reigate Road, Ewell, Surrey KT17 3DE
☎ (020) 8393 4265   **Fax:** (020) 8393 4265
Contact: C Kimber
Opening Times: 1000-1700 May-Sep.
1000-1600 Oct-Apr, B/hols & Suns. Closed
Xmas-New Year & Aug.
Mail Order: None
Cat. Cost: 2 x 1st class
Credit Cards: Visa, Switch, MasterCard
Specialities: Conifers & alpines.
Map Ref: L, C3

LBlo **TERENCE BLOCH - PLANTSMAN** ✉ UK
9 Colberg Place, Stamford Hill, London
N16 5RA
☎ (020) 8802 2535
Contact: Mr T Bloch
Opening Times: Mail order only.
Min. Mail Order UK: £15.00 + p&p
Cat. Cost: £3.30 incl p&p. Cheque/postal
order only*
Credit Cards: None
Specialities: Tropical plants for the
conservatory/home; rarer tropical fruiting
species for the conservatory/greenhouse.
Plants for sub-tropical summer bedding.
*Note: each season a new, A4 sized,
fully descriptive, colour catalogue is
produced.

LBmB **BLOMS BULBS** ✉ EU 📧 €
Primrose Nurseries, Melchbourne, Bedford,
Bedfordshire MK44 1ZZ
☎ (01234) 709099   **Fax:** (01234) 709799
E-mail: omiblom@aol.com
Web Site: www.blomsbulbs.co.uk
Contact: R J M Blom
Opening Times: 0900-1700 for phone
enquiries or to collect orders. Nursery not
open to the public, mail order only.
Min. Mail Order UK: No minimum charge
Min. Mail Order EU: Nmc
Cat. Cost: Free
Credit Cards: Visa, MasterCard
Specialities: Spring & summer flowering
bulbs, hardy border plants. Note: exports
bulbs only worldwide.
Map Ref: L, A3

LBow **RUPERT BOWLBY** ✉ EU
Gatton, Reigate, Surrey RH2 0TA
☎ (01737) 642221   **Fax:** (01737) 642221
Contact: Rupert Bowlby
Opening Times: Sat & Sun pm in Mar &
Sep-Oct.
Min. Mail Order UK: No minimum charge
Min. Mail Order EU: Nmc
Cat. Cost: 3 x 2nd class

Credit Cards: None
Specialities: Unusual bulbs & corms.
Map Ref: L, C4

LBra **S & N BRACKLEY** ✉ EU 📧 📧
117 Winslow Road, Wingrave, Aylesbury,
Buckinghamshire HP22 4QB
☎ (01296) 681384   **Fax:** (01296) 681384
Contact: Mrs S Brackley/Mrs K Earwicker
Opening Times: Please phone for appt.
Min. Mail Order UK: No minimum charge*
Min. Mail Order EU: Nmc
Cat. Cost: 1st class Sae.
Credit Cards: MasterCard, Visa
Specialities: Sweet pea plants (for collection
only). *Note: onion & leek plants by mail
order. Seeds only by mail to EU. Credit cards
accepted for minimum of £12.
Map Ref: L, B3

LBre **BRESSINGHAM PLANT CENTRE**
(DORNEY) ◆
Dorney, Windsor, Buckinghamshire SL4 6QP
☎ (01628) 669999   **Fax:** (01628) 669693
Contact: Malcolm Martin
Opening Times: 0900-1700 Nov-Feb, 0900-
1800 Mar-Oct 7 days.
Mail Order: None
Cat. Cost: None issued
Credit Cards: Delta, Switch, MasterCard, Visa
Specialities: Very wide general range. Many
own varieties. Focus on hardy ornamental
plants & grasses. Perennials.
Map Ref: L, B3

LBSe **BLOOMS OF BRESSINGHAM**
(BLETCHWORTH) ◆
Michael Seymour Garden Centre,
Station Road, Bletchworth, Surrey RH3 7LX
☎ (01737) 842099   **Fax:** (01737) 843829
Contact: Norma Moore
Opening Times: 0900-1700 1st Nov-31st
Mar, 0900-1800 1st Apr-31st Oct 7 days.
Mail Order: None
Cat. Cost: None issued.
Credit Cards: Visa, Delta, Switch, MasterCard
Specialities: Very wide general range. Many
own varieties. Focus on hardy ornamental
plants & grasses. Perennials & trees.
Map Ref: L, C4

LBuc **BUCKINGHAM NURSERIES** ✉ EU ◆
14 Tingewick Road, Buckingham,
Buckinghamshire MK18 4AE
☎ (01280) 813556   **Fax:** (01280) 815491
E-mail: enquiries@bucknur.com
Contact: R J & P L Brown
Opening Times: 0830-1730 (1800 in
summer) Mon-Fri, 1000-1600 Sun. Late

night opening Thu 1930 (2000 in summer).
Min. Mail Order UK: No minimum charge
Min. Mail Order EU: Nmc
Cat. Cost: Free
Credit Cards: Visa, MasterCard, Switch
Specialities: Bare rooted and container grown hedging. Trees, shrubs, herbaceous perennials, alpines, grasses & ferns.
Map Ref: L, A2

LBut   BUTTERFIELDS NURSERY ⊠ EU ▨ ▨
Harvest Hill, Bourne End, Buckinghamshire
SL8 5JJ
☎ (01628) 525455
Contact: I Butterfield
Opening Times: 0900-1300 & 1400-1700.
Please phone beforehand in case we are attending shows.
Min. Mail Order UK: No minimum charge
Min. Mail Order EU: £30.00 + p&p
Cat. Cost: 2 x 2nd class
Credit Cards: None
Specialities: Only *Pleione* by mail order. *Dahlia* for collection. National Collection of *Pleione*.
Map Ref: L, B3

LCaP   CARPENDERS PARK NURSERY ▨
Little Oxhey Lane, Watford, Hertfordshire
WD1 5BA
☎ (020) 8420 1959   **Fax:** (020) 8420 1958
E-mail: enquiries@carpenders.co.uk
Web Site: www.carpenders.co.uk
Contact: Mark Sage
Opening Times: 0900-1830 Mon-Sun.
Mail Order: None
Cat. Cost: £1.50 inc p&p
Credit Cards: Visa, MasterCard, Switch, Delta, American Express
Specialities: Herbaceous perennials incl. many unusual varieties. Large range of unusual hostas. Over 500 ornamental & fruit trees in stock incl. specimens.
Map Ref: L, B3

LCha   CHASE ORGANICS (GB) LTD ⊠ EU ▨
Riverdene Estate, Molesey Road, Hersham,
Surrey KT12 4RG
☎ (01932) 253666   **Fax:** (01932) 252707
E-mail: chaseorg@aol.com
Contact: S Bossard
Opening Times: 0930-1630 Mon-Fri.
Min. Mail Order UK: 80p p&p under
£17.50*
Min. Mail Order EU: No minimum charge
(seed only).
Cat. Cost: Free
Credit Cards: Visa, Access, Switch
Specialities: 'The Organic Gardening Catalogue' offers vegetable, herb & flower

seeds & garden sundries especially for organic gardeners. *Note: mail order plants only to UK, seeds to EU. Outside EU by arrangement.
Map Ref: L, C3

LChe   CHESSINGTON NURSERIES LTD ⊠ EU
Leatherhead Road, Chessington, Surrey
KT19 2NG
☎ (01372) 725638   **Fax:** (01372) 740859
Contact: Jim Knight
Opening Times: 0900-1800 Mon-Sat,
1000-1600 Sun.
Min. Mail Order UK: No minimum charge
Min. Mail Order EU: Nmc
Cat. Cost: 6 x 1st class
Credit Cards: MasterCard, Visa
Specialities: Conservatory plants esp. *Citrus, Hoya* & *Passiflora*.
Map Ref: L, C3

LChw   CHADWELL SEEDS ⊠ EU ▨
81 Parlaunt Road, Slough, Berkshire SL3 8BE
☎ (01753) 542823   **Fax:** (01753) 542823
Contact: Chris Chadwell
Min. Mail Order UK: No minimum charge
Min. Mail Order EU: Nmc
Cat. Cost: 3 x 2nd class
Credit Cards: None
Specialities: Seed collecting expedition to the Himalayas. Separate general seed list of Japanese, N. American & Himalayan plants.

LCla   CLAY LANE NURSERY
3 Clay Lane, South Nutfield, Nr Redhill,
Surrey RH1 4EG
☎ (01737) 823307
E-mail: ken.claylane@talk21.com
Contact: K W Belton
Opening Times: 0900-1700 Thu-Sun 1st Feb-31st Aug. Other times by appt. Please phone before travelling.
Mail Order: None
Cat. Cost: 3 x 1st class
Credit Cards: None
Specialities: *Fuchsia*.
Map Ref: L, C4

LCns   THE CONSERVATORY ⊠ EU
Gomshall Gallery, Gomshall, Surrey GU5 9LB
☎ (01483) 203019   **Fax:** (01483) 203282
E-mail: pf@conservatoryplants.com
Web Site: www.conservatoryplants.com
Contact: Marceline Siddons
Opening Times: 1000-1730 Mon-Sat all year, 1400-1700 Sun Apr-Oct. Phone to check Xmas & B/hols.
Min. Mail Order UK: No minimum charge
Min. Mail Order EU: Nmc

L

Cat. Cost: 3 x 2nd class
Credit Cards: Visa, MasterCard, Switch, Delta
Specialities: Wide range of conservatory &
house plants incl. *Citrus* & *Bougainvillea*.
Map Ref: L, C3

LCon   THE CONIFER GARDEN ✉ UK
Hare Lane Nursery, Little Kingshill, Great
Missenden, Buckinghamshire HP16 0EF
☎ (01494) 862086 (0900-1800)
Fax: (01494) 862086
E-mail: e mail conifers@hireintelligence.co.uk
Web Site: www.powel.freeserve.co.uk/conifer/
Contact: Mr & Mrs M P S Powell
Opening Times: Usually 1100-1600 Tue-
Wed, Fri & Sat (1100-1300 Dec-Jan & Jul-
Aug). Please phone first.
Min. Mail Order UK: £6.00
Cat. Cost: 2 x 1st class for list only
Credit Cards: None
Specialities: Conifers only - over 500
varieties always in stock.
Map Ref: L, B3

LCot   COTTAGE GARDEN PLANTS
9 Buckingham Road, Newbury, Berkshire
RG14 6DH
☎ (01635) 31941
Contact: Mrs Hannah Billcliffe
Opening Times: 1000-1700 Wed-Sat Mar-
Jul & Sep-Oct.
Mail Order: None
Cat. Cost: Sae + 1 x 1st class
Credit Cards: None
Specialities: Wide range of unusual perennials.
Map Ref: L, C2

LCTD   CTDA ✉ EU 🖼
174 Cambridge Street, London SW1V 4QE
☎ (020) 7976 5115
Contact: Basil Smith
Opening Times: Not open.
Min. Mail Order UK: £15.00 + p&p
Min. Mail Order EU: £15 + p&p
Cat. Cost: Free
Credit Cards: None
Specialities: Hardy *Cyclamen* for the garden,
named *Helleborus, Dierama* & *Aquilegia*
species. Also seeds.

LCtg   COTTAGE GARDEN NURSERY ◆
Barnet Road, Arkley, Barnet, Hertfordshire
EN5 3JX
☎ (020) 8441 8829   Fax: (020) 8531 3178
Contact: David and Wendy Spicer
Opening Times: 0930-1700 Wed-Sat Mar-
Oct, 0930-1600 Wed-Sat Nov-Feb, 1000-
1600 Sun all year.
Mail Order: None

Cat. Cost: None issued
Credit Cards: Visa, Access, MasterCard,
Switch, Solo, Delta
Specialities: General range of hardy shrubs,
trees & perennials. Architectural & exotics,
Fuchsia, seasonal bedding, patio plants.
Map Ref: L, B3

LDea   DEREK LLOYD DEAN ✉ EU 🖼
8 Lynwood Close, South Harrow, Middlesex
HA2 9PR
☎ (020) 8864 0899
Contact: Derek Lloyd Dean
Opening Times: Mail order only.
Min. Mail Order UK: £2.50 + p&p
Min. Mail Order EU: £2.50 + p&p
Cat. Cost: 2 x 1st class
Credit Cards: None
Specialities: Regal, angel, ivy & scented leaf
Pelargonium. National Collection of Angel
Pelargoniums.

LEar   EARLSTONE NURSERY ✉ UK 🖼
Earlstone Manor Farm, Burghclere,
Newbury, Berkshire RG20 9NG
☎ (01635) 278648   Fax: (01635) 278672
E-mail: ginsberg@dial.pipex.com
Contact: B C Ginsberg
Opening Times: By appt.
Min. Mail Order UK: £30.00 + p&p
Cat. Cost: Free
Credit Cards: None
Specialities: All varieties of *Buxus.* Topiary.
Taxus baccata & other varieties of *Taxus.*
Various varieties of *Ilex.*
Map Ref: L, C2

LEdu   EDULIS ✉ EU 🖼
1 Flowers Piece, Ashampstead, Berkshire
RG8 8SG
☎ (01635) 578113   Fax: (01635) 578113
E-mail: edulis2000@hotmail.com
Contact: Paul Barney
Opening Times: Mail order only.
Min. Mail Order UK: £30.00 + p&p
Min. Mail Order EU: £50.00 + p&p
Cat. Cost: 6 x 1st class
Credit Cards: None
Specialities: Unusual edibles, architectural
plants, permaculture plants.
Map Ref: L, B2

LEur   THE EUROPA NURSERY ✉ EU 🖼
PO Box 17589, London E1 4YN
☎ (020) 7265 8131   Fax: (020) 7366 9892
E-mail: europanurs@aol.com
Web Site: www.europa-nursery.co.uk
Contact: Tim Branney & Adam Draper
Opening Times: Not open to the public.

Min. Mail Order UK: No minimum charge
Min. Mail Order EU: Nmc
Cat. Cost: 2 x 1st class
Credit Cards: None
Specialities: Extensive range of *Aquilegia*, *Arisaema, Arum, Asarum, Disporum*, *Epimedium*, hardy gingers, *Paris*, *Polygonatum, Smilacina, Tricyrtis*. Many very rare & new introductions.

LFis   KAYTIE FISHER NURSERY ⊠ UK
South End Cottage, Long Reach, Ockham, Surrey GU23 6PF
☎ (01483) 282304 **Fax:** (01483) 282304
Contact: Kaytie Fisher
Opening Times: 1000-1700 Wed-Sun, 0800-2000 Thu Apr-Jun. 1000-1700 Wed-Fri Mar & Jul-Oct. Nov-Feb by appt. only.
Min. Mail Order UK: £11.95. Courier up to 20kg.
Cat. Cost: 3 x 1st class
Credit Cards: None
Specialities: Mainly hardy herbaceous, alpines, *Clematis* species, shrubs. Old shrub roses & climbing roses. Nursery 1 mile south east of RHS Wisley.
Map Ref: L, C3

LFox   FOXGROVE PLANTS ⊠ EU
Foxgrove, Enborne, Nr Newbury, Berkshire RG14 6RE
☎ (01635) 40554 **Fax:** (01635) 30555
Contact: Mrs Louise Peters
Opening Times:
Min. Mail Order UK: No minimum charge*
Min. Mail Order EU: Nmc
Cat. Cost: £1.00
Credit Cards: None
Specialities: Hardy & unusual plants, including *Galanthus*, hellebores, grasses, *Penstemon*, alpines.
*Note: mail order for *Galanthus* only.
Map Ref: L, C2

LGod   GODLY'S ROSES ⊠ EU ▣
Redbourn, St Albans, Hertfordshire AL3 7PS
☎ (01582) 792255 **Fax:** (01582) 794267
Contact: Colin Godly
Opening Times: 0900-1900 summer, 0900-dusk winter, Mon-Fri. 0900-1800 Sat & Sun.
Min. Mail Order UK: £4.50 + p&p
Min. Mail Order EU: £50.00 + p&p
Cat. Cost: Free
Credit Cards: Visa, Access, American Express, Switch
Specialities: Roses.
Map Ref: L, B3

LGre   GREEN FARM PLANTS
Bury Court, Bentley, Farnham, Surrey GU10 5LZ
☎ (01420) 23202 **Fax:** (01420) 22382
E-mail: GreenFarmPlants.Marina.Christopher @Care4free.net
Contact: M Christopher & J Coke
Opening Times: 1000-1800 Thu-Sat 23 Mar-28 Oct 2000, 22 Mar-27 Oct 2001.
Mail Order: None
Cat. Cost: 3 x 1st class
Credit Cards: Visa, MasterCard, JCB, Switch, Visa, Delta, Electron, Solo
Specialities: Small shrubs, sub-shrubs & perennials. Many uncommon. *Cistus*, *Prostanthera, Achillea, Eryngium, Monarda, Phlox*, grasses.
Map Ref: L, C3

LGro   GROWING CARPETS ⊠ UK ◆
Christmas Tree House, High Street, Guilden Morden, Nr Royston, Hertfordshire SG8 0JP
☎ (01763) 852705
Contact: Mrs E E Moore
Opening Times: 1100-1700 Mon-Sat 18 Mar-28 Oct 2000.
Min. Mail Order UK: No minimum charge*
Cat. Cost: 5 x 2nd class
Credit Cards: None
Specialities: Wide range of ground-covering plants. *Note: in order to avoid bad weather conditions, plants are only despatched in Apr, Sep & Oct on a first-come first-served basis.
Map Ref: L, A4

LGuA   GUILDFORD AQUATIC CENTRE
West Horsley Garden Centre, Epsom Road, West Horsley, Surrey KT24 6AR
☎ (01483) 281678 **Fax:** (01483) 285579
Web Site: www.fishkeeper.co.uk/guildford
Contact: Thomas Williams
Opening Times: 0900-1800 Mon-Sat, 1030-1630 Sun.
Mail Order: None
Credit Cards: Visa, Switch, MasterCard
Specialities: A wide variety of aquatic, marginal & bog plants. Tropical aquatic plants suitable for the aquarium also carried in stock. Please check current availability.
Map Ref: L, C3

LHer   HERONS BONSAI ⊠ UK ▣ €
Wiremill Lane, Newchapel, Lingfield, Surrey RH7 6HJ

KEY	
⊠ Mail order to UK or EU	
▧ Exports beyond EU	€ Euro accepted
▣ Also supplies Wholesale	◆ See Display advertisement

L

☎ (01342) 832657   Fax: (01342) 832025
E-mail: herons.bonsai@virgin.net
Web Site: www.herons.co.uk
Contact: Peter Chan
Opening Times: 0930-1730 Mon-Sat,
1030-1600 Sun.
Min. Mail Order UK: £20.00 + p&p
Cat. Cost: Sae
Credit Cards: Visa, MasterCard, Switch
Specialities: Japanese maple varieties,
Japanese cherries, *Wisteria,* Japanese *Iris,*
bamboos & esp. bonsai, plus very large
Japanese garden trees of Japanese white pine,
yew and maples.
Map Ref: L, C4

LHil   BRIAN HILEY ⊠ EU
25 Little Woodcote Estate, Wallington,
Surrey SM5 4AU
☎ (020) 8647 9679
Contact: Brian & Heather Hiley
Opening Times: 0900-1700 Wed-Sat (excl.
B/hols). Please check beforehand.
Min. Mail Order UK: No minimum charge
Min. Mail Order EU: Nmc
Cat. Cost: 3 x 1st class
Credit Cards: None
Specialities: *Penstemon, Salvia, Canna,* tender
& unusual plants. Ornamental grasses & ferns.
Map Ref: L, C4

LHkn   R HARKNESS & CO. LTD. ⊠ EU ▣ ▣ €
The Rose Gardens, Cambridge Road,
Hitchin, Hertfordshire SG4 0JT
☎ (01462) 420402   Fax: (01462) 422170
E-mail: harkness@roses.co.uk
Web Site: www.roses.co.uk
Contact: Owen Pope
Opening Times: 0900-1730 Mon-Fri.
Min. Mail Order UK: No minimum charge
Min. Mail Order EU: Nmc
Cat. Cost: Free
Credit Cards: American Express, Visa, Access,
Switch, Delta
Specialities: Roses.
Map Ref: L, A3

LHop   HOPLEYS PLANTS LTD ⊠ UK ▣
High Street, Much Hadham, Hertfordshire
SG10 6BU
☎ (01279) 842509   Fax: (01279) 843784
E-mail: hopleys@compuserve.com
Web Site: www.hopleys.co.uk
Contact: Aubrey Barker
Opening Times: 0900-1700 Mon & Wed-
Sat, 1400-1700 Sun. Closed Jan & Feb.
Min. Mail Order UK: No minimum charge
Cat. Cost: 5 x 1st class
Credit Cards: Visa, Access, Switch

Specialities: Wide range of hardy & half-
hardy shrubs & perennials.
Map Ref: L, A4

LHos   THE HOSTA GARDEN ⊠ EU ▣
47 Birch Grove, London W3 9SP
☎ (020) 8248 1300   Fax: (020) 8248 1300
E-mail: hostagarden@hotmail.com
Web Site: www.bcity.com/thehostagarden
Contact: Ian Toop
Opening Times: Mail order only.
Min. Mail Order UK: No minimum charge
Min. Mail Order EU: £20.00 + p&p
Cat. Cost: 4 x 1st class
Credit Cards: None
Specialities: *Hosta.*
Map Ref: L, B3

LHpC   MARTIN HARWOOD BULBS ⊠ EU
Hope Cottage, Halebourne Lane, Chobham,
Surrey GU24 8SL
☎ (01276) 857106
Contact: Martin Harwood
Min. Mail Order UK: No minimum charge
Min. Mail Order EU: Nmc
Cat. Cost: 1 x 1st class
Credit Cards: None
Specialities: *Narcissus, Allium, Crocus,
Fritillaria, Hyacinthus, Iris, Muscari, Scilla,
Tulipa* & other miscellaneous bulbs. National
Collection of *Narcissus.*

LHrt   HORTUS NURSERY
80 Old Charlton Road, Shepperton,
Middlesex TW17 8BS
☎ (01932) 242216   Fax: (01932) 241694
Contact: Marie-Elaine Houghton
Opening Times: 1000-1900 every Fri Mar-
Oct or by appt. at other times.
Mail Order: None
Cat. Cost: 2 x 1st class
Credit Cards: None
Specialities: Ornamental grasses & perennials.
Map Ref: L, C3

LHyd   HYDON NURSERIES ⊠ EU ▣ ▣ ◆ €
Clock Barn Lane, Hydon Heath, Godalming,
Surrey GU8 4AZ
☎ (01483) 860252   Fax: (01483) 419937
Contact: A F George, Rodney Longhurst &
Mrs A M George
Opening Times: 0800-1245 & 1400-1700
Mon-Sat. Sun during May & by appt. Open
B/hols.
Min. Mail Order UK: No minimum charge
Min. Mail Order EU: £25.00 + p&p
Cat. Cost: £1.50 or 6 x 1st class or 8 x 2nd
class
Credit Cards: None

Specialities: Large and dwarf *Rhododendron,* yakushimanum hybrids, azaleas (deciduous & evergreen), *Camellia* & other trees & shrubs. Specimen rhododendrons.
Map Ref: L, C3

LHyr **HYRONS TREES** ⊠ UK ▣
The Green, Sarratt, Rickmansworth, Hertfordshire WD3 6BL
☎ (01923) 263000   **Fax:** (01923) 270625
E-mail: peiser@hyronstrees.demon.co.uk
Contact: Graham Peiser
Opening Times: 0900-1300 Mon-Fri, but please check first.
Min. Mail Order UK: £30.00*
Cat. Cost: 4 x 1st class
Credit Cards: Delta, Switch
Specialities: Broadleaved trees (from whips to extra heavy standards), topiary & hedging. All available in containers. Hedging also available bare-root. *Note: mail order only for topiary & bare-root hedging.
Map Ref: L, B3

LIck **LOWER ICKNIELD FARM NURSERIES** ⊠ UK ◆
Lower Icknield Way, Great Kimble, Aylesbury, Buckinghamshire HP17 9TX
☎ (01844) 343436 mobile 0780 3979993
Contact: S Baldwin, D Baldwin
Opening Times: 0900-1730 7 days excl. Xmas-New Year.
Min. Mail Order UK: £14*
Cat. Cost: 3 x 1st class argyranthemums only
Credit Cards: None
Specialities: National Collection of *Argyranthemum.* Patio & basket plants. Tender & hardy perennials. Salvias. Grasses. *Note: mail order argyranthemums only.
Map Ref: L, B3

LIri **THE IRIS GARDEN** ⊠ EU ◆
47 Station Road, Barnet, Hertfordshire EN5 1PR
☎ (020) 8441 1300
Fax: (020) 8441 1300
E-mail: iris1992@aol.com
Contact: Clive Russell
Opening Times: Nursery not open. Visit our iris exhibits at shows. Please phone for show details.
Min. Mail Order UK: £15.00 + p&p*
Min. Mail Order EU: £25.00 + p&p
Cat. Cost: 6 x 1st class.
Credit Cards: None
Specialities: Modern tall bearded *Iris* from breeders in UK, USA, France & Australia. *Note: order must be received by end of June.

LJus **JUST BAMBOO LTD** ⊠ EU ▣ ▣ €
109 Hayes Lane, Bromley, Kent BR2 9EF
☎ (020) 8462 1800, mobile 07071 226266
Fax: (020) 8462 1800
E-mail: mikejames@justbamboo.com
Web Site: www.justbamboo.com
Contact: Mike James
Opening Times: By appt. only 1400-1800 Tue-Fri, 1000-1700 Sat, 1000-1300 Sun.
Min. Mail Order UK: £20.00 + p&p
Min. Mail Order EU: £60.00 + p&p
Cat. Cost: Sae + 2 x 1st class
Credit Cards: None
Specialities: *Bamboo,* ferns & grasses.
Map Ref: L, C4

LKna **KNAP HILL & SLOCOCK NURSERIES** ⊠ EU ▣ ▣
Barrs Lane, Knaphill, Woking, Surrey GU21 2JW
☎ (01483) 481214/5   **Fax:** (01483) 797261
Contact: Mrs Joy West
Opening Times: 0900-1700 Mon-Fri by appt. only.
Min. Mail Order UK: No minimum charge
Min. Mail Order EU: Nmc
Cat. Cost: 3 x 1st class
Credit Cards: Visa, Access
Specialities: Wide variety of rhododendrons & azaleas.
Map Ref: L, C3

LLin **LINCLUDEN NURSERY** ⊠ EU ▣ ▣
Bisley Green, Bisley, Woking, Surrey GU24 9EN
☎ (01483) 797005   **Fax:** (01483) 474015
Contact: Mr & Mrs J A Tilbury
Opening Times: 0930-1630 Mon-Sat all year excl. B/hols.
Min. Mail Order UK: No minimum charge
Min. Mail Order EU: Nmc
Cat. Cost: 3 x 1st class
Credit Cards: Visa, MasterCard
Specialities: Dwarf, slow-growing & unusual conifers.
Map Ref: L, C3

LLWG **LILIES-WATER-GARDENS** ⊠ UK ◆
Tarn-Hows, Broad Lane, Newdigate, Surrey RH5 5AT
☎ (01306) 631064
Fax: (01306) 631693
Contact: Simon Harman
Opening Times: By appt. only.
Min. Mail Order UK: £20.00
Cat. Cost: 5 x 1st class
Credit Cards: MasterCard, Visa, Delta, JCB, Maestro
Specialities: Waterlilies & marginal plants.

Tropical marginal plants suitable for conservatories.
Map Ref: L, C3

LLWP   L W Plants ⊠ UK
23 Wroxham Way, Harpenden, Hertfordshire AL5 4PP
☎ (01582) 768467
E-mail: lwplants@waitrose.com
Web Site: www.users.waitrose.com/~lwplants
Contact: Mrs M Easter
Opening Times: 1000-1700 most days, but please phone first.
Min. Mail Order UK: £15.00 + p&p*
Cat. Cost: A5 Sae + 5 x 2nd class
Credit Cards: None
Specialities: Unusual hardy perennials & herbs esp. *Diascia, Geranium, Penstemon* & *Thymus*. National Collection of *Thymus*.
*Note: mail order late Sep-Apr.
Map Ref: L, B3

LMil   Millais Nurseries ⊠ EU ◆ 🖪 🖾
Crosswater Lane, Churt, Farnham, Surrey GU10 2JN
☎ (01252) 792698   Fax: (01252) 792526
E-mail: sales@rhododendrons.co.uk
Web Site: www.rhododendrons.co.uk
Contact: David Millais
Opening Times: 1000-1300 & 1400-1700 Mon-Fri. Sat spring & autumn daily in May and early June.
Min. Mail Order UK: £25.00 + p&p*
Min. Mail Order EU: £60.00 + p&p
Cat. Cost: 4 x 1st class
Credit Cards: Visa, Switch, Delta, MasterCard
Specialities: Rhododendrons & azaleas.
*Note: mail order Oct-April only.
Map Ref: L, C3

LMor   Morehavens ⊠ EU 🖪
Sandpit Hill, Buckland Common, Tring, Hertfordshire HP23 6NG
☎ (01494) 758642
Contact: B Farmer
Opening Times: Only for collection.
Min. Mail Order UK: £11.50 incl. p&p
Min. Mail Order EU: £11.50
Cat. Cost: Free
Credit Cards: None
Specialities: *Camomile* 'Treneague'.
Map Ref: L, B3

LNet   Nettletons Nursery ⊠ UK 🖪 ◆
Ivy Mill Lane, Godstone, Surrey RH9 8NF
☎ (01883) 742426   Fax: (01883) 742426
Contact: Jonathan Nettleton
Opening Times: 0900-1300 & 1400-1700 Mon Tue Thu-Sat. In winter please phone first.

Min. Mail Order UK: *
Cat. Cost: 3 x 1st class
Credit Cards: Visa, Access
Specialities: Trees & shrubs esp. conifers, rhododendrons & azaleas, climbers, *Camellia*. 100 Japanese *Acer*. 35 *Wisteria*.
*Note: mail order, only 1 year grafted wisterias sent by post, other stock is too big.
Map Ref: L, C4

LNor   Northview Perennials ⊠ EU 🖪
27 Clifton Road, Henlow, Bedfordshire SG16 6BL
☎ (01462) 814509   Fax: (01462) 814509
Contact: N K Wake
Opening Times: By appt. only.
Min. Mail Order UK: No minimum charge*
Min. Mail Order EU: Nmc
Cat. Cost: 4 x 1st class
Credit Cards: None
Specialities: Herbaceous perennials. *Note: mail order dormant season only, normally mid-Oct to mid-Mar.
Map Ref: L, A3

LPal   The Palm Centre ⊠ EU 🖾 🖪
Ham Central Nursery, opposite Riverside Drive, Ham Street, Ham, Richmond, Surrey TW10 7HA
☎ (020) 8255 6191
Fax: (020) 8255 6192/6193
E-mail: mail@palmcentre.co.uk
Web Site: www.palmcentre.co.uk
Contact: Martin Gibbons
Opening Times: 1000-1800 (dusk in winter) 7 days.
Min. Mail Order UK: £10.00 + p&p
Min. Mail Order EU: £10.00 + p&p
Cat. Cost: Free
Credit Cards: Visa, MasterCard
Specialities: Palms & cycads, exotic & sub-tropical, hardy, half-hardy & tropical. Seedlings to mature trees. Also bamboo, tree ferns & other exotics.
Map Ref: L, B3

LPan   Pantiles Plant & Garden Centre ⊠ EU ◆ 🖪 🖾
Almners Road, Lyne, Chertsey, Surrey KT16 0BJ
☎ (01932) 872195   Fax: (01932) 874030
E-mail: pantiles@telinco.co.uk
Web Site: www.pantiles.co.uk
Contact: Steve Jeffries
Opening Times: 0900-1730 Mon-Sat, 0900-1700 Sun.
Min. Mail Order UK: £100.00 + p&p
Min. Mail Order EU: £100.00 + p&p
Cat. Cost: Free

Credit Cards: Visa, Switch, MasterCard
Specialities: Large trees, shrubs, conifers &
climbers in containers. Australasian & other
unusual plants.
Map Ref: L, C3

LPBA   PAUL BROMFIELD - AQUATICS
⊠ EU ◪ ◪ €
Maydencroft Lane, Gosmore, Hitchin,
Hertfordshire SG4 7QD
☎ (01462) 457399   **Fax:** (01462) 422652
Contact: P Bromfield
Opening Times: 0900-1300 & 1400-1730 7
days Feb-Oct. 1000-1300 Sat-Sun Nov-Jan.
Please ring first.
Min. Mail Order UK: £10.00 incl.
Min. Mail Order EU: £50.00 incl.
Cat. Cost: 2 x 1st class
Credit Cards: Visa, MasterCard, Delta, JCB,
Switch
Specialities: Water lilies, marginals & bog.
Map Ref: L, A3

LPen   PENSTEMONS BY COLOUR ⊠ EU ◪
76 Grove Avenue, Hanwell, London W7 3ES
☎ (020) 8840 3199   **Fax:** (020) 8840 6415
E-mail: debra.hughes1@virgin.net
Contact: Debra Hughes
Opening Times: Any time by appt.
Min. Mail Order UK: £5.00 + p&p
Min. Mail Order EU: £10.00 + p&p
Cat. Cost: Free
Credit Cards: None
Specialities: *Penstemon.*
Map Ref: L, B3

LPio   PIONEER NURSERY ⊠ EU ◪ €
Baldock Lane, Willian, Letchworth,
Hertfordshire SG6 2AE
☎ (01462) 675858   **Fax:** (01462) 675596
E-mail: pioneer@nursery.dircon.co.uk
Web Site: www.pioneerplants.com
Contact: Nick Downing
Opening Times: 0930-1800 Tue-Sun Feb-Dec.
Min. Mail Order UK: £15.00 + p&p
Min. Mail Order EU: 30 Euros
Cat. Cost: Free
Credit Cards: MasterCard, Visa
Specialities: *Salvia,* tender perennials,
Nerium oleander. Wide range of hard-to-find
perennials & bulbs.
Map Ref: L, A3

LPJP   PJ'S PALMS AND EXOTICS ⊠ EU €
41 Salcombe Road, Ashford, Middlesex
TW15 3BS
☎ (01784) 250181
Contact: Peter Jenkins
Opening Times: Mail order only 1st Mar-

30th Nov. Visits by arrangement.
Min. Mail Order UK: No minimum charge
Min. Mail Order EU: Nmc
Cat. Cost: 2 x 1st class
Credit Cards: None
Specialities: Palms & other exotic foliage
plants, hardy & half-hardy.
Map Ref: L, B3

LPlm   A J PALMER & SON ⊠ EU ◪
Denham Court Nursery, Denham Court
Drive, Denham, Uxbridge, Middlesex
UB9 5PG
☎ (01895) 832035   **Fax:** (01895) 832035
Contact: Sheila Palmer
Opening Times: 0900-dusk 7 days Jul-Oct,
rose field viewing. 0900-1700 Mon-Sat,
1000-1300 Sun Nov. Dec-Jun phone.
Min. Mail Order UK: No minimum charge
Min. Mail Order EU: Nmc
Cat. Cost: Free
Credit Cards: None
Specialities: Roses. Note: main showfield on
the A40 near Denham Roundabout
(junction 1 M40) unstaffed.
Map Ref: L, B3

LPri   PRIORSWOOD CLEMATIS ⊠ EU ◪ ◪
Priorswood, Widbury Hill, Ware,
Hertfordshire SG12 7QH
☎ (01920) 461543   **Fax:** (01920) 461543
Contact: G S Greenway
Opening Times: 0800-1700 Tue-Sun &
B/hol Mons.
Min. Mail Order UK: £10.00 + p&p
Min. Mail Order EU: £30.00 + p&p
Cat. Cost: Free plant list; catalogue/growing
guide £2.
Credit Cards: Visa, Access
Specialities: *Clematis* & other climbing
plants. *Lonicera, Parthenocissus, Solanum,
Passiflora, Vitis* etc.
Map Ref: L, B4

LPVe   PLANTA VERA ⊠ EU ◪
Lyne Hill Nursery, Farm Close, Lyne
Crossing Road, Chertsey, Surrey KT16 0AT
☎ (01932) 563011   **Fax:** (01932) 563011
Contact: Morris May
Opening Times: By arrangement.
Min. Mail Order UK: £24.00 (12 plants)
Min. Mail Order EU: £24 (12 plants)
Cat. Cost: 5 x 2nd class
Credit Cards: None

Specialities: 415 named violas & violettas.
National Collection status (provisional).
Map Ref: L, C3

LRHS   WISLEY PLANT CENTRE (RHS)
RHS Garden, Wisley, Woking, Surrey
GU23 6QB
☎ (01483) 211113 Fax: (01483) 212372
Opening Times: 1000-1800 Mon-Sat 1100-
1700 Sun summer, 1000-1730 Mon-Sat
1000-1600 Sun winter. Closed Easter Sun.
Mail Order: None
Cat. Cost: None issued
Credit Cards: MasterCard, Access, American
Express, Switch, Visa
Specialities: Very wide range, many rare &
unusual.
Map Ref: L, C3

LRot   ROTHERSTONE LOCKSIDE PLANTS ⊠ UK
Mapledurham Lock, Mapledurham Drive,
Purley-on-Thames, Reading, Berkshire
RG8 8BE
☎ (01189) 420239
Contact: J H Over
Opening Times: 1000-1800 all year.
Min. Mail Order UK: No minimum charge
Cat. Cost: Free
Credit Cards: None
Specialities: Perennials, grasses & ferns.
Map Ref: L, B2

LSee   SEEDS BY SIZE ⊠ EU ☒ €
45 Crouchfield, Boxmoor, Hemel
Hempstead, Hertfordshire HP1 1PA
☎ (01442) 251458
E-mail: john-robert-size@seeds-by-size.co.uk
Web Site: www.seeds-by-size.co.uk
Contact: Mr John Robert Size
Opening Times: Not open.
Min. Mail Order UK: No minimum charge
Min. Mail Order EU: Nmc
Cat. Cost: Sae
Credit Cards: None
Specialities: Flowers & vegetables. 1,400
varieties of vegetable, (175 cabbage, 99
cauliflower, 70 onion, 100 tomatoes) &
4,900 flowers such as 291 varieties of sweet
pea, 100 herbs.

**LSiH   SINO-HIMALAYAN PLANT
ASSOCIATION ⊠ UK ☒**
81 Parlaunt Road, Slough, Berkshire
SL3 8BE
☎ (01753) 542823 Fax: (01753) 542823
Contact: Chris Chadwell
Min. Mail Order UK: No minimum charge
Cat. Cost: None issued
Credit Cards: None

Specialities: Seed available for exchange to
members. Please apply for membership.

LSpr   SPRINGLEA NURSERY
Springlea, Seymour Plain, Marlow, Bucks
SL7 3BZ
☎ (01628) 473366 (mobile) 078085 12815
Contact: Mary Dean
Opening Times: Apr-Sep. Please check before
visiting. Garden open, see NGS for details.
Mail Order: None
Cat. Cost: None issued
Credit Cards: None
Specialities: Wide range of rare & unusual
shrubs & perennials incl. hardy *Geranium,
Pulmonaria, Primula,* bog plants, ground
cover & shade loving plants.
Map Ref: L, B3

LStr   HENRY STREET NURSERY ⊠ EU ☒
Swallowfield Road, Arborfield, Reading,
Berkshire RG2 9JY
☎ (0118) 9761223 Fax: (0118) 9761417
Contact: Mr M C Goold
Opening Times: 0900-1730 Mon-Sat,
1000-1600 Sun.
Min. Mail Order UK: No minimum charge
Min. Mail Order EU: Nmc
Cat. Cost: Free
Credit Cards: Visa, Access, Switch
Specialities: Roses.
Map Ref: L, D3

LSur   SURREY PRIMROSES ⊠ EU
Merriewood, Sandy Lane, Milford,
Godalming, Surrey GU8 5BJ
☎ (01483) 416747
Contact: Val & Geoff Yates
Opening Times: Not open to the public.
Min. Mail Order UK: No minimum charge
Min. Mail Order EU: Nmc
Cat. Cost: Sae
Credit Cards: None
Specialities: Primroses, old named varieties.
Map Ref: L, C3

LSyl   SYLVATICA NURSERY ⊠ EU €
Crosswater Farm, Crosswater Lane, Churt,
Farnham, Surrey GU10 2JN
☎ (01252) 792775 · Fax: (01252) 792526
E-mail: johnmillais@sylvatica.fsnet.co.uk
Contact: John Millais
Opening Times: By appt.
Min. Mail Order UK: No minimum charge
Min. Mail Order EU: Nmc
Cat. Cost: 5 x 1st class
Credit Cards: None
Specialities: *Sorbus* & woodland perennials.
Map Ref: L, C3

LToo   TOOBEES EXOTICS ✉ EU ▦
(Office) 20 Inglewood, St Johns, Woking,
Surrey GU21 3HX
☎ (01483) 797534 (nursery)
Fax: (01483) 751995
E-mail: bbpotter@compuserve.com
Web Site: www.cactus-mall.com/toobees
Contact: Bob Potter
Opening Times: 1000-1700 Wed-Sun &
B/hol Mons 4th Mar-1st Oct 2000.
Min. Mail Order UK: No minimum charge
Min. Mail Order EU: Nmc
Cat. Cost: Sae
Credit Cards: MasterCard, Visa, Delta,
Switch
Specialities: South African & Madagascan
succulents, many rare & unusual species.
Palms, tree ferns, air plants, carnivorous
plants, *Euphorbia, Pachypodium*. Note:
nursery is at Blackhorse Road, Brookwood,
Woking, Surrey GU22 0QT.
Map Ref: L, C3

LTor   TORHILL NURSERY ✉ EU ▦
3 The Avenue, Hertford, Hertfordshire
SG14 3DG
☎ (01920) 823623
Fax: (01763) 848909
E-mail: torhill.topiary@dial.pipex.com
Web Site: www.yew.co.uk or
www.torhill.co.uk
Contact: Chris Gates
Opening Times: By appt. only.
Min. Mail Order UK: No minimum charge
Min. Mail Order EU: Nmc
Cat. Cost: Free
Credit Cards: None
Specialities: Yew (*Taxus*) hedging & topiary,
box (*Buxus*) hedging, *Gunnera manicata*.

LVER   THE VERNON GERANIUM NURSERY
✉ EU
Cuddington Way, Cheam, Sutton, Surrey
SM2 7JB
☎ (020) 8393 7616
Fax: (020) 8786 7437
E-mail: mrgeranium@aol.com
Web Site: www.geraniumsuk.com
Contact: Philip James & Liz Sims
Opening Times: 0930-1730 Mon-Sat,
1000-1600 Sun, 1st Mar-31st Jul.
Min. Mail Order UK: No minimum charge
Min. Mail Order EU: Nmc
Cat. Cost: £2.00 UK*
Credit Cards: Visa, MasterCard, Switch
Specialities: *Pelargonium* & *Fuchsia*.
*Note: illustrated colour catalogue. £2.50 for
overseas.
Map Ref: L, C3

MIDLANDS

MAAq   AVON AQUATICS ✉ UK ▦
(Office) Sweet Knowle Farm, Preston-on-
Stour, Stratford-upon-Avon, Warwickshire
CV37 8NR
☎ (01789) 450638   Fax: (01789) 450967
E-mail: avonaquatics@btinternet.com
Web Site: www.avonaquatics.com
Contact: Rex Harding
Opening Times: 0900-1700 Mon-Sat 1000-
1600 Sun.
Min. Mail Order UK: £50.00 + p&p
Cat. Cost: No catalogue
Credit Cards: Visa, MasterCard, Switch
Specialities: Water lilies (70 varieties of
Nymphaea), marginals (native), oxygenators
& bog plants. Note: nursery is at Ilmington
Road Wimpstone, Stratford upon Avon.
Map Ref: M, C2

MAld   ALDERTON PLANT NURSERY
Spring Lane, Alderton, Towcester,
Northamptonshire NN12 7LW
☎ (01327) 811253
Contact: Tom Hutchinson
Opening Times: 1000-1630 Tue-Sun &
B/hol Mons. Closed Jan.
Mail Order: None
Cat. Cost: 2 x 1st class
Credit Cards: None
Specialities: *Fuchsia*.
Map Ref: M, C3

MAnH   ARN HILL PLANTS
62 West Lockinge, Wantage, Oxfordshire
OX12 8QE
☎ 01235 834312   Fax: 01235 862361
E-mail: arnhill@cs.com
Contact: Sally Hall
Opening Times: 1000-1300 Sat 15th Apr-
14th Oct 2000, 14th Apr-13th Oct 2001.
Other times by appt.
Mail Order: None
Cat. Cost: 3 x 1st class
Credit Cards: None
Specialities: Wide range of hardy perennials
& grasses.
Map Ref: M, D2

MArl   ARLEY HALL NURSERY
Arley Hall Nursery, Northwich, Cheshire
CW9 6NA
☎ (01565) 777479/777231
Fax: (01565) 777465
E-mail: janefoster@btinternet.com
Contact: Jane Foster
Opening Times: 1200-1730 Tue-Sun Easter-
end Sep. Also B/hol Mons.

M

M

Mail Order: None
Cat. Cost: 4 x 1st class
Credit Cards: None
Specialities: Wide range of herbaceous incl.
many unusual varieties.
Map Ref: M, A1

MAsh   ASHWOOD NURSERIES LTD ⊠ EU ▣
Greensforge, Kingswinford, West Midlands
DY6 0AE
☎ (01384) 401996   Fax: (01384) 401108
E-mail: ashwoodnurs@hotmail.com
Contact: John Massey & Philip Baulk
Opening Times: 0900-1800 Mon-Sat &
1100-1700 Sun excl. Xmas & Boxing Day.
Min. Mail Order UK: No minimum charge*
Min. Mail Order EU: Nmc
Cat. Cost: 4 x 1st class
Credit Cards: Visa, Access, MasterCard
Specialities: Large range of hardy plants &
dwarf conifers. National Collections of
Lewisia & *Cyclamen* species. Hellebores,
Hepatica. *Note: mail order for seeds, &
special offers only.
Map Ref: M, C2

MAus   DAVID AUSTIN ROSES LTD ⊠ EU ▣ ▣
Bowling Green Lane, Albrighton,
Wolverhampton, West Midlands WV7 3HB
☎ (01902) 376376   Fax: (01902) 372142
E-mail: retail@david-austin.simplyonline.co.uk
Web Site: www.davidaustinroses.com
Contact: Office Reception
Opening Times: 0900-1700 Mon-Fri, 1000-
1800 Sat, Sun & B/hols. Until dusk Nov-Mar.
Min. Mail Order UK: No minimum charge
Min. Mail Order EU: Nmc
Cat. Cost: Free
Credit Cards: Access, Switch, Visa
Specialities: Roses. National Collection of
English roses. Also hardy perennials at Claire
Austin Hardy Plants at same site.
Map Ref: M, B2

MAvo   AVONDALE NURSERY
(Office) 3 Avondale Road, Earlsdon,
Coventry, Warwickshire CV5 6DZ
☎ (024) 766 73662 (mobile) 0797 909 3096
Fax: (024) 766 73662
E-mail: avondalenursery@yahoo.co.uk
Web Site:
www.x28800.demon.co.uk/avondalenursery
Contact: Brian Ellis
Opening Times: 1000-1230, 1400-1700 7
days Mar-Oct. Closed Sun pm Jul-Aug.
Other times by appt.
Mail Order: None
Cat. Cost: 4 x 1st class
Credit Cards: None

Specialities: Rare & unusual perennials esp.
*Campanula, Eryngium, Leucanthemum,
Geum, Crocosmia, Pulmonaria* & grasses. Note:
nursery is at Smith's Nursery, 3 Stoneleigh
Road, Baginton, Nr Coventry CV8 3BA.
Map Ref: M, C2

MBar   BARNCROFT NURSERIES ⊠ UK ▣
Dunwood Lane, Longsdon, Nr Leek, Stoke-
on-Trent, Staffordshire ST9 9QW
☎ (01538) 384310   Fax: (01538) 384310
Web Site: www.barncroftnurseries.co.uk
Contact: S Warner
Opening Times: 0900-1700 or dusk if
earlier Fri-Sun all year, plus Mon-Thu 0900-
1700 Mar-Dec.
Min. Mail Order UK: No minimum charge
Cat. Cost: £1.50 incl. p&p
Credit Cards: None
Specialities: Extensive range of over 2000
heathers, conifers, shrubs, trees, climbers &
rhododendrons. Display garden containing
400 heather cvs.
Map Ref: M, B2

MBBe   BLOOMS OF BRESSINGHAM (RUGBY) ◆
Bernhards Garden Centre, Bilton Road,
Rugby, Warwickshire CV22 7DT
☎ (01788) 522005
Fax: (01788) 522855/816803
Contact: Brian O'Callaghan
Opening Times: 0900-1700 1st Nov-31st
Mar, 0900-1800 1st Apr-31 Oct 7 days.
Mail Order: None
Cat. Cost: none issued.
Credit Cards: Visa, Delta, Switch, MasterCard
Specialities: Very wide general range. Many
own varieties. Focus on hardy ornamental
plants & grasses. Perennials & trees.
Map Ref: M, C3

**MBct   BARCOTE GARDEN HERBACEOUS
PLANTS**
Barcote Garden, Faringdon, Oxon SN7 8PP
☎ (01367) 870600
E-mail: garden@barcote.free-online.co.uk
Contact: Christine Smith
Opening Times: By arrangement Mar-Oct.
Closed Nov-Feb.
Mail Order: None
Cat. Cost: Sae for plant list.
Credit Cards: None
Specialities: Herbaceous perennials.
Map Ref: M, D2

MBel   BELLHOUSE NURSERY
Bellhouse Lane, Moore, Nr Warrington,
Cheshire WA4 6TR
☎ (01925) 740874   Fax: (01925) 740672

Contact: Elaine Soens & Doreen Scott
Opening Times: 1000-1700 Wed-Mon Mar-Oct. Closed Nov-Feb & every Tue.
Mail Order: None
Cat. Cost: £1.00
Credit Cards: None
Specialities: Wide range of herbaceous plants & shrubs. Good selection of unusual varieties.
Map Ref: M, A1

MBlu   BLUEBELL NURSERY ⊠ EU ▣ €
Annwell Lane, Smisby, Nr Ashby de la Zouch LE65 2TA
☎ (01530) 413700   **Fax:** (01530) 417600
E-mail: sales@bluebellnursery.com
Web Site: www.bluebellnursery.com
Contact: Robert & Suzette Vernon
Opening Times: 0900-1700 Mon-Sat & 1030-1630 Sun Mar-Oct, 0900-1600 Mon-Sat (not Sun) Nov-Feb. Closed 24th Dec-4th Jan. Closed Easter Sun.
Min. Mail Order UK: No minimum charge
Min. Mail Order EU: Nmc
Cat. Cost: £1.00 + 2 x 1st class
Credit Cards: Visa, Access, Switch
Specialities: Uncommon trees & shrubs. Display garden & arboretum.
Map Ref: M, B2

MBNS   BARNSDALE GARDENS
Exton Avenue, Exton, Oakham, Rutland LE15 8AH
☎ (01572) 813200   **Fax:** (01572) 813346
E-mail: info@barnsdalegardens.co.uk
Web Site: www.barnsdalegardens.co.uk
Contact: Nick or Sue Hamilton
Opening Times: 1000-1700 1st Mar-31st Oct gardens & nursery, 1000-1600 1st Nov-28/29th Feb nursery only. Closed Xmas & New Year.
Mail Order: None
Cat. Cost: A5 + 5 x 2nd class
Credit Cards: Visa, Access, MasterCard, Switch, Delta
Specialities: Choice & unusual garden plants. Over 70 varieties of *Penstemon,* large collection of *Hemerocallis.*
Map Ref: M, B3

MBri   BRIDGEMERE NURSERIES ▣ ◆
Bridgemere, Nr Nantwich, Cheshire CW5 7QB
☎ (01270) 521100   **Fax:** (01270) 520215
Contact: Keith Atkey
Opening Times: 0900-2000 Mon-Sat, 1000-2000 Sun summer, until 1700 in winter.
Mail Order: None
Cat. Cost: None issued
Credit Cards: Visa, Access, MasterCard, Switch

Specialities: Perennials, shrubs, trees, roses, climbers, rhododendrons & azaleas, alpines, heathers, ferns, grasses, aquatics & house plants.
Map Ref: N, B1

MBrN   BRIDGE NURSERY ▣ €
Tomlow Road, Napton-on-the-hill, Nr Rugby, Warwickshire CV23 8HX
☎ (01926) 812737
Contact: Christine Dakin & Philip Martino
Opening Times: 1000-1600 Fri-Sun Apr-Oct. Other times by appt.
Mail Order: None
Cat. Cost: 4 x 1st class
Credit Cards: None
Specialities: Ornamental grasses, sedges & bamboos. Also range of shrubs & perennials.
Map Ref: M, C2

MBro   BROADSTONE NURSERIES
13 The Nursery, High Street, Sutton Courtenay, Abingdon, Oxfordshire OX14 4UA
☎ (01235) 847557 (evenings preferred)
Contact: J Shackleton
Opening Times: 1400-1700 Tue, 1400-1800 Sat (except show days). By appt. on other days/times.
Mail Order: None
Cat. Cost: 3 x 1st class
Credit Cards: None
Specialities: Plants for rock gardens, scree, troughs & borders. Lime tolerant hardy alpines, perennials & unusual plants. Small selection choice shrubs.
Map Ref: M, D3

MBur   BURROWS ROSES ⊠ EU
Meadow Croft, Spondon Road, Dale Abbey, Derby, Derbyshire DE7 4PQ
☎ (01332) 668289   **Fax:** (01332) 668289
Contact: Stuart & Diane Burrows
Opening Times: Mail order only.
Min. Mail Order UK: £4.00 + p&p, no min. order, up to 3 plants £2.00 p&p
Min. Mail Order EU: £4.00 + p&p
Cat. Cost: 2 x 1st class
Credit Cards: None
Specialities: Roses only.

MCad   CADDICK'S CLEMATIS NURSERIES ⊠ EU ◆
Lymm Road, Thelwall, Warrington, Cheshire WA13 0UF
☎ (01925) 757196

M

KEY	
⊠ Mail order to UK or EU	
▣ Exports beyond EU	€ Euro accepted
▣ Also supplies Wholesale	◆ See Display advertisement

M

Web Site: www.caddicks-clematis.co.uk
Contact: Mrs D Caddick
Opening Times: 1000-1700 Tue-Sat 8th Feb-31st Oct, 1100-1600 Sun. Nov by arrangement. 1100-1600 B/hols. Closed Dec & Jan.
Min. Mail Order UK: £12.60 + p&p
Min. Mail Order EU: £12.60 + p&p
Cat. Cost: £1.20 cheque/PO UK, £1.50 EC & Eire
Credit Cards: Visa, Access, MasterCard, Switch
Specialities: *Clematis.*
Map Ref: M, A1

MCAu CLAIRE AUSTIN HARDY PLANTS ✉ EU
Bowling Green Lane, Albrighton, Wolverhampton, West Midlands WV7 3HB
☎ (01902) 376333 Fax: (01902) 372142
E-mail: retail@david-austin.simplyonline.co.uk
Contact: Claire Austin
Opening Times: 0900-1700 Mon-Fri.
Min. Mail Order UK: No minimum charge
Min. Mail Order EU: £50.00 + p&p
Cat. Cost: Free
Credit Cards: MasterCard, Visa, Switch
Specialities: *Paeonia, Iris, Hemerocallis* & hardy plants.
Map Ref: M, B2

MCCP COLLECTORS CORNER PLANTS ✉ UK
33 Rugby Road, Clifton-upon-Dunsmore, Rugby, Warwickshire CV23 0DE
☎ (01788) 571881
Contact: Pat Neesam
Opening Times: By appt. only.
Min. Mail Order UK: £10
Cat. Cost: 6 x 1st class
Credit Cards: None
Specialities: General range of choice herbaceous perennials, grasses, shrubs, palms & ferns.
Map Ref: M, C3

MChe CHESHIRE HERBS ✉ EU ◆
Fourfields, Forest Road, Nr Tarporley, Cheshire CW6 9ES
☎ (01829) 760578 Fax: (01829) 760354
Contact: Mr & Mrs Ted Riddell
Opening Times: 1000-1700 7 days 3rd Jan-24th Dec.
Min. Mail Order UK: No minimum charge*
Min. Mail Order EU: Nmc
Cat. Cost: 2 x 1st class
Credit Cards: Access, Visa, Switch
Specialities: Display herb garden & Elizabethan knot garden. *Note: mail order seeds only (not plants).
Map Ref: M, B1

MChl CHARLECOTE FRUIT & FLOWERS
✉ EU 🅖
Dog Kennel Close, Charlecote, Warwickshire CV35 9ER
☎ (01789) 840601, (01789) 842674
Fax: (01789) 842588
E-mail: flowers@free4all
Web Site: www.charlecote.co.uk
Contact: John and Mark Williams
Opening Times: 1000-1800 7 days Mar-Oct.
Min. Mail Order UK: £10.00
Min. Mail Order EU: £10.00
Cat. Cost: 2 x 1st class
Credit Cards: Visa, Access
Specialities: Perennial herbaceous, vegetatively propagated, field-grown.
Map Ref: M, C2

MCli CLIPSTON NURSERY
Naseby Road, Clipston, Market Harborough, Leicestershire LE16 9RZ
☎ (01858) 525567 Fax: (01858) 525567
Contact: Kate Hayward
Opening Times: 1000-1800 7 days Mar-Sep.
Mail Order: None
Cat. Cost: 2 x 2nd class
Credit Cards: Visa
Specialities: Perennials incl. many unusual varieties.
Map Ref: M, C3

MCLN COUNTRY LADY NURSERY
Lilac Cottage, Chapel Lane, Gentleshaw, Nr Rugeley, Staffordshire WS15 4ND
☎ (01543) 675520
Fax: (01543) 675520
Contact: Mrs Sylvia Nunn
Opening Times: 1000-1700 Wed-Sun & B/hol Mons Mar-end Sep. Other times by appt.
Mail Order: None
Cat. Cost: A5 Sae + 2 x 1st class
Credit Cards: None
Specialities: Wide range of unusual perennials incl. hardy *Geranium, Heuchera, Penstemon* & *Primula.* 1 acre show garden.
Map Ref: M, B2

MCol COLLINWOOD NURSERIES ✉ UK
Mottram St Andrew, Macclesfield, Cheshire SK10 4QR
☎ (01625) 582272
Contact: A Wright
Opening Times: 0830-1730 Mon-Sat 1300-1730 Sun. Closed Sun in Jan-Mar.
Min. Mail Order UK: No minimum charge*
Cat. Cost: 1 x 1st class
Credit Cards: None
Specialities: *Chrysanthemum (Dendranthema).*

*Note: mail order plants available for despatch March, April & May only.
Map Ref: M, A2

MCoo   COOL TEMPERATE ⊠ EU ▣
5 Colville Villas, Nottingham NG1 4HN
☎ (0115) 947 4977   **Fax:** (0115) 947 4977
E-mail: philip.corbett@btinternet.com
Contact: Phil Corbett
Opening Times: Mail order only.
Min. Mail Order UK: No minimum charge
Min. Mail Order EU: Nmc
Cat. Cost: 2 x 1st class
Credit Cards: None
Specialities: Tree fruit, soft fruit, nitrogen-fixers, hedging, own-root fruit trees.

MCre   CRESCENT PLANTS ⊠ EU
34 The Crescent, Cradley Heath, West Midlands B64 7JS
☎ (0121) 550 2628   **Fax:** (0121) 550 2732
E-mail: ian@auriculas.co.uk
Web Site: www.auriculas.co.uk
Contact: Ian Goddard
Opening Times: By appt.
Min. Mail Order UK: No minimum charge
Min. Mail Order EU: Nmc
Cat. Cost: 2 x 1st class
Credit Cards: None
Specialities: Named varieties of *Primula auricula* incl. show, alpine, double, striped & border types. Also seed.

MDCh   DAVID CHESHIRE SEEDS ⊠ EU ▣ ▣
85 Grasmere Cres, Nuneaton, Warwickshire CV11 6EB
☎ (01203) 328891 (mobile) 07932 084655
E-mail: davidcheshire@Seed78.fsnet.co.uk
Contact: David Cheshire
Min. Mail Order UK: £5.00
Min. Mail Order EU: £5.00
Cat. Cost: 2 x 1st class
Credit Cards: None
Specialities: Seeds. Rare plants. Plants from wild collected seeds.

MDHE   DHE PLANTS ⊠ UK
(Office) Rose Lea, Darley House Estate, Darley Dale, Matlock, Derbyshire DE4 2QH
☎ (01629) 732512
Contact: Peter M Smith
Opening Times: 1000-1700 Tue-Sat, 1030-1630 Sun. Advance phone call desirable.
Min. Mail Order UK: No minimum charge*
Cat. Cost: 2 x 1st class
Credit Cards: None
Specialities: Alpines esp. *Erodium, Helianthemum, Saxifraga* & *Sisyrinchium.*
*Note: mail order Oct-Mar only. Nursery

stock is at Robert Young Garden Centre, Bakewell Rd, Matlock.
Map Ref: M, B2

MDun   DUNGE VALLEY GARDENS ▣
Windgather Rocks, Kettleshulme, High Peak SK23 7RF
☎ (01663) 733787   **Fax:** (01663) 733787
E-mail: xon74@dial.pipex.com
Contact: David Ketley
Opening Times: 1030-1800 1st Apr-31st Aug or by appt. Closed Mon except B/hols. Open w/ends Mar & Sep.
Mail Order: None
Cat. Cost: A4 Sae
Credit Cards: MasterCard, Visa
Specialities: *Rhododendron* species & hybrids. Magnolias, trees, shrubs & perennials, some rare & wild collected. *Meconopsis* & *Trillium.*
Map Ref: M, A2

MFie   FIELD HOUSE NURSERIES ⊠ EU ▣
Leake Road, Gotham, Nottinghamshire NG11 0JN
☎ (0115) 9830278   **Fax:** (0115) 9831486
E-mail: dlvwjw@field-house-alpines.fsbusiness.co.uk
Contact: Doug Lochhead & Valerie A Woolley
Opening Times: 0900-1700 Fri-Wed or by appt.
Min. Mail Order UK: No minimum charge*
Min. Mail Order EU: 4 plants
Cat. Cost: 4 x 1st or 4 x IRCs
Credit Cards: Visa, Access
Specialities: *Primula*, auriculas, alpines & rock plants. *Note: mail order for *Primula,* auriculas & seeds only. 3 National Collections of *Primula* & *P. auricula.*
Map Ref: M, B3

MFir   THE FIRS NURSERY
Chelford Road, Henbury, Macclesfield, Cheshire SK10 3LH
☎ (01625) 426422   **Fax:** (01625) 426422
Contact: Fay J Bowling
Opening Times: 1000-1700 Mon/Tue Fri/Sat, 1000-1900 Thu Mar-Sep.
Mail Order: None
Cat. Cost: 2 x 1st class
Credit Cards: None
Specialities: Wide range of herbaceous perennials, many unusual.
Map Ref: M, A2

MFry   FRYER'S NURSERIES LTD ⊠ EU ▣ ▣ €
Manchester Road, Knutsford, Cheshire WA16 0SX
☎ (01565) 755455   **Fax:** (01565) 653755
E-mail: garethfryer@fryers-roses.co.uk

Web Site: www.fryers-roses.co.uk
Contact: Gareth Fryer
Opening Times: 0900-1730 Mon-Sat &
1030-1630 Sun & 1000-1730 B/hols.
Min. Mail Order UK: No minimum charge
Min. Mail Order EU: Nmc
Cat. Cost: Free
Credit Cards: Visa, Access, Switch
Specialities: Extensive rose nursery & garden
centre producing over half a million bushes
annually. Rose fields in bloom Jun-Oct.
Map Ref: M, A1

M

MGan GANDY'S (ROSES) LTD ⊠ EU 🞐
North Kilworth, Nr Lutterworth,
Leicestershire LE17 6HZ
☎ (01858) 880398 Fax: (01858) 880433
Contact: Miss R D Gandy
Opening Times: 0900-1700 Mon-Sat &
1400-1700 Sun.
Min. Mail Order UK: No minimum charge
Min. Mail Order EU: £25.00 + p&p
Cat. Cost: Free
Credit Cards: None
Specialities: 580 rose varieties.
Map Ref: M, C3

**MGas LINDA GASCOIGNE WILD FLOWERS
⊠ EU**
17 Imperial Road, Kibworth Beauchamp,
Leicestershire LE8 0HR
☎ (0116) 2793959
Contact: Linda Gascoigne
Opening Times: By appt. only.
Min. Mail Order UK: £5.00 + p&p
Min. Mail Order EU: £10.00 + p&p
Cat. Cost: 3 x 1st class
Credit Cards: None
Specialities: Wide range of wild flowers &
plants to attract wildlife. No peat used.
Map Ref: M, C3

MGed GEDDINGTON GARDENS
The Spinney, Grafton Road, Geddington,
Northants NN14 1AJ
☎ (01536) 461020
Contact: Christine Sturman
Opening Times: 1000-1700 Wed-Sun
1st Mar-29 Oct 2000.
Mail Order: None
Cat. Cost: Not available
Credit Cards: None
Specialities: Hardy perennials, cottage garden
plants. *Penstemon.*
Map Ref: M, C3

MGos GOSCOTE NURSERIES LTD ⊠ EU ◆ €
Syston Road, Cossington, Leicestershire
LE7 4UZ

☎ (01509) 812121 Fax: (01509) 814231
E-mail: sales@goscote.co.uk
Web Site: www.goscote.co.uk
Contact: D C Cox & F J Toone
Opening Times: 7 days, closed between
Xmas & New Year.
Min. Mail Order UK: £25.00 + p&p
Min. Mail Order EU: £100.00 + p&p
Cat. Cost: 5 x 1st class
Credit Cards: Visa, Access, MasterCard,
Delta, Switch
Specialities: Japanese maples,
rhododendrons & azaleas, *Magnolia,
Camellia, Pieris* & other *Ericaceae.*
Ornamental trees & shrubs, conifers, fruit,
heathers, alpines, *Clematis* & unusual
climbers. Show garden to visit.
Map Ref: M, B3

MGrG GRANBY GARDENS
Granby House, 8 Long Acre, Bingham,
Nottinghamshire NG13 8BG
☎ (01949) 837696, Fax: (01949) 837696
(mobile) 07713 258668
Contact: Maureen Gladwin
Opening Times: 0900-1700 Mon-Wed.
Closed Aug. When open Sat & Sun 1000-
1600, but please phone first.
Mail Order: None
Cat. Cost: 2 x 2nd class stamps.
Credit Cards: None
Specialities: A wide range of herbaceous
perennials, shrubs & climbers. Some rare &
unusual.
Map Ref: M, B3

MHar HARTS GREEN NURSERY
89 Harts Green Road, Harborne,
Birmingham B17 9TZ
☎ (0121) 427 5200
Contact: B Richardson
Opening Times: 1400-1730 Wed Apr-Jul &
Sep. Other times, excl. Aug, by appt.
Mail Order: None
Cat. Cost: 2 x 1st class
Credit Cards: None
Specialities: Alpines & hardy perennials.
Some in small quantities only.
Map Ref: M, C2

MHer THE HERB NURSERY ◆
Thistleton, Oakham, Rutland LE15 7RE
☎ (01572) 767658 Fax: (01572) 768021
Contact: Peter Bench
Opening Times: 0900-1800 (or dusk) 7
days excl. Xmas-New Year.
Mail Order: None
Cat. Cost: A5 Sae
Credit Cards: None

Specialities: Herbs, wild flowers, cottage garden plants, scented-leaf pelargoniums.
Map Ref: M, B3

MHew HEWTHORN HERBS & WILD FLOWERS ⊠ EU
82 Julian Road, West Bridgford, Nottingham NG2 5AN
☎ (0115) 981 2861
Contact: Julie Palmer
Opening Times: By appt. only.
Min. Mail Order UK: No minimum charge
Min. Mail Order EU: £10.00 + p&p
Cat. Cost: 3 x 1st class
Credit Cards: None
Specialities: Native wild flowers, dye plants, native medicinal herbs. All organically grown.
Map Ref: M, B3

MHom HOMESTEAD PLANTS ⊠ UK
The Homestead, Normanton, Bottesford, Nottingham, Nottinghamshire NG13 0EP
☎ (01949) 842745   Fax: (01949) 842745
Contact: Mrs S Palmer
Opening Times: By appt.
Min. Mail Order UK: No minimum charge*
Cat. Cost: 4 x 2nd class
Credit Cards: None
Specialities: Hellebore species, hostas, jovibarbas & sempervivums, *Paeonia* species. Other herbaceous perennials in small numbers. *Note: mail order for hostas, jovibarbas, sempervivums & peonies only.
Map Ref: M, B3

MInt INTAKES FARM
Sandy Lane, Longsdon, Stoke-on-Trent, Staffordshire ST9 9QQ
☎ (01538) 398452
Contact: Mrs Kathleen Inman
Opening Times: By appt. only.
Mail Order: None
Cat. Cost: None issued
Credit Cards: None
Specialities: Double, variegated & unusual forms of British natives & cottage garden plants.
Map Ref: M, B2

MJac JACKSON'S NURSERIES ▣
Clifton Campville, Nr Tamworth, Staffordshire B79 0AP
☎ (01827) 373307   Fax: (01827) 373307
Contact: N Jackson
Opening Times: 0900-1800 Mon Wed-Sat, 1000-1700 Sun.
Mail Order: None
Cat. Cost: 2 x 1st class

Credit Cards: None
Specialities: *Fuchsia.*
Map Ref: M, B2

MJon C & K JONES ⊠ EU ▣▣
Golden Fields Nurseries, Barrow Lane, Tarvin, Cheshire CH3 8JF
☎ (01829) 740663   Fax: (01829) 741877
E-mail: keith@ckjones.freeserve.co.uk
Web Site: www.jonestherose.co.uk
Contact: Keith Jones/P Woolley
Opening Times: 0900-1630 Fri-Mon. Closed Tue, Wed & Thu.
Min. Mail Order UK: 1 plant + p&p
Min. Mail Order EU: 1 plant + p&p
Cat. Cost: £1.00
Credit Cards: MasterCard, Delta, Switch, Visa
Specialities: Roses.
Map Ref: M, B1

MKay KAYES GARDEN NURSERY
1700 Melton Road, Rearsby, Leicestershire LE7 4YR
☎ (01664) 424578
Contact: Hazel Kaye
Opening Times: 1000-1700 Tue-Sat & B/hols 1000-1200 Sun Mar-Oct. 1000-1600 Fri & Sat Nov, Dec & Feb. Closed Jan.
Mail Order: None
Cat. Cost: 2 x 1st class
Credit Cards: None
Specialities: Herbaceous, climbers & aquatic plants.
Map Ref: M, B3

MLan LANE END NURSERY
Old Cherry Lane, Lymm, Cheshire WA13 0TA
☎ (01925) 752618
E-mail: sawyer@laneend.u-net.com
Web Site: www.laneend.u-net.com
Contact: I Sawyer
Opening Times: 0930-1730 Thu-Tue Mar-Dec.
Mail Order: None
Cat. Cost: None issued
Credit Cards: None
Specialities: Award of Garden Merit plants with a wide range of choice & unusual shrubs, trees, perennials & ferns.
Map Ref: M, A1

MLea LEA RHODODENDRON GARDENS LTD ⊠ EU ▣
Lea, Matlock, Derbyshire DE4 5GH

K E Y	⊠ Mail order to UK or EU	
	▣ Exports beyond EU	€ Euro accepted
	▣ Also supplies Wholesale	◆ See Display advertisement

M

☎ (01629) 534380/534260
Fax: (01629) 534260
Contact: Jon Tye
Opening Times: 1000-1730 7 days 20 Mar-30 Jun. Out of season by appt.
Min. Mail Order UK: £15.00 + p&p
Min. Mail Order EU: £15.00 + p&p
Cat. Cost: 30p + Sae
Credit Cards: None
Specialities: Rhododendrons & azaleas.
Map Ref: M, B2

MLit   LITTLEWOOD FARM NURSERY
Cheddleton, Nr Leek, Staffordshire
ST13 7LB
☎ (01538) 360478   Fax: (01538) 360923
E-mail: chris@bloor0.freeserve.co.uk
Contact: Nanette Bloore
Opening Times: 1000-1800 Tue-Sun & B/hols 15th Mar-Oct.
Mail Order: None
Credit Cards: None
Specialities: Unusual hardy herbaceous plants incl. hardy *Geranium, Campanula, Hosta* & *Pulmonaria.* Also grasses & alpines.
Map Ref: M, B2

MLLN   LODGE LANE NURSERY & GARDENS
Lodge Lane, Dutton, Nr Warrington, Cheshire WA4 4HP
☎ (01928) 713718   Fax: (01928) 713718
Contact: Rod or Diane Casey
Opening Times: 1000-1700 Wed-Sun & B/hols, mid Mar-mid Sep. By appt. outside these dates.
Mail Order: None
Cat. Cost: 3 x 1st class
Credit Cards: None
Specialities: Unusual perennials & shrubs. Many *Aquilegia, Achillea, Allium, Aster, Campanula, Nepeta, Penstemon, Salvia, Euphorbia, Geranium.*
Map Ref: M, A1

MLov   LOVERS KNOT NURSERY ⊠ EU ◆
Woodside, Langley Road, Langley, Macclesfield, Cheshire SK11 0DG
☎ (01260) 253308   Fax: (01260) 253308
Contact: Ian Coppack
Opening Times: Mail order only.
Min. Mail Order UK: £5.00 + p&p
Min. Mail Order EU: £5.00 + p&p
Cat. Cost: 2 x 1st class
Credit Cards: None
Specialities: *Hosta.*

MMal   MALCOFF COTTAGE GARDEN NURSERY ⊠ UK
Malcoff, Chapel-en-le-Frith, High Peak,

Derbyshire SK23 0QR
☎ (01663) 751969   Fax: (01663) 751969
E-mail: malcoffcot@aol.com
Contact: Julie Norfolk
Opening Times: 1000-1700 Thu-Sun & B/hols 1st Mar-30th Sep. Other times by appt. Visitors are advised to phone for directions.
Min. Mail Order UK: £10.00 + p&p
Cat. Cost: 3 x 1st class
Credit Cards: None
Specialities: Herbs, wild flowers & hardy cottage garden plants incl. some old roses.
Map Ref: M, A2

MMat   MATTOCK'S ROSES ⊠ EU ⊠ ▣
Freepost, The Rose Nurseries, Nuneham Courtenay, Oxfordshire OX44 9PY
☎ (01865) 343265, (0345) 585652 (retail order line)   Fax: (01865) 343166
E-mail: roses@mattocks.co.uk
Web Site: www.mattocks.co.uk
Contact: Sales Office
Opening Times: 0900-1730 Mon-Sat (closes 1700 Nov-Feb), 1100-1700 Sun.
Min. Mail Order UK: No minimum charge
Min. Mail Order EU: Nmc
Cat. Cost: Free
Credit Cards: Visa, MasterCard
Specialities: Roses.
Map Ref: M, D3

MMea   MEARS ASHBY NURSERIES LTD ⊠ UK ⊠ ▣
Glebe House, Glebe Road, Mears Ashby, Northamptonshire NN6 0DL
☎ (01604) 812371/811811
Fax: (01604) 812353
E-mail: 106612.1047@compuserve.com
Contact: John B & J E Gaggini
Opening Times: 0800-1730 Mon-Fri (retail & w/sale). 0900-1730 Sat & Sun. (retail only).
Min. Mail Order UK: £8.00 + p&p*
Cat. Cost: £1.00 please state retail or w/sale cat.
Credit Cards: Visa, Access, Switch, MasterCard, Diners
Specialities: Specialist growers of container trees, shrubs, conifers & fruit, esp. *Wisteria.*
*Note: mail order for *Wisteria* only.
Map Ref: M, C3

MMHG   MORTON HALL GARDENS ⊠ EU
Morton Hall, Ranby, Retford, Nottingham DN22 8HW
☎ (01777) 702530
Contact: Gill McMaster
Opening Times: 0900-1600 Mon-Fri, 1400-1700 Sat, Sun & B/hols Mar-Nov.
Min. Mail Order UK: £5.00 + p&p
Min. Mail Order EU: £10.00 + p&p

Cat. Cost: 3 x 1st class
Credit Cards: None
Specialities: Shrubs & perennials.
Map Ref: M, A3

MMil   MILL HILL PLANTS ⊠ UK ◆
Mill Hill House, Elston Lane, East Stoke,
Newark, Nottinghamshire NG23 5QJ
☎ (01636) 525460
E-mail: millhill@talk21.com
Web Site: www.pgmail.clara.net/mhpg/
Contact: G M Gregory
Opening Times: 1000-1800 Wed-Sun &
B/hols Mar-Sep, Fri-Sun in Oct & by appt.
Min. Mail Order UK: No minimum charge*
Cat. Cost: Sae for *Iris* list. No catalogue.
Credit Cards: None
Specialities: Hardy perennials, many unusual
& bearded *Iris*. National Collection of
Berberis. *Note: mail order for *Iris* only.
Map Ref: M, B3

MMiN   MILLFIELD NURSERIES ⊠ EU ▣ €
Mill Lane, South Leverton, Nr Retford,
Nottinghamshire DN22 0DA
☎ (01427) 880422   Fax: (01427) 880422
E-mail: simon@millfieldhostas.f9.co.uk
Web Site: www.millfieldhostas.f9.co.uk
Contact: Mr S G Clark
Opening Times: By appt. only.
Min. Mail Order UK: £10.00 + p&p
Min. Mail Order EU: £25.00 + p&p
Cat. Cost: £1.00 discounted against order
Credit Cards: None
Specialities: *Hosta.*
Map Ref: M, A3

MMoz   MOZART HOUSE NURSERY GARDEN
⊠ UK ◆
84 Central Avenue, Wigston, Leicestershire
LE18 2AA
☎ (0116) 288 9548
Contact: Des Martin
Opening Times: By appt. only.
Min. Mail Order UK: £15.00 + p&p*
Cat. Cost: £1.00 + 30p postage.
Credit Cards: None
Specialities: *Bamboo,* ornamental grasses,
rushes & sedges, *Hosta.* *Note: mail order to
UK & Ireland only.
Map Ref: M, C3

MNaF   NATIONAL FOREST PLANT CENTRE ▣
Enterprise Glade, Bath Lane, Moira,
Swadlincote, Derbyshire DE12 6BD
☎ (01283) 558140   Fax: (01283) 210321
E-mail: Stephen.J.Pain@talk21.com
Contact: Stephen Pain
Opening Times: 1000-1800 Easter-30th

Sep, 1000-1600 Oct-Easter. Closed Mon
except B/hols.
Mail Order: None
Cat. Cost: None
Credit Cards: MasterCard, Delta, JCB,
Switch, Visa, Solo
Specialities: *Quercus,* acers (ornamental trees),
wild flowers.
Map Ref: M, B2

MNan   NANNEY'S BRIDGE NURSERY ▣ €
Church Minshull, Nantwich, Cheshire
CW5 6DY
☎ (01270) 522239   Fax: (01270) 522523
Contact: D Dickinson
Opening Times: By appt. only.
Mail Order: None
Cat. Cost: 3 x 1st class
Credit Cards: None
Specialities: Hardy perennials and ornamental
grasses.
Map Ref: M, B1

MNes   NESS GARDENS
Univ. of Liverpool Botanic Gdns., Ness,
Neston, South Wirral, Cheshire CH64 4AY
☎ (0151) 353 0123
Fax: (0151) 353 1004
E-mail: peter.cunnington@liverpool.ac.uk
Web Site:
www.merseyworld.com/nessgardens/
Contact: D Maher
Opening Times: 0930-1700 7 days Apr-Oct,
1000-1600 7 days Nov-Mar.
Mail Order: None
Cat. Cost: None issued
Credit Cards: Delta, Switch, Visa
Specialities: *Rhododendron, Primula,
Meconopsis, Penstemon* & *Camellia.*
Map Ref: M, A1

MNew   NEWINGTON NURSERIES ⊠ UK
Newington, Wallingford, Oxfordshire
OX10 7AW
☎ (01865) 400533   Fax: (01865) 891766
E-mail: newington.nurseries@btinternet.com
Contact: Mrs A T Hendry
Opening Times: 1000-1700 Tues-Sun Mar-
Oct, 1000-1600 Tues-Sun Nov-Feb.
Min. Mail Order UK: Please enquire for
details.
Cat. Cost: £1.00 + 2nd class A5 Sae
Credit Cards: Access, MasterCard, Visa,
Switch
Specialities: Unusual cottage garden plants,
old-fashioned roses, conservatory plants &
herbs. National Collection of *Alocasia
(Araceae).*
Map Ref: M, D3

M

M

MNFA   THE NURSERY FURTHER AFIELD ✉ EU
Evenley Road, Mixbury, Nr Brackley,
Northamptonshire NN13 5YR
☎ (01280) 848808/848539 (evenings)
Fax: (01280) 848864
Contact: Gerald Sinclair
Opening Times: 1000-1300 & 1400-1700
Wed-Sat mid Mar-early Oct. Sun afternoons
in Jul. Special open days as advertised. By
appt. for collection of orders.
Min. Mail Order UK: £15.00 + p&p*
Min. Mail Order EU: £25.00 + p&p
Cat. Cost: A5 Sae
Credit Cards: None
Specialities: Hardy herbaceous perennials,
geraniums, *Hemerocallis*. National Collection
of *Hemerocallis*. *Note: mail order for
Hemerocallis only. (Mixbury is in Oxfordshire.)
Map Ref: M, C3

MNrw   NORWELL NURSERIES ✉ UK 🖪 ◆
Woodhouse Road, Norwell, Newark,
Nottinghamshire NG23 6JX
☎ (01636) 636337
E-mail: wardha@aol.com
Contact: Dr Andrew Ward
Opening Times: 1000-1700 Mon, Wed-Fri
& Sun (Wed-Mon May & Jun). By appt.
Aug & 20th Oct-1st Mar.
Min. Mail Order UK: £10.00 + p&p
Cat. Cost: 3 x 1st class
Credit Cards: None
Specialities: A large collection of unusual &
choice herbaceous perennials & alpines esp.
Penstemon, hardy *Geranium, Campanula,
Geum,* summer bulbs & grasses. Gardens
open.
Map Ref: M, B3

MOke   OKELL'S NURSERIES 🖪
Duddon Heath, Nr Tarporley, Cheshire
CW6 0EP
☎ (01829) 741512   Fax: (01829) 741587
E-mail: heather@okells nurseries.sagehost.co.uk
Contact: Tim Okell
Opening Times: 0900-1700 7 days (retail)
0830-1700 5 days (wholesale).
Mail Order: None
Cat. Cost: Free
Credit Cards: Visa, Access, Switch, MasterCard
Specialities: Heathers & alpines.
Map Ref: M, B1

MOne   ONE HOUSE NURSERY ✉ UK ◆
Buxton New Road, Macclesfield, Cheshire
SK11 0AD
☎ (01625) 427087
Contact: Miss J L Baylis
Opening Times: 1000-1700 Tue-Sun &

B/hol Mons Mar-Oct, Nov-Feb ring for
opening times.
Min. Mail Order UK: No minimum charge*
Cat. Cost: 3 x 1st class
Credit Cards: None
Specialities: Alpines & perennials. Good range
of *Primula, Sempervivum,* dwarf
Rhododendron, dwarf conifers, bulbs &
gentians. *Note: mail order for sempervivums
& double primroses only.
Map Ref: M, A2

MOsc   OSCROFT'S DAHLIAS ✉ EU 🖪
Woodside, Warwick Road, Chadwick End,
Nr Solihull, West Midlands B93 0BP
☎ (01564) 782450
Contact: June & Fred Oscroft
Opening Times: 0900-1700 7 days.
Min. Mail Order UK: 6 plants or 2 tubers.
Min. Mail Order EU: Tubers only. Nmc.
Cat. Cost: 1 x 1st class
Credit Cards: None
Specialities: *Dahlia*. Note: second nursery at
Sprotborough Road, Doncaster, S. Yorks,
DN5 8BE. Tel (01302) 785026.
Map Ref: M, C2

**MPet   PETER GRAYSON
(SWEET PEA SEEDSMAN) ✉ EU 🖪 🖪**
34 Glenthorne Close, Brampton, Chesterfield,
Derbyshire S40 3AR
☎ (01246) 278503   Fax: (01246) 278503
Web Site: www.igarden.co.uk/petergrayson/
Contact: Peter Grayson
Opening Times: Not open, mail order only.
Min. Mail Order UK: No minimum charge
Min. Mail Order EU: Nmc
Cat. Cost: A5 Sae (20p stamp)
Credit Cards: None
Specialities: *Lathyrus* species & cvs. Very large
collection of old-fashioned sweet peas & over
100 Spencer sweet peas incl. our own
cultivars.

MPEx   PLANTA EXOTICA ✉ EU 🖪
11 Heath Close, Banbury, Oxon OX15 4RZ
☎ (01295) 721989   Fax: (01295) 721989
Contact: Mrs M Hill
Opening Times: Mar-Sep by appt.
Min. Mail Order UK: £3.95 + p&p
Min. Mail Order EU: £3.95 + p&p
Cat. Cost: 2 x 1st class
Credit Cards: Visa, MasterCard
Specialities: Rainforest plants, alpines.
Map Ref: M, C2

MPhe   PHEDAR NURSERY ✉ EU 🖪 🖪
Bunkers Hill, Romiley, Stockport, Cheshire
SK6 3DS

☎ (0161) 430 3772
Fax: (0161) 430 3772
Contact: Will McLewin
Opening Times: Frequent esp. in spring but very irregular. Please phone to arrange appt.
Min. Mail Order UK: No minimum charge
Min. Mail Order EU: Nmc
Cat. Cost: 3 x A5 AE or address labels + 4 x 1st class
Credit Cards: None
Specialities: *Helleborus, Paeonia*. Note: non-EU exports subject to destination. Limited stock of some rare items.
Map Ref: M, A2

MPot   POTS OF PLANTS ⊠UK ◨
154 Percival Road, Rugby, Warwickshire CV22 5JX
☎ (01788) 565276
Contact: A & S Webb
Opening Times: By appt. only.
Min. Mail Order UK: No minimum charge
Cat. Cost: 2 x 1st class
Credit Cards: None
Specialities: Ornamental grasses & bamboos.

MRav   RAVENSTHORPE NURSERY ⊠EU
6 East Haddon Road, Ravensthorpe, Northamptonshire NN6 8ES
☎ (01604) 770548   Fax: (01604) 770548
E-mail: Plants:6raventhorpe.freeserve.co.uk
Contact: Jean & Richard Wiseman
Opening Times: 1000-1800 (dusk if earlier) Tue-Sun. Also B/hol Mons.
Min. Mail Order UK: No minimum charge
Min. Mail Order EU: Nmc
Cat. Cost: 4 x 1st class
Credit Cards: Visa, MasterCard
Specialities: Over 2,600 different trees, shrubs & perennials with many unusual varieties. Search & delivery service for large orders, winter months only.
Map Ref: M, C3

MRod   RODBASTON COLLEGE ⊠EU ◨
Rodbaston, Penkridge, Staffordshire ST19 5PH
☎ (01785) 712209
Fax: (01785) 715701
E-mail: rodplants@hotmail.com
Web Site: www.rodbaston.ac.uk
Contact: Yoke van der Meer
Opening Times: By appt.
Min. Mail Order UK: £10.00
Min. Mail Order EU: £15.00
Cat. Cost: 2 x 1st class
Credit Cards: None
Specialities: Salvias, pelargoniums, general.
Map Ref: M, B2

MS&S   S & S PERENNIALS
24 Main Street, Normanton Le Heath, Leicestershire LE67 2TB
☎ (01530) 262250
Contact: Shirley Pierce
Opening Times: Afternoons only, otherwise please phone.
Mail Order: None
Cat. Cost: 2 x 1st class
Credit Cards: None
Specialities: *Erythronium, Fritillaria,* hardy *Cyclamen,* dwarf *Narcissus, Hepatica, Anemone* & *Ranunculus.*
Map Ref: M, B2

MSal   SALLEY GARDENS ⊠EU ◨ €
32 Lansdowne Drive, West Bridgford, Nottinghamshire NG2 7FJ
☎ (0115) 9233878 evenings
Contact: Richard Lewin
Opening Times: By appt.
Min. Mail Order UK: No minimum charge
Min. Mail Order EU: Nmc
Cat. Cost: Sae
Credit Cards: None
Specialities: Medicinal plants esp. from North America & China. Dye plants, herbs, spices, seeds.
Map Ref: M, B3

MSCN   STONYFORD COTTAGE NURSERY ◨
Stonyford Lane, Cuddington, Northwich, Cheshire CW8 2TF
☎ (01606) 888128   Fax: (01606) 888312
E-mail: sales@stonyford.u-net.com
Web Site: www.gardenchoice.co.uk
Contact: F A Overland
Opening Times: 1000-1730 Tue-Sun & B/hol Mons 1 Mar-31 Oct.
Mail Order: None
Cat. Cost: 4 x 1st class
Credit Cards: None
Specialities: Wide range of herbaceous perennials, *Diascia, Salvia* & hardy *Geranium.*
Map Ref: M, B1

MSph   SPRINGHILL PLANTS
(Office) 18 Westfields, Abingdon, Oxford OX14 1BA
☎ (01235) 530889 before 0930 only, or mobile 0779 0863378.
Contact: Caroline Cox
Opening Times: Apr-Sep by appt. only.

M

⊠	Mail order to UK or EU	
⊠	Exports beyond EU	€ Euro accepted
◨	Also supplies Wholesale	◆ See Display advertisement

M

Please telephone first.
Mail Order: None
Cat. Cost: 75p or 3 x 1st class
Credit Cards: None
Specialities: Small nursery offering a wide range of unusual & garden-worthy perennials & shrubs. Many AGM & rare plants available.
Note: nursery is at Buildings Farm, Gozzard's Ford, Nr Marcham, Abingdon, OX13 6QH.
Map Ref: M, D2

MSta STAPELEY WATER GARDENS LTD
⊠ EU ⊠ 🖴
London Road, Stapeley, Nantwich, Cheshire CW5 7LH
☎ (01270) 623868   **Fax:** (01270) 624919
E-mail: stapeleywg@btinternet.com
Contact: Mr Dean Barratt
Opening Times: From 0900 Mon-Fri, 1000 Sat, Sun & B/hols all year excl. Xmas Day. Please check closing times.
Min. Mail Order UK: No minimum charge
Min. Mail Order EU: Nmc
Cat. Cost: £2.00 handbook, price list free
Credit Cards: Visa, Access, MasterCard, Switch
Specialities: World's largest water garden centre. Full range of hardy water lilies, aquatic, bog & poolside plants. Also large general stock. National Collection of *Nymphaea* (UK & France).
Map Ref: M, B1

MSte STEVENTON ROAD NURSERIES ⊠ EU 🖴
Steventon Road, East Hanney, Wantage, Oxfordshire OX12 0HS
☎ (01235) 868828   **Fax:** (01235) 763670
Contact: John Graham
Opening Times: 1000-1630 Mon-Fri, 1000-1700 Sat & Sun 4th Mar-5th Nov 2000, 3rd Mar-4th Nov 2001.
Min. Mail Order UK: £15.00 + p&p
Min. Mail Order EU: £30.00 + p&p
Cat. Cost: 4 x 1st class
Credit Cards: None
Specialities: Tender & hardy perennials.
Map Ref: M, D2

MTed TED BROWN UNUSUAL PLANTS €
1 Croftway, Markfield, Leicester LE67 9UG
☎ (01530) 244517
Contact: Ted Brown
Opening Times: From 1000 Sat, Sun & B/hols Mar-Nov. Other times by appt.
Mail Order: None
Cat. Cost: None issued
Credit Cards: None
Specialities: Mainly herbaceous, many unusual. Bamboos.
Map Ref: M, B3

MTho A & A THORP
Bungalow No 5, Main Street, Theddingworth, Leicestershire LE17 6QZ
☎ (01858) 880496
Contact: Anita & Andrew Thorp
Opening Times: Dawn to dusk all year.
Mail Order: None
Cat. Cost: 50p + Sae
Credit Cards: None
Specialities: Unusual plants or those in short supply.
Map Ref: M, C3

MTis TISSINGTON NURSERY
Tissington, Nr Ashbourne, Derbyshire DE6 1RA
☎ (01335) 390650
Fax: (01335) 390693
Contact: Mrs Sue Watkins
Opening Times: 1000-1800 daily except Mons 1st Mar-31st Oct. Also closed Tue in Mar, Sept & Oct. Open B/hols.
Mail Order: None
Cat. Cost: 3 x 1st class
Credit Cards: Visa, MasterCard
Specialities: Perennials, shrubs & climbers incl. unusual varieties.
Map Ref: M, B2

MTPN THE PLANT NURSERY ⊠ UK
Sandy Hill Lane, off Overstone Road, Moulton, Northampton NN3 7JB
☎ (01604) 491941 after 6pm
Contact: Mrs B Jeyes
Opening Times: 1000-1700 Fri-Sun & B/hols Mar-Oct. 1000-1600 Sun only Nov & Dec.
Min. Mail Order UK: No minimum charge*
Cat. Cost: 3 x 1st class
Credit Cards: None
Specialities: Wide range of herbaceous, alpines, shrubs, grasses, hardy *Geranium*, *Sempervivum* & succulents.
*Note: mail order of *Sempervivum*, succulents only.
Map Ref: M, C3

MWar WARD FUCHSIAS ⊠ UK
5 Pollen Close, Sale, Cheshire M33 3LS
☎ (0161) 282 7434
Contact: K Ward
Opening Times: 0930-1700 Tue-Sun Feb-Jun incl. B/hols.
Min. Mail Order UK: No minimum charge
Cat. Cost: Free*
Credit Cards: None
Specialities: *Fuchsia*. *Note: catalogue includes cultural information.
Map Ref: M, A1

MWat   **WATERPERRY GARDENS LTD** ✉ UK
Waterperry, Nr Wheatley, Oxfordshire
OX33 1JZ
☎ (01844) 339226/254
Fax: (01844) 339883
Contact: Mr R Jacobs
Opening Times: 0900-1730 Mon-Fri, 0900-
1800 Sat & Sun summer. 0900-1700 winter.
Min. Mail Order UK: No minimum charge*
Cat. Cost: 75p
Credit Cards: Visa, MasterCard, Switch,
American Express
Specialities: General plus National
Collection of *Saxifraga (Porophyllum)*. *Note:
limited mail order, please phone for further
information and credit card facilities.
Map Ref: M, D3

MWgw   **WINGWELL NURSERY** ✉ UK
Top Street, Wing, Oakham, Rutland LE15 8SE
☎ (01572) 737727
Fax: (01572) 737788
E-mail: dejardin.design@btinternet.com
Contact: Rose Dejardin
Opening Times: 1000-1700 Wed-Sun &
B/hol Mons Mar-Dec excl. Aug.
Min. Mail Order UK: No minimum charge*
Cat. Cost: £1 for descriptive cat. please.
Credit Cards: None
Specialities: Herbaceous perennials.
*Note: mail order Oct-Mar.
Map Ref: M, B3

MWhe   **A D & N WHEELER**
Pye Court, Willoughby, Rugby, Warwickshire
CV23 8BZ
☎ (01788) 890341   **Fax:** (01788) 890341
Contact: Mrs N Wheeler
Opening Times: 1000-1630 7 days mid
Feb-late Jun. Other times please phone first
for appt.
Mail Order: None
Cat. Cost: 3 x 1st class
Credit Cards: None
Specialities: *Fuchsia, Pelargonium* & hardy
Geranium.
Map Ref: M, C3

MWhi   **WHITEHILL FARM NURSERY** ✉ EU
Whitehill Farm, Burford, Oxon OX18 4DT
☎ (01993) 823218   **Fax:** (01993) 822894
Contact: P J M Youngson
Opening Times: 0900-1800 (or dusk if
earlier) 7 days.
Min. Mail Order UK: £5.00 + p&p
Min. Mail Order EU: £5.00 + p&p
Cat. Cost: 4 x 1st class (£1.00 refunded on
1st order)
Credit Cards: None

Specialities: Grasses & bamboos, less
common shrubs, perennials & trees.
Map Ref: M, D2

MWht   **WHITELEA NURSERY** ✉ UK
Whitelea Lane, Tansley, Matlock, Derbyshire
DE4 5FL
☎ (01629) 55010
E-mail: whitelea@nursery-stock.freeserve.co.uk
Web Site: www.nursery-stock.freeserve.co.uk
Contact: David Wilson
Opening Times: By appt.
Min. Mail Order UK: No minimum charge
Cat. Cost: 1 x 2nd class or Sae.
Credit Cards: None
Specialities: *Bamboo,* ivies. Substantial
quantities of 15 cultivars & species of
bamboo, remainder stocked only in small
numbers for specialist collectors.
Map Ref: M, B2

MWll   **THE WALLED GARDEN** ✉ EU 🖪 €
2 Castle Road, Shirburn, Watlington,
Oxfordshire OX9 5DJ
☎ (01491) 612882, (01491) 612117
evenings
E-mail: thewalledgarden@myoffice.ltd.uk.
Contact: Bridget Gaisburgh-Watkyn
Opening Times: 1000-1800 Thu-Tue
Mar-Nov.
Min. Mail Order UK: £5.00 + p&p
Min. Mail Order EU: £250.00
Cat. Cost: 4 x 1st class
Credit Cards: None
Specialities: Wild flowers, unusual
herbaceous perennials & white flowering
herbaceous plants.
Map Ref: M, D3

MWoo   **WOODFIELD BROS** ✉ UK 🖪
Wood End, Clifford Chambers, Stratford-on-
Avon, Warwickshire CV37 8HR
☎ (01789) 205618
Contact: B Woodfield
Opening Times: 1000-1630 Mon-Fri, 1000-
1600 Sat & 0900-1200 Sun for plant
collection only.
Min. Mail Order UK: See list for details
Cat. Cost: Sae
Credit Cards: None
Specialities: Lupins & *Delphinium,* plants
& seeds.
Map Ref: M, C2

MWrn   **WARREN HILLS NURSERY**
Warren Hills Cottage, Warren Hills Road,
Coalville, Leicestershire LE67 4UY
☎ (01530) 812350
E-mail: warrenhills@tinyworld.co.uk

M

Contact: Penny Waters or Bob Taylor
Opening Times: By appt. only.
Mail Order: None
Cat. Cost: 2 x 1st class
Credit Cards: None
Specialities: *Astrantia, Campanula, Geranium, Aquilegia, Penstemon, Salvia, Heuchera, Pulmonaria.*
Map Ref: M, B2

MWst   WOODSHOOT NURSERIES ⊠ UK 🖾
King's Bromley, Burton-upon-Trent, Staffordshire DE13 7HN
☎ (01543) 472233   **Fax:** (01543) 472115
Web Site: www.plants-for-all-reasons.co.uk
Contact: Janice Rea
Opening Times: Mail order only for retail sales. Wholesale on site, please phone for details.
Min. Mail Order UK: £20*
Cat. Cost: 2 x 1st class
Credit Cards: None
Specialities: Phoriums, alstromerias, *Pittosporum, Tropaeolum.*
*Note: mail order only for retail sales.

NORTHERN

NArc   ARCADIA NURSERIES LTD ⊠ EU 🖾
Brasscastle Lane, Nunthorpe, Middlesborough, Cleveland TS8 9EB
☎ (01642) 310782   **Fax:** (01642) 300817
E-mail: sales@arcadianurseries.co.uk
Contact: Mr P Birch
Opening Times: Garden centre 0900-1700 spring-autumn, 0900-1500 winter. Mail order office 0900-1700 all year.
Min. Mail Order UK: 6 plants or 1 collection.
Min. Mail Order EU: 6 plants or 1 collection.
Cat. Cost: Free on request
Credit Cards: Visa, Access, EuroCard, Switch, MasterCard
Specialities: *Fuchsia* & auriculas.
Map Ref: N, C2

NArg   ARGHAM VILLAGE NURSERY ⊠ EU
Argham Grange, Grindale, Bridlington, East Yorkshire YO16 4XZ
☎ (01723) 892141   **Fax:** (01723) 892141
E-mail: geoffpickering@arghamvillage
Web Site: www.arghamvillage.co.uk
Contact: Geoff Pickering
Opening Times: 1000-1700 Mar-Oct, 1130-1500 Nov-Feb, 7 days.
Min. Mail Order UK: £20.00 + p&p
Min. Mail Order EU: £50.00 + p&p
Cat. Cost: 4 x 1st class
Credit Cards: Visa, MasterCard, Delta
Specialities: Herbaceous perennials.
Map Ref: N, C3

NAsh   ASHTONS NURSERY GARDENS ⊠ UK 🖾
Mythop Road, Lytham, Lytham St Annes, Lancashire FY8 4JP
☎ (01253) 736627/794808
Fax: (01253) 735311
E-mail: ashtonsnursery@compuserve.com
Web Site: www.ashtons-lytham.co.uk
Contact: T M Ashton
Opening Times: 0900-1700 daily.
Min. Mail Order UK: No minimum charge
Cat. Cost: 2 x 1st class
Credit Cards: MasterCard, Visa, Switch, Delta, American Express
Specialities: Herbaceous plants. Hardy shrubs.
Map Ref: N, D1

NBat   BATTERSBY ROSES ⊠ EU
Peartree Cottage, Old Battersby, Great Ayton, Cleveland TS9 6LU
☎ (01642) 723402
Contact: Eric & Avril Stainthorpe
Opening Times: 1000-dusk most days.
Min. Mail Order UK: No minimum charge
Min. Mail Order EU: Nmc
Cat. Cost: Sae
Credit Cards: None
Specialities: Exhibition roses incl. some American miniatures.
Map Ref: N, C2

NBea   BEAMISH CLEMATIS NURSERY
Burntwood Cottage, Stoney Lane, Beamish, Co. Durham DH9 0SJ
☎ (0191) 370 0202
Fax: (0191) 370 0202
Contact: Colin Brown or Jan Wilson
Opening Times: 0900-1700 7 days Feb-Nov.
Mail Order: None
Cat. Cost: 3 x 1st class
Credit Cards: None
Specialities: *Clematis,* climbers, shrubs & ornamental trees.
Map Ref: N, B2

NBee   BEECHCROFT NURSERIES ⊠ UK
Bongate, Appleby-in-Westmorland, Cumbria CA16 6UE
☎ (01768) 351201
Fax: (01768) 351201
Contact: Roger Brown
Opening Times: 0900-1700 7 days.
Min. Mail Order UK: No minimum charge*
Cat. Cost: Sae for tree list.
Credit Cards: None
Specialities: Hardy field-grown trees & shrubs.
*Note: mail order trees Nov-Mar only.
Map Ref: N, C1

NBid   BIDE-A-WEE COTTAGE GARDENS ⊠ UK
Stanton, Netherwitton, Morpeth,
Northumberland NE65 8PR
☎ (01670) 772262
E-mail: bideaweecg@aol.com
Contact: Mark Robson
Opening Times: 1330-1700 Sat & Wed 29th
Apr-2nd Sep 2000, 28th Apr-1st Sep 2001.
Min. Mail Order UK: £10.00 + p&p
Cat. Cost: 3 x 1st class
Credit Cards: None
Specialities: Unusual herbaceous perennials,
Primula, grasses.
Map Ref: N, B2

NBir   BIRKHEADS COTTAGE GARDEN
NURSERY ⊠ UK
Nr Causey Arch, Sunniside, Newcastle upon
Tyne, Tyne & Wear NE16 5EL
☎ (01207) 232262, 0378 447920
Fax: (01207) 232262
E-mail: birkheads@breathemail.net
Contact: Mrs Christine Liddle
Opening Times: 1000-1700 every day Mar-
end Oct. Winter opening 1000-1500 (please
phone first). Groups by appt.
Min. Mail Order UK: £10.00*
Cat. Cost: None issued
Credit Cards: None
Specialities: Hardy herbaceous perennials,
grasses, bulbs & herbs. *Allium, Campanula,
Digitalis, Euphorbia, Geranium, Meconopsis,
Primula.* *Note: mail order from Sep 2000.
Map Ref: N, B2

NBlu   BLUNDELL'S NURSERIES ▣
68 Southport New Road, Tarleton, Preston,
Lancashire PR4 6HY
☎ (01772) 815442
E-mail: jerplusjeff@netscapeonline.co.uk
Contact: Any member of staff
Opening Times: 0900-1700 daily except
Weds. Closed Dec-Feb.
Mail Order: None
Cat. Cost: No catalogue issued
Credit Cards: None
Map Ref: N, D1

NBrk   T H BARKER & SONS ⊠ UK ◆
Baines Paddock Nursery, Haverthwaite,
Ulverston, Cumbria LA12 8PF
☎ (015395) 58236
E-mail: rachel@thbarker.demon.co.uk
Contact: W E Thornley
Opening Times: 0930-1730 Wed-Sun 1st
Feb-30th Nov.
Min. Mail Order UK: 2 plants + p&p
Cat. Cost: £1.00 (*Clematis* & climbers)
Credit Cards: None

Specialities: *Clematis, Lonicera* & other
climbers. Cottage garden plants esp. hardy
Geranium, Aster, Ranunculus, Iris & *Viola.*
Many rare. Most stock grown on the nursery.
Map Ref: N, C1

NBro   BROWNTHWAITE HARDY PLANTS
Fell Yeat, Casterton, Kirkby Lonsdale,
Lancashire LA6 2JW
☎ (015242) 71340 after 1800.
Contact: Chris Benson
Opening Times: Tue-Sun 1st Apr-30th Sep.
Mail Order: None
Cat. Cost: 3 x 1st class
Credit Cards: None
Specialities: Herbaceous perennials & grasses
incl. *Geranium, Campanula, Iris,* especially
*Iris ensata, Primula auricula, Primula
sieboldii* & *Penstemon.* National Collection
of *Ligularia.*
Map Ref: N, C1

NBur   BURTON AGNES HALL NURSERY ⊠ EU
Burton Agnes Hall Preservation Trust Ltd,
Estate Office, Burton Agnes, Driffield, East
Yorkshire YO25 0ND
☎ (01262) 490324   Fax: (01262) 490513
Contact: Mrs S Cunliffe-Lister
Opening Times: 1100-1700 Apr-Oct.
Min. Mail Order UK: £15.00 + p&p*
Min. Mail Order EU: £15.00 + p&p
Cat. Cost: 4 x 1st class
Credit Cards: None
Specialities: Large range perennials &
alpines. Many unusual varieties esp.
*Penstemon, Osteospermum, Digitalis, Anemone,
Geranium.* National Collection of *Campanula.*
*Note: mail order Nov-Mar only.
Map Ref: N, C3

NBus   BUSH GREEN COTTAGE NURSERY
⊠ UK ▣
Foxfield Road, Broughton-in-Furness,
Cumbria LA20 6BY
☎ (01229) 716724
Contact: Jim Haunch
Opening Times: 1000-1700 Tue-Sun &
B/hols. For garden see NGS handbook.
Min. Mail Order UK: No minimum charge
Cat. Cost: 4 x 1st class
Credit Cards: None
Specialities: Hardy *Geranium, Hosta,*
interesting hardy perennials & ferns. Grasses.
Map Ref: N, C1

K E Y	
⊠ Mail order to UK or EU	
⊠ Exports beyond EU	€ Euro accepted
▣ Also supplies Wholesale	◆ See Display advertisement

NCat CATFORTH GARDENS
Roots Lane, Catforth, Preston, Lancashire
PR4 0JB
☎ (01772) 690561/690269
Contact: Judith Bradshaw & Chris Moore
Opening Times: 1030-1700 1 April-end
Aug 2000.
Mail Order: None
Cat. Cost: 5 x 1st class
Credit Cards: None
Specialities: National Collection of hardy
Geranium. 3 gardens open every day. Over
1500 varieties of herbaceous plants.
Map Ref: N, D1

NChi CHIPCHASE CASTLE NURSERY
Chipchase Castle, Wark, Hexham,
Northumberland NE48 3NT
☎ (01434) 230083
Contact: Suzanne Newell & Janet Beakes
Opening Times: 1000-1700 Thu-Sun &
B/hol Mons Easter (or 1st Apr)-mid Oct.
Mail Order: None
Cat. Cost: A5 Sae for list
Credit Cards: None
Specialities: Unusual herbaceous esp.
Erodium, Eryngium, Geranium, Penstemon
& *Viola*.
Map Ref: N, B2

NChl CHILTERN SEEDS ✉ EU ◆ ☒
Bortree Stile, Ulverston, Cumbria
LA12 7PB
☎ (01229) 581137 (24 hrs)
Fax: (01229) 584549
E-mail: info@chilternseeds.co.uk
Web Site: www.chilternseeds.co.uk
Contact: G D Bowden
Opening Times: Normal office hours,
Mon-Fri.
Min. Mail Order UK: No minimum charge
Min. Mail Order EU: Nmc
Cat. Cost: 3 x 2nd class
Credit Cards: Visa, Access, American
Express, Switch, MasterCard, EuroCard
Specialities: Almost 4,600 items of all kinds -
wild flowers, trees, shrubs, cacti, annuals,
house plants, vegetables & herbs.

NCiC CICELY'S COTTAGE GARDEN PLANTS
43 Elmers Green, Skelmersdale, Lancashire
WN8 6SG
☎ (01695) 720790
Contact: Maureen Duncan
Opening Times: By appt. only. Please phone.
Mail Order: None
Cat. Cost: 4 x 1st class
Credit Cards: None
Specialities: Perennials & shrubs incl.

Diascia, Osteospermum, Penstemon, Viola,
Hedera & *Hebe*.
Map Ref: N, D1

NCot COTTAGE GARDEN PLANTS ✉ UK
1 Sycamore Close, Whitehaven, Cumbria
CA28 6LE
☎ (01946) 695831
E-mail: jeanp@compuserve.com
Web Site: http://ourworld.compuserve.com-
/homepages/jeanp
Contact: Mrs J Purkiss
Opening Times: By appt. only.
Min. Mail Order UK: No minimum charge
Cat. Cost: None issued.
Credit Cards: None
Specialities: Hardy perennials incl. *Corydalis,*
Dicentra, Geranium, Meconopsis, Polemonium,
Primula & *Pulmonaria*.
Map Ref: N, C1

NCra CRAVEN'S NURSERY ✉ EU ☒ ☒
1 Foulds Terrace, Bingley, West Yorkshire
BD16 4LZ
☎ (01274) 561412   Fax: (01274) 561412
Contact: S R Craven & M Craven
Opening Times: By appt. only.
Min. Mail Order UK: £10.00 + p&p
Min. Mail Order EU: £50.00 + p&p
Cat. Cost: 4 x 1st class
Credit Cards: None
Specialities: Show auriculas, alpines, *Primula,*
Sempervivum, Jovibarba & specialist seeds.
Map Ref: N, D2

NCro CROSTON CACTUS ✉ EU
43 Southport Road, Eccleston, Chorley,
Lancashire PR7 6ET
☎ (01257) 452555
E-mail: desert.plants@lineone.net
Contact: John Henshaw
Opening Times: 0930-1700 Wed-Sat &
by appt.
Min. Mail Order UK: £5.00 + p&p
Min. Mail Order EU: £10.00 + p&p
Cat. Cost: 2 x 1st or 2 x IRCs
Credit Cards: None
Specialities: Mexican cacti, *Echeveria* hybrids
& some bromeliads & *Tillandsia*.
Map Ref: N, D1

NCut CUTTING EDGE NURSERY ◆
Highfield Farm, Knowle Road, off Upper
Sheffield Road, Barnsley, Yorkshire S70 4AW
☎ (01226) 730292   Fax: (01226) 280256
Contact: Brian B Cockerline
Opening Times: 0900-1700 Mon-Sat,
1000-1600 Sun.
Mail Order: None

Cat. Cost: 2 x 1st class
Credit Cards: None
Specialities: Wide selection of perennials, many uncommon.
Map Ref: N, D2

NDea   DEANSWOOD PLANTS
Potteries Lane, Littlethorpe, Ripon, North Yorkshire HG4 3LF
☎ (01765) 603441
Contact: Jacky Barber
Opening Times: 1000-1700 Tue-Sun 1st Apr-30th Sep.
Mail Order: None
Cat. Cost: List 2 x 25p
Credit Cards: None
Specialities: Pond, marginals & bog plants.
Map Ref: N, C2

NDlv   DALESVIEW NURSERY ✉ EU 📷 📓
24 Braithwaite Edge Road, Keighley, West Yorkshire BD22 6RA
☎ (01535) 606531
Contact: David Ellis & Eileen Morgan
Opening Times: 1000-1700 Wed-Sun & B/hols.
Min. Mail Order UK: No minimum charge
Min. Mail Order EU: Nmc
Cat. Cost: 4 x 1st class
Credit Cards: None
Specialities: Dwarf *Hebe*, *Saxifraga*, *Primula*, *Rhododendron* & conifers.
Map Ref: N, D2

NDov   DOVE COTTAGE PLANTS ✉ UK
23 Shibden Hall Road, Halifax, West Yorkshire HX3 9XA
☎ (01422) 203553
Contact: Stephen & Kim Rogers
Opening Times: 1000-1800 Tue-Sun & B/hols Feb-Nov.
Min. Mail Order UK: No minimum charge
Cat. Cost: Sae + 2 x 1st class
Credit Cards: Switch
Specialities: *Helleborus*, *Pulmonaria*, *Epimedium*, hardy *Geranium*, *Primula*, *Achillea*, bamboo, grasses & other perennials.
Map Ref: N, D2

NEgg   EGGLESTON HALL
Barnard Castle, Co. Durham DL12 0AG
☎ (01833) 650403, gardeners' 650115
Fax: (01833) 650378
Contact: Mrs R H Gray
Opening Times: 1000-1700 7 days.
Mail Order: None
Cat. Cost: £1.50 + Sae
Credit Cards: EuroCard, Maestro, Visa, Electron, Switch, Solo, JCB

Specialities: Rare & unusual plants with particular emphasis on flower arranging.
Map Ref: N, C2

NEqu   EQUATORIAL PLANT CO. ✉ EU 📓 📷 €
7 Gray Lane, Barnard Castle, Co. Durham DL12 8PD
☎ (01833) 690519   Fax: (01833) 690519
E-mail: equatorialplants@onyxnet.co.uk
Contact: Richard Warren PhD
Opening Times: By appt. only.
Min. Mail Order UK: No minimum charge
Min. Mail Order EU: Nmc
Cat. Cost: Free
Credit Cards: Visa, Access
Specialities: Laboratory-raised orchids only.

NFai   FAIRY LANE NURSERIES
Fairy Lane, Sale, Greater Manchester M33 2JT
☎ (0161) 905 1137, (0161) 969 5594
Contact: Mrs J Coxon
Opening Times: 1200-1700 Thu-Mon Mar-Oct.
Mail Order: None
Cat. Cost: None issued
Credit Cards: Access, Visa
Specialities: Hardy & tender perennials, herbs, *Hebe* & less usual shrubs. National garden gift tokens.
Map Ref: N, D2

NFir   FIR TREES PELARGONIUM NURSERY ✉ EU
Stokesley, Middlesbrough, Cleveland TS9 5LD
☎ (01642) 713066   Fax: (01642) 713066
E-mail: firtre@globalnet.co.uk
Web Site: www.users.globalnet.co.uk/~firtre
Contact: Helen Bainbridge
Opening Times: 1000-1600 7 days 15th Mar-30th Sep, 1000-1600 Mon-Fri 1st Oct-15th Mar.
Min. Mail Order UK: £2.00 + p&p
Min. Mail Order EU: £2.00 + p&p
Cat. Cost: 4 x 1st class
Credit Cards: MasterCard, Visa
Specialities: All types of *Pelargonium* - fancy leaf, regal, decorative regal, oriental regal, angel, miniature, zonal, ivy leaf, stellar, scented, dwarf, unique, golden stellar & species.
Map Ref: N, C2

NFla   FLAXTON HOUSE NURSERY ✉ UK
Flaxton, York, North Yorkshire Y060 7RJ
☎ (01904) 468753
Contact: Mrs H Williams
Opening Times: 1000-1700 Tue-Sun 1st Mar-31st Oct.
Min. Mail Order UK: £7.50 +p&p*
Cat. Cost: 2 x 1st class

N

Credit Cards: None
Specialities: Wide general range of shrubs &
herbaceous with many unusual plants. *Note:
mail order Sep-Mar only.
Map Ref: N, C3

NFor   FORD NURSERY ⊠UK ◆
Castle Gardens, Ford, Berwick-upon-Tweed,
Northumberland TD15 2PZ
☎ (01890) 820379
Fax: (01890) 820594
E-mail: Ford.nursery@which.net
Contact: Marjorie Spark & Roy Harmeston
Opening Times: 1000-1800 7 days Mar-
Oct, 1000-1630 Mon-Fri Nov-Feb.
Min. Mail Order UK: No minimum charge
Cat. Cost: Free
Credit Cards: Visa, Access, Switch
Specialities: Over 1200 different species of
container-grown hardy ornamental shrubs,
perennials, trees & herbs, climbers & grasses.
Map Ref: N, A2

NGCt   GARTH COTTAGE NURSERY ⊠UK ▣
Garth Cottage, Newby Wiske, Northallerton,
North Yorkshire DL7 9ET
☎ (01609) 777233 incl. answerphone service
Fax: (01609) 775777
Contact: Paul & Christine Turner
Opening Times: At present by prior
arrangement only.
Min. Mail Order UK: No minimum charge
Cat. Cost: 2 x 1st class for each of 3 (herbs,
ivies, lavenders)
Credit Cards: None
Specialities: 200+ varieties of herbs, with
emphasis on culinary incl. mint, rosemary,
sage, basil, oregano & thyme. 70+ varieties of
lavender & 300+ ivies. Also ground cover,
topiarised & cane-grown climbing ivies.
Large specimen plants.
Map Ref: N, C2

NGdn   GARDEN HOUSE NURSERIES
The Square, Dalston, Carlisle, Cumbria
CA5 7LL
☎ (01228) 710297
E-mail: gardenhousenursery@btinternet.com
Web Site:
www.btinternet.com/~gardenhousenursery
Contact: David Hickson
Opening Times: 0900-1700 7 days Mar-Oct.
Mail Order: None
Cat. Cost: None issued, plant list is on web
site.
Credit Cards: None
Specialities: *Geranium, Hosta, Hemerocallis,
Iris,* grasses & *Penstemon.*
Map Ref: N, B1

NGHP   GREEN GARDEN HERBS & PLANTS
⊠EU ▣
73 Alma Road, Leeds, Yorks LS6 2AH
☎ (0113) 274 7940
Contact: Sarah Clark
Opening Times: Please phone for appt.
Min. Mail Order UK: No minimum charge*
Min. Mail Order EU: Nmc
Cat. Cost: 3 x 2nd class
Credit Cards: None
Specialities: Herbs. *Note: mail order only if
essential. Nursery located at Greenscapes
Horticultural Centre, Brandon Cres,
Shadwell, Leeds LS17 9JH.
Map Ref: N, D2

NGil   GILLIES CARNATIONS ⊠EU ◆ ▣ ▣
22 Chetwyn Avenue, Bromley Cross, Bolton,
Lancashire BL7 9BN
☎ (01204) 306273   Fax: (01204) 306273
E-mail: gillies.carnations@cwcom.net
Web Site: www. gillies-carnations.co.uk
Contact: R & T Gillies
Opening Times: By appt. only.
Min. Mail Order UK: No minimum charge
Min. Mail Order EU: £15.00 + p&p
Cat. Cost: 1 x 1st class
Credit Cards: Visa, MasterCard
Specialities: Pinks, perpetual flowering
carnations. Also seeds.
Map Ref: N, D1

NHal   HALLS OF HEDDON ⊠EU ▣ ▣
(Office) West Heddon Nurseries,
Heddon-on-the-Wall, Newcastle-upon-Tyne,
Northumberland NE15 0JS
☎ (01661) 852445
Contact: Judith Lockey
Opening Times: 0900-1700 Mon-Sat 1000-
1700 Sun.
Min. Mail Order UK: No minimum charge*
Min. Mail Order EU: £25.00 + p&p*
Cat. Cost: 3 x 2nd class
Credit Cards: None
Specialities: *Chrysanthemum* & *Dahlia*. Wide
range of herbaceous.
*Note: mail order *Dahlia* & *Chrysanthemum*
only. EU & export *Dahlia* tubers only.
Map Ref: N, B2

NHar   HARTSIDE NURSERY GARDEN ⊠EU ▣
Nr Alston, Cumbria CA9 3BL
☎ (01434) 381372   Fax: (01434) 381372
Contact: S L & N Huntley
Opening Times: 0930-1630 Mon-Fri, 1230-
1600 Sat, Sun & B/hols, 1st Mar-31st Oct.
By appt. 1st Nov-28th Feb.
Min. Mail Order UK: No minimum charge
Min. Mail Order EU: £50.00 + p&p

Cat. Cost: 4 x 1st class or 3 x IRC
Credit Cards: Visa, Access, American Express
Specialities: Alpines grown at altitude of 1100
feet in Pennines. *Primula*, ferns, *Gentian* &
Meconopsis.
Map Ref: N, B1

NHaw   THE HAWTHORNES NURSERY ⊠ UK
Marsh Road, Hesketh Bank, Nr Preston,
Lancashire PR4 6XT
☎ (01772) 812379
Contact: Irene & Richard Hodson
Opening Times: 0900-1800 7 days 1st Mar-
30th Jun, Thu-Sun July-Oct. Gardens open
for NGS.
Min. Mail Order UK: £10.00
Cat. Cost: 5 x 1st class
Credit Cards: None
Specialities: *Clematis,* honeysuckle, choice
selection of shrub & climbing roses, extensive
range of perennials, mostly on display in the
garden.
Map Ref: N, D1

NHer   HERTERTON HOUSE GARDEN
NURSERY
Hartington, Cambo, Morpeth,
Northumberland NE61 4BN
☎ (01670) 774278
Contact: Mrs M Lawley & Mr Frank Lawley
Opening Times: 1330-1730 Mon Wed Fri-
Sun 1st Apr-end Sep. (Earlier or later in the
year weather permitting.)
Mail Order: None
Cat. Cost: None issued
Credit Cards: None
Specialities: *Achillea, Aquilegia, Geum,
Polemonium.* Country garden flowers.
Map Ref: N, B2

NHex   HEXHAM HERBS
Chesters Walled Garden, Chollerford,
Hexham, Northumberland NE46 4BQ
☎ (01434) 681483
Contact: Susie & Kevin White
Opening Times: 1000-1700 7 days Mar-end
Oct. Please phone for winter times.
Mail Order: None
Cat. Cost: None issued.
Credit Cards: None
Specialities: Extensive range of herbs.
National Collections of *Thymus* & *Origanum.*
Wild flowers, grasses & unusual perennials
esp. *Geranium, Epilobium* & variegated plants.
Map Ref: N, B2

NHHG   HARDSTOFT HERB GARDEN
Hall View Cottage, Hardstoft, Pilsley,
Nr Chesterfield, Derbyshire S45 8AH

☎ (01246) 854268
Contact: Lynne & Steve Raynor
Opening Times: 1000-1700 daily 15th
Mar-15th Sep. Closed Tue excl. Easter &
B/hol weeks.
Mail Order: None
Cat. Cost: Free
Credit Cards: MasterCard, Switch, Delta, Visa
Specialities: Very wide range of herb plants.
Over 40 lavenders & 12 rosemary. Scented
pelargoniums.
Map Ref: N, D2

NHlc   HALECAT NURSERIES
Witherslack, Grange over Sands, Cumbria
LA11 6RU
☎ (01539) 552229   Fax: (01539) 52227
Contact: Carl Harrison
Opening Times: 0900-1630 Mon-Fri all
year, 1400-1600 Sun Apr-Oct. Parties by appt.
Mail Order: None
Cat. Cost: None issued
Credit Cards: Visa, MasterCard, Access
Specialities: *Hosta, Hydrangea, Euphorbia,*
grey foliage and perennial border plants.
Map Ref: N, C1

NHol   HOLDEN CLOUGH NURSERY
⊠ EU ◆ 🗗 🗷
Holden, Bolton-by-Bowland, Clitheroe,
Lancashire BB7 4PF
☎ (01200) 447615   Fax: (01200) 447615
E-mail: enquiries@holdencloughnursery.co.uk
Web Site: www.holdencloughnursery.co.uk
Contact: P J Foley
Opening Times: 0900-1630 Mon-Sat all
year, 0900-1630 B/hol Mons, 1300-1630
Easter Sun & Suns of May B/hol w/ends.
Note: closed 25th Dec-2nd Jan 2001 &
Good Fri.
Min. Mail Order UK: No minimum charge
Min. Mail Order EU: Nmc
Cat. Cost: £1.40
Credit Cards: None
Specialities: Large general list incl. *Primula,
Saxifraga, Sempervivum, Pulmonaria, Astilbe,*
grasses, *Hosta,* heathers & *Rhododendron.*
Map Ref: N, C2

NHor   HORN'S GARDEN CENTRE ⊠ UK €
Dixon Estate, Shotton Colliery, Nr Peterlee,
Co. Durham DH6 2PX
☎ (0191) 5262987   Fax: (0191) 5262987
Contact: G Horn & Theresa Horn

Opening Times: 0900-1730 Mon-Sat 1000-1600 Sun, all year excl. Easter Mon.
Min. Mail Order UK: £6.25 + p&p
Cat. Cost: 2 x 1st class
Credit Cards: Visa, EuroCard, MasterCard, Access, Switch, American Express, Delta
Specialities: *Coleus (Solenostemon), Streptocarpus, Fuchsia* & *Pelargonium.*
Map Ref: N, B2

NLan   LANDLIFE WILDFLOWERS LTD ⊠ UK ▣
National Wildflower Centre, Court Hey Park, Liverpool, Merseyside L16 3NA
☎ (0151) 737 1819
Fax: (0151) 737 1820
E-mail: info@landlife.org.uk
Web Site: www.wildflower.org.uk
Contact: Gillian Watson
Opening Times: By appt. for collection only.
Min. Mail Order UK: £24.00
Cat. Cost: Sae + 2 x 2nd class
Credit Cards: Visa, Delta, Access
Specialities: Wild herbaceous plants & seeds.
Map Ref: N, D1

NLAp   LANESIDE ALPINES
(Office) 74 Croston Road, Garstang, Preston, Lancashire PR3 1HR
☎ (01772) 863081   Fax: (01772) 866320
E-mail: JcrHutch@aol
Contact: Jeff Hutchings
Opening Times: 0900-1700, 1100-1600 Sun.
Mail Order: None
Credit Cards: None
Specialities: Alpines. Note: nursery is at Ribblesdale Nurseries, Newsham Hall Lane, Woodplumpton, Preston, PR4 0AS.
Map Ref: N, D1

NLar   LARCH COTTAGE NURSERIES ⊠ EU ◆
Melkinthorpe, Penrith, Cumbria CA10 2DR
☎ (01931) 712404   Fax: (01931) 712727
E-mail: Briony@larchcottage.freeserve.co.uk
Contact: Joanne McCullock or Briony Stott
Opening Times: 1000-1730 daily.
Min. Mail Order UK: No minimum charge
Min. Mail Order EU: Nmc
Cat. Cost: 7 x 2nd class
Credit Cards: Visa, Access, Switch, Delta, American Express, Solo
Specialities: Unusual & old fashioned perennials. Rare & dwarf conifers. Unusual shrubs & trees. Aquatics & water lilies.
Map Ref: N, C1

NMar   J & D MARSTON ⊠ EU ◆ €
Culag, Green Lane, Nafferton, Driffield, East Yorkshire YO25 0LF
☎ (01377) 254487   Fax: (01377) 254487

Contact: J & D Marston
Opening Times: 1350-1700 Sat & Sun Easter-mid Sep. Other times by appt.
Min. Mail Order UK: £15.00 + p&p
Min. Mail Order EU: Price on application
Cat. Cost: 5 x 1st class
Credit Cards: None
Specialities: Hardy & greenhouse ferns only.
Map Ref: N, C3

NMen   MENDLE NURSERY ⊠ EU
Holme, Scunthorpe DN16 3RF
☎ (01724) 850864
Contact: Mrs A Earnshaw
Opening Times: 1000-1600 Tue-Sun.
Min. Mail Order UK: No minimum charge
Min. Mail Order EU: Nmc
Cat. Cost: 3 x 2nd class
Credit Cards: None
Specialities: Many unusual alpines esp. *Saxifraga* & *Sempervivum.*
Map Ref: N, D3

NMGW   MGW PLANTS ⊠ UK
45 Potovens Lane, Lofthouse Gate, Wakefield, Yorkshire WF3 3JE
☎ (01924) 820096
Contact: Michael G Wilson
Opening Times: 1000-dusk Wed-Sat 1st Feb-31st Oct.
Min. Mail Order UK: £10.00 + p&p
Cat. Cost: 1 x 1st class
Credit Cards: None
Specialities: Alpines incl. *Campanula* & *Geranium.* Bulbs incl. *Colchicum* & *Crocus.* Herbaceous incl. *Geranium* & *Iris.*
Map Ref: N, D2

NMir   MIRES BECK NURSERY ⊠ EU ▣
Low Mill Lane, North Cave, Brough, North Humberside HU15 2NR
☎ (01430) 421543
Contact: Irene Tinklin & Martin Rowland
Opening Times: 1000-1600 Thu-Sat 1st Mar-31st Jul. 1000-1500 Thu-Fri 1st Aug-28th Feb & by appt.
Min. Mail Order UK: £15.00 + p&p*
Min. Mail Order EU: £15.00 + p&p
Cat. Cost: 3 x 1st class
Credit Cards: None
Specialities: Wild flower plants of Yorkshire provenance. *Note: mail order for wild flower plants, plugs & seeds only.
Map Ref: N, D3

NMoo   MOOR MONKTON NURSERIES ⊠ UK
Moor Monkton, Nr York, North Yorkshire YO25 8JJ
☎ (01904) 738319   Fax: (01904) 738319

E-mail: sales@bamboo-uk.co.uk
Web Site: www.bamboo-uk.co.uk
Contact: Peter Owen
Opening Times: 0900-1700.
Min. Mail Order UK: £20.00 + p&p
Cat. Cost: Bamboo list available, e-mail
for details
Credit Cards: None
Specialities: Bamboos, palms, unusual trees,
shrubs & perennials.
Map Ref: N, C2

NMos STANLEY MOSSOP ✉ EU ⚅ ▣
Boonwood Garden Centre, Gosforth,
Seascale, Cumbria CA20 1BP
☎ (01946) 725330
Fax: (01946) 725829
Contact: Stanley, Gary & Kay Mossop.
Opening Times: 1000-1700 7 days.
Min. Mail Order UK: No minimum
charge
Min. Mail Order EU: £50.00 + p&p
Cat. Cost: Free
Credit Cards: None
Specialities: *Achimenes, Achimenantha,
Eucodonia, Gloxinia* (incl. species) &
Smithiantha.
Map Ref: N, C1

NMun MUNCASTER CASTLE ✉ EU ⚅
Ravenglass, Cumbria CA18 1RQ
☎ (01229) 717357
Fax: (01229) 717010
E-mail: acrhodos@globalnet.co.uk
Web Site: www.users.globalnet.co.uk/~acrhodos
Contact: Alan J Clark
Opening Times: 1000-1700 7 days 1st Apr-
31st Oct. All other times by appt.
Min. Mail Order UK: £20.00 + p&p
Min. Mail Order EU: £50.00 + p&p
Cat. Cost: 3 x 1st class
Credit Cards: Access, Visa, not for
telephone orders
Specialities: Rhododendrons & azaleas.
Map Ref: N, C1

NNew NEWTON HILL ALPINES ▣
335 Leeds Road, Newton Hill, Wakefield,
Yorkshire WF1 2JH
☎ (01924) 377056
Contact: Sheena Vigors
Opening Times: 0900-1700 Fri-Wed all
year. Closed Thu. Please phone first.
Mail Order: None
Cat. Cost: 2 x 1st class
Credit Cards: None
Specialities: Alpines esp. *Saxifraga,* also *Erica,*
conifers & dwarf shrubs.
Map Ref: N, D2

NNor NORCROFT NURSERIES ✉ UK ▣
St Owen's, Cargorigg, Carlisle, Cumbria
CA6 4AL
☎ (01228) 674705
(mobile) 078877 81555
Fax: (01228) 674705
Contact: Keith Bell
Opening Times: Every afternoon except
Mon but open B/hols.
Min. Mail Order UK: No minimum
charge
Cat. Cost: 2 x 2nd class
Credit Cards: None
Specialities: Hardy herbaceous & ornamental
grasses.
Map Ref: N, B1

NNrd NORDEN ALPINES ✉ EU ▣
Hirst Road, Carlton, Nr Goole, Humberside
DN14 9PX
☎ (01405) 861348
Contact: Norma & Denis Walton
Opening Times: 1000-1700 Fri-Mon incl.
or by appt.
Min. Mail Order UK: £10.00 + p&p
Min. Mail Order EU: £10.00 + p&p
Cat. Cost: 3 x 2nd class
Credit Cards: None
Specialities: Many unusual alpines - over
2000 esp. auriculas, *Campanula, Primula* &
Saxifraga.
Map Ref: N, D3

NOaD OAK DENE NURSERIES ✉ UK
10 Back Lane West, Royston, Barnsley,
Yorkshire S71 4SB
☎ (01226) 722253   Fax: (01226) 722253
Contact: J Foster or Mr G Foster
Opening Times: 1000-1600 1st Apr-30th
Sep, 0900-1800 1st Oct-31st Mar. (Closed
12.30-13.30.)
Min. Mail Order UK: Please phone for
further info.
Cat. Cost: None issued
Credit Cards: None
Specialities: Cacti, succulents & South
African *Lachenalia* bulbs.
Map Ref: N, D2

NOak OAK TREE NURSERY ✉ UK
Mill Lane, Barlow, Selby, North Yorkshire
YO8 8EY
☎ (01757) 618409
Contact: Gill Plowes
Opening Times: 1000-1630 Tue-Sun mid
Mar-end Sep.
Min. Mail Order UK: £10.00 + p&p
Cat. Cost: 2 x 1st class
Credit Cards: None

Specialities: Cottage garden plants, grasses & ferns.
Map Ref: N, D3

NOGN   The Ornamental Grass Nursery ⊠ UK
Church Farm, Westgate, Rillington, Malton, N. Yorkshire YO17 8LN
☎ (01944) 758247   **Fax:** (01944) 758247
Contact: Angela Kilby
Opening Times: 1000-1600 Tue, Wed & Thu 1st Apr-1st Oct.
Min. Mail Order UK: No minimum charge*
Cat. Cost: 4 x 1st class
Credit Cards: None
Specialities: Ornamental grasses, bamboos and ferns. *Note: no mail order for bamboos.
Map Ref: N, C3

NOrc   Orchard House Nursery ▣
Orchard House, Wormald Green, Nr Harrogate, North Yorks HG3 3PX
☎ (01765) 677541   **Fax:** (01765) 677541
Contact: Mr B M Corner
Opening Times: 0800-1630 Mon-Fri.
Mail Order: None
Cat. Cost: 4 x 1st class
Credit Cards: None
Specialities: Herbaceous perennials, ferns, grasses, water plants & unusual cottage garden plants.
Map Ref: N, C2

NPal   The Palm Farm ⊠ EU ▣ €
Thornton Hall Gardens, Station Road, Thornton Curtis, Nr Ulceby, Humberside DN39 6XF
☎ (01469) 531232   **Fax:** (01469) 531232
Contact: W W Spink
Opening Times: 1400-1700 7 days in summer. Please phone for winter times.
Min. Mail Order UK: £11.00 + p&p
Min. Mail Order EU: £25.00 + p&p
Cat. Cost: 1 x 2nd class
Credit Cards: None
Specialities: Hardy & half-hardy palms, unusual trees, shrubs & conservatory plants. Note: payment in Euros accepted only if purchaser pays bank commission.
Map Ref: N, D3

NPar   Gerry Parker Plants ⊠ EU
9 Cotherstone Road, Newton Hall, Durham DH1 5YN
☎ (0191) 386 8749
Contact: G Parker
Opening Times: Open by appt.
Min. Mail Order UK: No minimum charge
Min. Mail Order EU: Nmc

Cat. Cost: 3 x 1st class
Credit Cards: None
Specialities: Woodland plants, bulbs, border plants, all suited to clay soils.
Map Ref: N, B2

NPer   Perry's Plants ◆
The River Garden, Sleights, Whitby, North Yorkshire YO21 1RR
☎ (01947) 810329   **Fax:** (01947) 810940
E-mail: perry@rivergardens.fsnet.co.uk
Contact: Pat & Richard Perry
Opening Times: 1000-1700 mid-March to Oct.
Mail Order: None
Cat. Cost: Large (A4) Sae
Credit Cards: None
Specialities: *Lavatera, Malva, Erysimum, Euphorbia, Anthemis, Osteospermum* & *Hebe*. Also uncommon hardy & container plants.
Map Ref: N, C3

NPoe   Poets Cottage Shrub Nursery ◆
Lealholm, Whitby, North Yorkshire YO21 2AQ
☎ (01947) 897424
Contact: Hilda Rees
Opening Times: 0900-1700 Mar-Christmas, 1300-1530 Jan & Feb, 7 days.
Mail Order: None
Cat. Cost: None issued.
Credit Cards: None
Specialities: Dwarf conifers, *Acer* & herbaceous.
Map Ref: N, C3

NPri   Primrose Cottage Nursery ◆
Ringway Road, Moss Nook, Wythenshawe, Manchester M22 5WF
☎ (0161) 437 1557   **Fax:** (0161) 499 9932
E-mail: caroline@primrosenursery.freeserve.co.uk
Web Site: www.primrosenursery.freeserve.co.uk
Contact: Caroline Dumville
Opening Times: 0815-1800 Mon-Sat, 0930-1730 Sun.
Mail Order: None
Cat. Cost: 1 x 1st class
Credit Cards: Visa, Access, Switch, MasterCard
Specialities: Hardy herbaceous perennials, alpines, herbs, roses, patio & hanging basket plants. Shrubs.
Map Ref: N, D2

NPro   ProudPlants
Shadyvale Nurseries, Ainstable, Carlisle, Cumbria CA4 9QN
☎ (01768) 896604
Contact: Roger Proud
Opening Times: 0900-1800 7 days Mar-

Nov. Other times by appt.
Mail Order: None
Cat. Cost: None issued
Credit Cards: None
Specialities: Interesting & unusual shrubs & perennials esp. dwarf & ground cover plants.
Map Ref: N, C1

NPSI   PLANTS OF SPECIAL INTEREST ◆
4 High Street, Braithwell, Nr Rotherham, South Yorkshire S66 7AL
☎ (01709) 790642   **Fax:** (01709) 790342
Contact: Rita Ann Dunstan
Opening Times: 1000-1700 Tue-Sun Feb-Nov.
Mail Order: None
Cat. Cost: 3 x 1st class
Credit Cards: Access, Switch
Specialities: Wide selection of herbaceous plants esp. *Zantedeschia* & grasses. Also specimen trees & shrubs.
Map Ref: N, D2

NRar   RARER PLANTS
Ashfield House, Austfield Lane, Monk Fryston, Leeds, North Yorkshire LS25 5EH
☎ (01977) 682263
Contact: Anne Watson
Opening Times: 1000-1600 Sat & Sun 1st Feb-1st May.
Mail Order: None
Cat. Cost: Sae
Credit Cards: None
Specialities: *Helleborus* & unusual plants.
Map Ref: N, D2

NRib   RIBBLESDALE NURSERIES ⊠ €
Newsham Hall Lane, Woodplumpton, Preston, Lancashire PR4 0AS
☎ (01772) 863081
E-mail: ribblesdale99@hotmail.com
Contact: James Hart
Opening Times: 0900-1730 daily. 0900-1900 Thu Apr-Jul.
Mail Order: None
Credit Cards: Visa, MasterCard, Delta, Switch
Specialities: Trees, shrubs & perennials. Conifers, hedging, alpines, fruit, climbers, herbs, aquatics, ferns & conservatory plants.
Map Ref: N, D1

NRob   W ROBINSON & SONS LTD
⊠ EU ◪ ⊠ €
Sunny Bank, Forton, Nr Preston, Lancashire PR3 0BN
☎ (01524) 791210   **Fax:** (01524) 791933
Contact: Miss Robinson
Opening Times: 0900-1700 7 days Mar-Jun, 0800-1700 Mon-Fri Jul-Feb.

Min. Mail Order UK: No minimum charge
Min. Mail Order EU: Nmc
Cat. Cost: Free
Credit Cards: Visa, Access, American Express, Switch
Specialities: Mammoth vegetable seed. Onions, leeks, tomatoes & beans.

NRog   R V ROGER LTD ⊠ EU ◪
The Nurseries, Malton Road (A.169), Pickering, North Yorkshire YO18 7HG
☎ (01751) 472226   **Fax:** (01751) 476749
E-mail: ian@clivia.demon.co.uk
Web Site: www.ian@clivia.demon.co.uk
Contact: A G & I M Roger
Opening Times: 0900-1700 Mon-Sat, 1300-1700 Sun. Closed 25th Dec-2nd Jan.
Min. Mail Order UK: No minimum charge
Min. Mail Order EU: Nmc
Cat. Cost: £1.50
Credit Cards: Visa, Access, Switch
Specialities: General list, hardy in north of England.
Map Ref: N, C3

NRya   RYAL NURSERY ⊠ EU ◪
East Farm Cottage, Ryal, Northumberland NE20 0SA
☎ (01661) 886562
Fax: (01661) 886918
E-mail: alpines@ryal.freeserve.co.uk
Contact: R F Hadden
Opening Times: Mar-Jul 1300-1600 Mon-Tue but please phone first, 1000-1600 Sun & by appt.
Min. Mail Order UK: £5.00 + p&p
Min. Mail Order EU: £5.00 + p&p
Cat. Cost: Sae
Credit Cards: None
Specialities: Alpine & woodland plants.
Map Ref: N, B2

NSla   SLACK TOP ALPINES ◪
Hebden Bridge, West Yorkshire HX7 7HA
☎ (01422) 845348
Contact: M R or R Mitchell
Opening Times: 1000-1800 Wed-Sun & B/hol Mons 1st Mar-31st Oct.
Mail Order: None
Cat. Cost: Sae
Credit Cards: None
Specialities: Alpine & rockery plants. *Gentiana, Saxifraga, Primula* & *Pulsatilla*.
Map Ref: N, D2

NSpr **SPRINGWOOD PLEIONES** ✉ EU
35 Heathfield, Leeds, West Yorkshire
LS16 7AB
☎ (0113) 261 1781
E-mail: simon@zoom.co.uk
Web Site:
http://pages.zoom.co.uk\simonr\springwood\
Contact: Ken Redshaw
Opening Times: By appt. only.
Min. Mail Order UK: £3.00 + p&p
Min. Mail Order EU: £3.00 + p&p
Cat. Cost: 1 x 1st class
Credit Cards: None
Specialities: *Pleione*.
Map Ref: N, D2

N **NSti** **STILLINGFLEET LODGE NURSERIES** ✉ UK
Stillingfleet, Yorkshire YO19 6HP
☎ (01904) 728506   Fax: (01904) 728506
E-mail: vanessa.cook@still-lodge.freeserve.co.uk
Contact: Vanessa Cook
Opening Times: 1000-1600 Tue Wed Fri &
Sat 1st Apr-18th Oct.
Min. Mail Order UK: No minimum charge
Cat. Cost: 8 x 2nd class
Credit Cards: None
Specialities: Foliage & unusual perennials.
Hardy *Geranium, Pulmonaria*, variegated
plants & grasses. National Collection of
Pulmonaria.
Map Ref: N, D2

NSwl **SWANLAND NURSERIES** ✉ EU
Beech Hill Road, Swanland, Nr Hull, East
Yorkshire HU14 3QY
☎ (01482) 633670   Fax: (01482) 634064
E-mail: swanland@aol.com
Web Site: www.swanland.co.uk/nurseries
Contact: Debbie Naulls
Opening Times: 0900-1700 Mon-Sat,
1030-1630 Sun year round excl. Xmas &
New Year B/hols.
Min. Mail Order UK: 6 plants
Min. Mail Order EU: 6 plants
Cat. Cost: £1 cheque/Postal Order
Credit Cards: Visa, American Express,
MasterCard
Specialities: Pelargoniums. The North of
England *Pelargonium* Collection (over 800
varieties).
Map Ref: N, D3

NTay **TAYLORS NURSERIES** ✉ UK ◆
Sutton Road, Sutton, Doncaster, Yorkshire
DN6 9JZ
☎ (01302) 700716   Fax: (01302) 708415
E-mail: tayclem@easicom.com
Contact: Julie Taylor
Opening Times: 0900-1700 daily. Closed

Xmas & Boxing Day & New Year's Day.
Min. Mail Order UK: 1 plant + p&p
Cat. Cost: 6 x 1st class
Credit Cards: Visa, Access, MasterCard,
Delta, Switch, Solo
Specialities: *Clematis* (over 300 varieties).
Map Ref: N, D2

NTow **TOWN FARM NURSERY** ✉ EU
Whitton, Stockton on Tees, Cleveland
TS21 1LQ
☎ (01740) 631079
E-mail: David.Baker@themail.co.uk
Contact: F D Baker
Opening Times: 1000-1800 Sat & Sun Feb-
Jun. After Jun 2000 by appt. only.
Min. Mail Order UK: £5.00 + p&p
Min. Mail Order EU: £20.00 + p&p
Cat. Cost: Sae
Credit Cards: None
Specialities: Unusual alpines, border
perennials & shrubs. Also seed.
Map Ref: N, C2

NVic **THE VICARAGE GARDEN** ✉ UK ▣
Carrington, Urmston, Manchester M31 4AG
☎ (0161) 775 2750   Fax: (0161) 775 3679
Contact: Chris Goodman
Opening Times: 0900-1700 Mon-Sat,
closed Thu. 1000-1630 Sun all year. Closed
weekdays 1230-1330 Sep-Mar.
Min. Mail Order UK: £10.00 + p&p
Cat. Cost: 5 x 1st class or list 2 x 2nd class
Credit Cards: Visa, MasterCard
Specialities: Herbaceous, alpines, grasses,
ferns. Free admission to 7 acre gardens.
Map Ref: N, D2

NWCA **WHITE COTTAGE ALPINES** ✉ EU
Sunnyside Nurseries, Hornsea Road,
Sigglesthorne, East Yorkshire HU11 5QL
☎ (01964) 542692   Fax: (01964) 542692
E-mail: NWCA@whitcottalpines.demon.co.uk
Contact: Sally E Cummins
Opening Times: 1000-1700 (or dusk) Thu-
Sun & B/hol Mons Feb-Nov.
Min. Mail Order UK: £7.50 + p&p
Min. Mail Order EU: £15.00 + p&p
Cat. Cost: 4 x 1st class
Credit Cards: Visa, MasterCard, Switch, JCB
Specialities: Alpines & rockery plants. Over
500 species incl. American, dwarf *Salix* &
Helichrysum.
Map Ref: N, C3

NWea **WEASDALE NURSERIES** ✉ EU €
Newbiggin-on-Lune, Kirkby Stephen,
Cumbria CA17 4LX
☎ (01539) 623246   Fax: (01539) 623277

E-mail: sales@weasdale.com
Web Site: www.weasdale.com
Contact: Andrew Forsyth
Opening Times: 0900-1700 Mon-Fri.
Closed w/ends, B/hols, Xmas-New Year.
Min. Mail Order UK: No minimum
charge
Min. Mail Order EU: Nmc
Cat. Cost: £1 (£1.50 by credit card) or 5 x
2nd or 4 x 1st class stamps
Credit Cards: Visa, MasterCard, Switch,
Delta, Access, Solo
Specialities: Hardy forest trees, hedging,
broadleaved & conifers. Specimen trees &
shrubs grown at 850 feet. Mail order a
speciality.
Map Ref: N, C2

NWit   D S WITTON ☒ UK
26 Casson Drive, Harthill, Sheffield, Yorks
S26 7WA
☎ (01909) 771366
Contact: Don Witton
Opening Times: By appt. only.
Min. Mail Order UK: No minimum charge*
Cat. Cost: 1 x 1st class + sae
Credit Cards: None
Specialities: Hardy *Euphorbia*. National
Collection of hardy *Euphorbia*, over 120
different varieties.
*Note: mail order *Euphorbia* seed only.
Map Ref: N, D2

NWoo   WOODLANDS COTTAGE NURSERY
Summerbridge, Harrogate, North Yorkshire
HG3 4BT
☎ (01423) 780765   **Fax:** (01423) 781390
E-mail: j.stark@btinternet.com
Contact: Mrs Ann Stark
Opening Times: 1030-1800 Mon Wed Fri
Sat mid Mar-end Sep.
Mail Order: None
Cat. Cost: 2 x 1st class
Credit Cards: None
Specialities: Herbs, plants for shade & hardy
perennials.
Map Ref: N, C2

NYoL   YORKSHIRE LAVENDER
The Yorkshire Lavender Farm, Terrington,
York, North Yorkshire YO60 6QB
☎ (01653) 648430, (01653) 648008
Fax: (01653) 648430
E-mail: albayork@netscapeonline.co.uk
Contact: Nigel W B Goodwill
Opening Times: 1030-1630 7 days
Easter-30th Sep.
Mail Order: None
Cat. Cost: None issued

Credit Cards: None
Specialities: *Lavandula*.
Map Ref: N, C3

NZep   ZEPHYRWUDE IRISES ☒ EU
48 Blacker Lane, Crigglestone, Wakefield,
West Yorkshire WF4 3EW
☎ (01924) 252101
Contact: Richard L Brook
Opening Times: Mail order only.
Viewing by appt. 0900-dusk most days May-
early June, peak late May. Phone 0900-2300.
Min. Mail Order UK: £15.00 + p&p
Min. Mail Order EU: £15.00 + p&p
Cat. Cost: 1 x 1st class
Credit Cards: None
Specialities: Bearded *Iris,* 1970s-80s hybrids
only. Mainly 12" dwarf & intermediate, a
few tall. Catalogue available Apr-15th Sep.
Delivery Aug-Oct only.
Map Ref: N, A2

SOUTHERN

SAft   AFTON PARK NURSERY
Newport Road, Afton, Freshwater, Isle of
Wight PO40 9XR
☎ (01983) 755774,
mobile 0966 543031
Fax: (01983) 756661
E-mail: Chris@skyroots.demon.co.uk
Web Site: www.skyroots.demon.co.uk
Contact: Chris Barnes
Opening Times: 0930-1700 Mon-Sat,
1030-1630 Sun Mar-Oct.
Mail Order: None
Cat. Cost: 4 x 1st class
Credit Cards: Visa, MasterCard
Specialities: Wide general range, emphasis
on unusual perennials and coastal shrubs.
Grasses, wild flowers & plants for
Mediterranean gardens.
Map Ref: S, D2

SAga   AGAR'S NURSERY €
Agars Lane, Hordle, Lymington, Hampshire
SO41 0FL
☎ (01590) 683703
Contact: Mrs Diana Tombs
Opening Times: 1000-1700 Fri-Wed
Mar-Oct, 1000-1600 Fri-Wed Nov, Dec
& Feb.
Mail Order: None
Cat. Cost: None issued
Credit Cards: None
Specialities: *Penstemon* & *Salvia*. Also wide
range of hardy plants incl. shrubs, climbers
& herbaceous.
Map Ref: S, D2

S

SAll ALLWOOD BROS ✉ EU
London Road, Hassocks, West Sussex
BN6 9NB
☎ (01273) 844229 **Fax:** (01273) 846022
Contact: David James
Opening Times: 0900-1600 Mon-Fri.
Min. Mail Order UK: No minimum charge
Min. Mail Order EU: Nmc
Cat. Cost: 2 x 1st class
Credit Cards: Access, Visa, MasterCard, Switch
Specialities: *Dianthus* incl. hardy border
carnations, pinks, perpetual & *Allwoodii,*
some available as seed. Note: exports seed only.
Map Ref: S, D4

**SAPC ARCHITECTURAL PLANTS
(CHICHESTER) LTD** ✉ EU ◆ 🔲 🔳
Lidsey Road Nursery, Westergate, Nr
Chichester, West Sussex PO20 6SU
☎ (01243) 545008 **Fax:** (01243) 545009
Web Site: http://members.aol.com/-
gshaw29868/archplnt.htm
Contact: Christine Shaw
Opening Times: 1000-1600 Sun-Fri all year.
Closed on Sat.
Min. Mail Order UK: No minimum charge
Min. Mail Order EU: £150.00 + p&p
Cat. Cost: Free
Credit Cards: Visa, Access, EuroCard,
Switch, Delta, Electron, JCB, MasterCard,
American Express
Specialities: Architectural plants & hardy
exotics esp. evergreen broadleaved trees &
seaside exotics. Note: second nursery near
Horsham, Code SArc.
Map Ref: S, D3

SApp APPLE COURT ✉ ◆ 🔳
Hordle Lane, Hordle, Lymington,
Hampshire SO41 0HU
☎ (01590) 642130 **Fax:** (01590) 644220
E-mail: applecourt@btinternet.com
Web Site: www.applecourt.com
Contact: Diana Grenfell, Roger Grounds
Opening Times: Daily excl. Wed Mar-Sep.
Closed Oct-Feb.
Min. Mail Order UK: £15.00 + p&p
Min. Mail Order EU: £50.00 + p&p
Cat. Cost: 4 x 1st class
Credit Cards: None
Specialities: *Hosta,* grasses, ferns,
Hemerocallis. National Collection of
Woodwardia, Rohdea, & *Hosta.*
Map Ref: S, D2

SApu APULDRAM ROSES ✉ EU 🔲
Apuldram Lane, Dell Quay, Chichester,
Sussex PO20 7EF
☎ (01243) 785769 **Fax:** (01243) 536973
E-mail: d.sawday@virgin.net
Web Site: www.gardening-uk.com/apuldram/
Contact: Mrs Sawday
Opening Times: 0900-1700 Mon-Sat, 1030-
1630 Sun & B/hols excl. 23rd Dec-5th Jan.
Min. Mail Order UK: £4.50 + p&p
Min. Mail Order EU: £4.50 + p&p
Cat. Cost: 2 x 1st class
Credit Cards: Switch, MasterCard, Visa
Specialities: Roses.
Map Ref: S, D3

SArc ARCHITECTURAL PLANTS ✉ EU ◆ 🔲 🔳
Cooks Farm, Nuthurst, Horsham, West
Sussex RH13 6LH
☎ (01403) 891772 **Fax:** (01403) 891056
E-mail: architecturalplants@horsham.-
intelynx.net
Contact: Sarah Chandler & Monique
Gudgeon
Opening Times: 0900-1700 Mon-Sat.
Min. Mail Order UK: No minimum charge
Min. Mail Order EU: £150.00 + p&p
Cat. Cost: Free
Credit Cards: American Express, Access,
EuroCard, Switch, Delta, Electron,
JCB, Visa
Specialities: Architectural plants & hardy
exotics. Note: second nursery near
Chichester, Code SAPC.
Map Ref: S, C3

SAsh ASHENDEN NURSERY
Cranbrook Road, Benenden, Cranbrook,
Kent TN17 4ET
☎ (01580) 241792 **Fax:** (01580) 241792
Contact: Kevin McGarry
Opening Times: By appt. Please phone.
Mail Order: None
Cat. Cost: 1 x 1st class sae
Credit Cards: None
Specialities: Rock garden plants, perennials
& ornamental grasses.
Map Ref: S, C5

SBai STEVEN BAILEY LTD ✉ EU 🔲
Silver Street, Sway, Lymington, Hampshire
SO41 6ZA
☎ (01590) 682227 **Fax:** (01590) 683765
Contact: Fiona Whittles
Opening Times: 1000-1300 & 1400-1630
Mon-Fri all year. 1000-1300 & 1400-1600
Sat Mar-Jun excl. B/hols.
Min. Mail Order UK: Quote available
Min. Mail Order EU: Quote available
Cat. Cost: 2 x 2nd class
Credit Cards: Visa, Access
Specialities: Carnations, pinks & *Alstroemeria.*
Map Ref: S, D5

SBea **BEAN PLACE NURSERY** ▣
(Office) 52 Gladstone Road, South
Willesborough, Ashford, Kent TN24 0BY
☎ (01233) 631550 **Fax:** (01233) 631550
Contact: Miss A Jefford
Opening Times: 1000-1600 Sun-Tue 1st
Mar-1st Nov. Other times by appt.
Mail Order: None
Cat. Cost: 3 x 1st class
Credit Cards: None
Specialities: Ornamental grasses, herbaceous
perennials & cottage garden plants. Note:
nursery is at Bean Place, Ashford Road,
Bethersden.
Map Ref: S, C5

SBir **BIRCHFLEET NURSERY** ⊠ EU ▣ ▣
Nyewood, Petersfield, Hampshire
GU31 5JQ
☎ (01730) 821636 **Fax:** (01730) 821636
E-mail: gammoak@aol.com
Contact: John & Daphne Gammon
Opening Times: By appt. only. Please phone.
Min. Mail Order UK: £20.00 + p&p
Min. Mail Order EU: £30.00 + p&p
Credit Cards: None
Specialities: Oaks. National Collection of
Liquidambar.
Map Ref: S, C3

SBla **BLACKTHORN NURSERY**
Kilmeston, Alresford, Hampshire SO24 0NL
☎ (01962) 771796 **Fax:** (01962) 771071
Contact: A R & S B White
Opening Times: 0900-1700 Thu-Sun Feb-
Jun 2000. 0900-1700 every Fri & Sat
Mar-June 2001.
Mail Order: None
Cat. Cost: Info. sheets available at nursery
Credit Cards: None
Specialities: Choice perennials & alpines, esp.
Daphne, Epimedium, Helleborus & Hepatica.
Map Ref: S, C2

SBod **BODIAM NURSERY** ⊠ UK ▣ €
Ockham House, Bodiam, Robertsbridge,
East Sussex TN32 5RA
☎ (01580) 830811/830649
Fax: (01580) 830071
Contact: Richard Biggs and Mike Gornert
Opening Times: 0900-1700 or by appt.
Min. Mail Order UK: £15.00 + p&p
Cat. Cost: 4 x 1st class
Credit Cards: Visa, MasterCard, EuroCard,
American Express
Specialities: Heathers, herbaceous perennials,
grasses, conifers, azaleas, *Camellia* &
climbers.
Map Ref: S, C5

SBra **J BRADSHAW & SON** ⊠ EU ▣ ▣ ◆
Busheyfield Nursery, Herne, Herne Bay,
Kent CT6 7LJ
☎ (01227) 375415 **Fax:** (01227) 375415
Contact: D J Bradshaw & Martin Bradshaw
Opening Times: 1000-1700 Tue-Sat 1st
Mar-31st Oct. Other times by appt. only.
Min. Mail Order UK: 2 plants + p&p
Min. Mail Order EU: 2 plants + p&p
Cat. Cost: Sae + 2 x 1st class
Credit Cards: None
Specialities: *Clematis, Lonicera, Rosa,
Banksia,* other climbers & wall shrubs.
Map Ref: S, C5

SBre **BRESSINGHAM PLANT CENTRE
(HAYWARDS HEATH)** ◆
Borde Hill, Haywards Heath, West Sussex
RH16 1XP
☎ (01444) 414151 **Fax:** (01444) 454367
Contact: Norma Moore
Opening Times: 0900-1700 1st Nov-31st
Mar, 0900-1800 1st Apr-31st Oct 7 days.
Mail Order: None
Cat. Cost: None issued
Credit Cards: Delta, Switch, MasterCard, Visa
Specialities: Very wide general range. Many
own varieties. Focus on hardy ornamental
plants & grasses.
Map Ref: S, C4

SBrk **BROOKSIDE NURSERY** ⊠ EU ▣ €
Elderberry Farm, Bognor Road, Rowhook,
Horsham, West Sussex RH12 3PS
☎ (01403) 790996 **Fax:** (01403) 790195
E-mail: alanbutler1@compuserve.com
Web Site: www.cactus-
mall.com/nursery/brooksid.html
Contact: A J Butler
Opening Times: 1000-1700 Thu-Sun &
B/hol Mons. Please phone first.
Min. Mail Order UK: No minimum charge
Min. Mail Order EU: Nmc
Cat. Cost: 1 x 1st class
Credit Cards: Visa, MasterCard, Switch
Specialities: Cacti & succulent plants.
National Collection of *Sansevieria.*
Map Ref: S, C3

SBro **RON & WENDY MITCHELL** ⊠ EU ▣ ▣
Rapallo, 9 Palmers Road, Wootton Bridge,
Isle of Wight PO33 4NA
☎ (01983) 884282
Contact: Mrs W M Mitchell

S

Opening Times: By appt. only.
Min. Mail Order UK: No minimum charge
Min. Mail Order EU: Nmc*
Cat. Cost: 3 x 2nd class
Credit Cards: None
Specialities: Miniature & dwarf *Pelargonium*.
*Note: unrooted cuttings only to EU.

SBrw   BROADWATER PLANTS
(Office) Coblands Nursery, Trench Road,
Tonbridge, Kent TN10 3HQ
☎ (01892) 534760   Fax: (01892) 534760
E-mail: broadwater@coblands.co.uk
Web Site: www.coblands.co.uk
Contact: John Moaby
Opening Times: 0900-1630 Mon-Fri, 0900-
1600 Sat 1st Mar-30th Jun.
Mail Order: None
Cat. Cost: 3 x 1st class
Credit Cards: MasterCard, Visa
Specialities: *Rhododendron, Camellia* &
ericaceous incl. many unusual species. Field-
grown *Rhododendron* (hardy hybrids)
available at specimen sizes. Min. order £100
home counties, other areas Poa. Note:
nursery is at Fairview Lane, Tunbridge Wells,
TN3 9LU.
Map Ref: S, C4

SCam   CAMELLIA GROVE NURSERY ⊠ EU ▣ ▣
Market Garden, Lower Beeding, West Sussex
RH13 6PX
☎ (01403) 891143   Fax: (01403) 891336
E-mail: rhs20@camellia-grove.com
Contact: Antonia Loder
Opening Times: 7 days, by appt. only. This
is so we can give you our undivided attention.
Min. Mail Order UK: No minimum charge
Min. Mail Order EU: £100.00 +p&p
Cat. Cost: 2 x 1st class
Credit Cards: Access, Visa
Specialities: Camellias & azaleas.
Map Ref: S, C3

SChr   JOHN CHURCHER PLANTS ⊠ EU ▣
47 Grove Avenue, Portchester, Fareham,
Hampshire PO16 9EZ
☎ (023) 9232 6740
Contact: John Churcher
Opening Times: By appt. only. Please
phone.
Min. Mail Order UK: No minimum charge
Min. Mail Order EU: Nmc*
Cat. Cost: Sae for list
Credit Cards: None
Specialities: *Opuntia, Agave*, succulents,
palms, plus small general range, hardy &
half-hardy. *Note: exports seed only.
Map Ref: S, D2

**SChu   CHURCH HILL COTTAGE
          GARDENS ⊠ UK**
Charing Heath, Ashford, Kent TN27 0BU
☎ (01233) 712522   Fax: (01233) 712522
Contact: Mr M & J & Mrs M Metianu
Opening Times: 1000-1700 1st Feb-30th Nov
Tue-Sun & B/hol Mons. Other times by appt.
Min. Mail Order UK: £10.00 + p&p
Cat. Cost: 4 x 1st class
Credit Cards: None
Specialities: Unusual hardy plants, *Dianthus,
Hosta*, ferns & *Viola*, alpines & shrubs.
Map Ref: S, C5

SCit   THE CITRUS CENTRE ⊠ EU ▣ ▣ €
West Mare Lane, Marehill, Pulborough, West
Sussex RH20 2EA
☎ (01798) 872786   Fax: (01798) 874880
E-mail: enquiries@citruscentre.co.uk
Web Site: www.citruscentre.co.uk
Contact: Amanda & Chris Dennis
Opening Times: 0930-1730 Wed-Sun.
Phone for Xmas & B/hol opening times.
Min. Mail Order UK: No minimum charge
Min. Mail Order EU: Nmc
Cat. Cost: Sae
Credit Cards: Visa, Access
Specialities: *Citrus* & citrus relatives.
Map Ref: S, D3

SCko   COOKOO BOX NURSERY ⊠ EU ▣ ▣
Longfield, 63 Charlesford Avenue,
Kingswood, Maidstone, Kent ME17 3PH
☎ (01622) 844866
Contact: Mr P Cook
Opening Times: By appt. only.
Min. Mail Order UK: No minimum charge
Min. Mail Order EU: Nmc
Cat. Cost: 2 x 1st class
Credit Cards: None
Specialities: A family run nursery with an
increasing range of grasses, cottage garden
perennials, *Salvia, Phlox, Hosta, Penstemon*
(some unusual), & spring, summer &
autumn bedding.
Map Ref: S, C5

SCob   COBLANDS NURSERY ▣
(Office) Trench Road, Tonbridge, Kent
TN10 3HQ
☎ (01732) 770999   Fax: (01732) 770271
E-mail: plants@coblands.co.uk
Web Site: www.coblands.co.uk
Contact: Nick Coslett
Opening Times: 0830-1600 Mon-Fri.
Mail Order: None
Cat. Cost: W/sale cat. only
Credit Cards: Visa, MasterCard
Specialities: General range esp. herbaceous,

common & unusual, many in large quantities. Bamboos, grasses & ferns. Note: nursery is at Back Lane, Ivy Hatch, Ightham, Sevenoaks, Kent.
Map Ref: S, C4

SCog   COGHURST NURSERY ⊠ EU 🔳
Ivy House Lane, Nr Three Oaks, Hastings, East Sussex TN35 4NP
☎ (01424) 756228   **Fax:** (01424) 428944
E-mail: rotherview@supa net.com
Contact: J Farnfield & L A Edgar
Opening Times: 0930-1600 7 days.
Min. Mail Order UK: No minimum charge
Min. Mail Order EU: Nmc
Cat. Cost: 2 x 2nd class for availability list.
Credit Cards: None
Specialities: *Camellia.*
Map Ref: S, D5

SCoo   COOLING'S NURSERIES LTD
Rushmore Hill, Knockholt, Sevenoaks, Kent TN14 7NN
☎ (01959) 532269   **Fax:** (01959) 534092
Contact: M Hooker
Opening Times: 0900-1700 Mon-Sat & 1000-1630 Sun.
Mail Order: None
Cat. Cost: 4 x 1st class
Credit Cards: Visa, Access, Switch, Electron, Delta
Specialities: Large range of perennials, conifers & bedding plants. Some unusual shrubs.
Map Ref: S, C4

SCou   COOMBLAND GARDENS ⊠ EU 🔳
Coombland, Coneyhurst, Billingshurst, West Sussex RH14 9DG
☎ (01403) 741727   **Fax:** (01403) 741079
Contact: David Browne
Opening Times: 1400-1600 Mon-Fri Mar-end Oct. B/hols & other times by appt. only.
Min. Mail Order UK: £20.00 + p&p
Min. Mail Order EU: 8 plants + p&p*
Cat. Cost: 5 x 1st class
Credit Cards: None
Specialities: National Collection of hardy geraniums. Choice herbaceous. Also seeds. *Note: hardy geraniums only to EU.
Map Ref: S ,C3

SCrf   CROFTERS NURSERIES 🔳
Church Hill, Charing Heath, Nr Ashford, Kent TN27 0BU
☎ (01233) 712798   **Fax:** (01233) 712798
E-mail: croftersch@hotmail.com
Contact: John Webb
Opening Times: 1000-1700. Closed Mon & Thu and Aug. Please check first.

Mail Order: None
Cat. Cost: 3 x 1st class
Credit Cards: None
Specialities: Fruit and ornamental trees and conifers. Old apple varieties. Small number of *Prunus serrula* with grafted ornamental heads.
Map Ref: S, C5

SCro   CROFTWAY NURSERY ⊠ EU 🔳 €
Yapton Road, Barnham, Bognor Regis, West Sussex PO22 0BH
☎ (01243) 552121   **Fax:** (01243) 552125
E-mail: sales@croftway.co.uk
Web Site: www.croftway.co.uk
Contact: Graham Spencer
Opening Times: 0900-1700 Mon-Sat, 1000-1600 Sun. Closed 1st Dec-28th Feb except by appt.
Min. Mail Order UK: No minimum charge*
Min. Mail Order EU: Nmc
Cat. Cost: 4 x 1st class
Credit Cards: Visa, Access, Switch, American Express
Specialities: Wide general range, emphasis on perennials. Specialists in *Iris* & hardy *Geranium*. *Note: mail order for *Iris* & *Geranium* & selected other plants only.
Map Ref: S, D3

SDay   A LA CARTE DAYLILIES ⊠ EU ♦ €
Little Hermitage, St Catherine's Down, Nr Ventnor, Isle of Wight PO38 2PD
☎ (01983) 730512
Contact: Jan & Andy Wyers
Opening Times: By appt. only.
Min. Mail Order UK: No minimum charge
Min. Mail Order EU: Nmc
Cat. Cost: 3 x 1st class
Credit Cards: None
Specialities: *Hemerocallis.* National Collections of miniature & small flowered *Hemerocallis* & large flowered *Hemerocallis* (post-1960 award-winning cultivars).
Map Ref: S, D2

SDea   DEACON'S NURSERY ⊠ EU ♦ 🔳 🔳
Moor View, Godshill, Isle of Wight PO38 3HW
☎ (01983) 840750 (24 hrs), (01983) 522243
Fax: (01983) 523575
Contact: G D & B H W Deacon
Opening Times: 0800-1600 Mon-Fri May-Sep, 0800-1700 Mon-Fri 0800-1200 Sat Oct-Apr.
Min. Mail Order UK: No minimum charge
Min. Mail Order EU: Nmc
Cat. Cost: Stamp appreciated
Credit Cards: Visa, Access, Switch

S

S

Specialities: Over 300 varieties of apple, old & new plus pears, plums, gages, damsons & cherries. Fruit & nut trees, triple peaches, ballerinas. Modern soft fruit. Grapes & hops. Combinations of "family trees". Family trees - blueberries/nuts/asparagus.
Map Ref: S, D2

SDeJ   DE JAGER & SONS ☒ EU ☒ ⬛
The Nurseries, Marden, Kent TN12 9BP
☎ (01622) 831235   Fax: (01622) 832416
E-mail: PdeJag@aol.com
Contact: Mrs J Williams
Opening Times: 0900-1700 Mon-Fri
Min. Mail Order UK: £15.00 + p&p
Min. Mail Order EU: £15.00 + p&p
Cat. Cost: Free
Credit Cards: Visa, Access
Specialities: Wide general range esp. bulbs. *Lilium, Tulipa, Narcissus* species & miscellaneous. Large range of perennials.
Map Ref: S, C5

SDix   GREAT DIXTER NURSERIES ☒ EU
Northiam, Rye, East Sussex TN31 6PH
☎ (01797) 253107   Fax: (01797) 252879
E-mail: greatdixter@compuserve.com
Contact: K Leighton
Opening Times: 0900-1230 & 1330-1700 Mon-Fri, 0900-1200 Sat all year. Also 1400-1700 Sat, Sun & B/hols Apr-Oct.
Min. Mail Order UK: £15.00 + p&p
Min. Mail Order EU: £15.00 + p&p
Cat. Cost: 4 x 1st class
Credit Cards: Access, Switch, Visa
Specialities: *Clematis*, shrubs and plants. Gardens open.
Map Ref: S, C5

SDnm   DENMANS GARDEN (JOHN BROOKES LTD)
Clock House, Denmans, Fontwell, Nr Arundel, West Sussex BN18 0SU
☎ (01243) 542808   Fax: (01243) 544064
E-mail: denmans@cwcom.net
Web Site: www.denmans-garden.co.uk
Contact: Michael Neve
Opening Times: 0900-1700 7 days 1st Mar-31st Oct.
Mail Order: None
Cat. Cost: £2.50
Credit Cards: Visa, MasterCard
Specialities: Rare and unusual plants.
Map Ref: S, D3

SDow   DOWNDERRY NURSERY ☒ EU ☒ ⬛
Pillar Box Lane, Hadlow, Nr Tonbridge, Kent TN11 9SW
☎ (01732) 810081   Fax: (01732) 811398

E-mail: simon@downderry-nursery.co.uk
Web Site: www.downderry-nursery.co.uk
Contact: Dr S J Charlesworth
Opening Times: 1000-1700 Wed-Sat & 1100-1700 Sun & B/hols May-Nov & by appt.
Min. Mail Order UK: No minimum charge
Min. Mail Order EU: Nmc
Cat. Cost: 4 x 1st class
Credit Cards: Delta, MasterCard, Switch, Visa
Specialities: National Collections of *Lavandula* and *Rosmarinus*.
Map Ref: S, C4

SDry   DRYSDALE GARDEN EXOTICS ☒ EU
Bowerwood Road, Fordingbridge, Hampshire SP6 1BN
☎ (01425) 653010
Contact: David Crampton
Opening Times: 0930-1730 Wed-Fri, 1000-1730 Sun. Closed 24th Dec-2nd Jan incl.
Min. Mail Order UK: £10.00 + p&p
Min. Mail Order EU: £15.00 + p&p
Cat. Cost: 3 x 1st class
Credit Cards: None
Specialities: Plants for exotic & foliage effect. Plants for Mediterranean gardens. National Collection of bamboos.
Map Ref: S, D1

SDys   DYSONS NURSERY ☒ UK
Great Comp Garden, Platt, Sevenoaks, Kent TN15 8QS
☎ (01732) 886154
E-mail: William.Dyson@ukgateway.net
Contact: William T Dyson
Opening Times: 1100-1800 7 days 1st Apr-31st Oct. Other times by appt.
Min. Mail Order UK: £15.00 + p&p
Cat. Cost: 2 x 1st class
Credit Cards: None
Specialities: Wide range of choice & unusual plants esp. *Salvia, Sempervivum, Geranium* & *Crocosmia*.
Map Ref: S, C4

SEas   EASTFIELD PLANT CENTRE
Paice Lane, Medstead, Alton, Hampshire GU34 5PR
☎ (01420) 563640
Fax: (01420) 563640
Contact: D M & P Barton
Opening Times: 0900-1700 7 days 1st Feb-20th Dec or by appt.
Mail Order: None
Cat. Cost: None issued
Credit Cards: None
Specialities: General range.
Map Ref: S, C2

SEND **EAST NORTHDOWN FARM** ⊠ UK 🖾 ◆
Margate, Kent CT9 3TS
☎ (01843) 862060
Fax: (01843) 860206
E-mail: friend.northdown@ukonline.co.uk
Web Site: www.botanyplants.co.uk
Contact: Louise & William Friend
Opening Times: 0900-1700 Mon-Sat,
1000-1700 Sun all year. Closed Xmas week
& Easter Sun.
Min. Mail Order UK: £25.00*
Cat. Cost: None issued
Credit Cards: Visa, Switch, MasterCard
Specialities: Chalk & coast-loving plants.
*Note: mail order service Sep-Feb only.
Map Ref: S, B6

SFam **FAMILY TREES** ⊠ EU ◆
Sandy Lane, Shedfield, Hampshire SO32 2HQ
☎ (01329) 834812
Contact: Philip House
Opening Times: 0930-1230 Wed & Sat mid
Oct-mid Apr.
Min. Mail Order UK: No minimum charge
Min. Mail Order EU: Nmc
Cat. Cost: Free
Credit Cards: None
Specialities: Fruit & ornamental trees.
Trained fruit tree specialists - standards,
espaliers, cordons etc. Other trees, old-
fashioned & climbing roses & evergreens.
Map Ref: S, D2

SFor **FORWARD NURSERIES** ⊠ UK 🖾
Borough Green Road, Ightham, Sevenoaks,
Kent TN15 9JA
☎ (01732) 884726   Fax: (01732) 886626
Contact: Paul van Leeuwen
Opening Times: 0800-1700 Mon-Fri, 1000-
1600 Sat & Sun.
Min. Mail Order UK: No minimum charge
Cat. Cost: Free
Credit Cards: Visa, MasterCard, Switch,
American Express
Specialities: *Hedera.*
Map Ref: S, C4

SFur **FURZEY GARDENS NURSERY** ⊠ EU 🖾 🖾
(Office) The Minstead Training Project,
Minstead Lodge, Minstead, Nr Lyndhurst,
Hampshire SO43 7FT
☎ (023) 8081 4134   Fax: (023) 8081 2297
Contact: Peter White
Opening Times: Nursery 1000-1700 7 days
Mar-Dec. Mail order all year.
Min. Mail Order UK: £20.00 + p&p
Min. Mail Order EU: £20.00 + p&p
Cat. Cost: 1 x 2nd class
Credit Cards: None

Specialities: *Acer.* Note: nursery is at Furzey
Gardens, Minstead, Nr Lyndhurst.
Map Ref: S, D2

SGar **GARDEN PLANTS** 🖾
Windy Ridge, Victory Road, St Margarets-at-
Cliffe, Dover, Kent CT15 6HF
☎ (01304) 853225   Fax: (01304) 853225
E-mail: GardenPlants@tks.u-net.com
Contact: Teresa Ryder
Opening Times: 1000-1700 (closed Wed)
Mail Order: None
Cat. Cost: 2 x 1st class + A5 Sae
Credit Cards: None
Specialities: Unusual perennials,
penstemons, salvias and diascias. Plantsman's
garden open to view. Map essential for
first visit.
Map Ref: S, C6

SGrm **GRIMSDYKE HOUSE** ⊠ EU 🖾 🖾
12 Southcourt Avenue, Bexhill-on-Sea, East
Sussex TN39 3AR
☎ (01424) 221452   Fax: (01424) 221452
Contact: A P Hamilton
Opening Times: 0900-1700 Mon-Fri,
0900-1200 Sat & Sun.
Min. Mail Order UK: £6.00
Min. Mail Order EU: £6.00
Cat. Cost: 3 x 1st class
Credit Cards: None
Specialities: *Bougainvillea.* Note: export only
express airmail and phyto certificate, all
costed individually.
Map Ref: S, D5

SHar **HARDY'S COTTAGE GARDEN
PLANTS** ⊠ EU 🖾
Freefolk Priors, Freefolk, Whitchurch,
Hampshire RG28 7NJ
☎ (01256) 896533
Fax: (01256) 896572
E-mail:
hardy@cottagegardenplants01.freeserve.co.uk
Contact: Rosy Hardy
Opening Times: 1000-1700 7 days 1st Mar-
31st Oct.
Min. Mail Order UK: No minimum charge
Min. Mail Order EU: Nmc
Cat. Cost: 5 x 1st class.
Credit Cards: Visa, Access
Specialities: Hardy *Geranium* & other
herbaceous both old & new.
Map Ref: S, C2

K E Y	⊠ Mail order to UK or EU
	🖾 Exports beyond EU € Euro accepted
	🖾 Also supplies Wholesale ◆ See Display advertisement

S

SHay   HAYWARD'S CARNATIONS ✉ EU ▣
The Chace Gardens, Stakes Road, Purbrook,
Waterlooville, Hampshire PO7 5PL
☎ (023) 9226 3047   **Fax:** (023) 9226 3047
Contact: A N Hayward
Opening Times: 0930-1700 Mon-Fri.
Min. Mail Order UK: £10.00 + p&p
Min. Mail Order EU: £50.00 + p&p
Cat. Cost: 1 x 1st class
Credit Cards: None
Specialities: Hardy pinks & border carnations
(Dianthus). Greenhouse perpetual carnations.
Map Ref: S, D2

SHDw   HIGHDOWN NURSERY ✉ EU ▣ ▣ €
New Hall Lane, Small Dole, Nr Henfield,
West Sussex BN5 9YH
☎ (01273) 492976   **Fax:** (01273) 492976
Contact: A G & J H Shearing
Opening Times: 0900-1700 7 days.
Min. Mail Order UK: £10.00 + p&p
Min. Mail Order EU: £10.00 + p&p
Cat. Cost: 3 x 1st class
Credit Cards: Visa, MasterCard, Delta,
JCB, EuroCard
Specialities: Herbs.
Map Ref: S, D3

SHel   HELLYER'S GARDEN PLANTS ✉ UK ◆
Orchards, off Wallage Lane*, Rowfant,
Nr Crawley, Sussex RH10 4NJ
☎ (01342) 718280
E-mail: penelope.hellyer@hellyers.co.uk
Contact: Penelope Hellyer
Opening Times: 1000-1700 Wed-Sat Mar-
Oct & by prior appt.
Min. Mail Order UK: No minimum charge
Cat. Cost: 3 x 1st + A5 Sae. Mail order list
1 x 1st + A5 Sae.
Credit Cards: None
Specialities: Unusual hardy plants for
sun/shade. Small selection of climbers &
shrubs. Over 100 varieties of hardy *Geranium.*
*Note: Wallage Lane is off the B2028
equidistant Crawley Down & Turners Hill.
Map Ref: S, C4

SHFr   SUE HARTFREE ✉ EU
25 Crouch Hill Court, Lower Halstow, Nr
Sittingbourne, Kent ME9 7EJ
☎ (01795) 842426
Contact: Sue Hartfree
Opening Times: Any time by appt. Please
phone first.
Min. Mail Order UK: £15.00 + p&p*
Min. Mail Order EU: £20.00 + p&p*
Cat. Cost: A5 Sae + 4 x 1st class
Credit Cards: None
Specialities: Unusual & interesting shrubs,

hardy & half-hardy perennials incl. *Salvia,
Lobelia, Penstemon & Lysimachia.* All can be
seen growing in the garden. *Note: mail
order Oct-Mar.
Map Ref: S, C5

SHHo   HIGHFIELD HOLLIES ✉ UK ◆
Highfield Farm, Hatch Lane, Liss,
Hampshire GU33 7NH
☎ (01730) 892372   **Fax:** (01730) 894853
E-mail: louise@bendall.prestel.co.uk
Web Site: www.commercepark.co.uk/bendall/
Contact: Mrs Louise Bendall
Opening Times: By appt.
Min. Mail Order UK: No minimum charge
Cat. Cost: 2 x 1st class
Credit Cards: None
Specialities: *Ilex* - over 100 species &
cultivars incl. many specimen trees & topiary.
Map Ref: S, C3

SHmp   HAMPSHIRE CARNIVOROUS PLANTS
✉ EU ▣ ▣
Ya-Mayla, Allington Lane, West End,
Southampton, Hampshire SO30 3HQ
☎ (023) 8047 3314, mobile 07703 258296
Fax: (023) 8047 3314
E-mail: matthew@msoper.freesave.co.uk
Contact: Matthew Soper
Opening Times: By appt. only.
Min. Mail Order UK: No minimum charge
Min. Mail Order EU: £50.00 + p&p
Cat. Cost: 2 x 2nd class
Credit Cards: None
Specialities: Carnivorous plants esp.
Nepenthes, Heliamphora, Sarracenia.

SHvs   HARVEST NURSERIES ✉ EU
Harvest Cottage, Boonshill Farm, Iden, Nr
Rye, East Sussex TN31 7QA
☎ (01797) 230583
E-mail: derek@harvest99.freeserve.co.uk
Contact: D A Smith
Opening Times: Mail order only.
Min. Mail Order UK: No minimum charge
Min. Mail Order EU: £20.00 + p&p
Cat. Cost: 2 x 1st class
Credit Cards: None
Specialities: *Epiphyllum* & wide range of
succulents. Descriptive catalogue.

SHya   BRENDA HYATT ✉ EU
1 Toddington Crescent, Bluebell Hill,
Chatham, Kent ME5 9QT
☎ (01634) 863251
Contact: Mrs Brenda Hyatt
Opening Times: By appt. only.
Min. Mail Order UK: No minimum charge
Min. Mail Order EU: Nmc

Cat. Cost: £1.00
Credit Cards: None
Specialities: Show auriculas. Holder
of National Collection of Show
green/grey/white edged & fancy auriculas,
incl. the Douglas Collection.
Map Ref: S, C5

SIde   IDEN CROFT HERBS ✉ EU ◆ ▣
Frittenden Road, Staplehurst, Kent
TN12 0DH
☎ (01580) 891432
Fax: (01580) 892416
E-mail: idencroft.herbs@dial.pipex.com
Web Site: www./oxalis.co.uk/ic.htm
Contact: Rosemary & D Titterington
Opening Times: 0900-1700 Mon-Sat all
year. 1100-1700 Sun & B/hols 1st Mar-
30th Sep.
Min. Mail Order UK: No minimum charge
Min. Mail Order EU: Nmc*
Cat. Cost: 2 x 1st class for descriptive list.
Credit Cards: Visa, Access, Delta, JCB,
EuroCard, Switch
Specialities: Herbs, aromatic & wild flower
plants & plants for bees & butterflies.
National Collections of *Mentha* &
Origanum.
*Note: exports seed only.
Map Ref: S, C5

SIng   W E TH. INGWERSEN LTD
Birch Farm Nursery, Gravetye, East
Grinstead, West Sussex RH19 4LE
☎ (01342) 810236
Contact: M P & M R Ingwersen
Opening Times: 0900-1300 & 1330-1600
7 days 1st Mar-30th Sep. 0900-1300 &
1330-1600 Mon-Fri Oct-Feb.
Mail Order: None
Cat. Cost: 2 x 1st class
Credit Cards: None
Specialities: Very wide range of hardy plants
mostly alpines. Also seed.
Map Ref: S, C4

SJus   JUST ROSES ✉ EU
Beales Lane, Northiam, Nr Rye, East Sussex
TN31 6QY
☎ (01797) 252355
Contact: Mr J Banham
Opening Times: 0900-1200 & 1300-1700
Tue-Fri, 0900-1200 & 1300-1600 Sat & Sun.
Min. Mail Order UK: 1 plant + p&p
Min. Mail Order EU: No minimum charge
Cat. Cost: Free
Credit Cards: None
Specialities: Roses.
Map Ref: S, C5

SKCa   KENT CACTI ✉ EU
(Office) 35 Rutland Way, Orpington, Kent
BR5 4DY
☎ (01689) 836249, mobile 07767 881981
Fax: (01689) 830157
Contact: Mr D Sizmur
Opening Times: 1000-1700 most days.
Please phone first.
Min. Mail Order UK: No minimum charge
Min. Mail Order EU: Nmc
Cat. Cost: A5 Sae. No list for carnivorous
plants.
Credit Cards: None
Specialities: *Agave, Astrophytum,
Conophytum, Crassula, Echeveria*, small
Opuntia, Mammillaria etc. Note: nursery is
at Woodlands Farm, Shire Lane,
Farnborough, Kent, BR6 7HH.
Map Ref: S, C4

SKee   KEEPERS NURSERY ✉ UK
Gallants Court, Gallants Lane, East Farleigh,
Maidstone, Kent ME15 0LE
☎ (01622) 726465   Fax: (01622) 726465
E-mail: keepers.nursery@talk21.com
Web Site: www.keepers-nursery.co.uk
Contact: Hamid Habibi
Opening Times: All reasonable hours by appt.
Min. Mail Order UK: £10.00 + p&p
Cat. Cost: 2 x 1st class. Free by e-mail
Credit Cards: None
Specialities: Old & unusual top fruit
varieties. Top fruit propagated to order.
Map Ref: S, C4

SKen   KENT STREET NURSERIES ✉ EU ▣
Sedlescombe, Battle, East Sussex TN33 0SF
☎ (01424) 751134   Fax: (01424) 751499
E-mail: Peter@Stapleyp.freeserve.co.uk
Web Site: www.1066-countryplants.co.uk
Contact: Mrs D Downey
Opening Times: 0900-1800 7 days.
Min. Mail Order UK: £7.50
Min. Mail Order EU: No minimum charge
Cat. Cost: 2 x 1st class*
Credit Cards: MasterCard, Visa
Specialities: *Fuchsia, Pelargonium*, bedding
& perennials. *Note: separate *Fuchsia* &
Pelargonium lists - please specify which
required.
Map Ref: S, C5

SLan   LANGLEY BOXWOOD NURSERY
✉ EU ◆ ▣ ▣
Rake, Nr Liss, Hampshire GU33 7JL
☎ (01730) 894467   Fax: (01730) 894703
E-mail: langbox@msn.com.uk
Web Site: www.boxwood.co.uk
Contact: Elizabeth Braimbridge

S

Opening Times: Mon-Fri. Sat please ring first. Please phone for directions.
Min. Mail Order UK: £20.00 + p&p
Min. Mail Order EU: £100.00 + p&p
Cat. Cost: 4 x 1st class
Credit Cards: None
Specialities: *Buxus* species, cultivars & hedging. Good range of topiary. *Taxus*. National Collection of *Buxus*.
Map Ref: S, C3

SLau   THE LAURELS NURSERY ▣
Benenden, Cranbrook, Kent TN17 4JU
☎ (01580) 240463   **Fax:** (01580) 240463
Contact: Peter or Sylvia Kellett
Opening Times: 0800-1700 Mon-Thu, 0800-1600 Fri, 0900-1200 Sat. Sun by appt. only.
Mail Order: None
Cat. Cost: Free
Credit Cards: None
Specialities: Open ground & container ornamental trees, shrubs & climbers incl. flowering cherries, birch & *Wisteria*.
Map Ref: S, C5

SLBF   LITTLE BROOK FUCHSIAS ▣
Ash Green Lane West, Ash Green, Nr Aldershot, Hampshire GU12 6HL
☎ (01252) 329731
E-mail: carolgubler@business.ntl.com
Contact: Carol Gubler
Opening Times: 0900-1700 Wed-Sun 1st Jan-9th Jul.
Mail Order: None
Cat. Cost: 50p + Sae
Credit Cards: None
Specialities: Fuchsias old & new.
Map Ref: S, C3

SLdr   LODER PLANTS ⊠ EU ▣ ▣ €
Market Garden, Lower Beeding, West Sussex RH13 6PX
☎ (01403) 891412   **Fax:** (01403) 891336
E-mail: loder@rhododendrons.com
Web Site: www.rhododendrons.com
Contact: Chris Loder
Opening Times: 7 days, by appt. only. This is so we can give you our undivided attention.
Min. Mail Order UK: No minimum charge
Min. Mail Order EU: £100.00 + p&p
Cat. Cost: 2 x 1st class
Credit Cards: Visa, Access
Specialities: Rhododendrons & azaleas in all sizes. *Camellia, Acer*.
Map Ref: S, C3

SLim   LIME CROSS NURSERY ◆ ▣ ▣
Herstmonceux, Hailsham, East Sussex BN27 4RS

☎ (01323) 833229   **Fax:** (01323) 833944
E-mail: LimeCross@aol.com
Contact: J A Tate, G Monk
Opening Times: 0830-1700 Mon-Sat, 1000-1600 Sun.
Mail Order: None
Cat. Cost: 5 x 2nd class
Credit Cards: Visa, MasterCard, Delta, Switch
Specialities: Conifers, trees & shrubs, climbers. Note: export for large orders only.
Map Ref: S, D4

SLod   THE LODGE NURSERY ⊠ UK
Cottage Lane, Westfield, Nr Hastings, East Sussex TN35 4RP
☎ (01424) 870186
Contact: Mrs Sandra Worley
Opening Times: 1030-1700 Wed-Sun mid Mar-end Oct & all B/hols.
Min. Mail Order UK: No minimum charge
Cat. Cost: £1.25
Credit Cards: None
Specialities: Small nursery with a wide variety of mainly herbaceous perennials.
Map Ref: S, D5

SLon   LONGSTOCK PARK NURSERY
Longstock, Stockbridge, Hampshire SO20 6EH
☎ (01264) 810894
Fax: (01264) 810924
Contact: Peter Moore
Opening Times: 0830-1630 Mon-Sat all year excl. Xmas & New Year, & 1400-1700 Sun Mar-Oct.
Mail Order: None
Cat. Cost: £2 cheque includes postage.
Credit Cards: Visa, Access, Switch, MasterCard
Specialities: A wide range, over 2000 varieties, of trees, shrubs, perennials, climbers, aquatics & ferns. Increasing range of *Daphne*. National Collection of *Buddleja*.
Map Ref: S, C2

SLPI   LANDSCAPE PLANTS ⊠ EU ▣ ▣
Cattamount, Grafty Green, Maidstone, Kent ME17 2AP
☎ (01622) 850245
Fax: (01622) 858063
Contact: Tom La Dell
Opening Times: By appt. only.
Min. Mail Order UK: £100.00 + p&p
Min. Mail Order EU: £200.00 + p&p
Cat. Cost: 2 x 1st class
Credit Cards: None
Specialities: Shrubs & perennials for low maintenance planting.
Map Ref: S, C5

S

SMac MACGREGORS PLANTS ✉ UK ▣
Carters Clay Road, Lockerley, Romsey,
Hampshire SO51 0GL
☎ (01794) 340256 **Fax:** (01794) 341828
Contact: Irene & Stuart Bowron
Opening Times: 1000-1600 Fri-Sun &
B/hol Mons Mar-Sep. Other times by appt.
Min. Mail Order UK: No minimum charge*
Cat. Cost: 3 x 1st class
Credit Cards: None
Specialities: Less common shrubs &
perennials, particularly for shade. National
Collection of *Phygelius*. Limited stocks of
rarer plants may be reserved prior to
propagation.
*Note: mail order restricted to small numbers
of plants sent by 24 hour carrier.
Map Ref: S, C2

SMad MADRONA NURSERY ✉ EU
Pluckley Road, Bethersden, Kent TN26 3DD
☎ (01233) 820100 **Fax:** (01233) 820091
Contact: Liam MacKenzie
Opening Times: 1000-1700 Sat-Tue 18th
Mar-31st Oct. Closed 7th-26th Aug.
Min. Mail Order UK: No minimum charge
Min. Mail Order EU: Nmc
Cat. Cost: Free
Credit Cards: Visa, MasterCard, American
Express, JCB, Switch
Specialities: Unusual shrubs, conifers &
perennials.
Map Ref: S, C5

SMcB MCBEANS ORCHIDS ✉ EU ▣ ▣
Cooksbridge, Lewes, Sussex BN8 4PR
☎ (01273) 400228 **Fax:** (01273) 401181
Contact: Jim Durrant
Opening Times: 1030-1600 7 days excl.
Xmas & Boxing Day, New Year & Good Fri.
Min. Mail Order UK: £29.95 incl.
Min. Mail Order EU: £100.00 + p&p
Cat. Cost: Free
Credit Cards: Visa, American Express, Access
Specialities: Orchids - *Cymbidium,
Odontoglossum, Phalaenopsis, Paphiopedilum,
Miltonia, Cattleya* & other genera.
Map Ref: S, D4

**SMer MERRYFIELD NURSERIES
(CANTERBURY) LTD** ✉ UK
Stodmarsh Road, Canterbury, Kent CT3 4AP
☎ (01227) 462602
E-mail: merry-field@tinyonline.co.uk
Contact: Mrs A Downs
Opening Times: 1000-1600 Mon, 0900-1730
Tue-Sat, 1000-1700 Sun & B/hol Mons.
Min. Mail Order UK: £10.00 + p&p
Cat. Cost: None issued at present

Credit Cards: Access, Visa, Switch
Specialities: Herbaceous & conifers.
Map Ref: S, C5

SMHT MOUNT HARRY TREES ◆
Offham, Lewes, East Sussex BN7 3QW
☎ (01273) 474 456 **Fax:** (01273) 474 266
Contact: A Renton
Opening Times: By appt.
Mail Order: None
Cat. Cost: 2 x 1st class
Credit Cards: None
Specialities: Full list of deciduous trees,
specialising in heavy-standard to semi-mature
sizes, incl. *Sophora japonica, Aesculus indica,
Tilia mongolica, Paulownia tomentosa, Sorbus
hupehensis.*
Map Ref: S, D4

SMrm MERRIMENTS GARDENS €
Hawkhurst Road, Hurst Green, East Sussex
TN19 7RA
☎ (01580) 860666 **Fax:** (01580) 860324
E-mail: info@merriments.co.uk
Web Site: www.merriments.co.uk
Contact: Mark & Amanda Buchele
Opening Times: 0930-1730 Mon-Sat,
1030-1730 Sun (or dusk in winter).
Mail Order: None
Cat. Cost: £1.00 + 2 x 1st class
Credit Cards: Visa, Access, American Express
Specialities: Unusual shrubs. Tender & hardy
perennials.
Map Ref: S, C4

SMur MURRELLS PLANT & GARDEN CENTRE
Broomers Hill Lane, Pulborough, West
Sussex RH20 2DU
☎ (01798) 875508 **Fax:** (01798) 872695
Contact: Clive Mellor
Opening Times: 0900-1730 summer,
0900-1700 winter, 1000-1600 Sun.
Mail Order: None
Cat. Cost: 3 x 1st class
Credit Cards: Switch, MasterCard, Visa, Solo
Specialities: Shrubs, trees & herbaceous
plants incl. many rare & unusual varieties.
Map Ref: S, D3

SNut NUTLIN NURSERY
Crowborough Road, Nutley, Nr Uckfield,
Sussex TN22 3HU
☎ (01825) 712670 **Fax:** (01825) 712670
Contact: Mrs Morven Cox

KEY		
✉	Mail order to UK or EU	
▣	Exports beyond EU	€ Euro accepted
▣	Also supplies Wholesale	◆ See Display advertisement

S

Opening Times: Phone in evening before visiting.
Mail Order: None
Cat. Cost: 1 x 1st class
Credit Cards: None
Specialities: *Hydrangea* & *Wisteria* and hardy ferns.
Map Ref: S, C4

SOkd OAKDENE NURSERY ⊠ EU ▣
Street End Lane, Broad Oak, Heathfield, East Sussex TN21 8TU
☎ (01435) 864382
Contact: David Sampson
Opening Times: 0900-1700 Wed-Sat excl. B/hols. Sun by appt.
Min. Mail Order UK: £10.00
Min. Mail Order EU: £25.00
Cat. Cost: 3 x 2nd class
Credit Cards: None
Specialities: Rare and unusual alpines. Woodland plants.
Map Ref: S, C4

SOkh OAKHURST NURSERY
Mardens Hill, Crowborough, East Sussex TN6 1XL
☎ (01892) 653273   **Fax:** (01892) 653273
E-mail: baileyp4@compuserve.com
Contact: Stephanie Colton
Opening Times: 1100-1700 most days mid Apr-mid Sep. Other times, & if travelling, please phone first esp. at w/ends.
Mail Order: None
Cat. Cost: 2 x 1st class
Credit Cards: None
Specialities: Common & uncommon herbaceous perennials.
Map Ref: S, C4

SOWG THE OLD WALLED GARDEN ▣
Oxonhoath, Hadlow, Kent TN11 9SS
☎ (01732) 810012   **Fax:** (01732) 810012
E-mail: amyrtle@aol.com
Contact: John & Heather Angrave
Opening Times: 0900-1700 Mon-Fri. W/ends by appt.
Mail Order: None
Credit Cards: None
Specialities: Many rare & unusual shrubs. Wide range of conservatory plants esp. Australian. National Collection of *Callistemon*.
Map Ref: S, C4

SPan PANDORA NURSERY
(Office) 17 Quail Way, Horndean, Waterlooville, Hampshire PO8 9YN
☎ (023) 9259 7323, mobile 07767 606053/54

E-mail: Paul@pandoranursery.demon.co.uk
Contact: Paul & Amanda O'Carroll
Opening Times: 1000-1600 Wed-Fri Mar-end Oct. Also by appt.
Mail Order: None
Cat. Cost: 2 x 1st class & C5 Sae.
Credit Cards: None
Specialities: *Cistus* & *Euphorbia,* plus expanding range of garden-worthy shrubs & climbers. *Lonicera,* shrubby, *Ozothamnus, Olearia, Spiraca, Callistemon.* Note: nursery is at The Walled Garden, Bury Lodge Estate, West Street, Hambledon, Hants.
Map Ref: S, D2

SPar THE PARADISE GARDEN ▣
The Courtyard, at Stable Antiques, 46 West Street, Storrington, West Sussex RH20 4EE
☎ (01903) 740540
Fax: (01903) 740441
E-mail: pargard@aol.com
Contact: Clive Parker
Opening Times: 1000-1800 Wed-Sun British Summer Time, 1000-dusk Fri-Sun winter. Please phone before visiting.
Mail Order: None
Cat. Cost: None issued
Credit Cards: Visa, MasterCard, Access, American Express, Switch, Delta
Specialities: Architectural & foliage plants.
Map Ref: S, D3

SPer PERRYHILL NURSERIES ▣
Hartfield, East Sussex TN7 4JP
☎ (01892) 770377   **Fax:** (01892) 770929
Contact: P J Chapman (Manager)
Opening Times: 0900-1700 7 days 1st Mar-31st Oct. 0900-1630 1st Nov-28th Feb.
Mail Order: None
Cat. Cost: £1.65
Credit Cards: Visa, Access, MasterCard, EuroCard, Switch
Specialities: Wide range of trees, shrubs, conifers, *Rhododendron* etc. Over 1300 herbaceous varieties, over 500 varieties of roses. Note: export for large orders only.
Map Ref: S, C4

SPet PETTET'S NURSERY ▣
Poison Cross, Eastry, Sandwich, Kent CT13 0EA
☎ (01304) 613869   **Fax:** (01304) 613869
E-mail: pettetsnursery@eastrysandwich.-freeserve.co.uk
Contact: T & EHP Pettet
Opening Times: 0900-1700 daily Mar-June. 1000-1600 daily July-Dec.
Mail Order: None

Credit Cards: None
Specialities: Climbers, shrubs, herbaceous perennials & alpines, pelargoniums & fuchsias.
Map Ref: S, C6

SPla   PLAXTOL NURSERIES ⊠ EU
The Spoute, Plaxtol, Sevenoaks, Kent TN15 0QR
☎ (01732) 810550
Fax: (01732) 810149
E-mail: info@plaxtol-nurseries.co.uk
Web Site: www.plaxtol-nurseries.co.uk
Contact: Tessa, Donald & Jenny Forbes
Opening Times: 1000-1700 7 days. Closed 2 weeks from Xmas Eve.
Min. Mail Order UK: £10.00 + p&p*
Min. Mail Order EU: £30.00 + p&p
Cat. Cost: 2 x 1st class
Credit Cards: Visa, American Express, MasterCard
Specialities: Hardy shrubs & herbaceous esp. for flower arrangers. Old-fashioned roses, ferns & climbers.
*Note: mail order Nov-Mar only.
Map Ref: S, C4

SPlb   PLANTBASE ⊠ UK
(Office) 37 Forest Road, Hawkenbury, Tunbridge Wells, Kent TN2 5AL
☎ (01892) 617011
Fax: (01892) 617011
E-mail: graham@plantbase.freeserve.co.uk
Contact: Graham Blunt
Opening Times: Not open to the public.
Mail Order: Only
Cat. Cost: 2 x 1st class
Credit Cards: None
Specialities: A wide range of alpines, perennials, shrubs, climbers, waterside plants, herbs & Australasian shrubs.

SPLN   PAULS LANE NURSERY ⊡
Hollybush Cottage, Pauls Lane, Sway, Lymington, Hampshire SO41 6BR
☎ (01590) 683864
Fax: (01590) 683864
E-mail: Paulsnursery@farmersweekly.net
Contact: F R Toyne
Opening Times: 1000-1700 w/ends Mar-Oct. 1100-1500 w/ends Nov-Dec. Other times by appt.
Mail Order: None
Cat. Cost: 2 x 1st class
Credit Cards: None
Specialities: Ornamental grasses and plants for the Mediterranean look. Note: nursery is 300 yards down the lane from the cottage.
Map Ref: S, D2

SPop   POPS PLANTS ⊠ EU ⊡
Pops Cottage, Barford Lane, Downton, Salisbury, Wiltshire SP5 3PZ
☎ (01725) 511421   Fax: (01425) 653472
E-mail: pops@downton51.freeserve.co.uk
Contact: G Dawson
Opening Times: Strictly by appt. only.
Min. Mail Order UK: No minimum charge
Min. Mail Order EU: Nmc
Cat. Cost: 1 x 1st class
Credit Cards: Visa, Switch, MasterCard
Specialities: *Primula auricula.* Please note new location.

SRCN   ROSE COTTAGE NURSERY ⊠ EU
Rose Cottage, Kingsley Common, Nr Bordon, Hampshire GU35 9NF
☎ (01420) 489071   Fax: (01420) 476629
E-mail: elliot@wordshop.co.uk
Web Site: www.hyperstore.co.uk/rose
Contact: Ian Elliot
Opening Times: Open by appt. Mar-Oct.
Min. Mail Order UK: No minimum charge
Min. Mail Order EU: £20.00 + p&p
Cat. Cost: 3 x 1st class
Credit Cards: None
Specialities: Drought tolerant plants, mainly fully hardy. Suit most conditions but ideal for Mediterranean or gravel gardens.
Map Ref: S, C3

SReu   G REUTHE LTD ⊠ EU
Crown Point Nursery, Sevenoaks Road, Ightham, Nr Sevenoaks, Kent TN15 0HB
☎ (01732) 810694   Fax: (01732) 862166
Contact: C Tomlin & P Kindley
Opening Times: 0900-1630 Mon-Sat. 1000-1630 Sun & B/hols Apr & May only, occasionally in June, please check. Closed Jan, Jul & Aug.
Min. Mail Order UK: £25.00 + p&p
Min. Mail Order EU: £500.00*
Cat. Cost: £2.00
Credit Cards: Visa, Access
Specialities: Rhododendrons & azaleas, trees, shrubs & climbers. *Note: certain plants only to EU & export.
Map Ref: S, C4

SRGP   ROSIE'S GARDEN PLANTS ⊠ EU ⊡
Rochester Road, Aylesford, Kent ME20 7EB
☎ (01622) 715777   Fax: (01622) 715777
E-mail: JC Aviolet@aol.com
Contact: J C A'violét
Opening Times: 1000-1700 Wed-Sat 1st Mar-30 Sep 2000.
Min. Mail Order UK: No minimum charge
Min. Mail Order EU: Nmc
Cat. Cost: 2 x 1st class

S

Credit Cards: Visa, MasterCard, Switch
Specialities: Hardy *Geranium*.
Map Ref: S, C5

SRiv   RIVER GARDEN NURSERIES ✉ EU ▣
Troutbeck, Otford, Sevenoaks, Kent
TN14 5PH
☎ (01959) 525588   Fax: (01959) 525810
E-mail: alban@atlas.co.uk
Contact: Jenny Alban Davies
Opening Times: By appt. only.
Min. Mail Order UK: £10.00 + p&p
Min. Mail Order EU: £50.00 + p&p
Cat. Cost: 2 x 1st class
Credit Cards: None
Specialities: *Buxus* species, cultivars &
hedging. *Buxus* topiary.
Map Ref: S, C4

S **SRms   RUMSEY GARDENS** ✉ EU ▣ ◆
117 Drift Road, Clanfield, Waterlooville,
Hampshire PO8 0PD
☎ (023) 9259 3367
E-mail: info@rumsey-gardens.co.uk
Web Site: www.rumsey-gardens.co.uk
Contact: Mr N R Giles
Opening Times: 0900-1700 Mon-Sat,
1000-1700 Sun & B/hols.
Min. Mail Order UK: No minimum charge
Min. Mail Order EU: Nmc
Cat. Cost: See web site
Credit Cards: None
Specialities: Wide general range. National
Collection of *Cotoneaster*.
Map Ref: S, D2

SRob   ROBINS NURSERY
Coldharbour Road, Upper Dicker, Hailsham,
East Sussex BN27 3PY
☎ (01323) 844734
E-mail: robnurse@robnurse.free-online.co.uk
Web Site: www.robnurse.free-online.co.uk
Contact: Stuart Dye
Opening Times: 1100-1700 Thu-Sun &
B/hol Mons Mar-Oct.
Mail Order: None
Cat. Cost: Free
Credit Cards: MasterCard, Visa
Specialities: Small retail nursery specialising
in herbaceous plants & shrubs incl. *Aquilegia,
Alcea, Digitalis, Viburnum & Verbascum*, plus
a good selection of kitchen herbs.
Map Ref: S, D4

SRos   ROSEWOOD DAYLILIES ✉ UK
70 Deansway Avenue, Sturry, Nr Canterbury,
Kent CT2 0NN
☎ (01227) 711071
Contact: Chris Searle

Opening Times: By appt. only. Please phone.
Min. Mail Order UK: No minimum charge
Cat. Cost: 2 x 1st class
Credit Cards: None
Specialities: *Hemerocallis*, mainly newer
American varieties.
Map Ref: S, C5

SRot   ROTHERVIEW NURSERY ✉ EU ▣
Ivy House Lane, Three Oaks, Hastings, East
Sussex TN35 4NP
☎ (01424) 717141/756228
Fax: (01424) 428944
E-mail: rotherview@supanet.com
Contact: Ray Bates
Opening Times: 1000-1700 Mar-Oct,
1000-1530 Nov-Feb, 7 days.
Min. Mail Order UK: £10.00 + p&p
Min. Mail Order EU: £20.00 + p&p
Cat. Cost: 2 x 1st class
Credit Cards: None
Specialities: Alpines.
Map Ref: S, D5

**SRPl   ROGER PLATTS GARDEN DESIGN &
NURSERIES**
Stick Hill, Edenbridge, Kent TN8 5NH
☎ (01732) 863318   Fax: (01732) 863318
E-mail: plattsgdn@aol.com
Contact: Patricia Marchant
Opening Times: 0900-1700 7 days.
Mail Order: None
Cat. Cost: Available shortly
Credit Cards: Access, Visa, American Express
Specialities: Perennials, roses, shrubs,
specimen sized plants.
Map Ref: S, C4

SRum   RUMWOOD NURSERIES ✉ EU ▣
Langley, Maidstone, Kent ME17 3ND
☎ (01622) 861477   Fax: (01622) 863123
Contact: Mr R Fermor or Mr J Fermor
Opening Times: 0900-1700 Mon-Sat,
1000-1600 Sun.
Min. Mail Order UK: No minimum charge
Min. Mail Order EU: Nmc
Cat. Cost: 1 x 2nd class
Credit Cards: Visa, Access, American
Express, Switch, Solo
Specialities: Roses, trees, shrubs & conifers.
Map Ref: S, C5

SSad   MRS JANE SADLER
Ingrams Cottage, Wisborough Green,
Billingshurst, West Sussex RH14 0ER
☎ (01403) 700234   Fax: (01403) 700234
Contact: Mrs Jane Sadler
Opening Times: Irregular. Please phone first.
Mail Order: None

Cat. Cost: Sae
Credit Cards: None
Specialities: Small nursery specialising in less common varieties esp. auriculas, *Lavandula* & *Pelargonium*.
Map Ref: S, C3

SSca   SCALERS HILL NURSERY
Scalers Hill, Cobham, Nr Gravesend, Kent DA12 3BH
☎ (01474) 822856
Contact: Mrs Ann Booth
Opening Times: 0900-1600 Wed-Sat mid Mar-end Oct, or by appt.
Mail Order: None
Cat. Cost: 2 x 1st class
Credit Cards: None
Specialities: Unusual perennials & alpines.
Map Ref: S, B4

SScr   SCREE GARDENS €
56 Valley Drive, Loose, Maidstone, Kent ME15 9TL
☎ (01622) 746941
Contact: Michael Brett
Opening Times: 1000-1700 Sat & Sun Apr-Aug. Garden open under NGS. Due to occasional absence at shows, please phone first.
Mail Order: None
Cat. Cost: None issued
Credit Cards: None
Specialities: Rock garden, scree, trough & herbaceous plants.
Map Ref: S, C5

SSea   SEALE NURSERIES ⊠ EU ◆
Seale Lane, Seale, Farnham, Surrey GU10 1LD
☎ (01252) 782410   Fax: (01252) 783038
E-mail: plants@sealenurseries.demon.co.uk
Web Site: www.sealenurseries.demon.co.uk
Contact: David May
Opening Times: 0900-1700 7 days.
Min. Mail Order UK: £10.00 + p&p
Min. Mail Order EU: £10.00 + p&p
Cat. Cost: 2 x 2nd class
Credit Cards: Visa, Switch, Access
Specialities: *Pelargonium, Fuchsia,* roses, herbaceous.
Map Ref: S, C3

SSht   STONEHURST NURSERY ⊠ UK ▣
Little Stonehurst Farm, Pottens Mill Lane, Broad Oak, Heathfield, East Sussex TN21 8UA
☎ (01435) 810124   Fax: (01435) 810124
E-mail: sales@stonehurstnursery.co.uk
Web Site: www.stonehurstnursery.co.uk
Contact: Mr Brian Lewington
Opening Times: Not open to the public.

E-mail, fax or phone at all reasonable times.
Min. Mail Order UK: No minimum charge
Cat. Cost: Free
Credit Cards: Visa, MasterCard, Electron, Switch, Solo, JCB, Maestro
Specialities: Interesting & unusual selection of shrubs, specialising in acid lovers. Wide variety of field & container-grown hedging plants suitable for inland & coastal areas.

SSmi   ALAN C SMITH ⊠ UK
127 Leaves Green Road, Keston, Kent BR2 6DG
☎ (01959) 572531
Contact: Alan C Smith
Opening Times: By appt. only.
Min. Mail Order UK: No minimum charge
Cat. Cost: 50p
Credit Cards: None
Specialities: *Sempervivum* & *Jovibarba*.
Map Ref: S, C4

SSmt   PETER J SMITH ⊠ EU ▣
Chanctonbury Nurseries, Rectory Lane, Ashington, Pulborough, Sussex RH20 3AS
☎ (01903) 892870   Fax: (01903) 893036
E-mail: petersmith@plillies.globalnet.co.uk
Contact: Sales Dept. (Valerie)
Opening Times: 1000-1300 Mon-Fri 1st Apr-30th Sep.
Min. Mail Order UK: £6.00 + p&p
Min. Mail Order EU: £30.00 + p&p
Cat. Cost: 1 x 1st class
Credit Cards: Visa, Access, MasterCard
Specialities: The Princess & Little Princess ranges of hybrid *Alstroemeria* for conservatory & garden. Also hybrid *Limonium* & *Freesia*. Gipsy *Dianthus. Euphorbia molii*.
Map Ref: S, D3

SSoC   SOUTHCOTT NURSERY ⊠ UK
Southcott, South Street, Lydd, Romney Marsh, Kent TN29 9DQ
☎ (01797) 321848
Fax: (01797) 321848
E-mail: southcottnursery@yahoo.co.uk
Contact: Suzy Clark
Opening Times: 1300-1730 Tues-Sat.
Min. Mail Order UK: £10.00 + p&p
Cat. Cost: 3 x 1st class
Credit Cards: None
Specialities: Unusual hardy & half-hardy perennials & shrubs.
Map Ref: S, C5

K E Y		
	⊠ Mail order to UK or EU	
	✈ Exports beyond EU	€ Euro accepted
	▣ Also supplies Wholesale	◆ See Display advertisement

S

SSpe   SPELDHURST NURSERIES
Langton Road, Speldhurst, Tunbridge Wells,
Kent TN3 0NR
☎ (01892) 862682   **Fax:** (01892) 862682
Contact: Christine & Stephen Lee
Opening Times: 1000-1700 Wed-Sat excl.
Jan. 1000-1600 Sun Mar-Jul & Sep-Oct.
Mail Order: None
Cat. Cost: 4 x 1st class for list.
Credit Cards: MasterCard, Visa, Switch,
Delta, American Express
Specialities: Herbaceous.
Map Ref: S, C4

SSpi   SPINNERS GARDEN €
Boldre, Lymington, Hampshire SO41 5QE
☎ (01590) 673347
Contact: Peter Chappell & Kevin Hughes
Opening Times: 1000-1700 Tue-Sat. Sun &
Mon by appt. only.
Mail Order: None
Cat. Cost: 3 x 1st class
Credit Cards: None
Specialities: Less common trees & shrubs
esp. *Acer, Magnolia,* species & lace-cap
Hydrangea. Woodland & bog plants.
National Collection of *Trillium.*
Map Ref: S, D2

SSpr   SPRINGBANK NURSERIES ⊠ EU ◪
Winford Road, Newchurch, Sandown, Isle of
Wight PO36 0JX
☎ (01983) 865444   **Fax:** (01983) 868688
Contact: K Hall
Opening Times: 7 days Sep-Oct. Collections
by appt. Specific open days to be advertised.
Min. Mail Order UK: £10.00 + p&p
Min. Mail Order EU: £25.00 + p&p
Cat. Cost: £1.50
Credit Cards: None
Specialities: *Nerine sarniensis* hybrids (over
600 varieties) & some species. National
Collection of *Nerine sarniensis.*
Map Ref: S, D2

SSta   STARBOROUGH NURSERY ⊠ EU
Starborough Road, Marsh Green,
Edenbridge, Kent TN8 5RB
☎ (01732) 865614
Fax: (01732) 862166
Contact: C Tomlin & P Kindley
Opening Times: 1000-1600 Mon-Sat.
Closed Jan, Jul & Aug & most Weds.
Min. Mail Order UK: £25.00 + p&p
Min. Mail Order EU: £500.00*
Cat. Cost: £2.00
Credit Cards: Visa, Access
Specialities: Rare and unusual shrubs esp.
Daphne, Acer, rhododendrons & azaleas,
Magnolia & *Hamamelis.* *Note: certain
plants only to EU.
Map Ref: S, C4

SSte   STENBURY NURSERY ⊠ UK €
Smarts Cross, Southford, Nr Whitwell, Isle
of Wight PO38 2AG
☎ (01983) 840115   **Fax:** (01983) 811861
E-mail: stenburynursery@netscapeonline.co.uk
Contact: Mr B Clarke
Opening Times: 0900-1730 summer, 0930-
1600 winter Mon, Fri, Sat & Sun.
Min. Mail Order UK: No minimum charge
Cat. Cost: 2 x 1st class stamps
Credit Cards: None
Specialities: Passifloras, melaleucas,
callistemons and other Australian plants,
solanums, aquilegias, *Digitalis,* salvias, asclepias
and lobelias.
Map Ref: S, D2

SStn   STONEHURST NURSERIES ⊠ EU ◪ ◪
Selsfield Road, Ardingly, Haywards Heath,
Sussex RH17 6TN
☎ (01444) 892488   **Fax:** (01444) 892488
E-mail: stonehurst@compuserve.com
Web Site: www.stonehurstnurseries.com
Contact: N. Creek (camellias), A Bannister
(orchids)
Opening Times: 0900-1300 & 1400-1700
Tue-Sun. Open B/hol Mons.
Min. Mail Order UK: £5.00 + p&p
Min. Mail Order EU: £5.00 + p&p
Cat. Cost: 2 x 1st class
Credit Cards: Visa, MasterCard
Specialities: Orchids & camellias.
Map Ref: S, C4

SSww   SOUTHVIEW NURSERIES ⊠ UK ◆ €
Chequers Lane, Eversley Cross, Hook,
Hampshire RG27 0NT
☎ (0118) 9732206
Contact: Mark & Elaine Trenear
Opening Times: 1000-1630 Wed-Sat
1st Mar-30 Sep. Please phone first.
Min. Mail Order UK: No minimum charge
Cat. Cost: Free
Credit Cards: None
Specialities: Unusual hardy plants, specialising
in old fashioned pinks & period plants.
National Collection of old pinks.
Map Ref: S, C3

STes   TEST VALLEY NURSERY
Stockbridge Road, Timsbury, Romsey,
Hampshire SO51 0NG
☎ (01794) 368881
Contact: Julia Benn
Opening Times: 1000-1600 Tue-Fri,

1100-1700 Sat & Sun Mar-Oct.
Mail Order: None
Cat. Cost: 3 x 2nd class
Credit Cards: None
Specialities: Small nursery with range of herbaceous perennials, specialising in unusual & new varieties. Limited quantities of some varieties. Please phone first to avoid disappointment.
Map Ref: S, C2

STil TILE BARN NURSERY ⊠ EU ▣ ▣
Standen Street, Iden Green, Benenden, Kent TN17 4LB
☎ (01580) 240221 **Fax:** (01580) 240221
Contact: Peter Moore
Opening Times: 0900-1700 Wed-Sat.
Min. Mail Order UK: £10.00 + p&p
Min. Mail Order EU: £25.00 + p&p
Cat. Cost: Sae
Credit Cards: None
Specialities: *Cyclamen* species.
Map Ref: S, C5

STre PETER TRENEAR ⊠ EU
Chantreyland, Chequers Lane, Eversley Cross, Hampshire RG27 0NX
☎ (0118) 9732300
E-mail: petertrenear@bonsai2.demon.co.uk
Contact: Peter Trenear
Opening Times: 0900-1630 Mon-Sat.
Min. Mail Order UK: £5.00 + p&p
Cat. Cost: 1 x 1st class
Credit Cards: None
Specialities: Trees, shrubs, conifers & *Pinus*.
Map Ref: S, C3

SUsu USUAL & UNUSUAL PLANTS
Onslow House, Magham Down, Hailsham, East Sussex BN27 1PL
☎ (01323) 840967 **Fax:** (01323) 844725
E-mail: jennie@onslow.clara.net
Contact: Jennie Maillard
Opening Times: 0930-1730 Wed-Sat & B/hol Mons 1st Mar-31st Oct.
Mail Order: None
Cat. Cost: Sae + 50p
Credit Cards: None
Specialities: Small quantities of a wide variety of unusual perennials esp. *Diascia, Erysimum, Euphorbia,* hardy *Geranium, Salvia* & grasses.
Map Ref: S, D4

SVal VALE NURSERY ⊠ EU
Heath Cottage, Hayes Lane, Stockbury Valley, Sittingbourne, Kent ME9 7QH
☎ (01795) 844004 **Fax:** (01795) 842991
E-mail: info@valenursery.co.uk
Web Site: www.valenursery.co.uk

Contact: Anthony Clarke
Opening Times: Not open to the public. Mail order only.
Min. Mail Order UK: £5.00
Cat. Cost: 2 x 1st class
Credit Cards: None
Specialities: Herbaceous perennials.

SVen VENTNOR BOTANIC GARDEN
Undercliff Drive, Ventnor, Isle of Wight PO38 1UL
☎ (01983) 852198 **Fax:** (01983) 856154
E-mail: simon@vbg1.demon.co.uk
Web Site: http://botanic.co.uk
Contact: Simon Goodenough & Jan Wyers
Opening Times: 1000-1700 7 days Mar-Oct.
Mail Order: None
Credit Cards: MasterCard, Visa
Map Ref: S, D2

SVil THE VILLAGE NURSERIES ◆
Sinnocks, West Chiltington, Pulborough, West Sussex RH20 2JX
☎ (01798) 813040 **Fax:** (01798) 813040
Contact: Peter Manfield
Opening Times: 0900-1800 or dusk, 7 days.
Mail Order: None
Cat. Cost: Free plant list for hardy perennials & grasses.
Credit Cards: Visa, Delta, MasterCard, Switch
Specialities: Retail nursery specialising in a wide range of hardy perennials & grasses, incl. many new varieties. Also, selected shrubs, conifers, climbers, roses & trees.
Map Ref: S, D3

SWal WALLACE PLANTS
Lewes Road Nursery, Lewes Road, Laughton, East Sussex BN8 6BN
☎ (01323) 811729
Contact: Simon Wallace
Opening Times: 0930-1800 or dusk if earlier.
Mail Order: None
Cat. Cost: 3 x 1st class
Credit Cards: None
Specialities: Ornamental grasses, hebes, fuchsias, hardy geraniums, salvias, penstemons, some unusual plants.
Map Ref: S, D4

SWat WATER MEADOW
NURSERY ⊠ EU ▣ ▣ €
Cheriton, Nr Alresford, Hampshire SO24 0QB
☎ (01962) 771895, (01962) 771895
Fax: (01962) 771895
E-mail: watermeadowplants@msn.com
Web Site: www.plantaholic.co.uk
Contact: Mrs Sandy Worth
Opening Times: 0900-1700 Wed-Sat Mar-

Oct or by appt.
Min. Mail Order UK: £10.00 + p&p
Min. Mail Order EU: £50.00 + p&p
Cat. Cost: 4 x 1st class or £1.00 cheque
Credit Cards: Visa, MasterCard
Specialities: Water lilies, extensive water garden plants, unusual herbaceous perennials, aromatic herbs & wild flowers. National Collection of *Papaver orientale* group.
Map Ref: S, C2

SWCr   WYCH CROSS NURSERIES
Wych Cross, Forest Row, East Sussex
RH18 5JW
☎ (01342) 822705   **Fax:** (01342) 825329
E-mail: roses@wychcross.co.uk
Web Site: www.wychcross.co.uk
Contact: J Paisley
Opening Times: 0900-1730 Mon-Sat.
Mail Order: None
Cat. Cost: Free catalogue
Credit Cards: Visa, MasterCard, Delta, Switch
Specialities: Roses.
Map Ref: S, C4

SWyc   WYCHWOOD WATERLILY & CARP FARM ⊠ EU ⊠
Farnham Road, Odiham, Hook, Hampshire
RG29 1HS
☎ (01256) 702800   **Fax:** (01256) 701001
E-mail: cnhenley@aol.com
Contact: Reg, Ann & Clair Henley
Opening Times: 1000-1800 7 days
Min. Mail Order UK: £1.00 + p&p
Min. Mail Order EU: £1.00 + p&p
Cat. Cost: 2 x 1st class
Credit Cards: Visa, Access, Switch, Solo
Specialities: Aquatics. *Nymphaea*, moisture loving, marginals & oxygenating plants. Moist & water *Iris* incl. American *I. ensata*. National Collection of *Nymphaea*.
Map Ref: S, C3

SYvo   YVONNE'S PLANTS
66 The Ridgway, Woodingdean, Brighton, East Sussex BN2 6PD
☎ (01273) 300883
E-mail: yvonnesplants@cdlaw.freeserve.co.uk
Web Site:
www.cdlaw.freeserve.co.uk/yvonnes plants
Contact: Yvonne Law
Opening Times: Mar-Oct by appt. only.
Mail Order: None
Cat. Cost: None issued.
Credit Cards: None
Specialities: Conservatory, tender & herbaceous perennials, incl. *Abutilon, Cestrum, Agapanthus, Canna, Fuchsia, Hedychium*.
Map Ref: S, D4

WALES AND THE WEST

WAba   ABACUS NURSERIES ⊠ EU ⊠
Drummau Road, Skewen, Neath, Wales
SA10 6NW
☎ (01792) 817994 (evenings)
E-mail: plants@abacus-dahlias.co.uk
Web Site: www.abacus-dahlias.co.uk
Contact: David Hill
Opening Times: Not open to the public. Collection by arrangement.
Min. Mail Order UK: No minimum charge
Min. Mail Order EU: Nmc
Cat. Cost: 1 x 2nd class
Credit Cards: None
Specialities: *Dahlia*.
Map Ref: W, D3

WAbb   ABBEY DORE COURT GARDENS
Abbeydore, Nr Hereford, Herefordshire
HR2 0AD
☎ (01981) 240419
Fax: (01981) 240419
Contact: Mrs C Ward
Opening Times: 1100-1800 daily. Closed Mon excl. B/hols. Wed 8th Apr-30th Sep. Parties by arrangement. Suns in Oct.
Mail Order: None
Cat. Cost: None issued
Credit Cards: None
Specialities: Shrubs & hardy perennials, many unusual, which may be seen growing in the garden.
Map Ref: W, C4

WAbe   ABERCONWY NURSERY
Graig, Glan Conwy, Colwyn Bay, Conwy, Wales LL28 5TL
☎ (01492) 580875
Contact: Dr & Mrs K G Lever
Opening Times: 1000-1700 Tue-Sun Feb-Oct. W/ends only Nov-Jan.
Mail Order: None
Cat. Cost: 2 x 2nd class
Credit Cards: Visa, MasterCard
Specialities: Alpines, including specialist varieties, esp. autumn gentians, *Saxifraga* & dwarf ericaceous. Shrubs, conifers & woodland plants incl. *Helleborus* & *Epimedium*.
Map Ref: W, A3

WAct   ACTON BEAUCHAMP ROSES ⊠ EU ⊠
Acton Beauchamp, Worcester, Worcestershire
WR6 5AE
☎ (01531) 640433   **Fax:** (01531) 640802
Contact: Lindsay Bousfield
Opening Times: 1000-1700 summer 1000-1600 winter Tue-Sat & B/hol Mons, 1400-1700 Sun May-Sep.

Min. Mail Order UK: No minimum charge
Min. Mail Order EU: Nmc
Cat. Cost: 3 x 1st class
Credit Cards: Visa, MasterCard, EuroCard
Specialities: Species roses, old roses, modern shrub, English, climbers, ramblers & ground-cover roses.
Map Ref: W, C4

WAlt ALTERNATIVES ⊠ UK
The Brackens, Yorkley Wood, Nr Lydney, Gloucestershire GL15 4TU
☎ (01594) 562457
E-mail: altern@lineone.net
Web Site: www.website.lineone.net/~altern
Contact: Mrs Rosemary Castle
Opening Times: Mail order only.
Min. Mail Order UK: £4.50*
Cat. Cost: 3 x 1st class
Credit Cards: None
Specialities: Unusual forms of common British natives incl. *Bellis, Ranunculus, Trifolium* & *Urtica*. *Note: small stocks, spring/autumn supply only.

WAul AULDEN FARM
Aulden, Leominster, Herefordshire HR6 0JT
☎ (01568) 720129
E-mail: pf@auldenfarm.co.uk
Web Site: www.auldenfarm.co.uk
Contact: Alun & Jill Whitehead
Opening Times: 1200-1700 Tue & Thu Apr-Sep.
Mail Order: None
Cat. Cost: Sae
Credit Cards: None
Specialities: Hardy herbaceous perennials & some shrubs with a special interest in *Hemerocallis* & *Iris ensata*.
Map Ref: W, C4

WBaG BALMER GROVE PLANTS
Welshampton,, Shropshire SY12 0PP
☎ (01948) 710403
Contact: Nick & Gill Eleftheriou
Opening Times: 0930-1800 most days (except Thu) Mar-Oct, please phone to check times.
Mail Order: None
Cat. Cost: None issued
Credit Cards: None
Specialities: Selected unusual hardy garden plants, mainly herbaceous perennials, all carefully home-grown in loam-based compost.
Map Ref: W, B4

WBar BARNCROFT NURSERIES ⊠ UK ▣
Olden Lane, Ruyton-xi-Towns, Shrewsbury, Shropshire SY4 1JD

☎ (01939) 261619
Contact: Mrs R E Eccleston
Opening Times: 1000-1730 Tue-Sat, 1000-1600 Sun. Closed throughout Jan.
Min. Mail Order UK: £10.00 + p&p
Cat. Cost: 2 x 1st class
Credit Cards: None
Specialities: Wide range of unusual herbaceous plants, shrubs, water plants and ferns, as well as cottage garden favourites.
Map Ref: W, B4

WBcn BEACON'S NURSERIES
Tewkesbury Road, Eckington, Nr Pershore, Worcestershire WR10 3DE
☎ (01386) 750359
Contact: Jonathan Beacon
Opening Times: 0900-1300 & 1400-1700 Mon-Sat, 1400-1700 Sun. (Closed 25th Dec-1st Jan.)
Mail Order: None
Cat. Cost: 4 x 1st class
Credit Cards: None
Specialities: Shrubs, camellias, herbaceous, aquatics, conifers, climbing plants & roses.
Map Ref: W, B5

WBea BEACONS' BOTANICALS ⊠ UK
Banc-y-Felin, Carregsawdde, Llangadog, Carmarthenshire, Wales SA19 9DA
☎ (01550) 777992
Contact: Mrs S H Williams
Opening Times: Most w/days, phone first.
Min. Mail Order UK: £10.00 + p&p
Cat. Cost: 2 x 1st class
Credit Cards: None
Specialities: Hardy *Geranium, Allium, Campanula, Persicaria*, unusual mints & hardy bulbs, *Veronica*. Extensive range of rare & unusual herbaceous plants.
Map Ref: W, C3

WBod BODNANT GARDEN NURSERY LTD ⊠ EU ▣
Tal-y-Cafn, Colwyn Bay, Clwyd, Wales LL28 5RE
☎ (01492) 650731 Fax: (01492) 650863
E-mail: sales@bodnant.co.uk
Web Site: www.bodnant.co.uk
Contact: Sian Grindley
Opening Times: All year.
Min. Mail Order UK: No minimum charge
Min. Mail Order EU: Nmc
Cat. Cost: £2 refundable with first order

K E Y	
⊠	Mail order to UK or EU
▣	Exports beyond EU € Euro accepted
▣	Also supplies Wholesale ◆ See Display advertisement

W

Credit Cards: Visa, MasterCard, Switch, Connect, American Express
Specialities: *Rhododendron, Camellia* & *Magnolia.* Wide range of unusual trees and shrubs.
Map Ref: W, A3

WBor   BORDERVALE PLANTS
Nantyderi, Sandy Lane, Ystradowen, Cowbridge, Vale of Glamorgan, Wales CF71 7SX
☎ (01446) 774036
Contact: Claire E Jenkins
Opening Times: 1000-1700 Fri-Sun & B/hols Apr-Sep. 1000-1700 Sat & Sun Oct. Other times by appt.
Mail Order: None
Cat. Cost: 1st class Sae
Credit Cards: None
Specialities: Unusual herbaceous perennials & cottage garden plants, many displayed in the garden.
Map Ref: W, D3

WBou   BOUTS COTTAGE NURSERIES ✉ EU
Bouts Lane, Inkberrow, Worcestershire WR7 4HP
☎ (01386) 792923
Contact: M & S Roberts
Opening Times: Not open to the public.
Min. Mail Order UK: No minimum charge
Min. Mail Order EU: Nmc
Cat. Cost: Sae
Credit Cards: None
Specialities: *Viola.*

WBrE   BRON EIFION NURSERY ✉ UK
Bron Eifion, Criccieth, Gwynedd LL52 0SA
☎ (01766) 522890
Contact: Suzanne Evans
Opening Times: 1000-dusk 7 days 1st Mar-31st Oct. 1st Nov-29th Feb by appt. only.
Min. Mail Order UK: £30.00 + p&p
Cat. Cost: 4 x 2nd class
Credit Cards: None
Specialities: *Kalmia, Embothrium,* plants for coastal regions & wide range of hardy plants.
Map Ref: W, B2

WBro   BROOK FARM PLANTS ✉ UK
Boulsdon Lane, Newent, Gloucestershire GL18 1JH
☎ (01531) 822534
E-mail: sally@brookfarm.fsbusiness.co.uk
Web Site: www.brookfarm.fsbusiness.co.uk
Contact: Mrs S E Keene
Opening Times: 1400-1700 Wed-Sat Apr-Oct. Most other times by appt.
Min. Mail Order UK: No minimum charge

Cat. Cost: 2 x 2nd class
Credit Cards: None
Specialities: *Digitalis, Papaver, Schizostylis* & other unusual perennials.
Map Ref: W, C4

WBry   JULIA'S GARDEN
(Office) Bryn Tirion, Pen-y-felin, Nannerch, Flintshire, Wales CH7 5RW
☎ (01352) 741498   Fax: (01352) 741498
E-mail: jon03@globalnet.co.uk
Contact: Julia White
Opening Times: 1000-1600 Sat & Sun 6th May-17th Sep 2000, 5th May-16th Sep 2001.
Mail Order: None
Cat. Cost: 2 x 1st class
Credit Cards: None
Specialities: *Alcea, Mentha, Origanum, Digitalis* & *Angelica.* Note: nursery is at Bryn Ffynnon Fields Nursery, Bontuchel, Ruthin, LL15 2BL.
Map Ref: W, A3

WBuc   BUCKNELL NURSERIES 🌿
Bucknell, Shropshire SY7 0EL
☎ (01547) 530606   Fax: (01547) 530699
Contact: A N Coull
Opening Times: 0800-1700 Mon-Fri, 1000-1300 Sat.
Mail Order: None
Cat. Cost: Free
Credit Cards: None
Specialities: Bare-rooted hedging conifers & forest trees.
Map Ref: W, C4

WByw   BYEWAYS
Daisy Lane, Whittington, Oswestry, Shropshire SY11 4EA
☎ (01691) 659539
Contact: Barbara Molesworth
Opening Times: By appt. only. Please phone first.*
Mail Order: None
Cat. Cost: Sae + 1 x 2nd class
Credit Cards: None
Specialities: *Aster, Campanula,* hardy *Geranium* & *Pulmonaria.* *Note: also at Newtown Market on Tue.
Map Ref: W, B4

WCDu   CASTELL DU PLANTS ✉ UK 🌿
Castell Du, Dolgran, Pencader, Carmarthenshire, Wales SA39 9BX
☎ (01559) 384535
E-mail: annellio@castelldu-plants.co.uk
Contact: Nick & Ann Elliott
Opening Times: By appt. only.
Min. Mail Order UK: No minimum charge

Cat. Cost: 2 x 1st class
Credit Cards: None
Specialities: *Agapanthus, Alchemilla, Allium, Asphodeline, Farfugium, Gaura, Geranium, Iris, Libertia, Roscoea, Thalictrum, Tulbaghia, Uvularia* & *Verbascum.*
Map Ref: W, C2

WCel   CELYN VALE EUCALYPTUS NURSERIES
☒ EU ◆ ▣ ☒
Carrog, Corwen, Clwyd LL21 9LD
☎ (01490) 430671   **Fax:** (01490) 430671
E-mail: info@eucalyptus.co.uk
Web Site: www.eucalyptus.co.uk
Contact: Andrew McConnell & Paul Yoxall
Opening Times: 0900-1600 Mon-Fri Mar-end Oct. Please phone first outside these days.
Min. Mail Order UK: 3 plants + p&p
Min. Mail Order EU: 3 plants + p&p
Cat. Cost: 2 x 1st class
Credit Cards: Switch, Delta, Solo, Electron, MasterCard, Visa
Specialities: Hardy *Eucalyptus* & *Acacia.*
Map Ref: W, A3

WCer   CERNEY HOUSE GARDENS
North Cerney, Cirencester, Gloucestershire
GL7 7BX
☎ (01285) 831205   **Fax:** (01285) 831676
E-mail: cerneygardens@hotmail.com
Contact: Barbara Johnson
Opening Times: Tue, Wed & Fri Apr-Sep, or by appt.
Mail Order: None
Credit Cards: None
Specialities: Herbs, hardy *Geranium, Ajuga, Pulmonaria, Vinca, Tradescantia* & *Symphytum.*
Map Ref: W, D5

WCFE   CHARLES F ELLIS
(Office) Barn House, Wormington, Nr Broadway, Worcestershire WR12 7NL
☎ (01386) 584077 (nursery)
Contact: Charles Ellis
Opening Times: 1000-1600 7 days
1st Apr-30th Sep.
Mail Order: None
Cat. Cost: None issued.
Credit Cards: None
Specialities: Wide range of more unusual shrubs, conifers & climbers. Note: nursery is at Oak Piece Farm Nursery, Stanton, Broadway, Worcs.
Map Ref: W, B5

WCGr   CARROB GROWERS ☒ EU
Llangunville, Llanrothal, Nr Monmouth, Monmouthshire NP25 5QL
☎ Not yet available

Contact: R & C Boyle
Opening Times: By appt. only.
Min. Mail Order UK: No minimum charge
Min. Mail Order EU: Nmc
Cat. Cost: 1 x 1st class
Credit Cards: None
Specialities: Old & modern varieties of peonies of particular garden worthiness. Please note new location from June 2000.
Map Ref: W, D4

WCHb   THE COTTAGE HERBERY
Mill House, Boraston, Nr Tenbury Wells, Worcestershire WR15 8LZ
☎ (01584) 781575   **Fax:** (01584) 781483
Contact: K & R Hurst
Opening Times: 1000-1800 Sun & by appt. May-end Jul.
Mail Order: None
Cat. Cost: 4 x 2nd class
Credit Cards: None
Specialities: Over 600 varieties of herbs. Aromatic & scented foliage plants esp. *Symphytum, Pulmonaria, Lamium, Monarda, Ajuga, Salvia, Lobelia* & *Crocosmia.* Also seeds.
Map Ref: W, C4

WChG   CHENNELS GATE GARDENS & NURSERY
Eardisley, Herefordshire HR3 6LJ
☎ (01544) 327288
Contact: Mark Dawson
Opening Times: 1000-1700 7 days Mar-Dec.
Mail Order: None
Cat. Cost: 2 x 2nd class
Credit Cards: None
Specialities: Interesting & unusual cottage garden plants, grasses, hedging & shrubs.
Map Ref: W, C4

WCil   CILWERN PLANTS
Cilwern, Talley, Llandeilo, Carmarthenshire, Wales SA19 7YH
☎ (01558) 685526
Contact: Anne Knatchbull-Hugessen
Opening Times: 1100-1800 Tue-Sun & B/hol Mons Mar-Oct. Nov-Feb by appt.
Mail Order: None
Cat. Cost: Sae for list
Credit Cards: None
Specialities: Hardy perennials esp. *Geranium.*
Map Ref: W, C3

WClu   CLUN HILLS NURSERY
Crossways, Newcastle on Clun, Craven Arms, Shropshire SY7 8QT
☎ (01686) 670890
Contact: R G Smith or P J Smith
Opening Times: 1400-1700 Sun, other

W

times by prior appt.
Mail Order: None
Cat. Cost: 2 x 1st class
Credit Cards: None
Specialities: Hardy perennials esp. *Geranium*.
Note: nursery is at 1400 feet.
Map Ref: W, B4

WCot　COTSWOLD GARDEN FLOWERS
⊠ EU ▣ ⊠ €
Sands Lane, Badsey, Evesham, Worcestershire
WR11 5EZ
☎ (01386) 422829 mail order (01386)
422829　**Fax:** (01386) 47337
E-mail: cgf@star.co.uk
Web Site: www.cgf.net
Contact: Bob Brown, Vicky Parkhouse,
Gareth Miller (mail order)
Opening Times: 0900-1730 Mon-Fri all
year, 1000-1730 Sat & Sun Mar-Sep. Sat &
Sun Oct-Feb by appt.
Min. Mail Order UK: No minimum charge
Min. Mail Order EU: Nmc
Cat. Cost: Free
Credit Cards: None, Visa*
Specialities: Easy & unusual perennials.
*Note: credit cards not accepted for UK
sales, Visa accepted for overseas sales.
Map Ref: W, C5

WCra　CRANESBILL NURSERY ⊠ EU
White Cottage, Stock Green, Nr Redditch,
Worcestershire B96 6SZ
☎ (01386) 792414　**Fax:** (01386) 792280
Contact: Mrs S M Bates
Opening Times: 1000-1700 15th Apr-30th
Sep. Closed Wed & Thu. August by appt.
only. Please contact for w/end opening.
Min. Mail Order UK: No minimum charge*
Min. Mail Order EU: Nmc
Cat. Cost: 4 x 1st class
Credit Cards: None
Specialities: Hardy geraniums & other
herbaceous plants.
*Note: mail order autumn only.
Map Ref: W, C5

WCru　CRÛG FARM PLANTS ▣ ◆
Griffith's Crossing, Nr Caernarfon,
Gwynedd, Wales LL55 1TU
☎ (01248) 670232　**Fax:** (01248) 670232
E-mail: bleddyn&sue@crug-farm.demon.co.uk
Web Site: www.crug-farm.demon.co.uk
Contact: Mr B & Mrs S Wynn-Jones
Opening Times: 1000-1800 Thu-Sun last
Sat Feb-last Sun Sep, plus B/hols.
Mail Order: None
Cat. Cost: Sae + 2 x 2nd class
Credit Cards: Visa, Access, Delta, MasterCard

Specialities: Shade plants, climbers, hardy
Geranium, Pulmonaria, rare shrubs,
Tropaeolum, herbaceous & bulbous incl. self-
collected new introductions from the Far East.
Map Ref: W, A2

WCwm　CWMRHAIADR NURSERY ⊠ UK
Glaspwll, Machynlleth, Powys, Wales
SY20 8UB
☎ (01654) 702223
Contact: Glynne Jones
Opening Times: By appt. only. Please phone.
Min. Mail Order UK: £20.00*
Cat. Cost: 2 x 1st class
Credit Cards: None
Specialities: Rarer conifer species & clones.
Magnolia. Trees & shrubs for autumn colour.
Increasing range of rarer trees & shrubs from
seed. Camellias. *Note: mail order Nov &
Mar only.
Map Ref: W, B3

WDCP　DAVID CARTWRIGHT PLANTS
⊠ EU ▣ €
Chapel Farm Bungalow, Rhydspence,
Whitney-on-Wye, Herefordshire HR3 6EU
☎ (01497) 831689
E-mail: d.cart.plants@care4free.net
Contact: David Cartwright
Opening Times: Not open to the public.
Min. Mail Order UK: No minimum charge
Min. Mail Order EU: Nmc
Cat. Cost: 1 x 1st class
Credit Cards: None
Specialities: *Eucalyptus, Digitalis.*

WDib　DIBLEY'S NURSERIES ⊠ EU ▣ ◆
Llanelidan, Ruthin, Denbighshire LL15 2LG
☎ (01978) 790677　**Fax:** (01978) 790668
E-mail: sales@dibleys.com
Web Site: www.dibleys.com
Contact: R Dibley
Opening Times: 1000-1700 7 days Mar-Oct.
Min. Mail Order UK: No minimum charge
Min. Mail Order EU: £20.00 + p&p
Cat. Cost: Free
Credit Cards: Visa, Access, Switch, Electron,
Solo
Specialities: *Streptocarpus, Columnea,
Solenostemon* & other gesneriads & *Begonia.*
National Collection of *Streptocarpus.*
Map Ref: W, A3

WDin　DINGLE NURSERIES ▣
Welshpool, Powys, Wales SY21 9JD
☎ (01938) 555145　**Fax:** (01938) 555778
Contact: Kerry Hamer
Opening Times: 0900-1700 Wed-Mon.
(W/sale Mon-Sat only.)

Mail Order: None
Cat. Cost: Free plant list
Credit Cards: MasterCard, Switch,
EuroCard, Delta, Visa
Specialities: Largest range of trees & shrubs
in Wales. Wide seasonal selection of all plants
for the garden incl. roses, herbaceous
perennials, conifers & bare-rooted forestry,
hedging & fruit. All sizes, incl. many mature
specimens.
Map Ref: W, B4

WDyG   DYFFRYN GWYDDNO NURSERY ⊠ UK
Dyffryn Farm, Lampeter Velfrey, Narberth,
Pembrokeshire SA67 8UN
☎ (01834) 861684
E-mail: sally.polson@virgin.net
Contact: Mrs S.L. Polson
Opening Times: 1300-1500 Mon-Sat
1st May-1st Oct.
Min. Mail Order UK: £20.00*
Cat. Cost: 2 x 2nd class
Credit Cards: None
Specialities: Eclectic, yet wide-ranging, from
tender salvias & grasses to bog. *Note: mail
order Nov-Mar, order incl. min. postage
charge of £10.00.
Map Ref: W, D2

**WEas   EASTGROVE COTTAGE GARDEN
NURSERY**
Sankyns Green, Little Witley, Worcestershire
WR6 6LQ
☎ (01299) 896389
Web Site: www.hughesmedia.co.uk/eastgrove/
Contact: Malcolm & Carol Skinner
Opening Times: 1400-1700 Thu-Mon 1st
Apr-31st Jul. Closed Aug. 1400-1700 Thu-
Sat 1st Sep-14th Oct, 1400-1700 Sun 24th
Sep. Thu by appt. throughout winter.
Mail Order: None
Cat. Cost: Available on web site
Credit Cards: None
Specialities: Unique cottage garden &
arboretum open. A wide range of *Viola,
Iris,* hardy *Chrysanthemum, Dianthus,
Pelargonium* & many exciting tender
conservatory plants.
Map Ref: W, C5

WEll   ELLWOOD PENSTEMONS ⊠ UK
Ellwood House, Fern Road, Ellwood, Coleford,
Forest of Dean, Gloucestershire GL16 7LY
☎ (01594) 833839
Contact: Yvonne Shorthouse
Opening Times: Most times Mon-Sat all
year by appt. only, please phone first.
Min. Mail Order UK: No minimum charge
Cat. Cost: 2 x 2nd class

Credit Cards: None
Specialities: Penstemons, hardy geraniums.
Map Ref: W, D4

WElm   THE GARDEN AT THE ELMS NURSERY
Frenchlands Lane, Lower Broadheath,
Worcestershire WR2 6QU
☎ (01905) 640841   Fax: (01905) 640675
E-mail: www.gardenattheelms.co.uk
Contact: Emma Stewart
Opening Times: 1000-1700 Wed-Sat 24th
Mar-30th Sep 2000, 30th Mar-29th Sep 2001.
Mail Order: None
Cat. Cost: 3 x 1st class (plant list)
Credit Cards: None
Specialities: Unusual hardy plants & cottage
garden favourites, most grown on the nursery
from stock in an old farmhouse garden
which is open by appt.
Map Ref: W, C5

WFar   FARMYARD NURSERIES ⊠ EU ◆ ▣ ▣
Llandysul, Dyfed, Wales SA44 4RL
☎ (01559) 363389, (01267) 220259
Fax: (01559) 362200
E-mail: richard@farmyardnurseries.co.uk
Web Site: www.farmyardnurseries.co.uk
Contact: Richard Bramley
Opening Times: 1000-1700 7 days excl.
Xmas, Boxing Day & New Year's Day.
Min. Mail Order UK: No minimum charge
Min. Mail Order EU: £50.00 + p&p
Cat. Cost: 4 x 1st class
Credit Cards: Visa, Switch, MasterCard
Specialities: Excellent general range esp.
Helleborus, Hosta, Tricyrtis & *Schizostylis.*
General shrubs, trees, climbers, alpines &
esp. herbaceous. National Collection of
Tricyrtis.
Map Ref: W, C2

WFib   FIBREX NURSERIES LTD ⊠ EU ▣
Honeybourne Road, Pebworth, Stratford-on-
Avon, Warwickshire CV37 8XP
☎ (01789) 720788   Fax: (01789) 721162
Contact: H M D Key & R L Godard-Key
Opening Times: 1030-1700 Mon-Fri, 1200-
1700 Sat & Sun Mar-Jul. 1030-1700 Mon-
Fri Aug-Feb. Office hours 0930-1700 Mon-
Fri all year excl. last 2 weeks Dec & first
week Jan.
Min. Mail Order UK: £10.00 + p&p
Min. Mail Order EU: £20.00 + p&p
Cat. Cost: 2 x 2nd class

Credit Cards: MasterCard, Visa
Specialities: *Hedera,* ferns, *Pelargonium* &
Helleborus. Note: plant collections subject to
time of year, please check by phone. National
Collections of pelargoniums & *Hedera.*
Map Ref: W, B5

WFoF   FLOWERS OF THE FIELD ⬛
Field Farm, Weobley, Herefordshire HR4 8QJ
☎ (01544) 318262   Fax: (01544) 318262
Contact: Kathy Davies
Opening Times: 0900-1900 7 days.
Mail Order: None
Cat. Cost: 2 x 1st class
Credit Cards: None
Specialities: Cut flowers eg lilies,
chrysanthemums, carnations & gladioli.
Traditional & unusual perennials and grasses,
shrubs, trees & herbs. Summer & winter
hanging baskets & bedding.
Map Ref: W, C4

WFro   FRON NURSERY ✉ EU ⬛ ⬛
Fron Issa, Rhiwlas, Oswestry, Shropshire
SY10 7JH
☎ (01691) 600605 evenings
Contact: Thoby Miller
Opening Times: By appt. only. Please
phone first.
Min. Mail Order UK: £20.00 + p&p
Min. Mail Order EU: £50.00 + p&p
Cat. Cost: 2 x 1st class
Credit Cards: None
Specialities: Rare and unusual trees, shrubs
& perennials.
Map Ref: W, B4

WGei   W G GEISSLER
Winsford, Kingston Road, Slimbridge,
Gloucestershire GL2 7BW
☎ (01453) 890340   Fax: (01453) 890340
E-mail: w.geissler@virgin.net
Web Site:
www.t.mann.taylor.clara.net/ptero.html
Contact: W G Geissler
Opening Times: 0900-1700 (2000 in
summer) Mar-Nov.
Mail Order: None
Cat. Cost: None issued.
Credit Cards: None
Specialities: Hardy cacti & succulents and
related books. National Collections of
Opuntia (sect. *Tephrocactus)* & P*terocactus.*
Map Ref: W, D4

WGer   GERDDI FRON GOCH
Pant Road, Llanfaglan, Caernarfon,
Gwynedd LL54 5RL
☎ (01286) 672212   Fax: (01286) 678912

Web Site: www.gerddifrongoch.wales.com
Contact: R A & Mrs V Williams
Opening Times: 0900-1800 Mon-Sat,
1000-1600 Sun all year.
Mail Order: None
Cat. Cost: None issued
Credit Cards: MasterCard, Switch, Visa
Specialities: Wide range of trees, shrubs,
conifers & herbaceous perennials, some ferns
& grasses. Emphasis on plants for coastal &
damp sites.
Map Ref: W, A2

WGor   GORDON'S NURSERY
1 Cefnpennar Cottages, Cefnpennar, Mountain
Ash, Mid Glamorgan, Wales CF45 4EE
☎ (01443) 474593   Fax: (01443) 475835
E-mail: 101716.2661@compuserve.com
Web Site: http://ourworld.compuserve.com/
homepages/gordonsnursery
Contact: D A Gordon
Opening Times: 1000-1800 7 days 1st Mar-
31st Oct. 1100-1600 Sat & Sun 1st Nov-
28th Feb.
Mail Order: None
Cat. Cost: 3 x 1st class
Credit Cards: Visa, MasterCard
Specialities: Shrubs, perennials, alpines &
dwarf conifers.
Map Ref: W, D3

WGra   GRANGE FARM NURSERY ◆
Guarlford, Malvern, Worcestershire
WR13 6NY
☎ (01684) 562544   Fax: (01684) 562544
Contact: Mrs C Nicholls
Opening Times: 0900-1730 daily summer.
0900-1700 daily winter excl. Xmas & first
2 weeks in Jan.
Mail Order: None
Cat. Cost: Free pamphlet
Credit Cards: Visa, Access, Switch
Specialities: Wide general range of container-
grown hardy shrubs, trees, conifers, heathers,
alpines & herbaceous. Shrub, climbing &
bush roses.
Map Ref: W, C5

WGwG   GWYNFOR GROWERS ✉ UK
Gwynfor, Pontgarreg, Llangranog, Llandysul,
Ceredigion, Wales SA44 6AU
☎ (01239) 654151   Fax: (01239) 654152
E-mail: anne@gwynfor-growers.freeserve.co.uk
Contact: Anne & Bob Seaman
Opening Times: 1000-1600 Wed-Mon
winter. 1000-1800 7 days rest of year.
Min. Mail Order UK: £30.00 + p&p
Cat. Cost: 4 x 1st class
Credit Cards: None

Specialities: Good general range specialising in herbaceous plants, *Fuchsia* & herbs.
Map Ref: W, C2

WGWT   GRAFTED WALNUT TREES ⊠ UK 🖪 €
(Office) Bramley Cottage, Wyck Rissington, Cheltenham, Glos GL54 2PN
☎ (01451) 822098
Web Site: www.georgesnuts.co.uk
Contact: George Latham
Opening Times: Not open.
Min. Mail Order UK: No minimum charge
Cat. Cost: 3 x 1st class
Credit Cards: None
Specialities: Grafted walnut trees incl. nut bearing varieties of English walnut, ornamental forms of English & black walnut, minor species & hybrids. Note: this address is for correspondence and collection of orders- nursery at other sites.
Map Ref: W, B5

WGwy   GWYDIR PLANTS ⊠ UK
Snowdon View, Dolwyddelan, North Wales LL25 0UJ
☎ (01690) 750379   **Fax:** (01690) 750379
E-mail: snowdonview@btinternet.com
Contact: Mrs D Southgate
Opening Times: By appt. only.
Min. Mail Order UK: £5.00
Cat. Cost: 2 x 1st class
Credit Cards: None
Specialities: Hardy perennials, wild flowers, native trees & shrubs, herbs; incl. some noteworthy but hard-to-find plants. Please phone for market days & plant fairs.
Map Ref: W, A3

WHal   HALL FARM NURSERY
Vicarage Lane, Kinnerley, Nr Oswestry, Shropshire SY10 8DH
☎ (01691) 682135   **Fax:** (01691) 682135
Contact: Christine Ffoulkes-Jones
Opening Times: 1000-1700 Tue-Sat 3rd Mar-14th Oct 2000. 2001 may differ.
Mail Order: None
Cat. Cost: 4 x 1st class
Credit Cards: None
Specialities: Unusual herbaceous plants incl. hardy *Geranium, Pulmonaria,* grasses & many others.
Map Ref: W, B4

WHar   HARLEY NURSERY
Harley, Shropshire SY5 6LP
☎ (01952) 510241   **Fax:** (01952) 510222
Contact: Duncan Murphy
Opening Times: 0900-1730 Mon-Sat, 1000-1750 Sun & B/hols.

Mail Order: None
Cat. Cost: 2 x 1st class
Credit Cards: Visa, Access
Specialities: Wide range of ornamental & fruit trees. Also own-grown shrubs, climbing & hedging plants. Many unusual varieties.
Map Ref: W, B4

WHbs   HERBS AT MYDDFAI
Beiliglas, Myddfai, Nr Llandovery, Carmarthenshire SA20 0QB
☎ (01550) 720494
E-mail: beiliglas@aol.com
Contact: Gill Swan
Opening Times: 1400-1800 Tue-Sat Apr-Oct, or by appt.
Mail Order: None
Cat. Cost: 2 x 1st class
Credit Cards: None
Specialities: Herbs & wild flowers. Organic.
Map Ref: W, C3

WHCG   HUNTS COURT GARDEN & NURSERY   **W**
North Nibley, Dursley, Gloucestershire GL11 6DZ
☎ (01453) 547440   **Fax:** (01453) 547944
E-mail: keith@huntscourt.fsnet.co.uk
Contact: T K & M M Marshall
Opening Times: Nursery & garden 0900-1700 Tue-Sat excl. Aug. Also by appt. See NGS for Sun openings.
Mail Order: None
Cat. Cost: 5 x 2nd class
Credit Cards: None
Specialities: Old rose species & climbers. Hardy *Geranium, Penstemon* & unusual shrubs.
Map Ref: W, D5

WHCr   HERGEST CROFT GARDENS
Kington, Herefordshire HR5 3EG
☎ (01544) 230160   **Fax:** (01544) 230160
Contact: Stephen Lloyd
Opening Times: 1330-1830 7 days Apr-Oct.
Mail Order: None
Cat. Cost: None issued
Credit Cards: None
Specialities: *Acer, Betula* & unusual woody plants.
Map Ref: W, C4

WHen   HENLLYS LODGE PLANTS
Henllys Lodge, Beaumaris, Anglesey, Gwynedd, Wales LL58 8HU
☎ (01248) 810106
Contact: Mrs E Lane
Opening Times: 1100-1700 Mon, Wed, Fri, Sat & Sun, & by appt. Apr-Oct.
Mail Order: None

W

Cat. Cost: 2 x 1st class
Credit Cards: None
Specialities: Hardy *Geranium,* ground cover &
cottage style perennials.
Map Ref: W, A3

WHer   THE HERB GARDEN & HISTORICAL
PLANT NURSERY ⊠ EU
Pentre Berw, Gaerwen, Anglesey, Wales
LL60 6LF
Contact: Corinne & David Tremaine-
Stevenson
Opening Times: 0900-1700 7 days excl. Tue.
Open all B/hols.
Min. Mail Order UK: £15.00 + p&p
Min. Mail Order EU: £50.00 + p&p
sterling only.
Cat. Cost: List £2.00 in stamps
Credit Cards: None
Specialities: Wide range of herbs, rare natives
& wild flowers; rare & unusual perennials,
scented *Pelargonium* & old roses.
Map Ref: W, A2

WHil   HILLVIEW HARDY PLANTS ⊠ EU ◆ 🅶 🅵
Worfield, Nr Bridgnorth, Shropshire
WV15 5NT
☎ (01746) 716454
Fax: (01746) 716454
Contact: Ingrid Millington
Opening Times: 0900-1700 Mon-Sat
Mar-mid Oct. At all other times, please
phone first.
Min. Mail Order UK: £10.00 + p&p
Min. Mail Order EU: £10.00 + p&p
Cat. Cost: 4 x 2nd class
Credit Cards: None
Specialities: Choice herbaceous perennials
incl. *Auricula, Primula, Monarda, Dierama,
Crocosmia, Watsonia, Eucomis, Phlox,* grasses &
ferns. Contract growing for wholesale.
Map Ref: W, B4

WHoo   HOO HOUSE NURSERY 🅶 ◆
Hoo House, Gloucester Road, Tewkesbury,
Gloucestershire GL20 7DA
☎ (01684) 293389
Fax: (01684) 293389
E-mail: nursery@hoohouse.totalserve.co.uk
Contact: Robin & Julie Ritchie
Opening Times: 1400-1700 Mon-Sat.
Mail Order: None
Cat. Cost: 3 x 1st class
Credit Cards: None
Specialities: Wide range of herbaceous &
alpines - many unusual - incl. *Campanula,
Geranium* & *Penstemon.* National Collections
of *Platycodon* & *Gentiana asclepiadea* cvs.
Map Ref: W, B5

WIvo   IVOR MACE NURSERIES ⊠ UK
2 Mace Lane, Ynyswen, Treorci, Rhondda,
Mid Glamorgan, Wales CF42 6DS
☎ (01443) 775531
Contact: I Mace
Opening Times: Not open to the public.
Min. Mail Order UK: £5.00 + p&p*
Cat. Cost: Sae
Credit Cards: None
Specialities: Large exhibition chrysanthemums.
*Note: delivery by mail order or collection
during Feb & Mar only.

WIvy   IVYCROFT PLANTS
Upper Ivington, Leominster, Herefordshire
HR6 0JN
☎ (01568) 720344
Contact: Roger Norman
Opening Times: 0900-1600 Wed & Thu
Mar-Sep. Other times by appt., please phone.
Mail Order: None
Cat. Cost: 2 x 1st class
Credit Cards: None
Specialities: *Cyclamen, Viola,* alpines &
herbaceous.
Map Ref: W, C4

WJas   PAUL JASPER TREES ⊠ EU 🅶
The Lighthouse, Bridge Street, Leominster,
Herefordshire HR6 8DX
Fax: (01568) 616499 for orders.
E-mail: pjasper253@aol.com
Contact: Paul Jasper
Opening Times: Not open for retail sales.
Min. Mail Order UK: £30.00 + p&p
Min. Mail Order EU: £100.00 + p&p
Cat. Cost: 2 x 1st class
Credit Cards: None
Specialities: Full range of fruit & ornamental
trees. Over 100 modern and traditional apple
varieties, plus 220 others all direct from the
grower. Many unusual varieties of *Malus
domestica.*
Map Ref: W, C4

WJek   JEKKA'S HERB FARM ⊠ EU 🅶 🅶
Rose Cottage, Shellards Lane, Alveston,
Bristol, Avon BS35 3SY
☎ (01454) 418878   Fax: (01454) 411988
E-mail: farm@jekkasherb.demon.co.uk
Web Site: www.jekkasherb.demon.co.uk
Contact: Jekka McVicar
Opening Times: By appt. only.
Min. Mail Order UK: No minimum charge
Min. Mail Order EU: Nmc*
Cat. Cost: 4 x 1st class
Credit Cards: Visa, MasterCard
Specialities: Culinary, medicinal, aromatic,
decorative herbs, native wild flowers. *Note:

individual quotations for EU sales. Organic Food Federation symbol.
Map Ref: W, D4

WJun JUNGLE GIANTS ⊠ EU ☒ ⬛
Burford House Gardens, Tenbury Wells, Worcestershire WR15 8HQ
☎ (01584) 819885   **Fax:** (01584) 819779
E-mail: bamboo@junglegiants.co.uk
Web Site: www.junglegiants.co.uk
Contact: Michael Brisbane & Bym Welthy
Opening Times: 7 days. By appt. only please.
Min. Mail Order UK: £20.00 + p&p
Min. Mail Order EU: £25.00 + p&p
Cat. Cost: £5.75 incl. p+p for full info. pack
Credit Cards: None
Specialities: *Bamboo.*
Map Ref: W, C4

WKif KIFTSGATE COURT GARDENS
Kiftsgate Court, Chipping Camden, Gloucestershire GL55 6LW
☎ (01386) 438777   **Fax:** (01386) 438777
Contact: Mrs J Chambers
Opening Times: 1400-1800 Wed, Thu & Sun 1st Apr-30th Sep & B/hol Mons. Also Sat in Jun & Jul.
Mail Order: None
Cat. Cost: None issued
Credit Cards: None
Specialities: Small range of unusual plants.
Map Ref: W, C5

WKin KINGSTONE COTTAGE PLANTS ⊠ EU
Weston-under-Penyard, Ross-on-Wye, Herefordshire HR9 7NT
☎ (01989) 565267
E-mail: S.hughes@kingstone.fs.business.co.uk
Contact: Mr M Hughes
Opening Times: By appt. & as under NGS.
Min. Mail Order UK: No minimum charge
Min. Mail Order EU: Nmc
Cat. Cost: 2 x 1st class
Credit Cards: None
Specialities: National Collection of *Dianthus.*
Map Ref: W, C4

WLeb LEBA ORCHARD - GREEN'S LEAVES ⊠ UK ⬛
Lea Bailey, Nr Ross-on-Wye, Herefordshire HR9 5TY
☎ (01989) 750303
Contact: Paul Green
Opening Times: By appt. only, w/ends preferred.
Min. Mail Order UK: £10.00 + p&p
Cat. Cost: 2 x 2nd class
Credit Cards: None
Specialities: Ivies, ornamental grasses, sedges

& phormiums. Increasing range of rare & choice shrubs, also some perennials.
Map Ref: W, C4

WLin LINGEN NURSERY AND GARDEN ⊠ EU ⬛
Lingen, Nr Bucknell, Shropshire SY7 0DY
☎ (01544) 267720   **Fax:** (01544) 267720
E-mail: kim&maggie@lingen.freeserve.co.uk
Contact: Kim W Davis
Opening Times: 1000-1700 7 days Feb-Oct. Fri-Sun Nov-Jan by appt.
Min. Mail Order UK: No minimum charge
Min. Mail Order EU: £20.00 + p&p
Cat. Cost: 3 x 1st class
Credit Cards: Visa, MasterCard
Specialities: Alpines, rock plants & herbaceous esp. *Androsace, Aquilegia, Campanula, Iris, Primula,* auriculas & *Penstemon.* National Collection of herbaceous *Campanula* & housing that of *Iris sibirica.*
Map Ref: W, C3

WLow LOWER SPRING NURSERY ⬛
Kenley, Shrewsbury, Shropshire SY5 6PA
☎ (01952) 510589
Contact: Bob Hemmings
Opening Times: Sat & Sun Mar-Sep. Winter w/ends by arrangement.
Mail Order: None
Cat. Cost: 2 x 1st class
Credit Cards: None
Specialities: A good range of cacti & succulents, plus herbaceous, alpines & shrubs.
Map Ref: W, B4

WLRN LITTLE RHYNDASTON NURSERIES
Hayscastle, Haverfordwest, Pembrokeshire SA62 5PT
☎ (01437) 710656
Contact: D A & P Baster
Opening Times: 0900-1700 Mon-Sat, 1100-1700 Sun. Closed Aug.
Mail Order: None
Cat. Cost: None issued
Credit Cards: Visa, MasterCard, Switch
Specialities: Herbaceous perennials, conifers, shrubs, alpines, climbers, patio plants, many suitable for coastal locations.
Map Ref: W, C1

WMal MARSHALL'S MALMAISON ⊠ EU ⬛ ☒ €
4 The Damsells, Tetbury, Gloucestershire GL8 8JA
☎ (01666) 502589

KEY		
⊠	Mail order to UK or EU	
☒	Exports beyond EU	€ Euro accepted
⬛	Also supplies Wholesale	◆ See Display advertisement

W

Contact: J M Marshall
Opening Times: By appt. only.
Min. Mail Order UK: £16.50 incl. p&p
Min. Mail Order EU: £16.50 incl. p&p
Cat. Cost: 1st class Sae
Credit Cards: None
Specialities: National Collection of malmaison carnations.
Map Ref: W, D5

WMaN THE MARCHES NURSERY ⊠ EU
Presteigne, Powys, Wales LD8 2HG
☎ (01544) 260474
Fax: (01544) 260474
Contact: Jane Cooke
Opening Times: Mail order only.
Min. Mail Order UK: No minimum charge*
Min. Mail Order EU: Nmc
Cat. Cost: 3 x 1st class
Credit Cards: None
Specialities: An increasing range of choice perennials, many uncommon, incl. *Achillea, Chrysanthemum, Erysimum, Geranium, Papaver, Penstemon* & *Phlox*.
*Note: mail order mainly in spring.

WMAq MEREBROOK WATER PLANTS ⊠ EU
Merebrook Farm, Hanley Swan, Worcester, Worcestershire WR8 0DX
☎ (01684) 310950
Fax: (01684) 310034
E-mail: enquiries@pondplants.co.uk
Web Site: www.pondplants.co.uk
Contact: Roger Kings & Biddi Kings
Opening Times: 1000-1700 Thu-Tue Easter-Sep.
Min. Mail Order UK: No minimum charge
Min. Mail Order EU: £20.00
Cat. Cost: Free
Credit Cards: Access, Visa, Switch, Delta
Specialities: *Nymphaea* (water lilies) & other aquatic plants.
Map Ref: W, B5

WMEx MARSTON EXOTICS ⊠ UK 🗹 🖾
Brampton Lane, Madley, Herefordshire HR2 9LX
☎ (01981) 251659,
mobile 0798 0354076
Fax: (01981) 251649
Web Site: http://freespace.virgin.net/carnivorous.connection/
Contact: Jackie Gardner
Opening Times: By appointment only.
Min. Mail Order UK: See list for details
Cat. Cost: List 3 x 1st class*
Credit Cards: None
Specialities: Carnivorous plants. National

Collection of *Sarracenia*. Also large collection of seeds.
*Note: price list & Growers Guide £2.85.
Map Ref: W, C4

WMoo MOORLAND COTTAGE PLANTS ⊠ UK
Rhyd-y-Groes, Brynberian, Crymych, Pembrokeshire, Wales SA41 3TT
☎ (01239) 891363
Contact: Jennifer Matthews
Opening Times: 1000-1800 Thu-Tue end Feb-end Sept. Other times by appt.
Min. Mail Order UK: See cat. for details.
Cat. Cost: 4 x 1st class
Credit Cards: None
Specialities: Traditional & unusual hardy perennials incl. *Aster, Astilbe, Campanula, Crocosmia, Geranium, Geum, Persicaria, Potentilla, Sedum, Sidalcea, Veronica,* grasses, cottage garden plants, woodland plants & colourful ground cover.
Map Ref: W, C2

WMou MOUNT PLEASANT TREES 🖾
Rockhampton, Berkeley, Gloucestershire GL13 9DU
☎ (01454) 260348
Contact: P & G Locke
Opening Times: By appt. only.
Mail Order: None
Cat. Cost: 3 x 2nd class
Credit Cards: None
Specialities: Wide range of trees for forestry, hedging, woodlands & gardens esp. *Tilia* & *Populus*.
Map Ref: W, D4

WMul MULU NURSERIES ⊠ EU 🗹 🖾 €
Burford House, Tenbury Wells, Worcestershire WR15 8HQ
☎ (01584) 811592   Fax: (01584) 819301
E-mail: plants@mulu.co.uk
Web Site: www.mulu.co.uk
Contact: Andy Bateman, Helen Lane
Opening Times: 1000-1800 or dusk 7 days. Phone first Nov-Mar.
Min. Mail Order UK: No minimum charge
Min. Mail Order EU: £25.00 + p&p
Cat. Cost: 4 x 1st class
Credit Cards: Visa, MasterCard, Delta
Specialities: Exotic plants, hardy & tender incl. bananas, gingers, palms, tree ferns, aroids etc.
Map Ref: W, C4

WNor NORFIELDS ⊠ EU 🗹 🖾
Llangwm Arboretum, Usk, Monmouthshire NP15 1NQ
☎ (01291) 650306   Fax: (01291) 650577

Contact: Andrew Norfield
Opening Times: Not open.
Min. Mail Order UK: £3.00 + p&p
Min. Mail Order EU: £3.00 + p&p
Cat. Cost: 1 x 1st class
Credit Cards: None
Specialities: Wide range of tree seedlings for growing on. *Acer, Betula, Stewartia* & pregerminated seed.

WOak   OAK COTTAGE HERBS ⊠ UK ◆
(Office) Oak House, Astley, Shrewsbury, Shropshire SY4 4BP
☎ (01939) 210219   **Fax:** (01939) 210219
Contact: Jane & Edward Bygott.
Opening Times: Plant sales & display gardens at Pimhill Organic Farm Shop, 1000-1700 daily Apr to mid-Sep.
Min. Mail Order UK: No minimum charge
Cat. Cost: 3 x 1st class
Credit Cards: None
Specialities: Beneficial plants, herbs, wild flowers. Vegetable plants to Soil Association standard.
Map Ref: W, B4

WOFF   OLD FASHIONED FLOWERS ⊠ EU
Cleeway, Eardington, Bridgnorth, Shropshire WV16 5JT
☎ (01746) 766909
E-mail: jsnocken@brier.dudley.gov.uk
Contact: John Snocken
Opening Times: By appt. only.
Min. Mail Order UK: No minimum charge
Min. Mail Order EU: Nmc
Cat. Cost: 2 x 2nd class
Credit Cards: None
Specialities: Show pansies, fancy pansies & exhibition violas. National Collection of florists' violas and pansies.
Map Ref: W, B4

WOld   OLD COURT NURSERIES ⊠ EU €
Colwall, Nr Malvern, Worcestershire WR13 6QE
☎ (01684) 540416   **Fax:** (01684) 565314
E-mail: picton@dircon.co.uk
Web Site: www.autumnasters.co.uk
Contact: Paul & Meriel Picton
Opening Times: 1100-1730 Wed-Sun Apr-Oct, 7 days 2nd week Sep-2nd week Oct.
Min. Mail Order UK: No minimum charge*
Min. Mail Order EU: Nmc
Cat. Cost: 2 x 1st class
Credit Cards: None
Specialities: National Collection of michaelmas daisies. Herbaceous perennials.
*Note: mail order for *Aster* only.
Map Ref: W, C4

WOrn   ORNAMENTAL TREE NURSERIES
⊠ UK 🖳
Broomy Hill Gardens, Cobnash, Kingsland, Herefordshire HR6 9QZ
☎ (01568) 708016   **Fax:** (01568) 709022
E-mail: enquiries@ornamental-trees.co.uk
Web Site: www.ornamental-trees.co.uk
Contact: Russell Mills
Opening Times: 0900-1700 Mon-Sat.
Min. Mail Order UK: £17.50
Cat. Cost: 2 x 2nd class
Credit Cards: Visa, Switch, MasterCard, Access, Delta
Specialities: Ornamental trees.
Map Ref: W, C4

WOTO   OGON TORA ORIENTAL NURSERY 🖳
12 Pikes Pool Lane, Burcot, Bromsgrove, Worcestershire B60 1LJ
☎ (0121) 445 3114
Contact: Mr J M Hall
Opening Times: 1000-1630 Sat, Sun & B/hols. Mon-Fri by appt. only. Please phone. Closed Xmas-New Year's Day incl.
Mail Order: None
Cat. Cost: None issued.
Credit Cards: None
Specialities: Choice & unusual shrubs, trees, perennials, ferns & bamboos. Particularly plants from Japan & China. Nursery also grows trees & shrubs esp. for the production of *Bonsai*.
Map Ref: W, C5

WOut   OUT OF THE COMMON WAY ⊠ EU
(Office) Penhyddgan, Boduan, Pwllheli, Gwynedd, Wales LL53 8YH
☎ (01758) 721577 (Office), (01407) 720431 (Nursery)
Contact: Joanna Davidson (nursery) Margaret Mason (office & mail order)
Opening Times: By arrangement.
Min. Mail Order UK: No minimum charge
Min. Mail Order EU: Nmc
Cat. Cost: Sae
Credit Cards: None
Specialities: *Nepeta, Geranium, Salvia, Viola, Digitalis, Lavandula, Stachys* & *Veronica*.
Note: nursery is at Pandy Treban, Bryngwran, Anglesey, LL65 3YW.
Map Ref: W, A2

WOve   OVERCOURT GARDEN NURSERY
Sutton St Nicholas, Hereford HR1 3AY
☎ (01432) 880845
E-mail: harpers@harpover.freeserve.co.uk
Contact: Nicola Harper
Opening Times: 0930-1630 Wed-Sat 1st Mar-31st Oct. Closed 5th-20th Aug.

W

Mail Order: None
Cat. Cost: 3 x 2nd class
Credit Cards: None
Specialities: Hardy perennials, many unusual. Garden open under NGS. Groups welcome by appt.
Map Ref: W, C4

WOVN THE OLD VICARAGE NURSERY ⊠ UK
Lucton, Leominster, Herefordshire HR6 9PN
☎ (01568) 780538
Fax: (01568) 780818
Contact: Mrs R M Flake
Opening Times: 1000-1700 most days, but please phone first to be sure.
Min. Mail Order UK: No minimum charge
Cat. Cost: 2 x 1st class
Credit Cards: None
Specialities: Roses - old roses, climbers & ramblers, species & ground cover. *Euphorbia* & half-hardy *Salvia*.
Map Ref: W, C4

WPat CHRIS PATTISON ⊠ EU 🖥
Brookend, Pendock, Gloucestershire GL19 3PL
☎ (01531) 650480
Fax: (01531) 650480
E-mail: cpplants@redmarley.freeserve.co.uk
Web Site: www.redmarley.freeserve.co.uk
Contact: Chris Pattison
Opening Times: 0900-1700 Mon-Fri. W/ends by appt. only.
Min. Mail Order UK: £10.00 +p&p*
Min. Mail Order EU: £10.00
Cat. Cost: 3 x 1st class
Credit Cards: None
Specialities: Choice & rare shrubs and alpines. Grafted stock esp. Japanese maples & *Liquidambar*. Wide range of *Viburnum*, dwarf willows & dwarf ericaceous shrubs. *Note: mail order Nov-Mar only.
Map Ref: W, D5

WPen PENPERGWM PLANTS
Penpergwm Lodge, Abergavenny, Gwent, Wales NP7 9AS
☎ (01873) 840422/840208
Fax: (01873) 840470/840208
E-mail: penpergwmplants@dial.pipex.com
Web Site: www.penplants.com
Contact: Mrs J Kerr, Mrs S Boyle
Opening Times: Thu-Sun 1400-1800 30th Mar-1st Oct 2000, 29th Mar-30th Sep 2001.
Mail Order: None
Cat. Cost: 2 x 1st class
Credit Cards: None
Specialities: Hardy perennials.
Map Ref: W, D4

WPer PERHILL NURSERIES ⊠ EU 🖥
Worcester Road, Great Witley, Worcestershire WR6 6JT
☎ (01299) 896329 Fax: (01299) 896990
E-mail: PerhillP@aol.com
Web Site: www.hartlana.co.uk/perhill/
Contact: Duncan Straw
Opening Times: 0900-1700 Mon-Sat, 1000-1600 Sun 1st Feb-15th Oct & by appt.
Min. Mail Order UK: No minimum charge
Min. Mail Order EU: £10.00
Cat. Cost: 6 x 2nd class
Credit Cards: MasterCard, Delta, Switch, EuroCard, Visa
Specialities: Over 2500 varieties of rare & unusual alpines & herbaceous perennials incl. *Penstemon, Campanula, Salvia, Thymus*, herbs & *Veronica*.
Map Ref: W, C4

WPGP PAN-GLOBAL PLANTS ⊠ UK
Spoonbed Nursery, Rococo Garden, Painswick, Glos GL6 6TH
☎ (01452) 814242 Fax: (01453) 768858
Contact: N Macer
Opening Times: 1100-1700 Wed-Sun 2nd Wed in Jan-30th Nov. Also B/hols.
Min. Mail Order UK: Please enquire*
Cat. Cost: 3 x 1st class
Credit Cards: MasterCard, Visa
Specialities: Rare, unusual & hard to find trees, shrubs & herbaceous esp. *Hydrangea* & *Magnolia*, many collected in the wild.
*Note: mail order for reasonable quantities only.
Map Ref: W, D5

WPhl JUST PHLOMIS ⊠ EU
Sunningdale, Grange Court, Westbury-on-Severn, Gloucestershire GL14 1PL
☎ (01452) 760268 Fax: (01452) 760268
E-mail: j.mann.taylor@clara.co.uk
Web Site: www.j.mann.taylor.clara.net/phlomis.html
Contact: J Mann Taylor
Opening Times: By appt. only.
Min. Mail Order UK: £7.50 + p&p
Min. Mail Order EU: £7.50 + p&p
Cat. Cost: 2 x 2nd class
Credit Cards: None
Specialities: National Collection of *Phlomis*.
Map Ref: W, D4

WPic THE PICTON CASTLE TRUST NURSERY ⊠ EU
Picton Castle, Haverfordwest, Pembrokeshire SA62 4AS
☎ (01437) 751326 Fax: (01437) 751326
E-mail: pct@pictoncastle.freeserve.co.uk

Web Site: www.pictoncastle.co.uk
Contact: D L Pryse Lloyd
Opening Times: 1030-1700 7 days except
Mon Apr-Oct. Other times by arrangement.
Min. Mail Order UK: No minimum charge
Cat. Cost: 1 x 1st class
Credit Cards: None
Specialities: Woodland & unusual shrubs.
Herbs.
Map Ref: W, D2

WPnn   THE PERENNIAL NURSERY
Rhosygilwen, Llanrhian Road, St Davids,
Pembrokeshire SA62 6DB
☎ (01437) 721954   Fax: (01437) 721954
E-mail: Rhosygilwendairy@ukgateway.net
Contact: Mrs Philipa Symons
Opening Times: 0930-1730 every day
Mar-Oct. Nov-Apr by appt.
Mail Order: None
Cat. Cost: None issued.
Credit Cards: None
Specialities: Herbaceous perennials & alpines
esp. *Erodium.* Tender perennials esp.
Argyranthemum.
Map Ref: W, C1

WPnP   PENLAN PERENNIALS ⊠ EU ▣ €
Penlan Farm, Penrhiwpal, Llandysul,
Ceredigion, Wales SA44 5QH
☎ (01239) 851244   Fax: (01239) 851244
E-mail:
penlanperennials@penlanfm.freeserve.co.uk
Web Site: www.penlanfm.freeserve.co.uk
Contact: Richard & Jane Cain
Opening Times: 0930-1730 Wed-Sun
Mar-Oct & B/hols.
Min. Mail Order UK: No minimum charge*
Min. Mail Order EU: Nmc
Cat. Cost: 3 x 1st class
Credit Cards: None
Specialities: Hardy *Geranium* (195). Dry &
moist shade lovers & woodland plants, incl.
bulbs, climbers & shrubs but especially
herbaceous perennials.
*Note: mail order all year. Next day delivery.
Map Ref: W, C2

WPrP   PRIME PERENNIALS ⊠ EU
Llety Moel, Rhos-y-Garth, Llanilar, Nr
Aberystwyth, Ceredigion SY23 4SG
☎ (01974) 241505
Contact: Elizabeth Powney
Opening Times: Not open to the public.
Min. Mail Order UK: £14.00 + p&p or 6
plants
Min. Mail Order EU: £40.00 + p&p
Cat. Cost: 4 x 1st class
Credit Cards: None

Specialities: Unusual & interesting perennials.
Hardy *Geranium, Thalictrum, Pulmonaria* &
grasses, grown 650ft above sea level.
Map Ref: W, C3

WPry   THE PRIORY
Kemerton, Tewkesbury, Gloucestershire
GL20 7JN
☎ (01386) 725258   Fax: (01386) 725258
Contact: Mrs P Healing
Opening Times: 1400-1900 Thu.
Mail Order: None
Cat. Cost: None issued
Credit Cards: Visa, Access, American
Express, Diners
Specialities: *Datura,* rare & unusual plants.
Map Ref: W, B5

WPyg   THE PYGMY PINETUM
Cannop Crossroads, Nr Coleford, Forest of
Dean, Gloucestershire GL15 7EQ
☎ (01594) 833398   Fax: (01594) 810815
E-mail: ppnursery@aol.com
Contact: Keith Parker
Opening Times: 0900-1730 7 days.
Mail Order: None
Cat. Cost: 3 x 2nd class
Credit Cards: Visa, MasterCard, Switch
Specialities: Unusual shrubs, alpines &
herbaceous. Wide range of trees, heathers,
ferns, top fruit, water plants & climbers.
Map Ref: W, D4

WRha   RHANDIRMWYN PLANTS
8 Pannau Street, Rhandirmwyn, Nr
Llandovery, Carmarthenshire,
Wales SA20 0NP
☎ (01550) 760220   Fax: (01550) 760398
Contact: Sara Fox/Thomas Sheppard
Opening Times: Open most days from
Apr-end Sep, but please ring first to avoid
disappointment.
Mail Order: None
Credit Cards: None
Specialities: Old-fashioned cottage garden
plants, over 400 varieties. *Geranium,
Helleborus, Primula* (double), *Pulmonaria,
Salvia.* Note: nursery is now at 8 Pannau
Street, Rhandirmwyn.
Map Ref: W, C3

WRHF   RED HOUSE FARM
Flying Horse Lane, Bradley Green, Nr
Redditch, Worcestershire B96 6QT

W

K E Y	⊠ Mail order to UK or EU	
	▣ Exports beyond EU	€ Euro accepted
	▣ Also supplies Wholesale	◆ See Display advertisement

☎ (01527) 821269
Fax: (01527) 821674
Contact: Mrs Maureen Weaver
Opening Times: 0900-1700 Mon-Sat all
year. 1000-1700 Sun & B/hols.
Mail Order: None
Cat. Cost: 2 x 1st class
Credit Cards: None
Specialities: Cottage garden perennials.
Map Ref: W, B5

WRic RICKARD'S HARDY FERNS ⊠ EU
Kyre Park, Kyre, Tenbury Wells,
Worcestershire WR15 8RP
☎ (01885) 410282, (01885) 410729
Fax: (01885) 410729
Contact: Martin Rickard
Opening Times: Wed-Mon all year but
appt. advisable Nov-Feb.
Min. Mail Order UK: £20.00 + p&p*
Min. Mail Order EU: £50.00 + p&p
Cat. Cost: 5 x 1st class or 6 x 2nd class
Credit Cards: None
Specialities: Ferns, hardy & half-hardy, tree
ferns. National Collections of *Polypodium,
Cystopteris* & *Thelypteroid* ferns.
*Note: UK customers please order with a
limited cheque. EU customers please write &
confirm availability before ordering.
Map Ref: W, C4

WRos ROSEMARY'S FARMHOUSE NURSERY
Llwyn-y-moel-gau, Llanfihangel, Llanfyllin,
Powys SY22 5JE
☎ (01691) 648196   Fax: (01691) 648196
E-mail: rosemary@farmhouse-
nursery.fsnet.co.uk
Contact: Rosemary Pryce
Opening Times: 1000-1700 most days all
year, but advisable to phone to confirm.
Mail Order: None
Cat. Cost: None issued.
Credit Cards: None
Specialities: Unusual perennials &
ornamental grasses. Hardy geraniums.
Map Ref: W, B3

WRus RUSHFIELDS OF LEDBURY ▣
Ross Road, Ledbury, Herefordshire HR8 2LP
☎ (01531) 632004
Fax: (01531) 633454
E-mail: rush01531@aol.com
Contact: B & J Homewood
Opening Times: 1100-1700 Wed-Sat. Other
times by appt.
Mail Order: None
Cat. Cost: A5 Sae 31p + £1.00
Credit Cards: Visa, Access
Specialities: Unusual herbaceous incl.

Euphorbia, hardy *Geranium, Helleborus, Hosta,
Osteospermum, Penstemon,* primroses & grasses.
Map Ref: W, C4

WSan SANDSTONES COTTAGE GARDEN
PLANTS ⊠ EU
58 Bolas Heath, Great Bolas, Shropshire TF6
6PS
☎ (01952) 541657   Fax: (01952) 541657
E-mail: pbrelsforth@cwcom.net
Web Site: www.sandstonesplants.mcmail.com
Contact: Joanne Brelsforth
Opening Times: Tues & Wed May-Sep or
by appt.
Min. Mail Order UK: £10.00 + p&p
Min. Mail Order EU: £25.00 + p&p
Cat. Cost: 4 x 1st class
Credit Cards: None
Specialities: Unusual & interesting hardy
perennials. Also large range of variegated
varieties.
Map Ref: W, B4

WSel SELSLEY HERB FARM
Waterlane, Selsley, Stroud, Gloucestershire
GL5 5LW
☎ (01453) 766682   Fax: (01453) 753674
Contact: Rob Wimperis
Opening Times: 1000-1700 Tue-Sat,
1400-1700 Sun & B/hols Apr-Sep.
Mail Order: None
Cat. Cost: None issued
Credit Cards: None
Specialities: Culinary, aromatic & medicinal
herbs & selected garden plants.
Map Ref: W, D5

WSHC STONE HOUSE COTTAGE NURSERIES
Stone, Nr Kidderminster, Worcestershire
DY10 4BG
☎ (01562) 69902   Fax: (01562) 69960
E-mail: louisa@shcn.co.uk
Contact: J F & L N Arbuthnott
Opening Times: 1000-1730 Wed-Sat. For
Sun see NGS for details. By appt. only
Oct-Mar.
Mail Order: None
Cat. Cost: Sae
Credit Cards: None
Specialities: Small general range esp. wall
shrubs, climbers & unusual plants.
Map Ref: W, B5

WShe SHERBORNE GARDENS ▣
Sherborne, Cheltenham, Gloucestershire
GL54 3DW
☎ (01451) 844522, (01451) 844248
Fax: (01451) 844695
E-mail: sherborne.gardens@dial.pipex.com

Contact: John E M Hill
Opening Times: 0800-1700 Mon-Sat
Mar-Oct & Mon-Fri Nov-Feb.
Mail Order: None
Cat. Cost: 2 x 1st class
Credit Cards: None
Map Ref: W, D5

WShi   JOHN SHIPTON (BULBS) ⊠ EU 🔲 ⊠ €
Y Felin, Henllan Amgoed, Whitland, Dyfed,
Wales SA34 0SL
☎ (01994) 240125
Fax: (01994) 241180
E-mail: bluebell@zoo.co.uk
Web Site: www.bluebellbulbs.co.uk
Contact: John Shipton
Opening Times: By appt. only.
Min. Mail Order UK: No minimum charge
Min. Mail Order EU: Nmc
Cat. Cost: Sae
Credit Cards: None
Specialities: Native British bulbs, and bulbs
& plants for naturalising.
Map Ref: W, D2

WSpi   SPINNEYWELL NURSERY ⊠ EU 🔲 ◆
Waterlane, Oakridge, Bisley,
Glos GL6 7PH
☎ (01452) 770092   Fax: (01452) 770151
E-mail: spinneywell@tesco.net
Web Site: www.goto.nu/spinneywell
Contact: Wendy Asher
Opening Times: 1000-1700 7 days Mar-
Dec. 1000-1600 Mon, Wed, Thu, Fri &
1400-1600 Sun Jan & Feb.
Min. Mail Order UK: £10.00 + p&p
Min. Mail Order EU: £30.00 + p&p
Cat. Cost: 6 x 1st class
Credit Cards: None
Specialities: *Buxus, Taxus* & unusual
herbaceous & shrubs. Hellebores,
euphorbias, *Ceanothus,* hardy geraniums.
Map Ref: W, D5

WSPU   PERSHORE COLLEGE OF
HORTICULTURE 🔲
Specialist Plant Unit & Plant Centre,
Avonbank, Pershore, Worcestershire
WR10 3JP
☎ (01386) 561385   Fax: (01386) 555601
Contact: Lucy Allum (Plant Centre)
Opening Times: (Plant Centre) 0900-1700
Mon-Sat, 1000-1600 Sun.
Mail Order: None
Cat. Cost: £1.00
Credit Cards: Visa, Access
Specialities: National Collection of *Penstemon.*
Open for viewing 0800-1630 Mon-Fri.
Map Ref: W, B5

WStl   ST ISHMAEL'S NURSERIES
Haverfordwest, Pembrokeshire SA62 3SX
☎ (01646) 636343
Fax: (01646) 636343
Contact: Mr D & Mrs H Phippen
Opening Times: 0900-1730 7 days summer.
0900-1700 7 days winter.
Mail Order: None
Cat. Cost: None issued
Credit Cards: Visa, Diners, Access, Switch,
Delta, MasterCard, EuroCard
Specialities: Wide general range.
Map Ref: W, D1

WSuF   SUNNYBANK VINE NURSERY ⊠ EU 🔲 🔲
The Old Trout Inn, Dulas, Herefordshire
HR2 0HL
☎ (01981) 240256
Contact: B R Edwards
Opening Times: Mail order only.
Min. Mail Order UK: £8.00 incl. p&p
Min. Mail Order EU: £10.00 incl. p&p*
Cat. Cost: Sae
Credit Cards: None
Specialities: Vines. *Note: EU sales by
arrangement.
Map Ref: W, D4

WTin   TINPENNY PLANTS
Tinpenny Farm, Fiddington, Tewkesbury,
Gloucestershire GL20 7BJ
☎ (01684) 292668
E-mail: plants@tinpenny.totalserve.co.uk
Contact: Elaine Horton
Opening Times: 1200-1700 Tue-Thu or
by appt.
Mail Order: None
Cat. Cost: 2 x 1st class
Credit Cards: None
Specialities: Wide range of hardy garden-
worthy plants esp. *Helleborus, Iris* &
Sempervivum.
Map Ref: W, B5

WTre   TREASURES OF TENBURY LTD ⊠ EU
Burford House Gardens, Tenbury Wells,
Worcestershire WR15 8HQ
☎ (01584) 810777
Fax: (01584) 810673
E-mail: treasures@burford.co.uk
Contact: Mr Charles Chesshire
Opening Times: 1000-1800 (dusk in
winter) 7 days.
Min. Mail Order UK: No minimum charge*
Min. Mail Order EU: Nmc
Cat. Cost: Free *Clematis* list
Credit Cards: Visa, Access, Switch
Specialities: *Clematis* and herbaceous,
conservatory plants, bamboos, trees &

shrubs. National Collection of *Clematis.*
*Note: mail order only between Oct-Mar.
Map Ref: W, C4

WTro   TROED-Y-RHIW TREES & SHRUBS
⊠ UK
Abercregan, Cymmer, Port Talbot, West
Glamorgan, Wales SA13 3LG
☎ (01639) 850503
E-mail: joseph.latham@btinternet.com
Contact: F A Latham
Opening Times: By arrangement.
Min. Mail Order UK: £10.00 + p&p
Cat. Cost: 2 x 1st class
Credit Cards: None
Specialities: Hardy trees & shrubs.
Map Ref: W, D3

WTus   MARTIN TUSTIN ▣
Bowers Hill Nursery, Willersey Road, Badsey,
Nr Evesham, Worcestershire WR11 5HG
☎ (01386) 832124   Fax: (01386) 832124
Contact: Martin Tustin
Opening Times: 0900-1800 7 days excl.
Xmas week. By appt. only.
Mail Order: None
Cat. Cost: 2 x 1st class
Credit Cards: None
Specialities: Lavenders.
Map Ref: W, B5

WUnu   UNUSUAL PLANTS ◆
Mork Road, St Briavels, Lydney,
Gloucestershire GL15 6QE
☎ (01594) 530561
Fax: c/o (01291) 630413
Contact: Norman D Heath
Opening Times: 1100-1800 Sat, Sun &
B/hols. Evenings by arrangement.
Mail Order: None
Cat. Cost: None issued
Credit Cards: None
Specialities: Hardy perennials, alpines &
rockery plants.
Map Ref: W, D4

WViv   VIV MARSH POSTAL PLANTS
⊠ EU ◆ ▣ €
Walford Heath, Shrewsbury, Shropshire
SY4 2HT
☎ (01939) 291475   Fax: (01939) 290743
E-mail: mail@PostalPlants.co.uk
Web Site: www.PostalPlants.co.uk
Contact: Mr Viv Marsh
Opening Times: Not open to the public.
Min. Mail Order UK: £5.00 + p&p
Min. Mail Order EU: £10.00 + p&p
Cat. Cost: 5 x 1st class or 2 x IRCs (£1
refund on first order)

Credit Cards: Visa, MasterCard
Specialities: Rare & routine herbaceous
perennials. Note: mail order beyond Europe
in Oct-Feb only when plants are dormant.

WWal   THE WALLED GARDEN AT
PIGEONSFORD ⊠ UK ▣ €
Llangranog, Llandysul, Ceredigion, Wales
SA44 6AF
☎ (01239) 654360   Fax: (01239) 654360
E-mail: pigeonsford@llangrannog.com
Web Site: www.llangrannog.com/pigeonsford
Contact: David & Hilary Pritchard
Opening Times: 1000-1800 Easter-end Oct.
Phone for appt. Nov-Easter.
Min. Mail Order UK: £6.00 + p&p
Cat. Cost: 4 x 1st class
Credit Cards: None
Specialities: Good general range specialising
in herbaceous plants esp. hardy *Geranium* &
Primula. Camellia.
Map Ref: W, C2

WWat   WATERWHEEL NURSERY
Bully Hole Bottom, Usk Road, Shirenewton,
Chepstow, Monmouthshire, Wales NP6 6SA
☎ (01291) 641577   Fax: (01291) 641851
E-mail: dte@waterwheelnursery.freeserve.co.uk
Web Site:
www.waterwheelnursery.freeserve.co.uk
Contact: Desmond & Charlotte Evans
Opening Times: 0900-1800 Tue-Sat, also
B/hol Mons. From 28th Oct 2000 open by
appt. only until Mar 2001 when the nursery
will be permanently closed.
Mail Order: None
Cat. Cost: 2 x 1st class
Credit Cards: None
Specialities: Unusual & choice garden-
worthy plants esp. shrubs. Also trees,
climbers, perennials, grasses etc. Over 1600
in all. Note: write for list with map, or phone
for directions, before visiting.
Map Ref: W, D4

WWeb   WEBBS OF WYCHBOLD ▣ ◆ €
Wychbold, Droitwich, Worcestershire
WR9 0DG
☎ (01527) 861777   Fax: (01527) 861284
E-mail:
carole@webbsofwychbold.demon.co.uk
Contact: David Smith, Olly Spencer
Opening Times: 0900-1800 Mon-Fri
winter. 0900-2000 Mon-Fri summer. 0900-
1800 Sat & 1030-1630 Sun all year.
Mail Order: None
Cat. Cost: None issued
Credit Cards: Visa, Access, American Express
Specialities: Hardy trees & shrubs, climbers,

conifers, alpines, heathers, herbaceous, herbs, roses, fruit & aquatics. National Collection of shrubby *Potentilla*.
Map Ref: W, B5

WWes   WESTONBIRT ARBORETUM ⊠ UK
(Forest Enterprise), Tetbury, Gloucestershire GL8 8QS
☎ (01666) 880544   **Fax:** (01666) 880386
Contact: Glyn R Toplis
Opening Times: 1000-1730 7 days summer. 1000-1700 winter.
Min. Mail Order UK: No minimum charge*
Cat. Cost: None issued
Credit Cards: Visa, Access
Specialities: Trees & shrubs, many choice & rare. *Note: mail order Nov-Mar only.
Map Ref: W, D5

WWhi   WHIMBLE NURSERY
Kinnerton, Presteigne, Powys LD8 2PD
☎ (01547) 560413
E-mail: nursery@whimble.totalserve.co.uk
Contact: Liz Taylor
Opening Times: 1100-1730 Wed, Thurs, Fri & Sun. Sat & evenings by appt.
Mail Order: None
Cat. Cost: 5 x 1st class*
Credit Cards: None
Specialities: Mainly herbaceous, some unusual. Small collections of *Achillea, Crocosmia, Dianthus, Geranium, Penstemon, Viola*. *Note: send Sae for plant list (no descriptions).
Map Ref: W, C4

WWin   WINTERGREEN NURSERIES
Bringsty Common, Worcestershire WR6 5UJ
☎ (01886) 821858 eves.
Contact: S Dodd
Opening Times: 1000-1730 Wed-Sun 1st Mar-31st Oct & by appt.
Mail Order: None
Cat. Cost: 2 x 2nd class
Credit Cards: None
Specialities: General esp. alpines & herbaceous.
Map Ref: W, C4

WWol   WOOLMANS PLANTS LTD ⊠ EU ▤ €
The Plant Centre, Knowle Hill, Evesham, Worcestershire WR11 5EN
☎ (01386) 833022   **Fax:** (01386) 832915
E-mail: sales@woolman.co.uk
Web Site: www.woolman.co.uk
Contact: John Woolman
Opening Times: 0900-1700 Mon-Sun.
Min. Mail Order UK: No minimum charge
Min. Mail Order EU: Nmc

Cat. Cost: Free
Credit Cards: MasterCard, Visa, Switch
Specialities: *Chrysanthemum,* hanging basket & patio plants, *Dahlia,* perennials.
Map Ref: W, B5

WWoo   WOODLANDS NURSERIES ▤
Woodlands View, Blakemere, Herefordshire HR2 9PY
☎ (01981) 500306   **Fax:** (01981) 500184
E-mail: larry@lowther1.fsnet.co.uk
Contact: Larry & Mal Lowther
Opening Times: By appt. only.
Mail Order: None
Cat. Cost: 2 x 1st class
Credit Cards: None
Specialities: Common & unusual herbaceous perennials, shrubs, ferns, trees & grasses.
Map Ref: W, C4

WWpP   WATERPUMP PLANTS
Waterpump Farm, Ryeford, Ross-on-Wye, Herefordshire HR9 7PU
☎ (01989) 750177
Contact: Mrs E Sugden
Opening Times: 1100-1800 Tue-Sat Apr-Sep or by appt.
Mail Order: None
Cat. Cost: None at present.
Credit Cards: None
Specialities: Herbaceous, hardy geraniums, moisture loving & marginal pond plants. Organically grown.
Map Ref: W, C4

WWst   WESTONBIRT PLANTS ⊠ EU
9 Westonbirt Close, Worcester, Worcestershire WR5 3RX
☎ (01905) 350429 (answerphone)
Fax: (01905) 350429
Contact: Garry Dickerson
Opening Times: Not open, strictly mail order only.
Min. Mail Order UK: No minimum charge
Min. Mail Order EU: Nmc
Cat. Cost: 2 x 1st class
Credit Cards: None
Specialities: *Iris, Fritillaria, Erythronium,* particular interest in *Iris* species, plus *Crocus, Corydalis* & *Lilium*.

WWye   WYE VALLEY PLANTS ◆
The Nurtons, Tintern, Chepstow, Gwent, Wales NP16 7NX

KEY		
⊠	Mail order to UK or EU	
▣	Exports beyond EU	€ Euro accepted
▤	Also supplies Wholesale	◆ See Display advertisement

W

☎ (01291) 689253   **Fax:** (01291) 689253
Contact: Adrian & Elsa Wood
Opening Times: 1030-1700 Wed-Mon
mid Feb-mid Oct. Other times by appt.
Mail Order: None
Cat. Cost: 3 x 1st class
Credit Cards: None
Specialities: Wide range of unusual
perennials, aromatic and medicinal herbs,
Salvia, Origanum, grasses & sedges. Soil
Association symbol. Cert UK 5.
Map Ref: W, D4

ABROAD

XB&T   **B & T WORLD SEEDS** ✉ EU 🖪 ☑ €
Paguignan, 34210 Olonzac, France
☎ (0033) 0468912963
Fax: (0033) 0468913039
E-mail: ralph@b-and-t-world-seeds.com
Web Site: www.b-and-t-world-seeds.com
Contact: Lesley Sleigh & Ralph Wheatley
Opening Times:
Min. Mail Order UK: £5.00
Min. Mail Order EU: £5.00
Cat. Cost: £10 Europe, £14 elsewhere.
Credit Cards: Visa, MasterCard
Specialities: Master list contains over 40,000
items. 199 sub-lists available. Lists to
specification. Note: exports seed only.
Catalogue/botanical reference system
available on CD Rom. SeedyRom (TM)
catalogue £20 worldwide.

XFro   **FROSCH EXCLUSIVE PERENNIALS**
✉ EU 🖪 ☑ €
Am Brunnen 14, 85551 Kirchheim, Germany
☎ 00 49 89 9043190
Fax: 00 49 89 9037683
E-mail: info@cypripedium.de
Web Site: www.cypripedium.de
Contact: Michael Weinert
Opening Times: Mail order only. 0700-2200.
Min. Mail Order UK: £60.00 + p&p
Min. Mail Order EU: £60.00 + p&p
Cat. Cost: None issued
Credit Cards: None
Specialities: *Cypripedium* hybrids. Hardy
orchids. Note: exports beyond the EU.

XJel   **JELITTO PERENNIAL SEED** ✉ EU ☑ ♦ €
PO Box 1264, D-29685 Schwarmstedt,
Germany
☎ 00 49 50 71-98 29-0
Fax: 00 49 50 71-98 29-27
E-mail: info@jelitto.com
Web Site: www.jelitto.com
Contact: Ulrich Schamp, Georg Uebelhart
Opening Times: Not open to the public.
Min. Mail Order UK:
Min. Mail Order EU: £32.00 + p&p
Cat. Cost: Free
Credit Cards: Visa, MasterCard
Specialities: Seeds of alpines, perennials,
herbs, wild flowers, ornamental grasses;
more than 2500 varieties.

SPECIALIST NURSERIES

Nurseries have classified themselves under the following headings where they *exclusively* or *predominantly* supply this range of plants. Plant groups are set out in alphabetical order. Refer to

Nursery Details by Code on page 796 for details of the nurseries whose codes are listed under the plant group which interests you. See page 793 for a fuller explanation.

ACID LOVING PLANTS

CMac CTrh CWCL EPar
GCrs GDra GGGa GGar
IBlr ISea LMil LSyl MBar
MGos NLAp SBrw SCam
SHmp SLdr SOkd SRCN
SRot SSht WAbe WPic

ALPINES/ROCK PLANTS

CAvo CCha CCpl CGra
CInt CLyd CMea CNic
CPBP CPri CStu CWes
CWil EBur ECho EEls
EHyt EMNN EPot GCrs
GDra GFle GGGa GTou
IBlr ITim LBmB LBee
LPVe LTor MCre MDCh
MNew MOne MTho NBro
NCra NDlv NHar NHol
NLAp NMen NNew NRya
NSla NTow NWCA SIng
SOkd SPop SRms SRot
WAbe WGor WHoo WLin
WPat WPer WUnu

AQUATICS

CBen CCuc CRow CWtG
EHon EMFW EPar GGar
LGuA LLWG LPBA MAAq
MHew MSta NOrc SLon
SWat SWyc WHer WLin
WMAq

BAMBOOS

CDDB COld EFul EGln
EOas EPVP EPla ERod
GBin ISta LEdu LHer LJus
MBrN MCCP MMoz MTed
MWht NMoo NOGN NPal
SAPC SCob SDry WMul

WJun WMEx WNor WPGP

BULBOUS PLANTS

CAvo CBro CElm CGrW
CLAP CLCN CMea CQua
CStu CWoo EBot EHyt
EMon EMui EPar EPot
ERos ETub GCrs GEve
GTou IBal IBlr IDun
LBmB LBlo LBow LHpC
LPJP MNrw MS&S MTho
NMen NOaD SDeJ STil
WShi WWst

CACTI & SUCCULENTS

CCpl CPhi CTrC CTrF
CWil EGln EOas EPln
ESou EYou LToo NCro
NOaD SChr SBrk SHvs
SKCa WGei WLow

CARNIVOROUS

CSWC EAnd GTro SHmp
SKCa WMEx

CLIMBERS

CJas CPlN CRHN CSPN
CTri CWhi ECot EOrc
EPla ERea ERob ESCh
ETho LPri MBar MKay
MNew NAsh NBea NBrk
NSti NTay SAPC SApu
SBra SLau SLim SLon
SPla SRum WBuc WHar
WSHC WSpi WTre

CONIFERS

CKen CLnd CSli CTho
ECho EHul EMac EOrn

EPot GChr GPin GTre
LBee LCon LLin MAsh
MBar MGos NAsh NMoo
NOGN SCoo SCrf SLim
SRum WGor

CONSERVATORY PLANTS

CBrP CCpl CPlN CRHN
CRoM CSpe CTbh CTrC
CWDa EBSP EBak ECon
EEls EOHP EPVP ERea
GGGa LBlo LCns LDea
LToo MNew NAsh NFir
NPal SGrm SLdr SOWG
SYvo WDib WMal WMul
WRic

FERNS

CCuc CLAP COld CTbh
CWtG EFer EHon EMon
EPVP GBin GOrP LCaP
LJus MCCP NBro NBus
NDlv NHar NHol NMar
NOak NOrc SApp SChu
SCob SLon SNut SPla
SRms SRot WRic

FRUIT

CAgr CCAT CGOG CTho
CTri EMac EMui ERea
GTre GTwe LBlo MCoo
SCrf SDea SFam SKee
WBuc WHar WJas WSuF

GRASSES

CBrm CCuc CInt CKno
CMea CWes EBur ECGN
EFul EHoe EHon EHul
EMon EPGN EPPr EPla
EWsh GBin GCal GDea

GIBF GKir GOrn GOrP
LCaP LEdu LGre LJus MBel
MBrN MCCP MKay MMoz
MNan MNrw MPot NBea
Nbro NBus NHex NHol
NMoo NNor NOak NOGN
NOrc NPSI NSti SApp SBea
SCob SPla SWal WHal
WHer WLeb WMEx WPer
WPrP WWye

HEDGING PLANTS

CArn CDul CKin CLnd
CSil CTrC CTrF CTrG
CTri ECot EMac ERom
GChr GTre IClo IMGH
ISsi LBuc LCon LEar LHyr
LPan LTor MBar MCoo
MGos NGCt SCam SFor
SHHo SLan SRiv SRum
SSht WBuc WDin WHar
WMou WOrn WSpi WTus
WWeb

HERBS

CAgr CArn CCha COld
CSev EBot EEls ELau
EOHP GBar GPoy IIve ILis
LEdu LLWP LMor MChe
MHer MHew MSal NGCt
NGHP NHex NHHG
NWoo SHDw SIde SWat
WBry WCHb WGwG

WHbs WJek WOak WPer
WSel WUnu WWye

ORCHIDS

CBur CHdy EFEx GUzu
NEqu NSpr SMcB SStn
WHer XFro

ORNAMENTAL TREES

CAgr CCAT CDul CEnd
CLnd CMFo CTho ECho
ECot ECrN EMac EMui
ERav ERod GChr GIBF
GKir GTre ISea LHer LHyr
LPan LSyl MDCh MGos
NBea NBee NPSI SBir
SFam SFur SLau SLim
SMHT SRum WBuc WCel
WHar WJas WMou WNor
WOrn WPGP

SEEDS

CDob CGGs CGrW CJas
CKin CPas CPla CSut CTrF
CTuc EDrk EMcA EMsh
ET&M GDra GIBF GOrP
GPoy LBra LCha LChw
LCTD LSee LSiH MAsh
MDCh MPet MPhe NChl
NCra NLan NRob SCou
SHmp SIde SWyc WJek
WNor XB&T XJel

SPECIMEN SIZE PLANTS

CArn CDul CSil CTho
CTrG ECho ECon ECot
ECrN EGln EHul ELau
EPVP ERom GIBF GTre
IHar IMGH ISta LCns
LCon LEar LEdu LHyd
LHyr LLin LMil LNet LPVe
LPan LTor NCro NGCt
NMar NOrc SAPC SBrw
SCam SCob SCrf SFor
SHHo SLdr SMHT SRum
WDin WHar WHer WJun
WMul WPat WSpi WTus
WWeb

TOPIARY

CWes ECot ERea ERom
IHar LEar LHyr LPan LTor
NGCt SFor SHHo SLan
SRiv WSpi WWeb

WILD FLOWERS

CArn CKin CNat EWFC
IIve LPJP MGas MHer
MHew MInt NHex NHHG
NLan NMir SIde SWat
WAlt WHbs WJek WOak
WShi WUnu

NURSERY INDEX BY NAME

Nurseries that are included in the *RHS Plant Finder* for the first time this year (or have been reintroduced) are marked in **bold type**. Full details of the nurseries will be found in

Nursery Details by Code on page 796. For a key to the geographical codes, see the reverse of the card insert at the start of **Nurseries**.

Bodiam Nursery	**SBod**
Bodmin Plant and Herb Nursery	**CBod**
Bodnant Garden Nursery Ltd	**WBod**
Bonhard Nursery	**GBon**
Bordervale Plants	**WBor**
Bosvigo Plants	**CBos**
The Botanic Nursery	**CBot**
Botanicus	**EBot**
Bouts Cottage Nurseries	**WBou**
Ann & Roger Bowden	**CBdn**
Rupert Bowlby	**LBow**
S & N Brackley	**LBra**
J Bradshaw & Son	**SBra**
Bramley Lodge Garden Nursery	**CBrm**
Bregover Plants	**CBre**
Blooms of Bressingham (Bletchworth)	**LBSe**
Bressingham Plant Centre (Clandon)	**LBCl**
Bressingham Plant Centre (Diss)	**EBre**
Bressingham Plant Centre (Dorney)	**LBre**
Bressingham Plant Centre (Elton)	**EBrP**
Bressingham Plant Centre (Haywards Heath)	**SBre**
Blooms of Bressingham (Rugby)	**MBBe**
Bridge End Nurseries	**GBri**
Bridge Nursery	**MBrN**
Bridgemere Nurseries	**MBri**
Broadleas Gardens Ltd	**CBrd**
Broadleigh Gardens	**CBro**
Broadstone Nurseries	**MBro**
Broadwater Plants	**SBrw**
Iain Brodie of Falsyde	**GIBF**
Paul Bromfield - Aquatics	**LPBA**
Bron Eifion Nursery	**WBrE**
Brook Farm Plants	**WBro**
Brooklands Plants	**CBrP**
Brookside Nursery	**SBrk**
Brookwood Nurseries	**IBro**
Ted Brown Unusual Plants	**MTed**
Brownthwaite Hardy Plants	**NBro**
Buckingham Nurseries	**LBuc**
Buckland Plants	**GBuc**
Bucknell Nurseries	**WBuc**
Jenny Burgess	**EBur**
Burncoose & South Down Nurseries	**CB&S**
Burnham Nurseries	**CBur**
Burrows Roses	**MBur**
Burton Agnes Hall Nursery	**NBur**
Bush Green Cottage Nursery	**NBus**
Butterfields Nursery	**LBut**
Byeways	**WByw**
Caddick's Clematis Nurseries	**MCad**
Cally Gardens	**GCal**
Cambridge Garden Plants	**ECGP**
Camellia Grove Nursery	**SCam**
Candacraig Gardens	**GCan**
Carncairn Daffodils	**ICar**
Carpenders Park Nursery	**LCaP**
Carrob Growers	**WCGr**
Castell Du Plants	**WCDu**

Catforth Gardens	**NCat**
Celyn Vale Eucalyptus Nurseries	**WCel**
Cerney House Gardens	**WCer**
Chadwell Seeds	**LChw**
Chapel Farm House Nursery	**CCha**
Chapel-Uny Nursery	**CCpl**
Sheila Chapman Clematis	**ESCh**
Charlecote Fruit & Flowers	**MChl**
Charter House Nursery	**GCHN**
Chase Organics (GB) Ltd	**LCha**
The Beth Chatto Gardens Ltd	**ECha**
Chennels Gate Gardens & Nursery	**WChG**
Cherry Tree Nursery	**CChe**
Cheshire Herbs	**MChe**
Chessington Nurseries Ltd	**LChe**
Chew Valley Trees	**CCVT**
Chiltern Seeds	**NChl**
Chipchase Castle Nursery	**NChi**
Choice Landscapes	**ECho**
Choice Plants	**EChP**
Christie's Nursery	**GCrs**
Christie Elite Nurseries	**GChr**
Church Hill Cottage Gardens	**SChu**
John Churcher Plants	**SChr**
Churchtown Nurseries	**CCtw**
Cicely's Cottage Garden Plants	**NCiC**
Cider Apple Trees	**CCAT**
Cilwern Plants	**WCil**
The Citrus Centre	**SCit**
Clay Lane Nursery	**LCla**
Cley Nurseries Ltd	**ECle**
Clipston Nursery	**MCli**
Clonmel Garden Centre	**IClo**
Clun Hills Nursery	**WClu**
Coblands Nursery	**SCob**
James Cocker & Sons	**GCoc**
Coghurst Nursery	**SCog**
Cold Harbour Nursery	**CCol**
Collectors Corner Plants	**MCCP**
Collinwood Nurseries	**MCol**
The Conifer Garden	**LCon**
The Conservatory	**LCns**
Conservatory PlantLine	**ECon**
The Contented Gardener Nursery	**ECGN**
Cookoo Box Nursery	**SCko**
Cool Temperate	**MCoo**
Cooling's Nurseries Ltd	**SCoo**
Coombland Gardens	**SCou**
Patricia Cooper	**ECoo**
Cotswold Garden Flowers	**WCot**
Cotswold Hardy Plants Ltd	**CCHP**
Cottage Garden Nursery	**LCtg**
Cottage Garden Plants (Whitehaven)	**NCot**
Cottage Garden Plants (Newbury)	**LCot**
Cottage Gardens	**ECot**
The Cottage Herbery	**WCHb**
Cottage Nurseries	**ECtt**
Country Lady Nursery	**MCLN**

County Park Nursery	ECou	Elworthy Cottage Plants	CElw
Cranesbill Nursery	WCra	Endsleigh Gardens	CEnd
Craven's Nursery	NCra	Equatorial Plant Co.	NEqu
Creake Plant Centre	ECre	Equatorial Plant Co. (Vireyas)	CEqu
Crescent Plants	MCre	The Europa Nursery	LEur
Crocknafeola Nursery	ICro	**Evelix Daffodils**	GEve
Crofters Nurseries	SCrf	Fairhaven Nursery	CFai
Croftway Nursery	SCro	Fairy Lane Nurseries	NFai
Croston Cactus	NCro	Family Trees	SFam
Crown Nursery	ECrN	Farmyard Nurseries	WFar
Crûg Farm Plants	WCru	Feebers Hardy Plants	CFee
CTDA	LCTD	The Fern Nursery	EFer
Cuckoo Mill Nursery	CCuc	Fernwood Nursery	CWil
Cutting Edge Nursery	NCut	Fibrex Nurseries Ltd	WFib
Cwmrhaiadr Nursery	WCwm	Field House Nurseries	MFie
Dalesview Nursery	NDlv	Fillan's Plants	CFil
D'Arcy & Everest	EDAr	Fir Tree Farm Nursery	CFir
David Cartwright Plants	WDCP	Fir Trees Pelargonium Nursery	NFir
David Cheshire Seeds	MDCh	**Firecrest (Trees & Shrubs Nursery)**	EMac
De Jager & Sons	SDeJ	The Firs Nursery	MFir
Deacon's Nursery	SDea	Kaytie Fisher Nursery	LFis
Derek Lloyd Dean	LDea	Flaxton House Nursery	NFla
Deanston Nursery	GDea	Fleurs Plants	GFle
Deanswood Plants	NDea	Flora Exotica	EFEx
Deelish Garden Centre	IDee	**The Flower Bower**	CFwr
Denmans Garden (John Brookes Ltd)	SDnm	Flowers of the Field	WFoF
Devon & Dorset Bamboo	CDDB	Ford Nursery	NFor
Devon Violet Nursery	CDev	**Forward Nurseries**	SFor
DHE Plants	MDHE	Four Seasons	EFou
Dibley's Nurseries	WDib	Foxgrove Plants	LFox
Dickson Nurseries Ltd	IDic	Friars Way Nursery	CFri
Dingle Nurseries	WDin	Fron Nursery	WFro
Samuel Dobie & Son	CDob	Frosch Exclusive Perennials	XFro
Dove Cottage Plants	NDov	Fryer's Nurseries Ltd	MFry
Downderry Nursery	SDow	Fulbrooke Nursery	EFul
Messrs. Jack Drake	GDra	Rodney Fuller	CFul
John Drake	EDrk	Furzey Gardens Nursery	SFur
Drysdale Garden Exotics	SDry	Gandy's (Roses) Ltd	MGan
Duchy of Cornwall	CDoC	Garden Cottage Nursery	GGar
Dulford Nurseries	CDul	Garden House Nurseries	NGdn
Brian Duncan	IDun	**Garden Plants**	SGar
Dunge Valley Gardens	MDun	Gardiner's Hall Plants	EGar
Dysons Nursery	SDys	**Garth Cottage Nursery**	NGCt
Dyffryn Gwyddno Nursery	WDyG	Linda Gascoigne Wild Flowers	MGas
Earlstone Nursery	LEar	Geddington Gardens	MGed
East Northdown Farm	SEND	W G Geissler	WGei
Eastfield Plant Centre	SEas	Gerddi Fron Goch	WGer
Eastgrove Cottage Garden Nursery	WEas	Gillies Carnations	NGil
Edulis	LEdu	Glebe Cottage Plants	CGle
Eggesford Gardens	CEgg	Glen Chantry	EGle
Eggleston Hall	NEgg	Glendoick Gardens Ltd	GGGa
Eildon Plants	GEil	Glenhirst Cactus Nursery	EGln
Charles F Ellis	WCFE	Global Orange Groves UK	CGOG
Ellwood Penstemons	WEll	Godly's Roses	LGod
Elm House Nursery	EElm	**Godolphin Nurseries**	CGdn
Elm Tree Nursery	CElm	Goldbrook Plants	EGol
The Garden at The Elms Nursery	WElm	Elisabeth Goodwin Nurseries	EGoo
Elsworth Herbs	EEls	Gordon's Nursery	WGor

Langley Boxwood Nursery	SLan	Meadow Cottage Plants	CMCo
Langthorns Plantery	ELan	Meadows Nursery	CMdw
The Lanhydrock Gardens (NT)	CLan	Mears Ashby Nurseries Ltd	MMea
Larch Cottage Nurseries	NLar	Mendle Nursery	NMen
The Laurels Nursery	SLau	Merebrook Water Plants	WMAq
Laurel Farm Herbs	ELau	Merriments Gardens	SMrm
Lea Rhododendron Gardens Ltd	MLea	Merryfield Nurseries (Canterbury) Ltd	SMer
Leba Orchard - Green's Leaves	WLeb	Mickfield Fish & Watergarden Centre	EMFW
Lilies-Water-Gardens	LLWG	Mickfield Hostas	EMic
Lilliesleaf Nursery	GLil	Mill Cottage Plants	CMil
Lime Cross Nursery	SLim	Mill Hill Plants	MMil
Lincluden Nursery	LLin	Mill Race Nursery	EMil
Lingen Nursery and Garden	WLin	Millais Nurseries	LMil
Liscahane Nursery	ILsc	Millfield Nurseries	MMiN
Lisdoonan Herbs	ILis	Mills' Farm Plants & Gardens	EMFP
Little Brook Fuchsias	SLBF	Milton Garden Plants	CMGP
Little Creek Nursery	CLCN	Mires Beck Nursery	NMir
Little Rhyndaston Nurseries	WLRN	**Ron & Wendy Mitchell**	SBro
Little Treasures	CLTr	Monksilver Nursery	EMon
Littlewood Farm Nursery	MLit	Moor Monkton Nurseries	NMoo
C S Lockyer	CLoc	Moorland Cottage Plants	WMoo
Loder Plants	SLdr	Morehavens	LMor
Lodge Lane Nursery & Gardens	MLLN	John Morley	EMor
The Lodge Nursery	SLod	Morton Hall Gardens	MMHG
Long Acre Plants	CLAP	Stanley Mossop	NMos
Longhall Nursery	CLon	Frances Mount Perennial Plants	EMou
Longstock Park Nursery	SLon	**Mount Harry Trees**	SMHT
Lovers Knot Nursery	MLov	Mount Pleasant Trees	WMou
Lower Icknield Farm Nurseries	LIck	Mozart House Nursery Garden	MMoz
Lower Severalls Nursery	CSev	Ken Muir	EMui
Lower Spring Nursery	WLow	Mulu Nurseries	WMul
Lydford Alpine Nursery	CLyd	Muncaster Castle	NMun
Lynash Nurseries	CLyn	Kathleen Muncaster Fuchsias	EKMF
M & M Plants	CM&M	Murrells Plant & Garden Centre	SMur
M G H Nurseries	IMGH	Nanney's Bridge Nursery	MNan
MGW Plants	NMGW	**National Forest Plant Centre**	MNaF
Mac Foliage	CMFo	Natural Selection	CNat
Ivor Mace Nurseries	WIvo	Ness Gardens	MNes
Elizabeth MacGregor	GMac	Nettletons Nursery	LNet
MacGregors Plants	SMac	Newington Nurseries	MNew
Macpennys Nurseries	CMac	Newton Hill Alpines	NNew
Macplants	GMaP	Nicky's Rock Garden Nursery	CNic
Madrona Nursery	SMad	**Norcroft Nurseries**	NNor
Malcoff Cottage Garden Nursery	MMal	Norden Alpines	NNrd
Mallet Court Nursery	CMCN	Norfields	WNor
Manor Nursery	EMan	Norfolk Lavender	ENor
The Marches Nursery	WMaN	Northview Perennials	LNor
Lesley Marshall	EMar	Sheila Northway Auriculas	GNor
S E Marshall & Co Ltd.	EMsh	Norwell Nurseries	MNrw
Marshall's Malmaison	WMal	Notcutts Nurseries	ENot
J & D Marston	NMar	**The Nursery Further Afield**	MNFA
Marston Exotics	WMEx	Nutlin Nursery	SNut
Martin Nest Nurseries	EMNN	Oak Cottage Herbs	WOak
Marwood Hill Gardens	CMHG	Oak Dene Nurseries (Barnsley)	NOaD
Mattock's Roses	MMat	Oak Tree Nursery	NOak
S M McArd (Seeds)	EMcA	**Oakdene Nursery (Broad Oak)**	SOkd
McBeans Orchids	SMcB	Oakhurst Nursery	SOkh
The Mead Nursery	CMea	Oasis	EOas

Roseholme Nursery	ERos	Stenbury Nursery	SSte
Roseland House Nursery	CRHN	Steventon Road Nurseries	MSte
Rosemary's Farmhouse Nursery	WRos	Stillingfleet Lodge Nurseries	NSti
Rosewarne Collections	CRsw	Stone House Cottage Nurseries	WSHC
Rosewood Daylilies	SRos	**Stone Lane Gardens**	CSto
Rosie's Garden Plants	SRGP	Stonehurst Nurseries (Ardingly)	SStn
Rotherstone Lockside Plants	LRot	**Stonehurst Nursery (Broad Oak)**	SSht
Rotherview Nursery	SRot	Stonyford Cottage Nursery	MSCN
Rougham Hall Nurseries	ERou	Henry Street Nursery	LStr
Rowde Mill Nursery	CRde	Sue Strickland Plants	CStr
Rowden Gardens	CRow	**Stuckey's Alpines**	CStu
Rumsey Gardens	SRms	Brian Sulman	EBSP
Rumwood Nurseries	SRum	Pearl Sulman	ESul
Rushfields of Ledbury	WRus	Sunnybank Vine Nursery	WSuF
Ryal Nursery	NRya	Surrey Primroses	LSur
Ryans Nurseries	IRya	Suttons Seeds	CSut
S & S Perennials	MS&S	**Swanland Nurseries**	NSwl
Mrs Jane Sadler	SSad	Sylvatica Nursery	LSyl
St Ishmael's Nurseries	WStI	Taylors Nurseries	NTay
Salley Gardens	MSal	Test Valley Nursery	STes
Sampford Shrubs	CSam	Thompson & Morgan (UK) Ltd	ET&M
Sandstones Cottage Garden Plants	WSan	Thorncroft Clematis Nursery	ETho
Scalers Hill Nursery	SSca	Thornhayes Nursery	CTho
Scree Gardens	SScr	A & A Thorp	MTho
Seaforde Gardens	ISea	Three Counties Nurseries	CThr
Seagate Irises	ESgI	Tile Barn Nursery	STil
Seale Nurseries	SSea	Timpany Nurseries & Gardens	ITim
Seaside Nursery	ISsi	Tinpenny Plants	WTin
Seeds by Size	LSee	Tissington Nursery	MTis
Selsley Herb Farm	WSel	Toobees Exotics	LToo
Sherborne Gardens	WShe	The Torbay Palm Farm	CTor
Sherston Parva Nursery Ltd	CSPN	Torhill Nursery	LTor
John Shipton (Bulbs)	WShi	Tough Alpine Nursery	GTou
Shrubland Park Nurseries	EShb	Town Farm Nursery	NTow
Silver Dale Nurseries	CSil	Treasures of Tenbury Ltd	WTre
Clive Simms	ESim	Trebah Enterprises Ltd	CTbh
Sino-Himalayan Plant Association	LSiH	**Treepac**	GTre
Siskin Plants	ESis	Tregothnan Nursery	CTrG
Skipness Plants	GSki	Trehane Camellia Nursery	CTrh
Slack Top Alpines	NSla	Peter Trenear	STre
Slipps Garden Centre	CSli	Tresidder Farm Plants	CTrF
Alan C Smith	SSmi	Trevena Cross Nurseries	CTrC
Peter J Smith	SSmt	Trewidden Estate Nursery	CTre
South West Carnivorous Plants	CSWC	Trewithen Nurseries	CTrw
Southcott Nursery	SSoC	Triscombe Nurseries	CTri
Southfield Nurseries	ESou	Troed-y-Rhiw Trees & Shrubs	WTro
Southview Nurseries	SSvw	Tropic House	GTro
Special Plants	CSpe	Edwin Tucker & Sons	CTuc
Speldhurst Nurseries	SSpe	Martin Tustin	WTus
Spinners Garden	SSpi	J Tweedie Fruit Trees	GTwe
Spinneywell Nursery	WSpi	Unusual Plants	WUnu
Springbank Nurseries	SSpr	Usual & Unusual Plants	SUsu
Springhill Plants	MSph	Uzumara Orchids	GUzu
Springlea Nursery	LSpr	**Vale Nursery**	SVal
Springwood Pleiones	NSpr	Van Tubergen UK Ltd	ETub
Stam's Bamboo Nursery Ltd	ISta	Ventnor Botanic Garden	SVen
Stapeley Water Gardens Ltd	MSta	**Veritas Nursery**	GVer
Starborough Nursery	SSta	The Vernon Geranium Nursery	LVER

INDEX MAP

The maps on the following pages
show the approximate location of
the nurseries whose details are
listed in this directory.

Orkney Islands

Shetland Islands

G *MAP 7*
SCOTLAND
Page 931

N *MAP 6*
NORTHERN
Page 930

I *MAP 8*
N. IRELAND & REPUBLIC
Page 932

M *MAP 4*
MIDLANDS
Page 928

E *MAP 5*
EASTERN
Page 929

W *MAP 3*
WALES AND THE WEST
Page 926

L *MAP 2*
LONDON AREA
Page 924

C *MAP 1*
SOUTH WEST
Page 922

S *MAP 2*
SOUTHERN
Page 924

Isles of Scilly

Channel Islands

KEY

CRow Details of nurseries with letter Codes in
boxes are given in the Nursery Details by
Code Index starting on page 796.

Motorways
Primary routes
Other 'A' roads

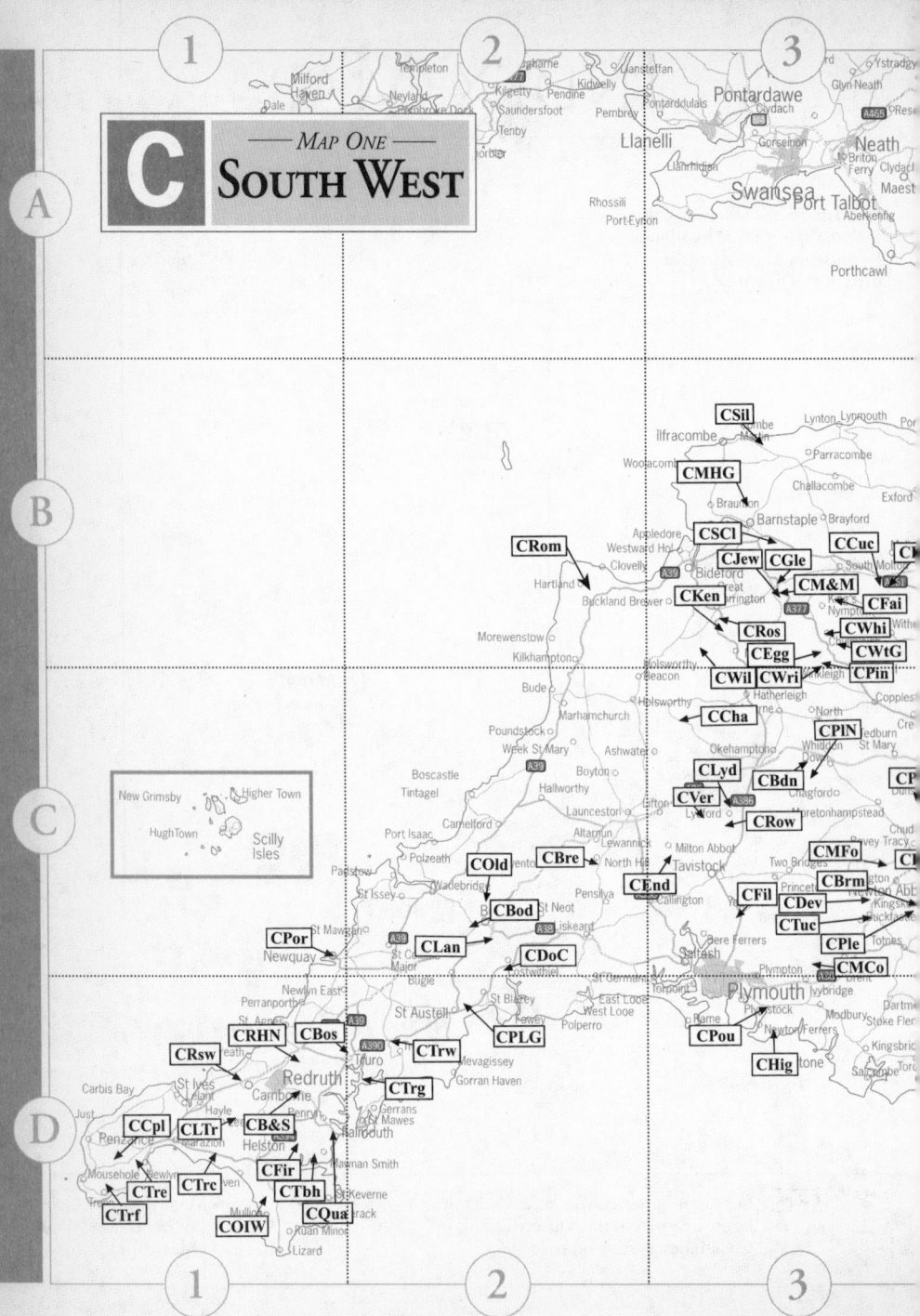

C

— MAP ONE —
SOUTH WEST

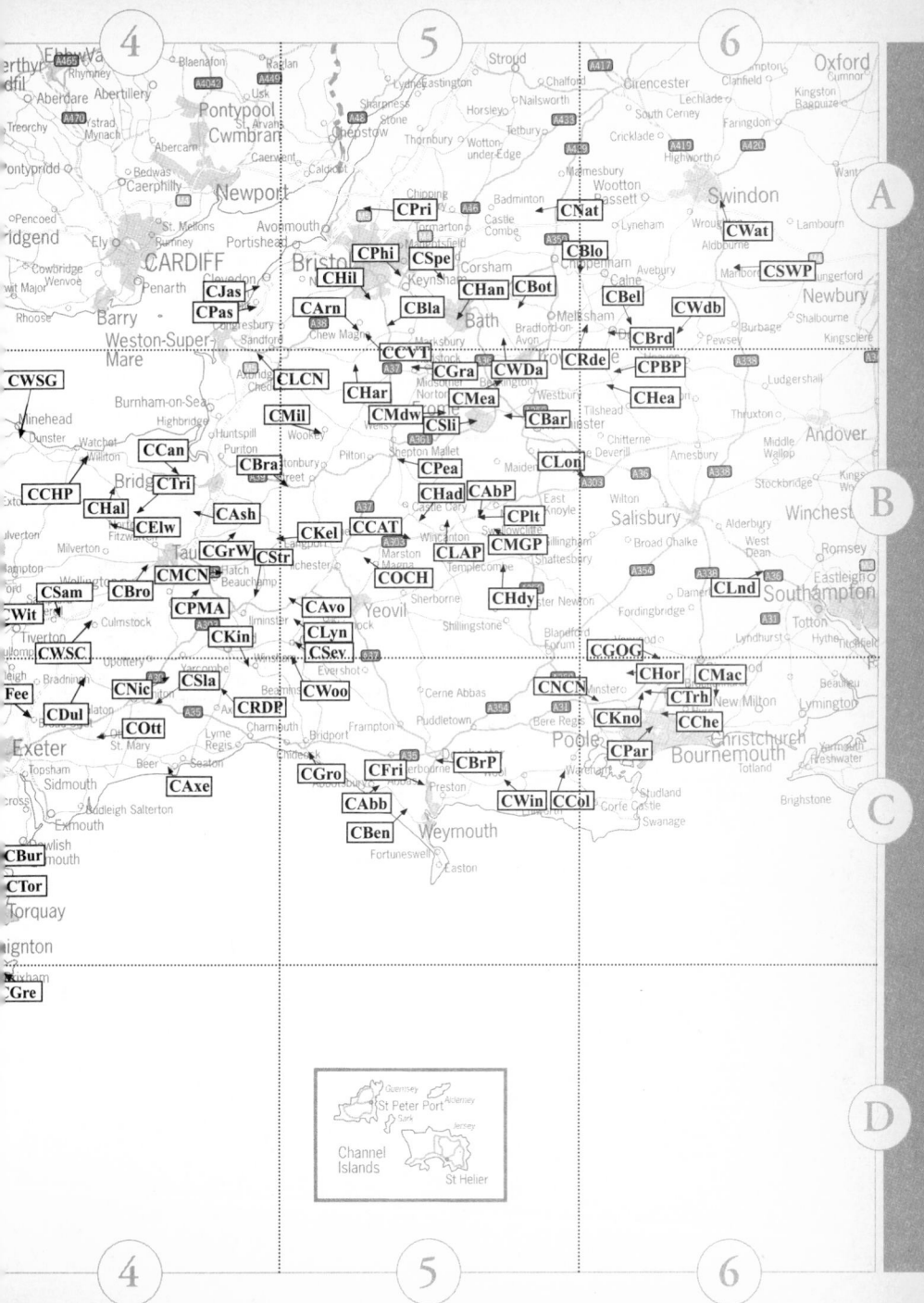

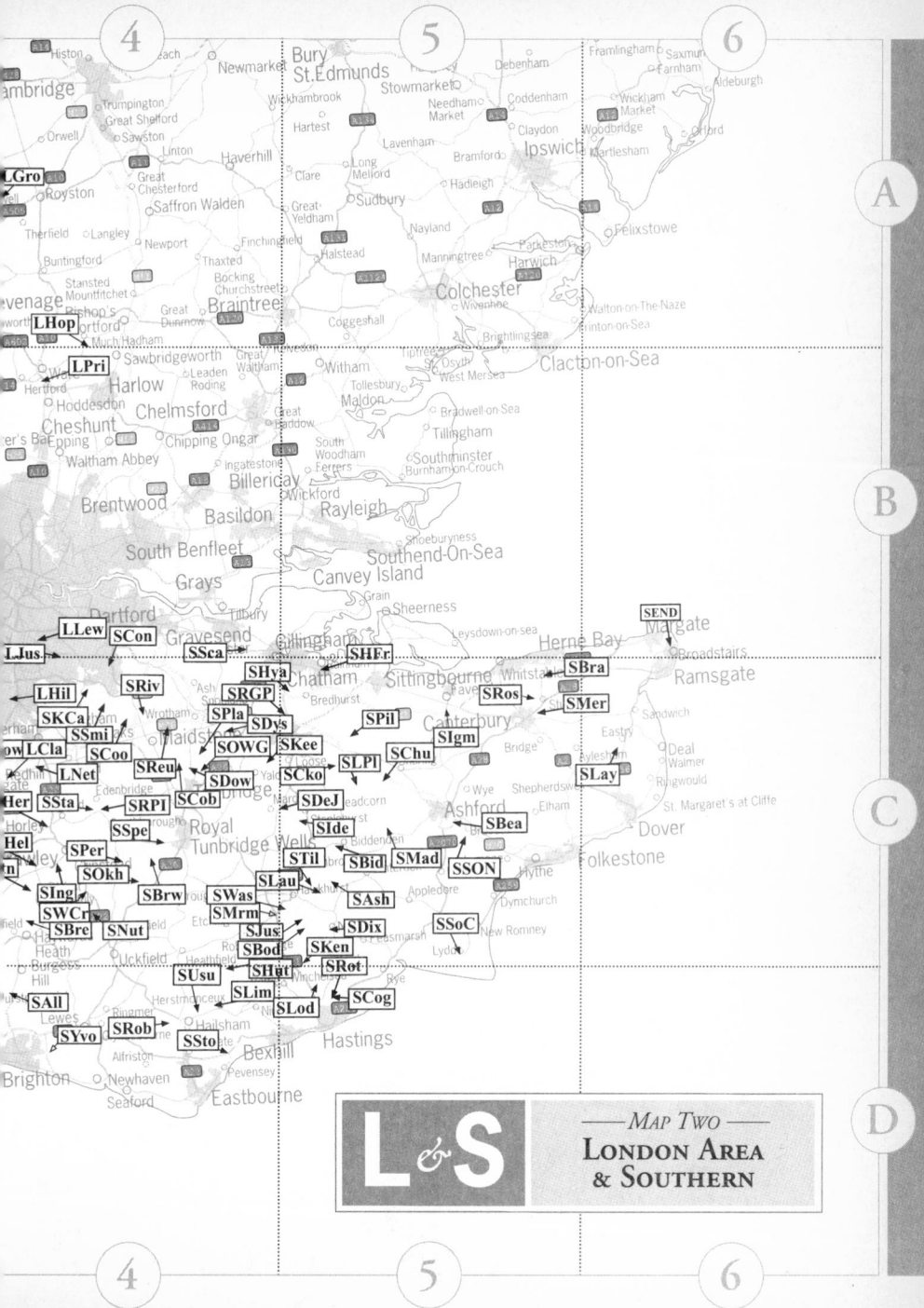

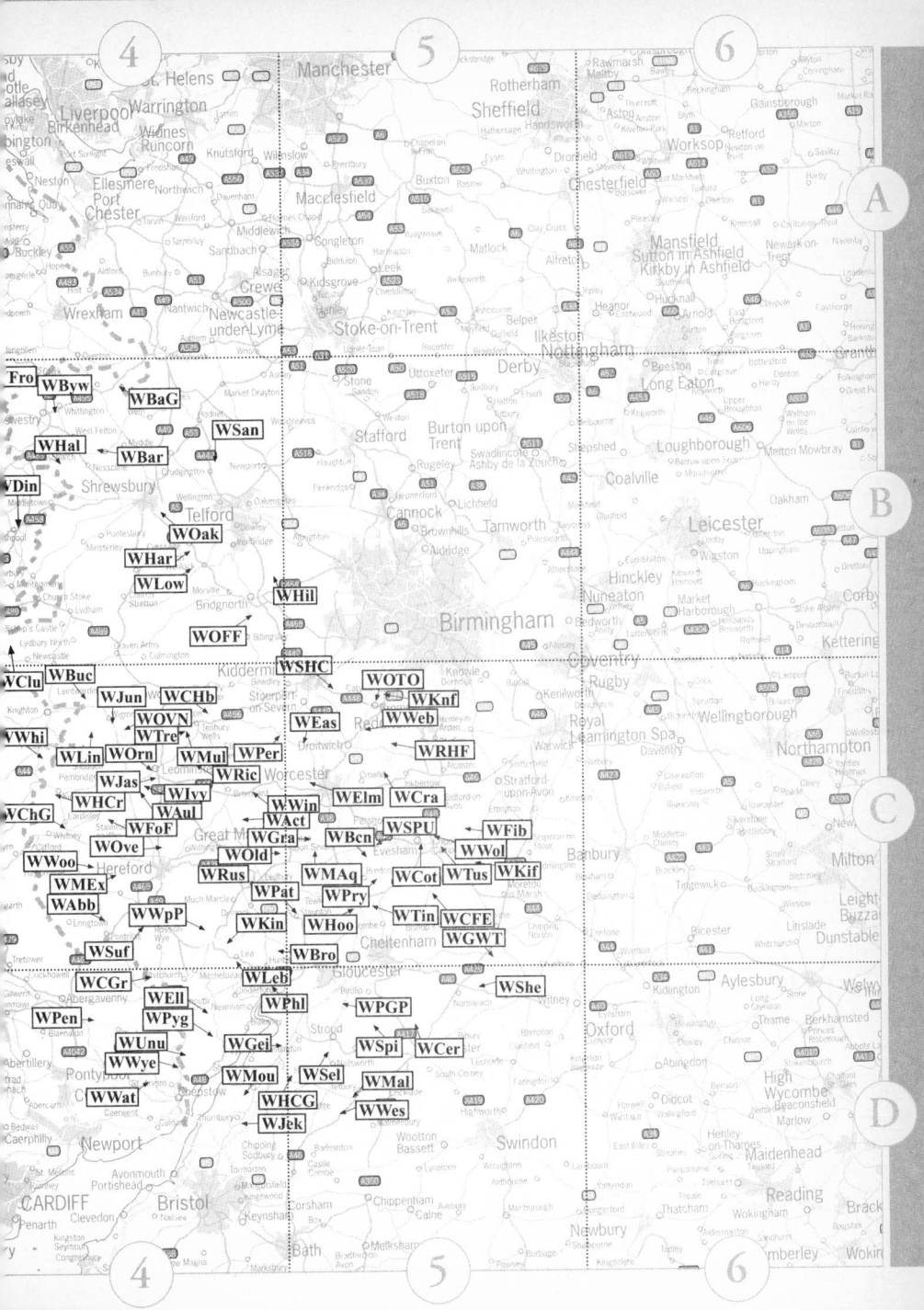

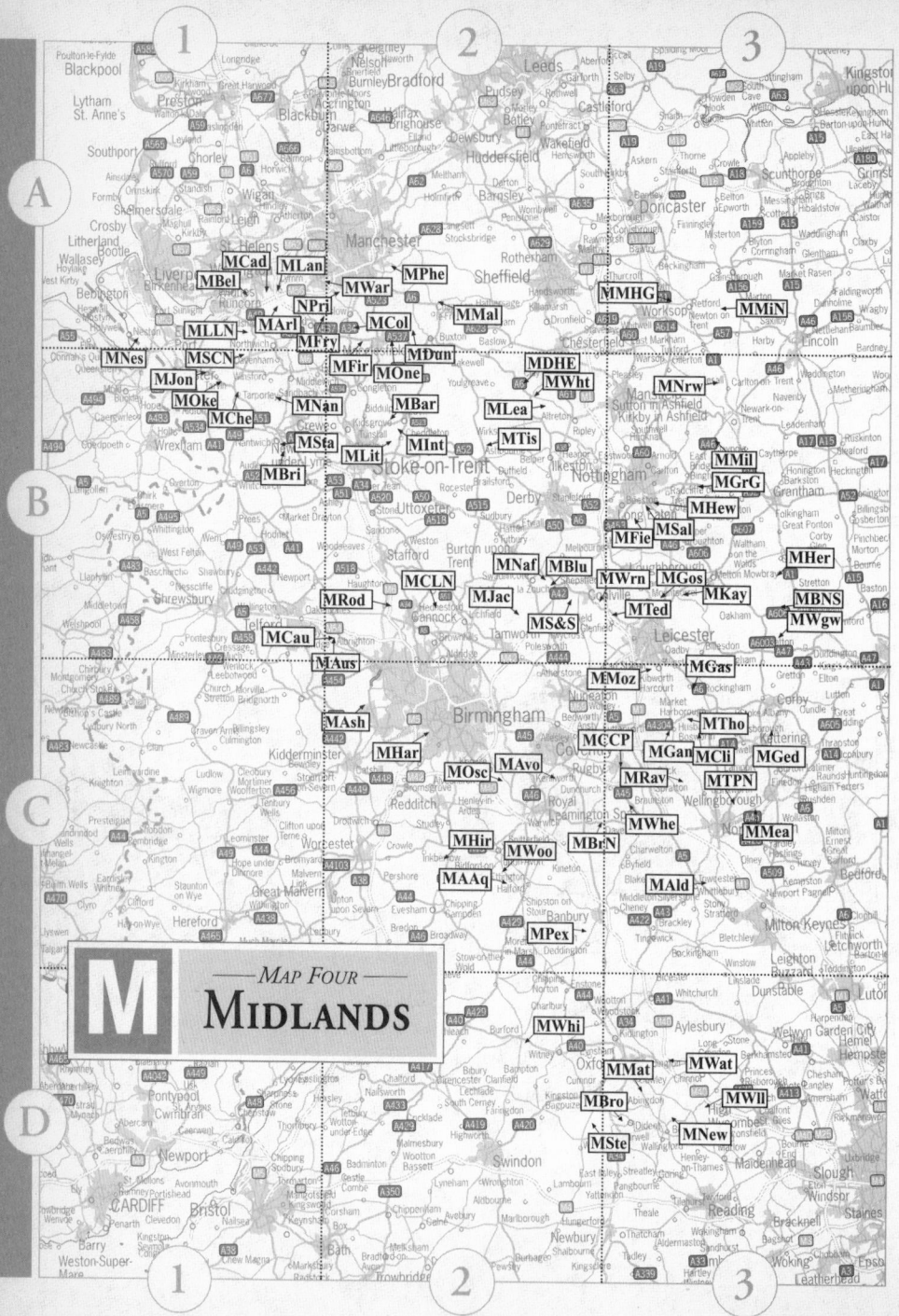

MAP FOUR

MIDLANDS

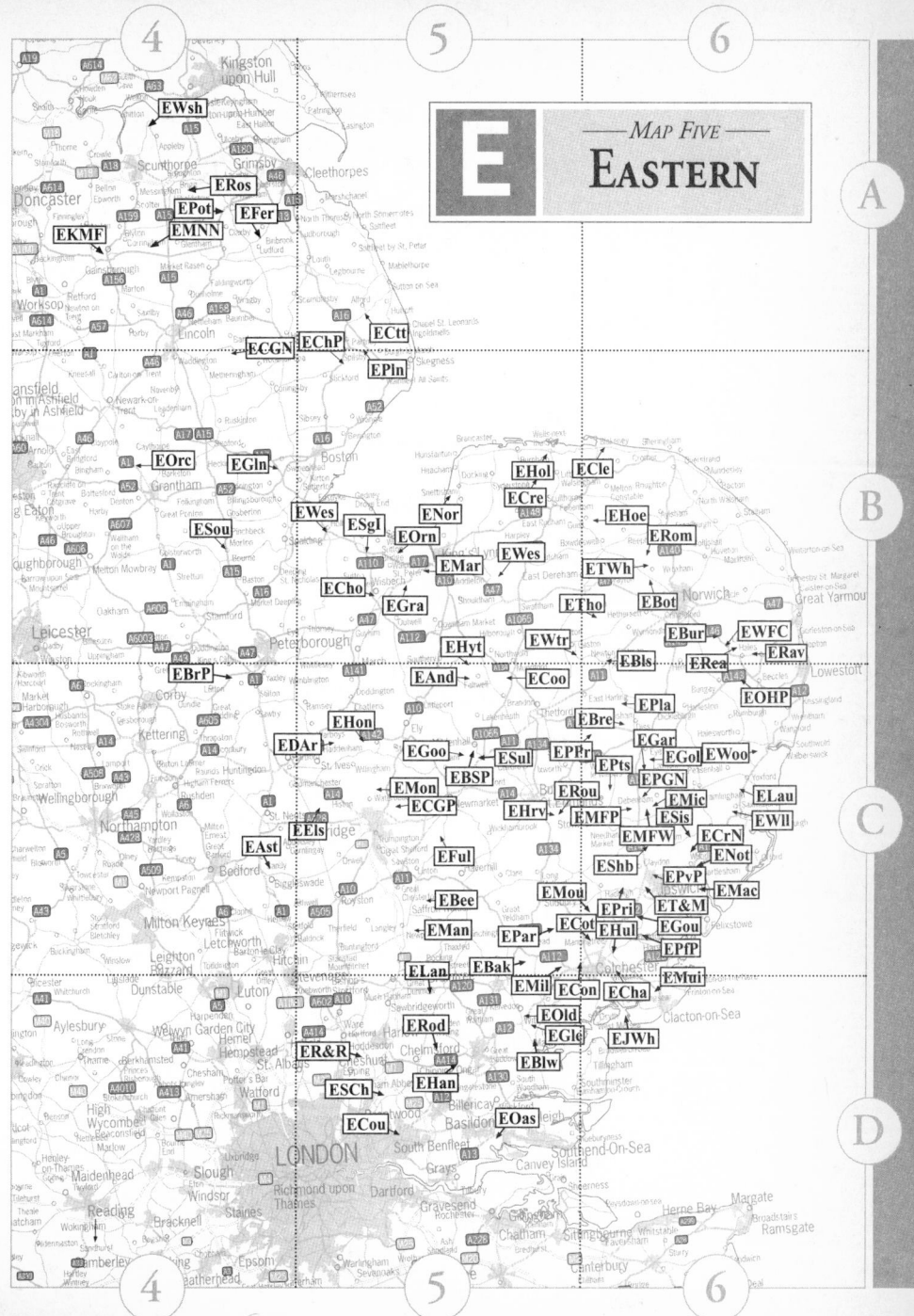

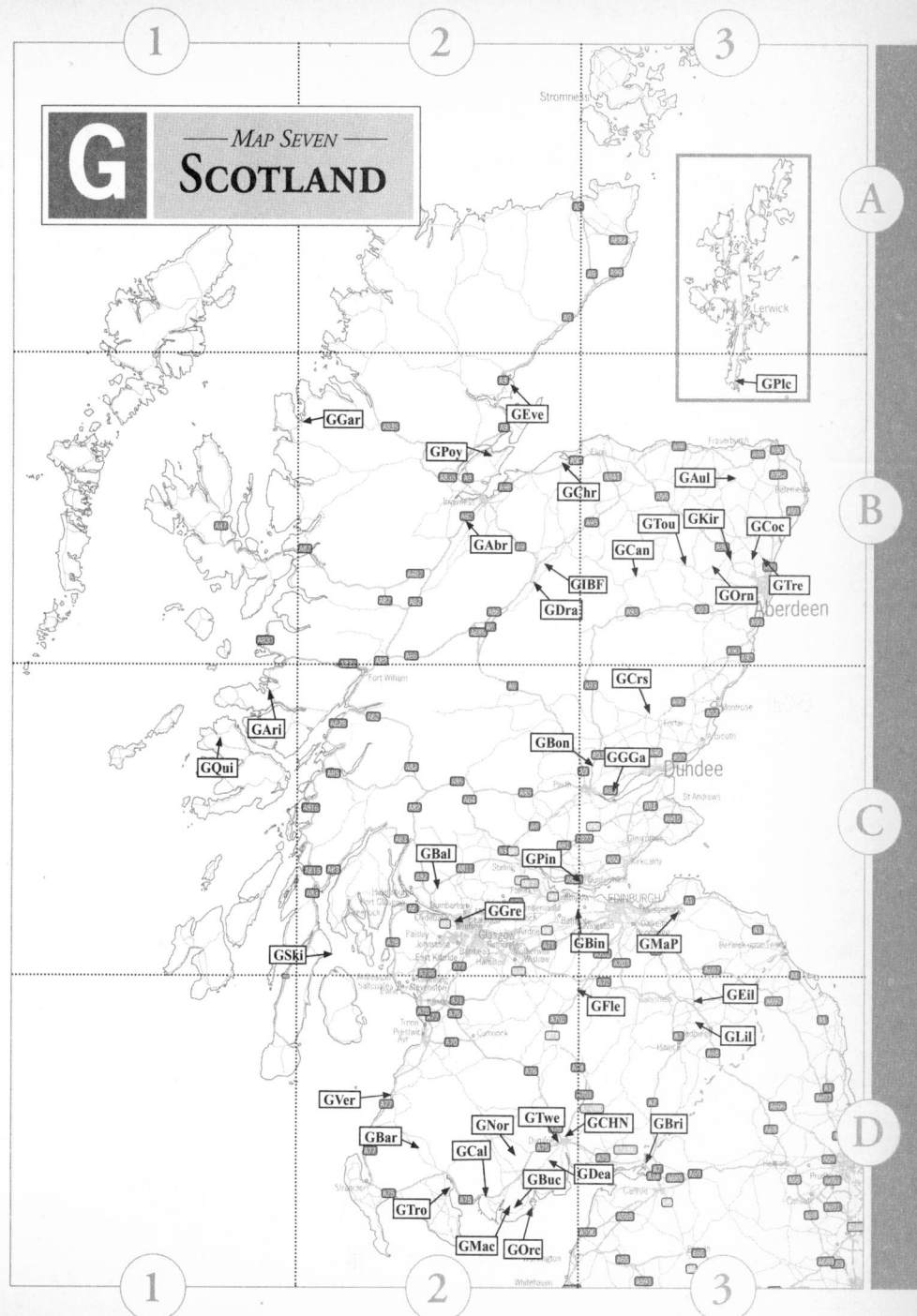

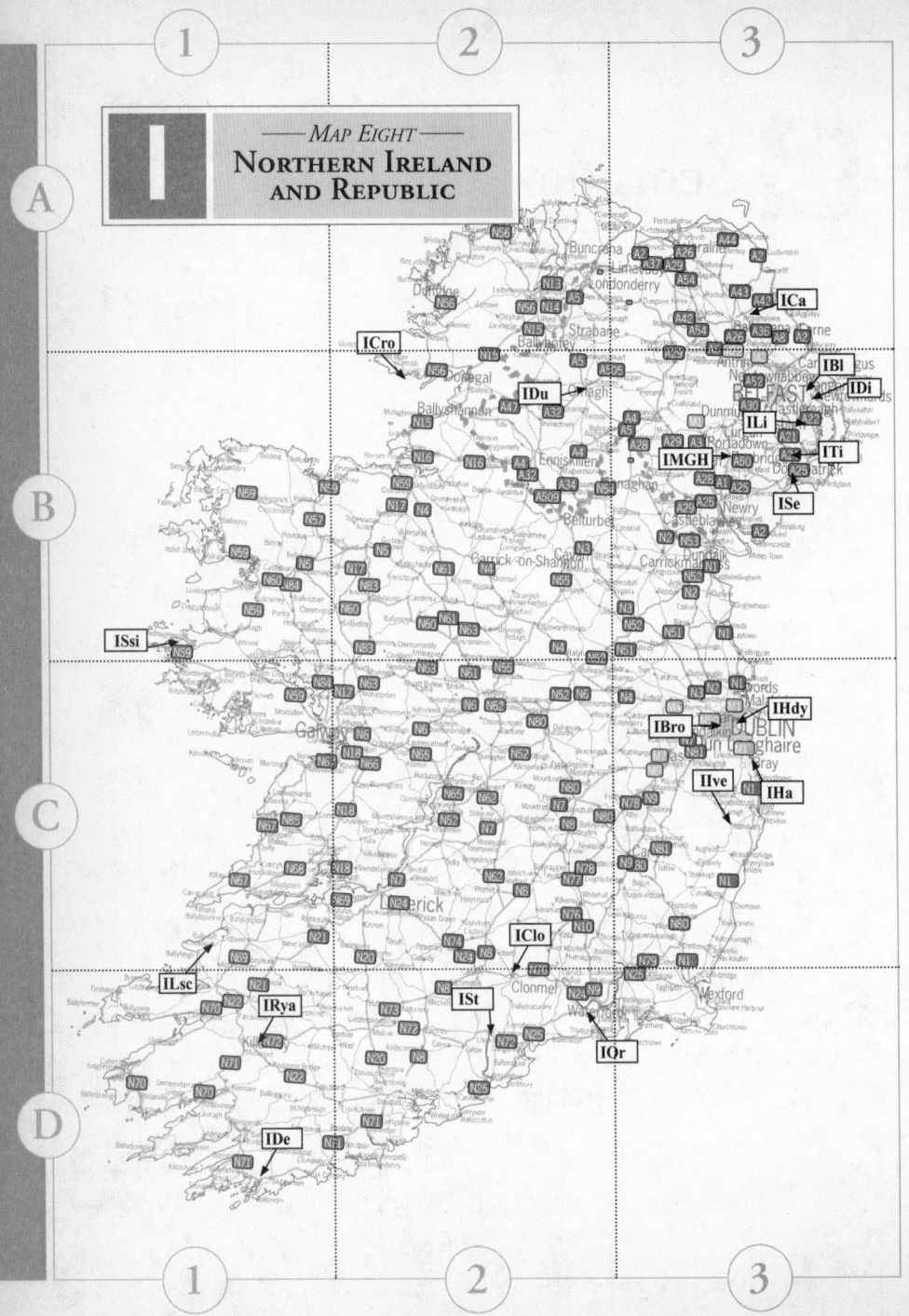

1 — *MAP EIGHT*
NORTHERN IRELAND
AND REPUBLIC

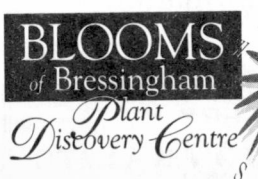

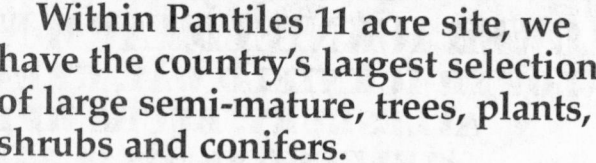

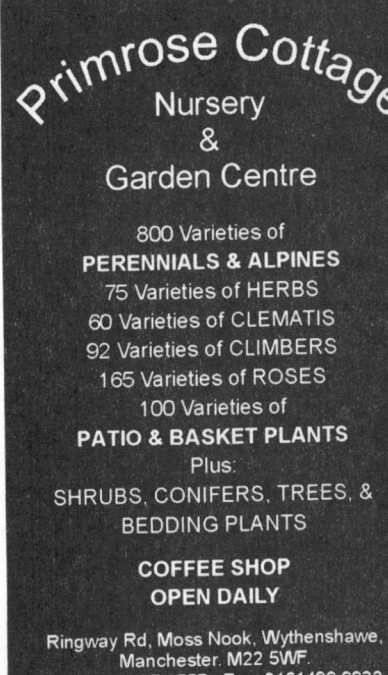

946

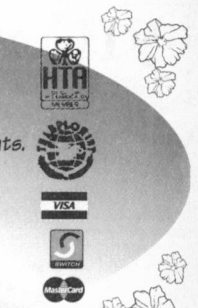

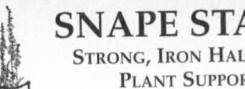

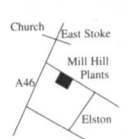

954

INDEX OF ADVERTISERS

The HARDY PLANT SOCIETY

Explores, encourages and conserves all that is best in gardens

The Hardy Plant Society encourages interest in growing hardy perennial plants and provides members with information about familiar and less well known perennial plants that flourish in our gardens, how to grow them and where they may obtained. This friendly society offers a range of activities locally and nationally, giving members plenty of opportunity to meet other keen gardeners to share ideas and information in a convivial atmosphere. The activities and work of the Society inform and encourage the novice gardener, stimulate and enlighten the more knowledgeable, and entertain and enthuse all gardeners bonded by a love for, and an interest in, hardy perennial plants.

LOCAL GROUPS

There are over 40 local groups across the UK and national members are invited to join the group nearest to them. Each group offers a wide range of gardening activities including informative lectures, garden visits and plant plus educational and social events throughout the year. Most groups produce their own newsletters. Full details of how to join a local group are sent out to new members.

SPECIALIST GROUPS AND GARDENING BY POST

Specialist Groups produce their own newsletters and organise meetings and events for fellow enthusiasts. The Correspondents Group ensures that members who are unable to attend meetings can exchange gardening ideas and information.

SEED DISTRIBUTION

Every member can join in the annual Seed Distribution Scheme by obtaining or donating hardy perennial seed. The Seed List offers over 2,500 tempting varieties of rare, unusual and familiar seeds and is sent to every member in December.

Please see overleaf for an application form

SHOWS AND EVENTS

Exhibits at major shows throughout the country let visitors see hardy plants in bloom and leaf in their natural season and more information about the work of the Society is available. Events hosted by local group members are also organised, from plant study days to residential weekends to garden visits. The Society also organises overseas garden tours.

CONSERVATION

The Hardy Plant Society is concerned about the conservation of garden plants and is working towards ensuring that older, rarer and lesser-known perennial plants are conserved and made available to gardeners generally.

PUBLICATIONS AND THE SLIDE LIBRARY

The Society's journal, *The Hardy Plant*, is published twice a year and regular newsletters provide information on all the Society's events, activities, interests and group contacts. The Society also publishes a series of booklets on special plant families which include Hardy Geraniums, Penstemons, Pulmonarias, Hostas and Success with Seed. Other publications for members include a B&B list and a mail order book service. The Slide Library has a wide range of hardy plant slides available on loan.

INFORMATION ABOUT THE SOCIETY IS AVAILABLE FROM:

The Administrator
Mrs Pam Adams
The Hardy Plant Society
Little Orchard
Great Comberton
Pershore
Worcestershire WR10 3DP

Tel: 01386 710317, Fax: 01386 710117
E-mail: admin@hardy-plant.org.uk
Website: www.hardy-plant.org.uk

The HARDY PLANT SOCIETY

MEMBERSHIP APPLICATION FOR 2000

The Annual Subscriptions are:
Single £10.00 per year (one member)
Joint £12.00 per year (two members at the same address)

- Subscriptions are renewable annually on **1 January**.
- Subscriptions of members joining after 1 October are valid until the end of the following year.
- Overseas members are requested to pay in pounds sterling by International Money Order or by credit card. An optional charge of £6.00 is made for airmail postage outside Western Europe of all literature, if preferred.

Please fill in the details in BLOCK CAPITALS, tear off this form and send it with your payment to the Administrator or telephone the Administrator with details of your credit card.

Please tick the type of membership required

☐   Single £10.00 per year (one member)

☐   Joint £12.00 per year (two members at one address)

☐   Airmail postage £6.00 per year (optional for members outside Western Europe)

NAME/S ....

ADDRESS ....

....

.... POST CODE ....

TELEPHONE NUMBER ....

I enclose a cheque/postal order* payable to **THE HARDY PLANT SOCIETY** (in pounds sterling ONLY) for £ ....

OR
Please debit my Visa/Master Card* by the sum of £ ....
(* delete as required)

CARD NUMBER   ☐☐☐☐   ☐☐☐☐   ☐☐☐☐   ☐☐☐☐

EXPIRY DATE   ☐☐☐☐

Name as embossed on card ....

Signature ....

Please print your name and address clearly, tear out the page and send it to
The Administrator at the address overleaf

The Hardy Plant Society is a Registered Charity, number 208080

The Royal Horticultural Society
- inspiration for all gardeners

For practical advice, ideas and information join the RHS and take advantage of nearly 200 years of horticultural expertise.

Let the RHS help you with your garden and enjoy all the benefits that Membership brings:

- RHS Gardens Wisley, Rosemoor and Hyde Hall and free access to 37 other gardens

- 20 RHS Flower Shows, including Chelsea, Hampton Court Palace and RHS Flower Show at Tatton Park

- Monthly Members' magazine *The Garden*

- Discounted tickets to RHS lectures, events and garden tours across Britain

- RHS experts' gardening advice service

RHS Membership Special Offer - Save £7

RHS Membership is normally £35 (including a one-off £7 joining fee) but you can save £7 and pay just £28 by joining by direct debit on the form overleaf.

To join, simply complete the application form overleaf or call

Membership Hotline on 020 7821 3000

and quote code 1587

THE ROYAL
HORTICULTURAL
SOCIETY

Subscription rate valid until 31 October 2000   Registered charity no. 222879

The Royal Horticultural Society Membership
Application form

Please return to:
Membership Department, The Royal Horticultural Society,
PO BOX 313, London SW1P 2PE

Save £7 when you join by direct debit

I would like to become a Member of The Royal Horticultural Society

☐ Direct debit at £28

☐ Cheque and credit card at £35
(includes a £7 joining fee)

code 1588

(BLOCK CAPITALS PLEASE)

Title

Surname

Initial(s)

Address

Postcode

Daytime Tel No.

Payment Details

Payment by credit card | £35.00 |

☐ Please charge to my credit card

☐ RHS Mastercard ☐ Mastercard ☐ Visa ☐ Amex ☐

Card number

☐☐☐☐ ☐☐☐☐ ☐☐☐☐ ☐☐☐☐

Expiry Date /   Date

Cardholder's name

Signature

Payment by Cheque (sterling only)

☐ I enclose a cheque made payable to The Royal Horticultural Society for | £35.00 |

Payment by Direct Debit (UK only) | £28.0 |

☐ Please complete the Direct Debit mandate below

THE ROYAL HORTICULTURAL SOCIETY

Instruction to your Bank or Building Society
to pay by Direct Debit (UK only)

DIREC Deb

1. Name and full postal address of your UK Bank or Building Society

The Manager   Bank/Building Society

Address

Postcode

2. Name(s) of Account Holder(s)

3. Bank sort code (from the right hand corner of your cheque) ☐☐☐☐☐☐

4. Bank or Building Society account number ☐☐☐☐☐☐☐☐

Originator's number | 9 | 9 | 8 | 9 | 7 |

RHS reference
(for RHS use only)

Instruction to your Bank or Building Society

Please pay The Royal Horticultural Society Direct Debits from the account detailed in the instruction subject to the safeguards assured by the Direct Debit Guarantee. I understand that the instruction may remain with The Royal Horticultural Society and if so, details will be passed electronically to my Bank/Building Society.

5. Signature

Date

Banks and Building Societies may not accept Direct Debit instructions for some type of accounts